Blackstone's
EC Legislation Handbook

Edited by

Nigel G. Foster, BA, LLM, Dip German
Senior Lecturer in Law, University of Wales, College of Cardiff
Director, Law and German Degree

BLACKSTONE
PRESS LIMITED

First published in Great Britain 1998 by Blackstone Press Limited, Aldine Place, London W12 8AA. Telephone 0181-740 2277

© Nigel G. Foster, 1998

ISBN: 1 85431 623 0

British Library Cataloguing in Publication Data
A CIP catalogue record for this book is available from the British Library

Typeset by Montage Studios Limited, Tonbridge, Kent
Printed by Bell & Bain Limited, Glasgow

CONTENTS

EDITOR'S PREFACE

This collection of legislation is intended to cater for practitioners who need to consult a wide range of EC legislative material. Access to up-to-date and accurate versions of Community legislation can be difficult. The aim of this volume is to present Community legislation in updated and consolidated versions. References are given to the provisions of UK national legislation transforming EC Directives in a cross reference table at the front of the volume.

Part of the reason for deciding to edit a printed collection in this technological era, is that most persons do not have access to the voluminous *Official Journal* legislation series and electronic databases which contain the collection are not always as up to date or as complete or accurate as they should be. Some consist merely of abstracts of the most important provisions rather than full text. Printing and downloading can also often present further problems rather than providing an instant and accurate copy of the desired legislation and, in particular, information from the 'C' series, often vital for interpreting actual provisions of legislation, can be even more difficult to find and obtain. It can also be difficult to work with electronic databases and material on screen. Hence, a portable version of Community law will be an invaluable tool for the practising lawyer who requires a practical and accessible form of the most popular and necessary EC legislation.

The original decision to edit a compilation was prompted partly by the many suggestions received from practitioners, especially those who commented via book reviews in professional journals on possible additions to the material included in the Blackstone's *EC Legislation* volume. This was rarely possible, because I considered that that publication, designed primarily for law students, would be in danger of expanding so much, it would lose sight of its prime objective, namely to provide a collection of core materials which will assist the study of EC law and may be taken into examinations. As a result, many of the requests for particular provisions could not be acceded to. This present volume, in contrast, is able to contain a comprehensive range of EC legislative material, likely to be the subject of attention of practitioners. However, it cannot be exhaustive bearing in mind the now myriad Community legislative measures. The selection will cover the most common subject areas of litigation. The exclusions from this collection are as follows, although it may be that in future some adjustment will be made according to representations received.

Although increasingly of historical interest, the parts of the EEC Treaty which were subject to amendment by the Treaty on European Union have been reproduced in Annex 1 as they may still feature in some of the long running disputes involving articles of the Treaty. Representing the other end of the scale in the development of the European Union is the Treaty of Amsterdam which is reproduced in Annex 2. As this has not been ratified yet by the Member States and is not in force, I have not included the many declarations and protocols attached to it.

Selection has been exercised in the area of competition law by cutting out most provisions on transport (air, rail and sea). The areas of agriculture, fisheries, foodstuffs and pharmaceutical products have been excluded. Not all health and safety and consumer protection legislation has been included, which although appearing very important hardly register as sources of litigation. Until it becomes clear whether the more recent information technology legislation enactments are widely consulted, these are also omitted. The section on financial services does not extend to stock exchange and share requirements, as these are better catered for in specialist publications on company law, as is company law legislation itself, which is also excluded. I have been selective in the vast area of telecommunications legislation and only the most popular are included; others are left for the specialist telecommunications treatments. Other omissions are in the areas of economic and monetary union, motor insurance and taxation. Most environmental law is excluded at this stage. Following the near demise of EFTA and thus the importance of the EEA, I have decided not to include the EEA Treaty. All text that is included is full text, including preambles and annexes.

I was assisted initially in preparing this volume by Caroline J. Fletcher who worked as a research assistant in the Law School and at a later stage by Joanne Berryman, research assistant. Thanks to both for their help. Thanks also to Ian Thomson of the EDC in Cardiff and my secretary, Linda Mackleworth, for additional assistance in tracking down elusive EC materials and in the preparation of text. Once more, thanks to the staff and agents of Blackstone Press, in particular Heather Saward, Paula Doolan and Linda Murdoch the typesetter, for yet another smooth production process. A number of individuals and firms have also been very helpful in commenting on my earlier draft contents lists and have made numerous helpful suggestions. In particular, I am grateful to: Stephanie Beaumont and colleagues at Clifford Chance; Nigel Cooper, Barrister; Duncan Grehan of Duncan Grehan and Partners, Solicitors; Pamela Kiesselbach and Dorothy Livingston of Herbert Smith; Iain Morrison of Kennedy's; and Ernest Schneider of Schneider & Co., Solicitors. They have helped me shape the final product but bear no responsibility for any errors or omissions which may appear.

Finally, I should like to acknowledge and thank the forebearance of my wife Dawn and children Lynsey and Alexander for my absence for the many more hours this project took than anticipated.

I have tried to present the law as it stands on 17 November 1997. I acknowledge with grateful thanks the source of the material contained within this volume, taken from the *Official Journal of the European Communities*. Where noticed, errors and omissions in this material were corrected. All other errors and omissions are down to me. I would be extremely grateful to any reader who spots 'one of those which got away', if they would take the time and trouble to point it or them out to me or my publisher. Thanks in advance.

Nigel Foster
Pontprennau
(a little known area of Cardiff)
20 January 1998

TABLE ONE OF CROSS REFERENCES[1]

EC DIRECTIVES   UK IMPLEMENTING LEGISLATION

Directive	OJ No.	UK Legislation Title	SI No.
Free movement of persons			
64/221	L56/50	The Immigration (European Economic Area) Order	1994/1895
68/360	L257/13	The Immigration (European Economic Area) Order	1994/1895
73/148	L172/14	The Immigration (European Economic Area) Order	1994/1895
75/34	L14/10	The Immigration (European Economic Area) Order	1994/1895
77/249	L78/17	European Communities (Services of Lawyers) Order 1978	1978/1910
89/48	L19/16	EC (Recognition of professional qualifications) Regulations	1991/824
90/364	L180/26	Immigration (EEA) Order 1994	1994/1895
90/365	L180/28	Immigration (EEA) Order 1994	1994/1895
93/96	L317/59	Immigration (EEA) Order 1994	1994/1895
Social Policy: Equal Pay and Treatment			
75/117	L45/19	Equal Pay Act 1970	
		Equal Pay (Amendment) Regulations	1983/1794
		Sex Discrimination and Equal Pay (Remedies) Regulations	1993/2798
		Employment Protection (Part-time) Employees Regulations	1995/31
		Sex Discrimination and Equal Pay (Miscellaneous Amendments) Regulations	1996/438
76/207	L39/40	Sex Discrimination Act 1975	
		Sex Discrimination (Amendment) Order	1988/249
		Sex Discrimination and Equal Pay (Remedies) Regulations	1993/2798
		Sex Discrimination Act 1975 (Application to Armed Forces) Regulations	1994/3276
		Employment Protection (Part-time) Employees Regulations	1995/31
		Sex Discrimination and Equal Pay (Miscellaneous Amendments) Regulations	1996/438
79/7	L6/24	Social Security Act 1989	
		Social Security (Severe Disabilities Allowances) Amendment Regulations	1993/3194
		Social Security (Severe Disabilities Allowances and Invalid Care Allowances) Amendment Regulations	1994/2556

Note

[1]A Directive year is denoted by the first two digits in the reference, e.g., 70 relates to 1970. Only principal instruments or latest versions are listed and those relating to sub-divisions only of the UK are omitted and some less important Regulations and orders are also omitted in order to avoid overloading this table. Some directives have been implemented in.

Directive	OJ No.	UK Legislation Title	SI No.
		Management of Health and Safety at Work (Amendment) Regulations	1994/2865
93/104	L307/18	No UK reference available yet	
94/33	L216/12	The Health and Safety (Young Persons) Regulations 1997	1997/135

Competition

86/653	L382/17	The Commercial Agents Regulations	1993/3053

Intellectual Property

89/104	L40/1	Trade Marks Act 1994	
92/100	L346/61	Copyright and Related Rights Regulations	1996/2967
93/83	L248/15	Copyright and Related Rights Regulations	1996/2967
93/98	L290/9	Duration of Copyright and Rights in Performances Regulations	1995/3297

Information Technology and Telecommunications

89/552	L298/23	Broadcasting Act 1990	
91/250	L122/42	Copyright (Computer Programmes) Regulations	1992/3233
96/9	L77/20	Copyrights, Designs and Patents Act 1988 (Subject to possible amendment)	
97/36	L202/60	No Reference available yet.	

Public Undertakings

89/655	L395/33	Public Works Contracts Regulations	1991/2680
		Public Supply Contracts Regulations	1991/2679
		Public Services Contracts Regulations	1993/3228
92/13	L76/14	Utilities Supply and Works Contracts Regulations	1992/3279
92/50	L209/1	Public Services Contracts Regulations	1993/3228
93/36	L 199/1	Public Supply Contracts Regulations	1995/201
93/37	L 199/54	Public Works Contracts Regulations	1991/2679
		Public Works Contracts Regulations	1991/2680
		Public Supply Contracts Regulations	1995/201

Environmental Provisions

75/442	L194/39	Control of Pollution Act 1974	
as amended by		Food & Environment Protection Act 1985	
91/156	L78/32	Control of Pollution (Amendment) Act 1989	
		Environmental Protection Act 1990	
		Town & Country Planning Act 1990	
		Control of Pollution (Special Waste) Regulations	1980/1709
		Control of Pollution (landed ships' waste) Regulations	1987/402
		Control of Pollution (Special Waste) Amendment Regulations	1988/1790
		Collection and Disposal of Waste Regulations	1988/819
		Town & Country Planning (assessment of environmental effects) Regulations	1988/1199
		Deposit in the Sea (exemptions) Order	1988/1699
		Control of Pollution (landed ship's waste) (Amendment) Regulations	1989/65
		Environmental Protection (Prescribed processes & substances) Regulations	1991/472

Directive OJ No.		UK Legislation Title	SI No.
		Town & Country Planning (Assessment of Environmental Effects) (Amendment) Regulations 1992	1992/1494
		Town & Country Planning (Assessment of Environmental Effects) (Amendment) Regulations 1994	1994/677
		Highways (Assessment of Environmental Effects) Regulations	1994/1002
		Town and Country Planning (General Development) (Amendment) Order	1994/678
		Town and Country Planning (Environmental Assesment and unauthorised Development) Regulations	1995/2258
		Land Drainage Improvement Works (Assessment of Environmental Effects) (Amendment) Regulations 1995	1995/2195

Consumer Protection

84/450	L250/17	Consumer Protection the control of misleading advertising Regulations	1988/915
		Financial Services Act 1986 Order 198	1988/740
85/374	L210/29	Consumer Protection Act 1987	
85/577	L372/31	Consumer Protection (Cancellation of Contracts concluded away from business premises) Regulations	1988/958
87/102	L42/48	Consumer Credit Act 1974	
		Consumer Credit (Total charge for credit) Regulations	1980/51
		Consumer Credit (Agreements) Regulations	1983/1553
		Consumer Credit (Agreements) (Amendment) Regulations	1984/1600
		Consumer Credit (Total charge for credit) (Amendment) Regulations	1985/1192
		Consumer Credit (Total charge for credit and rebate on early settlement) (Amendment) Regulations	1989/596
88/378 amended by	L187/1	Toys (Safety) Regulations	1989/1275
93/68	L220/1	Toys (Safety) Regulations	1995/204
90/314	L158/59	Package Holidays and package Tours Regulations	1992/3288
92/59	L288/24	The General Product Safety Regulations	1994/2328
		Simple Pressure Vessels (Safety) (Amendment) Regulations	1994/3098
		Construction Products (Amendment) Regulations	1994/3051
		Electromagnetic Compatibility (Amendment) Regulations	1994/3080
		Supply of Machinery (Safety) (Amendment) Regulations	1994/2063
		Personal Protective Equipment (EC Directive) (Amendment) Regulations	1994/2326
		Non-automatic Weighing Instruments (EEC Requirements) Regulations	1995/1907
		Active Implantable Medical Devices (Amendment and Transitional Provisions) Regulations	1995/1671
		The Gas Appliances (Safety) Regulations	1995/1629
		Telecommunications Terminal Equipment (Amendment and Extension) Regulations	1994/3129
		Boiler (Efficiency) Regulations	1993/3083
		Boiler (Efficiency) (Amendment) Regulations	1994/3083
		Electrical Equipment (Safety) Regulations	1994/3260
93/13	L95/29	Unfair Terms in Consumer Contracts Regulations	1994/3159

Financial Services
Banking and Finance

73/183	L 194/1	Public Trustee (Custodian Trustee) Rules	1975/1189
		Authorised Unit Trust Schemes Regulations	1976/195

Directive	OJ No.	UK Legislation Title	SI No.
77/780	L322/30	Banking Act 1979	
		Banking Regulations	1979/938
		Banking Act 1987	
89/299	L 124/16	Notice Bank of England BSD/1990/2	
		Prudential Note 1992/1 of the Building Societies Commission under the Building Societies Act 1986	
89/646	L386/1	Banking Co-ordination (Second Council Directive) Regulations	1992/3218
		Banking Co-ordination (Second Council Directive) (Amendment) Regulations	1992/3225
89/647	L386/14	Notice to Institutions authorised under the Banking Act 1987 (BSD/1990/3) 01/12/90	
		Amendments to the Bank 'Statute Notice implementation in the UK of the Solvency Ratio Directive (BSD1990/3)	
		Prudential Note 1992/1 under the Building Societies Act 1986	
		1992/1611, 1992/1612, 1988/777, 1991/702, 1991/1729	
91/308	L166/77	Money Laundering Regulations	1993/1933
		Criminal Justice Act 1993	
97/5	L43/25	Value Added Tax Act 1994 (and amendments to be made)	

Insurance Sector: Non Life

Directive	OJ No.	UK Legislation Title	SI No.
73/239	L228/3	Insurance Companies (Classes of General Business) Regulations	1977/1552
amended by		Insurance Companies (Solvency: General Business) Regulations	1977/1553
76/580	L189/13	Insurance Companies (Authorisation and Accounts: General Business) Regulations	1978/720
84/641	L339/21		1978/917
87/343	L185/72	Insurance Companies (Deposits) Regulations	
87/344	1185/77	Lloyd's (General Business) Regulations	1979/956
90/618	L330/44	Insurance (Transfer of General Business) Regulations	1980/956
90/619	L330/50	Insurance Companies Act 1981	
92/49	L228/1	Insurance Companies Regulations	1981/1654
		Lloyd's (Financial Resources) Regulations	1981/1655
		Insurance Companies (Assistance) Regulations	1987/2130
		Insurance Companies (Credit Insurance) Regulations	1990/1159
		Insurance Companies (legal expenses insurance) Regulation	1990/1160
		Insurance companies (legal expenses insurance) (application for authorisation) Regulations	1990/1181
		Insurance Companies (Amendment) Regulations	1990/1333
		Insurance Companies (credit insurance) Regulations	1993/2519
		Friendly Societies (insurance business No. 2) Regulations	1993/2520
		Friendly Societies (Authorisation No. 2) Regulations	1993/2521
		Friendly Societies (Insurance Business) Regulations	1994/1981
		Friendly Societies (Authorisation) Regulations	1994/1982
		Insurance Companies (Reserves) Regulations	1996/1181
		Insurance Companies Ordinance (General Insurance and Long Term Insurance Directives) Regulations of 1996	

Directive	OJ No.	UK Legislation Title	SI No.
78/473	L151/25	Co-Insurance (Determination of Certain Liabilities) Regulations	1981/710
		Insurance Companies Regulations	1981/1654
		Insurance Companies Act 1982	
84/641	L339/21	Insurance companies (assistance) Regulations 1987	1987/2130
87/344	L185/77	Insurance companies (credit insurance) Regulations	1990/1159
		Insurance companies (legal expenses insurance) Regulations	1990/1160
88/357	L 172/1	Insurance Companies(Amendment) Regulations	1990/1333
amended by		Friendly Societies (Amendment) Regulations	1993/2519
90/618	L330/49	Friendly Societies (Insurance Business No. 2) Regulations	1993/2520
and		Friendly Societies (Insurance Business) Regulations	1994/1981
92/49	L228/1	Friendly Societies (Amendment) Regulations	1994/1984
		Insurance Companies Ordinance (General Insurance and Long Term Insurance Directives) Regulations of 1996	1996/944
92/49	L228/1	Insurance Companies (Accounts and Statements) (Amendment) Regulations	1994/1515
		Insurance Companies Regulations 199	1994/1516
		Private Medical Insurance (Tax Relief) (Amendment) Regulations	1994/1527
		Insurance Companies (Third Insurance Directives) Regulations	1994/1696
		Insurance Premium Tax (Taxable Insurance Contracts) Order	1994/1698
		Friendly Societies (Insurance Business) Regulations	1994/1981
		Friendly Societies (Authorisation) Regulations	1994/1982
		Friendly Societies (Amendment) Regulations	1994/1983
		Friendly Societies (Amendment) Regulations	1994/1984
		Insurance Companies (Amendment) Regulations	1994/3132
		Insurance Companies (Amendment No. 2) Regulations	1994/3133
		Insurance Companies Ordinance (General Insurance and Long Term Insurance Directives) Regulations of 1996	1996/944

Insurance: Life

Directive	OJ No.	UK Legislation Title	SI No.
79/267	L63/1	Insurance Companies Act 1981	
amended by		Insurance Companies Regulations	1981/1654
90/619	L330/50	Lloyd's (Financial Resources) Regulations	1981/1655
and		Friendly Societies (Long Term Insurance Business) Regulations	1987/2132
92/96	L360/1	Insurance Companies (Transfer of Long Term Business) Regulations	1990/1207
		Friendly Societies (Amendment) Regulations	1993/2519
		Friendly Societies (Insurance Business No. 2) Regulations	1993/2520
		Friendly Societies(Authorisation No. 2) Regulations	1993/2521
		Friendly Societies (Insurance Business) Regulations	1994/1981
		Friendly Societies (Authorisation) Regulations	1994/1982
90/619	L330/50	Insurance Companies (Amendment) Regulations	1992/2890
amended by		Insurance Companies (Amendment) Regulations	1993/174
92/96	L360/1	Insurance Companies(Cancellation) Regulations	1993/1327
		Friendly Societies (Amendment) Regulations	1993/2519
		Friendly Societies (Insurance Business) Regulations	1994/1981
		Friendly Societies (Amendment) Regulations	1994/1984
		Insurance companies ordinance (General insurance and long term insurance directives) Regulations of 1996	1996/944

TABLE TWO OF CROSS REFERENCES[1]

UK IMPLEMENTING LEGISLATION   EC DIRECTIVES

UK Legislation Title	SI No.	Directive	OJ No.
Free movement of persons			
The Immigration (European Economic Area) Order	1994/1895	64/221	L56/50
The Immigration (European Economic Area) Order	1994/1895	68/360	L257/13
The Immigration (European Economic Area) Order	1994/1895	73/148	L172/14
The Immigration (European Economic Area) Order	1994/1895	75/34	L14/10
European Communities (Services of Lawyers) Order 1978	1978/1910	77/249	L78/17
EC (Recognition of professional qualifications) Regulations	1991/824	89/48	L19/16
Immigration (EEA) Order 1994	1994/1895	90/364	L180/26
Immigration (EEA) Order 1994	1994/1895	90/365	L180/28
Immigration (EEA) Order 1994	1994/1895	93/96	L317/59
Social Policy: Equal Pay and Treatment			
Equal Pay Act 1970		75/117	L45/19
Equal Pay (Amendment) Regulations	1983/1794		
Sex Discrimination and Equal Pay (Remedies) Regulations	1993/2798		
Employment Protection (Part-time) Employees Regulations	1995/31		
Sex Discrimination and Equal Pay (Miscellaneous Amendments) Regulations	1996/438		
Sex Discrimination Act 1975		76/207	L39/40
Sex Discrimination (Amendment) Order	1988/249		
Sex Discrimination and Equal Pay (Remedies) Regulations	1993/2798		
Sex Discrimination Act 1975 (Application to Armed Forces) Regulations	1994/3276		
Employment Protection (Part-time) Employees Regulations	1995/31		
Sex Discrimination and Equal Pay (Miscellaneous Amendments) Regulations	1996/438		

Note

[1]Where only one corresponding EC directive reference is given for a number of UK references, this indicates that the content of the Directive has been enacted or deemed already in force in part in all of these pieces of legislation.

UK Legislation Title	SI No.	Directive	OJ No.
Social Security Act 1989		79/7	L6/24
Social Security (Severe Disabilities Allowances) Amendment Regulations	1993/3194		
Social Security (Severe Disabilities Allowances and Invalid Care Allowances) Amendment Regulations	1994/2556		
Pneumonconisosis, Byssiniosis and Miscellaneous Diseases Benefit (Amendment) Scheme	1987/400		
National Health Service (Charges for Drugs and Appointments) Amendment No. 2 Regulations	1995/2737		
Social Security Act 1989		86/378	L225/40
Sex Discrimination Act 1975		86/613	L359/56
Equal Pay Act 1971			
Social Security Act 1975			
Sex Discrimination Act 1986			
Sex Discrimination (Amendment) Order 1988	1988/249		
No reference yet available.		96/97	L46/20
Social Policy: Worker Protection			
Trade Union and Labour Relations (Consolidation) Act 1992		75/129 amended by	L48/29
Trade Union Reform and Employment Rights Act 1993 S.34		92/56	L245/3
Transfer of Undertakings (Protection of Employment) Regulations	1981/1794	77/187	L61/26
Transfer of Undertakings (Protection of Employment) (Amendment) Regulations 1987	1987/442		
Collective Redundancies and Transfer of Undertakings (Protection of Employment) (Amendment) Regulations 1995	1995/2587		
Insolvency Regulations of 1983,		80/987	L283/23
Statutory Rules of Northern Ireland number 282 of 1983		as amended by	
The European Community Act 1978		87/164	L66/11
Health and Safety at Work Act 1974		89/391	L183/1
Employment Protection (Consolidation) Act 1978			
Trade Union Reform and Employment Rights Act 1993			
Health and Safety (First-Aid) Regulations	1981/917		
Reporting of Injuries, Diseases and Dangerous Occurrences Regulations	1985/2023		
The Health and Safety (Miscellaneous Modifications) Regulations	1989/1141		
Management of Health and Safety at Work Regulations	1992/2051		
Workplace (Health, Safety and Welfare) Regulations	1992/3004		
Provision and Use of Work Equipement Regulations	1992/2932		
Personal Protective Equipment at Work Regulations	1992/2966		
Manual Handling Operations Regulations	1992/2793		
Health and Safety (Consultation with Employees) Regulations	1996/1513		
The Fire Precautions (Workplace) Regulations 1997	1997/1840		
Trade Union Reform and Employment Rights Act 1993		91/533	L288/32

UK Legislation Title	SI No.	Directive	OJ No.
Construction (Design and Management) Regulations	1994/3140	92/57	L245/1
Construction (Health, Safety and Welfare) Regulations	1996/1592		
Social Security Contributions and Benefits Act 1992		92/85	L348/1
Trade Union Reform and Employment Rights Act 1993			
Trade Union Reform and Employment Rights Act 1993 (Commencement No. 3 and Transitional Provisions) Order	1994/1365		
Social Security Maternity Benefits and Statutory Sick Pay (Amendment) Regulations	1994/1367		
Maternity Allowance and Statutory Sick Pay Regulations	1994/1230		
The Suspension from Work (on Maternity Grounds) Order	1994/2930		
Management of Health and Safety at Work Regulations	1992/2051		
Management of Health and Safety at Work (Amendment) Regulations	1994/2865		
No reference available yet		93/104	L307/18
The Health and Safety (Young Persons) Regulations 1997	1997/135	94/33	L216/12
Competition			
The Commercial Agents Regulations	1993/3053	86/653	L382/17
Intellectual Property			
Trade Marks Act 1994		89/104	L40/1
Copyright and Related Rights Regulations	1996/2967	92/100	L346/61
Copyright and Related Rights Regulations	1996/2967	93/83	L248/15
Duration of Copyright and Rights in Performances Regulations	1995/3297	93/98	L290/9
Information Technology and Telecommunications			
Broadcasting Act 1990		89/552	L298/23
Copyright (Computer Programmes) Regulations	1992/3233	91/250	L122/42
Copyrights, Designs and Patents Act 1988 (Subject to possible amendment)		96/9	L77/20
No UK Reference available yet.		97/36	L202/60
Public Undertakings			
Public Works Contracts Regulations	1991/2680	89/655	L395/33
Public Supply Contracts Regulations	1991/2679		
Public Services Contracts Regulations	1993/3228		
Utilities Supply and Works Contracts Regulations	1992/3279	92/13	L76/14
Public Services Contracts Regulations	1993/3228	92/50	L209/1
Public Supply Contracts Regulations	1995/201	93/36	L199/1

UK Legislation Title	SI No.	Directive	OJ No.
Public Works Contracts Regulations	1991/2679	93/37	L199/54
Public Works Contracts Regulations	1991/2680		
Public Supply Contracts Regulations	1995/201		
Environmental Provisions			
Control of Pollution Act 1974		75/442	L194/39
Food & Environment Protection Act 1985		as amended by	
Control of Pollution (amendment) Act 1989		91/156	L78/32
Environmental Protection Act 1990			
Town & Country Planning Act 1990			
Control of Pollution (Special Waste) Regulations	1980/1709		
Control of Pollution (landed ships' waste) Regulations	1987/402		
Control of Pollution (Special Waste) Amendment Regulations	1988/1790		
Collection and Disposal of Waste Regulations	1988/819		
Town & Country Planning (assessment of environmental effects) Regulations	1988/1199		
Deposit in the Sea (exemptions) Order	1988/1699		
Control of Pollution (landed ship's waste) (amendment) Regulations	1989/65		
Environmental Protection (Prescribed processes & substances) Regulations	1991/472		
Controlled Waste (Registration of carriers & seizure of vehicles) Regulations	1991/1624		
Control of Pollution (Silage, Slurry & agricultural Fuel oil) Regulations	1991/324		
Disposal of Controlled Waste (Exceptions) Regulations 1991	1991/508		
EP (applications, appeals & registers) and Duty of Care Regulations	1991/2839		
Controlled Waste Regulations	1992/588		
Waste Management Licensing Regulations	1994/1056		
Transfrontier Shipment of Waste Regulations	1994/1137		
Waste Management Regulations	1996/634		
Control of Pollution (Silage, Slurry and Agriculture Fuel Oil) (Amendment) Regulations 1996	1996/2044		
Special Waste Regulations 1996	1996/972		
Control of Pollution (Silage, Slurry and Agricultural Fuel Oil) (Amendment) Regulations 1997	1997/547		
Countryside Act 1968		85/337	L175/40
Control of Pollution Act of 1974, Section 30(1)			
Environmental Protection Act 1990			
Town and Country Planning Act 1990 (and numerous Regulations made under this Act)			
Public Health Act 1936 and the Definitions Of 'Drain' And 'Sewer' In Public Health Act 1875			
Water Act 1973 p. 29			
Water Act 1989 Schedule 8 p. 3 and Schedule 27, Part I			
Water Consolidation (Consequential Provisions) Act 1991, Schedule 1 Paragraph 2(4) Transport and Works Act 1992 (and numerous Regulations issued under it)			
Criminal Damage Act 1971			
Wildlife and Countryside (Service of Notices) Act Order	1988/1249		
Wildlife and Countryside (Amendment) Act 1991			
Wildlife and Countryside (Amendment) Act 1985			
Control Of Pollution (Special Waste) Regulations	1980/1709		

UK Legislation Title	SI No.	Directive	OJ No.
Town and Country Planning (Assessment of Environmental Effects) Regulations	1988/1199		
Environmental Assessment (Afforestation) Regulations	1988/1207		
Environmental Assessment (Salmon Farming in Marine Waters) Regulations	1988/1218		
Land Drainage Improvment (Assessment of Environmental Effects) Regulations	1988/1217		
Highways (Assessment of Environmental Effects) Regulations	1988/1241		
Town and Country Development (Amendment) Order	1988/1272		
Harbour Works (Assessment of Environmental Effects) Regulations	1988/1336		
Transfrontier Shipment of Hazardous Waste Regulations 1988	1988/1562		
Transfrontier Shipment of Waste Regulations 1994	1994/1137		
Electronic and Pipe-Line Works (Assessment of Environmental Effects) Regulations	1989/167		
Electricity & Pipe-Line Works (Assessment of Environmental Effects) Regulations 1990	1990/442		
Harbour Works (Assessment of Environmental Effects) (No. 2) Regulations	1989/424		
Harbour Works (Assessment of Environmental Effects) (Amendment) Regulations 1996	1996/1946		
Town & Country Planning (Assessment of Environmental Effects) (Amendment) Regulations 1990	1990/367		
Town & Country Planning (Assessment of Environmental Effects) (Amendment) Regulations 1992	1992/1494		
The Town & Country Planning (Assessment of Environmental Effects) (Amendment) Regulations 1994	1994/677		
Highways (Assessment of Environmental Effects) Regulations	1994/1002		
Town and Country Planning (General Development) (Amendment) Order	1994/678		
Town and Country Planning (Environmental Assesment and unauthorised Development) Regulations	1995/2258		
Land Drainage Improvement Works (Assessment of Environmental Effects) (Amendment) Regulations 1995	1995/2195		
Consumer Protection			
Consumer Protection the control of misleading advertising Regulations	1988/915	84/450	L250/17
Financial Services Act 1986 Order 198	1988/740		
Consumer Protection Act 1987		85/374	L210/29
Consumer Protection (Cancellation of Contracts concluded away from business premises) Regulations	1988/958	85/577	L372/31
Consumer Credit Act 1974		87/102	L42/48
Consumer Credit (Total charge for credit) Regulations	1980/51		
Consumer Credit (Agreements) Regulations	1983/1553		
Consumer Credit (Agreements) (Amendment) Regulations	1984/1600		
Consumer Credit (Total charge for credit) (Amendment) Regulations	1985/1192		
Consumer Credit (Total charge for credit and rebate on early settlement) (Amendment) Regulations	1989/596		
Toys (Safety) Regulations	1989/1275	88/378 amended by	L187/1
Toys (Safety) Regulations	1995/204	93/68	L220/1

UK Legislation Title	SI No.	Directive	OJ No.
Package Holidays and package Tours Regulations	1992/3288	90/314	L158/59
The General Product Safety Regulations	1994/2328	92/59	L288/24
Simple Pressure Vessels (Safety) (Amendment) Regulations	1994/3098		
Construction Products (Amendment) Regulations	1994/3051		
Electromagnetic Compatibility (Amendment) Regulations	1994/3080		
Supply of Machinery (Safety) (Amendment) Regulations	1994/2063		
Personal Protective Equipment (EC Directive) (Amendment) Regulations	1994/2326		
Non-automatic Weighing Instruments (EEC Requirements) Regulations	1995/1907		
Active Implantable Medical Devices (Amendment and Transitional Provisions) Regulations	1995/1671		
The Gas Appliances (Safety) Regulations	1995/1629		
Telecommunications Terminal Equipment (Amendment and Extension) Regulations	1994/3129		
Boiler (Efficiency) Regulations	1993/3083		
Boiler (Efficiency) (Amendment) Regulations	1994/3083		
Electrical Equipment (Safety) Regulations	1994/3260		
Unfair Terms in Consumer Contracts Regulations	1994/3159	93/13	L95/29
Financial Services			
Banking and Finance			
Public Trustee (Custodian Trustee) Rules	1975/1189	73/183	L194/1
Authorised Unit Trust Schemes Regulations	1976/195		
Banking Act 1979		77/780	L322/30
Banking Regulations	1979/938		
Banking Act 1987			
Notice Bank of England BSD/1990/2		89/299	L124/16
Prudential Note 1992/1 of the Building Societies Commission under the Building Societies Act 1986			
Banking Co-ordination (Second Council Directive) Regulations	1992/3218	89/646	L386/1
Banking Co-ordination (Second Council Directive) (Amendment) Regulations	1992/3225		
Notice to Institutions authorised under the Banking Act 1987 (BSD/1990/3) 01/12/90		89/647	L386/14
Amendments to the Bank Statute Notice implementation in the UK of the Solvency Ratio Directive (BSD1990/3)			
Prudential Note 1992/1 under the Building Societies Act 1986 1992/1611, 1992/1612, 1988/777, 1991/702, 1991/1729			
Money Laundering Regulations	1993/1933	91/308	L166/77
Criminal Justice Act 1993			
Value Added Tax Act 1994 (and amendments to be made)		97/5	L43/25
Insurance Sector: Non Life			
Insurance Companies (Classes of General Business) Regulations	1977/1552	73/239	L228/3

UK Legislation Title	SI No.	Directive	OJ No.
Insurance Companies (Solvency: General Business) Regulations	1977/1553	amended by	
Insurance Companies (Authorisation and Accounts: General Business) Regulations		76/580	L189/13
	1978/720	84/641	L339/21
Insurance Companies (Deposits) Regulations	1978/917	87/343	L185/72
Lloyd's (General Business) Regulations	1979/956	87/344	1185/77
Insurance (Transfer of General Business) Regulations	1980/956	90/618	L330/44
Insurance Companies Act 1981		90/619	L330/50
Insurance Companies Regulations	1981/1654	92/49	L228/1
Lloyd's (Financial Resources) Regulations	1981/1655		
Insurance Companies (Assistance) Regulations	1987/2130		
Insurance Companies (Credit Insurance) Regulations	1990/1159		
Insurance Companies (legal expenses insurance) Regulation	1990/1160		
Insurance companies (legal expenses insurance) (application for authorisation) Regulations	1990/1181		
Insurance Companies (Amendment) Regulations	1990/1333		
Insurance Companies (credit insurance) Regulations	1993/2519		
Friendly Societies (Insurance Business No. 2) Regulations	1993/2520		
Friendly Societies (Authorisation No. 2) Regulations	1993/2521		
Friendly Societies (Insurance Business) Regulations	1994/1981		
Friendly Societies (Authorisation) Regulations	1994/1982		
Insurance Companies (Reserves) Regulations	1996/1181		
Insurance Companies Ordinance (General Insurance and Long Term Insurance Directives) Regulations of 1996			
Co-Insurance (Determination of Certain Liabilities) Regulations	1981/710	78/473	L151/25
Insurance Companies Regulations	1981/1654		
Insurance Companies Act 1982			
Insurance companies (assistance) Regulations 1987	1987/2130	84/641	L339/21
Insurance companies (credit insurance) Regulations	1990/1159	87/344	L185/77
Insurance companies (legal expenses insurance) Regulations	1990/1160		
Insurance Companies (Amendment) Regulations	1990/1333	88/357	L172/1
Friendly Societies (Amendment) Regulations	1993/2519	amended by	
Friendly Societies (Insurance Business No. 2) Regulations	1993/2520	90/618	L330/49
Friendly Societies (Insurance Business) Regulations	1994/1981	and	
Friendly Societies (Amendment) Regulations	1994/1984	92/49	L228/1
Insurance Companies Ordinance (General Insurance and Long Term Insurance Directives) Regulations of 1996	1996/944		
Insurance Companies (Accounts and Statements) (Amendment) Regulations	1994/1515	92/49	L228/1
Insurance Companies Regulations 1994	1994/1516		
Private Medical Insurance (Tax Relief) (Amendment) Regulations	1994/1527		
Insurance Companies (Third insurance Directives) Regulations	1994/1696		
Insurance Premium Tax (Taxable Insurance Contracts) Order	1994/1698		
Friendly Societies (Insurance Business) Regulations	1994/1981		
Friendly Societies (Authorisation) Regulations	1994/1982		
Friendly Societies (Amendment) Regulations	1994/1983		
Friendly Societies (Amendment) Regulations	1994/1984		

UK Legislation Title	SI No.	Directive OJ No.	
Insurance Companies (Amendment) Regulations	1994/3132		
Insurance Companies (Amendment No. 2) Regulations	1994/3133		
Insurance Companies Ordinance (General Insurance and Long Term Insurance Directives) Regulations of 1996	1996/944		
Insurance: Life			
Insurance Companies Act 1981	79/267	L63/1	
Insurance Companies Regulations	1981/1654	amended by	
Lloyd's (Financial Resources) Regulations	1981/1655	90/619	L330/50
Friendly Societies (Long Term Insurance Business) Regulations	1987/2132	and	
Insurance Companies (Transfer of Long Term Business) Regulations	1990/1207	92/96	L360/1
Friendly Societies (Amendment) Regulations	1993/2519		
Friendly Societies (Insurance Business No. 2) Regulations	1993/2520		
Friendly Societies(Authorisation No. 2) Regulations	1993/2521		
Friendly Societies (Insurance Business) Regulations	1994/1981		
Friendly Societies (Authorisation) Regulations	1994/1982		
Insurance Companies (Amendment) Regulations	1992/2890	90/619	L330/50
Insurance Companies (Amendment) Regulations	1993/174	amended by	
Insurance Companies(Cancellation) Regulations	1993/1327	92/96	L360/1
Friendly Societies (Amendment) Regulations	1993/2519		
Friendly Societies (Insurance Business) Regulations	1994/1981		
Friendly Societies (Amendment) Regulations	1994/1984		
Insurance companies ordinance (General insurance and long term insurance directives) Regulations of 1996	1996/944		
The insurance companies (accounts and statements) (amendment) Regulation	1994/1515	92/96	L360/1
Insurance Companies Regulations	1994/1516		
Insurance Companies (Third insurance Directives) Regulations	1994/1696		
Friendly Societies (Insurance Business) Regulations	1994/1981		
Friendly Societies (Authorisation) Regulations	1994/1982		
Friendly Societies (Amendment) Regulations	1994/1984		
Insurance Companies (Amendment) Regulations 1994	1994/3132		
Insurance companies (Amendment No. 2) Regulations 1994	1994/3133		
Insurance companies ordinance (general insurance and long term insurance directives) Regulations	1996/944		

PRIMARY LEGISLATION

TREATY ESTABLISHING THE EUROPEAN COMMUNITY[1]

His Majesty the King of the Belgians,
The President of the Federal Republic of Germany,
The President of the French Republic,
The President of the Italian Republic,
His Royal Highness the Grand Duke of Luxembourg,
Her Majesty the Queen of the Netherlands,

DETERMINED to lay the foundations of an ever closer union among the peoples of Europe,

RESOLVED to ensure the economic and social progress of their countries by common action to eliminate the barriers which divide Europe,

AFFIRMING as the essential objective of their efforts the constant improvement of the living and working conditions of their peoples,

RECOGNISING that the removal of existing obstacles calls for concerted action in order to guarantee steady expansion, balanced trade and fair competition,

ANXIOUS to strengthen the unity of their economies and to ensure their harmonious development by reducing the differences existing between the various regions and the backwardness of the less favoured regions,

DESIRING to contribute, by means of a common commercial policy, to the progressive abolition of restrictions on international trade,

INTENDING to confirm the solidarity which binds Europe and the overseas countries and desiring to ensure the development of their prosperity, in accordance with the principles of the Charter of the United Nations,

Note

[1]Title as amended by the Treaty amending Certain Financial Provisions, the Single European Act, the Merger Treaty, the Greenland Treaty, and Acts of Accession and Article G(1) of the Treaty on European Union (hereinafter referred to as 'TEU'). The reader will find in the following pages a complete, amended version of the Treaty establishing the European Economic Community as it has emerged following the 'entry into force of Title II of the TEU: Provisions amending the Treaty establishing the European Economic Community with a view to establishing the European Community' (Articles G(1) to (84)).

RESOLVED by thus pooling their resources to preserve and strengthen peace and liberty, and calling upon the other peoples of Europe who share their ideal to join in their efforts,

HAVE DECIDED to create a European Community and to this end have designated as their Plenipotentiaries:

His Majesty the King of the Belgians:
Mr Paul-Henri Spaak,
Minister for Foreign Affairs,
Baron J. Ch. Snoy et d'Oppuers,
Secretary-General of the Ministry of Economic Affairs, Head of the Belgian Delegation to the Intergovernmental Conference;
The President of the Federal Republic of Germany:
Dr Konrad Adenauer,
Federal Chancellor,
Professor Dr Walter Hallstein,
State Secretary of the Federal Foreign Office;
The President of the French Republic:
Mr Christian Pineau,
Minister for Foreign Affairs,
Mr Maurice Faure,
Under-Secretary of State for Foreign Affairs;
The President of the Italian Republic:
Mr Antonio Segni,
President of the Council of Ministers,
Professor Gaetano Martino,
Minister for Foreign Affairs;
Her Royal Highness the Grand Duchess of Luxembourg:
Mr Joseph Bech,
President of the Government, Minister for Foreign Affairs,
Mr Lambert Schaus,
Ambassador, Head of the Luxembourg Delegation of the Intergovernmental Conference;
Her Majesty the Queen of the Netherlands:
Mr Joseph Luns,
Minister for Foreign Affairs,
Mr J. Linthorst Homan,
Head of the Netherlands Delegation to the Intergovernmental Conference;

WHO, having exchanged their Full Powers, found in good and due form, have agreed as follows.

PART ONE   PRINCIPLES

Article 1
By this Treaty, the High Contracting Parties establish among themselves a *European Community*.

Article 2[1]
The Community shall have as its task, by establishing a common market *and an economic and monetary union and by implementing the common*

Note
[1] As amended by Article G(2) TEU.

policies or activities referred to in Articles 3 and 3a, to promote throughout the Community a harmonious *and balanced* development of economic activities, *sustainable and non-inflationary growth respecting the environment, a high degree of convergence of economic performance, a high level of employment and of social protection, the raising of the standard of living and quality of life, and economic and social cohesion and solidarity among Member States*.

Article 3[1]
For the purposes set out in Article 2, the activities of the Community shall include, as provided in this Treaty and in accordance with the timetable set out therein:

    (a)   the elimination, as between Member States, of customs duties and quantitative restrictions on the import and export of goods, and of all other measures having equivalent effect;

    (b)   *a common commercial policy;*

    (c)   *an internal market characterised by* the abolition, as between Member States, of obstacles to the free movement of goods, persons, services and capital;

    (d)   *measures concerning the entry and movement of persons in the internal market as provided for in Article 100c;*

    (e)   *a common policy in the sphere of agriculture and fisheries;*

    (f)   *a common policy in the sphere of transport;*

    (g)   *a system ensuring that competition in the internal market is not distorted;*

    (h)   the approximation of the laws of Member States to the extent required for the functioning of the common market;

    (i)   *a policy in the social sphere comprising a European Social Fund;*

    (j)   *the strengthening of economic and social cohesion;*

    (k)   *a policy in the sphere of the environment;*

    (l)   *the strengthening of the competitiveness of Community industry;*

    (m)   *the promotion of research and technological development;*

    (n)   *encouragement for the establishment and development of trans-European networks;*

    (o)   *a contribution to the attainment of a high level of health protection;*

    (p)   *a contribution to education and training of quality and to the flowering of the cultures of the Member States;*

    (q)   *a policy in the sphere of development cooperation;*

    (r)   *the association of the overseas countries and territories in order to increase trade and promote jointly economic and social development;*

    (s)   *a contribution to the strengthening of consumer protection;*

    (t)   *measures in the spheres of energy, civil protection and tourism.*

Note
[1]As amended by Article G(3) TEU.

Article 3a[1]

1.   For the purposes set out in Article 2, the activities of the Member States and the Community shall include, as provided in this Treaty and in accordance with the timetable set out therein, the adoption of an economic policy which is based on the close coordination of Member States' economic policies, on the internal market and on the definition of common objectives, and conducted in accordance with the principle of an open market economy with free competition.

2.   Concurrently with the foregoing, and as provided in this Treaty and in accordance with the timetable and the procedures set out therein, these activities shall include the irrevocable fixing of exchange rates leading to the introduction of a single currency, the ECU, and the definition and conduct of a single monetary policy and exchange rate policy the primary objective of both of which shall be to maintain price stability and, without prejudice to this objective, to support the general economic policies in the Community, in accordance with the principle of an open market economy with free competition.

3.   These activities of the Member States and the Community shall entail compliance with the following guiding principles; stable prices, sound public finances and monetary conditions and a sustainable balance of payments.

Note
[1]As inserted by Article G(4) TEU.

Article 3b[1]

The Community shall act within the limits of the powers conferred upon it by this Treaty and of the objectives assigned to it therein.

In areas which do not fall within its exclusive competence, the Community shall take action, in accordance with the principle of subsidiarity, only if and in so far as the objectives of the proposed action cannot be sufficiently achieved by the Member States and can therefore, by reason of the scale or effects of the proposed action, be better achieved by the Community.

Any action by the Community shall not go beyond what is necessary to achieve the objectives of this Treaty.

Note
[1]As inserted by Article G(5) TEU.

Article 4[1]

1.   The tasks entrusted to the Community shall be carried out by the following institutions:
   — a European Parliament,
   — a Council,
   — a Commission,
   — a Court of Justice,
   — *a Court of Auditors.*

Each institution shall act within the limits of the powers conferred upon it by this Treaty.

Note
[1]As amended by Article G(6) TEU.

2. The Council and the Commission shall be assisted by an Economic and Social Committee *and a Committee of the Regions* acting in an advisory capacity.

Article 4a[1]

A European System of Central Banks (hereinafter referred to as 'ESCB') and a European Central Bank (hereinafter referred to as 'ECB') shall be established in accordance with the procedures laid down in this Treaty; they shall act within the limits of the powers conferred upon them by this Treaty and by the Statute of the ESCB and of the ECB (hereinafter referred to as 'Statute of the ESCB') annexed thereto.

Note
[1]As inserted by Article G(7) TEU.

Article 4b[1]

A European Investment Bank is hereby established, which shall act within the limits of the powers conferred upon it by this Treaty and the Statute annexed thereto.

Note
[1]As inserted by Article G(7) TEU.

Article 5

Member States shall take all appropriate measures, whether general or particular, to ensure fulfilment of the obligations arising out of this Treaty or resulting from action taken by the institutions of the Community. They shall facilitate the achievement of the Community's tasks.

They shall abstain from any measure which could jeopardise the attainment of the objectives of this Treaty.

Article 6[1]

Within the scope of application of this Treaty, and without prejudice to any special provisions contained therein, any discrimination on grounds of nationality shall be prohibited.

The Council, acting in accordance with the procedure referred to in Article 189c, may adopt rules designed to prohibit such discrimination.

Note
[1]As amended by Article G(8) TEU.

Article 7[1]

1. The common market shall be progressively established during a transitional period of twelve years.

This transitional period shall be divided into three stages of four years each; the length of each stage may be altered in accordance with the provisions set out below.

2. To each stage there shall be assigned a set of actions to be initiated and carried through concurrently.

Note
[1]Articles 7, 7a, 7b and 7c: former Articles 8, 8a, 8b and 8c (Article G(9) TEU).

3.   Transition from the first to the second stage shall be conditional upon a finding that the objectives specifically laid down in this Treaty for the first stage have in fact been attained in substance and that, subject to the exceptions and procedures provided for in this Treaty, the obligations have been fulfilled.

This finding shall be made at the end of the fourth year by the Council, acting unanimously on a report from the Commission. A Member State may not, however, prevent unanimity by relying upon the non-fulfilment of its own obligations. Failing unanimity, the first stage shall automatically be extended for one year.

At the end of the fifth year, the Council shall make its finding under the same conditions. Failing unanimity, the first stage shall automatically be extended for a further year.

At the end of the sixth year, the Council shall make its finding, acting by a qualified majority on a report from the Commission.

4.   Within one month of the last-mentioned vote any Member State which voted with the minority or, if the required majority was not obtained, any Member State shall be entitled to call upon the Council to appoint an arbitration board whose decision shall be binding upon all Member States and upon the institutions of the Community. The arbitration board shall consist of three members appointed by the Council acting unanimously on a proposal from the Commission.

If the Council has not appointed the members of the arbitration board within one month of being called upon to do so, they shall be appointed by the Court of Justice within a further period of one month.

The arbitration board shall elect its own Chairman.

The board shall make its award within six months of the date of the Council vote referred to in the last subparagraph of paragraph 3.

5.   The second and third stages may not be extended or curtailed except by a decision of the Council, acting unanimously on a proposal from the Commission.

6.   Nothing in the preceding paragraphs shall cause the transitional period to last more than fifteen years after the entry into force of this Treaty.

7.   Save for the exceptions or derogations provided for in this Treaty, the expiry of the transitional period shall constitute the latest date by which all the rules laid down must enter into force and all the measures required for establishing the common market must be implemented.

Article 7a

The Community shall adopt measures with the aim of progressively establishing the internal market over a period expiring on 31 December 1992, in accordance with the provisions of this Article and of Articles 7b, 7c, 28, 57(2), 59, 70(1), 84, 99, 100a and 100b and without prejudice to the other provisions of this Treaty.

The internal market shall comprise an area without internal frontiers in which the free movement of goods, persons, services and capital is ensured in accordance with the provisions of this Treaty.[1]

Note

[1] See in this respect the Regulation 2317/95 (OJ L234/1) in respect of visa requirements for nationals of third countries.

Article 7b

The Commission shall report to the Council before 31 December 1988 and again before 31 December 1990 on the progress made towards achieving the internal market within the time limit fixed in Article 7a.

The Council, acting by a qualified majority on a proposal from the Commission, shall determine the guidelines and conditions necessary to ensure balanced progress in all the sectors concerned.

Article 7c

When drawing up its proposals with a view to achieving the objectives set out in Article 7a, the Commission shall take into account the extent of the effort that certain economies showing differences in development will have to sustain during the period of establishment of the internal market and it may propose appropriate provisions.

If these provisions take the form of derogations, they must be of a temporary nature and must cause the least possible disturbance to the functioning of the common market.

PART TWO[1]   CITIZENSHIP OF THE UNION

Article 8

1. *Citizenship of the Union is hereby established.*
Every person holding the nationality of a Member State shall be a citizen of the Union.

2. *Citizens of the Union shall enjoy the rights conferred by this Treaty and shall be subject to the duties imposed thereby.*

Article 8a

1. *Every citizen of the Union shall have the right to move and reside freely within the territory of the Member States, subject to the limitations and conditions laid down in this Treaty and by the measures adopted to give it effect.*

2. *The Council may adopt provisions with a view to facilitating the exercise of the rights referred to in paragraph 1; save as otherwise provided in this Treaty, the Council shall act unanimously on a proposal from the Commission and after obtaining the assent of the European Parliament.*

Note
[1]Part Two as inserted by Article G.C TEU.

Article 8b

1. *Every citizen of the Union residing in a Member State of which he is not a national shall have the right to vote and to stand as a candidate at municipal elections in the Member State in which he resides, under the same conditions as nationals of that State. This right shall be exercised subject to detailed arrangements to be adopted before 31 December 1994 by the Council, acting unanimously on a proposal from the Commission and after consulting the European Parliament; these arrangements may provide for derogations where warranted by problems specific to a Member State.[1]*

Note
[1]Editor's Note: These arrangements are contained in Directive 94/80 (OJ 1994 L368) which came into force on 1 January 1996.

2. *Without prejudice to Article 138(3) and to the provisions adopted for its implementation, every citizen of the Union residing in a Member State of which he is not a national shall have the right to vote and to stand as a candidate in elections to the European Parliament in the Member State in which he resides, under the same conditions as nationals of that State. This right shall be exercised subject to detailed arrangements to be adopted before 31 December 1993 by the Council, acting unanimously on a proposal from the Commission and after consulting the European Parliament; these arrangements may provide for derogations where warranted by problems specific to a Member State.[2]*

Article 8c
Every citizen of the Union shall, in the territory of a third country in which the Member State of which he is a national is not represented, be entitled to protection by the diplomatic or consular authorities of any Member State, on the same conditions as the nationals of that State. Before 31 December 1993, Member States shall establish the necessary rules among themselves and start the international negotiations required to secure this protection.

Article 8d
Every citizen of the Union shall have the right to petition the European Parliament in accordance with Article 138d.
    Every citizen of the Union may apply to the Ombudsman established in accordance with Article 138e.

Article 8e
The Commission shall report to the European Parliament, to the Council and to the Economic and Social Committee before 31 December 1993 and then every three years on the application of the provisions of this Part. This report shall take account of the development of the Union.
    On this basis, and without prejudice to the other provisions of this Treaty, the Council, acting unanimously on a proposal from the Commission and after consulting the European Parliament, may adopt provisions to strengthen or to add to the rights laid down in this Part, which it shall recommend to the Member States for adoption in accordance with their respective constitutional requirements.

Notes
[2]Editor's Note: These arrangements are contained in Council Directive 93/109 (OJ 1993 L329/34) which is in force from the date of publication.

PART THREE[3]   COMMUNITY POLICIES
TITLE I   FREE MOVEMENT OF GOODS

Article 9
    1. The Community shall be based upon a customs union which shall cover all trade in goods and which shall involve the prohibition between Member States of customs duties on imports and exports and of all charges having

Note
[3]Part Three, regrouping former Parts Two and Three (Article G.D TEU).

equivalent effect, and the adoption of a common customs tariff in their relations with third countries.

2. The provisions of Chapter 1, Section 1, and of Chapter 2 of this Title shall apply to products originating in Member States and to products coming from third countries which are in free circulation in Member States.

Article 10

1. Products coming from a third country shall be considered to be in free circulation in a Member State if the import formalities have been complied with and any customs duties or charges having equivalent effect which are payable have been levied in that Member State, and if they have not benefited from a total or partial drawback of such duties or charges.

2. The Commission shall, before the end of the first year after the entry into force of this Treaty, determine the methods of administrative cooperation to be adopted for the purpose of applying Article 9(2), taking into account the need to reduce as much as possible formalities imposed on trade.

Before the end of the first year after the entry into force of this Treaty, the Commission shall lay down the provisions applicable, as regards trade between Member States, to goods originating in another Member State in whose manufacture products have been used on which the exporting Member State has not levied the appropriate customs duties or charges having equivalent effect, or which have benefited from a total or partial drawback of such duties or charges.

In adopting these provisions, the Commission shall take into account the rules for the elimination of customs duties within the Community and for the progressive application of the common customs tariff.

Article 11

Member States shall take all appropriate measures to enable Governments to carry out, within the periods of time laid down, the obligations with regard to customs duties which devolve upon them pursuant to this Treaty.

CHAPTER 1 THE CUSTOMS UNION
SECTION 1 ELIMINATION OF CUSTOMS DUTIES BETWEEN MEMBER STATES

Article 12

Member States shall refrain from introducing between themselves any new customs duties on imports or exports or any charges having equivalent effect, and from increasing those which they already apply in their trade with each other.

Article 13

1. Customs duties on imports in force between Member States shall be progressively abolished by them during the transitional period in accordance with Articles 14 and 15.

2. Charges having an effect equivalent to customs duties on imports, in force between Member States, shall be progressively abolished by them during the transitional period. The Commission shall determine by means of directives the timetable for such abolition. It shall be guided by the rules contained in Article 14(2) and (3) and by the directives issued by the Council pursuant to Article 14(2).

Article 14

1. For each product, the basic duty to which the successive reductions shall be applied shall be the duty applied on 1 January 1957.

2. The timetable for the reductions shall be determined as follows:

(a) during the first stage, the first reduction shall be made one year after the date when this Treaty enters into force; the second reduction, eighteen months later; the third reduction, at the end of the fourth year after the date when this Treaty enters into force;

(b) during the second stage, a reduction shall be made eighteen months after that stage begins; a second reduction, eighteen months after the preceding one; a third reduction, one year later;

(c) any remaining reductions shall be made during the third stage; the Council shall, acting by a qualified majority on a proposal from the Commission, determine the timetable therefor by means of directives.

3. At the time of the first reduction, Member States shall introduce between themselves a duty on each product equal to the basic duty minus 10%.

At the time of each subsequent reduction, each Member State shall reduce its customs duties as a whole in such manner as to lower by 10% its total customs receipts as defined in paragraph 4 and to reduce the duty on each product by at least 5% of the basic duty.

In the case, however, of products on which the duty is still in excess of 30%, each reduction must be at least 10% of the basic duty.

4. The total customs receipts of each Member State, as referred to in paragraph 3, shall be calculated by multiplying the value of its imports from other Member States during 1956 by the basic duties.

5. Any special problems raised in applying paragraphs 1 to 4 shall be settled by directives issued by the Council acting by a qualified majority on a proposal from the Commission.

6. Member States shall report to the Commission on the manner in which effect has been given to the preceding rules for the reduction of duties. They shall endeavour to ensure that the reduction made in the duties on each product shall amount:

— at the end of the first stage, to at least 25% of the basic duty;

— at the end of the second stage, to at least 50% of the basic duty.

If the Commission finds that there is a risk that the objectives laid down in Article 13, and the percentages laid down in this paragraph, cannot be attained, it shall make all appropriate recommendations to Member States.

7. The provisions of this Article may be amended by the Council, acting unanimously on a proposal from the Commission and after consulting the European Parliament.

Article 15

1. Irrespective of the provisions of Article 14, any Member State may, in the course of the transitional period, suspend in whole or in part the collection of duties applied by it to products imported from other Member States. It shall inform the other Member States and the Commission thereof.

2. The Member States declare their readiness to reduce customs duties against the other Member States more rapidly than is provided for in Article 14 if their general economic situation and the situation of the economic sector concerned so permit.

To this end, the Commission shall make recommendations to the Member States concerned.

Article 16
Member States shall abolish between themselves customs duties on exports and charges having equivalent effect by the end of the first stage at the latest.

Article 17
1. The provisions of Articles 9 to 15(1) shall also apply to customs duties of a fiscal nature. Such duties shall not, however, be taken into consideration for the purpose of calculating either total customs receipts or the reduction of customs duties as a whole as referred to in Article 14(3) and (4).

Such duties shall, at each reduction, be lowered by not less than 10% of the basic duty. Member States may reduce such duties more rapidly than is provided for in Article 14.

2. Member States shall, before the end of the first year after the entry into force of this Treaty, inform the Commission of their customs duties of a fiscal nature.

3. Member States shall retain the right to substitute for these duties an internal tax which complies with the provisions of Article 95.

4. If the Commission finds that substitution for any customs duty of a fiscal nature meets with serious difficulties in a Member State, it shall authorise that State to retain the duty on condition that it shall abolish it not later than six years after the entry into force of this Treaty. Such authorisation must be applied for before the end of the first year after the entry into force of this Treaty.

SECTION 2   SETTING UP OF THE COMMON CUSTOMS TARIFF

Article 18
The Member States declare their readiness to contribute to the development of international trade and the lowering of barriers to trade by entering into agreements designed, on a basis of reciprocity and mutual advantage, to reduce customs duties below the general level of which they could avail themselves as a result of the establishment of a customs union between them.

Article 19
1. Subject to the conditions and within the limits provided for hereinafter, duties in the common customs tariff shall be at the level of the arithmetical average of the duties applied in the four customs territories comprised in the Community.

2. The duties taken as the basis for calculating this average shall be those applied by Member States on 1 January 1957.

In the case of the Italian tariff, however, the duty applied shall be that without the temporary 10% reduction. Furthermore, with respect to items on which the Italian tariff contains a conventional duty, this duty shall be substituted for the duty applied as defined above, provided that it does not exceed the latter by more than 10%. Where the conventional duty exceeds the duty applied as defined above by more than 10%, the latter duty plus 10% shall be taken as the basis for calculating the arithmetical average.

With regard to the tariff hearing in List A, the duties shown in that List shall, for the purpose of calculating the arithmetical average, be substituted for the duties applied.

3.   The duties in the common customs tariff shall not exceed:
  (a)   3% for products within the tariff headings in List B;
  (b)   10% for products within the tariff headings in List C;
  (c)   15% for products within the tariff headings in List D;
  (d)   25% for products within the tariff headings in List E; where in respect
of such products, the tariff of the Benelux countries contains a duty not
exceeding 3%, such duty shall, for the purpose of calculating the arithmetical
average, be raised to 12%.

4.   List F prescribes the duties applicable to the products listed therein.

5.   The Lists of tariff headings referred to in this Article and in Article 20 are
set out in Annex I to this Treaty.

Article 20

The duties applicable to the products in List G shall be determined by
negotiation between the Member States. Each Member State may add further
products to this List to a value not exceeding 2% of the total value of its imports
from third countries in the course of the year 1956.

The Commission shall take all appropriate steps to ensure that such
negotiations shall be undertaken before the end of the second year after the
entry into force of this Treaty and be concluded before the end of the first stage.

If, for certain products, no agreement can be reached within these periods,
the Council shall, on a proposal from the Commission, acting unanimously
until the end of the second stage and by a qualified majority thereafter,
determine the duties in the common customs tariff.

Article 21

1.   Technical difficulties which may arise in applying Articles 19 and 20
shall be resolved, within two years of the entry into force of this Treaty, by
directives issued by the Council acting by a qualified majority on a proposal
from the Commission.

2.   Before the end of the first stage, or at latest when the duties are
determined, the Council shall, acting by a qualified majority on a proposal from
the Commission, decide on any adjustments required in the interests of the
internal consistency of the common customs tariff as a result of applying the
rules set out in Articles 19 and 20, taking account in particular of the degree of
processing undergone by the various goods to which the common tariff applies.

Article 22

The Commission shall, within two years of the entry into force of this Treaty,
determine the extent to which the customs duties of a fiscal nature referred to
in Article 17(2) shall be taken into account in calculating the arithmetical
average provided for in Article 19(1). The Commission shall take account of
any protective character which such duties may have.

Within six months of such determination, any Member State may request
that the procedure provided for in Article 20 should be applied to the product
in question, but in this event the percentage limit provided in that Article shall
not be applicable to that State.

Article 23

1.   For the purpose of the progressive introduction of the common customs
tariff, Member States shall amend their tariffs applicable to third countries as
follows:

(a)   in the case of tariff headings on which the duties applied in practice on 1 January 1957 do not differ by more than 15% in either direction from the duties in the common customs tariff, the latter duties shall be applied at the end of the fourth year after the entry into force of this Treaty;

(b)   in any other case, each Member State shall, as from the same date, apply a duty reducing by 30% the difference between the duty applied in practice on 1 January 1957 and the duty in the common customs tariff;

(c)   at the end of the second stage this difference shall again be reduced by 30%;

(d)   in the case of tariff headings for which the duties in the common customs tariff are not yet available at the end of the first stage, each Member State shall, within six months of the Council's action in accordance with Article 20, apply such duties as would result from application of the rules contained in this paragraph.

2.   Where a Member State has been granted an authorisation under Article 17(4), it need not, for as long as that authorisation remains valid, apply the preceding provisions to the tariff headings to which the authorisation applies. When such authorisation expires, the Member State concerned shall apply such duty as would have resulted from application of the rules contained in paragraph 1.

3.   The common custom tariff shall be applied in its entirety by the end of the transitional period at the latest.

Article 24
Member States shall remain free to change their duties more rapidly than is provided for in Article 23 in order to bring them into line with the common customs tariff.

Article 25
1.   If the Commission finds that the production in Member States of particular products contained in Lists B, C and D is insufficient to supply the demands of one of the Member States, and that such supply traditionally depends to a considerable extent on imports from third countries, the Council shall, acting by a qualified majority on a proposal from the Commission, grant the Member State concerned tariff quotas at a reduced rate of duty or duty free.

Such quotas may not exceed the limits beyond which the risk might arise of activities being transferred to the detriment of other Member States.

2.   In the case of the products in List E, and of those in List G for which the rates of duty have been determined in accordance with the procedure provided for in the third paragraph of Article 20, the Commission shall, where a change in sources of supply or shortage of supplies within the Community is such as to entail harmful consequences for the processing industries of a Member State, at the request of that Member State, grant it tariff quotas at a reduced rate of duty or duty free.

Such quotas may not exceed the limits beyond which the risk might arise of activities being transferred to the detriment of other Member States.

3.   In the case of the products listed in Annex II to this Treaty, the Commission may authorise any Member State to suspend, in whole or in part, collection of the duties applicable or may grant such Member State tariff quotas at a reduced rate of duty or duty free, provided that no serious disturbance of the market of the products concerned results therefrom.

4. The Commission shall periodically examine tariff quotas granted pursuant to this Article.

Article 26
The Commission may authorise any Member State encountering special difficulties to postpone the lowering or raising of duties provided for in Article 23 in respect of particular headings in its tariff.

Such authorisation may only be granted for a limited period and in respect of tariff headings which, taken together, represent for such State not more than 5% of the value of its imports from third countries in the course of the latest year for which statistical data are available.

Article 27
Before the end of the first stage, Member States shall, in so far as may be necessary, take steps to approximate their provisions laid down by law, regulation or administrative action in respect of customs matters. To this end, the Commission shall make all appropriate recommendations to Member States.

Article 28
Any autonomous alteration or suspension of duties in the common customs tariff shall be decided by the Council acting by a qualified majority on a proposal from the Commission.

Article 29
In carrying out the tasks entrusted to it under this Section the Commission shall be guided by:

    (a) the need to promote trade between Member States and third countries;

    (b) developments in conditions of competition within the Community in so far as they lead to an improvement in the competitive capacity of undertakings;

    (c) the requirements of the Community as regards the supply of raw materials and semi-finished goods; in this connection the Commission shall take care to avoid distorting conditions of competition between Member States in respect of finished goods;

    (d) the need to avoid serious disturbances in the economies of Member States and to ensure rational development of production and an expansion of consumption within the Community.

CHAPTER 2   ELIMINATION OF QUANTITATIVE RESTRICTIONS BETWEEN MEMBER STATES

Article 30
Quantitative restrictions on imports and all measures having equivalent effect shall, without prejudice to the following provisions, be prohibited between Member States.

Article 31
Member States shall refrain from introducing between themselves any new quantitative restrictions or measures having equivalent effect.

This obligation shall, however, relate only to the degree of liberalisation attained in pursuance of the decisions of the Council of the Organisation for

European Economic Cooperation of 14 January 1955. Member States shall supply the Commission, not later than six months after the entry into force of this Treaty, with lists of the products liberalised by them in pursuance of these decisions. These lists shall be consolidated between Member States.

Article 32
In their trade with one another Member States shall refrain from making more restrictive the quotas and measures having equivalent effect existing at the date of the entry into force of this Treaty.

These quotas shall be abolished by the end of the transitional period at the latest. During that period, they shall be progressively abolished in accordance with the following provisions.

Article 33
1. One year after the entry into force of this Treaty, each Member State shall convert any bilateral quotas open to any other Member States into global quotas open without discrimination to all other Member States.

On the same date, Member States shall increase the aggregate of the global quotas so established in such a manner as to bring about an increase of not less than 20% in their total value as compared with the preceding year. The global quota for each product, however, shall be increased by not less than 10%.

The quotas shall be increased annually in accordance with the same rules and in the same proportions in relation to the preceding year.

The fourth increase shall take place at the end of the fourth year after the entry into force of this Treaty; the fifth, one year after the beginning of the second stage.

2. Where, in the case of a product which has not been liberalised, the global quota does not amount to 3% of the national production of the State concerned, a quota equal to not less than 3% of such national production shall be introduced not later than one year after the entry into force of this Treaty. This quota shall be raised to 4% at the end of the second year, and to 5% at the end of the third. Thereafter, the Member State concerned shall increase the quota by not less than 15% annually.

Where there is no such national production, the Commission shall take a decision establishing an appropriate quota.

3. At the end of the tenth year, each quota shall be equal to not less than 20% of the national production.

4. If the Commission finds by means of a decision that during two successive years the imports of any product have been below the level of the quota opened, this global quota shall not be taken into account in calculating the total value of the global quotas. In such case, the Member State shall abolish quota restrictions on the product concerned.

5. In the case of quotas representing more than 20% of the national production of the product concerned, the Council may, acting by a qualified majority on a proposal from the Commission, reduce the minimum percentage of 10% laid down in paragraph 1. This alteration shall not, however, affect the obligation to increase the total value of global quotas by 20% annually.

6. Member States which have exceeded their obligations as regards the degree of liberalisation attained in pursuance of the decisions of the Council of the Organisation for European Economic Cooperation of 14 January 1955 shall be entitled, when calculating the annual total increase of 20% provided for

in paragraph 1, to take into account the amount of imports liberalised by autonomous action. Such calculation shall be submitted to the Commission for its prior approval.

7. The Commission shall issue directives establishing the procedure and timetable in accordance with which Member States shall abolish, as between themselves, any measures in existence when this Treaty enters into force which have an effect equivalent to quotas.

8. If the Commission finds that the application of the provisions of this Article, and in particular of the provisions concerning percentages, makes it impossible to ensure that the abolition of quotas provided for in the second paragraph of Article 32 is carried out progressively, the Council may, on a proposal from the Commission, acting unanimously during the first stage and by a qualified majority thereafter, amend the procedure laid down in this Article and may, in particular, increase the percentages fixed.

Article 34
1. Quantitative restrictions on exports, and all measures having equivalent effect, shall be prohibited between Member States.

2. Member States shall, by the end of the first stage at the latest, abolishing all quantitative restrictions on exports and any measures having equivalent effect which are in existence when this Treaty enters into force.

Article 35
The Member States declare their readiness to abolish quantitative restrictions on imports from and exports to other Member States more rapidly than is provided for in the preceding Articles, if their general economic situation and the situation of the economic sector concerned so permit.

To this end, the Commission shall make recommendations to the Member States concerned.

Article 36
The provisions of Articles 30 to 34 shall not preclude prohibitions or restrictions on imports, exports or goods in transit justified on grounds of public morality, public policy or public security; the protection of health and life of humans, animals or plants; the protection of national treasures possessing artistic, historic or archaeological value; or the protection of industrial and commercial property. Such prohibitions or restrictions shall not, however, constitute a means of arbitrary discrimination or a disguised restriction on trade between Member States.

Article 37
1. Member States shall progressively adjust any State monopolies of a commercial character so as to ensure that when the transitional period has ended no discrimination regarding the conditions under which goods are procured and marketed exists between nationals of Member States.

The provisions of this Article shall apply to any body through which a Member State, in law or in fact, either directly or indirectly supervises, determines or appreciably influences imports or exports between Member States. These provisions shall likewise apply to monopolies delegated by the State to others.

2. Member States shall refrain from introducing any new measure which is contrary to the principles laid down in paragraph 1 or which restricts the scope

of the Articles dealing with the abolition of customs duties and quantitative restrictions between Member States.

3. The timetable for the measures referred to in paragraph 1 shall be harmonised with the abolition of quantitative restrictions on the same products provided for in Articles 30 to 34.

If a product is subject to a State monopoly of a commercial character in only one or some Member States, the Commission may authorise the other Member States to apply protective measures until the adjustment provided for in paragraph 1 has been effected; the Commission shall determine the conditions and details of such measures.

4. If a State monopoly of a commercial character has rules which are designed to make it easier to dispose of agricultural products or obtain for them the best return, steps should be taken in applying the rules contained in this Article to ensure equivalent safeguards for the employment and standard of living of the producers concerned, account being taken of the adjustments that will be possible and the specialisation that will be needed with the passage of time.

5. The obligtations on Member States shall be binding only in so far as they are compatible with existing international agreements.

6. With effect from the first stage the Commission shall make recommendations as to the manner in which and the timetable according to which the adjustment provided for in this Article shall be carried out.

TITLE II AGRICULTURE

Article 38

1. The common market shall extend to agriculture and trade in agricultural products. 'Agricultural products' means the products of the soil, of stockfarming and of fisheries and products of first-stage processing directly related to these products.

2. Save as otherwise provided in Articles 39 to 46, the rules laid down for the establishment of the common market shall apply to agricultural products.

3. The products subject to the provisions of Articles 39 to 46 are listed in Annex II to this Treaty. Within two years of the entry into force of this Treaty, however, the Council shall, acting by a qualified majority on a proposal from the Commission, decide what products are to be added to this list.

4. The operation and development of the common market for agricultural products must be accompanied by the establishment of a common agricultural policy among the Member States.

Article 39

1. The objectives of the common agricultural policy shall be:

(a) to increase agricultural productivity by promoting technical progress and by ensuring the rational development of agricultural production and the optimum utilisation of the factors of production, in particular labour;

(b) thus to ensure a fair standard of living for the agricultural community, in particular by increasing the individual earnings of persons engaged in agriculture;

(c) to stabilise markets;

(d) to assure the availability of supplies;

(e) to ensure that supplies reach consumers at reasonable prices.

2.   In working out the common agricultural policy and the special methods for its application, account shall be taken of:

(a)   the particular nature of agricultural activity, which results from the social structure of agriculture and from structural and natural disparities between the various agricultural regions;

(b)   the need to effect the appropriate adjustments by degrees;

(c)   the fact that in the Member States agriculture constitutes a sector closely linked with the economy as a whole.

Article 40

1.   Member States shall develop the common agricultural policy by degrees during the transitional period and shall bring it into force by the end of that period at the latest.

2.   In order to attain the objectives set out in Article 39 a common organisation of agricultural markets shall be established.

This organisation shall take one of the following forms, depending on the product concerned:

(a)   common rules on competition;

(b)   compulsory coordination of the various national market organisations;

(c)   European market organisation.

3.   The common organisation established in accordance with paragraph 2 may include all measures required to attain the objectives set out in Article 39, in particular regulation of prices, aids for the production and marketing of the various products, storage and carryover arrangements and common machinery for stabilising imports or exports.

The common organisation shall be limited to pursuit of the objectives set out in Article 39 and shall exclude any discrimination between producers or consumers within the Community.

Any common price policy shall be based on common criteria and uniform methods of calculation.

4.   In order to enable the common organisation referred to in paragraph 2 to attain its objectives, one or more agricultural guidance and guarantee funds may be set up.

Article 41

To enable the objectives set out in Article 39 to be attained, provision may be made within the framework of the common agricultural policy for measures such as:

(a)   an effective coordination of efforts in the spheres of vocational training, of research and of the dissemination of agricultural knowledge; this may include joint financing of projects or institutions;

(b)   joint measures to promote consumption of certain products.

Article 42

The provisions of the Chapter relating to rules on competition shall apply to production of and trade in agricultural products only to the extent determined by the Council within the framework of Article 43(2) and (3) and in accordance with the procedure laid down therein, account being taken of the objectives set out in Article 39.

The Council may, in particular, authorise the granting of aid:

(a)   for the protection of enterprises handicapped by structural or natural conditions;

(b)   within the framework of economic development programmes.

Article 43

1.   In order to evolve the broad lines of a common agricultural policy, the Commission shall, immediately this Treaty enters into force, convene a conference of the Member States with a view to making a comparison of their agricultural policies, in particular by producing a statement of their resources and needs.

2.   Having taken into account the work of the conference provided for in paragraph 1, after consulting the Economic and Social Committee and within two years of the entry into force of this Treaty, the Commission shall submit proposals for working out and implementing the common agricultural policy, including the replacement of the national organisations by one of the forms of common organisation provided for in Article 40(2), and for implementing the measures specified in this Title.

These proposals shall take account of the interdependence of the agricultural matters mentioned in this Title.

The Council shall, on a proposal from the Commission and after consulting the European Parliament, acting unanimously during the first two stages and by a qualified majority thereafter, make regulations, issue directives, or take decisions, without prejudice to any recommendations it may also make.

3.   The Council may, acting by a qualified majority and in accordance with paragraph 2, replace the national market organisations by the common organisation provided for in Article 40(2) if:

(a)   the common organisation offers Member States which are opposed to this measure and which have an organisation of their own for the production in question equivalent safeguards for the employment and standard of living of the producers concerned, account being taken of the adjustments that will be possible and the specialisation that will be needed with the passage of time;

(b)   such an organisation ensures conditions for trade within the Community similar to those existing in a national market.

4.   If a common organisation for certain raw materials is established before a common organisation exists for the corresponding processed products, such raw materials as are used for processed products intended for export to third coutries may be imported from outside the Community.

Article 44

1.   In so far as progressive abolition of customs duties and quantitative restrictions between Member States may result in prices likely to jeopardise the attainment of the objectives set out in Article 39, each Member State shall, during the transitional period, be entitled to apply to particular products, in a non-discriminatory manner and in substitution for quotas and to such an extent as shall not impede the expansion of the volume of trade provided for in Article 45(2), a system of minimum prices below which imports may be either:

— temporarily suspended or reduced; or

— allowed, but subjected to the condition that they are made at a price higher than the minimum price for the product concerned.

In the latter case the minimum prices shall not include customs duties.

2.   Minimum prices shall neither cause a reduction of the trade existing between Member States when this Treaty enters into force nor form an obstacle

to progressive expansion of this trade. Minimum prices shall not be applied so as to form an obstacle to the development of a natural preference between Member States.

3. As soon as this Treaty enters into force the Council shall, on a proposal from the Commission, determine objective criteria for the establishment of minimum price systems and for the fixing of such prices.

These criteria shall in particular take account of the average national production costs in the Member State applying the minimum price, of the position of the various undertakings concerned in relation to such average production costs, and of the need to promote both the progressive improvement of agricultural practice and the adjustment and specialisation needed within the common market.

The Commission shall further propose a procedure for revising these criteria in order to allow for and speed up technical progress and to approximate prices progressively within the common market.

These criteria and the procedure for revising them shall be determined by the Council acting unanimously within three years of the entry into force of this Treaty.

4. Until the decision of the Council takes effect, Member States may fix minimum prices on condition that these are communicated beforehand to the Commission and to the other Member States so that they may submit their comments.

Once the Council has taken its decision. Member States shall fix minimum prices on the basis of the criteria determined as above.

The Council may, acting by a qualified majority on a proposal from the Commission, rectify any decisions taken by Member States which do not conform to the criteria defined above.

5. If it does not prove possible to determine the said objective criteria for certain products by the beginning of the third stage, the Council may, acting by a qualified majority on a proposal from the Commission, vary the minimum prices applied to these products.

6. At the end of the transitional period, a table of minimum prices still in force shall be drawn up. The Council shall, acting on a proposal from the Commission and by a majority of nine votes in accordance with the weighting laid down in the first subparagraph of Article 148(2), determine the system to be applied within the framework of the common agricultural policy.

Article 45

1. Until national market organisations have been replaced by one of the forms of common organisation referred to in Article 40(2), trade in products in respect of which certain Member States:

— have arrangements designed to guarantee national producers a market for their products; and

— are in need of imports,

shall be developed by the conclusion of long-term agreements or contracts between importing and exporting Member States.

These agreements or contracts shall be directed towards the progressive abolition of any discrimination in the application of these arrangements of the various producers within the Community.

Such agreements or contracts shall be concluded during the first stage; account shall be taken of the principle of reciprocity.

2. As regards quantities, these agreements or contracts shall be based on the average volume of trade between Member States in the products concerned during the three years before the entry into force of this Treaty and shall provide for an increase in the volume of trade within the limits of existing requirements, account being taken of traditional patterns of trade.

As regards prices, these agreements or contracts shall enable producers to dispose of the agreed quantities at prices which shall be progressively approximated to those paid to national producers on the domestic market of the purchasing country.

This approximation shall proceed as steadily as possible and shall be completed by the end of the transitional period at the latest.

Prices shall be negotiated between the parties concerned within the framework of directives issued by the Commission for the purpose of implementing the two preceding subparagraphs.

If the first stage is extended, these agreements or contracts shall continue to be carried out in accordance with the conditions applicable at the end of the fourth year after the entry into force of this Treaty, the obligation to increase quantities and to approximate prices being suspended until the transition to the second stage.

Member States shall avail themselves of any opportunity open to them under their legislation, particularly in respect of import policy, to ensure the conclusion and carrying out of these agreements or contracts.

3. To the extent that Member States require raw materials for the manufacture of products to be exported outside the Community in competition with products of third countries, the above agreements or contracts shall not form an obstacle to the importation of raw materials from this purpose from third countries. This provision shall not, however, apply if the Council unanimously decides to make provision for payments required to compensate for the higher price paid on goods imported for this purpose on the basis of these agreements or contracts in relation to the delivered price of the same goods purchased on the world market.

Article 46

Where in a Member State a product is subject to a national market organisation or to internal rules having equivalent effect which affect the competitive position of similar production in another Member State, a countervailing charge shall be applied by Member States to imports of the product coming from the Member State where such organisation or rules exist, unless that State applies a countervailing charge on export.

The Commission shall fix the amount of these charges at the level required to redress the balance; it may also authorise other measures, the conditions and details of which it shall determine.

Article 47

As to the functions to be performed by the Economic and Social Committee in pursuance of this Title, its agricultural section shall hold itself at the disposal of the Commission to prepare, in accordance with the provisions of Articles 197 and 198, the deliberations of the Committee.

TITLE III　FREE MOVEMENT OF PERSONS, SERVICES AND CAPITAL
CHAPTER 1　WORKERS

Article 48

1.　Freedom of movement for workers shall be secured within the Community by the end of the transitional period at the latest.

2.　Such freedom of movement shall entail the abolition of any discrimination based on nationality between workers of the Member States as regards employment, remuneration and other conditions of work and employment.

3.　It shall entail the right, subject to limitations justified on grounds of public policy, public security or public health:

(a)　to accept offers of employment actually made;

(b)　to move freely within the territory of Member States for this purpose;

(c)　to stay in a Member State for the purpose of employment in accordance with the provisions governing the employment of nationals of that State laid down by law, regulation or administrative action;

(d)　to remain in the territory of a Member State after having been employed in that State, subject to conditions which shall be embodied in implementing regulations to be drawn up by the Commission.

4.　The provisions of this Article shall not apply to employment in the public service.[1]

Note

[1](Editor's Note) Commission Notice 88/C 72/02 [OJ 1988 C72/2] provides an interpretation of Art. 48(4).

Article 49

As soon as this Treaty enters into force, the Council shall, *acting in accordance with the procedure referred to in Article 189b* and after consulting the Economic and Social Comittee, issue directives or make regulations setting out the measures required to bring about, by progressive stages, freedom of movement for workers, as defined in Article 48, in particular.[1]

(a)　by ensuring close cooperation between national employment services;

(b)　by systematically and progressively abolishing those administrative procedures and practices and those qualifying periods in respect of eligibility for available employment, whether resulting from national legislation or from agreements previously concluded between Member States, the maintenance of which would form an obstacle to liberalisation of the movement of workers;

(c)　by systematically and progressively abolishing all such qualifying periods and other restrictions provided for either under national legislation or under agreements previously concluded between Member States as imposed on workers of other Member States conditions regarding the free choice of employment other than those imposed on workers of the State concerned;

(d)　by setting up appropriate machinery to bring offers of employment into touch with applications for employment and to facilitate the achievement of a balance between supply and demand in the employment market in such a way as to avoid serious threats to the standard of living and level of employment in the various regions and industries.

Note

[1]Introductory words amended by Article G(10) TEU.

Article 50
Member States shall, within the framework of a joint programme, encourage the exchange of young workers.

Article 51
The Council shall, acting unanimously on a proposal from the Commission, adopt such measures in the field of social security as are necessary to provide freedom of movement for workers; to this end, it shall make arrangements to secure for migrant workers and their dependants:

(a)   aggregation, for the purpose of acquiring and retaining the right to benefit and of calculating the amount of benefit, of all periods taken into account under the laws of the several countries;

(b)   payment of benefits to persons resident in the territories of Member States.

CHAPTER 2   RIGHT OF ESTABLISHMENT

Article 52
Within the framework of the provisions set out below, restrictions on the freedom of establishment of nationals of a Member State in the territory of another Member State shall be abolished by progressive stages in the course of the transitional period. Such progressive abolition shall also apply to restrictions on the setting up of agencies, branches or subsidiaries by nationals of any Member State established in the territory of any Member State.

Freedom of establishment shall include the right to take up and pursue activities as self-employed persons and to set up and manage undertakings, in particular companies or firms within the meaning of the second paragraph of Article 58, under the conditions laid down for its own nationals by the law of the country where such establishment is effected, subject to the provisions of the Chapter relating to capital.

Article 53
Member States shall not introduce any new restrictions on the right of establishment in their territories of nationals of other Member States, save as otherwise provided in this Treaty.

Article 54
1.   Before the end of the first stage, the Council shall, acting unanimously on a proposal from the Commission and after consulting the Economic and Social Committee and the European Parliament, draw up a general programme for the abolition of existing restrictions on freedom of establishment within the Community. The Commission shall submit its proposal to the Council during the first two years of the first stage.

The programme shall set out the general conditions under which freedom of establishment is to be attained in the case of each type of activity and in particular the stages by which it is to be attained.

2.   In order to implement this general programme or, in the absence of such programme, in order to achieve a stage in attaining freedom of establishment as regards a particular activity, the Council, *acting in accordance with the procedure referred to in Article 189b* and after consulting the Economic and Social Committee, shall act by means of directives.[1]

Note
[1]Paragraph 2 as amended by Article G(11) TEU.

3.   The Council and the Commission shall carry out the duties devolving upon them under the preceding provisions, in particular:

(a)   by according, as a general rule, priority treatment to activities where freedom of establishment makes a particularly valuable contribution to the development of production and trade;

(b)   by ensuring close cooperation between the competent authorities in the Member States in order to ascertain the particular situation within the Community of the various activities concerned;

(c)   by abolishing those administrative procedures and practices, whether resulting from national legislation or from agreements previously concluded between Member States, the maintenance of which would form an obstacle to freedom of establishment;

(d)   by ensuring that workers of one Member State employed in the territory of another Member State may remain in that territory for the purpose of taking up activities therein as self-employed persons, where they satisfy the conditions which they would be required to satisfy if they were entering that State at the time when they intended to take up such activities;

(e)   by enabling a national of one Member State to acquire and use land and buildings situated in the territory of another Member State, in so far as this does not conflict with the principles laid down in Article 39(2);

(f)   by effecting the progressive abolition of restriction on freedom of establishment in every branch of activity under consideration, both as regards the conditions for setting up agencies, branches or subsidiaries in the territory of a Member State and as regards the subsidiaries in the territory of a Member State and as regards the conditions governing the entry of personnel belonging to the main establishment into managerial or supervisory posts in such agencies, branches or subsidiaries;

(g)   by coordinating to the necessary extent the safeguards which, for the protection of the interests of members and others, are required by Member States of companies or firms within the meaning of the second paragraph of Article 58 with a view to making such safeguards equivalent throughout the Community;

(h)   by satisfying themselves that the conditions of establishment are not distorted by aids granted by Member States.

Article 55

The provisions of this Chapter shall not apply, so far as any given Member State is concerned, to activities which in that State are connected, even occasionally with the exercise of official authority.

The Council may, acting by a qualified majority on a proposal from the Commission, rule that the provisions of this Chapter shall not apply to certain activities.

Article 56

1.   The provisions of this Chapter and measures taken in pursuance thereof shall not prejudice the applicability of provisions laid down by law, regulation or administrative action providing for special treatment for foreign nationals on grounds of public policy, public security or public health.

2.   Before the end of the transitional period, the Council shall, acting unanimously on a proposal from the Commission and after consulting the European Parliament, issue directives for the coordination of the

abovementioned provisions laid down by law, regulation or administrative action. After the end of the second stage, however, the Council shall, *acting in accordance with the procedure referred to in Article 189b,* issue directives for the coordination of such provisions as, in each Member State, are a matter for regulation or administrative action.[1]

Note
[1]Paragraph 2 as amended by Article G(12) TEU.

Article 57[1]

1.   In order to make it easier for persons to take up and pursue activities as self-employed persons, the Council shall, *acting in accordance with the procedure referred to in Article 189b,* issue directives for the mutual recognition of diplomas, certificates and other evidence of formal qualifications.

2.   *For the same purpose, the Council shall, before the end of the transitional period, issue directives for the coordination of the provisions laid down by law, regulation or administrative action in Member States concerning the taking up and pursuit of activities as self-employed persons. The Council, acting unanimously on a proposal from the Commission and after consulting the European Parliament, shall decide on directives the implementation of which involves in at least one Member State amendment of the existing principles laid down by law governing the professions with respect to training and conditions of access for natural persons. In other cases the Council shall act in accordance with the procedure referred to in Article 189b.*

3.   In the case of the medical and allied and pharmaceutical professions, the progressive abolition of restrictions shall be dependent upon coordination of the conditions for their exercise in the various Member States.

Note
[1]As amended by Article G(13) TEU.

Article 58

Companies or firms formed in accordance with the law of a Member State and having their registered office, central administration or principal place of business within the Community shall, for the purposes of this Chapter, be treated in the same way as natural persons who are nationals of Member States.

'Companies or firms' means companies or firms constituted under civil or commercial law, including cooperative societies, and other legal persons governed by public or private law, save for those which are non-profitmaking.

CHAPTER 3   SERVICES

Article 59

Within the framework of the provisions set out below, restrictions on freedom to provide services within the Community shall be progressively abolished during the transitional period in respect of nationals of Member States who are established in a State of the Community other than that of the person for whom the services are intended.

The Council may, acting by a qualified majority on a proposal from the Commission, extend the provisions of the Chapter to nationals of a third country who provide services and who are established within the Community.

Article 60

Services shall be considered to be 'services' within the meaning of this Treaty where they are normally provided for remuneration, in so far as they are not governed by the provisions relating to freedom of movement for goods, capital and persons.

'Services' shall in particular include:
- (a)   activities of an industrial character;
- (b)   activities of a commercial character;
- (c)   activities of craftsmen;
- (d)   activities of the professions.

Without prejudice to the provisions of the Chapter relating to the right of establishment, the person providing a service may, in order to do so, temporarily pursue his activity in the State where the service is provided, under the same conditions as are imposed by the State on its own nationals.

Article 61

1.   Freedom to provide services in the field of transport shall be governed by the provisions of the Title relating to transport.

2.   The liberalisation of banking and insurance services connected with movements of capital shall be effected in step with the progressive liberalisation of movement of capital.

Article 62

Save as otherwise provided in this Treaty, Member States shall not introduce any new restriction on the freedom to provide services which have in fact been attained at the date of the entry into force of this Treaty.

Article 63

1.   Before the end of the first stage, the Council shall, acting unanimously on a proposal from the Commission and after consulting the Economic and Social Committee and the European Parliament, draw up a general programme for the abolition of existing restrictions on freedom to provide services within the Community. The Commission shall submit its proposal to the Council during the first two years of the first stage.

The programme shall set out the general conditions under which and the stages by which each type of service is to be liberalised.

2.   In order to implement the general programme or, in the absence of such programme, in order to achieve a stage in the liberalisation of a specific service, the Council shall, on a proposal from the Commission and after consulting the Economic and Social Committee and the European Parliament, issue directives acting unanimously until the end of the first stage and by a qualified majority thereafter.

3.   As regards the proposals and decisions referred to in paragraphs 1 and 2, priority shall as a general rule be given to those services which directly affect production costs or the liberalisation of which helps to promote trade in goods.

Article 64

The Member States declare their readiness to undertake the liberalisation of services beyond the extent required by the directives issued pursuant to Article 63(2), if their general economic situation and the situation of the economic sector concerned so permit.

To this end, the Commission shall make recommendations to the Member States concerned.

Article 65

As long as restrictions on freedom to provide services have not been abolished, each Member State shall apply such restrictions without distinction on grounds of nationality or residence to all persons providing services within the meaning of the first paragraph of Article 59.

Article 66

The provisions of Articles 55 to 58 shall apply to the matters covered by this Chapter.

CHAPTER 4   CAPITAL AND PAYMENTS[1]

Note
[1]Title as amended by Article G(14) TEU.

Articles 67–73

(Repealed. See Article 73a.)

Article 73a[1]

As from 1 January 1994, Articles 67 to 73 shall be replaced by Articles 73b, c, d, e, f and g.

Article 73b[1]

1.   Within the framework of the provisions set out in this Chapter, all restrictions on the movement of capital between Member States and between Member States and third countries shall be prohibited.

2.   Within the framework of the provisions set out in this Chapter, all restrictions on payments between Member States and between Member States and third countries shall be prohibited.

Article 73c[1]

1.   The provisions of Article 73b shall be without prejudice to the application to third countries of any restrictions which exist on 31 December 1993 under national or Community law adopted in respect of the movement of capital to or from third countries involving direct investment — including in real estate —, establishment, the provision of financial services or the admission of securities to capital markets.

2.   Whilst endeavouring to achieve the objective of free movement of capital between Member States and third countries to the greatest extent possible and without prejudice to the other Chapters of this Treaty, the Council may, acting by a qualified majority on a proposal from the Commission, adopt measures on the movement of capital to or from third countries involving direct investment — including investment in real estate —, establishment, the provision of financial services or the admission of securities to capital markets. Unanimity shall be required for measures under this paragraph which constitute a step back in Community law as regards the liberalisation of the movement of capital to or from third countries.

Article 73d[1]

1.   The provisions of Article 73b shall be without prejudice to the right of Member States:

(a)   to apply the relevant provisions of their tax law which distinguish between tax-payers who are not in the same situation with

regard to their place of residence or with regard to the place where their capital is invested;

(b)   to take all requisite measures to prevent infringements of national law and regulations, in particular in the field of taxation and the prudential supervision of financial institutions, or to lay down procedures for the declaration of capital movements for purposes of administrative or statistical information, or to take measures which are justified on grounds of public policy or public security.

2.   The provisions of this Chapter shall be without prejudice to the applicability of restrictions on the right of establishment which are compatible with this Treaty.

3.   The measures and procedures referred to in paragraphs 1 and 2 shall not constitute a means of arbitrary discrimination or a disguised restriction on the free movement of capital and payments as defined in Article 73b.

Article 73e[1]

By way of derogation from Article 73b, Member States which, on 31 December 1993, enjoy a derogation on the basis of existing Community law, shall be entitled to maintain, until 31 December 1995 at the latest, restrictions on movements of capital authorised by such derogation as exist on that date.

Article 73f[1]

Where, in exceptional circumstances, movements of capital to or from third countries cause, or threaten to cause, serious difficulties for the operation of economic and monetary union, the Council, acting by a qualified majority on a proposal from the Commission and after consulting the ECB, may take safeguard measures with regard to third countries for a period not exceeding six months if such measures are strictly necessary.

Article 73g[1]

1.   If, in the cases envisaged in Article 228a, action by the Community is deemed necessary, the Council may, in accordance with the procedure provided for in Article 228a, take the necessary urgent measures on the movement of capital and on payments as regards the third countries concerned.

2.   Without prejudice to Article 224 and as long as the Council has not taken measures pursuant to paragraph 1, a Member State may, for serious political reasons and on grounds of urgency, take unilateral measures against a third country with regard to capital movements and payments. The Commission and the other Member States shall be informed of such measures by the date of their entry into force at the latest.

The Council may, acting by a qualified majority on a proposal from the Commission, decide that the Member State concerned shall amend or abolish such measures. The President of the Council shall inform the European Parliament of any such decision taken by the Council.

Article 73h[1]

Until 1 January 1994, the following provisions shall be applicable:

(1)   Each Member State undertakes to authorise, in the currency of the Member State in which the creditor or the beneficiary resides, any payments connected with the movement of goods, services or capital, and any transfers of capital and earnings, to the extent that the movement of goods, services, capital and persons between Member States has been liberalised pursuant to this Treaty.

The Member States declare their readiness to undertake the liberalisation of payments beyond the extent provided in the preceding subparagraph, in so far as their economic situation in general and the state of their balance of payments in particular so permit.

(2)   In so far as movements of goods, services and capital are limited only by restrictions on payments connected therewith, these restrictions shall be progressively abolished by applying, mutatis mutandis, the provisions of this Chapter and the Chapters relating to the abolition of quantitative restrictions and to the liberalisation of services.

(3)   Member States undertake not to introduce between themselves any new restrictions on transfers connected with the invisible transactions listed in Annex III to this Treaty.

The progressive abolition of existing restrictions shall be effected in accordance with the provisions of Articles 63 to 65, in so far as such abolition is not governed by the provisions contained in paragraphs 1 and 2 or by the other provisions of this Chapter.

(4)   If need be, Member States shall consult each other on the measures to be taken to enable the payments and transfers mentioned in this Article to be effected; such measures shall not prejudice the attainment of the objectives set out in this Treaty.

Note
[1]Articles 73a to 73h as inserted by Article G(15) TEU.

TITLE IV   TRANSPORT

Article 74
The objectives of this Treaty shall, in matters governed by this Title, be pursued by Member States within the framework of a common transport policy.

Article 75[1]
1.   For the purpose of implementing Article 74, and taking into account the distinctive features of transport, the Council shall, *acting in accordance with the procedure referred to in Article 189c* and after consulting the Economic and Social Committee, lay down:

(a)   common rules applicable to international transport to or from the territory of a Member State or passing across the territory of one or more Member States;

(b)   the conditions under which non-resident carriers may operate transport services within a Member State;

(c)   measures to improve transport safety;

(d)   any other appropriate provisions.

Note
[1]As amended by Article G(16) TEU.

2.   The provisions referred to in (a) and (b) of paragraph 1 shall be laid down during the transitional period.

3.   By way of derogation from the procedure provided for in paragraph 1, where the application of provisions concerning the principles of the regulatory system for transport would be liable to have a serious effect on the standard of living and on employment in certain areas and on the operation of transport facilities, they shall be laid down by the Council acting unanimously *on a proposal from the Commission, after consulting the European Parliament and the Economic and Social Committee.* In so doing, the Council shall take into account the need for adaptation to the economic development which will result from establishing the common market.

Article 76
Until the provisions referred to in Article 75(1) have been laid down, no Member State may, without the unanimous approval of the Council, make the various provisions governing the subject when this Treaty enters into force less favourable in their direct or indirect effect on carriers of other Member States as compared with carriers who are nationals of that State.

Article 77
Aids shall be compatible with this Treaty if they meet the needs of coordination of transport or if they represent reimbursement for the discharge of certain obligations inherent in the concept of a public service.

Article 78
Any measures taken within the framework of this Treaty in respect of transport rates and conditions shall take account of the economic circumstances of carriers.

Article 79
1.   In the case of transport within the Community, discrimination which takes the form of carriers charging different rates and imposing different conditions for the carriage of the same goods over the same transport links on grounds of the country of origin or of destination of the goods in question, shall be abolished, at the latest, before the end of the second stage.

2.   Paragraph 1 shall not prevent the Council from adopting other measures in pursuance of Article 75(1).

3.   Within two years of the entry into force of this Treaty, the Council shall, acting by a qualified majority on a proposal from the Commission and after consulting the Economic and Social Committee, lay down rules for implementing the provisions of paragraph 1.

The Council may in particular lay down the provisions needed to enable the institutions of the Community to secure compliance with the rule laid down in paragraph 1 and to ensure that users benefit from it to the full.

4.   The Commission shall, acting on its own initiative or on application by a Member State, investigate any cases of discrimination falling within paragraph 1 and, after consulting any Member State concerned, shall take the

necessary decisions within the framework of the rules laid down in accordance with the provisions of paragraph 3.

Article 80

1.   The imposition by a Member State, in respect of transport operations carried out within the Community, of rates and conditions involving any element of support or protection in the interest of one or more particular undertakings or industries shall be prohibited as from the beginning of the second stage, unless authorised by the Commission.

2.   The Commission shall, acting on its own initiative or on application by a Member State, examine the rates and conditions referred to in paragraph 1, taking account in particular of the requirements of an appropriate regional economic policy, the needs of underdeveloped areas and the problems of areas seriously affected by political circumstances on the one hand, and of the effects of such rates and conditions on competition between the different modes of transport on the other.

After consulting each Member State concerned, the Commission shall take the necessary decisions.

3.   The prohibition provided for in paragraph 1 shall not apply to tariffs fixed to meet competition.

Article 81

Charges or dues in respect of the crossing of frontiers which are charged by a carrier in addition to the transport rates shall not exceed a reasonable level after taking the costs actually incurred thereby into account.

Member States shall endeavour to reduce these costs progressively.

The Commission may make recommendations to Member States for the application of this Article.

Article 82

The provisions of this Title shall not form an obstacle to the application of measures taken in the Federal Republic of Germany to the extent that such measures are required in order to compensate for the economic disadvantages caused by the division of Germany to the economy of certain areas of the Federal Republic affected by that division.

Article 83

An Advisory Committee consisting of experts designated by the Governments of Member States, shall be attached to the Commission. The Commission, whenever it considers it desirable, shall consult the Committee on transport matters without prejudice to the powers of the transport section of the Economic and Social Committee.

Article 84

1.   The provisions of this Title shall apply to transport by rail, road and inland waterway.

2.   The Council may, acting by a qualified majority, decide whether, to what extent and by what procedure appropriate provisions may be laid down for sea and air transport.

The procedural provisions of Article 75(1) and (3) shall apply.

TITLE V COMMON RULES ON COMPETITION, TAXATION AND APPROXIMATION OF LAWS[1]
CHAPTER 1 RULES ON COMPETITION
SECTION 1 RULES APPLYING TO UNDERTAKINGS

Article 85

1. The following shall be prohibited as incompatible with the common market: all agreements between undertakings, decisions by associations of undertakings and concerted practices which may affect trade between Member States and which have as their object or effect the prevention, restriction or distortion of competition within the common market, and in particular those which:

(a) directly or indirectly fix purchase or selling prices or any other trading conditions;

(b) limit or control production, markets, technical development, or investment;

(c) share markets or sources of supply;

(d) apply dissimilar conditions to equivalent transactions with other trading parties, thereby placing them at a competitive disadvantage;

(e) make the conclusion of contracts subject to acceptance by the other parties of supplementary obligations which, by their nature or according to commercial usage, have no connection with the subject of such contracts.

2. Any agreements or decisions prohibited pursuant to this Article shall be automatically void.

3. The provisions of paragraph 1 may, however, be declared inapplicable in the case of:

— any agreement or category of agreements between undertakings;

— any decision or category of decisions by associations of undertakings;

— any concerted practice or category of concerted practices;

which contributes to improving the production or distribution of goods or to promoting technical or economic progress, while allowing consumers a fair share of the resulting benefit, and which does not;

(a) impose on the undertakings concerned restrictions which are not indispensable to the attainment of these objectives;

(b) afford such undertakings the possibility of eliminating competition in respect of a substantial part of the products in question.

Note
[1]Title introduced by Article G(17) TEU.

Article 86
Any abuse by one or more undertakings of a dominant position within the common market or in a substantial part of it shall be prohibited as incompatible with the common market in so far as it may affect trade between Member States.

Such abuse may, in particular, consist in:

(a) directly or indirectly imposing unfair purchase or selling prices or other unfair trading conditions;

(b) limiting production, markets or technical development to the prejudice of consumers;

(c) applying dissimilar conditions to equivalent transactions with other trading parties, thereby placing them at a competitive disadvantage;

(d)   making the conclusion of contracts subject to acceptance by the other parties of supplementary obligations which, by their nature or according to commercial usage, have no connection with the subject of such contracts.

Article 87

1.   Within three years of the entry into force of this Treaty the Council shall, acting unanimously on a proposal from the Commission and after consulting the European Parliament, adopt any appropriate regulations or directives to give effect to the principles set out in Articles 85 and 86.

If such provisions have not been adopted within the period mentioned, they shall be laid down by the Council, acting by a qualified majority on a proposal from the Commission and after consulting the European Parliament.

2.   The regulations or directives referred to in paragraph 1 shall be designed in particular:

(a)   to ensure compliance with the prohibitions laid down in Article 85(1) and in Article 86 by making provision for fines and periodic penalty payments;

(b)   to lay down detailed rules for the application of Article 85(3), taking into account the need to ensure effective supervision on the one hand, and to simplify administration to the greater possible extent on the other;

(c)   to define, if need be, in the various branches of the economy, the scope of the provisions of Articles 85 and 86;

(d)   to define the respective functions of the Commission and of the Court of Justice in applying the provisions laid down in this paragraph;

(e)   to determine the relationship between national laws and the provisions contained in this Section or adopted pursuant to this Article.

Article 88

Until the entry into force of the provisions adopted in pursuance of Article 87, the authorities in Member States shall rule on the admissibility of agreements, decisions and concerted practices and on abuse of a dominant position in the common market in accordance with the law of their country and with the provisions of Article 85, in particular paragraph 3, and of Article 86.

Article 89

1.   Without prejudice to Article 88, the Commission shall, as soon as it takes up its duties, ensure the application of the principles laid down in Articles 85 and 86. On application by a Member State or on its own initiative, and in cooperation with the competent authorities in the Member States, who shall give it their assistance, the Commission shall investigate cases of suspected infringement of these principles. If it finds that there has been an infringement, it shall propose appropriate measures to bring it to an end.

2.   If the infringement is not brought to an end, the Commission shall record such infringement of the principles in a reasoned decision. The Commission may publish its decision and authorise Member States to take the measures, the conditions and details of which it shall determine, needed to remedy the situation.

Article 90

1.   In the case of public undertakings and undertakings to which Member States grant special or exclusive rights, Member States shall neither enact nor maintain in force any measure contrary to the rules contained in this Treaty, in particular to those rules provided for in Article 6 and Articles 85 to 94.

2.   Undertakings entrusted with the operation of services of general economic interest or having the character of a revenue-producing monopoly shall be subject to the rules contained in this Treaty, in particular to the rules on competition, in so far as the application of such rules does not obstruct the performance, in law or in fact, of the particular tasks assigned to them. The development of trade must not be affected to such an extent as would be contrary to the interests of the Community.

3.   The Commission shall ensure the application of the provisions of this Article and shall, where necessary, address appropriate directives or decisions to Member States.

SECTION 2   DUMPING

Article 91

1.   If during the transitional period, the Commission, on application by a Member State or by any other interested party, finds that dumping is being practised within the common market, it shall address recommendations to the person or persons with whom such practices originate for the purpose of putting an end to them.

Should the practices continue, the Commission shall authorise the injured Member State to take protective measures, the conditions and details of which the Commission shall determine.

2.   As soon as this Treaty enters into force, products which originate in or are in free circulation in one Member State and which have been exported to another Member State shall, on reimportation, be admitted into the territory of the first-mentioned State free of all customs duties, quantitative restrictions or measures having equivalent effect. The Commission shall lay down appropriate rules for the application of this paragraph.

SECTION 3   AIDS GRANTED BY STATES

Article 92

1.   Save as otherwise provided in this Treaty, any aid granted by a Member State or through State resources in any form whatsoever which distorts or threatens to distort competition by favouring certain undertakings or the production of certain goods shall, in so far as it affects trade between Member States, be incompatible with the common market.

2.   The following shall be compatible with the common market:

(a)   aid having a social character, granted to individual consumers, provided that such aid is granted without discrimination related to the origin of the products concerned;

(b)   aid to make good the damage caused by natural disasters or exceptional occurrences;

(c)   aid granted to the economy of certain areas of the Federal Republic of Germany affected by the division of Germany, in so far as such aid is required in order to compensate for the economic disadvantages caused by that division.

3.   The following may be considered to be compatible with the common market:

(a)   aid to promote the economic development of areas where the standard of living is abnormally low or where there is serious underemployment;

(b) aid to promote the execution of an important project of common European interest or to remedy a serious disturbance in the economy of a Member State;

(c) aid to facilitate the development of certain economic activities or of certain economic areas, where such aid does not adversely affect trading conditions to an extent contrary to the common interest. However, the aids granted to shipbuilding as of 1 January 1957 shall, in so far as they serve only to compensate for the absence of customs protection, be progressively reduced under the same conditions as apply to the elimination of customs duties, subject to the provisions of this Treaty concerning common commercial policy towards third countries;

(d) aid to promote culture and heritage conservation where such aid does not affect trading conditions and competition in the Community to an extent that is contrary to the common interest;[1]

(e) such other categories of aid as may be specified by decision of the Council acting by a qualified majority on a proposal from the Commission.

Note
[1]Point (d) as inserted by Article G(18) TEU.

Article 93

1. The Commission shall, in cooperation with Member States, keep under constant review all systems of aid existing in those States. It shall propose to the latter any appropriate measures required by the progressive development or by the functioning of the common market.

2. If, after giving notice to the parties concerned to submit their comments, the Commission finds that aid granted by a State or through State resources is not compatible with the common market having regard to Article 92, or that such aid is being misused, it shall decide that the State concerned shall abolish or alter such aid within a period of time to be determined by the Commission.

If the State concerned does not comply with this decision within the prescribed time, the Commission or any other interested State may, in derogation from the provisions of Articles 169 and 170, refer the matter to the Court of Justice direct.

On application by a Member State, the Council, may, acting unanimously, decide that aid which that State is granting or intends to grant shall be considered to be compatible with the common market, in derogation from the provisions of Article 92 or from the regulations provided for in Article 94, if such a decision is justified by exceptional circumstances. If, as regards the aid in question, the Commission has already initiated the procedure provided for in the first subparagraph of this paragraph, the fact that the State concerned has made its application to the Council shall have the effect of suspending that procedure until the Council has made its attitude known.

If, however, the Council has not made its attitude known within three months of the said application being made, the Commission shall give its decision on the case.

3. The Commission shall be informed, in sufficient time to enable it to submit its comments, of any plans to grant or alter aid. If it considers that any such plan is not compatible with the common market having regard to Article 92, it shall without delay initiate the procedure provided for in paragraph 2. The Member State concerned shall not put its proposed measures into effect until this procedure has resulted in a final decision.

Article 94

The Council, acting by a qualified majority on a proposal from the Commission *and after consulting the European Parliament*, may make any appropriate regulations for the application of Articles 92 and 93 and may in particular determine the conditions in which Article 93(3) shall apply and the categories of aid exempted from this procedure.

Note
[1]As amended by Article G(19) TEU.

CHAPTER 2   TAX PROVISIONS

Article 95

No Member State shall impose, directly or indirectly, on the products of other Member States any internal taxation of any kind in excess of that imposed directly or indirectly on similar domestic products.

Further, no Member State shall impose on the products of other Member States any internal taxation of such a nature as to afford indirect protection to other products.

Member States shall, not later than at the beginning of the second stage, repeal or amend any provisions existing when this Treaty enters into force which conflict with the preceding rules.

Article 96

Where products are exported to the territory of any Member State, any repayment of internal taxation shall not exceed the internal taxation imposed on them whether directly or indirectly.

Article 97

Member States which levy a turnover tax calculated on a cumulative multi-stage tax system may, in the case of internal taxation imposed by them on imported products or of repayments allowed by them on exported products, establish average rates for products or groups of products, provided that there is no infringement of the principles laid down in Articles 95 and 96.

Where the average rates established by a Member State do not conform to these principles, the Commission shall address appropriate directives or decisions to the State concerned.

Article 98

In the case of charges other than turnover taxes, excise duties and other forms of indirect taxation, remissions and repayments in respect of exports to other Member States may not be granted and countervailing charges in respect of imports from Member States may not be imposed unless the measures contemplated have been previously approved for a limited period by the Council acting by a qualified majority on a proposal from the Commission.

Article 99[1]

The Council shall, acting unanimously on a proposal from the Commission and after consulting the European Parliament *and the Economic and Social Committee*, adopt provisions for the harmonisation of legislation concerning turnover taxes, excise duties and other forms of indirect taxation to the extent

Note
[1]As amended by Article G(20) TEU.

that such harmonisation is necessary to ensure the establishment and the functioning of the internal market within the time limit laid down in Article 7a.

CHAPTER 3   APPROXIMATION OF LAWS

Article 100[1]

The Council shall, acting unanimously on a proposal from the Commission and after consulting the European Parliament and the Economic and Social Committee, issue directives for the approximation of such laws, regulations or administrative provisions of the Member States as directly affect the establishment or functioning of the common market.

Note
[1]As amended by Article G(21) TEU.

Article 100a

1.   By way of derogation from Article 100 and save where otherwise provided in this Treaty, the following provisions shall apply for the achievement of the objectives set out in Article *7a.* The Council shall, *acting in accordance with the procedure referred to in Article 189b* and after consulting the Economic and Social Committee adopt the measures for the approximation of the provisions laid down by law, regulation or administrative action in Member States which have as their object the establishment and functioning of the internal market.[1]

2.   Paragraph 1 shall not apply to fiscal provisions, to those relating to the free movement of persons nor to those relating to the rights and interests of employed persons.

3.   The Commission, in its proposals envisaged in paragraph 1 concerning health, safety, environmental protection and consumer protection, will take as a base a high level of protection.

4.   If, after the adoption of a harmonisation measure by the Council acting by a qualified majority, a Member State deems it necessary to apply national provisions on grounds of major needs referred to in Article 36, or relating to protection of the environment or the working environment, it shall notify the Commission of these provisions.

The Commission shall confirm the provisions involved after having verified that they are not a means of arbitrary discrimination or a disguised restriction on trade between Member States.

By way of derogation from the procedure laid down in Articles 169 and 170, the Commission or any Member State may bring the matter directly before the Court of Justice if it considers that another Member State is making improper use of the powers provided for in this Article.

5.   The harmonisation measures referred to above shall, in appropriate cases, include a safeguard clause authorising the Member States to take, for one or more of the non-economic reasons referred to in Article 36, provisional measures subject to a Community control procedure.

Note
[1]Paragraph 1 as amended by Article G(22) TEU.

Article 100b

1.   During 1992, the Commission shall, together with each Member State draw up an inventory of national laws, regulations and administrative

provisions which fall under Article 100a and which have not been harmonised pursuant to that Article.

The Council, acting in accordance with the provisions of Article 100a, may decide that the provisions in force in a Member State must be recognised as being equivalent to those applied by another Member State.

2.   The provisions of Article 100a(4) shall apply by analogy.

3.   The Commission shall draw up the inventory referred to in the first subparagraph of paragraph 1 and shall submit appropriate proposals in good time to allow the Council to act before the end of 1992.

Article 100c[1]

1.   The Council, acting unanimously on a proposal from the Commission and after consulting the European Parliament, shall determine the third countries whose nationals must be in possession of a visa when crossing the external borders of the Member States.

2.   However, in the event of an emergency situation in a third country posing a threat of a sudden inflow of nationals from that country into the Community, the Council, acting by a qualified majority on a recommendation from the Commission, may introduce, for a period not exceeding six months, a visa requirement for nationals from the country in question. The visa requirements established under this paragraph may be extended in accordance with the procedure referred to in paragraph 1.

3.   From 1 January 1996, the Council shall adopt the decisions referred to in paragraph 1 by a qualified majority. The Council shall, before that date, acting by a qualified majority on a proposal from the Commission and after consulting the European Parliament, adopt measures relating to a uniform format for visas.

4.   In the areas referred to in this Article, the Commission shall examine any request made by a Member State that it submit a proposal to the Council.

5.   This Article shall be without prejudice to the exercise of the responsibilities incumbent upon the Member States with regard to the maintenance of law and order and the safeguarding of internal security.

6.   This Article shall apply to other areas if so decided pursuant to Article K.9 of the provisions of the Treaty on European Union which relate to cooperation in the fields of justice and home affairs, subject to the voting conditions determined at the same time.

7.   The provisions of the conventions in force between the Member States governing areas covered by this Article shall remain in force until their content has been replaced by directives or measures adopted pursuant to this Article.

Note
[1]As inserted by Article G(23) TEU.

Article 100d[1]
The Coordinating Committee consisting of senior officials set up by Article K.4 of the Treaty on European Union shall contribute, without

Note
[1]As inserted by Article G(24) TEU.

prejudice to the provisions of Article 151, to the preparation of the proceedings of the Council in the fields referred to in Article 100c.

Article 101

Where the Commission finds that a difference between the provisions laid down by law, regulation or administrative action in Member States is distorting the conditions of competition in the common market and that the resultant distortion needs to be eliminated, it shall consult the Member States concerned.

If such consultation does not result in an agreement eliminating the distortion in question, the Council shall, on a proposal from the Commission, acting unanimously during the first stage and by a qualified majority thereafter, issue the necessary directives. The Commission and the Council may take any other appropriate measures provided for in this Treaty.

Article 102

1.   Where there is a reason to fear that the adoption or amendment of a provision laid down by law, regulation or administrative action may cause distortion within the meaning of Article 101, a Member State desiring to proceed therewith shall consult the Commission. After consulting the Member States, the Commission shall recommend to the States concerned such measures as may be appropriate to avoid the distortion in question.

2.   If a State desiring to introduce or amend its own provisions does not comply with the recommendation addressed to it by the Commission, other Member States shall not be required, in pursuance of Article 101, to amend their own provisions in order to eliminate such distortion. If the Member State which has ignored the recommendation of the Commission causes distortion detrimental only to itself, the provisions of Article 101 shall not apply.

TITLE VI[1]   ECONOMIC AND MONETARY POLICY
CHAPTER 1   ECONOMIC POLICY

Article 102a

Member States shall conduct their economic policies with a view to contributing to the achievement of the objectives of the Community, as defined in Article 2, and in the context of the broad guidelines referred to in Article 103(2). The Member States and the Community shall act in accordance with the principle of an open market economy with free competition, favouring an efficient allocation of resources, and in compliance with the principles set out in Article 3a.

Note
[1]New title as inserted by Article G(25) TEU, replacing Title II, Articles 102a to 109.

Article 103

1.   Member States shall regard their economic policies as a matter of common concern and shall coordinate them within the Council, in accordance with the provisions of Article 102a.

2.   The Council shall, acting by a qualified majority on a recommendation from the Commission, formulate a draft for the broad guidelines of the economic policies of the Member States and of the Community, and shall report its findings to the European Council.

The European Council shall, acting on the basis of the report from the Council, discuss a conclusion on the broad guidelines of the economic policies of the Member States and of the Community.

On the basis of this conclusion, the Council shall, acting by a qualified majority, adopt a recommendation setting out these broad guidelines. The Council shall inform the European Parliament of its recommendation.

3.   In order to ensure closer coordination of economic policies and sustained convergence of the economic performances of the Member States, the Council shall, on the basis of reports submitted by the Commission, monitor economic developments in each of the Member States and in the Community as well as the consistency of economic policies with the broad guidelines referred to in paragraph 2, and regularly carry out an overall assessment.

For the purpose of this multilateral surveillance, Member States shall forward information to the Commission about important measures taken by them in the field of their economic policy and such other information as they deem necessary.

4.   Where it is established, under the procedure referred to in paragraph 3, that the economic policies of a Member State are not consistent with the broad guidelines referred to in paragraph 2 or that they risk jeopardising the proper functioning of economic and monetary union, the Council may, acting by a qualified majority on a recommendation from the Commission, make the necessary recommendations to the Member State concerned. The Council may, acting by a qualified majority on a proposal from the Commission, decide to make its recommendations public.

The President of the Council and the Commission shall report to the European Parliament on the results of multilateral surveillance. The President of the Council may be invited to appear before the competent Committee of the European Parliament if the Council has made its recommendations public.

5.   The Council, acting in accordance with the procedure referred to in Article 189c, may adopt detailed rules for the multilateral surveillance procedure referred to in paragraphs 3 and 4 of this Article.

Article 103a

1.   Without prejudice to any other procedures provided for in this Treaty, the Council may, acting unanimously on a proposal from the Commission, decide upon the measures appropriate to the economic situation, in particular if severe difficulties arise in the supply of certain products.

2.   Where a Member State is in difficulties or is seriously threatened with severe difficulties caused by exceptional occurrences beyond its control, the Council may, acting unanimously on a proposal from the Commission, grant, under certain conditions, Community financial assistance to the Member State concerned. Where the severe difficulties are caused by natural disasters, the Council shall act by qualified majority. The President of the Council shall inform the European Parliament of the decision taken.

from the ECB and after consulting the Commission or unanimously on a proposal from the Commission and after consulting the ECB. In either case, the assent of the European Parliament shall be required.

6. *The Council, acting by a qualified majority either on a proposal from the Commission and after consulting the European Parliament and the ECB or on a recommendation from the ECB and after consulting the European Parliament and the Commission, shall adopt the provisions referred to in Articles 4, 5.4, 19.2, 20, 28.1, 29.2, 30.4 and 34.3 of the Statute of the ESCB.*

Article 107

When exercising the powers and carrying out the tasks and duties conferred upon them by this Treaty and the Statute of the ESCB, neither the ECB, nor a national central bank, nor any member of their decision-making bodies shall seek or take instructions from Community institutions or bodies, from any government of a Member State or from any other body. The Community institutions and bodies and the governments of the Member States undertake to respect this principle and not to seek to influence the members of the decision-making bodies of the ECB or of the national central banks in the performance of their tasks.

Article 108

Each Member State shall ensure, at the latest at the date of the establishment of the ESCB, that its national legislation including the statutes of its national central bank is compatible with this Treaty and the Statute of the ESCB.

Article 108a

1. *In order to carry out the tasks entrusted to the ESCB, the ECB shall, in accordance with the provisions of this Treaty and under the conditions laid down in the Statute of the ESCB:*

    —make regulations to the extent necessary to implement the tasks, defined in Article 3.1, first indent, Articles 19.1, 22 and 25.2 of the Statute of the ESCB and in cases which shall be laid down in the acts of the Council referred to in Article 106(6);

    —take decisions necessary for carrying out the tasks entrusted to the ESCB under this Treaty and the Statute of the ESCB;

    —make recommendations and deliver opinions.

2. *A regulation shall have general application. It shall be binding in its entirety and directly applicable in all Member States.*

    Recommendations and opinions shall have no binding force.

    A decision shall be binding in its entirety upon those to whom it is addressed.

    Articles 190 to 192 shall apply to regulations and decisions adopted by the ECB.

    The ECB may decide to publish its decisions, recommendations and opinions.

3. *Within the limits and under the conditions adopted by the Council under the procedure laid down in Article 106(6), the ECB shall be entitled to impose fines or periodic penalty payments on*

undertakings for failure to comply with obligations under its regulations and decisions.

Article 109

1. *By way of derogation from Article 228, the Council may, acting unanimously on a recommendation from the ECB or from the Commission, and after consulting the ECB in an endeavour to reach a consensus consistent with the objective of price stability, after consulting the European Parliament, in accordance with the procedure in paragraph 3 for determining the arrangements, conclude formal agreements on an exchange rate system for the ECU in relation to non-Community currencies. The Council may, acting by a qualified majority on a recommendation from the ECB or from the Commission, and after consulting the ECB in an endeavour to reach a consensus consistent with the objective of price stability, adopt, adjust or abandon the central rates of the ECU within the exchange rate system. The President of the Council shall inform the European Parliament of the adoption, adjustment or abandonment of the ECU central rates.*

2. *In the absence of an exchange rate system in relation to one or more non-Community currencies as referred to in paragraph 1, the Council, acting by a qualified majority either on a recommendation from the Commission and after consulting the ECB or on a recommendation from the ECB, may formulate general orientations for exchange rate policy in relation to these currencies. These general orientations shall be without prejudice to the primary objective of the ESCB to maintain price stability.*

3. *By way of derogation from Article 228, where agreements concerning monetary or foreign exchange regime matters need to be negotiated by the Community with one or more States or international organisations, the Council, acting by a qualified majority on a recommendation from the Commission and after consulting the ECB, shall decide the arrangements for the negotiation and for the conclusion of such agreements. These arrangements shall ensure that the Community expresses a single position. The Commission shall be fully associated with the negotiations.*

Agreements concluded in accordance with this paragraph shall be binding on the institutions of the Community, on the ECB and on Member States.

4. *Subject to paragraph 1, the Council shall, on a proposal from the Commission and after consulting the ECB, acting by a qualified majority decide on the position of the Community at international level as regards issues of particular relevance to economic and monetary union and, acting unanimously, decide its representation in compliance with the allocation of powers laid down in Articles 103 and 105.*

5. *Without prejudice to Community competence and Community agreements as regards economic and monetary union, Member States may negotiate in international bodies and conclude international agreements.*

CHAPTER 3   INSTITUTIONAL PROVISIONS

Article 109a

1.   The Governing Council of the ECB shall comprise the members of the Executive Board of the ECB and the Governors of the national central banks.

2.   (a)   The Executive Board shall comprise the President, the Vice-President and four other members.

(b)   The President, the Vice-President and the other members of the Executive Board shall be appointed from among persons of recognised standing and professional experience in monetary or banking matters by common accord of the Governments of the Member States at the level of Heads of State or of Government, on a recommendation from the Council, after it has consulted the European Parliament and the Governing Council of the ECB.

Their term of office shall be eight years and shall not be renewable.

Only nationals of Member States may be members of the Executive Board.

Article 109b

1.   The President of the Council and a member of the Commission may participate, without having the right to vote, in meetings of the Governing Council of the ECB.

The President of the Council may submit a motion for deliberation to the Governing Council of the ECB.

2.   The President of the ECB shall be invited to participate in Council meetings when the Council is discussing matters relating to the objectives and tasks of the ESCB.

3.   The ECB shall address an annual report on the activities of the ESCB and on the monetary policy of both the previous and current year to the European Parliament, the Council and the Commission, and also to the European Council. The President of the ECB shall present this report to the Council and to the European Parliament, which may hold a general debate on that basis.

The President of the ECB and the other members of the Executive Board may, at the request of the European Parliament or on their own initiative, be heard by the competent Committees of the European Parliament.

Article 109c

1.   In order to promote coordination of the policies of Member States to the full extent needed for the functioning of the internal market, a Monetary Committee with advisory status is hereby set up.

It shall have the following tasks:

— to keep under review the monetary and financial situation of the Member States and of the Community and the general payments system of the Member States and to report regularly thereon to the Council and to the Commission;

— to deliver opinions at the request of the Council or of the Commission, or on its own initiative for submission to those institutions;

— without prejudice to Article 151, to contribute to the preparation of the work of the Council referred to in Articles 73f, 73g, 103(2), (3), (4) and (5), 103a, 104a, 104b, 104c, 109e(2), 109f(6), 109h, 109i, 109j(2) and 109k(1);

— to examine, at least once a year, the situation regarding the movement of capital and the freedom of payments, as they result from the application of this Treaty and of measures adopted by the Council; the examination shall cover all measures relating to capital movements and payments; the Committee shall report to the Commission and to the Council on the outcome of this examination.

The Member States and the Commission shall each appoint two members of the Monetary Committee.

2.   At the start of the third stage, an Economic and Financial Committee shall be set up. The Monetary Committee provided for in paragraph 1 shall be dissolved.

The Economic and Financial Committee shall have the following tasks:

— to deliver opinions at the request of the Council or of the Commission, or on its own initiative for submission to those institutions;

— to keep under review the economic and financial situation of the Member States and of the Community and to report regularly thereon to the Council and to the Commission, in particular on financial relations with third countries and international institutions;

— without prejudice to Article 151, to contribute to the preparation of the work of the Council referred to in Articles 73f, 73g, 103(2), (3), (4) and (5), 103a, 104a, 104b, 104c, 105(6), 105a(2), 106(5) and (6), 109, 109h, 109i(2) and (3), 109k(2), 109l(4) and (5), and to carry out other advisory and preparatory tasks assigned to it by the Council;

— to examine, at least once a year, the situation regarding the movement of capital and the freedom of payments, as they result from the application of this Treaty and of measures adopted by the Council; the examination shall cover all measures relating to capital movements and payments; the Committee shall report to the Commission and to the Council on the outcome of this examination.

The Member States, the Commission and the ECB shall each appoint no more than two members of the Committee.

3.   The Council shall, acting by a qualified majority on a proposal from the Commission and after consulting the ECB and the Committee referred to in this Article, lay down detailed provisions concerning the composition of the Economic and Financial Committee. The President of the Council shall inform the European Parliament of such a decision.

4.   In addition to the tasks set out in paragraph 2, if and as long as there are Member States with a derogation as referred to in Articles 109k and 109l, the Committee shall keep under review the monetary and financial situation and the general payments system of those Member States and report regularly thereon to the Council and to the Commission.

Article 109d
For matters within the scope of Articles 103(4), 104c with the exception of paragraph 14, 109, 109j, 109k and 109l(4) and (5), the Council or a Member State may request the Commission to make a recommendation or a proposal, as appropriate. The Commission shall examine this request and submit its conclusions to the Council without delay.

CHAPTER 4 TRANSITIONAL PROVISIONS

Article 109e
1. The second stage for achieving economic and monetary union shall begin on 1 January 1994.
2. Before that date
(a) each Member State shall
—adopt, where necessary, appropriate measures to comply with the prohibitions laid down in Article 73b, without prejudice to Article 73e, and in Articles 104 and 104a(1);
—adopt, if necessary, with a view to permitting the assessment provided for in subparagraph (b), multiannual programmes intended to ensure the lasting convergence necessary for the achievement of economic and monetary union, in particular with regard to price stability and sound public finances;
(b) the Council shall, on the basis of a report from the Commission, assess the progress made with regard to economic and monetary convergence, in particular with regard to price stability and sound public finances, and the progress made with the implementation of Community law concerning the internal market.
3. The provisions of Articles 104, 104a(1), 104b(1) and 104c with the exception of paragraphs 1, 9, 11 and 14 shall apply from the beginning of the second stage.
The provisions of Articles 103a(2), 104c(1), (9) and (11), 105, 105a, 107, 109, 109a, 109b and 109c(2) and (4) shall apply from the beginning of the third stage.
4. In the second stage, Member States shall endeavour to avoid excessive government deficits.
5. During the second stage, each Member State shall, as appropriate, start the process leading to the independence of its central bank, in accordance with Article 108.

Article 109f
1. At the start of the second stage, a European Monetary Institute (hereinafter referred to as 'EMI') shall be established and take up its duties; it shall have legal personality and be directed and managed by a Council, consisting of a President and the Governors of the national central banks, one of whom shall be Vice-President.
The President shall be appointed by common accord of the Governments of the Member States at the level of Heads of State or of Government, on a recommendation from, as the case may be, the Committee of Governors of the central banks of the Member States (hereinafter referred to as 'Committee of Governors') or the Council of the EMI, and after consulting the European Parliament and the Council, the President shall be selected from among persons of

recognised standing and professional experience in monetary or banking matters. Only nationals of Member States may be President of the EMI. The Council of the EMI shall appoint the Vice-President.

The Statute of the EMI is laid down in a Protocol annexed to this Treaty.

The Committee of Governors shall be dissolved at the start of the second stage.

2.   The EMI shall:

*   —strengthen cooperation between the national central banks;*
*   —strengthen the coordination of the monetary policies of the Member States, with the aim of ensuring price stability;*
*   —monitor the functioning of the European Monetary System;*
*   —hold consultations concerning issues falling within the competence of the national central banks and affecting the stability of financial institutions and markets;*
*   —take over the tasks of the European Monetary Cooperation Fund, which shall be dissolved; the modalities of dissolution are laid down in the Statute of the EMI;*
*   —facilitate the use of the ECU and oversee its development, including the smooth functioning of the ECU clearing system.*

3.   For the preparation of the third stage, the EMI shall:

*   —prepare the instruments and the procedures necessary for carrying out a single monetary policy in the third stage;*
*   —promote the harmonisation, where necessary, of the rules and practices governing the collection, compilation and distribution of statistics in the areas within its field of competence;*
*   —prepare the rules for operations to be undertaken by the national central banks within the framework of the ESCB;*
*   —promote the efficiency of cross-border payments;*
*   —supervise the technical preparation of ECU bank notes.*

At the latest by 31 December 1996, the EMI shall specify the regulatory, organisational and logistical framework necessary for the ESCB to perform its tasks in the third stage. This framework shall be submitted for decision to the ECB at the date of its establishment.

4.   The EMI, acting by a majority of two thirds of the members of its Council, may:

*   —formulate opinions or recommendations on the overall orientation of monetary policy and exchange rate policy as well as on related measures introduced in each Member State;*
*   —submit opinions or recommendations to Governments and to the Council on policies which might affect the internal or external monetary situation in the Community and, in particular, the functioning of the European Monetary System;*
*   —make recommendations to the monetary authorities of the Member States concerning the conduct of their monetary policy.*

5.   The EMI, acting unanimously, may decide to publish its opinions and its recommendations.

6.   The EMI shall be consulted by the Council regarding any proposed Community act within its field of competence.

Within the limits and under the conditions set out by the Council, acting by a qualified majority on a proposal from the Commission and after consulting the European Parliament and the EMI, the EMI shall be consulted by the authorities of the Member States on any draft legislative provision within its field of competence.

7. *The Council may, acting unanimously on a proposal from the Commission and after consulting the European Parliament and the EMI, confer upon the EMI other tasks for the preparation of the third stage.*

8. *Where this Treaty provides for a consultative role for the ECB, references to the ECB shall be read as referring to the EMI before the establishment of the ECB.*

Where this Treaty provides for a consultative role for the EMI, references to the EMI shall be read, before 1 January 1994, as referring to the Committee of Governors.

9. *During the second stage, the term 'ECB' used in Articles 173, 175, 176, 177, 180 and 215 shall be read as referring to the EMI.*

Article 109g
The currency composition of the ECU basket shall not be changed.

From the start of the third stage, the value of the ECU shall be irrevocably fixed in accordance with Article 109l(4).

Article 109h
1. *Where a Member State is in difficulties or is seriously threatened with difficulties as regards its balance of payments either as a result of an overall disequilibrium in its balance of payments, or as a result of the type of currency at its disposal, and where such difficulties are liable in particular to jeopardise the functioning of the common market or the progressive implementation of the common commercial policy, the Commission shall immediately investigate the position of the State in question and the action which, making use of all the means at its disposal, that State has taken or may take in accordance with the provisions of this Treaty. The Commission shall state what measures it recommends the State concerned to take.*

If the action taken by a Member State and the measures suggested by the Commission do not prove sufficient to overcome the difficulties which have arisen or which threaten, the Commission shall, after consulting the Committee referred to in Article 109c, recommend to the Council the granting of mutual assistance and appropriate methods therefor.

The Commission shall keep the Council regularly informed of the situation and of how it is developing.

2. *The Council, acting by a qualified majority, shall grant such mutual assistance; it shall adopt directives or decisions laying down the conditions and details of such assistance, which may take such forms as:*

(a) a concerted approach to or within any other international organisations to which Member States may have recourse;

(b) measures needed to avoid deflection of trade where the State which is in difficulties maintains or reintroduces quantitative restrictions against third countries;

(c) the granting of limited credits by other Member States, subject to their agreement.

3.   *If the mutual assistance recommended by the Commission is not granted by the Council or if the mutual assistance granted and the measures taken are insufficient, the Commission shall authorise the State which is in difficulties to take protective measures, the conditions and details of which the Commission shall determine.*

Such authorisation may be revoked and such conditions and details may be changed by the Council acting by a qualified majority.

4.   *Subject to Article 109k(6), this Article shall cease to apply from the beginning of the third stage.*

Article 109i

1.   *Where a sudden crisis in the balance of payments occurs and a decision within the meaning of Article 109h(2) is not immediately taken, the Member State concerned may, as a precaution, take the necessary protective measures. Such measures must cause the least possible disturbance in the functioning of the common market and must not be wider in scope than is strictly necessary to remedy the sudden difficulties which have arisen.*

2.   *The Commission and the other Member States shall be informed of such protective measures not later than when they enter into force. The Commission may recommend to the Council the granting of mutual assistance under Article 109h.*

3.   *After the Commission has delivered an opinion and the Committee referred to in Article 109c has been consulted, the Council may, acting by a qualified majority, decide that the State concerned shall amend, suspend or abolish the protective measures referred to above.*

4.   *Subject to Article 109k(6), this Article shall cease to apply from the beginning of the third stage.*

Article 109j

1.   *The Commission and the EMI shall report to the Council on the progress made in the fulfilment by the Member States of their obligations regarding the achievement of economic and monetary union. These reports shall include an examination of the compatibility between each Member State's national legislation, including the statutes of its national central bank, and Articles 107 and 108 of this Treaty and the Statute of the ESCB. The reports shall also examine the achievement of a high degree of sustainable convergence by reference to the fulfilment by each Member State of the following criteria:*

— *the achievement of a high degree of price stability; this will be apparent from a rate of inflation which is close to that of, at most, the three best performing Member States in terms of price stability;*

— *the sustainability of the government financial position; this will be apparent from having achieved a government budgetary position without a deficit that is excessive as determined in accordance with Article 104c(6);*

— *the observance of the normal fluctuation margins provided for by the Exchange Rate Mechanism of the European Monetary System, for at least two years, without devaluing against the currency of any other Member State;*

— the durability of convergence achieved by the Member State and of its participation in the Exchange Rate Mechanism of the European Monetary System being reflected in the long-term interest rate levels.

The four criteria mentioned in this paragraph and the relevant periods over which they are to be respected are developed further in a Protocol annexed to this Treaty. The reports of the Commission and the EMI shall also take account of the development of the ECU, the results of the integration of markets, the situation and development of the balances of payments on current account and an examination of the development of unit labour costs and other price indices.

2.   On the basis of these reports, the Council, acting by a qualified majority on a recommendation from the Commission, shall assess:

— for each Member State, whether it fulfils the necessary conditions for the adoption of a single currency;

— whether a majority of the Member States fulfil the necessary conditions for the adoption of a single currency,

and recommend its findings to the Council, meeting in the composition of the Heads of State or of Government. The European Parliament shall be consulted and forward its opinion to the Council, meeting in the composition of the Heads of State or of Government.

3.   Taking due account of the reports referred to in paragraph 1 and the opinion of the European Parliament referred to in paragraph 2, the Council, meeting in the composition of Heads of State or of Government, shall, acting by a qualified majority, not later than 31 December 1996:

— decide, on the basis of the recommendations of the Council referred to in paragraph 2, whether a majority of the Member States fulfil the necessary conditions for the adoption of a single currency;

— decide whether it is appropriate for the Community to enter the third stage,

and if so

— set the date for the beginning of the third stage.

4.   If by the end of 1997 the date for the beginning of the third stage has not been set, the third stage shall start on 1 January 1999. Before 1 July 1998, the Council, meeting in the composition of Heads of State or of Government, after a repetition of the procedure provided for in paragraphs 1 and 2, with the exception of the second indent of paragraph 2, taking into account the reports referred to in paragraph 1 and the opinion of the European Parliament, shall, acting by a qualified majority and on the basis of the recommendations of the Council referred to in paragraph 2, confirm which Member States fulfil the necessary conditions for the adoption of a single currency.

Article 109k

1.   If the decision has been taken to set the date in accordance with Article 109j(3), the Council shall, on the basis of its recommendations referred to in Article 109j(2), acting by a qualified majority on a recommendation from the Commission, decide whether any, and if so which, Member States shall have a derogation as defined in paragraph 3 of this Article. Such Member States shall in this Treaty be referred to as 'Member States with a derogation'.

If the Council has confirmed which Member States fulfil the necessary conditions for the adoption of a single currency, in accordance with Article 109j(4), those Member States which do not fulfil the conditions shall have a derogation as defined in paragraph 3 of this Article. Such Member States shall in this Treaty be referred to as 'Member States with a derogation'.

2.   At least once every two years, or at the request of a Member State with a derogation, the Commission and the ECB shall report to the Council in accordance with the procedure laid down in Article 109j(1). After consulting the European Parliament and after discussion in the Council, meeting in the composition of the Heads of State or of Government, the Council shall, acting by a qualified majority on a proposal from the Commission, decide which Member States with a derogation fulfil the necessary conditions on the basis of the criteria set out in Article 109j(1), and abrogate the derogations of the Member States concerned.

3.   A derogation referred to in paragraph 1 shall entail that the following Articles do not apply to the Member State concerned: Articles 104c(9) and (11), 105(1), (2), (3) and (5), 105a, 108a, 109, and 109a(2)(b). The exclusion of such a Member State and its national central bank from rights and obligations within the ESCB is laid down in Chapter IX of the Statute of the ESCB.

4.   In Articles 105(1), (2) and (3), 105a, 108a, 109 and 109a(2)(b), 'Member States' shall be read as 'Member States without a derogation'.

5.   The voting rights of Member States with a derogation shall be suspended for the Council decisions referred to in the Articles of this Treaty mentioned in paragraph 3. In that case, by way of derogation from Articles 148 and 189a(1), a qualified majority shall be defined as two thirds of the votes of the representatives of the Member States without a derogation weighted in accordance with Article 148(2), and unanimity of those Member States shall be required for an act requiring unanimity.

6.   Articles 109h and 109i shall continue to apply to a Member State with a derogation.

Article 109l

1.   Immediately after the decision on the date for the beginning of the third stage has been taken in accordance with Article 109j(3), or, as the case may be, immediately after 1 July 1998:

*   —the Council shall adopt the provisions referred to in Article 106(6);*

*   —the governments of the Member States without a derogation shall appoint, in accordance with the procedure set out in Article 50 of the Statute of the ESCB, the President, the Vice-President and the other members of the Executive Board of the ECB. If there are Member States with a derogation, the number of members of the Executive*

Board may be smaller than provided for in Article 11.1 of the Statute of the ESCB, but in no circumstances shall it be less than four.

As soon as the Executive Board is appointed, the ESCB and the ECB shall be established and shall prepare for their full operation as described in this Treaty and the Statute of the ESCB. The full exercise of their powers shall start from the first day of the third stage.

2. As soon as the ECB is established, it shall, if necessary take over tasks of the EMI. The EMI shall go into liquidation upon the establishment of the ECB; the modalities of liquidation are laid down in the Statute of the EMI.

3. If and as long as there are Member States with a derogation, and without prejudice to Article 106(3) of this Treaty, the General Council of the ECB referred to in Article 45 of the Statute of the ESCB shall be constituted as a third decision-making body of the ECB.

4. At the starting date of the third stage, the Council shall, acting with the unanimity of the Member States without a derogation, on a proposal from the Commission and after consulting the ECB, adopt the conversion rates at which their currencies shall be irrevocably fixed and at which irrevocably fixed rate the ECU shall be substituted for these currencies, and the ECU will become a currency in its own right. This measure shall by itself not modify the external value of the ECU. The Council shall, acting according to the same procedure, also take the other measures necessary for the rapid introduction of the ECU as the single currency of those Member States.

5. If it is decided, according to the procedure set out in Article 109k(2), to abrogate a derogation, the Council shall, acting with the unanimity of the Member States without a derogation and the Member State concerned, on a proposal from the Commission and after consulting the ECB, adopt the rate at which the ECU shall be substituted for the currency of the Member State concerned, and take the other measures necessary for the introduction of the ECU as the single currency in the Member State concerned.

Article 109m

1. Until the beginning of the third stage, each Member State shall treat its exchange rate policy as a matter of common interest. In so doing, Member States shall take account of the experience acquired in cooperation within the framework of the European Monetary System (EMS) and in developing the ECU, and shall respect existing powers in this field.

2. From the beginning of the third stage and for as long as a Member State has a derogation, paragraph 1 shall apply by analogy to the exchange rate policy of that Member State.

TITLE VII[1]   COMMON COMMERCIAL POLICY

Article 110

By establishing a customs union between themselves Member States aim to contribute, in the common interest, to the harmonious development of world

Note

[1]New title as inserted by Article G(26) TEU, replacing Chapter 4 of Title II, Articles 110 to 116.

trade, the progressive abolition of restrictions on international trade and the lowering of customs barriers.

The common commercial policy shall take into account the favourable effect which the abolition of customs duties between Member States may have on the increase in the competitive strength of undertakings in those States.

Article 111
(repealed)

Article 112

1. Without prejudice to obligations undertaken by them within the framework of other international organisations, Member States shall, before the end of the transitional period, progressively harmonise the systems whereby they grant aid for exports to third countries, to the extent necessary to ensure that competition between undertakings of the Community is not distorted.

On a proposal from the Commission, the Council, shall, acting unanimously until the end of the second stage and by a qualified majority thereafter, issue any directives needed for this purpose.

2. The preceding provisions shall not apply to such drawback of customs duties or charges having equivalent effect nor to such repayment of indirect taxation including turnover taxes, excise duties and other indirect taxes as is allowed when goods are exported from a Member State to a third country, in so far as such drawback or repayment does not exceed the amount imposed, directly or indirectly, on the products exported.

Article 113[1]

1. The common commercial policy shall be based on uniform principles, particularly in regard to changes in tariff rates, the conclusion of tariff and trade agreements, the achievement of uniformity in measures of liberalisation, export policy and measures to protect trade such as those to be taken in the event of dumping or subsidies.

2. The commission shall submit proposals to the Council for implementing the common commercial policy.

3. Where agreements with *one or more States or international or-ganisations* need to be negotiated, the Commission shall make recommendations to the Council, which shall authorise the Commission to open the necessary negotiations.

The Commission shall conduct these negotiations in consultation with a special committee appointed by the Council to assist the Commission in this task and within the framework of such directives as the Council may issue to it. *The relevant provisions of Article 228 shall apply.*

4. In exercising the powers conferred upon it by this Article, the Council shall act by a qualified majority.

Note
[1]As amended by Article G(28) TEU.

Article 114
(repealed)

Article 115[1]

To order to ensure that the execution of measures of commercial policy taken in accordance with this Treaty by any Member State is not obstructed by deflection of trade, or where differences between such measures lead to economic difficulties in one or more Member States, the Commission shall recommend the methods for the requisite cooperation between Member States. Failing this, the Commission *may authorise* Member States to take the necessary protective measures, the conditions and details of which it shall determine.

In case of urgency, Member States shall request authorisation to take the necessary measures themselves from the Commission, which shall take a decision as soon as possible; the Member States concerned shall then notify the measures to the other Member States. The Commission may decide at any time that the Member States concerned shall amend or abolish the measures in question.

In the selection of such measures, priority shall be given to those which cause the least disturbance of the functioning of the common market.

Note

[1]As amended by Article G(30) TEU.

Article 116

(repealed)

TITLE VIII   SOCIAL POLICY, EDUCATION, VOCATIONAL TRAINING AND YOUTH[1]
CHAPTER 1   SOCIAL PROVISIONS

Article 117

Member States agree upon the need to promote improved working conditions and an improved standard of living for workers, so as to make possible their harmonisation while the improvement is being maintained.

They believe that such a development will ensue not only from the functioning of the common market, which will favour the harmonisation of social systems, but also from the procedures provided for in this Treaty and from the approximation of provisions laid down by law, regulation or administrative action.

Note

[1]Title as introduced by Article G(32) TEU.

Article 118

Without prejudice to the other provisions of this Treaty and in conformity with its general objectives, the Commission shall have the task of promoting close cooperation between Member States in the social field, particularly in matters relating to:

— employment;
— labour law and working conditions;
— basic and advanced vocational training;
— social security;
— prevention of occupational accidents and diseases;
— occupational hygiene;

— the right of association, and collective bargaining between employers and workers.

To this end, the Commission shall act in close contact with Member States by making studies, delivering opinions and arranging consultations both on problems arising at national level and on those of concern to international organisations.

Before delivering the opinions provided for in this Article, the Commission shall consult the Economic and Social Committee.

Article 118a

1.   Member States shall pay particular attention to encouraging improvements, especially in the working environment, as regards the health and safety of workers, and shall set as their objective the harmonisation of conditions in this area, while maintaining the improvements made.

2.   In order to help achieve the objective laid down in the first paragraph, the Council, *acting in accordance with the procedure referred to in Article 189c* and after consulting the Economic and Social Committee, shall adopt by means of directives, minimum requirements for gradual implementation, having regard to the conditions and technical rules obtaining in each of the Member States.[1]

Such directives shall avoid imposing administrative, financial and legal constraints in a way which would hold back the creation and development of small and medium-sized undertakings.

3.   The provisions adopted pursuant to this Article shall not prevent any Member State from maintaining or introducing more stringent measures for the protection of working conditions compatible with this Treaty.

Note
[1]First subparagraph as amended by Article G(33) TEU.

Article 118b

The Commission shall endeavour to develop the dialogue between management and labour at European level which could, if the two sides consider it desirable, lead to relations based on agreement.

Article 119

Each Member State shall during the first stage ensure and subsequently maintain the application of the principle that men and women should receive equal pay for equal work.

For the purpose of this Article, 'pay' means the ordinary basic or minimum wage or salary and any other consideration, whether in cash or in kind, which the worker receives, directly or indirectly, in respect of his employment from his employer.

Equal pay without discrimination based on sex means:

(a)   that pay for the same work at piece rates shall be calculated on the basis of the same unit of measurement;

(b)   that pay for work at time rates shall be the same for the same job.

Article 120

Member States shall endeavour to maintain the existing equivalence between paid holiday schemes.

Article 121

The Council may, acting unanimously and after consulting the Economic and Social Committee, assign to the Commission tasks in connection with the implementation of common measures, particularly as regards social security for the migrant workers referred to in Articles 48 to 51.

Article 122

The Commission shall include a separate chapter on social developments within the Community in its annual report to the European Parliament.

The European Parliament may invite the Commission to draw up reports on any particular problems concerning social conditions.

CHAPTER 2   THE EUROPEAN SOCIAL FUND

Article 123[1]

In order to improve employment opportunities for workers in the *internal* market and to contribute thereby to raising the standard of living, a European Social Fund is hereby established in accordance with the provisions set out below; *it shall aim* to render the employment of workers easier and to increase their geographical and occupational mobility within the Community, *and to facilitate their adaptation to industrial changes and to changes in production systems, in particular through vocational training and retraining*.

Note
[1]As amended by Article G(34) TEU.

Article 124

The Fund shall be administered by the Commission.

The Commission shall be assisted in this task by a Committee presided over by a member of the Commission and composed of representatives of Governments, trade unions and employers' organisations.

Article 125[1]

The Council, acting in accordance with the procedure referred to in Article 189c and after consulting the Economic and Social Committee, shall adopt implementing decisions relating to the European Social Fund.

Note
[1]As amended by Article G(35) TEU.

CHAPTER 3[1]   EDUCATION, VOCATIONAL TRAINING AND YOUTH

Article 126

1.   The Community shall contribute to the development of quality education by encouraging cooperation between Member States and, if necessary, by supporting and supplementing their action, while fully respecting the responsibility of the Member States for the content of teaching and the organisation of education systems and their cultural and linguistic diversity.

Note
[1]Chapter 3 (Articles 126 and 127) as introduced by Article G(36) TEU. Former Articles 126 and 127 null and void.

2.   *Community action shall be aimed at:*

    — *developing the European dimension in education, particularly through the teaching and dissemination of the languages of the Member States;*

    — *encouraging mobility of students and teachers, inter alia by encouraging the academic recognition of diplomas and periods of study;*

    — *promoting cooperation between educational establishments;*

    — *developing exchanges of information and experience on issues common to the education systems of the Member States;*

    — *encouraging the development of youth exchanges and of exchanges of socio-educational instructors;*

    — *encouraging the development of distance education.*

3.   *The Community and the Member States shall foster co-operation with third countries and the competent international organisations in the field of education, in particular the Council of Europe.*

4.   *In order to contribute to the achievement of the objectives referred to in this Article, the Council:*

    — *acting in accordance with the procedure referred to in Article 189b, after consulting the Economic and Social Committee and the Committee of the Regions, shall adopt incentive measures, excluding any harmonisation of the laws and regulations of the Member States;*

    — *acting by a qualified majority on a proposal from the Commission, shall adopt recommendations.*

Article 127

1.   *The Community shall implement a vocational training policy which shall support and supplement the action of the Member States, while fully respecting the responsibility of the Member States for the content and origination of vocational training.*

2.   *Community action shall aim to:*

    — *facilitate adaptation to industrial changes, in particular through vocational training and retraining;*

    — *improve initial and continuing vocational training in order to facilitate vocational integration and reintegration into the labour market;*

    — *facilitate access to vocational training and encourage mobility of instructors and trainees and particularly young people;*

    — *stimulate cooperation on training between educational or training establishments and firms;*

    — *develop exchanges of information and experience on issues common to the training systems of the Member States.*

3.   *The Community and the Member States shall foster cooperation with third countries and the competent international organisations in the sphere of vocational training.*

4.   *The Council, acting in accordance with the procedure referred to in Article 189c and after consulting the Economic and Social Committee, shall adopt measures to contribute to the achievement of the objectives referred to in this Article, excluding any harmonisation of the laws and regulations of the Member States.*

TITLE IX[1]   CULTURE

Article 128

1.   *The Community shall contribute to the flowering of the cultures of the Member States, while respecting their national and regional diversity and at the same time bringing the common cultural heritage to the fore.*

2.   *Action by the Community shall be aimed at encouraging cooperation betweeen Member States and, if necessary, supporting and supplementing their action in the following areas:*

    —improvement of the knowledge and dissemination of the culture and history of the European peoples;

    —conservation and safeguarding of cultural heritage of European significance;

    —non-commercial cultural exchanges;

    —artistic and literary creation, including in the audio-visual sector.

3.   *The Community and the Member States shall foster cooperation with third countries and the competent international organisations in the sphere of culture, in particular the Council of Europe.*

4.   *The Community shall take cultural aspects into account in its action under other provisions of this Treaty.*

5.   *In order to contribute to the achievement of the objectives referred to in this Article, the Council:*

    —acting in accordance with the procedure referred to in Article 189b and after consulting the Committee of the Regions, shall adopt incentive measures, excluding any harmonisation of the laws and regulations of the Member States. The Council shall act unanimously throughout the procedures referred to in Article 189b;

    —acting unanimously on a proposal from the Commission, shall adopt recommendations.

Note
[1]As inserted by Article G(37) TEU. Former Article 128 null and void. Former Articles 129 and 130 have become Articles 198d and 198e.

TITLE X[1]   PUBLIC HEALTH

Article 129

1.   *The Community shall contribute towards ensuring a high level of human health protection by encouraging cooperation between the Member States and, if necessary, lending support to their action.*

Community action shall be directed towards the prevention of diseases, in particular the major health scourges, including drug dependence, by promoting research into their causes and their transmission, as well as health information and education.

Health protection requirements shall form a constituent part of the Community's other policies.

2.   *Member States shall, in liaison with the Commission, coordinate among themselves their policies and programmes in the areas*

Note
[1]As inserted by Article G(38) TEU.

referred to in paragraph 1. The Commission may, in close contact with the Member States, take any useful initiative to promote such coordination.

3. The Community and the Member States shall foster cooperation with third countries and the competent international organisations in the sphere of public health.

4. In order to contribute to the achievement of the objectives referred to in this Article, the Council:

—acting in accordance with the procedure referred to in Article 189b, after consulting the Economic and Social Committee and the Committee of the Regions, shall adopt incentive measures, excluding any harmonisation of the laws and regulations of the Member States;

—acting by a qualified majority on a proposal from the Commission, shall adopt recommendations.

TITLE XI[1]   CONSUMER PROTECTION

Article 129a

1. The Community shall contribute to the attainment of a high level of consumer protection through:

(a) measures adopted pursuant to Article 100a in the context of the completion of the internal market;

(b) specific action which supports and supplements the policy pursued by the Member States to protect the health, safety and economic interests of consumers and to provide adequate information to consumers.

2. The Council, acting in accordance with the procedure referred to in Article 189b and after consulting the Economic and Social Committee, shall adopt the specific action referred to in paragraph 1(b).

3. Action adopted pursuant to paragraph 2 shall not prevent any Member State from maintaining or introducing more stringent protective measures. Such measures must be compatible with this Treaty. The Commission shall be notified of them.

Note
[1]As inserted by Article G(38) TEU.

TITLE XII[1]   TRANS-EUROPEAN NETWORKS

Article 129b

1. To help achieve the objectives referred to in Articles 7a and 130a and to enable citizens of the Union, economic operators and regional and local communities to derive full benefit from the setting up of an area without internal frontiers, the Community shall contribute to the establishment and development of trans-European networks in the areas of transport, telecommunications and energy infrastructures.

2. Within the framework of a system of open and competitive markets, action by the Community shall aim at promoting the interconnection and inter-operability of national networks as well as access to such networks. It shall take account in particular of the need to link island, landlocked and peripheral regions with the central regions of the Community.

Note
[1]As inserted by Article G(38) TEU.

Article 129c

1. In order to achieve the objectives referred to in Article 129b, the Community:

—shall establish a series of guidelines covering the objectives, priorities and broad lines of measures envisaged in the sphere of trans-European networks; these guidelines shall identify projects of common interest;

—shall implement any measures that may prove necessary to ensure the inter-operability of the networks, in particular in the field of technical standardisation;

—may support the financial efforts made by the Member States for projects of common interest financed by Member States, which are identified in the framework of the guidelines referred to in the first indent, particularly through feasibility studies, loan guarantees or interest rate subsidies; the Community may also contribute, through the Cohesion Fund to be set up no later than 31 December 1993 pursuant to Article 130d, to the financing of specific projects in Member States in the area of transport infrastructure.

The Community's activities shall take into account the potential economic viability of the projects.

2. Member States shall, in liaison with the Commission, coordinate among themselves the policies pursued at national level which may have a significant impact on the achievement of the objectives referred to in Article 129b. The Commission may, in close cooperation with the Member States, take any useful initiative to promote such coordination.

3. The Community may decide to cooperate with third countries to promote projects of mutual interest and to ensure the inter-operability of networks.

Article 129d

The guidelines referred to in Article 129c(1) shall be adopted by the Council, acting in accordance with the procedure referred to in Article 189b and after consulting the Economic and Social Committee and the Committee of the Regions.

Guidelines and projects of common interest which relate to the territory of a Member State shall require the approval of the Member State concerned.

The Council, acting in accordance with the procedure referred to in Article 189c and after consulting the Economic and Social Committee and the Committee of the Regions, shall adopt the other measures provided for in Article 129c(1).

TITLE XIII[1] INDUSTRY

Article 130

1. The Community and the Member States shall ensure that the conditions necessary for the competitiveness of the Community's industry exist.

Note

[1]As inserted by Article G(38) TEU.

For that purpose, in accordance with a system of open and competitive markets, their action shall be aimed at:
    — speeding up the adjustment of industry to structural changes;
    — encouraging an environment favourable to initiative and to the development of undertakings throughout the Community, particularly small and medium-sized undertakings;
    — encouraging an environment favourable to cooperation between undertakings;
    — fostering better exploitation of the industrial potential of policies of innovation, research and technological development.
    2.   The Member States shall consult each other in liaison with the Commission and, where necessary, shall coordinate their action. The Commission may take any useful initiative to promote such coordination.
    3.   The Community shall contribute to the achievement of the objectives set out in paragraph 1 through the policies and activities it pursues under other provisions of this Treaty. The Council, acting unanimously on a proposal from the Commission, after consulting the European Parliament and the Economic and Social Committee, may decide on specific measures in support of action taken in the Member States to achieve the objectives set out in paragraph 1.
    This Title shall not provide a basis for the introduction by the Community of any measure which could lead to a distortion of competition.

TITLE XIV[1]   ECONOMIC AND SOCIAL COHESION

Article 130a
In order to promote its overall harmonious development, the Community shall develop and pursue its actions leading to the strengthening of its economic and social cohesion.

    In particular, the Community shall aim at reducing disparities between *the levels of development of* the various regions and the backwardness of the least-favoured regions, *including rural areas*.

Note
[1]Former Title V, as amended by Article G(38) TEU.

Article 130b
Member States shall conduct their economic policies and shall coordinate them in such a way as, in addition, to attain the objectives set out in Article 130a. *The formulation* and implementation of the Community's policies and actions and the implementation of the internal market shall take into account the objectives set out in Article 130a and shall contribute to their achievement. The Community shall also support the achievement of these objectives by the action it takes through the Structural Funds (European Agricultural Guidance and Guarantee Fund, Guidance Section; European Social Fund; European Regional Development Fund), the European Investment Bank and the other existing financial instruments.

    The Commission shall submit a report to the European Parliament, the Council, the Economic and Social Committee and the Committee of the Regions every three years on the progress made towards achieving economic and social cohesion and on the manner in which the various means provided for in this Article have contributed to it. This report shall, if necessary, be accompanied by appropriate proposals.

If specific actions prove necessary outside the Funds and without prejudice to the measures decided upon within the framework of the other Community policies, such actions may be adopted by the Council acting unanimously on a proposal from the Commission and after consulting the European Parliament, the Economic and Social Committee and the Committee of the Regions.

Article 130c
The European Regional Development Fund is intended to help to redress the main regional imbalances in the Community through participation in the development and structural adjustment of regions whose development is lagging behind and in the conversion of declining industrial regions.

Article 130d
Without prejudice to Article 130e, the Council, acting unanimously on a proposal from the Commission and after obtaining the assent of the European Parliament and consulting the Economic and Social Committee and the Committee of the Regions, shall define the tasks, priority objectives and the organisation of the Structural Funds, which may involve grouping the Funds. The Council, acting by the same procedure, shall also define the general rules applicable to them and the provisions necessary to ensure their effectiveness and the coordination of the Funds with one another and with the other existing financial instruments.

The Council, acting in accordance with the same procedure, shall before 31 December 1993 set up a Cohesion Fund to provide a financial contribution to projects in the fields of environment and trans-European networks in the area of transport infrastructure.

Article 130e
Implementing decisions relating to the European Regional Development Fund shall be taken by the Council, acting in accordance with the procedure referred to in Article 189c and after consulting the Economic and Social Committee and the Committee of the Regions.

With regard to the European Agricultural Guidance and Guarantee Fund, Guidance Section, and the European Social Fund, *Articles 43 and 125* respectively shall continue to apply.

TITLE XV[1]   RESEARCH AND TECHNOLOGICAL DEVELOPMENT

Article 130f
1.   The Community *shall have* the objective of strengthening the scientific and technological bases of Community industry and encouraging it to become more competitive at international level, *while promoting all the research activities deemed necessary by virtue of other Chapters of this Treaty.*

Note
[1]Former Title VI, as amended by Article G(38) TEU.

2.   *For this purpose* the Community shall, throughout the Community, encourage undertakings, including small and medium-sized undertakings, research centres and universities in their research and technological development activities *of high quality;* it shall support their efforts to cooperate with one another, aiming, notably, at enabling undertakings to exploit the internal market potential to the full, in particular through the opening up of national public contracts, the definition of common standards and the removal of legal and fiscal obstacles to that cooperation.

3.   *All Community activities under this Treaty in the area of research and technological development, including demonstration projects, shall be decided on and implemented in accordance with the provisions of this Title.*

Article 130g
In pursuing these objectives, the Community shall carry out the following activities, complementing the activities carried out in the Member States:

(a)   implementation of research, technological development and demonstration programmes, by promoting cooperation with and between undertakings, research centres and universities;

(b)   promotion of cooperation in the field of Community research, technological development and demonstration with third countries and international organisations;

(c)   dissemination and optimisation of the results of activities in Community research, technological development and demonstration;

(d)   stimulation of the training and mobility of researchers in the Community.

Article 130h
1.   *The Community and the Member States shall coordinate their research and technological development activities so as to ensure that national policies and Community policy are mutually consistent.*

2.   *In close cooperation with the Member States, the Commission may take any useful initiative to promote the coordination referred to in paragraph 1.*

Article 130i
1.   *A multiannual framework programme, setting out all the activities of the Community, shall be adopted by the Council, acting in accordance with the procedure referred to in Article 189b after consulting the Economic and Social Committee. The Council shall act unanimously throughout the procedures referred to in Article 189b.*

The framework programme shall:

—establish the scientific and technological objectives to be achieved by the activities provided for in Article 130g and fix the relevant priorities;

—indicate the broad lines of such activities;

—fix the maximum overall amount and the detailed rules for Community financial participation in the framework programme and the respective shares in each of the activities provided for.

2.   *The framework programme shall be adapted or supplemented as the situation changes.*

3. The framework programme shall be implemented through specific programmes developed within each activity. Each specific programme shall define the detailed rules for implementing it, fix its duration and provide for the means deemed necessary. The sum of the amounts deemed necessary, fixed in the specific programmes, may not exceed the overall maximum amount fixed for the framework programme and each activity.

4. The Council, acting by a qualified majority on a proposal from the Commission and after consulting the European Parliament and the Economic and Social Committee, shall adopt the specific programmes.

Article 130j
For the implementation of the multiannual framework programme the Council shall:

—determine the rules for the participation of undertakings, research centres and universities;

—lay down the rules governing the dissemination of research results.

Article 130k
In implementing the multiannual framework programme, supplementary programmes may be decided on involving the participation of certain Member States only, which shall finance them subject to possible Community participation.

The Council shall adopt the rules applicable to supplementary programmes, particularly as regards the dissemination of knowledge and access by other Member States.

Article 130l
In implementing the multiannual framework programme the Community may make provision, in agreement with the Member States concerned, for participation in research and development programmes undertaken by several Member States, including participation in the structures created for the execution of those programmes.

Article 130m
In implementing the multiannual framework programme the Community may make provision for cooperation in Community research, technological development and demonstration with third countries or international organisations.

The detailed arrangements for such cooperation may be the subject of agreements between the Community and the third parties concerned, which shall be negotiated and concluded in accordance with Article 228.

Article 130n
The Community may set up joint undertakings or any other structure necessary for the efficient execution of Community research, technological development and demonstration programmes.

Article 130o
The Council, acting unanimously on a proposal from the Commission and after consulting the European Parliament and the Economic and Social Committee, shall adopt the provisions referred to in Article 130n.

The Council, acting in accordance with the procedure referred to in Article 189c and after consulting the Economic and Social Committee, shall adopt the provisions referred to in Articles 130j to l. Adoption of the supplementary programmes shall require the agreement of the Member States concerned.

Article 130p
At the beginning of each year the Commission shall send a report to the European Parliament and the Council. The report shall include information on research and technological development activities and the dissemination of results during the previous year, and the work programme for the current year.

Article 130q
(repealed)

TITLE XVI[1]   ENVIRONMENT

Article 130r
1.   Community policy on the environment *shall contribute to pursuit of the following objectives:*
—preserving, protecting and improving the quality of the environment;
—protecting human health;
—prudent and rational utilisation of natural resources;
—promoting measures at international level to deal with regional or worldwide environmental problems.
2.   *Community policy on the environment shall aim at a high level of protection taking into account the diversity of situations in the various regions of the Community. It shall be based on the precautionary principle and on the principles that preventive action should be taken, that environmental damage should as a priority be rectified at source and that the polluter should pay. Environmental protection requirements must be integrated into the definition and implementation of other Community policies.*
In this context, harmonisation measures answering these requirements shall include, where appropriate, a safeguard clause allowing Member States to take provisional measures, for non-economic environmental reasons, subject to a Community inspection procedure.
3.   *In preparing its policy on the environment, the Community shall take account of:*
—available scientific and technical data;
—environmental conditions in the various regions of the Community;
—the potential benefits and costs of action or lack of action;
—the economic and social development of the Community as a whole and the balanced development of its regions.
4.   Within their respective spheres of competence, the Community and the Member States shall cooperate with third countries and with the competent

Note
[1]Former Title VII, as amended by Article G(38) TEU.

international organisations. The arrangements for Community cooperation may be the subject of agreements between the Community and the third parties concerned, which shall be negotiated and concluded in accordance with Article 228.

The previous subparagraph shall be without prejudice to Member States' competence to negotiate in international bodies and to conclude international agreements.

Article 130s

1.   The Council, acting in accordance with the procedure referred to in Article 189c and after consulting the Economic and Social Committee, shall decide what action is to be taken by the Community in order to achieve the objectives referred to in Article 130r.

2.   By way of derogation from the decision-making procedure provided for in paragraph 1 and without prejudice to Article 100a, the Council, acting unanimously on a proposal from the Commission and after consulting the European Parliament and the Economic and Social Committee, shall adopt:

—provisions primarily of a fiscal nature;

—measures concerning town and country planning, land use with the exception of waste management and measures of a general nature, and management of water resources;

—measures significantly affecting a Member State's choice between different energy sources and the general structure of its energy supply.

The Council may, under the conditions laid down in the preceding subparagraph, define those matters referred to in this paragraph on which decisions are to be taken by a qualified majority.

3.   In other areas, general action programmes setting out priority objectives to be attained shall be adopted by the Council, acting in accordance with the procedure referred to in Article 189b and after consulting the Economic and Social Committee.

The Council, acting under the terms of paragraph 1 or paragraph 2 according to the case, shall adopt the measures necessary for the implementation of these programmes.

4.   Without prejudice to certain measures of a Community nature, the Member States shall finance and implement the environment policy.

5.   Without prejudice to the principle that the polluter should pay, if a measure based on the provisions of paragraph 1 involves costs deemed disproportionate for the public authorities of a Member State, the Council shall, in the act adopting that measure, lay down appropriate provisions in the form of:

—temporary derogations and/or

—financial support from the Cohesion Fund to be set up no later than 31 December 1993 pursuant to Article 130d.

Article 130t

The protective measures adopted pursuant to Article 130s shall not prevent any Member State from maintaining or introducing more stringent protective measures. *Such measures must be compatible with this Treaty. They shall be notified to the Commission.*

TITLE XVII[1]   DEVELOPMENT COOPERATION

Article 130u

1.   Community policy in the sphere of development cooperation, which shall be complementary to the policies pursued by the Member States, shall foster:

— the sustainable economic and social development of the developing countries, and more particularly the most disadvantaged among them;

— the smooth and gradual integration of the developing countries into the world economy;

— the campaign against poverty in the developing countries.

2.   Community policy in this area shall contribute to the general objective of developing and consolidating democracy and the rule of law, and to that of respecting human rights and fundamental freedoms.

3.   The Community and the Member States shall comply with the commitments and take account of the objectives they have approved in the context of the United Nations and other competent international organisations.

Note

[1]As inserted by Article G(38) TEU.

Article 130v

The Community shall take account of the objectives referred to in Article 130u in the policies that it implements which are likely to affect developing countries.

Article 130w

1.   Without prejudice to the other provisions of this Treaty the Council, acting in accordance with the procedure referred to in Article 189c, shall adopt the measures necessary to further the objectives referred to in Article 130u. Such measures may take the form of multiannual programmes.

2.   The European Investment Bank shall contribute, under the terms laid down in its Statute, to the implementation of the measures referred to in paragraph 1.

3.   The provisions of this Article shall not affect cooperation with the African, Caribbean and Pacific countries in the framework of the ACP-EEC Convention.

Article 130x

1.   The Community and the Member States shall coordinate their policies on development cooperation and shall consult each other on their aid programmes, including in international organisations and during international conferences. They may undertake joint action. Member States shall contribute if necessary to the implementation of Community aid programmes.

2.   The Commission may take any useful initiative to promote the coordination referred to in paragraph 1.

Article 130y
Within their respective spheres of competence, the Community and the
Member States shall cooperate with third countries and with the
competent international organisations. The arrangements for Com-
munity cooperation may be the subject of agreements between the
Community and the third parties concerned, which shall be negotiated
and concluded in accordance with Article 228.

The previous paragraph shall be without prejudice to Member
States' competence to negotiate in international bodies and to con-
clude international agreements.

PART FOUR ASSOCIATION OF THE OVERSEAS COUNTRIES AND TERRITORIES

Article 131
The Member States agree to associate with the Community the non-European countries and territories which have special relations with Belgium, Denmark, France, Italy, the Netherlands and the United Kingdom. These countries and territories (hereinafter called the 'countries and territories') are listed in Annex IV to this Treaty.

The purpose of association shall be to promote the economic and social development of the countries and territories and to establish close economic relations between them and the Community as a whole.

In accordance with the principles set out in the Preamble to this Treaty, association shall serve primarily to further the interests and prosperity of the inhabitants of these countries and territories in order to lead them to the economic, social and cultural development to which they aspire.

Article 132
Association shall have the following objectives:
1. Member States shall apply to their trade with the countries and territories the same treatment as they accord each other pursuant to this Treaty.
2. Each country or territory shall apply to its trade with Member States and with the other countries and territories the same treatment as that which it applies to the European State with which it has special relations.
3. The Member States shall contribute to the investments required for the progressive development of these countries and territories.
4. For investments financed by the Community, participation in tenders and supplies shall be open on equal terms to all natural and legal persons who are nationals of a Member State or of one of the countries and territories.
5. In relations between Member States and the countries and territories the right of establishment of nationals and companies or firms shall be regulated in accordance with the provisions and procedures laid down in the Chapter relating to the right of establishment and on a non-discriminatory basis, subject to any special provisions laid down pursuant to Article 136.

Article 133
1. Customs duties on imports into the Member States of goods originating in the countries and territories shall be completely abolished in conformity with the progressive abolition of customs duties between Member States in accordance with the provisions of this Treaty.

2.   Customs duties on imports into each country or territory from Member States or from the other countries or territories shall be progressively abolished in accordance with the provisions of Articles 12, 13, 14, 15 and 17.

3.   The countries and territories may, however, levy customs duties which meet the needs of their development and industrialisation or produce revenue for their budgets.

The duties referred to in the preceding subparagraph shall nevertheless be progressively reduced to the level of those imposed on imports of products from the Member State with which each country or territory has special relations. The percentages and the timetable of the reductions provided for under this Treaty shall apply to the difference between the duty imposed on a product coming from the Member State which has special relations with the country or territory concerned and the duty imposed on the same product coming from within the Community on entry into the importing country or territory.

4.   Paragraph 2 shall not apply to countries and territories which, by reason of the particular international obligations by which they are bound, already apply a non-discriminatory customs tariff when this Treaty enters into force.

5.   The introduction of or any change in customs duties imposed on goods imported into the countries and territories shall not, either in law or in fact, give rise to any direct or indirect discrimination between imports from the various Member States.

Article 134

If the level of the duties applicable to goods from a third country on entry into a country or territory is liable, when the provisions of Article 133(1) have been applied, to cause deflections of trade to the detriment of any Member State, the latter may request the Commission to propose to the other Member States the measures needed to remedy the situation.

Article 135

Subject to the provisions relating to public health, public security or public policy, freedom of movement within Member States for workers from the countries and territories, and within the countries and territories for workers from Member States, shall be governed by agreements to be concluded subsequently with the unanimous approval of Member States.

Article 136

For an initial period of five years after the entry into force of this Treaty, the details of and procedure for the association of the countries and territories with the Community shall be determined by an Implementing Convention annexed to this Treaty.

Before the Convention referred to in the preceding paragraph expires, the Council shall, acting unanimously, lay down provisions for a further period, on the basis of the experience acquired and of the principles set out in this Treaty.

Article 136a

The provisions of Articles 131 to 136 shall apply to Greenland, subject to the specific provisions for Greenland set out in the Protocol on special arrangements for Greenland, annexed to this Treaty.

PART FIVE INSTITUTIONS OF THE COMMUNITY
TITLE I PROVISIONS GOVERNING THE INSTITUTIONS
CHAPTER 1 THE INSTITUTIONS
SECTION 1 THE EUROPEAN PARLIAMENT

Article 137[1]
The European Parliament, which shall consist of representatives of the peoples of the States brought together in the Community, shall exercise the powers conferred upon it by this Treaty.

Note
[1]As amended by Article G(39) TEU.

Article 138
(Paragraphs 1 and 2 lapsed on 17 July 1979 in accordance with Article 14 of the Act concerning the election of the representatives of the European Parliament)
[See Article 1 of that Act which reads as follows:
1.   The representatives in the European Parliament of the peoples of the States brought together in the Community shall be elected by direct universal suffrage.]
[See Article 2 of that Act which reads as follows:
2.   The number of representatives elected in each Member State is as follows:

Belgium	25
Denmark	16
Germany	99
Greece	25
Spain	64
France	87
Ireland	15
Italy	87
Luxembourg	6
Netherlands	31
Austria	21
Portugal	25
Finland	16
Sweden	22
United Kingdom	87].[1]

3.   The European Parliament shall draw up proposals for elections by direct universal suffrage in accordance with a uniform procedure in all Member States.
The Council shall, acting unanimously after obtaining the assent of the European Parliament, which shall act by a majority of its component members, lay down the appropriate provisions, which it shall recommend to Member States for adoption in accordance with their respective constitutional requirements.[2]

Notes
[1]As amended by Council Decision 95/1 (OJ 1995 L1/1) adjusting the Treaty of Accession of the three new Member States.
[2]Second subparagraph as amended by Article G(40) TEU.

Article 138a[1]
Political parties at European level are important as a factor for integration within the Union. They contribute to forming a European awareness and to expressing the political will of the citizens of the Union.

Note
[1]As inserted by Article G(41) TEU.

Article 138b[1]
In so far as provided in this Treaty, the European Parliament shall participate in the process leading up to the adoption of Community acts by exercising its powers under the procedures laid down in Articles 189b and 189c and by giving its assent or delivering advisory opinions.

The European Parliament may, acting by a majority of its members, request the Commission to submit any appropriate proposal on matters on which it considers that a Community act is required for the purpose of implementing this Treaty.

Note
[1]As inserted by Article G(41) TEU.

Article 138c[1]
In the course of its duties, the European Parliament may, at the request of a quarter of its members, set up a temporary Committee of Inquiry to investigate, without prejudice to the powers conferred by this Treaty on other institutions or bodies, alleged contraventions or maladministration in the implementation of Community law, except where the alleged facts are being examined before a court and while the case is still subject to legal proceedings.

The temporary Committee of Inquiry shall cease to exist on the submission of its report.

The detailed provisions governing the exercise of the right of inquiry shall be determined by common accord of the European Parliament, the Council and the Commission.[2]

Notes
[1]As inserted by Article G(41) TEU.
[2]Further details to be found in Decision 95/167 (OJ L113/2).

Article 138d[1]
Any citizen of the Union, and any natural or legal person residing or having its registered office in a Member State, shall have the right to address, individually or in association with other citizens or persons, a petition to the European Parliament on a matter which comes within the Community's fields of activity and which affects him, her or it directly.

Note
[1]As inserted by Article G(41) TEU.

Article 138e[1]

1. *The European Parliament shall appoint an Ombudsman empowered to receive complaints from any citizen of the Union or any natural or legal person residing or having its registered office in a Member State concerning instances of maladministration in the activities of the Community institutions or bodies, with the exception of the Court of Justice and the Court of First Instance acting in their judicial role.*

In accordance with his duties, the Ombudsman shall conduct inquiries for which he finds grounds, either on his own initiative or on the basis of complaints submitted to him direct or through a member of the European Parliament, except where the alleged facts are or have been the subject of legal proceedings. Where the Ombudsman establishes an instance of maladministration, he shall refer the matter to the institution concerned, which shall have a period of three months in which to inform him of its views. The Ombudsman shall then forward a report to the European Parliament and the institution concerned. The person lodging the complaint shall be informed of the outcome of such inquiries.[2]

The Ombudsman shall submit an annual report to the European Parliament on the outcome of his inquiries.

2. *The Ombudsman shall be appointed after each election of the European Parliament for the duration of its term of office. The Ombudsman shall be eligible for reappointment.*

The Ombudsman may be dismissed by the Court of Justice at the request of the European Parliament if he no longer fulfils the conditions required for the performance of his duties or if he is guilty of serious misconduct.

3. *The Ombudsman shall be completely independent in the performance of his duties. In the performance of those duties he shall neither seek nor take instructions from any body. The Ombudsman may not, during his term of office, engage in any other occupation, whether gainful or not.*

4. *The European Parliament shall, after seeking an opinion from the Commission and with the approval of the Council acting by a qualified majority, lay down the regulations and general conditions governing the performance of the Ombudsman's duties.*

Notes
[1] As inserted by Article G(41) TEU.
[2] Appointment noted in E.P. Decision 95/376 (OJ L225/17).

Article 139[1]
The European Parliament shall hold an annual session. It shall meet, without requiring to be convened, on the second Tuesday in March.

The European Parliament may meet in extraordinary session at the request of a majority of its members or at the request of the Council or of the Commission.

Note
[1] With regard to the second sentence of this subparagraph, see also Article 10(3) of the Act concerning the election of the representatives of the European Parliament.

Article 140
The European Parliament shall elect its President and its officers from among its members.

Members of the Commission may attend all meetings and shall, at their request, be heard on behalf of the Commission.

The Commission shall reply orally or in writing to questions put to it by the European Parliament or by its members.

The Council shall be heard by the European Parliament in accordance with the conditions laid down by the Council in its rules of procedure.

Article 141
Save as otherwise provided in this Treaty, the European Parliament shall act by an absolute majority of the votes cast.

The rules of procedure shall determine the quorum.

Article 142
The European Parliament shall adopt its rules of procedure, acting by a majority of its members.

The proceedings of the European Parliament shall be published in the manner laid down in its rules of procedure.

Article 143
The European Parliament shall discuss in open session the annual general report submitted to it by the Commission.

Article 144
If a motion of censure on the activities of the Commission is tabled before it, the European Parliament shall not vote thereon until at least three days after the motion has been tabled and only by open vote.

If the motion of censure is carried by a two-thirds majority of the votes cast, representing a majority of the members of the European Parliament, the members of the Commission shall resign as a body. They shall continue to deal with current business until they are replaced in accordance with Article 158. *In this case, the term of office of the members of the Commission appointed to replace them shall expire on the date on which the term of office of the members of the Commission obliged to resign as a body would have expired.[1]*

Note
[1]Third sentence of the second subparagraph as inserted by Article G(42) TEU.

SECTION 2   THE COUNCIL

Article 145
To ensure that the objectives set out in this Treaty are attained, the Council shall, in accordance with the provisions of this Treaty:

— ensure coordination of the general economic policies of the Member States;

— have power to take decisions;

— confer on the Commission, in the acts which the Council adopts, powers for the implementation of the rules which the Council lays down. The Council may impose certain requirements in respect of the exercise of these powers. The Council may also reserve the right, in specific cases, to exercise directly implementing powers itself. The procedures referred to above must be consonant with principles and rules to be laid down in advance by the Council, acting unanimously on a proposal from the Commission and after obtaining the Opinion of the European Parliament.

Article 146[1]
The Council shall consist of a representative of each Member State at ministerial level, authorised to commit the government of that Member State.

The office of President shall be held in turn by each Member State in the Council for a term of six months, in the following order of Member States:

—for a first cycle of six years: Belgium, Denmark, Germany, Greece, Spain, France, Ireland, Italy, Luxembourg, Netherlands, Portugal, United Kingdom;

—for the following cycle of six years: Denmark, Belgium, Greece, Germany, France, Spain, Italy, Ireland, Netherlands, Luxembourg, United Kingdom, Portugal.

Note
[1]See Council Decision 95/2 determining the order in which the Presidency of the Council shall be held (OJ 1995 L1/220).

Article 147
The Council shall meet when convened by its President on his own initiative or at the request of one of its members or of the Commission.

Article 148
1. Save as otherwise provided in this Treaty, the Council shall act by a majority of its members.
2. Where the Council is required to act by a qualified majority, the votes of its members shall be weighted as follows:

Belgium	5
Denmark	3
Germany	10
Greece	5
Spain	8
France	10
Ireland	3
Italy	10
Luxembourg	2
Netherlands	5
Austria	4
Portugal	5
Finland	3
Sweden	4
United Kingdom	10

For their adoption, acts of the Council shall require at least:
—62 votes in favour where this Treaty requires them to be adopted on a proposal from the Commission,

— 62 votes in favour, cast by at least 10 members, in other cases.[1]

3. Abstentions by members present in person or represented shall not prevent the adoption by the Council of acts which required unanimity.

Note
[1]As amended by Council Decision 95/1 (OJ 1995 L1/1) adjusting the Treaty of Accession of the three new Member States.

Article 149
(repealed)

Article 150
Where a vote is taken, any member of the Council may also act on behalf of not more than one other member.

Article 151[1]
   1.   A committee consisting of the Permanent Representatives of the Member States shall be responsible for preparing the work of the Council and for carrying out the tasks assigned to it by the Council.
   2.   The Council shall be assisted by a General Secretariat, under the direction of a Secretary-General. The Secretary-General shall be appointed by the Council acting unanimously.
   The Council shall decide on the organisation of the General Secretariat.
   3.   The Council shall adopt its rules of procedure.

Note
[1]As amended by Article G(46) TEU.

Article 152
The Council may request the Commission to undertake any studies the Council considers desirable for the attainment of the common objectives, and to submit to it any appropriate proposals.

Article 153
The Council shall, after receiving an opinion from the Commission, determine the rules governing the committees provided for in this Treaty.

Article 154
The Council shall, acting by a qualified majority, determine the salaries, allowances and pensions of the President and members of the Commission, and of the President, Judges, Advocates-General and Registrar of the Court of Justice. It shall also, again by a qualified majority, determine any payment to be made instead of remuneration.

SECTION 3   THE COMMISSION

Article 155
In order to ensure the proper functioning and development of the common market, the Commission shall:
   — ensure that the provisions of this Treaty and the institutions pursuant thereto are applied;
   — formulate recommendations or deliver opinions on matters dealt with in this Treaty, if it expressly so provides or if the Commission considers it necessary;

— have its own power of decision and participate in the shaping of measures taken by the Council and by the European Parliament in the manner provided for in this Treaty;

— exercise the powers conferred on it by the Council for the implementation of the rules laid down by the latter.

Article 156

The Commission shall publish annually, not later than one month before the opening of the session of the European Parliament, a general report on the activities of the Community.

Article 157

1. The Commission shall consist of 20 members, who shall be chosen on the grounds of their general competence and whose independence is beyond doubt.[1]

The number of members of the Commission may be altered by the Council, acting unanimously.

Only nationals of Member States may be members of the Commission.

The Commission must include at least one national of each of the Member States, but may not include more than two members having the nationality of the same State.

2. The members of the Commission shall, in the general interest of the Community, be completely independent in the performance of their duties.

In the performance of these duties, they shall neither seek nor take instructions from any government or from any other body. They shall refrain from any action incompatible with their duties. Each Member State undertakes to respect this principle and not to seek to influence the members of the Commission in the performance of their tasks.

The members of the Commission may not, during their term of office, engage in any other occupation, whether gainful or not. When entering upon their duties they shall give a solemn undertaking that, both during and after their term of office, they will respect the obligations arising therefrom and in particular their duty to behave with integrity and discretion as regards the acceptance, after they have ceased to hold office, of certain appointments or benefits. In the event of any breach of these obligations, the Court of Justice may, on application by the Council or the Commission, rule that the member concerned be, according to the circumstances, either compulsorily retired in accordance with Article 160 or deprived of his right to a pension or other benefits in its stead.

Note

[1] As amended by Council Decision 95/1 (OJ 1995 L1/1) adjusting the Treaty of Accession of the three new Member States.

Article 158[1]

1. The members of the Commission shall be appointed, in accordance with the procedure referred to in paragraph 2, for a period of five years, subject, if need be, to Article 144.

Note

[1] As amended by Article G(48) TEU.

Their term of office shall be renewable.

2.   The governments of the Member States shall nominate by common accord, after consulting the European Parliament, the person they intend to appoint as President of the Commission.

The governments of the Member States shall, in consultation with the nominee for President, nominate the other persons whom they intend to appoint as members of the Commission.

The President and the other members of the Commission thus nominated shall be subject as a body to a vote of approval by the European Parliament. After approval by the European Parliament, the President and the other members of the Commission shall be appointed by common accord of the government of the Member States.

3.   Paragraphs 1 and 2 shall be applied for the first time to the President and the other members of the Commission whose term of office begins on 7 January 1995.

The President and the other members of the Commission whose term of office begins on 7 January 1993 shall be appointed by common accord of the governments of the Member States. Their term of office shall expire on 6 January 1995.

Article 159[1]
Apart from normal replacement, or death, the duties of a member of the Commission shall end when he resigns or is compulsorily retired.

The vacancy thus caused shall be filled for the remainder of the member's term of office by a new member appointed by common accord of the governments of the Member States. The Council may, acting unanimously, decide that such a vacancy need not be filled.

In the event of resignation, compulsory retirement or death, the President shall be replaced for the remainder of his term of office. The procedure laid down in Article 158(2) shall be applicable for the replacement of the President.

Save in the case of compulsory retirement under Article 160, members of the Commission shall remain in office until they have been replaced.

Note
[1]As amended by Article G(48) TEU.

Article 160
If any member of the Commission no longer fulfils the conditions required for the performance of his duties or if he has been guilty of serious misconduct, the Court of Justice may, on application by the Council or the Commission, compulsorily retire him.

Article 161[1]
The Commission may appoint a Vice-President or two Vice-Presidents from among its members.

Note
[1]As amended by Article G(48) TEU.

Article 162

1. The Council and the Commission shall consult each other and shall settle by common accord their methods of cooperation.

2. The Commission shall adopt its rules of procedure so as to ensure that both it and its departments operate in accordance with the provisions of this Treaty. It shall ensure that these rules are published.

Article 163

The Commission shall act by a majority of the number of members provided for in Article 157.

A meeting of the Commission shall be valid only if the number of members laid down in its rules of procedure is present.

SECTION 4   THE COURT OF JUSTICE

Article 164

The Court of Justice shall ensure that in the interpretation and application of this Treaty the law is observed.

Article 165[1]

The Court of Justice shall consist of 15 Judges.[2]

The Court of Justice shall sit in plenary session. It may, however, form chambers, each consisting of three or five judges, either to undertake certain preparatory inquiries or to adjudicate on particular categories of cases in accordance with rules laid down for these purposes.

The Court of Justice shall sit in plenary session when a Member State or a Community institution that is a party to the proceedings so requests.

Should the Court of Justice so request, the Council may, acting unanimously, increase the number of judges and make the necessary adjustments to the second and third paragraphs of this Article and to the second paragraph of Article 167.

Notes

[1]As amended by Article G(49) TEU.
[2]As amended by Council Decision 95/1 (OJ 1995 L1/1) adjusting the Treaty of Accession of the three new Member States.

Article 166

The Court of Justice shall be assisted by eight Advocates-General. However, a ninth Advocate-General shall be appointed as from the date of accession until 6 October 2000.[1]

It shall be the duty of the Advocate-General, acting with complete impartiality and independence, to make, in open court, reasoned submissions on cases brought before the Court of Justice, in order to assist the Court in the performance of the task assigned to it in Article 164.

Should the Court of Justice so request, the Council may, acting unanimously, increase the number of Advocates-General and make the necessary adjustments to the third paragraph of Article 167.

Note

[1]As amended by Council Decision 95/1 (OJ 1995 L1/1) adjusting the Treaty of Accession of the three new Member States.

Article 167

The Judges and Advocates-General shall be chosen from persons whose independence is beyond doubt and who possess the qualifications required for appointment to the highest judicial offices in their respective countries or who are jurisconsults of recognised competence; they shall be appointed by common accord of the Governments of the Member States for a term of six years.

Every three years there shall be a partial replacement of the Judges. Eight and seven Judges shall be replaced alternately.[1]

Every three years there shall be a partial replacement of the Advocates-General. Four Advocates-General shall be replaced on each occasion.[2]

Retiring Judges and Advocates-General shall be eligible for reappointment.

The Judges shall elect the President of the Court of Justice from among their number for a term of three years. He may be re-elected.

Notes

[1-2]As amended by Council Decision 95/1 (OJ 1995 L1/1) adjusting the Treaty of Accession of the three new Member States.

Article 168

The Court of Justice shall appoint its Registrar and lay down the rules governing his service.

Article 168a[1]

1.   A Court of First Instance shall be attached to the Court of Justice with jurisdiction to hear and determine at first instance, subject to a right of appeal to the Court of Justice on points of law only and in accordance with the conditions laid down by the Statute, certain classes of action or proceeding defined in accordance with the conditions laid down in paragraph 2. The Court of First Instance shall not be competent to hear and determine questions referred for a preliminary ruling under Article 177.

2.   At the request of the Court of Justice and after consulting the European Parliament and the Commission, the Council, acting unanimously, shall determine the classes of action or proceeding referred to in paragraph 1 and the composition of the Court of First Instance and shall adopt the necessary adjustments and additional provisions to the Statute of the Court of Justice. Unless the Council decides otherwise, the provisions of this Treaty relating to the Court of Justice, in particular the provisions of the Protocol on the Statute of the Court of Justice, shall apply to the Court of First Instance.

3.   The members of the Court of First Instance shall be chosen from persons whose independence is beyond doubt and who possess the ability required for appointment to judicial office; they shall be appointed by common accord of the governments of the Member States for a term of six years. The membership shall be partially renewed every three years. Retiring members shall be eligible for re-appointment.

4.   The Court of First Instance shall establish its rules of procedure in agreement with the Court of Justice. Those rules shall require the unanimous approval of the Council.

Note

[1]As amended by Article G(50) TEU.

Article 169

If the Commission considers that a Member State has failed to fulfil an obligation under this Treaty, it shall deliver a reasoned opinion on the matter after giving the State concerned the opportunity to submit its observations.

If the State concerned does not comply with the opinion within the period laid down by the Commission, the latter may bring the matter before the Court of Justice.

Article 170

A Member State which considers that another Member State has failed to fulfil an obligation under this Treaty may bring the matter before the Court of Justice.

Before a Member State brings an action against another Member State for an alleged infringement of an obligation under this Treaty, it shall bring the matter before the Commission.

The Commission shall deliver a reasoned opinion after each of the States concerned has been given the opportunity to submit its own case and its observations on the other party's case both orally and in writing.

If the Commission has not delivered an opinon within three months of the date on which the matter was brought before it, the absence of such opinion shall not prevent the matter from being brought before the Court of Justice.

Article 171[1]

1.   If the Court of Justice finds that a Member State has failed to fulfil an obligation under this Treaty, the State shall be required to take the necessary measures to comply with the judgment of the Court of Justice.

2.   *If the Commission considers that the Member State concerned has not taken such measures it shall, after giving that State the opportunity to submit its observations, issue a reasoned opinion specifying the points on which the Member State concerned has not complied with the judgment of the Court of Justice.*

If the Member State concerned fails to take the necessary measures to comply with the Court's judgment within the time-limit laid down by the Commission, the latter may bring the case before the Court of Justice. In so doing it shall specify the amount of the lump sum or penalty payment to be paid by the Member State concerned which it considers appropriate in the circumstances.

If the Court of Justice finds that the Member State concerned has not complied with its judgment it may impose a lump sum or penalty payment on it.

This procedure shall be without prejudice to Article 170.

Note
[1]As amended by Article G(51) TEU.

Article 172[1]

Regulations *adopted jointly by the European Parliament and the Council, and* by the Council, pursuant to the provisions of this Treaty, may give the Court of Justice unlimited jurisdiction with regard to the penalties provided for in such regulations.

Note
[1]As amended by Article G(52) TEU.

Article 173[1]
The Court of Justice shall review the legality of acts adopted jointly by the European Parliament and the Council, of acts of the Council, of the Commission and of the ECB, other than recommendations and opinions, and of acts of the European Parliament intended to produce legal effects vis-à-vis third parties.

It shall for this purpose have jurisdiction in actions brought by a Member State, the Council or the Commission on grounds of lack of competence, infringement of an essential procedural requirement, infringement of this Treaty or of any rule of law relating to its application, or misuse of powers.

The Court shall have jurisdiction under the same conditions in actions brought by the European Parliament and by the ECB for the purpose of protecting their prerogatives.

Any natural or legal person may, under the same conditions, institute proceedings against a decision addressed to that person or against a decision which, although in the form of a regulation or a decision addressed to another person, is of direct and individual concern to the former.

The proceedings provided for in this Article shall be instituted within two months of the publication of the measure, or of its notification to the plaintiff, or, in the absence thereof, of the day on which it came to the knowledge of the latter, as the case may be.

Note
[1]As amended by Article G(53) TEU.

Article 174
If the action is well founded, the Court of Justice shall declare the act concerned to be void.

In the case of a regulation, however, the Court of Justice shall, if it considers this necessary, state which of the effects of the regulation which it has declared void shall be considered as definitive.

Article 175[1]
Should *the European Parliament,* the Council or the Commission, in infringement of this Treaty, fail to act, the Member States and the other institutions of the Community may bring an action before the Court of Justice to have the infringement established.

The action shall be admissible only if the institution concerned has first been called upon to act. If, within two months of being so called upon, the institution concerned has not defined its position, the action may be brought within a further period of two months.

Any natural or legal person may, under the conditions laid down in the preceding paragraphs, complain to the Court of Justice that an institution of the Community has failed to address to that person any act other than a recommendation or an opinion.

The Court of Justice shall have jurisdiction, under the same conditions, in actions or proceedings brought by the ECB in the areas falling within the latter's field of competence and in actions or proceedings brought against the latter.

Note
[1]As amended by Article G(54) TEU.

Article 176[1]
The institution or institutions whose act has been declared void or whose failure to act has been declared contrary to this Treaty shall be required to take the necessary measures to comply with the judgment of the Court of Justice.

The obligation shall not affect any obligation which may result from the application of the second paragraph of Article 215.

This Article shall also apply to the ECB.

Note
[1]As amended by Article G(55) TEU.

Article 177[1]
The Court of Justice shall have jurisdiction to give preliminary rulings concerning:

(a)   the interpretation of this Treaty;

(b)   the validity and interpretation of acts of the institutions of the Community *and of the ECB;*

(c)   the interpretation of the statutes of bodies established by an act of the Council, where those statutes so provide.

Where such a question is raised before any court or tribunal of a Member State, that court or tribunal may, if it considers that a decision on the question is necessary to enable it to give judgment, request the Court of Justice to give a ruling thereon.

Where any such question is raised in a case pending before a court or tribunal of a Member State against whose decisions there is no judicial remedy under national law, that court or tribunal shall bring the matter before the Court of Justice.

Note
[1]As amended by Article G(56) TEU.

Article 178
The Court of Justice shall have jurisdiction in disputes relating to compensation for damage provided for in the second paragraph of Article 215.

Article 179
The Court of Justice shall have jurisdiction in any dispute between the Community and its servants within the limits and under the conditions laid down in the Staff Regulations or the Conditions of Employment.

Article 180[1]
The Court of Justice shall, within the limits hereinafter laid down, have jurisdiction in disputes concerning:

(a)   the fulfilment by Member States of obligations under the Statute of the European Investment Bank. In this connection, the Board of Directors of the Bank shall enjoy the powers conferred upon the Commission by Article 169;

(b)   measures adopted by the Board of Governors of the European Investment Bank. In this connection, any Member State, the Commission or the Board of Directors of the Bank may institute proceedings under the conditions laid down in Article 173;

Note
[1]As amended by Article G(57) TEU.

(c) measures adopted by the Board of Directors of the European Investment Bank. Proceedings against such measures may be instituted only by Member States or by the Commission, under the conditions laid down in Article 173, and solely on the grounds of non-compliance with the procedure provided for in Article 21(2), (5), (6) and (7) of the Statute of the Bank;

(d)   the fulfilment by national central banks of obligations under this Treaty and the Statute of the ESCB. In this connection the powers of the Council of the ECB in respect of national central banks shall be the same as those conferred upon the Commission in respect of Member States by Article 169. If the Court of Justice finds that a national central bank has failed to fulfil an obligation under this Treaty, that bank shall be required to take the necessary measures to comply with the judgment of the Court of Justice.

Article 181
The Court of Justice shall have jurisdiction to give judgment pursuant to any arbitration clause contained in a contract concluded by or on behalf of the Community, whether that contract be governed by public or private law.

Article 182
The Court of Justice shall have jurisdiction in any dispute between Member States which relates to the subject matter of this Treaty if the dispute is submitted to it under a special agreement between the parties.

Article 183
Save where jurisdiction is conferred on the Court of Justice by this Treaty, disputes to which the Community is a party shall not on that ground be excluded from the Jurisdiction of the courts or tribunals of the Member States.

Article 184[1]
Notwithstanding the expiry of the period laid down in *the fifth paragraph of* Article 173, any party may, in proceedings in which *a regulation adopted jointly by the European Parliament and the Council, or* a regulation of the Council, of the Commission, or of the ECB is at issue, plead the grounds specified in *the second paragraph of* Article 173 in order to invoke before the Court of Justice the inapplicability of that regulation.

Note
[1]As amended by Article G(58) TEU.

Article 185
Actions brought before the Court of Justice shall not have suspensory effect. The Court of Justice may, however, if it considers that circumstances so require, order that application of the contested act be suspended.

Article 186
The Court of Justice may in any cases before it prescribe any necessary interim measures.

Article 187
The judgments of the Court of Justice shall be enforceable under the conditions laid down in Article 192.

Article 188

The Statute of the Court of Justice is laid down in a separate Protocol.

The Council may, acting unanimously at the request of the Court of Justice and after consulting the Commission and the European Parliament, amend the provisions of Title III of the Statute.

The Court of Justice shall adopt its rules of procedure. These shall require the unanimous approval of the Council.

SECTION 5[1]   THE COURT OF AUDITORS

Article 188a
The Court of Auditors shall carry out the audit.

Note
[1]Section 5 (Articles 188a to 188c) formerly Articles 206 and 206a as inserted by Article G(59) TEU.

Article 188b

1.   The Court of Auditors shall consist of 15 members.[1]

2.   The members of the Court of Auditors shall be chosen from among persons who belong or have belonged in their respective countries to external audit bodies or who are especially qualified for this office. Their independence must be beyond doubt.

3.   The members of the Court of Auditors shall be appointed for a term of six years by the Council, acting unanimously after consulting the European Parliament.

However, when the first appointments are made, four members of the Court of Auditors, chosen by lot, shall be appointed for a term of office of four years only.

The members of the Court of Auditors shall be eligible for reappointment.

They shall elect the President of the Court of Auditors from among their number for a term of three years. The President may be re-elected.

4.   The members of the Court of Auditors shall, in the general interest of the Community, be completely independent in the performance of their duties.

In the performance of these duties, they shall neither seek nor take instructions from any government or from any other body. They shall refrain from any action incompatible with their duties.

5.   The members of the Court of Auditors may not, during their term of office, engage in any other occupation, whether gainful or not. When entering upon their duties they shall give a solemn undertaking that, both during and after their term of office, they will respect the obligations arising therefrom and in particular their duty to behave with integrity and discretion as regards the acceptance, after they have ceased to hold office, of certain appointments or benefits.

6.   Apart from normal replacement, or death, the duties of a member of the Court of Auditors shall end when he resigns, or is

Note
[1]As amended by Council Decision 95/1 (OJ 1995 L1/1) adjusting the Treaty of Accession of the three new Member States.

compulsorily retired by a ruling of the Court of Justice pursuant to paragraph 7.

The vacancy thus caused shall be filled for the remainder of the member's term of office.

Save in the case of compulsory retirement, members of the Court of Auditors shall remain in office until they have been replaced.

7. A member of the Court of Auditors may be deprived of his office or of his right to a pension or other benefits in its stead only if the Court of Justice, at the request of the Court of Auditors, finds that he no longer fulfils the requisite conditions or meets the obligations arising from his office.

8. The Council, acting by a qualified majority, shall determine the conditions of employment of the President and the members of the Court of Auditors and in particular their salaries, allowances and pensions. It shall also, by the same majority, determine any payment to be made instead of remuneration.

9. The provisions of the Protocol on the Privileges and Immunities of the European Communities applicable to the Judges of the Court of Justice shall also apply to the members of the Court of Auditors.

Article 188c

1. The Court of Auditors shall examine the accounts of all revenue and expenditure of the Community. It shall also examine the accounts of all revenue and expenditure of all bodies set up by the Community in so far as the relevant constituent instrument does not preclude such examination.

The Court of Auditors shall provide the European Parliament and the Council with a statement of assurance as to the reliability of the accounts and the legality and regularity of the underlying transactions.

2. The Court of Auditors shall examine whether all revenue has been received and all expenditure incurred in a lawful and regular manner and whether the financial management has been sound.

The audit of revenue shall be carried out on the basis both of the amounts established as due and the amounts actually paid to the Community.

The audit of expenditure shall be carried out on the basis both of commitments undertaken and payments made.

These audits may be carried out before the closure of accounts for the financial year in question.

3. The audit shall be based on records and, if necessary, performed on the spot in the other institutions of the Community and in the Member States. In the Member States the audit shall be carried out in liaison with the national audit bodies or, if these do not have the necessary powers, with the competent national departments. These bodies or departments shall inform the Court of Auditors whether they intend to take part in the audit.

The other institutions of the Community and the national audit bodies or, if these do not have the necessary powers, the competent national departments, shall forward to the Court of Auditors, at its request, any document or information necessary to carry out its task.

4.   *The Court of Auditors shall draw up an annual report after the close of each financial year. It shall be forwarded to the other institutions of the Community and shall be published, together with the replies of these institutions to the observations of the Court of Auditors, in the Official Journal of the European Communities.*

The Court of Auditors may also, at any time, submit observations, particularly in the form of special reports, on specific questions and deliver opinions at the request of one of the other institutions of the Community.

It shall adopt its annual reports, special reports or opinions by a majority of its members.

It shall assist the European Parliament and the Council in exercising their powers of control over the implementation of the budget.

CHAPTER 2   PROVISIONS COMMON TO SEVERAL INSTITUTIONS

Article 189[1]

In order to carry out their task and in accordance with the provisions of this Treaty, *the European Parliament acting jointly with the Council,* the Council and the Commission shall make regulations and issue directives, take decisions, make recommendations or deliver opinions.

A regulation shall have general application. It shall be binding in its entirety and directly applicable in all Member States.

A directive shall be binding, as to the result to be achieved, upon each Member State to which it is addressed, but shall leave to the national authorities the choice of form and methods.

A decision shall be binding in its entirety upon those to whom it is addressed.

Recommendations and opinions shall have no binding force.

Note
[1]As amended by Article G(60) TEU.

Article 189a[1]

1.   *Where, in pursuance of this Treaty, the Council acts on a proposal from the Commission, unanimity shall be required for an act constituting an amendment to that proposal, subject to Article 189b(4) and (5).*

2.   *As long as the Council has not acted, the Commission may alter its proposal at any time during the procedures leading to the adoption of a Community act.*

Note
[1]As inserted by Article G(61) TEU.

Article 189b[1]

1.   *Where reference is made in this Treaty to this Article for the adoption of an act, the following procedure shall apply.*

2.   *The Commission shall submit a proposal to the European Parliament and the Council.*

Note
[1]As inserted by Article G(61) TEU.

The Council, acting by a qualified majority after obtaining the opinion of the European Parliament, shall adopt a common position. The common position shall be communicated to the European Parliament. The Council shall inform the European Parliament fully of the reasons which led it to adopt its common position. The Commission shall inform the European Parliament fully of its position.

If within three months of such communication, the European Parliament:

(a) approves the common position, the Council shall definitively adopt the act in question in accordance with that common position;

(b) has not taken a decision, the Council shall adopt the act in question in accordance with its common position;

(c) indicates, by an absolute majority of its component members, that it intends to reject the common position, it shall immediately inform the Council. The Council may convene a meeting of the Conciliation Committee referred to in paragraph 4 to explain further its position. The European Parliament shall thereafter either confirm, by an absolute majority of its component members, its rejection of the common position, in which event the proposed act shall be deemed not to have been adopted, or propose amendments in accordance with subparagraph (d) of this paragraph;

(d) proposes amendments to the common position by an absolute majority of its component members, the amended text shall be forwarded to the Council and to the Commission, which shall deliver an opinion on those amendments.

3. If, within three months of the matter being referred to it, the Council, acting by a qualified majority, approves all the amendments of the European Parliament, it shall amend its common position accordingly and adopt the act in question; however, the Council shall act unanimously on the amendments on which the Commission has delivered a negative opinion. If the Council does not approve the act in question, the President of the Council, in agreement with the President of the European Parliament, shall forthwith convene a meeting of the Conciliation Committee.

4. The Conciliation Committee, which shall be composed of the members of the Council or their representatives and an equal number of represenatives of the European Parliament, shall have the task of reaching agreement on a joint text, by a qualified majority of the members of the Council or their representatives and by a majority of the representatives of the European Parliament. The Commission shall take part in the Conciliation Committee's proceedings and shall take all the necessary initiatives with a view to reconciling the positions of the European Parliament and the Council.

5. If, within six weeks of its being convened, the Conciliation Committee approves a joint text, the European Parliament, acting by an absolute majority of the votes cast, and the Council, acting by a qualified majority, shall have a period of six weeks from that approval in which to adopt the act in question in accordance with the joint text. If one of the two institutions fails to approve the proposed act, it shall be deemed not to have been adopted.

6.   *Where the Conciliation Committee does not approve a joint text, the proposed act shall be deemed not to have been adopted unless the Council, acting by a qualified majority within six weeks of expiry of the period granted to the Conciliation Committee, confirms the common position to which it agreed before the conciliation procedure was initiated, possibly with amendments proposed by the European Parliament. In this case, the act in question shall be finally adopted unless the European Parliament, within six weeks of the date of confirmation by the Council, rejects the text by an absolute majority of its component members, in which case the proposed act shall be deemed not to have been adopted.*

7.   *The periods of three months and six weeks referred to in this Article may be extended by a maximum of one month and two weeks respectively by common accord of the European Parliament and the Council. The period of three months referred to in paragraph 2 shall be automatically extended by two months where paragraph 2(c) applies.*

8.   *The scope of the procedure under this Article may be widened, in accordance with the procedure provided for in Article N(2) of the Treaty on European Union, on the basis of a report to be submitted to the Council by the Commission by 1996 at the latest.*

Article 189c[1]
Where reference is made in this Treaty to this Article for the adoption of an act, the following procedure shall apply:

(a)   The Council, acting by a qualified majority on a proposal from the Commission and after obtaining the opinion of the European Parliament, shall adopt a common position.

(b)   The Council's common position shall be communicated to the European Parliament. The Council and the Commission shall inform the European Parliament fully of the reasons which led the Council to adopt its common position and also of the Commission's position.

If, within three months of such communication, the European Parliament approves this common position or has not taken a decision within that period, the Council shall definitively adopt the act in question in accordance with the common position.

(c)   The European Parliament may, within the period of three months, referred to in point (b), by an absolute majority of its component members, propose amendments to the Council's common position. The European Parliament may also, by the same majority, reject the Council's common position. The result of the proceedings shall be transmitted to the Council and the Commission.

If the European Parliament has rejected the Council's common position, unanimity shall be required for the Council to act on a second reading.

(d)   The Commission shall, within a period of one month, re-examine the proposal on the basis of which the Council adopted its common position, by taking into account the amendments proposed by the European Parliament.

Note
[1]As inserted by Article G(61) TEU.

The Commission shall forward to the Council, at the same time as its re-examined proposal, the amendments of the European Parliament which it has not accepted, and shall express its opinion on them. The Council may adopt these amendments unanimously.

(e)   The Council, acting by a qualified majority, shall adopt the proposal as re-examined by the Commission.

Unanimity shall be required for the Council to amend the proposal as re-examined by the Commission.

(f)   In the cases referred to in points (c), (d) and (e), the Council shall be required to act within a period of three months. If no decision is taken within this period, the Commission proposal shall be deemed not to have been adopted.

(g)   The periods referred to in points (b) and (f) may be extended by a maximum of one month by common accord between the Council and the European Parliament.

Article 190[1]
Regulations, directives and decisions adopted jointly by the European Parliament and the Council, and such acts adopted by the Council or the Commission, shall state the reasons on which they are based and shall refer to any proposals or opinions which were required to be obtained pursuant to this Treaty.

Note
[1]As amended by Article G(62) TEU.

Article 191[1]
1.   Regulations, directives and decisions adopted in accordance with the procedure referred to in Article 189b shall be signed by the President of the European Parliament and by the President of the Council and published in the Official Journal of the Community. They shall enter into force on the date specified in them or, in the absence thereof, on the twentieth day following that of their publication.

2.   Regulations of the Council and of the Commission, as well as directives of those institutions which are addressed to all Member States, shall be published in the Official Journal of the Community. They shall enter into force on the date specified in them or, in the absence thereof, on the twentieth day following that of their publication.

3.   Other directives, and decisions, shall be notified to those to whom they are addressed and shall take effect upon such notification.

Note
[1]As amended by Article G(63) TEU.

Article 192
Decisions of the Council or of the Commission which impose a pecuniary obligation on persons other than States, shall be enforceable.

Enforcement shall be governed by the rules of civil procedure in force in the State in the territory of which it is carried out. The order for its enforcement shall be appended to the decision, without other formality than verification of the authenticity of the decision, by the national authority which the Government of each Member State shall designate for this purpose and shall make known to the Commission and to the Court of Justice.

When these formalities have been completed on application by the party concerned, the latter may proceed to enforcement in accordance with the national law, by bringing the matter directly before the competent authority.

Enforcement may be suspended only by a decision of the Court of Justice. However, the courts of the country concerned shall have jurisdiction over complaints that enforcement is being carried out in an irregular manner.

CHAPTER 3   THE ECONOMIC AND SOCIAL COMMITTEE

Article 193
An Economic and Social Committe is hereby established. It shall have advisory status.

The Committee shall consist of representatives of the various categories of economic and social activity, in particular, representatives of producers, farmers, carriers, workers, dealers, craftsmen, professional occupations and representatives of the general public.

Article 194[1]
The number of members of the Economic and Social Committee shall be as follows:

Belgium	12
Denmark	9
Germany	24
Greece	12
Spain	21
France	24
Ireland	9
Italy	24
Luxembourg	6
Netherlands	12
Austria	12
Portugal	12
Finland	9
Sweden	12
United Kingdom	24

The members of the committee shall be appointed by the Council, acting unanimously, for four years. Their appointments shall be renewable.[2]

The members of the Committee may not be bound by any mandatory instructions. They shall be completely independent in the performance of their duties, in the general interest of the Community.

The Council acting by a qualified majority, shall determine the allowances of members of the Committee.

Notes
[1]As amended by Article G(64) TEU.
[2]As amended by Council Decision 95/1 (OJ 1995 L1/1) adjusting the Treaty of Accession of the three new Member States.

Article 195

1. For the appointment of the members of the Committee, each Member State shall provide the Council with a list containing twice as many candidates as there are seats allotted to its nationals.

The composition of the Committee shall take account of the need to ensure adequate representation of the various categories of economic and social activity.

2. The Council shall consult the Commission. It may obtain the opinion of European bodies which are representative of the various economic and social sectors to which the activities of the Community are of concern.

Article 196[1]

The Committee shall elect its chairman and officers from among its members for a term of two years.

It shall adopt its rules of procedure.

The Committee shall be convened by its chairman at the request of the Council of the Commission. *It may also meet on its own initiative.*

Note

[1]As amended by Article G(65) TEU.

Article 197

The Committee shall include specialised sections for the principal fields covered by this Treaty.

In particular, it shall contain an agricultural section and a transport section, which are the subject of special provisions in the Titles relating to agriculture and transport.

These specialised sections shall operate within the general terms of reference of the Committee. They may not be consulted independently of the Committee.

Sub-committees may also be established within the Committee to prepare on specific questions or in specific fields, draft opinions to be submitted to the Committee for its consideration.

The Rules of procedure shall lay down the methods of composition and the terms of reference of the specialised sections and of the sub-committees.

Article 198[1]

The Committee must be consulted by the Council or by the Commission where this Treaty so provides. The Committee may be consulted by these institutions in all cases in which they consider it appropriate. *It may issue an opinion on its own initiative in cases in which it considers such action appropriate.*

The Council or the Commission shall, if it considers it necessary, set the Committee, for the submission of its opinion, a time-limit which may not be less than one month from the date on which the chairman receives notification to this effect. Upon expiry of the time-limit, the absence of an opinion shall not prevent further action.

The opinion of the Committee and that of the specialised section, together with a record of the proceedings, shall be forwarded to the Council and to the Commission.

Note

[1]As amended by Article G(66) TEU.

CHAPTER 4[1]   THE COMMITTEE OF THE REGIONS

Article 198a
A Committee consisting of representatives of regional and local bodies, hereinafter referred to as 'the Committee of the Regions', is hereby established with advisory status.

The number of members of the Committee of the Regions shall be as follows:

Belgium	12
Denmark	9
Germany	24
Greece	12
Spain	21
France	24
Ireland	9
Italy	24
Luxembourg	6
Netherlands	12
Austria	12
Portugal	12
Finland	9
Sweden	12
United Kingdom	24

The members of the Committee and an equal number of alternate members shall be appointed for four years by the Council acting unanimously on proposals from the respective Member States. Their term of office shall be renewable.[2]

The members of the Committee may not be bound by any mandatory instructions. They shall be completely independent in the performance of their duties, in the general interest of the Community.

Notes
[1]Chapter 4 (Articles 198a to 198c) as inserted by Article G(67) TEU.
[2]As amended by Council Decision 95/1 (OJ 1995 L1/1) adjusting the Treaty of Accession of the three new Member States.

Article 198b
The Committee of the Regions shall elect its chairman and officers from among its members for a term of two years.

It shall adopt its rules of procedure and shall submit them for approval to the Council, acting unanimously.

The Committee shall be convened by its chairman at the request of the Council or of the Commission. It may also meet on its own initiative.

Article 198c
The Committee of the Regions shall be consulted by the Council or by the Commission where this Treaty so provides and in all other cases in which one of these two institutions considers it appropriate.

The Council or the Commission shall, if it considers it necessary, set the Committee, for the submission of its opinion, a time-limit which may not be less than one month from the date on which the chairman receives notification to this effect. Upon expiry of the time-limit, the absence of an opinion shall not prevent further action.

Where the Economic and Social Committee is consulted pursuant to Article 198, the Committee of the Regions shall be informed by the Council or the Commission of the request for an opinion. Where it considers that specific regional interests are involved, the Committee of the Regions may issue an opinion on the matter.

It may issue an opinion on its own initiative in cases in which it considers such action appropriate.

The opinion of the Committee, together with a record of the proceedings, shall be forwarded to the Council and to the Commission.

CHAPTER 5[1] EUROPEAN INVESTMENT BANK

Article 198d

The European Investment Bank shall have legal personality.

The members of the European Investment Bank shall be the Member States.

The Statute of the European Investment Bank is laid down in a Protocol annexed to this Treaty.

Note
[1]Chapter 5 (Articles 198d and 198e, formerly Articles 129 and 130) as inserted by Article G(68) TEU.

Article 198e

The task of the European Investment Bank shall be to contribute, by having recourse to the capital market and utilising its own resources, to the balanced and steady development of the common market in the interest of the Community. For this purpose the Bank shall, operating on a non-profit-making basis, grant loans and give guarantees which in all sectors of the economy:

(a)   projects for developing less-developed regions;

(b)   projects for modernising or converting undertakings or for developing fresh activities called for by the progressive establishment of the common market, where these projects are of such a size or nature that they cannot be entirely financed by the various means available in the individual Member States;

(c)   projects of common interest to several Member States which are of such a size or nature that they cannot be entirely financed by the various means available in the individual Member States.

In carrying out its task, the Bank shall facilitate the financing of investment programmes in conjunction with assistance from the structural Funds and other Community financial instruments.

TITLE II   FINANCIAL PROVISIONS

Article 199[1]

All items of revenue and expenditure of the Community, including those relating to the European Social Fund, shall be included in estimates to be drawn up for each financial year and shall be shown in the budget.

Note
[1]As amended by Article G(69) TEU.

Administrative expenditure occasioned for the institutions by the provisions of the Treaty on European Union relating to common foreign and security policy and to cooperation in the fields of justice and home affairs shall be charged to the budget. The operational expenditure occasioned by the implementation of the said provisions may, under the conditions referred to therein, be charged to the budget.

The revenue and expenditure shown in the budget shall be in balance.

Article 200
(repealed)

Article 201[1]
Without prejudice to other revenue, the budget shall be financed wholly from own resources.

The Council, acting unanimously on a proposal from the Commission and after consulting the European Parliament, shall lay down provisions relating to the system of own resources of the Community, which it shall recommend to the Member States for adoption in accordance with their respective constitutional requirements.

Note
[1]As amended by Article G(71) TEU.

Article 201a[1]
With a view to maintaining budgetary discipline, the Commission shall not make any proposal for a Community act, or alter its proposal, or adopt any implementing measure which is likely to have appreciable implications for the budget without providing the assurance that that proposal or that measure is capable of being financed within the limit of the Community's own resources arising under provisions laid down by the Council pursuant to Article 201.

Note
[1]As inserted by Article G(72) TEU.

Article 202
The expenditure shown in the budget shall be authorised for one financial year, unless the regulations made pursuant to Article 209 provide otherwise.

In accordance with conditions to be laid down pursuant to Article 209, any appropriations, other than those relating to staff expenditure, that are unexpended at the end of the financial year may be carried forward to the next financial year only.

Appropriations shall be classified under different chapters grouping items of expenditure according to their nature or purpose and subdivided, as far as may be necessary, in accordance with the regulations made pursuant to Article 209.

The expenditure of the European Parliament, the Council, the Commission and the Court of Justice shall be set out in separate parts of the budget, without prejudice to special arrangements for certain common items of expenditure.

Article 203
1. The financial year shall run from 1 January to 31 December.
2. Each institution of the Community shall, before 1 July, draw up estimates of its expenditure. The Commission shall consolidate these estimates

in a preliminary draft budget. It shall attach thereto an opinion which may contain different estimates.

The preliminary draft budget shall contain an estimate of revenue and an estimate of expenditure.

3.   The Commission shall place the preliminary draft budget before the Council not later than 1 September of the year preceding that in which the budget is to be implemented.

The Council shall consult the Commission and, where appropriate, the other institutions concerned whenever it intends to depart from the preliminary draft budget.

The Council, acting by a qualified majority, shall establish the draft budget and forward it to the European Parliament.

4.   The draft budget shall be placed before the European Parliament not later than 5 October of the year preceding that in which the budget is to be implemented.

The European Parliament shall have the right to amend the draft budget, acting by a majority of its members, and to propose to the Council, acting by an absolute majority of the votes cast, modifications to the draft budget relating to expenditure necessarily resulting from this Treaty or from acts adopted in accordance therewith.

If, within 45 days of the draft budget being placed before it, the European Parliament has given its approval, the budget shall stand as finally adopted. If within this period the European Parliament has not amended the draft budget nor proposed any modifications thereto, the budget shall be deemed to be finally adopted.

If within this period the European Parliament has adopted amendments or proposed modifications, the draft budget together with the amendments or proposed modifications shall be forwarded to the Council.

5.   After discussing the draft budget with the Commission and, where appropriate, with the other institutions concerned, the Council shall act under the following conditions:

(a)   The Council may, acting by a qualified majority, modify any of the amendments adopted by the European Parliament;

(b)   With regard to the proposed modifications:

—where a modification proposed by the European Parliament does not have the effect of increasing the total amount of the expenditure of an institution, owing in particular to the fact that the increase in expenditure which it would involve would be expressly compensated by one or more proposed modifications correspondingly reducing expenditure, the Council may, acting by a qualified majority, reject the proposed modification. In the absence of a decision to reject it, the proposed modification shall stand as accepted;

—where a modification proposed by the European Parliament has the effect of increasing the total amount of the expenditure of an institution, the Council may, acting by a qualified majority, accept this proposed modification. In the absence of a decision to accept it, the proposed modification shall stand as rejected;

—where, in pursuance of one of the two preceding subparagraphs, the Council has rejected a proposed modification, it may, acting by a qualified majority, either retain the amount shown in the draft budget or fix another amount.

The draft budget shall be modified on the basis of the proposed modifications accepted by the Council.

If, within 15 days of the draft being placed before it, the Council has not modified any of the amendments adopted by the European Parliament and if the modifications proposed by the latter have been accepted, the budget shall be deemed to be finally adopted. The Council shall inform the European Parliament that it has not modified any of the amendments and that the proposed modifications have been accepted.

If within this period the Council has modified one or more of the amendments adopted by the European Parliament or if the modifications proposed by the latter have been rejected or modified, the modified draft budget shall again be forwarded to the European Parliament. The Council shall inform the European Parliament of the results of its deliberations.

6. Within 15 days of the draft budget being placed before it, the European Parliament, which shall have been notified of the action taken on its proposed modifications, may, acting by a majority of its members and three-fifths of the votes cast, amend or reject the modifications to its amendments made by the Council and shall adopt the budget accordingly. If within this period the European Parliament has not acted, the budget shall be deemed to be finally adopted.

7. When the procedure provided for in this Article has been completed, the President of the European Parliament shall declare that the budget has been finally adopted.

8. However, the European Parliament, acting by a majority of its members and two-thirds of the votes cast, may, if there are important reasons, reject the draft budget and ask for a new draft to be submitted to it.

9. A maximum rate of increase in relation to the expenditure of the same type to be incurred during the current year shall be fixed annually for the total expenditure other than that necessarily resulting from this Treaty or from acts adopted in accordance therewith.

The Commission shall, after consulting the Economic Policy Committee, declare what this maximum rate is as it results from:

— the trend, in terms of volume, of the gross national product within the Community;

— the average variation in the budgets of the Member States; and

— the trend of the cost of living during the preceding financial year.

The maximum rate shall be communicated, before 1 May, to all the institutions of the Community. The latter shall be required to conform to this during the budgetary procedure, subject to the provisions of the fourth and fifth subparagraphs of this paragraph.

If, in respect of expenditure other than that necessarily resulting from this Treaty or from acts adopted in accordance therewith, the actual rate of increase in the draft budget, established by the Council is over half the maximum rate, the European Parliament may, exercising its right of amendment, further increase the total amount of that expenditure to a limit not exceeding half the maximum rate.

Where the European Parliament, the Council or the Commission consider that the activities of the Communities require that the rate determined according to the procedure laid down in this paragraph should be exceeded, another rate may be fixed by agreement between the Council, acting by a qualified majority, and the European Parliament, acting by a majority of its members and three-fifths of the votes cast.

10.   Each institution shall exercise the powers conferred upon it by this Article, with due regard for the provisions of the Treaty and for acts adopted in accordance therewith, in particular those relating to the Community's own resources and to the balance between revenue and expenditure.

Article 204

If at the beginning of a financial year, the budget has not yet been voted, a sum equivalent to not more than one-twelfth of the budget appropriations for the preceding financial year may be spent each month in repect of any chapter or other subdivision of the budget in accordance with the provisions of the Regulations made pursuant to Article 209; this arrangement shall not, however, have the effect of placing at the disposal of the Commission appropriations in excess of one-twelfth of those provided for in the draft budget in course of preparation.

The Council may, acting by a qualified majority, provided that the other conditions laid down in the first subparagraph are observed, authorise expenditure in excess of one-twelfth.

If the decision relates to expenditure which does not necessarily result from this Treaty or from acts adopted in accordance therewith, the Council shall forward it immediately to the European Parliament; within 30 days the European Parliament, acting by a majority of its members and three-fifths of the votes cast, may adopt a different decision on the expenditure in excess of the one-twelfth referred to in the first subparagraph. This part of the decision of the Council shall be suspended until the European Parliament has taken its decision. If within the said period the European Parliament has not taken a decision which differs from the decision of the Council, the latter shall be deemed to be finally adopted.

The decisions referred to in the second and third subparagraphs shall lay down the necessary measures relating to resources to ensure application of this Article.

Article 205[1]

The Commission shall implement the budget, in accordance with the provisions of the regulations made pursuant to Article 209, on its own responsibility and within the limits of the appropriations, *have regard to the principles of sound financial management.*

The regulations shall lay down detailed rules for each institution concerning its part in effecting its own expenditure.

Within the budget, the Commission may, subject to the limits and conditions laid down in the regulations made pursuant to Article 209, transfer appropriations from one chapter to another or from one subdivision to another.

Note
[1]As amended by Article G(73) TEU.

Article 205a

The commission shall submit annually to the Council and to the European Parliament the accounts of the preceding financial year relating to the implementation of the budget. The Commission shall also forward to them a financial statement of the assets and liabilities of the Community.

Article 206[1]

1.   The European Parliament, acting on a recommendation from the Council which shall act by a qualified majority, shall give a discharge to the Commission in respect of the implementation of the budget. To this end, the Council and the European Parliament in turn shall examine the accounts and the financial statement referred to in Article 205a, the annual report by the Court of Auditors together with the replies of the institutions under audit to the observations of the Court of Auditors and any relevant special reports by the Court of Auditors.

2.   Before giving a discharge to the Commission, or for any other purpose in connection with the exercise of its powers over the implementation of the budget, the European Parliament may ask to hear the Commission give evidence with regard to the execution of expenditure or the operation of financial control systems. The Commission shall submit any necessary information to the European Parliament at the latter's request.

3.   The Commission shall take all appropriate steps to act on the observations in the decisions giving discharge and on other observations by the European Parliament relating to the execution of expenditure, as well as on comments accompanying the recommendations on discharge adopted by the Council.

At the request of the European Parliament or the Council, the Commission shall report on the measures taken in the light of these observations and comments and in particular on the instructions given to the departments which are responsible for the implementation of the budget. These reports shall also be forwarded to the Court of Auditors.

Note
[1]Former Article 206b, as amended by Article G(74) TEU.

Article 206a and 206b
(repealed)

Article 207
The budget shall be drawn up in the unit of account determined in accordance with the provisions of the regulations made pursuant to Article 209.

The financial contributions provided for in Article 200(1) shall be placed at the disposal of the Community by the Member States in the national currencies.

The available balances of these contributions shall be deposited with the Treasuries of Member States or with bodies designated by them. While on deposit, such funds shall retain the value corresponding to the parity, at the date of deposit, in relation to the unit of account referred to in the first paragraph.

The balances may be invested on terms to be agreed between the Commission and the Member State concerned.

The regulations made pursuant to Article 209 shall lay down the technical conditions under which financial operations relating to the European Social Fund shall be carried out.

Article 208

The Commission may, provided it notifies the competent authorities of the Member States concerned, transfer into the currency of one of the Member States its holdings in the currency of another Member State, to the extent necessary to enable them to be used for purposes which come within the scope of this Treaty. The Commission shall as far as possible avoid making such transfers if it possesses cash or liquid assets in the currencies which it needs.

The Commission shall deal with each Member State through the authority designated by the State concerned. In carrying out financial operations the Commission shall employ the services of the bank of issue of the Member State concerned or of any other financial institution approved by that State.

Article 209[1]

The Council, acting unanimously on a proposal from the Commission and after consulting the European Parliament and obtaining the opinion of the Court of Auditors, shall:

(a)   make Financial Regulations specifying in particular the procedure to be adopted for estabishing and implementing the budget and for presenting and auditing accounts;

(b)   determine the methods and procedure whereby the budget revenue provided under the arrangements relating to the Community's own resources shall be made available to the Commission, and determine the measures to be applied, if need be, to meet cash requirements;

(c)   lay down rules concerning the responsibility of *financial controllers,* authorising officers and accounting officers, and concerning appropriate arrangements for inspection.

Note
[1]As amended by Article G(76) TEU.

Article 209a[1]
Member States shall take the same measures to counter fraud affecting the financial interests of the Community as they take to counter fraud affecting their own financial interests.

Without prejudice to other provisions of this Treaty, Member States shall coordinate their action aimed at protecting the financial interests of the Community against fraud. To this end they shall organise, with the help of the Commission, close and regular cooperation between the competent departments of their administrations.

Note
[1]As inserted by Article G(77) TEU.

PART SIX   GENERAL AND FINAL PROVISIONS

Article 210

The Community shall have legal personality.

Article 211

In each of the Member States, the Community shall enjoy the most extensive legal capacity accorded to legal persons under their laws; it may, in particular, acquire or dispose of movable and immovable property and may be a party to legal proceedings. To this end, the Community shall be represented by the Commission.

Article 212
(Article repealed by Article 24(2) of the Merger Treaty)
[See Article 24(1) of the Merger Treaty, which reads as follows:
1. The officials and other servants of the European Coal and Steel Community, the European Economic Community and the European Atomic Energy Community shall, at the date of entry into force of this Treaty, become officials and other servants of the European Communities and form part of the single administration of those Communities.

The Council shall, acting by a qualified majority on a proposal from the Commission and after consulting the other institutions concerned, lay down the Staff Regulations of officials of the European Communities and the conditions of Employment of other servants of those communities.]

Article 213
The Commission may, within the limits and under conditions laid down by the Council in accordance with the provisions of this Treaty, collect any information and carry out any checks required for the performance of the tasks entrusted to it.

Article 214
The members of the institutions of the Community, the members of committees, and the officials and other servants of the Community shall be required, even after their duties have ceased, not to disclose information of the kind covered by the obligation of professional secrecy, in particular information about undertakings, their business relations or their cost components.

Article 215[1]
The contractual liability of the Community shall be governed by the law applicable to the contract in question.

In the case of non-contractual liability, the Community shall, in accordance with the general principles common to the laws of the Member States, make good any damage caused by its institutions or by its servants in the performance of their duties.

The preceding paragraph shall apply under the same conditions to damage caused by the ECB or by its servants in the performance of their duties.

The personal liability of its servants towards the Community shall be governed by the provisions laid down in their Staff Regulations or in the Conditions of Employment applicable to them.

Note
[1]As amended by Article G(78) TEU.

Article 216
The seat of the institutions of the Community shall be determined by common accord of the Governments of the Member States.

Article 217
The rules governing the languages of the institutions of the Community shall, without prejudice to the provisions contained in the rules of procedure of the Court of Justice, be determined by the Council, acting unanimously.

Article 218
(Article repealed by the second paragraph of Article 28 of the Merger Treaty)
[See the first paragraph of Article 28 of the Merger Treaty, which reads as follows:

The European Communities shall enjoy in the territories of the Member States such privileges and immunities as are necessary for the performance of their tasks, under the conditions laid down in the Protocol annexed to this Treaty. The same shall apply to the European Investment Bank.]

Article 219
Member States undertake not to submit a dispute concerning the interpretation or application of this Treaty to any method of settlement other than those provided for therein.

Article 220
Member States shall, so far as is necessary, enter into negotiations with each other with a view to securing for the benefit of their nationals:
— the protection of persons and the enjoyment and protection of rights under the same conditions as those accorded by each State to its own nationals;
— the abolition of double taxation within the Community;
— the mutual recognition of companies or firms within the meaning of the second paragraph of Article 58, the retention of legal personality in the event of transfer of their seat from one country to another, and the possibility of mergers between companies or firms governed by the laws of different countries;
— the simplification of formalities governing the reciprocal recognition and enforcement of judgments of courts or tribunals and of arbitration awards.

Article 221
Within three years of the entry into force of this Treaty, Member States shall accord nationals of the other Member States the same treatment as their own nationals as regards participation in the capital of companies or firms within the meaning of Article 58, without prejudice to the application of the other provisions of this Treaty.

Article 222
This Treaty shall in no way prejudice the rules in Member States governing the system of property ownership.

Article 223
1.   The provisions of this Treaty shall not preclude the application of the following rules:
  (a)   No Member State shall be obliged to supply information the disclosure of which it considers contrary to the essential interests of its security;
  (b)   Any Member State may take such measures as it considers necessary for the protection of the essential interests of its security which are connected with the production of or trade in arms, munitions and war material; such measures shall not adversely affect the conditions of competition in the common market regarding products which are not intended for specifically military purposes.
2.   During the first years after the entry into force of this Treaty, the Council shall, acting unanimously, draw up a list of products to which the provisions of paragraph 1(b) shall apply.

3. The Council may, acting unanimously on a proposal from the Commission, make changes in this list.

Article 224

Member States shall consult each other with a view to taking together the steps needed to prevent the functioning of the common market being affected by measures which a Member State may be called upon to take in the event of serious internal disturbances affecting the maintenance of law and order, in the event of war, serious international tension constituting a threat of war, or in order to carry out obligations it has accepted for the purpose of maintaining peace and international security.

Article 225

If measures taken in the circumstances referred to in Articles 223 and 224 have the effect of distorting the conditions of competition in the common market, the Commission shall, together with the State concerned, examine how these measures can be adjusted to the rules laid down in this Treaty.

By way of derogation from the procedure laid down in Articles 169 and 170, the Commission or any Member State may bring the matter directly before the Court of Justice if it considers that another Member State is making improper use of the powers provided for in Articles 223 and 224. The Court of Justice shall give its ruling in camera.

Article 226

1. If, during the transitional period, difficulties arise which are serious and liable to persist in any sector of the economy or which could bring about serious deterioration in the economic situation of a given area, a Member State may apply for authorisation to take protective measures in order to rectify the situation and adjust the sector concerned to the economy of the common market.

2. On application by the State concerned, the Commission shall, by emergency procedure, determine without delay the protective measures which it considers necessary, specifying the circumstances and the manner in which they are to be put into effect.

3. The measures authorised under paragraph 2 may involve derogations from the rules of this Treaty, to such an extent and for such periods as are strictly necessary in order to attain the objectives referred to in paragraph 1. Priority shall be given to such measures as will least disturb the functioning of the common market.

Article 227[1]

1. This Treaty shall apply to the Kingdom of Belgium, the Kingdom of Denmark, the Federal Republic of Germany, the Hellenic Republic, the Kingdom of Spain, the French Republic, Ireland, the Italian Republic, the Grand Duchy of Luxembourg, the Kingdom of the Netherlands, the Republic of Austria, the Portuguese Republic, the Republic of Finland, the Kingdom of Sweden and the United Kingdom of Great Britain and Northern Ireland.[2]

2. *With regard to the French overseas departments, the general and particular provisions of this Treaty relating to:*

Notes
[1] As amended by Article G(79) TEU.
[2] As amended by Council Decision 95/1 (OJ 1995 L1/1) adjusting the Treaty of Accession of the three new Member States.

— the free movement of goods;
— agriculture, save for Article 40(4);
— the liberalisation of services;
— the rules on competition;
— the protective measures provided for in Articles 109h, 109i and
226;
— the institutions.
shall apply as soon as this Treaty enters into force.

The conditions under which the other provisions of this Treaty are to
apply shall be determined, within two years of the entry into force of
this Treaty, by decisions of the Council, acting unanimously on a
proposal from the Commission.

The institutions of the Community will, within the framework of the
procedures provided for in this Treaty, in particular Article 226, take
care that the economic and social development of these areas is made
possible.

3.   The special arrangements for association set out in Part Four of this
Treaty shall apply to the overseas countries and territories listed in Annex IV to
this Treaty.

This Treaty shall not apply to those overseas countries and territories having
special relations with the United Kingdom of Great Britain and Northern
Ireland which are not included in the aforementioned list.

4.   The provisions of this Treaty shall apply to the European Territories for
whose external relations a Member State is responsible.

5.   Notwithstanding the preceding paragraphs:
    (a)   This Treaty shall not apply to the Faroe Islands.
    (b)   This Treaty shall not apply to the Sovereign Base Areas of the United
Kingdom of Great Britain and Northern Ireland in Cyprus.
    (c)   This Treaty shall apply to the Channel Islands and the Isle of Man
only to the extent necessary to ensure the implementation of the arrangements
for those islands set out in the Treaty concerning the accession of new Member
States to the European Economic Community and to the European Atomic
Energy Community signed on 22 January 1972.

This Treaty shall not apply to the Åland islands. The Government of Finland
may, however, give notice, by a declaration deposited when ratifying this Treaty
with the Government of the Italian Republic, that the Treaty shall apply to the
Åland islands in accordance with the provisions set out in Protocol No. 2 to the
Act concerning the conditions of accession of the Republic of Austria, the
Republic of Finland and the Kingdom of Sweden and the adjustments to the
Treaties on which the European Union is founded. The Government of the
Italian Republic shall transmit a certified copy of any such declaration to the
Member States.[3]

Note
[3]As amended by Council Decision 95/1 [OJ 1995 L1/1] adjusting the Treaty of
Accession of the three new Member States.

Article 228[1]
    1.   Where this Treaty provides for the conclusion of agreements
between the Community and/or more States or international

Note
[1]As amended by Article G(80) TEU.

organisations, the Commission shall make recommendations to the Council, which shall authorise the Commission to open the necessary negotiations. The Commission shall conduct these negotiations in consultation with special committees appointed by the Council to assist it in this task and within the framework of such directives as the Council may issue to it.

In exercising the powers conferred upon it by this paragraph, the Council shall act by a qualified majority, except in the cases provided for in the second sentence of paragraph 2, for which it shall act unanimously.

2.   Subject to the powers vested in the Commission in this field, the agreements shall be concluded by the Council, acting by a qualified majority on a proposal from the Commission. The Council shall act unanimously when the agreement covers a field for which unanimity is required for the adoption of internal rules, and for the Agreements referred to in Article 238.

3.   The Council shall conclude agreements after consulting the European Parliament, except for the agreements referred to in Article 113(3), including cases where the agreement covers a field for which the procedure referred to in Article 189b or that referred to in Article 189c is required for the adoption of internal rules. The European Parliament shall deliver its opinion within a time limit which the Council may lay down according to the urgency of the matter. In the absence of an opinion within that time limit, the Council may act.

By way of derogation from the previous subparagraph, agreements referred to in Article 238, other agreements establishing a specific institutional framework by organising cooperation procedures, agreements having important budgetary implications for the Community and agreements entailing amendment of an act adopted under the procedure referred to in Article 189b shall be concluded after the assent of the European Parliament has been obtained.

The Council and the European Parliament may, in an urgent situation, agree upon a time limit for the assent.

4.   When concluding an agreement, the Council may, by way of derogation from paragraph 2, authorise the Commission to approve modifications on behalf of the Community where the agreement provides for them to be adopted by a simplified procedure or by a body set up by the agreement; it may attach specific conditions to such authorisation.

5.   When the Council envisages concluding an agreement which calls for amendments to this Treaty, the amendments must first be adopted in accordance with the procedure laid down in Article N of the Treaty of the European Union.

6.   The Council, the Commission or a Member State may obtain the opinion of the Court of Justice as to whether an agreement envisaged is compatible with the provisions of this Treaty. Where the opinion of the Court of Justice is adverse, the agreement may enter into force only in accordance with Article N of the Treaty on European Union.

7.   Agreements concluded under the conditions set out in this Article shall be binding on the institutions of the Community and on Member States.

Article 228a[1]
Where it is provided, in a common position or in a joint action adopted according to the provisions of the Treaty on European Union relating to the common foreign and security policy, for an action by the Community to interrupt or to reduce, in part or completely, economic relations with one or more third countries, the Council shall take the necessary urgent measures. The Council shall act by a qualified majority on a proposal from the Commission.

Note
[1]As inserted by Article G(81) TEU.

Article 229
It shall be for the Commission to ensure the maintenance of all appropriate relations with the organs of the United Nations, of its specialised agencies and of the General Agreement on Tariffs and Trade.

The Commission shall also maintain such relations as are appropriate with all international organisations.

Article 230
The Community shall establish all appropriate forms of cooperation with the Council of Europe.

Article 231[1]
The Community shall establish close cooperation with *the Organisation for Economic Cooperation and Development,* the details of which shall be determined by common accord.

Note
[1]As amended by Article G(82) TEU.

Article 232
1.   The provisions of this Treaty shall not affect the provisions of the Treaty establishing the European Coal and Steel Community, in particular as regards the rights and obligations of Member States, the powers of the institutions of that Community and the rules laid down by that Treaty for the functioning of the common market in coal and steel.

2.   The provisions of this Treaty shall not derogate from those of the Treaty establishing the European Atomic Energy Community.

Article 233
The provisions of this Treaty shall not preclude the existence or completion of regional unions between Belgium and Luxembourg, or between Belgium, Luxembourg and the Netherlands, to the extent that the objectives of these regional unions are not attained by application of this Treaty.

Article 234
The rights and obligations arising from agreements concluded before the entry into force of this Treaty between one or more Member States on the one hand, and one or more third countries on the other, shall not be affected by the provisions of this Treaty.

To the extent that such agreements are not compatible with this Treaty, the Member State or States concerned shall take all appropriate steps to eliminate the incompatibilities established. Member States shall, where necessary, assist each other to this end and shall, where appropriate, adopt a common attitude.

In applying the agreements referred to in the first paragraph, Member States shall take into account the fact that the advantages accorded under this Treaty by each Member State form an integral part of the establishment of the Community and are thereby inseparably linked with the creation of common institutions, the conferring of powers upon them and the granting of the same advantages by all the other Member States.

Article 235
If action by the Community should prove necessary to attain, in the course of the operation of the common market, one of the objectives of the Community and this Treaty has not provided the necessary powers, the Council shall, acting unanimously on a proposal from the Commission and after consulting the European Parliament, take the appropriate measures.

Article 236
(repealed)

Article 237
(repealed)

Article 238[1]
The Community may conclude *with one or more States or international organisations* agreements establishing an association involving reciprocal rights and obligations, common action and special procedure.

Note
[1]As amended by Article G(84) TEU.

Article 239
The protocols annexed to this Treaty by common accord of the Member States shall form an integral part thereof.

Article 240
This Treaty is concluded for an unlimited period.

SETTING UP OF THE INSTITUTIONS

Article 241
The Council shall meet within one month of the entry into force of this Treaty.

Article 242
The Council shall, within three months of its first meeting, take all appropriate measures to constitute the Economic and Social Committee.

Article 243
The Assembly[1] shall meet within two months of the first meeting of the Council, having been convened by the President of the Council, in order to elect its officers and draw up its rules of procedure. Pending the election of its officers, the oldest member shall take the chair.

Note
[1]Notwithstanding the provisions of Article 3 of the SEA, and for historical reasons, the term 'Assembly' has not been replaced by the terms 'European Parliament'.

Article 244

The Court of Justice shall take up its duties as soon as its members have been appointed. Its first President shall be appointed for three years in the same manner as its members.

The Court of Justice shall adopt its rules of procedure within three months of taking up its duties.

No matter may be brought before the Court of Justice until its rules of procedure have been published. The time within which an action must be brought shall run only from the date of this publication.

Upon his appointment, the President of the Court of Justice shall exercise the powers conferred upon him by this Treaty.

Article 245

The Commission shall take up its duties and assume the responsibilities conferred upon it by this Treaty as soon as its members have been appointed.

Upon taking up its duties, the Commission shall undertake the studies and arrange the contracts needed for making an overall survey of the economic situation of the Community.

Article 246

1. The first financial year shall run from the date on which this Treaty enters into force until 31 December following. Should this Treaty, however, enter into force during the second half of the year, the first financial year shall run until 31 December of the following year.

2. Until the budget for the first financial year has been established, Member States shall make the Community interest-free advances which shall be deducted from their financial contributions to the implementation of the budget.

3. Until the Staff Regulations of officials and the Conditions of Employment of other servants of the Community provided for in Article 212 have been laid down, each institution shall recruit the Staff it needs and to this end conclude contracts of limited duration.

Each institution shall examine together with the Council any question concerning the number, remuneration and distribution of posts.

FINAL PROVISIONS

Article 247

This Treaty shall be ratified by the High Contracting Parties in accordance with their respective constitutional requirements. The instruments of ratification shall be deposited with the Government of the Italian Republic.

This Treaty shall enter into force on the first day of the month following the deposit of the instrument of ratification by the last signatory State to take this step. If, however, such deposit is made less than fifteen days before the beginning of the following month, this Treaty shall not enter into force until the first day of the second month after the date of such deposit.

Article 248

This Treaty, drawn up in a single original in the Dutch, French, German and Italian languages, all four texts being equally authentic, shall be deposited in the archives of the Government of the Italian Republic, which shall transmit a certified copy to each of the Governments of the other signatory States.

In witness whereof, the undersigned Plenipotentiaries have signed this Treaty.

Done at Rome this twenty-fifth day of March in the year one thousand nine hundred and fifty-seven.

P. H. SPAAK	J. Ch SNOY ET D'OPPUERS
ADENAUER	HALLSTEIN
PINEAU	M. FAURE
Antonio SEGNI	Gaetano MARTINO
BECH	Lambert SCHAUS
J. LUNS	J. LINTHORST HOMAN

ANNEX I
LISTS A TO G REFERRED TO IN ARTICLES 19 AND 20 OF THIS TREATY

LIST G

List of tariff headings in respect of which the rates of duty in the common customs tariff are to be negotiated between the Member States

-1-*   -2-*

No in the Brussels Nomenclature * Description of products *

ex 03.01 * Saltwater fish, fresh (live or dead), chilled or frozen *

03.02 * Fish, salted, in brine, dried or smoked *

04.04 * Cheese and curd *

11.02 * Cereal groats and cereal meal; other worked cereal grains (for example, rolled, flaked, polished, pearled or kibbled, but not further prepared), except husked, glazed, polished or broken rice; gern of cereals, whole, rolled, flaked or ground *

11.07 * Malt, roasted or not *

ex 15.01 * Lard and other rendered pig fat *

15.02 * Unrendered fats of bovine cattle, sheep or goats; tallow (including 'premier jus') produced from those fats *

15.03 * Lard stearin, oleostearin and tallow stearin; lard oil, oleo-oil and tallow oil, not emulsified or mixed or prepared in any way *

ex 15.04 * Whale oil, whether or not refined *

15.07 * Fixed vegetable oils, fluid or solid, crude, refined or purified *

15.12 * Animal or vegetable fats and oils, hydrogenated, whether or not refined, but not further prepared *

18.03 * Cocoa paste (in bulk or in block), whether or not defatted *

18.04 * Cocoa butter (fat or oil) *

18.05 * Cocoa powder, unsweetened *

18.06 * Chocolate and other food preparations containing cocoa *

19.07 * Bread, ships' biscuits and other ordinary bakers' wares, not containing sugar, honey, eggs, fats, cheese or fruit *

19.08 * Pastry, biscuits, cakes and other fine bakers' wares, whether or not containing cocoa in any proportion *

21.02 * Extracts, essences or concentrates, of coffee, tea or maté; preparations with a basis of those extracts, essences or concentrates *

22.05 * Wine of fresh grapes; grape must with fermentation arrested by the addition of alcohol *

22.08 * Ethyl alcohol or neutral spirits, undenatured, of a strength of 80 degrees or higher; denatured spirits (including ethyl alcohol and neutral spirits) of any strength *

22.09 * Spirits (other than those of heading No 22.08); liqueurs and other spirituous beverages; compound alcoholic preparations (known as 'concentrated extracts') for the manufacture of beverages *

25.01 * Common salt (including rock salt, sea salt and table salt); pure sodium chloride; salt liquors, sea water *

25.03 * Sulphur of all kinds, other than sublimed sulphur, precipitated sulphur and colloidal sulphur *

25.30 * Crude natural borates and concentrates thereof (calcined or not), but not including borates separated from natural brine; crude natural boric acid containing not more than 85 per cent of H3BO3 calculated on the dry weight *

ex 26.01 * Lead ores and zinc ores *

ex 26.03 * Ash and residues, containing zinc *

27.10 * Petroleum and shale oils, other than crude; preparations not elsewhere specified or included, containing not less than 70 per cent by weight of petroleum or shale oils, these oils being the basic constituents of the preparations *

27.11 * Petroleum gases and other gaseous hydrocarbons *

27.12 * Petroleum jelly *

ex 27.13 * Paraffin wax, micro-crystalline wax, slack wax and other mineral wax, whether or not coloured, except ozokerite, lignite wax and peat wax *

ex 28.01 * Iodine, crude, and bromine *

28.02 * Sulphur, sublimed or precipitated; celloidal sulphur *

ex 28.11 * Arsenic pentoxide *

28.12 * Boric oxide and boric acid *

28.33 * Bromides, oxybromides, bromates and perbromates, and hypobromites *

ex 28.34 * Iodides and iodates *

28.46 * Borates and perborates *

ex 29.04 * Butyl and isobutyl alcohols (other than tertbutyl alcohol) *

ex 29.06 * Phenol, cresols and xylenols *

ex 32.01 * Extracts of quebracho and of wattle (mimosa) *

40.02 * Synthetic rubbers, including synthetic latex, whether or not stabilised; factice derived from oils *

44.03 * Wood in the rough, whether or not stripped of its bark or merely roughed down *

44.04 * Wood, roughly squared or half-squared, but not further manufactured *

44.05 * Wood sawn lengthwise, sliced or peeled, but not further prepared, of a thickness exceeding 5 millimetres *

45.01 * Natural cork, unworked, crushed, granulated or ground; waste cork *

45.02 * Natural cork in blocks, plates, sheets or strips (including cubes or square slabs, cut to size for corks or stoppers) *

47.01 * Pulp derived by mechanical or chemical means from any fibrous vegetable material *

50.02 * Raw silk (not thrown) *

50.03 * Silk waste (including cocoons unsuitable for reeling, silk noils and pulled or garnetted rags) *

50.04 * Silk yarn, other than yarn of noil or other waste silk, not put up for retail sale *

50.05 * Yarn spun from silk waste other than noil, not put up for retail sale *

ex 62.03 * Used sacks and bags, of jute, of a kind used for the packing of goods *

ex 70.19 * Glass beads, imitation pearls, imitation precious and semi-precious stones, imitation synthetic stones and similar fancy or decorative glass smallwares *

ex 73.02 * Ferro-alloys (other than high carbon ferro-manganese) *

76.01 * Unwrought aluminium; aluminium waste and scrap (1) *

77.01 * Unwrought magnesium; magnesium waste (excluding shavings of uniform size) and scrap (1) *

78.01 * Unwrought lead (including argentiferous lead); lead waste and scrap (1) *

79.01 * Zinc spelter; unwrought zinc; zinc waste and scrap (1) *

ex 81.01 * Tungsten (wolfram) unwrought, in powder (1) *

ex 81.02 * Molybdenum, unwrought (1) *

ex 81.03 * Tantalum, unwrought (1) *

ex 81.04 * Other base metals, unwrought (1) *

ex 84.06 * Engines for motor vehicles, flying machines and ships, boats and other vessels, and parts of such engines *

ex 84.08 * Reaction engines, and parts and accessories thereof*

84.45 * Machine-tools for working metal or metallic carbides, not being machines falling within heading No 84.49 or 84.50 *

84.48 * Accessories and parts suitable for use solely or principally with the machines falling within headings Nos 84.45 to 84.47, including work and tool holders, self-opening dieheads, dividing heads and other appliances for machine-tools; tool holders for the mechanical hand tools of heading No 82.04, 84.49 or 85.05 *

ex 84.63 * Transmission components for engines of motor vehicles *

87.06 * Parts and accessories of the motor vehicles falling within heading No 87.01, 87.02 or 87.03 *

88.02 * Flying machines, gliders and kites; rotochutes *

ex 88.03 * Parts of flying machines, gliders and kites *

(1) The rates of duty applicable to semi-finished products are to be reviewed in the light of the rate fixed for the unwrought metal, in accordance with the procedure laid down in Article 21(2) of this Treaty

ANNEX II
LIST REFERRED TO IN ARTICLE 38 OF THIS TREATY

         -1- *   -2- *

No in the Brussels Nomenclature * Description of products *

CHAPTER 1 * Live animals *

CHAPTER 2 * Meat and edible meat offals *

CHAPTER 3 * Fish, crustaceans and molluscs *

CHAPTER 4 * Dairy produce; birds' eggs; natural honey *

CHAPTER 5 * *

05.04 * Guts, bladders and stomachs of animals (other than fish), whole and pieces thereof *

05.15 * Animal products not elswhere specified or included; dead animals of Chapter 1 or Chapter 3, unfit for human consumption *

CHAPTER 6 * Live trees and other plants; bulbs, roots and the like; cut flowers and ornamental foliage *

CHAPTER 7 * Edible vegetables and certain roots and tubers *

CHAPTER 8 * Edible fruit and nuts; peel of melons or citrus fruit *

CHAPTER 9 * Coffee, tea and spices, excluding maté (heading No 09.03) *

CHAPTER 10 * Cereals *

CHAPTER 11 * Products of the milling industry; malt and starches; gluten; inulin *

CHAPTER 12 * Oil seeds and oleaginous fruit; miscellaneous grains, seeds and fruit; industrial and medical plants; straw and fodder *

CHAPTER 13 * *

ex 13.03 * Pectin *

CHAPTER 15 * *

15.01 * Lard and other rendered pig fat; rendered poultry fat *

15.02 * Unrendered fats of bovine cattle, sheep or goats; tallow (including 'premier jus') produced from those fats *

15.03 * Lard stearin, oleostearin and tallow stearin; lard oil, oleo-oil and tallow oil, not emulsified or mixed or prepared in any way *

15.04 * Fats and oil, of fish and marine mammals, whether or not refined *

15.07 * Fixed vegetable oils, fluid or solid, crude, refined or purified *

15.12 * Animal or vegetable fats and oils, hydrogenated, whether or not refined, but not further prepared *

15.13 * Margarine, imitation lard and other prepared edible fats *

15.17 * Residues resulting from the treatment of fatty substances or animal or vegetable waxes *

CHAPTER 16 * Preparations of meat, of fish, of crustaceans or molluscs *

CHAPTER 17 * *

17.01 * Beet sugar and cane sugar, solid *

17.02 * Other sugars; sugar syrups; artificial honey (whether or not mixed with natural honey); caramel *

17.03 * Molasses, whether or not decolourised *

17.05 (*) * Flavoured or coloured sugars, syrups and molasses, but not including fruit juices containing added sugar in any proportion *

CHAPTER 18 * *

18.01 * Cocoa beans, whole or broken, raw or roasted *

18.02 * Cocoa shells, husks, skins and waste *

CHAPTER 20 * Preparations of vegetables, fruit or other parts of plants *

CHAPTER 22 * *

22.04 * Grape must, in fermentation or with fermentation arrested otherwise than by the addition of alcohol *

22.05 * Wine of fresh grapes; grape must with fermentation arrested by the addition of alcohol *

22.07 * Other fermented beverages (for example, cider, perry and mead) *

ex 22.08 (*), ex 22.09 (*) * Ethyl alcohol or neutral spirits, whether or not denatured, of any strength, obtained from agricultural products listed in Annex

II to the Treaty, excluding liqueurs and other spirituous beverages and compound alcoholic preparations (known as 'concentrated extracts') for the manufacture of beverages *

22.10 (*) * Vinegar and substitutes for vinegar *

CHAPTER 23 * Residues and waste from the food industries; prepared animal fodder *

CHAPTER 24 * *

24.01 * Unmanufactured tobacco; tobacco refuse *

CHAPTER 45 * *

45.01 * Natural cork, unworked, crushed, granulated or ground; waste cork *

CHAPTER 54 * *

54.01 * Flax, raw or processed but not spun; flax tow and waste (including pulled or garnetted rags) *

CHAPTER 57 * *

57.01 * True hemp (Cannabis sativa), raw or processed but not spun; tow and waste of true hemp (including pulled or garnetted rags or ropes) *

ANNEX III
LIST OF INVISIBLE TRANSACTIONS REFERRED TO IN ARTICLE 106 OF THIS TREATY

— Maritime freights, including chartering, harbour expenses, disbursements for fishing vessels, etc.

— Inland waterway freights, including chartering.

— Road transport: passengers and freights, including chartering.

— Air transport: passengers and freights, including chartering.

Payment by passengers of international air tickets and excess luggage charges; payment of international air freight charges and chartered flights.

Receipts from the sale of international air tickets, excess luggage charges, international air freight charges, and chartered flights.

— For all means of maritime transport: harbour services (bunkering and provisioning, maintenance, repairs, expenses for crews, etc.).

For all means of inland waterway transport: harbour services (bunkering and provisioning, maintenance and minor repairs of equipment, expenses for crews, etc.).

For all means of commercial road transport: fuel, oil, minor repairs, garaging, expenses for drivers and crews, etc.

For all means of air transport: operating costs and general overheads, including repairs to aircraft and to air transport equipment.

— Warehousing and storage charges, customs clearance.

— Customs duties and fees.

— Transit charges.

— Repair and assembly charges.

Processing, finishing, processing of work under contract, and other services of the same nature.

— Repair of ships.

Repair of means of transport other than ships and aircraft.

— Technical assistance (assistance relating to the production and distribution of goods and services at all stages, given over a period limited according to the specific purpose of such assistance, and including e.g. advice or visits by experts, preparation of plans and blueprints, supervision of manufacture, market research, training of personnel).

— Commission and brokerage.

Profits arising out of transit operations or sales of trans-shipment.

Banking commissions and charges.

Representation expenses.

— Advertising by all media.

— Business travel.

— Participation by subsidiary companies and branches in overhead expenses of parent companies situated abroad and vice-versa.

— Contracting (construction and maintenance of buildings, roads, bridges, ports, etc. carried out by specialised firms, and, generally, at fixed prices after open tender).

— Differences, margins and deposits due in respect of operations on commodity terminal markets in conformity with normal bona fide commercial practice.

— Tourism.

— Travel for private reasons (education).

— Travel for private reasons (health).

— Travel for private reasons (family).

— Subscriptions to newspapers, periodicals, books, musical publications.

Newspapers, periodicals, books, musical publications and records.

— Printed films, commercial, documentary, educational, etc. (rentals, dues, subscriptions, reproduction and synchronisation fees, etc.).

— Membership fees.

— Current maintenance and repair of private property abroad.

— Government expenditure (official representation abroad, contributions to international organisations).

— Taxes, court expenses, registration fees for patents and trade marks.

Claims for damages.

Refunds in the case of cancellation of contracts and refunds of uncalled-for payments.

Fines.

—Periodical settlements in connection with public transport and postal, telegraphic and telephone services.

—Exchange authorisations granted to own or foreign nationals emigrating.

Exchange authorisations granted to own or foreign nationals returning to their country of origin.

—Salaries and wages (of frontier or seasonal workers and of other non-residents, without prejudice to the right of a country to regulate terms of employment of foreign nationals).

—Emigrants' remittances (without prejudice to the right of a country to regulate immigration).

—Fees.

—Dividends and shares in profits.

—Interest on debentures, mortgages, etc.

—Rent.

—Contractual amortisation (with the exception of transfers in connection with amortisation having the character either of anticipated repayments or of the discharge of accumulated arrears).

—Profits from business activity.

—Authors' royalties.

Patents, designs, trade marks and inventions (the assignment and licensing of patent rights, designs, trade marks and inventions, whether or not legally protected, and transfers arising out of such assignment or licensing).

—Consular receipts.

—Pensions and other income of a similar nature.

Maintenance payments resulting from a legal obligation or from a decision of a court and financial assistance in cases of hardship.

Transfers by instalments of assets deposited in one member country by persons residing in another member country whose personal income in that country is not sufficient to cover their living expenses.

—Transactions and transfers in connection with direct insurance.

—Transactions and transfers in connection with reinsurance and retrocession.

—Opening and reimbursement of commercial or industrial credits.

—Transfers of minor amounts abroad.

— Charges for documentation of all kinds incurred on their own account by authorised dealers in foreign exchange.

— Sports prizes and racing earnings.

— Inheritances.

— Dowries.

ANNEX IV OVERSEAS COUNTRIES AND TERRITORIES TO WHICH THE PROVISIONS OF PART IV OF THIS TREATY APPLY[1, 2, 3]

French West Africa: Senegal, French Sudan, French Guinea, Ivory Coast, Dahomey, Mauritania, Niger and Upper Volta;[4]

French Equatorial Africa: Middle Congo, Ubangi-Shari, Chad and Gabon;[4]

Saint Pierre and Miquelon,[5] the Comoro Archipelago,[6] Madagascar[4] and dependencies,[4] French Somaliland,[4] New Caledonia and dependencies, French Settlements in Oceania,[7] Southern and Antarctic Territories;[8]

The autonomous Republic of Togoland;[4]

The trust territory of the Cameroons under French administration;[4]

The Belgian Congo and Ruanda-Urundi;[4]

The trust territory of Somaliland under Italian administration;[4]

Netherlands New Guinea;[4]

The Netherlands Antilles;[9]

Anglo-French Condominium of the New Hebrides;[4]

The Bahamas;[4]

Bermuda;[10]

Brunei;[11]

Associated States in the Caribbean: Antigua, Dominica, Grenada, St Lucia, St Vincent, St Christopher, Nevis, Anguilla;[12]

British Honduras;[4]

Cayman Islands;

Falkland Islands and Dependencies;[13]

Gilbert and Ellice Islands;[4]

Central and Southern Line Islands;[10]

British Solomon Islands;[4]

Turks and Caicos Islands;

British Virgin Islands;

Montserrat;

Pitcairn;

St Helena and Dependencies;

The Seychelles;[4]

British Antarctic Territory;

British Indian Ocean Territory;

Greenland.[14]

Notes

[1]As amended by

— Article 1 of the Convention of 13 November 1962 amending the Treaty establishing the European Economic Community (*Official Journal of the European Communities*, No 150, 1 October 1964, p. 2414) and

— Article 24(2) of the Act of Accession DK/IRL/UK, modified by Article 13 of the AD AA DK/IRL/UK,

—The Treaty of 13 March 1984 amending, with regard to Greenland, the Treaties establishing the European Communities (*Official Journal of the European Communities,* No L 29, 1 February 1985).

[2]Council Decision 86/283/EEC of 30 June 1986 on the association of the overseas countries and territories with the European Economic Community (*Official Journal of the European Communities,* No L 175, 1 July 1986) contains a list of overseas countries and territories to which the provisions of Part Four of the Treaty apply.

[3]The provisions of Part Four of the Treaty applied to Surinam, by virtue of a Supplementary Act of the Kingdom of the Netherlands to complete its instruments of ratification, from 1 September 1962 to 16 July 1976.

[4]The provisions of Part Four of the Treaty no longer apply to these countries and territories, which have become independent and whose names may have been changed.

The relations between the European Economic Community and certain African States and Madagascar were the subject of the Conventions of Association signed at Yaoundé on 20 July 1963 and 29 July 1969. The relations with certain African, Caribbean and Pacific States were subsequently the subject of:

—the ACP-EEC Convention of Lomé, signed on 28 February 1975 (*Official Journal of the European Communities,* No L 25, 30 January 1976), which entered into force on 1 April 1976,

—the Second ACP-EEC Convention, signed at Lomé on 31 October 1979 (*Official Journal of the European Communities,* No L 347, 22 December 1980), which entered into force on 1 January 1981,

—the Third ACP-EEC Convention, signed at Lomé on 8 December 1984 (*Official Journal of the European Communities,* No L 86, 31 March 1986), which entered into force on 1 May 1986.

—the Fourth ACP-EEC Convention, signed at Lomé on 15 December 1989 (*Official Journal of the European Communities,* No L 229, 17 August 1991), which entered into force on 1 September 1991.

[5]Has become a French overseas department.

[6]The provisions of Part Four of the Treaty no longer apply to this Archipelago, except for the territorial collectivity of Mayotte which has remained on the list of overseas countries and territories (see note 2).

[7]New name: Overseas territory of French Polynesia,
            Overseas territory of the Wallis and Futuna Islands.

[8]New name: French Southern and Antarctic Territories.

[9]New name: Overseas countries of the Kingdom of the Netherlands:
            —Aruba
            —the Netherlands Antilles
              —Bonaire,
              —Curaçao,
              —Saba,
              —Sint Eustatius,
              —Sint Maarten.

[10]These territories are not included in the overseas countries and territories covered by Council Decision 86/283/EEC of 30 June 1986 (see note 2).

[11]The provisions of Part Four of the Treaty no longer apply to this territory, which became independent on 31 December 1983.

[12]The associated States, as a constitutional group, no longer exist. All the component territories have become independent, except Anguilla, to which the provisions of Part Four of the Treaty continue to apply.

[13]The dependencies of the Falkland Islands changed their name to South Georgia and the South Sandwich Islands on 3 October 1985 on ceasing to be dependencies of the Falkland Islands.

[14]Entry added by Article 4 of the Greenland Treaty.

TREATY ON EUROPEAN UNION[1]

His Majesty the King of the Belgians,
Her Majesty the Queen of Denmark,
The President of the Federal Republic of Germany,
The President of the Hellenic Republic,
His Majesty the King of Spain,
The President of the French Republic,
The President of Ireland,
The President of the Italian Republic,
His Royal Highness the Grand Duke of Luxembourg,
Her Majesty the Queen of the Netherlands,
The President of the Portuguese Republic,
Her Majesty the Queen of the United Kingdom of Great Britain and Northern Ireland,

RESOLVED to mark a new stage in the process of European integration undertaken with the establishment of the European Communities,

RECALLING the historic importance of the ending of the division of the European Continent and the need to create firm bases for the construction of the future Europe,

CONFIRMING their attachment to the principles of liberty, democracy and respect for human rights and fundamental freedoms and of the rule of law,

DESIRING to deepen the solidarity between their peoples while respecting their history, their culture and their traditions,

DESIRING to enhance further the democratic and efficient functioning of the institutions so as to enable them better to carry out, within a single institutional framework, the tasks entrusted to them,

RESOLVED to achieve the strengthening and the convergence of their economies and to establish an economic and monetary union including, in accordance with the provisions of this Treaty, a single and stable currency,

DETERMINED to promote economic and social progress for their peoples, within the context of the accomplishment of the internal market and of reinforced cohesion and environmental protection, and to implement policies ensuring that advances in economic integration are accompanied by parallel progress in other fields,

RESOLVED to establish a citizenship common to nationals of the countries,

RESOLVED to implement a common foreign and security policy including the eventual framing of a common defence policy, which might in time lead to a common defence, thereby reinforcing the European identity and its independence in order to promote peace, security and progress in Europe and in the world,

REAFFIRMING their objective to facilitate the free movement of persons, while ensuring the safety and security of their peoples, by including provisions on justice and home affairs in this Treaty,

RESOLVED to continue the process of creating an ever closer union among the peoples of Europe, in which decisions are taken as closely as possible to the citizen in accordance with the principle of subsidiarity,

Note
[1] As taken from OJ 1993 C 224.

IN VIEW of further steps to be taken in order to advance European integration,

HAVE DECIDED to establish a European Union and to this end have designated as their plenipotentiaries:

(List of Government representatives omitted.)

WHO, having exchanged their full powers, found in good and due form, have agreed as follows

TITLE I   COMMON PROVISIONS

Article A
By this Treaty, the High Contracting Parties establish among themselves a European Union, hereinafter called 'the Union'.

This Treaty marks a new stage in the process of creating an ever closer union among the peoples of Europe, in which decisions are taken as closely as possible to the citizen.

The Union shall be founded on the European Communities, supplemented by the policies and forms of cooperation established by this Treaty. Its task shall be to organise, in a manner demonstrating consistency and solidarity, relations between the Member States and between their peoples.

Article B
The Union shall set itself the following objectives:

— to promote economic and social progress which is balanced and sustainable, in particular through the creation of an area without internal frontiers, through the strengthening of economic and social cohesion and through the establishment of economic and monetary union, ultimately including a single currency in accordance with the provisions of this Treaty;

— to assert its identity on the international scene, in particular through the implementation of a common foreign and security policy including the eventual framing of a common defence policy, which might in time lead to a common defence;

— to strengthen the protection of the rights and interests of the nationals of its Member States through the introduction of a citizenship of the Union;

— to develop close cooperation on justice and home affairs;

— to maintain in full the 'acquis communautaire' and build on it with a view to considering, through the procedure referred to in Article N(2), to what extent the policies and forms of cooperation introduced by this Treaty may need to be revised with the aim of ensuring the effectiveness of the mechanisms and the institutions of the Community.

The objectives of the Union shall be achieved as provided in this Treaty and in accordance with the conditions and the timetable set out therein while respecting the principle of subsidiarity as defined in Article 3b of the Treaty establishing the European Community.

Article C
The Union shall be served by a single institutional framework which shall ensure the consistency and the continuity of the activities carried out in order to attain its objectives while respecting and building upon the 'acquis communautaire'.

The Union shall in particular ensure the consistency of its external activities as a whole in the context of its external relations, security, economic and development policies. The Council and the Commission shall be responsible for ensuring such consistency. They shall ensure the implementation of these policies, each in accordance with its respective powers.

Article D

The European Council shall provide the Union with the necessary impetus for its development and shall define the general political guidelines thereof.

The European Council shall bring together the Heads of State or of Government of the Member States and the President of the Commission. They shall be assisted by the Ministers for Foreign Affairs of the Member States and by a Member of the Commission. The European Council shall meet at least twice a year, under the chairmanship of the Head of State or of Government of the Member State which holds the Presidency of the Council.

The European Council shall submit to the European Parliament a report after each of its meetings and a yearly written report on the progress achieved by the Union.

Article E

The European Parliament, the Council, the Commission and the Court of Justice shall exercise their powers under the conditions and for the purposes provided for, on the one hand, by the provisions of the Treaties establishing the European Communities and of the subsequent Treaties and Acts modifying and supplementing them and, on the other hand, by the other provisions of this Treaty.

Article F

1. The Union shall respect the national identities of its Member States, whose systems of government are founded on the principles of democracy.

2. The Union shall respect fundamental rights, as guaranteed by the European Convention for the Protection of Human Rights and Fundamental Freedoms signed in Rome on 4 November 1950 and as they result from the constitutional traditions common to the Member States, as general principles of Community law.

3. The Union shall provide itself with the means necessary to attain its objectives and carry through its policies.

TITLE V   PROVISIONS ON A COMMON FOREIGN AND SECURITY POLICY

Article J

A common foreign and security policy is hereby established which shall be governed by the following provisions.

Article J.1

1. The Union and its Member States shall define and implement a common foreign and security policy, governed by the provisions of this Title and covering all areas of foreign and security policy.

2. The objectives of the common foreign and security policy shall be:

—to safeguard the common values, fundamental interests and independence of the Union;

— to strengthen the security of the Union and its Member States in all ways;

— to preserve peace and strengthen international security, in accordance with the principles of the United Nations Charter as well as the principles of the Helsinki Final Act and the objectives of the Paris Charter;

— to promote international cooperation;

— to develop and consolidate democracy and the rule of law, and respect for human rights and fundamental freedoms.

3.   The Union shall pursue these objectives:

— by establishing systematic cooperation between Member States in the conduct of policy, in accordance with Article J.2;

— by gradually implementing, in accordance with Article J.3, joint action in the areas in which the Member States have important interests in common.

4.   The Member States shall support the Union's external and security policy actively and unreservedly in a spirit of loyalty and mutual solidarity. They shall refrain from an action which is contrary to the interests of the Union or likely to impair its effectiveness as a cohesive force in international relations. The Council shall ensure that these principles are complied with.

Article J.2

1.   Member States shall inform and consult one another within the Council on any matter of foreign and security policy of general interest in order to ensure that their combined influence is exerted as effectively as possible by means of concerted and convergent action.

2.   Whenever it deems it necessary, the Council shall define a common position.

Member States shall ensure that their national policies conform to the common positions.

3.   Member States shall coordinate their action in international organisations and at international conferences. They shall uphold the common positions in such fora.

In international organisations and at international conferences where not all the Member States participate, those which do take part shall uphold the common positions.

Article J.3

The procedure for adopting joint action in matters covered by the foreign and security policy shall be the following:

1.   The council shall decide, on the basis of general guidelines from the European Council, that a matter should be the subject of joint action.

Whenever the Council decides on the principle of joint action, it shall lay down the specific scope, the Union's general and specific objectives in carrying out such action, if necessary its duration, and the means, procedures and conditions for its implementation.

2.   The Council shall, when adopting the joint action and at any stage during its development, define those matters on which decisions are to be taken by a qualified majority.

Where the Council is required to act by a qualified majority pursuant to the preceding subparagraph, the votes of its members shall be weighted in accordance with Article 148(2) of the Treaty establishing the European

Community, and for their adoption, acts of the Council shall require at least 62 votes in favour, cast by at least 10 members.[1]

3.   If there is a change in circumstances having a substantial effect on a question subject to joint action, the Council shall review the principles and objectives of that action and take the necessary decisions. As long as the Council has not acted, the joint action shall stand.

4.   Joint actions shall commit the Member States in the positions they adopt and in the conduct of their activity.

5.   Whenever there is any plan to adopt a national position or take national action pursuant to a joint action, information shall be provided in time to allow, if necessary, for prior consultations within the Council. The obligation to provide prior information shall not apply to measures which are merely a national transposition of Council decisions.

6.   In cases of imperative need arising from changes in the situation and failing a Council decision, Member States may take the necessary measures as a matter of urgency having regard to the general objectives of the joint action. The Member State concerned shall inform the Council immediately of any such measures.

7.   Should there be any major difficulties in implementing a joint action, a Member State shall refer them to the Council which shall discuss them and seek appropriate solutions. Such solutions shall not run counter to the objectives of the joint action or impair its effectiveness.

Note
[1]As amended by Council Decision 95/1 (OJ 1995 L1/1) adjusting the Treaty of Accession of the three new Member States.

Article J.4
1.   The common foreign and security policy shall include all questions related to the security of the Union, including the eventual framing of a common defence policy, which might in time lead to a common defence.

2.   The Union requests the Western European Union (WEU), which is an integral part of the development of the Union, to elaborate and implement decisions and actions of the Union which have defence implications. The Council shall, in agreement with the institutions of the WEU, adopt the necessary practical arrangements.

3.   Issues having defence implications dealt with under this Article shall not be subject to the procedures set out in Article J.3.

4.   The policy of the Union in accordance with this Article shall not prejudice the specific character of the security and defence policy of certain Member States and shall respect the obligations of certain Member States under the North Atlantic Treaty and be compatible with the common security and defence policy established within that framework.

5.   The provisions of this Article shall not prevent the development of closer cooperation between two or more Member States on a bilateral level, in the framework of the WEU and the Atlantic Alliance, provided such cooperation does not run counter to or impede that provided for in this Title.

6.   With a view to furthering the objective of this Treaty, and having in view the date of 1998 in the context of Article XII of the Brussels Treaty, the provisions of this Article may be revised as provided for in Article N(2) on the basis of a report to be presented in 1996 by the Council to the European

Council, which shall include an evaluation of the progress made and the experience gained until then.

Article J.5

1. The Presidency shall represent the Union in matters coming within the common foreign and security policy.

2. The Presidency shall be responsible for the implementation of common measures; in that capacity it shall in principle express the position of the Union in international organisations and international conferences.

3. In the tasks referred to in paragraphs 1 and 2, the Presidency shall be assisted if need be by the previous and next Member States to hold the Presidency. The Commission shall be fully associated in these tasks.

4. Without prejudice to Article J.2(3) and Article J.3(4), Member States represented in international organisations or international conferences where not all the Member States participate shall keep the latter informed of any matter of common interest.

Member States which are also members of the United Nations Security Council will concert and keep the other Member States fully informed. Member States which are permanent members of the Security Council will, in the execution of their functions, ensure the defence of the positions and the interests of the Union, without prejudice to their responsibilities under the provisions of the United Nations Charter.

Article J.6

The diplomatic and consular missions of the Member States and the Commission Delegations in third countries and international conferences, and their representations to international organisations, shall cooperate in ensuring that the common positions and common measures adopted by the Council are complied with and implemented.

They shall step up cooperation by exchanging information, carrying out joint assessments and contributing to the implementation of the provisions referred to in Article 8c of the Treaty establishing the European Community.

Article J.7

The Presidency shall consult the European Parliament on the main aspects and the basic choices of the common foreign and security policy and shall ensure that the views of the European Parliament are duly taken into consideration. The European Parliament shall be kept regularly informed by the Presidency and the Commission of the development of the Union's foreign and security policy.

The European Parliament may ask questions of the Council or make recommendations to it. It shall hold an annual debate on progress in implementing the common foreign and security policy.

Article J.8

1. The European Council shall define the principles of and general guidelines for the common foreign and security policy.

2. The Council shall take the decisions necessary for defining and implementing the common foreign and security policy on the basis of the general guidelines adopted by the European Council. It shall ensure the unity, consistency and effectiveness of action by the Union.

The Council shall act unanimously, except for procedural questions and in the case referred to in Article J.3(2).

3. Any Member State or the Commission may refer to the Council any question relating to the common foreign and security policy and may submit proposals to the Council.

4. In cases requiring a rapid decision, the Presidency, of its own motion, or at the request of the Commission or a Member State, shall convene an extraordinary Council meeting within forty-eight hours or, in an emergency, within a shorter period.

5. Without prejudice to Article 151 of the Treaty establishing the European Community, a Political Committee consisting of Political Directors shall monitor the international situation in the areas covered by common foreign and security policy and contribute to the definition of policies by delivering opinions to the Council at the request of the Council or on its own initiative. It shall also monitor the implementation of agreed policies, without prejudice to the responsibility of the Presidency and the Commission.

Article J.9
The Commission shall be fully associated with the work carried out in the common foreign and security policy field.

Article J.10
On the occasion of any review of the security provisions under Article J.4, the Conference which is convened to that effect shall also examine whether any other amendments need to be made to provisions relating to the common foreign and security policy.

Article J.11
1. The provisions referred to in Articles 137, 138, 139 to 142, 146, 147, 150 to 153, 157 to 163 and 217 of the Treaty establishing the European Community shall apply to the provisions relating to the areas referred to in this Title.

2. Administrative expenditure which the provisions relating to the areas referred to in this Title entail for the institutions shall be charged to the budget of the European Communities.

The Council may also:

— either decide unanimously that operational expenditure to which the implementation of those provisions gives rise is to be charged to the budget of the European Communities; in that event, the budgetary procedure laid down in the Treaty establishing the European Community shall be applicable;

— or determine that such expenditure shall be charged to the Member States, where appropriate in accordance with a scale to be decided.

TITLE VI PROVISIONS ON COOPERATION IN THE FIELDS OF JUSTICE AND HOME AFFAIRS

Article K
Cooperation in the fields of justice and home affairs shall be governed by the following provisions.

Article K.1
For the purposes of achieving the objectives of the Union, in particular the free movement of persons, and without prejudice to the powers of the European

Community, Member States shall regard the following areas as matters of common interest:

1. asylum policy;
2. rules governing the crossing by persons of the external borders or the Member States and the exercise of controls thereon;
3. immigration policy and policy regarding nationals of third countries:

   (a) conditions of entry and movement by nationals of third countries on the territory of Member States;

   (b) conditions of residence by nationals of third countries on the territory of Member States, including family reunion and access to employment;

   (c) combating unauthorised immigration, residence and work by nationals of third countries on the territory of Member States;

4. combating drug addiction in so far as this is not covered by 7 to 9;
5. combating fraud on an international scale in so far as this is not covered by 7 to 9;
6. judicial cooperation in civil matters;
7. judicial cooperation in criminal matters;
8. customs cooperation;
9. police cooperation for the purposes of preventing and combating terrorism, unlawful drug trafficking and other serious forms of international crime, including if necessary certain aspects of customs cooperation, in connection with the organisation of a Union-wide system for exchanging information within a European Police Office (Europol).

Article K.2

1. The matters referred to in Article K.1 shall be dealt with in compliance with the European Convention for the Protection of Human Rights and Fundamental Freedoms of 4 November 1950 and the Convention relating to the Status of Refugees of 28 July 1951 and having regard to the protection afforded by Member States to persons persecuted on political grounds.

2. This Title shall not affect the exercise of the responsibilities incumbent upon Member States with regard to the maintenance of law and order and the safeguarding of internal security.

Article K.3

1. In the areas referred to in Article K.1, Member States shall inform and consult one another within the Council with a view to coordinating their action. To that end, they shall establish collaboration between the relevant departments of their administrations.

2. The Council may:

   — on the initiative of any Member State or of the Commission, in the areas referred to in Article K.1(1) to (6);

   — on the initiative of any Member State, in the areas referred to in Article K.1(7) to (9):

   (a) adopt joint positions and promote, using the appropriate form and procedures, any cooperation contributing to the pursuit of the objectives of the Union;

   (b) adopt joint action in so far as the objectives of the Union can be attained better by joint action than by the Member State acting individually on account of the scale or effects of the action envisaged; it may decide that measures implementing joint action are to be adopted by a qualified majority;

    (c) without prejudice to Article 220 of the Treaty establishing the European Community, draw up conventions which it shall recommend to the Member States for adoption in accordance with their respective constitutional requirements.

Unless otherwise provided by such conventions, measures implementing them shall be adopted within the Council by a majority of two-thirds of the High Contracting Parties.

Such conventions may stipulate that the Court of Justice shall have jurisdiction to interpret their provisions and to rule on any disputes regarding their application, in accordance with such arrangements as they may lay down.

Article K.4

1.   A Coordinating Committee shall be set up consisting of senior officials. In addition to its coordinating role, it shall be the task of the Committee to:

— give opinions for the attention of the Council, either at the Council's request or on its own initiative;

— contribute, without prejudice to Article 151 of the Treaty establishing the European Community, to the preparation of the Council's discussions in the areas referred to in Article K.1 and, in accordance with the conditions laid down in Article 100d of the Treaty establishing the European Community, in the areas referred to in Article 100c of that Treaty.

2.   The Commission shall be fully associated with the work in the areas referred to in this Title.

3.   The Council shall act unanimously, except on matters of procedure and in cases where Article K.3 expressly provides for other voting rules.

Where the Council is required to act by a qualified majority, the votes of its members shall be weighted as laid down in Article 148(2) of the Treaty establishing the European Community, and for their adoption, acts of the Council shall require at least 62 votes in favour, cast by at least 10 members.[1]

Note
[1]As amended by Council Decision 95/1 (OJ 1995 L1/1) adjusting the Treaty of Accession of the three new Member States.

Article K.5

Within international organisations and at international conferences in which they take part, Member States shall defend the common positions adopted under the provisions of this Title.

Article K.6

The Presidency and the Commission shall regularly inform the European Parliament of discussions in the areas covered by this Title.

The Presidency shall consult the European Parliament on the principal aspects of activities in the areas referred to in this Title and shall ensure that the views of the European Parliament are duly taken into consideration.

The European Parliament may ask questions of the Council or make recommendations to it. Each year, it shall hold a debate on the progress made in implementation of the areas referred to in this Title.

Article K.7
The provisions of this Title shall not prevent the establishment or development of closer cooperation between two or more Member States in so far as such cooperation does not conflict with, or impede, that provided for in this Title.

Article K.8
1.   The provisions referred to in Articles 137, 138, 139 to 142, 146, 147, 150 to 153, 157 to 163 and 217 of the Treaty establishing the European Community shall apply to the provisions relating to the areas referred to in this Title.

2.   Administrative expenditure which the provisions relating to the areas referred to in this Title entail for the institutions shall be charged to the budget of the European Communities.

The Council may also:

— either decide unanimously that operational expenditure to which the implementation of those provisions gives rise is to be charged to the budget of the European Communities; in that event, the budgetary procedure laid down in the Treaty establishing the European Community shall be applicable;

— or determine that such expenditure shall be charged to the Member States, where appropriate in accordance with a scale to be decided.

Article K.9
The council, acting unanimously on the initiative of the Commission or a Member State, may decide to apply Article 100c of the Treaty establishing the European Commuinity to action in areas referred to in Article K.1(1) to (6), and at the same time determine the relevant voting conditions relating to it. It shall recommend the Member States to adopt the decision in accordance with their respective constitutional requirements.

TITLE VII   FINAL PROVISIONS

Article L
The provisions of the Treaty establishing the European Community, the Treaty establishing the European Coal and Steel Community and the Treaty establishing the European Atomic Energy Community concerning the powers of the Court of Justice of the European Communities and the exercise of those powers shall apply only to the following provisions of this Treaty:

(a)   provisions amending the Treaty establishing the European Economic Community with a view to establishing the European Community, the Treaty establishing the European Coal and Steel Community and the Treaty establishing the European Atomic Energy Community;

(b)   the third subparagraph of Article K.3(2)(c);

(c)   Articles L to S.

Article M
Subject to the provisions amending the Treaty establishing the European Economic Community with a view to establishing the European Community, the Treaty establishing the European Coal and Steel Community and the Treaty establishing the European Atomic Energy Community, and to these final provisions, nothing in this Treaty shall affect the Treaties establishing the European Communities or the subsequent Treaties and Acts modifying or supplementing them.

Article N

1.   The Government of any Member State or the Commisison may submit to the Council proposals for the Amendment of the Treaties on which the Union is founded.

If the Council, after consulting the European Parliament and, where appropriate, the Commission, delivers an opinion in favour of calling a conference of representatives of the governments of the Member States, the conference shall be convened by the President of the Council for the purpose of determining by common accord the amendments to be made to those Treaties. The European Central Bank shall also be consulted in the case of institutional changes in the monetary area.

The amendments shall enter into force after being ratified by all the Member States in accordance with their respective constitutional requirements.

2.   A conference of representatives of the governments of the Member States shall be convened in 1996 to examine those provisions of this Treaty for which revision is provided, in accordance with the objectives set out in Articles A and B.

Article O

Any European State may apply to become a Member of the Union. It shall address its application to the Council, which shall act unanimously after consulting the Commission and after receiving the assent of the European Parliament, which shall act by an absolute majority of its component members.

The conditions of admission and the adjustments to the Treaties on which the Union is founded which such admission entails shall be the subject of an agreement between the Member States and the applicant State. This agreement shall be submitted for ratification by all the Contracting States in accordance with their respective constitutional requirements.

Article P

1.   Articles 2 to 7 and 10 to 19 of the Treaty establishing a single Council and a single Commission of the European Communities, signed in Brussels on 8 April 1965, are hereby repealed.

2.   Article 2, Article 3(2) and Title III of the Single European Act signed in Luxembourg on 17 February 1986 and in The Hague on 28 February 1986 are hereby repealed.

Article Q

This Treaty is concluded for an unlimited period.

Article R

1.   This Treaty shall be ratified by the High Contracting Parties in accordance with their respective constitutional requirements. The instruments of ratification shall be deposited with the government of the Italian Republic.

2.   This Treaty shall enter into force on 1 January 1993, provided that all the instruments of ratification have been deposited, or, failing that, on the first day of the month following the deposit of the instrument of ratification by the last signatory State to take this step.

Article S

This Treaty, drawn up in a single original in the Danish, Dutch, English, French, German, Greek, Irish, Italian, Portuguese and Spanish languages, the texts in each of these languages being equally authentic, shall be deposited in the archives of the government of the Italian Republic, which will transmit a certified copy to each of the governments of the other signatory States.

In witness whereof the undersigned Plenipotentiaries have signed this Treaty.

Done at Maastricht on the seventh day of February in the year one thousand nine hundred and ninety-two.

(Signatures omitted.)

COMMUNITY CHARTER OF THE FUNDAMENTAL SOCIAL RIGHTS OF WORKERS
(Text taken from Social Europe 1/90, pp. 46-50.)

The Heads of State or Government of the Member States of the European Community meeting at Strasbourg on 9 December 1989[1]

Whereas, under the terms of Article 117 of the EEC Treaty, the Member States have agreed on the need to promote improved living and working conditions for workers so as to make possible their harmonisation while the improvement is being maintained;

Whereas following on from the conclusions of the European Councils of Hanover and Rhodes the European Council of Madrid considered that, in the context of the establishment of the single European market, the same importance must be attached to the social aspects as to the economic aspects and whereas, therefore, they must be developed in a balanced manner;

Having regard to the Resolutions of the European Parliament of 15 March 1989, 14 September 1989 and 22 November 1989, and to the Opinion of the Economic and Social Committee of 22 February 1989;

Whereas the completion of the internal market is the most effective means of creating employment and ensuring maximum well-being in the Community; whereas employment development and creation must be given first priority on the completion of the internal market; whereas it is for the Community to take up the challenges of the future with regard to economic competitiveness, taking into account, in particular, regional imbalances;

Whereas the social consensus contributes to the strengthening of the competitiveness of undertakings, of the economy as a whole and to the creation of employment; whereas in this respect it is an essential condition for ensuring sustained economic development;

Whereas the completion of the internal market must favour the approximation of improvements in living and working conditions, as well as economic and social cohesion within the European Community while avoiding distortions of competition;

Whereas the completion of the internal market must offer improvements in the social field for workers of the European Community, especially in terms of freedom of movement, living and working conditions, health and safety at work, social protection, education and training;

Note
[1]Text adopted by the Heads of State or Government of 11 Member States.

Whereas, in order to ensure equal treatment, it is important to combat every form of discrimination, including discrimination on grounds of sex, colour, race, opinions and beliefs, and whereas, in a spirit of solidarity, it is important to combat social exclusion;

Whereas it is for Member States to guarantee that workers from non-member countries and members of their families who are legally resident in a Member State of the European Community are able to enjoy, as regards their living and working conditions, treatment comparable to that enjoyed by workers who are nationals of the Member State concerned;

Whereas inspiration should be drawn from the Convention of the International Labour Organisation and from the European Social Charter of the Council of Europe;

Whereas the Treaty, as amended by the Single European Act, contains provisions laying down the powers of the Community relating *inter alia* to the freedom of movement of workers (Articles 7, 48 to 51), the right of establishment (Articles 52 to 58), the social field under the conditions laid down in Articles 117 to 122 — in particular as regards the improvement of health and safety in the working environment (Article 118a), the development of the dialogue between management and labour at European level (Article 118b), equal pay for men and women for equal work (Article 119) — the general principles for implementing a common vocational training policy (Article 128), economic and social cohesion (Articles 130a to 130e) and, more generally, the approximation of legislation (Articles 100, 100a and 235); whereas the implementation of the Charter must not entail an extension of the Community's powers as defined by the Treaties;

Whereas the aim of the present Charter is on the one hand to consolidate the progress made in the social field, through action by the Member States, the two sides of industry and the Community;

Whereas its aim is on the other hand to declare solemnly that the implementation of the Single European Act must take full account of the social dimension of the Community and that it is necessary in this context to ensure at appropriate levels the development of the social rights of workers of the European Community, especially employed workers and self-employed persons;

Whereas, in accordance with the conclusions of the Madrid European Council, the respective roles of Community rules, national legislation and collective agreements must be clearly established;

Whereas, by virtue of the principle of subsidiarity, responsibility for the initiatives to be taken with regard to the implementation of these social rights lies with the Member States or their constituent parts and, within the limits of its powers, with the European Community; whereas such implementation may take the form of laws, collective agreements or existing practices at the various appropriate levels and whereas it requires in many spheres the active involvement of the two sides of industry;

Whereas the solemn proclamation of fundamental social rights at European Community level may not, when implemented, provide grounds for any retrogression compared with the situation currently existing in each Member State;

Have adopted the following Declaration constituting the 'Community Charter of the Fundamental Social Rights of Workers':

TITLE I   FUNDAMENTAL SOCIAL RIGHTS OF WORKERS

Freedom of movement

1.   Every worker of the European Community shall have the right to freedom of movement throughout the territory of the Community, subject to restrictions justified on grounds of public order, public safety or public health.

2.   The right to freedom of movement shall enable any worker to engage in any occupation or profession in the Community in accordance with the principles of equal treatment as regards access to employment, working conditions and social protection in the host country.

3.   The right of freedom of movement shall also imply:

— harmonisation of conditions of residence in all Member States, particularly those concerning family reunification;

— elimination of obstacles arising from the non-recognition of diplomas or equivalent occupational qualifications;

— improvement of the living and working conditions of frontier workers.

Employment and remuneration

4.   Every individual shall be free to choose and engage in an occupation according to the regulations governing each occupation.

5.   All employment shall be fairly remunerated.

To this end, in accordance with arrangements applying in each country:

— workers shall be assured of an equitable wage, i.e., a wage sufficient to enable them to have a decent standard of living;

— workers subject to terms of employment other than an open-ended full-time contract shall benefit from an equitable reference wage;

— wages may be withheld, seized or transferred only in accordance with national law; such provisions should entail measures enabling the worker concerned to continue to enjoy the necessary means of subsistence for him- or herself and his or her family.

6.   Every individual must be able to have access to public placement services free of charge.

Improvement of living and working conditions

7.   The completion of the internal market must lead to an improvement in the living and working conditions of workers in the European Community. This process must result from an approximation of these conditions while the improvement is being maintained, as regards in particular the duration and organisation of working time and forms of employment other than open-ended contracts, such as fixed-term contracts, part-time working, temporary work and seasonal work.

The improvement must cover, where necessary, the development of certain aspects of employment regulations such as procedures for collective redundancies and those regarding bankruptcies.

8.   Every worker of the European Community shall have a right to a weekly rest period and to annual paid leave, the duration of which must be progressively harmonised in accordance with national practices.

9.   The conditions of employment of every worker of the European Community shall be stipulated in laws, a collective agreement or a contract of employment, according to arrangements applying in each country.

Social protection

According to the arrangements applying in each country:

10. Every worker of the European Community shall have a right to adequate social protection and shall, whatever his status and whatever the size of the undertaking in which he is employed, enjoy an adequate level of social security benefits.

Persons who have been unable either to enter or re-enter the labour market and have no means of subsistence must be able to receive sufficient resources and social assistance in keeping with their particular situation.

Freedom of association and collective bargaining

11. Employers and workers of the European Community shall have the right of association in order to constitute professional organisations or trade unions of their choice for the defence of their economic and social interests.

Every employer and every worker shall have the freedom to join or not to join such organisations without any personal or occupational damage being thereby suffered by him.

12. Employers or employers' organisations, on the one hand, and workers' organisations, on the other, shall have the right to negotiate and conclude collective agreements under the conditions laid down by national legislation and practice.

The dialogue between the two sides of industry at European level which must be developed, may, if the parties deem it desirable, result in contractual relations in particular at inter-occupational and sectoral level.

13. The right to resort to collective action in the event of a conflict of interests shall include the right to strike, subject to the obligations arising under national regulations and collective agreements.

In order to facilitate the settlement of industrial disputes the establishment and utilisation at the appropriate levels of conciliation, mediation and arbitration procedures should be encouraged in accordance with national practice.

14. The internal legal order of the Member States shall determine under which conditions and to what extent the rights provided for in Articles 11 to 13 apply to the armed forces, the police and the civil service.

Vocational training

15. Every worker of the European Community must be able to have access to vocational training and to benefit therefrom throughout his working life. In the conditions governing access to such training there may be no discrimination on grounds of nationality.

The competent public authorities, undertakings or the two sides of industry, each within their own sphere of competence, should set up continuing and permanent training systems enabling every person to undergo retraining more especially through leave for training purposes, to improve his skills or to acquire new skills, particularly in the light of technical developments.

Equal treatment for men and women

16. Equal treatment for men and women must be assured. Equal opportunities for men and women must be developed.

To this end, action should be intensified to ensure the implementation of the principle of equality between men and women as regards in particular access to employment, remuneration, working conditions, social protection, education, vocational training and career development.

Measures should also be developed enabling men and women to reconcile their occupational and family obligations.

Information, consultation and participation for workers

17.   Information, consultation and participation for workers must be developed along appropriate lines, taking account of the practices in force in the various Member States.

This shall apply especially in companies or groups of companies having establishments or companies in two or more Member States of the European Community.

18.   Such information, consultation and participation must be implemented in due time, particularly in the following cases;

— when technological changes which, from the point of view of working conditions and work organisation, have major implications for the workforce, are introduced into undertakings;

— in connection with restructuring operations in undertakings or in cases of mergers having an impact on the employment of workers;

— in cases of collective redundancy procedures;

— when transfrontier workers in particular are affected by employment policies pursued by the undertaking where they are employed.

Health protection and safety at the workplace

19.   Every worker must enjoy satisfactory health and safety conditions in his working environment. Appropriate measures must be taken in order to achieve further harmonisation of conditions in this area while maintaining the improvements made.

These measures shall take account, in particular, of the need for the training, information, consultation and balanced participation of workers as regards the risks incurred and the steps taken to eliminate or reduce them.

The provisions regarding implementation of the internal market shall help to ensure such protection.

Protection of children and adolescents

20.   Without prejudice to such rules as may be more favourable to young people, in particular those ensuring their preparation for work through vocational training, and subject to derogations limited to certain light work, the minimum employment age must not be lower than the minimum school-leaving age and, in any case, not lower than 15 years.

21.   Young people who are in gainful employment must receive equitable remuneration in accordance with national practice.

22.   Appropriate measures must be taken to adjust labour regulations applicable to young workers so that their specific development and vocational training and access to employment needs are met. The duration of work must, in particular, be limited — without it being possible to circumvent this limitation through recourse to overtime — and night work prohibited in the case of workers of under 18 years of age, save in the case of certain jobs laid down in national legislation or regulations.

23.   Following the end of compulsory education, young people must be entitled to receive initial vocational training of a sufficient duration to enable

them to adapt to the requirements of their future working life; for young workers, such training should take place during working hours.

Elderly persons

According to the arrangements applying in each country:

24. Every worker of the European Community must, at the time of retirement, be able to enjoy resources affording him or her a decent standard of living.

25. Any person who has reached retirement age but who is not entitled to a pension or who does not have other means of subsistence, must be entitled to sufficient resources and to medical and social assistance specifically suited to his needs.

Disabled persons

26. All disabled persons, whatever the origin and nature of their disablement, must be entitled to additional concrete measures aimed at improving their social and professional integration.

These measures must concern, in particular, according to the capacities of the beneficiaries, vocational training, ergonomics, accessibility, mobility, means of transport and housing.

TITLE II IMPLEMENTATION OF THE CHARTER

27. It is more particularly the responsibility of the Member States, in accordance with national practices, notably through legislative measures or collective agreements, to guarantee the fundamental social rights in this Charter and to implement the social measures indispensable to the smooth operation of the internal market as part of a strategy of economic and social cohesion.

28. The European Council invites the Commission to submit as soon as possible initiatives which fall within its powers, as provided for in the Treaties, with a view to the adoption of legal instruments for the effective implementation, as and when the internal market is completed, of those rights which come within the Community's area of competence.

29. The Commission shall establish each year, during the last three months, a report on the application of the Charter by the Member States and by the European Community.

30. The report of the Commission shall be forwarded to the European Council, the European Parliament and the Economic and Social Committee.

PROTOCOL ON SOCIAL POLICY

THE HIGH CONTRACTING PARTIES,

NOTING that eleven Member States, that is to say the Kingdom of Belgium, the Kingdom of Denmark, the Federal Republic of Germany, the Hellenic Republic, the Kingdom of Spain, the French Republic, Ireland, the Italian Republic, the Grand Duchy of Luxembourg, the Kingdom of the Netherlands, the Portuguese Republic, wish to continue along the path laid down in the 1989 Social Charter; that they have adopted among themselves an Agreement to this end; that this Agreement is annexed to this Protocol; that this Protocol and the said Agreement are without prejudice to the provisions of this Treaty, particularly those which relate to social policy which constitute an integral part of the 'acquis communautaire':

1. Agree to authorise those eleven Member States to have recourse to the institutions, procedures and mechanisms of the Treaty for the purposes of taking among themselves and applying as far as they are concerned the acts and decisions required for giving effect to the above-mentioned Agreement.

2. The United Kingdom of Great Britain and Northern Ireland shall not take part in the deliberations and the adoption by the Council of Commission proposals made on the basis of this Protocol and the above-mentioned Agreement.

By way of derogation from Article 148(2) of the Treaty, acts of the Council which are made pursuant to this Protocol and which must be adopted by a qualified majority shall be deemed to be so adopted if they have received at least 52 votes in favour. The unanimity of the members of the Council, with the exception of the United Kingdom of Great Britain and Northern Ireland, shall be necessary for acts of the Council which must be adopted unanimously and for those amending the Commission proposal.[1]

Acts adopted by the Council and any financial consequences other than administrative costs entailed for the institutions shall not be applicable to the United Kingdom of Great Britain and Northern Ireland.

3. This Protocol shall be annexed to the Treaty establishing the European Community.

Note
[1]As amended by Council Decision 95/1 (OJ 1995 L1/1) adjusting the Treaty of Accession of the three new Member States.

AGREEMENT ON SOCIAL POLICY CONCLUDED BETWEEN THE MEMBER STATES OF THE EUROPEAN COMMUNITY WITH THE EXCEPTION OF THE UNITED KINGDOM OF GREAT BRITAIN AND NORTHERN IRELAND

The undersigned eleven HIGH CONTRACTING PARTIES, that is to say the Kingdom of Belgium, the Kingdom of Denmark, the Federal Republic of Germany, the Hellenic Republic, the Kingdom of Spain, the French Republic, Ireland, the Italian Republic, the Grand Duchy of Luxembourg, the Kingdom of the Netherlands and the Portuguese Republic (hereinafter referred to as 'the Member States'),

WISHING to implement the 1989 Social Charter on the basis of the 'acquis communautaire',

CONSIDERING the Protocol on social policy,

HAVE AGREED as follows:

Article 1
The Community and the Member States shall have as their objectives the promotion of employment, improved living and working conditions, proper social protection, dialogue between management and labour, the development of human resources with a view to lasting high employment and the combating of exclusion. To this end the Community and the Member States shall implement measures which take account of the diverse forms of national practice, in particular in the field of contractual relations, and the need to maintain the competitiveness of the Community economy.

Article 2

1.   With a view to achieving the objectives of Article 1, the Community shall support and complement the activities of the Member States in the following fields:
— improvement in particular of the working environment to protect workers' health and safety;
— working conditions;
— the information and consultation of workers;
— equality between men and women with regard to labour market opportunities and treatment at work;
— the integration of persons excluded from the labour market, without prejudice to Article 127 of the Treaty establishing the European Community (hereinafter referred to as "the Treaty").

2.   To this end, the Council may adopt, by means of directives, minimum requirements for gradual implementation, having regard to the conditions and technical rules obtaining in each of the Member States. Such directives shall avoid imposing administrative, financial and legal constraints in a way which would hold back the creation and development of small and medium-sized undertakings.

The Council shall act in accordance with the procedure referred to in Article 198c of the Treaty after consulting the Economic and Social Committee.

3.   However, the Council shall act unanimously on a proposal from the Commission, after consulting the European Parliament and the Economic and Social Committee, in the following areas:
— social security and social protection of workers;
— protection of workers where their employment contract is terminated;
— representation and collective defence of the interests of workers and employers, including co-determination, subject to paragraph 6;
— conditions of employment for third-country nationals legally residing in Community territory;
— financial contributions for promotion of employment and job-creation, without prejudice to the provisions relating to the Social Fund.

4.   A Member State may entrust management and labour, at their joint request, with the implementation of directives adopted pursuant to paragraphs 2 and 3.

In this case, it shall ensure that, no later than the date on which a directive must be transposed in accordance with Article 189, management and labour have introduced the necessary measures by agreement, the Member State concerned being required to take any necessary measure enabling it at any time to be in a position to guarantee the results imposed by that directive.

5.   The provisions adopted pursuant to this Article shall not prevent any Member State from maintaining or introducing more stringent preventive measures compatible with the Treaty.

6.   The provisions of this Article shall not apply to pay, the right of association, the right to strike or the right to impose lock-outs.

Article 3

1.   The Commission shall have the task of promoting the consultation of management and labour at Community level and shall take any relevant measure to facilitate their dialogue by ensuring balanced support for the parties.

2.   To this end, before submitting proposals in the social policy field, the Commission shall consult management and labour on the possible direction of Community action.

3.   If, after such consultation, the Commission considers Community action advisable, it shall consult management and labour on the content of the envisaged proposal. Management and labour shall forward to the Commission an opinion or, where appropriate, a recommendation.

4.   On the occasion of such consultation, management and labour may inform the Commission of their wish to initiate the process provided for in Article 4. The duration of the procedure shall not exceed nine months, unless the management and labour concerned and the Commission decide jointly to extend it.

Article 4

1.   Should management and labour so desire, the dialogue between them at Community level may lead to contractual relations, including agreements.

2.   Agreements concluded at Community level shall be implemented either in accordance with the procedures and practices specific to management and labour and the Member States or, in matters covered by Article 2, at the joint request of the signatory parties, by a Council decision on a proposal from the Commission.

The Council shall act by qualified majority, except where the agreement in question contains one or more provisions relating to one of the areas referred to in Article 2(3), in which case it shall act unanimously.

Article 5

With a view to achieving the objectives of Article 1 and without prejudice to the other provisions of the Treaty, the Commission shall encourage cooperation between the Member States and facilitate the coordination of their action in all social policy fields under this Agreement.

Article 6

1.   Each Member State shall ensure that the principle of equal pay for male and female workers for equal work is applied.

2.   For the purpose of this Article, 'pay' means the ordinary basic or minimum wage or salary and any other consideration, whether in cash or in kind, which the worker receives directly or indirectly, in respect of his employment, from his employer.

Equal pay without discrimination based on sex means:

(a)   that pay for the same work at piece rates shall be calculated on the basis of the same unit of measurement;

(b)   that pay for work at time rates shall be the same for the same job.

3.   This Article shall not prevent any Member State from maintaining or adopting measures providing for specific advantages in order to make it easier for women to pursue a vocational activity or to prevent or compensate for disadvantages in their professional careers.

Article 7

The Commission shall draw up a report each year on progress in achieving the objectives of Article 1, including the demographic situation in the Community. It shall forward the report to the European Parliament, the Council and the Economic and Social Committee.

The European Parliament may invite the Commission to draw up reports on particular problems concerning the social situation.

DECLARATIONS

1. Declaration on Article 2(2)

The eleven High Contracting Parties note that in the discussions on Article 2(2) of the Agreement it was agreed that the Community does not intend, in laying down minimum requirements for the protection of the safety and health of employees, to discriminate in a manner unjustified by the circumstances against employees in small and medium-sized undertakings.

2. Declaration on Article 4(2)

The eleven High Contracting Parties declare that the first of the arrangements for application of the agreements between management and labour Community-wide — referred to in Article 4(2) — will consist in developing, by collective bargaining according to the rules of each Member State, the content of the agreements, and that consequently this arrangement implies no obligation on the Member States to apply the agreements directly or to work out rules for their transposition, nor any obligation to amend national legislation in force to facilitate their implementation.

LEGISLATION AND AGREEMENTS AFFECTING THE INSTITUTIONS

JOINT DECLARATION OF THE EUROPEAN PARLIAMENT, THE COUNCIL AND THE COMMISSION ON THE CONCILIATION PROCEDURE OF 1975
[OJ 1975, No. C89/1]

The European Parliament, the Council and the Commission,

Whereas from 1 January 1975, the Budget of the Communities will be financed entirely from the Communities' own resources;

Whereas in order to implement this system the European Parliament will be given increased budgetary powers;

Whereas the increase in the budgetary powers of the European Parliament must be accompanied by effective participation by the latter in the procedure for preparing and adopting decisions which give rise to important expenditure or revenue to be charged or credited to the budget of the European Communities,

Have agreed as follows:

1. A conciliation procedure between the European Parliament and the Council with the active assistance of the Commission is hereby instituted.

2. This procedure may be followed for Community acts of general application which have appreciable financial implications, and of which the adoption is not required by virtue of acts already in existence.

3. When submitting its proposal the Commission shall indicate whether the act in question is, in its opinion, capable of being the subject of the conciliation procedure. The European Parliament, when giving its Opinion, and the Council may request that this procedure be initiated.

4. The procedure shall be initiated if the criteria laid down in paragraph 2 are met and if the Council intends to depart from the Opinion adopted by the European Parliament.

5. The conciliation shall take place in a 'Conciliation Committee' consisting of the Council and representatives of the European Parliament. The Commission shall participate in the work of the Conciliation Committee.

6. The aim of the procedure shall be to seek an agreement between the European Parliament and the Council. The procedure should normally take place during a period not exceeding three months, unless the act in question has to be adopted before a specific date or if the matter is urgent, in which case the Council may fix an appropriate time limit.

7.   When the positions of the two institutions are sufficiently close, the European Parliament may give a new Opinion, after which the Council shall take definitive action.

Done at Brussels, 4 March 1975.

COUNCIL DECISION OF 24 JUNE 1988 ON THE SYSTEM OF THE COMMUNITIES' OWN RESOURCES (88/376/EEC, EURATOM) [OJ 1988, L185/24][1]

THE COUNCIL OF THE EUROPEAN COMMUNITIES,

Having regard to the Treaty establishing the European Economic Community, and in particular Articles 199 and 201 thereof,

Having regard to the Treaty establishing the European Atomic Energy Community, and in particular Articles 171(1) and 173 thereof,

Having regard to the proposal from the Commission,[2]

Having regard to the opinion of the European Parliament,[3]

Having regard to the opinion of the Economic and Social Committee,[4]

Whereas Council Decision 85/257/EEC, Euratom of 7 May 1985 on the Communities' system of own resources,[5] as last amended by the Single European Act, raised to 1.4% the limit for each Member State on the rate applied to the uniform value-added tax (VAT) base previously set at 1% by the Council Decision of 21 April 1970 on the replacement of financial contributions from Member States by the Communities' own resources[6] hereinafter referred to as 'the Decision of 21 April 1970';

Whereas the resources available within the limit of 1.4% are no longer sufficient to cover the estimates of Community expenditure;

Whereas the Single European Act opens up new possibilities to the Community; whereas Article 8a of the Treaty establishing the European Economic Community provides for the completion of the internal market by 31 December 1992;

Whereas the Community must possess stable and guaranteed revenue enabling it to stabilise the present situation and operate the common policies; whereas this revenue must be based on the expenditure deemed necessary to this end which was determined in the financial estimates in the Inter-institutional Agreement between the European Parliament, the Council and the Commission, which will take effect on 1 July 1988;

Whereas the European Council meeting in Brussels on 11, 12 and 13 February 1988 reached certain conclusions;

Whereas, in accordance with these conclusions, the Community will, by 1992, be assigned a maximum amount of own resources corresponding to 1.2% of the total of the Member States' gross national product for the year at market prices, hereinafter referred to as GNP;

Notes
[1]Editor's Note: Repealed by Decision 94/728 but parts transitionally remain in force.
[2]OJ No. C102, 16.4.1988, p. 8.
[3]Opinion delivered on 15 June 1988 (not yet published in the *Official Journal*).
[4]OJ No. C175, 4.7.1988.
[5]OJ No. L128/14.
[6]OJ No. L94/19.

Whereas observance of this ceiling requires that the total amount of own resources at the Community's disposal for the period 1988 to 1992 does not in any one year exceed a specified percentage of the sum of the Community's GNP for the year in question; whereas that percentage shall correspond to application of the guidelines established for growth in Community expenditure as laid down in the European Council conclusions concerning budgetary discipline and budget management, and a safety margin of .003% of Community GNP aimed at coping with unforeseen expenditure;

Whereas a global ceiling of 1.30% of the Member States' GNP is set for commitment appropriations; whereas an orderly progression of commitment appropriations and payment appropriations must be ensured;

Whereas these ceilings should remain applicable until this Decision is amended;

Whereas, with a view to matching the resources paid by each Member State more closely with its ability to contribute, the compositon of Community own resources should be amended and enlarged; whereas it is necessary for this purpose:

— to fix at 1.4% the maximum rate to be applied to each Member State's uniform base for value added tax, limited where appropriate to 55% of its GNP;

— to introduce an additional type of own resource to balance budget revenue and expenditure, based on the sum of Member States' GNP; for this purpose, the Council will adopt a Directive on the harmonisation of the compilation of gross national product at market prices;

Whereas the customs duties on products coming under the Treaty establishing the European Coal and Steel Community should be included in Community own resources;

Whereas the conclusions of the European Council of 25 and 26 June 1984 on the correction of budgetary imbalances continue to apply for the duration of this Decision's validity; whereas the present compensation mechanism must, however, be adjusted to take account of the capping of the VAT base and the introduction of an additional resource and must provide for financing of the correction on the basis of a GNP key; whereas this adjustment should ensure that the VAT share of the United Kingdom is replaced by its share of payments under the third and fourth resources (those provided by VAT and GNP respectively) and that the effect on the United Kingdom, in respect of a given year, of the capping of the VAT base and of the introduction of the fourth resource which is not compensated by this change will be offset by an adjustment to the compensation in respect of that year; whereas the contributions of Spain and Portugal should be reduced in accordance with the rebates provided for in Articles 187 and 374 of the 1985 Act of Accession;

Whereas the budgetary imbalances should be corrected in such a way as not to affect the own resources available for the Community's policies;

Whereas the conclusions of the European Council of 11, 12 and 13 February 1988 provided for the creation, in the Community budget, of a monetary reserve, hereinafter referred to as 'the EAGGF monetary reserve', to offset the impact of significant and unforeseen fluctuations in the ECU/dollar parity on the expenditure under the Guarantee Section of the European Agricultural Guidance and Guarantee Fund (EAGGF); whereas that reserve should be covered by specific provisions;

Whereas provisions must be laid down to cover the changeover from the system introduced by Decision 85/257/EEC, Euratom to that arising from this Decision;

Whereas the European Council of 11, 12 and 13 February 1988 provided that this Decision should take effect on 1 January 1988,

Has laid down these provisions, which it recommends to the Member States for adoption:

Article 1

The Communities shall be allocated resources of their own in accordance with the following Articles in order to ensure the financing of their budget.

The budget of the Communities shall, irrespective of other revenue, be financed entirely from the Communities' own resources.

Article 2

1. Revenue from the following shall constitute own resources entered in the budget of the Communities:

(a) levies, premiums, additional or compensatory amounts, additional amounts or factors and other duties established or to be established by the institutions of the Communities in respect of trade with non-member countries within the framework of the common agricultural policy, and also contributions and other duties provided for within the framework of the common organisation of the markets in sugar;

(b) Common Customs Tariff duties and other duties established or to be established by the institutions of the Communities in respect of trade with non-member countries and customs duties on products coming under the Treaty establishing the European Coal and Steel Community;

(c) the application of a uniform rate valid for all Member States to the VAT assessment base which is determined in a uniform manner for Member States according to Community rules; however, the assessment base for any Member State to be taken into account for the purposes of this Decision shall not exceed 55% of its GNP;

(d) the application of a rate — to be determined under the budgetary procedure in the light of the total of all other revenue — to the sum of all the Member States' GNP established in accordance with Community rules to be laid down in a Directive adopted under Article 8(2) of this Decision.

2. Revenue deriving from any new charges introduced within the framework of a common policy, in accordance with the Treaty establishing the European Economic Community or the Treaty establishing the European Atomic Energy Community, provided the procedure laid down in Article 201 of the Treaty establishing the European Economic Community or in Article 173 of the Treaty establishing the European Atomic Energy Community has been followed, shall also constitute own resources entered in the budget of the Communities.

3. Member States shall retain, by way of collection costs, 10% of the amounts paid under 1(a) and (b).

4. The uniform rate referred to in 1(c) shall correspond to the rate resulting from:

(a) the application of 1.4% to the VAT assessment base for the Member States, and

(b) the deduction of the gross amount of the reference compensation referred to in Article 4(2). The gross amount shall be the compensation amount adjusted for the fact that the United Kingdom is not participating in the financing of its own compensation and the Federal Republic of Germany's share is reduced by one-third. It shall be calculated as if the reference compensation amount were financed by Member States according to their VAT assessment bases established in accordance with Article 2(1)(c). For 1988, the gross amount of the reference compensation shall be reduced by 780 million ECU.

5. The rate fixed under paragraph 1(d) shall apply to the GNP of each Member State.

6. If, at the beginning of the financial year, the budget has not been adopted, the previous uniform VAT rate and the rate applicable to Member States' GNP, without prejudice to whatever provisions may be adopted in accordance with Article 8(2) by reason of the entry of an EAGGF monetary reserve in the budget, shall remain applicable until the entry into force of the new rates.

7. By way of derogation from 1(c), if, on 1 January of the financial year in question, the rules for determining the uniform basis for assessing VAT are not yet applied in all the Member States, the financial contribution which a Member State not yet applying this uniform basis is to make to the budget of the Communities in lieu of VAT shall be determined according to the proportion of its gross national product at market prices to the sum total of the gross national product of the Member States at market prices in the first three years of the five-year period preceding the year in question. This derogation shall cease to have effect as soon as the rules for determining the uniform basis for assessing VAT are applied in all Member States.

8. For the purposes of applying this Decision, GNP shall mean gross national product for the year at market prices.

Article 3

1. The total amount of own resources assigned to the Communities may not exceed 1.20% of the total GNP of the Community for payment appropriations.

The total amount of own resources assigned to the Communities may not, for any of the years during the 1988 to 1992 period, exceed the following percentages of the total GNP of the Community for the year in question:
— 1988: 1.15,
— 1989: 1.17,
— 1990: 1.18,
— 1991: 1.19,
— 1992: 1.20.

2. The commitment appropriations entered in the general budget of the Communities over the period 1988 to 1992 must follow an orderly progression resulting in a total amount which does not exceed 1.30% of the total GNP of the Community in 1992. A precise ratio between commitment appropriations and payment appropriations shall be maintained to guarantee their compatibility and to enable the ceiling mentioned in paragraph 1 to be observed in subsequent years.

3. The overall ceilings referred to in paragraphs 1 and 2 shall continue to apply until such time as this Decision is amended.

Article 4

The United Kingdom shall be granted a correction in respect of budgetary imbalances. This correction shall consist of a basic amount and an adjustment. The adjustment shall correct the basic amount to a reference compensation amount.

1. The basic amount shall be established by:

   (a)   calculating the difference, in the preceding financial year, between:

— the percentage share of the United Kingdom in the sum total of the payments referred to in Article 2(1)(c) and (d) made during the financial year, including adjustments at the uniform rate in respect of earlier financial years, and

— the percentage share of the United Kingdom in total allocated expenditure;

   (b)   applying the difference thus obtained to total allocated expenditure;

   (c)   multiplying the result by 0.66.

2. The reference compensation shall be the correction resulting from application of (a), (b) and (c) below, corrected by the effects arising for the United Kingdom from the changeover to capped VAT and the payments referred to in Article 2(1)(d).

It shall be established by:

   (a)   calculating the difference, in the preceding financial year, between:

— the percentage share of the United Kingdom in the sum total of VAT payments which would have been made during that financial year, including adjustments in respect of earlier financial years, for the amounts financed by the resources referred to in Article 2(1)(c) and (d) if the uniform VAT rate had been applied to non-capped bases, and

— the percentage share of the United Kingdom in total allocated expenditure;

   (b)   applying the difference thus obtained to total allocated expenditure;

   (c)   multiplying the result by 0.66;

   (d)   subtracting the payments by the United Kingdom taken into account in the first indent of 1(a) from those taken into account in the first indent of 2(a);

   (e)   subtracting the amount calculated at (d) from the amount calculated at (c).

3. The basic amount shall be adjusted in such a way as to correspond to the reference compensation amount.

Article 5

1. The cost of the correction shall be borne by the other Member States in accordance with the following arrangements:

The distribution of the cost shall first be calculated by reference to each Member State's share of the payments referred to in Article 2(1)(d), the United Kingdom being excluded; it shall then be adjusted in such a way as to restrict the share of the Federal Republic of Germany to two-thirds of the share resulting from this calculation.

2. The correction shall be granted to the United Kingdom by a reduction in its payments resulting from the application of Article 2(1)(c). The costs borne by the other Member States shall be added to their payments resulting from the application for each Member State of Article 2(1)(c) up to a 1.4% VAT rate and Article 2(1)(d).

3.   The Commission shall perform the calculations required for the application of Article 4 and this Article.

4.   If, at the beginning of the financial year, the budget has not been adopted, the correction granted to the United Kingdom and the costs borne by the other Member States as entered in the last budget finally adopted shall remain applicable.

Article 6

The revenue referred to in Article 2 shall be used without distinction to finance all expenditure entered in the budget of the Communities. However, the revenue needed to cover in full or in part the EAGGF monetary reserve, entered in the budget of the Communities, shall not be called up from the Member States until the reserve is implemented. Provisions for the operation of that reserve shall be adopted as necessary in accordance with Article 8(2).

The preceding subparagraph shall be without prejudice to the treatment of contributions by certain Member States to supplementary programmes provided for in Article 130l of the Treaty establishing the European Economic Community.

Article 7

Any surplus of the Communities' revenue over total actual expenditure during a financial year shall be carried over to the following financial year. However, any surplus generated by a transfer from EAGGF Guarantee chapters to the monetary reserve shall be regarded as constituting own resources.

Article 8

1.   The Community own resources referred to in Article 2(1)(a) and (b) shall be collected by the Member States in accordance with the national provisions imposed by law, regulation or administrative action, which shall, where appropriate, be adopted to meet the requirements of Community rules. The Commission shall examine at regular intervals the national provisions communicated to it by the Member States, transmit to the Member States the adjustments it deems necessary in order to ensure that they comply with Community rules and report to the budget authority. Member States shall make the resources under Article 2(1)(a) to (d) available to the Commission.

2.   Without prejudice to the auditing of the accounts and to checks that they are lawful and regular and as laid down in Article 206a of the Treaty establishing the European Economic Community, such auditing and checks being mainly concerned with the reliability and effectiveness of national systems and procedures for determining the base for own resources accruing from VAT and GNP and without prejudice to the inspection arrangements made pursuant to Article 209(c) of that Treaty, the Council shall, acting unanimously on a proposal from the Commission and after consulting the European Parliament, adopt the provisions necessary to apply this Decision and to make possible the inspection of the collection, the making available to the Commission and payment of the revenue referred to in Articles 2 and 5.

Article 9

The mechanism for the graduated fund of own resources accruing from VAT or GNP-based financial contributions introduced for the Kingdom of Spain and the Portuguese Republic up to 1991 by Articles 187 and 374 of the 1985 Act of Accession shall apply to the own resources accruing from VAT and the

GNP-based resource referred to in Article 2(1)(c) and (d) of this Decision. It shall also apply to payments by these two Member States in accordance with Article 5(2) of this Decision. In the latter case the rate of refund shall be that applicable for the year in respect of which the correction is granted.

Article 10

The Commission shall submit, by the end of 1991, a report on the operation of the system, including a re-examination of the correction of budgetary imbalances granted to the United Kingdom, established by this Decision.

Article 11

1. Member States shall be notified of this Decision by the Secretary-General of the Council of the European Communities; it shall be published in the Official Journal of the European Communities.

Member States shall notify the Secretary-General of the Council of the European Communities without delay of the completion of the procedures for the adoption of this Decision in accordance with their respective constitutional requirements.

This Decision shall enter into force on the first day of the month following receipt of the last of the notifications referred to in the second subparagraph. It shall take effect on 1 January 1988.

2. Subject to (b) and (c), Decision 85/257/EEC, Euratom shall be repealed as of 1 January 1988. Any references to the Decision of 21 April 1970 or to Decision 85/257/EEC, Euratom shall be construed as references to this Decision.

(b) Article 3 of Decision 85/257/EEC, Euratom shall continue to apply to the calculation and adjustment of revenue accruing from the application of rates to the uncapped uniform assessment basis for value added tax in 1987 and earlier years. For 1988 the deduction in favour of the United Kingdom in respect of previous financial years shall be calculated in accordance with points (b)(i), (ii) and (iii) of Article 3(3) of the said Decision. The distribution of the cost of financing it shall be calculated in accordance with Article 5(1) of this Decision. The amounts corresponding to the deduction and the distribution of the cost of financing it shall be dealt with in accordance with Article 5(2) of this Decision. When Article 2(7) has to be applied, the value added tax payments shall be replaced by financial contributions in the calculations referred to in this paragraph for any Member State concerned; this system shall also apply to the payment of adjustments of corrections for earlier years.

(c) Article 4(2) of Decision 85/257/EEC, Euratom shall continue to apply to the financial contributions needed to finance the completion of the supplementary programme for the operation of the HFR (high-flux reactor) reactor of 1984 to 1987.

Done at Luxembourg, 24 June 1988.
For the Council
The President
M. BANGEMANN

Editor's Note: Regulation 1552/89 (OJ 1989 L155/1) provides rules for the implementation of Decision 88/376.

**COUNCIL DECISION OF 31 OCTOBER 1994 ON THE SYSTEM OF
THE EUROPEAN COMMUNITIES' OWN RESOURCES
(94/728/EC, EURATOM) AS CORRECTED
[OJ 1994, L293/9]**

THE COUNCIL OF THE EUROPEAN UNION,

Having regard to the Treaty establishing the European Community, and in
particular Article 201 thereof,

Having regard to the Treaty establishing the European Atomic Energy
Community, and in particular Article 173 thereof,

Having regard to the proposal from the Commission,[1]

Having regard to the opinion of the European Parliament,[2]

Having regard to the opinion of the Economic and Social Committee,[3]

Whereas Council Decision 88/376/EEC, Euratom of 24 June 1988 on the
system of the Communities' own resources[4] expanded and amended the
composition of own resources by capping the VAT resources base at 55% of
gross national product ('GNP') for the year at market prices, with the
maximum call-in rate being maintained at 1.4%, and by introducing an
additional resource based on the total GNP of the Member States;

Whereas the European Council meeting in Edinburgh on 11 and 12
December 1992 reached certain conclusions;

Whereas the Communities must have adequate resources to finance their
policies;

Whereas, in accordance with these conclusions, the Communities will, by
1999, be assigned a maximum amount of own resources corresponding to
1.27% of the total of the Member States' GNPs for the year at market prices;

Whereas observance of this ceiling requires that the total amount of own
resources at the Community's disposal for the period 1995 to 1999 does not in
any one year exceed a specified percentage of the sum of the Member States'
GNPs for the year in question;

Whereas an overall ceiling of 1.335% of the Member States' GNPs is set for
commitment appropriations; whereas an orderly progression of commitment
appropriations and payment appropriations should be ensured;

Whereas these ceilings should remain applicable until this Decision is
amended;

Whereas, in order to make allowance for each Member State's ability to
contribute to the system of own resources and to correct the regressive aspects
of the current system for the least prosperous Member States, in accordance
with the Protocol on economic and social cohesion annexed to the Treaty on
European Union, the Communities' financing rules should be further amended:

— by lowering the ceiling for the uniform rate to be applied to the uniform
value added tax base of each Member State from 1.4 to 1.0% in equal steps
between 1995 and 1999,

Notes
[1] OJ No. C300, 6.11.1993, p. 17.
[2] OJ No. C61, 28.2.1994, p. 105.
[3] OJ No. C52, 19.2.1994, p. 1.
[4] OJ No. L185, 15.7.1988, p. 24.

— by limiting at 50% of GNP from 1995 onwards the value added tax base of the Member States whose per capita GNP in 1991 was less than 90% of the Community average, i.e., Greece, Spain, Ireland and Portugal, and by reducing the base from 55 to 50% in equal steps over the period 1995 to 1999 for the other Member States;

Whereas the European Council has examined the correction of budgetary imbalances on numerous occasions, particularly at its meeting on 25 and 26 June 1984;

Whereas the European Council of 11 and 12 December 1992 confirmed the formula for calculating the correction of budgetary imbalances defined in Decision 8/376/EEC, Euratom;

Whereas the budgetary imbalances should be corrected in such a way as not to affect the own resources available for Community policies;

Whereas the monetary reserve, hereinafter referred to as 'the EAGGF monetary reserve', is covered by specific provisions;

Whereas the conclusions of the European Council provided for the creation in the budget of two reserves, one for the financing of the Loan Guarantee Fund, and the other the emergency aid in non-member countries; whereas these reserves should be covered by specific provisions;

Whereas the Commission will by the end of 1999 submit a report on the operation of the system, which will contain a review of the mechanism for correcting budgetary imbalances granted to the United Kingdom; whereas it will also by the end of 1999 present a report containing the results of a study on the feasibility of creating a new own resource, as well as on arrangements for the possible introduction of a fixed uniform rate applicable to the VAT base;

Whereas provisions must be laid down to cover the changeover from the system introduced by Decision 88/376/EEC, Euratom to that arising from this Decision;

Whereas the European Council provided that this Decision should take effect on 1 January 1995,

HAS LAID DOWN THESE PROVISIONS, WHICH IT RECOMMENDS TO THE MEMBER STATES FOR ADOPTION:

Article 1

The Communities shall be allocated resources of their own in accordance with the detailed rules laid down in the following Articles in order to ensure the financing of their budget.

The budget of the Communities shall, without prejudice to other revenue, be financed wholly from the Communities' own resources.

Article 2

1. Revenue from the following shall constitute own resources entered in the budget of the Communities:

(a) levies, premiums, additional or compensatory amounts, additional amounts or factors and other duties established or to be established by the institutions of the Communities in respect of trade with non-member countries within the framework of the common agricultural policy, and also contributions and other duties provided for within the framework of the common organisation of the markets in sugar;

(b)   Common Customs Tariff duties and other duties established or to be established by the institutions of the Communities in respect of trade with non-member countries and customs duties on products coming under the Treaty establishing the European Coal and Steel Community;

(c)   the application of a uniform rate valid for all Member States to the VAT assessment base which is determined in a uniform manner for Member States according to Community rules. However, the assessment base to be taken into account for the purposes of this Decision shall, from 1995, not exceed 50% of GNP in the case of Member States whose per capita GNP, in 1991 was less than 90% of the Community average; for the other Member States the assessment base to be taken into account shall not exceed:

— 54% of their GNP in 1995,
— 53% of their GNP in 1996,
— 52% of their GNP in 1997,
— 51% of their GNP in 1998,
— 50% of their GNP in 1999,

The cap of 50% of their GNP to be introduced for all Member States in 1999 shall remain applicable until such time as this Decision is amended;

(d)   the application of a rate — to be determined pursuant to the budgetary procedure in the light of the total of all other revenue — to the sum of all the Member States' GNP established in accordance with the Community rules laid down in Directive 89/130/EEC, Euratom.[5]

Note
[5] OJ No. L49, 21.2.1989, p. 26.

2.   Revenue deriving from any new charges introduced within the framework of a common policy, in accordance with the Treaty establishing the European Community or the Treaty establishing the European Atomic Energy Community, provided the procedure laid down in Article 201 of the Treaty establishing the European Community or in Article 173 of the Treaty establishing the European Atomic Energy Community has been followed, shall also constitute own resources entered in the budget of the Communities.

3.   Member States shall retain, by way of collection costs, 10% of the amounts paid under 1(a) and (b).

4.   The uniform rate referred to in paragraph 1(c) shall correspond to the rate resulting from:

(a)   the application to the VAT assessment base for the Member States of:
— 1.32% in 1995,
— 1.24% in 1996,
— 1.16% in 1997,
— 1.08% in 1998,
— 1.00% in 1999.

The 1.00% rate in 1999 shall remain applicable until such time as this decision is amended;

(b)   the deduction of the gross amount of the reference compensation referred to in Article 4(2). The gross amount shall be the compensation amount adjusted for the fact that the United Kingdom is not participating in the financing of its own compensation and the Federal Republic of Germany's share is reduced by one-third. It shall be calculated as if the reference compensation amount were financed by Member States according to their VAT assessment bases established in accordance with Article 2(1)(c).

5. The rate fixed under paragraph 1(d) shall apply to the GNP of each Member State.

6. If, at the beginning of the financial year, the budget has not been adopted, the previous uniform VAT rate and rate applicable to Member States' GNPs, without prejudice to the provisions adopted in accordance with Article 8(2) as regards the EAGGF monetary reserve, the reserve for financing the Loan Guarantee Fund and the reserve for emergency aid in third world countries, shall remain applicable until the entry into force of the new rates.

7. For the purposes of applying this Decision, GNP shall mean gross national product for the year at market prices.

Article 3

1. The total amount of own resources assigned to the Communities may not exceed 1.27% of the total GNPs of the Member States for payment appropriations.

The total amount of own resources assigned to the Communities may not, for any of the years during the period 1995 to 1999, exceed the following percentages of the total GNPs of the Member States for the year in question:

— 1995: 1.21,
— 1996: 1.22,
— 1997: 1.24,
— 1998: 1.26,
— 1999: 1.27.

2. The commitment appropriations entered in the general budget of the Communities over the period 1995 to 1999 must follow an orderly progression resulting in a total amount which does not exceed 1.335% of the total GNPs of the Member States in 1999. An orderly ratio between commitment appropriations and payment appropriations shall be maintained to guarantee their compatibility and to enable the ceilings mentioned in paragraph 1 to be observed in subsequent years.

3. The overall ceilings referred to in paragraphs 1 and 2 shall remain applicable until such time as this Decision is amended.

Article 4

The United Kingdom shall be granted a correction in respect of budgetary imbalances. This correction shall consist of a basic amount and an adjustment. The adjustment shall correct the basic amount to a reference compensation amount.

1. The basic amount shall be established by:

(a) calculating the difference in the preceding financial year, between:

— the percentage share of the Untied Kingdom in the sum total of the payments referred to in Article 2(1)(c) and (d) made during the financial year, including adjustments at the uniform rate in respect of earlier financial years, and

— the percentage share of the United Kingdom in total allocated expenditure;

(b) applying the difference thus obtained to total allocated expenditure;

(c) multiplying the result by 0.66.

2. The reference compensation shall be the correction resulting from application of (a), (b) and (c) of this paragraph, corrected by the effects arising

for the United Kingdom from the changeover to capped VAT and the payments referred to in Article 2(1)(d).

It shall be established by:

(a)   calculating the difference, in the preceding financial year, between:

— the percentage share of the United Kingdom in the sum total of VAT payments which would have been made during that financial year, including adjustments in respect of earlier financial years, for the amounts financed by the resources referred to in Article 2(1)(c) and (d) if the uniform VAT rate had been applied to non-capped bases, and

— the percentage share of the United Kingdom in total allocated expenditure;

(b)   applying the difference thus obtained to total allocated expenditure;

(c)   multiplying the result by 0.66;

(d)   subtracting the payments by the United Kingdom taken into account in the first indent of point 1(a) from those taken into account in point (a), first indent of this subparagraph;

(e)   subtracting the amount calculated at (d) from the amount calculated at (c).

3.   The basic amount shall be adjusted in such a way as to correspond to the reference compensation amount.

Article 5

1.   The cost of the correction shall be borne by the other Member States in accordance with the following arrangements.

The distribution of the cost shall first be calculated by reference to each Member State's share of the payments referred to in Article 2(1)(d), the United Kingdom being excluded; it shall then be adjusted in such a way as to restrict the share of the Federal Republic of Germany to two-thirds of the share resulting from this calculation.

2.   The correction shall be granted to the United Kingdom by a reduction in its payments resulting from the application of Article 2(1)(c) and (d). The costs borne by the other Member States shall be added to their payments resulting from the application for each Member State of Article 2(1)(c) and (d).

3.   The Commission shall perform the calculations required for the application of Article 4 and this Article.

4.   If, at the beginning of the financial year, the budget has not been adopted, the correction granted to the United Kingdom and the costs borne by the other Member States as entered in the last budget finally adopted shall remain applicable.

Article 6

The revenue referred to in Article 2 shall be used without distinction to finance all expenditure entered in the budget. However, the revenue needed to cover in full or in part the EAGGF monetary reserve, the reserve for the financing of the Loan Guarantee Fund and the reserve for emergency aid in third countries, entered in the budget shall not be called up from the Member States until the reserves are implemented. Provisions for the operation of those reserves shall be adopted as necessary in accordance with Article 8(2).

The first paragraph shall be without prejudice to the treatment of contributions by certain Member States to supplementary programmes provided for in Article 130l of the Treaty establishing the European Community.

Article 7

Any surplus of the Communities' revenue over total actual expenditure during a financial year shall be carried over to the following financial year.

Any surpluses generated by a transfer from EAGGF Guarantee Section chapters, or surplus from the Guarantee Fund arising from external measures, transferred to the revenue account in the budget, shall be regarded as constituting own resources.

Article 8

1.   The Community own resources referred to in Article 2(1)(a) and (b) shall be collected by the Member States in accordance with the national provisions imposed by law, regulation or administrative action, which shall, where appropriate, be adapted to meet the requirements of Community rules. The Commission shall examine at regular intervals the national provisions communicated to it by the Member States, transmit to the Member States the adjustments it deems necessary in order to ensure that they comply with Community rules and report to the budget authority. Member States shall make the resources provided for in Article 2(1)(a) to (d) available to the Commission.

2.   Without prejudice to the auditing of the accounts and to checks that they are lawful and regular as laid down in Article 188c of the Treaty establishing the European Community, such auditing and checks being mainly concerned with the reliability and effectiveness of national systems and procedures for determining the base for own resources accruing from VAT and GNP and without prejudice to the inspection arrangements made pursuant to Article 209(c) of that Treaty, the Council shall, acting unanimously on a proposal from the Commission and after consulting the European Parliament, adopt the provisions necessary to apply this Decision and to make possible the inspection of the collection, the making available to the Commission and payment of the revenue referred to in Articles 2 and 5.

Article 9

The mechanism for the graduated refund of own resources accruing from VAT or GNP-based financial contributions introduced for Greece up to 1985 by Article 127 of the 1979 Act of Accession and for Spain and Portugal up to 1991 by Articles 187 and 374 of the 1985 Act of Accession shall apply to the own resources accruing from VAT and the GNP-based resources referred to in Article 2(1)(c) and (d) of the Decision. It shall also apply to payments by the two last-named Member States in accordance with Article 5(2) of this Decision. In the latter case the rate of refund shall be that applicable for the year in respect of which the correction is granted.

Article 10

The Commission shall submit, by the end of 1999, a report on the operation of the system, including a re-examination of the correction of budgetary imbalances granted to the United Kingdom, established by this Decision. It shall also by the end of 1999 submit a report on the findings of a study on the feasibility of creating a new own resource, as well as on arrangements for the possible introduction of a fixed uniform rate applicable to the VAT base.

Article 11

1.   Member States shall be notified of this Decision by the Secretary-General of the Council and the Decision shall be published in the Official Journal of the European Communities.

Member States shall notify the Secretary-General of the Council without delay of the completion of the procedures for the adoption of this Decision in accordance with their respective constitutional requirements.

This Decision shall enter into force on the first day of the month following receipt of the last of the notifications referred to in the second subparagraph. It shall take effect on 1 January 1995.

2. (a)   Subject to (b), Decision 88/376/EEC, Euratom shall be repealed as of 1 January 1995. Any references to the Council Decision of 21 April 1970 on the replacement of financial contributions from Member States by the Communities own resources,[6] to Council Decision 85/257/EEC, Euratom of 7 May 1985 on the Communities' system of own resources,[7] or to Decision 88/376/EEC, Euratom shall be construed as references to this Decision.

(b)   Article 3 of Decision 85/257/EEC, Euratom shall continue to apply to the calculation and adjustment of revenue from the application of rates to the uncapped uniform VAT base for 1987 and earlier years.

Articles 2, 4 and 5 of Decision 88/376/EEC, Euratom shall continue to apply to the calculation and adjustment of revenue accruing from the application of a uniform rate valid for all Member States to the VAT base determined in a uniform manner and limited to 55% of the GNP of each Member State and to the calculation of the correction of buggetary imbalances granted to the United Kingdom for the years 1988 to 1994. When Article 2(7) of that Decision has to be applied, the value added tax payments shall be replaced by financial contributions in the calculations referred to in this paragraph for any Member State concerned; this system shall also apply to the payment of adjustments of corrections for earlier years.

Done at Luxembourg, 31 October 1994.
For the Council
The President
K. KINKEL

Notes
[6]OJ No. L94, 28.4.1970, p. 19.
[7]OJ No. L128, 14.5.1985, p. 15. Decision repealed by Decision 88/376/EC, Euratom.

COUNCIL DECISION OF 13 JULY 1987 LAYING DOWN THE PROCEDURES FOR THE EXERCISE OF IMPLEMENTING POWERS CONFERRED ON THE COMMISSION (87/373/EEC)
[OJ 1987, No. L197/33]

THE COUNCIL OF THE EUROPEAN COMMUNITIES,

Having regard to the Treaty establishing the European Economic Community, and in particular Article 145 thereof,

Having regard to the proposal from the Commission,

Having regard to the opinion of the European Parliament,

Whereas, in the acts which it adopts, the Council confers on the Commission powers for the implementation of the rules which the Council lays down; whereas the Council may impose certain requirements in respect of the exercise of these powers; whereas it may also reserve the right, in specific cases, to exercise directly implementing powers itself;

Whereas, in order to improve the efficiency of the Community's decision-making process, the types of procedure to which it may henceforth have recourse should be limited; whereas certain rules governing any new provision introducing procedures for the exercise of implementing powers conferred by the Council on the Commission should therefore be laid down;

Whereas this Decision must not affect procedures for implementing Commission powers contained in acts which predate its entry into force; whereas it must be possible, when amending or extending such acts, to adapt the procedures to conform with those set out in this Decision or to retain the existing procedures,

HAS DECIDED AS FOLLOWS:

Article 1

Other than in specific cases where it reserves the right to exercise directly implementing powers itself, the Council shall, in the acts which it adopts, confer on the Commission powers for the implementation of the rules which it lays down. The Council shall specify the essential elements of these powers.

The Council may impose requirements in respect of the exercise of these powers, which must be in conformity with the procedures set out in Articles 2 and 3.

Article 2
Procedure I

The Commission shall be assisted by a committee of an advisory nature composed of the representatives of the Member States and chaired by the representative of the Commission.

The representative of the Commission shall submit to the committee a draft of the measures to be taken. The committee shall deliver its opinion on the draft, within a time limit which the chairman may lay down according to the urgency of the matter, if necessary by taking a vote.

The opinion shall be recorded in the minutes; in addition, each Member State shall have the right to ask to have its position recorded in the minutes.

The Commission shall take the utmost account of the opinion delivered by the committee. It shall inform the committee of the manner in which its opinion has been taken into account.

Procedure II

The Commission shall be assisted by a committee composed of the representatives of the Member States and chaired by the representative of the Commission.

The representative of the Commission shall submit to the committee a draft of the measures to be taken. The committee shall deliver its opinion on the draft within a time limit which the chairman may lay down according to the urgency of the matter. The opinion shall be delivered by the majority laid down in Article 148(2) of the Treaty in the case of decisions which the Council is required to adopt on a proposal from the Commission. The votes of the representatives of the Member States within the committee shall be weighted in the manner set out in that Article. The chairman shall not vote.

The Commission shall adopt measures which shall apply immediately. However, if these measures are not in accordance with the opinion of the committee, they shall be communicated by the Commission to the Council forthwith. In that event:

Variant (a)

The Commission may defer application of the measures which it has decided for a period of not more than one month from the date of such communication;

The Council, acting by a qualified majority, may take a different decision within the time limit referred to in the previous paragraph.

Variant (b)

The Commission shall defer application of the measures which it has decided for a period to be laid down in each act adopted by the Council, but which may in no case exceed three months from the date of communication.

The Council, acting by a qualified majority, may take a different decision within the time limit referred to in the previous paragraph.

Procedure III

The Commission shall be assisted by a committee composed of the representatives of the Member States and chaired by the representative of the Commission.

The representative of the Commission shall submit to the committee a draft of the measures to be taken. The committee shall deliver its opinion on the draft within a time limit which the chairman may lay down according to the urgency of the matter. The opinion shall be delivered by the majority laid down in Article 148(2) of the Treaty in the case of decisions which the Council is required to adopt on a proposal from the Commission. The votes of the representatives of the Member States within the committee shall be weighted in the manner set out in that Article. The chairman shall not vote.

The Commission shall adopt the measures envisaged if they are in accordance with the opinion of the committee.

If the measures envisaged are not in accordance with the opinion of the committee, or if no opinion is delivered, the Commission shall, without delay, submit to the Council a proposal relating to the measures to be taken. The Council shall act by a qualified majority.

Variant (a)

If, on the expiry of a period to be laid down in each act to be adopted by the Council under this paragraph but which may in no case exceed three months from the date of referral to the Council, the Council has not acted, the proposed measures shall be adopted by the Commission.

Variant (b)

If, on the expiry of a period to be laid down in each act to be adopted by the Council under this paragraph but which may in no case exceed three months from the date of referral to the Council, the Council has not acted, the proposed measures shall be adopted by the Commission, save where the Council has decided against the said measures by a simple majority.

Article 3

The following procedure may be applied where the Council confers on the Commission the power to decide on safeguard measures:

— the Commission shall notify the Council and the Member States of any decision regarding safeguard measures.

It may be stipulated that before adopting this decision the Commission shall consult the Member States in accordance with procedures to be determined in each case,

— any Member State may refer the Commission's decision to the Council within a time limit to be determined in the act in question.

Variant (a)

The Council, acting by a qualified majority, may take a different decision within a time limit to be determined in the act in question.

Variant (b)

The Council, acting by a qualified majority, may confirm, amend or revoke the decision adopted by the Commission. If the Council has not taken a decision within a time limit to be determined in the act in question, the decision of the Commission is deemed to be revoked.

Article 4

This Decision shall not affect the procedures for the exercise of the powers conferred on the Commission in acts which predate its entry into force.

Where such acts are amended or extended the Council may adapt the procedures laid down by these acts to conform with those set out in Articles 2 and 3 or retain the existing procedures.

Article 5

The Council shall review the procedures provided for in this Decision on the basis of a report submitted by the Commission before 31 December 1990.

PROTOCOL ON THE PRIVILEGES AND IMMUNITIES OF THE EUROPEAN COMMUNITIES
[Annex to the Merger Treaty (OJ 1967, No. 152, 13 July 1967)][1]

The High Contracting Parties,

Considering that, in accordance with Article 28 of the Treaty establishing a Single Council and a Single Commission of the European Communities, these Communities and the European Investment Bank shall enjoy in the territories of the Member States such privileges and immunities as are necessary for the performance of their tasks,

Have agreed upon the following provisions, which shall be annexed to this Treaty:

[1]Editor's Note: As amended by the Treaty on European Union Protocol.

CHAPTER I   PROPERTY, FUNDS, ASSETS AND OPERATIONS OF THE EUROPEAN COMMUNITIES

Article 1

The premises and buildings of the Communities shall be inviolable. They shall be exempt from search, requisition, confiscation or expropriation. The property and assets of the Communities shall not be the subject of any administrative or legal measure of constraint without the authorisation of the Court of Justice.

Article 2
The archives of the Communities shall be inviolable.

Article 3
The Communities, their assets, revenues and other property shall be exempt from all direct taxes.

The Governments of the Member States shall, wherever possible, take the appropriate measures to remit or refund the amount of indirect taxes or sales taxes included in the price of movable or immovable property, where the Communities make, for their official use, substantial purchases the price of which includes taxes of this kind. These provisions shall not be applied, however, so as to have the effect of distorting competition within the Communities.

No exemption shall be granted in respect of taxes and dues which amount merely to charges for public utility services.

Article 4
The Communities shall be exempt from all customs duties, prohibitions and restrictions on imports and exports in respect of articles intended for their official use: articles so imported shall not be disposed of, whether or not in return for payment, in the territory of the country into which they have been imported, except under conditions approved by the Government of that country.

The Communities shall also be exempt from any customs duties and any prohibitions and restrictions on imports and exports in respect of their publications.

Article 5
The European Coal and Steel Community may hold currency of any kind and operate accounts in any currency.

CHAPTER II   COMMUNICATIONS AND LAISSEZ-PASSER

Article 6
For their official communications and the transmission of all their documents, the institutions of the Communities shall enjoy in the territory of each Member State the treatment accorded by that State to diplomatic missions.

Official correspondence and other official communications of the institutions of the Communities shall not be subject to censorship.

Article 7
1.   Laissez-passer in a form to be prescribed by the Council, which shall be recognised as valid travel documents by the authorities of the Member States, may be issued to members and servants of the institutions of the Communities by the Presidents of these institutions. The laissez-passer shall be issued to officials and other servants under conditions laid down in the Staff Regulations of officials and the Conditions of Employment of other servants of the Communities.

The Commission may conclude agreements for these laissez-passer to be recognised as valid travel documents within the territory of third countries.

2. The provisions of Article 6 of the Protocol on the Privileges and Immunities of the European Coal and Steel Community shall, however, remain applicable to members and servants of the institutions who are at the date of entry into force of this Treaty in possession of the laissez-passer provided for in that Article, until the provisions of paragraph 1 of this Article are applied.

CHAPTER III MEMBERS OF THE EUROPEAN PARLIAMENT

Article 8

No administrative or other restriction shall be imposed on the free movement of members of the European Parliament travelling to or from the place of meeting of the European Parliament.

Members of the European Parliament shall, in respect of customs and exchange control, be accorded:

(a) by their own Government, the same facilities as those accorded to senior officials travelling abroad on temporary official missions;

(b) by the Governments of other Member States, the same facilities as those accorded to representatives of foreign Governments on temporary official missions.

Article 9

Members of the European Parliament shall not be subject to any form of inquiry, detention or legal proceedings in respect of opinions expressed or votes cast by them in the performance of their duties.

Article 10

During the sessions of the European Parliament, its members shall enjoy:

(a) in the territory of their own State, the immunities accorded to members of their parliament;

(b) in the territory of any other Member State, immunity from any measure of detention and from legal proceedings.

Immunity shall likewise apply to members while they are travelling to and from the place of meeting of the European Parliament.

Immunity cannot be claimed when a member is found in the act of committing an offence and shall not prevent the European Parliament from exercising its right to waive the immunity of one of its members.

CHAPTER IV REPRESENTATIVES OF MEMBER STATES TAKING PART IN THE WORK OF THE INSTITUTIONS OF THE EUROPEAN COMMUNITIES

Article 11

Representatives of Member States taking part in the work of the institutions of the Communities, their advisers and technical experts shall, in the performance of their duties and during their travel to and from the place of meeting, enjoy the customary privileges, immunities and facilities.

This Article shall also apply to members of the advisory bodies of the Communities.

CHAPTER V OFFICIALS AND OTHER SERVANTS OF THE EUROPEAN COMMUNITIES

Article 12

In the territory of each Member State and whatever their nationality, officials and other servants of the Communities shall:

(a)   subject to the provisions of the Treaties relating, on the one hand, to the rules on the liability of officials and other servants towards the Communities and, on the other hand, to the jurisdiction of the Court in disputes between the Communities and their officials and other servants, be immune from legal proceedings in respect of acts performed by them in their official capacity, including their words spoken or written. They shall continue to enjoy this immunity after they have ceased to hold office.

(b)   together with their spouses and dependent members of their families, not be subject to immigration restrictions or to formalities for the registration of aliens;

(c)   in respect of currency or exchange regulations, be accorded the same facilities as are customarily accorded to officials of international organisations;

(d)   enjoy the right to import free of duty their furniture and effects at the time of first taking up their post in the country concerned, and the right to re-export free of duty their furniture and effects, on termination of their duties in that country, subject in either case to the conditions considered to be necessary by the Government of the country in which this right is exercised;

(e)   have the right to import free of duty a motor car for their personal use, acquired either in the country of their last residence or in the country of which they are nationals on the terms ruling in the home market in that country, and to re-export it free of duty, subject in either case to the conditions considered to be necessary by the Government of the country concerned.

Article 13

Officials and other servants of the Communities shall be liable to a tax for the benefit of the Communities on salaries, wages and emoluments paid to them by the Communities, in accordance with the conditions and procedure laid down by the Council, acting on a proposal from the Commission.

They shall be exempt from national taxes on salaries, wages and emoluments paid by the Communities.

Article 14

In the application of income tax, wealth tax and death duties and in the application of conventions on the avoidance of double taxation concluded between Member States of the Communities, officials and other servants of the Communities who, solely by reason of the performance of their duties in the service of the Communities, establish their residence in the territory of a Member State other than their country of domicile for tax purposes at the time of entering the service of the Communities, shall be considered, both in the country of their actual residence and in the country of domicile for tax purposes, as having maintained their domicile in the latter country provided that it is a member of the Communities. This provision shall also apply to a spouse, to the extent that the latter is not separately engaged in a gainful occupation, and to children dependent on and in the care of the persons referred to in this Article.

Movable property belonging to persons referred to in the preceding paragraph and situated in the territory of the country where they are staying shall be exempt from death duties in that country; such property shall, for the assessment of such duty, be considered as being in the country of domicile for tax purposes, subject to the rights of third countries and to the possible application of provisions of international conventions on double taxation.

Any domicile acquired solely by reason of the performance of duties in the service of other international organisations shall not be taken into consideration in applying the provisions of this Article.

Article 15
The Council shall, acting unanimously on a proposal from the Commission, lay down the scheme of social security benefits for officials and other servants of the Communities.

Article 16
The Council shall, acting on a proposal from the Commission and after consulting the other institutions concerned, determine the categories of officials and other servants of the Communities to whom the provisions of Article 12, the second paragraph of Article 13, and Article 14 shall apply, in whole or in part.

The names, grades and addresses of officials and other servants included in such categories shall be communicated periodically to the Governments of the Member States.

CHAPTER VI PRIVILEGES AND IMMUNITIES OF MISSIONS OF THIRD COUNTRIES ACCREDITED TO THE EUROPEAN COMMUNITIES

Article 17
The Member State in whose territory the Communities have their seat shall accord the customary diplomatic immunities and privileges to missions of third countries accredited to the Communities.

CHAPTER VII GENERAL PROVISIONS

Article 18
Privileges, immunities and facilities shall be accorded to officials and other servants of the Communities solely in the interests of the Communities.

Each institution of the Communities shall be required to waive the immunity accorded to an official or other servant wherever that institution considers that the waiver of such immunity is not contrary to the interests of the Communities.

Article 19
The institutions of the Communities shall, for the purpose of applying this Protocol, cooperate with the responsible authorities of the Member States concerned.

Article 20
Articles 12 to 15 and Article 18 shall apply to members of the Commission.

Article 21
Articles 12 to 15 and Article 18 shall apply to the Judges, the Advocates-General, the Registrar and the Assistant Rapporteurs of the Court of Justice, without prejudice to the provisions of Article 3 of the Protocols on the Statute of the Court of Justice concerning immunity from legal proceedings of Judges and Advocates-General.

Article 22
This Protocol shall also apply to the European Investment Bank, to the members of its organs, to its staff and to the representatives of the Member

States taking part in its activities, without prejudice to the provisions of the Protocol on the Statute of the Bank.

The European Investment Bank shall in addition be exempt from any form of taxation or imposition of a like nature on the occasion of any increase in its capital and from the various formalities which may be connected therewith in the State where the Bank has its seat. Similarly, its dissolution or liquidation shall not give rise to any imposition. Finally, the activities of the Bank and of its organs carried on in accordance with its Statute shall not be subject to any turnover tax.

Article 23

The Protocol shall also apply to the European Central Bank, to the members of its organs and to its staff, without prejudice to the provisions of the Protocol on the Statute of the European System of Central Banks and the European Central Bank.

The European Central Bank shall, in addition, be exempt from any form of taxation or imposition of a like nature on the occasion of any increase in its capital and from the various formalities which may be connected therewith in the State where the bank has its seat. The activities of the Bank and of its organs carried on in accordance with the Statute of the European System of Central Banks and of the European Central Bank shall not be subject to any turnover tax.

The above provisions shall also apply to the European Monetary Institute. Its dissolution or liquidation shall not give rise to any imposition.

(Signatures omitted.)

PROTOCOL ON THE STATUTE OF THE COURT OF JUSTICE OF THE EUROPEAN ECONOMIC COMMUNITY[1]

Note
As amended by Council Decision 94/993 (OJ (1994) L379/1).

(Recitals omitted.)

Article 1
The Court established by Article 4 of this Treaty shall be constituted and shall function in accordance with the provisions of this Treaty and of this Statute.

TITLE I   JUDGES AND ADVOCATES-GENERAL

Article 2
Before taking up his duties each Judge shall, in open court, take an oath to perform his duties impartially and conscientiously and to preserve the secrecy of the deliberations of the Court.

Article 3
The Judges shall be immune from legal proceedings. After they have ceased to hold office, they shall continue to enjoy immunity in respect of acts performed by them in their official capacity including words spoken or written.

The Court, sitting in plenary session, may waive the immunity.

Where immunity has been waived and criminal proceedings are instituted against a Judge, he shall be tried, in any of the Member States, only by the Court competent to judge the members of the highest national judiciary.

Article 4

The Judges may not hold any political or administrative office.

They may not engage in any occupation, whether gainful or not, unless exemption is exceptionally granted by the Council.

When taking up their duties, they shall give a solemn undertaking that, both during and after their term of office, they will respect the obligations arising therefrom, in particular the duty to behave with integrity and discretion as regards the acceptance, after they have ceased to hold office, of certain appointments or benefits.

Any doubt on this point shall be settled by decision of the Court.

Article 5

Apart from normal replacement, or death, the duties of a Judge shall end when he resigns.

Where a Judge resigns, his letter of resignation shall be addressed to the President of the Court for transmission to the President of the Council. Upon this notification a vacancy shall arise on the bench.

Save where Article 6 applies, a Judge shall continue to hold office until his successor takes up his duties.

Article 6

A Judge may be deprived of his office or of his right to a pension or other benefits in its stead only if, in the unanimous opinion of the Judges and Advocates-General of the Court, he no longer fulfils the requisite conditions or meets the obligations arising from his office. The Judge concerned shall not take part in any such deliberations.

The Registrar of the Court shall communicate the decision of the Court to the President of the European Parliament and to the President of the Commission and shall notify it to the President of the Council.

In the case of a decision depriving a Judge of his office, a vacancy shall arise on the bench upon this later notification.

Article 7

A Judge who is to replace a member of the Court whose term of office has not expired shall be appointed for the remainder of his predecessor's term.

Article 8

The provisions of Articles 2 to 7 shall apply to the Advocates-General.

TITLE II   ORGANISATION

Article 9

The Registrar shall take an oath before the Court to perform his duties impartially and conscientiously and to preserve the secrecy of the deliberations of the Court.

Article 10

The Court shall arrange for replacement of the Registrar on occasions when he is prevented from attending the Court.

Article 11

Officials and other servants shall be attached to the Court to enable it to function. They shall be responsible to the Registrar under the authority of the President.

Article 12

On a proposal from the Court, the Council may, acting unanimously, provide for the appointment of Assistant Rapporteurs and lay down the rules governing their service. The Assistant Rapporteurs may be required, under conditions laid down in the rules of procedure, to participate in preparatory inquiries in cases pending before the Court and to cooperate with the Judge who acts as Rapporteur.

The Assistant Rapporteurs shall be chosen from persons whose independence is beyond doubt and who possess the necessary legal qualifications; they shall be appointed by the Council. They shall take an oath before the Court to perform their duties impartially and conscientiously and to preserve the secrecy of the deliberations of the Court.

Article 13

The Judges, the Advocates-General and the Registrar shall be required to reside at the place where the Court has its seat.

Article 14

The Court shall remain permanently in session. The duration of the judicial vacations shall be determined by the Court with due regard to the needs of its business.

Article 15[1]

Decisions of the Court shall be valid only when an uneven number of its members is sitting in the deliberations. Decisions of the full Court shall be valid if seven members are sitting. Decisions of the Chambers shall be valid only if three Judges are sitting; in the event of one of the Judges of a Chamber being prevented from attending, a Judge of another Chamber may be called upon to sit in accordance with conditions laid down in the rules of procedure.

Note
[1]Text as amended by Article 20 of the Act of Accession DK/IRL/UK.

Article 16

No Judge or Advocate-General may take part in the disposal of any case in which he has previously taken part as agent or adviser or has acted for one of the parties, or in which he has been called upon to pronounce as a Member of the court or tribunal, of a commission of inquiry or in any other capacity.

If, for some special reason, any Judge or Advocate-General considers that he should not take part in the judgment or examination of a particular case, he shall so inform the President. If, for some special reason, the President considers that any Judge or Advocate-General should not sit or make submissions in a particular case, he shall notify him accordingly.

Any difficulty arising as to the application of this Article shall be settled by decision of the Court.

A party may not apply for a change in the composition of the Court or of one of its Chambers on the grounds of either the nationality of a Judge or the absence from the Court or from the Chamber of a Judge of the nationality of that party.

TITLE III   PROCEDURE

Article 17

The States and the institutions of the Community shall be represented before the Court by an agent appointed for each case; the agent may be assisted by an adviser or by a lawyer.

The States, other than the Member States, which are parties to the Agreement on the European Economic Area, and also the EFTA Surveillance Authority referred to in that Agreement, shall be represented in same manner.

Other parties must be represented by a lawyer.

Only a lawyer authorised to practise before a court of a Member State or of another State which is a party to the Agreement on the European Economic Area may represent or assist a party before the court.

Such agents, advisers and lawyers shall, when they appear before the Court, enjoy the rights and immunities necessary to the independent exercise of their duties, under conditions laid down in the rules of procedure.

As regards such advisers and lawyers who appear before it, the Court shall have the powers normally accorded to courts of law, under conditions laid down in the rules of procedure.

University teachers being nationals of a Member State whose law accords them a right of audience shall have the same rights before the Court as are accorded by this Article to lawyers entitled to practise before a court of a Member State.

Article 18

The procedure before the Court shall consist of two parts: written and oral.

The written procedure shall consist of the communication to the parties and to the institutions of the Community whose decisions are in dispute, of applications, statements of case, defences and observations, and of replies, if any, as well as of all papers and documents in support or of certified copies of them.

Communications shall be made by the Registrar in the order and within the time laid down in the rules of procedure.

The oral procedure shall consist of the reading of the report presented by a judge acting as Rapporteur, the hearing by the Court of agents, advisers and lawyers entitled to practise before a court of a Member State and of the submissions of the Advocate-General, as well as the hearing, if any, of witnesses and experts.

Article 19

A case shall be brought before the Court by a written application addressed to the Registrar. The application shall contain the applicant's name and permanent address and the description of the signatory, the name of the party or names of the parties against whom the application is made, the subject matter of the dispute, the form of the order sought and a brief statement of the pleas in law on which the application is based.

The application shall be accompanied, where appropriate, by the measure the annulment of which is sought or, in the circumstances referred to in Article 175 of this Treaty, by documentary evidence of the date on which an institution was, in accordance with that Article, requested to act. If the documents are not submitted with the application, the Registrar shall ask the party concerned to produce them within a reasonable period, but in that event the rights of the party shall not lapse even if such documents are produced after the time limit for bringing proceedings.

Article 20
In the cases governed by Article 177 of this Treaty, the decision of the court or tribunal of a Member State which suspends its proceedings and refers a case to the Court shall be notified to the Court by the court or tribunal concerned. The decision shall then be notified by the Registrar of the Court to the parties, to the Member States and to the Commission, and also to the Council or to the European Central Bank if the act the validity or interpretation of which is in dispute originates from one of them, and to the European Parliament and the Council if the act the validity or interpretation of which is in dispute was adopted jointly by those two institutions.

Within two months of this notification, the parties, the Member States, the Commission and, where appropriate, the European Parliament, the Council and the European Central Bank, shall be entitled to submit statements of case or written observations to the Court.

The decision of the aforesaid court or tribunal shall, moreover, be notified by the Registrar of the Court to the States, other than the Member States, which are parties to the Agreement of the European Economic Area and also to the EFTA Surveillance Authority referred to in that Agreement which may, within two months of notification, where one of the fields of application of that Agreement is concerned, submit statements of case or written observations to the Court.

Article 21
The Court may require the parties to produce all documents and to supply all information which the Court considers desirable. Formal note shall be taken of any refusal.

The Court may also require the Member States and institutions not being parties to the case to supply all information which the Court considers necessary for the proceedings.

Article 22
The Court may at any time entrust any individual, body, authority, committee or other organisation it chooses with the task of giving an expert opinion.

Article 23
Witnesses may be heard under conditions laid down in the rules of procedure.

Article 24
With respect to defaulting witnesses the Court shall have the powers generally granted to courts and tribunals and may impose pecuniary penalties under conditions laid down in the rules of procedure.

Article 25
Witnesses and experts may be heard on oath taken in the form laid down in the rules of procedure or in the manner laid down by the law of the country of the witness or expert.

Article 26
The Court may order that a witness or expert be heard by the judicial authority of his place of permanent residence.

The order shall be sent for implementation to the competent judicial authority under conditions laid down in the rules of procedure. The documents drawn up in compliance with the letters rogatory shall be returned to the Court under the same conditions.

The Court shall defray the expenses, without prejudice to the right to charge them, where appropriate, to the parties.

Article 27

A Member State shall treat any violation of an oath by a witness or expert in the same manner as if the offence had been committed before one of its courts with jurisdiction in civil proceedings. At the instance of the Court, the Member State concerned shall prosecute the offender before its competent court.

Article 28

The hearing in court shall be public, unless the Court, of its own motion or on application by the parties, decides otherwise for serious reasons.

Article 29

During the hearings the Court may examine the experts, the witnesses and the parties themselves. The latter, however, may address the Court only through their representatives.

Article 30

Minutes shall be made of each hearing and signed by the President and the Registrar.

Article 31

The case list shall be established by the President.

Article 32

The deliberations of the Court shall be and shall remain secret.

Article 33

Judgments shall state the reasons on which they are based. They shall contain the names of the Judges who took part in the deliberations.

Article 34

Judgments shall be signed by the President and the Registrar. They shall be read in open court.

Article 35

The Court shall adjudicate upon costs.

Article 36

The President of the Court may, by way of summary procedure, which may, in so far as necessary, differ from some of the rules contained in this Statute and which shall be laid down in the rules of procedure, adjudicate upon applications to suspend execution, as provided for in Article 185 of this Treaty, or to prescribe interim measures in pursuance of Article 186, or to suspend enforcement in accordance with the last paragraph of Article 192.

Should the President be prevented from attending, his place shall be taken by another Judge under conditions laid down in the rules of procedure.

The ruling of the President or of the Judge replacing him shall be provisional and shall in no way prejudice the decision of the Court on the substance of the case.

Article 37

Member States and institutions of the Community may intervene in cases before the Court.

The same right shall be open to any other person establishing an interest in the result of any case submitted to the Court, save in cases between Member States, between institutions of the Community or between Member States and institutions of the Community.

Without prejudice to the preceding paragraph, the States, other than the Member States, which are parties to the Agreement on the European Economic Area, and also the EFTA Surveillance Authority referred to in that Agreement, may intervene in cases before the Court where one of the fields of application of that Agreement is concerned.

An application to intervene shall be limited to supporting the form of order sought by one of the parties.

Article 38

Where the defending party, after having been duly summoned, fails to file written submissions in defence, judgment shall be given against that party by default. An objection may be lodged against the judgment within one month of it being notified. The objection shall not have the effect of staying enforcement of the judgment by default unless the Court decides otherwise.

Article 39

Member States, institutions of the Community and any other natural or legal persons may, in cases and under conditions to be determined by the rules of procedure, institute third-party proceedings to contest a judgment rendered without their being heard, where the judgment is prejudicial to their rights.

Article 40

If the meaning or scope of a judgment is in doubt, the Court shall construe it on application by any party or any institution of the Community establishing an interest therein.

Article 41

An application for revision of a judgment may be made to the Court only on discovery of a fact which is of such a nature as to be a decisive factor, and which, when the judgment was given, was unknown to the Court and to the party claiming the revision.

The revision shall be opened by a judgment of the Court expressly recording the existence of a new fact, recognising that it is of such a character as to lay the case open to revision and declaring the application admissible on this ground.

No application for revision may be made after the lapse of ten years from the date of the judgment.

Article 42

Periods of grace based on considerations of distance shall be determined by the rules of procedure.

No right shall be prejudiced in consequence of the expiry of a time limit if the party concerned proves the existence of unforeseeable circumstances or of *force majeure*.

Article 43

Proceedings against the Community in matters arising from non-contractual liability shall be barred after a period of five years from the occurrence of the event giving rise thereto. The period of limitation shall be interrupted if proceedings are instituted before the Court or if prior to such proceedings an application is made by the aggrieved party to the relevant institution of the Community. In the latter event the proceedings must be instituted within the period of two months provided for in Article 173; the provisions of the second paragraph of Article 175 shall apply where appropriate.

(Signatures omitted.)

RULES OF PROCEDURE OF THE COURT OF JUSTICE OF THE EUROPEAN COMMUNITIES OF 19 JUNE 1991
[OJ 1991, No. L176/7][1]

CONTENTS

Note

[1]As corrected by OJ 1992 L383/117 and amended by OJ 1995 L44/61, OJ 1997 103/1 and Decision 97/419 OJ 1997 L103/3.

The Court of Justice,

Having regard to the powers conferred on the Court of Justice by the Treaty establishing the European Coal and Steel Community, the Treaty establishing the European Economic Community and the Treaty establishing the European Atomic Energy Community (Euratom),

Having regard to Article 55 of the Protocol on the Statute of the Court of Justice of the European Coal and Steel Community,

Having regard to the third paragraph of Article 188 of the Treaty establishing the European Economic Community,

Having regard to the third paragraph of Article 160 of the Treaty establishing the European Atomic Energy Community (Euratom),

Whereas it is necessary to revise the text of its Rules of Procedure in the various languages in order to ensure coherence and uniformity between those language versions;

With the unanimous approval of that revision, given by the Council on 29 April 1991;

And whereas, after the numerous amendments to its Rules of Procedure, it is necessary, in the interests of clarity and simplicity to establish a coherent authentic text,

With the unanimous approval of the Council, given on 7 June 1991,

REPLACES ITS RULES OF PROCEDURE BY THE FOLLOWING RULES:

INTERPRETATION

Article 1
In these Rules:
— 'EC Treaty' means the Treaty establishing the European Community,
— 'EC Statute' means the Protocol on the Statute of the Court of Justice of the European Community,

— 'ECSC Treaty' means the Treaty establishing the European Coal and Steel Community,
— 'ECSC Statute' means the Protocol on the Statute of the Court of Justice of the European Coal and Steel Community,
— 'Euratom Treaty' means the Treaty establishing the European Atomic Energy Community (Euratom),
— 'Euratom Statute' means the Protocol on the Statute of the Court of Justice of the European Atomic Energy Community,
— 'EEA Agreement' means the Agreement on the European Economic Area.

For the purposes of these Rules:
— 'Institutions' means the institutions of the Communities and bodies which are established by the Treaties, or by an act adopted in implementation thereof, and which may be parties before the Court,
— 'EFTA Surveillance Authority' means the surveillance authority referred to in the EEA Agreement.

TITLE I   ORGANIZATION OF THE COURT
CHAPTER 1   JUDGES AND ADVOCATES-GENERAL

Article 2
The term of office of a Judge shall begin on the date laid down in his instrument of appointment. In the absence of any provisions regarding the date, the term shall begin on the date of the instrument.

Article 3
1.   Before taking up his duties, a Judge shall at the first public sitting of the Court which he attends after his appointment take the following oath: 'I swear that I will perform my duties impartially and conscientiously; I swear that I will preserve the secrecy of the deliberations of the Court'.
2.   Immediately after taking the oath, a Judge shall sign a declaration by which he solemnly undertakes that, both during and after his term of office, he will respect the obligations arising therefrom, and in particular the duty to behave with integrity and discretion as regards the acceptance, after he has ceased to hold office, of certain appointments and benefits.

Article 4
When the Court is called upon to decide whether a Judge no longer fulfils the requisite conditions or no longer meets the obligations arising from his office, the President shall invite the Judge concerned to make representations to the Court, in closed session and in the absence of the Registrar.

Article 5
Articles 2, 3 and 4 of these Rules shall apply in a corresponding manner to Advocates-General.

Article 6
Judges and Advocates-General shall rank equally in precedence according to their seniority in office. Where there is equal seniority in office, precedence shall be determined by age. Retiring Judges and Advocates-General who are reappointed shall retain their former precedence.

CHAPTER 2 PRESIDENCY OF THE COURT AND CONSTITUTION OF THE CHAMBERS

Article 7

1. The Judges shall, immediately after the partial replacement provided for in Article 167 of the EC Treaty, Article 32b of the ECSC Treaty and Article 139 of the Euratom Treaty, elect one of their number as President of the Court for a term of three years.

2. If the office of the President of the Court falls vacant before the normal date of expiry thereof, the Court shall elect a successor for the remainder of the term.

3. The elections provided for in this Article shall be by secret ballot. If a Judge obtains an absolute majority he shall be elected. If no Judge obtains an absolute majority, a second ballot shall be held and the Judge obtaining the most votes shall be elected. Where two or more Judges obtain an equal number of votes the oldest of them shall be deemed elected.

Article 8

The President shall direct the judicial business and the administration of the Court; he shall preside at hearings and deliberations.

Article 9

1. The Court shall set up Chambers in accordance with the provisions of the second paragraph of Article 165 of the EC Treaty, the second paragraph of Article 32 of the ECSC Treaty and the second paragraph of Article 137 of the Euratom Treaty and shall decide which Judges shall be attached to them. The composition of the Chambers shall be published in the Official Journal of the European Communities.

2. As soon as an application initiating proceedings has been lodged, the President shall assign the case to one of the Chambers for any preparatory inquiries and shall designate a Judge from that Chamber to act as Rapporteur.

3. The Court shall lay down criteria by which, as a rule, cases are to be assigned to Chambers.

4. These Rules shall apply to proceedings before the Chambers. In cases assigned to a Chamber the powers of the President of the Court shall be exercised by the President of the Chamber.

Article 10

1. The Court shall appoint for a period of one year the Presidents of the Chambers and the First Advocate General.

The provisions of Article 7(2) and (3) shall apply.

Appointments made in pursuance of this paragraph shall be published in the Official Journal of the European Communities.

2. The First Advocate-General shall assign each case to an Advocate-General as soon as the Judge-Rapporteur has been designated by the President. He shall take the necessary steps if an Advocate-General is absent or prevented from acting.

Article 11

When the President of the Court is absent or prevented from attending or when the office of President is vacant, the functions of President shall be exercised by a President of a Chamber according to the order of precedence laid down in Article 6 of these Rules.

If the President of the Court and the President of the Chambers are all prevented from attending at the same time, or their posts are vacant at the same time, the functions of President shall be exercised by one of the other Judges according to the order of precedence laid down in Article 6 of these Rules.

CHAPTER 3   REGISTRY
SECTION 1   THE REGISTRAR AND ASSISTANT REGISTRAR

Article 12

1.   The Court shall appoint the Registrar. Two weeks before the date fixed for making the appointment, the President shall inform the Members of the Court of the applications which have been made for the post.

2.   An application shall be accompanied by full details of the candidate's age, nationality, university degrees, knowledge of any languages, present and past occupations and experience, if any, in judicial and international fields.

3.   The appointment shall be made following the procedure laid down in Article 7(3) of these Rules.

4.   The Registrar shall be appointed for a term of six years. He may be reappointed.

5.   The Registrar shall take the oath in accordance with Article 3 of these Rules.

6.   The Registrar may be deprived of his office only if he no longer fulfils the requisite conditions or no longer meets the obligations arising from his office; the Court shall take its decision after giving the Registrar an opportunity to make representations.

7.   If the office of Registrar falls vacant before the normal date of expiry of the term thereof, the Court shall appoint a new Registrar for a term of six years.

Article 13

The Court may, following the procedure laid down in respect of the Registrar, appoint one or more Assistant Registrars to assist the Registrar and to take his place in so far as the Instructions to the Registrar referred in Article 15 of these Rules allow.

Article 14

Where the Registrar and the Assistant Registrar are absent or prevented from attending or their posts are vacant, the President shall designate an official to carry out temporarily the duties of Registrar.

Article 15

Instructions to the Registrar shall be adopted by the Court acting on a proposal from the President.

Article 16

1.   There shall be kept in the Registry, under the control of the Registrar, a register initialled by the President, in which all pleadings and supporting documents shall be entered in the order in which they are lodged.

2.   When a document has been registered, the Registrar shall make a note to that effect on the original and, if a party so requests, on any copy submitted for the purpose.

3.   Entries in the register and the notes provided for in the preceding paragraph shall be authentic.

4.   Rules for keeping the register shall be prescribed by the Instructions to the Registrar referred to in Article 15 of the Rules.

5.   Persons having an interest may consult the register at the Registry and may obtain copies or extracts on payment of a charge on a scale fixed by the Court on a proposal from the Registrar.

The parties to a case may on payment of the appropriate charge also obtain copies of pleadings and authenticated copies of judgments and orders.

6.   Notice shall be given in the Official Journal of the European Communities of the date of registration of an application initiating proceedings, the names and addresses of the parties, the subject-matter of the proceedings, the form of order sought by the applicant and a summary of the pleas in law and of the main supporting arguments.

7.   Where the Council or the Commission is not a party to a case, the Court shall send to it copies of the application and of the defence, without the annexes thereto, to enable it to assess whether the inapplicability of one of its acts is being invoked under the third paragraph of Article 184 of the EC Treaty, Article 36 of the ECSC Treaty or Article 156 of the Euratom Treaty.

Article 17
1.   The Registrar shall be responsible, under the authority of the President, for the acceptance, transmission and custody of documents and for effecting service as provided for by these Rules.

2.   The Registrar shall assist the Court, the Chambers, the President and the Judges in all their official functions.

Article 18
The Registrar shall have custody of the seals. He shall be responsible for the records and be in charge of the publications of the Court.

Article 19
Subject to Articles 4 and 27 of these Rules, the Registrar shall attend the sittings of the Court and of the Chambers.

SECTION 2   OTHER DEPARTMENTS

Article 20
1.   The official and other servants of the Court shall be appointed in accordance with the provisions of the Staff Regulations.

2.   Before taking up his duties, an official shall take the following oath before the President, in the presence of the Registrar:

'I swear that I will perform loyally, discreetly and conscientiously the duties assigned to me by the Court of Justice of the European Communities'.

Article 21
The organization of the departments of the Court shall be laid down, and may be modified, by the Court on a proposal from the Registrar.

Article 22
The Court shall set up a translating service staffed by experts with adequate legal training and a thorough knowledge of several official languages of the Court.

Article 23
The Registrar shall be responsible, under the authority of the President, for the administration of the Court, its financial management and its accounts; he shall be assisted in this by an administrator.

CHAPTER 4   ASSISTANT RAPPORTEURS

Article 24

1.   Where the Court is of the opinion that the consideration of and preparatory inquiries in cases before it so require, it shall, pursuant to Article 2 of the EC Statute, Article 16 of the ECSC Statute and Article 2 of the Euratom Statute, propose the appointment of Assistant Rapporteurs.

2.   Assistant Rapporteurs shall in particular assist the President in connection with applications for the adoption of interim measures and assist the Judge-Rapporteurs in their work.

3.   In the performance of their duties the Assistant Rapporteurs shall be responsible to the President of the Court, the President of a Chamber or a Judge-Rapporteur, as the case may be.

4.   Before taking up his duties, an Assistant Rapporteur shall take before the Court the oath set out in Article 3 of these Rules.

CHAPTER 5   THE WORKING OF THE COURT

Article 25

1.   The dates and times of the sittings of the Court shall be fixed by the President.

2.   The dates and times of the sittings of the Chambers shall be fixed by their respective Presidents.

3.   The Court and the Chambers may choose to hold one or more sittings in a place other than that in which the Court has its seat.

Article 26

1.   Where, by reason of a Judge being absent or prevented from attending, there is an even number of Judges, the most junior Judge within the meaning of Article 6 of these Rules shall abstain from taking part in the deliberations unless he is the Judge-Rapporteur. In that case the Judge immediately senior to him shall abstain from taking part in the deliberations.

2.   If, after the Court has been convened, it is found that the quorum referred to in Article 15 of the EC Statute, Article 18 of the ECSC Statute and Article 15 of the Euratom Statute has not been attained, the President shall adjourn the sitting until there is a quorum.

3.   If, in any Chamber, the quorum referred to in Article 15 of the EC Statute, Article 1 of the ECSC Statute and Article 15 of the Euratom Statute has not been attained, the President of that Chamber shall so inform the President of the Court who shall designate another Judge to complete the Chamber.

Article 27

1.   The Court and Chambers shall deliberate in closed session.

2.   Only those Judges who were present at the oral proceedings and the Assistant Rapporteur, if any, entrusted with the consideration of the case may take part in the deliberations.

3.   Every Judge taking part in the deliberations shall state his opinion and the reasons for it.

4.   Any Judge may require that any questions be formulated in the language of his choice and communicated in writing to the Court or Chamber before being put to the vote.

5.   The conclusions reached by the majority of the Judges after final discussion shall determine the decision of the Court. Votes shall be cast in reverse order to the order of precedence laid down in Article 6 of these Rules.

6.   Differences of view on the substance, wording or order of questions, or on the interpretation of the voting shall be settled by decision of the Court or Chamber.

7.   Where the deliberations of the Court concern questions of its own administration, the Advocates-General shall take part and have a vote. The Registrar shall be present, unless the Court decides to the contrary.

8.   Where the court sits without the Registrar being present it shall, if necessary, instruct the most junior Judge within the meaning of Article 6 of these rules to draw up minutes. The minutes shall be signed by this Judge and by the President.

Article 28

1.   Subject to any special decision of the Court, its vacations shall be as follows:

—from 18 December to 10 January,

—from the Sunday before Easter to the second Sunday after Easter,

—from 15 July to 15 September.

During the vacations, the functions of President shall be exercised at the place where the Court has its seat either by the President himself, keeping in touch with the Registrar, or by a President of Chamber or other Judge invited by the President to take his place.

2.   In a case of urgency, the President may convene the Judges and the Advocates-General during the vacations.

3.   The Court shall observe the official holidays of the place where it has its seat.

4.   The Court may, in proper circumstances, grant leave of absence to any Judge or Advocate-General.

CHAPTER 6   LANGUAGES

Article 29

1.   The language of a case shall be Danish, Dutch, English, Finnish, French, German, Greek, Irish, Italian, Portuguese, Spanish or Swedish.

2.   The language of the case shall be chosen by the applicant, except that:

(a)   where the defendant is a Member State or a natural or legal person having the nationality of a Member State, the language of the case shall be the official language of that State; where that State has more than one official language, the applicant may choose between them;

(b)   at the joint request of the parties the use of another of the languages mentioned in paragraph 1 for all or part of the proceedings may be authorized;

(c)   at the request of one of the parties, and after the opposite party and the Advocate-General have been heard, the use of another of the languages mentioned in paragraph 1 as the language of the case for all or part of the proceedings may be authorized by way of derogation from subparagraphs (a) and (b).

In cases to which Article 103 of these Rules applies, the language of the case shall be the language of the national court or tribunal which refers the matter to the Court.

At the duly substantiated request of one of the parties to the main proceedings, and after the opposite party and the Advocate-General have been heard, the use of another of the languages mentioned in paragraph 1 may be authorised for the oral procedure. Requests as above may be decided on by the President; the latter may and, where he wishes to accede to a request without the agreement of all the parties, must refer the request to the Court.

3.   The language of the case shall be used in the written and oral pleadings of the parties and in supporting documents, and also in the minutes and decisions of the Court.

Any supporting documents expressed in another language must be accompanied by a translation into the language of the case.

In the case of lengthy documents, translations may be confined to extracts. However, the Court or Chamber may, of its own motion or at the request of a party, at any time call for a complete or fuller translation.

Notwithstanding the foregoing provisions, a Member State shall be entitled to use its official language when intervening in a case before the Court or when taking part in any reference of a kind mentioned in Article 103. This provision shall apply both to written statements and to oral addresses. The Registrar shall cause any such statement or address to be translated into the language of the case.

The States, other than the Member States, which are parties to the EEA Agreement, and also the EFTA Surveillance Authority, may be authorized to use one of the languages mentioned in paragraph 1, other than the language of the case, when they intervene in a case before the Court or participate in preliminary ruling proceedings envisaged by Article 20 of the EC Statute. This provision shall apply both to written statements and oral addresses. The Registrar shall cause any such statement or address to be translated into the language of the case.

4.   Where a witness or expert states that he is unable adequately to express himself in one of the languages referred to in paragraph (1) of this Article, the Court or Chamber may authorize him to give his evidence in another language. The Registrar shall arrange for translation into the language of the case.

5.   The President of the Court and the Presidents of Chambers in conducting oral proceedings, the Judge Rapporteur both in his preliminary report and in his report for the hearing, Judges and Advocates-General in putting questions and Advocates-General in delivering their opinions may use one of the languages referred to in paragraph (1) of this Article other than the language of the case. The Registrar shall arrange for translation into the language of the case.

Article 30

1.   The Registrar shall, at the request of any Judge, of the Advocate-General or of a party, arrange for anything said or written in the course of the proceedings before the Court or a Chamber to be translated into the languages he chooses from those referred to in Article 29(1).

2.   Publications of the Court shall be issued in the languages referred to in Article 1 of Council Regulation No 1.

Article 31

The texts of documents drawn up in the language of the case or in any other language authorized by the Court pursuant to Article 29 of these rules shall be authentic.

CHAPTER 7   RIGHTS AND OBLIGATIONS OF AGENTS, ADVISERS AND LAWYERS

Article 32

1.   Agents, advisers and lawyers, appearing before the Court or before any judicial authority to which the Court has addressed letters rogatory, shall enjoy immunity in respect of words spoken or written by them concerning the case or the parties.

2.   Agents, advisers and lawyers shall enjoy the following further privileges and facilities:

(a)   papers and documents relating to the proceedings shall be exempt from both search and seizure; in the event of a dispute the customs officials or police may seal those papers and documents; they shall then be immediately forwarded to the Court for inspection in the presence of the Registrar and of the person concerned;

(b)   agents, advisers and lawyers shall be entitled to such allocation of foreign currency as may be necessary for the performance of their duties;

(c)   agents, advisers and lawyers shall be entitled to travel in the course of duty without hindrance.

Article 33

In order to qualify for the privileges, immunities and facilities specified in Article 32, persons entitled to them shall furnish proof of their status as follows:

(a)   agents shall produce an official document issued by the party for whom they act, and shall forward without delay a copy thereof to the Registrar;

(b)   advisers and lawyers shall produce a certificate signed by the Registrar. The validity of this certificate shall be limited to a specified period, which may be extended or curtailed according to the length of the proceedings.

Article 34

The privileges, immunities and facilities specified in Article 32 of these Rules are granted exclusively in the interests of the proper conduct of proceedings. The Court may waive the immunity where it considers that the proper conduct of proceedings will not be hindered thereby.

Article 35

1.   Any adviser or lawyer whose conduct towards the Court, a Chamber, a Judge, an Advocate-General or the Registrar is incompatible with the dignity of the Court, or who uses his rights for purposes other than those for which they were granted, may at any time be excluded from the proceedings by an order of the Court or Chamber, after the Advocate-General has been heard; the person concerned shall be given an opportunity to defend himself. The order shall have immediate effect.

2.   Where an adviser or lawyer is excluded from the proceedings, the proceedings shall be suspended for a period fixed by the President in order to allow the party concerned to appoint another adviser or lawyer.

3.   Decisions taken under this Article may be rescinded.

Article 36

The provisions of this Chapter shall apply to university teachers who have a right of audience before the Court in accordance with Article 17 of the EC Statute, Article 20 of the ECSC Statute and Article 17 of the Euratom Statute.

TITLE II PROCEDURE
CHAPTER 1 WRITTEN PROCEDURE

Article 37

1.   The original of every pleading must be signed by the party's agent or lawyer.

The original, accompanied by all annexes referred to therein, shall be lodged together with five copies for the Court and a copy for every other party to the proceedings. Copies shall be certified by the party lodging them.

2.   Institutions shall in addition produce, within time-limits laid down by the Court, translations of all pleadings into the other languages provided for by Article 1 of Council Regulation No 1. The second subparagraph of paragraph (1) of this Article shall apply.

3.   All pleadings shall bear a date. In the reckoning of time-limits for taking steps in proceedings, only the date of lodgment at the Registry shall be taken into account.

4.   To every pleading there shall be annexed a file containing the documents relied on in support of it, together with a schedule listing them.

5.   Where in view of the length of a document only extracts from it are annexed to the pleading, the whole document or a full copy of it shall be lodged at the Registry.

Article 38

1.   An application of the kind referred to in Article 19 of the EC Statute, Article 22 of the ECSC Statute and Article 19 of the Euratom Statute shall state:

    (a)   the name and address of the applicant;

    (b)   the designation of the party against whom the application is made;

    (c)   the subject-matter of the proceedings and a summary of the pleas in law on which the application is based;

    (d)   the form of order sought by the applicant;

    (e)   where appropriate, the nature of any evidence offered in support.

2.   For the purpose of the proceedings, the application shall state an address for service in the place where the Court has its seat and the name of the person who is authorized and has expressed willingness to accept service.

If the application does not comply with these requirements, all service on the party concerned for the purpose of the proceedings shall be effected, for so long as the defect has not been cured, by registered letter addressed to the agent or lawyer of that party. By way of derogation from Article 79, service shall then be deemed to be duly effected by the lodging of the registered letter at the post office of the place where the Court has its seat.

3.   The lawyer acting for a party must lodge at the Registry a certificate that he is authorized to practise before a court of a Member State or of another State which is a party to the EEA Agreement.

4.   The application shall be accompanied, where appropriate, by the documents specified in the second paragraph of Article 19 of the EC Treaty, Article 22 of the ECSC Statute and in the second paragraph of Article 19 of the Euratom Statute.

5.   An application made by a legal person governed by private law shall be accompanied by:

(a)   the instrument or instruments constituting or regulating that legal person or a recent extract from the register of companies, firms or associations or any other proof of its existence in law;

(b)   proof that the authority granted to the applicant's lawyer has been properly conferred on him by someone authorized for the purpose.

6.   An application submitted under Articles 181 and 182 of the EEC Treaty, Articles 42 and 89 of the ECSC Treaty and Articles 153 and 154 of the Euratom Treaty shall be accompanied by a copy of the arbitration clause contained in the contract governed by private or public law entered into by the Communities or on their behalf, or, as the case may be, by a copy of the special agreement concluded between the Member States concerned.

7.   If an application does not comply with the requirements set out in paragraphs (3) to (6) of this Article, the Registrar shall prescribe a reasonable period within which the applicant is to comply with them whether by putting the application itself in order or by producing any of the abovementioned documents. If the applicant fails to put the application in order or to produce the required documents within the time prescribed, the Court shall, after hearing the Advocate-General, decide whether the noncompliance with these conditions renders the application formally inadmissible.

Article 39

The application shall be served on the defendant. In a case where Article 38(7) applies, service shall be effected as soon as the application has been put in order or the Court has declared it admissible notwithstanding the failure to observe the formal requirements set out in that Article.

Article 40

1.   Within one month after service on him of the application, the defendant shall lodge a defence, stating:

(a)   the name and address of the defendant;
(b)   the arguments of fact and law relied on;
(c)   the form of order sought by the defendant;
(d)   the nature of any evidence offered by him.

The provisions af Article 38(2) to (5) of these Rules shall apply to the defence.

2.   The time-limit laid down in paragraph (1) of this Article may be extended by the President on a reasoned application by the defendant.

Article 41

1.   The application initiating the proceedings and the defence may be supplemented by a reply from the applicant and by a rejoinder from the defendant.

2.   The President shall fix the time-limits within which these pleadings are to be lodged.

Article 42

1.   In reply or rejoinder a party may offer further evidence. The party must, however, give reasons for the delay in offering it.

2.   No new plea in law may be introduced in the course of proceedings unless it is based on matters of law or of fact which come to light in the course of the procedure.

If in the course of the procedure one of the parties puts forward a new plea in law which is so based, the President may, even after the expiry of the normal procedural time-limits, acting on a report of the Judge-Rapporteur and after hearing the Advocate-General, allow the other party time to answer on that plea.

The decision on the admissibility of the plea shall be reserved for the final judgment.

Article 43

The Court may, at any time, after hearing the parties and the Advocate-General, if the assignment referred to in Article 10(2) has taken place, order that two or more cases concerning the same subject-matter shall, on account of the connection between them, be joined for the purposes of the written or oral procedure or of the final judgment. The cases may subsequently be disjoined.

The President may refer these matters to the Court.

Article 44

1. After the rejoinder provided for in Article 41(1) of these Rules has been lodged, the President shall fix a date on which the Judge-Rapporteur is to present his preliminary report to the Court. The report shall contain recommendations as to whether a preparatory inquiry or any other preparatory step should be undertaken and whether the case should be referred to the Chamber to which it has been assigned under Article 9(2).

The Court shall decide, after hearing the Advocate-General, what action to take upon the recommendations of the Judge-Rapporteur.

The same procedure shall apply:

(a) where no reply or no rejoinder has been lodged within the time-limit fixed in accordance with Article 41(2) of these Rules;

(b) where the party concerned waives his right to lodge a reply or rejoinder.

2. Where the Court orders a preparatory inquiry and does not undertake it itself, it shall assign the inquiry to the Chamber. Where the Court decides to open the oral procedure without an inquiry, the President shall fix the opening date.

Article 44(a)

Without prejudice to any special provisions laid down in these Rules, and except in the specific cases in which, after the pleadings referred to in Article 40(1) and, as the case may be, in Article 41(1) have been lodged, the Court, acting on a report from the Judge-Rapporteur, after hearing the Advocate-General and with the express consent of the parties, decides otherwise, the procedure before the Court shall also include an oral part.

CHAPTER 2   PREPARATORY INQUIRIES
SECTION 1   MEASURES OF INQUIRY

Article 45

1. The Court, after hearing the Advocate-General, shall prescribe the measures of inquiry that it considers appropriate by means of an order setting out the facts to be proved. Before the Court decides on the measures of inquiry referred to in paragraph (2)(c), (d) and (e) the parties shall be heard.

The order shall be served on the parties.

2. Without prejudice to Articles 21 and 22 of the EC Statute, Articles 24 and 25 of the ECSC Statute or Articles 22 and 23 of the Euratom Statute, the following measures of inquiry may be adopted:

    (a)   the personal appearance of the parties;
    (b)   a request for information and production of documents;
    (c)   oral testimony;
    (d)   the commissioning of an expert's report;
    (e)   an inspection of the place or thing in question.

3.   The measures of inquiry which the Court has ordered may be conducted by the Court itself, or be assigned to the Judge-Rapporteur.

The Advocate-General shall take part in the measures of inquiry.

4.   Evidence may be submitted in rebuttal and previous evidence may be amplified.

Article 46

1.   A Chamber to which a preparatory inquiry has been assigned may exercise the powers vested in the Court by Articles 45 and 47 to 53 of these Rules; the powers vested in the President of the Court may be exercised by the President of the Chamber.

2.   Articles 56 and 57 of the Rules shall apply in a corresponding manner to proceedings before the Chamber.

3.   The parties shall be entitled to attend the measures of inquiry.

SECTION 2   THE SUMMONING AND EXAMINATION OF WITNESSES AND EXPERTS

Article 47

1.   The Court may, either of its own motion or an application by a party, and after hearing the Advocate-General, order that certain facts be proved by witnesses. The order of the Court shall set out the facts to be established.

The Court may summon a witness of its own motion or on application by a party or at the instance of the Advocate-General.

An application by a party for the examination of a witness shall state precisely about what facts and for what reasons the witness should be examined.

2.   The witness shall be summoned by an order of the Court containing the following information:

    (a)   the surname, forenames, description and address of the witness;
    (b)   an indication of the facts about which the witness is to be examined;
    (c)   where appropriate, particulars of the arrangements made by the Court for reimbursement of expenses incurred by the witness, and of the penalties which may be imposed on defaulting witnesses.

The order shall be served on the parties and the witnesses.

3.   The Court may make the summoning of a witness for whose examination a party has applied conditional upon the deposit with the cashier of the Court of a sum sufficient to cover the taxed costs thereof; the Court shall fix the amount of the payment.

The cashier shall advance the funds necessary in connection with the examination of any witness summoned by the Court of its own motion.

4.   After the identity of the witness has been established, the President shall inform him that he will be required to vouch the truth of his evidence in the manner laid down in these Rules.

The witness shall give his evidence to the Court, the parties having been given notice to attend. After the witness has given his main evidence the President may, at the request of a party or of his own motion, put questions to him.

The other Judges and the Advocate-General may do likewise. Subject to the control of the President, questions may be put to witnesses by the representatives of the parties.

5.   After giving his evidence, the witness shall take the following oath:
'I swear that I have spoken the truth, the whole truth and nothing but the truth.'

The Court may, after hearing the parties, exempt a witness from taking the oath.

6.   The Registrar shall draw up minutes in which the evidence of each witness is reproduced.

The minutes shall be signed by the President or by the Judge-Rapporteur responsible for conducting the examination of the witness, and by the Registrar. Before the minutes are thus signed, witnesses must be given an opportunity to check the content of the minutes and to sign them.

The minutes shall constitute an official record.

Article 48

1.   Witnesses who have been duly summoned shall obey the summons and attend for examination.

2.   If a witness who has been duly summoned fails to appear before the Court, the Court may impose upon him a pecuniary penalty not exceeding ECU 5,000 and may order that a further summons be served on the witness at his own expense.

The same penalty may be imposed upon a witness who, without good reason, refuses to give evidence or to take the oath or where appropriate to make a solemn affirmation equivalent thereto.

3.   If the witness proffers a valid excuse to the Court, the pecuniary penalty imposed on him may be cancelled. The pecuniary penalty imposed may be reduced at the request of the witness where he establishes that it is disproportionate to his income.

4.   Penalties imposed and other measures ordered under this Article shall be enforced in accordance with Articles 187 and 192 of the EC Treaty, Articles 44 and 92 of the ECSC Treaty and Articles 159 and 164 of the Euratom Treaty.

Article 49

1.   The Court may order that an expert's report be obtained. The order appointing the expert shall define his task and set a time-limit within which he is to make his report.

2.   The expert shall receive a copy of the order, together with all the documents necessary for carrying out his task. He shall be under the supervision of the Judge-Rapporteur, who may be present during his investigation and who shall be kept informed of his progress in carrying out his task.

The Court may request the parties or one of them to lodge security for the costs of the expert's report.

3.   At the request of the expert, the Court may order the examination of witnesses. Their examination shall be carried out in accordance with Article 47 of these Rules.

4.   The expert may give his opinion only on points which have been expressly referred to him.

5.   After the expert has made his report, the Court may order that he be examined, the parties having been given notice to attend. Subject to the control

of the President, questions may be put to the expert by the representatives of the parties.

6.   After making his report, the expert shall take the following oath before the Court:

'I swear that I have conscientiously and impartially carried out my task.'

The Court may, after hearing the parties, exempt the expert from taking the oath.

Article 50

1.   If one of the parties objects to a witness or to an expert on the ground that he is not a competent or proper person to act as witness or expert or for any other reason, or if a witness or expert refuses to give evidence, to take the oath or to make a solemn affirmation equivalent thereto, the matter shall be resolved by the Court.

2.   An objection to a witness or to an expert shall be raised within two weeks after service of the order summoning the witness or appointing the expert; the statement of objection must set out the grounds of objection and indicate the nature of any evidence offered.

Article 51

1.   Witnesses and experts shall be entitled to reimbursement of their travel and subsistence expenses. The cashier of the Court may make a payment to them towards these expenses in advance.

2.   Witnesses shall be entitled to compensation for loss of earnings, and experts to fees for their services. The cashier of the Court shall pay witnesses and experts their compensation or fees after they have carried out their respective duties or tasks.

Article 52

The Court may, on application by a party or of its own motion, issue letters rogatory for the examination of witnesses or experts, as provided for in the supplementary rules mentioned in Article 125 of these Rules.

Article 53

1.   The Registrar shall draw up minutes of every hearing. The minutes shall be signed by the President and by the Registrar and shall constitute an official record.

2.   The parties may inspect the minutes and any expert's report at the Registry and obtain copies at their own expense.

SECTION 3   CLOSURE OF THE PREPARATORY INQUIRY

Article 54

Unless the Court prescribes a period within which the parties may lodge written observations, the President shall fix the date for the opening of the oral procedure after the preparatory inquiry has been completed. Where a period had been prescribed for the lodging of written observations, the President shall fix the date for the opening of the oral procedure after that period has expired.

CHAPTER 3   ORAL PROCEDURE

Article 55

1.   Subject to the priority of decisions provided for in Article 85 of these Rules, the Court shall deal with the cases before it in the order in which the

preparatory inquiries in them have been completed. Where the preparatory inquiries in several cases are completed simultaneously, the order in which they are to be dealt with shall be determined by the dates of entry in the register of the applications initiating them respectively.

2. The President may in special circumstances order that a case be given priority over others.

The President may in special circumstances, after hearing the parties and the Advocate-General, either on his own initiative or at the request of one of the parties, defer a case to be dealt with at a later date. On a joint application by the parties the President may order that a case be deferred.

Article 56

1. The proceedings shall be opened and directed by the President, who shall be responsible for the proper conduct of the hearing.

2. The oral proceedings in cases heard in camera shall not be published.

Article 57

The President may in the course of the hearing put questions to the agents, advisers or lawyers of the parties.

The other Judges and the Advocate-General may do likewise.

Article 58

A party may address the Court only through his agent, adviser or lawyer.

Article 59

1. The Advocate-General shall deliver his opinion orally at the end of the oral procedure.

2. After the Advocate-General has delivered his opinion, the President shall declare the oral procedure closed.

Article 60

The Court may at any time, in accordance with Article 45(1), after hearing the Advocate-General, order any measure of inquiry to be taken or that a previous inquiry be repeated or expanded. The Court may direct the Chamber or the Judge-Rapporteur to carry out the measures so ordered.

Article 61

The Court may after hearing the Advocate-General order the reopening of the oral procedure.

Article 62

1. The Registrar shall draw up minutes of every hearing. The minutes shall be signed by the President and by the Registrar and shall constitute an official record.

2. The parties may inspect the minutes at the Registry and obtain copies at their own expense.

CHAPTER 4   JUDGMENTS

Article 63

The judgment shall contain:
— a statement that it is the judgment of the Court,
— the date of its delivery,
— the names of the President and of the Judges taking part in it,

— the name of the Advocate-General,
— the name of the Registrar,
— the description of the parties,
— the names of the agents, advisers and lawyers of the parties,
— a statement of the forms of order sought by the parties,
— a statement that the Advocate-General has been heard,
— a summary of the facts,
— the grounds for the decision,
— the operative part of the judgment, including the decision as to costs.

Article 64

1.   The judgment shall be delivered in open court; the parties shall be given notice to attend to hear it.

2.   The original of the judgment, signed by the President, by the Judges who took part in the deliberations and by the Registrar, shall be sealed and deposited at the Registry; the parties shall be served with certified copies of the judgment.

3.   The Registrar shall record on the original of the judgment the date on which it was delivered.

Article 65

The judgment shall be binding from the date of its delivery.

Article 66

1.   Without prejudice to the provisions relating to the interpretation of judgments the Court may, of its own motion or on application by a party made within two weeks after the delivery of a judgment, rectify clerical mistakes, errors in calculation and obvious slips in it.

2.   The parties, whom the Registrar shall duly notify, may lodge written observations within a period prescribed by the President.

3.   The Court shall take its decision in closed session after hearing the Advocate-General.

4.   The original of the rectification order shall be annexed to the original of the rectified judgment. A note of this order shall be made in the margin of the original of the rectified judgment.

Article 67

If the Court should omit to give a decision on a specific head of claim or on costs, any party may within a month after service of the judgment apply to the Court to supplement its judgment.

The application shall be served on the opposite party and the President shall prescribe a period within which that party may lodge written observations. After these observations have been lodged, the Court shall, after hearing the Advocate-General, decide both on the admissibility and on the substance of the application.

Article 68

The Registrar shall arrange for the publication of reports of cases before the Court.

CHAPTER 5   COSTS

Article 69

1.   A decision as to costs shall be given in the final judgment or in the order which closes the proceedings.

2.   The unsuccessful party shall be ordered to pay the costs if they have been applied for in the successful party's pleadings. Where there are several unsuccessful parties the Court shall decide how the costs are to be shared.

3.   Where each party succeeds on some and fails on other heads, or where the circumstances are exceptional, the Court may order that the costs be shared or that the parties bear their own costs. The Court may order a party, even if successful, to pay costs which the Court considers that party to have unreasonably or vexatiously caused the opposite party to incur.

4.   The Member States and institutions which intervene in the proceedings shall bear their own costs. The States, other than Member States, which are parties to the EEA Agreement, and also the EFTA Surveillance Authority, shall bear their own costs if they intervene in the proceedings. The Court may order an intervener other than those mentioned in the preceding subparagraph to bear his own costs.

5.   A party who discontinues or withdraws from proceedings shall be ordered to pay the costs if they have been applied for in the other party's observations on the discontinuance pleadings. However, upon application by the party who discontinues or withdraws from proceedings, the costs shall be borne by the other party if this appears justified by the conduct of that party. Where the parties have come to an agreement on costs, the decision as to costs shall be in accordance with that agreement.

If costs are not applied for, the parties shall bear their own costs.

6.   Where a case does not proceed to judgment the costs shall be in the discretion of the Court.

Article 70
Without prejudice to the second subparagraph of Article 69(3) of these Rules, in proceedings between the Communities and their servants the institutions shall bear their own costs.

Article 71
Costs necessarily incurred by a party in enforcing a judgment or order of the Court shall be refunded by the opposite party on the scale in force in the State where the enforcement takes place.

Article 72
Proceedings before the Court shall be free of charge, except that:

(a)   where a party has caused the Court to incur avoidable costs the Court may, after hearing the Advocate General, order that party to refund them;

(b)   where copying or translation work is carried out at the request of a party, the cost shall, in so far as the Registrar considers it excessive, be paid for by that party on the scale of charges referred to in Article 16(5) of these Rules.

Article 73
Without prejudice to the preceding Article, the following shall be regarded as recoverable costs:

(a)   sums payable to witnesses and experts under Article 51 of these Rules;

(b)   expenses necessarily incurred by the parties for the purpose of the proceedings, in particular the travel and subsistence expenses and the remuneration of agents, advisers or lawyers.

Article 74

1.   If there is a dispute concerning the costs to be recovered, the Chamber to which the case has been assigned shall, on application by the party concerned and after hearing the opposite party and the Advocate-General, make an order, from which no appeal shall lie.

2.   The parties may, for the purposes of enforcement, apply for an authenticated copy of the order.

Article 75

1.   Sums due from the cashier of the Court shall be paid in the currency of the country where the Court has its seat.

At the request of the person entitled to any sum, it shall be paid in the currency of the country where the expenses to be refunded were incurred or where the steps in respect of which payment is due were taken.

2.   Other debtors shall make payment in the currency of their country of origin.

3.   Conversions of currency shall be made at the official rates of exchange ruling on the day of payment in the country where the Court has its seat.

CHAPTER 6   LEGAL AID

Article 76

1.   A party who is wholly or in part unable to meet the costs of the proceedings may at any time apply for legal aid.

The application shall be accompanied by evidence of the applicant's need of assistance, and in particular by a document from the competent authority certifying his lack of means.

2.   If the application is made prior to proceedings which the applicant wishes to commence, it shall briefly state the subject of such proceedings.

The application need not be made through a lawyer.

3.   The President shall designate a Judge to act as Rapporteur. The Chamber to which the latter belongs shall, after considering the written observations of the opposite party and after hearing the Advocate-General, decide whether legal aid should be granted in full or in part, or whether it should be refused. The Chamber shall consider whether there is manifestly no cause of action.

The Chamber shall make an order without giving reasons, and no appeal shall lie thereform.

4.   The Chamber may at any time, either of its own motion or on application, withdraw legal aid if the circumstances which led to its being granted alter during the proceedings.

5.   Where legal aid is granted, the cashier of the Court shall advance the funds necessary to meet the expenses. In its decision as to costs the Court may order the payment to the cashier of the Court of the whole or any part of amounts advanced as legal aid.

The Registrar shall take steps to obtain the recovery of these sums from the party ordered to pay them.

CHAPTER 7   DISCONTINUANCE

Article 77

If, before the Court has given its decision, the parties reach a settlement of their dispute and intimate to the Court the abandonment of their claims, the

President shall order the case to be removed from the register and shall give a decision as to costs in accordance with Article 69(5), having regard to any proposals made by the parties on the matter.

This provision shall not apply to proceedings under Articles 173 and 175 of the EC Treaty, Articles 33 and 35 of the ECSC Treaty or Articles 146 and 148 of the Euratom Treaty.

Article 78

If the applicant informs the Court in writing that he wishes to discontinue the proceedings, the President shall order the case to be removed from the register and shall give a decision as to costs in accordance with Article 69(5).

CHAPTER 8   SERVICE

Article 79

Where these Rules require that a document be served on a person, the Registrar shall ensure that service is effected at that person's address for service either by the dispatch of a copy of the document by registered post with a form for acknowledgement of receipt or by personal delivery of the copy against a receipt.

The Registrar shall prepare and certify the copies of documents to be served, save where the parties themselves supply the copies in accordance with Article 37(1) of these Rules.

CHAPTER 9   TIME LIMITS

Article 80

1.   Any period of time prescribed by the EC, ECSC or Euratom Treaties, the Statutes of the Court or these Rules for the taking of any procedural step shall be reckoned as follows:

(a)   where a period expressed in days, weeks, months or years is to be calculated from the moment at which an event occurs or an action takes place, the day during which that event occurs or that action takes place shall not be counted as falling within the period in question;

(b)   a period expressed in weeks, months or in years shall end with the expiry of whichever day in the last week, month or year is the same day of the week, or falls on the same date, as the day during which the event or action from which the period is to be calculated occurred or took place. If, in a period expressed in months or in years, the day on which it should expire does not occur in the last month, the period shall end with the expiry of the last day of that month;

(c)   where a period is expressed in months and days, it shall first be reckoned in whole months, then in days;

(d)   periods shall include official holidays, Sundays and Saturdays;

(e)   periods shall not be suspended during the judicial vacations.

2.   If the period would otherwise end on a Saturday, Sunday or an official holiday, it shall be extended until the end of the first following working day.

A list of official holidays drawn up by the Court shall be published in the Official Journal of the European Communities.

Article 81

1.   Where the period of time allowed for initiating proceedings against a measure adopted by an institution runs from the publication of that measure,

that period shall be calculated, for the purposes of Article 80(1)(a), from the end of the 14th day after publication thereof in the *Official Journal of the European Communities*.

2.   The extensions, on account of distance, of prescribed time limits shall be provided for in a decision of the Court which shall be published in the Official Journal of the European Communities.

Article 82
Any time limit prescribed pursuant to these Rules may be extended by whoever prescribed it.

The President and the Presidents of Chambers may delegate to the Registrar power of signature for the purpose of fixing time limits which, pursuant to these Rules, it falls to them to prescribe or of extending such time limits.

CHAPTER 10   STAY OF PROCEEDINGS

Article 82a
1.   The proceedings may be stayed:

   (a)   in the circumstances specified in the third paragraph of Article 47 of the EC Statute, the third paragraph of Article 47 of the ECSC Statute and the third paragraph of Article 48 of the Euratom Statute, by order of the Court or of the Chamber to which the case has been assigned, made after hearing the Advocate-General;

   (b)   in all other cases, by decision of the President adopted after hearing the Advocate-General and, save in the case of references for a preliminary ruling as referred to in Article 103, the parties.

The proceedings may be resumed by order or decision, following the same procedure.

The orders or decisions referred to in this paragraph shall be served on the parties.

2.   The stay of proceedings shall take effect on the date indicated in the order or decision of stay or, in the absence of such indication, on the date of that order or decision.

While proceedings are stayed time shall cease to run for the purposes of prescribed time limits for all parties.

3.   Where the order or decision of stay does not fix the length of stay, it shall end on the date indicated in the order or decision of resumption or, in the absence of such indication, on the date of the order or decision of resumption.

From the date of resumption time shall begin to run afresh for the purposes of the time limits.

TITLE III   SPECIAL FORMS OF PROCEDURE
CHAPTER 1   SUSPENSION OF OPERATION OR ENFORCEMENT AND OTHER INTERIM MEASURES

Article 83
1.   An application to suspend the operation of any measure adopted by an institution, made pursuant to Article 185 of the EC Treaty, the second paragraph of Article 39 of the ECSC Treaty or Article 157 of the Euratom Treaty, shall be admissible only if the applicant is challenging that measure in proceedings before the Court.

An application for the adoption of any other interim measure referred to in the third paragraph of Article 39 of the ECSC Treaty, Article 186 of the EEC Treaty or Article 158 of the Euratom Treaty shall be admissible only if it is made by a party to a case before the Court and relates to that case.

2.   An application of a kind referred to in paragraph (1) of this Article shall state the subject-matter of the proceedings, the circumstances giving rise to urgency and the pleas of fact and law establishing a prima facie case for the interim measures applied for.

3.   The application shall be made by a separate document and in accordance with the provisions of Articles 37 and 38 of these Rules.

Article 84

1.   The application shall be served on the opposite party, and the President shall prescribe a short period within which that party may submit written or oral observations.

2.   The President may order a preparatory inquiry.

The President may grant the application even before the observations of the opposite party have been submitted. This decision may be varied or cancelled even without any application being made by any party.

Article 85

The President shall either decide on the application himself or refer it to the Court.

If the President is absent or prevented from attending, Article 11 of these Rules shall apply.

Where the application is referred to it, the Court shall postpone all other cases, and shall give a decision after hearing the Advocate-General. Article 84 shall apply.

Article 86

1.   The decision on the application shall take the form of a reasoned order, from which no appeal shall lie. The order shall be served on the parties forthwith.

2.   The enforcement of the order may be made conditional on the lodging by the applicant of security, of an amount and nature to be fixed in the light of the cirumstances.

3.   Unless the order fixes the date on which the interim measure is to lapse, the measure shall lapse when final judgment is delivered.

4.   The order shall have only an interim effect, and shall be without prejudice to the decision of the Court on the substance of the case.

Article 87

On application by a party, the order may at any time be varied or cancelled on account of a change in circumstances.

Article 88

Rejection of an application for an interim measure shall not bar the party who made it from making a further application on the basis of new facts.

Article 89

The provisions of this Chapter shall apply to applications to suspend the enforcement of a decision of the Court or of any measure adopted by another institution, submitted pursuant to Articles 187 and 192 of the EC Treaty,

Articles 44 and 92 of the ECSC Treaty or Articles 159 and 164 of the Euratom Treaty.

The order granting the application shall fix, where appropriate, a date on which the interim measure is to lapse.

Article 90

1. An application of a kind referred to in the third and fourth paragraphs of Article 81 of the Euratom Treaty shall contain:

(a) the names and addresses of the persons or undertakings to be inspected;

(b) an indication of what is to be inspected and of the purpose of the inspection.

2. The President shall give his decision in the form of an order. Article 86 of these Rules shall apply.

If the President is absent or prevented from attending, Article 11 of these Rules shall apply.

CHAPTER 2   PRELIMINARY ISSUES

Article 91

1. A party applying to the Court for a decision on a preliminary objection or other preliminary plea not going to the substance of the case shall make the application by a separate document.

The application must state the pleas of fact and law relied on and the form of order sought by the applicant; any supporting documents must be annexed to it.

2. As soon as the application has been lodged, the President shall prescribe a period within which the opposite party may lodge a document containing a statement of the form of order sought by that party and its pleas in law.

3. Unless the Court decides otherwise, the remainder of the proceedings shall be oral.

4. The Court shall, after hearing the Advocate-General, decide on the application or reserve its decision for the final judgment.

If the Court refuses the application or reserves its decision, the President shall prescribe new time-limits for the further steps in the proceedings.

Article 92

1. Where it is clear that the Court has no jurisdiction to take cognizance of an action or where the action is manifestly inadmissible, the Court may, by reasoned order, after hearing the Advocate-General and without taking further steps in the proceedings, give a decision on the action.

2. The Court may at any time of its own motion consider whether there exists any absolute bar to proceeding with a case or declare, after hearing the parties, that the action has become devoid of purpose and that there is no need to adjudicate on it, it shall give its decision in accordance with Article 91 (3) and (4) of these Rules.

CHAPTER 3   INTERVENTION

Article 93

1. An application to intervene must be made within three months of the publication of the notice referred to in Article 16 (6) of these Rules.

The application shall contain:

    (a)   the description of the case;

    (b)   the description of the parties;

    (c)   the name and address of the intervener;

    (d)   the intervener's address for service at the place where the Court has its seat;

    (e)   the form of order sought, by one or more of the parties, in support of which the intervener is applying for leave to intervene;

    (f)   a statement of the circumstances establishing the right to intervene, where the application is submitted pursuant to the second or third paragraph of Article 37 of the EC Statute, Article 34 of the ECSC Statute or the second paragraph of Article 38 of the Euratom Statute;

The intervener shall be represented in accordance with Article 17 of the EC Statute, Article 20 of the ECSC Statute and Article 17 of the Euratom Statutes.

Articles 37 and 38 of these Rules shall apply.

2.   The application shall be served on the parties.

The President shall give the parties an opportunity to submit their written or oral observations before deciding on the application.

The President shall decide on the application by order or shall refer the application to the Court.

3.   If the President allows the intervention, the intervener shall receive a copy of every document served on the parties. The President may, however, on application by one of the parties, omit secret or confidential documents.

4.   The intervener must accept the case as he finds it at the time of his intervention.

5.   The President shall prescribe a period within which the intervener may submit a statement in intervention.

The statement in intervention shall contain:

    (a)   a statement of the form of order sought by the intervener in support of or opposing, in whole or in part, the form of order sought by one of the parties;

    (b)   the pleas in law and arguments relied on by the intervener;

    (c)   where appropriate, the nature of any evidence offered.

6.   After the statement in intervention has been lodged, the President shall, where necessary, prescribe a time-limit within which the parties may reply to that statement.

CHAPTER 4   JUDGMENTS BY DEFAULT AND APPLICATIONS TO SET THEM ASIDE

Article 94

1.   If a defendant on whom an application initiating proceedings has been duly served fails to lodge a defence to the application in the proper form within the time prescribed, the applicant may apply for judgment by default. The application shall be served on the defendant. The President shall fix a date for the opening of the oral procedure.

2.   Before giving judgment by default the Court shall, after hearing the Advocate-General, consider whether the application initiating proceedings is admissible, whether the appropriate formalities have been complied with, and whether the application appears well founded. The Court may decide to open the oral procedure on the application.

3.   A judgment by default shall be enforceable. The Court may, however, grant a stay of execution until the Court has given its decision on any application under paragraph (4) to set aside the judgment, or it may make execution subject to the provision of security of an amount and nature to be fixed in the light of the circumstances; this security shall be released if no such application is made or if the application fails.

4.   Application may be made to set aside a judgment by default. The application to set aside the judgment must be made within one month from the date of service of the judgment and must be lodged in the form prescribed by Articles 37 and 38 of these Rules.

5.   After the application has been served, the President shall prescribe a period within which the other party may submit his written observations. The proceedings shall be conducted in accordance with Articles 44 et seq. of these Rules.

6.   The Court shall decide by way of a judgment which may not be set aside. The original of this judgment shall be annexed to the original of the judgment by default. A note of the judgment on the application to set aside shall be made in the margin of the original of the judgment by default.

CHAPTER 5   CASES ASSIGNED TO CHAMBERS

Article 95

1.   The Court may assign any case brought before it to a Chamber insofar as the difficulty or importance of the case or particular circumstances are not such as to require that the Court decide it in plenary session.

2.   The decision so to assign a case shall be taken by the Court at the end of the written procedure upon consideration of the preliminary report presented by the Judge-Rapporteur and after the Advocate-General has been heard. However, a case may not be so assigned if a Member State or an institution of the Communities, being a party to the proceedings, has requested that the case be decided in plenary session. In this subparagraph the expression 'party to the proceedings' means any Member State or any institution which is a party to or an intervener in the proceedings or which has submitted written observations in any reference of a kind mentioned in Article 103 of these Rules.

The request referred to in the preceding subparagraph may not be made in proceedings between the Communities and their servants.

3.   A Chamber may at any stage refer a case back to the Court.

Article 96
(repealed)

CHAPTER 6   EXCEPTIONAL REVIEW PROCEDURES
SECTION 1   THIRD-PARTY PROCEEDINGS

Article 97

1.   Articles 37 and 38 of these Rules shall apply to an application initiating third-party proceedings. In addition such an application shall:

(a)   specify the judgment contested;

(b)   state how that judgment is prejudicial to the rights of the third party;

(c)   indicate the reasons for which the third party was unable to take part in the original case.

The application must be made against all the parties to the original case. Where the judgment has been published in the Official Journal of the European

Communities, the application must be lodged within two months of the publication.

2.   The Court may, on application by the third party, order a stay of execution of the judgment. The provisions of Title III, Chapter 1, of these Rules shall apply.

3.   The contested judgment shall be varied on the points on which the submissions of the third party are upheld.

The original of the judgment in the third-party proceedings shall be annexed to the original of the contested judgment. A note of the judgment in the third-party proceedings shall be made in the margin of the original of the contested judgment.

SECTION 2   REVISION

Article 98

An application for revision of a judgment shall be made within three months of the date on which the facts on which the application is based came to the applicant's knowledge.

Article 99

1.   Articles 37 and 38 of these Rules shall apply to an application for revision. In addition such an application shall:

(a)   specify the judgment contested;

(b)   indicate the points on which the judgment is contested;

(c)   set out the facts on which the application is based;

(d)   indicate the nature of the evidence to show that there are facts justifying revision of the judgment, and that the time-limit laid down in Article 98 has been observed.

2.   The application must be made against all parties to the case in which the contested judgment was given.

Article 100

1.   Without prejudice to its decision on the substance, the Court, in closed session, shall, after hearing the Advocate-General and having regard to the written observations of the parties, give in the form of a judgment its decision on the admissibility of the application.

2.   If the Court finds the application admissible, it shall proceed to consider the substance of the application and shall give its decision in the form of a judgment in accordance with these Rules.

3.   The original of the revising judgment shall be annexed to the original of the judgment revised. A note of the revising judgment shall be made in the margin of the original of the judgment revised.

CHAPTER 7   APPEALS AGAINST DECISIONS OF THE ARBITRATION COMMITTEE

Article 101

1.   An application initiating an appeal under the second paragraph of Article 18 of the Euratom Treaty shall state:

(a)   the name and address of the applicant;

(b)   the description of the signatory;

(c)   a reference to the arbitration committee's decision against which the appeal is made;

    (d)   the description of the parties;

    (e)   a summary of the facts;

    (f)   the pleas in law of and the form of order sought by the applicant.

2.   Articles 37 (3) and (4) and 38 (2), (3) and (5) of these Rules shall apply. A certified copy of the contested decision shall be annexed to the application.

3.   As soon as the application has been lodged, the Registrar of the Court shall request the arbitration committee registry to transmit to the Court the papers in the case.

4.   Articles 39, 40, 55 et seq. of these Rules shall apply to these papers.

5.   The Court shall give its decision in the form of a judgment. Where the Court sets aside the decision of the arbitration committee it may refer the case back to the committee.

CHAPTER 8   INTERPRETATION OF JUDGMENTS

Article 102

1.   An application for interpretation of a judgment shall be made in accordance with Articles 37 and 38 of these Rules. In addition it shall specify:

    (a)   the judgment in question;

    (b)   the passages of which interpretation is sought.

The application must be made against all the parties to the case in which the judgment was given.

2.   The Court shall give its decision in the form of a judgment after having given the parties an opportunity to submit their observations and after hearing the Advocate-General.

The original of the interpreting judgment shall be annexed to the original of the judgment interpreted. A note of the interpreting judgment shall be made in the margin of the original of the judgment interpreted.

CHAPTER 9   PRELIMINARY RULINGS AND OTHER REFERENCES FOR INTERPRETATION

Article 103

1.   In cases governed by Article 20 of the EC Statute and Article 21 of the Euratom Statute, the procedure shall be governed by the provisions of these Rules, subject to adaptations necessitated by the nature of the reference for a preliminary ruling.

2.   The provisions of paragraph (1) shall apply to the references for a preliminary ruling provided for in the Protocol concerning the interpretation by the Court of Justice of the Convention of 29 February 1968 on the mutual recognition of companies and legal persons and the Protocol concerning the interpretation by the Court of Justice of the Convention of 27 September 1968 on jurisdiction and the enforcement of judgments in civil and commercial matters, signed at Luxembourg on 3 June 1971, and to the references provided for by Article 4 of the latter Protocol.

The provisions of paragraph (1) shall apply also to references for interpretation provided for by other existing or future agreements.

3.   In cases provided for in Article 41 of the ECSC Treaty, the text of the decision to refer the matter shall be served on the parties in the case, the Member States, the Commission and the Council.

These parties, States and institutions may, within two months from the date of such service, lodge written statements of case or written observations.

The provisions of paragraph (1) shall apply.

Article 104

1.   The decisions of national courts or tribunals referred to in Article 103 shall be communicated to the Member States in the original version, accompanied by a translation into the official language of the State to which they are addressed.

In the cases governed by Article 20 of the EC Statute, the decisions of national courts or tribunals shall be notified to the States, other than the Member States, which are parties to the EEA Agreement, and also to the EFTA Surveillance Authority, in the original version, accompanied by a translation into one of the languages mentioned in Article 29(1), to be chosen by the addressee of the notification.

2.   As regards the representation and attendance of the parties to the main proceedings in the preliminary ruling procedure the Court shall take account of the rules of procedure of the national court or tribunal which made the reference.

3.   Where a question referred to the Court for a preliminary ruling is manifestly identical to a question on which the Court has already ruled, the Court may, after informing the court or tribunal which referred the question to it, hearing any observations submitted by the persons referred to in Article 20 of the EC Statute, Article 21 of the Euratom Statute and Article 103 (3) of these Rules and hearing the Advocate-General, give its decision by reasoned order in which reference is made to its previous judgment.

4.   Without prejudice to paragraph (3) of this Article, the procedure before the Court in the case of a reference for a preliminary ruling shall also include an oral part. However, after the statements of case or written observations referred to in Article 20 of the EC Statute, Article 21 of the Euratom Statute and Article 103(3) of these Rules have been submitted, the Court, acting on a report from the Judge-Rapporteur, after informing the persons who under the aforementioned provisions are entitled to submit such statements or observations, may, after hearing the Advocate-General, decide otherwise, provided that none of those persons has asked to present oral argument.

5.   It shall be for the national court or tribunal to decide as to the costs of the reference.

In special circumstances the Court may grant, by way of legal aid, assistance for the purpose of facilitating the representation or attendance of a party.

CHAPTER 10   SPECIAL PROCEDURES UNDER ARTICLES 103 TO 105 OF THE EURATOM TREATY

Article 105

1.   Four certified copies shall be lodged of an application under the third paragraph of Article 103 of the Euratom Treaty. The Commission shall be served with a copy.

2.   The application shall be accompanied by the draft of the agreement or contract in question, by the observations of the Commission addressed to the State concerned and by all other supporting documents.

The Commission shall submit its observations to the Court within a period of 10 days, which may be extended by the President after the State concerned has been heard.

A certified copy of the observations shall be served on that State.

3.   As soon as the application has been lodged the President shall designate a Judge to act as Rapporteur.

The First Advocate-General shall assign the case to an Advocate-General as soon as the Judge-Rapporteur has been designated.

4.   The decision shall be taken in closed session after the Advocate-General has been heard.

The agents and advisers of the State concerned and of the Commission shall be heard if they so request.

Article 106

1.   In cases provided for in the last paragraph of Article 104 and the last paragraph of Article 105 of the Euratom Treaty, the provisions of Articles 37 et seq. of these Rules shall apply.

2.   The application shall be served on the State to which the respondent person or undertaking belongs.

CHAPTER 11   OPINIONS

Article 107

1.   A request by the Council for an opinion pursuant to Article 228 of the EC Treaty shall be served on the Commission and on the European Parliament. Such a request by the Commission shall be served on the Council, on the European Parliament and or the Member States. Such a request by a Member State shall be served on the Council, on the European Parliament and or the Member States. Such a request by a Member State shall be served on the Council, on the Commission, on the European Parliament and the other Member States.

The President shall prescribe a period within which the institutions and Member States which have been served with a request may submit their written observations.

2.   The Opinion may deal not only with the question whether the envisaged agreement is compatible which the provisions of the EC Treaty but also with the question whether the Community or any Community institution has the power to enter into that agreement.

Article 108

1.   As soon as the request for an Opinion has been lodged, the President shall designate a Judge to act as Rapporteur.

2.   The Court sitting in closed session shall, after hearing the Advocates-General, deliver a reasoned Opinion.

3.   The Opinion, signed by the President, by the Judges who took part in the deliberations and by the Registrar, shall be served on the Council, the Commission, the European Parliament and the Member States.

Article 109

Requests for the Opinion of the Court under the fourth paragraph of Article 95 of the ECSC Treaty shall be submitted jointly by the Commission and the Council.

The Opinion shall be delivered in accordance with the provisions of the preceding Article. It shall be communicated to the Commission, the Council and the European Parliament.

TITLE IV   APPEALS AGAINST DECISIONS OF THE COURT
OF FIRST INSTANCE

Article 110

Without prejudice to the arrangements laid down in Article 29 (2) (b) and (c) and the fourth subparagraph of Article 29 (3) of these Rules, in appeals against decisions of the Court of First Instance as referred to in Articles 49 and 50 of the EC Statute, Articles 49 and 50 of the ECSC Statute and Articles 50 and 51 of the Euratom Statute, the language of the case shall be the language of the decision of the Court of First Instance against which the appeal is brought.

Article 111

1.   An appeal shall be brought by lodging an application at the Registry of the Court of Justice or of the Court of First Instance.

2.   The Registry of the Court of First Instance shall immediately transmit to the Registry of the Court of Justice the papers in the case at first instance and, where necessary, the appeal.

Article 112

1.   An appeal shall contain:

(a)   the name and address of the appellant;

(b)   the names of the other parties to the proceedings before the Court of First Instance;

(c)   the pleas in law and legal arguments relied on;

(d)   the form or order sought by the appellant.

Article 37 and Article 38 (2) and (3) of these Rules shall apply to appeals.

2.   The decision of the Court of First Instance appealed against shall be attached to the appeal. The appeal shall state the date on which the decision appealed against was notified to the appellant.

3.   If an appeal does not comply with Article 38 (3) or with paragraph (2) of this Article, Article 38 (7) of these Rules shall apply.

Article 113

1.   An appeal may seek:

— to set aside, in whole or in part, the decision of the Court of First Instance;

— the same form of order, in whole or in part, as that sought at first instance and shall not seek a different form of order.

2.   The subject-matter of the proceedings before the Court of First Instance may not be changed in the appeal.

Article 114

Notice of the appeal shall be served on all the parties to the proceedings before the Court of First Instance. Article 39 of these Rules shall apply.

Article 115

1.   Any party to the proceedings before the Court of First Instance may lodge a response within two months after service on him of notice of the appeal. The time-limit for lodging a response shall not be extended.

2. A response shall contain:

(a)   the name and address of the party lodging it;

(b)   the date on which notice of the appeal was served on him;

(c)   the pleas in law and legal arguments relied on;

(d)   the form of order sought by the respondent.

Article 38 (2) and (3) of these Rules shall apply.

Article 116

1.   A response may seek:

— to dismiss, in whole or in part, the appeal or to set aside, in whole or in part, the decision of the Court of First Instance;

— the same form of order, in whole or in part, as that sought at first instance and shall not seek a different form of order.

2.   The subject-matter of the proceedings before the Court of First Instance may not be changed in the response.

Article 117

1.   The appeal and the response may be supplemented by a reply and a rejoinder or any other pleading, where the President expressly, on application made within seven days of service of the response or of the reply, considers such further pleading necessary and expressly allows it in order to enable the party concerned to put forward its point of view or in order to provide a basis for the decision on the appeal.

2.   Where the response seeks to set aside, in whole or in part, the decision of the Court of First Instance on a plea in law which was not raised in the appeal, the appellant or any other party may submit a reply on that plea alone within two months of the service of the response in question. Paragraph (1) shall apply to any further pleading following such a reply.

3.   Where the President allows the lodging of a reply and a rejoinder, or any other pleading, he shall prescribe the period within which they are to be submitted.

Article 118

Subject to the following provisions, Articles 42 (2), 43, 44, 55 to 90, 93, 95 to 100 and 102 of these Rules shall apply to the procedure before the Court of Justice on appeal from a decision of the Court of First Instance.

Article 119

Where the appeal is, in whole or in part, clearly inadmissible or clearly unfounded, the Court may at any time, acting on a report from the Judge-Rapporteur and after hearing the Advocate-General, by reasoned order dismiss the appeal in whole or in part.

Article 120

After the submission of pleadings as provided for in Articles 115 (1) and, if any, Article 117 (1) and (2) of these Rules, the Court may, acting on a report from the Judge-Rapporteur and after hearing the Advocate-General and the parties, decide to dispense with the oral part of the procedure unless one of the parties objects on the ground that the written procedure did not enable him fully to defend his point of view.

Article 121

The report referred to in Article 44 (1) shall be presented to the Court after the pleadings provided for in Article 115 (1) and Article 117 (1) and (2) of these Rules have been lodged. The report shall contain, in addition to the recommendations provided for in Article 44 (1), a recommendation as to whether Article 120 of these Rules should be applied. Where no such pleadings are lodged, the same procedure shall apply after the expiry of the period prescribed for lodging them.

Article 122
Where the appeal is unfounded or where the appeal is well founded and the Court itself gives final judgment in the case, the Court shall make a decision as to costs.

In proceedings between the Communities and their servants:

— Article 70 of these Rules shall apply only to appeals brought by?

— by way of derogation from Article 69 (2) of these Rules, the Court may, in appeals brought by officials or other servants of an institution, order the parties to share the costs where equity so requires.

If the appeal is withdrawn Article 69 (5) shall apply.

When an appeal brought by a Member State or an institution which did not intervene in the proceedings before the Court of First Instance is well founded, the Court of Justice may order that the parties share the costs or that the successful appellant pay the costs which the appeal has caused an unsuccessful party to incur.

Article 123
An application to intervene made to the Court in appeal proceedings shall be lodged before the expiry of a period of one month running from the publication referred to in Article 16(6).

TITLE V   PROCEDURES PROVIDED FOR BY THE EEA AGREEMENT

Article 123a
1.   In the case governed by Article 111(3) of the EEA Agreement, the matter shall be brought before the Court by a request submitted by the Contracting Parties to the dispute. The request shall be served on the other Contracting Parties, on the Commission, on the EFTA Surveillance Authority and, where appropriate, on the other persons to whom a reference for a preliminary ruling raising the same question of interpretation of Community legislation would be notified.

The President shall prescribe a period within which the Contracting Parties and the other persons on whom the request has been served may submit written observations. The request shall be made in one of the languages mentioned in Article 29(1). Paragraphs (3) and (5) of that Article shall apply. The provsions of Article 104(1) shall apply mutatis mutandis.

2.   As soon as the request referred to in paragraph 1 of this Article has been submitted, the President shall appoint a Judge-Rapporteur. The First Advocate-General shall, immediately afterwards, assign the request to an Advocate-General.

The Court shall, after hearing the Advocate-General give a reasoned decision on the request in closed session.

3.   The decision of the Court, signed by the President, by the Judges who took part in the deliberations and by the Registrar, shall be served on the Contracting Parties and on the other persons referred to in paragraph 1.

Article 123b
In the case governed by Article 1 of Protocol 34 to the EEA Agreement, the request of a court or tribunal of an EFTA State shall be served on the parties to the case, on the Contracting Parties, on the Commission, on the EFTA Surveillance Authority and, where appropriate, on the other persons to whom

a reference for a preliminary ruling raising the same question of interpretation of Community legislation would be notified.

If the request is not submitted in one of the languages mentioned in Article 29(1), it shall be accompanied by a translation into one of those languages.

Within two months of this notification, the parties to the case, the Contracting Parties and the other persons referred to in the first paragraph shall be entitled to submit statements of case or written observations.

The procedure shall be governed by the provisions of these Rules, subject to the adaptations called for by the nature of the request.

MISCELLANEOUS PROVISIONS

Article 124

1.   The President shall instruct any person who is required to take an oath before the Court, as witness or expert, to tell the truth or to carry out his task conscientiously and impartially, as the case may be, and shall warn him of the criminal liability provided for in his national law in the event of any breach of this duty.

2.   The witness shall take the oath either in accordance with the first subparagraph of Article 47 (5) of these Rules or in the manner laid down by his national law.

Where his national law provides the opportunity to make, in judicial proceedings, a solemn affirmation equivalent to an oath as well as or instead of taking an oath, the witness may make such an affirmation under the conditions and in the form prescribed in his national law. Where his national law provides neither for taking an oath nor for making a solemn affirmation, the procedure described in paragraph (1) shall be followed.

3.   Paragraph (2) shall apply mutatis mutandis to experts, a reference to the first subparagraph of Article 49 (6) replacing in this case the reference to the first subparagraph of Article 47 (5) of these Rules.

Article 125

Subject to the provisions of Article 188 of the EC Treaty and Article 160 of the Euratom Treaty and after consultation with the Governments concerned, the Court shall adopt supplementary rules concerning its practice in relation to:

(a)   letters rogatory;

(b)   applications for legal aid;

(c)   reports of perjury by witnesses or experts, delivered pursuant to Article 27 of the EEC Statute and Article 28 of the ECSC and Euratom Statutes.

Article 126

These Rules replace the Rules of Procedure of the Court of Justice of the European Communities adopted on 4 December 1974 (Official Journal of the European Communities No L 350 of 28 December 1974, p. 1), as last amended on 15 May 1991.

Article 127

These Rules, which are authentic in the languages mentioned in Article 29 (1) of these Rules, shall be published in the Official Journal of the European Communities and shall enter into force on the first day of the second month following their publication.

Done at Luxembourg, 19 June 1991.

ANNEX I
DECISION ON OFFICIAL HOLIDAYS

THE COURT OF JUSTICE OF THE EUROPEAN COMMUNITIES

Having regard to Article 80(2) of the Rules of Procedure, which requires the Court to draw up a list of official holidays;

DECIDES:

Article 1

For the purposes of Article 80(2) of the Rules of Procedure the following shall be official holidays:

New Year's Day;
Easter Monday;
1 May;
Ascension Day;
Whit Monday;
23 June;
24 June, where 23 June is a Sunday;
15 August;
1 November;
25 December;
26 December.

The official holidays referred to in the first paragraph hereof shall be those observed at the place where the Court of Justice has its seat.

Article 2

Article 80(2)

The Rules of Procedure shall apply only to the official holidays mentioned in Article 1 of this Decision.

Article 3

This Decision, which shall constitute Annex I to the Rules of Procedure, shall enter into force on the same day as those Rules.

It shall be published in the Official Journal of the European Communities.

Done at Luxembourg, 19 June 1991.

ANNEX II
DECISION ON EXTENSION OF TIME LIMITS ON ACCOUNT OF DISTANCE

THE COURT OF JUSTICE OF THE EUROPEAN COMMUNITIES,

Having regard to Article 81 (2) of the Rules of Procedure relating to the extension, on account of distance, of prescribed time limits;

DECIDES:

Article 1

In order to take account of distance, procedural time limits for all parties save those habitually resident in the Grand Duchy of Luxembourg shall be extended as follows:

—for the Kingdom of Belgium: two days,

— for the Federal Republic of Germany, the European territory of the French Republic and the European territory of the Kingdom of the Netherlands: six days,

— for the European territory of the Kingdom of Denmark, for the Kingdom of Spain, for Ireland, for the Hellenic Republic, for the Republic of Austria, for the Portuguese Republic (with the exception of the Azores and Madeira), for the Republic of Finland, for the Kingdom of Sweden and for the United Kingdom: 10 days,

— for other European countries and territories: two weeks,

— for the autonomous regions of the Azores and Madeira of the Portuguese Republic: three weeks,

— for other countries, departments and territories: one month.

Article 2
This Decision, which shall constitute Annex II to the Rules of Procedure, shall enter into force on the same day as those Rules.

It shall be published in the Official Journal of the European Communities.

COUNCIL DECISION OF 24 OCTOBER 1988 ESTABLISHING A COURT OF FIRST INSTANCE OF THE EUROPEAN COMMUNITIES (88/591/ ECSC, EEC, EURATOM) as corrected by Corrigendum No. L241 [OJ 1989, No. C215/1] as amended by the Council Decision 93/350[1] [OJ 1993, No. L144/21])

THE COUNCIL OF THE EUROPEAN COMMUNITIES,

Having regard to the Treaty establishing the European Coal and Steel Community, and in particular Article 32d thereof,

Having regard to the Treaty establishing the European Economic Community, and in particular Article 168a thereof,

Having regard to the Treaty establishing the European Atomic Energy Community, and in particular Article 140a thereof,

Having regard to the Protocol on the Statute of the Court of Justice of the European Coal and Steel Community, signed in Paris on 18 April 1951,

Having regard to the Protocol on the Statute of the Court of Justice of the European Economic Community, signed in Brussels on 17 April 1957,

Having regard to the Protocol on the Statute of the Court of Justice of the European Atomic Energy Community, signed in Brussels on 17 April 1957,

Having regard to the Protocol on Privileges and Immunities of the European Communities, signed in Brussels on 8 April 1965,

Having regard to the request of the Court of Justice,

Having regard to the opinion of the Commission,

Having regard to the opinion of the European Parliament,[2]

Whereas Article 32d of the ECSC Treaty, Article 168a of the EEC Treaty and Article 140a of the EAEC Treaty empower the Council to attach to the Court of Justice a Court of First Instance called upon to exercise important

Notes
[1]**Editor's Note**: Itself subsequently amended by COUNCIL DECISION 94/149.
[2]OJ No. C187, 18.7.1988 p. 227.

judicial functions and whose members are independent beyond doubt and possess the ability required for performing such functions;

Whereas the aforesaid provisions empower the Council to give the Court of First Instance jurisdiction to hear and determine at first instance, subject to a right of appeal to the Court of Justice on points of law only and in accordance with the conditions laid down by the Statutes, certain classes of action or proceeding brought by natural or legal persons;

Whereas, pursuant to the aforesaid provisions, the Council is to determine the composition of that court and adopt the necessary adjustments and additional provisions to the Statutes of the Court of Justice;

Whereas, in respect of actions requiring close examination of complex facts, the establishment of a second court will improve the judicial protection of individual interests;

Whereas it is necessary, in order to maintain the quality and effectiveness of judicial review in the Community legal order, to enable the Court to concentrate its activities on its fundamental task of ensuring uniform interpretation of Community law;

Whereas it is therefore necessary to make use of the powers granted by Article 32d of the ECSC Treaty, Article 168a of the EEC Treaty and Article 140a of the EAEC Treaty and to transfer to the Court of First Instance jurisdiction to hear and determine at first instance certain classes of action or proceeding which frequently require an examination of complex facts, that is to say actions or proceedings brought by servants of the Communities and also, in so far as the ECSC Treaty is concerned, by undertakings and associations in matters concerning levies, production, prices, restrictive agreements, decisions or practices and concentrations, and so far as the EEC Treaty is concerned, by natural or legal persons in competition matters,

HAS DECIDED AS FOLLOWS:

Article 1
A Court, to be called the Court of First Instance of the European Communities, shall be attached to the Court of Justice of the European Communities. Its seat shall be at the Court of Justice.

Article 2
1. The Court of First Instance shall consist of 12 members.
2. The members shall elect the President of the Court of First Instance from among their number for a term of three years. He may be re-elected.
3. The members of the Court of First Instance may be called upon to perform the task of an Advocate-General.

It shall be the duty of the Advocate-General, acting with complete impartiality and independence, to make, in open court, reasoned submissions on certain cases brought before the Court of First Instance in order to assist the Court of First Instance in the performance of its task.

The criteria for selecting such cases, as well as the procedures for designating the Advocates-General, shall be laid down in the Rules of Procedure of the Court of First Instance.

A member called upon to perform the task of Advocate-General in a case may not take part in the judgment of the case.

4.   The Court of First Instance shall sit in chambers of three or five judges. The composition of the chambers and the assignment of cases to them shall be governed by the Rules of Procedure. In certain cases governed by the Rules of Procedure the Court of First Instance may sit in plenary session.

5.   Article 21 of the Protocol on Privileges and Immunities of the European Communities and Article 6 of the Treaty establishing a Single Council and a Single Commission of the European Communities shall apply to the members of the Court of First Instance and to its Registrar.

Article 3

1.   The Court of First Instance shall exercise at first instance the jurisdiction conferred on the Court of Justice by the Treaties establishing the Communities and by the acts adopted in implementation thereof, however, in respect of actions brought by natural or legal persons pursuant to the second paragraph of Article 33, Article 35 and the first and second paragraphs of Article 40 of the ECSC Treaty and which concern acts relating to the application of Article 74 of the said Treaty and in respect of actions brought by natural or legal persons pursuant to the fourth paragraph of Article 173, the third paragraph of Article 175 and Article 178 of the EC Treaty and relating to measures to protect trade within the meaning of Article 113 of that Treaty in the case of dumping and subsidies, its entry into force shall be fixed at 15 March 1994.

(a)   in disputes as referred to in Article 179 of the EEC Treaty and in Article 152 of the EAEC Treaty;

(b)   in actions brought by natural or legal persons pursuant to the second paragraph of Article 33, Article 35, the first and second paragraphs of Article 40 and Article 42 of the ECSC Treaty;

(c)   in actions brought by natural or legal persons pursuant to the second paragraph of Article 173, the third paragraph of Article 175 and Articles 178 and 181 of the EEC Treaty;

(d)   in actions brought by natural or legal persons pursuant to the second paragraph of Article 146, the third paragraph of Article 148 and Articles 151 and 153 of the EAEC Treaty.

Article 4

Save as hereinafter provided, Articles 34, 36, 39, 44 and 92 of the ECSC Treaty, Articles 172, 174, 176, 184 to 187 and 192 of the EEC Treaty and Articles 49, 83, 144b, 147, 149, 156 to 159 and 164 of the Euratom Treaty shall apply to the Court of First Instance.

Articles 5 and 6

(Omitted)[1]

Note

[1]Editor's Note: The contents of Articles 5 and 6 are omitted as they introduce further new Articles 44-54 to the Protocol on the Statute of the Court of Justice of the European Coal and Steel Community, which is not reproduced in this volume.

Article 7

The following provisions shall be inserted after Article 43 of the Protocol on the Statute of the Court of Justice of the European Economic Community:

[TITLE IV:

THE COURT OF FIRST INSTANCE OF THE EUROPEAN COMMUNITIES

Article 44

Articles 2 to 8, and 13 to 16 of this Statute shall apply to the Court of First Instance and its members. The oath referred to in Article 2 shall be taken before the Court of Justice and the decisions referred to in Articles 3, 4 and 6 shall be adopted by that Court after hearing the Court of First Instance.

Article 45

The Court of First Instance shall appoint its Registrar and lay down the rules governing his service. Articles 9, 10 and 13 of this Statute shall apply to the Registrar of the Court of First Instance mutatis mutandis.

The President of the Court of Justice and the President of the Court of First Instance shall determine, by common accord, the conditions under which officials and other servants attached to the Court of Justice shall render their services to the Court of First Instance to enable it to function. Certain officials or other servants shall be responsible to the Registrar of the Court of First Instance under the authority of the President of the Court of First Instance.

Article 46

The procedure before the Court of First Instance shall be governed by Title III of this Statute, with the exception of Article 20.

Such further and more detailed provisions as may be necessary shall be laid down in the Rules of Procedure established in accordance with Article 168a (4) of this Treaty.

Notwithstanding the fourth paragraph of Article 18 of this Statute, the Advocate-General may make his reasoned submissions in writing.

Article 47

Where an application or other procedural document addressed to the Court of First Instance is lodged by mistake with the Registrar of the Court of Justice it shall be transmitted immediately by that Registrar to the Registrar of the Court of First Instance; likewise, where an application or other procedural document addressed to the Court of Justice is lodged by mistake with the Registrar of the Court of First Instance, it shall be transmitted immediately by that Registrar to the Registrar of the Court of Justice.

Where the Court of First Instance finds that it does not have jurisdiction to hear and determine an action in respect of which the Court of Justice has jurisdiction, it shall refer that action to the Court of Justice; likewise, where the Court of Justice finds that an action falls within the jurisdiction of the Court of First Instance, it shall refer that action to the Court of First Instance, whereupon that Court may not decline jurisdiction.

Where the Court of Justice and the Court of First Instance are seised of cases in which the same relief is sought, the same issue of interpretation is raised or the validity of the same act is called in question, the Court of First Instance may, after hearing the parties, stay the proceedings before it until such time as the Court of Justice shall have delivered judgment. Where applications are made for the same act to be declared void, the Court of First

Instance may also decline jurisdiction in order that the Court of Justice may rule on such applications. In the cases referred to in this subparagraph, the Court of Justice may also decide to stay the proceedings before it; in that event, the proceedings before the Court of First Instance shall continue.

Article 48

Final decisions of the Court of First Instance, decisions disposing of the substantive issues in part only or disposing of a procedural issue concerning a plea of lack of competence. or inadmissibility, shall be notified by the Registrar of the Court of First Instance to all parties as well as all Member States and the Community institutions even if they did not intervene in the case before the Court of First Instance.

Article 49

An appeal may be brought before the Court of Justice, within two months of the notification of the decision appealed against, against final decisions of the Court of First Instance and decisions of that Court disposing of the substantive issues in part only or disposing of a procedural issue concerning a plea of lack of competence or inadmissibility.

Such an appeal may be brought by any party which has been unsuccessful, in whole or in part, in its submissions. However, interveners other than the Member States and the Community institutions may bring such an appeal only where the decision of the Court of First Instance directly affects them.

With the exception of cases relating to disputes between the Communities and its servants, an appeal may also be brought by Member States and Community institutions which did not intervene in the proceedings before the Court of First Instance. Such Member States and institutions shall be in the same position as Member States or institutions which intervened at first instance.

Article 50

Any person whose application to intervene has been dismissed by the Court of First Instance may appeal to the Court of Justice within two weeks of the notification of the decision dismissing the application.

The parties to the proceedings may appeal to the Court of Justice against any decision of the Court of First Instance made pursuant to Article 185 or 186 or the fourth paragraph of Article 192 of this Treaty within two months from their notification.

The appeal referred to in the first two paragraphs of this Article shall be heard and determined under the procedure referred to in Article 36 of this Statute.

Article 51

An appeal to the Court of Justice shall be limited to points of law. It shall lie on the grounds of lack of competence of the Court of First Instance, a breach of procedure before it which adversely affects the interests of the appellant as well as the infringement of Community law by the Court of First Instance.

No appeal shall lie regarding only the amount of the costs or the party ordered to pay them.

Article 52

Where an appeal is brought against a decision of the Court of First Instance, the procedure before the Court of Justice shall consist of a written part and an oral part. In accordance with conditions laid down in the Rules of Procedure the Court of Justice, having heard the Advocate-General and the parties, may dispense with the oral procedure.

Article 53

Without prejudice to Articles 185 and 186 of this Treaty, an appeal shall not have suspensory effect.

By way of derogation from Article 187 of the Treaty, decisions of the Court of First Instance declaring a regulation to be void shall take effect only as from the date of expiry of the period referred to in the first paragraph of Article 49 of this Statute or, if an appeal shall have been brought within that period, as from the date of dismissal of the appeal, without prejudice, however, to the right of a party to apply to the Court of Justice, pursuant to Articles 185 and 186 of this Treaty, for the suspension of the effects of the regulation which has been declared void or for the prescription of any other interim measure.

Article 54

If the appeal is well founded, the Court of Justice shall quash the decision of the Court of First Instance. It may itself give final judgment in the matter, where the state of the proceedings so permits, or refer the case back to the Court of First Instance for judgment.

Where a case is referred back to the Court of First Instance, that Court shall be bound by the decision of the Court of Justice on points of law.

When an appeal brought by a Member State or a Community institution, which did not intervene in the proceedings before the Court of First Instance, is well founded the Court of Justice may, if it considers this necessary, state which of the effects of the decision of the Court of First Instance which has been quashed shall be considered as definitive in respect of the parties to the litigation.]

Article 8

The former Articles 44, 45 and 46 of the Protocol on the Statute of the Court of Justice of the European Economic Community shall become Articles 55, 56 and 57 respectively.

Articles 9 and 10

(Omitted)[1]

Note

[1]These relate to the EURATOM Treaty, likewise not reproduced in this volume.

Article 11

The first President of the Court of First Instance shall be appointed for three years in the same manner as its members. However, the Governments of the Member States may, by common accord, decide that the procedure laid down in Article 2(2) shall be applied. The Court of First Instance shall adopt its Rules of Procedure immediately upon its constitution. Until the entry into force of the Rules of Procedure of the Court of First Instance, the Rules of Procedure of the Court of Justice shall apply mutatis mutandis.

Article 12

Immediately after all members of the Court of First Instance have taken oath, the President of the Council shall proceed to choose by lot the members of the

Court of First Instance whose terms of office are to expire at the end of the first three years in accordance with Article 32d(3) of the ECSC Treaty, Article 168a(3) of the EEC Treaty, and Article 140a(3) of the EAEC Treaty.

Article 13
This Decision shall enter into force on the day following its publication in the Official Journal of the European Communities, with the exception of Article 3, which shall enter into force on the date of the publication in the Official Journal of the European Communities of the ruling by the President of the Court of Justice that the Court of First Instance has been constituted in accordance with law.

Article 14
Cases referred to in Article 3 of which the Court of Justice is seised on the date on which that Article enters into force but in which the preliminary report provided for in Article 44 (1) of the Rules of Procedure of the Court of Justice has not yet been presented shall be referred back to the Court of First Instance.

Done at Luxembourg, 24 October 1988.
For the Council
The President
Th. PANGALOS

RULES OF PROCEDURE OF THE COURT OF FIRST INSTANCE OF THE EUROPEAN COMMUNITIES OF 2 MAY 1991
[OJ 1991 L136/1][1]

TABLE OF CONTENTS

Note
[1]As corrected by OJ 1991 L317/34 and amended by OJ 1994 L249/17, OJ 1995 L44/64, OJ 1995 L172/3 and OJ 1997 L103/6.

THE COURT OF FIRST INSTANCE OF THE EUROPEAN COMMUNITIES,

Having regard to Article 32d of the Treaty establishing the European Coal and Steel Community,

Having regard to Article 168a of the Treaty establishing the European Economic Community,

Having regard to Article 140a of the Treaty establishing the European Atomic Energy Community,

Having regard to the Protocol on the Statute of the Court of Justice of the European Coal and Steel Community, signed in Paris on 18 April 1951,

Having regard to the Protocol on the Statute of the Court of Justice of the European Economic Community, signed in Brussels on 17 April 1957,

Having regard to the Protocol on the Statute of the Court of Justice of the European Atomic Energy Community, signed in Brussels on 17 April 1957,

Having regard to Council Decision 88/591/ECSC, EEC, Euratom of 24 October 1988 establishing a Court of First Instance of the European Communities (OJ No. L319 of 25 November 1988, with corrigendum in OJ No. L241 of 17 August 1989), and in particular Article 11 thereof,

Having regard to the agreement of the Court of Justice,

Having regard to the unanimous approval of the Council, given on 21 December 1990 and 29 April 1991,

Whereas the Court of First Instance is to establish its rules of procedure in agreement with the Court of Justice and with the unanimous approval of the Council and to adopt them immediately upon its constitution;

Whereas it is necessary to adopt the provisions laid down for the functioning of the Court of First Instance by the Treaties, by the Protocols on the Statutes of the Court of Justice and by the Council Decision of 24 October 1988 establishing a Court of First Instance of the European Communities and to adopt any other provisions necessary for applying and, where required, supplementing those instruments;

Whereas it is necessary to lay down for the Court of First Instance procedures adapted to the duties of such a court and to the task entrusted to the Court of First Instance of ensuring effective judicial protection of individual interests in cases requiring close examination of complex facts;

Whereas it is, moreover, desirable that the rules applicable to the procedure before the Court of First Instance should not differ more than is necessary from the rules applicable to the procedure before the Court of Justice under its Rules of Procedure adopted on 4 December 1974 (OJ No. L350 of 28 December 1974), as subsequently amended, adopts the following

RULES OF PROCEDURE
INTERPRETATION

Article 1

In these Rules:

'EC Treaty' means the Treaty establishing the European Community,

'EC Statute' means the Protocol on the Statute of the Court of Justice of the European Community,

'ECSC Treaty' means the Treaty establishing the European Coal and Steel Community,

'ECSC statute' means the Protocol on the Statute of the Court of Justice of the European Coal and Steel Community,

'Euratom Treaty' means the Treaty establishing the European Atomic Energy Community (Euratom),

'Euratom Statute' means the Protocol on the Statute of the Court of Justice of the European Atomic Energy Community,

'EEA Agreement' means the Agreement on the European Economic Area.

For the purpose of these Rules:

'institutions' means the institutions of the Communities and bodies which are established by the Treaties, or by an act adopted in implementation thereof, and which may be parties before the Court of First Instance,

'EFTA Surveillance Authority' means the surveillance authority referred to in the EEA Agreement.

TITLE I   ORGANIZATION OF THE COURT OF FIRST INSTANCE
CHAPTER 1   PRESIDENT AND MEMBERS OF THE COURT OF FIRST INSTANCE

Article 2

1. Every Member of the Court of First Instance shall, as a rule, perform the function of Judge. Members of the Court of First Instance are hereinafter referred to as 'Judges'.

2. Every Judge, with the exception of the President, may, in the circumstances specified in Articles 17 to 19, perform the function of Advocate-General in a particular case. References to the Advocate-General in these Rules shall apply only where a Judge has been designated as Advocate-General.

Article 3

The term of office of a Judge shall begin on the date laid down in his instrument of appointment. In the absence of any provision regarding the date, the term shall begin on the date of the instrument.

Article 4

1.   Before taking up his duties, a Judge shall take the following oath before the Court of Justice of the European Communities: 'I swear that I will perform my duties impartially and conscientiously; I swear that I will preserve the secrecy of the deliberations of the Court.'

2.   Immediately after taking the oath, a Judge shall sign a declaration by which he solemnly undertakes that, both during and after his term of office, he will respect the obligations arising therefrom, and in particular the duty to behave with integrity and discretion as regards the acceptance, after he has ceased to hold office, of certain appointments and benefits.

Article 5

When the Court of Justice is called upon to decide, after consulting the Court of First Instance, whether a Judge of the Court of First Instance no longer fulfils the requisite conditions or no longer meets the obligations arising from his office, the President of the Court of First Instance shall invite the Judge concerned to make representations to the Court of First Instance, in closed session and in the absence of the Registrar. The Court of First Instance shall state the reasons for its opinion. An opinion to the effect that a Judge of the Court of First Instance no longer fulfils the requisite conditions or no longer meets the obligations arising from his office must receive the votes of at least seven Judges of the Court of First Instance. In that event, particulars of the voting shall be communicated to the Court of Justice. Voting shall be by secret ballot; the Judge concerned shall not take part in the deliberations.

Article 6

With the exception of the President of the Court of First Instance and of the Presidents of the Chambers, the Judges shall rank equally in precedence according to their seniority in office. Where there is equal seniority in office, precedence shall be determined by age. Retiring Judges who are reappointed shall retain their former precedence.

Article 7

1.   The Judges shall, immediately after the partial replacement provided for in Article 168(a) of the EC Treaty, Article 32(d) of the ECSC Treaty and Article 140(a) of the Euratom Treaty, elect one of their number as President of the Court of First Instance for a term of three years.

2.   If the office of President of the Court of First Instance falls vacant before the normal date of expiry thereof, the Court of First Instance shall elect a successor for the remainder of the term.

3.   The elections provided for in this Article shall be by secret ballot. If a Judge obtains an absolute majority he shall be elected. If no Judge obtains an absolute majority, a second ballot shall be held and the Judge obtaining the most votes shall be elected. Where two or more Judges obtain an equal number of votes the oldest of them shall be deemed elected.

Article 8
The President of the Court of First Instance shall direct the judicial business and the administration of the Court of First Instance. He shall preside at plenary sittings and deliberations.

Article 9
When the President of the Court of First Instance is absent or prevented from attending or when the office of President is vacant, the functions of President shall be exercised by a President of a Chamber according to the order of precedence laid down in Article 6. If the President of the Court and the Presidents of the Chambers are all prevented from attending at the same time, or their posts are vacant at the same time, the functions of President shall be exercised by one of the other Judges according to the order of precedence laid down in Article 6.

CHAPTER 2   CONSTITUTION OF THE CHAMBERS AND DESIGNATION OF JUDGE-RAPPORTEURS AND ADVOCATES-GENERAL

Article 10
1.   The Court of First Instance shall set up Chambers composed of three or five Judges and shall decide which Judges shall be attached to them.

2.   The composition of the Chambers shall be published in the Official Journal of the European Communities.

Article 11
1.   Cases before the Court of First Instance shall be heard by Chambers composed in accordance with Article 10. Cases may be heard by the Court of First Instance sitting in plenary session under the conditions laid down in Articles 14, 51, 106, 118, 124, 127 and 129.

2.   In cases coming before a Chamber, the term 'Court of First Instance' in these Rules shall designate that Chamber.

Article 12
1.   Subject to the provisions of Article 14, disputes between the Communities and their servants shall be assigned to Chambers of three Judges. Other cases shall, subject to the provisions of Article 14, be assigned to Chambers of five Judges.

2.   The Court of First Instance shall lay down criteria by which, as a rule, cases are to be assigned to Chambers composed of the same number of Judges.

Article 13
1.   As soon as the application initiating proceedings has been lodged, the President of the Court of First Instance shall assign the case to one of the Chambers.

2.   The President of the Chamber shall propose to the President of the Court of First Instance, in respect of each case assigned to the Chamber, the designation of a Judge to act as Rapporteur; the President of the Court of First Instance shall decide on the proposal.

Article 14
Whenever the legal difficulty or the importance of the case or special circumstances so justify, a case may be referred to the Court of First Instance

sitting in plenary session or to a Chamber composed of a different number of Judges. Any decision to refer a case shall be taken under the conditions laid down in Article 51.

Article 15

The Court of First Instance shall appoint for a period of one year the Presidents of the Chambers. The provisions of Article 7(2) and (3) shall apply. The appointments made in pursuance of this Article shall be published in the Official Journal of the European Communities.

Article 16

In cases coming before a Chamber the powers of the President shall be exercised by the President of the Chamber.

Article 17

When the Court of First Instance sits in plenary session, it shall be assisted by an Advocate-General designated by the President of the Court of First Instance.

Article 18

A Chamber of the Court of First Instance may be assisted by an Advocate-General if it is considered that the legal difficulty or the factual complexity of the case so requires.

Article 19

The decision to designate an Advocate-General in a particular case shall be taken by the Court of First Instance sitting in plenary session at the request of the Chamber before which the case comes. The President of the Court of First Instance shall designate the Judge called upon to perform the function of Advocate-General in that case.

CHAPTER 3   REGISTRY
SECTION 1   THE REGISTRAR

Article 20

1. The Court of First Instance shall appoint the Registrar. Two weeks before the date fixed for making the appointment, the President of the Court of First Instance shall inform the Judges of the applications which have been submitted for the post.

2. An application shall be accompanied by full details of the candidate's age, nationality, university degrees, knowledge of any languages, present and past occupations and experience, if any, in judicial and international fields.

3. The appointment shall be made following the procedure laid down in Article 7(3).

4. The Registrar shall be appointed for a term of six years. He may be reappointed.

5. Before he takes up his duties the Registrar shall take the oath before the Court of First Instance in accordance with Article 4.

6. The Registrar may be deprived of his office only if he no longer fulfils the requisite conditions or no longer meets the obligations arising from his office; the Court of First Instance shall take its decision after giving the Registrar an opportunity to make representations.

7.   If the office of Registrar falls vacant before the usual date of expiry of the term thereof, the Court of First Instance shall appoint a new Registrar for a term of six years.

Article 21
The Court of First Instance may, following the procedure laid down in respect of the Registrar, appoint one or more Assistant Registrars to assist the Registrar and to take his place in so far as the Instructions to the Registrar referred in Article 23 allow.

Article 22
Where the Registrar is absent or prevented from attending and, if necessary, where the Assistant Registrar is absent or so prevented, or where their posts are vacant, the President of the Court of First Instance shall designate an official or servant to carry out the duties of Registrar.

Article 23
Instructions to the Registrar shall be adopted by the Court of First Instance acting on a proposal from the President of the Court of First Instance.

Article 24
1.   There shall be kept in the Registry, under the control of the Registrar, a register initialled by the President of the Court of First Instance, in which all pleadings and supporting documents shall be entered in the order in which they are lodged.

2.   When a document has been registered, the Registrar shall make a note to that effect on the original and, if a party so requests, on any copy submitted for the purpose.

3.   Entries in the register and the notes provided for in the preceding paragraph shall be authentic.

4.   Rules for keeping the register shall be prescribed by the Instructions to the Registrar referred to in Article 23.

5.   Persons having an interest may consult the register at the Registry and may obtain copies or extracts on payment of a charge on a scale fixed by the Court of First Instance on a proposal from the Registrar. The parties to a case may on payment of the appropriate charge also obtain copies of pleadings and authenticated copies of orders and judgments.

6.   Notice shall be given in the Official Journal of the European Communities of the date of registration of an application initiating proceedings, the names and addresses of the parties, the subject-matter of the proceedings, the form of order sought by the applicant and a summary of the pleas in law and of the main supporting arguments.

7.   Where the Council or the Commission is not a party to a case, the Court of First Instance shall send to it copies of the application and of the defence, without the annexes thereto, to enable it to assess whether the inapplicability of one of its acts is being invoked under Article 184 of the EC Treaty, the third paragraph of Article 36 of the ECSC Treaty or Article 156 of the Euratom Treaty.

Article 25
1.   The Registrar shall be responsible, under the authority of the President, for the acceptance, transmission and custody of documents and for effecting service as provided for by these Rules.

2.   The Registrar shall assist the Court of First Instance, the Chambers, the President and the Judges in all their official functions.

Article 26
The Registrar shall have custody of the seals. He shall be responsible for the records and be in charge of the publications of the Court of First Instance.

Article 27
Subject to Articles 5 and 33, the Registrar shall attend the sittings of the Court of First Instance and of the Chambers.

SECTION 2   OTHER DEPARTMENTS

Article 28
The officials and other servants whose task is to assist directly the President, the Judges and the Registrar shall be appointed in accordance with the Staff Regulations. They shall be responsible to the Registrar, under the authority of the President of the Court of First Instance.

Article 29
The officials and other servants referred to in Article 28 shall take the oath provided for in Article 20(2) of the Rules of Procedure of the Court of Justice before the President of the Court of First Instance in the presence of the Registrar.

Article 30
The Registrar shall be responsible, under the authority of the President of the Court of First Instance, for the administration of the Court of First Instance, its financial management and its accounts; he shall be assisted in this by the departments of the Court of Justice.

CHAPTER 4   THE WORKING OF THE COURT OF FIRST INSTANCE

Article 31
1.   The dates and times of the sittings of the Court of First Instance shall be fixed by the President.
2.   The Court of First Instance may choose to hold one or more sittings in a place other than that in which the Court of First Instance has its seat.

Article 32
1.   Where, by reason of a Judge being absent or prevented from attending, there is an even number of Judges, the most junior Judge within the meaning of Article 6 shall abstain from taking part in the deliberations unless he is the Judge Rapporteur. Where, following the designation of an Advocate-General pursuant to Article 17, there is an even number of Judges in the Court of First Instance sitting in plenary session, the President of the Court shall designate, before the hearing and in accordance with a rota established in advance by the Court of First Instance and published in the Official Journal of the European Communities, the Judge who will not take part in the judgment of the case. In this case, the Judge immediately senior to him shall abstain from taking part in the deliberations.
2.   If, after the Court of First Instance has been convened in plenary session, it is found that the quorum of nine Judges has not been attained, the

President of the Court of First Instance shall adjourn the sitting until there is a quorum.

3.   If in any Chamber the quorum of three Judges has not been attained, the President of that Chamber shall so inform the President of the Court of First Instance who shall designate another Judge to complete the Chamber.

4.   If in any Chamber of three or five Judges the number of Judges assigned to that Chamber is higher than three or five respectively, the President of the Chamber shall decide which of the Judges will be called upon to take part in the judgment of the case.

Article 33

1.   The Court of First Instance shall deliberate in closed session.

2.   Only those Judges who were present at the oral proceedings may take part in the deliberations.

3.   Every Judge taking part in the deliberations shall state his opinion and the reasons for it.

4.   Any Judge may require that any question be formulated in the language of his choice and communicated in writing to the other Judges before being put to the vote.

5.   The conclusions reached by the majority of the Judges after final discussion shall determine the decision of the Court of First Instance. Votes shall be cast in reverse order to the order of precedence laid down in Article

6.   6. Differences of view on the substance, wording or order of questions, or on the interpretation of a vote shall be settled by decision of the Court of First Instance.

7.   Where the deliberations of the Court of First Instance concern questions of its own administration, the Registrar shall be present, unless the Court of First Instance decides to the contrary.

8.   Where the Court of First Instance sits without the Registrar being present it shall, if necessary, instruct the most junior Judge within the meaning of Article 6 to draw up minutes. The minutes shall be signed by this Judge and by the President.

Article 34

1.   Subject to any special decision of the Court of First Instance, its vacations shall be as follows:

—from 18 December to 10 January,

—from the Sunday before Easter to the second Sunday after Easter,

—from 15 July to 15 September.

During the vacations, the functions of President shall be exercised at the place where the Court of First Instance has its seat either by the President himself, keeping in touch with the Registrar, or by a President of Chamber or other Judge invited by the President to take his place.

2.   In a case of urgency, the President may convene the Judges during the vacations.

3.   The Court of First Instance shall observe the official holidays of the place where it has its seat.

4.   The Court of First Instance may, in proper circumstances, grant leave of absence to any Judge.

CHAPTER 5   LANGUAGES

Article 35

1.   The language of a case shall be Danish, Dutch, English, Finnish, French, German, Greek, Irish, Italian, Portuguese, Spanish or Swedish.

2.   The language of the case shall be chosen by the applicant, except that:

(a)   at the joint request of the parties, the use of another of the languages mentioned in paragraph 1 for all or part of the proceedings may be authorized;

(b)   at the request of one of the parties, and after the opposite party and the Advocate-General have been heard, the use of another of the languages mentioned in paragraph 1 as the language of the case for all or part of the proceedings may be authorized by way of derogation from subparagraph (a). Requests as above may be decided on by the President; the latter may and, where he proposes to accede to a request without the agreement of all the parties, must refer the request to the Court of First Instance.

3.   The language of the case shall be used in the written and oral pleadings of the parties and in supporting documents, and also in the minutes and decisions of the Court of First Instance.

Any supporting documents expressed in another language must be accompanied by a translation into the language of the case. In the case of lengthy documents, translations may be confined to extracts. However, the Court of First Instance may, of its own motion or at the request of a party, at any time call for a complete or fuller translation.

Notwithstanding the foregoing provisions, a Member State shall be entitled to use its official language when intervening in a case before the Court of First Instance. This provision shall apply both to written statements and to oral addresses. The Registrar shall cause any such statement or address to be translated into the language of the case. The States, other than the Member States, which are parties to the EEA Agreement, and also the EFTA Surveillance Authority, may be authorised to use one of the languages mentioned in paragraph 1, other than the language of the case, when they intervene in a case before the Court of First Instance. This provision shall apply both to written statements and oral addresses. The Registrar shall cause any such statement or address to be translated into the language of the case.

4.   Where a witness or expert states that he is unable adequately to express himself in one of the languages referred to in paragraph (1) of this Article, the Court of First Instance may authorise him to give his evidence in another language. The Registrar shall arrange for translation into the language of the case.

5.   The President in conducting oral proceedings, the Judge Rapporteur both in his preliminary report and in his report for the hearing, Judges and the Advocate-General in putting questions and the Advocate-General in delivering his opinion may use one of the languages referred to in paragraph (1) of this Article other than the language of the case. The Registrar shall arrange for translation into the language of the case.

Article 36

1.   The Registrar shall, at the request of any Judge, of the Advocate-General or of a party, arrange for anything said or written in the course of the proceedings before the Court of First Instance to be translated into the languages he chooses from those referred to in Article 35(1).

2.   Publications of the Court of First Instance shall be issued in the language referred to in Article 1 of Council Regulation No 1.

Article 37
The texts of documents drawn up in the language of the case or in any other language authorised by the Court of First Instance pursuant to Article 35 shall be authentic.

CHAPTER 6   RIGHTS AND OBLIGATIONS OF AGENTS, ADVISERS AND LAWYERS

Article 38
1.   Agents, advisers and lawyers, appearing before the Court of First Instance or before any judicial authority to which it has addressed letters rogatory, shall enjoy immunity in respect of words spoken or written by them concerning the case or the parties.

2.   Agents, advisers and lawyers shall enjoy the following further privileges and facilities:

(a)   papers and documents relating to the proceedings shall be exempt from both search and seizure; in the event of a dispute the customs officials or police may seal those papers and documents; they shall then be immediately forwarded to the Court of First Instance for inspection in the presence of the Registrar and of the person concerned;

(b)   agents, advisers and lawyers shall be entitled to such allocation of foreign currency as may be necessary for the performance of their duties;

(c)   agents, advisers and lawyers shall be entitled to travel in the course of duty without hindrance.

Article 39
In order to qualify for the privileges, immunities and facilities specified in Article 38, persons entitled to them shall furnish proof of their status as follows:

(a)   agents shall produce an official document issued by the party for whom they act and shall forward without delay a copy thereof to the Registrar.

(b)   advisers and lawyers shall produce a certificate signed by the Registrar. The validity of this certificate shall be limited to a specified period, which may be extended or curtailed according to the length of the proceedings.

Article 40
The privileges, immunities and facilities specified in Article 38 are granted exclusively in the interests of the proper conduct of proceedings. The Court of First Instance may waive the immunity where it considers that the proper conduct of proceedings will not be hindered thereby.

Article 41
1.   Any adviser or lawyer whose conduct towards the Court of First Instance, the President, a Judge or the Registrar is incompatible with the dignity of the Court of First Instance, or who uses his rights for purposes other than those for which they were granted, may at any time be excluded from the proceedings by an order of the Court of First Instance; the person concerned shall be given an opportunity to defend himself. The order shall have immediate effect.

2.   Where an adviser or lawyer is excluded from the proceedings, the proceedings shall be suspended for a period fixed by the President in order to allow the party concerned to appoint another adviser or lawyer.

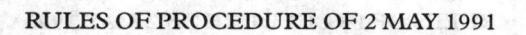

3.   Decisions taken under this Article may be rescinded.

Article 42
The provisions of this Chapter shall apply to university teachers who have a right of audience before the Court of First Instance in accordance with Article 17 of the EC Statute, Article 20 of the ECSC Statute and Article 17 of the Euratom Statute.

TITLE II   PROCEDURE
CHAPTER 1   WRITTEN PROCEDURE

Article 43
1.   The original of every pleading must be signed by the party's agent or lawyer. The original, accompanied by all annexes referred to therein, shall be lodged together with five copies for the Court of First Instance and a copy for every other party to the proceedings. Copies shall be certified by the party lodging them.
2.   Institutions shall in addition produce, within time-limits laid down by the Court of First Instance, translations of all pleadings into the other languages provided for by Article 1 of Council Regulation No. 1. The second subparagraph of paragraph (1) of this Article shall apply.
3.   All pleadings shall bear a date. In the reckoning of time-limits for taking steps in proceedings only the date of lodgment at the Registry shall be taken into account.
4.   To every pleading there shall be annexed a file containing the documents relied on in support of it, together with a schedule listing them.
5.   Where in view of the length of a document only extracts from it are annexed to the pleading, the whole document or a full copy of it shall be lodged at the Registry.

Article 44
1.   An application of the kind referred to in Article 19 of the EC Statute, Article 22 of the ECSC Statute and Article 19 of the Euratom Statute shall state:
    (a)   the name and address of the applicant;
    (b)   the designation of the party against whom the application is made;
    (c)   the subject-matter of the proceedings and a summary of the pleas in law on which the application is based;
    (d)   the form of order sought by the applicant;
    (e)   where appropriate, the nature of any evidence offered in support.
2.   For the purpose of the proceedings, the application shall state an address for service in the place where the Court of First Instance has its seat and the name of the person who is authorised and has expressed willingness to accept service. If the application does not comply with these requirements, all service on the party concerned for the purposes of the proceedings shall be effected, for so long as the defect has not been cured, by registered letter addressed to the agent or lawyer of that party. By way of derogation from Article 100, service shall then be deemed to have been duly effected by the lodging of the registered letter at the post office of the place where the Court of First Instance has its seat.
3.   The lawyer acting for a party must lodge at the Registry a certificate that he is authorised to practise before a Court of a Member State or of another State which is a party to the EEA Agreement.

4. The application shall be accompanied, where appropriate, by the documents specified in the second paragraph of Article 19 of the EC Statute, in the second paragraph of Article 22 of the ECSC and in the second paragraph of Article 19 of the Euratom Statute.

5. An application made by a legal person governed by private law shall be accompanied by:

(a)   the instrument or instruments constituting and regulating that legal person or a recent extract from the register of companies, firms or associations or any other proof of its existence in law;

(b)   proof that the authority granted to the applicant's lawyer has been properly conferred on him by someone authorised for the purpose.

6. If an application does not comply with the requirements set out in paragraphs (3) to (5) of this Article, the Registrar shall prescribe a reasonable period within which the applicant is to comply with them whether by putting the application itself in order or by producing any of the abovementioned documents. If the applicant fails to put the application in order or to produce the required documents within the time prescribed, the Court of First Instance shall decide whether the non-compliance with these conditions renders the application formally inadmissible.

Article 45

The application shall be served on the defendant. In a case where Article 44(6) applies, service shall be effected as soon as the application has been put in order or the Court of First Instance has declared it admissible notwithstanding the failure to observe the formal requirements set out in that Article.

Article 46

1. Within one month after service on him of the application, the defendant shall lodge a defence, stating:

(a)   the name and address of the defendant;

(b)   the arguments of fact and law relied on;

(c)   the form of order sought by the defendant;

(d)   the nature of any evidence offered by him. The provisions of Article 44(2) to (5) shall apply to the defence.

2. In proceedings between the Communities and their servants the defence shall be accompanied by the complaint within the meaning of Article 90(2) of the Staff Regulations of Officials and by the decision rejecting the complaint together with the dates on which the complaint was submitted and the decision notified.

3. The time-limit laid down in paragraph (1) of this Article may be extended by the President on a reasoned application by the defendant.

Article 47

1. The application initiating the proceedings and the defence may be supplemented by a reply from the applicant and by a rejoinder from the defendant.

2. The President shall fix the time-limits within which these pleadings are to be lodged.

Article 48

1. In reply or rejoinder a party may offer further evidence. The party must, however, give reasons for the delay in offering it.

2.   No new plea in law may be introduced in the course of proceedings unless it is based on matters of law or of fact which come to light in the course of the procedure. If in the course of the procedure one of the parties puts forward a new plea in law which is so based, the President may, even after the expiry of the normal procedural time-limits, acting on a report of the Judge-Rapporteur and after hearing the Advocate-General, allow the other party time to answer on that plea. Consideration of the admissibility of the plea shall be reserved for the final judgment.

Article 49
At any stage of the proceedings the Court of First Instance may, after hearing the Advocate-General, prescribe any measure of organization of procedure or any measure of inquiry referred to in Articles 64 and 65 or order that a previous inquiry be repeated or expanded.

Article 50
The President may, at any time, after hearing the parties and the Advocate-General, order that two or more cases concerning the same subject-matter shall, on account of the connection between them, be joined for the purposes of the written or oral procedure or of the final judgment. The cases may subsequently be disjoined. The President may refer those matters to the Court of First Instance.

Article 51
In the cases specified in Article 14, and at any stage in the proceedings, the Chamber hearing the case may, either on its own initiative or at the request of one of the parties, propose to the Court of First Instance sitting in plenary session that the case be referred to the Court of First Instance sitting in plenary session or to a Chamber composed of a different number of Judges. The Court of First Instance sitting in plenary session shall, after hearing the parties and the Advocate-General, decide whether or not to refer a case.

Article 52
1.   Without prejudice to the application of Article 49, the President shall, after the rejoinder has been lodged, fix a date on which the Judge-Rapporteur is to present his preliminary report to the Court of First Instance. The report shall contain recommendations as to whether measures of organization of procedure or measures of inquiry should be undertaken and whether the case should be referred to the Court of First Instance sitting in plenary session or to a Chamber composed of a different number of Judges.

2.   The Court of First Instance shall decide, after hearing the Advocate-General, what action to take upon the recommendations of the Judge-Rapporteur. The same procedure shall apply:

(a)   where no reply or no rejoinder has been lodged within the time-limit fixed in accordance with Article 47(2);

(b)   where the party concerned waives his right to lodge a reply or rejoinder.

Article 53
Where the Court of First Instance decides to open the oral procedure without undertaking measures of organization of procedure or ordering a preparatory inquiry, the President of the Court of First Instance shall fix the opening date.

Article 54

Without prejudice to any measures of organization of procedure or measures of inquiry which may be arranged at the stage of the oral procedure, where, during the written procedure, measures of organization of procedure or measures of inquiry have been instituted and completed, the President shall fix the date for the opening of the oral procedure.

CHAPTER 2   ORAL PROCEDURE

Article 55

1.   Subject to the priority of decisions provided for in Article 106, the Court of First Instance shall deal with the cases before it in the order in which the preparatory inquiries in them have been completed. Where the preparatory inquiries in several cases are completed simultaneously, the order in which they are to be dealt with shall be determined by the dates of entry in the register of the applications initiating them respectively.

2.   The President may in special circumstances order that a case be given priority over others. The President may in special circumstances, after hearing the parties and the Advocate-General, either on his own initiative or at the request of one of the parties, defer a case to be dealt with at a later date. On a joint application by the parties the President may order that a case be deferred.

Article 56

The proceedings shall be opened and directed by the President, who shall be responsible for the proper conduct of the hearing.

Article 57

The oral proceedings in cases heard in camera shall not be published.

Article 58

The President may in the course of the hearing put questions to the agents, advisers or lawyers of the parties. The other Judges and the Advocate-General may do likewise.

Article 59

A party may address the Court of First Instance only through his agent, adviser or lawyer.

Article 60

Where an Advocate-General has not been designated in a case, the President shall declare the oral procedure closed at the end of the hearing.

Article 61

1.   Where the Advocate-General delivers his opinion in writing, he shall lodge it at the Registry, which shall communicate it to the parties.

2.   After the delivery, orally or in writing, of the opinion of the Advocate-General the President shall declare the oral procedure closed.

Article 62

The Court of First Instance may, after hearing the Advocate-General, order the re-opening of the oral procedure.

Article 63

1.   The Registrar shall draw up minutes of every hearing. The minutes shall be signed by the President and by the Registrar and shall constitute an official record.

2.   The parties may inspect the minutes at the Registry and obtain copies at their own expense.

CHAPTER 3   MEASURES OF ORGANIZATION OF PROCEDURE AND MEASURES OF INQUIRY
SECTION 1   MEASURES OF ORGANIZATION OF PROCEDURE

Article 64

1.   The purpose of measures of organization of procedure shall be to ensure that cases are prepared for hearing, procedures carried out and disputes resolved under the best possible conditions. They shall be prescribed by the Court of First Instance, after hearing the Advocate-General.

2.   Measures of organization of procedure shall, in particular, have as their purpose:

(a)   to ensure efficient conduct of the written and oral procedure and to facilitate the taking of evidence;

(b)   to determine the points on which the parties must present further argument or which call for measures of inquiry;

(c)   to clarify the forms of order sought by the parties, their pleas in law and arguments and the points at issue between them;

(d)   to facilitate the amicable settlement of proceedings.

3.   Measures of organization of procedure may, in particular, consist of:

(a)   putting questions to the parties;

(b)   inviting the parties to make written or oral submissions on certain aspects of the proceedings;

(c)   asking the parties or third parties for information or particulars;

(d)   asking for documents or any papers relating to the case to be produced;

(e)   summoning the parties' agents or the parties in person to meetings.

4.   Each party may, at any stage of the procedure, propose the adoption or modification of measures of organization of procedure. In that case, the other parties shall be heard before those measures are prescribed. Where the procedural circumstances so require, the Registrar shall inform the parties of the measures envisaged by the Court of First Instance and shall give them an opportunity to submit comments orally or in writing.

5.   If the Court of First Instance sitting in plenary session decides to prescribe measures of organization of procedure and does not undertake such measures itself, it shall entrust the task of so doing to the Chamber to which the case was originally assigned or to the Judge-Rapporteur. If a Chamber prescribes measures of organization of procedure and does not undertake such measures itself, it shall entrust the task to the Judge-Rapporteur. The Advocate-General shall take part in measures of organization of procedure.

SECTION 2   MEASURES OF INQUIRY

Article 65

Without prejudice to Articles 21 and 22 of the EC Statute, Articles 24 and 25 of the ECSC Statute and Articles 22 and 23 of the Euratom Statute, the following measures of inquiry may be adopted:

(a)   the personal appearance of the parties;

(b)   a request for information and production of documents;

(c)   oral testimony;

(d) the commissioning of an expert's report;

(e) an inspection of the place or thing in question.

Article 66

1. The Court of First Instance, after hearing the Advocate General, shall prescribe the measures of inquiry that it considers appropriate by means of an order setting out the facts to be proved. Before the Court of First Instance decides on the measures of inquiry referred to in Article 65(c), (d) and (e) the parties shall be heard. The order shall be served on the parties.

2. Evidence may be submitted in rebuttal and previous evidence may be amplified.

Article 67

1. Where the Court of First Instance sitting in plenary session orders a preparatory inquiry and does not undertake such an inquiry itself, it shall entrust the task of so doing to the Chamber to which the case was originally assigned or to the Judge-Rapporteur. Where a Chamber orders a preparatory inquiry and does not undertake such an inquiry itself, it shall entrust the task of so doing to the Judge-Rapporteur. The Advocate-General shall take part in the measures of inquiry.

2. The parties may be present at the measures of inquiry.

SECTION 3   THE SUMMONING AND EXAMINATION OF WITNESSES AND EXPERTS

Article 68

1. The Court of First Instance may, either of its own motion or on application by a party, and after hearing the Advocate-General and the parties, order that certain facts be proved by witnesses. The order shall set out the facts to be established. The Court of First Instance may summon a witness of its own motion or on application by a party or at the instance of the Advocate-General. An application by a party for the examination of a witness shall state precisely about what facts and for what reasons the witness should be examined.

2. The witness shall be summoned by an order containing the following information:

(a) the surname, forenames, description and address of the witness;

(b) an indication of the facts about which the witness is to be examined;

(c) where appropriate, particulars of the arrangements made by the Court of First Instance for reimbursement of expenses incurred by the witness, and of the penalties which may be imposed on defaulting witnesses. The order shall be served on the parties and the witnesses.

3. The Court of First Instance may make the summoning of a witness for whose examination a party has applied conditional upon the deposit with the cashier of the Court of First Instance of a sum sufficient to cover the taxed costs thereof; the Court of First Instance shall fix the amount of the payment. The cashier of the Court of First Instance shall advance the funds necessary in connection with the examination of any witness summoned by the Court of First Instance of its own motion.

4. After the identity of the witness has been established, the President shall inform him that he will be required to vouch the truth of his evidence in the manner laid down in paragraph (5) of this Article and in Article 71. The witness shall give his evidence to the Court of First Instance, the parties having been

given notice to attend. After the witness has given his main evidence the President may, at the request of a party or of his own motion, put questions to him. The other Judges and the Advocate-General may do likewise. Subject to the control of the President, questions may be put to witnesses by the representatives of the parties.

5.   Subject to the provisions of Article 71, the witness shall, after giving his evidence, take the following oath: 'I swear that I have spoken the truth, the whole truth and nothing but the truth.' The Court of First Instance may, after hearing the parties, exempt a witness from taking the oath.

6.   The Registrar shall draw up minutes in which the evidence of each witness is reproduced. The minutes shall be signed by the President or by the Judge-Rapporteur responsible for conducting the examination of the witness, and by the Registrar. Before the minutes are thus signed, witnesses must be given an opportunity to check the content of the minutes and to sign them. The minutes shall constitute an official record.

Article 69

1.   Witnesses who have been duly summoned shall obey the summons and attend for examination.

2.   If a witness who has been duly summoned fails to appear before the Court of First Instance, the latter may impose upon him a pecuniary penalty not exceeding 5,000 ECU and may order that a further summons be served on the witness at his own expense. The same penalty may be imposed upon a witness who, without good reason, refuses to give evidence or to take the oath or where appropriate to make a solemn affirmation equivalent thereto.

3.   If the witness proffers a valid excuse to the Court of First Instance, the pecuniary penalty imposed on him may be cancelled. The pecuniary penalty imposed may be reduced at the request of the witness where he establishes that it is disproportionate to his income.

4.   Penalties imposed and other measures ordered under this Article shall be enforced in accordance with Articles 187 and 192 of the EC Treaty, Articles 44 and 92 of the ECSC Treaty and Articles 159 and 164 of the Euratom Treaty.

Article 70

1.   The Court of First Instance may order that an expert's report be obtained. The order appointing the expert shall define his task and set a time-limit within which he is to make his report.

2.   The expert shall receive a copy of the order, together with all the documents necessary for carrying out his task. He shall be under the supervision of the Judge-Rapporteur, who may be present during his investigation and who shall be kept informed of his progress in carrying out his task. The Court of First Instance may request the parties or one of them to lodge security for the costs of the expert's report.

3.   At the request of the expert, the Court of First Instance may order the examination of witnesses. Their examination shall be carried out in accordance with Article 68.

4.   The expert may give his opinion only on points which have been expressly referred to him.

5.   After the expert has made his report, the Court of First Instance may order that he be examined, the parties having been given notice to attend. Subject to the control of the President, questions may be put to the expert by the representatives of the parties.

6.   Subject to the provisions of Article 71, the expert shall, after making his report, take the following oath before the Court of First Instance:

'I swear that I have conscientiously and impartially carried out my task.'

The Court of First Instance may, after hearing the parties, exempt the expert from taking the oath.

Article 71

1.   The President shall instruct any person who is required to take an oath before the Court of First Instance, as witness or expert, to tell the truth or to carry out his task conscientiously and impartially, as the case may be, and shall warn him of the criminal liability provided for in his national law in the event of any breach of this duty.

2.   Witnesses and experts shall take the oath either in accordance with the first subparagraph of Article 68(5) and the first subparagraph of Article 70(6) or in the manner laid down by their national law.

3.   Where the national law provides the opportunity to make, in judicial proceedings, a solemn affirmation equivalent to an oath as well as or instead of taking an oath, the witnesses and experts may make such an affirmation under the conditions and in the form prescribed in their national law. Where their national law provides neither for taking an oath nor for making a solemn affirmation, the procedure described in the first paragraph of this Article shall be followed.

Article 72

1.   The Court of First Instance may, after hearing the Advocate-General, decide to report to the competent authority referred to in Annex III to the Rules supplementing the Rules of Procedure of the Court of Justice of the Member State whose courts have penal jurisdiction in any case of perjury on the part of a witness or expert before the Court of First Instance, account being taken of the provisions of Article 71.

2.   The Registrar shall be responsible for communicating the decision of the Court of First Instance. The decision shall set out the facts and circumstances on which the report is based.

Article 73

1.   If one of the parties objects to a witness or to an expert on the ground that he is not a competent or proper person to act as witness or expert or for any other reason, or if a witness or expert refuses to give evidence, to take the oath or to make a solemn affirmation equivalent thereto, the matter shall be resolved by the Court of First Instance.

2.   An objection to a witness or to an expert shall be raised within two weeks after service of the order summoning the witness or appointing the expert; the statement of objection must set out the grounds of objection and indicate the nature of any evidence offered.

Article 74

1.   Witnesses and experts shall be entitled to reimbursement of their travel and subsistence expenses. The cashier of the Court of First Instance may make a payment to them towards these expenses in advance.

2.   Witnesses shall be entitled to compensation for loss of earnings, and experts to fees for their services. The cashier of the Court of First Instance shall pay witnesses and experts their compensation or fees after they have carried out their respective duties or tasks.

Article 75

1. The Court of First Instance may, on application by a party or of its own motion, issue letters rogatory for the examination of witnesses or experts.

2. Letters rogatory shall be issued in the form of an order which shall contain the name, forenames, description and address of the witness or expert, set out the facts on which the witness or expert is to be examined, name the parties, their agents, lawyers or advisers, indicate their addresses for service and briefly describe the subject-matter of the proceedings. Notice of the order shall be served on the parties by the Registrar.

3. The Registrar shall send the order to the competent authority named in Annex I to the Rules supplementing the Rules of Procedure of the Court of Justice of the Member State in whose territory the witness or expert is to be examined. Where necessary, the order shall be accompanied by a translation into the official language or languages of the Member State to which it is addressed. The authority named pursuant to the first paragraph shall pass on the order to the judicial authority which is competent according to its national law. The competent judicial authority shall give effect to the letters rogatory in accordance with its national law. After implementation the competent judicial authority shall transmit to the authority named pursuant to the first paragraph the order embodying the letters rogatory, any documents arising from the implementation and a detailed statement of costs. These documents shall be sent to the Registrar. The Registrar shall be responsible for the translation of the documents into the language of the case.

4. The Court of First Instance shall defray the expenses occasioned by the letters rogatory without prejudice to the right to charge them, where appropriate, to the parties.

Article 76

1. The Registrar shall draw up minutes of every hearing. The minutes shall be signed by the President and by the Registrar and shall constitute an official record.

2. The parties may inspect the minutes and any expert's report at the Registry and obtain copies at their own expense.

CHAPTER 4   STAY OF PROCEEDINGS AND DECLINING OF JURISDICTION BY THE COURT OF FIRST INSTANCE

Article 77

Without prejudice to Article 123(4), Article 128 and Article 129(4), proceedings may be stayed:

(a) in the circumstances specified in the third paragraph of Article 47 of the EC Statute, the third paragraph of Article 47 of the ECSC Statute and the third paragraph of Article 48 of the Euratom Statute;

(b) where an appeal is brought before the Court of Justice against a decision of the Court of First Instance disposing of the substantive issues in part only, disposing of a procedural issue concerning a plea of lack of competence or inadmissibility or dismissing an application to intervene;

(c) at the joint request of the parties.

Article 78

The decision to stay the proceedings shall be made by order of the President after hearing the parties and the Advocate-General; the President may refer the matter to the Court of First Instance. A decision ordering that the proceedings be resumed shall be adopted in accordance with the same procedure. The orders referred to in this Article shall be served on the parties.

Article 79

1. The stay of proceedings shall take effect on the date indicated in the order of stay or, in the absence of such an indication, on the date of that order. While proceedings are stayed time shall, except for the purposes of the time-limit prescribed in Article 115(1) for an application to intervene, cease to run for the purposes of prescribed time-limits for all parties.

2. Where the order of stay does not fix the length of the stay, it shall end on the date indicated in the order of resumption or, in the absence of such indication, on the date of the order of resumption. From the date of resumption time shall begin to run afresh for the purposes of the time-limits.

Article 80

Decisions declining jurisdiction in the circumstances specified in the third paragraph of Article 47 of the EC Statute, the third paragraph of Article 47 of the ECSC Statute and the third paragraph of Article 48 of the Euratom Statute shall be made by the Court of First Instance by way of an order which shall be served on the parties.

CHAPTER 5   JUDGMENTS

Article 81

The judgment shall contain:
— a statement that it is the judgment of the Court of First Instance,
— the date of its delivery,
— the names of the President and of the Judges taking part in it,
— the name of the Advocate-General, if designated,
— the name of the Registrar,
— the description of the parties,
— the names of the agents, advisers and lawyers of the parties,
— a statement of the forms of order sought by the parties,
— a statement, where appropriate, that the Advocate-General delivered his opinion,
— a summary of the facts,
— the grounds for the decision,
— the operative part of the judgment, including the decision as to costs.

Article 82

1. The judgment shall be delivered in open court; the parties shall be given notice to attend to hear it.

2. The original of the judgment, signed by the President, by the Judges who took part in the deliberations and by the Registrar, shall be sealed and deposited at the Registry; the parties shall be served with certified copies of the judgment.

3. The Registrar shall record on the original of the judgment the date on which it was delivered.

Article 83

Subject to the provisions of the second paragraph of Article 53 of the EC Statute, the second paragraph of Article 53 of the ECSC Statute and the second paragraph of Article 54 of the Euratom Statute, the judgment shall be binding from the date of its delivery.

Article 84

1. Without prejudice to the provisions relating to the interpretation of judgments, the Court of First Instance may, of its own motion or on application by a party made within two weeks after the delivery of a judgment, rectify clerical mistakes, errors in calculation and obvious slips in it.

2. The parties, whom the Registrar shall duly notify, may lodge written observations within a period prescribed by the President.

3. The Court of First Instance shall take its decision in closed session.

4. The original of the rectification order shall be annexed to the original of the rectified judgment. A note of this order shall be made in the margin of the original of the rectified judgment.

Article 85

If the Court of First Instance should omit to give a decision on costs, any party may within a month after service of the judgment apply to the Court of First Instance to supplement its judgment. The application shall be served on the opposite party and the President shall prescribe a period within which that party may lodge written observations. After these observations have been lodged, the Court of First Instance shall decide both on the admissibility and on the substance of the application.

Article 86

The Registrar shall arrange for the publication of cases before the Court of First Instance.

CHAPTER 6   COSTS

Article 87

1. A decision as to costs shall be given in the final judgment or in the order which closes the proceedings.

2. The unsuccessful party shall be ordered to pay the costs if they have been applied for in the successful party's pleadings. Where there are several unsuccessful parties the Court of First Instance shall decide how the costs are to be shared.

3. Where each party succeeds on some and fails on other heads, or where the circumstances are exceptional, the Court of First Instance may order that the costs be shared or that each party bear its own costs. The Court of First Instance may order a party, even if successful, to pay costs which it considers that party to have unreasonably or vexatiously caused the opposite party to incur.

4. The Member States and institutions which intervened in the proceedings shall bear their own costs. The States, other than the Member States, which are parties to the EEA Agreement, and also the EFTA Surveillance Authority, shall bear their own costs if they intervene in the proceedings. The Court of First Instance may order an intervener other than those mentioned in the preceding subparagraph to bear his own costs.

5. A party who discontinues or withdraws from proceedings shall be ordered to pay the costs if they have been applied for in the observations of the other party on the discontinuence. However, upon application by the party who discontinues or withdraws from proceedings, the costs shall be borne by the other party if this appears justified by the conduct of that party. Where the parties have come to an agreement on costs, the decision as to costs shall be in

accordance with that agreement. If costs are not applied for, the parties shall bear their own costs.

6.   Where a case does not proceed to judgment, the costs shall be in the discretion of the Court of First Instance.

Article 88
Without prejudice to the second subparagraph of Article 87(3), in proceedings between the Communities and their servants the institutions shall bear their own costs.

Article 89
Costs necessarily incurred by a party in enforcing a judgment or order of the Court of First Instance shall be refunded by the opposite party on the scale in force in the State where the enforcement takes place.

Article 90
Proceedings before the Court of First Instance shall be free of charge, except that:

(a)   where a party has caused the Court of First Instance to incur avoidable costs, the Court of First Instance may order that party to refund them;

(b)   where copying or translation work is carried out at the request of a party, the cost shall, in so far as the Registrar considers it excessive, be paid for by that party on the scale of charges referred to in Article 24(5).

Article 91
Without prejudice to the preceding Article, the following shall be regarded as recoverable costs:

(a)   sums payable to witnesses and experts under Article 74;

(b)   expenses necessarily incurred by the parties for the purpose of the proceedings, in particular the travel and subsistence expenses and the remuneration of agents, advisers or lawyers.

Article 92
1.   If there is a dispute concerning the costs to be recovered, the Court of First Instance hearing the case shall, on application by the party concerned and after hearing the opposite party, make an order, from which no appeal shall lie.

2.   The parties may, for the purposes of enforcement, apply for an authenticated copy of the order.

Article 93
1.   Sums due from the cashier of the Court of First Instance shall be paid in the currency of the country where the Court of First Instance has its seat. At the request of the person entitled to any sum, it shall be paid in the currency of the country where the expenses to be refunded were incurred or where the steps in respect of which payment is due were taken.

2.   Other debtors shall make payment in the currency of their country of origin.

3.   Conversions of currency shall be made at the official rates of exchange ruling on the day of payment in the country where the Court of First Instance has its seat.

CHAPTER 7   LEGAL AID

Article 94

1.   A party who is wholly or in part unable to meet the costs of the proceedings may at any time apply for legal aid. The application shall be accompanied by evidence of the applicant's need of assistance, and in particular by a document from the competent authority certifying his lack of means.

2.   If the application is made prior to proceedings which the applicant wishes to commence, it shall briefly state the subject of such proceedings. The application need not be made through a lawyer. The President of the Court of First Instance shall designate a Judge to act as Rapporteur. The President shall, after considering the written observations of the opposite party, decide whether legal aid should be granted in full or in part, or whether it should be refused. He shall consider whether there is manifestly no cause of action. He may refer the matter to the Court of First Instance. The Decision shall be taken by way of an order without giving reasons, and no appeal shall lie therefrom.

Article 95

1.   The Court of First Instance, by any order by which it decides that a person is entitled to receive legal aid, shall order that a lawyer be appointed to act for him.

2.   If the person does not indicate his choice of lawyer, or if the Court of First Instance considers that his choice is unacceptable, the Registrar shall send a copy of the order and of the application for legal aid to the authority named in Annex II to the Rules supplementing the Rules of Procedure of the Court of Justice, being the competent authority of the State concerned.

3.   The Court of First Instance, in the light of the suggestions made by that authority, shall of its own motion appoint a lawyer to act for the person concerned.

4.   An order granting legal aid may specify an amount to be paid to the lawyer appointed to act for the person concerned or fix a limit which the lawyer's disbursements and fees may not, in principle, exceed.

Article 96

The Court of First Instance may at any time, either of its own motion or on application, withdraw legal aid if the circumstances which led to its being granted alter during the proceedings.

Article 97

1.   Where legal aid is granted, the cashier of the Court of First Instance shall advance the funds necessary to meet the expenses.

2.   The President, who may refer the matter to the Court of First Instance shall adjudicate on the lawyer's disbursements and fees; he may, on application by the lawyer, order that he receive an advance.

3.   In its decision as to costs the Court of First Instance may order the payment to the cashier of the Court of First Instance of the whole or any part of amounts advanced as legal aid. The Registrar shall take steps to obtain the recovery of these sums from the party ordered to pay them.

CHAPTER 8   DISCONTINUANCE

Article 98

If, before the Court of First Instance has given its decision, the parties reach a settlement of their dispute and intimate to the Court of First Instance the abandonment of their claims, the President shall order the case to be removed from the register and shall give a decision as to costs in accordance with Article 87(5) having regard to any proposals made by the parties on the matter. This provision shall not apply to proceedings under Articles 173 and 175 of the EC Treaty, Articles 33 and 35 of the ECSC Treaty or Articles 146 and 148 of the Euratom Treaty.

Article 99

If the applicant informs the Court of First Instance in writing that he wishes to discontinue the proceedings, the President shall order the case to be removed from the register and shall give a decision as to costs in accordance with Article 87(5).

CHAPTER 9   SERVICE

Article 100

Where these Rules require that a document be served on a person, the Registrar shall ensure that service is effected at that person's address for service either by the dispatch of a copy of the document by registered post with a form for acknowledgement of receipt or by personal delivery of the copy against a receipt. The Registrar shall prepare and certify the copies of documents to be served, save where the parties themselves supply the copies in accordance with Article 43(1).

CHAPTER 10   TIME-LIMITS

Article 101

1. Any period of time prescribed by the EC, ECSC or Euratom Treaties, the Statutes of the Court of Justice or these Rules for the taking of any procedural step shall be reckoned as follows:

(a) Where a period expressed in days, weeks, months or years is to be calculated from the moment at which an event occurs or an action takes place, the day during which that event occurs or that action takes place shall not be counted as falling within the period in question;

(b) A period expressed in weeks, months or in years shall end with the expiry of whichever day in the last week, month or year is the same day of the week, or falls on the same date, as the day during which the event or action from which the period is to be calculated occurred or took place. If, in a period expressed in months or in years, the day on which it should expire does not occur in the last month, the period shall end with the expiry of the last day of that month;

(c) Where a period is expressed in months and days, it shall first be reckoned in whole months, then in days;

(d) Periods shall include official holidays, Sundays and Saturdays;

(e) Periods shall not be suspended during the judicial vacations.

2. If the period would otherwise end on a Saturday, Sunday or official holiday, it shall be extended until the end of the first following working day. The list of official holidays drawn up by the Court of Justice and published in the Official Journal of the European Communities shall apply to the Court of First Instance.

Article 102

1. Where the period of time allowed for commencing proceedings against a measure adopted by an institution runs from the publication of that measure,

that period shall be calculated, for the purposes of Article 101(1), from the end of the 14th day after publication thereof in the *Official Journal of the European Communities*.

2. The extensions, on account of distance, of prescribed time-limits provided for in a decision of the Court of Justice and published in the Official Journal of the European Communities shall apply to the Court of First Instance.

Article 103

1. Any time-limit prescribed pursuant to these Rules may be extended by whoever prescribed it.

2. The President may delegate power of signature to the Registrar for the purpose of fixing time-limits which, pursuant to these Rules, it falls to the President to prescribe, or of extending such time-limits.

TITLE III   SPECIAL FORMS OF PROCEDURE
CHAPTER 1   SUSPENSION OF OPERATION OR ENFORCEMENT AND OTHER INTERIM MEASURES

Article 104

1. An application to suspend the operation of any measure adopted by an institution, made pursuant to Article 185 of the EC Treaty, the second paragraph of Article 39 of the ECSC Treaty or Article 157 of the Euratom Treaty, shall be admissible only if the applicant is challenging that measure in proceedings before the Court of First Instance. An application for the adoption of any other interim measure referred to in Article 186 of the EC Treaty, the third paragraph of Article 39 of the ECSC Treaty and or Article 158 of the Euratom Treaty shall be admissible only if it is made by a party to a case before the Court of First Instance and relates to that case.

2. An application of a kind referred to in paragraph (1) of this Article shall state the subject-matter of the proceedings, the circumstances giving rise to urgency and the pleas of fact and law establishing a prima facie case for the interim measures applied for.

3. The application shall be made by a separate document and in accordance with the provisions of Articles 43 and 44.

Article 105

1. The application shall be served on the opposite party, and the President of the Court of First Instance shall prescribe a short period within which that party may submit written or oral observations.

2. The President of the Court of First Instance may order a preparatory inquiry. The President of the Court of First Instance may grant the application even before the observations of the opposite party have been submitted. This decision may be varied or cancelled even without any application being made by any party.

Article 106

The President of the Court of First Instance shall either decide on the application himself or refer it to the Chamber to which the case has been assigned in the main proceedings or to the Court of First Instance sitting in plenary session if the case has been assigned to it. If the President of the Court of First Instance is absent or prevented from attending, he shall be replaced by the President or the most senior Judge, within the meaning of Article 6, of the bench of the Court of First Instance to which the case has been assigned. Where the application is referred to a bench of the Court of First Instance, that bench shall postpone all other cases and shall give a decision. Article 105 shall apply.

Article 107

1. The decision on the application shall take the form of a reasoned order. The order shall be served on the parties forthwith.

2. The enforcement of the order may be made conditional on the lodging by the applicant of security, of an amount and nature to be fixed in the light of the circumstances.

3. Unless the order fixes the date on which the interim measure is to lapse, the measure shall lapse when final judgment is delivered.

4. The order shall have only an interim effect, and shall be without prejudice to the decision on the substance of the case by the Court of First Instance.

Article 108

On application by a party, the order may at any time be varied or cancelled on account of a change in circumstances.

Article 109

Rejection of an application for an interim measure shall not bar the party who made it from making a further application on the basis of new facts.

Article 110

The provisions of this Chapter shall apply to applications to suspend the enforcement of a decision of the Court of First Instance or of any measure adopted by another institution, submitted pursuant to Articles 187 and 192 of the EC Treaty, Articles 44 and 92 of the ECSC Treaty or Articles 159 and 164 of the Euratom Treaty. The order granting the application shall fix, where appropriate, a date on which the interim measure is to lapse.

CHAPTER 2   PRELIMINARY ISSUES

Article 111

Where it is clear that the Court of First Instance has no jurisdiction to take cognisance of an action or where the action is manifestly inadmissible or manifestly lacking any foundation in law, the Court of First Instance may, by reasoned order, after hearing the Advocate-General and without taking further steps in the proceedings, give a decision on the action.

Article 112

The decision to refer an action to the Court of Justice, pursuant to the second paragraph of Article 47 of the EC Statute, the second paragraph of Article 47 of the ECSC Statute and the second paragraph of Article 48 of the Euratom Statute, shall, in the case of manifest lack of competence, be made by reasoned order and without taking any further steps in the proceedings.

Article 113

The Court of First Instance may at any time of its own motion consider whether there exists any absolute bar to proceeding with an action or declare, after hearing the parties, that the action has become devoid of purpose and that there is no need to adjudicate on it; it shall give its decision in accordance with Article 114(3) and (4).

Article 114

1. A party applying to the Court of First Instance for a decision on admissibility, on lack of competence or other preliminary plea not going to the substance of the case shall make the application by a separate document. The application must contain the pleas of fact and law relied on and the form of order sought by the applicant; any supporting documents must be annexed to it.

2. As soon as the application has been lodged, the President shall prescribe a period within which the opposite party may lodge a document containing a statement of the form of order sought by that party and its pleas in law.

3. Unless the Court of First Instance otherwise decides, the remainder of the proceedings shall be oral.

4. The Court of First Instance shall, after hearing the Advocate-General, decide on the application or reserve its decision for the final judgment. It shall refer the case to the Court of Justice if the case falls within the jurisdiction of that Court. If the Court of First Instance refuses the application or reserves its decision, the President shall prescribe new time-limits for further steps in the proceedings.

CHAPTER 3   INTERVENTION

Article 115

1. An application to intervene must be made within three months of the publication of the notice referred to in Article 24(6).

2. The application shall contain:

    (a)   the description of the case;

    (b)   the description of the parties;

    (c)   the name and address of the intervener;

    (d)   the intervener's address for service at the place where the Court of First Instance has its seat;

    (e)   the form of order sought, by one or more of the parties, in support of which the intervener is applying for leave to intervene;

    (f)   A statement of the circumstances establishing the right to intervene, where the application is submitted pursuant to the second or third paragraph of Article 37 of the EC Statute, Article 34 of the ECSC Statute or the second paragraph of Article 38 of the Euratom Statute. Articles 43 and 44 shall apply.

3. The intervener shall be represented in accordance with Article 17 of the EC Statute, the first and second paragraphs of Article 20 of the ECSC Statute and Article 17 of the Euratom Statute.

Article 116

1. The application shall be served on the parties. The President shall give the parties an opportunity to submit their written or oral observations before deciding on the application. The President shall decide on the application by order or shall refer the decision to the Court of First Instance. The order must be reasoned if the application is dismissed.

2. If the President allows the intervention, the intervener shall receive a copy of every document served on the parties. The President may, however, on application by one of the parties, omit secret or confidential documents.

3. The intervener must accept the case as he finds it at the time of his intervention.

4. The President shall prescribe a period within which the intervener may submit a statement in intervention. The statement in intervention shall contain:

(a) a statement of the form of order sought by the intervener in support of or opposing, in whole or in part, the form of order sought by one of the parties;

(b) the pleas in law and arguments relied on by the intervener;

(c) where appropriate, the nature of any evidence offered.

5. After the statement in intervention has been lodged, the President shall, where necessary, prescribe a time-limit within which the parties may reply to that statement.

CHAPTER 4   JUDGMENTS OF THE COURT OF FIRST INSTANCE DELIVERED AFTER ITS DECISION HAS BEEN SET ASIDE AND THE CASE REFERRED BACK TO IT

Article 117

Where the Court of Justice sets aside a judgment or an order of the Court of First Instance and refers the case back to that Court, the latter shall be seised of the case by the judgment so referring it.

Article 118

1. Where the Court of Justice sets aside a judgment or an order of a Chamber, the President of the Court of First Instance may assign the case to another Chamber composed of the same number of Judges.

2. Where the Court of Justice sets aside a judgment delivered or an order made by the Court of First Instance sitting in plenary session, the case shall be assigned to that Court as so constituted.

3. In the cases provided for in paragraphs (1) and (2) of this Article, Articles 13(2), 14 and 51 shall apply.

Article 119

1. Where the written procedure before the Court of First Instance has been completed when the judgment referring the case back to it is delivered, the course of the procedure shall be as follows:

(a) Within two months from the service upon him of the judgment of the Court of Justice the applicant may lodge a statement of written observations.

(b) In the month following the communication to him of that statement, the defendant may lodge a statement of written observations. The time allowed to the defendant for lodging it may in no case be less than two months from the service upon him of the judgment of the Court of Justice.

(c) In the month following the simultaneous communication to the intervener of the observations of the applicant and the defendant, the intervener may lodge a statement of written observations. The time allowed to the intervener for lodging it may in no case be less than two months from the service upon him of the judgment of the Court of Justice.

2. Where the written procedure before the Court of First Instance had not been completed when the judgment referring the case back to the Court of First Instance was delivered, it shall be resumed, at the stage which it had reached, by means of measures of organization of procedure adopted by the Court of First Instance.

3.   The Court of First Instance may, if the circumstances so justify, allow supplementary statements of written observations to be lodged.

Article 120
The procedure shall be conducted in accordance with the provisions of Title II of these Rules.

Article 121
The Court of First Instance shall decide on the costs relating to the proceedings instituted before it and to the proceedings on the appeal before the Court of Justice.

CHAPTER 5   JUDGMENTS BY DEFAULT AND APPLICATIONS TO SET THEM ASIDE

Article 122
1.   If a defendant on whom an application initiating proceedings has been duly served fails to lodge a defence to the application in the proper form within the time prescribed, the applicant may apply to the Court of First Instance for judgment by default. The application shall be served on the defendant. The Court of First Instance may decide to open the oral procedure on the application.
2.   Before giving judgment by default the Court of First Instance shall consider whether the application initiating proceedings is admissible, whether the appropriate formalities have been complied with, and whether the application appears well founded. It may order a preparatory inquiry.
3.   A judgment by default shall be enforceable. The Court of First Instance may, however, grant a stay of execution until it has given its decision on any application under paragraph (4) of this Article to set aside the judgment, or it may make execution subject to the provision of security of an amount and nature to be fixed in the light of the circumstances; this security shall be released if no such application is made or if the application fails.
4.   Application may be made to set aside a judgment by default. The application to set aside the judgment must be made within one month from the date of service of the judgment and must be lodged in the form prescribed by Articles 43 and 44.
5.   After the application has been served, the President shall prescribe a period within which the other party may submit his written observations. The proceedings shall be conducted in accordance with the provisions of Title II of these Rules.
6.   The Court of First Instance shall decide by way of a judgment which may not be set aside. The original of this judgment shall be annexed to the original of the judgment by default. A note of the judgment on the application to set aside shall be made in the margin of the original of the judgment by default.

CHAPTER 6   EXCEPTIONAL REVIEW PROCEDURES
SECTION 1   THIRD-PARTY PROCEEDINGS

Article 123
1.   Articles 43 and 44 shall apply to an application initiating third-party proceedings. In addition such an application shall:

(a) specify the judgment contested;

(b) state how that judgment is prejudicial to the rights of the third party;

(c) indicate the reasons for which the third party was unable to take part in the original case before the Court of First Instance. The application must be made against all the parties to the original case. Where the judgment has been published in the Official Journal of the European Communities, the application must be lodged within two months of the publication.

2. The Court of First Instance may, on application by the third party, order a stay of execution of the judgment. The provisions of Title III, Chapter 1, shall apply.

3. The contested judgment shall be varied on the points on which the submissions of the third party are upheld. The original of the judgment in the third-party proceedings shall be annexed to the original of the contested judgment. A note of the judgment in the third-party proceedings shall be made in the margin of the original of the contested judgment.

4. Where an appeal before the Court of Justice and an application initiating third-party proceedings before the Court of First Instance contest the same judgment of the Court of First Instance, the Court of First Instance may, after hearing the parties, stay the proceedings until the Court of Justice has delivered its judgment.

Article 124

The application initiating third-party proceedings shall be assigned to the Chamber which delivered the judgment which is the subject of the application; if the Court of First Instance sitting in plenary session delivered the judgment, the application shall be assigned to it.

SECTION 2 REVISION

Article 125

Without prejudice to the period of ten years prescribed in the third paragraph of Article 41 of the EC Statute, the third paragraph of Article 38 of the ECSC Statute and the third paragraph of Article 42 of the Euratom Statute, an application for revision of a judgment shall be made within three months of the date on which the facts on which the application is based came to the applicant's knowledge.

Article 126

1. Articles 43 and 44 shall apply to an application for revision. In addition such an application shall:

(a) specify the judgment contested;

(b) indicate the points on which the application is based;

(c) set out the facts on which the application is based;

(d) indicate the nature of the evidence to show that there are facts justifying revision of the judgment, and that the time-limits laid down in Article 125 have been observed.

2. The application must be made against all parties to the case in which the contested judgment was given.

Article 127

1. The application for revision shall be assigned to the Chamber which delivered the judgment which is the subject of the application; if the Court of

First Instance sitting in plenary session delivered the judgment, the application shall be assigned to it.

2.   Without prejudice to its decision on the substance, the Court of First Instance shall, after hearing the Advocate-General, having regard to the written observations of the parties, give its decision on the admissibility of the application.

3.   If the Court of First Instance finds the application admissible, it shall proceed to consider the substance of the application and shall give its decision in the form of a judgment in accordance with these Rules.

4.   The original of the revising judgment shall be annexed to the original of the judgment revised. A note of the revising judgment shall be made in the margin of the original of the judgment revised.

Article 128
Where an appeal before the Court of Justice and an application for revision before the Court of First Instance concern the same judgment of the Court of First Instance, the Court of First Instance may, after hearing the parties, stay the proceedings until the Court of Justice has delivered its judgment.

SECTION 3   INTERPRETATION OF JUDGMENTS
Article 129
1.   An application for interpretation of a judgment shall be made in accordance with Articles 43 and 44. In addition it shall specify:
    (a)   the judgment in question;
    (b)   the passages of which interpretation is sought. The application must be made against all the parties to the case in which the judgment was given.

2.   The application for interpretation shall be assigned to the Chamber which delivered the judgment which is the subject of the application; if the Court of First Instance sitting in plenary session delivered the judgment, the application shall be assigned to it.

3.   The Court of First Instance shall give its decision in the form of a judgment after having given the parties an opportunity to submit their observations and after hearing the Advocate General. The original of the interpreting judgment shall be annexed to the original of the judgment interpreted. A note of the interpreting judgment shall be made in the margin of the original of the judgment interpreted.

4.   Where an appeal before the Court of Justice and an application for interpretation before the Court of First Instance concern the same judgment of the Court of First Instance, the Court of First Instance may, after hearing the parties, stay the proceedings until the Court of Justice has delivered its judgment.

TITLE IV   PROCEEDINGS RELATING TO INTELLECTUAL
PROPERTY RIGHTS

Article 130
1.   Subject to the special provisions of this Title, the provisions of these Rules of Procedure shall apply to proceedings brought against the Office for Harmonization in the Internal Market (Trade Marks and Designs) and against the Community Plant Variety Office, (both hereinafter referred to as 'the Office'), and concerning the application of the rules relating to an intellectual property regime.

2.   The provisions of this Title shall not apply to actions brought directly against the Office without prior proceedings before a Board of Appeal.

Article 131

1.   The application shall be drafted in one of the languages described in Article 35(1), according to the applicant's choice.

2.   The language in which the application is drafted shall become the language of the case if the applicant was the only party to the proceedings before the Board of Appeal or if another party to those proceedings does not object to this within a period laid down for that purpose by the Registrar after the application has been lodged. If, within that period, the parties to the proceedings before the Board of Appeal inform the Registrar of their agreement on the choice, as the language of the case, of one of the languages referred to in Article 35(1), that language shall become the language of the case before the Court of First Instance. In the event of an objection to the choice of the language of the case made by the applicant within the period referred to above and in the absence of an agreement on the matter between the parties to the proceedings before the Board of Appeal, the language in which the application for registration in question was filed at the Office shall become the language of the case. If, however, on a reasoned request by any party and after hearing the other parties, the President finds that the use of that language would not enable all parties to the proceedings before the Board of Appeal to follow the proceedings and defend their interests and that only the use of another language from among those mentioned in Article 35(1) makes it possible to remedy that situation, he may designate that other language as the language of the case; the President may refer the matter to the Court of First Instance.

3.   In the pleadings and other documents addressed to the Court of First Instance and during the oral procedure, the applicant may use the language chosen by him in accordance with paragraph 1 and each of the other parties may use a language chosen by that party from those mentioned in Article 35(1).

4.   If, by virtue of paragraph 2, a language other than that in which the application is drafted becomes the language of the case, the Registrar shall cause the application to be translated into the language of the case. Each party shall be required, within a reasonable period to be prescribed for that purpose by the Registrar, to produce a translation into the language of the case of the pleadings or documents other than the application that are lodged by that party in a language other than the language of the case pursuant to paragraph 3. The party producing the translation, which shall be authentic within the meaning of Article 37, shall certify its accuracy. If the translation is not produced within the period prescribed, the pleading or the procedural document in question shall be removed from the file. The Registrar shall cause everything said during the oral procedure to be translated into the language of the case and, at the request of any party, into the language used by that party in accordance with paragraph 3.

Article 132

1.   Without prejudice to Article 44, the application shall contain the names of all the parties to the proceedings before the Board of Appeal and the addresses which they had given for the purposes of the notifications to be effected in the course of those proceedings. The contested decision of the

Board of Appeal shall be appended to the application. The date on which the applicant was notified of that decision must be indicated.

2.   If the application does not comply with paragraph 1, Article 44(6) shall apply.

Article 133

1.   The Registrar shall inform the Office and all the parties to the proceedings before the Board of Appeal of the lodging of the application. He shall arrange for service of the application after determining the language of the case in accordance with Article 131(2).

2.   The application shall be served on the Office, as defendant, and on the parties to the proceedings before the Board of Appeal other than the applicant. Service shall be effected in the language of the case. Service of the application on a party to the proceedings before the Board of Appeal shall be effected by registered post with a form of acknowledgment of receipt at the address given by the party concerned for the purposes of the notifications to be effected in the course of the proceedings before the Board of Appeal.

3.   Once the application has been served, the Office shall forward to the Court of First Instance the file relating to the proceedings before the Board of Appeal.

Article 134

1.   The parties to the proceedings before the Board of Appeal other than the applicant may participate, as interveners, in the proceedings before the Court of First Instance.

2.   The interveners referred to in paragraph 1 shall have the same procedural rights as the main parties. They may support the form of order sought by a main party and they may apply for a form of order and put forward pleas in law independently of those applied for and put forward by the main parties.

3.   An intervener, as referred to in paragraph 1, may, in his response lodged in accordance with Article 135(1), seek an order annulling or altering the decision of the Board of Appeal on a point not raised in the application and put forward pleas in law not raised in the application. Such submissions seeking orders or putting forward pleas in law in the intervener's response shall cease to have effect should the applicant discontinue the proceedings.

4.   In derogation from Article 122, the default procedure shall not apply where an intervener, as referred to in paragraph 1 of this Article, has responded to the application in the manner and within the period prescribed.

Article 135

1.   The Office and the interveners referred to in Article 134(1) may submit responses to the application within a period of two months from the service of the application. Article 46 shall apply to the responses.

2.   The application and the responses may be supplemented by replies and rejoinders by the parties, including the interveners referred to in Article 134(1), where the President, on a reasoned application made within two weeks of service of the responses or replies, considers such further pleading necessary and allows it in order to enable the party concerned to put forward its point of view. The President shall prescribe the period within which such pleadings are to be submitted.

3.   Without prejudice to the foregoing, in the cases referred to in Article 134(3), the other parties may, within a period of two months of service upon them of the response, submit a pleading confined to responding to the form of order sought and the pleas in law submitted for the first time in the response of a intervener. That period may be extended by the President on a reasoned application from the party concerned.

4.   The parties' pleadings may not change the subject-matter of the proceedings before the Board of Appeal.

Article 136

1.   Where an action against a decision of a Board of Appeal is successful, the Court of First Instance may order the Office to bear only its own costs.

2.   Costs necessarily incurred by the parties for the purposes of the proceedings before the Board of Appeal and costs incurred for the purposes of the production, prescribed by the second subparagraph of Article 131(4), of translations of pleadings or other documents into the language of the case shall be regarded as recoverable costs. In the event of inaccurate translations being produced, the second subparagraph of Article 87(3) shall apply.

MISCELLANEOUS PROVISIONS

Article 137

These Rules, which are authentic in the languages mentioned in Article 35(1), shall be published in the Official Journal of the European Communities. They shall enter into force on the first day of the second month from the date of their publication.

Done at Luxembourg on 2 May 1991.
H. JUNG, Registrar
J. L. CRUZ VILAÇA, President

RULES OF PROCEDURE OF THE COMMISSION OF 17 FEBRUARY 1993 (COMMISSION DECISION 93/492) [OJ NO 1993 L 230/15][1]

THE COMMISSION OF THE EUROPEAN COMMUNITIES,

Having regard to the Treaty establishing a Single Council and a Single Commission of the European Communities, and in particular Article 16 thereof,

HAS ADOPTED THESE RULES OF PROCEDURE:

CHAPTER I   THE COMMISSION

Article 1
The Commission shall act collectively in accordance with these Rules.

Article 2
Commission decisions shall be adopted:

Note
[1]Amended by Commission Decision 95/148/EC/ECSC/Euratom (OJ No. L097, 29/04/1995 p. 0082)

(a) at the Commission's meetings; or
(b) by written procedure, in accordance with Article 10; or
(c) by delegation, in accordance with Article 11.

SECTION I   MEETINGS OF THE COMMISSION

Article 3

Meetings of the Commission shall be convened by the President.

The Commission shall, as a general rule, meet at least once a week. It shall hold additional meetings whenever necessary.

Article 4

Each year the Commission shall adopt an annual programme. The President shall adopt the agenda for each meeting in the light of this programme and a quarterly rolling programme which will normally include any items requiring a Commission decision.

If a Member of the Commission requests the inclusion of an item that is not covered by the quarterly programme, it shall be placed on the agenda provided, save in exceptional circumstances, nine days' notice is given. The agenda and the necessary working documents shall be circulated to the Members of the Commission within the time limit and in the working languages prescribed by the Commission in accordance with Article 24.

Any Member of the Commission may request or, in his absence, have a request made for an item to be withdrawn from the agenda, in which case the item shall be held over for a later meeting, but an item shall not be withdrawn if the effect would be to prevent the Commission from meeting a deadline where failure to meet it would have legal consequences. If any objection is raised to a further request for withdrawal of the same item, the Commission shall decide the matter. The Commission may decide by majority vote to discuss any question which is not on the agenda or for which the necessary working documents have been distributed late. It may decide by majority vote not to discuss any item on the agenda.

Article 5

The number of Members present required to constitute a quorum shall be equal to a majority of the number of Members specified in the Treaty.

Article 6

The Commission takes decisions on a proposal from one or more of its Members.

A vote shall be taken if any Member so requests. The vote may be on a proposal as originally made or as amended by the Member or Members responsible or by the President.

Commission decisions shall be adopted if a majority of the number of Members specified in the Treaty vote in favour. This provision shall apply to decisions of all kinds, subject to the first sentence of the fifth paragraph of Article 4.

Article 7

Meetings of the Commission shall not be public. Discussions shall be confidential.

Article 8

Save as otherwise decided by the Commission, the Secretary-General shall attend meetings. Attendance of other persons shall be determined in accordance with rules to give effect to these Rules of Procedure.

In the absence of a Member of the Commission, his chef de cabinet may attend the meeting and, at the invitation of the President, state the views of the absent Member.

The Commission may, by way of exception, decide to hear any other person.

Article 9

Minutes shall be taken of all meetings of the Commission.

The draft minutes shall be submitted to the Commission for approval at a subsequent meeting. The approved minutes shall be authenticated by the signatures of the President and the Secretary-General.

SECTION II   OTHER DECISION-MAKING PROCEDURES

Article 10

The agreement of the Commission to a proposal by one or more of its Members may be obtained by means of a written procedure, provided the Directorates-General directly involved are in agreement and the proposal has been endorsed by the Legal Service.

For this purpose, the text of the proposal shall be circulated in writing to all Members of the Commission, in the languages prescribed by the Commission in accordance with Article 24, with a time limit within which Members must make known any reservations or amendments they wish to make.

Any Member of the Commission may, in the course of the written procedure, request that the proposal be discussed. In such case, the matter shall be placed on the agenda of the next meeting of the Commission.

A proposal on which no Member of the Commission has made a reservation and maintained it up to the time limit set for a written procedure shall be deemed to be agreed by the Commission. Proposals adopted shall be recorded in a day note which shall be noted in the minutes of the next meeting.

Article 11

The Commission may, provided the principle of collective responsibility is fully respected, empower one or more of its Members to take, on its behalf and under its responsibility, clearly defined management or administrative measures, including instruments preparatory to a decision to be taken by the Commission collectively at a later time.

The Commission may also instruct one or more of its Members, with the agreement of the President, to adopt the definitive text of any instrument as defined in the first paragraph or of any proposal to be presented to other institutions the substance of which has already been determined in discussion.

Decisions adopted by delegation procedure shall be recorded in a day note which shall be noted in the minutes of the next meeting.

Powers conferred in this way may be subdelegated only as expressly provided in the enabling decision. The provisions of the first to fourth paragraphs shall be without prejudice to the rules concerning delegation in respect of financial matters or the powers conferred on the appointing authority and the authority empowered to conclude contracts of employment.

SECTION III   PREPARATION AND IMPLEMENTATION OF COMMISSION DECISIONS

Article 12

The Commission may assign to its Members areas in which they will have special responsibility for preparing the Commission's business and for implementing its decisions.

A Member of the Commission to whom an area of responsibility is so assigned shall give instructions to the relevant department or departments.

Article 13

The Commission may set up working groups of its Members; it shall appoint the chairman of any such group.

Article 14

Members of the Commission may each appoint personal staff to assist them in their work and in preparing Commission decisions.

Article 15

The Secretary-General shall assist the President in preparing the proceedings and meetings of the Commission.

He shall ensure that decision-making procedures are properly implemented and that effect is given to the decisions referred to in Article 2.

He shall ensure the necessary coordination between departments in preparing the proceedings of the Commission and that the rules for submission of documents to the Commission are complied with.

He shall take the necessary steps to ensure official notification and publication of Commission instruments in the Official Journal of the European Communities and that the documents of the Commission and its departments are transmitted to the other institutions of the European Communities.

He shall be responsible for official relations with the other institutions of the European Communities, subject to any decision by the Commission to exercise any function itself or to assign it to its Members or departments. He shall monitor the proceedings of the other institutions of the European Communities and keep the Commission informed.

Article 16

Instruments adopted by the Commission in the course of a meeting shall be attached, in the authentic language or languages, in such a way that they cannot be separated, to the minutes of the meeting at which they were adopted. They shall be authenticated by the signatures of the President and the Secretary-General on the first page of the minutes.

Instruments adopted by written procedure shall be attached, in the authentic language or languages, in such a way that they cannot be separated, to the day note referred to in Article 10. They shall be authenticated by the signature of the Secretary-General on the last page of the day note.

Instruments adopted by delegation procedure shall be attached, in the authentic language or languages, in such a way that they cannot be separated, to the day note referred to in Article 11. They shall be authenticated by the signature of the Secretary-General on the last page of the day note.

For the purposes of these Rules, 'instruments' means any instrument as referred to in Article 14 of the ECSC Treaty, Article 189 of the EC Treaty or Article 161 of the Euratom Treaty.

For the purposes of these Rules, 'authentic language or languages' means all the official languages of the Communities in the case of instruments of general application and, in other cases, the languages of those to whom they are addressed.

CHAPTER II   COMMISSION DEPARTMENTS

Article 17
A number of departments forming a single administrative service shall assist the Commission in the performance of its official functions.

The first paragraph is without prejudice to the provisions of Article 12.

Article 18
The administrative service of the Commission shall consist of Directorates-General and equivalent departments.

Directorates-General and equivalent departments shall normally be divided into Directorates, and Directorates into Units.

Article 19
The Commission may, in special cases, set up temporary structures to deal with particular matters and shall determine their responsibilities and method of operation.

Article 20
Departments involved in the preparation or implementation of Commission decisions shall work together as closely as possible.

Before submitting a document to the Commission, the department responsible shall, in sufficient time, consult other departments which are associated or concerned by virtue of their powers or responsibilities or the nature of the subject. The Legal Service shall be consulted on all drafts of or proposals for legal instruments and on all documents which may have legal implications. The Directorates-General responsible for the budgets, for personnel and for the administration shall be consulted on all documents which may have implications concerning the budget and finances or personnel and administration respectively. The Directorate-General responsible for financial control shall likewise be consulted, as need be.

The department responsible shall endeavour to frame a proposal that has the agreement of the departments consulted. In the event of disagreement, it shall append to its proposal the different views expressed by these departments, subject to the provisions of Article 10.

CHAPTER III   DEPUTIZING

Article 21
If the President is prevented from exercising his functions, they shall be exercised by one of the Vice-Presidents or Members chosen in the order laid down by the Commission.

Article 22
Where the Secretary-General is prevented from exercising his functions, they shall be exercised by the Deputy Secretary-General or, where this is not possible, by an official designated by the Commission.

Article 23

Save as otherwise decided by the Commission, where any superior is prevented from exercising his functions, his place shall be taken by the longest-serving subordinate present, or (in the event of equal length of service) by the person who is the senior by age, in the highest category and grade.

In the absence of the Head of one of the external delegations, the Director-General with responsibility for the delegation is empowered to appoint, with the agreement of the relevant Member of the Commission, a Chargé d'affaires who need not satisfy the conditions set out in the first paragraph.

FINAL PROVISIONS

Article 24

The Commission shall determine, as necessary, rules to give effect to these Rules of Procedure.

Article 25

The provisional Rules of Procedure of 6 July 1967 are hereby repealed.

Article 26

These Rules of Procedure shall enter into force on 11 September 1993.

Article 27

These Rules of Procedure shall be published in the Official Journal of the European Communities.

Done at Brussels, 17 February 1993.
For the Commission
The President
Jacques DELORS

SECONDARY LEGISLATION

FREE MOVEMENT OF GOODS

COMMISSION DIRECTIVE OF 22 DECEMBER 1969 BASED ON THE PROVISIONS OF ARTICLE 33(7), ON THE ABOLITION OF MEASURES WHICH HAVE AN EFFECT EQUIVALENT TO QUANTITATIVE RESTRICTIONS ON IMPORTS AND ARE NOT COVERED BY OTHER PROVISIONS ADOPTED IN PURSUANCE OF THE EEC TREATY (70/50/EEC)
[OJ Sp. Ed. 1970, I No. L13/29, p. 17]

THE COMMISSION OF THE EUROPEAN COMMUNITIES,

Having regard to the provisions of the Treaty establishing the European Economic Community, and in particular Article 33(7) thereof;

Whereas for the purpose of Article 30 *et seq.* 'measures' means laws, regulations, administrative provisions, administrative practices, and all instruments issuing from a public authority, including recommendations;

Whereas for the purposes of this Directive 'administrative practices' means any standard and regularly followed procedure of a public authority; whereas 'recommendations' means any instruments issuing from a public authority which, while not legally binding on the addressees thereof, cause them to pursue a certain conduct;

Whereas the formalities to which imports are subject do not as a general rule have an effect equivalent to that of quantitative restrictions and, consequently, are not covered by this Directive;

Whereas certain measures adopted by Member States, other than those applicable equally to domestic and imported products, which were operative at the date of entry into force of the Treaty and are not covered by other provisions adopted in pursuance of the Treaty, either preclude importation or make it more difficult or costly than the disposal of domestic production;

Whereas such measures must be considered to include those which make access of imported products to the domestic market, at any marketing stage, subject to a condition which is not laid down for domestic products or to a condition differing from that laid down for domestic products, and more difficult to satisfy, so that a burden is thus placed on imported products only;

Whereas such measures must also be considered to include those which, at any marketing stage, grant to domestic products a preference, other than an aid, to which conditions may or may not be attached, and where such measures totally or partially preclude the disposal of imported products;

Whereas such measures hinder imports which could otherwise take place, and thus have an effect equivalent to quantitative restrictions on imports;

Whereas effects on the free movement of goods of measures which relate to the marketing of products and which apply equally to domestic and imported products are not as a general rule equivalent to those of quantitative restrictions, since such effects are normally inherent in the disparities between rules applied by Member States in this respect;

Whereas, however, such measures may have a restrictive effect on the free movement of goods over and above that which is intrinsic to such rules;

Whereas such is the case where imports are either precluded or made more difficult or costly than the disposal of domestic production and where such effect is not necessary for the attainment of an objective within the scope of the powers for the regulation of trade left to Member States by the Treaty; whereas such is in particular the case where the said objective can be attained just as effectively by other means which are less of a hindrance to trade; whereas such is also the case where the restrictive effect of these provisions on the free movement of goods is out of proportion to their purpose;

Whereas these measures accordingly have an effect equivalent to that of quantitative restrictions on imports;

Whereas the customs union cannot be achieved without the abolition of such measures having an equivalent effect to quantitative restrictions on imports;

Whereas Member States must abolish all measures having equivalent effect by the end of the transitional period at the latest, even if no Commission Directive expressly requires them to do so;

Whereas the provisions concerning the abolition of quantitative restrictions and measures having equivalent effect between Member States apply both to products originating in and exported by Member States and to products originating in third countries and put into free circulation in the other Member States;

Whereas Article 33(7) does not apply to measures of the kind referred to which fall under other provisions of the Treaty, and in particular those which fall under Articles 37(1) and 44 of the Treaty or form an integral part of a national organisation of an agricultural market;

Whereas Article 33(7) does not apply to the charges and taxation referred to in Article 12 *et seq.* and Article 95 *et seq.* or to the aids mentioned in Article 92;

Whereas the provisions of Article 33(7) do not prevent the application, in particular, of Articles 36 and 223;

HAS ADOPTED THIS DIRECTIVE:

Article 1
The purpose of this Directive is to abolish the measures referred to in Articles 2 and 3, which were operative at the date of entry into force of the EEC Treaty.

Article 2
1.   This Directive covers measures, other than those applicable equally to domestic or imported products, which hinder imports which could otherwise take place, including measures which make importation more difficult or costly than the disposal of domestic production.

2.   In particular, it covers measures which make imports or the disposal, at any marketing stage, of imported products subject to a condition — other than a formality — which is required in respect of imported products only, or a condition differing from that required for domestic products and more difficult to satisfy. Equally, it covers, in particular, measures which favour domestic products or grant them a preference, other than an aid, to which conditions may or may not be attached.

3.   The measures referred to must be taken to include those measures which:

(a)   lay down, for imported products only, minimum or maximum prices below or above which imports are prohibited, reduced or made subject to conditions liable to hinder importation;

(b)   lay down less favourable prices for imported products than for domestic products;

(c)   fix profit margins or any other price components for imported products only or fix these differently for domestic products and for imported products, to the detriment of the latter;

(d)   preclude any increase in the price of the imported product corresponding to the supplementary costs and charges inherent in importation;

(e)   fix the prices of products solely on the basis of the cost price or the quality of domestic products at such a level as to create a hindrance to importation;

(f)   lower the value of an imported product, in particular by causing a reduction in its intrinsic value, or increase its costs;

(g)   make access of imported products to the domestic market conditional upon having an agent or representative in the territory of the importing Member State;

(h)   lay down conditions of payment in respect of imported products only, or subject imported products to conditions which are different from those laid down for domestic products and more difficult to satisfy;

(i)   require, for imports only, the giving of guarantees or making of payments on account;

(j)   subject imported products only to conditions, in respect, in particular of shape, size, weight, composition, presentation, identification or putting up, or subject imported products to conditions which are different from those for domestic products and more difficult to satisfy;

(k)   hinder the purchase by private individuals of imported products only, or encourage, require or give preference to the purchase of domestic products only;

(l)   totally or partially preclude the use of national facilities or equipment in respect of imported products only, or totally or partially confine the use of such facilities or equipment to domestic products only;

(m)   prohibit or limit publicity in respect of imported products only, or totally or partially confine publicity to domestic products only;

(n)   prohibit, limit or require stocking in respect of imported products only; totally or partially confine the use of stocking facilities to domestic products only, or make the stocking of imported products subject to conditions which are different from those required for domestic products and more difficult to satisfy;

(o)   make importation subject to the granting of reciprocity by one or more Member States;

(p) prescribe that imported products are to conform, totally or partially, to rules other than those of the importing country;

(q) specify time limits for imported products which are insufficient or excessive in relation to the normal course of the various transactions to which these time limits apply;

(r) subject imported products to controls or, other than those inherent in the customs clearance procedure, to which domestic products are not subject or which are stricter in respect of imported products than they are in respect of domestic products, without this being necessary in order to ensure equivalent protection;

(s) confine names which are not indicative of origin or source to domestic products only.

Article 3

This Directive also covers measures governing the marketing of products which deal, in particular, with shape, size, weight, composition, presentation, identification or putting up and which are equally applicable to domestic and imported products, where the restrictive effect of such measures on the free movement of goods exceeds the effects intrinsic to trade rules.

This is the case, in particular, where:

— the restrictive effects on the free movement of goods are out of proportion to their purpose;

— the same objective can be attained by other means which are less of a hindrance to trade.

Article 4

1. Member States shall take all necessary steps in respect of products which must be allowed to enjoy free movement pursuant to Articles 9 and 10 of the Treaty to abolish measures having an effect equivalent to quantitative restrictions on imports and covered by this Directive.

2. Member States shall inform the Commission of measures taken pursuant to this Directive.

Article 5

1. This Directive does not apply to measures:

(a) which fall under Article 37(1) of the EEC Treaty;

(b) which are referred to in Article 44 of the EEC Treaty or form an integral part of a national organisation of an agricultural market not yet replaced by a common organisation.

2. This Directive shall apply without prejudice to the application, in particular, of Articles 36 and 223 of the EEC Treaty.

Article 6

This Directive is addressed to the Member States.

Done at Brussels, 22 December 1969,
For the Commission
The President
Jean REY

COMMISSION PRACTICE NOTE ON IMPORT PROHIBITIONS

COMMUNICATION FROM THE COMMISSION CONCERNING THE CONSEQUENCES OF THE JUDGMENT GIVEN BY THE COURT OF JUSTICE ON 20 FEBRUARY 1979 IN CASE 120/78 ('CASSIS DE DIJON')
[OJ 1980, No. C256/2]

The following is the text of a letter which has been sent to the Member States; the European Parliament and the Council have also been notified of it.

In the Commission's Communication of 6 November 1978 on 'Safeguarding free trade within the Community', it was emphasised that the free movement of goods is being affected by a growing number of restrictive measures.

The judgment delivered by the Court of Justice on 20 February 1979 in Case 120/78 (the 'Cassis de Dijon' case), and recently reaffirmed in the judgment of 26 June 1980 in Case 788/79, has given the Commission some interpretative guidance enabling it to monitor more strictly the application of the Treaty rules on the free movement of goods, particularly Articles 30 to 36 of the EEC Treaty.

The Court gives a very general definition of the barriers to free trade which are prohibited by the provisions of Article 30 *et seq.* of the EEC Treaty. These are taken to include 'any national measure capable of hindering, directly or indirectly, actually or potentially, intra-Community trade'.

In its judgment of 20 February 1979 the Court indicates the scope of this definition as it applies to technical and commercial rules.

Any product lawfully produced and marketed in one Member State must, in principle, be admitted to the market of any other Member State.

Technical and commercial rules, even those equally applicable to national and imported products, may create barriers to trade only where those rules are necessary to satisfy mandatory requirements and to serve a purpose which is in the general interest and for which they are an essential guarantee. This purpose must be such as to take precedence over the requirements of the free movement of goods, which constitutes one of the fundamental rules of the Community.

The conclusions in terms of policy which the Commission draws from this new guidance are set out below.

— Whereas Member States may, with respect to domestic products and in the absence of relevant Community provisions, regulate the terms on which such products are marketed, the case is different for products imported from other Member States.

Any product imported from another Member State must in principle be admitted to the territory of the importing Member State if it has been lawfully produced, that is, conforms to the rules and processes of manufacture that are customarily and traditionally accepted in the exporting country, and is marketed in the territory of the latter.

This principle implies that Member States, when drawing up commercial or technical rules liable to affect the free movement of goods, may not take an exclusively national viewpoint and take account only of requirements confined to domestic products. The proper functioning of the common market demands that each Member State also give consideration to the legitimate requirements of the other Member States.

— Only under very strict conditions does the Court accept exceptions to this principle; barriers to trade resulting from differences between commercial and technical rules are only admissible:

— if the rules are necessary, that is appropriate and not excessive, in order to satisfy mandatory requirements (public health, protection of consumers or the environment, the fairness of commercial transactions, etc.);

— if the rules serve a purpose in the general interest which is compelling enough to justify an exception to a fundamental rule of the Treaty such as the free movement of goods;

— if the rules are essential for such a purpose to be attained, i.e., are the means which are the most appropriate and at the same time least hinder trade.

The Court's interpretation has induced the Commission to set out a number of guidelines.

— The principles deduced by the Court imply that a Member State may not in principle prohibit the sale in its territory of a product lawfully produced and marketed in another Member State even if the product is produced according to technical or quality requirements which differ from those imposed on its domestic products. Where a product 'suitably and satisfactorily' fulfils the legitimate objective of a Member State's own rules (public safety, protection of the consumer or the environment, etc.), the importing country cannot justify prohibiting its sale in its territory by claiming that the way it fulfils the objective is different from that imposed on domestic products.

In such a case, an absolute prohibition of sale could not be considered 'necessary' to satisfy a 'mandatory requirement' because it would not be an 'essential guarantee' in the sense defined in the Court's judgment.

The Commission will therefore have to tackle a whole body of commercial rules which lay down that products manufactured and marketed in one Member State must fulfil technical or qualitative conditions in order to be admitted to the market of another and specifically in all cases where the trade barriers occasioned by such rules are inadmissible according to the very strict criteria set out by the Court.

The Commission is referring in particular to rules covering the composition, designation, presentation and packaging of products as well as rules requiring compliance with certain technical standards.

— The Commission's work of harmonisation will henceforth have to be directed mainly at national laws having an impact on the functioning of the common market where barriers to trade to be removed arise from national provisions which are admissible under the criteria set by the Court.

The Commission will be concentrating on sectors deserving priority because of their economic relevance to the creation of a single internal market.

To forestall later difficulties, the Commission will be informing Member States of potential objections, under the terms of Community law, to provisions they may be considering introducing which come to the attention of the Commission.

It will be producing suggestions soon on the procedures to be followed in such cases.

The Commission is confident that this approach will secure greater freedom of trade for the Community's manufacturers, so strengthening the industrial base of the Community, while meeting the expectations of consumers.

FREE MOVEMENT OF PERSONS

REGULATION (EEC) NO 1612/68 OF THE COUNCIL OF 15 OCTOBER 1968 ON FREEDOM OF MOVEMENT FOR WORKERS WITHIN THE COMMUNITY AS AMENDED[1]
[OJ Sp. Ed. 1968, No. L257/2, p. 475]

THE COUNCIL OF THE EUROPEAN COMMUNITIES,

Having regard to the Treaty establishing the European Economic Community, and in particular Article 49 thereof;

Having regard to the proposal from the Commission;

Having regard to the Opinion of the European Parliament;[2]

Having regard to the Opinion of the Economic and Social Committee;[3]

Whereas freedom of movement for workers should be secured within the Community by the end of the transitional period at the latest; whereas the attainment of this objective entails the abolition of any discrimination based on nationality between workers of the Member States as regards employment, remuneration and other conditions of work and employment, as well as the right of such workers to move freely within the Community in order to pursue activities as employed persons subject to any limitations justified on grounds of public policy, public security or public health;

Whereas by reason in particular of the early establishment of the customs union and in order to ensure the simultaneous completion of the principal foundations of the Community, provisions should be adopted to enable the objectives laid down in Articles 48 and 49 of the Treaty in the field of freedom of movement to be achieved and to perfect measures adopted successively under Regulation No. 15[4] on the first steps for attainment of freedom of movement and under Council Regulation No. 38/54/EEC[5] of 25 March 1964 on freedom of movement for workers within the Community;

Whereas freedom of movement constitutes a fundamental right of workers and their families; whereas mobility of labour within the Community must be

Notes

[1]Editor's Note. As Amended by Regulations 312/76 [OJ 1976, No. L39/2] and 2434/92 [OJ 1992, No. L245/1]

[2]OJ No. 268, 6.11.1967, p. 9.

[3]OJ No. 298, 7.12.1967, p. 10.

[4]OJ No. 57, 26.8.1961, p. 1073/61.

[5]OJ No. 62, 17.4.1964, p. 965/64.

one of the means by which the worker is guaranteed the possibility of improving his living and working conditions and promoting his social advancement, while helping to satisfy the requirements of the economies of the Member States; whereas the right of all workers in the Member States to pursue the activity of their choice within the Community should be affirmed;

Whereas such right must be enjoyed without discrimination by permanent, seasonal and frontier workers and by those who pursue their activities for the purpose of providing services;

Whereas the right of freedom of movement, in order that it may be exercised, by objective standards, in freedom and dignity, requires that equality of treatment shall be ensured in fact and in law in respect of all matters relating to the actual pursuit of activities as employed persons and to eligibility for housing, and also that obstacles to the mobility of workers shall be eliminated, in particular as regards the worker's right to be joined by his family and the conditions for the integration of that family into the host country;

Whereas the principle of non-discrimination between Community workers entails that all nationals of Member States have the same priority as regards employment as is enjoyed by national workers;

Whereas it is necessary to strengthen the machinery for vacancy clearance, in particular by developing direct co-operation between the central employment services and also between the regional services, as well as by increasing and co-ordinating the exchange of information in order to ensure in a general way a clearer picture of the labour market; whereas workers wishing to move should also be regularly informed of living and working conditions; whereas, furthermore, measures should be provided for the case where a Member State undergoes or foresees disturbances on its labour market which may seriously threaten the standard of living and level of employment in a region or an industry; whereas for this purpose the exchange of information, aimed at discouraging workers from moving to such a region or industry, constitutes the method to be applied in the first place but, where necessary, it should be possible to strengthen the results of such exchange of information by temporarily suspending the abovementioned machinery, any such decision to be taken at Community level;

Whereas close links exist between freedom of movement for workers, employment and vocational training, particularly where the latter aims at putting workers in a position to take up offers of employment from other regions of the Community; whereas such links make it necessary that the problems arising in this connection should no longer be studied in isolation but viewed as inter-dependent, account also being taken of the problems of employment at the regional level; and whereas it is therefore necessary to direct the efforts of Member States toward coordinating their employment policies at Community level;

Whereas the Council, by its Decision of 15 October 1968[1] made Articles 48 and 49 of the Treaty and also the measures taken in implementation thereof applicable to the French overseas departments;

Note
[1]OJ No. L257, 19.10.1968, p. 1.

HAS ADOPTED THIS REGULATION:

PART I   EMPLOYMENT AND WORKERS' FAMILIES
TITLE I   ELIGIBILITY FOR EMPLOYMENT

Article 1

1.   Any national of a Member State, shall, irrespective of his place of residence, have the right to take up an activity as an employed person, and to pursue such activity, within the territory of another Member State in accordance with the provisions laid down by law, regulation or administrative action governing the employment of nationals of that State.

2.   He shall, in particular, have the right to take up available employment in the territory of another Member State with the same priority as nationals of that State.

Article 2

Any national of a Member State and any employer pursuing an activity in the territory of a Member State may exchange their applications for and offers of employment, and may conclude and perform contracts of employment in accordance with the provisions in force laid down by law, regulation or administrative action, without any discrimination resulting therefrom.

Article 3

1.   Under this Regulation, provisions laid down by law, regulation or administrative action or administrative practices of a Member State shall not apply:

—where they limit application for and offers of employment, or the right of foreign nationals to take up and pursue employment or subject these to conditions not applicable in respect of their own nationals; or

—where, though applicable irrespective of nationality, their exclusive or principal aim or effect is to keep nationals of other Member States away from the employment offered.

This provision shall not apply to conditions relating to linguistic knowledge required by reason of the nature of the post to be filled.

2.   There shall be included in particular among the provisions or practices of a Member State referred to in the first subparagraph of paragraph 1 those which:

(a)   prescribe a special recruitment procedure for foreign nationals;

(b)   limit or restrict the advertising or vacancies in the press or through any other medium or subject it to conditions other than those applicable in respect of employers pursuing their activities in the territory of that Member State;

(c)   subject eligibility for employment to conditions of registration with employment offices or impede recruitment of individual workers, where persons who do not reside in the territory of that State are concerned.

Article 4

1.   Provisions laid down by law, regulation or administrative action of the Member States which restrict by number of percentage the employment of foreign nationals in any undertaking, branch of activity or region, or at a national level, shall not apply to nationals of the other Member States.

2.   When in a Member State the granting of any benefit to undertakings is subject to a minimum percentage of national workers being employed, nationals of the other Member States shall be counted as national workers, subject to the provisions of the Council Directive of 15 October 1963.

Article 5

A national of a Member State who seeks employment in the territory of another Member State shall receive the same assistance there as that afforded by the employment offices in that State to their own nationals seeking employment.

Article 6

1. The engagement and recruitment of a national of one Member State for a post in another Member State shall not depend on medical, vocational or other criteria which are discriminatory on grounds of nationality by comparison with those applied to nationals of the other Member State who wish to pursue the same activity.

2. Nevertheless, a national who holds an offer in his name from an employer in a Member State other than that of which he is a national may have to undergo a vocational test, if the employer expressly requests this when making his offer of employment.

TITLE II   EMPLOYMENT AND EQUALITY OF TREATMENT

Article 7

1. A worker who is a national of a Member State may not, in the territory of another Member State, be treated differently from national workers by reason of his nationality in respect of any conditions of employment and work, in particular as regards remuneration, dismissal, and should he become unemployed, reinstatement or re-employment;

2. He shall enjoy the same social and tax advantages as national workers.

3. He shall also, by virtue of the same right and under the same conditions as national workers, have access to training in vocational schools and retraining centres.

4. Any clause of a collective or individual agreement or of any other collective regulation concerning eligibility for employment, employment, remuneration and other conditions of work or dismissal shall be null and void in so far as it lays down or authorises discriminatory conditions in respect of workers who are nationals of the other Member States.

Article 8

1. A worker who is a national of a Member State and who is employed in the territory of another Member State shall enjoy equality of treatment as regards membership of trade unions and the exercise of rights attaching thereto, including the right to vote and to be eligible for the administration or management posts of a trade union; he may be excluded from taking part in the management of bodies governed by public law and from holding an office governed by public law. Furthermore, he shall have the right of eligibility for workers' representative bodies in the undertaking. The provisions of this Article shall not affect laws or regulations in certain Member States which grant more extensive rights to workers coming from the other Member States.

2. This Article shall be reviewed by the Council on the basis of a proposal from the Commission which shall be submitted within not more than two years.

Article 9

1. A worker who is a national of a Member State and who is employed in the territory of another Member State shall enjoy all the rights and benefits

accorded to national workers in matters of housing, including ownership of the housing he needs.

2.   Such worker may, with the same right as nationals, put his name down on the housing lists in the region in which he is employed, where such lists exist; he shall enjoy the resultant benefits and priorities.

If his family has remained in the country whence he came, they shall be considered for this purpose as residing in the said region, where national workers benefit from a similar presumption.

TITLE III   WORKERS' FAMILIES

Article 10

1.   The following shall, irrespective of their nationality, have the right to install themselves with a worker who is a national of one Member State and who is employed in the territory of another Member State:

(a)   his spouse and their descendants who are under the age of 21 years or are dependants;

(b)   dependent relatives in the ascending line of the worker and his spouse.

2.   Member States shall facilitate the admission of any member of the family not coming within the provisions of paragraph 1 if dependent on the worker referred to above or living under his roof in the country whence he comes.

3.   For the purposes of paragraphs 1 and 2, the worker must have available for his family housing considered as normal for national workers in the region where he is employed; this provision, however must not give rise to discrimination between national workers and workers from the other Member States.

Article 11

Where a national of a Member State is pursuing an activity as an employed or self-employed person in the territory of another Member State, his spouse and those of the children who are under the age of 21 years or dependent on him shall have the right to take up any activity as an employed person throughout the territory of that same State, even if they are not nationals of any Member State.

Article 12

The children of a national of a Member State who is or has been employed in the territory of another Member State shall be admitted to that State's general educational, apprenticeship and vocational training courses under the same conditions as the nationals of that State, if such children are residing in its territory.

Member States shall encourage all efforts to enable such children to attend these courses under the best possible conditions.

PART II   CLEARANCE OF VACANCIES AND APPLICATIONS FOR EMPLOYMENT
TITLE I   CO-OPERATION BETWEEN THE MEMBER STATES AND WITH THE COMMISSION

Article 13

1.   The Member States of the Commission shall instigate or together undertake any study of employment or unemployment which they consider necessary for securing freedom of movement for workers within the Community.

The central employment services of the Member States shall co-operate closely with each other and with the Commission with a view to acting jointly as regards the clearing of vacancies and applications for employment within the Community and the resultant placing of workers in employment.

2.   To this end the Member States shall designate specialist services which shall be entrusted with organising work in the fields referred to above and co-operating with each other and with the departments of the Commission.

The Member States shall notify the Commission of any change in the designation of such services; the Commission shall publish details thereof for information in the *Official Journal of the European Communities.*

Article 14

1.   The Member States shall send to the Commission information on problems arising in connection with the freedom of movement and employ- ment of workers and particulars of the state and development of employment by region.

2.   The Commission, taking the utmost account of the opinion of the Technical Committee, shall determine the manner in which the information referred to in paragraph 1 is to be drawn up.

3.   In accordance with the procedure laid down by the Commission in agreement with the Technical Committee, the specialist service of each Member State shall send to the specialist services of the other Member States and to the European Co-ordination Office such information concerning living and working conditions and the state of the labour market as is likely to be of guidance to workers from the other Member States. Such information shall be brought up to date regularly.

The specialist services of the other Member States shall ensure that wide publicity is given to such information, in particular by circulating it among the appropriate employment services and by all suitable means of communication for informing the workers concerned.

TITLE II   MACHINERY FOR VACANCY CLEARANCE

Article 15

1.   The specialist service of each Member State shall regularly send to the specialist services of the other Member States and to the European Coordina- tion Office:

(a)   details of vacancies which could be filled by nationals of other Member States;

(b)   details of vacancies addressed to non-Member States;

(c)   details of applications for employment by those who have formally expressed a wish to work in another Member State;

(d)   information, by region and by branch of activity, on applicants who have declared themselves actually willing to accept employment in another country. The specialist service of each Member State shall forward this information to the appropriate employment services and agencies as soon as possible.

2.   The details of vacancies and applications referred to in paragraph 1 shall be circulated according to a uniform system to be established by the European Coordination Office in collaboration with the Technical Committee. If

necessary, the European Coordination Office may adapt this system in collaboration with the Technical Committee.

Article 16

1.   Any vacancy within the meaning of Article 15 communicated to the employment services of a Member State shall be notified to and processed by the competent employment services of the other Member States concerned. Such services shall forward to the services of the first Member State the details of suitable applications.

2.   The applications for employment referred to in Article 15(1)(c) shall be responded to by the relevant services of the Member States within a reasonable period, not exceeding one month.

3.   The employment services shall grant workers who are nationals of the Member States the same priority as the relevant measures grant to nationals vis-à-vis workers from non-Member States.

Article 17

1.   The provisions of Article 16 shall be implemented by the specialist services. However, in so far as they have been authorised by the central services and in so far as the organisation of the employment services of a Member State and the placing techniques employed make it possible:

(a)   the regional employment services of the Member States shall:

(i)   on the basis of the returns referred to in Article 15, on which appropriate action will be taken, directly bring together and clear vacancies and applications for employment;

(ii)   established direct relations for clearance:

— of vacancies offered to a named worker;

— of individual applications for employment sent either to a specific employment service or to an employer pursuing his activity within the area covered by such a service;

— where the clearing operations concern seasonal workers who must be recruited as quickly as possible;

(b)   the services territorially responsible for the border regions of two or more Member States shall regularly exchange data relating to vacancies and applications for employment in their area and, acting in accordance with their arrangements with the other employment services of their countries, shall directly bring together and clear vacancies and applications for employment. If necessary, the services territorially responsible for border regions shall also set up cooperation and service structures to provide:

— users with as much practical information as possible on the various aspects of mobility, and

— management and labour, social services (in particular public, private or those of public interest) and all institutions concerned, with a framework of coordinated measures relating to mobility;

(c)   official employment services which specialise in certain occupations or specific categories of persons shall cooperate directly with each other.

2.   The Member States concerned shall forward to the Commission the list, drawn up by common accord, of services referred to in paragraph 1; the Commission shall publish such list, and any amendment thereto, in the *Official Journal of the European Communities*.

Article 18
Adoption of recruiting procedures as applied by the implementing bodies provided for under agreements concluded between two or more Member States shall not be obligatory.

TITLE III MEASURES FOR CONTROLLING THE BALANCE OF THE LABOUR MARKET

Article 19
1. On the basis of a report from the Commission drawn up from information supplied by the Member States, the latter and the Commission shall at least once a year analyse jointly the results of Community arrangements regarding vacancies and applications.

2. The Member States shall examine with the Commission all the possibilities of giving priority to nationals of Member States when filling employment vacancies in order to achieve a balance between vacancies and applications for employment within the Community. They shall adopt all measures necessary for this purpose.

3. Every two years the Commission shall submit a report to the European Parliament, the Council and the Economic and Social Committee on the implementation of Part II of this Regulation, summarising the information required and the data obtained from the studies and research carried out and highlighting any useful points with regard to developments on the Community's labour market.

Article 20
(repealed)

TITLE IV EUROPEAN CO-ORDINATION OFFICE

Article 21
The European Office for Co-ordinating the Clearance of Vacancies and Applications for Employment, established within the Commission (called in the Regulation the 'European Co-ordination Office'), shall have the general task of promoting vacancy clearance at Community level. It shall be responsible in particular for all the technical duties in this field which, under the provisions of this Regulation, are assigned to the Commission, and especially for assisting the national employment services.

It shall summarise the information referred to in Articles 14 and 15 and the data arising out of the studies and research carried out pursuant to Article 13, so as to bring to light any useful facts about foreseeable developments on the Community labour market; such facts shall be communicated to the specialist services of the Member States and to the Advisory and Technical Committees.

Article 22
1. The European Co-ordination Office shall be responsible, in particular, for:

(a) co-ordinating the practical measures necessary for vacancy clearance at Community level and for analysing the resulting movements of workers;

(b) contributing to such objectives by implementing, in co-operation with the Technical Committee, joint methods of action at administrative and technical levels;

(c)   carrying out, where a special need arises, and in agreement with the specialist services, the bringing togther of vacancies and applications for employment for clearance by these specialist services.

2.   It shall communicate to the specialist services vacancies and applications for employment sent directly to the Commission, and shall be informed of the action taken thereon.

Article 23

The Commission may, in agreement with the competent authority of each Member State, and in accordance with the conditions and procedures which it shall determine on the basis of the Opinion of the Technical Committee, organise visits and assignments for officials of other Member States, and also advanced programmes for specialist personnel.

PART III   COMMITTEES FOR ENSURING CLOSE CO-OPERATION BETWEEN THE MEMBER STATES IN MATTERS CONCERNING THE FREEDOM OF MOVEMENT OF WORKERS AND THEIR EMPLOYMENT
TITLE I   THE ADVISORY COMMITTEE

Article 24

The Advisory Committee shall be responsible for assisting the Commission in the examination of any questions arising from the application of the Treaty and measures take in pursuance therof, in matters concerning the freedom of movement of workers and their employment.

Article 25

The Advisory Committee shall be responsible in particular for:

(a)   examining problems concerning freedom of movement and employment within the framework of national manpower policies, with a view to co-ordinating the employment policies of the Member States at Community level, thus contributing to the development of the economies and to an improved balance of the labour market;

(b)   making a general study of the effects of implementing this Regulation and any supplementary measures;

(c)   submitting to the Commission any reasoned proposals for revising this Regulation;

(d)   delivering, either at the request of the Commission or on its own initiative, reasoned opinions on general questions or on questions of principle, in particular on exchange of information concerning developments in the labour market, on the movement of workers between Member States, on programmes or measures to develop vocational guidance and vocational training which are likely to increase the possibilities of freedom of movement and employment, and on all forms of assistance to workers and their families, including social assistance and the housing of workers.

Article 26

1.   The Advisory Committee shall be composed of six members for each Member State, two of whom shall represent the government, two the trade unions and two the employers' associations.

2.   For each of the categories referred to in paragraph 1, one alternate member shall be appointed by each Member State.

3.   The term of office of the members and their alternates shall be two years. Their appointments shall be renewable.

On expiry of their term of office, the members and their alternates shall remain in office until replaced or until their appointments are renewed.

Article 27

The members of the Advisory Committee and their alternates shall be appointed by the Council which shall endeavour, when selecting representatives of trade unions and employers' associations, to achieve adequate representation on the Committee of the various economic sectors concerned.

The list of members and their alternates shall be published by the Council for information in the *Official Journal of the European Communities*.

Article 28

The Advisory Committee shall be chaired by a member of the commission or his alternate. The Chairman shall not vote. The Committee shall meet at least twice a year. It shall be convened by its Chairman, either on his own initiative, or at the request of at least one third of the members. Secretarial services shall be provided for the Committee by the Commission.

Article 29

The chairman may invite individuals or representatives of bodies with wide experience in the field of employment or movement of workers to take part in meetings as observers or as experts. The Chairman may be assisted by expert advisers.

Article 30

1.   An opinion delivered by the Committee shall not be valid unless two-thirds of the members are present.

2.   Opinions shall state the reasons on which they are based; they shall be delivered by an absolute majority of the votes validly cast; they shall be accompanied by a written statement of the views expressed by the minority, when the latter so requests.

Article 31

The Advisory Committee shall establish its working methods by rules of procedure which shall enter into force after the Council, having received an opinion from the Commission, has given its approval. The entry into force of any amendment that the Committee decides to make thereto shall be subject to the same procedure.

TITLE II   THE TECHNICAL COMMITTEE

Article 32

The Technical Committee shall be responsible for assisting the Commission to prepare, promote and follow up all technical work and measures for giving effect to this Regulation and any supplementary measures.

Article 33

The Technical Committee shall be responsible in particular for:

(a)   promoting and advancing co-operation between the public authorities concerned in the Member States on all technical questions relating to freedom of movement of workers and their employment;

(b)   formulating procedures for the organisation of the joint activities of the public authorities concerned;

(c)   facilitating the gathering of information likely to be of use to the Commission and for the studies and research provided for in this Regulation, and encouraging exchange of information and experience between the administrative bodies concerned;

(d)   investigating at a technical level the harmonisation of the criteria by which Member States assess the state of their labour markets.

Article 34

1.   The Technical Committee shall be composed of representatives of the Governments of the Member States. Each Government shall appoint as member of the Technical Committee one of the members who represent it on the Advisory Committee.

2.   Each government shall appoint an alternate from among its other representatives — members or alternates — on the Advisory Committee.

Article 35

The Technical Committee shall be chaired by a member of the Commission or his representative. The Chairman shall not vote. The Chairman and the members of the Committee may be assisted by expert advisers.

Secretarial services shall be provided for the Committee by the Commission.

Article 36

The proposals and opinions formulated by the Technical Committee shall be submitted to the Commission, and the Advisory Committee shall be informed thereof. Any such proposals and opinions shall be accompanied by a written statement of the views expressed by the various members of the Technical Committee, when the latter so request.

Article 37

The Technical Committee shall establish its working methods by rules of procedure which shall enter into force after the Council, having received an opinion from the Commission, has given its approval. The entry into force of any amendment which the Committee decides to make thereto shall be subject to the same procedure.

PART IV   TRANSITIONAL AND FINAL PROVISIONS
TITLE I   TRANSITIONAL PROVISIONS

Article 38

Until the adoption by the Commission of the uniform system referred to in Article 15(2), the European Co-ordination Office shall propose any measures likely to be of use in drawing up and circulating the returns referred to in Article 15(1).

Article 39

The rules of procedure of the Advisory Committee and the Technical Committee in force at the time of entry into force of this Regulation shall continue to apply.

Article 40

Until the entry into force of the measures to be taken by Member States in pursuance of the Council Directive of 15 October 1968[1] and where, under the measures taken by the Member States in pursuance of the Council Directive of 25 March 1964[2] the work permit provided for in Article 22 of Regulation No. 38/64/EEC is necessary to determine the period of validity and extension of the residence permit, written confirmation of engagement from the employer or a certificate of employment stating the period of employment may be substituted for such work permit. Any written confirmation by the employer or certificate of employment showing that the worker has been engaged for an indefinite period shall have the same effect as that of a permanent work permit.

Notes
[1] OJ No. L257, 19.10.1968, p. 13.
[2] OJ No. 62, 17.4.1964, p. 981/64.

Article 41

If, by reason of the abolition of the work permit, a Member State can no longer compile certain statistics on the employment of foreign nationals, such Member State may, for statistical purposes, retain the work permit in respect of nationals of the other Member States until new statistical methods are introduced, but no later than 31 December 1969. The work permit must be issued automatically and must be valid until the actual abolition of work permits in such Member State.

TITLE II   FINAL PROVISIONS

Article 42

1.   This Regulation shall not affect the provisions of the Treaty establishing the European Coal and Steel Community which relate to workers with recognised qualifications in coalmining or steelmaking, nor those of the Treaty establishing the European Atomic Energy Community which deal with eligibility for skilled employment in the field of nuclear energy, nor any measures taken in pursuance of those Treaties.

Nevertheless, this Regulation shall apply to categories of workers referred to in the first subparagraph and to members of their families in so far as their legal position is not governed by the above-mentioned Treaties or measures.

2.   This Regulation shall not affect measures taken in accordance with Article 51 of the Treaty.

3.   This Regulation shall not affect the obligations of Member States arising out of:

—special relations or future agreements with certain non-European countries or territories, based on institutional ties existing at the time of the entry into force of this Regulation; or

—agreements in existence at the time of the entry into force of this Regulation with certain non-European countries or territories, based on institutional ties between them.

Workers from such countries or territories who, in accordance with this provision, are pursuing activities as employed persons in the territory of one of those Member States may not invoke the benefit of the provisions of this Regulation in the territory of the other Member States.

Article 43

Member States shall, for information purposes, communicate to the Commission the texts of agreements, conventions or arrangements concluded between them in the manpower field between the date of their being signed and that of their entry into force.

Article 44

The Commission shall adopt measures pursuant to this Regulation for its implementation. To this end it shall act in close co-operation with the central public authorities of the Member States.

Article 45

The Commission shall submit to the Council proposals aimed at abolishing, in accordance with the conditions of the Treaty, restrictions on eligibility for employment of workers who are nationals of Member States, where the absence of mutual recognition of diplomas, certificates or other evidence of formal qualifications may prevent freedom of movement for workers.

Article 46

The administrative expenditure of the Committees referred to in Part III shall be included in the budget of the European Communities in the section relating to the Commission.

Article 47

This Regulation shall apply to the territories of the Member States and to their nationals, without prejudice to Articles 2, 3, 10 and 11.

Article 48

Regulation No. 38/64/EEC shall cease to have effect when this Regulation enters into force.

This Regulation shall be binding in its entirety and directly applicable in all Member States.

Done at Luxembourg, 15 October 1968.
For the Council
The President
G. SEDATI

**COUNCIL DIRECTIVE OF 25 FEBRUARY 1964 ON THE
CO-ORDINATION OF SPECIAL MEASURES CONCERNING THE
MOVEMENT AND RESIDENCE OF FOREIGN NATIONALS
WHICH ARE JUSTIFIED ON GROUNDS OF PUBLIC POLICY,
PUBLIC SECURITY OR PUBLIC HEALTH (64/221/EEC)
[OJ Sp. Ed. 1964, No. 850/64, p. 117]***

THE COUNCIL OF THE EUROPEAN ECONOMIC COMMUNITY

Having regard to the Treaty establishing the European Economic Community, and in particular Article 56(2) thereof;

Notes

*Editor's note: Reference may be necessary to Directives 72/194 (OJ L121/32) and 75/35 (OJ L14/14) which extended the scope of the Directive 64/221 to the members of the family of workers and the self-employed respectively.

Having regard to Council Regulation No. 15 of 16 August 1961[1] on initial measures to bring about free movement of workers within the Community, and in particular Article 47 thereof;

Having regard to Council Directive of 16 August 1961[2] on administrative procedures and practices governing the entry into and employment and residence in a Member State of workers and their families from other Member States of the Community;

Having regard to the General Programmes[3] for the abolition of restrictions on freedom of establishment and on freedom to provide services, and in particular Title II of each such programme;

Having regard to the Council Directive of 25 February 1964[4] on the abolition of restrictions on movement and resident within the Community for nationals of Member States with regard to establishment and the provision of services;

Having regard to the proposal from the Commission;

Having regard to the Opinion of the European Parliament;[5]

Having regard to the Opinion of the Economic and Social Committee;[6]

Whereas co-ordination of provisions laid down by law, regulation or administrative action which provide for special treatment for foreign nationals on grounds of public policy, public security or public health should in the first place deal with the conditions for entry and residence of nationals of Member States moving within the Community either in order to pursue activities as employed or self-employed persons, or as recipients of services;

Whereas such co-ordination presupposes in particular an approximation of the procedures followed in each Member State when invoking grounds of public policy, public security or public health in matters connected with the movement or residence of foreign nationals;

Whereas, in each Member State, nationals of other Member States should have adequate legal remedies available to them in respect of the decisions of the Administration in such matters;

Whereas it would be of little practical use to compile a list of diseases and disabilities which might endanger public health, public policy or public security and it would be difficult to make such a list exhaustive; whereas it is sufficient to classify such diseases and disabilities in groups;

HAS ADOPTED THIS DIRECTIVE:

Notes
[1]OJ No. 57, 26.8.1961, p. 1073/61.
[2]OJ No. 80, 13.12.1961, p. 1513/61.
[3]OJ No. 2, 15.1.1962, pp. 32/62 and 36/62.
[4]OJ No. 56, 4.4.1964, p. 845/64.
[5]OJ No. 134, 14.12.1962, p. 2861/62.
[6]OJ No. 56, 4.4.1964, p. 856/64.

Article 1

1.   The provisions of this Directive shall apply to any national of a Member State who resides in or travels to another Member State of the Community, either in order to pursue an activity as an employed or self-employed person, or as a recipient of services.

2.   These provisions shall apply also to the spouse and to members of the family who come within the provisions of the regulations and directives adopted in this field in pursuance of the Treaty.

Article 2

1.   This Directive relates to all measures concerning entry into their territory, issue or renewal of residence permits, or expulsion from their territory, taken by Member States on grounds of public policy, public security or public health.

2.   Such grounds shall not be invoked to service economic ends.

Article 3

1.   Measures taken on grounds of public policy or of public security shall be based exclusively on the personal conduct of the individual concerned.

2.   Previous criminal convictions shall not in themselves constitute grounds for the taking of such measures.

3.   Expiry of the identity card or passport used by the person concerned to enter the host country and to obtain a residence permit shall not justify expulsion from the territory.

4.   The State which issued the identity card or passport shall allow the holder of such document to re-enter its territory without any formality even if the document is no longer valid or the nationality of the holder is in dispute.

Article 4

1.   The only diseases or disabilities justifying refusal of entry into a territory or refusal to issue a first residence permit shall be those listed in the Annex to this Directive.

2.   Diseases or disabilities occurring after a first residence permit has been issued shall not justify refusal to renew the residence permit or expulsion from the territory.

3.   Member States shall not introduce new provisions or practices which are more restrictive than those in force at the date of notification of this Directive.

Article 5

1.   A decision to grant or to refuse a first residence permit shall be taken as soon as possible and in any event not later than six months from the date of application for the permit.

The person concerned shall be allowed to remain temporarily in the territory pending a decision either to grant or to refuse a residence permit.

2.   The host country may, in cases where this is considered essential, request the Member State of origin of the applicant, and if need be other Member States, to provide information concerning any previous police record. Such enquiries shall not be made as a matter of routine. The Member State consulted shall give its reply within two months.

Article 6

The person concerned shall be informed of the grounds of public policy, public security, or public health upon which the decision taken in his case is based, unless this is contrary to the interests of the security of the State involved.

Article 7

The person concerned shall be officially notified of any decision to refuse the issue or renewal of a residence permit or to expel him from the territory. The period allowed for leaving the territory shall be stated in this notification. Save in cases of urgency, this period shall be not less than fifteen days if the person concerned has not yet been granted a residence permit and not less than one month in all other cases.

Article 8

The person concerned shall have the same legal remedies in respect of any decision concerning entry, or refusing the issue or renewal of a residence permit, or ordering expulsion from the territory, as are available to nationals of the State concerned in respect of acts of the administration.

Article 9

1.   Where there is no right of appeal to a court of law, or where such appeal may be only in respect of the legal validity of the decision, or where the appeal cannot have suspensory effect, a decision refusing renewal of a residence permit or ordering the expulsion of the holder of a residence permit from the territory shall not be taken by the administrative authority, save in cases of urgency, until an opinion has been obtained from a competent authority of the host country before which the person concerned enjoys such rights of defence and of assistance or representation as the domestic law of that country provides for.

This authority shall not be the same as that empowered to take the decision refusing renewal of the residence permit or ordering expulsion.

2.   Any decision refusing the issue of a first residence permit or ordering expulsion of the person concerned before the issue of the permit shall, where that person so requests, be referred for consideration to the authority whose prior opinion is required under paragraph 1. The person concerned shall then be entitled to submit his defence in person, except where this would be contrary to the interests of national security.

Article 10

1.   Member States shall within six months of notification of this Directive put into force the measures necessary to comply with its provisions and shall forthwith inform the Commission thereof.

2.   Member States shall ensure that the texts of the main provisions of national law which they adopt in the field governed by this Directive are communicated to the Commission.

Article 11

This Directive is addressed to the Member States.

Done at Brussels, 25 February 1964.

ANNEX

A.   *Diseases which might endanger public health:*

1.   Diseases subject to quarantine listed in International Health Regulation No. 2 of the World Health Organisation of 25 May 1951;

2.   Tuberculosis of the respiratory system in an active state or showing a tendency to develop;

3.   Syphilis;

4.   Other infectious diseases or contagious parasitic diseases if they are the subject of provisions for the protection of nationals of the host country.

B. *Diseases and disabilities which might threaten public policy or public security:*
1. Drug addiction;
2. Profound mental disturbance; manifest conditions of psychotic disturbance with agitation, delirium, hallucinations or confusion.

COUNCIL DIRECTIVE OF 15 OCTOBER 1968 ON THE ABOLITION OF RESTRICTIONS ON MOVEMENT AND RESIDENCE WITHIN THE COMMUNITY FOR WORKERS OF MEMBER STATES AND THEIR FAMILIES (68/360/EEC)[1]
[OJ Sp. Ed. 1968, No. L257/13, p. 485]

THE COUNCIL OF THE EUROPEAN COMMUNITIES,

Having regard to the Treaty establishing the European Economic Community, and in particular Article 49 thereof;

Having regard to the proposal from the Commission;

Having regard to the Opinion of the European Parliament;[2]

Having regard to the Opinion of the Economic and Social Committee;[3]

Whereas Council Regulation (EEC) No. 1612/68[4] fixed the provisions governing freedom of movement for workers within the Community; whereas, consequently, measures should be adopted for the abolition of restrictions which still exist concerning movement and residence within the Community, which conform to the rights and privileges accorded by the said Regulation to nationals of any Member State who move in order to pursue activities as employed persons and to members of their families;

Whereas the rules applicable to residence should, as far as possible, bring the position of workers from other Member States and members of their families into line with that of nationals;

Whereas the co-ordination of special measures relating to the movement and residence of foreign nationals, justified on grounds of public policy, public security or public health, is the subject of the Council Directive of 25 February 1964,[5] adopted in application of Article 56(2) of the Treaty;

HAS ADOPTED THIS DIRECTIVE:

Notes
[1] As amended by Decision 95/1 OJ 1995 No. L1/1.
[2] OJ No. 268, 6.11.1967, p. 10.
[3] OJ No. 298, 7.12.1967, p. 10.
[4] OJ No. L257, 19.10.1968, p. 2.
[5] OJ No. 56, 4.4.1964, p. 850/64.

Article 1
Member States shall, acting as provided in this Directive, abolish restrictions on the movement and residence of nationals of the said States and of members of their families to whom Regulation (EEC) No 1612/68 applies.

Article 2
1. Member States shall grant the nationals referred to in Article 1 the right to leave their territory in order to take up activities as employed persons and to pursue such activities in the territory of another Member State. Such right shall be exercised simply on production of a valid identity card or passport. Members of the family shall enjoy the same right as the national on whom they are dependent.

2.   Member States shall, acting in accordance with their laws, issue to such nationals, or renew, an identity card or passport, which shall state in particular the holder's nationality.

3.   The passport must be valid at least for all Member States and for countries through which the holder must pass when travelling between Member States. Where a passport is the only document on which the holder may lawfully leave the country, its period of validity shall be not less than five years.

4.   Member States may not demand from the nationals referred to in Article 1 any exit visa or any equivalent document.

Article 3

1.   Member States shall allow the persons referred to in Article 1 to enter their territory simply on production of a valid identity card or passport.

2.   No entry visa or equivalent document may be demanded save from members of the family who are not nationals of a Member State. Member States shall accord to such persons every facility for obtaining any necessary visas.

Article 4

1.   Member States shall grant the right of residence in their territory to the persons referred to in Article 1 who are able to produce the documents listed in paragraph 3.

2.   As proof of the right of residence, a document entitled 'Residence Permit for a National of a Member State of the EEC' shall be issued. This document must include a statement that it has been issued pursuant to Regulation (EEC) No 1612/68 and to the measures taken by the Member States for the implementation of the present Directive. The text of such statement is given in the Annex to this Directive.

3.   For the issue of a Residence Permit for a National of a Member State of the EEC, Member States may require only the production of the following documents;

— by the worker:

(a)   the document with which he entered their territory;

(b)   a confirmation of engagement from the employer or a certificate of employment;

— by the members of the worker's family:

(c)   the document with which they entered the territory;

(d)   a document issued by the competent authority of the State of origin or the State whence they came, proving their relationship;

(e)   in the cases referred to in Article 10(1) and (2) of Regulation (EEC) No 1612/68, a document issued by the competent authority of the State of origin or the State whence they came, testifying that they are dependent on the worker or that they live under his roof in such country.

4.   A member of the family who is not a national of a Member State shall be issued with a residence document which shall have the same validity as that issued to the worker on whom he is dependent.

Article 5

Completion of the formalities for obtaining a residence permit shall not hinder the immediate beginning of employment under a contract concluded by the applicants.

Article 6

1.   The residence permit:

(a)   must be valid throughout the territory of the Member State which issued it;

(b)   must be valid for at least five years from the date of issue and be automatically renewable.

2.   Breaks in residence not exceeding six consecutive months and absence on military service shall not affect the validity of a residence permit.

3.   Where a worker is employed for a period exceeding three months but not exceeding a year in the service of an employer in the host State or in the employ of a person providing services, the host Member State shall issue him a temporary residence permit, the validity of which may be limited to the expected period of the employment.

Subject to the provisions of Article 8(1)(c), a temporary residence permit shall be issued also to a seasonal worker employed for a period of more than three months. The period of employment must be shown in the documents referred to in paragraph 4(3)(b).

Article 7

1.   A valid residence permit may not be withdrawn from a worker solely on the grounds that he is no longer in employment, either because he is temporarily incapable of work as a result of illness or accident, or because he is involuntarily unemployed, this being duly confirmed by the competent employment office.

2.   When the residence permit is renewed for the first time, the period of residence may be restricted, but not to less than twelve months, where the worker has been involuntarily unemployed in the Member State for more than twelve consecutive months.

Article 8

1.   Member States shall, without issuing a residence permit, recognise the right of residence in their territory of:

(a)   a worker pursuing an activity as an employed person, where the activity is not expected to last for more than three months. The document with which the person concerned entered the territory and a statement by the employer on the expected duration of the employment shall be sufficient to cover his stay; a statement by the employer shall not, however, be required in the case of workers coming within the provisions of the Council Directive of 25 February 1964[1] on the attainment of freedom of establishment and freedom to provide services in respect of the activities of intermediaries in commerce, industry and small craft industries.

(b)   a worker who, while having his residence in the territory of a Member State to which he returns as a rule, each day or at least once a week, is employed in the territory of another Member State. The competent authority of the State where he is employed may issue such worker with a special permit valid for five years and automatically renewable;

(c)   a seasonal worker who holds a contract of employment stamped by the competent authority of the Member State on whose territory he has come to pursue his activity.

Note
[1]OJ No. 56, 4.4.1964, p. 869/64.

2.   In all cases referred to in paragraph 1, the competent authorities of the host Member State may require the worker to report his presence in the territory.

Article 9

1.   The residence documents granted to nationals of a Member State of the EEC referred to in this Directive shall be issued and renewed free of charge or on payment of an amount not exceeding the dues and taxes charged for the issue of identity cards to nationals.

2.   The visa referred to in Article 3(2) and the stamp referred to in Article 8(1)(c) shall be free of charge.

3.   Member States shall take the necessary steps to simplify as much as possible the formalities and procedure for obtaining the documents mentioned in paragraph 1.

Article 10

Member States shall not derogate from the provisions of this Directive save on grounds of public policy, public security or public health.

Article 11

1.   This Directive shall not affect the provisions of the Treaty establishing the European Coal and Steel Community which relate to workers with recognised skills in coal mining and steel making, or the provisions of the Treaty establishing the European Atomic Energy Community which deal with the right to take up skilled employment in the field of nuclear energy, or any measures taken in implementation of those Treaties.

2.   Nevertheless, this Directive shall apply to the categories of workers referred to in paragraph 1, and to members of their families, in so far as their legal position is not governed by the above-mentioned Treaties or measures.

Article 12

1.   Member States shall, within nine months of notification of this Directive, bring into force the measures necessary to comply with its provisions and shall forthwith inform the Commission thereof.

2.   They shall notify the Commission of amendments made to provisions imposed by law, regulation or administrative action for the simplification of the formalities and procedure for issuing such documents as are still necessary for the entry, exit and residence of workers and members of their families.

Article 13

1.   The Council Directive of 25 March 1964[1] on the abolition of restrictions on movement and on residence within the Community of workers and their families shall continue to have effect until this Directive is implemented by the Member States.

2.   Residence permits issued pursuant to the Directive referred to in Paragraph 1 shall remain valid until the date on which they next expire.

Note

[1] OJ No. 62, 17.4.1964, p. 981/64.

Article 14
This Directive is addressed to the Member States.

Done at Luxembourg, 15 October 1968.
For the Council
The President
G. SEDATI

ANNEX

Text of the statement referred to in Article 4(2):
'This permit is issued pursuant to Regulation (EEC) No. 1612/68 of the Council of the European Communities of 15 October 1968 and to the measures taken in implementation of the Council Directive of 15 October 1968.

In accordance with the provisions of the above-mentioned Regulation, the holder of this permit has the right to take up and pursue an activity as an employed person in ....[1] territory under the same conditions as ....[1] workers.'

Note
[1]Austrian, Belgian, British, Danish, Finnish, German, Greek, Irish, French, Italian, Luxembourg, Netherlands, Portuguese, Spanish, Swedish, according to the country issuing the permit.

REGULATION (EEC) No 1251/70 OF THE COMMISSION OF 29 JUNE 1970 ON THE RIGHT OF WORKERS TO REMAIN IN THE TERRITORY OF A MEMBER STATE AFTER HAVING BEEN EMPLOYED IN THAT STATE
[OJ Sp. Ed. 1970, No. L142/24, p. 402]

THE COMMISSION OF THE EUROPEAN COMMUNITIES,

Having regard to the Treaty establishing the European Economic Community, and in particular Article 48(3)(d) thereof, and Article 2 of the Protocol on the Grand Duchy of Luxembourg;
Having regard to the Opinion of the European Parliament;[1]
Whereas Council Regulation (EEC) No. 1612/68[2] of 15 October 1968 and Council Directive No. 68/360/EEC of 15 October 1968[3] enabled freedom of movement for workers to be secured at the end of a series of measures to be achieved progressively; whereas the right of residence acquired by workers in active employment has as a corollary the right, granted by the Treaty to such workers, to remain in the territory of a Member State after having been employed in that State; whereas it is important to lay down the conditions for the exercise of such right;
Whereas the said Council Regulation and Council Directive contain the appropriate provisions concerning the right of workers to reside in the territory of a Member State for the purposes of employment; whereas the right to

Notes
[1]OJ No. C65, 5.6.1970, p. 16.
[2]OJ No. L257, 19.10.1968, p. 2.
[3]OJ No. L257, 19.10.1968, p. 13.

remain, referred to in Article 48(3)(d) of the Treaty, is interpreted therefore as the right of the worker to maintain his residence in the territory of a Member State when he ceases to be employed there;

Whereas the mobility of labour in the Community requires that workers may be employed successively in several Member States without thereby being placed at a disadvantage;

Whereas it is important, in the first place, to guarantee to the worker residing in the territory of a Member State the right to remain in that territory when he ceases to be employed in that State because he has reached retirement age or by reason of permanent incapacity to work; whereas, however, it is equally important to ensure that right for the worker who, after a period of employment and residence in the territory of a Member State, works as an employed person in the territory of another Member State, while still retaining his residence in the territory of the first State;

Whereas, to determine the conditions under which the right to remain arises, account should be take of the reasons which have led to the termination of employment in the territory of the Member State concerned and, in particular, of the difference between retirement, the normal and foreseeable end of working life, and incapacity to work which leads to a premature and unforeseeable termination of activity; whereas special conditions must be laid down where termination of activity is the result of an accident at work or occupational disease, or where the worker's spouse is or was a national of the Member State concerned;

Whereas the worker who has reached the end of his working life should have sufficient time in which to decide where he wishes to establish his final residence;

Whereas the exercise by the worker of the right to remain entails that such right shall be extended to members of his family; whereas in the case of the death of the worker during his working life, maintenance of the right of residence of the members of his family must also be recognised and be the subject of special conditions;

Whereas persons to whom the right to remain applies must enjoy equality of treatment with national workers who have ceased their working lives;

HAS ADOPTED THIS REGULATION

Article 1
The provisions of this Regulation shall apply to nationals of a Member State who have worked as employed persons in the territory of another Member State and to members of their families, as defined in Article 10 of Council Regulation (EEC) No 1612/68 on freedom of movement for workers within the Community.

Article 2
1. The following shall have the right to remain permanently in the territory of a Member State:

(a) a worker who, at the time of termination of his activity, has reached the age laid down by the law of that Member State for entitlement to an old-age pension and who has been employed in that State for at least the last twelve months and has resided there continuously for more than three years;

(b)   a worker who, having resided continuously in the territory of that State for more than two years, ceases to work there as an employed person as a result of permanent incapacity to work. If such incapacity is the result of an accident at work or an occupational disease entitling him to a pension for which an institution of that State is entirely or partially responsible, no condition shall be imposed as to length of residence;

(c)   a worker who, after three years' continuous employment and residence in the territory of that State, works as an employed person in the territory of another Member State, while retaining his residence in the territory of the first State, to which he returns, as a rule, each day or at least once a week.

Periods of employment completed in this way in the territory of the other Member State shall, for the purposes of entitlement to the rights referred to in subparagraphs (a) and (b), be considered as having been completed in the territory of the State of residence.

2.   The conditions as to length of residence and employment laid down in paragraph 1(a) and the condition as to length of residence laid down in paragraph 1(b) shall not apply if the worker's spouse is a national of the Member State concerned or has lost the nationality of that State by marriage to that worker.

Article 3

1.   The members of a worker's family referred to in Article 1 of this Regulation who are residing with him in the territory of a Member State shall be entitled to remain there permanently if the worker has acquired the right to remain in the territory of that State in accordance with Article 2, and to do so even after his death.

2.   If, however, the worker dies during his working life and before having acquired the right to remain in the territory of the State concerned, members of his family shall be entitled to remain there permanently on condition that:

— the worker, on the date of his decease, had resided continuously in the territory of that Member State for at least 2 years; or

— his death resulted from an accident at work or an occupational disease; or

— the surviving spouse is a national of the State of residence or lost the nationality of that State by marriage to that worker.

Article 4

1.   Continuity of residence as provided for in Articles 2(1) and 3(2) may be attested by any means of proof in use in the country of residence. It shall not be affected by temporary absences not exceeding a total of three months per year, nor by longer absences due to compliance with the obligations of military service.

2.   Periods of involuntary unemployment, duly recorded by the competent employment office, and absences due to illness or accident shall be considered as periods of employment within the meaning of Article 2(1).

Article 5

1.   The person entitled to the right to remain shall be allowed to exercise it within two years from the time of becoming entitled to such right pursuant to

Article 2(1)(a) and (b) and Article 3. During such period he may leave the territory of the Member State without adversely affecting such right.

2.   No formality shall be required on the part of the person concerned in respect of the exercise of the right to remain.

Article 6

1.   Persons coming under the provisions of this Regulation shall be entitled to a residence permit which:

(a)   shall be issued and renewed free of charge or on payment of a sum not exceeding the dues and taxes payable by nationals for the issue or renewal of identity documents;

(b)   must be valid throughout the territory of the Member State issuing it;

(c)   must be valid for at least five years and be renewable automatically.

2.   Periods of non-residence not exceeding six consecutive months shall not affect the validity of the residence permit.

Article 7

The right to equality of treatment, established by Council Regulation (EEC) No 1612/68, shall apply also to persons coming under the provisions of this Regulation.

Article 8

1.   This Regulation shall not affect any provisions laid down by law, regulation or administrative action of one Member State which would be more favourable to nationals of other Member States.

2.   Member States shall facilitate re-admission to their territories of workers who have left those territories after having resided there permanently for a long period and having been employed there and who wish to return there when they have reached retirement age or are permanently incapacitated for work.

Article 9

1.   The Commission may, taking account of developments in the demographic situation of the Grand Duchy of Luxembourg, lay down, at the request of that State, different conditions from those provided for in this Regulation, in respect of the exercise of the right to remain in Luxembourg territory.

2.   Within two months after the request supplying all appropriate details has been put before it, the Commission shall take a decision, stating the reasons on which it is based.

It shall notify the Grand Duchy of Luxembourg of such decision and inform the other Member States thereof;

This Regulation shall be binding in its entirety and directly applicable in all Member States.

Done at Brussels, 29 June 1970.

For the Commission

The President

Jean REY

COUNCIL DIRECTIVE OF 21 MAY 1973 ON THE ABOLITION OF RESTRICTIONS ON MOVEMENT AND RESIDENCE WITHIN THE COMMUNITY FOR NATIONALS OF MEMBER STATES WITH REGARD TO ESTABLISHMENT AND THE PROVISION OF SERVICES (73/148/EEC)
[OJ 1973, No. L172/14]

THE COUNCIL OF THE EUROPEAN COMMUNITIES

Having regard to the Treaty establishing the European Economic Community, and in particular Article 54(2) and Article 63(2) thereof;

Having regard to the General Programmes for the abolition of restrictions on freedom of establishment and freedom to provide services,[1] and in particular Title II thereof;

Having regard to the proposal from the Commission;

Having regard to the Opinion of the European Parliament;[2]

Having regard to the Opinion of the Economic and Social Committee;[3]

Whereas freedom of movement of persons as provided for in the Treaty and the General Programmes for the abolition of restrictions on freedom of establishment and on freedom to provide services entails the abolition of restrictions on movement and residence within the Community for nationals of Member States wishing to establish themselves or to provide services within the territory of another Member State;

Whereas freedom of establishment can be fully attained only if a right of permanent residence is granted to the persons who are to enjoy freedom of establishment; whereas freedom to provide services entails that persons providing and receiving services should have the right of residence for the time during which the services are being provided;

Whereas Council Directive of 25 February 1964[4] on the abolition of restrictions on movement and residence within the Community for nationals of Member States with regard to establishment and the provision of services laid down the rules applicable in this area to activities as self-employed persons;

Whereas Council Directive of 15 October 1968[5] on the abolition of restrictions on movement and residence within the Community for workers of Member States and their families, which replaced the Directive of 25 March 1964[6] bearing the same title, has in the meantime amended the rules applicable to employed persons;

Whereas the provisions concerning movement and residence within the Community of self-employed persons and their families should likewise be improved;

HAS ADOPTED THIS DIRECTIVE:

Notes
[1] OJ No. 2, 15.1.1962, p. 32/62 and 36/62.
[2] OJ No. C19, 28.2.1972, p. 5.
[3] OJ No. C67, 24.6.1972, p. 7.
[4] OJ No. 56, 4.4.1964, p. 845/64.
[5] OJ No. L257, 19.10.1968, p. 13.
[6] OJ No. 62, 17.4.1964, p. 981/64.

Whereas the coordination of special measures concerning the movement and residence of foreign nationals, justified on grounds of public policy, public security or public health, is already the subject of the Council Directive of 25 February 1964;[7]

Notes
[7] OJ No. 56, 4.4.1964, p. 850/64.

Article 1

1.   The Member States shall, acting as provided in this Directive, abolish restrictions on the movement and residence of:

(a)   nationals of a Member State who are established or who wish to establish themselves in another Member State in order to pursue activities as self-employed persons, or who wish to provide services in that State;

(b)   nationals of Member States wishing to go to another Member State as recipients of services;

(c)   the spouse and the children under twenty-one years of age of such nationals, irrespective of their nationality;

(d)   the relatives in the ascending and descending lines of such nationals and of the spouse of such nationals, which relatives are dependent on them, irrespective of their nationality.

2.   Member States shall favour the admission of any other member of the family of a national referred to in paragraph 1(a) and (b) or of the spouse of that national, which member is dependent on that national or spouse of that national or who in the country of origin was living under the same roof.

Article 2

1.   Member States shall grant the persons referred to in Article 1 the right to leave their territory. Such right shall be exercised simply on production of a valid identity card or passport. Members of the family shall enjoy the same right as the national on whom they are dependent.

2.   Member States shall, acting in accordance with their laws, issue to their nationals, or renew, an identity card or passport, which shall state in particular the holder's nationality.

3.   The passport must be valid at least for all Member States and for countries through which the holder must pass when travelling between Member States. Where a passport is the only document on which the holder may lawfully leave the country, its period of validity shall be not less than five years.

4.   Member States may not demand from the persons referred to in Article 1 any exit visa or any equivalent requirement.

Article 3

1.   Member States shall grant to the persons referred to in Article 1 right to enter their territory merely on production of a valid identity card or passport.

2.   No entry visa or equivalent requirement may be demanded save in respect of members of the family who do have the nationality of a Member State. Member States shall afford to such persons every facility for obtaining any necessary visas.

Article 4

1.   Each Member State shall grant the right of permanent residence to nationals of other Member States who establish themselves within its territory

in order to pursue activities as self-employed persons, when the restrictions on these activities have been abolished pursuant to the Treaty.

As proof of the right of residence, a document entitled 'Residence Permit for a National of a Member State of the European Communities' shall be issued. This document shall be valid for not less than five years from the date of issue and shall be automatically renewable.

Breaks in residence not exceeding six consecutive months and absence on military service shall not affect the validity of a residence permit.

A valid residence permit may not be withdrawn from a national referred to in Article 1(1)(a) solely on the grounds that he is no longer in employment because he is temporarily incapable of work as a result of illness or accident.

Any national of a Member State who is not specified in the first subparagraph but who is authorised under the laws of another Member State to pursue an activity within its territory shall be granted a right of abode for a period not less than that of the authorisation granted for the pursuit of the activity in question.

However, any national referred to in subparagraph 1 and to whom the provisions of the preceding subparagraph apply as a result of a change of employment shall retain his residence permit until the date on which it expires.

2.   The right of residence for persons providing and receiving services shall be of equal duration with the period during which the services are provided.

Where such period exceeds three months, the Member State in the territory of which the services are performed shall issue a right of abode as proof of the right of residence.

Where the period does not exceed three months, the identity card or passport with which the person concerned entered the territory shall be sufficient to cover his stay. The Member State may, however, require the person concerned to report his presence in the territory.

3.   A member of the family who is not a national of a Member State shall be issued with a residence document which shall have the same validity as that issued to that national on whom he is dependent.

Article 5
The right of residence shall be effective throughout the territory of the Member State concerned.

Article 6
An applicant for a residence permit or right of abode shall not be required by a Member State to produce anything other than the following, namely:

(a)   the identity card or passport with which he or she entered its territory;

(b)   proof that he or she comes within one of the classes of person referred to in Articles 1 and 4.

Article 7
1.   The residence documents granted to nationals of a Member State shall be issued and renewed free of charge or on payment of an amount not exceeding the dues and taxes charged for the issue of identity cards to nationals. These provisions shall also apply to documents and certificates required for the issue and renewal of such residence documents.

2.   The visas referred to in Article 3(2) shall be free of charge.

3.   Member States shall take the necessary steps to simplify as much as possible the formalities and the procedure for obtaining the documents mentioned in paragraph 1.

Article 8
Member States shall not derogate from the provisions of this Directive save on grounds of public policy, public security or public health.

Article 9
1.   Member States shall, within six months of notification of this Directive, bring into force the measures necessary to comply with its provisions and shall forthwith inform the Commission thereof.
2.   They shall notify the Commission of amendments made to provisions imposed by law, regulation or administrative action for the simplification with regard to establishment and the provision of services of the formalities and procedure for issuing such documents as are still necessary for the movement and residence of persons referred to in Article 1.

Article 10
1.   The Council Directive of 25 February 1964 on the abolition of restrictions on movement and residence within the Community for nationals of Member States with regard to establishment and the provision of services shall remain applicable until this Directive is implemented by the Member States.
2.   Residence documents issued pursuant to the Directive referred to in paragraph 1 shall remain valid until the date on which they next expire.

Article 11
This Directive is addressed to the Member States.

Done at Brussels, 21 May 1973.
For the Council
The President
E. GLINNE

COUNCIL DIRECTIVE OF 17 DECEMBER 1974 CONCERNING THE RIGHT OF NATIONALS OF A MEMBER STATE TO REMAIN IN THE TERRITORY OF ANOTHER MEMBER STATE AFTER HAVING PURSUED THEREIN AN ACTIVITY IN A SELF-EMPLOYED CAPACITY (75/34/EEC)
[OJ 1975, No. L14/10]

THE COUNCIL OF THE EUROPEAN COMMUNITIES.

Having regard to the Treaty establishing the European Economic Community, and in particular Article 235 thereof;
Having regard to the General Programme for the abolition of restrictions on freedom of establishment,[1] and in particular Title II thereof;
Having regard to the proposal from the Commission;
Having regard to the Opinion of the European Parliament;[2]
Having regard to the Opinion of the Economic and Social Committee;[3]

Notes
[1]OJ No. 2, 15.1.1962, p. 36/62.
[2]OJ No. C14, 27.3.1973, p. 20.
[3]OJ No. C142, 31.12.1972, p. 12.

Whereas pursuant to Council Directive No. 73/148/EEC[4] of 21 May 1973 on the abolition of restrictions on movement and residence within the Community for nationals of Member States with regard to establishment and the provision of services, each Member State grants the right of permanent residence to nationals of other Member States who establish themselves within its territory in order to pursue activities as self-employed persons, when the restrictions on these activities have been abolished pursuant to the Treaty;

Whereas it is normal for a person to prolong a period of permanent residence in the territory of a Member State by remaining there after having pursued an activity there; whereas the absence of a right so to remain in such circumstances is an obstacle to the attainment of freedom of establishment; whereas, as regards employed persons, the conditions under which such a right may be exercised have already been laid down by Regulation (EEC) No. 1251/70;[5]

Notes
[4] OJ No. L172, 28.6.1973, p. 14.
[5] OJ No. L142, 30.6.1970, p. 24.

Whereas Article 48(3)(d) of the Treaty recognises the right of workers to remain in the territory of a Member State after having been employed in the State; whereas Article 54(2) does not expressly provide a similar right for self-employed persons; whereas, nevertheless, the nature of establishment, together with attachments formed to the countries in which they have pursued their activities, means that such persons have a definite interest in enjoying the same right to remain as that granted to workers; whereas in justification of this measure reference should be made to the Treaty provision enabling it to be taken;

Whereas freedom of establishment within the Community requires that nationals of Member States may pursue self-employed activities in several Member States in succession without thereby being placed at a disadvantage;

Whereas a national of a Member State residing in the territory of another Member State should be guaranteed the right to remain in that territory when he ceases to pursue an activity as a self-employed person in that State because he has reached retirement age or by reason of permanent incapacity to work; whereas such a right should also be guaranteed to the national of a member State who, after a period of activity in a self-employed capacity and residence in the territory of a second Member State, pursues an activity in the territory of a third Member State while still retaining his residence in the territory of the second State;

Whereas, to determine the conditions under which the right to remain arises, account should be taken of the reasons which have led to the termination of activity in the territory of the Member State concerned and, in particular, of the difference between retirement, the normal and foreseeable end of working life, and permanent incapacity to work which leads to a premature and unforeseeable termination of activity; whereas special conditions must be laid down where the spouse is or was a national of the member State concerned, or where termination of activity is the result of an accident at work or occupational illness;

Whereas a national of a Member State who has reached the end of his working life, after working in a self-employed capacity in the territory of another Member State, should have sufficient time in which to decide where he wishes to establish his final residence;

Whereas the exercise of the right to remain by a national of a Member State working in a self-employed capacity entails extension of such right to the members of his family; whereas in the case of the death of a national of a Member State working in a self-employed capacity during his working life the right of residence of the members of his family must also be recognised and be the subject of special conditions;

Whereas persons to whom the right to remain applies must enjoy equality of treatment with nationals of the State concerned who have reached the end of their working lives,

HAS ADOPTED THIS DIRECTIVE:

Article 1

Member States shall, under the conditions laid down in this Directive, abolish restrictions on the right to remain in their territory in favour of nationals of another Member State who have pursued activities as self-employed persons in their territory, and members of their families, as defined in Article 1 of Directive No 73/148/EEC.

Article 2

1. Each Member State shall recognise the right to remain permanently in its territory of:

(a)   any person who, at the time of termination of his activity, has reached the age laid down by the law of that State for entitlement to an old-age pension and who has pursued his activity in that State for at least the previous twelve months and has resided there continuously for more than three years.

Where the law of that Member State does not grant the right to an old-age pension to certain categories of self-employed workers, the age requirement shall be considered as satisfied when the beneficiary reaches 65 years of age;

(b)   any person who, having resided continuously in the territory of that State for more than two years, ceases to pursue his activity there as a result of permanent incapacity to work.

If such incapacity is the result of an accident at work or an occupational illness entitling him to a pension which is payable in whole or in part by an institution of that State no condition shall be imposed as to length of residence;

(c)   any person who, after three years' continuous activity and residence in the territory of that State, pursues his activity in the territory of another Member State, while retaining his residence in the territory of the first State, to which he returns, as a rule, each day or at least once a week.

Periods of activity so completed in the territory of the other Member State shall, for the purposes of entitlement to the rights referred to in (a) and (b), be considered as having been completed in the territory of the State of residence.

2. The conditions as to length of residence and activity laid down in paragraph 1(a) and the condition as to length of residence laid down in paragraph 1(b) shall not apply if the spouse of the self-employed person is a national of the Member State concerned or has lost the nationality of that State by marriage to that person.

Article 3

1. Each Member State shall recognise the right of the members of the self-employed person's family referred to in Article 1 who are residing with him in the territory of that State to remain there permanently, if the person

concerned has acquired the right to remain in the territory of that State in accordance with Article 2. This provision shall continue to apply even after the death of the person concerned.

2. If, however, the self-employed person dies during his working life and before having acquired the right to remain in the territory of the State concerned, that State shall recognise the right of the members of his family to remain there permanently on condition that:

— the person concerned, on the date of his decease, had resided continuously in its territory for at least two years; or

— his death resulted from an accident at work or an occupational illness; or

— the surviving spouse is a national of that State or lost such nationality by marriage to the person concerned.

Article 4

1. Continuity of residence as provided for in Articles 2(1) and 3(2) may be attested by any means of proof in use in the country of residence. It may not be affected by temporary absences not exceeding a total of three months per year, nor by longer absences due to compliance with the obligations of military service.

2. Periods of inactivity due to circumstances outside the control of the person concerned or of inactivity owing to illness or accident must be considered as periods of activity within the meaning of Article 2(1).

Article 5

1. Member States shall allow the person entitled to the right to remain to exercise such right within two years from the time of becoming entitled thereto pursuant to Article 2(1)(a) and (b) and Article 3. During this period the beneficiary must be able to leave the territory of the Member State without adversely affecting such right.

2. Member States shall not require the person concerned to comply with any particular formality in order to exercise the right to remain.

Article 6

1. Member States shall recognise the right of persons having the right to remain in their territory to a residence permit, which must:

(a) be issued and renewed free of charge or on payment of a sum not exceeding the dues and taxes payable by nationals for the issue or renewal of identity cards;

(b) be valid throughout the territory of the Member State issuing it;

(c) be valid for five years and renewable automatically.

2. Periods of non-residence not exceeding six consecutive months and longer absences due to compliance with the obligations of military service may not affect the validity of a residence permit.

Article 7

Member States shall apply to persons having the right to remain in their territory the right of equality of treatment recognised by the Council Directives on the abolition of restrictions on freedom of establishment pursuant to Title III of the General Programme which provides for such abolition.

Article 8
1.   This Directive shall not affect any provisions laid down by law, regulation or administrative action of any Member State which would be more favourable to nationals of other Member States.

2.   Member States shall facilitate re-admission to their territories of self-employed persons who left those territories after having resided there permanently for a long period while pursuing an activity there and who wish to return when they have reached retirement age as defined in Article 2(1)(a) or are permanently incapacitated for work.

Article 9
Member States may not derogate from the provisions of this Directive save on grounds of public policy, public security or public health.

Article 10
1.   Member States shall, within twelve months of notification of this Directive, bring into force the measures necessary to comply with its provisions and shall forthwith inform the Commission thereof.

2.   Following notification of this Directive, Member States shall further ensure that the Commission is informed, in sufficient time for it to submit its comments, of all proposed laws, regulations or administrative provisions which they intend to adopt in the field covered by this Directive.

Article 11
This Directive is addressed to the Member States.

Done at Brussels, 17 December 1974.
For the Council
The President
M. DURAFOUR

COUNCIL DIRECTIVE OF 22 MARCH 1977 TO FACILITATE THE EFFECTIVE EXERCISE BY LAWYERS OF FREEDOM TO PROVIDE SERVICES (77/249/EEC)
[OJ 1977, No. L78/17][1]

THE COUNCIL OF THE EUROPEAN COMMUNITIES,

Having regard to the Treaty establishing the European Economic Community, and in particular Articles 57 and 66 thereof,

Having regard to the proposal from the Commission,

Having regard to the opinion of the European Parliament,[2]

Having regard to the opinion of the Economic and Social Committee,[3]

Whereas, pursuant to the Treaty, any restriction on the provision of services which is based on nationality or on conditions of residence has been prohibited since the end of the transitional period;

Whereas this Directive deals only with measures to facilitate the effective pursuit of the activities of lawyers by way of provision of services; whereas more detailed measures will be necessary to facilitate the effective exercise of the right of establishment;

Notes
[1] As amended to OJ 1995 L1/1.
[2] OJ No. C103, 5.10.1972, p. 19 and OJ No. C53, 8.3.1976, p. 33.
[3] OJ No. C36, 28.3.1970, p. 37 and OJ No. C50, 4.3.1976, p. 17.

Whereas if lawyers are to exercise effectively the freedom to provide services host Member States must recognise as lawyers those persons practising the profession in the various Member States;

Whereas, since this Directive solely concerns provision of services and does not contain provisions on the mutual recognition of diplomas, a person to whom the Directive applies must adopt the professional title used in the Member State in which he is established, hereinafter referred to as 'the Member State from which he comes',

HAS ADOPTED THIS DIRECTIVE:

Article 1

1.   This Directive shall apply, within the limits and under the conditions laid down herein, to the activities of lawyers pursued by way of provision of services.

Notwithstanding anything contained in this Directive, Member States may reserve to prescribed categories of lawyers the preparation of formal documents for obtaining title to administer estates of deceased persons, and the drafting of formal documents creating or transferring interests in land.

2.   'Lawyers' means any person entitled to pursue his professional activities under one of the following designations:[1]

Note

[1] As amended by the Accession Acts.

Austria:	Rechtsanwalt
Belgium:	Avocat — Advocaat
Denmark:	Advokat
Germany:	Rechtsanwalt
Greece:	Dikigoros
France:	Avocat
Finland:	Asianajaja/Advokat
Ireland:	Barrister
	Solicitor
Italy:	Avvocato
Luxembourg:	Avocat-avoué
Netherlands:	Advocaat
Portugal	Advogado
Spain	Abogado
Sweden:	Advokat
United Kingdom:	Advocate
	Barrister
	Solicitor.

Article 2

Each Member State shall recognise as a lawyer for the purpose of pursuing the activities specified in Article 1(1) any person listed in paragraph 2 of that Article.

Article 3

A person referred to in Article 1 shall adopt the professional title used in the Member State from which he comes, expressed in the language or one of the languages, of that State, with an indication of the professional organisation by

which he is authorised to practise or the court of law before which he is entitled
to practise pursuant to the laws of that State.

Article 4

1. Activities relating to the representation of a client in legal proceedings or
before public authorities shall be pursued in each host Member State under the
conditions laid down for lawyers established in that State, with the exception of
any conditions requiring residence, or registration with a professional organisation, in that State.

2. A lawyer pursuing these activities shall observe the rules of professional
conduct of the host Member State, without prejudice to his obligations in the
Member State from which he comes.

3. When these activities are pursued in the United Kingdom, 'rules of
professional conduct of the host Member State' means the rules of professional
conduct applicable to solicitors, where such activities are not reserved for
barristers and advocates. Otherwise the rules of professional conduct applicable to the latter shall apply. However, barristers from Ireland shall always be
subject to the rules of professional conduct applicable in the United Kingdom
to barristers and advocates.

When these activities are pursued in Ireland 'rules of professional conduct of
the host Member State' means, in so far as they govern the oral presentation of
a case in court, the rules of professional conduct applicable to barristers. In all
other cases the rules of professional conduct applicable to solicitors shall apply.
However, barristers and advocates from the United Kingdom shall always be
subject to the rules of professional conduct applicable in Ireland to barristers.

4. A lawyer pursuing activities other than those referred to in paragraph 1
shall remain subject to the conditions and rules of professional conduct of the
Member State from which he comes without prejudice to respect for the rules,
whatever their source, which govern the profession in the host Member State,
especially those concerning the incompatibility of the exercise of the activities of
a lawyer with the exercise of other activities in that State, professional secrecy,
relation with other lawyers, the prohibition on the same lawyer acting for parties
with mutually conflicting interests, and publicity. The latter rules are applicable
only if they are capable of being observed by a lawyer who is not established in
the host Member State and to the extent to which their observance is objectively
justified to ensure, in that State, the proper exercise of a lawyer's activities, the
standing of the profession and respect for the rules concerning incompatibility.

Article 5

For the pursuit of activities relating to the representation of a client in legal
proceedings, a Member State may require lawyers to whom Article 1 applies:

— to be introduced, in accordance with local rules or customs, to the
presiding judge and, where appropriate, to the President of the relevant Bar in
the host Member State;

— to work in conjunction with a lawyer who practises before the judicial
authority in question and who would, where necessary, be answerable to that
authority, or with an 'avoué' or 'procuratore' practising before it.

Article 6

Any Member State may exclude lawyers who are in the salaried employment of
a public or private undertaking from pursuing activities relating to the

representation of that undertaking in legal proceedings in so far as lawyers established in that State are not permitted to pursue those activities.

Article 7

1. The competent authority of the host Member State may request the person providing the services to establish his qualifications as a lawyer.

2. In the event of non-compliance with the obligations referred to in Article 4 and in force in the host Member State, the competent authority of the latter shall determine in accordance with its own rules and procedures the consequences of such non-compliance, and to this end may obtain an appropriate professional information concerning the person providing services. It shall notify the competent authority of the Member State from which the person comes of any decision taken. Such exchanges shall not affect the confidential nature of the information supplied.

Article 8

1. Member States shall bring into force the measures necessary to comply with this Directive within two years of its notification and shall forthwith inform the Commission thereof.

2. Member States shall communicate to the Commission the texts of the main provisions of national law which they adopt in the field covered by this directive.

Article 9

This Directive is addressed to the Member States.

Done at Brussels, 22 March 1977.
For the Council
The President
Judith HART

COUNCIL DIRECTIVE OF 21 DECEMBER 1988 ON A GENERAL SYSTEM FOR THE RECOGNITION OF HIGHER-EDUCATION DIPLOMAS AWARDED ON COMPLETION OF PROFESSIONAL EDUCATION AND TRAINING OF AT LEAST THREE YEARS' DURATION (89/48/EEC)
[OJ 1989, No. L19/16]

THE COUNCIL OF THE EUROPEAN COMMUNITIES,

Having regard to the Treaty establishing the European Economic Community, and in particular Articles 49, 57(1) and 66 thereof,
    Having regard to the proposal from the Commission,[1]
    In cooperation with the European Parliament,[2]
    Having regard to the opinion of the Economic and Social Committee,[3]

Notes
[1]OJ No. C217, 28.8.1985, p. 3 and OJ No. C143, 10.6.1986, p. 7.
[2]OJ No. C345, 31.12.1985, p. 80 and OJ No. C309, 5.12.1988.
[3]OJ No. C75, 3.4.1986, p. 5.

Whereas, pursuant to Article 3(c) of the Treaty the abolition, as between Member States, of obstacles to freedom of movement for persons and services constitutes one of the objectives of the Community; whereas, for nationals of the Member States, this means in particular the possibility of pursuing a profession, whether in a self-employed or employed capacity, in a Member State other than that in which they acquired their professional qualifications;

Whereas the provisions so far adopted by the Council, and pursuant to which Member States recognise mutually and for professional purposes higher-education diplomas issued within their territory, concern only a few professions; whereas the level and duration of the education and training governing access to those professions have been regulated in a similar fashion in all the Member States or have been the subject of the minimal harmonisation needed to establish sectoral systems for the mutual recognition of diplomas;

Whereas, in order to provide a rapid response to the expectations of nationals of Community countries who hold higher-education diplomas awarded on completion of professional education and training issued in a Member State other than that in which they wish to pursue their profession, another method of recognition of such diplomas should also be put in place such as to enable those concerned to pursue all those professional activities which in a host Member State are dependent on the completion of post-secondary education and training, provided they hold such a diploma preparing them for those activities awarded on completion of a course of studies lasting at least three years and issued in another Member State;

Whereas this objective can be achieved by the introduction of a general system for the recognition of higher-education diplomas awarded on completion of professional education and training of at least three years' duration;

Whereas, for those professions for the pursuit of which the Community has not laid down the necessary minimum level of qualification, Member States reserve the option of fixing such a level with a view to guaranteeing the quality of services provided in their territory; whereas, however, they may not, without infringing their obligations laid down in Article 5 of the Treaty, require a national of a Member State to obtain those qualifications which in general they determine only by reference to diplomas issued under their own national education systems, where the person concerned has already acquired all or part of those qualifications in another Member State; whereas, as a result, any host Member State in which a profession is regulated is required to take account of qualifications acquired in another Member State and to determine whether those qualifications correspond to the qualifications which the Member State concerned requires;

Whereas collaboration between the Member States is appropriate in order to facilitate their compliance with those obligations; whereas, therefore, the means of organising such collaboration should be established;

Whereas the term 'regulated professional activity' should be defined so as to take account of differing national sociological situations; whereas the term should cover not only professional activities access to which is subject, in a Member State, to the possession of a diploma, but also professional activities, access to which is unrestricted when they are practised under a professional title reserved for the holders of certain qualifications; whereas the professional associations and organisations which confer such titles on their members and are recognised by the public authorities cannot invoke their private status to avoid application of the system provided for by this Directive;

Whereas it is also necessary to determine the characteristics of the professional experience or adaptation period which the host Member State may require of the person concerned in addition to the higher-education diploma, where the person's qualifications do not correspond to those laid down by national provisions;

Whereas an aptitude test may also be introduced in place of the adaptation period; whereas the effect of both will be to improve the existing situation with regard to the mutual recognition of diplomas between Member States and therefore to facilitate the free movement of persons within the Community; whereas their function is to assess the ability of the migrant, who is a person who has already received his professional training in another Member State, to adapt to this new professional environment; whereas, from the migrant's point of view, an aptitude test will have the advantage of reducing the length of the practice period; whereas, in principle, the choice between the adaptation period and the aptitude test should be made by the migrant; whereas, however, the nature of certain professions is such that Member States must be allowed to prescribe, under certain conditions, either the adaptation period or the test; whereas, in particular, the differences between the legal systems of the Member States, whilst they may vary in extent from one Member State to another, warrant special provisions since, as a rule, the education or training attested by the diploma, certificate or other evidence of formal qualifications in a field of law in the Member State of origin does not cover the legal knowledge required in the host Member State with respect to the corresponding legal field;

Whereas, moreover, the general system for the recognition of higher-education diplomas is intended neither to amend the rules, including those relating to professional ethics, applicable to any person pursuing a profession in the territory of a Member State nor to exclude migrants from the application of those rules; whereas that system is confined to laying down appropriate arrangements to ensure that migrants comply with the professional rules of the host Member State;

Whereas Articles 49, 57(1) and 66 of the Treaty empower the Community to adopt provisions necessary for the introduction and operation of such a system;

Whereas the general system for the recognition of higher-education diplomas is entirely without prejudice to the application of Article 48(4) and Article 55 of the Treaty;

Whereas such a system, by strengthening the right of a Community national to use his professional skills in any Member State, supplements and reinforces his right to acquire such skills wherever he wishes;

Whereas this system should be evaluated, after being in force for a certain time, to determine how efficiently it operates and in particular how it can be improved or its field of application extended,

HAS ADOPTED THIS DIRECTIVE:

Article 1

For the purposes of this Directive the following definitions shall apply:

(a) diploma: any diploma, certificate or other evidence of formal qualifications or any set of such diplomas, certificates or other evidence:

— which has been awarded by a competent authority in a Member State, designated in accordance with its own laws, regulations or administrative provisions;

— which shows that the holder has successfully completed a post-secondary course of at least three years' duration, or of an equivalent duration part-time, at a university or establishment of higher education or another establishment of similar level and, where appropriate, that he has successfully completed the professional training required in addition to the post-secondary course, and

— which shows that the holder has the professional qualifications required for the taking up or pursuit of a regulated profession in that Member State, provided that the education and training attested by the diploma, certificate or other evidence of formal qualifications were received mainly in the Community, or the holder thereof has three years' professional experience certified by the Member State which recognised a third-country diploma, certificate or other evidence of formal qualifications.

The following shall be treated in the same way as a diploma, within the meaning of the first sub-paragraph: any diploma, certificate or other evidence of formal qualifications or any set of such diplomas, certificates or other evidence awarded by a competent authority in a Member State if it is awarded on the successful completion of education and training received in the Community and recognised by a competent authority in that Member State as being of an equivalent level and if it confers the same rights in respect of the taking up and pursuit of a regulated profession in that Member State;

(b)   host Member State: any Member State in which a national of a Member State applies to pursue a profession subject to regulation in that Member State, other than the State in which he obtained his diploma or first pursued the profession in question;

(c)   a regulated profession: the regulated professional activity or range of activities which constitute this profession in a Member State;

(d)   regulated professional activity: a professional activity, in so far as the taking up or pursuit of such activity or one of its modes of pursuit in a Member State is subject, directly or indirectly by virtue of laws, regulations or administrative provisions, to the possession of a diploma. The following in particular shall constitute a mode of pursuit of a regulated professional activity:

— pursuit of an activity under a professional title, in so far as the use of such a title is reserved to the holders of a diploma governed by laws, regulations or administrative provisions,

— pursuit of a professional activity relating to health, in so far as remuneration and/or reimbursement for such an activity is subject by virtue of national social security arrangements to the possession of a diploma.

Where the first subparagraph does not apply, a professional activity shall be deemed to be a regulated professional activity if it is pursued by the members of an association or organisation the purpose of which is, in particular, to promote and maintain a high standard in the professional field concerned and which, to achieve that purpose, is recognised in a special form by a Member State and:

— awards a diploma to its members,

— ensures that its members respect the rules of professional conduct which it prescribes, and

— confers on them the right to use a title or designatory letters, or to benefit from a status corresponding to that diploma.

A non-exhaustive list of associations or organisations which, when this Directive is adopted, satisfy the conditions of the second subparagraph is contained in the Annex. Whenever a Member State grants the recognition referred to in the second subparagraph to an association or organisation, it shall inform the Commission thereof, which shall publish this information in the *Official Journal of the European Communities*.

(e) professional experience: the actual and lawful pursuit of the profession concerned in a Member State;

(f) adaptation period: the pursuit of a regulated profession in the host Member State under the responsibility of a qualified member of that profession, such period of supervised practice possibly being accompanied by further training. This period of supervised practice shall be the subject of an assessment. The detailed rules governing the adaptation period and its assessment as well as the status of a migrant person under supervision shall be laid down by the competent authority in the host Member States;

(g) aptitude test: a test limited to the professional knowledge of the applicant, made by the competent authorities of the host Member State with the aim of assessing the ability of the applicant to pursue a regulated profession in that Member State.

In order to permit this test to be carried out, the competent authorities shall draw up a list of subjects which, on the basis of a comparison of the education and training required in the Member State and that received by the applicant, are not covered by the diploma or other evidence of formal qualifications possessed by the applicant.

The aptitude test must take account of the fact that the applicant is a qualified professional in the Member State of origin or the Member State from which he comes. It shall cover subjects to be selected from those on the list, knowledge of which is essential in order to be able to exercise the profession in the host Member State. The test may also include knowledge of the professional rules applicable to the activities in question in the host Member State. The detailed application of the aptitude test shall be determined by the competent authorities of that State with due regard to the rules of Community law.

The status, in the host Member State, of the applicant who wishes to prepare himself for the aptitude test in that State shall be determined by the competent authorities in that State.

Article 2

This Directive shall apply to any national of a Member State wishing to pursue a regulated profession in a host Member State in a self-employed capacity or as an employed person.

This Directive shall not apply to professions which are the subject of a separate Directive establishing arrangements for the mutual recognition of diplomas by Member States.

Article 3

Where, in a host Member State, the taking up or pursuit of a regulated profession is subject to possession of a diploma, the competent authority may not, on the grounds of inadequate qualifications, refuse to authorise a national of a Member State to take up or pursue that profession on the same conditions as apply to its own nationals:

(a) if the applicant holds the diploma required in another Member State for the taking up or pursuit of the profession in question in its territory, such diploma having been awarded in a Member State; or

(b)   if the applicant has pursued the profession in question full-time for two years during the previous ten years in another Member State which does not regulate that profession, within the meaning of Article 1(c) and the first subparagraph of Article 1(d), and possesses evidence of one or more formal qualifications:

— which have been awarded by a competent authority in a Member State, designated in accordance with the laws, regulations or administrative provisions of such State,

— which show that the holder has successfully completed a post-secondary course of at least three years' duration, or of an equivalent duration part-time, at a university or establishment of higher education or another establishment of similar level of a Member State and, where appropriate, that he has successfully completed the professional training required in addition to the post-secondary course and

— which have prepared the holder for the pursuit of his profession.

The following shall be treated in the same way as the evidence of formal qualifications referred to in the first subparagraph: any formal qualifications or any set of such formal qualifications awarded by a competent authority in a Member State if it is awarded on the successful completion of training received in the Community and is recognised by that Member State as being of an equivalent level, provided that the other Member States and the Commission have been notified of this recognition.

Article 4

1.   Notwithstanding Article 3, the host Member State may also require the applicant:

(a)   to provide evidence of professional experience, where the duration of the education and training adduced in support of his application, as laid down in Article 3(a) and (b), is at least one year less than that required in the host Member State. In this event, the period of professional experience required:

— may not exceed twice the shortfall in duration of education and training where the shortfall relates to post-secondary studies and/or to a period of probationary practice carried out under the control of a supervising professional person and ending with an examination,

— may not exceed the shortfall where the shortfall relates to professional practice acquired with the assistance of a qualified member of the profession.

In the case of diplomas within the meaning of the last subparagraph of Article 1(a), the duration of education and training recognised as being of an equivalent level shall be determined as for the education and training defined in the first subparagraph of Article 1(a).

When applying these provisions, account must be taken of the professional experience referred to in Article 3(b).

At all events, the provisions, experience required may not exceed four years;

(b)   to complete an adaptation period not exceeding three years or take an aptitude test:

— where the matters covered by the education and training he has received as laid down in Article 3 (a) and (b), differ substantially from those covered by the diploma required in the host Member State, or

— where, in the case referred to in Article 3(a), the profession regulated in the host Member State comprises one or more regulated professional activities which are not in the profession regulated in the Member State from which the applicant originates or comes and that difference corresponds to specific education and training required in the host Member State and covers matters which differ substantially from those covered by the diploma adduced by the applicant, or

— where, in the case referred to in Article 3(b), the profession regulated in the host Member State comprises one or more regulated professional activities which are not in the profession pursued by the applicant in the Member State from which he originates or comes, and that difference corresponds to specific education and training required in the host Member State and covers matters which differ substantially from those covered by the evidence of formal qualifications adduced by the applicant.

Should the host Member State make use of this possibility, it must give the applicant the right to choose between an adaptation period and an aptitude test. By way of derogation from this principle, for professions whose practice requires precise knowledge of national law and in respect of which the provision of advice and/or assistance concerning national law is an essential and constant aspect of the professional activity, the host Member State may stipulate either an adaptation period or an aptitude test. Where the host Member State intends to introduce derogations for other professions as regards an applicant's right to choose, the procedure laid down in Article 10 shall apply.

2.   However, the host Member State may not apply the provisions of paragraph 1(a) and (b) cumulatively.

Article 5

Without prejudice to Articles 3 and 4, a host Member State may allow the applicant, with a view to improving his possibilities of adapting to the professional environment in that State, to undergo there, on the basis of equivalence, that part of his professional education and training represented by professional practice, acquired with the assistance of a qualified member of the profession, which he has not undergone in his Member State of origin or the Member State from which he has come.

Article 6

1.   Where the competent authority of a host Member State requires of persons wishing to take up a regulated profession proof that they are of good character or repute or that they have not been declared bankrupt, or suspends or prohibits the pursuit of this profession in the event of serious professional misconduct or a criminal offence, that State shall accept as sufficient evidence, in respect of nationals of Member States wishing to pursue that profession in its territory, the production of documents issued by competent authorities in the Member State of origin or the Member State from which the foreign national comes showing that those requirements are met.

Where the competent authorities of the Member State of origin or of the Member State from which the foreign national comes do not issue the documents referred to in the first subparagraph, such documents shall be replaced by a declaration on oath — or, in States where there is no provision for declaration on oath, by a solemn declaration — made by the person concerned before a competent judicial or administrative authority or, where appropriate, a notary or qualified professional body of the Member State of origin or the

Member State from which the person comes; such authority or notary shall issue a certificate attesting the authenticity of the declaration on oath or solemn declaration.

2. Where the competent authority of a host Member State requires of nationals of that Member State wishing to take up or pursue a regulated profession a certificate of physical or mental health, that authority shall accept as sufficient evidence in this respect the production of the document required in the Member State of origin or the Member State from which the foreign national comes.

Where the Member State of origin or the Member State from which the foreign national comes does not impose any requirements of this nature on those wishing to take up or pursue the profession in question, the host Member State shall accept from such nationals a certificate issued by a competent authority in that State corresponding to the certificates issued in the host Member State.

3. The competent authorities of host Member States may require that the documents and certificates referred to in paragraphs 1 and 2 are presented no more than three months after their date of issue.

4. Where the competent authority of a host Member State requires nationals of that Member State wishing to take up or pursue a regulated profession to take an oath or make a solemn declaration and where the form of such oath or declaration cannot be used by nationals of other Member States, that authority shall ensure that an appropriate and equivalent form of oath or declaration is offered to the person concerned.

Article 7

1. The competent authorities of host Member States shall recognise the right of nationals of Member States who fulfil the conditions for the taking up and pursuit of a regulated profession in their territory to use the professional title of the host Member State corresponding to that profession.

2. The competent authorities of host Member States shall recognise the right of nationals of Member States who fulfil the conditions for the taking up and pursuit of a regulated profession in their territory to use their lawful academic title and, where appropriate, the abbreviation thereof deriving from their Member State of origin or the Member State from which they come, in the language of that State. Host Member State may require this title to be followed by the name and location of the establishment or examining board which awarded it.

3. Where a profession is regulated in the host Member State by an association or organisation referred to in Article 1(d), nationals of Member States shall only be entitled to use the professional title or designatory letters conferred by that organisation or association on proof of membership.

Where the association or organisation makes membership subject to certain qualification requirements, it may apply these to nationals of other Member States who are in possession of a diploma within the meaning of Article 1(a) or a formal qualification within the meaning of Article 3(b) only in accordance with this Directive, in particular Articles 3 and 4.

Article 8

1. The host Member State shall accept as proof that the conditions laid down in Articles 3 and 4 are satisfied the certificates and documents issued by

the competent authorities in the Member States, which the person concerned shall submit in support of his application to pursue the profession concerned.

2. The procedure for examining an application to pursue a regulated profession shall be completed as soon as possible and the outcome communicated in a reasoned decision of the competent authority in the host Member State not later than four months after presentation of all the documents relating to the person concerned. A remedy shall be available against this decision, or the absence thereof, before a court or tribunal in accordance with the provisions of national law.

Article 9

1. Member States shall designate, within the period provided for in Article 12, the competent authorities empowered to receive the applications and take the decisions referred to in this Directive.

They shall communicate this information to the other Member States and to the Commission.

2. Each Member State shall designate a person responsible for coordinating the activities of the authorities referred to in paragraph 1 and shall inform the other Member States and the Commission to that effect. His role shall be to promote uniform application of this Directive to all the professions concerned. A coordinating group shall be set up under the aegis of the Commission, composed of the coordinators appointed by each Member State or their deputies and chaired by a representative of the Commission.

The task of this group shall be:

— to facilitate the implementation of this Directive,

— to collect all useful information for its application in the Member States.

The group may be consulted by the Commission on any changes to the existing system that may be contemplated.

3. Member States shall take measures to provide the necessary information on the recognition of diplomas within the framework of this Directive. They may be assisted in this task by the information centre on the academic recognition of diplomas and periods of study established by the Member States within the framework of the Resolution of the Council and the Ministers of Education meeting within the Council of 9 February 1976[1] and, where appropriate, the relevant professional associations or organisations. The Commission shall take the necessary initiatives to ensure the development and coordination of the communication of the necessary information.

Note
[1] OJ No. C38, 19.2.1976, p. 1.

Article 10

1. If, pursuant to the third sentence of the second subparagraph of Article 4(1)(b), a Member State proposes not to grant applicants the right to choose between an adaptation period and an aptitude test in respect of a profession within the meaning of this Directive, it shall immediately communicate to the Commission the corresponding draft provision. It shall at the same time notify the Commission of the grounds which make the enactment of such a provision necessary.

The Commission shall immediately notify the other Member States of any draft it has received; it may also consult the coordinating group referred to in Article 9(2) of the draft.

2. Without prejudice to the possibility for the Commission and the other Member States of making comments on the draft, the Member State may adopt the provision only if the Commission has not taken a decision to the contrary within three months.

3. At the request of a Member State or the Commission, Member States shall communicate to them, without delay, the definitive text of a provision arising from the application of this Article.

Article 11

Following the expiry of the period provided for in Article 12, Member States shall communicate to the Commission, every two years, a report on the application of the system introduced.

In addition to general remarks, this report shall contain a statistical summary of the decisions taken and a description of the main problems arising from application of the Directive.

Article 12

Member States shall take the measures necessary to comply with this Directive within two years of its notification.[1] They shall forthwith inform the Commission thereof.

Member States shall communicate to the Commission the texts of the main provisions of national law which they adopt in the field governed by this Directive.

Note

[1] This directive was notified to Member States on 4 January 1989.

Article 13

Five years at the latest following the date specified in Article 12, the Commission shall report to the European Parliament and the Council on the state of application of the general system for the recognition of higher-education diplomas awarded on completion of professional education and training of at least three years' duration.

After conducting all necessary consultations, the Commission shall, on this occasion, present its conclusions as to any changes that need to be made to the system as it stands. At the same time the Commission shall, where appropriate, submit proposals for improvements in the present system in the interest of further facilitating the freedom of movement, right of establishment and freedom to provide services of the persons covered by this Directive.

Article 14

The Directive is addressed to the Member States

Done at Brussels, 21 December 1988.

ANNEX

List of professional associations or organisations which satisfy the conditions of the second subparagraph of Article 1(d)

IRELAND[1]

1. The Institute of Chartered Accountants in Ireland[2]
2. The Institute of Certified Public Accountants in Ireland[2]
3. The Association of Certified Accountants[2]
4. Institution of Engineers of Ireland
5. Irish Planning Institute

UNITED KINGDOM

1. Institute of Chartered Accountants in England and Wales
2. Institute of Chartered Accountants of Scotland
3. Institute of Chartered Accountants in Ireland
4. Chartered Association of Certified Accounts
5. Chartered Institute of Loss Adjusters
6. Chartered Institute of Management Accounts
7. Institute of Chartered Secretaries and Administrators
8. Chartered Insurance Institute
9. Institute of Actuaries
10. Faculty of Actuaries
11. Chartered Institute of Bankers
12. Institute of Bankers in Scotland
13. Royal Institution of Chartered Surveyors
14. Roya Town Planning Institute
15. Chartered Society of Physiotherapy
16. Royal Society of Chemistry
17. British Psychological Society
18. Library Association
19. Institute of Chartered Foresters
20. Chartered Institute of Building
21. Engineering Council
22. Institute of Energy
23. Institution of Structural Engineers
24. Institution of Civil Engineers
25. Institution of Mining Engineers
26. Institution of Mining and Metallurgy

Notes

[1]Irish nationals are also members of the following United Kingdom chartered bodies:
Institute of Chartered Accountants in England and Wales
Institute of Chartered Accountants of Scotland
Institute of Actuaries
Faculty of Actuaries
The Chartered Institute of Management Accountants
Institute of Chartered Secretaries and Administrators
Royal Town Planning Institute
Royal Institution of Chartered Surveyors
Chartered Institute of Building.
[2]For the purposes of the activity of Auditing only.

STATEMENT BY THE COUNCIL AND THE COMMISSION

Re Article 9(1)
'The Council and the Commission agree that professional bodies and higher-education establishments should be consulted or be involved in an appropriate way in the decision-making process.'

27.   Institution of Electrical Engineers
28.   Institution of Gas Engineers
29.   Institution of Mechanical Engineers
30.   Institution of Chemical Engineers
31.   Institution of Production Engineers
32.   Institution of Marine Engineers
33.   Royal Institution of Naval Architects
34.   Royal Aeronautical Society
35.   Institute of Metals
36.   Chartered Institution of Building Services Engineers
37.   Institute of Measurement and Control
38.   British Computer Society.

COUNCIL RECOMMENDATION OF 21 DECEMBER 1988 CONCERNING NATIONALS OF MEMBER STATES WHO HOLD A DIPLOMA CONFERRED IN A THIRD STATE (89/49/EEC)
[OJ 1989, No. L19/24]

THE COUNCIL OF THE EUROPEAN COMMUNITIES,

Approving Council Directive 89/48/EEC of 21 December 1988 on a general system for the recognition of higher-education diplomas awarded on completion of professional education and training of at least three years' duration;

Noting that this Directive refers only to diplomas, certificates and other evidence of formal qualifications awarded in Member States to nationals of Member States;

Anxious, however, to take account of the special position of nationals of Member States who hold diplomas, certificates or other evidence of formal qualifications awarded in third States and who are thus in a position comparable to one of those described in Article 3 of the Directive,

Hereby recommends:

that the Governments of the Member States should allow the persons referred to above to take up and pursue regulated professions within the Community by recognising these diplomas, certificates and other evidence of formal qualifications in their territories.

Done at Brussels, 21 December 1988.

COUNCIL DIRECTIVE OF 28 JUNE 1990 ON THE RIGHT OF RESIDENCE (90/364/EEC)
[OJ 1990, No. L180/26]

THE COUNCIL OF THE EUROPEAN COMMUNITIES,

Having regard to the Treaty establishing the European Economic Community, and in particular Article 235 thereof,

Having regard to the proposal from the Commission,[1]

Having regard to the opinion of the European Parliament,[2]

Notes
[1]OJ No. C191, 28.7.1989, p. 5; and OJ No. C26, 3.2.1990, p. 22.
[2]Opinion delivered on 13 June 1990 (not yet published in the Official Journal).

Having regard to the opinion of the Economi and Social Committee,[3]

Whereas Article 3(c) of the Treaty provides that the activities of the Community shall include, as provided in the Treaty, the abolition, as between Member States, of obstacles to freedom of movement for persons;

Whereas Article 8a of the Treaty provides that the internal market must be established by 31 December 1992; whereas the internal market comprises an area without internal frontiers in which the free movement of goods, persons, services and capital is ensured in accordance with the provisions of the Treaty;

Whereas national provisions on the right of nationals of the Member States to reside in a Member State other than their own must be harmonized to ensure such freedom of movement;

Whereas beneficiaries of the right of residence must not become an unreasonable burden on the public finances of the host Member State;

Whereas this right can only be genuinely exercised if it is also granted to members of the family;

Whereas the beneficiaries of this Directive should be covered by administrative arrangements similar to those laid down in particular in Directive 68/360/EEC[4] and Directive 64/221/EEC;[5]

Whereas the Treaty does not provide, for the action concerned, powers other than those of Article 235,

Notes
[3] OJ No. C329, 30.12.1989, p. 25.
[4] OJ No. L257, 19.10.1968, p. 13.
[5] OJ No. 56, 4.4.1964, p. 850/64.

HAS ADOPTED THIS DIRECTIVE:

Article 1

1.   Member States shall grant the right of residence to nationals of Member States who do not enjoy this right under other provisions of Community law and to members of their families as defined in paragraph 2, provided that they themselves and the members of their families are covered by sickness insurance in respect of all risks in the host Member State and have sufficient resources to avoid becoming a burden on the social assistance system of the host Member State during their period of residence.

The resources referred to in the first subparagraph shall be deemed sufficient where they are higher than the level of resources below which the host Member State may grant social assistance to its nationals, taking into account the personal circumstances of the applicant and, where appropriate, the personal circumstances of persons admitted pursuant to paragraph 2.

Where the second subparagraph cannot be applied in a Member State, the resources of the applicant shall be deemed sufficient if they are higher than the level of the minimum social security pension paid by the host Member State.

2.   The following shall, irrespective of their nationality, have the right to install themselves in another Member State with the holder of the right of residence:

(a)   his or her spouse and their descendants who are dependants;

(b)   dependent relatives in the ascending line of the holder of the right of residence and his or her spouse.

Article 2

1.   Exercise of the right of residence shall be evidenced by means of the issue of a document known as a 'Residence permit for a national of a Member State of the EEC', the validity of which may be limited to five years on a renewable basis. However, the Member States may, when they deem it to be necessary, require revalidation of the permit at the end of the first two years of residence. Where a member of the family does not hold the nationality of a Member State, he or she shall be issued with a residence document of the same validity as that issued to the national on whom he or she depends.

For the purpose of issuing the residence permit or document, the Member State may require only that the applicant present a valid identity card or passport and provide proof that he or she meets the conditions laid down in Article 1.

2.   Articles 2, 3, 6(1)(a) and (2) and Article 9 of Directive 68/360/EEC shall apply mutatis mutandis to the beneficiaries of this Directive.

The spouse and the dependent children of a national of a Member State entitled to the right of residence within the territory of a Member State shall be entitled to take up any employed or self-employed activity anywhere within the territory of that Member State, even if they are not nationals of a Member State.

Member States shall not derogate from the provisions of this Directive save on grounds of public policy, public security or public health. In that event, Directive 64/221/EEC shall apply.

3.   This Directive shall not affect existing law on the acquisition of second homes.

Article 3

The right of residence shall remain for as long as beneficiaries of that right fulfil the conditions laid down in Article 1.

Article 4

The Commission shall, not more than three years after the date of implementation of this Directive, and at three-yearly intervals thereafter, draw up a report on the application of this Directive and submit it to the European Parliament and the Council.

Article 5

Member States shall bring into force the laws, regulations and administrative provisions necessary to comply with this Directive not later than 30 June 1992.

They shall forthwith inform the Commission thereof.

Article 6

This Directive is addressed to the Member States.

Done at Luxembourg, 28 June 1990.

(Signature omitted.)

**COUNCIL DIRECTIVE OF 28 JUNE 1990 ON THE RIGHT OF
RESIDENCE FOR EMPLOYEES AND SELF-EMPLOYED
PERSONS WHO HAVE CEASED THEIR OCCUPATIONAL
ACTIVITY (90/365/EEC)
[OJ 1990, No. L180/28]**

THE COUNCIL OF THE EUROPEAN COMMUNITIES,

Having regard to the Treaty establishing the European Economic Community, and in particular Article 235 thereof,

Having regard to the proposal from the Commission,[1]

Having regard to the opinion of the European Parliament,[2]

Having regard to the opinion of the Economic and Social Committee,[3]

Whereas Article 3(c) of the Treaty provides that the activities of the Community shall include, as provided in the Treaty, the abolition, as between Member States, of obstacles to freedom of movement for persons;

Whereas Article 8a of the Treaty provides that the internal market must be established by 31 December 1992; whereas the internal market comprises an area without internal frontiers in which the free movement of goods, persons, services and capital is ensured, in accordance with the provisions of the Treaty;

Whereas Articles 48 and 52 of the Treaty provide for freedom of movement for workers and self-employed persons, which entails the right of residence in the Member States in which they pursue their occupational activity; whereas it is desirable that this right of residence also be granted to persons who have ceased their occupational activity even if they have not exercised their right to freeedom of movement during their working life;

Whereas beneficiaries of the right of residence must not become an unreasonable burden on the public finances of the host Member State;

Whereas under Article 10 of Regulation (EEC) No. 1408/71,[4] as amended by Regulation (EEC) No. 1390/81,[5] recipients of invalidity or old age cash benefits or pensions for accidents at work or occupational diseases are entitled to continue to receive these benefits and pensions even if they reside in the territory of a Member State other than that in which the institution responsible for payment is situated;

Whereas this right can only be genuinely exercised if it is also granted to members of the family;

Whereas the beneficiaries of this Directive should be covered by administrative arrangements similar to those laid down in particular by Directive 68/630/EEC[6] and Directive 64/221/EEC;[7]

Whereas the Treaty does not provide, for the action concerned, powers other than those of Article 235,

HAS ADOPTED THIS DIRECTIVE:

Notes
[1] OJ No. C191, 28.7.1989, p. 3; and OJ No. C26, 3.2.1990, p. 19.
[2] Opinion delivered on 13 June 1990 (not yet published in the Official Journal).
[3] OJ No. C329, 30.12.1989, p. 25.
[4] OJ No. L149, 5.7.1971, p. 2.
[5] OJ No. 143, 29.5.1981, p. 1.
[6] OJ No. L257, 19.10.1968, p. 13.
[7] OJ No. 56, 4.4.1964, p. 850/64.

Article 1

1. Member States shall grant the right of residence to nationals of Member States who have pursued an activity as an employee or self-employed person and to members of their families as defined in paragraph 2, provided that they are recipients of an invalidity or early retirement pension, or old age benefits, or of a pension in respect of an industrial accident or disease of an amount sufficient to avoid becoming a burden on the social security system of the host Member State during their period of residence and provided they are covered by sickness insurance in respect of all risks in the host Member State.

The resources of the applicant shall be deemed sufficient where they are higher than the level of resources below which the host Member State may grant social assistance to its nationals, taking into account the personal circumstances of persons admitted pursuant to paragraph 2.

Where the second subparagraph cannot be applied in a Member State, the resources of the applicant shall be deemed sufficient if they are higher than the level of the minimum social security pension paid by the host Member State.

2. The following shall, irrespective of their nationality, have the right to install themselves in another Member State with the holder of the right of residence:

    (a)   his or her spouse and their descendants who are dependants;

    (b)   dependent relatives in the ascending line of the holder of the right of residence and his or her spouse.

Article 2

1. Exercise of the right of residence shall be evidenced by means of the issue of a document known as a 'Residence permit for a national of a Member State of the EEC', whose validity may be limited to five years on a renewable basis. However, the Member States may, when they deem it to be necessary, require revalidation of the permit at the end of the first two years of residence. Where a member of the family does not hold the nationality of a Member State, he or she shall be issued with a residence document of the same validity as that issued to the national on whom he or she depends.

For the purposes of issuing the residence permit or document, the Member State may require only that the applicant present a valid identity card or passport and provide proof that he or she meets the conditions laid down in Article 1.

2. Articles 2, 3, 6(1)(a) and (2) and Article 9 of Directive 68/360/EEC shall apply mutatis mutandis to the beneficiaries of this Directive.

The spouse and the dependent children of a national of a Member State entitled to the right of residence within the territory of a Member State shall be entitled to take up any employed or self-employed activity anywhere within the territory of that Member State, even if they are not nationals of a Member State.

Member States shall not derogate from the provisions of this Directive save on grounds of public policy, public security or public health. In that event, Directive 64/221/EEC shall apply.

3. This Directive shall not affect existing law on the acquisition of second homes.

Article 3

The right of residence shall remain for as long as beneficiaries of that right fulfil the conditions laid down in Article 1.

Article 4
The Commission shall, not more than three years after the date of implementation of this Directive, and at three-yearly intervals thereafter, draw up a report on the application of this Directive and submit it to the European Parliament and the Council.

Article 5
Member States shall bring into force the laws, regulations and administrative provisions necessary to comply with this Directive not later than 30 June 1992.
   They shall forthwith inform the Commission thereof.

Article 6
This Directive is addressed to the Member States.

Done at Luxembourg, 28 June 1990.

(Signature omitted.)

COUNCIL DIRECTIVE OF 29 OCTOBER 1993 ON THE RIGHT OF RESIDENCE FOR STUDENTS (93/96/EEC)
[OJ 1993, No. L317/59]

THE COUNCIL OF THE EUROPEAN COMMUNITIES,

Having regard to the Treaty establishing the European Economic Community, and in particular the second paragraph of Article 7 thereof,
   Having regard to the proposal from the Commission,[1]
   In cooperation with the European Parliament,[2]
   Having regard to the opinion of the Economic and Social Committee,[3]
   Whereas Article 3(c) of the Treaty provides that the activities of the Community shall include, as provided in the Treaty, the abolition, as between Member States, of obstacles to freedom of movement for persons;
   Whereas Article 8a of the Treaty provides that the internal market must be established by 31 December 1992; whereas the internal market comprises an area without internal frontiers in which the free movement of goods, persons, services and capital is ensured in accordance with the provisions of the Treaty;
   Whereas, as the Court of Justice has held, Articles 128 and 7 of the Treaty prohibit any discrimination between nationals of the Member States as regards access to vocational training in the Community;
   Whereas access by a national of one Member State to vocational training in another Member State implies, for that national, a right of residence in that other Member State;
   Whereas, accordingly, in order to guarantee access to vocational training, the conditions likely to facilitate the effective exercise of that right of residence should be laid down;
   Whereas the right of residence for students forms part of a set of related measures designed to promote vocational training;

Notes
[1] OJ No. C166, 17.6.1993, p. 16.
[2] OJ No. C255, 20.9.1993, p. 70 and OJ No. C315, 22.11.1993.
[3] OJ No. C304, 10.11.1993, p. 1.

Whereas beneficiaries of the right of residence must not become an unreasonable burden on the public finances of the host Member State;

Whereas, in the present state of Community law, as established by the case law of the Court of Justice, assistance granted to students does not fall within the scope of the Treaty within the meaning of Article 7 thereof;

Whereas the right of residence can only be genuinely exercised if it is also granted to the spouse and their dependent children;

Whereas the beneficiaries of this Directive should be covered by administrative arrangements similar to those laid down in particular in Council Directive 68/360/EEC of 15 October 1968 on the abolition of restrictions on movement and residence within the Community for workers of Member States and their families[4] and Council Directive 64/221/EEC of the 25 February 1964 on the coordination of special measures concerning the movement and residence of foreign nationals which are justified on grounds of public policy, public security or public health;[5]

Whereas this Directive does not apply to students who enjoy the right of residence by virtue of the fact that they are or have been effectively engaged in economic activities or are members of the family of a migrant worker;

Whereas, by its judgment of 7 July 1992 in Case C-295/90, the Court of Justice annulled Council Directive 90/366/EEC of 28 June 1990 on the right of residence for students,[6] while maintaining the effects of the annulled Directive until the entry into force of a directive adopted on the appropriate legal basis;

Whereas the effects of Directive 90/366/EEC should be maintained during the period up to 31 December 1993, the date by which Member States are to have adopted the laws, regulations and administrative provisions necessary to comply with this Directive,

HAS ADOPTED THIS DIRECTIVE:

Notes
[4]OJ No. L257, 19.10.1968, p. 13. Directive as last amended by the Act of Accession of 1985.
[5]OJ No. 56, 4.4.1964, p. 850/64.
[6]OJ No. L180, 13.7.1990, p. 30.

Article 1
In order to lay down conditions to facilitate the exercise of the right of residence and with a view to guaranteeing access to vocational training in a non-discriminatory manner for a national of a Member State who has been accepted to attend a vocational training course in another Member State, the Member States shall recognise the right of residence for any student who is a national of a Member State and who does not enjoy that right under other provisions of Community law, and for the student's spouse and their dependent children, where the student assures the relevant national authority, by means of a declaration or by such alternative means as the student may choose that are at least equivalent, that he has sufficient resources to avoid becoming a burden on the social assistance system of the host Member State during their period of residence, provided that the student is enrolled in a recognised educational establishment for the principal purpose of following a vocational training course there and that he is covered by sickness insurance in respect of all risks in the host Member State.

Article 2

1. The right of residence shall be restricted to the duration of the course of studies in question.

The right of residence shall be evidenced by means of the issue of a document known as a 'residence permit for a national of a Member State of the Community', the validity of which may be limited to the duration of the course of studies or to one year where the course lasts longer; in the latter event it shall be renewable annually. Where a member of the family does not hold the nationality of a Member State, he or she shall be issued with a residence document of the same validity as that issued to the national on whom he or she depends.

For the purpose of issuing the residence permit or document, the Member State may require only that the applicant present a valid identity card or passport and provide proof that he or she meets the conditions laid down in Article 1.

2. Articles 2, 3 and 9 of Directive 68/360/EEC shall apply *mutatis mutandis* to the beneficiaries of this Directive.

The spouse and the dependent children of a national of a Member State entitled to the right of residence within the territory of a Member State shall be entitled to take up any employed or self-employed activity anywhere within the territory of that Member State, even if they are not nationals of a Member State.

Member States shall not derogate from the provisions of this directive save on grounds of public policy, public security or public health: in that event, Articles 2 to 9 of Directive 64/221/EEC shall apply.

Article 3

This Directive shall not establish any entitlement to the payment of maintenance grants by the host Member State on the part of students benefiting from the right of residence.

Article 4

The right of residence shall remain for as long as beneficiaries of that right fulfil the conditions laid down in Article 1.

Article 5

The Commission shall, not more than three years after the date of implementation of this Directive, and at three-yearly intervals thereafter, draw up a report on the application of this Directive and submit it to the European Parliament and the Council.

The Commission shall pay particular attention to any difficulties to which the implementation of Article 1 might give rise in the Member States; it shall, if appropriate, submit proposals to the Council with the aim of remedying such difficulties.

Article 6

Member States shall bring into force the laws, regulations and administrative provisions necessary to comply with this Directive not later than 31 December 1993.

They shall forthwith inform the Commission thereof.

For the period preceding that date, the effects of Directive 90/366/EEC shall be maintained.

When Member States adopt those measures, they shall contain a reference to this Directive or shall be accompanied by such a reference on the occasion of their official publication.

The methods of making such references shall be laid down by the Member States.

Article 7
This Directive is addressed to the Member States.

Done at Brussels, 29 October 1993.
For the Council
The President
R. URBAIN

SOCIAL SECURITY

COUNCIL REGULATION (EEC) No. 1408/71 ON THE APPLICATION OF SOCIAL SECURITY SCHEMES TO EMPLOYED PERSONS, TO SELF-EMPLOYED PERSONS AND TO MEMBERS OF THEIR FAMILIES MOVING WITHIN THE COMMUNITY
[OJ 1997, No. L28/4][1]

Note

[1]Editor's Note: This is now the latest version to appear in which the Regulation has been re-issued in a consolidated form as an annex to Regulation 118/97 [OJ 1997, No. L28/1]. This includes all amendments up to and including Regulation 118/97 and replaces the consolidation which previously appeared in OJ 1992, No. C325/1

TABLE OF CONTENTS

ANNEXES

Annex IV — Legislation referred to in Article 37(1)of the Regulation under which the amount of invalidity benefits is independent of the length of periods of insurance — Special schemes for self-employed persons within the meaning of Articles 38(3) and 45(3) of Regulation No. 1408/71 — Cases referred to in Article 46(1)(b) of the Regulation where the calculation of benefit in accordance with Article 46(2) of the Regulation may be waived — Benefits and agreements referred to in Article 46b(2) of the Regulation

Annex V — Concordance between the legislation of Member States on conditions relating to the degree of invalidity

Annex VI — Special procedures for applying the legislation of certain Member States

Annex VII — Instances in which a person shall be simultaneously subject to the legislation of two Member States

THE COUNCIL OF THE EUROPEAN UNION,

Having regard to the Treaty establishing the European Community, and in particular Articles 51 and 235 thereof,

Having regard to the proposal from the Commission,

Having regard to the opinion of the European Parliament,

Having regard to the opinion of the Economic and Social Committee,

Whereas the provisions for the coordination of national social security legislations fall within the framework of freedom of movement for workers who are nationals of Member States and should contribute towards the improvement of their standard of living and conditions of employment;

Whereas freedom of movement for persons, which is one of the cornerstones of the Community, is not confined to employed persons but also extends to self-employed persons in the framework of the freedom of establishment and the freedom to supply services;

Whereas the considerable differences existing between national legislations as regards the persons to whom they apply make it preferable to establish the principle that the Regulation applies to all persons insured under social security schemes for employed persons and for self-employed persons or by virtue of pursuing employment or self-employment;

Whereas it is necessary to respect the special characteristics of national social security legislations and to draw up only a system of coordination;

Whereas it is necessary, within the framework of that coordination, to guarantee within the Community equality of treatment under the various national legislations to workers living in the Member States and their dependants and their survivors;

Whereas the provisions for coordination must guarantee that workers moving within the Community and their dependants and their survivors retain the rights and the advantages acquired and in the course of being acquired;

Whereas these objectives must be attained in particular by aggregation of all the periods taken into account under the various national legislations for the purpose of acquiring and retaining the right to benefits and of calculating the amount of benefits, and by the provision of benefits for the various categories of persons covered by the Regulation regardless of their place of residence within the Community;

Whereas employed persons and self-employed persons moving within the Community should be subject to the social security scheme of only one single Member State in order to avoid overlapping of national legislations applicable and the complications which could result therefrom;

Whereas employed persons and self-employed persons moving within the Community should be subject to the social security scheme of only one single Member State in order to avoid overlapping of national legislations applicable and the complications which could result therefrom;

Whereas the instances in which a person should be subject simultaneously to the legislation of two Member States as an exception to the general rule should be as limited in number and scope as possible;

Whereas with a view to guaranteeing the equality of treatment of all workers occupied on the territory of a Member State as effectively as possible, it is appropriate to determine as the legislation applicable, as a general rule, that of the Member State in which the person concerned pursues employment of self-employment;

Whereas in certain situations which justify other criteria of applicability, it is possible to derogate from this general rule;

Whereas certain benefits foreseen under national laws may fall simultaneously within social security and social assistance, because of the personal scope of their application, their objectives and their manner of application, it is necessary to lay down a system of coordination, which takes into account the special characteristics of the benefits concerned, that should be included in the Regulation in order to protect the interests of migrant workers in accordance with the provisions of the Treaty;

Whereas such benefits should be granted, in respect of persons falling within the scope of this Regulation, solely in accordance with the legislation of the country of residence of the person concerned or of the members of his or her family, with such aggregation of periods of residence completed in any other Member State as is necessary and without discrimination on grounds fo nationality;

Whereas it is necessary to lay down specific rules, in particular in the field of sickness and unemployment, for frontier workers and seasonal workers, taking account of the specific nature of their situation;

Whereas in the field of sickness and maternity benefits, it is necessary to guarantee the protection of persons living or staying in a Member State other than the competent Member State;

Whereas the specific position of pension claimants and pensioners and the members of their families calls for the provisions governing sickness insurance to adapted to their situation;

Whereas for invalidity benefits a system of coordination should be drawn up which respects the specific characteristics of national legislations; whereas it is therefore necessary to make a distinction between legislations under which the amount of invalidity benefit is independent of the length of insurance and legislations under which the amount depends on the aforementioned length;

Whereas the differences between the schemes in the Member States call for the adoption of rules of coordination which are applicable in the case of aggravation of invalidity;

Whereas it is expedient that a system for the award of old-age benefits and survivors benefits be worked out where the employed or self-employed person has been subject to the legislation of one or more Member States;

Whereas there is a need to determine the amount of a pension calculated in accordance with the method used for aggregation and pro rata calculation and guaranteed by Community law where the application of national legislation, including provisions concerning reduction, suspension or withdrawal, is less favourable than the aforementioned method;

Whereas to protect migrant workers and their survivors against an excessively stringent application of the national provisions concerning reduction, suspension or withdrawal, it is necessary to include provisions laying down strict rules for the application of these provisions;

Whereas, in respect of benefits for accidents at work and occupational diseases, it is necessary, for the purpose of affording protection, that rules be laid down covering the situation of persons residing or staying in a Member State other than the competent Member State;

Whereas it is necessary to lay down specific provisions for death grants;

Whereas, in order to secure mobility of labour under improved conditions, it is necessary henceforth to ensure closer coordination between the unemployment insurance schemes and the unemployment assistance schemes of all the Member States;

Whereas it is therefore particularly appropriate, in order to facilitate search for employment in the various Member States, to grant to an unemployed worker, for a limited period, the unemployment benefits provided for by the legislation of the Member State to which he was last subject;

Whereas, with a view to determining the legislation applicable to family benefits, the criterion of employment ensures equal treatment between all workers subject to the same legislation;

Whereas, in order to avoid unwarranted overlapping of benefits, there is a need to provide for rules of priority in the case of overlapping of the right to family benefits under the legislation of the competent State and under the legislation of the country of residence of the members of the family;

Whereas the legislations of the Member States differ from each other and are specific in nature, it is considered necessary to draw up specific rules for the coordination of the national schemes providing benefits for dependent children of pensioners and for orphans;

Whereas it is necessary to establish an Administrative Commission consisting of a government representative from each of the Member States, charged in particular with dealing with all administrative questions or questions of interpretation arising from the provisions of this Regulation, and to further cooperation between the Member States;

Whereas it is desirable, within the framework of an Advisory Committee, to have the representatives of workers and employers examine the issues treated by the Administrative Commission;

Whereas it is necessary to lay down special provisions which correspond to the special characteristics of the national legislations in order to facilitate the application of the rules of coordination,

HAS ADOPTED THIS REGULATION:

TITLE I   GENERAL PROVISIONS

Article 1(7)[1]   Definitions

For the purpose of this Regulation:

(a) 'employed person' and 'self-employed person' mean respectively:

(i)   any person who is insured, compulsorily or on an optional continued basis, for one or more of the contingencies covered by the branches of a social security scheme for employed or self-employed persons;

(ii)   any person who is compulsorily insured for one or more of the contingencies covered by the branches of social security dealt with in this Regulation, under a social security scheme for all residents or for the whole working population, if such person:

— can be identified as an employed or self-employed person by virtue of the manner in which such scheme is administered or financed, or,

— failing such criteria, is insured for some other contingency specified in Annex I under a scheme for employed or self-employed persons, or under a scheme referred to in (iii), either compulsorily or on an optional continued basis, or, as no such scheme exists in the Member State concerned, complies with the definition given in Annex I;

(iii)   any person who is compulsorily insured for several of the contingencies covered by the branches dealt with in this Regulation, under a standard social security scheme for the whole rural population in accordance with the criteria laid down in Annex I;

(iv)   any person who is voluntarily insured for one or more of the contingencies covered by the branches dealt with in this Regulation, under a security scheme of a Member State for employed or self-employed persons or for all residents or for certain categories of residents:

— if such person carries out an activity as an employed or self-employed person, or

— if such person has previously been compulsorily insured for the same contingency under a scheme for employed or self-employed persons of the same Member State;

(b) 'frontier worker' means any employed or self-employed person who pursues his occupation in the territory of a Member State and resides in the territory of another Member State to which he returns as a rule daily or at least once a week; however, a frontier worker who is posed elsewhere in the territory of the same or another Member State by the undertaking to which he is normally attached, or who engages in the provision of services elsewhere in the territory of the same or another Member State, shall retain the status of frontier worker for a period not exceeding four months, even if he is prevented, during that period, from returning daily or at least once a week to the place where he resides;

(c) 'seasonal worker' means any employed person who goes to the territory of a Member State other than the one in which he is resident to do work there of a seasonal nature for an undertaking or an employer of that State for a period which may on no account exceed eight months, and who stays in

Note

[1]Editor's Note: The numbers appearing in brackets following the Article Numbers refer to the Acts amending Regulations 1408/71 and 574/72 as appear in Annex B (OJ 1997 L28/228-229). Annex B is reproduced below at the start of the annexes.

the territory of the said State for the duration of this work; work of a seasonal nature shall be taken to mean work which, being dependent on the succession of the seasons, automatically recurs each year;

(d) 'refugee' shall have the meaning assigned to it in Article 1 of the Convention on the Status of Refugees, signed at Geneva on 28 July 1951;

(e) 'stateless person' shall have the meaning assigned to it in Article 1 of the Convention on the Status of Stateless Persons, signed in New York on 28 September 1954;

(f) (i) 'member of the family' means any person defined or recognised as a member of the family or designated as a member of the household by the legislation under which benefits are provided or, in the case referred to in Articles 22(1)(a) and 31, by the legislation of the Member State in whose territory such person resides; where, however, the said legislation regards as a member of the family or a member of the household only a person living under the same roof as the employed or self-employed person, this condition shall be considered satisfied if the person in question is mainly dependent on that person. Where the legislation of a Member State on sickness or maternity benefits in kind does not enable members of the family to be distinguished from the other persons to whom it applies, the term 'member of the family' shall have the meaning given to it in Annex I;

(ii) where, however, the benefits concerned are benefits for disabled persons granted under the legislation of a Member State to all nationals of that State who fulfil the prescribed conditions, the term 'member of the family' means at least the spouse of an employed or self-employed person and the children of such person who are either minors or dependent upon such person;

(g) 'survivor' means any person defined or recognised as such by the legislation under which the benefits are granted; where, however, the said legislation regards as a survivor only a person who was living under the same roof as the deceased, this condition shall be considered satisfied if such person was mainly dependent on the deceased;

(h) 'residence' means habitual residence;

(i) 'stay' means temporary residence;

(j) 'legislation' means in respect of each Member State statutes, regulations and other provisions and all other implementing measures, present or future, relating to the branches and schemes of social security covered by Article 4(1) and (2) or those special non-contributory benefits covered by Article 4(2a). The term excludes provisions of existing or future industrial agreements, whether or not they have been the subject of a decision by the authorities rendering them compulsory or extending their scope. However, in so far as such provisions

(i) serve to put into effect compulsory insurance imposed by the laws and regulations referred to in the preceding subparagraph; or

(ii) set up a scheme administered by the same institution as that which administers the schemes set up by the laws and regulations referred to in the preceding subparagraph.

The limitation on the term may at any time be lifted by a declaration of the Member State concerned specifying the schemes of such a kind to which this Regulation applies. Such a declaration shall be notified and published in accordance with the provisions of Article 97.

The provisions of the preceding subparagraph shall not have effect of exempting from the application of this Regulation the schemes to which Regulation No. 3 applies.

The term 'legislation' also excludes provisions governing special schemes for self-employed persons the creation of which is left to the initiatives of those concerned or which apply only to a part of the territory of the Member State concerned, irrespective of whether or not the authorities decided to make them compulsory or extend their scope. The special schemes in question are specified in Annex II;

(k) 'social security convention' means any bilateral or multilateral instrument which binds or will bind two or more Member States exclusively, and any other multilateral instrument which binds or will bind at least two Member States and one or more other States in the field of social security, for all or part of the branches and schemes set out in Article 4(1) and (2), together with agreements, of whatever kind, concluded pursuant to the said instruments;

(l) 'competent authority' means, in respect of each Member State, the Minister, Ministers or other equivalent authority responsible for social security schemes throughout or in any part of the territory of the State in question;

(m) 'Administrative Commission' means the commission referred to in Article 80;

(n) 'institution' means, in respect of each member State the body or authority responsible for administering all or part of the legislation;

(o) 'competent institution' means:

(i)   the institution with which the person concerned is insured at the time of the application for benefit; or

(ii)   the institution from which the person concerned is entitled or would be entitled to benefits if he or a member or members of his family were resident in the territory of the Member State in which the institution is situated; or

(iii) the institution designated by the competent authority of the Member State concerned; or

(iv)   in the case of a scheme relating to an employer's liability in respect of the benefits set out in Article 4(1), either the employer or the insurer involved or, in default thereof, a body or authority designated by the competent authority of the Member State concerned;

(p) 'institution of the place of residence' and 'institution of the place of stay' mean respectively the institution which is competent to provide benefits in the place where the person concerned resides and the institution which is competent to provide benefits in the place where the person concerned is staying, under the legislation administered by that institution or, where no such institution exists, the institution designated by the competent authority of the Member State in question;

(q) 'competent State' means the Member State in whose territory the competent institution is situated;

(r) 'periods of insurance' means periods of contribution or periods of employment or self-employment as defined or recognised as periods of insurance by the legislation under which they were completed or considered as completed, and all periods treated as such, where they are regarded by the said legislation as equivalent to periods of insurance;

(s) 'periods of employment' and 'periods of self-employment' means periods so defined or recognised by the legislation under which they were completed, and all periods treated as such, where they are regarded by the said legislation as equivalent to periods of employment or of self-employment;

(sa) 'periods of residence' means periods as defined or recognised as such by the legislation under which they were completed or considered as completed;

(t) 'benefits' and 'pensions' mean all benefits and pensions, including all elements thereof payable out of public funds, revalorisation increases and supplementary allowances, subject to the provisions of Title III, as also lump-sum benefits which may be paid in lieu of pensions, and payments made by way of reimbursement of contributions;

(u) (i) the term 'family benefits' means all benefits in kind or in cash intended to meet family expenses under the legislation provided for in Article 4(1)(h), excluding the special childbirth allowances mentioned in Annex II;[1]

(ii) 'family allowances' means periodical cash benefits granted exclusively by reference to the number and, where appropriate, the age of members of the family;

(v) 'death grants' means any once-for-all payment in the event of death exclusive of the lump-sum benefits referred to in subparagraph (t).

Note
[1]Amended by Regulation 3096/95 of 22 December 1995 [OJ 1995, No. L335/10].

Article 2   Persons covered

1. This Regulation shall apply to employed or self-employed persons who are or have been subject to the legislation of one or more Member States and who are nationals of one of the Member States or who are stateless persons or refugees residing within the territory of one of the Member States, as well as to the members of their families and their survivors.

2. In addition, this Regulation shall apply to the survivors of employed or self-employed persons who have been subject to the legislation of one or more Member States, irrespective of the nationality of such employed or self-employed persons, where their survivors are nationals of one of the member States, or stateless persons or refugees residing within the territory of one of the Member States.

3. This Regulation shall apply to civil servants and to persons who, in accordance with the legislation applicable, are treated as such, where they are or have been subject to the legislation of a Member State to which this Regulation applies.

Article 3   Equality of treatment

1. Subject to the special provisions of this Regulation, persons resident in the territory of one of the Member States to whom this Regulation applies shall be subject to the same obligations and enjoy the same benefits under the legislation of any Member State as the nationals of that State.

2. The provisions of paragraph 1 shall apply to the right to elect members of the organs of social security institutions or to participate in their nomination, but shall not affect the legislative provisions of any Member State relating to eligibility or methods of nomination of persons concerned to those organs.

3. Save as provided in Annex III, the provisions of social security conventions which remain in force pursuant to Article 7(2)(c) and the provisions of conventions concluded pursuant to Article 8(1), shall apply to all persons to whom this Regulation applies.

Article 4(7)   Matters covered

1. This Regulation shall apply to all legislation concerning the following branches of social security:

(a)   sickness and maternity benefits;

(b)   invalidity benefits, including those intended for the maintenance or improvement of earning capacity;

(c)   old-age benefits;

(d)   survivor's benefits;

(e)   benefits in respect of accidents at work and occupational diseases;

(f)   death grants;

(g)   unemployment benefits;

(h)   family benefits.

2. This Regulation shall apply to all general and special social security schemes, whether contributory or non-contributory, and to schemes concerning the liability of an employer or shipowner in respect of the benefits referred to in paragraph 1.

2a. This Regulation shall also apply to special non-contributory benefits which are provided under legislation or schemes other than those referred to in paragraph 1 or excluded by virtue of paragraph 4, where such benefits are intended:

(a)   either to provide supplementary, substitute or ancillary cover against the risks covered by the branches of social security referred to in paragraph 1(a) to (h), or

(b)   solely as specific protection for the disabled.

2b. This Regulation shall not apply to the provisions in the legislation of a Member State concerning special non-contributory benefits, referred to in Annex II, Section III, the validity of which is confined to part of its territory.

3. The provisions of Title III of this Regulation shall not, however, affect the legislative provisions of any Member State concerning a shipowner's liability.

4. This Regulation shall not apply to social and medical assistance, to benefit schemes for victims of war or its consequences, or to special schemes for civil servants and persons treated as such.

Article 5(7)   Declarations by the Member States on the scope of this Regulation

The Member States shall specify the legislation and schemes referred to in Article 4(1) and (2), the special non-contributory benefits referred to in Article 4(2a), the minimum benefits referred to in Article 50 and the benefits referred to in Articles 77 and 78 in declarations to be notified and published in accordance with Article 97.

Article 6   Social security conventions replaced by this Regulation

Subject to the provisions of Articles 7, 8 and 46(4), this Regulation shall, as regards persons and matters which it covers, replace the provisions of any social security convention binding either:

(a)   two or more Member States exclusively; or

(b)   at least two Member States and one or more other States, where settlement of the cases concerned does not involve any institution of one of the latter States.

Article 7(4)   International provisions not affected by this Regulation

1.   This Regulation shall not affect obligations arising from:

(a)   any convention adopted by the International Labour Conference which, after ratification by one or more Member States, has entered into force;

(b)   the European Interim Agreements on Social Security of 11 December 1953 concluded between the Member States of the Council of Europe.

2.   The provisions of Article 6 notwithstanding, the following shall continue to apply:

(a)   the provisions of the Agreements of 27 July 1950 and 30 November 1979 concerning social security for Rhine boatmen;

(b)   the provisions of the European Convention of 9 July 1956 concerning social security for workers in international transport;

(c)   the provisions of the social security conventions listed in Annex III.

Article 8   Conclusion of conventions between Member States

1.   Two or more Member States may, as need arises, conclude conventions with each other based on the principles and in the spirit of this Regulation.

2.   Each Member State shall notify, in accordance with the provisions of Article 97(1), any convention concluded with another Member State under the provisions of paragraph 1.

Article 9   Admission to voluntary or optional continued insurance

1.   The provisions of the legislation of any Member State which make admission to voluntary or optional continued insurance conditional upon residence in the territory of that State shall not apply to persons resident in the territory of another Member State, provided that at some time in their past working life they were subject to the legislation of the first State as employed or as self-employed persons.

2.   Where, under the legislation of a Member State, admission to voluntary or optional continued insurance is conditional upon completion of periods of insurance, the periods of insurance or residence completed under the legislation of another Member State shall be taken into account, to the extent required, as if they were completed under the legislation of the first State.

Article 9a(4)   Prolongation of the reference period

Where, under the legislation of a Member State recognition of entitlement to a benefit is conditional upon completion of a minimum period of insurance during a specific period preceding the contingency insured against (reference period) and where the aforementioned legislation provides that the periods during which the benefits have been granted under the legislation of that Member State or periods devoted to the upbringing of children in the territory of that Member State shall give rise to prolongation of the reference period, periods during which invalidity pensions or old-age pensions or sickness benefits, unemployment benefits or benefits for accidents at work (except for pensions) have been awarded under the legislation of another Member State and periods devoted to the upbringing of children in the territory of another Member State shall likewise give rise to prolongation of the aforesaid reference period.

Article 10   Waiving of residence clauses — Effect of compulsory insurance on reimbursement of contributions

1.   Save as otherwise provided in this Regulation invalidity, old-age or survivors' cash benefits, pensions for accidents at work or occupational diseases and death grants acquired under the legislation of one or more Member States shall not be subject to any reduction, modification, suspension, withdrawal or confiscation by reason of the fact that the recipient resides in the territory of a Member State other than that in which the institution responsible for payment is situated.

The preceding subparagraph shall also apply to lump-sum benefits granted in cases of remarriage of a surviving spouse who was entitled to a survivor's pension.

2.   Where under the legislation of a Member State reimbursement of contributions is conditional upon the person concerned having ceased to be subject to compulsory insurance, this condition shall not be considered satisfied as long as the person concerned is subject to compulsory insurance as an employed or self-employed person under the legislation of another Member State.

Article 10a(7)   Special non-contributory benefits

1.   Notwithstanding the provisions of Article 10 and Title III, persons to whom this Regulation applies shall be granted the special contributory cash benefits referred to in Article 4(2a) exclusively in the territory of the Member state in which they reside, in accordance with the legislation of that State, provided tht such benefits are listed in Annex IIa. Such benefits shall be granted by and at the expense of the institution of the place of residence.

2.   The institution of a Member State under whose legislation entitlement to benefits covered by paragraph 1 is subject to the completion of periods of employment, self-employment or residence shall regard, to the extent necess-ary, periods of employment, self-employment or residence completed in the territory of any other Member State as periods completed in the territory of the first Member State.

3.   Where entitlement to a benefit covered by paragraph 1 but granted in the form of a supplement is subject, under the legislation of a Member State, to receipt of a benefit covered by Article 4(1)(a) to (h), and no such benefit is due under that legislation, any corresponding benefit granted under the legislation of any other Member State shall be treated as a benefit granted under the legislation of the first Member State for the purposes of entitlement to the supplement.

4.   Where the granting of a disability or invalidity benefit covered by paragraph 1 is subject, under the legislation of a Member State to the condition that the disability or invalidity should be diagnosed for the first time in the territory of that Member State, this condition shall be deemed to be fulfilled where such diagnosis is made for the first time in the territory of another Member State.

Article 11   Revalorisation of benefits

Rules for revalorisation provided by the legislation of a Member State shall apply to benefits due under that legislation taking into account the provisions of this Regulation.

Article 12(6)(8)   Prevention of overlapping of benefits

1.   This Regulation can neither confer nor maintain the right to several benefits of the same kind for one and the same period of compulsory insurance. However, this provision shall not apply to benefits in respect of invalidity, old age, death (pensions) or occupational disease which are awarded by the institutions of two or more Member States, in accordance with the provisions of Article 41, 43(2) and (3), 46, 50 and 51 or Article 60(1)(b).

2.   Save as otherwise provided in this Regulation, the provisions of the legislation of a Member State governing the reduction, suspension or withdrawal of benefits in cases of overlapping with other social security benefits or any other form of income may be invoked even where such benefits were acquired under the legislation of another Member State or where such income was acquired in the territory of another Member State.

3.   The provisions of the legislation of a Member State for reduction, suspension or withdrawal of benefit in the case of a person in receipt of invalidity benefits or anticipatory old-age benefits pursuing a professional or trade activity may be invoked against such person even though he is pursuing his activity in the territory of another Member State.

4.   An invalidity pension payable under Netherlands legislation shall, in a case where the Netherlands institution is bound under the provisions of Article 57(5) or 60(2)(b) to contribute also to the cost of benefits for occupational disease granted under the legislation of another Member State be reduced by the amount payable to the institution of the other Member State which is responsible for granting the benefits for occupational disease.

TITLE II   DETERMINATION OF THE LEGISLATION APPLICABLE

Article 13(6)   General rules

1.   Subject to Article 4(c), persons to whom this Regulation applies shall be subject to the legislation of a single Member State only. That legislation shall be determined in accordance with the provisions of this Title.

2.   Subject to Articles 14 to 17:

    (a)   a person employed in the territory of one Member State shall be subject to the legislation of that State even if he resides in the territory of another Member State or if the registered office or place of business of the undertaking or individual employing him is situated in the territory of another Member State;

    (b)   a person who is self-employed in the territory of one Member State shall be subjected to the legislation of that State even if he resides in the territory of another Member State;

    (c)   a person employed on board a vessel flying the flag of a Member State shall be subject to the legislation of that State;

    (d)   civil servants and persons treated as such shall be subject to the legislation of the Member State to which the administration employing them is subject;

    (e)   a person called up or recalled for service in the armed forces, or for civilian service, of a Member State shall be subject to the legislation of that State. If entitlement under that legislation is subject to the completion of periods of insurance before entry into or after release from such military or civilian service, periods of insurance completed under the legislation of any other Member State shall be taken into account, to the extent necessary, as if they were periods of insurance completed under the legislation of the first State. The employed or self-employed or self-employed person called up or recalled for service in the armed forces or for civilian service shall retain the status of employed or self-employed person;

(f)   a person to whom the legislation of a Member State ceases to be applicable, without the legislation of another Member State becoming applicable to him in accordance with one of the rules laid down in the aforegoing subparagraphs or in accordance with one of the exceptions or special provisions laid down in Articles 14 to 17 shall be subject to the legislation of the Member State in whose territory he resides in accordance with the provisions of that legislation alone.

Article 14   Special rules applicable to persons, other than mariners, engaged in paid employment

Article 13(2)(a) shall apply subject to the following exceptions and circumstances:

1.   (a)   A person employed in the territory of a Member State by an undertaking to which he is normally attached who is posted by that undertaking to the territory of another Member State to perform work there for that undertaking shall continue to be subject to the legislation of the first Member State, provided that the anticipated duration of that work does not exceed 12 months and that he is not sent to replace another person who has completed his term of posting.

(b)   If the duration of the work to be done extends beyond the duration originally anticipated, owing to unforeseeable circumstances, and exceeds 12 months, the legislation of the first Member State shall continue to apply until the completion of such work, provided that the competent authority of the Member State in whose territory the person concerned is posted or the body designated by that authority gives its consent; such consent must be requested before the end of the initial 12-month period. Such consent cannot, however, be given for a period exceeding 12 months.

2.   A person normally employed in the territory of two or more Member States shall be subject to the legislation determined as follows:

(a)   A person who is a member of the travelling or flying personnel of an undertaking which, for hire or reward or on its own account, operates international transport services for passengers or goods by rail, road, air or inland waterway and has its registered office or place of business in the territory of a Member State shall be subject to the legislation of the latter State, with the following restrictions:

(i)   where the said undertaking has a branch or permanent representation in the territory of a Member State other than that in which it has its registered office or place of business, a person employed by such branch or permanent representtion shall be subject to the legislation of the Member State in whose territory such branch or permanent representation is situated;

(ii)   where a person is employed principally in the territory of the Member State in which he resides, he shall be subject to the legislation of that State, even if the undertaking which employs him has no registered office or place of business or branch or permanent representation in that territory.

(b)   A person other than that referred to in (a) shall be subject:

(i)   to the legislation of the Member State in whose territory he resides, if he pursues his activity partly in that territory or if he is attached to several undertakings or several employers who have their registered offices or places of business in the territory of different Member States;

(ii)   to the legislation of the Member State in whose territory is situated the registered office or place of business of the undertaking or individual employing him, if he does not reside in the territory of any of the Member States where he is pursuing his activity.

3.   A person who is employed in the territory of one Member State by an undertaking which has its registered office or place of business in the territory of another Member State and which straddles the common frontier of these States shall be subject to the legislation of the Member State in whose territory the undertaking has its registered office or place of business.

Article 14a   Special rules applicable to persons, other than mariners, who are self-employed (Article 13(2)(b)) shall apply subject to the following exceptions and circumstances

1.   (a)   A person normally self-employed in the territory of a Member State and who performs work in the territory of another Member State shall continue to be subject to the legislation of the first Member State, provided that the anticipated duration of the work does not exceed 12 months.

(b)   If the duration of the work to be done extends beyond the duration originally anticipated, owing to unforeseeable circumstances, and exceeds 12 months, the legislation of the first Member State shall continue to apply until the completion of such work, provided that the competent authority of the Member State in whose territory the person concerned has entered to perform the work in question or the body appointed by that authority gives its consent; such consent must be requested before the end of the initial 12-month period. Such consent cannot, however, be given for a period exceeding 12 months.

2.   A person normally self-employed in the territory of two or more Member States shall be subject to the legislation of the Member State in whose territory he resides if he pursues any part of his activity in the territory of that Member State. If he does not pursue any activity in the territory of the Member State in which he resides, he shall be subject to the legislation of the Member State in whose territory he pursues his main activity. The criteria used to determine the principal activity are laid down in the Regulation referred to in Article 98.

3.   A person who is self-employed in an undertaking which has its registered office or place of business in the territory of one Member State and which straddles the common frontier of two Member States shall be subject to the legislation of the Member State in whose territory the undertaking has its registered office or place of business.

4.   If the legislation to which a person should be subject in accordance with paragraphs 2 or 3 does not enable that person, even on a voluntary basis, to join a pension scheme, the person concerned shall be subject to the legislation of the other Member State which would apply apart from these particular provisions, or should the legislation of two or more Member States apply in this way, he shall be subject to the legislation decided on by common agreement amongst the Member States concerned or their competent authorities.

Article 14b   Special rules applicable to mariners

Article 13(2)(c) shall apply subject to the following exceptions and circumstances:

1.   A person employed by an undertaking to which he is normally attached, either in the territory of a Member State or on board a vessel flying the flag of a Member State who is posted by that undertaking on board a vessel flying the flag of another Member State to perform work there for that undertaking shall, subject to the conditions provided in Article 14(1), continue to be subject to the legislation of the first Member State.

2.   A person normally self-employed, either in the territory of a Member State or on board a vessel flying the flag of a Member State and who performs work on his own account on board a vessel flying the flag of another Member State shall, subject to the conditions provided in Article 14a(1), continue to be subject to the legislation of the first Member State.

3.   A person who, while not being normally employed at sea, performs work in the territorial waters or in a port of a Member State on a vessel flying the flag of another Member State within those territorial waters or in that port, but is not a member of the crew of the vessel, shall be subject to the legislation of the first Member State.

4.   A person employed on board a vessel flying the flag of a Member State and remunerated for such employment by an undertaking or a person whose registered office or place of business is in the territory of another Member State shall be subject to the legislation of the latter State if he is resident in the territory of that State; the undertaking or person paying the remuneration shall be considered as the employer for the purposes of the said legislation.

Article 14c(2)   Special rules applicable to persons who are simultaneously employed in the territory of one Member State and self-employed in the territory of another Member State

A person who is simultaneously employed in the territory of one Member State and self-employed in the territory of another Member State shall be subject:

(a)   save as otherwise provided in subparagraph (b) to the legislation of the Member State in the territory of which he is engaged in paid employment or, where he pursues such an activity in the territory of two or more Member States, to the legislation determined in accordance with Article 14(2) or (3);

(b)   in the cases mentioned in Annex VII:

— to the legislation of the Member State in the territory of which he is engaged in paid employment, that legislation having been determined in accordance with the provisions of Article 14(2) or (3), where he pursues such an activity in the territory of two or more Member States, and

— to the legislation of the Member State in the territory of which he is self-employed, that legislation having been determined in accordance with Article 14a(2), (3) or (4), where he pursues such an activity in the territory of two or more Member States.

Article 14d(2)   Miscellaneous provisions

1.   The person referred to in Article 14(2) and (3), 14a(2), (3) and (4) and 14c(a) shall be treated, for the purposes of application of the legislation laid down in accordance with these provisions, as if he pursued all his professional activity or activities in the territory of the Member State concerned.

2.   The person referred to in Article 14c(b) shall be treated, for the purposes of determining the rates of contributions to be charged to self-employed workers under the legislation of the Member State in whose territory he is self-employed, as if he pursued his paid employment in the territory of the Member State concerned.

3.   The provisions of the legislation of a Member State under which a pensioner who is pursuing a professional or trade activity is not subject to compulsory insurance in respect of such activity shall also apply to a pensioner whose pension was acquired under the legislation of another Member State, unless the person concerned expressly asks to be so subject by applying to the institution designated by the competent authority of the first Member State and named in Annex 10 to the Regulation referred to in Article 98.

Article 15   Rules concerning voluntary insurance or optional continued insurance

1.   Articles 13 to 14d shall not apply to voluntary insurance or to optional insurance unless, in respect of one of the branches referred to in Article 4, there exists in any Member State only a voluntary scheme of insurance.

2.   Where application of the legislation of two or more Member States entails overlapping of insurance:

— under a compulsory insurance scheme and one or more voluntary or optional continued insurance schemes, the person concerned shall be subject exclusively to the compulsory insurance scheme,

— under two or more voluntary or optional continued insurance schemes, the person concerned may join only the voluntary or optional continued insurance scheme for which he has opted.

3.   However, in respect of invalidity, old age and death (pensions), the person concerned may join the voluntary or optional continued insurance scheme of a Member State, even if he is compulsorily subject to the legislation of another Member State, to the extent that such overlapping is explicitly or implicitly admitted in the first Member State.

Article 16   Special rules regarding persons employed by diplomatic missions and consular posts, and auxiliary staff of the European Communities

1.   The provisions of Article 13(2)(a) shall apply to persons employed by diplomatic missions and consular posts and to the private domestic staff of agents of such missions or posts.

2.   However, employed persons covered by paragraph 1 who are nationals of the member State which is the accrediting or sending State may opt to be subject to the legislation of that State. Such right of option may be renewed at the end of each calendar year and shall not have retrospective effect.

3.   Auxiliary staff of the European Communities may opt to be subject to the legislation of the Member State in whose territory they are emplyed, to the legislation of the Member State to which they were last subject or to the legislation of the Member State whose nationals they are, in respect of provisions other than those relating to family allowances, the granting of which is governed by the conditions of employment applicable to such staff. This right of option, which may be exercised once only, shall take effect from the date of entry into employment.

Article 17(6)   Exceptions to Articles 13 to 16

Two or more Member States, the competent authorities of these States or the bodies designated by these authorities may by common agreement provide for exceptions to the provisions of Articles 13 to 16 in the interest of certain categories of persons or of certain persons.

Article 17a(6)　Special rules concerning recipients of pensions due under the legislation of one or more Member States

The recipient of a pension due under the legislation of a Member State or of pensions due under the legislation of several Member States who resides in the territory of another Member State may at his request be exempted from the legislation of the latter State provided that he is not subject to that legislation because of the pursuit of an occupation.

TITLE III　SPECIAL PROVISIONS RELATING TO THE VARIOUS CATEGORIES OF BENEFITS
CHAPTER I　SICKNESS AND MATERNITY
SECTION 1　COMMON PROVISIONS

Article 18　Aggregation of periods of insurance, employment or residence

1.　The competent institution of a Member State whose legislation makes the acquisition, retention or recovery of the right to benefits conditional upon the completion of periods of insurance, employment or residence shall, to the extent necessary, take account of periods of insurance, employment or residence completed under the legislation of any other Member State as if they were periods completed under the legislation which it administers.

2.　The provisions of paragraph 1 shall apply to seasonal workers, even in repect of periods prior to any break in insurance exceeding the period allowed by the legislation of the competent State, provided, however, that the person concerned has not ceased to be insured for a period exceeding four months.

SECTION 2　EMPLOYED OR SELF-EMPLOYED PERSONS AND MEMBERS OF THEIR FAMILIES

Article 19　Residence in a Member State other than the competent State — General rules

1.　An employed or self-employed person residing in the territory of a Member State other than the competent State, who satisfies the conditions of the legislation of the competent State for entitlement to benefits, taking account where appropriate of the provisions of Article 18, shall receive in the State in which he is resident:

(a)　benefits in kind provided on behalf of the competent institution by the institution of the place of residence in accordance with the provisions of the legislation administered by that institution as though he were insured with it;

(b)　cash benefits provided by the competent institution in accordance with the legislation which it administers. However, by agreement between the competent institution and the institution of the place of residence, such benefits may be provided by the latter institution on behalf of the former, in accordance with the legislation of the competent State.

2.　The provisions of paragraph 1 shall apply by analogy to members of the family who reside in the territory of a Member State other than the competent

State in so far as they are not entitled to such benefits under the legislation of the State in whose territory they reside.

Where the members of the family reside in the territory of a Member State under whose legislation the right to receive benefits in kind is not subject to condition of insurance or employment, benefits in kind which they receive shall be considered as being on behalf of the institution with which the employed or self-employed person is insured, unless the spouse or the person looking after the children pursues a professional or trade activity in the territory of the said Member State.

Article 20   Frontier workers and members of their families — Special rules

A frontier worker may also obtain benefits in the territory of the competent State. Such benefits shall be provided by the competent institution in accordance with the provisions of the legislation of that State, as though the person concerned were resident in that State. Members of his family may receive benefits under the same conditions; however, receipt of such benefits shall, except in urgent cases, be conditional upon an agreement between the States concerned or between the competent authorities of those States or, in its absence, on prior authorisation by the competent institution.

Article 21   Stay in or transfer of residence to the competent State

1.   The employed or self-employed person referred to in Article 19(1) who is staying in the territory of the competent State shall receive benefits in accordance with the provisions of the legislation of that State as though he were resident there, even if he has already received benefits for the same case of sickness or maternity before his stay.

2.   Paragraph 1 shall apply by analogy to the members of the family referred to in Article 19(2). However, where the latter reside in the territory of a Member State other than the one in whose territory the employed or self-employed person resides, benefits in kind shall be provided by the institution of the place of stay on behalf of the institution of the place of residence of the persons concerned.

3.   Paragraphs 1 and 2 shall not apply to frontier workers and the members of their families.

4.   An employed or self-employed person and members of his family referred to in Article 19 who transfer their residence to the territory of the competent State shall receive benefits in accordance with the provisions of the legislation of that State even if they have already received benefits for the same case of sickness or maternity before transferring their residence.

Article 22   Stay outside the competent State — Return to or transfer of residence to another Member State during sickness or maternity — Need to go to another Member State in order to receive appropriate treatment

1.   An employed or self-employed person who satisfies the conditions of the legislation of the competent State for entitlement to benefits, taking account where appropriate of the provisions of Article 18, and:

(a)   whose condition necessitates immediate benefits during a stay in the territory of another Member State; or

(b) who, having become entitled to benefits chargeable to the competent institution, is authorised by that institution to return to the territory of the Member State where he resides, or to transfer his residence to the territory of another Member State; or

(c) who is authorised by the competent institution to go to the territory of another Member State to receive there the treatment appropriate to his condition, shall be entitled:

(i) to benefits in kind provided on behalf of the competent institution by the institution of the place of stay or residence in accordance with the provisions of the legislation which it administers, as though he were insured with it; the length of the period during which benefits are provided shall be governed, however, by the legislation of the competent State;

(ii) to cash benefits provided by the competent institution in accordance with the provisions of the legislation which it administers. However, by agreement between the competent institution and the institution of the place of stay or residence, such benefits may be provided by the latter institution on behalf of the former, in accordance with the provisions of the legislation of the competent State.

2. The authorisation required under paragraph 1(b) may be refused only if it is established that movement of the person concerned would be prejudicial to his state of health or the receipt of medical treatment.

The authorisation required under paragraph 1(c) may not be refused where the treatment in question is among the benefits provided for by the legislation of the Member State on whose territory the person concerned resides and where he cannot be given such treatment within the time normally necessary for obtaining the treatment in question in the Member State of residence taking account of his current state of health and the probable course of the disease.

3. The provisions of paragraphs 1 and 2 shall apply by analogy to members of the family of an employed or self-employed person. However, for the purpose of applying paragraph 1(a) and (c)(i) to the members of the family referred to in Article 19(2) who reside in the territory of a Member State other than the one in whose territory the employed or self-employed person resides:

(a) benefits in kind shall be provided on behalf of the institution of the Member State in whose territory the members of the family are residing by the institution of the place of stay in accordance with the provisions of the legislation which it administers as if the employed or self-employed person were insured there. The period during which benefits are provided shall, however, be that laid down under the legislation of the Member State in whose territory the members of the family are residing;

(b) the authorisation required under paragraph 1(c) shall be issued by the institution of the Member State in whose territory the members of the family are residing.

4. The fact that the provisions of paragraph 1 apply to an employed or self-employed person shall not affect the right to benefit of members of his family.

Article 22A   Special Rules for certain categories of persons

Notwithstanding Article 2 of this Regulation, Article 22(1)(a) and (c) shall also apply to persons who are nationals of a Member State and are insured under the legislation of a Member State and to the members of their families residing with them.

Article 22B   Employment in a Member State other than the competent State — Stay in the State of Employment[1]

The employed or self-employed person referred to in Articles 13(2)(d), 14, 14a, 14b, 14c(a) or 17, and members of the family accompanying him, shall benefit from the provisions of Article 22(1)(a) for any condition requiring benefits during a stay in the territory of the Member State in which the worker is employed or whose flag the vessel aboard which the worker is employed is flying.

Note

[1]Inserted by Regulation 3096/95 of 22 December 1995 [OJ 1995, L335/10].

Article 23   Calculation of cash benefits

1.   The competent institution of a Member State whose legislation provides that the calculation of cash benefits shall be based on average earnings or on average contributions, shall determine such average earnings or contributions exclusively by reference to earnings or contributions completed under the said legislation.

2.   The competent institution of a Member State whose legislation provides that the calculation of cash benefits shall be based on standard earnings, shall take account exclusively of the standard earnings or, where appropriate, of the average of standard earnings for the periods completed under the said legislation.

3.   The competent institution of a Member State under whose legislation the amount of cash benefits varies with the number of members of the family, shall also take into account the members of the family of the person concerned who are resident in the territory of another Member State as if they were resident in the territory of the competent State.

Article 24   Substantial benefits in kind

1.   Where the right of an employed or self-employed person or a member of his family to a prosthesis, a major appliance or other substantial benefits in kind has been recognised by the institution of a Member State before he becomes insured with the institution of another Member State, the said employed or self-employed person shall receive such benefits at the expense of the first institution, even if they are granted after he becomes insured with the second institution.

2.   The Administrative Commission shall draw up the list of benefits to which the provisions of paragraph 1 apply.

SECTION 3   UNEMPLOYED PERSONS AND MEMBERS OF THEIR FAMILIES

Article 25

1.   An unemployed person who was formerly employed or self-employed, to whom the provisions of Article 69(1) or the second sentence of Article 71(1)(b)(ii) apply, and who satisfies the conditions of the legislation of the competent State for entitlement to benefits in kind and in cash, taking account where appropriate of the provisions of Article 18, shall receive for the period provided under Article 69(1)(c):

(a)   benefits in kind provided on behalf of the competent institution by the institution of the Member State in which he seeks employment in accordance with the provisions of the legislation which the later institution administers, as though he were insured with it;

(b)   cash benefits provided by the competent institution in accordance with the provisions of the legislation which it administers. However, by agreement between the competent institution and the institution of the Member State in which the unemployed person seeks employment, benefits may be provided by the latter institution on behalf of the former institution in accordance with the provisions of the legislation of the competent State. Unemployment benefits under Article 69(1) shall not be granted for the period during which cash benefits are received.

2.   A totally unemployed person who was formerly employed and to whom the provisions of Article 71(1)(a)(ii) or the first sentence of Article 71(1)(b)(ii) apply, shall receive benefits in kind and in cash in accordance with the provisions of the legislation of the Member State in whose territory he resides, as though he had been subject to that legislation during his last employment, taking account where appropriate of the provisions of Article 18; the cost of such benefits shall be met by the institution of the country of residence.

3.   Where an unemployed person satisfies the conditions of the legislation of the Member State which is responsible for the cost of unemployment benefits for entitlement to sickness and maternity benefits, taking account where appropriate of the provisions of Article 18, the members of his family shall receive these benefits, irrespective of the Member State in whose territory they reside or are staying. Such benefits shall be provided:

(i)   with regard to the benefits in kind, by the institution of the place of residence or stay in accordance with the provisions of the legislation which it administers, on behalf of the competent institution of the Member State which is responsible for the cost of unemployment benefits;

(ii)   with regard to cash benefits, by the competent institution of the Member State which is responsible for the cost of unemployment benefits, in accordance with the legislation which it administers.

4.   Without prejudice to any provisions of the legislation of a Member State which permit an extension of the period during which sickness benefits may be granted, the period provided for in paragraph 1 may, in cases of force majeure, be extended by the competent institution within the limit fixed by the legislation administered by that institution.

Article 25A   Contributions payable by wholly unemployed persons
The institution which is responsible for granting benefits in kind and cash benefits to the unemployed persons referred to in Article 25(2) and which belongs to a Member State whose legislation provides for deduction of contributions payable by unemployed persons to cover sickness and maternity benefits shall be authorised to make such deductions in accordance with the provisions of its legislation.

SECTION 4   PENSION CLAIMANTS AND MEMBERS OF THEIR FAMILIES

Article 26   Right to benefits in kind in cases of cessation of the right to benefits from the institution which was last competent
1.   An employed or self-employed person, members of his family or his survivors who, during the investigation of a claim for pension, cease to be

entitled to benefits in kind under the legislation of the Member State last competent, shall nevertheless receive such benefits under the following conditions: benefits in kind shall be provided in accordance with the provisions of the legislation of the Member State in whose territory the person or persons concerned reside, provided that they are entitled to such benefits under that legislation or would be entitled to them under the legislation of another Member State if they were residing in the territory of that State, taking account where appropriate of the provisions of Article 18.

2. A pension claimant who is entitled to benefits in kind under the legislation of a Member State which obliges the person concerned to pay sickness insurance contributions himself during the investigation of his pension claim shall cease to be entitled to benefits in kind at the end of the second month for which he has not paid the contributions due.

3. Benefits in kind provided in accordance with the provisions of paragraph 1 shall be chargeable to the institution which has collected contributions in accordance with the provisions of paragraph 2; where no contributions are payable under the provisions of paragraph 2, the institution responsible for the cost of the benefits in kind after awarding the pension in accordance with the provisions of Article 28 shall refund the amount of the benefits provided to the institution of the place of residence.

SECTION 5 PENSIONERS AND MEMBERS OF THEIR FAMILIES

Article 27 Pensions payable under the legislation of several States where there is a right to benefits in the country of residence

A pensioner who is entitled to draw pensions under the legislation of two or more Member States, of which one is that of the Member State in whose territory he resides, and who is entitled to benefits under the legislation of the latter Member State, taking account where appropriate of the provisions of Article 18 and Annex VI, shall, with members of his family, receive such benefits from the institution of the place of residence and at the expense of that institution as though the person concerned were a pensioner whose pension was payable solely under the legislation of the latter Member State.

Article 28 Pensions payable under the legislation of one or more States, in cases where there is no right to benefits in the country of residence

1. A pensioner who is entitled to a pension under the legislation of one Member State or to pensions under the legislation of two or more Member States and who is not entitled to benefits under the legislation of the Member State in whose territory he resides shall nevertheless receive such benefits for himself and for members of his family, in so far as he would, taking account where appropriate of the provisions of Article 18 and Annex VI, be entitled thereto under the legislation of the Member State or of at least one of the Member States competent in respect of pensions if he were resident in the territory of such State. The benefits shall be provided under the following conditions:

(a) benefits in kind shall be provided on behalf of the institution referred to in paragraph 2 by the institution of the place of residence as though the person concerned were a pensioner under the legislation of the State in whose territory he resides and were entitled to such benefits;

(b)   cash benefits shall, where appropriate, be provided by the competent institution as determined by the rules of paragraph 2, in accordance with the legislation which it administers. However, upon agreement between the competent institution and the institution of the place of residence, such benefits may be provided by the latter institution on behalf of the former, in accordance with the legislation of the competent State.

2.   In the case covered by paragraph 1, the cost of benefits in kind shall be borne by the institution as determined according to the following rules:

(a)   where the pensioner is entitled to the said benefits under the legislation of a single Member State, the cost shall be borne by the competent institution of that State;

(b)   where the pensioner is entitled to the said benefits under the legislation of two or more Member States, the cost thereof shall be borne by the competent institution of the Member State to whose legislation the pensioner has been subject for the longest period of time; should the application of this rule result in several institutions being responsible for the cost of benefits the cost shall be borne by the institution administering the legislation to which the pensioner was last subject.

Article 28a   Pensions payable under the legislation of one or more of the Member States other than the country of residence where there is a right to benefits in the latter country

Where the pensioner entitled to a pension under the legislation of one Member State, or to pensions under the legislation of two or more Member States, resides in the territory of a Member State under whose legislation the right to receive benefits in kind is not subject to conditions of insurance or employment, nor is any pension payable, the cost of benefits in kind provided to him and to members of his family shall be borne by the institution of one of the Member States competent in respect of pensions, determined according to the rules laid down in Article 28(2), to the extent that the pensioner and members of his family would have been entitled to such benefits under the legislation administered by the said institutions if they resided in the territory of the Member State where that institution is situated.

Article 29   Residence of members of the family in a State other than the one in which the pensioner resides — Transfer of residence to the State where the pensioner resides

1.   Members of the family of a pensioner entitled to a pension under the legislation of one Member State or to pensions under the legislation of two or more Member States who reside in the territory of a Member State other than the one in which the pensioner resides shall, where he is entitled to benefits under the legislation of one Member State, receive benefits as though the pensioner were resident in the same territory as themselves. Benefits shall be provided under the following conditions:

(a)   benefits in kind shall be provided by the institution of the place of residence of the members of the family in accordance with the provisions of the legislation which that institution administers, the cost being borne by the institution of the pensioner's place of residence.

(b)   cash benefits shall, where appropriate, be provided by the competent institution as determined by the provisions of Article 27 or 28(2), in accordance with the provisions of the legislation which it administers.

However, upon agreement between the competent institution and the institution of the place of residence of the members of the family, such benefits may be provided by the latter institution on behalf of the former, in accordance with the provisions of the legislation of the competent State.

2.   Members of the family referred to in paragraph 1 who transfer their residence to the territory of the Member State where the pensioner resides, shall receive:

(a)   benefits in kind under the provisions of the legislation of that State, even if they have already received benefits for the same case of sickness or maternity before transferring their residence;

(b)   cash benefits provided where appropriate by the competent institution determined by the provisions of Article 27 or 28(2), in accordance with the legislation which it administers. However, upon agreement between the competent institution and the institution of the place of residence of the pensioner, such benefits may be provided by the latter institution on behalf of the former, in accordance with the provisions of the legislation of the competent State.

Article 30   Substantial benefits in kind
The provisions of Article 24 shall apply by analogy to pensioners.

Article 31   Stay of the pensioner and/or members of his family in a State other than the State in which they reside
A pensioner entitled to a pension or pensions under the legislation of one Member State or to pensions under the legislation of two or more Member States who is entitled to benefits under the legislation of one of those States shall, with members of his family who are staying in the territory of a Member State other than the one in which they reside, receive:

(a)   benefits in kind provided by the institution of the place of stay in accordance with the provisions of the legislation which it administers, the cost being borne by the institution of the pensioner's place of residence;

(b)   cash benefits provided, where appropriate, by the competent institution as determined by the provisios of Article 27 or 28(2), in accordance with the provisions of the legislation which it administers. However, upon agreement between the competent institution and the institution of the place of stay, these benefits may be provided by the latter institution on behalf of the former, in accordance with the provisions of the legislation of the competent State.

Article 32
Repealed[1]

Note
[1]Repealed by Regulation 3096/95 of 22 December 1995 [OJ 1995, L335/10].

Article 33(4)   Contributions payable by pensioners
1.   The institution of a Member State which is responsible for payment of a pension and whch administers legislation providing for deductions from pensions in respect of contributions for sickness and maternity shall be authorised to make such deductions, calculated in accordance with the legislation concerned, from the pension payable by such institution, to the extent that the cost of the benefits under Articles 27, 28, 28a, 29, 31 and 32 is to be borne by an institution of the said Member State.

2.   Where, in the case referred to in Article 28a, the acquisition of benefits in respect of sickness and maternity is subject to the payment of contributions or similar payments under the legislation of a Member State in whose territory the pensioner in question resides, by virtue of such residence, these contributions shall not be payable.

Article 34   General provisions
1.   For the purposes of Articles 28, 28a, 29 and 31, a pensioner who is in receipt of two or more pensions due under the legislation of a single Member State shall be regarded as a pensioner entitled to draw a pension under the legislation of one Member State, within the meaning of these provisions.
2.   Articles 27 to 33 shall not apply to a pensioner or to members of his family who are entitled to benefits under the legislation of a Member State as a result of pursuing a professional or trade activity. In such a case, the person concerned shall, for the purposes of the implementation of this chapter, be considered as an employed or self-employed person or as a member of an employed or self-employed person's family.

SECTION 6   MISCELLANEOUS PROVISIONS

Article 35   Scheme applicable where there are a number of schemes in the country of residence or stay — Previous illness — Maximum period during which benefits are granted
1.   Subject to paragraph 2, where the legislation of the country of stay or residence contains several sickness or maternity insurance schemes, the provisions applicable under Articles 19, 21(1), 22, 25, 26, 28(1), 29(1) or 31 shall be those of the scheme covering manual workers in the steel industry. Where, however, the said legislation includes a special scheme for workers in mines and similar undertakings, the provisions of such scheme shall apply to that category of workers and members of their families provided the institution of the place of stay or residence to which application is made is competent to admiister such scheme.
2.   Where the legislation of the country of stay or residence includes one or more special schemes, covering all or most occupational categories of self-employed persons, which grant benefits in kind less favourable than those granted to employed persons, the provisions applicable to the person concerned and the members of his family pursuant to Articles 19(1)(a) and (2), 22(1) (under (i)) and (3), 28(1)(a) and 31(a) shall be those of the scheme or schemes determined by the implementing Regulation referred to in Article 98:
    (a)   where, in the competent State, the person concerned is insured under a special scheme for self-employed persons which also grants less favourable benefits in kind than those granted to employed person, or
    (b)   where a person in receipt of one or more pensions is, under the pensions legislation of the competent Member State or Member States, entitled only to the benefits in kind provided for by a special scheme for self-employed persons which also grants less favourable benefits in kind than those granted to employed persons.
3.   Where, under the legislation of a Member State, the granting of benefits is conditional upon the origin of the illness, that condition shall apply neither to employed or self-employed persons nor to the members of their families to whom this Regulation applies, regardless of the Member State in whose territory they reside.

4. Where the legislation of a Member State fixes a maximum period for the granting of benefits, the institution which administers that legislation may, where appropriate, take account of the period during which the benefits have already been provided by the institution of another Member State for the same case of sickness or maternity.

SECTION 7   REIMBURSEMENT BETWEEN INSTITUTIONS

Article 36[1]

1. Benefits in kind provided in accordance with the provisions of this chapter by the institution of one Member State on behalf of the institution of another Member State shall be fully refunded.

2. The refunds referred to in paragraph 1 shall be determined and made in accordance with the procedure provided for by the implementing Regulation referred to in Article 98, either on production of proof of actual expenditure or on the basis of lump-sum payments. In the latter case, the lump-sum payments shall be such as to ensure that the refund is as close as possible to actual expenditure.

3. Two or more Member States, or the competent authorities of those States, may provide for other methods of reimbursement or may waive all reimbursement between institutions under their jurisdiction.

Note
[1]Amended by Regulation 3096/95 of 22 December 1995 [OJ 1995, L335/10].

CHAPTER 2(8)   INVALIDITY
SECTION 1   EMPLOYED PERSONS OR SELF-EMPLOYED PERSONS SUBJECT ONLY TO LEGISLATION UNDER WHICH THE AMOUNT OF INVALIDITY BENEFITS IS INDEPENDENT OF THE DURATION OF PERIODS OF INSURANCE

Article 37(8)   General provisions

1. An employed person or a self-employed person who has been successively or alternately subject to the legislation of two or more Member States and who has completed periods of insurance exclusively under legislation according to which the amount of invalidity benefits is independent of the duration of periods of insurance shall receive benefits in accordance with Article 39.

This Article shall not affect pension increases or supplements in respect of chidren, granted in accordance with Chapter 8.

2. Annex IV, part A, lists legislation of the kind mentioned in paragraph 1 which are in force in the territory of each of the Member States concerned.

Article 38(8)   Consideration of periods of insurance or of residence completed under the legislation to which an employed person or a self-employed person was subject for the acquisition, retention or recovery of the right to benefits

1. Where the legislation of a Member State makes the acquisition, retention or recovery of the right to benefits, under a scheme which is not a special scheme within the meaning of paragraphs 2 or 3, subject to the completion of periods of insurance or of residence, the competent institution of that Member State shall take account, where necessary, of the periods of insurance or of residence completed under the legislation of any other Member

State, be it under a general scheme or under a special scheme and either as an employed person or as a self-employed person. For that purpose, it shall take account of these periods as if they had been completed under its own legislation.

2.   Where the legislation of a Member State makes the granting of certain benefits conditional upon the periods of insurance having been completed only in an occupation which is subject to a special scheme for employed persons or, where appropriate, in a specific employment, periods completed under the legislation of other Member States shall be taken into account for the granting of these benefits only if completed under a corresponding scheme or, failing that, in the same occupation or, where appropriate, in the same employment.

If, account having been taken of the periods thus completed, the person concerned does not satisfy the conditions for receipt of these benefits, these periods shall be taken into account for the granting of the benefits under the general scheme or, failing that, under the scheme applicable to manual or clerical workers, as the case may be, subject to the condition that the person concerned has been affiliated to one or other of these schemes.

3.   Where the legislation of a Member State makes the granting of certain benefits conditional upon the period of insurance having completed only in an occupation subject to a special scheme for self-employed persons, periods completed under the legislation of other Member States shall be taken into account for the granting of these benefits only if completed under a corresponding scheme or, failing that, in the same occupation. The special schemes for self-employed persons referred to in this paragraph are listed in Annex IV, part B, for each Member State concerned. If, account having been taken of the periods thus completed, the person concerned does not satisfy the conditions for receipt of these benefits, these periods shall be taken into account for the granting of the benefits under the general scheme or, failing that, under the scheme applicable to manual or clerical workers, as the case may be, subject to the condition that the person concerned has been affiliated to one or other of these schemes.

Article 39(8)   Award of benefits

1.   The institution of a Member State whose legislation was applicable at the time when incapacity for work followed by invalidity occurred shall determine, in accordance with that legislation, whether the person concerned satisfies the conditions for entitlement to benefits, taking account, where appropriate, of Article 38.

2.   A person who satisfies the conditions referred to in paragraph 1 shall receive the benefits only from the said institution, in accordance with the provisions of the legislation which it administers.

3.   A person who is not entitled to benefits under paragraph 1 shall receive the benefits to which he is still entitled under the legislation of another Member State taking account, where appropriate, of Article 38.

4.   If the legislation referred to in paragraphs 2 or 3 provides that the amount of the benefits shall be determined taking into account the existence of members of the family other than the children, the competent institution shall also take into consideration those members of the family of the person concerned who are residing in the territory of another Member State, as if they were residing in the territory of the competent State.

5.   If the legislation referred to in paragraph 2 or 3 lays down provisions for the reduction, suspension or withdrawal of benefits in the case of overlapping with other income or with benefits of a different kind within the meaning of Article 46a(2), Article 46a(3) and Article 46c(5) shall apply mutatis mutandis.

6.   A wholly unemployed employee to whom Article 71(1)(a)(ii) or the first sentence of Article 71(1)(b)(ii) applies shall receive the invalidity benefits provided by the competent institution of the Member State in whose territory he resides, in accordance with the legislation which it administers, as though he had been subject to that legislation during his last employment, account being taken, where appropriate, of Article 38 and/or Article 25(2).

Where that institution applies legislation providing for deduction of contributions payable by unemployed persons to cover invalidity benefits, it shall be authorised to make such deductions in accordance with the provisions of its legislation.[1]

Note

[1]Inserted by Regulation 3095/95 of 22 December 1995 [OJ 1995, L335/1].

The institution of the country of residence shall be responsible for paying these benefits. If the legislation which that institution administers provides for the calculation of benefits to be based on wages or salaries, the institution shall take into account the wages or salaries received in the last country of employment and in the country of residence in accordance with the legislation which it administers. Where no wage or salary has been received in the country of residence, the competent institution shall refer, as necessary and in accordance with the rules laid down in its legislation, to the salaries received in the last country of employment.

SECTION 2(8)   EMPLOYED PERSONS OR SELF-EMPLOYED PERSONS SUBJECT EITHER ONLY TO LEGISLATION UNDER WHICH THE AMOUNT OF INVALIDITY BENEFIT DEPENDS ON THE DURATION OF PERIODS OF INSURANCE OR RESIDENCE OR THE LEGISLATION OF THIS TYPE AND OF THE TYPE REFERRED TO IN SECTION 1

Article 40(8)   General provisions

1.   An employed person or a self-employed person who has been successively or alternately subject to the legislation of two or more Member States, of which at least one is not of the type referred to in Article 37(1), shall receive benefits under the provisions of Chapter 3, which shall apply mutatis mutandis, taking into account the provisions of paragraph 4.

2.   However, an employed or self-employed person who suffers incapacity for work leading to invalidity while subject to a legislation listed in Annex IV, part A, shall receive benefits in accordance with the provisions of Article 37(1) on the following conditions:

— that he satisfied the conditions of that legislation or other legislation of the same type, taking account where appropriate of Article 38, but without having recourse to periods of insurance completed under legislation not listed in Annex IV, part A, and

— that he does not satisfy the conditions required for the acquisition of the right to invalidity benefits under a legislation not listed in Annex IV, part A, and

—that he does not assert any claims to old-age benefits, account being taken of the second sentence of Article 44(2).

3. (a) For the purpose of determining the right to benefits under the legislation of a Member State, listed in Annex IV, part A, which makes the granting of invalidity benefits conditional upon the person concerned having received cash sickness benefits or having been incapable of work during a specified period, where an employed person or a self-employed person who has been subject to that legislation suffers incapacity for work leading to invalidity while subject to the legislation of another Member Sttae, account shall be taken of the following, without prejudice to Article 37(1):

(i)   any period during which, in respect of that incapacity for work, he has, under the legislation of the second Member State, received cash sickness benefits, or, in lieu thereof, continued to receive a wage or salary;

(ii)   any period during which, in respect of the invalidity which followed that incapacity for work, he has received benefits within the meaning of Chapters 2 and 3 of Title III of the Regulation granted in respect of invalidity under the legislation of the second Member State, as if it were a period during which cash sickness benefits were paid to him under the legislation of the first Member State or during which he was incapable of working within the meaning of that legislation.

(b) The right to invalidity benefits under the legislation of the first member State shall be acquired either upon expiry of the preliminary period of compensation for sickness as required by that legislation or upon expiry of the preliminary period of incapcaity of work as required by that legislation, but not before:

(i)   the date of acquisition of the right to invalidity benefits referred to in subparagraph (a)(ii) under the legislation of the second Member State, or

(ii)   the day following the last day on which the person concerned is entitled to cash sickness benefits under the legislation of the second Member State.

4. A decision taken by an institution of a Member State concerning the degree of invalidity of a claimant shall be binding on the institution of any other Member State concerned, provided that the concordance between the legislation of these States on conditions relating to the degree of invalidity is acknowledged in Annex V.

SECTION 3(8)   AGGRAVATION OF INVALIDITY

Article 41

1. In the case of aggravation of an invalidity for which an employed person or a self-employed person is receiving benefits under the legislation of a single Member State, the following provision shall apply:

(a) if the person concerned has not been subject to the legislation of another Member State since receiving benefits, the competent institution of the first State shall grant the benefits, taking the aggravation into account, in accordance with the provisions of the legislation which it administers;

(b) if the person concerned has been subject to the legislation of one or more of the other Member States since receiving benefits, the benefits shall be granted to him, taking the aggravation into account, in accordance with Article 37(1) or 40(1) or (2), as appropriate;

(c) if the total amount of the benefit or benefits payable under subparagraph (b) is lower than the amount of the benefit which the person concerned was receiving at the expense of the institution previously liable for payment, such institution shall pay him a supplement equal to the difference between the two amounts;

(d) if, in the case referred to in subparagraph (b), the institution responsible for the initial incapacity is a Dutch institution, and if:

(i) the illness which caused the aggravation is the same as the one which gave rise to the granting of benefits under Dutch legislation;

(ii) this illness is an occupational disease within the meaning of the legislation of the Member State to which the person concerned was last subject and entitles him to payment of the supplement referred to in Article 60(1)(b), and

(iii) the legislation or legislation to which the person concerned has been subject since receiving benefits is or are listed in Annex IV, part A, the Dutch institution shall continue to provide the initial benefit after the aggravation occurs, and the benefit due under the legislation of the last Member State to which the person concerned was subject shall be reduced by the amount of the Dutch benefit;

(e) if, in the case referred to in subparagraph (b), the person concerned is not entitled to benefits at the expense of an institution of another member State, the competent institution of the first State shall grant the benefits, according to the provisions of the legislation of the State, taking into account the aggravation and, where appropriate, Article 38.

2. In the case of aggravation of an invalidity for which an employed person or a self-employed person is receiving benefits under the legislation of two or more Member States, the benefits shall be granted to him, taking the aggravation into account, in accordance with Article 40(1).

SECTION 4(8) RESUMPTION OF PROVISION OF BENEFITS AFTER SUSPENSION OR WITHDRAWAL — CONVERSION OF INVALIDITY BENEFITS INTO OLD-AGE BENEFITS — RECALCULATION OF BENEFITS GRANTED UNDER ARTICLE 39

Article 42(8) Determination of the institution responsible for the provision of benefits where provision of invalidity benefits is resumed

1. If provision of benefits is to be resumed after suspension, such provision shall, without prejudice to Article 43, be the responsibility of the institution or institutions which were responsible for provision of the benefits at the time of their suspension.

2. If, after withdrawal of benefits, the condition of the person concerned warrants the granting of further benefits, they shall be granted in accordance with Article 37(1) or Article 40(1) or (2), as appropriate.

Aarticle 43(8) Conversion of invalidity benefits into old-age benefits — Recalculation of benefits granted under Article 39

1. Invalidity benefits shall be converted into old-age benefits, where appropriate, under the conditions laid down by the legislation or legislation under which they were granted, and in accordance with Chapter 3.

2. Where a person receiving invalidity benefits can establish a claim to old-age benefits under the legislation of one or more Member States, in accordance with Article 49, any institution which is responsible for providing invalidity benefits under the legislation of a Member State shall continue to

provide such person with the invalidity benefits to which he is entitled under the legislation which it administers until the provisions of paragraph 1 become applicable as regards that institution or so long as the person concerned fulfils the conditions for such benefits.

3. Where invalidity benefits granted in accordance with Article 39 under the legislation of a Member State are converted into old-age benefits and where the person concerned does not yet satisfy the conditions required by one or more national legislation to receive these benefits, the person concerned shall receive, from this or these Member States, from the date of the conversion, invalidity benefits granted in accordance with Chapter 3 as if that Chapter had been applicable at the time when his incapacity for work leading to invalidity occurred, until the person concerned satisfies the qualifying conditions for old-age benefit laid down by the national legislation or legislation concerned or, where such conversion is not provided for, as long as he has a right to invalidity benefits under the legislation or legislation concerned.

4. The invalidity benefits provided under Article 39 shall be recalculated pursuant to Chapter 3 as soon as the beneficiary satisfies the qualifying conditions for invalidity benefits laid down by a legislation not listed in Annex IV, part A, or as soon as he receives old-age benefits under the legislation of another Member State.

CHAPTER 3   OLD AGE AND DEATH (PENSIONS)

Article 44(8)   General provisions for the award of benefits where an employed or self-employed person has been subject to the legislation of two or more Member States

1. The right to benefits of an employed or self-employed person who has been subject to the legislation of two or more Member States, or of his survivors, shall be determined in accordance with the provisions of this Chapter.

2. Save as otherwise provided in Article 49, the processing of a claim for an award submitted by the person concerned shall have regard to all the legislation to which the employed or self-employed person has been subject.

Exception shall be made to this rule if the person concerned expressly asks for postponement of the award of old-age benefits to which he would be entitled under the legislation of one or more Member States.

3. This Chapter shall not apply to increase in pensions or to supplements for pensions in respect of children or to orphans' pensions granted in accordance with the provisions of Chapter 8.

Article 45(8)   Consideration of periods of insurance or of residence completed under the legislation to which an employed person or self-employed person was subject, for the acquisition, retention or recovery of the right to benefits

1. Where the legislation of a Member State makes the acquisition, retention or recovery of the right to benefits, under a scheme which is not a special scheme within the meaning of paragraphs 2 or 3, subject to the completion of periods of insurance or of residence, the competent institution of that Member State shall take account, where necessary, of the periods of insurance or of residence under the legislation of any other Member State, be it under a general scheme or under a special scheme and either as an employed

person or a self-employed person. For that purpose, it shall take account of these periods as if they had been completed under its own legislation.

2.   Where the legislation of a Member State makes the granting of certain benefit conditional upon the periods of insurance having been completed only in an occupation which is subject to a special scheme for employed persons or, where appropriate, in a specific employment, periods completed under the legislation of other Member States shall be taken into account for the granting of these benefits only if completed under a corresponding scheme or, failing that, in the same occupation or, where appropriate, in the same employment. If, account having been taken of the periods thus completed, the person concerned does not satisfy the conditions for receipt of these benefits, these periods shall be taken into account for the granting of the benefits under the general scheme or, failing that, under the scheme applicable to manual or clerical workers, as the case may be, subject to the condition that the person has been affiliated to one or other of these schemes.

3.   Where the legislation of a Member State makes the granting of certain benefits conditional upon the periods of insurance having been completed only in an occupation subject to a special scheme for self-employed persons, periods completed under the legislation of other Member States shall be taken into account for the granting of these benefits only if completed under a corresponding scheme or, failing that, in the same occupation. The special schemes for self-employed persons referred to in this paragraph are listed in Annex I, part B, for each Member State concerned. If, account having been taken of the periods referred to in this paragraph, the person concerned does not satisfy the conditions for receipt of these benefits, these periods shall be taken into account for the granting of the benefits under the general scheme or, failing this, under the scheme applicable to manual or clerical workers, as the case may be, subject to the condition that the person concerned has been affiliated to one or other of these schemes.

4.   The periods of insurance completed under a special scheme of a Member State shall be taken into account under the general scheme or, failing that, under the scheme applicable to manual or clerical workers, as the case may be, of another Member State for the acquisition, retention or recovery of the right to benefits, subject to the condition that the person concerned has been affiliated to one or other of these schemes, even if these periods have already been taken into account in the latter State under a scheme referred to in paragraph 2 or in the first sentence of paragraph 3.

5.   Where the legislation of a Member State makes the acquisition, retention or recovery of the right to benefits conditional upon the person concerned being insured at the time of the materialisation of the risk, this condition shall be regarded as having been satisfied in the case of insurance under the legislation of another Member State, in accordance with the procedures provided for in Annex VI for each Member State concerned.

6.   A period of full employment of a worker to whom Article 71(1)(a)(ii) or (b)(ii), first sentence, applies shall be taken into account by the competent institution of the Member State in whose territory the worker concerned resides in accordance with the legislation administered by that institution, as if that legislation applied to him during his last employment.

Where the institution applies legislation providing for deduction of contributions payable by unemployed persons to cover old age pensions and death, it shall be authorised to make such deductions in accordance with the provisions of its legislation.[1]

If the period of full unemployment in the country of residence of the person concerned can be taken into account only if contribution periods have been completed in that country, this condition shall be deemed to be fulfilled if the contribution periods have been completed in another Member State.

Note

[1]Inserted by Regulation 3095/95 of 22 December 1995 [OJ 1995 L335/1].

Article 46(8)   Award of benefits

1.   Where the conditions required by the legislation of a Member State for entitlement to benefits have been satisfied without having to apply Article 45 or Article 40(3), the following rules shall apply:

(a)   the competent institution shall calculate the amount of the benefit that would be due:

(i)   on the one hand, only under the provisions of the legislation which it administers;

(ii)   on the other hand, pursuant to paragraph 2;

(b)   the competent institution may, however, waive the calculation to be carried out in accordance with (a)(ii) if the result of this calculation, apart from differences arising from the use of round figures, is equal to or lower than the result of the calculation carried out in accordance with (a)(i), insofar as that institution does not apply any legislation containing rules against overlapping as referred to in Articles 46b and 46c or if the afore-entioned institution applies a legislation containing rules against overlapping in the case referred to in Article 46c, provided that the said legislation lays down that benefits of a different kind shall be taken into consideration only on the basis of the relation of the periods of insurance or of residence completed under that legislation alone to the periods of insurance or of residence required by that legislation in order to qualify for full benefit entitlement.

Annex IV, part C, lists for each Member State concerned the cases where the two calculations would lead to a result of this kind.

2.   Where the conditions required by the legislation of a Member State for entitlement to benefits are satisfied only after application of Article 45 and/or Article 40(3), the following rules shall apply:

(a)   the competent institution shall calculate the theoretical amount of the benefit to which the person concerned could lay claim provided all periods of insurance and/or of residence, which have been completed under the legislation of the Member States to which the employed person or self-employed person was subject, have been completed in the State in question under the legislation which it administers on the date of the award of the benefit.

If, under the legislation, the amount of the benefit is independent of the duration of the periods completed, the amount shall be regarded as being the theoretical amount referred to in this paragraph;

(b)   the competent institution shall subsequently determine the actual amount of the benefit on the basis of the theoretical amount referred to in the preceding paragraph in accordance with the ratio of the duration of the periods of insurance or of residence completed before the materialisation of the risk under the legislation which it administers to the total duration of the periods of insurance and of residence completed before the materialisation of the risk under the legislation of all the Member States concerned.

3.   The person concerned shall be entitled to the highest amount calculated in accordance with paragraphs 1 and 2 from the competent institution of each Member State without prejudice to any application of the provisions concerning reduction, suspension or withdrawal provided for by the legislation under which this benefit is due.

Where that is the case, the comparison to be carried out shall relate to the amounts determind after the application of the said provisions.

4.   When, in the case of invalidity, old-age or survivor's pensions, the total of the benefits due from the competent institutions of two or more Member States under the provisions of a multilateral social security convention referred to in Article 6(b) does not exceed the total which would be due from such Member States under paragraphs 1 to 3, the person concerned shall benefit from the provisions of this Chapter.

Article 46a(8)   General provisions relating to reduction, suspension or withdrawal applicable to benefits in respect of invalidity, old age or survivors under the legislation of the Member States

1.   For the purposes of this Chapter, overlapping of benefits of the same kind shall have the following meaning: all overlapping of benefits in respect of invalidity, old age and survivors calculated or provided on the basis of periods of insurance and/or residence completed by one and the same person.

2.   For the purposes of this Chapter, overlapping of benefits of different kinds means all overlapping of benefits that cannot be regarded as being of the same kind within the meaning of paragraph 1.

3.   The following rules shall be applicable for the application of provisions on reduction, suspension or withdrawal laid down by the legislation of a Member State in the case of overlapping of a benefit in respect of invalidity, old age or survivors with a benefit of the same kind or a benefit of a different kind or with other income:

(a)   account shall be taken of the benefits acquired under the legislation of another Member State or of other income acquired in another Member State only where the legislation of the first Member State provides for the taking into account of benefits or income acquired abroad;

(b)   account shall be taken of the amount of benefits to be granted by another Member State before deduction of taxes, social security contributions and other individual levies or deductions;

(c)   no account shall be taken of the amount of benefits acquired under the legislation of another Member State which are awarded on the basis of voluntary insurance or continued optional insurance;

(d)   where provisions on reduction, suspension or withdrawal are applicable under the legislation of only one Member State on account of the fact that the person concerned receives benefits of a similar or different kind payable under the legislation of other Member States or other income acquired within the territory of other Member States, the benefit payable under the legislation of the first Member State may be reduced only within the limit of the amount of the benefits payable under the legislation or the income acquired within the territory of other Member States.

Article 46b(8)   Special provisions applicable in the case of overlapping of benefits of the same kind under the legislation of two or more Member States

1.   The provisions on reduction, suspension or withdrawal laid down by the legislation of a Member State shall not be applicable to a benefit calculated in accordance with Article 46(2).

2.   The provisions on reduction, suspension or withdrawal laid down by the legislation of a Member State shall apply to a benefit calculated in accordance with Article 46(1)(a)(i) only if the benefit concerned is:

(a)   either a benefit, which is referred to in Annex IV, part D, the amount of which does not depend on the length of the periods of insurance or of residence completed, or

(b)   a benefit, the amount of which is determined on the basis of a credited period deemed to have been completed between the date on which the risk materialised and a later date. In the latter case, the said provisions shall apply in the case of overlapping of such a benefit:

(i)   either with a benefit of the same kind, except where an agreement has been concluded between two or more Member States providing that one and the same credited period may not be taken into account two or more times;

(ii)   or with a benefit of the type referred to in (a). The benefits and agreements referred to in (b) are mentioned in Annex IV, part D.

Article 46c(8)   Special provisions applicable in the case of overlapping of one or more benefits referred to in Article 46a(1) with one or more benefits of a different kind or with other income, where two or more Member States are concerned

1.   If the receipt of benefits of a different kind or other income entails the reduction, suspension or withdrawal of two or more benefits referred to in Article 46(1)(a)(i), the amounts which would not be paid in strict application of the provisions concerning reduction, suspension or withdrawal provided for by the legislation of the Member States concerned shall be divided by the number of benefits subject to reduction, suspension or withdrawal.

2.   Where the benefit in question is calculated in accordance with Article 46(2), the benefit or benefits of a different kind from other Member States or other income and all other elements provided for by the legislation of the Member State for the application of the provisions in respect of reduction, suspension or withdrawal shall be taken into account in proportion to the periods of insurance and/or residence referred to in Article 46(2)(b), and shall be used for the calculation of the said benefit.

3.   If the receipt of benefits of a different kind or of other income entails the reduction, suspension or withdrawal of one or more benefits referred to in Article 46(1)(a)(i), and of one or more benefits referred to in Article 46(2), the following rules shall apply:

(a)   where in a case of a benefit or benefits referred to in Article 46(1)(a)(i), the amounts which would not be paid in strict application of the provisions concerning reduction, suspension or withdrawal provided for by the legislation of the Member States concerned shall be divided by the number of benefits subject to reduction, suspension or withdrawal;

(b)   where in a case of a benefit or benefits calculated in accordance with Article 46(2), the reduction, suspension or withdrawal shall be carried out in accordance with paragraph 2.

4.   Where, in the case referred to in paragraph 1 and 3(a), the legislation of a Member State provides that, for the application of provisions concerning reduction, suspension or withdrawal, account shall be taken of benefits of a different kind and/or other income and all other elements in proportion to the periods of insurance referred to in Article 46(2)(b), the division provided for in the said paragraphs shall not apply in respect of that Member State.

5.   All the abovementioned provisions shall apply mutatis mutandis where the legislation of one or more Member States provides that the right to a benefit cannot be acquired in the case where the person concerned is in receipt of a benefit of a different kind, payable under the legislation of another Member State, or of other income.

Article 47(8)   Additional provisions for the calculation of benefits

1.   For the calculation of the theoretical and pro rata amounts referred to in Article 46(2), the following rules shall apply:

(a)   where the total length of the periods of insurance and of residence completed before the risk materialised under the legislation of all the Member States concerned is longer than the maximum period required by the legislation of one of these States for receipt of full benefit, the competent institution of that State shall take into consideration this maximum period instead of the total length of the periods completed; this method of calculation must not result in the imposition on that institution of the cost of a benefit greater than the full benefit provided for by the legislation which it administers. This provision shall not apply to benefits, the amount of which does not depend on the length of insurance;

(b)   the procedure for taking account of overlapping periods is laid down in the implementing Regulation referred to in Article 98;

(c)   where, under the legislation of a Member State, benefits are calculated on the basis of average earnings, an average contribution, an average increase or on the relation which existed, during the periods of insurance, between the claimant's gross earnings and the average gross earnings of all insured persons other than apprentices, such average figures or relations shall be determined by the competent institution of that State solely on the basis of the periods of insurance completed under the legislation of the said State, or the gross earnings received by the person concerned during those periods only;

(d)   where, under the legislation of a Member State, benefits are calculated on the basis of the amount of earnings, contributions or increases, the competent institution of that State shall determine the earnings, contributions and increases to be taken into account in respect of the periods of insurance or residence completed under the legislation of other Member States on the basis of the average earnings, contributions or increases recorded in respect of the periods of insurance completed under the legislation which it administers;

(e)   where, under the legislation of a Member State, benefits are calculated on the basis of standard earnings or a fixed amount, the competent institutions of that State shall consider the standard earnings or the fixed amount to be taken into account by it in respect of periods of insurance or residence completed under the legislation of other Member States as being equal to the standard earnings or fixed amount or, where appropriate, to the average of the standard earnings or the fixed amount corresponding to the periods of insurance completed under the legislation which it administers;

(f) where, under the legislation of a Member State, benefits are calculated for some periods on the basis of the amount of earnings and, for other periods, on the basis of standard earnings or a fixed amount, the competent institution of that State shall, in respect of periods of insurance or residence completed under the legislation of other Member States, take into account the earnings or fixed amounts determined in accordance with the provisions referred to in (d) or (e) or, as appropriate, the average of these earnings or fixed amounts, where benefits are calculated on the basis of standard earnings or a fixed amount for all the periods completed under the legislation which it administers, the competent institution shall consider the earnings to be taken into account in respect of the periods of insurance or residence completed under the legislation of other Member States as being equal to the national earnings corresponding to the standard earnings or fixed amount;

(g) Where, under the legislation of a Member State, benefits are calculated on the basis of average contributions, the competent institution shall determine that average by reference only to those periods of insurance completed under the legislation of the said State.

2. The provisions of the legislation of a Member State concerning the revalorisation of the factors taken into account for the calculation of benefits shall apply, as appropriate, to the factors to be taken into account by the competent institution of that State, in accordance with paragraph 1, in respect of the periods of insurance or residence completed under the legislation of other Member States.

3. If, under the legislation of a Member State, the amount of benefits is determined taking into account the existence of members of the family other than children, the competent institution of that State shall also take into consideration those members of the family of the person concerned who are residing in the territory of another Member State as if they were residing in the territory of the competent State.

4. If the legislation which the competent institution of a Member State administers requires a salary to be taken into account for the calculation of benefits, where the first and second subparagraphs of Article 45(6) have been applied, and if, in this Member State, only periods of full unemployment with benefit in accordance with Article 71(1)(a)(ii) or the first sentence of Article 71(1)(b)(ii) are taken into consideration for the payment of pensions, the competent institution of that Member State shall pay the pension on the basis of the salary it used as the reference for providing that unemployment benefit in accordance with the legislation which it administers.

Article 48 (8)   Periods of insurance or of residence of less than one year

1. Notwithstanding Article 46(2), the institution of a Member State shall not be required to award benefits in respect of periods completed under the legislation it administers, which are taken into account when the risk materialises, if:

— the duration of the said periods does not amount to one year, and

— taking only these periods into consideration, no right to benefit is acquired by virtue of the provisions of that legislation.

2. The competent institution of each of the Member States concerned shall take into account the periods referred to in paragraph 1, for the purposes of applying Article 46(2) excepting subparagraph (b).

3. If the effect of applying paragraph 1 would be to relieve all the institutions of the Member States concerned of their obligations, benefits shall be awarded exclusively under the legislation of the last of those States whose conditions are satisfied, as if all the periods of insurance and residence completed and taken into account in accordance with Article 45(1) to (4) had been completed under the legislation of that State.

Article 49(8)   Calculation of benefits where the person concerned does not simultaneously satisfy the conditions laid down by all the legislation under which periods of insurance or of residence have been completed or when he has expressly requested a postponement of the award of old-age benefits

1. If, at a given time, the person concerned does not satisfy the conditions laid down for the provision of benefits by all the legislation of the Member States to which he has been subject, taking into account where appropriate Article 40(3), but satisfies the conditions or one or more of them only, the following provisions shall apply:

(a)   each of the competent institutions administering a legislation whose conditions are satisfied shall calculate the amount of the benefit due, in accordance with Article 46;

(b)   however:[1]

(i)   if the person concerned satisfies the conditions of at least two legislations without having recourse to periods of insurance or residence completed under the legislation whose conditions are not satisfied, these periods shall not be taken into account for the purposes of Article 46(2) unless taking into account of the said periods makes it possible to determine a higher amount of benefit;

(ii)   if the person concerned satisfies the conditions of one legislation only without having recourse to periods of insurance or residence completed under the legislation whose conditions are not satisfied, the amount of the benefit due shall, in accordance with Article 46(1)(a)(i), be calculated in accordance with the provisions of that legislation whose conditions are satisfied, taking account of the periods completed under that legislation only, unless taking account of the periods completed under the legislation whose conditions are not satisfied makes it possible, in accordance with Article 46(1)(a)(i), to determine a higher amount of benefit.

The provisions of this paragraph shall apply mutatis mutandis where the person concerned has expressly requested the postponement of the award of old-age benefits, in accordance with the second sentence of Article 44(2).

2. The benefit or benefits awarded under one or more of the legislations in question, in the case referred to in paragraph 1, shall be recalculated

Note

[1]Amended by Regulation 3096/95 of 22 December 1995 [OJ 1995 L335/10].

automatically in accordance with Article 46, as and when the conditions required by one or more of the other legislations to which the person concerned has been subject are satisfied, taking into account, where appropriate, Article 45 and taking into account once again, where appropriate paragraph 1. This paragraph shall apply mutatis mutandis where a person requests the award of old-age benefits acquired under the legislation of one or more Member States which had until then been postponed in accordance with the second sentence of Article 44(2).

3.   A recalculation shall automatically be made in accordance with paragraph 1, without prejudice to Article 40(2), where the conditions required by one or more of the legislations concerned are no longer satisfied.

Article 50(8) Award of a supplement where the total of benefits payable under the legislation of the various Member States does not amount to the minimum laid down by the legislation of the State in whose territory the recipient resides

A recipient of benefits to whom this Chapter applies may not, in the State in whose territory he resides and under whose legislation a benefit is payable to him, be awarded a benefit which is less than the minimum benefit fixed by that legislation for a period of insurance or residence equal to all the periods of insurance taken into account for the payment in accordance with the preceding Articles. The competent institution of the State shall, if necessary, pay him throughout the period of his residence in its territory a supplement equal to the difference between the total of the benefits payable under this Chapter and the amount of the minimum benefit.

Article 51(8)   Revalorisation and recalculation of benefits

1.   If, by reason of an increase in the cost of living or changes in the level of wages or salaries or other reasons for adjustment, the benefits of the States concerned are altered by a fixed percentage or amount, such percentage or amount must be applied directly to the benefits determined under Article 46, without the need for a recalculation in accordance with that Article.

2.   On the other hand, if the method of determining benefits or the rules for calculating benefits should be altered, a recalculation shall be carried out in accordance with Article 46.

CHAPTER 4   ACCIDENTS AT WORK AND OCCUPATIONAL DISEASES
SECTION 1   RIGHT TO BENEFITS

Article 52   Residence in a Member State other than the competent State — General rules

An employed or self-employed person who sustains an accident at work or contracts an occupational disease, and who is residing in the territory of a Member State other than the competent State, shall receive in the State in which he is residing:

(a)   benefits in kind, provided on behalf of the competent institution by the institutions of his place of residence in accordance with the provisions of the legislation which it administers as if he were insured with it;

(b)   cash benefits provided by the competent institution in accordance with the provisions of the legislation which it administers. However, by agreement between the competent institution and the institution of the place of residence, these benefits may be provided by the latter institution on behalf of the former in accordance with the legislation of the competent State.

Article 53   Frontier workers — Special rule

A frontier worker may also obtain benefits in the territory of the competent State. Such benefits shall be provided by the competent institution in accordance with the provisions of the legislation of that State, as if the person concerned were residing there.

Article 54   Stay in or transfer of residence to the competent State

1.   An employed or self-employed person covered by Article 52 who is staying in the teritory of the competent State shall receive benefits in accordance with the provisions of the legislation of that State, even if he has already received benefits before his stay. This provision shall not, however, apply to frontier workers.

2.   An employed or self-employed person covered by Article 52 who transfers his place of residence to the territory of the competent State shall receive benefits in accordance with the provisions of the legislation of that State, even if he has already received benefits before transferring his residence.

Article 55   Stay outside the competent State — Return to or transfer of residence to another Member State after sustaining an accident or contracting an occupational disease — Need to go to another Member State in order to receive appropriate treatment

1.   An employed or self-employed person who sustains an accident at work or contracts an occupational disease and:

(a)   who is staying in the territory of a Member State other than the competent State; or

(b)   who, after having become entitled to benefits chargeable to the competent institution, is authorised by that institution to return to the territory of the Member State where he is resident, or to transfer his place of reswidence to the territory of another Member State; or

(c)   who is authorised by the competent institution to go to the territory of another Member State in order to receive there the treatment appropriate to his condition, shall be entitled:

(i)   to benefits in kind provided on behalf of the competent institution by the institution of the place of stay or residence in accordance with the provisions of the legislation administered by that institution as though he were insured with it, the period during which benefits are provided shall, however, be governed by the legislation of the competent State;

(ii)   to cash benefits provided by the competent institution in accordance with the legislation which it administers. However, by agreement between the competent institution and the institutionof the place of stay or residence, those benefits may be provided by the latter institution on behalf of the former institution, in accordance with the legislation of the competent State.

2.   The authorisation required under paragraph 1(b) may be refused only if it is established that movement of the person concerned would be prejudicial to his state of health or to the medical treatment being given.

The authorisation required under paragraph 1(c) may not be refused where the treatment in question cannot be given to the person concerned in the territory of the Member State in which he resides.

Article 56   Accidents while travelling

An accident while travelling which occurs in the territory of a Member State other than the competent State shall be deemed to have occurred in the territory of the competent State.

Article 57(4)   Benefits for an occupational disease where the person concerned has been exposed to the same risk in several Member States

1. When a person who has contracted an occupational disease has, under the legislation of two or more Member States, pursued an activity which by its nature is likely to cause that disease, the benefits that he or his survivors may claim shall be awarded exclusively under the legislation of the last of those States whose conditions are satisfied, taking into account, where appropriate, paragraphs 2 to 5.

2. If, under the legislation of a Member State, the granting of benefits in respect of an occupational disease is subject to the condition that the disease in question was first diagnosed within its territory, such condition shall be deemed to be satisfied if the disease was first diagnosed in the territory of another Member State.

3. If, under the legislation of a Member State, the granting of benefits in respect of an occupational disease is subject to the condition that the disease in question was diagnosed within a specific time limit following cessation of the last activity which was likely to cause such a disease, the competent institution of that State, when checking the time at which such activity was pursued, shall take into account, to the extent necessary, similar activities pursued under the legislation of any other Member State, as if they had been pursued under the legislation of the first State.

4. If, under the legislation of a Member State, the granting of benefits in respect of an occupational disease is subject to the condition that an activity likely to cause the disease in question was pursued for a certain length of time, the competent institution of the State shall take into account, to the extent necessary, periods during which such activity was pursued under the legislation of any other Member State, as if it had been pursued under the legislation of the first State.

5. In cases of sclerogenic pneumoconiosis, the cost of cash benefits, including pensions, shall be divided among the competent institutions of the Member States in whose territory the person concerned pursued an activity likely to cause the disease. This division shall be carried out on the basis of the ratio which the length of the periods of old-age insurance or residence referred to in Article 45(1) completed under the legislation of each of the States bears to the total length of the periods of old-age insurance or residence completed under the legislation of all the States at the dates on which the benefits commenced.

6. The Council shall determine unanimously, on a proposal from the Commission, the occupational diseases to which the provisions of paragraph 5 shall be extended.

Article 58   Calculation of cash benefits

1. The competent institution of a Member State whose legislation provides that the calculation of cash benefits shall be based on average earnings shall determine such average earnings exclusively by reference to earnings confirmed as having been paid during the periods completed under the said legislation.

2.   The competent institution of a Member State whose legislation provides that the calculation of cash benefits shall be based on standard earnings shall take account exclusively of the standard earnings, or where appropriate, of the average of standard earnings for the periods completed under the said legislation.

3.   The competent institution of a Membr State whose legislation provides that the amount of cash benefits shall vary with the number of members in the family shall take into account also the members of the family of the person concerned who are residing in the teritory of another Member State, as if they were residing in the territory of the competent State.

Article 59   Costs of transporting a person who has sustained an accident at work or is suffering from an occupational disease

1.   The competent institution of a Member State whose legislation provides for meeting the costs of transporting a person who has sustained an accident at work or is suffering from an occupational disease, either to his place of residence or to a hospital, shall meet such costs to the corresponding place in the territory of another Member State where the person resides, provided that that institution gives prior authorisation for such transport, duly taking into account the reasons justifying it. Such authorisation shall not be required in the case of a frontier worker.

2.   The competent institution of a Member State whose legislation provides for the costs of transporting the body of a person killed in an accident at work to the place of burial shall, in accordance with the provisions of the legislation which it administers, meet such costs to the corresponding place in the territory of another Member State, where the person was residing at the time of the accident.

SECTION 2   AGGRAVATION OF AN OCCUPATIONAL DISEASE FOR WHICH THE BENEFIT HAS BEEN AWARDED

Article 60(4)(8)

1.   In the event of aggravation of an occupational disease for which an employed or self-employed person has received or is receiving benefit under the legislation of a Member State, the following rules shall apply:

(a)   if the person concerned has not, while in receipt of benefits, been engaged in an occupation under the legislation of another Member State likely to cause or aggrvate the disease in question, the competent institution of the first Member State shall be bound to meet the cost of the benefits under the provisions of the legislation which it administers taking into account the aggrevation;

(b)   if the person concerned, while in receipt of benefits, has pursued such an activity under the legislation of another Member State, the competent institution of the first Member State shall be bound to meet the cost of the benefits under the legislation which it administers without taking the aggrava-tion into account. The competent institution of the second Member State shall grant a supplement to the person concerned, the amount of which shall be equal to the difference between the amount of benefits due after the aggravation and the amount which would have been due prior to the aggravation under the legislation which it administers if the disease in question had occurred under the legislation of that Member State;

(c) if, in the case covered by subparagraph (b), an employed or self-employed person suffering from sclerogenic pneumoconiosis or from a disease determined under Article 57(6) is not entitled to benefits under the legislation of the second Member State, the competent institution of the first Member State shall be bound to provide benefits under the legislation which it administers, taking the aggravation into account. The competent institution of the second Member State shall, however, meet the cost of the difference between the amount of cash benefits, including pensions, due from the competent institution of the first Member State, taking the aggravation into account, and the amount of the corresponding benefits which were due prior to the aggravation;

(d) the provisions for reduction, suspension or withdrawal laid down by the legislation of a Member State shall not apply to persons receiving benefits awarded by institutions of two Member States in accordance with subparagraph (b).

2. In the event of aggravation of an occupational disease giving rise to the application of the provisions of Article 57(5), the following provisions shall apply:

(a) the competent institution with granted the benefits in accordance with the provisions of Article 57(1) shall be bound to provide benefits under the legislation which it administers taking the aggravation into account;

(b) the cost of cash benefits, including pensions, shall continue to be divided between the institutions which shared the costs of former benefits in accordance with the provisions of Article 57(5). Where, however, the person has again pursued an activity likely to cause or to aggravate the occupational disease in question, either under the legislation of one of the Member States in which he had already pursued an activity of the same nature or under the legislation of another Member State, the competent institution of such State shall meet the cost of the difference between the amount of benefits due, taking account of the aggravation, and the amount of benefits due prior to the aggravation.

SECTION 3   MISCELLANEOUS PROVISIONS

Article 61   Rules for taking into account the special features of certain legislation

1. If there is no insurance against accidents at work or occupational diseases in the territory of the Member State in which the person concerned happens to be, or if such insurance exists but there is no institution responsible for providing benefits in kind, those benefits shall be provided by the institution of the place of stay or residence responsible for providing benefit in kind in the event of sickness.

2. Where the legislation of the competent State makes wholly cost-free benefits in kind conditional upon use of the medical service organised by the employer, benefits in kind provided in the cases referred to in Articles 52 and 55(1) shall be deemed to have been provided by such a medical service.

3. Where the legislation of the competent State includes a scheme relating to the obligations of the employer, benefits in kind provided in the case referred to in Articles 52 and 55(1) shall be deemed to have been provided at the request of the competent institution.

4.　Where the nature of the scheme of the competent State relating to compensation for accidents at work is not that of compulsory insurance, the provision of benefits in kind shall be made directly by the employer or by the insurer involved.

5.　Where the legislation of a Member State provides expressly or by implication that accidents at work or occupational diseases which have occurred or have been confirmed previously shall be taken into consideration in order to assess the degree of incapacity, to establish a right to any benefit, or to determine the amount of benefit, the competent institution of that Member State shall also take into consideration accidents at work or occupational diseases which have occurred or have been confirmed previously under the legislation of another Member State as if they had occurred or had been confirmed under the legislation which it administers.

6.　Where the legislation of a Member State provides expressly or by implication that accidents at work or occupational diseases which have occurred or have been confirmed subsequently shall be taken into consideration in order to assess the degree of incapacity, to establish the right to any benefit, or to determine the amount of such benefit, the competent institution of that Member State shall also take into consideration accidents at work or occupational diseases which have occurred or have been confirmed subsequently under the legislation of another Member State as if they had occurred or had been confirmed under the legislation which it administers, but only where:

(1)　no compensation is due in respect of the accident at work or the occupational disease which had occurred or had been confirmed previously under the legislation which it administers; and

(2)　no compensation is due by virtue of the legislation of the other Member State under which the accident at work or the occupational disease occurred or was confirmed subsequently, account having been taken of the provisions of paragraph 5, in respect of that accident at work or that occupational disease.

Article 62　Scheme applicable where there are several schemes in the country of stay or residence — Maximum duration of benefits

1.　If the legislation of the country of stay or residence has several insurance schemes, the provisions applicable under Article 52 or 55(1) shall be those of the scheme for manual workers in the steel industry. However, if that legislation includes a special scheme for workers in mines and similar undertakings, the provisions of that scheme shall apply to that category of workers where the institution of the place of stay or residence to which they submit their claim is competent to administer that scheme.

2.　If the legislation of a Member State fixes a maximum period during which benefits may be granted, the institution which administers that legislation may take into account any period during which the benefits have already been provided by the institution of another Member State.

SECTION 4　REIMBURSEMENTS BETWEEN INSTITUTIONS

Article 63

1.　The competent institution shall be obliged to reimburse the amount of benefits in kind provided on its behalf in accordance with the provisions of Articles 52 and 55(1).

2.   The reimbursements referred to in paragraph 1 shall be determined and made in accordance with the procedures laid down by the implementing Regulation referred to in Article 98, on proof of actual expenditure.

3.   Two or more member States, or the competent authorities of such States, may provide for other methods of reimbursement or waive reimbursement between the institutions coming under their jurisdiction.

CHAPTER 5   DEATH GRANTS

Article 64   Aggregation of periods of insurance or residence

The competent institution of a Member State whose legislation makes the acquisition, retention or recovery of the right to death grants subject to the completion of periods of insurance or residence shall take account, to the extent necessary, of periods of insurance or residence completed under the legislation of any other Member State as though they had been completed under the legislation which it administers.

Article 65   Right to grants where death occurs in, or where the person entitled resides in, a Member State other than the competent State

1.   When an employed or self-employed person, a pensioner or a pension claimant, or a member of his family, dies in the territory of a Member State other than the competent State, the death shall be deemed to have occurred in the territory of the competent State.

2.   The competent institution shall be obliged to award death grants payable under the legislation which it administers, even if the person entitled resides in the territory of a Member State other than the competent State.

3.   The provisions of paragraphs 1 and 2 shall also apply when the death is the result of an accident at work or an occupational disease.

Article 66   Provision of benefits in the event of the death of a pensioner who had resided in a Member State other than the one whose institution was responsible for providing benefits in kind

In the event of the death of a pensioner who was entitled to a pension under the legislation of one Member State, or to pensions under the legislation of two or more Member States, when such pensioner was residing in the territory of a Member State other than the one whose institution was responsible for providing him with benefits in kind under the provisions of Article 28, the death grants payable under the legislation administered by that institution shall be provided by that institution at its own expense as though the pensioner had been residing in the teritory of the Member State of that institution at the time of his death.

The provisions of the preceding paragraph shall apply by analogy to the members of the family of a pensioner.

CHAPTER 6   UNEMPLOYMENT BENEFITS

SECTION 1   COMMON PROVISIONS

Article 67   Aggregation or periods of insurance or employment

1.   The competent institution of a Member State whose legislation makes the acquisition, retention or recovery of the right to benefits subject to the completion of periods of insurance shall take into account, to the extent

necessary, periods of insurance or employment completed as an employed person under the legislation of any other Member State, as though they were periods of insurance completed under the legislation which it administers, provided, however, that the periods of employment would have been counted as periods of insurance had they been completed under that legislation.

2. The competent institution of a Member State whose legislation makes the acquisition, retention or recovery of the right to benefits subject to the completion of periods of employment shall take into account, to the extent necessary, periods of insurance or employment completed as an employed person under the legislation of any other Member State, as though they were periods of employment completed under the legislation which it administers.

3. Except in the cases referred to in Article 71(1)(a)(ii) and (b)(ii), application of the provisions of paragraphs 1 and 2 shall be subject to the condition that the person concerned should have completed lastly:

— in the case of paragraph 1, periods of insurance,

— in the case of paragraph 2, periods of employment, in accordance with the provisions of the legislation under which the benefits are claimed.

4. Where the length of the period during which benefits may be granted depends on the length of periods of insurance or employment, the provisions of paragraph 1 or 2 shall apply, as appropriate.

Article 68   Calculation of benefits

1. The competent institution of a Member State whose legislation provides that the calculation of benefits should be based on the amount of the previous wage or salary shall take into account exclusively the wage or salary received by the person concerned in respect of his last employment in the territory of that State. However, if the person concerned had been in his last employment in that territory for less than four weeks, the benefits shall be calculated on the basis of the normal wage or salary corresponding, in the place where the unemployed person is residing or staying, to an equivalent or similar employment to his last employment in the territory of another Member State.

2. The competent institution of a Member State whose legislation provides that the amount of benefits varies with the number of members of the family, shall take into account also members of the family of the person concerned who are residing in the territory of another Member State, as though they were residing in the territory of the competent State. This provision shall not apply if, in the country of residence of the members of the family, another person is entitled to unemployment benefits for the calculation of which the members of the family are taken into consideration.

SECTION 2   UNEMPLOYED PERSONS GOING TO A MEMBER STATE OTHER THAN THE COMPETENT STATE

Article 69   Conditions and limits for the retention of the right to benefits

1. An employed or self-employed person who is wholly unemployed and who satisfies the conditions of the legislation of a Member State for entitlement to benefits and who goes to one or more other Member State in order to seek

employment there shall retain his entitlement to such benefits under the following conditions and within the following limits:

(a) Before his departure, he must have been registered as a person seeking work and have remained available to the employment services of the competent State for at least four weeks after becoming unemployed. However, the competent services or institutions may authorise his departure before such time has expired.

(b) He must register as a person seeking work with the employment services of each of the Member States to which he goes and be subject to the control procedure organised therein. This condition shall be considered satisfied for the period before registration if the person concerned registered within seven days of the date when he ceased to be available to the employment services of the State he left. In exceptional cases, this period may be extended by the competent services or institutions.

(c) Entitlement to benefits shall continue for a maximum period of three months from the date when the person concerned ceased to be available to the employment services of the State which he left, provided that the total duration of the benefits does not exceed the duration of the period of benefits he was entitled to under the legislation of that State. In the case of a seasonal worker such duration shall, moreover, be limited to the period remaining until the end of the season for which he was engaged.

2. If the person concerned returns to the competent State before the expiry of the period during which he is entitled to benefits under the provisions of paragraph 1(c), he shall continue to be entitled to benefits under the legislation of that State; he shall lose all entitlement to benefits under the legislation of the competent State if he does not return there before the expiry of that period. In exceptional cases, this time limit may be extended by the competent services or institutions.

3. The provisions of paragraph 1 may be invoked only once between two periods of employment.

4. Where the competent State is Belgium, an unemployed person who returns there after the expiry of the three month period laid down in paragraph 1(c), shall not requalify for benefits in that country until he has been employed there for at least three months.

Article 70   Provision of benefits and reimbursements

1. In the cases referred to in Article 69(1), benefits shall be provided by the institution of each of the States to which an unemployed person goes to seek employment. The competent institution of the Member State to whose legislation an employed or self-employed person was subject at the time of his last employment shall be obliged to reimburse the amount of such benefits.

2. The reimbursements referred to in paragraph 1 shall be determined and made in accordance with the procedure laid down by the implementing Regulation referred to in Article 98, on proof of actual expenditure, or by lump sum payments.

3. Two or more Member States, or the competent authorities of those States, may provide for other methods of reimbursement or payment, or may waive all reimbursement betwen the institutions coming under their jurisdiction.

SECTION 3   UNEMPLOYED PERSONS WHO, DURING THEIR LAST EMPLOYMENT, WERE RESIDING IN A MEMBER STATE OTHER THAN THE COMPETENT STATE

Article 71

1.   An unemployed person who was formerly employed and who, during his last employment, was residing in the territory of a Member State other than the competent State shall receive benefits in accordance with the following provisions:

(a)   (i)   A frontier worker who is partially or intermittently unemployed in the undertaking which employs him, shall receive benefits in accordance with the provisions of the legislation of the competent State as if he were residing in the territory of that State; these benefits shall be provided by the competent institution.

(ii)   A frontier worker who is wholly unemployed shall receive benefits in accordance with the provisions of the legislation of the Member State in whose territory he resides as though he had been subject to that legislation while last employed; these benefits shall be provided by the institution of the place of residence at its own expense.

(b)   (i)   An employed person, other than a frontier worker, who is partially, intermittently or wholly unemployed and who remains available to his employer or to the employment services in the territory of the competent State shall receive benefits in accordance with the provisions of the legislation of that State as though he were residing in its territory; these benefits shall be provided by the competent institution.

(i)   An employed person, other than a frontier worker, who is wholly unemployed and who makes himself available for work to the employment services in the territory of the Member State in which he resides, or who returns to that territory, shall receive benefits in accordance with the legislation of that State as if he had last been employed there; the institution of the place of residence shall provide such benefits at its own expense. However, if such an employed person has become entitled to benefits at the expense of the competent institution of the Member State to whose legislation he was last subject, he shall receive benefits under the provisions of Article 69. Receipt of benefits under the legislation of the State in which he resides shall be suspended for any period during which the unemployed person may, under the provisions of Article 69, make a claim for benefits under the legislation to which he was last subject.

2.   An unemployed person may not claim benefits under the legislation of the Member State in whose territory he resides while he is entitled to benefits under the provisions of paragraph 1(a)(i) or (b)(i).

CHAPTER 7   FAMILY BENEFITS

Article 72(5)   Aggregation of periods of insurance, employment or self-employment

Where the legislation of a Member State makes acquisition of the right to benefits conditional upon completion of periods of insurance, employment or self-employment, the competent institution of that State shall take into account for this purpose, to the extent necessary, periods of insurance, employment or self-employment completed in any other Member State, as if they were periods completed under the legislation which it administers.

Article 72a(6)　Employed persons who have become fully unemployed

An employed person who has become fully unemployed and to whom Article 71(1)(a)(ii) or (b)(ii), first sentence, apply shall, for the members of his family residing in the territory of the same Member State as he, receive family benefits in accordance with the legislation of that State, as if he had been subject to that legislation during his last employment, taking account, where appropriate, of the provisions of Article 72. These benefits shall be provided by, and at the expense of, the institution of the place of residence.

Where that institution applies legislation providing for deduction of contributions payable by unemployed persons to cover family benefits, it shall be authorised to make such deductions in accordance with the provisions of its legislation.[1]

Note
[1]Inserted by Regulation 3095/95 of 22 December 1995 [OJ 1995 L335/1].

Article 73(5)　Employed or self-employed persons the members of whose families reside in a Member State other than the competent State

An employed or self-employed person subject to the legislation of a Member State shall be entitled, in respect of the members of his family who are residing in another Member State, to the family benefits provided for by the legislation of the former State, as if they were residing in that State, subject to the provisions of Annex VI.

Article 74(5)　Unemployed persons the members of whose families reside in a Member State other than the competent State

An unemployed person who was formerly employed or self-employed and who draws unemployment benefits under the legislation of a Member State shall be entitled, in respect of the members of his family residing in another Member State, to the family benefits provided for by the legislation of the former State, as if they were residing in that State, subject to the provisions of Annex VI.

Article 75(5)　Provisions of benefits

1.　Family benefits shall be provided, in the cases referred to in Article 73, by the competent institution of the State to the legislation of which the employed or self-employed person is subject and, in the cases referred to in Article 74, by the competent institution of the State under the legislation of which an unemployed person who was formerly employed or self-employed receives unemployment benefits. They shall be provided in accordance with the provisions administered by such institutions, whether or not the natural or legal person to whom such benefits are payable is residing or staying in the territory of the competent State or in that of another Member State.

2.　However, if the family benefits are not used by the person to whom they should be provided for the maintenance of the members of the family, the competent institution shall discharge its legal obligations by providing the said benefits to the natural or legal person actually maintaining the members of the family, at the request of, and through the agency of, the institution of their place of residence or of the designated institution or body appointed for this purpose by the competent authority of the country of their residence.

3.   Two or more Member States may agree, in accordance with the provisions of Article 8, that the competent institution shall provide the family benefits due under the legislation of those States or of one of those States to the natural or legal person actually maintaining the members of the family, either directly or through the agency of the institution of their place of residence.

Article 76(5)   Rules of priority in cases of overlapping entitlement to family benefits under the legislation of the competent State and under the legislation of the Member State of residence of the members of the family

1.   Where, during the same period, for the same family member and by reason of carrying on an occupation, family benefits are provided for by the legislation of the Member State in whose territory the members of the family are residing, entitlement to the family benefits due in accordance with the legislation of another Member State, if appropriate under Articles 73 or 74, shall be suspended up to the amount provided for in the legislation of the first Member State.

2.   If an application for benefits is not made in the Member States in whose territory the members of the family are residing, the competent institution of the other Member State may apply the provisions of paragraph 1 as if benefits were granted in the first Member State.

CHAPTER 8   BENEFITS FOR DEPENDENT CHILDREN OF PENSIONERS AND FOR ORPHANS

Article 77   Dependent children of pensioners

1.   The term 'benefits', for the purposes of this Article, shall mean family allowances for persons receiving pensions for old age, invalidity or an accident at work or occupational disease, and increases or supplements to such pensions in respect of the children of such pensioners, with the exception of supplements granted under insurance schemes for accidents at work and occupational diseases.

2.   Benefits shall be granted in accordance with the following rules, irrespective of the Member State in whose territory the pensioner or the children are residing:

(a)   to a pensioner who draws a pension under the legislation of one Member State only, in accordance with the legislation of the Member State responsible for the pension;

(b)   to a pensioner who draws pensions under the legislation of more than one Member State:

(i)   in accordance with the legislation of whichever of these States he resides in provided that, taking into account, where appropriate, the provisions of Article 79(1)(a), a right to one of the benefits referred to in paragraph 1 is acquired under the legislation of that State; or

(ii)   in other cases in accordance with the legislation of the Member State to which he has been subject for the longest period of time, provided that, taking into account, where appropriate, the provisions of Article 79(1)(a), a right to one of the benefits referred to in paragraph 1 is acquired under such legislation; if no right to benefit is acquired under that legislation, the conditions for the acquisition of such right under the legislation of the other Member States concerned shall be examined in decreasing order of the length of periods of insurance or residence completed under the legislation of those Member States.

Article 78 Orphans

1. The term 'benefits', for the purposes of this Article, means family allowances and, where appropriate, supplementary or special allowances for orphans and orphans' pensions except those granted under insurance schemes for accidents at work and occupational diseases.

2. Orphans' benefits shall be granted in accordance with the following rules, irrespective of the Member State in whose territory the orphan or the natural or legal person actually maintaining him is resident:

(a) for the orphan of a deceased employed or self-employed person who was subject to the legislation of one Member State only in accordance with the legislation of that State;

(b) for the orphan of a deceased employed or self-employed person who was subject to the legislation of several Member States;

(i) in accordance with the legislation of the Member State in whose territory the orphan resides provided that, taking into account, where appropriate, the provisions of Article 79(1)(a), a right to one of the benefits referred to in paragraph 1 is acquired under the legislation of that State; or

(ii) in other cases in accordance with the legislation of the Member State to which the deceased had been subject for the longest period of time, provided that, taking into account, where appropriate, the provisions of Article 79(1)(a), the right to one of the benefits referred to in paragraph 1 is acquired under the legislation of that State; if no right is acquired under that legislation, the conditions for the acquisition of such right under the legislation of the other Member States shall be examined in decreasing order of the length of periods of insurance or residence completed under the legislation of those Member States.

However, the legislation of the Member State applicable in respect of provision of the benefits referred to in Article 77 for a pensioner's children shall remain applicable after the death of the said pensioner in respect of the provision of the benefits to his orphans.

Article 79(4) Provisions common to benefits for dependent children of pensioners and for orphans

1. Benefits, within the meaning of Articles 77 and 78, shall be provided in accordance with the legislation determined by applying the provisions of those Articles by the institution responsible for administering such legislation and at its expense as if the pensioner or the deceased had been subject only to the legislation of the competent State. However:

(a) if that legislation provides that the acquisition, retention or recovery of the right to benefits shall be dependent on the length of periods of insurance, employment, self-employment or residence such length shall be determined taking into account, where appropriate, the provisions of Article 45 or, as the case may be, Article 72;

(b) if that legislation provides that the amount of benefits shall be calculated on the basis of the amount of the pension, or shall depend on the length of periods of insurance the amount of these benefits shall be calculated on the basis of the theoretical amount determined in accordance with the provisions of Article 46(2).

2. In a case where the effect of applying the rule laid down in Articles 77(2)(b)(ii) and 78(2)(b)(ii) would be to make several Member States competent, the length of the periods being equal, benefits within the meaning of Article 77 or 78, as the case may be, shall be granted in accordance with the legislation of the Member States to which the pensioner or the deceased was last subject.

3. Th right to benefits due only under the national legislation or under the provisions of paragraph 2 and under Articles 77 and 78 shall be suspended if the children become entitled to family benefits or family allowances under the legislation of a Member State by virtue of the pursuit of a professional or trade activity. In such a case, the persons concerned shall be considered as members of the family of an employed or self-employed person.

TITLE IV   ADMINISTRATIVE COMMISSION ON SOCIAL SECURITY FOR MIGRANT WORKERS

Article 80   Composition and working methods

1. There shall be attached to the Commission of the European Communities, an Administrative Commission on Social Security for Migrant Workers (hereinafter called 'the Administrative Commission') made up of a government representative of each of the Member States, assisted, where necessary, by expert advisers. A representative of the Commission of the European Communities shall attend the meetings of the Administrative Commission in an advisory capacity.

2. The Administrative Commission shall be assisted in technical matters by the International Labour Office under the terms of the agreements concluded to that end between the European Economic Community and the International Labour Organisation.

3. The rules of the Administrative Commission shall be drawn up by mutual agreement among its members.

Decisions on questions of interpretation referred to in Article 81(a) shall be unanimous. They shall be given the necessary publicity.

4. Secretarial services shall be provided for the Administrative Commission by the Commission of the European Communities.

Article 81   Tasks of the Administrative Commission

The Administrtive Commission shall have the following duties:

(a)   to deal with all administrative questions and questions of interpretation arising from the provisions of this Regulation and subsequent Regulations, or from any agreement or arrangement concluded thereunder, without prejudice to the right of the authorities, institutions and persons concerned to have recourse to the procedures and tribunals provided for by the legislation of Member States, by this Regulation or by the Treaty;

(b)   to carry out all translations of documents relating to the implementation of this Regulation at the request of the competent authorities, institutions and tribunals of the Member States, and in particular translations of claims submitted by persons who may be entitled to benefit under the provisions of this Regulation;

(c)   to foster and develop cooperation between Member States in social security matters, particularly in respect of health and social measures of common interest;

(d) to foster and develop cooperation between Member States with a view to expediting, taking into account developments in administrative management techniques, the award of benefits, in particular those due under the provisions of this Regulation for invalidity, old age and death (pensions);

(e) to assemble the factors to be taken into consideration for drawing up accounts relating to the costs to be borne by the institutions of the Member States under the provisions of this Regulation and to adopt the annual accounts between the said institutions;

(f) to undertake any other function coming within its competence under the provisions of this and of subsequent Regulations or any agreement or arrangement made thereunder;

(g) to submit proposals to the Commission of the European Economic Community for working out subsequent Regulations and for the revision of this and subsequent Regulations.

TITLE V ADVISORY COMMITTEE ON SOCIAL SECURITY FOR MIGRANT WORKERS

Article 82(A)[1] Establishment, composition and working methods

1. An Advisory Committee on Social Security for Migrant Workers (hereinafter called 'the Advisory Committee') is hereby established, with 72 members comprising, from each Member State:

(a) two representatives of the government, of whom one at least must be a member of the Administrative Commission;

(b) two representatives of trade unions;

(c) two representatives of employers' organisations.

For each of the categories referred to above, an alternate member shall be appointed for each Member State.

Note
[1]Amended by Regulation 118/97 of 3 December 1996 [OJ No. L28/1]

2. Members of the Advisory Committee and their alternates shall be appointed by the Council which shall endeavour, when selecting representatives of trade unions and employers' organisations, to achieve an equitable representation on the Committee of the various sectors concerned.

The list of members and their alternates shall be published by the Council in the Official Journal of the European Communities.

3. The term of office for members ad alternates shall be two years. Their appointments may be renewed. On expiry of their term of office, members and alternates shall remain in office until they are replaced or until their appointments are renewed.

4. The Advisory Committee shall be chaired by a representative of the Commission. The chairman shall not vote.

5. The Advisory Committee shall meet at least once each year. It shall be convened by its chairman, either on his own initiative or on written application to him by at least one-third of the members. Such application must include concrete proposals concerning the agenda.

6. Acting on a proposal from its chairman, the Advisory Committee may decide, in exceptional circumstances, to take advice from any persons or representatives of organisations with extensive experience in social security matters. Furthermore, the Committee shall receive technical assistance from

the International Labour Office under the same conditions as the Administrative Commission, under the terms of the agreement concluded between the European Economic Community and the International Labour Organisation.

7. The opinions and proposals of the Advisory Committee must state the reasons on which they are based. They shall be delivered by an absolute majority of the votes validly cast.

The Committee shall, by a majority of its members, draw up its rules of procedure which shall be approved by the Council, after receiving the opinion of the Commission.

8. Secretarial services shall be provided for the Advisory Committee by the Commission of the European Communities.

Article 83   Tasks of the Advisory Committee

The Advisory Committee shall be empowered, at the request of the Commission of the European Communities, of the Administrative Commission or on its own initiative:

(a) to examine general questions or questions of principle and problems arising from the implementation of the Regulations adopted within the framework of the provisions of Article 51 of the Treaty;

(b) to formulate opinions on the subject for the Administrative Commission and proposals for any revision of the Regulations.

TITLE VI   MISCELLANEOUS PROVISIONS

Article 84(4)   Cooperation between competent authorities

1. The competent authorities of Member States shall communicate to each other all information regarding:

(a) measures taken to implement this Regulation;

(b) changes in their legislation which are likely to affect the implementation of this Regulation.

2. For the purposes of implementing this Regulation, the authorities and institutions of Member States shall lend their good offices and act as though implementing their own legislation. The administrative assistance furnished by the said authorities and institutions shall, as a rule, be free of charge. However, the competent authorities of the Member States may agree to certain expenses being reimbursed.

3. The authorities and institutions of Member States may, for the purpose of implementing this Regulation, communicate directly with one another and with the persons concerned or their representatives.

4. The authorities, institutions and tribunals of one Member State may not reject claims or other documents submitted to them on the grounds that they are written in an official language of another Member State. They shall have recourse where appropriate to the provsions of Article 81(b).

5. (a) Where, under this Regulation or under the implementing Regulation referred to in Article 98, the authorities or institutions of a Member State communicate personal data to the authorities or institutions of another Member State, that communication shall be subject to the legal provisions governing protection of data laid down by the Member State providing the data.

Any subsequent transmission as well as the storage, alteration and destruction of the data shall be subject to the provisions of the legislation on data protection of the receiving Member State.

(b) The use of personal data for purposes other than those of social security shall be subject to the approval of the person concerned or in accordance with the other guarantees provided for by national legislation.

Article 85 Exemptions from or reductions of taxes — Exempt from authentication

1. Any exemption from or reduction of taxes, stamp duty, notarial or registration fees provided for in the legislation of one Member State in respect of certificates or documents reuired to be produced for the purposes of the legislation of that State shall be extended to similar documents required to be produced for the purposes of the legislation of another Member State or of this Regulation.

2. All statements, documents and certificates of any kind whatsoever required to be produced for the purposes of this Regulation shall be exempt from authentication by diplomatic or consular authorities.

Article 86 Claims, declarations or appeals submitted to an authority, institution or tribunal of a Member State other than the competent State

1. Any claim, declaration or appeal which should have been submitted, in order to comply with the legislation of one Member State, within a specified period to an authority, institution or tribunal of that State shall be admissible if it is submitted within the same period to a corresponding authority, institution or tribunal of another Member State. In such a case the authority, institution, or tribunal receiving the claim, declaration or appeal shall forward it without delay to the competent authority, institution or tribunal of the former State either directly or through the competent authorities of the Member State concerned. The date on which such claims, declarations or appeals were submitted to the authority, institution or tribunal of the second State shall be considered as the date of their submission to the competent authority, institution or tribunal.

2. Where a person entitled to do so under the legislation of a Member State has submitted to that State a claim for family benefits even though that State is not competent by priority right, the date on which the first application was made shall be considered as the date on which it was submitted to the competent authority, institution or tribunal, provided that a new application is submitted in the Member State which is competent by priority right by a person entitled to do so under the legislation of that State. The second application must be submitted within a period of one year after notification of the rejection of the first application or the cessation of payment of benefits in the first Member State.[1]

Note
[1] Inserted by Regulation 3095/95 of 22 December 1995 [OJ 1995 L335/1].

Article 87 Medical examinations

1. Medical examinations provided for by the legislaton of one Member State may be carried out at the request of the competent institution, in the territory of another Member State, by the institution of the place of stay or residence of the person entitled to benefits, under conditions laid down in the implementing Regulation referred to in Article 98 or, failing these, under

conditions agreed upon between the competent authorities of the Member States concerned.

2. Medical examinations carried out under the conditions laid down in paragraph 1 shall be considered as having been carried out in the territory of the competent State.

Article 88[1]   Transfers from one Member State to another of sums of money payable pursuant to this Regulation

Where appropriate, money transfers effected in accordance with this Regulation shall be made in accordance with the relevant agreements in force between the Member States concerned at the time of transfer. Where no such agreements are in force between two Member States, the competent authorities of the said States or the authorities responsible for international payments shall, by mutual agreement, determine the measures necessary for effecting such transfers.

Note
[1]Amended by Regulation 118/97 of 2 December 1996 [OJ No. L28/1].

Article 89   Special procedures for implementing certain legislation

Special procedures for implementing the legislation of certain Member States are set out in Annex VI.

Article 90(5)

. . .

Article 91   Contributions chargeable to employers or undertakings not established in the competent State

An employer shall not be bound to pay increased contributions by reason of the fact that his place of business or the registered office or place of business of his undertaking is in the territory of a Member State other than the competent State.

Article 92   Collection of contributions

1. Contributions payable to an institution of one Member State may be collected in the territory of another Member State in accordance with the administrative procedure and with the guarantees and privileges applicable to the collection of contributions payable to the corresponding institution of the latter State.

2. The procedure for the implementation of the provisions of paragraph 1 shall be governed, in so far as is necessary, by the implementing Regulation referred to in Article 98 or by means of agreements between Member States. Such implementing procedure may also cover procedure for enforcing payment.

Article 93   Rights of institutions responsible for benefits against liable third parties

1. If a person receives benefits under the legislation of one Member State in respect of an injury resulting from an occurrence in the territory of another State, any rights of the institution responsible for benefits against a third party bound to compensate for the injury shall be governed by the following rules:

(a) Where the institution responsible for benefits is, by virtue of the legislation which it administers, subrogated to the rights which the recipient has against the third party, such subrogation shall be recognised by each Member State.

(b)   Where the said institution has direct rights against the third party, such rights shall be recognised by each Member State.

2.   If a person receives benefits under the legislation of one Member State in respect of an injury resulting from an occurrence in the territory of another Member State, the provisions of the said legislation which determine in which cases the civil liability of employers or of the persons employed by them is to be excluded shall apply with regard to the said person or to the competent institution.

The provisions of paragraph 1 shall also apply to any rights of the institution responsible for benefit against an employer or the persons employed by him in cases where their liability is not excluded.

3.   Where, in accordance with the provisions of Article 36(3) and/or Article 63(3), two or more Member States or the competent authorities of those States have concluded an agreement to waive reimbursement between institutions under their jurisdiction, any rights arising against a liable third party shall be governed by the following rules:

(a)   Where the institution of the Member State of stay or residence awards benefits to a person in respect of an injury which was sustained within its territory, that institution, in accordance with the legislation which it administers, shall exercise the right to subrogation or direct action against the third party liable to provide compensation for the injury.

(b)   For the purpose of implementing (a):

(i)   the person receiving benefits shall be deemed to be insured with the institution of the place of stay or residence, and

(ii)   that institution shall be deemed to be the debtor institution.

(c)   The provisions of paragraphs 1 and 2 shall remain applicable in respect of any benefits not covered by the waiver agreement referred to in this paragraph.

TITLE VII   TRANSITIONAL AND FINAL PROVISIONS

Article 94(4)(5)(6)(8)(9)   Transitional provisions for employed persons

1.   No right shall be acquired under this Regulation in respect of a period prior to 1 October 1972 or to the date of its application in the territory of the Member State concerned or in a part of the territory of that State.

2.   All periods of insurance and, where appropriate, all periods of employment or residence completed under the legislation of a Member State before October 1972 or before the date of its application in the territory of that Member State or in a part of the territory of that State shall be taken into consideration for the determination of rights acquired under the provisions of this Regulation.

3.   Subject to the provisions of paragraph 1, a right shall be acquired under this Regulation even though it relates to a contingency which materialised prior to 1 October 1972 or to the date of its application in the territory of the Member State concerned or in a part of the territory of that State.

4.   Any benefit which has not been awarded or which has been suspended by reason of the nationality or place of residence of the person concerned shall,

on the application of the person concerned, be awarded or resumed with effect from 1 October 1972 or the date of its application in the territory of the Member State concerned or in a part of the territory of that State, provided that the rights previously determined have not given rise to a lump sum payment.

5.   The rights of a person to whom a pension was awarded prior to 1 October 1972 or to the date of its application in the territory of the Member State concerned or in a part of the territory of that State may, on the application of the person concerned, be reviewed, taking into account the provisions of this Regulation. This provision shall also apply to the other benefits referred to in Article 78.

6.   If an application referred to in paragraph 4 or 5 is submitted within two years from 1 October 1972 or from the date of its application in the territory of the Member State concerned, the rights acquired under this Regulation shall have effect from that date, and the provisions of the legislation of any Member State concerning the forfeiture or limitation of rights may not be invoked against the persons concerned.

The same provisions shall apply as regards the application of this Regulation in those territories which became a part of the Federal Republic of Germany on 3 October 1990 provided that the application referred to in paragraph 4 or 5 is submitted within two years of 1 June 1992.

7.   If an application referred to in paragraph 4 or 5 is submitted after the expiry of the two-year period after 1 October 1972 or following the date of its application in the territory of the Member State concerned, rights which have not been forfeited or which are not time barred shall have effect from the date on which the application was submitted, except where more favourable provisions of the legislation of any Member State apply.

The same provisions shall aply as regards the application of this Regulation in those territories which became a part of the Federal Republic of Germany on 3 October 1990 provided that the application referred to in paragraph 4 or 5 is submitted after two years have elapsed from 1 June 1992.

8.   In cases of sclerogenic pneumoconiosis, the provision of Article 57(5) shall apply to cash benefits for an occupational disease the expense of which, in the absence of agreement between the institutions concerned, could not be divided between those institutions before 1 October 1972.

9.   The family allowances received by employed persons employed in France or unemployed workers receiving unemployment benefits under French legislation in respect of the members of their families residing in another Member State on the date of 15 November 1989 shall continue to be paid at the rates, within the limits and according to the procedures applicable on that date as long as their amount exceeds that of the benefits that would be due as from the date of 16 November 1989 and as long as the persons concerned are subject to French legislation. Account shall not be taken of interruptions lasting less than one month, nor of periods during which unemployment or sickness benefit is drawn. The procedure for implementing this paragraph and in particular the sharing of the cost of these allowances shall be determined by mutual agreement between the Member States concerned or by their competent authorities, after the Administrative Commission has delivered an opinion.

10. The rights of persons to whom a pension was awarded prior to the entry into force of Article 45(6) may be reviewed at their request subject to the provisions of Article 45(6).

Article 95(3)(9)   Transitional provisions for self-employed persons

1. No right shall be acquired under this Regulation in respect of a period prior to 1 July 1982 or to the date of its implementation in the territory of the Member State concerned or in a part of the territory of that State.

2. All insurance periods and, where appropriate, all periods of employment, of self-employment or of residence completed under the legislation of a Member State before 1 July 1982 or before the date of implementation of this Regulation in the territory of that Member State or in a part of the territory of that State shall be taken into consideration for the determination of rights acquired under this Regulation.

3. Subject to paragraph 1, a right shall be acquired under this Regulation even though it relates to a contingency which materialised prior to 1 July 1982 or to the date of implementation of this Regulation in the territory of the Member State concerned or in a part of the territory of that State.

4. Any benefit which has not been awarded or which has been suspended by reason of the nationality or place of residence of the person concerned shall, on the application of the person concerned, be awarded or resumed with effect from 1 July 1982 or from the date of implementation of this Regulation in the territory of the Member State concerned or in a part of the territory of that State, provided that the rights previously determined have not given rise to a lump-sum payment.

5. The rights of a person to whom a pension was awarded prior to 1 July 1982 or to the date of implementation of this Regulation in the territory of the Member State concerned or in a part of the territory of that State may, on the application of the person concerned, be reviewed, taking into account this Regulation. This provision shall also apply to the other benefits referred to in Article 78.

6. If an application referred to in paragraph 4 or 5 is submitted within two years of 1 July 1982 or of the date of implementation of this Regulation in the territory of the Member State concerned, the rights acquired under this Regulation shall have effect from that date, and the provisions of the legislation of any Member State concerning the forfeiture or limitation of rights may not be invoked against the persons concerned. The same provisions shall apply as regards the application of this Regulation in those territories which became a part of the Federal Republic of Germany on 3 October 1990 provided that the application referred to in paragraph 4 or 5 is submitted within two years of 1 June 1992.

7. If an application referred to in paragraph 4 or 5 is submitted after the expiry of the two-year period from 1 July 1982 or following the date of implementation of this Regulation in the territory of the Member State concerned, rights which have not been forfeited or are not barred by limitation shall have effect from the date on which the application was submitted, except where more favourable provisions of the legislation of any Member State apply. The same provisions shall apply as regards the application of this Regulation in those territories which became a part of the Federal Republic of Germany on 3 October 1990 provided that the application referred to in paragraph 4 or 5 is submitted after two years have elapsed from 1 June 1992.

Article 95a(8)   Transitional provisions for application of Regulation (EEC) No. 1248/92[1]

1.   Under Regulation (EEC) No. 1248/92 no right shall be acquired for a period prior to 1 June 1992.

2.   All insurance periods or periods of residence completed under the legislation of a Member State before 1 June 1992 shall be taken into consideration for the determination of rights to benefits pursuant to Regulation (EEC) No. 1248/92.

3.   Subject to paragraph 1, a right shall be acquired under Regulation (EEC) No. 1248/92 even though relating to a contingency which materialised prior to 1 June 1992.

4.   The rights of a person to whom a pension was awarded prior to 1 June 1992 may, on the application of the person concerned, be reviewed, taking intop account the provisions of Regulation (EEC) No. 1248/92.

5.   If an application referred to in paragraph 4 is submitted within two years from 1 June 1992 the rights acquired under Regulation (EEC) No. 1248/92 shall have effect from that date, and the provisions of the legislation of any Member State concerning the forfeiture or limitation of rights may not be invoked against the persons concerned.

6.   If the application referred to in paragraph 4 is submitted after the expiry of the two-year period after 1 June 1992, rights which have not been forfeited or not barred by limitation shall have effect from the date on which the application was submitted, except where more favourable provisions of the legislation of any Member State apply.

Note
[1] OJ No. L136, 19.5.1992, p. 7.

Article 95b   Transitional provisions for application of Regulation (EEC) No. 1247/92[1]

1.   Regulation (EEC) No. 1247/92 shall not provide any entitlement for periods prior to 1 June 1992.

2.   The periods of residence and periods of employment or of self-employment completed on the territory of a Member State before 1 June 1992 shall be taken into consideration for the determination of rights acquired under the provisions of Regulation (EEC) No. 1247/92.

3.   Subject to paragraph 1, a right shall be acquired pursuant to Regulation (EEC) 1247/92 even where it relates to a contingency that occurred before 1 June 1992.

4.   All special non-contributory benefits which have not been awarded or which have been suspended by reason of the nationality of the person concerned shall, on the application of the person concerned, be awarded or resumed with effect from 1 June 1992, provided that the rights previously determined have not given rise to a lump-sum payment.

5.   The rights of persons to whom a pension was awarded prior to 1 June 1992, may, on the application of the persons concerned, be reviewed, taking account of the provision of Regulation (EEC) No. 1247/92.

Note
[1] Inserted by Regulation 3095/95 of 22 December 1995 [OJ 1995 L335/1].

6.   If an application referred to in paragraph 4 or 5 is submitted within two years from 1 June 1992, the rights acquired pursuant to Regulation (EEC) No. 1247/92 shall have effect from that date, and the provisions of the legislation of any Member State concerning the forfeiture of limitation of rights may not be invoked against the person concerned.

7.   If an application referred to in paragraph 4 or 5 is submitted after the expiry of the two year period after 1 June 1992, rights which have not been forfeited or which are not time-barred shall have effect from the date on which the application was submitted, except where more favourable provisions of the legislation of any Member State apply.

8.   The application of Article 1 of Regulation (EEC) No. 1247/92 may not result in the withdrawal of benefits which are awarded before 1 June 1992 by the competent institutions of the Member States under Title III of Regulation (EEC) No. 1408/71 to which Article 10 of the latter regulation is applicable.

9.   The application of Article 1 of Regulation (EEC) No. 1247/92 may not result in the rejection of an application for a special non-contributory benefit awarded as a supplement to a pension, which was submitted by the person concerned who had satisfied the conditions for the award of this benefit before 1 June 1992, even where the person concerned resides on the territory of a Member State other than the competent Member State, provided that the application for the benefit is submitted within a period of five years starting from 1 June 1992.

10.   Notwithstanding the provisions of paragraph 1, any special non-contributory benefit, granted as a supplement to a pension, which has not been awarded or which has been suspended by reason of the residence of the person concerned on the territory of a Member State other than the competent Member State, shall on the application of the person concerned, be awarded or resumed with effect from 1 June 1992, in the first case from the date on which the benefits should have been awarded, and in the second case on the date of suspension of the benefit.

11.   Where special non-contributory benefits as referred to in Article 4(2a) of Regulation (EEC) No. 1408/71 may, during the same period and for the same person, be granted pursuant to Article 10a of that Regulation by the competent institution of the Member State in the territory of which that person is resident and pursuant to paragraphs 1 to 10 of this Article by the competent institution of another Member State, the person concerned may only aggregate those benefits up to the limit of the highest amount of the special benefit he could claim under one of the legislations in question.

12.   The detailed rules of application of paragraph 11 and in particular the application, with regard to the benefits referred to in that paragraph, of the clauses for reduction, suspension or abolition provided for under the legislation of one or more Member States and the allocation of the differential additional amounts shall be set by decision of the Administrative Commission on Social Security for Migrant Workers and, where appropriate, by common accord of the Member States concerned or their competent authorities.

Article 96   Agreements relating to reimbursement between institutions

The Agreements concluded pursuant to Articles 36(3), 63(3) and 70(3) before 1 July 1982 shall apply likewise to persons to whom the scope of the present

Regulation was extended on that date, except in the event of an objection by one of the contracting Member States to these Agreements.

This objection shall be taken into account if the competent authority of that Member State informs the competent authority of the other Member State(s) concerned in writing before 1 October 1983. A copy of this communication shall be forwarded to the Administrative Commission.

Article 97   Notification pursuant to certain provisions

1.   The notifications referred to in Articles 1(j), 5 and 8(2) shall be addressed to the President of the Council of the European Communities. They shall indicate the date of entry into force of the laws and schemes in question or, in the case of the notifications referred to in Article 1(j), the date from which this Regulation shall apply to the schemes mentioned in the declarations of the Member States.

2.   Notifications received in accordance with the provisions of paragraph 1 shall be published in the Official Journal of the European Communities.

Article 98   Implementing Regulation

A further Regulation shall lay down the procedure for implementing this Regulation.

Article 99(5)

. . .

Article 100[1]   Repeal of previous Regulations

Deleted.

Note

[1]Amended by Regulation 118/97 of 2nd December 1996 [OJ No. L28/1].

ANNEX B   LISTS OF ACTS AMENDING REGULATIONS (EEC) NO. 1408/71 AND (EEC) NO. 574/72

A.   Act of Accession of Spain and Portugal [OJ No. L302, 15.11.1985, p. 23)

B.   Act of Accession of Austria, Finland and Sweden [OJ No. C241, 29.8.1994, p. 9] as adjusted by Council Decision 95/1/EC [OJ No. L1, 1.1.1995, p. 1]

1.   Made up to date by Council Regulation (EEC) No. 2001/83 of 2 June 1983 [OJ No. L230, 22.8.1983, p. 6].

2.   Council Regulation (EEC) No. 1660/85 of 13 June 1985 amending Regulation (EEC) No. 1408/71 on the application of social security schemes to employed persons, to self-employed persons and to members of their families moving within the Community and Regulation (EEC) No. 574/72 laying down the procedure for implementing Regulation (EEC) No. 1408/71 [OJ No. L160, 20.6.1985, p. 1; Spanish text: DO Edicíon especial, 1985 (05.V4), p. 142; Portuguese text; OJ DO Edição Especial, 1985 (05.V4), p. 142; Swedish text: EGT, Specialutgåva 1994, område 05 (04), p. 61; Finnish text: EYVL:n erityispainos 1994, alue 05 (04), p. 61].

3.   Council Regulation (EEC) No. 1661/85 of 13 June 1985 laying down the technical adaptations to the Community rules on social security for migrant workers with regard to Greenland [OJ No. L160, 20.6.1985, p. 7; Spanish text: DO Edicíon especial, 1985 (05.V4), p. 148; Portuguese text; OJ Edição

Especial, 1985 (05.04), p. 148; Swedish text: EGT, Specialutgåva 1994, område 05 (04), p. 67; Finnish text: EYVL:n erityispainos 1994, alue 05 (04), p. 67].

4. Commission Regulation (EEC) No. 513/86 of 26 February 1986 amending Annexes 1, 4, 5 and 6 to Council Regulation (EEC) No. 574/72 laying down the procedure for implementing Regulation (EEC) No. 1408/71 on the application of social security schemes to employed persons, to self-employed persons and to members of their families moving within the Community [OJ No. L51, 28.2.1986, p. 44; Swedish text: EGT, Specialutgåva 1994, område 05 (04), p. 73; Finnish text: EYVL:n erityispainos 1994, alue 05 (04), p. 73].

5. Council Regulation (EEC) No. 3811/86 of 11 December 1986 amending Regulation (EEC) No. 1408/71 on the application of social security schemes to employed persons, to self-employed persons and to members of their families moving within the Community and Regulation (EEC) No. 574/72 laying down the procedure for implementing Regulation (EEC) No. 1408/71 [OJ No. L355, 16.12.1986, p. 5; Swedish text: EGT, Specialutgåva 1994, område 05 (04), p. 86; Finnish text: EYVL:n erityispainos 1994, alue 05 (04), p. 86].

6. Council Regulation (EEC) No. 1305/89 of 11 May 1989 amending Regulation (EEC) No. 1408/71 on the application of social security schemes to employed persons, to self-employed persons and to members of their families moving within the Community and Regulation (EEC) No. 574/72 laying down the procedure for implementing Regulation (EEC) No. 1408/71 [OJ No. L131, 13.5.1985, p. 1; Swedish text: EGT, Specialutgåva 1994, område 05 (04), p. 143; Finnish text: EYVL:n erityispainos 1994, alue 05 (04), p. 143].

7. Council Regulation (EEC) No. 2332/89 of 18 July 1989 amending Regulation (EEC) No. 1408/71 on the application of social security schemes to employed persons, to self-employed persons and to members of their families moving within the Community and Regulation (EEC) No. 574/72 laying down the procedure for implementing Regulation (EEC) No. 1408/71 [OJ No. L224, 2.8.1989, p. 1; Swedish text: EGT, Specialutgåva 1994, område 05 (04), p. 154; Finnish text: EYVL:n erityispainos 1994, alue 05 (04), p. 154].

8. Council Regulation (EEC) No. 3427/89 of 30 October 1989 amending Regulation (EEC) No. 1408/71 on the application of social security schemes to employed persons, to self-employed persons and to members of their families moving within the Community and Regulation (EEC) No. 574/72 laying down the procedure for implementing Regulation (EEC) No. 1408/71 [OJ No. L331, 16.11.1989, p. 1; Swedish text: EGT, Specialutgåva 1994, område 05 (04), p. 165; Finnish text: EYVL:n erityispainos 1994, alue 05 (04), p. 165].

9. Council Regulation (EEC) No. 2195/91 of 25 June 1991 amending Regulation (EEC) No. 1408/71 on the application of social security schemes to employed persons, to self-employed persons and to members of their families moving within the Community and Regulation (EEC) No. 574/72 laying down the procedure for implementing Regulation (EEC) No. 1408/71 [OJ No. L206, 29.7.1991, p. 2; Swedish text: EGT, Specialutgåva 1994, område 05 (05), p. 46; Finnish text: EYVL:n erityispainos 1994, alue 05 (05), p. 46].

10. Council Regulation (EEC) No. 1247/92 of 30 April 1992 amending Regulation (EEC) No. 1408/71 on the application of social security schemes to employed persons, to self-employed persons and to members of their families

moving within the Community and Regulation (EEC) No. 574/72 laying down the procedure for implementing Regulation (EEC) No. 1408/71 [OJ No. L136, 19.5.1992, p. 1; Swedish text: EGT, Specialutgåva 1994, område 05 (05), p. 124; Finnish text: EYVL:n erityispainos 1994, alue 05 (05), p. 124].

11. Council Regulation (EEC) No. 1248/92 of 30 April 1992 amending Regulation (EEC) No. 1408/71 on the application of social security schemes to employed persons, to self-employed persons and to members of their families moving within the Community and Regulation (EEC) No. 574/72 laying down the procedure for implementing Regulation (EEC) No. 1408/71 [OJ No. L136, 19.5.1992, p. 7; Swedish text: EGT, Specialutgåva 1994, område 05 (05), p. 130; Finnish text: EYVL:n erityispainos 1994, alue 05 (05), p. 130].

12. Council Regulation (EEC) No. 1249/92 of 30 April 1992 amending Regulation (EEC) No. 1408/71 on the application of social security schemes to employed persons, to self-employed persons and to members of their families moving within the Community and Regulation (EEC) No. 574/72 laying down the procedure for implementing Regulation (EEC) No. 1408/71 [OJ No. L136, 19.5.1992, p. 28; Swedish text: EGT, Specialutgåva 1994, område 05 (05), p. 151; Finnish text: EYVL:n erityispainos 1994, alue 05 (05), p. 151].

13. Council Regulation (EEC) No. 1245/93 of 30 June 1993 amending Regulation (EEC) No. 1408/71 on the application of social security schemes to employed persons, to self-employed persons and to members of their families moving within the Community, Regulation (EEC) No. 574/72 laying down the procedure for implementing Regulation (EEC) No. 1408/71 and Regulation (EEC) No. 1247/92 amending Regulation (EEC) No. 1408/71 [OJ No. L181, 23.7.1993, p. 1; Swedish text: EGT, Specialutgåva 1994, område 05 (06), p. 63; Finnish text: EYVL:n erityispainos 1994, alue 05 (06), p. 63].

14. Council Regulation (EEC) No. 3095/95 of 22 December 1995 amending Regulation (EEC) No. 1408/71 on the application of social security schemes to employed persons, to self-employed persons and to members of their families moving within the Community, Regulation (EEC) No. 574/72 fixing the procedure for implementing Regulation (EEC) No. 1408/71, Regulation (EEC) No. 1247/92 amending Regulation (EEC) No. 1408/71 and Regulation (EEC) No. 1945/93 amending Regulation (EEC) No. 1247/92 [OJ No. L335, 30.12.1995, p. 1].

15. Council Regulation (EC) No. 3096/95 of 22 December 1995 amending Regulation (EEC) No. 1408/71 on the application of social security schemes to employed persons, to self-employed persons and to members of their families moving within the Community and Regulation (EEC) No. 574/72 laying down the procedure for implementing Regulation (EEC) No. 1408/71 [OJ No. L335, 30.12.1995, p. 10].

ANNEX I(A)(8)(9)(13)(14)(15) PERSONS COVERED BY THE REGULATION

I. Employed persons and/or self-employed persons (Article 1(a)(ii) and (iii) of the Regulation)

A. BELGIUM
Does not apply.

B. DENMARK

1.   Any person who, from the fact of pursuing an activity as an employed person, is subject:

(a)   to the legislation on accidents at work and occupational diseases for the period prior to 1 September 1977;

(b)   to the legislation on supplementary pensions for employed persons (arbejdsmarkedets tillaegspension, ATP) for a period commencing on or after 1 September 1977, shall be considered as an employed person within the meaning of Article 1(a)(ii) of the Regulation.

2.   Any person who, pursuant to the law on daily cash benefits in the event of sickness or maternity, is entitled to such benefits on the basis of an earned income other than a wage or salary shall be considered a self-employed person within the meaning of Article 1(a)(ii) of the Regulation.

C. GERMANY

If the competent institution for granting family benefits in accordance with Chapter 7 of Title III of the Regulation is a German institution, then within the meaning of Article 1(a)(ii) of the Regulation:

(a)   'employed person' means compulsorily insured against unemployment or any person who, as a result of such insurance, obtains cash benefits under sickness insurance or comparable benefits;

(b)   'self-employed person' means any person pursuing self-employment which is bound:

— to join, or pay contributions in respect of, an old-age insurance within a scheme for self-employed persons, or

— to join a scheme within the framework of compulsory pension insurance.

D. SPAIN

Does not apply.

E. FRANCE

If a French institution is the competent institution for the grant of family benefits in accordance with Title III, Chapter 7 of the Regulation:

1.   'employed person' within the meaning of Article 1(a)(ii) of the Regulation shall be deemed to mean any person who is compulsorily insured under the social security scheme in accordance with Article L 311-2 of the Social Security Code and who fulfils the minimum conditions regarding work or remuneration provided for in Article L 313-1 of the Social Security Code in order to benefit from cash benefits under sickness insurance, maternity and invalidity cover or the person who benefits from these cash benefits;

2.   'self-employed person' within the meaning of Article 1(a)(ii) of the Regulation shall be deemed to mean any person who performs a self-employed activity and who is required to take out insurance and to pay old-age benefit contributions to a self-employed persons' scheme.

F. GREECE

1.   Persons insured under the OGA scheme who pursue exclusively activities as employed persons or who are or have been subject to the legislation of another Member State and who consequently are or have been 'employed persons within the meaning of Article 1(a) of the Regulation are considered as employed persons within the meaning of Article 1(a)(iii) of the Regulation.

2.   For the purposes of granting the national family allowances, persons referred to in Article 1(a)(i) and (iii) of the Regulation are considered as employed persons within the meaning of Article 1(a)(ii) of the Regulation.

G.   IRELAND

1.   Any person who is compulsorily or voluntarily insured pursuant to the provisions of Sections 5 and 37 of the Social Welfare (Consolidation) Act 1981 shall be considered an employed person within the meaning of Article 1(a)(ii) of the Regulation.

2.   Any person who is pursuing a professional or trade activity without a contract of employment or who has retired from such activity shall be considered a self-employed person within the meaning of Article 1(a)(ii) of the Regulation. As regards sickness benefits in kind, the person concerned must also be entitled to such benefits under Section 45 or 46 of the Health Act 1970.

H.   ITALY
Does not apply.

I.   LUXEMBOURG
Does not apply.

J.   NETHERLANDS
Any person pursuing an activity or occupation without a contract of employment shall be considered a self-employed person within the meaning of Article 1(a)(ii) of the Regulation.

K.   AUSTRIA
Does not apply.

L.   PORTUGAL
Does not apply.

M.   FINLAND
Any person who is an employed or self-employed person within the meaning of the legislation on the Employment Pensions Scheme shall be considered respectively as employed or self-employed within the meaning of Article 1(a)(ii) of the Regulation.

N.   SWEDEN
Any person who is an employed or self-employed person within the meaning of the legislation on work injury insurance shall be considered respectively as employed or self-employed within the meaning of Article 1(a)(ii) of the Regulation.

O.   UNITED KINGDOM
Any person who is an 'employed earner' or a 'self-employed earner' within the meaning of the legislation of Great Britain or of the legislation of Northern Ireland shall be regarded respectively as an employed person or a self-employed person within the meaning of Article 1(a)(ii) of the Regulation. Any person in respect of whom contributions are payable as an 'employed person' or a 'self-employed person' in accordance with the legislation of Gibraltar shall be regarded respectively as an employed person or a self-employed person within the meaning of Article 1(a)(ii) of the Regulation.

II. Members of the family   (Second sentence of Article 1(f) of the Regulation)

A. BELGIUM
Does not apply.

B. DENMARK
For the purpose of determining a right to sickness or maternity benefits in kind existing pursuant to Articles 22(1)(a) and 31 of the Regulation, the expression 'member of the family' shall mean:

1. The spouse of an employed person, a self-employed person or other entitled person under the terms of the Regulation, in so far as they are not themselves entitled persons under the terms of the Regulation; or

2. a child under 18 years of age in the care of someone who is an entitled person under the terms of the Regulation.

C. GERMANY
Does not apply.

D. SPAIN
Does not apply.

E. FRANCE
The term 'member of the family' means any person mentioned in Article L 512-3 of the Social Security Code.

F. GREECE
Does not apply.

G. IRELAND
For the purpose of determining entitlement to benefits in kind pursuant to Articles 22(1)(a) and 31 of the Regulation, 'member of the family' means any person regarded as a dependant of the employed or self-employed person for the purposes of the Health Acts 1947 to 1970.

H. ITALY
Does not apply.

I. LUXEMBOURG
Does not apply.

J. NETHERLANDS
Does not apply.

K. AUSTRIA
Does not apply.

L. PORTUGAL
Does not apply.

M. FINLAND
For the purpose of determining entitlement to benefits in kind pursuant to the provisions of chapter 1 of Title III of the Regulation, 'member of the family' means a spouse or a child as defined by the Sickness Insurance Act.

N.   SWEDEN
For the purpose of determining entitlement to benefits in kind pursuant to the
provisions of chapter 1 of Title III of the Regulation, 'member of the family'
means a spouse or a child under the age of 18.

O.   UNITED KINGDOM
For the purpose of determining entitlement to benefits in kind the term
'member of the family' means:
   1.   As regards the legislation of Great Britain and Northern Ireland:
  (1)   a spouse provided that:
   (a)   that person, whether employed or self-employed, or another person
entitled under the Regulation, is:
    (i)   residing with the spouse; or
    (ii)   contributing to the maintenance of the spouse; and
  (b)   the spouse does not:
    (i)   have earnings as an employed or self-employed person or income
as a person entitled under the Regulation; or
    (ii)   receive a social security benefit or pension based on the spouse's
own insurance;
  (2)   a person having care of a child, provided that:
   (a)   the employed or self-employed person or person entitled under the
Regulation is:
    (i)   living together with the person as though husband and wife; or
    (ii)   contributing to the maintenance of the person; and
  (b)   the person does not:
    (i)   have earnings as an employed or self-employed worker or income
as a person entitled under the Regulation: or
    (ii)   receive a social security benefit or pension based on the person's
own insurance:
  (3)   a child in respect of whom that person, the employed or self-employed
person, or another person entitled under the Regulation is or could be paid
child-benefit.
   2.   As regards the legislation of Gibraltar:
any person regarded as dependent within the meaning of the Group practice
Scheme Ordinance, 1973.

ANNEX II (A) (8) (10) (15)
(Article 1 (j) and (u) of the Regulation)

**I.   Special schemes for self-employed persons excluded from the
scope of the Regulation pursuant to the fourth sub-paragraph of Article
1 (j)**

A.   BELGIUM
Does not apply.

B.   DENMARK
Does not apply.

C.   GERMANY
Insurance and welfare institutions (Versicherungs- und Versorgungswerke)
for doctors, dentists, veterinary surgeons, dispensing chemists, barristers
and counsel, patent agents (Patentanwaelte), notaries public, auditors

(Wirtschaftspruefer), tax consultants and advisers (Steuerbevollmaechtigte), sea pilots (Seelotsen) and architects, set up pursuant to legislation of the Laender, and other insurance and welfare institutions, in particular welfare (Fuersorgeeinrichtungen) and the system for extending fee-sharing (erweiterte Honorarverteilung).

D. SPAIN

1. Free welfare systems, which complement or supplement the social security systems, administered by institutions governed by the General Law on Social Security of 6 December 1941 and its Regulation of 26 May 1943:

(a) either with regard to benefits which complement or supplement those of social security, or

(b) with regard to mutual insurance associations for whose integration into the social security system there is no provision under point 7 of the sixth transitional provision of the General Law on Social Security of 30 May 1974, and which consequently are not substituted for the institutions of the compulsory social security system.

2. Welfare system and/or with the character of social assistance or a charity, managed by institutions not subject to the General Law on Social Security or to the Law of 6 December 1941.

E. FRANCE

1. Self-employed persons outside the agricultural sphere:

(a) The supplementary old-age insurance schemes and the invalidity and death insurance schemes for self-employed persons, such as are mentioned in Articles L 658, L 659, L 663-11, L 663-12, L 682 and L 683-1 of the Social Security Code.

(b) The additional benefits referred to in Article 9 of Law No. 66.509 of 12 July 1966.

2. Self-employed persons in agriculture: The types of insurance set out in Articles 1049 and 1234.19 of the Rural Code, concerning, on the one hand, sickness, maternity and old-age, on the other, accidents at work and occupational diseases of self-employed persons in agriculture.

F. GREECE
Does not apply.

G. IRELAND
Does not apply.

H. ITALY
Does not apply.

I. LUXEMBOURG
Does not apply.

J. NETHERLANDS
Does not apply.

K. AUSTRIA
Insurance and welfare institutions (Versicherungs- und Versorgungswerke), 'welfare in particular funds' (Fürsorgeeinrichtungen) and the system for extending fee-sharing (erweiterte Honarverteilung) for doctors, veterinary surgeons, barristers and counsel, and civil engineers (Ziviltechniker).

L. PORTUGAL
Does not apply.

M. FINLAND
Does not apply.

N. SWEDEN
Does not apply.

O. UNITED KINGDOM
Does not apply.

II. Special childbirth or adoption allowances excluded from the scope of the Regulation under the terms of Article 1(u)(i)[1]

A. BELGIUM
  (a) Childbirth allowance
  (b) Adoption premium

B. DENMARK
None.

C. GERMANY
None.

D. SPAIN
None.

E. FRANCE
  (a) The allowance for young children up to the age of three months.
  (b) Adoption allowance

F. GREECE
None.

G. IRELAND
None.

H. ITALY
None.

I. LUXEMBOURG
  (a) antenatal allowance;
  (b) childbirth allowance.

J. NETHERLANDS
None.

K. AUSTRIA
The general part of childbirth allowance.

L. PORTUGAL
None.

M. FINLAND
The Maternity package or the maternity lump-sum grant pursuant to the Maternity Grant Act.

N. SWEDEN
None.

O. UNITED KINGDOM
None.

Note
[1]Amended by Regulation 3096/95 of 22nd December 1995 (OJ 1995 L335/10).

III. Special non-contributory benefits within the meaning of Article 4(2b) which do not fall within the scope of the Regulation

A. BELGIUM
None.

B. DENMARK
None.

C. GERMANY
(a) Benefits granted under Laender legislation for the disabled, and in particular for the blind.

(b) The social supplement under the Law of 28 June 1990 on the alignment of pensions.

D. SPAIN
None.

E. FRANCE
None.

F. GREECE
None.

G. IRELAND
None.

H. ITALY
None.

I. LUXEMBOURG
None.

J. NETHERLANDS
None.

K. AUSTRIA
Benefits granted under Bundesländer legislation for disabled persons in the need of care.

L. PORTUGAL
None.

M. FINLAND
None.

N. SWEDEN
None.

O. UNITED KINGDOM
None.

ANNEX IIa (10)(12)(13)(14)(15)
(Article 10a of the Regulation)

A. BELGIUM
(a) Allowances for disabled persons (Law of 27 February 1987).
(b) Guaranteed income for elderly persons (Law of 1 April 1969).
(c) Guaranteed family benefits (Law of 20 July 1971).

B. DENMARK[1]
Accommodation expenses for pensioners (Law on individual accommodation assistance, consolidated by Law No. 204 of 29 March 1995).

Note
[1]Amended by Regulation 3096/95 of 22nd December 1995 (OJ 1995 L335/10).

C. GERMANY
None.

D. SPAIN
(a) Benefits under the Law on the social integration of disabled persons (Law No. 13/82 of 7 April 1982).
(b) Cash benefits to assist the elderly and invalids unable to work (Royal Decree No. 2620/81 of 24 July 1984).
(c) Non-contributory disablement and retirement pensions and dependent child benefits as provided for in Articles 132(1), 136a, 137a, 138a, 154a, 155a, 156a, 167, 168(2), 169 and 170 of the General Law on Social Security, as amended by Law No 26/90 of 20 December 1990 establishing non-contributory social security benefits.

E. FRANCE
(a) Supplementary allowance from the National Solidarity Fund (Law of 30 June 1956).
(b) Disabled adults' allowance (Law of 30 June 1975).
(c) The special allowance (Law of 10 July 1952).

F. GREECE
(a) Special benefits for elderly persons (Law 1296/82).
(b) Allowance for children of non-working mothers whose husbands have been called up for military service (Law 1483/84, Article 23(1)).
(c) Allowance for children of non-working mothers whose husbands are in prison (Law 1483/84, Article 23(2)).
(d) Allowance for persons suffering from congenital hemolytic anaemia (Decree-law 321/69; common ministerial order G4a/F.222/oik.2204).
(e) Allowance for the deaf and dumb (Exceptional law 421/37; common ministerial order G4b/F.422/oik.2205).
(f) Allowance for seriously disabled persons (Decree-law 162/73; common ministerial order G4a/F.225//oik.161).
(g) Allowance for spasmophiliacs (Decree-law 162/72; common ministerial order G4a/F.224/oik.2207).
(h) Allowance for persons suffering from a serious mental disability (Decree-law 162/73; common ministerial order G4b/423/oik.2208).
(i) Allowance for the blind (Law 958/79; common ministerial order G4b/F.421/oik.2209).

G. IRELAND

(a) Unemployment assistance (Social Welfare (Consolidation) Act 1981, Part II32519I, Chapter 2).

(b) Old age and blind pensions (non-contributory)(Social Welfare (Consolidation) Act 1981, Part III, Chapter 3).

(c) Widows' and orphans' pensions (non-contributory)(Social Welfare (Consolidation) Act 1981, Part III, Chapter 4).

(d) Lone parent's allowance (Social Welfare Act 1990, Part III).

(e) Carer's allowance (Social Welfare Act 1990, Part IV).

(f) Family income supplement (Social Welfare Act 1984, Part III).

(g) Disabled person's maintenance allowance (Health Act 1970, Section 69).

(h) Mobility allowance (Health Act 1970, Section 61).

(i) Infectious diseases maintenance allowance (Health Act 1947, Sections 5 and 44(5)).

(j) Domiciliary care allowance (Health Act 1970, Section 61).

(k) Blind welfare allowance (Blind Persons Act 1920, Chapter 49).

(l) Disabled person's rehabilitation allowance (Health Act 1970, Sections 68, 69 and 72).

H. ITALY

(a) Social pensions for persons without means (Law No. 153 of 30 April 1969).

(b) Pensions and allowances for the civilian disabled or invalids (Laws No. 118 of 30 March 1974, No. 18 of 11 February 1980 and No. 508 of 23 November 1988).

(c) Pensions and allowances for the deaf and dumb (Laws No. 381 of 26 May 1970 and No. 508 of 23 November 1988).

(d) Pensions and allowances for the civilian blind (Laws No. 382 of 27 May 1970 and No. 508 of 23 November 1988).

(e) Benefits supplementing the minimum pension (Laws No. 638 of 11 November 1983 and No. 407 of 29 December 1990).

(f) Benefits supplementing disability allowances (Law No. 222 of 12 June 1984).

(g) Monthly allowances for continuous personal assistance for those receiving pensions for incapacity for work (Law No. 222 of 12 June 1984).

I. LUXEMBOURG

(a) Compensatory cost of living allowance (Law of 13 June 1975).

(b) Special severe disablement allowance (Law of 16 April 1979).

(c) Maternity allowance (Law of 30 April 1980).

J. NETHERLANDS
None.

K. AUSTRIA

(a) Compensatory supplement (Federal Act of 9 September 1955 on General Social Insurance — ASVG, Federal Act of 11 October 1978 on Social Insurance For Persons engaged in Trade and Commerce — GSVG and Federal Act of 11 October 1978 on Social Insurance for Farmers — BSVG).

(b) Care allowance (Pflegegeld) under the Austrian Federal Care Allowance Act (Bundespflegegeldgesetz) with the exception of care allowance granted by accident insurance institutions where the handicap is caused by an accident at work of occupational disease.

L. PORTUGAL

(a) Non-contributory family allowances (Decree-Law No. 160/80 of 27 May 1980).

(b) Nursing mother's allowance (Decree-Law No. 160/80 of 27 May 1980).

(c) Supplementary allowance for disabled children and young people (Decree-Law No. 160/80 of 27 May 1980).

(d) Allowance for attendance at special schools (Decree-Law No. 160/80 of 27 May 1980).

(e) Non-contributory orphan's pension (Decree-Law No. 160/80 of 27 May 1980).

(f) Non-contributory invalidity pension (Decree-Law No. 464/80 of 13 October 1980).

(g) Non-contributory old-age pension (Decree-Law No. 464/80 of 13 October 1980).

(h) Supplementary severe invalidity pension (Decree-Law No. 160/80 of 27 May 1980).

(i) Non-contributory widow's pension (Regulatory Decree No. 52/81 of 11 November 1981).

M. FINLAND

(a) Child-care allowance (Child-care Allowances Act, 444/69).

(b) Disability allowance (Disability Allowance Act, 124/88).

(c) Housing allowance for pensioners (Act concerning Housing Allowance for Pensioners, 591/78).

(d) Basic employment allowance (Unemployment Allowance Act, 602/84) in cases where a person does not fulfil the corresponding conditions for the earning-related unemployment allowance.

N. SWEDEN

(a) Municipal Housing Supplements to basic pensions (LAW 1962: 392, reprinted 1976: 1014).

(b) Handicap allowances which are not paid to a person receiving a pension (Law 1962: 381 reprinted 1982: 120).

(c) Care allowance for handicapped children (Law 1962: 381 reprinted 1982: 120).

O. UNITED KINGDOM

(a) Mobility allowance (Social Security Act 1975 of 20 March 1975, Section 37A, and Social Security (Northern Ireland) Act 1975 of 20 March 1975, Section 37A).

(b) Invalid care allowance (Social Security Act 1975 of 20 March 1975, Section 37, and Social Security (Northern Ireland) Act 1975 of 20 March 1975, Section 37).

(c) Family credit (Social Security Act 1986 of 25 July 1986, Sections 20 to 22, and Social Security (Northern Ireland) Order 1986 of 5 November 1986, Articles 21 to 23).

(d) Attendance allowance (Social Security Act 1975 of 20 March 1975, Section 35, and Social Security (Northern Ireland) Act 1975 of 20 March 1975, Section 35).

(e)   Income support (Social Security Act 1986 of 25 July 1986, Sections 20 to 22 and Section 23, and Social Security (Northern Ireland) Order 1986 of 5 November 1986, Articles 21 to 28).

(f)   Disability living allowance (Disability Living Allowance and Disability Working Allowance Act 1991 of 27 June 1991, Section 1 and Disability Living Allowance and Disability Working Allowance (Northern Ireland) Order 1991 of 24 July 1991, Article 3).

(g)   Disability working allowance (Disability Living Allowance and Disability Working Allowance Act 1991 of 27 June 1991, Section 6, and Disability Living Allowance and Disability Working Allowance (Northern Ireland) Order 1991 of 24 July 1991, Article 8).

(h)   Income based allowances for jobseekers (Jobseekers Act 1995, 28 June 1995, Sections 1(2)(d)(ii) and 3, and Jobseekers (Northern Ireland) Order 1995, 18 October 1995, Articles 3(2)(d)(ii) and 5.)

Note
[1]Amended by Regulation 3096/95 of 22nd December 1995 (OJ 1995 L335/10).

ANNEX III(A)(6)(7)(12)(14)(15)
PROVISIONS OF SOCIAL SECURITY CONVENTIONS REMAINING APPLICABLE NOTWITHSTANDING ARTICLE 6 OF THE REGULATION — PROVISIONS OF SOCIAL SECURITY CONVENTIONS WHICH DO NOT APPLY TO ALL PERSONS TO WHOM THE REGULATION APPLIES
(Articles 7(2)(c) and 3(3) of the Regulation)

General comments
1.   In so far as the provisions contained in this Annex provide for references to the provisions of other conventions, those references shall be replaced by references to the corresponding provisions of this Regulation, unless the provisions of the conventions in question are themselves contained in this Annex.
2.   The termination clause provided for in a social security convention, some of whose provisions are contained in this Annex, shall continue to apply as regards those provisions.

A.   Provisions of social security conventions remaining applicable notwithstanding Article 6 of the Regulation (Article 7(2)(c) of the Regulation)

1.   BELGIUM-DENMARK
No convention.
2.   BELGIUM-GERMANY
(a)   Articles 3 and 43 of the Final Protocol of 7 December 1957 to the General Convention of that date, as in the Complementary Protocol of 10 November 1960.
(b)   Complementary Agreement No. 3 of 7 December 1957 to the General Convention of the same date, as in the Complementary Protocol of 10 November 1960 (payment of pensions for the period preceding the entry into force of the General Convention).
3.   BELGIUM-SPAIN
None.

4. BELGIUM-FRANCE

(a) Articles 13, 16 and 23 of the Complementary Agreement of 17 January 1948 to the General Convention of that date (workers in mines and similar undertakings).

(b) The exchange of letters of 27 February 1953 (application of Article 4(2) of the General Convention of 17 January 1948).

(c) The exchange of letters of 29 July 1953 on allowances to elderly employed persons.

5. BELGIUM-GREECE

Articles 15(2), 35(2) and 37 of the General Convention of 1 April 1958.

6. BELGIUM-IRELAND

No convention.

7. BELGIUM-ITALY

Article 29 of the Convention of 30 April 1948.

8. BELGIUM-LUXEMBOURG

(a) Articles 3, 4, 5, 6 and 7 of the Convention of 16 November 1959, as in the Convention of 12 February 1964 (frontier workers).

(b) The exchange of letters of 10 and 12 July 1968 concerning self-employed persons.

9. BELGIUM-NETHERLANDS

Articles 2 and 4 of the Agreement of 27 October 1971 (Overseas social insurance).

10. BELGIUM-AUSTRIA

(a) Article 4 of the Convention on social security of 4 April 1977 as regards persons residing in a third State.

(b) Point III of the Final Protocol to the said Convention as regards persons residing in a third State.

11. BELGIUM-PORTUGAL

Articles 1 and 5 of the Convention of 13 January 1965 (social security for employees in the Belgian Congo and Rwanda-Urundi), in the wording contained in the Agreement concluded by an exchange of letters dated 18 June 1982.

12. BELGIUM-FINLAND

No Convention.

13. BELGIUM-SWEDEN

No Convention.

14. BELGIUM-UNITED KINGDOM

None.

15. DENMARK-GERMANY

(a) Point 15 of the Final Protocol to the Convention on social insurances of 14 August 1953.

(b) The Complementary Agreement of 14 August 1953 to the Convention mentioned above.

16. DENMARK-SPAIN

No convention.

17. DENMARK-FRANCE

None.

18. DENMARK-GREECE

No convention.

19. DENMARK-IRELAND

No convention.

20. DENMARK-ITALY
No convention.
21. DENMARK-LUXEMBOURG
No convention.
22. DENMARK-NETHERLANDS
No convention.
23. DENMARK-AUSTRIA
   (a) Article 4 of the Convention on social security of 16 June 1987 as regards persons residing in a third State.
   (b) Point I of the Final Protocol to the said Convention as regards persons residing in a third State.
24. DENMARK-PORTUGAL
No Convention.
25. DENMARK-FINLAND
Article 10 of the Nordic Convention on social security of 15 June 1992.
26. DENMARK-SWEDEN
Article 10 of the Nordic Convention on social security of 15 June 1992.
27. DENMARK-UNITED KINGDOM
None.
28. GERMANY-SPAIN
Articles 4(1) and 45(2) of the Social Security Convention of 4 December 1973.
29. GERMANY-FRANCE
   (a) Articles 11(1), 16 (second paragraph) and 19 of the General Convention of 10 July 1950.
   (b) Article 9 of Complementary Agreement No. 1 of 10 July 1950 to the General Convention of the same date (workers in mines and similar undertakings).
   (c) Complementary Agreement No. 4 of 10 July 1950 to the General Convention of the same date, as in added Section No. 2 of 18 June 1955.
   (d) Titles I and III of added Section No. 2 of 18 June 1955.
   (e) Points 6, 7 and 8 of the General Protocol of 10 July 1950 to the General Convention of the same date.
   (f) Titles II, III and IV of the Agreement of 20 December 1963 (social security in the Saar).
30. GERMANY-GREECE
   (a) Article 5(2) of the General Convention of 25 April 1961.
   (b) Articles 8(1), (2)(b) and (3), 9 to 11 and Chapters I and IV, in so far as they concern these Articles, of the Convention on unemployment insurance of 31 May 1961, together with the note in the minutes of 14 June 1980.
   (c) Protocol of 7 October 1991 in conjunction with the Agreement of 6 July 1984 between the Government of the German Democratic Republic and the Government of the Hellenic republic on the settlement of problems relating to pensions.
31. GERMANY-IRELAND
No convention.
32. GERMANY-ITALY
   (a) Articles 3(2), 23(2), 26 and 36(3) of the Convention of 5 May 1953 (social insurance).
   (b) The Complementary Agreement of 12 May 1953 to the Convention of 5 May 1953 (payment of pensions for the period preceding the entry into force of the Convention).

33. GERMANY-LUXEMBOURG

Articles 4, 5, 6 and 7 of the Treaty of 11 July 1959 (Ausgleichsvertrag)(settlement of the dispute between Germany and Luxembourg).

34. GERMANY-NETHERLANDS

(a) Article 3(2) of the Convention of 29 March 1951.

(b) Articles 2 and 3 of Complementary Agreement No 4 of 21 December 1956 to the Convention of 29 March 1951 (settlement of rights acquired under the German social insurance scheme by Dutch workers between 13 May 1940 and 1 September 1945).

35. GERMANY-AUSTRIA

(a) Article 41 of the Convention on social security of 22 December 1966 as amended by Complementary Conventions No 1 of 10 April 1969, No 2 of 20 March 1974 and No 3 of 29 August 1980.

(b) Paragraphs 3(c), 3(d), 17, 20(a) and 21 of the Final Protocol to the said Convention.

(c) Article 3 of the said Convention as regards persons residing in a third State.

(d) Paragraph 3(g) of the Final Protocol to the said Convention as regards persons residing in a third State.

(e) Article 4(1) of the Convention as regards the German legislation, under which accidents (and occupational diseases) occuring outside the territory of the Federal Republic of Germany, and periods completed outside that territory, do not give rise to payment of benefits or only give rise to payment of benefits, under certain conditions, when those entitled to the reside outside the territory of the Federal Republic of Germany, in cases in which:

(i) the benefit has already been paid or is payable on 1 January 1994;

(ii) the beneficiary has established his habitual residence in Austria before 1 January 1994 and the payment of pensions due under the pension and accident insurance begins prior to 31 December 1994; this shall also apply to periods during which another pension, including a survivor's pension was collected, replacing the initial one, where the periods of collection follow each other without interruption.

(f) Paragraph 19(b) of the Final Protocol to the said Convention. In applying Number 3(c) of this provision the amount taken into account by the competent institution shall not exceed the amount, which is due in respect of the corresponding periods to be remunerated by this institution.

(g) Article 2 of Complementary Convention No. 1 of 10 April 1969 to the said Convention.

(h) Article 1(5) and 8 of the said Convention on unemployment insurance of 19 July 1978.

(i) Paragraph 10 of the Final Protocol to the said Convention.

36. GERMANY-PORTUGAL

Article 5(2) of the Convention of 6 November 1964.

37. GERMANY-FINLAND

(a) Article 4 of the Convention on social security of 23 April 1979.

(b) Point 9(a) of the Final Protocol to the said Convention.

38. GERMANY-SWEDEN

(a) Article 4(2) of the Convention on social security of 27 February 1976.

(b) Point 8(a) of the Final Protocol of the said Convention.

39.   GERMANY-UNITED KINGDOM

(a)   Articles 3(1) and (6) and 7(2) to (6) of the Convention on social security of 20 April 1960.

(b)   Articles 2 to 7 of the Final Protocol to the Convention on social security of 20 April 1960.

(c)   Articles 2(5) and 5(2) to (6) of the Convention on unemployment insurance of 20 April 1960.

40.   SPAIN-FRANCE

None.

41.   SPAIN-GREECE

No convention.

42.   SPAIN-IRELAND

No convention.

43.   SPAIN-ITALY

Articles 5, 18(1)(c) and 23 of the Convention on social security of 30 October 1979.

44.   SPAIN-LUXEMBOURG

(a)   Article 5(2) of the Convention of 8 May 1969.

(b)   Article 1 of the Administrative Arrangement of 27 June 1975 for the application of the Convention of 8 May 1969 to self-employed persons.

45.   SPAIN-NETHERLANDS

Article 23(2) of the Convention on social security of 5 February 1974.

46.   SPAIN-AUSTRIA

(a)   Article 4 of the Convention on social security of 6 November 1981 as regards persons residing in a third State.

(b)   Point II of the Final Protocol to the said Convention as regards persons residing in a third State.

47.   SPAIN-PORTUGAL

Articles 4(2), 16(2) and 22 of the General Convention of 11 June 1969.

48.   SPAIN-FINLAND

Article 5(2) of the Convention on social security of 19 December 1985.

49.   SPAIN-SWEDEN.

Articles 5(2) and 16 of the Convention on social security of 4 February 1983.

50.   SPAIN-UNITED KINGDOM

None.

51.   FRANCE-GREECE

Articles 16 (fourth subparagraph) and 30 of the General Convention of 19 April 1958.

52.   FRANCE-IRELAND

No convention.

53.   FRANCE-ITALY

(a)   Articles 20 and 24 of the General Convention of 31 March 1948.

(b)   The exchange of letters of 3 March 1956 (sickness benefits for seasonal workers employed in agriculture).

54.   FRANCE-LUXEMBOURG

Articles 11 and 14 of the Complementary Agreement of 12 November 1949 to the General Convention of the same date (workers in mines and similar undertakings).

55.   FRANCE-NETHERLANDS

Article 11 of the Complementary Agreement of 1 June 1954 to the General Convention of 7 January 1950 (workers in mines and similar undertakings).

56.   FRANCE-AUSTRIA
None.

57.   FRANCE-PORTUGAL
None.

58.   FRANCE-FINLAND
None.

59.   FRANCE-SWEDEN
None.

60.   FRANCE-UNITED KINGDOM
The exchange of letters of 27 and 30 July 1970 concerning the position with regard to social security of United Kingdom teachers temporarily pursuing their profession in France by virtue of the Cultural Convention of 2 March 1948.

61.   GREECE-IRELAND
No convention.

62.   GREECE-ITALY
No convention.

63.   GREECE-LUXEMBOURG
No convention.

64.   GREECE-NETHERLANDS
Article 4(2) of the General Convention of 13 September 1966.

65.   GREECE-AUSTRIA
      (a)   Article 4 of the Convention on social security of 14 December 1979 as amended by the Complementary Convention of 21 May 1986 as regards persons residing in a third State.
      (b)   Point II of the Final Protocol to the said Convention as regards persons residing in a third State.

66.   GREECE-PORTUGAL
No convention.

67.   GREECE-FINLAND
Articles 5(2) and 21 of the Convention on social security of 21 March 1988.

68.   GREECE-SWEDEN
Articles 5(2) and 23 of the Convention on social security of 5 May 1978 as amended by the Complementary Convention of 14 September 1984.

69.   GREECE-UNITED KINGDOM
No convention.

70.   IRELAND-ITALY
No convention.

71.   IRELAND-LUXEMBOURG
No convention.

72.   IRELAND-NETHERLANDS
No convention.

73.   IRELAND-AUSTRIA
Article 4 of the Convention on social security of 30 September 1988 as regards persons residing in a third State.

74.   IRELAND-PORTUGAL
No convention.

75.   IRELAND-FINLAND
No Convention.

76.   IRELAND-SWEDEN
No Convention

77.   IRELAND-UNITED KINGDOM
Article 8 of the Agreement of 14 September 1971 on social security.
78.   ITALY-LUXEMBOURG
Articles 18(2) and 24 of the General Convention of 29 May 1951.
79.   ITALY-NETHERLANDS
Article 21(2) of the General Convention of 28 October 1952.
80.   ITALY-AUSTRIA
     (a)   Articles 5(3) and 9(2) of the Convention on social security of 21 January 1981.
     (b)   Article 4 of the said Convention and paragraph 2 of the Final Protocol to the said Convention as regards persons residing in a third State.
81.   ITALY-PORTUGAL
No convention.
82.   ITALY-FINLAND
No Convention.
83.   ITALY-SWEDEN
Article 20 of the Convention on social security of 25 September 1979.
84.   ITALY-UNITED KINGDOM
None.
85.   LUXEMBOURG-NETHERLANDS
None.
86.   LUXEMBOURG-AUSTRIA
     (a)   Article 5(2) of the Convention on social security of 21 December 1971 as amended by the Complementary Conventions No. 1 of 16 May 1973 and No. 2 of 9 October 1978.
     (b)   Article 3(2) of the Convention as regards persons residing in a third State.
     (c)   Point III of the Final Protocol to the said Convention as regards persons residing in a third State.
87.   LUXEMBOURG-PORTUGAL
Article 3(2) of the Convention of 12 February 1965.
88.   LUXEMBOURG-FINLAND
Article 5(2) of the Convention on social security of 15 September 1988.
89.   LUXEMBOURG-SWEDEN
     (a)   Articles 4 and 29(1) of the Convention on social security of 21 February 1985 as regards persons residing in a third State.
     (b)   Article 30 of the said Convention.
90.   LUXEMBOURG-UNITED KINGDOM
None.
91.   LUXEMBOURG-AUSTRIA
     (a)   Article 3 of the Convention on social security of 7 March 1974 as amended by the Complementary Convention of 5 November 1980 as regards persons residing in a third State.
     (b)   Point II of the Final Protocol to the said Convention as regards persons residing in a third State.
92.   NETHERLANDS-PORTUGAL
Articles 5(2) and 31 of the Convention of 18 July 1979.
93.   NETHERLANDS-FINLAND
No Convention

94.   NETHERLANDS-SWEDEN
Articles 4 and 24(3) of the Convention on social security of 2 July 1976 as regards persons residing in a third State.

95.   NETHERLANDS-UNITED KINGDOM
None.

96.   AUSTRIA-PORTUGAL
None.

97.   AUSTRIA-FINLAND
   (a)   Article 4 of the Convention on social security of 11 December 1985 as amended by the Complementary Convention of 9 March 1993 as regards persons residing in a third State.

98.   AUSTRIA-SWEDEN
   (a)   Articles 4 and 24(1) of the Convention on social security of 11 November 1975 as amended by the Complementary Convention of 21 October 1982 as regards persons residing in a third State.
   (b)   Point II of the Final Protocol to the said Convention as regards persons residing in a third State.

99.   AUSTRIA-UNITED KINGDOM
   (a)   Article 3 of the Convention on social security of 22 July 1980 as amended by the Complementary Conventions No 1 of 9 December 1985 and No 2 of 13 October 1992 as regards persons residing in a third State.
   (b)   Protocol concerning benefits in kind to the said Convention with the exception of Article 2(3) as regards persons who cannot claim treatment under Chaper 1 of Title III of the Regulation.

100.   PORTUGAL-FINLAND
None.

101.   PORTUGAL-SWEDEN
Article 6 of the Convention on social security of 25 October 1978.

102.   PORTUGAL-UNITED KINGDOM
   (a)   Article 2(1) of the Protocol on medical treatment of 15 November 1978.
   (b)   As regards Portuguese employed persons, and for the period from 22 October 1987 to the end of the transitional period provided for in Article 220(1) of the Act relating to the conditions of accession of Spain and Portugal: Article 26 of the Social Security Convention of 15 November 1978, as amended by the Exchange of Letters of 28 September 1987.

103.   FINLAND-SWEDEN.
Article 10 of the Nordic Convention on social security of 15 June 1992.

104.   FINLAND-UNITED KINGDOM
None.

105.   SWEDEN-UNITED KINGDOM
Article 4(3) of the Convention on social security of 29 June 1987.

B.   Provisions of Conventions which do not apply to all persons to whom the Regulation applies (Article 3(3) of the Regulation)

1.   BELGIUM-DENMARK
No convention.

2.   ...

3.   BELGIUM-SPAIN
None.

4.   BELGIUM-FRANCE

  (a)   The exchange of letters of 29 July 1953 on allowances to elderly employed persons.

  (b)   The exchange of letters of 27 February 1953 (application of Article 4(2) of the General Convention of 17 January 1948).

5.   BELGIUM-GREECE

None.

6.   BELGIUM-IRELAND

None.

7.   BELGIUM-ITALY

None.

8.   BELGIUM-LUXEMBOURG

Articles 2 and 4 of the Agreement on 27 October 1971 (overseas social security).

9.   BELGIUM-NETHERLANDS

Articles 2 and 4 of the Agreement of 4 February 1969 (overseas occupation).

10.   BELGIUM-AUSTRIA

  (a)   Article 4 of the Convention on social security of 4 April 1977 as regards persons residing in a third State.

  (b)   Point III of the Final Protocol to the said Convention as regards persons residing in a third State.

11.   BELGIUM-PORTUGAL

Articles 1 and 5 of the Convention of 13 January 1965 (social security for employees of the Belgian Congo and Rwanda-Urundi) in the wording that appears in the Agreement concluded by exchange of letters dated 18 June 1982.

12.   BELGIUM-FINLAND

No Convention.

13.   BELGIUM-SWEDEN

No Convention.

14.   BELGIUM-UNITED KINGDOM

None.

15.   DENMARK-GERMANY

  (a)   Point 15 of the Final Protocol to the Convention on social insurances of 14 August 1953.

  (b)   The Complementary Agreement of 14 August 1953 to the Convention mentioned above.

16.   DENMARK-SPAIN

No convention.

17.   DENMARK-FRANCE

None.

18.   DENMARK-GREECE

No convention.

19.   DENMARK-IRELAND

No convention.

20.   DENMARK-ITALY

No convention.

21.   DENMARK-LUXEMBOURG

No convention.

22.   DENMARK-NETHERLANDS

No convention.

23.   DENMARK-AUSTRIA
   (a)   Article 4 of the Convention on social security of 16 June 1987 as regards persons residing in a third State.
   (b)   Point I of the Final Protocol to the said Convention as regards persons residing in a third State.

24.   DENMARK-PORTUGAL
No convention.

25.   DENMARK-FINLAND
No Convention.

26.   DENMARK-SWEDEN
None.

27.   DENMARK-UNITED KINGDOM
None.

28.   GERMANY-SPAIN
Articles 4(1) and 45(2) of the Social Security Convention of 4 December 1973.

29.   GERMANY-FRANCE
   (a)   Articles 16 (second paragraph) and 19 of the General Convention of 10 July 1950.
   (b)   Complementary Agreement No. 4 of 10 July 1950 to the General Convention of the same date, as in added Section No. 2 of 18 June 1955.
   (c)   Titles I and III of added Section No. 2 of 18 June 1955.
   (d)   Points 6, 7 and 8 of the General Protocol of 10 July 1950 to the General Convention of the same date.
   (e)   Titles II, III and IV of the Agreement of 20 December 1963 (social security in the Saar).

30.   GERMANY-GREECE
Protocol of 7 October 1991 in conjunction with the Agreement of 6 July 1984 between the Government of the German Democratic Republic and the Government of the Hellenic Republic on the settlement of problems relating to pensions.

31.   GERMANY-IRELAND
No convention.

32.   GERMANY-ITALY
   (a)   Articles 3(2), 26 of the Convention of 5 May 1953 (social insurance).
   (b)   The Complementary Agreement of 12 May 1953 to the Convention of 5 May 1953 (payment of pensions for the period prior to the entry into force of the Convention).

33.   GERMANY-LUXEMBOURG
Articles 4, 5, 6 and 7 of the Treaty of 11 July 1959 (settlement of the dispute between Germany and Luxembourg).

34.   GERMANY-NETHERLANDS
   (a)   Article 3(2) of the Convention of 29 March 1951.
   (b)   Articles 2 and 3 of Complementary Agreement No. 4 of 21 December 1956 to the Convention of 29 March 1951 (settlement of rights acquired under the German social insurance scheme by Dutch workers between 13 May 1940 and 1 September 1945).

35.   GERMANY-AUSTRIA
   (a)   Article 41 of the Convention on social security of 22 December 1966 as amended by Complementary Conventions No 1 of 10 April 1969, No. 2 of 20 March 1974 and No. 3 of 29 August 1980.

(b)   Paragraphs 20(a) of the Final Protocol to the said Convention.

(c)   Article 3 of the said Convention as regards persons residing in a third State.

(d)   Paragraph 3(g) of the Final Protocol to the said Convention.

(e)   Article 4(1) of the Convention as regards the German legislation, under which accidents (and occupational diseases) occurring outside the territory of the Federal Republic of Germany, and periods completed outside that territory, do not give rise to payment of benefits or only give rise to payment of benefits under certain conditions, when those entitled to them reside outside the territory of the Federal Republic of Germany, in cases in which:

(i)   the benefit has already been paid or is payable on 1 January 1994;

(ii)   the beneficiary has established his habitual residence in Austria before 1 January 1994 and the payment of pensions due under the pension and accident insurance begins prior to 31 December 1994; this shall also apply to periods during which another pension, including a survivor's pension was collected, replacing the initial one, where the periods of collection follow each other without interruption.

(f)   Paragraph 19(b) of the Final Protocol to the said Convention. In applying Number 3(c) of this provision the amount taken into account by the competent institution shall not exceed the amount, which is due in respect of the corresponding periods to be remunerated by this institution.

36.   GERMANY-PORTUGAL

Article 5(2) of the Convention of 6 November 1964.

37.   GERMANY-FINLAND

Article 4 of the Convention on social security of 23 April 1979.

38.   GERMANY-SWEDEN

Article 4(2) of the Convention on social security of 27 February 1976.

39.   GERMANY-UNITED KINGDOM

(a)   Articles 3(1) and (6) and 7(2) to (6) of the Convention on social security of 20 April 1960.

(b)   Articles 2 to 7 of the Final Protocol to the Convention on social security of 20 April 1960.

(c)   Articles 2(5) and 5(2) to (6) of the Convention on unemployment insurance of 20 April 1960.

40.   SPAIN-FRANCE

None.

41.   SPAIN-GREECE

No convention.

42.   SPAIN-IRELAND

No convention.

43.   SPAIN-ITALY

Articles 5, 18(1)(c) and 23 of the Convention on social security of 30 October 1979.

44.   SPAIN-LUXEMBOURG

(a)   Article 5(2) of the Convention of 8 May 1969.

(b)   Article 1 of the Administrative Arrangement of 27 June 1975 for the application of the Convention of 8 May 1969 to self-employed persons.

45.   SPAIN-NETHERLANDS

Article 23(2) of the Convention on social security of 5 February 1974.

46.   SPAIN-AUSTRIA

    (a)   Article 4 of the Convention on social security of 6 November 1981 as regards persons residing in a third State.

    (b)   Point II of the Final Protocol to the said Convention as regards persons residing in a third State.

47.   SPAIN-PORTUGAL

Articles 4(2), 16(2) and 22 of the General Convention of 11 June 1969.

48.   SPAIN-FINLAND

Article 5(2) of the Convention on social security of 19 December 1985.

49.   SPAIN-SWEDEN.

Articles 5(2) and 16 of the Convention on social security of 4 February 1983.

50.   SPAIN-UNITED KINGDOM

None.

51.   FRANCE-GREECE

None.

52.   FRANCE-IRELAND

No convention.

53.   FRANCE-ITALY

Articles 20 and 24 of the General Convention of 31 March 1948.

54.   FRANCE-LUXEMBOURG

None.

55.   FRANCE-NETHERLANDS

None.

56.   FRANCE-AUSTRIA

None.

57.   FRANCE-PORTUGAL

None.

58.   FRANCE-FINLAND

No Convention.

59.   FRANCE-SWEDEN

None.

60.   FRANCE-UNITED KINGDOM

The exchange of letters of 27 and 30 July 1970 concerning the position with regard to social security of United Kingdom teachers temporarily pursuing their profession in France by virtue of the Cultural Convention of 2 March 1948.

61.   GREECE-IRELAND

No convention.

62.   GREECE-ITALY

No convention.

63.   GREECE-LUXEMBOURG

No convention.

64.   GREECE-NETHERLANDS

None.

65.   GREECE-AUSTRIA

    (a)   Article 4 of the Convention on social security of 14 December 1979 as amended by the Complementary Convention of 21 May 1986 as regards persons residing in a third State.

    (b)   Point II of the Final Protocol to the said Convention as regards persons residing in a third State.

66.   GREECE-PORTUGAL
No convention.
67.   GREECE-FINLAND
Article 5(2) of the Convention on social security of 21 March 1988.
68.   GREECE-SWEDEN
Article 5(2) of the Convention on social security of 5 May 1978 as amended by
the Complementary Convention of 14 September 1984.
69.   GREECE-UNITED KINGDOM
No convention.
70.   IRELAND-ITALY
No convention.
71.   IRELAND-LUXEMBOURG
No convention.
72.   IRELAND-NETHERLANDS
No convention.
73.   IRELAND-AUSTRIA
Article 4 of the Convention on social security of 30 September 1988 as regards
persons residing in a third State.
74.   IRELAND-PORTUGAL
No convention.
75.   IRELAND-FINLAND
No Convention.
76.   IRELAND-SWEDEN
No Convention
77.   IRELAND-UNITED KINGDOM
None.
78.   ITALY-LUXEMBOURG
None.
79.   ITALY-NETHERLANDS
None.
80.   ITALY-AUSTRIA
        (a)   Articles 5(3) and 9(2) of the Convention on social security of 21
January 1981.
        (b)   Article 4 of the said Convention and paragraph 2 of the Final
Protocol to the said Convention as regards persons residing in a third State.
81.   ITALY-PORTUGAL
No convention.
82.   ITALY-FINLAND
No Convention.
83.   ITALY-SWEDEN
Article 20 of the Convention on social security of 25 September 1979.
84.   ITALY-UNITED KINGDOM
None.
85.   LUXEMBOURG-NETHERLANDS
None.
86.   LUXEMBOURG-AUSTRIA
        (a)   Article 5(2) of the Convention on social security of 21 December
1971 as amended by the Complementary Conventions No. 1 of 16 May 1973
and No. 2 of 9 October 1978.

(b)   Article 3(2) of the Convention as regards persons residing in a third State.

(c)   Point III of the Final Protocol to the said Convention as regards persons residing in a third State.

87.   LUXEMBOURG-PORTUGAL

Article 3(2) of the Convention of 12 February 1965.

88.   LUXEMBOURG-FINLAND

Article 5(2) of the Convention on social security of 15 September 1988.

89.   LUXEMBOURG-SWEDEN

Articles 4 and 29(1) of the Convention on social security of 21 February 1985 as regards persons residing in a third State.

90.   LUXEMBOURG-UNITED KINGDOM

None.

91.   NETHERLANDS-AUSTRIA

(a)   Article 3 of the Convention on social security of 7 March 1974 as amended by the Complementary Convention of 5 November 1980 as regards persons residing in a third State.

(b)   Point II of the Final Protocol to the said Convention as regards persons residing in a third State.

92.   NETHERLANDS-PORTUGAL

Articles 5(2) and 31 of the Convention of 18 July 1979.

93.   NETHERLANDS-FINLAND

No Convention

94.   NETHERLANDS-SWEDEN

Articles 4 and 24(3) of the Convention on social security of 2 July 1976 as regards persons residing in a third State.

95.   NETHERLANDS-UNITED KINGDOM

None.

96.   AUSTRIA-PORTUGAL

None.

97.   AUSTRIA-FINLAND

(a)   Article 4 of the Convention on social security of 11 December 1985 as amended by the Complementary Convention of 9 March 1993 as regards persons residing in a third State.

98.   AUSTRIA-SWEDEN

(a)   Articles 4 and 24(1) of the Convention on social security of 11 November 1975 as amended by the Complementary Convention of 21 October 1982 as regards persons residing in a third State.

(b)   Point II of the Final Protocol to the said Convention as regards persons residing in a third State.

99.   AUSTRIA-UNITED KINGDOM

(a)   Article 3 of the Convention on social security of 22 July 1980 as amended by the Complementary Conventions No. 1 of 9 December 1985 and No. 2 of 13 October 1992 as regards persons residing in a third State.

(b)   Protocol concerning benefits in kind to the said Convention with the exception of Article 2(3) as regards persons who cannot claim treatment under Chapter 1 of Title III of the Regulation.

100.   PORTUGAL-FINLAND

None.

101.   PORTUGAL-SWEDEN
Article 6 of the Convention on social security of 25 October 1978.
102.   PORTUGAL-UNITED KINGDOM
Article 2(1) of the Protocol on medical treatment of 15 November 1978.
103.   FINLAND-SWEDEN.
None.
104.   FINLAND-UNITED KINGDOM
None.
105.   SWEDEN-UNITED KINGDOM
Article 4(3) of the Convention on social security of 29 June 1987.

ANNEX IV(B)(11)(13)(15)
(Articles 37(2), 38(3), 45(3), 46(1)(b) and 46b(2) of the Regulation)

A.   Legislations referred to in Article 37(1) of the Regulation under which the amount of invalidity benefits is independent of the length of periods of insurance

A.   BELGIUM
  (a)   Legislation relating to the general invalidity scheme, the special invalidity scheme for miners and the special scheme for merchant navy mariners.
  (b)   Legislation on insurance for self-employed persons against incapacity to work.
  (c)   Legislation relating to invalidity in the overseas social insurance scheme and the invalidity scheme for former employees of the Belgian Congo and Rwanda-Urundi.

B.   DENMARK
None.

C.   GERMANY
None.

D.   SPAIN
Legislation relating to invalidity insurance under the general scheme and under the special schemes.

E.   FRANCE
  1.   *Employed persons*
All legislations on invalidity insurance, except for the legislation concerning the invalidity insurance of the social security scheme for miners.
  2.   *Self-employed persons*
The legislation on invalidity insurance for persons self-employed in agriculture.

F.   GREECE
Legislation relating to the agricultural insurance scheme.

G.   IRELAND
Chapter 10 of Part II of the Social Welfare (Consolidation) Act 1981.

H.   ITALY
None.

I.   LUXEMBOURG
None.

J. NETHERLANDS

(a) The law of 18 February 1966 on insurance against incapacity for work, as amended.

(b) The law of 11 December 1975 on general insurance against incapacity for work, as amended.

K. AUSTRIA
None.

L. PORTUGAL
None.

M. FINLAND
National pensions to persons who are born disabled or become disabled at an early age (the National Pensions Act (547/93)).

N. SWEDEN
None.

O. UNITED KINGDOM

(a) *Great Britain*

Sections 15 and 36 of the Social Security Act 1975.
Sections 14, 15 and 16 of the Social Security Pensions Act 1975.

(b) *Northern Ireland*

Sections 15 and 36 of the Social Security (Northern Ireland) Act 1975.
Articles 16, 17 and 18 of the Social Security Pensions (Northern Ireland) Order 1975.

B. Special schemes for self-employed persons within the meaning of Articles 38(3) and 45(3) of Regulation No. 1408/71.

A. BELGIUM
None.

B. DENMARK
None.

C. GERMANY
Old-age insurance for farmers (Alterssicherung für Landwirte).

D. SPAIN
Scheme for lowering the retirement age of self-employed persons engaged in seafaring activities as described in Royal Decree No. 2309 of 23 July 1970.

E. FRANCE
None.

F. GREECE
None.

G. IRELAND
None.

H. ITALY
Pension insurance schemes for (Assicurazione pensioni per):
— medical practitioners (medici),
— pharmacists (farmacisti),

— veterinarians (veterinari),
— midwives (ostetriche),
— engineers and architects (ingegneri ed architetti),
— surveyors (geometri),
— solicitors and barristers (avvocati e procuratori),
— economists (dottori commercialisti),
— accountants and industrial experts (rabionieri e periti commerciali),
— employment consultants (consulenti del lavoro),
— notaries (notai),
— customs agents (spedizionieri doganali).

I. LUXEMBOURG
None.

J. THE NETHERLANDS
None.

K. AUSTRIA
None.

L. PORTUGAL
None.

M. FINLAND
None.

N. SWEDEN
None.

O. UNITED KINGDOM
None.

C. Cases referred to in Article 46(1)(b) of the Regulation where the calculation of benefit in accordance with Article 46(2) of the Regulation may be waived.

A. BELGIUM
None.

B. DENMARK
All applications for pensions referred to in the law on social pensions, except for pensions mentioned in Annex IV part D.

C. GERMANY
None.

D. SPAIN
None.

E. FRANCE
None.

F. GREECE
None.

G. IRELAND
All applications for retirement pensions, contributory old-age pensions and windows' pensions.

H.　ITALY
Invalidity, retirement and survivors pensions for employed persons and for the following categories of self-employed persons: farmers farming directly, share-croppers, farmers, craftsmen and persons engaged in commercial activities.

I.　LUXEMBOURG
None.

J.　THE NETHERLANDS
All applications for old-age pensions under the law of 31 May 1956 governing general old-age insurance, as amended.

K.　AUSTRIA
None.

L. PORTUGAL
Invalidity, old-age and widows' pensions.

M.　FINLAND
None.

N.　SWEDEN
All applications for old-age basic and supplementary pensions except pensions mentioned in Annex IV D.

O.　UNITED KINGDOM
All applications for retirement and widow's pension determined pursuant to the provisions of Title III, Chapter 3 of the Regulation, with the exception of those for which:

(a)　during a tax year beginning on or after 6 April 1975:

(i)　the party concerned had completed periods of insurance, employment or residence under the legislation of the United Kingdom and of another Member State; and

(ii)　one (or more) of the tax years referred to in (i) was not considered a qualifying year within the meaning of the legislation of the United Kingdom;

(b)　the periods of insurance completed under the legislation in force in the United Kingdom for the periods prior to 5 July 1948 would be taken into account for the purposes of Article 46(2) of the Regulation by application of the periods of insurance, employment or residence under the legislation of another Member State.

D.　Benefits and agreements referred to in Article 46b(2) of the Regulation.

1.　*Benefits referred to in Article 46b(2)(a) of the Regulation, the amount of which is independent of the length of periods of insurance or residence completed:*

(a)　The invalidity benefits provided for by the legislations referred to in part A of this Annex.

(b)　The full Danish national old-age pension acquired after 10 years' residence by persons who will have been awarded a pension by 1 October 1989 at the latest.

(c)　The Spanish death allowances and survivors' pensions granted under the general and special schemes.

(d)   The widows' allowance under the widowhood insurance of the French general social security system or the agricultural workers' system.

(e)   The widowers' or widows' invalidity pension under the French general social security system or the agricultural workers' system, when calculated on the basis of the invalidity pension of a deceased spouse, paid in accordance with Article 46(1)(a)(i).

(f)   The Netherlands widows' pension under the law of 9 April 1959 governing the general insurance for widows and orphans, as amended.

(g)   Finnish national pensions determined according to the National Pensions Act of 8 June 1956 and awarded under the transitional rules of the National Pensions Act (547/93).

(h)   The full Swedish basic pension awarded under the basic pension legislation which applied before 1 January 1993 and the full basic pension awarded under the transitional rules to the legislation applying from that date.

2.   *Benefits referred to in Article 46b(2)(b) of the Regulation, the amount of which is determined by reference to a credited period deemed to have been completed between the date on which the risk materialised and a later date:*

(a)   Danish early-retirement pensions, the amount of which is determined in accordance with legislation in force before 1 October 1984.

(b)   German invalidity and survivors' pensions, for which account is taken of a supplementary period, and German old-age pensions, for which account is taken of a supplementary period already acquired.

(c)   Italian pensions for total incapacity for work (inabilità).

(d)   Luxembourg invalidity and survivors' pensions.

(e)   Finnish employment pensions for which account is taken of future periods according to the national legislation.

(f)   Swedish invalidity and survivors' pensions for which account is taken of a credited period of insurance and Swedish old-age pensions for which account is taken of credited periods already acquired.

3.   *Agreements referred to in Article 46b(2)(b)(i) of the Regulation intended to prevent the same credited period being taken into account two or more times:*
Agreement of 20 July 1978 between the Government of the Grand Duchy of Luxembourg and Government of the Federal Republic of Germany concerning various social security matters.

Nordic Convention of 15 June 1992 on social security.

ANNEX V(15)

CONCORDANCE BETWEEN THE LEGISLATION OF MEMBER STATES ON CONDITIONS RELATING TO THE DEGREE OF INVALIDITY

(Article 40(4) of the Regulation)

BELGIUM

Member States	Schemes administered by Member States' institutions who have taken a decision recognising the degree of invalidity	Schemes administered by Belgian institutions on which the decision is binding in cases of concordance				
		General scheme	Miner's scheme		Mariners' scheme	Ossom
			General invalidity	Occupational invalidity		
FRANCE	1. General scheme: — Group III (constant attendance) — Group II — Group I	Concordance	Concordance	Concordance	No concordance	No concordance
	2. Agricultural scheme: — Total, general invalidity — Two-thirds general invalidity — Constant attendance	Concordance	Concordance	Concordance	No concordance	No concordance
	3. Miners' scheme: — Partial, general invalidity — Constant attendance — Occupational invalidity	No concordance	Concordance	Concordance	No concordance	No concordance
	4. Mariners' scheme: — General invalidity — Constant attendance — Occupational invalidity	No concordance	No concordance	No concordance	Concordance	No concordance
ITALY	1. General scheme: — Invalidity — manual workers — Invalidity — clerical staff	No concordance	Concordance	Concordance	No concordance	No concordance
	2. Mariners' scheme: — Unfitness for seafaring	No concordance	No concordance	No concordance	Concordance	No concordance
LUXEMBOURG	Worker's invalidity — manual workers Invalidity — clerical staff	Concordance	Concordance	Concordance	No concordance	No concordance

FRANCE

Schemes administered by French institutions on which the decision is binding in cases of concordance

Member States	Schemes administered by Member States' institutions having taken a decision recognising the degree of invalidity	General scheme			Agricultural scheme			Miner's scheme			Mariner's scheme		
		Group I	Group II	Group III Constant attendance	2/3 Invalidity	Total invalidity	Constant attendance	2/3 General invalidity	Constant attendance	Occupational invalidity	2/3 General invalidity	Total occupational invalidity	Constant attendance
BELGIUM	1. General scheme	Concordance	No concordance	No concordance	Concordance	No concordance	No concordance	Concordance	No concordance	No concordance	No concordance	No concordance	No concordance
	2. Miner's scheme: —partial general invalidity	Concordance	No concordance	No concordance	Concordance	No concordance	No concordance	Concordance	No concordance	No concordance	No concordance	No concordance	No concordance
	—occupational invalidity	No concordance	No concordance	No concordance	No concordance	No concordance	No concordance	No concordance[1]	No concordance	Concordance[2]	No concordance	No concordance	No concordance
	3. Mariner's scheme	Concordance[1]	No concordance	No concordance	Concordance[1]	No concordance	No concordance	Concordance[1]	No concordance	No concordance	No concordance	No concordance	No concordance
ITALY	1. General scheme: —invalidity — manual workers	Concordance	No concordance	No concordance	Concordance	No concordance	No concordance	Concordance	No concordance	No concordance	No concordance	No concordance	No concordance
	—invalidity — clerical staff	Concordance	No concordance	No concordance	Concordance	No concordance	No concordance	Concordance	No concordance	No concordance	No concordance	No concordance	No concordance
	2. Mariner's scheme: —unfitness for seafaring	No concordance	No concordance	No concordance	No concordance	No concordance	No concordance	No concordance	No concordance	No concordance	No concordance	No concordance	No concordance
LUXEMBOURG	Invalidity — manual workers	Concordance	No concordance	No concordance	Concordance	No concordance	No concordance	Concordance	No concordance	No concordance	No concordance	No concordance	No concordance
	Invalidity — clerical staff	No concordance	No concordance	No concordance	No concordance	No concordance	No concordance	No concordance	No concordance	No concordance	No concordance	No concordance	No concordance

[1] In so far as the invalidity recognised by the Belgian institutions is general invalidity.
[2] Only if the Belgian institution has recognised that the worker is unfit for work underground or at ground level.

ITALY

Schemes administered by Italian institutions on which the decision is binding in cases of concordance

Member States	Schemes administered by Member States' institutions who have taken a decision recognising the degree of invalidity	General scheme — Manual workers	General scheme — Clerical staff	Mariners' unfitness for navigation
BELGIUM	1. General scheme	No concordance	No concordance	No concordance
	2. Miners' scheme			
	— partial general invalidity	Concordance	Concordance	No concordance
	— occupational invalidity	No concordance	No concordance	No concordance
	3. Mariners' scheme	No concordance	No concordance	No concordance
FRANCE	1. General scheme			
	— Group III (constant attendance)	Concordance	Concordance	No concordance
	— Group II	Concordance	Concordance	No concordance
	— Group I	Concordance	Concordance	No concordance
	2. Agricultural scheme:			
	— total, general invalidity	Concordance	Concordance	No concordance
	— partial general invalidity	Concordance	Concordance	No concordance
	— constant attendance	No concordance	No concordance	No concordance
	3. Miners' scheme:			
	— partial, general invalidity	Concordance	Concordance	No concordance
	— constant attendance	No concordance	No concordance	No concordance
	— Occupational invalidity	No concordance	No concordance	No concordance
	4. Mariners' scheme:			
	— general invalidity	No concordance	No concordance	No concordance
	— constant attendance	No concordance	No concordance	No concordance

LUXEMBOURG

Member States	Schemes administered by institutions of Member States who have taken a decision recognising the degree of invalidity	Schemes administered by Italian institutions on which the decision is binding in cases of concordance	
		Invalidity — manual workers	Invalidity — clerical staff
BELGIUM	1. General scheme	Concordance	Concordance
	2. Miners' scheme		
	— partial general invalidity	No concordance	No concordance
	— occupational invalidity	No concordance	No concordance
	3. Mariners' scheme	Concordance[1]	Concordance[1]
FRANCE	1. General scheme		
	— Group III (constant attendance)		
	— Group II	} Concordance	Concordance
	— Group I		
	2. Agricultural scheme:		
	— total, general invalidity		
	— two-thirds general invalidity	} Concordance	Concordance
	— constant attendance		
	3. Miners' scheme:		
	— two-thirds general invalidity	} Concordance	Concordance
	— constant attendance		
	— occupational invalidity	No concordance	No concordance
	4. Mariners' scheme:		
	— partial general invalidity	} Concordance	Concordance
	— constant attendance		
	— occupational invalidity	No concordance	No concordance

[1] In so far as the invalidity recognised by the Belgian institution is general invalidity.

ANNEX VI(A)(b)(2)(7)(8)(9)(11)(12)(13)(14)(15)
SPECIAL PROCEDURES FOR APPLYING THE LEGISLATIONS
OF CERTAIN MEMBER STATES
(Article 89 of the Regulation)

A. BELGIUM

1.   Persons whose entitlement to sickness insurance benefits in kind derives from the provisions of the Belgian compulsory sickness and invalidity scheme applicable to self-employed persons shall be eligible under the provisions of Chapter 1 of Title III of the Regulation, including Article 35(1), under the following conditions:

(a)   In the event that they are temporarily resident in the territory of a Member State other than Belgium, the persons concerned shall be entitled:

(i)   to the benefits in kind provided for under the legislation of the Member State of temporary residence in respect of hospitalisation care;

(ii)   to reimbursement in respect of other benefits in kind provided for under the Belgian scheme by the relevant Belgian institution at the rate provided for under the legislation of the State of temporary residence.

(b)   In the event that they are permanently resident in the territory of a Member State other than Belgium, the persons concerned shall be entitled to the benefits in kind provided for under the legislation of the Member State of permanent residence provided that they pay the relevant Belgian institution the appropriate additional contribution provided for under Belgian regulations.

2.   For the application of the provisions of Chapters 7 and 8 of Title III of the Regulation by the competent Belgian institution, a child shall be considered to have been brought up in the Member State in whose territory he resides.

3.   For the purposes of Article 46(2) of the Regulation, periods of old-age insurance completed under Belgian legislation before 1 January 1945 shall also be considered as periods of insurance completed under the Belgian legislation on the general invalidity scheme and the mariners' scheme.

4.   In applying Article 40(3)(a)(ii), account shall only be taken of periods during which the employed or self-employed person was incapable of work within the meaning of Belgian legislation.

5.   For the purposes of Article 46(2) of the Regulation, periods of old-age insurance completed by self-employed persons under Belgian legislation, prior to the entry into force of the legislation on the incapacity for work of self-employed persons, shall be considered as periods completed under the latter legislation.

6.   In order to establish whether the requirements imposed by Belgian legislation for entitlement to unemployment benefits are fulfilled, account shall be taken only of days of paid employment; however, account shall be taken of days accepted as equivalent within the meaning of the said legislation only in so far as the days worked which preceded them were days of paid employment.

7.   Pursuant to Articles 72 and 79(1)(a) of the Regulation, account shall be taken of periods of employment and/or periods of insurance completed under the legislation of another Member State where entitlement to benefit under Belgian legislation is subject to the condition that, for a specified previous period, the qualifying conditions for family benefits in the framework of the scheme for employment persons have been met.

8.   For the purposes of applying Article 14a(2), (3) and (4), 14c(a) and 14d of Regulation (EEC) No. 1408/71, business revenues in the reference year

which serve as a basis for determining the contributions due by virtue of the social arrangements for self-employed persons shall be calculated using the mean annual rate for the year during which this income was received.

The rate of conversion is the annual mean of the conversion rates published in the *Official Journal of the European Communities* pursuant to Article 107(5) of Regulation (EEC) No. 547/72.

9. In the calculation of the theoretical amount of an invalidity pension, as referred to in Article 46(2) of the Regulation, the competent Belgian institution shall take as its basis the income received in the profession last exercised by the person concerned.

10. Any employed person or self-employed person who is no longer insured in Belgium under the sickness and invalidity insurance legislation — which also makes the grant of the right to benefits conditional upon the person concerned being insured when the risk materialises — shall be considered to be still insured when the risk materialises, for the purposes of implementation of Chapter 3 of Title III of the Regulation, if he is insured for the same risks under the legislation of another Member State.

11. If the person concerned is entitled to a Belgian invalidity benefit under Article 45 of the Regulation, that benefit shall be awarded in accordance with the rules laid down by Article 46(2) of the Regulation:

(a) In accordance with the provisions laid down by the Law of 9 August 1963 on the establishment and organisation of a compulsory sickness and invalidity insurance scheme if, at the time of occurrence of the incapacity for work, he was insured for the same risk under the legislation of another Member State as an employed person within the meaning of Article 1(a) of the Regulation.

(b) In accordance with the provisions laid down by the Royal Decree of 20 July 1971 on the establishment of an insurance scheme against incapacity for work for self-employed persons if, at the time of occurrence of the incapacity for work, he was a self-employed person within the meaning of Article 1(a) of the Regulation.

B. DENMARK

1. Completed periods of insurance, employment or self-employment in a Member State other than Denmark shall be taken into account for admission to membership of an approved unemployment insurance fund in the same way as if they were periods of employment or self-employment completed in Denmark.

2. Employed or self-employed persons, pension claimants and pensioners, and members of their families referred to in Articles 19, 22(1) and (3), 25(1) and (3), 26(1), 28a, 29 and 31 of the Regulation, resident or staying in Denmark, shall be entitled to benefits in kind on the same terms as those laid down by Danish legislation for persons who, under the law on the public health service (lov om offentlig sygesikring), belong to class 1.

3. (a) The provisions of Danish legislation on social pensions that stipulate that the right to pension is subject to the claimant being resident in Denmark are not applicable to employed or self-employed persons or their survivors who reside in the territory of a Member State other than Denmark.

(b) For the purpose of calculating the pension, periods of employment or self-employment completed in Denmark by a frontier worker or a seasonal worker are regarded as periods of residence completed in Denmark by the surviving spouse in so far as the surviving spouse was during these periods, linked to the frontier worker or seasonal worker by marriage without separation from bed and board or *de facto* separation on grounds of incompatibility and provided that during these periods the spouse resided in the territory of another Member State.

(c)   For the purpose of calculating the pension, periods of employment or self-employment completed in Denmark before 1 January 1984 by an employed or self-employed person other than a frontier worker or seasonal worker shall be regarded as periods of residence completed in Denmark by the surviving spouse, in so far as the surviving spouse was during these periods, linked to the employed or self-employed person by marriage without separation from bed and board or *de facto* separation on grounds of incompatibility, and provided that during these periods the spouse resided in the territory of another Member State.

(d)   Periods to be taken into account under the terms of (b) and (c) shall not be taken into consideration if they coincide with the periods taken into account for the calculation of the pension due to the person concerned under the legislation on compulsory insurance of another Member State or with the periods during which the person concerned received a pension under such legislation.

These periods shall, however, be taken into consideration if the annual amount of the said pension is less than half the basic amount of the social pension.

4.   The terms of the Regulation shall be without prejudice to the provisional rules under the Danish laws of 7 June 1972 on the pension rights of Danish nationals having their effective residence in Denmark for a specified period immediately preceding the date of the claim. However, a pension shall be granted under those conditions laid down for Danish nationals to nationals of other Member States having their effective residence in Denmark during the year immediately preceding the date of claim.

5.   (a)   The periods during which a frontier worker residing within the territory of a Member State other than Denmark has pursued his professional or trade activity in Denmark are to be considered as periods of residence for the purposes of Danish legislation. The same shall apply to periods in which a frontier worker is posted to or provides services in a Member State other than Denmark.

(b)   The periods during which a seasonal worker residing within the territory of a Member State other than Denmark has pursued his occupation in Denmark are to be considered as periods of residence for the purposes of Danish legislation. The same applies to periods during which a seasonal worker is posted to the territory of a Member State other than Denmark.

6.   In order to determine whether or not conditions for entitlement to daily allowances in the case of sickness or maternity laid down by the law of 20 December 1989 on daily allowances in the case of sickness or maternity have been satisfied, where the person concerned is no longer subject to Danish legislation during the periods of reference fixed by the above-mentioned law:

(a)   account shall be taken of the insurance periods and employment periods fulfilled under the legislation of a Member State other than Denmark during the abovementioned reference periods during which the person concerned was not covered by Danish legislation, as if they are periods completed under the latter legislation, and

(b)   during the periods taken into account, a self-employed person or an employed person (in cases where, for the latter, remuneration cannot serve as a basis for calculating the daily allowances) are regarded as having had an average remuneration or salary of an amount equal to that on the basis of which the cash allowances are calculated in respect of the periods completed under Danish legislation during the reference periods.

7.   Article 46a(3)(d) and Article 46c(1) and (3) of the Regulation and Article 7(1) of the implementing Regulation shall not be applied to pensions awarded in the context of Danish legislation.

8.   For the purpose of applying Article 67 of the Regulation, unemployment benefits for self-employed persons insured in Denmark shall be calculted in accordance with Danish legislation.

9.   Where the beneficiary of a Danish retirement pension or early retirement pension is also entitled to a survivor's pension from another Member State, these pensions, for the implementation of Danish legislation shall be regarded as benefits of the same kind within the meaning of Article 46a(1) of the Regulation, subject to the condition, however, that the person whose periods of insurance or of residence serve as the basis for the calculation of the survivor's pension has also completed periods of residence in Denmark.

C.   GERMANY

1.   The provisions of Article 10 of the Regulation are without prejudice to the provisions under which accidents (and occupational diseases) occurring outside the territory of the Federal Republic of Germany, and periods completed outside that territory, do not give grounds for benefits, or do so only subject to certain conditions, when the persons concerned are resident outside the territory of the Federal Republic of Germany.

2.   (a)   The standard period for allocation (pauschale Anrechnungszeit) shall be determined exclusively with reference to German periods.

(b)   For the purpose of taking into account German pension periods for miners' pension insurance, only German legislation shall apply.

(c)   For the purpose of taking into account German substitute periods (Ersatzzeiten), only German legislation shall apply.

3.   If application of the Regulation or later regulations on social security places an exceptional burden on certain sickness insurance institutions, that shall be compensated for in full or in part. The Federal Association of Local General Funds, as liaison body (sickness insurance), shall take decisions regarding such compensation by common agreement with the other central federations of sickness funds. The resources necessary to implement the compensation shall be provided by taxes levied on all the sickness insurance institutions in proportion to the average number of members over the previous years, with the exception of retired members.

4.   Article 7 of Book VI of the Social Code shall apply to nationals of the other Member States and to stateless persons and refugees residing in the territory of other Member States, according to the following rules.

If the general conditions are fulfilled, voluntary contributions may be paid to the German pension insurance scheme:

(a)   if the person concerned is domiciled or resident in the territory of the Federal Republic of Germany;

(b)   if the party concerned is domiciled or resident in the territory of another Member State and has at some point previously contributed, either compulsorily or voluntarily, to the German pension insurance scheme;

(c)   if the party concerned is a national of another Member State, is domiciled or resident in the territory of a third Member State, has contributed for at least 60 months to the German pension insurance scheme or was eligible for voluntary insurance pursuant to Article 232 of Book VI of the Social Code, and is not compulsorily or voluntarily insured under the legislation of another Member State.

5.   ...

6.   ...

7.   ...

8.   ...

9.   Where the costs of benefits in kind which are granted by German institutions of the place of residence to pensioners or members of their family who are insured with competent institutions of other Member States must be refunded on the basis of monthly lump sums, such costs shall, for the purpose of financial equalisation among German institutions of sickness insurance for pensioners, be treated as expenditure on the German sickness insurance scheme for pensioners. The lump sums refunded to the German institutions of the place of residence by the competent institutions of other Member States shall be regarded as receipts which must be taken into account in the aforementioned financial equalisation.

10.   In the case of self-employed persons, the award of unemployment assistance (Arbeitslosenhilfe) shall be conditional on the person concerned having, before reporting himself unemployed, worked for at least a year mainly as a self-employed person in the territory of the Federal Republic of Germany, and not having simply left that work temporarily.

11.   Periods of insurance completed under the legislation of another Member State, under a special old-age insurance scheme for farmers or, if no such scheme exists, as farmers under the general scheme, shall be taken into account to satisfy the conditions of minimum length of insurance required for the person to be subject to contribution within the meaning of Article 27 of the law on old-age insurance for farmers (Gesetz über die Alterssicherung der Landwirte — GAL), always providing that:

(a)   the declaration on which the obligation to pay contributions is based shall have been lodged within the prescribed time, and

(b)   before lodging the declaration, the person concerned shall have been last subject to contribution under the old-age insurance scheme for farmers in the territory of the Federal Republic of Germany.

12.   Periods of compulsory insurance completed under the legislation of another Member State, either under a special scheme for craftsmen, or, if no such scheme exists, under a special scheme for self-employed persons or under the general scheme, shall be taken into account to justify the existence of the 18 years of compulsory contributions required for exemption from compulsory affiliation to pension insurance for self-employed craftsmen.

13.   For the purpose of applying German legislation on compulsory sickness insurance of pensioners as provided for in Article 5(1)(ii) of Volume V

of the Social Insurance Code (Fünftes Sozialgesetzbuch — SGB V) and Article 56 of the Sickness Insurance Reform Law (Gesundheitsreformgesetz), periods of insurance of residence completed under the legislation of another Member State during which the person concerned was entitled to sickness benefits in kind are taken into account, in so far as is necessary, as periods of insurance completed under German legislation provided they do not overlap with periods of insurance completed under that legislation.

14.   For the grant of cash benefits pursuant to Article 47(1) of Volume V of the German Social Insurance Code (SGB V) and Articles 200(2) and 561(1) of the German Law on Social Insurance (Reichsversicherungsordnung — RVO), the German institutions shall determine the net remuneration to be taken into account for the calculation of the benefits as though the insured persons resided in the Federal Republic of Germany.

15.   Greek teachers who have civil servant status and who, by the fact that they have taught in German schools, have contributed to the compulsory German pension insurance scheme as well as to the special Greek civil servant scheme and who ceased to be covered by compulsory German insurance after 31 December 1978 may, on request, have the compulsory contributions reimbursed in accordance with Article 210 of Book VI of the Social Code. Applications for reimbursement of contributions are to be introduced during the course of the year following the date of entry into force of this provision. The party concerned may also pursue his claim within the six calendar months following the date on which he ceased to be subject to compulsory insurance.

Article 210(6) of Book VI of the Social Code shall only apply with regard to the periods during which compulsory contributions to the pension insurance scheme were paid in addition to contributions to the special Greek civil servant scheme and with regard to the allocation periods immediately following the periods during which these compulsory contributions were paid.

16.   ...

17.   For the grant of benefits to persons requiring in-depth and constant care under Articles 53 *et seq.* of Volume V of the German Social Insurance Code (SGB V), the institution of the place of residence shall, for the provision of assistance in the form of benefits in kind, take account of periods of insurance, employment or residence completed under the legislation of another Member State as if they were periods completed under the legislation applicable to the institution.

18.   A person in receipt of a pension under German legislation and a pension under the legislation of another Member State shall be deemed, for the purposes of applying Article 27 of the Regulation, to be entitled to sickness and maternity benefits in kind if, under Article 8(1), point 4, of Volume V of the German Social Insurance Code (SGB V), that person is exempted from compulsory sickness insurance (Krankenversicherung).

19.   A period of insurance for child-rearing under German legislation is valid even for a period during which the employed person concerned brought up the child in another Member State provided that person was unable to engage in occupational activity by virtue of Article 6(1) of the Protection of Mothers Law (Mutterschutzgesetz) or took parental leave under Article 15 of the federal Child-rearing Allowance Law (Bundeserziehungsgeldgesetz) and did not engage in any minor (geringfügig) employment within the meaning of Article 8 of SGB IV.

20.   Where the provisions of German pension law in force on 31 December 1991 apply, the provisions of Annex VI shall also apply in the version thereof in force on 31 December 1991.

D.   SPAIN

1.   The condition either of carrying on the activity of an employed or of a self-employed person, or the condition of having previously been compulsorily insured against the same contingency under a scheme organised for the benefit of employed or self-employed persons of the same Member State, laid down in Article 1(a)(iv) of the Regulation, may not be relied upon against persons who, in accordance with the provisions of Royal Decree No. 2805/1979 of 7 December 1979, are affiliated voluntarily to the general social security scheme in their capacity as an official or employee serving an international intergovernmental organisation.

2.   The provisions of Royal Decree No. 2805/1979 of 7 December 1979 apply to nationals of the Member State and to refugees and stateless persons:

   (a)   where they are resident in Spanish territory, or

   (b)   where they are resident in the territory of another Member State and where they have been previously, at some time, compulsorily affiliated to the Spanish social security scheme, or

   (c)   where they are resident in the territory of a third State and have paid contributions for at least 1800 days to the Spanish social security scheme and where they are not insured either compulsorily or voluntarily by virtue of the legislation of another Member State.

3.   Any employed person or self-employed person who is no longer insured under Spanish legislation shall be considered to be still insured, when the risk materialises, for the purposes of implementing the provisions of Chapter 3 of Title III of the Regulation, if he is insured, under the legislation of another Member State at the time of materialisation of the risk or, failing that, in the case where a benefit is due for the same risk in pursuance of the legislation of another Member State. The latter condition shall be deemed to have been fulfilled, however, in the case referred to in Article 48(1).

4.   (a)   Under Article 47 of the Regulation, the calculation of the theoretical Spanish benefit shall be carried out on the basis of the actual contributions of the insured person during the years immediately preceding payment of the last contribution to the Spanish social security.

   (b)   The amount of the pension obtained shall be increased by the amount of the increases and revalorisations calculated for each year after and up to the year preceding the materialisation of the risk for pensions of the same kind.

E.   FRANCE

1.   (a)   The allowance for elderly employed persons, together with the allowance for elderly self-employed persons, and the agricultural old-age allowance shall be granted, under the conditions laid down for French workers by French legislation to all employed or self-employed persons who are nationals of other Member States and who, at the time of making their claim, are resident in French territory.

   (b)   The same shall apply to refugees and stateless persons.

   (c)   The provisions of the Regulation shall not affect the provisions of French legislation under which only periods of work as employed persons or periods treated as such or, as appropriate, periods of work as self-employed persons in the territories of the European departments and the overseas departments (Guadeloupe, Guyana, Martinique and Réunion) of the French Republic shall be taken into consideration for acquisition of the right to the allowance for elderly employed persons.

2.   The special allowance and cumulative indemnity provided for by the special legislation for social security in the mines shall be provided only for workers employed in French mines.

3.   Law No. 65-555 of 10 July 1965 which grants to French nationals, who are pursuing, or who have pursued, a professional or trade activity abroad, the right to join the voluntary old-age insurance scheme, shall apply to nationals of other Member States under the following conditions:

— the professional or trade activity giving rise to voluntary insurance under the French system should not be, or have been, pursued either on French territory or on the territory of the Member State of which the employed or self-employed person is a national,

— the employed or self-employed person must produce evidence, when making his claim, either that he has resided in France for at least 10 years, consecutive or not, or that he has been continuously subject to French legislation on a compulsory or optional basis for the same length of time.

4.   A person who is subject to French legislation pursuant to Article 14(1) or Article 14a(1) of the Regulation shall be entitled, in respect of the members of his family accompanying him in the territory of the Member State in which he is pursuing an occupation, to the following family benefits:

(a)   the allowance for young children provided until the age of three months;

(b)   the family benefits provided in accordance with Article 73 of the Regulation.

5.   For the calculation of the theoretical amounts referred to in Article 46(2)(a) of the Regulation, in schemes in which old-age pensions are calculated on the basis of retirement points, the competent institution shall take into account, in respect of each of the years of insurance completed under the legislation of any other Member State, the member of retirement points arrived at by dividing the number of retirement points acquired under the legislation it applies by the number of years corresponding to these points.

6.   (a)   Frontier workers who pursue the activities of employed persons in the territory of a Member State other than France and who reside in the French departments of Haut-Rhin, Bas-Rhin and Moselle, shall be entitled in the territory of those departments to the benefits in kind provided for by the local Alsace-Lorraine scheme set up by Laws No. 46-1428 of 12 June 1946 and No. 67-814 of 25 September 1967, pursuant to Article 19 of the Regulation.

(b)   These provisions shall apply by analogy to those entitled under Articles 25(2) and (3) and 28 and 29 of the Regulation.

7.   Notwithstanding Articles 73 and 74 of the Regulation, the housing allowances, the home child-care allowance and the parental child-rearing allowance shall be granted only to persons concerned and to members of their families standing residing in French territory.

8.   Any employed person who is no longer subject to French legislation governing widowhood insurance under the French general social security system or the agricultural workers' system shall be deemed to have the status of

an insured person under such legislation when the risk materialises, for the purposes of the implementation of the provisions of Chapter 3 of Title III of the Regulation, if that person is insured as an employed person under the legislation of another Member State at the time of the materialisation of the risk or, failing that, in the case where a survivor's benefit is due in pursuance of the legislation on employed persons of another Member State. This condition shall be deemed to have been fulfilled, however, in the case referred to in Article 48(1).

F.   GREECE

1.   ...

2.   Law No. 1469/84 concerning voluntary affiliation to the pension insurance scheme for Greek nationals and foreign nationals of Greek origin, is applicable to nationals of other Member States, stateless persons and refugees residing in the territory of a Member State in accordance with the second subparagraph.

Subject to the other conditions of this law being met, contributions may be made:

(a)   where the person concerned is domiciled or resides in the territory of a Member State and has at some time in the past been compulsorily affiliated to the Greek pension insurance scheme, or

(b)   regardless of the place of domicile or residence, where the person concerned has either previously resided in Greece for 10 years, whether consecutive or not, or has previously been subject to Greek legislation whether compulsorily or voluntarily for a period of 1,500 days.

3.   Notwithstanding the relevant provisions applied by the OGA Regulations, the periods during which benefits payable in respect of an accident at work or of an occupational disease as defined in the legislation of Member States, which makes separate provision for such risks, provided that they coincide with periods of employment in the agricultural sector in Greece, shall be regarded as periods of insurance under the legislation applied by the OGA within the meaning of Article 1(r) of the Regulation.

4.   In the context of Greek legislation, the application of Article 49(2) of the Regulation is subject to the condition that the new calculation referred to in the aforementioned Article shall not adversely affect the interests of the person concerned.

5.   Where the rules of the Greek auxiliary pension funds ('επικουρικℵ ταμεία') make provision for the recognition of compulsory old age pension insurance periods completed with statutory Greek insurance institutions ('κℵριας ασφℵλισης') these rules shall also apply to compulsory pension insurance periods in the pension branch completed under the legislation of any other Member State falling within the scope of the Regulation.

6.   Employed persons who were compulsorily affiliated until 31 December 1992 to a pension insurance scheme of a Member State other than Greece and who are subject to compulsory Greek social insurance (base statutory scheme) for the first time after 1 January 1993, shall be regarded as 'formerly insured persons' in accordance with the provisions of Law No. 2084/92.

G.   IRELAND

1.   Employed or self-employed persons, unemployed persons, pension claimants and pensioners, together with members of their families, referred to

in Articles 19(1), 22(1) and (3), 25(1) and (3), 26(1), 28a, 29 and 31 of the Regulation, who are residing or staying in Ireland, shall be entitled free of charge to all medical treatment provided for by Irish legislation where the cost of this treatment is payable by the institution of a Member State other than Ireland.

2.   The members of the family of an employed or self-employed person who is subject to the legislation of a Member State other than Ireland and who satisfies the conditions laid down by that legislation for entitlement to benefits, account being taken, where appropriate, of Article 18 of the Regulation, shall be entitled free of charge, if they are resident in Ireland, to all medical treatment provided for by Irish legislation.

The cost of such benefits shall be payable by the institution with which the employed or self-employed person is insured.

However, where the spouse of the employed or self-employed person or the person looking after the children pursues a professional or trade activity in Ireland, benefits for members of the family shall remain payable by the Irish institution to the extent that entitlement to such benefits is granted solely under the provisions of Irish legislation.

3.   If an employed person subject to Irish legislation has left the territory of a Member State to proceed, in the course of his employment, to the territory of another Member State and sustains an accident before arriving there, his entitlement to benefit in respect of the said accident shall be established:

(a)   as if this accident had occurred on the territory of Ireland, and

(b)   without taking into consideration his absence from the territory of Ireland, when determining whether, by virtue of his employment, he was insured under the said legislation.

4.   ...

5.   For the purpose of calculating the earnings for the granting of the pay-related benefit payable under Irish legislation with unemployment benefit, an amount equal to the average weekly wage in that year of male or female employed persons, as applicable, shall, notwithstanding Articles 23(1) and 68(1) of the Regulation be credited to the employed person in respect of each week of employment completed as an employed person under the legislation of another Member State during the relevant income tax year.

6.   In applying Article 40(3)(a)(ii), account shall only be taken of periods during which the employed or self-employed person was incapable of work within the meaning of Irish legislation.

7.   For the purposes of Article 44(2), an employed person shall be deemed to have expressly asked for postponement of the award of an old-age pension to which he would be entitled under the legislation of Ireland if, where retirement is a condition for receiving the old-age pension, he has not retired.

8.   ...

9.   An unemployed person returning to Ireland at the end of the period of three months for which he continued to receive benefits under the legislation of Ireland in application of Article 69(1) of the Regulation shall be entitled to apply for unemployment benefits notwithstanding Article 69(2) if he satisfies the conditions laid down in the aforementioned legislation.

10.   A period of subjection to Irish legislation in accordance with Article 13(2)(f) of the Regulation may not:

(i)   be taken into account under that provision as a period of subjection to Irish legislation for the purposes of Title III of the Regulation, nor

(ii)   make Ireland the competent State for the provision of benefits provided for in Article 18, 38 or 39(1) of the Regulation.

H.   ITALY
None.

I.   LUXEMBOURG

1.   Notwithstanding Article 94(2) of the Regulation, periods of insurance or periods treated as such completed by employed persons or self-employed persons under Luxembourg legislation for invalidity, old-age or death pensions insurance either before 1 January 1946 or before an earlier date stipulated by a bilateral convention shall be taken into consideration for the purpose of applying this legislation only if the person concerned demonstrates that he has completed six months of insurance under the Luxembourg scheme after the date in question. Where several bilateral conventions apply, periods of insurance or periods treated as such shall be taken into consideration as from the earliest of these dates.

2.   For the purpose of granting the fixed part of Luxembourg pensions, periods of insurance completed under Luxembourg legislation by employed or self-employed persons not residing in Luxembourg territory shall, as from 1 October 1972, be treated as periods of residence.

3.   The second subparagraph of Article 22(2) of the Regulation does not affect the provisions of Luxembourg legislation pursuant to which authorisation by the Sickness Fund for treatment abroad cannot be refused where the required treatment cannot be provided in the Grand Duchy.

4.   For the purpose of taking the insurance period provided for in Article 171(7) of the Social Insurance Code (Code des Assurances Sociales) into account, the Luxembourg institution shall recognise periods of insurance completed by the person concerned under the legislation of any other Member State as if they were periods completed under the legislation which it administers. Application of the foregoing provision shall be subject to the condition that the person concerned last completed insurance periods under Luxembourg legislation.

J.   NETHERLANDS

1.   *Insurance for medical expenses*

(a)   As regards entitlement to benefits in kind under Netherlands legislation, persons entitled to benefits in kind shall mean persons who are insured or co-insured under the insurance scheme covered by the Netherlands law on sickness insurance funds for the purpose of the implementation of Chapter 1 of Title III.

(b)   ...

(c)   For the purposes of Articles 27 to 34 of the Regulation, the following pensions shall be treated as pensions payable under the legal provisions mentioned in subparagraphs (b) (invalidity) and (c) (old age) of the declaration of the Kingdom of the Netherlands under Article 5 of the Regulation:

— pensions awarded under the Law of 6 January 1966 (*Staatsblad* 6) on a new ruling in respect of civil servants and their survivors (Netherlands Civil Service Pensions Act) (Algemene burgerlijke pensioenwet),

— pensions awarded under the Law of 6 October 1966 (*Staatsblad* 445) on a new ruling in respect of pensions for military personnel and their survivors (Military Pensions Act) (Algemene militaire pensioenwet),

—pensions awarded under the Law of 15 February 1967 (*Staatsblad* 138) on a new ruling in respect of pensions for employees of the NV Nederlandse Spoorwegen (Netherlands Railway Company) and their survivors (Railway Pensions Act) (Spoorwegpensioenwet),

—pensions awarded under the Regulation governing conditions of employment of the Netherlands Railway Company (Règlement Dienstvoorwaarden Nederlandse Spoorwegen) (RDV 1964 NS), or

—benefits in respect of a pension before the age of 65 under a pension scheme designed to provide old-age assistance to workers and former workers, or benefits in respect of an early retirement pension from work under a scheme for early retirement set up by the State or by or under an industrial agreement, or a scheme to be designated by the Sickness Fund Council.

(d)   Members of the family as referred to in Article 19(2) who reside in the Netherlands and employed or self-employed workers and the members of their families as referred to in Article 22(1)(b) and (3) read in conjunction with Article 22(1)(b), and Articles 25 and 26 who are entitled to benefits under the legislation of another Member State shall not be insured under the Algemene Wet Bijzondere Ziektekosten (Law on general insurance against special medical expenses) (AWBZ).

2.   *Application of Netherlands legislation on general old-age insurance (Toepassing van de Nederlandse Algemene Ouderdomswet) (AOW)*

(a)   The reduction referred to in Article 13(1) of the AOW shall not be applied for calendar years or parts thereof before 1 January 1957 during which a recipient, not satisfying the conditions permitting him to have such years treated as periods of insurance, resided in the territory of the Netherlands between the ages of 15 years and 65 years, or during which, whilst residing in the territory of another Member State, he pursued an activity as an employed person in the Netherlands for an employer established in that country.

By way of derogation from Article 7 of the AOW, persons who resided or worked in accordance with the abovementioned conditions only prior to 1 January 1957 shall also be regarded as being entitled to a pension.

(b)   The reduction referred to in Article 13(1) of the AOW shall not apply to calendar years or parts thereof prior to 2 August 1989 during which, between his 15th and 65th birthdays the person who is or was married was not insured under the abovementioned legislation despite being resident in the territory of a Member State other than the Netherlands, if these calendar years or parts thereof coincide, on the one hand, with the periods of insurance completed by the person's spouse under that legislation provided that the couple's marriage subsisted during these periods, and, on the other, with the calendar years or parts thereof to be taken into account under subparagraph (a).

By way of derogation from Article 7 of the AOW, this person shall be considered a pensioner.

(c)   The reduction referred to in Article 13(2) of the AOW shall not apply to calendar years or parts thereof prior to 1 January 1957 during which the spouse of a pensioner who fails to satisfy the conditions for having these years treated as periods of insurance resided in the Netherlands between the spouse's 15th and 65th birthdays or during which, despite being resident in the territory of another Member State, the spouse pursued an activity as an employed person in the Netherlands for an employer established in the Netherlands.

(d)   The reduction referred to in Article 13(2) of the AOW shall not apply to calendar years or parts thereof prior to 2 August 1989 during which, between his 15th and 65th birthdays, the pensioner's spouse was resident in a Member State other than the Netherlands and was not insured under the abovementioned legislation if these calendar years or parts thereof coincide, on the one hand, with the periods of insurance completed by the spouse under that legislation provided that the couple's marriage subsisted during these periods, and, on the other, with the calendar years or parts thereof to be taken into account under subparagraph (a).

(e)   The provisions referred to in (a), (b), (c) and (d) shall be applied only if the person concerned has resided for six years in the territory of one or more Member States after the age of 59 years and for as long as that person is residing in the territory of one of these Member States.

(f)   By way of derogation from the provisions of Article 45(1) of the law on general old-age insurance (AOW), and Article 47(1) of the law on general insurance for orphans and widows (AWW), the spouse of an employed person or of a self-employed person covered by a compulsory insurance scheme, residing in a Member State other than the Netherlands, shall be authorised to take out voluntary insurance under that legislation but only for the periods after 2 August 1989 during which the employed person or self-employed person is or was compulsorily insured under the abovementioned legislation. This authorisation ceases on the date of termintaion of the compulsory insurance of the employed person or self-employed person.

The abovementioned authorisation shall not cease, however, where the compulsory insurance of the employed person or the self-employed person is terminated as a result of his death and where his widow receives only a pension under the Netherlands legislation on general insurance for widows and orphans (AWW).

In any event, the authorisation in respect of voluntary insurance ceases on the date on which the voluntarily insured person reaches the age of 65 years.

The contribution which has to be paid for the aforementioned voluntary insurance shall be determined for the spouse of an employed person or of a self-employed person who is compulsorily insured under the Netherlands legislation on general old-age insurance (AOW) and the Netherlands legislation on general insurance for widows and orphans (AWW) in accordance with the provisions relating to the determination of the contribution of compulsory insurance, subject to the condition that his/her income shall be deemed to have been received in the Netherlands.

For the spouse for an employed person or of a self-employed person who was compulsorily insured on or after 2 August 1989 the contribution shall be determined in accordance with the provisions relating to the determination of the contribution for voluntary insurance under the Netherlands legislation on general old-age insurance and the Netherlands legislation on general insurance for widows and orphans.

(g)   The authorisation referred to in (f) shall be granted only if the spouse of an employed person or of a self-employed person has informed the *Sociale Verzekeringsbank* (Social Insurance Bank) not later than one year after commencement of his/her compulsory insurance period of the intention to take out voluntary insurance.

For the spouse of an employed person or of a self-employed person who was compulsorily insured immediately prior to or on 2 August 1989, the period of one year shall commence on the date of 2 August 1989.

The authorisation referred to in point 4 of (f) may not be granted to a spouse not residing in the Netherlands of an employed or self-employed person to whom the provisions of Article 14(1), Article 14a(1) or Article 17 of the Regulation apply if that spouse, in accordance with the provisions of Netherlands legislation alone, is or was authorised to take out voluntary insurance.

(h)   Points (a), (b), (c), (d) and (f) shall not apply either to those periods which coincide with periods which may be taken into account for calculating pension rights under the old-age insurance legislation of a Member State other than the Netherlands or to those periods during which the person concerned has drawn an old-age pension under such legislation.

(i)   For the purposes of Article 46(2) of the Regulation, only periods of insurance completed after the age of 15 years under the Netherlands General Law on Old-Age Insurance (AOW) shall be taken into account as periods of insurance.

3.   (a)   Any employed person or self-employed person who is no longer subject to Dutch legislation governing widowhood insurance shall be deemed to be insured under such legislation when the risk materialises, for the purposes of the implementation of the provisions of Chapter 3 of Title III of the Regulation, if that person is insured under the legislation of another Member State for the same risk or, failing that, in the case where a survivor's benefit is due in pursuance of the legislation of another Member State. The later condition shall be deemed to have been fulfilled, however, in the case referred to in Article 48(1).

(b) Where, pursuant to subparagraph (a), a widow has the right to a widow's pension under Dutch legislation relating to general insurance for widows and for orphans, that pension shall be calculated in accordance with Article 46(2) of the Regulation.

For the application of these provisions, the periods of insurance completed before 1 October 1959 during which the employed person or self-employed person resided in the territory of the Netherlands before attaining the age of 15 years or during which, while still resident on the territory of another Member State, he carried out a gainful activity in the Netherlands for an employer established in that country, shall also be regarded as periods of insurance completed under the aforementioned Dutch legislation.

(c)   Account shall not be taken of the periods to be taken into consideration under subparagrpah (b), which coincide with periods of insurance completed under the legislation of another Member State in respect of survivors' pensions.

(d)   For the purposes of Article 46(2) of the Regulation, only periods of insurance completed after the age of 15 years under the General Law on Insurance for Widows and Orphans (AWW) shall be taken into account as periods of insurance.

4.   (a)   Any employed person or self-employed person who is no longer insured under the Law of 18 February 1966 relating to insurance against incapacity for work (WAO) and/or under the Law of 11 December 1975 relating to incapacity for work (AAW) shall be considered to be still insured at the time of the materialisation of the risk for the purposes of the implementa-

tion of the provisions of Chapter 3 of Title III of the Regulation, if he is insured for the same risk under the legislation of another Member State or, failing that, in the case where a benefit is due under the legislation of another Member State for the same risk. The latter condition shall be considered to be fulfilled, however, in the case referred to in Article 48(1).

(b) If, pursuant to subparagraph (a), the person concerned is entitled to a Dutch invalidity benefit, that benefit shall be awarded in accordance with rules laid down by Article 46(2) of the Regulation:

(i)   in accordance with the provisions laid down by the abovementioned Law of 18 February 1966 (WAO), if, at the time of occurrence of the incapacity for work he was insured for the same risk under the legislation of another Member State as an employed person within the meaning of Article 1(a) of the Regulation;

(ii)   in accordance with the provisions laid down by the abovementioned law of 11 December 1975 (AAW) if, when the incapacity for work arose, he:

—was insured for the risk under the legislation of another Member State but not in the capacity of employed person within the meaning of Article 1(a) of the Regulation, or

—was not insured for the risk under the legislation of another Member State but can assert a claim to benefits under the legislation of another Member State.

If the amount of the benefit calculated pursuant to the provisions of (i) is less than that resulting from application of the provisions of (ii), the last-mentioned benefit shall be payable.

(c) In the calculation of the benefits awarded in accordance with the abovementioned Law of 18 February 1966 (WAO) or in accordance with the abovementioned law of 11 December 1975 (AAW), the Dutch institutions shall take account of:

—periods of paid employment and periods treated as such completed in the Netherlands before 1 July 1967,

—periods of insurance completed under the abovementioned Law of 18 February 1966 (WAO),

—periods of insurance completed by the person concerned after the age of 15 years under the abovementioned Law of 11 December 1975 (AAW) in so far as these do not coincide with the periods of insurance completed under the abovementioned law of 18 February 1966 (WAO).

(d) In the calculation of the Netherlands invalidity benefit pursuant to Article 40(1) of the Regulation, the Dutch institutions do not take account of any supplements to be awarded under the provision of the Law on supplements. The right to that supplement and the amount thereof are calculated only on the basis of the Law on supplements.

5.   *Application of Netherlands legislation on family allowances*

(a)   An employed or self-employed person to whom Netherlands legislation on family benefits becomes applicable during a quarter and who was, on the first day of that quarter, subject to the corresponding legislation of another Member State, shall be considered as being insured as from that first day under Netherlands law.

(b)   The amount of the family benefits which may be claimed by an employed or self-employed person who is considered, pursuant to (a), as being insured under Netherlands legislation on family benefits shall be fixed in accordance with the detailed arrangements laid down in the implementing Regulation referred to in Article 98 of the Regulation.

6. *Application of certain transitional provisions*

Article 45(1) shall not apply to the assessment of entitlement to benefits under the transitional provisions of the legislation on general old-age insurance (Article 46), on general insurance for widows and orphans and on general insurance against incapacity for work.

K. AUSTRIA

1. For the purpose of applying Chapter 1 of Title III of the Regulation, a person receiving a civil servant's pension shall be considered to be a pensioner.

2. For the purpose of applying Article 46(2) of the Regulation, increments for contributions for supplementary insurance and the miner's supplementary benefit under Austrian legislation shall be disregarded. In these cases the amount calculated according to Article 46(2) of the Regulation shall be increased by increments for contributions for supplementary insurance and the miner's supplementary benefit.

3. For the purpose of applying Article 46(2) of the Regulation, in applying Austrian legislation the day relevant for a pension (Stichtag) shall be considered as the date when the risk materialises.

4. The application of the provisions of the Regulation shall not have the effect of reducing any entitlement to benefits by virtue of Austrian legislation with regard to persons who have suffered in their social security situation for political or religious reasons or for reasons of their descent.

L. PORTUGAL

Serving or retired civil servants, and members of their families, covered by a special health care scheme, may receive sickness and maternity benefits in kind in the event of immediate need during a stay in the territory of another Member State or when travelling there to receive care appropriate to their state of health with the prior authorisation of the competent Portuguese institution, in accordance with the procedures laid down in Article 22(1)(a) and (c), the second sentence of paragraph 2 and paragraph 3 and in Article 31(1) of Regulation (EEC) No. 1408/71, under the same conditions as employed and self-employed persons covered by the general social security scheme.

M. FINLAND

1. In order to determine whether the period between the occurrence of the pension contingency and the pensionable age (future period) should be taken into account when calculating the amount of the Finnish employment pension, the periods of insurance or residence under the legislation of another Member State shall be taken into consideration for the condition relating to residence in Finland.

2. Where employment or self-employment in Finland has terminated and the contingency occurs during employment or self-employment in another Member State and where the pension according to the Finnish employment pension legislation no longer includes the period between the contingency and the pensionable age (future period), periods of insurance under the legislation of another Member State shall be taken into consideration for the requirement of the future period as if they were periods of insurance in Finland.

3. When, under the legislation of Finland, an increment is payable by an institution in Finland because of a delay in processing a claim for a benefit, a claim submitted to an institution of another Member State shall, for the purpose of applying the provisions of the Finnish legislation relating to such increment, be considered to have been presented on the date when that claim, along with all necessary enclosures, reaches the competent institution in Finland.

N. SWEDEN

1. When applying Article 18(1) for the purpose of establishing a person's entitlement to a parental benefit a period of insurance completed under the legislation of another Member State than Sweden shall be considered to be based on the same average earnings as the Swedish periods of insurance to which they are aggregated.

2. The provisions of the Regulation on the aggregation of insurance or residence periods shall not apply to the transitional rules of the Swedish legislation on the right to a more favourable calculation of basic pensions for persons residing in Sweden for a specified period preceding the date of the claim.

3. For the purpose of establishing the entitlement to an invalidity or survivor's pension partly based on future assumed insurance periods a person shall be considered to meet the insurance and income requirements of the Swedish legislation when covered as an employed or self-employed person by an insurance or residence scheme of another Member State.

4. Years of care of small children shall, according to prescribed conditions of the Swedish legislation, be considered as insurance periods for supplementary pension purposes even when the child and the person concerned are residing in another Member State, provided that the person taking care of the child is on parental leave under the provisions of the Law on Right to Leave for Child Rearing.

O. UNITED KINGDOM

1. When a person who is normally resident in Gibraltar, or who has been required, since he last arrived in Gibraltar, to pay contributions under the legislation of Gibraltar as an employed person, applies, as a result of incapacity to work, maternity or unemployment, for exemption from the payment of contributions over a certain period, and asks for contributions for that period to be credited to him, any period during which that person has been working in the territory of a Member State other than the United Kingdom shall, for the purposes of his application, be regarded as a period during which he has been employed in Gibraltar and for which he has paid contributions as an employed person in accordance with the legislation of Gibraltar.

2. Where, in accordance with United Kigndom legislation, a person may be entitled to a retirement pension if:

(a) the contributions of a former spouse are taken into account as if they were that person's own contributions, or

(b) the relevant contribution conditions are satisfied by that person's spouse or former spouse,

then provided, in each case, that the spouse or former spouse is or was an employed or self-employed person who had been subject to the legislation of two or more Member States, the provisions of Chapter 3 of Title III of the

Regulation shall apply in order to determine entitlement under United Kingdom legislation. In this case, references in the said Chapter 3 to 'periods of insurance' shall be construed as references to periods of insurance completed by:

(i)   a spouse or former spouse, where a claim is made by a married woman, a man who is widowed or a person whose marriage has terminated otherwise than by the death of the spouse, or

(ii)   a former spouse, where a claim is made by a widow, who was not in receipt of a survivor's benefit immediately before reaching pensionable age or who is only in receipt of an age-related widow's pension calculated pursuant to Article 46(2) of the Regulation.

3.   (a)   If unemployment benefit provided under United Kingdom legislation is paid to a person pursuant to Article 71(1)(a)(ii) or (b)(ii) of the Regulation, then for the purpose of satisfying the conditions imposed by United Kingdom legislation in relation to child benefit concerning a period of presence within Great Britain or, as the case may be, Northern Ireland, periods of insurance, employment or self-employment completed by that person under the legislation of another Member State shall be regarded as periods of presence in Great Britain or, as the case may be, Northern Ireland.

(b)   If, pursuant to Title II of the Regulation, excluding Article 13(2)(f), United Kingdom legislation is applicable in respect of an employed or self-employed person who does not satisfy the condition imposed by United Kingdom legislation in relation to child benefit concerning:

(i)   presence within Great Britain or, as the case may be, Northern Ireland, he shall be regarded, for the purpose of satisfying such condition, as being so present;

(ii)   a period of presence within Great Britain, or, as the case may be, Northern Ireland, periods of insurance, employment or self-employment completed by the said worker under the legislation of another Member State shall, for the purpose of satisfying such conditions, be regarded as periods of presence in Great Britain or, as the case may be, Northern Ireland.

(c)   In respect of claims to family allowances under the legislation of Gibraltar the foregoing provisions of subparagraphs (a) and (b) shall apply by analogy.

4.   The widow's payment provided under United Kingdom legislation shall be treated, for the purposes of Chapter 3 of the Regulation, as a survivor's pension.

5.   For the purposes of applying Article 10a(2) to the provisions governing entitlement to attendance allowance, invalid care allowance and disability living allowance, a period of employment, self-employment or residence completed in the territory of a Member State other than the United Kingdom shall be taken into account insofar as is necessary to satisfy conditions as to presence in the United Kingdom, prior to the day on which entitlement to the benefit in question first arises.

6.   In the event of an employed person subject to United Kingdom legislation being the victim of an accident after leaving the territory of one Member State while travelling, in the course of this employment, to the territory of another Member State, but before arriving there, his entitlement to benefits in respect of that accident shall be established:

(a)   as if the accident had occurred within the territory of the United Kingdom, and

(b)   for the purpose of determining whether he was an employed earner under the legislation of Great Britain or the legislation of Northern Ireland or an employed person under the legislation of Gibraltar, by disregrding his absence from those territories.

7.   This Regulation does not apply to those provisions of United Kingdom legislation which are intended to bring into force any social security agreement concluded between the United Kingdom and a third State.

8.   For the purposes of Chapter 3 of Title III of the Regulation no account shall be taken of graduated contributions paid by the insured person under United Kingdom legislation or of graduated retirement benefits payable under that legislation. The amount of the graduated benefits shall be added to the amount of the benefit due under the United Kingdom legislation as determined in accordance with the said chapter. The total of these two amounts shall constitute the benefit actually due to the person concerned.

9. ...

10.   For the purpose of applying the Non-Contributory Social Insurance Benefit and Unemployment Insurance Ordinance (Gibraltar), any person to whom this Regulation is applicable shall be deemed to be ordinarily resident in Gibraltar if he resides in a Member State.

11.   For the purpose of Articles 10, 27, 28, 28a, 29, 30 and 31 of the Regulation, the attendance allowance granted to an employed or self-employed person under United Kingdom legislation shall be considered as an invalidity benefit.

12.   For the purpose of Article 10(1) of the Regulation any beneficiary under United Kingdom legislation who is staying in the territory of another Member State shall, during that stay, be considered as if he resided in the territory of that other Member State.

13.1   For the purpose of calculating an earnings factor with a view to determining the right to benefits under United Kingdom legislation, subject to point 15, each week during which an employed or self-employed person has been subject to the legislation of another Member State and which commenced during the relevant income tax year within the meaning of United Kingdom legislation shall be taken into account in the following way:

(a)   Periods between 6 April 1975 and 5 April 1987:

(i)   for each week of insurance, employment or residence as an employed person, the person concerned shall be deemed to have paid contributions as an employed earner on the basis of earnings equivalent to two-thirds of that year's upper earnings limit;

(ii)   for each week of insurance, self-employment or residence as a self-employed person the person concerned shall be deemed to have paid class 2 contributions as a self-employed earner.

(b)   Periods from 6 April 1987 onwards:

(i)   for each week of insurance, employment or residence as an employed person, the person concerned shall be deemed to have received, and paid contributions as an employed earner, for, weekly earnings equivalent to two-thirds of that week's upper earnings limit;

(ii)   for each week of insurance, self-employment or residence as a self-employed person the person concerned shall be deemed to have paid class 2 contributions as a self-employed earner.

(c)   For each full week during which he has completed a period treated as a period of insurance, employment, self-employment or residence, the person concerned shall be deemed to have had contributions or earnings credited to him as appropriate, but only to the extent required to bring his total earnings factor for that tax year to the level required to make that tax year a reckonable year within the meaning of the United Kingdom legislation governing the crediting of contributions or earnings.

13.2   For the purposes of Article 46(2)(b) of the Regulation, where:

(a)   if in any income tax year starting on or after 6 April 1975, an employed person has completed periods of insurance, employment or residence exclusively in a Member State other than the United Kingdom, and the application of paragraph 1(a)(i) or paragraph 1(b)(i) results in that year being counted as a qualifying year within the meaning of United Kingdom legislation for the purposes of Article 46(2)(a) of the Regulation, he shall be deemed to have been insured for 52 weeks in that year in that other Member State:

(b)   any income tax year starting on or after 6 April 1975 does not count as a qualifying year within the meaning of United Kingdom legislation for the purposes of Article 46(2)(a) of the Regulation, any periods of insurance, employment or residence completed in that year shall be disregarded.

13.3   For the purpose of converting an earnings factor into periods of insurance the earnings factor achieved in the relevant income tax year within the meaning of United Kingdom legislation shall be divided by that year's lower earnings limit. The result shall be expressed as a whole number, any remaining fraction being ignored. The figure so calculated shall be treated as representing the number of weeks of insurance completed under United Kingdom legislation during that year provided that such figure shall not exceed the number of weeks during which in that year that person was subject to that legislation.

14.   In applying Article 40(3)(a)(ii), account shall only be taken of periods during which the employed or self-employed person was incapable of work within the meaning of United Kingdom legislation.

15.1   For the purpose of calculating, under Article 46(2)(a) of the Regulation, the theoretical amount of that part of the pension which consists of an additional component under United Kingdom legislation:

(a)   the expression 'earnings, contributions or increases' in Article 47(1)(b) of the Regulation shall be construed as meaning surpluses in earnings factors as defined in the Social Security Pensions Act 1975 or, as the case may be, the Social Security Pensions (Northern Ireland) Order 1975;

(b)   an average of the surpluses in earnings factor shall be calculated in accordance with Article 47(1)(b) of the Regulation as construed in subparagraph (a) above by dividing the aggregated surpluses recorded under United Kingdom legislation by the number of income tax years within the meaning of United Kingdom legislation (including part income tax years) completed under that legislation since 6 April 1978 which occur within the relevant period of insurance.

15.2   The expression 'periods of insurance or residence' in Article 46(2) of the Regulation shall be construed, for the purpose of assessing the amount of that part of the pension which consists of an additional component under United Kingdom legislation, as meaning periods of insurance or residence which have been completed since 6 April 1978.

16.   An unemployed person returning to the United Kingdom after the end of the period of three months during which he continued to receive benefits

under the legislation of the United Kingdom pursuant to Article 69(1) of the Regulation shall continue to be entitled to unemployment benefits by way of derogation from Article 69(2) if he satisfies the conditions in the aforementioned legislation.

17. For the purposes of entitlement to severe disablement allowance any employed or self-employed person who is, or has been, subject to United Kingdom legislation in accordance with Title II of the Regulation, excluding Article 13(2)(f):

(a) shall, for the entire period during which he was employed or self-employed and subject to United Kingdom legislation whilst present or resident in another Member State, be treated as having been present or resident in the United Kingdom;

(b) shall be entitled to have periods of insurance as an employed or self-employed person completed in the territory and under the legislation of another Member State treated as periods of presence or residence in the United Kingdom.

18. A period of subjection to United Kingdom legislation in accordance with Article 13(2)(f) of the Regulation may not:

(i) be taken into account under that provision as a period of subjection to United Kingdom legislation for the purposes of Title III of the Regulation, nor

(ii) make the United Kingdom the competent State for the provision of the benefits provided for in Article 18, 38 or 39(1) of the Regulation.

19. Subject to any conventions concluded with individual Member States, for the purposes of Article 13(2)(f) of the Regulation and Article 10b of the Implementing Regulation, United Kingdom legislation shall cease to apply at the end of the day on the latest of the following three days to any person previously subject to United Kingdom legislation as an employed or self-employed person:

(a) the day on which residence is transferred to the other Member State referred to in Article 13(2)(f);

(b) the day of cessation of the employment or self-employment, whether permanent or temporary, during which that person was subject to United Kingdom legislation;

(c) the last day of any period of receipt of United Kingdom sickness or maternity benefit (including benefits in kind for which the United Kingdom is the competent State) or unemployment benefit which

(i) began before the date of transfer of residence to another Member State or, if later,

(ii) immediately followed employment or self-employment in another Member State while that person was subject to United Kingdom legislation.

20. The fact that a person has become subject to the legislation of another Member State in accordance with Article 13(2)(f) of the Regulation, Article 10b of the Implementing Regulation and point 19 above, shall not prevent:

(a) the application to him by the United Kingdom as the competent State of the provisions relating to employed or self-employed persons of Title III, Chapter 1 and Chapter 2, Section 1 or Article 40(2) of the Regulation if he remains an employed or self-employed person for those purposes and was last so insured under the legislation of the United Kingdom;

(b) his treatment as an employed or self-employed person for the purposes of Chapters 7 and 8 of Title III of the Regulation or Articles 10 or 10a of the Implementing Regulation, provided United Kingdom benefit under Chapter 1 of Title III is payable to him in accordance with paragraph (a).

ANNEX VII(B)(2)(5)(6)(15)
INSTANCES IN WHICH A PERSON SHALL BE SIMULTANEOUSLY SUBJECT TO THE LEGISLATION OF TWO MEMBER STATES
(Article 14c(1)(b) of the Regulation)

1. Where he is self-employed in Belgium and gainfully employed in any other Member State.

2. Where a person resident in Denmark is self-employed in Denmark and gainfully employed in any other Member State.

3. For the agricultural accident insurance scheme and the old-age insurance scheme for farmers: where he is self-employed in farming in Germany and gainfully employed in any other Member State.

4. Where a person resident in Spain is self-employed in Spain and gainfully employed in any other Member State.

5. Where he is self-employed in France and gainfully employed in any other Member State, except Luxembourg.

6. Where he is self-employed in farming in France and gainfully employed in Luxembourg.

7. For the pension insurance scheme for self-employed persons: where he is self-employed in Greece and gainfully employed in any other Member State.

8. Where he is self-employed in Italy and gainfully employed in any other Member State.

9. Where a person is self-employed in Austria and gainfully employed in any other Member State.

10. Where he is self-employed in Portugal and gainfully employed in any other Member State.

11. Where a person resident in Finland is self-employed in Finland and gainfully employed in any other Member State.

12. Where a person resident in Sweden is self-employed in Sweden and gainfully employed in any other Member State.

SOCIAL POLICY: EQUAL PAY AND TREATMENT

COUNCIL DIRECTIVE OF 10 FEBRUARY 1975 ON THE APPROXIMATION OF THE LAWS OF THE MEMBER STATES RELATING TO THE APPLICATION OF THE PRINCIPLE OF EQUAL PAY FOR MEN AND WOMEN (75/117/EEC)

[OJ 1975, No. L45/19]

THE COUNCIL OF THE EUROPEAN COMMUNITIES,

Having regard to the Treaty establishing the European Economic Community, and in particular Article 100 thereof;

Having regard to the proposal from the Commission;

Having regard to the Opinion of the European Parliament;[1]

Having regard to the Opinion of the Economic and Steel Community;[2]

Whereas implementation of the principle that men and women should receive equal pay contained in Article 119 of the Treaty is an integral part of the establishment and functioning of the common market;

Whereas it is primarily the responsibility of the Member States to ensure the application of this principle by means of appropriate laws, regulations and administrative provision;

Whereas the Council resolution of 21 January 1974[3] governing a social action programme, aimed at making it possible to harmonise living and working conditions while the improvement is being maintained and at achieving a balanced social and economic development of the Community, recognised that priority should be given to action taken on behalf of women as regards access to employment and vocational training and advancement, and as regards working conditions, including pay;

Whereas it is desirable to reinforce the basic laws by standards aimed at facilitating the practical application of the principle of equality in such a way that all employees in the Community can be protected in these matters;

Whereas differences continue to exist in the various Member States despite the efforts made to apply the resolution of the conference of the Member States of 30 December 1961 on equal pay for men and women and whereas, therefore, the national provisions should be approximated as regards applications of the principle of equal pay,

HAS ADOPTED THIS DIRECTIVE:

Notes
[1] OJ No. C55, 13.5.1974, p. 43.
[2] OJ No. C88, 26.7.1974, p. 7.
[3] OJ No. C13, 12.2.1974, p. 1.

Article 1

The principle of equal pay for men and women outlined in Article 119 of the Treaty, hereinafter called 'principle of equal pay', means, for the same work or for work to which equal value is attributed, the elimination of all discrimination on grounds of sex with regard to all aspects and conditions of remuneration.

In particular, where a job classification system is used for determining pay, it must be based on the same criteria for both men and women and so drawn up as to exclude any discrimination on grounds of sex.

Article 2

Member States shall introduce into their national legal systems such measures as are necessary to enable all employees who consider themselves wronged by failure to apply the principle of equal pay to pursue their claims by judicial process after possible recourse to other competent authorities.

Article 3

Member States shall abolish all discrimination between men and women arising from laws, regulations or administrative provisions which is contrary to the principle of equal pay.

Article 4

Member States shall take the necessary measures to ensure that provisions appearing in collective agreements, wage scales, wage agreements or individual contracts of employment which are contrary to the principle of equal pay shall be, or may be declared, null and void or may be amended.

Article 5

Member States shall take the necessary measures to protect employees against dismissal by the employer as a reaction to a complaint within the undertaking or to any legal proceedings aimed at enforcing compliance with the principle of equal pay.

Article 6

Member States shall, in accordance with their national circumstances and legal systems, take the measures necessary to ensure that the principle of equal pay is applied. They shall see that effective means are available to take care that this principle is observed.

Article 7

Member States shall take care that the provisions adopted pursuant to this Directive, together with the relevant provisions already in force, are brought to the attention of employees by all appropriate means, for example at their place of employment.

Article 8

1.   Member States shall put into force the laws, regulations and administrative provisions necessary in order to comply with this Directive within one year of its notification and shall immediately inform the Commission thereof.

2.   Member States shall communicate to the Commission the texts of the laws, regulations and administrative provisions which they adopt in the field covered by this Directive.

Article 9

Within two years of the expiry of the one-year period referred to in Article 8, Member States shall forward all necessary information to the Commission to enable it to draw up a report on the application of the Directive for submission to the Council.

Article 10
This Directive is addressed to the Member States.

Done at Brussels, 10 February 1975.
For the Council
The President
G. FITZGERALD

COUNCIL DIRECTIVE OF 9 FEBRUARY 1976 ON THE IMPLEMENTATION OF THE PRINCIPLE OF EQUAL TREATMENT FOR MEN AND WOMEN AS REGARDS ACCESS TO EMPLOYMENT, VOCATIONAL TRAINING AND PROMOTION, AND WORKING CONDITIONS (76/207/EEC)
[OJ 1976, No. L39/40]

THE COUNCIL OF THE EUROPEAN COMMUNITIES,

Having regard to the Treaty establishing the European Economic Community, and in particular Article 235 thereof,
    Having regard to the proposal from the Commission,
    Having regard to the opinion of the European Parliament,[1]
    Having regard to the opinion of the Economic and Social Committee,[2]
    Whereas the Council, in its resolution of 21 January 1974 concerning a social action programme,[3] included among the priorities action for the purpose of achieving equality between men and women as regards access to employment and vocational training and promotion and as regards working conditions, including pay;
    Whereas, with regard to pay, the Council adopted on 10 February 1975 Directive 75/117/EEC on the approximation of the laws of the Member States relating to the application of the principle of equal pay for men and women;[4]
    Whereas Community action to achieve the principle of equal treatment for men and women in respect of access to employment and vocational training and promotion and in respect of other working conditions also appears to be necessary; whereas, equal treatment for male and female workers constitutes one of the objectives of the Community, in so far as the harmonisation of living and working conditions while maintaining their improvement are *inter alia* to be furthered; whereas the Treaty does not confer the necessary specific powers for this purpose;
    Whereas the definition and progressive implementation of the principle of equal treatment in matters of social security should be ensured by means of subsequent instruments,

HAS ADOPTED THIS DIRECTIVE:

Notes
[1] OJ No. C111, 20.5.1975, p. 14.
[2] OJ No. C286, 15.12.1975, p. 8.
[3] OJ No. C13, 12.2.1974, p. 1.
[4] OJ No. L45, 19.2.1975, p. 19.

Article 1

1.   The purpose of this Directive is to put into effect in the Member States the principle of equal treatment for men and women as regards access to employment, including promotion, and to vocational training and as regards working conditions and, on the conditions referred to in paragraph 2, social security. This principle is hereinafter referred to as 'the principle of equal treatment'.

2.   With a view to ensuring the progressive implementation of the principle of equal treatment in matters of social security, the Council, acting on a proposal from the Commission, will adopt provisions defining its substance, its scope and the arrangements for its application.

Article 2

1.   For the purposes of the following provisions, the principle of equal treatment shall mean that there shall be no discrimination whatsoever on grounds of sex either directly or indirectly by reference in particular to marital or family status.

2.   This Directive shall be without prejudice to the right of Member States to exclude from its field of application those occupational activities and, where appropriate, the training leading thereto, for which, by reason of their nature or the context in which they are carried out, the sex of the worker constitutes a determining factor.

3.   This Directive shall be without prejudice to provisions concerning the protection of women, particularly as regards pregnancy and maternity.

4.   This Directive shall be without prejudice to measures to promote equal opportunity for men and women, in particular by removing existing inequalities which affect women's opportunities in the areas referred to in Article 1(1).

Article 3

1.   Application of the principle of equal treatment means that there shall be no discrimination whatsoever on grounds of sex in the conditions, including selection criteria, for access to all jobs or posts, whatever the sector or branch of activity, and to all levels of the occupational hierarchy.

2.   To this end, Member States shall take the measures necessary to ensure that:

(a)   any laws, regulations and administrative provisions contrary to the principle of equal treatment shall be abolished;

(b)   any provisions contrary to the principle of equal treatment which are included in collective agreements, individual contracts of employment, internal rules of undertakings or in rules governing the independent occupations and professions shall be, or may be declared, null and void or may be amended;

(c)   those laws, regulations and administrative provisions contrary to the principle of equal treatment when the concern for protection which originally inspired them is no longer well founded shall be revised; and that where similar provisions are included in collective agreements labour and management shall be requested to undertake the desired revision.

Article 4

Application of the principle of equal treatment with regard to access to all types and to all levels, of vocational guidance, vocational training, advanced vocational training and retraining, means that Member States shall take all necessary measure to ensure that:

(a)   any laws, regulations and administrative provisions contrary to the principle of equal treatment shall be abolished;

(b)   any provisions contrary to the principle of equal treatment which are included in collective agreements, individual contracts of employment, internal rules of undertakings or in rules governing the independent occupations and professions shall be, or may be declared, null and void or may be amended;

(c)   without prejudice to the freedom granted in certain Member States to certain private training establishments, vocational guidance, vocational training, advanced vocational training and retraining shall be accessible on the basis of the same criteria and at the same levels without any discrimination on grounds of sex.

Article 5

1.   Application of the principle of equal treatment with regard to working conditions, including the conditions governing dismissal, means that men and women shall be guaranteed the same conditions without discrimination on grounds of sex.

2.   To this end, Member States shall take the measures necessary to ensure that:

(a)   any laws, regulations and administrative provisions contrary to the principle of equal treatment shall be abolished;

(b)   any provisions contrary to the principle of equal treatment which are included in collective agreements, individual contracts of employment, internal rules of undertakings or in rules governing the independent occupations and professions shall be, or may be declared, null and void or may be amended;

(c)   those laws, regulations and administrative provisions contrary to the principle of equal treatment when the concern for protection which originally inspired them is no longer well founded shall be revised; and that where similar provisions are included in collective agreements labour and management shall be requested to undertake the desired revision.

Article 6

Member States shall introduce into their national legal systems such measures as are necessary to enable all persons who consider themselves wronged by failure to apply to them the principle of equal treatment within the meaning of Articles 3, 4 and 5 to pursue their claims by judicial process after possible recourse to other competent authorities.

Article 7

Member States shall take the necessary measures to protect employees against dismissal by the employer as a reaction to a complaint within the undertaking or to any legal proceedings aimed at enforcing compliance with the principle of equal treatment.

Article 8

Member States shall take care that the provisions adopted pursuant to this Directive, together with the relevant provisions already in force, are brought to the attention of employees by all appropriate means, for example at their place of employment.

Article 9

1.   Member States shall put into force the laws, regulations and administrative provisions necessary in order to comply with this Directive within 30

months of its notification and shall immediately inform the Commission thereof.

However, as regards the first part of Article 3(2)(c) and the first part of Article 5(2)(c), Member States shall carry out a first examination and if necessary a first revision of the laws, regulations and administrative provisions referred to therein within four years of notification of this Directive.

2.   Member States shall periodically assess the occupational activities referred to in Article 2(2) in order to decide, in the light of social developments, whether there is justification for maintaining the exclusions concerned. They shall notify the Commission of the results of this assessment.

3.   Member States shall also communicate to the Commission the texts of laws, regulations and administrative provisions which they adopt in the field covered by this Directive.

Article 10
Within two years following expiry of the 30-month period laid down in the first subparagraph of Article 9(1), Member States shall forward all necessary information to the Commission to enable it to draw up a report on the application of this Directive for submission to the Council.

Article 11
This Directive is addressed to the Member States.

Done at Brussels, 9 February 1976.
For the Council
The President
G. THORN

COUNCIL DIRECTIVE OF 19 DECEMBER 1978 ON THE PROGRESSIVE IMPLEMENTATION OF THE PRINCIPLE OF EQUAL TREATMENT FOR MEN AND WOMEN IN MATTERS OF SOCIAL SECURITY (79/7/EEC)
[OJ 1979, No. L6/24]

THE COUNCIL OF THE EUROPEAN COMMUNITIES,

Having regard to the Treaty establishing the European Economic Community, and in particular Article 235 thereof,
  Having regard to the proposal from the Commission,[1]
  Having regard to the opinion of the European Parliament,[2]
  Having regard to the opinion of the Economic and Social Committee,[3]
  Whereas Article 1(2) of Council Directive 76/207/EEC of 9 February 1976 on the implementation of the principle of equal treatment for men and women as regards access to employment, vocational training and promotion, and working conditions[4] provides that, with a view to ensuring the progressive implementation of the principle of equal treatment in matters of social security,

Notes
[1]OJ No. C34, 11.2.1977, p. 3.
[2]OJ No. C299, 12.12.1977, p. 13.
[3]OJ No. C180, 28.7.1977, p. 36.
[4]OJ No. L36, 14.2.1976, p. 40.

the Council, acting on a proposal from the Commission, will adopt provisions defining its substance, its scope and the arrangements for its application; whereas the Treaty does not confer the specific powers required for this purpose;

Whereas the principle of equal treatment in matters of social security should be implemented in the first place in the statutory schemes which provide protection against the risks of sickness, invalidity, old age, accidents at work, occupational diseases and unemployment, and in social assistance in so far as it is intended to supplement or replace the abovementioned schemes;

Whereas the implementation of the principle of equal treatment in matters of social security does not prejudice the provisions relating to the protection of women on the ground of maternity; whereas, in this respect, Member States may adopt specific provisions for women to remove existing instances of unequal treatment,

HAS ADOPTED THIS DIRECTIVE:

Article 1

The purpose of this Directive is the progressive implementation, in the field of social security and other elements of social protection provided for in Article 3, of the principle of equal treatment for men and women in matters of social security, hereinafter referred to as 'the principle of equal treatment'.

Article 2

This Directive shall apply to the working population—including self-employed persons, workers and self-employed persons whose activity is interrupted by illness, accident or involuntary unemployment and persons seeking employment—and to retired or invalided workers and self-employed persons.

Article 3

1.   This Directive shall apply to:

(a)   statutory schemes which provide protection against the following risks:

- — sickness,
- — invalidity,
- — old age,
- — accidents at work and occupational diseases,
- — unemployment;

(b)   social assistance, in so far as it is intended to supplement or replace the schemes referred to in (a).

2.   This Directive shall not apply to the provisions concerning survivors' benefits nor to those concerning family benefits, except in the case of family benefits granted by way of increases of benefits due in respect of the risks referred to in paragraph 1(a).

3.   With a view to ensuring implementation of the principle of equal treatment in occupational schemes, the Council, acting on a proposal from the Commission, will adopt provisions defining its substance, its scope and the arrangements for its application.

Article 4

1.   The principle of equal treatment means that there shall be no discrimination whatsoever on ground of sex either directly, or indirectly by reference in particular to marital or family status, in particular as concerns:

— the scope of the schemes and the conditions of access thereto,
— the obligation to contribute and the calculation of contributions,
— the calculation of benefits including increases due in respect of a spouse and for dependants and the conditions governing the duration and retention of entitlement to benefits.

2. The principle of equal treatment shall be without prejudice to the provisions relating to the protection of women on the grounds of maternity.

Article 5
Member States shall take the measures necessary to ensure that any laws, regulations and administrative provisions contrary to the principle of equal treatment are abolished.

Article 6
Member States shall introduce into their national legal systems such measures as are necessary to enable all persons who consider themselves wronged by failure to apply the principle of equal treatment to pursue their claims by judicial process, possibly after recourse to other competent authorities.

Article 7
1. This Directive shall be without prejudice to the right of Member States to exclude from its scope:

(a) the determination of pensionable age for the purposes of granting old-age and retirement pensions and the possible consequences thereof for other benefits;

(b) advantages in respect of old-age pension schemes granted to persons who have brought up children; the acquisition of benefit entitlements following periods of interruption of employment due to the bringing up of children;

(c) the granting of old-age or invalidity benefit entitlements by virtue of the derived entitlements of a wife;

(d) the granting of increases of long-term invalidity, old-age, accidents at work and occupational disease benefits for a dependent wife;

(e) the consequences of the exercise, before the adoption of this Directive, of a right of option not to acquire rights or incur obligations under a statutory scheme.

2. Member States shall periodically examine matters excluded under paragraph 1 in order to ascertain, in the light of social developments in the matter concerned, whether there is justification for maintaining the exclusions concerned.

Article 8
1. Member States shall bring into force the laws, regulations and administrative provisions necessary to comply with this Directive within six years of its notification. They shall immediately inform the Commission thereof.

2. Member States shall communicate to the Commission the text of laws, regulations and administrative provisions which they adopt in the field covered by this Directive, including measures adopted pursuant to Article 7(2).

They shall inform the Commission of their reasons for maintaining any existing provisions on the matters referred to in Article 7(1) and of the possibilities for reviewing them at a later date.

Article 9

Within seven years of notification of this Directive, Member States shall forward all information necessary to the Commission to enable it to draw up a report on the application of this Directive for submission to the Council and to propose such further measures as may be required for the implementation of the principle of equal treatment.

Article 10

This Directive is addressed to the Member States.

Done at Brussels, 19 December 1978.

COUNCIL DIRECTIVE OF 24 JULY 1986 ON THE IMPLEMENTATION OF THE PRINCIPLE OF EQUAL TREATMENT FOR MEN AND WOMEN IN OCCUPATIONAL SOCIAL SECURITY SCHEMES (86/378/EEC)
[OJ 1986, No. L225/40][1]

THE COUNCIL OF THE EUROPEAN COMMUNITIES,

Having regard to the Treaty establishing the European Economic Community, and in particular Articles 100 and 235 thereof,

Having regard to the proposal from the Commission,[2]

Having regard to the opinion of the European Parliament,[3]

Having regard to the opinion of the Economic and Social Committee,[4]

Whereas the Treaty provides that each Member State shall ensure the application of the principle that men and women should receive equal pay for equal work; whereas 'pay' should be taken to mean the ordinary basic or minimum wage or salary and any other consideration, whether in cash or in kind, which the worker receives, directly or indirectly, from his employer in respect of his employment;

Whereas, although the principle of equal pay does indeed apply directly in cases where discrimination can be determined solely on the basis of the criteria of equal treatment and equal pay, there are also situations in which implementation of this principle implies the adoption of additional measures which more clearly define its scope;

Whereas Article 1(2) of Council Directive 76/207/EEC of 9 February 1976 on the implementation of the principle of equal treatment for men and women as regards access to employment, vocational training and promotion, and working conditions[5] provides that, with a view to ensuring the progressive implementation of the principle of equal treatment in matters of social security, the Council, acting on a proposal from the Commission, will adopt provisions defining its substance, its scope and the arrangements for its application;

Notes

[1]Editor's Note: As amended by Corrigendum 1986 L283/27 and Directive 96/97 (OJ 1997 L46/20). The non-amending parts of the Directive 96/97 are reproduced following Directive 86/613 below.

[2]OJ No. C134, 21.5.1983, p. 7.

[3]OJ No. C117, 30.4.1984, p. 169.

[4]OJ No. C35, 9.2.1984, p. 7.

[5]OJ No. L39, 14.2.1976, p. 40.

whereas the Council adopted to this end Directive 79/7/EEC of 19 December 1978 on the progressive implementation of the principle of equal treatment for men and women in matters of social security;[6]

Whereas Article 3(3) of Directive 79/7/EEC provides that, with a view to ensuring implementation of the principle of equal treatment in occupational schemes, the Council, acting on a proposal from the Commission, will adopt provisions defining its substance, its scope and the arrangements for its application;

Whereas the principle of equal treatment should be implemented in occupational social security schemes which provide protection against the risks specified in Article 3(1) of Directive 79/7/EEC as well as those which provide employees with any other consideration in cash or in kind within the meaning of the Treaty;

Whereas implementation of the principle of equal treatment does not prejudice the provisions relating to the protection of women by reason of maternity,

HAS ADOPTED THIS DIRECTIVE:

Note
[6]OJ No. C6, 10.1.1979, p. 24.

Article 1
The object of this Directive is to implement, in occupational social security schemes, the principle of equal treatment for men and women, hereinafter referred to as 'the principle of equal treatment'.

Article 2
1.   'Occupational social security schemes' means schemes not governed by Directive 79/7/EEC whose purpose is to provide workers, whether employees or self-employed, in an undertaking or group of undertakings, area of economic activity, occupational sector or group of such sectors with benefits intended to supplement the benefits provided by statutory social security schemes or to replace them, whether membership of such schemes is compulsory or optional.
2.   This Directive does not apply to:
  (a)   individual contracts for self-employed workers;
  (b)   schemes for self-employed workers having only one member;
  (c)   insurance contracts to which the employer is not a party, in the case of salaried workers;
  (d)   optional provisions of occupational schemes offered to participants individually to guarantee them:
    — either additional benefits, or
    — a choice of date on which the normal benefits for self-employed workers will start, or a choice between several benefits;
  (e)   occupational schemes in so far as benefits are financed by contributions paid by workers on a voluntary basis.
3.   This Directive does not preclude an employer granting to persons who have already reached the retirement age for the purposes of granting a pension by virtue of an occupational scheme, but who have not yet reached the retirement age for the purposes of granting a statutory retirement pension, a pension supplement, the aim of which is to make equal or more nearly equal the overall amount of benefit paid to these persons in relation to the amount

paid to persons of the other sex in the same situation who have already reached the statutory retirement age, until the persons benefiting from the supplement reach the statutory retirement age.

Article 3

This Directive shall apply to members of the working population including self-employed persons, persons whose activity is interrupted by illness, maternity, accident or involuntary unemployment and persons seeking employment, to retired and disabled workers and to those claiming under them, in accordance with national law and/or practice.

Article 4

This Directive shall apply to:

(a) occupational schemes which provide protection against the following risks:

— sickness,
— invalidity,
— old age, including early retirement,
— industrial accidents and occupational diseases,
— unemployment;

(b) occupational schemes which provide for other social benefits, in cash or in kind, and in particular survivors' benefits and family allowances, if such benefits are accorded to employed persons and thus constitute a consideration paid by the employer to the worker by reason of the latter's employment.

Article 5

1. Under the conditions laid down in the following provisions, the principle of equal treatment implies that there shall be no discrimination on the basis of sex, either directly or indirectly, by reference in particular to marital or family status, especially as regards:

— the scope of the schemes and the conditions of access to them;
— the obligation to contribute and the calculation of contributions;
— the calculation of benefits, including supplementary benefits due in respect of a spouse or dependants, and the conditions governing the duration and retention of entitlement to benefits.

2. The principle of equal treatment shall not prejudice the provisions relating to the protection of women by reason of maternity.

Article 6

1. Provisions contrary to the principle of equal treatment shall include those based on sex, either directly or indirectly, in particular by reference to marital or status family for:

(a) determining the persons who may participate in an occupational scheme;

(b) fixing the compulsory or optional nature of participation in an occupational scheme;

(c) laying down different rules as regards the age of entry into the scheme or the minimum period of employment or membership of the scheme required to obtain the benefits thereof;

(d) laying down different rules, except as provided for in points (h) and (i), for the reimbursement of contributions when a worker leaves a scheme without having fulfilled the conditions guaranteeing him a deferred right to long-term benefits;

(e)   setting different conditions for the granting of benefits of restricting such benefits to workers of one or other of the sexes;

(f)   fixing different retirement ages;

(g)   suspending the retention or acquisition of rights during periods of maternity leave or leave for family reasons which are granted by law or agreement and are paid by the employer;

(h)   setting different levels of benefit, except insofar as may be necessary to take account of actuarial calculation factors which differ according to sex in the case of defined contribution schemes;

In the case of funded defined-benefit schemes, certain elements (examples of which are annexed) may be unequal where the inequality of the amounts results from the effects of the use of actuarial factors differing according to sex at the time when the scheme's funding is implemented;

(i)   setting different levels of worker contribution;
setting different levels of employers' contribution, except:

— in the case of defined-contribution schemes if the aim is to equalise the amount of the final benefits or to make them more nearly equal for both sexes,

— in the case of funded defined-benefit schemes where the employer's contributions are intended to ensure the adequacy of the funds necessary to cover the cost of the benefits defined,

(j)   laying down different standards or standards applicable only to workers of a specified sex, except as provided for in subparagraphs (h) and (i), as regards the guarantee or retention of entitlement to deferred benefits when a worker leaves a scheme.

2.   Where the granting of benefits within the scope of this Directive is left to the discretion of the scheme's management bodies, the latter must comply with the principle of equal treatment.

Article 7
Member States shall take all necessary steps to ensure that:

(a)   provisions contrary to the principle of equal treatment in legally compulsory collective agreements, staff rules of undertakings or any other arrangements relating to occupational schemes are null and void, or may be declared null and void or amended;

(b)   schemes containing such provisions may not be approved or extended by administrative measures.

Article 8
1.   Member States shall take the necessary steps to ensure that the provisions of occupational schemes for self-employed workers contrary to the principle of equal treatment are revised with effect from 1 January 1993 at the latest.

2.   This Directive shall not preclude rights and obligations relating to a period of membership of an occupational scheme for self-employed workers prior to revision of that scheme from remaining subject to the provisions of the scheme in force during that period.

Article 9
As regards schemes for self-employed workers, Member States may defer compulsory application of the principle of equal treatment with regard to:

(a)   determination of pensionable age for the granting of old-age or retirement pensions, and the possible implications for other benefits:
— either until the date on which such equality is achieved in statutory schemes,
— or, at the latest, until such equality is required by a directive.

(b)   survivors' pensions until community law establishes the principle of equal treatment in statutory social security schemes in that regard;

(c)   the application of the first subparagraph of point (i) of Article 6(1) to take account of the different actuarial calculation factors, at the latest until 1 January 1999.

Article 9a

Where men and women may claim a flexible pensionable age under the same conditions, this shall not be deemed to be incompatible with this Directive.

Article 10

Member States shall introduce into their national legal systems such measures as are necessary to enable all persons who consider themselves injured by failure to apply the principle of equal treatment to pursue their claims before the courts, possibly after bringing the matters before other competent authorities.

Article 11

Member States shall take all the necessary steps to protect worker against dismissal where this constitutes a response on the part of the employer to a complaint made at undertaking level or to the institution of legal proceedings aimed at enforcing compliance with the principle of equal treatment.

Article 12

1.   Member States shall bring into force such laws, regulations and administrative provisions as are necessary in order to comply with this Directive at the latest three years after notification thereof. They shall immediately inform the Commission thereof.

2.   Member States shall communicate to the Commission at the latest five years after notification of this Directive all information necessary to enable the Commission to draw up a report on the application of this Directive for submission to the Council.

Article 13

This Directive is addressed to the Member States.

Done at Brussels, 24 July 1986.

ANNEX

Examples of elements which may be unequal, in respect of funded defined-benefit schemes, as referred to in Article 6(h):
— conversion into a capital sum of part of a periodic pension,
— transfer of pension rights,
— a reversionary pension payable to a dependant in return for the surrender of part of a pension,
— a reduced pension where the worker opts to take early retirement.

**COUNCIL DIRECTIVE 86/613 OF 11 DECEMBER 1986 ON THE
APPLICATION OF THE PRINCIPLE OF EQUAL TREATMENT
BETWEEN MEN AND WOMEN ENGAGED IN AN ACTIVITY,
INCLUDING AGRICULTURE, IN A SELF-EMPLOYED
CAPACITY, AND ON THE PROTECTION OF SELF-EMPLOYED
WOMEN DURING PREGNANCY AND MOTHERHOOD**
(86/613/EEC)
[OJ 1986, No. L359/56]

THE COUNCIL OF THE EUROPEAN COMMUNITIES,

Having regard to the Treaty establishing the European Economic Community,
and in particular Articles 100 and 235 thereof,

Having regard to the proposal from the Commission,[1]

Having regard to the opinion of the European Parliament,[2]

Having regard to the opinion of the Economic and Social Committee,[3]

Whereas, in its resolution of 12 July 1982 on the promotion of equal
opportunities for women,[4] the Council approved the general objectives of the
Commission communication concerning a new Community action programme on the promotion of equal opportunities for women (1982 to 1985)
and expressed the will to implement appropriate measures to achieve them;

Whereas action 5 of the programme referred to above concerns the
application of the principle of equal treatment to self-employed women and to
women in agriculture;

Whereas the implementation of the principle of equal pay for men and
women workers, as laid down in Article 119 of the Treaty, forms an integral
part of the establishment and functioning of the common market;

Whereas on 10 February 1975 the Council adopted Directive 75/117/EEC
on the approximation of the laws of the Member States relating to the
application of the principle of equal pay for men and women;[5]

Whereas, as regards other aspects of equality of treatment between men and
women, on 9 February 1976 the Council adopted Directive 76/207/EEC on
the implementation of the principle of equal treatment for men and women as
regards access to employment, vocational training and promotion, and working
conditions[6] and on 19 December 1978 Directive 79/7/EEC on the progressive
implementation of the principle of equal treatment for men and women in
matters of social security;[7]

Whereas, as regards persons engaged in a self-employed capacity, in
an activity in which their spouses are also engaged, the implementation of
the principle of equal treatment should be pursued through the adoption
of detailed provisions designed to cover the specific situation of these
persons;

Notes
[1] OJ No. C113, 27.4.1984, p. 4.
[2] OJ No. C172, 2.7.1984, p. 90.
[3] OJ No. C343, 24.12.1984, p. 1.
[4] OJ No. L186, 21.7.1982, p. 3.
[5] OJ No. L45, 19.2.1975, p. 19.
[6] OJ No. L39, 14.2.1975, p. 40.
[7] OJ No. L6, 10.1.1979, p. 24.

Whereas differences persist between the Member States in this field, whereas, therefore it is necessary to approximate national provisions with regard to the application of the principle of equal treatment;

Whereas in certain respects the Treaty does not confer the powers necessary for the specific actions required;

Whereas the implementation of the principle of equal treatment is without prejudice to measures concerning the protection of women during pregnancy and motherhood,

HAS ADOPTED THIS DIRECTIVE:

SECTION I   AIMS AND SCOPE

Article 1

The purpose of this Directive is to ensure, in accordance with the following provisions, application in the Member States of the principle of equal treatment as between men and women engaged in an activity in a self-employed capacity, or contributing to the pursuit of such an activity, as regards those aspects not covered by Directives 76/207/EEC and 79/7/EEC.

Article 2

This Directive covers:

(a)   self-employed workers, i.e., all persons pursuing a gainful activity for their own account, under the conditions laid down by national law, including farmers and members of the liberal professions;

(b)   their spouses, not being employees or partners, where they habitually, under the conditions laid down by national law, participate in the activities of the self-employed worker and perform the same tasks or ancillary tasks.

Article 3

For the purposes of this Directive the principle of equal treatment implies the absence of all discrimination on grounds of sex, either directly or indirectly, by reference in particular to marital or family status.

SECTION II EQUAL TREATMENT BETWEEN SELF-EMPLOYED MALE AND FEMALE WORKERS—POSITION OF THE SPOUSES WITHOUT PROFESSIONAL STATUS OF SELF-EMPLOYED WORKERS—PROTECTION OF SELF-EMPLOYED WORKERS OR WIVES OF SELF-EMPLOYED WORKERS DURING PREGNANCY AND MOTHERHOOD

Article 4

As regards self-employed persons, Member States shall take the measures necessary to ensure the elimination of all provisions which are contrary to the principle of equal treatment as defined in Directive 76/207/EEC, especially in respect of the establishment, equipment or extension of a business or the launching or extension of any other form of self-employed activity including financial facilities.

Article 5

Without prejudice to the specific conditions for access to certain activities which apply equally to both sexes, Member States shall take the measures necessary to ensure that the conditions for the formation of a company between spouses are not more restrictive than the conditions for the formation of a company between unmarried persons.

Article 6

Where a contributory social security system for self-employed workers exists in a Member State, that Member State shall take the necessary measures to enable the spouses referred to in Article 2(b) who are not protected under the self-employed worker's social security scheme to join a contributory social security scheme voluntarily.

Article 7

Member States shall undertake to examine under what conditions recognition of the work of the spouses referred to in Article 2(b) may be encouraged and, in the light of such examination, consider any appropriate steps for encouraging such recognition.

Article 8

Member States shall undertake to examine whether, and under what conditions, female self-employed workers and the wives of self-employed workers may, during interruptions in their occupational activity owing to pregnancy or motherhood,

— have access to services supplying temporary replacements or existing national social services, or

— be entitled to cash benefits under a social security scheme or under any other public social protection system.

SECTION III   GENERAL AND FINAL PROVISIONS

Article 9

Member States shall introduce into their national legal systems such measures as are necessary to enable all persons who consider themselves wronged by failure to apply the principle of equal treatment in self-employed activities to pursue their claims by judicial process, possibly after recourse to other competent authorities.

Article 10

Member States shall ensure that the measures adopted pursuant to this Directive, together with the relevant provisions already in force, are brought to the attention of bodies representing self-employed workers and vocational training centres.

Article 11

The Council shall review this Directive, on a proposal from the Commission, before 1 July 1993.

Article 12

1.   Member States shall bring into force the laws, regulations and administrative provisions necessary to comply with this Directive not later than 30 June 1989.

However, if a Member State which, in order to comply with Article 5 of this Directive, has to amend its legislation on matrimonial rights and obligations, the date on which such Member State must comply with Article 5 shall be 30 June 1991.

2.   Member States shall immediately inform the Commission of the measures taken to comply with this Directive.

Article 13
Member States shall forward to the Commission, not later than 30 June 1991, all the information necessary to enable it to draw up a report on the application of this directive for submission to the Council.

Article 14
This Directive is addressed to the Member States.

Done at Brussels, 11 December 1986.

COUNCIL DIRECTIVE 96/97/EC OF 20 DECEMBER 1996 AMENDING DIRECTIVE 86/378/EEC ON THE IMPLEMENTATION OF THE PRINCIPLE OF EQUAL TREATMENT FOR MEN AND WOMEN IN OCCUPATIONAL SOCIAL SECURITY SCHEMES
[OJ 1997, No. L46/20]

THE COUNCIL OF THE EUROPEAN UNION,

Having regard to the Treaty establishing the European Community, and in particular Article 100 thereof,
   Having regard to the proposal from the Commission,[1]
   Having regard to the opinion of the European Parliament,[2]
   Having regard to the opinion of the Economic and Social Committee,[3]
   Whereas Article 119 of the Treaty provides that each Member State shall ensure the application of the principle that men and women should receive equal pay for equal work; whereas 'pay' should be taken to mean the ordinary basic or minimum wage or salary and any other consideration, whether in cash or in kind, which the worker receives, directly or indirectly, from his employer in respect of his employment;
   Whereas, in its judgment of 17 May 1990, in Case 262/88: *Barber* v *Guardian Royal Exchange Assurance Group,*[4] the Court of Justice of the European Communities acknowledges that all forms of occupational pension constitute an element of pay within the meaning of Article 119 of the Treaty;
   Whereas, in the abovementioned judgment, as clarified by the judgment of 14 December 1993 (Case C-110/91: *Moroni* v *Collo GmbH*),[5] the Court interprets Article 119 of the Treaty in such a way that discrimination between men and women in occupational social security schemes is prohibited in general and not only in respect of establishing the age of entitlement to a pension or when an occupational pension is offered by way of compensation for compulsory retirement on economic grounds;
   Whereas, in accordance with Protocol 2 concerning Article 119 of the Treaty annexed to the Treaty establishing the European Community, benefits under

Notes
[1] OJ No. C218, 23.8.1995, p. 5.
[2] Opinion delivered on 12 November 1996 [OJ No. C362, 2.12.1996].
[3] OJ No. C18, 22.1.1996, p. 132.
[4] [1990] ECR I-1889.
[5] [1993] ECR I-6591.

occupational social security schemes shall not be considered as remuneration if and in so far as they are attributable to periods of employment prior to 17 May 1990, except in the case of workers or those claiming under them who have, before that date, initiated legal proceedings or raised an equivalent claim under the applicable national law;

Whereas, in its judgments of 28 September 1994[6] (Case C-57/93: *Vroege* v *NCIV Instituut voor Volkshuisvesting BV* and Case C-128/93: *Fisscher* v *Voorhuis Hengelo BV*), the Court ruled that the abovementioned Protocol did not affect the right to join an occupational pension scheme, which continues to be governed by the judgment of 13 May 1986 in Case 170/84: *Bilka-Kaufhaus GmbH* v *Hartz*,[7] and that the limitation of the effects in time of the judgment of 17 May 1990 in Case C-262/88: *Barber* v *Guardian Royal Exchange Assurance Group* does not apply to the right to join an occupational pension scheme; whereas the Court also ruled that the national rules relating to time limits for bringing actions under national law may be relied on against workers who assert their right to join an occupational pension scheme, provided that they are not less favourable for that type of action than for similar actions of a domestic nature and that they do not render the exercise of rights conferred by Community law impossible in practice; whereas the Court has also pointed out that the fact that a worker can claim retroactively to join an occupational pension scheme does not allow the worker to avoid paying the contributions relating to the period of membership concerned;

Whereas the exclusion of workers on the grounds of the nature of their work contracts from access to a company or sectoral social security scheme may constitute indirect discrimination against women;

Whereas, in its judgment of 9 November 1993 (Case C-132/92: *Birds Eye Walls Ltd* v *Friedel M. Roberts*),[8] the Court has also specified that it is not contrary to Article 119 of the Treaty, when calculating the amount of a bridging pension which is paid by an employer to male and female employees who have taken early retirement on grounds of ill health and which is intended to compensate, in particular, for loss of income resulting from the fact that they have not yet reached the age required for payment of the State pension which they will subsequently receive and to reduce the amount of the bridging pension accordingly, even though, in the case of men and women aged between 60 and 65, the result is that a female ex-employee receives a smaller bridging pension than that paid to her male counterpart, the difference being equal to the amount of the State pension to which she is entitled as from the age of 60 in respect of the periods of service completed with that employer;

Whereas, in its judgment of 6 October 1993 (Case C-109/91: *Ten Oever* v *Stichting Bedrijfpensioenfonds voor het Glazenwassers- en Schoonmaakbedrijf*)[9] and in its judgments of 14 December 1993 (Case C-110/91: *Moroni* v *Collo GmbH*), 22 December 1993 (Case C-152/91: *Neath* v *Hugh Steeper Ltd*)[10] and 28 Septmber 1994 (Case C-200/91: *Coloroll Pension Trustees Limited* v *Russell*

Notes
[6][1994] ECR I-4541 and (1994) ECR I-483, respectively.
[7][1996] ECR I-1607.
[8][1993] ECR I-5579.
[9][1993] ECR I-4879.
[10][1993] ECR I-6953.

and Others),[11] the Court confirms that, by virtue of the judgment of 17 May 1990 (Case C-262/88: *Barber* v *Guardian Royal Exchange Assurance Group*), the direct effect of Article 119 of the Treaty may be relied on, for the purpose of claiming equal treatment in the matter of occupational pensions, only in relation to benefits payable in respect of periods of service subsequent to 17 May 1990, except in the case of workers or those claiming under them who have, before that date, initiated legal proceedings or raised an equivalent claim under the applicable national law;

Whereas, in its abovementioned judgments (Case C-109/91: *Ten Oever* v *Stichting Bedrijfpensioenfonds voor het Glazenwassers- en Schoonmaakbedrijf* and Case C-200/91: *Coloroll Pension Trustees Limited* v *Russell and Others*), the Court confirms that the limitation of the effects in time of the Barber judgment applies to survivors' pensions and, consequently, equal treatment in this matter may be claimed only in relation to periods of service subsequent to 17 May 1990, except in the case of those who have, before that date, initiated legal proceedings or raised an equivalent claim under the applicable national law;

Whereas, moreover, in its judgments in Case C-152/91 and Case C-200/91, the Court specifies that the contributions of male and female workers to a defined-benefit pension scheme must be the same, since they are covered by Article 119 of the Treaty, whereas inequality of employers' contributions paid under funded defined-benefit schemes, which is due to the use of actuarial factors differing according to sex, is not to be assessed in the light of that same provision;

Whereas, in its judgments of 28 September 1994[12] (Case C-408/92: *Smith* v *Advel Systems* and Case C-28/93: *Van den Akker* v *Stichting Shell Pensioenfonds*), the Court points out that Article 119 of the Treaty precludes an employer who adopts measures necessary to comply with the *Barber* judgment of 17 May 1990 (C-262/88) from raising the retirement age for women to that which exists for men in relation to periods of service completed between 17 May 1990 and the date on which those measures come into force; on the other hand, as regards periods of service completed after the latter date, Article 119 does not prevent an employer from taking that step; as regards periods of service prior to 17 May 1990, Community law imposed no obligation which would justify retroactive reduction of the advantages which women enjoyed;

Whereas, in its abovementioned judgment in Case C-200/91: *Coloroll Pension Trustees Limited* v *Russell and Others*), the Court ruled that additional benefits stemming from contributions paid by employees on a purely voluntary basis are not covered by Article 119 of the Treaty;

Whereas, among the measures included in its third medium-term action programme on equal opportunities for women and men (1991 to 1995),[13] the Commission emphasises once more the adoption of suitable measures to take account of the consequences of the judgment of 17 May 1990 in Case 262/88 (*Barber* v *Guardian Royal Exchange Assurance Group*);

Notes
[11][1994] ECR I-4389.
[12][1994] ECR I-4435 and [1994] ECR I-4527, respectively.
[13]OJ No. C142, 31.5.1991, p. 1.

Whereas that judgment automatically invalidates certain provisions of Council Directive 86/378/EEC of 24 July 1986 on the implementation of the principle of equal treatment for men and women in occupational social security schemes[14] in respect of paid workers;

Whereas Article 119 of the Treaty is directly applicable and can be invoked before the national courts against any employer, whether a private person or a legal person, and whereas it is for these courts to safeguard the rights which that provision confers on individuals;

Whereas, on grounds of legal certainty, it is necesary to amend Directive 86/378/EEC in order to adapt the provisions which are affected by the Barber case-law,

Notes

[14]OJ No. L225, 12.8.1986, p. 40.

HAS ADOPTED THIS DIRECTIVE

Article 1[1]

Note

Editor's Note: Article 1 amended Directive 86/378 and is not reproduced here.

Article 2

1. Any measure implementing this Directive, as regards paid workers, must cover all benefits derived from periods of employment subsequent to 17 May 1990 and shall apply retroactively to that date, without prejudice to workers or those claiming under them who have, before that date, initiated legal proceedings or raised an equivalent claim under national law. In that event, the implementation measures must apply retroactively to 8 April 1976 and must cover all the benefits derived from periods of employment after that date. For Member States which acceded to the Community after 8 April 1976, that date shall be replaced by the date on which Article 119 of the Treaty became applicable on their territory.

2. The second sentence of paragraph 1 shall not prevent national rules relating to time limits for bringing actions under national law from being relied on against workers or those claiming under them who initiated legal proceedings or raise an equivalent claim under national law before 17 May 1990, provided that they are not less favourable for that type of action than for similar actions of a domestic nature and that they do not render the exercise of Commnity law impossible in practice.

3. For Member States whose accession took place after 17 May 1990 and who were on 1 January 1994 Contracting Parties to the Agreement on the European Economic Area, the date of 17 May 1990 in paragraph 1 and 2 of this Directive is replaced by 1 January 1994.

Article 3

1. Member States shall bring into force the laws, regulations and administrative provisions necessary to comply with this Directive by 1 July 1997. They shall forthwith inform the Commission thereof.

When Member States adopt these provisions, they shall contain a reference to this Directive or be accompanied by such reference on the occasion of their official publication. The methods of making such a reference shall be laid down by the Member States.

2.   Member States shall communicate to the Commission, at the latest two years after the entry into force of this Directive, all information necessary to enable the Commission to draw up a report on the application of this Directive.

Article 4
This Directive shall enter into force on the 20th day following that of its publication in the *Official Journal of the European Communities*.

Article 5
This Directive is addressed to the Member States.

Done at Brussels, 20 December 1996.
For the Council
The President
S. BARRETT

SOCIAL POLICY: WORKER PROTECTION AND HEALTH AND SAFETY

COUNCIL DIRECTIVE OF 17 FEBRUARY 1975 ON THE APPROXIMATION OF THE LAWS OF THE MEMBER STATES RELATING TO COLLECTIVE REDUNDANCIES (75/129/EEC) [OJ 1975, No. L48/29] AS AMENDED BY COUNCIL DIRECTIVE OF 24 JUNE 1992 (92/56/EEC) [OJ 1992, No. L245/3]

THE COUNCIL OF THE EUROPEAN COMMUNITIES,

Having regard to the Treaty establishing the European Economic Community, and in particular Article 100 thereof;

Having regard to the proposal from the Commission;

Having regard to the opinion of the European Parliament;[1]

Having regard to the opinion of the Economic and Social Committee;[2]

Whereas it is important that greater protection should be afforded to workers in the event of collective redundancies while taking into account the need for balanced economic and social development within the community;

Whereas, despite increasing convergence, differences still remain between the provisions in force in the Member States of the Community concerning the practical arrangements and procedures for such redundancies and the measures designed to alleviate the consequences of redundancy for workers;

Whereas these differences can have a direct effect on the functioning of the common market;

Whereas the Council Resolution of 21 January 1974[3] concerning a social action programme makes provision for a directive on the approximation of Member States' legislation on collective redundancies;

Whereas this approximation must therefore be promoted while the improvement is being maintained within the meaning of Article 117 of the treaty,

Notes
[1]OJ No. C19, 12.4.1973, p. 10.
[2]OJ No. C100, 22.11.1973, p. 11.
[3]OJ No. C13, 12.2.1974, p. 1.

HAS ADOPTED THIS DIRECTIVE:

SECTION I   DEFINITIONS AND SCOPE

Article 1
1.   For the purposes of this Directive:

(a) 'collective redundancies' means dismissals effected by an employer for one or more reasons not related to the individual workers concerned where, according to the choice of the Member States, the number of redundancies is:
— either, over a period of 30 days:
      (1)   at least 10 in establishments normally employing more than 20 and less than 100 workers;
      (2)   at least 10% of the number of workers in establishments normally employing at least 100 but less than 300 workers;
      (3)   at least 30 in establishments normally employing 300 workers or more;
— or, over a period of 90 days, at least 20, whatever the number of workers normally employed in the establishments in question;

(b) 'workers' representatives' means the workers' representatives provided for by the laws or practices of the Member States. For the purpose of calculating the number of redundancies provided for in the first subparagraph of point (a), terminations of an employment contract which occur to the individual workers concerned shall be assimilated to redundancies, provided that there are at least five redundancies.

2. This Directive shall not apply to:

(a) collective redundancies affected under contracts of employment concluded for limited periods of time or for specific tasks except where such redundancies take place prior to the date of expiry or the completion of such contracts;

(b) workers employed by public administrative bodies or by establishments governed by public law (or, in Member States where this concept is unknown, by equivalent bodies);

(c) the crews of sea-going vessels;

(d) workers affected by the termination of an establishment's activities where that is the result of a judicial decision.

SECTION II   INFORMATION AND CONSULTATION

Article 2

1. Where an employer is contemplating collective redundancies, he shall begin consultations with the workers' representatives in good time with a view to reaching an agreement.

2. These consultations shall, at least, cover ways and means of avoiding collective redundancies or reducing the number of workers affected, and of mitigating the consequences by recourse to accompanying social measures aimed, *inter alia*, at aid for redeploying or retraining workers made redundant. Member States may provide that the workers' representatives may call upon the services of experts in accordance with national legislation and/or practice.

3. To enable the workers' representatives to make constructive proposals, the employers shall in good time during the course of the consultations:
    (a)   supply them with all relevant information and
    (b)   in any event notify them in writing of:
       (i)   the reasons for the projected redundancies;
      (ii)   the number of categories of workers to be made redundant;
    (iii)   the number and categories of workers normally employed;
    (iv)   the period over which the projected redundancies are to be effected;

(v)   the criteria proposed for the selection of the workers to be made redundant in so far as national legislation and/or practice confers the power therefor upon the employer;

(vi)   the method for calculating any redundancy payments other than those arising out of national legislation and/or practice.

The employer shall forward to the competent public authority a copy of, at least, the elements of the written communication which are provided for in the first subparagraph, point (b), subpoints (i) to (v).

4.   The obligations laid down in paragraphs 1, 2 and 3 shall apply irrespective of whether the decision regarding collective redundancies is being taken by the employer or by an undertaking controlling the employer.

In considering alleged breaches of the information, consultation and notification requirements laid down by this Directive, account shall not be taken of any defence on the part of the employer on the ground that the necessary information has not been provided to the employer by the undertaking which took the decision leading to collective redundancies.

SECTION III   PROCEDURE FOR COLLECTIVE REDUNDANCIES

Article 3

1.   Employers shall notify the competent public authority in writing of any projected collective redundancies. However, Member States may provide that in the case of planned collective redundancies arising from termination of the establishment's activities as a result of a judicial decision, the employer shall be obliged to notify the competent public authority in writing only if the latter so requests.

This notification shall contain all relevant information concerning the projected collective redundancies and the consultations with workers' representatives provided for in Article 2, and particularly the reasons for the redundancies, the number of workers to be made redundant, the number of workers normally employed and the period over which the redundancies are to be effected.

2.   Employers shall forward to the workers' representatives a copy of the notification provided for in paragraph 1.

The workers' representatives may send any comments they may have to the competent public authority.

Article 4

1.   Projected collective redundancies notified to the competent public authority shall take effect not earlier than 30 days after the notification referred to in Article 3(1) without prejudice to any provisions governing individual rights with regard to notice of dismissal.

Member States may grant the competent public authority the power to reduce the period provided for in the preceding subparagraph.

2.   The period provided for in paragraph 1 shall be used by the competent public authority to seek solutions in the problems raised by the projected collective redundancies.

3.   Where the initial period provided for in paragraph 1 is shorter than 60 days, Member States may grant the competent public authority the power to extend the initial period to 60 days following notification where the problems raised by the projected collective redundancies are not likely to be solved within the initial period.

4.   Member States need not apply this Article to collective redundancies arising from termination of the establishment's activities where this is the result of a judicial decision.

Member States may grant the competent public authority wider powers of extension.

The employer must be informed of the extension and the grounds for it before expiry of the initial period provided for in paragraph 1.

SECTION IV   FINAL PROVISIONS

Article 5
This Directive shall not affect the right of Member States to apply or to introduce laws, regulations or administrative provisions which are more favourable to workers or to promote or to allow the application of collective agreements more favourable to workers.

Article 5a
Member States shall ensure that judicial and/or administrative procedures for the enforcement of obligations under this Directive are available to the workers' representatives and/or workers.

Article 6
1.   Member States shall bring into force the laws, regulations and administrative provisions needed in order to comply with this Directive within two years following its notification and shall forthwith inform the Commission thereof.

2.   Member States shall communicate to the Commission the texts of the laws, regulations and administrative provisions which they adopt in the field covered by this Directive.

Article 7
Within two years following expiry of the two year period laid down in Article 6, Member States shall forward all relevant information to the Commission to enable it to draw up a report for submission to the Council on the application of this Directive.

Article 8
This Directive is addressed to the Member States.
Done at Brussels, 17 February 1975.

(Signature omitted.)

COUNCIL DIRECTIVE OF 14 FEBRUARY 1977 ON THE APPROXIMATION OF THE LAWS OF THE MEMBER STATES RELATING TO THE SAFEGUARDING OF EMPLOYEES' RIGHTS IN THE EVENT OF TRANSFERS OF UNDERTAKINGS, BUSINESSES OR PARTS OF BUSINESSES (77/187/EEC) [OJ 1977, No. L61/27][1]

THE COUNCIL OF THE EUROPEAN COMMUNITIES,
   Having regard to the Treaty establishing the European Economic Community, and in particular Article 100 thereof,

Notes
[1]Article 11 of Directive 82/891 [OJ 1982, No. L378/47] applies the provisions of this Directive to Public Limited Liability Companies.

Having regard to the proposal from the Commission,

Having regard to the opinion of the European Parliament,[2]

Having regard to the opinion of the Economic and Social Committee,[3]

Whereas economic trends are bringing in their wake, at both national and Community level, changes in the structure of undertakings, through transfers of undertakings, businesses or parts of businesses to other employers as a result of legal transfers or mergers;

Whereas it is necessary to provide for the protection of employees in the event of a change of employer, in particular, to ensure that their rights are safeguarded;

Whereas differences still remain in the Member States as regards the extent of the protection of employees in this respect and these differences should be reduced;

Whereas these differences can have a direct effect on the functioning of the common market;

Whereas it is therefore necessary to promote the approximation of laws in this field while maintaining the improvement described in Article 117 of the Treaty,

HAS ADOPTED THIS DIRECTIVE:

Notes

[2]OJ No. C95, 28.4.1975, p. 17.

[3]OJ No. C225, 7.11.1975, p. 25.

SECTION I   SCOPE AND DEFINITIONS

Article 1

This Directive shall apply to the transfer of an undertaking, business or part of a business to another employer as a result of a legal transfer or merger.

2.   This Directive shall apply where and in so far as the undertaking, business or part of the business to be transferred is situated within the territorial scope of the Treaty.

3.   This Directive shall not apply to sea-going vessels.

Article 2

For the purposes of this Directive:

(a)   'transferor' means any natural or legal person who, by reason of a transfer within the meaning of Article 1(1), ceases to be the employer in respect of the undertaking, business or part of the business;

(b)   'transferee' means any natural or legal person who, by reason of a transfer within the meaning of Article 1(1), becomes the employer in respect of the undertaking, business or part of the business;

(c)   'representatives of the employees' means the representatives of the employees provided for by the laws or practice of the Member States, with the exception of members of administrative, governing or supervisory bodies of companies who represent employees on such bodies in certain Member States.

SECTION II   SAFEGUARDING OF EMPLOYEES' RIGHTS

Article 3

1.   The transferor's rights and obligations arising from a contract of employment or from an employment relationship existing on the date of a

transfer within the meaning of Article 1(1) shall, by reason of such transfer, be transferred to the transferee.

Member States may provide that, after the date of transfer within the meaning of Article 1(1) and in addition to the transferee, the transferor shall continue to be liable in respect of obligations which arose from a contract of employment or an employment relationship.

2.   Following the transfer within the meaning of Article 1(1), the transferee shall continue to observe the terms and conditions agreed in any collective agreement on the same terms applicable to the transferor under that agreement, until the date of termination or expiry of the collective agreement or the entry into force or application of another collective agreement.

Member States may limit the period for observing such terms and conditions, with the proviso that it shall not be less than one year.

3.   Paragraphs 1 and 2 shall not cover employees' rights to old-age, invalidity or survivors' benefits under supplementary company or inter-company pension schemes outside the statutory social security schemes in Member States.

Member States shall adopt the measures necessary to protect the interests of employees and of persons no longer employed in the transferor's business at the time of the transfer within the meaning of Article 1(1) in respect of rights conferring on them immediate or prospective entitlement to old-age benefits, including survivors' benefits, under supplementary schemes referred to in the first subparagraph.

Article 4

1.   The transfer of an undertaking, business or part of a business shall not in itself constitute grounds for dismissal by the transferor or the transferee. This provision shall not stand in the way of dismissals that may take place for economic, technical or organisational reasons entailing changes in the workforce.

Member States may provide that the first subparagraph shall not apply to certain specific categories of employees who are not covered by the laws or practice of the Member States in respect of protection against dismissal.

2.   If the contract of employment or the employment relationship is terminated because the transfer within the meaning of Article 1(1) involves a substantial change in working conditions to the detriment of the employee, the employer shall be regarded as having been responsible for termination of the contract of employment or of the employment relationship.

Article 5

1.   If the business preserves its autonomy, the status and function, as laid down by the laws, regulations or administrative provisions of the Member States, of the representatives or of the representation of the employees affected by the transfer within the meaning of Article 1(1) shall be preserved.

The first subparagraph shall not apply if, under the laws, regulations, administrative provisions or practice of the Member States, the conditions necessary for the re-appointment of the representatives of the employees or for the reconstitution of the representation of the employees are fulfilled.

2.   If the term of office of the representatives of the employees affected by a transfer within the meaning of Article 1(1) expires as a result of the transfer, the representatives shall continue to enjoy the protection provided by the laws, regulations, administrative provisions or practice of the Member States.

SECTION III   INFORMATION AND CONSULTATION

Article 6

1.   The transferor and the transferee shall be required to inform the representatives of their respective employees affected by a transfer within the meaning of Article 1(1) of the following:
— the reasons for the transfer,
— the legal, economic and social implications of the transfer for the employees,
— measures envisaged in relation to the employees.

The transferor must give such information to the representatives of his employees in good time before the transfer is carried out.

The transferee must give such information to the representatives of his employees in good time, and in any event before his employees are directly affected by the transfer as regards their conditions of work and employment.

2.   If the transferor or the transferee envisages measures in relation to his employees, he shall consult his representatives of the employees in good time on such measures with a veiw to seeking agreement.

3.   Member States whose laws, regulations or administrative provisions provide that representatives of the employees may have recourse to an arbitration board to obtain a decision on the measures to be taken in relation to employees may limit the obligations laid down in paragraphs 1 and 2 to cases where the transfer carried out gives rise to a change in the business likely to entail serious disadvantages for a considerable number of the employees.

The information and consultations shall cover at least the measures envisaged in relation to the employees.

The information must be provided and consultations take place in good time before the change in the business as referred to in the first subparagraph is effected.

4.   Member States may limit the obligations laid down in paragraphs 1, 2 and 3 to undertakings or businesses which, in respect of the number of employees, fulfil the conditions for the election or designation of a collegiate body representing the employees.

5.   Member States may provide that where there are no representatives of the employees in an undertaking or business, the employees concerned must be informed in advance when a transfer within the meaning of Article 1(1) is about to take place.

SECTION IV   FINAL PROVISIONS

Article 7

This Directive shall not affect the right of Member States to apply or introduce laws, regulations or administrative provisions which are more favourable to employees.

Article 8

1.   Member States shall bring into force the laws regulations and administrative provisions needed to comply with this Directive within two years of its notification and shall forthwith inform the Commission thereof.

2.   Member States shall communicate to the Commission the texts of the laws, regulations and administrative provisions which they adopt in the field covered by this Directive.

Article 9
Within two years following expiry of the two-year period laid down in Article 8, Member States shall forward all relevant information to the Commission in order to enable it to draw up a report on the application of this Directive for submission to the Council.

Article 10
This Directive is addressed to the Member States.
Done at Brussels, 14 February 1977.

(Signature omitted.)

COUNCIL DIRECTIVE OF 20 OCTOBER 1980 ON THE APPROXIMATION OF THE LAWS OF THE MEMBER STATES RELATING TO THE PROTECTION OF EMPLOYEES IN THE EVENT OF THE INSOLVENCY OF THEIR EMPLOYER
(80/987/EEC)
[OJ 1980, No. L283/23]*

THE COUNCIL OF THE EUROPEAN COMMUNITIES,
Having regard to the Treaty establishing the European Economic Community, and in particular Article 100 thereof,
Having regard to the proposal from the Commission,[1]
Having regard to the opinion of the European Parliament,[2]
Having regard to the opinion of the Economic and Social Committee,[3]
Whereas it is necessary to provide for the protection of employees in the event of the insolvency of their employer, in particular in order to guarantee payment of their outstanding claims, while taking account of the need for balanced economic and social development in the Community;
Whereas differences still remain between the member states as regards the extent of the protection of employees in this respect; whereas efforts should be directed towards reducing these differences, which can have a direct effect on the functioning of the common market;
Whereas the approximation of laws in this field should, therefore, be promoted while the improvement within the meaning of Article 117 of the Treaty is maintained;
Whereas as a result of the geographical situation and the present job structures in that area, the labour market in Greenland is fundamentally different from that of the other areas of the Community;
Whereas to the extent that the Hellenic Republic is to become a member of the European Economic Community on 1 January 1981 in acordance with the act concerning the conditions of accession of the Hellenic Republic and the adjustments to the Treaties, it is appropriate to stipulate in the annex to the Directive under the heading 'Greece', those categories of employees whose claims may be excluded in accordance with Article 1(2) of the Directive,

HAS ADOPTED THIS DIRECTIVE:

Note
*As amended by Directive 87/164 [OJ 1987 No. L66/11]
[1]OJ No. C135, 9.6.1978, p. 2.
[2]OJ No. C39, 12.2.1979, p. 26.
[3]OJ No. C105, 26.4.1979, p. 15.

SECTION I SCOPE AND DEFINITIONS

Article 1

1. This Directive shall apply to employees' claims arising from contracts of employment or employment relationships and existing against employers who are in a state of insolvency within the meaning of Article 2(1).

2. Member States may, by way of exception, exclude claims by certain categories of employee from the scope of this Directive, by virtue of the special nature of the employee's contract of employment or employment relationship or of the existence of other forms of guarantee offering the employee protection equivalent to that resulting from this Directive.

The categories of employee referred to in the first subparagraph are listed in the Annex.

3. This Directive shall not apply to Greenland. This exception shall be re-examined in the event of any development in the job structures in that region.

Article 2

1. For the purposes of this Directive, an employer shall be deemed to be in a state of insolvency:

(a) where a request has been made for the opening of proceedings involving the employer's assets, as provided for under the laws, regulations and administrative provisions of the Member State concerned, to satisfy collectively the claims of creditors and which make it possible to take into consideration the claims referred to in Article 1(1), and

(b) where the authority which is competent pursuant to the said laws, regulations and administrative provisions has:

— either decided to open the proceedings,

— or established that the employer's undertaking or business has been definitively closed down and that the available assets are insufficient to warrant the opening of the proceedings.

2. This Directive is without prejudice to national law as regards the definition of the terms 'employee', 'employer', 'pay', 'right conferring immediate entitlement' and 'right conferring prospective entitlement'.

SECTION II PROVISIONS CONCERNING GUARANTEE INSTITUTIONS

Article 3

1. Member States shall take the measures necessary to ensure that guarantee institutions guarantee, subject to Article 4, payment of employees' outstanding claims resulting from contracts of employment or employment relationships and relating to pay for the period prior to a given date.

2. At the choice of the Member States, the date referred to in paragraph 1 shall be:

— either that of the onset of the employer's insolvency;

— or that of the notice of dismissal issued to the employee concerned on account of the employer's insolvency;

— or that of the onset of the employer's insolvency or that on which the contract of employment or the employment relationship with the employee concerned was discontinued on account of the employer's insolvency.

Article 4

1. Member States shall have the option to limit the liability of guarantee institutions, referred to in Article 3.

2. When Member States exercise the option referred to in paragraph 1, they shall:

— in the case referred to in Article 3(2), first indent, ensure the payment of outstanding claims relating to pay for the last three months of the contract of employment or employment relationship occurring within a period of six months preceding the date of the onset of the employer's insolvency;

— in the case referred to in Article 3(2), second indent, ensure the payment of outstanding claims relating to pay for the last three months of the contract of employment or employment relationship preceding the date of the notice of dismissal issued to the employee on account of the employer's insolvency;

— in the case referred to in Article 3(2), third indent, ensure the payment of outstanding claims relating to pay for the last 18 months of the contract of employment or employment relationship preceding the date of the onset of the employer's insolvency or the date on which the contract of employment or the employment relationship with the employee was discontinued on account of the employer's insolvency. In this case, Member States may limit the liability to make payment to pay corresponding to a period of eight weeks or to several shorter periods totalling eight weeks.

3. However, in order to avoid the payment of sums going beyond the social objective of this Directive, Member States may set a ceiling to the liability for employees' outstanding claims.

When Member States exercise this option, they shall inform the Commission of the methods used to set the ceiling.

Article 5

Member States shall lay down detailed rules for the organisation, financing and operation of the guarantee institutions, complying with the following principles in particular:

(a) the assets of the institutions shall be independent of the employers' operating capital and be inaccessible to proceedings for insolvency;

(b) employers shall contribute to financing, unless it is fully covered by the public authorities;

(c) the institutions' liabilities shall not depend on whether or not obligations to contribute to financing have been fulfilled.

SECTION III   PROVISIONS CONCERNING SOCIAL SECURITY

Article 6

Member States may stipulate that Articles 3, 4 and 5 shall not apply to contributions due under national statutory social security schemes or under supplementary company or inter-company pension schemes outside the national statutory social security schemes.

Article 7

Member States shall take the measures necessary to ensure that non-payment of compulsory contributions due from the employer, before the onset of his insolvency, to their insurance institutions under national statutory social security schemes does not adversely affect employees' benefit entitlement in respect of these insurance institutions inasmuch as the employees' contributions were deducted at source from the remuneration paid.

Article 8

Member States shall ensure that the necessary measures are taken to protect the interests of employees and of persons having already left the employer's undertaking or business at the date of the onset of the employer's insolvency in respect of rights conferring on them immediate or prospective entitlement to old-age benefits, including survivors' benefits, under supplementary company or inter-company pension schemes outside the national statutory social security schemes.

SECTION IV   GENERAL AND FINAL PROVISIONS

Article 9

This Directive shall not affect the option of Member States to apply or introduce laws, regulations or administrative provisions which are more favourable to employees.

Article 10

This Directive shall not affect the option of Member States:
    (a)   to take the measures necessary to avoid abuses;
    (b)   to refuse or reduce the liability referred to in Article 3 or the guarantee obligation referred to in Article 7 if it appears that fulfilment of the obligation is unjustifiable because of the existence of special links beween the employee and the employer and of common interests resulting in collusion between them.

Article 11

    1.   Member States shall bring into force the laws, regulations and administrative provisions necessary to comply with this Directive within 36 months of its notification. They shall forthwith inform the Commission thereof.
    2.   Member States shall communicate to the Commission the texts of the laws, regulations and administrative provisions which they adopt in the field governed by this Directive.

Article 12

Within 18 months of the expiry of the period of 36 months laid down in Article 11(1), Member States shall forward all relevant information to the Commission in order to enable it to draw up a report on the application of this Directive for submission to the Council.

Article 13

This Directive is addressed to the Member States.
  Done at Luxembourg, 20 October 1980.

(Signature omitted.)

ANNEX

Categories of employee whose claims may be excluded from the scope of this Directive, in accordance with Article 1 (2)

I.   Employees having a contract of employment, or an employment relationship, of a special nature

A.   GREECE

The master and the members of a crew of a fishing vessel, if and to the extent that they are remunerated by a share in the profits or gross earnings of the vessel.

B. SPAIN
Domestic servants employed by a natural person.

C. IRELAND
    1.   Out-workers (i.e., persons doing piece-work in their own homes), unless they have a written contract of employment.
    2.   Close relatives of the employer, without a written contract of employment, whose work has to do with a private dwelling or farm in, or on, which the employer and the close relatives reside.
    3.   Persons who normally work for less than 18 hours a week for one or more employers and who do not derive their basic means of subsistence from the pay for this work.
    4.   Persons engaged in share fishing on a seasonal, casual or part-time basis.
    5.   The spouse of the employer.

D. NETHERLANDS
Domestic servants employed by a natural person and working less than three days a week for the natural person in question.

E. UNITED KINGDOM
    1.   The master and the members of the crew of a fishing vessel who are remunerated by a share in the profits or gross earnings of the vessel.
    2.   The spouse of the employer.

F. AUSTRIA
    1.   Members of the authority of a body corporate, which is responsible for the statutory representation of that body.
    2.   Associates entitled to exercise dominant influence in the association, even if this influence is based on fiduciary disposition.

G. SWEDEN
An employee, or the survivors of an employee, who on his own or together with his close relatives was the owner of an essential part of the employer's undertaking or business and had a considerable influence on its activities. This shall apply also when the employer is a legal person without an undertaking or business.

II.   Employees covered by other forms of guarantee

A. GREECE
The crews of sea-going vessels.

B. IRELAND
    1.   Permanent and pensionable employees of local or other public authorities or statutory transport undertakings.
    2.   Pensionable teachers employed in the following: national schools, secondary schools, comprehensive schools, teachers' training colleges.
    3.   Permanent and pensionable employees of one of the voluntary hospitals funded by the Exchequer.

C. ITALY
    1.   Employees covered by benefits laid down by law guaranteeing that their wages will continue to be paid in the event that the undertaking is hit by an economic crisis.

2.   The crews of sea-going vessels.

D.   UNITED KINGDOM
1.   Registered dock workers other than those wholly or mainly engaged in work which is not dock work.
2.   The crews of sea-going vessels.

COUNCIL DIRECTIVE 89/391/EEC OF 12 JUNE 1989 ON THE INTRODUCTION OF MEASURES TO ENCOURAGE IMPROVEMENTS IN THE SAFETY AND HEALTH OF WORKERS AT WORK
[OJ 1989, No. L183/1]

THE COUNCIL OF THE EUROPEAN COMMUNITIES,

Having regard to the Treaty establishing the European Economic Community, and in particular Article 118a thereof,

Having regard to the proposal from the Commission,[1] drawn up after consultation with the Advisory Committee on Safety, Hygiene and Health Protection at Work,

In cooperation with the European Parliament,[2]

Having regard to the opinion of the Economic and Social Committee,[3]

Whereas Article 118a of the Treaty provides that the Council shall adopt, by means of Directives, minimum requirements for encouraging improvements, especially in the working environment, to guarantee a better level of protection of the safety and health of workers;

Whereas this Directive does not justify any reduction in levels of protection already achieved in individual Member States, the Member State being committed, under the Treaty, to encouraging improvements in conditions in this area and to harmonizing conditions while maintaining the improvements made;

Whereas it is known that workers can be exposed to the effects of dangerous environmental factors at the work place during the course of their working life;

Whereas, pursuant to Article 118a of the Treaty, such Directives must avoid imposing administrative, financial and legal constraints which would hold back the creation and development of small and medium-sized undertakings;

Whereas the communication from the Commission on its programme concerning safety, hygiene and health at work[4] provides for the adoption of Directives designed to guarantee the safety and health of workers;

Whereas the Council, in its resolution of 21 December 1987 on safety, hygiene and health at work,[5] took note of the Commission's intention to submit to the Council in the near future a Directive on the organization of the safety and health of workers at the work place;

Notes
[1] OJ No. C141, 30.5.1988, p. 1.
[2] OJ No. C326, 19.12.1988, p. 102, and OJ No. C158, 26.6.1989.
[3] OJ No. C175, 4.7.1988, p. 22.
[4] OJ No. C28, 3.2.1988, p. 3.
[5] OJ No. C28, 3.2.1988, p. 1.

Whereas in February 1988 the European Parliament adopted four resolutions following the debate on the internal market and worker protection; whereas these resolutions specifically invited the Commission to draw up a framework Directive to serve as a basis for more specific Directives covering all the risks connected with safety and health at the work place;

Whereas Member States have a responsibility to encourage improvements in the safety and health of workers on their territory; whereas taking measures to protect the health and safety of workers at work also helps, in certain cases, to preserve the health and possibly the safety of persons residing with them;

Whereas Member States' legislative systems covering safety and health at the work place differ widely and need to be improved; whereas national provisions on the subject, which often include technical specifications and/or self-regulatory standards, may result in different levels of safety and health protection and allow competition at the expense of safety and health;

Whereas the incidence of accidents at work and occupational diseases is still too high; whereas preventive measures must be introduced or improved without delay in order to safeguard the safety and health of workers and ensure a higher degree of protection;

Whereas, in order to ensure an improved degree of protection, workers and/or their representatives must be informed of the risks to their safety and health and of the measures required to reduce or eliminate these risks; whereas they must also be in a position to contribute, by means of balanced participation in accordance with national laws and/or practices, to seeing that the necessary protective measures are taken;

Whereas information, dialogue and balanced participation on safety and health at work must be developed between employers and workers and/or their representatives by means of appropriate procedures and instruments, in accordance with national laws and/or practices;

Whereas the improvement of workers' safety, hygiene and health at work is an objective which should not be subordinated to purely economic considerations;

Whereas employers shall be obliged to keep themselves informed of the latest advances in technology and scientific findings concerning work-place design, account being taken of the inherent dangers in their undertaking, and to inform accordingly the workers' representatives exercising participation rights under this Directive, so as to be able to guarantee a better level of protection of workers' health and safety;

Whereas the provisions of this Directive apply, without prejudice to more stringent present or future Community provisions, to all risks, and in particular to those arising from the use at work of chemical, physical and biological agents covered by Directive 80/1107/EEC,[6] as last amended by Directive 88/642/EEC;[7]

Whereas, pursuant to Decision 74/325/EEC,[8] the Advisory Committee on Safety, Hygiene and Health Protection at Work is consulted by the Commission on the drafting of proposals in this field;

Notes
[6] OJ No. L327, 3.12.1980, p. 8.
[7] OJ No. L356, 24.12.1988, p. 74.
[8] OJ No. L185, 9.7.1974, p. 15.

Whereas a Committee composed of members nominated by the Member States needs to be set up to assist the Commission in making the technical adaptations to the individual Directives provided for in this Directive.

HAS ADOPTED THIS DIRECTIVE:

SECTION I   GENERAL PROVISIONS

Article 1   Object

1.   The object of this Directive is to introduce measures to encourage improvements in the safety and health of workers at work.

2.   To that end it contains general principles concerning the prevention of occupational risks, the protection of safety and health, the elimination of risk and accident factors, the informing, consultation, balanced participation in accordance with national laws and/or practices and training of workers and their representatives, as well as general guidelines for the implementation of the said principles.

3.   This Directive shall be without prejudice to existing or future national and Community provisions which are more favourable to protection of the safety and health of workers at work.

Article 2   Scope

1.   This Directive shall apply to all sectors of activity, both public and private (industrial, agricultural, commercial, administrative, service, educational, cultural, leisure, etc.).

2.   This Directive shall not be applicable where characteristics peculiar to certain specific public service activities, such as the armed forces or the police, or to certain specific activities in the civil protection services inevitably conflict with it. In that event, the safety and health of workers must be ensured as far as possible in the light of the objectives of this Directive.

Article 3   Definitions

For the purposes of this Directive, the following terms shall have the following meanings:

(a)   worker: any person employed by an employer, including trainees and apprentices but excluding domestic servants;

(b)   employer: any natural or legal person who has an employment relationship with the worker and has responsibility for the undertaking and/or establishment;

(c)   workers' representative with specific responsibility for the safety and health of workers: any person elected, chosen or designated in accordance with national laws and/or practices to represent workers where problems arise relating to the safety and health protection of workers at work;

(d)   prevention: all the steps or measures taken or planned at all stages of work in the undertaking to prevent or reduce occupational risks.

Article 4

1.   Member States shall take the necessary steps to ensure that employers, workers and workers' representatives are subject to the legal provisions necessary for the implementation of this Directive.

2.   In particular, Member States shall ensure adequate controls and supervision.

SECTION II   EMPLOYERS' OBLIGATIONS

Article 5   General provision

1.   The employer shall have a duty to ensure the safety and health of workers in every aspect related to the work.

2.   Where, pursuant to Article 7(3), an employer enlists competent external services or persons, this shall not discharge him from his responsibilities in this area.

3.   The workers' obligations in the field of safety and health at work shall not affect the principle of the responsibility of the employer.

4.   This Directive shall not restrict the option of Member States to provide for the exclusion or the limitation of employers' responsibility where occurrences are due to unusual and unforeseeable circumstances, beyond the employers' control, or to exceptional events, the consequences of which could not have been avoided despite the exercise of all due care.

Member States need not exercise the option referred to in the first subparagraph.

Article 6   General obligations on employers

1.   Within the context of his responsibilities, the employer shall take the measures necessary for the safety and health protection of workers, including prevention of occupational risks and provision of information and training, as well as provision of the necessary organization and means.

The employer shall be alert to the need to adjust these measures to take account of changing circumstances and aim to improve existing situations.

2.   The employer shall implement the measures referred to in the first subparagraph of paragraph 1 on the basis of the following general principles of prevention:

(a)   avoiding risks;

(b)   evaluating the risks which cannot be avoided:

(c)   combating the risks at source;

(d)   adapting the work to the individual, especially as regards the design of work places, the choice of work equipment and the choice of working and production methods, with a view, in particular, to alleviating monotonous work and work at a predetermined work-rate and to reducing their effect on health.

(e)   adapting to technical progress;

(f)   replacing the dangerous by the non-dangerous or the less dangerous;

(g)   developing a coherent overall prevention policy which covers technology, organization of work, working conditions, social relationships and the influence of factors related to the working environment;

(h)   giving collective protective measures priority over individual protective measures;

(i)   giving appropriate instructions to the workers.

3.   Without prejudice to the other provisions of this Directive, the employer shall, taking into account the nature of the activities of the enterprise and/or establishment:

(a)   evaluate the risks to the safety and health of workers, inter alia in the choice of work equipment, the chemical substances or preparations used, and the fitting-out of work places.

Subsequent to this evaluation and as necessary, the preventive measures and the working and production methods implemented by the employer must:

— assure an improvement in the level of protection afforded to workers with regard to safety and health,

— be integrated into all the activities of the undertaking and/or establishment and at all hierarchical levels;

(b) where he entrusts tasks to a worker, take into consideration the worker's capabilities as regards health and safety;

(c) ensure that the planning and introduction of new technologies are the subject of consultation with the workers and/or their representatives, as regards the consequences of the choice of equipment, the working conditions and the working environment for the safety and health of workers;

(d) take appropriate steps to ensure that only workers who have received adequate instructions may have access to areas where there is serious and specific danger.

4. Without prejudice to the other provisions of this Directive, where several undertakings share a work place, the employers shall cooperate in implementing the safety, health and occupational hygiene provisions and, taking into account the nature of the activities, shall coordinate their actions in matters of the protection and prevention of occupational risks, and shall inform one another and their respective workers and/or workers' representatives of these risks.

5. Measures related to safety, hygiene and health at work may in no circumstances involve the workers in financial cost.

Article 7   Protective and preventive services

1. Without prejudice to the obligations referred to in Articles 5 and 6, the employer shall designate one or more workers to carry out activities related to the protection and prevention of occupational risks for the undertaking and/or establishment.

2. Designated workers may not be placed at any disadvantage because of their activities related to the protection and prevention of occupational risks. Designated workers shall be allowed adequate time to enable them to fulfil their obligations arising from this Directive.

3. If such protective and preventive measures cannot be organised for lack of competent personnel in the undertaking and/or establishment, the employer shall enlist competent external services or persons.

4. Where the employer enlists such services or persons, he shall inform them of the factors known to affect, or suspected of affecting, the safety and health of the workers and they must have access to the information referred to in Article 10(2).

5. In all cases:

— the workers designated must have the necessary capabilities and the necessary means,

— the external services or persons consulted must have the necessary aptitudes and the necessary personal and professional means, and

— the workers designated and the external services or persons consulted must be sufficient in number to deal with the organization of protective and preventive measures, taking into account the size of the undertaking and/or establishment and/or the hazards to which the workers are exposed and their distribution throughout the entire undertaking and/or establishment.

6. The protection from, and prevention of, the health and safety risks which form the subject of this Article shall be the responsibility of one or more workers, of one service or of separate services whether from inside or outside the undertaking and/or establishment.

The worker(s) and/or agency(ies) must work together whenever necessary.

7. Member States may define, in the light of the nature of the activities and size of the undertakings, the categories of undertakings in which the employer, provided he is competent, may himself take responsibility for the measures referred to in paragraph 1.

8. Member States shall define the necessary capabilities and aptitudes referred to in paragraph 5.

They may determine the sufficient number referred to in paragraph 5.

Article 8   First aid, fire-fighting and evacuation of workers, serious and imminent danger

1. The employer shall:

— take the necessary measures for first aid, fire-fighting and evacuation of workers, adapted to the nature of the activities and the size of the undertaking and/or establishment and taking into account other persons present,

— arrange any necessary contacts with external services, particularly as regards first aid, emergency medical care, rescue work and fire-fighting.

2. Pursuant to paragraph 1, the employer shall, inter alia, for first aid, fire-fighting and the evacuation of workers, designate the workers required to implement such measures.

The number of such workers, their training and the equipment available to them shall be adequate, taking account of the size and/or specific hazards of the undertaking and/or establishment.

3. The employer shall:

(a)   as soon as possible, inform all workers who are, or may be, exposed to serious and imminent danger of the risk involved and of the steps taken or to be taken as regards protection;

(b)   take action and give instructions to enable workers in the event of serious, imminent and unavoidable danger to stop work and/or immediately to leave the work place and proceed to a place of safety;

(c)   save in exceptional cases for reasons duly substantiated, refrain from asking workers to resume work in a working situation where there is still a serious and imminent danger.

4. Workers who, in the event of serious, imminent and unavoidable danger, leave their workstation and/or a dangerous area may not be placed at any disadvantage because of their action and must be protected against any harmful and unjustified consequences, in accordance with national laws and/or practices.

5. The employer shall ensure that all workers are able, in the event of serious and imminent danger to their own safety and/or that of other persons, and where the immediate superior responsible cannot be contacted, to take the appropriate steps in the light of their knowledge and the technical means at their disposal, to avoid the consequences of such danger.

Their actions shall not place them at any disadvantage, unless they acted carelessly or there was negligence on their part.

Article 9   Various obligations on employers

1.   The employer shall:

(a)   be in possession of an assessment of the risks to safety and health at work, including those facing groups of workers exposed to particular risks;

(b)   decide on the protective measures to be taken and, if necessary, the protective equipment to be used;

(c)   keep a list of occupational accidents resulting in a worker being unfit for work for more than three working days;

(d)   draw up, for the responsible authorities and in accordance with national laws and/or practices, reports on occupational accidents suffered by his workers.

2.   Member States shall define, in the light of the nature of the activities and size of the undertakings, the obligations to be met by the different categories of undertakings in respect of the drawing-up of the documents provided for in paragraph 1(a) and

(b)   and when preparing the documents provided for in paragraph 1(c) and (d).

Article 10   Worker information

1.   The employer shall take appropriate measures so that workers and/or their representatives in the undertaking and/or establishment receive, in accordance with national laws and/or practices which may take account, inter alia, of the size of the undertaking and/or establishment, all the necessary information concerning:

(a)   the safety and health risks and protective and preventive measures and activities in respect of both the undertaking and/or establishment in general and each type of workstation and/or job;

(b)   the measures taken pursuant to Article 8(2).

2.   The employer shall take appropriate measures so that employers of workers from any outside undertakings and/or establishments engaged in work in his undertaking and/or establishment receive, in accordance with national laws and/or practices, adequate information concerning the points referred to in paragraph 1(a) and

(b)   which is to be provided to the workers in question.

3.   The employer shall take appropriate measures so that workers with specific functions in protecting the safety and health of workers, or workers' representatives with specific responsibility for the safety and health of workers shall have access, to carry out their functions and in accordance with national laws and/or practices, to:

(a)   the risk assessment and protective measures referred to in Article 9(1)(a) and (b);

(b)   the list and reports referred to in Article 9(1)(c) and (d);

(c)   the information yielded by protective and preventive measures, inspection agencies and bodies responsible for safety and health.

Article 11   Consultation and participation of workers

1.   Employers shall consult workers and/or their representatives and allow them to take part in discussions on all questions relating to safety and health at work.

This presupposes:

— the consultation of workers,

— the right of workers and/or their representatives to make proposals,

— balanced participation in accordance with national laws and/or practices.

2.   Workers or workers' representatives with specific responsibility for the safety and health of workers shall take part in a balanced way, in accordance with national laws and/or practices, or shall be consulted in advance and in good time by the employer with regard to:

(a)   any measure which may substantially affect safety and health;

(b)   the designation of workers referred to in Articles 7(1) and 8(2) and the activities referred to in Article 7(1);

(c)   the information referred to in Articles 9(1) and 10;

(d)   the enlistment, where appropriate, of the competent services or persons outside the undertaking and/or establishment, as referred to in Article 7(3);

(e)   the planning and organization of the training referred to in Article 12.

3.   Workers' representatives with specific responsibility for the safety and health of workers shall have the right to ask the employer to take appropriate measures and to submit proposals to him to that end to mitigate hazards for workers and/or to remove sources of danger.

4.   The workers referred to in paragraph 2 and the workers' representatives referred to in paragraphs 2 and 3 may not be placed at a disadvantage because of their respective activities referred to in paragraphs 2 and 3.

5.   Employers must allow workers' representatives with specific responsibility for the safety and health of workers adequate time off work, without loss of pay, and provide them with the necessary means to enable such representatives to exercise their rights and functions deriving from this Directive.

6.   Workers and/or their representatives are entitled to appeal, in accordance with national law and/or practice, to the authority responsible for safety and health protection at work if they consider that the measures taken and the means employed by the employer are inadequate for the purposes of ensuring safety and health at work.

Workers' representatives must be given the opportunity to submit their observations during inspection visits by the competent authority.

Article 12   Training of workers

1.   The employer shall ensure that each worker receives adequate safety and health training, in particular in the form of information and instructions specific to his workstation or job:

— on recruitment,

— in the event of a transfer or a change of job,

— in the event of the introduction of new work equipment or a change in equipment,

— in the event of the introduction of any new technology.

The training shall be:

— adapted to take account of new or changed risks, and

— repeated periodically if necessary.

2.   The employer shall ensure that workers from outside undertakings and/or establishments engaged in work in his undertaking and/or establishment

have in fact received appropriate instructions regarding health and safety risks during their activities in his undertaking and/or establishment.

3.   Workers' representatives with a specific role in protecting the safety and health of workers shall be entitled to appropriate training.

4.   The training referred to in paragraphs 1 and 3 may not be at the workers' expense or at that of the workers' representatives.

The training referred to in paragraph 1 must take place during working hours.

The training referred to in paragraph 3 must take place during working hours or in accordance with national practice either within or outside the undertaking and/or the establishment.

SECTION III   WORKERS' OBLIGATIONS

Article 13

1.   It shall be the responsibility of each worker to take care as far as possible of his own safety and health and that of other persons affected by his acts or Commissions at work in accordance with his training and the instructions given by his employer.

2.   To this end, workers must in particular, in accordance with their training and the instructions given by their employer:

(a)   make correct use of machinery, apparatus, tools, dangerous substances, transport equipment and other means of production;

(b)   make correct use of the personal protective equipment supplied to them and, after use, return it to its proper place;

(c)   refrain from disconnecting, changing or removing arbitrarily safety devices fitted, e.g. to machinery, apparatus, tools, plant and buildings, and use such safety devices correctly;

(d)   immediately inform the employer and/or the workers with specific responsibility for the safety and health of workers of any work situation they have reasonable grounds for considering represents a serious and immediate danger to safety and health and of any shortcomings in the protection arrangements;

(e)   cooperate, in accordance with national practice, with the employer and/or workers with specific responsibility for the safety and health of workers, for as long as may be necessary to enable any tasks or requirements imposed by the competent authority to protect the safety and health of workers at work to be carried out;

(f)   cooperate, in accordance with national practice, with the employer and/or workers with specific responsibility for the safety and health of workers, for as long as may be necessary to enable the employer to ensure that the working environment and working conditions are safe and pose no risk to safety and health within their field of activity.

SECTION IV   MISCELLANEOUS PROVISIONS

Article 14   Health surveillance

1.   To ensure that workers receive health surveillance appropriate to the health and safety risks they incur at work, measures shall be introduced in accordance with national law and/or practices.

2.   The measures referred to in paragraph 1 shall be such that each worker, if he so wishes, may receive health surveillance at regular intervals.

3.   Health surveillance may be provided as part of a national health system.

Article 15   Risk groups

Particularly sensitive risk groups must be protected against the dangers which specifically affect them.

Article 16   Individual Directives — Amendments — General scope of this Directive

1.   The Council, acting on a proposal from the Commission based on Article 118a of the Treaty, shall adopt individual Directives, inter alia, in the areas listed in the Annex.

2.   This Directive and, without prejudice to the procedure referred to in Article 17 concerning technical adjustments, the individual Directives may be amended in accordance with the procedure provided for in Article 118a of the Treaty.

3.   The provisions of this Directive shall apply in full to all the areas covered by the individual Directives, without prejudice to more stringent and/or specific provisions contained in these individual Directives.

Article 17   Committee

1.   For the purely technical adjustments to the individual Directives provided for in Article 16(1) to take account of:
— the adoption of Directives in the field of technical harmonization and standardisation, and/or
— technical progress, changes in international regulations or specifications, and new findings,
the Commission shall be assisted by a committee composed of the representatives of the Member States and chaired by the representative of the Commission.

2.   The representative of the Commission shall submit to the committee a draft of the measures to be taken.

The committee shall deliver its opinion on the draft within a time limit which the chairman may lay down according to the urgency of the matter.

The opinion shall be delivered by the majority laid down in Article 148(2) of the Treaty in the case of decisions which the Council is required to adopt on a proposal from the Commission.

The votes of the representatives of the Member States within the committee shall be weighted in the manner set out in that Article. The chairman shall not vote.

3.   The Commission shall adopt the measures envisaged if they are in accordance with the opinion of the committee.

If the measures envisaged are not in accordance with the opinion of the committee, or if no opinion is delivered, the Commission shall, without delay, submit to the Council a proposal relating to the measures to be taken. The Council shall act by a qualified majority.

If, on the expiry of three months from the date of the referral to the Council, the Council has not acted, the proposed measures shall be adopted by the Commission.

Article 18   Final provisions

1.   Member States shall bring into force the laws, regulations and administrative provisions necessary to comply with this Directive by 31 December 1992.

They shall forthwith inform the Commission thereof.

2.   Member States shall communicate to the Commission the texts of the provisions of national law which they have already adopted or adopt in the field covered by this Directive.

3.   Member States shall report to the Commission every five years on the practical implementation of the provisions of this Directive, indicating the points of view of employers and workers.

The Commission shall inform the European Parliament, the Council, the Economic and Social Committee and the Advisory Committee on Safety, Hygiene and Health Protection at Work.

4.   The Commission shall submit periodically to the European Parliament, the Council and the Economic and Social Committee a report on the implementation of this Directive, taking into account paragraphs 1 to 3.

Article 19
This Directive is addressed to the Member States.

Done at Luxembourg, 12 June 1989.
For the Council
The President
M. CHAVES GONZALES

ANNEX

List of areas referred to in Article 16(1)
— Work places
— Work equipment
— Personal protective equipment
— Work with visual display units
— Handling of heavy loads involving risk of back injury
— Temporary or mobile work sites
— Fisheries and agriculture

COUNCIL DIRECTIVE OF 14 OCTOBER 1991 ON AN EMPLOYER'S OBLIGATION TO INFORM EMPLOYEES OF THE CONDITIONS APPLICABLE TO THE CONTRACT OR EMPLOYMENT RELATIONSHIP (91/533/EEC)
[OJ 1991, No. L288/32]

THE COUNCIL OF THE EUROPEAN COMMUNITIES,

Having regard to the Treaty establishing the European Economic Community, and in particular Article 100 thereof,

Having regard to the proposal from the Commission,[1]
Having regard to the opinion of the European Parliament,[2]
Having regard to the opinion of the Economic and Social Committee,[3]

Whereas the development, in the Member States, of new forms of work has led to an increase in the number of types of employment relationship;

Notes
[1] OJ No. C24, 31.1.1991, p. 3.
[2] OJ No. C240, 16.9.1991, p. 21.
[3] OJ No. C159, 17.6.1991, p. 32.

Whereas, faced with this development, certain Member States have considered it necessary to subject employment relationships to formal requirements; whereas these provisions are designed to provide employees with improved protection against possible infringements of their rights and to create greater transparency on the labour market;

Whereas the relevant legislation of the Member States differs considerably on such fundamental points as the requirement to inform employees in writing of the main terms of the contract or employment relationship;

Whereas differences in the legislation of Member States may have a direct effect on the operation of the common market;

Whereas Article 117 of the Treaty provides for the Member States to agree upon the need to promote improved working conditions and an improved standard of living for workers, so as to make possible their harmonisation while the improvement is being maintained;

Whereas point 9 of the Community Charter of Fundamental Social Rights for Workers, adopted at the Strasbourg European Council on 9 December 1989 by the Heads of State and Government of 11 Member States, states:

'The conditions of employment of every worker of the European Community shall be stipulated in laws, a collective agreement or a contract of employment according to arrangements applying in each country.';

Whereas it is necessary to establish at Community level the general requirement that every employee must be provided with a document containing information on the essential elements of his contract or employment relationship;

Whereas, in view of the need to maintain a certain degree of flexibility in employment relationships, Member States should be able to exclude certain limited cases of employment relationship from this Directive's scope of application;

Whereas the obligation to provide information may be met by means of a written contract, a letter of appointment or one or more other documents or, if they are lacking, a written statement signed by the employer;

Whereas, in the case of expatriation of the employee, the latter must, in addition to the main terms of his contract or employment relationship, be supplied with relevant information connected with his secondment;

Whereas, in order to protect the interests of employees with regard to obtaining a document, any change in the main terms of the contract or employment relationship must be communicated to them in writing;

Whereas it is necessary for Member States to guarantee that employees can claim the rights conferred on them by this Directive;

Whereas Member States are to adopt the laws, regulations and legislative provisions necessary to comply with this Directive or are to ensure that both sides of industry set up the necessary provisions by agreement, with Member States being obliged to take the necessary steps enabling them at all times to guarantee the results imposed by the Directive,

HAS ADOPTED THIS DIRECTIVE

Article 1   Scope

1.   This Directive shall apply to every paid employee having a contract or employment relationship defined by the law in force in a Member State and/or governed by the law in force in a Member State.

2. Member States may provide that this Directive shall not apply to employees having a contract or employment relationship:

(a) — with a total duration not exceeding one month, and/or

    — with a working week not exceeding eight hours; or

(b) of a causal and/or specific nature provided, in these cases, that its non-application is justified by objective considerations.

Article 2   Obligation to provide information

1. An employer shall be obliged to notify an employee to whom this Directive applies, hereinafter referred to as 'the employee', of the essential aspects of the contract or employment relationship.

2. The information referred to in paragraph 1 shall cover at least the following:

(a) the identities of the parties;

(b) the place of work; where there is no fixed or main place of work, the principle that the employee is employed at various places and the registered place of business or, where appropriate, the domicile of the employer;

(c) (i) the title, grade, nature or category of the work for which the employee is employed; or

    (ii) a brief specification or description of the work;

(d) the date of commencement of the contract or employment relationship;

(e) in the case of a temporary contract or employment relationship, the expected duration thereof;

(f) the amount of paid leave to which the employee is entitled or, where this cannot be indicated when the information is given, the procedures for allocating and determining such leave;

(g) the length of the periods of notice to be observed by the employer and the employee should their contract or employment relationship be terminated or, where this cannot be indicated when the information is given, the method for determining such periods of notice;

(h) the initial basic amount, the other component elements and the frequency of payment of the remuneration to which the employee is entitled;

(i) the length of the employee's normal working day or week;

(j) where appropriate;

    (i) the collective agreements governing the employee's conditions of work; or

    (ii) in the case of collective agreements concluded outside the business by special joint bodies or institutions, the name of the competent body or joint institution within which the agreements were concluded.

3. The information referred to in paragraph 2(f), (g), (h) and (i) may, where appropriate, be given in the form of a reference to the laws, regulations and administrative or statutory provisions or collective agreements governing those particular points.

Article 3   Means of information

1. The information referred to in Article 2(2) may be given to the employee, not later than two months after the commencement of employment, in the form of:

(a) a written contract of employment; and/or

(b) a letter of engagement; and/or

(c)   one or more other written documents, where one of these documents contains at least all the information referred to in Article 2(2)(a), (b), (c), (d), (h) and (i).

2.   Where none of the documents referred to in paragraph 1 is handed over to the employee within the prescribed period, the employer shall be obliged to give the employee, not later than two months after the commencement of employment, a written declaration signed by the employer and containing at least the information referred to in Article 2(2).

Where the document(s) referred to in paragraph 1 contain only part of the information required, the written declaration provided for in the first sub-paragrph of this paragraph shall cover the remaining information.

3.   Where the contract or employment relationship comes to an end before expiry of a period of two months as from the date of the start of work, the information provided for in Article 2 and in this Article must be made available to the employee by the end of this period at the latest.

Article 4   Expatriate employees

1.   Where an employee is required to work in a country or countries other than the Member State whose law and/or practice governs the contract or employment relationship, the document(s) referred to in Article 3 must be in his/her possession before his/her departure and must include at least the following additional information:

(a)   the duration of the employment abroad;

(b)   the currency to be used for the payment of remuneration;

(c)   where appropriate, the benefits in cash or kind attendant on the employment abroad;

(d)   where appropriate, the conditions governing the employee's repatriation.

2.   The information referred to in paragraph 1(b) and (c) may, where appropriate, be given in the form of a reference to the laws, regualtions and administrative or statutory provisions or collective agreements governing those particular points.

3.   Paragraphs 1 and 2 shall not apply if the duration of the employment outside the country whose law and/or practice governs the contract or employment relationship is one month or less.

Article 5   Modification of aspects of the contract or employment relationship

1.   Any change in the details referred to in Articles 2(2) and 4(1) must be the subject of a written document to be given by the employer to the employee at the earliest opportunity and not later than one month after the date of entry into effect of the change in question.

2.   The written document referred to in paragraph 1 shall not be compulsory in the event of a change in the laws, regulations and administrative or statutory provisions or collective agreements cited in the documents referred to in Article 3, supplemented, where appropriate, pursuant to Article 4(1).

Article 6   Form and proof of the existence of a contract or employment relationship and procedural rules

This Directive shall be without prejudice to national law and practice concerning;

— the form of the contract or employment relationship,
— proof as regards the existence and content of a contract or employment relationship,
— the relevant procedural rules.

Article 7   More favourable provisions
This Directive shall not affect Member States' prerogative to apply or to introduce laws, regulations or administrative provisions which are more favourable to employees or to encourage or permit the application of agreements which are more favourable to employees.

Article 8   Defence of rights
1.   Member States shall introduce into their national legal systems such measures as are necessary to enable all employees who consider themselves wronged by failure to comply with the obligations arising from this Directive to pursue their claims by judicial process after possible recourse to other competent authorities.

2.   Member States may provide that access to the means of redress referred to in paragraph 1 are subject to the notification of the employer by the employee and the failure by the employer to reply within 15 days of notification.

However, the formality of prior notification may in no case be required in the cases referred to in Article 4, neither for workers with a temporary contract or employment relationship, nor for employees not covered by a collective agreement or by collective agreements relating to the employment relationship.

Article 9   Final provisions
1.   Member States shall adopt the laws, regulations and administrative provisions necessary to comply with this Directive no later than 30 June 1993 or shall ensure by that date that the employers' and workers' representatives introduce the required provisions by way of agreement, the Member States being obliged to take the necessary steps enabling them at all times to guarantee the results imposed by this Directive.

They shall forthwith inform the Commission thereof.

2.   Member States shall take the necessary measures to ensure that, in the case of employment relationships in existence upon entry into force of the provisions that they adopt, the employer gives the employee, on request, within two months of receiving that request, any of the documents referred to in Article 3, supplemented, where appropriate, pursuant to Article 4(1).

3.   When Member States adopt the measures referred to in paragraph 1, such measures shall contain a reference to this Directive or shall be accompanied by such reference on the occasion of their official publication. The methods of making such a reference shall be laid down by the Member States.

4.   Member States shall forthwith inform the Commission of the measures they take to implement this Directive.

Article 10
This Directive is addressed to the Member States.

Done at Luxembourg, 14 October 1991.
For the Council
The President
B. de VRIES

COUNCIL DIRECTIVE 92/57/EEC OF 24 JUNE 1992 ON THE IMPLEMENTATION OF MINIMUM SAFETY AND HEALTH REQUIREMENTS AT TEMPORARY OR MOBILE CONSTRUCTION SITES (EIGHTH INDIVIDUAL DIRECTIVE WITHIN THE MEANING OF ARTICLE 16(1) OF DIRECTIVE 89/391/EEC) [OJ 1992, No. L245/1][1]

THE COUNCIL OF THE EUROPEAN COMMUNITIES,

Having regard to the Treaty establishing the European Economic Community, and in particular Article 118a thereof,

Having regard to the proposal from the Commission,[2] submitted after consulting the Advisory Committee on Safety, Hygiene and Health Protection at Work,

In cooperation with the European Parliament,[3]

Having regard to the opinion of the Economic and Social Committee,[4]

Whereas Article 118a of the Treaty provides that the Council shall adopt, by means of directives, minimum requirements for encouraging improvements, especially in the working environment, to ensure a better level of protection of the safety and health of workers;

Whereas, under the terms of that Article, those directives are to avoid imposing administrative, financial and legal constraints in a way which would hold back the creation and development of small and medium-sized undertakings;

Whereas the communication from the Commission on its programme concerning safety, hygiene and health at work[5] provides for the adoption of a Directive designed to guarantee the safety and health of workers at temporary or mobile construction sites;

Whereas, in its resolution of 21 December 1987 on safety, hygiene and health at work,[6] the Council took note of the Commission's intention of submitting to the Council in the near future minimum requirements concerning temporary or mobile construction sites;

Whereas temporary or mobile construction sites constitute an area of activity that exposes workers to particularly high levels of risk;

Whereas unsatisfactory architectural and/or organisational options or poor planning of the works at the project preparation stage have played a role in more than half of the occupational accidents occurring on construction sites in the Community;

Whereas in each Member State the authorities responsible for safety and health at work must be informed, before the beginning of the works, of the execution of works the scale of which exceeds a certain threshold;

Whereas, when a project is being carried out, a large number of occupational accidents may be caused by inadequate coordination, particularly where

Notes
[1] As corrected by OJ 1993, No. L15 and 33.
[2] OJ No. C213, 28.8.1990, p. 2 and OJ No. C112, 27.4.1991, p. 4.
[3] OJ No. C78, 18.3.1990, p. 172 and OJ No. C150, 15.6.1992.
[4] OJ No. C120, 6.5.1991, p. 24.
[5] OJ No. C28, 3.2.1988, p. 3.
[6] OJ No. C28, 3.2.1988, p. 1.

various undertakings work simultaneously or in succession at the same temporary or mobile construction site;

Whereas it is therefore necessary to improve coordination between the various parties concerned at the project preparation stage and also when the work is being carried out;

Whereas compliance with the minimum requirements designed to guarantee a better standard of safety and health at temporary or mobile construction sites is essential to ensure the safety and health of workers;

Whereas, moreover, self-employed persons and employers, where they are personally engaged in work activity, may, through their activities on a temporary or mobile construction site, jeopardise the safety and health of workers;

Whereas it is therefore necessary to extend to self-employed persons and to employers where they are personally engaged in work activity on the site certain relevant provisions of Council Directive 89/655/EEC of 30 November 1989 concerning the minimum safety and health requirements for the use of work equipment by workers at work (second individual Directive),[7] and of Council Directive 89/656/EEC of 30 November 1989 on the minimum health and safety requirements for the use by workers of personal protective equipment at the workplace (third individual Directive);[8]

Whereas this Directive is an individual Directive within the meaning of Article 16(1) of Council Directive 89/391/EEC of 12 June 1989 on the introduction of measures to encourage improvements in the safety and health of workers at work;[9] whereas, therefore, the provisions of the said Directive are fully applicable to temporary or mobile construction sites, without prejudice to more stringent and/or specific provisions contained in this Directive;

Whereas this Directive constitutes a practical step towards the achievement of the social dimension of the internal market with special reference to the subject matter of Council Directive 89/106/EEC of 21 December 1988 on the approximation of laws, regulations and administrative provisions of the Member States relating to construction products[10] and the subject matter covered by Council Directive 89/440/EEC of 18 July 1989 amending Directive 71/305/EEC concerning coordination of procedures for the award of public work contracts;[11]

Whereas, pursuant to Council Decision 74/325/EEC,[12] the Advisory Committee on Safety, Hygiene and Health Protection at Work is consulted by the Commission with a view to drawing up proposals in this field,

Notes
[7]OJ No. L393, 30.12.1989, p. 13.
[8]OJ No. L393, 30.12.1989, p. 18.
[9]OJ No. L183, 29.6.1989, p. 1.
[10]OJ No. L40, 11.2.1989, p. 12.
[11]OJ No. L210, 21.7.1989, p. 1. Amended by Commission Decision 90/380/EEC (OJ No. L187, 19.7.1990, p. 55)
[12]OJ No. L185, 9.7.1974, p. 15. Last amended by the 1985 Act of Accession.

HAS ADOPTED THIS DIRECTIVE:

Article 1   Subject
1. This Directive, which is the eighth individual Directive within the meaning of Article 16(1) of Directive 89/391/EEC, lays down minimum safety

and health requirements for temporary or mobile construction sites, as defined in Article 2(a).

2.   This Directive shall not apply to drilling and extraction in the extractive industries within the meaning of Article 1(2) of Council Decision 74/326/EEC of 27 June 1974 on the extension of the responsibilities of the Mines Safety and Health Commission to all mineral-extracting industries.[1]

3.   The provisions of Directive 89/391/EEC are fully applicable to the whole scope referred to in paragraph 1, without prejudice to more stringent and/or specific provisions contained in this Directive.

Note
[1]OJ No. L185, 9.7.1974, p. 18.

Article 2   Definitions
For the purposes of this Directive:

(a)   'temporary or mobile construction sites' (hereinafter referred to as 'construction sites') means any construction site at which building or civil engineering works are carried out; a non-exhaustive list of such works is given in Annex I;

(b)   'client' means any natural or legal person for whom a project is carried out;

(c)   'project supervisor' means any natural or legal person responsible for the design and/or execution and/or supervision of the execution of a project, acting on behalf of the client;

(d)   'self-employed person' means any person other than those referred to in Article 3(a) and (b) of Directive 89/391/EEC whose professional activity contributes to the completion of a project;

(e)   'coordinator for safety and health matters at the project preparations stage' means any natural or legal person entrusted by the client and/or project supervisor, during the project preparation stage, with performing the duties referred to in Article 5;

(f)   'coordinator for safety and health matters at the project execution stage' means any natural or legal person entrusted by the client and/or project supervisor, during execution of the project, with performing the duties referred to in Article 6.

Article 3   Appointment of coordinators — Safety and health plan — Prior notice
1.   The client or the project supervisor shall appoint one or more coordinators for safety and health matters, as defined in Article 2(e) and (f), for any construction site on which more than one contractor is present.

2.   The client or the project supervisor shall ensure that prior to the setting up of a construction site a safety and health plan is drawn up in accordance with Article 5(b).

The Member States may, after consulting both management and the workforce, allow derogations from the provisions of the first subparagraph, except where it is a question of:

— work involving particular risks as listed in Annex II, or

— work for which prior notice is required pursuant to paragraph 3 of this Article.

3.   In the case of construction sites:

— on which work is scheduled to last longer than 30 working days and on which more than 20 workers are occupied simultaneously, or

— on which the volume of work is scheduled to exceed 500 person-days, the client or the project supervisor shall communicate a prior notice drawn up in accordance with Annex III to the competent authorities before work starts. The prior notice must be clearly displayed on the construction site and, if necessary, periodically updated.

Article 4   Project preparation stage: general principles

The project supervisor, or where appropriate the client, shall take account of the general principles of prevention concerning safety and health referred to in Directive 89/391/EEC during the various stages of designing and preparing the project, in particular:

— when architectural, technical and/or organisational aspects are being decided, in order to plan the various items or stages of work which are to take place simultaneously or in succession,

— when estimating the period required for completing such work or work stages.

Account shall also be taken, each time this appears necessary, of all safety and health plans and of files drawn up in accordance with Article 5(b) or (c) or adjusted in accordance with Article 6(c).

Article 5   Project preparation stage: duties of coordinators

The coordinator(s) for safety and health matters during the project preparation stage appointed in accordance with Article 3(1) shall:

(a)   coordinate implementation of the provisions of Article 4;

(b)   draw up, or cause to be drawn up, a safety and health plan setting out the rules applicable to the construction site concerned, taking into account where necessary the industrial activities taking place on the site; this plan must also include specific measures concerning work which falls within one or more of the categories of Annex II;

(c)   prepare a file appropriate to the characteristics of the project containing relevant safety and health information to be taken into account during any subsequent works.

Article 6   Project execution stage: duties of coordinators

The coordinator(s) for safety and health matters during the project execution stage appointed in accordance with Article 3(1) shall:

(a)   coordinate implementation of the general principles of prevention and safety:

— when technical and/or organisational aspects are being decided, in order to plan the various items or stages of work which are to take place simultaneously or in succession,

— when estimating the period required for completing such work or work stages;

(b)   coordinate implementation of the relevant provisions in order to ensure that employers and, if necessary for the protection of workers, self-employed persons:

— apply the principles referred to in Article 8 in a consistent manner,

— where required, follow the safety and health plan referred to in Article 5(b);

    (c)   make, or cause to be made, any adjustments required to the safety and health plan referred to in Article 5(b) and the file referred to in Article 5(c) to take account of the progress of the work and any changes which have occurred;

    (d)   organise cooperation between employers, including successive employers on the same site, coordination of their activities with a view to protecting workers and preventing accidents and occupational health hazards and reciprocal information as provided for in Article 6(4) of Directive 89/391/EEC, ensuring that self-employed persons are brought into this process where necessary;

    (e)   coordinate arrangements to check that the working procedures are being implemented correctly;

    (f)   take the steps necessary to ensure that only authorised persons are allowed onto the construction site.

Article 7 Responsibilities of clients, project supervisors and employers

1. Where a client or project supervisor has appointed a coordinator or coordinators to perform the duties referred to in Articles 5 and 6, this does not relieve the client or project supervisor of his responsibilities in that respect.

2. The implementation of Articles 5 and 6, and of paragraph 1 of this Article shall not affect the principle of employers' responsibility as provided for in Directive 89/391/EEC.

Article 8 Implementation of Article 6 of Directive 89/391/EEC

When the work is being carried out, the principles set out in Article 6 of Directive 89/391/EEC shall be applied, in particular as regards:

    (a)   keeping the construction site in good order and in a satisfactory state of cleanliness;

    (b)   choosing the location of workstations bearing in mind how access to these workplaces is obtained, and determining routes or areas for the passage and movement of equipment;

    (c)   the conditions under which various materials are handled;

    (d)   technical maintenance, pre-commissioning checks and regular checks on installations and equipment with a view to correcting any faults which might affect the safety and health of workers;

    (e)   the demarcation and laying-out of areas for the storage of various materials, in particular where dangerous materials or substances are concerned;

    (f)   the conditions under which the dangerous materials used are removed;

    (g)   the storage and disposal or removal of waste and debris;

    (h)   the adaptation, based on progress made with the site, of the actual period to be allocated for the various types of work or work stages;

    (i)   cooperation between employers and self-employed persons;

    (j)   interaction with industrial activities at the place within which or in the vicinity of which the construction site is located.

Article 9   Obligations of employers

In order to preserve safety and health on the construction site, under the conditions set out in Article 6 and 7, employers shall:

(a)   in particular when implementing Article 8, take measures that are in line with the minimum requirements set out in Annex IV;

(b)   take into account directions from the coordinator(s) for safety and health matters.

Article 10   Obligations of other groups of persons

1.   In order to preserve safety and health on the construction site, self-employed persons shall:

(a)   comply in particular with the following, mutatis mutandis:

(i)   the requirements of Article 6(4) and Article 13 of Directive 89/391/EEC and Article 8 and Annex IV of this Directive;

(ii)   Article 4 of Directive 89/655/EEC and the relevant provisions of the Annex thereto;

(iii)   Article 3, Article 4(1) to (4) and (9) and Article 5 of Directive 89/656/EEC;

(b)   take into account directions from the coordinator(s) for safety and health matters.

2.   In order to preserve safety and health on the site, where employers are personally engaged in work activity on the construction site, they shall:

(a)   comply in particular with the following, mutatis mutandis:

(i)   Article 13 of Directive 89/391/EEC;

(ii)   Article 4 of Directive 89/655/EEC and the relevant provisions of the Annex thereto;

(iii)   Articles 3, 4(1), (2), (3), (4), (9) and 5 of Directive 89/656/EEC;

(b)   take account of the comments of the coordinator(s) for safety and health.

Article 11   Information for workers

1.   Without prejudice to Article 10 of Directive 89/391/EEC, workers and/or their representatives shall be informed of all the measures to be taken concerning their safety and health on the construction site.

2.   The information must be comprehensible to the workers concerned.

Article 12   Consultation and participation of workers

Consultation and participation of workers and/or of their representatives shall take place in accordance with Article 11 of Directive 89/391/EEC on matters covered by Articles 6, 8 and 9 of this Directive, ensuring whenever necessary proper coordination between workers and/or workers' representatives in undertakings carrying out their activities at the workplace, having regard to the degree of risk and the size of the work site.

Article 13   Amendment of the Annexes

1.   Amendments to Annexes I, II and III shall be adopted by the Council in accordance with the procedure laid down in Article 118a of the Treaty.

2.   Strictly technical adaptations of Annex IV as a result of:

— the adoption of directives on technical harmonization and standardisation regarding temporary or mobile construction sites, and/or

— technical progress, changes in international regulations or specifications or knowledge in the field of temporary or mobile construction sites shall be adopted in accordance with the procedure laid down in Article 17 of Directive 89/391/EEC.

Article 14   Final provisions

1.   Member States shall bring into force the laws, regulations and administrative provisions necessary to comply with this Directive by 31 December 1993 at the latest.

They shall forthwith inform the Commission thereof.

2.   When Member States adopt these measures, they shall contain a reference to this Directive or be accompanied by such reference on the occasion of their official publication. The methods of making such a reference shall be laid down by the Member States.

3.   Member States shall communicate to the Commission the texts of the provisions of national law which they have already adopted or adopt in the field governed by this Directive.

4.   Member States shall report to the Commission every four years on the practical implementation of the provisions of this Directive, indicating the points of view of employers and workers.

The Commission shall inform the European Parliament, the Council, the Economic and Social Committee and the Advisory Committee on Safety, Hygiene and Health Protection at Work.

5.   The Commission shall submit periodically to the European Parliament, the Council and the Economic and Social Committee a report on the implementation of this Directive, taking into account paragraphs 1, 2, 3 and 4.

Article 15

This Directive is addressed to the Member States.

Done at Luxembourg, 24 June 1992.
For the Council
The President
Jos da SILVA PENEDA

ANNEX I   NON-EXHAUSTIVE LIST OF BUILDING AND CIVIL ENGINEERING WORKS REFERRED TO IN ARTICLE 2(a) OF THE DIRECTIVE

1.   Excavation
2.   Earthworks
3.   Construction
4.   Assembly and disassembly of prefabricated elements
5.   Conversion or fitting-out
6.   Alterations
7.   Renovation
8.   Repairs
9.   Dismantling
10.   Demolition
11.   Upkeep
12.   Maintenance — Painting and cleaning work
13.   Drainage

ANNEX II   NON-EXHAUSTIVE LIST OF WORK INVOLVING PARTICULAR RISKS TO THE SAFETY AND HEALTH OF WORKERS REFERRED TO IN ARTICLE 3(2), SECOND PARAGRAPH OF THE DIRECTIVE

1.   Work which puts workers at risk of burial under earthfalls, engulfment in swampland or falling from a height, where the risk is particularly aggravated by the nature of the work or processes used or by the environment at the place of work or site.[1]

2.   Work which puts workers at risk from chemical or biological substances constituting a particular danger to the safety and health of workers or involving a legal requirement for health monitoring.

3.   Work with ionising radiation requiring the designation of controlled or supervised areas as defined in Article 20 of Directive 80/836/Euratom.[2]

4.   Work near high voltage power lines.

5.   Work exposing workers to the risk of drowning.

6.   Work on wells, underground earthworks and tunnels.

7.   Work carried out by divers having a system of air supply.

8.   Work carried out by workers in caissons with a compressed-air atmosphere.

9.   Work involving the use of explosives.

10.   Work involving the assembly or dismantling of heavy prefabricated components.

Notes

[1]In implementing point 1, Member States have the option of setting figures for individual situations.

[2]OJ No. L246, 17.9.1980, p. 1. Last amended by Directive 84/467/Euratom (OJ No. L265, 5.10.1984, p. 4).

ANNEX III   CONTENT OF THE PRIOR NOTICE REFERRED TO IN ARTICLE 3(3), FIRST PARAGRAPH OF THE DIRECTIVE

1.   Date of forwarding:.

2.   Exact address of the construction site:.

3.   Client(s) (name(s) and address(es)):.

4.   Type of project:.

5.   Project supervisor(s) (name(s) and address(es)):.

6.   Safety and health coordinators(s) during the project preparation stage (name(s) and address(es)):.

7.   Coordinator(s) for safety and health matters during the project execution stage (name(s) and address(es)):.

8.   Date planned for start of work on the construction site:.

9.   Planned duration of work on the construction site:.

10.   Estimated maximum number of workers on the construction site:.

11.   Planned number of contractors and self-employed persons on the construction site:.

12.   Details of contractors already chosen:.

ANNEX IV   MINIMUM SAFETY AND HEALTH REQUIREMENTS FOR CONSTRUCTION SITES

Referred to in Article 9(a) and Article 10(1)(a)(i) of the Directive Preliminary remarks.

The obligations laid down in this Annex apply wherever required by the features of the construction site, the activity, the circumstances or a hazard. For the purposes of this Annex, 'rooms' covers, inter alia, hutted accommodation.

PART A   GENERAL MINIMUM REQUIREMENTS FOR ON-SITE WORKPLACES

1.   Stability and solidity

1.1   Materials, equipment and, more generally, any component which, when moving in any way, may affect the safety and health of workers must be stabilised in an appropriate and safe manner.

1.2   Access to any surface involving insufficiently resistant materials is not authorised unless appropriate equipment or means are provided to enable the work to be carried out safely.

2.   Energy distribution installations

2.1   The installations must be designed, constructed and used so as not to present a fire or explosion hazard; persons must be adequately protected against the risk of electrocution caused by direct or indirect contact.

2.2   The design, construction and choice of equipment and protection devices must take account of the type and power of the energy distributed, external conditions and the competence of persons with access to parts of the installation.

3.   Emergency routes and exits

3.1   Emergency routes and exits must remain clear and lead as directly as possible to a safe area.

3.2   In the event of danger, it must be possible for workers to evacuate all workstations quickly and as safely as possible.

3.3   The number, distribution and dimensions of emergency routes and exits depend on the use, equipment and dimensions of the site and of the rooms and the maximum number of persons that may be present.

3.4   Specific emergency routes and exits must be indicated by signs in accordance with the national regulations implementing Directive 77/576/EEC.[1] Such signs must be sufficiently resistant and be placed at appropriate points.

3.5   Emergency routes and exits, and the traffic routes and doors giving access to them, must be free from obstruction so that they can be used at any time without hindrance.

3.6   Emergency routes and exits requiring illumination must be provided with emergency lighting of adequate intensity in case the lighting fails.

Notes
[1]OJ No. L229, 7.9.1977, p. 12. Last amended by Directive 79/640/EEC (OJ No. L183, 19.7.1979, p. 1).

4.   Fire detection and fire fighting

4.1   Depending of the characteristics of the site, the dimensions and use of the rooms, the on-site equipment, the physical and chemical properties of the substances present and the maximum potential number of people present, an adequate number of appropriate fire-fighting devices and, where required, fire detectors and alarm systems must be provided.

4.2   These fire-fighting devices, fire detectors and alarm systems must be regularly checked and maintained.

Appropriate tests and drills must take place at regular intervals.

4.3   Non-automatic fire-fighting equipment must be easily accessible and simple to use.

The equipment must be indicated by signs in accordance with the national regulations implementing Directive 77/576/EEC.

Such signs must be sufficiently resistant and placed at appropriate points.

5.   Ventilation

Steps shall be taken to ensure that there is sufficient fresh air, having regard to the working methods used and the physical demands placed on the workers. If a forced ventilation system is used, it must be maintained in working order and must not expose workers to draughts which are harmful to health.

Any breakdown must be indicated by a control system where this is necessary for workers' health.

6.   Exposure to particular risks

6.1   Workers must not be exposed to harmful levels of noise or to harmful external influences (e.g. gases, vapours, dust).

6.2   If workers have to enter an area where the atmosphere is liable to contain a toxic or harmful substance or to have an insufficient oxygen level or to be inflammable, the confined atmosphere must be monitored and appropriate steps taken to prevent any hazards.

6.3   A worker may not in any circumstances be exposed to a high-risk confined atmosphere.

He must at least be watched at all times from outside and all appropriate precautions must be taken to ensure that he can be assisted effectively and immediately.

7.   Temperature

During working hours, the temperature must be appropriate for human beings, having regard to the working methods used and the physical demands placed on the workers.

8.   Natural and artificial lighting of workstations, rooms and traffic routes on the site

8.1   Workstations, rooms and traffic routes must as far as possible have sufficient natural lighting and be provided with appropriate and sufficient artificial lighting at night and when natural daylight is inadequate; where necessary, portable light sources that are protected against impact must be used.

The colour of artificial light used must not alter or affect the perception of signals or signposts.

8.2   Lighting installations for rooms, workstations and traffic routes must be placed in such a way that there is no risk of accident to workers as a result of the type of lighting fitted.

8.3   Rooms, workstations and traffic routes where workers are especially exposed to risks in the event of failure of artificial lighting must be provided with emergency lighting of adequate intensity.

9. Doors and gates

9.1   Sliding doors must be fitted with a safety device to prevent them from being derailed and falling over.

9.2   Doors and gates opening upwards must be fitted with a mechanism to secure them against falling back.

9.3   Doors and gates along escape routes must be appropriately marked.

9.4   In the immediate vicinity of gates intended primarily for vehicle traffic, there must be doors for pedestrian traffic unless it is safe for pedestrians to cross; such doors must be clearly marked and kept free at all times.

9.5   Mechanical doors and gates must operate without any risk of accident to workers.

They must be fitted with emergency stop devices which are easily identifiable and accessible and, unless they open automatically in the event of a power-cut, it must be possible for them to be opened manually.

10 Traffic routes — danger areas

10.1   Traffic routes, including stairs, fixed ladders and loading bays and ramps, must be calculated, located, laid out and made negotiable to ensure easy, safe and appropriate access in such a way as not to endanger workers employed in the vicinity of these traffic routes.

10.2   Routes used for pedestrian traffic and/or goods traffic including those used for loading and unloading must be dimensioned in accordance with the number of potential users and the type of activity concerned.

If means of transport are used on traffic routes, a sufficient safety clearance or adequate protective devices must be provided for other site users.

Routes must be clearly marked, regularly checked and properly maintained.

10.3   Sufficient clearance must be allowed between vehicle traffic routes and doors, gates, passages for pedestrians, corridors and staircases.

10.4   If the site includes limited-access areas, these must be equipped with devices to prevent unauthorised workers from entering.

Appropriate measures must be taken to protect workers who are authorised to enter the danger areas.

Danger areas must be clearly signposted.

11. Loading bays and ramps

11.1   Loading bays and ramps must be suitable for the dimensions of the loads to be transported.

11.2   Loading bays must have at least one exit point.

11.3   Loading ramps must be sufficiently safe to prevent workers from falling off.

12. Freedom of movement at the workstation

The floor area at the workstation must be such as to allow workers sufficient freedom of movement to perform their work, taking account of any necessary equipment or appliances present.

13. First aid

13.1   The employer must ensure that first aid can be provided, and that the staff trained to provide it can be called upon, at any time.

Measures must be taken to ensure that workers who have had an accident or have suddenly been taken ill can be removed for medical treatment.

13.2   One or more first-aid rooms must be provided where the scale of the works or the types of activity being carried out so require.

13.3   First-aid rooms must be fitted with essential first-aid installations and equipment and be easily accessible to stretchers.

They must be signposted in accordance with the national regulations implementing Directive 77/576/EEC.

13.4   In addition, first-aid equipment must be available at all places where working conditions so require.

This equipment must be suitably marked and easily accessible.

The address and telephone number of the local emergency service must be clearly displayed.

14. Sanitary equipment

14.1   Changing rooms and lockers.

14.1.1   Appropriate changing rooms must be provided for workers if they have to wear special work clothes and if, for reasons of health or propriety, they cannot be expected to change in another area.

Changing rooms must be easily accessible, be of sufficient capacity and be provided with seating.

14.1.2   Changing rooms must be sufficiently large and have facilities to enable each worker, where necessary, to dry his working clothes as well as his own clothing and personal effects and to lock them away. If circumstances so require (e.g. dangerous substances, humidity, dirt), facilities must be provided to enable working clothes to be kept in a place separate from workers' own clothes and personal effects.

14.1.3   Provision must be made for separate changing rooms or separate use of changing rooms for men and women.

14.1.4   If changing rooms are not required as referred to in point 14.1.1, first paragraph, each worker must be provided with a place in which he can lock away his own clothes and personal effects.

14.2   Showers and washbasins.

14.2.1   Suitable showers in sufficient numbers must be provided for workers if required by the nature of the work or for health reasons. Provision must be made for separate shower rooms or separate use of shower rooms for men and women.

14.2.2   The shower rooms must be sufficiently large to permit each worker to wash without hindrance in conditions of an appropriate standard of hygiene. The showers must be equipped with hot and cold running water.

14.2.3   Where showers are not required under the first paragraph of 14.2.1, a sufficient number of suitable washbasins with running water (hot water if necessary) must be provided in the vicinity of the workstations and the changing rooms. Provision must be made for separate washbasins, or separate use of washbasins for men and women when so required for reasons of propriety.

14.2.4   Where the rooms housing the showers or washbasins are separate from the changing rooms, there must be easy communication between the two.

14.3   Lavatories and washbasins. Special facilities with an adequate number of lavatories and washbasins must be provided for workers in the vicinity of workstations, rest rooms, changing rooms and rooms housing showers or washbasins. Provision must be made for separate lavatories or separate use of lavatories for men and women.

15.   Rest rooms and/or accommodation areas

15.1   Where the safety or health of workers, in particular because of the type of activity carried out or the presence of more than a certain number of employees as well as the remote nature of the site, so require, workers must be provided with easily accessible rest rooms and/or accommodation areas.

15.2   Rest rooms and/or accommodation areas must be large enough and equipped with an adequate number of tables and seats with backs for the number of workers concerned.

15.3   If there are no facilities of this kind, other facilities must be provided in which workers can stay during interruptions in work.

15.4   Fixed accommodation areas unless used only in exceptional cases, must have sufficient sanitary equipment, a rest room and a leisure room.

They must be equipped with beds, cupboards, tables and seats with backs taking account of the number of workers, and be allocated taking account, where appropriate, of the presence of workers of both sexes.

15.5   Appropriate measures should be taken for the protection of non-smokers against discomfort caused by tobacco smoke in rest rooms and/or accommodation areas.

16.   Pregnant women and nursing mothers

Pregnant women and nursing mothers must be able to lie down to rest in appropriate conditions.

17.   Handicapped workers

Workplaces must be organised to take account of handicapped workers, if necessary.

The provision applies in particular to the doors, passageways, staircases, showers, washbasins, lavatories and workstations used or occupied directly by handicapped persons.

18.   Miscellaneous provisions

18.1   The surroundings and the perimeter of the site must be signposted and laid out so as to be clearly visible and identifiable.

18.2   Workers must be provided at the site with a sufficient quantity of drinking water and possibly another suitable non-alcoholic beverage both in occupied rooms and in the vicinity of workstations.

18.3   Workers must:

—be provided with facilities enabling them to take their meals in satisfactory conditions,

—where appropriate, be provided with facilities enabling them to prepare their meals in satisfactory conditions.

PART B   SPECIFIC MINIMUM REQUIREMENTS FOR ON-SITE WORKSTATIONS

Preliminary remark

If special situations so dictate, the classification of these minimum requirements into two sections, as below, should not regarded as binding.

SECTION I   ON-SITE INDOOR WORKSTATIONS

1.   Stability and solidity

Premises must have a structure and stability appropriate to the nature of their use.

2. Emergency doors
Emergency doors must open outwards.

Emergency doors must not be so locked or fastened that they cannot be easily and immediately opened by any person who may require to use them in an emergency. Sliding or revolving doors are not permitted if intended as emergency exits.

3. Ventilation
If air-conditioning or mechanical ventilation installations are used, they must operate in such a way that workers are not exposed to draughts which cause discomfort.

Any deposit or dirt likely to create an immediate danger to the health of workers by polluting the atmosphere must be removed without delay.

4. Temperature
4.1 The temperature in rest areas, rooms for duty staff, sanitary facilities, canteens and first-aid rooms must be appropriate to the particular purpose of such areas.

4.2 Windows, skylights and glass partitions should allow excessive effects of sunlight to be avoided, having regard to the nature of the work and the use of the room.

5. Natural and artificial lighting
Workplaces must as far as possible have sufficient natural light and be equipped with the means of providing artificial lighting which is adequate for the purposes of protecting workers' safety and health.

6. Floors, walls, ceilings and roofs of rooms
6.1 The floors of workplaces must have no dangerous bumps, holes or slopes and must be fixed, stable and not slippery.

6.2 The surfaces of floors, walls and ceilings in rooms must be such that they can be cleaned or refurbished to an appropriate standard of hygiene.

6.3 Transparent or translucent walls, in particular all-glass partitions, in rooms or in the vicinity of workplaces and traffic routes must be clearly indicated and made of safety material or be shielded from such places or traffic routes to prevent workers from coming into contact with walls or being injured should the walls shatter.

7. Windows and skylights
7.1 It must be possible for workers to open, close, adjust or secure windows, skylights and ventilators in a safe manner. When open, they must not be positioned so as to constitute a hazard to workers.

7.2 Windows and skylights must be designed in conjunction with equipment or otherwise fitted with devices allowing them to be cleaned without risk to the workers carrying out this work or to workers present.

8. Doors and Gates
8.1 The position, number and dimensions of doors and gates, and the materials used in their construction, are determined by the nature and use of the rooms or areas.

8.2 Transparent doors must be appropriately marked at a conspicuous level.

8.3 Swing doors and gates must be transparent or have see-through panels.

8.4   If transparent or translucent surfaces in doors and gates are not made of safety material and if there is a danger that workers may be injured if a door or gate should shatter, the surfaces must be protected against breakage.

9.   Traffic routes
Where the use and equipment of rooms so requires for the protection of workers, traffic routes must be clearly identified.

10.   Specific measures for escalators and travelators
Escalators and travelators must function safely.

They must be equipped with any necessary safety devices.

They must be fitted with easily identifiable and accessible emergency shut-down devices.

11.   Room dimensions and air space in rooms
Workrooms must have sufficient surface area and height to allow workers to perform their work without risk to their safety, health or well-being.

SECTION II   ON-SITE OUTDOOR WORKSTATIONS

1.   Stability and solidity
1.1   High-level or low-level movable or fixed workstations must be solid and stable, taking account of:
   — the number of workers occupying them,
   — the maximum loads they may have to bear and the weight distribution,
   — the outside influences to which they may be subject.

If the support and the other components of these workstations are not intrinsically stable, their stability will have to be ensured by appropriate and safe methods of fixing to avoid any untimely or spontaneous movement of the whole or of parts of the workstations.

1.2   Checking

Stability and solidity must be checked appropriately and especially after any change in the height or depth of the workstation.

2.   Energy distribution installations
2.1   On-site energy distribution installations, especially those subject to outside influences, must be regularly checked and maintained.

2.2   Installations existing before the site began must be identified, checked and clearly signposted.

2.3   Whenever possible, where overhead electric power lines exist, either they must be redirected away from the area of the site or else the current must be cut off.

If this is not possible, there will be barriers or notices to ensure that vehicles and installations are kept away.

Suitable warnings and suspended protections must be provided where vehicles have to pass beneath the lines.

3.   Atmospheric influences
Workers must be protected against atmospheric influences which could affect their health and safety.

4. Falling objects

Wherever technically feasible, workers must be protected by collective methods against falling objects.

Materials and equipment must be laid out or stacked in such a way as to prevent their collapsing or overturning.

Where necessary, there must be covered passageways on the site or access to danger areas must be made impossible.

5. Falls from a height

5.1 Falls from a height must be physically prevented in particular by means of solid cradles which are sufficiently high and have at least an end-board, a main handrail and an intermediate handrail or an equivalent alternative.

5.2 In principle, work at a height must be carried out only with appropriate equipment or using collective protection devices such as cradles, platforms or safety nets.

If the use of such equipment is not possible because of the nature of the work, suitable means of access must be provided and safety harnesses or other anchoring safety methods must be used.

6. Scaffolding and leaders[1]

6.1 All scaffolding must be properly designed, constructed and maintained to ensure that it does not collapse or move accidentally.

6.2 Work platforms, gangways and scaffolding stairways must be constructed, dimensioned, protected and used in such a way as to prevent people from falling or being exposed to falling objects.

6.3 Scaffolding must be inspected by a competent person:
    (a)   before being put into service;
    (b)   subsequently, at periodic intervals;
    (c)   after any modification, period without use, exposure to bad weather or seismic tremors, or any other circumstance which may have affected its strength or stability.

6.4 Ladders must be sufficiently strong and correctly maintained. They must be correctly used, in appropriate places and in accordance with their intended purpose.

6.5 Mobile scaffolding must be secured against spontaneous movements.

Note
[1]This point will be specified in the framework of the future Directive amending Directive 89/655/EEC, particularly with a view to supplementing point 3 of the Annex thereto.

7. Lifting equipment[1]

7.1 All lifting devices and accessories, including their component parts, attachments, anchorings and supports, must be:
    (a)   properly designed and constructed and sufficiently strong for the use to which they are put;
    (b)   correctly installed and used;
    (c)   maintained in good working order;

Note
[1]This point will be specified in the framework of the future Directive amending Directive 89/655/EEC, particularly with a view to supplementing point 3 of the Annex thereto.

(d)   checked and subjected to periodic tests and inspections in accordance with current legislation;

(e)   operated by qualified workers who have received appropriate training.

7.2   All lifting devices and accessories must clearly display their maximum load values.

7.3   Lifting equipment and accessories may not be used for other than their intended purposes.

8.   Excavating and materials-handling vehicles and machinery[1]

8.1   All excavating and materials-handling vehicles and machinery must be:

(a)   properly designed and constructed taking account, as far as possible, of the principles of ergonomics;

(b)   kept in good working order;

(c)   used correctly.

8.2   Drivers and operators of excavating and materials-handling vehicles and machinery must be specially trained.

8.3   Preventive measures must be taken to ensure that excavating and materials-handling vehicles and machinery do not fall into the excavations or into water.

8.4   Where appropriate, excavating machinery and materials-handling machinery must be fitted with structures to protect the driver against being crushed if the machine overturns, and against falling objects.

Note

[1]This point will be specified in the framework of the future Directive amending Directive 89/655/EEC, particularly with a view to supplementing point 3 of the Annex thereto.

9.   Installations, machinery, equipment[1]

9.1   Installations, machinery and equipment, including hand tools whether power-driven or not, must be:

(a)   properly designed and constructed taking account, as far as possible, of the principles of ergonomics;

(b)   kept in good working order;

(c)   used solely for the work for which they were designed;

(d)   operated by workers who have received appropriate training.

9.2   Installations and equipment under pressure must be checked and subjected to regular tests and inspections in accordance with existing legislation.

Note

[1]This point will be specified in the framework of the future Directive amending Directive 89/655/EEC, particularly with a view to supplementing point 3 of the Annex thereto.

10.   Excavations, wells, underground works, tunnels and earthworks

10.1   Suitable precautions must be taken in an excavation, well, underground working or tunnel:

(a)   using an appropriate support or embankment;

(b)   to prevent hazards entailed in the fall of a person, materials or objects, or flooding;

(c)   to provide sufficient ventilation at all workstations so as to ensure a breathable atmosphere which is not dangerous or harmful to health;

(d)   to enable workers to reach safety in the event of fire or inrush of water or materials.

10.2   Before excavation starts, measures must be taken to identify and reduce to a minimum any hazard due to underground cables and other distribution systems.

10.3   Safe routes into and out of the excavation must be provided.

10.4   Piles of earth, materials and moving vehicles must be kept away from the excavation; appropriate barriers must be built if necessary.

11.   Demolition work
Where the demolition of a building or construction may present a danger:

(a)   appropriate precautions, methods and procedures must be adopted;

(b)   the work must be planned and undertaken only under the supervision of a competent person.

12.   Metal or concrete frameworks, shutterings and heavy prefabricated components
12.1   Metal or concrete frameworks and their components, shutterings, prefabricated components or temporary supports, and buttresses must be erected and dismantled only under the supervision of a competent person.

12.2   Adequate precautions must be taken to protect workers against risks arising from the temporary fragility or instability of a structure.

12.3   Shutterings, temporary supports and buttresses must be devised and designed, installed and maintained so as to safely withstand any strains and stresses which may be placed on them.

13.   Cofferdams and caissons
13.1   All cofferdams and caissons must be:

(a)   well constructed, of appropriate, solid materials of adequate strength;

(b)   appropriately equipped so that workers can gain shelter in the event of an irruption of water and materials.

13.2   The construction, installation, transformation or dismantling of a cofferdam or caisson must take place only under the supervision of a competent person.

13.3   All cofferdams and caissons must be inspected by a competent person at regular intervals.

14.   Work on roofs
14.1   Where necessary to avert a risk or where the height or the slope exceed values set by the Member States, collective preventive measures must be taken to prevent workers, and tools or other objects or materials, from falling.

14.2   Where workers have to work on or near a roof or any other surface made of fragile materials through which it is possible to fall, preventive measures must be taken to ensure that they do not inadvertently walk on the surface made of fragile materials, or fall to the ground.

COUNCIL DIRECTIVE 92/85 OF 19 OCTOBER 1992 ON THE INTRODUCTION OF MEASURES TO ENCOURAGE IMPROVEMENTS IN THE SAFETY AND HEALTH AT WORK OF PREGNANT WORKERS AND WORKERS WHO HAVE RECENTLY GIVEN BIRTH OR ARE BREASTFEEDING (TENTH INDIVIDUAL DIRECTIVE WITHIN THE MEANING OF ARTICLE 16(1) OF DIRECTIVE 89/391/EEC)
[OJ 1992, No. L348/1]

THE COUNCIL OF THE EUROPEAN COMMUNITIES,

Having regard to the Treaty establishing the European Economic Community, and in particular Article 118a thereof,

Having regard to the proposal from the Commission, drawn up after consultation with the Advisory Committee on Safety, Hygiene and Health Protection at work,[1]

In cooperation with the European Parliament,[2]

Having regard to the opinion of the Economic and Social Committee,[3]

Whereas Article 118a of the Treaty provides that the Council shall adopt, by means of directives, minimum requirements for encouraging improvements, especially in the working environment, to protect the safety and health of workers;

Whereas this Directive does not justify any reduction in levels of protection already achieved in individual Member States, the Member States being committed, under the Treaty, to encouraging improvements in conditions in this area and to harmonising conditions while maintaining the improvements made;

Whereas, under the terms of Article 118a of the Treaty, the said directives are to avoid imposing administrative, financial and legal constraints in a way which would hold back the creation and development of small and medium-sized undertakings;

Whereas, pursuant to Decision 74/325/EEC,[4] as last amended by the 1985 Act of Accession, the Advisory Committee on Safety, Hygiene and Health protection at Work is consulted by the Commission on the drafting of proposals in this field;

Whereas the Community Charter of the fundamental social rights of workers, adopted at the Strasbourg European Council on 9 December 1989 by the Heads of State or Government of 11 Member States, lays down, in paragraph 19 in particular, that:

'Every worker must enjoy satisfactory health and safety conditions in his working environment. Appropriate measures must be taken in order to achieve further harmonisation of conditions in this area while maintaining the improvements made';

Whereas the Commission, in its action programme for the implementation of the Community Charter of the fundamental social rights of workers, has

Notes
[1] OJ No. C281, 9 November 1990, p. 3 and OJ No. C25 1 February 1991, p. 9.
[2] OJ No. C19, 28 January 1992, p. 177 and OJ No. C150, 15 June 1992, p. 99.
[3] OJ No. C41, 18 February 1991, p. 29.
[4] OJ No. L185, 9 July 1974, p. 15.

included among its aims the adoption by the Council of a Directive on the protection of pregnant women at work;

Whereas Article 15 of Council Directive 89/391/EEC of 12 June 1989 on the introduction of measures to encourage improvements in the safety and health of workers at work[5] provides that particularly sensitive risk groups must be protected against the dangers which specifically affect them;

Whereas pregnant workers, workers who have recently given birth or who are breastfeeding must be considered a specific risk group in many respects, measures must be taken with regard to their safety and health;

Whereas the protection of the safety and health of pregnant workers, workers who have recently given birth or workers who are breastfeeding should not treat women on the labour market unfavourably nor work to the detriment of directives concerning equal treatment for men and women;

Whereas some types of activities may pose a specific risk, for pregnant workers, workers who have recently given birth or workers who are breast-feeding, of exposure to dangerous agents, processes or working conditions; whereas such risks must therefore be assessed and the result of such assessment communicated to female workers and/or their representatives;

Whereas, further, should the result of this assessment reveal the existence of a risk to the safety or health of the female worker, provision must be made for such worker to be protected;

Whereas pregnant workers and workers who are breastfeeding must not engage in activities which have been assessed as revealing a risk of exposure, jeopardizing safety and health, to certain particularly dangerous agents or working conditions;

Whereas provision should be made for pregnant workers, workers who have recently given birth or workers who are breastfeeding not to be required to work at night where such provision is necessary from the point of view of their safety and health;

Whereas the vulnerability of pregnant workers, workers who have recently given birth or who are breastfeeding makes it necessary for them to be granted the right to maternity leave of at least 14 continuous weeks, allocated before and/or after confinement, and renders necessary the compulsory nature of maternity leave of at least two weeks, allocated before and/or after confinement;

Whereas the risk of dismissal for reasons associated with their condition may have harmful effects on the physical and mental state of pregnant workers, workers who have recently given birth or who are breastfeeding; whereas provision should be made for such dismissal to be prohibited;

Whereas measures for the organisation of work concerning the protection of the health of pregnant workers, workers who have recently given birth or workers who are breastfeeding would serve no purpose unless accompanied by the maintenance of rights linked to the employment contract, including maintenance of payment and/or entitlement to an adequate allowance;

Whereas, moreover, provision concerning maternity leave would also serve no purpose unless accompanied by the maintenance of rights linked to the employment contract and or entitlement to an adequate allowance;

Note
[5] OJ No. L183, 29 June 1989, p. 1.

Whereas the concept of an adequate allowance in the case of maternity leave must be regarded as a technical point of reference with a view to fixing the minimum level of protection and should in no circumstances be interpreted as suggesting an analogy between pregnancy and illness,

HAS ADOPTED THIS DIRECTIVE:

SECTION I   PURPOSE AND DEFINITIONS

Article 1   Purpose

1.   The purpose of this Directive, which is the tenth individual Directive within the meaning of Article 16(1) of Directive 89/391/EEC, is to implement measures to encourage improvements in the safety and health at work of pregnant workers and workers who have recently given birth or who are breastfeeding.

2.   The provisions of Directive 89/391/EEC, except for Article 2(2) thereof, shall apply in full to the whole area covered by paragraph 1, without prejudice to any more stringent and/or specific provisions contained in this Directive.

3.   This Directive may not have the effect of reducing the level of protection afforded to pregnant workers, workers who have recently given birth or who are breastfeeding as compared with the situation which exists in each Member State on the date on which this Directive is adopted.

Article 2   Definitions

For the purposes of this Directive:

(a)   *pregnant worker* shall mean a pregnant worker who informs her employer of her condition, in accordance with national legislation and/or national practice;

(b)   *worker who has recently given birth* shall mean a worker who has recently given birth within the meaning of national legislation and/or national practice and who informs her employer of her condition, in accordance with that legislation and/or practice;

(c)   *worker who is breastfeeding* shall mean a worker who is breastfeeding within the meaing of national legislation and/or national practice and who informs her employer of her condition, in accordance with that legislation and/or practice.

SECTION II   GENERAL PROVISIONS

Article 3   Guidelines

1.   In consultation with the Member States and assisted by the Advisory Committee on Safety, Hygiene and Health Protection at Work, the Commission shall draw up guidelines on the assessment of the chemical, physical and biological agents and industrial processes considered hazardous for the safety or health of workers within the meaning of Article 2.

The guidelines referred to in the first subparagraph shall also cover movements and postures, mental and physical fatigue and other types of physical and mental stress connected with the work done by workers within the meaning of Article 2.

2.   The purpose of the guidelines referred to in paragraph 1 is to serve as a basis for the assessment referred to in Article 4(1).

To this end, Member States shall bring these guidelines to the attention of all employers and all female workers and/or their representatives in the respective Member State.

Article 4   Assessment and information
1.   For all activities liable to involve a specific risk of exposure to the agents, processes or working conditions of which a non-exhaustive list is given in Annex I, the employer shall assess the nature, degree and duration of exposure, in the undertaking and/or establishment concerned, of workers within the meaning of Article 2, either directly or by way of the protective and preventive services referred to in Article 7 of Directive 89/391/EEC, in order to:
— assess any risks to the safety or health and any possible effect on the pregnancy or breastfeeding of workers within the meaning of Article 2.
— decide what measures should be taken.
2.   Without prejudice to Article 10 of Directive 89/391/EEC, workers within the meaning of Article 2 and workers likely to be in one of the situations referred to in Article 2 in the undertaking and/or establishment concerned and/or their representatives shall be informed of the results of the assessment referred to in paragraph 1 and of all measures to be taken concerning health and safety at work.

Article 5   Action further to the results of the assessment
1.   Without prejudice to Article 6 of Directive 89/391/EEC, if the results of the assessment referred to in Article 4(1) reveal risk to the safety or health or an effect on the pregnancy or breastfeeding of a worker within the meaning of Article 2, the employer shall take the necessary measures to ensure that, by temporarily adjusting the working conditions and/or the working hours of the worker concerned, the exposure of that worker to such risks is avoided.
2.   If the adjustment of her working conditions and/or working hours is not technically and/or objectively feasible, or cannot reasonably be required on duly substantiated grounds, the employer shall take the necessary measures to move the worker concerned to another job.
3.   If moving her to another job is not technically and/or objectively feasible or cannot reasonably be required on duly substantiated grounds, the worker concerned shall be granted leave in accordance with national legislation and/or national practice for the whole of the period necessary to protect her safety or health.
4.   The provisions of this Article shall apply *mutatis mutandis* to the case where a worker pursuing an activity which is forbidden pursuant to Article 6 becomes pregnant or starts breastfeeding and informs her employer thereof.

Article 6   Cases in which exposure is prohibited
In addition to the general provisions concerning the protection of workers, in particular those relating to the limit values for occupational exposure:
1.   pregnant workers within the meaning of Article 2(a) may under no circumstances be obliged to perform duties for which the assessment has revealed a risk of exposure, which would jeopardise safety or health, to the agents and working conditions listed in Annex II, Section A;
2.   workers who are breastfeeding, within the meaning of Article 2(c), may under no circumstances be obliged to perform duties for which the assessment has revealed a risk of exposure, which would jeopardise safety or health, to the agents and working conditions listed in Annex II, Section B.

Article 7   Night work
1.   Member States shall take the necessary measures to ensure that workers referred to in Article 2 are not obliged to perform night work during their

pregnancy and for a period following childbirth which shall be determined by the national authority competent for safety and health, subject to submission, in accordance with the procedures laid down by the Member States, of a medical certificate stating that this is necessary for the safety or health of the worker concerned.

2. The measures referred to in paragraph 1 must entail the possibility, in accordance with national legislation and/or national practice, of:

(a) transfer to daytime work; or

(b) leave from work or extension of maternity leave where such a transfer is not technically and/or objectively feasible or cannot reasonably be required on duly substantiated grounds.

Article 8   Maternity leave

1. Member States shall take the necessary measures to ensure that workers within the meaning of Article 2 are entitled to a continuous period of maternity leave of at least 14 weeks allocated before and/or after confinement in accordance with national legislation and/or practice.

2. The maternity leave stipulated in paragraph 1 must include compulsory maternity leave of at least two weeks allocated before and/or after confinement in accordance with national legislation and/or practice.

Article 9   Time off for ante-natal examinations

Member States shall take the necessary measures to ensure that pregnant workers within the meaning of Article 2(a) are entitled to, in accordance with national legislation and/or practice, time off, without loss of pay, in order to attend ante-natal examinations, if such examinations have to take place during working hours.

Article 10   Prohibition of dismissal

In order to guarantee workers, within the meaning of Article 2, the exercise of their health and safety protection rights as recognised under this Article, it will be provided that:

1. Member States shall take the necessary measures to prohibit the dismissal of workers, within the meaning of Article 2, during the period from the beginning of their pregnancy to the end of the maternity leave referred to in Article 8(1), save in exceptional cases not connected with their condition which are permitted under national legislation and/or practice and, where applicable, provided that the competent authority has given its consent;

2. if a worker, within the meaning of Article 2, is dismissed during the period referred to in point 1, the employer must cite duly substantiated grounds for her dismissal in writing;

3. Member States shall take the necessary measures to protect workers, within the meaning of Article 2, from consequences of dismissal which is unlawful by virtue of point 1.

Article 11   Employment rights

In order to guarantee workers within the meaning of Article 2 the exercise of their health and safety protection rights as recognised in this Article, it shall be provided that:

1.   in the cases referred to in Articles 5, 6 and 7, the employment rights relating to the employment contract, including the maintenance of a payment to, and/or entitlement to an adequate allowance for, workers within the meaning of Article 2, must be ensured in accordance with national legislation and/or national practice;

2.   in the case referred to in Article 8, the following must be ensured:

(a)   the rights connected with the employment contract of workers within the meaning of Article 2, other than those referred to in point (b) below;

(b)   maintenance of a payment to, and/or entitlement to an adequate allowance for, workers within the meaning of Article 2;

3.   the allowance referred to in point 2(b) shall be deemed adequate if it guarantees income at least equivalent to that which the worker concerned would receive in the event of a break in her activities on grounds connected with her state of health, subject to any ceiling laid down under national legislation;

4.   Member States may make entitlement to pay or the allowance referred to in points 1 and 2(b) conditional upon the worker concerned fulfilling the conditions of eligibility for such benefits laid down under national legislation.

These conditions may under no circumstances provide for periods of previous employment in excess of 12 months immediately prior to the presumed date of confinement.

Article 12   Defence of rights

Member States shall introduce into their national legal systems such measures as are necessary to enable all workers who should themselves wronged by failure to comply with the obligations arising from the Directive to pursue their claims by judicial process (and/or, in accordance with national laws and/or practice) by recourse to other competent authorities.

Article 13   Amendments to the Annexes

1.   Strictly technical adjustments to Annex I as a result of technical progress, changes in international regulations or specifications and new findings in the area covered by this Directive shall be adopted in accordance with the procedure laid down in Article 17 of Directive 89/391/EEC.

2.   Annex II may be amended only in accordance with the procedure laid down in Article 118a of the Treaty.

Article 14   Final provisions

1.   Member States shall bring into force the laws, regulations and administrative provisions necessary to comply with this Directive not later than two years after the adoption thereof or ensure, at the latest two years after adoption of this Directive, that the two sides of industry introduce the requisite provisions by means of collective agreements, with Member States being required to make all the necessary provisions to enable them at all times to guarantee the results laid down by this Directive. They shall forthwith inform the Commission thereof.

2.   When Member States adopt the measures referred to in paragraph 1, they shall contain a reference to this Directive or shall be accompanied by such

reference on the occasion of their official publication. The methods of making such a reference shall be laid down by the Member States.

3. Member States shall communicate to the Commission the texts of the essential provisions of national law which they have already adopted or adopt in the field governed by this Directive.

4. Member States shall report to the Commission every five years on the practical implementation of the provisions of this Directive, indicating the points of view of the two sides of industry.

However, Member States shall report for the first time to the Commission on the practical implementation of the provisions of this Directive, indicating the points of view of the two sides of industry, four years after its adoption.

The Commission shall inform the European Parliament, the Council, the Economic and Social Committee and the Advisory Committee on Safety, Hygiene and Health Protection at Work.

5. The Commission shall periodically submit to the European Parliament, the Council and the Economic and Social Committee a report on the implementation of this Directive, taking into account paragraphs 1, 2 and 3.

6. The Council will re-examine the Directive, on the basis of an assessment carried out on the basis of the reports referred to in the second subparagraph of paragraph 4 and, should the need arise, of a proposal, to be submitted by the Commission at the latest five years after adoption of the Directive.

Article 15
This Directive is addressed to the Member States.

Done at Luxembourg, 19 October 1992.
For the Council,
The President,
D. CURRY

ANNEX I   NON-EXHAUSTIVE LIST OF AGENTS, PROCESSES AND WORKING CONDITIONS REFERRED TO IN ARTICLE 4(1)

A.   Agents
1. *Physical agents* where these are regarded as agents causing foetal lesions and/or likely to disrupt placental attachment, and in particular:
  (a)   shocks, vibration or movement;
  (b)   handling of loads entailing risks, particularly of a dorsolumbar nature;
  (c)   noise;
  (d)   ionizing radiation;
  (e)   non-ionizing radiation;
  (f)   extremes of cold or heat;
  (g)   movements and postures, travelling — either inside or outside the establishment — mental and physical fatigue and other physical burdens connected with the activity of the worker within the meaning of Article 2 of the Directive.

  2. *Biological agents*
Biological agents of risk groups 2, 3 and 3 within the meaning of Article 2(d) numbers 2, 3 and 4 of Directive 90/679/EEC, in so far as it is known that these

agents or the therapeutic measures necessitated by such agents endanger the health of pregnant women and the unborn child and in so far as they do not yet appear in Annex II.

3.   *Chemical agents*

The following chemical agents in so far as it is known that they endanger the health of pregnant women and the unborn child and in so far as they do not yet appear in Annex II:

    (a)   substances labelled R 40, R 45, R 46, and R 47 under Directive 67/548/EEC in so far as they do not yet appear in Annex II;

    (b)   chemical agents in Annex I to Directive 90/394/EEC;

    (c)   mercury and mercury derivatives;

    (d)   antimitotic drugs;

    (e)   carbon monoxide;

    (f)   chemical agents of known and dangerous percutaneous absorption.

B.   Processes

Industrial processes listed in Annex I to Directive 90/394/EEC.

C.   Working conditions

Underground mining work.

ANNEX II   NON-EXHAUSTIVE LIST OF AGENTS AND WORKING CONDITIONS REFERRED TO IN ARTICLE 6

A.   Pregnant workers within the meaning of Article 2(a)

1.   *Agents*

    (a)   Physical agents

Work in hyperbaric atmosphere, e.g., pressurised enclosures and underwater diving.

    (b)   Biological agents

The following biological agents:

— toxoplasma,

— rubella virus,

unless the pregnant workers are proved to be adequately protected against such agents by immunisation.

    (c)   Chemical agents

Lead and lead derivatives in so far as these agents are capable of being absorbed by the human organism.

2.   *Working conditions*

Underground mining work.

B.   Workers who are breastfeeding within the meaning of Article 2(c)

1.   *Agents*

    (a)   Chemical agents

Lead and lead derivatives in so far as these agents are capable of being absorbed by the human organism.

2.   *Working conditions*

Underground mining work.

COUNCIL DIRECTIVE (EC) 93/104 OF 23 NOVEMBER 1993 CONCERNING CERTAIN ASPECTS OF THE ORGANISATION OF WORKING TIME
[OJ 1993, No. L307/18]

THE COUNCIL OF THE EUROPEAN UNION,

Having regard to the Treaty establishing the European Community, and in particular Article 118a thereof,

Having regard to the proposal from the Commission,[1]

In cooperation with the European Parliament,[2]

Having regard to the opinion of the Economic and Social Committee,[3]

Whereas Article 118a of the Treaty provides that the Council shall adopt, by means of directives, minimum requirements for encouraging improvements, especially in the working environment, to ensure a better level of protection of the safety and health of workers;

Whereas, under the terms of that Article, those directives are to avoid imposing administrative, financial and legal constraints in a way which would hold back the creation and development of small and medium-sized undertakings;

Whereas the provisions of Council Directive 89/391/EEC of 12 June 1989 on the introduction of measures to encourage improvements in the safety and health of workers at work[4] are fully applicable to the areas covered by this Directive without prejudice to more stringent and/or specific provisions contained therein;

Whereas the Community Charter of the Fundamental Social Rights of Workers, adopted at the meeting of the European Council held at Strasbourg on 9 December 1989 by the Heads of State or of Government of 11 Member States, and in particular points 7, first subparagraph, 8 and 19, first subparagraph, thereof, declared that:

'7.   The completion of the internal market must lead to an improvement in the living and working conditions of workers in the European Community. This process must result from an approximation of these conditions while the improvement is being maintained, as regards in particular the duration and organisation of working time and forms of employment other than open-ended contracts, such as fixed-term contracts, part-time working, temporary work and seasonal work.

8.   Every worker in the European Community shall have a right to a weekly rest period and to annual paid leave, the duration of which must be progressively harmonised in accordance with national practices.

19.   Every worker must enjoy satisfactory health and safety conditions in his working environment. Appropriate measures must be taken in order to achieve further harmonisation of conditions in this area while maintaining the improvements made.';

Notes
[1] OJ No. C254, 9.10.1990, p. 4.
[2] OJ No. C72, 18.3.1991, p. 95; and Decision of 27 October 1993 (not yet published in the Official Journal).
[3] OJ No. C60, 8.3.1991, p. 26.
[4] OJ No. L183, 29.6.1989, p. 1.

Whereas the improvement of workers' safety, hygiene and health at work is an objective which should not be subordinated to purely economic considerations;

Whereas this Directive is a practical contribution towards creating the social dimension of the internal market;

Whereas laying down minimum requirements with regard to the organisation of working time is likely to improve the working conditions of workers in the Community;

Whereas, in order to ensure the safety and health of Community workers, the latter must be granted minimum daily, weekly and annual periods of rest and adequate breaks; whereas it is also necessary in this context to place a maximum limit on weekly working hours;

Whereas account should be taken of the principles of the International Labour Organisation with regard to the organisation of working time, including those relating to night work;

Whereas, with respect to the weekly rest period, due account should be taken of the diversity of cultural, ethnic, religious and other factors in the Member States; whereas, in particular, it is ultimately for each Member State to decide whether Sunday should be included in the weekly rest period, and if so to what extent;

Whereas research has shown that the human body is more sensitive at night to environmental disturbances and also to certain burdensome forms of work organisation and that long periods of night work can be detrimental to the health of workers and can endanger safety at the workplace;

Whereas there is a need to limit the duration of periods of night work, including overtime, and to provide for employers who regularly use night workers to bring this information to the attention of the competent authorities if they so request;

Whereas it is important that night workers should be entitled to a free health assessment prior to their assignment and thereafter at regular intervals and that whenever possible they should be transferred to day work for which they are suited if they suffer from health problems;

Whereas the situation of night and shift workers requires that the level of safety and health protection should be adapted to the nature of their work and that the organisation and functioning of protection and prevention services and resources should be efficient;

Whereas specific working conditions may have detrimental effects on the safety and health of workers; whereas the organisation of work according to a certain pattern must take account of the general principle of adapting work to the worker;

Whereas, given the specific nature of the work concerned, it may be necessary to adopt separate measures with regard to the organisation of working time in certain sectors or activities which are excluded from the scope of this Directive;

Whereas, in view of the question likely to be raised by the organisation of working time within an undertaking, it appears desirable to provide for flexibility in the application of certain provisions of this Directive, whilst ensuring compliance with the principles of protecting the safety and health of workers;

Whereas it is necessary to provide that certain provisions may be subject to derogations implemented, according to the case, by the Member States or the

two sides of industry; whereas, as a general rule, in the event of a derogation, the workers concerned must be given equivalent compensatory rest
periods,

HAS ADOPTED THIS DIRECTIVE:

SECTION I   SCOPE AND DEFINITIONS

Article 1   Purpose and scope

1.   This Directive lays down minimum safety and health requirements for
the organisation of working time.

2.   This Directive applies to:

(a)   minimum periods of daily rest, weekly rest and annual leave, to
breaks and maximum weekly working time; and

(b)   certain aspects of night work, shift work and patterns of work.

3.   This Directive shall apply to all sectors of activity, both public and
private, within the meaning of Article 2 of Directive 89/391/EEC, without
prejudice to Article 17 of this Directive, with the exception of air, rail, road, sea,
inland waterway and lake transport, sea fishing, other work at sea and the
activities of doctors in training;

4.   The provisions of Directive 89/391/EEC are fully applicable to the
matters referred to in paragraph 2, without prejudice to more stringent and/or
specific provisions contained in this Directive.

Article 2   Definitions

For the purposes of this Directive, the following definitions shall apply:

1.   working time shall mean any period during which the worker is working,
at the employer's disposal and carrying out his activity or duties, in accordance
with national laws and/or practice;

2.   rest period shall mean any period which is not working time;

3.   night time shall mean any period of not less than seven hours, as defined
by national law, and which must include in any case the period between
midnight and 5 a. m.;

4.   night worker shall mean:

(a)   on the one hand, any worker, who, during night time, works at least
three hours of his daily working time as a normal course; and

(b)   on the other hand, any worker who is likely during night time to work
a certain proportion of his annual working time, as defined at the choice of the
Member State concerned:

(i)   by national legislation, following consultation with the two sides
of industry; or

(ii)   by collective agreements or agreements concluded between the
two sides of industry at national or regional level;

5.   shift work shall mean any method of organising work in shifts whereby
workers succeed each other at the same work stations according to a certain
pattern, including a rotating pattern, and which may be continuous or
discontinuous, entailing the need for workers to work at different times over a
given period of days or weeks;

6.   shift worker shall mean any worker whose work schedule is part of
shift work.

SECTION II   MINIMUM REST PERIODS — OTHER ASPECTS OF THE ORGANISATION OF WORKING TIME

Article 3   Daily rest

Member States shall take the measures necessary to ensure that every worker is entitled to a minimum daily rest period of 11 consecutive hours per 24-hour period.

Article 4   Breaks

Member States shall take the measures necessary to ensure that, where the working day is longer than six hours, every worker is entitled to a rest break, the details of which, including duration and the terms on which it is granted, shall be laid down in collective agreements or agreements between the two sides of industry or, failing that, by national legislation.

Article 5   Weekly rest period

Member States shall take the measures necessary to ensure that, per each seven-day period, every worker is entitled to a minimum uninterrupted rest period of 24 hours plus the 11 hours' daily rest referred to in Article 3.

The minimum rest period referred to in the first subparagraph shall in principle include Sunday.[1]

If objective, technical or work organisation conditions so justify, a minimum rest period of 24 hours may be applied.

Note
[1]This sentence has been annulled by the Court of Justice in the case *UK* v *Council*, 12 November 1996 (Case C-84/94).

Article 6   Maximum weekly working time

Member States shall take the measures necessary to ensure that, in keeping with the need to protect the safety and health of workers:

1.   the period of weekly working time is limited by means of laws, regulations or administrative provisions or by collective agreements or agreements between the two sides of industry;

2.   the average working time for each seven-day period, including overtime, does not exceed 48 hours.

Article 7   Annual leave

1.   Member States shall take the measures necessary to ensure that every worker is entitled to paid annual leave of at least four weeks in accordance with the conditions for entitlement to, and granting of, such leave laid down by national legislation and/or practice.

2.   The minimum period of paid annual leave may not be replaced by an allowance in lieu, except where the employment relationship is terminated.

SECTION III   NIGHT WORK — SHIFT WORK — PATTERNS OF WORK

Article 8   Length of night work

Member States shall take the measures necessary to ensure that:

1.   normal hours of work for night workers do not exceed an average of eight hours in any 24-hour period;

2.   night workers whose work involves special hazards or heavy physical or mental strain do not work more than eight hours in any period of 24 hours during which they perform night work.

For the purposes of the aforementioned, work involving special hazards or heavy physical or mental strain shall be defined by national legislation and/or practice or by collective agreements or agreements concluded between the two sides of industry, taking account of the specific effects and hazards of night work.

Article 9   Health assessment and transfer of night workers to day work

1.   Member States shall take the measures necessary to ensure that:

(a)   night workers are entitled to a free health assessment before their assignment and thereafter at regular intervals;

(b)   night workers suffering from health problems recognised as being connected with the fact that they perform night work are transferred whenever possible to day work to which they are suited.

2.   The free health assessment referred to in paragraph 1(a) must comply with medical confidentiality.

3.   The free health assessment referred to in paragraph 1(a) may be conducted within the national health system.

Article 10   Guarantees for night-time working

Member States may make the work of certain categories of night workers subject to certain guarantees, under conditions laid down by national legislation and/or practice, in the case of workers who incur risks to their safety or health linked to night-time working.

Article 11   Notification of regular use of night workers

Member States shall take the measures necessary to ensure that an employer who regularly uses night workers brings this information to the attention of the competent authorities if they so request.

Article 12   Safety and health protection

Member States shall take the measures necessary to ensure that:

1.   night workers and shift workers have safety and health protection appropriate to the nature of their work;

2.   appropriate protection and prevention services or facilities with regard to the safety and health of night workers and shift workers are equivalent to those applicable to other workers and are available at all times.

Article 13   Pattern of work

Member States shall take the measures necessary to ensure that an employer who intends to organise work according to a certain pattern takes account of the general principle of adapting work to the worker, with a view, in particular, to alleviating monotonous work and work at a predetermined work-rate, depending on the type of activity, and of safety and health requirements, especially as regards breaks during working time.

SECTION IV   MISCELLANEOUS PROVISIONS

Article 14   More specific Community provisions

The provisions of this Directive shall not apply where other Community instruments contain more specific requirements concerning certain occupations or occupational activities.

Article 15   More favourable provisions

This Directive shall not affect Member States' right to apply or introduce laws, regulations or administrative provisions more favourable to the protection of the safety and health of workers or to facilitate or permit the application of collective agreements or agreements concluded between the two sides of industry which are more favourable to the protection of the safety and health of workers.

Article 16   Reference periods
Member States may lay down:

1.   for the application of Article 5 (weekly rest period), a reference period not exceeding 14 days;

2.   for the application of Article 6 (maximum weekly working time), a reference period not exceeding four months.

The periods of paid annual leave, granted in accordance with Article 7, and the periods of sick leave shall not be included or shall be neutral in the calculation of the average;

3.   for the application of Article 8 (length of night work), a reference period defined after consultation of the two sides of industry or by collective agreements or agreements concluded between the two sides of industry at national or regional level.

If the minimum weekly rest period of 24 hours required by Article 5 falls within that reference period, it shall not be included in the calculation of the average.

Article 17   Derogations
1.   With due regard for the general principles of the protection of the safety and health of workers, Member States may derogate from Article 3, 4, 5, 6, 8 or 16 when, on account of the specific characteristics of the activity concerned, the duration of the working time is not measured and/or predetermined or can be determined by the workers themselves, and particularly in the case of:

(a)   managing executives or other persons with autonomous decision-taking powers;

(b)   family workers; or

(c)   workers officiating at religious ceremonies in churches and religious communities.

2.   Derogations may be adopted by means of laws, regulations or administrative provisions or by means of collective agreements or agreements between the two sides of industry provided that the workers concerned are afforded equivalent periods of compensatory rest or that, in exceptional cases in which it is not possible, for objective reasons, to grant such equivalent periods of compensatory rest, the workers concerned are afforded appropriate protection:

2.1   from Articles 3, 4, 5, 8 and 16:

(a)   in the case of activities where the worker's place of work and his place of residence are distant from one another or where the worker's different places of work are distant from one another;

(b)   in the case of security and surveillance activities requiring a permanent presence in order to protect property and persons, particularly security guards and caretakers or security firms;

(c)   in the case of activities involving the need for continuity of service or production, particularly:

(i)   services relating to the reception, treatment and/or care provided by hospitals or similar establishments, residential institutions and prisons;

(ii)   dock or airport workers;

    (iii)   press, radio, television, cinematographic production, postal and telecommunications services, ambulance, fire and civil protection services;

    (iv)   gas, water and electricity production, transmission and distribution, household refuse collection and incineration plants;

    (v)   industries in which work cannot be interrupted on technical grounds;

    (vi)   research and development activities;

    (vii)   agriculture;

  (d)   where there is a foreseeable surge of activity, particularly in:

    (i)   agriculture;

    (ii)   tourism;

    (iii)   postal services;

  2.2   from Articles 3, 4, 5, 8 and 16:

  (a)   in the circumstances described in Article 5 (4) of Directive 89/391/EEC;

  (b)   in cases of accident or imminent risk of accident;

  2.3   from Articles 3 and 5:

  (a)   in the case of shift work activities, each time the worker changes shift and cannot take daily and/or weekly rest periods between the end of one shift and the start of the next one;

  (b)   in the case of activities involving periods of work split up over the day, particularly those of cleaning staff.

  3.   Derogations may be made from Articles 3, 4, 5, 8 and 16 by means of collective agreements or agreements concluded between the two sides of industry at national or regional level or, in conformity with the rules laid down by them, by means of collective agreements or agreements concluded between the two sides of industry at a lower level.

Member States in which there is no statutory system ensuring the conclusion of collective agreements or agreements concluded between the two sides of industry at national or regional level, on the matters covered by this Directive, or those Member States in which there is a specific legislative framework for this purpose and within the limits thereof, may, in accordance with national legislation and/or practice, allow derogations from Articles 3, 4, 5, 8 and 16 by way of collective agreements or agreements concluded between the two sides of industry at the appropriate collective level.

The derogations provided for in the first and second subparagraphs shall be allowed on condition that equivalent compensating rest periods are granted to the workers concerned or, in exceptional cases where it is not possible for objective reasons to grant such periods, the workers concerned are afforded appropriate protection.

Member States may lay down rules:

  — for the application of this paragraph by the two sides of industry, and

  — for the extension of the provisions of collective agreements or agreements concluded in conformity with this paragraph to other workers in accordance with national legislation and/or practice.

  4.   The option to derogate from point 2 of Article 16, provided in paragraph 2, points 2.1. and 2.2. and in paragraph 3 of this Article, may not result in the establishment of a reference period exceeding six months.

However, Member States shall have the option, subject to compliance with the general principles relating to the protection of the safety and health of workers, of allowing, for objective or technical reasons or reasons concerning the organisation of work, collective agreements or agreements concluded between the two sides of industry to set reference periods in no event exceeding 12 months.

Before the expiry of a period of seven years from the date referred to in Article 18 (1) (a), the Council shall, on the basis of a Commission proposal accompanied by an appraisal report, re-examine the provisions of this paragraph and decide what action to take.

Article 18   Final provisions

1.   (a)   Member States shall adopt the laws, regulations and administrative provisions necessary to comply with this Directive by 23 November 1996, or shall ensure by that date that the two sides of industry establish the necessary measures by agreement, with Member States being obliged to take any necessary steps to enable them to guarantee at all times that the provisions laid down by this Directive are fulfilled.

(b)   (i)   However, a Member State shall have the option not to apply Article 6, while respecting the general principles of the protection of the safety and health of workers, and provided it takes the necessary measures to ensure that:

—no employer requires a worker to work more than 48 hours over a seven-day period, calculated as an average for the reference period referred to in point 2 of Article 16, unless he has first obtained the worker's agreement to perform such work,

—no worker is subjected to any detriment by his employer because he is not willing to give his agreement to perform such work,

—the employer keeps up-to-date records of all workers who carry out such work,

—the records are placed at the disposal of the competent authorities, which may, for reasons connected with the safety and/or health of workers, prohibit or restrict the possibility of exceeding the maximum weekly working hours,

—the employer provides the competent authorities at their request with information on cases in which agreement has been given by workers to perform work exceeding 48 hours over a period of seven days, calculated as an average for the reference period referred to in point 2 of Article 16.

Before the expiry of a period of seven years from the date referred to in (a), the Council shall, on the basis of a Commission proposal accompanied by an appraisal report, re-examine the provisions of this point

(i)   and decide on what action to take.

(ii)   Similarly, Member States shall have the option, as regards the application of Article 7, of making use of a transitional period of not more than three years from the date referred to in (a), provided that during that transitional period:

—every worker receives three weeks' paid annual leave in accordance with the conditions for the entitlement to, and granting of, such leave laid down by national legislation and/or practice, and

—the three-week period of paid annual leave may not be replaced by an allowance in lieu, except where the employment relationship is terminated.

(c)   Member states shall forthwith inform the Commission thereof.

2.   When Member States adopt the measures referred to in paragraph 1, they shall contain a reference to this Directive or shall be accompanied by such reference on the occasion of their official publication. The methods of making such a reference shall be laid down by the Member States.

3.   Without prejudice to the right of Member States to develop, in the light of changing circumstances, different legislative, regulatory or contractual provisions in the field of working time, as long as the minimum requirements provided for in this Directive are complied with, implementation of this Directive shall not constitute valid grounds for reducing the general level of protection afforded to workers.

4.   Member States shall communicate to the Commission the texts of the provisions of national law already adopted or being adopted in the field governed by this Directive.

5.   Member States shall report to the Commission every five years on the practical implementation of the provisions of this Directive, indicating the viewpoints of the two sides of industry.

The Commission shall inform the European Parliament, the Council, the Economic and Social Committee and the Advisory Committee on Safety, Hygiene and Health Protection at Work thereof.

6.   Every five years the Commission shall submit to the European Parliament, the Council and the Economic and Social Committee a report on the application of this Directive taking into account paragraphs 1, 2, 3, 4 and 5.

Article 19
This Directive is addressed to the Member States.

Done at Brussels, 23 November 1993.
For the Council
The President
M. SMET

COUNCIL DIRECTIVE 94/33/ EC OF 22 JUNE 1994 ON THE PROTECTION OF YOUNG PEOPLE AT WORK
[OJ 1994, No. L216/12]

THE COUNCIL OF THE EUROPEAN UNION,

Having regard to the Treaty establishing the European Community, and in Particular Article 118a thereof,

Having regard to the proposal from the Commission,[1]

Having regard to the opinion of the Economic and Social Committee,[2]

Acting in accordance with the procedure referred to in Article 189c of the Treaty,[3]

Notes
[1] OJ No. C84, 4.4.1992, p. 7.
[2] OJ No. C313, 30.11.1992, p. 70.
[3] Opinion of the European Parliament of 17 December 1992 (OJ No. C21, 25.1.1993, p. 167). Council Common Position of 23 November 1993 (not yet published in the Official Journal) and Decision of the European Parliament of 9 March 1994 (OJ No. C91, 28.3.1994, p. 89).

Whereas Article 118a of the Treaty provides that the Council shall adopt, by means of directives, minimum requirements to encourage improvements, especially in the working environment, as regards the health and safety of workers;

Whereas, under that Article, such directives must avoid imposing administrative, financial and legal constraints in a way which would hold back the creation and development of small and medium-sized undertakings;

Whereas points 20 and 22 of the Community Charter of the Fundamental Social Rights of Workers, adopted by the European Council in Strasbourg on 9 December 1989, state that:

'20.   Without prejudice to such rules as may be more favourable to young people, in particular those ensuring their preparation for work through vocational training, and subject to derogations limited to certain light work, the minimum employment age must not be lower than the minimum school-leaving age and, in any case, not lower than 15 years;

22.   Appropriate measures must be taken to adjust labour regulations applicable to young workers so that their specific development and vocational training and access to employment needs are met. The duration of work must, in particular, be limited — without it being possible to circumvent this limitation through recourse to overtime — and night work prohibited in the case of workers of under eighteen years of age, save in the case of certain jobs laid down in national legislation or regulations.';

Whereas account should be taken of the principles of the International Labour Organization regarding the protection of young people at work, including those relating to the minimum age for access to employment or work;

Whereas, in this Resolution on child labour,[4] the European Parliament summarised the various aspects of work by young people and stressed its effects on their health, safety and physical and intellectual development, and pointed to the need to adopt a Directive harmonizing national legislation in the field;

Whereas Article 15 of Council Directive 89/391/EEC of 12 June 1989 on the introduction of measures to encourage improvements in the safety and health of workers at work[5] provides that particularly sensitive risk groups must be protected against the dangers which specifically affect them;

Whereas children and adolescents must be considered specific risk groups, and measures must be taken with regard to their safety and health;

Whereas the vulnerability of children calls for Member States to prohibit their employment and ensure that the minimum working or employment age is not lower than the minimum age at which compulsory schooling as imposed by national law ends or 15 years in any event; whereas derogations from the prohibition on child labour may be admitted only in special cases and under the conditions stipulated in this Directive; whereas, under no circumstances, may such derogations be detrimental to regular school attendance or prevent children benefiting fully from their education;

Whereas, in view of the nature of the transition from childhood to adult life, work by adolescents should be strictly regulated and protected;

Whereas every employer should guarantee young people working conditions appropriate to their age;

Notes
[4] OJ No. C190, 20.7.1987, p. 44.
[5] OJ No. L183, 29.6.1989, p. 1.

Whereas employers should implement the measures necessary to protect the safety and health of young people on the basis of an assessment of work-related hazards to the young;

Whereas Member States should protect young people against any specific risks arising from their lack of experience, absence of awareness of existing or potential risks, or from their immaturity;

Whereas Member States should therefore prohibit the employment of young people for the work specified by this Directive;

Whereas the adoption of specific minimal requirements in respect of the organization of working time is likely to improve working conditions for young people;

Whereas the maximum working time of young people should be strictly limited and night work by young people should be prohibited, with the exception of certain jobs specified by national legislation or rules;

Whereas Member States should take the appropriate measures to ensure that the working time of adolescents receiving school education does not adversely affect their ability to benefit from that education;

Whereas time spent on training by young persons working under a theoretical and/or practical combined work/training scheme or an in-plant work-experience should be counted as working time;

Whereas, in order to ensure the safety and health of young people, the latter should be granted minimum daily, weekly and annual periods of rest and adequate breaks;

Whereas, with respect to the weekly rest period, due account should be taken of the diversity of cultural, ethnic, religious and other factors prevailing in the Member States; whereas in particular, it is ultimately for each Member State to decide whether Sunday should be included in the weekly rest period, and if so to what extent;

Whereas appropriate work experience may contribute to the aim of preparing young people for adult working and social life, provided it is ensured that any harm to their safety, health and development is avoided;

Whereas, although derogations from the bans and limitations imposed by this Directive would appear indispensable for certain activities or particular situations, applications thereof must not prejudice the principles underlying the established protection system;

Whereas this Directive constitutes a tangible step towards developing the social dimension of the internal market;

Whereas the application in practice of the system of protection laid down by this Directive will require that Member States implement a system of effective and proportionate measures;

Whereas the implementation of some provisions of this Directive poses particular problems for one Member State with regard to its system of protection for young people at work; whereas that Member State should therefore be allowed to refrain from implementing the relevant provisions for a suitable period,

HAS ADOPTED THIS DIRECTIVE:

SECTION I

Article 1   Purpose

1. Member States shall take the necessary measures to prohibit work by children. They shall ensure, under the conditions laid down by this Directive,

that the minimum working or employment age is not lower than the minimum age at which compulsory full-time schooling as imposed by national law ends or 15 years in any event.

2.   Member States shall ensure that work by adolescents is strictly regulated and protected under the conditions laid down in this Directive.

3.   Member States shall ensure in general that employers guarantee that young people have working conditions which suit their age. They shall ensure that young people are protected against economic exploitation and against any work likely to harm their safety, health or physical, mental, moral or social development or to jeopardise their education.

Article 2   Scope

1.   This Directive shall apply to any person under 18 years of age having an employment contract or an employment relationship defined by the law in force in a Member State and/or governed by the law in force in a Member State.

2.   Member States may make legislative or regulatory provision for this Directive not to apply, within the limits and under the conditions which they set by legislative or regulatory provision, to occasional work or short-term work involving:

(a)   domestic service in a private household, or

(b)   work regarded as not being harmful, damaging or dangerous to young people in a family undertaking.

Article 3   Definitions

For the purposes of this Directive:

(a)   'young person' shall mean any person under 18 years of age referred to in Article 2(1);

(b)   'child' shall mean any young person of less than 15 years of age or who is still subject to compulsory full-time schooling under national law;

(c)   'adolescent' shall mean any young person of at least 15 years of age but less than 18 years of age who is no longer subject to compulsory full-time schooling under national law;

(d)   'light work' shall mean all work which, on account of the inherent nature of the tasks which it involves and the particular conditions under which they are performed:

(i)   is not likely to be harmful to the safety, health or development of children, and

(ii)   is not such as to be harmful to their attendance at school, their participation in vocational guidance or training programmes approved by the competent authority or their capacity to benefit from the instruction received;

(e)   'working time' shall mean any period during which the young person is at work, at the employer's disposal and carrying out his activity or duties in accordance with national legislation and/or practice;

(f)   'rest period' shall mean any period which is not working time.

Article 4   Prohibition of work by children

1.   Member States shall adopt the measures necessary to prohibit work by children.

2.   Taking into account the objectives set out in Article 1, Member States may make legislative or regulatory provision for the prohibition of work by children not to apply to:

(a)   children pursuing the activities set out in Article 5;

(b)   children of at least 14 years of age working under a combined work/training scheme or an in-plant work-experience scheme, provided that such work is done in accordance with the conditions laid down by the competent authority;

(c)   children of at least 14 years of age performing light work other than that covered by Article 5; light work other than that covered by Article 5 may, however, be performed by children of 13 years of age for a limited number of hours per week in the case of categories of work determined by national legislation.

3.   Member States that make use of the opinion referred to in paragraph 2(c) shall determine, subject to the provisions of this Directive, the working conditions relating to the light work in question.

Article 5   Cultural or similar activities

1.   The employment of children for the purposes of performance in cultural, artistic, sports or advertising activities shall be subject to prior authorisation to be given by the competent authority in individual cases.

2.   Member States shall by legislative or regulatory provision lay down the working conditions for children in the cases referred to in paragraph 1 and the details of the prior authorisation procedure, on condition that the activities:

(i)   are not likely to be harmful to the safety, health or development of children, and

(ii)   are not such as to be harmful to their attendance at school, their participation in vocational guidance or training programmes approved by the competent authority or their capacity to benefit from the instruction received.

3.   By way of derogation from the procedure laid down in paragraph 1, in the case of children of at least 13 years of age, Member States may authorise, by legislative or regulatory provision, in accordance with conditions which they shall determine, the employment of children for the purposes of performance in cultural, artistic, sports or advertising activities.

4.   The Member States which have a specific authorisation system for modelling agencies with regard to the activities of children may retain that system.

SECTION II

Article 6   General obligations on employers

1.   Without prejudice to Article 4(1), the employer shall adopt the measures necessary to protect the safety and health of young people, taking particular account of the specific risks referred to in Article 7(1).

2.   The employer shall implement the measures provided for in paragraph 1 on the basis of an assessment of the hazards to young people in connection with their work.

The assessment must be made before young people begin work and when there is any major change in working conditions and must pay particular attention to the following points:

(a)   the fitting-out and layout of the workplace and the workstation;

(b)   the nature, degree and duration of exposure to physical, biological and chemical agents;

(c)   the form, range and use of work equipment, in particular agents, machines, apparatus and devices, and the way in which they are handled;

(d)   the arrangement of work processes and operations and the way in which these are combined (organization of work);

(e)   the level of training and instruction given to young people.

Where this assessment shows that there is a risk to the safety, the physical or mental health or development of young people, an appropriate free assessment and monitoring of their health shall be provided at regular intervals without prejudice to Directive 89/391/EEC.

The free health assessment and monitoring may form part of a national health system.

3.   The employer shall inform young people of possible risks and of all measures adopted concerning their safety and health. Furthermore, he shall inform the legal representatives of children of possible risks and of all measures adopted concerning children's safety and health.

4.   The employer shall involve the protective and preventive services referred to in Article 7 of Directive 89/391/EEC in the planning, implementation and monitoring of the safety and health conditions applicable to young people.

Article 7   Vulnerability of young people — Prohibition of work

1.   Member States shall ensure that young people are protected from any specific risks to their safety, health and development which are a consequence of their lack of experience, of absence of awareness of existing or potential risks or of the fact that young people have not yet fully matured.

2.   Without prejudice to Article 4(1), Member States shall to this end prohibit the employment of young people for:

(a)   work which is objectively beyond their physical or psychological capacity;

(b)   work involving harmful exposure to agents which are toxic, carcinogenic, cause heritable genetic damage, or harm to the unborn child or which in any other way chronically affect human health;

(c)   work involving harmful exposure to radiation;

(d)   work involving the risk of accidents which it may be assumed cannot be recognised or avoided by young persons owing to their insufficient attention to safety or lack of experience or training; or

(e)   work in which there is a risk to health from extreme cold or heat, or from noise or vibration. Work which is likely to entail specific risks for young people within the meaning of paragraph 1 includes:

— work involving harmful exposure to the physical, biological and chemical agents referred to in point I of the Annex, and

— processes and work referred to in point II of the Annex.

3.   Member States may, by legislative or regulatory provision, authorise derogations from paragraph 2 in the case of adolescents where such derogations are indispensable for their vocational training, provided that protection of their safety and health is ensured by the fact that the work is performed under the supervision of a competent person within the meaning of Article 7 of Directive 89/391/EEC and provided that the protection afforded by that Directive is guaranteed.

SECTION III

Article 8   Working time

1.   Member States which make use of the option in Article 4(2)(b) or (c) shall adopt the measures necessary to limit the working time of children to:

(a)   eight hours a day and 40 hours a week for work performed under a combined work/training scheme or an in-plant work-experience scheme;

(b)   two hours on a school day and 12 hours a week for work performed in term-time outside the hours fixed for school attendance, provided that this is not prohibited by national legislation and/or practice; in no circumstances may the daily working time exceed seven hours; this limit may be raised to eight hours in the case of children who have reached the age of 15;

(c)   seven hours a day and 35 hours a week for work performed during a period of at least a week when school is not operating; these limits may be raised to eight hours a day and 40 hours a week in the case of children who have reached the age of 15;

(d)   seven hours a day and 35 hours a week for light work performed by children no longer subject to compulsory full-time schooling under national law.

2.   Member States shall adopt the measures necessary to limit the working time of adolescents to eight hours a day and 40 hours a week.

3.   The time spent on training by a young person working under a theoretical and/or practical combined work/training scheme or an in-plant work-experience scheme shall be counted as working time.

4.   Where a young person is employed by more than one employer, working days and working time shall be cumulative.

5.   Member States may, by legislative or regulatory provision, authorise derogations from paragraph 1(a) and paragraph 2 either by way of exception or where there are objective grounds for so doing.

Member States shall, by legislative or regulatory provision, determine the conditions, limits and procedure for implementing such derogations.

Article 9   Night work

1.   (a) Member States which make use of the option in Article 4(2)(b) or (c) shall adopt the measures necessary to prohibit work by children between 8 p.m. and 6 a.m.

(b)   Member States shall adopt the measures necessary to prohibit work by adolescents either between 10 p.m. and 6 a.m. or between 11 p.m. and 7 a.m.

2.   (a) Member States may, by legislative or regulatory provision, authorise work by adolescents in specific areas of activity during the period in which night work is prohibited as referred to in paragraph 1(b). In that event, Member States shall take appropriate measures to ensure that the adolescent is supervised by an adult where such supervision is necessary for the adolescent's protection.

(b)   If point (a) is applied, work shall continue to be prohibited between midnight and 4 a.m. However, Member States may, by legislative or regulatory provision, authorise work by adolescents during the period in which night work is prohibited in the following cases, where there are objective grounds for so doing and provided that adolescents are allowed suitable compensatory rest time and that the objectives set out in Article 1 are not called into question:

—work performed in the shipping or fisheries sectors;
—work performed in the context of the armed forces or the police;
—work performed in hospitals or similar establishments;
—cultural, artistic, sports or advertising activities.

3.   Prior to any assignment to night work and at regular intervals thereafter, adolescents shall be entitled to a free assessment of their health and capacities, unless the work they do during the period during which work is prohibited is of an exceptional nature.

Article 10   Rest period

1.   (a)   Member States which make use of the option in Article 4(2)(b) or (c) shall adopt the measures necessary to ensure that, for each 24-hour period, children are entitled to a minimum rest period of 14 consecutive hours.

(b)   Member States shall adopt the measures necessary to ensure that, for each 24-hour period, adolescents are entitled to a minimum rest period of 12 consecutive hours.

2.   Member States shall adopt the measures necessary to ensure that, for each seven-day period:
—children in respect of whom they have made use of the option in Article 4(2)(b) or (c), and
—adolescents are entitled to a minimum rest period of two days, which shall be consecutive if possible.

Where justified by technical or organization reasons, the minimum rest period may be reduced, but may in no circumstances be less than 36 consecutive hours.

The minimum rest period referred to in the first and second subparagraphs shall in principle include Sunday.

3.   Member States may, by legislative or regulatory provision, provide for the minimum rest periods referred to in paragraphs 1 and 2 to be interrupted in the case of activities involving periods of work that are split up over the day or are of short duration.

4.   Member States may make legislative or regulatory provision for derogations from paragraph 1(b) and paragraph 2 in respect of adolescents in the following cases, where there are objective grounds for so doing and provided that they are granted appropriate compensatory rest time and that the objectives set out in Article 1 are not called into question:

(a)   work performed in the shipping or fisheries sectors;
(b)   work performed in the context of the armed forces or the police;
(c)   work performed in hospitals or similar establishments;
(d)   work performed in agriculture;
(e)   work performed in the tourism industry or in the hotel, restaurant and café sector;
(f)   activities involving periods of work split up over the day.

Article 11   Annual rest

Member States which make use of the option referred to in Article 4(2)(b) or (c) shall see to it that a period free of any work is included, as far as possible, in the school holidays of children subject to compulsory full-time schooling under national law.

Article 12   Breaks
Member States shall adopt the measures necessary to ensure that, where daily working time is more than four and a half hours, young people are entitled to a break of at least 30 minutes, which shall be consecutive if possible.

Article 13   Work by adolescents in the event of force majeure
Member States may, by legislative or regulatory provision, authorise derogations from Article 8(2), Article 9(1)(b), Article 10(1)(b) and, in the case of adolescents, Article 12, for work in the circumstances referred to in Article 5(4) of Directive 89/391/EEC, provided that such work is of a temporary nature and must be performed immediately, that adult workers are not available and that the adolescents are allowed equivalent compensatory rest time within the following three weeks.

SECTION IV

Article 14   Measures
Each Member State shall lay down any necessary measures to be applied in the event of failure to comply with the provisions adopted in order to implement this Directive; such measures must be effective and proportionate.

Article 15   Adaptation of the Annex
Adaptations of a strictly technical nature to the Annex in the light of technical progress, changes in international rules or specifications and advances in knowledge in the field covered by this Directive shall be adopted in accordance with the procedure provided for in Article 17 of Directive 89/391/EEC.

Article 16   Non-reducing clause
Without prejudice to the right of Member States to develop, in the light of changing circumstances, different provisions on the protection of young people, as long as the minimum requirements provided for by this Directive are complied with, the implementation of this Directive shall not constitute valid grounds for reducing the general level of protection afforded to young people.

Article 17   Final provisions
1.   (a)   Member States shall bring into force the laws, regulations and administrative provisions necessary to comply with this Directive not later than 22 June 1996 or ensure, by that date at the latest, that the two sides of industry introduce the requisite provisions by means of collective agreements, with Member States being required to make all the necessary provisions to enable them at all times to guarantee the results laid down by this Directive.

(b)   The United Kingdom may refrain from implementing the first subparagraph of Article 8(1)(b) with regard to the provision relating to the maximum weekly working time, and also Article 8(2) and Article 9(1)(b) and (2) for a period of four years from the date specified in subparagraph (a).

The Commission shall submit a report on the effects of this provision.

The Council, acting in accordance with the conditions laid down by the Treaty, shall decide whether this period should be extended.

(c)   Member States shall forthwith inform the Commission thereof.

2.   When Member States adopt the measures referred to in paragraph 1, such measures shall contain a reference to this Directive or shall be accompanied by such reference on the occasion of their official publication. The methods of making such reference shall be laid down by Member States.

3.   Member States shall communicate to the Commission the texts of the main provisions of national law which they have already adopted or adopt in the field governed by this Directive.

4.   Member States shall report to the Commission every five years on the practical implementation of the provisions of this Directive, indicating the viewpoints of the two sides of industry.

The Commission shall inform the European Parliament, the Council and the Economic and Social Committee thereof.

5.   The Commission shall periodically submit to the European Parliament, the Council and the Economic and Social Committee a report on the application of this Directive taking into account paragraphs 1, 2, 3 and 4.

Article 18

This Directive is addressed to the Member States.

Done at Luxembourg, 22 June 1994.

For the Council

The President

E. YIANNOPOULOS

ANNEX   NON-EXHAUSTIVE LIST OF AGENTS, PROCESSES AND WORK (ARTICLE 7(2), SECOND SUBPARAGRAPH)

I   AGENTS

1.   Physical agents

  (a)   Ionizing radiation;

  (b)   Work in a high-pressure atmosphere, e.g. in pressurised containers, diving.

2.   Biological agents

  (a)   Biological agents belonging to groups 3 and 4 within the meaning of Article 2(d) of Council Directive 90/679/EEC of 26 November 1990 on the protection of workers from risks related to exposure to biological agents at work (Seventh individual Directive within the meaning of Article 16(1) of Directive 89/391/EEC).[1]

3.   Chemical agents

  (a)   Substances and preparations classified according to Council Directive 67/548/EEC of 27 June 1967 on the approximation of laws, regulations and administrative provisions relating to the classification, packaging and labelling of dangerous substances[2] with amendments and Council Directive 88/379/EEC of 7 June 1988 on the approximation of the laws, regulations and administrative provisions of the Member States relating to the classification, packaging and labelling of dangerous preparations[3] as toxic (T), very toxic (Tx), corrosive (C) or explosive (E);

  (b)   Substances and preparations classified according to Directives 67/548/EEC and 88/379/EEC as harmful (Xn) and with one or more of the following risk phrases:

Notes

[1]OJ No. L374, 31.12.1990, p. 1.

[2]OJ No. 196, 16.8.1967, p. 1. Directive as last amended by Directive 93/679/EEC (OJ No. L268, 29.10.1993, p. 71).

[3]OJ No. L187, 16.7.1988, p. 14. Directive as last amended by Directive 93/18/EEC (OJ No. L104, 29.4.1993, p. 46).

—danger of very serious irreversible effects (R39),
—possible risk of irreversible effects (R40),
—may cause sensitisation by inhalation (R42),
—may cause sensitisation by skin contact (R43),
—may cause cancer (R45),
—may cause heritable genetic damage (R46),
—danger of serious damage to health by prolonged exposure (R48),
—may impair fertility (R60),
—may cause harm to the unborn child (R61);

   (c)   Substances and preparations classified according to Directives 67/
548/EEC and 88/379/EEC as irritant (Xi) and with one or more of the
following risk phrases:
—highly flammable (R12);
—may cause sensitisation by inhalation (R42),
—may cause sensitisation by skin contact (R43),

   (d)   Substances and preparations referred to Article 2(c) of Council
Directive 90/394/EEC of 28 June 1990 on the protection of workers from the
risks related to exposure to carcinogens at work (Sixth individual Directive
within the meaning of Article 16(1) of Directive 89/391/EEC;[4]

   (e)   Lead and compounds thereof, inasmuch as the agents in question are
absorbable by the human organism;

   (f)   Asbestos.

Note
[4]OJ No. L196, 26.7.1990, p. 1.

II   PROCESSES AND WORK

   1.   Processes at work referred to in Annex I to Directive 90/394/EEC.
   2.   Manufacture and handling of devices, fireworks or other objects
containing explosives.
   3.   Work with fierce or poisonous animals.
   4.   Animal slaughtering on an industrial scale.
   5.   Work involving the handling of equipment for the production, storage or
application of compressed, liquified or dissolved gases.
   6.   Work with vats, tanks, reservoirs or carboys containing chemical agents
referred to in 1.3.
   7.   Work involving a risk of structural collapse.
   8.   Work involving high-voltage electrical hazards.
   9.   Work the pace of which is determined by machinery and involving
payment by results.

COMPETITION

REGULATION NO 17. FIRST REGULATION IMPLEMENTING ARTICLES 85 AND 86 OF THE TREATY
[OJ Sp. Ed. 1962, No. 204/62, p. 87][1]

THE COUNCIL OF THE EUROPEAN ECONOMIC COMMUNITY,

Having regard to the Treaty establishing the European Economic Community, and in particular Article 87 thereof;

Having regard to the proposal from the Commission;

Having regard to the opinion of the Economic and Social Committee;

Having regard to the opinion of the European Parliament;

Whereas, in order to establish a system ensuring that competition shall not be distorted in the common market, it is necessary to provide for balanced application of Articles 85 and 86 in a uniform manner in the Member States;

Whereas in establishing the rules for applying Article 85(3) account must be taken of the need to ensure effective supervision and to simplify administration to the greatest possible extent;

Whereas it is accordingly necessary to make it obligatory, as a general principle, for undertakings which seek application of Article 85(3) to notify to the Commission their agreements, decisions and concerted practices;

Whereas, on the one hand, such agreements, decisions and concerted practices are probably very numerous and cannot therefore all be examined at the same time and, on the other hand, some of them have special features which may make them less prejudicial to the development of the common market;

Whereas there is consequently a need to make more flexible arrangements for the time being in respect of certain categories of agreement, decision and concerted practice without prejudging their validity under Article 85;

Whereas it may be in the interest of undertakings to know whether any agreements, decisions or practices to which they are party, or propose to become party, may lead to action on the part of the Commission pursuant to Article 85(1) or Article 86;

Whereas, in order to secure uniform application of Articles 85 and 86 in the common market, rules must be made under which the Commission, acting in close and constant liaison with the competent authorities of the Member States, may take the requisite measures for applying those Articles;

Note
[1] As amended up to OJ 1995 L1/1.

Whereas for this purpose the Commission must have the co-operation of the competent authorities of the Member States and be empowered, throughout the common market, to require such information to be supplied and to undertake such investigations as are necessary to bring to light any agreement, decision or concerted practice prohibited by Article 85(1) or any abuse of a dominant position prohibited by Article 86:

Whereas, in order to carry out its duty of ensuring that the provisions of the Treaty are applied, the Commission must be empowered to address to undertakings or associations of undertakings Recommendations and Decisions for the purpose of bringing to an end infringements of Articles 85 and 86;

Whereas compliance with Articles 85 and 86 and the fulfilment of obligations imposed on undertakings and associations of undertakings under this regulation must be enforceable by means of fines and periodic penalty payments;

Whereas undertakings concerned must be accorded the right to be heard by the Commission, third parties whose interests may be affected by a decision must be given the opportunity of submitting their comments beforehand, and it must be ensured that wide publicity is given to decisions taken;

Whereas all decisions taken by the Commission under this Regulation are subject to review by the Court of Justice under the conditions specified in the Treaty;

Whereas it is moreover desirable to confer upon the Court of Justice, pursuant to Article 172, unlimited jurisdiction in respect of decisions under which the Commission imposes fines or periodic penalty payments;

Whereas this regulation may enter into force without prejudice to any other provisions that may hereinafter be adopted pursuant to Article 87;

HAS ADOPTED THIS REGULATION:

Article 1   Basic provision
Without prejudice to Articles 6, 7 and 23 of this Regulation, agreements, decisions and concerted practices of the kind described in Article 85(1) of the Treaty and the abuse of a dominant position in the market, within the meaning of Article 86 of the Treaty, shall be prohibited, no prior decision to that effect being required.

Article 2   Negative clearance
Upon application by the undertakings or associations of undertakings concerned, the Commission may certify that, on the basis of the facts in its possession, there are no grounds under Article 85(1) or Article 86 of the Treaty for action on its part in respect of an agreement, decision or practice.

Article 3   Termination of infringements
1.   Where the Commission, upon application or upon its own initiative, finds that there is infringement of Article 85 or Article 86 of the Treaty, it may by decision require the undertakings or associations of undertakings concerned to bring such infringement to an end.

2.   Those entitled to make application are:
   (a)   Member States;
   (b)   natural or legal persons who claim a legitimate interest.

3. Without prejudice to the other provisions of this Regulation, the Commission may, before taking a decision under paragraph 1, address to the undertakings or associations of undertakings concerned recommendations for termination of the infringement.

Article 4 Notification of new agreements, decisions and practices

1. Agreements, decisions and concerted practices of the kind described in Article 85(1) of the Treaty which come into existence after the entry into force of this Regulation and in respect of which the parties seek application of Article 85(3) must be notified to the Commission. Until they have been notified, no decision in application of Article 85(3) may be taken.

2. Paragraph 1 shall not apply to agreements, decisions or concerted practices where:

(1) the only parties thereto are undertakings from one Member State and the agreements, decisions or practices do not relate either to imports or to exports between Member States;

(2) not more than two undertakings are party thereto, and the agreements only:

(a) restrict the freedom of one party to the contract in determining the prices or conditions of business upon which the goods which he has obtained from the other party to the contract may be resold; or

(b) impose restrictions on the exercise of the rights of the assignee or user of industrial property rights — in particular patents, utility models, designs or trade marks — or of the person entitled under a contract to the assignment, or grant, of the right to use a method of manufacture or knowledge relating to the use and to the application of industrial processes;

(3) they have as their sole object:

(a) the development or uniform application of standards or types; or

(b) joint research and development;

(c) specialisation in the manufacture of products, including agreements necessary for achieving this,

— where the products which are the subject of specialisation do not, in a substantial part of the common market, represent more than 15% of the volume of business done in identical products or those considered by consumers to be similar by reason of their characteristics, price and use, and

— where the total annual turnover of the participating undertakings does not exceed 200 million units of account.

These agreements, decisions and practices may be notified to the Commission.

Article 5 Notification of existing agreements, decisions and practices

1. Agreements, decisions and concerted practices of the kind described in Article 85(1) of the Treaty which are in existence at the date of entry into force of this Regulation and in respect of which the parties seek application of Article 85(3) shall be notified to the Commission before 1 November 1962.

However, notwithstanding the foregoing provisions, any agreements, decisions and concerted practices to which not more than two undertakings are party shall be notified before 1 February 1963.

2. Paragraph 1 shall not apply to agreements, decisions or concerted practices falling within Article 4(2); these may be notified to the Commission.

Article 6   Decisions pursuant to Article 85(3)

1.   Whenever the Commission takes a decision pursuant to Article 85(3) of the Treaty, it shall specify therein the date from which the decision shall take effect. Such date shall not be earlier than the date of notification.

2.   The second sentence of paragraph 1 shall not apply to agreements, decisions or concerted practices falling within Article 4(2) and Article 5(2), nor to those falling within Article 5(1) which have been notified within the time limit specified in Article 5(1).

Article 7   Special provisions for existing agreements, decisions and practices

1.   Where agreements, decisions and concerted practices in existence at the date of entry into force of this Regulation and notified within the time limits specified in Article 5(1) do not satisfy the requirements of Article 85(3) of the Treaty and the undertakings or associations of undertakings concerned cease to give effect to them or modify them in such manner that they no longer fall within the prohibition contained in Article 85(1) or that they satisfy the requirements of Article 85(3), the prohibition contained in Article 85(1) shall apply only for a period fixed by the Commission. A decision by the Commission pursuant to the foregoing sentence shall not apply as against undertakings and associations of undertakings which did not expressly consent to the notification.

2.   Paragraph 1 shall apply to agreements, decisions and concerted practices falling within Article 4(2) which are in existence at the date of entry into force of this Regulation if they are notified before 1 January 1967.

Article 8   Duration and revocation of decisions under Article 85(3)

1.   A decision in application of Article 85(3) of the Treaty shall be issued for a specified period and conditions and obligations may be attached thereto.

2.   A decision may on application be renewed if the requirements of Article 85(3) of the Treaty continue to be satisfied.

3.   The Commission may revoke or amend its decision or prohibit specified acts by the parties:

   (a)   where there has been a change in any of the facts which were basic to the making of the decision;

   (b)   where the parties commit a breach of any obligation attached to the decision;

   (c)   where the decision is based on incorrect information or was induced by deceit;

   (d)   where the parties abuse the exemption from the provisions of Article 85(1) of the Treaty granted to them by the decision.

   In cases to which subparagraphs (b), (c) or (d) apply, the decision may be revoked with retroactive effect.

Article 9   Powers

1.   Subject to review of its decision by the Court of Justice, the Commission shall have sole power to declare Article 85(1) inapplicable pursuant to Article 85(3) of the Treaty.

2.   The Commission shall have power to apply Article 85(1) and Article 86 of the Treaty; this power may be exercised notwithstanding that the time limits specified in Article 5(1) and in Article 7(2) relating to notification have not expired.

3.   As long as the Commission has not initiated any procedure under Articles 2, 3 or 6, the authorities of the Member States shall remain competent to apply Article 85(1) and Article 86 in accordance with Article 88 of the Treaty; they shall remain competent in this respect notwithstanding that the time limits specified in Article 5(1) and in Article 7(2) relating to notification have not expired.

Article 10   Liaison with the authorities of the Member States

1.   The Commission shall forthwith transmit to the competent authorities of the Member States a copy of the applications and notifications together with copies of the most important documents lodged with the Commission for the purpose of establishing the existence of infringements of Articles 85 or 86 of the Treaty or of obtaining negative clearance or a decision in application of Article 85(3).

2.   The Commission shall carry out the procedure set out in paragraph 1 in close and constant liaison with the competent authorities of the Member States; such authorities shall have the right to express their views upon the procedure.

3.   An Advisory Committee on Restrictive Practices and Monopolies shall be consulted prior to the taking of any decision following upon a procedure under paragraph 1, and of any decision concerning the renewal, amendment or revocation of a decision pursuant to Article 85(3) of the Treaty.

4.   The Advisory Committee shall be composed of officials competent in the matter of restrictive practices and monopolies. Each Member State shall appoint an official to represent it who, if prevented from attending, may be replaced by another official.

5.   The consultation shall take place at a joint meeting convened by the Commission; such meeting shall be held not earlier than fourteen days after dispatch of the notice convening it. The notice shall, in respect of each case to be examined, be accompanied by a summary of the case together with an indication of the most important documents, and a preliminary draft decision.

6.   The Advisory Committee may deliver an opinion notwithstanding that some of its members or their alternates are not present. A report of the outcome of the consultative proceedings shall be annexed to the draft decision. It shall not be made public.

Article 11   Requests for information

1.   In carrying out the duties assigned to it by Article 89 and by provisions adopted under Article 87 of the Treaty, the Commission may obtain all necessary information from the Governments and competent authorities of the Member States and from undertakings and associations of undertakings.

2.   When sending a request for information to an undertaking or association of undertakings, the Commission shall at the same time forward a copy of the request to the competent authority of the Member State in whose territory the seat of the undertaking or association of undertakings is situated.

3.   In its request the Commission shall state the legal basis and the purpose of the request and also the penalties provided for in Article 15(1)(b) for supplying incorrect information.

4.   The owners of the undertakings or their representatives and, in the case of legal persons, companies or firms, or of associations having no legal personality, the persons authorised to represent them by law or by their constitution shall supply the information requested.

5. Where an undertaking or association of undertakings does not supply the information requested within the time limit fixed by the Commission, or supplies incomplete information, the Commission shall by decision require the information to be supplied. The decision shall specify what information is required, fix an appropriate time limit within which it is to be supplied and indicate the penalties provided for in Article 15(1)(b) and Article 16(1)(c) and the right to have the decision reviewed by the Court of Justice.

6. The Commission shall at the same time forward a copy of its decision to the competent authority of the Member State in whose territory the seat of the undertaking or association of undertakings is situated.

Article 12   Inquiry into sectors of the economy

1. If in any sector of the economy the trend of trade between Member States, price movements, inflexibility of prices or other circumstances suggest that in the economic sector concerned competition is being restricted or distorted within the common market, the Commission may decide to conduct a general inquiry into that economic sector and in the course thereof may request undertakings in the sector concerned to supply the information necessary for giving effect to the principles formulated in Article 85 and 86 of the Treaty and for carrying out the duties entrusted to the Commission.

2. The Commission may in particular request every undertaking or association of undertakings in the economic sector concerned to communicate to it all agreements, decisions and concerted practices which are exempt from notification by virtue of Article 4(2) and Article 5(2).

3. When making inquiries pursuant to paragraph 2, the Commission shall also request undertakings or groups of undertakings whose size suggests that they occupy a dominant position within the common market or a substantial part thereof to supply to the Commission and such particulars of the structure of the undertakings and of their behaviour as are requisite to an appraisal of their position in the light of Article 86 of the Treaty.

4. Article 10(3) to (6) and Articles 11, 13 and 14 shall apply correspondingly.

Article 13   Investigations by the authorities of the Member States

1. At the request of the Commission, the competent authorities of the Member States shall undertake the investigations which the Commission considers to be necessary under Article 14(1), or which it has ordered by decision pursuant to Article 14(3). The officials of the competent authorities of the Member States responsible for conducting these investigations shall exercise their powers upon production of an authorisation in writing issued by the competent authority of the Member State in whose territory the investigation is to be made. Such authorisation shall specify the subject matter and purpose of the investigation.

2. If so requested by the Commission or by the competent authority of the Member State in whose territory the investigation is to be made, the officials of the Commission may assist the officials of such authorities in carrying out their duties.

Article 14   Investigating powers of the Commission

1. In carrying out the duties assigned to it by Article 89 and by provisions adopted under Article 87 of the Treaty, the Commission may undertake all

necessary investigations into undertakings and associations of undertakings. To this end the officials authorised by the Commission are empowered:

(a)   to examine the books and other business records;

(b)   to take copies of or extracts from the books and business records;

(c)   to ask for oral explanations on the spot;

(d)   to enter any premises; land and means of transport of undertakings.

2.   The officials of the Commission authorised for the purpose of these investigations shall exercise their powers upon production of an authorisation in writing specifying the subject matter and purpose of the investigation and the penalties provided for in Article 15(1)(c) in cases where production of the required books or other business records is incomplete. In good time before the investigation, the Commission shall inform the competent authority of the Member State in whose territory the same is to be made of the investigation and of the identity of the authorised officials.

3.   Undertakings and associations of undertakings shall submit to investigations ordered by decision of the Commission. The decision shall specify the subject matter and purpose of the investigation, appoint the date on which it is to begin and indicate the penalties provided for in Article 15(1)(c) and Article 16(1)(d) and the right to have the decision reviewed by the Court of Justice.

4.   The Commission shall take decisions referred to in paragraph 3 after consultation with the competent authority of the Member State in whose territory the investigation is to be made.

5.   Officials of the competent authority of the Member State in whose territory the investigation is to be made may, at the request of such authority or of the Commission, assist the officials of the Commission in carrying out their duties.

6.   Where an undertaking opposes an investigation ordered pursuant to this Article, the Member State concerned shall afford the necessary assistance to the officials authorised by the Commission to enable them to make their investigation. Member States shall, after consultation with the Commission, take the necessary measures to this end before 1 October 1962.

Article 15   Fines

1.   The Commission may by decision impose on undertakings or associations of undertakings fines of from 100 to 5,000 units of account where, intentionally or negligently:

(a)   they supply incorrect or misleading information in an application pursuant to Article 2 or in a notification pursuant to Articles 4 or 5; or

(b)   they supply incorrect information in response to a request made pursuant to Article 11(3) or (5) or to Article 12, or do not supply information within the time limit fixed by a decision taken under Article 11(5); or

(c)   they produce the required books or other business records in incomplete form during investigations under Article 13 or 14, or refuse to submit to an investigation ordered by decision issued in implementation of Article 14(3).

2.   The Commission may by decision impose on undertakings or associations of undertakings fines of from 1,000 to 1,000,000 units of account, or a sum in excess thereof but not exceeding 10% of the turnover in the preceding business year of each of the undertakings participating in the infringement where, either intentionally or negligently:

(a)   they infringe Article 85(1) or Article 86 of the Treaty; or

(b)   they commit a breach of any obligation imposed pursuant to Article 8(1).

In fixing the amount of the fine, regard shall be had both to the gravity and to the duration of the infringement.

3.   Article 10(3) to (6) shall apply.

4.   Decisions taken pursuant to paragraphs 1 and 2 shall not be of a criminal law nature.

5.   The fines provided for in paragraph 2(a) shall not be imposed in respect of acts taking place:

(a)   after notification to the Commission and before its decision in application of Article 85(3) of the Treaty, provided they fall within the limits of the activity described in the notification;

(b)   before notification and in the course of agreements, decisions or concerted practices in existence at the date of entry into force of this Regulation, provided that notification was effected within the time limits specified in Article 5(1) and Article 7(2).

6.   Paragraph 5 shall not have effect where the Commission has informed the undertakings concerned that after preliminary examination it is of opinion that Article 85(1) of the Treaty applies and that application of Article 85(3) is not justified.

Article 16   Periodic penalty payments

1.   The Commission may by decision impose on undertakings or associations of undertakings periodic penalty payments of from 50 to 1,000 units of account per day, calculated from the date appointed by the decision, in order to compel them:

(a)   to put an end to an infringement of Article 85 or 86 of the Treaty, in accordance with a decision taken pursuant to Article 3 of this Regulation;

(b)   to refrain from any act prohibited under Article 8(3);

(c)   to supply complete and correct information which it has requested by decision taken pursuant to Article 11(5);

(d)   to submit to an investigation which it has ordered by decision taken pursuant to Article 14(3).

2.   Where the undertakings or associations of undertakings have satisfied the obligation which it was the purpose of the periodic penalty payment to enforce, the Commission may fix the total amount of the periodic penalty payment at a lower figure than that which would arise under the original decision.

3.   Article 10(3) to (6) shall apply.

Article 17   Review by the Court of Justice

The Court of Justice shall have unlimited jurisdiction within the meaning of Article 172 of the Treaty to review decisions whereby the Commission has fixed a fine or periodic penalty payment; it may cancel, reduce or increase the fine or periodic penalty payment imposed.

Article 18   Unit of account

For the purposes of applying Articles 15 to 17 the unit of account shall be that adopted in drawing up the budget of the Community in accordance with Articles 207 and 209 of the Treaty.

Article 19   Hearing of the parties and of third persons
1.   Before taking decisions as provided for in Articles 2, 3, 6, 7, 8, 15 and 16, the Commission shall give the undertakings or associations of undertakings concerned the opportunity of being heard on the matters to which the Commission has taken objection.
2.   If the Commission or the competent authorities of the Member State consider it necessary, they may also hear other natural or legal persons. Applications to be heard on the part of such persons shall, where they show a sufficient interest, be granted.
3.   Where the Commission intends to give negative clearance pursuant to Article 2 or take a decision in application of Article 85(3) of the Treaty, it shall publish a summary of the relevant application or notification and invite all interested third parties to submit their observations within a time limit which it shall fix being not less than one month. Publication shall have regard to the legitimate interest of undertakings in the protection of their business secrets.

Article 20   Professional secrecy
1.   Information acquired as a result of the application of Articles 11, 12, 13 and 14 shall be used only for the purpose of the relevant request or investigation.
2.   Without prejudice to the provisions of Articles 19 and 21, the Commission and the competent authorities of the Member States, their officials and other servants shall not disclose information acquired by them as a result of the application of this Regulation and of the kind covered by the obligation of professional secrecy.
3.   The provisions of paragraphs 1 and 2 shall not prevent publication of general information or surveys which do not contain information relating to particular undertakings or associations of undertakings.

Article 21   Publication of decisions
1.   The Commission shall publish the decisions which it takes pursuant to Articles 2, 3, 6, 7 and 8.
2.   The publication shall state the names of the parties and the main content of the decisions; it shall have regard to the legitimate interest of undertakings in the protection of their business secrets.

Article 22   Special provisions
1.   The Commission shall submit to the Council proposals for making certain categories of agreement, decision and concerted practice falling within Article 4(2) or Article 5(2) compulsorily notifiable under Article 4 or 5.
2.   Within one year from the date of entry into force of this Regulation, the Council shall examine, on a proposal from the Commission, what special provisions might be made for exempting from the provisions of this Regulation agreements, decisions and concerted practices falling within Article 4(2) or Article 5(2).

Article 23 Transitional provisions applicable to decisions of authorities of the Member States.
1.   Agreements, decisions and concerted practices of the kind described in Article 85(1) of the Treaty to which, before the entry into force of this Regulation, the competent authority of a Member State has declared Article 85(1) to be inapplicable pursuant to Article 85(3) shall not be subject to

compulsory notification under Article 5. The decision of the competent authority of the Member State shall be deemed to be a decision within the meaning of Article 6; it shall cease to be valid upon expiration of the period fixed by such authority but in any event not more than three years after the entry into force of this Regulation. Article 8(3) shall apply.

2.   Applications for renewal of decisions of the kind described in paragraph 1 shall be decided upon by the Commission in accordance with Article 8(2).

Article 24   Implementing provisions

The Commission shall have power to adopt implementing provisions concerning the form, content and other details of applications pursuant to Articles 2 and 3 and of notifications pursuant to Articles 4 and 5, and concerning hearings pursuant to Article 19(1) and (2).

Article 25

1.   As regards agreements, decisions and concerted practices to which Article 85 of the Treaty applies by virtue of accession, the date of accession shall be substituted for the date of entry into force of this Regulation in every place where reference is made in this Regulation to this latter date.

2.   Agreements, decisions and concerted practices existing at the date of accession to which Article 85 of the Treaty applies by virtue of accession shall be notified pursuant to Article 5(1) or Article 7(1) and (2) witin six months from the date of accession.

3.   Fines under Article 15(2)(a) shall not be imposed in respect of any act prior to notification of the agreements, decisions and practices to which paragraph 2 applies and which have been notified within the period therein specified.

4.   New Member States shall take the measures referred to in Article 14(6) within six months from the date of accession after consulting the Commission.

5.   The provisions of paragraphs 1 to 4 above still apply in the same way in the case of the accession of the Hellenic Republic, the Kingdom of Spain and the Portuguese Republic.

6.   The provisions of paragraphs 1 to 4 still apply in the same way in the case of the accession of Austria, Finland and Sweden. However, they do not apply to agreements, decisions and concerted practices which at the date of accession already fall under Article 54 of the EEA Agreement.

This Regulation shall be binding in its entirety and directly applicable in all Member States.

(Signature omitted.)

EEC COUNCIL: REGULATION NO 26 APPLYING CERTAIN RULES OF COMPETITION TO PRODUCTION OF AND TRADE IN AGRICULTURAL PRODUCTS
[OJ No. 30, 20/04/1962, p. 0993][1]

THE COUNCIL OF THE EUROPEAN ECONOMIC COMMUNITY,

Having regard to the Treaty establishing the European Economic Community, and in particular Articles 42 and 43 thereof;

Having regard to the proposal from the Commission;

Note
[1]Amended by Regulation 49 (OJ No. L53, 01.7.1962, p. 1571).

Having regard to the opinion of the European Parliament;

Whereas by virtue of Article 42 of the treaty one of the matters to be decided under the Common Agricultural Policy is whether the rules on competition laid down in the treaty are to apply to production of and trade in agricultural products, and accordingly the provisions hereinafter contained will have to be supplemented in the light of developments in that policy;

Whereas the proposals submitted by the Commission for the formulation and implementation of the Common Agricultural Policy show that certain rules on competition must forthwith be made applicable to production of and trade in agricultural products in order to eliminate practices contrary to the principles of the Common Market and prejudicial to attainment of the objectives set out in Article 39 of the treaty and in order to provide a basis for the future establishment of a system of competition adapted to the development of the Common Agricultural Policy;

Whereas the rules on competition relating to the agreements, decisions and practices referred to in Article 85 of the treaty and to the abuse of dominant positions must be applied to production of and trade in agricultural products, in so far as their application does not impede the functioning of national organisations of agricultural markets or jeopardise attainment of the objectives of the Common Agricultural Policy;

Whereas special attention is warranted in the case of farmers' organisations which are particularly concerned with the joint production or marketing of agricultural products or the use of joint facilities, unless such joint action excludes competition or jeopardises attainment of the objectives of Article 39 of the treaty;

Whereas, in order both to avoid compromising the development of a Common Agricultural Policy and to ensure certainty in the law and non-discriminatory treatment of the undertakings concerned, the Commission must have sole power, subject to review by the Court of Justice, to determine whether the conditions provided for in the two preceding recitals are fulfilled as regards the agreements, decisions and practices referred to in Article 85 of the treaty;

Whereas, in order to enable the specific provisions of the treaty regarding agriculture, and in particular those of Article 39 thereof, to be taken into consideration, the Commission must, in questions of dumping, assess all the causes of the practices complained of and in particular the price level at which products from other sources are imported into the market in question;

Whereas it must, in the light of its assessment, make recommendations and authorise protective measures as provided in Article 91(1) of the treaty;

Whereas, in order to implement, as part of the development of the Common Agricultural Policy, the rules on aids for production of or trade in agricultural products, the Commission should be in a position to draw up a list of existing, new or proposed aids, to make appropriate observations to the Member States and to propose suitable measures to them;

HAS ADOPTED THIS REGULATION:

Article 1

From the entry into force of this Regulation, Articles 85 to 90 of the treaty and provisions made in implementation thereof shall, subject to Article 2 below, apply to all agreements, decisions and practices referred to in Articles 85(1) and 86 of the treaty which relate to production of or trade in the products listed in Annex II to the treaty;

Article 2

1. (Declared void by the Court of Justice: E.C.R. (1962) 491)[1]

2. After consulting the Member States and hearing the undertakings or associations of undertakings concerned and any other natural or legal person that it considers appropriate, the Commission shall have sole power, subject to review by the Court of Justice, to determine, by decision which shall be published, which agreements, decisions and practices fulfil the conditions specified in Paragraph 1.

3. The Commission shall undertake such determination either on its own initiative or at the request of a competent authority of a Member State or of an interested undertaking or association of undertakings.

4. The publication shall state the names of the parties and the main content of the decision; it shall have regard to the legitimate interest of undertakings in the protection of their business secrets.

Editors Note: This is for the purposes of information only. Declared void by the Court of Justice (article 2(1))

Article 85(1) of the treaty shall not apply to such of the agreements, decisions and practices referred to in the preceding article as form an integral part of a national market organisation or are necessary for attainment of the objectives set out in article 39 of the treaty. in particular, it shall not apply to agreements, decisions and practices of farmers, farmers' associations, or associations of such associations belonging to a single member state which concern the production or sale of agricultural products or the use of joint facilities for the storage, treatment or processing of agricultural products, and under which there is no obligation to charge identical prices, unless the commission finds that competition is thereby excluded or that the objectives of article 39 of the treaty are jeopardised.

Article 3

1. Without prejudice to Article 46 of the treaty, article 91 (1) thereof shall apply to trade in the products listed in Annex II to the treaty.

2. With due regard for the provisions of the treaty relating to agriculture, and in particular those of Article 39, the Commission shall assess all the causes of the practices complained of, in particular the price level at which products from other sources are imported into the market in question.

In the light of its assessment, it shall make recommendations and authorise protective measures as provided in Article 91(1) of the treaty.

Article 4

The provisions of Article 93(1) and of the first sentence of Article 93(3) of the treaty shall apply to aids granted for production of or trade in the products listed in Annex IIi to the treaty.

Article 5

This Regulation shall enter into force on the day following its publication in the Official Journal of the European Communities, with the exception of articles 1 to 3, which shall enter into force on 1 July 1962.

This regulation shall be binding in its entirety and directly applicable in all Member States.

Done at Brussels, 4 April 1962.
For the Council,
The President,
M. COUVE DE MURVILLE

REGULATION NO 99/63/EEC OF THE COMMISSION OF 25 JULY 1963 ON THE HEARINGS PROVIDED FOR IN ARTICLE 19(1) AND (2) OF COUNCIL REGULATION NO 17
[OJ Sp. Ed. 1963, No. 2268/63, p. 47]

THE COMMISSION OF THE EUROPEAN ECONOMIC COMMUNITY,

Having regard to the Treaty establishing the European Economic Community, and in particular Articles 87 and 155 thereof;

Having regard to Article 24 of Council Regulation No. 17(1) of 6 February 1962 (first Regulation implementing Articles 85 and 86 of the Treaty);

Whereas the Commission has power under Article 24 of Council Regulation No. 17 to lay down implementing provisions concerning the hearings provided for in Article 19(1) and (2) of that Regulation;

Whereas in most cases the Commission will in the course of its inquiries already be in close touch with the undertakings or associations of undertakings which are the subject thereof and they will accordingly have the opportunity of making known their views regarding the objections raised against them;

Whereas, however, in accordance with Article 19(1) of Regulation No. 17 and with the rights of defence, the undertakings and associations of undertakings concerned must have the right on conclusion of the inquiry to submit their comments on the whole of the objections raised against them which the Commission proposes to deal with in its decisions;

Whereas persons other than the undertakings or associations of undertakings which are the subject of the inquiry may have an interest in being heard;

Whereas, by the second sentence of Article 19(2) of Regulation No. 17, such persons must have the opportunity of being heard if they apply and show that they have a sufficient interest;

Whereas it is desirable to enable persons who, pursuant to Article 3(2) of Regulation No. 17, have applied for an infringement to be terminated to submit their comments where the Commission considers that on the basis of the information in its possession there are insufficient grounds for granting the application;

Whereas the various persons entitled to submit comments must do so in writing, both in their own interest and in the interests of good administration, without prejudice to oral procedure where appropriate to supplement the written evidence;

Whereas it is necessary to define the rights of persons who are to be heard, and in particular the conditions upon which they may be represented or assisted and the setting and calculation of time limits;

Whereas the advisory committee on restrictive practices and monopolies delivers its opinion on the basis of a preliminary draft decision;

Whereas it must therefore be consulted concerning a case after the inquiry in respect thereof has been completed;

Whereas such consultation does not prevent the Commission from reopening an inquiry if need be;

HAS ADOPTED THIS REGULATION:

Article 1
Before consulting the Advisory Committee on Restrictive Practices and Monopolies, the Commission shall hold a hearing pursuant to Article 19(1) of Regulation No 17.

Article 2
1. The Commission shall inform undertakings and associations of undertakings in writing of the objections raised against them. The communication shall be addressed to each of them or to a joint agent appointed by them.

2. The Commission may inform the parties by giving notice in the *Official Journal of the European Communities,* if from the circumstances of the case this appears appropriate, in particular where notice is to be given to a number of undertakings but no joint agent has been appointed. The notice shall have regard to the legitimate interest of the undertakings in the protection of their business secrets.

3. A fine or a periodic penalty payment may be imposed on an undertaking or association of undertakings only if the objections were notified in the manner provided for in paragraph 1.

4. The Commission shall when giving notice of objections fix a time limit up to which the undertakings and associations of undertakings may inform the Commission of their views.

Article 3
1. Undertakings and associations of undertakings shall, within the appointed time limit, make known in writing their views concerning the objections raised against them.

2. They may in their written comments set out all matters relevant to their defence.

3. They may attach any relevant documents in proof of the facts set out. They may also propose that the Commission hear persons who may corroborate those facts.

Article 4
The Commission shall in its decisions deal only with those objections raised against undertakings and associations of undertakings in respect of which they have been afforded the opportunity of making known their views.

Article 5
If natural or legal persons showing a sufficient interest apply to be heard pursuant to Article 19(2) of Regulation No 17, the Commission shall afford them the opportunity of making known their views in writing within such time limit as it shall fix.

Article 6
Where the Commission, having received an application pursuant to Article (2) of Regulation No 17, considers that on the basis of the information in its possession there are insufficient grounds for granting the application, it shall

inform the applicants of its reasons and fix a time limit for them to submit any further comments in writing.

Article 7

1. The Commission shall afford to persons who have so requested in their written comments the opportunity to put forward their arguments orally, if those persons show a sufficient interest or if the Commission proposes to impose on them a fine or periodic penalty payment.

2. The Commission may likewise afford to any other person the opportunity of orally expressing his views.

Article 8

1. The Commission shall summon the persons to be heard to attend on such date as it shall appoint.

2. It shall forthwith transmit a copy of the summons to the competent authorities of the Member States, who may appoint an official to take part in the hearing.

Article 9

1. Hearing shall be conducted by the persons appointed by the Commission for that purpose.

2. Persons summoned to attend shall appear either in person or be represented by legal representatives or by representatives authorised by their constitution. Undertakings and associations of undertakings may moreover be represented by a duly authorised agent appointed from among their permanent staff.

Persons heard by the Commission may be assisted by lawyers or university teachers who are entitled to plead before the Court of Justice of the European Communities in accordance with Article 17 of the Protocol on the Statute of the Court, or by other qualified persons.

3. Hearings shall not be public. Persons shall be heard separately or in the presence of other persons summoned to attend. In the latter case, regard shall be had to the legitimate interest of the undertakings in the protection of their business secrets.

4. The essential content of the statements made by each person heard shall be recorded in minutes which shall be read and approved by him.

Article 10

Without prejudice to Article 2(2), information and summonses from the Commission shall be sent to the addressees by registered letter with acknowledgement of receipt, or shall be delivered by hand against receipt.

Article 11

1. In fixing the time limits provided for in Articles 2, 5 and 6, the Commission shall have regard both to the time required for preparation of comments and to the urgency of the case. The time limit shall be not less than two weeks; it may be extended.

2. Time limits shall run from the day following receipt of a communication or delivery thereof by hand.

3. Written comments must reach the Commission or be dispatched by registered letter before expiry of the time limit. Where the time limit would expire on a Sunday or public holiday, it shall be extended up to the end of the

next following working day. For the purpose of calculating this extension, public holidays shall, in cases where the relevant date is the date of receipt of written comments, be those set out in the Annex to this Regulation, and in cases where the relevant date is the date of dispatch, those appointed by law in the country of dispatch.

This Regulation shall be binding in its entirety and Directly applicable in all member states.

Done at Brussels, 25 July 1963.
For the Commission,
The President,
Walter HALLSTEIN

Annex referred to in the third sentence of Article 11(3)
(list of public holidays)
New year * 1 Jan.
Good Friday *
Easter Saturday *
Easter Monday *
Labour day * 1 May
Schuman plan day * 9 May
Ascension day *
Whit Monday *
Belgian national day * 21 July
Assumption * 15 Aug.
All saints * 1 Nov.
All souls * 2 Nov.
Christmas eve * 24 Dec.
Christmas day * 25 Dec.
The day following Christmas day * 26 Dec.
New year's eve * 31 Dec.

COMMISSION REGULATION (EC) NO 3385/94 of 21 DECEMBER 1994 ON THE FORM, CONTENT AND OTHER DETAILS OF APPLICATIONS AND NOTIFICATIONS PROVIDED FOR IN COUNCIL REGULATION NO 17
[OJ 1994, No. L377/28]

THE COMMISSION OF THE EUROPEAN COMMUNITIES,

Having regard to the Treaty establishing the European Community,
    Having regard to the Agreement on the European Economic Area,
    Having regard to Council Regulation No 17 of 6 February 1962, First Regulation implementing Articles 85 and 86 of the Treaty,[1] as last amended by the Act of Accession of Spain and Portugal, and in particular Article 24 thereof,
    Whereas Commission Regulation No. 27 of 3 May 1962, First Regulation implementing Council Regulation No. 17,[2] as last amended by Regulation (EC) No. 3666/93,[3] no longer meets the requirements of efficient administrative procedure; whereas it should therefore be replaced by a new Regulation;

Notes
[1]OJ No. 13, 21.2.1962, p. 204/62.
[2]OJ No. 35, 10.5.1962, p. 1118/62.
[3]OJ No. L336, 31.12.1993, p.1.

Whereas, on the one hand, applications for negative clearance under Article 2 and notifications under Articles 4, 5 and 25 of Regulation No 17 have important legal consequences, which are favourable to the parties to an agreement, a decision or a practice, while, on the other hand, incorrect or misleading information in such applications or notifications may lead to the imposition of fines and may also entail civil law disadvantages for the parties; whereas it is therefore necessary in the interests of legal certainty to define precisely the persons entitled to submit applications and notifications, the subject matter and content of the information which such applications and notifications must contain, and the time when they become effective;

Whereas each of the parties should have the right to submit the application or the notification to the Commission; whereas, furthermore, a party exercising the right should inform the other parties in order to enable them to protect their interests; whereas applications and notifications relating to agreements, decisions or practices of associations of undertakings should be submitted only by such association;

Whereas it is for the applicants and the notifying parties to make full and honest disclosure to the Commission of the facts and circumstances which are relevant for coming to a decision on the agreements, decisions or practices concerned;

Whereas, in order to simplify and expedite their examination, it is desirable to prescribe that a form be used for applications for negative clearance relating to Article 85(1) and for notifications relating to Article 85(3); whereas the use of this form should also be possible in the case of applications for negative clearance relating to Article 86;

Whereas the Commission, in appropriate cases, will give the parties, if they so request, an opportunity before the application or the notification to discuss the intended agreement, decision or practice informally and in strict confidence; whereas, in addition, it will, after the application or notification, maintain close contact with the parties to the extent necessary to discuss with them any practical or legal problems which it discovers on a first examination of the case and if possible to remove such problems by mutual agreement;

Whereas the provisions of this Regulation must also cover cases in which applications for negative clearance relating to Article 53(1) or Article 54 of the EEA Agreement, or notifications, relating to Article 53(3) of the EEA Agreement are submitted to the Commission,

HAS ADOPTED THIS REGULATION:

Article 1   Persons entitled to submit applications and notifications

1.   The following may submit an application under Article 2 of Regulation No. 17 relating to Article 85(1) of the Treaty or a notification under Articles 4, 5 and 25 of Regulation No. 17:

(a)   any undertaking and any association of undertakings being a party to agreements or to concerted practices; and

(b)   any association of undertakings adopting decisions or engaging in practices;
which may fall within the scope of Article 85(1).

Where the application or notification is submitted by some, but not all, of the parties, referred to in point (a) of the first subparagraph, they shall give notice to the other parties.

2.   Any undertaking which may hold, alone or with other undertakings, a dominant position within the common market or in a substantial part of it, may submit an application under Article 2 of Regulation No. 17 relating to Article 86 of the Treaty.

3.   Where the application or notification is signed by representatives of persons, undertakings or associations of undertakings, such representatives shall produce written proof that they are authorised to act.

4.   Where a joint application or notification is made, a joint representative should be appointed who is authorised to transmit and receive documents on behalf of all the applicants or notifying parties.

Article 2   Submission of applications and notifications

1.   Applications under Article 2 of Regulation No. 17 relating to Article 85(1) of the Treaty and notifications under Articles 4, 5 and 25 of Regulation No. 17 shall be submitted in the manner prescribed by Form A/B as shown in the Annex to this Regulation. Form A/B may also be used for applications under Article 2 of Regulation No. 17 relating to Article 86 of the Treaty. Joint applications and joint notifications shall be submitted on a single form.

2.   Seventeen copies of each application and notification and three copies of the Annexes thereto shall be submitted to the Commission at the address indicated in Form A/B.

3.   The documents annexed to the application or notification shall be either originals or copies of the originals; in the latter case the applicant or notifying party shall confirm that they are true copies of the originals and complete.

4.   Applications and notifications shall be in one of the official languages of the Community. This language shall also be the language of the proceeding for the applicant or notifying party. Documents shall be submitted in their original language. Where the original language is not one of the official languages, a translation into the language of the proceeding shall be attached.

5.   Where applications for negative clearance relating to Article 53(1) or Article 54 of the EEA Agreement or notifications relating to Article 53(3) of the EEA Agreement are submitted, they may also be in one of the official languages of the EFTA States or the working language of the EFTA Surveillance Authority. If the language chosen for the application or notification is not an official language of the Community, the applicant or notifying party shall supplement all documentation with a translation into an official language of the Community. The language which is chosen for the translation shall be the language of the proceeding for the applicant or notifying party.

Article 3   Content of applications and notifications

1.   Applications and notifications shall contain the information, including documents, required by Form A/B. The information must be correct and complete.

2.   Applications under Article 2 of Regulation No. 17 relating to Article 86 of the Treaty shall contain a full statement of the facts, specifying, in particular, the practice concerned and the position of the undertaking or undertakings within the common market or a substantial part thereof in regard to the products or services to which the practice relates.

3.   The Commission may dispense with the obligation to provide any particular information, including documents, required by Form A/B where the

Commission considers that such information is not necessary for the examination of the case.

4. The Commission shall, without delay, acknowledge in writing to the applicant or notifying party receipt of the application or notification, and of any reply to a letter sent by the Commission pursuant to Article 4(2).

Article 4   Effective date of submission of applications and notifications

1. Without prejudice to paragraphs 2 to 5, applications and notifications shall become effective on the date on which they are received by the Commission. Where, however, the application or notification is sent by registered post, it shall become effective on the date shown on the postmark of the place of posting.

2. Where the Commission finds that the information, including documents, contained in the application or notification is incomplete in a material respect, it shall, without delay, inform the applicant or notifying party in writing of this fact and shall fix an appropriate time limit for the completion of the information. In such cases, the application or notification shall become effective on the date on which the complete information is received by the Commission.

3. Material changes in the facts contained in the application or notification which the applicant or notifying party knows or ought to know must be communicated to the Commission voluntarily and without delay.

4. Incorrect or misleading information shall be considered to be incomplete information.

5. Where, at the expiry of a period of one month following the date on which the application or notification has been received, the Commission has not provided the applicant or notifying party with the information referred to in paragraph 2, the application or notification shall be deemed to have become effective on the date of its receipt by the Commission.

Article 5   Repeal
Regulation No. 27 is repealed.

Article 6   Entry into force
This Regulation shall enter into force on 1 March 1995.

This Regulation shall be binding in its entirety and directly applicable in all Member States.

Done at Brussels, 21 December 1994.
For the Commission,
Karel VAN MIERT,
Member of the Commission

FORM A/B INTRODUCTION

Form A/B, as its Annex, is an integral part of the Commission Regulation (EC) No. 3385/94 of 21 December 1994 on the form, content and other details of applications and notifications provided for in Council Regulation No. 17 (hereinafter referred to as 'the Regulation'). It allows undertakings and associations of undertakings to apply to the Commission for negative clearance agreements or practices which may fall within the prohibitions of Article 85(1) and Article 86 of the EC Treaty, or within Articles 53(1) and 54 of the EEA

Agreement or to notify such agreement and apply to have it exempted from the prohibition set out in Article 85(1) by virtue of the provisions of Article 85(3) of the EC Treaty or from the prohibition of Article 53(1) by virtue of the provisions of Article 53(3) of the EEA Agreement. To facilitate the use of the Form A/B the following pages set out:

— in which situations it is necessary to make an application or a notification (Point A),

— to which authority (the Commission or the EFTA Surveillance Authority) the application or notification should be made (Point B),

— for which purposes the application or notification can be used (Point C),

— what information must be given in the application or notification (Points D, E and F),

— who can make an application or notification (Point G),

— how to make an application or notification (Point H),

— how the business secrets of the undertakings can be protected (Point I),

— how certain technical terms used in the operational part of the Form A/B should be interpreted (Point J), and

— the subsequent procedure after the application or notification has been made (Point K).

A.   IN WHICH SITUATIONS IS IT NECESSARY TO MAKE AN APPLICATION OR A NOTIFICATION?
I.   PURPOSE OF THE COMPETITION RULES OF THE EC TREATY AND THE EEA AGREEMENT

1.   Purpose of the EC Competition Rules

The purpose of the competition rules is to prevent the distortion of competition in the common market by restrictive practices or the abuse of dominant positions. They apply to any enterprise trading directly or indirectly in the common market, wherever established.

Article 85(1) of the EC Treaty prohibits restrictive agreements, decisions or concerted practices (arrangements) which may affect trade between Member States, and Article 85(2) declares agreements and decisions containing such restrictions void (although the Court of Justice has held that if restrictive terms of agreements are severable, only those terms are void); Article 85(3), however, provides for exemption of arrangements with beneficial effects, if its conditions are met. Article 86 prohibits the abuse of a dominant position which may affect trade between Member States. The original procedures for implementing these Articles, which provide for 'negative clearance' and exemption pursuant to Article 85(3),were laid down in Regulation No. 17.

2.   Purpose of the EEA competition rules

The competition rules of the Agreement on the European Economic Area (concluded between the Community, the Member States and the EFTA States)[1] are based on the same principles as those contained in the Community competition rules and have the same purpose, i.e. to prevent the distortion of competition in the EEA territory by cartels or the abuse of dominant position. They apply to any enterprise trading directly or indirectly in the EEA territory, wherever established.

Article 53(1) of the EEA Agreement (the text of Articles 53, 54 and 56 of the EEA Agreement is reproduced in Annex I) prohibits restrictive agreements, decisions or concerted practices (arrangements) which may affect trade between the Community and one or more EFTA States (or between EFTA States), and Article 53(2) declares agreements or decisions containing such restrictions void; Article 53(3), however, provides for exemption of arrangements with beneficial effects, if its conditions are met.

Article 54 prohibits the abuse of a dominant position which may affect trade between the Community and one or more EFTA States (or between EFTA States). The procedures for implementing these Articles, which provide for 'negative clearance' and exemption pursuant to Article 53(3), are laid down in Regulation No. 17, supplemented for EEA purposes, by Protocols 21, 22 and 23 to the EEA Agreement.[2]

Notes
[1]See list of Member States and EFTA States in Annex III.
[2]Reproduced in Annex I.

II. THE SCOPE OF THE COMPETITION RULES OF THE EC TREATY AND THE EEA AGREEMENT

The applicability of Articles 85 and 86 of the EC Treaty and Articles 53 and 54 of the EEA Agreement depends on the circumstances of each individual case. It presupposes that the arrangement or behaviour satisfies all the conditions set out in the relevant provisions. This question must consequently be examined before any application for negative clearance or any notification is made.

1. Negative clearance

The negative clearance procedure allows undertakings to ascertain whether the Commission considers that their arrangement or their behaviour is or is not prohibited by Article 85(1), or Article 86 of the EC Treaty or by Article 53(1) or Article 54 of the EEA Agreement. This procedure is governed by Article 2 of Regulation No. 17. The negative clearance takes the form of a decision by which the Commission certifies that, on the basis of the facts in its possession, there are no grounds pursuant to Article 85(1) or Article 86 of the EC Treaty or under Article 53(1) or Article 54 of the EEA Agreement for action on its part in respect of the arrangement or behaviour. There is, however, no point in making an application when the arrangements or the behaviour are manifestly not prohibited by the abovementioned provisions. Nor is the Commission obliged to give negative clearance. Article 2 of Regulation No. 17 states that '. . . the Commission may certify . . .'. The Commission issues negative clearance decisions only where an important problem of interpretation has to be solved. In the other cases it reacts to the application by sending a comfort letter.

The Commission has published several notices relating the interpretation of Article 85(1) of the EC Treaty. They define certain categories of agreements which, by their nature or because of their minor importance, are not caught by the prohibition.[1]

Note
[1]See Annex II.

2. Exemption

The procedure for exemption pursuant to Article 85(3) of the EC Treaty and Article 53(3) of the EEA Agreement allows companies to enter into arrangements which, in fact, offer economic advantages but which, without exemption, would be prohibited by Article 85(1) of the EC Treaty or by Article 53(1) of the EEA Agreement. This procedure is governed by Articles 4, 6 and 8 and, for the new Member States, also by Articles 5, 7 and 25 of Regulation No. 17. The exemption takes the form of a decision by the Commission declaring Article 85(1) of the EC Treaty or Article 53(1) of the EEA Agreement to be inapplicable to the arrangements described in the decision. Article 8 requires the Commission to specify the period of validity of any such decision, allows the Commission to attach conditions and obligations and provides for decisions to be amended or revoked or specified acts by the parties to be prohibited in certain circumstances, notably if the decisions were based on incorrect information or if there is any material change in the facts.

The Commission has adopted a number of regulations granting exemptions to categories of agreements.[1] Some of these regulations provide that some agreements may benefit from exemption only if they are notified to the Commission pursuant to Article 4 or 5 of Regulation No. 17 with a view to obtaining exemption, and the benefit of the opposition procedure is claimed in the notification. A decision granting exemption may have retroactive effect, but, with certain exceptions, cannot be made effective earlier than the date of notification (Article 6 of Regulation No. 17). Should the Commission find that notified arrangements are indeed prohibited and cannot be exempted and, therefore, take a decision condemning them, the participants are nevertheless protected, between the date of the notification and the date of the decision, against fines for any infringement described in the notification (Article 3 and Article 15 (5) and (6) of Regulation No. 17). Normally the Commission issues exemption decisions only in cases of particular legal, economic or political importance. In the other cases it terminates the procedure by sending a comfort letter.

Note
[1]See Annex II.

B.   TO WHICH AUTHORITY SHOULD APPLICATION OR NOTIFICATION BE MADE?

The applications and notifications must be made to the authority which has competence for the matter. The Commission is responsible for the application of the competition rules of the EC Treaty. However there is shared competence in relation to the application of the competition rules of the EEA agreement.

The competence of the Commission and of the EFTA Surveillance Authority to apply the EEA competition rules follows from Article 56 of the EEA Agreement. Applications and notifications relating to agreements, decisions or concerted practices liable to affect trade between Member States should be addressed to the Commission unless their effects on trade between Member States or on competition within the Community are not appreciable within the meaning of the Commission notice of 1986 on agreements of minor importance.[1] Furthermore, all restrictive agreements, decisions or concerted practices affecting trade between one Member State and one or more EFTA States fall within the competence of the Commission, provided that the undertakings concerned achieve more than 67% of their combined EEA-wide turnover

Notes
[1]OJ No. C 231, 12.9.1986, p. 2.

within the Community.[2] However, if the effects of such agreements, decisions or concerted practices on trade between Member States or on competition within the Community are not appreciable, the notification should, where necessary, be addressed to the EFTA Surveillance Authority. All other agreements, decisions and concerted practices falling under Article 53 of the EEA Agreement should be notified to the EFTA Surveillance Authority (the address of which is given in Annex III).

Applications for negative clearance regarding Article 54 of the EEA Agreement should be lodged with the Commission if the dominant position exists only in the Community, or with the EFTA Surveillance Authority, if the dominant position exists only in the whole of the territory of the EFTA States, or a substantial part of it. Only where the dominant position exists within both territories should the rules outlined above with respect to Article 53 be applied. The Commission will apply, as a basis for appraisal, the competition rules of the EC Treaty. Where the case falls under the EEA Agreement and is attributed to the Commission pursuant to Article 56 of that Agreement, it will simultaneously apply the EEA rules.

Notes
[2]For a definition of 'turnover' in this context, see Articles 2, 3 and 4 of Protocol 22 to the EEA Agreement reproduced in Annex I.

C.   THE PURPOSE OF THIS FORM

Form A/B lists the questions that must be answered and the information and documents that must be provided when applying for the following:

— a negative clearance with regard to Article 85(1) of the EC Treaty and/or Article 53(1) of the EEA Agreement, pursuant to Article 2 of Regulation No. 17, with respect to agreements between undertakings, decisions by associations of undertakings and concerted practices,

— an exemption pursuant to Article 85(3) of the EC Treaty and/or Article 53(3) of the EEA Agreement with respect to agreements between undertakings, decisions by associations of undertakings and concerted practices,

— the benefit of the opposition procedure contained in certain Commission regulations granting exemption by category.

This form allows undertakings applying for negative clearance to notify, at the same time, in order to obtain an exemption in the event that the Commission reaches the conclusion that no negative clearance can be granted. Applications for negative clearance and notifications relating to Article 85 of the EC Treaty shall be submitted in the manner prescribed by form A/B (see Article 2(1), first sentence of the Regulation). This form can also be used by undertakings that wish to apply for a negative clearance from Article 86 of the EC Treaty or Article 53 of the EEA Agreement, pursuant to Article 2 of Regulation No. 17. Applicants requesting negative clearance from Article 86 are not required to use form A/B. They are nonetheless strongly recommended to give all the information requested below to ensure that their application gives a full statement of the facts (see Article 2(1), second sentence of the Regulation).

The applications or notifications made on the form A/B issued by the EFTA side are equally valid. However, if the agreements, decisions or practices concerned fall solely within Articles 85 or 86 of the EC Treaty, i. e. have no

EEA relevance whatsoever, it is advisable to use the present form established by the Commission.

D.   WHICH CHAPTERS OF THE FORM SHOULD BE COMPLETED?

The operational part of this form is sub-divided into four chapters.

Undertakings wishing to make an application for a negative clearance or a notification must complete Chapters I, II and IV. An exception to this rule is provided for in the case where the application or notification concerns an agreement concerning the creation of a cooperative joint venture of a structural character if the parties wish to benefit from an accelerated procedure. In this situation Chapters I, III and IV should be completed.

In 1992, the Commission announced that it had adopted new internal administrative rules that provided that certain applications and notifications — those of cooperative joint ventures which are structural in nature — would be dealt with within fixed deadlines. In such cases the services of the Commission will, within two months of receipt of the complete notification of the agreement, inform the parties in writing of the results of the initial analysis of the case and, as appropriate, the nature and probable length of the administrative procedure they intend to engage. The contents of this letter may vary according to the characteristics of the case under investigation:

—in cases not posing any problems, the Commission will send a comfort letter confirming the compatibility of the agreement with Article 85(1) or (3),

—if a comfort letter cannot be sent because of the need to settle the case by formal decision, the Commission will inform the undertakings concerned of its intention to adopt a decision either granting or rejecting exemption,

—if the Commission has serious doubts as to the compatibility of the agreement with the competition rules, it will send a letter to the parties giving notice of an in-depth examination which may, depending on the case, result in a decision either prohibiting, exempting subject to conditions and obligations, or simply exempting the agreement in question.

This new accelerated procedure, applicable since 1 January 1993, is based entirely on the principle of self-discipline. The deadline of two months from the complete notification — intended for the initial examination of the case — does not constitute a statutory term and is therefore in no way legally binding. However, the Commission will do its best to abide by it. The Commission reserves the right, moreover, to extend this accelerated procedure to other forms of cooperation between undertakings.

A cooperative joint venture of a structural nature is one that involves an important change in the structure and organization of the business assets of the parties to the agreement. This may occur because the joint venture takes over or extends existing activities of the parent companies or because it undertakes new activities on their behalf. Such operations are characterised by the commitment of significant financial, material and/or non-tangible assets such as intellectual property rights and knowhow. Structural joint ventures are therefore normally intended to operate on a medium- or long-term basis.

This concept includes certain 'partial function' joint ventures which take over one or several specific functions within the parents' business activity without access to the market, in particular research and development and/or production. It also covers those 'full function' joint ventures which give rise to coordination of the competitive behaviour of independent undertakings, in particular between the parties to the joint venture or between them and the joint venture.

In order to respect the internal deadline, it is important that the Commission has available on notification all the relevant information reasonably available to the notifying parties that is necessary for it to assess the impact of the operation in question on competition. Form A/B therefore contains a special section (Chapter III) that must be completed only by persons notifying cooperative joint ventures of a structural character that wish to benefit from the accelerated procedure.

Persons notifying joint ventures of a structural character that wish to claim the benefit of the aforementioned accelerated procedure should therefore complete Chapters I, III and IV of this form. Chapter III contains a series of detailed questions necessary for the Commission to assess the relevant market(s) and the position of the parties to the joint venture on that (those) market(s).

Where the parties do not wish to claim the benefit of an accelerated procedure for their joint ventures of a structural character they should complete Chapters I, II and IV of this form. Chapter II contains a far more limited range of questions on the relevant market(s) and the position of the parties to the operation in question on that (those) market(s), but sufficient to enable the Commission to commence its examination and investigation.

E.   THE NEED FOR COMPLETE INFORMATION

The receipt of a valid notification by the Commission has two main consequences.

First, it affords immunity from fines from the date that the valid notification is received by the Commission with respect to applications made in order to obtain exemption (see Article 15 (5) of Regulation No. 17). Second, until a valid notification is received, the Commission cannot grant an exemption pursuant to Article 85(3) of the EC Treaty and/or Article 53(3) of the EEA Agreement, and any exemption that is granted can be effective only from the date of receipt of a valid notification.[1] Thus, whilst there is no legal obligation to notify as such, unless and until an arrangement that falls within the scope of Article 85(1) and/or Article 53(1) has not been notified and is, therefore, not capable of being exempted, it may be declared void by a national court pursuant to Article 85(2) and/or Article 53(2).[2]

Where an undertaking is claiming the benefit of a group exemption by recourse to an opposition procedure, the period within which the Commission must oppose the exemption by category only applies from the date that a valid notification is received. This is also true of the two months' period imposed on the Commission services for an initial analysis of applications for negative clearance and notifications relating to cooperative joint ventures of a structural character which benefit from the accelerated procedure.

A valid application or notification for this purpose means one that is not incomplete (see Article 3(1) of the Regulation). This is subject to two

Notes
[1] Subject to the qualification provided for in Article 4(2) of Regulation No. 17.
[2] For further details of the consequences of non-notification see the Commission notice on cooperation between national Courts and the Commission (OJ No. C39, 13.2.1993, p. 6).

qualifications. First, if the information or documents required by this form are not reasonably available to you in part or in whole, the Commission will accept that a notification is complete and thus valid notwithstanding the failure to provide such information, providing that you give reasons for the unavailability of the information, and provide your best estimates for missing data together with the sources for the estimates. Indications as to where any of the requested information or documents that are unavailable to you could be obtained by the Commission must also be provided.

Second, the Commission only requires the submission of information relevant and necessary to its inquiry into the notified operation. In some cases not all the information required by this form will be necessary for this purpose. The Commission may therefore dispense with the obligation to provide certain information required by this form (see Article 3(3) of the Regulation. This provision enables, where appropriate, each application or notification to be tailored to each case so that only the information strictly necessary for the Commission's examination is provided. This avoids unnecessary administrative burdens being imposed on undertakings, in particular on small and medium-sized ones. Where the information or documents required by this form are not provided for this reason, the application or notification should indicate the reasons why the information is considered to be unnecessary to the Commission's investigation.

Where the Commission finds that the information contained in the application or notification is incomplete in a material respect, it will, within one month from receipt, inform the applicant or the notifying party in writing of this fact and the nature of the missing information. In such cases, the application or notification shall become effective on the date on which the complete information is received by the Commission. If the Commission has not informed the applicant or the notifying party within the one month period that the application or notification is incomplete in a material respect, the application or notification will be deemed to be complete and valid (see Article 4 of the Regulation). It is also important that undertakings inform the Commission of important changes in the factual situation including those of which they become aware after the application or notification has been submitted. The Commission must, therefore, be informed immediately of any changes to an agreement, decision or practice which is the subject of an application or notification (see Article 4(3) of the Regulation). Failure to inform the Commission of such relevant changes could result in any negative clearance decision being without effect or in the withdrawal of any exemption decision[3] adopted by the Commission on the basis of the notification.

Note

[3] See point (a) of Article 8(3) of Regulation No. 17.

F. THE NEED FOR ACCURATE INFORMATION

In addition to the requirement that the application or notification be complete, it is important that you ensure that the information provided is accurate (see Article 3(1) of the Regulation). Article 15(1)(a) of Regulation No. 17 states that the Commission may, by decision, impose on undertakings or associations of undertakings fines of up to ECU 5,000 where, intentionally or negligently, they supply incorrect or misleading information in an application for negative clearance or notification. Such information is, moreover, considered to be incomplete (see Article 4(4) of the Regulation), so that the parties cannot benefit from the advantages of the opposition procedure or accelerated procedure (see above, Point E).

G. WHO CAN LODGE AN APPLICATION OR A NOTIFICATION?

Any of the undertakings party to an agreement, decision or practice of the kind described in Articles 85 or 86 of the EC Treaty and Articles 53 or 54 of the EEA Agreement may submit an application for negative clearance, in relation to Article 85 and Article 53, or a notification requesting an exemption. An association of undertakings may submit an application or a notification in relation to decisions taken or practices pursued into in the operation of the association.

In relation to agreements and concerted practices between undertakings it is common practice for all the parties involved to submit a joint application or notification. Although the Commission strongly recommends this approach, because it is helpful to have the views of all the parties directly concerned at the same time, it is not obligatory. Any of the parties to an agreement may submit an application or notification in their individual capacities, but in such circumstances the notifying party should inform all the other parties to the agreement, decision or practice of that fact (see Article 1(3) of the Regulation). They may also provide them with a copy of the completed form, where relevant once confidential information and business secrets have been deleted (see below, operational part, question 1.2).

Where a joint application or notification is submitted, it has also become common practice to appoint a joint representative to act on behalf of all the undertakings involved, both in making the application or notification, and in dealing with any subsequent contacts with the Commission (see Article 1(4) of the Regulation). Again, whilst this is helpful, it is not obligatory, and all the undertakings jointly submitting an application or a notification may sign it in their individual capacities.

H. HOW TO SUBMIT AN APPLICATION OR NOTIFICATION

Applications and notifications may be submitted in any of the official languages of the European Community or of an EFTA State (see Article 2(4) and (5) of the Regulation). In order to ensure rapid proceedings, it is, however, recommended to use, in case of an application or notification to the EFTA Surveillance Authority one of the official languages of an EFTA State or the working language of the EFTA Surveillance Authority, which is English, or, in case of an application or notification to the Commission, one of the official languages of the Community or the working language of the EFTA Surveillance Authority. This language will thereafter be the language of the proceeding for the applicant or notifying party.

Form A/B is not a form to be filled in. Undertakings should simply provide the information requested by this form, using its sections and paragraph numbers, signing a declaration as stated in Section 19 below, and annexing the required supporting documentation. Supporting documents shall be submitted in their original language; where this is not an official language of the Community they must be translated into the language of the proceeding. The supporting documents may be originals or copies of the originals (see Article

2(4) of the Regulation). All information requested in this form shall, unless otherwise stated, relate to the calendar year preceding that of the application or notification. Where information is not reasonably available on this basis (for example if accounting periods are used that are not based on the calendar year, or the previous year's figures are not yet available) the most recently available information should be provided and reasons given why figures on the basis of the calendar year preceding that of the application or notification cannot be provided.

Financial data may be provided in the currency in which the official audited accounts of the undertaking(s) concerned are prepared or in ECUS. In the latter case the exchange rate used for the conversion must be stated. Seventeen copies of each application or notification, but only three copies of all supporting documents must be provided (see Article 2(2) of the Regulation).

The application or notification is to be sent to:

Commission of the European Communities,
Directorate-General for Competition (DG IV),
The Registrar,
200, Rue de la Loi,
B-1049 Brussels.

or be delivered by hand during Commission working days and official working hours at the following address:

Commission of the European Communities,
Directorate-General for Competition (DG IV),
The Registrar,
158, Avenue de Cortenberg,
B-1040 Brussels.

I. CONFIDENTIALITY

Article 214 of the EC Treaty, Article 20 of Regulation No. 17, Article 9 of Protocol 23 to the EEA Agreement, Article 122 of the EEA Agreement and Articles 20 and 21 of Chapter II of Protocol 4 to the Agreement between the EFTA States on the establishment of a Surveillance Authority and of a Court of Justice require the Commission, the Member States, the EEA Surveillance Authority and EFTA States not to disclose information of the kind covered by the obligation of professional secrecy. On the other hand, Regulation No. 17 requires the Commission to publish a summary of the application or notification, should it intend to take a favourable decision. In this publication, the Commission '. . . shall have regard to the legitimate interest of undertakings in the protection of their business secrets' (Article 19(3) of Regulation No. 17; see also Article 21(2) in relation to the publication of decisions). In this connection, if an undertaking believes that its interests would be harmed if any of the information it is asked to supply were to be published or otherwise divulged to other undertakings, it should put all such information in a separate annex with each page clearly marked 'Business Secrets'. It should also give reasons why any information identified as confidential or secret should not be divulged or published. (See below, Section 5 of the operational part that requests a non-confidential summary of the notification).

J. SUBSEQUENT PROCEDURE

The application or notification is registered in the Registry of the Directorate-General for Competition (DG IV). The date of receipt by the Commission (or the date of posting if sent by registered post) is the effective date of the submission (see Article 4(1) of the Regulation). However, special rules apply to incomplete applications and notifications (see above under Point E). The Commission will acknowledge receipt of all applications and notifications in writing, indicating the case number attributed to the file. This number must be used in all future correspondence regarding the notification. The receipt of acknowledgement does not prejudge the question whether the application or notification is valid. Further information may be sought from the parties or from third parties (Articles 11 to 14 of Regulation No. 17) and suggestions might be made as to amendments to the arrangements that might make them acceptable. Equally, a short preliminary notice may be published in the C series of the Official Journal of the European Communities, stating the names of the interested undertakings, the groups to which they belong, the economic sectors involved and the nature of the arrangements, and inviting third party comments (see below, operational part, Section 5).

Where a notification is made together for the purpose of the application of the opposition procedure, the Commission may oppose the grant of the benefit of the group exemption with respect to the notified agreement. If the Commission opposes the claim, and unless it subsequently withdraws its opposition, that notification will then be treated as an application for an individual exemption. If, after examination, the Commission intends to grant the application for negative clearance or exemption, it is obliged (by Article 19(3) of Regulation No. 17) to publish a summary and invite comments from third parties.

Subsequently, a preliminary draft decision has to be submitted to and discussed with the Advisory Committee on Restrictive Practices and Dominant Positions composed of officials of the competent authorities of the Member States in the matter of restrictive practices and monopolies (Article 10 of Regulation No. 17) and attended, where the case falls within the EEA Agreement, by representatives of the EFTA Surveillance Authority and the EFTA States which will already have received a copy of the application or notification. Only then, and providing nothing has happened to change the Commission's intention, can it adopt the envisaged decision.

Files are often closed without any formal decision being taken, for example, because it is found that the arrangements are already covered by a block exemption, or because they do not call for any action by the Commission, at least in circumstances at that time. In such cases comfort letters are sent. Although not a Commission decision, a comfort letter indicates how the Commission's departments view the case on the facts currently in their possession which means that the Commission could where necessary — for example, if it were to be asserted that a contract was void under Article 85(2) of the EC Treaty and/or Article 53(2) of the EEA Agreement — take an appropriate decision to clarify the legal situation.

K.   DEFINITIONS USED IN THE OPERATIONAL PART OF THIS FORM

Agreement: The word 'agreement' is used to refer to all categories of arrangements, i.e. agreements between undertakings, decisions by associations of undertakings and concerted practices.

Year: All references to the word 'year' in this form shall be read as meaning calendar year, unless otherwise stated.

Group: A group relationship exists for the purpose of this form where one undertaking:

— owns more than half the capital or business assets of another undertaking, or

— has the power to exercise more than half the voting rights in another undertaking, or

— has the power to appoint more than half the members of the supervisory board, board of directors or bodies legally representing the undertaking, or

— has the right to manage the affairs of another undertaking.

An undertaking which is jointly controlled by several other undertakings (joint venture) forms part of the group of each of these undertakings.

Relevant product market: questions 6.1 and 11.1 of this form require the undertaking or individual submitting the notification to define the relevant product and/or service market(s) that are likely to be affected by the agreement in question. That definition(s) is then used as the basis for a number of other questions contained in this form. The definition(s) thus submitted by the notifying parties are referred to in this form as the relevant product market(s). These words can refer to a market made up either of products or of services.

Relevant geographic market: questions 6.2 and 11.2 of this form require the undertaking or individual submitting the notification to define the relevant geographic market(s) that are likely to be affected by the agreement in question. That definition(s) is then used as the basis for a number of other questions contained in this form. The definition(s) thus submitted by the notifying parties are referred to in this form as the relevant geographic market(s).

Relevant product and geographic market: by virtue of the combination of their replies to questions 6 and 11 the parties provide their definition of the relevant market(s) affected by the notified agreement(s). That (those) definition(s) is (are) then used as the basis for a number of other questions contained in this form. The definition(s) thus submitted by the notifying parties is referred to in this form as the relevant geographic and product market(s).

Notification: this form can be used to make an application for negative clearance and/or a notification requesting an exemption. The word 'notification' is used to refer to either an application or a notification.

Parties and notifying party: the word 'party' is used to refer to all the undertakings which are party to the agreement being notified. As a notification may be submitted by only one of the undertakings which are party to an agreement, 'notifying party' is used to refer only to the undertaking or undertakings actually submitting the notification.

OPERATIONAL PART

PLEASE MAKE SURE THAT THE FIRST PAGE OF YOUR APPLICATION OR NOTIFICATION CONTAINS THE WORDS 'APPLICATION FOR NEGATIVE CLEARANCE/NOTIFICATION IN ACCORDANCE WITH FORM A/B'

CHAPTER I

Sections concerning the parties, their groups and the agreement (to be completed for all notifications)

Section 1   Identity of the undertakings or persons submitting the notification

1.1   Please list the undertakings on behalf of which the notification is being submitted and indicate their legal denomination or commercial name, shortened or commonly used as appropriate (if it differs from the legal denomination).

1.2   If the notification is being submitted on behalf of only one or some of the undertakings party to the agreement being notified, please confirm that the remaining undertakings have been informed of that fact and indicate whether they have received a copy of the notification, with relevant confidential information and business secrets deleted.[1] (In such circumstances a copy of the edited copy of the notification which has been provided to such other undertakings should be annexed to this notification.)

1.3   If a joint notification is being submitted, has a joint representative[2] been appointed?[3]

If yes, please give the details requested in 1.3.1 to 1.3.3 below.

If no, please give details of any representatives who have been authorised to act for each or either of the parties to the agreement indicating who they represent.

1.3.1   Name of representative.

1.3.2   Address of representative.

1.3.3   Telephone and fax number of representative.

1.4   In cases where one or more representatives have been appointed, an authority to act on behalf of the undertaking(s) submitting the notification must accompany the notification.

Notes

[1]The Commission is aware that in exceptional cases it may not be practicable to inform non-notifying parties to the notified agreement of the fact that it has been notified, or to provide them a copy of the notification. This may be the case, for example, where a standard agreement is being notified that is concluded with a large number of undertakings. Where this is the case you should state the reasons why it has not been practicable to follow the standard procedure set out in this question.

[2]For the purposes of this question a representative means an individual or undertaking formally appointed to make the notification or application on behalf of the party or parties submitting the notification. This should be distinguished from the situation where the notification is signed by an officer of the company or companies in question. In the latter situation no representative is appointed.

[3]It is not mandatory to appoint representatives for the purpose of completing and/or submitting this notification. This question only requires the identification of representatives where the notifying parties have chosen to appoint them.

Section 2 Information on the parties to the agreement and the groups to which they belong

2.1 State the name and address of the parties to the agreement being notified, and the country of their incorporation.

2.2 State the nature of the business of each of the parties to the agreement being notified.

2.3 For each of the parties to the agreement, give the name of a person that can be contacted, together with his or her name, address, telephone number, fax number and position held in the undertaking.

2.4 Identify the corporate groups to which the parties to the agreement being notified belong. State the sectors in which these groups are active, and the world-wide turnover of each group.[1]

Note

[1]For the calculation of turnover in the banking and insurance sectors see Article 3 of Protocol 22 to the EEA Agreement.

Section 3 Procedural matters

3.1 Please state whether you have made any formal submission to any other competition authorities in relation to the agreement in question. If yes, state which authorities, the individual or department in question, and the nature of the contact. In addition to this, mention any earlier proceedings or informal contacts, of which you are aware, with the Commission and/or the EFTA Surveillance Authority and any earlier proceedings with any national authorities or courts in the Community or in EFTA concerning these or any related agreements.

3.2 Please summarise any reasons for any claim that the case involves an issue of exceptional urgency.

3.3 The Commission has stated that where notifications do not have particular political, economic or legal significance for the Community they will normally be dealt with by means of comfort letter.[1] Would you be satisfied with a comfort letter? If you consider that it would be inappropriate to deal with the notified agreement in this manner, please explain the reasons for this view.

3.4 State whether you intend to produce further supporting facts or arguments not yet available and, if so, on which points.[2]

Notes

[1]See paragraph 14 of the notice on cooperation between national courts and the Commission in applying Articles 85 and 86 of the EC Treaty (OJ No. C39, 13.2.1993, p. 6).

[2]In so far as the notifying parties provide the information required by this form that was reasonably available to them at the time of notification, the fact that the parties intend to provide further supporting facts or documentation in due course does not prevent the notification being valid at the time of notification and, in the case of structural joint ventures where the accelerated procedure is being claimed, the two month deadline commencing.

Section 4 Full details of the arrangements

4.1 Please summarise the nature, content and objectives pursued by the agreement being notified.

4.2 Detail any provisions contained in the agreements which may restrict the parties in their freedom to take independent commercial decisions, for example regarding:

— buying or selling prices, discounts or other trading conditions,
— the quantities of goods to be manufactured or distributed or services to be offered,
— technical development or investment,
— the choice of markets or sources of supply,
— purchases from or sales to third parties,
— whether to apply similar terms for the supply of equivalent goods or services,
— whether to offer different services separately or together.

If you are claiming the benefit of the opposition procedure, identify in this list the restrictions that exceed those automatically exempted by the relevant regulation.

4.3 State between which Member States of the Community and/or EFTA States[1] trade may be affected by the arrangements. Please give reasons for your reply to this question, giving data on trade flows where relevant. Furthermore please state whether trade between the Community or the EEA territory and any third countries is affected, again giving reasons for your reply.

Note
[1] See list in Annex II.

Section 5 Non-confidential Summary

Shortly following receipt of a notification, the Commission may publish a short notice inviting third party comments on the agreement in question.[1] As the objective pursued by the Commission in publishing an informal preliminary notice is to receive third party comments as soon as possible after the notification has been received, such a notice is usually published without first providing it to the notifying parties for their comments. This section requests the information to be used in an informal preliminary notice in the event that the Commission decides to issue one. It is important, therefore, that your replies to these questions do not contain any business secrets or other confidential information.

1. State the names of the parties to the agreement notified and the groups of undertakings to which they belong.
2. Give a short summary of the nature and objectives of the agreement. As a guideline this summary should not exceed 100 words.
3. Identify the product sectors affected by the agreement in question.

Note
[1] An example of such a notice figures in annex 1 to this Form. Such a notice should be distinguished from a formal notice published pursuant to Article 19(3) of Regulation No. 17. An Article 19(3) notice is relatively detailed, and gives an indication of the Commission's current approach in the case in question. Section 5 only seeks information that will be used in a short preliminary notice, and not a notice published pursuant to Article 19(3).

CHAPTER II SECTION CONCERNING THE RELEVANT MARKET

(to be completed for all notifications except those relating to structural joint ventures for which accelerated treatment is claimed)

Section 6 The relevant market

A relevant product market comprises all those products and/or services which are regarded as interchangeable or substitutable by the consumer, by reason of the products' characteristics, their prices and their intended use. The following factors are normally considered to be relevant to the determination of the relevant product market and should be taken into account in this analysis:[1]

— the degree of physical similarity between the products/services in question,

— any differences in the end use to which the goods are put,

— differences in price between two products,

— the cost of switching between two potentially competing products,

— established or entrenched consumer preferences for one type or category of product over another,

— industry-wide product classifications (e.g. classifications maintained by trade associations). The relevant geographic market comprises the area in which the undertakings concerned are involved in the supply of products or services, in which the conditions of competition are sufficiently homogeneous and which can be distinguished from neighbouring areas because, in particular, conditions of competition are appreciably different in those areas. Factors relevant to the assessment of the relevant geographic market include[2] the nature and characteristics of the products or services concerned, the existence of entry barriers or consumer preferences, appreciable differences of the undertakings' market share or substantial price differences between neighbouring areas, and transport costs.

6.1   In the light of the above please explain the definition of the relevant product market or markets that in your opinion should form the basis of the Commission's analysis of the notification. In your answer, please give reasons for assumptions or findings, and explain how the factors outlined above have been taken into account. In particular, please state the specific products or services directly or indirectly affected by the agreement being notified and identify the categories of goods viewed as substitutable in your market definition. In the questions figuring below, this (or these) definition(s) will be referred to as 'the relevant product market(s)'.

6.2   Please explain the definition of the relevant geographic market or markets that in your opinion should form the basis of the Commission's analysis of the notification. In your answer, please give reasons for assumptions or findings, and explain how the factors outlined above have been taken into account. In particular, please identify the countries in which the parties are active in the relevant product market(s), and in the event that you consider the relevant geographic market to be wider than the individual Member States of the Community or EFTA on which the parties to the agreement are active, give the reasons for this.

In the questions below, this (or these) definition(s) will be referred to as 'the relevant geographic market(s)'.

Notes
[1]This list is not, however, exhaustive, and notifying parties may refer to other factors.
[2]This list is not, however, exhaustive, and notifying parties may refer to other factors.

Section 7   Group members operating on the same markets as the parties

7.1   For each of the parties to the agreement being notified, provide a list of all undertakings belonging to the same group which are:

7.1.1   active in the relevant product market(s);

7.1.2   active in markets neighbouring the relevant product market(s) (i.e. active in products and/or services that represent imperfect and partial substitutes for those included in your definition of the relevant product market(s)).

Such undertakings must be identified even if they sell the product or service in question in other geographic areas than those in which the parties to the notified agreement operate. Please list the name, place of incorporation, exact product manufactured and the geographic scope of operation of each group member.

Section 8   The position of the parties on the affected relevant product markets

Information requested in this section must be provided for the groups of the parties as a whole. It is not sufficient to provide such information only in relation to the individual undertakings directly concerned by the agreement.

8.1   In relation to each relevant product market(s) identified in your reply to question 6.1 please provide the following information:

8.1.1   the market shares of the parties on the relevant geographic market during the previous three years;

8.1.2   where different, the market shares of the parties in

(a)   the EEA territory as a whole,

(b)   the Community,

(c)   the territory of the EFTA States and

(d)   each EC Member State and EFTA State during the previous three years.[1]

For this section, where market shares are less than 20%, please state simply which of the following bands are relevant: 0 to 5%, 5 to 10%, 10 to 15%, 15 to 20%.

For the purpose of answering these questions, market share may be calculated either on the basis of value or volume. Justification for the figures provided must be given. Thus, for each answer, total market value/volume must be stated, together with the sales/turnover of each of the parties in question. The source or sources of the information should also be given (e.g. official statistics, estimates, etc.), and where possible, copies should be provided of documents from which information has been taken.

Note

[1]Where the relevant geographic market has been defined as world wide, these figures must be given regarding the EEA, the Community, the territory of the EFTA States, and each EC Member State. Where the relevant geographic market has been defined as the Community, these figures must be given for the EEA, the territory of the EFTA States, and each EC Member State. Where the market has been defined as national, these figures must be given for the EEA, the Community and the territory of the EFTA States.

Section 9   The position of competitors and customers on the relevant product market(s)

Information requested in this section must be provided for the group of the parties as a whole and not in relation to the individual companies directly concerned by the agreement notified.

For the (all) relevant product and geographic market(s) in which the parties have a combined market share exceeding 15%, the following questions must be answered.

9.1   Please identify the five main competitors of the parties. Please identify the company and give your best estimate as to their market share in the relevant geographic market(s). Please also provide address, telephone and fax number, and, where possible, the name of a contact person at each company identified.

9.2   Please identify the five main customers of each of the parties. State company name, address, telephone and fax numbers, together with the name of a contact person.

Section 10   Market entry and potential competition in product and geographic terms

For the (all) relevant product and geographic market(s) in which the parties have a combined market share exceeding 15%, the following questions must be answered.

10.1   Describe the various factors influencing entry in product terms into the relevant product market(s) that exist in the present case (i.e. what barriers exist to prevent undertakings that do not presently manufacture goods within the relevant product market(s) entering this market(s)). In so doing take account of the following where appropriate:

— to what extent is entry to the markets influenced by the requirement of government authorisation or standard setting in any form? Are there any legal or regulatory controls on entry to these markets?

— to what extent is entry to the markets influenced by the availability of raw materials?

— to what extent is entry to the markets influenced by the length of contracts between an undertaking and its suppliers and/or customers?

— describe the importance of research and development and in particular the importance of licensing patents, know-how and other rights in these markets.

10.2   Describe the various factors influencing entry in geographic terms into the relevant geographic market(s) that exist in the present case (i.e. what barriers exist to prevent undertakings already producing and/or marketing products within the relevant product market(s) but in areas outside the relevant geographic market(s) extending the scope of their sales into the relevant geographic market(s)?). Please give reasons for your answer, explaining, where relevant, the importance of the following factors:

— trade barriers imposed by law, such as tariffs, quotas etc.,

— local specification or technical requirements,

— procurement policies,

— the existence of adequate and available local distribution and retailing facilities,

— transport costs,

— entrenched consumer preferences for local brands or products,

— language.

Have any new undertakings entered the relevant product market(s) in geographic areas where the parties sell during the last three years? Please provide this information with respect to both new entrants in product terms and new entrants in geographic terms. If such entry has occurred, please identify the undertaking(s) concerned (name, address, telephone and fax numbers, and, where possible, contact person), and provide your best estimate of their market share in the relevant product and geographic market(s).

CHAPTER III   SECTION CONCERNING THE RELEVANT MARKET ONLY FOR STRUCTURAL JOINT VENTURES FOR WHICH ACCELERATED TREATMENT IS CLAIMED

Section 11   The relevant market

A relevant product market comprises all those products and/or services which are regarded as interchangeable or substitutable by the consumer, by reason of the products' characteristics, their prices and their intended use.

The following factors are normally considered to be relevant[1] to the determination of the relevant product market and should be taken into account in this analysis:

— the degree of physical similarity between the products/services in question,

— any differences in the end use to which the goods are put,

— differences in price between two products,

— the cost of switching between two potentially competing products,

— established or entrenched consumer preferences for one type or category of product over another,

— different or similar industry-wide product classifications (e.g. classifications maintained by trade associations).

The relevant geographic market comprises the area in which the undertakings concerned are involved in the supply of products or services, in which the conditions of competition are sufficiently homogeneous and which can be distinguished from neighbouring areas because, in particular, conditions of competition are appreciably different in those areas.

Factors relevant to the assessment of the relevant geographic market include[2] the nature and characteristics of the products or services concerned, the existence of entry barriers or consumer preferences, appreciable differences of the undertakings' market share or substantial price differences between neighbouring areas, and transport costs.

11.1   The notifying parties' analysis of the relevant market.

11.1.1   In the light of the above, please explain the definition of the relevant product market or markets that in the opinion of the parties should form the basis of the Commission's analysis of the notification. In your answer, please give reasons for assumptions or findings, and explain how the factors outlined above have been taken into account.

In the questions figuring below, this (or these) definition(s) will be referred to as 'the relevant product market(s)'.

11.1.2   Please explain the definition of the relevant geographic market or markets that in the opinion of the parties should form the basis of the Commission's analysis of the notification.

In your answer, please give reasons for assumptions or findings, and explain how the factors outlined above have been taken into account.

11.2   Questions on the relevant product and geographic market(s).

Answers to the following questions will enable the Commission to verify whether the product and geographic market definitions put forward by you in Section 11.1 are compatible with definitions figuring above.

Notes
[1]This list is not, however, exhaustive, and notifying parties may refer to other factors.
[2]This list is not, however, exhaustive, and notifying parties may refer to other factors.

Product market definition

11.2.1   List the specific products or services directly or indirectly affected by the agreement being notified.

11.2.2   List the categories of products and/or services that are, in the opinion of the notifying parties, close economic substitutes for those identified in the reply to question 11.2.1. Where more than one product or service has been identified in the reply to question 11.2.1, a list for each product must be provided for this question.

The products identified in this list should be ordered in their degree of substitutability, first listing the most perfect substitute for the products of the parties, finishing with the least perfect substitute.[3] Please explain how the factors relevant to the definition of the relevant product market have been taken into account in drawing up this list and in placing the products/services in their correct order.

Note

[3]Close economic substitute; most perfect substitute; least perfect substitute these definitions are only relevant to those filling out Chapter III of the form, i.e. those notifying structural joint ventures requesting the accelerated procedure. For any given product (for the purposes of this definition 'product' is used to refer to products or services) a chain of substitutes exists. This chain is made up of all conceivable substitutes for the product in question, i.e. all those products that will, to a greater or lesser extent, fulfil the needs of the consumer in question. The substitutes will range from very close (or perfect) ones (products to which consumers would turn immediately in the event of, for example, even a very small price increase for the product in question) to very distant (or imperfect) substitutes (products to which customers would only turn in the event of a very large price rise for the product in question). When defining the relevant market, and calculating market shares, the Commission only takes into account close economic substitutes of the products in question. Close economic substitutes are ones to which customers would turn to in response to a small but significant price increase for the product in question (say 5%). This enables the Commission to assess the market power of the notifying companies in the context of a relevant market made up of all those products that consumers of the products in question could readily and easily turn to. However, this does not mean that the Commission fails to take into account the constraints on the competitive behaviour of the parties in question resulting from the existence of imperfect substitutes (those to which a consumer could not turn in response to a small but significant price increase (say 5%) for the products in question). These effects are taken into account once the market has been defined, and the market shares determined.

It is therefore important for the Commission to have information regarding both close economic substitutes for the products in question, as well as less perfect substitutes. For example, assume two companies active in the luxury watch sector conclude a research and development agreement. They both manufacture watches costing ECU 1,800 to 2,000. Close economic substitutes are likely to be watches of other manufactures in the same or similar price category, and these will be taken into account when defining the relevant product market. Cheaper watches, and in particular disposable plastic watches, will be imperfect substitutes, because it is unlikely that a potential purchaser of a ECU 2,000 watch will turn to one costing ECU 20 if the expensive one increased its price by 5%.

Geographic market definition

11.2.3   List all the countries in which the parties are active in the relevant product market(s). Where they are active in all countries within any given groups of countries or trading area (e.g. the whole Community or EFTA, the EEA countries, world-wide) it is sufficient to indicate the area in question.

11.2.4   Explain the manner in which the parties produce and sell the goods and/or services in each of these various countries or areas. For example, do they manufacture locally, do they sell through local distribution facilities, or do they distribute through exclusive, or non-exclusive, importers and distributors?

11.2.5   Are there significant trade flows in the goods/services that make up the relevant product market(s) (i) between the EC Member States (please specify which and estimate the percentage of total sales made up by imports in each Member State in which the parties are active), (ii) between all or part of the EC Member States and all or part of the EFTA States (again, please specify and estimate the percentage of total sales made up by imports), (iii) between the EFTA States (please specify which and estimate the percentage of total sales made up by imports in each such State in which the parties are active), and (iv) between all or part of the EEA territory and other countries? (again, please specify and estimate the percentage of total sales made up by imports.)

11.2.6   Which producer undertakings based outside the Community or the EEA territory sell within the EEA territory in countries in which the parties are active in the affected products? How do these undertakings market their products? Does this differ between different EC Member States and/or EFTA States?

Section 12   Group members operating on the same markets as the parties to the notified agreement

12.1   For each of the parties to the agreement being notified, provide a list of all undertakings belonging to the same group which are:

12.1.1   active in the relevant product market(s);

12.1.2   active in markets neighbouring the relevant product market(s) (i.e. active in products/services that represent imperfect and partial substitutes[1] for those included in your definition of the relevant product market(s);

12.1.3   active in markets upstream and/or downstream from those included in the relevant product market(s). Such undertakings must be identified even if they sell the product or service in question in other geographic areas than those in which the parties to the notified agreement operate. Please list the name, place of incorporation, exact product manufactured and the geographic scope of operation of each group member.

Note
[1]The following are considered to be partial substitutes: products and services which may replace each other solely in certain geographic areas, solely during part of the year or solely for certain uses.

Section 13   The position of the parties on the relevant product market(s)

Information requested in this section must be provided for the group of the parties as a whole and not in relation to the individual companies directly concerned by the agreement notified.

13.1   In relation to each relevant product market(s), as defined in your reply to question 11.1.2, please provide the following information:

13.1.1   the market shares of the parties on the relevant geographic market during the previous three years;

13.1.2   where different, the market shares of the parties in (a) the EEA territory as a whole, (b) the Community, (c) the territory of the EFTA States and (d) each EC Member State and EFTA State during the previous three years.[1] For this section, where market shares are less than 20%, please state simply which of the following bands are relevant: 0 to 5%, 5 to 10%, 10 to 15%, 15 to 20% in terms of value or volume.

For the purpose of answering these questions, market share may be calculated either on the basis of value or volume. Justification for the figures provided must be given. Thus, for each answer, total market value/volume must be stated, together with the sales/turnover of each the parties in question. The source or sources of the information should also be given, and where possible, copies should be provided of documents from which information has been taken.

13.2   If the market shares in question 13.1 were to be calculated on a basis other than that used by the parties, would the resultant market shares differ by more than 5% in any market (i.e. if the parties have calculated market shares on the basis of volume, what would be the relevant figure if it was calculated on the basis of value?) If the figure were to differ by more than 5% please provide the information requested in question 13.1 on the basis of both value and volume.

13.3   Give your best estimate of the current rate of capacity utilisation of the parties and in the industry in general in the relevant product and geographic market(s).

Note
[1]Where the relevant geographic market has been defined as world wide, these figures must be given regarding the EEA, the Community, the territory of the EFTA States, and each EC Member State and EFTA State. Where the relevant geographic market has been defined as the Community, these figures must be given for the EEA, the territory of the EFTA States, and each EC Member State and EFTA State. Where the market has been defined as national, these figures must be given for the EEA, the Community and the territory of the EFTA States.

Section 14   The position of competitors and customers on the relevant product market(s)

Information requested in this section must be provided for the group of the parties as a whole and not in relation to the individual companies directly concerned by the agreement notified. For the (all) relevant product market(s) in which the parties have a combined market share exceeding 10% in the EEA as a whole, the Community, the EFTA territory or in any EC Member State or EFTA Member State, the following questions must be answered.

14.1   Please identify the competitors of the parties on the relevant product market(s) that have a market share exceeding 10% in any EC Member State, EFTA State, in the territory of the EFTA States, in the EEA, or world-wide. Please identify the company and give your best estimate as to their market share in these geographic areas. Please also provide the address, telephone and fax numbers, and, where possible, the name of a contact person at each company identified.

14.2   Please describe the nature of demand on the relevant product market(s). For example, are there few or many purchasers, are there different categories of purchasers, are government agencies or departments important purchasers?

14.3   Please identify the five largest customers of each of the parties for each relevant product market(s). State company name, address, telephone and fax numbers, together with the name of a contact person.

Section 15   Market entry and potential competition

For the (all) relevant product market(s) in which the parties have a combined market share exceeding 10% in the EEA as a whole, the Community, the EFTA territory or in any EC Member State or EFTA State, the following questions must be answered.

15.1   Describe the various factors influencing entry into the relevant product market(s) that exist in the present case. In so doing take account of the following where appropriate:

— to what extent is entry to the markets influenced by the requirement of government authorisation or standard setting in any form? Are there any legal or regulatory controls on entry to these markets?

— to what extent is entry to the markets influenced by the availability of raw materials?

— to what extent is entry to the markets influenced by the length of contracts between an undertaking and its suppliers and/or customers?

— what is the importance of research and development and in particular the importance of licensing patents, know-how and other rights in these markets?

15.2   Have any new undertakings entered the relevant product market(s) in geographic areas where the parties sell during the last three years? If so, please identify the undertaking(s) concerned (name, address, telephone and fax numbers, and, where possible, contact person), and provide your best estimate of their market share in each EC Member State and EFTA State that they are active and in the Community, the territory of the EFTA States and the EEA territory as a whole.

15.3   Give your best estimate of the minimum viable scale for the entry into the relevant product market(s) in terms of appropriate market share necessary to operate profitably.

15.4   Are there significant barriers to entry preventing companies active on the relevant product market(s):

15.4.1   in one EC Member State or EFTA State selling in other areas of the EEA territory;

15.4.2   outside the EEA territory selling into all or parts of the EEA territory? Please give reasons for your answers, explaining, where relevant, the importance of the following factors:

— trade barriers imposed by law, such as tariffs, quotas etc.,

— local specification or technical requirements,

— procurement policies,

— the existence of adequate and available local distribution and retailing facilities,

— transport costs,

— entrenched consumer preferences for local brands or products,

— language.

CHAPTER IV   FINAL SECTIONS

To be completed for all notifications

Section 16   Reasons for the application for negative clearance

If you are applying for negative clearance state:

16.1   why, i.e. state which provision or effects of the agreement or behaviour might, in your view, raise questions of compatibility with the Community's and/or the EEA rules of competition. The object of this subheading is to give the Commission the clearest possible idea of the doubts you have about your agreement or behaviour that you wish to have resolved by a negative clearance. Then, under the following three references, give a statement of the relevant facts and reasons as to why you consider Article 85(1) or 86 of the EC Treaty and/or Article 53(1) or 54 of the EEA Agreement to be inapplicable, i.e.:

16.2   why the agreements or behaviour do not have the object or effect of preventing, restricting or distorting competition within the common market or within the territory of the EFTA States to any appreciable extent, or why your undertaking does not have or its behaviour does not abuse a dominant position; and/or

16.3   why the agreements or behaviour do not have the object or effect of preventing, restricting or distorting competition within the EEA territory to any appreciable extent, or why your undertaking does not have or its behaviour does not abuse a dominant position; and/or

16.4   why the agreements or behaviour are not such as may affect trade between Member States or between the Community and one or more EFTA States, or between EFTA States to any appreciable extent.

Section 17   Reasons for the application for exemption

If you are notifying the agreement, even if only as a precaution, in order to obtain an exemption under Article 85(3) of the EC Treaty and/or Article 53(3) of the EEA Agreement, explain how:

17.1   the agreement contributes to improving production or distribution, and/or promoting technical or economic progress. In particular, please explain the reasons why these benefits are expected to result from the collaboration; for example, do the parties to the agreement possess complementary technologies or distribution systems that will produce important synergies? (if, so, please state which). Also please state whether any documents or studies were drawn up by the notifying parties when assessing the feasibility of the operation and the benefits likely to result therefrom, and whether any such documents or studies provided estimates of the savings or efficiencies likely to result. Please provide copies of any such documents or studies;

17.2   a proper share of the benefits arising from such improvement or progress accrues to consumers;

17.3   all restrictive provisions of the agreement are indispensable to the attainment of the aims set out under 17.1 (if you are claiming the benefit of the opposition procedure, it is particularly important that you should identify and justify restrictions that exceed those automatically exempted by the relevant Regulations). In this respect please explain how the benefits resulting from the agreement identified in your reply to question 17.1 could not be achieved, or could not be achieved so quickly or efficiently or only at higher cost or with less certainty of success (i) without the conclusion of the agreement as a whole and (ii) without those particular clauses and provisions of the agreement identified in your reply to question 4.2;

17.4 the agreement does not eliminate competition in respect of a substantial part of the goods or services concerned.

Section 18   Supporting documentation

The completed notification must be drawn up and submitted in one original. It shall contain the last versions of all agreements which are the subject of the notification and be accompanied by the following:

(a)   sixteen copies of the notification itself;

(b)   three copies of the annual reports and accounts of all the parties to the notified agreement, decision or practice for the last three years;

(c)   three copies of the most recent in-house or external long-term market studies or planning documents for the purpose of assessing or analysing the affected markets) with respect to competitive conditions, competitors (actual and potential), and market conditions. Each document should indicate the name and position of the author;

(d)   three copies of reports and analyses which have been prepared by or for any officer(s) or director(s) for the purposes of evaluating or analysing the notified agreement.

Section 19   Declaration

The notification must conclude with the following declaration which is to be signed by or on behalf of all the applicants or notifying parties.[1]

'The undersigned declare that the information given in this notification is correct to the best of their knowledge and belief, that complete copies of all documents requested by form A/B have been supplied to the extent that they are in the possession of the group of undertakings to which the applicant(s) or notifying party(ies) belong(s) and are accessible to the latter, that all estimates are identified as such and are their best estimates of the underlying facts and that all the opinions expressed are sincere.

They are aware of the provisions of Article 15(1)(a) of Regulation No. 17.

Place and date:

Signatures:'

Please add the name(s) of the person(s) signing the application or notification and their function(s).

Note

[1]Applications and notifications which have not been signed are invalid.

ANNEX I   TEXT OF ARTICLES 85 AND 86 OF THE EC TREATY (Omitted), ARTICLES 53, 54 AND 56 OF THE EEA AGREEMENT, AND OF ARTICLES 2, 3 AND 4 OF PROTOCOL 22 TO THAT AGREEMENT

ARTICLE 53 OF THE EEA AGREEMENT

1.   The following shall be prohibited as incompatible with the functioning of this Agreement: all agreements between undertakings, decisions by associations of undertakings and concerted practices which may affect trade between Contracting Parties and which have as their object or effect the prevention, restriction or distortion of competition within the territory covered by this Agreement, and in particular those which:

(a)   directly or indirectly fix purchase or selling prices or any other trading conditions;

(b)   limit or control production, markets, technical development, or investment;

(c)   share markets or sources of supply;

(d)   apply dissimilar conditions to equivalent transactions with other trading parties, thereby placing them at a competitive disadvantage;

(e)   make the conclusion of contracts subject to acceptance by the other parties of supplementary obligations which, by their nature or according to commercial usage, have no connection with the subject of such contracts.

2.   Any agreements or decisions prohibited pursuant to this Article shall be automatically void.

3.   The provisions of paragraph 1 may, however, be declared inapplicable in the case of:

— any agreement or category of agreements between undertakings,

— any decision or category of decisions by associations of undertakings,

— any concerted practice or category of concerted practices, which contributes to improving the production or distribution of goods or to promoting technical or economic progress, while allowing consumers a fair share of the resulting benefit, and which does not:

(a)   impose on the undertakings concerned restrictions which are not indispensable to the attainment of these objectives;

(b)   afford such undertakings the possibility of eliminating competition in respect of a substantial part of the products in question.

ARTICLE 54 OF THE EEA AGREEMENT

Any abuse by one or more undertakings of a dominant position within the territory covered by this agreement or in a substantial part of it shall be prohibited as incompatible with the functioning of this Agreement in so far as it may affect trade between Contracting Parties. Such abuse may, in particular, consist in:

(a)   directly or indirectly imposing unfair purchase or selling prices or other unfair trading conditions;

(b)   limiting production, markets or technical development to the prejudice of consumers;

(c)   applying dissimilar conditions to equivalent transactions with other trading parties, thereby placing them at a competitive disadvantage;

(d)   making the conclusion of contracts subject to acceptance by the other parties of supplementary obligations which, by their nature or according to commercial usage, have no connection with the subject of such contracts.

ARTICLE 56 OF THE EEA AGREEMENT

1.   Individual cases falling under Article 53 shall be decided upon by the surveillance authorities in accordance with the following provisions:

(a)   individual cases where only trade between EFTA States is affected shall be decided upon by the EFTA Surveillance Authority;

(b)   without prejudice to subparagraph (c), the EFTA Surveillance Authority decides, as provided for in the provisions set out in Article 58, Protocol 21 and the rules adopted for its implementation, Protocol 23 and Annex XIV, on cases where the turnover of the undertakings concerned in the territory of the EFTA States equals 33% or more of their turnover in the territory covered by this Agreement;

(c)   the EC Commission decides on the other cases as well as on cases under (b) where trade between EC Member States is affected, taking into account the provisions set out in Article 58, Protocol 21, Protocol 23 and Annex XIV.

2.   Individual cases falling under Article 54 shall be decided upon by the surveillance authority in the territory of which a dominant position is found to exist. The rules set out in paragraph 1 (b) and (c) shall apply only if dominance exists within the territories of both surveillance authorities.

3.   Individual cases falling under paragraph 1(c), whose effects on trade between EC Member States or on competition within the Community are not appreciable, shall be decided upon by the EFTA Surveillance Authority.

4.   The terms 'undertaking' and 'turnover' are, for the purpose of this Article, defined in Protocol 22.

ARTICLES 2, 3 AND 4 OF PROTOCOL 22 TO THE EEA AGREEMENT

Article 2

'Turnover' within the meaning of Article 56 of the Agreement shall comprise the amounts derived by the undertaking concerned, in the territory covered by this Agreement, in the preceding financial year from the sale of products and the provision of services falling within the undertaking's ordinary scope of activities after deduction of sales rebates and of value-added tax and other taxes directly related to turnover.

Article 3

In place of turnover the following shall be used:

(a)   for credit institutions and other financial institutions, their total assets multiplied by the ratio between loans and advances to credit institutions and customers in transactions with residents in the territory covered by this Agreement and the total sum of those loans and advances;

(b)   for insurance undertakings, the value of gross premiums received from residents in the territory covered by this Agreement, which shall comprise all amounts received and receivable in respect of insurance contracts issued by or on behalf of the insurance undertakings, including also outgoing reinsurance premiums, and after deduction of taxes and parafiscal contributions or levies charged by reference to the amounts of individual premiums or the total value of premiums.

Article 4

1.   In derogation of the definition of the turnover relevant for the application of Article 56 of the Agreement, as contained in Article 2 of this Protocol, the relevant turnover shall be constituted:

(a)   as regards agreements, decisions of associations of undertakings and concerted practices related to distribution and supply arrangements between non-competing undertakings, of the amounts derived from the sale of goods or the provision of services which are the subject matter of the agreements, decisions or concerted practices, and from the other goods or services which are considered by users to be equivalent in view of their characteristics, price and intended use;

(b)   as regards agreements, decisions of associations of undertakings and concerted practices related to arrangements on transfer of technology between non-competing undertakings, of the amounts derived from the sale of goods or the provision of services which result from the technology which is the subject matter of the agreements, decisions or concerted practices, and of the amounts derived from the sale of those goods or the provision of those services which that technology is designed to improve or replace.

2.   However, where at the time of the coming to existence of arrangements as described in paragraph 1(a) and (b) turnover as regards the sale of products or the provision of services is not in evidence, the general provision as contained in Article 2 shall apply.

ANNEX II   LIST OF RELEVANT ACTS
(as of 1 March 1995)

(If you think it possible that your arrangements do not need to be notified by virtue of any of these regulations or notices it may be worth your while to obtain a copy.)

IMPLEMENTING REGULATIONS

(1) Council Regulation No. of 6 February 1992: First Regulation implementing Articles 85 and 86 of the Treaty (OJ No. 13, 21.2.1962, p. 204/62, English Special Edition 1959-1962, November 1972, p. 87) as amended (OJ No. 58, 10.7.1962, p. 1655/62; OJ No. 162, 7.11.1963, p. 2696/63; OJ No. L 285, 29.12.1971, p. 49; OJ No. L73, 27.3.1972, p. 92; OJ No. L291, 19.11.1979, p. 94 and OJ No. L302, 15.11.1985, p. 165).

Commission Regulation (EC) No. 3385/94 of 21 December 1994 on the form, content and other details of applications and notifications provided for in Council Regulation No. 17.

REGULATIONS GRANTING BLOCK EXEMPTION IN RESPECT OF A WIDE RANGE OF AGREEMENTS

Commission Regulation (EC) No. 1983/83 of 22 June 1983 on the application of Article 85(3) of the Treaty to categories of exclusive distribution agreements (OJ No. L173, 30.6.1983, p. 1, as corrected in OJ No. L281, 13. 10. 1983, p. 24), as well as this Regulation as adapted for EEA purposes (see point 2 of Annex XIV to the EEA Agreement).

Commission Regulation (EEC) No. 1984/83 of 22 June 1983 on the application of Article 85(3) of the Treaty to categories of exclusive purchasing agreements (OJ No. L173, 30.6.1983, p. 5, as corrected in OJ No. L281, 13. 10. 1983, p. 24), as well as this Regulation as adapted for EEA purposes (see point 3 of Annex XIV to the EEA Agreement).

See also the Commission notices concerning Regulations (EEC) No. 1983/93 and (EEC) No. 1984/83 (OJ No. C101, 13.4.1984, p. 2 and OJ No. C121, 13.5.1992, p. 2).

Commission Regulation (EEC) No. 2349/84 of 23 July 1984 on the application of Article 85(3) of the Treaty to certain categories of patent licensing agreements (OJ No. L219, 16.8.1984, p. 15, as corrected in OJ No. L113, 26.4.1985, p. 34), as amended (OJ No. L12, 18.1.1995, p. 13), as well as this Regulation as adapted for EEA purposes (see point 5 of Annex XIV to the EEA Agreement). Article 4 of this Regulation provides for an opposition procedure.

Commission Regulation (EEC) No. 123/85 of 12 December 1984 on the application of Article 85(3) of the Treaty to certain categories of motor vehicle distributing and servicing agreements (OJ No. L15, 18.1.1985, p.16); as well as this Regulation as adapted for EEA purposes (see point 4 of Annex XIV to the EEA Agreement).

See also the Commission notices concerning this Regulation (OJ No. C17, 18.1.1985, p. 4 and OJ No. C329, 18.12.1991, p. 20).

Commission Regulation (EEC) No. 417/85 of 19 December 1984 on the application of Article 85(3) of the Treaty to categories of specialization agreements (OJ No. L53, 22.2.1985, p. 1), as amended (OJ No. L21, 29.1.1993, p. 8), as well as this Regulation as adapted for EEA purposes (see point 6 of Annex XIV to the EEA Agreement). Article 4 of this Regulation provides for an opposition procedure.

Commission Regulation (EEC) No. 418/85 of 19 December 1984 on the application of Article 85(3) of the Treaty to categories of research and development cooperation agreements (OJ No. L53, 22.2.1985, p. 5), as amended (OJ No. L21, 29.1.1993, p. 8), as well as this Regulation as adapted for EEA purposes (see point 7 of Annex XIV to the EEA Agreement). Article 7 of this Regulation provides for an opposition procedure.

Commission Regulation (EEC) No. 4087/88 of 30 November 1988 on the application of Article 85(3) of the Treaty to categories of franchise agreements (OJ No. L359, 28.12.1988, p. 46), as well as this Regulation as adapted for EEA purposes (see point 8 of Annex XIV to the EEA Agreement). Article 6 of this Regulation provides for an opposition procedure.

Commission Regulation (EEC) No. 556/89 of 30 November 1988 on the application of Article 85(3) of the Treaty to certain categories of know-how licensing agreements (OJ No. L61, 4.3.1989, p. 1), as amended (OJ No. L21, 29.1.1993, p. 8), as well as this Regulation as adapted for EEA purposes (see point 9 of Annex XIV to the EEA Agreement). Article 4 of this Regulation provides for an opposition procedure.

Commission Regulation (EEC) No. 3932/92 of 21 December 1992 on the application of Article 85(3) of the Treaty to certain categories of agreements, decisions and concerted practices in the insurance sector (OJ No. L398, 31.12.1992, p. 7). This Regulation will be adapted for EAA purposes.

NOTICES OF A GENERAL NATURE

(2) Commission notice on exclusive dealing contracts with commercial agents (OJ No. 139, 24.12.1962, p. 2921/62). This states that the Commission does not consider most such agreements to fall under the prohibition of Article 85(1).

Commission notice concerning agreements, decisions and concerted practices in the field of cooperation between enterprises (OJ No. C75, 29.7.1968, p. 3, as corrected in OJ No. C84, 28.8.1968, p. 14). This defines the sorts of cooperation on market studies, accounting, R & D, joint use of production, storage or transport, ad hoc consortia, selling or after-sales service, advertising or quality labelling that the Commission considers not to fall under the prohibition of Article 85(1).

Commission notice concerning its assessment of certain subcontracting agreements in relation to Article 85(1) of the Treaty (OJ No. C1, 3.1.1979, p. 2).

Commission notice on agreements, decisions and concerted practices of minor importance which do not fall under Article 85(1) of the Treaty (OJ No. C231, 12.9.1986, p. 2) as amended by Commission notice (OJ No. C368, 23.12.1994, p. 20) — in the main, those where the parties have less than 5% of the market between them, and a combined annual turnover of less than ECU 300 million.

Commission guidelines on the application of EEC competition rules in the telecommunications sector (OJ No. C233, 6.9. 1991, p. 2). These guidelines aim at clarifying the application of Community competition rules to the market participants in the telecommunications sector.

Commission notice on cooperation between national courts and the Commission in applying Articles 85 and 86 (OJ No. C39, 13.2.1993, p. 6). This notice sets out the principles on the basis of which such cooperation takes place.

Commission notice concerning the assessment of cooperative joint ventures pursuant to Article 85 of the EC Treaty (OJ No. C43, 16.2.1993, p. 2). This notice sets out the principles on the assessment of joint ventures.

A collection of these texts (as at 31 December 1989) was published by the Office for Official Publications of the European Communities (references Vol I: ISBN 92-826-1307-0, catalogue No: CV-42-90-001-EN-C). An updated collection is in preparation.

Pursuant to the Agreement, these texts will also cover the European Economic Area.

(1) As regards procedural rules applied by the EFTA Surveillance Authority, see Article 3 of Protocol 21 to the EEA Agreement and the relevant provisions in Protocol 4 to the Agreement between the EFTA States on the establishment of a Surveillance Authority and a Court of Justice.

(2) See also the corresponding notices published by the EFTA Surveillance Authority.

ANNEX III   LIST OF MEMBER STATES AND EFTA STATES, ADDRESS OF THE COMMISSION AND OF THE EFTA SURVEILLANCE AUTHORITY, LIST OF COMMISSION INFORMATION OFFICES WITHIN THE COMMUNITY AND IN EFTA STATES AND ADDRESSES OF COMPETENT AUTHORITIES IN EFTA STATES

The Member States as at the date of this Annex are: Austria, Belgium, Denmark, Finland, France, Germany, Greece, Ireland, Italy, Luxembourg, the Netherlands, Portugal, Spain, Sweden and the United Kingdom.

The EFTA States which will be Contracting Parties of the EEA Agreement, as at the date of this Annex, are: Iceland, Liechtenstein and Norway.

The address of the Commission's Directorate-General for Competition is:

Commission of the European Communities
Directorate-General for Competition
200 rue de la Loi
B-1049 Brussels
Tel. (322) 299 11 11

The address of the EFTA Surveillance Authority's Competition Directorate is:

EFTA Surveillance Authority
Competition Directorate
1-3 rue Marie-Thérèse
B-1040 Brussels
Tel. (322) 286 17 11

The addresses of the Commission's Information Offices in the Community are:

BELGIUM
73 rue Archimède
B-1040 Bruxelles
Tel. (322) 299 11 11

DENMARK
Hoejbrohus
OEstergade 61 Postboks 144
DK-1004 Koebenhavn K
Tel. (4533) 14 41 40

FEDERAL REPUBLIC OF GERMANY
Zitelmannstrasse 22
D-53113 Bonn
Tel. (49228) 53 00 90
Kurfuerstendamm 102
D-10711 Berlin 31
Tel. (4930) 896 09 30
Erhardtstrasse 27
D-80331 Muenchen
Tel. (4989) 202 10 11

GREECE
2 Vassilissis Sofias
Case Postale 11002
GR-Athina 10674
Tel. (301) 724 39 82/83/84

SPAIN
Calle de Serrano 41
5a Planta
E-28001 Madrid
Tel. (341) 435 17 00
Av. Diagonal, 407 bis
18 Planta
E-08008 Barcelona
Tel. (343) 415 81 77

FRANCE
288, boulevard Saint-Germain
F-75007 Paris
Tel. (331) 40 63 38 00
CMCI 2,
rue Henri Barbusse
F-13241 Marseille, Cedex 01
Tel. (3391) 91 46 00

IRELAND
39 Molesworth Street
IRL-Dublin 2
Tel. (3531) 71 22 44

ITALY
Via Poli 29
I-00187 Roma
Tel. (396) 699 11 60
Corso Magenta 61
I-20123 Milano
Tel. (392) 480 15 05

LUXEMBURG
Bâtiment Jean-Monnet
rue Alcide de Gasperi
L-2920 Luxembourg
Tel. (352) 430 11

NETHERLANDS
Postbus 30465
NL-2500 GL Den Haag
Tel. (3170) 346 93 26

AUSTRIA
Hoyosgasse 5
A-1040 Wien
Tel. (431) 505 33 79

PORTUGAL
Centro Europeu Jean Monnet
Largo Jean Monnet, 1-10°
P-1200 Lisboa
Tel. (3511) 54 11 44

FINLAND
31 Pohjoisesplanadi
00100 Helsinki
Tel. (3580) 65 64 20

SWEDEN
PO Box 16396
Hamngatan 6
11147 Stockholm
Tel. (468) 611 11 72

UNITED KINGDOM
8 Storey's Gate
UK-London SW1P 3AT
Tel. (4471) 973 19 92
Windsor House
9/15 Bedford Street
UK-Belfast BT2 7EG

Tel. (44232) 24 07 08
4 Cathedral Road
UK-Cardiff CF1 9SG
Tel. (44222) 37 16 31
9 Alva Street
UK-Edinburgh EH2 4PH
Tel. (4431) 225 20 58

The addresses of the Commission's Information Offices in the EFTA States are:

NORWAY
Postboks 1643 Vika 0119 Oslo 1
Haakon's VII Gate No. 6
0161 Oslo 1
Tel. (472) 83 35 83

Forms for notifications and applications, as well as more detailed information on the EEA competition rules, can also be obtained from the following offices:

AUSTRIA
Federal Ministry for Economic Affairs
Tel. (431) 71 100

FINLAND
Office of Free Competition
Tel. (3580) 73 141

ICELAND
Directorate of Competition and Fair Trade
Tel. (3541) 27 422

LIECHTENSTEIN
Office of National Economy
Division of Economy and Statistics
Tel. (4175) 61 11

NORWAY
Price Directorate
Tel. (4722) 40 09 00

SWEDEN
Competition Authority
Tel. (468) 700 16

**COUNCIL DIRECTIVE OF 18 DECEMBER 1986 ON THE
COORDINATION OF THE LAWS OF THE MEMBER STATE
RELATING TO SELF-EMPLOYED COMMERCIAL AGENTS**
(86/653/ EEC)
[OJ 1986, No. L382/17]

THE COUNCIL OF THE EUROPEAN COMMUNITIES,

Having regard to the Treaty establishing the European Economic Community, and in particular Articles 57(2) and 100 thereof,

Having regard to the proposal from the Commission,[1]
Having regard to the opinion of the European Parliament,[2]
Having regard to the opinion of the Economic and Social Committee,[3]
Whereas the restrictions on the freedom of establishment and the freedom to provide services in respect of activities of intermediaries in commerce, industry and small craft industries were abolished by Directive 64/224/EEC;[4]

Whereas the differences in national laws concerning commercial representation substantially affect the conditions of competition and the carrying on of that activity within the Community and are detrimental both to the protection available to commercial agents vis-à-vis their principals and to the security of commercial transactions; whereas moreover those differences are such as to inhibit substantially the conclusion and operation of commercial representation contracts where principal and commercial agents are established in different Member States;

Whereas trade in goods between Member States should be carried on under conditions which are similar to those of a single market, and this necessitates approximation of the legal systems of the Member States to the extent required for the proper functioning of the common market; whereas in this regard the rules concerning conflict of laws do not, in the matter of commercial representation, remove the inconsistencies referred to above, nor would they even if they were made uniform, and accordingly the proposed harmonization is necessary notwithstanding the existence of those rules;

Whereas in this regard the legal relationship between commercial agent and principal must be given priority;

Whereas it is appropriate to be guided by the principles of Article 117 of the Treaty and to maintain improvements already made, when harmonizing the laws of the Member States relating to commercial agents;

Whereas additional transitional periods should be allowed for certain Member States which have to make a particular effort to adapt their regulations, especially those concerning indemnity for termination of contract between the principal and the commercial agent, to the requirements of this Directive,

Notes
[1] OJ 1979 C56/5.
[2] OJ 1978 C239/17.
[3] OJ 1978 C59/31.
[4] OJ 1964 L56/869.

HAS ADOPTED THIS DIRECTIVE:

CHAPTER I   SCOPE

Article 1

1.   The harmonization measures prescribed by this Directive shall apply to the laws, regulations and administrative provisions of the Member States governing the relations between commercial agents and their principals.

2.   For the purposes of this Directive, 'commercial agent' shall mean a self-employed intermediary who has continuing authority to negotiate the sale or the purchase of goods on behalf of another person, hereinafter called the 'principal', or to negotiate and conclude such transactions on behalf of and in the name of that principal.

3.   A commercial agent shall be understood within the meaning of this Directive as not including in particular:
— a person who, in his capacity as an officer, is empowered to enter into commitments binding on a company or association,
— a partner who is lawfully authorised to enter into commitments binding on his partners,
— a receiver, a receiver and manager, a liquidator or a trustee in bankruptcy.

Article 2
1.   This Directive shall not apply to:
— commercial agents when they operate on commodity exchanges or in the commodity market, or
— the body known as the Crown Agents for Overseas Governments and Administrations, as set up under the Crown Agents Act 1979 in the United Kingdom, or its subsidiaries.
2.   Each of the Member States shall have the right to provide that the Directive shall not apply to those persons whose activities as commercial agents are considered secondary by the law of that Member State.

CHAPTER II   RIGHTS AND OBLIGATIONS

Article 3
1.   In performing his activities a commercial agent must look after his principal's interests and act dutifully and in good faith.
2.   In particular, a commercial agent must:
(a)   make proper efforts to negotiate and, where appropriate, conclude the transactions he is instructed to take care of;
(b)   communicate to his principal all the necessary information available to him;
(c)   comply with reasonable instructions given by his principal.

Article 4
1.   In his relations with his commercial agent a principal must act dutifully and in good faith.
2.   A principal must in particular:
(a)   provide his commercial agent with the necessary documentation relating to the goods concerned;
(b)   obtain for his commercial agent the information necessary for the performance of the agency contract, and in particular notify the commercial agent within a reasonable period once he anticipates that the volume of commercial transactions will be significantly lower than that which the commercial agent could normally have expected.
3.   A principal must, in addition, inform the commercial agent within a reasonable period of his acceptance, refusal, and of any non-execution of a commercial transaction which the commercial agent has procured for the principal.

Article 5
The parties may not derogate from the provisions of Articles 3 and 4.

CHAPTER III   REMUNERATION

Article 6

1.   In the absence of any agreement on this matter between the parties, and without prejudice to the application of the compulsory provisions of the Member States concerning the level of remuneration, a commercial agent shall be entitled to the remuneration that commercial agents appointed for the goods forming the subject of his agency contract are customarily allowed in the place where he carries on his activities. If there is no such customary practice a commercial agent shall be entitled to reasonable remuneration taking into account all the aspects of the transaction.

2.   Any part of the remuneration which varies with the number or value of business transactions shall be deemed to be commission within the meaning of this Directive.

3.   Articles 7 to 12 shall not apply if the commercial agent is not remunerated wholly or in part by commission.

Article 7

1.   A commercial agent shall be entitled to commission on commercial transactions concluded during the period covered by the agency contract:

   (a)   where the transaction has been concluded as a result of his action; or

   (b)   where the transaction is concluded with a third party whom he has previously acquired as a customer for transactions of the same kind.

2.   A commercial agent shall also be entitled to commission on transactions concluded during the period covered by the agency contract:

   — either where he is entrusted with a specific geographical area or group of customers,

   — or where he has an exclusive right to a specific geographical area or group of customers, and where the transaction has been entered into with a customer belonging to that area or group.

Member States shall include in their legislation one of the possibilities referred to in the above two indents.

Article 8

A commercial agent shall be entitled to commission on commercial transactions concluded after the agency contract has terminated:

   (a)   if the transaction is mainly attributable to the agency contract and if the transaction was entered into within a reasonable period after that contract terminated; or

   (b)   if, in accordance with the conditions mentioned in Article 7, the order of the third party reached the principal or the commercial agent before the agency contract terminated.

Article 9

A commercial agent shall not be entitled to the commission referred to in Article 7, if that commission is payable, pursuant to Article 8, to the previous commercial agent, unless it is equitable because of the circumstances for the commission to be shared between the commercial agents.

Article 10

1.   The commission shall become due as soon as and to the extent that one of the following circumstances obtains:

(a)   the principal has executed the transaction; or

(b)   the principal should, according to his agreement with the third party, have executed the transaction; or

(c)   the third party has executed the transaction.

2.   The commission shall become due at the latest when the third party has executed his part of the transaction or should have done so if the principal had executed his part of the transaction, as he should have.

3.   The commission shall be paid not later than on the last day of the month following the quarter in which it became due.

4.   Agreements to derogate from paragraphs 2 and 3 to the detriment of the commercial agent shall not be permitted.

Article 11

1.   The right to commission can be extinguished only if and to the extent that:

—it is established that the contract between the third party and the principal will not be executed, and

—that fact is due to a reason for which the principal is not to blame.

2.   Any commission which the commercial agent has already received shall be refunded if the right to it is extinguished.

3.   Agreements to derogate from paragraph 1 to the detriment of the commercial agent shall not be permitted.

Article 12

1.   The principal shall supply his commercial agent with a statement of the commission due, not later than the last day of the month following the quarter in which the commission has become due. This statement shall set out the main components used in calculating the amount of commission.

2.   A commercial agent shall be entitled to demand that he be provided with all the information, and in particular an extract from the books, which is available to his principal and which he needs in order to check the amount of the commission due to him.

3.   Agreements to derogate from paragraphs 1 and 2 to the detriment of the commercial agent shall not be permitted.

4.   This Directive shall not conflict with the internal provisions of Member States which recognise the right of a commercial agent to inspect a principal's books.

CHAPTER IV   CONCLUSION AND TERMINATION OF THE AGENCY CONTRACT

Article 13

1.   Each party shall be entitled to receive from the other on request a signed written document setting out the terms of the agency contract including any terms subsequently agreed. Waiver of this right shall not be permitted.

2.   Notwithstanding paragraph 1 a Member State may provide that an agency contract shall not be valid unless evidenced in writing.

Article 14

An agency contract for a fixed period which continues to be performed by both parties after that period has expired shall be deemed to be converted into an agency contract for an indefinite period.

Article 15

1.   Where an agency contract is concluded for an indefinite period either party may terminate it by notice.

2.   The period of notice shall be one month for the first year of the contract, two months for the second year commenced, and three months for the third year commenced and subsequent years. The parties may not agree on shorter periods of notice.

3.   Member States may fix the period of notice at four months for the fourth year of the contract years. They may decide that the parties may not agree to shorter periods.

4.   If the parties agree on longer periods than those laid down in paragraphs 2 and 3, the period of notice to be observed by the principal must not be shorter than that to be observed by the commercial agent.

5.   Unless otherwise agreed by the parties, the end of the period of notice must coincide with the end of a calendar month.

6.   The provision of this Article shall apply to an agency contract for a fixed period where it is converted under Article 14 into an agency contract for an indefinite period, subject to the proviso that the earlier fixed period must be taken into account in the calculation of the period of notice.

Article 16

Nothing in this Directive shall affect the application of the law of the Member States where the latter provides for the immediate termination of the agency contract:

(a)   because of the failure of one party to carry out all or part of his obligations;

(b)   where exceptional circumstances arise.

Article 17

1.   Member States shall take the measures necessary to ensure that the commercial agent is, after termination of the agency contract, indemnified in accordance with paragraph 2 or compensated for damage in accordance with paragraph 3.

2.   (a)   The commercial agent shall be entitled to an indemnity if and to the extent that:

—he has brought the principal new customers or has significantly increased the volume of business with existing customers and the principal continues to derive substantial benefits from the business with such customers, and

—the payment of this indemnity is equitable having regard to all the circumstances and, in particular, the commission lost by the commercial agent on the business transacted with such customers. Member States may provide for such circumstances also to include the application or otherwise of a restraint of trade clause, within the meaning of Article 20;

(b)   The amount of the indemnity may not exceed a figure equivalent to an indemnity for one year calculated from the commercial agent's average annual remuneration over the preceding five years and if the contract goes back less than five years the indemnity shall be calculated on the average for the period in question;

(c)   The grant of such an indemnity shall not prevent the commercial agent from seeking damages.

3. The commercial agent shall be entitled to compensation for the damage he suffers as a result of the termination of his relations with the principal. Such damage shall be deemed to occur particularly when the termination takes place in circumstances:

— depriving the commercial agent of the commission which proper performance of the agency contract would have procured him whilst providing the principal with substantial benefits linked to the commercial agent's activities,

— and/or which have not enabled the commercial agent to amortise the costs and expenses that he had incurred for the performance of the agency contract on the principal's advice.

4. Entitlement to the indemnity as provided for in paragraph 2 or to compensation for damage as provided for under paragraph 3, shall also arise where the agency contract is terminated as a result of the commercial agent's death.

5. The commercial agent shall lose his entitlement to the indemnity in the instances provided for in paragraph 2 or to compensation for damage in the instances provided for in paragraph 3, if within one year following termination of the contract he has not notified the principal that he intends pursuing his entitlement.

6. The Commission shall submit to the Council, within eight years following the date of notification of this Directive, a report on the implementation of this Article, and shall if necessary submit to it proposals for amendments.

Article 18
The indemnity or compensation referred to in Article 17 shall not be payable:

(a) where the principal has terminated the agency contract because of default attributable to the commercial agent which would justify immediate termination of the agency contract under national law;

(b) where the commercial agent has terminated the agency contract, unless such termination is justified by circumstances attributable to the principal or on grounds of age, infirmity or illness of the commercial agent in consequence of which he cannot reasonably be required to continue his activities;

(c) where, with the agreement of the principal, the commercial agent assigns his rights and duties under the agency contract to another person.

Article 19
The parties may not derogate from Articles 17 and 18 to the detriment of the commercial agent before the agency contract expires.

Article 20
1. For the purposes of this Directive an agreement restricting the business activities of a commercial agent following termination of the agency contract is hereinafter referred to as a restraint of trade clause.

2. A restraint of trade clause shall be valid only if and to the extent that:

(a) it is concluded in writing; and

(b) it relates to the geographical area or the group of customers and the geographical area entrusted to the commercial agent and to the kind of goods covered by his agency under the contract.

3.   A restraint of trade clause shall be valid for not more than two years after termination of the agency contract.

4.   This Article shall not affect provisions of national law which impose other restrictions on the validity or enforceability of restraint of trade clauses or which enable the courts to reduce the obligations on the parties resulting from such an agreement.

CHAPTER V   GENERAL AND FINAL PROVISIONS

Article 21

Nothing in this Directive shall require a Member State to provide for the disclosure of information where such disclosure would be contrary to public policy.

Article 22

1.   Member States shall bring into force the provisions necessary to comply with this Directive before 1 January 1990. They shall forthwith inform the Commission thereof. Such provisions shall apply at least to contracts concluded after their entry into force. They shall apply to contracts in operation by 1 January 1994 at the latest.

2.   As from the notification of this Directive, Member States shall communicate to the Commission the main laws, regulations and administrative provisions which they adopt in the field governed by this Directive.

3.   However, with regard to Ireland and the United Kingdom, 1 January 1990 referred to in paragraph 1 shall be replaced by 1 January 1994. With regard to Italy, 1 January 1990 shall be replaced by 1 January 1993 in the case of the obligations deriving from Article 17.

Article 23

This Directive is addressed to the Member States

Done at Brussels, 18 December 1986
For the Council
The President
M. JOPLING

COUNCIL REGULATION (EC) NO 384/96 OF 22 DECEMBER 1995 ON PROTECTION AGAINST DUMPED IMPORTS FROM COUNTRIES NOT MEMBERS OF THE EUROPEAN COMMUNITY
[OJ 1996 L56/1][1]

THE COUNCIL OF THE EUROPEAN UNION,

Having regard to the Treaty establishing the European Community, and in particular Article 113 thereof,

    Having regard to the Regulations establishing the common organization of agricultural markets and the Regulations adopted pursuant to Article 235 of

Note

[1]As amended by Regulation 2331/96 [OJ 1996 L317/1]. This replaces Regulations 3283/94 OJ 1994 L349/1 and 2176/84 L173/5). See also Decision 2277/96 which applies Regulation 384/96 to the ECSC Treaty OJ 1996 L308/11.

the Treaty applicable to goods manufactured from agricultural products, and in particular the provisions of those Regulations which allow for derogation from the general principle that protective measures at frontiers may be replaced solely by the measures provided for in those Regulations,

Having regard to the proposal from the Commission,[2]

Having regard to the opinion of the European Parliament,[3]

(1)   Whereas, by Regulation (EC) No. 2423/88,[4] the Council adopted common rules for protection against dumped or subsidised imports from countries which are not members of the European Community;

(2)   Whereas those rules were adopted in accordance with existing international obligations, in particular those arising from Article VI of the General Agreement on Tariffs and Trade (hereinafter referred to as 'GATT'), from the Agreement on Implementation of Article VI of the GATT (1979 Anti-Dumping Code) and from the Agreement on Interpretation and Application of Articles VI, XVI and XXIII of the GATT (Code on Subsidies and Countervailing Duties);

(3)   Whereas the multilateral trade negotiations concluded in 1994 have led to new Agreements on the implementation of Article VI of GATT and it is therefore appropriate to amend the Community rules in the light of these new Agreements; whereas is it also desirable, in the light of the different nature of the new rules for dumping and subsidies respectively, to have a separate body of Community rules in each of those two areas; whereas, consequently, the new rules on protection against subsidies and countervailing duties are contained in a separate Regulation;

(4)   Whereas, in applying the rules it is essential, in order to maintain the balance of rights and obligations which the GATT Agreement establishes, that the Community take account of how they are interpreted by the Community's major trading partners;

(5)   Whereas the new agreement on dumping, namely, the Agreement on Implementation of Article VI of the General Agreement on Tariffs and Trade 1994 (hereinafter referred to as 'the 1994 Anti-Dumping Agreement'), contains new and detailed rules, relating in particular to the calculation of dumping, procedures for initiating and pursuing an investigation, including the establishment and treatment of the facts, the imposition of provisional measures, the imposition and collection of anti-dumping duties, the duration and review of anti-dumping measures and the public disclosure of information relating to anti-dumping investigations; whereas, in view of the extent of the changes and to ensure a proper and transparent application of the new rules, the language of the new agreements should be brought into Community legislation as far as possible;

(6)   Whereas it is desirable to lay down clear and detailed rules on the calculation of normal value; whereas in particular such value should in all cases be based on representative sales in the ordinary course of trade in the exporting country; whereas it is expedient to define the circumstances in which domestic

Notes
[2]OJ No. C319, 30.11.1995.
[3]OJ No. C17, 22.1.1996.
[4]OJ No. L209, 2.8.1988, p. 1, as last amended by Regulation (EC) No. 522/94 (OJ No. L66, 10.3.1994, p. 10).

sales may be considered to be made at a loss and may be disregarded, and in which recourse may be had to remaining sales, or to constructed normal value, or to sales to a third country; whereas it is also desirable to provide for a proper allocation of costs, even in start-up situations; whereas it is also appropriate to lay down guidance as to definition of start-up and the extent and method of allocation; whereas it is also necessary, when constructing normal value, to indicate the methodology that is to be applied in determining the amounts for selling, general and administrative costs and the profit margin that should be included in such value;

(7)   Whereas when determining normal value for non-market economy countries, it appears prudent to set out rules for choosing the appropriate market-economy third country that is to be used for such purpose and, where it is not possible to find a suitable third country, to provide that normal value may be established on any other reasonable basis;

(8)   Whereas it is expedient to define the export price and to enumerate the adjustments which are to be made in those cases where a reconstruction of this price from the first open-market price is deemed necessary;

(9)   Whereas, for the purpose of ensuring a fair comparison between export price and normal value, it is advisable to list the factors which may affect prices and price comparability and to lay down specific rules as to when and how the adjustments should be made, including the fact that any duplication of adjustments should be avoided; whereas it is also necessary to provide that comparison may be made using average prices although individual export prices may be compared to an average normal value where the former vary by customer, region or time period;

(10)   Whereas it is desirable to lay down clear and detailed guidance as to the factors which may be relevant for the determination of whether the dumped imports have caused material injury or are threatening to cause injury; whereas, in demonstrating that the volume and price levels of the imports concerned are responsible for injury sustained by a Community industry, attention should be given to the effect of other factors and in particular prevailing market conditions in the Community;

(11)   Whereas it is advisable to define the term 'Community industry' and to provide that parties related to exporters may be excluded from such industry and to define the term 'related'; whereas, it is also necessary to provide for anti-dumping action to be taken on behalf of producers in a region of the Community and to lay down guidelines on the definition of such region;

(12)   Whereas it is necessary to lay down who may lodge an anti-dumping complaint, including the extent to which it should be supported by the Community industry, and the information on dumping, injury and causation which such complaint should contain; whereas it is also expedient to specify the procedures for the rejection of complaints or the initiation of proceedings;

(13)   Whereas it is necessary to lay down the manner in which interested parties should be given notice of the information which the authorities require, and should have ample opportunity to present all relevant evidence and to defend their interests, whereas it is also desirable to set out clearly the rules and procedures to be followed during the investigation, in particular the rules whereby interested parties are to make themselves known, present their views and submit information within specified time limits, if such views and information are to be taken into account, whereas it is also appropriate to set

out the conditions under which an interested party may have access to, and comment on, information presented by other interested parties; whereas there should also be cooperation between the Member States and the Commission in the collection of information;

(14)   Whereas it is necessary to lay down the conditions under which provisional duties may be imposed, including the condition that they may be imposed no earlier than 60 days from initiation and not later than nine months thereafter, whereas for administrative reasons it is also necessary to provide that such duties may in all cases be imposed by the Commission, either directly for a nine-month period or in two stages of six and three months;

(15)   Whereas it is necessary to specify procedures for accepting undertakings which eliminate dumping and injury instead of imposing provisional or definitive duties; whereas it is also appropriate to lay down the consequences of breach or withdrawal of undertakings and that provisional duties may be imposed in cases of suspected violation or where further investigation is necessary to supplement the findings; whereas, in accepting undertakings, care should be taken that the proposed undertakings, and their enforcement, do not lead to anti-competitive behaviour;

(16)   Whereas it is necessary to provide that the termination of cases should, irrespective of whether definitive measures are adopted or not, normally take place within 12 months, and in no case later than 15 months, from the initiation of the investigation; whereas investigations or proceedings should be terminated where the dumping is de minimis or the injury is negligible, and it is appropriate to define those terms; whereas, where measures are to be imposed, it is necessary to provide for the termination of investigations and to lay down that measures should be less than the margin of dumping if such lesser amount would remove the injury, as well as to specify the method of calculating the level of measures in cases of sampling;

(17)   Whereas it is necessary to provide for retroactive collection of provisional duties if that is deemed appropriate and to define the circumstances which may trigger the retroactive application of duties to avoid the undermining of the definitive measures to be applied; whereas it is also necessary to provide that duties may be applied retroactively in cases of breach or withdrawal of undertakings;

(18)   Whereas it is necessary to provide that measures are to lapse after five years unless a review indicates that they should be maintained; whereas it is also necessary to provide, in cases where sufficient evidence is submitted of changed circumstances, for interim reviews or for investigations to determine whether refunds of anti-dumping duties are warranted; whereas it is also appropriate to lay down that in any recalculation of dumping which necessitates a reconstruction of export prices, duties are not to be treated as a cost incurred between importation and resale where the said duty is being reflected in the prices of the products subject to measures in the Community;

(19)   Whereas it is necessary to provide specifically for the reassessment of export prices and dumping margins where the duty is being absorbed by the exporter through a form of compensatory arrangement and the measures are not being reflected in the prices of the products subject to measures in the Community;

(20)   Whereas the 1994 Anti-Dumping Agreement does not contain provisions regarding the circumvention of anti-dumping measures, though a

separate GATT Ministerial Decision recognises circumvention as a problem and has referred it to the GATT Anti-dumping Committee for resolution; whereas given the failure of the multilateral negotiations so far and pending the outcome of the referral to the GATT Anti-Dumping Committee, it is necessary to introduce new provisions into Community legislation to deal with practices, including mere assembly of goods in the Community or a third country, which have as their main aim the circumvention of anti-dumping measures;

(21) Whereas it is expedient to permit suspension of anti-dumping measures where there is a temporary change in market conditions which makes the continued imposition of such measures temporarily inappropriate;

(22) Whereas it is necessary to provide that imports under investigation may be made subject to registration upon importation in order to enable measures to be applied subsequently against such imports;

(23) Whereas in order to ensure proper enforcement of measures, it is necessary that Member States monitor, and report to the Commission, the import trade of products subject to investigation or subject to measures, and also the amount of duties collected under this Regulation;

(24) Whereas it is necessary to provide for consultation of an Advisory Committee at regular and specified stages of the investigation; whereas, the Committee should consist of representatives of Member States with a representative of the Commission as chairman;

(25) Whereas it is expedient to provide for verification visits to check information submitted on dumping and injury, such visits being, however, conditional on proper replies to questionnaires being received;

(26) Whereas it is essential to provide for sampling in cases where the number of parties or transactions is large in order to permit completion of investigations within the appointed time limits;

(27) Whereas it is necessary to provide that where parties do not cooperate satisfactorily other information may be used to establish findings and that such information may be less favourable to the parties than if they had cooperated;

(28) Whereas provision should be made for the treatment of confidential information so that business secrets are not divulged;

(29) Whereas it is essential that provision be made for proper disclosure of essential facts and considerations to parties which qualify for such treatment and that such disclosure be made, with due regard to the decision-making process in the Community, within a time period which permits parties to defend their interests;

(30) Whereas it is prudent to provide for an administrative system under which arguments can be presented as to whether measures are in the Community interest, including the consumers' interest, and to lay down the time periods within which such information has to be presented as well as the disclosure rights of the parties concerned;

(31) Whereas, by Regulation (EC) No. 3283/94 of 22 December 1994 on protection against dumped imports from countries not members of the European Community,[1] the Council repealed Regulation (EEC) No. 2423/88

Note
[1] OJ No. L349, 31.12.1994, p. 1. Regulation as last amended by Regulation (EC) No. 1251/95 (OJ No. L122, 2.6.1995, p. 1).

and instituted a new common system of defence against dumped imports from countries not members of the European Community;

(32)   Whereas significant errors in the text of Regulation (EC) No. 3283/94 became apparent on publication;

(33)   Whereas, moreover, that Regulation has already been twice amended;

(34)   Whereas, in the interests of clarity, transparency and legal certainty, that Regulation should therefore be repealed and replaced, without prejudice to the anti-dumping proceedings already initiated under it or under Regulation (EEC) No. 2423/88,

HAS ADOPTED THIS REGULATION:

Article 1   Principles

1.   An anti-dumping duty may be applied to any dumped product whose release for free circulation in the Community causes injury.

2.   A product is to be considered as being dumped if its export price to the Community is less than a comparable price for the like product, in the ordinary course of trade, as established for the exporting country.

3.   The exporting country shall normally be the country of origin. However, it may be an intermediate country, except where, for example, the products are merely transhipped through that country, or the products concerned are not produced in that country, or there is no comparable price for them in that country.

4.   For the purpose of this Regulation, the term 'like product' shall be interpreted to mean a product which is identical, that is to say, alike in all respects, to the product under consideration, or in the absence of such a product, another product which although not alike in all respects, has characteristics closely resembling those of the product under consideration.

Article 2   Determination of dumping

A.   NORMAL VALUE

1.   The normal value shall normally be based on the prices paid or payable, in the ordinary course of trade, by independent customers in the exporting country. However, where the exporter in the exporting country does not produce or does not sell the like product, the normal value may be established on the basis of prices of other sellers or producers. Prices between parties which appear to be associated or to have a compensatory arrangement with each other may not be considered to be in the ordinary course of trade and may not be used to establish normal value unless it is determined that they are unaffected by the relationship.

2.   Sales of the like product intended for domestic consumption shall normally be used to determine normal value if such sales volume constitutes 5% or more of the sales volume of the product under consideration to the Community. However, a lower volume of sales may be used when, for example, the prices charged are considered representative for the market concerned.

3.   When there are no or insufficient sales of the like product in the ordinary course of trade, or where because of the particular market situation such sales do not permit a proper comparison, the normal value of the like product shall be calculated on the basis of the cost of production in the country of origin plus a reasonable amount for selling, general and administrative costs and for

profits, or on the basis of the export prices, in the ordinary course of trade, to an appropriate third country, provided that those prices are representative.

4.   Sales of the like product in the domestic market of the exporting country, or export sales to a third country, at prices below unit production costs (fixed and variable) plus selling, general and administrative costs may be treated as not being in the ordinary course of trade by reason of price, and may be disregarded in determining normal value, only if it is determined that such sales are made within an extended period in substantial quantities, and are at prices which do not provide for the recovery of all costs within a reasonable period of time. If prices which are below costs at the time of sale are above weighted average costs for the period of investigation, such prices shall be considered to provide for recovery of costs within a reasonable period of time. The extended period of time shall normally be one year but shall in no case be less than six months, and sales below unit cost shall be considered to be made in substantial quantities within such a period when it is established that the weighted average selling price is below the weighted average unit cost, or that the volume of sales below unit cost is not less than 20% of sales being used to determine normal value.

5.   Costs shall normally be calculated on the basis of records kept by the party under investigation, provided that such records are in accordance with the generally accepted accounting principles of the country concerned and that it is shown that the records reasonably reflect the costs associated with the production and sale of the product under consideration. Consideration shall be given to evidence submitted on the proper allocation of costs, provided that it is shown that such allocations have been historically utilised. In the absence of a more appropriate method, preference shall be given to the allocation of costs on the basis of turnover. Unless already reflected in the cost allocations under this subparagraph, costs shall be adjusted appropriately for those non-recurring items of cost which benefit future and/or current production. Where the costs for part of the period for cost recovery are affected by the use of new production facilities requiring substantial additional investment and by low capacity utilisation rates, which are the result of start-up operations which take place within or during part of the investigation period, the average costs for the start-up phase shall be those applicable, under the abovementioned allocation rules, at the end of such a phase, and shall be included at that level, for the period concerned, in the weighted average costs referred to in the second sub-paragraph of paragraph 4. The length of a start-up phase shall be determined in relation to the circumstances of the producer or exporter concerned, but shall not exceed an appropriate initial portion of the period for cost recovery. For this adjustment to costs applicable during the investigation period, information relating to a start-up phase which extends beyond that period shall be taken into account where it is submitted prior to verification visits and within three months of the initiation of the investigation.

6.   The amounts for selling, for general and administrative costs and for profits shall be based on actual data pertaining to production and sales, in the ordinary course of trade, of the like product, by the exporter or producer under investigation. When such amounts cannot be determined on this basis, the amounts may be determined on the basis of:

(a)   the weighted average of the actual amounts determined for other exporters or producers subject to investigation in respect of production and sales of the like product in the domestic market of the country of origin;

(b) the actual amounts applicable to production and sales, in the ordinary course of trade, of the same general category of products for the exporter or producer in question in the domestic market of the country of origin;

(c) any other reasonable method, provided that the amount for profit so established shall not exceed the profit normally realised by other exporters or producers on sales of products of the same general category in the domestic market of the country of origin.

7. In the case of imports from non-market economy countries and, in particular, those to which Council Regulation (EC) No 519/94[1] applies, normal value shall be determined on the basis of the price or constructed value in a market economy third country, or the price from such a third country to other countries, including the Community, or where those are not possible, on any other reasonable basis, including the price actually paid or payable in the Community for the like product, duly adjusted if necessary to include a reasonable profit margin. An appropriate market economy third country shall be selected in a not unreasonable manner, due account being taken of any reliable information made available at the time of selection. Account shall also be taken of time limits; where appropriate, a market economy third country which is subject to the same investigation shall be used. The parties to the investigation shall be informed shortly after its initiation of the market economy third country envisaged and shall be given 10 days to comment.

Note
[1] OJ No. L67, 10.3.1994, p. 89.

B.   EXPORT PRICE

8. The export price shall be the price actually paid or payable for the product when sold for export from the exporting country to the Community.

9. In cases where there is no export price or where it appears that the export price is unreliable because of an association or a compensatory arrangement between the exporter and the importer or a third party, the export price may be constructed on the basis of the price at which the imported products are first resold to an independent buyer, or, if the products are not resold to an independent buyer, or are not resold in the condition in which they were imported, on any reasonable basis. In these cases, adjustment for all costs, including duties and taxes, incurred between importation and resale, and for profits accruing, shall be made so as to establish a reliable export price, at the Community frontier level. The items for which adjustment shall be made shall include those normally borne by an importer but paid by any party, either inside or outside the Community, which appears to be associated or to have a compensatory arrangement with the importer or exporter, including usual transport, insurance, handling, loading and ancillary costs; customs duties, any anti-dumping duties, and other taxes payable in the importing country by reason of the importation or sale of the goods; and a reasonable margin for selling, general and administrative costs and profit.

C.   COMPARISON

10. A fair comparison shall be made between the export price and the normal value. This comparison shall be made at the same level of trade and in respect of sales made at as nearly as possible the same time and with due

account taken of other differences which affect price comparability. Where the normal value and the export price as established are not on such a comparable basis due allowance, in the form of adjustments, shall be made in each case, on its merits, for differences in factors which are claimed, and demonstrated, to affect prices and price comparability. Any duplication when making adjustments shall be avoided, in particular in relation to discounts, rebates, quantities and level of trade. When the specified conditions are met, the factors for which adjustment can be made are listed as follows:

(a)   Physical characteristics

An adjustment shall be made for differences in the physical characteristics of the product concerned. The amount of the adjustment shall correspond to a reasonable estimate of the market value of the difference.

(b)   Import charges and indirect taxes

An adjustment shall be made to normal value for an amount corresponding to any import charges or indirect taxes borne by the like product and by materials physically incorporated therein, when intended for consumption in the exporting country and not collected or refunded in respect of the product exported to the Community.

(c)   Discounts, rebates and quantities

An adjustment shall be made for differences in discounts and rebates, including those given for differences in quantities, if these are properly quantified and are directly linked to the sales under consideration. An adjustment may also be made for deferred discounts and rebates if the claim is based on consistent practice in prior periods, including compliance with the conditions required to qualify for the discount or rebates.

(d)   Level of trade

(i)   An adjustment for differences in levels of trade, including any differences which may arise in OEM (Original Equipment Manufacturer) sales, shall be made where, in relation to the distribution chain in both markets, it is shown that the export price, including a constructed export price, is at a different level of trade from the normal value and the difference has affected price comparability which is demonstrated by consistent and distinct differences in functions and prices of the seller for the different levels of trade in the domestic market of the exporting country. The amount of the adjustment shall be based on the market value of the difference.

(ii)   However, in circumstances not envisaged under (i), when an existing difference in level of trade cannot be quantified because of the absence of the relevant levels on the domestic market of the exporting countries, or where certain functions are shown clearly to relate to levels of trade other than the one which is to be used in the comparison, a special adjustment may be granted.

(e)   Transport, insurance, handling, loading and ancillary costs

An adjustment shall be made for differences in the directly related costs incurred for conveying the product concerned from the premises of the exporter to an independent buyer, where such costs are included in the prices charged. Those costs shall include transport, insurance, handling, loading and ancillary costs.

(f)   Packing

An adjustment shall be made for differences in the directly related packing costs for the product concerned.

(g)   Credit

An adjustment shall be made for differences in the cost of any credit granted for the sales under consideration, provided that it is a factor taken into account in the determination of the prices charged.

(h)   After-sales costs

An adjustment shall be made for differences in the direct costs of providing warranties, guarantees, technical assistance and services, as provided for by law and/or in the sales contract.

(i)   Commissions

An adjustment shall be made for differences in commissions paid in respect of the sales under consideration.

(j)   Currency conversions

When the price comparison requires a conversion of currencies, such conversion shall be made using the rate of exchange on the date of sale, except that when a sale of foreign currency on forward markets is directly linked to the export sale involved, the rate of exchange in the forward sale shall be used. Normally, the date of sale shall be the date of invoice but the date of contract, purchase order or order confirmation may be used if these more appropriately establish the material terms of sale. Fluctuations in exchange rates shall be ignored and exporters shall be granted 60 days to reflect a sustained movement in exchange rates during the investigation period.

(k)   Other factors

An adjustment may also be made for differences in other factors not provided for under subparagraphs (a) to (j) if it is demonstrated that they affect price comparability as required under this paragraph, in particular that customers consistently pay different prices on the domestic market because of the difference in such factors.

D.   DUMPING MARGIN

11.   Subject to the relevant provisions governing fair comparison, the existence of margins of dumping during the investigation period shall normally be established on the basis of a comparison of a weighted average normal value with a weighted average of prices of all export transactions to the Community, or by a comparison of individual normal values and individual export prices to the Community on a transaction-to-transaction basis. However, a normal value established on a weighted average basis may be compared to prices of all individual export transactions to the Community, if there is a pattern of export prices which differs significantly among different purchasers, regions or time periods, and if the methods specified in the first sentence of this paragraph would not reflect the full degree of dumping being practised. This paragraph shall not preclude the use of sampling in accordance with Article 17.

12.   The dumping margin shall be the amount by which the normal value exceeds the export price. Where dumping margins vary, a weighted average dumping margin may be established.

Article 3   Determination of injury

1.   Pursuant to this Regulation, the term 'injury' shall, unless otherwise specified, be taken to mean material injury to the Community industry, threat of material injury to the Community industry or material retardation of the establishment of such an industry and shall be interpreted in accordance with the provisions of this Article.

2.   A determination of injury shall be based on positive evidence and shall involve an objective examination of both (a) the volume of the dumped imports and the effect of the dumped imports on prices in the Community market for like products; and (b) the consequent impact of those imports on the Community industry.

3.   With regard to the volume of the dumped imports, consideration shall be given to whether there has been a significant increase in dumped imports, either in absolute terms or relative to production or consumption in the Community. With regard to the effect of the dumped imports on prices, consideration shall be given to whether there has been significant price undercutting by the dumped imports as compared with the price of a like product of the Community industry, or whether the effect of such imports is otherwise to depress prices to a significant degree or prevent price increases, which would otherwise have occurred, to a significant degree. No one or more of these factors can necessarily give decisive guidance.

4.   Where imports of a product from more than one country are simultaneously subject to anti-dumping investigations, the effects of such imports shall be cumulatively assessed only if it is determined that (a) the margin of dumping established in relation to the imports from each country is more than de minimis as defined in Article 9(3) and that the volume of imports from each country is not negligible; and (b) a cumulative assessment of the effects of the imports is appropriate in light of the conditions of competition between imported products and the conditions of competition between the imported products and the like Community product.

5.   The examination of the impact of the dumped imports on the Community industry concerned shall include an evaluation of all relevant economic factors and indices having a bearing on the state of the industry, including the fact that an industry is still in the process of recovering from the effects of past dumping or subsidisation, the magnitude of the actual margin of dumping, actual and potential decline in sales, profits, output, market share, productivity, return on investments, utilisation of capacity; factors affecting Community prices; actual and potential negative effects on cash flow, inventories, employment, wages, growth, ability to raise capital or investments. This list is not exhaustive, nor can any one or more of these factors necessarily give decisive guidance.

6.   It must be demonstrated, from all the relevant evidence presented in relation to paragraph 2, that the dumped imports are causing injury within the meaning of this Regulation. Specifically, this shall entail a demonstration that the volume and/or price levels identified pursuant to paragraph 3 are responsible for an impact on the Community industry as provided for in paragraph 5, and that this impact exists to a degree which enables it to be classified as material.

7.   Known factors other than the dumped imports which at the same time are injuring the Community industry shall also be examined to ensure that injury caused by these other factors is not attributed to the dumped imports under paragraph 6. Factors which may be considered in this respect include the volume and prices of imports not sold at dumping prices, contraction in demand or changes in the patterns of consumption, restrictive trade practices of, and competition between, third country and Community producers, developments in technology and the export performance and productivity of the Community industry.

8.   The effect of the dumped imports shall be assessed in relation to the production of the Community industry of the like product when available data permit the separate identification of that production on the basis of such criteria as the production process, producers' sales and profits. If such separate identification of that production is not possible, the effects of the dumped imports shall be assessed by examination of the production of the narrowest group or range of products, which includes the like product, for which the necessary information can be provided.

9.   A determination of a threat of material injury shall be based on facts and not merely on allegation, conjecture or remote possibility. The change in circumstances which would create a situation in which the dumping would cause injury must be clearly foreseen and imminent. In making a determination regarding the existence of a threat of material injury, consideration should be given to such factors as:

   (a)   a significant rate of increase of dumped imports into the Community market indicating the likelihood of substantially increased imports;

   (b)   sufficient freely disposable capacity of the exporter or an imminent and substantial increase in such capacity indicating the likelihood of substantially increased dumped exports to the Community, account being taken of the availability of other export markets to absorb any additional exports;

   (c)   whether imports are entering at prices that would, to a significant degree, depress prices or prevent price increases which otherwise would have occurred, and would probably increase demand for further imports; and

   (d)   inventories of the product being investigated. No one of the factors listed above by itself can necessarily give decisive guidance but the totality of the factors considered must lead to the conclusion that further dumped exports are imminent and that, unless protective action is taken, material injury will occur.

Article 4   Definition of Community industry

1.   For the purposes of this Regulation, the term 'Community industry' shall be interpreted as referring to the Community producers as a whole of the like products or to those of them whose collective output of the products constitutes a major proportion, as defined in Article 5(4), of the total Community production of those products, except that:

   (a)   when producers are related to the exporters or importers or are themselves importers of the allegedly dumped product, the term 'Community industry' may be interpreted as referring to the rest of the producers;

   (b)   in exceptional circumstances the territory of the Community may, for the production in question, be divided into two or more competitive markets and the producers within each market may be regarded as a separate industry if

   (i)   the producers within such a market sell all or almost all of their production of the product in question in that market; and

   (ii)   the demand in that market is not to any substantial degree supplied by producers of the product in question located elsewhere in the Community. In such circumstances, injury may be found to exist even where a major portion of the total Community industry is not injured, provided there is a concentration of dumped imports into such an isolated market and provided further that the dumped imports are causing injury to the producers of all or almost all of the production within such a market.

2.   For the purpose of paragraph 1, producers shall be considered to be related to exporters or importers only if (a) one of them directly or indirectly controls the other; or (b) both of them are directly or indirectly controlled by a third person; or (c) together they directly or indirectly control a third person provided that there are grounds for believing or suspecting that the effect of the relationship is such as to cause the producer concerned to behave differently from non-related producers. For the purpose of this paragraph, one shall be deemed to control another when the former is legally or operationally in a position to exercise restraint or direction over the latter.

3.   Where the Community industry has been interpreted as referring to the producers in a certain region, the exporters shall be given an opportunity to offer undertakings pursuant to Article 8 in respect of the region concerned. In such cases, when evaluating the Community interest of the measures, special account shall be taken of the interest of the region. If an adequate undertaking is not offered promptly or the situations set out in Article 8(9) and (10) apply, a provisional or definitive duty may be imposed in respect of the Community as a whole. In such cases, the duties may, if practicable, be limited to specific producers or exporters.

4.   The provisions of Article 3(8) shall be applicable to this Article.

Article 5   Initiation of proceedings

1.   Except as provided for in paragraph 6, an investigation to determine the existence, degree and effect of any alleged dumping shall be initiated upon a written complaint by any natural or legal person, or any association not having legal personality, acting on behalf of the Community industry.

The complaint may be submitted to the Commission, or to a Member State, which shall forward it to the Commission. The Commission shall send Member States a copy of any complaint it receives. The complaint shall be deemed to have been lodged on the first working day following its delivery to the Commission by registered mail or the issuing of an acknowledgement of receipt by the Commission.

Where, in the absence of any complaint, a Member State is in possession of sufficient evidence of dumping and of resultant injury to the Community industry, it shall immediately communicate such evidence to the Commission.

2.   A complaint under paragraph 1 shall include evidence of dumping, injury and a causal link between the allegedly dumped imports and the alleged injury. The complaint shall contain such information as is reasonably available to the complainant on the following:

(a)   identity of the complainant and a description of the volume and value of the Community production of the like product by the complainant. Where a written complaint is made on behalf of the Community industry, the complaint shall identify the industry on behalf of which the complaint is made by a list of all known Community producers of the like product (or associations of Community producers of the like product) and, to the extent possible, a description of the volume and value of Community production of the like product accounted for by such producers;

(b)   a complete description of the allegedly dumped product, the names of the country or countries of origin or export in question, the identity of each known exporter or foreign producer and a list of known persons importing the product in question;

(c) information on prices at which the product in question is sold when destined for consumption in the domestic markets of the country or countries of origin or export (or, where appropriate, information on the prices at which the product is sold from the country or countries of origin or export to a third country or countries or on the constructed value of the product) and information on export prices or, where appropriate, on the prices at which the product is first resold to an independent buyer in the Community;

(d) information on changes in the volume of the allegedly dumped imports, the effect of those imports on prices of the like product on the Community market and the consequent impact of the imports on the Community industry, as demonstrated by relevant factors and indices having a bearing on the state of the Community industry, such as those listed in Article 3(3) and (5).

3. The Commission shall, as far as possible, examine the accuracy and adequacy of the evidence provided in the complaint to determine whether there is sufficient evidence to justify the initiation of an investigation.

4. An investigation shall not be initiated pursuant to paragraph 1 unless it has been determined, on the basis of an examination as to the degree of support for, or opposition to, the complaint expressed by Community producers of the like product, that the complaint has been made by or on behalf of the Community industry. The complaint shall be considered to have been made by or on behalf of the Community industry if it is supported by those Community producers whose collective output constitutes more than 50% of the total production of the like product produced by that portion of the Community industry expressing either support for or opposition to the complaint. However, no investigation shall be initiated when Community producers expressly supporting the complaint account for less than 25% of total production of the like product produced by the Community industry.

5. The authorities shall avoid, unless a decision has been made to initiate an investigation, any publicising of the complaint seeking the initiation of an investigation. However, after receipt of a properly documented complaint and before proceeding to initiate an investigation, the government of the exporting country concerned shall be notified.

6. If in special circumstances, it is decided to initiate an investigation without having received a written complaint by or on behalf of the Community industry for the initiation of such investigation, this shall be done on the basis of sufficient evidence of dumping, injury and a causal link, as described in paragraph 2, to justify such initiation.

7. The evidence of both dumping and injury shall be considered simultaneously in the decision on whether or not to initiate an investigation. A complaint shall be rejected where there is insufficient evidence of either dumping or of injury to justify proceeding with the case. Proceedings shall not be initiated against countries whose imports represent a market share of below 1%, unless such countries collectively account for 3% or more of Community consumption.

8. The complaint may be withdrawn prior to initiation, in which case it shall be considered not to have been lodged.

9. Where, after consultation, it is apparent that there is sufficient evidence to justify initiating a proceeding, the Commission shall do so within 45 days of the lodging of the complaint and shall publish a notice in the *Official Journal of*

the European Communities. Where insufficient evidence has been presented, the complainant shall, after consultation, be so informed within 45 days of the date on which the complaint is lodged with the Commission.

10. The notice of initiation of the proceedings shall announce the initiation of an investigation, indicate the product and countries concerned, give a summary of the information received, and provide that all relevant information is to be communicated to the Commission; it shall state the periods within which interested parties may make themselves known, present their views in writing and submit information if such views and information are to be taken into account during the investigation; it shall also state the period within which interested parties may apply to be heard by the Commission in accordance with Article 6(5).

11. The Commission shall advise the exporters, importers and representative associations of importers or exporters known to it to be concerned, as well as representatives of the exporting country and the complainants, of the initiation of the proceedings and, with due regard to the protection of confidential information, provide the full text of the written complaint received pursuant to paragraph 1 to the known exporters and to the authorities of the exporting country, and make it available upon request to other interested parties involved. Where the number of exporters involved is particularly high, the full text of the written complaint may instead be provided only to the authorities of the exporting country or to the relevant trade association.

12. An anti-dumping investigation shall not hinder the procedures of customs clearance.

Article 6   The investigation

1. Following the initiation of the proceeding, the Commission, acting in cooperation with the Member States, shall commence an investigation at Community level. Such investigation shall cover both dumping and injury and these shall be investigated simultaneously. For the purpose of a representative finding, an investigation period shall be selected which, in the case of dumping shall, normally, cover a period of not less than six months immediately prior to the initiation of the proceeding. Information relating to a period subsequent to the investigation period shall, normally, not be taken into account.

2. Parties receiving questionnaires used in an anti-dumping investigation shall be given at least 30 days to reply. The time limit for exporters shall be counted from the date of receipt of the questionnaire, which for this purpose shall be deemed to have been received one week from the day on which it was sent to the exporter or transmitted to the appropriate diplomatic representative of the exporting country. An extension to the 30 day period may be granted, due account being taken of the time limits of the investigation, provided that the party shows due cause for such extension, in terms of its particular circumstances.

3. The Commission may request Member States to supply information, and Member States shall take whatever steps are necessary in order to give effect to such requests. They shall send to the Commission the information requested together within the results of all inspections, checks or investigations carried out. Where this information is of general interest or where its transmission has been requested by a Member State, the Commission shall forward it to the Member States, provided it is not confidential, in which case a non-confidential summary shall be forwarded.

4.   The Commission may request Member States to carry out all necessary checks and inspections, particularly amongst importers, traders and Community producers, and to carry out investigations in third countries, provided that the firms concerned give their consent and that the government of the country in question has been officially notified and raises no objection. Member States shall take whatever steps are necessary in order to give effect to such requests from the Commission. Officials of the Commission shall be authorised, if the Commission or a Member State so requests, to assist the officials of Member States in carrying out their duties.

5.   The interested parties which have made themselves known in accordance with Article 5(10) shall be heard if they have, within the period prescribed in the notice published in the Official Journal of the European Communities, made a written request for a hearing showing that they are an interested party likely to be affected by the result of the proceeding and that there are particular reasons why they should be heard.

6.   Opportunities shall, on request, be provided for the importers, exporters, representatives of the government of the exporting country and the complainants, which have made themselves known in accordance with Article 5(10), to meet those parties with adverse interests, so that opposing views may be presented and rebuttal arguments offered. Provision of such opportunities must take account of the need to preserve confidentiality and of the convenience to the parties. There shall be no obligation on any party to attend a meeting, and failure to do so shall not be prejudicial to that party's case. Oral information provided under this paragraph shall be taken into account in so far as it is subsequently confirmed in writing.

7.   The complainants, importers and exporters and their representative associations, users and consumer organisations, which have made themselves known in accordance with Article 5(10), as well as the representatives of the exporting country may, upon written request, inspect all information made available by any party to an investigation, as distinct from internal documents prepared by the authorities of the Community or its Member States, which is relevant to the presentation of their cases and not confidential within the meaning of Article 19, and that it is used in the investigation. Such parties may respond to such information and their comments shall be taken into consideration, wherever they are sufficiently substantiated in the response.

8.   Except in the circumstances provided for in Article 18, the information which is supplied by interested parties and upon which findings are based shall be examined for accuracy as far as possible.

9.   For proceedings initiated pursuant to Article 5(9), an investigation shall, whenever possible, be concluded within one year. In any event, such investigations shall in all cases be concluded within 15 months of initiation, in accordance with the findings made pursuant to Article 8 for undertakings or the findings made pursuant to Article 9 for definitive action.

Article 7   Provisional measures

1.   Provisional duties may be imposed if proceedings have been initiated in accordance with Article 5, if a notice has been given to that effect and interested parties have been given adequate opportunities to submit information and make comments in accordance with Article 5(10), if a provisional affirmative determination has been made of dumping and consequent injury to the

Community industry, and if the Community interest calls for intervention to prevent such injury. The provisional duties shall be imposed no earlier than 60 days from the initiation of the proceedings but not later than nine months from the initiation of the proceedings.

2. The amount of the provisional anti-dumping duty shall not exceed the margin of dumping as provisionally established, but it should be less than the margin if such lesser duty would be adequate to remove the injury to the Community industry.

3. Provisional duties shall be secured by a guarantee, and the release of the products concerned for free circulation in the Community shall be conditional upon the provision of such guarantee.

4. The Commission shall take provisional action after consultation or, in cases of extreme urgency, after informing the Member States. In this latter case, consultations shall take place 10 days, at the latest, after notification to the Member States of the action taken by the Commission.

5. Where a Member State requests immediate intervention by the Commission and where the conditions in paragraph 1 are met, the Commission shall within a maximum of five working days of receipt of the request, decide whether a provisional anti-dumping duty shall be imposed.

6. The Commission shall forthwith inform the Council and the Member States of any decision taken under paragraphs 1 to 5. The Council, acting by a qualified majority, may decide differently.

7. Provisional duties may be imposed for six months and extended for a further three months or they may be imposed for nine months. However, they may only be extended, or imposed for a nine-month period, where exporters representing a significant percentage of the trade involved so request or do not object upon notification by the Commission.

Article 8   Undertakings

1. Investigations may be terminated without the imposition of provisional or definitive duties upon receipt of satisfactory voluntary undertakings from any exporter to revise its prices or to cease exports to the area in question at dumped prices, so that the Commission, after consultation, is satisfied that the injurious effect of the dumping is eliminated. Price increases under such undertakings shall not be higher than necessary to eliminate the margin of dumping and they should be less than the margin of dumping if such increases would be adequate to remove the injury to the Community industry.

2. Undertakings may be suggested by the Commission, but no exporter shall be obliged to enter into such an undertaking. The fact that exporters do not offer such undertakings, or do not accept an invitation to do so, shall in no way prejudice consideration of the case. However, it may be determined that a threat of injury is more likely to be realised if the dumped imports continue. Undertakings shall not be sought or accepted from exporters unless a provisional affirmative determination of dumping and injury caused by such dumping has been made. Save in exceptional circumstances, undertakings may not be offered later than the end of the period during which representations may be made pursuant to Article 20(5).

3. Undertakings offered need not be accepted if their acceptance is considered impractical, if such as where the number of actual or potential exporters is too great, or for other reasons, including reasons of general policy.

The exporter concerned may be provided with the reasons for which it is proposed to reject the offer of an undertaking and may be given an opportunity to make comments thereon. The reasons for rejection shall be set out in the definitive decision.

4.   Parties which offer an undertaking shall be required to provide a non-confidential version of such undertaking, so that it may be made available to interested parties to the investigation.

5.   Where undertakings are, after consultation, accepted and where there is no objection raised within the Advisory Committee, the investigation shall be terminated. In all other cases, the Commission shall submit to the Council forthwith a report on the results of the consultation, together with a proposal that the investigation be terminated. The investigation shall be deemed terminated if, within one month, the Council, acting by a qualified majority, has not decided otherwise.

6.   If the undertakings are accepted, the investigation of dumping and injury shall normally be completed. In such a case, if a negative determination of dumping or injury is made, the undertaking shall automatically lapse, except in cases where such a determination is due in large part to the existence of an undertaking. In such cases it may be required that an undertaking be maintained for a reasonable period. In the event that an affirmative determination of dumping and injury is made, the undertaking shall continue consistent with its terms and the provisions of this Regulation.

7.   The Commission shall require any exporter from which an undertaking has been accepted to provide, periodically, information relevant to the fulfilment of such undertaking, and to permit verification of pertinent data. Non-compliance with such requirements shall be construed as a breach of the undertaking.

8.   Where undertakings are accepted from certain exporters during the course of an investigation, they shall, for the purpose of Article 11, be deemed to take effect from the date on which the investigation is concluded for the exporting country.

9.   In case of breach or withdrawal of undertakings by any party, a definitive duty shall be imposed in accordance with Article 9, on the basis of the facts established within the context of the investigation which led to the undertaking, provided that such investigation was concluded with a final determination as to dumping and injury and that the exporter concerned has, except where he himself has withdrawn the undertaking, been given an opportunity to comment.

10.   A provisional duty may, after consultation, be imposed in accordance with Article 7 on the basis of the best information available, where there is reason to believe that an undertaking is being breached, or in case of breach or withdrawal of an undertaking where the investigation which led to the undertaking has not been concluded.

Article 9   Termination without measures; imposition of definitive duties

1.   Where the complaint is withdrawn, the proceeding may be terminated unless such termination would not be in the Community interest.

2.   Where, after consultation, protective measures are unnecessary and there is no objection raised within the Advisory Committee, the investigation

or proceeding shall be terminated. In all other cases, the Commission shall submit to the Council forthwith a report on the results of the consultation, together with a proposal that the proceeding be terminated. The proceeding shall be deemed terminated if, within one month, the Council, acting by a qualified majority, has not decided otherwise.

3.   For a proceeding initiated pursuant to Article 5(9), injury shall normally be regarded as negligible where the imports concerned represent less than the volumes set out in Article 5(7). For the same proceeding, there shall be immediate termination where it is determined that the margin of dumping is less than 2%, expressed as a percentage of the export price, provided that it is only the investigation that shall be terminated where the margin is below 2% for individual exporters and they shall remain subject to the proceeding and may be reinvestigated in any subsequent review carried out for the country concerned pursuant to Article 11.

4.   Where the facts as finally established show that there is dumping and injury caused thereby, and the Community interest calls for intervention in accordance with Article 21, a definitive anti-dumping duty shall be imposed by the Council, acting by simple majority on a proposal submitted by the Commission after consultation of the Advisory Committee. Where provisional duties are in force, a proposal for definitive action shall be submitted to the Council not later than one month before the expiry of such duties. The amount of the anti-dumping duty shall not exceed the margin of dumping established but it should be less than the margin if such lesser duty would be adequate to remove the injury to the Community industry.

5.   An anti-dumping duty shall be imposed in the appropriate amounts in each case, on a non-discriminatory basis on imports of a product from all sources found to be dumped and causing injury, except as to imports from those sources from which undertakings under the terms of this Regulation have been accepted. The Regulation imposing the duty shall specify the duty for each supplier or, if that is impracticable, and as a general rule in the cases referred to in Article 2(7), the supplying country concerned.

6.   When the Commission has limited its examination in accordance with Article 17, any anti-dumping duty applied to imports from exporters or producers which have made themselves known in accordance with Article 17 but were not included in the examination shall not exceed the weighted average margin of dumping established for the parties in the sample. For the purpose of this paragraph, the Commission shall disregard any zero and de minimis margins, and margins established in the circumstances referred to in Article 18. Individual duties shall be applied to imports from any exporter or producer which is granted individual treatment, as provided for in Article 17.

Article 10   Retroactivity

1.   Provisional measures and definitive anti-dumping duties shall only be applied to products which enter free circulation after the time when the decision taken pursuant to Articles 7(1) or 9(4), as the case may be, enters into force, subject to the exceptions set out in this Regulation.

2.   Where a provisional duty has been applied and the facts as finally established show that there is dumping and injury, the Council shall decide, irrespective of whether a definitive anti-dumping duty is to be imposed, what proportion of the provisional duty is to be definitively collected. For this

purpose, 'injury' shall not include material retardation of the establishment of a Community industry, nor threat of material injury, except where it is found that this would, in the absence of provisional measures, have developed into material injury. In all other cases involving such threat or retardation, any provisional amounts shall be released and definitive duties can only be imposed from the date that a final determination of threat or material retardation is made.

3.   If the definitive anti-dumping duty is higher than the provisional duty, the difference shall not be collected. If the definitive duty is lower than the provisional duty, the duty shall be recalculated. Where a final determination is negative, the provisional duty shall not be confirmed.

4.   A definitive anti-dumping duty may be levied on products which were entered for consumption not more than 90 days prior to the date of application of provisional measures but not prior to the initiation of the investigation, provided that imports have been registered in accordance with Article 14(5), the Commission has allowed the importers concerned an opportunity to comment, and:

(a)   there is, for the product in question, a history of dumping over an extended period, or the importer was aware of, or should have been aware of, the dumping as regards the extent of the dumping and the injury alleged or found; and

(b)   in addition to the level of imports which caused injury during the investigation period, there is a further substantial rise in imports which, in the light of its timing and volume and other circumstances, is likely to seriously undermine the remedial effect of the definitive anti-dumping duty to be applied.

5.   In cases of breach or withdrawal of undertakings, definitive duties may be levied on goods entered for free circulation not more than 90 days before the application of provisional measures, provided that imports have been registered in accordance with Article 14(5), and that any such retroactive assessment shall not apply to imports entered before the breach or withdrawal of the undertaking.

Article 11   Duration, reviews and refunds

1.   An anti-dumping measure shall remain in force only as long as, and to the extent that, it is necessary to counteract the dumping which is causing injury.

2.   A definitive anti-dumping measure shall expire five years from its imposition or five years from the date of the conclusion of the most recent review which has covered both dumping and injury, unless it is determined in a review that the expiry would be likely to lead to a continuation or recurrence of dumping and injury. Such an expiry review shall be initiated on the initiative of the Commission, or upon request made by or on behalf of Community producers, and the measure shall remain in force pending the outcome of such review. An expiry review shall be initiated where the request contains sufficient evidence that the expiry of the measures would be likely to result in a continuation or recurrence of dumping and injury. Such a likelihood may, for example, be indicated by evidence of continued dumping and injury or evidence that the removal of injury is partly or solely due to the existence of measures or evidence that the circumstances of the exporters, or market

conditions, are such that they would indicate the likelihood of further injurious dumping. In carrying out investigations under this paragraph, the exporters, importers, the representatives of the exporting country and the Community producers shall be provided with the opportunity to amplify, rebut or comment on the matters set out in the review request, and conclusions shall be reached with due account taken of all relevant and duly documented evidence presented in relation to the question as to whether the expiry of measures would be likely, or unlikely, to lead to the continuation or recurrence of dumping and injury. A notice of impending expiry shall be published in the Official Journal of the European Communities at an appropriate time in the final year of the period of application of the measures as defined in this paragraph. Thereafter, the Community producers shall, no later than three months before the end of the five-year period, be entitled to lodge a review request in accordance with the second sub-paragraph. A notice announcing the actual expiry of measures pursuant to this paragraph shall also be published.

3. The need for the continued imposition of measures may also be reviewed, where warranted, on the initiative of the Commission or at the request of a Member State or, provided that a reasonable period of time of at least one year has elapsed since the imposition of the definitive measure, upon a request by any exporter or importer or by the Community producers which contains sufficient evidence substantiating the need for such an interim review. An interim review shall be initiated where the request contains sufficient evidence that the continued imposition of the measure is no longer necessary to offset dumping and/or that the injury would be unlikely to continue or recur if the measure were removed or varied, or that the existing measure is not, or is no longer, sufficient to counteract the dumping which is causing injury. In carrying out investigations pursuant to this paragraph, the Commission may, inter alia, consider whether the circumstances with regard to dumping and injury have changed significantly, or whether existing measures are achieving the intended results in removing the injury previously established under Article 3. In these respects, account shall be taken in the final determination of all relevant and duly documented evidence.

4. A review shall also be carried out for the purpose of determining individual margins of dumping for new exporters in the exporting country in question which have not exported the product during the period of investigation on which the measures were based. The review shall be initiated where a new exporter or producer can show that it is not related to any of the exporters or producers in the exporting country which are subject to the anti-dumping measures on the product, and that it has actually exported to the Community following the abovementioned investigation period, or where it can demonstrate that it has entered into an irrevocable contractual obligation to export a significant quantity to the Community. A review for a new exporter shall be initiated, and carried out on an accelerated basis, after consultation of the Advisory Committee and after Community producers have been given an opportunity to comment. The Commission Regulation initiating a review shall repeal the duty in force with regard to the new exporter concerned by amending the Regulation which has imposed such duty, and by making imports subject to registration in accordance with Article 14(5) in order to ensure that, should the review result in a determination of dumping in respect of such an exporter, anti-dumping duties can be levied retroactively to the date of the initiation of

the review. The provisions of this paragraph shall not apply where duties have been imposed under Article 9(6).

5.   The relevant provisions of this Regulation with regard to procedures and the conduct of investigations, excluding those relating to time limits, shall apply to any review carried out pursuant to paragraphs 2, 3 and 4. Any such review shall be carried out expeditiously and shall normally be concluded within 12 months of the date of initiation of the review.

6.   Reviews pursuant to this Article shall be initiated by the Commission after consultation of the Advisory Committee. Where warranted by reviews, measures shall be repealed or maintained pursuant to paragraph 2, or repealed, maintained or amended pursuant to paragraphs 3 and 4, by the Community institution responsible for their introduction. Where measures are repealed for individual exporters, but not for the country as a whole, such exporters shall remain subject to the proceeding and may, automatically, be reinvestigated in any subsequent review carried out for that country pursuant to this Article.

7.   Where a review of measures pursuant to paragraph 3 is in progress at the end of the period of application of measures as defined in paragraph 2, such review shall also cover the circumstances set out in paragraph 2. Notwithstanding paragraph 2, an importer may request reimbursement of duties collected where it is shown that the dumping margin, on the basis of which duties were paid, has been eliminated, or reduced to a level which is below the level of the duty in force.

8.   In requesting a refund of anti-dumping duties, the importer shall submit an application to the Commission. The application shall be submitted via the Member State of the territory in which the products were released for free circulation, within six months of the date on which the amount of the definitive duties to be levied was duly determined by the competent authorities or of the date on which a decision was made definitively to collect the amounts secured by way of provisional duty. Member States shall forward the request to the Commission forthwith. An application for refund shall only be considered to be duly supported by evidence where it contains precise information on the amount of refund of anti-dumping duties claimed and all customs documentation relating to the calculation and payment of such amount. It shall also include evidence, for a representative period, of normal values and export prices to the Community for the exporter or producer to which the duty applies. In cases where the importer is not associated with the exporter or producer concerned and such information is not immediately available, or where the exporter or producer is unwilling to release it to the importer, the application shall contain a statement from the exporter or producer that the dumping margin has been reduced or eliminated, as specified in this Article, and that the relevant supporting evidence will be provided to the Commission. Where such evidence is not forthcoming from the exporter or producer within a reasonable period of time the application shall be rejected. The Commission shall, after consultation of the Advisory Committee, decide whether and to what extent the application should be granted, or it may decide at any time to initiate an interim review, whereupon the information and findings from such review carried out in accordance with the provisions applicable for such reviews, shall be used to determine whether and to what extent a refund is justified. Refunds of duties shall normally take place within 12 months, and in

no circumstances more than 18 months after the date on which a request for a refund, duly supported by evidence, has been made by an importer of the product subject to the anti-dumping duty. The payment of any refund authorised should normally be made by Member States within 90 days of the abovementioned decision.

9. In all review or refund investigations carried out pursuant to this Article, the Commission shall, provided that circumstances have not changed, apply the same methodology as in the investigation which led to the duty, with due account being taken of Article 2, and in particular paragraphs 11 and 12 thereof, and of Article 17.

10. In any investigation carried out pursuant to this Article, the Commission shall examine the reliability of export prices in accordance with Article 2. However, where it is decided to construct the export price in accordance with Article 2(9), it shall calculate it with no deduction for the amount of anti-dumping duties paid when conclusive evidence is provided that the duty is duly reflected in resale prices and the subsequent selling prices in the Community.

Article 12

1. Where the Community industry submits sufficient information showing that measures have led to no movement, or insufficient movement, in resale prices or subsequent selling prices in the Community, the investigation may, after consultation, be reopened to examine whether the measure has had effects on the abovementioned prices.

2. During a reinvestigation pursuant to this Article, exporters, importers and Community producers shall be provided with an opportunity to clarify the situation with regard to resale prices and subsequent selling prices: if it is concluded that the measure should have led to movements in such prices, then, in order to remove the injury previously established in accordance with Article 3, export prices shall be reassessed in accordance with Article 2 and dumping margins shall be recalculated to take account of the reassessed export prices. Where it is considered that a lack of movement in the prices in the Community is due to a fall in export prices which has occurred prior to or following the imposition of measures, dumping margins may be recalculated to take account of such lower export prices.

3. Where a reinvestigation pursuant to this Article shows increased dumping the measures in force shall be amended by the Council, by simple majority on a proposal from the Commission, in accordance with the new findings on export prices.

4. The relevant provisions of Articles 5 and 6 shall apply to any review carried out pursuant to this Article, except that such review shall be carried out expeditiously and shall normally be concluded within six months of the date of initiation of the reinvestigation.

5. Alleged changes in normal value shall only be taken into account under this Article where complete information on revised normal values, duly substantiated by evidence, is made available to the Commission within the time limits set out in the notice of initiation of an investigation. Where an investigation involves a re-examination of normal values, imports may be made subject to registration in accordance with Article 14(5) pending the outcome of the reinvestigation.

Article 13   Circumvention

1.   Anti-dumping duties imposed pursuant to this Regulation may be extended to imports from third countries of like products, or parts thereof, when circumvention of the measures in force is taking place. Circumvention shall be defined as a change in the pattern of trade between third countries and the Community which stems from a practice, process or work for which there is insufficient due cause or economic justification other than the imposition of the duty, and where there is evidence that the remedial effects of the duty are being undermined in terms of the prices and/or quantities of the like products and there is evidence of dumping in relation to the normal values previously established for the like or similar products.

2.   An assembly operation in the Community or a third country shall be considered to circumvent the measures in force where:

   (a)   the operation started or substantially increased since, or just prior to, the initiation of the anti-dumping investigation and the parts concerned are from the country subject to measures; and

   (b)   the parts constitute 60% or more of the total value of the parts of the assembled product, except that in no case shall circumvention be considered to be taking place where the value added to the parts brought in, during the assembly or completion operation, is greater than 25% of the manufacturing cost, and

   (c)   the remedial effects of the duty are being undermined in terms of the prices and/or quantities of the assembled like product and there is evidence of dumping in relation to the normal values previously established for the like or similar products.

3.   Investigations shall be initiated pursuant to this Article where the request contains sufficient evidence regarding the factors set out in paragraph 1. Initiations shall be made, after consultation of the Advisory Committee, by Commission Regulation which shall also instruct the customs authorities to make imports subject to registration in accordance with Article 14(5) or to request guarantees. Investigations shall be carried out by the Commission, which may be assisted by customs authorities and shall be concluded within nine months. When the facts as finally ascertained justify the extension of measures, this shall be done by the Council, acting by simple majority and on a proposal from the Commission, from the date on which registration was imposed pursuant to Article 14(5) or on which guarantees were requested. The relevant procedural provisions of this Regulation with regard to initiations and the conduct of investigations shall apply pursuant to this Article.

4.   Products shall not be subject to registration pursuant to Article 14(5) or measures where they are accompanied by a customs certificate declaring that the importation of the goods does not constitute circumvention. These certificates may be issued to importers, upon written application following authorisation by decision of the Commission after consultation of the Advisory Committee or decision of the Council imposing measures and they shall remain valid for the period, and under the conditions, set down therein.

5.   Nothing in this Article shall preclude the normal application of the provisions in force concerning customs duties.

Article 14   General provisions

1.   Provisional or definitive anti-dumping duties shall be imposed by Regulation, and collected by Member States in the form, at the rate specified

and according to the other criteria laid down in the Regulation imposing such duties. Such duties shall also be collected independently of the customs duties, taxes and other charges normally imposed on imports. No product shall be subject to both anti-dumping and countervailing duties for the purpose of dealing with one and the same situation arising from dumping or from export subsidisation.

2. Regulations imposing provisional or definitive anti-dumping duties, and Regulations or Decisions accepting undertakings or terminating investigations or proceedings, shall be published in the Official Journal of the European Communities. Such Regulations or Decisions shall contain in particular and with due regard to the protection of confidential information, the names of the exporters, if possible, or of the countries involved, a description of the product and a summary of the material facts and considerations relevant to the dumping and injury determinations. In each case, a copy of the Regulation or Decision shall be sent to known interested parties. The provisions of this paragraph shall apply mutatis mutandis to reviews.

3. Special provisions, in particular with regard to the common definition of the concept of origin, as contained in Council Regulation (EEC) No. 2913/92,[1] may be adopted pursuant to this Regulation.

4. In the Community interest, measures imposed pursuant to this Regulation may, after consultation of the Advisory Committee, be suspended by a decision of the Commission for a period of nine months. The suspension may be extended for a further period, not exceeding one year, if the Council so decides, acting by simple majority on a proposal from the Commission. Measures may only be suspended where market conditions have temporarily changed to an extent that injury would be unlikely to resume as a result of the suspension, and provided that the Community industry has been given an opportunity to comment and these comments have been taken into account. Measures may, at any time and after consultation, be reinstated if the reason for suspension is no longer applicable.

5. The Commission may, after consultation of the Advisory Committee, direct the customs authorities to take the appropriate steps to register imports, so that measures may subsequently be applied against those imports from the date of such registration. Imports may be made subject to registration following a request from the Community industry which contains sufficient evidence to justify such action. Registration shall be introduced by Regulation which shall specify the purpose of the action and, if appropriate, the estimated amount of possible future liability. Imports shall not be made subject to registration for a period longer than nine months.

6. Member States shall report to the Commission every month, on the import trade in products subject to investigation and to measures, and on the amount of duties collected pursuant to this Regulation.

Note
[1] OJ No. L302, 19.10.1992, p. 1.

Article 15 Consultations

1. Any consultations provided for in this Regulation shall take place within an Advisory Committee, which shall consist of representatives of each Member State, with a representative of the Commission as chairman. Consultations shall be held immediately at the request of a Member State or on the initiative

of the Commission and in any event within a period of time which allows the time limits set by this Regulation to be adhered to.

2. The Committee shall meet when convened by its chairman. He shall provide the Member States, as promptly as possible, with all relevant information.

3. Where necessary, consultation may be in writing only; in that event, the Commission shall notify the Member States and shall specify a period within which they shall be entitled to express their opinions or to request an oral consultation which the chairman shall arrange, provided that such oral consultation can be held within a period of time which allows the time limits set by this Regulation to be adhered to.

4. Consultation shall cover, in particular:

(a) the existence of dumping and the methods of establishing the dumping margin;

(b) the existence and extent of injury;

(c) the causal link between the dumped imports and injury;

(d) the measures which, in the circumstances, are appropriate to prevent or remedy the injury caused by dumping and the ways and means of putting such measures into effect.

Article 16   Verification visits

1. The Commission shall, where it considers it appropriate, carry out visits to examine the records of importers, exporters, traders, agents, producers, trade associations and organisations and to verify information provided on dumping and injury. In the absence of a proper and timely reply, a verification visit may not be carried out.

2. The Commission may carry out investigations in third countries as required, provided that it obtains the agreement of the firms concerned, that it notifies the representatives of the government of the country in question and that the latter does not object to the investigation. As soon as the agreement of the firms concerned has been obtained the Commission should notify the authorities of the exporting country of the names and addresses of the firms to be visited and the dates agreed.

3. The firms concerned shall be advised of the nature of the information to be verified during verification visits and of any further information which needs to be provided during such visits, though this should not preclude requests made during the verification for further details to be provided in the light of information obtained.

4. In investigations carried out pursuant to paragraphs 1, 2 and 3, the Commission shall be assisted by officials of those Member States who so request.

Article 17   Sampling

1. In cases where the number of complainants, exporters or importers, types of product or transactions is large, the investigation may be limited to a reasonable number of parties, products or transactions by using samples which are statistically valid on the basis of information available at the time of the selection, or to the largest representative volume of production, sales or exports which can reasonably be investigated within the time available.

2. The final selection of parties, types of products or transactions made under these sampling provisions shall rest with the Commission, though

preference shall be given to choosing a sample in consultation with, and with the consent of, the parties concerned, provided such parties make themselves known and make sufficient information available, within three weeks of initiation of the investigation, to enable a representative sample to be chosen.

3.   In cases where the examination has been limited in accordance with this Article, an individual margin of dumping shall, nevertheless, be calculated for any exporter or producer not initially selected who submits the necessary information within the time limits provided for in this Regulation, except where the number of exporters or producers is so large that individual examinations would be unduly burdensome and would prevent completion of the investigation in good time.

4.   Where it is decided to sample and there is a degree of non-cooperation by some or all of the parties selected which is likely to materially affect the outcome of the investigation, a new sample may be selected. However, if a material degree of non-cooperation persists or there is insufficient time to select a new sample, the relevant provisions of Article 18 shall apply.

Article 18   Non-cooperation

1.   In cases in which any interested party refuses access to, or otherwise does not provide, necessary information within the time limits provided in this Regulation, or significantly impedes the investigation, provisional or final findings, affirmative or negative, may be made on the basis of the facts available. Where it is found that any interested party has supplied false or misleading information, the information shall be disregarded and use may be made of facts available. Interested parties should be made aware of the consequences of non-cooperation.

2.   Failure to give a computerised response shall not be deemed to constitute non-cooperation, provided that the interested party shows that presenting the response as requested would result in an unreasonable extra burden or unreasonable additional cost.

3.   Where the information submitted by an interested party is not ideal in all respects it should nevertheless not be disregarded, provided that any deficiencies are not such as to cause undue difficulty in arriving at a reasonably accurate finding and that the information is appropriately submitted in good time and is verifiable, and that the party has acted to the best of its ability.

4.   If evidence or information is not accepted, the supplying party shall be informed forthwith of the reasons therefor and shall be granted an opportunity to provide further explanations within the time limit specified. If the explanations are considered unsatisfactory, the reasons for rejection of such evidence or information shall be disclosed and given in published findings.

5.   If determinations, including those regarding normal value, are based on the provisions of paragraph 1, including the information supplied in the complaint, it shall, where practicable and with due regard to the time limits of the investigation, be checked by reference to information from other independent sources which may be available, such as published price lists, official import statistics and customs returns, or information obtained from other interested parties during the investigation.

6.   If an interested party does not cooperate, or cooperates only partially, so that relevant information is thereby withheld, the result may be less favourable to the party than if it had cooperated.

Article 19   Confidentiality

1.   Any information which is by nature confidential, (for example, because its disclosure would be of significant competitive advantage to a competitor or would have a significantly adverse effect upon a person supplying the information or upon a person from whom he has acquired the information) or which is provided on a confidential basis by parties to an investigation shall, if good cause is shown, be treated as such by the authorities.

2.   Interested parties providing confidential information shall be required to furnish non-confidential summaries thereof. Those summaries shall be in sufficient detail to permit a reasonable understanding of the substance of the information submitted in confidence. In exceptional circumstances, such parties may indicate that such information is not susceptible of summary. In such exceptional circumstances, a statement of the reasons why summarisation is not possible must be provided.

3.   If it is considered that a request for confidentiality is not warranted and if the supplier of the information is either unwilling to make the information available or to authorise its disclosure in generalised or summary form, such information may be disregarded unless it can be satisfactorily demonstrated from appropriate sources that the information is correct. Requests for confidentiality shall not be arbitrarily rejected.

4.   This Article shall not preclude the disclosure of general information by the Community authorities and in particular of the reasons on which decisions taken pursuant to this Regulation are based, or disclosure of the evidence relied on by the Community authorities in so far as is necessary to explain those reasons in court proceedings. Such disclosure must take into account the legitimate interests of the parties concerned that their business secrets should not be divulged.

5.   The Council, the Commission and Member States, or the officials of any of these, shall not reveal any information received pursuant to this Regulation for which confidential treatment has been requested by its supplier, without specific permission from the supplier. Exchanges of information between the Commission and Member States, or any information relating to consultations made pursuant to Article 15, or any internal documents prepared by the authorities of the Community or its Member States, shall not be divulged except as specifically provided for in this Regulation.

6.   Information received pursuant to this Regulation shall be used only for the purpose for which it was requested.

Article 20   Disclosure

1.   The complainants, importers and exporters and their representative associations, and representatives of the exporting country, may request disclosure of the details underlying the essential facts and considerations on the basis of which provisional measures have been imposed. Requests for such disclosure shall be made in writing immediately following the imposition of provisional measures, and the disclosure shall be made in writing as soon as possible thereafter.

2.   The parties mentioned in paragraph 1 may request final disclosure of the essential facts and considerations on the basis of which it is intended to recommend the imposition of definitive measures, or the termination of an investigation or proceedings without the imposition of measures, particular

attention being paid to the disclosure of any facts or considerations which are different from those used for any provisional measures.

3. Requests for final disclosure, as defined in paragraph 2, shall be addressed to the Commission in writing and be received, in cases where a provisional duty has been applied, not later than one month after publication of the imposition of that duty. Where a provisional duty has not been applied, parties shall be provided with an opportunity to request final disclosure within time limits set by the Commission.

4. Final disclosure shall be given in writing. It shall be made, due regard being had to the protection of confidential information, as soon as possible and, normally, not later than one month prior to a definitive decision or the submission by the Commission of any proposal for final action pursuant to Article 9. Where the Commission is not in a position to disclose certain facts or considerations at that time, these shall be disclosed as soon as possible thereafter. Disclosure shall not prejudice any subsequent decision which may be taken by the Commission or the Council but where such decision is based on any different facts and considerations, these shall be disclosed as soon as possible.

5. Representations made after final disclosure is given shall be taken into consideration only if received within a period to be set by the Commission in each case, which shall be at least 10 days, due consideration being given to the urgency of the matter.

Article 21   Community interest

1. A determination as to whether the Community interest calls for intervention shall be based on an appreciation of all the various interests taken as a whole, including the interests of the domestic industry and users and consumers; and a determination pursuant to this Article shall only be made where all parties have been given the opportunity to make their views known pursuant to paragraph 2. In such an examination, the need to eliminate the trade distorting effects of injurious dumping and to restore effective competition shall be given special consideration. Measures, as determined on the basis of the dumping and injury found, may not be applied where the authorities, on the basis of all the information submitted, can clearly conclude that it is not in the Community interest to apply such measures.

2. In order to provide a sound basis on which the authorities can take account of all views and information in the decision as to whether or not the imposition of measures is in the Community interest, the complainants, importers and their representative associations, representative users and representative consumer organisations may, within the time limits specified in the notice of initiation of the anti-dumping investigation, make themselves known and provide information to the Commission. Such information, or appropriate summaries thereof, shall be made available to the other parties specified in this Article, and they shall be entitled to respond to such information.

3. The parties which have acted in conformity with paragraph 2 may request a hearing. Such requests shall be granted when they are submitted within the time limits set in paragraph 2, and when they set out the reasons, in terms of the Community interest, why the parties should be heard.

4. The parties which have acted in conformity with paragraph 2 may provide comments on the application of any provisional duties imposed. Such

comments shall be received within one month of the application of such measures if they are to be taken into account and they, or appropriate summaries thereof, shall be made available to other parties who shall be entitled to respond to such comments.

5. The Commission shall examine the information which is properly submitted and the extent to which it is representative and the results of such analysis, together with an opinion on its merits, shall be transmitted to the Advisory Committee. The balance of views expressed in the Committee shall be taken into account by the Commission in any proposal made pursuant to Article 9.

6. The parties which have acted in conformity with paragraph 2 may request the facts and considerations on which final decisions are likely to be taken to be made available to them. Such information shall be made available to the extent possible and without prejudice to any subsequent decision taken by the Commission or the Council.

7. Information shall only be taken into account where it is supported by actual evidence which substantiates its validity.

Article 22   Final provisions
This Regulation shall not preclude the application of:

(a)   any special rules laid down in agreements concluded between the Community and third countries;

(b)   the Community Regulations in the agricultural sector and Council Regulations (EC) No. 3448/93,[1] (EEC) No. 2730/75[2] and (EEC) No. 2783/75;[3] this Regulation shall operate by way of complement to those Regulations and in derogation from any provisions thereof which preclude the application of anti-dumping duties;

(c)   special measures, provided that such action does not run counter to obligations pursuant to the GATT.

Note
[1] OJ No. L318, 20.12.1993, p. 18.
[2] OJ No. L281, 1.11.1975, p. 20. Regulation as amended by Commission Regulation (EEC) No. 222/88 (OJ No. L28, 1.2.1988, p. 1).
[3] OJ No. L282, 1.11.1975, p. 104. Regulation as last amended by Regulation (EEC) No. 3290/94 (OJ No. L349, 31.12.1994, p. 105).

Article 23   Repeal of existing legislation and transitional measures
Regulation (EC) No. 3283/94 is hereby repealed, with the exception of the first paragraph of Article 23 thereof. However, the repeal of Regulation (EC) No. 3283/94 shall not prejudice the validity of proceedings initiated thereunder. References to Regulation (EEC) No. 2423/88 and to Regulation (EC) No. 3283/94 shall be construed as references to this Regulation, where appropriate.

Article 24   Entry into force
This Regulation shall enter into force on the day of its publication in the Official Journal of the European Communities. However, the time limits provided for in Articles 5(9), 6(9) and 7(1) shall apply to complaints lodged under Article 5(9) as from 1 September 1995 and investigations initiated pursuant to such complaints.

This Regulation shall be binding in its entirety and directly applicable in all Member States.

Done at Brussels, 22 December 1995.
For the Council,
L. ATIENZA SERNA,
The President

COMMISSION NOTICES

NOTICE OF DECEMBER 24, 1962
ON EXCLUSIVE AGENCY CONTRACTS MADE WITH
COMMERCIAL AGENTS
[JO 139/62]

I.   The Commission considers that contracts made with commercial agents, in which those agents undertake, for a specified part of the territory of the Common Market:
    — to negotiate transactions on behalf of an enterprise, or
    — to conclude transactions in the name and on behalf of an enterprise, or
    — to conclude transactions in their own name and on behalf of this enterprise,
are not covered by the prohibition laid down in Article 85, paragraph (1) of the Treaty.

It is essential in this case that the contracting party, described as a commercial agent, should, in fact, be such, by the nature of his functions and that he should neither undertake nor engage in activities proper to an independent trader in the course of commercial operations. The Commission regards as the decisive criterion, which distinguishes the commercial agent from the independent trader, the agreement — express or implied — which deals with responsibility for the financial risks bound up with the sale or with the performance of the contract. Thus the Commission's assessment is not governed by the way the 'representative' is described. Except for the usual *del credere* guarantee, a commercial agent must not, by the nature of his functions, assume any risk resulting from the transaction. If he does assume such risks his function becomes economically akin to that of an independent and he must therefore be treated as such for the purposes of the rules of competition. In such circumstances exclusive agency contracts must be regarded as agreements made with independent traders.

The Commission considers that an 'independent trader' is most likely to be involved where the contracting party described as a commercial agent:
    — is required to keep or does in fact keep, as his own property, a considerable stock of the products covered by the contract, or
    — is required to organise, maintain or ensure at his own expense a substantial service to customers free of charge, or does in fact organise, maintain or ensure such a service, or
    — can determine or does in fact determine prices or terms of business.

II.   In contrast to what is envisaged in this announcement about contracts made with commercial agents, the possibility that Article 85, paragraph (1), may be applicable to exclusive agency contracts with independent traders cannot be ruled out. In the case of such exclusive contracts the restriction of competition lies either in the limitation of supply, when the vendor undertakes to supply a given product only to one purchaser, or in the limitation of demand, when the purchaser undertakes to obtain a given product only from one vendor. In the case of reciprocal undertakings there will be such restrictions of competition on both sides. The question whether a restriction of competition of this nature is liable to affect trade between Member States depends on the circumstances of the case.

On the other hand, in the Commission's opinion, the conditions for the prohibition laid down in Article 85, paragraph (1), are not fulfilled by exclusive agency contracts made with commercial agents, since they have neither the object nor the effect of preventing, restricting or distorting competition within the common market. The commercial agent only performs an auxiliary function in the commodity market. In that market he acts on the instructions and in the interest of the enterprise on whose behalf he is operating. Unlike the independent trader, he himself is neither a purchaser nor a vendor, but seeks purchasers or vendors in the interest of the other party to the contract, who is the person doing the buying or selling. In this type of exclusive representation contract, the selling or buying enterprise does not cease to be a competitor; it merely uses an auxiliary, i.e. the commercial agent, to dispose of or acquire products on the market.

The legal status of commercial agents is determined, more or less uniformly, by statute in most of the member countries and by case law in others. The characteristic feature which all commercial agents have in common is their function as auxiliaries in the negotiation of business deals. The powers of commercial agents are subject to the rules laid down in civil law on 'mandate' and 'procuration'. Within the limits of those provisions the other party to the contract — who is the person selling or buying — is free to decide the product and the territory in respect of which he is willing to assign those functions to his agent.

Apart from the competitive situation on those markets where the commercial agent functions as an auxiliary to the other party to the contract, one has to consider the particular market on which commercial agents offer their services for the negotiation or conclusion of transactions. The obligation assumed by the agent — to work exclusively for one principal for a certain period of time — entails a limitation of supply on that market; the obligation assumed by the other party to the contract — to appoint him sole agent for a given territory — involves a limitation of demand on the market. Nevertheless, the Commission views these restrictions as a result of the special obligation between the commercial agent and his principal to protect each other's interests and therefore considers that they involve no restriction of competition.

The object of this Notice is to give enterprises some indication of the consideration by which the Commission will be guided when interpreting Article 85(1) of the Treaty and applying it to exclusive dealing contracts with commercial agents. The situation having thus been clarified, it will as a general rule no longer be useful for enterprises to obtain negative clearance for the agreements mentioned, nor will it be necessary to have the legal position established through a Commission decision on an individual case; this also means that notification will no longer be necessary for agreements of this type.

This Notice is without prejudice to any interpretation that may be given by other competent authorities and in particular by the courts.

COMMISSION NOTICE ON COOPERATION AGREEMENTS[1]

Concerning agreements, decisions and concerted practices in the field of co-operation between enterprises.

Questions are frequently put to the Commission of the European Communities on the attitude it intends to take up, within the framework of the implementation of the competition rules contained in the Treaties of Rome and Paris, with regard to co-operation between enterprises. In this Notice, it endeavours to provide guidance which, though not exhaustive, could prove useful to enterprises in the correct interpretation, in particular, of Article 85(1) of the EEC Treaty and Article 65(1) of the ECSC Treaty.

Note
[1] OJ 1968 C75/3 of 23 July 1968.

I   The Commission welcomes co-operation among small and medium-sized enterprises where such co-operation enables them to work more rationally and increase their productivity and competitiveness on a larger market. The Commission considers that it is its task to facilitate co-operation among small and medium-sized enterprises in particular. However, co-operation among large enterprises, too, can be economically justifiable without presenting difficulties from the angle of competition policy.

Article 85(1) of the Treaty establishing the European Economic Community (EEC Treaty), and Article 65(1) of the Treaty establishing the European Coal and Steel Community (ECSC Treaty) provide that all agreements, decisions and concerted practices (hereafter referred to as 'agreements') which have as their object or result the prevention, restriction or distortion of competition (hereafter referred to as 'restraints of competition') in the Common Market are incompatible with the Common Market and are forbidden; under Article 85(1) of the EEC Treaty this applies, however, only if these agreements are liable to impair trade between the member-States.

The Commission feels that in the interest of the small and medium-sized enterprises in particular it should make known the considerations by which it will be guided when interpreting Article 85(1) of the EEC Treaty and Article 65(1) of the ECSC Treaty and applying them to certain co-operation arrangements between enterprises, and indicate which of these arrangements in its opinion do not come under these provisions. This notice applies to all enterprises, irrespective of their size.

There may also be forms of co-operation between enterprises other than the forms of co-operation listed below which are not prohibited by Article 85(1) of the EEC Treaty or Article 65(1) of the ECSC Treaty. This applies in particular if the market position of the enterprises co-operating with each other is in the aggregate too weak to lead, through the agreements between them, to an appreciable restraint of competition in the Common Market and — for Article 85 of the EEC Treaty — impair trade between the member-States.

It is also pointed out, in respect of other forms of co-operation between enterprises or agreements containing additional clauses, that where the rules of competition of the Treaties apply, such forms of co-operation or agreements can be exempted by virtue of Article 85(3) of the EEC Treaty or be authorised by virtue of Article 65(2) of the ECSC Treaty.

The Commission intends to establish rapidly, by means of suitable decisions in individual cases or by general notices, the status of the various forms of co-operation in relation to the provisions of the Treaty.

No general statement can be made at this stage on the application of Article 86 of the EEC Treaty on the abuse of dominant positions within the Common Market or within a part of it. The same applies to Article 66(7) of the ECSC Treaty.

As a result of this notice, as a general rule, it will no longer be useful for enterprises to obtain negative clearance, as defined by Article 2 of Regulation 17, for the agreements listed, nor should it be necessary for the legal situation to be clarified through a Commission decision on an individual case; this also means that notification will no longer be necessary for agreements of this type. However, if it is doubtful whether in an individual case an agreement between enterprises restricts competition or if other forms of co-operation between enterprises which in the view of the enterprises do not restrict competition are not listed here, the enterprises are free to apply, where the matter comes under Article 85(1) of the EEC Treaty, for negative clearance, or to file as a precautionary measure, where Article 65(1) of the ECSC Treaty is the relevant clause, an application on the basis of Article 65(2) of the ECSC Treaty.

This notice does not prejudice interpretation by the Court of Justice of the European Communities.

The Commission takes the view that the following agreements do not restrict competition.

(1) *Agreements having as their sole object:*
   (a) *An exchange of opinion or experience,*
   (b) *Joint market research,*
   (c) *The joint carrying out of comparative studies of enterprises or industries,*
   (d) *The joint preparation of statistics and calculation models.*

Agreements whose sole purpose is the joint procurement of information which the various enterprises need to determine their future market behaviour freely and independently, or the use by each of the enterprises of a joint advisory body, do not have as their object or result the restriction of competition. But if the scope of action of the enterprises is limited or if the market behaviour is co-ordinated either expressly or through concerted parties, there may be restraint of competition. This is in particular the case where concrete recommendations are made or where conclusions are given such a form that they induce at least some of the participating enterprises to behave in an identical manner on the market.

The exchange of information can take place between the enterprises themselves or through a body acting as an intermediary. It is, however, particularly difficult to distinguish between information which has no bearing on competition on the one hand and behaviour in restraint of competition on the other, if there are special bodies which have to register orders, turnover figures, investment figures, and prices, so that it can as a rule not be automatically assumed that Article 85(1) of the EEC Treaty or Article 65(1) of the ECSC Treaty do not apply to them. A restraint of competition may occur in particular on an oligopolist market for homogenous products.

In the absence of more far-reaching co-operation between the participating enterprises, joint market research and comparative studies of different enterprises and industries to collect information and ascertain facts and market conditions do not in themselves impair competition. Other arrangements of this type, as for instance the joint establishment of economic and structural analyses, so obviously do not impair competition that there is no need to mention them specifically.

Calculation models containing specified rates of calculation are to be regarded as recommendations that may lead to restraints of competition.

(2) *Agreements having as their sole object:*
   (a) *Co-operation in accounting matters,*
   (b) *Joint provision of credit guarantees,*
   (c) *Joint debt-collecting associations,*
   (d) *Joint business or tax consultant agencies.*

These are cases of co-operation relating to fields that do not concern the supply of goods and services and the economic decisions of the enterprises involved, so that they cannot lead to restraints of competition.

Co-operation in accounting matters is neutral from the point of view of competition as it only serves for the technical handling of the accounting work. Nor is the creation of credit guarantee associations affected by the competition rules, since it does not modify the relationship between supply and demand.

Debt-collecting associations whose work is not confined to the collection of outstanding payments in line with the intentions and conditions of the participating enterprises, or which fix prices or exert in any other way an influence on price formation, may restrict competition. Application of uniform conditions by all participating firms may constitute a case of concerted practices, as may joint comparison of prices. In this connection, no objection can be raised against the use of standardised printed forms; their use must, however, not be combined with an understanding of tacit agreement on uniform prices, rebates or conditions of sale.

(3) *Agreements having as their sole object:*
   (a) *The joint implementation of research and development projects,*
   (b) *The joint placing of research and development contracts,*
   (c) *The sharing out of research and development projects among the participating enterprises.*

In the field of research, too, the mere exchange of experience and results serves for information only and does not restrict competition. It therefore need not be mentioned expressly.

Agreements on the joint execution of research work or the joint development of the results of research up to the stage of industrial application do not affect the competitive position of the parties. This also applies to the sharing of research fields and development work if the results are available to all participating enterprises. However, if the enterprises enter into commitments which restrict their own research and development activity or the utilisation of the results of joint work so that they do not have a free hand with regard to their own research and development outside the joint projects, this can constitute an infringement of the rules of competition of the Treaties. Where firms do not carry out joint research work, contractual obligations or concerted parties binding them to refrain from research work of their own either completely or in certain sectors may result in a restraint of competition. The sharing out of sectors of research without an understanding providing for mutual access to the results is to be regarded as a case of specialisation that may restrict competition.

There may also be a restraint of competition if agreements are concluded or corresponding concerted practices applied with regard to the practical exploitation of the results of research and development work carried out jointly, particularly if the participating enterprises undertake or agree to manufacture only products or the types of product developed jointly or to share out future production among themselves.

It is of the essence of joint research that the results should be exploited by the participating enterprises in proportion to their participation. If the participation of certain enterprises is confined to a specific sector of the common research project or to the provision of only limited financial assistance, there is no restraint of competition — in so far as there has been any joint research at all — if the results of research are made available to these enterprises only in proportion to the degree of their participation. There may, however, be a restraint of competition if certain participating enterprises are excluded from the exploitation of the results, either entirely or to an extent not commensurate with their participation.

If the granting of licences to third parties is expressly or tacitly excluded, there may be a restraint of competition; the fact that research is carried out jointly justifies, however, arrangements binding the enterprises to grant licences to third parties only by common agreement or by majority decision.

For the assessment of the compatibility of the agreement with the rules of competition, it does not matter what legal form the common research and development work takes.

(4)   *Agreements which have as their only object the joint use of production facilities and storing and transport equipment:*

These forms of co-operation do not restrict competition because they are confined to organisational and technical arrangements for the use of the facilities. There may be a restraint of competition if the enterprises involved do not bear the cost of utilisation of the installation or equipment themselves or if agreements are concluded or concerted practices applied regarding joint production or the sharing out of production or the establishment or running of a joint enterprise.

(5)   *Agreements having as their sole object the setting up of working partnerships for the common execution of orders, where the participating enterprises do not compete with each other as regards the work to be done or where each of them by itself is unable to execute the orders:*

Where enterprises do not compete with each other they cannot restrict competition by setting up associations. This applies in particular to enterprises belonging to different industries but also to firms of the same industry to the extent that their contribution under the working partnership consists only of goods or services. It is not a question of whether the enterprises compete with each other in other industries so much as whether in the light of the concrete circumstances of a particular case there is a possibility that in the foreseeable future they may compete with each other with regard to the products or services involved. If the absence of competition between the enterprises and the maintenance of this situation are based on agreements or concerted practices, there may be a restraint of competition.

But even in the case of associations formed by enterprises which compete with each other there is no restraint of competition if the participating enterprises cannot execute the specific order by themselves. This applies in particular if, for lack of experience, specialised knowledge, capacity or financial resources these enterprises, when working alone, have no chance of success or cannot finish the work within the required time-limit or cannot bear the financial risk. Nor is there a restraint of competition if it is only by the setting up of an association that the enterprises are put in a position to make a promising offer. There may, however, be a restraint of competition if the enterprises undertake to work solely in the framework of an association.

(6) *Agreements having as their sole object:*

(a) *Joint selling arrangements,*

(b) *Joint after-sales and repair service, provided the participating enter-prises are not competitors with regard to the products or services covered by the agreement.*

As already explained in detail under Section 5, co-operation between enterprises cannot restrict competition if the firms do not compete with each other.

Very often joint selling by small or medium-sized enterprises — even if they are competing with each other — does not entail an appreciable restraint of competition; it is, however, impossible to establish in this Notice any general criteria or to specify what enterprises may be deemed 'small or medium-sized'.

There is no joint after-sales and repair service if several manufacturers, without acting in concert with each other, arrange for an after-sales and repair service for their product to be provided by an enterprise which is independent. In such a case there is no restraint of competition, even if the manufacturers are competitors.

(7) *Agreements having as their sole object joint advertising.*

Joint advertising is designed to draw the buyers' attention to the products of an industry or to a common brand; as such it does not restrict competition between the participating enterprises. However, if the participating enterprises are partly or wholly prevented, by agreements or concerted practices, from themselves advertising or if they are subjected to other restrictions, there may be a restraint of competition.

(8) *Agreements having as their sole object the use of a common label to designate a certain quality, where the label is available to all competitors on the same conditions.*

Such associations for the joint use of a quality label do not restrict competition if other competitors, whose products objectively meet the stipulated quality requirements, can use the label on the same conditions as the members. Nor do the obligations to accept quality control of the products provided with the label, to issue uniform instructions for use, or to use the label for the products meeting the quality standards constitute restraints of competition. But there may be restraint of competition if the right to use the label is linked to obligations regarding production, marketing, price formation or obligations of any other type, as is for instance the case when the participating enterprises are obliged to manufacture or sell only products of guaranteed quality.

COMMISSION NOTICE OF 18 DECEMBER 1978 CONCERNING ITS ASSESSMENT OF CERTAIN SUBCONTRACTING AGREEMENTS IN RELATION TO ARTICLE 85(1) OF THE EEC TREATY
[OJ 1979 C1/2]

1. In this notice the Commission of the European Communities gives its view as to subcontracting agreements in relation to Article 85(1) of the Treaty establishing the European Economic Community. This class of agreement is at the present time a form of work distribution which concerns firms of all sizes, but which offers opportunities for development in particular to small and medium sized firms.

The Commission considers that agreements under which one firm, called 'the contractor', whether or not in consequence of a prior order from a third party, entrusts to another, called 'the subcontractor', the manufacture of goods, the supply of services or the performance of work under the contractor's instructions, to be provided to the contractor or performed on his behalf, are not of themselves caught by the prohibition in Article 85(1).

To carry out certain subcontracting agreements in accordance with the contractor's instructions, the subcontractor may have to make use of particular technology or equipment which the contractor will have to provide. In order to protect the economic value of such technology or equipment, the contractor may wish to restrict their use by the subcontractor to whatever is necessary for the purpose of the agreement. The question arises whether such restrictions are caught by Article 85(1). They are assessed in this notice with due regard to the purpose of such agreements, which distinguishes them from ordinary patent and know-how licensing agreements.

2. In the Commission's view, Article 85(1) does not apply to clauses whereby:

— technology or equipment provided by the contractor may not be used except for the purposes of the subcontracting agreement,

— technology or equipment provided by the contractor may not be made available to third parties,

— the goods, services or work resulting from the use of such technology or equipment may be supplied only to the contractor or performed on his behalf, provided that and in so far as this technology or equipment is necessary to enable the subcontractor under reasonable conditions to manufacture the goods, to supply the services or to carry out the work in accordance with the contractor's instructions. To that extent the subcontractor is providing goods, services or work in respect of which he is not an independent supplier in the market.

The above proviso is satisfied where performance of the subcontracting agreement makes necessary the use by the subcontractor of:

— industrial property rights of the contractor or at his disposal, in the form of patents, utility models, designs protected by copyright, registered designs or other rights, or

— secret knowledge or manufacturing processes (know-how) of the contractor or at his disposal, or of

— studies, plans or documents accompanying the information given which have been prepared by or for the contractor, or

—dies, patterns or tools, and accessory equipment that are distinctively the contractor's,

which, even though not covered by industrial property rights nor containing any element of secrecy, permit the manufacture of goods which differ in form, function or composition from other goods manufactured or supplied on the market.

However, the restrictions mentioned above are not justifiable where the subcontractor has at his disposal or could under reasonable conditions obtain access to the technology and equipment needed to produce the goods, provide the services or carry out the work. Generally, this is the case when the contractor provides no more than general information which merely describes the work to be done. In such circumstances the restrictions could deprive the subcontractor of the possibility of developing his own business in the fields covered by the agreement.

3. The following restrictions in connection with the provision of technology by the contractor may in the Commission's view also be imposed by subcontracting agreements without giving grounds for objection under Article 85(1):

—an undertaking by either of the parties not to reveal manufacturing processes or other know-how of a secret character, or confidential information given by the other party during the negotiation and performance of the agreement, as long as the know-how or information in question has not become public knowledge,

—an undertaking by the subcontractor not to make use, even after expiry of the agreement, of manufacturing processes or other know-how of a secret character received by him during the currency of the agreement, as long as they have not become public knowledge,

—an undertaking by the subcontractor to pass on to the contractor on a non-exclusive basis any technical improvements which he has made during the currency of the agreement, or, where a patentable invention has been discovered by the subcontractor, to grant non-exclusive licences in respect of inventions relating to improvements and new applications of the original invention to the contractor for the term of the patent held by the latter.

This undertaking by the subcontractor may be exclusive in favour of the contractor in so far as improvements and inventions made by the subcontractor during the currency of the agreement are incapable of being used independently of the contractor's secret know-how or patent, since this does not constitute an appreciable restriction of competition.

However, any undertaking by the subcontractor regarding the right to dispose of the results of his own research and development work may restrain competition, where such results are capable of being used independently. In such circumstances, the subcontracting relationship is not sufficient to displace the ordinary competition rules on the disposal of industrial property rights or secret know-how.

4. Where the subcontractor is authorised by a subcontracting agreement to use a specified trade mark, trade name or get up, the contractor may at the same time forbid such use by the subcontractor in the case of goods, services or work which are not to be supplied to the contractor.

5. Although this notice should in general obviate the need for firms to obtain a ruling on the legal position by an individual Commission Decision, it

does not affect the right of the firms concerned to apply for negative clearance as defined by Article 2 of Regulation No. 17 or to notify the agreement to the Commission under Article 4(1) of that Regulation.[1]

The 1968 notice on cooperation between enterprises,[2] which lists a number of agreements that by their nature are not to be regarded as anti-competitive, is thus supplemented in the subcontracting field. The Commission also reminds firms that, in order to promote cooperation between small and medium sized businesses, it has published a notice concerning agreements of minor importance which do not fall under Article 85(1) of the Treaty establishing the European Economic Community.[3]

This notice is without prejudice to the view that may be taken of subcontracting agreements by the Court of Justice of the European Communities.

Note
[1]First Regulation implementing Article 85 and 86 of the EEC Treaty [OJ No. 13, 21.2.1962, p. 204/62].
[2]Notice concerning agreements, decisions and concerted practices relating to cooperation between enterprises [OJ No. C75, 29.7.1968, p. 3].
[3]OJ No. C313, 29.12.1977, p. 3.

COMMISSION NOTICE OF 3 SEPTEMBER 1986 ON AGREEMENTS OF MINOR IMPORTANCE WHICH DO NOT FALL UNDER ARTICLE 85(1) OF THE TREATY ESTABLISHING THE EUROPEAN ECONOMIC COMMUNITY (86/C231/02)
[OJ 1986, No. C231/2][1]

I

1.   The Commission considers it important to facilitate cooperation between undertakings where such cooperation is economically desirable without presenting difficulties from the point of view of competition policy, which is particularly true of cooperation between small and medium-sized undertakings. To this end it published the 'Notice concerning agreements, decisions and concerted practices in the field of cooperation between undertakings' listing a number of agreements that by their nature cannot be regarded as restraints of competition. Furthermore, in the Notice concerning its assessment of certain subcontracting agreements the Commission considered that this type of contract which offers opportunities for development, in particular, to small and medium-sized undertakings is not in itself caught by the prohibition in Article 85(1). By issuing the present Notice, the Commission is taking a further step towards defining the field of application of Article 85(1), in order to facilitate cooperation between small and medium-sized undertakings.

2.   In the Commission's opinion, agreements whose effects on trade between Member States or on competition are negligible do not fall under the ban on restrictive agreements contained in Article 85(1). Only those agreements are prohibited which have an appreciable impact on market conditions, in that they appreciably alter the market position, in other words the sales or supply possibilities, of third undertakings and of users.

Note
[1]Editor's Note: As amended by Commission Notice of 23.12.94, OJ 1994 C368/20.

3.   In the present Notice the Commission, by setting quantitative criteria and by explaining their application, has given a sufficiently concrete meaning to the concept 'appreciable' for undertakings to be able to judge for themselves whether the agreements they have concluded with other undertakings, being of minor importance, do not fall under Article 85(1). The quantitative definition of 'appreciable' given by the Commission is, however, no absolute yardstick; in fact, in individual cases even agreements between undertakings which exceed these limits may still have only a negligible effect on trade between Member States or on competition, and are therefore not caught by Article 85(1).

4.   As a result of this Notice, there should no longer be any point in undertakings obtaining negative clearance, as defined by Article 2 of the Council Regulation No. 17, for the agreements covered, nor should it be necessary to have the legal position established through Commission decisions in individual cases; notification with this end in view will no longer be necessary for such agreements. However, if it is doubtful whether in an individual case an agreement appreciably affects trade between Member States or competition, the undertakings are free to apply for negative clearance or to notify the agreement.

5.   In cases covered by the present Notice the Commission, as a general rule, will not open proceedings under Regulation No. 17, either upon application or upon its own initiative. Where, due to exceptional circumstances, an agreement which is covered by the present Notice nevertheless falls under Article 85(1), the Commission will not impose fines. Where undertakings have failed to notify an agreement falling under Article 85(1) because they wrongly assumed, owing to a mistake in calculating their market share or aggregate turnover, that the agreement was covered by the present Notice, the Commission will not consider imposing fines unless the mistake was due to negligence.

6.   This Notice is without prejudice to the competence of national courts to apply Article 85(1) on the basis of their own jurisdiction, although it constitutes a factor which such courts may take into account when deciding a pending case. It is also without prejudice to any interpretation which may be given by the Court of Justice of the European Communities.

II

7.   The Commission holds the view that agreements between undertakings engaged in the production or distribution of goods or in the provision of services generally do not fall under the prohibition of Article 81(1) if:

— the goods or services which are the subject of the agreement (hereinafter referred to as 'the contract products') together with the participating undertakings' other goods or services which are considered by users to be equivalent in view of their characteristics, price and intended use, do not represent more than 5% of the total market for such goods or services (hereinafter referred to as 'products') in the area of the common market affected by the agreement and

— the aggregate annual turnover of the participating undertakings does not exceed 300 million ECU.

8.   The Commission also holds the view that the said agreements do not fall under the prohibition of Article 85(1) if the abovementioned market share of turnover is exceeded by not more than one tenth during two successive financial years.

9.   For the purposes of this Notice, participating undertakings are:

(a)   undertakings party to the agreement;

(b)   undertakings in which a party to the agreement, directly or indirectly,

—owns more than half the capital or business assets or

—has the power to exercise more than half the voting rights, or

—has the power to appoint more than half the members of the supervisory board, board of management or bodies legally representing the undertakings, or

—has the right to manage the affairs;

(c)   undertakings which directly or indirectly have in or over a party to the agreement the rights or powers listed in (b);

(d)   undertakings in or over which an undertaking referred to in (c) directly or indirectly has the rights or powers listed in (b).

Undertakings in which several undertakings as referred to in (a) to (d) jointly have, directly or indirectly, the rights or powers set out in (b) shall also be considered to be participating undertakings.

10.   In order to calculate the market share, it is necessary to determine the relevant market. This implies the definition of the relevant product market and the relevant geographical market.

11.   The relevant product market includes besides the contract products any other products which are identical or equivalent to them. This rule applies to the products of the participating undertakings as well as to the market for such products. The products in question must be interchangeable. Whether or not this is the case must be judged from the vantage point of the user, normally taking the characteristics, price and intended use of the goods together. In certain cases, however, products can form a separate market on the basis of their characteristics, their price or their intended use alone. This is true especially where consumer preferences have developed.

12.   Where the contract products are components which are incorporated into another product by the participating undertakings, reference should be made to the market for the latter product, provided that the components represent a significant part of it. Where the contract products are components which are sold to third undertakings, reference should be made to the market for the components. In cases where both conditions apply, both markets should be considered separately.

13.   The relevant geographical market is the area within the Community in which the agreement produces its effects. This area will be the whole common market where the contract products are regularly bought and sold in all Member States. Where the contract products cannot be bought and sold in a part of the common market, or are bought and sold only in limited quantities or at irregular intervals in such a part, that part should be disregarded.

14.   The relevant geographical market will be narrower than the whole common market in particular where:

—the nature and characteristics of the contract product, e.g., high transport costs in relation to the value of the product, restrict its mobility; or

—movement of the contract product within the common market is hindered by barriers to entry to national markets resulting from State intervention, such as quantitative restrictions, severe taxation differentials and non-tariff barriers, e.g., type approvals or safety standard certifications. In such cases the national territory may have to be considered as the relevant geographical market. However, this will only be justified if the existing barriers to entry cannot be overcome by reasonable effort and at an acceptable cost.

15.   Aggregate turnover includes the turnover in all goods and services, excluding tax, achieved during the last financial year by the participating undertaking. In cases where an undertaking has concluded similar agreements with various other undertakings in the relevant market, the turnover of all participating undertakings should be taken together. The aggregate turnover shall not include dealings between participating undertakings.

16.   The present Notice shall not apply where in a relevant market competition is restricted by the cumulative effects of parallel networks of similar agreements established by several manufacturers or dealers.

17.   The present Notice is likewise applicable to decisions by associations of undertakings and to concerted practices.

NOTICE ON COOPERATION BETWEEN NATIONAL COURTS AND THE COMMISSION IN APPLYING ARTICLES 85 AND 86 OF THE EEC TREATY
[93/C 39/06]

I.   INTRODUCTION

1.   The abolition of internal frontiers enables firms in the Community to embark on new activities and Community consumers to benefit from increased competition. The Commission considers that these advantages must not be jeopardised by restrictive or abusive practices of undertakings and that the completion of the internal market thus reaffirms the importance of the Community's competition policy and competition law.

2.   A number of national and Community institutions have contributed to the formulation of Community competition law and are responsible for its day-to-day application. For this purpose, the national competition authorities, national and Community courts and the Commission each assume their own tasks and responsibilities, in line with the principles developed by the case-law of the Court of Justice of the European Communities.

3.   If the competition process is to work well in the internal market, effective cooperation between these institutions must be ensured. The purpose of this Notice is to achieve this in relations between national courts and the Commission. It spells out how the Commission intends to assist national courts by closer cooperation in the application of Articles 85 and 86 of the EEC Treaty in individual cases.

II.   POWERS

4.   The Commission is the administrative authority responsible for the implementation and for the thrust of competition policy in the Community and for this purpose has to act in the public interest. National courts, on the other hand, have the task of safeguarding the subjective rights of private individuals in their relations with one another.[1]

Notes
[1] Case C-234/89, *Delimitis* v *Henninger Bräu* [1991] ECR I-935, paragraph 44; Case T-24/90, *Automec* v *Commission*, judgment of 17 September 1992, paragraphs 73 and 85 (not yet reported).

5.   In performing these different tasks, national courts and the Commission possess concurrent powers for the application of Article 85(1) and Article 86 of the Treaty. In the case of the Commission, the power is conferred by Article 89 and by the provisions adopted pursuant to Article 87. In the case of the national courts, the power derives from the direct effect of the relevant Community rules. In *BRT* v *Sabam*, the Court of Justice considered that 'as the prohibitions of Articles 85(1) and 86 tend by their very nature to produce direct effects in relations between individuals, these Articles create direct rights in respect of the individuals concerned which the national courts must safeguard'.[2]

6.   In this way, national courts are able to ensure, at the request of the litigants or on their own initiative, that the competition rules will be respected for the benefit of private individuals. In addition, Article 85(2) enables them to determine, in accordance with the national procedural law applicable, the civil law effects of the prohibition set out in Article 85.[3]

7.   However, the Commission, pursuant to Article 9 of Regulation No. 17,[4] has sole power to exempt certain types of agreements, decisions and concerted practices from this prohibition. The Commission may exercise this power in two ways. It may take a decision exempting a specific agreement in an individual case. It may also adopt regulations granting block exemptions for certain categories of agreements, decisions or concerted practices, where it is authorised to do so by the Council, in accordance with Article 87.

8.   Although national courts are not competent to apply Article 85(3), they may nevertheless apply the decisions and regulations adopted by the Commission pursuant to that provision. The Court has on several occasions confirmed that the provisions of a regulation are directly applicable.[5] The Commission considers that the same is true for the substantive provisions of an individual exemption decision.

9.   The powers of the Commission and those of national courts differ not only in their objective and content, but also in the ways in which they are exercised. The Commission exercises its powers according to the procedural rules laid down by Regulation No. 17, whereas national courts exercise theirs in the context of national procedural law.

10.   In this connection, the Court of Justice has laid down the principles which govern procedures and remedies for invoking directly applicable Community law.

'Although the Treaty has made it possible in a number of instances for private persons to bring a direct action, where appropriate, before the Court of Justice, it was not intended to create new remedies in the national courts to ensure the observance of Community law other than those already laid down by national law. On the other hand ... it must be possible for every type of

Notes
[2]Case 127/73, *BRT* v *Sabam* [1974] ECR 51, paragraph 16.
[3]Case 56/65, *LTM* v *MBU* [1996] ECR 337; Case 48/72, *Brasserie De Haecht* v *Wilkin-Janssen* [1973] ECR 77; Case 319/82, *Ciments et Bétons* v *Kerpen & Kerpen* [1983] ECR 4173.
[4]Council Regulation No. 17 of 6 February 1962; First Regulation implementing Articles 85 and 86 of the Treaty [OJ No. 13, 21.2.1962, p. 204/62; Special Edition 1959-62, p. 87].
[5]Case 63/75, *Fonderies Roubaix* v *Fonderies Roux* [1976] ECR 111; Case C-234/89, *Delimitis* v *Henninger Bräu* [1991] ECR I-935.

action provided for by national law to be available for the purpose of ensuring observance of Community provisions having direct effect, on the same conditions concerning the admissibility and procedure as would apply were it a question of ensuring observance of national law.'[1]

11. The Commission considers that these principles apply in the event of breach of the Community competition rules; individuals and companies have access to all procedural remedies provided for by national law on the same conditions as would apply if a comparable breach of national law were involved. This equality of treatment concerns not only the definitive finding of a breach of competition rules, but embraces all the legal means capable of contributing to effective legal protection. Consequently, it is the right of parties subject to Community law that national courts should take provisional measures, that an effective end should be brought, by injunction, to the infringement of Community competition rules of which they are victims, and that compensation should be awarded for the damage suffered as a result of infringements, where such remedies are available in proceedings relating to similar national law.

12. Here the Commission would like to make it clear that the simultaneous application of national competition law is compatible with the application of Community law, provided that it does not impair the effectiveness and uniformity of Community competition rules and the measures taken to enforce them. Any conflicts which may arise when national and Community competition law are applied simultaneously must be resolved in accordance with the principle of the precedence of Community law.[2] The purpose of this principle is to rule out any national measure which could jeopardise the full effectiveness of the provisions of Community law.

III. THE EXERCISE OF POWERS BY THE COMMISSION

13. As the administrative authority responsible for the Community's competition policy, the Commission must serve the Community's general interest. The administrative resources at the Commission's disposal to perform its task are necessarily limited and cannot be used to deal with all the cases brought to its attention. The Commission is therefore obliged, in general, to take all organisational measures necessary for the performance of its task and, in particular, to establish priorities.[3]

14. The Commission intends, in implementing its decision-making powers, to concentrate on notifications, complaints and own-initiative proceedings having particular political, economic or legal significance for the Community. Where these features are absent in a particular case, notifications will normally be dealt with by means of comfort letter and complaints should, as a rule, be handled by national courts or authorities.

Notes
[1]Case 158/80, *Rewe* v *Hauptzollamt Kiel* [1981] ECR 1805, paragraph 44; see also Case 33/76, *Rewe* v *Landwirtschaftskammer Saarland* [1976] ECR 1989; Case 79/83, *Harz* v *Deutsche Tradax* [1984] ECR 1921; Case 199/82, *Amministrazione delle Finanze dello Stato* v *San Giorgio* [1983] ECR 3595.
[2]Case 14/68, *Walt Wilhelm and Others* v *Bundeskartellamt* [1969] ECR 1; Joined Cases 253/78 and 1 to 3/79, *Procureur de la République* v *Giry and Guerlain* [1980] ECR 2327.
[3]Case T-24/90, *Automec* v *Commission*, judgment of 17 September 1992, paragraph 77 (not yet reported).

15.   The Commission considers that there is not normally a sufficient Community interest in examining a case when the plaintiff is able to secure adequate protection of his rights before the national courts.[4] In these circumstances the complaint will normally be filed.

16.   In this respect the Commission would like to make it clear that the application of Community competition law by the national courts has considerable advantages for individuals and companies:

—the Commission cannot award compensation for loss suffered as a result of an infringement of Article 85 or Article 86. Such claims may be brought only before the national courts. Companies are more likely to avoid infringements of the Community competition rules if they risk having to pay damages or interest in such an event,

—national courts can usually adopt interim measures and order the ending of infringements more quickly than the Commission is able to do,

—before national courts, it is possible to combine a claim under Community law with a claim under national law. This is not possible in a procedure before the Commission,

—in some Member States, the courts have the power to award legal costs to the successful applicant. This is never possible in the administrative procedure before the Commission.

Notes
[4]Case T-24/90, cited above, paragraphs 91 to 94.

IV.   APPLICATION OF ARTICLES 85 AND 86 BY NATIONAL COURTS

17.   The national court may have to reach a decision on the application of Articles 85 and 86 in several procedural situations. In the case of civil law proceedings, two types of action are particularly frequent: actions relating to contracts and actions for damages. Under the former, the defendant usually relies on Article 85(2) to dispute the contractual obligations invoked by the plaintiff. Under the latter, the prohibitions contained in Articles 85 and 86 are generally relevant in determining whether the conduct which has given rise to the alleged injury is illegal.

18.   In such situations, the direct effect of Article 85(1) and Article 86 gives national courts sufficient powers to comply with their obligation to hand down judgment. Nevertheless, when exercising these powers, they must take account of the Commission's powers in order to avoid decisions which could conflict with those taken or envisaged by the Commission in applying Article 85(1) and Article 86, and also Article 85(3).[1]

19.   In its case-law the Court of Justice has developed a number of principles which make it possible for such contradictory decisions to be avoided.[2] The Commission feels that national courts could take account of these principles in the following manner.

Notes
[1]Case C-234/89, *Delimitis* v *Henninger Bräu* [1991] ECR I-935, paragraph 47.
[2]Case 48/72, *Brasserie de Haecht* v *Wilkin-Janssen* [1973] ECR 77; Case 127/73, *BRT* v *Sabam* [1974] ECR 51; Case C-234/89, *Delimitis* v *Henninger Bräu* [1991] ECR I-935.

1. *Application of Article 85(1) and (2) and Article 86*

20. The first question which national courts have to answer is whether the agreement, decision or concerted practice at issue infringes the prohibitions laid down in Article 85(1) or Article 86. Before answering this question, national courts should ascertain whether the agreement, decision or concerted practice has already been the subject of a decision, opinion or other official statement issued by an administrative authority and in particular by the Commission. Such statements provide national courts with significant information for reaching a judgment, even if they are not formally bound by them. It should be noted in this respect that not all procedures before the Commission lead to an official decision, but that cases can also be closed by comfort letters. Whilst it is true that the Court of Justice has ruled that this type of letter does not bind national courts, it has nevertheless stated that the opinion expressed by the Commission constitutes a factor which the national courts may take into account in examining whether the agreements or conduct in question are in accordance with the provisions of Article 85.[3]

21. If the Commission has not ruled on the same agreement, decision or concerted practice, the national courts can always be guided, in interpreting the Community law in question, by the case-law of the Court of Justice and the existing decisions of the Commission. It is with this in view that the Commission has, in a number of general notices,[4] specified categories of agreements that are not caught by the ban laid down in Article 85(1).

22. On these bases, national courts should generally be able to decide whether the conduct at issue is compatible with Article 85(1) and Article 86. Nevertheless, if the Commission has initiated a procedure in a case relating to the same conduct, they may, if they consider it necessary for reasons of legal certainty, stay the proceedings while awaiting the outcome of the Commission's action.[5] A stay of proceedings may also be envisaged where national courts wish to seek the Commission's views in accordance with the arrangements referred to in this Notice.[6] Finally, where national courts have persistent doubts on questions of compatibility, they may stay proceedings in order to bring the matter before the Court of Justice, in accordance with Article 177 of the Treaty.

23. However, where national courts decide to give judgment and find that the conditions for applying Article 85(1) or Article 86 are not met, they should pursue their proceedings on the basis of such a finding, even if the agreement,

Notes

[3] Case 99/79, *Lancôme v Etos* (1980) ECR 2511, paragraph 11.
[4] See the notices on:

— exclusive dealing contracts with commercial agents [OJ No. 139, 24.12.1962, p. 2921/62],

— agreements, decisions and concerted practices in the field of cooperation between enterprises [OJ No. C75 29.7.1968, p. 3, as corrected in OJ No. C84, 28.8.1968, p. 14],

— assessment of certain subcontracting agreements [OJ No. C231, 12.9.1986, p. 2].

[5] Case 127/73, *BRT v Sabam* [1974] ECR 51, paragraph 21. The procedure before the Commission is initiated by an authoritative act. A simple acknowledgement of receipt cannot be considered an authoritative act as such; Case 48/72, *Brasserie de Haecht v Wilkin-Janssen* [1973] ECR 77, paragraphs 16 and 17.

[6] Case C-234/89, *Delimitis v Henninger Bräu* [1991] ECR I-935, paragraph 53, Part V of this Notice.

decision or concerted practice at issue has been notified to the Commission. Where the assessment of the facts shows that the conditions for applying the said Articles are met, national courts must rule that the conduct at issue infringes Community competition law and take the appropriate measures, including those relating to the consequences that attach to infringement of a statutory prohibition under the civil law applicable.

2.   *Application of Article 85(3)*

24.   If the national court concludes that an agreement, decision or concerted practice is prohibited by Article 85(1), it must check whether it is or will be the subject of an exemption by the Commission under Article 85(3). Here several situations may arise.

25.   (a)   The national court is required to respect the exemption decisions taken by the Commission. Consequently, it must treat the agreement, decision or concerted practice at issue as compatible with Community law and fully recognise its civil law effects. In this respect mention should be made of comfort letters in which the Commission services state that the conditions for applying Article 85(3) have been met. The Commission considers that national courts may take account of these letters as factual elements.

26.   (b)   Agreements, decisions and concerted practices which fall within the scope of application of a block exemption regulation are automatically exempted from the prohibition laid down in Article 85(1) without the need for a Commission decision or comfort letter.[1]

27.   (c)   Agreements, decisions and concerted practices which are not covered by a block exemption regulation and which have not been the subject of an individual exemption decision or a comfort letter must, in the Commission's view, be examined in the following manner.

28.   The national court must first examine whether the procedural conditions necessary for securing exemption are fulfilled, notably whether the agreement, decision or concerted practice has been duly notified in accordance with Article 4(1) of Regulation No. 17. Where no such notification has been made, and subject to Article 4(2) of Regulation No. 17, exemption under Article 85(3) is ruled out, so that the national court may decide, pursuant to Article 85(2), that the agreement, decision or concerted practice is void.

29.   Where the agreement, decision or concerted practice has been duly notified to the Commission, the national court will assess the likelihood of an exemption being granted in the case in question in the light of the relevant criteria developed by the case law of the Court of Justice and the Court of First Instance and by previous regulations and decisions of the Commission.

30.   Where the national court has in this way ascertained that the agreement, decision or concerted practice at issue cannot be the subject of an individual exemption, it will take the measures necessary to comply with the requirements of Article 85(1) and (2). On the other hand, if it takes the view that individual exemption is possible, the national court should suspend the proceedings while awaiting the Commission's decision. If the national court does suspend the proceedings, it nevertheless remains free, according to the rules of the applicable national law, to adopt any interim measures it deems necessary.

Notes

[1] A list of the relevant regulations and of the official explanatory comments relating to them is given in the Annex to this Notice.

31.   In this connection, it should be made clear that these principles do not apply to agreements, decisions and concerted practices which existed before Regulation No. 17 entered into force or before that Regulation became applicable as a result of the accession of a new Member State and which were duly notified to the Commission. The national courts must consider such agreements, decisions and concerted practices to be valid so long as the Commission or the authorities of the Member States have not taken a prohibition decision or sent a comfort letter to the parties informing them that the file has been closed.[2]

32.   The Commission realises that the principles set out above for the application of Articles 85 and 86 by national courts are complex and sometimes insufficient to enable those courts to perform their judicial function properly. This is particularly so where the practical application of Article 85(1) and Article 86 gives rise to legal or economic difficulties, where the Commission has initiated a procedure in the same case or where the agreement, decision or concerted practice concerned may become the subject of an individual exemption within the meaning of Article 85(3). National courts may bring such cases before the Court of Justice for a preliminary ruling, in accordance with Article 177. They may also avail themselves of the Commission's assistance according to the procedures set out below.

Note
[2]Case 48/72, *Brasserie de Haecht* v *Wilkin-Janssen* [1973] ECR 77; Case 59/77, *De Bloss* v *Bouyer* [1977] ECR 2359; Case 99/79, *Lancôme* v *Etos* [1980] ECR 2511.

V.   COOPERATION BETWEEN NATIONAL COURTS AND THE COMMISSION

33.   Article 5 of the EEC Treaty establishes the principle of constant and sincere cooperation between the Community and the Member States with a view to attaining the objectives of the Treaty, including implementation of Article 3(f), which refers to the establishment of a system ensuring that competition in the common market is not distorted. This principle involves obligations and duties of mutual assistance, both for the Member States and for the Community institutions. The Court has thus ruled that, under Article 5 of the EEC Treaty, the Commission has a duty of sincere cooperation *vis-à-vis* judicial authorities of the Member States, who are responsible for ensuring that Community law is applied and respected in the national legal system.[1]

34.   The Commission considers that such cooperation is essential in order to guarantee the strict, effective and consistent application of Community competition law. In addition, more effective participation by the national courts in the day-to-day application of competition law gives the Commission more time to perform its administrative task, namely to steer competition policy in the Community.

35.   In the light of these considerations, the Commission intends to work towards closer cooperation with national courts in the following manner.

36.   The Commission conducts its policy so as to give the parties concerned useful pointers to the application of competition rules. To this end, it will

Notes
[1]Case C-2/88 Imm., *Zwartveld* [1990] ECR I-3365, paragraph 18; Case C-234/89, *Delimitis* v *Henninger Bräu* [1991] ECR I-935, paragraph 53.

continue its policy in relation to block exemption regulations and general notices. These general texts, the case-law of the Court of Justice and the Court of First Instance, the decisions previously taken by the Commission and the annual reports on competition policy are all elements of secondary legislation or explanations which may assist national courts in examining individual cases.

37.   If these general pointers are insufficient, national courts may, within the limits of their national procedural law, ask the Commission and in particular its Directorate-General for Competition for the following information.

First, they may ask for information of a procedural nature to enable them to discover whether a certain case is pending before the Commission, whether a case has been the subject of a notification, whether the Commission has officially initiated a procedure or whether it has already taken a position through an official decision or through a comfort letter sent by its services. If necessary, national courts may also ask the Commission to give an opinion as to how much time is likely to be required for granting or refusing individual exemption for notified agreements or practices, so as to be able to determine the conditions for any decision to suspend proceedings or whether interim measures need to be adopted.[2] The Commission, for its part, will endeavour to give priority to cases which are the subject of national proceedings suspended in this way, in particular when the outcome of a civil dispute depends on them.

38.   Next, national courts may consult the Commission on points of law. Where the application of Article 85(1) and Article 86 causes them particular difficulties, national courts may consult the Commission on its customary practice in relation to the Community law at issue. As far as Articles 85 and 86 are concerned, these difficulties relate in particular to the conditions for applying these Articles as regards the effect on trade between Member States and as regards the extent to which the restriction of competition resulting from the practices specified in these provisions is appreciable. In its replies, the Commission does not consider the merits of the case. In addition, where they have doubts as to whether a contested agreement, decision or concerted practice is eligible for an individual exemption, they may ask the Commission to provide them with an interim opinion. If the Commission says that the case in question is unlikely to qualify for an exemption, national courts will be able to waive a stay of proceedings and rule on the validity of the agreement, decision or concerted practice.

39.   The answers given by the Commission are not binding on the courts which have requested them. In its replies the Commission makes it clear that its view is not definitive and that the right for the national court to refer to the Court of Justice, pursuant to Article 177, is not affected. Nevertheless, the Commission considers that it gives them useful guidance for resolving disputes.

40.   Lastly, national courts can obtain information from the Commission regarding factual data: statistics, market studies and economic analyses. The Commission will endeavour to communicate these data, within the limits laid down in the following paragraph, or will indicate the source from which they can be obtained.

41.   It is in the interests of the proper administration of justice that the Commission should answer requests for legal and factual information in the

Notes
[2] See paragraphs 22 and 30 of this Notice.

shortest possible time. Nevertheless, the Commission cannot accede to such requests unless several conditions are met. First, the requisite data must actually be at its disposal. Secondly, the Commission may communicate this data only in so far as permitted by the general principle of sound administrative practice.

42. For example, Article 214 of the Treaty, as spelt out in Article 20 of Regulation No. 17 for the purposes of the competition rules, requires the Commission not to disclose information of a confidential nature. In addition, the duty of sincere cooperation deriving from Article 5 is one applying to the relationship between national courts and the Commission and cannot concern the position of the parties to the dispute pending before those courts. As *amicus curiae*, the Commission is obliged to respect legal neutrality and objectivity. Consequently, it will not accede to requests for information unless they come from a national court, either directly, or indirectly through parties which have been ordered by the court concerned to provide certain information. In the latter case, the Commission will ensure that its answer reaches all the parties to the proceedings.

43. Over and above such exchange of information, required in specific cases, the Commission is anxious to develop as far as possible a more general information policy. To this end, the Commission intends to publish an explanatory booklet regarding the application of the competition rules at national level.

44. Lastly, the Commission also wishes to reinforce the effect of national competition judgments. To this end, it will study the possibility of extending the scope of the Convention on jurisdiction and the enforcement of judgments in civil and commercial matters to competition cases assigned to administrative courts.[1] It should be noted that, in the Commission's view, competition judgments are already governed by this Convention where they are handed down in cases of a civil and commercial nature.

Note
[1] Convention of 27 September 1968 [OJ No. L304, 30.10.1978, p. 77].

VI. FINAL REMARKS

45. This Notice does not relate to the competition rules governing the transport sector.[1] Nor does it relate to the competition rules laid down in the Treaty establishing the European Coal and Steel Community.

46. This Notice is issued for guidance and does not in any way restrict the rights conferred on individuals or companies by Community law.

Note
[1] Regulation No. 141/62 of the Council of 26 November 1962 exempting transport from the application of Council Regulation No. 17 [OJ No. 124, 28.11.1962, p. 2751/62], as amended by Regulations Nos 165/65/EEC [OJ No. 210, 11.12.1963, p. 3141/65] and 1002/67/EEC [OJ No. 306, 16.12.1967, p. 1]; Regulation (EEC) No. 1017/68 of the Council of 19 July 1968 applying rules of competition to transport by rail, road and inland waterway [OJ No. L175, 23.7.1968, p. 1]; Council Regulation (EEC) No. 4056/86 of 22 December 1986 laying down detailed rules for the application of Articles 85 and 86 of the Treaty to maritime transport [OJ No. L378, 31.12.1986, p. 4]; Council Regulation (EEC) No. 3975/87 of 14 December 1987 laying down the procedure for the application of the rules on competition to undertakings in the air transport sector [OJ No. L374, 31.12.1987, p. 1].

47. This Notice is without prejudice to any interpretation of the Community competition rules which may be given by the Court of Justice of the European Communities.

48. A summary of the answers given by the Commission pursuant to this Notice will be published annually in the Competition Report.

ANNEX   BLOCK EXEMPTIONS

A.   ENABLING COUNCIL REGULATIONS

I.   Vertical agreements (see under B. I and B. II)

Council Regulation No. 19/65/EEC of 2 March 1965 on the application of Article 85(3) of the Treaty to certain categories of agreements and concerted practices [OJ, Special Edition 1965–66, p. 35].

II.   Horizontal agreements (see under B. III)

Council Regulation (EEC) No. 2821/71 of 20 December 1971 on the application of Article 85(3) of the Treaty to categories of agreements, decisions and concerted practices [OJ, Special Edition 1971–III, p. 1032], modified by Regulation (EEC) No. 2743/72 of 19 December 1972 [OJ, Special Edition 1972, 28–30.12.1972, p. 60].

B.   COMMISSION BLOCK EXEMPTION REGULATIONS AND EXPLANATORY NOTICES

I.   Distribution agreements

1.   Commission Regulation (EEC) No. 1983/83 of 22 June 1983 concerning exclusive distribution agreements [OJ No. L173, 30.6.1983, p. 1].

2.   Commission Regulation (EEC) No. 1984/83 of 22 June 1983 concerning exclusive purchasing agreements [OJ No. L173, 30.6.1983, p. 5].

3.   Commission Notice concerning Commission Regulations (EEC) No. 1983/83 and (EEC) No. 1984/83 [OJ No. C101, 13.4.1984, p. 2].

4.   Commission Regulation (EEC) No. 123/85 of 12 December 1984 concerning motor vehicle distribution and servicing agreements [OJ No. L15, 18.1.1985, p. 16].

5.   Commission Notice concerning Regulation (EEC) No. 123/85 [OJ No. C17, 18.1.1985, p. 4].

6.   Commission Notice on the clarification of the activities of motor vehicle intermediaries [OJ No. C329, 18.12.1991, p. 20].

II.   Licensing and franchising agreements

1.   Commission Regulation (EEC) No. 2349/84 of 23 July 1984 concerning patent licensing agreements [OJ No. L219, 16.8.1984, p. 15; corrigendum OJ No. L280, 22.10.1985, p. 32].

2.   Commission Regulation (EEC) No. 4087/88 of 30 November 1988 concerning franchising agreements [OJ No. L359, 28.12.1988, p. 46].

3.   Commission Regulation (EEC) No. 556/89 of 30 November 1988 concerning know-how licensing agreements [OJ No. L61, 4.3.1989, p. 1].

III.   Cooperative agreements

1.   Commission Regulation (EEC) No. 417/85 of 19 December 1984 concerning specialisation agreements [OJ No. L53, 22.2.1985, p. 1].

2.   Commission Regulation (EEC) No. 418/85 of 19 December 1984 concerning research and development agreements [OJ No. L53, 22.2.1985, p. 5].

COMMISSION NOTICE CONCERNING THE ASSESSMENT OF COOPERATIVE JOINT VENTURES PURSUANT TO ARTICLE 83 OF THE EEC TREATY

[93/C 43/02]

I. INTRODUCTION

1. Joint Ventures (JVs), as referred to in this Notice, embody a special, institutionally fixed form of cooperation between undertakings. They are versatile instruments at the disposal of the parents, with the help of which different goals can be pursued and attained.

2. JVs can form the basis and the framework for cooperation in all fields of business activity. Their potential area of application includes, *inter alia*, the procuring and processing of data, the organisation of working systems and procedures, taxation and business consultancy, the planning and financing of investment, the implementation of research and development plans, the acquisition and granting of licences for the use of intellectual property rights, the supply of raw materials or semi-finished products, the manufacture of goods, the provision of services, advertising, distribution and customer service.

3. JVs can fulfil one or more of the aforementioned tasks. Their activity can be limited in time or be of an unlimited duration. The broader the concrete and temporal framework of the cooperation, the stronger it will influence the business policy of the parents in relation to each other and to third parties. If the JV concerns market-orientated matters such as purchasing, manufacturing, sales or the provision of services, it will normally lead to coordination, if not even to a uniformity of the competitive behaviour of the parents at that particular economic level. This is all the more true where a JV fulfils all the functions of a normal undertaking and consequently behaves on the market as an independent supplier or purchaser. The creation of a JV which combines wholly or in part the existing activities of the parents in a particular economic area or takes over new activities for the parents, brings, over and above that, a change in the structure of the participating enterprises.

4. The assessment of cooperative joint ventures pursuant to Article 85(1) and (3) does not depend on the legal form which the parents choose for their cooperation. The applicability of the prohibition of restrictive practices depends, on the contrary, on whether the creation or the activities of the JV may affect trade between Member States and have as their object or effect the prevention, restriction or distortion of competition within the common market. The question whether an exemption can be granted to a JV will depend on the one hand on its overall economic benefits and on the other hand on the nature and scope of the restrictions of competition it entails.

5. In view of the variety of situations which come into consideration it is impossible to make general comments on the compliance of JVs with competition law. For a large proportion of JVs, whether or not they fall within the scope of application of Article 85 depends on their particular activity.[1] For other JVs, prohibition will occur only if particular legal and factual circumstances coincide, the existence of which must be determined on a case-by-case basis.[2] Exemptions from the prohibition are based on the analysis of the overall

Notes
[1] See below III. 1, point 15.
[2] See below III. 2 and 3, points 17 *et seq.* and 32 *et seq.*

economic balance, the result of which can turn out differently.[3] Cooperative joint ventures can however be divided into different categories, which are each open to the same competition law analysis.

6.   In the Commission Notice of 1968 concerning agreements, decisions and concerted practices in the field of cooperation between enterprises,[4] the Commission listed a series of types of cooperation which *by their nature* are not prohibited because they do not have as their object or effect the restriction of competition within the meaning of Article 85(1). The 1986 Notice on agreements of minor importance[5] sets out quantitative criteria for those arrangements which are not prohibited because they have no *appreciable* impact on competition or inter-State trade. Both Notices apply to JVs. Commission Regulations (EEC) No. 417/85, (EEC) No. 418/85, (EEC) No. 2349/84 and (EEC) No. 556/89 on the application of Article 85(3) of the Treaty to specialisation agreements,[6] research and development agreements,[7] patent licensing agreements[8] and know-how licensing agreements,[9] as amended by Regulation (EEC) No. 151/93,[10] include JVs amongst the beneficiaries of these group exemptions.[11] Further general indications on the assessment of cooperative JVs for competition purposes can be found in the numerous decisions and notices of the Commission in individual cases.[12]

7.   The Commission will hereinafter summarise its administrative practice to date. In this way undertakings will be informed about both the legal and economic criteria which will guide the Commission in the future application of Article 85(1) and (3) to cooperative joint ventures. This Notice applies to all JVs which do not fall within the scope of application of Article 3 of Council Regulation (EEC) No. 4064/89 of 21 December 1989 on the control of concentrations between undertakings.[13] It forms the counterpart of the Notice regarding concentrative and cooperative operations[14] and the Notice on restrictions ancillary to concentrations[15] which clarify the abovementioned Regulation. Links between undertakings other than JVs will not be dealt with in this Notice, even though they often have similar effects on competition in the common market and on trade between Member States. Having regard to the experience of the Commission, however, no generally applicable conclusions can yet be drawn.

8.   This notice is without prejudice to the power of national courts in the Member States to apply Article 85(1) and group exemptions under Article 85(3) on the basis of their own jurisdiction. Nevertheless it constitutes a factor

Notes
[3]See below IV. 1 and 2, points 43 *et seq.* and 52 *et seq.*
[4]OJ No. C75, 29.7.1968, p. 3; corrected by OJ No. C84, 28.8.1968, p. 14.
[5]OJ No. C231, 12.9.1986, p. 2.
[6]OJ No. L53, 22.2.1985, p. 1.
[7]OJ No. L53, 22.2.1985, p. 5.
[8]OJ No. L219, 16.8.1984, p. 15; corrected by OJ No. L280, 22.10.1985, p. 32.
[9]OJ No. L61, 4.3.1989, p. 1.
[10]OJ No. L21, 23.12.1992, p. 8.
[11]See below IV. 1, points 43 *et seq.*
[12]For references and summaries see the Commission Competition Policy Reports.
[13]OJ No. L395, 30.12.1989, p. 1; corrected by OJ No. L257, 21.9.1990, p. 13.
[14]OJ No. C203, 14.8.1990, p. 10.
[15]OJ No. C203, 14.8.1990, p. 5.

which the national courts can take into account when deciding a dispute before them. It is also without prejudice to any interpretation which may be given by the Court of Justice of the European Communities.

II. THE CONCEPT OF COOPERATIVE JOINT VENTURES

9. The concept of cooperative joint ventures can be derived from Regulation (EEC) No. 4064/89. According to Article 3(1), a JV is an undertaking under the joint control of several other undertakings, the parents. Control, according to Article 3(3), consists of the possibility of exercising a decisive influence on the activities of the undertaking. Whether joint control, the prerequisite of every JV, exists, is determined by the legal and factual circumstances of the individual case. For details refer to the Notice regarding concentrative and cooperative operations.[1]

10. According to Article 3(2) of Regulation (EEC) No. 4064/89, any JV which does not fulfil the criteria of a concentration, is cooperative in nature. Under the second subparagraph, this applies to:

— all JVs, the activities of which are not to be performed on a lasting basis, especially those limited in advance by the parents to a short time period,

— JVs which do not perform all the functions of an autonomous economic entity, especially those charged by their parents simply with the operation of particular functions of an undertaking (partial-function JVs),

— JVs which perform all the functions of an autonomous economic entity (full-function JVs) where they give rise to coordination of competitive behaviour by the parents in relation to each other or to the JV.

The delimitation of cooperative and concentrative operations can be difficult in individual cases. The abovementioned Commission Notice[2] contains detailed instructions for the solution of this problem. Additional indications can also be gained from the practice of the Commission under Regulation (EEC) No. 4064/89.[3]

11. Cooperative JVs are outside the scope of the provisions on merger control. The determination of the cooperative character of a JV has however no substantive legal effects. It simply means that the JV is subject to the procedures set out in Regulation No. 17[4] or Regulations (EEC) No. 1017/68,[5] (EEC)

Notes

[1]See points 6 to 14.

[2]See points 15 and 16.

[3]See on the one hand Decisions (pursuant to Article 6(1)(a) of Regulation (EEC) No. 4064/89); Renault/Volvo; Baxter/Nestlé/Salvia; Apollinaris/Schweppes; Elf/Enterprise; Sunrise; BSN/Nestlé/Cokoladovny; Flachglas/Vegla; Eureko, Herba/IRR; Koipe-Tabacalera/Elosua; on the other hand Decisions (pursuant to Article 6(1)(b) of Regulation (EEC) No. 4064/89): Sanofi/Sterling Drugs; Elf/BC/Cepsa; Dräger/IBM/ HMP; Thomson/Pilkington; UAP/Transatlantic/Sun Life; TNT/GD Net; Lucas/ Eaton; Courtaulds/SNIA; Volvo/Atlas; Ericsson/Kolbe; Spar/Dansk Supermarket; Generali/BCHA; Mondi/Frantschach; Eucom/Digital; Ericsson/Ascom; Thomas Cook/LTU/West LB; Elf-Atochem/Rohm & Haas; Rhône-Poulenc/SNIA; Northern Telecom/Matra Telecommunications; Avesta/British Steel, NCC/AGA/Axel Johnson; References and summaries in the Commission Competition Policy Reports).

[4]OJ No. 13, 21.2.1962, p. 204/62.

[5]OJ No. L175, 23.7.1968, p. 10.

No. 4056/86[6] or (EEC) No. 3975/87[7] in the determination of its compliance with Article 85(1) and (3).

Notes
[6]OJ No. L378, 31.12.1986, p. 4.
[7]OJ No. L374, 31.12.1987, p. 1.

III.   ASSESSMENT PURSUANT TO ARTICLE 85

1.   General comments

12.   JVs can be caught by the prohibition of cartels only where they fulfil all the requisite elements pursuant to Article 85(1).

13.   The creation of a JV is usually based on an agreement between undertakings and sometimes on a decision of an association of undertakings. The exercise of control as well as the management of the business is likewise usually governed by contract. Where there is no agreement, which is the case for instance in the acquisition of a joint controlling interest in an existing company by the purchase of shares on the stock exchange, the continued existence of the JV depends on the parent companies' coordinating their policy towards the JV and their manner of controlling it.

14.   Whether the aforementioned agreements, decisions or concerted practices are likely to affect trade between Member States, can be decided only on a case-by-case basis. Where the JV's actual or foreseeable effects on competition are limited to the territory of one Member State or to territories outside the Community, Article 85(1) will not apply.

15.   Article 85(1) does not therefore apply to certain categories of JV because they do not have as their object or effect the prevention, restriction or distortion of competition. This is particularly true for:

— JVs formed by parents which all belong to the same group and which are not in a position freely to determine their market behaviour: in such a case its creation is merely a matter of internal organisation and allocation of tasks within the group,

— JVs of minor economic importance within the meaning of the 1986 Notice;[1] there is no *appreciable* restriction of competition where the combined turnover of the participating undertakings does not exceed ECU 200 million and their market share is not more than 5%,

— JVs with activities neutral to competition within the meaning of the 1968 Notice on cooperation between enterprises:[2] the types of cooperation referred to therein do not restrict competition because:

— they have as their sole object the procurement of non-confidential information and therefore serve in the preparation of autonomous decisions of the participating enterprises,[3]

— they have as their sole object management cooperation;[4]

Notes
[1]OJ No. C231, 12.9.1986, p. 2.
[2]OJ No. C75, 29.7.1968, p. 3; corrected by OJ No. C93, 18.9.1968, p. 14.
[3]See II, point 1.
[4]See II, point 2.

— they have as their sole object cooperation in fields removed from the market,[5]

— they are concerned solely with technical and organisational arrangements;[6]

— they concern solely arrangements between non-competitors,[7]

— even though they concern arrangements between competitors, they neither limit the parties' competitive behaviour nor affect the market position of third parties.[8]

The aforementioned characteristics for distinguishing between conduct restrictive of competition and conduct which is neutral from a competition point of view are not fixed, but form part of the general development of Community law. They must therefore be construed and applied in the light of the case-law of the Court of Justice as well as of the Commission's decisions. In addition, general Commission notices are modified from time to time in order to adapt them to the evolution of the law.

16.   JVs which do not fall into any of the abovementioned categories must be individually examined to see whether they have the object or effect of restricting competition. The basic principles of the Notice on cooperation can be useful in such examination. The Commission will explain below on what criteria it assesses the restrictive character of a JV.

Notes
[5]See II, point 3.
[6]See II, point 4.
[7]See II, points 5 and 6.
[8]See II, points 7 and 8.

2.   Criteria for the establishment of restrictions of competition

17.   The appraisal of a cooperative JV in the light of the competition rules will focus on the relationship between the enterprises concerned and on the effects of their cooperation on third parties. In this respect the first task is to check whether the creation or operation of the JV is likely to prevent, restrict or distort competition between the parents. Secondly, it is necessary to examine whether the operation in question is likely to affect appreciably the competitive position of third parties, especially with regard to supply and sales possibilities. The relationship of the parents to the JV requires a separate legal assessment only if the JV is a full-function undertaking. However, even here the assessment must always take into account the relationship of the parents to each other and to third parties. Prevention, restriction or distortion of competition will be brought about by a JV only if its creation or activity affects the conditions of competition on the relevant market. The evaluation of a JV pursuant to Article 85(1) therefore always implies defining the relevant geographic and product market. The criteria to apply in that process are to be drawn from the *de minimis* Notice and the Commission's previous decisions. Special attention must be paid to networks of JVs which are set up by the same parents, by one parent with different partners or by different parents in parallel. They form an important element of the market structure and may therefore be of decisive influence in determining whether the creation of a JV leads to restrictions of competition.

(a) *Competition between parent companies*

18.   Competition between parent companies can be prevented, restricted or distorted through cooperation in a JV only to the extent that companies are already actual or potential competitors. The assumption of potential competitive circumstances presupposes that each parent alone is in a position to fulfil the tasks assigned to the JV and that it does not forfeit its capabilities to do so by the creation of the JV. An economically realistic approach is necessary in the assessment of any particular case.

19.   The Commission has developed a set of questions, which aim to clarify the theoretical and practical existing possibilities for the parents to perform the tasks individually instead of together.[1] Although these questions are designed to apply in particular to the case of manufacturing of goods, they are also relevant to the provision of services. They are as follows:

— *Contribution to the JV*
Does each parent company have sufficient financial resources to carry out the planned investment? Does each parent company have sufficient managerial qualifications to run the JV? Does each parent company have access to the necessary input products?

— *Production of the JV*
Does each parent know the production technique? Does each parent make the upstream or downstream products himself and does it have access to the necessary production facilities?

— *Sales by the JV*
Is actual or potential demand such as to enable each parent company to manufacture the product on its own? Does each parent company have access to the distribution channels needed to sell the product manufactured by the JV?

— *Risk factors*
Can each parent company on its own bear the technical and financial risks associated with the production operations of the JV?

— *Access to the relevant market*
What is the relevant geographic and product market? What are the barriers to entry into the market? Is each parent company capable of entering that market on its own? Can each parent overcome existing barriers within a reasonable time and without undue effort or cost?

20.   The parents of a JV are potential competitors, in so far as in the light of the above factors, which may be given different weight from case to case, they could reasonably be expected to act autonomously. In that connection, analysis must focus on the various stages of the activity of an undertaking. The economic pressure towards cooperation at the R&D stage does not normally eliminate the possibility of competition between the participating undertakings at the production and distribution stages. The pooling of the production capacity of several undertakings, when it is economically unavoidable and thus unobjectionable as regards competition law, does not necessarily imply that these undertakings should also cooperate in the distribution of the products concerned.

Note
[1] See Thirteenth Competition Policy Report (1983), point 55.

(b) *Competition between the parent companies and the JV*

21.   The relationship between the parents and the JV takes a specific significance when the JV is a full-function JV and is in competition with, or is a supplier or a customer of, at least one of the parents. The applicability of the prohibition on cartels depends on the circumstances of the individual case. As anti-competitive behaviour between the parents will as a rule also influence business relationships between the parents and the JV and conversely, anti-competitive behaviour by the JV and one of the parents will always affect relationships between the parents, a global analysis of all the different relationships is necessary. The Commission's decisions offer plenty of examples of this.

22.   The restriction of competition, within the meaning of Article 85(1), between parents and JVs typically manifests itself in the division of geographical markets, product markets (especially through specialisation) or customers. In such cases the participating undertakings reduce their activity to the role of potential competitors. If they remain active competitors, they will usually be tempted to reduce the intensity of competition by coordinating their business policy, especially as to prices and volume of production or sales or by voluntarily restraining their efforts.

(c) *Effects of the JV on the position of third parties*

23.   The restrictive effect on third parties depends on the JV's activities in relation to those of its parents and on the combined market power of the undertakings concerned.

24.   Where the parent companies leave it to the JV to handle their purchases or sales, the choice available to suppliers or customers may be appreciably restricted. The same is true when the parents arrange for the JV to manufacture primary or intermediate products or to process products which they themselves have produced. The creation of a JV may even exclude from the market the parents' traditional suppliers and customers. That risk increases in step with the degree of oligopolisation of the market and the existence of exclusive or preferential links between the JV and its parents.

25.   The existence of a JV in which economically significant undertakings pool their respective market power may even be a barrier to market entry by potential competitors and/or impede the growth of the parents' competitors.

(d) *Assessment of the appreciable effect of restrictions of competition*

26.   The scale of a JV's effects on competition depends on a number of factors, the most important of which are:
— the market shares of the parent companies and the JV, the structure of the relevant market and the degree of concentration in the sector concerned,
— the economic and financial strength of the parent companies, and any commercial or technical edge which they may have in comparison to their competitors,
— the market proximity of the activities carried out by the JV,
— whether the fields of activity of the parent companies and the JV are identical or interdependent,
— the scale and significance of the JV's activities in relation to those of its parents,

—the extent to which the arrangements between the firms concerned are restrictive,

—the extent to which market access by third parties is restricted.

(e)   *JV networks*

27.   JV networks can particularly restrict competition because they increase the influence of the individual JV on the business policy of the parents and on the market position of third parties. The assessment under competition law must take into account the different ways of arranging JV networks just as much as the cumulative effects of parallel existing networks.

28.   Often competing parent companies set up several JVs which are active in the same product market but in different geographical markets. On the top of the restrictions of competition which can already be attributed to each JV, there will then be those which arise in the relationships between the individual JVs. The ties between the parents are strengthened by the creation of every further JV so that any competition which still exists between them will be further reduced.

29.   The same is true in the case where competing parents set up several JVs for complementary products which they themselves intend to process or for non-complementary products which they themselves distribute. The extent and intensity of the restrictive effects on competition are also increased in such cases. Competition is most severely restricted where undertakings competing within the same oligopolistic economic sector set up a multitude of JVs for related products or for a great variety of intermediate products. These considerations are also valid for the service sector.

30.   Even where a JV is created by non-competing undertakings and does not, on its own, cause any restriction of competition, it can be anti-competitive if it belongs to a network of JVs set up by one of the parents for the same product market with different partners, because competition between the JVs may then be prevented, restricted or distorted.[1] If the different partners are actual or potential competitors, there will additionally be restrictive effects in the relationships between them.

31.   Parallel networks of JVs, involving different parent companies, simply reveal the degree of personal and financial connection between the undertakings of an economic sector or between several economic sectors. They form, in so far as they are comparable to the degree of concentration on the relevant market, an important aspect of the economic environment which has to be taken into account in the assessment from a competition point of view of both the individual networks and the participating JVs.

Note
[1]See Decision Optical Fibres, OJ No. L236, 22.8.1986, p. 30.

3.   Assessment of the most important types of JV

(a)   *Joint ventures between non-competitors*

32.   This group rarely causes problems for competition, whether the JV fulfils merely partial or the full functions of an undertaking. In the first case one must simply examine whether market access of third parties is significantly

affected by the cooperation between the parents.[1] In the second case the emphasis of the examination is on the same question and the problem of competition restrictions between one of the parent and the JV[2] is usually only of secondary significance.

33.   JVs between non-competitors created for research and development, for production or for distribution of goods including customer service do not in principle fall within Article 85(1). The non-application of the prohibition is justified by the combination of complementary knowledge, products and services in the JV. That is, however, subject to the reservation that there remains room for a sufficient number of R&D centres, production units and sales channels in the respective area of economic activity of the JV.[3] The same reasoning also applies to the assessment of purchasing JVs for customers from different business sectors. Such JVs are unobjectionable from a competition point of view as long as they leave suppliers with sufficient possibilities of customer choice.

34.   JVs which manufacture exclusively for their parents primary or intermediate products or undertake processing for one or more of their parents do not, as a rule, restrict competition. A significant restriction of the supply and sales possibilities of third parties, a prerequisite for the application of the prohibition, can occur only if the parents have a strong market position in the supply or demand of the relevant products.

35.   In the assessment of a full-function JV it is essential whether the activities the JV pursues are closely linked to those of the parents. In addition, the relationship of the activities of the parents to each other is of importance. If the JV trades in a product market which is upstream or downstream of the market of a parent, restrictions of competition can occur in relation to third parties, if the participants are undertakings with market power.[4] If the market of the JV is upstream of the market of one of the parents and at the same time downstream of the market of another parent, the JV functions as a connection between the two parents and also possibly as a vertical multi-level integration instrument. In such a situation the exclusive effects with regard to third parties are reinforced. Whether it fulfils the requisite minimum degree for the application of Article 85(1) can be decided only on an individual basis. If the JV and one of the parents trade in the same product market, then coordination of their market behaviour is probable if not inevitable.[5]

Notes

[1] See above III. 2(c) points 23, 24 and 25.
[2] See above III. 2(b) points 21 and 22.
[3] See Section II of the Notice on cooperation, points 3 and 6, and regulation (EEC) No. 418/85 on the application of Article 85(3) of the Treaty to categories of research and development agreements, OJ No. L53, 22.2.1985, p. 5.
[4] No negative effect was found by the Commission in Decision 86/405/EEC (Optical Fibres), OJ No. L236, 22.8.1986, p. 30, and in Decision 90/410/EEC (Elopak/Metal Box-Odin), OJ No. L209, 8.8.1990, p. 15.
[5] See above III. 2(b) point 22, and Decision 87/100/EEC (Mitchell Cotts/Sofiltra), OJ No. L41, 11.2.1987, p. 31.

(b)   *Joint ventures by competitors*

36.   In this situation the effects of the JV on competition between the parents and on the market position of third parties must be analysed. The

relationship between the activities of the JV and those of the parents is of decisive importance. In the absence of any interplay, Article 85(1) will usually not be applicable. The competition law assessment of the different types of JV leads to the following results.

37. A research and development JV may, in exceptional cases, restrict competition if it excludes individual activity in this area by the parents or if competition by the parents on the market for the resulting products will be restricted. This will normally be the case where the JV also assumes the exploitation of the newly developed or improved products or processes.[1] Whether the restriction of competition between the parents and the ensuing possible secondary effects on third parties are appreciable can be decided only on a case-by-case basis.

38. Sales JVs, selling the products of competing manufacturers, restrict competition between the parents on the supply side and limit the choice of purchasers. They belong to the category of traditional horizontal cartels which are subject to the prohibition of Article 85(1),[2] when they have an appreciable effect on the market.

39. Purchasing JVs set up by competitors can give the participants an advantageous position on the demand side and reduce the choice of suppliers. Depending on the importance of the jointly-sold products to the production and sales activities of the parents, the cooperation can also lead to a considerable weakening of price competition between the participating undertakings. This applies even more so when the purchase price makes up a significant part of the total cost of the products distributed by the parents. The application of Article 85(1) depends on the circumstances of the individual case.[3]

40. JVs which manufacture primary or intermediate products for competing parent companies, which are further processed by them into the final product, must be assessed on the same principles. On the other hand, if the JV undertakes the processing of basic materials supplied by the parents, or the processing of half-finished into fully-finished products, with the aim of resupplying the parents, then competition between the participating undertakings, taking into consideration the market proximity of their cooperation and the inherent tendency to align prices, will usually exist only in a weaker form.[4] This is particularly so when the entire production activities of the parents are concentrated in the JV and the parents withdraw to the role of pure distributors. This leads to the standardisation of manufacturing costs and the quality of the products so that essentially the only competition between the

Notes

[1] See Notice in cooperation, II, point 3 and Regulation (EEC) No. 418/85 (cited in footnote 7).

[2] See the following decisions: NCH, OJ No. L22, 26.1.1972, p. 16; Cementregeling voor Nederland, OJ No. L303, 31.12.1972, p. 7; Cimbel, OJ No. L303, 31.12.1972, p. 24; CSV, OJ No. L242, 4.9.1978, p. 15; UIP, OJ No. L226, 3.8.1989, p. 25 and Astra, OJ No. L....

[3] See the following decisions: Socemas, OJ No. L201, 12.8.1968, p. 4; Intergroup, OJ No. L212, 9.8.1975, p. 23; National Sulphuric Acid Association I, OJ No. L260, 3.10.1980, p. 24 and (II) OJ No. L190, 5.7.1989, p. 25; Filmeinkauf Deutscher Fernsehanstalten, OJ No. L284, 3.10.1989, p. 36; and IJsselcentrale, OJ No. L28, 2.2.1991, p. 32.

[4] See Notice in Exxon/Shell, OJ 1989 No. L74/21.

parents is on trade margins. This is a considerable restriction of competition which cannot be remedied by the parents marketing the products under different brand names.[5]

41. Different situations must be distinguished when assessing full-function JVs between competing undertakings.[6]

—Where the JV operates on the same market as its parents, the normal consequence is that competition between all participating undertakings will be restricted.

—Where the JV operates on a market upstream or downstream of that of the parents with which it has supply or delivery links, the effects on competition will be the same as in the case of a production JV.

—Where the JV operates on a market adjacent to that of its parents, competition can only be restricted when there is a high degree of interdependence between the two markets. This is especially the case when the JV manufactures products which are complementary to those of its parents.

Combinations of various types of JV are often found in economic life so that an overall assessment of the resultant restrictions of competition between participating undertakings and the consequences of the cooperation on third parties must be carried out. In addition the economic circumstances must be taken into account, especially the association of a JV to a network with other JVs and the existence of several parallel JV networks within the same economic sector.[7]

42. Even JVs between competitors, which are usually caught by the prohibition in Article 85(1), must be examined to see whether in the actual circumstances of the individual case they have as their object or effect the restriction, prevention or distortion of competition. This will not be the case where cooperation in the form of a JV can objectively be seen as the only possibility for the parents to enter a new market or to remain in their existing market, provided that their presence will strengthen competition or prevent it from being weakened. Under these conditions the JV will neither reduce

Notes

[5]See Decision 91/38/EEC (KSB/Goulds/Lowara/ITT), OJ No. L19, 25.1.1991, p. 25; the anti-competitive character of joint economic production is acknowledged in principle in Regulation (EEC) 417/85 on the application of Article 85(3) of the EEC Treaty to categories of specialisation agreements, OJ No. L53, 22.2.1985, p. 1.

[6]See in particular the following decisions: Bayer/Gist-Brocades, OJ No. L30, 5.2.1976, p. 13; United Reprocessors and KEWA, OJ No. L51, 26.2.1976, pp. 7, 15; Vacuum Interrupters I, OJ No. L48, 19.2.1977, p. 32, and II, OJ No. L383, 31.12.1980, p. 1; De Laval/Stork I, OJ No. L215, 23.8.1977, p. 11, and II, OJ No. L59, 4.3.1988, p. 32; GEC/Weir, OJ No. L327, 20.12.1977, p. 26; WANO/Schwarzpulver, OJ No. L322, 16.11.1978, p. 26; Langenscheidt/Hachette, OJ No. L39, 11.2.1982, p. 25; Amersham/Buchler, OJ No. L314, 10.11.1982, p. 34; Rockwell/Iveco, OJ No. L 224, 17.8.1983, p. 19; Carbon Gas Technologie, OH No. L376, 31.12.1983, p. 17; Enichem/ICI, OJ No. L150, 24.2.1988, p. 18; Bayer/BP Chemicals, OJ No. L150, 16.6.1988, p. 35; Iveco/Ford, OJ No. L230, 19.8.1988, p. 39; Alcatel Espace/ANT, OJ No. L32, 3.2.1990, p. 19; Konsortium ECR 900, OJ No. L228, 22.8.1990, p. 31; Screensport/EBU — Eurosport, OJ No. L63, 9.3.1991, p. 32; Eirpage, OJ No. L306, 7.11.1991, p. 22; Procter and Gamble/Finaf, OJ No. C3, 7.1.1992, p. 2 and Infonet, OH No. C7, 11.1.1992, p. 3.

[7]See above III. 2(e), points 27 to 31.

existing competition nor prevent potential competition from being realised. The prohibition in Article 85(1) will therefore not apply.[8]

Note

[8]See the following decisions: Alliance des constructeurs français de machines-outils, OJ No. L201, 12.8.1968, p. 1; SAFCO, OJ No. L13, 17.1.1972, p. 44; Metaleurop, OJ No. L179, 12.7.1990, p. 41; Elopak/Metal Box-Odin, OJ No. L209, 8.8.190, p. 15; Konsortium ECR 900, OJ No. L228, 22.8.1990, p. 31.

IV.   ASSESSMENT PURSUANT TO ARTICLE 85(3)

1.   Group exemptions

43.   JVs falling within the scope of Article 85(1) are exempted from the prohibition if they fulfil the conditions of a group exemption. Two Commission regulations legalise cooperation between undertakings in the form of JVs. Two other Commission regulations authorise certain restrictive agreements on the transfer of technology to a JV by its parents. The field of application of these group exemption regulations will be considerably expanded, notably for JVs, by Regulation (EEC) No. 151/93.[1]

(a)   *Specialisation Regulation*

44.   Regulation (EEC) No. 417/85 on the application of Article 85(3) to categories of specialisation agreements[2] includes, *inter alia*, agreements whereby several undertakings leave the manufacture of certain products to a JV set up by them. This transfer can be for existing or future production. The creation and use of production JVs are exempted only if the aggregate market share of the participating undertakings does not exceed 20% and the cumulated turnover does not exceed ECU 1,000 million. Agreements between more sizeable undertakings, the turnover of which exceeds ECU 1,000 million, also benefit from the group exemption if they are properly notified and the Commission does not object to the agreement within six months. This procedure is not applicable when the market share threshold is exceeded.

45.   The abovementioned rules apply exclusively to cooperation at the production level. The JV must supply all its production — which can include primary, intermediate or finished products — to its parents. The latter are not permitted to be active as manufacturers in the JV's area of production, but they may manufacture other products belonging to that product market. Products made by the JV are then sold by the parents, each of which can deal as exclusive distributor for a given territory.

46.   Agreements in which the parents entrust JVs with the distribution of the contract products are also covered by the group exemption, though only under more rigorous conditions. The aggregate market share of the participating undertakings must not exceed 10%. In this case also, there is a turnover threshold of ECU 1,000 million, the effect of which undertakings can avoid by resorting to the opposition procedure. Regulation (EEC) No. 417/85 leaves the undertakings concerned free to organise their cooperation at the production and distribution stages. It allows for separate production followed by joint distribution of the contract products through a sales JV, as well as for the

Notes

[1]OJ No. L21, 23.12.1992, p. 8.
[2]OJ No. L53, 22.2.1985, p. 1.

merging of production and distribution in a full-function JV, or the separation of both functions through the creation of a production JV and a sales JV. The production and/or distribution of the contract products can be entrusted to several JVs instead of one, which may, as the case may be, fulfil their function on the basis of exclusive contracts in various territories.

(b)   *Research and Development Regulation*

47.   Regulation (EEC) No. 418/85 on the application of Article 85(3) to categories of research and development agreements[1] provides for the exemption of JVs whose activities can range from R&D to the joint exploitation of results. The term exploitation covers the manufacture of new or improved products as well as the use of new or improved production processes, the marketing of products derived from R&D activities and the granting of manufacturing, use or distribution licences to third parties. The exemption is subject to the requirement that the joint R&D contributes substantially to technical or economic progress and is essential to the manufacture of new or improved products.

48.   Regulation (EEC) No. 418/85 also links exemption from the prohibition to quantitative conditions in the form of a two-fold market share limit. Cooperation in the form of a JV dealing with R&D, production and licensing policy will be permitted for parents who have an aggregate market share of up to 20%. In the area of R&D as well as manufacture, the Regulation allows all forms of coordination of behaviour because it does not require specialisation. The parents can themselves remain or become active within the field of activity of the JV. They are also allowed to determine in what way they wish to use the possibilities of production by themselves or the licensing of third parties. By the allocation of contract territories the parents can protect themselves for the duration of the contract from the manufacture and use of the contract products by other partners in the reserved territories; furthermore, they can prevent other partners from pursuing an active marketing policy in those territories for five years after the introduction of the new or improved product into the common market. If, on the contrary, the partners entrust one or more JVs with the distribution of the contract products, a market share threshold of 10% is applicable to the whole of their cooperation. As Regulation (EEC) No. 418/85 does not provide for a turnover threshold, all undertakings regardless of their size can benefit from the group exemption.

Note
[1] OJ No. L53, 22.2.1985, p. 5.

(c)   *Patent-licensing and know-how licensing Regulations*

49.   Regulation (EEC) No. 2349/84 on the application of Article 85(3) of the Treaty to categories of patent licensing agreements[1] applies also to such agreements between any one of the parents and the JV affecting the activities of the JV. If the parents are competitors on the market of the contract products, the group exemption applies only up to a certain market share limit. This is 20% if the JV simple carries on manufacturing or 10% if it carries on the manufacture and marketing of the licensed products.

Notes
[1] OJ No. L219, 16.8.1984, p. 15.

50.   Regulation (EEC) No. 2349/84 also permits the granting of exclusive territorial manufacture and distribution licences to the JV, the protection of the licence territories of the JV and of the parents against active and passive competition by other participants for the duration of the contract and the protection of the licence territory of the JV against other licensees. The parents can protect the JV from an active distribution policy by other licensees for the full duration of the contract. During an initial five-year period from the introduction of a product into the common market, it is possible to forbid direct imports of contract products by other licensees into the JV's licensed territory.

51.   Regulation (EEC) No. 556/89 on the application of Article 85(3) of the Treaty to certain categories of know-how licensing agreements[2] contains similar provisions, except that the territorial protection between the JV and the parents is limited to 10 years, being from the signature of the first know-how agreement concluded for a territory inside the Community. This point in time also marks the beginning of the period for which the JV can be protected against active competition (10 years) and passive competition (five years) by other licensees.

Note
[2]OJ No. L61, 4.3.1989, p. 1.

2.   Individual Exemptions

(a)   *General comments*

52.   JVs which fall within Article 85(1) without fulfilling the conditions for the application of a group exemption regulation are not inevitably unlawful. They can be exempted by an individual decision of the Commission in so far as they fulfil the four conditions of Article 85(3). According to Articles 4, 5 and 15 of Regulation No. 17 an individual exemption can be issued only if the participating undertakings have notified the agreement, decision or concerned practice on which cooperation is based, to the Commission. Certain arrangements which are less harmful to the development of the common market are dispensed from the requirement to notify by Article 4(2) of Regulation No. 17. They can therefore be exempted without prior notification. The same applies to transport cartels within the meaning of Regulations (EEC) No. 1017/68, (EEC) No. 4056/86 and (EEC) No. 3975/87.

53.   The Commission must, pursuant to Article 85(3), examine:
— whether the JV contributes to improving the production or distribution of goods or to promoting technical or economic progress,
— whether consumers are allowed a fair share of the resulting benefit,
— whether the parents or the JV are subject to restrictions which are not indispensable for the attainment of these objectives, and
— whether the cooperation in the JV affords the undertakings concerned the possibility of eliminating competition in respect of a substantial part of the products or services in question.

An exemption from the prohibition in Article 85(1) can be issued only if the answer to the first two questions is in the affirmative and the answer to the second two questions is negative.

(b) *Principles of assessment*

54. In order to fulfil the first two conditions of Article 85(3) the JV must bring appreciable objective advantages for third parties, especially consumers, which at least equal the consequent detriment to competition.

55. Advantages in the abovementioned sense, which can be pursued and attained with the aid of a JV, include, in the Commission's opinion, in particular, the development of new or improved products and processes which are marketed by the originator or by third parties under licence. In addition, measures opening up new markets, leading to the sales expansion of the undertaking in new territories or the enlargement of its supply range by new products, will in principle be assessed favourably. In all these cases the undertakings in question contribute to dynamic competition, consolidating the internal market and strengthening the competitiveness of the relevant economic sector. Production and sales increases can also be a pre-competitive stimulant. On the other hand, the rationalisation of production activities and distribution networks are rather a means of adapting supply to a shrinking or stagnant demand. It leads, however, to cost savings which, under effective competition, are usually passed on to customers as lower prices. Plans for the reduction of production capacity however lead mostly to price rises. Agreements of this latter type will be judged favourably only if they serve to overcome a structural crisis, to accelerate the removal of unprofitable production capacity from the market and thereby to reestablish competition in the medium term.

56. The Commission will give a negative assessment to agreements which have as their main purpose the coordination of actual or potential competition between the participating undertakings. This is especially so for joint price-fixing, the reduction of production and sales by establishing quotas, the division of markets and contractual prohibitions or restrictions on investment. JVs which are created or operated essentially to achieve such aims are nothing but classic cartels the anticompetitive effects of which are well known.

57. The pros and cons of a JV will be weighed against each other on an overall economic balance, by means of which the type and the extent of the respective advantages and risks can be assessed. If the parents are economically and financially powerful and have, over and above that a high market-share, their exemption applications will need a rigorous examination. The same applies to JVs which reinforce an existing narrow oligopoly or belong to a network of JVs.

58. The acceptance pursuant to Article 85(3)(a) of restrictions on the parents or the JV depends above all on the type and aims of the cooperation. In this context, the decisive factor is usually whether the contractual restriction on the parties' economic freedom is directly connected with the creation of the JV and can be considered indispensable for its existence.[1] It is only for the restriction of global competition that Article 85(3)(b) sets an absolute limit. Competition must be fully functioning at all times. Agreements which endanger its effectiveness cannot benefit from individual exemption. This category includes JVs which, through the combination of activities of the parents, achieve, consolidate or strengthen a dominant position.

Note
[1] See below V. 2, point 70 *et seq.*

(c)   *Assessment of the most important types of JV*

59.   Pure research and development JVs which do not fulfil the conditions for group exemption under Regulation (EEC) No. 418/85 can still in general be viewed positively. This type of cooperation normally offers important economic benefits without adversely affecting competition. That is also the case where the parents entrust the JV with the further task of granting licences to third parties. If the JV also takes on the manufacture of the jointly researched and developed product, the assessment for the purpose of exemption must include the principles which apply to production JVs.[1] JVs which are responsible for R&D, licensing, production and distribution are full-function JVs and must be analysed accordingly.[2]

60.   Sales JVs belong to the category of classic horizontal cartels. They have as a rule the object and effect of coordinating the sales policy of competing manufacturers. In this way they not only close off price competition between the parents but also restrict the volume of goods to be delivered by the participants within the framework of the system for allocating orders. The Commission will therefore in principle assess sales JVs negatively.[3] The Commission takes a positive view however of those cases where joint distribution of the contract products is part of a global cooperation project which merits favourable treatment pursuant to Article 85(3) and for the success of which it is indispensable. The most important examples are sales JVs between manufacturers who have concluded a reciprocal specialisation agreement, but wish to continue to offer the whole range of products concerned, or sales JVs set up for the joint exploitation of the results of joint R&D, even at the distribution stage. In other cases, an exemption can be envisaged only in certain specific circumstances.[4]

61.   Purchasing JVs contribute to the rationalisation of ordering and to the better use of transport and store facilities but are at the same time an instrument for the setting of uniform purchase prices and conditions and often of purchase quotas. By combining their demand power in a JV, the parents can obtain a position of excessive influence *vis-à-vis* the other side of the market and distort competition between suppliers. Consequently, the disadvantages often outweigh the possible benefits which can accompany purchasing JVs, particularly those between competing producers. The Commission is correspondingly prepared to grant exemptions only in exceptional cases and then only if the parents retain the possibility of purchasing individually.[5] No decision has, however, concerned the most important of the purchasing JVs so far.

62.   Production JVs can serve different economic purposes. They will often be set up to create new capacity for the manufacture of particular products

Notes
[1]See below points 62 and 63.
[2]See below point 64.
[3]See the NCH, Cementregeling voor Nederland, Cimbel and CSV decisions (all cited in footnote to point 39).
[4]See Decision 89/467/EEC (UIP) (cited in footnote to point 39).
[5]See the National Sulphuric Acid Association, Filmeinkauf Deutscher Fernsehanstalten, IJsselcentrale decisions (all cited in footnote to point 40).

which are also manufactured by the parents.[6] In other cases the JV will be entrusted with the manufacture of a new product in the place of the parents.[7] Finally, the JV can be entrusted with the combination of the production capacities of the parents and their expansion or reduction as necessary.

63. In view of the various tasks of production JVs their assessment for exemption purposes will be carried out according to different yardsticks. JVs, for the expansion of production capacity or product range, can contribute not only to the prevention of parallel investment — which results in costs savings — but also to the stimulation of competition. The combination or reduction of existing product capacity is primarily a rationalisation measure and is usually of a defensive nature. It is not always obvious that measures of this kind benefit third parties, especially consumers and they must therefore be justified individually. Generally applicable quantitative thresholds, for instance in the form of market share limits, cannot be fixed for production JVs. The more the competition between the parents is restricted, the more emphasis must be put on the maintenance of competition with third parties. The market share limit of 20% in the group exemption regulations can serve as a starting point for the assessment of production JVs in individual cases.

64. Full-function JVs, in so far as they are not price-fixing, quota-fixing or market-sharing cartels or vehicles for a coordination of the investment policies conducted by the parents which goes beyond the individual case, often form elements of dynamic competition and then deserve a favourable assessment.[8] As cooperation also includes distribution, the Commission has to take special care in assessing individual cases that no position of market power will be created or strengthened by entrusting the JV with all the functions of an undertaking combined with the placing at its disposal of all the existing resources of the parents. To assess whether a full-function JV raises problems of compatibility with the competition rules or not, an important point of reference is the aggregate market share limit of 10% contained in the group exemption regulations. Below this threshold it can be assumed that the effect of exclusion from the market of third parties and the danger of creating or reinforcing barriers to market entry will be kept within justifiable limits. A prerequisite is however that the market structure will continue to guarantee effective competition. If the said threshold is exceeded, an exemption will be considered only after a careful examination of each individual case.

Notes

[6] See Exxon/Shell (footnote to point 41).

[7] See the KSB/Goulds/Lowara/ITT decision (cited in footnote to point 42).

[8] See the following decisions: Amersham/Buchler, OJ No. L314, 10.11.1982, p. 34; Rockwell/Iveco, OJ No. L224, 17.8.1983, p. 19; Carbon Gas Technologie, OJ No. L376, 31.12.1983, p. 17; Enichem/ICI, OJ No. L50, 24.2.1988, p. 18; Bayer/BP Chemicals, OJ No. L150, 16.6.1988, p. 35; Iveco/ANT, OJ No. L230, 19.8.1988, p. 39; Alcatel Espace/ANT, OJ No. L32, 3.2.1990, p. 19; Eirpage, OJ No. L306, 7.11.1991, p. 22; Bayer/Gist-Brocades, OJ No. L30, 5.2.1976, p. 13; United Reprocessors and KEWA, OH No. L51, 26.2.1976, p. 7; Vacuum Interrupters I, OJ No. L48, 19.2.1977, p. 32 and II, OJ No. L383, 31.12.1980, p. 1; De Laval/Stork I, OJ No. L215, 23.8.1977, p. 11 and II, OJ No. L59, 4.3.1988, p. 32; GEC/Weir, OJ No. L327, 20.12.1977, p. 26; Langenscheidt/Hachette, OJ No. L39, 11.2.1982, p. 25; Procter and Gamble/Finaf, OJ No. C3, 7.1.1992, p. 2; and INFONET, OJ No. C7, 11.1.1992, p. 3.

V. ANCILLARY RESTRICTIONS

1. Principles of assessment

65. A distinction must be made between restrictions of competition which arise from the creation and operation of a JV, and additional agreements which would, on their own, also constitute restrictions of competition by limiting the freedom of action in the market of the participating undertakings. Such additional agreements are either directly related to and necessary for the establishment and operation of the JV in so far as they cannot be dissociated from it without jeopardising its existence, or are simply concluded at the same time as the JV's creation without having those features.

66. Additional agreements which are directly related to the JV and necessary for its existence must be assessed together with the JV. They are treated under the rules of competition as ancillary restrictions if they remain subordinate in importance to the main object of the JV. In particular, in determining the 'necessity' of the restriction, it is proper not only to take account of its nature, but equally to ensure that its duration, subject matter and geographical field of application do not exceed what the creation and operation of the JV normally requires.

67. If a JV does not fall within the scope of Article 85(1), then neither do any additional agreements which, while restricting competition on their own, are ancillary to the JV in the manner described above. Conversely, if a JV falls within the scope of Article 85(1), then so will any ancillary restrictions. The exemption from prohibition is based for both on the same principles. Ancillary restrictions require no special justification under Article 85(3). They will generally be exempted for the same period as the JV.

68. Additional agreements which are not ancillary to the JV normally fall within the scope of Article 85(1), even though the JV itself may not. For them to be granted an exemption under Article 85(3), a specific assessment of their benefits and disadvantages must be made. This assessment must be carried out separately from that of the JV.

69. In view of the diversity of JVs and of the additional restrictions that may be linked to them, only a few examples can be given of the application of existing principles. They are drawn from previous Commission practice.

2. Assessment of certain additional restrictions

70. Assessment of whether additional restrictions constitute an ancillary agreement must distinguish between those which affect the JV and those which affect the parents.

(a) Restrictions on the JV

71. Of the restrictions which affect the JV, those which give concrete expression to its object, such as contract clauses which specify the product range or the location of production, may be regarded as ancillary. Additional restrictions which go beyond the definition of the venture's object and which relate to quantities, prices or customers may not. The same can be said for export bans.

72. When the setting-up of the JV involves the creation of new production capacity or the transfer of technology from the parent, the obligation imposed on the JV not to manufacture or market products competing with the licensed

products may usually be regarded as ancillary. The JV must seek to ensure the success of the new production unit, without depriving the parent companies of the necessary control over exploitation and dissemination of their technology.[1]

73.   In certain circumstances, other restrictions on the JV can be classified as ancillary such as contract clauses which limit the cooperation to a certain area or to a specific technical application of the transferred technology. Such restrictions must be seen as the inevitable consequences of the parent's wish to limit the cooperation to a specific field of activity without jeopardising the object and existence of the JV.[2]

74.   Lastly, where the parent companies assign to the JV certain stages of production or the manufacture of certain products, obligations on the JV to purchase from or supply its parents may also be regarded as ancillary, at least during the JV's starting-up period.

Notes
[1]Mitchell Cotts/Sofiltra (footnote to point 37).
[2]Elopak/Metal Box-Odin (footnote to point 36).

(b)   *Restrictions on the parent companies*

75.   Restrictions which prohibit the parent companies from competing with the JV or from actively competing with it in its area of activity, may be regarded as ancillary at least during the JV's starting-up period. Additional restrictions relating to quantities, prices or customers, and export bans obviously go beyond what is required for the setting-up and operation of the JV.

76.   The Commission has in one case regarded as ancillary, a territorial restriction imposed on a parent company where the JV was granted an exclusive manufacturing licence in respect of fields of technical application and product markets in which both the JV and the parent were to be active.[1] This decision was limited, however, to the starting-up period of the JV and appeared necessary for the parents to become established in a new geographical market with the help of the JV. In another case, the grant to the JV of an exclusive exploitation licence without time-limit was regarded as indispensable for its creation and operation. In this case the parent company granting the licence was not active in the same field of application or on the same product market as that for which the licence was granted.[2] This will generally be the case with JVs undertaking new activities in respect of which the parent companies are neither actual not potential competitors.

Notes
[1]Mitchell Cotts/Sofiltra (footnote to point 37).
[2]Elopak/Metal Box-Odin (footnote to point 36).

CONCENTRATIONS/MERGERS

COUNCIL REGULATION (EEC) NO 4064/89 OF 21 DECEMBER 1989 ON THE CONTROL OF CONCENTRATIONS BETWEEN UNDERTAKINGS (AS CORRECTED)[1]
[OJ 1989, No. L257/13]

THE COUNCIL OF THE EUROPEAN COMMUNITIES,

Having regard to the Treaty establishing the European Economic Community, and in particular Articles 87 and 235 thereof,

Having regard to the proposal from the Commission,[2]

Having regard to the opinion of the European Parliament,[3]

Having regard to the opinion of the Economic and Social Committee,[4]

(1) Whereas, for the achievement of the aims of the Treaty establishing the European Economic Community, Article 3(f) gives the Community the objective of instituting 'a system ensuring that competition in the common market is not distorted';

(2) Whereas this system is essential for the achievement of the internal market by 1992 and its further development;

(3) Whereas the dismantling of internal frontiers is resulting and will continue to result in major corporate reorganisations in the Community, particularly in the form of concentrations;

(4) Whereas such a development must be welcomed as being in line with the requirements of dynamic competition and capable of increasing the competitiveness of European industry, improving the conditions of growth and raising the standard of living in the Community;

(5) Whereas, however, it must be ensured that the process of reorganisation does not result in lasting damage to competition; whereas Community law must therefore include provisions governing those concentrations which may significantly impede effective competition in the common market or in a substantial part of it;

(6) Whereas Articles 85 and 86, while applicable, according to the case-law of the Court of Justice, to certain concentrations, are not, however, sufficient to

Notes
[1]by Corrigendum to OJ 1989 No. L395/1 and amended by, OJ 1994 C241/57, Decision 95/1 [OJ 1995 L1/1] and Regulation 1310/97 [OJ 1997 L180/1].
[2]OJ No. C130, 19.5.1988, p. 4.
[3]OJ No. C309, 5.12.1988, p. 55.
[4]OJ No. C208, 8.8.1988, p. 11.

control all operations which may prove to be incompatible with the system of undistorted competition envisaged in the Treaty;

(7)   Whereas a new legal instrument should therefore be created in the form of a Regulation to permit effective control of all concentrations from the point of view of their effect on the structure of competition in the Community and to be the only instrument applicable to such concentrations;

(8)   Whereas this Regulation should therefore be based not only on Article 87 but, principally, on Article 235 of the Treaty, under which the Community may give itself the additional powers of action necessary for the attainment of its objectives, including with regard to concentrations on the markets for agricultural products listed in Annex II to the Treaty;

(9)   Whereas the provisions to be adopted in this Regulation should apply to significant structural changes the impact of which on the market goes beyond the national borders of any one Member State;

(10)   Whereas the scope of application of this Regulation should therefore be defined according to the geographical area of activity of the undertakings concerned and be limited by quantitative thresholds in order to cover those concentrations which have a Community dimension; whereas, at the end of an initial phase of the application of this Regulation, these thresholds should be reviewed in the light of the experience gained;

(11)   Whereas a concentration with a Community dimension exists where the combined aggregate turnover of the undertakings concerned exceeds given levels worldwide and within the Community and where at least two of the undertakings concerned have their sole or main fields of activities in different Member States or where, although the undertakings in question act mainly in one and the same Member State, at least one of them has substantial operations in at least one other Member State; whereas that is also the case where the concentrations are effected by undertakings which do not have their principal fields of activities in the Community but which have substantial operations there;

(12)   Whereas the arrangements to be introduced for the control of concentrations should, without prejudice to Article 90(2) of the Treaty, respect the principle of non-discrimination between the public and the private sectors; whereas, in the public sector, calculation of the turnover of an undertaking concerned in a concentration needs, therefore, to take account of undertakings making up an economic unit with an independent power of decision, irrespective of the way in which their capital is held or of the rules of administrative supervision applicable to them;

(13)   Whereas it is necessary to establish whether concentrations with a Community dimension are compatible or not with the common market from the point of view of the need to maintain and develop effective competition in the common market; whereas, in so doing, the Commission must place its appraisal within the general framework of the achievement of the fundamental objectives referred to in Article 2 of the Treaty, including that of strengthening the Community's economic and social cohesion, referred to in Article 130a;

(14)   Whereas this Regulation should establish the principle that a concentration with a Community dimension which creates or strengthens a position as a result of which effective competition in the common market or in a substantial part of it is significantly impeded is to be declared incompatible with the common market;

(15) Whereas concentrations which, by reason of the limited market share of the undertakings concerned, are not liable to impede effective competition may be presumed to be compatible with the common market; whereas, without prejudice to Articles 85 and 86 of the Treaty, an indication to this effect exists, in particular, where the market share of the undertakings concerned does not exceed 25% either in the common market or in a substantial part of it;

(16) Whereas the Commission should have the task of taking all the decisions necessary to establish whether or not concentrations with a Community dimension are compatible with the common market, as well as decisions designed to restore effective competition;

(17) Whereas to ensure effective control undertakings should be obliged to give prior notification of concentrations with a Community dimension and provision should be made for the suspension of concentrations for a limited period, and for the possibility of extending or waiving a suspension where necessary; whereas in the interests of legal certainty the validity of transactions must nevertheless be protected as much as necessary;

(18) Whereas a period within which the Commission must initiate proceedings in respect of a notified concentration and periods within which it must give a final decision on the compatibility or incompatibility with the common market of a notified concentration should be laid down;

(19) Whereas the undertakings concerned must be afforded the right to be heard by the Commission when proceedings have been initiated; whereas the members of the management and supervisory bodies and the recognised representatives of the employees of the undertakings concerned, and third parties showing a legitimate interest, must also be given the opportunity to be heard;

(20) Whereas the Commission should act in close and constant liaison with the competent authorities of the Member States from which it obtains comments and information;

(21) Whereas, for the purposes of this Regulation, and in accordance with the case-law of the Court of Justice, the Commission must be afforded the assistance of the Member States and must also be empowered to require information to be given and to carry out the necessary investigations in order to appraise concentrations;

(22) Whereas compliance with this Regulation must be enforceable by means of fines and periodic penalty payments; whereas the Court of Justice should be given unlimited jurisdiction in that regard pursuant to Article 172 of the Treaty;

(23) Whereas it is appropriate to define the concept of concentration in such a manner as to cover only operations bringing about a lasting change in the structure of the undertakings concerned; whereas it is therefore necessary to exclude from the scope of this Regulation those operations which have as their object or effect the coordination of the competitive behaviour of undertakings which remain independent, since such operations fall to be examined under the appropriate provisions of the Regulations implementing Articles 85 and 86 of the Treaty; whereas it is appropriate to make this distinction specifically in the case of the creation of joint ventures;

(24) Whereas there is no coordination of competitive behaviour within the meaning of this Regulation where two or more undertakings agree to acquire

jointly control of one or more other undertakings with the object and effect of sharing amongst themselves such undertakings or their assets;

(25)   Whereas this Regulation should still apply where the undertakings concerned accept restrictions directly related and necessary to the implementation of the concentration;

(26)   Whereas the Commission should be given exclusive competence to apply this Regulation, subject to review by the Court of Justice;

(27)   Whereas the Member States may not apply their national legislation on competition to concentrations with a Community dimension, unless this Regulation makes provision therefor; whereas the relevant powers of national authorities should be limited to cases where, failing intervention by the Commission, effective competition is likely to be significantly impeded within the territory of a Member State and where the competition interests of that Member State cannot be sufficiently protected otherwise by this Regulation; whereas the Member States concerned must act promptly in such cases; whereas this Regulation cannot, because of the diversity of national law, fix a single deadline for the adoption of remedies;

(28)   Whereas, furthermore, the exclusive application of this Regulation to concentrations with a Community dimension is without prejudice to Article 223 of the Treaty, and does not prevent the Member States from taking appropriate measures to protect legitimate interests other than those pursued by this Regulation, provided that such measures are compatible with the general principles and other provisions of Community law;

(29)   Whereas concentrations not covered by this Regulation come, in principle, within the jurisdiction of the Member States; whereas, however, the Commission should have the power to act, at the request of a Member State concerned, in cases where effective competition could be significantly impeded within that Member State's territory;

(30)   Whereas the conditions in which concentrations involving Community undertakings are carried out in non-member countries should be observed, and provision should be made for the possibility of the Council giving the Commission an appropriate mandate for negotiation with a view to obtaining non-discriminatory treatment for Community undertakings;

(31)   Whereas this Regulation in no way detracts from the collective rights of employees as recognised in the undertakings concerned,

HAS ADOPTED THIS REGULATION:

Article 1   Scope

1.   Without prejudice to Article 22, this Regulation shall apply to all concentrations with a Community dimension as defined in paragraphs 2 and 3.

2.   For the purposes of this Regulation, a concentration has a Community dimension where:

(a)   the combined aggregate worldwide turnover of all the undertakings concerned is more than ECU 5,000 million; and

(b)   the aggregate Community-wide turnover of each of at least two of the undertakings concerned is more than ECU 250 million, unless each of the undertakings concerned achieves more than two-thirds of its aggregate Community-wide turnover within one and the same Member State.

3. For the purposes of this Regulation, a concentration that does not meet the thresholds laid down in paragraph 2 has a Community dimension where:

(a) the combined aggregate worldwide turnover of all the undertakings concerned is more than ECU 2,500 million;

(b) in each of at least three Member States, the combined aggregate turnover of all the undertakings concerned is more than ECU 100 million;

(c) in each of at least three Member States included for the purpose of point (b), the aggregate turnover of each of at least two of the undertakings concerned is more than ECU 25 million; and

(d) the aggregate Community-wide turnover of each of at least two of the undertakings concerned is more than ECU 100 million;

unless each of the undertakings concerned achieves more than two-thirds of its aggregate Community-wide turnover within one and the same Member State.

(4) Before 1 July 2000 the Commission shall report to the Council on the operation of the thresholds and criteria set out in paragraphs 2 and 3.

5. Following the report referred to in paragraph 4 and on a proposal from the Commission, the Council, acting by a qualified majority, may revise the thresholds and criteria mentioned in paragraph 3.

Article 2 Appraisal of concentrations

1. Concentrations within the scope of this Regulation shall be appraised in accordance with the following provisions with a view to establishing whether or not they are compatible with the common market.

In making this appraisal, the Commission shall take into account:

(a) the need to maintain and develop effective competition within the common market in view of, among other things, the structure of all the markets concerned and the actual or potential competition from undertakings located either within or without the Community;

(b) the market position of the undertakings concerned and their economic and financial power, the alternatives available to suppliers and users, their access to supplies or markets, any legal or other barriers to entry, supply and demand trends for the relevant goods and services, the interests of the intermediate and ultimate consumers, and the development of technical and economic progress provided that it is too consumers' advantage and does not form an obstacle to competition.

2. A concentration which does not create or strengthen a dominant position as a result of which effective competition would be significantly impeded in the common market or in a substantial part of it shall be declared compatible with the common market.

3. A concentration which creates or strengthens a dominant position as a result of which effective competition would be significantly impeded in the common market or in a substantial part of it shall be declared incompatible with the common market.

4. To the extent that the creation of a joint venture constituting a concentration pursuant to Article 3 has as its object or effect the coordination of the competitive behaviour of undertakings that remain independent, such coordination shall be appraised in accordance with the criteria of Article 85(1) and (3) of the Treaty, with a view to establishing whether or not the operation is compatible with the common market.

In making this appraisal, the Commission shall take into account in particular:

—whether two or more parent companies retain to a significant extent activities in the same market as the joint venture or in a market which is downstream or upstream from that of the joint venture or in a neighbouring market closely related to this market,

—whether the coordination which is the direct consequence of the creation of the joint venture affords the undertakings concerned the possibility of eliminating competition in respect of a substantial part of the products or services in question.

Article 3   Definition of concentration

1.   A concentration shall be deemed to arise where:

    (a)   two or more previously independent undertakings merge, or

    (b)   one or more persons already controlling at least one undertaking, or one or more undertakings acquire, whether by purchase of securities or assets, by contract or by any other means, direct or indirect control of the whole or parts of one or more other undertakings.

2.   The creation of a joint venture performing on a lasting basis all the functions of an autonomous economic entity, shall constitute a concentration within the meaning of paragraph 1(b).

3.   For the purposes of this Regulation, control shall be constituted by rights, contracts or any other means which, either separately or in combination and having regard to the considerations of fact or law involved, confer the possibility of exercising decisive influence on an undertaking, in particular by:

    (a)   ownership or the right to use all or part of the assets of an undertaking;

    (b)   rights or contracts which confer decisive influence on the composition, voting or decisions of the organs of an undertaking.

4.   Control is acquired by persons or undertakings which:

    (a)   are holders of the rights or entitled to rights under the contracts concerned; or

    (b)   while not being holders of such rights or entitled to rights under such contracts, have the power to exercise the rights deriving therefrom.

5.   A concentration shall not be deemed to arise where:

    (a)   credit institutions or other financial institutions or insurance companies, the normal activities of which include transactions and dealing in securities for their own account or for the account of others, hold on a temporary basis securities which they have acquired in an undertaking with a view to reselling them, provided that they do not exercise voting rights in respect of those securities with a view to determining the competitive behaviour of that undertaking or provided that they exercise such voting rights only with a view to preparing the disposal of all or part of that undertaking or of its assets or the disposal of those securities and that any such disposal takes place within one year of the date of acquisition; that period may be extended by the Commission on request where such institutions or companies can show that the disposal was not reasonably possible within the period set;

    (b)   control is acquired by an office-holder according to the law of a Member State relating to liquidation, winding up, insolvency, cessation of payments, compositions or analogous proceedings;

(c)   the operations referred to in paragraph 1(b) are carried out by the financial holding companies referred to in Article 5(3) of the Fourth Council Directive 78/660/EEC of 25 July 1978 on the annual accounts of certain types of companies,[1] as last amended by Directive 84/569/EEC,[2] provided however that the voting rights in respect of the holding are exercised, in particular in relation to the appointment of members of the management and supervisory bodies of the undertakings in which they have holdings, only to maintain the full value of those investments and not to determine directly or indirectly the competitive conduct of those undertakings.

Notes
[1]OJ 1978 L222/11.
[2]OJ 1984 L314/28.

Article 4   Prior notification of concentrations

1.   Concentrations with a Community dimension defined in this Regulation shall be notified to the Commission not more than one week after the conclusion of the agreement, or the announcement of the public bid, or the acquisition of a controlling interest. That week shall begin when the first of those events occurs.

2.   A concentration which consists of a merger within the meaning of Article 3(1)(a) or in the acquisition of joint control within the meaning of Article 3(1)(b) shall be notified jointly by the parties to the merger or by those acquiring joint control as the case may be. In all other cases, the notification shall be effected by the person or undertaking acquiring control of the whole or parts of one or more undertakings.

3.   Where the Commission finds that a notified concentration falls within the scope of this Regulation, it shall publish the fact of the notification, at the same time indicating the names of the parties, the nature of the concentration and the economic sectors involved. The Commission shall take account of the legitimate interest of undertakings in the protection of their business secrets.

Article 5   Calculation of turnover

1.   Aggregate turnover within the meaning of Article 1(2) shall comprise the amounts derived by the undertakings concerned in the preceding financial year from the sale of products and the provision of services falling within the undertakings' ordinary activities after deduction of sales rebates and of value added tax and other taxes directly related to turnover. The aggregate turnover of an undertaking concerned shall not include the sale of products or the provision of services between any of the undertakings referred to in paragraph 4. Turnover, in the Community or in a Member State, shall comprise products sold and services provided to undertakings or consumers, in the Community or in that Member State as the case may be.

2.   By way of derogation from paragraph 1, where the concentration consists in the acquisition of parts, whether or not constituted as legal entities, of one or more undertakings, only the turnover relating to the parts which are the subject of the transaction shall be taken into account with regard to the seller or sellers. However, two or more transactions within the meaning of the first subparagraph which take place within a two-year period between the same persons or undertakings shall be treated as one and the same concentration arising on the date of the last transaction.

3.   In place of turnover the following shall be used:

(a) for credit institutions and other financial institutions, as regards Article 1(2) and (3), the sum of the following income items as defined in Council Directive 86/635/EEC of 8 December 1986 on the annual accounts and consolidated accounts of banks and other financial institutions,[1] after deduction of value added tax and other taxes directly related to those items, where appropriate:

    (i)   interest income and similar income;

    (ii)   income from securities:

— income from shares and other variable yield securities,

— income from participating interests,

— income from shares in affiliated undertakings;

    (iii)   commissions receivable;

    (iv)   net profit on financial operations;

    (v)   other operating income.

The turnover of a credit or financial institution in the Community or in a Member State shall comprise the income items, as defined above, which are received by the branch or division of that institution established in the Community or in the Member State in question, as the case may be;

(b) for insurance undertakings, the value of gross premiums written which shall comprise all amounts received and receivable in respect of insurance contracts issued by or on behalf of the insurance undertakings, including also outgoing reinsurance premiums, and after deduction of taxes and parafiscal contributions or levies charged by reference to the amounts of individual premiums or the total volume of premiums; as regards Article 1(2)(b) and (3)(b), (c) and (d) and the final part of Article 1(2) and (3), gross premiums received from Community residents and from residents of one Member State respectively shall be taken into account.

Note

[1] OJ No. L372, 31.12.1986, p. 1.

4. Without prejudice to paragraph 2, the aggregate turnover of an undertaking concerned within the meaning of Article 1(2) and (3) shall be calculated by adding together the respective turnovers of the following:

    (a)   the undertaking concerned;

    (b)   those undertakings in which the undertaking concerned, directly or indirectly:

— owns more than half the capital or business assets, or

— has the power to exercise more than half the voting rights, or

— has the power to appoint more than half the members of the supervisory board, the administrative board or bodies legally representing the undertakings, or

— has the right to manage the undertakings' affairs;

    (c)   those undertakings which have in the undertaking concerned the rights or powers listed in (b);

    (d)   those undertakings in which an undertaking as referred to in (c) has the rights or powers listed in (b);

    (e)   those undertakings in which two or more undertakings as referred to in (a) to (d) jointly have the rights or powers listed in (b).

5. Where undertakings concerned by the concentration jointly have the rights or powers listed in paragraph 4(b), in calculating the aggregate turnover of the undertakings concerned for the purposes of Article 1(2) and (3):

    (a)   no account shall be taken of the turnover resulting from the sale of products or the provision of services between the joint undertaking and each of the undertakings concerned or any other undertaking connected with any one of them, as set out in paragraph 4(b) to (e);

(b)   account shall be taken of the turnover resulting from the sale of products and the provision of services between the joint undertaking and any third undertakings. This turnover shall be apportioned equally amongst the undertakings concerned.

Article 6   Examination of the notification and initiation of proceedings

1.   The Commission shall examine the notification as soon as it is received.

(a)   Where it concludes that the concentration notified does not fall within the scope of this Regulation, it shall record that finding by means of a decision.

(b)   Where it finds that the concentration notified, although falling within the scope of this Regulation, does not raise serious doubts as to its compatibility with the common market, it shall decide not to oppose it and shall declare that it is compatible with the common market. The decision declaring the concentration compatible shall also cover restrictions directly related and necessary to the implementation of the concentration.

(c)   Without prejudice to paragraph 1(a), where the Commission finds that the concentration notified falls within the scope of this Regulation and raises serious doubts as to its compatibility with the common market, it shall decide to initiate proceedings.

1a.   Where the Commission finds that, following modification by the undertakings concerned, a notified concentration no longer raises serious doubts within the meaning of paragraph 1(c), it may decide to declare the concentration compatible with the common market pursuant to paragraph 1(b).

The Commission may attach to its decision under paragraph 1(b) conditions and obligations intended to ensure that the undertakings concerned comply with the commitments they have entered into *vis-à-vis* the Commission with a view to rendering the concentration compatible with the common market.

1b.   The Commission may revoke the decision it has taken pursuant to paragraph 1(a) or (b) where:

(a)   the decision is based on incorrect information for which one of the undertakings is responsible or where it has been obtained by deceit, or

(b)   the undertakings concerned commit a breach of an obligation attached to the decision.

1c.   In the case referred to in paragraph 1(b), the Commission may take a decision under paragraph 1, without being bound by the deadlines referred to in Article 10(1).

2.   The Commission shall notify its decision to the undertakings concerned and the competent authorities of the Member States without delay.

Article 7   Suspension of concentrations

1.   A concentration as defined in Article 1 shall not be put into effect either before its notification or until it has been declared compatible with the common market pursuant to a decision under Article 6(1)(b) or Article 8(2) or on the basis of a presumption according to Article 10(6).

3.   Paragraph 1 shall not prevent the implementation of a public bid which has been notified to the Commission in accordance with Article 4(1), provided

that the acquirer does not exercise the voting rights attached to the securities in question or does so only to maintain the full value of those investments and on the basis of a derogation granted by the Commission under paragraph 4.

4.   The Commission may, on request, grant a derogation from the obligations imposed in paragraphs 1 or 3. The request to grant a derogation must be reasoned. In deciding on the request, the Commission shall take into account inter alia the effects of the suspension on one or more undertakings concerned by a concentration or on a third party and the threat to competition posed by the concentration. That derogation may be made subject to conditions and obligations in order to ensure conditions of effective competition. A derogation may be applied for and granted at any time, even before notification or after the transaction.

5.   The validity of any transaction carried out in contravention of paragraph 1 shall be dependent on a decision pursuant to Article 6(1)(b) or Article 8(2) or (3) or on a presumption pursuant to Article 10(6). This Article shall, however, have no effect on the validity of transactions in securities including those convertible into other securities admitted to trading on a market which is regulated and supervised by authorities recognised by public bodies, operates regularly and is accessible directly or indirectly to the public, unless the buyer and seller knew or ought to have known that the transaction was carried out in contravention of paragraph 1.

Article 8   Powers of decision of the Commission

1.   Without prejudice to Article 9, all proceedings initiated pursuant to Article 6(1)(c) shall be closed by means of a decision as provided for in paragraphs 2 to 5.

2.   Where the Commission finds that, following modification by the undertakings concerned if necessary, a notified concentration fulfils the criterion laid down in Article 2(2) and, in the cases referred to in Article 2(4), the criteria laid down in Article 85(3) of the Treaty, it shall issue a decision declaring the concentration compatible with the common market. It may attach to its decision conditions and obligations intended to ensure that the undertakings concerned comply with the commitments they have entered into a vis-à-vis the Commission with a view to rendering the concentration compatible with the common market. The decision declaring the concentration compatible shall also cover restrictions directly related and necessary to the implementation of the concentration.

3.   Where the Commission finds that a concentration fulfils the criterion defined in Article 2(3) or, in the cases referred to in Article 2(4), does not fulfil the criteria laid down in Article 85(3) of the Treaty, it shall issue a decision declaring that the concentration is incompatible with the common market.

4.   Where a concentration has already been implemented, the Commission may, in a decision pursuant to paragraph 3 or by separate decision require the undertakings or assets brought together to be separated or the cessation of joint control or any other action that may be appropriate in order to restore conditions of effective competition.

5.   The Commission may revoke the decision it has taken pursuant to paragraph 2 where:

(a)   the declaration of compatibility is based on incorrect information for which one of the undertakings is responsible or where it has been obtained by deceit; or

(b) the undertakings concerned commit a breach of an obligation attached to the decision.

6.   In the case referred to in paragraph 5, the Commission may take a decision under paragraph 3, without being bound by the deadline referred to in Article 10(3).

Article 9   Referral to the competent authorities of the Member States

1.   The Commission may, by means of a decision notified without delay to the undertakings concerned and the competent authorities of the other Member States, refer a notified concentration to the competent authorities of the Member State concerned in the following circumstances.

2.   Within three weeks of the date of receipt of the copy of the notification a Member State may inform the Commission, which shall inform the undertakings concerned, that:

(a) a concentration threatens to create or to strengthen a dominant position as a result of which effective competition will be significantly impeded on a market within that Member State, which presents all the characteristics of a distinct market, or

(b) a concentration affects competition on a market within that Member State, which presents all the characteristics of a distinct market and which does not constitute a substantial part of the common market.

3.   If the Commission considers that, having regard to the market for the products or services in question and the geographical reference market within the meaning of paragraph 7, there is such a distinct market and that such a threat exists, either:

(a) it shall itself deal with the case in order to maintain or restore effective competition on the market concerned; or

(b) it shall refer the case or part of the case to the competent authorities of the Member State concerned with a view to the application of that State's national competition law. In cases where a Member State informs the Commission that a concentration affects competition in a distinct market within its territory that does not form a substantial part of the common market, the Commission shall refer the whole or part of the case relating to the distinct market concerned, if it considers that such a distinct market is affected.

If, however, the Commission considers that such a distinct market or threat does not exist it shall adopt a decision to that effect which it shall address to the Member State concerned.

4.   A decision to refer or not to refer pursuant to paragraph 3 shall be taken:

(a) as a general rule within the six-week period provided for in Article 10(1), second subparagraph, where the Commission, pursuant to Article 6(1)(b), has not initiated proceedings; or

(b) within three months at most of the notification of the concentration concerned where the Commission has initiated proceedings under Article 6(1)(c), without taking the preparatory steps in order to adopt the necessary measures under Article 8(2), second subparagraph, (3) or (4) to maintain or restore effective competition on the market concerned.

5.   If within the three months referred to in paragraph 4(b) the Commission, despite a reminder from the Member State concerned, has not taken a decision on referral in accordance with paragraph 3 nor has taken the

preparatory steps referred to in paragraph 4(b), it shall be deemed to have taken a decision to refer the case to the Member State concerned in accordance with paragraph 3(b).

6.   The publication of any report or the announcement of the findings of the examination of the concentration by the competent authority of the Member State concerned shall be effected not more than four months after the Commission's referral.

7.   The geographical reference market shall consist of the area in which the undertakings concerned are involved in the supply and demand of products or services, in which the conditions of competition are sufficiently homogeneous and which can be distinguished from neighbouring areas because, in particular, conditions of competition are appreciably different in those areas. This assessment should take account in particular of the nature and characteristics of the products or services concerned, of the existence of entry barriers or consumer preferences, of appreciable differences of the undertakings' market shares between the area concerned and neighbouring areas or of substantial price differences.

8.   In applying the provisions of this Article, the Member State concerned may take only the measures strictly necessary to safeguard or restore effective competition on the market concerned.

9.   In accordance with the relevant provisions of the Treaty, any Member State may appeal to the Court of Justice, and in particular request the application of Article 186, for the purpose of applying its national competition law.

10.   This Article may be re-examined at the same time as the thresholds referred to in Article 1.

Article 10   Time limits for initiating proceedings and for decisions

1.   The decisions referred to in Article 6(1) must be taken within one month at most. That period shall begin on the day following that of the receipt of a notification or, if the information to be supplied with the notification is incomplete, on the day following that of the receipt of the complete information or where, after notification of a concentration, the undertakings concerned submit commitments pursuant to Article 6(1a), which are intended by the parties to form the basis for a decision pursuant to Article 6(1)(b).

That period shall be increased to six weeks if the Commission receives a request from a Member State in accordance with Article 9(2).

2.   Decisions taken pursuant to Article 8(2) concerning notified concentrations must be taken as soon as it appears that the serious doubts referred to in Article 6(1)(c) have been removed, particularly as a result of modifications made by the undertakings concerned, and at the latest by the deadline laid down in paragraph 3.

3.   Without prejudice to Article 8(6), decisions taken pursuant to Article 8(3) concerning notified concentrations must be taken within not more than four months of the date on which proceedings are initiated.

4.   The periods set by paragraphs 1 and 3 shall exceptionally be suspended where, owing to circumstances for which one of the undertakings involved in the concentration is responsible, the Commission has had to request information by decision pursuant to Article 11 or to order an investigation by decision pursuant to Article 13.

5. Where the Court of Justice gives a Judgment which annuls the whole or part of a Commission decision taken under this Regulation, the periods laid down in this Regulation shall start again from the date of the Judgment.

6. Where the Commission has not taken a decision in accordance with Article 6(1)(b) or (c) or Article 8(2) or (3) within the deadlines set in paragraphs 1 and 3 respectively, the concentration shall be deemed to have been declared compatible with the common market, without prejudice to Article 9.

Article 11   Requests for information

1. In carrying out the duties assigned to it by this Regulation, the Commission may obtain all necessary information from the Governments and competent authorities of the Member States, from the persons referred to in Article 3(1)(b), and from undertakings and associations of undertakings.

2. When sending a request for information to a person, an undertaking or an association of undertakings, the Commission shall at the same time send a copy of the request to the competent authority of the Member State within the territory of which the residence of the person or the seat of the undertaking or association of undertakings is situated.

3. In its request the Commission shall state the legal basis and the purpose of the request and also the penalties provided for in Article 14(1)(c) for supplying incorrect information.

4. The information requested shall be provided, in the case of undertakings, by their owners or their representatives and, in the case of legal persons, companies or firms, or of associations having no legal personality, by the persons authorised to represent them by law or by their statutes.

5. Where a person, an undertaking or an association of undertakings does not provide the information requested within the period fixed by the Commission or provides incomplete information, the Commission shall by decision require the information to be provided. The decision shall specify what information is required, fix an appropriate period within which it is to be supplied and state the penalties provided for in Articles 14(1)(c) and 15(1)(a) and the right to have the decision reviewed by the Court of Justice.

6. The Commission shall at the same time send a copy of its decision to the competent authority of the Member State within the territory of which the residence of the person or the seat of the undertaking or association of undertakings is situated.

Article 12   Investigations by the authorities of the Member States

1. At the request of the Commission, the competent authorities of the Member States shall undertake the investigations which the Commission considers to be necessary under Article 13(1), or which it has ordered by decision pursuant to Article 13(3). The officials of the competent authorities of the Member States responsible for conducting those investigations shall exercise their powers upon production of an authorisation in writing issued by the competent authority of the Member State within the territory of which the investigation is to be carried out. Such authorisation shall specify the subject matter and purpose of the investigation.

2. If so requested by the Commission or by the competent authority of the Member State within the territory of which the investigation is to be carried

out, officials of the Commission may assist the officials of that authority in carrying out their duties.

Article 13   Investigative powers of the Commission

1.   In carrying out the duties assigned to it by this Regulation, the Commission may undertake all necessary investigations into undertakings and associations of undertakings.

To that end the officials authorised by the Commission shall be empowered:

(a)   to examine the books and other business records;

(b)   to take or demand copies of or extracts from the books and business records;

(c)   to ask for oral explanations on the spot;

(d)   to enter any premises, land and means of transport of undertakings.

2.   The officials of the Commission authorised to carry out the investigations shall exercise their powers on production of an authorisation in writing specifying the subject matter and purpose of the investigation and the penalties provided for in Article 14(1)(d) in cases where production of the required books or other business records is incomplete. In good time before the investigation, the Commission shall inform, in writing, the competent authority of the Member State within the territory of which the investigation is to be carried out of the investigation and of the identities of the authorised officials.

3.   Undertakings and associations of undertakings shall submit to investigations ordered by decision of the Commission. The decision shall specify the subject matter and purpose of the investigation, appoint the date on which it shall begin and state the penalties provided for in Articles 14(1)(d) and 15(1)(b) and the right to have the decision reviewed by the Court of Justice.

4.   The Commission shall in good time and in writing inform the competent authority of the Member State within the territory of which the investigation is to be carried out of its intention of taking a decision pursuant to paragraph 3.

It shall hear the competent authority before taking its decision.

5.   Officials of the competent authority of the Member State within the territory of which the investigation is to be carried out may, at the request of that authority or of the Commission, assist the officials of the Commission in carrying out their duties.

6.   Where an undertaking or association of undertakings opposes an investigation ordered pursuant to this Article, the Member State concerned shall afford the necessary assistance to the officials authorised by the Commission to enable them to carry out their investigation. To this end the Member States shall, after consulting the Commission, take the necessary measures within one year of the entry into force of this Regulation.

Article 14   Fines

1.   The Commission may by decision impose on the persons referred to in Article 3(1)(b), undertakings or associations of undertakings fines of from ECU 1,000 to 50,000 where intentionally or negligently:

(a)   they fail to notify a concentration in accordance with Article 4;

(b)   they supply incorrect or misleading information in a notification pursuant to Article 4;

(c)   they supply incorrect information in response to a request made pursuant to Article 11 or fail to supply information within the period fixed by a decision taken pursuant to Article 11;

(d) they produce the required books or other business records in incomplete form during investigations under Article 12 or 13, or refuse to submit to an investigation ordered by decision taken pursuant to Article 13.

2. The Commission may by decision impose fines not exceeding 10% of the aggregate turnover of the undertakings concerned within the meaning of Article 5 on the persons or undertakings concerned where, either intentionally or negligently, they:

(a) fail to comply with an obligation imposed by decision pursuant to Article 7(4) or 8(2), second subparagraph;

(b) put into effect a concentration in breach of Article 7(1) or disregard a decision taken pursuant to Article 7(2);

(c) put into effect a concentration declared incompatible with the common market by decision pursuant to Article 8(3) or do not take the measures ordered by decision pursuant to Article 8(4).

3. In setting the amount of a fine, regard shall be had to the nature and gravity of the infringement.

4. Decisions taken pursuant to paragraphs 1 and 2 shall not be of criminal law nature.

Article 15   Periodic penalty payments

1. The Commission may by decision impose on the persons referred to in Article 3(1)(b), undertakings or associations of undertakings concerned periodic penalty payments of up to ECU 25,000 for each day of delay calculated from the date set in the decision, in order to compel them:

(a) to supply complete and correct information which it has requested by decision pursuant to Article 11;

(b) to submit to an investigation which it has ordered by decision pursuant to Article 13.

2. The Commission may by decision impose on the persons referred to in Article 3(1)(b) or on undertakings periodic penalty payments of up to ECU 100,000 for each day of delay calculated from the date set in the decision, in order to compel them:

(a) to comply with an obligation imposed by decision pursuant to Article 7(4) or Article 8(2), second subparagraph, or

(b) to apply the measures ordered by decision pursuant to Article 8(4).

3. Where the persons referred to in Article 3(1)(b), undertakings or associations of undertakings have satisfied the obligation which it was the purpose of the periodic penalty payment to enforce, the Commission may set the total amount of the periodic penalty payments at a lower figure than that which would arise under the original decision.

Article 16   Review by the Court of Justice

The Court of Justice shall have unlimited jurisdiction within the meaning of Article 172 of the Treaty to review decisions whereby the Commission has fixed a fine or periodic penalty payments; it may cancel, reduce or increase the fine or periodic penalty payments imposed.

Article 17   Professional secrecy

1. Information acquired as a result of the application of Articles 11, 12, 13 and 18 shall be used only for the purposes of the relevant request, investigation or hearing.

2.   Without prejudice to Articles 4(3), 18 and 20, the Commission and the competent authorities of the Member States, their officials and other servants shall not disclose information they have acquired through the application of this Regulation of the kind covered by the obligation of professional secrecy.

3.   Paragraphs 1 and 2 shall not prevent publication of general information or of surveys which do not contain information relating to particular undertakings or associations of undertakings.

Article 18   Hearing of the parties and of third persons

1.   Before taking any decision provided for in Articles 7(4), Article 8(2), second subparagraph, and (3) to (5) and Articles 14 and 15, the Commission shall give the persons, undertakings and associations of undertakings concerned the opportunity, at every stage of the procedure up to the consultation of the Advisory Committee, of making known their views on the objections against them.

2.   By way of derogation from paragraph 1, a decision to grant a derogation from suspension as referred to in Article 7(4) may be taken provisionally, without the persons, undertakings or associations of undertakings concerned being given the opportunity to make known their views beforehand, provided that the Commission gives them that opportunity as soon as possible after having taken its decision.

3.   The Commission shall base its decision only on objections on which the parties have been able to submit their observations. The rights of the defence shall be fully respected in the proceedings. Access to the file shall be open at least to the parties directly involved, subject to the legitimate interest of undertakings in the protection of their business secrets.

4.   In so far as the Commission or the competent authorities of the Member States deem it necessary, they may also hear other natural or legal persons. Natural or legal persons showing a sufficient interest and especially members of the administrative or management bodies of the undertakings concerned or the recognised representatives of their employees shall be entitled, upon application, to be heard.

Article 19   Liaison with the authorities of the Member States

1.   The Commission shall transmit to the competent authorities of the Member States copies of notifications within three working days and, as soon as possible, copies of the most important documents lodged with or issued by the Commission pursuant to this Regulation. Such documents shall include commitments which are intended by the parties to form the basis for a decision pursuant to Articles 6(1)(b) or 8(2).

2.   The Commission shall carry out the procedures set out in this Regulation in close and constant liaison with the competent authorities of the Member States, which may express their views upon those procedures. For the purposes of Article 9 it shall obtain information from the competent authority of the Member State as referred to in paragraph 2 of that Article and give it the opportunity to make known its views at every stage of the procedure up to the adoption of a decision pursuant to paragraph 3 of that Article; to that end it shall give it access to the file.

3.   An Advisory Committee on concentrations shall be consulted before any decision is taken pursuant to Article 8(2) to (5), 14 or 15, or any provisions are adopted pursuant to Article 23.

4.   The Advisory Committee shall consist of representatives of the authorities of the Member States. Each Member State shall appoint one or two representatives; if unable to attend, they may be replaced by other representatives. At least one of the representatives of a Member State shall be competent in matters of restrictive practices and dominant positions.

5.   Consultation shall take place at a joint meeting convened at the invitation of and chaired by the Commission. A summary of the case, together with an indication of the most important documents and a preliminary draft of the decision to be taken for each case considered, shall be sent with the invitation. The meeting shall take place not less than 14 days after the invitation has been sent. The Commission may in exceptional cases shorten that period as appropriate in order to avoid serious harm to one or more of the undertakings concerned by a concentration.

6.   The Advisory Committee shall deliver an opinion on the Commission's draft decision, if necessary by taking a vote. The Advisory Committee may deliver an opinion even if some members are absent and unrepresented. The opinion shall be delivered in writing and appended to the draft decision. The Commission shall take the utmost account of the opinion delivered by the Committee. It shall inform the Committee of the manner in which its opinion has been taken into account.

7.   The Advisory Committee may recommend publication of the opinion. The Commission may carry out such publication. The decision to publish shall take due account of the legitimate interest of undertakings in the protection of their business secrets and of the interest of the undertakings concerned in such publication's taking place.

Article 20   Publication of decisions

1.   The Commission shall publish the decisions which it takes pursuant to Article 8(2) to (5) in the *Official Journal of the European Communities*.

2.   The publication shall state the names of the parties and the main content of the decision; it shall have regard to the legitimate interest of undertakings in the protection of their business secrets.

Article 21   Jurisdiction

1.   Subject to review by the Court of Justice, the Commission shall have sole jurisdiction to take the decisions provided for in this Regulation.

2.   No Member State shall apply its national legislation on competition to any consideration that has a Community dimension. The first subparagraph shall be without prejudice to any Member State's power to carry out any enquiries necessary for the application of Article 9(2) or after referral, pursuant to Article 9(3), first subparagraph, indent (b), or (5), to take the measures strictly necessary for the application of Article 9(8).

3.   Notwithstanding paragraphs 1 and 2, Member States may take appropriate measures to protect legitimate interests other than those taken into consideration by this Regulation and compatible with the general principles and other provisions of Community law.

Public security, plurality of the media and prudential rules shall be regarded as legitimate interests within the meaning of the first subparagraph.

Any other public interest must be communicated to the Commission by the Member State concerned and shall be recognised by the Commission after an assessment of its compatibility with the general principles and other provisions of Community law before the measures referred to above may be taken. The Commission shall inform the Member State concerned of its decision within one month of that communication.

Article 22   Application of the Regulation

1.   This Regulation alone shall apply to concentrations as defined in Article 3, and Regulations No. 17(1), (EEC) No. 1017/68(2), (EEC) No. 4056/86(3) and (EEC) No. 3975/87(4) shall not apply, except in relation to joint ventures that do not have a Community dimension and which have their object or effect the coordination of the competitive behaviour of undertakings that remain independent.

3.   If the Commission finds, at the request of a Member State or at the joint request of two or more Member States, that a concentration as defined in Article 3 that has no Community dimension within the meaning of Article 1 creates or strengthens a dominant position as a result of which effective competition would be significantly impeded within the territory of the Member State or States making the joint request it may, in so far as the concentration affects trade between Member States, adopt the decisions provided for in Article 8(2), second subparagraph, (3) and (4).

4.   Articles 2(1)(a) and (b), 5, 6, 8 and 10 to 20 shall apply to a request made pursuant to paragraph 3. Article 7 shall apply to the extent that the concentration has not been put into effect on the date on which the Commission informs the parties that a request has been made. The period within which proceedings may be initiated pursuant to Article 10(1) shall begin on the day following that of the receipt of the request from the Member State or States concerned. The request must be made within one month at most of the date on which the concentration was made known to the Member State or to all Member States making a joint request or effected. This period shall begin on the date of the first of those events.

5.   Pursuant to paragraph 3 the Commission shall take only the measures strictly necessary to maintain or restore effective competition within the territory of the Member State or States at the request of which it intervenes.

Article 23   Implementing provisions

The Commission shall have the power to adopt implementing provisions concerning the form, content and other details of notifications pursuant to Article 4, time limits pursuant to Articles 7, 9, 10 and 22, and hearings pursuant to Article 18. The Commission shall have the power to lay down the procedure and time limits for the submission of commitments pursuant to Articles 6(1a) and 8(2).

Article 24   Relations with non-member countries

1.   The Member States shall inform the Commission of any general difficulties encountered by their undertakings with concentrations as defined in Article 3 in a non-member country.

2. Initially not more than one year after the entry into force of this Regulation and thereafter periodically the Commission shall draw up a report examining the treatment accorded to Community undertakings, in the terms referred to in paragraphs 3 and 4, as regards concentrations in non-member countries. The Commission shall submit those reports to the Council, together with any recommendations.

3. Whenever it appears to the Commission, either on the basis of the reports referred to in paragraph 2 or on the basis of other information, that a non-member country does not grant Community undertakings treatment comparable to that granted by the Community to undertakings from that non-member country, the Commission may submit proposals to the Council for an appropriate mandate for negotiation with a view to obtaining comparable treatment for Community undertakings.

4. Measures taken under this Article shall comply with the obligations of the Community or of the Member States, without prejudice to Article 234 of the Treaty, under international agreements, whether bilateral or multilateral.

Article 25   Entry into force[1]

1. This Regulation shall enter into force on 21 September 1990.

2. This Regulation shall not apply to any concentration which was the subject of an agreement or announcement or where control was acquired within the meaning of Article 4(1) before the date of this Regulation's entry into force and it shall not in any circumstances apply to any concentration in respect of which proceedings were initiated before that date by a Member State's authority with responsibility for competition.

3. As regards concentrations to which this regulation applies by virtue of accession, the date of accession shall be substituted for the date of entry into force of this Regulation. The provision of paragraph 2, second alternative, applies in the same way to proceedings initiated by a competition authority of the new Member States or by the EFTA Surveillance Authority.

This Regulation shall be binding in its entirety and directly applicable in all Member States.

Done at Brussels, 21 December 1989.

(Signature omitted.)

Note

[1]Articles 2 and 3 of Regulation 1310/97 concerned with applicability and entry into force of the new rules are reproduced here:

Article 2

This Regulation shall not apply to any concentration which was the subject of an agreement or announcement or where control was acquired within the meaning of Article 4(1) of Regulation (EEC) No. 4064/89, before 1 March 1998 and it shall not in any circumstances apply to any concentration in respect of which proceedings were initiated before 1 March 1998 by a Member State's authority with responsiblity for competition.

Article 3

This Regulation shall enter into force on 1 March 1998.

This Regulation shall be binding in its entirety and directly applicable in all Member States.

COMMISSION REGULATION (EC) NO. 3384/94 OF 21 DECEMBER 1994 ON THE NOTIFICATIONS, TIME LIMITS AND HEARINGS PROVIDED FOR IN COUNCIL REGULATION (EEC) NO. 4064/89 ON THE CONTROL OF CONCENTRATIONS BETWEEN UNDERTAKINGS
[OJ 1994, No. L377/1]

THE COMMISSION OF THE EUROPEAN COMMUNITIES,

Having regard to the Treaty establishing the European Community and the Agreement on the European Economic Area,

Having regard to the Agreement on the European Economic Area,

Having regard to Council Regulation (EEC) No. 4064/89 of 21 December 1989 on the control of concentrations between undertakings,[1] and in particular Article 23 thereof,

Having regard to Council Regulation No. 17 of 6 February 1962, First Regulation implementing Articles 85 and 86 of the Treaty,[2] as last amended by the Act of Accession of Spain and Portugal, and in particular Article 24 thereof,

Having regard to Council Regulation (EEC) No. 1017/68 of 19 July 1968 applying rules of competition to transport by rail, road and inland waterway,[3] as last amended by the Act of Accession of Greece, and in particular Article 29 thereof,

Having regard to Council Regulation (EEC) No. 4056/86 of 22 December 1986 laying down detailed rules for the application of Articles 85 and 86 of the Treaty to maritime transport,[4] and in particular Article 26 thereof,

Having regard to Council Regulation (EEC) No. 3975/87 of 14 December 1987 laying down detailed rules for the application of the competition rules to undertakings in air transport,[5] as last amended by Regulation (EEC) No. 2410/92,[6] and in particular Article 19 thereof,

Having consulted the Advisory Committee on Concentrations,

(1) Whereas experience in the application of Commission Regulation (EEC) No. 2367/90,[7] as amended by Regulation (EC) No. 3666/93[8] which implements Regulation (EEC) No. 4064/89, has shown the need to improve certain procedural aspects thereof, whereas it should therefore be replaced by a new regulation;

(2) Whereas Regulation (EEC) No. 4064/89 is based on the principle of compulsory notification of concentrations before they are put into effect; whereas, on the one hand, a notification has important legal consequences which are favourable to the parties to the concentration plan, while, on the other hand, failure to comply with the obligation to notify renders the parties liable to a fine and may also entail civil law disadvantages for them; whereas it

Notes
[1] OJ No. L395, 30.12.1989, p. 1.
[2] OJ No. 13, 21.2.1962, p. 204/62.
[3] OJ No. L175, 23.7.1968, p. 1.
[4] OJ No. L378, 31.12.1986, p. 4.
[5] OJ No. L374, 31.12.1987, p. 1.
[6] OJ No. L140, 24.8.1992, p. 18.
[7] OJ No. L219, 14.8.1990, p. 5.
[8] OJ No. L336, 31.12.1993, p. 7.

is therefore necessary in the interests of legal certainty to define precisely the subject matter and content of the information to be provided in the notification;

(3)   Whereas it is for the notifying parties to make full and honest disclosure to the Commission of the facts and circumstances which are relevant for taking a decision on the notified concentration;

(4)   Whereas in order to simplify and expedite examination of the notification it is desirable to prescribe that a form be used;

(5)   Whereas since notification sets in motion legal time limits for initiating proceedings and for decisions, the conditions governing such time limits and the time when they become effective must also be determined;

(6)   Whereas rules must be laid down in the interests of legal certainty for calculating the time limits provided for in Regulation (EEC) No. 4064/89, and whereas in particular, the beginning and end of the period and the circumstances suspending the running of the period must be determined, with due regard to the requirements resulting from the exceptionally short legal time limits referred to above; whereas in the absence of specific provisions the determination of rules applicable to periods, dates and time limits should be based on the principles of Council Regulation (EEC, Euratom) No. 1182/71;[1]

(7)   Whereas the provisions relating to the Commission's procedure must be framed in such a way as to safeguard fully the right to be heard and the rights of defence; whereas for these purposes the Commission should distinguish between the parties who notify the concentration, other parties involved in the concentration plan, third parties and parties regarding whom the Commission intends to take a decision imposing a fine or periodic penalty payments;

(8)   Whereas the Commission will give the notifying parties and other parties involved, if they so request, an opportunity before notification to discuss the intended concentration informally and in strict confidence; whereas in addition it will, after notification, maintain close contact with those parties to the extent necessary to discuss with them any practical or legal problems which it discovers on a first examination of the case and if possible to remove such problems by mutual agreement;

(9)   Whereas in accordance with the principle of the rights of defence, the notifying parties must be given the opportunity to submit their comments on all the objections which the Commission proposes to take into account in its decisions; whereas other parties involved should also be informed of the Commission's objections and granted the opportunity to express their views;

(10)   Whereas third parties having sufficient interest must also be given the opportunity of expressing their views where they make a written application;

(11)   Whereas the various persons entitled to submit comments should do so in writing, both in their own interest and in the interest of good administration, without prejudice to their right to request a formal oral hearing where appropriate to supplement the written procedure; whereas in urgent cases, however, the Commission must be able to proceed immediately to formal oral hearings of the notifying parties, other parties involved or third parties;

Note
[1] OJ No. L124, 86.1971, p. 1.

(12)   Whereas it is necessary to define the rights of persons who are to be heard, to what extent they should be granted access to the Commission's file and on what conditions they may be represented or assisted;

(13)   Whereas the Commission must respect the legitimate interest of undertakings in the protection of their business secrets;

(14)   Whereas, in order to enable the Commission to carry out a proper assessment of modifications to the original concentration plan, and to ensure due consultation with other parties involved, third parties and the authorities of the Member States as provided for in Regulation (EEC) No. 4064/89, in particular Article 18(1) and (4) thereof, a time limit for submitting modifications to the concentration plan as provided for in Article 10(2) of Regulation (EEC) No. 4064/89 must be laid down;

(15)   Whereas it is also necessary to define the rules for fixing and calculating the time limits for reply fixed by the Commission;

(16)   Whereas the Advisory Committee on Concentrations must deliver its opinion on the basis of a preliminary draft decision; whereas it must therefore be consulted on a case after the inquiry into that case has been completed; whereas such consultation does not, however, prevent the Commission from reopening an inquiry if need be,

HAS ADOPTED THIS REGULATION:

SECTION I   NOTIFICATIONS

Article 1   Persons entitled to submit notifications

1.   Notifications shall be submitted by the persons or undertakings referred to in Article 4(2) of Regulation (EEC) No. 4064/89.

2.   Where notifications are signed by representatives of persons or of undertakings, such representatives shall produce written proof that they are authorised to act.

3.   Joint notifications should be submitted by a joint representative who is authorised to transmit and to receive documents on behalf of all notifying parties.

Article 2   Submission of notifications

1.   Notifications shall be submitted in the manner prescribed by Form CO as shown in Annex I. Joint notifications shall be submitted on a single form.

2.   Twenty-four copies of each notification and 19 copies of the supporting documents shall be submitted to the Commission at the address indicated in Form CO.

3.   The supporting documents shall be either originals or copies of the originals; in the latter case the notifying parties shall confirm that they are true and complete.

4.   Notifications shall be in one of the official languages of the Community. This language shall also be the language of the proceeding for the notifying parties. Supporting documents shall be submitted in their original language. Where the original language is not one of the official languages, a translation into the language of the proceeding shall be attached.

5.   Where notifications are made pursuant to Article 57 of the EEA Agreement, they may also be in one of the official languages of the EFTA States or the working language of the EFTA Surveillance Authority. If the language chosen for the notifications is not an official language of the Community, the

notifying parties shall simultaneously supplement all documentation with a translation into an official language of the Community. The language which is chosen for the translation shall determine the language used by the Commission as the language of the proceedings for the notifying parties.

Article 3   Information and documents to be provided

1.   Notifications shall contain the information, including documents, requested by Form CO. The information must be correct and complete.

2.   The Commission may dispense with the obligation to provide any particular information, including documents, requested by Form CO where the Commission considers that such information is not necessary for the examination of the case.

3.   The Commission shall without delay acknowledge in writing to the notifying parties or their representatives receipt of the notification and of any reply to a letter sent by the Commission pursuant to Article 4(2) and 4(4).

Article 4   Effective date of notification

1.   Subject to paragraphs 2, 3 and 4, notifications shall become effective on the date on which they are received by the Commission.

2.   Where the information, including documents, contained in the notification is incomplete in a material respect, the Commission shall without delay inform the notifying parties or their representatives in writing and shall set an appropriate time limit for the completion of the information. In such cases, the notification shall become effective on the date on which the complete information is received by the Commission.

3.   Material changes in the facts contained in the notification which the notifying parties know or ought to have known must be communicated to the Commission voluntarily and without delay. In such cases, when these material changes could have a significant effect on the appraisal of the concentration, the notification may be considered by the Commission as becoming effective on the date on which the information on the material changes is received by the Commission; the Commission shall inform the notifying parties or their representatives of this in writing and without delay.

4.   Incorrect or misleading information shall be considered to be incomplete information.

5.   When the Commission publishes the fact of the notification pursuant to Article 4(3) of Regulation (EEC) No. 4064/89, it shall specify the date upon which the notification has been received. Where, further to the application of paragraphs 2, 3 and 4, the effective date of notification is later than the date specified in this publication, the Commission shall issue a further publication in which it will state the later date.

Article 5   Conversion of notifications

1.   Where the Commission finds that the operation notified does not constitute a concentration within the meaning of Article 3 of Regulation (EEC) No. 4064/89 it shall inform the notifying parties or their representatives in writing. In such a case, the Commission shall, if requested by the notifying parties, as appropriate and subject to paragraph 2, treat the notification as an application within the meaning of Article 2 or a notification within the meaning of Article 4 of Regulation No. 17, as an application within the meaning of Article 12 or a notification within the meaning of Article 14 of Regulation

(EEC) No. 1017/68, as an application within the meaning of Article 12 of Regulation (EEC) No. 4056/86 or as an application within the meaning of Article 3(2) or of Article 5 of Regulation (EEC) No. 3975/87.

2. In cases referred to in paragraph 1, second sentence, the Commission may require that the information given in the notification be supplemented within an appropriate time limit fixed by it in so far as this is necessary for assessing the operation on the basis of the abovementioned Regulations. The application or notification shall be deemed to fulfil the requirements of such Regulations from the date of the original notification where the additional information is received by the Commission within the time limit fixed.

SECTION II   TIME LIMITS FOR INITIATING PROCEEDINGS AND FOR DECISIONS

Article 6   Beginning of the time period

1. The periods referred to in Article 10(1) of Regulation (EEC) No. 4064/89 shall start at the beginning of the working day (as defined under Article 22) following the effective date of the notification, within the meaning of Article 4 of this Regulation.

2. The period referred to in Article 10(3) of Regulation (EEC) No. 4064/89 shall start at the beginning of the working day (as defined under Article 22) following the day on which proceedings were initiated.

Article 7   End of the time period

1. The time period referred to in Article 10(1) first subparagraph of Regulation (EEC) No. 4064/89 shall end with the expiry of the day which in the month following that in which the time period began falls on the same date as the day from which the period runs. Where such a day does not occur in that month, the period shall end with the expiry of the last day of that month.

2. The time period referred to in Article 10(1) second subparagraph of Regulation (EEC) No. 4064/89 shall end with the expiry of the day which in the sixth week following that in which the period began is the same day of the week as the day from which the period runs.

3. The time period referred to in Article 10(3) of Regulation (EEC) No. 4064/89 shall end with the expiry of the day which in the fourth month following that in which the period began falls on the same date as the day from which the period runs. Where such a day does not occur in that month, the period shall end with the expiry of the last day of that month.

4. Where the last day of the period is not a working day within the meaning of Article 22, the period shall end with the expiry of the following working day.

Article 8   Recovery of holidays

Once the end of the time period has been determined in accordance with Article 7, if public holidays or other holidays of the Commission as defined in Article 22 fall within the periods referred to in Article 10(1) and in Article 10(3) of Regulation (EEC) No. 4064/89, a corresponding number of working days shall be added to those periods.

Article 9   Suspension of the time limit

1. The period referred to in Article 10(3) of Regulation (EEC) No. 4064/89 shall be suspended where the Commission, pursuant to Articles 11(5) and 13(3) of the same Regulation, has to take a decision because:

(a)   information which the Commission has requested pursuant to Article 11(1) of Regulation (EEC) No. 4064/89 from one of the notifying parties or another involved party (as defined in Article 11 of this Regulation) is not provided or not provided in full within the time limit fixed by the Commission;

(b)   one of the notifying parties or another involved party (as defined in Article 11 of this Regulation) has refused to submit to an investigation deemed necessary by the Commission on the basis of Article 13(1) of Regulation (EEC) No. 4064/89 or to cooperate in the carrying out of such an investigation in accordance with the abovementioned provision;

(c)   the notifying parties have failed to inform the Commission of material changes in the facts contained in the notification.

2.   The period referred to in Article 10(3) of Regulation (EEC) No. 4064/89 shall be suspended:

(a)   in the cases referred to in subparagraph 1(a), for the period between the end of the time limit fixed in the request for information and the receipt of the complete and correct information required by decision;

(b)   in the cases referred to in subparagraph 1(b), for the period between the unsuccessful attempt to carry out the investigation and the completion of the investigation ordered by decision;

(c)   in the cases referred to in subparagraph 1(c), for the period between the occurrence of the change in the facts referred to therein and the receipt of the complete and correct information requested by decision or the completion of the investigation ordered by decision.

3.   The suspension of the time limit shall begin on the day following that on which the event causing the suspension occurred. It shall end with the expiry of the day on which the reason for suspension is removed. Where such a day is not a working day within the meaning of Article 22, the suspension of the time limit shall end with the expiry of the following working day.

Article 10   Compliance with the time limit

The time limits referred to in Article 10(1) and (3) of Regulation (EEC) No. 4064/89 shall be met where the Commission has taken the relevant decision before the end of the period. Notification of the decision to the notifying parties must follow without delay.

SECTION III   HEARING OF THE PARTIES AND OF THIRD PARTIES

Article 11   Parties to be heard

For the purposes of the rights to be heard pursuant to Article 18 of Regulation (EEC) No. 4064/89, the following parties are distinguished:

(a)   notifying parties, that is, persons or undertakings submitting a notification pursuant to Article 4(2) of Regulation (EEC) No. 4064/89;

(b)   other involved parties, that is, parties to the concentration plan other than the notifying parties, such as the seller and the undertaking which is the target of the concentration;

(c)   third parties, that is, natural or legal persons showing a sufficient interest, including customers, suppliers and competitors, and especially members of the administration or management organs of the undertakings concerned or recognised workers' representatives of those undertakings;

(d) parties regarding whom the Commission intends to take a decision pursuant to Article 14 or Article 15 of Regulation (EEC) No. 4064/89.

Article 12   Decisions on the suspension of concentrations

1. Where the Commission intends to take a decision pursuant to Article 7(2) of Regulation (EEC) No. 4064/89 or a decision pursuant to Article 7(4) of that Regulation which adversely affects the parties, it shall, pursuant to Article 18(1) of that Regulation, inform the notifying parties and other involved parties in writing of its objections and shall fix a time limit within which they may make known their views.

2. Where the Commission pursuant to Article 18(2) of Regulation (EEC) No. 4064/89 has taken a decision referred to in paragraph 1 provisionally without having given the notifying parties and other involved parties the opportunity to make known their views, it shall without delay and in any event before the expiry of the suspension send them the text of the provisional decision and shall fix a time limit within which they may make known their views. Once the notifying parties and other involved parties have made known their views, the Commission shall take a final decision annulling, amending or confirming the provisional decision. Where they have not made known their views within the time limit fixed, the Commission's provisional decision shall become final with the expiry of that period.

3. The notifying parties and other involved parties shall make known their views in writing or orally within the time limit fixed. They may confirm their oral statements in writing.

Article 13   Decisions on the substance of the case

1. Where the Commission intends to take a decision pursuant to Article 8(2), second subparagraph, Article 8(3), (4) or (5) of Regulation (EEC) No. 4064/89 it shall, before consulting the Advisory Committee on Concentrations, hear the parties pursuant to Article 18(1) and (3) of that Regulation.

2. (a) The Commission shall address its objections in writing to the notifying parties. The Commission shall, when giving notice of objections, set a time limit within which the notifying parties may inform the Commission of their views in writing.

(b) The Commission shall inform other involved parties in writing of these objections. The Commission shall also set a time limit within which these other involved parties may inform the Commission of their views in writing.

3. (a) After having addressed its objections to the notifying parties, the Commission shall, upon request, give them access to the file for the purpose of enabling them to exercise their rights of defence.

(b) The Commission shall, upon request, also give the other involved parties who have been informed of the objections access to the file in so far as this is necessary for the purposes of preparing their observations.

4. The parties to whom the Commission's objections have been addressed or who have been informed of these objections shall, within the time limit fixed, make known in writing their views on the objections. In their written comments, they may set out all matters relevant to the case and may attach any relevant documents in proof of the facts set out. They may also propose that the Commission hear persons who may corroborate those facts.

5. Where the Commission intends to take a decision pursuant to Article 14 or Article 15 of Regulation (EEC) No. 4064/89 it shall, before consulting the

Advisory Committee on Concentrations, hear (pursuant to Article 18(1) and (3) of that Regulation) the parties regarding whom the Commission intends to take such a decision.

The procedure provided pursuant to subparagraphs 2(a), 3(a), and paragraph 4 is applicable, mutatis mutandis.

Article 14   Oral hearings

1.   The Commission shall afford the notifying parties who have so requested in the written comments the opportunity to put forward their arguments orally in a formal hearing if such parties show a sufficient interest. It may also in other cases afford such parties the opportunity of expressing their views orally.

2.   The Commission shall afford other involved parties who have so requested in their written comments the opportunity to express their views orally in a formal hearing if they show a sufficient interest. It may also in other cases afford such parties the opportunity of expressing their views orally.

3.   The Commission shall afford parties in relation to whom it proposes to impose a fine or periodic penalty payment who have so requested in their written comments the opportunity to put forward their arguments orally in a formal hearing. It may also in other cases afford such parties the opportunity of expressing their views orally.

4.   The Commission shall summon the persons to be heard to attend on such date as it shall appoint.

5.   The Commission shall immediately transmit a copy of the summons to the competent authorities of the Member States, who may appoint an official to take part in the hearing.

Article 15   Conduct of formal oral hearings

1.   Hearings shall be conducted by persons appointed by the Commission for that purpose.

2.   Persons summoned to attend shall either appear in person or be represented by legal representatives or by representatives authorised by their constitution. Undertakings and associations of undertakings may be represented by a duly authorised agent appointed from among their permanent staff.

3.   Persons heard by the Commission may be assisted by lawyers or university teachers who are entitled to plead before the Court of Justice of the European Communities in accordance with Article 17 of the Protocol on the Statute of the Court of Justice, or by other qualified persons.

4.   Hearings shall not be public. Persons shall be heard separately or in the presence of other persons summoned to attend. In the latter case, regard shall be had to the legitimate interest of the undertakings in the protection of their business secrets.

5.   The statements made by each person heard shall be recorded.

Article 16   Hearing of third parties

1.   If third parties apply in writing to be heard pursuant to Article 18(4) of Regulation (EEC) No. 4064/89, the Commission shall inform them in writing of the nature and subject matter of the procedure and shall fix a time limit within which they may make known their views.

2.   The third parties referred to in paragraph 1 shall make known their views in writing within the time limit fixed. The Commission may, where

appropriate, afford the parties who have so requested in their written comments, the opportunity to participate in a formal hearing. It may also in other cases afford such parties the opportunity of expressing their views orally.

3. The Commission may likewise afford to any other third parties the opportunity of expressing their views.

Article 17   Confidential information

Information, including documents, shall not be communicated or made accessible in so far as it contains business secrets of any person or undertaking, including the notifying parties, other involved parties or of third parties, or other confidential information the disclosure of which is not considered necessary by the Commission for the purpose of the procedure, or where internal documents of the authorities are concerned.

SECTION IV   MODIFICATIONS OF THE CONCENTRATION PLAN

Article 18   Time limit for modifications to the concentration plan

1. The modifications to the original concentration plan made by the undertakings concerned as provided for pursuant to Article 10(2) of Regulation (EEC) No. 4064/89 which are intended by the parties to form the basis for a decision pursuant to Article 8(2) shall be submitted to the Commission within not more than three months of the date on which proceedings were initiated. The Commission may in exceptional circumstances extend this period.

2. The time period referred to in paragraph 1 shall be determined according to the same rules as those contained in Articles 6 to 9 of this Regulation.

SECTION V   MISCELLANEOUS PROVISIONS

Article 19   Transmission of documents

1. Transmission of documents and summonses from the Commission to the addressees may be effected in any of the following ways:
   (a)   delivery by hand against receipt;
   (b)   registered letter with acknowledgment of receipt;
   (c)   telefax with a request for acknowledgment of receipt;
   (d)   telex;
   (e)   electronic mail with a request for acknowledgment of receipt.

2. Subject to Article 21(1), paragraph 1 also applies to the transmission of documents from the notifying parties, from other involved parties or from third parties to the Commission.

3. Where a document is sent by telex, by telefax or by electronic mail, it shall be presumed that it has been received by the addressee on the day on which it was sent.

Article 20   Setting of time limits

1. In fixing the time limits provided for pursuant to Article 4(2), 5(2), 12(1) and (2), 13(2) and 16(1), the Commission shall have regard to the time required for preparation of statements and to the urgency of the case. It shall also take account of working days as defined under Article 22 as well as public holidays in the country of receipt of the Commission's communication.

2. These time limits shall be set in terms of a precise calendar date.

Article 21 Receipt of documents by the Commission

1. Subject to the provisions of Article 4(1) of this Regulation, notifications must be delivered to the Commission at the address indicated in Form CO or have been dispatched by registered letter to the address indicated in Form CO before the expiry of the period referred to in Article 4(1) of Regulation (EEC) No. 4064/89.

Additional information requested to complete notifications pursuant to Article 4(2) and (4) or to supplement notifications pursuant to Article 5(2) of this Regulation must reach the Commission at the aforesaid address or have been dispatched by registered letter before the expiry of the time limit fixed in each case.

Written comments on Commission communications pursuant to Articles 12(1) and (2), 13(2) and 16(1) must be delivered to the Commission or must have reached the Commission at the aforesaid address before the expiry of the time limit fixed in each case.

2. Time limits referred to in subparagraphs two and three of paragraph 1 shall be determined in accordance with Article 20.

3. Should the last day of a time limit fall on a day which is not a working day (as defined under Article 22), or which is a public holiday in the country of dispatch, the time limit expires on the following working day.

Article 22 Definition of working days

The expression 'working days' in this Regulation means all days other than Saturdays, Sundays, public holidays and other holidays as determined by the Commission and published in the Official Journal of the European Communities before the beginning of each year.

Article 23 Repeal

Regulation (EEC) No. 2367/90 is repealed.

Article 24 Entry into force

This Regulation shall enter into force on 1 March 1995. This Regulation shall be binding in its entirety and directly applicable in all Member States.

Done at Brussels, 21 December 1994
For the Commission,
Karel VAN MIERT,
Member of the Commission

ANNEX FORM CO RELATING TO THE NOTIFICATION OF A CONCENTRATION PURSUANT TO REGULATION (EEC) NO. 4064/89

INTRODUCTION

A. The purpose of this Form

This Form specifies the information that must be provided by an undertaking or undertakings when notifying the Commission of a concentration with a Community dimension. A 'concentration' is defined in Article 3 and 'Community dimension' by Article 1 of Regulation (EEC) No. 4064/89.

Your attention is drawn to Regulation (EEC) No. 4064/89 and to Regulation (EC) No. 3385/94, (hereinafter referred to as the 'Implementing Regulation') and to the corresponding provisions of the Agreement on the European

Economic Area. Experience has shown that prenotification meetings are extremely valuable to both the notifying party(ies) and the Commission in determining the precise amount of information required in a notification and, in the large majority of cases, will result in a significant reduction of the information required. Accordingly, notifying parties are encouraged to consult the Commission regarding the possibility of dispensing with the obligation to provide certain information (see Section B (b) discussing the possibility of waivers).

B. The need for a correct and complete notification

All information required by this Form must be correct and complete (Article 4 of the Implementing Regulation). In particular you should note that:

(a)   if the information required by this Form is not reasonably available to you in part or in whole (for example, because of the unavailability of information on a target company during a contested bid), the Commission will accept that the notification is complete and thus valid notwithstanding the failure to provide such information, providing that you give reasons for the unavailability of said information, and provide your best estimates for missing data together with the sources for the estimates. Where possible, indications as to where any of the requested information that is unavailable to you could be obtained by the Commission should also be provided; unless all material information required by this Form is supplied in full or good reasons are given explaining why this has not been possible the notification will be incomplete and will only become effective on the date on which all such information required is received;

(b)   the Commission only requires the submission of information relevant and necessary to its inquiry into the notified operation. If you consider that any particular information requested by this Form, in the full- or short-form version, may not be necessary for the Commission's examination of the case, you may explain this in your notification and ask the Commission to dispense with the obligation to provide that information, pursuant to Article 3(2) of the Implementing Regulation;

(c)   incorrect or misleading information in the notification will be considered to be incomplete information. In such cases, the Commission will inform the notifying parties or their representatives of this in writing and without delay. The notification will only become effective on the date on which the complete and accurate information is received by the Commission (Article 4(2) and (4) of the Implementing Regulation). Article 14(1)(b) of Regulation (EEC) No. 4064/89 provides that incorrect or misleading information where supplied intentionally or negligently can make the notifying party or parties liable to fines of up to ECU 50,000. In addition, pursuant to point (a) of Article 8(5) of Regulation (EEC) No. 4064/89 the Commission may also revoke its decision on the compatibility of a notified concentration where it is based on incorrect information for which one of the undertakings is responsible.

C. Notification in short-form

(a)   In cases where a joint venture has no, or de minimis, actual or foreseen activities within the EEA territory, the Commission intends to allow notification of the operation by means of short-form. Such cases occur where joint control is acquired by two or more undertakings, and where:

(i)   the turnover of the joint venture and/or the turnover of the contributed activities, is less than ECU 100 million in the EEA territory; and

(ii)   the total value of assets transferred to the joint venture is less than ECU 100 million in the EEA territory.

(b) If you consider that the operation to be notified meets these qualifications, you may explain this in your notification and ask the Commission to dispense with the obligation to provide the full-form notification, pursuant to Article 3(2) of the Implementing Regulation, and to allow you to notify by means of short-form.

(c)   Short-form notification allows the notifying parties to limit the information provided in the notification to the following sections and questions:

— Section 1,
— Section 2, except questions 2.1 (a, b and d), 2.3.4, and 2.3.5,
— Section 3, only question 3.1 and 3.2 (a),
— Section 5, only questions 5.1 and 5.3,
— Section 6,
— Section 10, and
— Section 9, only questions 9.5 and 9.6 (optional for the convenience of the parties).

(d)   In addition, with respect to the affected markets of the joint venture as defined below in Section 6, indicate the following for the EEA territory, for the Community as a whole, for each Member State and EFTA State, and where different, in the opinion of the notifying parties, for the relevant geographic market:

— the sales in value and volume, as well as the market shares, for the year preceding the operation, and

— the five largest customers and the five largest competitors in the affected markets in which the joint venture will be active. Provide the name, address, telephone number, fax number and appropriate contact person of each such customer and competitor.

(e)   The Commission may require full, or where appropriate partial, notification under the Form CO where:

— the notified operation does not meet the short-form thresholds, or

— this appears to be necessary for an adequate investigation with respect to possible competition problems on affected markets.

In such cases, the notification may be considered incomplete in a material respect pursuant to Article 4(2) of the Implementing Regulation. The Commission will inform the notifying parties or their representatives of this in writing and without delay and will fix a deadline for the submission of a full or, where appropriate partial, notification. The notification will only become effective on the date on which all information required is received.

D.   Who must notify

In the case of a merger within the meaning of Article 3(1)(a) or the acquisition of joint control in an undertaking within the meaning of Article 3(1)(b), the notification shall be completed jointly by the parties to the merger or by those acquiring joint control as the case may be. In case of the acquisition of a controlling interest in an undertaking by another, the acquirer must complete the notification.

In the case of a public bid to acquire an undertaking, the bidder must complete the notification.

Each party completing the notification is responsible for the accuracy of the information which it provides.

E.   How to notify

The notification must be completed in one of the official languages of the European Community. This language shall thereafter be the language of the proceedings for all notifying parties. Where notifications are made in accordance with Article 12 of Protocol 24 to the EEA Agreement in an official language of an EFTA State which is not an official language of the Community, the notification shall simultaneously be supplemented with a translation into an official language of the Community.

The information requested by this Form is to be set out using the sections and paragraph numbers of the Form, signing a declaration as provided in Section 10, and annexing supporting documentation.

Supporting documents shall be submitted in their original language; where this is not an official language of the Community they shall be translated into the language of the proceeding (Article 2(4) of the Implementing Regulation). Requested documents may be originals or copies of the originals. In the latter case the notifying party shall confirm that they are true and complete. Twenty-four copies of each notification and 19 copies of all supporting documentation must be provided.

The notification should be delivered by registered mail or by hand (or courier service) during normal Commission working hours at the following address:

Commission of the European Communities,
Directorate-General for Competition (DG IV),
Merger Task Force,
150 avenue de Cortenberg/Kortenberglaan 150,
B-1049 Brussels.

F.   Confidentiality

Article 214 of the Treaty and Article 17(2) of Regulation (EEC) No. 4064/89 as well as the corresponding provisions of the EEA Agreement require the Commission, the Member States, the EFTA Surveillance Authority and the EFTA States, their officials and other servants not to disclose information they have acquired through the application of the Regulation of the kind covered by the obligation of professional secrecy. The same principle must also apply to protect confidentiality between notifying parties.

If you believe that your interests would be harmed if any of the information you are asked to supply were to be published or otherwise divulged to other parties, submit this information separately with each page clearly marked 'Business Secrets'. You should also give reasons why this information should not be divulged or published. In the case of mergers or joint acquisitions, or in other cases where the notification is completed by more than one of the parties, business secrets may be submitted under separate cover, and referred to in the notification as an annex. All such annexes must be included in the submission in order for a notification to be considered complete.

G.   Definitions and instructions for purposes of this Form

Notifying party or parties: in cases where a notification is submitted by only one of the undertakings party to an operation, 'notifying parties' is used to refer only to the undertaking actually submitting the notification. Party(ies) to the concentration or parties: these terms relate to both the acquiring and acquired parties, or to the merging parties, including all undertakings in which a controlling interest is being acquired or which is the subject of a public bid.

Except where otherwise specified, the terms 'notifying party(ies)' and 'party(ies) to the concentration' include all the undertakings which belong to the same groups as those 'parties'.

Affected markets: Section 6 of this Form requires the notifying parties to define the relevant product and/or service markets, and further to identify which of those relevant markets are likely to be affected by the notified operation. This definition of affected market is used as the basis for requiring information for a number of other questions contained in this Form. The definitions thus submitted by the notifying parties are referred to in this Form as the affected market(s). This term can refer to a relevant market made up either of products or of services.

Year: all references to the word 'year' in this Form shall be read as meaning calendar year, unless otherwise stated. All information requested in this Form shall, unless otherwise specified, relate to the year preceding that of the notification.

The financial data requested in Section 2.4 must be provided in ECUs at the average conversion rates prevailing for the years or other periods in question. All references contained in this Form are to the relevant Articles and paragraphs of Council Regulation (EEC) No. 4064/89, unless otherwise stated.

SECTION 1   BACKGROUND INFORMATION

1.1   Information on notifying party (or parties)
Give details of:

   1.1.1   name and address of undertaking;

   1.1.2   nature of the undertaking's business;

   1.1.3   name, address, telephone number, fax number and/or telex of, and position held by, the appropriate contact person.

1.2   Information on other parties to the concentration
For each party to the concentration (except the notifying party or parties) give details of:

   1.2.1   name and address of undertaking;

   1.2.2   nature of undertaking's business;

   1.2.3   name, address, telephone number, fax number and/or telex of, and position held by the appropriate contact person.

1.3   Address for service
Give an address (in Brussels if available) to which all communications may be made and documents delivered.

1.4   Appointment of representatives
Where notifications are signed by representatives of undertakings, such representatives shall produce written proof that they are authorised to act. If a joint notification is being submitted, has a joint representative been appointed?

If yes, please give the details requested in Sections 1.4.1 to 1.4.4.

If no, please give details of information of any representatives who have been authorised to act for each of the parties to the concentration, indicating whom they represent:

1.4.1 name of representative;

1.4.2 address of representative;

1.4.3 name of person to be contacted (and address, if different from 1.4.2);

1.4.4 telephone number, fax number and/or telex.

SECTION 2   DETAILS OF THE CONCENTRATION

2.1   Briefly describe the nature of the concentration being notified. In doing so state:

(a) whether the proposed concentration is a full legal merger, an acquisition of sole or joint control, a concentrative joint venture or a contract or other means of conferring direct or indirect control within the meaning of Article 3(3);

(b) whether the whole or parts of parties are subject to the concentration;

(c) a brief explanation of the economic and financial structure of the concentration;

(d) whether any public offer for the securities of one party by another party has the support of the former's supervisory boards of management or other bodies legally representing that party;

(e) the proposed or expected date of any major events designed to bring about the completion of the concentration;

(f) the proposed structure of ownership and control after the completion of the concentration;

(g) any financial or other support received from whatever source (including public authorities) by any of the parties and the nature and amount of this support.

2.2   List the economic sectors involved in the concentration.

2.3   For each of the undertakings concerned by the concentration provide the following data for the last financial year:

2.3.1   world-wide turnover;

2.3.2   Community-wide turnover;

2.3.3   EFTA-wide turnover;

2.3.4   turnover in each Member State;

2.3.5   turnover in each EFTA State;

2.3.6   the Member State, if any, in which more than two-thirds of Community-wide turnover is achieved;

2.3.7   the EFTA State, if any, in which more than two-thirds of EFTA-wide turnover is achieved.

2.4   Provide the following information with respect to the last financial year:

2.4.1   does the combined turnover of the undertakings concerned in the territory of the EFTA States equal 25% or more of their total turnover in the EEA territory?

2.4.2   does each of at least two undertakings concerned have a turnover exceeding ECU 250 million in the territory of the EFTA States?

SECTION 3   OWNERSHIP AND CONTROL

For each of the parties to the concentration provide a list of all undertakings belonging to the same group.

This list must include:

3.1 all undertakings or persons controlling these parties, directly or indirectly;

3.2 all undertakings active on any affected market that are controlled, directly or indirectly:

    (a) by these parties;

    (b) by any other undertaking identified in 3.1.

For each entry listed above, the nature and means of control shall be specified. The information sought in this section may be illustrated by the use of organization charts or diagrams to show the structure of ownership and control of the undertakings.

SECTION 4   PERSONAL AND FINANCIAL LINKS AND PREVIOUS ACQUISITIONS

With respect to the parties to the concentration and each undertaking or person identified in response to Section 3 provide:

4.1 a list of all other undertakings which are active on affected markets (affected markets are defined in Section 6) in which the undertakings, or persons, of the group hold individually or collectively 10% or more of the voting rights, issued share capital or other securities; in each case identify the holder and state the percentage held;

4.2 a list for each undertaking of the members of their boards of management who are also members of the boards of management or of the supervisory boards of any other undertaking which is active on affected markets; and (where applicable) for each undertaking a list of the members of their supervisory boards who are also members of the boards of management of any other undertaking which is active on affected markets; in each case identify the name of the other undertaking and the positions held;

4.3 details of acquisitions made during the last three years by the groups identified above (Section 3) of undertakings active in affected markets as defined in Section 6.

Information provided here may be illustrated by the use of organisation charts or diagrams to give a better understanding.

SECTION 5   SUPPORTING DOCUMENTATION

Notifying parties shall provide the following:

5.1 copies of the final or most recent versions of all documents bringing about the concentration, whether by agreement between the parties to the concentration, acquisition of a controlling interest or a public bid;

5.2 in a public bid, a copy of the offer document, if unavailable on notification, should be submitted as soon as possible and not later than when it is posted to shareholders);

5.3 copies of the most recent annual reports and accounts of all the parties to the concentration;

5.4 where at least one affected market is identified: copies of analyses, reports, studies and surveys submitted to or prepared for any member(s) of the board of directors, the supervisory board, or the shareholders' meeting, for the purpose of assessing or analysing the concentration with respect to competitive conditions, competitors (actual and potential), and market conditions.

SECTION 6   MARKET DEFINITIONS

The relevant product and geographic markets determine the scope within which the market power of the new entity resulting from the concentration must be assessed.

The notifying party or parties shall provide the data requested having regard to the following definitions:

I.   Relevant product markets

A relevant product market comprises all those products and/or services which are regarded as interchangeable or substitutable by the consumer, by reason of the products' characteristics, their prices and their intended use. A relevant product market may in some cases be composed of a number of individual products and/or services which present largely identical physical or technical characteristics and are interchangeable.

Factors relevant to the assessment of the relevant product market include the analysis of why the products or services in these markets are included and why others are excluded by using the above definition, and having regard to, e.g. substitutability, conditions of competition, prices, cross-price elasticity of demand or other factors relevant for the definition of the product markets.

II.   Relevant geographic markets

The relevant geographic market comprises the area in which the undertakings concerned are involved in the supply of relevant products or services, in which the conditions of competition are sufficiently homogeneous and which can be distinguished from neighbouring geographic areas because, in particular, conditions of competition are appreciably different in those areas.

Factors relevant to the assessment of the relevant geographic market include the nature and characteristics of the products or services concerned, the existence of entry barriers, consumer preferences, appreciable differences of the undertakings' market shares between neighbouring geographic areas or substantial price differences.

III.   Affected markets

For purposes of information required in this Form, affected markets consist of relevant product markets where in the EEA territory, in the Community, in the territory of the EFTA States, in any Member State or in any EFTA State:

(a)   two or more of the parties to the concentration are engaged in business activities in the same product market and where the concentration will lead to a combined market share of 15% or more. These are horizontal relationships;

(b)   one or more of the parties to the concentration are engaged in business activities in a product market, which is upstream or downstream of a product market in which any other party to the concentration is engaged, and any of their individual or combined market share is 25% or more, regardless of whether there is or is not any existing supplier/customer relationship between the parties to the concentration. These are vertical relationships.

On the basis of the above definitions and market share thresholds, provide the following information:

6.1   Identify each affected market within the meaning of Section III, within the EEA territory, the Community, the territory of the EFTA States, in any Member State or in any EFTA State.

6.2   Briefly describe the relevant product and geographic markets concerned by the notified operation, including those which are closely related to the relevant product market(s) concerned (in upstream, downstream and horizontal neighbouring markets), where two or more of the parties to the concentration are active and which are not affected markets within the meaning of Section III.

SECTION 7   INFORMATION ON AFFECTED MARKETS

For each affected relevant product market, for each of the last three financial years:

(a)   for the EEA territory;

(b)   for the Community as a whole;

(c)   for the territory of the EFTA States as a whole;

(d)   individually for each Member State and EFTA State where the parties to the concentration do business;

(e)   and, where in the opinion of the notifying parties, the relevant geographic market is different; provide the following:

7.1   an estimate of the total size of the market in terms of sales value (in ECUs) and volume (units). Indicate the basis and sources for the calculations and provide documents where available to confirm these calculations;

7.2   the sales in value and volume, as well as an estimate of the market shares, of each of the parties to the concentration;

7.3   an estimate of the market share in value (and where appropriate volume) of all competitors (including importers) having at least 10% of the geographic market under consideration. Provide documents where available to confirm the calculation of these market shares and provide the name, address, telephone number, fax number and appropriate contact person, of these competitors;

7.4   an estimate of the total value and volume and source of imports from outside the EEA territory and identify:

(a)   the proportion of such imports that are derived from the groups to which the parties to the concentration belong;

(b)   an estimate of the extent to which any quotas, tariffs or non-tariff barriers to trade, affect these imports, and

(c)   an estimate of the extent to which transportation and other costs affect these imports;

7.5   the extent to which trade among States within the EEA territory is affected by:

(a)   transportation and other costs; and

(b)   other non-tariff barriers to trade;

7.6   the manner in which the parties to the concentration produce and sell the products and/or services; for example, whether they manufacture locally, or sell through local distribution facilities;

7.7   a comparison of price levels in each Member State and EFTA State by each party to the concentration and a similar comparison of price levels between the Community, the EFTA States and other areas where these products are produced (e.g. eastern Europe, the United States of America, Japan, or other relevant areas);

7.8   the nature and extent of vertical integration of each of the parties to the concentration compared with their largest competitors.

SECTION 8   GENERAL CONDITIONS IN AFFECTED MARKETS

8.1   Identify the five largest suppliers to the notifying parties and their individual shares of purchases from each of these suppliers (or raw materials or goods used for purposes of producing the relevant products). Provide the name, address, telephone number, fax number and appropriate contact person, of these suppliers.

Structure of supply in affected markets

8.2   Explain the distribution channels and service networks that exist on the affected markets. In so doing, take account of the following where appropriate:

(a)   the distribution systems prevailing on the market and their importance. To what extent is distribution performed by third parties and/or undertakings belonging to the same group as the parties identified in Section 3?

(b)   the service networks (for example, maintenance and repair) prevailing and their importance in these markets. To what extent are such services performed by third parties and/or undertakings belonging to the same group as the parties identified in Section 3?

8.3   Where appropriate, provide an estimate of the total Community-wide and EFTA-wide capacity for the last three years. Over this period what proportion of this capacity is accounted for by each of the parties to the concentration, and what have been their respective rates of capacity utilisation.

Structure of demand in affected markets

8.4   Identify the five largest customers of the notifying parties in each affected market and their individual share of total sales for such products accounted for by each of those customers. Provide the name, address, telephone number, fax number and appropriate contact person, of each of these customers.

8.5   Explain the structure of demand in terms of:

(a)   the phases of the markets in terms of, for example, take-off, expansion, maturity and decline, and a forecast of the growth rate of demand;

(b)   the importance of customer preferences, in terms of brand loyalty, products differentiation and the provision of a full range of products;

(c)   the degree of concentration or dispersion of customers;

(d)   segmentation of customers into different groups and describe the 'typical customer' of each group;

(e)   the importance of exclusive distribution contracts and other types of long-term contracts;

(f)   the extent to which public authorities, government agencies, state enterprises or similar bodies are important participants as a source of demand.

Market entry

8.6   Over the last five years, has there been any significant entry into any affected markets? If the answer is 'yes', where possible provide their name, address, telephone number, fax number and appropriate contact person, and an estimate of their current market shares.

8.7   In the opinion of the notifying parties are there undertakings (including those at present operating only in extra-Community or extra-EEA markets) that are likely to enter the market? If the answer is 'yes', please explain why and identify such entrants by name, address, telephone number, fax number and appropriate contact person, and an estimate of the time within which such entry is likely to occur.

8.8   Describe the various factors influencing entry into affected markets that exist in the present case, examining entry from both a geographical and product viewpoint. In so doing, take account of the following where appropriate:

(a)   the total costs of entry (R & D, establishing distribution systems, promotion, advertising, servicing, etc.) on a scale equivalent to a significant viable competitor, indicating the market share of such a competitor;

(b)   any legal or regulatory barriers to entry, such as government authorisation or standard setting in any form;

(c)   any restrictions created by the existence of patents, know-how and other intellectual property rights in these markets and any restrictions created by licensing such rights;

(d)   the extent to which each of the parties to the concentration are licensees or licensors of patents, know-how and other rights in the relevant markets;

(e)   the importance of economies of scale for the production of products in the affected markets;

(f)   access to sources of supply, such as availability of raw materials.

Research and development

8.9   Give an account of the importance of research and development in the ability of a firm operating on the relevant market(s) to compete in the long-term. Explain the nature of the research and development in affected markets carried out by the undertakings to the concentration. In so doing, take account of the following, where appropriate:

(a)   the research and development intensities for these markets and the relevant research and development intensities for the parties to the concentration;

(b)   the course of technological development for these markets over an appropriate time period (including developments in products and/or services, production processes, distribution systems, etc.);

(c)   the major innovations that have been made in these markets and the undertakings responsible for these innovations;

(d)   the cycle of innovation in these markets and where the parties are in this cycle of innovation.

Cooperative Agreements

8.10   To what extent do cooperative agreements (horizontal or vertical) exist in the affected markets?

8.11   Give details of the most important cooperative agreements engaged in by the parties to the concentration in the affected markets, such as research and development, licensing, joint production, specialization, distribution, long-term supply and exchange of information agreements.

Trade associations

8.12   With respect to the trade associations in the affected markets:

(a)   identify those in which the parties to the concentration are members;

(b)   identify the most important trade associations to which the customers and suppliers of the parties to the concentration belong. Provide the

name, address, telephone number, fax number and appropriate contact person
of all trade associations listed above.

SECTION 9   GENERAL MATTERS

Market data on conglomerate aspects

Where any of the parties to the concentration hold individually a
market share of 25% or more for any product market in which there is
no horizontal or vertical relationship as described above, provide the
following information:

9.1   a description of each product market and explain why the products
and/or services in these markets are included (and why others are excluded) by
reasons of their characteristics, prices and their intended use;

9.2   an estimate of the value of the market and the market shares of each of
the groups to which the parties belong for each product market identified in 9.1
for the last financial year:

    (a)   for the EEA territory as a whole;

    (b)   for the Community as a whole;

    (c)   for the territory of the EFTA States as a whole;

    (d)   individually for each Member State and EFTA State where the
groups to which the parties belong do business;

    (e)   and where different, for the relevant geographic market.

Overview of the markets

9.3   Describe the world-wide context of the proposed concentration,
indicating the position of each of the parties to the concentration outside of the
EEA territory in terms of size and competitive strength.

9.4   Describe how the proposed concentration is likely to affect the interests
of intermediate and ultimate consumers and the development of technical and
economic progress.

Ancillary restraints

9.5   Operations which have as their object or effect the coordination of the
competitive behaviour of undertakings which remain independent fall, in
principle, within Articles 85 and 86 of the Treaty of Rome. However, if the
parties to the concentration, and/or other involved parties (including the seller
and minority shareholders), enter into ancillary restrictions directly related and
necessary to the implementation of the concentration, these restrictions may be
assessed in conjunction with the concentration itself (see in particular the 25th
recital to Regulation (EEC) No. 4064/89 and Commission notice on restrictions ancillary to concentrations.

    (a)   Identify each ancillary restriction in the agreements provided with
the notification for which you request an assessment in conjunction with the
concentration; and

    (b)   explain why these are directly related and necessary to the implemen-
tation of the concentration.

Transfer of notification

9.6   In the event that the Commission finds that the operation notified does
not constitute a concentration within the meaning of Article 3 of Regulation
(EEC) No. 4064/89 do you request that it be treated as an application for
negative clearance from, or a notification to obtain an exemption from Article
85 of the Treaty of Rome?

SECTION 10   DECLARATION

Article 1(2) of the Implementing Regulation states that where notifications are signed by representatives of undertakings, such representatives shall produce written proof that they are authorised to act. Such written authorisation must accompany the notification.

The notification must conclude with the following declaration which is to be signed by or on behalf of all the notifying parties.

The undersigned declare that, to the best of their knowledge and belief, the information given in this notification is true, correct, and complete, that complete copies of documents required by Form CO, have been supplied, and that all estimates are identified as such and are their best estimates of the underlying facts and that all the opinions expressed are sincere.

They are aware of the provisions of Article 14(1)(b) of Regulation (EEC) No. 4064/89.

Place and date:

Signatures:

(Guidance Notes omitted)

COMMISSION NOTICES

COMMISSION NOTICE REGARDING RESTRICTIONS ANCILLARY TO CONCENTRATIONS

(90/C 203/05)

I. INTRODUCTION

1. Council Regulation (EEC) No. 4264/89 of 21 December 1989 on the control of concentrations between undertakings ('the Regulation')[1] states in its 25th recital that its application is not excluded where the undertakings concerned accept restrictions which are directly related and necessary to the implementation of the concentration, hereinafter referred to as 'ancillary restrictions'. In the scheme of the Regulation, such restrictions are to be assessed together with the concentration itself. It follows, as confirmed by Article 8(2), second subparagraph, last sentence of the Regulation, that a decision declaring the concentration compatible also covers these restrictions. In this situation, under the provisions of Article 22, paragraphs 1 and 2, the Regulation is solely applicable, to the exclusion of Regulation No. 17[2] as well as Regulations (EEC) No. 1017/68,[3] (EEC) No. 4056/86[4] and (EEC) No. 3975/87.[5] This avoids parallel Commission proceedings, one concerned with the assessment of the concentration under the Regulation, and the other aimed at the application of Articles 85 and 86 to the restrictions which are ancillary to the concentration.

2. In this notice, the Commission sets out to indicate the interpretation it gives to the notion of 'restrictions directly related and necessary to the implementation of the concentration'. Under the Regulation such restrictions must be assessed in relation to the concentration, whatever their treatment might be under Articles 85 and 86 if they were to be considered in isolation or in a different economic context. The Commission endeavours, within the limits set by the Regulation, to take the greatest account of business practice and of the conditions necessary for the implementation of concentrations.

This notice is without prejudice to the interpretation which may be given by the Court of Justice of the European Communities.

Notes
[1] OJ No. L395, 30.12.1989, p. 1.
[2] OJ No. L13, 21.2.1962, p. 204/62.
[3] OJ No. L175, 23.7.1968, p. 1.
[4] OJ No. L378, 31.12.1986, p. 4.
[5] OJ No. L374, 31.12.1987, p. 1.

II.   PRINCIPLES OF EVALUATION

3.   The 'restrictions' meant are those agreed on between the parties to the concentration which limit their own freedom of action in the market. They do not include restrictions to the detriment of third parties. If such restrictions are the inevitable consequences of the concentration itself, they must be assessed together with it under the provisions of Article 2 of the Regulation. If, on the contrary, such restrictive effects on third parties are separable from the concentration they may, if appropriate, be the subject of an assessment of compatibility with Articles 85 and 86 of the EEC Treaty.

4.   For restrictions to be considered 'directly related' they must be ancillary to the implementation of the concentration, that is to say subordinate in importance to the main object of the concentration. They cannot be substantial restrictions wholly different in nature from those which result from the concentration itself. Neither are they contractual arrangements which are among the elements constituting the concentration, such as those establishing economic unity between previously independent parties, or organising joint control by two undertakings of another undertaking. As integral parts of the concentration, the latter arrangements constitute the very subject matter of the evaluation to be carried out under the Regulation.

Also excluded, for concentrations which are carried out in stages, are the contractual arrangements relating to the stages before the establishment of control within the meaning of Article 33, paragraphs 1 and 3 of the Regulation. For these, Articles 85 and 86 remain applicable as long as the conditions set out in Article 3 are not fulfilled.

The notion of directly related restrictions likewise excludes from the application of the Regulation additional restrictions agreed at the same time which have no direct link with the concentration. It is not enough that the additional restrictions exist in the same context as the concentration.

5.   The restrictions must likewise be 'necessary to the implementation of the concentration', which means that in their absence the concentration could not be implemented or could only be implemented under more uncertain conditions, at substantially higher cost, over an appreciably longer period or with considerably less probability of success. This must be judged on an objective basis.

6.   The question of whether a restriction meets these conditions cannot be answered in general terms. In particular as concerns the necessity of the restriction, it is proper not only to take account of its nature, but equally to ensure, in applying the rule of proportionality, that its duration and subject matter, and geographic field of application, do not exceed what the implementation of the concentration reasonably requires. If alternatives are available for the attainment of the legitimate aim pursued, the undertakings must choose the one which is objectively the least restrictive of competition.

These principles will be followed and further developed by the Commission's practice in individual cases. However, it is already possible, on the basis of past experience, to indicate the attitude the Commission will take to those restrictions most commonly encountered in relation to the transfer of undertakings or parts of undertakings, the division of undertakings or of their assets following a joint acquisition of control, or the creation of concentrative joint ventures.

III. EVALUATION OF COMMON ANCILLARY RESTRICTIONS IN CASES OF THE TRANSFER OF AN UNDERTAKING

A. *Non-competition clauses*

1.   Among the ancillary restrictions which meet the criteria set out in the Regulation are contractual prohibitions on competition which are imposed on the vendor in the context of a concentration achieved by the transfer of an undertaking or part of an undertaking. Such prohibitions guarantee the transfer to the acquirer of the full value of the assets transferred, which in general include both physical assets and intangible assets such as the goodwill which the vendor has accumulated or the know-how he has developed. These are not only directly related to the concentration, but are also necessary for its implementation because, in their absence, there would be reasonable grounds to expect that the sale of the undertaking or part of an undertaking could not be accomplished satisfactorily. In order to take over fully the value of the assets transferred, the acquirer must be able to benefit from some protection against competitive acts of the vendor in order to gain the loyalty of customers and to assimilate and exploit the know-how. Such protection cannot generally be considered necessary when *de facto* the transfer is limited to physical assets (such as land, buildings or machinery) or to exclusive industrial and commercial property rights (the holders of which could immediately take action against infringements by the transferor of such rights).

However, such a prohibition on competition is justified by the legitimate objective sought of implementing the concentration only when its duration, its geographical field of application, its subject matter and the persons subject to it do not exceed what is reasonably necessary to that end.

2.   With regard to the acceptable duration of a prohibition on competition, a period of five years has been recognised as appropriate when the transfer of the undertaking includes the goodwill and know-how, and a period of two years when it includes only the goodwill. However, these are not absolute rules; they do not preclude a prohibition of longer duration in particular circumstances, where for example the parties can demonstrate that customer loyalty will persist for a period longer than two years or that the economic life cycle of the products concerned is longer than five years and should be taken into account.

3.   The geographic scope of the non-competition clause must be limited to the area where the vendor had established the products or services before the transfer. It does not appear objectively necessary that the acquirer be protected from competition by the vendor in territories which the vendor had not previously penetrated.

4.   In the same manner, the non-competition clause must be limited to products and services which form the economic activity of the undertaking transferred. In particular, in the case of a partial transfer of assets, it does not appear that the acquirer needs to be protected from the competition of the vendor in the products or services which constitute the activities which the vendor retains after the transfer.

5.   The vendor may bind himself, his subsidiaries and commercial agents. However, an obligation to impose similar restrictions on others would not qualify as an ancillary restriction. This applies in particular to clauses which would restrict the scope for resellers or users to import or export.

6.   Any protection of the vendor is not normally an ancillary restriction and is therefore to be examined under Articles 85 and 86 of the EEC Treaty.

B.   *Licences of industrial and commercial property rights and of know-how*

1.   The implementation of a transfer of an undertaking or part of an undertaking generally includes the transfer to the acquirer, with a view to the full exploitation of the assets transferred, of rights to industrial or commercial property or know-how. However, the vendor may remain the owner of the rights in order to exploit them for activities other than those transferred. In these cases, the usual means for ensuring that the acquirer will have the full use of the assets transferred is to conclude licensing agreements in his favour.

2.   Simple or exclusive licences of patents, similar rights or existing know-how can be accepted as necessary for the completion of the transaction, and likewise agreements to grant such licences. They may be limited to certain fields of use, to the extent that they correspond to the activities of the undertaking transferred. Normally it will not be necessary for such licences to include territorial limitations on manufacture which reflect the territory of the activity transferred. Licences may be granted for the whole duration of the patent or similar rights or the duration of the normal economic life of the know-how. As such licences are economically equivalent to a partial transfer of rights, they need not be limited in time.

3.   Restrictions in licence agreements, going beyond what is provided above, fall outside the scope of the Regulation. They must be assessed on their merits according to Article 85(1) and (3). Accordingly, where they fulfil the conditions required, they may benefit from the block exemptions provided for by Regulation (EEC) No. 2349/84 on patent licences[1] or Regulation (EEC) No. 559/89 on know-how licences.[2]

4.   The same principles are to be applied by analogy in the case of licences of trademarks, business names or similar rights. There may be situations where the vendor wishes to remain the owner of such rights in relation to activities retained, but the acquirer needs the rights to use them to market the products constituting the object of the activity of the undertaking or part of an undertaking transferred.

In such circumstances, the conclusion of agreements for the purpose of avoiding confusion between trademarks may be necessary.

Notes
[1] OJ No. L219, 16.8.1984, p. 15.
[2] OJ No. L61, 4.3.1989, p. 1.

C.   *Purchase and supply agreements*

1.   In many cases, the transfer of an undertaking or part of an undertaking can entail the disruption of traditional lines of internal procurement and supply resulting from the previous integration of activities within the economic entity of the vendor. To make possible the break up of the economic unity of the vendor and the partial transfer of the assets to the acquirer under reasonable conditions, it is often necessary to maintain, at least for a transitional period, similar links between the vendor and the acquirer. This objective is normally attained by the conclusion of purchase and supply agreements between the vendor and the acquirer of the undertaking or part of an undertaking. Taking account of the particular situation resulting from the break up of the economic unity of the vendor such obligations, which may lead to restrictions of competition, can be recognised as ancillary. They may be in favour of the vendor as well as the acquirer.

2.   The legitimate aim of such obligations may be to ensure the continuity of supply to one or other of the parties of products necessary to the activities retained (for the vendor) or taken over (for the acquirer). Thus, there are grounds for recognising, for a transitional period, the need for supply obligations aimed at guaranteeing the quantities previously supplied within the vendor's integrated business or enabling their adjustment in accordance with the development of the market.

Their aim may also be to provide continuity of outlets for one or the other of the parties, as they were previously assured within the single economic entity. For the same reason, obligations providing for fixed quantities, possibly with a variation clause, may be recognised as necessary.

3.   However, there does not appear to be a general justification for exclusive purchase or supply obligations. Save in exceptional circumstances, for example resulting from the absence of a market or the specificity of products, such exclusivity is not objectively necessary to permit the implementation of a concentration in the form of a transfer of an undertaking or part of an undertaking.

In any event, in accordance with the principle of proportionality, the undertakings concerned are bound to consider whether there are no alternative means to the ends pursued, such as agreements for fixed quantities, which are less restrictive than exclusivity.

4.   As for the duration of procurement and supply obligations, this must be limited to a period necessary for the replacement of the relationship of dependency by autonomy in market. The duration of such a period must be objectively justified.

IV.   EVALUATION OF ANCILLARY RESTRICTIONS IN THE CASE OF A JOINT ACQUISITION

1.   As set out in the 24th recital, the Regulation is applicable when two or more undertakings agree to acquire jointly the control of one or more other undertakings, in particular by means of a public tender offer, where the object or effect is the division among themselves of the undertakings or their assets. This is a concentration implemented in two successive stages; the common strategy is limited to the acquisition of control. For the transaction to be concentrative, the joint acquisition must be followed by a clear separation of the undertakings or assets concerned.

2.   For this purpose, an agreement by the joint acquirers of an undertaking to abstain from making separate competing offers for the same undertaking, or otherwise acquiring control, may be considered an ancillary restriction.

3.   Restrictions limited to putting the division into effect are to be considered directly related and necessary to the implementation of the concentration. This will apply to arrangements made between the parties for the joint acquisition of control in order to divide among themselves the production facilities or the distribution networks together with the existing trademarks of the undertaking acquired in common. The implementation of this division may not in any circumstances lead to the coordination of the future behaviour of the acquiring undertakings.

4.   To the extent that such a division involves the break up of a pre-existing economic entity, arrangements that make the break up possible under reasonable conditions must be considered ancillary. In this regard, the

principles explained above in relation to purchase and supply arrangements over a transitional period in cases of transfer of undertakings should be applied by analogy.

V.   EVALUATION OF ANCILLARY RESTRICTIONS IN CASES OF CONCENTRATIVE JOINT VENTURES WITHIN THE MEANING OF ARTICLE 3(2) SUBPARAGRAPH 2 OF THE REGULATION

This evaluation must take account of the characteristics peculiar to concentrative joint ventures, the constituent elements of which are the creation of an autonomous economic entity exercising on a long-term basis all the functions of an undertaking, and the absence of coordination of competitive behaviour between the parent undertakings and between them and the joint venture. This condition implies in principle the withdrawal of the parent undertakings from the market assigned to the joint venture and, therefore, their disappearance as actual or potential competitors of the new entity.

A.   Non-competition obligations
To the extent that a prohibition on the parent undertakings competing with the joint venture aims at expressing the reality of the lasting withdrawal of the parents from the market assigned to the joint venture, it will be recognised as an integral part of the concentration.

B.   Licences for industrial and commercial property rights and know-how
The creation of a new autonomous economic entity usually involves the transfer of the technology necessary for carrying on the activities assigned to it, in the form of a transfer of rights and related know-how. Where the parent undertakings intend nonetheless to retain the property rights, particularly with the aim of exploitation in other fields of use, the transfer of technology to the joint venture may be accomplished by means of licences. Such licences may be exclusive, without having to be limited in duration or territory, for they serve only as a substitute for the transfer of property rights. They must therefore be considered necessary to the implementation of the concentration.

C.   Purchase and supply obligations
If the parent undertakings remain present in a market upstream or downstream of that of the joint venture, any purchase and supply agreements are to be examined in accordance with the principles applicable in the case of the transfer of an undertaking.

COMMISSION NOTICE ON THE DISTINCTION BETWEEN CONCENTRATIVE AND COOPERATIVE JOINT VENTURES UNDER COUNCIL REGULATION (EEC) NO. 4064/89 OF 21 DECEMBER 1989 ON THE CONTROL OF CONCENTRATIONS BETWEEN UNDERTAKINGS
(94/C 385/01)

I.   INTRODUCTION

1.   The purpose of this notice is to provide guidance as to how the Commission interprets Article 3 of Regulation (EEC) No. 4064/89[1] (hereinafter referred to as 'the Merger Regulation') in relation to joint ventures.

Notes
[1]OJ No. C395, 30.12.1989, p. 1, corrected version OJ No. L257, 21.9.1990, p. 13.

2. This notice replaces the notice on the same subject adopted by the Commission on 25 July 1990.[2] Changes made in the current notice reflect the experience gained by the Commission in applying the Merger Regulation since its entry into force on 21 September 1990. The principles set out in this notice will be followed and further developed by the Commission's practice in individual cases.

3. Under the Community competition rules joint ventures are undertakings which are jointly controlled by two or more other undertakings.[3] In practice joint ventures encompass a broad range of operations, from merger-like operations to cooperation for particular functions such as R&D, production or distribution.

4. Joint ventures fall within the scope of the Merger Regulation if they meet the requirements of a concentration set out in Article 3 thereof.

5. According to recital 23 of the Merger Regulation 'it is appropriate to define the concept of concentration in such a manner as to cover only operations bringing about a lasting change in the structure of the undertakings concerned ... it is therefore necessary to exclude from the scope of this Merger Regulation those operations which have as their object or effect the coordination of competitive behaviour of undertakings which remain independent ...'

6. The structural changes brought about by concentrations frequently reflect a dynamic process of restructuring in the markets concerned. They are permitted under the Merger Regulation unless they result in serious damage to the structure of competition by creating or strengthening a dominant position.

In this respect concentrations are to be contrasted with arrangements between independent undertakings whereby they coordinate their competitive behaviour. The latter do not, in principle, involve a lasting change in structure of undertakings. It is therefore appropriate to submit such arrangements to the prohibition laid down in Article 85(1) of the EEC Treaty where they affect trade between Member States and have as their object or effect the prevention, restriction or distortion of competition within the common market, and they can be exempted from this prohibition only where they fulfil the requirements of Article 85(3). For this reason, cooperative arrangements are dealt with under Regulation (EEC) No. 17,[4] (EEC) No. 1017/68,[5] (EEC) No. 4056/86[6] or (EEC) No. 3975/87[7] implementing Article 85 and 86.[8]

7. The Merger Regulation deals with the distinction between concentrative and cooperative operations in Article 3(2)[9] as follows:

Notes
[2]OJ No. C203, 14.8.1990, p. 10.
[3]The concept of joint control is set out in the notice on the notion of a concentration.
[4]OJ No. 13, 21.2.1962, p. 204/62.
[5]OJ No. L175, 23.7.1968, p. 1.
[6]OJ No. L378, 31.12.1986, p. 4.
[7]OJ No. L374, 31.12.1987, p. 1.
[8]See Commission Notice concerning the assessment of cooperative joint ventures pursuant to Article 85 of the EEC Treaty, OJ No. C43, 16.2.1993, p. 2.
[9]Whilst Article 3(2) first subparagraph, is not confined to joint ventures, its application to operations other than joint ventures is not dealt with in the context of the present notice.

'An operation, including the creation of a joint venture, which has as its object or effect the coordination of the competitive behaviour of undertakings which remain independent shall not constitute a concentration within the meaning of paragraph 1(b).

The creation of a joint venture performing on a lasting basis all the functions of an autonomous economic entity, which does not give rise to coordination of the competitive behaviour of the parties amongst themselves or between them and the joint venture, shall constitute a concentration within the meaning of paragraph 1(b).'

8.   Although Article 3(2), second subparagraph, refers to coordination between parent companies and the joint venture, this has to be interpreted in the light of recital 23 and Article 3(2), first subparagraph, the purpose of which is to exclude from the scope of the Merger Regulation operations which lead to the coordination of behaviour between 'undertakings which remain independent'. For the purposes of the distinction between cooperative and concentrative joint ventures therefore, the coordination between the parent companies and the joint venture referred to in the second subparagraph is relevant only in so far as it is an instrument for producing or reinforcing the coordination between the parent companies.

II.   JOINT VENTURES UNDER ARTICLE 3 OF THE MERGER REGULATION

9.   In order to be a concentration within the meaning of Article 3 of the Merger Regulation an operation must fulfil the following requirements:

1.   Joint control

10.   A joint venture may fall within the scope of the Merger Regulation where there is an acquisition of joint control by two or more undertakings, that is, its parent companies (Article 3(1)(b)). The concept of control is set out in Article 3(3). This provides that control is based on the possibility of exercising decisive influence on an undertaking, which is determined by both legal and factual considerations.

11.   The principles for determining joint control are set out in detail in the Commission's notice on the notion of concentration.[1]

Note
[1]Paragraphs 18 to 39.

2.   Structural change of the undertakings

12.   Article 3(2), second subparagraph stipulates that the joint venture must perform, on a lasting basis, all the functions of an autonomous economic entity.

13.   Essentially this means that the joint venture must operate on a market, performing the functions normally carried out by other undertakings operating on the same market. In order to do so the joint venture must have sufficient financial and other resources including finance, staff, and assets (tangible and intangible) in order to operate a business activity on a lasting basis. In respect of intellectual property rights it is sufficient that these rights are licensed to the joint venture for its duration.[1] Joint ventures which satisfy this requirement are commonly described as 'full-function' joint ventures.

Notes
[1]Case IV/M.236, Ericsson/Ascom of 8 July 1992 (paragraph 11).

14.   A joint venture is not a full-function venture if it only takes over one specific function within the parent companies' business activities without access to the market. This is the case, for example, for joint ventures limited to R&D or production. Such joint ventures are auxiliary to their parent companies' business activities. This is also the case where a joint venture is essentially limited to the distribution or sales of its parent companies' products and, therefore, acts principally as a sales agency. However, the fact that a joint venture makes use of the distribution network or outlet of one or more of its parent companies, normally will not disqualify it as 'full-function' as long as the parent companies are acting only as agents of the joint venture.[2]

15.   The strong presence of the parent companies in upstream or downstream markets is a factor to be taken into consideration in assessing the full-function character of a joint venture where this presence leads to substantial sales or purchases between the parent companies and the joint venture. The fact that the joint venture relies almost entirely on sales to its parent companies or purchases from them only for an initial start-up period does not normally affect the full-function character of the joint venture. Such a start-up period may be necessary in order to establish the joint venture on a market. It will normally not exceed a time period of three years, depending on the specific conditions of the market in question.[3]

Where sales from the joint venture to the parent companies are intended to be made on a lasting basis the essential question is whether regardless of these sales the joint venture is geared to play an active role on the market. In this respect the relative proportion of these sales compared with the total production of the joint venture is an important factor. Another factor is that sales to the parent companies are made on the basis of normal commercial conditions.[4]

In relation to purchases made by the joint venture from its parent companies, the full-function character of the joint venture is questionable in particular where little value is added to the products or services concerned at the level of the joint venture itself. In such a situation, the joint venture may be closer to a joint sales agency. However, in contrast to this situation where a joint venture is active in a trade market and performs the normal functions of a trading company in such a market, it normally will not be an auxiliary sales agency but a full-function joint venture. A trade market is characterised by the existence of companies which specialise in the selling and distribution of products without being vertically integrated in addition to those which may be integrated, and where different sources of supply are available for the products in question. In addition, many trade markets may require operators to invest in specific facilities such as outlets, stockholding, warehouses, depots, transport fleets and sales personnel. In order to constitute a full-function joint venture in a trading market, it must have the necessary facilities and be likely to obtain a substantial

Notes
[2]Case IV/M.102, TNT/Canada Post etc. of 2 December 1991; Case IV/M.149, Lucas/Eaton of 9 December 1991.
[3]Case IV/M.394, Mannesmann/RWE/Deutsche Bank of 22 December 1983 (paragraph 9).
[4]Case IV/M.266, Rhône-Poulenc Chimie/SITA of 26 November 1992 (paragraph 15), to be contrasted with Case IV/M.168, Flachglas/VEGLA of 13 April 1992.

proportion of its supplies not only from its parent companies but also from other competing sources.[1]

16. Furthermore, the joint venture must be intended to operate on a lasting basis. The fact that the parent companies commit to the joint venture the resources described above normally demonstrates that this is the case. In addition, agreements setting up a joint venture often provide for certain contingencies, for example, the failure of the joint venture or fundamental disagreement as between the parent companies.[2] This may be achieved by the incorporation of provisions for the eventual dissolution of the joint venture itself or the possibility for one or more parent companies to withdraw from the joint venture. This kind of provision does not prevent the joint venture from being considered as operating on a lasting basis. The same is normally true where the agreement specifies a period for the duration of the joint venture where this period is sufficiently long in order to bring about a lasting change in the structure of the undertaking concerned,[3] or where the agreement provides for the possible continuation of the joint venture beyond this period. By contrast, the joint venture will not be considered to operate on a lasting basis where it is established for a short finite duration. This would be the case, for example, where a joint venture is established in order to construct a specific project such as a power plant, but it will not be involved in the operation of the plant once its construction has been completed.

Notes

[1] Case IV/M.179, Spar/Dansk Supermarked of 3 February 1992 (food retail); Case IV/M.326, Toyota Motor Corp./Walter Frey Holding/Toyota France of 1 July 1993 (car distribution).
[2] Case IV/M.408, RWE/Mannesmann of 28 February 1994 (paragraph 6).
[3] Case IV/M.259, British Airways /TAT of 27 October 1992 (paragraph 10).

3. Cooperative aspects

17. The creation of a full-function joint venture normally constitutes a concentration within the meaning of Article 3 of the Merger Regulation under its object or effect is coordination of the competitive behaviour of independent undertaking which is likely to result in a restriction of competition within the meaning of Article 85(1). In order to assess whether a joint venture is cooperative in nature it is necessary to determine whether there is coordination between the parent companies in relation to prices, markets, output or innovation. The coordination between the parent companies and the joint venture referred to in the second subparagraph of Article 3(2) is relevant only in so far as it is an instrument for producing or reinforcing the coordination between the parent companies. Where there is a restriction of competition of this kind the Commission will have to examine the applicability of Article 85 to the whole operation by means of Regulation No. 17. Where the factors leading to this restriction of competition can be separated from the creation of the joint venture itself, the former will be assessed under Regulation No. 17, the latter under the rules on merger control.[1]

Note

[1] Case IV/M.179, Spar/Dansk Supermarked of 3 February 1992 (paragraph 8).
Case IV/M.263, Ahold/Jeronimo Martins of 29 September 1992 (paragraph 8).

3.1 *Product market*

18. The following typical situations illustrate where coordination of the competitive behaviour of the parent companies resulting in an appreciable restriction of competition may or may not occur:

— there is no possibility of coordination of the competitive behaviour of independent undertakings where the parent companies transfer their entire business activities to the joint venture or their total activities in a given industrial sector,

— coordination can normally be excluded where the parent companies are not active in the market of the joint venture or transfer to the joint venture all their activities in this market or where only one parent company remains active in the joint venture's market. The same is true where the parent companies retain only minor activities in the market of the joint venture,

— by contrast to the above, there is normally a high probability of coordination where two or more parent companies retain to a significant extent activities in the same product market as the joint venture itself in so far as these activities are in the same geographic market.[1]

— There is also a probability of coordination where the parent companies or the joint venture specialise in specific segments of an overall product market, unless these segments are of minor importance in view of the main activities of the parent companies or the joint venture respectively or there are objective reasons for the parent companies to retain their activities outside the joint venture, e.g., technology related to other activities of the parent companies. In the latter case each of the parent companies retains a genuine interest in their specific segments. The existence of the joint venture therefore does not normally of itself justify the assumption that they would coordinate their behaviour with regard to these activities,

— where a network of cooperative links already exists between the parent companies in the joint venture's market the main object or effect of the joint venture may be to add a further link and thereby strengthen already existing coordination of competitive behaviour,[2]

— where the parent companies are active in a market which is downstream from the joint venture's market coordination of their competitive behaviour may occur where the joint venture is their main supplier and relatively little further value is added at the level of the parent companies; equally, where the parent companies are active in a market which is upstream from the joint venture's market coordination of their competitive behaviour may occur where their main customer is the joint venture either in general or in a particular geographic market,

Notes
[1] Case IV/M.088, Elf Enterprise of 24 July 1991 (paragraph 6); Case IV/M.117 Koipe — Tabacalera/Elosua of 28 July 1992 (paragraphs 10 to 14). In principle, the same would apply where, following the creation of the joint venture, the parent companies, while no longer active in the joint venture's market, nevertheless remain potential competitors in this market. However, this can normally be excluded since it is unlikely that the parents would re-enter the market on their own, in particular, where they have transferred their respective activities to the joint venture, or where they commit significant investment to the joint venture.
[2] Case IV/M.176, Sunrise of 13 January 1992 (paragraph 34).

—where two or more parent companies have a significant activity in a neighbouring market and this neighbouring market is of significant economic importance compared with that of the joint venture, the collaboration within the joint venture may lead to the coordination of the parent companies' competitive behaviour on this neighbouring market.[3] In this context a neighbouring market is a separate but closely related market to the market of the joint venture, both markets having common characteristics including technology, customers or competitors.

Note

[3]Case IV/M.293, Philips/Thomson/SAGEM of 18 January 1993 (paragraph 19).

3.2 *Geographic market*

19.   The parent companies and the joint venture may be active in the same product market but in different geographic markets. In this context two situations may be particularly relevant: the parent companies and the joint venture are each in different geographic markets, or the parent companies are in the same geographic market which is nevertheless different from that of the joint venture. In these situations coordination may or may not occur as follows:

—where the parent companies and the joint venture are all in different geographic makets, the Commission will examine closely the likelihood of coordination between the parent companies. In doing so the Commission will consider interaction between markets, and foreseeable developments in the emergence of wider geographic markets particularly in the light of the market integration process in the Community.[1] The same applies where one parent company and the joint venture are in the same geographic market while the other parent companies are all in different geographic markets,

—where the parent companies are in the same geographic market, which is different from that of the joint venture, there is scope for coordination of the competitive behaviour of the parent companies where the joint venture's activities have a substantial economic importance when compared with the parent companies' activities on their home market and where there is interaction between the parent companies' and joint venture's markets or such interaction is likely to evolve in the near future. By contrast, where the joint venture's activities account for only a small proportion of the overall activities of the parent companies in the products concerned, the conclusion that collaboration in the joint venture would lead to coordination on the parent companies' market would be justified only in exceptional cases,

—in any event, where the coordination of competitive behaviour of the parent companies takes place on geographic markets outside the Community or the EEA and has no appreciable effect on competition within the Community/ EEA the joint venture is considered to be concentrative despite this coordination.

20.   In relation to the abovementioned paragraphs, the fact that a joint venture leads to coordination of the competitive behaviour of the parent companies does not prevent the assumption of a concentration where these cooperative elements are only of minor economic importance relative to the operation as a whole (*de minimis*).

Note

[1]See Case IV/M.207, Eureko of 27 April 1992 (paragraph 16(b)) which can be contrasted with Case IV/M.319, BHF/CCF/Charterhouse of 30 August 1993 (paragraph 6).

However a high accumulation of minor elements of coordination may lead to a situation where the operation as a whole has to be considered as cooperative.

III. FINAL

21. The Commission's interpretation of Article 3 with respect to joint ventures is without prejudice to the interpretation which may be given by the Court of Justice or the Court of First Instance of the European Communities.

COMMISSION NOTICE ON THE NOTION OF A CONCENTRATION UNDER COUNCIL REGULATION (EEC) NO. 4064/89 OF 21 DECEMBER 1989 ON THE CONTROL OF CONCENTRATIONS BETWEEN UNDERTAKINGS
(94/C 385/05)

I. INTRODUCTION

1. The purpose of this notice is to provide guidance as to how the Commission interprets the notion of a concentration under Article 3 of Regulation (EEC) No. 4064/89[1] (hereinafter referred to as the 'Merger Regulation'). It forms part of the initiatives which the Commission envisaged in its report[2] to the Council of Ministers of 28 July 1993 in order to improve the transparency and legal security of all decisions taken in application of the Regulation. This formal guidance on the interpretation of Article 3 should enable firms to establish more quickly whether and to what extent their operations may be covered by Community merger control in advance of any contact with the Commission's services.

2. This notice deals with paragraphs (1), (3), (4) and (5) of Article 3. The interpretation of Article 3 in relation to joint ventures, dealt with in particular under Article 3(2), is set out in the Commission's notice on the distinction between concentrative and cooperative joint ventures.[3]

3. According to recital 23 of the Merger Regulation the concept of a concentration is defined as covering only operations which bring about a lasting change in the structure of the undertakings concerned. Article 3(1) provides that such a structural change is brought about either by a merger between two previously independent undertakings or by the acquisition of control over the whole or part of another undertaking.

4. The determination of the existence of a concentration under the Merger Regulation is based upon qualititative rather than quantitative criteria, focusing on the notion of control. These criteria include considerations of both law and fact. It follows, therefore, that a concentration may occur on a legal or a *de facto* basis.

5. Article 3(1) of the Regulation defines two categories of concentration:
   — those arising from a merger between previously independent undertakings (point (a));

Notes
[1] OJ No. L395, 30.12.1989, p. 1, corrected version OJ No. L257, 21.9.1990, p. 13.
[2] Doc. COM(93) 385 final, as amended by COM(93) 385 final /2.
[3] Commission notice regarding the distinction between concentrative and cooperative joint ventures under Council Regulation (EEC) No. 4064/89 of 21 December 1989 on the control of concentrations between undertakings.

— those arising from an acquisition of control (point (b)).
These are treated respectively in sections II and III below.

II. MERGERS BETWEEN PREVIOUSLY INDEPENDENT UNDERTAKINGS

6.   A merger within the meaning of point (a) of Article 3(1) of the Merger Regulation occurs when two or more independent undertakings amalgamate into a new undertaking and cease to exist as different legal entities. A merger may also occur when an undertaking is absorbed by another, the latter retaining its legal identity while the former ceases to exist as a legal entity.

7.   A merger within the meaning of point (a) of Article 3(1) may also occur where, in the absence of a legal merger, the combining of the activities of previously independent undertakings results in the creation of a single economic unit.[1] This may arise in particular where two or more undertakings, while retaining their individual legal personalities, establish contractually a common economic management.[2] If this leads to a *de facto* amalgamation of the undertakings concerned into a genuine common economic unit, the operation is considered to be a merger. A prerequisite for the determination of a common economic unit is the existence of a permanent, single economic management. Other relevant factors may include internal profit and loss compensation as between the various undertakings within the group, and their joint liability externally. The *de facto* amalgamation may be reinforced by cross-shareholdings between the undertakings forming the economic unit.

Notes

[1] In determining the previous independence of undertakings the issue of control may be relevant. Control is considered generally in paragraphs 12, *et seq.* below. For this specific issue minority shareholders are deemed to have control if they have previously obtained a majority of votes on major decisions at shareholders' meetings. The reference period in this context is normally three years.

[2] This could apply for example, in the case of a 'Gleichordnungskonzern' in German law, certain 'Groupements d'Intérêts Economiques' in French law, and certain partnerships.

III. ACQUISITION OF CONTROL

8.   Point (b) of Article 3(1) provides that a concentration occurs in the case of an acquisition of control. Such control may be acquired by one undertaking acting alone or by two or more undertakings acting jointly.

Control may also be acquired by a person in circumstances where that person already controls (whether solely or jointly) at least one other undertaking or, alternatively, by a combination of persons (which control another undertaking) and/or undertakings. The term 'person' in this context extends to public bodies[1] and private entities, as well as individuals.

As defined, a concentration within the meaning of the Merger Regulation is limited to changes in control. Internal restructuring within a group of companies, therefore, cannot constitute a concentration.

An exceptional situation exists where both the acquiring and acquired undertakings are public companies owned by the same State (or by the same public body). In this case, whether the operation is to be considered as an internal restructuring or not depends in turn on the question whether both undertakings were formerly part of the same economic unit within the meaning of recital 12 of the Merger Regulation. Where the undertakings were formerly part of different economic units having an independent power of decision the operation will be deemed to constitute a concentration and not an internal restructuring.[2] Such independent power of decision does not normally exist, however, where the undertakings are within the same holding company.

9.   Whether an operation gives rise to an acquisition of control depends on a number of legal and/or factual elements. The acquisition of property rights and shareholders' agreements are important but are not the only elements involved: purely economic relationships may also be determinant. Therefore, in exceptional circumstances a situation of economic dependence may lead to control on a factual basis where, for example, very important long term-supply agreements or credits provided by suppliers or customers, coupled with structural links, confer decisive influence.[3]

There may also be acquisition of control even if it is not the declared intention of the parties.[4] Moreover the Merger Regulation clearly defines control as 'having the possibility of exercising decisive influence' rather than the actual exercise of such influence.

10.   Control is nevertheless normally acquired by persons or undertakings which are the holders of the rights or are entitled to rights conferring control (point (a) of Article 3(4)). There may be exceptional situations where the formal holder of a controlling interest differs from the person or undertaking having in fact the real power to exercise the rights resulting from this interest. This may be the case, for example, where an undertaking uses another person or undertaking for the acquisition of a controlling interest and exercises the rights through this person or undertaking, even though the latter is formally the holder of the rights. In such a situation control is acquired by the undertaking which in reality is behind the operation and in fact enjoys the power to control the target undertaking (point (b) of Article 3(4)). The evidence needed to establish this type of indirect control may include factors such as the source of financing or family links.

11.   The object of control can be one or more undertakings which constitute legal entities, or the assets of such entities, or only some of these assets.[5] In the last mentioned situation, which could apply to brands or licences, the assets in question must constitute a business to which a market turnover can be clearly attributed.

12.   The acquisition of control may be of sole or joint control. In both cases control is defined as the possibility to exercise decisive influence on an undertaking on the basis of rights, contracts or any other means (Article 3(3)).

Notes
[1]Including the State itself, e.g., Case IV/M.157 — Air France/Sabena, of 5 October 1992 in relation to the Belgian State, or other public bodies such as the Treuhand in Cases IV/M.308 — Kali und Salz/MDK/Treuhand, of 14 December 1993.
[2]Case IV/M.097 — Péchinery/Usinor, of 24 June 1991; IV/M.216 — CEA Industrie/France Télécom/SGS-Thomson, 22 February 1993.
[3]For example in the Usinor/Bamesa decision adopted by the Commission under the ECSC Treaty, See also Case IV/M.258 CCIE/GTE, of 25 September 1992.
[4]Case IV/M.157 — Air France/Sabena, of 5 October 1992.
[5]Case IV/M.286 Zürich/MMI, of 2 April 1993.

1. Sole control

13.   Sole control is normally acquired on a legal basis where an undertaking acquires a majority of the voting rights of a company. It is not in itself significant that the acquired shareholding is 50% of the share capital plus one share[1] or that it is 100% of the share capital.[2] In the absence of other elements an acquisition which does not include a majority of the voting rights does not normally confer control even if it involves the acquisition of a majority of the share capital.

14.   Sole control may also be acquired in the case of a 'qualified minority'. This can be established on a legal and/or de facto basis.

On a legal basis it can occur where specific rights are attached to the minority shareholding. These may be preferential shares leading to a majority of the voting rights or other rights enabling the minority shareholder to determine the strategic commercial behaviour of the target company, such as the power to appoint more than half of the members of the supervisory board or the administrative board.

A minority shareholder may also be deemed to have sole control on a de facto basis. This is the case, for example, where the shareholder is highly likely to achieve a majority in the shareholders' meeting, given that the remaining shares are widely dispersed.[3] In such a situation it is unlikely that all the smaller shareholders will be present or represented at the shareholders' meeting. The determination of whether or not sole control exists in a particular case is based on the evidence resulting from the presence of shareholders in previous years. Where, on the basis of the number of shareholders attending the shareholders' meeting, a minority shareholder has a stable majority of the votes in this meeting, then the large minority shareholder is taken to have sole control.[4]

Sole control can also be exercised by a minority shareholder who has the right to manage the activities of the company and to determine its business policy.

15.   An option to purchase or convert shares cannot in itself confer sole control unless the option will be exercised in the near future according to legally binding agreements.[5] However the likely exercise of such an option can be taken into account as an additional element which, together with other elements, may lead to the conclusion that there is sole control.

16.   A change from joint to sole control of an undertaking is deemed to be a concentration within the meaning of the Merger Regulation because decisive influence exercised solely is substantially different to decisive influence exercised jointly.[6] For the same reason, an operation involving the acquisition of joint control of one part of an undertaking and sole control of another part, are in principle regarded as two separate concentrations under the Merger Regulation.[7]

Notes

[1]Case IV/M.296 — Crédit Lyonnais/BFG Bank, of 11 January 1993.
[2]Case IV/M.299 Sara Lee/BP Food Division, of 8 February 1993.
[3]Case IV/M.025 Arjomari/Wiggins Teape, of 10 February 1990.
[4]Case IV/M.343 — Société Générale de Belgique/Générale de Banque, of 3 August 1993.
[5]Case T-2/93 Air France v Commission (judgment of 19 May 1994, not yet published).
[6]This issue is dealt with in paragraphs 30 to 32 of the notice on the notion of undertakings concerned.
[7]Case IV/M.409 ABB/Renault Automation, of 9 March 1994.

17.   The concept of control under the Merger Regulation may be different from that applied in specific areas of legislation concerning, for example, prudential rules, taxation, air transport or media. In addition, national legislation within a Member State may provide specific rules on the structure of bodies representing the organisation of decision-making within an undertaking, in particular, in relation to the rights of representatives of employees. While such legislation may confer a certain power of control upon persons other than the shareholders, the concept of control under the Merger Regulation is related only to the means of influence normally enjoyed by the owners of an undertaking. Finally, the prerogatives exercised by a State acting as a public authority rather than as a shareholder, in so far as they are limited to the protection of the public interest, do not constitute control within the meaning of the Merger Regulation to the extent that they have neither the aim nor the affect of enabling the State to exercise a decisive influence over the activity of the undertaking.[8]

Note
[8]Case IV/M.493 — Tractebel/Distrigaz II, of 1 September 1994.

2. Joint control

18.   As in the case of sole control, the acquisition of joint control (which includes changes from sole control to joint control) can also be established on a legal or *de facto* basis. There is joint control if the shareholders (the parent companies) must reach agreement on major decisions concerning the controlled undertaking (the joint venture).

19.   Joint control exists where two or more undertakings or persons have the possibility to exercise decisive influence over another undertaking. Decisive influence in this sense normally means the power to block actions which determine the strategic commercial behaviour of an undertaking. Unlike sole control, which confers the power upon a specific shareholder to determine the strategic decisions in an undertaking, joint control is characterised by the possibility of a deadlock situation resulting from the power of two or more parent companies to reject proposed strategic decisions. It follows, therefore, that these shareholders must reach a common understanding in determining the commercial policy of the joint venture.

2.1   *Equality in voting rights or appointment to decision-making bodies*

20.   The clearest form of joint control exists where there are only two parent companies which share equally the voting rights to the joint venture. In this case it is not necessary for a formal agreement to exist between them. However, where there is a formal agreement, it must not contradict the principle of equality between the parent companies, by laying down, for example, that each is entitled to the same number of representatives in the management bodies and that none of the members has a casting vote.[1] Equality may also be achieved where both parent companies have the right to appoint an equal number of members to the decision-making bodies of the joint venture.

Note
[1]Case IV/M.272 Matra/CAP Gemini Sogeti, of 17 March 1993.

2.2   *Veto rights*

21.   Joint control may exist even where there is no equality between the two parent companies in votes or in representation in decision-making bodies or

where there are more than two parent companies. This is the case where minority shareholders have additional rights which allow them to veto decisions which are essential for the strategic commercial behaviour of the joint venture.[1] These veto rights may be set out in the statute of the joint venture or conferred by agreement between its parent companies. The veto rights themselves may operate by means of a specific quorum required for decisions taken in the shareholders' meeting or in the board of directors to the extent that the parent companies are represented on this board. It is also possible that strategic decisions are subject to approval by a body, e.g., supervisory board, where the minority shareholders are represented and form part of the quorum needed for such decisions.

22.   These veto rights must be related to strategic decisions on the business policy of the joint venture. They must go beyond the veto rights normally accorded to minority shareholders in order to protect their financial interests as investors in the joint venture. This normal protection of the rights of minority shareholders is related to decisions on the essence of the joint venture, such as, changes in the statute, increase or decrease of the capital or liquidation. A veto right, for example, which prevents the sale or winding up of the joint venture, does not confer joint control on the minority shareholder concerned.[2]

23.   In contrast, veto rights which confer joint control typically include decisions and issues such as the budget, the business plan, major investments or the appointment of senior management. The acquisition of joint control, however, does not require that the acquiror has the power to exercise decisive influence on the day-to-day running of an undertaking. The crucial element is that the veto rights are sufficient to enable the parent companies to exercise such influence in relation to the strategic business behaviour of the joint venture. Moreover, it is not necessary to establish that an acquiror of joint control of the joint venture will actually make use of its decisive influence. The possibility to use this influence and, hence, the mere existence of the veto rights, is sufficient.

24.   In order to acquire joint control, it is not necessary for a minority shareholder to have all the veto rights mentioned above. It may be sufficient that only some, or even one such right, exists. Whether or not this is the case depends upon the precise content of the veto right itself and also the importance of this right in the context of the specific business of the joint venture.

Notes
[1] Case T-2/93, *Air France* v *Commission* (ibid). Case IV/M.0010 Conagra/Idea, of 3 May 1991.
[2] Case IV/M.062 — Eridania/ISL, of 30 July 1991.

Appointment of management and determination of budget

25.   Normally the most important veto rights are those concerning decisions on the appointment of the management and the budget. The power to co-determine the structure of the management confers upon the holder the power to exercise decisive influence on the commercial policy of an undertaking. The same is true with respect to decisions on the budget since the budget determines the precise framework of the activities of the joint venture and, in particular, the investments it may make.

Business plan

26. The business plan normally provides details of the aims of a company together with the measures to be taken in order to achieve those aims. A veto right over this type of business plan may be sufficient to confer joint control even in the absence of any other veto right. In contrast, where the business plan contains merely general declarations concerning the business aims of the joint venture, the existence of a veto right will be only one element in the general assessment of joint control but will not, on its own, be sufficient to confer joint control.

Investments

27. In the case of a veto right on investments the importance of this right depends on, first, the level of investments which are subject to the approval of the parent companies and secondly, the extent to which investments constitute an essential feature of the market in which the joint venture is active. In relation to the first, where the level of investments necessitating parental approval is extremely high, this veto right may be closer to the normal protection of the interests of a minority shareholder than to a right conferring a power of co-determination over the commercial policy of the joint venture. With regard to the second, the investment policy of an undertaking normally is an important element in assessing whether or not there is joint control. However, there may be some markets where investment does not play a significant role in the market behaviour of an undertaking.

Market-specific rights

28. Apart from the typical veto rights mentioned above, there exist a number of other veto rights related to specific decisions which are important in the context of the particular market on the joint venture. One example is the decision on the technology to be used by the joint venture where technology is a key feature of the joint venture's activities. Another example relates to markets characterised by product differentiation and a significant degree of innovation. In such markets a veto right over decisions relating to new product lines to be developed by the joint venture may also be an important element in establishing the existence of joint control.

Overall context

29. In assessing the relative importance of veto rights, where there are a number of them, these rights should not be evaluated in isolation. On the contrary, the determination of the existence or not of joint control is based upon an assessment of these rights as a whole. However, a veto right which does not relate either to commercial policy and strategy or to the budget of business plan cannot be regarded as giving joint control to its owner.[1]

Note

[1] Case IV/M.295 — SITA-RPC/SCORI, of 10 March 1993.

2.3 Common exercise of voting rights

30. Even in the absence of specific veto rights, two or more undertakings acquiring minority shareholdings in another undertaking may obtain joint control. This may be the case where the minority shareholdings together provide the means for controlling the target undertaking. This means that the minority shareholders, together, will have a majority of the voting rights; and

they will act together in exercising these voting rights. This can result from a legally binding agreement to this effect, or it may be established on a *de facto* basis.

31.   The legal means to ensure the common exercise of voting rights can be in the form of a holding company to which the minority shareholders transfer their rights, or an agreement by which they engage themselves to act in the same way (pooling agreement).

32.   Very exceptionally, collective action can occur on a *de facto* basis where strong common interests exist between the minority shareholders to the effect that they would not act against each other in exercising their rights in relation to the joint venture.

33.   In the case of acquisitions of minority shareholdings the prior existence of links between the minority shareholders or the acquisition of the shareholdings by means of concerted action will be factors indicating such a common interest.

34.   In the case where a new joint venture is established, as opposed to the acquisition of minority shareholdings in an already existing company, there is a higher probability that the parent companies are carrying out a deliberate common policy. This is true, in particular, where each parent company provides a contribution to the joint venture which is vital for its operation (e.g., specific technologies, local know-how or supply agreements). In these circumstances the parent companies may be able to operate the joint venture in full cooperation only with each other's agreement on the most important strategic decisions even if there is no express provision for any veto rights. The greater the number of parent companies involved in such a joint venture, however, the likelihood of this situation occurring becomes increasingly remote.

35.   In the absence of strong common interests such as those outlined above, the possibility of changing coalitions between minority shareholders will normally exclude the assumption of joint control. Where there is no stable majority in the decision-making procedure and the majority can on each occasion be any of the various combinations possible amongst the minority shareholders, it cannot be assumed that the minority shareholders will jointly control the undertaking. In this context, it is not sufficient that there are agreements between two or more parties having an equal shareholding in the capital of an undertaking which establish identical rights and powers between the parties. For example, in the case of an undertaking where three shareholders each own a third of the share capital and each elect a third of the members of the Board of Directors, the shareholders do not have joint control since decisions are required to be taken on the basis of a simple majority. The same considerations also apply in more complex structures, for example, where the capital of an undertaking is equally divided between three shareholders and whose Board of Management is composed of 12 members of which two are each elected by shareholders A, B and C, two by A, B and C jointly, and the remaining four by the other eight members. In this case also there is no joint control, and hence no control at all within the meaning of the Merger Regulation.

2.4   *Other considerations related to joint control*

36.   Joint control is not incompatible with the fact that one of the parent companies enjoys specific knowledge of and experience in the business of the

joint venture. In such a case, the other parent company can play a modest or even non-existent role in the daily management of the joint venture where its presence is motivated by considerations of a financial, long-term strategy, brand image or general policy nature. Nevertheless, it must always retain the real possibility of contesting the decision taken by the other parent company, without which there would be sole control.

37.   For joint control to exist, there should not be a casting vote for one parent company only. However, there can be joint control when this casting vote can be exercised only after a series of stages of arbitration and attempts at reconciliation or in a very limited field.[1]

Note
[1]Case IV/M.425 — British Telecom/Banco Santander, of 28 March 1994.

2.5   Joint control for a limited period
38.   Where an operation leads to joint control for a starting-up period[1] but, according to legally binding agreements, this joint control will be converted to sole control by one of the shareholders, the whole operation will normally be considered as an acquisition of sole control.

Note
[1]This starting-up period must not exceed three years. Case IV/M.425 — British Telecom/Banco Santander, ibid.

3.   Control by a single shareholder on the basis of veto rights
39.   An exceptional situation exists where, in the course of an acquisition, only one shareholder is able to veto strategic decisions in an undertaking but this shareholder does not have the power, on his own, to impose such decisions. This situation occurs either where one shareholder holds 50% in an undertaking whilst the remaining 50% is held by two or more minority shareholders, or where there is a quorum required for strategic decisions which in fact confers a veto right upon only one minority shareholder.[1] In these circumstances, a single shareholder possesses the same level of influence as that normally enjoyed by several jointly-controlling shareholders, i.e., the power to block the adoption of strategic decisions. However, this shareholder does not enjoy the powers which are normally conferred on an undertaking with sole control, i.e., the power to impose strategic decisions. Since this shareholder can produce the same deadlock situation as in the normal cases of joint control he acquires decisive influence and therefore control within the meaning of the Merger Regulation.[2]

Notes
[1]Case IV/M.258 — CCIE/GTE, of 25 September 1992, where the veto rights of only one shareholder were exercisable through a member of the board appointed by this shareholder.
[2]Since this shareholder is the only undertaking acquiring a controlling influence only this shareholder is obliged to submit a notification under the Merger Regulation.

4.   Changes in the structure of control
40.   A concentration may also occur where an operation leads to a change in the structure of control. This includes the change from joint control to sole control as well as an increase in the number of shareholders exercising joint control. The principles of determining the existence of a concentration in these

circumstances are set out in detail in the notice on the notion of undertakings concerned.[1]

Note
[1]Paragraphs 30 to 48.

IV. EXCEPTIONS

41.   Article 3(5) sets out three exceptional situations where the acquisition of a controlling interest does not constitute a concentration under the Merger Regulation.

42.   First, the acquisition of securities by companies, the normal activities of which include transactions and dealings for their own account or for the account of others, is not deemed to constitute a concentration if such an acquisition is made in the framework of these businesses and where the securities are held only on a temporary basis (point (a) of Article 3(5)). In order to fall within this exception, the following requirements must be fulfilled:

— the acquiring undertaking must be a credit or other financial institution or insurance company the normal activities of which are described above,

— the securities must be acquired with a view to their resale,

— the acquiring undertaking must not exercise the voting rights with a view to determining the strategic commercial behaviour of the target or must exercise these rights at least only with a view to preparing the total or partial disposal of the undertaking, its assets or securities,

— the acquiring undertaking must dispose of its controlling interest within one year of the date of the acquisition, that is, it must reduce its shareholding within this one-year period at least to a level which no longer confers control. This period, however, may be extended by the Commission where the acquiring undertaking can show that the disposal was not reasonably possible within the one-year period.

43.   Secondly, there is no change of control, and so no concentration within the meaning of the Merger Regulation, where control is acquired by an office-holder according to the law of a Member State relating to liquidation, winding-up, insolvency, cessation of payments, compositions or analogous proceedings (point (b) of Article 3(5));

44.   Thirdly, a concentration does not arise where a financial holding company within the meaning of the Fourth Council Directive 78/660/EEC[1] acquires control, provided that this company exercises its voting rights only to maintain the full value of its investment and does not otherwise determine directly or indirectly the strategic commercial conduct of the controlled undertaking.

45.   In the context of the exceptions under Article 3(5), the question may arise whether a rescue operation constitutes a concentration under the Merger Regulation. A rescue operation typically involves the conversion of existing debt into a new company, through which a syndicate of banks may acquire joint

Notes
[1]OJ No. L222, 14.8.1978, p. 11, as last amended by Directive 84/569/EEC, OJ No. L314, 4.12.1984, p. 28. Article 5(3) of this Directive defines financial holding companies as 'those companies the sole objective of which is to acquire holdings in other undertakings, and to manage such holdings and turn them to profit, without involving themselves directly or indirectly in the management of those undertakings, the aforegoing without prejudice to their rights as shareholders'.

control of the company concerned. Where such an operation meets the criteria for joint control, as outlined above, it will normally be considered to be a concentration.[2] Although the primary intention of the banks is to restructure the financing of the undertaking concerned for its subsequent resale, the exception set out in point (a) of Article 3(5) is normally not applicable to such an operation. This is so because the restructuring programme normally requires the controlling banks to determine the strategic commercial behaviour of the rescued undertaking. Furthermore, it is not normally realistic to transfer a rescued company into a commercially viable entity and to resell it within the permitted one-year period. Moreover, the length of time needed to achieve this aim may be so uncertain that it would be difficult to grant an extension of the disposal period.

Notes

[2]Case IV/M.116 — Kelt/American Express, of 28 August 1991.

V. FINAL

46.   The Commission's interpretation of Article 3 as set out in this notice is without prejudice to the interpretation which may be given by the Court of Justice or the Court of First Instance of the European Communities.

COMMISSION NOTICE ON THE NOTION OF UNDERTAKINGS CONCERNED UNDER COUNCIL REGULATION (EEC) NO. 4064/89 OF 21 DECEMBER 1989 ON THE CONTROL OF CONCENTRATIONS BETWEEN UNDERTAKINGS
(94/C 385/12)

I.   INTRODUCTION

1.   This Commission notice aims at clarifying the Commission's interpretation of the notion of undertakings concerned in Articles 1 and 5 of Regulation (EEC) No. 4064/89,[1] as well as at helping to identify the undertakings concerned in the most typical situations which have arisen in cases dealt with by the Commission to date. The principles set out in this notice will be followed and further developed by the Commission's practice in individual cases.

2.   According to Article 1 of the Merger Regulation, this Regulation only applies to operations that satisfy a double condition. First, several undertakings must merge, or one or more undertakings must acquire control of the whole or part of other undertakings through the proposed operation, which must qualify as concentrations within the meaning of Article 3 of the Regulation. Secondly, those undertakings must meet the three turnover thresholds set out in Article 1.

3.   From the point of view of determining jurisdiction, the undertakings concerned are, broadly speaking, the actors in the transaction in so far as they are the merging, or acquiring and acquired parties; in addition, their total aggregate economic size in terms of turnover will be decisive to determine whether the thresholds are fulfilled. The concept of undertakings concerned is used only for the purposes of determining jurisdiction, as the Commission's

Note

[1]Council Regulation (EEC) No. 4064/89 of 21 December 1989 on the control of concentrations between undertakings (hereafter referred to as 'the Merger Regulation'), OJ No. L395, 30.12.1989, p. 1, corrected version OJ No. L257, 21.9.1990.

assessment of the competitive impact of the operation on the market place will then focus not only on the activities of those undertakings concerned party to the concentration, but also on the activities of the groups to which these undertakings belong.

4.   The Commission's interpretation of Articles 1 and 5 with respect to the notion of undertakings concerned is without prejudice to the interpretation which may be given by the Court of Justice or by the Court of First Instance of the European Communities.

II.   THE NOTION OF UNDERTAKING CONCERNED

5.   Undertakings concerned are the direct participants in a merger or acquisition of control. In this respect, Article 3(1) of the Merger Regulation provides that:

A concentration shall be deemed to arise where:

    (a)   two or more previously independent undertakings merge, or

    (b)   — one or more persons already controlling at least one undertaking, or

    — one or more undertakings

acquire, whether by purchase of securities or assets, by contract or by any other means, direct or indirect control of the whole or parts of one or more undertakings.

6.   In the case of a merger, the undertakings concerned will be the undertakings that are merging.

7.   In the remaining cases, it is the concept of 'acquiring control' that will determine which are the undertakings concerned. On the acquiring side, there can be one or several companies acquiring sole or joint control. On the acquired side, there can be one or more companies as a whole or parts thereof, when only one of their subsidiaries or some of their assets are the subject of the transaction. As a general rule, each of these companies will be an undertaking concerned within the meaning of the Merger Regulation. However, the particular features of specific transactions require a certain refinement of this principle, as will be seen below when analysing different possible scenarios.

8.   In those concentrations other than mergers or the setting up of new joint ventures, i.e., in cases of sole or joint acquisition of pre-existing companies or part of them, there is an important party to the agreement that gives rise to the operation who is to be ignored when identifying the undertakings concerned: the seller. Although it is clear that the operation cannot proceed without its consent, its role ends when the transaction is completed since, by definition, from the moment the seller has relinquished all control over the company, its links with it disappear. Where the seller retains joint control with the acquiring company (or companies) it will be considered as one of the undertakings concerned.

9.   Once the undertakings concerned have been identified in a given transaction, their turnover for the purposes of determining jurisdiction should be calculated according to the rules set out in Article 5 of the Merger Regulation.[1] One of the main provisions of Article 5 is that where the

Note

[1]The rules for calculating turnover in accordance with Article 5 are detailed in the Commission Notice on Calculation of Turnover.

undertaking concerned belongs to a group, the turnover of the whole group should be included in the calculation. All references to the turnover of the undertakings concerned in Article 1 should be therefore understood as the turnover of their entire respective groups.

10.   The same can be said with repect to the substantive appraisal of the impact of a concentration in the market place. When Article 2 of the Merger Regulation provides that the Commission shall take into account 'the market position of the undertakings concerned and their economic and financial power', this includes the groups to which they belong.

11.   It is important not to confuse the concept of undertakings concerned under Articles 1 and 5, with those other terms used in the Merger Regulation and in the Implementing Regulation[2] in referring to the various undertakings which may be involved in a procedure. These other notions are notifying parties, other involved parties, third parties and parties who may be subject to fines or periodic penalty payments. They are defined in Section III of the Implementing Regulation, along with their respective rights and duties.

Note
[2]Commission Regulation (EC) No. 3384/94 of 21 December 1994 on the notifications, time limits and hearings provided for in Council Regulation (EEC) No. 4064/89 (hereinafter referred to as the 'Implementing Regulation') [OJ No. L377, 31.12.1994].

III.   IDENTIFYING THE UNDERTAKINGS CONCERNED IN DIFFERENT TYPES OF OPERATIONS

1.   Mergers

12.   In a merger, several previously independent companies come together to create a new company or, while remaining separate legal entities, to create a single economic unit. As mentioned earlier, the undertakings concerned are each of the merging entities.

2.   Acquisition of sale control

2.1   *Acquisition of sole control of the whole company*

13.   Acquisition of sole control of the whole company is the most straightforward case of acquisition of control; the undertakings concerned will be the acquiring company and the acquired or target company.

2.2   *Acquisition of sale control of part of a company*

14.   The first subparagraph of Article 5(2) of the Merger Regulation stipulates that when the operation concerns the acquisition of parts of one or more undertakings, only those parts which are the subject of the transaction shall be taken into account with regard to the seller. The concept of 'parts' is to be understood as one or more separate legal entities (such as subsidiaries), internal subdivisions within the seller (such as a division or unit), or specific assets which in themselves could constitute a business (e.g., in certain cases brands or licences) to which a market turnover can clearly be attributed. In this case, the undertakings concerned will be the acquirer and the acquired part(s) of the target company.

15.   The second subparagrph of Article 5(2) includes a special provision on staggered operations or follow-up deals, whereby if several acquisitions of parts by the same purchaser from the same seller occur within a two-year period, these transactions shall be treated as one and the same operation arising

on the date of the last transaction. In this case, the undertakings concerned are the acquirer and the different acquired part(s) of the target company taken as a whole.

2.3   Acquisition of sole control of previously reduced or enlarged companies

16.   The undertakings concerned are the acquiring company and the target company(ies), in their configuration at the date of the operation.

17.   The Commission bases itself on the configuration of the undertakings concerned at the date of the event triggering the obligation to notify under Article 4(1) of the Merger Regulation, namely the conclusion of the agreement, the announcement of the public bid, or the acquisition of a controlling interest. If the target company has divested an entity or closed a business prior to the date of the event triggering notification or where such a divestment or closure is a pre-condition for the operation,[1] then sales of the divested entity or closed business would not be included when calculating turnover. Conversely if the target company has acquired an entity prior to the date of the event triggering notification, the sales of the latter would be added.[2]

Notes
[1]See Judgment of the Court of First Instance of 24 March 1994 in Case T-3/93 — *Air France* v *Commission* (not yet published).
[2]The calculation of turnover in the case of acquisitions or divestments subsequently to the date of the last audited accounts is dealt with the Commission Notice on Calculation of Turnover, paragraph 27.

2.4   Acquisition of sole control through a subsidiary of a group

18.   Where the target company is acquired by a group through one of its subsidiaries, the undertakings concerned for the purpose of calculating turnover are the target company and the acquiring subsidiary. However, regarding the actual notification, this can be made by the subsidiary concerned or by its parent company.

19.   All the companies within a group (parent companies, subsidiaries, etc.) constitute a single economic entity, and therefore there can only be one undertaking concerned within the one group — i.e., the subsidiary and the parent company cannot each be considered as separate undertakings concerned, either for the purposes of ensuring that the threshold requirements are fulfilled (for example, if the target company does not meet the ECU 250 million Community-turnover threshold), or that they are not (for example if a group was split into two companies each with a Community turnover below ECU 250 million).

20.   However, even though there can only be one undertaking concerned within a group, Article 5(4) of the Merger Regulation provides that it is the turnover of the whole group to which the undertaking concerned belongs that will be included in the threshold calculations.[1]

Note
[1]The calculation of turnover in the case of company groups is dealt with in the Commission Notice on Calculation of Turnover, paragraphs 36 to 42.

3.   Acquisition of joint control

3.1   Acquisition of joint control of a newly-created company

21.   In the case of acquisition of joint control of a newly-created company, the undertakings concerned are each of the companies acquiring control of the

newly set-up joint venture (which, as it does not yet exist, cannot yet be considered as an undertaking concerned and furthermore has no turnover of its own yet).

3.2 Acquisition of joint control of a pre-existing company

22.   In the case of acquisition of joint control of a pre-existing company or business,[1] the undertakings concerned are each of the companies acquiring joint control on the one hand, and the pre-existing acquired company on the other.

23.   Where the pre-existing company was under the sole control of one company and one or several new shareholders acquire joint control but the initial parent company remains, the undertakings concerned are each of the jointly-controlling companies (including this initial shareholder) and the target company. This situation is a passage from sole to joint control. In so far as sole control and joint control have a different nature, the Commission has consistently considered that passing from one type of control to another normally constitutes a concentration.

Note
[1] I.e., two or more companies (companies A, B, etc.) acquire a pre-existing company (company X). For changes in the shareholding in cases of joint control of an existing joint venture see Section III.6.

3.3 Acquisition of joint control in order to split assets immediately

24.   In the case where several undertakings come together solely for the purpose of acquiring another company and agree to divide up the acquired assets according to a pre-existing plan immediately upon completion of the transaction, there is no effective concentration of economic power between the acquirers and the target company as the assets acquired are only jointly held and controlled for a 'legal instant'. This type of acquisition in order to split assets up immediately will in fact be considered as several operations, whereby each of the acquiring companies acquires its relevant part of the target company. For each of these operations, the undertakings concerned will therefore be the acquiring company, and that part of the target which it is acquiring (just as if there was an acquisition of sole control of part of a company).

25.   This scenario is referred to in the recital 24 of the Merger Regulation, which stipulates that the Merger Regulation applies to agreements whose sole object is to divide up the assets acquired immediately after the acquisition.

4.   Acquisition of control by a joint venture

26.   In transactions where a joint venture acquires control of another company, the question arises whether or not, from the point of view of the acquiring party, the joint venture should be taken as a single undertaking concerned (the turnover of which would include the turnover of its parent companies), or whether each of its parent companies should individually be considered as undertakings concerned. In other words, the issue is whether or not to 'lift the corporate veil' of the intermediate undertaking (the vehicle). In principle, the undertaking concerned is the direct participant in the acquisition of control. However, there may be circumstances where companies set up 'shell' companies, which have no or insignificant turnover of their own, or use an existing joint venture which is operating on a different market from that of

the target company in order to carry out acquisitions on behalf of the parent companies. Where the acquired or target company has a Community turnover of less than ECU 250 million the question of determining the undertakings concerned may be decisive for jurisdictional purposes.[1] In this type of situation the Commission will look at the economic reality of the operation to determine which are the undertakings concerned.

27.   Where the acquisition is carried out by a full-function joint venture, i.e., a joint venture which has sufficient financial and other resources to operate a business activity on a lasting basis,[2] which is already operating on a market, the Commission will normally consider the joint venture itself and the target company to be the undertakings concerned (and not the joint venture's parent companies).

28.   Conversely, where the joint venture can be regarded as a vehicle for an acquisition by the parent companies, the Commission will consider each of the parent companies themselves to be the undertakings concerned, rather than the joint venture, together with the target company. This is the case in particular where the joint venture is set up especially for the purpose of acquiring the target company, where the joint venture has not yet started to operate, where an existing joint venture has no legal personality or full-function character as referred to above; or where the joint venture is an association of undertakings. The same applies where there are elements which demonstrate that the parent companies are in fact the real players behind the operation. These elements may include a significant involvement by the parent companies themselves in the initiative, organisation and financing of the operation. Moreover, where the acquisition leads to a substantial diversification in the nature of the joint venture's activities this may also indicate that the parent companies are the real players in the operation. This will normally be the case when the joint venture acquires a target company operating on a different product market. In those cases the parent companies should be regarded as undertakings concerned.

29.   In the TNT case,[3] joint control over a joint venture (JVC) was to be acquired by a joint venture (GD NET BV) between five postal administrations and another acquiring company (TNT Ltd) (see below). In this case, the Commission considered that the joint venture GD NET BV was simply a

Notes

[1] The target company hypothetically has an aggregate Community turnover of less than ECU 250 million, and the acquiring parties are two (or more) undertakings, each with a Community turnover exceeding ECU 250 million. If the target is acquired by a 'shell' company set up between the acquiring undertakings, there would be only one company (the 'shell' company) with a Community turnover exceeding ECU 250 million and thus one of the cumulative threshold conditions for Community jurisdiction would fail to be fulfilled (namely, the existence at least two undertakings with a Community turnover exceeding ECU 250 million). Conversely, if instead of acting through a 'shell' company, the acquiring undertakings acquire the target company themselves, then the turnover threshold would be met and the Merger Regulation would apply to this transaction.

[2] The rules determining the full-function nature of a joint venture are contained in the Commission Notice regarding the distinction between concentrative and cooperative joint ventures, paragraphs 13 to 15.

[3] Case IV/M.102 — TNT/Canada Post, DBP Postdienst, La Poste, PTT Post and Sweden Post, of 2 December 1991.

vehicle set up to enable the parent companies (the five postal administrations) to participate in the resulting JVC joint venture in order to facilitate decision-making amongst themselves and to ensure that the parent companies spoke and acted as one; this configuration would ensure that the parent companies could exercise a decisive influence with the other acquiring company, TNT, over the resulting joint venture JVC and would avoid the situation where that other acquirer could exercise sole control because of the postal administrations' inability to reach a unified position on any decision.

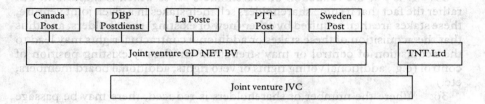

5. Passage from joint control to sole control

30. In the case of passage from joint control to sole control, one shareholder acquires the stake previously held by the other shareholder(s). In the case of two shareholders, each of them has joint control over the entire joint venture, and not sole control over 50% of the joint venture; hence the sale of all of his shares by one shareholder to the other does not lead the sole remaining shareholder to pass from sole control over 50% to sole control over 100% of the joint venture, but rather to pass from joint control to sole control of the entire company (which, subsequently to the operation, ceases to be a 'joint' venture).

31. In this situation, the undertakings concerned are the remaining (acquiring) shareholder and the joint venture. As is case for any other seller, the 'exiting' shareholder is not an undertaking concerned.

32. The ICI/Tioxide case[1] was precisely such a passage from joint (50/50) control to sole control. The Commission considered that '. . . decisive influence exercised solely is substantially different to decisive influence exercised jointly, since the latter has to take into account the potentially different interests of the other party or parties concerned ... By changing the quality of decisive influence exercised by ICI on Tioxide, the transaction will bring about a durable change of the structure of the concerned parties . . .'. In this case, the undertakings concerned were held to be ICI (as acquirer) and Tioxide as a whole (as acquired), but not the seller Cookson.

Note
[1] Case IV/M.023 — ICI/Tioxide, of 28 November 1990.

6. Change in the shareholding in cases of joint control of an existing joint venture

33. The decisive element in assessing in the shareholding of a company is whether the operation leads to a change in the quality of control. The Commission assesses each operation on a case-by-case basis, but in certain hypotheses, there will be a presumption that the given operation leads, or respectively does not lead, to such a change in the quality of control, and thus constitutes a notifiable concentration.

34.   A distinction must be made according to the circumstances of the change in the shareholding; first, one or more existing shareholder(s) can exit; secondly, one or more new additional shareholder(s) can enter, and thirdly, one or more existing shareholder(s) can be replaced by one or more new shareholder(s).

6.1   *Reduction in the number of shareholders leading to passage from joint to sole control*

35.   It is not the reduction of shareholders *per se* which is important, but rather the fact that if some shareholders sell their stakes in a given joint venture, these stakes are then acquired by other (new or existing) shareholders, and thus that the acquisition of these stakes or additional contractual rights may lead to the acquisition of control or may strengthen an already existing position of control (e.g., additional voting rights or veto rights, additional board members, etc.).

36.   Where the number of shareholders is reduced, there may be passage from joint control to sole control (see Section III.5. also), in which case the remaining shareholder acquires sole control of the company. The undertakings concerned will be the remaining (acquiring) shareholder and the acquired company (previously the joint venture).

37.   In addition to the shareholder with sole control of the company, there may be other shareholders, for example with minority stakes, but who do not have a controlling interest in the company; these shareholders are not undertakings concerned as they do not exercise control.

6.2   *Reduction in the number of shareholders not leading to passage from joint to sole control*

38.   Where the operation involves a reduction in the number of shareholders having joint control, without leading to the passage from joint to sole control and without any new entry or substitution of shareholders acquiring control (see Section III.6.3.), the proposed transaction will normally be presumed not to lead to a change in the quality of control, and therefore not be a notifiable concentration. This would be the case where, for example, five shareholders initially have equal stakes of 20% each, and where after the operation, one shareholder would exit, and the remaining four shareholders would each have equal stakes of 25%.

39.   However, this situation would be different where there is a significant change in the quality of control such as where the reduction of shareholders gives the remaining shareholders additional veto rights or additional board members which create a new acquisition of control by at least one of the shareholders, either through the application of the existing or a new shareholders' agreement. In this case, the undertakings concerned will be each of the remaining shareholders which exercise joint control and the joint venture. In Avesta II,[1] the fact that the number of major shareholders decreased from four to three led to one of the remaining shareholders acquiring negative veto rights (which it had not previously enjoyed) because of the provisions of the

Notes
[1] Case IV/M.452 — Avesta II, of 9 June 1994.

shareholders' agreement which remained in force.[2] This acquisition of full veto rights was considered by the Commission to represent a change in the quality of control.

Note
[2]In this case, a shareholder party to the shareholders' agreement sold its stake of approximately 7%. As the exiting shareholder had shared veto rights with another shareholder who remained, and as the shareholders' agreement remained unchanged, the remaining shareholder now acquired full veto rights.

6.3 *Any other changes in the composition of the shareholding*

40. Finally, in the case where following changes in the shareholding, one or more shareholders acquire control, the operation will constitute a notifiable operation as there is a presumption that the operation will normally lead to a change in the quality of control.

41. Irrespective of whether the number of shareholders decreases, increases or remains the same subsequent to the operation, this acquisition of control can take any of the following forms:

— entry of new shareholder(s) (either leading to the passage from sole to joint control, or situation of joint control both before and after the operation);

— acquisition of a controlling interest by minority shareholder(s) (either leading to the passage from sole to joint control, or situation of joint control both before and after the operation);

— substitution of shareholder(s) (situation of joint control both before and after the operation).

42. The question is whether the undertakings concerned are the joint venture and the new shareholder(s) who would together acquire control of a pre-existing company, or whether all of the shareholders (existing and new) are to be considered as undertakings concerned acquiring control of a new joint venture. This question is particularly relevant when there is no express agreement between one (or several) of the existing shareholders and the new shareholder(s), who might only have had an agreement with the 'exiting' shareholder(s), i.e., the seller(s).

43. A change in the shareholding through the entry or substitution of shareholders is considered as leading to a change in the quality of control. This is because the entry of a new parent company, or the substitution of one parent company for another, is not comparable to the simple acquisition of part of a business as it implies a change in the nature and quality of control of the whole joint venture, even when, both before and after the operation, joint control is exercised by a given number of shareholders.

44. The Commission therefore considers that the undertakings concerned in cases where there are changes in the shareholding are the shareholders (both existing and new) who exercise joint control and the joint venture itself. As mentioned earlier, non-controlling shareholders are not undertakings concerned.

45. An example of such a change in the shareholding is the Synthomer/Yule Catto case,[1] in which one of two parent companies with joint control over the pre-existing joint venture was replaced by a new parent company. Both parent companies with joint control (the existing one and the new one) and the joint venture were considered as undertakings concerned.

Note
[1]Case IV/M.376 — Synthomer/Yule Catto, of 22 October 1993.

7. 'Demergers' and the break-up of companies

46. When two undertakings merge or set up a joint venture, then subsequently de-merge or break up their joint venture, and the assets[1] are split between the 'demerging' parties differently from under the original configuration, there will normally be more than one acquisition of control (see the Annex).

47. For example, undertakings A and B merge and then subsequently demerge with a new asset configuarion. There will be the acquisition by undertaking A of various assets (which may have been previously owned by itself, as well as assets previously owned by undertaking B and assets jointly acquired by the entity resulting from the merger), with similar acquisitions for undertaking B. Similarly, a break-up of a joint venture can be considered as the passage from joint control over the joint venture's entire assets to sole control over the divided assets (see Solvay-Laporte/Interox).[2]

48. A break-up of a company in this way is 'asymmetrical'. For such a demerger, the undertakings concerned (for each break-up operation) will be, on the one hand, the original parties to the merger and on the other, the assets that each original party is acquiring. For the break-up of a joint venture, the undertakings concerned (for each break-up operation) will be, on the one hand, the original parties to the joint venture, each as acquirer, and on the other, that part of the joint venture that each original party is acquiring.

Notes

[1] By 'assets', reference is made to specific assets which in themselves could constitute a business (e.g., a subsidiary, a division of a company, in some cases brands or licences, etc.) to which a market turnover can clearly be attributed.

[2] Case No. IV/M.197 — Solvay-Laporte/Interox, of 30 April 1992.

8. Swaps of Assets[1]

49. In those transactions where two (or more) companies exchange assets, regardless of whether these constitute legal entities or not, each acquisition of control constitutes an independent concentration. Although it is true that both transfers of assets in a swap are usually considered by the parties to be interdependent, that they are often agreed in a single document, and that they may even take place simultaneously, the purpose of the Merger Regulation is to assess the impact of the operation resulting from the acquisition of control by each of the companies. The legal or even economic link between those operations is not sufficient for them to qualify as a single concentration.

50. Hence the undertakings concerned will for each property transfer be the acquiring companies, and the acquired companies or assets.

Note

[1] See footnote 15.

9. Acquisitions of control by individual persons

51. Article 3(1) of the Merger Regulation specifically provides that a concentration shall be deemed to arise, *inter alia*, where 'one or more persons already controlling at least one undertaking' acquire control of the whole or parts of one or more undertakings. This text indicates that acquisitions of control by individuals will only bring about a lasting change in the structure of the companies concerned if those individuals carry out economic activities of their own. The Commission considers that the undertakings concerned are the

target company and the individual acquirer (with the turnover of the undertaking(s) controlled by that individual being included in the calculation of turnover).

52.   This was the view taken in the Commission decision in the Asko/Jacobs/Adia case,[1] where Asko, a German holding company with substantial retailing assets, and Mr Jacobs, a private Swiss investor, acquired joint control of Adia, a Swiss company active mainly in personnel services. Mr Jacobs was considered to be an undertaking concerned because of the economic interests he held in the industrial chocolate, sugar confectionery and coffee sectors.

Note
[1]Case IV/M.082 — Asko/Jacobs/Adia, of 16 May 1991.

10.   Management buy-outs

53.   An acquisition of control of a company by its own managers is also an acquisition by individuals, and what has been said above is therefore also applicable here. However, the management of the company may pool its interests through a 'vehicle company', so that it acts with a single voice and also to facilitate decision making. Such a vehicle company may be, but is not necessarily, an undertaking concerned. The general rule on acquisitions of control by a joint venture applies here (see Section III.4.).

54.   With or without a vehicle company, the management may also look for investors in order to finance the operation. Very often, the rights granted to these investors according to their shareholding may be such that control within the meaning of Article 3 of the Merger Regulation will be conferred on them and not on the management itself, which may simply enjoy minority rights. In the CWB/Goldman Sachs/Tarkett decision,[1] the two companies managing the investment funds taking part in the transaction were in fact those acquiring joint control, and not the managers.

Note
[1]Case IV/M.395 — CWB/Goldman Sachs/Tarkett, of 21 February 1994.

11.   Acquisition of control by a State-owned company

55.   In those situations where a state-owned company merges with or acquires control of another company controlled by the same State,[1] the question arises as to whether these transactions really constitute concentrations within the meaning of Article 3 of the Regulation or rather internal restructuring operations of the 'public sector group of companies'.[2] In this respect, recital 12 of the Merger Regulation sets forth the principle of non-discrimination between the public and the private sectors and declares that 'in the public sector, calculation of the turnover of an undertaking concerned in a concentration needs, therefore, to take account of undertakings making up an economic unit with an independent power of decision, irrespective of the way in which their capital is held or of the rules of administrative supervision applicable to them'.

56.   A merger or acquisition of control arising between two companies owned by the same State may constitute a concentration and, if it does, both of

Notes
[1]By 'State', reference is made to any legal public entity, i.e., Member States but also regional or local public entities such as provinces, departments, Länder, etc.
[2]See also Commission Notice on the notion of a concentration, paragraph 8.

them will qualify as undertakings concerned, since the mere fact that two companies are both owned by the same State does not necessarily mean that they belong to the same 'group'. Indeed, the decisive issue will be whether or not these companies are both part of the same industrial holding and are subject to a certain coordinated strategy. This was the approach taken in the SGS/Thomson decision.[3]

Note

[3]Case IV/M.216 — CEA Industrie/France Telecom/Finmeccanica/SGS-Thomson, of 22 February 1993.

ANNEX
'DEMERGERS' AND BREAK-UP OF COMPANIES[1]

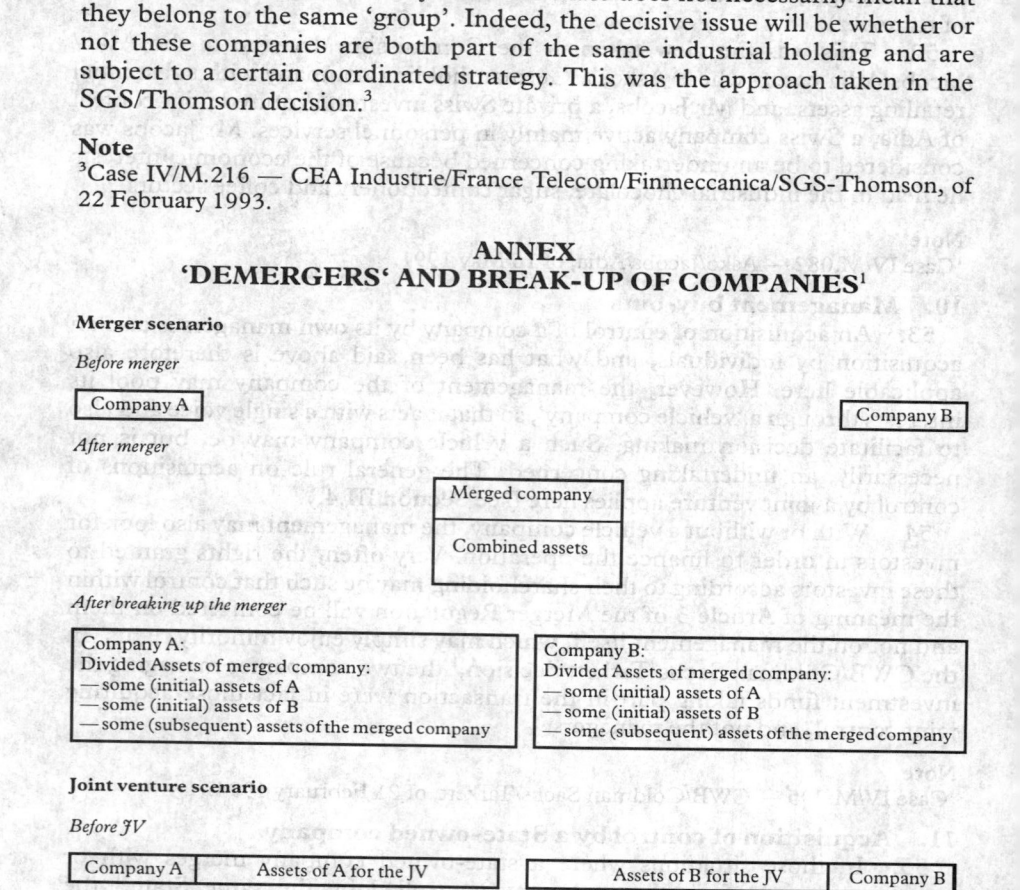

Merger scenario

Before merger

Company A   Company B

After merger

Merged company

Combined assets

After breaking up the merger

Company A:
Divided Assets of merged company:
— some (initial) assets of A
— some (initial) assets of B
— some (subsequent) assets of the merged company

Company B:
Divided Assets of merged company:
— some (initial) assets of A
— some (initial) assets of B
— some (subsequent) assets of the merged company

Joint venture scenario

Before JV

Company A   Assets of A for the JV   Assets of B for the JV   Company B

After JV

Company A   Joint venture   Company B

Combined assets

After breaking up the JV

Company A   Divided Assets of joint venture
             —some (initial) assets of A
             —some (initial) assets of B
             —some (subsequent) assets of the JV

Company B   Divided Assets of joint venture
             —some (initial) assets of A
             —some (initial) assets of B
             —some (subsequent) assets of the JV

Note

[1]By 'assets', reference is made to specific assets which in themselves could constitute a business (e.g., a subsidiary, a division of a company, in certain cases brands or licences) to which a market turnover can clearly be attributed.

COMMISSION NOTICE ON CALCULATION OF TURNOVER UNDER COUNCIL REGULATION (EEC) NO. 4064/89 OF 21 DECEMBER 1989 ON THE CONTROL OF CONCENTRATIONS BETWEEN UNDERTAKINGS[1]
[94/C 385/21]

1.   The purpose of this notice is to expand upon the text of Articles 1 and 5 of Council Regulation (EEC) No. 4064/89 (hereinafter referred to as 'the Merger Regulation') and in so doing to elucidate certain procedural and practical questions which have caused doubt or difficulty.

2.   This notice is based on the experience gained by the Commission in applying the Merger Regulation to date. The principles it sets out will be followed and further developed by the Commission's practice in individual cases.

3.   The Merger Regulation has a two-fold test for Commission jurisdiction. One test is that the transaction must be a concentration within the meaning of Article 3.[2] The second comprises the three turnover thresholds contained in Article 1 and which are designed to identify those transactions which have an impact upon the Community and can be deemed to be of 'Community interest'. In particular, the world-wide turnover threshold is intended to measure the overall dimension of the undertakings concerned, the Community turnover threshold seeks to determine whether they carry on a minimum level of activities in the Community and the two-thirds rule aims to exclude purely domestic transactions from Community jurisdiction. Turnover is used as a proxy for the economic resources and activity being combined in a concentration, and it is allocated geographically to reflect the geographic distribution of these resources and activity.

4.   The thresholds as such are designed to establish jurisdiction and not to assess the market position of the parties to the concentration nor the impact of the operation. In so doing they include turnover derived from, and thus the resources devoted to, all areas of activity of the parties, and not just those directly involved in the concentration. Article 1 of the Merger Regulation sets out the thresholds to be used to determine a concentration of 'Community dimension' while Article 5 explains how turnover should be calculated.

5.   The fact that the thresholds of Article 1 of the Merger Regulation are purely quantitative, since they are only based on turnover calculation instead of market share or other criteria, shows that their aim is to provide a simple and objective mechanism that can be easily handled by the companies involved in a merger in order to determine if their transaction is of Community dimension and therefore notifiable.

6.   The decisive issue for Article 1 of the Merger Regulation is to measure the economic strength of the undertakings concerned as reflected in their respective turnover figures, regardless of the sector where such turnover was achieved and of whether those sectors will be at all affected by the transaction in question. The Merger Regulation has thereby given priority to the determination of the overall economic and financial resources that are being

Notes
[1]OJ No. L395, 30.12.1989, p. 1, corrected version OJ No. L257, 21.9.1990.
[2]The concept of concentration is defined in the Notice on 'the notion of concentration'.

combined through the merger in order to decide whether the latter is of Community interest.

7. In this context, it is clear that turnover should reflect as accurately as possible the economic strength of the undertakings involved in a transaction. This is the purpose of the set of rules contained in Article 5 of the Merger Regulation which are designed to ensure that the resulting figures are a true representation of economic reality.

8. The Commission's interpretation of Articles 1 and 5 with respect to calculation of turnover is without prejudice to the interpretation which may be given by the Court of Justice or the Court of First Instance of the European Communities.

I. 'ACCOUNTING' CALCULATION OF TURNOVER

1. Turnover as a reflection of activity

1.1 *The concept of turnover*

9. The concept of turnover as used in Article 5 of the Merger Regulation refers explicitly to 'the amounts derived from the sale of products and the provision of services'. Sale, as a reflection of the undertaking's activity, is thus the essential criterion for calculating turnover, whether for products or the provision of services. 'Amounts derived from sale' generally appear in company accounts under the heading 'sales'.

10. In the case of products, turnover can be determined without difficulty, namely by identifying each commercial act involving a transfer of ownership.

11. In the case of services, the factors to be taken into account in calculating turnover are much more complex, since the commercial act involves a transfer of 'value'.

12. Generally speaking, the method of calculating turnover in the case of services does not differ from that used in the case of products: the Commission takes into consideration the total amount of sales. Where the service provided is sold directly by the provider to the customer, the turnover of the undertaking concerned consists of the total amount of sales for the provision of services in the last financial year.

13. Because of the complexity of the service sector, this general principle may have to be adapted to the specific conditions of the service provided. Thus, in certain sectors of activity (such as tourism and advertising), the service may be sold through the intermediary of other suppliers. Because of the diversity of such sectors, many different situations may arise. For example, the turnover of a service undertaking which acts as an intermediary may consist solely of the amount of commissions which it receives.

14. Similarly, in a number of areas such as credit, financial services and insurance, technical problems in calculating turnover arise which will be dealt with in section III.

1.2 *Ordinary activities*

15. Article 5(1) states that the amounts to be included in the calculation of turnover must correspond to the 'ordinary activities' of the undertakings concerned.

16. With regard to aid granted to undertakings by public bodies, any aid relating to one of the ordinary activities of an undertaking concerned is liable to be included in the calculation of turnover if the undertaking is itself the

recipient of the aid and if the aid is directly linked to the sale of products and the provision of services by the undertaking and is therefore reflected in the price.[1] For example, aid towards the consumption of a product allows the manufacturer to sell at a higher price than that actually paid by consumers.

17.   With regard to services, the Commission looks at the undertaking's ordinary activities involved in establishing the resources required for providing the service. In its Decision in the Accor/Wagons-Lits case,[2] the Commission decided to take into account the item 'other operating proceeds' included in Wagons-Lits' profit and loss account. The Commission considered that the components of this item which incuded certain income from its car-hire activities were derived from the sale of products and the provision of services by Wagons-Lits and were part of its ordinary activities.

Notes
[1] See Case IV/M.156 — Cereol/Continentale Italiana of 27 November 1991. In this case, the Commission excluded Community aid from the calculation of turnover because the aid was not intended to support the sale of products manufactured by one of the undertakings involved in the merger, but the producers of the raw materials (grain) used by the undertaking, which specialised in the crushing of grain.
[2] Case IV/M.126 — Accor/Wagons-Lits, of 28 April 1992.

2.   'Net' turnover
18.   The turnover to be taken into account is 'net' turnover, after deduction of a number of components specified in the Regulation. The Commission's aim is to adjust turnover in such a way as to enable it to decide on the real economic weight of the undertaking.

2.1   *The deduction of rebates and taxes*
19.   Article 5(1) provides for the 'deduction of sales rebates and of value added tax and other taxes directly related to turnover'. The deductions thus relate to business components (sales rebates) and tax components (value added tax and other taxes directly related to turnover).

20.   'Sales rebates' should be taken to mean all rebates or discounts which are granted by the undertakings during their business negotiations with their customers and which have a direct influence on the amounts of sales.

21.   As regards the deduction of taxes, the Merger Regulation refers to VAT and 'other taxes directly related to turnover'. As far as VAT is concerned, its deduction does not in general pose any problem. The concept of 'taxes directly related to turnover' is a clear reference to indirect taxation since it is directly linked to turnover, such as, for example, taxes on alcoholic beverages.

2.2   *The deduction of 'internal' turnover*
22.   The first subparagraph of Article 5(1) states that 'the aggregate turnover of an undertaking concerned shall not include the sale of products or the provision of services between any of the undertakings referred to in paragraph 4', i.e., those which have links with the undertaking concerned (essentially parent companies or subsidiaries).

23.   The aim is to exclude the proceeds of business dealings within a group so as to take account of the real economic weight of each entity. Thus, the 'amounts' taken into account by the Merger Regulation reflect only the transactions which take place between the group of undertakings on the one hand and third parties on the other.

3.   Adjustment of turnover calculation rules for the different types of operations

3.1   *The general rule*

24.   According to Article 5(1) of the Merger Regulation 'aggregate turnover within the meaning of Article 1(2) shall comprise the amounts derived by the undertakings concerned in the preceding financial year from the sale of products and the provision of services . . .'. The basic principle is thus that for each undertaking concerned the turnover to be taken into account is the turnover of the closest financial year to the date of the transaction.

25.   This provision shows that since there are usually no audited accounts of the year ending the day before the transaction, the closest representation of a whole year of activity of the company in question is the one given by the turnover figures of the most recent financial year.

26.   The Commission seeks to base itself upon the most accurate and reliable figures available. As a general rule therefore, the Commission will refer to audited or other definitive accounts. However, in cases where major differences between the Community's accounting standards and those of a non-member country are observed, the Commission may consider it necessary to restate these accounts in accordance with the Community standards in respect of turnover. The Commission is, in any case, reluctant to rely on provisional, management or any other form of provisional accounts in any but exceptional circumstances (see the next paragraph). Where a concentration takes place within the first months of the year and audited accounts are not yet available for the most recent financial year, the figures to be taken into account are those relating to the previous year. Where there is a major divergence between the two sets of accounts, and in particular, when the final draft figures for the most recent years are available, the Commission may decide to take those draft figures into account.

27.   Notwithstanding paragraph 26, an adjustment must always be made to account for acquisitions or divestments subsequent to the date of the audited accounts. This is necessary if the true resources being concentrated are to be identified. Thus if a company disposes of a subsidiary or closes a factory at any time before the signature of the final agreement or the announcement of the public bid or the acquisition of a controlling interest bringing about a concentration, or where such a divestment or closure is a pre-condition for the operation[1] the turnover generated by that subsidiary or factory must be subtracted from the turnover of the notifying party as shown in its last audited accounts. Conversely, the turnover generated by assets of which control has been acquired subsequent to the preparation of the most recent audited accounts must be added to a company's turnover for notification purposes.

28.   Other factors that may affect turnover on a temporary basis such as a decrease of the orders of the product or a slow-down of the production process within the period prior to the transaction will be ignored for the purposes of calculating turnover. No adjustment to the definitive accounts will be made to incorporate them.

Note

[1] See Judgment of 24 March 1994 of the Court of First Instance in Case T-3/93 — *Air France* v *Commission* (not yet published).

29. Regarding the geographical allocation of turnover, since audited accounts often do not provide a geographical breakdown of the sort required by the Merger Regulation, the Commission will rely on the best figures available provided by the companies in accordance with the rule laid down in Article 5(1) of the Merger Regulation (see Section II.1).

3.2 Acquisitions of parts of companies

30. Article 5(2) of the Merger Regulation provides that 'where the concentration consists in the acquisition of parts, whether or not constituted as legal entities, of one or more undertakings only the turnover relating to the parts which are the subject of the transcation shall be taken into account with regard to the seller or sellers'.

31. This provision states that when the acquiror does not purchase an entire group, but only one or part of its businesses, whether or not constituted as a subsidiary, only the turnover of the part effectively acquired should be included in the turnover calculation. In fact, although in legal terms the seller as a whole (with all its subsidiaries) is an essential party to the transaction, since the sale-purchaser agreement cannot be concluded without him, he plays no role one the agreement has been implemented. The possible impact of the transaction in the marketplace will exclusively depend on the combination of the economic and financial resources that are the subject of a property transfer with those of the acquiror and not on the part of the seller who remains independent.

3.3 Suggested operations

32. Sometimes certain successive transactions are only individual steps within a wider strategy between the same parties. Considering each transaction alone, even if only for determining jurisdiction, would imply ignoring economic reality. At the same time, whereas none of these suggested operations may be designed in this fashion because they will better meet the needs of the parties, it is not excluded that others could be structured like this in order to circumvent the application of the Merger Regulation.

33. The Merger Regulation has foreseen these scenarios in Article 5(2), second subparagraph, which provides that 'two or more transactions within the meaning of the first subparagraph which take place within a two-year period between the same persons or undertakings shall be treated as one and the same concentration arising on the date of the last transaction'.

34. In practical terms, this provision means that if company A buys a subsidiary of company B that represents 50% of the overall activity of B and one year later it acquires the other subsidiary (the remaining 50% of B), both transactions will be taken as one. Assuming that each of the subsidiaries only attained a turnover in the Community of ECU 200 million, the first transaction would not be notifiable. However, since the second takes place within the two-year-period, both have to be notified as a single transaction when the second occurs.

35. The importance of the provision is that previous transactions (within two years) become notifiable with the most recent transactions once the thresholds are cumulatively met.

3.4 *Turnover of groups*

36. When an undertaking concerned in a concentration within the meaning of Article 1 of the Merger Regulation[1] belongs to a group, the turnover of the group as a whole is to be taken into account in order to determine whether the thresholds are met. The aim is again to capture the total volume of the economic resources that are being combined through the operation.

37. The Merger Regulation does not define the concept of group in abstract terms but focuses on whether the companies have the right to manage the undertaking's affairs as the yardstick to determine which of the companies that have some direct or indirect links with an undertaking concerned should be regarded as part of its group.

38. Article 5(4) of the Merger Regulation provides the following:
'Without prejudice to paragraph 2 (acquisitions of parts) the aggregate turnover of an undertaking concerned within the meaning of Article 1(2) shall be calculated by adding together the respective turnovers of the following:

    (a) the undertaking concerned;

    (b) those undertakings in which the undertaking concerned directly or indirectly:

      — owns more than half the capital or business assets, or

      — has the power to exercise more than half the voting rights, or

      — has the power to appoint more than half the members of the supervisory board, the administrative board or bodies legally representing the undertakings, or

      — has the right to manage the undertakings' affairs;

    (c) those undertakings which have in the undertaking concerned the rights or powers listed in (b);

    (d) those undertakings in which an undertaking as referred to in (c) has the rights or powers listed in (b);

    (e) those undertakings in which two or more undertakings as referred to in (a) to (d) jointly have the rights or powers listed in (b).'

This means that the turnover of the company directly involved in the transaction (subparagraph (a)) should include its subsidiaries (b), its parent companies (c), the other subsidiaries of its parent companies (d) and any other undertaking jointly controlled by two or more of the companies belonging to the group (e). A graphic example is as follows:

Note
[1]See Commission Notice on the notion of undertakings concerned.

The undertaking concerned and its group:

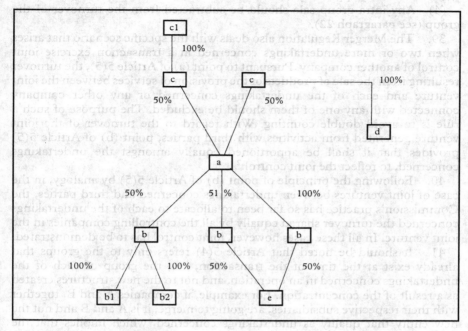

a: The undertaking concerned
b: Is subsidiaries and their own subsidiaries (b1 and b2)
c: Its parent companies and their own parent companies (c1)
d: Other subsidiaries of the parent companies of the undertaking concerned
e: Companies jointly controlled by two (or more) companies of the group

Note: These letters correspond to the relevant subparagraphs of Article 5(4).

Several remarks can be made from this chart:

(1)   As long as the test of control of subparagraph (b) is fulfilled, the whole turnover of the subsidiary in question will be taken into account regardless of the actual shareholding of the controlling company. In the example, the whole turnover of the three subsidiaries (called b) of the undertaking concerned (a) will be included.

(2)   When any of the companies identified as belonging to the group also control others, these should also be incorporated into the calculation. In the example, one of the subsidiaries of a (called b) has in turn its own subsidiaries b1 and b2.

(3)   When two or more companies jointly control the undertaking concerned (a) in the sense that the agreement of each and all of them is needed in order to manage the undertaking's affairs, the turnover of all of them should be included.[1] In the example, the two parent companies (c) of the undertaking concerned (a) would be taken into account as well as their own parent companies (c1 in the example). Although the Merger Regulation does not explicitly mention this rule for those cases where the undertaking concerned is in fact a joint venture, it is inferred from the text of subparagraph (c), which

uses the plural when referring to the parent companies. This interpretation has been consistently applied by the Commission.

(4)   Any intra-group sale should be subtracted from the turnover of the group (see paragraph 22).

39.   The Merger Regulation also deals with the specific scenario that arises when two or more undertakings concerned in a transaction exercise joint control of another company. Pursuant to point (a) of Article 5(5), the turnover resulting from the sale of products or the provision of services between the joint venture and each of the undertakings concerned or any other company connected with any one of them should be excluded. The purpose of such a rule is to avoid double counting. With regard to the turnover of the joint venture generated from activities with third parties, point (b) of Article 5(5) provides that it shall be apportioned equally amongst the undertakings concerned, to reflect the joint control.[2]

40.   Following the principle of point (b) of Article 5(5) by analogy, in the case of joint ventures between undertakings concerned and third parties, the Commission's practice has so far been to allocate to each of the undertakings concerned the turnover shared equally by all the controlling companies in the joint venture. In all these cases however, joint control has to be demonstrated.

41.   It should be noted that Article 5(4) refers only to the groups that already exist at the time of the transaction, i.e., the group of each of the undertakings concerned in an operation, and not to the new structures created as a result of the concentration. For example, if companies A and B, together with their respective subsidiaries, are going to merge, it is A and B and not the new entity that qualify as undertakings concerned, which implies that the turnover of each of the two groups should be calculated independently.

42.   Since the aim of this provision is simply to identify the companies belonging to the existing groups for the purposes of turnover calculation, the test of having the right to manage the undertaking's affairs in Article 5(4) is somewhat different to the test of control set out in Article 3(3), which refers to the acquisition of control carried out by means of the transaction subject to examination. Whereas the former is simpler and easier to prove on the basis of factual evidence, the latter is more demanding because in the absence of an acquisition of control no concentration arises.

Note

[1]See Commission Notice on the notion of undertakings concerned for acquisitions of control by a joint venture (paragraphs 26 to 29).

[2]For example, company A and company B set up a joint venture C. These two parent companies exercise at the same time joint control of company D, although A has 60% and B 40% of the capital. When calculating the turnover of A and B at the time they set up the new joint venture C, the turnover of D with third parties is attributed in equal parts to A and B.

3.5   *Turnover of State-owned companies*

43.   While Article 5(4) sets out the method to determine the economic grouping to which an undertaking concerned belongs for the purpose of calculating turnover, the Article's provisions should be read in conjunction with recital 12 of the Regulation in respect of State-owned enterprises. This recital states that in order to avoid discrimination between the public and private sector, account should be taken 'of undertakings making up an

economic unit with an independent power of decision irrespective of the way in which their capital is held or of the rules of administrative supervision applicable to them'. Thus the mere fact that two companies are both State-owned should not automatically lead to the conclusion that they are part of a group for Article 5 purposes. Rather it should be considered whether there are grounds to consider that both companies constitute an independent economic unit.

44.		Thus where a State-owned company is not part of an overall industrial holding company and is not subject to any coordination with other State-controlled holdings, it should be treated as an independent group for the purposes of Article 5, and the turnover of other companies owned by that State should not be taken into account. Where, however, a Member State's interests are grouped together in holding companies, are managed together, or where for other reasons it is clear that State-owned companies form part of an 'economic unit with an independent power of decision', then the turnover of those businesses should be considered part of the undertaking concerned's group for the purposes of Article 5.

II.   GEOGRAPHICAL ALLOCATION OF TURNOVER

1.   General rule

45.		The second and third thresholds set by Article 1 select cases which have sufficient Community turnover to be of Community interest and which are primarily cross-border in nature. They both require turnover to be allocated geographically to achieve this. The second subparagraph of Article 5(1) provides that the location of turnover is determined by the location of the customer at the time of the transaction.

'Turnover, in the Community or in a Member State, shall comprise products sold and services provided to undertakings or consumers, in the Community or in that Member State as the case may be.'

46.		The reference to 'products sold' and 'services provided' is not intended to discriminate between goods and services by focusing on where the sale takes place in the case of goods but the place where a service is provided (which might be different from where the service was sold) in the case of services. In both cases turnover should be attributed to the place where the customer is located because that is, in most circumstances, where a deal was made, where the turnover for the supplier in question was generated and where competition with alternative suppliers took place.[1] The second subparagraph of Article 5(1) does not focus on where a good or service is enjoyed or the benefit of the good or service derived. In the case of a mobile good, a motor car may well be driven across Europe by its purchaser but it was purchased at only one place — Paris, Berlin or Madrid, say. This is also true in the case of those services where it is possible to separate the purchase of a service from its delivery. Thus in the case of package holidays, competition for the sale of holidays through travel agents takes place locally, as with retail shopping, even though the service may be provided in a number of distant locations. This turnover is however, earned locally and not at the site of an eventual holiday.

Note
[1]Where the place where the customer was located when purchasing the goods or service and the place where the billing was subsequently made are different, turnover should be allocated to the former.

47.   This applies even where a multinational corporation has a Community buying strategy and sources all its requirements for a good or service from one location. The fact that the components are susequently used in 10 different plants in a variety of Member States does not alter the fact that the transaction with a company outside the group occurred in only one country. The subsequent distribution to other sites is purely an internal question for the company concerned.

48.   Certain sectors do, however, pose very particular problems with regard to the geogrpahical allocation of turnover (see Section III).

2.   Conversion of turnover into ecus

49.   When converting turnover figures into ecus great care should be taken with the exchange rate used. The annual turnover of a company should be converted at the average rate for the 12 months concerned. This average can be obtained from the Commission. The audited annual turnover figures should not be broken down into component quarterly, monthly, or weekly sales figures and converted individually at the corresponding average quarterly, monthly or weekly rates and then the ecus figures summed to give a total for the year.

50.   When a company has sales in a range of currencies, the procedure is no different. The total turnover given in the consolidated audited accounts and in that company's reporting currency is converted into ecus at the average rate for the 12 months. Local currency sales should not be converted directly into ecus since these figures are not from the consolidated audited accounts of the company.

III.   CREDIT AND OTHER FINANCIAL INSTITUTIONS AND INSURANCE UNDERTAKINGS

1.   Definitions

51.   The specific nature of banking and insurance activities is formally recognised by the Merger Regulation which includes specific provisions dealing with the calculation of turnover for these sectiors.[1] Although the Merger Regulation does not provide a definition of the terms, 'credit institutions and other financial institutions' within the meaning of point (a) of Article 5(3), the Commission in its practice has consistently adopted the definitions provided in the first and second banking directives:

— 'Credit institution means an undertaking whose business is to receive deposits or other repayable funds from the public and to grant credits for its own account'.[2]

— 'Financial institution shall mean an undertaking other than a credit institution, the principal activity of which is to acquire holdings or to carry on one or more of the activities listed in points 2 to 12 in the Annex'.[3]

Notes

[1] See Article 5(3) of the Merger Regulation.

[2] First Council Directive (77/780/EEC) of 12 December 1977 on the coordination of laws, regulations and administrative provisions relating to the taking up and pursuit of the business of credit institutions, Article 1 [OJ No. L322, 17.12.1977, p. 30].

[3] Second Council Directive (89/646/EEC) of 15 December 1989 on the coordination of laws, regulations and administrative provisions relating to the taking up and pursuit of the business of credit institutions, Article 1(6) [OJ No. L386, 30.12.1989, p. 1].

52. From the definition of 'financial institution' given above it is clear that on the one hand holding companies shall be considered as financial institutions and, on the other hand, that undertakings which perform on a regular basis as a principal activity one or more activities expressly mentioned in points 2 to 12 of the abovementioned Annex shall also be considered as financial institutions within the meaning of point (a) of Article 5(3) of the Merger Regulation. These activities include:

— lending (*inter alia*, consumer credit, mortgage credit, factoring, . . .),

— financial leasing,

— money transmission services,

— issuing and managing instruments of payment (credit cards, travellers' cheques and bankers' drafts),

— guarantees and commitments,

— trading on own account or on account of customers in money market instruments, foreign exchange, financial futures and options, exchange and interest rate instruments, and transferable securities,

— participation in share issues and the provision of services related to such issues,

— advice to undertakings on capital structure, industrial strategy and related questions and advice and services relating to mergers and the purchase of undertakings,

— money broking,

— portfolio management and advice,

— safekeeping and administration of securities.

2. Calculation of turnover

53. The methods of calculation of turnover for credit and other financial institutions and for insurance undertakings are described in Article 5(3) of the Merger Regulation and examples are provided in guidance notes one and two respectively, annexed to Form CO. These provisions remain in force. The purpose of this section is to provide an answer to supplementary questions related to turnover calculation for the abovementioned types of undertaking which were raised during the first years of the application of the Merger Regulation.

2.1 *Credit and financial institutions (other than financial holding companies)*

2.1.1 General

54. There are normally no particular difficulties in applying the rule of one-tenth of total assets for the definition of the world-wide turnover to credit institutions and other kinds of financial institutions. However, difficulties may arise with regard to the calculation of Community-wide turnover and the determination of the turnover within Member States for the purpose of application of the two-thirds rule.

55. Difficulties also arise with some financial institutions which do not provide loans and advances '*stricto sensu*', or when the credit granted, if any exists, is not a relevant indicator of the economic activity and weight of the undertakings concerned. This is the case, for example, with asset management companies, merchant banks, credit card companies, trading in foreign exchange, money market instruments, financial futures and options, as the companies in question are mainly firms providing financial services rather than

granting credit to business or individuals. In such cases, the determination of Community-wide turnover using the criteria established by the Merger Regulation cannot be applied meaningfully.

56. Therefore, with regard to the calculation of Community-wide turnover and turnover within a Member State, the concept of 'loans and advances' should be interpreted broadly in order to include any kind of activity which could be assimilated to some form of credit activity. For example, the fact that a financial institution has a portfolio of bonds and other interest-bearing securities has been assimilated for the purpose of the application of the Merger Regulation to a means of granting credit and therefore the securities held have been considered as loans and advances.[1]

Note
[1]See Case IV/M.166 — Torras/Sarrió., of 24 February 1992.

2.1.2 Turnover of leasing companies

57. There is a fundamental distinction to be made, for the purpose of application of point (a) of Article 5(3) of the Merger Regulation, between financial leases and operating leases. Basically, financial leases are made for longer periods than operating leases and ownership is generally transferred to the lessee at the end of the lease term by means of a bargain purchase option included in the lease contract. Under an operating lease, on the contrary, ownership is not transferred to the lessee at the end of the lease term and the cost of maintenance, repair and insurance of the leased equipment are included in the lease payments. A financial lease therefore functions as a loan by the lessor to enable the lessee to purchase a given asset. A financial leasing company is thus a financial institution within the meaning of point (a) of Article 5(3) and its turnover has to be calculated by applying the specific rules related to the calculation of turnover for credit and other financial institutions. Given that operational leasing activities do not have this lending function, they are not considered as carried out by financial institutions, at least as primary activities, and therefore the general turnover calculation rules of Article 5(1) should apply.[1]

Note
[1]See Case IV/M.234 — GECC/Avis Lease, 15 July 1992.

2.1.3 Turnover of fund management companies

58. In the case of a fund management company, the relevant assets to be taken into account in the calculation of turnover by the one-tenth of assets rule are only those belonging to the fund management company itself and not the assets being managed on behalf of clients. The assets being managed do not belong to the fund management company; they are held on a fiduciary basis and therefore either they are booked in 'off balance sheet' accounts (not included in the total assets figure of the fund management company) or they have to be booked in financial statements completely independent of the accounts of the fund management company. However, commission generated by asset management should be counted, as such, as turnover of a fund management company. Hence the turnover of a fund management company, which manages both its own assets and assets belonging to clients, will be calculated as follows:

Own assets $\times \frac{1}{10}$ = x

Commission or fees generated by management of clients' assets   = y

Total turnover   = x + y

2.2 Insurance undertakings

2.2.1 Gross premium written

59.   The application of the concept of gross premiums written as a measure of turnover for insurance undertakings has raised supplementary questions notwithstanding the definition provided in point (b) of Article 5(3) of the Merger Regulation. The following clarifications are appropriate:

— 'gross' premiums written is the sum of received premiums (which may include received reinsurance premiums if the undertaking concerned has activities in the field of reinsurance). Outgoing or outward reinsurance premiums, i.e., all amounts paid and payable by the undertaking concerned to get reinsurance cover, are already included in the gross premiums written within the meaning of the Merger Regulation,

— wherever the word 'premiums' is used (gross *premiums*, net (earned *premiums*, outgoing reinsurance *premiums* etc.) these premiums are related not only to new insurance contracts made during the accounting year being considered but also to all premiums related to contracts made in previous years which remain in force during the period taken into consideration.

2.2.2 Investments of insurance undertakings

60.   In order to constitute appropriate reserves allowing for the reimbursement of claims, insurance undertakings, which are also considered as institutional investors, usually hold a huge portfolio of investments in shares, interest-bearing securities, land and property and other assets which provide an annual revenue which is not considered as turnover for insurance undertakings.

61.   However, with regard to the application of the Merger Regulation, a major distinction should be made between pure financial investments, in which the insurance undertaking is not involved in the management of the undertakings where the investments have been made, and those investments leading to the acquisition of a controlling interest in a given undertaking thus allowing the insurance undertaking to exert a decisive influence on the business conduct of the subsidiary or affiliated company concerned. In such cases Article 5(4) of the Merger Regulation would apply, and the turnover of the subsidiary or affiliated company should be added to the turnover of the insurance undertaking for the determination of the thresholds laid down in the Merger Regulation.[1]

Note
[1]See Case IV/M.018 — AG/AMEV, of 21 November 1990.

2.3 Financial holding companies

62.   A financial holding company is a financial institution and therefore the calculation of its turnover should follow the criteria established in point (a) of Article 5(3) for the calculationof turnover for credit and other financial institutions. However, as the main purpose of a financial holding is to acquire and manage participation in other undertakings, Article 5(4) also applies (as for insurance undertakings, with regard to those participations allowing the financial holding company to exercise a decisive influence on the business

conduct to exercise a decisive influence on the business conduct of the undertakings in question. In such cases, the turnover figures of those undertakings obtained directly from the audited financial statements, or requiring special calculations (for example, turnover of banking and insurance undertakings) are simply added together in order to obtain the relevant turnover which will be used to determine whether the case falls under the Merger Regulation.

63.   In these cases different accounting rules, in particular those related to the preparation of consolidated accounts, which are to some extent harmonised but not identical within the Community, may need to be taken into consideration. This applies to any type of undertaking concerned by the Merger Regulation but it is particularly important in the case of financial holding companies[1] where the number and the diversity of enterprises controlled and the degree of control the holding holds on its subsidiaries, affiliated and participated companies requires careful examination.

64.   This method of calculation, of which an example is given in the following paragraphs, may in practice prove onerous. Therefore a strict and detailed application of this method will be necessary only in cases where it seems that the turnover of a financial holding company is likely to be close to the Merger Regulation thresholds; in other cases it may well be obvious that the turnover is far from the thresholds of the Merger Regulation, and therefore the published accounts are adequate for the establishment of jurisdiction.

Note
[1]See for example Case IV/M.166 — Torras/Sarrió, of 24 February 1992, Case IV/M.213 — Hong Kong and Shanghai Bank/Midland, of 21 May 1992, IV/M.192 — Banesto/Totta, of 14 April 1992.

Example of the calculation of turnover of financial holding companies
   (a)   Initially, it is necessary to consider the non-consolidated balance sheet of the financial holding company instead of the group consolidated accounts. Although this type of undertaking may have assets such as cash, plant property and equipment, the major part of the assets of a financial holding company are normally constituted by investments in shares, bonds and other interest bearing securities.

At the end of the most recent financial year the non-consolidated balance sheet of a financial holding company may be presented as follows, according to published financial statements:

			(ECU million)
Assets		Liabilities	
Marketable Securities	2,000[1]	Debt	1,500
Participations	2,000[2]	Equity	2,500
Total Assets	4,000	Total Liabilities	4,000

[1]Marketable Securities are constituted by bonds and other interest bearing securities and shares held as pure financial investments in undertakings on which the holding company does not exercise any kind of influence.
[2]Participants represent investment in shares on a long-term basis in companies on which the holding company exerts some kind of influence.

(b)   As the assets as presented do not provide the necessary information for the calculation of turnover under the Merger Regulation, a different breakdown of assets is required:

		(ECU million)
(i)	Bonds and other interest bearing securities	1,500
(ii)	Shares in undertakings not controlled by the financial holding[1]	1,500
		3,000
(iii)	Shareholding in undertakings controlled:	
	of which insurance undertakings	500
	industrial undertakings	500
		1,000
	Total Assets	4,000

The following additional details are required:

Total value of gross premiums written by insurance undertakings controlled (excluding intra-group contracts and after deduction of taxes	ECU 300 Million
Total turnover of industrial undertakings controlled (not including intra-group sales and excluding VAT)	ECU 2,000 Million

(c)   To calculate the aggregate world-wide turnover of the financial holding company account should be taken separately of the turnover of the different activities of the group (industrial, financial and insurance) and then the amounts should be added in order to get the final amount. Turnover for insurance and industrial activities are already given (ECU 300 million and 2,000 million respectively). Assets which are not related to shareholding in undertakings controlled amount to ECU 3,000 million (see (i) and (ii) above). Therefore total world-wide turnover is as follows:

		(ECU million)
— Turnover related to financial activities $\frac{1}{10} \times 3,000$	=	300
— Turnover related to insurance activities gross premiums written	=	300
— Turnover of industrial activities		2,000
Total worldwide turnover Group ABC		2,600

Community-wide turnover and turnover in Member States calculations should follow the same principle. For Community-wide and Member States turnover calculations related to financial activities, bonds and other interest-bearing securities should be considered as loans and advances.

Note
[1]'Controlled' in the sense of Article 5(4)(b) of the Merger Regulation.

3. Geographical allocation of turnover of banking and insurance undertakings

65.   The geographical turnover of banking and insurance undertakings is in principle allocated according to the place of residence of the beneficiaries of loans and advances for credit and other financial institutions, and of customers who pay insurance premiums in the case of insurance undertakings as stated in Article 5(3) of the Merger Regulation.

66.   A particular problem which arises with financial institutions is how to allocate loans, and in particular the frequently large volumes of overnight interbank loans when the client is not a subsidiary as such, but a branch or division of a company or bank incorporated in a different country. Since the branch or division to which the loan is made is most likely to be the place where the loan will be used, it is only rational to allocate geographically that loan to the branch or division rather than the place of incorporation of the debtor company or bank, even if this is what the banks themselves take into account for risk assessment purposes.[1]

67.   The current practice of the Commission is to consider, for banking and insurance undertakings, that branches, divisions and other undertakings operating on a lasting basis but not having a legal personality should be considered as residents in the countries in which they have been established.

Note

[1] See Case IV/M.213 — Hong Kong and Shanghai Bank/Midland, of 21 May 1992.

4. ECU exchange rate applicable to credit and financial institutions

68.   The question of the appropriateness of average annual exchange rates for financial institutions arises, since for such institutions turnover calculations are based on data derived from the balance sheet, which represents a financial situation at a particular date, rather than the profit and loss account which represents financial flows through time. However, in order to avoid using a separate method for this particular sector, the balance sheet asset values should be converted at the average rate for the 12 months preceding the balance sheet date, in conformity with the general rule.

COMMISSION NOTICE ON THE INTERNAL RULES OF PROCEDURE FOR PROCESSING REQUESTS FOR ACCESS TO THE FILE IN CASES PURSUANT TO ARTICLES 85 AND 86 OF THE EC TREATY, ARTICLES 65 AND 66 OF THE ECSC TREATY AND COUNCIL REGULATION (EEC) NO. 4064/89
(97/C 23/03)

INTRODUCTION

Access to the file is an important procedural stage in all contentious competition cases (prohibitions with or without a fine, prohibitions of mergers, rejection of complaints, etc.). The Commission's task in this area is to reconcile two opposing obligations, namely that of safeguarding the rights of the defence and that of protecting confidential information concerning firms.

The purpose of this notice is to ensure compatibility beween current administrative practice regarding access to the file and the case-law of the Court of Justice of the European Communities and the Court of First Instance, in particular the 'Soda-ash' cases.[1] The line of conduct thus laid down concerns cases dealt with on the basis of the competition rules applicable to enterprises: Articles 85 and 86, of the EC Treaty, Regulation (EEC) No. 4064/89[2] (hereinafter 'the Merger Regulation'), and Articles 65 and 66 of the ECSC Treaty.

Access to the file, which is one of the procedural safeguards designed to ensure effective exercise of the right to be heard[3] provided for in Article 19(1) and (2) of Council Regulation No. 17[4] and Article 2 of Commission Regulation No. 99/63/EEC,[5] as well as in the corresponding provisions of the Regulations governing the application of Articles 85 and 86 in the field of transport, must be arranged in all cases involving decisions on infringements, decisions rejecting complaints, decisions imposing interim measures and decisions adopted on the basis of Article 15(6) of Regulation No. 17.

The guidelines set out below, however, essentially relate to the rights of the undertakings which are the subject of investigations into alleged infringements; they do not relate to the rights of third parties, and complainants in particular.

In merger cases, access to the file by parties directly concerned is expressly provided for in Article 18(3) of the Merger Regulation and in Article 13(3)(a) of Regulation (EC) No. 3384/94[6] ('the Implementing Regulation').

Notes
[1]Court of First Instance judgments in Cases T-30/91, *Solvay v Commission*, T-36/91, *ICI v Commission*, and T-37/91, *ICI v Commission* [1995] ECR II-1775, II-1847 and II-1901.
[2]OJ No. L395, 30.12.1989, p. 1, as corrected in OJ No. L257, 21.9.1990, p. 13.
[3]Judgment of the Court of First Instance in Joined Cases T-10, 11, 12 and 15/92, CBR and Others [1992] ECR II-2667, at paragraph 38.
[4]OJ No. 13, 21.2.1962, p. 204/62.
[5]OJ No. 127, 20.8.1963, p. 2268/63.
[6]OJ No. L377, 31.12.1994, p. 1.

I. SCOPE AND LIMITS OF ACCESS TO THE FILE

As the purpose of providing access to the file is to enable the addressees of a statement of objections to express their views on the conclusions reached by the Commission, the firms in question must have access to all the documents making up the 'file' of the Commission (DG IV), apart from the categories of documents identified in the Hercules judgment,[1] namely the business secrets of other undertakings, internal Commission documents[2] and other confidential information.

Thus not all the documents collected in the course of an investigation are communicable and a distinction must be made between non-communicable and communicable documents.

Notes
[1]Court of First Instance judgment in Case T-7/89, *Hercules Chemicals v Commission* [1991] ECR II-1711, paragraph 54.
[2]Internal Commission documents do not form part of the investigation file and are placed in the file of internal documents relating to the case under examination (see points I.A.3 and II.A.2 below).

A. Non-communicable documents

1. *Business secrets*

Business secrets mean information (documents or parts of documents) for which an undertaking has claimed protection as 'business secrets', and which are recognised as such by the Commission.

The non-communicability of such information is intended to protect the legitimate interest of firms in preventing third parties from obtaining strategic information on their essential interests and on the operation or development of their business.[1]

The criteria for determining what constitutes a business secret have not as yet been defined in full. Reference may be made, however, to the case-law, especially the Akzo and the BAT and Reynolds judgments,[2] to the criteria used in anti-dumping procedures,[3] and to decisions on the subject by the Hearing Officer. The term 'business secret' must be construed in its broader sense: according to Akzo, Regulation No. 17 requires the Commission to have regard to the legitimate interest of firms in the protection of their business secrets.

Business secrets need no longer be protected when they are known outside the firm (or group or association of firms) to which they relate. Nor can facts remain business secrets if, owing to the passage of time or for any other reason, they are no longer commercially important.

Where business secrets provide evidence of an infringement or tend to exonerate a firm, the Commission must reconcile the interest in the protection of sensitive information, the public interest in having the infringement of the competition rules terminated, and the rights of the defence. This calls for an assessment of:

    (i)   the relevance of the information to determining whether or not an infringement has been committed;

    (ii)   its probative value;

    (iii) whether it is indispensable;

    (iv) the degree of sensitivity involved (to what extent would disclosure of the information harm the interests of the firm?);

    (v)   the seriousness of the infringement.

Each document must be assessed individually to determine whether the need to disclose it is greater than the harm which might result from disclosure.

Notes

[1]For example methods of assessing manufacturing and distribution costs, production secrets and processes, supply sources, quantities produced and sold, market shares, customer and distributor lists, marketing plants, cost price structure, sales policy, and information on the internal organisation of the firm.

[2]Case 53/85, Akzo [1986] ECR 1965, paragraphs 24 to 28, and paragraph 28 in particular on pp. 1991-1992. Cases 142 and 156/84, *BAT and Reynolds* v *Commission* [1987] ECR 4487, paragraph 21.

[3]Order of the Court of 30.3.1982 in Case 236/81, *Celanese* v *Commission and Council* [1982] ECR 1183.

2. *Confidential documents*

It is also necessary to protect information for which confidentiality has been requested.

This category includes information making it possible to identify the suppliers of the information who wish to remain anonymous to the other parties, and certain types of information communicated to the Commission on condition that confidentiality is observed, such as documents obtained during an investigation which form part of a firm's property and are the subject of a non-disclosure request (such as a market study commissioned by the firm and forming part of its property). As in the preceding case (business secrets), the Commission must reconcile the legitimate interest of the firm in protecting its assets, the public interest in having breaches of the competition rules terminated, and the rights of the defence. Military secrets also belong in the category of 'other confidential information'.

As a rule, the confidential nature of documents is not a bar to their disclosure[1] if the information in question is necessary in order to prove an alleged infringement ('inculpatory documents') or if the papers invalidate or rebut the reasoning of the Commission set out in its statement of objections ('exculpatory documents').

Note
[1]Here the procedure described in point II.A.1.3 should be followed.

3. *Internal documents*

Internal documents are, by their nature, not the sort of evidence on which the Commission can rely in its assessment of a case. For the most part they consist of drafts, opinions or memos from the departments concerned and relating to ongoing procedures.

The Commission departments must be able to express themselves freely within their institution concerning ongoing cases. The disclosure of such documents could also jeopardise the secrecy of the Commission's deliberations.

It should, moreover, be noted that the secrecy of proceedings is also protected by the code of conduct on public access to Commission and Council documents as set out in Commission Decision 94/90/ECSC, EC, Euratom,[1] as amended by Decision 96/567/ECSC, EC, Euratom[2] as are internal documents relating to inspections and investigations and those whose disclosure could jeopardize the protection of individual privacy, business and industrial secrets or the confidentiality requested by a legal or natural person.

These considerations justify the non-disclosure of this category of documents, which will, in future, be placed in the file of internal documents relating to cases under investigation, which is, as a matter of principle, inaccessible (see point II.A.2).

Notes
[1]OJ No. L46, 18.2.1994, p. 58.
[2]OJ No. L247, 28.9.1996, p. 45.

B. Communicable documents

All documents not regarded as 'non-communicable' under the above-mentioned criteria are accessible to the parties concerned.

Thus, access to the file is not limited to documents which the Commission regards as 'relevant' to an undertaking's rights of defence.

The Commission does not select accessible documents in order to remove those which may be relevant to the defence of an undertaking. This concept, already outlined in the Court of First Instance judgments in Hercules and

Cimenteries CBR,[1] was confirmed and developed in the Soda-ash case, where the Court held that 'in the defended proceedings for which Regulation No. 17 provides it cannot be for the Commission alone to decide which documents are of use for the defence.... The Commission must give the advisers of the undertaking concerned the opportunity to examine documents which may be relevant so that their probative value for the defence can be assessed'. (Case T-30/91, paragraph 81).

Note
[1]In paragraph 54 of Hercules, referred to in paragraph 41 of the Cimenteries judgment, the Court of First Instance held that the Commission has an obligation to make available to the undertakings all documents, whether in their favour or otherwise, which it has obtained during the course of the investigation, save where the business secrets of other undertakings, the internal documents of the Commission or other confidential information are involved.

Special note concerning studies:
It should be stressed that studies commissioned in connection with proceedings or for a specific file, whether used directly or indirectly in the proceedings, must be made accessible irrespective of their intrinsic value. Access must be given not only to the results of a study (reports, statistics, etc.), but also to the Commission's correspondence with the contractor, the tender specifications and the methodology of the study;[1]

However, correspondence relating to the financial aspects of a study and the references concerning the contractor remain confidential in the interests of the latter.

Note
[1]As a result of this provision, it is necessary, when drawing up a study contract, to include a specific clause stipulating that the study and the relevant documents (methodology, correspondence with the Commission) may be disclosed by the Commission to third parties.

II.   PROCEDURES FOR IMPLEMENTING ACCESS TO THE FILE

A.   Preparation procedure — Cases investigated pursuant to Articles 85 and 86

1.   *Investigation file*

1.1   *Return of certain documents after inspection visits*
In the course of its investigations pursuant to Article 14(2) and (3) of Regulation No. 17, the Commission obtains a considerable number of documents, some of which may, following a detailed examination, prove to be irrelevant to the case in question. Such documents are normally returned to the firm as rapidly as possible.

1.2   *Request for a non-confidential version of a document*
In order to facilitate access to the file at a later stage in proceedings, the undertakings concerned will be asked systematically to:

— detail the information (documents or parts of documents) which they regard as business secrets and the confidential documents whose disclosure would injure them,

— substantiate their claim for confidentiality in writing,

— give the Commission a non-confidential version of their confidential documents (where confidential passages are deleted).

As regards documents taken during an inspection (Article 14(2) and (3)), requests are made only after the inspectors have returned from their mission.

When an undertaking, in response to a request from the Commission, claims that the information supplied is confidential, the following procedure will be adopted:

(a)   at the stage of the proceedings, claims of confidentiality which at first sight seem justified will be accepted provisionally. The Commission reserves the right, however, to reconsider the matter at a later stage of the proceedings;

(b)   where it is apparent that the claim of confidentiality is clearly unjustified, for example where it relates to a document already published or distributed extensively, or is excessive where it covers all, or virtually all the documents obtained or sent without any plausible justification, the firm concerned will be informed that the Commission does not agree with the scope of the confidentiality that is claimed. The matter will be dealt with when the final assessment is made of the accessibility of the documents (see below).

1.3   Final assessment of the accessibility of documents

It may prove necessary to grant other undertakings involved access to a document even where the undertaking that has issued it objects, if the document serves as a basis for the decision[1] or is clearly an exculpatory document.

If an undertaking states that a document is confidential but does not submit a non-confidential version, the following procedure applies:

— the undertaking claiming confidentiality will be contacted again and asked for a reasonably coherent non-confidential version of the document,

— if the undertaking continues to object to the disclosure of the information, the competent department applies to the Hearing Officer, who will if necessary implement the procedure leading to a decision pursuant to Article 5(4) of Commission Decision 94/810/ECSC, EC of 12 December 1994 on the terms of reference of hearing officers in competition procedures before the Commission.[2] The undertaking will be informed by letter that the Hearing Officer is examining the question.

Notes

[1] For example, documents which help to define the scope, duration and nature of the infringement, the identity of participants, the harm to competition, the economic context, etc.

[2] OJ No. L330, 21.12.1994, p. 67.

1.4   Enumerative list of documents

An enumerative list of documents should be drawn up according to the following principles:

(a)   the list should include uninterupted numbering of all the pages in the investigation file and an indication (using a classification code) of the degree of accessibility of the document and the parties with authorised access;

(b)   an access code is given to each document on the list:

— accessible document

— partially accessible document

— non-accessible document;

(c)   the category of completely non-accessible documents essentially consists of documents containing 'business secrets' and other confidential documents. In view of the 'Soda-ash' case-law, the list will include a summary enabling the content and subject of the documents to be identified, so that any firm having requested access to the file is able to determine in full knowledge of the facts whether the documents are likely to be relevant to its defence and to decide whether to request access despite that classification;

(d) accessible and partially accessible documents do not call for a description of their content in the list as they can be 'physically' consulted by all firms, either in their full version or in their non-confidential version. In the latter event, only the sensitive passages are deleted in such a way that the firm with access is not able to determine the nature of the information deleted (e.g., turnover).

2. *File of internal documents relating to ongoing cases*

In order to simplify administration and increase efficiency, internal documents will, in future, be placed in the file of internal documents relating to cases under investigation (non-accessible) containing all internal documents in chronological order. Classification in this category is subject to the control of the Hearing Officer, who will if necessary certify that the papers contained therein are 'internal documents'.

The following, for example, will be deemed to be internal documents:

(a) requests for instructions made to, and instructions received from, hierarchical superiors on the treatment of cases;

(b) consultations with other Commission departments on a case;

(c) correspondence with other public authorities concerning a case;[1]

(d) drafts and other working documents;

(e) individual technical assistance contracts (languages, computing, etc.) relating to a specific aspect of a case.

Note

[1]It is necessary to protect the confidentiality of documents obtained from public authorities; this rule applies not only to documents from competition authorities, but also to those from other public authorities, Member States or non-member countries.

Any exception to the principle of non-disclosure of these documents must be firmly justified on the grounds of safe-guarding the rights of the defence (e.g., complaint lodged by a Member State pursuant to Article 3 of Regulation No. 17). Letters simply expressing interest, whether from a public authority of a Member State or of a third country, are non-communicable in principle.

A distinction must be made, however, between the opinions or comments expressed by other public authorities, which are afforded absolute protection, and any specific documents they may have furnished, which are not always covered by the exception. In the latter case, it is advisable in any event to proceed with circumspection, especially if the documents are from a non-member country, as it is considered of prime importance for the development of international cooperation in the application of the competition rules, to safeguard the relationship of trust between the Commission and non-member countries.

There are two possibilities in this context:

(a) There may already be an agreement governing the confidentiality of the information exchanged.

Article VIII(2) of the Agreement between the European Communities and the Government of the United States of America regarding the application of their competition laws [OJ No. L95, 27.4.1995, p. 45] stipulates that exchanges of information and information received under the Agreement must be protected 'to the fullest extent possible'. The article lays down a point of international law which must be complied with.

(b) If there is no such agreement, the same principle of guaranteed confidentiality should be observed.

B. Preparatory procedure — Cases examined within the meaning of the Merger Regulation

1. *Measures common to the preparatory procedure in cases investigated pursuant to Articles 85 and 86*

(a) *Return of certain documents after an inspection*
On-the-spot inspections are specifically provided for the Article 13 of the Merger Regulation: in such cases, the procedure provided for in point II.A.1.1 for cases examined on the basis of Articles 85 and 86 is applicable.

(b) *Enumerative list of documents*
The enumerative list of the documents in the Commission file with the access codes will be drawn up in accordance with the criteria set out in point II.A.1.4.

(c) *Request for a non-confidential version of a document*
In order to facilitate access to the file, firms being investigated will be asked to:
— detail the information (documents or parts of documents) they regard as business secrets and the confidential documents whose disclosure would injure them,
— substantiate their request for confidentiality in writing,
— give the Commission a reasonably coherent non-confidential version of their confidential documents (where confidential passages are deleted).

This procedure will be followed in stage II cases (where the Commission initiates proceedings in respect of the notifying parties) and in stage I cases (giving rise to a Commission decision without initiation of proceedings).

2. *Measures specific to preparatory procedures in merger cases*

(a) *Subsequent procedure in stage II cases*
In stage II cases the subsequent procedure is as follows:
Where a firm states that all or part of the documents it has provided are business secrets, the following steps should be taken:
— if the claim appears to be justified, the documents or parts of documents concerned will be regarded as non-accessible to third parties,
— if the claim does not appear to be justified, the competent Commission department will ask the firm, in the course of the investigation and no later then the time at which the statement of objections is sent, to review its position. The firm must either state in writing which documents or parts of documents must be regarded as confidential, or send a non-confidential version of the documents.

If disagreement regarding the extent of the confidentiality persists, the competent department refers the matter to the Hearing Officer, who may if necessary take the decision provided for in Article 5(4) of Decision 94/810/ECSC, EC.

(b) *Specific cases*
Article 9(1) of the Merger Regulation provides that 'the Commission may, by means of a decision notified without delay to the undertakings concerned ... refer a notified concentration to the competent authorities of the Member State concerned'. In the context of access to the file, the parties concerned should, as a general rule be able to see the request for referral from a national authority, with the exception of any business secrets or other confidential information it may contain.

Article 22(3) of the Merger Regulation provides that 'If the Commission finds, at the request of a Member State, that a concentration (. . .) that has no Community dimension (. . .) creates or strengthens a dominant position (. . .) it may (. . .) adopt the decision provided for in the second subparagraph of Article 8(2), (3) and (4)'. Such requests have the effect of empowering the Commission to deal with mergers which would normally fall outside its powers of review. Accordingly, the parties concerned should be granted right of access to the letter from the Member State requesting referral, after deletion of any business secrets or other confidential information.

C. Practical arrangements for access to the file

1. *General rule: access by way of consultation on the Commission's premises*
Firms are invited to examine the relevant files on the Commission's premises.

If the firm considers, on the basis of the list of documents it has received, that it requires certain non-accessible documents for its defence, it may make a reasoned request to that end to the Hearing Officer.[1]

2.   If the file is not too bulky, however, the firm has the choice of being sent all the accessible documents, apart from those already sent with the statement of objections or the letter rejecting the complaint, or of consulting the file on the Commission's premises.

As regards Articles 85 and 86 cases, contrary to a common previous practice, the statement of objections or letter of rejection will in future be accompanied only by the evidence adduced and documents cited on which the objections/ rejection letter is based.

Any request for access made prior to submission of the statement of objections will in principle be inadmissible.

Note
[1]Special procedure provided for in Decision 94/810/ECSC, EC.

D. Particular questions which may arise in connection with complaints and procedures relating to abuse of a dominant position (Articles 85 and 86)

1. *Complaints*
While complainants may properly be involved in proceedings, they do not have the same rights and guarantees as the alleged infringers. A complainant's right to consult the files does not share the same basis as the rights of defence of the addresses of a statement of objections, and there are no grounds for treating the rights of the complainant as equivalent to those of the firms objected to.

Nevertheless, a complainant who has been informed of the intention to reject his complaint may request access to the documents on which the Commission based its position. Complainants may not, however, have access to any confidential information or other business secrets belonging to the firms complained of, or to third-party firms, which the Commission has obtained in the course of its investigations (Articles 11 and 14 of Regulation No. 17).

Clearly, it is even more necessary here to respect the principle of confidentiality as there is no presumption of infringement. In accordance with the judgment in Fedetab,[1] Article 19(2) of Regulation No. 17 gives complainants a right to be heard and not a right to receive confidential information.

Notes
[1]Cases 209-215 and 218/78, Fedetab [1980] ECR 3125, paragraph 46.

2. *Procedures in cases of abuse of a dominant position*

The question of procedures in cases of abuse of a dominant position was referred to by the Court of First Instance and the Court of Justice in the *BPB Industries and British Gypsum* v *Commission* case.[2]

By definition, firms in a dominant position on a market are able to place very considerable economic or commercial pressure on their competitors or on their trading partners, customers or suppliers.

The Court of First Instance and the Court of Justice thus acknowledged the legitimacy of the reluctance displayed by the Commission in revealing certain letters received from customers of the firm being investigated.

Although it is of value to the Commission for giving a better understanding of the market concerned, the information does not in any way constitute inculpatory evidence, and its disclosure to the firm concerned might easily expose the authors to the risk of retaliatory measures.

Notes
[2]Judgment of the Court of First Instance in Case T-65/89, BPB Industries and British Gypsum [1993] ECR II-389, and judgment of the Court of Justice in Case C-310/93 P in BPB Industries and British Gypsum [1995] EC I-865.

INTELLECTUAL PROPERTY

FIRST COUNCIL DIRECTIVE OF 21 DECEMBER 1988 TO APPROXIMATE THE LAWS OF THE MEMBER STATES RELATING TO TRADE MARKS (89/104/EEC) [OJ 1988, No. L40/1] AS AMENDED BY DIRECTIVE 92/10
[OJ 1992 No. L6/35]

THE COUNCIL OF THE EUROPEAN COMMUNITIES,

Having regard to the Treaty establishing the European Economic Community, and in particular Article 100a thereof,

Having regard to the proposal from the Commission,[1]

In cooperation with the European Parliament,[2]

Having regard to the opinion of the Economic and Social Committee,[3]

Whereas the trade mark laws at present applicable in the Member States contain disparities which may impede the free movement of goods and freedom to provide services and may distort competition within the common market;

Whereas it is therefore necessary, in view of the establishment and functioning of the internal market, to approximate the laws of Member States;

Whereas it is important not to disregard the solutions and advantages which the Community trade mark system may afford to undertakings wishing to acquire trade marks;

Whereas it does not appear to be necessary at present to undertake full-scale approximation of the trade mark laws of the Member States and it will be sufficient if approximation is limited to those national provisions of law which most directly affect the functioning of the internal market;

Whereas the Directive does not deprive the Member States of the right to continue to protect trade marks acquired through use but takes them into account only in regard to the relationship between them and trade marks acquired by registration;

Whereas Member States also remain free to fix the provisions of procedure concerning the registration, the revocation and the invalidity of trade marks acquired by registration; whereas they can, for example, determine the form of trade mark registration and invalidity procedures, decide whether earlier rights should be invoked either in the registration procedure or in the invalidity

Notes

[1] OJ 1980 No. C351/1 and OJ 1985 No. C351/4.

[2] OJ 1983 No. C307/66 and OJ 1988 No. C309.

[3] OJ 1981 No. C310/22.

procedure or in both and, if they allow earlier rights to be invoked in the registration procedure, have an opposition procedure or an ex officio examination procedure or both; whereas Member States remain free to determine the effects of revocation or invalidity of trade marks;

Whereas this Directive does not exclude the application to trade marks of provisions of law of the Member States other than trade mark law, such as the provisions relating to unfair competition, civil liability or consumer protection;

Whereas attainment of the objectives at which this approximation of laws is aiming requires that the conditions for obtaining and continuing to hold a registered trade mark are, in general, identical in all Member States; whereas, to this end, it is necessary to list examples of signs which may constitute a trade mark, provided that such signs are capable of distinguishing the goods or services of one undertaking from those of other undertakings; whereas the grounds for refusal or invalidity concerning the trade mark itself, for example, the absence of any distinctive character, or concerning conflicts between the trade mark and earlier rights, are to be listed in an exhaustive manner, even if some of these grounds are listed as an option for the Member States which will therefore be able to maintain or introduce those grounds in their legislation; whereas Member States will be able to maintain or introduce into their legislation grounds of refusal or invalidity linked to conditions for obtaining and continuing to hold a trade mark for which there is no provision of approximation, concerning, for example, the eligibility for the grant of a trade mark, the renewal of the trade mark or rules on fees, or related to the non-compliance with procedural rules;

Whereas in order to reduce the total number of trade marks registered and protected in the Community and, consequently, the number of conflicts which arise between them, it is essential to require that registered trade marks must actually be used or, if not used, be subject to revocation; whereas it is necessary to provide that a trade mark cannot be invalidated on the basis of the existence of a non-used earlier trade mark, while the Member States remain free to apply the same principle in respect of the registration of a trade mark or to provide that a trade mark may not be successfully invoked in infringement proceedings if it is established as a result of a plea that the trade mark could be revoked; whereas in all these cases it is up to the Member States to establish the applicable rules of procedure;

Whereas it is fundamental, in order to facilitate the free circulation of goods and services, to ensure that henceforth registered trade marks enjoy the same protection under the legal systems of all the Member States; whereas this should however not prevent the Member States from granting at their option extensive protection to those trade marks which have a reputation;

Whereas the protection afforded by the registered trade mark, the function of which is in particular to guarantee the trade mark as an indication of origin, is absolute in the case of identity between the mark and the sign and goods or services; whereas the protection applies also in cases of similarity between the mark and the sign and the goods or services; whereas it is indispensable to give an interpretation of the concept of similarity in relation to the likelihood of confusion; whereas the likelihood of confusion, the appreciation of which depends on numerous elements and, in particular, on the recognition of the trade mark on the market, of the association which can be made with the used or registered sign, of the degree of similarity between the trade mark and the sign and between the goods or services identified, constitutes the specific condition for such protection; whereas the ways in which likelihood of confusion may be established, and in particular the onus of proof, are a matter for national procedural rules which are not prejudiced by the Directive;

Whereas it is important, for reasons of legal certainty and without inequitably prejudicing the interests of a proprietor of an earlier trade mark, to provide that the latter may no longer request a declaration of invalidity nor may he oppose the use of a trade mark subsequent to his own of which he has knowingly tolerated the use for a substantial length of time, unless the application for the subsequent trade mark was made in bad faith:

Whereas all Member States of the Community are bound by the Paris Convention for the Protocol of Industrial Property; whereas it is necessary that the provisions of this Directive are entirely consistent with those of the Paris Convention; whereas the obligations of the Member States resulting from this Convention are not affected by this Directive; whereas, where appropriate, the second subparagraph of Article 234 of the Treaty is applicable,

HAS ADOPTED THIS DIRECTIVE:

Article 1
Scope.

This Directive shall apply to every trade mark in respect of goods or services which is the subject of registration or of an application in a Member State for registration as an individual trade mark, a collective mark or a guarantee or certification mark, or which is the subject of a registration or an application for registration in the Benelux Trade Mark Office or of an international registration having effect in a Member State.

Article 2
Signs of which a trade mark may consist.

A trade mark may consist of any sign capable of being represented graphically, particularly words, including personal names, designs, letters, numerals, the shape of goods or of their packaging, provided that such signs are capable of distinguishing the goods or services of one undertaking from those of other undertakings.

Article 3
Grounds for refusal or invalidity.

1. The following shall not be registered or if registered shall be liable to be declared invalid:

    (a) signs which cannot constitute a trade mark;

    (b) trade marks which are devoid of any distinctive character;

    (c) trade marks which consist exclusively of signs or indications which may serve, in trade, to designate the kind, quality, quantity, intended purpose, value, geographical origin, or the time of production of the goods or of rendering of the service, or other characteristics of the goods or service;

    (d) trade marks which consist exclusively of signs or indications which have become customary in the current language or in the bona fide and established practices of the trade;

    (e) signs which consist exclusively of:

        — the shape which results from the nature of the goods themselves, or

        — the shape of goods which is necessary to obtain a technical result, or

— the shape which gives substantial value to the goods;

(f)   trade marks which are contrary to public policy or to accepted principles of morality;

(g)   trade marks which are of such a nature as to deceive the public, for instance as to the nature, quality or geographical origin of the goods or service;

(h)   trade marks which have not been authorised by the competent authorities and are to be refused or invalidated pursuant to Article 6 ter of the Paris Convention for the Protection of Industrial Property, hereinafter referred to as the 'Paris Convention'.

2.   Any Member State may provide that a trade mark shall not be registered or, if registered, shall be liable to be declared invalid where and to the extent that:

(a)   the use of that trade mark may be prohibited pursuant to provisions of law other than trade mark law of the Member State concerned or of the Community;

(b)   the trade mark covers a sign of high symbolic value, in particular a religious symbol;

(c)   the trade mark includes badges, emblems and escutcheons other than those covered by Article 6 ter of the Paris Convention and which are of public interest, unless the consent of the appopriate authorities to its registration has been given in conformity with the legislation of the Member State;

(d)   the application for registration of the trade mark was made in bad faith.

3.   A trade mark shall not be refused registration or be declared invalid in accordance with paragraph 1(b), (c) or (d) if, before the date of application for registration and following the use which has been made of it, it has acquired a distinctive character. Any Member State may in addition provide that this provision shall also apply where the distinctive character was acquired after the date of application for registration or after the date of registration.

4.   Any Member State may provide that, by derogation from the preceding paragraphs, the grounds of refusal of registration or invalidity in force in that State prior to the date on which the provisions necessary to comply with the Directive enter into force, shall apply to trade marks for which application has been made prior to that date.

Article 4
Further grounds for refusal or invalidity concerning conflicts with earlier rights.

1.   A trade mark shall not be registered or, if registered, shall be liable to be declared invalid:

(a)   if it is identical with an earlier trade mark, and the goods or services for which the trade mark is applied for or is registered are identical with the goods or services for which the earlier trade mark is protected;

(b)   if because of its identity with, or similarity to, the earlier trade mark and the identity or similarity of the goods or services covered by the trade marks, there exists a likelihood of confusion on the part of the public, which includes the likelihood of association with the earlier trade mark.

2.   'Earlier trade marks' within the meaning of paragraph 1 means:

(a)   trade marks of the following kinds with a date of application for registration which is earlier than the date of application for registration of the trade mark, taking account, where appropriate, of the priorities claimed in respect of those trade marks;

    (i)   Community trade marks;

    (ii)   trade marks registered in the Member State or, in the case of Belgium, Luxembourg or the Netherlands, at the Benelux Trade Mark Office;

    (iii)   trade marks registered under international arrangements which have effect in the Member State;

    (b)   Community trade marks which validly claim seniority, in accordance with the Regulation on the Community trade mark, from a trade mark referred to in (a)(ii) and (iii), even when the latter trade mark has been surrendered or allowed to lapse;

    (c)   applications for the trade marks referred to in (a) and (b), subject to their registration;

    (d)   trade marks which, on the date of application for registration of the trade mark, or, where appropriate, of the priority claimed in respect of the application of registration of the trade mark, are well known in a Member State, in the sense in which the words 'well known' are used in Article 6 bis of the Paris Convention.

3.   A trade mark shall furthermore not be registered or, if registered, shall be liable to be declared invalid if it is identical with, or similar to, an earlier Community trade mark within the meaning of paragraph 2 and is to be, or has been, registered for goods or services which are not similar to those for which the earlier Community trade mark is registered, where the earlier Community trade mark has a reputation in the Community and where the use of the later trade mark without due cause would take unfair advantage of, or be detrimental to, the distinctive character or the repute of the earlier Community trade mark.

4.   Any Member State may furthermore provide that a trade mark shall not be registered or, if registered, shall be liable to be declared invalid where, and to the extent that:

    (a)   the trade mark is identical with, or similar to, an earlier national trade mark within the meaning of paragraph 2 and is to be, or has been, registered for goods or services which are not similar to those for which the earlier trade mark is registered, where the earlier trade mark has a reputation in the Member State concerned and where the use of the later trade mark without due cause would take unfair advantage of, or be detrimental to, the distinctive character or the repute of the earlier trade mark;

    (b)   rights to a non-registered trade mark or to another sign used in the course of trade were acquired prior to the date of application for registration of the subsequent trade mark, or the date of the priority claimed for the application for registration of the subsequent trade mark and that non-registered trade mark or other sign confers on its proprietor the right to prohibit the use of a subsequent trade mark;

    (c)   the use of the trade mark may be prohibited by virtue of an earlier right other than the rights referred to in paragraphs 2 and 4(b) and in particular:

        (i)   a right to a name;

        (ii)   a right of personal portrayal;

        (iii)   a copyright;

        (iv)   an industrial property right;

(d)   the trade mark is identical with, or similar to, an earlier collective trade mark conferring a right which expired within a period of a maximum of three years preceding application;

(e)   the trade mark is identical with, or similar to, an earlier guarantee or certification mark conferring a right which expired within a period preceding application the length of which is fixed by the Member State;

(f)   the trade mark is identical with, or similar to, an earlier trade mark which was registered for identical or similar goods or services and conferred on them a right which has expired for failure to renew within a period of a maximum of two years preceding application, unless the proprietor of the earlier trade mark gave his agreement to the registration of the later mark or did not use his trade mark;

(g)   the trade mark is liable to be confused with a mark which was in use abroad on the filing date of the application and which is still in use there, provided that at the date of the application the applicant was acting in bad faith.

5.   The Member States may permit that in appropriate circumstances registration need not be refused or the trade mark need not be declared invalid where the proprietor of the earlier trade mark or other earlier right consents to the registration of the later trade mark.

6.   Any Member State may provide that, by derogation from paragraphs 1 to 5, the grounds for refusal of registration or invalidity in force in that State prior to the date on which the provisions necessary to comply with this Directive enter into force, shall apply to trade marks for which application has been made prior to that date.

Article 5
Rights conferred by a trade mark.

1.   The registered trade mark shall confer on the proprietor exclusive rights therein. The proprietor shall be entitled to prevent all third parties not having his consent from using in the course of trade:

(a)   any sign which is identical with the trade mark in relation to goods or services which are identical with those for which the trade mark is registered;

(b)   any sign where, because of its identity with, or similarity to, the trade mark and the identity or similarity of the goods or services covered by the trade mark and the sign, there exists a likelihood of confusion on the part of the public, which includes the likelihood of association between the sign and the trade mark.

2.   Any Member State may also provide that the proprietor shall be entitled to prevent all third parties not having his consent from using in the course of trade any sign which is identical with, or similar to, the trade mark in relation to goods or services which are not similar to those for which the trade mark is registered, where the latter has a reputation in the Member State and where use of that sign without due cause takes unfair advantage of, or is detrimental to, the distinctive character or the repute of the trade mark.

3.   The following, inter alia, may be prohibited under paragraphs 1 and 2:

(a)   affixing the sign to the goods or to the packaging thereof;

(b)   offering the goods, or putting them on the market or stocking them for these purposes under that sign, or offering or supplying services thereunder;

(c)   importing or exporting the goods under the sign;

(d)   using the sign on business papers and in advertising.

4. Where, under the law of the Member State, the use of a sign under the conditions referred to in 1(b) or 2 could not be prohibited before the date on which the provisions necessary to comply with this Directive entered into force in the Member State concerned, the rights conferred by the trade mark may not be relied on to prevent the continued use of the sign.

5. Paragraphs 1 to 4 shall not affect provisions in any Member State relating to the protection against the use of a sign other than for the purposes of distinguishing goods or services, where use of that sign without due cause takes unfair advantage of, or is detrimental to, the distinctive character or the repute of the trade mark.

Article 6
Limitation of the effects of a trade mark.

1. The trade mark shall not entitle the proprietor to prohibit a third party from using, in the course of trade,

(a) his own name or address;

(b) indications concerning the kind, quality, quantity, intended purpose, value, geographical origin, the time of production of goods or of rendering of the service, or other characteristics of goods or services;

(c) the trade mark where it is necessary to indicate the intended purpose of a product or service, in particular as accessories or spare parts; provided he uses them in accordance with honest practices in industrial or commercial matters.

2. The trade mark shall not entitle the proprietor to prohibit a third party from using, in the course of trade, an earlier right which only applies in a particular locality if that right is recognised by the laws of the Member State in question and within the limits of the territory in which it is recognised.

Article 7
Exhaustion of the rights conferred by a trade mark.

1. The trade mark shall not entitle the proprietor to prohibit its use in relation to goods which have been put on the market in the Community under that trade mark by the proprietor or with his consent.

2. Paragraph 1 shall not apply where there exist legitimate reasons for the proprietor to oppose further commercialisation of the goods, especially where the condition of the goods is changed or impaired after they have been put on the market.

Article 8
Licensing.

1. A trade mark may be licensed for some or all of the goods or services for which it is registered and for the whole or part of the Member State concerned. A licence may be exclusive or non-exclusive.

2. The proprietor of a trade mark may invoke the rights conferred by that trade mark against a licensee who contravenes any provision in his licensing contract with regard to its duration, the form covered by the registration in which the trade mark may be used, the scope of the goods or services for which the licence is granted, the territory in which the trade mark may be affixed, or the quality of the goods manufactured or of the services provided by the licensee.

Article 9
Limitation in consequence of acquiescence.

1. Where, in a Member State, the proprietor of an earlier trade mark as referred to in Article 4(2) has acquiesced, for a period of five successive years, in the use of a later trade mark registered in that Member State while being aware of such use, he shall no longer be entitled on the basis of the earlier trade mark either to apply for a declaration that the later trade mark is invalid or to oppose the use of the later trade mark in respect of the goods or services for which the later trade mark has been used, unless registration of the later trade mark was applied for in bad faith.

2. Any Member State may provide that paragraph 1 shall apply mutatis mutandis to the proprietor of an earlier trade mark referred to in Article 4 (4)(a) or an other earlier right referred to in Article 4 (4)(b) or (c).

3. In the cases referred to in paragraphs 1 and 2, the proprietor of a later registered trade mark shall not be entitled to oppose the use of the earlier right, even though that right may no longer be invoked against the later trade mark.

Article 10
Use of trade marks.

1. If, within a period of five years following the date of the completion of the registration procedure, the proprietor has not put the trade mark to genuine use in the Member State in connection with the goods or services in respect of which it is registered, or if such use has been suspended during an uninterrupted period of five years, the trade mark shall be subject to the sanctions provided for in this Directive, unless there are proper reasons for non-use.

2. The following shall also constitute use within the meaning of paragraph 1:

    (a) use of the trade mark in a form differing in elements which do not alter the distinctive character of the mark in the form in which it was registered;

    (b) affixing of the trade mark to goods or to the packaging thereof in the Member State concerned solely for export purposes.

3. Use of the trade mark with the consent of the proprietor or by any person who has authority to use a collective mark or a guarantee or certification mark shall be deemed to constitute use by the proprietor.

4. In relation to trade marks registered before the date on which the provisions necessary to comply with this Directive enter into force in the Member State concerned:

    (a) where a provision in force prior to that date attaches sanctions to non-use of a trade mark during an uninterrupted period, the relevant period of five years mentioned in paragraph 1 shall be deemed to have begun to run at the same time as any period of non-use which is already running at that date;

    (b) where there is no use provision in force prior to that date, the periods of five years mentioned in paragraph 1 shall be deemed to run from that date at the earliest.

Article 11
Sanctions for non-use of a trade mark in legal or administrative proceedings.

1. A trade mark may not be declared invalid on the ground that there is an earlier conflicting trade mark if the latter does not fulfil the requirements of use set out in Article 10(1), (2) and (3) or in Article 10(4), as the case may be.

2. Any Member State may provide that registration of a trade mark may not be refused on the ground that there is an earlier conflicting trade mark if the latter does not fulfil the requirements of use set out in Article 10(1), (2) and (3) or in Article 10(4), as the case may be.

3. Without prejudice to the application of Article 12, where a counter-claim for revocation is made, any Member State may provide that a trade mark may not be successfully invoked in infringement proceedings if it is established as a result of a plea that the trade mark could be revoked pursuant to Article 12(1).

4. If the earlier trade mark has been used in relation to part only of the goods or services for which it is registered, it shall, for purposes of applying paragraphs 1, 2 and 3, be deemed to be registered in respect only of that part of the goods or services.

Article 12
Grounds for revocation.

1. A trade mark shall be liable to revocation if, within a continuous period of five years, it has not been put to genuine use in the Member State in connection with the goods or services in respect of which it is registered, and there are no proper reasons for non-use; however, no person may claim that the proprietor's rights in a trade mark should be revoked where, during the interval between expiry of the five-year period and filing of the application for revocation, genuine use of the trade mark has been started or resumed; the commencement or resumption of use within a period of three months preceding the filing of the application for revocation which began at the earliest on expiry of the continuous period of five years of non-use, shall, however, be disregarded where preparations for the commencement or resumption occur only after the proprietor becomes aware that the application for revocation may be filed.

2. A trade mark shall also be liable to revocation if, after the date on which it was registered,

    (a) in consequence of acts or inactivity of the proprietor, it has become the common name in the trade for a product or service in respect of which it is registered;

    (b) in consequence of the use made of it by the proprietor of the trade mark or with his consent in respect of the goods or services for which it is registered, it is liable to mislead the public, particularly as to the nature, quality or geographical origin of those goods or services.

Article 13
Grounds for refusal or revocation or invalidity relating to only some of the goods or services.

Where grounds for refusal of registration or for revocation or invalidity of a trade mark exist in respect of only some of the goods or services for which that trade mark has been applied for or registered, refusal of registration or revocation or invalidity shall cover those goods or services only.

Article 14
Establishment a posteriori of invalidity or revocation of a trade mark.

Where the seniority of an earlier trade mark which has been surrendered or allowed to lapse, is claimed for a Community trade mark, the invalidity or revocation of the earlier trade mark may be established a posteriori.

Article 15
Special provisions in respect of collective marks, guarantee marks and certification marks.

1. Without prejudice to Article 4, Member States whose laws authorise the registration of collective marks or of guarantee or certification marks may provide that such marks shall not be registered, or shall be revoked or declared invalid, on grounds additional to those specified in Articles 3 and 12 where the function of those marks so requires.

2. By way of derogation from Article 3(1)(c), Member States may provide that signs or indications which may serve, in trade, to designate the geographical origin of the goods or services may constitute collective, guarantee or certification marks. Such a mark does not entitle the proprietor to prohibit a third party from using in the course of trade such signs or indications, provided he uses them in accordance with honest practices in industrial or commercial matters; in particular, such a mark may not be invoked against a third party who is entitled to use a geographical name.

Article 16
National provisions to be adopted pursuant to this Directive.

1. The Member States shall bring into force the laws, regulations and administrative provisions necessary to comply with this Directive not later than 31 December 1992. They shall immediately inform the Commission thereof.

2. Acting on a proposal from the Commission, the Council, acting by qualified majority, may defer the date referred to in paragraph 1 until 31 December 1992 at the latest.

3. Member State shall communicate to the Commission the text of the main provisions of national law which they adopt in the field governed by this Directive.

Article 17
Addressees.

This Directive is addressed to the Member States.

Done at Brussels, 21 December 1988.
For the Council.
The President
V. PAPANDREOU

COUNCIL REGULATION (EC) 40/94 OF 20 DECEMBER 1993 ON THE COMMUNITY TRADE MARK
[OJ 1994, No. L11/1]*

THE COUNCIL OF THE EUROPEAN UNION,

Having regard to the Treaty Establishing the European Community, and in particular Article 235 thereof,
Having regard to the proposal from the Commission,[1]
Having regard to the opinion of the European Parliament,[2]
Having regard to the opinion of the Economic and Social Committee,[3]

Notes
*as amended by Council Regulation (EC) No. 3288/94 of 22 December 1994 [OJ 1994 L349/83]
[1]OJ No. C351, 31 December 1980, p. 1 and OJ No. C230 31 August 1984, p. 1.
[2]OJ No. C307, 14 November 1983, p. 46 and OJ No. C280, 28 October 1991, p. 153.
[3]OJ No. C310, 30 November 1981, p. 22.

Whereas it is desirable to promote throughout the Community a harmonious development of economic activities and a continuous and balanced expansion by completing an internal market which functions properly and offers conditions which are similar to those obtaining in a national market; whereas in order to create a market of this kind and make it increasingly a single market, not only must be barriers to free movement of goods and services be removed and arrangements be instituted which ensure that competition is not distorted, but, in addition, legal conditions must be created which enable undertakings to adapt their activities to the scale of the Community, whether in manufacturing and distributing goods or in providing services; whereas for those purposes, trade marks enabling the products and services of undertakings to be distinguished by identical means throughout the entire Community, regardless of frontiers, should feature amongst the legal instruments which undertakings have at their disposal;

Whereas action by the Community would appear to be necessary for the purpose of attaining the Community's said objectives; whereas such action involves the creation of Community arrangements for trade marks whereby undertakings can by means of one procedural system obtain Community trade marks to which uniform protection is given and which produce their effects throughout the entire area of the Community; whereas the principle of the unitary character of the Community trade mark thus stated will apply unless otherwise provided for in this Regulation;

Whereas the barrier of territoriality of the rights conferred on proprietors of trade marks by the laws of the Member States cannot be removed by approximation of laws; whereas in order to open up unrestricted economic activity in the whole of the common market for the benefit of undertakings, trade marks need to be created which are governed by a uniform Community law directly applicable in all Member States;

Whereas since the Treaty has not provided the specific powers to establish such a legal instrument, Article 235 of the Treaty should be applied;

Whereas the Community law relating to trade marks nevertheless does not replace the laws of the Member States on trade marks; whereas it would not in fact appear to be justified to require undertakings to apply for registration of their trade marks as Community trade marks; whereas national trade marks continue to be necessary for those undertakings which do not want protection of their trade marks at Community level;

Whereas the rights in a Community trade mark may not be obtained otherwise than by registration, and registration is to be refused in particular if the trade mark is not distinctive, if it is unlawful or if it conflicts with earlier rights;

Whereas the protection afforded by a Community trade mark, the function of which is in particular to guarantee the trade mark as an indication of origin, is absolute in the case of identity between the mark and the sign and the goods or services; whereas the protection applies also in cases of similarity between the mark and the sign and the goods or services; whereas an interpretation should be given of the concept of similarity in relation to the likelihood of confusion; whereas the likelihood of confusion, the appreciation of which depends on numerous elements and, in particular, on the recognition of the trade mark on the market, the association which can be made with the used or registered sign, the degree of similarity between the trade mark and the sign and between the goods or services identified, constitutes the specific condition for such protection;

Whereas it follows from the principle of free flow of goods that the proprietor of a Community trade mark must not be entitled to prohibit its use by a third party in relation to goods which have been put into circulation in the Community, under the trade mark, by him or with his consent, save where there exist legitimate reasons for the proprietor to oppose further commercialisation of the goods;

Whereas there is no justification for protection Community trade marks or, as against them, any trade mark which has been registered before them, except where the trade marks are actually used;

Whereas a Community trade mark is to be regarded as an object of property which exists separately from the undertakings whose goods or services are designated by it; whereas accordingly, it must be capable of being transferred, subject to the overriding need to prevent the public being misled as a result of the transfer. It must also be capable of being charged as security in favour of a third party and of being the subject matter of licences;

Whereas administrative measures are necessary at Community level for implementing in relation to every trade mark the trade mark law created by this Regulation; whereas it is therefore essential, while retaining the Community's existing institutional structure and balance of powers, to establish an Office for Harmonisation in the Internal Market (trade marks and designs) which is independent in relation to technical matters and has legal, administrative and financial autonomy; whereas to this end it is necessary and appropriate that it should be a body of the Community having legal personality and exercising the implementing powers which are conferred on it by this Regulation, and that it should operate within the framework of Community law without detracting from the competencies exercised by the Community institutions;

Whereas it is necessary to ensure that parties who are affected by decisions made by the Office are protected by the law in a manner which is suited to the special character of trade mark law; whereas to that end provision is made for an appeal to lie from decisions of the examiners and of the various divisions of the Office; whereas if the department whose decision is contested does not rectify its decision it is to remit the appeal to a Board of Appeal of the Office, which is to decide on it; whereas decisions of the Boards of Appeal are, in turn, amenable to actions before the Court of Justice of the European Communities, which has jurisdiction to annul or to alter the contested decision;

Whereas under Council Decision 88/591/ECSC, EEC, Euratom of 24 October 1988 establishing a Court of First Instance of the European Communities,[4] as amended by Decision 93/250/Euratom, ECSC, EEC of 8 June 1993,[5] that Court shall exercise at the first instance the jurisdiction conferred on the Court of Justice by the Treaties establishing the Communities — with particular regard to appeals lodged under the second subparagraph of Article 173 of the EC Treaty — and by the acts adopted in implementation thereof, save as otherwise provided in an act setting up a body governed by Community law; whereas the jurisdiction which this Regulation confers on the

Notes
[4] OJ No. L319, 25 November 1988, p. 1 and corrigendum in OJ No. L241, 17 August 1989, p. 4.
[5] OJ No. L144, 16 June 1993, p. 21.

Court of Justice to cancel and reform decisions of the appeal courts shall accordingly be exercised at the first instance by the Court in accordance with the above Decision;

Whereas in order to strengthen the protection of Community trade marks the Member States should designate, having regard to their own national system, as limited a number as possible of national courts of first and second instance having jurisdiction in matters of infringement and validity of Community trade marks;

Whereas decisions regarding the validity and infringement of Community trade marks must have effect and cover the entire area of the Community, as this is the only way of preventing inconsistent decisions on the part of the courts and the Office and of ensuring that the unitary character of Community trade marks is not undermined; whereas the rules contained in the Brussels Convention of Jurisdiction and the Enforcement of Judgments in Civil and Commercial Matters will apply to all actions at law relating to Community trade marks, save where this Regulation derogates from those rules;

Whereas contradictory judgments should be avoided in actions which involve the same acts and the same parties and which are brought on the basis of a Community trade mark and parallel national trade marks; whereas for this purpose, when the actions are brought in the same Member State, the way in which this is to be achieved is a matter for national procedural rules, which are not prejudiced by this Regulation, whilst when the actions are brought in different Member States, provisions modelled on the rules on *lis pendens* and related actions of the above-mentioned Brussels Convention appear appropriate;

Whereas in order to guarantee the full autonomy and independence of the Office, it is considered necessary to grant it an autonomous budget whose revenue comes principally from fees paid by the users of the system; whereas however, the Community budgetary procedure remains applicable as far as any subsidies chargeable the general budget of the European Communities are concerned; whereas moreover, the auditing of accounts should be undertaken by the Court of Auditors;

Whereas implementing measures are required for the Regulation's application, particularly as regards the adoption and amendment of fees regulations and an Implementing Regulation; whereas such measures should be adopted by the Commission, assisted by a Committee composed of representatives of the Member States, in accordance with the procedural rules laid down in Article 2, procedure III(b), of Council Decisions 87/373/EEC of 13 July 1987 laying down the procedures for the exercise of implementing powers conferred on the Commission,[6]

HAS ADOPTED THIS REGULATION:

Note

[6]OJ No. L197, 18 July 1987, p. 33.

TITLE I   GENERAL PROVISIONS

Article 1   Community trade mark

1.   A trade mark for goods or services which is registered in accordance with the conditions contained in this Regulation and in the manner herein provided is hereinafter referred to as a 'Community trade mark'.

2.   A Community trade mark shall have a unitary character. It shall have equal effect throughout the Community: it shall not be registered, transferred or surrendered or be the subject of a decision revoking the rights of the proprietor or declaring it invalid, nor shall its use be prohibited, save in respect of the whole Community. This principle shall apply unless otherwise provided in this Regulation.

Article 2   Office
An Office for Harmonisation in the Internal Market (trade marks and designs), hereinafter referred to as 'the Office', is hereby established.

Article 3   Capacity to act
For the purpose of implementing this Regulation, companies or firms and other legal bodies shall be regarded as legal persons if, under the terms of the law governing them, they have the capacity in their own name to have rights and obligations of all kinds, to make contracts or accomplish other legal acts and to sue and be sued.

TITLE II   THE LAW RELATING TO TRADE MARKS
SECTION 1   DEFINITION OF A COMMUNITY TRADE MARK; OBTAINING A COMMUNITY TRADE MARK

Article 4   Signs of which a Community trade mark may consist
A Community trade mark may consist of any signs capable of being represented graphically, particularly words, including personal names, designs, letters, numerals, the shape of goods or of their packaging, provided that such signs are capable of distinguishing the goods or services of one undertaking from those of other undertakings.

Article 5   Persons who can be proprietors of Community trade marks
   1.   The following natural or legal persons, including authorities established under public law, may be proprietors of Community trade marks:
      (a)   nationals of the Member States; or
      (b)   nationals of other States which are parties to the Paris Convention for the protection of industrial property, hereinafter referred to as 'the Paris Convention', or to the Agreement establishing the World Trade Organisation;
      (c)   nationals of States which are not parties to the Paris Convention who are domiciled or have their seat or who have real and effective industrial or commercial establishments within the territory of the Community or of a State which is party to the Paris Convention; or
      (d)   nationals, other than those referred to under subparagraph (c), of any State which is not party to the Paris Convention or to the Agreement establishing the World Trade Organisation and which, according to published findings, accords to nationals of all the Member States the same protection for trade marks as it accords to its own nationals and, if nationals of the Member States are required to prove registration in the country of origin, recognises the registration of Community trade marks as such proof.
   2.   With respect to the application of paragraph 1, stateless persons as defined by Article 1 of the Convention relating to the Status of Stateless Persons signed at New York on 28 September 1954, and refugees as defined by Article 1 of the Convention relating to the Status of Refugees signed at Geneva on 28 July 1951 and modified by the Protocol relating to the Status of Refugees

signed at New York on 31 January 1967, shall be regarded as nationals of the country in which they have their habitual residence.

3. Persons who are nationals of a State covered by paragraph 1(d) must prove that the trade mark for which an application for a Community trade mark has been submitted is registered in the State of origin, unless, according to published findings, the trade marks of nationals of the Member States are registered in the State of origin in question without proof of prior registration as a Community trade mark or as a national trade mark in a Member State.

Article 6   Means whereby a Community trade mark is obtained
A Community trade mark shall be obtained by registration.

Article 7   Absolute grounds for refusal
1.   The following shall not be registered:
 (a)   signs which do not conform to the requirements of Article 4;
 (b)   trade marks which are devoid of any distinctive character;
 (c)   trade marks which consist exclusively of signs or indications which may serve, in trade, to designate the kind, quality, quantity, intended purpose, value, geographical origin or the time of production of the goods or of rendering of the service, or other characteristics of the goods or service;
 (d)   trade marks which consist exclusively of signs or indications which have become customary in the current language or in the bona fide and established practices of the trade;
 (e)   signs which consist exclusively of:
  (i)   the shape which results from the nature of the goods themselves; or
  (ii)   the shape of goods which is necessary to obtain a technical result; or
  (iii)   the shape which gives substantial value to the goods;
 (f)   trade marks which are contrary to public policy or to accepted principles of morality;
 (g)   trade marks which are of such a nature as to deceive the public, for instance as to the nature, quality or geographical origin of the goods or service;
 (h)   trade marks which have not been authorised by the competent authorities and are to be refused pursuant to Article 6ter of the Paris Convention;
 (i)   trade marks which include badges, emblems or escutcheons other than those covered by Article 6 of the Paris Convention and which are of particular public interest, unless the consent of the appropriate authorities to their registration has been given.
 (j)   trade marks for wines which contain or consist of a geographical indication identifying wines or for spirits which contain or consist of a geographical indication identifying spirits with respect to such wines or spirits not having that origin.
2.   Paragraph 1 shall apply notwithstanding that the grounds of non-registrability obtain in only part of the Community.
3.   Paragraph 1(b), (c) and (d) shall not apply if the trade mark has become distinctive in relation to the goods or services for which registration is requested in consequence of the use which has been made of it.

Article 8   Relative grounds for refusal

1.   Upon opposition by the proprietor of an earlier trade mark, the trade mark applied for shall not be registered;

(a)   if it is identical with the earlier trade mark and the goods or services for which registration is applied for are identical with the goods or services for which the eralier trade mark is protected;

(b)   If because of its identity with or similarity to the earlier trade mark and the identity or similarity of the goods or services covered by the trade marks there exists a likelihood of confusion on the part of the public in the territory in which the earlier trade mark is protected; the likelihood of confusion includes the likelihood of association with the earlier trade mark.

2.   For the purposes of paragraph 1, 'Earlier trade marks' means:

(a)   trade marks of the following kinds with a date of application for registration which is earlier than the date of application for registration of the Community trade mark, taking account, where appropriate, of the priorities claimed in respect of those trade marks:

(i)   Community trade marks;

(ii)   trade marks registered in a Member State, or, in the case of Belgium, the Netherlands or Luxembourg, at the Benelux Trade Mark Office;

(iii)   trade marks registered under international arrangements which have effect in a Member State;

(b)   applications for the trade marks referred to in subparagraph (a), subject to their registration;

(c)   trade marks which, on the date of application for registration of the Community trade mark, or, where appropriate, of the priority claimed in respect of the application for registration of the Community trade mark, are well known in a Member State, in the sense in which the words 'well known' are used in Article 6bis of the Paris Convention.

3.   Upon opposition by the proprietor of the trade mark, a trade mark shall not be registered where an agent or representative of the proprietor of the trade mark applies for registration thereof in his own name without the proprietor's consent, unless the agent or representative justifies his action.

4.   Upon opposition by the proprietor of a non-registered trade mark or of another sign used in the course of trade of more than mere local significance, the trade mark applied for shall not be registered where and to the extent that, pursuant to the law of the Member State governing that sign,

(a)   rights to that sign were acquired prior to the date of application for registration of the Community trade mark, or the date of the priority claimed for the application for registration of the Community trade mark;

(b)   that sign confers on its proprietor the right to prohibit the use of a subsequent trade mark.

5.   Furthermore, upon opposition by the proprietor of an earlier trade mark within the meaning of paragraph 2, the trade mark applied for shall not be registered where it is identical with or similar to the earlier trade mark and is to be registered for goods or services which are not similar to those for which the earlier trade mark is registered, where in the case of an earlier Community trade mark the trade mark has a reputation in the Community and, in the case of an earlier national trade mark, the trade mark has a reputation in the Member State concerned and where the use without due cause of the trade mark applied

for would take unfair advantage of, or be detrimental to, the distinctive character or the repute of the earlier trade mark.

SECTION 2   EFFECTS OF COMMUNITY TRADE MARKS

Article 9   Rights conferred by a Community trade mark

1.   A Community trade mark shall confer on the proprietor exclusive rights therein. The proprietor shall be entitled to prevent all third parties not having his consent from using in the course of trade:

(a)   any sign which is identical with the Community trade mark in relation to goods or services which are identical with those for which the Community trade mark is registered;

(b)   any sign where, because of its identity with or similarity to the Community trade mark and the identity or similarity of the goods or services covered by the Community trade mark and the sign, there exists a likelihood of confusion on the part of the public; the likelihood of confusion includes the likelihood of association between the sign and the trade mark;

(c)   any sign which is identical with or similar to the Community trade mark in relation to goods or services which are not similar to those for which the Community trade mark is registered, where the latter has a reputation in the Community and where use of that sign without due cause takes unfair advantage of, or is detrimental to, the distinctive character or the repute of the Community trade mark.

2.   The following, inter alia, may be prohibited under paragraph 1:

(a)   affixing the sign to the goods or to the packaging thereof;

(b)   offering the goods, putting them on the market or stocking them for these purposes under that sign, or offering or supplying services thereunder;

(c)   importing or exporting the goods under that sign;

(d)   using the sign on business papers and in advertising.

3.   The rights conferred by a Community trade mark shall prevail against third parties from the date of publication of registration of the trade mark. Reasonable compensation may, however, be claimed in respect of matters arising after the date of publication of a Community trade mark application, which matters would, after publication of the registration of the trade mark, be prohibited by virtue of that publication. The court seized of the case may not decide upon the merits of the case until the registration has been published.

Article 10   Reproduction of Community trade marks in dictionaries

If the reproduction of a Community trade mark in a dictionary, encyclopaedia or similar reference work gives the impression that it constitutes the generic name of the goods or services for which the trade mark is registered, the publisher of the work shall, at the request of the proprietor of the Community trade mark, ensure that the reproduction of the trade mark at the latest in the next edition of the publication is accompanied by an indication that it is a registered trade mark.

Article 11   Prohibition on the use of a Community trade mark registered in the name of an agent or representative

Where a Community trade mark is registered in the name of the agent or representative of a person who is the proprietor of that trade mark, without the proprietor's authorisation, the latter shall be entitled to oppose the use of his mark by his agent or representative if he has not authorised such use, unless the agent or representative justifies his action.

Article 12   Limitation of the effects of a Community trade mark

A Community trade mark shall not entitle the proprietor to prohibit a third party from using in the course of trade:

    (a)   his own name or address;

    (b)   indications concerning the kind, quality, quantity, intended purpose, value, geographical origin, the time of production of the goods or of rendering of the service, or other characteristics of the goods or service;

    (c)   the trade mark where it is necessary to indicate the intended purpose of a product or service, in particular as accessories or spare parts, provided he uses them in accordance with honest practices in industrial or commercial matters.

Article 13   Exhaustion of the rights conferred by a Community trade mark

1.   A Community trade mark shall not entitle the proprietor to prohibit its use in relation to goods which have been put on the market in the Community under that trade mark by the proprietor or with his consent.

2.   Paragraph 1 shall not apply where there exist legitimate reasons for the proprietor to oppose further commercialisation of the goods, especially where the condition of the goods is changed or impaired after they have been put on the market.

Article 14   Complementary application of national law relating to infringement

1.   The effects of Community trade marks shall be governed solely by the provisions of this Regulation. In other respects, infringement of a Community trade mark shall be governed by the national law relating to infringement of a national trade mark in accordance with the provisions of Title X.

2.   This Regulation shall not prevent actions concerning a Community trade mark being brought under the law of Member States relating in particular to civil liability and unfair competition.

3.   The rules of procedure to be applied shall be determined in accordance with the provisions of Title X.

SECTION 3   USE OF COMMUNITY TRADE MARKS

Article 15   Use of Community trade marks

1.   If, within a period of five years following registration, the proprietor has not put the Community trade mark to genuine use in the Community in connection with the goods or services in respect of which it is registered, or if such use has been suspended during an uninterrupted period of five years, the Community trade mark shall be subject to the sanctions provided for in this Regulation, unless there are proper reasons for non-use.

2.   The following shall also constitute use within the meaning of paragraph 1:

    (a)   use of the Community trade mark in a form differing in elements which do not alter the distinctive character of the mark in the form in which it was registered;

    (b)   affixing of the Community trade mark to goods or to the packaging thereof in the Community solely for export purposes.

3.   Use of the Community trade mark with the consent of the proprietor shall be deemed to constitute use by the proprietor.

SECTION 4   COMMUNITY TRADE MARKS AS OBJECTS OF PROPERTY

Article 16   Dealing with Community trade marks as national trade marks

1.   Unless Articles 17 to 24 provide otherwise, a Community trade mark as an object of property shall be dealt with in its entirety, and for the whole area of the Community, as a national trade mark registered in the Member State in which, according to the Register of Community trade marks,

(a)   the proprietor has his seat or his domicile on the relevant date; or

(b)   where subparagraph (a) does not apply, the proprietor has an establishment on the relevant date.

2.   In cases which are not provided for by paragraph 1, the Member State referred to in that paragraph shall be the Member State in which the seat of the Office is situated.

3.   If two or more persons are mentioned in the Register of Community trade marks as joint proprietors, paragraph 1 shall apply to the joint proprietor first mentioned; failing this, it shall apply to the subsequent joint proprietors in the order in which they are mentioned. Where paragraph 1 does not apply to any of the joint proprietors, paragraph 2 shall apply.

Article 17   Transfer

1.   A Community trade mark may be transferred, separately from any transfer of the undertaking, in respect of some or all of the goods or services for which it is registered.

2.   A transfer of the whole of the undertaking shall include the transfer of the Community trade mark except where, in accordance with the law governing the transfer, there is agreement to the contrary or circumstances clearly dictate otherwise. This provision shall apply to the contractual obligation to transfer the undertaking.

3.   Without prejudice to paragraph 2, an assignment of the Community trade mark shall be made in writing and shall require the signature of the parties to the contract, except when it is a result of a judgment; otherwise it shall be void.

4.   Where it is clear from the transfer documents that because of the transfer the Community trade mark is likely to mislead the public concerning the nature, quality or geographical origin of the goods or services in respect of which it is registered, the Office shall not register the transfer unless the successor agrees to limit registration of the Community trade mark to goods or services in respect of which it is not likely to mislead.

5.   On request of one of the parties a transfer shall be entered in the Register and published.

6.   As long as the transfer has not been entered in the Register, the successor in title may not invoke the rights arising from the registration of the Community trade mark.

7.   Where there are time limits to be observed vis-à-vis the Office, the successor in title may make the corresponding statements to the Office once the request for registration of the transfer has been received by the Office.

8.   All documents which require notification to the proprietor of the Community trade mark in accordance with Article 77 shall be addressed to the person registered as proprietor.

Article 18   Transfer of a trade mark registered in the name of an agent
Where a Community trade mark is registered in the name of the agent or representative of a person who is the proprietor of that trade mark, without the proprietor's authorisation, the latter shall be entitled to demand the assignment in his favour of the said registration, unless such agent or representative justifies his action.

Article 19   Rights in rem
1.   A Community trade mark may, independently of the undertaking, be given as security or be the subject of rights in rem.
2.   On request of one of the parties, rights mentioned in paragraph 1 shall be entered in the Register and published.

Article 20   Levy of execution
1.   A Community trade mark may be levied in execution.
2.   As regards the procedure for levy of execution in respect of a Community trade mark, the courts and authorities of the Member States determined in accordance with Article 16 shall have exclusive jurisdiction.
3.   On request of one of the parties, levy of execution shall be entered in the Register and published.

Article 21   Bankruptcy or like proceedings
1.   Until such time as common rules for the Member States in this field enter into force, the only Member State in which a Community trade mark may be involved in bankruptcy or like proceedings shall be that in which such proceedings are first brought within the meaning of national law or of conventions applicable in this field.
2.   Where a Community trade mark is involved in bankruptcy or like proceedings, on request of the competent national authority an entry to this effect shall be made in the Register and published.

Article 22   Licensing
1.   A Community trade mark may be licensed for some or all of the goods or services for which it is registered and for the whole or part of the Community. A licence may be exclusive or non-exclusive.
2.   The proprietor of a Community trade mark may invoke the rights conferred by the trade mark against a licensee who contravenes any provision in his licensing contract with regard to its duration, the form covered by the registration in which the trade mark may be used, the scope of the goods or services for which the licence is granted, the territory in which the trade mark may be affixed, or the quality of the goods manufactured or of the services provided by the licensee.
3.   Without prejudice to the provisions of the licensing contract, the licensee may bring proceedings for infringement of a Community trade mark only if its proprietor consents thereto. However, the holder of an exclusive licence may bring such proceedings if the proprietor of the trade mark, after formal notice, does not himself bring infringement proceedings within an appropriate period.
4.   A licensee shall, for the purpose of obtaining compensation for damage suffered by him, be entitled to intervene in infringement proceedings brought by the proprietor of the Community trade mark.

5. On request of one of the parties the grant or transfer of a licence in respect of a Community trade mark shall be entered in the Register and published.

Article 23   Effects vis-à-vis third parties

1. Legal acts referred to in Articles 17, 19 and 22 concerning a Community trade mark shall only have effects vis-à-vis third parties in all the Member States after entry in the Register. Nevertheless, such an act, before it is so entered, shall have effect vis-à-vis third parties who have acquired rights in the trade mark after the date of that act but who knew of the act at the date on which the rights were acquired.

2. Paragraph 1 shall not apply in the case of a person who acquires the Community trade mark or a right concerning the Community trade mark by way of transfer of the whole of the undertaking or by any other universal succession.

3. The effects vis-à-vis third parties of the legal acts referred to in Article 20 shall be governed by the law of the Member State determined in accordance with Article 16.

4. Until such time as common rules for the Member States in the field of bankruptcy enter into force, the effects vis-à-vis third parties of bankruptcy or like proceedings shall be governed by the law of the Member State in which such proceedings are first brought within the meaning of national law or of conventions applicable in this field.

Article 24   The application for a Community trade mark as an object of property

Articles 16 to 23 shall apply to applications for Community trade marks.

TITLE III   APPLICATION FOR COMMUNITY TRADE MARKS
SECTION 1   FILING OF APPLICATIONS AND THE CONDITIONS WHICH GOVERN THEM

Article 25   Filing of applications

1. An application for a Community trade mark shall be filed, at the choice of the applicant,

  (a)   at the Office; or

  (b)   at the central industrial property office of a Member State or at the Benelux Trade Mark Office. An application filed in this way shall have the same effect as if it had been filed on the same date at the Office.

2. Where the application is filed at the central industrial property office of a Member State or at the Benelux Trade Mark Office, that office shall take all steps to forward the application to the Office within two weeks after filing. It may charge the applicant a fee which shall not exceed the administrative costs of receiving and forwarding the application.

3. Applications referred to in paragraph 2 which reach the Office more than one month after filing shall be deemed withdrawn.

4. Ten years after the entry into force of this Regulation, the Commission shall draw up a report on the operation of the system of filing applications for Community trade marks, together with any proposal for modifying this system.

Article 26   Conditions with which applications must comply

1. An application for a Community trade mark shall contain:

    (a)   a request for the registration of a Community trade mark;
    (b)   information identifying the applicant;
    (c)   a list of the goods or services in respect of which the registration is requested;
    (d)   a representation of the trade mark.
    2.   The application for a Community trade mark shall be subject to the payment of the application fee and, when appropriate, of one or more class fees.
    3.   An application for a Community trade mark must comply with the conditions laid down in the implementing Regulation referred to in Article 140.

Article 27   Date of filing
The date of filing of a Community trade mark application shall be the date on which documents containing the information specified in Article 26(1) are filed with the Office by the applicant or, if the application has been filed with the central office of a Member State or with the Benelux Trade Mark Office, with that office, subject to payment of the application fee within a period of one month of filing the above mentioned documents.

Article 28   Classification
Goods and services in respect of which Community trade marks are applied for shall be classified in conformity with the system of classification specified in the Implementing Regulation.

SECTION 2   PRIORITY

Article 29   Right of priority
    1.   A person who has duly filed an application for a trade mark in or for any State party to the Paris Convention or to the Agreement establishing the World Trade Organisation, or his successors in title, shall enjoy, for the purpose of filing a Community trade mark application for the same trade mark in respect of goods or services which are identical with or contained within those for which the application has been filed, a right or priority during a period of six months from the date of filing of the first application.
    2.   Every filing that is equivalent to a regular national filing under the national law of the State where it was made or under bilateral or multilateral agreements shall be recognised as giving rise to a right of priority.
    3.   By a regular national filing is meant any filing that is sufficient to establish the date on which the application was filed, whatever may be the outcome of the application.
    4.   A subsequent application for a trade mark which was the subject of a previous first application in respect of the same goods or services, and which is filed in or in respect of the same State shall be considered as the first application for the purposes of determining priority, provided that, at the date of filing of the subsequent application, the previous application has been withdrawn, abandoned or refused, without being open to public inspection and without leaving any rights outstanding, and has not served as a basis for claiming a right of priority. The previous application may not thereafter serve as a basis for claiming a right of priority.
    5.   If the first filing has been made in a State which is not a party to the Paris Convention or to the Agreement establishing the world Trade Organisation, paragraphs 1 to 4 shall apply only in so far as that State, according to published findings, grants, on the basis of the first filing made at the Office and subject to

conditions equivalent to those laid down in this Regulation, a right of priority having equivalent effect.

Article 30   Claiming priority

An applicant desiring to take advantage of the priority of a previous application shall file a declaration of priority and a copy of the previous application. If the langauge of the latter is not one of the languages of the Office, the applicant shall file a translation of the previous application in one of those languages.

Article 31   Effect of priority right

The right of priority shall have the effect that the date of priority shall count as the date of filing of the Community trade mark application for the purposes of establishing which rights take precedence.

Article 32   Equivalence of Community filing with national filing

A Community trade mark application which has been accorded a date of filing shall, in the Member States, be equivalent to a regular national filing, where appropriate with the priority claimed for the Community trade mark application.

SECTION 3   EXHIBITION PRIORITY

Article 33   Exhibition priority

1.   If an applicant for a Community trade mark has displayed goods or services under the mark applied for, at an official or officially recognised international exhibition falling within the terms of the Convention on International Exhibitions signed at Paris on 22 November 1928 and last revised on 30 November 1972, he may, if he files the application within a period of six months from the date of the first display of the goods or services under the mark applied for, claim or right of priority from that date within the meaning of Article 31.

2.   An applicant who wishes to claim priority pursuant to paragraph 1 must file evidence of the display of goods or services under the mark applied for under the conditions laid down in the Implementing Regulation.

3.   An exhibition priority granted in a Member State or in a third country does not extend the period of priority laid down in Article 29.

SECTION 4   CLAIMING THE SENIORITY OF A NATIONAL TRADE MARK

Article 34   Claiming the seniority of a national trade mark

1.   The proprietor of an earlier trade mark registered in a Member State, including a trade mark registered in the Benelux countries, or registered under international arrangements having effect in a Member State, who applies for an identical trade mark for registration as a Community trade mark for goods or services which are identical with or contained within those for which the earlier trade mark has been registered, may claim for the Community trade mark the seniority of the earlier trade mark in respect of the Member State in or for which it is registered.

2.   Seniority shall have the sole effect under this Regulation that, where the proprietor of the Community trade mark surrenders the earlier trade mark or allows it to lapse, he shall be deemed to continue to have the same rights as he would have had if the earlier trade mark had continued to be registered.

3. The seniority claimed for the Community trade mark shall lapse if the earlier trade mark the seniority of which is claimed is declared to have been revoked or to be invalid or if it is surrendered prior to the registration of the Community trade mark.

Article 35   Claiming seniority after registration of the Community trade mark

1. The proprietor of a Community trade mark who is the proprietor of an earlier identical trade mark registered in a Member State, including a trade mark registered in the Benelux countries, or of a trade mark registered under international arrangements having effect in a Member State, for identical goods or services, may claim the seniority of the earlier trade mark in respect of the Member State in or for which it is registered.

2. Article 34(2) and (3) shall apply.

TITLE IV   REGISTRATION PROCEDURE
SECTION 1   EXAMINATION OF APPLICATIONS

Article 36   Examination of the conditions of filing

1. The Office shall examine whether:

(a) the Community trade mark application satisfies the requirements for the accordance of a date of filing in accordance with Article 27;

(b) the Community trade mark application complies with the conditions laid down in the Implementing Regulation;

(c) where appropriate, the class fees have been paid within the prescribed period.

2. Where the Community trade mark application does not satisfy the requirements referred to in paragraph 1, the Office shall request the applicant to remedy the deficiencies or the default on payment within the prescribed period.

3. If the deficiencies or the default on payment established pursuant to paragraph 1(a) are not remedied within this period, the application shall not be dealt with as a Community trade mark application. If the applicant complies with the Office's request, the Office shall accord as the date of filing of the application the date on which the deficiencies or the default on payment established are remedied.

4. If the deficiencies established pursuant to paragraph 1(b) are not remedied within the prescribed period, the Office shall refuse the application.

5. If the default on payment established pursuant to paragraph 1(c) is not remedied within the prescribed period, the application shall be deemed to be withdrawn unless it is clear which categories of goods or services the amount paid is intended to cover.

6. Failure to satisfy the requirements concerning the claim to priority shall result in loss of the right of priority for the application.

7. Failure to satisfy the requirements concerning the claiming of seniority of a national trade mark shall result in loss of the right for the application.

Article 37   Examination of the conditions relating to the entitlement of the proprietor

1. Where, pursuant to Article 5, the applicant may not be the proprietor of a Community trade mark, the application shall be refused.

2.   The application may not be refused before the applicant has been given the opportunity to withdraw his application or submit his observations.

Article 38   Examination as to absolute grounds for refusal

1.   Where, under Article 7, a trade mark is ineligible for registration in respect of some or all of the goods or services covered by the Community trade mark application, the application shall be refused as regards those goods or services.

2.   Where the trade mark contains an element which is not distinctive, and where the inclusion of said element in the trade mark could give rise to doubts as to the scope of protection of the trade mark, the Office may request, as a condition for registration of said trade mark, that the applicant state that he disclaims any exclusive right to such element. Any disclaimer shall be published together with the application or the registration of the Community trade mark, as the case may be.

3.   The application shall not be refused before the applicant has been allowed the opportunity of withdrawing or amending the application or of submitting his observations.

SECTION 2   SEARCH

Article 39   Search

1.   Once the Office has accorded a date of filing to a Community trade mark application and has established that the applicant satisfies the conditions referred to in Article 5, it shall draw up a Community search report citing those earlier Community trade marks or Community trade mark applications discovered which may be invoked under Article 8 against the registration of the Community trade mark applied for.

2.   As soon as a Community trade mark application has been accorded a date of filing, the Office shall transmit a copy thereof to the central industrial property office of each Member State which has informed the Office of its decision to operate a search in its own register of trade marks in respect of Community trade mark applications.

3.   Each of the central industrial property offices referred to in paragraph 2 shall communicate to the Office within three months as from the date on which it received the Community trade mark application a search report which shall either cite those earlier national trade marks or trade mark applications discovered which may be invoked under Article 8 against the registration of the Community trade mark applied for, or state that the search has revealed no such rights.

4.   An amount shall be paid by the Office to each central industrial property office for each search report provided by that office in accordance with paragraph 3. The amount, which shall be the same for each office, shall be fixed by the Budget Committee by means of a decision adopted by a majority of three-quarters of the representatives of the Member States.

5.   The Office shall transmit without delay to the applicant for the Community trade mark the Community search report and the national search reports received within the time limit laid down in paragraph 3.

6.   Upon publication of the Community trade mark application, which may not take place before the expiry of a period of one month as from the date on which the Office transmits the search reports to the applicant, the Office shall

inform the proprietors of any earlier Community trade marks or Community trade mark applications cited in the Community search report of the publication of the Community trade mark application.

7.   The Commission shall, five years after the opening of the Office for the filing of applications, submit to the Council a report on the operation of the system of searching resulting from this Article, including the payments made to Member States under paragraph 4, and, if necessary, appropriate proposals for amending this Regulation with a view to adapting the system of searching on the basis of the experience gained and bearing in mind developments in searching techniques.

SECTION 3   PUBLICATION OF THE APPLICATION

Article 40   Publication of the application

1.   If the conditions which the application for a Community trade mark must satisfy have been fulfilled and if the period referred to in Article 39(6) has expired, the application shall be published to the extent that it has not been refused pursuant to Articles 37 and 38.

2.   Where, after publication, the application is refused under Articles 37 and 38, the decision that it has been refused shall be published upon becoming final.

SECTION 4   OBSERVATIONS BY THIRD PARTIES AND OPPOSITION

Article 41   Observations by third parties

1.   Following the publication of the Community trade mark application, any natural or legal person and any group or body representing manufacturers, producers, suppliers of services, traders or consumers may submit to the Office written observations, explaining on which grounds under Article 7, in particular, the trade mark shall not be registered ex officio. They shall not be parties to the proceedings before the Office.

2.   The observations referred to in paragraph 1 shall be communicated to the applicant who may comment on them.

Article 42   Opposition

1.   Within a period of three months following the publication of a Community trade mark application, notice of opposition to registration of the trade mark may be given on the grounds that it may not be registered under Article 8:

(a)   by the proprietors of earlier trade marks referred to in Article 8(2) as well as licensees authorised by the proprietors of those trade marks, in respect of Article 8(1) and (5);

(b)   by the proprietors of trade marks referred to in Article 8(3);

(c)   by the proprietors of earlier marks or signs referred to in Article 8(4) and by persons authorised under the relevant national law to exercise these rights.

2.   Notice of opposition to registration of the trade mark may also be given, subject to the conditions laid down in paragraph 1, in the event of the publication of an amended application in accordance with the second sentence of Article 44(2).

3.   Opposition must be expressed in writing and must specify the grounds on which it is made. It shall not be treated as duly entered until the opposition fee has been paid. Within a period fixed by the Office, the opponent may submit in support of his case facts, evidence and arguments.

Article 43   Examination of opposition

1.   In the examination of the opposition the Office shall invite the parties, as often as necessary, to file observations, within a period set them by the Office, on communications from the other parties or issued by itself.

2.   If the applicant so requests, the proprietor of an earlier Community trade mark who has given notice of opposition shall furnish proof that, during the period of five years preceding the date of publication of the Community trade mark application, the earlier Community trade mark has been put to genuine use in the Community in connection with the goods or services in respect of which it is registered and which he cites as justification for his opposition, or that there are proper reasons for non-use, provided the earlier Community trade mark has at that date been registered for not less than five years. In the absence of proof to this effect, the opposition shall be rejected. If the earlier Community trade mark has been used in relation to part only of the goods or services for which it is registered it shall, for the purposes of the examination of the opposition, be deemed to be registered in respect only of that part of the goods or services.

3.   Paragraph 2 shall apply to earlier national trade marks referred to in Article 8(2)(a), by substituting use in the Member State in which the earlier national trade mark is protected for use in the Community.

4.   The Office may, if it thinks fit, invite the parties to make a friendly settlement.

5.   If examination of the opposition reveals that the trade mark may not be registered in respect of some or all of the goods or services for which the Community trade mark application has been made, the application shall be refused in respect of those goods or services. Otherwise the opposition shall be rejected.

6.   The decision refusing the application shall be published upon becoming final.

SECTION 5   WITHDRAWAL, RESTRICTION AND AMENDMENT OF THE APPLICATION

Article 44   Withdrawal, restriction and amendment of the application

1.   The applicant may at any time withdraw his Community trade mark application or restrict the list of goods or services contained therein. Where the application has already been published, the withdrawal or restriction shall also be published.

2.   In other respects, a Community trade mark application may be amended, upon request of the applicant, only by correcting the name and address of the applicant, errors of wording or of copying, or obvious mistakes, provided that such correction does not substantially change the trade mark or extend the list of goods or services. Where the amendments affect the representation of the trade mark or the list of goods or services and are made after publication of the application, the trade mark application shall be published as amended.

SECTION 6   REGISTRATION

Article 45   Registration

Where an application meets the requirements of this Regulation and where no notice of opposition has been given within the period referred to in Article 42(1) or where opposition has been rejected by a definitive decision, the trade mark shall be registered as a Community trade mark, provided that the registration fee has been paid within the period prescribed. If the fee is not paid within this period the application shall be deemed to be withdrawn.

TITLE V   DURATION, RENEWAL AND ALTERATION OF COMMUNITY TRADE MARKS

Article 46   Duration of registration

Community trade marks shall be registered for a period of ten years from the date of filing of the application. Registration may be renewed in accordance with Article 47 for further periods of ten years.

Article 47   Renewal

1.   Registration of the Community trade mark shall be renewed at the request of the proprietor of the trade mark or any person expressly authorised by him, provided that the fees have been paid.

2.   The Office shall inform the proprietor of the Community trade mark, and any person having a registered right in respect of the Community trade mark, of the expiry of the registration in good time before the said expiry. Failure to give such information shall not involve the responsibility of the Office.

3.   The request for renewal shall be submitted within a period of six months ending on the last day of the month in which protection ends. The fees shall also be paid within this period. Failing this, the request may be submitted and the fees paid within a further period of six months following the day referred to in the first sentence, provided that an additional fee is paid within this further period.

4.   Where the request is submitted or the fees paid in respect of only some of the goods or services for which the Community trade mark is registered, registration shall be renewed for those goods or services only.

5.   Renewal shall take effect from the day following the date on which the existing registration expires. The renewal shall be registered.

Article 48   Alteration

1.   The Community trade mark shall not be altered in the register during the period of registration or on renewal thereof.

2.   Nevertheless, where the Community trade mark includes the name and address of the proprietor, any alteration thereof not substantially affecting the identity of the trade mark as originally registered may be registered at the request of the proprietor.

3.   The publication of the registration of the alteration shall contain a representation of the Community trade mark as altered. Third parties whose rights may be affected by the alteration may challenge the registration thereof within a period of three months following publication.

TITLE VI   SURRENDER, REVOCATION AND INVALIDITY
SECTION 1   SURRENDER

Article 49   Surrender

1.   A Community trade mark may be surrendered in respect of some or all of the goods or services for which it is registered.

2.   The surrender shall be declared to the Office in writing by the proprietor of the trade mark. It shall not have effect until it has been entered in the Register.

3.   Surrender shall be entered only with the agreement of the proprietor of a right entered in the Register. If a licence has been registered, surrender shall only be entered in the Register if the proprietor of the trade mark proves that he has informed the licensee of his intention to surrender; this entry shall be made on expiry of the period prescribed by the Implementing Regulation.

SECTION 2   GROUNDS FOR REVOCATION

Article 50   Grounds for revocation

1.   The rights of the proprietor of the Community trade mark shall be declared to be revoked on application to the Office or on the basis of a counterclaim in infringement proceedings:

(a)   if, within a continuous period of five years, the trade mark has not been put to genuine use in the Community in connection with the goods or services in respect of which it is registered, and there are no proper reasons for non-use; however, no person may claim that the proprietor's rights in a Community trade mark should be revoked where, during the interval between expiry of the five-year period and filing of the application or counterclaim, genuine use of the trade mark has been started or resumed; the commencement or resumption of use within a period of three months preceding the filing of the application or counterclaim which began at the earliest on expiry of the continuous period of five years of non-use shall, however, be disregarded where preparations for the commencement or resumption occur only after the proprietor becomes aware that the application or counterclaim may be filed;

(b)   if, in consequence of acts or inactivity of the proprietor, the trade mark has become the common name in the trade for a product or service in respect of which it is registered;

(c)   if, in consequence of the use made of it by the proprietor of the trade mark or with his consent in respect of the goods or services for which it is registered, the trade mark is liable to mislead the public, particularly as to the nature, quality or geographical origin of those goods or services;

(d)   if the proprietor of the trade mark no longer satisfies the conditions laid down by Article 5.

2.   Where the grounds for revocation of rights exist in respect of only some of the goods or services for which the Community trade mark is registered, the rights of the proprietor shall be declared to be revoked in respect of those goods or services only.

SECTION 3   GROUNDS FOR INVALIDITY

Article 51   Absolute grounds for invalidity

1.   A Community trade mark shall be declared invalid on application to the Office or on the basis of a counterclaim in infringement proceedings,

(a)   where the Community trade mark has been registered in breach of the provisions of Article 5 or of Article 7;

(b)   where the applicant was acting in bad faith when he filed the application for the trade mark.

2.   Where the Community trade mark has been registered in breach of the provisions of Article 7(1)(b), (c) or (d), it may nevertheless not be declared invalid if, in consequence of the use which has been made of it, it has after registration acquired a distinctive character in relation to the goods or services for which it is registered.

3.   Where the ground for invalidity exists in respect of only some of the goods or services for which the Community trade mark is registered, the trade mark shall be declared invalid as regards those goods or services only.

Article 52   Relative grounds for invalidity

1.   A Community trade mark shall be declared invalid on application to the Office or on the basis of a counterclaim in infringement proceedings:

(a)   where there is an earlier trade mark as referred to in Article 8(2) and the conditions set out in paragraph 1 or paragraph 5 of that Article are fulfilled;

(b)   where there is a trade mark as referred to in Article 8(3) and the conditions set out in that paragraph are fulfilled;

(c)   where there is an earlier right as referred to in Article 8(4) and the conditions set out in that paragraph are fulfilled.

2.   A Community trade mark shall also be declared invalid on application to the Office or on the basis of a counterclaim in infringement proceedings where the use of such trade mark may be prohibited pursuant to the national law governing the protection of any other earlier right and in particular:

(a)   a right to a name;

(b)   a right of personal portrayal;

(c)   a copyright;

(d)   an industrial property right.

3.   A Community trade mark may not be declared invalid where the proprietor of a right referred to in paragraphs 1 or 2 consents expressly to the registration of the Community trade mark before submission of the application for a declaration of invalidity or the counterclaim.

4.   Where the proprietor of one of the rights referred to in paragraphs 1 or 2 has previously applied for a declaration that a Community trade mark is invalid or made a counterclaim in infringement proceedings, he may not submit a new application for a declaration of invalidity or lodge a counterclaim on the basis of another of the said rights which he could have invoked in support of his first application or counterclaim.

5.   Article 51(3) shall apply.

Article 53   Limitation in consequence of acquiescence

1.   Where the proprietor of a Community trade mark has acquiesced, for a period of five successive years, in the use of a later Community trade mark in the Community while being aware of such use, he shall no longer be entitled on the basis of the earlier trade mark either to apply for a declaration that the later trade mark is invalid or to oppose the use of the later trade mark in respect of the goods or services for which the later trade mark has been used, unless registration of the later Community trade mark was applied for in bad faith.

2.   Where the proprietor of an earlier national trade mark as referred to in Article 8(2) or of another earlier sign referred to in Article 8(4) has acquiesced, for a period of five successive years, in the use of a later Community trade mark in the Member State in which the earlier trade mark or the other earlier sign is protected while being aware of such use, he shall no longer be entitled on the basis of the earlier trade mark or of the other earlier sign either to apply for a declaration that the later trade mark is invalid or to oppose the use of the later trade mark in respect of the goods or services for which the later trade mark has been used, unless registration of the later Community trade mark was applied for in bad faith.

3.   In the cases referred to in paragraphs 1 and 2, the proprietor of a later Community trade mark shall not be entitled to oppose the use of the earlier right, even though that right may no longer be invoked against the later Community trade mark.

SECTION 4   CONSEQUENCES OF REVOCATION AND INVALIDITY

Article 54   Consequences of revocation and invalidity

1.   The Community trade mark shall be deemed not to have had, as from the date of the application for revocation or of the counterclaim, the effects specified in this Regulation, to the extent that the rights of the proprietor have been revoked. An earlier date, on which one of the grounds for revocation occurred, may be fixed in the decision at the request of one of the parties.

2.   The Community trade mark shall be deemed not to have had, as from the outset, the effects specified in this Regulation, to the extent that the trade mark has been declared invalid.

3.   Subject to the national provisions relating either to claims for compensation for damage caused by negligence or lack of good faith on the part of the proprietor of the trade mark, or to unjust enrichment, the retroactive effect of revocation or invalidity of the trade mark shall not affect:

(a)   any decision on infringement which has acquired the authority of a final decision and been enforced prior to the revocation or invalidity decision;

(b)   any contract concluded prior to the revocation or invalidity decision, in so far as it has been performed before that decision; however, repayment, to an extent justified by the circumstances, of sums paid under the relevant contract, may be claimed on grounds of equity.

SECTION 5   PROCEEDINGS IN THE OFFICE IN RELATION TO REVOCATION OR INVALIDITY

Article 55   Application for revocation or for a declaration of invalidity

1.   An application for revocation of the rights of the proprietor of a Community trade mark or for a declaration that the trade mark is invalid may be submitted to the Office:

(a)   where Articles 50 and 51 apply, by any natural or legal person and any group or body set up for the purpose of representing the interests of manufacturers, producers, suppliers of services, traders or consumers, which under the terms of the law governing it has the capacity in its own name to sue and be sued;

(b)   where Article 52(1) applies, by the persons referred to in Article 42(1);

(c)   where Article 52(2) applies, by the owners of the earlier rights referred to in that provision or by the persons who are entitled under the law of the Member State concerned to exercise the rights in question.

2.   The application shall be filed in a written reasoned statement. It shall not be deemed to have been filed until the fee has been paid.

3.   An application for revocation or for a declaration of invalidity shall be inadmissible if an application relating to the same subject matter and cause of action, and involving the same parties, has been adjudicated on by a court in a Member State and has acquired the authority of a final decision.

Article 56   Examination of the application

1.   In the examination of the application for revocation of rights or for a declaration of invalidity, the Office shall invite the parties, as often as necessary, to file observations, within a period to be fixed by the Office, on communications from the other parties or issued by itself.

2.   If the proprietor of the Community trade mark so requests, the proprietor of an earlier Community trade mark, being a party to the invalidity proceedings, shall furnish proof that, during the period of five years preceding the date of the application for a declaration of invalidity, the earlier Community trade mark has been put to genuine use in the Community in connection with the goods or services in respect of which it is registered and which he cites as justification for his application, or that there are proper reasons for non-use, provided the earlier Community trade mark has at that date been registered for non-use, provided the earlier Community trade mark has at that date been registered for not less than five years. If, at the date on which the Community trade mark application was published, the earlier Community trade mark had been registered for not less than five years, the proprietor of the earlier Community trade mark shall furnish proof that, in addition, the conditions contained in Article 43(2) were satisfied at that date. In the absence of proof to this effect the application for a declaration of invalidity shall be rejected. If the earlier Community trade mark has been used in relation to part only of the goods or services for which it is registered it shall, for the purpose of the examination of the application for a declaration of invalidity, be deemed to be registered in respect only of that part of the goods or services.

3.   Paragraph 2 shall apply to earlier national trade marks referred to in Article 8(2)(a), by substituting use in the Member State in which the earlier national trade mark is protected for use in the Community.

4.   The Office may, if it thinks fit, invite the parties to make a friendly settlement.

5.   If the examination of the application for revocation of rights or for a declaration of invalidity reveals that the trade mark should not have been registered in respect of some or all of the goods or services for which it is registered, the rights of the proprietor of the Community trade mark shall be revoked or it shall be declared invalid in respect of those goods or services. Otherwise the application for revocation of rights or for a declaration of invalidity shall be rejected.

6.   The decision revoking the rights of the proprietor of the Community trade mark or declaring it invalid shall be entered in the Register upon becoming final.

TITLE VII   APPEALS

Article 57   Decisions subject to appeal

1.   An appeal shall lie from decisions of the examiners, Opposition Divisions, Administration of Trade Marks and Legal Division and Cancellation Divisions. It shall have suspensive effect.

2.   A decision which does not terminate proceedings as regards one of the parties can only be appealed together with the final decision, unless the decision allows separate appeal.

Article 58   Persons entitled to appeal and to be parties to appeal proceedings

Persons entitled to appeal and to be parties to appeal proceedings. Any party to proceedings adversely affected by a decision may appeal. Any other parties to the proceedings shall be parties to the appeal proceedings as of right.

Article 59   Time Limit and form of appeal

Notice of appeal must be filed in writing at the Office within two months after the date of notification of the decision appealed from. The notice shall be deemed to have been filed only when the fee for appeal has been paid. Within four months after the date of notification of the decision, a written statement setting out the grounds of appeal must be filed.

Article 60   Interlocutory revision

1.   If the department whose decision is contested considers the appeal to be admissible and well founded, it shall rectify its decision. This shall not apply where the appellant is opposed by another party to the proceedings.

2.   If the decision is not rectified within one month after receipt of the statement of grounds, the appeal shall be remitted to the Board of Appeal without delay, and without comment as to its merit.

Article 61   Examination of appeals

1.   If the appeal is admissible, the Board of Appeal shall examine whether the appeal is allowable.

2.   In the examination of the appeal, the Board of Appeal shall invite the parties, as often as necessary, to file observations, within a period to be fixed by the Board of Appeal, on communications from the other parties or issued by itself.

Article 62   Decisions in respect of appeals

1.   Following the examination as to the allowability of the appeal, the Board of Appeal shall decide on the appeal. The Board of Appeal may either exercise any power within the competence of the department which was responsible for the decision appealed or remit the case to that department for further prosecution.

2.   If the Board of Appeal remits the case for further prosecution to the department whose decision was appealed, the department shall be bound by the ratio decidendi of the Board of Appeal, in so far as the facts are the same.

3.   The decisions of the Boards of Appeal shall take effect only as from the date of expiration of the period referred to in Article 63(5) or, if an action has been brought before the Court of Justice within that period, as from the date of rejection of such action.

Article 63   Actions before the Court of Justice

1.   Actions may be brought before the Court of Justice against decisions of the Boards of Appeal on appeals.

2.   The action may be brought on grounds of lack of competence, infringement of an essential procedural requirement, infringement of the Treaty, of this Regulation or of any rule of law relating to their application or misuse of power.

3.   The Court of Justice has jurisdiction to annul or to alter the contested decision.

4.   The action shall be open to any party to proceedings before the Board of Appeal adversely affected by its decision.

5.   The action shall be brought before the Court of Justice within two months of the date of notification of the decision of the Board of Appeal.

6.   The Office shall be required to take the necessary measures to comply with the judgment of the Court of Justice.

TITLE VIII   COMMUNITY COLLECTIVE MARKS

Article 64   Community collective marks

1.   A Community collective mark shall be a Community trade mark which is described as such when the mark is applied for and is capable of distinguishing the goods or services of the members of the association which is the proprietor of the mark from those of other undertakings. Associations of manufacturers, producers, suppliers of services, or traders which, under the terms of the law governing them, have the capacity in their own name to have rights and obligations of all kinds, to make contracts or accomplish other legal acts and to sue and be sued, as well as legal persons governed by public law, may apply for Community collective marks.

2.   In derogation from Article 7(1)(c), signs or indications which may serve, in trade, to designate the geographical origin of the goods or services may constitute Community collective marks within the meaning of paragraph 1. A collective mark shall not entitle the proprietor to prohibit a third party from using in the course of trade such signs or indications, provided he uses them in accordance with honest practices in industrial or commercial matters; in particular, such a mark may not be invoked against a third party who is entitled to use a geographical name.

3.   The provisions of this Regulation shall apply to Community collective marks, unless Articles 65 to 72 provide otherwise.

Article 65   Regulations governing use of the mark

1.   An applicant for a Community collective mark must submit regulations governing its use within the period prescribed.

2.   The regulations governing use shall specify the persons authorised to use the mark, the conditions of membership of the association and, where they exist, the conditions of use of the mark including sanctions. The regulations governing use of a mark referred to in Article 64(2) must authorise any person whose goods or services originate in the geographical area concerned to become a member of the association which is the proprietor of the mark.

Article 66   Refusal of the application

1.   In addition to the grounds for refusal of a Community trade mark application provided for in Articles 36 and 38, an application for a Community

collective mark shall be refused where the provisions of Article 64 and 65 are not satisfied, or where the regulations governing use are contrary to public policy or to accepted principles of morality.

2. An application for a Community collective mark shall also be refused if the public is liable to be misled as regards the character or the significance of the mark, in particular if it is likely to be taken to be something other than a collective mark.

3. An application shall not be refused if the applicant, as a result of amendment of the regulations governing use, meets the requirements of paragraphs 1 and 2.

Article 67   Observations by third parties

Apart from the cases mentioned in Article 41, any person, group or body referred to in that Article may submit to the Office written observations based on the particular grounds on which the application for a Community collective mark should be refused under the terms of Article 66.

Article 68   Use of marks

Use of a Community collective mark by any person who has authority to use it shall satisfy the requirements of this Regulation, provided that the other conditions which this Regulation imposes with regard to the use of Community trade marks are fulfilled.

Article 69   Amendment of the regulations governing use of the mark

1. The proprietor of a Community collective mark must submit to the Office any amended regulations governing use.

2. The amendment shall not be mentioned in the Register if the amended regulations do not satisfy the requirements of Article 65 or involve one of the grounds for refusal referred to in Article 66.

3. Article 67 shall apply to amended regulations governing use.

4. For the purposes of applying this Regulation, amendments to the regulations governing use shall take effect only from the date of entry of the mention of the amendment in the Register.

Article 70   Persons who are entitled to bring an action for infringement

1. The provisions of Article 22(3) and (4) concerning the rights of licensees shall apply to every person who has authority to use a Community collective mark.

2. The proprietor of a Community collective mark shall be entitled to claim compensation on behalf of persons who have authority to use the mark where they have sustained damage in consequence of unauthorised use of the mark.

Article 71   Grounds for revocation

Apart from the grounds for revocation provided for in Article 50, the rights of the proprietor of a Community collective mark shall be revoked on application to the Office or on the basis of a counterclaim in infringement proceedings, if:

(a) the proprietor does not take reasonable steps to prevent the mark being used in a manner incompatible with the conditions of use, where these exist, laid down in the regulations governing use, amendments to which have, where appropriate, been mentioned in the Register;

(b)   the manner in which the mark has been used by the proprietor has caused it to become liable to mislead the public in the manner referred to in Article 66(2);

(c)   an amendment to the regulations governing use of the mark has been mentioned in the Register in breach of the provisions of Article 69(2), unless the proprietor of the mark, by further amending the regulations governing use, complies with the requirements of those provisions.

Article 72   Grounds for invalidity

Apart from the grounds for invalidity provided for in Articles 51 and 52, a Community collective mark which is registered in breach of the provisions of Article 66 shall be declared invalid on application to the Office or on the basis of a counterclaim in infringement proceedings, unless the proprietor of the mark, by amending the regulations governing use, complies with the requirements of those provisions.

TITLE IX   PROCEDURE
SECTION 1   GENERAL PROVISIONS

Article 73   Statement of reasons on which decisions are based

Decisions of the Office shall state the reasons on which they are based. They shall be based only on reasons or evidence on which the parties concerned have had no opportunity to present their comments.

Article 74   Examination of the facts by the Office of its own motion

1.   In proceedings before it the Office shall examine the facts of its own motion; however, in proceedings relating to relative grounds for refusal of registration, the Office shall be restricted in this examination to the facts, evidence and arguments provided by the parties and the relief sought.

2.   The Office may disregard facts or evidence which are not submitted in due time by the parties concerned.

Article 75   Oral proceedings

1.   If the Office considers that oral proceedings would be expedient they shall be held either at the instance of the Office or at the request of any party to the proceedings.

2.   Oral proceedings before the examiners, the Opposition Division and the Administration of Trade Marks and Legal Division shall not be public.

3.   Oral proceedings, including delivery of the decision, shall be public before the Cancellation Division and the Boards of Appeal, in so far as the department before which the proceedings are taking place does not decide otherwise in cases where admission of the public could have serious and unjustified disadvantages, in particular for a party to the proceedings.

Article 76   Taking of evidence

1.   In any proceedings before the Office, the means of giving or obtaining evidence shall include the following:
   (a)   hearing the parties;
   (b)   requests for information;
   (c)   the production of documents and items of evidence;
   (d)   hearing witnesses;
   (e)   opinions by experts;

(f) statements in writing sworn or affirmed or having a similar effect under the law of the State in which the statement is drawn up.

2. The relevant department may commission one of its members to examine the evidence adduced.

3. If the Office considers it necessary for a party, witness or expert to give evidence orally, it shall issue a summons to the person concerned to appear before it.

4. The parties shall be informed of the hearing of a witness or expert before the Office. They shall have the right to be present and to put questions to the witness or expert.

Article 77   Notification

The Office shall, as a matter of course, notify those concerned of decisions and summonses and of any notice or other communication from which a time limit is reckoned, or of which those concerned must be notified under other provisions of this Regulation or of the Implementing Regulation, or of which notification has been ordered by the President of the Office.

Article 78   Restitutio in integrum

1. The applicant for or proprietor of a Community trade mark or any other party to proceedings before the Office who, in spite of all due care required by the circumstances having been taken, was unable to observe a time limit *vis-à-vis* the Office shall, upon application, have his rights re-established if the non-observance in question has the direct consequence, by virtue of the provisions of this Regulation, of causing the loss of any right or means of redress.

2. The application must be filed in writing within two months from the removal of the cause of non-compliance with the time limit. The omitted act must be completed within this period. The application shall only be admissible within the year immediately following the expiry of the unobserved time limit. In the case of non-submission of the request for renewal of registration or of non-payment of a renewal fee, the further period of six months provided in Article 47(3), third sentence, shall be deducted from the period of one year.

3. The application must state the grounds on which it is based and must set out the facts on which it relies. It shall not be deemed to be filed until the fee for re-establishment of rights has been paid.

4. The department competent to decide on the omitted act shall decide upon the application.

5. The provisions of this Article shall not be applicable to the time limits referred to in paragraph 2 of this Article, Articles 29(1) and 42(1).

6. Where the applicant for or proprietor of a Community trade mark has his rights re-established, he may not invoke his rights *vis-à-vis* a third party who, in good faith, has put goods on the market or supplied services under a sign which is identical with or similar to the Community trade mark in the course of the period between the loss of rights in the application or in the Community trade mark and publication of the mention of re-establishment of those rights.

7. A third party who may avail himself of the provisions of paragraph 6 may bring third party proceedings against the decision re-establishing the rights of the applicant for or proprietor of a Community trade mark within a period of two months as from the date of publication of the mention of re-establishment of those rights.

8.   Nothing in this Article shall limit the right of a Member State to grant restitutio in intergrum in respect of time limits provided for in this Regulation and to be observed *vis-à-vis* the authorities of such State.

Article 79   Reference to general principles
In the absence of procedural provisions in this Regulation, the Implementing Regulation, the fees regulations or the rules of procedure of the Boards of Appeal, the Office shall take into account the principles of procedural law generally recognised in the Member States.

Article 80   Termination of financial obligations
1.   Rights of the Office to the payment of a fee shall be extinguished after four years from the end of the calendar year in which the fee fell due.
2.   Rights against the Office for the refunding of fees or sums of money paid in excess of a fee shall be extinguished after four years from the end of the calendar year in which the right arose.
3.   The period laid down in paragraphs 1 and 2 shall be interrupted in the case covered by paragraph 1 by a request for payment of the fee and in the case covered by paragraph 2 by a reasoned claim in writing. On interruption it shall begin again immediately and shall end at the latest six years after the end of the year in which it originally began, unless, in the meantime, judicial proceedings to enforce the right have begun; in this case the period shall end at the earliest one year after the judgment has acquired the authority of a final decision.

SECTION 2   COSTS

Article 81   Costs
1.   The losing party in opposition proceedings, proceedings for revocation, proceedings for a declaration of invalidity or appeal proceedings shall bear the fees incurred by the other party as well as all costs, without prejudice to Article 115(6), incurred by him essential to the proceedings, including travel and subsistence and the remuneration of an agent, adviser or advocate, within the limits of the scales set for each category of costs under the conditions laid down in the Implementing Regulation.
2.   However, where each party succeeds on some and fails on other heads, or if reasons of equity so dictate, the Opposition Division, Cancellation Division or Board of Appeal shall decide a different apportionment of costs.
3.   The party who terminates the proceedings by withdrawing the Community trade mark application, the opposition, the application for revocation of rights, the application for a declaration of invalidity or the appeal, or by not renewing registration of the Community trade mark or by surrendering the Community trade mark, shall bear the fees and the costs incurred by the other party as stipulated in paragraphs 1 and 2.
4.   Where a case does not proceed to judgment the costs shall be at the discretion of the Opposition Division, Cancellation Division or Board of Appeal.
5.   Where the parties conclude before the Opposition Division, Cancellation Division or Board of Appeal a settlement of costs differing from that provided for in the preceding paragraphs, the department concerned shall take note of that agreement.
6.   On request the registry of the Opposition Division or Cancellation Division or Board of Appeal shall fix the amount of the costs to be paid

pursuant to the preceding paragraphs. The amount so determined may be reviewed by a decision of the Opposition Division or Cancellation Division or Board of Appeal on a request filed within the prescribed period.

Article 82   Enforcement of decisions fixing the amount of costs

1.   Any final decision of the Office fixing the amount of costs shall be enforceable.

2.   Enforcement shall be governed by the rules of civil procedure in force in the State in the territory of which it is carried out. The order for its enforcement shall be appended to the decision, without other formality than verification of the authenticity of the decision, by the national authority which the Government of each Member State shall designate for this purpose and shall make known to the Office and to the Court of Justice.

3.   When these formalities have been completed on application by the party concerned, the latter may proceed to enforcement in accordance with the national law, by bringing the matter directly before the competent authority.

4.   Enforcement may be suspended only by a decision of the Court of Justice. However, the courts of the country concerned shall have jurisdiction over complaints that enforcement is being carried out in an irregular manner.

SECTION 3   INFORMATION OF THE PUBLIC AND OF THE OFFICIAL AUTHORITIES OF THE MEMBER STATES

Article 83   Register of Community trade marks

The Office shall keep a register to be known as the Register of Community trade marks, which shall contain those particulars the registration or inclusion of which is provided for by this Regulation or by the Implementing Regulation. The Register shall be open to public inspection.

Article 84   Inspection of files

1.   The files relating to Community trade mark applications which have not yet been published shall not be made available for inspection without the consent of the applicant.

2.   Any person who can prove that the applicant for a Community trade mark has stated that after the trade mark has been registered he will invoke the rights under it against him may obtain inspection of the files prior to the publication of the application and without the consent of the applicant.

3.   Subsequent to the publication of the Community trade mark application, the files relating to such application and the resulting trade mark may be inspected on request.

4.   However, where the files are inspected pursuant to paragraphs 2 or 3, certain documents in the file may be withheld from inspection in accordance with the provisions of the Implementing Regulation.

Article 85   Periodical publications

The Office shall periodically publish:

   (a)   a Community Trade Marks Bulletin containing entries made in the Register of Community trade marks as well as other particulars the publication of which is prescribed by this Regulation or by the Implementing Regulation;

   (b)   an Official Journal containing notices and information of a general character issued by the President of the Office, as well as any other information relevant to this Regulation or its implementation.

Article 86   Administrative cooperation

Unless otherwise provided in this Regulation or in national laws, the Office and the courts or authorities of the Member States shall on request give assistance to each other by communicating information or opening files for inspection. Where the Office lays files open to inspection by courts, Public Prosecutors' Offices or central industrial property offices, the inspection shall not be subject to the restrictions laid down in Article 84.

Article 87   Exchange of publications

1.   The Office and the central industrial property offices of the Member States shall despatch to each other on request and for their own use one or more copies of their respective publications free of charge.

2.   The Office may conclude agreements relating to the exchange or supply of publications.

SECTION 4   REPRESENTATION

Article 88   General principles of representation

1.   Subject to the provisions of paragraph 2, no person shall be compelled to be represented before the Office.

2.   Without prejudice to paragraph 3, second sentence, natural or legal persons not having either their domicile or their principal place of business or a real and effective industrial or commercial establishment in the Community must be represented before the Office in accordance with Article 89(1) in all proceedings established by this Regulation, other than in filing an application for a Community trade mark; the Implementing Regulation may permit other exceptions.

3.   Natural or legal persons having their domicile or principal place of business or a real and effective industrial or commercial establishment in the Community may be represented before the Office by an employee, who must file with it a signed authorisation for insertion on the files, the details of which are set out in the Implementing Regulation. An employee of a legal person to which this paragraph applies may also represent other legal persons which have economic connections with the first legal person, even if those other legal persons have neither their domicile nor their principal place of business not a real and effective industrial or commercial establishment within the Community.

Article 89   Professional representatives

1.   Representation of natural or legal persons before the Office may only be undertaken by;

(a)   any legal practitioner qualified in one of the Member States and having his place of business within the Community, to the extent that he is entitled, within the said State, to act as a representative in trade mark matters; or

(b)   professional representatives whose names appear on the list maintained for this purpose by the Office.

Representatives acting before the Office must file with it a signed authorisation for insertion on the files, the details of which are set out in the Implementing Regulation.

2.   Any natural person who fulfils the following conditions may be entered on the list of professional representatives;

(a) he must be a national of one of the Member States;

(b) he must have his place of business or employment in the Community;

(c) he must be entitled to represent natural or legal persons in trade mark matters before the central industrial property office of the Member State in which he has his place of business or employment. Where, in that State, the entitlement is not conditional upon the requirement of special professional qualifications, persons applying to be entered on the list who act in trade mark matters before the central industrial property office of the said State must have habitually so acted for at least five years. However, persons whose professional qualification to represent natural or legal persons in trade mark matters before the central industrial property office of one of the Member States is officially recognised in accordance with the regulations laid down by such State shall not be subject to the condition of having exercised the profession.

3. Entry shall be effected upon request, accompanied by a certificate furnished by the central industrial property office of the Member State concerned, which must indicate that the conditions laid down in paragraph 2 are fulfilled.

4. The President of the Office may grant exemption from:

(a) the requirement of paragraph 2(c), second sentence, if the applicant furnishes proof that he has acquired the requisite qualification in another way;

(b) the requirement of paragraph 2(a) in special circumstances.

5. The conditions under which a person may be removed from the list of professional representatives shall be laid down in the Implementing Regulations.

TITLE X   JURISDICTION AND PROCEDURE IN LEGAL ACTIONS RELATING TO COMMUNITY TRADE MARKS
SECTION 1   APPLICATION OF THE CONVENTION ON JURISDICTION AND ENFORCEMENT

Article 90   Application of the Convention on Jurisdiction and Enforcement

1. Unless otherwise specified in this Regulation, the Convention on Jurisdiction and the Enforcement of Judgments in Civil and Commercial Matters, signed in Brussels on 27 September 1968, as amended by the Conventions on the Accession to that Convention of the States acceding to the European Communities, the whole of which Convention and of which Conventions of Accession are hereinafter referred to as the 'Convention on Jurisdiction and Enforcement', shall apply to proceedings relating to Community trade marks and applications for Community trade marks, as well as to proceedings relating to simultaneous and successive actions on the basis of Community trade marks and national trade marks.

2. In the case of proceedings in respect of the actions and claims referred to in Article 92:

(a) Articles 2, 4, 5(1), (3), (4) and (5) and Article 24 of the Convention on Jurisdiction and Enforcement shall not apply;

(b) Articles 17 and 18 of that Convention shall apply subject to the limitations in Article 93(4) of this Regulation;

(c) the provisions of Title II of that Convention which are applicable to persons domiciled in a Member State shall also be applicable to persons who do not have a domicile in any Member State but have an establishment therein.

SECTION 2   DISPUTES CONCERNING THE INFRINGEMENT AND VALIDITY OF COMMUNITY TRADE MARKS

Article 91   Community trade mark courts

1.   The Member States shall designate in their territories as limited a number as possible of national courts and tribunals of first and second instance, hereinafter referred to as 'Community trade mark courts', which shall perform the functions assigned to them by this Regulation.

2.   Each Member State shall communicate to the Commission within three years of the entry into force of this Regulation a list of Community trade mark courts indicating their names and their territorial jurisdiction.

3.   Any change made after communication of the list referred to in paragraph 2 in the number, names or territorial jurisdiction of the courts shall be notified without delay by the Member State concerned to the Commission.

4.   The information referred to in paragraphs 2 and 3 shall be notified by the Commission to the Member States and published in the *Official Journal of the European Communities*.

5.   As long as a Member State has not communicated the list as stipulated in paragraph 2, jurisdiction for any proceedings resulting from an action or application covered by Article 92, and for which the courts of that State have jurisdiction under Article 93, shall lie with that court of the State in question which would have jurisdiction *ratione loci* and *ratione materiae* in the case of proceedings relating to a national trade mark registered in that State.

Article 92   Jurisdiction over infringement and validity

The Community trade mark courts shall have exclusive jurisdiction:

(a)   for all infringement actions and — if they are permitted under national law — actions in respect of threatened infringement relating to Community trade marks;

(b)   for actions for declaration of non-infringement, if they are permitted under national law;

(c)   for all actions brought as a result of acts referred to in Article 9(3), second sentence;

(d)   for counterclaims for revocation or for a declaration of invalidity of the Community trade mark pursuant to Article 96.

Article 93   International jurisdiction

1.   Subject to the provisions of this Regulation as well as to any provisions of the Convention on Jurisdiction and Enforcement applicable by virtue of Article 90, proceedings in respect of the actions and claims referred to in Article 92 shall be brought in the courts of the Member State in which the defendant is domiciled or, if he is not domiciled in any of the Member States, in which he has an establishment.

2.   If the defendant is neither domiciled nor has an establishment in any of the Member States, such proceedings shall be brought in the courts of the Member State in which the plaintiff is domiciled or, if he is not domiciled in any of the Member States, in which he has an establishment.

3.   If neither the defendant nor the plaintiff is so domiciled or has such an establishment, such proceedings shall be brought in the courts of the Member State where the Office has its seat.

4.   Notwithstanding the provisions of paragraphs 1, 2 and 3:

(a)   Article 17 of the Convention on Jurisdiction and Enforcement shall apply if the parties agree that a different Community trade mark court shall have jurisdiction;

(b)   Article 18 of that Convention shall apply if the defendant enters an appearance before a different Community trade mark court.

5.   Proceedings in respect of the actions and claims referred to in Article 92, with the exception of actions for a declaration of non-infringement of a Community trade mark, may also be brought in the courts of the Member State in which the act of infringement has been committed or threatened, or in which an act within the meaning of Article 9(3), second sentence, has been committed.

Article 94   Extent of jurisdiction

1.   A Community trade mark court whose jurisdiction is based on Article 93(1) to (4) shall have jurisdiction in respect of:

— acts of infringement committed or threatened within the territory of any of the Member States,

— acts within the meaning of Article 9(3), second sentence, committed within the territory of any of the Member States.

2.   A Community trade mark court whose jurisdiction is based on Article 93(5) shall have jurisdiction only in respect of acts committed or threatened within the territory of the Member State in which that court is situated.

Article 95   Presumption of validity — Defence as to the merits

1.   The Community trade mark courts shall treat the Community trade mark as valid unless its validity is put in issue by the defendant with a counterclaim for revocation or for a declaration of invalidity.

2.   The validity of a Community trade mark may not be put in issue in an action for a declaration of non-infringement.

3.   In the actions referred to in Article 92(a) and (c) a plea relating to revocation or invalidity of the Community trade mark submitted otherwise than by way of a counterclaim shall be admissible in so far as the defendant claims that the rights of the proprietor of the Community trade mark could be revoked for lack of use or that Community trade mark could be declared invalid on account of an earlier right of the defendant.

Article 96   Counterclaims

1.   A counterclaim for revocation or for a declaration of invalidity may only be based on the grounds for revocation or invalidity mentioned in this Regulation.

2.   A Community trade mark court shall reject a counterclaim for revocation or for a declaration of invalidity if a decision taken by the Office relating to the same subject matter and cause of action and involving the same parties has already become final.

3.   If the counterclaim is brought in a legal action to which the proprietor of the trade mark is not already a party, he shall be informed thereof and may be joined as a party to the action in accordance with the conditions set out in national law.

4.   The Community trade mark court with which a counterclaim for revocation or for a declaration of invalidity of the Community trade mark has been filed shall inform the Office of the date on which the counterclaim was

filed. The latter shall record this fact in the Register of Community trade marks.

5.   Article 56(3), (4), (5) and (6) shall apply.

6.   Where a Community trade mark court has given a judgment which has become final on a counterclaim for revocation or for invalidity of a Community trade mark, a copy of the judgment shall be sent to the Office. Any party may request information about such transmission. The Office shall mention the judgment in the Register of Community trade marks in accordance with the provisions of the Implementing Regulation.

7.   The Community trade mark court hearing a counterclaim for revocation or for a declaration of invalidity may stay the proceedings on application by the proprietor of the Community trade mark and after hearing the other parties and may request the defendant to submit an application for revocation or for a declaration of invalidity to the Office within a time limit which it shall determine. If the application is not made within the time limit, the proceedings shall continue; the counterclaim shall be deemed withdrawn. Article 100(3) shall apply.

Article 97   Applicable law

1.   The Community trade mark courts shall apply the provisions of this Regulation.

2.   On all matters not covered by this Regulation a Community trade mark court shall apply its national law, including its private international law.

3.   Unless otherwise provided in this Regulation, a Community trade mark court shall apply the rules of procedure governing the same type of action relating to a national trade mark in the Member State where it has its seat.

Article 98   Sanctions

1.   Where a Community trade mark court finds that the defendant has infringed or threatened to infringe a Community trade mark, it shall, unless there are special reasons for not doing so, issue an order prohibiting the defendant from proceeding with the acts which infringed or would infringe the Community trade mark. It shall also take such measures in accordance with its national law as are aimed at ensuring that this prohibition is complied with.

2.   In all other respects the Community trade mark court shall apply the law of the Member State to which the acts of infringement or threatened infringement were committed, including the private international law.

Article 99   Provisional and protective measures

1.   Application may be made to the courts of a Member State, including Community trade mark courts, for such provisional, including protective, measures in respect of a Community trade mark or Community trade mark application as may be available under the law of that State in respect of a national trade mark, even if, under this Regulation, a Community trade mark court of another Member State has jurisdiction as to the substance of the matter.

2.   A Community trade mark court whose jurisdiction is based on Article 93(1), (2), (3) or (4) shall have jurisdiction to grant provisional and protective measures which, subject to any necessary procedure for recognition and enforcement pursuant to Title III of the Convention on Jurisdiction and

Enforcement, are applicable in the territory of any Member State. No other court shall have such jurisdiction.

Article 100   Specific rules on related actions

1.   A Community trade mark court hearing an action referred to in Article 92, other than an action for a declaration of non-infringement shall, unless there are special grounds for continuing the hearing, of its own motion after hearing the parties or at the request of one of the parties and after hearing the other parties, stay the proceedings where the validity of the Community trade mark is already in issue before another Community trade mark court on account of a counterclaim or where an application for revocation or for a declaration of invalidity has already been filed at the Office.

2.   The Office, when hearing an application for revocation or for a declaration of invalidity shall, unless there are special grounds for continuing the hearing, of its own motion after hearing the parties or at the request of one of the parties and after hearing the other parties, stay the proceedings where the validity of the Community trade mark is already in issue on account of a counterclaim before a Community trade mark court. However, if one of the parties to the proceedings before the Community trade mark court so requests, the court may, after hearing the other parties to these proceedings, stay the proceedings. The Office shall in this instance continue the proceedings pending before it.

3.   Where the Community trade mark court stays the proceedings it may order provisional and protective measures for the duration of the stay.

Article 101   Jurisdiction of Community trade mark courts of second instance — Further appeal

1.   An appeal to the Community trade mark courts of second instance shall lie from judgments of the Community trade mark courts of first instance in respect of proceedings arising from the actions and claims referred to in Article 92.

2.   The conditions under which an appeal may be lodged with a Community trade mark court of second instance shall be determined by the national law of the Member State in which that court is located.

3.   The national rules concerning further appeal shall be applicable in respect of judgments of Community trade mark courts of second instance.

SECTION 3   OTHER DISPUTES CONCERNING COMMUNITY TRADE MARKS

Article 102   Supplementary provisions on the jurisdiction of national courts other than Community trade mark courts

1.   Within the Member State whose courts have jurisdiction under Article 90(1) those courts shall have jurisdiction for actions other than those referred to in Article 92, which would have jurisdiction *ratione loci* and *ratione materiae* in the case of actions relating to a national trade mark registerd in that State.

2.   Actions relating to a Community trade mark, other than those referred to in Article 92, for which no court has jurisdiction under Article 90(1) and paragraph 1 of this Article may be heard before the courts of the Member State in which the Office has its seat.

Article 103   Obligation of the national court

A national court which is dealing with an action relating to a Community trade mark, other than the action referred to in Article 92, shall treat the trade mark as valid.

SECTION 4   TRANSITIONAL PROVISION

Article 104   Transitional provision relating to the application of the Convention on Jurisdiction and Enforcement

The provisions of the Convention on Jurisdiction and Enforcement which are rendered applicable by the preceding Articles shall have effect in respect of any Member State solely in the text of the Convention which is in force in respect of that State at any given time.

TITLE XI   EFFECTS ON THE LAWS OF THE MEMBER STATES
SECTION 1   CIVIL ACTIONS ON THE BASIS OF MORE THAN ONE TRADE MARK

Article 105   Simultaneous and successive civil actions on the basis of Community trade marks and national trade marks

1.   Where actions for infringement involving the same cause of action and between the same parties are brought in the courts of different Member States, one seized on the basis of a Community trade mark and the other seized on the basis of a national trade mark:

(a)   the court other than the court first seized shall of its own motion decline jurisdiction in favour of that court where the trade marks concerned are identical and valid for identical goods or services. The court which would be required to decline jurisdiction may stay its proceedings if the jurisdiction of the other court is contested;

(b)   the court other than the court first seized may stay its proceedings where the trade marks concerned are identical and valid for similar goods or services and where the trade marks concerned are similar and valid for identical or similar goods or services.

2.   The court hearing an action for infringement on the basis of a Community trade mark shall reject the action if a final judgment on the merits has been given on the same cause of action and between the same parties on the basis of an identical national trade mark valid for identical goods or services.

3.   The court hearing an action for infringement on the basis of a national trade mark shall reject the action if a final judgment on the merits has been given on the same cause of action and between the same parties on the basis of an identical Community trade mark valid for identical goods or services.

4.   Paragraphs 1, 2 and 3 shall not apply in respect of provisional, including protective, measures.

SECTION 2   APPLICATION OF NATIONAL LAWS FOR THE PURPOSE OF PROHIBITING THE USE OF COMMUNITY TRADE MARKS

Article 106   Prohibition of use of Community trade marks

1.   This Regulation shall, unless otherwise provided for, not affect the right existing under the laws of the Member States to invoke claims for infringement of earlier rights within the meaning of Article 8 or Article 52(2) in relation to the use of a later Community trade mark. Claims for infringement of earlier

rights within the meaning of Article 8(2) and (4) may, however, no longer be invoked if the proprietor of the earlier right may no longer apply for a declaration that the Community trade mark is invalid in accordance with Article 53(2).

2.   This Regulation shall, unless otherwise provided for, not affect the right to bring proceedings under the civil, administrative or criminal law of a Member State or under provisions of Community law for the purpose of prohibiting the use of a Community trade mark to the extent that the use of a national trade mark may be prohibited under the law of that Member State or under Community law.

Article 107   Prior rights applicable to particular localities

1.   The proprietor of an earlier right which only applies to a particular locality may oppose the use of the Community trade mark in the territory where his right is protected in so far as the law of the Member State concerned so permits.

2.   Paragraph 1 shall cease to apply if the proprietor of the earlier right has acquiesced in the use of the Community trade mark in the territory where his right is protected for a period of five successive years, being aware of such use, unless the Community trade mark was applied for in bad faith.

3.   The proprietor of the Community trade mark shall not be entitled to oppose use of the right referred to in paragraph 1 even though that right may no longer be invoked against the Community trade mark.

SECTION 3   CONVERSION INTO A NATIONAL TRADE MARK APPLICATION

Article 108   Request for the application of national procedure

1.   The applicant for or proprietor of a Community trade mark may request the conversion of his Community trade mark application or Community trade mark into a national trade mark application

(a)   to the extent that the Community trade mark application is refused, withdrawn, or deemed to be withdrawn;

(b)   to the extent that the Community trade mark ceases to have effect.

2.   Conversion shall not take place:

(a)   where the rights of the proprietor of the Community trade mark have been revoked on the grounds of non-use, unless in the Member State for which conversion is requested the Community trade mark has been put to use which would be considered to be genuine use under the laws of that Member State;

(b)   for the purpose of protection in a Member State in which, in accordance with the decision of the Office or of the national court, grounds for refusal of registration or grounds for revocation or invalidity apply to the Community trade mark application or Community trade mark.

3.   The national trade mark application resulting from the conversion of a Community trade mark application or a Community trade mark shall enjoy in respect of the Member State concerned the date of filing or the date of priority of that application or trade mark and, where appropriate, the seniority of a trade mark of that State claimed under Article 34 or 35.

4.   Where:

—the Community trade mark application is deemed to be withdrawn or is refused by a decision of the Office which was become final,

— the Community trade mark ceases to have effect as a result of a decision of the Office which has become final or as a result of registration of surrender of the Community trade mark,

the Office shall notify to the appliant or proprietor a communication fixing a period of three months from the date of that communication in which a request for conversion may be filed.

5. Where the Community trade mark application is withdrawn or the Community trade mark ceases to have effect as a result of failure to renew the registration, the request for conversion shall be filed within three months after the date on which the Community trade mark application is withdrawn or on which the registration of the Community trade mark expires.

6. Where the Community trade mark ceases to have effect as a result of a decision of a national court, the request for conversion shall be filed within three months after the date on which that decision acquired the authority of a final decision.

7. The effect referred to in Article 32 shall lapse if the request is not filed in due time.

Article 109 Submission, publication and transmission of the request for conversion

1. A request for conversion shall be filed with the Office and shall specify the Member States in which application of the procedure for registration of a national trade mark is desired. The request shall not be deemed to be filed until the conversion fee has been paid.

2. If the Community trade mark application has been published, receipt of any such request shall be recorded in the Register of Community trade marks and the request for conversion shall be published.

3. The Office shall check whether conversion may be requested in accordance with Article 108(1), whether the request has been filed within the period laid down in Article 108(4), (5) or (6), as the case may be, and whether the conversion fee has been paid. If these conditions are fulfilled, the Office shall transmit the request to the central industrial property offices of the States specified therein. At the request of the central industrial property office of a State concerned, the Office shall give it any information enabling that office to decide as to the admissibility of the request.

Article 110 Formal requirements for conversion

1. Any central industrial property office to which the request is transmitted shall decide as to its admissibility.

2. A Community trade mark application or a Community trade mark transmitted in accordance with Article 109 shall not be subjected to formal requirements of national law which are different from or additional to those provided for in this Regulation or in the Implementing Regulation.

3. Any central industrial property office to which the request is transmitted may require that the applicant shall, within not less than two months:

    (a)   pay the national application fee;

    (b)   file a translation in one of the official languages of the State in question of the request and of the documents accompanying it;

    (c)   indicate an address for service in the State in question;

    (d)   supply a representation of the trade mark in the number of copies specified by the State in question.

TITLE XII   THE OFFICE
SECTION 1   GENERAL PROVISIONS

Article 111   Legal status

1. The Office shall be a body of the Community. It shall have legal personality.

2. In each of the Member States the Office shall enjoy the most extensive legal capacity accorded to legal persons under their laws; it may, in particular, acquire or dispose of movable and immovable property and may be a party to legal proceedings.

3. The Office shall be represented by its President.

Article 112   Staff

1. The Staff Regulations of officials of the European Communities, the Conditions of Employment of other servants of the European Communities, and the rules adopted by agreement between the Institutions of the European Communities for giving effect to those Staff Regulations and Conditions of Employment shall apply to the staff of the Office, without prejudice to the application of Article 131 to the members of the Boards of Appeal.

2. Without prejudice to Article 120, the powers conferred on each Institution by the Staff Regulations and by the Conditions of Employment of other servants shall be exercised by the Office in respect of its staff.

Article 113   Privileges and immunities

The Protocol on the Privileges and Immunities of the European Communities shall apply to the Office.

Article 114   Liability

1. The contractual liability of the Office shall be governed by the law applicable to the contract in question.

2. The Court of Justice shall be competent to give judgment pursuant to any arbitration clause contained in a contract concluded by the Office.

3. In the case of non-contractual liability, the Office shall, in accordance with the general principles common to the laws of the Member States, make good any damage caused by its departments or by its servants in the performance of their duties.

4. The Court of Justice shall have jurisdiction in disputes relating to compensation for the damage referred to in paragraph 3.

5. The personal liability of its servants towards the Office shall be governed by the provisions laid down in their Staff Regulations or in the Conditions of Employment applicable to them.

Article 115   Languages

1. The application for a Community trade mark shall be filed in one of the official languages of the European Community.

2. The languages of the Office shall be English, French, German, Italian and Spanish.

3. The applicant must indicate a second language which shall be a language of the Office the use of which he accepts as a possible language of proceedings for opposition, revocation or invalidity proceedings.

If the application was filed in a language which is not one of the languages of the Office, the Office shall arrange to have the application, as described in Article 26(1), translated into the language indicated by the applicant.

4.   Where the applicant for a Community trade mark is the sole party to proceedings before the Office, the language of proceedings shall be the language used for filing the application for a Community trade mark. If the application was made in a language other than the languages of the Office, the Office may send written communications to the applicant in the second language indicated by the applicant in his application.

5.   The notice of opposition and an application for revocation or invalidity shall be filed in one of the languages of the Office.

6.   If the language chosen, in accordance with paragraph 5, for the notice of opposition or the application for revocation or invalidity is the language of the application for a trade mark or the second language indicated when the application was filed, that language shall be the language of the proceedings.

If the language chosen, in accordance with paragraph 5, for the notice of opposition or the application for revocation or invalidity is neither the language of the application for a trade mark nor the second language indicated when the application was filed, the opposing party or the party seeking revocation or invalidity shall be required to produce, at his own expense, a translation of his application either into the language of the application for a trade mark, provided that it is a language of the Office, or into the second language indicated when the application was filed. The translation shall be produced within the period prescribed in the implementing regulation. The language into which the application has been translated shall then become the language of the proceedings.

7.   Parties to opposition, revocation, invalidity or appeal proceedings may agree that a different official language of the European Community is to be the language of the proceedings.

Article 116   Publication; entries in the Register

1.   An application for a Community trade mark, as described in Article 26(1), and all other information the publication of which is prescribed by this Regulation or the implementing regulation, shall be published in all the official languages of the European Community.

2.   All entries in the Register of Community trade marks shall be made in all the official languages of the European Community.

3.   In cases of doubt, the text in the language of the Office in which the application for the Community trade mark was filed shall be authentic. If the application was filed in an official language of the European Community other than one of the languages of the Office, the text in the second language indicated by the applicant shall be authentic.

Article 117

The translation services required for the functioning of the Office shall be provided by the Translation Centre of the Bodies of the Union once this begins operation.

Article 118   Control of legality

1.   The Commission shall check the legality of those acts of the President of the Office in respect of which Community law does not provide for any check

on legality by another body and of acts of the Budget Committee attached to the Office pursuant to Article 133.

2.   It shall require that any unlawful acts as referred to in paragraph 1 be altered or annulled.

3.   Member States and any person directly and personally involved may refer to the Commission any act as referred to in paragraph 1, whether express or implied, for the Commission to examine the legality of that act. Referral shall be made to the Commission within 15 days of the day on which the party concerned first became aware of the act in question. The Commission shall take a decision within one month. If no decision has been taken within this period, the case shall be deemed to have been dismissed.

SECTION 2   MANAGEMENT OF THE OFFICE

Article 119   Powers of the President

1.   The Office shall be managed by the President.

2.   To this end the President shall have in particular the following functions and powers:

(a)   he shall take all necessary steps, including the adoption of internal administrative instructions and the publication of notices, to ensure the functioning of the Office;

(b)   he may place before the Commission any proposal to amend this Regulation, the Implementing Regulation, the rules of procedure of the Boards of Appeal, the fees regulations and any other rules applying to Community trade marks after consulting the Administrative Board and, in the case of the fees regulations and the budgetary provisions of this Regulation, the Budget Committee;

(c)   he shall draw up the estimates of the revenue and expenditure of the Office and shall implement the budget;

(d)   he shall submit a management report to the Commission, the European Parliament and the Administrative Board each year;

(e)   he shall exercise in respect of the staff the powers laid down in Article 112(2);

(f)   he may delegate his powers.

3.   The President shall be assisted by one or more Vice-Presidents. If the President is absent or indisposed, the Vice-President or one of the Vice-Presidents shall take his place in accordance with the procedure laid down by the Administrative Board.

Article 120   Appointment of senior officials

1.   The President of the Office shall be appointed by the Council from a list of at most three candidates, which shall be prepared by the Administrative Board. Power to dismiss the President shall lie with the Council, acting on a proposal from the Administrative Board.

2.   The term of office of the President shall not exceed five years. This term of office shall be renewable.

3.   The Vice-President or Vice-Presidents of the Office shall be appointed or dismissed as in paragraph 1, after consultation of the President.

4.   The Council shall exercise disciplinary authority over the officials referred to in paragraphs 1 and 3 of this Article.

SECTION 3   ADMINISTRATIVE BOARD

Article 121   Creation and powers

1.   An Administrative Board is hereby set up, attached to the Office. Without prejudice to the powers attributed to the Budget Committee in Section 5 — budget and financial control — the Administrative Board shall have the powers defined below.

2.   The Administrative Board shall draw up the lists of candidates provided for in Article 120.

3.   It shall fix the date for the first filing of Community trade mark applications, pursuant to Article 143(3).

4.   It shall advise the President on matters for which the Office is responsible.

5.   It shall be consulted before adoption of the guidelines for examination in the Office and in the other cases provided for in this Regulation.

6.   It may deliver opinions and requests for information to the President and to the Commission where it considers that this is necessary.

Article 122   Composition

1.   The Administrative Board shall be composed of one representative of each Member State and one representative of the Commission and their alternates.

2.   The members of the Administrative Board may, subject to the provisions of its rules of procedure, be assisted by advisers or experts.

Article 123   Chairmanship

1.   The Administrative Board shall elect a chairman and a deputy chairman from among its members. The deputy chairman shall *ex officio* replace the chairman in the event of his being prevented from attending to his duties.

2.   The duration of the terms of office of the chairman and the deputy chairman shall be three years. The terms of office shall be renewable.

Article 124   Meetings

1.   Meetings of the Administrative Board shall be convened by its chairman.

2.   The President of the Office shall take part in the deliberations, unless the Administrative Board decides otherwise.

3.   The Administrative Board shall hold an ordinary meeting once a year; in addition, it shall meet on the initiative of its chairman or at the request of the Commission or of one-third of the Member States.

4.   The Administrative Board shall adopt rules of procedure.

5.   The Administrative Board shall take its decisions by a simple majority of the representatives of the Member States. However, a majority of three-quarters of the representatives of the Member States shall be required for the decisions which the Administrative Board is empowered to take under Article 120(1) and (3). In both cases each Member State shall have one vote.

6.   The Administrative Board may invite observers to attend its meetings.

7.   The Secretariat for the Administrative Board shall be provided by the Office.

SECTION 4   IMPLEMENTATION OF PROCEDURES

Article 125   Competence

For taking decisions in connection with the procedures laid down in this Regulation, the following shall be competent:

(a)   Examiners;
(b)   Opposition Divisions;
(c)   an Administration of Trade Marks and Legal Division;
(d)   Cancellation Divisions;
(e)   Boards of Appeal.

Article 126   Examiners

An examiner shall be responsible for taking decisions on behalf of the Office in relation to an application for registration of a Community trade mark, including the matters referred to in Articles 36, 37, 38 and 66, except in so far as an Opposition Division is responsible.

Article 127   Opposition Divisions

1.   An Opposition Division shall be responsible for taking decisions on an opposition to an application to register a Community trade mark.

2.   An Opposition Division shall consist of three members. At least one of the members must be legally qualified.

Article 128   Administration of Trade Marks and Legal Division

1.   The Administration of Trade Marks and Legal Division shall be responsible for those decisions required by this Regulation which do not fall within the competence of an examiner, an Opposition Division or a Cancellation Division. It shall in particular be responsible for decisions in respect of entries in the Register of Community trade marks.

2.   It shall also be responsible for keeping the list of professional representatives which is referred to in Article 89.

3.   A decision of the Division shall be taken by one member.

Article 129   Cancellation Divisions

1.   A Cancellation Division shall be responsible for taking decisions in relation to an application for the revocation or declaration of invalidity of a Community trade mark.

2.   A Cancellation Division shall consist of three members. At least one of the members must be legally qualified.

Article 130   Boards of Appeal

1.   The Boards of Appeal shall be responsible for deciding on appeals from decisions of the examiners, Opposition Divisions, Administration of Trade Marks and Legal Division and Cancellation Divisions.

2.   A Board of Appeal shall consist of three members. At least two of the members must be legally qualified.

Article 131   Independence of the members of the Boards of Appeal

1.   The members, including the chairmen, of the Boards of Appeal shall be appointed, in accordance with the procedure laid down in Article 120, for the appointment of the President of the Office, for a term of five years. They may not be removed from office during this term, unless there are serious grounds for such removal and the Court of Justice, on application by the body which appointed them, takes a decision to this effect. Their term of office shall be renewable.

2.   The members of the Boards of Appeal shall be independent. In their decisions they shall not be bound by any instructions.

3.   The members of the Boards of Appeal may not be examiners or members of the Opposition Divisions, Administration of Trade Marks and Legal Division or Cancellation Divisions.

Article 132   Exclusion and objection

1.   Examiners and members of the Divisions set up within the Office or of the Boards of Appeal may not take part in any proceedings if they have any personal interest therein, or if they have previously been involved as representatives of one of the parties. Two of the three members of an Opposition Division shall not have taken part in examining the application. Members of the Cancellation Divisions may not take part in any proceedings if they have participated in the final decision on the case in the proceedings for registration or opposition proceedings. Members of the Boards of Appeal may not take part in appeal proceedings if they participated in the decision under appeal.

2.   If, for one of the reasons mentioned in paragraph 1 or for any other reason, a member of a Division or of a Board of Appeal considers that he should not take part in any proceedings, he shall inform the Division or Board accordingly.

3.   Examiners and members of the Divisions or of a Board of Appeal may be objected to be any party for one of the reasons mentioned in paragraph 1, or if suspected of partiality. An objection shall not be admissible if, while being aware of a reason for objection, the party has taken a procedural step. No objection may be based upon the nationality of examiners or members.

4.   The Divisions and the Boards of Appeal shall decide as to the action to be taken in the cases specified in paragraphs 2 and 3 without the participation of the member concerned. For the purposes of taking this decision the member who withdraws or has been objected to shall be replaced in the Division or Board of Appeal by his alternate.

SECTION 5   BUDGET AND FINANCIAL CONTROL

Article 133   Budget Committee

1.   A Budget Committee is hereby set up, attached to the Office. The Budget Committee shall have the powers assigned to it in this Section and in Article 39(4).

2.   Articles 121(6), 122, 123 and 124(1) to (4), (6) and (7) shall apply to the Budget Committee *mutatis mutandis*.

3.   The Budget Committee shall take its decisions by a simple majority of the representatives of the Member States. However, a majority of three-quarters of the representatives of the Member States shall be required for the decisions which the Budget Committee is empowered to take under Articles 39(4), 135(3) and 138. In both cases each Member State shall have one vote.

Article 134   Budget

1.   Estimates of all the Office's revenue and expenditure shall be prepared for each financial year and shall be shown in the Office's budget, and each financial year shall correspond with the calendar year.

2.   The revenue and expenditure shown in the budget shall be in balance.

3.   Revenue shall comprise, without prejudice to other types of income, total fees payable under the fees regulations, and, to the extent necessary, a subsidy entered against a specific heading of the general budget of the European Communities, Commission Section.

Article 135   Preparation of the budget

1.   The President shall draw up each year an estimate of the Office's revenue and expenditure for the following year and shall send it to the Budget Committee not later than 31 March in each year, together with a list of posts.

2.   Should the budget estimates provide for a Community subsidy, the Budget Committee shall immediately forward the estimate to the Commission, which shall forward it to the budget authority of the Communities. The Commission may attach an opinion on the estimate along with an alternative estimate.

3.   The Budget Committee shall adopt the budget, which shall include the Office's list of posts. Should the budget estimates contain a subsidy from the general budget of the Communities, the Office's budget shall, if necessary, be adjusted.

Article 136   Financial control

Control of commitment and payment of all expenditure and control of the existence and recovery of all revenue of the Office shall be carried out by the Financial Controller appointed by the Budget Committee.

Article 137   Auditing of accounts

1.   Not later than 31 March in each year the President shall transmit to the Commission, the European Parliament, the Budget Committee and the Court of Auditors accounts of the Office's total revenue and expenditure for the preceding financial year. The Court of Auditors shall examine them in accordance with Article 188c of the Treaty.

2.   The Budget Committee shall give a discharge to the President of the Office in respect of the implementation of the budget.

Article 138   Financial provisions

The Budget Committee shall, after consulting the Court of Auditors of the European Communities and the Commission, adopt internal financial provisions specifying, in particular, the procedure for establishing and implementing the Office's budget. As far as is compatible with the particular nature of the Office, the financial provisions shall be based on the financial regulations adopted for other bodies set up by the Community.

Article 139   Fees regulations

1.   The fees regulations shall determine in particular the amounts of the fees and the ways in which they are to be paid.

2.   The amounts of the fees shall be fixed at such a level as to ensure that the revenue in respect thereof is in principle sufficient for the budget of the Office to be balanced.

3.   The fees regulations shall be adopted and amended in accordance with the procedure laid down in Article 141.

TITLE XIII   FINAL PROVISIONS

Article 140   Community implementing provisions

1.   The rules implementing this Regulation shall be adopted in an Implementing Regulation.

2.   In addition to the fees provided for in the preceding Articles, fees shall be charged, in accordance with the detailed rules of application laid down in the Implementing Regulation, in the cases listed below:

1.   alteration of the representation of a Community trade mark;
2.   late payment of the registration fee;
3.   issue of a copy of the certificate of registration;
4.   registration of the transfer of a Community trade mark;
5.   registration of a licence or another right in respect of a Community trade mark;
6.   registration of a licence or another right in respect of an application for a Community trade mark;
7.   cancellation of the registration of a licence or another right;
8.   alteration of a registered Community trade mark;
9.   issue of an extract from the Register;
10. inspection of the files;
11. issue of copies of file documents;
12. issue of certified copies of the application;
13. communication of information in a file;
14. review of the determination of the procedural costs to be refunded.

3.   The Implementing Regulation and the rules of procedure of the Boards of Appeal shall be adopted and amended in accordance with the procedure laid down in Article 141.

Article 141   Establishment of a committee and procedure for the adoption of implementing regulations

1.   The Commission shall be assisted by a Committee on Fees, Implementation Rules and the Procedure of the Boards of Appeal of the Office for Harmonisation in the Internal Market (trade marks and designs), which shall be composed of representatives of the Member States and chaired by a representative of the Commission.

2.   The representative of the Commission shall submit to the Committee a draft of the measures to be taken. The Committee shall deliver its opinion on the draft within a time limit which the chairman may lay down according to the urgency of the matter. The opinion shall be delivered by the majority laid down in Article 148(2) of the Treaty in the case of decisions which the Council is required to adopt on a proposal from the Commission. The votes of the representatives of the Member States within the Committee shall be weighted in the manner set out in that Article. The chairman shall not vote.

The Commission shall adopt the measures envisaged if they are in accordance with the opinion of the Committee.

If the measures envisaged are not in accordance with the opinion of the Committee, or if no opinion is delivered, the Commission shall, without delay, submit to the Council a proposal relating to the measures to be taken. The Council shall act by a qualified majority.

If, on the expiry of a period of three months from the date of referral to the Council, the Council has not acted, the proposed measures shall be adopted by the Commission, save where the Council has decided against the measures by a simple majority.

Article 142   Compatibility with other Community legal provisions

This Regulation shall not affect Council Regulation (EEC) No. 2081/92 on the protection of geographical indications and designations of origin for agricultural products and foodstuffs[1] of 14 July 1992, and in particular Article 14 thereof.

Note
[1]OJ No. L208, 24.7.1992, p. 1.

Article 143   Entry into force
1.   This Regulation shall enter into force on the 60th day following that of its publication in the *Office Journal of the European Communities.*
2.   The Member States shall within three years following entry ito force of this Regulation take the necessary measures for the purpose of implementing Articles 91 and 110 hereof and shall forthwith inform the Commission of those measures.
3.   Applications for Community trade marks may be filed at the Office from the date fixed by the Administrative Board on the recommendation of the President of the Office.
4.   Applications for Community trade marks filed within three months before the date referred to in paragraph 3 shall be deemed to have been filed on that date.

This Regulation shall be binding in its entirety and directly applicable in all Member States.

Done at Brussels, 20 December 1993.

COUNCIL DIRECTIVE 92/100/EEC OF 19 NOVEMBER 1992 ON RENTAL RIGHT AND LENDING RIGHT AND ON CERTAIN RIGHTS RELATED TO COPYRIGHT IN THE FIELD OF INTELLECTUAL PROPERTY
[OJ 1992 No. L 346/61]

THE COUNCIL OF THE EUROPEAN COMMUNITIES,

Having regard to the Treaty establishing the European Economic Community, and in particular Articles 57(2), 66 and 100a thereof,
  Having regard to the proposal from the Commission,[1]
  In cooperation with the European Parliament,[2]
  Having regard to the opinion of the Economic and Social Committee,[3]
  Whereas differences exist in the legal protection provided by the laws and practices of the Member States for copyright works and subject matter of related rights protection as regards rental and lending; whereas such differences are sources of barriers to trade and distortions of competition which impede the achievement and proper functioning of the internal market;
  Whereas such differences in legal protection could well become greater as Member States adopt new and different legislation or as national case-law interpreting such legislation develops differently;

Note
[1]OJ No. C53, 28.2.1991, p. 35 and OJ No. C128, 20.5.1992, p. 8.
[2]OJ No. C67, 16.3.1992, p. 92 and Decision of 28 October 1992 (not yet published in the Official Journal).
[3]OJ No. C269, 14.10.1991, p. 54.

Whereas such differences should therefore be eliminated in accordance with the objective of introducing an area without internal frontiers as set out in Article 8a of the Treaty so as to institute, pursuant to Article 3(f) of the Treaty, a system ensuring that competition in the common market is not distorted;

Whereas rental and lending of copyright works and the subject matter of related rights protection is playing an increasingly important role in particular for authors, performers and producers of phonograms and films; whereas piracy is becoming an increasing threat;

Whereas the adequate protection of copyright works and subject matter of related rights protection by rental and lending rights as well as the protection of the subject matter of related rights protection by the fixation right, reproduction right, distribution right, right to broadcast and communication to the public can accordingly be considered as being of fundamental importance for the Community's economic and cultural development;

Whereas copyright and related rights protection must adapt to new economic developments such as new forms of exploitation;

Whereas the creative and artistic work of authors and performers necessitates an adequate income as a basis for further creative and artistic work, and the investments required particularly for the production of phonograms and films are especially high and risky;

Whereas the possibility for securing that income and recouping that investment can only effectively be guaranteed through adequate legal protection of the rightholders concerned;

Whereas these creative, artistic and entrepreneurial activities are, to a large extent, activities of self-employed persons; whereas the pursuit of such activities must be made easier by providing a harmonized legal protection within the Community;

Whereas, to the extent that these activities principally constitute services, their provision must equally be facilitated by the establishment in the Community of a harmonized legal framework;

Whereas the legislation of the Member States should be approximated in such a way so as not to conflict with the international conventions on which many Member States' copyright and related rights laws are based;

Whereas the Community's legal framework on the rental right and lending right and on certain rights related to copyright can be limited to establishing that Member States provide rights with respect to rental and lending for certain groups of rightholders and further to establishing the rights of fixation, reproduction, distribution, broadcasting and communication to the public for certain groups of rightholders in the field of related rights protection;

Whereas it is necessary to define the concepts of rental and lending for the purposes of this Directive;

Whereas it is desirable, with a view to clarity, to exclude from rental and lending within the meaning of this Directive certain forms of making available, as for instance making available phonograms or films (cinematographic or audiovisual works or moving images, whether or not accompanied by sound) for the purpose of public performance or broadcasting, making available for the purpose of exhibition, or making available for on-the-spot reference use;

Whereas lending within the meaning of this Directive does not include making available between establishments which are accessible to the public;

Whereas, where lending by an establishment accessible to the public gives rise to a payment the amount of which does not go beyond what is necessary to cover the operating costs of the establishment, there is no direct or indirect economic or commercial advantage within the meaning of this Directive;

Whereas it is necessary to introduce arrangements ensuring that an unwaivable equitable remuneration is obtained by authors and performers who must retain the possibility to entrust the administration of this right to collecting societies representing them;

Whereas the equitable remuneration may be paid on the basis of one or several payments at any time on or after the conclusion of the contract;

Whereas the equitable remuneration must take account of the importance of the contribution of the authors and performers concerned to the phonogram or film;

Whereas it is also necessary to protect the rights at least of authors as regards public lending by providing for specific arrangements; whereas, however, any measures based on Article 5 of this Directive have to comply with Community law, in particular with Article 7 of the Treaty;

Whereas the provisions of Chapter II do not prevent Member States from extending the presumption set out in Article 2(5) to the exclusive rights included in that chapter; whereas furthermore the provisions of Chapter II do not prevent Member States from providing for a rebuttable presumption of the authorization of exploitation in respect of the exclusive rights of performers provided for in those articles, in so far as such presumption is compatible with the International Convention for the Protection of Performers, Producers of Phonograms and Broadcasting Organizations (hereinafter referred to as the Rome Convention);

Whereas Member States may provide for more far-reaching protection for owners of rights related to copyright than that required by Article 8 of this Directive;

Whereas the harmonized rental and lending rights and the harmonized protection in the field of rights related to copyright should not be exercised in a way which constitutes a disguised restriction on trade between Member States or in a way which is contrary to the rule of media exploitation chronology, as recognized in the Judgment handed down in *Société Cinéthèque v FNCF*,[1]

Note
[1]Cases 60/84 and 61/84, ECR 1985, p. 2605.

HAS ADOPTED THIS DIRECTIVE:

CHAPTER I   RENTAL AND LENDING RIGHT

Article 1   Object of harmonization

1.   In accordance with the provisions of this Chapter, Member States shall provide, subject to Article 5, a right to authorize or prohibit the rental and lending of originals and copies of copyright works, and other subject matter as set out in Article 2(1).

2.   For the purposes of this Directive, 'rental' means making available for use, for a limited period of time and for direct or indirect economic or commercial advantage.

3.   For the purposes of this Directive, 'lending' means making available for use, for a limited period of time and not for direct or indirect economic or

commercial advantage, when it is made through establishments which are accessible to the public.

4. The rights referred to in paragraph 1 shall not be exhausted by any sale or other act of distribution of originals and copies of copyright works and other subject matter as set out in Article 2(1).

Article 2   Rightholders and subject matter of rental and lending right

1. The exclusive right to authorize or prohibit rental and lending shall belong:

— to the author in respect of the original and copies of his work,

— to the performer in respect of fixations of his performance,

— to the phonogram producer in respect of his phonograms, and

— to the producer of the first fixation of a film in respect of the original and copies of his film. For the purposes of this Directive, the term 'film' shall designate a cinematographic or audiovisual work or moving images, whether or not accompanied by sound.

2. For the purposes of this Directive the principal director of a cinematographic or audiovisual work shall be considered as its author or one of its authors. Member States may provide for others to be considered as its co-authors.

3. This Directive does not cover rental and lending rights in relation to buildings and to works of applied art.

4. The rights referred to in paragraph 1 may be transferred, assigned or subject to the granting of contractual licences.

5. Without prejudice to paragraph 7, when a contract concerning film production is concluded, individually or collectively, by performers with a film producer, the performer covered by this contract shall be presumed, subject to contractual clauses to the contrary, to have transferred his rental right, subject to Article 4.

6. Member States may provide for a similar presumption as set out in paragraph 5 with respect to authors.

7. Member States may provide that the signing of a contract concluded between a performer and a film producer concerning the production of a film has the effect of authorizing rental, provided that such contract provides for an equitable remuneration within the meaning of Article 4. Member States may also provide that this paragraph shall apply mutatis mutandis to the rights included in Chapter II.

Article 3   Rental of computer programs

This Directive shall be without prejudice to Article 4(c) of Council Directive 91/250/EEC of 14 May 1991 on the legal protection of computer programs.[1]

Note
[1]OJ No. L122, 17.5.1991, p. 42.

Article 4   Unwaivable right to equitable remuneration

1. Where an author or performer has transferred or assigned his rental right concerning a phonogram or an original or copy of a film to a phonogram or film producer, that author or performer shall retain the right to obtain an equitable remuneration for the rental.

2. The right to obtain an equitable remuneration for rental cannot be waived by authors or performers.

3. The administration of this right to obtain an equitable remuneration may be entrusted to collecting societies representing authors or performers.

4. Member States may regulate whether and to what extent administration by collecting societies of the right to obtain an equitable remuneration may be imposed, as well as the question from whom this remuneration may be claimed or collected.

Article 5   Derogation from the exclusive public lending right

1. Member States may derogate from the exclusive right provided for in Article 1 in respect of public lending, provided that at least authors obtain a remuneration for such lending. Member States shall be free to determine this remuneration taking account of their cultural promotion objectives.

2. When Member States do not apply the exclusive lending right provided for in Article 1 as regards phonograms, films and computer programs, they shall introduce, at least for authors, a remuneration.

3. Member States may exempt certain categories of establishments from the payment of the remuneration referred to in paragraphs 1 and 2.

4. The Commission, in cooperation with the Member States, shall draw up before 1 July 1997 a report on public lending in the Community. It shall forward this report to the European Parliament and to the Council.

CHAPTER II   RIGHTS RELATED TO COPYRIGHT

Article 6   Fixation right

1. Member States shall provide for performers the exclusive right to authorize or prohibit the fixation of their performances.

2. Member States shall provide for broadcasting organizations the exclusive right to authorize or prohibit the fixation of their broadcasts, whether these broadcasts are transmitted by wire or over the air, including by cable or satellite.

3. A cable distributor shall not have the right provided for in paragraph 2 where it merely retransmits by cable the broadcasts of broadcasting organizations.

Article 7   Reproduction right

1. Member States shall provide the exclusive right to authorize or prohibit the direct or indirect reproduction:

— for performers, of fixations of their performances,

— for phonogram producers, of their phonograms,

— for producers of the first fixations of films, in respect of the original and copies of their films, and

— for broadcasting organizations, of fixations of their broadcasts, as set out in Article 6(2).

2. The reproduction right referred to in paragraph 1 may be transferred, assigned or subject to the granting of contractual licences.

Article 8   Broadcasting and communication to the public

1. Member States shall provide for performers the exclusive right to authorize or prohibit the broadcasting by wireless means and the communication to the public of their performances, except where the performance is itself already a broadcast performance or is made from a fixation.

2. Member States shall provide a right in order to ensure that a single equitable remuneration is paid by the user, if a phonogram published for commercial purposes, or a reproduction of such phonogram, is used for broadcasting by wireless means or for any communication to the public, and to ensure that this remuneration is shared between the relevant performers and phonogram producers. Member States may, in the absence of agreement between the performers and phonogram producers, lay down the conditions as to the sharing of this remuneration between them.

3. Member States shall provide for broadcasting organizations the exclusive right to authorize or prohibit the rebroadcasting of their broadcasts by wireless means, as well as the communication to the public of their broadcasts if such communication is made in places accessible to the public against payment of an entrance fee.

Article 9   Distribution right

1. Member States shall provide
— for performers, in respect of fixations of their performances,
— for phonogram producers, in respect of their phonograms,
— for producers of the first fixations of films, in respect of the original and copies of their films,
— for broadcasting organizations, in respect of fixations of their broadcast as set out in Article 6(2), the exclusive right to make available these objects, including copies thereof, to the public by sale or otherwise, hereafter referred to as the 'distribution right'.

2. The distribution right shall not be exhausted within the Community in respect of an object as referred to in paragraph 1, except where the first sale in the Community of that object is made by the rightholder or with his consent.

3. The distribution right shall be without prejudice to the specific provisions of Chapter I, in particular Article 1(4).

4. The distribution right may be transferred, assigned or subject to the granting of contractual licences.

Article 10   Limitations to rights

1. Member States may provide for limitations to the rights referred to in Chapter II in respect of:
    (a)   private use;
    (b)   use of short excerpts in connection with the reporting of current events;
    (c)   ephemeral fixation by a broadcasting organization by means of its own facilities and for its own broadcasts;
    (d)   use solely for the purposes of teaching or scientific research.

2. Irrespective of paragraph 1, any Member State may provide for the same kinds of limitations with regard to the protection of performers, producers of phonograms, broadcasting organizations and of producers of the first fixations of films, as it provides for in connection with the protection of copyright in literary and artistic works. However, compulsory licences may be provided for only to the extent to which they are compatible with the Rome Convention.

3. Paragraph 1(a) shall be without prejudice to any existing or future legislation on remuneration for reproduction for private use.

CHAPTER III   DURATION

Article 11
(Repealed)

Article 12¹
(Repealed)

Note
¹Articles 11 and 12 repealed by Directive 93/98 [OJ 1993 L209/9].

CHAPTER IV   COMMON PROVISIONS

Article 13   Application in time

1.   This Directive shall apply in respect of all copyright works, performances, phonograms, broadcasts and first fixations of films referred to in this Directive which are, on 1 July 1994, still protected by the legislation of the Member States in the field of copyright and related rights or meet the criteria for protection under the provisions of this Directive on that date.

2.   This Directive shall apply without prejudice to any acts of exploitation performed before 1 July 1994.

3.   Member States may provide that the rightholders are deemed to have given their authorization to the rental or lending of an object referred to in Article 2(1) which is proven to have been made available to third parties for this purpose or to have been acquired before 1 July 1994. However, in particular where such an object is a digital recording, Member States may provide that rightholders shall have a right to obtain an adequate remuneration for the rental or lending of that object.

4.   Member States need not apply the provisions of Article 2(2) to cinematographic or audiovisual works created before 1 July 1994.

5.   Member States may determine the date as from which the Article 2(2) shall apply, provided that that date is no later than 1 July 1997.

6.   This Directive shall, without prejudice to paragraph 3 and subject to paragraphs 8 and 9, not affect any contracts concluded before the date of its adoption.

7.   Member States may provide, subject to the provisions of paragraphs 8 and 9, that when rightholders who acquire new rights under the national provisions adopted in implementation of this Directive have, before 1 July 1994, given their consent for exploitation, they shall be presumed to have transferred the new exclusive rights.

8.   Member States may determine the date as from which the unwaivable right to an equitable remuneration referred to in Article 4 exists, provided that that date is no later than 1 July 1997.

9.   For contracts concluded before 1 July 1994, the unwaivable right to an equitable remuneration provided for in Article 4 shall apply only where authors or performers or those representing them have submitted a request to that effect before 1 January 1997. In the absence of agreement between rightholders concerning the level of remuneration, Member States may fix the level of equitable remuneration.

Article 14   Relation between copyright and related rights

Protection of copyright-related rights under this Directive shall leave intact and shall in no way affect the protection of copyright.

Article 15   Final provisions

1.   Member States shall bring into force the laws, regulations and administrative provisions necessary to comply with this Directive not later than 1 July 1994. They shall forthwith inform the Commission thereof.

When Member States adopt these measures, they shall contain a reference to this Directive or shall be accompanied by such reference at the time of their official publication.

The methods of making such a reference shall be laid down by the Member States.

2.   Member States shall communicate to the Commission the main provisions of domestic law which they adopt in the field covered by this Directive.

Article 16

This Directive is addressed to the Member States.

Done at Brussels, 19 November 1992.
For the Council
The President
E. LEIGH

COUNCIL DIRECTIVE 93/83/EEC OF 27 SEPTEMBER 1993 ON THE COORDINATION OF CERTAIN RULES CONCERNING COPYRIGHT AND RIGHTS RELATED TO COPYRIGHT APPLICABLE TO SATELLITE BROADCASTING AND CABLE RETRANSMISSION
[OJ 1993 No. L248/15]

THE COUNCIL OF THE EUROPEAN COMMUNITIES,

Having regard to the Treaty establishing the European Economic Community, and in particular Articles 57(2) and 66 thereof,
  Having regard to the proposal from the Commission,[1]
  In cooperation with the European Parliament,[2]
  Having regard to the opinion of the Economic and Social Committee,[3]

(1)   Whereas the objectives of the Community as laid down in the Treaty include establishing an ever closer union among the peoples of Europe, fostering closer relations between the States belonging to the Community and ensuring the economic and social progress of the Community countries by common action to eliminate the barriers which divide Europe;
(2)   Whereas, to that end, the Treaty provides for the establishment of a common market and an area without internal frontiers; whereas measures to achieve this include the abolition of obstacles to the free movement of services and the institution of a system ensuring that competition in the common market is not distorted;

Note
[1]OJ No. C255, 1.10.1991, p. 3 and OJ No. C25, 28.1.1993, p. 43.
[2]OJ No. C305, 23.11.1992, p. 129 and OJ No. C255, 20.9.1993.
[3]OJ No. C98, 21.4.1992, p. 44.

Whereas, to that end, the Council may adopt directives for the coordination of the provisions laid down by law, regulation or administrative action in Member States concerning the taking up and pursuit of activities as self-employed persons;

(3)   Whereas broadcasts transmitted across frontiers within the Community, in particular by satellite and cable, are one of the most important ways of pursuing these Community objectives, which are at the same time political, economic, social, cultural and legal;

(4)   Whereas the Council has already adopted Directive 89/552/EEC of 3 October 1989 on the coordination of certain provisions laid down by law, regulation or administrative action in Member States concerning the pursuit of television broadcasting activities,[1] which makes provision for the promotion of the distribution and production of European television programmes and for advertising and sponsorship, the protection of minors and the right of reply;

(5)   Whereas, however, the achievement of these objectives in respect of cross-border satellite broadcasting and the cable retransmission of programmes from other Member States is currently still obstructed by a series of differences between national rules of copyright and some degree of legal uncertainty; whereas this means that holders of rights are exposed to the threat of seeing their works exploited without payment of remuneration or that the individual holders of exclusive rights in various Member States block the exploitation of their rights; whereas the legal uncertainty in particular constitutes a direct obstacle in the free circulation of programmes within the Community;

(6)   Whereas a distinction is currently drawn for copyright purposes between communication to the public by direct satellite and communication to the public by communications satellite; whereas, since individual reception is possible and affordable nowadays with both types of satellite, there is no longer any justification for this differing legal treatment;

(7)   Whereas the free broadcasting of programmes is further impeded by the current legal uncertainty over whether broadcastsing by a satellite whose signals can be received directly affects the rights in the country of transmission only or in all countries of reception together; whereas, since communications satellites and direct satellites are treated alike for copyright purposes, this legal uncertainty now affects almost all programmes broadcast in the Community by satellite;

(8)   Whereas, furthermore, legal certainty, which is a prerequisite for the free movement of broadcasts within the Community, is missing where programmes transmitted across frontiers are fed into and retransmitted through cable networks;

(9)   Whereas the development of the acquisition of rights on a contractual basis by authorization is already making a vigorous contribution to the creation of the desired European audiovisual area; whereas the continuation of such contractual agreements should be ensured and their smooth application in practice should be promoted wherever possible;

(10)   Whereas at present cable operators in particular cannot be sure that they have actually acquired all the programme rights covered by such an agreement;

Note
[1] OJ No. L298, 17.10.1989, p. 23.

(11)   Whereas, lastly, parties in different Member States are not all similarly bound by obligations which prevent them from refusing without valid reason to negotiate on the acquisition of the rights necessary for cable distribution or allowing such negotiations to fail;

(12)   Whereas the legal framework for the creation of a single audiovisual area laid down in Directive 89/552/EEC must, therefore, be supplemented with reference to copyright;

(13)   Whereas, therefore, an end should be put to the differences of treatment of the transmission of programmes by communications satellite which exist in the Member States, so that the vital distinction throughout the Community becomes whether works and other protected subject matter are communicated to the public; whereas this will also ensure equal treatment of the suppliers of cross-border broadcasts, regardless of whether they use a direct broadcasting satellite or a communications satellite;

(14)   Whereas the legal uncertainty regarding the rights to be acquired which impedes cross-border satellite broadcasting should be overcome by defining the notion of communication to the public by satellite at a Community level; whereas this definition should at the same time specify where the act of communication takes place; whereas such a definition is necessary to avoid the cumulative application of several national laws to one single act of broadcasting; whereas communication to the public by satellite occurs only when, and in the Member State where, the programme-carrying signals are introduced under the control and responsibility of the broadcasting organization into an uninterrupted chain of communication leading to the satellite and down towards the earth; whereas normal technical procedures relating to the programme-carrying signals should not be considered as interruptions to the chain of broadcasting;

(15)   Whereas the acquisition on a contractual basis of exclusive broadcasting rights should comply with any legislation on copyright and rights related to copyright in the Member State in which communication to the public by satellite occurs;

(16)   Whereas the principle of contractual freedom on which this Directive is based will make it possible to continue limiting the exploitation of these rights, especially as far as certain technical means of transmission or certain language versions are concerned;

(17)   Whereas, in arriving at the amount of the payment to be made for the rights acquired, the parties should take account of all aspects of the broadcast, such as the actual audience, the potential audience and the language version;

(18)   Whereas the application of the country-of-origin principle contained in this Directive could pose a problem with regard to existing contracts; whereas this Directive should provide for a period of five years for existing contracts to be adapted, where necessary, in the light of the Directive; whereas the said country-of-origin principle should not, therefore, apply to existing contracts which expire before 1 January 2000; whereas if by that date parties still have an interest in the contract, the same parties should be entitled to renegotiate the conditions of the contract;

(19)   Whereas existing international co-production agreements must be interpreted in the light of the economic purpose and scope envisaged by the parties upon signature; whereas in the past international co-production agreements have often not expressly and specifically addressed communication to the public by satellite within the meaning of this Directive a particular form

of exploitation; whereas the underlying philosophy of many existing international co-production agreements is that the rights in the co-production are exercised separately and independently by each co-producer, by dividing the exploitation rights between them along territorial lines;

Whereas, as a general rule, in the situation where a communication to the public by satellite authorized by one co-producer would prejudice the value of the exploitation rights of another co-producer, the interpretation of such an existing agreement would normally suggest that the latter co-producer would have to give his consent to the authorization, by the former co-producer, of the communication to the public by satellite;

Whereas the language exclusivity of the latter co-producer will be prejudiced where the language version or versions of the communication to the public, including where the version is dubbed or subtitled, coincide(s) with the language or the languages widely understood in the territory allotted by the agreement to the latter co-producer;

Whereas the notion of exclusivity should be understood in a wider sense where the communication to the public by satellite concerns a work which consists merely of images and contains no dialogue or subtitles;

Whereas a clear rule is necessary in cases where the international co-production agreement does not expressly regulate the division of rights in the specific case of communication to the public by satellite within the meaning of this Directive;

(20)   Whereas communications to the public by satellite from non-member countries will under certain conditions be deemed to occur within a Member State of the Community;

(21)   Whereas it is necessary to ensure that protection for authors, performers, producers of phonograms and broadcasting organizations is accorded in all Member States and that this protection is not subject to a statutory licence system;

Whereas only in this way is it possible to ensure that any difference in the level of protection within the common market will not create distortions of competition;

(22)   Whereas the advent of new technologies is likely to have an impact on both the quality and the quantity of the exploitation of works and other subject matter;

(23)   Whereas in the light of these developments the level of protection granted pursuant to this Directive to all rightholders in the areas covered by this Directive should remain under consideration;

(24)   Whereas the harmonization of legislation envisaged in this Directive entails the harmonization of the provisions ensuring a high level of protection of authors, performers, phonogram producers and broadcasting organizations;

Whereas this harmonization should not allow a broadcasting organization to take advantage of differences in levels of protection by relocating activities, to the detriment of audiovisual productions;

(25)   Whereas the protection provided for rights related to copyright should be aligned on that contained in Council Directive 92/100/EEC of 19 November 1992 on rental right and lending right and on certain rights related to copyright in the field of intellectual property[2] for the purposes of communication to the public by satellite;

Note
[2]OJ No. L346, 27.11.1992, p. 61.

Whereas, in particular, this will ensure that performers and phonogram producers are guaranteed an appropriate remuneration for the communication to the public by satellite of their performances or phonograms;

(26) Whereas the provisions of Article 4 do not prevent Member States from extending the presumption set out in Article 2(5) of Directive 92/100/EEC to the exclusive rights referred to in Article 4;

Whereas, furthermore, the provisions of Article 4 do not prevent Member States from providing for a rebuttable presumption of the authorization of exploitation in respect of the exclusive rights of performers referred to in that Article, in so far as such presumption is compatible with the International Convention for the Protection of Performers, Producers of Phonograms and Broadcasting Organizations;

(27) Whereas the cable retransmission of programmes from other Member States is an act subject to copyright and, as the case may be, rights related to copyright;

Whereas the cable operator must, therefore, obtain the authorization from every holder of rights in each part of the programme retransmitted;

Whereas, pursuant to this Directive, the authorizations should be granted contractually unless a temporary exception is provided for in the case of existing legal licence schemes;

(28) Whereas, in order to ensure that the smooth operation of contractual arrangements is not called into question by the intervention of outsiders holding rights in individual parts of the programme, provision should be made, through the obligation to have recourse to a collecting society, for the exclusive collective exercise of the authorization right to the extent that this is required by the special features of cable retransmission;

Whereas the authorization right as such remains intact and only the exercise of this right is regulated to some extent, so that the right to authorize a cable retransmission can still be assigned;

Whereas this Directive does not affect the exercise of moral rights;

(29) Whereas the exemption provided for in Article 10 should not limit the choice of holders of rights to transfer their rights to a collecting society and thereby have a direct share in the remuneration paid by the cable distributor for cable retransmission;

(30) Whereas contractual arrangements regarding the authorization of cable retransmission should be promoted by additional measures;

Whereas a party seeking the conclusion of a general contract should, for its part, be obliged to submit collective proposals for an agreement;

Whereas, furthermore, any party shall be entitled, at any moment, to call upon the assistance of impartial mediators whose task is to assist negotiations and who may submit proposals;

Whereas any such proposals and any opposition thereto should be served on the parties concerned in accordance with the applicable rules concerning the service of legal documents, in particular as set out in existing international conventions;

Whereas, finally, it is necessary to ensure that the negotiations are not blocked without valid justification or that individual holders are not prevented without valid justification from taking part in the negotiations;

Whereas none of these measures for the promotion of the acquisition of rights calls into question the contractual nature of the acquisition of cable retransmission rights;

(31) Whereas for a transitional period Member States should be allowed to retain existing bodies with jurisdiction in their territory over cases where the right to retransmit a programme by cable to the public has been unreasonably refused or offered on unreasonable terms by a broadcasting organization;

Whereas it is understood that the right of parties concerned to be heard by the body should be guaranteed and that the existence of the body should not prevent the parties concerned from having normal access to the courts;

(32) Whereas, however, Community rules are not needed to deal with all of those matters, the effects of which perhaps with some commercially insignificant exceptions, are felt only inside the borders of a single Member State;

(33) Whereas minimum rules should be laid down in order to establish and guarantee free and uninterrupted cross-border broadcasting by satellite and simultaneous, unaltered cable retransmission of programmes broadcast from other Member States, on an essentially contractual basis;

(34) Whereas this Directive should not prejudice further harmonization in the field of copyright and rights related to copyright and the collective administration of such rights;

Whereas the possibility for Member States to regulate the activities of collecting societies should not prejudice the freedom of contractual negotiation of the rights provided for in this Directive, on the understanding that such negotiation takes place within the framework of general or specific national rules with regard to competition law or the prevention of abuse of monopolies;

(35) Whereas it should, therefore, be for the Member States to supplement the general provisions needed to achieve the objectives of this Directive by taking legislative and administrative measures in their domestic law, provided that these do not run counter to the objectives of this Directive and are compatible with Community law;

(36) Whereas this Directive does not affect the applicability of the competition rules in Articles 85 and 86 of the Treaty,

HAS ADOPTED THIS DIRECTIVE:

CHAPTER I DEFINITIONS

Article 1 Definitions

1. For the purpose of this Directive, 'satellite' means any satellite operating on frequency bands which, under telecommunications law, are reserved for the broadcast of signals for reception by the public or which are reserved for closed, point-to-point communication. In the latter case, however, the circumstances in which individual reception of the signals takes place must be comparable to those which apply in the first case.

2. (a) For the purpose of this Directive, 'communication to the public by satellite' means the act of introducing, under the control and responsibility of the broadcasting organization, the programme-carrying signals intended for reception by the public into an uninterrupted chain of communication leading to the satellite and down towards the earth.

(b) The act of communication to the public by satellite occurs solely in the Member State where, under the control and responsibility of the broadcasting organization, the programme-carrying signals are introduced into an uninterrupted chain of communication leading to the satellite and down towards the earth.

(c) If the programme-carrying signals are encrypted, then there is communication to the public by satellite on condition that the means for decrypting the broadcast are provided to the public by the broadcasting organization or with its consent.

(d) Where an act of communication to the public by satellite occurs in a non-Community State which does not provide the level of protection provided for under Chapter II,

(i) if the programme-carrying signals are transmitted to the satellite from an uplink situation situated in a Member State, that act of communication to the public by satellite shall be deemed to have occurred in that Member State and the rights provided for under Chapter II shall be exercisable against the person operating the uplink station; or

(ii) if there is no use of an uplink station situated in a Member State but a broadcasting organization established in a Member State has commissioned the act of communication to the public by satellite, that act shall be deemed to have occurred in the Member State in which the broadcasting organization has its principal establishment in the Community and the rights provided for under Chapter II shall be exercisable against the broadcasting organization.

3. For the purposes of this Directive, 'cable retransmission' means the simultaneous, unaltered and unabridged retransmission by a cable or microwave system for reception by the public of an initial transmission from another Member State, by wire or over the air, including that by satellite, of television or radio programmes intended for reception by the public.

4. For the purposes of this Directive 'collecting society' means any organization which manages or administers copyright or rights related to copyright as its sole purpose or as one of its main purposes.

5. For the purposes of this Directive, the principal director of a cinematographic or audiovisual work shall be considered as its author or one of its authors. Member States may provide for others to be considered as its co-authors.

CHAPTER II BROADCASTING OF PROGRAMMES BY SATELLITE

Article 2 Broadcasting right
Member States shall provide an exclusive right for the author to authorize the communication to the public by satellite of copyright works, subject to the provisions set out in this chapter.

Article 3 Acquisition of broadcasting rights
1. Member States shall ensure that the authorization referred to in Article 2 may be acquired only by agreement.

2. A Member State may provide that a collective agreement between a collecting society and a broadcasting organization concerning a given category of works may be extended to rightholders of the same category who are not represented by the collecting society, provided that:

— the communication to the public by satellite simulcasts a terrestrial broadcast by the same broadcaster, and

— the unrepresented rightholder shall, at any time, have the possibility of excluding the extension of the collective agreement to his works and of exercising his rights either individually or collectively.

3.   Paragraph 2 shall not apply to cinematographic works, including works created by a process analogous to cinematography.

4.   Where the law of a Member State provides for the extension of a collective agreement in accordance with the provisions of paragraph 2, that Member State shall inform the Commission which broadcasting organizations are entitled to avail themselves of that law. The Commission shall publish this information in the Official Journal of the European Communities (C series).

Article 4   Rights of performers, phonogram producers and broadcasting organizations

1.   For the purposes of communication to the public by satellite, the rights of performers, phonogram producers and broadcasting organizations shall be protected in accordance with the provisions of Articles 6, 7, 8 and 10 of Directive 92/100/EEC.

2.   For the purposes of paragraph 1, 'broadcasting by wireless means' in Directive 92/100/EEC shall be understood as including communication to the public by satellite.

3.   With regard to the exercise of the rights referred to in paragraph 1, Articles 2(7) and 12 of Directive 92/100/EEC shall apply.

Article 5   Relation between copyright and related rights

Protection of copyright-related rights under this Directive shall leave intact and shall in no way affect the protection of copyright.

Article 6   Minimum protection

1.   Member States may provide for more far-reaching protection for holders of rights related to copyright than that required by Article 8 of Directive 92/100/EEC.

2.   In applying paragraph 1 Member States shall observe the definitions contained in Article 1(1) and (2).

Article 7   Transitional provisions

1.   With regard to the application in time of the rights referred to in Article 4(1) of this Directive, Article 13(1), (2), (6) and (7) of Directive 92/100/EEC shall apply. Article 13(4) and (5) of Directive 92/100/EEC shall apply mutatis mutandis.

2.   Agreements concerning the exploitation of works and other protected subject matter which are in force on the date mentioned in Article 14(1) shall be subject to the provisions of Articles 1(2), 2 and 3 as from 1 January 2000 if they expire after that date.

3.   When an international co-production agreement concluded before the date mentioned in Article 14(1) between a co-producer from a Member State and one or more co-producers from other Member States or third countries expressly provides for a system of division of exploitation rights between the co-producers by geographical areas for all means of communication to the public, without distinguishing the arrangement applicable to communication to the public by satellite from the provisions applicable to the other means of communication, and where communication to the public by satellite of the

co-production would prejudice the exclusivity, in particular the language exclusivity, of one of the co-producers or his assignees in a given territory, the authorization by one of the co-producers or his assignees for a communication to the public by satellite shall require the prior consent of the holder of that exclusivity, whether co-producer or assignee.

CHAPTER III   CABLE RETRANSMISSION

Article 8   Cable retransmission right

1.   Member States shall ensure that when programmes from other Member States are retransmitted by cable in their territory the applicable copyright and related rights are observed and that such retransmission takes place on the basis of individual or collective contractual agreements between copyright owners, holders of related rights and cable operators.

2.   Notwithstanding paragraph 1, Member States may retain until 31 December 1997 such statutory licence systems which are in operation or expressly provided for by national law on 31 July 1991.

Article 9   Exercise of the cable retransmission right

1.   Member States shall ensure that the right of copyright owners and holders or related rights to grant or refuse authorization to a cable operator for a cable retransmission may be exercised only through a collecting society.

2.   Where a rightholder has not transferred the management of his rights to a collecting society, the collecting society which manages rights of the same category shall be deemed to be mandated to manage his rights. Where more than one collecting society manages rights of that category, the rightholder shall be free to choose which of those collecting societies is deemed to be mandated to manage his rights. A rightholder referred to in this paragraph shall have the same rights and obligations resulting from the agreement between the cable operator and the collecting society which is deemed to be mandated to manage his rights as the rightholders who have mandated that collecting society and he shall be able to claim those rights within a period, to be fixed by the Member State concerned, which shall not be shorter than three years from the date of the cable retransmission which includes his work or other protected subject matter.

3.   A Member State may provide that, when a rightholder authorizes the initial transmission within its territory of a work or other protected subject matter, he shall be deemed to have agreed not to exercise his cable retransmission rights on an individual basis but to exercise them in accordance with the provisions of this Directive.

Article 10   Exercise of the cable retransmission right by broadcasting organisations

Member States shall ensure that Article 9 does not apply to the rights exercised by a broadcasting organization in respect of its own transmission, irrespective of whether the rights concerned are its own or have been transferred to it by other copyright owners and/or holders of related rights.

Article 11   Mediators

1.   Where no agreement is concluded regarding authorization of the cable retransmission of a broadcast, Member States shall ensure that either party may call upon the assistance of one or more mediators.

2.   The task of the mediators shall be to provide assistance with negotiation. They may also submit proposals to the parties.

3.   It shall be assumed that all the parties accept a proposal as referred to in paragraph 2 if none of them expresses its opposition within a period of three months. Notice of the proposal and of any opposition thereto shall be served on the parties concerned in accordance with the applicable rules concerning the service of legal documents.

4.   The mediators shall be so selected that their independence and impartiality are beyond reasonable doubt.

Article 12   Prevention of the abuse of negotiating positions

1.   Member States shall ensure by means of civil or administrative law, as appropriate, that the parties enter and conduct negotiations regarding authorization for cable retransmission in good faith and do not prevent or hinder negotiation without valid justification.

2.   A Member State which, on the date mentioned in Article 14(1), has a body with jurisdiction in its territory over cases where the right to retransmit a programme by cable to the public in that Member State has been unreasonably refused or offered on unreasonable terms by a broadcasting organization may retain that body.

3.   Paragraph 2 shall apply for a transitional period of eight years from the date mentioned in Article 14(1).

CHAPTER IV   GENERAL PROVISIONS

Article 13   Collective administration of rights
This Directive shall be without prejudice to the regulation of the activities of collecting societies by the Member States.

Article 14   Final provisions

1.   Member States shall bring into force the laws, regulations and administrative provisions necessary to comply with this Directive before 1 January 1995. They shall immediately inform the Commission thereof.

When Member States adopt these measures, the latter shall contain a reference to this Directive or shall be accompanied by such reference at the time of their official publication. The methods of making such a reference shall be laid down by the Member States.

2.   Member States shall communicate to the Commission the provisions of national law which they adopt in the field covered by this Directive.

3.   Not later than 1 January 2000, the Commission shall submit to the European Parliament, the Council and the Economic and Social Committee a report on the application of this Directive and, if necessary, make further proposals to adapt it to developments in the audio and audiovisual sector.

Article 15
This Directive is addressed to the Member States.

Done at Brussels, 27 September 1993.
For the Council
The President
R. URBAIN

COUNCIL DIRECTIVE 93/98/EEC OF 29 OCTOBER 1993 HARMONIZING THE TERM OF PROTECTION OF COPYRIGHT AND CERTAIN RELATED RIGHTS
[OJ 1993 NO. L 290/9]

THE COUNCIL OF THE EUROPEAN COMMUNITIES,

Having regard to the Treaty establishing the European Economic Community, and in particular Articles 57(2), 66 and 100a thereof,

Having regard to the proposal from the Commission,[1]

In cooperation with the European Parliament,[2]

Having regard to the opinion of the Economic and Social Committee,[3]

(1) Whereas the Berne Convention for the protection of literary and artistic works and the International Convention for the protection of performers, producers of phonograms and broadcasting organizations (Rome Convention) lay down only minimum terms of protection of the rights they refer to, leaving the Contracting States free to grant longer terms; whereas certain Member States have exercised this entitlement; whereas in addition certain Member States have not become party to the Rome Convention;

(2) Whereas there are consequently differences between the national laws governing the terms of protection of copyright and related rights, which are liable to impede the free movement of goods and freedom to provide services, and to distort competition in the common market; whereas therefore with a view to the smooth operation of the internal market, the laws of the Member States should be harmonized so as to make terms of protection identical throughout the Community;

(3) Whereas harmonization must cover not only the terms of protection as such, but also certain implementing arrangements such as the date from which each term of protection is calculated;

(4) Whereas the provisions of this Directive do not affect the application by the Member States of the provisions of Article 14a(2)(b), (c) and (d) and (3) of the Berne Convention;

(5) Whereas the minimum term of protection laid down by the Berne Convention, namely the life of the author and 50 years after his death, was intended to provide protection for the author and the first two generations of his descendants; whereas the average lifespan in the Community has grown longer, to the point where this term is no longer sufficient to cover two generations;

(6) Whereas certain Member States have granted a term longer than 50 years after the death of the author in order to offset the effects of the world wars on the exploitation of authors' works;

(7) Whereas for the protection of related rights certain Member States have introduced a term of 50 years after lawful publication or lawful communication to the public;

Note

[1] OJ No. C92, 11.4.1992, p. 6 and OJ No. C27, 30.1.1993, p. 7.

[2] OJ No. C337, 21.12.1992, p. 205 and Decision of 27 October 1993 (not yet published in the Official Journal).

[3] OJ No. C287, 4.11.1992, p. 53.

(8)   Whereas under the Community position adopted for the Uruguay Round negotiations under the General Agreement on Tariffs and Trade (GATT) the term of protection for producers of phonograms should be 50 years after first publication;

(9)   Whereas due regard for established rights is one of the general principles of law protected by the Community legal order; whereas, therefore, a harmonization of the terms of protection of copyright and related rights cannot have the effect of reducing the protection currently enjoyed by rightholders in the Community; whereas in order to keep the effects of transitional measures to a minimum and to allow the internal market to operate in practice, the harmonization of the term of protection should take place on a long term basis;

(10)   Whereas in its communication of 17 January 1991 'Follow-up to the Green Paper — Working programme of the Commission in the field of copyright and neighbouring rights' the Commission stresses the need to harmonize copyright and neighbouring rights at a high level of protection since these rights are fundamental to intellectual creation and stresses that their protection ensures the maintenance and development of creativity in the interest of authors, cultural industries, consumers and society as a whole;

(11)   Whereas in order to establish a high level of protection which at the same time meets the requirements of the internal market and the need to establish a legal environment conducive to the harmonious development of literary and artistic creation in the Community, the term of protection for copyright should be harmonized at 70 years after the death of the author or 70 years after the work is lawfully made available to the public, and for related rights at 50 years after the event which sets the term running;

(12)   Whereas collections are protected according to Article 2(5) of the Berne Convention when, by reason of the selection and arrangement of their content, they constitute intellectual creations; whereas those works are protected as such, without prejudice to the copyright in each of the works forming part of such collections, whereas in consequence specific terms of protection may apply to works included in collections;

(13)   Whereas in all cases where one or more physical persons are identified as authors the term of protection should be calculated after their death; whereas the question of authorship in the whole or a part of a work is a question of fact which the national courts may have to decide;

(14)   Whereas terms of protection should be calculated from the first day of January of the year following the relevant event, as they are in the Berne and Rome Conventions;

(15)   Whereas Article 1 of Council Directive 91/250/EEC of 14 May 1991 on the legal protection of computer programs[1] provides that Member States are to protect computer programs, by copyright, as literary works within the meaning of the Berne Convention; whereas this Directive harmonizes the term of protection of literary works in the Community; whereas Article 8 of Directive 91/250/EEC, which merely makes provisional arrangements governing the term of protection of computer programs, should accordingly be repealed;

(16)   Whereas Articles 11 and 12 of Council Directive 92/100/EEC of 19 November 1992 on rental right and lending right and on certain rights related

Note
[1] OJ No. L122, 17.5.1991, p. 42.

to copyright in the field of intellectual property[2] make provision for minimum terms of protection only, subject to any further harmonization; whereas this Directive provides such further harmonization; whereas these Articles should accordingly be repealed;

(17) Whereas the protection of photographs in the Member States is the subject of varying regimes; whereas in order to achieve a sufficient harmonization of the term of protection of photographic works, in particular of those which, due to their artistic or professional character, are of importance within the internal market, it is necessary to define the level of originality required in this Directive; whereas a photographic work within the meaning of the Berne Convention is to be considered original if it is the author's own intellectual creation reflecting his personality, no other criteria such as merit or purpose being taken into account; whereas the protection of other photographs should be left to national law;

(18) Whereas, in order to avoid differences in the term of protection as regards related rights it is necessary to provide the same starting point for the calculation of the term throughout the Community; whereas the performance, fixation, transmission, lawful publication, and lawful communication to the public, that is to say the means of making a subject of a related right perceptible in all appropriate ways to persons in general, should be taken into account for the calculation of the term of protection regardless of the country where this performance, fixation, transmission, lawful publication, or lawful communication to the public takes place;

(19) Whereas the rights of broadcasting organizations in their broadcasts, whether these broadcasts are transmitted by wire or over the air, including by cable or satellite, should not be perpetual; whereas it is therefore necessary to have the term of protection running from the first transmission of a particular broadcast only; whereas this provision is understood to avoid a new term running in cases where a broadcast is identical to a previous one;

(20) Whereas the Member States should remain free to maintain or introduce other rights related to copyright in particular in relation to the protection of critical and scientific publications; whereas, in order to ensure transparency at Community level, it is however necessary for Member States which introduce new related rights to notify the Commission;

(21) Whereas it is useful to make clear that the harmonization brought about by this Directive does not apply to moral rights;

(22) Whereas, for works whose country of origin within the meaning of the Berne Convention is a third country and whose author is not a Community national, comparison of terms of protection should be applied, provided that the term accorded in the Community does not exceed the term laid down in this Directive;

(23) Whereas where a rightholder who is not a Community national qualifies for protection under an international agreement the term of protection of related rights should be the same as that laid down in this Directive, except that it should not exceed that fixed in the country of which the rightholder is a national;

(24) Whereas comparison of terms should not result in Member States being brought into conflict with their international obligations;

Note
[2] OJ No L346, 27.11.1992, p. 61.

(25)   Whereas, for the smooth functioning of the internal market this Directive should be applied as from 1 July 1995;

(26)   Whereas Member States should remain free to adopt provisions on the interpretation, adaptation and further execution of contracts on the exploitation of protected works and other subject matter which were concluded before the extension of the term of protection resulting from this Directive;

(27)   Whereas respect of acquired rights and legitimate expectations is part of the Community legal order; whereas Member States may provide in particular that in certain circumstances the copyright and related rights which are revived pursuant to this Directive may not give rise to payments by persons who undertook in good faith the exploitation of the works at the time when such works lay within the public domain,

HAS ADOPTED THIS DIRECTIVE:

Article 1   Duration of authors' rights

1.   The rights of an author of a literary or artistic work within the meaning of Article 2 of the Berne Convention shall run for the life of the author and for 70 years after his death, irrespective of the date when the work is lawfully made available to the public.

2.   In the case of a work of joint authorship the term referred to in paragraph 1 shall be calculated from the death of the last surviving author.

3.   In the case of anonymous or pseudonymous works, the term of protection shall run for seventy years after the work is lawfully made available to the public. However, when the pseudonym adopted by the author leaves no doubt as to his identity, or if the author discloses his identity during the period referred to in the first sentence, the term of protection applicable shall be that laid down in paragraph 1.

4.   Where a Member State provides for particular provisions on copyright in respect of collective works or for a legal person to be designated as the rightholder, the term of protection shall be calculated according to the provisions of paragraph 3, except if the natural persons who have created the work as such are identified as such in the versions of the work which are made available to the public. This paragraph is without prejudice to the rights of identified authors whose identifiable contributions are included in such works, to which contributions paragraph 1 or 2 shall apply.

5.   Where a work is published in volumes, parts, instalments, issues or episodes and the term of protection runs from the time when the work was lawfully made available to the public, the term of protection shall run for each such item separately.

6.   In the case of works for which the term of protection is not calculated from the death of the author or authors and which have not been lawfully made available to the public within seventy years from their creation, the protection shall terminate.

Article 2   Cinematographic or audiovisual works

1.   The principal director of a cinematographic or audiovisual work shall be considered as its author or one of its authors. Member States shall be free to designate other co-authors.

2.   The term of protection of cinematographic or audiovisual works shall expire 70 years after the death of the last of the following persons to survive,

whether or not these persons are designated as co-authors: the principal director, the author of the screenplay, the author of the dialogue and the composer of music specifically created for use in the cinematographic or audiovisual work.

Article 3   Duration of related rights

1.   The rights of performers shall expire 50 years after the date of the performance. However, if a fixation of the performance is lawfully published or lawfully communicated to the public within this period, the rights shall expire 50 years from the date of the first such publication or the first such communication to the public, whichever is the earlier.

2.   The rights of producers of phonograms shall expire 50 years after the fixation is made. However, if the phonogram is lawfully published or lawfully communicated to the public during this period, the rights shall expire 50 years from the date of the first such publication or the first such communication to the public, whichever is the earlier.

3.   The rights of producers of the first fixation of a film shall expire 50 years after the fixation is made. However, if the film is lawfully published or lawfully communicated to the public during this period, the rights shall expire 50 years from the date of the first such publication or the first such communication to the public, whichever is the earlier. The term 'film' shall designate a cinematographic or audiovisual work or moving images, whether or not accompanied by sound.

4.   The rights of broadcasting organizations shall expire 50 years after the first transmission of a broadcast, whether this broadcast is transmitted by wire or over the air, including by cable or satellite.

Article 4   Protection of previously unpublished works

Any person who, after the expiry of copyright protection, for the first time lawfully publishes or lawfully communicates to the public a previously unpublished work, shall benefit from a protection equivalent to the economic rights of the author. The term of protection of such rights shall be 25 years from the time when the work was first lawfully published or lawfully communicated to the public.

Article 5   Critical and scientific publications

Member States may protect critical and scientific publications of works which have come into the public domain. The maximum term of protection of such rights shall be 30 years from the time when the publication was first lawfully published.

Article 6   Protection of photographs

Photographs which are original in the sense that they are the author's own intellectual creation shall be protected in accordance with Article 1. No other criteria shall be applied to determine their eligibility for protection. Member States may provide for the protection of other photographs.

Article 7   Protection vis-à-vis third countries

1.   Where the country of origin of a work, within the meaning of the Berne Convention, is a third country, and the author of the work is not a Community national, the term of protection granted by the Member States shall expire on the date of expiry of the protection granted in the country of origin of the work, but may not exceed the term laid down in Article 1.

2.   The terms of protection laid down in Article 3 shall also apply in the case of rightholders who are not Community nationals, provided Member States grant them protection. However, without prejudice to the international obligations of the Member States, the term of protection granted by Member States shall expire no later than the date of expiry of the protection granted in the country of which the rightholder is a national and may not exceed the term laid down in Article 3.

3.   Member States which, at the date of adoption of this Directive, in particular pursuant to their international obligations, granted a longer term of protection than that which would result from the provisions, referred to in paragraphs 1 and 2 may maintain this protection until the conclusion of international agreements on the term of protection by copyright or related rights.

Article 8   Calculation of terms

The terms laid down in this Directive are calculated from the first day of January of the year following the event which gives rise to them.

Article 9   Moral rights

This Directive shall be without prejudice to the provisions of the Member States regulating moral rights.

Article 10   Application in time

1.   Where a term of protection, which is longer than the corresponding term provided for by this Directive, is already running in a Member State on the date referred to in Article 13(1), this Directive shall not have the effect of shortening that term of protection in that Member State.

2.   The terms of protection provided for in this Directive shall apply to all works and subject matter which are protected in at least one Member State, on the date referred to in Article 13(1), pursuant to national provisions on copyright or related rights or which meet the criteria for protection under Directive 92/100/EEC.

3.   This Directive shall be without prejudice to any acts of exploitation performed before the date referred to in Article 13(1). Member States shall adopt the necessary provisions to protect in particular acquired rights of third parties.

4.   Member States need not apply the provisions of Article 2(1) to cinematographic or audiovisual works created before 1 July 1994.

5.   Member States may determine the date as from which Article 2(1) shall apply, provided that date is no later than 1 July 1997.

Article 11   Technical adaptation

1.   Article 8 of Directive 91/250/EEC is hereby repealed.

2.   Articles 11 and 12 of Directive 92/100/EEC are hereby repealed.

Article 12   Notification procedure

Member States shall immediately notify the Commission of any governmental plan to grant new related rights, including the basic reasons for their introduction and the term of protection envisaged.

Article 13   General provisions

1.   Member States shall bring into force the laws, regulations and adminis-trative provisions necessary to comply with Articles 1 to 11 of this Directive

before 1 July 1995. When Member States adopt these provisions, they shall contain a reference to this Directive or shall be accompanied by such reference at the time of their official publication. The methods of making such a reference shall be laid down by the Member States. Member States shall communicate to the Commission the texts of the provisions of national law which they adopt in the field governed by this Directive.

2.   Member States shall apply Article 12 from the date of notification of this Directive.

Article 14
This Directive is addressed to the Member States.

Done at Brussels, 29 October 1993.
For the Council
The President
R. URBAIN

THE BLOCK EXEMPTIONS (INCLUDING INTELLECTUAL PROPERTY AND INSURANCE)

COMMISSION REGULATION (EEC) NO. 1983/83 OF 22 JUNE 1983 ON THE APPLICATION OF ARTICLE 85(3) OF THE TREATY TO CATEGORIES OF EXCLUSIVE DISTRIBUTION AGREEMENTS
[OJ 1983 L173/1]*

Having regard to the Treaty establishing the European Economic Community,

Having regard to Council Regulation No. 19/65/EEC of 2 March 1965 on the application of Article 85(3) of the Treaty to certain categories of agreements and concerted practices,[1] as last amended by the act of Accession of Greece, and in particular Article 1 thereof,

Having published a draft of this regulation,[2] having consulted the advisory committee on restrictive practices and dominant positions,

(1)   Whereas regulation no 19/65/EEC empowers the commission to apply Article 85(3) of the Treaty by regulation to certain categories of bilateral exclusive distribution agreements and analogous concerted practices falling within Article 85(1);

(2)   Whereas experience to date makes it possible to define a category of agreements and concerted practices which can be regarded as normally satisfying the conditions laid down in Article 85(3);

(3)   Whereas exclusive distribution agreements of the category defined in Article 1 of this regulation may fall within the prohibition contained in Article 85(1) of the Treaty;

Whereas this will apply only in exceptional cases to exclusive agreements of this kind to which only undertakings from one member state are party and which concern the resale of goods within that member state;

Whereas, however, to the extent that such agreements may affect trade between member states and also satisfy all the requirements set out in this regulation there is no reason to withhold from them the benefit of the exemption by category;

(4)   Whereas it is not necessary expressly to exclude from the defined category those agreements which do not fulfil the conditions of Article 85(1) of the Treaty;

Note

*as corrected by OJ 1983 L281/24 and amended by OJ 1995 L1/1.
[1]OJ No. 36, 6.3.1965, p. 533/65.
[2]OJ No. C172, 10.7.1982, p. 3.

(5) Whereas exclusive distribution agreements lead in general to an improvement in distribution because the undertaking is able to concentrate its sales activities, does not need to maintain numerous business relations with a larger number of dealers and is able, by dealing with only one dealer, to overcome more easily distribution difficulties in international trade resulting from linguistic, legal and other differences;

(6) Whereas exclusive distribution agreements facilitate the promotion of sales of a product and lead to intensive marketing and to continuity of supplies while at the same time rationalizing distribution;

Whereas they stimulate competition between the products of different manufacturers;

Whereas the appointment of an Exclusive distributor who will take over sales promotion, customer services and carrying of stocks is often the most effective way, and sometimes indeed the only way, for the manufacturer to enter a market and compete with other manufacturers already present;

Whereas this is particularly so in the case of small and medium-sized undertakings;

Whereas it must be left to the contracting parties to decide whether and to what extent they consider it desirable to incorporate in the agreements terms providing for the promotion of sales;

(7) Whereas, as a rule, such exclusive distribution agreements also allow consumers a fair share of the resulting benefit as they gain directly from the improvement in distribution, and their economic and supply position is improved as they can obtain products manufactured in particular in other countries more quickly and more easily;

(8) Whereas this regulation must define the obligations restricting competition which may be included in exclusive distribution agreements;

Whereas the other restrictions on competition allowed under this regulation in addition to the exclusive supply obligation produce a clear division of functions between the parties and compel the exclusive distributor to concentrate his sales efforts on the contract goods and the contract territory;

Whereas they are, where they are agreed only for the duration of the agreement, generally necessary in order to attain the improvement in the distribution of goods sought through exclusive distribution;

Whereas it may be left to the contracting parties to decide which of these obligations they include in their agreements;

Whereas further restrictive obligations and in particular those which limit the exclusive distributor's choice of customers or his freedom to determine his prices and conditions of sale cannot be exempted under this regulation;

(9) Whereas the exemption by category should be reserved for agreements for which it can be assumed with sufficient certainty that they satisfy the conditions of Article 85(3) of the Treaty;

(10) Whereas it is not possible, in the absence of a case-by-case examination, to consider that adequate improvements in distribution occur where a manufacturer entrusts the distribution of his goods to another manufacturer with whom he is in competition;

Whereas such agreements should, therefore, be excluded from the exemption by category;

Whereas certain derogations from this rule in favour of small and medium-sized undertakings can be allowed;

(11)   Whereas consumers will be assured of a fair share of the benefits resulting from exclusive distribution only if parallel imports remain possible;

Whereas agreements relating to goods which the user can obtain only from the exclusive distributor should therefore be excluded from the exemption by category;

Whereas the parties cannot be allowed to abuse industrial property rights or other rights in order to create absolute territorial protection;

Whereas this does not prejudice the relationship between competition law and industrial property rights, since the sole object here is to determine the conditions for exemption by category;

(12)   Whereas, since competition at the distribution stage is ensured by the possibility of parallel imports, the exclusive distribution agreements covered by this regulation will not normally afford any possibility of eliminating competition in respect of a substantial part of the products in question;

Whereas this is also true of agreements that allot to the exclusive distributor a contract territory covering the whole of the common market;

(13)   Whereas, in particular cases in which agreements or concerted practices satisfying the requirements of this regulation nevertheless have effects incompatible with Article 85(3) of the Treaty, the commission may withdraw the benefit of the exemption by category from the undertakings party to them;

(14)   Whereas agreements and concerted practices which satisfy the conditions set out in this regulation need not be notified;

Whereas an undertaking may nonetheless in a particular case where real doubt exists, request the commission to declare whether its agreements comply with this regulation;

(15)   Whereas this regulation does not affect the applicability of commission regulation (EEC) No 3604/82 of 23 December 1982 on the application of Article 85(3) of the Treaty to categories of specialization agreements;[1]

Whereas it does not exclude the application of Article 86 of the Treaty,

Note
[1]OJ No. L376, 31.12.1982, p. 33.

HAS ADOPTED THIS REGULATION:

Article 1
Pursuant to Article 85(3) of the Treaty and subject to the provisions of this regulation, it is hereby declared that Article 85(1) of the Treaty shall not apply to agreements to which only two undertakings are party and whereby one party agrees with the other to supply certain goods for resale within the whole or a defined area of the common market only to that other.

Article 2
1.   Apart from the obligation referred to in Article 1 no restriction on competition shall be imposed on the supplier other than the obligation not to supply the contract goods to users in the contract territory.

2.   No restriction on competition shall be imposed on the exclusive distributor other than:

(a)   the obligation not to manufacture or distribute goods which compete with the contract goods;

(b)   the obligation to obtain the contract goods for resale only from the other party;

(c)   the obligation to refrain, outside the contract territory and in relation to the contract goods, from seeking customers, from establishing any branch and from maintaining any distribution depot.

3.   Article 1 shall apply notwithstanding that the exclusive distributor undertakes all or any of the following obligations:

(a)   to purchase complete ranges of goods or minimum quantities;

(b)   to sell the contract goods under trade marks or packed and presented as specified by the other party;

(c)   to take measures for promotion of sales, in particular:

— to advertise,

— to maintain a sales network or stock of goods,

— to provide customer and guarantee services,

— to employ staff having specialized or technical training.

Article 3

Article 1 shall not apply where:

(a)   manufacturers of identical goods or of goods which are considered by users as equivalent in view of their characteristics, price and intended use enter into reciprocal exclusive distribution agreements between themselves in respect of such goods;

(b)   manufacturers of identical goods or of goods which are considered by users as equivalent in view of their characteristics, price and intended use enter into a non-reciprocal exclusive distribution agreement between themselves in respect of such goods unless at least one of them has a total annual turnover of no more than 100 million ECU;

(c)   users can obtain the contract goods in the contract territory only from the exclusive distributor and have no alternative source of supply outside the contract territory;

(d)   one or both of the parties makes it difficult for intermediaries or users to obtain the contract goods from other dealers inside the common market or, in so far as no alternative source of supply is available there, from outside the common market, in particular where one or both of them:

1.   Exercises industrial property rights so as to prevent dealers or users from obtaining outside, or from selling in, the contract territory properly marked or otherwise properly marketed contract goods;

2.   Exercises other rights or takes other measures so as to prevent dealers or users from obtaining outside, or from selling in, the contract territory contract goods.

Article 4

1.   Article 3(a) and (b) shall also apply where the goods there referred to are manufactured by an undertaking connected with a party to the agreement.

2.   Connected undertakings are:

(a)   undertakings in which a party to the agreement, directly or indirectly:

— owns more than half the capital or business assets, or

— has the power to exercise more than half the voting rights, or

— has the power to appoint more than half the members of the supervisory board, board of directors or bodies legally representing the undertaking, or

— has the right to manage the affairs;

(b)   undertakings which directly or indirectly have in or over a party to the agreement the rights or powers listed in (a);

(c) undertakings in which an undertaking referred to in (b) directly or indirectly has the rights or powers listed in (a).

3. Undertakings in which the parties to the agreement or undertakings connected with them jointly have the rights or powers set out in paragraph 2(a) shall be considered to be connected with each of the parties to the agreement.

Article 5

1. For the purpose of Article 3(b), the ECU is the unit of account used for drawing up the budget of the community pursuant to Articles 207 and 209 of the Treaty.

2. Article 1 shall remain applicable where during any period of two consecutive financial years the total turnover referred to in Article 3(b) is exceeded by no more than 10%.

3. For the purpose of calculating total turnover within the meaning of Article 3(b), the turnovers achieved during the last financial year by the party to the agreement and connected undertakings in respect of all goods and services, excluding all taxes and other duties, shall be added together. For this purpose no account shall be taken of dealings between the party to the agreement and its connected undertakings or between its connected undertakings.

Article 6

The Commission may withdraw the benefit of this regulation, pursuant to Article 7 of Regulation No. 19/65/EEC, when it finds in a particular case that an agreement which is exempted by this regulation nevertheless has certain effects which are incompatible with the conditions set out in Article 85(3) of the Treaty, and in particular where:

(a) the contract goods are not subject, in the contract territory, to effective competition from identical goods or goods considered by users as equivalent in view of their characteristics, price and intended use;

(b) access by other suppliers to the different stages of distribution within the contract territory is made difficult to a significant extent;

(c) for reasons other than those referred to in Article 3(c) and (d) it is not possible for intermediaries or users to obtain supplies of the contract goods from dealers outside the contract territory on the terms there customary;

(d) the exclusive distributor:

1. Without any objectively justified reason refuses to supply in the contract territory categories of purchasers who cannot obtain contract goods elsewhere on suitable terms or applies to them differing prices or conditions of sale;

2. Sells the contract goods at excessively high prices.

Article 7

In the period 1 July 1983 to 31 December 1986, the prohibition in Article 85(1) of the Treaty shall not apply to agreements which were in force on 1 July 1983 or entered into force between 1 July and 31 December 1983 and which satisfy the exemption conditions of Regulation No. 67/67/EEC.[1]

The provisions of the preceding paragraph shall apply in the same way to agreements which were in force on the date of accession of the Kingdom of Spain and of the Portuguese Republic and which, as a result of accession, fall within the scope of Article 85(1) of the Treaty.

Note
[1] OJ No. 57, 25.3.1967, p. 849/67.

Article 7a
The prohibition in Article 85(1) of the Treaty shall not apply to agreements which were in existence at the date of accession of Austria, Finland, and Sweden and which, by reason of this accession, fall within the scope of Article 85(1) if, within six months from the date of accession, they are so amended that they comply with the conditions laid down in this Regulation.

However, this Article shall not apply to agreements which at the date of accession already fall under Article 53 of the EEA Agreement.

Article 8
This regulation shall not apply to agreements entered into for the resale of drinks in premises used for the sale and consumption of drinks or for the resale of petroleum products in service stations.

Article 9
This regulation shall apply mutatis mutandis to concerted practices of the type defined in Article 1.

Article 10
This regulation shall enter into force on 1 July 1983.

It shall expire on 31 December 1997.

This regulation shall be binding in its entirety and directly applicable in all member states.

Done at Brussels, 22 June 1983.
For the commission
Frans ANDRIESSEN
Member of the commission

COMMISSION REGULATION (EEC) NO. 1984/83 OF 22 JUNE 1983 ON THE APPLICATION OF ARTICLE 85(3) OF THE TREATY TO CATEGORIES OF EXCLUSIVE PURCHASING AGREEMENTS
[OJ 1983 L173/5]*

Having regard to the Treaty establishing the European Economic Community,

Having regard to Council Regulation No. 19/65/EEC of 2 March 1965 on the application of Article 85(3) of the Treaty to certain categories of agreements and concerted practices,[1] as last amended by the act of accession of Greece, and in particular Article 1 thereof,

Having published a draft of this Regulation,[2] having consulted the advisory committee on restrictive practices and dominant positions,

(1) Whereas Regulation No. 19/65/EEC empowers the Commission to apply Article 85(3) of the Treaty by Regulation to certain categories of bilateral exclusive purchasing agreements entered into for the purpose of the resale of goods and corresponding concerted practices falling within Article 85(1);

(2) Whereas experience to date makes it possible to define three categories of agreements and concerted practices which can be regarded as normally satisfying the conditions laid down in Article 85(3);

Note
*as corrected by OJ 1983 L281/24 and amended by OJ 1995 L1/1.
[1]OJ No. 36, 6.3.1965, p. 533/65.
[2]OJ No. C172, 10.7.1982, p. 7.

Whereas the first category comprises exclusive purchasing agreements of short and medium duration in all sectors of the economy;

Whereas the other two categories comprise long-term exclusive purchasing agreements entered into for the resale of beer in premises used for the sale and consumption of drinks (beer supply agreements) and of petroleum products in filling stations (service-station agreements);

(3) Whereas exclusive purchasing agreements of the categories defined in this Regulation may fall within the prohibition contained in Article 85(1) of the Treaty;

Whereas this will often be the case with agreements concluded between undertakings from different member states;

Whereas an exclusive purchasing agreement to which undertakings from only one member state are party and which concerns the resale of goods within that member state may also be caught by the prohibition;

Whereas this is in particular the case where it is one of a number of similar agreements which together may affect trade between member states;

(4) Whereas it is not necessary expressly to exclude from the defined categories those agreements which do not fulfil the conditions of Article 85(1) of the Treaty;

(5) Whereas the exclusive purchasing agreements defined in this Regulation lead in general to an improvement in distribution;

Whereas they enable the supplier to plan the sales of his goods with greater precision and for a longer period and ensure that the reseller's requirements will be met on a regular basis for the duration of the agreement;

Whereas this allows the parties to limit the risk to them of variations in market conditions and to lower distribution costs;

(6) Whereas such agreements also facilitate the promotion of the sales of a product and lead to intensive marketing because the supplier, in consideration for the exclusive purchasing obligation, is as a rule under an obligation to contribute to the improvement of the structure of the distribution network, the quality of the promotional effort or the sales success;

Whereas, at the same time, they stimulate competition between the products of different manufacturers;

Whereas the appointment of several resellers, who are bound to purchase exclusively from the manufacturer and who take over sales promotion, customer services and carrying of stock, is often the most effective way, and sometimes the only way, for the manufacturer to penetrate a market and compete with other manufacturers already present;

Whereas this is particularly so in the case of small and medium-sized undertakings;

Whereas it must be left to the contracting parties to decide whether and to what extent they consider it desirable to incorporate in their agreements terms concerning the promotion of sales;

(7) Whereas, as a rule, exclusive purchasing agreements between suppliers and resellers also allow consumers a fair share of the resulting benefit as they gain the advantages of regular supply and are able to obtain the contract goods more quickly and more easily;

(8) Whereas this Regulation must define the obligations restricting competition which may be included in an exclusive purchasing agreement;

Whereas the other restrictions of competition allowed under this Regulation in addition to the exclusive purchasing obligation lead to a clear division of functions between the parties and compel the reseller to concentrate his sales efforts on the contract goods;

Whereas they are, where they are agreed only for the duration of the agreement, generally necessary in order to attain the improvement in the distribution of goods sought through exclusive purchasing;

Whereas further restrictive obligations and in particular those which limit the reseller's choice of customers or his freedom to determine his prices and conditions of sale cannot be exempted under this Regulation;

(9)   Whereas the exemption by categories should be reserved for agreements for which it can be assumed with sufficient certainty that they satisfy the conditions of Article 85(3) of the Treaty;

(10)   Whereas it is not possible, in the absence of a case-by-case examination, to consider that adequate improvements in distribution occur where a manufacturer imposes an exclusive purchasing obligation with respect to his goods on a manufacturer with whom he is in competition;

Whereas such agreements should, therefore, be excluded from the exemption by categories;

Whereas certain derogations from this rule in favour of small and medium-sized undertakings can be allowed;

(11)   Whereas certain conditions must be attached to the exemption by categories so that access by other undertakings to the different stages of distribution can be ensured;

Whereas, to this end, limits must be set to the scope and to the duration of the exclusive purchasing obligation;

Whereas it appears appropriate as a general rule to grant the benefit of a general exemption from the prohibition on restrictive agreements only to exclusive purchasing agreements which are concluded for a specified product or range of products and for not more than five years;

(12)   Whereas, in the case of beer supply agreements and service-station agreements, different rules should be laid down which take account of the particularities of the markets in question;

(13)   Whereas these agreements are generally distinguished by the fact that, on the one hand, the supplier confers on the reseller special commercial or financial advantages by contributing to his financing, granting him or obtaining for him a loan on favourable terms, equipping him with a site or premises for conducting his business, providing him with equipment or fittings, or undertaking other investments for his benefit and that, on the other hand, the reseller enters into a long-term exclusive purchasing obligation which in most cases is accompanied by a ban on dealing in competing products;

(14)   Whereas beer supply and service-station agreements, like the other Exclusive purchasing agreements dealt with in this Regulation, normally produce an appreciable improvement in distribution in which consumers are allowed a fair share of the resulting benefit;

(15)   Whereas the commercial and financial advantages conferred by the supplier on the reseller make it significantly easier to establish, modernize, maintain and operate premises used for the sale and consumption of drinks and service stations;

Whereas the exclusive purchasing obligation and the ban on dealing in competing products imposed on the reseller incite the reseller to devote all the resources at his disposal to the sale of the contract goods;

Whereas such agreements lead to durable cooperation between the parties allowing them to improve or maintain the quality of the contract goods and of the services to the customer and sales efforts of the reseller;

Whereas they allow long-term planning of sales and consequently a cost effective organization of production and distribution;

Whereas the pressure of competition between products of different makes obliges the undertakings involved to determine the number and character of premises used for the sale and consumption of drinks and service stations, in accordance with the wishes of customers;

(16) Whereas consumers benefit from the improvements described, in particular because they are ensured supplies of goods of satisfactory quality at fair prices and conditions while being able to choose between the products of different manufacturers;

(17) Whereas the advantages produced by beer supply agreements and service-station agreements cannot otherwise be secured to the same extent and with the same degree of certainty;

Whereas the exclusive purchasing obligation on the reseller and the non-competition clause imposed on him are essential components of such agreements and thus usually indispensable for the attainment of these advantages;

Whereas, however, this is true only as long as the reseller's obligation to purchase from the supplier is confined in the case of premises used for the sale and consumption of drinks to beers and other drinks of the types offered by the supplier, and in the case of service stations to petroleum-based fuel for motor vehicles and other petroleum-based fuels;

Whereas the exclusive purchasing obligation for lubricants and related petroleum-based products can be accepted only on condition that the supplier provides for the reseller or finances the procurement of specific equipment for the carrying out of lubrication work;

Whereas this obligation should only relate to products intended for use within the service station;

(18) Whereas, in order to maintain the reseller's commercial freedom and to ensure access to the retail level of distribution on the part of other suppliers, not only the scope but also the duration of the purchasing obligation must be limited;

Whereas it appears appropriate to allow drinks suppliers a choice between a medium-term exclusive purchasing agreement covering a range of drinks and a long-term exclusive purchasing agreement for beer;

Whereas it is necessary to provide special rules for those premises used for the sale and consumption of drinks which the supplier lets to the reseller;

Whereas, in this case, the reseller must have the right to obtain from other undertakings, under the conditions specified in this Regulation, other drinks, except beer, supplied under the agreement or of the same type but bearing a different trademark;

Whereas a uniform maximum duration should be provided for service-station agreements, with the exception of tenancy agreements between the supplier and the reseller, which takes account of the long-term character of the relationship between the parties;

(19) Whereas to the extent that member states provide, by law or administrative measures, for the same upper limit of duration for the exclusive

purchasing obligation upon the reseller in service-station agreements as laid down in this Regulation but provide for a permissible duration which varies in proportion to the consideration provided by the supplier or generally provide for a shorter duration than that permitted by this Regulation, such laws or measures are not contrary to the objectives of this Regulation which, in this respect, merely sets an upper limit to the duration of service-station agreements;

Whereas the application and enforcement of such national laws or measures must therefore be regarded as compatible with the provisions of this Regulation;

(20)   Whereas the limitations and conditions provided for in this Regulation are such as to guarantee effective competition on the markets in question;

Whereas, therefore, the agreements to which the exemption by category applies do not normally enable the participating undertakings to eliminate competition for a substantial part of the products in question;

(21)   Whereas, in particular cases in which agreements or concerted practices satisfying the conditions of this Regulation nevertheless have effects incompatible with Article 85(3) of the Treaty, the Commission may withdraw the benefit of the exemption by category from the undertakings party thereto;

(22)   Whereas agreements and concerted practices which satisfy the conditions set out in this Regulation need not be notified;

Whereas an undertaking may nonetheless, in a particular case where real doubt exists, request the Commission to declare whether its agreements comply with this Regulation;

(23)   Whereas this Regulation does not affect the applicability of Commission Regulation (EEC) No. 3604/82 of 23 December 1982 on the application of Article 85(3) of the Treaty to categories of specialization agreements;[1]

Whereas it does not exclude the application of Article 86 of the Treaty,

Note
[1]OJ No. L376, 31.12.1982, p. 33.

HAS ADOPTED THIS REGULATION:

TITLE I   GENERAL PROVISIONS

Article 1
Pursuant to Article 85(3) of the Treaty, and subject to the conditions set out in Articles 2 to 5 of this Regulation, it is hereby declared that Article 85(1) of the Treaty shall not apply to agreements to which only two undertakings are party and whereby one party, the reseller, agrees with the other, the supplier, to purchase certain goods specified in the agreement for resale only from the supplier or from a connected undertaking or from another undertaking which the supplier has entrusted with the sale of his goods.

Article 2
1.   No other restriction of competition shall be imposed on the supplier than the obligation not to distribute the contract goods or goods which compete with the contract goods in the reseller's principal sales area and at the reseller's level of distribution.

2.   Apart from the obligation described in Article 1, no other restriction of competition shall be imposed on the reseller than the obligation not to manufacture or distribute goods which compete with the contract goods.

3. Article 1 shall apply notwithstanding that the reseller undertakes any or all of the following obligations;

(a) to purchase complete ranges of goods;

(b) to purchase minimum quantities of goods which are subject to the exclusive purchasing obligation;

(c) to sell the contract goods under trademarks, or packed and presented as specified by the supplier;

(d) to take measures for the promotion of sales, in particular:

— to advertise,

— to maintain a sales network or stock of goods,

— to provide customer and guarantee services,

— to employ staff having specialized or technical training.

Article 3

Article 1 shall not apply where:

(a) manufacturers of identical goods or of goods which are considered by users as equivalent in view of their characteristics, price and intended use enter into reciprocal exclusive purchasing agreements between themselves in respect of such goods;

(b) manufacturers of identical goods or of goods which are considered by users as equivalent in view of their characteristics, price and intended use enter into a non-reciprocal exclusive purchasing agreement between themselves in respect of such goods, unless at least one of them has a total annual turnover of no more than 100 million ECU;

(c) the exclusive purchasing obligation is agreed for more than one type of goods where these are neither by their nature nor according to commercial usage connected to each other;

(d) the agreement is concluded for an indefinite duration or for a period of more than five years.

Article 4

1. Article 3(a) and (b) shall also apply where the goods there referred to are manufactured by an undertaking connected with a party to the agreement.

2. Connected undertakings are:

(a) undertakings in which a party to the agreement, directly or indirectly:

— owns more than half the capital or business assets, or

— has the power to exercise more than half the voting rights, or

— has the power to appoint more than half the members of the supervisory board, board of directors or bodies legally representing the undertaking, or

— has the right to manage the affairs;

(b) undertakings which directly or indirectly have in or over a party to the agreement the rights or powers listed in (a);

(c) undertakings in which an undertaking referred to in (b) directly or ndirectly has the rights or powers listed in (a).

3. Undertakings in which the parties to the agreement or undertakings connected with them jointly have the rights or powers set out in paragraph 2(a) shall be considered to be connected with each of the parties to the agreement.

Article 5

1. For the purpose of Article 3(b), the ECU is the unit of account used for drawing up the budget of the Community pursuant to Articles 207 and 209 of the Treaty.

2.   Article 1 shall remain applicable where during any period of two consecutive financial years the total turnover referred to in Article 3(b) is exceeded by no more than 10%.

3.   For the purpose of calculating total turnover within the meaning of Article 3(b), the turnovers achieved during the last financial year by the party to the agreement and connected undertakings in respect of all goods and services, excluding all taxes and other duties, shall be added together. For this purpose no account shall be taken of dealings between the party to the agreement and its connected undertakings or between its connected undertakings.

TITLE II   SPECIAL PROVISIONS FOR BEER SUPPLY AGREEMENTS

Article 6

1.   Pursuant to Article 85(3) of the Treaty, and subject to Articles 7 to 9 of this Regulation, it is hereby declared that Article 85(1) of the Treaty shall not apply to agreements to which only two undertakings are party and whereby one party, the reseller, agrees with the other, the supplier, in consideration for the according of special commercial or financial advantages, to purchase only from the supplier, an undertaking connected with the supplier or another undertaking entrusted by the supplier with the distribution of his goods, certain beers, or certain beers and certain other drinks, specified in the agreement for resale in premises used for the sale and consumption of drinks and designated in the agreement.

2.   The declaration in paragraph 1 shall also apply where exclusive purchasing obligations of the kind described in paragraph 1 are imposed on the reseller in favour of the supplier by another undertaking which is itself not a supplier.

Article 7

1.   Apart from the obligation referred to in Article 6, no restriction on competition shall be imposed on the reseller other than:

(a)   the obligation not to sell beers and other drinks which are supplied by other undertakings and which are of the same type as the beers or other drinks supplied under the agreement in the premises designated in the agreement;

(b)   the obligation, in the event that the reseller sells in the premises designated in the agreement beers which are supplied by other undertakings and which are of a different type from the beers supplied under the agreement, to sell such beers only in bottles, cans or other small packages, unless the sale of such beers in draught form is customary or is necessary to satisfy a sufficient demand from consumers;

(c)   the obligation to advertise goods supplied by other undertakings within or outside the premises designated in the agreement only in proportion to the share of these goods in the total turnover realized in the premises.

2.   Beers or other drinks are of different types where they are clearly distinguishable by their composition, appearance or taste.

Article 8

1.   Article 6 shall not apply where:

(a)   the supplier or a connected undertaking imposes on the reseller exclusive purchasing obligations for goods other than drinks or for services;

(b)   the supplier restricts the freedom of the reseller to obtain from an undertaking of his choice either services or goods for which neither an exclusive purchasing obligation nor a ban on dealing in competing products may be imposed;

(c)   the agreement is concluded for an indefinite duration or for a period of more than five years and the exclusive purchasing obligation relates to specified beers and other drinks;

(d)   the agreement is concluded for an indefinite duration or for a period of more than 10 years and the exclusive purchasing obligation relates only to specified beers;

(e)   the supplier obliges the reseller to impose the exclusive purchasing obligation on his successor for a longer period than the reseller would himself remain tied to the supplier.

2.   Where the agreement relates to premises which the supplier lets to the reseller or allows the reseller to occupy on some other basis in law or in fact, the following provisions shall also apply:

(a)   notwithstanding paragraphs (1)(c) and (d), the exclusive purchasing obligations and bans on dealing in competing products specified in this title may be imposed on the reseller for the whole period for which the reseller in fact operates the premises;

(b)   the agreement must provide for the reseller to have the right to obtain:

— drinks, except beer, supplied under the agreement from other undertakings where these undertakings offer them on more favourable conditions which the supplier does not meet,

— drinks, except beer, which are of the same type as those supplied under the agreement but which bear different trade marks, from other undertakings where the supplier does not offer them.

Article 9
Articles 2(1) and (3), 3(a) and (b), 4 and 5 shall apply mutatis mutandis.

TITLE III   SPECIAL PROVISIONS FOR SERVICE-STATION AGREEMENTS

Article 10
Pursuant to Article 85(3) of the Treaty and subject to Articles 11 to 13 of this Regulation, it is hereby declared that Article 85(1) of the Treaty shall not apply to agreements to which only two undertakings are party and whereby one party, the reseller, agrees with the other, the supplier, in consideration for the according of special commercial or financial advantages, to purchase only from the supplier, an undertaking connected with the supplier or another undertaking entrusted by the supplier with the distribution of his goods, certain petroleum-based motor-vehicle fuels or certain petroleum-based motor-vehicle and other fuels specified in the agreement for resale in a service station designated in the agreement.

Article 11
Apart from the obligation referred to in Article 10, no restriction on competition shall be imposed on the reseller other than:

(a)   the obligation not to sell motor-vehicle fuel and other fuels which are supplied by other undertakings in the service station designated in the agreement;

(b) the obligation not to use lubricants or related petroleum-based products which are supplied by other undertakings within the service station designated in the agreement where the supplier or a connected undertaking has made available to the reseller, or financed, a lubrication bay or other motor-vehicle lubrication equipment;

(c) the obligation to advertise goods supplied by other undertakings within or outside the service station designated in the agreement only in proportion to the share of these goods in the total turnover realized in the service station;

(d) the obligation to have equipment owned by the supplier or a connected undertaking or financed by the supplier or a connected undertaking serviced by the supplier or an undertaking designated by him.

Article 12

1. Article 10 shall not apply where:

(a) the supplier or a connected undertaking imposes on the reseller exclusive purchasing obligations for goods other than motor-vehicle and other fuels or for services, except in the case of the obligations referred to in Article 11(b) and (d);

(b) the supplier restricts the freedom of the reseller to obtain from an undertaking of his choice goods or services for which under the provisions of this title neither an exclusive purchasing obligation nor a ban on dealing in competing products may be imposed;

(c) the agreement is concluded for an indefinite duration or for a period of more than 10 years;

(d) the supplier obliges the reseller to impose the exclusive purchasing obligation on his successor for a longer period than the reseller would himself remain tied to the supplier.

2. Where the agreement relates to a service station which the supplier lets to the reseller, or allows the reseller to occupy on some other basis, in law or in fact, exclusive purchasing obligations or bans on dealing in competing products specified in this Title may, notwithstanding paragraph 1(c), be imposed on the reseller for the whole period for which the reseller in fact operates the premises.

Article 13

Articles 2(1) and (3), 3(a) and (b), 4 and 5 of this Regulation shall apply mutatis mutandis.

TITLE IV   MISCELLANEOUS PROVISIONS

Article 14

The Commission may withdraw the benefit of this Regulation, pursuant to Article 7 of Regulation no 19/65/EEC, when it finds in a particular case that an agreement which is exempted by this Regulation nevertheless has certain effects which are incompatible with the conditions set out in Article 85(3) of the Treaty, and in particular where:

(a) the contract goods are not subject, in a substantial part of the common market, to effective competition from identical goods or goods considered by users as equivalent in view of their characteristics, price and intended use;

(b) access by other suppliers to the different stages of distribution in a substantial part of the common market is made difficult to a significant extent;

(c)   the supplier without any objectively justified reason:

1.   Refuses to supply categories of resellers who cannot obtain the contract goods elsewhere on suitable terms or applies to them differing prices or conditions of sale;

2.   Applies less favourable prices or conditions of sale to resellers bound by an exclusive purchasing obligation as compared with other resellers at the same level of distribution.

Article 15

1.   In the period 1 July 1983 to 31 December 1986, the prohibition in Article 85(1) of the Treaty shall not apply to agreements of the kind described in Article 1 which either were in force on 1 July 1983 or entered into force between 1 July and 31 December 1983 and which satisfy the exemption conditions of Regulation No. 67/67/EEC.[1]

2.   In the period 1 July 1983 to 31 December 1988, the prohibition in Article 85(1) of the Treaty shall not apply to agreements of the kinds described in Articles 6 and 10 which either were in force on 1 July 1983 or entered into force between 1 July and 31 December 1983 and which satisfy the exemption conditions of Regulation No. 67/67/EEC.

3.   In the case of agreements of the kinds described in Articles 6 and 10, which were in force on 1 July 1983 and which expire after 31 December 1988, the prohibition in Article 85(1) of the Treaty shall not apply in the period from 1 January 1989 to the expiry of the agreement but at the latest to the expiry of this Regulation to the extent that the supplier releases the reseller, before 1 January 1989, from all obligations which would prevent the application of the exemption under titles II and III.

4.   The provisions of the preceding paragraphs shall apply in the same way to the agreements referred to respectively in those paragraphs, which were in force on the date of accession of the Kingdom of Spain and of the Portuguese Republic and which, as a result of accession, fall within the scope of Article 85(1) of the Treaty.

Note
[1]OJ No. 57, 25.3.1967, p. 849/67.

Article 15a

The prohibition in Article 85(1) of the Treaty shall not apply to agreements which were in existence at the date of accession of Austria, Finland, and Sweden and which, by reason of this accession, fall within the scope of Article 85(1) if, within six months from the date of accession, they are so amended that they comply with the conditions laid down in this Regulation. However, this Article shall not apply to agreements which at the date of accession already fall under Article 53(1) of the EEA Agreement.

Article 16

This Regulation shall not apply to agreements by which the supplier undertakes with the reseller to supply only to the reseller certain goods for resale, in the whole or in a defined part of the Community, and the reseller undertakes with the supplier to purchase these goods only from the supplier.

Article 17

This Regulation shall not apply where the parties or connected undertakings, for the purpose of resale in one and the same premises used for the sale and consumption of drinks or service station, enter into agreements both of the kind referred to in title I and of a kind referred to in title II or III.

Article 18
This Regulation shall apply mutatis mutandis to the categories of concerted practices defined in Articles 1, 6 and 10.

Article 19
This Regulation shall enter into force on 1 July 1983.
   It shall expire on 31 December 1997.

This Regulation shall be binding in its entirety and directly applicable in all member states.

Done at Brussels, 22 June 1983.
For the Commission
Frans ANDRIESSEN
Member of the Commission

COMMISSION NOTICE CONCERNING COMMISSION REGULATIONS (EEC) NO. 1983/83 AND (EEC) NO. 1984/83 OF 22 JUNE 1983 ON THE APPLICATION OF ARTICLE 85(3) OF THE TREATY TO CATEGORIES OF EXCLUSIVE DISTRIBUTION AND EXCLUSIVE PURCHASING AGREEMENTS
[84/C 101/02]*

(This text replaces the previous text published in Official Journal of the European Communities No. C335 of 30 December 1983, page 7)

I.   INTRODUCTION

1.   Commission Regulation No. 67/67/EEC of 22 March 1967 on the application of Article 85(3) of the Treaty to certain categories of exclusive dealing agreements[1] expired on 30 June 1983 after being in force for over 15 years. With Regulations (EEC) No. 1983/83 and (EEC) No. 1984/83,[2] the Commission has adapted the block exemption of exclusive distribution agreements and exclusive purchasing agreements to the intervening developments in the common market and in Community law. Several of the provisions in the new Regulations are new. A certain amount of interpretative guidance is therefore called for. This will assist undertakings in bringing their agreements into line with the new legal requirements and will also help ensure that the Regulations are applied uniformly in all the Member States.
2.   In determining how a given provision is to be applied, one must take into account, in addition to the ordinary meaning of the words used, the intention of the provision as this emerges from the preamble. For further guidance, reference should be made to the principles that have been evolved in the case law of the Court of Justice of the European Communities and in the Commission's decisions on individual cases.

Note
*as modified by Commission Notice 1992 OJ C121/2.
[1]OJ No. 57, 25.3.1967, p. 849/67.
[2]OJ No. L173, 30.6.1983, pp. 1 and 5.

3.   This notice sets out the main considerations which will determine the
Commission's view of whether or not an exclusive distribution or purchasing
agreement is covered by the block exemption. The notice is without prejudice
to the jurisdiction of national courts to apply the Regulations, although it may
well be of persuasive authority in proceedings before such courts. Nor does the
notice necessarily indicate the interprtation which might be given to the
provisions by the Court of Justice.

II.   EXCLUSIVE DISTRIBUTION AND EXCLUSIVE PURCHASING AGREEMENTS (REGULATIONS (EEC) NO. 1983/83 AND (EEC) NO. 1984/83)

1.   *Similarities and differences*

4.   Regulations (EEC) No. 1983/83 and (EEC) No. 1984/83 are both
concerned with exclusive agreements between two undertakings for the
purpose of the resale of goods. Each deals with a particular type of
such agreements. Regulation (EEC) No. 1983/83 applies to exclusive
distribution agreements, Regulation (EEC) No. 1984/83 to exclusive
purchasing agreements. The distinguishing feature of exclusive distribution
agreements is that one party, the supplier, allots to the other, the reseller, a
defined territory (the contract territory) on which the reseller has to concentrate his sales effort, and in return undertakes not to supply any other reseller in
that territory. In exclusive purchasing agrements, the reseller agrees to
purchase the contract goods only from the other party and not from any other
supplier. The supplier is entitled to supply other resellers in the same sales area
and at the same level of distribution. Unlike an exclusive distributor, the tied
reseller is not protected against competition from other resellers who, like
himself, receive the contract goods direct from the supplier. On the other hand,
he is free of restrictions as to the area over which he may make his sales effort.
5.   In keeping with their common starting point, the Regulations have many
provisions that are the same or similar in both Regulations. This is true of the
basic provision in Article 1, in which the respective subject-matters of the block
exemption, the exclusive supply or purchasing obligation, are defined, and of
the exhaustive list of restrictions of competition which may be agreed in
addition to the exclusive supply or purchasing obligation (Article 2(1) and (2)),
the nonexhaustive enumeration of other obligations which do not prejudice the
block exemption (Article 2(3)), the inapplicability of the block exemption in
principle to exclusive agreements between competing manufacturers (Article
3(a) and (b), 4 and 5), the withdrawal of the block exemption in individual
cases (Article 6 of Regulations (EEC) No. 1983/83 and Article 14 of
Regulation (EEC) No. 1984/83), the transitional provisions (Article 7 of
Regulation (EEC) No. 1983/83 and Article 15(1) of Regulation (EEC) No.
1984/83), and the inclusion of concerted practices within the scope of the
Regulations (Article 9 of Regulation (EEC) No. 1983/83 and Article 18 of
Regulation (EEC) No. 1984/83). In so far as their wording permits, these
parallel provisions are to be interpreted in the same way.
6.   Different rules are laid down in the Regulations wherever they need to
take account of matters which are peculiar to the exlcusive distribution
agreements or exclusive purchasing agreements respectively. This applies in
Regulation (EEC) No. 1983/83, to the provisions regarding the obligation on

the exclusive distributor not actively to promote sales outside the contract territory (Article 2(2)(c) and the inapplicability of the block exemption to agreements which give the exclusive distributor absolute territorial protection (Article 3(c) and (d)) and, in Regulation (EEC) No. 1984/83, to the provisions limiting the scope and duration of the block exemption for exclusive purchasing agreements in general (Article 3(c) and (d)) and for beer-supply and service-station agreements in particular (Titles II and III).

7.   The scope of the two Regulations has been defined so as to avoid any overlap (Article 16 of Regulation (EEC) No. 1984/83).

2. *Basic Provision*
(Article 1)

8.   Both Regulations apply only to agreements entered into for the purpose of the resale of goods to which not more than two undertakings are party.

(a) 'For resale'

9.   The notion of resale requires that the goods concerned be disposed of by the purchasing party to others in return for consideration. Agreements on the supply or purchase of goods which the purchasing party transforms or processes into other goods or uses or consumes in manufacturing other goods are not agreements for resale. The same applies to the supply of components which are combined with other components into a different product. The criterion is that the goods distributed by the reseller are the same as those the other party has supplied to him for that purpose. The economic identity of the goods is not affected if the reseller merely breaks up and packages the goods in smaller quantities, or repackages them before resale.

10.   Where the reseller performs additional operations to improve the quality, durability, appearance or taste of the goods (such as rustproofing of metals, sterilisation of food or the addition of colouring matter or flavourings to drugs), the position will mainly depend on how much value the operation adds to the goods. Only a slight addition in value can be taken not to change the economc identity of the goods. In determining the precise dividing line in individual cases, trade usage in particular must be considered. The Commission applies the same principles to agreements under which the reseller is supplied with a concentrated extract for a drink which he has to dilute with water, pure alcohol or another liquid and to bottle before reselling.

(b) 'Goods'

11.   Exclusive agreements for the supply of services rather than the resale of goods are not covered by the Regulations. The block exemption still applies, however, where the reseller provides customer or after-sales services incidentally to the resale of the goods. Nevertheless, a case where the charge for the service is higher than the price of the goods would fall outside the scope of the Regulations.

12.   The hiring out of goods in return for payment comes closer, economically speaking, to a resale of goods than to provision of services. The Commission therefore regards exclusive agreements under which the purchasing party hires out or leases to others the goods supplied to him as covered by the Regulations.

(c)   'Only two undertakings party'

13.   To be covered by the block exemption, the exclusive distribution or purchasing agreement must be between only one supplier and one reseller in each case. Several undertakings forming one economic unit count as one undertaking.

14.   This limitation on the number of undertakings that may be party relates solely to the individual agreement. A supplier does not lose the benefit of the block exemption if he enters into exclusive distribution or purchasing agreements covering the same goods with several resellers.

15.   The supplier may delegate the performance of his contractual obligations to a connected or independent undertaking which he has entrusted with the distribution of his goods, so that the reseller has to purchase the contract goods from the latter undertaking. This principle is expressly mentioned only in Regulation (EEC) No. 1984/83 (Article 1, 6 and 10), because the question of delegation arises mainly in connection with exclusive purchasing agreements. It also applies, however, to exclusive distribution agreements under Regulation (EEC) No. 1983/83.

16.   The involvement of undertakings other than the contracting parties must be confined to the execution of deliveries. The parties may accept exclusive supply or purchase obligations only for themselves, and not impose them on third parties, since otherwise more than two undertakings would be party to the agreement. The obligation of the parties to ensure that the obligations they have accepted are respected by connected undertakings is, however, covered by the block exemption.

3.   *Other restrictions on competition that are exempted*
(Article 2(1) and (2))

17.   Apart from the exclusive supply obligation (Regulation (EEC) No. 1983/83) or exclusive purchase obligation (Regulation (EEC) No. 1984/83), obligations defined in Article 1 which must be present if the block exemption is to apply, the only other restrictions of competition that may be agreed by the parties are those set out in Article 2(1) and (2). If they agree on further obligations restrictive of competition, the agreement as a whole is no longer covered by the block exemption and requires individual exemption. For example, an agreement will exceed the bounds of the Regulations if the parties relinquish the possibility of independently determining their prices or conditions of business or undertake to refrain from, or even prevent, cross-border trade, which the Regulations expressly state must not be impeded. Among other clauses which in general are not permissible under the Regulations are those which impede the reseller in his free choice of customers.

18.   The obligations restrictive of competition that are exempted may be agreed only for the duration of the agreement. This also applied to restrictions accepted by the supplier or reseller on competing with the other party.

4.   *Obligations upon the reseller which do not prejudice the block exemption*
(Article 2(3))

19.   The obligations cited in this provision are examples of clauses which generally do not restrict competition. Undertakings are therefore free to include one, several or all of these obligations in their agreements. However,

the obligations may not be formulated or applied in such a way as to take on the character of restrictions of competition that are not permitted. To forestall this danger, Article 2(3)(b) of Regulation (EEC) No. 1984/83 expressly allows minimum purchase obligations only for goods that are subject to an exclusive purchasing obligation.

20. As part of the obligation to take measures for promotion of sales and in particular to maintain a distribution network (Article 2(3)(c) of Regulation (EEC) No. 1983/83 and Article 2(3)(d) of Regulation (EEC) No. 1984/83), the reseller may be forbidden to supply the contract goods to unsuitable dealers. Such clauses are unobjectionable if admission to the distribution network is based on objective criteria of a qualitative nature relating to the professional qualifications of the owner of the business or his staff or the suitability of his business premises, if the criteria are the same for all potential dealers, and if the criteria are actually applied in a nondiscriminatory manner. Distribution systems which do not fulfil these conditions are not covered by the block exemption.

5. *Inapplicability of the block exemption to exclusive agreements between competing manufacturers*
(Articles 3(a) and (b), 4 and 5)

21. The block exemption does not apply if either the parties themselves or undertakings connected with them are manufacturers, manufacture goods belonging to the same product market, and enter into exclusive distribution or purchasing agreements with one another in respect of those goods. Only identical or equivalent goods are regarded as belonging to the same product market. The goods in question must be interchangeable. Whether or not this is the case must be judged from the vantage point of the user, normally taking the characteristics, price and intended use of the goods together. In certain cases, however, goods can form a separate market on the basis of their characteristics, their price or their intended use alone. This is true especially where consumer preferences have developed. The above provisions are applicable regardless of whether or not the parties or the undertakings connected with them are based in the Community and whether or not they are already actually in competition with one another in the relevant goods inside or outside the Community.

22. In principle, both reciprocal and non-reciprocal exclusive agreements between competing manufacturers are not covered by the block exemption and are therefore subject to individual scrutiny of their compatibility with Article 85 of the Treaty, but there is an exception for non-reciprocal agreements of the abovementioned kind where one or both of the parties are undertakings with a total annual turnover of no more than 100 million ECU (Article 3(b)). Annual turnover is used as a measure of the economic strength of the undertakings involved. Therefore, the agregate turnover from goods and services of all types, and not only from the contract goods, is to be taken. Turnover taxes and other turnover-related levies are not included in turnover. Where a party belongs to a group of connected undertakings, the world-wide turnover of the group, excluding intra-group sales (Article 5(3)), is to be used.

23. The total turnover limit can be exceeded during any period of two successive financial years by up to 10% without loss of the block exemption. The block exemption is lost if, at the end of the second financial year, the total turnover over the preceding two years has been over 220 million ECU (Article 5(2)).

6. *Withdrawal of the block exemption in individual cases*
(Article 6 of Regulation (EEC) No. 1983/83 and Article 14 of Regulation (EEC) No. 1984/83)

24.   The situations described are meant as illustrations of the sort of situations in which the Commission can exercise its powers under Article 7 of Council Regulation No. 19/65/EEC[1] to withdraw a block exemption. The benefit of the block exemption can only be withdrawn by a decision in an individual case following proceedings under Regulation No. 17. Such a decision cannot have retroactive effect. It may be coupled with an individual exemption subject to conditions or obligations or, in an extreme case, with the finding of an infringement and an order to bring it to an end.

Note
[1]OJ No. 36, 6.3.1965, p. 533/65.

7. *Transitional provisions*
(Article 7 of Regulation (EEC) No. 1983/83 and Article 15(1) of Regulation (EEC) No. 1984/83)

25.   Exclusive distribution or exclusive purchasing agreements which were concluded and entered into force before 1 January 1984 continue to be exempted under the provisions of Regulation No. 67/67/EEC until 31 December 1986. Should the parties wish to apply such agreements beyond 1 January 1987, they will either have to bring them into line with the provisions of the new Regulations or to notify them to the Commission. Special rules apply in the case of beer-supply and service-station agreements (see paragraphs 64 and 65 below).

8. *Concerted practices*
(Article 9 of Regulation (EEC) No. 1983/83 and Article 18 of Regulation (EEC) No. 1984/83)

26.   These provisions bring within the scope of the Regulations exclusive distribution and purchasing arrangements which are operated by undertakings but are not the subject of a legally-binding agreement.

III.   EXCLUSIVE DISTRIBUTION AGREEMENTS (REGULATION (EEC) NO. 1983/83)

1. *Exclusive supply obligation*
(Article 1)

27.   The exclusive supply obligation does not prevent the supplier from providing the contract goods to other resellers who afterwards sell them in the exclusive distributor's territory. It makes no difference whether the other dealers concerned are established outside or inside the territory. The supplier is not in breach of his obligation to the exclusive distributor provided that he supplies the resellers who wish to sell the contract goods in the territory only at their request and that the goods are handed over outside the territory. It does not matter whether the reseller takes delivery of the goods himself or through an intermediary, such as a freight forwarder. However, supplies of this nature are only permissible if the reseller and not the supplier pays the transport costs of the goods into the contract territory.

28.　The goods supplied to the exclusive distributor must be intended for resale in the contract territory. This basic requirement does not, however, mean that the exclusive distributor cannot sell the contract goods to customers outside his contract territory should he receive orders from them. Under Article 2(2)(c), the supplier can prohibit him only from seeking customers in other areas, but not from supplying them.

29.　It would also be incompatible with the Regulation for the exclusive distributor to be restricted to suppying only certain categories of customers (e.g., specialist retailers in his contract territory and prohibited from supplying other categories (e.g., department stores), which are supplied by other resellers appointed by the supplier for that purpose.

2.　Restriction on competition by the supplier (Article 2(1))

30.　The restriction on the supplier himself supplying the contract goods to final users in the exclusive distributor's contract territory need not be absolute. Clauses permitting the supplier to supply certain customers in the territory — with or without payment of compensation to the exclusive distributor — are compatible with the block exemption provided the customers in question are not resellers. The supplier remains free to supply the contract goods outside the contract territory to final users based in the territory. In this case the position is the same as for dealers (see paragraph 27 above).

3.　Inapplicability of the block exemption in cases of absolute territorial protection (Articles 3(c) and (d))

31.　The block exemption cannot be claimed for agreements that give the exclusive distributor absolute territorial protection. If the situation described in Article 3(c) obtains, the parties must ensure either that the contract goods can be sold in the contract territory by parallel importers or that users have a real possibility of obtaining them from undertakings outside the contract territory, if necessary outside the Community, at the prices and on the terms there prevailing. The supplier can represent an alternative source of supply for the purposes of this provision if he is prepared to supply the contract goods on request to final users located in the contract territory.

32.　Article 3(d) is chiefly intended to safeguard the freedom of dealers and users to obtain the contract goods in other Member States. Action to impede imports into the Community from third countries will only lead to loss of the block exemption if there are no alternative sources of supply in the Community. This situation can arise especially where the exclusive distributor's contract territory covers the whole or the major part of the Community.

33.　The block exemption ceases to apply as from the moment that either of the parties takes measures to impede parallel imports into the contract territory. Agreements in which the supplier undertakes with the exclusive distributor to prevent his other customers from supplying into the contract territory are ineligible for the block exemption from the outset. This is true even if the parties agree only to prevent imports into the Community from third countries. In this case it is immaterial whether or not there are alternative sources of supply in the Community. The inapplicability of the block exemption follows from the mere fact that the agreement contains restrictions on competition which are not covered by Article 2(1).

IV. EXCLUSIVE PURCHASING AGREEMENTS (REGULATION (EEC) NO. 1984/83)

1. *Structure of the Regulation*

34. Title I of the Regulation contains general provisions for exclusive purchasing agreements and Titles II and III special provisions for beer-supply and service-station agreements. The latter types of agreement are governed exclusively by the special provisions, some of which (Articles 9 and 13), however, refer to some of the general provisions, Article 17 also excludes the combination of agreements of the kind referred to in Title I with those of the kind referred to in Titles II or III to which the same undertakings or undertakings connected with them are party. To prevent any avoidance of the special provisions for beer-supply and service-station agreements, it is also made clear that the provisions governing the exclusive distribution of goods do not apply to agreements entered into for the resale of drinks on premises used for the sale or consumption of beer or for the resale of petroleum products in service stations (Article 8 of Regulation (EEC) No. 1983/83).

2. *Exclusive purchasing obligation*
(Article 1)

35. The Regulation only covers agreements whereby the reseller agrees to purchase all his requirements for the contract goods from the other party. If the purchasing obligation relates to only part of such requirements, the block exemption does not apply. Clauses which allow the reseller to obtain the contract goods from other suppliers, should these sell them more cheaply or on more favourable terms than the other party are still covered by the block exemption. The same applies to clauses releasing the reseller from his exclusive purchasing obligation should the other party be unable to supply.

36. The contract goods must be specified by brand or denomination in the agreement. Only if this is done will it be possible to determine the precise scope of the reseller's exclusive purchasing obligation (Article 1) and of the ban on dealing in competing products (Article 2(2)).

3. *Restriction on competition by the supplier*
(Article 2(1))

37. This provision allows the reseller to protect himself against direct competition from the supplier in his principal sales area. The reseller's principal sales area is determined by his normal business activity. It may be more closely defined in the agreement. However, the supplier cannot be forbidden to supply dealers who obtain the contract goods outside this area and afterwards resell them to customers inside it or to appoint other resellers in the area.

4. *Limits of the block exemption*
(Article 3(c) and (d))

38. Article 3(c) provides that the exclusive purchasing obligation can be agreed for one or more products, but in the latter case the products must be so related as to be thought of as belonging to the same range of goods. The relationship can be found on technical (e.g., a machine, accessories and spare parts for it) or commercial grounds (e.g., several products used for the same

purpose) or on usage in the trade (different goods that are customarily offered for sale together). In the latter case, regard must be had to the usual practice at the reseller's level of distribution on the relevant market, taking into account all relevant dealers and not only particular forms of distribution. Exclusive purchasing agreements covering goods which do not belong together can only be exempted from the competition rules by an individual decision.

39.   Under Article 3(d), exclusion purchasing agreements concluded for an indefinite period are not covered by the block exemption. Agreements which specify a fixed term but are automatically renewable unless one of the parties gives notice to terminate are to be considered to have been concluded for an indefinite period.

V.   BEER-SUPPLY AGREEMENTS (TITLE II OF REGULATION (EEC) NO. 1984/83)

— 2.   Exclusive purchasing obligation
— 3.   Other restrictions of competition that are exempted
— 4.   Agreements excluded from the block exemption.

1.   *Agreements of minor importance*

40.   It is recalled that the Commission's notice on agreements of minor importance[1] states that the Commission holds the view that agreements between undertakings do not fall under the prohibition of Article 85(1) of the EEC Treaty if certain conditions as regards market share and turnover are met by the undertakings concerned. Thus, it is evident that when an undertaking, brewery or wholesaler, surpasses the limits as laid down in the above notice, the agreements concluded by it may fall under Article 85(1) of the EEC Treaty. The notice, however, does not apply where in a relevant market competition is restricted by the cumulative effects of parallel networks of similar agreements which would not individually fall under Article 85(1) of the EEC Treaty if the notice was applicable. Since the markets for beer will frequently be character-ised by the existence of cumulative effects, it seems appropriate to determine which agreements can nevertheless be considered *de minimis*.

Note
[1] OJ No. C231, 12.9.1986, p. 2.

The Commission is of the opinion that an exclusive beer supply agreement concluded by a brewery, in the sense of Article 6, and including Article 8(2) of Regulation (EEC) 1984/83 does not, in general, fall under Article 85(1) of the EEC Treaty if
— the market share of that brewery is not higher than 1% on the national market for the resale of beer in premises used for the sale and consumption of drinks, and
— if that brewery does not produe more than 200,000 hl of beer per annum.
However, these principles do not apply if the agreement in question is concluded for more than 7 and a half years in as far as it covers beer and other drinks, and for 15 years if it covers only beer.
In order to establish the market share of the brewery and its annual production, the provisions of Article 4(2) of Regulation (EEC) 1984/83 apply.

As regards exclusive beer supply agreements in the sense of Article 6, and including Article 8(2) of Regulation (EEC) 1984/83 which are concluded by wholesalers, the above principles apply *mutatis mutandis* by taking account of the position of the brewery whose beer is the main subject of the agreement in question.

The present communication does not preclude that in individual cases even agreements between undertakings which do not fulfil the above criteria, in particular where the number of outlets tied to them is limited as compared to the number of outlets existing on the market, may still have only a negligible effect on trade between Member States or on competition, and would therefore not be caught by Article 85(1) of the EEC Treaty.

Neither does this communication in any way Prejudge the application of national law to the agreements covered by it.

1.   Exclusive purchasing obligation
(Article 6)

41.   The beers and other drinks covered by the exclusive purchasing obligation must be specified by brand or denomination in the agreement. An exclusive purchasing obligation can only be imposed on the reseller for drinks which the supplier carries at the time the contract takes effect and provided that they are supplied in the quantities required, at sufficiently regular intervals and at prices and on conditions allowing normal sales to the consumer. Any extension of the exclusive purchasing obligation to drinks not specified in the agreement requires an additional agreement, which must likewise satisfy the requirements of Title II of the Regulation. A change in the brand or denomination of a drink which in other respects remains unchanged does not constitute such an extension of the exclusive purchasing obligation.

42.   The exclusive purchasing obligation can be agreed in respect of one or more premises used for the sale and consumption of drinks which the reseller runs at the time the contract takes effect. The name and location of the premises must be stated in the agreement. Any extension of the exclusive purchasing obligation to other such premises requires an additional agreement, which must likewise satisfy the provisions of Title II of the Regulation.

43.   The concept of 'premises used for the sale and consumption of drinks' covers any licensed premises used for this purpose. Private clubs are also included. Exclusive purchasing agreements between the supplier and the operator of an off-licence shop are governed by the provisions of Title I of the Regulation.

44.   Special commercial or financial advantages are those going beyond what the reseller could normally expect under an agreement. The explanations given in the 13th recital are illustrations. Whether or not the supplier is affording the reseller special advantages depends on the nature, extent and duration of the obligation undertaken by the parties. In doubtful cases usage in the trade is the decisive element.

45.   The reseller can enter into exclusive purchasing obligations both with a brewery in respect of beers of a certain type and with a drinks wholesaler in respect of beers of another type and/or other drinks. The two agreements can be combined into one document. Article 6 also covers cases where the drinks wholesaler performs several functions at once, signing the first agreement on the brewery's and the second on his own behalf and also undertaking delivery

of all the drinks. The provisions of Title II do not apply to the contractual relation between the brewery and the drinks wholesaler.

46.   Article 6(2) makes the block exemption also applicable to cases in which the supplier affords the owner of premises financial or other help in equipping them as a public house, restaurant, etc., and in return the owner imposes on the buyer or tenant of the premises an exclusive purchasing obligation in favour of the supplier. A similar situation, economically speaking, is the transmission of an exclusive purchasing obligation from the owner of a public house to his successor. Under Article 8(1)(e) this is also, in principle, permissible.

2.   *Other restrictions of competition that are exempted*
(Article 7)

47.   The list of permitted obligations given in Article 7 is exhaustive. If any further obligations restricting competition are imposed on the reseller, the exclusive purchasing agreement as a whole is no longer covered by the block exemption.

48.   The obligation referred to in paragraph 1(a) applies only so long as the supplier is able to supply the beers or other drinks specified in the agreement and subject to the exclusive purchasing obligation in sufficient quantities to cover the demand the reseller anticipates for the products from his customers.

49.   Under paragraph 1(b), the reseller is entitled to sell beer of other types in draught form if the other party has tolerated this in the past. If this is not the case, the reseller must indicate that there is sufficient demand from his customers to warrant the sale of other draught beers. The demand must be deemed sufficient if it can be satisfied without a simultaneous drop in sales of the beers specified in the exclusive purchasing agreement. It is definitely not sufficient if sales of the additional draught beer turn out to be so slow that there is a danger of its quality deteriorating. It is for the reseller to assess the potential demand of his customers for other types of beer; after all, he bears the risk if his forecasts are wrong.

50.   The provision in paragraph 1(c) is not only intended to ensure the possibility of advertising products supplied by other undertakings to the minimum extent necessary in any given circumstances. The advertising of such products should also reflect their relative importance *vis-à-vis* the competing products of the supplier who is party to the exclusive purchasing agreement. Advertising for products which the public house has just begun to sell may not be excluded or unduly impeded.

51.   The Commission believes that the designations of types customary in inter-State trade and within the individual Member States may afford useful pointers to the interpretation of Article 7(2). Nevertheless the alternative criteria stated in the provision itself are decisive. In doubtful cases, whether or not two beers are clearly distinguishable by their composition, appearance or taste depends on custom at the place where the public house is situated. The parties may, if they wish, jointly appoint an expert to decide the matter.

3.   *Agreements excluded from the block exemption*
(Article 8)

52.   The reseller's right to purchase drinks from third parties may be restricted only to the extent allowed by Articles 6 and 7. In his purchases of

goods other than drinks and in his procurement of services which are not directly connected with the supply of drinks by the other party, the reseller must remain free to choose his supplier. Under Article 8(1)(a) and (b), any action by the other party or by an undertaking connected with or appointed by him or acting at his instigation or with his agreement to prevent the reseller exercising his rights in this regard will entail the loss of the block exemption. For the purposes of these provisions it makes no difference whether the reseller's freedom is restricted by contract, informal understanding, economic pressures or other practical measures.

53.   The installation of amusement machines in tenanted public houses may by agreement be made subject to the owner's permission. The owner may refuse permission on the ground that this would impair the character of the premises or he may restrict the tenant to particular types of machines. However, the practice of some owners of tenanted public houses to allow the tenant to conclude contracts for the installation of such machines only with certain undertakings which the owner recommends is, as a rule, incompatible with this Regulation, unless the undertakings are selected on the basis of objective criteria of a qualitative nature that are the same for all potential providers of such equipment and are applied in a non-discriminatory manner. Such criteria may refer to the reliability of the undertaking and its staff and the quality of the services it provides. The supplier may not prevent a public house tenant from purchasing amusement machines rather than renting them.

54.   The limitation of the duration of the agreement in Article 8(1)(c) and (d) does not affect the parties' right to renew their agreement in accordance with the provisions of Title II of the Regulation.

55.   Article 8(2)(b) must be interpreted in the light both of the aims of the Community competition rules and of the general legal principle whereby contracting parties must exercise their rights in good faith.

56.   Whether or not a third undertaking offers certain drinks covered by the exclusive purchasing obligation on more favourable terms than the other party for the purposes of the first indent of Article 8(2)(b) is to be judged in the first instance on the basis of a comparison of prices. This should take into account the various factors that go to determine the prices. If a more favourable offer is available and the tenant wishes to accept it, he must inform the other party of his intentions without delay so that the other party has an opportunity of matching the terms offered by the third undertaking. If the other party refuses to do so or fails to let the tenant have his decision within a short period, the tenant is entitled to purchase the drinks from the other undertaking. The Commission will ensure that exercise of the brewery's or drinks wholesaler's right to match the prices quoted by another supplier does not make it significantly harder for other suppliers to enter the market.

57.   The tenant's right provided for in the second indent of Article 8(2)(b) to purchase drinks of another brand or denomination from third undertakings obtains in cases where the other party does not offer them. Here the tenant is not under a duty to inform the other party of his intentions.

58.   The tenant's rights arising from Article 8(2)(b) override any obligation to purchase minimum quantities imposed upon him under Article 9 in conjunction with Article 2(3)(b) to the extent that this is necessary to allow the tenant full exercise of those rights.

VI.   SERVICE-STATION AGREEMENTS (TITLE III OF REGULATION (EEC) NO. 1984/83)

1.   *Exclusive purchasing obligation*
(Article 10)

59.   The exclusive purchasing obligation can cover either motor vehicle fuels (e.g., heating oil, bottled gas, paraffin). All the goods concerned must be petroleum-based products.

60.   The motor vehicle fuels covered by the exclusive purchasing obligations must be for use in motor-powered land or water vehicles or aircraft. The term 'service station' is to be interpreted in a correspondingly wide sense.

61.   The Regulation applies to petrol stations adjoining public roads and fuelling installations on private property not open to public traffic.

2.   *Other restrictions on competition that are exempted*
(Article 11)

62.   Under Article 11(b) only the use of lubricants and related petroleum-based products supplied by other undertakings can be prohibited. This provision refers to the servicing and maintenance of motor vehicles, i.e., to the reseller's freedom to purchase the said products from other undertakings for resale in the service station. The petroleum-based products related to lubricants referred to in paragraph (b) are additives and brake fluids.

63.   For the interpretation of Article 11(c), the considerations stated in paragraph 49 above apply by analogy.

3.   *Agreements excluded from the block exemption*
(Article 12)

64.   These provisions are analogous to those of Article 8(1)(a), (b), (d) and (e) and 8(2)(a). Reference is therefore made to paragraphs 51 and 53 above.

VII.   TRANSITIONAL PROVISIONS FOR BEER-SUPPLY AND SERVICE-STATION AGREEMENTS (ARTICLE 15(2) AND (3))

65.   Under Article 15(2), all beer-supply and service-station agreements which were concluded and entered into force before 1 January 1984 remain covered by the provisions of Regulation No. 67/67/EEC until 31 December 1988. From 1 January 1989 they must comply with the provisions of Titles II and III of Regulation (EEC) No. 1984/83. Under Article 15(3), in the case of agreements which were in force on 1 July 1983, the same principle applies except that the 10-year maximum duration for such agreements laid down in Article 8(1)(d) and Article 12(1)(c) may be exceeded.

66.   The sole requirement for the eligible beer-supply and service-station agreements to continue to enjoy the block exemption beyond 1 January 1989 is that they be brought into line with the new provisions. It is left to the undertakings concerned how they do so. One way is for the parties to agree to amend the original agreement, another for the supplier unilaterally to release the reseller from all obligations that would prevent the application of the block exemption after 1 January 1989. The latter method is only mentioned in Article 15(3) in relation to agreements in force on 1 July 1983. However, there is no reason why this possibility should not also be open to parties to agreements entered into between 1 July 1983 and 1 January 1984.

67.   Parties lose the benefit of application of the transitional provisions if they extend the scope of their agreement as regards persons, places or subject matter, or incorporate into it additional obligations restrictive of competition. The agreement then counts as a new agreement. The same applies if the parties substantially change the nature or extent of their obligations to one another. A substantial change in this sense includes a revision of the purchase price of the goods supplied to the reseller or of the rent for a public house or service station which goes beyond mere adjustment to the changing economic environment.

COMMISSION REGULATION (EEC) NO 417/85 OF 19 DECEMBER 1984 ON THE APPLICATION OF ARTICLE 85(3) OF THE TREATY TO CATEGORIES OF SPECIALISATION AGREEMENTS [OJ 1985, No. L53/1] AS AMENDED BY COMMISSION REGULATION (EEC) OF 23 DECEMBER 1992 No. 151/93 [OJ 1992, No. L21/8]*

THE COMMISSION OF THE EUROPEAN COMMUNITIES,

Having regard to the Treaty establishing the European Economic Community,

Having regard to Council Regulation (EEC) No. 2821/71 of 20 December 1971 on the application of Article 85(3) of the Treaty to categories of agreements, decisions and concerted practices,[1] as last amended by the act of accession of Greece, and in particular Article 1 thereof,

Having published a draft of this Regulation,[2]

Having consulted the advisory committee on restrictive practices and dominant positions,

Whereas:

(1)   Regulation (EEC) No. 2821/71 empowers the Commission to apply Article 85(3) of the Treaty by Regulation to certain categories of agreements, decisions and concerted practices falling within the scope of Article 85(1) which relate to specialisation, including agreements necessary for achieving it.

(2)   Agreements on specialisation in present or future production may fall within the scope of Article 85(1).

(3)   Agreements on specialisation in production generally contribute to improving the production or distribution of goods, because undertakings concerned can concentrate on the manufacture of certain products and thus operate more efficiently and supply the products more cheaply. It is likely that, given effective competition, consumers will receive a fair share of the resulting benefit.

(4)   Such advantages can arise equally from agreements whereby each participant gives up the manufacture of certain products in favour of another participant and from agreements whereby the participants undertake to manufacture certain products or have them manufactured only jointly.

Notes
*and OJ 1995 L1/1.
[1]OJ No. L285, 29.12.1971, p. 46.
[2]OJ No. C211, 11.8.1984, p. 2.

(5)   The Regulation must specify what restrictions of competition may be included in specialisation agreements. The restrictions of competition that are permitted in the Regulation in addition to reciprocal obligations to give up manufacture are normally essential for the making and implementation of such agreements. These restrictions are therefore, in general, indispensable for the attainment of the desired advantages for the participating undertakings and consumers. It may be left to the parties to decide which of these provisions they include in their agreements.

(6)   The exemption must be limited to agreements which do not give rise to the possibility of eliminating competition in respect of a substantial part of the products in question. The Regulation must therefore apply only as long as the market share and turnover of the participating undertakings do not exceed a certain limit.

(7)   It is, however, appropriate to offer undertakings which exceed the turnover limit set in the Regulation a simplified means of obtaining the legal certainty provided by the block exemption. This must allow the Commission to exercise effective supervision as well as simplifying its administration of such agreements.

(8)   In order to facilitate the conclusion of long-term specialisation agreements, which can have a bearing on the structure of the participating undertakings, it is appropriate to fix the period of validity of the Regulation at 13 years. If the circumstances on the basis of which the Regulation was adopted should change significantly within this period, the Commission will make the necessary amendments.

(9)   Agreements, decisions and concerted practices which are automatically exempted pursuant to this Regulation need not be notified. Undertakings may none the less in an individual case request a decision pursuant to Council Regulation No. 17,[1] as last amended by the Act of Accession of Greece,

HAS ADOPTED THIS REGULATION:

Note
[1]OJ No. 13, 21.2.1962, p. 204/62.

Article 1
Pursuant to Article 85(3) of the Treaty and subject to the provisions of this Regulation, it is hereby declared that Article 85(1) of the Treaty shall not apply to agreements on specialisation whereby, for the duration of the agreement, undertakings accept reciprocal obligations:

(a)   not to manufacture certain products or to have them manufactured, but to leave it to other parties to manufacture the products or have them manufactured; or

(b)   to manufacture certain products or have them manufactured only jointly.

Article 2
1.   Article 1 shall also apply to the following restrictions of competition:

(a)   an obligation not to conclude with third parties specialisation agreements relating to identical products or to products considered by users to be equivalent in view of their characteristics, price and intended use;

(b)   an obligation to procure products which are the subject of the specialisation exclusively from another party, a joint undertaking or an undertaking jointly charged with their manufacture, except where they are obtainable on more favourable terms elsewhere and the other party, the joint undertaking or the undertaking charged with manufacture is not prepared to offer the same terms;

(c)   an obligation to grant other parties the exclusive right, within the whole or a defined area of the common market, to distribute products which are the subject of the specialisation, provided that intermediaries and users can also obtain the products from other suppliers and the parties do not render it difficult for intermediaries and users to thus obtain the products;

(d)   an obligation to grant one of the parties the exclusive right to distribute products which are the subject of the specialisation provided that that party does not distribute products of a third undertaking which compete with the contract products;

(e)   an obligation to grant the exclusive right to distribute products which are the subject of the specialisation to a joint undertaking or to a third undertaking, provided that the joint undertaking or third undertaking does not manufacture or distribute products which compete with the contract products;

(f)   an obligation to grant the exclusive right to distribute within the whole or a defined area of the common market the products which are the subject of the specialisation to joint undertakings or third undertakings which do not manufacture or distribute products which compete with the contract products, provided that users and intermediaries can also obtain the contract products from other suppliers and that neither the parties nor the joint undertakings or third undertakings entrusted with the exclusive distribution of the contract products render it difficult for users and intermediaties to thus obtain the contract products.

2.   Article 1 shall also apply where the parties undertake obligations of the types referred to in paragraph 1 but with a more limited scope than is permitted by that paragraph.

2a.   Article 1 shall not apply if restrictions of competition other than those set out in paragraphs 1 and 2 are imposed upon the parties by agreement, decision or concerted practice.

3.   Article 1 shall apply notwithstanding that any of the following obligations, in particular, are imposed:

(a)   an obligation to supply other parties with products which are the subject of the specialisation and in so doing to observe minimum standards of quality;

(b)   an obligation to maintain minimum stocks of products which are the subject of the specialisation and of replacement parts for them;

(c)   an obligation to provide customer and guarantee services for products which are the subject of the specialisation.

Article 3

1.   Article 1 shall apply only if:

(a)   the products which are the subject of the specialisation together with the participating undertakings' other products which are considered by users to be equivalent in view of their characteristics, price and intended use do not represent more than 20% of the market for all such products in the common market or a substantial part thereof; and

(b)   the aggregate turnover of all the participating undertakings does not exceed ECU 1,000 million.

2.   If pursuant to point (d), (e) or (f) of Article 2(1), one of the parties, a joint undertaking, a third undertaking or more than one joint undertaking or third undertaking are entrusted with the distribution of the products which are the subject of the specialisation, Article 1 shall apply only if:

(a)   the products which are the subject of the specialisation together with the participating undertakings' other products which are considered by users to be equivalent in view of their characteristics, price and intended use do not represent more than 10% of the market for all such products in the common market or a substantial part thereof; and

(b)   the aggregate annual turnover of all the participating undertakings does not exceed ECU 1,000 million.

3.   Article 1 shall continue to apply if the market shares and turnover referred to in paragraph 1 and 2 are exceeded during any period of two consecutive financial years by not more than one-tenth.

4.   Where the limits laid down in paragraph 3 are exceeded, Article 1 shall continue to apply for a period of six months following the end of the financial year during which they were exceeded.

Article 4

1.   The exemption provided for in Article 1 shall also apply to agreements involving participating undertakings, whose aggregate turnover exceeds the limits laid down in Article 3(1)(b), (2)(b) and (3); on condition that the agreements in question are notified to the Commission in accordance with the provisions of Commission Regulation No. 27,[1] and that the Commission does not oppose such exemption within a period of six months.

2.   The period of six months shall run from the date on which the notification is received by the Commission. Where, however, the notification is made by registered post, the period shall run from the date shown on the postmark of the place of posting.

3.   Paragraph 1 shall apply only if:

(a)   express reference is made to this Article in the notification or in a communication accompanying it; and

(b)   the information furnished with the notification is complete and in accordance with the facts.

4.   The benefit of paragraph 1 may be claimed for agreements notified before the entry into force of this Regulation by submitting a communication to the Commission referring expressly to this Article and to the notification. Paragraphs 2 and 3(b) shall apply *mutatis mutandis*.

5.   The Commission may oppose the exemption. It shall oppose exemption if it receives a request to do so from a Member State within three months of the forwarding to the Member State of the notification referred to in paragraph 1 or of the communication referred to in paragraph 4. This request must be justified on the basis of considerations relating to the competition rules of the Treaty.

6.   The Commission may withdraw the opposition to the exemption at any time. However, where the opposition was raised at the request of a Member State and this request is maintained, it may be withdrawn only after consultation of the Advisory Committee on Restrictive Practices and Dominant Positions.

Note
[1] OJ No. 35, 10.5.1962, p. 1118/62.

7. If the opposition is withdrawn because the undertakings concerned have shown that the conditions of Article 85(3) are fulfilled, the exemption shall apply from the date of notification.

8. If the opposition is withdrawn because the undertakings concerned have amended the agreement so that the conditions of Article 85(3) are fulfilled, the exemption shall apply from the date on which the amendments take effect.

9. If the Commission opposes exemption and the opposition is not withdrawn, the effects of the notification shall be governed by the provisions of Regulation No. 17.

Article 5

1. Information acquired pursuant to Article 4 shall be used only for the purposes of this Regulation.

2. The Commission and the authorities of the Member States, their officials and other servants shall not disclose information acquired by them pursuant to this Regulation of a kind that is covered by the obligation of professional secrecy.

3. Paragraphs 1 and 2 shall not prevent publication of general information or surveys which do not contain information relating to particular undertakings or associations of undertakings.

Article 6

For the purpose of calculating total annual turnover within the meaning of Article 3(1)(b) and (2)(b), the turnovers achieved during the last financial year by the participating undertakings in respect of all goods and services excluding tax shall be added together. For this purpose, no account shall be taken of dealings between the participating undertakings or between these undertakings and a third undertaking jointly charged with manufacture or sale.

Article 7

1. For the purposes of Article 3(1) and (2), and Article 6, participating undertakings are:
   (a) undertakings party to the agreement;
   (b) undertakings in which a party to the agreement, directly or indirectly:
         — owns more than half the capital or business assets,
         — has the power to exercise more than half the voting rights,
         — has the power to appoint at least half the members of the supervisory board, board of management or bodies legally representing the undertakings, or
         — has the right to manage the affairs;
   (c) undertakings which directly or indirectly have in or over a party to the agreement the rights or powers listed in (b);
   (d) undertakings in or over which an undertaking referred to in (c) directly or indirectly has the rights or powers listed in (b).

2. Undertakings in which the undertakings referred to in paragraph 1(a) to (d) directly or indirectly jointly have the rights or powers set out in paragraph 1(b) shall also be considered to be participating undertakings.

Article 8

The Commission may withdraw the benefit of this Regulation, pursuant to Article 7 of Regulation (EEC) No. 2821/71, where it finds in a particular case that an agreement exempted by this Regulation nevertheless has effects which are incompatible with the conditions set out in Article 85(3) of the Treaty, and in particular where:

(a)   the agreement is not yielding significant results in terms of rationalisation or consumers are not receiving a fair share of the resulting benefit; or

(b)   the products which are the subject of the specialisation are not subject in the common market or a substantial part thereof to effective competition from identical products or products considered by users to be equivalent in view of their characteristics, price and intended use.

Article 9

This Regulation shall apply *mutatis mutandis* to decisions of associations of undertakings and concerted practices.

Article 9a

The prohibition in Article 85(1) of the Treaty shall not apply to the specialisation agreements which were in existence at the date of the accession of the Kingdom of Spain and of the Portuguese Republic and which, by reason of this accession, fall within the scope of Article 85(1), if, before 1 July 1986, they are so amended that they comply with the conditions laid down in this Regulation.

As regards agreements to which Article 85 of the Treaty applies as a result of the accession of Austria, Finland and Sweden, the preceding paragraph shall apply *mutatus mutandis* on the understanding that the relevant dates shall be the date of accession of those countries and six months after the date of accession respectively. However, this paragraph shall not apply to agreements which at the date of accession already fall under Article 53(1) of the EEA Agreement.

Article 10

1.   This Regulation shall enter into force on 1 March 1985. It shall apply until 31 December 1997.

2.   Commission Regulation (EEC) No. 3604/82[1] is hereby repealed.

Done at Brussels, 19 December 1984

Note
[1]OJ No. L376, 31.12.1982, p. 33.

COMMISSION REGULATION (EEC) NO 418/85 OF 19 DECEMBER 1984 ON THE APPLICATION OF ARTICLE 85(3) OF THE TREATY TO CATEGORIES OF RESEARCH AND DEVELOPMENT AGREEMENTS [OJ 1985, No. L53/51] AS AMENDED BY COMMISSION REGULATION (EEC) No. 151/93 OF 23 DECEMBER 1992 [OJ 1992, No. L21/8]*

THE COMMISSION OF THE EUROPEAN COMMUNITIES,

Having regard to the Treaty establishing the European Economic Community,

Having regard to Council Regulation (EEC) No. 2821/71 of 20 December 1971 on the application of Articles 85(3) of the Treaty to categories of agreements, decisions and concerted practices,[1] as last amended by the Act of Accession of Greece, and in particular article 1 thereof,

Notes
*and Decision 95/1 [OJ 1995 L1/1].
[1]OJ No. L285, 29.12.1971, p. 46.

Having published a draft of this Regulation,[2]

Having consulted the advisory committee on restrictive practices and dominant positions.

Whereas:

(1)   Regulation (EEC) No. 2821/71 empowers the Commission to apply Article 85(3) of the Treaty by Regulation to certain categories of agreements, decisions and concerted practices falling within the scope of Article 85(1) which have as their object the research and development of products or processes up to the stage of industrial application, and exploitation of the results, including provisions regarding industrial property rights and confidential technical knowledge.

(2)   As stated in the Commission's 1968 notice concerning agreements, decisions and concerted practices in the field of cooperation between enterprises,[3] agreements on the joint execution of research work or the joint development of the results of the research, up to but not including the stage of industrial application, generally do not fall within the scope of Article 85(1) of the Treaty. In certain circumstances, however, such as where the parties agree not to carry out other research and development in the same field, thereby forgoing the opportunity of gaining competitive advantages over the other parties, such agreements may fall within Article 85(1) and should therefore not be excluded from this Regulation.

(3)   Agreements providing for both joint research and development and joint exploitation of the results may fall within Article 85(1) because the parties jointly determine how the products developed are manufactured or the processes developed are applied or how related intellectual property rights or know-how are exploited.

(4)   Cooperation in research and development and in the exploitation of the results generally promotes technical and economic progress by increasing the dissemination of technical knowledge between the parties and avoiding duplication of research and development work, by stimulating new advances through the exchange of complementary technical knowledge, and by rationalising the manufacture of the products or application of the processes arising out of the research and development. These aims can be achieved only where the research and development programme and its objectives are clearly defined and each of the parties is given the opportunity of exploiting any of the results of the programme that interest it; where universities or research institutes participate and are not interested in the industrial exploitation of the results, however, it may be agreed that they may use the said results solely for the purpose of further research.

(5)   Consumers can generally be expected to benefit from the increased volume and effectiveness of research and development through the introduction of new or improved products or services or the reduction of prices brought about by new or improved processes.

(6)   This Regulation must specify the restrictions of competition which may be included in the exempted agreements. The purpose of the permitted restrictions is to concentrate the research activities of the parties in order to

Notes
[2]OJ No. C16, 21.1.1984, p. 3.
[3]OJ No. C75, 29.7.1968, p. 3, corrected by OJ No. C84, 28.8.1968, p. 14.

improve their chances of success, and to facilitate the introduction of new products and services onto the market. These restrictions are generally necessary to secure the desired benefits for the parties and consumers.

(7)   The joint exploitation of results can be considered as the natural consequence of joint research and development. It can take different forms ranging from manufacture to the exploitation of intellectual property rights or know-how that substantially contributes to technical or economic progress. In order to attain the benefits and objectives described above and to justify the restrictions of competition which are exempted, the joint exploitation must relate to products or processes for which the use of the results of the research and development is decisive. Joint exploitation is not therefore justified where it relates to improvements which were not made within the framework of a joint research and development programme but under an agreement having some other principal objective, such as the licensing of intellectual property rights, joint manufacture or specialisation, and merely containing ancillary provisions on joint research and development.

(8)   The exemption granted under the Regulation must be limited to agreements which do not afford the undertakings the possibility of eliminating competition in respect of a substantial part of the products in question. In order to guarantee that several independent poles of research can exist in the common market in any economic sector, it is necessary to exclude from the block exemption agreements between competitors whose combined share of the market for products capable of being improved or replaced by the results of the research and development exceeds a certain level at the time the agreement is entered into.

(9)   In order to guarantee the maintenance of effective competition during joint exploitation of the results, it is necessary to provide that the block exemption will cease to apply if the parties' combined shares of the market for the products arising out of the joint research and development become too great. However, it should be provided that the exemption will continue to apply, irrespective of the parties' market shares, for a certain period after the commencement of joint exploitation, so as to await stabilisation of their market shares, particularly after the introduction of an entirely new product, and to guarantee a minimum period of return on the generally substantial investments involved.

(10)   Agreements between undertakings which do not fulfil the market share conditions laid down in the Regulation may, in appropriate cases, be granted an exemption by individual decision, which will in particular take account of world competition and the particular circumstances prevailing in the manufacture of high technology products.

(11)   It is desirable to list in the Regulation a number of obligations that are commonly found in research and development agreements but that are normally not restrictive of competition and to provide that, in the event that, because of the particular economic or legal circumstances, they should fall within Article 85(1), they also would be covered by the exemption. This list is not exhaustive.

(12)   The Regulation must specify what provisions may not be included in agreements if these are to benefit from the block exemption by virtue of the fact that such provisions are restrictions falling within Article 85(1) for which there can be no general presumption that they will lead to the positive effects required by Article 85(3).

(13) Agreements which are not automatically covered by the exemption because they include provisions that are not expressly exempted by the Regulation and are not expressly excluded from exemption are none the less capable of benefiting from the general presumption of compatibility with Article 85(3) on which the block exemption is based. It will be possible for the Commission rapidly to establish whether this is the case for a particular agreement. Such an agreement should therefore be deemed to be covered by the exemption provided for in this Regulation where it is notified to the Commission and the Commission does not oppose the application of the exemption within a specified period of time.

(14) Agreements covered by this Regulation may also take advantage of provisions contained in other block exemption Regulations of the Commission, and in particular Regulation (EEC) No. 417/85 on specialisation agreements, Regulation (EEC) No. 1983/83[1] on exclusive distribution agreements, Regulation (EEC) No. 1984/83,[2] on exclusive purchasing agreements and Regulation (EEC) No. 2349/84[3] on patent licensing agreements, if they fulfil the conditions set out in these Regulations. The provisions of the aforementioned Regulations are, however, not applicable in so far as this Regulation contains specific rules.

(15) If individual agreements exempted by this Regulation nevertheless have effects which are incompatible with Article 85(3), the Commission may withdraw the benefit of the block exemption.

(16) The Regulation should apply with retroactive effect to agreements in existence when the Regulation comes into force where such agreements already fulfil its conditions or are modified to do so. The benefit of these provisions may not be claimed in actions pending at the date of entry into force of this Regulation, nor may it be relied on as grounds for claims for damages against third parties.

(17) Since research and development cooperation agreements are often of a long-term nature, especially where the cooperation extends to the exploitation of the results, it is appropriate to fix the period of validity of the Regulation at 13 years. If the circumstances on the basis of which the Regulation was adopted should change significantly within this period, the Commission will make the necessary amendments.

(18) Agreements which are automatically exempted pursuant to this Regulation need not be notified. Undertakings may nevertheless in a particular case request a decision pursuant to Council Regulation No. 17,[4] as last amended by the Act of Accession of Greece,

Notes
[1]OJ No. L173, 30.6.1983, p. 1.
[2]OJ No. L173, 30.6.1983, p. 5.
[3]OJ No. L219, 16.8.1984, p. 15.
[4]OJ No. L3, 21.2.1962, p. 204/62.

HAS ADOPTED THIS REGULATION:

Article 1

1. Pursuant to Article 85(3) of the Treaty and subject to the provisions of this Regulation, it is hereby declared that Article 85(1) of the Treaty shall not apply to agreements entered into between undertakings for the purpose of:

(a) joint research and development of products or processes and joint exploitation of the results of that research and development;

(b) joint exploitation of the results of research and development of products or processes jointly carried out pursuant to a prior agreement between the same undertakings; or

(c) joint research and development of products or processes excluding joint exploitation of the results, in so far as such agreements fall within the scope of Article 85(1).

2.   For the purposes of this Regulation:

(a) *research and development of products or processes* means the acquisition of technical knowledge and the carrying out of theoretical analysis, systematic study or experimentation, including experimental production, technical testing of products or processes, the establishment of the necessary facilities and the obtaining of intellectual property rights for the results;

(b) *contract processes* means processes arising out of the research and development;

(c) *contract products* means products or services arising out of the research and development or manufactured or provided applying the contract processes;

(d) *exploitation of the results* means the manufacture of the contract products or the application of the contract processes or the assignment or licensing of intellectual property rights or the communication of know-how required for such manufacture or application;

(e) *technical knowledge* means technical knowledge which is either protected by an intellectual property right or is secret (know-how).

3.   Research and development of the exploitation of the results are carried out *jointly* where:

(a) the work involved is:
— carried out by a joint team, organisation or undertaking,
— jointly entrusted to a third party, or
— allocated between the parties by way of specialisation in research, development or production;

(b) the parties collaborate in any way in the assignment or the licensing of intellectual property rights or the communication of know-how, within the meaning of paragraph 2(d), to third parties.

Article 2

The exemption provided for in Article 1 shall apply on condition that:

(a) the joint research and development work is carried out within the framework of a programme defining the objectives of the work and the field in which it is to be carried out;

(b) all the parties have access to the results of the work;

(c) where the agreement provides only for joint research and development, each party is free to exploit the results of the joint research and development and any pre-existing technical knowledge necessary therefore independently;

(d) the joint exploitation relates only to results which are protected by intellectual property rights or constitute know-how which substantially contributes to technical or economic progress and that the results are decisive for the manufacture of the contract products or the application of the contract processes;

(e) (repealed)

(f)   undertakings charged with manufacture by way of specialisation in production are required to fulfil orders for supplies from all the parties.

Article 3

1.   Where the parties are not competing manufacturers of products capable of being improved or replaced by the contract products, the exemption provided for in Article 1 shall apply for the duration of the research and development programme and, where the results are jointly exploited, for five years from the time the contract products are first put on the market within the common market.

2.   Where two or more of the parties are competing manufacturers within the meaning of paragraph 1, the exemption provided for in Article 1 shall apply for the period specified in paragraph 1 only if, at the time the agreement is entered into, the parties' combined production of the products capable of being improved or replaced by the contract products does not exceed 20% of the market for such products in the common market or a substantial part thereof.

3.   After the end of the period referred to in paragraph 1, the exemption provided for in Article 1 shall continue to apply as long as the production of the contract products together with the parties' combined production of other products which are considered by users to be equivalent in view of their characteristics, price and intended use does not exceed 20% of the total market for such products in the common market or a substantial part thereof. Where contract products are components used by the parties of the manufacture of other products, reference shall be made to the markets for such of those latter products for which the components represent a significant part.

3a.   Where one of the parties, a joint undertaking, a third undertaking or more than one joint undertaking or third undertaking are entrusted with the distribution of the products which are the subject of the agreement under Article 4(1)(fa), (fb) or (fc), the exemption provided for in Article 1 shall apply only if the parties production of the products referred to in paragraphs 2 and 3 does not exceed 10% of the market for all such products in the common market or a substantial part thereof.

4.   The exemption provided for in Article 1 shall continue to apply where the market shares referred to in paragraphs 3 and 4 are exceeded during any period of two consecutive financial years by not more than one-tenth.

5.   Where the limits laid down in paragraph 5 are also exceeded, the exemption provided for in Article 1 shall continue to apply for a period of six months following the end of the financial year during which they were exceeded.

Article 4

1.   The exemption provided for in Article 1 shall also apply to the following restrictions of competition imposed on the parties:

(a)   an obligation not to carry out independently research and development in the field to which the programme relates or in a closely connected field during the execution of the programme;

(b)   an obligation not to enter into agreements with third parties on research and development in the field to which the programme relates or in a closely connected field during the execution of the programme;

(c)   an obligation to procure the contract products exclusively from parties, joint organisations or undertakings or third parties, jointly charged with their manufacture;

(d)   an obligation not to manufacture the contract products or apply the contract processes in territories reserved for other parties;

(e)   an obligation to restrict the manufacture of the contract products or application of the contract processes to one or more technical fields of application, except where two or more of the parties are competitors within the meaning of Article 3 at the time the agreement is entered into;

(f)   an obligation not to pursue, for a period of five years from the time the contract products are first put on the market within the common market, an active policy of putting the products on the market in territories reserved for other parties, and in particular not to engage in advertising specifically aimed at such territories or to establish any branch or maintain any distribution depot there for the distribution of the products, provided that users and intermediaries can obtain the contract products from other suppliers and the parties do not render it difficult for intermediaries and users to thus obtain the products;

(fa)   an obligation to grant one of the parties the exclusive right to distribute the contract products, provided that the party does not distribute products manufactured by a third producer which compete with the contract products;

(fb)   an obligation to grant the exclusive right to distribute the contract products to a joint undertaking or a third undertaking, provided that the joint undertaking or third undertaking does not manufacture or distribute products which compete with the contract products;

(fc)   an obligation to grant the exclusive right to distribute the contract products in the whole or a defined area of the common market to joint undertakings or third undertakings which do not manufacture or distribute products which compete with the contract products, provided that users and intermediaries are also able to obtain the contract products from other suppliers and neither the parties nor the joint undertakings or third undertakings entrusted with the exclusive distribution of the contract products render it difficult for users and intermediaries to thus obtain the contract products.

(g)   an obligation on the parties to communicate to each other any experience they may gain in exploiting the results and to grant each other non-exclusive licences for inventions relating to improvements or new applications.

2.   The exemption provided for in Article 1 shall also apply where in a particular agreement the parties undertake obligations of the types referred to in paragraph 1 but with a more limited scope than is permitted by that paragraph.

Article 5

1.   Article 1 shall apply notwithstanding that any of the following obligations, in particular, are imposed on the parties during the currency of the agreement:

(a)   an obligation to communicate patented or non-patented technical knowledge necessary for the carrying out of the research and development programme for the exploitation of its results;

(b)   an obligation not to use any know-how received from another party for purposes other than carrying out the research and development programme and the exploitation of its results;

(c)   an obligation to obtain and maintain in force intellectual property rights for the contract products or processes;

(d)   an obligation to preserve the confidentiality of any know-how received or jointly developed under the research and development programme; this obligation may be imposed even after the expiry of the agreement;
(e)   an obligation:
  (i)   to inform other parties of infringements of their intellectual property rights,
  (ii)   to take legal action against infringers, and
  (iii)   to assist in any such legal action or share with the other parties in the cost thereof
(f)   an obligation to pay royalties or render services to other parties to compensate for unequal contributions to the joint research and development or unequal exploitation of its results;
(g)   an obligation to share royalties received from third parties with other parties;
(h)   an obligation to supply other parties with minimum quantities of contract products and to observe minimum standards of quality.
2.   In the event that, because of particular circumstances, the obligations referred to in paragraph 1 fall within the scope of Article 85(1), they also shall be covered by the exemption. The exemption provided for in this paragraph shall also apply where in a particular agreement the parties undertake obligations of the types referred to in paragraph 1 but with a more limited scope than is permitted by that paragraph.

Article 6
The exemption provided for in Article 1 shall not apply where the parties, by agreement, decision or concerted practice:
(a)   are restricted in their freedom to carry out research and development independently or in cooperation with third parties in a field unconnected with that to which the programme relates or, after its completion, in the field to which the programme relates or in a connected field;
(b)   are prohibited after completion of the research and development programme from challenging the validity of intellectual property rights which the parties hold in the common market and which are relevant to the programme or, after the expiry of the agreement, from challenging the validity of intellectual property rights which the parties hold in the common market and which protect the results of the research and development;
(c)   are restricted as to the quantity of the contract products they may manufacture or sell or as to the number of operations employing the contract process they may carry out;
(d)   are restricted in their determination of prices, components of prices or discounts when selling the contract products to third parties;
(e)   are restricted as to the customers they may serve, without prejudice to Article 4(1)(e);
(f)   are prohibited from putting the contract products on the market or pursuing an active sales policy for them in territories within the common market that are reserved for other parties after the end of the period referred to in Article 4(1)(f);
(g)   are required not to grant licences to third parties to manufacture the contract products or to apply the contract processes even though the

exploitation by the parties themselves of the results of the joint research and development is not provided for or does not take place.

(h)   are required:

—to refuse without any objectively justified reason to meet demand from users or dealers established in their respective territories who would market the contract products in other territories within the common market, or

—to make it difficult for users or dealers to obtain the contract products from other dealers within the common market, and in particular to exercise intellectual property rights or take measures so as to prevent users or dealers from obtaining, or from putting on the market within the common market, products which have been lawfully put on the market within the common market by another party or with its consent.

Article 7

1.   The exemption provided for in this Regulation shall also apply to agreements of the kinds described in Article 1 which fulfil the conditions laid down in Articles 2 and 3 and which contain obligations restrictive of competition which are not covered by Articles 4 and 5 and do not fall within the scope of Article 6, on condition that the agreements in question are notified to the Commission in accordance with the provisions of Commission Regulation No 27,[1] and that the Commission does not oppose such exemption within a period of six months.

2.   The period of six months shall run from the date on which the notification is received by the Commission. Where, however, the notification is made by registered post, the period shall run from the date shown on the postmark of the place of posting.

3.   Paragraph 1 shall apply only if:

(a)   express reference is made to this Article in the notification or in a communication accompanying it, and

(b)   the information furnished with the notification is complete and in accordance with the facts.

4.   The benefit of paragraph 1 may be claimed for agreements notified before the entry into force of this Regulation by submitting a communication to the Commission referring expressly to this Article and to the notification. Paragraphs 2 and 3(b) shall apply *mutatis mutandis*.

5.   The Commission may oppose the exemption. It shall oppose exemption if it receives a request to do so from a Member State within three months of the forwarding to the Member State of the notification referred to in paragraph 1 or of the communication referred to in paragraph 4. This request must be justified on the basis of considerations relating to the competition rules of the Treaty.

6.   The Commission may withdraw the opposition to the exemption at any time. However, where the opposition was raised at the request of a Member State and this request is maintained, it may be withdrawn only after consultation of the Advisory Committee on Restrictive Practices and Dominant Positions.

7.   If the opposition is withdrawn because the undertakings concerned have shown that the conditions of Article 85(3) are fulfilled, the exemption shall apply from the date of notification.

8.   If the opposition is withdrawn because the undertakings concerned have amended the agreement so that the conditions of Article 85(3) are fulfilled, the exemption shall apply from the date on which the amendments take effect.

9.   If the Commission opposes exemption and the opposition is not withdrawn, the effects of the notification shall be governed by the provisions of Regulation No 17.

Note
[1]OJ No. 35, 10.5.1962, p. 1118/62.

Article 8

1.   Information acquired pursuant to Article 7 shall be used only for the purposes of this Regulation.

2.   The Commission and the authorities of the Member States, their officials and other servants shall not disclose information acquired by them pursuant to this Regulation of a kind that is covered by the obligation of professional secrecy.

3.   Paragraphs 1 and 2 shall not prevent publication of general information or surveys which do not contain information relating to particular undertakings or associations of undertakings.

Article 9

1.   The provisions of this Regulation shall also apply to rights and obligations which the parties create for undertakings connected with them. The market shares held and the actions and measures taken by connected undertakings shall be treated as those of the parties themselves.

2.   Connected undertakings for the purposes of this Regulation are:
   (a)   undertakings in which a party to the agreement, directly or indirectly:
       — owns more than half the capital or business assets,
       — has the power to exercise more than half the voting rights,
       — has the power to appoint more than half the members of the supervisory board, board of directors or bodies legally representing the undertakings, or
       — has the right to manage the affairs;
   (b)   undertakings which directly have in or over a party to the agreement the rights or powers listed in (a);
   (c)   undertakings in or over which an undertaking referred to in (b) directly or indirectly has the rights or powers listed in (a);

3.   Undertakings in which the parties to the agreement or undertakings connected with them jointly have, directly or indirectly, the rights or powers set out in paragraph 2(a) shall be considered to be connected with each of the parties to the agreement.

Article 10

The Commission may withdraw the benefit of this Regulation, pursuant to Article 7 of Regulation (EEC) No 2821/71, where it finds in a particular case that an agreement exempted by this Regulation nevertheless has certain effects which are incompatible with the conditions laid down in Article 85(3) of the Treaty, and in particular where:

   (a)   the existence of the agreement substantially restricts the scope for third parties to carry out research and development in the relevant field because of the limited research capacity available elsewhere;

(b)   because of the particular structure of supply, the existence of the agreement substantially restricts the access of third parties to the market for the contract products;

(c)   without any objectively valid reason, the parties do not exploit the results of the joint research and development;

(d)   the contract products are not subject in the whole or a substantial part of the common market to effective competition from identical products or products considered by users as equivalent in view of their characteristics, price and intended use.

Article 11

1.   In the case of agreements notified to the Commission before 1 March 1985, the exemption provided for in Article 1 shall have retroactive effect from the time at which the conditions for application of this Regulation were fulfilled or, where the agreement does not fall within Article 4(2)(3)(b) of Regulation No 17, not earlier than the date of notification.

2.   In the case of agreements existing on 13 March 1962 and notified to the Commission before 1 February 1963, the exemption shall have retroactive effect from the time at which the conditions for application of this Regulation were fulfilled.

3.   Where agreements which were in existence on 13 March 1962 and which were notified to the Commission before 1 February 1963, or which are covered by Article 4(2)(3)(b) of Regulation No 17 and were notified to the Commission before 1 January 1967, are amended before 1 September 1985 so as to fulfil the conditions for application of this Regulation, such amendment being communicated to the Commission before 1 October 1985, the prohibition laid down in Article 85(1) of the Treaty shall not apply in respect of the period prior to the amendment. The communication of amendments shall take effect from the date of their receipt by the Commission. Where the communication is sent by registered post, it shall take effect from the date shown on the postmark of the place of posting.

4.   In the case of agreements to which Article 85 of the Treaty applies as a result of the accession of the United Kingdom, Ireland and Denmark, paragraphs 1 to 3 shall apply except that the relevant dates shall be 1 January 1973 instead of 13 March 1962 and 1 July 1973 instead of 1 February 1963 and 1 January 1967.

5.   In the case of agreements to which Article 85 of the Treaty applies as a result of the accession of Greece, paragraphs 1 to 3 shall apply except that the relevant dates shall be 1 January 1981 instead of 13 March 1962 and 1 July 1981 instead of 1 February 1963 and 1 January 1967.

6.   As regards agreements to which Article 83 of the Treaty applies as a result of the accession of the Kingdom of Spain and of the Portuguese Republic, paragraphs 1 to 3 shall apply except that the relevant dates should be 1 January 1986 instead of 13 March 1962, 1 March 1985 and 1 September 1985. The amendment made to the agreements in accordance with the provisions of paragraph 3 need not be notified to the Commission.

7.   As regards agreements to which Article 85 of the Treaty applies as a result of the accession of Austria, Finland and Sweden, paragraphs 1 to 3 shall apply *mutatis mutandis* on the understanding that the relevant dates shall be the date of accession instead of 13 March 1962 and six months after the date of

accession instead of 1 February 1963, 1 January 1967, 1 March 1965 and 1 September 1985. The amendment made to these agreements in accordance with the provisions of paragraph 3 need not be notified to the Commission. However, this paragraph shall not apply to agreements which at the date of accession already fall under Article 53(1) of the EEA Agreement.

Article 12

This Regulation shall apply *mutatis mutandis* to decisions of associations of undertakings.

Article 13

This Regulation shall enter into force on 1 March 1985.

It shall apply until 31 December 1997.

This Regulation shall be binding in its entirety and directly applicable in all Member States.

Done at Brussels, 19 December 1984.
For the Commission
Frans ANDRIESSEN
Member of the Commission

COMMISSION REGULATION (EEC) NO 4087/88 OF 30 NOVEMBER 1988 ON THE APPLICATION OF ARTICLE 85(3) OF THE TREATY TO CATEGORIES OF FRANCHISE AGREEMENTS
[OJ 1988, No. L359/46]*

THE COMMISSION OF THE EUROPEAN COMMUNITIES,

Having regard to the Treaty establishing the European Economic Community,

Having regard to Council Regulation No. 19/65/EEC of 2 March 1965 on the application of Article 85(3) of the Treaty to certain categories of agreements and concerted practices,[1] as last amended by the Act of Accession of Spain and Portugal, and in particular Article 1 thereof,

Having published a draft of this Regulation,[2]

Having consulted the Advisory Committee on Restrictive Practices and Dominant Positions,

Whereas:

(1) Regulation No 19/65/EEC empowers the Commission to apply Article 85(3) of the Treaty by Regulation to certain categories of bilateral exclusive agreements falling within the scope of Article 85(1) which either have as their object the exclusive distribution or exclusive purchase of goods, or include restrictions imposed in relation to the assignment or use of industrial property rights.

(2) Franchise agreements consist essentially of licences of industrial or intellectual property rights relating to trade marks or signs and know-how,

Note

*as amended by Decision 95/1 [OJ 1995 L1/1].
[1] OJ No. 35, 10.5.1962, p. 1118/62.
[2] OJ No. C229, 27.8.1987, p. 3.

which can be combined with restrictions relating to supply or purchase of goods.

(3) Several types of franchise can be distinguished according to their object: industrial franchise concerns the manufacturing of goods, distribution franchise concerns the sale of goods, and service franchise concerns the supply of services.

(4) It is possible on the basis of the experience of the Commission to define categories of franchise agreements which fall under Article 85(1) but can normally be regarded as satisfying the conditions laid down in Article 85(3). This is the case for franchise agreements whereby one of the parties supplies goods or provides services to end users. On the other hand, industrial franchise agreements should not be covered by this Regulation. Such agreements, which usually govern relationships between producers, present different characteristics than the other types of franchise. They consist of manufacturing licences based on patents and/or technical know-how, combined with trade-mark licences. Some of them may benefit from other block exemptions if they fulfil the necessary conditions.

(5) This Regulation covers franchise agreements between two undertakings, the franchisor and the franchisee, for the retailing of goods or the provision of services to end users, or a combination of these activities, such as the processing or adaptation of goods to fit specific needs of their customers. It also covers cases where the relationship between franchisor and franchisees if made through a third undertaking, the master franchisee. It does not cover wholesale franchise agreements because of the lack of experience of the Commission in that field.

(6) Franchise agreements as defined in this Regulation can fall under Article 85(1). They may in particular affect intra-Community trade where they are concluded between undertakings from different Member States or where they form the basis of a network which extends beyond the boundaries of a single Member State.

(7) Franchise agreements as defined in this Regulation normally improve the distribution of goods and/or the provision of services as they give franchisors the possibility of establishing a uniform network with limited investments, which may assist the entry of new competitors on the market, particularly in the case of small and medium-sized undertakings, thus increasing interbrand competition. They also allow independent traders to set up outlets more rapidly and with higher chance of success than if they had to do so without the franchisor's experience and assistance. They have therefore the possibility of competing more efficiently with large distribution undertakings.

(8) As a rule, franchise agreements also allow consumers and other end users a fair share of the resulting benefit, as they combine the advantage of a uniform network with the existence of traders personally interested in the efficient operation of their business. The homogeneity of the network and the constant cooperation between the franchisor and the franchisees ensures a constant quality of the products and services. The favourable effect of franchising on interbrand competition and the fact that consumers are free to deal with any franchisee in the network guarantees that a reasonable part of the resulting benefits will be passed on to the consumers.

(9) This Regulation must define the obligations restrictive of competition which may be included in franchise agreements. This is the case in particular

for the granting of an exclusive territory to the franchisees combined with the prohibition on actively seeking customers outside that territory, which allows them to concentrate their efforts on their allotted territory. The same applies to the granting of an exclusive territory to a master franchisee combined with the obligation not to conclude franchise agreements with third parties outside that territory. Where the franchisees sell or use in the process of providing services, goods manufactured by the franchisor or according to its instructions and or bearing its trade mark, an obligation on the franchisees not to sell, or use in the process of the provision of services, competing goods, makes it possible to establish a coherent network which is identified with the franchised goods. However, this obligation should only be accepted with respect to the goods which form the essential subject-matter of the franchise. It should notably not relate to accessories or spare parts for these goods.

(10) The obligations referred to above thus do not impose restrictions which are not necessary for the attainment of the abovementioned objectives. In particular, the limited territorial protection granted to the franchisees is indispensable to protect their investment.

(11) It is desirable to list in the Regulation a number of obligations that are commonly found in franchise agreements and are normally not restrictive of competition and to provide that if, because of the particular economic or legal circumstances, they fall under Article 85(1), they are also covered by the exemption. This list, which is not exhaustive, includes in particular clauses which are essential either to preserve the common identity and reputation of the network or to prevent the know-how made available and the assistance given by the franchisor from benefiting competitors.

(12) The Regulation must specify the conditions which must be satisfied for the exemption to apply. To guarantee that competition is not eliminated for a substantial part of the goods which are the subject of the franchise, it is necessary that parallel imports remain possible. Therefore, cross deliveries between franchisees should always be possible. Furthermore, where a franchise network is combined with another distribution system, franchisees should be free to obtain supplies from authorised distributors. To better inform consumers, thereby helping to ensure that they receive a fair share of the resulting benefits, it must be provided that the franchisee shall be obliged to indicate its status as an independent undertaking, by any appropriate means which does not jeopardise the common identity of the franchised network. Furthermore, where the franchisees have to honour guarantees for the franchisor's goods, this obligation should also apply to goods supplied by the franchisor, other franchisees or other agreed dealers.

(13) The Regulation must also specify restrictions which may not be included in franchise agreements if these are to benefit from the exemption granted by the Regulation, by virtue of the fact that such provisions are restrictions falling under Article 85(1) for which there is no general presumption that they will lead to the positive effects required by Article 85(3). This applies in particular to market sharing between competing manufacturers, to clauses unduly limiting the franchisee's choice of suppliers or customers, and to cases where the franchisee is restricted in determining its prices. However, the franchisor should be free to recommend prices to the franchisees, where it is not prohibited by national laws and to the extent that it does not lead to concerted practices for the effective application of these prices.

(14) Agreements which are not automatically covered by the exemption because they contain provisions that are not expressly exempted by the Regulation and not expressly excluded from exemption may nonetheless generally be presumed to be eligible for application of Article 85(3). It will be possible for the Commission rapidly to establish whether this is the case for a particular agreement. Such agreements should therefore be deemed to be covered by the exemption provided for in this Regulation where they are notified to the Commission and the Commission does not oppose the application of the exemption within a specified period of time.

(15) If individual agreements exempted by this Regulation nevertheless have effects which are incompatible with Article 85(3), in particular as interpreted by the administrative practice of the Commission and the case law of the Court of Justice, the Commission may withdraw the benefit of the block exemption. This applies in particular where competition is significantly restricted because of the structure of the relevant market.

(16) Agreements which are automatically exempted pursuant to this Regulation need not be notified. Undertakings may nevertheless in a particular case request a decision pursuant to Council Regulation No 17[1] as last amended by the Act of Accession of Spain and Portugal.

(17) Agreements may benefit from the provisions either of this Regulation or of another Regulation, according to their particular nature and provided that they fulfil the necessary conditions of application. They may not benefit from a combination of the provisions of this Regulation with those of another block exemption Regulation,

Note
[1]OJ No. 13, 21.2.1962, p. 204/62.

HAS ADOPTED THIS REGULATION:

Article 1
1. Pursuant to Article 85(3) of the Treaty and subject to the provisions of this Regulation, it is hereby declared that Article 85(1) of the Treaty shall not apply to franchise agreements to which two undertakings are party, which include one or more of the restrictions listed in Article 2.

2. The exemption provided for in paragraph 1 shall also apply to master franchise agreements to which two undertakings are party. Where applicable, the provisions of this Regulation concerning the relationship between franchisor and franchisee shall apply *mutatis mutandis* to the relationship between franchisor and master franchisee and between master franchisee and franchisee.

3. For the purposes of this Regulation:
   (a) 'franchise' means a package of industrial or intellectual property rights relating to trade marks, trade names, shop signs, utility models, designs, copyrights, know-how or patents, to be exploited for the resale of goods or the provision of services to end users;
   (b) 'franchise agreement' means an agreement whereby one undertaking, the franchisor, grants the other, the franchisee, in exchange for direct or indirect financial consideration, the right to exploit a franchise for the purposes of marketing specified types of goods and/or services; it includes at least obligations relating to:

— the use of a common name or shop sign and a uniform presentation of contract premises and/or means of transport,

— the communication by the franchisor to the franchisee of know-how,

— the continuing provision by the franchisor to the franchisee or commercial or technical assistance during the life of the agreement;

(c) 'master franchise agreement' means an agreement whereby one undertaking, the franchisor, grants the other, the master franchisee, in exchange of direct or indirect financial consideration, the right to exploit a franchise for the purposes of concluding franchise agreements with third parties, the franchisees;

(d) 'franchisor's goods' means goods produced by the franchisor or according to its instructions, and/or bearing the franchisor's name or trade mark;

(e) 'contract premises' means the premises used for the exploitation of the franchise or, when the franchise is exploited outside those premises, the base from which the franchisee operates the means of transport used for the exploitation of the franchise (contract means of transport);

(f) 'know-how' means a package of non-patented practical information, resulting from experience and testing by the franchisor, which is secret, substantial and identified;

(g) 'secret' means that the know-how, as a body or in the precise configuration and assembly of its components, is not generally known or easily accessible; it is not limited in the narrow sense that each individual component of the know-how should be totally unknown or unobtainable outside the franchior's business;

(h) 'substantial' means that the know-how includes information which is of importance for the sale of goods or the provision of services to end users, and in particular for the presentation of goods for sale, the processing of goods in connection with the provision of services, methods of dealing with customers, and administration and financial management; the know-how must be useful for the franchisee by being capable, at the date of conclusion of the agreement, of improving the competitive position of the franchisee, in particular by improving the franchisee's performance or helping it to enter a new market;

(i) 'identified' means that the know-how must be described in a sufficiently comprehensive manner so as to make it possible to verify that it fulfils the criteria of secrecy and substantiality; the description of the know-how can either be set out in the franchise agreement or in a separate document or recorded in any other appropriate form.

Article 2
The exemption provided for in Article 1 shall apply to the following restrictions of competition:

(a) an obligation on the franchisor, in a defined area of the common market, the contract territory, not to:

— grant the right to exploit all or part of the franchise to third parties,

— itself exploit the franchise, or itself market the goods or services which are the subject-matter of the franchise under a similar formula.

— itself supply the franchisor's goods to third parties;

(b) an obligation on the master franchisee not to conclude franchise agreement with third parties outside its contract territory;

(c) an obligation on the franchisee to exploit the franchise only from the contract premises;

(d) an obligation on the franchisee to refrain, outside the contract territory, from seeking customers for the goods or the services which are the subject-matter of the franchise;

(e) an obligation on the franchisee not to manufacture, sell or use in the course of the provision of services, goods competing with the franchisor's goods which are the subject-matter of the franchise; where the subject-matter of the franchise is the sale or use in the course of the provision of services both certain types of goods and spare parts or accessories therefor, that obligation may not be imposed in respect of these spare parts or accessories.

Article 3

1. Article 1 shall apply notwithstanding the presence of any of the following obligations on the franchisee, in so far as they are necessary to protect the franchisor's industrial or intellectual property rights or to maintain the common identity and reputation of the franchised network:

(a) to sell, or use in the course of the provision of services, exclusively goods matching minimum objective quality specifications laid down by the franchisor;

(b) to sell, or use in the course of the provision of services, goods which are manufactured only by the franchisor or by third parties designed by it, where it is impracticable, owing to the nature of the goods which are the subject-matter of the franchise, to apply objective quality specifications;

(c) not to engage, directly or indirectly, in any similar business in a territory where it would compete with a member of the franchised network, including the franchisor; the franchisee may be held to this obligation after termination of the agreement, for a reasonable period which may not exceed one year, in the territory where it has exploited the franchise;

(d) not to acquire financial interests in the capital of a competing undertaking, which would give the franchisee the power to influence the economic conduct of such undertaking;

(e) to sell the goods which are the subject-matter of the franchise only to end users, to other franchisees and to resellers within other channels of distribution supplied by the manufacturer of these goods or with its consent;

(f) to use its best endeavours to sell the goods or provide the services that are the subject-matter of the franchise; to offer for sale a minimum range of goods, achieve a minimum turnover, plan its orders in advance, keep minimum stocks and provide customer and warranty services;

(g) to pay to the franchisor a specified proportion of its revenue for advertising and itself carry out advertising for the nature of which it shall obtain the franchisor's approval.

2. Article 1 shall apply notwithstanding the presence of any of the following obligations on the franchisee:

(a) not to disclose to third parties the know-how provided by the franchisor; the franchisee may be held to this obligation after termination of the agreement;

(b) to communicate to the franchisor any experience gained in exploiting the franchise and to grant it, and other franchisees, a non-exclusive licence for the know-how resulting from the experience;

(c) to inform the franchisor of infringements of licensed industrial or intellectual property rights, to take legal action against infringers or to assist the franchisor in any legal actions against infringers:

(d) not to use know-how licensed by the franchisor for purposes other than the exploitation of the franchise; the franchisee may be held to this obligation after termination of the agreement;

(e) to attend or have its staff attend training courses arranged by the franchisor;

(f) to apply the commercial methods devised by the franchisor, including any subsequent modification thereof, and use the licensed industrial or intellectual property rights;

(g) to comply with the franchisor's standards for the equipment and presentation of the contract premises and/or means of transport;

(h) to allow the franchisor to carry out checks of the contract premises and/or means of transport, including the goods sold and the services provided, and the inventory and accounts of the franchisee;

(i) not without the franchisor's consent to change the location of the contract premises;

(j) not without the franchisor's consent to assign the rights and obligations under the franchise agreement.

3. In the event that, because of particular circumstances, obligations referred to in paragraph 2 fall within the scope of Article 85(1), they shall also be exempted even if they are not accompanied by any of the obligations exempted by Article 1.

Article 4

The exemption provided for in Article 1 shall apply on condition that:

(a) the franchisee is free to obtain the goods that are the subject-matter of the franchise from other franchisees; where such goods are also distributed through another network of authorised distributors, the franchisee must be free to obtain the goods from the latter;

(b) where the franchisor obliges the franchisee to honour guarantees for the franchisor's goods, that obligation shall apply in respect of such goods supplied by any member of the franchised network or other distributors which give a similar guarantee, in the common market;

(c) the franchisee is obliged to indicate its status as an independent undertaking; this indication shall however not interfere with the common identity of the franchised network resulting in particular from the common name or shop sign and uniform appearance of the contract premises and/or means of transport.

Article 5

The exemption granted by Article 1 shall not apply where:

(a) undertakings producing goods or providing services which are identical or are considered by users as equivalent in view of their characteristics, price and intended use, enter into franchise agreements in respect of such goods or services;

(b) without prejudice to Article 2(e) and Article 3(1)(b), the franchisee is prevented from obtaining supplies of goods of a quality equivalent to those offered by the franchisor;

(c) without prejudice to Article 2(e), the franchisee is obliged to sell, or use in the process of providing services, goods manufactured by the franchisor or third parties designated by the franchisor and the franchisor refuses, for reasons other than protecting the franchisor's industrial or intellectual property rights, or maintaining the common identity and reputation of the franchised network, to designate as authorised manufacturers third parties proposed by the franchisee;

(d) the franchisee is prevented from continuing to use the licensed know-how after termination of the agreement where the know-how has become generally known or easily accessible, other than by breach of an obligation by the franchisee;

(e) the franchisee is restricted by the franchisor, directly or indirectly, in the determination of sale prices for the goods or services which are the subject-matter of the franchise, without prejudice to the possibility for the franchisor of recommending sale prices;

(f) the franchisor prohibits the franchisee from challenging the validity of the industrial or intellectual property rights which form part of the franchise, without prejudice to the possibility for the franchisor of terminating the agreement in such a case;

(g) franchisees are obliged not to supply within the common market the goods or services which are the subject-matter of the franchise to end users because of their place of residence.

Article 6

1. The exemption provided for in Article 1 shall also apply to franchise agreements which fulfil the conditions laid down in Article 4 and include obligations restrictive of competition which are not covered by Articles 2 and 3(3) and do not fall within the scope of Article 5, on condition that the agreements in question are notified to the Commission in accordance with the provisions of Commission Regulation No 27 and that the Commission does not oppose such exemption within a period of six months.

2. The period of six months shall run from the date on which the notification is received by the Commission. Where, however, the notification is made by registered post, the period shall run from the date shown on the postmark of the place of posting.

3. Paragraph 1 shall apply only if:

(a) express reference is made to this Article in the notification or in a communication accompanying it; and

(b) the information furnished with the notification is complete and in accordance with the facts.

4. The benefit of paragraph 1 can be claimed for agreements notified before the entry into force of this Regulation by submitting a communication to the Commission referring expressly to this Article and to the notification. Paragraphs 2 and 3(b) shall apply *mutatis mutandis*.

5. The Commission may oppose exemption. It shall oppose exemption if it receives a request to do so from a Member State within three months of the forwarding to the Member State of the notification referred to in paragraph 1 or the communication referred to in paragraph 4. This request must be justified on the basis of considerations relating to the competition rules of the Treaty.

6. The Commission may withdraw its opposition to the exemption at any time. However, where that opposition was raised at the request of a Member State, it may be withdrawn only after consultation of the Advisory Committee on Restrictive Practices and Dominant Positions.

7.   If the opposition is withdrawn because the undertakings concerned have shown that the conditions of Article 85(3) are fulfilled, the exemption shall apply from the date of the notification.

8.   If the opposition is withdrawn because the undertakings concerned have amended the agreement so that the conditions of Article 85(3) are fulfilled, the exemption shall apply from the date on which the amendments take effect.

9.   If the Commission opposes exemption and its opposition is not withdrawn, the effects of the notification shall be governed by the provisions of Regulation No 17.

Article 7

1.   Information acquired pursuant to Article 6 shall be used only for the purposes of this Regulation.

2.   The Commission and the authorities of the Member States, their officials and other servants shall not disclose information acquired by them pursuant to this Regulation of a kind that is covered by the obligation of professional secrecy.

3.   Paragraphs 1 and 2 shall not prevent publication of general information or surveys which do not contain information relating to particular undertakings or associations of undertakings.

Article 8

The Commission may withdraw the benefit of this Regulation, pursuant to Article 7 of Regulation No 19/65/EEC,[1] where it finds in a particular case that an agreement exempted by this Regulation nevertheless has certain effects which are incompatible with the conditions laid down in Article 85(3) of the EEC Treaty, and in particular where territorial protection is awarded to the franchisee and:

(a)   access to the relevant market or competition therein is significantly restricted by the cumulative effect of parallel networks of similar agreements established by competing manufacturers or distributors;

(b)   the goods or services which are the subject-matter of the franchise do not face, in a substantial part of the common market, effective competition from goods or services which are identical or considered by users as equivalent in view of their characteristics, price and intended use;

(c)   the parties, or one of them, prevent end users, because of their place of residence, from obtaining, directly or through intermediaries, the goods or services which are the subject-matter of the franchise within the common market, or use differences in specifications concerning those goods or services in different Member States, to isolate markets;

(d)   franchisees engage in concerted practices relating to the sale prices of the goods or services which are the subject-matter of the franchise;

(e)   the franchisor uses its right to check the contract premises and means of transport, or refuses its agreement to requests by the franchisee to move the contract premises or assign its rights and obligations under the franchise agreement, for reasons other than protecting the franchisor's industrial or intellectual property rights, maintaining the common identity and reputation of the franchised network or verifying that the franchisee abides by its obligations under the agreement.

Note
[1]OJ No. 36, 6.3.1965, p. 533/65.

Article 8a

The prohibition in Article 85(1) of the Treaty shall not apply to the franchise agreements which were in existence at the date of accession of Austria, Finland and Sweden and which, by reason of this accession, fall within the scope of Article 85(1) if, within six months from the date of accession, they are so amended that they comply with the conditions laid down in this Regulation.

However, this Article shall not apply to agreements which at the date of accession already fall under Article 53(1) of the EEA Agreement.

Article 9

This Regulation shall enter into force on 1 February 1989.

It shall remain in force until 31 December 1999.

This Regulation shall be binding in its entirety and directly applicable in all Member States.

Done at Brussels, 30 November 1988.

For the Commission
Peter SUTHERLAND
Member of the Commission

COMMISSION REGULATION (EC) NO. 1475/95 OF 28 JUNE 1995 ON THE APPLICATION OF ARTICLE 85(3) OF THE TREATY TO CERTAIN CATEGORIES OF MOTOR VEHICLE DISTRIBUTION AND SERVICING AGREEMENTS
[OJ 1995, No. L145/25]

THE COMMISSION OF THE EUROPEAN COMMUNITIES,

Having regard to the Treaty establishing the European Community,

Having regard to Council Regulation No. 19/65/EEC of 2 March 1965 on the application of Article 85(3) of the Treaty to certain categories of agreements and concerted practices,[1] as last amended by the Act of Accession of Austria, Finland and Sweden, and in particular Article 1 thereof,

Having published a draft of this Regulation,[2]

Having consulted the Advisory Committee on Restrictive Practices and Dominant Positions,

Whereas:

(1)   Under Regulation No. 19/65/EEC the Commission is empowered to declare by means of a Regulation that Article 85(3) of the Treaty applies to certain categories of agreements falling within Article 85(1) to which only two undertakings are party and by which one party agrees with the other to supply only to that other certain goods for resale within a defined area of the common market. The experience gained in dealing with many motor vehicle distribution and servicing agreements allows a category of agreement to be defined which can generally be regarded as satisfying the conditions laid down in Article 85(3).

These are agreements, for a definite or an indefinite period, by which the supplying party entrusts to the reselling party the task of promoting the

Note
[1] OJ No. 36, 6.3.1965, p. 533/65.
[2] OJ No. C379, 31.12.1994, p. 16.

distribution and servicing of certain products of the motor vehicle industry in a defined area and by which the supplier undertakes to supply contract goods for resale only to the dealer, or only to a limited number of undertakings within the distribution network besides the dealer, within the contract territory.

A list of definitions for the purpose of this Regulation is set out in Article 10.

(2) Notwithstanding that the obligations listed in Articles 1, 2 and 3 normally have as their object or effect the prevention, restriction or distortion of competition within the common market and are normally liable to affect trade between Member States, the prohibition in Article 85(1) of the Treaty may nevertheless be declared inapplicable to these agreements by virtue of Article 85(3), albeit only under certain restrictive conditions.

(3) The applicability of Article 85(1) of the Treaty to distribution and servicing agreements in the motor vehicle industry stems in particular from the fact that the restrictions on competition and obligations agreed within the framework of a manufacturer's distribution system, and listed in Articles 1 to 4 of this Regulation, are generally imposed in the same or similar form throughout the common market. The motor vehicle manufacturers cover the whole common market or substantial parts of it by means of a cluster of agreements involving similar restrictions on competition and affect in this way not only distribution and servicing within Member States but also trade between them.

(4) The exclusive and selective distribution clauses can be regarded as indispensable measures of rationalization in the motor vehicle industry, because motor vehicles are consumer durables which at both regular and irregular intervals require expert maintenance and repair, not always in the same place.

Motor vehicle manufacturers cooperate with the selected dealers and repairers in order to provide specialized servicing for the product. On grounds of capacity and efficiency alone, such a form of cooperation cannot be extended to an unlimited number of dealers and repairers. The linking of servicing and distribution must be regarded as more efficient than a separation between a distribution organization for new vehicles on the one hand and a servicing organization which would also distribute spare parts on the other, particularly as, before a new vehicle is delivered to the final consumer, the undertaking within the distribution system must give it a technical inspection according to the manufacturer's specification.

(5) However, obligatory recourse to the authorized network is not in all respects indispensable for efficient distribution. It should therefore be provided that the supply of contract goods to resellers may not be prohibited where they:

—belong to the same distribution system (Article 3(10)(a)), or

—purchase spare parts for their own use in effecting repairs or maintenance (Article 3(10)(b)).

Measures taken by a manufacturer or by undertakings within the distribution system with the object of protecting the selective distribution system are compatible with the exemption under this Regulation. This applies in particular to a dealer's obligation to sell vehicles to a final consumer using the services of an intermediary only where that consumer has authorized that intermediary to act as his agent (Article 3(11)).

(6) It should be possible to prevent wholesalers not belonging to the distribution system from reselling parts originating from motor vehicle

manufacturers. It may be supposed that the system, beneficial to the consumer, whereby spare parts are readily available across the whole contract range, including those parts with a low turnover, could not be maintained without obligatory recourse to the authorized network.

(7) The ban on dealing in competing products may be exempted on condition that it does not inhibit the dealer from distributing vehicles of other makes in a manner which avoids all confusion between makes (Article 3(3)). The obligation to refrain from selling products of other manufacturers other than in separate sales premises, under separate management, linked to the general obligation to avoid confusion between different makes, guarantees exclusivity of distribution for each make in each place of sale. This last obligation has to be implemented in good faith by the dealer so that the promotion, sale and after-sales service cannot, in any manner, cause confusion in the eyes of the consumer or result in unfair practices on the part of the dealer with regard to suppliers of competing makes. In order to maintain the competitiveness of competing products, the separate management of different sales premises has to be carried out by distinct legal entities. Such an obligation provides an incentive for the dealer to develop sales and servicing of contract goods and thus promotes competition in the supply of those products and competing products. These provisions do not prevent the dealer from offering and providing maintenance and repair services for competing makes of motor vehicle in the same workshop, subject to the option of obliging the dealer not to allow third parties to benefit unduly from investments made by the supplier (Article 3(4)).

(8) However, bans on dealing in competing products cannot be regarded in all circumstances as indispensable to efficient distribution. Dealers must be free to obtain from third parties supplies of parts which match the quality of those offered by the manufacturer, and to use and sell them. In this regard, it can be presumed that all parts coming from the same source of production are identical in characteristics and origin; it is for spare-part manufacturers offering parts to dealers to confirm, if need be, that such parts correspond to those supplied to the manufacturer of the vehicle. Moreover, dealers must retain their freedom to choose parts which are usable in motor vehicles within the contract range and which match or exceed the quality standard. Such a limit on the ban on dealing in competing products takes account of both the importance of vehicle safety and the maintenance of effective competition (Article 3(5) and Article 4(1)(6) and (7)).

(9) The restrictions imposed on the dealer's activities outside the allotted area lead to more intensive distribution and servicing efforts in an easily supervised contract territory, to knowledge of the market based on closer contact with consumers, and to more demand-orientated supply (Article 3(8) and (9)). However, demand for contract goods must remain flexible and should not be limited on a regional basis. Dealers must not be confined to satisfying the demand for contract goods within their contract territories, but must also be able to meet demand from persons and undertakings in other areas of the common market. Advertising by dealers in a medium which is directed at customers outside the contract territory should not be prevented, because it does not run counter to the obligation to promote sales within the contract territory. The acceptable means of advertising do not include direct personal contact with the customer, whether by telephone or other form of telecommunication, doorstep canvassing or by individual letter.

(10) So as to give firms greater legal certainty, certain obligations imposed on the dealer that do not stand in the way of exemption should be specified regarding the observation of minimum distribution and servicing standards (Article 4(1)(1)), regularity of orders (Article 4(1)(2)), the achievement of quantitative sales or stock targets agreed by the parties or determined by an expert third party in the event of disagreement (Article 4(1)(3) to (5)) and the arrangements made for after-sales service (Article 4(1)(6) to (9). Such obligations are directly related to the obligations in Articles 1, 2 and 3 and influence their restrictive effect. They may therefore be exempted, for the same reasons as the latter, where they fall in individual cases under the prohibition contained in Article 85(1) of the Treaty (Article 4(2)).

(11) Pursuant to Regulation No. 19/65/EEC, the conditions which must be satisfied if the declaration of inapplicability is to take effect must be specified.

(12) Under Article 5(1)(1)(a) and (b) it is a condition of exemption that the undertaking should honour the guarantee and provide free servicing, vehicle recall work, and repair and maintenance services necessary for the safe and reliable functioning of the vehicle, irrespective of where in the common market the vehicle was purchased. These provisions are intended to prevent limitation of the consumer's freedom to buy anywhere in the common market.

(13) Article 5(1)(2)(a) is intended to allow the manufacturer to build up a coordinated distribution system, but without hindering the relationship of confidence between dealers and sub-dealers. Accordingly, if the supplier reserves the right to approve appointments of sub-dealers by the dealer, he must not be allowed to withhold such approval arbitrarily.

(14) Article 5(1)(2)(b) requires the supplier not to impose on a dealer within the distribution system any requirements, as defined in Article 4(1), which are discriminatory or inequitable.

(15) Article 5(1)(2)(c) is intended to counter the concentration of the dealer's demand on the supplier which might follow from cumulation of discounts. The purpose of this provision is to allow spare-parts suppliers which do not offer as wide a range of goods as the manufacturer to compete on equal terms.

(16) Article 5(1)(2)(d) makes exemption subject to the condition that the dealer must be able to purchase for customers in the common market volume-produced passenger cars with the technical features appropriate to their place of residence or to the place where the vehicle is to be registered, in so far as the corresponding model is also supplied by the manufacturer through undertakings within the distribution system in that place (Article 10(10)). This provision obviates the danger that the manufacturer and undertakings within the distribution network might make use of product differentiation as between parts of the common market to partition the market.

(17) Article 5(2) makes the exemption dependent on other minimum conditions which aim to prevent the dealer, owing to the obligations which are imposed upon him, from becoming economically over-dependent on the supplier and from abandoning the competitive activity which is nominally open to him because to pursue it would be against the interests of the manufacturer or other undertakings within the distribution network.

(18) Under Article 5(2)(1), the dealer may, for objectively justified reasons, oppose the application of excessive obligations covered by Article 3(3).

(19) Article 5(2)(2) and (3) and Article 5(3) lay down minimum requirements for exemption concerning the duration and termination of the distribution and servicing agreement, because the combined effect of the investments the dealer makes in order to improve the distribution and servicing of contract goods and a short-term agreement or one terminable at short notice is greatly to increase the dealer's dependence on the supplier. In order to avoid obstructing the development of flexible and efficient distribution structures, however, the supplier should be entitled to terminate the agreement where there is a need to reorganize all or a substantial part of the network. To allow rapid settlement of any disputes, provision should be made for reference to an expert third party or arbitrator who will decide in the event of disagreement, without prejudice to the parties' right to bring the matter before a competent court in conformity with the relevant provisions of national law.

(20) Pursuant to Regulation No. 19/65/EEC, the restrictions or provisions which must not be contained in the agreements, if the declaration of inapplicability of Article 85(1) of the Treaty under this Regulation is to take effect, are to be specified (Article 6(1), (1) to (5)). Moreover, practices of the parties which lead to automatic loss of the benefit of exemption when committed systematically and repeatedly shall be defined (Article 6(1)(6) to (12)).

(21) Agreements under which one motor vehicle manufacturer entrusts the distribution of his products to another must be excluded from the block exemption, because of their far-reaching impact on competition (Article 6(1), (1)).

(22) In order to ensure that the parties remain within the limits of the Regulation, any agreements whose object goes beyond the products or services referred to in Article 1 or which stipulate restrictions of competition not exempted by this Regulation should also be excluded from the exemption (Article 6(1)(2) and (3)).

(23) The exemption similarly does not apply where the parties agree between themselves obligations concerning goods covered by this Regulation which would be acceptable in the combination of obligations which is exempted by Commission Regulation (EEC) No. 1983/83[1] or (EEC) No. 1984/83,[2] as last amended by the Act of Accession of Austria, Finland and Sweden, regarding the application of Article 85(3) of the Treaty to categories of exclusive distribution agreements and exclusive purchasing agreements respectively, but which go beyond the scope of the obligations exempted by this Regulation (Article 6(1)(4)).

(24) In order to protect dealers' investments and prevent any circumvention by suppliers of the rules governing the termination of agreements, it should be confirmed that the exemption does not apply where the supplier reserves the right to amend unilaterally during the period covered by the contract the terms of the exclusive territorial dealership granted to the dealer (Article 6(1)(5)).

(25) In order to maintain effective competition at the distribution stage, it is necessary to provide that the manufacturer or supplier will lose the benefit of exemption where he restricts the dealer's freedom to develop his own policy on resale prices (Article 6(1)(6)).

Note
[1]OJ No. L173, 30.6.1983, p. 1.
[2]OJ No. L173, 30.6.1983, p. 5.

(26) The principle of a single market requires that consumers shall be able to purchase motor vehicles wherever in the Community prices or terms are most favourable and even to resell them, provided that the resale is not effected for commercial purposes. The benefits of this Regulation cannot therefore be accorded to manufacturers or suppliers who impede parallel imports or exports through measures taken in respect of consumers, authorized intermediaries or undertakings within the network (Article 6(1)(7) and (8)).

(27) So as to ensure, in the interest of consumers, effective competition on the maintenance and repair markets, the exemption must also be withheld from manufacturers or suppliers who impede independent spare-part producers' and distributors' access to the markets or restrict the freedom of resellers or repairers, whether or not they belong to the network, to purchase and use such spare parts where they match the quality of the original spare parts. The dealer's right to procure spare parts with matching quality from external undertakings of his choice and the corresponding right for those undertakings to furnish spare parts to resellers of their choice, as well as their freedom to affix their trade mark or logo, are provided for subject to compliance with the industrial property rights applicable to those spare parts (Article 6(1)(9) to (11)).

(28) In order to give final consumers genuine opportunities of choice as between repairers belonging to the network and independent repairers, it is appropriate to impose upon manufacturers the obligation to give to repairers outside the network the technical information necessary for the repair and maintenance of their makes of car, whilst taking into account the legitimate interest of the manufacturer to decide itself the mode of exploitation of its intellectual property rights as well as its identified, substantial, secret know-how when granting licences to third parties. However, these rights must be exercised in a manner which avoids all discrimination or other abuse (Article 6(1)(12)).

(29) For reasons of clarity, the legal effects arising from inapplicability of the exemption in the various situations referred to in the Regulation should be defined (Article 6(2) and (3)).

(30) Distribution and servicing agreements can be exempted, subject to the conditions laid down in Articles 5 and 6, so long as the application of obligations covered by Articles 1 to 4 brings about an improvement in distribution and servicing to the benefit of the consumer and effective competition exists, not only between manufacturers' distribution systems but also to a certain extent within each system within the common market. As regards the categories of products set out in Article 1, the conditions necessary for effective competition, including competition in trade between Member States, may be taken to exist at present, so that European consumers may be considered in general to take an equitable share in the benefit from the operation of such competition.

(31) Since the provisions of Commission Regulation (EEC) No. 123/85 of 12 December 1984 on the application of Article 85(3) of the Treaty to certain categories of motor vehicle distribution and servicing agreements,[1] as last amended by the Act of Accession of Austria, Finland and Sweden, are applicable until 30 June 1995, provision should be made for transitional

Note
[1] OJ No. L15, 18.1.1985, p. 16.

arrangements in respect of agreements still running on that date which satisfy the exemption conditions laid down by that Regulation (Article 7). The Commission's powers to withdraw the benefit of exemption or to alter its scope in a particular case should be spelled out and several important categories of cases should be listed by way of example (Article 8). Where the Commission makes use of its power of withdrawal, as provided for in Article 8(2), it should take into account any price differentials which do not principally result from the imposition of national fiscal measures or currency fluctuations between the Member States (Article 8).

(32)   In accordance with Regulation No. 19/65/EEC, the exemption must be defined for a limited period. A period of seven years is appropriate for taking account of the specific characteristics of the motor vehicle sector and the foreseeable changes in competition in that sector. However, the Commission will regularly appraise the application of the Regulation by drawing up a report by 31 December 2000 (Articles 11 and 13).

(33)   Agreements which fulfil the conditions set out in this Regulation need not be notified. However, in the case of doubt undertakings are free to notify their agreements to the Commission in accordance with Council Regulation No. 17,[2] as last amended by the Act of Accession of Austria, Finland and Sweden.

(34)   The sector-specific character of the exemption by category for motor vehicles broadly rules out any regulations containing general exemptions by category as regards distribution. Such exclusion should be confirmed in respect of Commission Regulation (EEC) No. 4087/88 of 30 November 1988 concerning the application of Article 85(3) of the Treaty to categories of franchise agreements,[3] as last amended by the Act of Accession of Austria, Finland and Sweden, without prejudice to the right of undertakings to seek an individual exemption under Regulation No. 17. On the other hand, as regards Regulations (EEC) No. 1983/83 and (EEC) No. 1984/83, which make provision for a more narrowly drawn framework of exemptions for undertakings, it is possible to allow them to choose. As for Commission Regulations (EEC) No. 417/85[4] and (EEC) No. 418/85,[5] as last amended by the Act of Accession of Austria, Finland and Sweden, which relate to the application of Article 85(3) of the Treaty to categories of specialization agreements and to categories of research and development agreements, respectively, but whose emphasis is not on distribution, their applicability is not called in question (Article 12).

(35)   This Regulation is without prejudice to the application of Article 86 of the Treaty.

Notes
[2]OJ No. 13, 21.2.1962, p. 204/62.
[3]OJ No. L359, 28.12.1988, p. 46.
[4]OJ No. L53, 22.2.1985, p. 1.
[5]OJ No. L53, 22.2.1985, p. 5.

HAS ADOPTED THIS REGULATION:

Article 1
Pursuant to Article 85(3) of the Treaty it is hereby declared that subject to the conditions laid down in this Regulation Article 85(1) shall not apply to agreements to which only two undertakings are party and in which one

contracting party agrees to supply, within a defined territory of the common market

— only to the other party, or

— only to the other party and to a specified number of other undertakings within the distribution system, for the purpose of resale, certain new motor vehicles intended for use on public roads and having three or more road wheels, together with spare parts therefor.

Article 2

The exemption shall also apply where the obligation referred to in Article 1 is combined with an obligation on the supplier neither to sell contract goods to final consumers nor to provide them with servicing for contract goods in the contract territory.

Article 3

The exemption shall also apply where the obligation referred to in Article 1 is combined with an obligation on the dealer:

1. not, without the supplier's consent, to modify contract goods or corresponding goods, unless such modification has been ordered by a final consumer and concerns a particular motor vehicle within the range covered by the contract, purchased by that final consumer;

2. not to manufacture products which compete with contract goods;

3. not to sell new motor vehicles offered by persons other than the manufacturer except on separate sales premises, under separate management, in the form of a distinct legal entity and in a manner which avoids confusion between makes;

4. not to permit a third party to benefit unduly, through any after-sales service performed in a common workshop, from investments made by a supplier, notably in equipment or the training of personnel;

5. neither to sell spare parts which compete with contract goods without matching them in quality nor to use them for repair or maintenance of contract goods or corresponding goods;

6. without the supplier's consent, neither to conclude distribution or servicing agreements with undertakings operating in the contract territory for contract goods or corresponding goods nor to alter or terminate such agreements;

7. to impose upon undertakings with which the dealer has concluded agreements in accordance with point 6 obligations comparable to those which the dealer has accepted in relation to the supplier and which are covered by Articles 1 to 4 and are in conformity with Articles 5 and 6;

8. outside the contract territory:

(a) not to maintain branches or depots for the distribution of contract goods or corresponding goods,

(b) not to solicit customers for contract goods or corresponding goods, by personalized advertising;

9. not to entrust third parties with the distribution or servicing of contract goods or corresponding goods outside the contract territory;

10. not to supply to a reseller:

(a) contract goods or corresponding goods unless the reseller is an undertaking within the distribution system, or

(b) spare parts within the contract range unless the reseller uses them for the repair or maintenance of a motor vehicle;

11. not to sell motor vehicles within the contract range or corresponding goods to final consumers using the services of an intermediary unless that intermediary has prior written authority from such consumers to purchase a specified motor vehicle or where it is taken away by him, to collect it.

Article 4

1. The exemption shall apply notwithstanding any obligation whereby the dealer undertakes to:

(1) comply, in distribution, sales and after-sales servicing with minimum standards, regarding in particular;

(a) the equipment of the business premises and the technical facilities for servicing;

(b) the specialized, technical training of staff;

(c) advertising;

(d) the collection, storage and delivery of contract goods or corresponding goods and sales and after-sales servicing;

(e) the repair and maintenance of contract goods and corresponding goods, particularly as regards the safe and reliable functioning of motor vehicles;

(2) order contract goods from the supplier only at certain times or within certain periods, provided that the interval between ordering dates does not exceed three months;

(3) endeavour to sell, within the contract territory and during a specified period, a minimum quantity of contract goods, determined by the parties by common agreement or, in the event of disagreement between the parties as to the minimum number of contractual goods to be sold annually, by an expert third party, account being taken in particular of sales previously achieved in the territory and of forecast sales for the territory and at national level;

(4) keep in stock such quantity of contract goods as may be determined in accordance with the procedure in (3);

(5) keep such demonstration vehicles within the contract range, or such number thereof, as may be determined in accordance with the procedure in (3);

(6) perform work under guarantee, free servicing and vehicle-recall work for contract goods and corresponding goods;

(7) use only spare parts within the contract range or corresponding spare parts for work under guarantee, free servicing and vehicle-recall work in respect of contract goods or corresponding goods;

(8) inform customers, in a general manner, of the extent to which spare parts from other sources might be used for the repair or maintenance of contract goods or corresponding goods;

(9) inform customers whenever spare parts from other sources have been used for the repair or maintenance of contract goods or corresponding goods.

2. The exemption shall also apply to the obligations referred to in (1) above where such obligations fall in individual cases under the prohibition contained in Article 85(1).

Article 5

1. In all cases, the exemption shall apply only if:

(1) the dealer undertakes:

(a) in respect of motor vehicles within the contract range or corresponding thereto which have been supplied in the common market by another undertaking within the distribution network:

— to honour guarantees and to perform free servicing and vehicle-recall work to an extent which corresponds to the dealer's obligation covered by Article 4(1)(6),

— to carry out repair and maintenance work in accordance with Article 4(1)(1)(e);

(b) to impose upon the undertakings operating within the contract territory with which the dealer has concluded distribution and servicing agreements as provided for in Article 3(6) an obligation to honour guarantees and to perform free servicing and vehicle recall work at least to the extent to which the dealer himself is so obliged:

(2) the supplier:

(a) does not without objectively valid reasons withhold consent to conclude, alter or terminate sub-agreements referred to in Article 3(6);

(b) does not apply, in relation to the dealer's obligations referred to in Article 4(1), minimum requirements or criteria for estimates such that the dealer is subject to discrimination without objective reasons or is treated inequitably;

(c) distinguishes, in any scheme for aggregating quantities or values of goods obtained by the dealer from the supplier and from connected undertakings within a specified period for the purpose of calculating discounts, at least between supplies of

— motor vehicles within the contract range,

— spare parts within the contract range, for supplies of which the dealer is dependent on undertakings within the distribution network, and

— other goods;

(d) supplies to the dealer, for the purpose of performance of a contract of sale concluded between the dealer and a final customer in the common market, any passenger car which corresponds to a model within the contract range and which is marketed by the manufacturer or with the manufacturer's consent in the Member State in which the vehicle is to be registered.

2. Where the dealer has, in accordance with Article 4(1), assumed obligations for the improvement of distribution and servicing structures, the exemption shall apply provided that:

(1) the supplier releases the dealer from the obligations referred to in Article 3(3) where the dealer shows that there are objective reasons for doing so;

(2) the agreement is for a period of at least five years or, if for an indefinite period, the period of notice for regular termination of the agreement is at least two years for both parties; this period is reduced to at least one year where:

— the supplier is obliged by law or by special agreement to pay appropriate compensation on termination of the agreement, or

— the dealer is a new entrant to the distribution system and the period of the agreement, or the period of notice for regular termination of the agreement, is the first agreed by that dealer;

(3) each party undertakes to give the other at least six months' prior notice of intention not to renew an agreement concluded for a definite period.

3. The conditions for exemption laid down in (1) and (2) shall not affect;

— the right of the supplier to terminate the agreement subject to at least one year's notice in a case where it is necessary to reorganize the whole or a substantial part of the network,

—the right of one party to terminate the agreement for cause where the other party fails to perform one of its basic obligations. In each case, the parties must, in the event of disagreement, accept a system for the quick resolution of the dispute, such as recourse to an expert third party or an arbitrator, without prejudice to the parties' right to apply to a competent court in conformity with the provisions of national law.

Article 6

1. The exemption shall not apply where:

(1) both parties to the agreement or their connected undertakings are motor vehicle manufacturers; or

(2) the parties link their agreement to stipulations concerning products or services other than those referred to in this Regulation or apply their agreement to such products or services; or

(3) in respect of motor vehicles having three or more road wheels, spare parts or services therefor, the parties agree restrictions of competition that are not expressly exempted by this Regulation; or

(4) in respect of motor vehicles having three or more road wheels or spare parts therefor, the parties make agreements or engage in concerted practices which are exempted from the prohibition in Article 85(1) of the Treaty under Regulations (EEC) No. 1983/83 or (EEC) No. 1984/83 to an extent exceeding the scope of this Regulation; or

(5) the parties agree that the supplier reserves the right to conclude distribution and servicing agreements for contract goods with specified further undertakings operating within the contract territory, or to alter the contract territory; or

(6) the manufacturer, the supplier or another undertaking directly or indirectly restricts the dealer's freedom to determine prices and discounts in reselling contract goods or corresponding goods; or

(7) the manufacturer, the supplier or another undertaking within the network directly or indirectly restricts the freedom of final consumers, authorized intermediaries or dealers to obtain from an undertaking belonging to the network of their choice within the common market contract goods or corresponding goods or to obtain servicing for such goods, or the freedom of final consumers to resell the contract goods or corresponding goods, when the sale is not effected for commercial purposes; or

(8) the supplier, without any objective reason, grants dealers remunerations calculated on the basis of the place of destination of the motor vehicles resold or the place of residence of the purchaser; or

(9) the supplier directly or indirectly restricts the dealer's freedom under Article 3(5) to obtain from a third undertaking of his choice spare parts which compete with contract goods and which match their quality; or

(10) the manufacturer directly or indirectly restricts the freedom of suppliers of spare-parts to supply such products to resellers of their choice, including those which are undertakings within the distribution system, provided that such parts match the quality of contract goods; or

(11) the manufacturer directly or indirectly restricts the freedom of spare-part manufacturers to place effectively and in an easily visible manner their trade mark or logo on parts supplied for the initial assembly or for the repair or maintenance of contract goods or corresponding goods; or

(12) the manufacturer refuses to make accessible, where appropriate upon payment, to repairers who are not undertakings within the distribution system, the technical information required for the repair or maintenance of the contractual or corresponding goods or for the implementing of environmental protection measures, provided that the information is not covered by an intellectual property right or does not constitute identified, substantial, secret know-how; in such case, the necessary technical information shall not be withheld improperly.

2. Without prejudice to the consequences for the other provisions of the agreement, in the cases specified in paragraph 1(1) to (5), the inapplicability of the exemption shall apply to all the clauses restrictive of competition contained in the agreement concerned; in the cases specified in paragraph 1(6) to (12), it shall apply only to the clauses restrictive of competition agreed respectively on behalf of the manufacturer, the supplier or another undertaking within the network which is engaged in the practice complained of.

3. Without prejudice to the consequences for the other provisions of the agreement, in the cases specified in paragraph 1(6) to (12), the inapplicability of the exemption shall only apply to the clauses restrictive of competition agreed in favour of the manufacturer, the supplier or another undertaking within the network which appear in the distribution and servicing agreements concluded for a geographic area within the common market in which the objectionable practice distorts competition, and only for the duration of the practice complained of.

Article 7

The prohibition laid down in Article 85(1) of the Treaty shall not apply during the period from 1 October 1995 to 30 September 1996 to agreements already in force on 1 October 1995 which satisfy the conditions for exemption provided for in Commission Regulation (EEC) No. 123/85.

Article 8

The Commission may withdraw the benefit of the application of this Regulation, pursuant to Article 7 of Regulation No. 19/65/EEC, where it finds that in an individual case an agreement which falls within the scope of this Regulation nevertheless has effects which are incompatible with the provisions of Article 85(3) of the Treaty, and in particular:

(1) where, in the common market or a substantial part thereof, contract goods or corresponding goods are not subject to competition from products considered by consumers as similar by reason of their characteristics, price and intended use;

(2) where prices or conditions of supply for contract goods or for corresponding goods are continually being applied which differ substantially as between Member States, such substantial differences being chiefly due to obligations exempted by this Regulation;

(3) where the manufacturer or an undertaking within the distribution system in supplying the distributors with contract goods or corresponding goods apply, unjustifiably, discriminatory prices or sales conditions.

Article 9

This Regulation shall apply mutatis mutandis to concerted practices falling within the categories covered by this Regulation.

Article 10

For the purposes of this Regulation the following terms shall have the following meanings:

1. 'distribution and servicing agreements' are framework agreements between two undertakings, for a definite or indefinite period, whereby the party supplying goods entrusts to the other the distribution and servicing of those goods;

2. 'parties', are the undertakings which are party to an agreement within the meaning of Article 1: 'the supplier' being the undertaking which supplies the contract goods, and 'the dealer' the undertaking entrusted by the supplier with the distribution and servicing of contract goods;

3. the 'contract territory' is the defined territory of the common market to which the obligation of exclusive supply in the meaning of Article 1 applies;

4. 'contract goods' are new motor vehicles intended for use on public roads and having three or more road wheels, and spare parts therefor, which are the subject of an agreement within the meaning of Article 1;

5. the 'contract range' refers to the totality of the contract goods;

6. 'spare parts' are parts which are to be installed in or upon a motor vehicle so as to replace components of that vehicle. They are to be distinguished from other parts and accessories, according to trade usage;

7. the 'manufacturer' is the undertaking:

   (a) which manufactures or procures the manufacture of the motor vehicles in the contract range, or

   (b) which is connected with an undertaking described at (a);

8. 'connected undertakings' are:

   (a) undertakings one of which directly or indirectly:

   — holds more than half of the capital or business assets of the other, or

   — has the power to exercise more than half the voting rights in the other, or

   — has the power to appoint more than half the members of the supervisory board, board of directors or bodies legally representing the other, or

   — has the right to manage the affairs of the other;

   (b) undertakings in relation to which a third undertaking is able directly or indirectly to exercise such rights or powers as are mentioned in (a) above.

9. 'undertakings within the distribution system' are, besides the parties to the agreement, the manufacturer and undertakings which are entrusted by the manufacturer or with the manufacturer's consent with the distribution of servicing of contract goods or corresponding goods;

10. a 'passenger car which corresponds to a model within the contract range' is a passenger car:

   — manufactured or assembled in volume by the manufacturer, and

   — identical as to body style, drive-line, chassis, and type of motor with a passenger car within the contract range;

11. 'corresponding goods', 'corresponding motor vehicles' and 'corresponding parts' are those which are similar in kind to those in the contract range, are distributed by the manufacturer or with the manufacturer's consent, and are the subject of a distribution or servicing agreement with an undertaking within the distribution system;

12. 'resale' includes all transactions by which a physical or legal person
   — 'the reseller'
   — disposes of a motor vehicle which is still in a new condition and which he had previously acquired in his own name and on his own behalf, irrespective

of the legal description applied under civil law or the format of the transaction which effects such resale. The term resale shall include all leasing contracts which provide for a transfer of ownership or an option to purchase prior to the expiry of the contract;

13.   'distribute' and 'sell' include other forms of supply by the dealer such as leasing.

Article 11

1.   The Commission will evaluate on a regular basis the application of this Regulation, particularly as regards the impact of the exempted system of distribution on price differentials of contract goods between the different Member States and on the quality of service to final users.

2.   The Commission will collate the opinions of associations and experts representing the various interested parties, particularly consumer organizations.

3.   The Commission will draw up a report on the evaluation of this Regulation on or before 31 December 2000, particularly taking into account the criteria provided for in paragraph 1.

Article 12

Regulation (EEC) No. 4087/88 is not applicable to agreements concerning the products or services referred to in this Regulation.

Article 13

This Regulation shall enter into force on 1 July 1995. It shall apply from 1 October 1995 until 30 September 2002. The provisions of Regulation (EEC) No. 123/85 shall continue to apply until 30 September 1995.

This Regulation shall be binding in its entirety and directly applicable in all Member States.

Done at Brussels, 28 June 1995.
For the Commission
Karel VAN MIERT
Member of the Commission

CLARIFICATION OF THE ACTIVITIES OF MOTOR VEHICLE INTERMEDIARIES
(91/C 329/20)

This notice is to supplement the notice[1] published with Regulation (EEC) No. 123/85 in order to clarify the scope of the activities of the intermediaries mentioned in that Regulation. The relationship between an intermediary and the person for whom he or it is acting is primarily governed by their contract and by the national law applicable, and does not affect the rights and obligations of third parties to the contract. This notice does not therefore summarise all the obligations of an intermediary.

Note
[1]OJ No. C17, 18.1.1985.

1.   Principles

The following guidelines, which are in line with the balanced objectives pursued by Regulation (EEC) No. 123/85, are based on two principles. The first is that the intermediary referred to in the Regulation is a provider of services acting for the account of a purchaser and final user; he cannot assume risks normally associated with ownership, and is given prior written authority by an identified principal, whose name and address are given, to exercise such activity. The second is the principle of the transparency of the authorisation, and in particular the requirement that, under national law, the intermediary pass on to the purchaser all the benefits obtained in the negotiations carried out on his behalf.

In this context, three groups of criteria should be distinguished:

    (a)   with regard to the validity of the authorisation and to the provision of assistance;

    (b) with regard to the intermediary's scope for advertising;

    (c)   with regard to the intermediary's possibilities of supply.

The Commission's experience suggests that the following guidelines and criteria appear appropriate for dealing with the practical requirements. Activities which do not conform to these guidelines and criteria will justify the presumption, in the absence of evidence to the contrary, that an intermediary is acting beyond the limits set by Article 3(11) of Regulation (EEC) No. 123/85, or creating a confusion in the mind of the public on this point by giving the impression that he is a reseller.

2.   Practical criteria

(a)   *The validity of the authorisation and the service of assistance*

The intermediary is free to organise the structure of his activities. However, operations involving a network of independent undertakings using a common name or other common distinctive signs could create the misleading impression of an authorised distribution system.

An intermediary may use an outlet in the same building as a supermarket if the outlet is outside the premises where the principal activities of the supermarket are carried on, provided that he complies with the principles set out in the present notice.

Although he cannot assume the risks of ownership, the intermediary must be free to assume the transport and storage risks associated with the vehicle and the credit risks relating to the final purchaser for the financing of the purchase in a foreign country. The services must be provided in total transparency with regard to the various services offered and to payment, and this must be verifiable through the presentation of detailed and exhaustive accounts to the purchaser.

The intermediary must list in detail to the client, in a document which may be separable from the written authorisation, the various services offered to him and must give him the possibility to choose those which suit him. In this document, an intermediary not supplying the full range of services associated with the putting into circulation of an imported vehicle should state which services he is not supplying.

(b)   *Advertising by the intermediary*

The intermediary must be able to advertise, though without creating in potential purchasers' minds any confusion between himself and a reseller. Subject to this restriction, he should be able to:

— concentrate his activities, and thus his advertising, on a given brand or on a particular model, provided that he expressly adds an appropriate disclaimer indicating that he is not a reseller, but acts as an intermediary offering his services,

— provide full information on the price which he can obtain, making it clear that the price indicated is his best estimate,

— display cars which have been bought by his clients using his services, or a particular type or model which he can obtain for them, provided that he expressly and visibly makes it clear that he is acting as an intermediary offering his services and not as a reseller, and that types or models which he displays are not for sale,

— use all logos and brand names, in accordance with the applicable rules of law, but without creating any confusion in the mind of the public with regard to the fact that he is an intermediary and not part of the distribution network of the manufacturer or manufacturers concerned.

Where a supermarket carries on a distinct activity as an intermediary, all necessary measures must be taken to avoid confusion in the minds of buyers (final users) with its principal commercial activities conducted under its usual or distinctive sign.

(c)   *Supply of the intermediaries*

In general the intermediary is free to organise his business relationship with the various dealers in the distribution networks of the different manufacturers; this should not lead the intermediary to establish with such dealers a relationship which is privileged and contrary to contractual obligations accepted in accordance with Regulation (EEC) No. 123/85, especially Articles 3(8)(a) and (b), (9) and (4)(1)(3). In particular the intermediary must obtain supplies on conditions which are normal in the market, and he must not:

— make agreements by which he undertakes obligations to buy,

— receive discounts different from those which are customary on the market of the country in which the car is purchased.

In this context, sales of more than 10% of his annual sales by any one authorised dealer through any one intermediary would create the presumption of a privileged relationship contrary to the Articles cited above.

COMMISSION REGULATION (EC) NO. 240/96 OF 31 JANUARY 1996 ON THE APPLICATION OF ARTICLE 85(3) OF THE TREATY TO CERTAIN CATEGORIES OF TECHNOLOGY TRANSFER AGREEMENTS
[OJ 1996, No. L31/1]

THE COMMISSION OF THE EUROPEAN COMMUNITIES,

Having regard to the Treaty establishing the European Community,

Having regard to Council Regulation No. 19/65/EEC of 2 March 1965 on the application of Article 85(3) of the Treaty to certain categories of agreements and concerted practices,[1] as last amended by the Act of Accession of Austria, Finland and Sweden, and in particular Article 1 thereof,

Notes
[1] OJ No. 36, 6.3.1965, p. 533/65.

Having published a draft of this Regulation,[2] after consulting the Advisory Committee on Restrictive Practices and Dominant Positions,

Whereas:

(1)   Regulation No. 19/65/EEC empowers the Commission to apply Article 85(3) of the Treaty by regulation to certain categories of agreements and concerted practices falling within the scope of Article 85(1) which include restrictions imposed in relation to the acquisition or use of industrial property rights — in particular of patents, utility models, designs or trademarks — or to the rights arising out of contracts for assignment of, or the right to use, a method of manufacture of knowledge relating to use or to the application of industrial processes.

(2)   The Commission has made use of this power by adopting Regulation (EEC) No. 2349/84 of 23 July 1984 on the application of Article 85(3) of the Treaty to certain categories of patent licensing agreements,[3] as last amended by Regulation (EC) No. 2131/95,[4] and Regulation (EEC) No. 556/89 of 30 November 1988 on the application of Article 85(3) of the Treaty to certain categories of know-how licensing agreements,[5] as last amended by the Act of Accession of Austria, Finland and Sweden.

(3)   These two block exemptions ought to be combined into a single regulation covering technology transfer agreements, and the rules governing patent licensing agreements and agreements for the licensing of know-how ought to be harmonized and simplified as far as possible, in order to encourage the dissemination of technical knowledge in the Community and to promote the manufacture of technically more sophisticated products. In those circumstances Regulation (EEC) No. 556/89 should be repealed.

(4)   This Regulation should apply to the licensing of Member States' own patents, Community patents[6] and European patents[7] ('pure patent licensing agreements'). It should also apply to agreements for the licensing of non-patented technical information such as descriptions of manufacturing processes, recipes, formulae, designs or drawings, commonly termed 'know-how ('pure know-how licensing agreements'), and to combined patent and know-how licensing agreements ('mixed agreements'), which are playing an increasingly important role in the transfer of technology. For the purposes of this Regulation, a number of terms are defined in Article 10.

(5)   Patent or know-how licensing agreements are agreements whereby one undertaking which holds a patent or know-how ('the licensor') permits another undertaking ('the licensee') to exploit the patent thereby licensed, or communicates the know-how to it, in particular for purposes of manufacture, use or putting on the market. In the light of experience acquired so far, it is possible to define a category of licensing agreements covering all or part of the common market which are capable of falling within the scope of Article 85(1) but which can normally be regarded as satisfying the conditions laid down in

Notes
[2]OJ No. C178, 30.6.1994, p. 3.
[3]OJ No. L219, 16.8.1984, p. 15.
[4]OJ No. L214, 8.9. 1995, p. 6.
[5]OJ No. L61, 4.3.1989, p. 1.
[6]OJ No. L17, 15.12.1975, p. 1.
[7]European Patent Convention 5.10.1973.

Article 85(3), where patents are necessary for the achievement of the objects of the licensed technology by a mixed agreement or where know-how — whether it is ancillary to patents or independent of them — is secret, substantial and identified in any appropriate form. These criteria are intended only to ensure that the licensing of the know-how or the grant of the patent licence justifies a block exemption of obligations restricting competition. This is without prejudice to the right of the parties to include in the contract provisions regarding other obligations, such as the obligation to pay royalties, even if the block exemption no longer applies.

(6)   It is appropriate to extend the scope of this Regulation to pure or mixed agreements containing the licensing of intellectual property rights other than patents (in particular, trademarks, design rights and copyright, especially software protection), when such additional licensing contributes to the achievement of the objects of the licensed technology and contains only ancillary provisions.

(7)   Where such pure or mixed licensing agreements contain not only obligations relating to territories within the common market but also obligations relating to non-member countries, the presence of the latter does not prevent this Regulation from applying to the obligations relating to territories within the common market. Where licensing agreements for non-member countries or for territories which extend beyond the frontiers of the Community have effects within the common market which may fall within the scope of Article 85(1), such agreements should be covered by this Regulation to the same extent as would agreements for territories within the common market.

(8)   The objective being to facilitate the dissemination of technology and the improvement of manufacturing processes, this Regulation should apply only where the licensee himself manufactures the licensed products or has them manufactured for his account, or where the licensed product is a service, provides the service himself or has the service provided for his account, irrespective of whether or not the licensee is also entitled to use confidential information provided by the licensor for the promotion and sale of the licensed product. The scope of this Regulation should therefore exclude agreements solely for the purpose of sale. Also to be excluded from the scope of this Regulation are agreements relating to marketing know-how communicated in the context of franchising arrangements and certain licensing agreements entered into in connection with arrangements such as joint ventures or patent pools and other arrangements in which a licence is granted in exchange for other licences not related to improvements to or new applications of the licensed technology. Such agreements pose different problems which cannot at present be dealt with in a single regulation (Article 5).

(9)   Given the similarity between sale and exclusive licensing, and the danger that the requirements of this Regulation might be evaded by presenting as assignments what are in fact exclusive licenses restrictive of competition, this Regulation should apply to agreements concerning the assignment and acquisition of patents or know-how where the risk associated with exploitation remains with the assignor. It should also apply to licensing agreements in which the licensor is not the holder of the patent or know-how but is authorized by the holder to grant the licence (as in the case of sub-licences) and to licensing agreements in which the parties' rights or obligations are assumed by connected undertakings (Article 6).

(10)   Exclusive licensing agreements, i.e. agreements in which the licensor undertakes not to exploit the licensed technology in the licensed territory himself or to grant further licences there, may not be in themselves incompatible with Article 85(1) where they are concerned with the introduction and protection of a new technology in the licensed territory, by reason of the scale of the research which has been undertaken, of the increase in the level of competition, in particular inter-brand competition, and of the competitiveness of the undertakings concerned resulting from the dissemination of innovation within the Community. In so far as agreements of this kind fall, in other circumstances, within the scope of Article 85(1), it is appropriate to include them in Article 1 in order that they may also benefit from the exemption.

(11)   The exemption of export bans on the licensor and on the licensees does not prejudice any developments in the case law of the Court of Justice in relation to such agreements, notably with respect to Articles 30 to 36 and Article 85(1). This is also the case, in particular, regarding the prohibition on the licensee from selling the licensed product in territories granted to other licensees (passive competition).

(12)   The obligations listed in Article 1 generally contribute to improving the production of goods and to promoting technical progress. They make the holders of patents or know-how more willing to grant licences and licensees more inclined to undertake the investment required to manufacture, use and put on the market a new product or to use a new process. Such obligations may be permitted under this Regulation in respect of territories where the licensed product is protected by patents as long as these remain in force.

(13)   Since the point at which the know-how ceases to be secret can be difficult to determine, it is appropriate, in respect of territories where the licensed technology comprises know-how only, to limit such obligations to a fixed number of years. Moreover, in order to provide sufficient periods of protection, it is appropriate to take as the starting-point for such periods the date on which the product is first put on the market in the Community by a licensee.

(14)   Exemption under Article 85(3) of longer periods of territorial protection for know-how agreements, in particular in order to protect expensive and risky investment or where the parties were not competitors at the date of the grant of the licence, can be granted only by individual decision. On the other hand, parties are free to extend the term of their agreements in order to exploit any subsequent improvement and to provide for the payment of additional royalties. However, in such cases, further periods of territorial protection may be allowed only starting from the date of licensing of the secret improvements in the Community, and by individual decision. Where the research for improvements results in innovations which are distinct from the licensed technology the parties may conclude a new agreement benefiting from an exemption under this Regulation.

(15)   Provision should also be made for exemption of an obligation on the licensee not to put the product on the market in the territories of other licensees, the permitted period for such an obligation (this obligation would ban not just active competition but passive competition too) should, however, be limited to a few years from the date on which the licensed product is first put on the market in the Community by a licensee, irrespective of whether the licensed technology comprises know-how, patents or both in the territories concerned.

(16)　The exemption of territorial protection should apply for the whole duration of the periods thus permitted, as long as the patents remain in force or the know-how remains secret and substantial. The parties to a mixed patent and know-how licensing agreement must be able to take advantage in a particular territory of the period of protection conferred by a patent or by the know-how, whichever is the longer.

(17)　The obligations listed in Article 1 also generally fulfil the other conditions for the application of Article 85(3). Consumers will, as a rule, be allowed a fair share of the benefit resulting from the improvement in the supply of goods on the market. To safeguard this effect, however, it is right to exclude from the application of Article 1 cases where the parties agree to refuse to meet demand from users or resellers within their respective territories who would resell for export, or to take other steps to impede parallel imports. The obligations referred to above thus only impose restrictions which are indispensable to the attainment of their objectives.

(18)　It is desirable to list in this Regulation a number of obligations that are commonly found in licensing agreements but are normally not restrictive of competition, and to provide that in the event that because of the particular economic or legal circumstances they should fall within Article 85(1), they too will be covered by the exemption. This list, in Article 2, is not exhaustive.

(19)　This Regulation must also specify what restrictions or provisions may not be included in licensing agreements if these are to benefit from the block exemption. The restrictions listed in Article 3 may fall under the prohibition of Article 85(1), but in their case there can be no general presumption that, although they relate to the transfer of technology, they will lead to the positive effects required by Article 85(3), as would be necessary for the granting of a block exemption. Such restrictions can be declared exempt only by an individual decision, taking account of the market position of the undertakings concerned and the degree of concentration on the relevant market.

(20)　The obligations on the licensee to cease using the licensed technology after the termination of the agreement (Article 2(1)(3)) and to make improvements available to the licensor (Article 2(1)(4)) do not generally restrict competition. The post-term use ban may be regarded as a normal feature of licensing, as otherwise the licensor would be forced to transfer his know-how or patents in perpetuity. Undertakings by the licensee to grant back to the licensor a licence for improvements to the licensed know-how and/or patents are generally not restrictive of competition if the licensee is entitled by the contract to share in future experience and inventions made by the licensor. On the other hand, a restrictive effect on competition arises where the agreement obliges the licensee to assign to the licensor rights to improvements of the originally licensed technology that he himself has brought about (Article 3(6)).

(21)　The list of clauses which do not prevent exemption also includes an obligation on the licensee to keep paying royalties until the end of the agreement independently of whether or not the licensed know-how has entered into the public domain through the action of third parties or of the licensee himself (Article 2(1)(7)). Moreover, the parties must be free, in order to facilitate payment, to spread the royalty payments for the use of the licensed technology over a period extending beyond the duration of the licensed patents, in particular by setting lower royalty rates. As a rule, parties do not need to be protected against the foreseeable financial consequences of an agreement freely entered into, and they should therefore be free to choose the appropriate means of financing the technology transfer and sharing between them the risks of such use. However, the setting of rates of royalty so as to achieve one of the restrictions listed in Article 3 renders the agreement ineligible for the block exemption.

(22)   An obligation on the licensee to restrict his exploitation of the licensed technology to one or more technical fields of application ('fields of use') or to one or more product markets is not caught by Article 85(1) either, since the licensor is entitled to transfer the technology only for a limited purpose (Article 2(1)(8)).

(23)   Clauses whereby the parties allocate customers within the same technological field of use or the same product market, either by an actual prohibition on supplying certain classes of customer or through an obligation with an equivalent effect, would also render the agreement ineligible for the block exemption where the parties are competitors for the contract products (Article 3(4)). Such restrictions between undertakings which are not competitors remain subject to the opposition procedure. Article 3 does not apply to cases where the patent or know-how licence is granted in order to provide a single customer with a second source of supply. In such a case, a prohibition on the second licensee from supplying persons other than the customer concerned is an essential condition for the grant of a second licence, since the purpose of the transaction is not to create an independent supplier in the market. The same applies to limitations on the quantities the licensee may supply to the customer concerned (Article 2(1)(13)).

(24)   Besides the clauses already mentioned, the list of restrictions which render the block exemption inapplicable also includes restrictions regarding the selling prices of the licensed product or the quantities to be manufactured or sold, since they seriously limit the extent to which the licensee can exploit the licensed technology and since quantity restrictions particularly may have the same effect as export bans (Article 3(1) and (5)). This does not apply where a licence is granted for use of the technology in specific production facilities and where both a specific technology is communicated for the setting-up, operation and maintenance of these facilities and the licensee is allowed to increase the capacity of the facilities or to set up further facilities for its own use on normal commercial terms. On the other hand, the licensee may lawfully be prevented from using the transferred technology to set up facilities for third parties, since the purpose of the agreement is not to permit the licensee to give other producers access to the licensor's technology while it remains secret or protected by patent (Article 2(1)(12)).

(25)   Agreements which are not automatically covered by the exemption because they contain provisions that are not expressly exempted by this Regulation and not expressly excluded from exemption, including those listed in Article 4(2), may, in certain circumstances, nonetheless be presumed to be eligible for application of the block exemption. It will be possible for the Commission rapidly to establish whether this is the case on the basis of the information undertakings are obliged to provide under Commission Regulation (EC) No. 3385/94.[1] The Commission may waive the requirement to supply specific information required in form A/B but which it does not deem

Note
[1] OJ No. L377, 31.12.1994, p. 28.

necessary. The Commission will generally be content with communication of the text of the agreement and with an estimate, based on directly available data, of the market structure and of the licensee's market share. Such agreements should therefore be deemed to be covered by the exemption provided for in this Regulation where they are notified to the Commission and the Commission does not oppose the application of the exemption within a specified period of time.

(26) Where agreements exempted under this Regulation nevertheless have effects incompatible with Article 85(3), the Commission may withdraw the block exemption, in particular where the licensed products are not faced with real competition in the licensed territory (Article 7). This could also be the case where the licensee has a strong position on the market. In assessing the competition the Commission will pay special attention to cases where the licensee has more than 40% of the whole market for the licensed products and of all the products or services which customers consider interchangeable or substitutable on account of their characteristics, prices and intended use.

(27) Agreements which come within the terms of Articles 1 and 2 and which have neither the object nor the effect of restricting competition in any other way need no longer be notified. Nevertheless, undertakings will still have the right to apply in individual cases for negative clearance or for exemption under Article 85(3) in accordance with Council Regulation No. 17(2), as last amended by the Act of Accession of Austria, Finland and Sweden. They can in particular notify agreements obliging the licensor not to grant other licences in the territory, where the licensee's market share exceeds or is likely to exceed 40%,

HAS ADOPTED THIS REGULATION:

Article 1

1. Pursuant to Article 85(3) of the Treaty and subject to the conditions set out below, it is hereby declared that Article 85(1) of the Treaty shall not apply to pure patent licensing or know-how licensing agreements and to mixed patent and know-how licensing agreements, including those agreements containing ancillary provisions relating to intellectual property rights other than patents, to which only two undertakings are party and which include one or more of the following obligations:

(1) an obligation on the licensor not to license other undertakings to exploit the licensed technology in the licensed territory;

(2) an obligation on the licensor not to exploit the licensed technology in the licensed territory himself;

(3) an obligation on the licensee not to exploit the licensed technology in the territory of the licensor within the common market;

(4) an obligation on the licensee not to manufacture or use the licensed product, or use the licensed process, in territories within the common market which are licensed to other licensees;

(5) an obligation on the licensee not to pursue an active policy of putting the licensed product on the market in the territories within the common market which are licensed to other licensees, and in particular not to engage in advertising specifically aimed at those territories or to establish any branch or maintain any distribution depot there;

(6)   an obligation on the licensee not to put the licensed product on the market in the territories licensed to other licensees within the common market in response to unsolicited orders;

(7)   an obligation on the licensee to use only the licensor's trademark or get up to distinguish the licensed product during the term of the agreement, provided that the licensee is not prevented from identifying himself as the manufacturer of the licensed product;

(8)   an obligation on the licensee to limit his production of the licensed product to the quantities he requires in manufacturing his own products and to sell the licensed product only as an integral part of or a replacement part for his own products or otherwise in connection with the sale of his own products, provided that such quantities are freely determined by the licensee.

2.   Where the agreement is a pure patent licensing agreement, the exemption of the obligations referred to in paragraph 1 is granted only to the extent that and for as long as the licensed product is protected by parallel patents, in the territories respectively of the licensee (points (1), (2), (7) and (8)), the licensor (point (3)) and other licensees (points (4) and (5)). The exemption of the obligation referred to in point (6) of paragraph 1 is granted for a period not exceeding five years from the date when the licensed product is first put on the market within the common market by one of the licensees, to the extent that and for as long as, in these territories, this product is protected by parallel patents.

3.   Where the agreement is a pure know-how licensing agreement, the period for which the exemption of the obligations referred to in points (1) to (5) of paragraph 1 is granted may not exceed ten years from the date when the licensed product is first put on the market within the common market by one of the licensees.

The exemption of the obligation referred to in point (6) of paragraph 1 is granted for a period not exceeding five years from the date when the licensed product is first put on the market within the common market by one of the licensees.

The obligations referred to in points (7) and (8) of paragraph 1 are exempted during the lifetime of the agreement for as long as the know-how remains secret and substantial.

However, the exemption in paragraph 1 shall apply only where the parties have identified in any appropriate form the initial know-how and any subsequent improvements to it which become available to one party and are communicated to the other party pursuant to the terms of the agreement and to the purpose thereof, and only for as long as the know-how remains secret and substantial.

4.   Where the agreement is a mixed patent and know-how licensing agreement, the exemption of the obligations referred to in points (1) to (5) of paragraph 1 shall apply in Member States in which the licensed technology is protected by necessary patents for as long as the licensed product is protected in those Member States by such patents if the duration of such protection exceeds the periods specified in paragraph 3.

The duration of the exemption provided in point (6) of paragraph 1 may not exceed the five-year period provided for in paragraphs 2 and 3.

However, such agreements qualify for the exemption referred to in paragraph 1 only for as long as the patents remain in force or to the extent that the know-how is identified and for as long as it remains secret and substantial whichever period is the longer.

5.   The exemption provided for in paragraph 1 shall also apply where in a particular agreement the parties undertake obligations of the types referred to in that paragraph but with a more limited scope than is permitted by that paragraph.

Article 2

1.   Article 1 shall apply notwithstanding the presence in particular of any of the following clauses, which are generally not restrictive of competition:

(1)   an obligation on the licensee not to divulge the know-how communicated by the licensor; the licensee may be held to this obligation after the agreement has expired;

(2)   an obligation on the licensee not to grant sublicences or assign the licence;

(3)   an obligation on the licensee not to exploit the licensed know-how or patents after termination of the agreement in so far and as long as the know-how is still secret or the patents are still in force;

(4)   an obligation on the licensee to grant to the licensor a licence in respect of his own improvements to or his new applications of the licensed technology, provided:

— that, in the case of severable improvements, such a licence is not exclusive, so that the licensee is free to use his own improvements or to license them to third parties, in so far as that does not involve disclosure of the know-how communicated by the licensor that is still secret,

— and that the licensor undertakes to grant an exclusive or non-exclusive licence of his own improvements to the licensee;

(5)   an obligation on the licensee to observe minimum quality specifications, including technical specifications, for the licensed product or to procure goods or services from the licensor or from an undertaking designated by the licensor, in so far as these quality specifications, products or services are necessary for:

(a)   a technically proper exploitation of the licensed technology; or

(b)   ensuring that the product of the licensee conforms to the minimum quality specifications that are applicable to the licensor and other licensees; and to allow the licensor to carry out related checks;

(6)   obligations:

(a)   to inform the licensor of misappropriation of the know-how or of infringements of the licensed patents; or

(b)   to take or to assist the licensor in taking legal action against such misappropriation or infringements;

(7)   an obligation on the licensee to continue paying the royalties:

(a)   until the end of the agreement in the amounts, for the periods and according to the methods freely determined by the parties, in the event of the know-how becoming publicly known other than by action of the licensor, without prejudice to the payment of any additional damages in the event of the know-how becoming publicly known by the action of the licensee in breach of the agreement;

(b)   over a period going beyond the duration of the licensed patents, in order to facilitate payment;

(8)   an obligation on the licensee to restrict his exploitation of the licensed technology to one or more technical fields of application covered by the licensed technology or to one or more product markets;

(9)   an obligation on the licensee to pay a minimum royalty or to produce a minimum quantity of the licensed product or to carry out a minimum number of operations exploiting the licensed technology;

(10)   an obligation on the licensor to grant the licensee any more favourable terms that the licensor may grant to another undertaking after the agreement is entered into;

(11)   an obligation on the licensee to mark the licensed product with an indication of the licensor's name or of the licensed patent;

(12)   an obligation on the licensee not to use the licensor's technology to construct facilities for third parties; this is without prejudice to the right of the licensee to increase the capacity of his facilities or to set up additional facilities for his own use on normal commercial terms, including the payment of additional royalties;

(13)   an obligation on the licensee to supply only a limited quantity of the licensed product to a particular customer, where the licence was granted so that the customer might have a second source of supply inside the licensed territory; this provision shall also apply where the customer is the licensee, and the licence which was granted in order to provide a second source of supply provides that the customer is himself to manufacture the licensed products or to have them manufactured by a subcontractor;

(14)   a reservation by the licensor of the right to exercise the rights conferred by a patent to oppose the exploitation of the technology by the licensee outside the licensed territory;

(15)   a reservation by the licensor of the right to terminate the agreement if the licensee contests the secret or substantial nature of the licensed know-how or challenges the validity of licensed patents within the common market belonging to the licensor or undertakings connected with him;

(16)   a reservation by the licensor of the right to terminate the licence agreement of a patent if the licensee raises the claim that such a patent is not necessary;

(17)   an obligation on the licensee to use his best endeavours to manufacture and market the licensed product;

(18)   a reservation by the licensor of the right to terminate the exclusivity granted to the licensee and to stop licensing improvements to him when the licensee enters into competition within the common market with the licensor, with undertakings connected with the licensor or with other undertakings in respect of research and development, production, use or distribution of competing products, and to require the licensee to prove that the licensed know-how is not being used for the production of products and the provision of services other than those licensed.

2.   In the event that, because of particular circumstances, the clauses referred to in paragraph 1 fall within the scope of Article 85(1), they shall also be exempted even if they are not accompanied by any of the obligations exempted by Article 1.

3.   The exemption in paragraph 2 shall also apply where an agreement contains clauses of the types referred to in paragraph 1 but with a more limited scope than is permitted by that paragraph.

Article 3

Article 1 and Article 2(2) shall not apply where:

(1) one party is restricted in the determination of prices, components of prices or discounts for the licensed products;

(2) one party is restricted from competing within the common market with the other party, with undertakings connected with the other party or with other undertakings in respect of research and development, production, use or distribution of competing products without prejudice to the provisions of Article 2(1)(17) and (18);

(3) one or both of the parties are required without any objectively justified reason:

(a) to refuse to meet orders from users or resellers in their respective territories who would market products in other territories within the common market;

(b) to make it difficult for users or resellers to obtain the products from other resellers within the common market, and in particular to exercise intellectual property rights or take measures so as to prevent users or resellers from obtaining outside, or from putting on the market in the licensed territory products which have been lawfully put on the market within the common market by the licensor or with his consent; or do so as a result of a concerted practice between them;

(4) the parties were already competing manufacturers before the grant of the licence and one of them is restricted, within the same technical field of use or within the same product market, as to the customers he may serve, in particular by being prohibited from supplying certain classes of user, employing certain forms of distribution or, with the aim of sharing customers, using certain types of packaging for the products, save as provided in Article 1(1)(7) and Article 2(1)(13);

(5) the quantity of the licensed products one party may manufacture or sell or the number of operations exploiting the licensed technology he may carry out are subject to limitations, save as provided in Article (1)(8) and Article 2(1)(13);

(6) the licensee is obliged to assign in whole or in part to the licensor rights to improvements to or new applications of the licensed technology;

(7) the licensor is required, albeit in separate agreements or through automatic prolongation of the initial duration of the agreement by the inclusion of any new improvements, for a period exceeding that referred to in Article 1(2) and (3) not to license other undertakings to exploit the licensed technology in the licensed territory, or a party is required for a period exceeding that referred to in Article 1(2) and (3) or Article 1(4) not to exploit the licensed technology in the territory of the other party or of other licensees.

Article 4

1. The exemption provided for in Articles 1 and 2 shall also apply to agreements containing obligations restrictive of competition which are not covered by those Articles and do not fall within the scope of Article 3, on condition that the agreements in question are notified to the Commission in accordance with the provisions of Articles 1, 2 and 3 of Regulation (EC) No. 3385/94 and that the Commission does not oppose such exemption within a period of four months.

2. Paragraph 1 shall apply, in particular, where:

(a) the licensee is obliged at the time the agreement is entered into to accept quality specifications or futher licences or to procure goods or services which are not necessary for a technically satisfactory exploitation of the licensed technology or for ensuring that the production of the licensee conforms to the quality standards that are respected by the licensor and other licensees;

(b) the licensee is prohibited from contesting the secrecy or the substantiality of the licensed know-how or from challenging the validity of patents licensed within the common market belonging to the licensor or undertakings connected with him.

3. The period of four months referred to in paragraph 1 shall run from the date on which the notification takes effect in accordance with Article 4 of Regulation (EC) No. 3385/94.

4. The benefit of paragraphs 1 and 2 may be claimed for agreements notified before the entry into force of this Regulation by submitting a communication to the Commission referring expressly to this Article and to the notification. Paragraph 3 shall apply mutatis mutandis.

5. The Commission may oppose the exemption within a period of four months. It shall oppose exemption if it receives a request to do so from a Member State within two months of the transmission to the Member State of the notification referred to in paragraph 1 or of the communication referred to in paragraph 4.

This request must be justified on the basis of considerations relating to the competition rules of the Treaty.

6. The Commission may withdraw the opposition to the exemption at any time. However, where the opposition was raised at the request of a Member State and this request is maintained, it may be withdrawn only after consultation of the Advisory Committee on Restrictive Practices and Dominant Positions.

7. If the opposition is withdrawn because the undertakings concerned have shown that the conditions of Article 85(3) are satisfied, the exemption shall apply from the date of notification.

8. If the opposition is withdrawn because the undertakings concerned have amended the agreement so that the conditions of Article 85(3) are satisfied, the exemption shall apply from the date on which the amendments take effect.

9. If the Commission opposes exemption and the opposition is not withdrawn, the effects of the notification shall be governed by the provisions of Regulation No. 17.

Article 5

1. This Regulation shall not apply to:

(1) agreements between members of a patent or know-how pool which relate to the pooled technologies;

(2) licensing agreements between competing undertakings which hold interests in a joint venture, or between one of them and the joint venture, if the licensing agreements relate to the activities of the joint venture;

(3) agreements under which one party grants the other a patent and/or know-how licence and in exchange the other party, albeit in separate agreements or through connected undertakings, grants the first party a patent,

trademark or know-how licence or exclusive sales rights, where the parties are competitors in relation to the products covered by those agreements;

(4) licensing agreements containing provisions relating to intellectual property rights other than patents which are not ancillary;

(5) agreements entered into solely for the purpose of sale.

2. This Regulation shall nevertheless apply:

(1) to agreements to which paragraph 1(2) applies, under which a parent undertaking grants the joint venture a patent or know-how licence, provided that the licensed products and the other goods and services of the participating undertakings which are considered by users to be interchangeable or substitutable in view of their characteristics, price and intended use represent:

— in case of a licence limited to production, not more than 20%, and

— in case of a licence covering production and distribution, not more than 10% of the market for the licensed products and all interchangeable or substitutable goods and services;

(2) to agreements to which paragraph 1(1) applies and to reciprocal licences within the meaning of paragraph 1(3), provided the parties are not subject to any territorial restriction within the common market with regard to the manufacture, use or putting on the market of the licensed products or to the use of the licensed or pooled technologies.

3. This Regulation shall continue to apply where, for two consecutive financial years, the market shares in paragraph 2(1) are not exceeded by more than one-tenth; where that limit is exceeded, this Regulation shall continue to apply for a period of six months from the end of the year in which the limit was exceeded.

Article 6

This Regulation shall also apply to:

(1) agreements where the licensor is not the holder of the know-how or the patentee, but is authorized by the holder or the patentee to grant a licence;

(2) assignments of know-how, patents or both where the risk associated with exploitation remains with the assignor, in particular where the sum payable in consideration of the assignment is dependent on the turnover obtained by the assignee in respect of products made using the know-how or the patents, the quantity of such products manufactured or the number of operations carried out employing the know-how or the patents;

(3) licensing agreements in which the rights or obligations of the licensor or the licensee are assumed by undertakings connected with them.

Article 7

The Commission may withdraw the benefit of this Regulation, pursuant to Article 7 of Regulation No. 19/65/EEC, where it finds in a particular case that an agreement exempted by this Regulation nevertheless has certain effects which are incompatible with the conditions laid down in Article 85(3) of the Treaty, and in particular where:

(1) the effect of the agreement is to prevent the licensed products from being exposed to effective competition in the licensed territory from identical goods or services or from goods or services considered by users as interchangeable or substitutable in view of their characteristics, price and intended use, which may in particular occur where the licensee's market share exceeds 40%;

(2)   without prejudice to Article 1(1)(6), the licensee refuses, without any objectively justified reason, to meet unsolicited orders from users or resellers in the territory of other licensees;

(3)   the parties:

(a)   without any objectively justified reason, refuse to meet orders from users or resellers in their respective territories who would market the products in other territories within the common market; or

(b)   make it difficult for users or resellers to obtain the products from other resellers within the common market, and in particular where they exercise intellectual property rights or take measures so as to prevent resellers or users from obtaining outside, or from putting on the market in the licensed territory products which have been lawfully put on the market within the common market by the licensor or with his consent;

(4)   the parties were competing manufacturers at the date of the grant of the licence and obligations on the licensee to produce a minimum quantity or to use his best endeavours as referred to in Article 2(1), (9) and (17) respectively have the effect of preventing the licensee from using competing technologies.

Article 8

1.   For purposes of this Regulation:

(a)   patent applications;

(b)   utility models;

(c)   applications for registration of utility models;

(d)   topographies of semiconductor products;

(e)   certificats d'utilit and certificats d'addition under French law;

(f)   applications for certificats d'utilit and certificats d'addition under French law;

(g)   supplementary protection certificates for medicinal products or other products for which such supplementary protection certificates may be obtained;

(h)   plant breeder's certificates; shall be deemed to be patents.

2.   This Regulation shall also apply to agreements relating to the exploitation of an invention if an application within the meaning of paragraph 1 is made in respect of the invention for a licensed territory after the date when the agreements were entered into but within the time-limits set by the national law or the international convention to be applied.

3.   This Regulation shall furthermore apply to pure patent or know-how licensing agreements or to mixed agreements whose initial duration is automatically prolonged by the inclusion of any new improvements, whether patented or not, communicated by the licensor, provided that the licensee has the right to refuse such improvements or each party has the right to terminate the agreement at the expiry of the initial term of an agreement and at least every three years thereafter.

Article 9

1.   Information acquired pursuant to Article 4 shall be used only for the purposes of this Regulation.

2.   The Commission and the authorities of the Member States, their officials and other servants shall not disclose information acquired by them

pursuant to this Regulation of the kind covered by the obligation of professional secrecy.

3.   The provisions of paragraphs 1 and 2 shall not prevent publication of general information or surveys which do not contain information relating to particular undertakings or associations of undertakings.

Article 10

For purposes of this Regulation:

(1)   'know-how' means a body of technical information that is secret, substantial and identified in any appropriate form;

(2)   'secret' means that the know-how package as a body or in the precise configuration and assembly of its components is not generally known or easily accessible, so that part of its value consists in the lead which the licensee gains when it is communicated to him; it is not limited to the narrow sense that each individual component of the know-how should be totally unknown or unobtainable outside the licensor's business;

(3)   'substantial' means that the know-how includes information which must be useful, i.e. can reasonably be expected at the date of conclusion of the agreement to be capable of improving the competitive position of the licensee, for example by helping him to enter a new market or giving him an advantage in competition with other manufacturers or providers of services who do not have access to the licensed secret know-how or other comparable secret know-how;

(4)   'identified' means that the know-how is described or recorded in such a manner as to make it possible to verify that it satisfies the criteria of secrecy and substantiality and to ensure that the licensee is not unduly restricted in his exploitation of his own technology, to be identified the know-how can either be set out in the licence agreement or in a separate document or recorded in any other appropriate form at the latest when the know-how is transferred or shortly thereafter, provided that the separate document or other record can be made available if the need arises;

(5)   'necessary patents' are patents where a licence under the patent is necessary for the putting into effect of the licensed technology in so far as, in the absence of such a licence, the realization of the licensed technology would not be possible or would be possible only to a lesser extent or in more difficult or costly conditions. Such patents must therefore be of technical, legal or economic interest to the licensee;

(6)   'licensing agreement' means pure patent licensing agreements and pure know-how licensing agreements as well as mixed patent and know-how licensing agreements;

(7)   'licensed technology' means the initial manufacturing know-how or the necessary product and process patents, or both, existing at the time the first licensing agreement is concluded, and improvements subsequently made to the know-how or patents, irrespective of whether and to what extent they are exploited by the parties or by other licensees;

(8)   'the licensed products' are goods or services the production or provision of which requires the use of the licensed technology;

(9)   'the licensee's market share' means the proportion which the licensed products and other goods or services provided by the licensee, which are considered by users to be interchangeable or substitutable for the licensed

products in view of their characteristics, price and intended use, represent the entire market for the licensed products and all other interchangeable or substitutable goods and services in the common market or a substantial part of it;

(10) 'exploitation' refers to any use of the licensed technology in particular in the production, active or passive sales in a territory even if not coupled with manufacture in that territory, or leasing of the licensed products;

(11) 'the licensed territory' is the territory covering all or at least part of the common market where the licensee is entitled to exploit the licensed technology;

(12) 'territory of the licensor' means territories in which the licensor has not granted any licences for patents and/or know-how covered by the licensing agreement;

(13) 'parallel patents' means patents which, in spite of the divergences which remain in the absence of any unification of national rules concerning industrial property, protect the same invention in various Member States;

(14) 'connected undertakings' means:

(a)   undertakings in which a party to the agreement, directly or indirectly:
— owns more than half the capital or business assets, or
— has the power to exercise more than half the voting rights, or
— has the power to appoint more than half the members of the supervisory board, board of directors or bodies legally representing the undertaking, or
— has the right to manage the affairs of the undertaking;

(b)   undertakings which, directly or indirectly, have in or over a party to the agreement the rights or powers listed in (a);

(c)   undertakings in which an undertaking referred to in (b), directly or indirectly, has the rights or powers listed in (a);

(d)   undertakings in which the parties to the agreement or undertakings connected with them jointly have the rights or powers listed in (a): such jointly controlled undertakings are considered to be connected with each of the parties to the agreement;

(15) 'ancillary provisions' are provisions relating to the exploitation of intellectual property rights other than patents, which contain no obligations restrictive of competition other than those also attached to the licensed know-how or patents and exempted under this Regulation;

(16) 'obligation' means both contractual obligation and a concerted practice;

(17) 'competing manufacturers' or manufacturers of 'competing products' means manufacturers who sell products which, in view of their characteristics, price and intended use, are considered by users to be interchangeable or substitutable for the licensed products.

Article 11

1.   Regulation (EEC) No. 556/89 is hereby repealed with effect from 1 April 1996.

2.   Regulation (EEC) No. 2349/84 shall continue to apply until 31 March 1996.

3.   The prohibition in Article 85(1) of the Treaty shall not apply to agreements in force on 31 March 1996 which fulfil the exemption requirements laid down by Regulation (EEC) No. 2349/84 or (EEC) No. 556/89.

Article 12

1.   The Commission shall undertake regular assessments of the application of this Regulation, and in particular of the opposition procedure provided for in Article 4.

2.   The Commission shall draw up a report on the operation of this Regulation before the end of the fourth year following its entry into force and shall, on that basis, assess whether any adaptation of the Regulation is desirable.

Article 13

This Regulation shall enter into force on 1 April 1996.

It shall apply until 31 March 2006.

Article 11(2) of this Regulation shall, however, enter into force on 1 January 1996.

This Regulation shall be binding in its entirety and directly applicable in all Member States.

Done at Brussels, 31 January 1996.
For the Commission
Karel VAN MIERT
Member of the Commission

INSURANCE BLOCK EXEMPTIONS

COUNCIL REGULATION (EEC) NO. 1534/91 OF 31 MAY 1991 ON THE APPLICATION OF ARTICLE 85(3) OF THE TREATY TO CERTAIN CATEGORIES OF AGREEMENTS, DECISIONS AND CONCERTED PRACTICES IN THE INSURANCE SECTOR
[OJ 1991 L143/1]

THE COUNCIL OF THE EUROPEAN COMMUNITIES,

Having regard to the Treaty establishing the European Economic Community, and in particular Article 87 thereof,

Having regard to the proposal from the Commission,[1]

Having regard to the opinion of the European Parliament,[2]

Having regard to the opinion of the Economic and Social Committee,[3]

Whereas Article 85(1) of the Treaty may, in accordance with Article 85(3), be declared inapplicable to categories of agreements, decisions and concerted practices which satisfy the requirements of Article 85(3);

Whereas the detailed rules for the application of Article 85(3) of the Treaty must be adopted by way of a Regulation based on Article 87 of the Treaty;

Whereas cooperation between undertakings in the insurance sector is, to a certain extent, desirable to ensure the proper functioning of this sector and may at the same time promote consumers' interests;

Whereas the application of Council Regulation (EEC) No. 4064/89 of 21 December 1989 on the control of concentrations between undertakings[4] enables the Commission to exercise close supervision on issues arising from concentrations in all sectors, including the insurance sector;

Whereas exemptions granted under Article 85(3) of the Treaty cannot themselves affect Community and national provisions safeguarding consumers' interests in this sector;

Whereas agreements, decisions and concerted practices serving such aims may, in so far as they fall within the prohibition contained in Article 85(1) of the Treaty, be exempted therefrom under certain conditions; whereas this applies in particular to agreements, decisions and concerted practices relating to the establishment of common risk premium tariffs based on collectively

Notes
[1] OJ No. C16, 23.1.1990, p. 13.
[2] OJ No. C260, 15.10.1990, p.57.
[3] OJ No. C182, 23.7.1990, p. 27.
[4] OJ No. L395, 30.12.1989, p. 1.

ascertained statistics or the number of claims, the establishment of standard policy conditions, common coverage of certain types of risks, the settlement of claims, the testing and acceptance of security devices, and registers of, and information on, aggravated risks;

Whereas in view of the large number of notifications submitted pursuant to Council Regulation No. 17 of 6 February 1962: First Regulation implementing Articles 85 and 86 of the Treaty,[5] as last amended by the Act of Accession of Spain and Portugal, it is desirable that in order to facilitate the Commission's task, it should be enabled to declare, by way of Regulation, that the provisions of Article 85(1) of the Treaty are inapplicable to certain categories of agreements, decisions and concerted practices;

Whereas it should be laid down under which conditions the Commission, in close and constant liaison with the competent authorities of the Member States, may exercise such powers;

Whereas, in the exercise of such powers, the Commission will take account not only of the risk of competition being eliminated in a substantial part of the relevant market and of any benefit that might be conferred on policyholders resulting from the agreements, but also of the risk which the proliferation of restrictive clauses and the operation of accommodation companies would entail for policyholders;

Whereas the keeping of registers and the handling of information on aggravated risks should be carried out subject to the proper protection of confidentiality;

Whereas, under Article 6 of Regulation No. 17, the Commission may provide that a decision taken in accordance with Article 85(3) of the Treaty shall apply with retroactive effect; whereas the Commission should also be able to adopt provisions to such effect in a Regulation;

Whereas, under Article 7 of Regulation No. 17, agreements, decisions and concerted practices may, by decision of the Commission, be exempted from prohibition, in particular if they are modified in such manner that they satisfy the requirements of Article 85(3) of the Treaty;

Whereas it is desirable that the Commission be enabled to grant by Regulation like exemption to such agreements, decisions and concerted practices if they are modified in such manner as to fall within a category defined in an exempting Regulation;

Whereas it cannot be ruled out that, in specific cases, the conditions set out in Article 85(3) of the Treaty may not be fulfilled; whereas the Commission must have the power to regulate such cases pursuant to Regulation No. 17 by way of a Decision having effect for the future,

Note
[5] OJ No. 13, 21.2.1962, p. 204/62.

HAS ADOPTED THIS REGULATION:

Article 1

1. Without prejudice to the application of Regulation No. 17, the Commission may, by means of a Regulation and in accordance with Article 85(3) of the Treaty, declare that Article 85(1) shall not apply to categories of agreements between undertakings, decisions of associations of undertakings and concerted

practices in the insurance sector which have as their object cooperation with respect to:

    (a)   the establishment of common risk premium tariffs based on collectively ascertained statistics or the number of claims;

    (b)   the establishment of common standard policy conditions;

    (c)   the common coverage of certain types of risks;

    (d)   the settlement of claims;

    (e)   the testing and acceptance of security devices;

    (f)   registers of, and information on, aggravated risks, provided that the keeping of these registers and the handling of this information is carried out subject to the proper protection of confidentiality.

    2.   The Commission Regulation referred to in paragraph 1, shall define the categories of agreements, decisions and concerted practices to which it applies and shall specify in particular:

    (a)   the restrictions or clauses which may, or may not, appear in the agreements, decisions and concerted practices;

    (b)   the clauses which must be contained in the agreements, decisions and concerted practices or the other conditions which must be satisfied.

Article 2

Any Regulation adopted pursuant to Article 1 shall be of limited duration. It may be repealed or amended where circumstances have changed with respect to any of the facts which were essential to its being adopted; in such case, a period shall be fixed for modification of the agreements, decisions and concerted practices to which the earlier Regulation applies.

Article 3

A Regulation adopted pursuant to Article 1 may provide that it shall apply with retroactive effect to agreements, decisions and concerted practices to which, at the date of entry into force of the said Regulation, a Decision taken with retroactive effect pursuant to Article 6 of Regulation No. 17 would have applied.

Article 4

    1.   A Regulation adopted pursuant to Article 1 may provide that the prohibition contained in Article 85(1) of the Treaty shall not apply, for such period as shall be fixed in that Regulation, to agreements, decisions and concerted practices already in existence on 13 March 1962 which do not satisfy the conditions of Article 85(3) where:

    — within six months from the entry into force of the said Regulation, they are so modified as to satisfy the said conditions in accordance with the provisions of the said Regulation and

    — the modifications are brought to the notice of the Commission within the time limit fixed by the said Regulation.

    The provisions of the first subparagraph shall apply in the same way to those agreements, decisions and concerted practices existing at the date of accession of new Member States to which Article 85(1) of the Treaty applies by virtue of accession and which do not satisfy the conditions of Article 85(3).

    2.   Paragraph 1 shall apply to agreements, decisions and concerted practices which had to be notified before 1 February 1963, in accordance with Article 5

of Regulation No. 17, only where they have been so notified before that date. Paragraph 1 shall not apply to agreements, decisions and concerted practices existing at the date of accession of new Member States to which Article 85(1) of the Treaty applies by virtue of accession and which had to be notified within six months from the date of accession in accordance with Articles 5 and 25 of Regulation No. 17, unless they have been so notified within the said period.

3.   The benefit of provisions adopted pursuant to paragraph 1 may not be invoked in actions pending at the date of entry into force of a Regulation adopted pursuant to Article 1; neither may it be invoked as grounds for claims for damages against third parties.

Article 5

Where the Commission proposes to adopt a Regulation, it shall publish a draft thereof to enable all persons and organizations concerned to submit to it their comments within such time limit, being not less than one month, as it shall fix.

Article 6

1.   The Commission shall consult the Advisory Committee on Restrictive Practices and Monopolies:
    (a)   before publishing a draft Regulation;
    (b)   before adopting a Regulation.
2.   Article 10(5) and (6) of Regulation No. 17, relating to consultation of the Advisory Committee, shall apply. However, joint meetings with the Commission shall take place not earlier than one month after dispatch of the notice convening them.

Article 7

Where the Commission, either on its own initiative or at the request of a Member State or of natural or legal persons claiming a legitimate interest, finds that, in any particular case, agreements, decisions and concerted practices, to which a Regulation adopted pursuant to Article 1 applies, have nevertheless certain effects which are incompatible with the conditions laid down in Article 85(3) of the Treaty, it may withdraw the benefit of application of the said regulation and take a decision in accordance with Articles 6 and 8 of Regulation No. 17, without any notification under Article 4(1) of Regulation No. 17 being required.

Article 8

Not later than six years after the entry into force of the Commission Regulation provided for in Article 1, the Commission shall submit to the European Parliament and the Council a report on the functioning of this Regulation, accompanied by such proposals for amendments to this Regulation as may appear necessary in the light of experience. This Regulation shall be binding in its entirety and directly applicable in all Member States.

Done at Brussels, 31 May 1991.
For the Council
The President
A. BODRY

COMMISSION REGULATION (EEC) NO. 3932/92 OF 21 DECEMBER 1992 ON THE APPLICATION OF ARTICLE 85(3) OF THE TREATY TO CERTAIN CATEGORIES OF AGREEMENTS, DECISIONS AND CONCERTED PRACTICES IN THE INSURANCE SECTOR
[OJ 1992 L398/7]*

THE COMMISSION OF THE EUROPEAN COMMUNITIES,

Having regard to the Treaty establishing the European Economic Community,

Having regard to Council Regulation (EEC) No. 1534/91 of 31 May 1991 on the application of Article 85(3) of the Treaty to certain categories of agreements, decisions and concerted practices in the insurance sector,[1]

Having published a draft of this Regulation,[2]

Having consulted the Advisory Committee on Restrictive Practices and Dominant Positions,

Whereas:

(1) Regulation (EEC) No. 1534/91 empowers the Commission to apply Article 85(3) of the Treaty by regulation to certain categories of agreements, decisions and concerted practices in the insurance sector which have as their object:

(a) cooperation with respect to the establishment of common risk premium tariffs based on collectively ascertained statistics or the number of claims;

(b) the establishment of common standard policy conditions;

(c) the common coverage of certain types of risks;

(d) the settlement of claims;

(e) the testing and acceptance of security devices;

(f) registers of, and information on, aggravated risks.

(2) The Commission by now has acquired sufficient experience in handling individual cases to make use of such power in respect of the categories of agreements specified in points (a), (b), (c) and (e) of the list.

(3) In many cases, collaboration between insurance companies in the aforementioned fields goes beyond what the Commission has permitted in its notice concerning cooperation between enterprises,[3] and is caught by the prohibition in Article 85(1). It is therefore appropriate to specify the obligations restrictive of competition which may be included in the four categories of agreements covered by it.

(4) It is further necessary to specify for each of the four categories the conditions which must be satisfied before the exemption can apply. These conditions have to ensure that the collaboration between insurance undertakings is and remains compatible with Article 85(3).

Note

*As amended by the Decision 95/1 [OJ 1995 L1/1]
[1] OJ No. L143, 7.6.1991, p. 1.
[2] OJ No. C207, 14.8.1992, p. 2.
[3] OJ No. C75, 29.7.1968, p. 3; corrigendum OJ No. C84, 28.8.1968, p. 14.

(5) It is finally necessary to specify for each of these categories the situations in which the exemption does not apply. For this purpose it has to define the clauses which may not be included in the agreements covered by it because they impose undue restrictions on the parties, as well as other situations falling under Article 85(1) for which there is no general presumption that they will yield the benefits required by Article 85(3).

(6) Collaboration between insurance undertakings or within associations of undertakings in the compilation of statistics on the number of claims, the number of individual risks insured, total amounts paid in respect of claims and the amount of capital insured makes it possible to improve the knowledge of risks and facilitates the rating of risks for individual companies. The same applies to their use to establish indicative pure premiums or, in the case of insurance involving capitalization, frequency tables. Joint studies on the probable impact of extraneous circumstances that may influence the frequency or scale of claims, or the yield of different types of investments, should also be included. It is, however, necessary to ensure that the restrictions are only exempted to the extent to which they are necessary to attain these objectives. It is therefore appropriate to stipulate that concerted practices on commercial premiums — that is to say, the premiums actually charged to policyholders, comprising a loading to cover administrative, commercial and other costs, plus a loading for contingencies or profit margins — are not exempted, and that even pure premiums can serve only for reference purposes.

(7) Standard policy conditions or standard individual clauses for direct insurance and standard models illustrating the profits of a life assurance policy have the advantage of improving the comparability of cover for the consumer and of allowing risks to be classified more uniformly. However, they must not lead either to the standardization of products or to the creation of too captive a customer base. Accordingly, the exemptions should apply on condition that they are not binding, but serve only as models.

(8) Standard policy conditions may in particular not contain any systematic exclusion of specific types of risk without providing for the express possibility of including that cover by agreement and may not provide for the contractual relationship with the policyholder to be maintained for an excessive period or go beyond the initial object to the policy. This is without prejudice to obligations arising from Community or national law.

(9) In addition, it is necessary to stipulate that the common standard policy conditions must be generally accessible to any interested person, and in particular to the policyholder, so as to ensure that there is real transparency and therefore benefit for consumers.

(10) The establishment of co-insurance or co-reinsurance groups designed to cover an unspecified number of risks must be viewed favourably in so far as it allows a greater number of undertakings to enter the market and, as a result, increases the capacity for covering, in particular, risks that are difficult to cover because of their scale, rarity or novelty.

(11) However, so as to ensure effective competition it is appropriate to exempt such groups subject to the condition that the participants shall not hold a share of the relevant market in excess of a given percentage. The percentage of 15% appears appropriate in the case of co-reinsurance groups. The percentage should be reduced to 10% in the case of co-insurance groups. This

is because the mechanism of co-insurance requires uniform policy conditions and commercial premiums, with the result that residual competition between members of a co-insurance group is particularly reduced. As regards catastrophe risks or aggravated risks, those figures shall be calculated only with reference to the market share of the group itself.

(12) In the case of co-reinsurance groups, it is necessary to cover the determination of the risk premium including the probable cost of covering the risks. It is further necessary to cover the determination of the operating cost of the co-reinsurance and the remuneration of the participants in their capacity as co-reinsurers.

(13) It should be legitimate in both cases to declare group cover for the risks brought into the group to be subject to

(a) the application of common or accepted conditions of cover,

(b) the requirement that agreement be obtained prior to the settlement of all (or all large) claims,

(c) to joint negotiation of retrocession, and

(d) to a ban on retroceding individual shares. The requirement that all risks be brought into the group should however be excluded because that would be an excessive restriction of competition.

(14) The establishment of groups constituted only by reinsurance companies need not be covered by this Regulation due to lack of sufficient experience in this field.

(15) The new approach in the realm of technical harmonization and standardization, as defined in the Council resolution of 7 May 1985,[1] and also the global approach to certification and testing, which was presented by the Commission in its communication to the Council of 15 June 1989[2] and which was approved by the Council in its resolution of 21 December 1989,[3] are essential to the functioning of the internal market because they promote competition, being based on standard quality criteria throughout the Community.

(16) It is in the hope of promoting those standard quality criteria that the Commission permits insurance undertakings to collaborate in order to establish technical specifications and rules concerning the evaluation and certification of the compliance of security devices, which as far as possible should be uniform at a European level, thereby ensuring their use in practice.

(17) Cooperation in the evaluation of security devices and of the undertakings installing and maintaining them is useful in so far as it removes the need for repeated individual evaluation. Accordingly, the Regulation should define the conditions under which the formulation of technical specifications and procedures for certifying such security devices and the undertakings installing or maintaining them are authorized. The purpose of such conditions is to ensure that all manufacturers and installation and maintenance undertakings may apply for evaluation, and that the evaluation and certification are guided by objective and well-defined criteria.

Notes

[1] OJ No. C136, 4.6.1985, p. 1.
[2] OJ No. C267, 19.10.1989, p. 3.
[3] OJ No. C10, 16.1.1990, p. 1.

(18)   Lastly, such agreements must not result in an exhaustive list; each undertaking must remain free to accept devices and installation and maintenance undertakings not approved jointly.

(19)   If individual agreements exempted by this Regulation nevertheless have effects which are incompatible with Article 85(3), as interpreted by the administrative practice of the Commission and the case-law of the Court of Justice, the Commission must have the power to withdraw the benefit of the block exemption. This applies for example where studies on the impact of future developments are based on unjustifiable hypotheses; or where recommended standard policy conditions contain clauses which create, to the detriment of the policyholder, a significant imbalance between the rights and obligations arising from the contract; or where groups are used or managed in such a way as to give one or more participating undertakings the means of acquiring or reinforcing a preponderant influence on the relevant market, or if these groups result in market sharing, or if policyholders encounter unusual difficulties in finding cover for aggravated risks outside a group. This last consideration would normally not apply where a group covers less than 25% of those risks.

(20)   Agreements which are exempted pursuant to this Regulation need not be notified. Undertakings may nevertheless in cases of doubt notify their agreements pursuant to Council Regulation No. 17,[4] as last amended by the Act of Accession of Spain and Portugal,

Note
[4] OJ No. 13, 21.2.1962, p. 204/62.

HAS ADOPTED THIS REGULATION:

TITLE I   GENERAL PROVISIONS

Article 1
Pursuant to Article 85(3) of the Treaty and subject to the provisions of this Regulation, it is hereby declared that Article 85(1) of the Treaty shall not apply to agreements, decisions by associations of undertakings and concerted practices in the insurance sector which seek cooperation with respect to:

   (a)   the establishment of common risk-premium tariffs based on collectively ascertained statistics or on the number of claims;
   (b)   the establishment of standard policy conditions;
   (c)   the common coverage of certain types of risks;
   (d)   the establishment of common rules on the testing and acceptance of security devices.

TITLE II   CALCULATION OF THE PREMIUM

Article 2
The exemption provided for in Article 1(a) hereof shall apply to agreements, decisions and concerted practices which relate to:

   (a)   the calculation of the average cost of risk cover (pure premiums) or the establishment and distribution of mortality tables, and tables showing the frequency of illness, accident and invalidity, in connection with insurance involving an element of capitalization — such tables being based on the assembly of data, spread over a number of risk-years chosen as an observation period, which relate to identical or comparable risks in sufficient number to constitute a base which can be handled statistically and which will yield figures on (inter alia):

— the number of claims during the said period,

— the number of individual risks insured in each risk-year of the chosen observation period,

— the total amounts paid or payable in respect of claims arisen during the said period,

— the total amount of capital insured for each risk-year during the chosen observation period,

(b) the carrying-out of studies on the probable impact of general circumstances external to the interested undertakings on the frequency or scale of claims, or the profitability of different types of investment, and the distribution of their results.

Article 3

The exemption shall apply on condition that:

(a) the calculations, tables or study results referred to in Article 2, when compiled and distributed, include a statement that they are purely illustrative;

(b) the calculations or tables referred to in Article 2(a) do not include in any way loadings for contingencies, income deriving from reserves, administrative or commercial costs comprising commissions payable to intermediaries, fiscal or para-fiscal contributions or the anticipated profits of the participating undertakings;

(c) the calculations, tables or study results referred to in Article 2 do not identify the insurance undertakings concerned.

Article 4

The exemption shall not benefit undertakings or associations of undertakings which enter into an undertaking or commitment among themselves, or which oblige other undertakings, not to use calculations or tables that differ from those established pursuant to Article 2(a), or not to depart from the results of the studies referred to in Article 2(b).

TITLE III   STANDARD POLICY CONDITIONS FOR DIRECT INSURANCE

Article 5

1. The exemption provided for in Article 1(b) shall apply to agreements, decisions and concerted practices which have as their object the establishment and distribution of standard policy conditions for direct insurance.

2. The exemption shall also apply to agreements, decisions and concerted practices which have as their object the establishment and distribution of common models illustrating the profits to be realized from an insurance policy involving an element of capitalization.

Article 6

1. The exemption shall apply on condition that the standard policy conditions referred to in Article 5(1):

(a) are established and distributed with an explicit statement that they are purely illustrative; and

(b) expressly mention the possibility that different conditions may be agreed; and

(c) are accessible to any interested person and provided simply upon request.

2. The exemption shall apply on condition that the illustrative models referred to in Article 5(2) are established and distributed only by way of guidance.

Article 7

1. The exemption shall not apply where the standard policy conditions referred to in Article 5(1) contain clauses which:

(a) exclude from the cover losses normally relating to the class of insurance concerned, without indicating explicitly that each insurer remains free to extend the cover to such events;

(b) make the cover of certain risks subject to specific conditions, without indicating explicitly that each insurer remains free to waive them;

(c) impose comprehensive cover including risks to which a significant number of policyholders is not simultaneously exposed, without indicating explicitly that each insurer remains free to propose separate cover;

(d) indicate the amount of the cover or the part which the policyholder must pay himself (the 'excess');

(e) allow the insurer to maintain the policy in the event that he cancels part of the cover, increases the premium without the risk or the scope of the cover being changed (without prejudice to indexation clauses), or otherwise alters the policy conditions without the express consent of the policyholder;

(f) allow the insurer to modify the term of the policy without the express consent of the policyholder;

(g) impose on the policyholder in the non-life assurance sector a contract period of more than three years;

(h) impose a renewal period of more than one year where the policy is automatically renewed unless notice is given upon the expiry of a given period;

(i) require the policyholder to agree to the reinstatement of a policy which has been suspended on account of the disappearance of the insured risk, if he is once again exposed to a risk of the same nature;

(j) require the policyholder to obtain cover from the same insurer for different risks;

(k) require the policyholder, in the event of disposal of the object of insurance, to make the acquirer take over the insurance policy.

2. The exemption shall not benefit undertakings or associations of undertakings which concert or undertake among themselves, or oblige other undertakings not to apply conditions other than those referred to in Article 5(1).

Article 8

Without prejudice to the establishment of specific insurance conditions for particular social or occupational categories of the population, the exemption shall not apply to agreements, decisions and concerted practices which exclude the coverage of certain risk categories because of the characteristics associated with the policyholder.

Article 9

1. The exemption shall not apply where, without prejudice to legally imposed obligations, the illustrative models referred to in Article 5(2) include only specified interest rates or contain figures indicating administrative costs;

2. The exemption shall not benefit undertakings or associations of undertakings which concert or undertake among themselves, or oblige other undertakings not to apply models illustrating the benefits of an insurance policy other than those referred to in Article 5(2).

TITLE IV   COMMON COVERAGE OF CERTAIN TYPES OF RISKS

Article 10

1. The exemption under Article 1(c) hereof shall apply to agreements which have as their object the setting-up and operation of groups of insurance undertakings or of insurance undertakings and reinsurance undertakings for the common coverage of a specific category of risks in the form of co-insurance or co-reinsurance.

2. For the purposes of this Regulation:

(a) 'co-insurance groups' means groups set up by insurance undertakings which:

— agree to underwrite in the name and for the account of all the participants the insurance of a specified risk category, or

— entrust the underwriting and management of the insurance of a specified risk category in their name and on their behalf to one of the insurance undertakings, to a common broker or to a common body set up for this purpose;

(b) 'co-reinsurance groups' means groups set up by insurance undertakings, possibly with the assistance of one or more re-insurance undertakings:

— in order to reinsure mutually all or part of their liabilities in respect of a specified risk category,

— incidentally, to accept in the name and on behalf of all the participants the re-insurance of the same category of risks.

3. The agreements referred to in paragraph 1 may determine:

(a) the nature and characteristics of the risks covered by the co-insurance or co-reinsurance;

(b) the conditions governing admission to the group;

(c) the individual own-account shares of the participants in the risks co-insured or co-reinsured;

(d) the conditions for individual withdrawal of the participants;

(e) the rules governing the operation and management of the group.

4. The agreements alluded to in paragraph 2(b) may further determine:

(a) the shares in the risks covered which the participants do not pass on for co-reinsurance (individual retentions);

(b) the cost of co-reinsurance, which includes both the operating costs of the group and the remuneration of the participants in their capacity as co-reinsurers.

Article 11

1. The exemption shall apply on condition that:

(a) the insurance products underwritten by the participating undertakings or on their behalf do not, in any of the markets concerned, represent:

— in the case of co-insurance groups, more than 10% of all the insurance products that are identical or regarded as similar from the point of view of the risks covered and of the cover provided,

— in the case of co-reinsurance groups, more than 15% of all the insurance products that are identical or regarded as similar from the point of view of the risks covered and of the cover provided;

(b)   each participating undertaking has the right to withdraw from the group, subject to a period of notice of not more than six months, without incurring any sanctions.

2.   By way of derogation from paragraph 1, the respective percentages of 10 and 15% apply only to the insurance products brought into the group, to the exclusion of identical or similar products underwritten by the participating companies or on their behalf and which are not brought into the group, where this group covers:

— catastrophe risks where the claims are both rare and large,

— aggravated risks which involve a higher probability of claims because of the characteristics of the risk insured.

This derogation is subject to the following conditions:

— that none of the concerned undertakings shall participate in another group that covers risks on the same market, and

— with respect to groups which cover aggravated risks, that the insurance products brought into the group shall not represent more than 15% of all identical or similar products underwritten by the participating companies or on their behalf on the market concerned.

Article 12

Apart from the obligations referred to in Article 10, no restriction on competition shall be imposed on the undertakings participating in a co-insurance group other than:

(a)   the obligation, in order to qualify for the co-insurance cover within the group, to

— take preventive measures into account,

— use the general or specific insurance conditions accepted by the group,

— use the commercial premiums set by the group;

(b)   the obligation to submit to the group or approval any settlement of a claim relating to a co-insured risk;

(c)   the obligation to entrust to the group the negotiation of reinsurance agreements on behalf of all concerned;

(d)   a ban on reinsuring the individual share of the co-insured risk.

Article 13

Apart from the obligations referred to in Article 10, no restriction on competition shall be imposed on the undertakings participating in a co-reinsurance group other than:

(a)   the obligation, in order to qualify for the co-reinsurance cover, to

— take preventive measures into account,

— use the general or specific insurance conditions accepted by the group,

— use a common risk-premium tariff for direct insurance calculated by the group, regard being had to the probable cost of risk cover or, where there is not sufficient experience to establish such a tariff, a risk premium accepted by the group,

— participate in the cost of the co-reinsurance;

(b) the obligation to submit to the group for approval the settlement of claims relating to the co-reinsured risks and exceeding a specified amount, or to pass such claims on to it for settlement;

(c) the obligation to entrust to the group the negotiation of retrocession agreements on behalf of all concerned;

(d) a ban on reinsuring the individual retention or retroceding the individual share.

TITLE V   SECURITY DEVICES

Article 14

The exemption provided for in Article 1 (d) shall apply to agreements, decisions and concerted practices which have as their object the establishment, recognition and distribution of:

— technical specifications, in particular technical specifications intended as future European norms, and also procedures for assessing and certifying the compliance with such specifications of security devices and their installation and maintenance,

— rules for the evaluation and approval of installation undertakings or maintenance undertakings.

Article 15

The exemption shall apply on condition that:

(a) the technical specifications and compliancy assessment procedures are precise, technically justified and in proportion to the performance to be attained by the security device concerned;

(b) the rules for the evaluation of installation undertakings and maintenance undertakings are objective, relate to their technical competence and are applied in a non-discriminatory manner;

(c) such specifications and rules are established and distributed with the statement that insurance undertakings are free to accept other security devices or approve other installation and maintenance undertakings which do not comply with these technical specifications or rules;

(d) such specifications and rules are provided simply upon request to any interested person;

(e) such specifications include a classification based on the level of performance obtained;

(f) a request for an assessment may be submitted at any time by any applicant;

(g) the evaluation of conformity does not impose on the applicant any expenses that are disproportionate to the costs of the approval procedure;

(h) the devices and installation undertakings and maintenance undertakings that meet the assessment criteria are certified to this effect in a non-discriminatory manner within a period of six months of the date of application, except where technical considerations justify a reasonable additional period;

(i) the fact of compliance or approval is certified in writing;

(j) the grounds for a refusal to issue the ceritifcate of compliance are given in writing by attaching a duplicate copy of the records of the tests and controls that have been carried out;

(k) the grounds for a refusal to take into account a request for assessment are provided in writing;

(l) the specifications and rules are applied by bodies observing the appropriate provisions of norms in the series EN 45 000.

TITLE VI MISCELLANEOUS PROVISIONS

Article 16

1. The provisions of this Regulation shall also apply where the participating undertakings lay down rights and obligations for the undertakings connected with them. The market shares, legal acts or conduct of the connected undertakings shall be considered to be those of the participating undertakings.

2. 'Connected undertakings' for the purposes of this Regulation means:

(a) undertakings in which a participating undertaking, directly or indirectly:

— owns more than half the capital or business assets, or

— has the power to exercise more than half the voting rights, or

— has the power to appoint more than half the members of the supervisory board, board of directors or bodies legally representing the undertaking, or

— has the right to manage the affairs of the undertaking;

(b) undertakings which directly or indirectly have in or over a participating undertaking the rights or powers listed in (a);

(c) undertakings in which an undertaking referred to in (b) directly or indirectly has the rights or powers listed in (a).

3. Undertakings in which the participating undertakings or undertakings connected with them have directly or indirectly the rights or powers set out in paragraph 2(a) shall be considered to be connected with each of the participating undertakings.

Article 17

The Commission may withdraw the benefit of this Regulation, pursuant to Article 7 of 1534/91, where it finds in a particular case that an agreement, decision or concerted practice exempted under this Regulation nevertheless has certain effects which are incompatible with the conditions laid down in Article 85(3) of the EEC Treaty, and in particular where,

— in the cases referred to in Title II, the studies are based on unjustifiable hypotheses,

— in the cases referred to in Title III, the standard policy conditions contain clauses other than those listed in Article 7(1) which create, to the detriment of the policyholder, a significant imbalance between the rights and obligations arising from the contract,

— in the cases referred to in Title IV:

(a) the undertakings participating in a group would not, having regard to the nature, characteristics and scale of the risks concerned, encounter any significant difficulties in operating individually on the relevant market without organizing themselves in a group;

(b) one or more participating undertakings exercise a determining influence on the commercial policy of more than one group on the same market;

(c) the setting-up or operation of a group may, through the conditions governing admission, the definition of the risks to be covered, the agreements on retrocession or by any other means, result in the sharing of the markets for the insurance products concerned or form neighbouring products;

(d) an insurance group which benefits from the provisions of Article 11(2) has such a position with respect to aggravated risks that the policyholders encounter considerable difficulties in finding cover outside this group.

Article 18

1. As regards agreements existing on 13 March 1962 and notified before 1 February 1963 and agreements, whether notified or not, to which Article 4(2)(1) of Regulation No. 17 applies, the declaration of inapplicability of Article 85(1) of the Treaty contained in this Regulation shall have retroactive effect from the time at which the conditions for application of this Regulation were fulfilled.

2. As regards all other agreements notified before this Regulation entered into force, the declaration of inapplicability of Article 85(1) of the Treaty contained in this Regulation shall have retroactive effect from the time at which the conditions for application of this Regulation were fulfilled, or from the date of notification, whichever is later.

Article 19

If agreements existing on 13 March 1962 and notified before 1 February 1963, or agreements covered by Article 4(2)(1) of Regulation No. 17 and notified before 1 January 1967, are amended before 31 December 1993 so as to fulfil the conditions for application of this Regulation, and if the amendment is communicated to the Commission before 1 April 1994, the prohibition in Article 85(1) of the Treaty shall not apply in respect of the period prior to the amendment. The communication shall take effect from the time of its receipt by the Commission. Where the communication is sent by registered post, it shall take effect from the date shown on the postmark of the place of posting.

Article 20

1. As regards agreements covered by Article 85 of the Treaty as a result of the accession of the United Kingdom, Ireland and Denmark, Articles 18 and 19 shall apply, on the understanding that the relevant dates shall be 1 January 1973 instead of 13 March 1962 and 1 July 1973 instead of 1 February 1963 and 1 January 1967.

2. As regards agreements covered by Article 85 of the Treaty as a result of the accession of Greece, Articles 18 and 19 shall apply, on the understanding that the relevant dates shall be 1 January 1981 instead of 13 March 1962 and 1 July 1981 instead of 1 February 1963 and 1 January 1967.

3. As regards agreements covered by Article 85 of the Treaty as a result of the accession of Spain and Portugal, Articles 18 and 19 shall apply, on the understanding that the relevant dates shall be 1 January 1986 instead of 13 March 1962 and 1 July 1986 instead of 1 February 1963 and 1 January 1967.

4. As regards agreements covered by Article 85 of the Treaty as a result of the accession of Austria, Finland, and Sweden, Articles 18 and 19 shall apply

mutatis mutandis on the understanding that the relevant dates shall be the date of accession instead of 13 March 1962 and six months after the date of accession instead of 1 February 1963, 1 January 1967, 31 December 1993 and 1 April 1994. The amendments made to the agreements in accordance with Article 19 need not be notified to the Commission. However, the present paragraph shall not apply to agreements which at the date of accession already fall under Article 53(1) of the EEA Agreement.

Article 21

This Regulation shall enter into force on 1 April 1993.

It shall apply until 31 March 2003.

This Regulation shall be binding in its entirety and directly applicable in all Member States.

Done at Brussels, 21 December 1992.
For the Commission
Leon BRITTAN
Vice-President

INFORMATION TECHNOLOGY AND TELECOMMUNICATIONS

COUNCIL DIRECTIVE OF 3 OCTOBER 1989 ON THE COORDINATION OF CERTAIN PROVISIONS LAID DOWN BY LAW, REGULATION OR ADMINISTRATIVE ACTION IN MEMBER STATES CONCERNING THE PURSUIT OF TELEVISION BROADCASTING ACTIVITIES (89/552/ EEC)
[OJ 1989, No. L298/23]*

THE COUNCIL OF THE EUROPEAN COMMUNITIES,

Having regard to the Treaty establishing the European Economic Community, and in particular Articles 57(2) and 66 thereof,

Having regard to the proposal from the Commission,[1]

In cooperation with the European Parliament,[2]

Having regard to the opinion of the Economic and Social Committee,[3]

Whereas the objectives of the Community as laid down in the Treaty include establishing an even closer union among the peoples of Europe, fostering closer relations between the States belonging to the Community, ensuring the economic and social progress of its countries by common action to eliminate the barriers which divide Europe, encouraging the constant improvement of the living conditions of its peoples as well as ensuring the preservation and strengthening of peace and liberty;

Whereas the Treaty provides for the establishment of a common market, including the abolition, as between Member States, of obstacles to freedom of movement for services and the institution of a system ensuring that competition in the common market is not distorted;

Whereas broadcasts transmitted across frontiers by means of various technologies are one of the ways of pursuing the objectives of the Community; whereas measures should be adopted to permit and ensure the transition from national markets to a common programme production and distribution market

Note

*Editor's Note: This Directive has been amended extensively by Directive 97/36 [OJ No. L220/60] which entered into force on 30/07/1997. Member States have until 31 December 1998 to implement it. Until then, Directive 97/36 is reproduced below and no changes to the text of this Directive will be made.

[1]OJ No. C179, 17.7.1986, p. 4.

[2]OJ No. C49, 22.2.1988, p. 53, and OJ No. C158, 26.6.1989.

[3]OJ No. C232, 31.8.1987, p. 29.

and to establish conditions of fair competition without prejudice to the public interest role to be discharged by the television broadcasting services;

Whereas the Council of Europe has adopted the European Convention on Transfrontier Television;

Whereas the Treaty provides for the issuing of directives for the coordination of provisions to facilitate the taking up of activities as self-employed persons;

Whereas television broadcasting constitutes, in normal circumstances, a service within the meaning of the Treaty;

Whereas the Treaty provides for free movement of all services normally provided against payment, without exclusion on grounds of their cultural or other content and without restriction of nationals of Member States established in a Community country other than that of the person for whom the services are intended;

Whereas this right as applied to the broadcasting and distribution of television services is also a specific manifestation in Community law of a more general principle, namely the freedom of expression as enshrined in Article 10(1) of the Convention for the Protection of Human Rights and Fundamental Freedoms ratified by all Member States; whereas for this reason the issuing of directives on the broadcasting and distribution of television programmes must ensure their free movement in the light of the said Article and subject only to the limits set by paragraph 2 of that Article and by Article 56(1) of the Treaty;

Whereas the laws, regulations and administrative measures in Member States concerning the pursuit of activities as television broadcasters and cable operators contain disparities, some of which may impede the free movement of broadcasts within the Community and may distort competition within the common market;

Whereas all such restrictions on freedom to provide broadcasting services within the Community must be abolished under the Treaty;

Whereas such abolition must go hand in hand with coordination of the applicable laws; whereas this coordination must be aimed at facilitating the pursuit of the professional activities concerned and, more generally, the free movement of information and ideas within the Community;

Whereas it is consequently necessary and sufficient that all broadcasts comply with the law of Member State from which they emanate;

Whereas this Directive lays down the minimum rules needed to guarantee freedom of transmission in broadcasting; whereas, therefore, it does not affect the responsibility of the Member States and their authorities with regard to the organization — including the systems of licensing, administrative authorization or taxation — financing and the content of programmes; whereas the independence of cultural developments in the Member States and the preservation of cultural diversity in the Community therefore remain unaffected;

Whereas it is necessary, in the common market, that all broadcasts emanating from and intended for reception within the Community and in particular those intended for reception in another Member State, should respect the law of the originating Member State applicable to broadcasts intended for reception by the public in that Member State and the provisions of this Directive;

Whereas the requirement that the originating Member State should verify that broadcasts comply with national law as coordinated by this Directive is sufficient under Community law to ensure free movement of broadcasts without secondary control on the same grounds in the receiving Member States; whereas, however, the receiving Member State may, exceptionally and under specific conditions provisionally suspend the retransmission of televised broadcasts;

Whereas it is essential for the Member States to ensure the prevention of any acts which may prove detrimental to freedom of movement and trade in television programmes or which may promote the creation of dominant positions which would lead to restrictions on pluralism and freedom of televised information and of the information sector as a whole;

Whereas this Directive, being confined specifically to television broadcasting rules, is without prejudice to existing or future Community acts of harmonization, in particular to satisfy mandatory requirements concerning the protection of consumers and the fairness of commercial transactions and competition;

Whereas co-ordination is nevertheless needed to make it easier for persons and industries producing programmes having a cultural objective to take up and pursue their activities;

Whereas minimum requirements in respect of all public or private Community television programmes for European audio-visual productions have been a means of promoting production, independent production and distribution in the abovementioned industries and are complementary to other instruments which are already or will be proposed to favour the same objective;

Whereas it is therefore necessary to promote markets of sufficient size for television productions in the Member States to recover necessary investments not only by establishing common rules opening up national markets but also by envisaging for European productions where practicable and by appropriate means a majority proportion in television programmes of all Member States; whereas, in order to allow the monitoring of the application of these rules and the pursuit of the objectives, Member States will provide the Commission with a report on the application of the proportions reserved for European works and independent productions in this Directive; whereas for the calculation of such proportions account should be taken of the specific situation of the Hellenic Republic and the Portuguese Republic; whereas the Commission must inform the other Member States of these reports accompanied, where appropriate by an opinion taking account of, in particular, progress achieved in relation to previous years, the share of first broadcasts in the programming, the particular circumstances of new television broadcasters and the specific situation of countries with a low audio-visual production capacity or restricted language area;

Whereas for these purposes 'European works' should be defined without prejudice to the possibility of Member States laying down a more detailed definition as regards television broadcasters under their jurisdiction in accordance with Article 3(1) in compliance with Community law and account being taken of the objectives of this Directive;

Whereas it is important to seek appropriate instruments and procedures in accordance with Community law in order to promote the implementation of these objectives with a view to adopting suitable measures to encourage the activity and development of European audio-visual production and distribution, particularly in countries with a low production capacity or restricted language area;

Whereas national support schemes for the development of European production may be applied in so far as they comply with Community law;

Whereas a commitment, where practicable, to a certain proportion of broadcasts for independent productions, created by producers who are independent of broadcasters, will stimulate new sources of television production, especially the creation of small and medium-sized enterprises; whereas it will offer new opportunities and outlets to the marketing of creative talents of employment of cultural professions and employees in the cultural field; whereas the definition of the concept of independent producer by the Member States should take account of that objective by giving due consideration to small and medium-sized producers and making it possible to authorize financial participation by the coproduction subsidiaries of television organizations;

Whereas measures are necessary for Member States to ensure that a certain period elapses between the first cinema showing of a work and the first television showing;

Whereas in order to allow for an active policy in favour of a specific language, Member States remain free to lay down more detailed or stricter rules in particular on the basis of language criteria, as long as these rules are in conformity with Community law, and in particular are not applicable to the retransmission of broadcasts originating in other Member States;

Whereas in order to ensure that the interests of consumers as television viewers are fully and properly protected, it is essential for television advertising to be subject to a certain number of minimum rules and standards and that the Member States must maintain the right to set more detailed or stricter rules and in certain circumstances to lay down different conditions for television broadcasters under their jurisdiction;

Whereas Member States, with due regard to Community law and in relation to broadcasts intended solely for the national territory which may not be received, directly or indirectly, in one or more Member States, must be able to lay down different conditions for the insertion of advertising and different limits for the volume of advertising in order to facilitate these particular broadcasts;

Whereas it is necessary to prohibit all television advertising promoting cigarettes and other tobacco products including indirect forms of advertising which, whilst not directly mentioning the tobacco product, seek to circumvent the ban on advertising by using brand names, symbols or other distinctive features of tobacco products or of undertakings whose known or main activities include the production or sale of such products;

Whereas it is equally necessary to prohibit all television advertising for medicinal products and medical treatment available only on prescription in the Member State within whose jurisdiction the broadcaster falls and to introduce strict criteria relating to the television advertising of alcoholic products;

Whereas in view of the growing importance of sponsorship in the financing of programmes, appropriate rules should be laid down;

Whereas it is, furthermore, necessary to introduce rules to protect the physical, mental and moral development of minors in programmes and in television advertising;

Whereas although television broadcasters are normally bound to ensure that programmes present facts and events fairly, it is nevertheless important that they should be subject to specific obligations with respect to the right of reply or equivalent remedies so that any person whose legitimate interests have been damaged by an assertion made in the course of a broadcast television programme may effectively exercise such right or remedy.

HAS ADOPTED THIS DIRECTIVE:

CHAPTER I   DEFINITIONS

Article 1
For the purpose of this Directive:

(a) 'television broadcasting' means the initial transmission by wire or over the air, including that by satellite, in unencoded or encoded form, of television programmes intended for reception by the public. It includes the communication of programmes between undertakings with a view to their being relayed to the public. It does not include communication services providing items of information or other messages on individual demand such as telecopying, electronic data banks and other similar services;

(b) 'television advertising' means any form of announcement broadcast in return for payment or for similar consideration by a public or private undertaking in connection with a trade, business, craft or profession in order to promote the supply of goods or services, including immovable property, or rights and obligations, in return for payment. Except for the purposes of Article 18, this does not include direct offers to the public for the sale, purchase or rental of products or for the provision of services in return for payment;

(c) 'surreptitious advertising' means the representation in words or pictures of goods, services, the name, the trade mark or the activities of a producer of goods or a provider of services in programmes when such representation is intended by the broadcaster to serve advertising and might mislead the public as to its nature. Such representation is considered to be intentional in particular if it is done in return for payment or for similar consideration;

(d) 'sponsorship' means any contribution made by a public or private undertaking not engaged in television broadcasting activities or in the production of audio-visual works, to the financing of television programmes with a view to promoting its name, its trade mark, its image, its activities or its products.

CHAPTER II   GENERAL PROVISIONS

Article 2
1. Each Member State shall ensure that all television broadcasts transmitted
—by broadcasters under its jurisdiction, or
—by broadcasters who, while not being under the jurisdiction of any Member State, make use of a frequency or a satellite capacity granted by, or a satellite up-link situated in, that Member State, comply with the law applicable to broadcasts intended for the public in that Member State.

2. Member States shall ensure freedom of reception and shall not restrict retransmission on their territory of television broadcasts from other Member States for reasons which fall within the fields coordinated by this Directive. Member States may provisonally suspend retransmissions of television broadcasts if the following conditions are fulfilled:

(a)   a television broadcast coming from another Member State manifestly, seriously and gravely infringes Article 22;

(b)   during the previous 12 months, the broadcaster has infringed the same provision on at least two prior occasions;

(c)   the Member State concerned has notified the broadcaster and the Commission in writing of the alleged infringements and of its intention to restrict retransmission should any such infringement occur again;

(d)   consultations with the transmitting State and the Commission have not produced an amicable settlement within 15 days of the notification provided for in point (c), and the alleged infringement persists. The Commission shall ensure that the suspension is compatible with Community law. It may ask the Member State concerned to put an end to a suspension which is contrary to Community law, as a matter of urgency. This provision is without prejudice to the application of any procedure, remedy or sanction to the infringements in question in the Member State which has jurisdiction over the broadcaster concerned.

3.   This Directive shall not apply to broadcasts intended exclusively for reception in States other than Member States, and which are not received directly or indirectly in one or more Member States.

Article 3

1.   Member States shall remain free to require television broadcasters under their jurisdiction to lay down more detailed or stricter rules in the areas covered by this Directive.

2.   Member States shall, by appropriate means, ensure, within the framework of their legislation, that television broadcasters under their jurisdiction comply with the provisions of this Directive.

CHAPTER III   PROMOTION OF DISTRIBUTION AND PRODUCTION OF TELEVISION PROGRAMMES

Article 4

1.   Member States shall ensure where practicable and by appropriate means, that broadcasters reserve for European works, within the meaning of Article 6, a majority proportion of their transmission time, excluding the time appointed to news, sports events, games, advertising and teletext services. This proportion, having regard to the broadcaster's informational, educational, cultural and entertainment responsibilities to its viewing public, should be achieved progressively, on the basis of suitable criteria.

2.   Where the proportion laid down in paragraph 1 cannot be attained, it must not be lower than the average for 1988 in the Member State concerned.

However, in respect of the Hellenic Republic and the Portuguese Republic, the year 1988 shall be replaced by the year 1990.

3.   From 3 October 1991, the Member States shall provide the Commission every two years with a report on the application of this Article and Article 5.

That report shall in particular include a statistical statement on the achievement of the proportion referred to in this Article and Article 5 for each of the television programmes falling within the jurisdiction of the Member State concerned, the reasons, in each case, for the failure to attain that proportion and the measures adopted or envisaged in order to achieve it.

The Commission shall inform the other Member States and the European Parliament of the reports, which shall be accompanied, where appropriate, by an opinion.

The Commission shall ensure the application of this Article and Article 5 in accordance with the provisions of the Treaty. The Commission may take account in its opinion, in particular, of progress achieved in relation to previous years, the share of first broadcast works in the programming, the particular circumstances of new television broadcasters and the specific situation of countries with a low audiovisual production capacity or restricted language area.

4.   The Council shall review the implementation of this Article on the basis of a report from the Commission accompanied by any proposals for revision that it may deem appropriate no later than the end of the fifth year from the adoption of the Directive.

To that end, the Commission report shall, on the basis of the information provided by Member States under paragraph 3, take account in particular of developments in the Community market and of the international context.

Article 5

Member States shall ensure, where practicable and by appropriate means, that broadcasters reserve at least 10% of their transmission time, excluding the time appointed to news, sports events, games, advertising and teletext services, or alternately, at the discretion of the Member State, at least 10% of their programming budget, for European works created by producers who are independent of broadcasters. This proportion, having regard to broadcasters' informational, educational, cultural and entertainment responsibilities to its viewing public, should be achieved progressively, on the basis of suitable criteria; it must be achieved by earmarking an adequate proportion for recent works, that is to say works transmitted within five years of their production.

Article 6

1.   Within the meaning of this chapter, 'European works' means the following:

(a)   works originating from Member States of the Community and, as regards television broadcasters falling within the jurisdiction of the Federal Republic of Germany, works from German territories where the Basic Law does not apply and fulfilling the conditions of paragraph 2;

(b)   works originating from European third States party to the European Convention on Transfrontier Television of the Council of Europe and fulfilling the conditions of paragraph 2;

(c)   works originating from other European third countries and fulfilling the conditions of paragraph 3.

2.   The works referred to in paragraph 1(a) and (b) are works mainly made with authors and workers residing in one or more States referred to in paragraph 1(a) and (b) provided that they comply with one of the following three conditions:

(a)   they are made by one or more producers established in one or more of those States; or

(b)   production of the works is supervised and actually controlled by one or more producers established in one or more of those States; or

(c) the contribution of co-producers of those States to the total co-production costs is preponderant and the co-production is not controlled by one or more producers established outside those States.

3. The works referred to in paragraph 1(c) are works made exclusively or in co-production with producers established in one or more Member State by producers established in one or more European third countries with which the Community will conclude agreements in accordance with the procedures of the Treaty, if those works are mainly made with authors and workers residing in one or more European States.

4. Works which are not European works within the meaning of paragraph 1, but made mainly with authors and workers residing in one or more Member States, shall be considered to be European works to an extent corresponding to the proportion of the contribution of Community co-producers to the total production costs.

Article 7
Member States shall ensure that the television broadcasters under their jurisdiction do not broadcast any cinematographic work, unless otherwise agreed between its rights holders and the broadcaster, until two years have elapsed since the work was first shown in cinemas in one of the Member States of the Community; in the case of cinematographic works co-produced by the broadcaster, this period shall be one year.

Article 8
Where they consider it necessary for purposes of language policy, the Member States, whilst observing Community law, may as regards some or all pro-grammes of television broadcasters under their jurisdiction, lay down more detailed or stricter rules in particular on the basis of language criteria.

Article 9
This chapter shall not apply to local television broadcasts not forming part of a national network.

CHAPTER IV   TELEVISION ADVERTISING AND SPONSORSHIP

Article 10
1. Television advertising shall be readily recognizable as such and kept quite separate from other parts of the programme service by optical and/or acoustic means.

2. Isolated advertising spots shall remain the exception.

3. Advertising shall not use subliminal techniques.

4. Surreptitious advertising shall be prohibited.

Article 11
1. Advertisements shall be inserted between programmes. Provided the conditions contained in paragraphs 2 to 5 of this Article are fulfilled, advertisements may also be inserted during programmes in such a way that the integrity and value of the programme, taking into account natural breaks in and the duration and nature of the programme, and the rights of the rights holders are not prejudiced.

2. In programmes consisting of autonomous parts, or in sports pro-grammes and similarly structured events and performances comprising inter-vals, advertisements shall only be inserted between the parts or in the intervals.

3. The transmission of audiovisual works such as feature films and films made for television (excluding series, serials, light entertainment programmes and documentaries), provided their programmed duration is more than 45 minutes, may be interrupted once for each complete period of 45 minutes. A further interruption is allowed if their programmed duration is at least 20 minutes longer than two or more complete periods of 45 minutes.

4. Where programmes, other than those covered by paragraph 2, are interrupted by advertisements, a period of at least 20 minutes should elapse between each successive advertising break within the programme.

5. Advertisements shall not be inserted in any broadcast of a religious service. News and current affairs programmes, documentaries, religious programmes, and children's programmes, when their programmed duration is less than 30 minutes shall not be interrupted by advertisements. If their programmed duration is of 30 minutes or longer, the provisions of the previous paragraphs shall apply.

Article 12
Television advertising shall not:
  (a) prejudice respect for human dignity;
  (b) include any discrimination on grounds of race, sex or nationality;
  (c) be offensive to religious or political beliefs;
  (d) encourage behaviour prejudicial to health or to safety;
  (e) encourage behaviour prejudicial to the protection of the environment.

Article 13
All forms of television advertising for cigarettes and other tobacco products shall be prohibited.

Article 14
Television advertising for medicinal products and medical treatment available only on prescription in the Member State within whose jurisdiction the broadcaster falls shall be prohibited.

Article 15
Television advertising for alcoholic beverages shall comply with the following criteria:
  (a) it may not be aimed specifically at minors or, in particular, depict minors consuming these beverages;
  (b) it shall not link the consumption of alcohol to enhanced physical performance or to driving;
  (c) it shall not create the impression that the consumption of alcohol contributes towards social or sexual success;
  (d) it shall not claim that alcohol has therapeutic qualities or that it is a stimulant, a sedative or a means of resolving personal conflicts;
  (e) it shall not encourage immoderate consumption of alcohol or present abstinence or moderation in a negative light;
  (f) it shall not place emphasis on high alcoholic content as being a positive quality of the beverages.

Article 16
Television advertising shall not cause moral or physical detriment to minors, and shall therefore comply with the following criteria for their protection:

(a)   it shall not directly exhort minors to buy a product or a service by exploiting their inexperience or credulity;

(b)   it shall not directly encourage minors to persuade their parents or others to purchase the goods or services being advertised;

(c)   it shall not exploit the special trust minors place in parents, teachers or other persons;

(d)   it shall not unreasonably show minors in dangerous situations.

Article 17

1.   Sponsored television programmes shall meet the following requirements:

(a)   the content and scheduling of sponsored programmes may in no circumstances be influenced by the sponsor in such a way as to affect the responsibility and editorial independence of the broadcaster in respect of programmes;

(b)   they must be clearly identified as such by the name and/or logo of the sponsor at the beginning and/or the end of the programmes;

(c)   they must not encourage the purchase or rental of the products or services of the sponsor or a third party, in particular by making special promotional references to those products or services.

2.   Television programmes may not be sponsored by natural or legal persons whose principal activity is the manufacture or sale of products, or the provision of services, the advertising of which is prohibited by Article 13 or 14.

3.   News and current affairs programmes may not be sponsored.

Article 18

1.   The amount of advertising shall not exceed 15% of the daily transmission time. However, this percentage may be increased to 20% to include forms of advertisements such as direct offers to the public for the sale, purchase or rental of products or for the provision of services, provided the amount of spot advertising does not exceed 15%.

2.   The amount of spot advertising within a given one-hour period shall not exceed 20%.

3.   Without prejudice to the provisions of paragraph 1, forms of advertisements such as direct offers to the public for the sale, purchase or rental of products or for the provision of services shall not exceed one hour per day.

Article 19

Member States may lay down stricter rules than those in Article 18 for programming time and the procedures for television broadcasting for television broadcasters under their jurisdiction, so as to reconcile demand for televised advertising with the public interest, taking account in particular of:

(a)   the role of television in providing information, education, culture and entertainment;

(b)   the protection of pluralism of information and of the media.

Article 20

Without prejudice to Article 3, Member States may, with due regard for Community law, lay down conditions other than those laid down in Article 11 (2) to (5) and in Article 18 in respect of broadcasts intended solely for the national territory which may not be received, directly or indirectly, in one or more other Member States.

Article 21
Member States shall, within the framework of their laws, ensure that in the case of television broadcasts that do not comply with the provisions of this chapter, appropriate measures are applied to secure compliance with these provisions.

CHAPTER V   PROTECTION OF MINORS

Article 22
Member States shall take appropriate measures to ensure that television broadcasts by broadcasters under their jurisdiction do not include programmes which might seriously impair the physical, mental or moral development of minors, in particular those that involve pornography or gratuitous violence. This provision shall extend to other programmes which are likely to impair the physical, mental or moral development of minors, except where it is ensured, by selecting the time of the broadcast or by any technical measure, that minors in the area of transmission will not normally hear or see such broadcasts. Member States shall also ensure that broadcasts do not contain any incitement to hatred on grounds of race, sex, religion or nationality.

CHAPTER VI   RIGHT OF REPLY

Article 23
1.   Without prejudice to other provisions adopted by the Member States under civil, administrative or criminal law, any natural or legal person, regardless of nationality, whose legitimate interests, in particular reputation and good name, have been damaged by an assertion of incorrect facts in a television programme must have a right of reply or equivalent remedies.

2.   A right of reply or equivalent remedies shall exist in relation to all broadcasters under the jurisdiction of a Member State.

3.   Member States shall adopt the measures needed to establish the right of reply or the equivalent remedies and shall determine the procedure to be followed for the exercise thereof. In particular, they shall ensure that a sufficient time span is allowed and that the procedures are such that the right or equivalent remedies can be exercised appropriately by natural or legal persons resident or established in other Member States.

4.   An application for exercise of the right of reply or the equivalent remedies may be rejected if such a reply is not justified according to the conditions laid down in paragraph 1, would involve a punishable act, would render the broadcaster liable to civil law proceedings or would transgress standards of public decency.

5.   Provision shall be made for procedures whereby disputes as to the exercise of the right of reply or the equivalent remedies can be subject to judicial review.

CHAPTER VII   FINAL PROVISIONS

Article 24
In fields which this Directive does not coordinate, it shall not affect the rights and obligations of Member States resulting from existing conventions dealing with telecommunications or broadcasting.

Article 25
1.   Member States shall bring into force the laws, regulations and administrative provisions necessary to comply with this Directive not later than 3
October 1991. They shall forthwith inform the Commission thereof.
2.   Member States shall communicate to the Commission the text of the
main provisions of national law which they adopt in the fields governed by this
Directive.

Article 26
Not later than the end of the fifth year after the date of adoption of this
Directive and every two years thereafter, the Commission shall submit to the
European Parliament, the Council, and the Economic and Social Committee
a report on the application of this Directive and, if necessary, make further
proposals to adapt it to developments in the field of television broadcasting.

Article 27
This Directive is addressed to the Member States.

Done at Luxembourg, 3 October 1989.
For the Council
The President
R. DUMAS

**COUNCIL DIRECTIVE OF 14 MAY 1991 ON THE LEGAL
PROTECTION OF COMPUTER PROGRAMS (91/250/EEC)
[OJ 1991, No. L122/42]**

THE COUNCIL OF THE EUROPEAN COMMUNITIES,

Having regard to the Treaty establishing the European Economic Community
and in particular Article 100a thereof,
     Having regard to the proposal from the Commission,[1]
     In cooperation with the European Parliament,[2]
     Having regard to the opinion of the Economic and Social Committee,[3]

Notes
[1]OJ No. C91, 12.4.1989, p. 4; and OJ No. C320, 20.12.1990, p. 22.
[2]OJ No. C231, 17.9.1990, p. 78; and Decision of 17 April 1991, not yet published in
the Official Journal).
[3]OJ No. C329, 30.12.1989, p. 4.

Whereas computer programs are at present not clearly protected in all Member
States by existing legislation and such protection, where it exists, has different
attributes;
     Whereas the development of computer programs requires the investment of
considerable human, technical and financial resources while computer programs
can be copied at a fraction of the cost needed to develop them independently;
     Whereas computer programs are playing an increasingly important role in a
broad range of industries and computer program technology can accordingly
be considered as being of fundamental importance for the Community's
industrial development;
     Whereas certain differences in the legal protection of computer programs
offered by the laws of the Member States have direct and negative effects on the

functioning of the common market as regards computer programs and such differences could well become greater as Member States introduce new legislation on this subject;

Whereas existing differences having such effects need to be removed and new ones prevented from arising, while differences not adversely affecting the functioning of the common market to a substantial degree need not be removed or prevented from arising;

Whereas the Community's legal framework on the protection of computer programs can accordingly in the first instance be limited to establishing that Member States should accord protection to computer programs under copyright law as literary works and, further, to establishing who and what should be protected, the exclusive rights on which protected persons should be able to rely in order to authorise or prohibit certain acts and for how long the protection should apply;

Whereas, for the purpose of this Directive, the term 'computer program' shall include programs in any form, including those which are incorporated into hardware; whereas this term also includes preparatory design work leading to the development of a computer program provided that the nature of the preparatory work is such that a computer program can result from it at a later stage;

Whereas, in respect of the criteria to be applied in determining whether or not a computer program is an original work, no tests as to the qualitative or aesthetic merits of the program should be applied;

Whereas the Community is fully committed to the promotion of international standardisation;

Whereas the function of a computer program is to communicate and work together with other components of a computer system and with users and, for this purpose, a logical and, where appropriate, physical interconnection and interaction is required to permit all elements of software and hardware to work with other software and hardware and with users in all the ways in which they are intended to function;

Whereas the parts of the program which provide for such interconnection and interaction between elements of software and hardware are generally known as 'interfaces';

Whereas this functional interconnection and interaction is generally known as 'interoperability'; whereas such interoperability can be defined as the ability to exchange information and mutually to use the information which has been exchanged;

Whereas, for the avoidance of doubt, it has to be made clear that only the expression of a computer program is protected and that ideas and principles which underlie any element of a program, including those which underlie its interfaces, are not protected by copyright under this Directive;

Whereas, in accordance with this principle of copyright, to the extent that logic, algorithms and programming languages comprise ideas and principles, those ideas and principles are not protected under this Directive;

Whereas, in accordance with the legislation and jurisprudence of the Member States and the international copyright conventions, the expression of those ideas and principles is to be protected by copyright;

Whereas, for the purposes of this Directive, the term 'rental' means the making available for use, for a limited period of time and for profit-making purposes, of a computer program or a copy thereof; whereas this term does not include public lending, which, accordingly, remains outside the scope of this Directive;

Whereas the exclusive rights of the author to prevent the unauthorised reproduction of his work have to be subject to a limited exception in the case of a computer program to allow the reproduction technically necessary for the use of that program by the lawful acquirer;

Whereas this means that the acts of loading and running necessary for the use of a copy of a program which has been lawfully acquired, and the act of correction of its errors, may not be prohibited by contract; whereas, in the absence of specific contractual provisions, including when a copy of the program has been sold, any other act necessary for the use of the copy of a program may be performed in accordance with its intended purpose by a lawful acquirer of that copy;

Whereas a person having a right to use a computer program should not be prevented from performing acts necessary to observe, study or test the functioning of the program, provided that these acts do not infringe the copyright in the program;

Whereas the unauthorised reproduction, translation, adaptation or transformation of the form of the code in which a copy of a computer program has been made available constitutes an infringement of the exclusive rights of the author;

Whereas, nevertheless, circumstances may exist when such a reproduction of the code and translation of its form within the meaning of Article 4(a) and (b) are indispensable to obtain the necessary information to achieve the interoperability of an independently created program with other programs;

Whereas it has therefore to be considered that in these limited circumstances only, performance of the acts of reproduction and translation by or on behalf of a person having a right to use a copy of the program is legitimate and compatible with fair practice and must therefore be deemed not to require the authorisation of the rightholder;

Whereas an objective of this exception is to make it possible to connect all components of a computer system, including those of different manufacturers, so that they can work together;

Whereas such an exception to the author's exclusive rights may not be used in a way which prejudices the legitimate interests of the rightholder or which conflicts with a normal exploitation of the program;

Whereas, in order to remain in accordance with the provisions of the Berne Convention for the Protection of Literary and Artistic Works, the term of protection should be the life of the author and fifty years from the first of January of the year following the year of his death or, in the case of an anonymous or pseudonymous work, 50 years from the first of January of the year following the year in which the work is first published;

Whereas protection of computer programs under copyright laws should be without prejudice to the application, in appropriate cases, of other forms of protection; whereas, however, any contractual provisions contrary to Article 6 or to the exceptions provided for in Article 5(2) and (3) should be null and void;

Whereas the provisions of this Directive are without prejudice to the application of the competition rules under Articles 85 and 86 of the Treaty if a dominant supplier refuses to make information available which is necessary for interoperability as defined in this Directive;

Whereas the provisions of this Directive should be without prejudice to specific requirements of Community law already enacted in respect of the publication of interfaces in the telecommunications sector or Council Decisions relating to standardisation in the field of information technology and telecommunication;

Whereas this Directive does not affect derogations provided for under national legislation in accordance with the Berne Convention on points not covered by this Directive,

HAS ADOPTED THIS DIRECTIVE:

Article 1   Object of protection

1.   In accordance with the provisions of this Directive, Member States shall protect computer programs, by copyright, as literary works within the meaning of the Berne Convention for the Protection of Literary and Artistic Works. For the purposes of this Directive, the term 'computer programs' shall include their preparatory design material.

2.   Protection in accordance with this Directive shall apply to the expression in any form of a computer program. Ideas and principles which underlie any element of a computer program, including those which underlie its interfaces, are not protected by copyright under this Directive.

3.   A computer program shall be protected if it is original in the sense that it is the author's own intellectual creation. No other criteria shall be applied to determine its eligibility for protection.

Article 2   Authorship of computer programs

1.   The author of a computer program shall be the natural person or group of natural persons who has created the program or, where the legislation of the Member State permits, the legal person designated as the rightholder by that legislation. Where collective works are recognised by the legislation of a Member State, the person considered by the legislation of the Member State to have created the work shall be deemed to be its author.

2.   In respect of a computer program created by a group of natural persons jointly, the exclusive rights shall be owned jointly.

3.   Where a computer program is created by an employee in the execution of his duties or following the instructions given by his employer, the employer exclusively shall be entitled to exercise all economic rights in the program so created, unless otherwise provided by contract.

Article 3   Beneficiaries of protection

Protection shall be granted to all natural or legal persons eligible under national copyright legislation as applied to literary works.

Article 4   Restricted Acts

Subject to the provisions of Articles 5 and 6, the exclusive rights of the rightholder within the meaning of Article 2, shall include the right to do or to authorize:

(a)   the permanent or temporary reproduction of a computer program by any means and in any form, in part or in whole. Insofar as loading, displaying, running, transmission or storage of the computer program necessitate such reproduction, such acts shall be subject to authorisation by the rightholder;

(b)   the translation, adaptation, arrangement and any other alteration of a computer program and the reproduction of the results thereof, without prejudice to the rights of the person who alters the program;

(c)   any form of distribution to the public, including the rental, of the original computer program or of copies thereof. The first sale in the Community of a copy of a program by the rightholder or with his consent shall exhaust the distribution right within the Community of that copy, with the exception of the right to control further rental of the program or a copy thereof.

Article 5   Exceptions to the restricted acts

1.   In the absence of specific contractual provisions, the acts referred to in Article 4(a) and (b) shall not require authorisation by the rightholder where they are necessary for the use of the computer program by the lawful acquirer in accordance with its intended purpose, including for error correction.

2.   The making of a back-up copy by a person having a right to use the computer program may not be prevented by contract insofar as it is necessary for that use.

3.   The person having a right to use a copy of a computer program shall be entitled, without the authorisation of the rightholder, to observe, study or test the functioning of the program in order to determine the ideas and principles which underlie any element of the program if he does so while performing any of the acts of loading, displaying, running, transmitting or storing the program which he is entitled to do.

Article 6   Decompilation

The authorisation of the rightholder shall not be required where reproduction of the code and translation of its form within the meaning of Article 4(a) and (b) are indispensable to obtain the information necessary to achieve the interoperability of an independently created computer program with other programs, provided that the following conditions are met:

(a)   these acts are performed by the licensee or by another person having a right to use a copy of a program, or on their behalf by a person authorized to do so;

(b)   the information necessary to achieve interoperability has not previously been readily available to the persons referred to in subparagraph (a); and

(c)   these acts are confined to the parts of the original program which are necessary to achieve interoperability.

2.   The provisions of paragraph 1 shall not permit the information obtained through its application:

(a)   to be used for goals other than to achieve the interoperability of the independently created computer program;

(b)   to be given to others, except when necessary for the interoperability of the independently created computer program; or

(c)   to be used for the development, production or marketing of a computer program substantially similar in its expression, or for any other act which infringes copyright.

3.   In accordance with the provisions of the Berne Convention for the protection of Literary and Artistic Works, the provisions of this Article may not

be interpreted in such a way as to allow its application to be used in a manner which unreasonably prejudices the rightholder's legitimate interests or conflicts with a normal exploitation of the computer program.

Article 7   Special measures of protection

1.   Without prejudice to the provisions of Articles 4, 5 and 6, Member States shall provide, in accordance with their national legislation, appropriate remedies against a person committing any of the acts listed in subparagraphs (a), (b) and (c) below:

(a)   any act of putting into circulation a copy of a computer program knowing, or having reason to believe, that it is an infringing copy;

(b)   the possession, for commercial purposes, of a copy of a computer program knowing, or having reason to believe, that it is an infringing copy;

(c)   any act of putting into circulation, or the possession for commercial purposes of, any means the sole intended purpose of which is to facilitate the unauthorized removal or circumvention of any technical device which may have been applied to protect a computer program.

2.   Any infringing copy of a computer program shall be liable to seizure in accordance with the legislation of the Member State concerned.

3.   Member States may provide for the seizure of any means referred to in paragraph 1(c).

Article 8

Editor's Note: Repealed by art. 11 of Directive 93/98 (OJ 1993 L290/36).

Article 9   Continued application of other legal provisions

1.   The provisions of this Directive shall be without prejudice to any other legal provisions such as those concerning patent rights, trade-marks, unfair competition, trade secrets, protection of semi-conductor products or the law of contract. Any contractual provisions contrary to Article 6 or to the exceptions provided for in Article 5(2) and (3) shall be null and void.

2.   The provisions of this Directive shall apply also to programs created before 1 January 1993 without prejudice to any acts concluded and rights acquired before that date.

Article 10   Final provisions

1.   Member States shall bring into force the laws, regulations and administrative provisions necessary to comply with this Directive before 1 January 1993.

When Member States adopt these measures, the latter shall contain a reference to this Directive or shall be accompanied by such reference on the occasion of their official publication. The methods of making such a reference shall be laid down by the Member States.

2.   Member States shall communicate to the Commission the provisions of national law which they adopt in the field governed by this Directive.

Article 11

This Directive is addressed to the Member States.

Done at Brussels, 14 May 1991.

(Signature omitted.)

DIRECTIVE 96/9/EC OF THE EUROPEAN PARLIAMENT AND OF THE COUNCIL OF 11 MARCH 1996 ON THE LEGAL PROTECTION OF DATABASES
[OJ 1996, No. L77/20]

THE EUROPEAN PARLIAMENT AND THE COUNCIL OF THE EUROPEAN UNION,

Having regard to the Treaty establishing the European Community, and in particular Article 57(2), 66 and 100a thereof,

Having regard to the proposal from the Commission,[1]

Having regard to the opinion of the Economic and Social Committee,[2]

Acting in accordance with the procedure laid down in Article 189b of the Treaty,[3]

(1)   Whereas databases are at present not sufficiently protected in all Member States by existing legislation; whereas such protection, where it exists, has different attributes;

(2)   Whereas such differences in the legal protection of databases offered by the legislation of the Member States have direct negative effects on the functioning of the internal market as regards databases and in particular on the freedom of natural and legal persons to provide on-line database goods and services on the basis of harmonised legal arrangements throughout the Community; whereas such differences could well become more pronounced as Member States introduce new legislation in this field, which is now taking on an increasingly international dimension;

(3)   Whereas existing differences distorting the functioning of the internal market need to be removed and new ones prevented from arising, while differences not adversely affecting the functioning of the internal market or the development of an information market within the Community need not be removed or prevented from arising;

(4)   Whereas copyright protection for databases exists in varying forms in the Member States according to legislation or case-law, and whereas, if differences in legislation in the scope and conditions of protection remain between the Member States, such unharmonised intellectual property rights can have the effect of preventing the free movement of goods or services within the Community;

(5)   Whereas copyright remains an appropriate form of exclusive right for authors who have created databases;

(6)   Whereas, nevertheless, in the absence of a harmonised system of unfair-competition legislation or of case-law, other measures are required in addition to prevent the unauthorised extraction and/or re-utilisation of the contents of a database;

(7)   Whereas the making of databases requires the investment of considerable human, technical and financial resources while such databases can be copied or accessed at a fraction of the cost needed to design them independently;

Notes
[1]OJ 1992 C156/4 and OJ 1993 C308/1.
[2]OJ No. C19, 25.1.1993, p. 3.
[3]OJ 1993 C194/144, and OJ 1995 C288/14.

(8)   Whereas the unauthorised extraction and/or re-utilisation of the contents of a database constitute acts which can have serious economic and technical consequences;

(9)   Whereas databases are a vital tool in the development of an information market within the Community; whereas this tool will also be of use in many other fields;

(10)   Whereas the exponential growth, in the Community and worldwide, in the amount of information generated and processed annually in all sectors of commerce and industry calls for investment in all the Member States in advanced information processing systems;

(11)   Whereas there is at present a very great imbalance in the level of investment in the database sector both as between the Member States and between the Community and the world's largest database-producing third countries;

(12)   Whereas such an investment in modern information storage and processing systems will not take place within the Community unless a stable and uniform legal protection regime is introduced for the protection of the rights of makers of databases;

(13)   Whereas this Directive protects collections, sometimes called 'compilations', of works, data or other materials which are arranged, stored and accessed by means which include electronic, electromagnetic or electro-optical processes or analogous processes;

(14)   Whereas protection under this Directive should be extended to cover non-electronic databases;

(15)   Whereas the criteria used to determine whether a database should be protected by copyright should be defined to the fact that the selection or the arrangement of the contents of the database is the author's own intellectual creation; whereas such protection should cover the structure of the database;

(16)   Whereas no criterion other than originality in the sense of the author's intellectual creation should be applied to determine the eligibility of the database for copyright protection, and in particular no aesthetic or qualitative criteria should be applied;

(17)   Whereas the term 'database' should be understood to include literary, artistic, musical or other collections of works or collections of other material such as texts, sound, images, numbers, facts, and data; whereas it should cover collections of independent works, data or other materials which are systematically or methodically arranged and can be individually accessed; whereas this means that a recording or an audio-visual, cinematographic, literary or musical work as such does not fall within the scope of this Directive;

(18)   Whereas this Directive is without prejudice to the freedom of authors to decide whether, or in what manner, they will allow their works to be included in a database, in particular whether or not the authorisation given is exclusive; whereas the protection of databases by the sui generis right is without prejudice to existing rights over their contents, and whereas in particular where an author or the holder of a related right permits some of his works or subject matter to be included in a database pursuant to a non-exclusive agreement, a third party may make use of those works or subject matter subject to the required consent of the author or of the holder of the related right without the sui generis right of the maker of the database being invoked to prevent him doing so, on condition that those works or subject matter are neither extracted from the database nor re-utilised on the basis thereof;

(19)   Whereas, as a rule, the compilation of several recordings of musical performances on a CD does not come within the scope of this Directive, both because, as a compilation, it does not meet the conditions for copyright protection and because it does not represent a substantial enough investment to be eligible under the sui generis right;

(20)   Whereas protection under this Directive may also apply to the materials necessary for the operation or consultation of certain databases such as thesaurus and indexation systems;

(21)   Whereas the protection provided for in this Directive relates to databases in which works, data or other materials have been arranged systematically or methodically; whereas it is not necessary for those materials to have been physically stored in an organised manner;

(22)   Whereas electronic databases within the meaning of this Directive may also include devices such as CD-ROM and CD-i;

(23)   Whereas the term 'database' should not be taken to extend to computer programs used in the making or operation of a database, which are protected by Council Directive 91/250/ EEC of 14 May 1991 on the legal protection of computer programs;[1]

(24)   Whereas the rental and lending of databases in the field of copyright and related rights are governed exclusively by Council Directive 92/100/EEC of 19 November 1992 on rental right and lending right and on certain rights related to copyright in the field of intellectual property;[2]

(25)   Whereas the term of copyright is already governed by Council Directive 93/98/EEC of 29 October 1993 harmonizing the term of protection of copyright and certain related rights;[3]

(26)   Whereas works protected by copyright and subject matter protected by related rights, which are incorporated into a database, remain nevertheless protected by the respective exclusive rights and may not be incorporated into, or extracted from, the database without the permission of the rightholder or his successors in title;

(27)   Whereas copyright in such works and related rights in subject matter thus incorporated into a database are in no way affected by the existence of a separate right in the selection or arrangement of these works and subject matter in a database;

(28)   Whereas the moral rights of the natural person who created the database belong to the author and should be exercised according to the legislation of the Member States and the provisions of the Berne Convention for the Protection of Literary and Artistic Works; whereas such moral rights remain outside the scope of this Directive;

(29)   Whereas the arrangements applicable to databases created by employees are left to the discretion of the Member States; whereas, therefore nothing in this Directive prevents Member States from stipulating in their legislation that where a database is created by an employee in the execution of his duties or following the instructions given by his employer, the employer exclusively shall be entitled to exercise all economic rights in the database so created, unless otherwise provided by contract;

Notes

[1] OJ 1991 L122/42.
[2] OJ No. L346, 27.11.1992, p. 61.
[3] OJ No. L290, 24.11.1993, p. 9.

(30)   Whereas the author's exclusive rights should include the right to determine the way in which his work is exploited and by whom, and in particular to control the distribution of his work to unauthorised persons;

(31)   Whereas the copyright protection of databases includes making databases available by means other than the distribution of copies;

(32)   Whereas Member States are required to ensure that their national provisions are at least materially equivalent in the case of such acts subject to restrictions as are provided for by this Directive;

(33)   Whereas the question of exhaustion of the right of distribution does not arise in the case of on-line databases, which come within the field of provision of services; whereas this also applies with regard to a material copy of such a database made by the user of such a service with the consent of the rightholder; whereas, unlike CD-ROM or CD-i, where the intellectual property is incorporated in a material medium, namely an item of goods, every on-line service is in fact an act which will have to be subject to authorisation where the copyright so provides;

(34)   Whereas, nevertheless, once the rightholder has chosen to make available a copy of the database to a user, whether by an on-line service or by other means of distribution, that lawful user must be able to access and use the database for the purposes and in the way set out in the agreement with the rightholder, even if such access and use necessitate performance of otherwise restricted acts;

(35)   Whereas a list should be drawn up of exceptions to restricted acts, taking into account the fact that copyright as covered by this Directive applies only to the selection or arrangements of the contents of a database; whereas Member States should be given the option of providing for such exceptions in certain cases; whereas, however, this option should be exercised in accordance with the Berne Convention and to the extent that the exceptions relate to the structure of the database; whereas a distinction should be drawn between exceptions for private use and exceptions for reproduction for private purposes, which concerns provisions under national legislation of some Member States on levies on blank media or recording equipment;

(36)   Whereas the term 'scientific research' within the meaning of this Directive covers both the natural sciences and the human sciences;

(37)   Whereas Article 10(1) of the Berne Convention is not affected by this Directive;

(38)   Whereas the increasing use of digital recording technology exposes the database maker to the risk that the contents of his database may be copied and rearranged electronically, without his authorisation, to produce a database of identical content which, however, does not infringe any copyright in the arrangement of his database;

(39)   Whereas, in addition to aiming to protect the copyright in the original selection or arrangement of the contents of a database, this Directive seeks to safeguard the position of makers of databases against misappropriation of the results of the financial and professional investment made in obtaining and collecting the contents by protecting the whole or substantial parts of a database against certain acts by a user or competitor;

(40)   Whereas the object of this sui generis right is to ensure protection of any investment in obtaining, verifying or presenting the contents of a database for the limited duration of the right; whereas such investment may consist in

the deployment of financial resources and/or the expending of time, effort and energy;

(41) Whereas the objective of the sui generis right is to give the maker of a database the option of preventing the unauthorised extraction and/or re-utilisation of all or a substantial part of the contents of that database; whereas the maker of a database is the person who takes the initiative and the risk of investing; whereas this excludes subcontractors in particular from the definition of maker;

(42) Whereas the special right to prevent unauthorised extraction and/or re-utilisation relates to acts by the user which go beyond his legitimate rights and thereby harm the investment; whereas the right to prohibit extraction and/or re-utilisation of all or a substantial part of the contents relates not only to the manufacture of a parasitical competing product but also to any user who, through his acts, causes significant detriment, evaluated qualitatively or quantitatively, to the investment;

(43) Whereas, in the case of on-line transmission, the right to prohibit re-utilisation is not exhausted either as regards the database or as regards a material copy of the database or of part thereof made by the addressee of the transmission with the consent of the rightholder;

(44) Whereas, when on-screen display of the contents of a database necessitates the permanent or temporary transfer of all or a substantial part of such contents to another medium, that act should be subject to authorisation by the rightholder;

(45) Whereas the right to prevent unauthorised extraction and/or re-utilisation does not in any way constitute an extension of copyright protection to mere facts or data;

(46) Whereas the existence of a right to prevent the unauthorised extraction and/or re-utilisation of the whole or a substantial part of works, data or materials from a database should not give rise to the creation of a new right in the works, data or materials themselves;

(47) Whereas, in the interests of competition between suppliers of information products and services, protection by the sui generis right must not be afforded in such a way as to facilitate abuses of a dominant position, in particular as regards the creation and distribution of new products and services which have an intellectual, documentary, technical, economic or commercial added value; whereas, therefore, the provisions of this Directive are without prejudice to the application of Community or national competition rules;

(48) Whereas the objective of this Directive, which is to afford an appropriate and uniform level of protection of databases as a means to secure the remuneration of the maker of the database, is different from the aim of Directive 95/46/EC of the European Parliament and of the Council of 24 October 1995 on the protection of individuals with regard to the processing of personal data and on the free movement of such data,[1] which is to guarantee free circulation of personal data on the basis of harmonised rules designed to protect fundamental rights, notably the right to privacy which is recognised in Article 8 of the European Convention for the Protection of Human Rights and

Note
[1] OJ No. L281, 23.11.1995, p. 31.

Fundamental Freedoms; whereas the provisions of this Directive are without prejudice to data protection legislation;

(49) Whereas, notwithstanding the right to prevent extraction and/or re-utilisation of all or a substantial part of a database, it should be laid down that the maker of a database or rightholder may not prevent a lawful user of the database from extracting and re-utilising insubstantial parts; whereas, however, that user may not unreasonably prejudice either the legitimate interests of the holder of the sui generis right or the holder of copyright or a related right in respect of the works or subject matter contained in the database;

(50) Whereas the Member States should be given the option of providing for exceptions to the right to prevent the unauthorised extraction and/or re-utilisation of a substantial part of the contents of a database in the case of extraction for private purposes, for the purposes of illustration for teaching or scientific research, or where extraction and/or re-utilisation are/is carried out in the interests of public security or for the purposes of an administrative or judicial procedure; whereas such operations must not prejudice the exclusive rights of the maker to exploit the database and their purpose must not be commercial;

(51) Whereas the Member States, where they avail themselves of the option to permit a lawful user of a database to extract a substantial part of the contents for the purposes of illustration for teaching or scientific research, may limit that permission to certain categories of teaching or scientific research institution;

(52) Whereas those Member States which have specific rules providing for a right comparable to the sui generis right provided for in this Directive should be permitted to retain, as far as the new right is concerned, the exceptions traditionally specified by such rules;

(53) Whereas the burden of proof regarding the date of completion of the making of a database lies with the maker of the database;

(54) Whereas the burden of proof that the criteria exist for concluding that a substantial modification of the contents of a database is to be regarded as a substantial new investment lies with the maker of the database resulting from such investment;

(55) Whereas a substantial new investment involving a new term of protection may include a substantial verification of the contents of the database;

(56) Whereas the right to prevent unauthorised extraction and/or re-utilisation in respect of a database should apply to databases whose makers are nationals or habitual residents of third countries or to those produced by legal persons not established in a Member State, within the meaning of the Treaty, only if such third countries offer comparable protection to databases produced by nationals of a Member State or persons who have their habitual residence in the territory of the Community;

(57) Whereas, in addition to remedies provided under the legislation of the Member States for infringements of copyright or other rights, Member States should provide for appropriate remedies against unauthorised extraction and/or re-utilisation of the contents of a database;

(58) Whereas, in addition to the protection given under this Directive to the structure of the database by copyright, and to its contents against

unauthorised extraction and/or re-utilisation under the sui generis right, other legal provisions in the Member States relevant to the supply of database goods and services continue to apply;

(59) Whereas this Directive is without prejudice to the application to databases composed of audio-visual works of any rules recognised by a Member State's legislation concerning the broadcasting of audio-visual programmes;

(60) Whereas some Member States currently protect under copyright arrangements databases which do not meet the criteria for eligibility for copyright protection laid down in this Directive; whereas, even if the databases concerned are eligible for protection under the right laid down in this Directive to prevent unauthorised extraction and/or re-utilisation of their contents, the term of protection under that right is considerably shorter than that which they enjoy under the national arrangements currently in force; whereas harmonization of the criteria for determining whether a database is to be protected by copyright may not have the effect of reducing the term of protection currently enjoyed by the rightholders concerned; whereas a derogation should be laid down to that effect; whereas the effects of such derogation must be confined to the territories of the Member States concerned,

HAVE ADOPTED THIS DIRECTIVE:

CHAPTER I   SCOPE

Article 1   Scope
1.   This Directive concerns the legal protection of databases in any form.
2.   For the purposes of this Directive, 'database' shall mean a collection of independent works, data or other materials arranged in a systematic or methodical way and individually accessible by electronic or other means.
3.   Protection under this Directive shall not apply to computer programs used in the making or operation of databases accessible by electronic means.

Article 2   Limitations on the scope
This Directive shall apply without prejudice to Community provisions relating to:
    (a)   the legal protection of computer programs;
    (b)   rental right, lending right and certain rights related to copyright in the field of intellectual property;
    (c)   the term of protection of copyright and certain related rights.

CHAPTER II   COPYRIGHT

Article 3   Object of protection
1.   In accordance with this Directive, databases which, by reason of the selection or arrangement of their contents, constitute the author's own intellectual creation shall be protected as such by copyright. No other criteria shall be applied to determine their eligibility for that protection.
2.   The copyright protection of databases provided for by this Directive shall not extend to their contents and shall be without prejudice to any rights subsisting in those contents themselves.

Article 4   Database authorship

1.   The author of a database shall be the natural person or group of natural persons who created the base or, where the legislation of the Member States so permits, the legal person designated as the rightholder by that legislation.

2.   Where collective works are recognised by the legislation of a Member State, the economic rights shall be owned by the person holding the copyright.

3.   In respect of a database created by a group of natural persons jointly, the exclusive rights shall be owned jointly.

Article 5   Restricted acts

In respect of the expression of the database which is protectable by copyright, the author of a database shall have the exclusive right to carry out or to authorise:

(a)   temporary or permanent reproduction by any means and in any form, in whole or in part;

(b)   translation, adaptation, arrangement and any other alteration;

(c)   any form of distribution to the public of the database or of copies thereof. The first sale in the Community of a copy of the database by the rightholder or with his consent shall exhaust the right to control resale of that copy within the Community;

(d)   any communication, display or performance to the public;

(e)   any reproduction, distribution, communication, display or perform-ance to the public of the results of the acts referred to in (b).

Article 6   Exceptions to restricted acts

1.   The performance by the lawful user of a database or of a copy thereof of any of the acts listed in Article 5 which is necessary for the purposes of access to the contents of the databases and normal use of the contents by the lawful user shall not require the authorisation of the author of the database. Where the lawful user is authorised to use only part of the database, this provision shall apply only to that part.

2.   Member States shall have the option of providing for limitations on the rights set out in Article 5 in the following cases:

(a)   in the case of reproduction for private purposes of a non-electronic database;

(b)   where there is use for the sole purpose of illustration for teaching or scientific research, as long as the source is indicated and to the extent justified by the non-commercial purpose to be achieved;

(c)   where there is use for the purposes of public security or for the purposes of an administrative or judicial procedure;

(d)   where other exceptions to copyright which are traditionally authorised under national law are involved, without prejudice to points (a), (b) and (c).

3.   In accordance with the Berne Convention for the Protection of Literary and Artistic Works, this Article may not be interpreted in such a way as to allow its application to be used in a manner which unreasonably prejudices the rightholder's legitimate interests or conflicts with normal exploitation of the database.

CHAPTER III   SUI GENERIS RIGHT

Article 7   Object of protection

1.   Member States shall provide for a right for the maker of a database which shows that there has been qualitatively and/or quantitatively a substantial investment in either the obtaining, verification or presentation of the contents to prevent extraction and/or re-utilisation of the whole or of a substantial part, evaluated qualitatively and/or quantitatively, of the contents of that database.

2.   For the purposes of this Chapter:

(a)   'extraction' shall mean the permanent or temporary transfer of all or a substantial part of the contents of a database to another medium by any means or in any form;

(b)   're-utilisation' shall mean any form of making available to the public all or a substantial part of the contents of a database by the distribution of copies, by renting, by on-line or other forms of transmission. The first sale of a copy of a database within the Community by the rightholder or with his consent shall exhaust the right to control resale of that copy within the Community; Public lending is not an act of extraction or re-utilisation.

3.   The right referred to in paragraph 1 may be transferred, assigned or granted under contractual licence.

4.   The right provided for in paragraph 1 shall apply irrespective of the eligibility of that database for protection by copyright or by other rights. Moreover, it shall apply irrespective of eligibility of the contents of that database for protection by copyright or by other rights. Protection of databases under the right provided for in paragraph 1 shall be without prejudice to rights existing in respect of their contents.

5.   The repeated and systematic extraction and/or re-utilisation of insubstantial parts of the contents of the database implying acts which conflict with a normal exploitation of that database or which unreasonably prejudice the legitimate interests of the maker of the database shall not be permitted.

Article 8   Rights and obligations of lawful users

1.   The maker of a database which is made available to the public in whatever manner may not prevent a lawful user of the database from extracting and/or re-utilising insubstantial parts of its contents, evaluated qualitatively and/or quantitatively, for any purposes whatsoever. Where the lawful user is authorised to extract and/or re-utilise only part of the database, this paragraph shall apply only to that part.

2.   A lawful user of a database which is made available to the public in whatever manner may not perform acts which conflict with normal exploitation of the database or unreasonably prejudice the legitimate interests of the maker of the database.

3.   A lawful user of a database which is made available to the public in any manner may not cause prejudice to the holder of a copyright or related right in respect of the works or subject matter contained in the database.

Article 9   Exceptions to the sui generis right

Member States may stipulate that lawful users of a database which is made available to the public in whatever manner may, without the authorisation of its maker, extract or re-utilise a substantial part of its contents:

(a)   in the case of extraction for private purposes of the contents of a non-electronic database;

(b)   in the case of extraction for the purposes of illustration for teaching or scientific research, as long as the source is indicated and to the extent justified by the non-commercial purpose to be achieved;

(c)   in the case of extraction and/or re-utilisation for the purposes of public security or an administrative or judicial procedure.

Article 10   Term of protection

1.   The right provided for in Article 7 shall run from the date of completion of the making of the database. It shall expire fifteen years from the first of January of the year following the date of completion.

2.   In the case of a database which is made available to the public in whatever manner before expiry of the period provided for in paragraph 1, the term of protection by that right shall expire fifteen years from the first of January of the year following the date when the database was first made available to the public.

3.   Any substantial change, evaluated qualitatively or quantitatively, to the contents of a database, including any substantial change resulting from the accumulation of successive additions, deletions or alterations, which would result in the database being considered to be a substantial new investment, evaluated qualitatively or quantitatively, shall qualify the database resulting from that investment for its own term of protection.

Article 11   Beneficiaries of protection under the sui generis right

1.   The right provided for in Article 7 shall apply to databases whose makers or rightholders are nationals of a Member State or who have their habitual residence in the territory of the Community.

2.   Paragraph 1 shall also apply to companies and firms formed in accordance with the law of a Member State and having their registered office, central administration or principal place of business within the Community; however, where such a company or firm has only its registered office in the territory of the Community, its operations must be genuinely linked on an ongoing basis with the economy of a Member State.

3.   Agreements extending the right provided for in Article 7 to databases made in third countries and falling outside the provisions of paragraphs 1 and 2 shall be concluded by the Council acting on a proposal from the Commission. The term of any protection extended to databases by virtue of that procedure shall not exceed that available pursuant to Article 10.

CHAPTER IV   COMMON PROVISIONS

Article 12   Remedies

Member States shall provide appropriate remedies in respect of infringements of the rights provided for in this Directive.

Article 13   Continued application of other legal provisions

This Directive shall be without prejudice to provisions concerning in particular copyright, rights related to copyright or any other rights or obligations subsisting in the data, works or other materials incorporated into a database, patent rights, trade marks, design rights, the protection of national treasures, laws on restrictive practices and unfair competition, trade secrets, security, confidentiality, data protection and privacy, access to public documents, and the law of contract.

Article 14 Application over time

1. Protection pursuant to this Directive as regards copyright shall also be available in respect of databases created prior to the date referred to Article 16 (1) which on that date fulfil the requirements laid down in this Directive as regards copyright protection of databases.

2. Notwithstanding paragraph 1, where a database protected under copyright arrangements in a Member State on the date of publication of this Directive does not fulfil the eligibility criteria for copyright protection laid down in Article 3 (1), this Directive shall not result in any curtailing in that Member State of the remaining term of protection afforded under those arrangements.

3. Protection pursuant to the provisions of this Directive as regards the right provided for in Article 7 shall also be available in respect of databases the making of which was completed not more than fifteen years prior to the date referred to in Article 16 (1) and which on that date fulfil the requirements laid down in Article 7.

4. The protection provided for in paragraphs 1 and 3 shall be without prejudice to any acts concluded and rights acquired before the date referred to in those paragraphs.

5. In the case of a database the making of which was completed not more than fifteen years prior to the date referred to in Article 16 (1), the term of protection by the right provided for in Article 7 shall expire fifteen years from the first of January following that date.

Article 15 Binding nature of certain provisions

Any contractual provision contrary to Articles 6 (1) and 8 shall be null and void.

Article 16 Final provisions

1. Member States shall bring into force the laws, regulations and administrative provisions necessary to comply with this Directive before 1 January 1998.

When Member States adopt these provisions, they shall contain a reference to this Directive or shall be accompanied by such reference on the occasion of their official publication. The methods of making such reference shall be laid down by Member States.

2. Member States shall communicate to the Commission the text of the provisions of domestic law which they adopt in the field governed by this Directive.

3. Not later than at the end of the third year after the date referred to in paragraph 1, and every three years thereafter, the Commission shall submit to the European Parliament, the Council and the Economic and Social Committee a report on the application of this Directive, in which, inter alia, on the basis of specific information supplied by the Member States, it shall examine in particular the application of the sui generis right, including Articles 8 and 9, and shall verify especially whether the application of this right has led to abuse of a dominant position or other interference with free competition which would justify appropriate measures being taken, including the establishment of

non-voluntary licensing arrangements. Where necessary, it shall submit proposals for adjustment of this Directive in line with developments in the area of databases.

Article 17
This Directive is addressed to the Member States.

Done at Strasbourg, 11 March 1996.
For the European Parliament
The President
K. HAENSCH

For the Council
The President
L. DINI

DIRECTIVE 97/36/EC OF THE EUROPEAN PARLIAMENT AND OF THE COUNCIL OF 30 JUNE 1997 AMENDING COUNCIL DIRECTIVE 89/552/EEC ON THE COORDINATION OF CERTAIN PROVISIONS LAID DOWN BY LAW, REGULATION OR ADMINISTRATIVE ACTION IN MEMBER STATES CONCERNING THE PURSUIT OF TELEVISION BROADCASTING ACTIVITIES
[OJ 1997, No. L220/60]

THE EUROPEAN PARLIAMENT AND THE COUNCIL OF THE EUROPEAN UNION,

Having regard to the Treaty establishing the European Community, and in particular Articles 57(2) and 66 thereof,
    Having regard to the proposal from the Commission,[1]
    Having regard to the opinion of the Economic and Social Committee,[2]
    Acting in accordance with the procedure laid down in Article 189b of the Treaty[3] in the light of the joint text approved by the Conciliation Committee on 16 April 1997,

    (1)   Whereas Council Directive 89/552/EEC[4] constitutes the legal framework for television broadcasting in the internal market;
    (2)   Whereas Article 26 of Directive 89/552/EEC states that the Commission shall, not later than the end of the fifth year after the date of adoption of the Directive, submit to the European Parliament, the Council and the Economic and Social Committee a report on the application of the Directive and, if necessary, make further proposals to adapt it to developments in the field of television broadcasting;
    (3)   Whereas the application of Directive 89/552/EEC and the report on its application have revealed the need to clarify certain definitions or obligations on Member States under this Directive;

Notes
[1] OJ No. C185, 19.7.1995, p. 4 and OJ No. C221, 30.7.1996, p. 10.
[2] OJ No. C301, 13.11.1995, p. 35.
[3] Opinion of the European Parliament of 14 February 1996 [OJ No. C65, 4.3.1996, p. 113]. Council Common Position of 18 July 1996 [OJ No. C264, 11.9.1996, p. 52] and Decision of the European Parliament of 12 November 1996 [OJ No. C362, 2.12.1996, p. 56]. Decision of the European Parliament of 10 June 1997 and Decision of the Council of 19 June 1997.
[4] OJ No. L298, 17.10.1989, p. 23. Directive as amended by the 1994 Act of Accession.

(4)   Whereas the Commission, in its communication of 19 July 1994 entitled 'Europe's way to the information society: an action plan', underlined the importance of a regulatory framework applying to the content of audiovisual services which would help to safeguard the free movement of such services in the Community and be responsive to the opportunities for growth in this sector opened up by new technologies, while at the same time taking into account the specific nature, in particular the cultural and sociological impact, of audiovisual programmes, whatever their mode of transmission;

(5)   Whereas the Council welcomed this action plan at its meeting of 28 September 1994 and stressed the need to improve the competitiveness of the European audiovisual industry;

(6)   Whereas the Commission has submitted a Green Paper on the Protection of Minors and Human Dignity in audiovisual and information services and has undertaken to submit a Green Paper focusing on developing the cultural aspects of these new services;

(7)   Whereas any legislative framework concerning new audiovisual services must be compatible with the primary objective of this Directive which is to create the legal framework for the free movement of services;

(8)   Whereas it is essential that the Member States should take action with regard to services comparable to television broadcasting in order to prevent any breach of the fundamental principles which must govern information and the emergence of wide disparities as regards free movement and competition;

(9)   Whereas the Heads of State and Government meeting at the European Council in Essen on 9 and 10 December 1994 called on the Commission to present a proposal for a revision of Directive 89/552/EEC before their next meeting;

(10)   Whereas the application of Directive 89/552/EEC has revealed the need to clarify the concept of jurisdiction as applied specifically to the audiovisual sector; whereas, in view of the case law of the Court of Justice of the European Communities, the establishment criterion should be made the principal criterion determining the jurisdiction of a particular Member State;

(11)   Whereas the concept of establishment, according to the criteria laid down by the Court of Justice in its judgment of 25 July 1991 in the Factortame case,[5] involves the actual pursuit of an economic activity through a fixed establishment for an indefinite period;

(12)   Whereas the establishment of a television broadcasting organization may be determined by a series of practical criteria such as the location of the head office of the provider of services, the place where decisions on programming policy are usually taken, the place where the programme to be broadcast to the public is finally mixed and processed, and the place where a significant proportion of the workforce required for the pursuit of the television broadcasting activity is located;

(13)   Whereas the fixing of a series of practical criteria is designed to determine by an exhaustive procedure that one Member State and one only has jurisdiction over a broadcaster in connection with the provision of the services which this Directive addresses; nevertheless, taking into account the case law of the Court of Justice and so as to avoid cases where there is a vacuum of

Note
[5] Case C-221/89. *Queen* v *Secretary of State for Transport, ex parte Factortame Ltd and Others* (1991) ECR I-3905, paragraph 20.

jurisdiction it is appropriate to refer to the criterion of establishment within the meaning of Articles 52 and following of the Treaty establishing the European Community as the final criterion determining the jurisdiction of a Member State;

(14)   Whereas the Court of Justice has constantly held[6] that a Member State retains the right to take measures against a television broadcasting organization that is established in another Member State but directs all or most of its activity to the territory of the first Member State if the choice of establishment was made with a view to evading the legislation that would have applied to the organization had it been established on the territory of the first Member State;

(15)   Whereas Article F (2) of the Treaty on European Union stipulates that the Union shall respect fundamental rights as guaranteed by the European Convention for the Protection of Human Rights and Fundamental Freedoms as general principles of Community law; whereas any measure aimed at restricting the reception and/or suspending the retransmission of television broadcasts taken under Article 2a of Directive 89/552/EEC as amended by this Directive must be compatible with such principles;

(16)   Whereas it is necessary to ensure the effective application of the provisions of Directive 89/552/EEC as amended by this Directive throughout the Community in order to preserve free and fair competition between firms in the same industry;

(17)   Whereas directly affected third parties, including nationals of other Member States, must be able to assert their rights, according to national law, before competent judicial or other authorities of the Member State with jurisdiction over the television broadcasting organization that may be failing to comply with the national provisions arising out of the application of Directive 89/552/EEC as amended by this Directive;

(18)   Whereas it is essential that Member States should be able to take measures to protect the right to information and to ensure wide access by the public to television coverage of national or non-national events of major importance for society, such as the Olympic games, the football World Cup and European football championship; whereas to this end Member States retain the right to take measures compatible with Community law aimed at regulating the exercise by broadcasters under their jurisdiction of exclusive broadcasting rights to such events;

(19)   Whereas it is necessary to make arrangements within a Community framework, in order to avoid potential legal uncertainty and market distortions and to reconcile free circulation of television services with the need to prevent the possibility of circumvention of national measures protecting a legitimate general interest;

(20)   Whereas, in particular, it is appropriate to lay down in this Directive provisions concerning the exercise by broadcasters of exclusive broadcasting rights that they may have purchased to events considered to be of major importance for society in a Member State other than that having jurisdiction over the broadcasters, and whereas, in order to avoid speculative rights

Note
[6]See, in particular, the judgments in Case 33/74, *Van Binsbergen* ʌ *Bestuur van de Bedrijfsvereniging,* (1974) ECR 1299 and in Case C-23/93, *TV 10 SA* v *Commissariaat voor de Media,* (1994) ECR I-4795.

purchases with a view to circumvention of national measures, it is necessary to apply these provisions to contracts entered into after the publication of this Directive and concerning events which take place after the date of implementation, and whereas, when contracts that predate the publication of this Directive are renewed, they are considered to be new contracts;

(21) Whereas events of major importance for society should, for the purposes of this Directive, meet certain criteria, that is to say be outstanding events which are of interest to the general public in the European Union or in a given Member State or in an important component part of a given Member State and are organised in advance by an event organiser who is legally entitled to sell the rights pertaining to that event;

(22) Whereas, for the purposes of this Directive, 'free television' means broadcasting on a channel, either public or commercial, of programmes which are accessible to the public without payment in addition to the modes of funding of broadcasting that are widely prevailing in each Member State (such as licence fee and/or the basic tier subscription fee to a cable network);

(23) Whereas Member States are free to take whatever measures they deem appropriate with regard to broadcasts which come from third countries and which do not satisfy the conditions laid down in Article 2 of Directive 89/552/EEC as amended by this Directive, provided they comply with Community law and the international obligations of the Community;

(24) Whereas in order to eliminate the obstacles arising from differences in national legislation on the promotion of European works, Directive 89/552/EEC as amended by this Directive contains provisions aimed at harmonizing such legislation; whereas those provisions which, in general, seek to liberalise trade must contain clauses harmonizing the conditions of competition;

(25) Whereas, moreover, Article 128(4) of the Treaty establishing the European Community requires the Community to take cultural aspects into account in its action under other provisions of the Treaty;

(26) Whereas the Green Paper on 'Strategy options to strengthen the European programme industry in the context of the audiovisual policy of the European Union', adopted by the Commission on 7 April 1994, puts forward inter alia measures to promote European works in order to further the development of the sector; whereas the Media II programme, which seeks to promote training, development and distribution in the audiovisual sector, is also designed to enable the production of European works to be developed; whereas the Commission has proposed that production of European works should also be promoted by a Community mechanism such as a Guarantee Fund;

(27) Whereas broadcasting organisations, programme makers, producers, authors and other experts should be encouraged to develop more detailed concepts and strategies aimed at developing European audiovisual fiction films that are addressed to an international audience;

(28) Whereas, in addition to the considerations cited above, it is necessary to create conditions for improving the competitiveness of the programme industry; whereas the communications on the application of Articles 4 and 5 of Directive 89/552/EEC, adopted by the Commission on 3 March 1994 and 15 July 1996 pursuant to Article 4(3) of that Directive, draw the conclusion that measures to promote European works can contribute to such an improvement but that they need to take account of developments in the field of television broadcasting;

(29)   Whereas channels broadcasting entirely in a language other than those of the Member States should not be covered by the provisions of Articles 4 and 5; whereas, nevertheless, where such a language or languages represent a substantial part but not all of the channel's transmission time, the provisions of Articles 4 and 5 should not apply to that part of transmission time;

(30)   Whereas the proportions of European works must be achieved taking economic realities into account; whereas, therefore, a progressive system for achieving this objective is required;

(31)   Whereas, with a view to promoting the production of European works, it is essential that the Community, taking into account the audiovisual capacity of each Member State and the need to protect lesser used languages of the European Union, should promote independent producers; whereas Member States, in defining the notion of 'independent producer', should take appropriate account of criteria such as the ownership of the production company, the amount of programmes supplied to the same broadcaster and the ownership of secondary rights;

(32)   Whereas the question of specific time scales for each type of television showing of cinematographic works is primarily a matter to be settled by means of agreements between the interested parties or professionals concerned;

(33)   Whereas advertising for medicinal products for human use is subject to the provisions of Directive 92/28/EEC;[7]

(34)   Whereas daily transmission time allotted to announcements made by the broadcaster in connection with its own programmes and ancillary products directly derived from these, or to public service announcements and charity appeals broadcast free of charge, is not to be included in the maximum amounts of daily or hourly transmission time that may be allotted to advertising and teleshopping;

(35)   Whereas, in order to avoid distortions of competition, this derogation is limited to announcements concerning products that fulfil the dual condition of being both ancillary to and directly derived from the programmes concerned; whereas the term ancillary refers to products intended specifically to allow the viewing public to benefit fully from or to interact with these programmes;

(36)   Whereas in view of the development of teleshopping, an economically important activity for operators as a whole and a genuine outlet for goods and services within the Community, it is essential to modify the rules on transmission time and to ensure a high level of consumer protection by putting in place appropriate standards regulating the form and content of such broadcasts;

(37)   Whereas it is important for the competent national authorities, in monitoring the implementation of the relevant provisions, to be able to distinguish, as regards channels not exclusively devoted to teleshopping, between transmission time devoted to teleshopping spots, advertising spots and other forms of advertising on the one hand and, on the other, transmission time devoted to teleshopping windows; whereas it is therefore necessary and sufficient that each window be clearly identified by optical and acoustic means at least at the beginning and the end of the window;

(38)   Whereas Directive 89/552/EEC as amended by this Directive applies to channels exclusively devoted to teleshopping or self-promotion, without

Note
[7]OJ No. L113, 30.4.1992, p. 13.

conventional programme elements such as news, sports, films, documentaries and drama, solely for the purposes of these Directives and without prejudice to the inclusion of such channels in the scope of other Community instruments;

(39)   Whereas it is necessary to make clear that self-promotional activities are a particular form of advertising in which the broadcaster promotes its own products, services, programmes or channels; whereas, in particular, trailers consisting of extracts from programmes should be treated as programmes; whereas self-promotion is a new and relatively unknown phenomenon and provisions concerning it may therefore be particularly subject to review in future examinations of this Directive;

(40)   Whereas it is necessary to clarify the rules for the protection of the physical, mental and moral development of minors; whereas the establishment of a clear distinction between programmes that are subject to an absolute ban and those that may be authorised subject to the use of appropriate technical means should satisfy concern about the public interest expressed by Member States and the Community;

(41)   Whereas none of the provisions of this Directive that concern the protection of minors and public order requires that the measures in question must necessarily be implemented through the prior control of television broadcasts;

(42)   Whereas an investigation by the Commission, in liaison with the competent Member State authorities, of the possible advantages and drawbacks of further measures to facilitate the control exercised by parents or guardians over the programmes that minors may watch shall consider, inter alia, the desirability of:

— the requirement for new television sets to be equipped with a technical device enabling parents or guardians to filter out certain programmes,

— the setting up of appropriate rating systems,

— encouraging family viewing policies and other educational and awareness measures,

— taking into account experience gained in this field in Europe and elsewhere as well as the views of interested parties such as broadcasters, producers, educationalists, media specialists and relevant associations, with a view to presenting, if necessary before the deadline laid down in Article 26, appropriate proposals for legislative or other measures;

(43)   Whereas it is appropriate to amend Directive 89/552/EEC to allow natural or legal persons whose activities include the manufacture or the sale of medicinal products and medical treatment available only on prescription to sponsor television programmes, provided that such sponsorship does not circumvent the prohibition of television advertising for medicinal products and medical treatment available only on prescription;

(44)   Whereas the approach in Directive 89/552/EEC and this Directive has been adopted to achieve the essential harmonization necessary and sufficient to ensure the free movement of television broadcasts in the Community; whereas Member States remain free to apply to broadcasters under their jurisdiction more detailed or stricter rules in the fields co-ordinated by this Directive, including, inter alia, rules concerning the achievement of language policy goals, protection of the public interest in terms of television's role as a provider of information, education, culture and entertainment, the need to safeguard

pluralism in the information industry and the media, and the protection of competition with a view to avoiding the abuse of dominant positions and/or the establishment or strengthening of dominant positions by mergers, agreements, acquisitions or similar initiatives; whereas such rules must be compatible with Community law;

(45) Whereas the objective of supporting audiovisual production in Europe can be pursued within the Member States in the framework of the organization of their broadcasting services, inter alia, through the definition of a public interest mission for certain broadcasting organisations, including the obligation to contribute substantially to investment in European production;

(46) Whereas Article B of the Treaty on European Union states that one of the objectives the Union shall set itself is to maintain in full the 'acquis communautaire',

HAVE ADOPTED THIS DIRECTIVE:

Article 1

Directive 89/552/EEC is hereby amended as follows:

1. in Article 1:

   (a) the following new point (b) shall be inserted:

   '(b) "broadcaster" means the natural or legal person who has editorial responsibility for the composition of schedules of television programmes within the meaning of (a) and who transmits them or has them transmitted by third parties;'

   (b) the former point (b) shall become point (c) and shall read as follows:

   '(c) "television advertising" means any form of announcement broadcast whether in return for payment or for similar consideration or broadcast for self-promotional purposes by a public or private undertaking in connection with a trade, business, craft or profession in order to promote the supply of goods or services, including immovable property, rights and obligations, in return for payment;'

   (c) the former points (c) and (d) shall become points (d) and (e);

   (d) the following point shall be added:

   '(f) "teleshopping" means direct offers broadcast to the public with a view to the supply of goods or services, including immovable property, rights and obligations, in return for payment.';

2. Article 2 shall be replaced by the following:

'Article 2

1. Each Member State shall ensure that all television broadcasts transmitted by broadcasters under its jurisdiction comply with the rules of the system of law applicable to broadcasts intended for the public in that Member State.

2. For the purposes of this Directive the broadcasters under the jurisdiction of a Member State are:

   — those established in that Member State in accordance with paragraph 3;

   — those to whom paragraph 4 applies.

3. For the purposes of this Directive, a broadcaster shall be deemed to be established in a Member State in the following cases:

(a)   the broadcaster has its head office in that Member State and the editorial decisions about programme schedules are taken in that Member State;

(b)   if a broadcaster has its head office in one Member State but editorial decisions on programme schedules are taken in another Member State, it shall be deemed to be established in the Member State where a significant part of the workforce involved in the pursuit of the television broadcasting activity operates; if a significant part of the workforce involved in the pursuit of the television broadcasting activity operates in each of those Member States, the broadcaster shall be deemed to be established in the Member State where it has its head office; if a significant part of the workforce involved in the pursuit of the television broadcasting activity operates in neither of those Member States, the broadcaster shall be deemed to be established in the Member State where it first began broadcasting in accordance with the system of law of that Member State, provided that it maintains a stable and effective link with the economy of that Member State;

(c)   if a broadcaster has its head office in a Member State but decisions on programme schedules are taken in a third country, or vice-versa, it shall be deemed to be established in the Member State concerned, provided that a significant part of the workforce involved in the pursuit of the television broadcasting activity operates in that Member State.

4.   Broadcasters to whom the provisions of paragraph 3 are not applicable shall be deemed to be under the jurisdiction of a Member State in the following cases:

(a)   they use a frequency granted by that Member State;

(b)   although they do not use a frequency granted by a Member State they do use a satellite capacity appertaining to that Member State;

(c)   although they use neither a frequency granted by a Member State nor a satellite capacity appertaining to a Member State they do use a satellite up-link situated in that Member State.

5.   If the question as to which Member State has jurisdiction cannot be determined in accordance with paragraphs 3 and 4, the competent Member State shall be that in which the broadcaster is established within the meaning of Articles 52 and following of the Treaty establishing the European Community.

6.   This Directive shall not apply to broadcasts intended exclusively for reception in third countries, and which are not received directly or indirectly by the public in one or more Member States.';

3.   the following Article shall be inserted:

'**Article 2a**

1.   Member States shall ensure freedom of reception and shall not restrict retransmissions on their territory of television broadcasts from other Member States for reasons which fall within the fields co-ordinated by this Directive.

2.   Member States may, provisionally, derogate from paragraph 1 if the following conditions are fulfilled:

(a)   a television broadcast coming from another Member State manifestly, seriously and gravely infringes Article 22(1) or (2) and/or Article 22a;

(b)   during the previous 12 months, the broadcaster has infringed the provision(s) referred to in (a) on at least two prior occasions;

(c)   the Member State concerned has notified the broadcaster and the Commission in writing of the alleged infringements and of the measures it intends to take should any such infringement occur again;

(d)   consultations with the transmitting Member State and the Commission have not produced an amicable settlement within 15 days of the notification provided for in (c), and the alleged infringement persists.

The Commission shall, within two months following notification of the measures taken by the Member State, take a decision on whether the measures are compatible with Community law. If it decides that they are not, the Member State will be required to put an end to the measures in question as a matter of urgency.

3.   Paragraph 2 shall be without prejudice to the application of any procedure, remedy or sanction to the infringements in question in the Member State which has jurisdiction over the broadcaster concerned.';

4.   Article 3 shall be replaced by the following:

'**Article 3**

1.   Member States shall remain free to require television broadcasters under their jurisdiction to comply with more detailed or stricter rules in the areas covered by this Directive.

2.   Member States shall, by appropriate means, ensure, within the framework of their legislation, that television broadcasters under their jurisdiction effectively comply with the provisions of this Directive.

3.   The measures shall include the appropriate procedures for third parties directly affected, including nationals of other Member States, to apply to the competent judicial or other authorities to seek effective compliance according to national provisions.

Article 3a

1.   Each Member State may take measures in accordance with Community law to ensure that broadcasters under its jurisdiction do not broadcast on an exclusive basis events which are regarded by that Member State as being of major importance for society in such a way as to deprive a substantial proportion of the public in that Member State of the possibility of following such events via live coverage or deferred coverage on free television. If it does so, the Member State concerned shall draw up a list of designated events, national or non-national, which it considers to be of major importance for society. It shall do so in a clear and transparent manner in due and effective time. In so doing the Member State concerned shall also determine whether these events should be available via whole or partial live coverage, or where necessary or appropriate for objective reasons in the public interest, whole or partial deferred coverage.

2.   Member States shall immediately notify to the Commission any measures taken or to be taken pursuant to paragraph 1. Within a period of three months from the notification, the Commission shall verify that such measures are compatible with Community law and communicate them to the other Member States. It shall seek the opinion of the Committee established pursuant to Article 23a. It shall forthwith publish the measures taken in the Official Journal of the European Communities and at least once a year the consolidated list of the measures taken by Member States.

3. Member States shall ensure, by appropriate means, within the framework of their legislation that broadcasters under their jurisdiction do not exercise the exclusive rights purchased by those broadcasters following the date of publication of this Directive in such a way that a substantial proportion of the public in another Member State is deprived of the possibility of following events which are designated by that other Member State in accordance with the preceding paragraphs via whole or partial live coverage or, where necessary or appropriate for objective reasons in the public interest, whole or partial deferred coverage on free television as determined by that other Member State in accordance with paragraph 1.';

5. In Article 4(1), the words 'and teletext services' shall be replaced by the words 'teletext services and teleshopping';

6. In Article 5, the words 'and teletext services' shall be replaced by the words 'teletext services and teleshopping';

7. Article 6 shall be amended as follows:

(a) paragraph 1(a) shall be replaced by the following:

'(a) works originating from Member States';

(b) in paragraph 1, the following subparagraph shall be added:

'Application of the provisions of (b) and (c) shall be conditional on works originating from Member States not being the subject of discriminatory measures in the third countries concerned.';

(c) paragraph 3 shall be replaced by the following:

'3. The works referred to in paragraph 1(c) are works made exclusively or in co-production with producers established in one or more Member States by producers established in one or more European third countries with which the Community has concluded agreements relating to the audiovisual sector, if those works are mainly made with authors and workers residing in one or more European States.';

(d) paragraph 4 shall become paragraph 5 and the following paragraph shall be inserted:

'4. Works that are not European works within the meaning of paragraph 1 but that are produced within the framework of bilateral co-production treaties concluded between Member States and third countries shall be deemed to be European works provided that the Community co-producers supply a majority share of the total cost of the production and that the production is not controlled by one or more producers established outside the territory of the Member States.';

(e) in the new paragraph 5, the words 'paragraph 1' shall be replaced by the words 'paragraphs 1 and 4'.

8. Article 7 shall be replaced by the following:

'**Article 7**

Member States shall ensure that broadcasters under their jurisdiction do not broadcast cinematographic works outside periods agreed with the rights holders.';

9. Article 8 shall be deleted;

10. Article 9 shall be replaced by the following:

'**Article 9**

This Chapter shall not apply to television broadcasts that are intended for local audiences and do not form part of a national network.';

11. the title of Chapter IV shall be replaced by the following:

'Television advertising, sponsorship and teleshopping'.

12.   Article 10 shall be replaced by the following:

'**Article 10**

1.   Television advertising and teleshopping shall be readily recognisable as such and kept quite separate from other parts of the programme service by optical and/or acoustic means.

2.   Isolated advertising and teleshopping spots shall remain the exception.

3.   Advertising and teleshopping shall not use subliminal techniques.

4.   Surreptitious advertising and teleshopping shall be prohibited.';

13.   Article 11 shall be replaced by the following:

'**Article 11**

1.   Advertising and teleshopping spots shall be inserted between programmes. Provided the conditions set out in paragraphs 2 to 5 are fulfilled, advertising and teleshopping spots may also be inserted during programmes in such a way that the integrity and value of the programme, taking into account natural breaks in and the duration and nature of the programme, and the rights of the rights holders are not prejudiced.

2.   In programmes consisting of autonomous parts, or in sports programmes and similarly structured events and performances containing intervals, advertising and teleshopping spots shall only be inserted between the parts or in the intervals.

3.   The transmission of audiovisual works such as feature films and films made for television (excluding series, serials, light entertainment programmes and documentaries), provided their scheduled duration is more than 45 minutes, may be interrupted once for each period of 45 minutes. A further interruption shall be allowed if their scheduled duration is at least 20 minutes longer than two or more complete periods of 45 minutes.

4.   Where programmes, other than those covered by paragraph 2, are interrupted by advertising or teleshopping spots, a period of at least 20 minutes should elapse between each successive advertising break within the programme.

5.   Advertising and teleshopping shall not be inserted in any broadcast of a religious service. News and current affairs programmes, documentaries, religious programmes and children's programmes, when their scheduled duration is less than 30 minutes, shall not be interrupted by advertising or by teleshopping. If their scheduled duration is 30 minutes or longer, the provisions of the previous paragraphs shall apply.';

14.   In Article 12, the introductory words shall be replaced by the following: 'Television advertising and teleshopping shall not:';

15.   Article 13 shall be replaced by the following:

'**Article 13**

All forms of television advertising and teleshopping for cigarettes and other tobacco products shall be prohibited.';

16.   in Article 14, the present text shall become paragraph 1 and the following paragraph shall be added:

'2.   Teleshopping for medicinal products which are subject to a marketing authorisation within the meaning of Council Directive 65/65/EEC of 26 January 1965 on the approximation of provisions laid down by law, regulation or administrative action relating to medicinal products,* as well as teleshopping for medical treatment, shall be prohibited.'

17. In Article 15, the introductory words shall be replaced by the following: 'Television advertising and teleshopping for alcoholic beverages shall comply with the following criteria:';

18. In Article 16, the present text shall become paragraph 1 and the following paragraph shall be added:

'2. Teleshopping shall comply with the requirements referred to in paragraph 1 and, in addition, shall not exhort minors to contract for the sale or rental of goods and services.';

19. Article 17 shall be amended as follows:

(a) paragraph 2 shall be replaced by the following:

'2. Television programmes may not be sponsored by undertakings whose principal activity is the manufacture or sale of cigarettes and other tobacco products.';

(b) paragraph 3 shall become paragraph 4 and the following paragraph shall be inserted:

'3. Sponsorship of television programmes by undertakings whose activities include the manufacture or sale of medicinal products and medical treatment may promote the name or the image of the undertaking but may not promote specific medicinal products or medical treatments available only on prescription in the Member State within whose jurisdiction the broadcaster falls.';

20. Article 18 shall be replaced by the following:

'**Article 18**

1. The proportion of transmission time devoted to teleshopping spots, advertising spots and other forms of advertising, with the exception of teleshopping windows within the meaning of Article 18a, shall not exceed 20% of the daily transmission time. The transmission time for advertising spots shall not exceed 15% of the daily transmission time.

2. The proportion of advertising spots and teleshopping spots within a given clock hour shall not exceed 20%.

3. For the purposes of this Article, advertising does not include:

— announcements made by the broadcaster in connection with its own programmes and ancillary products directly derived from those programmes;

— public service announcements and charity appeals broadcast free of charge.';

21. The following Article shall be inserted:

'**Article 18a**

1. Windows devoted to teleshopping broadcast by a channel not exclusively devoted to teleshopping shall be of a minimum uninterrupted duration of 15 minutes.

2. The maximum number of windows per day shall be eight. Their overall duration shall not exceed three hours per day. They must be clearly identified as teleshopping windows by optical and acoustic means.';

Note

*OJ No. 22, 9.2.1965, p. 369. Directive as last amended by Directive 93/39/EEC [OJ No. L214, 24.8.1993, p. 22].

22.   Article 19 shall be replaced by the following:
'Article 19
Chapters I, II, IV, V, VI, VIa and VII shall apply mutatis mutandis to channels exclusively devoted to teleshopping. Advertising on such channels shall be allowed within the daily limits established by Article 18(1). Article 18(2) shall not apply.';

23.   The following Article shall be inserted:
'Article 19a
Chapters I, II, IV, V, VI, VIa and VII shall apply mutatis mutandis to channels exclusively devoted to self-promotion. Other forms of advertising on such channels shall be allowed within the limits established by Article 18(1) and (2). This provision in particular shall be subject to review in accordance with Article 26.';

24.   Article 20 shall be replaced by the following:
'Article 20
Without prejudice to Article 3, Member States may, with due regard for Community law, lay down conditions other than those laid down in Article 11(2) to (5) and Articles 18 and 18a in respect of broadcasts intended solely for the national territory which cannot be received, directly or indirectly by the public, in one or more other Member States.';

25.   Article 21 shall be deleted.

26.   The title of Chapter V shall be replaced by the following:
'Protection of minors and public order';

27.   Article 22 shall be replaced by the following:
'Article 22
   1.   Member States shall take appropriate measures to ensure that television broadcasts by broadcasters under their jurisdiction do not include any programmes which might seriously impair the physical, mental or moral development of minors, in particular programmes that involve pornography or gratuitous violence.
   2.   The measures provided for in paragraph 1 shall also extend to other programmes which are likely to impair the physical, mental or moral development of minors, except where it is ensured, by selecting the time of the broadcast or by any technical measure, that minors in the area of transmission will not normally hear or see such broadcasts.
   3.   Furthermore, when such programmes are broadcast in unencoded form Member States shall ensure that they are preceded by an acoustic warning or are identified by the presence of a visual symbol throughout their duration.';

28.   The following Article shall be inserted:
'Article 22a
Member States shall ensure that broadcasts do not contain any incitement to hatred on grounds of race, sex, religion or nationality.';

29.   The following Article shall be inserted:
'Article 22b
   1.   The Commission shall attach particular importance to application of this Chapter in the report provided for in Article 26.
   2. The Commission shall within one year from the date of publication of this Directive, in liaison with the competent Member State authorities, carry out an investigation of the possible advantages and drawbacks of further measures with a view to facilitating the control exercised by parents or

guardians over the programmes that minors may watch. This study shall consider, inter alia, the desirability of:

— the requirement for new television sets to be equipped with a technical device enabling parents or guardians to filter out certain programmes;

— the setting up of appropriate rating systems,

— encouraging family viewing policies and other educational and awareness measures,

— taking into account experience gained in this field in Europe and elsewhere as well as the views of interested parties such as broadcasters, producers, educationalists, media specialists and relevant associations.';

30.   Article 23(1) shall be replaced by the following:

'1.   Without prejudice to other provisions adopted by the Member States under civil, administrative or criminal law, any natural or legal person, regardless of nationality, whose legitimate interests, in particular reputation and good name, have been damaged by an assertion of incorrect facts in a television programme must have a right of reply or equivalent remedies. Member States shall ensure that the actual exercise of the right of reply or equivalent remedies is not hindered by the imposition of unreasonable terms or conditions. The reply shall be transmitted within a reasonable time subsequent to the request being substantiated and at a time and in a manner appropriate to the broadcast to which the request refers.';

31.   After Article 23, the following new Chapter VIa shall be inserted:

'CHAPTER VIa

Contact committee

Article 23a

1.   A contact committee shall be set up under the aegis of the Commission. It shall be composed of representatives of the competent authorities of the Member States. It shall be chaired by a representative of the Commission and meet either on his initiative or at the request of the delegation of a Member State.

2.   The tasks of this committee shall be:

(a)   to facilitate effective implementation of this Directive through regular consultation on any practical problems arising from its application, and particularly from the application of Article 2, as well as on any other matters on which exchanges of views are deemed useful;

(b)   to deliver own-initiative opinions or opinions requested by the Commission on the application by the Member States of the provisions of this Directive;

(c)   to be the forum for an exchange of views on what matters should be dealt with in the reports which Member States must submit pursuant to Article 4(3), on the methodology of these, on the terms of reference for the independent study referred to in Article 25a, on the evaluation of tenders for this and on the study itself;

(d)   to discuss the outcome of regular consultations which the Commission holds with representatives of broadcasting organisations, producers, consumers, manufacturers, service providers and trade unions and the creative community;

(e)   to facilitate the exchange of information between the Member States and the Commission on the situation and the development of regulatory activities regarding television broadcasting services, taking account of the Community's audiovisual policy, as well as relevant developments in the technical field;

(f) to examine any development arising in the sector on which an exchange of views appears useful.';

32. The following Article shall be inserted:

'**Article 25a**

A further review as provided for in Article 4 (4) shall take place before 30 June 2002. It shall take account of an independent study on the impact of the measures in question at both Community and national level.';

33. Article 26 shall be replaced by the following:

'**Article 26**

Not later than 31 December 2000, and every two years thereafter, the Commission shall submit to the European Parliament, the Council and the Economic and Social Committee a report on the application of this Directive as amended and, if necessary, make further proposals to adapt it to developments in the field of television broadcasting, in particular in the light of recent technological developments.

Article 2

1. Member States shall bring into force the laws, regulations and administrative provisions necessary to comply with this Directive not later than 31 December 1998. They shall immediately inform the Commission thereof.

When Member States adopt these measures, they shall contain a reference to this Directive or be accompanied by such reference on the occasion of their official publication. The methods of making such reference shall be laid down by Member States.

2. Member States shall communicate to the Commission the text of the main provisions of national law which they adopt in the field covered by this Directive.

Article 3

This Directive shall enter into force on the date of its publication in the Official Journal of the European Communities.

Article 4

This Directive is addressed to the Member States.

Done at Luxembourg, 30 June 1997.
For the Parliament
The President
J. M. GIL-ROBLES

For the Council
The President
A. NUIS

COMMISSION DECLARATION

Article 23a (1)
(Contact Committee)
The Commission undertakes, at its own responsibility, to inform the European Parliament's competent committee of the outcome of the meetings of the Contact Committee. It will provide that information in good time and in an appropriate manner.

PUBLIC UNDERTAKINGS

COUNCIL DIRECTIVE 89/665/EEC OF 21 DECEMBER 1989 ON THE COORDINATION OF THE LAWS, REGULATIONS AND ADMINISTRATIVE PROVISIONS RELATING TO THE APPLICATION OF REVIEW PROCEDURES TO THE AWARD OF PUBLIC SUPPLY AND PUBLIC WORKS CONTRACTS
[OJ 1989 L395/33]

THE COUNCIL OF THE EUROPEAN COMMUNITIES,

Having regard to the Treaty establishing the European Economic Community, and in particular Article 100a thereof,

Having regard to the proposal from the Commission,[1]

In cooperation with the European Parliament,[2]

Having regard to the opinion of the Economic and Social Committee,[3]

Whereas Community Directives on public procurement, in particular Council Directive 71/305/EEC of 26 July 1971 concerning the coordination of procedures for the award of public works contracts,[4] as last amended by Directive 89/440/EEC,[5] and Council Directive 77/62/EEC of 21 December 1976 coordinating procedures for the award of public supply contracts,[6] as last amended by Directive 88/295/EEC,[7] do not contain any specific provisions ensuring their effective application;

Whereas the existing arrangements at both national and Community levels for ensuring their application are not always adequate to ensure compliance with the relevant Community provisions particularly at a stage when infringements can be corrected;

Whereas the opening-up of public procurement to Community competition necessitates a substantial increase in the guarantees of transparency and non-discrimination; whereas, for it to have tangible effects, effective and rapid

Notes

[1] OJ No. C230, 28.8.1987, p. 6 and OJ No. C15, 19.1.1989, p. 8.

[2] OJ No. C167, 27.6.1988, p. 77 and OJ No. C323, 27.12.1989.

[3] OJ No. C347, 22.12.1987, p. 23.

[4] OJ No. L185, 16.8.1971, p. 5.

[5] OJ No. L210, 21.7.1989, p. 1.

[6] OJ No. L13, 15.1.1977, p. 1.

[7] OJ No. L127, 20.5.1988, p. 1.

remedies must be available in the case of infringements of Community law in the field of public procurement or national rules implementing that law;

Whereas in certain Member States the absence of effective remedies or inadequacy of existing remedies deter Community undertakings from submitting tenders in the Member State in which the contracting authority is established; whereas, therefore, the Member States concerned must remedy this situation;

Whereas, since procedures for the award of public contracts are of such short duration, competent review bodies must, among other things, be authorised to take interim measures aimed at suspending such a procedure or the implementation of any decisions which may be taken by the contracting authority; whereas the short duration of the procedures means that the aforementioned infringements need to be dealt with urgently;

Whereas it is necessary to ensure that adequate procedures exist in all the Member States to permit the setting aside of decisions taken unlawfully and compensation of persons harmed by an infringement;

Whereas, when undertakings do not seek review, certain infringements may not be corrected unless a specific mechanism is put in place;

Whereas, accordingly, the Commission, when it considers that a clear and manifest infringement has been committed during a contract award procedure, should be able to bring it to the attention of the competent authorities of the Member State and of the contracting authority concerned so that appropriate steps are taken for the rapid correction of any alleged infringement;

Whereas the application in practice of the provisions of this Directive should be re-examined within a period of four years of its implementation on the basis of information to be supplied by the Member States concerning the functioning of the national review procedures,

HAS ADOPTED THIS DIRECTIVE:

Article 1

1. The Member States shall take the measures necessary to ensure that, as regards contract award procedures falling within the scope of Directives 71/305/EEC and 77/62/EEC, decisions taken by the contracting authorities may be reviewed effectively and, in particular, as rapidly as possible in accordance with the conditions set out in the following Articles, and, in particular, Article 2(7) on the grounds that such decisions have infringed Community law in the field of public procurement or national rules implementing that law.

2. Member States shall ensure that there is no discrimination between undertakings claiming injury in the context of a procedure for the award of a contract as a result of the distinction made by this Directive between national rules implementing Community law and other national rules.

3. The Member States shall ensure that the review procedures are available, under detailed rules which the Member States may establish, at least to any person having or having had an interest in obtaining a particular public supply or public works contract and who has been or risks being harmed by an alleged infringement. In particular, the Member States may require that the person seeking the review must have previously notified the contracting authority of the alleged infringement and of his intention to seek review.

Article 2

1. The Member States shall ensure that the measures taken concerning the review procedures specified in Article 1 include provision for the powers to:

(a) take, at the earliest opportunity and by way of interlocutory procedures, interim measures with the aim of correcting the alleged infringement or preventing further damage to the interests concerned, including measures to suspend or to ensure the suspension of the procedure for the award of a public contract or the implementation of any decision taken by the contracting authority;

(b) either set aside or ensure the setting aside of decisions taken unlawfully, including the removal of discriminatory technical, economic or financial specifications in the invitation to tender, the contract documents or in any other document relating to the contract award procedure;

(c) award damages to persons harmed by an infringement.

2. The powers specified in paragraph 1 may be conferred on separate bodies responsible for different aspects of the review procedure.

3. Review procedures need not in themselves have an automatic suspensive effect on the contract award procedures to which they relate.

4. The Member States may provide that when considering whether to order interim measures the body responsible may take into account the probable consequences of the measures for all interests likely to be harmed, as well as the public interest, and may decide not to grant such measures where their negative consequences could exceed their benefits. A decision not to grant interim measures shall not prejudice any other claim of the person seeking these measures.

5. The Member States may provide that where damages are claimed on the grounds that a decision was taken unlawfully, the contested decision must first be set aside by a body having the necessary powers.

6. The effects of the exercise of the powers referred to in paragraph 1 on a contract concluded subsequent to its award shall be determined by national law.

Furthermore, except where a decision must be set aside prior to the award of damages, a Member State may provide that, after the conclusion of a contract following its award, the powers of the body responsible for the review procedures shall be limited to awarding damages to any person harmed by an infringement.

7. The Member States shall ensure that decisions taken by bodies responsible for review procedures can be effectively enforced.

8. Where bodies responsible for review procedures are not judicial in character, written reasons for their decisions shall always be given. Furthermore, in such a case, provision must be made to guarantee procedures whereby any allegedly illegal measure taken by the review body or any alleged defect in the exercise of the powers conferred on it can be the subject of judicial review or review by another body which is a court or tribunal within the meaning of Article 177 of the EEC Treaty and independent of both the contracting authority and the review body.

The members of such an independent body shall be appointed and leave office under the same conditions as members of the judiciary as regards the authority responsible for their appointment, their period of office, and their removal. At least the President of this independent body shall have the same legal and professional qualifications as members of the judiciary. The independent body shall take its decisions following a procedure in which both sides are heard, and these decisions shall, by means determined by each Member State, be legally binding.

Article 3

1. The Commission may invoke the procedure for which this Article provides when, prior to a contract being concluded, it considers that a clear and manifest infringement of Community provisions in the field of public procurement has been committed during a contract award procedure falling within the scope of Directives 71/305/EEC and 77/62/EEC.

2. The Commission shall notify the Member State and the contracting authority concerned of the reasons which have led it to conclude that a clear and manifest infringement has been committed and request its correction.

3. Within 21 days of receipt of the notification referred to in paragraph 2, the Member State concerned shall communicate to the Commission:

  (a) its confirmation that the infringement has been corrected; or

  (b) a reasoned submission as to why no correction has been made; or

  (c) a notice to the effect that the contract award procedure has been suspended either by the contracting authority on its own initiative or on the basis of the powers specified in Article 2(1)(a).

4. A reasoned submission in accordance with paragraph 3(b) may rely among other matters on the fact that the alleged infringement is already the subject of judicial or other review proceedings or of a review as referred to in Article 2(8). In such a case, the Member State shall inform the Commission of the result of those proceedings as soon as it becomes known.

5. Where notice has been given that a contract award procedure has been suspended in accordance with paragraph 3(c), the Member State shall notify the Commission when the suspension is lifted or another contract procedure relating in whole or in part to the same subject matter is begun. That notification shall confirm that the alleged infringement has been corrected or include a reasoned submission as to why no correction has been made.

Article 4

1. Not later than four years after the implementation of this Directive, the Commission, in consultation with the Advisory Committee for Public Contracts, shall review the manner in which the provisions of this Directive have been implemented and, if necessary, make proposals for amendments.

2. By 1 March each year the Member States shall communicate to the Commission information on the operation of their national review procedures during the preceding calendar year. The nature of the information shall be determined by the Commission in consultation with the Advisory Committee for Public Contracts.

Article 5

Member States shall bring into force, before 1 December 1991, the measures necessary to comply with this Directive. They shall communicate to the Commission the texts of the main national laws, regulations and administrative provisions which they adopt in the field governed by this Directive.

Article 6
This Directive is addressed to the Member States.

Done at Brussels, 21 December 1989.
For the Council,
The President,
É. CRESSON

COUNCIL DIRECTIVE 92/13/EEC OF 25 FEBRUARY 1992 COORDINATING THE LAWS, REGULATIONS AND ADMINISTRATIVE PROVISIONS RELATING TO THE APPLICATION OF COMMUNITY RULES ON THE PROCUREMENT PROCEDURES OF ENTITIES OPERATING IN THE WATER, ENERGY, TRANSPORT AND TELECOMMUNICATIONS SECTORS
[OJ 1992 L76/14]

THE COUNCIL OF THE EUROPEAN COMMUNITIES,

Having regard to the Treaty establishing the European Economic Community, and in particular Article 100a thereof,
  Having regard to the proposal from the Commission,[1]
  In cooperation with the European Parliament,[2]
  Having regard to the opinion of the Economic and Social Committee,[3]

Whereas Council Directive 90/531/EEC of 17 September 1990 on the procurement procedures of entities operating in the water, energy, transport and telecommunications sectors[4] lays down rules for procurement procedures to ensure that potential suppliers and contractors have a fair opportunity to secure the award of contracts, but does not contain any specific provisions ensuring its effective application;

  Whereas the existing arrangements at both national and Community levels for ensuring its application are not always adequate;

  Whereas the absence of effective remedies or the inadequacy of existing remedies could deter Community undertakings from submitting tenders; whereas, therefore, the Member States must remedy this situation;

  Whereas Council Directive 89/665/EEC of 21 December 1989 on the coordination of the laws, regulations and administrative provisions relating to the application of review procedures to the award of public supply and public works contracts[5] is limited to contract award procedures within the scope of Council Directive 71/305/EEC of 26 July 1971 concerning the coordination of procedures for the award of public works contracts,[6] as last amended by Directive 90/531/EEC, and Council Directive 77/62/EEC of 21 December 1976 coordinating procedures for the award of public supply contracts,[7] as last amended by Directive 90/531/EEC;

Notes
[1] OJ No. C216, 31.8.1990, p. 8; and OJ No. C179, 10.7.1991, p. 18.
[2] OJ No. C106, 22.4.1991, p. 82 and OJ No. C39, 17.2.1992.
[3] OJ No. C60, 8.3.1991, p. 16.
[4] OJ No. L297, 29.10.1990, p. 1.
[5] OJ No. L395, 30.12.1989, p. 33.
[6] OJ No. L185, 16.8.1971, p. 5.
[7] OJ No. L13, 15.1.1977, p. 1.

Whereas the opening-up of procurement in the sectors concerned to Community competition implies that provisions must be adopted to ensure that appropriate review procedures are made available to suppliers or contractors in the event of infringement of the relevant Community law or national rules implementing that law;

Whereas it is necessary to provide for a substantial increase in the guarantees of transparency and non-discrimination and whereas, for it to have tangible effects, effective and rapid remedies must be available;

Whereas account must be taken of the specific nature of certain legal orders by authorizing the Member States to choose between the introduction of different powers for the review bodies which have equivalent effects;

Whereas one of these options includes the power to intervene directly in the contracting entities' procurement procedures such as by suspending them, or by setting aside decisions or discriminatory clauses in documents or publications;

Whereas the other option provides for the power to exert effective indirect pressure on the contracting entities in order to make them correct any infringements or prevent them from committing infringements, and to prevent injury from occurring;

Whereas claims for damages must always be possible;

Whereas, where a claim is made for damages representing the costs of preparing a bid or of participating in an award procedure, the person making the claim is not be required, in order to obtain the reimbursement of his costs, to prove that the contract would have been awarded to him in the absence of such infringement;

Whereas the contracting entities which comply with the procurement rules may make this known through appropriate means; whereas this requires an examination, by independent persons, of procurement procedures and practices applied by those entities;

Whereas for this purpose an attestation system, allowing for a declaration on the correct application of the procurement rules, to be made in notices published in the Official Journal of the European Communities, is appropriate;

Whereas the contracting entities should have the opportunity of having recourse to the attestation system if they so wish; whereas the Member States must offer them the possibility of doing so; whereas they can do so either by setting up the system themselves or by allowing the contracting entities to have recourse to the attestation system established by another Member State; whereas they may confer the task of carrying out the examination under the attestation system to persons, professions or staff of institutions;

Whereas the necessary flexibility in the introduction of such a system is guaranteed by laying down the essential requirements for it in this Directive; whereas operational details should be provided in European Standards to which this Directive refers;

Whereas the Member States may need to determine operational details prior to, or in addition to, the rules contained in European Standards;

Whereas, when undertakings do not seek review, certain infringements may not be corrected unless a specific mechanism is put in place;

Whereas, accordingly, the Commission, when it considers that a clear and manifest infringement has been committed during a contract award procedure, should be able to bring it to the attention of the competent authorities of the

Member State and of the contracting entity concerned so that appropriate steps are taken for the rapid correction of that infringement;

Whereas it is necessary to provide for the possibility of conciliation at Community level to enable disputes to be settled amicably;

Whereas the application in practice of this Directive should be reviewed at the same time as that of Directive 90/531/EEC on the basis of information to be supplied by the Member States concerning the functioning of the national review procedures;

Whereas this Directive must be brought into effect at the same time as Directive 90/531/EEC;

Whereas it is appropriate that the Kingdom of Spain, the Hellenic Republic and the Portuguese Republic are granted adequate additional periods to transpose this Directive, taking account of the dates of application of Directive 90/531/EEC in those countries,

HAS ADOPTED THIS DIRECTIVE:

CHAPTER I   REMEDIES AT NATIONAL LEVEL

Article 1

1.   The Member States shall take the measures necessary to ensure that decisions taken by contracting entities may be reviewed effectively and, in particular, as rapidly as possible in accordance with the conditions set out in the following Articles and, in particular, Article 2(8), on the grounds that such decisions have infringed Community law in the field of procurement or national rules implementing that law as regards:

(a)   contract award procedures falling within the scope of Council Directive 90/531/EEC; and

(b)   compliance with Article 3(2)(a) of that Directive in the case of the contracting entities to which that provision applies.

2.   Member States shall ensure that there is no discrimination between undertakings likely to make a claim for injury in the context of a procedure for the award of a contract as a result of the distinction made by this Directive between national rules implementing Community law and other national rules.

3.   The Member States shall ensure that the review procedures are available, under detailed rules which the Member States may establish, at least to any person having or having had an interest in obtaining a particular contract and who has been or risks being harmed by an alleged infringement. In particular, the Member States may require that the person seeking the review must have previously notified the contracting entity of the alleged infringement and of his intention to seek review.

Article 2

1.   The Member States shall ensure that the measures taken concerning the review procedures specified in Article 1 include provision for the powers: either

(a)   to take, at the earliest opportunity and by way of interlocutory procedure, interim measures with the aim of correcting the alleged infringement or preventing further injury to the interests concerned, including measures to suspend or to ensure the suspension of the procedure for the award of a contract or the implementation of any decision taken by the contracting entity; and

(b)   to set aside or ensure the setting aside of decisions taken unlawfully, including the removal of discriminatory technical, economic or financial specifications in the notice of contract, the periodic indicative notice, the notice on the existence of a system of qualification, the invitation to tender, the contract documents or in any other document relating to the contract award procedure in question; or

(c)   to take, at the earliest opportunity, if possible by way of interlocutory procedures and if necessary by a final procedure on the substance, measures other than those provided for in points (a) and (b) with the aim of correcting any identified infringement and preventing injury to the interests concerned; in particular, making an order for the payment of a particular sum, in cases where the infringement has not been corrected or prevented.

Member States may take this choice either for all contracting entities or for categories of entities defined on the basis of objective criteria, in any event preserving the effectiveness of the measures laid down in order to prevent injury being caused to the interests concerned;

(d)   and, in both the above cases, to award damages to persons injured by the infringement. Where damages are claimed on the grounds that a decision has been taken unlawfully, Member States may, where their system of internal law so requires and provides bodies having the necessary powers for that purpose, provide that the contested decision must first be set aside or declared illegal.

2.   The powers referred to in paragraph 1 may be conferred on separate bodies responsible for different aspects of the review procedure.

3.   Review procedures need not in themselves have an automatic suspensive effect on the contract award procedures to which they relate.

4.   The Member States may provide that, when considering whether to order interim measures, the body responsible may take into account the probable consequences of the measures for all interests likely to be harmed, as well as the public interest, and may decide not to grant such measures where their negative consequences could exceed their benefits. A decision not to grant interim measures shall not prejudice any other claim of the person seeking these measures.

5.   The sum to be paid in accordance with paragraph 1(c) must be set at a level high enough to dissuade the contracting entity from committing or persisting in an infringement. The payment of that sum may be made to depend upon a final decision that the infringement has in fact taken place.

6.   The effects of the exercise of the powers referred to in paragraph 1 on a contract concluded subsequent to its award shall be determined by national law. Furthermore, except where a decision must be set aside prior to the award of damages, a Member State may provide that, after the conclusion of a contract following its award, the powers of the body responsible for the review procedures shall be limited to awarding damages to any person harmed by an infringement.

7.   Where a claim is made for damages representing the costs of preparing a bid or of participating in an award procedure, the person making the claim shall be required only to prove an infringement of Community law in the field of procurement or national rules implementing that law and that he would have had a real chance of winning the contract and that, as a consequence of that infringement, that chance was adversely affected.

8. The Member States shall ensure that decisions taken by bodies responsible for review procedures can be effectively enforced.

9. Whereas bodies responsible for review procedures are not judicial in character, written reasons for their decisions shall always be given. Furthermore, in such a case, provision must be made to guarantee procedures whereby any allegedly illegal measures taken by the review body or any alleged defect in the exercise of the powers conferred on it can be the subject of judicial review or review by another body which is a court or tribunal within the meaning of Article 177 of the Treaty and independent of both the contracting entity and the review body.

The members of the independent body referred to in the first paragraph shall be appointed and leave office under the same conditions as members of the judiciary as regards the authority responsible for their appointment, their period of office, and their removal. At least the President of this independent body shall have the same legal and professional qualifications as members of the judiciary. The independent body shall take its decisions following a procedure in which both sides are heard, and these decisions shall, by means determined by each Member State, be legally binding.

CHAPTER 2   ATTESTATION

Article 3

The Member States shall give contracting entities the possibility of having recourse to an attestation system in accordance with Articles 4 to 7.

Article 4

Contracting entities may have their contract award procedures and practices which fall within the scope of Directive 90/531/EEC examined periodically with a view to obtaining an attestation that, at that time, those procedures and practices are in conformity with Community law concerning the award of contracts and the national rules implementing the law.

Article 5

1. Attestors shall report to the contracting entity, in writing, on the results of their examination. They shall satisfy themselves, before delivering to the contracting entity the attestation referred to in Article 4, that any irregularities identified in the contracting entity's award procedures and practices have been corrected and measures have been taken to ensure that those irregularities are not repeated.

2. Contracting entities having obtained that attestation may include the following statement in a notice published in the Official Journal of the European Communities pursuant to Articles 16 to 18 of Directive 90/531/EEC:

'The contracting entity has obtained an attestation in accordance with Council Directive 92/13/EEC that, on ...., its contract award procedures and practices were in conformity with Community law and the national rules implementing that law.'

Article 6

1. Attestors shall be independent of the contracting entities and must be completely objective in carrying out their duties. They shall offer appropriate guarantees of relevant professional qualifications and experience.

2.   Member States may identify any persons, professions or institutions whose staff, called upon the act as attestors, they regard as fulfilling the requirements of paragraph 1. For these purposes, Member States may require professional qualifications, at least at the level of a higher education diploma within the meaning of Directive 89/48/EEC,[1] which they regard as relevant, or provide that particular examinations of professional competence organized or recognized by the State offer such guarantees.

Article 7
The provisions of Articles 4, 5 and 6 shall be considered as essential requirements for the development of European standards on attestation.

Note
[1]OJ No. L19, 24.1.1989, p. 16.

CHAPTER 3   CORRECTIVE MECHANISM

Article 8
1.   The Commission may invoke the procedures for which this Article provides when, prior to a contract being concluded, it considers that a clear and manifest infringement of Community provisions in the field of procurement has been committed during a contract award procedure falling within the scope of Directive 90/531/EEC or in relation to Article 3(2)(a) of that Directive in the case of the contracting entities to which that provision applies.
2.   The Commission shall notify the Member State and the contracting entity concerned of the reasons which have led it to conclude that a clear and manifest infringement has been committed and request its correction by appropriate means.
3.   Within 30 days of receipt of the notification referred to in paragraph 2, the Member State concerned shall communicate to the Commission:
   (a)   its confirmation that the infringement has been corrected; or
   (b)   a reasoned submission as to why no correction has been made; or
   (c)   a notice to the effect that the contract award procedure has been suspended either by the contracting entity on its own initiative or on the basis of the powers specified in Article 2(1)(a).
4.   A reasoned submission in accordance with paragraph 3(b) may rely among other matters on the fact that the alleged infringement is already the subject of judicial review proceedings or of a review as referred to in Article 2(9). In such a case, the Member State shall inform the Commission of the result of those proceedings as soon as it becomes known.
5.   Where notice has been given that a contract award procedure has been suspended in accordance with paragraph 3(c), the Member State concerned shall notify the Commission when the suspension is lifted or another contract procedure relating in whole or in part to the same subject matter is begun. That new notification shall confirm that the alleged infringement has been corrected or include an reasoned submission as to why no correction has been made.

CHAPTER 4   CONCILIATION

Article 9
1.   Any person having or having had an interest in obtaining a particular contract falling within the scope of Directive 90/531/EEC and who, in relation to the procedure for the award of that contract, considers that he has been or

risks being harmed by an alleged infringement of Community law in the field of procurement or national rules implementing that law may request the application of the conciliation procedure provided for in Articles 10 and 11.

2. The request referred to in paragraph 1 shall be addressed in writing to the Commission or to the national authorities listed in the Annex. These authorities shall forward requests to the Commission as quickly as possible.

Article 10

1. Where the Commission considers, on the basis of the request referred to in Article 9, that the dispute concerns the correct application of Community law, it shall ask the contracting entity to state whether it is willing to take part in the conciliation procedure. If the contracting entity declines to take part, the Commission shall inform the person who made the request that the procedure cannot be initiated. If the contracting entity agrees, paragraphs 2 to 7 shall apply.

2. The Commission shall propose, as quickly as possible, a conciliator drawn from a list of independent persons accredited for this purpose. This list shall be drawn up by the Commission, following consultation of the Advisory Committee for Public Contracts or, in the case of contracting entities the activities of which are defined in Article 2(2)(d) of Directive 90/531/EEC, following consultation of the Advisory Committee on Telecommunications Procurement.

Each party to the conciliation procedure shall declare whether it accepts the conciliator, and shall designate an additional conciliator. The conciliators may invite not more than two other persons as experts to advise them in their work. The parties to the conciliation procedure and the Commission may reject any expert invited by the conciliators.

3. The conciliators shall give the person requesting the application of the conciliation procedure, the contracting entity and any other candidate or tenderer participating in the relevant contract award procedure the opportunity to make representations on the matter either orally or in writing.

4. The conciliators shall endeavour as quickly as possible to reach an agreement between the parties which is in accordance with Community law.

5. The conciliators shall report to the Commission on their findings and on any result achieved.

6. The person requesting the application of the concilation procedure and the contracting entity shall have the right to terminate the procedure at any time.

7. Unless the parties decide otherwise, the person requesting the application of the conciliation procedure and the contracting entity shall be responsible for their own costs. In addition, they shall each bear half of the costs of the procedure, excluding the costs of intervening parties.

Article 11

1. Where, in relation to a particular contract award procedure, an interested person within the meaning of Article 9, other than the person requesting the conciliation procedure, is pursuing judicial review proceedings or other proceedings for review within the meaning of this Directive, the contracting entity shall inform the conciliators. These shall inform that person that a request has been made to apply the conciliation procedure and shall invite that person to indicate within a given time limit whether he agrees to participate in that procedure. If that person refuses to participate, the

conciliators may decide, acting if necessary by a majority, to terminate the conciliation procedure if they consider that the participation of this person is necessary to resolve the dispute. They shall notify their decision to the Committee and give the reasons for it.

2. Action taken pursuant to this Chapter shall be without prejudice to:

(a) any action that the Commission or any Member State might take pursuant to Articles 169 or 170 of the Treaty or pursuant to Chapter 3 of this Directive;

(b) the rights of the persons requesting the conciliation procedure, of the contracting entity or of any other person.

CHAPTER 5   FINAL PROVISIONS

Article 12

1. Not later than four years after the application of this Directive, the Commission, in consultation with the Advisory Committee for Public Contracts, shall review the manner in which the provisions of this Directive have been implemented and, in particular, the use of the European Standards and, if necessary, make proposals for amendments.

2. Before 1 March each year the Member States shall communicate to the Commission information on the operation of their national review procedures during the preceding calendar year. The nature of the information shall be determined by the Commission in consultation with the Advisory Committee for Public Contracts.

3. In the case of matters relating to contracting entities the activities of which are defined in Article 2(2)(d) of Directive 90/531/EEC, the Commission shall also consult the Advisory Committee on Telecommunications Procurement.

Article 13

1. Member States shall take, before 1 January 1993, the measures necessary to comply with this Directive. The Kingdom of Spain shall take these measures not later than 30 June 1995. The Hellenic Republic and the Portuguese Republic shall take these measures not later than 30 June 1997. They shall forthwith inform the Commission thereof.

When Member States adopt these measures, they shall contain an reference to this Directive or shall be accompanied by such reference on the occasion of their official publication. The methods of making such a reference shall be laid down by the Member States.

2. Member States shall bring into force the measures referred to in paragraph 1 on the same dates as those laid down in Directive 90/531/EEC.

3. Member States shall communicate to the Commission the texts of the main provisions of domestic law which they adopt in the field governed by this Directive.

Article 14

This Directive is addressed to the Member States.

Done at Brussels, 25 February 1992.
For the Council,
The President,
Victor MARTINS

ANNEX

National authorities to which requests for application of the conciliation procedure referred to in Article 9 may be addressed

Belgium:
Services du Premier Ministre
Diensten Van de Eerste Minister
Ministère des Affaires économiques
Ministerie van Economische Zaken

Denmark:
Industri- og Handelsstyrelsen (supply contracts)
Boligsministeriet (works contracts)

Germany:
Bundesministerium fuer Wirtschaft

Greece:
Ypoyrgeio Viomichanias, Energeias kai Technologias
Ypoyrgeio Emporioy Ypoyrgeio Perivallontos, Chorotaxias kai Dimosion Ergon

Spain:
Ministerio de Economía y Hacienda

France:
Commission centrale des marchés

Ireland:
Department of Finance

Italy:
Presidenza del Consiglio dei Ministri Politiche Comunitarie

Luxembourg:
Ministère des travaux publics

Netherlands:
Ministerie van Economische Zaken

Portugal:
Conselho de mercados de obras publicas e particulares

United Kingdom:
HM Treasury

Austria:
Bundesministerium fuer wirtschaftliche Angelegenheiten

Finland:
Kauppa- ja teollisuusministerioe/Handels- och industriministeriet

Sweden:
Naemnden foer offentlig upphandling.

COUNCIL DIRECTIVE 92/50/EEC OF 18 JUNE 1992 RELATING TO THE CO-ORDINATION OF PROCEDURES FOR THE AWARD OF PUBLIC SERVICE CONTRACTS
[OJ 1992 L209/1]

THE COUNCIL OF THE EUROPEAN COMMUNITIES,

Having regard to the Treaty establishing the European Economic Community, and in particular the last sentence of Article 57(2) and Article 66 thereof,

Having regard to the proposal from the Commission,[1]
In cooperation with the European Parliament,[2]
Having regard to the opinion of the Economic and Social Committee,[3]

Whereas the European Council has drawn conclusions on the need to complete the internal market;

Whereas measures aimed at progressively establishing the internal market during the period up to 31 December 1992 need to be taken; whereas the internal market is an area without internal frontiers in which the free movement of goods, persons, services and capital is ensured;

Whereas these objectives require the co-ordination of the procurement procedures for the award of public service contracts;

Whereas the White Paper on the completion of the internal market contains an action programme and a timetable for opening up public procurement, including in the field of services insofar as this is not already covered by Council Directive 71/305/EEC of 26 July 1971 concerning the co-ordination of procedures for the award of public works contracts[4] and Council Directive 77/62/EEC of 21 December 1976 co-ordinating procedures for the award of public supply contracts;[5]

Whereas this Directive should be applied by all contracting authorities within the meaning of Directive 71/305/EEC;

Whereas obstacles to the free movement of services need to be avoided; whereas, therefore, service providers may be either natural or legal persons; whereas this Directive shall not, however, prejudice the application, at national level, of rules concerning the conditions for the pursuit of an activity or a profession provided that they are compatible with Community law;

Whereas the field of services is best described, for the purpose of application of procedural rules and for monitoring purposes, by subdividing it into categories corresponding to particular positions of a common classification; whereas Annexes I A and I B of this Directive refer to the CPC nomenclature (common product classification) of the United Nations; whereas that nomenclature is likely to be replaced in the future by Community nomenclature; whereas provision should be made for adapting the CPC nomenclature in Annexes I A and B in consequence;

Whereas the provision of services is covered by this Directive only in so far as it is based on contracts; whereas the provision of services on other bases, such as law or regulations, or employment contracts, is not covered;

Whereas, in accordance with Article 130f of the Treaty, the encouragement of research and development is a means to strengthen the scientific and technological basis of European industry and the opening up of public contracts will contribute to this end; whereas contributions to the financing of research programmes should not be subject to this Directive; whereas research

Notes
[1] OJ No. C23, 31.1.1991, p. 1, and OJ No. C250, 25.9.1991, p. 4.
[2] OJ No. C158, 17.6.1991, p. 90, and OJ No. C150, 15.6.1992.
[3] OJ No. C191, 22.7.1991, p. 41.
[4] OJ No. L185, 16.8.1971, p. 5. Directive last amended by Directive 90/531/EEC (OJ No. L297, 29.10.1990, p. 1).
[5] OJ No. L13, 15.1.1977, p. 1. Directive last amended by Directive 90/531/EEC (OJ No. L297, 29.10.1990, p. 1).

and development service contracts other than those where the benefits accrue exclusively to the contracting authority for its use in the conduct of its own affairs, on condition that the service provided is wholly remunerated by the contracting authority, are not therefore covered by this Directive;

Whereas contracts relating to the acquisition or rental of immovable property or to rights thereon have particular characteristics, which make the application of procurement rules inappropriate;

Whereas the award of contracts for certain audiovisual services in the broadcasting field is governed by considerations which make the application of procurement rules inappropriate;

Whereas arbitration and conciliation services are usually provided by bodies or individuals which are agreed on, or selected, in a manner which cannot be governed by procurement rules;

Whereas for the purposes of this Directive financial services do not include the instruments of monetary, exchange rate, public debt, reserve management, and other policies involving transactions in securities and other financial instruments; whereas, therefore, contracts in connection with the issue, sale, purchase or transfer of securities and other financial instruments are not covered by this Directive; whereas central bank services are also excluded;

Whereas, in the field of services, the same derogations as in Directives 71/305/EEC and 77/62/EEC should apply as regards State security or secrecy and the priority of other procurement rules such as those pursuant to international agreements, those concerning the stationing of troops, or the rules of international organisations;

Whereas this Directive does not prejudice the application of, in particular, Articles 55, 56 and 66 of the Treaty;

Whereas public service contracts, particularly in the field of property management, may from time to time include some works; whereas it results from Directive 71/305/EEC that, for a contract to be a public works contract, its object must be the achievement of a work; whereas, in so far as these works are incidental rather than the object of the contract, they do not justify treating the contract as a public works contract;

Whereas the rules concerning service contracts as contained in Council Directive 90/531/EEC of 17 September 1990 on the procurement procedures of entities operating in the water, energy, transport and telecommunications sectors[6] should remain unaffected by this Directive;

Whereas contracts with a designated single source of supply may, under certain conditions, be fully or partly exempted from this Directive;

Whereas this Directive should not apply to small contracts below a certain threshold in order to avoid unnecessary formalities; whereas this threshold may in principle be the same as that for public supply contracts; whereas the calculation of the contract value, the publication and the method of adaptation of the thresholds should be the same as in the other Community procurement directives;

Whereas, to eliminate practices that restrict competition in general and participation in contracts by other Member States' nationals in particular, it is necessary to improve the access of service providers to procedures for the award of contracts;

Note
[6]OJ No. L297, 29.10.1990, p. 1.

Whereas full application of this Directive must be limited, for a transitional period, to contracts for those services where its provisions will enable the full potential for increased cross-frontier trade to be realised; whereas contracts for other services need to be monitored for a certain period before a decision is taken on the full application of this Directive; whereas the mechanism for such monitoring needs to be defined; whereas this mechanism should at the same time enable those interested to share the relevant information;

Whereas the rules for the award of public service contracts should be as close as possible to those concerning public supply contracts and public works contracts;

Whereas the procurement rules contained in Directives 71/305/EEC and 77/62/EEC can be appropriate, with necessary adaptations so as to take into account special aspects of procurement of services such as the choice of the negotiated procedure, design contests, variants, the legal form under which the service providers operate, the reservation of certain activities to certain professions, registration and quality assurance;

Whereas use may be made of the negotiated procedure with prior publication of a notice when the service to be provided cannot be specified with sufficient precision, particularly in the field of intellectual services, with the result that such a contract cannot be awarded by selection of the best tender in accordance with the rules governing the open and restricted procedures;

Whereas the relevant Community rules on mutual recognition of diplomas, certificates or other evidence of formal qualifications apply when evidence of a particular qualification is required for participation in an award procedure or a design contest;

Whereas the objectives of this Directive do not require any changes in the current situation at national level as regards price competition between service providers of certain services;

Whereas the operation of this Directive should be reviewed at the latest three years after the date set for procurement rules to be transposed into national law; whereas the review should extend in particular to the possibility of making the Directive fully applicable to a wider range of service contracts,

HAS ADOPTED THIS DIRECTIVE:

TITLE I   GENERAL PROVISIONS

Article 1

For the purposes of this Directive:

(a)   public service contracts shall mean contracts for pecuniary interest concluded in writing between a service provider and a contracting authority, to the exclusion of:

(i)   public supply contracts within the meaning of Article 1(a) of Directive 77/62/EEC or public works contracts within the meaning of Article 1(a) of Directive 71/305/EEC;

(ii)   contracts awarded in the fields referred to in Articles 2, 7, 8 and 9 of Directive 90/531/EEC or fulfilling the conditions in Article 6(2) of the same Directive;

(iii)   contracts for the acquisition or rental, by whatever financial means, of land, existing buildings, or other immovable property or concerning rights thereon; nevertheless, financial service contracts concluded at the same time as, before or after the contract of acquisition or rental, in whatever form, shall be subject to this Directive;

    (iv)   contracts for the acquisition, development, production or co-production of programme material by broadcasters and contracts for broadcasting time;

    (v)   contracts for voice telephony, telex, radiotelephony, paging and satellite services;

    (vi)   contracts for arbitration and conciliation services;

    (vii)   contracts for financial services in connection with the issue, sale, purchase or transfer of securities or other financial instruments, and central bank services;

    (viii)   employment contracts;

    (ix)   research and development service contracts other than those where the benefits accrue exclusively to the contracting authority for its use in the conduct of its own affairs, on condition that the service provided is wholly remunerated by the contracting authority;

    (b)   contracting authorities shall mean the State, regional or local authorities, bodies governed by public law, associations formed by one or more of such authorities or bodies governed by public law. 'Body governed by public law' means any body:

—established for the specific purpose of meeting needs in the general interest, not having an industrial or commercial character, and

—having legal personality and

—financed, for the most part, by the State, or regional or local authorities, or other bodies governed by public law; or subject to management supervision by those bodies; or having an administrative, managerial or supervisory board, more than half of whose members are appointed by the State, regional or local authorities or by other bodies governed by public law.

The lists of bodies or of categories of such bodies governed by public law which fulfil the criteria referred to in the second subparagraph of this point are set out in Annex I to Directive 71/305/EEC. These lists shall be as exhaustive as possible and may be reviewed in accordance with the procedure laid down in Article 30b of that Directive;

    (c)   'service provider' shall mean any natural or legal person, including a public body, which offers services.

A service provider who submits a tender shall be designated by the term tenderer and one who has sought an invitation to take part in a restricted or negotiated procedure by the term candidate;

    (d)   'open procedures' shall mean those national procedures whereby all interested service providers may submit a tender;

    (e)   'restricted procedures' shall mean those national procedures whereby only those service providers invited by the authority may submit a tender;

    (f)   'negotiated procedures' shall mean those national procedures whereby authorities consult service providers of their choice and negotiate the terms of the contract with one or more of them;

    (g)   'design contests' shall mean those national procedures which enable the contracting authority to acquire, mainly in the fields of area planning, town planning, architecture and civil engineering, or data processing, a plan or design selected by a jury after being put out to competition with or without the award of prizes.

Article 2

If a public contract is intended to cover both products within the meaning of Directive 77/62/EEC and services within the meaning of Annexes I A and I B to this Directive, it shall fall within the scope of this Directive if the value of the services in question exceeds that of the products covered by the contract.

Article 3

1. In awarding public service contracts or in organising design contests, contracting authorities shall apply procedures adapted to the provisions of this Directive.

2. Contracting authorities shall ensure that there is no discrimination between different service providers.

3. Member States shall take the necessary measures to ensure that the contracting authorities comply or ensure compliance with this Directive where they subsidise directly by more than 50% a service contract awarded by an entity other than themselves in connection with a works contract within the meaning of Article 1a(2) of Directive 71/305/EEC.

Article 4

1. This Directive shall apply to public service contracts awarded by contracting authorities in the field of defence, except for contracts to which the provisions of Article 223 of the Treaty apply.

2. This Directive shall not apply to services which are declared secret or the execution of which must be accompanied by special security measures in accordance with the laws, regulations or administrative provisions in force in the Member State concerned or when the protection of the basic interests of that State's security so requires.

Article 5

This Directive shall not apply to public contracts governed by different procedural rules and awarded:

(a) in pursuance of an international agreement concluded between a Member State and one or more third countries and covering services intended for the joint implementation or exploitation of a project by the signatory States; any agreement shall be communicated to the Commission, which may consult the Advisory Committee for Public Contracts set up by Council Decision 71/306/EEC;[1]

(b) to undertakings in a Member State or a third country in pursuance of an international agreement relating to the stationing of troops;

(c) pursuant to the particular procedure of an international organization.

Note

[1]OJ No. L185, 16.8.1971, p. 15. Decision amended by Decision 77/63/EEC (OJ No. L13, 15.1.1977, p. 15).

Article 6

This Directive shall not apply to public service contracts awarded to an entity which is itself a contracting authority within the meaning of Article 1(b) on the basis of an exclusive right which it enjoys pursuant to a published law, regulation or administrative provision which is compatible with the Treaty.

Article 7

1.   This Directive shall apply to public service contracts, the estimated value of which, net of VAT, is not less than ECU 200,000.

2.   For the purposes of calculating the estimated value of the contract, the contracting authority shall include the estimated total remuneration of the service provider, taking account of the provisions of paragraphs 3 to 8.

3.   The selection of the valuation method shall not be used with the intention of avoiding the application of this Directive, nor shall any procurement requirement for a given amount of services be split up with the intention of avoiding the application of this Article.

4.   For the purposes of calculating the estimated contract value for the following types of services, account shall be taken, where appropriate:

— as regards insurance services, of the premium payable,

— as regards banking and other financial services, of fees, commissions and interest as well as other types of remuneration,

— as regards contracts which involve design, of the fee or commission payable.

Where the services are subdivided into several lots, each one the subject of a contract, the value of each lot must be taken into account for the purpose of calculating the amount referred to above.

Where the value of the lots is not less than this amount, the provisions of this Directive shall apply to all lots. Contracting authorities may waive application of paragraph 1 for any lot which has an estimated value net of VAT of less than ECU 80,000, provided that the total value of such lots does not exceed 20% of the total value of all the lots.

5.   In the case of contracts which do not specify a total price, the basis for calculating the estimated contract value shall be:

— in the case of fixed-term contracts, where their term is 48 months or less, the total contract value for its duration;

— in the case of contracts of indefinite duration or with a term of more than 48 months, the monthly instalment multiplied by 48.

6.   In the case of regular contracts or of contracts which are to be renewed within a given time, the contract value may be established on the basis of:

— either the actual aggregate cost of similar contracts for the same categories of services awarded over the previous fiscal year or 12 months, adjusted, where possible, for anticipated changes in quantity or value over the twelve months following the initial contract,

— or the estimated aggregate cost during the twelve months following the first service performed or during the term of the contract, where this is greater than 12 months.

7.   Where a proposed contract provides for options, the basis for calculating the contract value shall be the maximum permitted total including use of the option clauses.

8.   The value of the thresholds in national currencies shall be revised every two years with effect from 1 January 1994. The calculation of these values shall be based on the average daily values of those currencies expressed in ECUs over the 24 months terminating on the last day of August immediately preceding the 1 January revision. The values shall be published in the Official Journal of the European Communities at the beginning of November.

Article 28

1.   The contracting authority may state in the contract documents, or be obliged by a Member State to do so, the authority or authorities from which a tenderer may obtain the appropriate information on the obligations relating to the employment protection provisions and the working conditions which are in force in the Member State, region or locality in which the services are to be performed and which shall be applicable to the services provided on site during the performance of the contract.

2.   The contracting authority which supplies the information referred to in paragraph 1 shall request the tenderers or those participating in the contract award procedure to indicate that they have taken account, when drawing up their tender, of the obligations relating to employment protection provisions and the working conditions which are in force in the place where the service is to be carried out. This shall be without prejudice to the application of the provisions of Article 37 concerning the examination of abnormally low tenders.

CHAPTER 2   CRITERIA FOR QUALITATIVE SELECTION

Article 29

Any service provider may be excluded from participation in a contract who:

(a)   is bankrupt or is being wound up, whose affairs are being administered by the court, who has entered into an arrangement with creditors, who has suspended business activities or who is in any analogous situation arising from a similar procedure under national laws and regulations;

(b)   is the subject of proceedings for a declaration of bankruptcy, for an order for compulsory winding-up or administration by the court or for an arrangement with creditors or of any other similar proceedings under national laws or regulations;

(c)   has been convicted of an offence concerning his professional conduct by a judgment which has the force of res judicata;

(d)   has been guilty of grave professional misconduct proven by any means which the contracting authorities can justify;

(e)   has not fulfilled obligations relating to the payment of social security contributions in accordance with the legal provisions of the country in which he is established or with those of the country of the contracting authority;

(f)   has not fulfilled obligations relating to the payment of taxes in accordance with the legal provisions of the country of the contracting authority;

(g)   is guilty of serious misrepresentation in supplying or failing to supply the information that may be required under this Chapter. Where the contracting authority requires of the service provider proof that none of the cases quoted in (a), (b), (c), (e), or (f) applies to him, it shall accept as sufficient evidence:

— for (a), (b) or (c), the production of an extract from the 'judicial record' or, failing this, of an equivalent document issued by a competent judicial or administrative authority in the country of origin or in the country whence that person comes showing that these requirements have been met,

— for (e) or (f), a certificate issued by the competent authority in the Member State concerned. Where the country concerned does not issue such

The method of calculation referred to in the preceding subparagraph shall be examined, on the Commission's initiative, within the Advisory Committee for Public Contracts in principle two years after its initial application.

TITLE II   TWO-TIER APPLICATION

Article 8

Contracts which have as their object services listed in Annex I A shall be awarded in accordance with the provisions of Titles III to VI.

Article 9

Contracts which have as their object services listed in Annex I B shall be awarded in accordance with Articles 14 and 16.

Article 10

Contracts which have as their object services listed in both Annexes I A and I B shall be awarded in accordance with the provisions of Titles III to VI where the value of the services listed in Annex I A is greater than the value of the services listed in Annex I B. Where this is not the case, they shall be awarded in accordance with Articles 14 and 16.

TITLE III   CHOICE OF AWARD PROCEDURES AND RULES GOVERNING DESIGN CONTESTS

Article 11

1.   In awarding public service contracts, contracting authorities shall apply the procedures defined in Article 1(d), (e) and (f), adapted for the purposes of this Directive.

2.   Contracting authorities may award their public service contracts by negotiated procedure, with prior publication of a contract notice in the following cases:

(a)   in the event of irregular tenders in response to an open or restricted procedure or in the event of tenders which are unacceptable under national provisions that are in accordance with Articles 23 to 28, insofar as the original terms of the contract are not substantially altered. Contracting authorities may in such cases refrain from publishing a contract notice where they include in the negotiated procedure all the tenderers who satisfy the criteria of Articles 29 to 35 and who, during the prior open or restricted procedure, have submitted tenders in accordance with the formal requirements of the tendering procedure;

(b)   in exceptional cases, when the nature of the services or the risks involved do not permit prior overall pricing;

(c)   when the nature of the services to be procured, in particular in the case of intellectual services and services falling within category 6 of Annex I A, is such that contract specifications cannot be established with sufficient precision to permit the award of the contract by selecting the best tender according to the rules governing open or restricted procedures.

3.   Contracting authorities may award public service contracts by negotiated procedure without prior publication of a contract notice in the following cases:

(a)   in the absence of tenders or of appropriate tenders in response to an open or restricted procedure provided that the original terms of the contract are not substantially altered and that a report is communicated to the Commission at its request;

(b) when, for technical or artistic reasons, or for reasons connected with the protection of exclusive rights, the services may be provided only by a particular service provider;

(c) where the contract concerned follows a design contest and must, under the rules applying, be awarded to the successful candidate or to one of the successful candidates. In the latter case, all successful candidates shall be invited to participate in the negotiations;

(d) in so far as is strictly necessary when, for reasons of extreme urgency brought about by events unforeseeable by the contracting authorities in question, the time limit for the open, restricted or negotiated procedures referred to in Articles 17 to 20 cannot be kept. The circumstances invoked to justify extreme urgency must not in any event be attributable to the contracting authorities;

(e) for additional services not included in the project initially considered or in the contract first concluded but which have, through unforeseen circumstances, become necessary for the performance of the service described therein, on condition that the award is made to the service provider carrying out such service:

— when such additional services cannot be technically or economically separated from the main contract without great inconvenience to the contracting authorities, or

— when such services, although separable from the performance of the original contract, are strictly necessary for its completion.

However, the aggregate estimated value of contracts awarded for additional services may not exceed 50 % of the amount of the main contract;

(f) for new services consisting in the repetition of similar services entrusted to the service provider to which the same contracting authorities awarded an earlier contract, provided that such services conform to a basic project for which a first contract was awarded according to the procedures referred to in paragraph 4. As soon as the first project is put up for tender, notice must be given that the negotiated procedure might be adopted and the total estimated cost of subsequent services shall be taken into consideration by the contracting authorities when they apply the provisions of Article 7. This procedure may be applied solely during the three years following the conclusion of the original contract.

4. In all other cases, the contracting authorities shall award their public service contracts by the open procedure or by the restricted procedure.

Article 12

1. The contracting authority shall, within fifteen days of the date on which the request is received, inform any eliminated candidate or tenderer who so requests in writing of the reasons for rejection of his application or his tender, and, in the case of a tender, the name of the successful tenderer.

2. The contracting authority shall inform candidates or tenderers who so request in writing of the grounds on which it decided not to award a contract in respect of which a prior call for competition was made, or to recommence the procedure. It shall also inform the Office for Official Publications of the European Communities of that decision.

3. For each contract awarded, the contracting authorities shall draw up a written report which shall include at least the following:

— the name and address of the contracting authority, the subject and value of the contract,

— the names of the candidates or tenderers admitted and the reasons for their selection,

— the names of the candidates or tenderers rejected and the reasons for their rejection,

— the name of the successful tenderer and the reasons why his tender was selected and, if known, the part of the contract which the successful tenderer intends to subcontract to third parties,

— for negotiated procedures, the circumstances referred to in Article 11 which justify the use of these procedures.

This report, or the main features of it, shall be communicated to the Commission at its request.

Article 13

1. This Article shall apply to design contests organised as part of a procedure leading to the award of a service contract whose estimated value net of VAT is not less than the value referred to in Article 7(1).

2. This Article shall apply to all design contests where the total amount of contest prizes and payments to participants is not less than ECU 200,000.

3. The rules for the organization of a design contest shall be in conformity with the requirements of this Article and shall be communicated to those interested in participating in the contest.

4. The admission of participants to design contests shall not be limited:

— by reference to the territory or part of the territory of a Member State,

— on the grounds that, under the law of the Member State in which the contest is organised, they would have been required to be either natural or legal persons.

5. Where design contests are restricted to a limited number of participants, the contracting authorities shall lay down clear and non-discriminatory selection criteria. In any event, the number of candidates invited to participate shall be sufficient to ensure genuine competition.

6. The jury shall be composed exclusively of natural persons who are independent of participants in the contest. Where a particular professional qualification is required from participants in a contest, at least a third of its members must have the same qualification or its equivalent. The jury shall be autonomous in its decisions or opinions. These shall be reached on the basis of projects submitted anonymously and solely on the grounds of the criteria indicated in the notice within the meaning of Article 15(3).

TITLE IV COMMON RULES IN THE TECHNICAL FIELD

Article 14

1. The technical specifications defined in Annex II shall be given in the general documents or the contractual documents relating to each contract.

2. Without prejudice to the legally binding national technical rules and insofar as these are compatible with Community law, such technical specifications shall be defined by the contracting authorities by reference to national standards implementing European standards or by reference to European technical approvals or by reference to common technical specifications.

3. A contracting authority may depart from paragraph 2 if:

(a) the standards, European technical approvals or common technical specifications do not include any provisions for establishing conformity, or technical means do not exist for establishing satisfactorily the conformity of a product with these standards, European technical approvals or common technical specifications;

(b) the application of paragraph 2 would prejudice the application of Council Directive 86/361/EEC of 24 July 1986 on the initial stage of the mutual recognition of type approval for telecommunications terminal equipment,[1] or Council Decision 87/95/EEC of 22 December 1986 on standardisation in the field of information technology and telecommunications[2] or other Community instrument in specific service or product areas;

(c) these standards, European technical approvals or common technical specifications would oblige the contracting authority to use products or materials incompatible with equipment already in use or would entail disproportionate costs or disproportionate technical difficulties, but only as part of a clearly defined and recorded strategy with a view to the transition, with a given period, to European standards, European technical approvals or common technical specifications;

(d) the project concerned is of a genuinely innovative nature for which use of existing European standards, European technical approvals or common technical specifications would not be appropriate.

4. Contracting authorities invoking paragraph 3 shall record, wherever possible, the reasons for doing so in the contract notice published in the Official Journal of the European Communities or in the contract documents and in all cases shall record these reasons in their internal documentation and shall supply such information on request to Member States and to the Commission.

5. In the absence of European standards or European technical approvals or common technical specifications, the technical specifications:

(a) shall be defined by reference to the national technical specifications recognised as complying with the basic requirements listed in the Community directives on technical harmonization, in accordance with the procedures laid down in those directives, and in particular in accordance with the procedures laid down in Directive 89/106/EEC;[3]

(b) may be defined by reference to national technical specifications relating to design and method of calculation and execution of works and use of materials;

(c) may be defined by reference to other documents. In this case, it is appropriate to make reference in order of preference to:

(i) national standards implementing international standards accepted by the country of the contracting authority;

(ii) other national standards and national technical approvals of the country of the contracting authority;

(iii) any other standard.

6. Unless it is justified by the subject of the contract, Member States shall prohibit the introduction into the contractual clauses relating to a given

Note

[1] OJ No. L217, 5.8.1986, p. 21. Amended by Directive 91/263/EEC (OJ No. L128, 23.5.1991, p. 1).

[2] OJ No. L36, 7.2.1987, p. 31.

[3] OJ No. L40, 11.2.1989, p. 12.

contract of technical specifications which mention products of a specific make or source or of a particular process and which therefore favour or eliminate certain service providers. In particular, the indication of trade marks, patents, types, or of specific origin or production shall be prohibited. However, if such indication is accompanied by the words 'or equivalent', it shall be authorised in cases where the contracting authorities are unable to give a description of the subject of the contract using specifications which are sufficiently precise and intelligible to all parties concerned.

TITLE V   COMMON ADVERTISING RULES

Article 15

1.   Contracting authorities shall make known, by means of an indicative notice to be published as soon as possible after the beginning of their budgetary year, the intended total procurement in each of the service categories listed in Annex I A which they envisage awarding during the subsequent 12 months where the total estimated value, taking account of the provisions of Article 7, is not less than ECU 750,000.

2.   Contracting authorities who wish to award a public service contract by open, restricted or, under the conditions laid down in Article 11, negotiated procedure, shall make known their intention by means of a notice.

3.   Contracting authorities who wish to carry out a design contest shall make known their intention by means of a notice.

Article 16

1.   Contracting authorities who have awarded a public contract or have held a design contest shall send a notice of the results of the results of the award procedure to the Office for Official Publication of the European Communities.

2.   The notices shall be published:
    —in the case of public contracts for services listed in Annex I A, in accordance with Articles 17 to 20,
    —in the case of design contests, in accordance with Article 17.

3.   In the case of public contracts for services listed in Annex I B, the contracting authorities shall indicate in the notice whether they agree on its publication.

4.   The Commission shall draw up the rules for establishing regular reports on the basis of the notices referred to in paragraph 3, and for the publication of such reports in accordance with the procedure laid down in Article 40(3).

5.   Where the release of information on the contract award would impede law enforcement or otherwise be contrary to the public interest or would prejudice the legitimate commercial interests of a particular enterprise, public or private, or might prejudice fair competition between service providers, such information need not be published.

Article 17

1.   The notices shall be drawn up in accordance with the models set out in Annexes III and IV and shall specify the information requested in those models. The contracting authorities may not require any conditions other than those specified in Articles 31 and 32 when requesting information concerning the economic and technical standards which they require of service providers

for their selection (section 13 of Annex III B, section 13 of Annex III C, and section 12 of Annex III D).

2. The contracting authorities shall send the notices as rapidly as possible and by the most appropriate channels to the Office for Official Publications of the European Communities. In the case of the accelerated procedure referred to in Article 20, the notice shall be sent by telex, telegram or fax.

The notice referred to in Article 15(1) shall be sent as soon as possible after the beginning of each budgetary year.

The notice referred to in Article 16(1) shall be sent at the latest forty-eight days after the award of the contract in question or the closure of the design contest in question.

3. The notices referred to in Articles 15(1) and 16(1) shall be published in full in the Official Journal of the European Communities and in the TED data bank in the official languages of the Communities, the text in the original language alone being authentic.

4. The notices referred to in Article 15(2) and (3) shall be published in full in the Official Journal of the European Communities and in the TED data bank in their original language. A summary of the important elements of each notice shall be published in the official languages of the Communities, the text in the original language alone being authentic.

5. The Office for Official Publications of the European Communities shall publish the notices not later than 12 days after their dispatch. In the case of the accelerated procedure referred to in Article 20, this period shall be reduced to five days.

6. The notices shall not be published in the official journals or in the press of the country of the contracting authority before the date of dispatch to the Office for Official Publications of the European Communities; they shall mention that date. They shall not contain information other than that published in the Official Journal of the European Communities.

7. The contracting authorities must be able to supply proof of the date of dispatch.

8. The cost of publication of the notices in the Official Journal of the European Communities shall be borne by the Communities. The length of the notice shall not be greater than one page of the Official Journal, or approximately 650 words. Each edition of the Official Journal containing one or more notices shall reproduce the model notice or notices on which the published notice or notices are based.

Article 18

1. In open procedures the time limit for the receipt of tenders shall be fixed by the contracting authorities at not less than 52 days from the date of dispatch of the notice.

2. The time limit for the receipt of tenders provided for in paragraph 1 may be reduced to 36 days where the contracting authorities have published the contract notice, drafted in accordance with the model in Annex III A provided for in Article 15(1), in the Official Journal of the European Communities.

3. Provided that they have been requested in good time, the contract documents and supporting documents shall be sent to the service providers by the contracting authorities or competent departments within six days of receipt of their application.

4.   Provided that it has been requested in good time, additional information relating to the contract documents shall be supplied by the contracting authorities not later than six days before the final date fixed for receipt of tenders.

5.   Where the contract documents, supporting documents or additional information are too bulky to be supplied within the time limits laid down in paragraph 3 or 4 or where the tenders can be made only after a visit to the site or after on-the-spot inspection of the documents supporting the contract documents, the time limits laid down in paragraph 1 and 2 shall be extended accordingly.

Article 19

1.   In restricted procedures and negotiated procedures within the meaning of Article 11(2), the time limit for receipt of requests to participate fixed by the contracting authorities shall be not less than 37 days from the date of dispatch of the notice.

2.   The contracting authorities shall simultaneously and in writing invite the selected candidates to submit their tenders. The letter of invitation shall be accompanied by the contract documents and supporting documents. It shall include at least the following information:

(a)   where appropriate, the address of the service from which the contract documents and supporting documents can be requested and the final date for making such a request; also the amount and terms of payment of any sum to be paid for such documents;

(b)   the final date for receipt of tenders, the address to which they must be sent and the language or languages in which they must be drawn up;

(c)   a reference to the contract notice published;

(d)   an indication of any documents to be annexed, either to support the verifiable statements furnished by the candidate in accordance with Article 17(1), or to supplement the information provided for in that Article under the same conditions as those laid down in Articles 31 and 32;

(e)   the criteria for the award of the contract if these are not given in the notice.

3.   In restricted procedures, the time limit for receipt of tenders fixed by the contracting authorities may not be less than forty days from the date of dispatch of the written invitation.

4.   The time limit for receipt of tenders laid down in paragraph 3 may be reduced to 26 days where the contracting authorities have published the contract notice, drafted according to the model in Annex III A provided for in Article 15(1), in the Official Journal of the European Communities.

5.   Requests to participate in procedures for the award of contracts may be made by letter, telegram, telex, fax or telephone. If by one of the last four, they must be confirmed by letter dispatched before the end of the period laid down in paragraph 1.

6.   Provided it has been requested in good time, additional information relating to the contract documents must be supplied by the contracting authorities not later than six days before the final date fixed for the receipt of tenders.

7.   Where tenders can be made only after a visit to the site or after on-the-spot inspection of the documents supporting the contract documents, the time limit laid down in paragraphs 3 and 4 shall be extended accordingly.

Article 20

1. In cases where urgency renders impracticable the time limits laid down in Article 19, the contracting authorities may fix the following time limits:

(a) a time limit for receipt of requests to participate which shall be not less than 15 days from the date of dispatch of the notice;

(b) a time limit for the receipt of tenders which shall be not less than 10 days from the date of the invitation to tender.

2. Provided it has been requested in good time, additional information relating to the contract documents must be supplied by the contracting authorities not later than four days before the final date fixed for the receipt of tenders.

3. Requests for participation in contracts and invitations to tender must be made by the most rapid means of communication possible. When requests to participate are made by telegram, telex, fax or telephone, they must be confirmed by letter dispatched before the expiry of the time limit referred to in paragraph 1.

Article 21

Contracting authorities may arrange for the publication in the Official Journal of the European Communities of notices announcing public service contracts which are not subject to the publication requirement laid down in this Directive.

Article 22

The conditions for the drawing up, transmission, receipt, translation, collection and distribution of the notices referred to in Articles 15, 16 and 17 and of the statistical reports provided for in Articles 16(4) and 39 and the nomenclature provided for in Annexes I A and B together with the reference in the notices to particular positions of the nomenclature within the categories of services listed in those Annexes may be modified in accordance with the procedure laid down in Article 40(3).

TITLE VI
CHAPTER 1   COMMON RULES ON PARTICIPATION

Article 23

Contracts shall be awarded on the basis of the criteria laid down in Chapter 3, taking into account Article 24, after the suitability of the service providers not excluded under Article 29 has been checked by the contracting authorities in accordance with the criteria referred to in Articles 31 and 32.

Article 24

1. Where the criterion for the award of the contract is that of the economically most advantageous tender, contracting authorities may take account of variants which are submitted by a tenderer and meet the minimum specifications required by such contracting authorities. The contracting authorities shall state in the contract documents the minimum specifications to be respected by the variants and any specific requirements for their presentation. They shall indicate in the contract notice if variants are not authorised. Contracting authorities may not reject the submission of a variant on the sole grounds that it has been drawn up with technical specifications defined by reference to national standards transposing European standards, to European

technical approvals or to common technical specifications referred to in Article 14(2) or even by reference to national technical specifications referred to in Article 14(5)(a)and (b).

2. Contracting authorities which have admitted variants pursuant to paragraph 1 may not reject a variant on the sole grounds that it would lead, if successful, to a supply contract rather than a public service contract within the meaning of this Directive.

Article 25

In the contract documents, the contracting authority may ask the tenderer to indicate in his tender any share of the contract he may intend to subcontract to third parties. This indication shall be without prejudice to the question of the principal service provider's liability.

Article 26

1. Tenders may be submitted by groups of service providers. These groups may not be required to assume a specific legal form in order to submit the tender; however, the group selected may be required to do so when it has been awarded the contract.

2. Candidates or tenderers who, under the law of the Member State in which they are established, are entitled to carry out the relevant service activity, shall not be rejected solely on the grounds that, under the law of the Member State in which the contract is awarded, they would have been required to be either natural or legal persons.

3. Legal persons may be required to indicate in the tender or the request for participation the names and relevant professional qualifications of the staff to be responsible for the performance of the service.

Article 27

1. In restricted and negotiated procedures the contracting authorities shall, on the basis of information given relating to the service provider's position as well as to the information and formalities necessary for the evaluation of the minimum conditions of an economic and technical nature to be fulfilled by him, select from among the candidates with the qualifications required by Articles 29 to 35 those whom they will invite to submit a tender or to negotiate.

2. Where the contracting authorities award a contract by restricted procedure, they may prescribe the range within which the number of service providers which they intend to invite will fall. In this case the range shall be indicated in the contract notice. The range shall be determined in the light of the nature of the service to be provided. The range must number at least five service providers and may be up to twenty. In any event, the number of candidates invited to tender shall be sufficient to ensure genuine competition.

3. Where the contracting authorities award a contract by negotiated procedure as referred to in Article 11(2), the number of candidates admitted to negotiate may not be less than three, provided that there is a sufficient number of suitable candidates.

4. Each Member State shall ensure that contracting authorities issue invitations without discrimination to those nationals of other Member States who satisfy the necessary requirements and under the same conditions as to its own nationals.

documents or certificates, they may be replaced by a declaration on oath made by the person concerned before a judicial or administrative authority, a notary or a competent professional or trade body, in the country of origin or in the country whence that person comes. Member States shall, within the time limit referred to in Article 44, designate the authorities and bodies competent to issue such documents or certificates and shall forthwith inform the other Member States and the Commission thereof.

Article 30

1. In so far as candidates for a public contract or tenderers have to possess a particular authorisation or to be members of a particular organization in their home country in order to be able to perform the service concerned, the contracting authority may require them to prove that they hold such authorisation or membership.

2. Any candidate or tenderer may be requested to prove his enrolment, as prescribed in his country of establishment, in one of the professional or trade registers or to provide a declaration or certificate as described in paragraph 3 below.

3. The relevant professional and trade registers or declarations or certificates are:

— in Belgium, the 'registre du commerce — Handelsregister' and the 'ordres professionels — Beroepsorden',

— in Denmark, the 'Erhvervs- og Selskabstyrelsen',

— in Germany, the 'Handelsregister', the 'Handwerksrolle' and the 'Vereinsregister',

— in Greece, the service provider may be asked to provide a declaration on the exercise of the profession concerned made on oath before a notary; in the cases provided for by existing national legislation, for the provision of research services as mentioned in Annex I A, the professional register 'Mhtrvo Melethtvn' and 'Mhtrvo Grafeivn Meletvn',

— in Spain, the 'Registro Central de Empresas Consultoras y de Servicios del Ministerio de Economía y Hacienda',

— in France, the 'registre du commerce' and the 'répertoire des métiers',

— in Italy, the 'Registro della Camera di commercio, industria, agricoltura e artigianato', the 'Registro delle commissioni provinciali per l'artigianato' or the 'Consiglio nazionale degli ordini professionali',

— in Luxembourg, the 'registre aux firmes' and the 'rôle de la Chambre des métiers',

— in the Netherlands, the 'Handelsregister',

— in Portugal, the 'Registro nacional das Pessoas Colectivas',

— in Austria, the Firmenbuch, the Gewerberegister, the Mitgliederverzeichnisse der Landeskammern;

— in Finland, Kaupparekisteri/Handelsregistret;

— in Sweden, aktiebolags-, handels- eller

— in the United Kingdom and Ireland, the service provider may be requested to provide a certificate from the Registrar of Companies or the Registrar of Friendly Societies or, if he is not so certified, a certificate stating that the person concerned has declared on oath that he is engaged in the profession in question in the country in which he is established in a specific place under a given business name.

Article 31

1. Proof of the service provider's financial and economic standing may, as a general rule, be furnished by one or more of the following references:

(a) appropriate statements from banks or evidence of relevant professional risk indemnity insurance;

(b) the presentation of the service provider's balance sheets or extracts therefrom, where publication of the balance sheets is required under company law in the country in which the service provider is established;

(c) a statement of the undertaking's overall turnover and its turnover in respect of the services to which the contract relates for the previous three financial years.

2. The contracting authorities shall specify in the contract notice or in the invitation to tender which reference or references mentioned in paragraph 1 they have chosen and which other references are to be produced.

3. If, for any valid reason, the service provider is unable to provide the references requested by the contracting authority, he may prove his economic and financial standing by any other document which the contracting authority considers appropriate.

Article 32

1. The ability of service providers to perform services may be evaluated in particular with regard to their skills, efficiency, experience and reliability.

2. Evidence of the service provider's technical capability may be furnished by one or more of the following means according to the nature, quantity and purpose of the services to be provided:

(a) the service provider's educational and professional qualifications and/or those of the firm's managerial staff and, in particular, those of the person or persons responsible for providing the services;

(b) a list of the principal services provided in the past three years, with the sums, dates and recipients, public or private, of the services provided;

— where provided to contracting authorities, evidence to be in the form of certificates issued or countersigned by the competent authority,

— where provided to private purchasers, delivery to be certified by the purchaser or, failing this, simply declared by the service provider to have been effected;

(c) an indication of the technicians or technical bodies involved, whether or not belonging directly to the service provider, especially those responsible for quality control;

(d) a statement of the service provider's average annual manpower and the number of managerial staff for the last three years;

(e) a statement of the tool, plant or technical equipment available to the service provider for carrying out the services;

(f) a description of the service provider's measures for ensuring quality and his study and research facilities;

(g) where the services to be provided are complex or, exceptionally, are required for a special purpose, a check carried out by the contracting authority or on its behalf by a competent official body of the country in which the service provider is established, subject to that body's agreement, on the technical capacities of the service provider and, if necessary, on his study and research facilities and quality control measures;

(h) an indication of the proportion of the contract which the service provider may intend to sub-contract.

3. The contracting authority shall specify, in the notice or in the invitation to tender, which references it wishes to receive.

4. The extent of the information referred to in Article 31 and in paragraphs 1, 2 and 3 of this Article must be confined to the subject of the contract; contracting authorities shall take into consideration the legitimate interests of the service providers as regards the protection of their technical or trade secrets.

Article 33

Where contracting authorities require the production of certificates drawn up by independent bodies for attesting conformity of the service with certain quality assurance standards, they shall refer to quality assurance systems based on the relevant EN 29,000 European standards series certified by bodies conforming to the EN 45,000 European standards series. They shall recognise equivalent certificates from bodies established in other Member States. They shall also accept other evidence of equivalent quality assurance measures from service providers who have no access to such certificates, or no possibility of obtaining them within the relevant time limits.

Article 34

Within the limits of Articles 29 to 32, contracting authorities may invite the service providers to supplement the certificates and documents submitted or to clarify them.

Article 35

1. Member States who have official lists of recognised service providers must adapt them to the provisions of Articles 29(a) to (d) and (g) and of Articles 30, 31 and 32.

2. Service providers registered in the official lists may, for each contract, submit to the contracting authority a certificate of registration issued by the competent authority. This certificate shall state the reference which enabled them to be registered in the list and the classification given in this list.

3. Certified registration in official lists of service providers by the competent bodies shall, for the contracting authorities of other Member States, constitute a presumption of suitability corresponding to the service provider's classification only as regards Article 29(a) to (d) and (g), Article 30, Article 31(b) and (c) and Article 32(a). Information which can be deduced from registration in official lists may not be questioned. However, with regard to the payment of social security contributions, an additional certificate may be required of any registered service provider whenever a contract is offered. The contracting authorities of other Member States shall apply the above provisions only in favour of service providers established in the Member State holding the official list.

4. When registering service providers from other Member States in an official list, no proof or statement can be required in addition to those required of national service providers and, in any case, none in addition to those required in Articles 29 to 33.

5. Member States which have official lists shall be obliged to inform the other Member States of the address of the body to which applications for registration should be sent.

CHAPTER 3   CRITERIA FOR THE AWARD OF CONTRACTS

Article 36

1.   Without prejudice to national laws, regulations or administrative provisions on the remuneration of certain services, the criteria on which the contracting authority shall base the award of contracts may be:

(a)   where the award is made to the economically most advantageous tender, various criteria relating to the contract: for example, quality, technical merit, aesthetic and functional characteristics, technical assistance and after-sales service, delivery date, delivery period or period of completion, price; or

(b)   the lowest price only.

2.   Where the contract is to be awarded to the economically most advantageous tender, the contracting authority shall state in the contract documents or in the tender notice the award criteria which it intends to apply, where possible in descending order of importance.

Article 37

If, for a given contract, tenders appear to be abnormally low in relation to the service to be provided, the contracting authority shall, before it may reject those tenders, request in writing details of the constituent elements of the tender which it considers relevant and shall verify those constituent elements taking account of the explanations received. The contracting authority may take into consideration explanations which are justified on objective grounds including the economy of the method by which the service is provided, or the technical solutions chosen, or the exceptionally favourable conditions available to the tenderer for the provision of the service, or the originality of the service proposed by the tenderer. If the documents relating to the contract provide for its award at the lowest price tendered, the contracting authority must communicate to the Commission the rejection of tenders which it considers to be too low.

TITLE VII   FINAL PROVISIONS

Article 38

The calculation of time limits shall be made in accordance with Council Regulation (EEC, Euratom) No 1182/71 of 3 June 1971 determining the rules applicable to periods, dates and time limits.[1]

Note
[1]OJ No. L124, 8.6.1971, p. 1.

Article 39

1.   In order to permit assessment of the results of applying the Directive, Member States shall, by 31 October 1995 at the latest for the preceding year and thereafter by 31 October of every second year, forward to the Commission a statistical report on the service contracts awarded by contracting authorities.

2.   This report shall detail at least the number and value of contracts awarded by each contracting authority or category of contracting authority above the threshold, subdivided as far as possible by procedure, category of service and the nationality of the service provider to whom the contract has been awarded and, in the case of negotiated procedures, subdivided in accordance with Article 11, listing the number and value of the contracts awarded to each Member State and to third countries.

3.   The Commission shall determine in accordance with the procedure laid down in Article 40(3) the nature of any statistical information which is required in accordance with this Directive.

Article 40
1.   The Commission shall be assisted by the Advisory Committee for Public Contracts set up by Decision 71/306/EEC.
2.   As regards telecommunications services falling within category 5 of Annex IA, the Commission shall also be assisted by the Advisory Committee on Telecommunications Procurement set up by Directive 90/531/EEC.
3.   Where reference is made to the procedure laid down in this paragraph, the representative of the Commission shall submit to the Committee a draft of the measures to be taken. The Committee shall deliver its opinion on the draft within a time limit which the chairman may lay down according to the urgency of the matter, if necessary by taking a vote. The opinion shall be recorded in the minutes; in addition, each Member State shall have the right to ask to have its position recorded in the minutes. The Commission shall take the utmost account of the opinion delivered by the Committee. It shall inform the Committee of the manner in which its opinion has been taken into account.
4.   The Committees mentioned in paragraphs 1 and 2 shall examine, on the initiative of the Commission or at the request of a Member State, any question relating to the application of the Directive.

Article 41
Article 1(1) of Council Directive 89/665/EEC of 21 December 1989 on the co-ordination of the laws, regulations and administrative provisions relating to the application of review procedures to the award of public supply and public works contracts[1] shall be replaced by the following:
   '1.   The Member States shall take the measures necessary to ensure that, as regards contract award procedures falling within the scope of Directives 71/305/EEC, 77/62/EEC, and 92/50/EEC,[2] decisions taken by the contracting authorities may be reviewed effectively and, in particular, as rapidly as possible in accordance with the conditions set out in the following Articles and, in particular, Article 2(7) on the grounds that such decisions have infringed Community law in the field of public procurement or national rules implementing that law.'

Notes
[1]OJ No. L395, 30.12.1989, p. 33.
[2]OJ No. L209, 24.7.1992, p. 1.

Article 42
Editor's Note: Repealed by Directive 93/36.

Article 43
Not later than three years after the time limit for compliance with this Directive, the Commission, acting in close cooperation with the Committees referred to in Article 40(1) and (2), shall review the way in which this Directive has operated, including the effects of the application of the Directive to procurement of the services listed in Annex I A and the provisions concerning technical standards. It shall evaluate, in particular, the prospects for the full application of the Directive to procurement of the other services listed in Annex

I B, and the effects of in-house performance of services on the effective opening-up of procurement in this area. It shall make the necessary proposals to adapt the Directive accordingly.

Article 44

1.   Member States shall bring into force the laws, regulations and administrative provisions necessary to comply with this Directive before 1 July 1993. They shall forthwith inform the Commission thereof. When Member States adopt these provisions, they shall contain a reference to this Directive or shall be accompanied by such reference on the occasion of their official publication. The methods of making such a reference shall be laid down by the Member States.

2.   Member States shall communicate to the Commission the texts of the main provisions of national law which they adopt in the field governed by this Directive.

Article 45

This Directive is addressed to the Member States.

Done at Luxembourg, 18 June 1992.
For the Council,
The President
Victor MARTINS

ANNEX I

A   Services within the meaning of Article 8

Category No	Subject CPC	Reference No
1.	Maintenance and repair services	6112, 6122, 633, 886
2.	Land transport services(^{1}), including armoured car services, and courier services, except transport of mail	712 (except 71235), 7512, 87304
3.	Air transport services of passengers and freight, except transport of mail 73	(except 7321)
4.	Transport of mail by land(^{1}) and by air	71235, 7321
5.	Telecommunications services(^{2})	752
6.	Financial services ex 81	
	(a) Insurance services	812, 814
	(b) Banking and investment services(^{3})	
7.	Computer and related services	84
8.	R & D services(^{4})	85
9.	Accounting, auditing and book-keeping services	862
10.	Market research and public opinion polling services	864
11.	Management consultant services(^{5}) and related services	865, 866
12.	Architectural services; engineering services and integrated engineering services; urban planning and landscape architectural services; related scientific and technical consulting services; technical testing and analysis services	867
13.	Advertising services	871
14.	Building-cleaning services and property management services	874 82201 to 82206

Category No	Subject CPC	Reference No
15.	Publishing and printing services on a fee or contract basis	88442
16.	Sewage and refuse disposal services; sanitation and similar services	94
17.(¹)	Except for rail transport services covered by Category	
18.(²)	Except voice telephony, telex, radiotelephony, paging and satellite services.(³) Except contracts for financial services in connection with the issue, sale, purchase or transfer of securities or other financial instruments, and central bank services.(⁴) Except research and development service contracts other than those where the benefits accrue exclusively to the contracting authority for its use in the conduct of its own affairs on condition that the service provided is wholly remunerated by the contracting authority.(⁵) Except arbitration and conciliation services.	

ANNEX I

B   Services within the meaning of Article 9

Category No	Subject CPC	Reference No.
17.	Hotel and restaurant services	64
18.	Rail transport services	711
19.	Water transport services	72
20.	Supporting and auxiliary transport services	74
21.	Legal services	861
22.	Personnel placement and supply services	872
23.	Investigation and security services, except armoured car services	873 (except 87304)
24.	Education and vocational education services	92
25.	Health and social services	93
26.	Recreational, cultural and sporting services	96
27.	Other services	

ANNEX II   DEFINITION OF CERTAIN TECHNICAL SPECIFICATIONS

For the purpose of this Directive the following terms shall be defined as follows:

1. Technical specifications: the totality of the technical prescriptions contained in particular in the tender documents, defining the characteristics required of a work, material, product or supply, which permits a work, a material, a product or a supply to be described in a manner such that it fulfils the use for which it is intended by the contracting authority. These technical prescriptions shall include levels of quality, performance, safety or dimensions, including the requirements applicable to the material, the product or to the supply as regards quality assurance, terminology, symbols, testing and test methods, packaging, marking or labelling. They shall also include rules relating to design and costing, the test, inspection and acceptance conditions for works and methods or techniques of construction and all other technical conditions which the contracting authority is in a position to prescribe, under general or

specific regulations, in relation to the finished works and to the materials or parts which they involve.

2. Standard: a technical specification approved by a recognised standardising body for repeated and continuous application, compliance with which is in principle not compulsory.

3. European standard: a standard approved by the European Committee for Standardisation (CEN) or by the European Committee for Electrotechnical Standardisation (Cenelec) as 'European Standards (EN)' or 'Harmonization documents (HD)' according to the common rules of these organisations or by the European Telecommunications Standards Institute (ETSI) as a 'European Telecommunication standard' (ETS).

4. European technical approval: a favourable technical assessment of the fitness for use of a product, based on fulfilment of the essential requirements for building works, by means of the inherent characteristics of the product and the defined conditions of applications and use. European approval shall be issued by an approval body designated for this purpose by the Member State;

5. Common technical specification: a technical specification laid down in accordance with a procedure recognised by the Member States to ensure uniform application in all Member States which has been published in the Official Journal of the European Communities.

6. Essential requirements: requirements regarding safety, health and certain other aspects in the general interest, that the construction works can meet.

ANNEX III MODEL CONTRACT NOTICES

A Prior information

1. Name, address, telegraphic address, telephone, telex and fax numbers of the contracting authority, and, if different, of the service from which additional information may be obtained.

2. Intended total procurement in each of the service categories listed in Annex I A.

3. Estimated date for initiating the award procedures, per category.

4. Other information.

5. Date of dispatch of the notice.

6. Date of receipt of the notice by the Office for Official Publications of the European Communities.

B Open procedure

1. Name, address, telegraphic address, telephone, telex and fax numbers of the contracting authority.

2. Category of service and description. CPC reference number.

3. Place of delivery.

4. (a) Indication of whether the execution of the service is reserved by law, regulation or administrative provision to a particular profession.

(b) Reference of the law, regulation or administrative provision.

(c) Indication of whether legal persons should indicate the names and professional qualifications of the staff to be responsible for the execution of the service.

5. Indication of whether service providers can tender for a part of the services concerned.

6. Where applicable, non-acceptance of variants.

7. Duration of contract or time limit for completion of the service.

8. (a) Name and address of the service from which the necessary documents may be requested.

(b) Final date for making such requests.

(c) Where applicable, the amount and terms of payment of any sum payable for such documents.

9. (a) Persons authorised to be present at the opening of tenders.

(b) Date, time and place of the opening.

10. Where applicable, any deposits and guarantees required.

11. Main terms concerning financing and payment and/or references to the relevant provisions.

12. Where applicable, the legal form to be taken by the grouping of service providers winning the contract.

13. Information concerning the service provider's own position, and information and formalities necessary for an appraisal of the minimum economic and technical standards required of him.

14. Period during which the tenderer is bound to keep open his tender.

15. Criteria for the award of the contract and, if possible, their order of importance. Criteria other than that of the lowest price shall be mentioned if they do not appear in the contract documents.

16. Other information.

17. Date of dispatch of the notice.

18. Date of receipt of the notice by the Office for Official Publications of the European Communities.

C   Restricted procedure

1. Name, address, telegraphic address, telephone, telex and fax number of the contracting authority.

2. Category of service and description. CPC reference number.

3. Place of delivery.

4. (a) Indication of whether the execution of the service is reserved by law, regulation or administrative provision to a particular profession.

(b) Reference of the law, regulation or administrative provision.

(c) Indication whether legal persons should indicate the names and professional qualifications of the staff to be responsible for the execution of the service.

5. Indication of whether the service provider can tender for a part of the services concerned.

6. Envisaged number or range of service providers which will be invited to tender.

7. Where applicable, non-acceptance of variants.

8. Duration of contract, or time limit for completion of the service.

9. Where applicable, the legal form to be assumed by the grouping of service providers winning the contract.

10. (a) Where applicable, justification for the use of the accelerated procedure.

(b) Final date for the receipt of requests to participate.

(c) Address to which they must be sent.

(d) Language(s) in which they must be drawn up.

11. Final date for the dispatch of invitations to tender.

12. Where applicable, any deposits and guarantees required.

13. Information concerning the service provider's own position, and the information and formalities necessary for an appraisal of the minimum economic and technical standards required of him.

14. Criteria for the award of the contract and, if possible, their order of importance if these are not stated in the invitation to tender.

15. Other information.

16. Date of dispatch of the notice.

17. Date of receipt of the notice by the Office for Official Publications of the European Communities.

D   Negotiated procedure

1. Name, address, telegraphic address, telephone, telex and fax number of the contracting authority.

2. Category of service and description. CPC reference number.

3. Place of delivery.

4. (a) Indication of whether the execution of the service is reserved by law, regulation or administrative provision to a particular profession.

(b) Reference of the law, regulation or administrative provision.

(c) Indication of whether legal persons should indicate the names and professional qualifications of the staff to be responsible for the execution of the service.

5. Indication of whether the service provider can tender for a part of the services concerned.

6. Envisaged number or range of service providers which will be invited to tender.

7. Where applicable, non-acceptance of variants.

8. Duration of contract, or time limit for completion of the service.

9. Where applicable, the legal form to be assumed by the grouping of service providers winning the contract.

10. (a) Where applicable, justification for the use of the accelerated procedure.

(b) Final date for the receipt of requests to participate.

(c) Address to which they must be sent.

(d) Language(s) in which they must be drawn up.

11. Where applicable, any deposits and guarantees required.

12. Information concerning the service provider's own position, and the information and formalities necessary for an appraisal of the minimum economic and technical standards required of him.

13. Where applicable, the names and addresses of service providers already selected by the contracting authority.

14. Other information.

15. Date of dispatch of the notice.

16. Date of receipt of the notice by the Office for Official Publications of the European Communities.

17. Previous date(s) of publication in the Official Journal of the European Communities.

E   Contract award notice

1. Name and address of the contracting authority.

2. Award procedure chosen. In the case of the negotiated procedure without prior publication of a tender notice, justification (Article 11(3)).

3. Category of service and description. CPC reference number.

4. Date of award of the contract.

5.   Criteria for award of the contract.
6.   Number of tenders received.
7.   Name and address of service provider(s).
8.   Price or range of prices (minimum/maximum) paid.
9.   Where appropriate, value and proportion of the contract which may be subcontracted to third parties.
10.   Other information.
11.   Date of publication of the contract notice in the Official Journal of the European Communities.
12.   Date of dispatch of the notice.
13.   Date of receipt of the notice by the Office for Official Publications of the European Communities.
14.   In the case of contracts for services listed in Annex I B, agreement by the contracting authority to publication of the notice (Article 16(3)).

ANNEX IV

A   Design contest notice
1.   Name, address, telegraphic address, telephone, telex and fax numbers of the contracting authority and of the service from which additional documents may be obtained.
2.   Project description.
3.   Nature of the contest: open or restricted.
4.   In the case of open contests: final date for receipt of projects.
5.   In the case of restricted contests:
   (a)   the number of participants envisaged;
   (b)   where applicable, names of participants already selected;
   (c)   criteria for the selection of participants;
   (d)   final date for receipt of requests to participate.
6.   Where applicable, indication of whether participation is reserved to a particular profession.
7.   Criteria to be applied in the evaluation of projects.
8.   Where applicable, names of the selected members of the jury.
9.   Indication of whether the decision of the jury is binding on the contracting authority.
10.   Where applicable, number and value of prizes.
11.   Where applicable, details of payments to all participants.
12.   Indication of whether the prize-winners are permitted any follow-up contracts.
13.   Other information.
14.   Date of dispatch of the notice.
15.   Date of receipt of the notice by the Office for Official Publications of the European Communities.

B   Results of design contest
1.   Name, address, telegraphic address, telephone, telex and fax numbers of the contracting authority.
2.   Project description.
3.   Total number of participants.
4.   Number of foreign participants.
5.   Winner(s) of the contest.
6.   Where applicable, the prize(s).
7.   Other information.
8.   Reference of the design contest notice.
9.   Date of dispatch of the notice.

10.   Date of receipt of the notice by the Office for Official Publications of the European Communities.

COUNCIL DIRECTIVE (EEC) 93/36 OF 14 JUNE 1993 COORDINATING PROCEDURES FOR THE AWARD OF PUBLIC SUPPLY CONTRACTS
[OJ 1993, No. L199/1]*

THE COUNCIL OF THE EUROPEAN COMMUNITIES,

Having regard to the Treaty establishing the European Economic Community, and in particular Article 100a thereof,
Having regard to the proposal from the Commission,[1]
In cooperation with the European Parliament,[2]
Having regard of the opinion of the Economic and Social Committee,[3]

Whereas Council Directive 77/62/EEC of 21 December 1976 coordinating procedures for the award of public supply contracts[4] has been amended on a number of occasions; whereas, on the occasion of further amendments, the said Directive should, for reasons of clarity be recast;

Whereas it seems important in particular to align the drafting of the present Directive, as far as possible, on the provisions on public procurement as contained in Council Directive 93/37/EEC concerning the coordination of procedures for the award of public works contracts[5] and Council Directive 92/50/EEC of 18 June 1992, relating to the coordination of procedures on the award of public service contracts[6]

Whereas the alignments to be introduced relate, in particular, to the introduction of the functional definition of contracting authorities, the option of recourse to the open or restricted procedure, the requirement to justify the refusal of candidates or tenderers, the rules for drawing up reports on the execution of the different award procedures, the conditions for referring to the common rules in the technical field, publication and participation, clarifications concerning award criteria and the introduction of the Advisory Committee procedure;

Whereas the attainment of freedom of movement of goods in respect of public supply contracts awarded in Member States on behalf of the State, or regional or local authorities or other bodies governed by public law entails not only the abolition of restrictions but also the coordination of national procedures for the award of public supply contracts;

Whereas such coordination should take into account as far as possible the procedures and administrative practices in force in each Member State;

Whereas the Community is a Party to the Agreement on government procurement,[7] hereinafter referred to as 'the GATT Agreement';

Notes
*As amended by the Act of Accession for Austria, Finland and Sweden [OJ 1994 C241/228] and Decision 95/1 [OJ 1995 L1/1].
[1]OJ No. C277, 26.10.1992, p. 1.
[2]OJ No. C72, 15.3.1993, p. 73 and Decision of 26.5.1993 (not yet published in the Official Journal).
[3]OJ No. C332, 16.12.1992, p. 72.
[4]OJ No. L13, 15.1.1977, p. 1. Directive as last amended by Directive 92/50//EEC (OJ No. L209, 24.7.1992, p. 1).
[5]See p. 54 of this Official Journal.
[6]OJ No. L209, 24.7.1992, p. 1.
[7]OJ No. L71, 17.3.1980, p. 44 and OJ No. L345, 9.12.1987, p. 24.

Whereas Annex I to this Directive sets out the lists of contracting authorities subject to the GATT Agreement; whereas it is necessary to update this Annex in accordance with amendments submitted by the Member States;

Whereas this Directive does not apply to certain supply contracts which are awarded in the water, energy, transport and telecommunication sectors covered by Directive 90/531/EEC.[8]

Whereas, without prejudice to the application of the threshold set out for supply contracts subject to the GATT Agreement, supply contracts of less than ECU 200,000 may be exempted from competition as provided under this Directive and it is appropriate to provide for their exemption from coordination measures;

Whereas provision must be made for exceptional cases where measures concerning the coordination of procedures may not necessarily be applied, but whereas such cases must be expressly limited;

Whereas the negotiated procedure should be considered to be exceptional and therefore applicable only in limited cases;

Whereas it is necessary to provide common rules in the technical field which take account of the Community policy on standards and specifications; Whereas, to ensure development of effective competition in the field of public contracts, it is necessary that contract notices drawn up by the contracting authorities of Member States be advertised throughout the Community; whereas the information contained in these notices must enable suppliers established in the Community to determine whether the proposed contracts are of interest to them; whereas, for this purpose, it is appropriate to give them adequate information about the goods to be supplied and the conditions attached to their supply; whereas, more particularly, in restricted procedures advertisement is intended to enable suppliers of Member States to express their interest in contracts by seeking from the contracting authorities invitations to tender under the required conditions;

Whereas additional information concerning contracts must, as is customary in Member States, be given in the contract documents for each contract or else in an equivalent document;

Whereas it is necessary to provide common rules for participation in public supply contracts, including both qualitative selection criteria and criteria for the award of the contracts;

Whereas it would be appropriate to enable certain technical conditions concerning notices and statistical reports required by this Directive to be adapted in the light of changing technical requirements; whereas Annex II to this Directive refers to a nomenclature, whereas the Community may, as required, revise or replace its common nomenclature and whereas it is necessary to make provision for the possibility of adapting the reference made to the nomenclature accordingly;

Whereas this Directive should not affect the obligations of the Member States concerning the deadlines for transposition into national law and for application indicated in Annex V,

HAS ADOPTED THIS DIRECTIVE:

Note
[8] OJ No. L297, 29.10.1990, p. 1.

GATT Agreement, its threshold expressed in ECUs shall be published in the Official Journal of the European Communities at the beginning of the month of November which follows the revision laid down in the first part of subparagraph (c).

2. In the case of contracts for the lease, rental or hire purchase of products, the basis for calculating the estimated contract value shall be:

— in the case of fixed-term contracts, where their term is 12 months or less the total contract value for its duration, or, where their term exceeds 12 months, its total value including the estimated residual value;

— in the case of contracts for an indefinite period or in cases where there is doubt as to the duration of the contracts the monthly value multiplied by 48.

3. In the case of regular contracts or of contracts which are to be renewed within a given time, the estimated contract value shall be established on the basis of:

— either the actual aggregate value of similar contracts concluded over the previous fiscal year or 12 months, adjusted where possible, for anticipated changes in quantity or value over the 12 months following the initial

— or the estimated aggregate value during the 12 months following the first delivery or during the term of the contract, where this is greater than 12 months. The selection of the valuation method shall not be used with the intention of avoiding the application of this Directive.

4. If a proposed procurement of supplies of the same type may lead to contracts being awarded at the same time in separate parts, the estimated value of the total sum of these parts must be taken as the basis for the application of paragraphs 1 and 2.

5. In the case where a proposed procurement specifies option clauses, the basis for calculating the estimated contract value shall be the highest possible total of the purchase, lease, rental, or hire-purchase permissible, inclusive of the option clauses.

6. No procurement requirement for a given quantity of supplies may be split up with the intention of avoiding the application of this Directive.

Article 6

1. In awarding public supply contracts the contracting authorities shall apply the procedures defined in Article 1(d), (e) and (f), in the cases set out below.

2. The contracting authorities may award their supply contracts by negotiated procedure in the case of irregular tenders in response to an open or restricted procedure or in the case of tenders which are unacceptable under national provisions that are in accordance with provisions of Title IV, in so far as the original terms for the contract are not substantially altered. The contracting authorities shall in these cases publish a tender notice unless they include in such negotiated procedures all the enterprises satisfying the criteria of Articles 20 to 24 which, during the prior open or restricted procedure, have submitted tenders in accordance with the formal requirements of the tendering procedure.

3. The contracting authorities may award their supply contracts by negotiated procedure without prior publication of a tender notice, in the following:

(a) in the absence of tenders or appropriate tenders in response to an open or restricted procedure insofar as the original terms of the contract are not substantially altered and provided that a report is communicated to the Commission;

(b)   when the products involved are manufactured purely for the purpose of research, experiment, study or development, this provision does not extend to quantity production to establish commercial viability or to recover research and development costs;

(c)   when, for technical or artistic reasons, or for reasons connected with protection of exclusive rights, the products supplied may be manufactured or delivered only by a particular supplier;

(d)   in so far as is strictly necessary when, for reasons of extreme urgency brought about by events unforeseeable by the contracting authorities in question, the time limit laid down for the open, restricted or negotiated procedures referred to in paragraph 2 cannot be kept. The circumstances invoked to justify extreme urgency must not in any event be attributable to the contracting authorities;

(e)   for additional deliveries by the original supplier which are intended either as a partial replacement of normal supplies or installations or as the extension of existing supplies or installations where a change of supplier would oblige the contracting authority to acquire material having different technical characteristics which would result in incompatibility or disproportionate technical difficulties in operation and maintenance. The length of such contracts as well as that of recurrent contracts may, as a general rule, not exceed three years.

4.   In all other cases, the contracting authorities shall award their supply contracts by the open procedure or by the restricted procedure.

Article 7

1.   The contracting authority shall, within 15 days of the date on which the request is received, inform any eliminated candidate or tenderer who so requests of the reasons for rejection of his application or his tender, and, in the case of a tender, the name of the successful tenderer.

2.   The contracting authority shall inform candidates or tenderers who so request of the grounds on which it decided not to award a contract in respect of which a prior call for competition was made, or to recommence the procedure. It shall also inform the Office for Official Publications of the European Communities of that decision.

3.   For each contract awarded the contracting authorities shall draw up a written report which shall include at least the following:

— the name and address of the contracting authority, the subject and value of the contract,

— the names of the candidates or tenderers admitted and the reasons for their selection,

— the names of the candidates or tenderers rejected and the reasons for their rejection,

— the name of the successful tenderer and the reasons for his tender having been selected and, if known, any share of the contract the successful tenderer may intend to subcontract to a third party,

— for negotiated procedures, the circumstances referred to in Article 6 which justify the use of these procedures.

This report, or the main features of it, shall be communicated to the Commission at its request.

TITLE II   COMMON RULES IN THE TECHNICAL FIELD

Article 8

1. The technical specifications defined in Annex III shall be given in the general or contractual documents relating to each contract.

2. Without prejudice to the legally binding national technical rules, in so far as these are compatible with Community law, the technical specifications mentioned in paragraph 1 shall be defined by the contracting authorities by reference to national standards implementing European standards, or by reference to European technical approvals or by reference to common technical specifications.

3. A contracting authority may depart from paragraph 2 if:

(a)   the standards, European technical approvals or common technical specifications do not include any provision for establishing conformity or technical means do not exist for establishing satisfactorily the conformity of a product to these standards, European technical approvals or common technical specifications;

(b)   the application of paragraph 2 would prejudice the application of Council Directive 86/361/EEC of 24 July 1986 on the initial stage of the mutual recognition of type approval for telecommunications terminal equipment[1] or Council Decision 87/95/EEC of 22 December 1986 on standardisation in the field of information technology and telecommunications[2] or other Community instruments in specific service or product areas;

(c)   use of these standards, European technical approvals or common technical specifications would oblige the contracting authority to acquire supplies incompatible with equipment already in use or would entail disproportionate costs or disproportionate technical difficulties, but only as part of a clearly defined and recorded strategy with a view to change-over, within a given period, to European standards, European technical approvals or common technical specifications;

(d)   the project concerned is of a genuinely innovative nature for which use of existing European standards, European technical approvals or common technical specifications would not be appropriate.

4. Contracting authorities invoking paragraph 3 shall record, wherever possible, the reasons for doing so in the tender notice published in the Official Journal of the European Communities or in the contract documents and in all cases shall record these reasons in their internal documentation and shall supply such information on request to Member States and to the Commission.

5. In the absence of European standards, European technical approvals or common technical specifications, the technical specifications:

(a)   shall be defined by reference to the national technical specifications recognised as complying with the basic requirements listed in the Community directives on technical harmonisation, in accordance with the procedures laid down in those directives, and in particular in accordance with the procedures laid down in Directive 89/106/EEC;[3]

Notes
[1]OJ No. L217, 5.8.1986, p. 21. Directive as amended by Directive 91/263/EEC (OJ No. L128, 23.5 1991, p. 1).
[2]OJ No. L36, 7.2.1987, p. 31.
[3]OJ No. L40, 11.2.1989, p. 12.

(b) may be defined by reference to national technical specifications relating to design and method of calculation and execution of works and use of materials;

(c) may be defined by reference to other documents. In this case, it is appropriate to make reference in order of preference to:

(i) national standards implementing international standards accepted by the country of the contracting authority;

(ii) other national standards and national technical approvals of the country of the contracting authority;

(iii) any other standard.

6. Unless such specifications are justified by the subject of the contract, Member States shall prohibit the introduction into the contractual clauses relating to a given contract of technical specifications which mention goods of specific make or source or of a particular process and which therefore favour or eliminate certain suppliers or products. In particular, the indication of trade marks, patents, types or of a specific origin or production shall be prohibited. However, if such indication is accompanied by the words 'or equivalent' it shall be authorised in cases where the contracting authorities are unable to give a description of the subject of the contract using specifications which are sufficiently precise and fully intelligible to all parties concerned.

TITLE III   COMMON ADVERTISING RULES

Article 9

1. The contracting authorities shall make known, as soon as possible after the beginning of their budgetary year, by means of an indicative notice, the total procurement by product area which they envisage awarding during the subsequent 12 months where the total estimated value, taking into account the provisions of Article 5, is equal to or greater than ECU 750,000.

The product area shall be established by the contracting authorities by means of reference to the nomenclature 'Classification of Products According to Activities (CPA)'. The Commission shall determine the conditions of reference in the notice to particular positions of the nomenclature in accordance with the procedure laid down in Article 32(2).

2. Contracting authorities who wish to award a public supply contract by open, restricted or negotiated procedure in the cases referred to in Article 6(2), shall make known their intention by means of a notice.

3. Contracting authorities who have awarded a contract shall make known the result by means of a notice. However, certain information on the contract award may, in certain cases, not be published where release of such information would impede law enforcement or otherwise be contrary to the public interest, would prejudice the legitimate commercial interests of particular enterprises, public or private, or might prejudice fair competition between suppliers.

4. The notices shall be drawn up in accordance with the models given in Annex IV and shall specify the information requested in those models. The contracting authorities may not require any conditions other than those specified in Articles 22 and 23 when requesting information concerning the economic and technical standards which they require of suppliers for their selection (Section 11 of Annex IV B, Section 9 of Annex IV C and Section 8 of Annex IV D).

5. The contracting authorities shall send the notices as rapidly as possible and by the most appropriate channels to the Office for Official Publications of

the European Communities. In the case of the accelerated procedure referred to in Article 12, the notice shall be sent by telex, telegram or telefax. The notice referred to in paragraph 1 shall be sent as soon as possible after the beginning of each budgetary year. The notice referred to in paragraph 3 shall be sent at the latest 48 days after the award of the contract in question.

6. The notices referred to in paragraphs 1 and 3 shall be published in full in the Official Journal of the European Communities and in the TED data bank in the official languages of the Communities, the text in the original language alone being authentic.

7. The notice referred to in paragraph 2 shall be published in full in the Official Journal of the European Communities and in the TED data bank in their original language. A summary of the important elements of each notice shall be published in the official languages of the Communities, the text in the original language alone being authentic.

8. The Office for Official Publications of the European Communities shall publish the notices not later than 12 days after their dispatch. In the case of the accelerated procedure referred to in Article 12, this period shall be reduced to five days.

9. The notices shall not be published in the Official Journals or in the press of the country of the contracting authority before the date of dispatch to the Office for Official Publications of the European Communities; they shall mention that date. They shall not contain information other than that published in the Official Journal of the European Communities.

10. The contracting authorities must be able to supply proof of the date of dispatch.

11. The cost of publication of the notices in the Official Journal of the European Communities shall be borne by the Communities. The length of the notice shall not be greater than one page of the Journal, or approximately 650 words. Each edition of the Journal containing one or more notices shall reproduce the model notice or notices on which the published notice or notices are based.

Article 10

1. In open procedures the time limit for the receipt of tenders, fixed by the contracting authorities, shall not be less than 52 days from the date of dispatch of the notice.

2. Provided they have been requested in good time, the contract documents and supporting documents must be sent to the suppliers by the contracting authorities or competent departments within six days of receiving their application.

3. Provided it has been requested in good time, additional information relating to the contract documents shall be supplied by the contracting authorities not later than six days before the final date fixed for receipt of tenders.

4. Where the contract documents, supporting documents or additional information are too bulky to be supplied within the time limits laid down in paragraph 2 or 3 or where tenders can be made only after a visit to the site or after on-the-spot inspection of the documents supporting the contract documents, the time limit laid down in paragraph 1 shall be extended accordingly.

Article 11

1. In restricted procedures and negotiated procedures as described in Article 6(2), the time limit for receipt of requests to participate fixed by the contracting authorities shall not be less than 37 days from the date of dispatch of the notice.

2. The contracting authorities shall simultaneously and in writing invite the selected candidates to submit their tenders. The letter of invitation shall be accompanied by the contract documents and supporting documents. It shall include at least the following information:

(a)   where appropriate, the address of the service from which the contract documents and supporting documents can be requested and the final date for making such a request; also the amount and terms of payment of any sum to be paid for such documents;

(b)   the final date for receipt of tenders, the address to which they must be sent and the language or languages in which they must be drawn up;

(c)   a reference to the contract notice published;

(d)   an indication of any documents to be annexed, either to support the verifiable statements furnished by the candidate in accordance with Article 9(4), or to supplement the information provided for in that Article under the same conditions as those laid down in Articles 22 and 23;

(e)   the criteria for the award of the contract if these are not given in the notice.

3. In restricted procedures, the time limit receipt of tenders fixed by the contracting authorities may not be less than 40 days from the date of dispatch of the written invitation.

4. Requests to participate in procedures for the award of contracts may be made by letter, by telegram, telex, telefax or by telephone. If by one of the last four, they must be confirmed by letter dispatched before the end of the period laid down in paragraph 1.

5. Provided it has been requested in good time, additional information relating to the contract documents must be supplied by the contracting authorities not later than six days before the final date fixed for receipt of tenders.

6. Where tenders can be made only after a visit to the site or after on-the-spot inspection of the documents supporting the contract documents, the time limit laid down in paragraph 3 shall be extended accordingly.

Article 12

1. In cases where urgency renders impracticable the time limits laid down in Article 11, the contracting authorities may fix the following time limits:

(a)   a time limit for the receipt of requests to participate which shall not be less than 15 days from the date of dispatch of the notice;

(b)   a time limit for the receipt of tenders which shall not be less than 10 days from the date of the invitation to tender.

2. Provided it has been requested in good time, additional information relating to the contract documents must be supplied by the contracting authorities not less than four days before the final date fixed for the receipt of tenders.

3. Requests for participation in contracts and invitations to tender must be made by the most rapid means of communication possible. When requests to

participate are made by telegram, telex, telefax or telephone, they must be confirmed by letter dispatched before the expiry of the time limit referred to in paragraph 1.

Article 13
Contracting authorities may arrange for the publication in the Official Journal of the European Communities of notices announcing public supply contracts which are not subject to the publication requirement laid down in this Directive.

Article 14
The conditions for the drawing up, transmission, receipt, translation, collection and distribution of the notices referred to in Article 9 and of the statistical reports provided for in Article 31 as well as the nomenclature provided for in Article 9 and in Annexes II and IV may be modified in accordance with the procedure laid down in Article 32(2). The conditions for referring in the notices to particular positions in the nomenclature may be determined pursuant to the same procedure.

TITLE IV
CHAPTER 1   COMMON RULES ON PARTICIPATION

Article 15
1.   Contracts shall be awarded on the basis for the criteria laid down in Chapter 3 of this Title, taking into account Article 16, after the suitability of the suppliers not excluded under Article 20 has been checked by the contracting authorities in accordance with the criteria of economic and financial standing and of technical capacity referred to in Articles 22, 23 and 24.
2.   The contracting authorities shall respect fully the confidential nature of any information furnished by the suppliers.

Article 16
1.   Where the criterion for the award of the contract is that of the most economically advantageous tender, contracting authorities may take account of variants which are submitted by a tenderer and meet the minimum specifications required by the contracting authorities.
   The contracting authorities shall state in the contract documents the minimum specifications to be respected by the variants and any specific requirements for their presentation. They shall indicate in the tender notice if variants are not permitted.
   Contracting authorities may not reject the submission of a variant of the sole grounds that it has been drawn up with technical specifications defined by reference to national standards transposing European standards, to European technical approvals or to common technical specifications referred to in Article 8(2), or again by reference to national technical specifications to in Article 8(5)(a)and (b).
2.   Contracting authorities which have admitted variants pursuant to paragraph 1 may not reject a variant on the sole grounds that it would lead, if successful, to a service contract rather than a public supply contract within the meaning of this Directive.

Article 17

In the contract documents, the contracting authority may ask the tenderer to indicate in his tender any share of the contract he may intend to subcontract to third parties.

This indication shall be without prejudice to the question of the principal supplier's liability.

Article 18

Tenders may be submitted by groups of suppliers. These groups may not be required to assume a specific legal form in order to submit the tender; however, the group selected may be required to do so when it has been awarded the contract, to the extent that this change is necessary for the satisfactory performance of the contract.

Article 19

1.   In restricted and negotiated procedures the contracting authorities shall, on the basis of information given relating to the supplier's personal position as well as to the information and formalities necessary for the evaluation of the minimum conditions of an economic and technical nature to be fulfilled by him, select from among the candidates with the qualifications required by Articles 20 to 24 those whom they will invite to submit a tender or to negotiate.

2.   Where the contracting authorities award a contact by restricted procedure, they may prescribe the range within which the number of suppliers which they intend to invite will fall. In this case the range shall be indicated in the contract notice. The range shall be determined in the light of the nature of the goods to be supplied. The range must number at least five suppliers and may be up to 20. In any event, the number of candidates invited to tender shall be sufficient to ensure genuine competition.

3.   Where the contracting authorities award a contract by negotiated procedure as referred to in Article 6(2), the number of candidates admitted to negotiate may not be less than three provided that there is a sufficient number of suitable candidates.

4.   Each Member State shall ensure that contracting authorities issue invitations without discrimination to those nationals of other Member States who satisfy the necessary requirements and under the same conditions as to its own nationals.

CHAPTER 2   CRITERIA FOR QUALITATIVE SELECTION

Article 20

1.   Any supplier may be excluded from participation in the contract who:

(a)   is bankrupt or is being wound up, whose affairs are being administered by the court, who has entered into an arrangement with creditors, who has suspended business activities or who is any analogous situation arising from a similar procedure under national laws and regulations;

(b)   is the subject of proceedings for a declaration of bankruptcy, for an order for compulsory winding up or administration by the court or for an arrangement with creditors or of any other similar proceedings under national laws and regulations;

(c)   has been convicted of an offence concerning his professional conduct by a judgment which has the force of res judicata;

(d) has been guilty of grave professional misconduct proven by any means which the contracting authorities can justify;

(e) has not fulfilled obligations relating to the payment of social security contributions in accordance with the legal provisions of the country in which he is established or with those of the country of the contracting authority;

(f) has not fulfilled obligations relating to the payment of taxes in accordance with the legal provisions of the country in which he is established or those of the country of the contracting authority;

(g) is guilty of serious misrepresentation in supplying the information required under this Chapter.

2. Where the contracting authority requires to the supplier proof that none of the cases quoted in (a), (b), (c), (e) or (f) of paragraph 1 applies to him, it shall accept as sufficient evidence:

— for points (a), (b) or (c), the production of an extract from the 'judicial record' or, failing this, of an equivalent document issued by a competent judicial or administrative authority in the country of origin in the country whence that person comes showing that these requirements have been met,

— for points (e) or (f), a certificate issued by the competent authority in the Member State concerned.

3. Where the country in question does not issue the documents or certificates referred to in paragraph 2 or where these do not cover all the cases quoted in (a), (b) or (c) of paragraph 1, they may be replaced by a declaration on oath or, in Member States where there is no provision for declarations on oath, by a solemn declaration made by the person concerned before a competent judicial or administrative authority, a notary or a competent professional or trade body, in the country of origin whence that person comes.

4. Member States shall designate the authorities and bodies competent to issue the documents, certificates or declarations referred to in paragraphs 2 and 3 and shall forthwith inform the other Member States and the Commission

Article 21

1. Any supplier wishing to take part in a public supply contract may be requested to prove his enrolment, as prescribed in his country of establishment, in one of the professional or trade registers or to provide a declaration on oath or certificate as described in paragraph 2 below.

2. The relevant professional and trade registers or declarations or certificates are:

— in Belgium: 'Registre du commerce/Handelsregister',

— in Denmark: 'Aktieselskabsregistret', 'Foreningsregistret' and 'Handelsregistret',

— in Germany: 'Handelsregister' and 'Handwerksrolle',

— in Greece: 'Viotechniko i Viomichaniko i Emporiko Epimelitirio',

— in Spain: 'Registro Mercantil' or, in the case of non-registered individuals, a certificate stating that the person concerned has declared on oath that he is engaged in the profession in question,

— in France: 'Registre du commerce' and 'répertoire des métiers',

— in Italy: 'Registro della Camera di commercio, industria, agricoltura e artigianato', and 'Registro delle Commissioni provinciali per l'artigianato',

— in Luxembourg: 'Registre aux firmes' and 'Rôle de la chambre des métiers',

— in the Netherlands: 'Handelsregister',

— in Portugal: 'Registo Nacional das Pessoas Colectivas',

— in the United Kingdom and Ireland, the supplier may be requested to provide a certificate from the Registrar of Companies or the Registrar of Friendly Societies, that he is certified as incorporated or registered or, if he is not so certified, a certificate stating that the person concerned has declared on oath that he is engaged in the profession in question in the country in which he is established in a specific place under a given business name and under a specific trading name,

— in Austria, the Firmenbuch, the Gewerberegister, the Mitgliederverzeichnisse der Landeskammern,

— in Finland, Kaupparekisteri/Handelsregistret,

— in Sweden, aktiebolags-, handels- eller foereningsregistren.

Article 22

1.   Evidence of the supplier's financial and economic standing may, as a general rule, be furnished by one or more of the following references:

(a)   appropriate statements from bankers;

(b)   the presentation of the supplier's balance-sheets or extracts from the balance-sheets, where publication of the balance-sheet is required under the law of the country in which the supplier is established;

(c)   a statement of the supplier's overall turnover and its turnover in respect of the products to which the contract relates for the three previous financial years.

2.   The contracting authorities shall specify in the notice or in the invitation to tender which reference or references mentioned in paragraph 1 they have chosen and which references other than those mentioned under paragraph 1 are to be produced.

3.   If, for any valid reason, the supplier is unable to provide the references requested by the contracting authority, he may prove his economic and financial standing by any other document which the contracting authority considers appropriate.

Article 23

1.   Evidence of the supplier's technical capacity may be furnished by one or more of the following means according to the nature, quantity and purpose of the products to be supplied:

(a)   a list of the principal deliveries effected in the past three years, with the sums, dates and recipients, public or private, involved:

— where effected to public authorities, evidence to be in the form of certificates issued or countersigned by the competent authority;

— where effected to private purchasers, delivery to be certified by the purchaser or, failing this, simply declared by the supplier to have been effected;

(b)   a description of the supplier's technical facilities, its measures for ensuring quality and its study and research facilities;

(c)   indication of the technicians or technical bodies involved, whether or not belonging directly to the supplier, especially those responsible for quality control;

(d)   samples, description and/or photographs of the products to be supplied, the authenticity of which must be certified if the contracting authority so requests;

(e)   certificates drawn up by official quality control institutes or agencies of recognised competence attesting conformity to certain specifications or standards of products clearly identified by references to specifications or standards;

(f)   where the products to be supplied are complex or, exceptionally, are required for a special purpose, a check carried out by the contracting authorities or on their behalf by a competent official body of the country in which the supplier is established, subject to that body's agreement, on the production capacities of the supplier and if necessary on his study and research facilities and quality control measures.

2.   The contracting authority shall specify, in the notice or in the invitation to tender, which references it wishes to receive.

3.   The extent of the information referred to in Article 22 and in paragraph 1 and 2 of this Article must be confined to the subject of the contract; the contracting authority shall take into consideration the legitimate interests of the suppliers as regards the protection of their technical or trade secrets.

Article 24
Within the limits of Articles 20 to 23 the contracting authority may invite the suppliers to supplement the certificates and documents submitted or to clarify them.

Article 25
1.   Member States who have official lists of recognised suppliers must adapt them to the provisions of points (a) to (d) and (g) of Article 20(1) and of Articles 21, 22 and 23.

2.   Suppliers registered in the official lists may, for each contract, submit to the contracting authority a certificate of registration issued by the competent authority. This certificate shall state the reference which enabled them to be registered in the list and the classification given in that list.

3.   Certified registration in official lists of suppliers by the competent bodies shall, for the contracting authorities of other Member States, constitute a presumption of suitability corresponding to the suppliers' classification only as regards Article 20(1)(a) to (d) and (g), Article 21, Article 22(1)(b) and (e) Article 23(1)(a).

Information which can be deduced from registration in official lists may not be questioned. However, with regard to the payment of social security contributions, an additional certificate may be required of any registered suppliers whenever a contract is offered.

The contracting authorities of other Member States shall apply the first and second subparagraph only in favour of suppliers established in the Member States holding the official list.

4.   For the registration of suppliers of other Member States in an official list, no further proof or statements can be required other than those requested of national suppliers and, in any event, only those provided for under Articles 20 to 23.

5.   Member States holding an official list shall communicate the address of the body to which requests for registration may be made to other Member States and to the Commission which shall ensure distribution.

CHAPTER 3   CRITERIA FOR THE AWARD OF CONTRACTS

Article 26

1.   The criteria on which the contracting authority shall base the award of contracts shall be:

    (a)   either the lowest price only;

    (b)   or, when award is made to the most economically advantageous tender, various criteria according to the contract in question: e.g. price, delivery date, running costs, cost-effectiveness, quality, aesthetic and functional characteristics, technical merit, after-sales service and technical assistance.

2.   In the case referred to in point (b) of paragraph 1, the contracting authority shall state in the contract documents or in the contract notice all the criteria they intend to apply to the award, where possible in descending order of importance.

Article 27

If, for a given contract, tenders appear to be abnormally low in relation to the goods to be supplied, the contracting authority shall, before it may reject those tenders, request in writing details of the constituent elements of the tender which it considers relevant and shall verify those constituent elements taking account of the explanations received.

The contracting authority may take into consideration explanations relating to the economics of the manufacturing process, or to the technical solutions chosen, or to the exceptionally favourable conditions available to the tenderer for the supply of the goods, or to the originality of the supplies proposed by the tenderer.

If the documents relating to the contract provide for its award at the lowest price tendered, the contracting authority must communicate to the Commission the rejection of tenders which it considers to be too low.

TITLE V   FINAL PROVISIONS

Article 28

For the purposes of the award of public contracts by the contracting authorities referred to in Annex I, and, to the extent that rectifications, modifications or amendments have been made thereto, by their successor authorities, Member States shall apply in their relations conditions as favourable as those which they grant to third countries in implementation of the GATT Agreement, in particular those in Articles V and VI of that Agreement, on the restricted procedure, information and review. The Member States shall to this end consult each other within the Advisory Committee for Public Contracts on the measures to be taken pursuant to the Agreement.

Article 29

1.   The Commission shall examine the application of this Directive in consultation with the Advisory Committee for Public Contracts and where appropriate shall submit new proposals to the Council with the aim in particular of harmonising the measures taken by the Member States for the implementation of this Directive.

2.   The Commission shall review this Directive and any new measures which may be adopted by virtue of paragraph 1, having regard to the results of the further negotiations provided for in Article IX(6) of the GATT Agreement and shall, if necessary, submit appropriate proposals to the Council.

3.   The Commission shall update Annex I on the basis of any rectifications, modifications or amendments referred to in Article 28 and shall have the updated version published in the Official Journal of the European Communities.

Article 30
The calculation of time limits shall be made in accordance with Council Regulation (EEC, Euratom) No 1182/71 of 3 June 1971 determining the rules applicable to periods, dates and time limits.[1]

Note
[1]OJ No. L124, 8.6.1971, p. 1.

Article 31
1.   In order to permit assessment of the results of applying this Directive, Member States shall forward to the Commission a statistical report relative to supply contract awards:
     (a)   not later than 31 October of each year for the preceding year in respect of the contracting authorities listed in Annex I;
     (b)   not later than 31 October 1991 and for the Hellenic Republic, the Kingdom of Spain and the Portuguese Republic 31 October 1995 and thereafter 31 October of each second year for the preceding year in respect of the other contracting authorities within the meaning of Article 1.
2.   The statistical report shall detail at least:
     (a)   the number and value of contracts awarded by each contracting authority above the threshold and, in the case of contracting authorities mentioned in Annex I, the value below the threshold;
     (b)   the number and value of contracts awarded by each contracting authority above the threshold, subdivided by procedure, product and the nationality of the supplier to whom the contract has been awarded, and in the case of negotiated procedures, subdivided in accordance with Article 6, listing the number and value of the contracts awarded to each Member State and to third countries, and in the case of contracting authorities referred to in Annex I, the number and value of the contracts awarded to each signatory to the GATT Agreement.
3.   The Commission shall determine in accordance with the procedure laid down in Article 32(2) the nature of any additional statistical information, which is required in accordance with this Directive.

Article 32
1.   The Commission shall be assisted by the Advisory Committee for Public Contracts set up by Decision 71/306/EEC.
2.   Where reference is made to the procedure laid down in this paragraph, the representative of the Commission shall submit to the Committee a draft of the measures to be taken. The Committee shall deliver its opinion on the draft within a time limit which the chairman may lay down according to the urgency of the matter, if necessary by taking a vote.
The opinion shall be recorded in the minutes; in addition, each Member State shall have the right to ask to have its position recorded in the minutes.
The Commission shall take the utmost account to the opinion delivered by the Committee. It shall inform the Committee of the manner in which its opinion has been taken into account.

3.   The Committee mentioned in paragraph 1 shall examine, on the initiative of the Commission or at the request of a Member State, any question relating to the application of this Directive.

Article 33
Directive 77/62/EEC[1] is hereby repealed, without prejudice to the obligation of the Member States concerning the deadlines for transposition into national law and for application indicated in Annex V. References to the repealed Directives shall be construed as reference to this Directive and should be read in accordance with the correlation table set out in Annex VI.

Note
[1]Including the provisions which amended this Directive, namely:
— Directive 80/767/EEC (OJ No. L215, 18.8.1980, p. 1),
— Directive 88/295/EEC (OJ No. L127, 20.5.1988, p. 1),
— Article 35(1) of Directive 90/531/EEC (OJ No. L297, 29.10.1990, p. 1),
— Article 42(1) of Directive 92/50/EEC (OJ No. L209, 24.7.1992, p. 1).

Article 34
1.   Member States shall bring into force the laws, regulations and administrative provisions necessary to comply with this Directive before 14 June 1994. They shall immediately inform the Commission thereof. When Member States adopt these measures, they shall contain a reference to this Directive or shall be accompanied by such reference on the occasion of their official publication. The methods for making such a reference shall be laid down by the Member States.

2.   Member States shall communicate to the Commission the texts of the main provisions of national law which they adopt in the field governed by this Directive.

Article 35
This Directive is addressed to the Member States.

Done at Luxembourg, 14 June 1993.
For the Council
The President
J. TROEJBORG

ANNEX I

LIST OF CONTRACTING AUTHORITIES SUBJECT TO THE GATT AGREEMENT ON GOVERNMENT PROCUREMENT
(United Kingdom Only)

UNITED KINGDOM
Cabinet Office
Civil Service College
Civil Service Commission
Civil Service Occupational Health Service
Office of the Minister for the Civil Service
Parliamentary Counsel Office
Central Office of Information
Charity Commission
Crown Prosecution Service

Crown Estate Commissioners
Customs and Excise Department
Department for National Savings
Department of Education and Science
University Grants Committee
Department of Employment
Employment Appeals Tribunal
Industrial Tribunals
Office of Manpower Economics
Department of Energy
Department of Health
Central Council for Education and Training in Social Work
Dental Estimates Board
English National Board for Nursing, Midwifery and Health Visitors
Medical Boards and Examining Medical Officers (War Pensions)
National Health Service Authorities
Prescriptions Pricing Authority
Public Health Laboratory Service Board
Regional Medical Service
United Kingdom Central Council for Nursing, Midwifery and Health
    Visiting
Department of Social Security
Attendance Allowance Board
Occupational Pensions Board
Social Security Advisory Committee
Supplementary Benefits Appeal Tribunals
Department of the Environment
Building Research Establishment
Commons Commissioners
Countryside Commission
Fire Research Station (Boreham Wood)
Historic Buildings and Monuments Commission
Local Valuation Panels
Property Services Agency
Rent Assessment Panels
Royal Commission on Environmental Pollution
Royal Commission on Historical Monuments of England
Royal Fine Art Commission (England)
Department of the Procurator General and Treasury Solicitor
Legal Secretariat to the Law Officers
Department of Trade and Industry
Laboratory of the Government Chemist
National Engineering Laboratory
National Physical Laboratory
Warren Spring Laboratory
National Weights and Measures Laboratory
Domestic Coal Consumers' Council
Electricity Consultative Councils for England and Wales
Gas Consumers' Council
Transport Users Consultative Committee

Monopolies and Mergers Commission
Patent Office
Department of Transport
Coastguard Services
Transport and Road Research Laboratory
Transport Tribunal
Export Credits Guarantee Department
Foreign and Commonwealth Office
Government Communications Headquarters
Wilton Park Conference Centre
Government Actuary's Department
Home Office
Boundary Commission for England
Gaming Board for Great Britain
Inspectors of Constabulary
Parole Board and Local Review Committees
House of Commons
House of Lords
Inland Revenue, Board of
Intervention Board for Agricultural Produce
Lord Chancellor's Department
Council on Tribunals
County Courts (England and Wales)
Immigration Appellate Authorities
Immigration Adjudicators
Immigration Appeals Tribunal
Judge Advocate-General and Judge Advocate of the Fleet
Lands Tribunal
Law Commission
Legal Aid Fund (England and Wales)
Pensions Appeals Tribunals
Public Trustee Office
Office of the Social Security Commissioners
Special Commissioners for Income Tax (England and Wales)
Supreme Court (England and Wales)
Court of Appeal: Civil and Criminal Divisions
Courts Martial Appeal Court
Crown Court
High Court
Value Added Tax Tribunals
Ministry of Agriculture, Fisheries and Food
Advisory Services
Agricultural Development and Advisory Service
Agricultural Dwelling House Advisory Committees
Agricultural Land Tribunals
Agricultural Science Laboratories
Agricultural Wages Board and Committees
Cattle Breeding Centre
Plant Variety Rights Office
Royal Botanic Gardens, Kew

Ministry of Defence(16)
Meteorological Office
Procurement Executive
National Audit Office
National Investment Loans Office
Northern Ireland Court Service
Coroners Courts
County Courts
Crown Courts
Enforcement of Judgements Office
Legal Aid Fund
Magistrates Courts
Pensions Appeals Tribunals
Supreme Court of Judicature and Courts of Criminal Appeal
Northern Ireland, Department of Agriculture
Northern Ireland, Department for Economic Development
Northern Ireland, Department of Education
Northern Ireland, Department of the Environment
Northern Ireland, Department of Finance and Personnel
Northern Ireland, Department of Health and Social Services
Northern Ireland Office
Crown Solicitor's Office
Department of the Director of Public Prosecutions for Northern Ireland
Northern Ireland Forensic Science Laboratory
Office of Chief Electoral Officer for Northern Ireland
Police Authority for Northern Ireland
Probation Board for Northern Ireland
State Pathologist Service
Office of Arts and Libraries
British Library
British Museum
British Museum (Natural History)
Imperial War Museum
Museums and Galleries Commission
National Gallery
National Maritime Museum
National Portrait Gallery
Science Museum
Tate Gallery
Victoria and Albert Museum
Wallace Collection
Office of Fair Trading
Office of Population Censuses and Surveys
National Health Service Central Register
Office of the Parliamentary Commissioner for Administration and Health
Service Commissioners
Overseas Development Administration
Overseas Development and National Research Institute
Paymaster General's Office
Postal Business of the Post Office

Privy Council Office
Public Record Office
Registry of Friendly Societies
Royal Commission on Historical Manuscripts
Royal Hospital, Chelsea
Royal Mint
Scotland, Crown Office and Procurator
Fiscal Service
Scotland, Department of the Registers of Scotland
Scotland, General Register Office
National Health Service Central Register
Scotland, Lord Advocate's Department
Scotland, Queen's and Lord Treasurer's Remembrancer
Scottish Courts Administration
Accountant of Court's Office
Court of Justiciary
Court of Session
Lands Tribunal for Scotland
Pensions Appeal Tribunals
Scottish Land Court
Scottish Law Commission
Sheriff Courts
Social Security Commissioners' Office
Scottish Office
Central Services
Department of Agriculture and Fisheries for Scotland
Artificial Insemination Service
Crofters Commission
Red Deer Commission
Royal Botanic Garden, Edinburgh
Industry Department for Scotland
Scottish Electricity Consultative Councils
Scottish Development Department
Rent Assessment Panel and Committees
Royal Commission on the Ancient and Historical Monuments of Scotland
Royal Fine Art Commission for Scotland
Scottish Education Department
National Galleries of Scotland
National Library of Scotland
National Museums of Scotland
Scottish and Health Departments
HM Inspectorate of Constabulary
Local Health Councils
Mental Welfare Commission for Scotland
National Board for Nursing, Midwifery and Health Visiting for Scotland
Parole Board for Scotland and Local Review Committees
Scottish Antibody Production Unit
Scottish Council for Postgraduate Medical Education
Scottish Crime Squad
Scottish Criminal Record Office

Scottish Fire Service Training School
Scottish Health Boards
Scottish Health Service - Common Services Agency
Scottish Health Service Planning Council
Scottish Police College
Scottish Record Office
HM Stationery Office
HM Treasury
Central Computer and Telecommunications Agency
Chessington Computer Centre
Civil Service Catering Organisation
National Economic Development Council
Rating of Government Property Department
Welsh Office
Ancient Monuments (Wales) Commission
Council for the Education and Training of Health Visitors
Local Government Boundary Commission for Wales
Local Valuation Panels and Courts
National Health Service Authorities
Rent Control Tribunals and Rent Assessment Panels and Committees

ANNEX II

LIST OF PRODUCTS REFERRED TO IN ARTICLE 5 CONCERNING THE AWARD OF CONTRACTS BY CONTRACTING AUTHORITIES IN THE FIELD OF DEFENCE

Chapter 25: Salt; sulphur; earths and stone; plastering materials, lime and cement

Chapter 26: Metallic ores, slag and ash

Chapter 27: Mineral fuels, mineral oils and products of their distillation; bituminous substances; mineral waxes except:

ex 2710: special engine fuels

Chapter 28: Inorganic chemicals; organic and inorganic compounds of precious metals, of rare-earth metals, of radioactive elements and of isotopes except:

ex 2809: explosives

ex 2813: explosives

ex 2814: tear gas

ex 2828: explosives

ex 2832: explosives

ex 2839: explosives

ex 2850: toxic products

ex 2851: toxic products

ex 2854: explosives

Chapter 29: Organic chemicals except:

ex 2903: explosives

ex 2904: explosives

ex 2907: explosives

ex 2908: explosives

ex 2911: explosives

ex 2912: explosives
ex 2913: toxic products
ex 2914: toxic products
ex 2915: toxic products
ex 2921: toxic products
ex 2922: toxic products
ex 2923: toxic products
ex 2926: explosives
ex 2927: toxic products
ex 2929: explosives
Chapter 30: Pharmaceutical products
Chapter 31: Fertilizers
Chapter 32: Tanning and dyeing extracts; tannings and their derivatives; dyes, colours, paints and varnishes; putty, fillers and stoppings; inks
Chapter 33: Essential oils and resinoids; perfumery, cosmetic or toilet preparations
Chapter 34: Soap, organic surface-active agents, washing preparations, lubricating preparations, artificial waxes, prepared waxes, polishing and scouring preparations, candles and similar articles, modelling pastes and 'dental waxes'
Chapter 35: Albuminoidal substances; glues; enzymes
Chapter 37: Photographic and cinematographic goods
Chapter 38: Miscellaneous chemical products except:
ex 3819: toxic products
Chapter 39: Artificial resins and plastic materials, celluloses, esters and ethers; articles thereof except:
ex 3903 explosives
Chapter 40: Rubber, synthetic rubber, factice, and articles thereof except:
ex 4011: bullet-proof tyres
Chapter 41: Raw hides and skins (other than furskins) and leather
Chapter 42: Articles of leather; saddlery and harness; travel goods, handbags and similar containers; articles of animal gut (other than silk-worm gut)
Chapter 43: Furskins and artificial fur; manufactures thereof
Chapter 44: Wood and articles of wood; wood charcoal
Chapter 45: Cork and articles of cork
Chapter 46: Manufactures of straw of esparto and of other plaiting materials; basketware and wickerwork
Chapter 47: Paper-making material
Chapter 48: Paper and paperboard; articles of paper pulp, of paper or of paperboard
Chapter 49: Printed books, newspapers, pictures and other products of the printing industry; manuscripts, typescripts and plans
Chapter 65: Headgear and parts thereof
Chapter 66: Umbrellas, sunshades, walking-sticks, whips, riding-crops and parts thereof
Chapter 67: Prepared feathers and down and articles made of feathers or of down; artificial flowers; articles of human hair
Chapter 68: Articles of stone, of plaster, of cement, of asbestos, of mica and of similar materials
Chapter 69: Ceramic products
Chapter 70: Glass and glassware

Chapter 71: Pearls, precious and semi-precious stones, precious metals, rolled precious metals, and articles thereof; imitation jewellery

Chapter 73: Iron and steel and articles thereof

Chapter 74: Copper and articles thereof

Chapter 75: Nickel and articles thereof

Chapter 76: Aluminium and articles thereof

Chapter 77: Magnesium and beryllium and articles thereof

Chapter 78: Lead and articles thereof

Chapter 79: Zinc and articles thereof

Chapter 80: Tin and articles thereof

Chapter 81: Other base metals employed in metallurgy and articles thereof

Chapter 82: Tools, implements, cutlery, spoons and forks, of base metal; parts thereof except:

ex 8205: tools

ex 8207: tools, parts

Chapter 83: Miscellaneous articles of base metal

Chapter 84: Boilers, machinery and mechanical appliances; parts thereof except:

ex 8406: engines

ex 8408: other engines

ex 8445: machinery

ex 8453: automatic data-processing machines

ex 8455: parts of machines under heading No 84.53

ex 8459: nuclear reactors

Chapter 85: Electrical machinery and equipment; parts thereof except:

ex 8513: telecommunication equipment

ex 8515: transmission apparatus

Chapter 86: Railway and tramway locomotives, rolling-stock and parts thereof; railway and tramway tracks fixtures and fittings; traffic signalling equipment of all kinds (not electrically powered) except:

ex 8602: armoured locomotives, electric

ex 8603: other armoured locomotives

ex 8605: armoured wagons

ex 8606: repair wagons

ex 8607: wagons

Chapter 87: Vehicles, other than railway or tramway rolling-stock, and parts thereof except:

ex 8701: tractors

ex 8702: military vehicles

ex 8703: breakdown lorries

ex 8708: tanks and other armoured vehicles

ex 8709: motorcycles

ex 8714: trailers

Chapter 89: Ships, boats and floating structures except:

ex 8901 A: warships

Chapter 90: Optical, photographic, cinematographic, measuring, checking, precision, medical and surgical instruments and apparatus; parts thereof except:

ex 9005: binoculars

ex 9013: miscellaneous instruments, lasers

ex 9014: telemeters
ex 9028: electrical and electronic measuring instruments
ex 9011: microscopes
ex 9017: medical instruments
ex 9018: mechano-therapy appliances
ex 9019: orthopaedic appliances
ex 9020: X-ray apparatus
Chapter 91: Clocks and watches and parts thereof
Chapter 92: Musical instruments; sound recorders or reproducers; television image and sound recorders or reproducers; parts and accessories of such articles
Chapter 94: Furniture and parts thereof; bedding, mattresses, mattress supports, cushions and similar stuffed furnishings except:
ex 9401 A: aircraft seats
Chapter 95: Articles and manufactures of carving or moulding material
Chapter 96: Brooms, brushes, powder-puffs and sieves
Chapter 98: Miscellaneous manufactured articles

ANNEX III

DEFINITION OF CERTAIN TECHNICAL SPECIFICATIONS

For the purposes of this Directive the following terms shall be defined as follows:

1. Technical specifications: the totality of the technical prescriptions contained in particular in the tender documents, defining the characteristics required of a material, product or supply, which permits a material, a product or a supply to be described in a manner such that it fulfils the use for which it is intended by the contracting authority. These technical prescriptions shall include levels of quality, performance, safety or dimensions, including the requirements applicable to the material, the product or the supply as regards quality assurance, terminology, symbols, testing and test methods, packaging, marking or labelling.

2. Standard: a technical specification approved by a recognized standardizing body for repeated and continuous application, compliance with which is in principle not compulsory.

3. European standard: a standard approved by the European Committee for standardization (CEN) or by the European Committee for Electrotechnical Standardization (Cenelec) as 'European standard (EN)' or 'Harmonization documents (HD)' according to the common rules of these organizations.

4. European technical approval: a favorable technical assessment of the fitness for use of a product, based on fulfilment of the essential requirements for building works, by means of the inherent characteristics of the product and the defined conditions of application and use. The European agreement shall be issued by an approval body designated for this purpose by the Member State.

5. Common technical specification: a technical specification laid down in accordance with a procedure recognized by the Member States to ensure uniform application in all Member States which has been published in the Official Journal of the European Communities.

ANNEX IV

MODEL NOTICES OF SUPPLY CONTRACTS

A   Prior information

1.   The name, address, telegraphic address, telephone, telex and telefax numbers of the contracting authority, and if different, of the service from which additional information may be obtained:

2.   The nature and quantity or value of the products to be supplied: CPA reference number:

3.   Estimated date for initiating the award procedures in respect of the contract or contracts (if known):

4.   Other information:

5.   Date of dispatch of the notice:

6.   Date of receipt of the notice by the Office for Official Publications of the European Communities:

B   Open procedures

1.   The name, address, telegraphic address, telephone, telex and telefax numbers of the contracting authority:

2.   (a)   The award procedure chosen:

  (b)   Form of the contract for which tenders are being requested:

3.   (a)   Place of delivery:

  (b)   The nature and quantity of the goods to be supplied: CPA reference number:

  (c)   Indication of whether the supplier can tender for a part of the goods required:

4.   Time limit for delivery, if any:

5.   (a)   Name and address of the service from which the contract documents and additional documents may be requested:

  (b)   The final date for making such requests:

  (c)   Where applicable, the amount and terms of payment of the sum to be paid to obtain such documents:

6.   (a)   The final date for receipt of tenders:

  (b)   The address to which they must be sent:

  (c)   The language or languages in which they must be drawn up:

7.   (a)   The persons authorized to be present at the opening of tenders:

  (b)   The date, hour and place of such opening:

8.   Where applicable, any deposits and guarantees required:

9.   The main terms concerning financing and payment and/or references to the provisions in which these are contained:

10.   Where applicable, the legal form to be taken by the grouping of suppliers to whom the contract is awarded:

11.   Information concerning the supplier's own position, and information and formalities necessary for an appraisal of the minimum economic and technical standards required of the supplier:

12.   Period during which the tenderer is bound to keep open his tender:

13.   The criteria for the award of the contract. Criteria other than that of the lowest price shall be mentioned if they do not appear in the contract documents:

14.   Where applicable, prohibition on variants:

15.   Other information:
16.   Date of publication of the prior information notice in the Official Journal of the European Communities or references to its non-publication:
17.   Date of dispatch of the notice:
18.   Date of receipt of the notice by the Office for Official Publications of the European Communities:

C   Restricted procedures
1.   The name, address, telegraphic address, telephone, telex and telefax numbers of the contracting authority:
2.   (a)   The award procedure chosen:
     (b)   Where applicable, justification for use of the accelerated procedure:
     (c)   Form of the contract for which tenders are being requested:
3.   (a)   Place of delivery:
     (b)   The nature and quantity of the goods to be supplied: CPA reference number:
     (c)   Indication of whether the supplier can tender for a part of the goods required:
4.   Time limit for delivery, if any:
5.   Where applicable, the legal form to be assumed by the grouping of suppliers to whom the contract is awarded:
6.   (a)   The final date for the receipt of requests to participate:
     (b)   The address to which they must be sent:
     (c)   The language or languages in which they must be drawn up:
7.   The final date for the dispatch of inventions to tender:
8.   Where applicable, any deposits and guarantees required:
9.   Information concerning the supplier's personal position, and the information and formalities necessary for an appraisal of the minimum economic and technical standards required of him:
10.   The criteria for the award of the contract where they are mentioned in the invitation to tender:
11.   Envisaged number or range of suppliers which will be invited to tender:
12.   Where applicable, prohibition on variants:
13.   Other information:
14.   Date of publication of the prior information notice in the Official Journal of the European Communities or references to its non-publication:
15.   Date of dispatch of the notice:
16.   Date of receipt of the notice by the Office for Official Publications of the European Communities:

D   Negotiated procedures
1.   The name, address, telegraphic address, telephone, telex and telefax numbers of the contracting authority:
2.   (a) The award procedure chosen:
     (b)   Where applicable, justification for use of the accelerated procedure:
     (c)   Where applicable, form of contract for which tenders are invited:
3.   (a)   Place of delivery:
     (b)   The nature and quantity of the goods to be supplied: CPA reference number:

(c)   Indication of whether the suppliers can tender for a part of the goods required:

4.   Time limit for delivery, if any:

5.   Where applicable, the legal form to be assumed by a grouping of suppliers to whom the contract is awarded:

6.   (a)   The final date for the receipt of requests to participate:

(b)   The address to which they must be sent:

(c)   The language or languages in whch they must be drawn up:

7.   Where applicable, any deposits and guarantees required:

8.   Information concerning the supplier's personal position, and the information and formalities necessary for an appraisal of the minimum economic and technical standards required of him:

9.   Envisaged number or range of suppliers which will be invited to tender:

10.   Where applicable, prohibition on variants:

11.   Where applicable, the names and addresses of suppliers already selected by the awarding authority:

12.   Where applicable, date(s) of previous publications in the *Official Journal of the European Communities*:

13.   Other information:

14.   Date of dispatch of the Notice:

16.   Date of receipt of the notice by the Office of Official Publications of the European Communities:

E   Contracts awards

1.   Name and address of awarding authority:

2.   Award procedure chosen. In the case of the negotiated procedure, without publication of a tender notice, justification (Article 6(3)):

3.   Date of award of contract:

4.   Criteria for award of contract:

5.   Number of tenders received:

6.   Name(s) and address(es) of supplier(s):

7.   The nature and quantity of goods supplied, where applicable, by supplier: CPA reference number:

8.   Price or range of prices (minimum/maximum) paid:

9.   Where appropriate, value and proportion of contract likely to be subcontracted to third parties:

10.   Other information:

11.   Date of publication of the tender notice in the *Official Journal of the European Communities*:

12.   Date of dispatch of the notice:

13.   Date of receipt of the notice by the Office for Official Publications of the European Communities:

ANNEX V

DEADLINES FOR APPLICATION OF TRANSPOSITION MEASURES

Directive 77/62/EEC[1]	amended by Directives				amended by Acts of Accession	
	80/767/EEC[2]	88/295/EEC[3]	90/531/EEC[4]	92/50/EEC[5]	GR[6]	ES/PO[7]
Article 1(a)		amended				
Article 1(b) and (c)						
Article 1(d) to (f)		amended				
Article 2(1)		deleted				
Article 2(2)		amended	amended			
Article 2(3)						
Article 2a		inserted				
Article 3						
Article 4		deleted				
Article 5		amended				
Article 5(1)(c)				amended		
Article 6		amended				
Article 7		amended				
Article 8						
Article 9		amended				
Article 10(1)		amended				
Article 10(2) to (4)						
Article 11(1) to (3)		amended				
Article 11(4) to (6)						
Article 12(1)		amended				
Article 12(2) to (3)						
Article 13		deleted				
Article 14		deleted				
Article 15		deleted				
Article 16						
Article 17						
Article 18						
Article 19(1)		amended				
Article 19(2)						
Article 20						
Article 21(1)						
Article 21(2)		amended				
Article 22						
Article 23						
Article 24						
Article 25						
Article 26		amended				
Article 27						
Article 28						
Article 29		amended				
Article 30						
Article 31						
Article 32						
Annex I		amended			amended	amended
Annex II		amended				
Annex III			amended			
	Article 1					
	Article 2	deleted				
	Article 3	deleted				
	Article 4	deleted				
	Article 5	deleted				
	Article 6	deleted				
	Article 7					
	Article 8					
	Article 9					
	Article 10					
	Article 11					
	Annex I					
	Annex II					

[1]EC–9: 24.6.1978
GR: 1.1.1983
ES, PO: 1.1.1986
[2]EC–9: 1.1.1981
GR: 1.1.1983
ES, PO: 1.1.1986

[3]EC–9: 1.1.1989
GR, ES, PO: 1.3.1992

[4]EC–9: 1.1.1983
ES: 1.1.1996
GR, PO: 1.1.1998

[5]EC–12: 1.7.1993
[6]EC–10: 1.1.1983
[7]EC–12: 1.1.1986

ANNEX VI
CORRELATION TABLE

This directive	77/62/EEC	80/767/EEC	88/295/EEC	90/531/EEC	92/50/EEC
Article 1	Article 1				
Article 2(1)	Article 2(2)			Article 35(1)	
Article 2(2)	Article 2(3)				
Article 3	Article 2a				
Article 4	Article 3				
Article 5(1)(a) and (b)	Article 5(1)(a) and (b)				
Article 5(1)(c) first sub-paragraph	Article 5(1)(c)				Article 42(1)
Article 5(1)(c) second sub-paragraph	Article 5(1)(d)				
Article 5(1)(d)	—				
Article 5(2–6)	Article 5(2–6)				
Article 6(1)	Article 6(1)				
—	Article 6(2)				
Article 6(2)	Article 6(3)				
Article 6(3)(a)–(e)	Article 6(4)(a)–(e)				
Article 6(4)	Article 6(5)				
Article 7(1–2)	(—)				
Article 7(3)	Article 6(6)				
Article 8(1–4)	Article 7(1–4)				
Article 8(5)(a) and (b)	(—)				
Article 8(5)(c)	Article 7(5)(a)–(c)				
Article 8(6)	Article 7(6)				
Article 9(1) first sub-paragraph	Article 9(1) first sub-paragraph				
(—)	Article 9(1) second sub-paragraph				
Article 9(1) second sub-paragraph	—				
Article 9(2) and (3)	Article 9(2) and (3)				
Article 9(4)	Article 9(5)				
Article 9(5)	Article 9(4)				
Article 9(6) and (7)	Article 9(6) first sub-paragraph				
Article 9(8)	Article 9(6) second sub-paragraph				
Article 9(9)	Article 9(7)				
Article 9(10)	Article 9(8)				
Article 9(11)	Article 9(9)				
Article 10	Article 10				
Article 11(1)	Article 11(1)				
Article 11(2)	Article 11(2)				
Article 11(2)(a)–(e)	(—)				
Article 11(3)	Article 11(3)				
Article 11(4)	Article 11(5)				

This directive	77/62/EEC	80/767/EEC	88/295/EEC	90/531/EEC	92/50/EEC
Article 11(5)	Article 11(4)				
Article 11(6)	Article 11(6)				
Article 12	Article 12				
Article 13	Article 16				
Article 14	(—)				
Article 15	Article 17				
Article 16(1)	Article 8				
Article 16(2)	(—)				
Article 17	(—)				
Article 18	Article 18				
Article 19(1)	Article 19(1)				
Article 19(2) and (3)	(—)				
Article 19(4)	Article 19(2)				
Article 20	Article 20				
Article 21(1) and (2)	Article 21				
Article 22	Article 22				
Article 23	Article 23				
Article 24	Article 24				
Article 25	(—)				
Article 26(1) and (2)	Article 25(1) and (2)				
(—)	Article 25(3) and (4)				
Article 27	Article 25(5) to (7)				
—	Article 26				
—	Article 27				
Article 28		Article 1(1) and 7			
Article 29(1) and (2)		Article 8(1) and (2)			
Article 29(3)		Article 1(2)			
Article 30	Article 28				
Article 31	Article 29				
Article 32	(—)				
Article 33	Article 30 and 31	Article 9 and 10	Article 20 and 21		
Article 34	(—)				
Article 35	(—)				
(—)	Annex I				
Annex I		Annex I			
Annex II		Annex II			
Annex III	Annex II				
point 1	point 1				
point 2	point 2				
point 3	point 3				
point 4	—				
point 5	point 4				
Annex IV	Annex III				
point A	point D				
point B	point A				
point C	point B				
point D	point C				
point E	point E				
Annex V	(—)				
Annex VI	(—)				

COUNCIL DIRECTIVE (EEC) 93/37 OF 14 JUNE 1993
CONCERNING THE COORDINATION OF PROCEDURES
FOR THE AWARD OF PUBLIC WORKS
CONTRACTS
[OJ 1993 No. L199/ 54]*

THE COUNCIL OF THE EUROPEAN COMMUNITIES,

Having regard to the Treaty establishing the European Economic Community, and in particular Articles 57(2), 66 and 100a thereof,

Having regard to the proposal from the Commission,[1]

In cooperation with the European Parliament,[2]

Having regard to the opinion of the Economic and Social Committee,[3]

Whereas Council Directive 71/305/EEC of 26 July 1971 concerning the coordination of procedures for the award of public works contracts[4] has been amended substantially and on a number of occasions; whereas, for reasons of clarity and better understanding, the said Directive should be

Whereas the simultaneous attainment of freedom of establishment and freedom to provide services in respect of public works contracts awarded in Member States on behalf of the State, or regional or local authorities or other bodies governed by public law entails not only the abolition of restrictions but also the coordination of national procedures for the award of public works contracts;

Whereas such coordination should take into account as far as possible the procedures and administrative practices in force in each Member State;

Whereas this Directive does not apply to certain works contracts which are awarded in the water, energy, transport and telecommunication sectors covered by Directive 90/531/EEC; Whereas, in view of the increasing importance of concession contracts in the public works area and of their specific nature, rules concerning advertising should be included in this Directive;

Whereas works contracts of less than ECU 5,000,000 may be exempted from competition as provided for under this Directive and it is appropriate to provide for their exemption from coordination measures;

Whereas provision must be made for exceptional cases where measures concerning the coordination of procedures need not be applied, but such cases must be expressly limited;

Whereas the negotiated procedure should be considered to be exceptional and therefore only applicable in certain limited cases;

Whereas it is necessary to provide common rules in the technical field which take account of the Community policy on standards and specifications;

Notes

*As corrected by OJ 1994 L111/15, and amended by the Act of Accession for Austria, Finland and Sweden [OJ 1994 C241/228] and amended by Decision 95/1 [OJ 1995 L1/1].

[1]OJ No. C46, 20.2.1992, p. 79.

[2]OJ No. C125, 18.5.1992, p. 171 and OJ No. C305, 23.11.1992, p. 73.

[3]OJ No. C106, 27.4.1992, p. 11.

[4]OJ No. L185, 16.8.1971, p. 15; Directive as last amended by Directive 93/4/EEC [OJ No. L38, 16.2.1993, p. 31].

Whereas, to ensure development of effective competition in the field of public contracts, it is necessary that contract notices drawn up by the contracting authorities of Member States be advertised throughout the Community; whereas the information contained in these notices must enable contractors established in the Community to determine whether the proposed contracts are of interest to them; whereas, for this purpose, it is appropriate to give them adequate information on the works undertaken and the conditions attached thereto; whereas, more particularly, in restricted procedures advertisement is intended to enable contractors of Member States to express their interest in contracts by seeking from the contracting authorities invitations to tender under the required conditions;

Whereas additional information concerning contracts must, as is customary in Member States, be given in the contract documents for each contract or else in an equivalent document;

Whereas it is necessary to provide common rules for participation in public works contracts, including both qualitative selection criteria and criteria for the award of the contract;

Whereas it would be appropriate to enable certain technical conditions concerning notices and statistical reports required by this Directive to be adapted in the light of changing technical requirements; whereas Annex II to this Directive refers to the General Industrial Classification of Economic Activities within the European Communities (NACE); whereas the Community may, as required, revise or replace its common nomenclature and whereas it is necessary to make provision for the possibility of adapting the reference made to the NACE nomenclature in the said Annex II accordingly;

Whereas this Directive should not affect the obligations of the Member States concerning the deadlines for transposition into national law and for application indicated in Annex VII,

HAS ADOPTED THIS DIRECTIVE:

TITLE I   GENERAL PROVISIONS

Article 1

For the purpose of this Directive:

(a) 'public works contracts' are contracts for pecuniary interest concluded in writing between a contractor and a contracting authority as defined in (b), which have as their object either the execution, or both the execution and design, of works related to one of the activities referred to in Annex II or a work defined in (c) below, or the execution, by whatever means, of a work corresponding to the requirements specified by the contracting authority;

(b) 'contracting authorities' shall be the State, regional or local authorities, bodies governed by public law, associations formed by one or several of such authorities or bodies governed by public law;

A 'body governed by public law' means any body:

— established for the specific purpose of meeting needs in the general interest, not having an industrial or commercial character, and

— having legal personality, and

— financed, for the most part, by the State, or regional or local authorities, or other bodies governed by public law, or subject to management supervision by those bodies, or having an administrative, managerial or supervisory board, more than half of whose members are appointed by the State, regional or local authorities or by other bodies governed by public law;

The lists of bodies and categories of bodies governed by public law which fulfil the criteria referred to in the second subparagraph are set out in Annex I. These lists shall be as exhaustive as possible and may be reviewed in accordance with the procedure laid down in Article 35. To this end, Member States shall periodically notify the Commission of any changes in their lists of bodies and categories of bodies;

(c) a 'work' means the outcome of building or civil engineering, works taken as a whole that is sufficient of itself to fulfil an economic and technical function;

(d) 'public works concession' is a contract of the same type as that indicated in (a) except for the fact that the consideration for the works to be carried out consists either solely in the right to exploit the construction or in this right together with payment;

(e) 'open procedures' are those national procedures whereby all interested contractors may submit tenders;

(f) 'restricted procedures' are those national procedures whereby only those contractors invited by the contracting authority may submit tenders;

(g) 'negotiated procedures' are those national procedures whereby contracting authorities consult contractors of their choice and negotiate the terms of the contract with one or more of them;

(h) a contractor who submits a tender shall be designated by the term 'tenderer' and one who has sought an invitation to take part in a restricted or negotiated procedure by the term 'candidate'.

Article 2

1. Member States shall take the necessary measures to ensure that the contracting authorities comply or ensure compliance with this Directive where they subsidize directly by more than 50% a works contract awarded by an entity other than themselves.

2. Paragraph 1 shall concern only contracts covered by Class 50, Group 502, of the general industrial classification of economic activities within the European Communities (NACE) nomenclature and contracts relating to building work for hospitals, facilities intended for sports, recreation and leisure, school and university buildings and buildings used for administrative purposes.

Article 3

1. Should contracting authorities conclude a public works concession contract, the advertising rules as described in Article 11(3), (6), (7) and (9) to (13), and in Article 15, shall apply to that contract when its value is not less than ECU 5,000,000.

2. The contracting authority may:

— either require the concessionnaire to award contracts representing a minimum of 30% of the total value of the work for which the concession contract is to be awarded, to third parties, at the same time providing the option for candidates to increase this percentage. This minimum percentage shall be specified in the concession contract,

— or request the candidates for concession contracts to specify in their tenders the percentage, if any, of the total value of the work for which the concession contract is to be awarded which they intend to assign to third parties.

3. When the concessionnaire is himself a contracting authority, as referred to in Article 1(b), he shall comply with the provisions of this Directive in the case of works to be carried out by third parties.

4. Member States shall take the necessary steps to ensure that a concessionnaire other than a contracting authority shall apply the advertising rules listed in Article 11(4), (6), (7), and (9) to (13), and in Article 16, in respect of the contracts which it awards to third parties when the value of the contracts is not less than ECU 5,000,000. An advertisement is not, however, required where works contracts meet the conditions laid down in Article 7(3).

Undertakings which have formed a group in order to obtain the concession contract, or undertakings affiliated to them, shall not be regarded as third parties.

An 'affiliated undertaking' means any undertaking over which the concessionnaire may exercise, directly or indirectly, a dominant influence or which may exercise a dominant influence over the concessionnaire or which, in common with the concessionnaire, is subject to the dominant influence of another undertaking by virtue of ownership, financial participation or the rules which govern it. A dominant influence on the part of an undertaking shall be presumed when, directly or indirectly in relation to another undertaking, it:

— holds the major part of the undertaking's subscribed capital, or

— controls the majority of the votes attaching to shares issued by the undertakings, or

— can appoint more than half of the members of the undertaking's administrative, managerial or supervisory body.

A comprehensive list of these undertakings shall be enclosed with the candidature for the concession. This list shall be brought up to date following any subsequent changes in the relationship between the undertakings.

Article 4
This Directive shall not apply to:

(a) contracts awarded in the fields referred to in Articles 2, 7, 8 and 9 of Directive 90/531/EEC or fulfilling the conditions in Article 6(2) of that Directive;

(b) works contracts which are declared secret or the execution of which must be accompanied by special security measures in accordance with the laws, regulations or administrative provisions in force in the Member State concerned or when the protection of the basic interests of the Member State's security so requires.

Article 5
This Directive shall not apply to public contracts governed by different procedural rules and awarded:

(a) in pursuance of an international agreement, concluded in conformity with the Treaty, between a Member State and one or more non-member countries and covering works intended for the joint implementation or exploitation of a project by the signatory States; all agreements shall be communicated to the Commission, which may consult the Advisory Committee for Public Contracts set up by Decision 71/306/EEC;[1]

Note
[1] OJ No. L185, 16.8.1971, p. 15; Decision as amended by Decision 77/63/EEC [OJ No. L13, 15.1.1977, p.15].

(b)   to undertakings in a Member State or a non-member country in pursuance of an international agreement relating to the stationing of troops;

(c)   pursuant to the particular procedure of an international organization.

Article 6

1.   The provisions of this Directive shall apply to public works contracts whose estimated value net of VAT is not less than ECU 5,000,000.

2.   (a)   The value of the threshold in national currencies shall normally be revised every two years with effect from 1 January 1992. The calculation of this value shall be based on the average daily values of these currencies expressed in ECUs over the 24 months terminating on the last day of August immediately preceding the 1 January revision. The exchange values shall be published in the Official Journal of the European Communities at the beginning of November.

(b)   The method of calculation laid down in subparagraph (a) shall be reviewed, on a proposal from the Commission, by the Advisory Committee for Public Contracts in principle two years after its initial application.

3.   Where a work is subdivided into several lots, each one the subject of a contract, the value of each lot must be taken into account for the purpose of calculating the amounts referred to in paragraph 1. Where the aggregate value of the lots is not less than the amount referred to in paragraph 1, the provisions of that paragraph shall apply to all lots. Contracting authorities shall be permitted to depart from this provision for lots whose estimated value net of VAT is less than ECU 1,000,000, provided that the total estimated value of all the lots exempted does not, in consequence, exceed 20% of the total estimated value of all lots.

4.   No work or contract my be split up with the intention of avoiding the application of this Directive.

5.   When calculating the amounts referred to in paragraph 1 and in Article 7, account shall be taken not only of the amount of the public works contracts but also of the estimated value of the supplies needed to carry out the works are made available to the contractor by the contracting authorities.

Article 7

1.   In awarding public works contracts the contracting authorities shall apply the procedures defined in Article 1(e), (f) and (g), adapted to this Directive.

2.   The contracting authorities may award their public works contracts by negotiated procedure, with prior publication of a contract notice and after having selected the candidates according to publicly known qualitative criteria, in the following cases:

(a)   in the event of irregular tenders in response to an open or restricted procedure or in the case of tenders which are unacceptable under national provisions that are in accordance with the provisions of Title IV, insofar as the original terms of the contract are not substantially altered. The contracting authorities shall not, in these cases, publish a contract notice where they include in such negotiated procedure all the enterprises satisfying the criteria of Articles 24 to 29 which, during the prior open or restricted procedure, have submitted tenders in accordance with the formal requirements of the tendering procedure;

(b)   when the works involved are carried out purely for the purpose of research, experiment or development, and not to establish commercial viability or to recover research and development costs;

(c) in exceptional cases, when the nature of the works or the risks attaching thereto do not permit prior overall pricing.

3. The contracting authorities may award their public works contracts by negotiated procedure without prior publication of a contract notice, in the following cases:

(a) in the absence of tenders or of appropriate tenders in response to an open or restricted procedure insofar as the original terms of the contract are not substantially altered and provided that a report is communicated to the Commission at its request;

(b) when, for technical or artistic reasons or for reasons connected with the protection of exclusive rights, the works may only be carried out by a particular contractor;

(c) insofar as is strictly necessary when, for reasons of extreme urgency brought about by events unforeseen by the contracting authorities in question, the time limit laid down for the open, restricted or negotiated procedures referred to in paragraph 2 cannot be kept. The circumstances invoked to justify extreme urgency must not in any event be attributable to the contracting authorities;

(d) for additional works not included in the project initially considered or in the contract first concluded but which have, through unforeseen circumstances, become necessary for the carrying out of the work described therein, on condition that the award is made to the contractor carrying out such work:

— when such works cannot be technically or economically separated from the main contract without great inconvenience to the contracting authorities, or

— when such works, although separable from the execution of the original contract, are strictly necessary to its later stages,

However, the aggregate amount of contracts awarded for additional works may not exceed 50% of the amount of the main contract;

(e) for new works consisting of the repetition of similar works entrusted to the undertaking to which the same contracting authorities awarded an earlier contact, provided that such works conform to a basic project for which a first contract was awarded according to the procedures referred to in paragraph 4. As soon as the first project is put up for tender, notice must be given that this procedure might be adopted and the total estimated cost of subsequent works shall be taken into consideration by the contracting authorities when they apply the provisions of Article 6. This procedure may only be adopted during the three years following the conclusion of the original contract.

4. In all other cases, the contracting authorities shall award their public works contracts by the open procedure or by the restricted procedure.

Article 8

1. The contracting authority shall, within 15 days of the date on which the request is received, inform any eliminated candidate or tenderer who so requests of the reasons for rejection of his application or his tender, and, in the case of a tenderer, the name of the successful tenderer.

2. The contracting authority shall inform candidates or tenderers who so request of the grounds on which it decided not to award a contract in respect of which a prior call for competition was made, or to recommence the procedure. It shall also inform the Office for Official Publications of the European Communities of that decision.

3.   For each contract awarded, the contracting authorities shall draw up a written report which shall include at least the following:
—the name and address of the contracting authority, the subject and value of the contract,
—the names of the candidates or tenderers admitted and the reasons for their selection,
—the names of the candidates or tenderers rejected and the reasons for their rejection,
—the name of the successful tenderer and the reasons for his tender having been selected and, if known, any share of the contract the successful tenderer may intend to subcontract to a third party,
—for negotiated procedures, the circumstances referred to in Article 7 which justify the use of these procedures. This report, or the main features of it, shall be communicated to the Commission at its request.

Article 9

In the case of contracts relating to the design and construction of a public housing scheme whose size and complexity, and the estimated duration of the work involved, require that planning be based from the outset on close collaboration within a team comprising representatives of the contracting authorities, experts and the contractor to be responsible for carrying out the works, a special award procedure may be adopted for selecting the contractor most suitable for integration into the team.

In particular, contracting authorities shall include in the contract notice as accurate as possible a description of the works to be carried out so as to enable interested contractors to form a valid idea of the project. Furthermore, contracting authorities shall, in accordance with Articles 24 to 29, set out in such a contract notice the personal, technical and financial conditions to be fulfilled by candidates.

Where such procedure is adopted, contracting authorities shall apply the common advertising rules relating to restricted procedure and to the criteria for qualitative selection.

TITLE II   COMMON RULES IN THE TECHNICAL FIELD

Article 10

1.   The technical specifications defined in Annex III shall be given in the general or contractual documents relating to each contract.
2.   Without prejudice to the legally binding national technical rules and insofar as these are compatible with Community law, the technical specifications shall be defined by the contracting authorities by reference to national standards implementing European standards, or by reference to European technical approvals or by reference to common technical specifications.
3.   A contracting authority may depart from paragraph 2 if:
(a)   the standards, European technical approvals or common technical specifications do not include any provision for establishing conformity, or, if technical means do not exist for establishing satisfactorily the conformity of a product to these standards, European technical approvals or common technical specifications;
(b)   use of these standards, European technical approvals or common technical specifications would oblige the contracting authority to acquire

products or materials incompatible with equipment already in use or would entail disproportionate costs or disproportionate technical difficulties, but only as part of a clearly defined and recorded strategy with a view to change-over, within a given period, to European standards, European technical approvals or common technical specifications;

(c)   the project concerned is of a genuinely innovative nature for which use of existing European standards, European technical approvals or common technical specifications would not be appropriate.

4.   Contracting authorities invoking paragraph 3 shall record, wherever possible, the reasons for doing so in the tender notice published in the Official Journal of the European Communities or in the contract documents and in all cases shall record these reasons in their internal documentation and shall supply such information on request to Member States and to the Commission.

5.   In the absence of European standards or European technical approvals or common technical specifications, the technical specifications:

(a)   shall be defined by reference to the national technical specifications recognized as complying with the basic requirements listed in the Community directives on technical harmonization, in accordance with the procedures laid down in those directives, and in particular in accordance with the procedures laid down in Council Directive 89/106/EEC of 21 December 1988 on the approximation of laws, regulations and administrative provisions of the Member States relating to construction products;[1]

(b)   may be defined by reference to national technical specifications relating to design and method of calculation and execution of works and use of materials;

(c)   may be defined by reference to other documents. In this case, it is appropriate to make reference in order of preference to:

(i)   national standards implementing international standards accepted by the country of the contracting authority;

(ii)   other national standards and national technical approvals of the country of the contracting authority;

(iii)   any other standard.

6.   Unless such specifications are justified by the subject of the contract, Member States shall prohibit the introduction into the contractual clauses relating to a given contract of technical specifications which mention products of a specific make or source or of a particular process and which therefore favour or eliminate certain undertakings. In particular, the indication of trade marks, patents, types, or of a specific origin or production shall be prohibited. However, if such indication is accompanied by the words 'or equivalent', it shall be authorized in cases where the contracting authorities are unable to give a description of the subject of the contract using specifications which are sufficiently precise and intelligible to all parties concerned.

Note
[1]OJ No. L40, 11.2.1989, p. 12.

TITLE III   COMMON ADVERTISING RULES

Article 11
1.   Contracting authorities shall make known, by means of an indicative notice, the essential characteristics of the works contracts which they intend to

award and the estimated value of which is not less than the threshold laid down in Article 6(1).

2. Contracting authorities who wish to award a public works contract by open, restricted or negotiated procedure referred to in Article 7(2), shall make known their intention by means of a notice.

3. Contracting authorities who wish to award a works concession contract shall make known their intention by means of a notice.

4. Works concessionnaires, other than a contracting authority, who wish to award works contracts to a third party within the meaning of Article 3(4), shall make known their intention by means of a notice.

5. Contracting authorities who have awarded a contract shall make known the result by means of a notice. However, certain information on the contract award may, in certain cases, not be published where release of such information would impede law enforcement or otherwise be contrary to the public interest, would prejudice the legitimate commercial interests of particular enterprises, public or private, or might prejudice fair competition between contractors.

6. The notices referred to in paragraphs 1 to 5 shall be drawn up in accordance with the models given in Annexes IV, V and VI, and shall specify the information requested in those Annexes.

The contracting authorities may not require any conditions but those specified in Articles 26 and 27 when requesting information concerning the economic and technical standards which they require of contracts for their selection (point 11 of Annex IV B, point 10 of Annex IV C and point 9 of Annex IV D).

7. The contracting authorities shall send the notices referred to in paragraphs 1 to 5 as rapidly as possible and by the most appropriate channels to the Office for Official Publications of the European Communities. In the case of the accelerated procedure referred to in Article 14, the notice shall be sent by telex, telegram or telefax.

The notice referred to in paragraph 1 shall be sent as soon as possible after the decision approving the planning of the works contracts that the contracting authorities intend to award.

The notice referred to in paragraph 5 shall be sent at the latest 48 days after the award of the contract in question.

8. The notices referred to in paragraphs 1 and 5 shall be published in full in the Official Journal of the European Communities and in the TED data bank in the official languages of the Communities, the original text alone being authentic.

9. The notices referred to in paragraphs 2, 3 and 4 shall be published in full in the Official Journal of the European Communities and in the TED data bank in the original languages. A summary of the important elements of each notice shall be published in the other official languages of the Community, the original text alone being authentic.

10. The Office for Official Publications of the European Communities shall publish the notices not later than 12 days after their dispatch. In the case of the accelerated procedure referred to in Article 14, this period shall be reduced to five days.

11. The notice shall not be published in the official journals or in the press of the country of the contracting authority before the date of dispatch to the Official Journal of the European Communities and it shall mention this date. It

shall not contain information other than that published in the Official Journal of the European Communities.

12.   The contracting authorities must be able to supply evidence of the date of dispatch.

13.   The cost of publication of the notices in the Official Journal of the European Communities shall be borne by the Communities. The length of the notice shall not be greater than one page of the Journal, or approximately 650 words. Each edition of the Journal containing one or more notices shall reproduce the model notice or notices on which the published notice or notices are based.

Article 12

1.   In open procedures the time limit for the receipt of tenders, fixed by the contracting authorities shall be not less than 52 days from the date of dispatch of the notice.

2.   The time limit for the receipt of tenders laid down in paragraph 1 may be reduced to 36 days where the contracting authorities have published the notice provided for in Article 11(1), drafted in accordance with the specimen in Annex IV A, in the Official Journal of the European Communities.

3.   Provided they have been requested in good time, the contract documents and supporting documents must be sent to the contractors by the contracting authorities or competent departments within six days of receiving their application.

4.   Provided it has been requested in good time, additional information relating to the contract documents shall be supplied by the contracting authorities not later than six days before the final date fixed for receipt of tenders.

5.   Where the contract documents, supporting documents or additional information are too bulky to be supplied within the time limits laid down in paragraph 3 or 4 or where tenders can only be made after a visit to the site or after on-the-spot inspection of the documents supporting the contract documents, the time limits laid down in paragraphs 1 and 2 shall be extended accordingly.

Article 13

1.   In restricted procedures and negotiated procedures as described in Article 7(2), the time limit for receipt of requests to participate fixed by the contracting authorities shall be not less than 37 days from the date of dispatch of the notice.

2.   The contracting authorities shall simultaneously and in writing invite the selected candidates to submit their tenders. The letter of invitation shall be accompanied by the contract documents and supporting documents. It shall include at least the following information:

(a)   where appropriate, the address of the service from which the contract documents and supporting documents can be requested and the final date for making such a request; also the amount and terms of any sum to be paid for such documents;

(b)   the final date for receipt of tenders, the address to which they must be sent and the language or languages in which they must be drawn up;

(c)   a reference to the contract notice published;

(d)   an indication of any documents to be annexed, either to support the verifiable statements furnished by the candidate in accordance with Article

11(7), or to supplement the information provided for in that Article under the same conditions as those laid down in Articles 26 and 27;

(e) the criteria for the award of the contract if these are not given in the notice.

3. In restricted procedures, the time limit for receipt of tenders fixed by the contracting authorities may not be less than 40 days from the date of dispatch of the written invitation.

4. The time limit for the receipt of tenders laid down in paragraph 3 may be reduced to 26 days where the contracting authorities have published the notice provided for in Article 11(1), drafted in accordance with the model in Annex IV A, in the Official Journal of the European Communities.

5. Requests to participate in procedures for the award of contracts may be made by letter, by telegram, telex, telefax or by telephone. If by one of the last four, they must be confirmed by letter dispatched before the end of the period laid down in paragraph 1.

6. Provided it has been requested in good time, additional information relating to the contract documents must be supplied by the contracting authorities not later than six days before the final date fixed for the receipt of tenders.

7. Where tenders can be made only after a visit to the site or after on-the-spot inspection of the documents supporting the contract documents, the time limit laid down in paragraphs 3 and 4 shall be extended accordingly.

Article 14

1. In cases where urgency renders impracticable the time limits laid down in Article 13, the contracting authorities may fix the following time limits:

(a) a time limit for receipt of requests to participate which shall be not less than 15 days from the date of dispatch of the notice;

(b) a time limit for the receipt of tenders which shall be not less than 10 days from the date of the invitation to tender.

2. Provided it has been requested in good time, additional information relating to the contract documents must be supplied by the contracting authorities not later than four days before the final date fixed for the receipt of tenders.

3. Requests for participation in contracts and invitations to tender must be made by the most rapid means of communication possible. When requests to participate are made by telegram, telex, telefax or telephone, they must be confirmed by letter dispatched before the expiry of the time limit referred to in paragraph 1.

Article 15

Contracting authorities who wish to award a works concession contract shall fix a time limit for receipt of candidatures for the concession, which shall not be less than 52 days from the date of dispatch of the notice.

Article 16

In works contracts awarded by a works concessionnaire other than a contracting authority, the time limit for the receipt of requests to participate, fixed by the concessionnaire, shall be not less than 37 days from the date of dispatch of the notice, and the time limit for the receipt of tenders not less than 40 days from the date of dispatch of the notice or the invitation to tender.

Article 17

Contracting authorities may arrange for the publication in the Official Journal of the European Communities of notices announcing public works contracts which are not subject to the publication requirement laid down in this Directive.

TITLE IV   COMMON RULES ON PARTICIPATION
CHAPTER 1   GENERAL PROVISIONS

Article 18

Contracts shall be awarded on the basis of the criteria laid down in Chapter 3 of this Title, taking into account Article 19, after the suitability of the contractors not excluded under Article 24 has been checked by contracting authorities in accordance with the criteria of economic and financial standing and of technical knowledge or ability referred to in Articles 26 to 29.

Article 19

Where the criterion for the award of the contract is that of the most economically advantageous tender, contracting authorities may take account of variants which are submitted by a tenderer and meet the minimum specifications required by the contracting authorities.

The contracting authorities shall state in the contract documents the minimum specifications to be respected by the variants and any specific requirements for their presentation. They shall indicate in the tender notice if variants are not permitted.

Contracting authorities may not reject the submission of a variant on the sole grounds that it has been drawn up with technical specifications defined by reference to national standards transposing European standards, to European technical approvals or to common technical specifications referred to in Article 10(2) or again by reference to national technical specifications referred to in Article 10(5)(a) and (b).

Article 20

In the contract documents, the contracting authority may ask the tenderer to indicate in his tender any share of the contract he may intend to subcontract to third parties.

This indication shall be without prejudice to the question of the principal contractor's liability.

Article 21

Tenders may be submitted by groups of contractors. These groups may not be required to assume a specific legal form in order to submit the tender; however, the group selected may be required to do so when it has been awarded the contract.

Article 22

1.   In restricted and negotiated procedures the contracting authorities shall, on the basis of information given relating to the contractor's personal position as well as to the information and formalities necessary for the evaluation of the minimum conditions of an economic and technical nature to be fulfilled by him, select from among the candidates with the qualifications required by Articles 24 to 29 those whom they will invite to submit a tender or to negotiate.

2.   Where the contracting authorities award a contract by restricted procedure, they may prescribe the range within which the number of undertakings which they intend to invite will fall. In this case the range shall be indicated in the contract notice. The range shall be indicated in the contract notice. The range shall be determined in the light of the nature of the work to be carried out. The range must number at least 5 undertakings and may be up to 20. In any event, the number of candidates invited to tender shall be sufficient to ensure genuine competition.

3.   Where the contracting authorities award a contract by negotiated procedure as referred to in Article 7(2), the number of candidates admitted to negotiate may not be less than three provided that there is a sufficient number of suitable candidates.

4.   Each Member State shall ensure that contracting authorities issue invitations without discrimination to those nationals of other Member States who satisfy the necessary requirements and under the same conditions as to its own nationals.

Article 23

1.   The contracting authority may state in the contract documents, or be obliged by a Member State to do so, the authority or authorities from which a tenderer may obtain the appropriate information on the obligations relating to the employment protection provisions and the working conditions which are in force in the Member State, region or locality in which the works are to be executed and which shall be applicable to the works carried out on site during the performance of the contract.

2.   The contracting authority which supplies the information referred to in paragraph 1 shall request the tenderers or those participating in the contract procedure to indicate that they have taken account, when drawing up their tender, of the obligations relating to employment protection provisions and the working conditions which are in force in the place where the work is to be carried out. This shall be without prejudice to the application of the provisions of Article 30(4) concerning the examination of abnormally low tenders.

CHAPTER 2   CRITERIA FOR QUALITATIVE SELECTION

Article 24

Any contractor may be excluded from participation in the contract who:

(a)   is bankrupt or is being wound up, whose affairs are being administered by the court, who has entered into an arrangement with creditors, who has suspended business activities or who is in any analogous situation arising from a similar procedure under national laws and regulations;

(b)   is the subject of proceedings for a declaration of bankruptcy, for an order for compulsory winding up or administration by the court or for an arrangement with creditors or of any other similar proceedings under national laws or regulations;

(c)   has been convicted of an offence concerning his professional conduct by a judgment which has the force of res judicata;

(d)   has been guilty of grave professional misconduct proved by any means which the contracting authorities can justify;

(e)   has not fulfilled obligations relating to the payment of social security contributions in accordance with the legal provisions of the country in which he is established or with those of the country of the contracting authority;

(f) has not fulfilled obligations relating to the payment of taxes in accordance with the legal provisions of the country in which he is established or those of the country of the contracting authority;

(g) is guilty of serious misrepresentation in supplying the information required under this Chapter.

Where the contracting authority requires of the contractor proof that none of the cases quoted in (a), (b), (c), (e) or (f) applies to him, it shall accept as sufficient evidence:

— for points (a), (b) or (c), the production of an extract from the 'judicial record' or, failing this, of an equivalent document issued by a competent judicial or administrative authority in the country of origin in the country whence that person comes showing that these requirements have been met;

— for points (e) or (f), a certificate issued by the competent authority in the Member State concerned.

Where the country concerned does not issue such documents or certificates, they may be replaced by a declaration on oath or, in Member States where there is no provision for declarations on oath, by a solemn declaration made by the person concerned before a judicial or administrative authority, a notary or a competent professional or trade body, in the country of origin or in the country whence that person comes.

Member States shall designate the authorities and bodies competent to issue these documents and shall forthwith inform the other Member States and the Commission thereof.

Article 25

Any contractor wishing to take part in a public works contract may be requested to prove his enrolment in the professional or trade register under the conditions laid down by the laws of the Member State in which he is established:

— in Belgium the 'Registre du Commerce — Handelsregister',

— in Denmark, the 'Handelsregistret, Aktieselskabesregistret' and the 'Erhvervsregistret',

— in Germany, the 'Handelsregister' and the 'Handwerksrolle',

— in Greece, the registrar of contractors' enterprises '(Mitroo Ergoliptikon Epicheiriseon)' of the Ministry for Environment, Town and Country Planning and Public Works,

— in Spain, the 'Registro Oficial de Contratistas del Ministerio de Industria, Comercio y Turismo',

— in France, the 'Registre du Commerce and the Répertoire des métiers',

— in Italy, the 'Registro della Camera di commercio, industria, agricoltura e artigianato',

— in Luxembourg, the 'Registre aux firmes and the Rôle de la Chambre des métiers',

— in the Netherlands, the 'Handelsregister',

— in Portugal, the 'Commissao de Alvarÿs de Empresas de Obras Públicas e Particulares (CAEOPP)',

— in the United Kingdom and Ireland, the contractor may be requested to provide a certificate from the Registrar of Companies or the Registrar of Friendly Societies or, if this is not the case, a certificate stating that the person concerned has declared on oath that he is engaged in the profession in question in the country in which he is established, in a specific place and under a given business name.

— in Austria, the Firmenbuch, the Gewerberegister, the Mitgliederverzeichnisse der Landeskammern,

— in Finland, Kaupparekisteri/Handelsregistret;

— in Sweden, aktiebolags-, handels- eller foereningsregistren.

Article 26

1. Evidence of the contractor's financial and economic standing may, as a general rule, be furnished by one or more of the following references:

(a) appropriate statements from bankers;

(b) the presentation of the firm's balance sheets or extracts from the balance sheets, where publication of the balance sheet is required under the law of the country in which the contractor is established;

(c) a statement of the firm's overall turnover and the turnover on construction works for the three previous financial years.

2. The contracting authorities shall specify in the notice or in the invitation to tender which reference or references they have chosen and what references other than those mentioned under paragraph 1(a), (b) or (c) are to be produced.

3. If, for any valid reason, the contractor is unable to supply the references requested by the contracting authorities, he may prove his economic and financial standing by any other document which the contracting authorities consider appropriate.

Article 27

1. Evidence of the contractor's technical capability may be furnished by:

(a) the contractor's educational and professional qualifications and/or those of the firm's managerial staff and, in particular, those of the person or persons responsible for carrying out the works;

(b) a list of the works carried out over the past five years, accompanied by certificates of satisfactory execution for the most important works. These certificates shall indicate the value, date and site of the works and shall specify whether they were carried out according to the rules of the trade and properly completed. Where necessary, the competent authority shall submit these certificates to the contracting authority direct;

(c) a statement of the tools, plant and technical equipment available to the contractor for carrying out the work;

(d) a statement of the firm's average annual manpower and the number of managerial staff for the last three years;

(e) a statement of the technicians or technical bodies which the contractor can call upon for carrying out the work, whether or not they belong to the firm.

2. The contracting authorities shall specify in the invitation to tender which of these references are to be produced.

Article 28

Within the limits of Articles 24 to 27, the contracting authority may invite the contractor to supplement the certificates and documents submitted or to clarify them.

Article 29

1.   Member States who have official lists of recognized contractors must adapt them to the provisions of Article 24(a) to (d) and (g) and of Articles 25, 26 and 27.

2.   Contractors registered in the official lists may, for each contract, submit to the contracting authority a certificate of registration issued by the competent authority. This certificate shall state the reference which enabled them to be registered in the list and the classification given in this list.

3.   Certified registration in the official lists by the competent bodies shall, for the contracting authorities of other Member States, constitute a presumption of suitability for works corresponding to the contractor's classification only as regards Articles 24(a) to (d) and (g), 25, 26(b) and (c) and 27(b) and (d). Information which can be deduced from registration in official lists may not be questioned. However, with regard to the payment of social security contributions, an additional certificate may be required of any registered contractor whenever a contract is offered.

The contracting authorities of other Member States shall apply the above provisions only in favour of contractors who are established in the country holding the official list.

4.   For the registration of contractors of other Member States in an official list, no further proofs and statements may be required other than those requested of nationals and, in any event, only those provided for under Articles 24 to 27.

5.   Member States holding an official list shall communicate to other Member States the address of the body to which requests for registration may be made.

CHAPTER 3   CRITERIA FOR THE AWARD OF CONTRACTS

Article 30

1.   The criteria on which the contracting authorities shall base the award of contracts shall be:

   (a)   either the lowest price only;

   (b)   or, when the award is made to the most economically advantageous tender, various criteria according to the contract: e.g. price, period for completion, running costs, profitability, technical merit.

2.   In the case referred to in paragraph 1(b), the contracting authority shall state in the contract documents or in the contract notice all the criteria it intends to apply to the award, where possible in descending order of importance.

3.   Paragraph 1 shall not apply when a Member State bases the award of contracts on other criteria, within the framework of rules in force at the time of the adoption of this Directive whose aim is to give preference to certain tenderers, on condition that the rules invoked are compatible with the EEC Treaty.

4.   If, for a given contract, tenders appear to be abnormally low in relation to the works, the contracting authority shall, before it may reject those tenders, request, in writing, details of the constituent elements of the tender which it considers relevant and shall verify those constituent elements taking account of the explanations received.

The contracting authority may take into consideration explanations which are justified on objective grounds including the economy of the construction method, or the technical solution chosen, or the exceptionally favourable conditions available to the tenderer for the execution of the work, or the originality of the work proposed by the tenderer.

If the documents relating to the contract provide for its award at the lowest price tendered, the contracting authority must communicate to the Commission the rejection of tenders which it considers to be too low.

However, until the end of 1992, if current national law so permits, the contracting authority may exceptionally, without any discrimination on grounds of nationality, reject tenders which are abnormally low in relation to the works, without being obliged to comply with the procedure provided for in the first subparagraph if the number of such tenders for a particular contract is so high that implementation of this procedure would lead to a considerable delay and jeopardize the public interest attaching to the execution of the contract in question. Recourse to this exceptional procedure shall be mentioned in the notice referred to in Article 11(5).

Article 31

1. Until 31 December 1992, this Directive shall not prevent the application of existing national provisions on the award of public works contracts which have as their objective the reduction of regional disparities and the promotion of job creation in regions whose development is lagging behind and in declining industrial regions, on condition that the provisions concerned are compatible with the Treaty, in particular with the principles of non-discrimination on grounds of nationality, freedom of establishment and freedom to provide services, and with the Community's international obligations.

2. Paragraph 1 shall be without prejudice to Article 30(3).

Article 32

1. Member States shall inform the Commission of national standards covered by Article 30(3) and Article 31 and of the rules for applying them.

2. Member States concerned shall forward to the Commission, every year, a report describing the practical application of the measures referred to in paragraph 1. The reports shall be submitted to the Advisory Committee for Public Contracts.

TITLE V   FINAL PROVISIONS

Article 33

The calculation of the time limit for receipt of tenders or requests to participate shall be made in accordance with Council Regulation (EEC, Euratom) No 1182/71 of 3 June 1971 determining the rules applicable to periods, dates and time limits.[1]

Note
[1]OJ No. L124, 8.6.1971, p. 1.

Article 34

1. In order to permit assessment of the results of applying the Directive, Member States shall forward to the Commission a statistical report on the contracts awarded by contracting authorities by 31 October 1993 at the latest for the preceding year and thereafter by 31 October of every second year. Nevertheless, for Greece, Spain and Portugal, the date of 31 October 1993 shall be replaced by 31 October 1995.

2.   The statistical reports shall detail at least the number and value of contracts awarded by each contracting authority or category of contracting authority above the threshold, subdivided as far as possible by procedure, category of work and the nationality of the contractor to whom the contract has been awarded, and in the case of negotiated procedures, subdivided in accordance with Article 7, listing the number and value of the contracts awarded to each Member State and to third countries.

3.   The Commission shall determine in accordance with the procedure laid down in Article 35(3) the nature of any additional statistical information, which is requested under the Directive.

Article 35

1.   Annex I shall be amended by the Commission, in accordance with the procedure laid down in paragraph 3, when, in particular on the basis of the notifications from the Member States, it appears necessary:

(a)   to remove from the said Annex bodies governed by public law which no longer fulfil the criteria laid down in Article 1(b);

(b)   to include in that Annex bodies governed by public law which meet those criteria.

2.   The conditions for the drawing up, transmission, receipt, translation, collection and distribution of the notices referred to in Article 11 and of the statistical reports provided for in Article 34, the nomenclature provided for in Annex II, as well as the reference in the notices to particular positions of the nomenclature, may be modified in accordance with the procedure laid down in paragraph 3.

3.   The chairman of the Advisory Committee for Public Contracts shall submit to the committee a draft of any measures to be taken. The committee shall deliver its opinion on the draft, if necessary by taking a vote, within a time limit to be fixed by the chairman in light of the urgency of the matter.

The opinion shall be recorded in the minutes. In addition, each Member State shall have the right to request that its position be recorded in the minutes.

The Commission shall take the fullest account of the opinion delivered by the committee. It shall inform the committee of the manner in which its opinion has been taken into account.

4.   Amended versions of Annexes I and II and of the conditions set out in paragraph 2 shall be published in the Official Journal of the European Communities.

Article 36

1.   Directive 71/305/EEC[1] is hereby repealed, without prejudice to the obligations of the Member States concerning the deadlines for transposition into national law and for application indicated in Annex VII.

Note
[1]including the provisions which amended this Directive, namely:
— Directive 78/669/EEC (OJ No. L225, 16.8.1978, p. 41),
— Directive 89/440/EEC (OJ No. L210, 21.7.1989, p. 1),
— Commission Decision 90/380/EEC (OJ No. L187, 19.7.1990, p. 55,
— Article 35(2) of Directive 90/531/EEC (OJ No. L 297, 29.10.1990, p. 1), and
— Directive 93/4/EEC (OJ No. L38, 16.2.1993, p. 31).

2. References to the repealed Directive shall be construed as references to this Directive and should be read in accordance with the correlation table given in Annex VIII.

Article 37

This Directive is addressed to the Member States.

Done at Luxembourg, 14 June 1993.
For the Council
The President
J. TROEJBORG

ANNEX I

LISTS OF BODIES AND CATEGORIES OF BODIES GOVERNED BY PUBLIC LAW REFERRED TO IN ARTICLE 1(b)

III. GERMANY

1. Legal persons governed by public law

Authorities, establishments and foundations governed by public law and created by federal, State or local authorities in particular in the following sectors:

1.1. Authorities

— Wissenschaftliche Hochschulen und verfasste Studentenschaften (universities and established student bodies),

— berufsstaendige Vereinigungen (Rechtsanwalts-, Notar-, Steuerberater-, Wirtschaftspruefer-, Architekten-, Aerzte- und Apothekerkammern) (professional associations representing lawyers, notaries, tax consultants, accountants, architects, medical practitioners and pharmacists),

— Wirtschaftsvereinigungen (Landwirtschafts-, Handwerks-, Industrie- und Handelskammern, Handwerksinnungen, Handwerkerschaften) (business and trade associations: agricultural and craft associations, chambers of industry and commerce, craftmen's guilds, tradesmen's associations),

— Sozialversicherungen (Krankenkassen, Unfall- und Rentenversicherungstraeger) (social security institutions: health, accident and pension insurance funds),

— kassenaerztliche Vereinigungen (associations of panel doctors),

— Genossenschaften und Verbaende (cooperatives and other associations).

1.2. Establishments and foundations

Non-industrial and non-commercial establishments subject to state control and operating in the general interest, particularly in the following fields:

— Rechtsfaehige Bundesanstalten (federal institutions having legal capacity),

— Versorgungsanstalten und Studentenwerke (pension organizations and students' unions),

— Kultur-, Wohlfahrts- und Hilfsstiftungen (cultural, welfare and relief foundations).

2. Legal persons governed by private law

Non-industrial and non-commercial establishments subject to State control and operating in the general interest (including 'kommunale Versorgungsunternehmen'

— municipal utilities), particularly in the following fields:

—Gesundheitswesen (Krankenhaeuser, Kurmittelbetriebe, medizinische Forschungseinrichtungen, Untersuchungs- und Tierkoerperbeseitigungsanstalten) (health: hospitals, health resort establishments, medical research institutes, testing and carcase-disposal establishments),

—Kultur (oeffentliche Buehnen, Orchester, Museen, Bibliotheken, Archive, zoologische und botanische Gaerten) (culture: public theatres, orchestras, museums, libraries, archives, zoological and botanical gardens),

—Soziales (Kindergaerten, Kindertagesheime, Erholungseinrichtungen, Kinder- und Jugendheime, Freizeiteinrichtungen, Gemeinschafts- und Buergerhaeuser, Frauenhaeuser, Altersheime, Obdachlosenunterkuenfte) (social welfare: nursery schools, children's playschools, rest-homes, children's homes, hostels for young people, leisure centres, community and civic centres, homes for battered wives, old people's homes, accommodation for the homeless),

—Sport (Schwimmbaeder, Sportanlagen und -einrichtungen) (sport: swimming baths, sports facilities),

—Sicherheit (Feuerwehren, Rettungsdienste) (safety: fire brigades, other emergency services),

—Bildung (Umschulungs-, Aus-, Fort- und Weiterbildungseinrichtungen, Volkshochschulen) (education: training, further training and retraining establishments, adult evening classes),

—Wissenschaft, Forschung und Entwicklung (Grossforschungseinrichtungen, wissenschaftliche Gesellschaften und Vereine, Wissenschaftsfoerderung) (science, research and development: large-scale research institutes, scientific societies and associations, bodies promoting science),

—Entsorgung (Strassenreinigung, Abfall- und Abwasserbeseitigung) (refuse and garbage disposal services: street cleaning, waste and sewage disposal),

—Bauwesen und Wohnungswirtschaft (Stadtplanung, Stadtentwicklung, Wohnungsunternehmen, Wohnraumvermittlung) (building, civil engineering and housing: town planning, urban development, housing enterprises, housing agency services),

—Wirtschaft (Wirtschaftsfoerderungsgesellschaften) (economy: organizations promoting economic development),

—Friedhofs- und Bestattungswesen (cemeteries and burial services),

—Zusammenarbeit mit den Entwicklungslaendern (Finanzierung, technische Zusammenarbeit, Entwicklungshilfe, Ausbildung) (cooperation with developing countries: financing, technical cooperation, development aid, training).

V. SPAIN

Categories

—Entidades Gestoras y Servicios Comunes de la Seguridad Social (administrative entities and common services of the health and social services)

—Organismos Autónomos de la Administración del Estado (independent bodies of the national administration)

—Organismos Autónomos de las Comunidades Autónomas (independent bodies of the autonomous communities)

—Organismos Autónomos de las Entidades Locales (independent bodies of local authorities)

—Otras entidades sometidas a la legislación de contratos del Estado español (other entities subject to Spanish State legislation on procurement).

VI. FRANCE

Bodies
1. National public bodies:
1.1. with scientific, cultural and professional character:
— Collège de France,
— Conservatoire national des arts et métiers,
— Observatoire de Paris.
1.2. Scientific and technological:
— Centre national de la recherche scientifique (CNRS),
— Institut national de la recherche agronomique,
— Institut national de la santé et de la recherche médicale,
— Institut français de recherche scientifique pour le développement en coopération (ORSTOM).
1.3. with administrative character:
— Agence nationale pour l'emploi,
— Caisse nationale des allocations familiales,
— Caisse nationale d'assurance maladie des travailleurs salariés,
— Caisse nationale d'assurance vieillesse des travailleurs salariés,
— Office national des anciens combattants et victimes de la guerre,
— Agences financières de bassins.

Categories
1. National public bodies:
— universités (universities),
— écoles normales d'instituteurs (teacher training colleges).
2. Administrative public bodies at regional, departmental and local level:
— collèges (secondary schools),
— lycées (secondary schools),
— établissements publics hospitaliers (public hospitals),
— offices publics d'habitations à loyer modéré (OPHLM) (public offices for low-cost housing).
3. Groupings of territorial authorities:
— syndicats de communes (associations of local authorities),
— districts (districts),
— communautés urbaines (municipalities),
— institutions interdépartementales et interrégionales (institutions common to more than one Département and interregional institutions).

VIII. ITALY

Bodies
— Agenzia per la promozione dello sviluppo nel Mezzogiorno.

Categories
— Enti portuali e aeroportuali (port and airport authorities),
— Consorzi per le opere idrauliche (consortia for water engineering works),
— Le università statali, gli istituti universitari statali, i consorzi per i lavori interessanti le università (State universities, State university institutes, consortia for university development work),

—Gli istituti superiori scientifici e culturali, gli osservatori astronomici, astrofisici, geofisici o vulcanologici (higher scientific and cultural institutes, astronomical, astrophysical, geophysical or vulcanological observatories),

—Enti di ricerca e sperimentazione (organizations conducting research and experimental work),

—Le istituzioni pubbliche di assistenza e di beneficenza (public welfare and benevolent institutions),

—Enti che gestiscono forme obbligatorie di previdenza e di assistenza (agencies administering compulsory social security and welfare schemes),

—Consorzi di bonifica (land reclamation consortia),

—Enti di sviluppo o di irrigazione (development or irrigation agencies),

—Consorzi per le aree industriali (associations for industrial areas),

—Comunità montane (groupings of municipalities in mountain areas),

—Enti preposti a servizi di pubblico interesse (organizations providing services in the public interest),

—Enti pubblici preposti ad attività di spettacolo, sportive, turistiche e del tempo libero (public bodies engaged in entertainment, sport, tourism and leisure activities),

—Enti culturali e di promozione artistica (organizations promoting culture and artistic activities).

XII.   THE UNITED KINGDOM

Bodies
- —Central Blood Laboratories Authority,
- —Design Council,
- —Health and Safety Executive,
- —National Research Development Corporation,
- —Public Health Laboratory Services Board,
- —Advisory, Conciliation and Arbitration Service,
- —Commission for the New Towns,
- —Development Board For Rural Wales,
- —English Industrial Estates Corporation,
- —National Rivers Authority,
- —Northern Ireland Housing Executive,
- —Scottish Enterprise,
- —Scottish Homes,
- —Welsh Development Agency.

Categories
- —Universities and polytechnics, maintained schools and colleges,
- —National Museums and Galleries,
- —Research Councils,
- —Fire Authorities,
- —National Health Service Authorities,
- —Police Authorities,
- —New Town Development Corporations,
- —Urban Development Corporations.

XIII.   AUSTRIA

All bodies subject to budgetary supervision by the 'Rechnungshof' (audit authority) not having an industrial or commercial character.

XIV. FINLAND

Public or publicly controlled entities or undertakings not having an industrial or commercial character.

XV. SWEDEN

All non-commercial bodies whose procurement is subject to supervision by the National Board for Public Procurement.

ANNEX II

LIST OF PROFESSIONAL ACTIVITIES AS SET OUT IN THE GENERAL INDUSTRIAL CLASSIFICATION OF ECONOMIC ACTIVITIES WITHIN THE EUROPEAN COMMUNITIES (NACE)

Classes	Groups	Subgroups and Items	Description
50			BUILDING AND CIVIL ENGINEERING
	500		General building and civil engineering work (without any particular specification) and demolition work
		500.1	General Building and civil engineering work (without any particular specification) Demolition work
	501		Construction of flats, office blocks, hospitals and other buildings, both residential and non-residential
		501.1	General building contractors
		501.2	Roofings
		501.3	Construction of chimneys, kilns and furnaces
		501.4	Water-proofing and damp-proofing
		501.5	Restorations and maintenance of outside walls (repointing, cleaning, etc.)
		501.6	Erection and dismantling of scaffolding
		501.7	Other specialised activities relating to construction work (including carpentry)
	502		Civil engineering: construction of roads, bridges, railways, etc.
		502.1	General civil engineering work
		502.2	Earth-moving (navvying)
		502.3	Construction of bridges, tunnels and shafts; drilling
		502.4	Hydraulic engineering (rivers, canals, harbours, flows, lochs and dams)
		502.5	Road building (including specialised construction of airports and runways)
		502.6	Specialised construction work relating to water (i.e., to irrigation, land drainage, water supply, sewage disposal, sewerage, etc.)
		502.7	Specialised activities in other areas of civil engineering
	503		Installation (fittings and fixtures)
		503.1	General installation work
		503.2	Gas fitting and plumbing, and the installation of sanitary equipment
		503.3	Installation of heating and ventilating apparatus (central heating, air-conditioning, ventilation)
		503.4	Sound and heat insulation; insulation against vibration
		503.5	Electrical fittings
		503.6	Installation of aerials, lightning conductors, telephones, etc.

Classes Groups	Subgroups and Items	Description
504		Building completion work
	504.1	General building completion work
	504.2	Plastering
	504.3	Joinery, primarily engaged in the after assembly and/or installation (including the laying of parquet flooring)
	504.4	Painting, glazing and paper-hanging
	504.5	Tiling and otherwise covering floors and walls
	504.6	Other building completion work (putting in fireplaces, etc.)

ANNEX III

DEFINITION OF CERTAIN TECHNICAL SPECIFICATIONS

For the purposes of this Directive the following terms shall be defined as follows:

1. 'Technical specifications': the totality of the technical prescriptions contained in particular in the tender documents, defining the characteristics required of a work, material, product or supply, which permits a work, a material, a product or a supply to be described in a manner such that it fulfils the use for which it is intended by the contracting authority. These technical prescriptions shall include levels of quality, performance, safety or dimensions, including the requirements applicable to the material, the product or to the supply as regards quality assurance, terminology, symbols, testing and test methods, packaging, marking or labelling. They shall also include rules relating to design and costing, the test, inspection and acceptances for works and methods or techniques of construction and all other technical conditions which the contracting authority is in a position to prescribe, under general or specific regulations, in relation to the finished works and to the materials or parts which they involve;

2. 'Standard': a technical specification approved by a recognized standardizing body for repeated and continuous application, compliance with which is in principle not compulsory;

3. 'European standard': a standard approved by the European Committee for Standardization (CEN) or by the European Committee for Electrotechnical Standardization (Cenelec) as 'European standards (EN)' or 'Harmonization documents (HD)' according to the common rules of these organizations;

4. 'European technical approval': a favourable technical assessment of the fitness for use of a product, based on fulfilment of the essential requirements for building works, by means of the inherent characteristics of the product and the defined conditions of application and use. The European agreement shall be issued by an approval body designated for this purpose by the Member State;

5. 'Common technical specification': a technical specification laid down in accordance with a procedure recognized by the Member States to ensure uniform application in all Member States which has been published in the Official Journal of the European Communities;

6. 'Essential requirements': requirements regarding safety, health and certain other aspects in the general interest, that the construction works must meet.

ANNEX IV

MODEL CONTRACT NOTICES

A.   Prior information

1.   Name, address, telephone number, telegraphic address, telex and facsimile numbers of the contracting authority.

2.   (a)   Site.

(b)   Nature and extent of the services to be provided and, where relevant, main characteristics of any lots by reference to the work.

(c)   If available, an estimate of the cost range of the proposed services.

3.   (a)   Estimated date for initiating the award procedures in respect of the contract or contracts.

(b)   If known, estimated date for the start of the work.

(c)   If known, estimated timetable for completion of the work.

4.   If known, terms of financing of the work and of price revision and/or references to the provisions in which these are contained.

5.   Other information.

6.   Date of dispatch of the notice.

7.   Date of receipt of the notice by the Office for Official Publications of the European Communities.

B.   Open procedures

1.   Name, address, telephone number, telegraphic address, telex and facsimile numbers of the contracting authority.

2.   (a)   Award procedure chosen.

(b)   Nature of the contract for which tenders are being requested:

3.   (a)   Site.

(b)   Nature and extent of the services to be provided and general nature of the work.

(c)   If the work or the contract is subdivided into several lots, the size of the different lots and the possibility of tendering for one, for several or for all of the lots.

(d)   Information concerning the purpose of the work or the contract where the latter also involves the drawing up of projects.

4.   Any time limit for completion.

5.   (a)   Name and address of the service from which the contract documents and additional documents may be requested.

(b)   Where applicable, the amount and terms of payment of the sum to be paid to obtain such documents.

6.   (a)   Final date for receipt of tenders.

(b)   Address to which tenders must be sent.

(c)   Language or languages in which tenders must be drawn up.

7.   (a)   Where applicable, the persons authorized to be present at the opening of tenders.

(b)   Date, hour and place of opening of tenders.

8.   Any deposit and guarantees required.

9.   Main terms concerning financing and payment and/or references to the provisions in which these are contained.

10.   Where applicable, the legal form to be taken by the grouping of contractors to whom the contract is awarded.

11. Minimum economic and technical standards required of the contractor to whom the contract is awarded.

12. Period during which the tenderer is bound to keep open his tender.

13. Criteria for the award of the contract. Criteria other than that of the lowest price shall be mentioned where they do not appear in the contract documents.

14. Where applicable, prohibition on variants.

15. Other information.

16. Date of publication of the prior information notice in the Official Journal of the European Communities or references to its non-publication.

17. Date of dispatch of the notice.

18. Date of receipt of the notice by the Office for Official Publications of the European Communities.

C. Restricted procedures

1. Name, address, telephone number, telegraphic address, telex and facsimile numbers of the contracting authority.

2. (a) Award procedure chosen.

(b) Where applicable, justification for the use of the accelerated procedure.

(c) Nature of the contract for which tenders are being requested.

3. (a) Site.

(b) Nature and extent of the services to be provided and general nature of the work.

(c) If the work of the contract is subdivided into several lots, the size of the different lots and the possibility of tendering for one, for several or for all of the lots.

(d) Information concerning the purpose of the work or the contract where the latter also involves the drawing up of projects.

4. Any time limit for completion.

5. Where applicable, the legal form to be taken by the grouping of contractors to whom the contract is awarded.

6. (a) Final date for receipt of requests to participate.

(b) Address to which requests must be sent.

(c) Language or languages in which requests must be drawn up.

7. Final date for dispatch of invitations to tender.

8. Any deposit and guarantees required.

9. Main terms concerning financing and payment and/or the provisions in which these are contained.

10. Information concerning the contractor's personal position and minimum economic and technical standards required of the contractor to whom the contract is awarded.

11. Criteria for the award of the contract where they are not mentioned in the invitation to tender.

12. Where applicable, prohibition on variants.

13. Other information.

14. Date of publication of the prior information notice in the Official Journal of the European Communities or reference to its non-publication.

15. Date of dispatch of the notice.

16. Date of receipt of the notice by the Office for Official Publications of the European Communities.

D.   Negotiated procedures

1.   Name, address, telephone number, telegraphic address, telex and facsimile numbers of the contracting authority.

2.   (a)   Award procedure chosen.

(b)   Where applicable, justification for the use of the accelerated procedure.

(c)   Nature of the contract for which tenders are being requested.

3.   (a)   Site.

(b)   Nature and extent of the services to be provided and general nature of the work.

(c)   If the work or the contract is subdivided into several lots, the size of the different lots and the possibility of tendering for one, for several or for all of the lots.

(d)   Information concerning the purpose of the work or the contract where the latter also involves the drawing up of projects.

4.   Any time limit.

5.   Where applicable, the legal form to be taken by the grouping of contractors to whom the contract is awarded.

6.   (a)   Final date for receipt of tenders.

(b)   Address to which tenders must be sent.

(c)   Language or languages in which tenders must be drawn up.

7.   Any deposit and guarantees required.

8.   Main terms concerning financing and payment and/or the provisions in which these are contained.

9.   Information concerning the contractor's personal position and information and formalities necessary in order to evaluate the minimum economic and technical standards required of the contractor to whom the contract is awarded.

10.   Where applicable, prohibition on variants.

11.   Where applicable, name and address of suppliers already selected by the awarding authority.

12.   Date(s) of previous publications in the Official Journal of the European Communities.

13.   Other information.

14.   Date of publication of the prior information notice in the Official Journal of the European Communities.

15.   Date of dispatch of the notice.

16.   Date of receipt of the notice by the Office for Official Publications of the European Communities.

E.   Contract awards

1.   Name and address of awarding authority.

2.   Award procedure chosen.

3.   Date of award of contract.

4.   Criteria for award of contract.

5.   Number of offers received.

6.   Name and address of successful contractor(s).

7.   Nature and extent of the services provided, general characteristics of the finished structure.

8.   Price or range of prices (minimum/maximum) paid.

9. Where appropriate, value and proportion of contract likely to be subcontracted to third parties.

10. Other information.

11. Date of publication of the tender notice in the Official Journal of the European Communities.

12. Date of dispatch of the notice.

13. Date of receipt of the notice by the Office for Official Publications of the European Communities.

ANNEX V
MODEL NOTICE OF PUBLIC WORKS CONCESSION

1. Name, address, telephone number, telegraphic address, telex and facsimile numbers of the contracting authority.

2. (a) Site.

(b) Subject of the concession, nature and extent of the services to be provided.

3. (a) Final date for receipt of candidatures.

(b) Address to which candidatures must be sent.

(c) Language or languages in which candidatures must be drawn up.

4. Personal, technical and financial conditions to be fulfilled by the candidates.

5. Criteria for award of contract.

6. Where applicable, the minimum percentage of the works contracts awarded to third parties.

7. Other information.

8. Date of dispatch of the notice.

9. Date of receipt of the notice by the Office for Official Publications of the European Communities.

ANNEX VI
MODEL NOTICE OF WORKS CONTRACTS AWARDED BY THE CONCESSIONNAIRE

1. (a) Site.

(b) Nature and extent of the services to be provided and the general nature of the work.

2. Any time limit for the completion of the works.

3. Name and address of the service from which the contract documents and additional documents may be requested.

4. (a) Final date for receipt of requests to participate and/or for receipt of tenders.

(b) Address to which requests must be sent.

(c) Language or languages in which requests must be drawn up.

5. Any deposit and guarantees required.

6. Economic and technical standards required of the contract.

7. Criteria for the award of the contract.

8. Other information.

9. Date of dispatch of the notice.

10. Date of receipt of the notice by the Office for Official Publications of the European Communities.

ANNEX VII

DEADLINES FOR TRANSPOSITION AND FOR APPLICATION

Directive 77/305/EEC[1]	amended by Directives				amended by Acts of Accession of	
	78/669/EEC[2]	89/440/EEC[3]	90/531/EEC[4]	DK, IRL, UK[5]	GR[6]	E, P[7]
Article 1		amended				
Article 1a		amended				
Article 1b		amended				
Article 2		amended				
Article 3(1)		deleted				
Article 3(2)		deleted				
Article 3(3)		deleted				
Article 3(4) and (5), sub-paragraphs (a) and (b)		deleted				
		amended				
Article 3(4) and (5), sub-paragraph (c)		amended				
Article 4		amended				
Article 4a		amended				
Article 5		amended				
Article 5a		amended				
Article 6		amended				
Article 7(1)	amended	deleted				
Article 7(2)		deleted				
Article 8		deleted				
Article 9		deleted				
Article 10		amended				
Article 11		deleted				
Article 12		amended				
Article 13		amended				
Article 14		amended				
Article 15		amended				
Article 15a		amended				
Article 15b		amended				
Article 16		deleted				
Article 17		deleted				
Article 18		deleted				
Article 19	amended	amended				
Article 20		amended				
Article 20a		amended				
Article 20b		amended				
Article 21						
Article 22		amended				
Article 22a		amended				
Article 23						
Article 24		amended		amended	amended	amended
Article 25						
Article 26						
Article 27						
Article 28						
Article 29(1)						
Article 29(2)						
Article 29(3)		deleted				
Article 29(4)		amended				
Article 29(5)		amended				
Article 29a		amended				
Article 29b		amended				
Article 30						
Article 30a		amended				
Article 30b		amended				
Article 31		deleted				
Article 32						
Article 33						
Article 34						
Annexes I to VI		I to VI		I	I	II

[1]EC–6: 30.7.1972
DK, IRL, UK: 1.1.1973
GR: 1.1.1981
E, P: 1.1.1986

[2]EC-9: 16.2.1979
GR: 1.1.1981
E, P: 1.1.1986

[3]EC-9: 19.7.1990
GR, E, P: 1.3.1992

[4]EC-9: 1.1.1993
E: 1.1.1996
GR, P: 1.1.1998

[5]EC-9: 1.1.1973
[6]EC-10: 1.1.1981
[7]EC-12: 1.1.1986

ANNEX VIII

CORRELATION TABLE

Directive 71/305/EEC	This directive				
Article 1	Article 1				
Article 1a	Article 2				
Article 1b	Article 3				
Article 2	—				
Article 3(1)	—				
Article 3(2)	—				
Article 3(3)	—				
Article 3(4) and (5), sub-paragraph (a) and (b)	Article 4, sub-paragraph (a)				
Article 3(4) and (5), sub-paragraph (c)	Article 4, sub-paragraph (b)				
Article 4	Article 5				
Article 4a	Article 6				
Article 5	Article 7				
Article 5a	Article 8				
Article 6	Article 9				
Article 7	—				
Article 8	—				
Article 9	—				
Article 10	Article 10				
Article 11	—				
Article 12	Article 11				
Article 13	Article 12				
Article 14	Article 13				
Article 15	Article 14				
Article 15a	Article 15				
Article 15b	Article 16				
Article 16	—				
Article 17	—				
Article 18	—				
Article 19	Article 17				
Article 20	Article 18				
Article 20a	Article 19				
Article 20b	Article 20				
Article 21	Article 21				
Article 22	Article 22				
Article 22a	Article 23				
Article 23	Article 24				
Article 24	Article 25				
Article 25	Article 26				
Article 26	Article 27				
Article 27	Article 28				
Article 28	Article 29				
Article 29(1)	Article 30(1)				
Article 29(2)	Article 30(2)				
Article 29(3)	—				
Article 29(4)	Article 30(3)				
Article 29(5)	Article 30(4)				
Article 29a	Article 31				
Article 29b	Article 32				
Article 30	Article 33				
Article 30a	Article 34				
Article 30b	Article 35				
Article 31	—				
—	Article 36				
Article 32	—				
Article 33	—				
—	Article 37				
Article 34	Article 38				
Annexes I to VI	Annexes I to VI				
—	Annexes VII and VIII				

ENVIRONMENTAL PROVISIONS

COUNCIL DIRECTIVE 75/442/EEC OF 15 JULY 1975 ON WASTE [OJ L194/39]*

THE COUNCIL OF THE EUROPEAN COMMUNITIES,

Having regard to the Treaty establishing the European Economic Community, and in particular Articles 100 and 235 thereof;

Having regard to the proposal from the Commission;

Having regard to the opinion of the European Parliament;[1]

Having regard to the opinion of the Economic and Social Committee;[2]

Whereas any disparity between the provisions on waste disposal already applicable or in preparation in the various member states may create unequal conditions of competition and thus directly affect the functioning of the common market;

Whereas it is therefore necessary to approximate laws in this field, as provided for in Article 100 of the Treaty;

Whereas it seems necessary for this approximation of laws to be accompanied by Community action so that one of the aims of the Community in the sphere of protection of the environment and improvement of the quality of life can be achieved by more extensive rules;

Whereas certain specific provisions to this effect should therefore be laid down;

Whereas Article 235 of the Treaty should be invoked as the powers required for this purpose have not been provided for by the Treaty;

Whereas the essential objective of all provisions relating to waste disposal must be the protection of human health and the environment against harmful effects caused by the collection, transport, treatment, storage and tipping of waste;

Whereas the recovery of waste and the use of recovered materials should be encouraged in order to conserve natural resources;

Whereas the programme of action of the European Communities on the environment,[3] stresses the need for Community action, including the harmonization of legislation;

Notes

*As amended by Directive 91/156 [OJ 1991 L78/32], Directive 91/692 [OJ 1991 L377/48] and Decision 96/350 [OJ 1996 L135/32].

[1]OJ No. C32, 11.2.1975, p. 36.

[2]OJ No. C16, 23.1.1975, p. 12.

[3]OJ No. C112, 20.12.1973, p. 3.

Whereas effective and consistent regulations on waste disposal which neither obstruct intra-Community trade nor affect conditions of competition should be applied to movable property which the owner disposes of or is required to dispose of under the provisions of national Law in force, with the exception of radioactive, mining and agricultural waste, animal carcasses, waste waters, gaseous effluents and waste covered by specific Community rules

Whereas, in order to ensure the protection of the environment, provision should be made for a system of permits for undertakings which treat, store or tip waste on behalf of third parties, for a supervisory system for undertakings which dispose of their own waste and for those which collect the waste of others, and for a plan embracing the essential factors to be taken into consideration in respect of the various waste disposal operations;

Whereas that proportion of the costs not covered by the proceeds of treating the waste must be defrayed in accordance with the 'polluter pays' principle,

HAS ADOPTED THIS DIRECTIVE:

Article 1
For the purposes of this Directive:

(a) 'waste' shall mean any substance or object in the categories set out in Annex I which the holder discards or intends or is required to discard. The Commission, acting in accordance with the procedure laid down in Article 18, will draw up, not later than 1 April 1993, a list of wastes belonging to the categories listed in Annex I. This list will be periodically reviewed and, if necessary, revised by the same procedure;

(b) 'producer' shall mean anyone whose activities produce waste ('original producer') and/or anyone who carries out pre-processing, mixing or other operations resulting in a change in the nature or composition of this waste;

(c) 'holder' shall mean the producer of the waste or the natural or legal person who is in possession of it;

(d) 'management' shall mean the collection, transport, recovery and disposal of waste, including the supervision of such operations and after-care of disposal sites;

(e) 'disposal' shall mean any of the operations provided for in Annex II A;

(f) 'recovery' shall mean any of the operations provided for in Annex II B;

(g) 'collection' shall mean the gathering, sorting and/or mixing of waste for the purpose of transport.

Article 2
1. The following shall be excluded from the scope of this Directive:

(a) gaseous effluents emitted into the atmosphere;

(b) where they are already covered by other legislation:

(i) radioactive waste;

(ii) waste resulting from prospecting, extraction, treatment and storage of mineral resources and the working of quarries;

(iii) animal carcasses and the following agricultural waste: faecal matter and other natural, non-dangerous substances used in farming;

(iv) waste waters, with the exception of waste in liquid form;

(v) decommissioned explosives.

2.   Specific rules for particular instances or supplementing those of this Directive on the management of particular categories of waste may be laid down by means of individual Directives.

Article 3

1.   Member States shall take appropriate measures to encourage:
(a)   firstly, the prevention or reduction of waste production and its harmfulness, in particular by:
—the development of clean technologies more sparing in their use of natural resources,
—the technical development and marketing of products designed so as to make no contribution or to make the smallest possible contribution, by the nature of their manufacture, use or final disposal, to increasing the amount or harmfulness of waste and pollution hazards,
—the development of appropriate techniques for the final disposal of dangerous substances contained in waste destined for recovery;
(b)   secondly:
(i)   the recovery of waste by means of recycling, re-use or reclamation or any other process with a view to extracting secondary raw materials, or
(ii)   the use of waste as a source of energy.
2.   Except where Council Directive 83/189/EEC of 28 March 1983 laying down a procedure for the provision of information in the field of technical standards and regulations[1] applies, Member States shall inform the Commission of any measures they intend to take to achieve the aims set out in paragraph 1. The Commission shall inform the other Member States and the committee referred to in Article 18 of such measures.

Note
[1]OJ No. L109, 26.4.1983, p. 8.

Article 4

Member States shall take the necessary measures to ensure that waste is recovered or disposed of without endangering human health and without using processes or methods which could harm the environment, and in particular:
—without risk to water, air, soil and plants and animals,
—without causing a nuisance through noise or odours,
—without adversely affecting the countryside or places of special interest.
Member States shall also take the necessary measures to prohibit the abandonment, dumping or uncontrolled disposal of waste.

Article 5

1.   Member States shall take appropriate measures, in cooperation with other Member States where this is necessary or advisable, to establish an integrated and adequate network of disposal installations, taking account of the best available technology not involving excessive costs. The network must enable the Community as a whole to become self-sufficient in waste disposal and the Member States to move towards that aim individually, taking into account geographical circumstances or the need for specialized installations for certain types of waste.
2.   The network must also enable waste to be disposed of in one of the nearest appropriate installations, by means of the most appropriate methods

and technologies in order to ensure a high level of protection for the environment and public health.

Article 6

Member States shall establish or designate the competent authority or authorities to be responsible for the implementation of this Directive.

Article 7

1. In order to attain the objectives referred to in Article 3, 4 and 5, the competent authority or authorities referred to in Article 6 shall be required to draw up as soon as possible one or more waste management plans. Such plans shall relate in particular to:
— the type, quantity and origin of waste to be recovered or disposed of,
— general technical requirements,
— any special arrangements for particular wastes,
— suitable disposal sites or installations. Such plans may, for example, cover:
— the natural or legal persons empowered to carry out the management of waste,
— the estimated costs of the recovery and disposal operations,
— appropriate measures to encourage rationalisation of the collection, sorting and treatment of waste.

2. Member States shall collaborate as appropriate with the other Member States concerned and the Commission to draw up such plans. They shall notify the Commission thereof.

3. Member States may take the measures necessary to prevent movements of waste which are not in accordance with their waste management plans. They shall inform the Commission and the Member States of any such measures.

Article 8

Member States shall take the necessary measures to ensure that any holder of waste:
— has it handled by a private or public waste collector or by an undertaking which carries out the operations listed in Annex II A or B, or
— recovers or disposes of it himself in accordance with the provisions of this Directive.

Article 9

1. For the purposes of implementing Articles 4, 5 and 7, any establishment or undertaking which carries out the operations specified in Annex II A must obtain a permit from the competent authority referred to in Article 6.
Such permit shall cover:
— the types and quantities of waste,
— the technical requirements,
— the security precautions to be taken,
— the disposal site,
— the treatment method.

2. Permits may be granted for a specified period, they may be renewable, they may be subject to conditions and obligations, or, notably, if the intended method of disposal is unacceptable from the point of view of environmental protection, they may be refused.

Article 10
For the purposes of implementing Article 4, any establishment or undertaking which carries out the operations referred to in Annex II B must obtain a permit.

Article 11
1.   Without prejudice to Council Directive 78/319/EEC of 20 March 1978 on toxic and dangerous waste,[1] as last amended by the Act of Accession of Spain and Portugal, the following may be exempted from the permit requirement imposed in Article 9 or Article 10:
    (a)   establishments or undertakings carrying out their own waste disposal at the place of production; and
    (b)   establishments or undertakings that carry out waste recovery.
   This exemption may apply only:
   — if the competent authorities have adopted general rules for each type of activity laying down the types and quantities of waste and the conditions under which the activity in question may be exempted from the permit requirements, and
   — if the types or quantities of waste and methods of disposal or recovery are such that the conditions imposed in Article 4 are complied with.
2.   The establishments or undertakings referred to in paragraph 1 shall be registered with the competent authorities.
3.   Member States shall inform the Commission of the general rules adopted pursuant to paragraph 1.

Note
[1]OJ No. L84, 31.3.1978, p. 43.

Article 12
Establishments or undertakings which collect or transport waste on a professional basis or which arrange for the disposal or recovery of waste on behalf of others (dealers or brokers), where not subject to authorisation, shall be registered with the competent authorities.

Article 13
Establishments or undertakings which carry out the operations referred to in Articles 9 to 12 shall be subject to appropriate periodic inspections by the competent authorities.

Article 14
All establishments or undertakings referred to in Articles 9 and 10 shall:
   — keep a record of the quantity, nature, origin, and, where relevant, the destination, frequency of collection, mode of transport and treatment method in respect of the waste referred to in Annex I and the operations referred to in Annex II A or B,
   — make this information available, on request, to the competent authorities referred to in Article 6. Member States may also require producers to comply with the provisions of this Article.

Article 15
In accordance with the 'polluter pays' principle, the cost of disposing of waste must be borne by:

—the holder who has waste handled by a waste collector or by an undertaking as referred to in Article 9, and/or

—the previous holders or the producer of the product from which the waste came.

Article 16

At intervals of three years Member States shall send information to the Commission on the implementation of this Directive, in the form of a sectoral report which shall also cover other pertinent Community Directives. The report shall be drawn up on the basis either of a questionnaire or outline drafted by the Commission in accordance with the procedure laid down in Article 6 of Directive 91/692/EEC.[1] The questionnaire or outline shall be sent to the Member States six months before the start of the period covered by the report. The report shall be made to the Commission within nine months of the end of the three-year period covered by it. The first report shall cover the period 1995 to 1997 inclusive. The Commission shall publish a Community report on the implementation of the Directive within nine months of receiving the reports from the Member States.

Note
[1]OJ No. L377, 31.12.1991, p. 48.

Article 17

The amendments necessary for adapting the Annexes to this Directive to scientific and technical progress shall be adopted in accordance with the procedure laid down in Article 18.

Article 18

The Commission shall be assisted by a committee composed of the representatives of the Member States and chaired by the representative of the Commission. The representative of the Commission shall submit to the committee a draft of the measures to be taken. The committee shall deliver its opinion on the draft within a time limit which the chairman may lay down according to the urgency of the matter. The opinion shall be delivered by the majority laid down in Article 148(2) of the EEC Treaty in the case of decisions which the Council is required to adopt on a proposal from the Commission. The votes of the representatives of the Member States within the committee shall be weighted in the manner set out in that Article. The chairman shall not vote. The Commission shall adopt the measures envisaged if they are in accordance with the opinion of the committee. If the measures envisaged are not in accordance with the opinion of the committee, or if no opinion is delivered, the Commission shall, without delay, submit to the Council a proposal relating to the measures to be taken. The Council shall act by a qualified majority. If, on the expiry of a period of three months from the date of referral to the Council, the Council has not acted, the proposed measures shall be adopted by the Commission.

Article 19

Member states shall bring into force the measures needed in order to comply with this Directive within 24 months of its notification and shall forthwith inform the Commission thereof.

Article 20

Member states shall communicate to the Commission the texts of the main provisions of national law which they adopt in the field covered by this Directive.

Article 21

This Directive is addressed to the member states.

Done at Brussels, 15 July 1975.
For the Council,
The President,
M. RUMOR.

ANNEX I   CATEGORIES OF WASTE

Q1   Production or consumption residues not otherwise specified below

Q2   Off-specification products

Q3   Products whose date for appropriate use has expired

Q4   Materials spilled, lost or having undergone other mishap, including any materials, equipment, etc., contaminated as a result of the mishap

Q5   Materials contaminated or soiled as a result of planned actions (e.g. residues from cleaning operations, packing materials, containers, etc.)

Q6   Unusable parts (e.g. reject batteries, exhausted catalysts, etc.)

Q7   Substances which no longer perform satisfactorily (e.g. contaminated acids, contaminated solvents, exhausted tempering salts, etc.)

Q8   Residues of industrial processes (e.g. slags, still bottoms, etc.)

Q9   Residues from pollution abatement processes (e.g. scrubber sludges, baghouse dusts, spent filters, etc.)

Q10   Machining/finishing residues (e.g. lathe turnings, mill scales, etc.)

Q11   Residues from raw materials extraction and processing (e.g. mining residues, oil field slops, etc.)

Q12   Adulterated materials (e.g. oils contaminated with PCBs, etc.)

Q13   Any materials, substances or products whose use has been banned by law

Q14   Products for which the holder has no further use (e.g. agricultural, household, office, commercial and shop discards, etc.)

Q15   Contaminated materials, substances or products resulting from remedial action with respect to land

Q16   Any materials, substances or products which are not contained in the above categories.

ANNEX IIA   DISPOSAL OPERATIONS

NB: This Annex is intended to list disposal operations such as they occur in practice. In accordance with Article 4 waste must be disposed of without endangering human health and without the use of processes or methods likely to harm the environment.

D 1   Deposit into or onto land (e.g. landfill, etc.)

D 2   Land treatment (e.g. biodegradation of liquid or sludgy discards in soils, etc.)

D 3   Deep injection (e.g. injection of pumpable discards into wells, salt domes or naturally occurring repositories, etc.)

D 4   Surface impoundment (e.g. placement of liquid or sludgy discards into pits, ponds or lagoons, etc.)

D 5   Specially engineered landfill (e.g. placement into lined discrete cells which are capped and isolated from one another and the environment, etc.)

D 6   Release into a water body except seas/oceans

D 7   Release into seas/oceans including sea-bed insertion

D 8   Biological treatment not specified elsewhere in this Annex which results in final compounds or mixtures which are discarded by means of any of the operations numbered D 1 to D 12

D 9   Physico-chemical treatment not specified elsewhere in this Annex which results in final compounds or mixtures which are discarded by means of any of the operations numbered D 1 to D 12 (e.g. evaporation, drying, calcination, etc.)

D 10   Incineration on land

D 11   Incineration at sea

D 12   Permanent storage (e.g. emplacement of containers in a mine, etc.)

D 13   Blending or mixing prior to submission to any of the operations numbered D 1 to D 12

D 14   Repackaging prior to submission to any of the operations numbered D 1 to D 13

D 15   Storage pending any of the operations numbered D 1 to D 14 (excluding temporary storage, pending collection, on the site where it is produced)

ANNEX IIB   RECOVERY OPERATIONS

NB: This Annex is intended to list recovery operations as they occur in practice. In accordance with Article 4 waste must be recovered without endangering human health and without the use of processes or methods likely to harm the environment.

R 1   Use principally as a fuel or other means to generate energy

R 2   Solvent reclamation/regeneration

R 3   Recycling/reclamation of organic substances which are not used as solvents (including composting and other biological transformation processes)

R 4   Recycling/reclamation of metals and metal compounds

R 5   Recycling/reclamation of other inorganic materials

R 6   Regeneration of acids or bases

R 7   Recovery of components used for pollution abatement

R 8   Recovery of components from catalysts

R 9   Oil re-refining or other reuses of oil

R 10   Land treatment resulting in benefit to agriculture or ecological improvement

R 11   Use of wastes obtained from any of the operations numbered R 1 to R 10

R 12   Exchange of wastes for submission to any of the operations numbered R 1 to R 11

R 13   Storage of wastes pending any of the operations numbered R 1 to R 12 (excluding temporary storage, pending collection, on the site where it is produced)

COUNCIL DIRECTIVE 85/337/EEC OF 27 JUNE 1985 ON THE ASSESSMENT OF THE EFFECTS OF CERTAIN PUBLIC AND PRIVATE PROJECTS ON THE ENVIRONMENT
[OJ 1985 L175/40]*

THE COUNCIL OF THE EUROPEAN COMMUNITIES,

Having regard to the Treaty establishing the European Economic Community, and in particular Articles 100 and 235 thereof,

Having regard to the proposal from the Commission,[1]

Having regard to the opinion of the European Parliament,[2]

Having regard to the opinion of the Economic and Social Committee,[3]

Whereas the 1973[4] and 1977[5] action programmes of the European Communities on the environment, as well as the 1983[6] action programme, the main outlines of which have been approved by the Council of the European Communities and the representatives of the Governments of the Member States, stress that the best environmental policy consists in preventing the creation of pollution or nuisances at source, rather than subsequently trying to counteract their effects;

Whereas they affirm the need to take effects on the environment into account at the earliest possible stage in all the technical planning and decision-making processes;

Whereas to that end, they provide for the implementation of procedures to evaluate such effects;

Whereas the disparities between the laws in force in the various Member States with regard to the assessment of the environmental effects of public and private projects may create unfavourable competitive conditions and thereby directly affect the functioning of the common market;

Whereas, therefore, it is necessary to approximate national laws in this field pursuant to Article 100 of the Treaty;

Whereas, in addition, it is necessary to achieve one of the Community's objectives in the sphere of the protection of the environment and the quality of life;

Whereas, since the Treaty has not provided the powers required for this end, recourse should be had to Article 235 of the Treaty;

Whereas general principles for the assessment of environmental effects should be introduced with a view to supplementing and coordinating development consent procedures governing public and private projects likely to have a major effect on the environment;

Whereas development consent for public and private projects which are likely to have significant effects on the environment should be granted only after prior assessment of the likely significant environmental effects of these projects has been carried out;

Notes
*As amended by Directive 97/11 [OJ 1997 L73/5].
[1]OJ No. C169, 9.7.1980, p. 14.
[2]OJ No. C66, 15.3.1982, p. 89.
[3]OJ No. C185, 27.7.1981, p. 8.
[4]OJ No. C112, 20.12.1973, p. 1.
[5]OJ No. C139, 13.6.1977, p. 1.
[6]OJ No. C46, 17.2.1983, p. 1.

Whereas this assessment must be conducted on the basis of the appropriate information supplied by the developer, which may be supplemented by the authorities and by the people who may be concerned by the project in question;

Whereas the principles of the assessment of environmental effects should be harmonised, in particular with reference to the projects which should be subject to assessment, the main obligations of the developers and the content of the assessment;

Whereas projects belonging to certain types have significant effects on the environment and these projects must as a rule be subject to systematic assessment;

Whereas projects of other types may not have significant effects on the environment in every case and whereas these projects should be assessed where the Member States consider that their characteristics so require;

Whereas, for projects which are subject to assessment, a certain minimal amount of information must be supplied, concerning the project and its effects;

Whereas the effects of a project on the environment must be assessed in order to take account of concerns to protect human health, to contribute by means of a better environment to the quality of life, to ensure maintenance of the diversity of species and to maintain the reproductive capacity of the ecosystem as a basic resource for life;

Whereas, however, this Directive should not be applied to projects the details of which are adopted by a specific act of national legislation, since the objectives of this Directive, including that of supplying information, are achieved through the legislative process;

Whereas, furthermore, it may be appropriate in exceptional cases to exempt a specific project from the assessment procedures laid down by this Directive, subject to appropriate information being supplied to the Commission,

HAS ADOPTED THIS DIRECTIVE:

Article 1

1.   This Directive shall apply to the assessment of the environmental effects of those public and private projects which are likely to have significant effects on the environment.

2.   For the purposes of this Directive:
   'project' means:
   — the execution of construction works or of other installations or schemes,
   — other interventions in the natural surroundings and landscape including those involving the extraction of mineral resources;
   'developer' means: the applicant for authorisation for a private project or the public authority which initiates a project;
   'development consent' means: the decision of the competent authority or authorities which entitles the developer to proceed with the project.

3.   The competent authority or authorities shall be that or those which the Member States designate as responsible for performing the duties arising from this Directive.

4.   Projects serving national defence purposes are not covered by this Directive.

5.   This Directive shall not apply to projects the details of which are adopted by a specific act of national legislation, since the objectives of this Directive, including that of supplying information, are achieved through the legislative process.

Article 2

1. Member States shall adopt all measures necessary to ensure that, before consent is given, projects likely to have significant effects on the environment by virtue inter alia, of their nature, size or location are made subject to an assessment with regard to their effects. These projects are defined in Article 4.

2. The environmental impact assessment may be integrated into the existing procedures for consent to projects in the Member States, or, failing this, into other procedures or into procedures to be established to comply with the aims of this Directive.

3. Member States may, in exceptional cases, exempt a specific project in whole or in part from the provisions laid down in this Directive. In this event, the Member States shall:

   (a) consider whether another form of assessment would be appropriate and whether the information thus collected should be made available to the public;

   (b) make available to the public concerned the information relating to the exemption and the reasons for granting it;

   (c) inform the Commission, prior to granting consent, of the reasons justifying the exemption granted, and provide it with the information made available, where appropriate, to their own nationals. The Commission shall immediately forward the documents received to the other Member States. The Commission shall report annually to the Council on the application of this paragraph.

Article 3

The environmental impact assessment will identify, describe and assess in an appropriate manner, in the light of each individual case and in accordance with the Articles 4 to 11, the direct and indirect effects of a project on the following factors:

   — human beings, fauna and flora,

   — soil, water, air, climate and the landscape,

   — the inter-action between the factors mentioned in the first and second indents,

   — material assets and the cultural heritage.

Article 4

1. Subject to Article 2(3), projects of the classes listed in Annex I shall be made subject to an assessment in accordance with Articles 5 to 10.

2. Projects of the classes listed in Annex II shall be made subject to an assessment, in accordance with Articles 5 to 10, where Member States consider that their characteristics so require. To this end Member States may inter alia specify certain types of projects as being subject to an assessment or may establish the criteria and/or thresholds necessary to determine which of the projects of the classes listed in Annex II are to be subject to an assessment in accordance with Articles 5 to 10.

Article 5

1. In the case of projects which, pursuant to Article 4, must be subjected to an environmental impact assessment in accordance with Articles 5 to 10, Member States shall adopt the necessary measures to ensure that the developer supplies in an appropriate form the information specified in Annex III inasmuch as:

(a) the Member States consider that the information is relevant to a given stage of the consent procedure and to the specific characteristics of a particular project or type of project and of the environmental features likely to be affected;

(b) the Member States consider that a developer may reasonably be required to compile this information having regard inter alia to current knowledge and methods of assessment.

2. The information to be provided by the developer in accordance with paragraph 1 shall include at least:

— a description of the project comprising information on the site, design and size of the project,

— a description of the measures envisaged in order to avoid, reduce and, if possible, remedy significant adverse effects,

— the data required to identify and assess the main effects which the project is likely to have on the environment,

— a non-technical summary of the information mentioned in indents 1 to 3.

3. Where they consider it necessary, Member States shall ensure that any authorities with relevant information in their possession make this information available to the developer.

Article 6

1. Member States shall take the measures necessary to ensure that the authorities likely to be concerned by the project by reason of their specific environmental responsibilities are given an opportunity to express their opinion on the request for development consent. Member States shall designate the authorities to be consulted for this purpose in general terms or in each case when the request for consent is made. The information gathered pursuant to Article 5 shall be forwarded to these authorities. Detailed arrangements for consultation shall be laid down by the Member States.

2. Member States shall ensure that:

— any request for development consent and any information gathered pursuant to Article 5 are made available to the public,

— the public concerned is given the opportunity to express an opinion before the project is initiated.

3. The detailed arrangements for such information and consultation shall be determined by the Member States, which may in particular, depending on the particular characteristics of the projects or sites concerned:

— determine the public concerned,

— specify the places where the information can be consulted,

— specify the way in which the public may be informed, for example by bill-posting within a certain radius, publication in local newspapers, organization of exhibitions with plans, drawings, tables, graphs, models,

— determine the manner in which the public is to be consulted, for example, by written submissions, by public enquiry,

— fix appropriate time limits for the various stages of the procedure in order to ensure that a decision is taken within a reasonable period.

Article 7

Where a Member State is aware that a project is likely to have significant effects on the environment in another Member State or where a Member State likely to be significantly affected so requests, the Member State in whose territory the project is intended to be carried out shall forward the information gathered pursuant to Article 5 to the other Member State at the same time as it makes it available to its own nationals. Such information shall serve as a basis for any consultations necessary in the framework of the bilateral relations between two Member States on a reciprocal and equivalent basis.

Article 8
Information gathered pursuant to Articles 5, 6 and 7 must be taken into consideration in the development consent procedure.

Article 9
When a decision has been taken, the competent authority or authorities shall inform the public concerned of:
    — the content of the decision and any conditions attached thereto,
    — the reasons and considerations on which the decision is based where the Member States' legislation so provides. The detailed arrangements for such information shall be determined by the Member States. If another Member State has been informed pursuant to Article 7, it will also be informed of the decision in question.

Article 10
The provisions of this Directive shall not affect the obligation on the competent authorities to respect the limitations imposed by national regulations and administrative provisions and accepted legal practices with regard to industrial and commercial secrecy and the safeguarding of the public interest. Where Article 7 applies, the transmission of information to another Member State and the reception of information by another Member State shall be subject to the limitations in force in the Member State in which the project is proposed.

Article 11
    1.   The Member States and the Commission shall exchange information on the experience gained in applying this Directive.
    2.   In particular, Member States shall inform the Commission of any criteria and/or thresholds adopted for the selection of the projects in question, in accordance with Article 4(2), or of the types of projects concerned which, pursuant to Article 4(2), are subject to assessment in accordance with Articles 5 to 10.
    3.   Five years after notification of this Directive, the Commission shall send the European Parliament and the Council a report on its application and effectiveness. The report shall be based on the aforementioned exchange of information.
    4.   On the basis of this exchange of information, the Commission shall submit to the Council additional proposals, should this be necessary, with a view to this Directive's being applied in a sufficiently coordinated manner.

Article 12
    1.   Member States shall take the measures necessary to comply with this Directive within three years of its notification.[1]

Note
[1]This Directive was notified to the Member States on 3 July 1985.

2. Member States shall communicate to the Commission the texts of the provisions of national law which they adopt in the field covered by this Directive.

Article 13
The provisions of this Directive shall not affect the right of Member States to lay down stricter rules regarding scope and procedure when assessing environmental effects.

Article 14
This Directive is addressed to the Member States.

Done at Luxembourg, 27 June 1985.
For the Council,
The President,
A. BIONDI.

Note
Editor's Note: The following material contains the significantly amended Article and Annexes of Directive 85/337 and Articles 2 and 3 of the amending Directive 97/11 providing the entry into force date and transitional rules.

Article 2
1. Member States shall adopt all measures necessary to ensure that, before consent is given, projects likely to have significant effects on the environment by virtue, inter alia, of their nature, size or location are made subject to a requirement for development consent and an assessment with regard to their effects. These projects are defined in Article 4.
2. The environmental impact assessment may be integrated into the existing procedures for consent to projects in the Member States, or, failing this, into other procedures or into procedures to be established to comply with the aims of this Directive.
2a. Member States may provide for a single procedure in order to fulfil the requirements of this Directive and the requirements of Council Directive 96/61/EC of 24 September 1996 on integrated pollution prevention and control.[1]
3. Without prejudice to Article 7, Member States may, in exceptional cases, exempt a specific project in whole or in part from the provisions laid down in this Directive. In this event, the Member States shall:
  (a) consider whether another form of assessment would be appropriate and whether the information thus collected should be made available to the public;
  (b) make available to the public concerned the information relating to the exemption and the reasons for granting it;
  (c) inform the Commission, prior to granting consent, of the reasons justifying the exemption granted, and provide it with the information made available, where applicable, to their own nationals. The Commission shall immediately forward the documents received to the other Member States. The Commission shall report annually to the Council on the application of this paragraph.

Note
[1] OJ No. L257, 10.10.1996, p. 26.

Article 3

The environmental impact assessment shall identify, describe and assess in an appropriate manner, in the light of each individual case and in accordance with Articles 4 to 11, the direct and indirect effects of a project on the following factors:

— human beings, fauna and flora;

— soil, water, air, climate and the landscape;

— material assets and the cultural heritage;

— the interaction between the factors mentioned in the first, second and third indents.

Article 4

1.   Subject to Article 2(3), projects listed in Annex I shall be made subject to an assessment in accordance with Articles 5 to 10.

2.   Subject to Article 2(3), for projects listed in Annex II, the Member States shall determine through:

(a)   a case-by-case examination, or

(b)   thresholds or criteria set by the Member State whether the project shall be made subject to an assessment in accordance with Articles 5 to 10. Member States may decide to apply both procedures referred to in (a) and (b).

3.   When a case-by-case examination is carried out or thresholds or criteria are set for the purpose of paragraph 2, the relevant selection criteria set out in Annex III shall be taken into account.

4.   Member States shall ensure that the determination made by the competent authorities under paragraph 2 is made available to the public.

Article 5

1.   In the case of projects which, pursuant to Article 4, must be subjected to an environmental impact assessment in accordance with Articles 5 to 10, Member States shall adopt the necessary measures to ensure that the developer supplies in an appropriate form the information specified in Annex IV inasmuch as:

(a)   the Member States consider that the information is relevant to a given stage of the consent procedure and to the specific characteristics of a particular project or type of project and of the environmental features likely to be affected;

(b)   the Member States consider that a developer may reasonably be required to compile this information having regard inter alia to current knowledge and methods of assessment.

2.   Member States shall take the necessary measures to ensure that, if the developer so requests before submitting an application for development consent, the competent authority shall give an opinion on the information to be supplied by the developer in accordance with paragraph 1. The competent authority shall consult the developer and authorities referred to in Article 6(1) before it gives its opinion. The fact that the authority has given an opinion under this paragraph shall not preclude it from subsequently requiring the developer to submit further information. Member States may require the competent authorities to give such an opinion, irrespective of whether the developer so requests.

3.   The information to be provided by the developer in accordance with paragraph 1 shall include at least:

—a description of the project comprising information on the site, design and size of the project,

—a description of the measures envisaged in order to avoid, reduce and, if possible, remedy significant adverse effects,

—the data required to identify and assess the main effects which the project is likely to have on the environment,

—an outline of the main alternatives studied by the developer and an indication of the main reasons for his choice, taking into account the environmental effects,

—a non-technical summary of the information mentioned in the previous indents.

4.   Member States shall, if necessary, ensure that any authorities holding relevant information, with particular reference to Article 3, shall make this information available to the developer.

Article 6

1.   Member States shall take the measures necessary to ensure that the authorities likely to be concerned by the project by reason of their specific environmental responsibilities are given an opportunity to express their opinion on the information supplied by the developer and on the request for development consent. To this end, Member States shall designate the authorities to be consulted, either in general terms or on a case-by-case basis. The information gathered pursuant to Article 5 shall be forwarded to those authorities. Detailed arrangements for consultation shall be laid down by the Member States.

2.   Member States shall ensure that any request for development consent and any information gathered pursuant to Article 5 are made available to the public within a reasonable time in order to give the public concerned the opportunity to express an opinion before the development consent is granted.

3.   The detailed arrangements for such information and consultation shall be determined by the Member States, which may in particular, depending on the particular characteristics of the projects or sites concerned:

—determine the public concerned,

—specify the places where the information can be consulted,

—specify the way in which the public may be informed, for example by bill-posting within a certain radius, publication in local newspapers, organization of exhibitions with plans, drawings, tables, graphs, models,

—determine the manner in which the public is to be consulted, for example, by written submissions, by public enquiry,

—fix appropriate time limits for the various stages of the procedure in order to ensure that a decision is taken within a reasonable period.

Article 7

1.   Where a Member State is aware that a project is likely to have significant effects on the environment in another Member State or where a Member State likely to be significantly affected so requests, the Member State in whose territory the project is intended to be carried out shall send to the affected Member State as soon as possible and no later than when informing its own public, inter alia:

(a)   a description of the project, together with any available information on its possible transboundary impact;

(b) information on the nature of the decision which may be taken, and shall give the other Member State a reasonable time in which to indicate whether it wishes to participate in the Environmental Impact Assessment procedure, and may include the information referred to in paragraph 2.

2. If a Member State which receives information pursuant to paragraph 1 indicates that it intends to participate in the Environmental Impact Assessment procedure, the Member State in whose territory the project is intended to be carried out shall, if it has not already done so, send to the affected Member State the information gathered pursuant to Article 5 and relevant information regarding the said procedure, including the request for development consent.

3. The Member States concerned, each insofar as it is concerned, shall also:

(a) arrange for the information referred to in paragraphs 1 and 2 to be made available, within a reasonable time, to the authorities referred to in Article 6(1) and the public concerned in the territory of the Member State likely to be significantly affected; and

(b) ensure that those authorities and the public concerned are given an opportunity, before development consent for the project is granted, to forward their opinion within a reasonable time on the information supplied to the competent authority in the Member State in whose territory the project is intended to be carried out.

4. The Member States concerned shall enter into consultations regarding, inter alia, the potential transboundary effects of the project and the measures envisaged to reduce or eliminate such effects and shall agree on a reasonable time frame for the duration of the consultation period.

5. The detailed arrangements for implementing the provisions of this Article may be determined by the Member States concerned.

Article 8

The results of consultations and the information gathered pursuant to Articles 5, 6 and 7 must be taken into consideration in the development consent procedure.

Article 9

1. When a decision to grant or refuse development consent has been taken, the competent authority or authorities shall inform the public thereof in accordance with the appropriate procedures and shall make available to the public the following information:

— the content of the decision and any conditions attached thereto,

— the main reasons and considerations on which the decision is based,

— a description, where necessary, of the main measures to avoid, reduce and, if possible, offset the major adverse effects.

2. The competent authority or authorities shall inform any Member State which has been consulted pursuant to Article 7, forwarding to it the information referred to in paragraph 1.

Article 10

The provisions of this Directive shall not affect the obligation on the competent authorities to respect the limitations imposed by national regulations and administrative provisions and accepted legal practices with regard to commercial and industrial confidentiality, including intellectual property, and the safeguarding of the public interest. Where Article 7 applies, the transmission of information to another Member State and the receipt of information by another Member State shall be subject to the limitations in force in the Member State in which the project is proposed.

Article 11

1.   The Member States and the Commission shall exchange information on the experience gained in applying this Directive.

2.   In particular, Member States shall inform the Commission of any criteria and/or thresholds adopted for the selection of the projects in question, in accordance with Article 4(2).

4.   On the basis of this exchange of information, the Commission shall submit to the Council additional proposals, should this be necessary, with a view to this Directive's being applied in a sufficiently coordinated manner.

Article 2 of Directive 97/11

Five years after the entry into force of this Directive, the Commission shall send the European Parliament and the Council a report on the application and effectiveness of Directive 85/337/EEC as amended by this Directive. The report shall be based on the exchange of information provided for by Article 11(1) and (2). On the basis of this report, the Commission shall, where appropriate, submit to the Council additional proposals with a view to ensuring further coordination in the application of this Directive.

Article 3 of Directive 97/11

1.   Member States shall bring into force the laws, regulations and administrative provisions necessary to comply with this Directive by 14 March 1999 at the latest. They shall forthwith inform the Commission thereof.

When Member States adopt these provisions, they shall contain a reference to this Directive or shall be accompanied by such reference at the time of their official publication. The procedure for such reference shall be adopted by Member States.

2.   If a request for development consent is submitted to a competent authority before the end of the time limit laid down in paragraph 1, the provisions of Directive 85/337/EEC prior to these amendments shall continue to apply.

ANNEX I   PROJECTS SUBJECT TO ARTICLE 4(1)

1.   Crude-oil refineries (excluding undertakings manufacturing only lubricants from crude oil) and installations for the gasification and liquefaction of 500 tonnes or more of coal or bituminous shale per day.

2.   Thermal power stations and other combustion installations with a heat output of 300 megawatts or more and nuclear power stations and other nuclear reactors (except research installations for the production and conversion of fissionable and fertile materials, whose maximum power does not exceed 1 kilowatt continuous thermal load).

3.   Installations solely designed for the permanent storage or final disposal of radioactive waste.

4.   Integrated works for the initial melting of cast-iron and steel.

5.   Installations for the extraction of asbestos and for the processing and transformation of asbestos and products containing asbestos: for asbestos-

cement products, with an annual production of more than 20,000 tonnes of finished products, for friction material, with an annual production of more than 50 tonnes of finished products, and for other uses of asbestos, utilisation of more than 200 tonnes per year.

6.   Integrated chemical installations.

7.   Construction of motorways, express roads[1] and lines for long-distance railway traffic and of airports[2] with a basic runway length of 2,100 m or more.

8.   Trading ports and also inland waterways and ports for inland-waterway traffic which permit the passage of vessels of over 1,350 tonnes.

9.   Waste-disposal installations for the incineration, chemical treatment or land fill of toxic and dangerous wastes.

Notes
[1]For the purposes of the Directive, 'express road' means a road which complies with the definition in the European Agreement on main international traffic arteries of 15 November 1975.
[2]For the purposes of this Directive, 'airport' means airports which comply with the definition in the 1944 Chicago Convention setting up the International Civil Aviation Organization (Annex 14).

ANNEX II   PROJECTS SUBJECT TO ARTICLE 4(2)

1.   Agriculture

(a)   Projects for the restructuring of rural land holdings.

(b)   Projects for the use of uncultivated land or semi-natural areas for intensive agricultural purposes.

(c)   Water-management projects for agriculture.

(d)   Initial afforestation where this may lead to adverse ecological changes and land reclamation for the purposes of conversion to another type of land use.

(e)   Poultry-rearing installations.

(f)   Pig-rearing installations.

(g)   Salmon breeding.

(h)   Reclamation of land from the sea.

2. Extractive industry

(a)   Extraction of peat.

(b)   Deep drillings with the exception of drillings for investigating the stability of the soil and in particular:
— geothermal drilling,
— drilling for the storage of nuclear waste material,
— drilling for water supplies.

(c)   Extraction of minerals other than metalliferous and energy-producing minerals, such as marble, sand, gravel, shale, salt, phosphates and potash.

(d)   Extraction of coal and lignite by underground mining.

(e)   Extraction of coal and lignite by open-cast mining.

(f)   Extraction of petroleum.

(g)   Extraction of natural gas.

(h)   Extraction of ores.

(i)   Extraction of bituminous shale.

(j)   Extraction of minerals other than metalliferous and energy-producing minerals by open-cast mining.

(k)   Surface industrial installations for the extraction of coal, petroleum, natural gas and ores, as well as bituminous shale.
(l)   Coke ovens (dry coal distillation).
(m) Installations for the manufacture of cement.

3.   Energy industry
(a)   Industrial installations for the production of electricity, steam and hot water (unless included in Annex I).
(b)   Industrial installations for carrying gas, steam and hot water; transmission of electrical energy by overhead cables.
(c)   Surface storage of natural gas.
(d)   Underground storage of combustible gases.
(e)   Surface storage of fossil fuels.
(f)   Industrial briquetting of coal and lignite.
(g)   Installations for the production or enrichment of nuclear fuels.
(h)   Installations for the reprocessing of irradiated nuclear fuels.
(i)   Installations for the collection and processing of radioactive waste (unless included in Annex I).
(j)   Installations for hydroelectric energy production.

4.   Processing of metals
(a)   Iron and steelworks, including foundries, forges, drawing plants and rolling mills (unless included in Annex I).
(b)   Installations for the production, including smelting, refining, drawing and rolling, of nonferrous metals, excluding precious metals.
(c)   Pressing, drawing and stamping of large castings.
(d)   Surface treatment and coating of metals.
(e)   Boilermaking, manufacture of reservoirs, tanks and other sheet-metal containers.
(f)   Manufacture and assembly of motor vehicles and manufacture of motor-vehicle engines.
(g)   Shipyards.
(h)   Installations for the construction and repair of aircraft.
(i)   Manufacture of railway equipment.
(j)   Swaging by explosives.
(k)   Installations for the roasting and sintering of metallic ores.

5.   Manufacture of glass

6.   Chemical industry
(a)   Treatment of intermediate products and production of chemicals (unless included in Annex I).
(b)   Production of pesticides and pharmaceutical products, paint and varnishes, elastomers and peroxides.
(c)   Storage facilities for petroleum, petrochemical and chemical products.

7.   Food industry
(a)   Manufacture of vegetable and animal oils and fats.
(b)   Packing and canning of animal and vegetable products.
(c)   Manufacture of dairy products.
(d)   Brewing and malting.

    (e)   Confectionery and syrup manufacture.
    (f)   Installations for the slaughter of animals.
    (g)   Industrial starch manufacturing installations.
    (h)   Fish-meal and fish-oil factories.
    (i)   Sugar factories.

8.   Textile, leather, wood and paper industries
    (a)   Wool scouring, degreasing and bleaching factories.
    (b)   Manufacture of fibre board, particle board and plywood.
    (c)   Manufacture of pulp, paper and board.
    (d)   Fibre-dyeing factories.
    (e)   Cellulose-processing and production installations.
    (f)   Tannery and leather-dressing factories.

9.   Rubber industry
Manufacture and treatment of elastomer-based products.

10.   Infrastructure projects
    (a)   Industrial-estate development projects.
    (b)   Urban-development projects.
    (c)   Ski-lifts and cable-cars.
    (d)   Construction of roads, harbours, including fishing harbours, and airfields (projects not listed in Annex I).
    (e)   Canalisation and flood-relief works.
    (f)   Dams and other installations designed to hold water or store it on a long-term basis.
    (g)   Tramways, elevated and underground railways, suspended lines or similar lines of a particular type, used exclusively or mainly for passenger transport.
    (h)   Oil and gas pipeline installations.
    (i)   Installation of long-distance aqueducts.
    (j)   Yacht marinas.

11.   Other projects
    (a)   Holiday villages, hotel complexes.
    (b)   Permanent racing and test tracks for cars and motor cycles.
    (c)   Installations for the disposal of industrial and domestic waste (unless included in Annex I).
    (d)   Waste water treatment plants.
    (e)   Sludge-deposition sites.
    (f)   Storage of scrap iron.
    (g)   Test benches for engines, turbines or reactors.
    (h)   Manufacture of artificial mineral fibres.
    (i)   Manufacture, packing, loading or placing in cartridges of gunpowder and explosives.
    (j)   Knackers' yards.

12.   Modifications to development projects included in Annex I and projects in Annex I undertaken exclusively or mainly for the development and testing of new methods or products and not used for more than one year.

ANNEX III   INFORMATION REFERRED TO IN ARTICLE 5(1)

1.   Description of the project, including in particular:
— a description of the physical characteristics of the whole project and the land-use requirements during the construction and operational phases,
— a description of the main characteristics of the production processes, for instance, nature and quantity of the materials used,
— an estimate, by type and quantity, of expected residues and emissions (water, air and soil pollution, noise, vibration, light, heat, radiation, etc.) resulting from the operation of the proposed project.

2.   Where appropriate, an outline of the main alternatives studied by the developer and an indication of the main reasons for his choice, taking into account the environmental effects.

3.   A description of the aspects of the environment likely to be significantly affected by the proposed project, including, in particular, population, fauna, flora, soil, water, air, climatic factors, material assets, including the architectural and archaeological heritage, landscape and the inter-relationship between the above factors.

4.   A description[1] of the likely significant effects of the proposed project on the environment resulting from:
— the existence of the project,
— the use of natural resources,
— the emission of pollutants, the creation of nuisances and the elimination of waste; and the description by the developer of the forecasting methods used to assess the effects on the environment.

5.   A description of the measures envisaged to prevent, reduce and where possible offset any significant adverse effects on the environment.

6.   A non-technical summary of the information provided under the above headings.

7.   An indication of any difficulties (technical deficiencies or lack of know-how) encountered by the developer in compiling the required information.

Note
[1]This description should cover the direct effects and any indirect, secondary, cumulative, short, medium and long-term, permanent and temporary, positive and negative effects of the project.

Editor's Note: these are the amended Annexes to Directive 85/337.

ANNEX I   PROJECTS SUBJECT TO ARTICLE 4(1)

1.   Crude-oil refineries (excluding undertakings manufacturing only lubricants from crude oil) and installations for the gasification and liquefaction of 500 tonnes or more of coal or bituminous shale per day.

2. — Thermal power stations and other combustion installations with a heat output of 300 megawatts or more, and
— nuclear power stations and other nuclear reactors including the dismantling or decommissioning of such power stations or reactors[1] (except

Note
[1]Nuclear power stations and other nuclear reactors cease to be such an installation when all nuclear fuel and other radioactively contaminated elements have been removed permanently from the installation site.

research installations for the production and conversion of fissionable and fertile materials, whose maximum power does not exceed 1 kilowatt continuous thermal load).

3. (a) Installations for the reprocessing of irradiated nuclear fuel.

(b) Installations designed:

— for the production or enrichment of nuclear fuel,

— for the processing of irradiated nuclear fuel or high-level radioactive waste,

— for the final disposal of irradiated nuclear fuel,

— solely for the final disposal of radioactive waste,

— solely for the storage (planned for more than 10 years) of irradiated nuclear fuels or radioactive waste in a different site than the production site.

4. — Integrated works for the initial smelting of cast-iron and steel;

— Installations for the production of non-ferrous crude metals from ore, concentrates or secondary raw materials by metallurgical, chemical or electrolytic processes.

5. Installations for the extraction of asbestos and for the processing and transformation of asbestos and products containing asbestos: for asbestos-cement products, with an annual production of more than 20,000 tonnes of finished products, for friction material, with an annual production of more than 50 tonnes of finished products, and for other uses of asbestos, utilization of more than 200 tonnes per year.

6. Integrated chemical installations, i.e., those installations for the manufacture on an industrial scale of substances using chemical conversion processes, in which several units are juxtaposed and are functionally linked to one another and which are:

(i) for the production of basic organic chemicals;

(ii) for the production of basic inorganic chemicals;

(iii) for the production of phosphorous-, nitrogen- or potassium-based fertilizers (simple or compound fertilizers);

(iv) for the production of basic plant health products and of biocides;

(v) for the production of basic pharmaceutical products using a chemical or biological process;

(vi) for the production of explosives.

7. (a) Construction of lines for long-distance railway traffic and of airports[2] with a basic runway length of 2,100 m or more;

(b) Construction of motorways and express roads;[3]

(c) Construction of a new road of four or more lanes, or realignment and/or widening of an existing road of two lanes or less so as to provide four or more lanes, where such new road, or realigned and/or widened section of road would be 10 km or more in a continuous length.

8. (a) Inland waterways and ports for inland-waterway traffic which permit the passage of vessels of over 1,350 tonnes;

Notes

[2]For the purposes of this Directive, 'airport' means airports which comply with the definition in the 1944 Chicago Convention setting up the International Civil Aviation Organization (Annex 14).

[3]For the purposes of the Directive, 'express road' means a road which complies with the definition in the European Agreement on Main International Traffic Arteries of 15 November 1975.

(b)   Trading ports, piers for loading and unloading connected to land and outside ports (excluding ferry piers) which can take vessels of over 1,350 tonnes.

9.   Waste disposal installations for the incineration, chemical treatment as defined in Annex IIA to Directive 75/442/EEC[4] under heading D9, or landfill of hazardous waste (i.e. waste to which Directive 91/689/EEC[5] applies).

10.   Waste disposal installations for the incineration or chemical treatment as defined in Annex IIA to Directive 75/442/EEC under heading D9 of non-hazardous waste with a capacity exceeding 100 tonnes per day.

11.   Groundwater abstraction or artificial groundwater recharge schemes where the annual volume of water abstracted or recharged is equivalent to or exceeds 10 million cubic metres.

12.   (a) Works for the transfer of water resources between river basins where this transfer aims at preventing possible shortages of water and where the amount of water transferred exceeds 100 million cubic metres/year;

(b)   In all other cases, works for the transfer of water resources between river basins where the multi-annual average flow of the basin of abstraction exceeds 2,000 million cubic metres/year and where the amount of water transferred exceeds 5% of this flow. In both cases transfers of piped drinking water are excluded.

13.   Waste water treatment plants with a capacity exceeding 150,000 population equivalent as defined in Article 2 point 6 of Directive 91/271/EEC.[6]

14.   Extraction of petroleum and natural gas for commercial purposes where the amount extracted exceeds 500 tonnes/day in the case of petroleum and 500,000 m³/day in the case of gas.

15.   Dams and other installations designed for the holding back or permanent storage of water, where a new or additional amount of water held back or stored exceeds 10 million cubic metres.

16.   Pipelines for the transport of gas, oil or chemicals with a diameter of more than 800 mm and a length of more than 40 km.

17.   Installations for the intensive rearing of poultry or pigs with more than:
(a)   85,000 places for broilers, 60,000 places for hens;
(b)   3,000 places for production pigs (over 30 kg); or
(c)   900 places for sows.

18.   Industrial plants for the
(a)   production of pulp from timber or similar fibrous materials;
(b)   production of paper and board with a production capacity exceeding 200 tonnes per day.

19.   Quarries and open-cast mining where the surface of the site exceeds 25 hectares, or peat extraction, where the surface of the site exceeds 150 hectares.

20.   Construction of overhead electrical power lines with a voltage of 220 kV or more and a length of more than 15 km.

21.   Installations for storage of petroleum, petrochemical, or chemical products with a capacity of 200,000 tonnes or more.

Notes
[4]OJ No. L194, 25.7.1975, p. 39. Directive as last amended by Commission Decision 94/3/EC [OJ No. L5, 7.1.1994, p. 15].
[5]OJ No. L377, 31.12.1991, p. 20. Directive as last amended by Directive 94/31/EC [OJ No. L168, 2.7.1994, p. 28].
[6]OJ No. L135, 30.5.1991, p. 40. Directive as last amended by the 1994 Act of Accession.

ANNEX II   PROJECTS SUBJECT TO ARTICLE 4(2)

1.   Agriculture, silviculture and aquaculture
    (a)   Projects for the restructuring of rural land holdings;
    (b)   Projects for the use of uncultivated land or semi-natural areas for intensive agricultural purposes;
    (c)   Water management projects for agriculture, including irrigation and land drainage projects;
    (d)   Initial afforestation and deforestation for the purposes of conversion to another type of land use;
    (e)   Intensive livestock installations (projects not included in Annex I);
    (f)   Intensive fish farming;
    (g)   Reclamation of land from the sea.
2.   Extractive industry
    (a)   Quarries, open-cast mining and peat extraction (projects not included in Annex I);
    (b)   Underground mining;
    (c)   Extraction of minerals by marine or fluvial dredging;
    (d)   Deep drillings, in particular:
      — geothermal drilling,
      — drilling for the storage of nuclear waste material,
      — drilling for water supplies, with the exception of drillings for investigating the stability of the soil;
    (e)   Surface industrial installations for the extraction of coal, petroleum, natural gas and ores, as well as bituminous shale.
3.   Energy industry
    (a)   Industrial installations for the production of electricity, steam and hot water (projects not included in Annex I);
    (b)   Industrial installations for carrying gas, steam and hot water; transmission of electrical energy by overhead cables (projects not included in Annex I);
    (c)   Surface storage of natural gas;
    (d)   Underground storage of combustible gases;
    (e)   Surface storage of fossil fuels;
    (f)   Industrial briquetting of coal and lignite;
    (g)   Installations for the processing and storage of radioactive waste (unless included in Annex I);
    (h)   Installations for hydroelectric energy production;
    (i)   Installations for the harnessing of wind power for energy production (wind farms).
4.   Production and processing of metals
    (a)   Installations for the production of pig iron or steel (primary or secondary fusion) including continuous casting;
    (b)   Installations for the processing of ferrous metals:
      (i)   hot-rolling mills;
      (ii)   smitheries with hammers;
      (iii)   application of protective fused metal coats;
    (c)   Ferrous metal foundries;

(d)   Installations for the smelting, including the alloyage, of non-ferrous metals, excluding precious metals, including recovered products (refining, foundry casting, etc.);

(e)   Installations for surface treatment of metals and plastic materials using an electrolytic or chemical process;

(f)   Manufacture and assembly of motor vehicles and manufacture of motor-vehicle engines;

(g)   Shipyards;

(h)   Installations for the construction and repair of aircraft;

(i)   Manufacture of railway equipment;

(j)   Swaging by explosives;

(k)   Installations for the roasting and sintering of metallic ores.

5.   Mineral industry

(a)   Coke ovens (dry coal distillation);

(b)   Installations for the manufacture of cement;

(c)   Installations for the production of asbestos and the manufacture of asbestos-products (projects not included in Annex I);

(d)   Installations for the manufacture of glass including glass fibre;

(e)   Installations for smelting mineral substances including the production of mineral fibres;

(f)   Manufacture of ceramic products by burning, in particular roofing tiles, bricks, refractory bricks, tiles, stoneware or porcelain.

6.   Chemical industry (Projects not included in Annex I)

(a)   Treatment of intermediate products and production of chemicals;

(b)   Production of pesticides and pharmaceutical products, paint and varnishes, elastomers and peroxides;

(c)   Storage facilities for petroleum, petrochemical and chemical products.

7.   Food industry

(a)   Manufacture of vegetable and animal oils and fats;

(b)   Packing and canning of animal and vegetable products;

(c)   Manufacture of dairy products;

(d)   Brewing and malting;

(e)   Confectionery and syrup manufacture;

(f)   Installations for the slaughter of animals;

(g)   Industrial starch manufacturing installations;

(h)   Fish-meal and fish-oil factories;

(i)   Sugar factories.

8.   Textile, leather, wood and paper industries

(a)   Industrial plants for the production of paper and board (projects not included in Annex I);

(b)   Plants for the pretreatment (operations such as washing, bleaching, mercerization) or dyeing of fibres or textiles;

(c)   Plants for the tanning of hides and skins;

(d)   Cellulose-processing and production installations.

9.   Rubber industry Manufacture and treatment of elastomer-based products.

10.   Infrastructure projects

(a)   Industrial estate development projects;

(b)   Urban development projects, including the construction of shopping centres and car parks;

(c) Construction of railways and intermodal transshipment facilities, and of intermodal terminals (projects not included in Annex I);

(d) Construction of airfields (projects not included in Annex I);

(e) Construction of roads, harbours and port installations, including fishing harbours (projects not included in Annex I);

(f) Inland-waterway construction not included in Annex I, canalization and flood-relief works;

(g) Dams and other installations designed to hold water or store it on a long-term basis (projects not included in Annex I);

(h) Tramways, elevated and underground railways, suspended lines or similar lines of a particular type, used exclusively or mainly for passenger transport;

(i) Oil and gas pipeline installations (projects not included in Annex I);

(j) Installations of long-distance aqueducts;

(k) Coastal work to combat erosion and maritime works capable of altering the coast through the construction, for example, of dykes, moles, jetties and other sea defence works, excluding the maintenance and reconstruction of such works;

(l) Groundwater abstraction and artificial groundwater recharge schemes not included in Annex I;

(m) Works for the transfer of water resources between river basins not included in Annex I.

11. Other projects

(a) Permanent racing and test tracks for motorized vehicles;

(b) installations for the disposal of waste (projects not included in Annex I);

(c) Waste-water treatment plants (projects not included in Annex I);

(d) Sludge-deposition sites;

(e) Storage of scrap iron, including scrap vehicles;

(f) Test benches for engines, turbines or reactors;

(g) Installations for the manufacture of artificial mineral fibres;

(h) Installations for the recovery or destruction of explosive substances;

(i) Knackers' yards.

12. Tourism and leisure

(a) Ski-runs, ski-lifts and cable-cars and associated developments;

(b) Marinas;

(c) Holiday villages and hotel complexes outside urban areas and associated developments;

(d) Permanent camp sites and caravan sites;

(e) Theme parks.

13. — Any change or extension of projects listed in Annex I or Annex II, already authorized, executed or in the process of being executed, which may have significant adverse effects on the environment;

— Projects in Annex I, undertaken exclusively or mainly for the development and testing of new methods or products and not used for more than two years.

ANNEX III   SELECTION CRITERIA REFERRED TO IN ARTICLE 4(3)

1. Characteristics of projects

The characteristics of projects must be considered having regard, in particular, to:

—the size of the project,
—the cumulation with other projects,
—the use of natural resources,
—the production of waste,
—pollution and nuisances,
—the risk of accidents, having regard in particular to substances or technologies used.

2.   Location of projects

The environmental sensitivity of geographical areas likely to be affected by projects must be considered, having regard, in particular, to:
—the existing land use,
—the relative abundance, quality and regenerative capacity of natural resources in the area,
—the absorption capacity of the natural environment, paying particular attention to the following areas:

(a)   wetlands;
(b)   coastal zones;
(c)   mountain and forest areas;
(d)   nature reserves and parks;
(e)   areas classified or protected under Member States' legislation; special protection areas designated by Member States pursuant to Directive 79/409/EEC and 92/43/EEC;
(f)   areas in which the environmental quality standards laid down in Community Legislation have already been exceeded;
(g)   densely populated areas;
(h)   landscapes of historical, cultural or archaeological significance.

3.   Characteristics of the potential impact

The potential significant effects of projects must be considered in relation to criteria set out under 1 and 2 above, and having regard in particular to:
—the extent of the impact (geographical area and size of the affected population),
—the transfrontier nature of the impact,
—the magnitude and complexity of the impact,
—the probability of the impact,
—the duration, frequency and reversibility of the impact.

ANNEX IV   INFORMATION REFERRED TO IN ARTICLE 5(1)

1.   Description of the project, including in particular:
—a description of the physical characteristics of the whole project and the land-use requirements during the construction and operational phases,
—a description of the main characteristics of the production processes, for instance, nature and quantity of the materials used,
—an estimate, by type and quantity, of expected residues and emissions (water, air and soil pollution, noise, vibration, light, heat, radiation, etc.) resulting from the operation of the proposed project.

2.   An outline of the main alternatives studied by the developer and an indication of the main reasons for this choice, taking into account the environmental effects.

3.   A description of the aspects of the environment likely to be significantly affected by the proposed project, including, in particular, population, fauna,

DIRECTIVE 85/337

flora, soil, water, air, climatic factors, material assets, including the architectural and archaeological heritage, landscape and the inter-relationship between the above factors.

4.   A description[1] of the likely significant effects of the proposed project on the environment resulting from:
—the existence of the project,
—the use of natural resources,
—the emission of pollutants, the creation of nuisances and the elimination of waste, and the description by the developer of the forecasting methods used to assess the effects on the environment.

5.   A description of the measures envisaged to prevent, reduce and where possible offset any significant adverse effects on the environment.

6.   A non-technical summary of the information provided under the above headings.

7.   An indication of any difficulties (technical deficiencies or lack of know-how) encountered by the developer in compiling the required information.

Note
[1]This description should cover the direct effects and any indirect, secondary, cumulative, short, medium and long-term, permanent and temporary, positive and negative effects of the project.

CONSUMER PROTECTION

COUNCIL DIRECTIVE OF 10 SEPTEMBER 1984 RELATING TO THE APPROXIMATION OF THE LAWS, REGULATIONS AND ADMINISTRATIVE PROVISIONS OF THE MEMBER STATES CONCERNING MISLEADING ADVERTISING (84/450/EEC)
[OJ 1984, No. L250/17]

THE COUNCIL OF THE EUROPEAN COMMUNITIES,

Having regard to the Treaty establishing the European Economic Community, and in particular Article 100 thereof,

Having regard to the proposal from the Commission,[1]

Having regard to the opinion of the European Parliament,[2]

Having regard to the opinion of the Economic and Social Committee,[3]

Whereas the laws against misleading advertising now in force in the Member States differ widely; whereas, since advertising reaches beyond the frontiers of individual Member States, it has a direct effect on the establishment and the functioning of the common market;

Whereas misleading advertising can lead to distortion of competition within the common market;

Whereas advertising, whether or not it induces a contract, affects the economic welfare of consumers;

Whereas misleading advertising may cause a consumer to take decisions prejudicial to him when acquiring goods or other property, or using services, and the differences between the laws of the Member States not only lead, in many cases, to inadequate levels of consumer protection, but also hinder the execution of advertising campaigns beyond national boundaries and thus affect the free circulation of goods and provision of services;

Whereas the second programme of the European Economic Community for a consumer protection and information policy[4] provides for appropriate action for the protection of consumers against misleading and unfair advertising;

Whereas it is in the interest of the public in general, as well as that of consumers and all those who, in competition with one another, carry on a

Notes
[1] OJ No. C70, 21. 3. 1978, p. 4.
[2] OJ No. C140, 5. 6. 1979, p. 23.
[3] OJ No. C171, 9. 7. 1979, p. 43.
[4] OJ No. C133, 3. 6. 1981, p. 1.

trade, business, craft or profession, in the common market, to harmonise in the first instance national provisions against misleading advertising and that, at a second stage, unfair advertising and, as far as necessary, comparative advertising should be dealt with, on the basis of appropriate Commission proposals;

Whereas minimum and objective criteria for determining whether advertising is misleading should be established for this purpose;

Whereas the laws to be adopted by Member States against misleading advertising must be adequate and effective;

Whereas persons or organisations regarded under national law as having a legitimate interest in the matter must have facilities for initiating proceedings against misleading advertising, either before a court or before an administrative authority which is competent to decide upon complaints or to initiate appropriate legal proceedings;

Whereas it should be for each Member State to decide whether to enable the courts or administrative authorities to require prior recourse to other established means of dealing with the complaint;

Whereas the courts or administrative authorities must have powers enabling them to order or obtain the cessation of misleading advertising;

Whereas in certain cases it may be desirable to prohibit misleading advertising even before it is published; whereas, however, this in no way implies that Member States are under an obligation to introduce rules requiring the systematic prior vetting of advertising;

Whereas provision should be made for accelerated procedures under which measures with interim or definitive effect can be taken;

Whereas it may be desirable to order the publication of decisions made by courts or administrative authorities or of corrective statements in order to eliminate any continuing effects of misleading advertising;

Whereas administrative authorities must be impartial and the exercise of their powers must be subject to judicial review;

Whereas the voluntary control exercised by self-regulatory bodies to eliminate misleading advertising may avoid recourse to administrative or judicial action and ought therefore to be encouraged;

Whereas the advertiser should be able to prove, by appropriate means, the material accuracy of the factual claims he makes in his advertising, and may in appropriate cases be required to do so by the court or administrative authority;

Whereas this Directive must not preclude Member States from retaining or adopting provisions with a view to ensuring more extensive protection of consumers, persons carrying on a trade, business, craft or profession, and the general public,

HAS ADOPTED THIS DIRECTIVE:

Article 1
The purpose of this Directive is to protect consumers, persons carrying on a trade or business or practising a craft or profession and the interests of the public in general against misleading advertising and the unfair consequences thereof.

Article 2
For the purposes of this Directive:

1. 'advertising' means the making of a representation in any form in connection with a trade, business, craft or profession in order to promote the

supply of goods or services, including immovable property, rights and obligations;

2. 'misleading advertising' means any advertising which in any way, including its presentation, deceives or is likely to deceive the persons to whom it is addressed or whom it reaches and which, by reason of its deceptive nature, is likely to affect their economic behaviour or which, for those reasons, injures or is likely to injure a competitor;

3. 'person' means any natural or legal person.

Article 3

In determining whether advertising is misleading, account shall be taken of all its features, and in particular of any information it contains concerning:

(a)   the characteristics of goods or services, such as their availability, nature, execution, composition, method and date of manufacture or provision, fitness for purpose, uses, quantity, specification, geographical or commercial origin or the results to be expected from their use, or the results and material features of tests or checks carried out on the goods or services;

(b)   the price or the manner in which the price is calculated, and the conditions on which the goods are supplied or the services provided;

(c)   the nature, attributes and rights of the advertiser, such as his identity and assets, his qualifications and ownership of industrial, commercial or intellectual property rights or his awards and distinctions.

Article 4

1.   Member States shall ensure that adequate and effective means exist for the control of misleading advertising in the interests of consumers as well as competitors and the general public. Such means shall include legal provisions under which persons or organisations regarded under national law as having a legitimate interest in prohibiting misleading advertising may:

(a)   take legal action against such advertising; and/or

(b)   bring such advertising before an administrative authority competent either to decide on complaints or to initiate appropriate legal proceedings. It shall be for each Member State to decide which of these facilities shall be available and whether to enable the courts or administrative authorities to require prior recourse to other established means of dealing with complaints, including those referred to in Article 5.

2.   Under the legal provisions referred to in paragraph 1, Member States shall confer upon the courts or administrative authorities powers enabling them, in cases where they deem such measures to be necessary taking into account all the interests involved and in particular the public interest:

— to order the cessation of, or to institute appropriate legal proceedings for an order for the cessation of, misleading advertising, or

— if misleading advertising has not yet been published but publication is imminent, to order the prohibition of, or to institute appropriate legal proceedings for an order for the prohibition of, such publication, even without proof of actual loss or damage or of intention or negligence on the part of the advertiser.

Member States shall also make provision for the measures referred to in the first subparagraph to be taken under an accelerated procedure:

— either with interim effect, or

— with definitive effect, on the understanding that it is for each Member State to decide which of the two options to select.

Furthermore, Member States may confer upon the courts or administrative authorities powers enabling them, with a view to eliminating the continuing effects of misleading advertising the cessation of which has been ordered by a final decision:

— to require publication of that decision in full or in part and in such form as they deem adequate,

— to require in addition the publication of a corrective statement.

3.   The administrative authorities referred to in paragraph 1 must:

(a)   be composed so as not to cast doubt on their impartiality;

(b)   have adequate powers, where they decide on complaints, to monitor and enforce the observance of their decisions effectively;

(c)   normally give reasons for their decisions.

Where the powers referred to in paragraph 2 are exercised exclusively by an administrative authority, reasons for its decisions shall always be given.

Furthermore in this case, provision must be made for procedures whereby improper or unreasonable exercise of its powers by the administrative authority or improper or unreasonable failure to exercise the said powers can be the subject of judicial review.

Article 5

This Directive does not exclude the voluntary control of misleading advertising by self-regulatory bodies and recourse to such bodies by the persons or organisations referred to in Article 4 if proceedings before such bodies are in addition to the court or administrative proceedings referred to in that Article.

Article 6

Member States shall confer upon the courts or administrative authorities powers enabling them in the civil or administrative proceedings provided for in Article 4:

(a)   to require the advertiser to furnish evidence as to the accuracy of factual claims in advertising if, taking into account the legitimate interests of the advertiser and any other party to the proceedings, such a requirement appears appropriate on the basis of the circumstances of the particular case; and

(b)   to consider factual claims as inaccurate if the evidence demanded in accordance with (a) is not furnished or is deemed insufficient by the court or administrative authority.

Article 7

This Directive shall not preclude Member States from retaining or adopting provisions with a view to ensuring more extensive protection for consumers, persons carrying on a trade, business, craft or profession, and the general public.

Article 8

Member States shall bring into force the measures necessary to comply with this Directive by 1 October 1986 at the latest. They shall forthwith inform the Commission thereof.

Member States shall communicate to the Commission the text of all provisions of national law which they adopt in the field covered by this Directive.

Article 9
This Directive is addressed to the Member States.

Done at Brussels, 10 September 1984.
For the Council,
The President,
P. O'TOOLE

COUNCIL DIRECTIVE OF 25 JULY 1985 ON THE APPROXIMATION OF THE LAWS, REGULATIONS AND ADMINISTRATIVE PROVISIONS OF THE MEMBER STATES CONCERNING LIABILITY FOR DEFECTIVE PRODUCTS (85/374/EEC)
[OJ 1985, No. L210/29]

THE COUNCIL OF THE EUROPEAN COMMUNITIES,

Having regard to the Treaty establishing the European Economic Community, and in particular Article 100 thereof,
    Having regard to the proposal from the Commission,[1]
    Having regard to the opinion of the European Parliament,[2]
    Having regard to the opinion of the Economic and Social Committee,[3]

Whereas approximation of the laws of the Member States concerning the liability of the producer for damage caused by the defectiveness of his products is necessary because the existing divergences may distort competition and affect the movement of goods within the common market and entail a differing degree of protection of the consumer against damage caused by a defective product to his health or property;

Whereas liability without fault on the part of the producer is the sole means of adequately solving the problem, peculiar to our age of increasing technicality, of a fair apportionment of the risks inherent in modern technological production;

Whereas liability without fault should apply only to movables which have been industrially produced; whereas, as a result, it is appropriate to exclude liability for agricultural products and game, except where they have undergone a processing of an industrial nature which could cause a defect in these products; whereas the liability provided for in this Directive should also apply to movables which are used in the construction of immovables or are installed in immovables;

Whereas protection of the consumer requires that all producers involved in the production process should be made liable, in so far as their finished product, component part or any raw material supplied by them was defective; whereas, for the same reason, liability should extend to importers of products into the Community and to persons who present themselves as producers by affixing their name, trade mark or other distinguishing feature or who supply a product the producer of which cannot be identified;

Notes
[1]OJ No. C241, 14.10.1976, p. 9 and OJ No. C271, 26.10.1979, p. 3.
[2]OJ No. C127, 21.5.1979, p. 61.
[3]OJ No. C114, 7.5.1979, p. 15.

Whereas, in situations where several persons are liable for the same damage, the protection of the consumer requires that the injured person should be able to claim full compensation for the damage from any one of them;

Whereas, to protect the physical well-being and property of the consumer, the defectiveness of the product should be determined by reference not to its fitness for use but to the lack of the safety which the public at large is entitled to expect; whereas the safety is assessed by excluding any misuse of the product not reasonable under the circumstances;

Whereas a fair apportionment of risk between the injured person and the producer implies that the producer should be able to free himself from liability if he furnishes proof as to the existence of certain exonerating circumstances;

Whereas the protection of the consumer requires that the liability of the producer remains unaffected by acts or omissions of other persons having contributed to cause the damage; whereas, however, the contributory negligence of the injured person may be taken into account to reduce or disallow such liability;

Whereas the protection of the consumer requires compensation for death and personal injury as well as compensation for damage to property; whereas the latter should nevertheless be limited to goods for private use or consumption and be subject to a deduction of a lower threshold of a fixed amount in order to avoid litigation in an excessive number of cases; whereas this Directive should not prejudice compensation for pain and suffering and other non-material damages payable, where appropriate, under the law appliable to the case;

Whereas a uniform period of limitation for the bringing of action for compensation is in the interests both of the injured person and of the producer;

Whereas products age in the course of time, higher safety standards are developed and the state of science and technology progresses; whereas, therefore, it would not be reasonable to make the producer liable for an unlimited period for the defectiveness of his product; whereas, therefore, liability should expire after a reasonable length of time, without prejudice to claims pending at law;

Whereas, to achieve effective protection of consumers, no contractual derogation should be permitted as regards the liability of the producer in relation to the injured person;

Whereas under the legal systems of the Member States an injured party may have a claim for damages based on grounds of contractual liability or on grounds of non-contractual liability other than that provided for in this Directive; in so far as these provisions also serve to attain the objective of effective protection of consumers, they should remain unaffected by this Directive; whereas, in so far as effective protection of consumers in the sector of pharmaceutical products is already also attained in a Member State under a special liability system, claims based on this system should similarly remain possible;

Whereas, to the extent that liability for nuclear injury or damage is already covered in all Member States by adequate special rules, it has been possible to exclude damage of this type from the scope of this Directive;

Whereas, since the exclusion of primary agricultural products and game from the scope of this Directive may be felt, in certain Member States, in view of what is expected for the protection of consumers, to restrict unduly such protection, it should be possible for a Member State to extend liability to such products;

Whereas, for similar reasons, the possibility offered to a producer to free himself from liability if he proves that the state of scientific and technical knowledge at the time when he put the product into circulation was not such as to enable the existence of a defect to be discovered may be felt in certain Member States to restrict unduly the protection of the consumer; whereas it should therefore be possible for a Member State to maintain in its legislation or to provide by new legislation that this exonerating circumstance is not admitted; whereas, in the case of new legislation, making use of this derogation should, however, be subject to a Community stand-still procedure, in order to raise, if possible, the level of protection in a uniform manner throughout the Community;

Whereas, taking into account the legal traditions in most of the Member States, it is inappropriate to set any financial ceiling on the producer's liability without fault; whereas, in so far as there are, however, differing traditions, it seems possible to admit that a Member State may derogate from the principle of unlimited liability by providing a limit for the total liability of the producer for damage resulting from a death or personal injury and caused by identical items with the same defect, provided that this limit is established at a level sufficiently high to guarantee adequate protection of the consumer and the correct functioning of the common market;

Whereas the harmonisation resulting from this cannot be total at the present stage, but opens the way towards greater harmonisation; whereas it is therefore necessary that the Council receive at regular intervals, reports from the Commission on the application of this Directive, accompanied, as the case may be, by appropriate proposals;

Whereas it is particularly important in this respect that a re-examination be carried out of those parts of the Directive relating to the derogations open to the Member States, at the expiry of a period of sufficient length to gather practical experience on the effects of these derogations on the protection of consumers and on the functioning of the common market,

HAS ADOPTED THIS DIRECTIVE:

Article 1

The producer shall be liable for damage caused by a defect in his product.

Article 2

For the purpose of this Directive 'product' means all movables, with the exception of primary agricultural products and game, even though incorporated into another movable or into an immovable. 'Primary agricultural products' means the products of the soil, of stock-farming and of fisheries, excluding products which have undergone initial processing. 'Product' includes electricity.

Article 3

1. 'Producer' means the manufacturer of a finished product, the producer of any raw material or the manufacturer of a component part and any person who, by putting his name, trade mark or other distinguishing feature on the product presents himself as its producer.

2. Without prejudice to the liability of the producer, any person who imports into the Community a product for sale, hire, leasing or any form of distribution in the course of his business shall be deemed to be a producer within the meaning of this Directive and shall be responsible as a producer.

3. Where the producer of the product cannot be identified, each supplier of the product shall be treated as its producer unless he informs the injured person, within a reasonable time, of the identity of the producer or of the person who supplied him with the product. The same shall apply, in the case of an imported product, if this product does not indicate the identity of the importer referred to in paragraph 2, even if the name of the producer is indicated.

Article 4
The injured person shall be required to prove the damage, the defect and the causal relationship between defect and damage.

Article 5
Where, as a result of the provisions of this Directive, two or more persons are liable for the same damage, they shall be liable jointly and severally, without prejudice to the provisions of national law concerning the rights of contribution or recourse.

Article 6
1. A product is defective when it does not provide the safety which a person is entitled to expect, taking all circumstances into account, including:
    (a)   the presentation of the product;
    (b)   the use to which it could reasonably be expected that the product would be put;
    (c)   the time when the product was put into circulation.
2. A product shall not be considered defective for the sole reason that a better product is subsequently put into circulation.

Article 7
The producer shall not be liable as a result of this Directive if he proves:
    (a)   that he did not put the product into circulation; or
    (b)   that, having regard to the circumstances, it is probable that the defect which caused the damage did not exist at the time when the product was put into circulation by him or that this defect came into being afterwards; or
    (c)   that the product was neither manufactured by him for sale or any form of distribution for economic purpose nor manufactured or distributed by him in the course of his business; or
    (d)   that the defect is due to compliance of the product with mandatory regulations issued by the public authorities; or
    (e)   that the state of scientific and technical knowledge at the time when he put the product into circulation was not such as to enable the existence of the defect to be discovered; or
    (f)   in the case of a manufacturer of a component, that the defect is attributable to the design of the product in which the component has been fitted or to the instructions given by the manufacturer of the product.

Article 8
1. Without prejudice to the provisions of national law concerning the right of contribution or recourse, the liability of the producer shall not be reduced

when the damage is caused both by a defect in product and by the act or omission of a third party.

2. The liability of the producer may be reduced or disallowed when, having regard to all the circumstances, the damage is caused both by a defect in the product and by the fault of the injured person or any person for whom the injured person is responsible.

Article 9
For the purpose of Article 1, 'damage' means:

(a)   damage caused by death or by personal injuries;

(b)   damage to, or destruction of, any item of property other than the defective product itself, with a lower threshold of 500 ECU, provided that the item of property:

(i)   is of a type ordinarily intended for private use or consumption, and

(ii)   was used by the injured person mainly for his own private use or consumption.

This Article shall be without prejudice to national provisions relating to non-material damage.

Article 10
1. Member States shall provide in their legislation that a limitation period of three years shall apply to proceedings for the recovery of damages as provided for in this Directive. The limitation period shall begin to run from the day on which the plaintiff became aware, or should reasonably have become aware, of the damage, the defect and the identity of the producer.

2. The laws of Member States regulating suspension or interruption of the limitation period shall not be affected by this Directive.

Article 11
Member States shall provide in their legislation that the rights conferred upon the injured person pursuant to this Directive shall be extinguished upon the expiry of a period of 10 years from the date on which the producer put into circulation the actual product which caused the damage, unless the injured person has in the meantime instituted proceedings against the producer.

Article 12
The liability of the producer arising from this Directive may not, in relation to the injured person, be limited or excluded by a provision limiting his liability or exempting him from liability.

Article 13
This Directive shall not affect any rights which an injured person may have according to the rules of the law of contractual or non-contractual liability or a special liability system existing at the moment when this Directive is notified.

Article 14
This Directive shall not apply to injury or damage arising from nuclear accidents and covered by international conventions ratified by the Member States.

Article 15

1. Each Member State may:

(a) by way of derogation from Article 2, provide in its legislation that within the meaning of Article 1 of this Directive 'product' also means primary agricultural products and game;

(b) by way of derogation from Article 7(e), maintain or, subject to the procedure set out in paragraph 2 of this Article, provide in this legislation that the producer shall be liable even if he proves that the state of scientific and technical knowledge at the time when he put the product into circulation was not such as to enable the existence of a defect to be discovered.

2. A Member State wishing to introduce the measure specified in paragraph 1(b) shall communicate the text of the proposed measure to the Commission. The Commission shall inform the other Member States thereof.

The Member State concerned shall hold the proposed measure in abeyance for nine months after the Commission is informed and provided that in the meantime the Commission has not submitted to the Council a proposal amending this Directive on the relevant matter. However, if within three months of receiving the said information, the Commission does not advise the Member State concerned that it intends submitting such a proposal to the Council, the Member State may take the proposed measure immediately.

If the Commission does submit to the Council such a proposal amending the Directive within the aforementioned nine months, the Member State concerned shall hold the proposed measure in abeyance for a further period of 18 months from the date on which the proposal is submitted.

3. Ten years after the date of notification of this Directive, the Commission shall submit to the Council a report on the effect that rulings by the courts as to the application of Article 7(e) and of paragraph 1(b) of this Article have on consumer protection and the functioning of the common market. In the light of this report the Council, acting on a proposal from the Commission and pursuant to the terms of Article 100 of the Treaty, shall decide whether to repeal Article 7(e).

Article 16

1. Any Member State may provide that a producer's total liability for damage resulting from a death or personal injury and caused by identical items with the same defect shall be limited to an amount which may not be less than 70 million ECU.

2. Ten years after the date of notification of this Directive, the Commission shall submit to the Council a report on the effect on consumer protection and the functioning of the common market of the implementation of the financial limit on liability by those Member States which have used the option provided for in paragraph 1. In the light of this report the Council, acting on a proposal from the Commission and pursuant to the terms of Article 100 of the Treaty, shall decide whether to repeal paragraph 1.

Article 17

This Directive shall not apply to products put into circulation before the date on which the provisions referred to in Article 19 enter into force.

Article 18

1. For the purposes of this Directive, the ECU shall be that defined by Regulation (EEC) No 3180/78,[1] as amended by Regulation (EEC) No 2626/84.[2] The equivalent in national currency shall initially be calculated at the rate obtaining on the date of adoption of this Directive.

2. Every five years the Council, acting on a proposal from the Commission, shall examine and, if need be, revise the amounts in this Directive, in the light of economic and monetary trends in the Community.

Article 19

1. Member States shall bring into force, not later than three years from the date of notification of this Directive, the laws, regulations and administrative provisions necessary to comply with this Directive. They shall forthwith inform the Commission thereof.[3]

2. The procedure set out in Article 15(2) shall apply from the date of notification of this Directive.

Article 20

Member States shall communicate to the Commission the texts of the main provisions of national law which they subsequently adopt in the field governed by this Directive.

Article 21

Every five years the Commission shall present a report to the Council on the application of this Directive and, if necessary, shall submit appropriate proposals to it.

Article 22

This Directive is addressed to the Member States.

Done at Brussels, 25 July 1985.

Notes
[1]OJ No. L379, 30.12.1978, p. 1.
[2]OJ No. L247, 16.9.1984, p. 1.
[3]This Directive was notified to the Member States on 30 July 1985.

COUNCIL DIRECTIVE OF 20 DECEMBER 1985 TO PROTECT THE CONSUMER IN RESPECT OF CONTRACTS NEGOTIATED AWAY FROM BUSINESS PREMISES (85/577/ EEC)
[OJ 1985, No. L372/31]

THE COUNCIL OF THE EUROPEAN COMMUNITIES,

Having regard to the Treaty establishing the European Economic Community, and in particular Article 100 thereof,

Having regard to the proposal from the Commission,[1]

Having regard to the opinion of the European Parliament,[2]

Having regard to the opinion of the Economic and Social Committee[3]

Notes
[1]OJ No. C22, 29.1.1977, p. 6; OJ No. C127, 1.6.1978, p. 6.
[2]OJ No. C241, 10.10.1977, p. 26.
[3]OJ No. C180, 18.7.1977, p. 39.

Whereas it is a common form of commercial practice in the Member States for the conclusion of a contract or a unilateral engagement between a trader and consumer to be made away from the business premises of the trader, and whereas such contracts and engagements are the subject of legislation which differs from one Member State to another;

Whereas any disparity between such legislation may directly affect the functioning of the common market; whereas it is therefore necessary to approximate laws in this field;

Whereas the preliminary programme of the European Economic Community for a consumer protection and information policy[4] provides inter alia, under paragraphs 24 and 25, that appropriate measures be taken to protect consumers against unfair commercial practices in respect of doorstep selling; whereas the second programme of the European Economic Community for a consumer protection and information policy[5] confirmed that the action and priorities defined in the preliminary programme would be pursued;

Whereas the special feature of contracts concluded away from the business premises of the trader is that as a rule it is the trader who initiates the contract negotiations, for which the consumer is unprepared or which he does not expect; whereas the consumer is often unable to compare the quality and price of the offer with other offers;

Whereas this surprise element generally exists not only in contracts made at the doorstep but also in other forms of contract concluded by the trader away from his business premises;

Whereas the consumer should be given a right of cancellation over a period of at least seven days in order to enable him to assess the obligations arising under the contract;

Whereas appropriate measures should be taken to ensure that the consumer is informed in writing of this period for reflection;

Whereas the freedom of Member States to maintain or introduce a total or partial prohibition on the conclusion of contracts away from business premises, inasmuch as they consider this to be in the interest of consumers, must not be affected;

Notes
[4] OJ No. C92, 25.4.1975, p. 2.
[5] OJ No. C133, 3.6.1981, p. 1.

HAS ADOPTED THIS DIRECTIVE:

Article 1
1.   This Directive shall apply to contracts under which a trader supplies goods or services to a consumer and which are concluded: — during an excursion organised by the trader away from his business premises, or — during a visit by a trader (i) to the consumer's home or to that of another consumer; (ii) to the consumer's place of work; where the visit does not take place at the express request of the consumer.

2.   This Directive shall also apply to contracts for the supply of goods or services other than those concerning which the consumer requested the visit of the trader, provided that when he requested the visit the consumer did not know, or could not reasonably have known, that the supply of those other goods or services formed part of the trader's commercial or professional activities.

3.   This Directive shall also apply to contracts in respect of which an offer was made by the consumer under conditions similar to those described in paragraph 1 or paragraph 2 although the consumer was not bound by that offer before its acceptance by the trader.

4.   This Directive shall also apply to offers made contractually by the consumer under conditions similar to those described in paragraph 1 or paragraph 2 where the consumer is bound by his offer.

Article 2

For the purposes of this Directive: 'consumer' means a natural person who, in transactions covered by this Directive, is acting for purposes which can be regarded as outside his trade or profession; 'trader' means a natural or legal person who, for the transaction in question, acts in his commercial or professional capacity, and anyone acting in the name or on behalf of a trader.

Article 3

1.   The Member States may decide that this Directive shall apply only to contracts for which the payment to be made by the consumer exceeds a specified amount. This amount may not exceed 60 ECU. The Council, acting on a proposal from the Commission, shall examine and, if necessary, revise this amount for the first time no later than four years after notification of the Directive and thereafter every two years, taking into account economic and monetary developments in the Community.

2.   This Directive shall not apply to:

(a)   contracts for the construction, sale and rental of immovable property or contracts concerning other rights relating to immovable property. Contracts for the supply of goods and for their incorporation in immovable property or contracts for repairing immovable property shall fall within the scope of this Directive;

(b)   contracts for the supply of foodstuffs or beverages or other goods intended for current consumption in the household and supplied by regular roundsmen;

(c)   contracts for the supply of goods or services, provided that all three of the following conditions are met:

(i)   the contract is concluded on the basis of a trader's catalogue which the consumer has a proper opportunity of reading in the absence of the trader's representative,

(ii)   there is intended to be continuity of contact between the trader's representative and the consumer in relation to that or any subsequent transaction,

(iii)   both the catalogue and the contract clearly inform the consumer of his right to return goods to the supplier within a period of not less than seven days of receipt or otherwise to cancel the contract within that period without obligation of any kind other than to take reasonable care of the goods;

(d)   insurance contracts;

(e)   contracts for securities.

3.   By way of derogation from Article 1 (2), Member States may refrain from applying this Directive to contracts for the supply of goods or services having a direct connection with the goods or services concerning which the consumer requested the visit of the trader.

Article 4

In the case of transactions within the scope of Article 1, traders shall be required to give consumers written notice of their right of cancellation within the period laid down in Article 5, together with the name and address of a person against whom that right may be exercised. Such notice shall be dated and shall state particulars enabling the contract to be identified. It shall be given to the consumer:

(a)   in the case of Article 1(1), at the time of conclusion of the contract;

(b)   in the case of Article 1(2), not later than the time of conclusion of the contract;

(c)   in the case of Article 1(3) and 1(4), when the offer is made by the consumer. Member States shall ensure that their national legislation lays down appropriate consumer protection measures in cases where the information referred to in this Article is not supplied.

Article 5

1.   The consumer shall have the right to renounce the effects of his undertaking by sending notice within a period of not less than seven days from receipt by the consumer of the notice referred to in Article 4, in accordance with the procedure laid down by national law. It shall be sufficient if the notice is dispatched before the end of such period.

2.   The giving of the notice shall have the effect of releasing the consumer from any obligations under the cancelled contract.

Article 6

The consumer may not waive the rights conferred on him by this Directive.

Article 7

If the consumer exercises his right of renunciation, the legal effects of such renunciation shall be governed by national laws, particularly regarding the reimbursement of payments for goods or services provided and the return of goods received.

Article 8

This Directive shall not prevent Member States from adopting or maintaining more favourable provisions to protect consumers in the field which it covers.

Article 9

1.   Member States shall take the measures necessary to comply with this Directive within 24 months of its notification.[1] They shall forthwith inform the Commission thereof.

2.   Member States shall ensure that the texts of the main provisions of national law which they adopt in the field covered by this Directive are communicated to the Commission.

Note

[1] This Directive was notified to the Member States on 23 December 1985.

Article 10

This Directive is addressed to the Member States.

Done at Brussels, 20 December 1985.
For the Council
The President
R. KRIEPS

COUNCIL DIRECTIVE OF 22 DECEMBER 1986 FOR THE APPROXIMATION OF THE LAWS, REGULATIONS AND ADMINISTRATIVE PROVISIONS OF THE MEMBER STATES CONCERNING CONSUMER CREDIT (87/102/ EEC) [OJ 1987, No. L42/48]*

THE COUNCIL OF THE EUROPEAN COMMUNITIES,

Having regard to the Treaty establishing the European Economic Community, and in particular Article 100 thereof,

Having regard to the proposal from the Commission,[1]

Having regard to the opinion of the European Parliament,[2]

Having regard to the opinion of the Economic and Social Committee,[3]

Whereas wide differences exist in the laws of the Member States in the field of consumer credit;

Whereas these differences of law can lead to distortions of competition between grantors of credit in the common market;

Whereas these differences limit the opportunities the consumer has to obtain credit in other Member States; whereas they affect the volume and the nature of the credit sought, and also the purchase of goods and services;

Whereas, as a result, these differences have an influence on the free movement of goods and services obtainable by consumers on credit and thus directly affect the functioning of the common market;

Whereas, given the increasing volume of credit granted in the Community to consumers, the establishment of a common market in consumer credit would benefit alike consumers, grantors of credit, manufacturers, wholesalers and retailers of goods and providers of services;

Whereas the programmes of the European Economic Community for a consumer protection and information policy[4] provide, inter alia, that the consumer should be protected against unfair credit terms and that a harmonization of the general conditions governing consumer credit should be undertaken as a priority;

Whereas differences of law and practice result in unequal consumer protection in the field of consumer credit from one Member State to another;

Whereas there has been much change in recent years in the types of credit available to and used by consumers; whereas new forms of consumer credit have emerged and continue to develop;

Whereas the consumer should receive adequate information on the conditions and cost of credit and on his obligations; whereas this information should include, inter alia, the annual percentage rate of charge for credit, or, failing that, the total amount that the consumer must pay for credit; whereas, pending a decision on a Community method or methods of calculating the annual percentage rate of charge, Member States should be able to retain existing

Notes

*As amended by Directive 90/88/EEC [OJ 1990 L61/14]

[1] OJ No. C80, 27.3.1979, p. 4 and OJ No. C183, 10.7.1984, p. 4.

[2] OJ No. C242, 12.9.1983, p. 10.

[3] OJ No. C113, 7.5.1980, p. 22.

[4] OJ No. C92, 25.4.1975, p. 1 and OJ No. C133, 3.6.1981, p. 1.

methods or practices for calculating this rate, or failing that, should establish provisions for indicating the total cost of the credit to the consumer;

Whereas the terms of credit may be disadvantageous to the consumer; whereas better protection of consumers can be achieved by adopting certain requirements which are to apply to all forms of credit;

Whereas, having regard to the character of certain credit agreements or types of transaction, these agreements or transactions should be partially or entirely excluded from the field of application of this Directive;

Whereas it should be possible for Member States, in consultation with the Commission, to exempt from the Directive certain forms of credit of a non-commercial character granted under particular conditions;

Whereas the practices existing in some Member States in respect of authentic acts drawn up before a notary or judge are such as to render the application of certain provisions of this Directive unnecessary in the case of such acts; whereas it should therefore be possible for Member States to exempt such acts from those provisions;

Whereas credit agreements for very large financial amounts tend to differ from the usual consumer credit agreements; whereas the application of the provisions of this Directive to agreements for very small amounts could create unnecessary administrative burdens both for consumers and grantors of credit; whereas therefore, agreements above or below specified financial limits should be excluded from the Directive;

Whereas the provision of information on the cost of credit in advertising and at the business premises of the creditor or credit broker can make it easier for the consumer to compare different offers;

Whereas consumer protection is further improved if credit agreements are made in writing and contain certain minimum particulars concerning the contractual terms;

Whereas, in the case of credit granted for the acquisition of goods, Member States should lay down the conditions in which goods may be repossessed, particularly if the consumer has not given his consent; whereas the account between the parties should upon repossession be made up in such manner as to ensure that the repossession does not entail any unjustified enrichment;

Whereas the consumer should be allowed to discharge his obligations before the due date; whereas the consumer should then be entitled to an equitable reduction in the total cost of the credit;

Whereas the assignment of the creditor's rights arising under a credit agreement should not be allowed to weaken the position of the consumer;

Whereas those Member States which permit consumers to use bills of exchange, promissory notes or cheques in connection with credit agreements should ensure that the consumer is suitably protected when so using such instruments;

Whereas, as regards goods or services which the consumer has contracted to acquire on credit, the consumer should, at least in the circumstances defined below, have rights vis-à-vis the grantor of credit which are in addition to his normal contractual rights against him and against the supplier of the goods or services; whereas the circumstances referred to above are those where the grantor of credit and the supplier of goods or services have a pre-existing agreement whereunder credit is made available exclusively by that grantor of credit to customers of that supplier for the purpose of enabling the consumer to acquire goods or services from the latter;

Whereas the ECU is as defined in Council Regulation (EEC) No 3180/78,[1] as last amended by Regulation (EEC) No 2626/84;[2] whereas Member States should to a limited extent be at liberty to round off the amounts in national currency resulting from the conversion of amounts of this Directive expressed in ECU; whereas the amounts in this Directive should be periodically re-examined in the light of economic and monetary trends in the Community, and, if need be, revised;

Whereas suitable measures should be adopted by Member States for authorising persons offering credit or offering to arrange credit agreements or for inspecting or monitoring the activities of persons granting credit or arranging for credit to be granted or for enabling consumers to complain about credit agreements or credit conditions;

Whereas credit agreements should not derogate, to the detriment of the consumer, from the provisions adopted in implementation of this Directive or corresponding to its provisions; whereas those provisions should not be circumvented as a result of the way in which agreements are formulated;

Whereas, since this Directive provides for a certain degree of approximation of the laws, regulations and administrative provisions of the Member States concerning consumer credit and for a certain level of consumer protection, Member States should not be prevented from retaining or adopting more stringent measures to protect the consumer, with due regard for their obligations under the Treaty;

Whereas, not later than 1 January 1995, the Commission should present to the Council a report concerning the operation of this Directive,

HAS ADOPTED THIS DIRECTIVE:

Note
[1] OJ No. L379, 30.12.1978, p. 1.
[2] OJ No. L247, 16.9.1984, p. 1.

Article 1
1. This Directive applies to credit agreements.
2. For the purpose of this Directive:
   (a) 'consumer' means a natural person who, in transactions covered by this Directive, is acting for purposes which can be regarded as outside his trade or profession;
   (b) 'creditor' means a natural or legal person who grants credit in the course of his trade, business or profession, or a group of such persons;
   (c) 'credit agreement' means an agreement whereby a creditor grants or promises to grant to a consumer a credit in the form of a deferred payment, a loan or other similar financial accommodation.

Agreements for the provision on a continuing basis of a service or a utility, where the consumer has the right to pay for them, for the duration of their provision, by means of instalments, are not deemed to be credit agreements for the purpose of this Directive;
   (d) 'total cost of the credit to the consumer' means all the costs, including interest and other charges, which the consumer has to pay for the credit';
   (e) 'annual percentage rate of charge' means the total cost of the credit to the consumer, expressed as an annual percentage of the amount of the credit granted and calculated in accordance with Article 1a.

Article 1a

1. (a) The annual percentage rate of charge, which shall be that equivalent, on an annual basis, to the present value of all commitments (loans, repayments and charges), future or existing, agreed by the creditor and the borrower, shall be calculated in accordance with the mathematical formula set out in Annex II.

(b) Four examples of the method of calculation are given in Annex III, by way of illustration.

2. For the purpose of calculating the annual percentage rate of charge, the 'total cost of the credit to the consumer' as defined in Article 1(2)(d) shall be determined, with the exception of the following charges:

(i) charges payable by the borrower for non-compliance with any of his commitments laid down in the credit agreement;

(ii) charges other than the purchase price which, in purchases of goods or services, the consumer is obliged to pay whether the transaction is paid in cash or by credit;

(iii) charges for the transfer of funds and charges for keeping an account intended to receive payments towards the reimbursement of the credit the payment of interest and other charges except where the consumer does not have reasonable freedom of choice in the matter and where such charges are abnormally high; this provision shall not, however, apply to charges for collection of such reimbursements or payments, whether made in cash or otherwise;

(iv) membership subscriptions to associations or groups and arising from agreements separate from the credit agreement, even though such subscriptions have an effect on the credit terms;

(v) charges for insurance or guarantees; included are, however, those designed to ensure payment to the creditor, in the event of the death, invalidity, illness or unemployment of the consumer, of a sum equal to or less than the total amount of the credit together with relevant interest and other charges which have to be imposed by the creditor as a condition for credit being granted.

3. (a) Where credit transactions referred to in this Directive are subject to the provisions of national laws in force on 1 March 1990 which impose maximum limits on the annual percentage rate of charge for such transactions and, where such provisions permit standard costs other than those described in paragraph 2(i) to (v) not to be included in those maximum limits, Member States may, solely in respect of such transactions, not include the aforementioned costs when calculating the annual percentage rate of charge, as stipulated in this Directive, provided that there is a requirement, in the cases mentioned in Article 3 and in the credit agreement, that the consumer be informed of the amount and inclusion thereof in the payments to be made.

(b) Member States may no longer apply point (a) from the date of entry into force of the single mathematical formula for calculating the annual percentage rate of charge in the Community, pursuant to the provisions of paragraph 5(c).

4. (a) The annual percentage rate of charge shall be calculated at the time the credit contract is concluded, without prejudice to the provisions of Article 3 concerning advertisements and special offers.

(b) The calculation shall be made on the assumption that the credit contract is valid for the period agreed and that the creditor and the consumer fulfil their obligations under the terms and by the dates agreed.

5. (a) As a transitional measure, notwithstanding the provisions of paragraph 1(a), Member States which, prior to 1 March 1990, applied legal provisions whereby a mathematical formula different from that given in Annex II could be used for calculating the annual percentage rate of charge, may continue applying that formula within their territory for a period of three years starting from 1 January 1993.

Member States shall take the appropriate measures to ensure that only one mathematical formula for calculating the annual percentage rate of charge is used within their territory.

(b) Six months before the expiry of the time limit laid down in point (a) the Commission shall submit to the Council a report, accompanied by a proposal, which will make it possible in the light of experience, to apply a single Community mathematical formula for calculating the annual percentage rate of charge.

(c) The Council shall, acting by a qualified majority on the basis of the proposal from the Commission, take a decision before 1 January 1996.

6. In the case of credit contracts containing clauses allowing variations in the rate of interest and the amount or level of other charges contained in the annual percentage rate of charge but unquantifiable at the time when it is calculated, the annual percentage rate of charge shall be calculated on the assumption that interest and other charges remain fixed and will apply until the end of the credit contract.

7. Where necessary, the following assumptions may be made in calculating the annual percentage rate of charge:

— if the contract does not specify a credit limit, the amount of credit granted shall be equal to the amount fixed by the relevant Member State, without exceeding a figure equivalent to ECU 2,000;

— if there is no fixed timetable for repayment, and one cannot be deduced from the terms of the agreement and the means for repaying the credit granted, the duration of the credit shall be deemed to be one year;

— unless otherwise specified, where the contract provides for more than one repayment date, the credit will be made available and the repayments made at the earliest time provided for in the agreement.

Article 2

1. This Directive shall not apply to:

(a) credit agreements or agreements promising to grant credit:

— intended primarily for the purpose of acquiring or retaining property rights in land or in an existing or projected building,

— intended for the purpose of renovating or improving a building as such;

(b) hiring agreements except where these provide that the title will pass ultimately to the hirer;

(c) credit granted or made available without payment of interest or any other charge;

(d) credit agreements under which no interest is charged provided the consumer agrees to repay the credit in a single payment;

(e)   credit in the form of advances on a current account granted by a credit institution or financial institution other than on credit card accounts. Nevertheless, the provisions of Article 6 shall apply to such credits;

(f)   credit agreements involving amounts less than 200 ECU or more than 20,000 ECU;

(g)   credit agreements under which the consumer is required to repay the credit:

— either, within a period not exceeding three months,

— or, by a maximum number of four payments within a period not exceeding 12 months.

2.   A Member State may, in consultation with the Commission, exempt from the application of this Directive certain types of credit which fulfil the following conditions:

— they are granted at rates of charge below those prevailing in the market, and

— they are not offered to the public generally.

3.   The provisions of Article 1a and of Articles 4 to 12 shall not apply to credit agreements or agreements promising to grant credit, secured by mortgage on immovable property, insofar as these are not already excluded from the Directive under paragraph 1(a).

4.   Member States may exempt from the provisions of Articles 6 to 12 credit agreements in the form of an authentic act signed before a notary or judge.

Article 3

Without prejudice to Council Directive 84/450/EEC of 10 September 1984 relating to the approximation of the laws, regulations and administrative provisions of the Member States concerning misleading advertising,[1] and to the rules and principles applicable to unfair advertising, any advertisement, or any offer which is displayed at business premises, in which a person offers credit or offers to arrange a credit agreement and in which a rate of interest or any figures relating to the cost of the credit are indicated, shall also include a statement of the annual percentage rate of charge, by means of a representative example if no other means is practicable.

Note
[1]OJ No. L250, 19.9.1984, p. 17.

Article 4

1.   Credit agreements shall be made in writing. The consumer shall receive a copy of the written agreement.

2.   The written agreement shall include:

(a)   a statement of the annual percentage rate of charge;

(b)   a statement of the conditions under which the annual percentage rate of charge may be amended. In cases where it is not possible to state the annual percentage rate of charge, the consumer shall be provided with adequate information in the written agreement. This information shall at least include the information provided for in the second indent of Article 6(1).

(c)   a statement of the amount, number and frequency or dates of the payments which the consumer must make to repay the credit, as well as of the payments for interest and other charges; the total amount of these payments should also be indicated where possible;

(d)   a statement of the cost items referred to in Article 1a(2) with the exception of expenditure related to the breach of contractual obligations which were not included in the calculation of the annual percentage rate of charge but which have to be paid by the consumer in given circumstances, together with a statement identifying such circumstances. Where the exact amount of those items is known, that sum is to be indicated; if that is not the case, either a method of calculation or as accurate an estimate as possible is to be provided where possible.

3.   The written agreement shall further include the other essential terms of the contract. By way of illustration, the Annex to this Directive contains a list of terms which Member States may require to be included in the written agreement as being essential.

Article 5
(deleted)

Article 6

1.   Notwithstanding the exclusion provided for in Article 2(1)(e), where there is an agreement between a credit institution or financial institution and a consumer for the granting of credit in the form of an advance on a current account, other than on credit card accounts, the consumer shall be informed at the time or before the agreement is concluded:

— of the credit limit, if any,

— of the annual rate of interest and the charges applicable from the time the agreement is concluded and the conditions under which these may be amended,

— of the procedure for terminating the agreement.

This information shall be confirmed in writing.

2.   Furthermore, during the period of the agreement, the consumer shall be informed of any change in the annual rate of interest or in the relevant charges at the time it occurs. Such information may be given in a statement of account or in any other manner acceptable to Member States.

3.   In Member States where tacitly accepted overdrafts are permissible, the Member States concerned shall ensure that the consumer is informed of the annual rate of interest and the charges applicable, and of any amendment thereof, where the overdraft extends beyond a period of three months.

Article 7

In the case of credit granted for the acquisition of goods, Member States shall lay down the conditions under which goods may be repossessed, in particular if the consumer has not given his consent. They shall further ensure that where the creditor recovers possession of the goods the account between the parties shall be made up so as to ensure that the repossession does not entail any unjustified enrichment.

Article 8

The consumer shall be entitled to discharge his obligations under a credit agreement before the time fixed by the agreement. In this event, in accordance with the rules laid down by the Member States, the consumer shall be entitled to an equitable reduction in the total cost of the credit.

Article 9

Where the creditor's rights under a credit agreement are assigned to a third person, the consumer shall be entitled to plead against that third person any defence which was available to him against the original creditor, including set-off where the latter is permitted in the Member State concerned.

Article 10

The Member States which, in connection with credit agreements, permit the consumer:

(a)   to make payment by means of bills of exchange including promissory notes;

(b)   to give security by means of bills of exchange including promissory notes and cheques, shall ensure that the consumer is suitably protected when using these instruments in those ways.

Article 11

1.   Member States shall ensure that the existence of a credit agreement shall not in any way affect the rights of the consumer against the supplier of goods or services purchased by means of such an agreement in cases where the goods or services are not supplied or are otherwise not in conformity with the contract for their supply.

2.   Where:

(a)   in order to buy goods or obtain services the consumer enters into a credit agreement with a person other than the supplier of them; and

(b)   the grantor of the credit and the supplier of the goods or services have a pre-existing agreement whereunder credit is made available exclusively by that grantor of credit to customers of that supplier for the acquisition of goods or services from that supplier; and

(c)   the consumer referred to in subparagraph (a) obtains his credit pursuant to that pre-existing agreement; and

(d)   the goods or services covered by the credit agreement are not supplied, or are supplied only in part, or are not in conformity with the contract for supply of them; and

(e)   the consumer has pursued his remedies against the supplier but has failed to obtain the satisfaction to which he is entitled, the consumer shall have the right to pursue remedies against the grantor of credit. Member States shall determine to what extent and under what conditions these remedies shall be exercisable.

3.   Paragraph 2 shall not apply where the individual transaction in question is for an amount less than the equivalent of 200 ECU.

Article 12

1.   Member States shall:

(a)   ensure that persons offering credit or offering to arrange credit agreements shall obtain official authorisation to do so, either specifically or as suppliers of goods and services; or

(b)   ensure that persons granting credit or arranging for credit to be granted shall be subject to inspection or monitoring of their activities by an institution or official body; or

(c) promote the establishment of appropriate bodies to receive complaints concerning credit agreements or credit conditions and to provide relevant information or advice to consumers regarding them.

2. Member States may provide that the authorisation referred to in paragraph 1(a) shall not be required where persons offering to conclude or arrange credit agreements satisfy the definition in Article 1 of the first Council Directive of 12 December 1977 on the coordination of laws, regulations and administrative provisions relating to the taking up and pursuit of the business of credit institutions[1] and are authorised in accordance with the provisions of that Directive.

Where persons granting credit or arranging for credit to be granted have been authorised both specifically, under the provisions of paragraph 1(a) and also under the provisions of the aforementioned Directive, but the latter authorisation is subsequently withdrawn, the competent authority responsible for issuing the specific authorisation to grant credit under paragraph 1(a) shall be informed and shall decide whether the persons concerned may continue to grant credit, or arrange for credit to be granted, or whether the specific authorisation granted under paragraph 1(a) should be withdrawn.

Note
[1] OJ No. L322, 17.12.1977, p. 30.

Article 13
1. For the purposes of this Directive, the ECU shall be that defined by Regulation (EEC) No 3180/78, as amended by Regulation (EEC) No 2626/84. The equivalent in national currency shall initially be calculated at the rate obtaining on the date of adoption of this Directive.

Member States may round off the amounts in national currency resulting from the conversion of the amounts in ECU provided such rounding off does not exceed 10 ECU.

2. Every five years, and for the first time in 1995, the Council, acting on a proposal from the Commission, shall examine and, if need be, revise the amounts in this Directive, in the light of economic and monetary trends in the Community.

Article 14
1. Member States shall ensure that credit agreements shall not derogate, to the detriment of the consumer, from the provisions of national law implementing or corresponding to this Directive.

2. Member States shall further ensure that the provisions which they adopt in implementation of this directive are not circumvented as a result of the way in which agreements are formulated, in particular by the device of distributing the amount of credit over several agreements.

Article 15
This Directive shall not preclude Member States from retaining or adopting more stringent provisions to protect consumers consistent with their obligations under the Treaty.

Article 16
1. Member States shall bring into force the measures necessary to comply with this Directive not later than 1 January 1990 and shall forthwith inform the Commission thereof.

2.   Member States shall communicate to the Commission the texts of the main provisions of national law which they adopt in the field covered by this Directive.

Article 17
Not later than 1 January 1995 the Commission shall present a report to the Council concerning the operation of this Directive.

Article 18
This Directive is addressed to the Member States.

Done at Brussels, 22 December 1986.
For the Council
The President
G. SHAW

ANNEX I   LIST OF TERMS REFERRED TO IN ARTICLE 4 (3)

1.   Credit agreements for financing the supply of particular goods or services:
1.2   (i) a description of the goods or services covered by the agreement; (ii) the cash price and the price payable under the credit agreement; (iii) the amount of the deposit, if any, the number and amount of instalments and the dates on which they fall due, or the method of ascertaining any of the same if unknown at the time the agreement is concluded; (iv) an indication that the consumer will be entitled, as provided in Article 8, to a reduction if he repays early; (v) who owns the goods (if ownership does not pass immediately to the consumer) and the terms on which the consumer becomes the owner of them; (vi) a description of the security required, if any; (vii) the cooling-off period, if any; (viii) an indication of the insurance(s) required, if any, and, when the choice of insurer is not left to the consumer, an indication of the cost thereof, (ix) the obligation on the consumer to save a certain amount of money which must be placed in a special account.
2.   Credit agreements operated by credit cards:
1.2   (i) the amount of the credit limit, if any; (ii) the terms of repayment or the means of determining them; (iii) the cooling-off period, if any.
3.   Credit agreements operated by running account which are not otherwise covered by the Directive:
1.2   (i) the amount of the credit limit, if any, or the method of determining it; (ii) the terms of use and repayment; (iii) the cooling-off period, if any.
4.   Other credit agreements covered by the Directive:
1.2   (i) the amount of the credit limit, if any; (ii) an indication of the security required, if any; (iii) the terms of repayment; (iv) the cooling-off period, if any; (v) an indication that the consumer will be entitled, as provided in Article 8, to a reduction if he repays early.

ANNEX II   THE BASIC EQUATION EXPRESSING THE
EQUIVALENCE OF LOANS ON THE ONE HAND, AND
REPAYMENTS AND CHARGES ON THE OTHER:

1.2.3.4.5.6 K = m K = 1 AK (1 i) tK = K' = m' K' = 1 A'K' (1 i) tK'

Meaning of letters and symbols:
1.2   K is the number of a loan K' is the number of a repayment or a payment of charges AK is the amount of loan number K A'K' is the amount of

repayment number K represents a sum m is the number of the last loan m' is the number of the last repayment or payment of charges tK is the interval, expressed in years and fractions of a year, between the date of loan No 1 and those of subsequent loans Nos. 2 to m tK' is the interval expressed in years and fractions of a year between the date of loan No 1 and those of repayments or payments of charges Nos. 1 to m i is the percentage rate that can be calculated (either by algebra, by successive approximations, or by a computer programme) where the other terms in the equation are known from the contract or otherwise.

Remarks

(a) The amounts paid by both parties at different times shall not necessarily be equal and shall not necessarily be paid at equal intervals.

(b) The starting date shall be that of the first loan.

(c) Intervals between dates used in the calculations shall be expressed in years or in fractions of a year.

ANNEX III   EXAMPLES OF CALCULATIONS

First example

Sum loaned S = ECU 1,000.

It is repaid in a single payment of ECU 1,200 made 18 months, i.e. 1.5 years, after the date of the loan.

1.2   The equation becomes 1,000 = 1,200 (1 i) 1.5 1.2.3 or (1 i) 1.5 = 1.2 1 i = 1.129243... i = 0.129243...

This amount will be rounded down to 12.9% or 12.92% depending on whether the State or habitual practice allows the percentage to be rounded off to the first or second decimal.

Second example

The sum agreed is S = ECU 1,000 but the creditor retains ECU 50 for enquiry and administrative expenses, so that the loan is in fact ECU 950; the repayment of ECU 1,200, as in the first example, is made 18 months after the date of the loan.

1.2   The equation becomes 950 = 1,200 (1 i) 1.5 1.2.3.4.5.6 or (1 i) 1.5 = 1,200,950 = 1.263157... 1.2.3.4.5,6 1 i = 1.16851... i = 0.16851... rounded off to 16.9% or 16.85%.

Third example

The sum lent is ECU 1,000, repayable in two amounts each of ECU 600, paid after one and two years respectively.

1.2.3.4 The equation becomes 1,000 = 600 1 i 600 (1 i) 2; it is solved by algebra and produces i = 0.1306623, rounded off to 13.1% or 13.07%.

Fourth example

The sum lent is ECU 1,000 and the amounts to be paid by the borrower are:

1.2.3 After three months (0.25 years) ECU 272 After six months (0.50 years) ECU 272 After twelve months (1 year) ECU 544 Total ECU 1,088

The equation becomes:

1.2.3.4.5.6 1 000 = 272 (1 i) 0.25 272 (1 o) 0.50 544 1 i

This equation allows i to be calculated by successive approximations, which can be programmed on a pocket computer.

The result is:

i = 0.1321 rounded off to 13.2 or 13.21%.

COUNCIL DIRECTIVE OF 3 MAY 1988 ON THE APPROXIMATION OF THE LAWS OF THE MEMBER STATES CONCERNING THE SAFETY OF TOYS (88/378/ EEC)
[OJ 1988, No. L187/1]*

THE COUNCIL OF THE EUROPEAN COMMUNITIES,

Having regard to the Treaty establishing the European Economic Community, and in particular Article 100a thereof,
Having regard to the proposal from the Commission,[1]
In cooperation with the European Parliament,[2]
Having regard to the opinion of the Economic and Social Committee,[3]

Whereas the laws, regulations and administrative provisions in force in the various Member States relating to the safety characteristics of toys differ in scope and content; whereas such disparities are liable to create barriers to trade and unequal conditions of competition within the internal market without necessarily affording consumers in the common market, especially children, effective protection against the hazards arising from the products in question;

Whereas these obstacles to the attainment of an internal market in which only sufficiently safe products would be sold should be removed; whereas, for this purpose, the marketing and free movement of toys should be made subject to uniform rules based on the objectives regarding protection of consumer health and safety as set out in the Council resolution of 23 June 1986 concerning the future orientation of the policy of the European Economic Community for the protection and promotion of consumer interests;[4]

Whereas, to facilitate proof of conformity with the essential requirements, it is necessary to have harmonised standards at European level which concern, in particular, the design and composition of toys so that products complying with them may be assumed to conform to the essential requirements; whereas these standards harmonised at European level are drawn up by private bodies and must remain non-mandatory texts; whereas for that purpose the European Committee for Standardisation (CEN) and the European Committee for Electrotechnical Standardisation (CENELEC) are recognised as the competent bodies for the adoption of harmonised standards in accordance with the general guidelines for cooperation between the Commission and those two bodies signed on 13 November 1984; whereas, for the purposes of this Directive, a harmonised standard is a technical specification (European standard or harmonization document) adopted by one or both of those bodies upon a remit from the Commission in accordance with the provisions of Council Directive 83/189/EEC of 28 March 1983 laying down a procedure for

Notes
*As corrected by OJ 1988 L282/55 and as amended by Directive 93/68/EEC [OJ 1993 L220/1].
[1] OJ No. C282, 8.11.1986, p. 4.
[2] OJ No. C246, 14.9.1987, p. 91 and Decision of 9 March 1988 (not yet published in the Official Journal).
[3] OJ No. C232, 31.8.1987, p. 22.
[4] OJ No. C167, 5.7.1986, p. 1.

the provision of information in the field of technical standards and regulations,[1] as last amended by the Act of Accession of Spain and Portugal, and on the basis of the general guidelines;

Whereas, in accordance with the Council resolution of 7 May 1985 on a new approach to technical harmonization and standards,[2] the harmonization to be achieved should consist in establishing the essential safety requirements to be satisfied by all toys if they are to be placed on the market;

Whereas, in view of the size and mobility of the toy market and the diversity of the products concerned, the scope of this Directive should be determined on the basis of a sufficiently broad definition of 'toys'; whereas, nevertheless, it should be made clear that some products are not to be regarded as toys for the purposes of this Directive either because they are not in fact intended for children or because they call for supervision or special conditions of use;

Whereas toys placed on the market should not jeopardise the safety and/or health either of users or of third parties; whereas the standard of safety of toys should be determined in relation to the criterion of the use of the product as intended, but allowance should also be made for any foreseeable use, bearing in mind the normal behaviour of children who do not generally show the same degree of care as the average adult user;

Whereas the standard of safety of the toy must be considered when it is marketed, bearing in mind the need to ensure that this standard is maintained throughout the foreseeable and normal period of use of the toy;

Whereas compliance with the essential requirements is likely to guarantee consumer health and safety; whereas all toys placed on the market must comply with these requirements and, if they do, no obstacle must be put in the way of their free movement;

Whereas toys may be presumed to comply with these essential requirements where they are in conformity with the harmonised standards, reference numbers of which have been published in the Official Journal of the European Communities;

Whereas toys that conform to a model approved by an approved body may also be regarded as complying with the essential requirements; whereas such conformity must be certified by the affixing of a European mark;

Whereas certification procedures must be established to define the way in which national approved bodies have to approve models of toys not in conformity with standards and issue type-examination certificates for them and for toys in conformity with standards, a model of which is submitted to them for approval;

Whereas adequate information for the Member States, the Commission and all the approved bodies must be provided for at the various stages of the certification and inspection procedures;

Whereas Member States must appoint bodies, called 'approved bodies', for the purposes of applying the system introduced for toys; whereas adequate information on these bodies must be provided and they must all comply with minimum criteria for their approval;

Note
[1] OJ No. L109, 26.4.1983, p. 8.
[2] OJ No. C136, 4.6.1985, p.1.

Whereas cases might arise where a toy does not satisfy the essential safety requirements; whereas, in such cases, the Member State which ascertains this fact must take all appropriate measures to withdraw the products from the market or to prohibit their being placed on the market; whereas a reason must be given for this decision and, where the reason is a shortcoming in the harmonised standards, these, or a part thereof, must be withdrawn from the list published by the Commission;

Whereas the Commission is to ensure that the harmonised European standards in all the areas covered by the essential requirements listed in Annex II are drawn up in sufficient time to enable Member States to adopt and publish the necessary provisions by 1 July 1989; whereas the national provisions adopted on the basis of this Directive should consequently become effective on 1 January 1990;

Whereas provision must be made for suitable action to be taken against anyone wrongfully affixing a mark of conformity;

Whereas checks on the safety of toys already on the market must be carried out by the competent authorities of the Member States;

Whereas, for some categories of toys that are particularly dangerous or intended for very young children, warnings or details of precautions to be taken must also be given;

Whereas the Commission must receive regular information on activities carried out under this Directive by the approved bodies;

Whereas those to whom any decision taken under this Directive is addressed must know the reason for that decision and the remedies open to them;

Whereas the opinion of the Scientific Advisory Committee for the evaluation of the toxicity and ecotoxicity of chemical compounds has been taken into account with respect to the health-based limits of bioavailability of metallic compounds in toys to children,

HAS ADOPTED THIS DIRECTIVE:

Article 1

1. This Directive shall apply to toys. A 'toy' shall mean any product or material designed or clearly intended for use in play by children of less than 14 years of age.

2. The products listed in Annex I shall not be regarded as toys for the purposes of this Directive.

Article 2

1. Toys may be placed on the market only if they do not jeopardise the safety and/or health of users or third parties when they are used as intended or in a foreseeable way, bearing in mind the normal behaviour of children.

2. In the condition in which it is placed on the market, taking account of the period of foreseeable and normal use, a toy must meet the safety and health conditions laid down in this Directive.

3. For the purposes of this Directive, the expression 'placed on the market' shall cover both sale and distribution free of charge.

Article 3

Member States shall take all steps necessary to ensure that toys cannot be placed on the market unless they meet the essential safety requirements set out in Annex II.

Article 4

Member States shall not impede the placing on the market on their territory of toys which satisfy the provisions of this Directive.

Article 5

1. Member States shall presume that toys bearing the CE marking laid down in Article 11 comply with all the provisions of this Directive, including the conformity assessment procedures referred to in Articles 8, 9 and 10. Conformity of toys with the national standards which transpose the harmonised standards the reference numbers of which have been published in the Official Journal of the European Communities shall result in a presumption of conformity to the essential safety requirements referred to in Article 3. Member States shall publish the reference numbers of such 'national standards';

2. Member States shall presume that toys in respect of which the manufacturer has not applied the standards referred to in paragraph 1, or has applied them only in part, or for which no such standards exist, satisfy the essential requirements referred to in Article 3 where, after receipt of an EEC type-examination certificate, their conformity with the approved model has been certified by the affixation of the CE marking.

3. (a) Where the toys are subject to other Directives covering other aspects and which also provide for the affixing of the CE marking, the latter shall indicate that the toys in question are also presumed to conform to the provisions of those other Directives.

(b) However, where one or more of these Directives allow the manufacturer, during a transitional period, to choose which arrangements to apply, the CE marking shall indicate conformity only to the Directives applied by the manufacturer. In this case, particulars of the Directives applied, as published in the Official Journal of the European Communities, must be given in the documents, notices or instructions required by the Directives and accompanying such toys or, failing that, on their packaging.

Article 6

1. Where a Member State or the Commission considers that the harmonised standards referred to in Article 5(1) do not entirely satisfy the essential requirements referred to in Article 3, the Commission or the Member State shall refer the matter to the Standing Committee set up under Directive 83/189/EEC, hereinafter referred to as 'the committee', setting out its reasons. The committee shall issue an opinion as a matter of urgency. After receiving the committee's opinion, the Commission shall notify the Member States whether or not the standards concerned or a part thereof have to be withdrawn from the publications referred to in Article 5(1).

2. The Commission shall inform the European standardisation body concerned and, if necessary, issue a new standardisation brief.

Article 7

1. Where a Member State ascertains that toys bearing the CE marking which are used as intended or in accordance with Article 2 are likely to jeopardise the safety and/or health of consumers and/or third parties, it shall take all appropriate measures to withdraw the products from the market, or to prohibit or restrict their placing on the market. The Member State shall inform

the Commission immediately of this measure and indicate the reasons for its decision, stating in particular whether the non-compliance results from:

(a)   failure to meet the essential requirements referred to in Article 3, if the toy does not meet the standards referred to in Article 5(1);

(b)   incorrect application of the standards referred to in Article 5(1);

(c)   shortcomings in the standards referred to in Article 5(1).

2.   The Commission shall enter into consultation with the parties concerned as soon as possible. Where, after such consultation, the Commission finds that any measure as referred to in paragraph 1 is justified, it shall forthwith so inform the Member State that took the action and the other Member States. Where the decision referred to in paragraph 1 is attributed to shortcomings in the standards, the Commission, after consulting the parties concerned, shall bring the matter before the Committee within two months if the Member State which has taken the measures intends to maintain them and shall initiate the procedures referred to in Article 6.

3.   Where the toy which does not comply with the requirements bears the CE marking, the competent Member State shall take appropriate measures and inform the Commission, which shall inform the other Member States.

4.   (deleted)[1]

Note

[1]By OJ 1988 L281/55.

Article 8

1.   (a)   Before being placed on the market, toys manufactured in accordance with the harmonised standards referred to in Article 5(1) must have affixed to them the CE marking by which the manufacturer or his authorised representative established within the Community confirms that the toys comply with those standards;

(b)   The manufacturer or his authorised representative established within the Community shall keep the following information available for inspection:

— a description of the means (such as the use of a test report or technical file) whereby the manufacturer ensures conformity of production with the standards referred to in Article 5(1) and, as appropriate: an EC type-certificate drawn up by an approved body; copies of the documents the manufacturer has submitted to the approved body; a description of the means whereby the manufacturer ensures conformity with the approved model,

— the addresses of the places of manufacture and storage,

— detailed information concerning the design and manufacture.

Where neither the manufacturer nor his authorised representative are established within the Community, the above obligation to keep a dossier available shall be the responsibility of the person who places the toy on the Community market.

2.   (a)   Toys which do not conform in whole or in part to the standards referred to in Article 5(1) must have affixed to them, before being placed on the market, the CE marking by which the manufacturer or his authorised representative established within the Community confirms that the toy concerned conforms to the model examined in accordance with the procedures laid down in Article 10 which an approved body has stated complies with the essential requirements referred to in Article 3;

(b) the manufacturer or his authorised representative established within the Community shall keep the following information available for inspection:

— a detailed description of manufacture,

— a description of the means (such as the use of a test report or technical file) whereby the manufacturer ensures conformity with the approved model,

— the addresses of the places of manufacture and storage,

— copies of the documents the manufacturer has submitted to an approved body in accordance with Article 10(2),

— the test certificate for the sample or a certified copy thereof.

Where neither the manufacturer nor his authorised representative is established within the Community, the above obligation to keep a dossier available shall be the responsibility of the person who places the toy on the market in the Community.

3. In the event of non-observance of the obligations laid down in paragraphs 1(b) and 2(b), the competent Member State shall take appropriate measures to ensure that those obligations are observed.

Where non-observance of the obligations is obvious, it may in particular require the manufacturer or his authorised representative established within the Community to have a test performed at his own expense within a specified period by an approved body in order to verify compliance with the harmonised standards and essential safety requirements.

Article 9

1. The minimum criteria which Member States must meet in order to appoint the approved bodies referred to in this Directive are contained in Annex III.

2. Member States shall notify the Commission and the other Member States of the bodies which they have appointed to carry out the EC type-examination referred to in Article 8(2) and Article 10 together with the specific tasks which these bodies have been appointed to carry out and the identification numbers assigned to them beforehand by the Commission.

The Commission shall publish in the Official Journal of the European Communities a list of the notified bodies with their identification number and the tasks for which they have been notified. The Commission shall ensure that this list is kept up to date.

3. A Member State which has approved a body shall withdraw approval if it finds that the body no longer meets the criteria listed in Annex III. It shall forthwith inform the Commission thereof.

Article 10

1. EC type-examination is the procedure by which an approved body ascertains and certifies that a model of a toy satisfies the essential requirements referred to in Article 3.

2. The application for EC type-examination shall be lodged with an approved body by the manufacturer or by his authorised representative established within the Community.

The application shall include:

— a description of the toy,

— the name and address of the manufacturer or of his authorised representative or representatives, and the place of manufacture of the toy,

— comprehensive manufacturing and design data; and shall be accompanied by a model of the toy to be manufactured.

3. The approved body shall carry out the EC type-examination in the manner described below:

— it shall examine the documents supplied by the applicant and establish whether they are in order,

— it shall check that the toy would not jeopardise safety and/or health, as provided for in Article 2,

— it shall carry out the appropriate examinations and tests — using as far as possible the harmonised standards referred to in Article 5(1) — in order to check whether the model meets the essential requirements referred to in Article 3,

— it may ask for further examples of the model.

4. If the model complies with the essential requirements referred to in Article 3, the approved body shall draw up an EC type-examination certificate which shall be notified to the applicant. This certificate shall state the conclusions of the examination, indicate any conditions attaching to it and be accompanied by the descriptions and drawings of the approved toy.

The Commission, the other approved bodies and the other Member States may obtain on request a copy of the certificate and, on reasoned request, a copy of the design and manufacturing schedule and the reports on the examinations and tests carried out.

5. An approved body which refuses to issue an EC type-examination certificate shall so inform the Member State which approved it and the Commission, giving the reasons for refusal.

Article 11

1. The CE marking referred to in Articles 5, 7 and 8 and the name and/or trade name and/or mark and address of the manufacturer or his authorised representative or the importer into the Community shall as a rule be affixed either to the toy or on the packaging in a visible, easily legible and indelible form. In the case of small toys and toys consisting of small parts these particulars may be affixed in the same way to the packaging, to a label or to a leaflet. Where the said particulars are not affixed to the toy, the consumer's attention must be drawn to the advisability of keeping them.

2. The CE conformity marking shall consist of the initials 'CE' taking the form of the specimen given in Annex V.

3. The affixing of markings on the toys which are likely to deceive third parties as to the meaning and form of the CE marking shall be prohibited. Any other marking may be affixed to the toys, their packaging or a label provided that the visibility and legibility of the EC marking is not thereby reduced.

4. The particulars referred to in paragraph 1 may be abbreviated provided that the abbreviation enables the manufacturer, his authorised representative or the importer into the Community to be identified.

5. Annex IV sets out the warnings and indications of precautions to be taken during use that have to be given for certain toys. Member States may require that these warnings and precautions, or some of them, together with the information specified in paragraph 4, be given in their own national language or languages when the toys are placed on the market.

Article 12

1.   Member States shall take the necessary measures to ensure that sample checks are carried out on toys which are on their market, so as to verify their conformity with this Directive.

The authority responsible for inspection:

— shall obtain access, on request, to the place of manufacture or storage and to the information referred to in Article 8(1)(b) and (2)(b),

— may ask the manufacturer, his authorised representative or the person responsible for marketing the toy established within the Community to supply the information as provided for in Article 8(1)(b) and (2)(b) within a period specified by the Member State,

— may select a sample and take it away for examination and testing.

1a.   Without prejudice to Article 7:

(a)   where a Member State establishes that the CE marking has been affixed unduly, the manufacturer or his authorised representative established within the Community shall be obliged to make the product conform as regards the provisions concerning the CE marking and to end the infringement under the conditions imposed by the Member State;

(b)   where non-conformity continues, the Member State must take all appropriate measures to restrict or prohibit the placing on the market of the product in question or to ensure that it is withdrawn from the market in accordance with the procedures laid down in Article 7.

2.   Every three years, Member States shall send the Commission a report on the application of this Directive.

3.   The Member States and the Commission shall take the necessary measures to guarantee confidentiality with regard to the forwarding of the copies relating to the EC type-examination referred to in Article 10(4).

Article 13

Member States shall regularly inform the Commission of the activities carried out in pursuance of this Directive by the bodies they have approved so that the Commission may ensure that the inspection procedures are implemented correctly and without discrimination.

Article 14

Any decision taken pursuant to this Directive and involving restrictions on the placing of the toy on the market shall state the exact grounds on which it is based. It shall be notified at the earliest opportunity to the party concerned, who shall at the same time be informed of the remedies available to him under the laws in force in the Member State in question and of the time limits applying to such remedies.

Article 15

1.   Member States shall adopt and publish by 30 June 1989 the provisions necessary to comply with this Directive. They shall forthwith inform the Commission thereof. They shall apply these provisions from 1 January 1990.

2.   Member States shall communicate to the Commission the texts of the provisions of national law which they adopt in the field covered by this Directive.

Article 16
This Directive is addressed to the Member States.

Done at Brussels, 3 May 1988.
For the Council
The President
M. BANGEMANN

ANNEX I   PRODUCTS NOT REGARDED AS TOYS FOR THE PURPOSE OF THIS DIRECTIVE (Article 1 (1))

1.   Christmas decorations
2.   Detailed scale models for adult collectors
3.   Equipment intended to be used collectively in playgrounds
4.   Sports equipment
5.   Aquatic equipment intended to be used in deep water
6.   Folk dolls and decorative dolls and other similar articles for adult collectors
7.   'Professional' toys installed in public places (shopping centres, stations, etc.)
8.   Puzzles with more than 500 pieces or without picture, intended for specialists
9.   Air guns and air pistols
10.   Fireworks, including percussion caps[1]
11.   Slings and catapults
12.   Sets of darts with metallic points
13.   Electric ovens, irons or other functional products operated at a nominal voltage exceeding 24 volts
14.   Products containing heating elements intended for use under the supervision of an adult in a teaching context
15.   Vehicles with combustion engines
16.   Toy steam engines
17.   Bicycles designed for sport or for travel on the public highway
18.   Video toys that can be connected to a video screen, operated at a nominal voltage exceeding 24 volts
19.   Babies' dummies
20.   Faithful reproductions of real fire arms
21.   Fashion jewellery for children

Note
With the exception of percussion caps specifically designed for use in toys without prejudice to more stringent provisions already existing in certain Member States.

ANNEX II   ESSENTIAL SAFETY REQUIREMENTS FOR TOYS

I.   GENERAL PRINCIPLES

1.   In compliance with the requirements of Article 2 of the Directive, the users of toys as well as third parties must be protected against health hazards and risk of physical injury when toys are used as intended or in a foreseeable way, bearing in mind the normal behaviour of children. Such risks are those:
    (a)   which are connected with the design, construction or composition of the toy;

(b) which are inherent in the use of the toy and cannot be completely eliminated by modifying the toy's construction and composition without altering its function or depriving it of its essential properties.

2. (a) The degree of risk present in the use of a toy must be commensurate with the ability of the users, and where appropriate their supervisors, to cope with it. This applies in particular to toys which, by virtue of their functions, dimensions and characteristics, are intended for use by children of under 36 months.

(b) To observe this principle, a minimum age for users of toys and/or the need to ensure that they are used only under adult supervision must be specified where appropriate.

3. Labels on toys and/or their packaging and the instructions for use which accompany them must draw the attention of users or their supervisors fully and effectively to the risks involved in using them and to the ways of avoiding such risks.

II. PARTICULAR RISKS

1. Physical and mechanical properties

(a) Toys and their parts and, in the case of fixed toys, their anchorages, must have the requisite mechanical strength and, where appropriate, stability to withstand the stresses to which they are subjected during use without breaking or becoming liable to distortion at the risk of causing physical injury.

(b) Accessible edges, protrusions, cords, cables and fastenings on toys must be so designed and constructed that the risks of physical injury from contact with them are reduced as far as possible.

(c) Toys must be so designed and constructed as to minimise the risk of physical injury which could be caused by the movement of their parts.

(d) Toys, and their component parts, and any detachable parts of toys which are clearly intended for use by children under 36 months must be of such dimensions as to prevent their being swallowed and/or inhaled.

(e) Toys, and their parts and the packaging in which they are contained for retail sale must not present risk of strangulation or suffocation.

(f) Toys intended for use in shallow water which are capable of carrying or supporting a child on the water must be designed and constructed so as to reduce as far as possible, taking into account the recommended use of the toy, any risk of loss of buoyancy of the toy and loss of support afforded to the child.

(g) Toys which it is possible to get inside and which thereby constitute an enclosed space for occupants must have a means of exit which the latter can open easily from the inside.

(h) Toys conferring mobility on their users must, as far as possible, incorporate a braking system which is suited to the type of toy and is commensurate with the kinetic energy developed by it. Such a system must be easy for the user to operate without risk of ejection or physical injury for the user or for third parties.

(i) The form and composition of projectiles and the kinetic energy they may develop when fired from a toy designed for that purpose must be such that, taking into account the nature of the toy, there is no unreasonable risk of physical injury to the user or to third parties.

(j) Toys containing heating elements must be so constructed as to ensure that:

— the maximum temperature of any accessible surfaces does not cause burns when touched,

— liquids and gases contained within toys do not reach temperatures or pressures which are such that their escape from a toy, other than for reasons essential to the proper functioning of the toy, might cause burns, scalds or other physical injury.

2. Flammability

(a) Toys must not constitute a dangerous flammable element in the child's environment. They must therefore be composed of materials which:

1. do not burn if directly exposed to a flame or spark or other potential seat of fire; or

2. are not readily flammable (the flame goes out as soon as the fire cause disappears); or

3. if they do ignite, burn slowly and present a low rate of spread of the flame; or

4. irrespective of the toy's chemical composition, are treated so as to delay the combustion process. Such combustible materials must not constitute a risk of ignition for other materials used in the toy.

(b) Toys which, for reasons essential to their functioning, contain dangerous substances or preparations as defined in Council Directive 67/548/EEC,[1] in particular materials and equipment for chemistry experiments, model assembly, plastic or ceramic moulding, enamelling, photography or similar activities, must not contain, as such, substances or preparations which may become flammable due to the loss of non-flammable volatile components.

(c) Toys must not be explosive or contain elements or substances likely to explode when used as specified in Article 2 (1) of the Directive. This provision does not apply to toy percussion caps, for which reference should be made to point 10 of Annex I and the related footnote.

(d) Toys and, in particular, chemical games and toys, must not contain as such substances or preparations:

— which, when mixed, may explode:

— through chemical reaction, or through heating,

— when mixed with oxidising substances,

— which contain volatile components which are flammable in air and liable to form flammable or explosive vapour/air mixture.

Notes
[1] OJ No. 196, 16.8.1967, p. 1/67.

3. Chemical properties

1. Toys must be so designed and constructed that, when used as specified in Article 2(1) of the Directive, they do not present health hazards or risks of physical injury by ingestion, inhalation or contact with the skin, mucous tissues or eyes. They must in all cases comply with the relevant Community legislation relating to certain categories of products or to the prohibition, restriction of use or labelling of certain dangerous substances and preparations.

2. In particular, for the protection of children's health, bioavailability resulting from the use of toys must not, as an objective, exceed the following levels per day:

0.2 mg for antimony,
0.1 mg for arsenic,
25.0 mg for barium,
0.6 mg for cadmium,
0.3 mg for chromium,
0.7 mg for lead,
0.5 mg for mercury,
5.0 mg for selenium,

or such other values as may be laid down for these or other substances in Community legislation based on scientific evidence.

The bioavailability of these substances means the soluble extract having toxicological significance.

3. Toys must not contain dangerous substances or preparations within the meaning of Directives 67/548/EEC and 88/379/EEC[1] in amounts which may harm the health of children using them. At all events it is strictly forbidden to include, in a toy, dangerous substances or preparations if they are intended to be used as such while the toy is being used.

However, where a limited number of substances or preparations are essential to the functioning of certain toys, in particular materials and equipment for chemistry experiments, model assembly, plastic or ceramic moulding, enamelling, photography or similar activities, they are permitted up to a maximum concentration level to be defined for each substance or preparation by mandate of the European Committee for Standardisation (CEN) according to the procedure of the committee set up by Directive 83/189/EEC, provided the permitted substances and preparations comply with the Community classification rules in respect of labelling, without prejudice to point 4 of Annex IV.

4. Electrical properties

(a) Electric toys must not be powered by electricity of a nominal voltage exceeding 24 volts and no part of the toy may exceed 24 volts.

(b) Parts of toys which are connected to, or liable to come into contact with a source of electricity capable of causing electric shock, together with the cables or other conductors through which electricity is conveyed to such parts, must be properly insulated and mechanically protected so as to prevent the risk of such shock.

(c) Electric toys must be so designed and constructed as to ensure that the maximum temperatures reached by all directly accessible surfaces are not such as to cause burns when touched.

5. Hygiene

Toys must be so designed and manufactured as to meet the requirements of hygiene and cleanliness in order to avoid any risk of infection, sickness and contamination.

6. Radioactivity

Toys must not contain radioactive elements or substances in forms or proportions likely to be detrimental to a child's health. Council Directive 80/836/Euratom shall apply.[2]

Notes
[1] See page 14 of this Official Journal.
[2] OJ No. L246, 17.9.1980, p. 1.

ANNEX III   CONDITIONS TO BE FULFILLED BY THE APPROVED BODIES (Article 9 (1))

The bodies designated by the Member States must fulfil the following minimum conditions:
1.   availability of personnel and of the necessary means and equipment;
2.   technical competence and professional integrity of personnel;
3.   independence, in carrying out the tests, preparing the reports, issuing the certificates and performing the surveillance provided for in this Directive, of staff and technical personnel in relation to all circles, groups or persons directly or indirectly concerned with toys;
4.   maintenance of professional secrecy by personnel;
5.   subscription of a civil liability insurance unless that liability is covered by the state under national law.

Fulfilment of the conditions under 1 and 2 shall be verified at intervals by the competent authorities of the Member States.

ANNEX IV   WARNINGS AND INDICATIONS OF PRECAUTIONS TO BE TAKEN WHEN USING TOYS (Article 11 (5))

Toys must be accompanied by appropriate clearly legible warnings in order to reduce inherent risks in their use as described in the essential requirements, and specifically:
1.   Toys not intended for children under 36 months

Toys which might be dangerous for children under 36 months of age shall bear a warning, for example: 'Not suitable for children under 36 months' or 'Not suitable for children under three years' together with a brief indication, which may also appear in the instructions for use, of the specific risks calling for this restriction.

This provision does not apply to toys which, on account of their function, dimensions, characteristics, properties or other cogent grounds, are manifestly unsuitable for children under 36 months.

2.   Slides, suspended swings and rings, trapezes, ropes and similar toys attached to a crossbeam

Such toys shall be accompanied by instructions drawing attention to the need to carry out checks and maintenance of the main parts (suspensions, fixings, anchorages, etc.) at intervals, and pointing out that, if these checks are not carried out, the toy may cause a fall or overturn. Instructions must also be given as to correct assembly of the toy, indicating those parts which can present dangers if it is incorrectly assembled.

3.   Functional toys

Functional toys or their packaging shall bear the marking 'Warning: to be used under the direct supervision of an adult'. In addition, these toys shall be accompanied by directions giving working instructions as well as the precautions to be taken by the user, with the warning that failure to take these precautions would expose the user to the hazards — to be specified — normally associated with the appliance or product of which the toy is a scale model or an imitation. It will also be indicated that the toy must be kept out of the reach of very young children.

'Functional toys' means toys which are used in the same way as, and are often scale models of, appliances or installations intended for adults.

4. Toys containing inherently dangerous substances or preparations. Chemical toys

(a) Without prejudice to the application of the provisions laid down in Community directives on the classification, packaging and labelling of dangerous substances or preparations, the instructions for use of toys containing inherently dangerous substances or preparations shall bear a warning of the dangerous nature of these substances or preparations and an indication of the precautions to be taken by the user in order to avoid hazards associated with them, which shall be specified concisely according to the type of toy. The first aid to be given in the event of serious accidents resulting from the use of this type of toy shall also be mentioned. It shall also be stated that the toys must be kept out of reach of very young children.

(b) In addition to the instructions provided for in (a), chemical toys shall bear the following marking on their packaging: 'Warning: for children over[1] years of age only. For use under adult supervision'. In particular, the following are regarded as chemical toys: chemistry sets, plastic embedding sets, miniature workshops for ceramics, enamelling or photography and similar toys.

Note
[1]Age to be decided by the manufacturer.

5. Skates and skateboards for children
If these products are offered for sale as toys they shall bear the marking:
'Warning: protective equipment should be worn'.
Moreover, the instructions for use shall contain a reminder that the toy must be used with caution, since it requires great skill, so as to avoid falls or collisions causing injury to the user and third parties. Some indication shall also be given as to recommended protective equipment (helmets, gloves, knee-pads, elbow-pads, etc.).

6. Toys intended for use in water
The toys intended for use in water defined in Section II.1 (f) of Annex II shall contain the warning in accordance with CEN's brief to adapt standard EN/71, parts 1 and 2:
'Warning ! Only to be used in water in which the child is within its depth and under supervision'.

ANNEX V   CE CONFORMITY MARKING

— The CE conformity marking shall consist of the initials 'CE' taking the following form:
— If the CE marking is reduced or enlarged the proportions given in the above graduated drawing must be respected.
— The various components of the CE marking must have substantially the same vertical dimension, which may not be less than 5 mm.

COUNCIL DIRECTIVE OF 13 JUNE 1990 ON PACKAGE TRAVEL, PACKAGE HOLIDAYS AND PACKAGE TOURS (90/314/ EEC) [OJ 1990, No. L158/59]

THE COUNCIL OF THE EUROPEAN COMMUNITIES,

Having regard to the Treaty establishing the European Economic Community, and in particular Article 100a thereof,

Having regard to the proposal from the Commission,[1]
In cooperation with the European Parliament,[2]
Having regard to the opinion of the Economic and Social Committee,[3]

Whereas one of the main objectives of the Community is to complete the internal market, of which the tourist sector is an essential part;

Whereas the national laws of Member States concerning package travel, package holidays and package tours, hereinafter referred to as 'packages', show many disparities and national practices in this field are markedly different, which gives rise to obstacles to the freedom to provide services in respect of packages and distortions of competition amongst operators established in different Member States;

Whereas the establishment of common rules on packages will contribute to the elimination of these obstacles and thereby to the achievement of a common market in services, thus enabling operators established in one Member State to offer their services in other Member States and Community consumers to benefit from comparable conditions when buying a package in any Member State;

Whereas paragraph 36(b) of the Annex to the Council resolution of 19 May 1981 on a second programme of the European Economic Community for a consumer protection and information policy[4] invites the Commission to study, inter alia, tourism and, if appropriate, to put forward suitable proposals, with due regard for their significance for consumer protection and the effects of differences in Member States' legislation on the proper functioning of the common market;

Whereas in the resolution on a Community policy on tourism on 10 April 1984[5] the Council welcomed the Commission's initiative in drawing attention to the importance of tourism and took note of the Commission's initial guidelines for a Community policy on tourism;

Whereas the Commission communication to the Council entitled 'A New Impetus for Consumer Protection Policy', which was approved by resolution of the Council on 6 May 1986,[6] lists in paragraph 37, among the measures proposed by the Commission, the harmonization of legislation on packages;

Whereas tourism plays an increasingly important role in the economies of the Member States; whereas the package system is a fundamental part of tourism; whereas the package travel industry in Member States would be stimulated to greater growth and productivity if at least a minimum of common rules were adopted in order to give it a Community dimension; whereas this would not only produce benefits for Community citizens buying packages organised on the basis of those rules, but would attract tourists from outside the Community seeking the advantages of guaranteed standards in packages;

Whereas disparities in the rules protecting consumers in different Member States are a disincentive to consumers in one Member State from buying packages in another Member State;

Notes
[1] OJ No. C96, 12.4.1988, p. 5.
[2] OJ No. C69, 20.3.1989, p. 102 and OJ No. C149, 18. 6. 1990.
[3] OJ No. C102, 24.4.1989, p. 27.
[4] OJ No. C165, 23. 6. 1981, p. 24.
[5] OJ No. C115, 30.4.1984, p. 1.
[6] OJ No. C118, 7.3.1986, p. 28.

Whereas this disincentive is particularly effective in deterring consumers from buying packages outside their own Member State, and more effective than it would be in relation to the acquisition of other services, having regard to the special nature of the services supplied in a package which generally involve the expenditure of substantial amounts of money in advance and the supply of the services in a State other than that in which the consumer is resident;

Whereas the consumer should have the benefit of the protection introduced by this Directive irrespective of whether he is a direct contracting party, a transferee or a member of a group on whose behalf another person has concluded a contract in respect of a package;

Whereas the organiser of the package and/or the retailer of it should be under obligation to ensure that in descriptive matter relating to packages which they respectively organise and sell, the information which is given is not misleading and brochures made available to consumers contain information which is comprehensible and accurate;

Whereas the consumer needs to have a record of the terms of contract applicable to the package; whereas this can conveniently be achieved by requiring that all the terms of the contract be stated in writing or such other documentary form as shall be comprehensible and accessible to him, and that he be given a copy thereof;

Whereas the consumer should be at liberty in certain circumstances to transfer to a willing third person a booking made by him for a package;

Whereas the price established under the contract should not in principle be subject to revision except where the possibility of upward or downward revision is expressly provided for in the contract; whereas that possibility should nonetheless be subject to certain conditions;

Whereas the consumer should in certain circumstances be free to withdraw before departure from a package travel contract;

Whereas there should be a clear definition of the rights available to the consumer in circumstances where the organiser of the package cancels it before the agreed date of departure;

Whereas if, after the consumer has departed, there occurs a significant failure of performance of the services for which he has contracted or the organiser perceives that he will be unable to procure a significant part of the services to be provided, the organiser should have certain obligations towards the consumer;

Whereas the organiser and/or retailer party to the contract should be liable to the consumer for the proper performance of the obligations arising from the contract; whereas, moreover, the organiser and/or retailer should be liable for the damage resulting for the consumer from failure to perform or improper performance of the contract unless the defects in the performance of the contract are attributable neither to any fault of theirs nor to that of another supplier of services;

Whereas in cases where the organiser and/or retailer is liable for failure to perform or improper performance of the services involved in the package, such liability should be limited in accordance with the international conventions governing such services, in particular the Warsaw Convention of 1929 on International Carriage by Air, the Berne Convention of 1961 on Carriage by Rail, the Athens Convention of 1974 on Carriage by Sea and the Paris Convention of 1962 on the Liability of Hotel-keepers; whereas, moreover, with regard to damage other than personal injury, it should be possible for liability also to be limited under the package contract provided, however, that such limits are not unreasonable;

Whereas certain arrangements should be made for the information of consumers and the handling of complaints;

Whereas both the consumer and the package travel industry would benefit if organisers and/or retailers were placed under an obligation to provide sufficient evidence of security in the event of insolvency;

Whereas Member States should be at liberty to adopt, or retain, more stringent provisions relating to package travel for the purpose of protecting the consumer,

HAS ADOPTED THIS DIRECTIVE:

Article 1
The purpose of this Directive is to approximate the laws, regulations and administrative provisions of the Member States relating to packages sold or offered for sale in the territory of the Community.

Article 2
For the purposes of this Directive:

1. 'package' means the pre-arranged combination of not fewer than two of the following when sold or offered for sale at an inclusive price and when the service covers a period of more than twenty-four hours or includes overnight accommodation:
   (a) transport;
   (b) accommodation;
   (c) other tourist services not ancillary to transport or accommodation and accounting for a significant proportion of the package.

The separate billing of various components of the same package shall not absolve the organiser or retailer from the obligations under this Directive;

2. 'organiser' means the person who, other than occasionally, organises packages and sells or offers them for sale, whether directly or through a retailer;

3. 'retailer' means the person who sells or offers for sale the package put together by the organiser;

4. 'consumer' means the person who takes or agrees to take the package ('the principal contractor'), or any person on whose behalf the principal contractor agrees to purchase the package ('the other beneficiaries') or any person to whom the principal contractor or any of the other beneficiaries transfers the package ('the transferee');

5. 'contract' means the agreement linking the consumer to the organiser and/or the retailer.

Article 3
1. Any descriptive matter concerning a package and supplied by the organiser or the retailer to the consumer, the price of the package and any other conditions applying to the contract must not contain any misleading information.

2. When a brochure is made available to the consumer, it shall indicate in a legible, comprehensible and accurate manner both the price and adequate information concerning:

(a)   the destination and the means, characteristics and categories of transport used;

(b)   the type of accommodation, its location, category or degree of comfort and its main features, its approval and tourist classification under the rules of the host Member State concerned;

(c)   the meal plan;

(d)   the itinerary;

(e)   general information on passport and visa requirements for nationals of the Member State or States concerned and health formalities required for the journey and the stay;

(f)   either the monetary amount or the percentage of the price which is to be paid on account, and the timetable for payment of the balance;

(g)   whether a minimum number of persons is required for the package to take place and, if so, the deadline for informing the consumer in the event of cancellation. The particulars contained in the brochure are binding on the organiser or retailer, unless:

— changes in such particulars have been clearly communicated to the consumer before conclusion of the contract, in which case the brochure shall expressly state so,

— changes are made later following an agreement between the parties to the contract.

Article 4

1.   (a)   The organiser and/or the retailer shall provide the consumer, in writing or any other appropriate form, before the contract is concluded, with general information on passport and visa requirements applicable to nationals of the Member State or States concerned and in particular on the periods for obtaining them, as well as with information on the health formalities required for the journey and the stay;

(b)   The organiser and/or retailer shall also provide the consumer, in writing or any other appropriate form, with the following information in good time before the start of the journey:

(i)   the times and places of intermediate stops and transport connections as well as details of the place to be occupied by the traveller, e.g. cabin or berth on ship, sleeper compartment on train;

(ii)   the name, address and telephone number of the organiser's and/or retailer's local representative or, failing that, of local agencies on whose assistance a consumer in difficulty could call. Where no such representatives or agencies exist, the consumer must in any case be provided with an emergency telephone number or any other information that will enable him to contract the organiser and/or the retailer;

(iii)   in the case of journeys or stays abroad by minors, information enabling direct contact to be established with the child or the person responsible at the child's place of stay;

(iv)   information on the optional conclusion of an insurance policy to cover the cost of cancellation by the consumer or the cost of assistance, including repatriation, in the event of accident or illness.

2.   Member States shall ensure that in relation to the contract the following principles apply:

(a)   depending on the particular package, the contract shall contain at least the elements listed in the Annex;

(b)   all the terms of the contract are set out in writing or such other form as is comprehensible and accessible to the consumer and must be communicated to him before the conclusion of the contract; the consumer is given a copy of these terms;

(c)   the provision under (b) shall not preclude the belated conclusion of last-minute reservations or contracts.

3.   Where the consumer is prevented from proceeding with the package, he may transfer his booking, having first given the organiser or the retailer reasonable notice of his intention before departure, to a person who satisfies all the conditions applicable to the package. The transferor of the package and the transferee shall be jointly and severally liable to the organiser or retailer party to the contract for payment of the balance due and for any additional costs arising from such transfer.

4.   (a)   The prices laid down in the contract shall not be subject to revision unless the contract expressly provides for the possibility of upward or downward revision and states precisely how the revised price is to be calculated, and solely to allow for variations in:

— transportation costs, including the cost of fuel,

— dues, taxes or fees chargeable for certain services, such as landing taxes or embarkation or disembarkation fees at ports and airports,

— the exchange rates applied to the particular package.

(b)   During the twenty days prior to the departure date stipulated, the price stated in the contract shall not be increased.

5.   If the organiser finds that before the departure he is constrained to alter significantly any of the essential terms, such as the price, he shall notify the consumer as quickly as possible in order to enable him to take appropriate decisions and in particular:

— either to withdraw from the contract without penalty,

— or to accept a rider to the contract specifying the alterations made and their impact on the price.

The consumer shall inform the organiser or the retailer of his decision as soon as possible.

6.   If the consumer withdraws from the contract pursuant to paragraph 5, or if, for whatever cause, other than the fault of the consumer, the organiser cancels the package before the agreed date of departure, the consumer shall be entitled:

(a)   either to take a substitute package of equivalent or higher quality where the organiser and/or retailer is able to offer him such a substitute. If the replacement package offered is of lower quality, the organiser shall refund the difference in price to the consumer;

(b)   or to be repaid as soon as possible all sums paid by him under the contract. In such a case, he shall be entitled, if appropriate, to be compensated by either the organiser or the retailer, whichever the relevant Member State's law requires, for non-performance of the contract, except where:

(i)   cancellation is on the grounds that the number of persons enrolled for the package is less than the minimum number required and the consumer is informed of the cancellation, in writing, within the period indicated in the package description; or

(ii)   cancellation, excluding overbooking, is for reasons of force majeure, i.e. unusual and unforeseeable circumstances beyond the control of the party by whom it is pleaded, the consequences of which could not have been avoided even if all due care had been exercised.

7.   Where, after departure, a significant proportion of the services contracted for is not provided or the organiser perceives that he will be unable to procure a significant proportion of the services to be provided, the organiser shall make suitable alternative arrangements, at no extra cost to the consumer, for the continuation of the package, and where appropriate compensate the consumer for the difference between the services offered and those supplied.

If it is impossible to make such arrangements or these are not accepted by the consumer for good reasons, the organiser shall, where appropriate, provide the consumer, at no extra cost, with equivalent transport back to the place of departure, or to another return-point to which the consumer has agreed and shall, where appropriate, compensate the consumer.

Article 5

1.   Member States shall take the necessary steps to ensure that the organiser and/or retailer party to the contract is liable to the consumer for the proper performance of the obligations arising from the contract, irrespective of whether such obligations are to be performed by that organiser and/or retailer or by other suppliers of services without prejudice to the right of the organiser and/or retailer to pursue those other suppliers of services.

2.   With regard to the damage resulting for the consumer from the failure to perform or the improper performance of the contract, Member States shall take the necessary steps to ensure that the organiser and/or retailer is/are liable unless such failure to perform or improper performance is attributable neither to any fault of theirs nor to that of another supplier of services, because:

—the failures which occur in the performance of the contract are attributable to the consumer,

—such failures are attributable to a third party unconnected with the provision of the services contracted for, and are unforeseeable or unavoidable,

—such failures are due to a case of force majeure such as that defined in Article 4(6), second subparagraph (ii), or to an event which the organiser and/or retailer or the supplier of services, even with all due care, could not foresee or forestall.

In the cases referred to in the second and third indents, the organiser and/or retailer party to the contract shall be required to give prompt assistance to a consumer in difficulty. In the matter of damages arising from the non-performance or improper performance of the services involved in the package, the Member States may allow compensation to be limited in accordance with the international conventions governing such services.

In the matter of damage other than personal injury resulting from the non-performance or improper performance of the services involved in the package, the Member States may allow compensation to be limited under the contract. Such limitation shall not be unreasonable.

3.   Without prejudice to the fourth subparagraph of paragraph 2, there may be no exclusion by means of a contractual clause from the provisions of paragraphs 1 and 2.

4.   The consumer must communicate any failure in the performance of a contract which he perceives on the spot to the supplier of the services concerned and to the organiser and/or retailer in writing or any other appropriate form at the earliest opportunity.

This obligation must be stated clearly and explicitly in the contract.

Article 6
In cases of complaint, the organiser and/or retailer or his local representative, if there is one, must make prompt efforts to find appropriate solutions.

Article 7
The organiser and/or retailer party to the contract shall provide sufficient evidence of security for the refund of money paid over and for the repatriation of the consumer in the event of insolvency.

Article 8
Member States may adopt or return more stringent provisions in the field covered by this Directive to protect the consumer.

Article 9
1.   Member States shall bring into force the measures necessary to comply with this Directive before 31 December 1992. They shall forthwith inform the Commission thereof.

2.   Member States shall communicate to the Commission the texts of the main provisions of national law which they adopt in the field governed by this Directive. The Commission shall inform the other Member States thereof.

Article 10
This Directive is addressed to the Member States.

Done at Luxembourg, 13 June 1990.

For the Council
The President
D. J. O'MALLEY

ANNEX

Elements to be included in the contract if relevant to the particular package:

(a)   the travel destination(s) and, where periods of stay are involved, the relevant periods, with dates;

(b)   the means, characteristics and categories of transport to be used, the dates, times and points of departure and return;

(c)   where the package includes accommodation, its location, its tourist category or degree of comfort, its main features, its compliance with the rules of the host Member State concerned and the meal plan;

(d)   whether a minimum number of persons is required for the package to take place and, if so, the deadline for informing the consumer in the event of cancellation;

(e)   the itinerary;

(f)   visits, excursions or other services which are included in the total price agreed for the package;

(g)   the name and address of the organiser, the retailer and, where appropriate, the insurer;

(h) the price of the package, an indication of the possibility of price revisions under Article 4(4) and an indication of any dues, taxes or fees chargeable for certain services (landing, embarkation or disembarkation fees at ports and airports, tourist taxes) where such costs are not included in the package;

(i) the payment schedule and method of payment;

(j) special requirements which the consumer has communicated to the organiser or retailer when making the booking, and which both have accepted;

(k) periods within which the consumer must make any complaint concerning failure to perform or improper performance of the contract.

COUNCIL DIRECTIVE 92/59/EEC OF 29 JUNE 1992 ON GENERAL PRODUCT SAFETY
[OJ 1992, No. L228/24]

THE COUNCIL OF THE EUROPEAN COMMUNITIES,

Having regard to the Treaty establishing the European Economic Community, and in particular Article 100a thereof,

Having regard to the proposal from the Commission,[1]

In cooperation with the European Parliament,[2]

Having regard to the opinion of the Economic and Social Committee,[3]

Whereas it is important to adopt measures with the aim of progressively establishing the internal market over a period expiring on 31 December 1992; whereas the internal market is to comprise an area without internal frontiers in which the free movement of goods, persons, services and capital is ensured;

Whereas some Member States have adopted horizontal legislation on product safety, imposing, in particular, a general obligation on economic operators to market only safe products; whereas those legislations differ in the level of protection afforded to persons; whereas such disparities and the absence of horizontal legislation in other Member States are liable to create barriers to trade and distortions of competition within the internal market;

Whereas it is very difficult to adopt Community legislation for every product which exists or may be developed; whereas there is a need for a broadly-based, legislative framework of a horizontal nature to deal with those products, and also to cover lacunae in existing or forthcoming specific legislation, in particular with a view to ensuring a high level of protection of safety and health of persons, as required by Article 100a(3) of the Treaty;

Whereas it is therefore necessary to establish on a Community level a general safety requirement for any product placed on the market that is intended for consumers or likely to be used by consumers; whereas certain second-hand goods should nevertheless be excluded by their nature;

Whereas production equipment, capital goods and other products used exclusively in the context of a trade or business are not covered by this Directive;

Notes
[1] OJ No. C156, 27.6.1990, p. 8.
[2] OJ No. C96, 17.4.1990, p. 283 and Decision of 11 June 1992 (not yet published in the Official Journal).
[3] OJ No. C75, 26.3.1990, p. 1.

Whereas, in the absence of more specific safety provisions, within the framework of Community regulations, covering the products concerned, the provisions of this Directive are to apply;

Whereas when there are specific rules of Community law, of the total harmonization type, and in particular rules adopted on the basis of the new approach, which lay down obligations regarding product safety, further obligations should not be imposed on economic operators as regards the placing on the market of products covered by such rules;

Whereas, when the provisions of specific Community regulations cover only certain aspects of safety or categories of risks in respect of the product concerned, the obligations of economic operators in respect of such aspects are determined solely by those provisions;

Whereas it is appropriate to supplement the duty to observe the general safety requirement by an obligation on economic operators to supply consumers with relevant information and adopt measures commensurate with the characteristics of the products, enabling them to be informed of the risks that these products might present;

Whereas in the absence of specific regulations, criteria should be defined whereby product safety can be assessed;

Whereas Member States must establish authorities responsible for monitoring product safety and with powers to take the appropriate measures;

Whereas it is necessary in particular for the appropriate measures to include the power for Member States to organise, immediately and efficiently, the withdrawal of dangerous products already placed on the market;

Whereas it is necessary for the preservation of the unity of the market to inform the Commission of any measure restricting the placing on the market of a product or requiring its withdrawal from the market except for those relating to an event which is local in effect and in any case limited to the territory of the Member State concerned; whereas such measures can be taken only in compliance with the provisions of the Treaty, and in particular Articles 30 to 36;

Whereas this Directive applies without prejudice to the notification procedures in Council Directive 83/189/EEC of 28 March 1983 laying down a procedure for the provision of information in the field of technical standards and regulations[1] and in Commission Decision 88/383/EEC of 24 February 1988 providing for the improvement of information on safety, hygiene and health at work;[2]

Whereas effective supervision of product safety requires the setting-up at national and Community levels of a system of rapid exchange of information in emergency situations in respect of the safety of a product and whereas the procedure laid down by Council Decision 89/45/EEC of 21 December 1988 on a Community system for the rapid exchange of information on dangers arising from the use of consumer products[3] should therefore be incorporated into this Directive and the above Decision should be repealed; whereas it is also advisable for this Directive to take over the detailed procedures adopted under the above Decision and to give the Commission, assisted by a committee, power to adapt them;

Notes
[1] OJ No. L109, 26.4.1983, p. 8
[2] OJ No. L183, 14.7.1988, p. 34.
[3] OJ No. L17, 21.1.1989, p. 51.

Whereas, moreover, equivalent notification procedures already exist for pharmaceuticals, which come under Directives 75/319/EEC[4] and 81/851/EEC[5] concerning animal diseases referred to in Directive 82/894/EEC[6] for products of animal origin covered by Directive 89/662/EEC[7] and in the form of the system for the rapid exchange of information in radiological emergencies under Decision 87/600/Euratom;[8]

Whereas it is primarily for Member States, in compliance with the Treaty and in particular with Articles 30 to 36 thereof, to take appropriate measures with regard to dangerous products located within their territory;

Whereas in such a situation the decision taken on a particular product could differ from one Member State to another; whereas such a difference may entail unacceptable disparities in consumer protection and constitute a barrier to intra-Community trade;

Whereas it may be necessary to cope with serious product-safety problems which affect or could affect, in the immediate future, all or a large part of the Community and which, in view of the nature of the safety problem posed by the product cannot be dealt with effectively in a manner commensurate with the urgency of the problem under the procedures laid down in the specific rules of Community law applicable to the products or category of products in question;

Whereas it is therefore necessary to provide for an adequate mechanism allowing, in the last resort, for the adoption of measures applicable throughout the Community, in the form of a decision addressed to the Member States, in order to cope with emergency situations as mentioned above; whereas such a decision is not of direct application to economic operators and must be incorporated into a national instrument; whereas measures adopted under such a procedure can be no more than interim measures that have to be taken by the Commission assisted by a committee of representatives of the Member States; whereas, for reasons of cooperation with the Member States, it is appropriate to provide for a regulatory committee according to procedure III(b) of Decision 87/373/EEC;[9]

Whereas this Directive does not affect victims' rights within the meaning of Council Directive 85/374/EEC of 25 July 1985 on the approximation of the laws, regulations and administrative provisions of the Member States concerning liability for defective products;[10]

Whereas it is necessary that Member States provide for appropriate means of redress before the competent courts in respect of measures taken by the competent authorities which restrict the placing on the market of a product or require its withdrawal;

Whereas it is appropriate to consider, in the light of experience, possible adaptation of this Directive, particularly as regards extension of its scope and provisions on emergency situations and intervention at Community level;

Whereas, in addition, the adoption of measures concerning imported products with a view to preventing risks to the safety and health of persons must comply with the Community's international obligations,

Notes
[4] OJ No. L147, 9. 6. 1975, p. 13.
[5] OJ No. L317, 6. 11. 1981, p. 1.
[6] OJ No. L378, 31. 12. 1982, p. 58.
[7] OJ No. L395, 30. 12. 1989, p. 13.
[8] OJ No. L371, 30. 12. 1987, p. 76.
[9] OJ No. L197, 18.7.1987, p. 33.
[10] OJ No. L210, 7.8.1985, p. 29.

HAS ADOPTED THIS DIRECTIVE:

TITLE I   OBJECTIVE — SCOPE — DEFINITIONS

Article 1

1.   The purpose of the provisions of this Directive is to ensure that products placed on the market are safe.

2.   The provisions of this Directive shall apply in so far as there are no specific provisions in rules of Community law governing the safety of the products concerned. In particular, where specific rules of Community law contain provisions imposing safety requirements on the products which they govern, the provisions of Articles 2 to 4 of this Directive shall not, in any event, apply to those products. Where specific rules of Community law contain provisions governing only certain aspects of product safety or categories of risks for the products concerned, those are the provisions which shall apply to the products concerned with regard to the relevant safety aspects or risks.

Article 2

For the purposes of this Directive:

(a)   'product' shall mean any product intended for consumers or likely to be used by consumers, supplied whether for consideration or not in the course of a commercial activity and whether new, used or reconditioned. However, this Directive shall not apply to second-hand products supplied as antiques or as products to be repaired or reconditioned prior to being used, provided that the supplier clearly informs the person to whom he supplies the product to that effect;

(b)   'safe product' shall mean any product which, under normal or reasonably foreseeable conditions of use, including duration, does not present any risk or only the minimum risks compatible with the product's use, considered as acceptable and consistent with a high level of protection for the safety and health of persons, taking into account the following points in particular:

— the characteristics of the product, including its composition, packaging, instructions for assembly and maintenance,

— the effect on other products, where it is reasonably foreseeable that it will be used with other products,

— the presentation of the product, the labelling, any instructions for its use and disposal and any other indication or information provided by the producer,

— the categories of consumers at serious risk when using the product, in particular children.

The feasibility of obtaining higher levels of safety or the availability of other products presenting a lesser degree of risk shall not constitute grounds for considering a product to be 'unsafe' or 'dangerous';

(c)   'dangerous product' shall mean any product which does not meet the definition of 'safe product' according to point (b) hereof;

(d)   'producer' shall mean:

— the manufacturer of the product, when he is established in the Community, and any other person presenting himself as the manufacturer by affixing to the product his name, trade mark or other distinctive mark, or the person who reconditions the product,

—the manufacturer's representative, when the manufacturer is not established in the Community or, if there is no representative established in the Community, the importer of the product,

—other professionals in the supply chain, insofar as their activities may affect the safety properties of a product placed on the market.

(e) 'distributor' shall mean any professional in the supply chain whose activity does not affect the safety properties of a product.

TITLE II GENERAL SAFETY REQUIREMENT

Article 3

1. Producers shall be obliged to place only safe products on the market.

2. Within the limits of their respective activities, producers shall:

—provide consumers with the relevant information to enable them to assess the risks inherent in a product throughout the normal or reasonably foreseeable period of its use, where such risks are not immediately obvious without adequate warnings, and to take precautions against those risks.

Provision of such warnings does not, however, exempt any person from compliance with the other requirements laid down in this Directive,

—adopt measures commensurate with the characteristics of the products which they supply, to enable them to be informed of risks which these products might present and to take appropriate action including, if necessary, withdrawing the product in question from the market to avoid these risks.

The above measures shall for example include, whenever appropriate, marking of the products or product batches in such a way that they can be identified, sample testing of marketed products, investigating complaints made and keeping distributors informed of such monitoring.

3. Distributors shall be required to act with due care in order to help to ensure compliance with the general safety requirement, in particular by not supplying products which they know or should have presumed, on the basis of the information in their possession and as professionals, do not comply with this requirement. In particular, within the limits of their respective activities, they shall participate in monitoring the safety of products placed on the market, especially by passing on information on product risks and cooperating in the action taken to avoid these risks.

Article 4

1. Where there are no specific Community provisions governing the safety of the products in question, a product shall be deemed safe when it conforms to the specific rules of national law of the Member State in whose territory the product is in circulation, such rules being drawn up in conformity with the Treaty, and in particular Articles 30 and 36 thereof, and laying down the health and safety requirements which the product must satisfy in order to be marketed.

2. In the absence of specific rules as referred to in paragraph 1, the conformity of a product to the general safety requirement shall be assessed having regard to voluntary national standards giving effect to a European standard or, where they exist, to Community technical specifications or, failing these, to standards drawn up in the Member State in which the product is in circulation, or to the codes of good practice in respect of health and safety in the sector concerned or to the state of the art and technology and to the safety which consumers may reasonably expect.

Article 9

If the Commission becomes aware, through notification given by the Member States or through information provided by them, in particular under Article 7 or Article 8, of the existence of a serious and immediate risk from a product to the health and safety of consumers in various Member States and if:

(a) one or more Member States have adopted measures entailing restrictions on the marketing of the product or requiring its withdrawal from the market, such as those provided for in Article 6(1)(d) to (h);

(b) Member States differ on the adoption of measures to deal with the risk in question;

(c) the risk cannot be dealt with, in view of the nature of the safety issue posed by the product and in a manner compatible with the urgency of the case, under the other procedures laid down by the specific Community legislation applicable to the product or category of products concerned; and

(d) the risk can be eliminated effectively only by adopting appropriate measures applicable at Community level, in order to ensure the protection of the health and safety of consumers and the proper functioning of the common market, the Commission, after consulting the Member States and at the request of at least one of them, may adopt a decision, in accordance with the procedure laid down in Article 11, requiring Member States to take temporary measures from among those listed in Article 6(1)(d) to (h).

Article 10

1. The Commission shall be assisted by a Committee on Product Safety Emergencies, hereinafter referred to as 'the Committee', composed of the representatives of the Member States and chaired by a representative of the Commission.

2. Without prejudice to Article 9(c), there shall be close cooperation between the Committee referred to in paragraph 1 and the other Committees established by specific rules of Community law to assist the Commission as regards the health and safety aspects of the product concerned.

Article 11

1. The Commission representative shall submit to the Committee a draft of the measures to be taken. The Committee, having verified that the conditions listed in Article 9 are fulfilled, shall deliver its opinion on the draft within a time limit which the Chairman may lay down according to the urgency of the matter but which may not exceed one month. The opinion shall be delivered by the majority laid down in Article 148(2) of the Treaty for adoption of decisions by the Council on a proposal from the Commission. The votes of the representatives of the Member States within the Committee shall be weighted in the manner set out in that Article. The Chairman shall not vote.

The Commission shall adopt the measures in question, if they are in accordance with the opinion of the Committee. If the measures proposed are not in accordance with the Committee's opinion, or in the absence of an opinion, the Commission shall forthwith submit to the Council a proposal regarding the measures to be taken. The Council shall act by a qualified majority.

If the Council has not acted within 15 days of the date on which the proposal was submitted to it, the measures proposed shall be adopted by the Commission unless the Council has decided against them by a simple majority.

2. Any measure adopted under this procedure shall be valid for no longer than three months. That period may be prolonged under the same procedure.

3. Member States shall take all necessary measures to implement the decisions adopted under this procedure within less than 10 days.

4. The competent authorities of the Member States responsible for carrying out measures adopted under this procedure shall, within one month, give the parties concerned an opportunity to submit their views and shall inform the Commission accordingly.

Article 12
The Member States and the Commission shall take the steps necessary to ensure that their officials and agents are required not to disclose information obtained for the purposes of this Directive which, by its nature, is covered by professional secrecy, except for information relating to the safety properties of a given product which must be made public if circumstances so require, in order to protect the health and safety of persons.

TITLE VI   MISCELLANEOUS AND FINAL PROVISIONS

Article 13
This Directive shall be without prejudice to Directive 85/374/EEC.

Article 14
1. Any decision adopted under this Directive and involving restrictions on the placing of a product on the market, or requiring its withdrawal from the market, must state the appropriate reasons on which it is based. It shall be notified as soon as possible to the party concerned and shall indicate the remedies available under the provisions in force in the Member State in question and the time limits applying to such remedies.

The parties concerned shall, whenever feasible, be given an opportunity to submit their views before the adoption of the measure. If this has not been done in advance because of the urgency of the measures to be taken, such opportunity shall be given in due course after the measure has been implemented.

Measures requiring the withdrawal of a product from the market shall take into consideration the need to encourage distributors, users and consumers to contribute to the implementation of such measures.

2. Member States shall ensure that any measure taken by the competent authorities involving restrictions on the placing of a product on the market or requiring its withdrawal from the market can be challenged before the competent courts.

3. Any decision taken by virtue of this Directive and involving restrictions on the placing of a product on the market or requiring its withdrawal from the market shall be entirely without prejudice to assessment of the liability of the party concerned, in the light of the national criminal law applying in the case in question.

Article 15
Every two years following the date of adoption, the Commission shall submit a report on the implementation of this Directive to the European Parliament and the Council.

Article 16

Four years from the date referred to in Article 17(1), on the basis of a Commission report on the experience acquired, together with appropriate proposals, the Council shall decide whether to adjust this Directive, in particular with a view to extending its scope as laid down in Article 1(1) and Article 2(a), and whether the provisions of Title V should be amended.

Article 17

1. Member States shall adopt the laws, regulations and administrative provisions necessary to comply with this Directive by 29 June 1994 at the latest. They shall forthwith inform the Commission thereof. The provisions adopted shall apply with effect from 29 June 1994.

2. When these measures are adopted by the Member States, they shall contain a reference to this Directive or be accompanied by such a reference on the occasion of their official publication. The methods of making such a reference shall be laid down by the Member States.

3. Member States shall communicate to the Commission the text of the provisions of national law which they adopt in the area covered by this Directive.

Article 18

Decision 89/45/EEC is hereby repealed on the date referred to in Article 17(1).

Article 19

This Directive is addressed to the Member States.

Done at Luxembourg, 29 June 1992.
For the Council
The President
Carlos BORREGO

ANNEX
DETAILED PROCEDURES FOR THE APPLICATION OF THE COMMUNITY SYSTEM FOR THE RAPID EXCHANGE OF INFORMATION PROVIDED FOR IN ARTICLE 8

1. The system covers products placed on the market as defined in Article 2(a) of this Directive.

Pharmaceuticals, which come under Directive 75/319/EEC and 81/851/EEC, and animals, to which Directive 82/894/EEC applies and products of animal origin, as far as they are covered by Directive 89/662/EEC, and the system for radiological emergencies which covers widespread contamination of products (Decision 87/600/Euratom), are excluded, since they are covered by equivalent notification procedures.

2. The system is essentially aimed at a rapid exchange of information in the event of a serious and immediate risk to the health and safety of consumers. It is impossible to lay down specific criteria as to what, precisely, constitutes an immediate and serious risk; in this regard, the national authorities will therefore judge each individual case on its merits. It should be noted that, as Article 8 of this Directive relates to immediate threats posed by a product to consumers, products involving possible long-term risks, which call for a study of possible technical changes by means of directives or standards are not concerned.

3.   As soon as a serious and immediate risk is detected, the national authority shall consult, insofar as possible and appropriate, the producer or distributor of the product concerned. Their point of view and the details which they supply may be useful both to the administrations of the Member States and to the Commission in determining what action should be taken to ensure that the consumer is protected with a minimum of commercial disruption. To these ends the Member States should endeavour to obtain the maximum of information on the products and the nature of the danger, without compromising the need for rapidity.

4.   As soon as a Member State has detected a serious and immediate risk, the effects of which extend or could extend beyond its territory, and measures have been taken or decided on, it shall immediately inform the Commission. The Member State shall indicate that it is notifying the Commission under Article 8 of this Directive. All available details shall be given, in particular on:

(a)   information to identify the product;

(b)   the danger involved, including the results of any tests/analyses which are relevant to assessing the level of risk;

(c)   the nature of the measures taken or decided on;

(d)   information on supply chains where such information is possible.

Such information must be transmitted in writing, preferably by telex or fax, but may be preceded by a telephone call to the Commission. It should be remembered that the speed with which the information is communicated is crucial.

5.   Without prejudice to point 4, Member States may, where appropriate, pass information to the Commission at the stage preceding the decision on the measures to be taken. Immediate contact, as soon as a risk is discovered or suspected, can in fact facilitate preventive action.

6.   If the Member State considers certain information to be confidential, it should specify this and justify its request for confidentiality, bearing in mind that the need to take effective measures to protect consumers normally outweighs considerations of confidentiality. It should also be remembered that precautions are taken in all cases, both by the Commission and by the members of the network responsible in the various Member States, to avoid any unnecessary disclosure of information likely to harm the reputation of a product or series of products.

7.   The Commission shall verify the conformity of the information received with Article 8 of this Directive, contact the notifying country, if necessary, and forward the information immediately by telex or fax to the relevant authorities in the other Member States with a copy to each permanent representative; these authorities may, at the same time as the transmission of the telex, be contacted by telephone. The Commission may also contact the Member State presumed to be the country or origin of the product to carry out the necessary verifications.

8.   At the same time the Commission, when it considers it to be necessary, and in order to supplement the information received, can in exceptional circumstances institute an investigation of its own motion and/or convene the Committee on Emergencies provided for in Article 10(1) of this Directive.

In the case of such an investigation Member States shall supply the Commission with the requested information to the best of their ability.

9.   The other Member States are requested, wherever possible, to inform the Commission without delay of the following:

(a)   whether the product has been marketed in its territory;

(b)   supplementary information it has obtained on the danger involved, including the results of any tests/analyses carried out to assess the level of risk, and in any case they must inform the Commission as soon as possible of the following:

(c)   the measures taken or decided on, of the type mentioned in Article 8(1) of this Directive;

(d)   when the product mentioned in this information has been found within their territory but no measures have been taken or decided on and the reasons why no measures are to be taken.

10.   The Commission may, in the light of the evolution of a case and the information received from Member States under point 9 above, convene the above Committee on Emergencies in order to exchange views on the results obtained and to evaluate the measures taken. The Committee on Emergencies may also be convened at the request of a representative of a Member State.

11.   The Commission shall, by means of its internal coordination procedures, endeavour to:

(a)   avoid unnecessary duplication in dealing with notifications;

(b)   make full use of the expertise available within the Commission;

(c)   keep the other services concerned fully informed;

(d)   ensure that discussions in the various relevant committees are held in accordance with Article 10 of this Directive.

12.   When a Member State intends, apart from any specific measures taken because of serious and immediate risks, to modify its legislation by adopting technical specifications, the latter must be notified to the Commission at the draft stage, in accordance with Directive 83/189/EEC, if necessary, quoting the urgent reasons set out in Article 9(3) of that Directive.

13.   To allow it to have an overview of the situation, the Committee on Emergencies shall be periodically informed of all the notifications received and of the follow-up. With regard to points 8 and 10 above, and in those cases which fall within the scope of procedures and/or committees provided for by Community legislation governing specific products or product sectors, those committees shall be involved. In cases where the Committee on Emergencies is not involved and no provisions are made under 11(d), the contact points shall be informed of any exchange of views within other committees.

14.   At present there are two networks of contact points: the food products network and the non-food products network. The list of contact points and officials responsible for the networks with telephone, telex and fax numbers and addresses is confidential and distributed to the members of the network only. This list enables contact to be established with the Commission and between Member States in order to facilitate clarification of points of detail. When such contacts between Member States give rise to new information of general interest, the Member States which initiated the bilateral contact shall inform the Commission. Only information received or confirmed through contact points in Member States may be considered as received through the rapid exchange of information procedure.

Every year the Commission shall carry out a review of the effectiveness of the network, of any necessary improvements and of the progress made in the communications technology between the authorities responsible for its operation.

COUNCIL DIRECTIVE 93/13/EEC OF 5 APRIL 1993 ON UNFAIR TERMS IN CONSUMER CONTRACTS
[OJ 1993, No. L95]

THE COUNCIL OF THE EUROPEAN COMMUNITIES,

Having regard to the Treaty establishing the European Economic Community, and in particular Article 100A thereof,

Having regard to the proposal from the Commission,[1]

In cooperation with the European Parliament,[2]

Having regard to the opinion of the Economic and Social Committee,[3]

Whereas it is necessary to adopt measures with the aim of progressively establishing the internal market before 31 December 1992; whereas the internal market comprises an area without internal frontiers in which goods, persons, services and capital move freely;

Whereas the laws of Member States relating to the terms of contract between the seller of goods or supplier of services, on the one hand, and the consumer of them, on the other hand, show many disparities, with the result that the national markets for the sale of goods and services to consumers differ from each other and that distortions of competition may arise amongst the sellers and suppliers, notably when they sell and supply in other Member States;

Whereas, in particular, the laws of Member States relating to unfair terms in consumer contracts show marked divergences;

Whereas it is the responsibility of the Member States to ensure that contracts concluded with consumers do not contain unfair terms;

Whereas, generally speaking, consumers do not know the rules of law which, in Member States other than their own, govern contracts for the sale of goods or services; whereas this lack of awareness may deter them from direct transactions for the purchase of goods or services in another Member State;

Whereas, in order to facilitate the establishment of the internal market and to safeguard the citizen in his role as consumer when acquiring goods and services under contracts which are governed by the laws of Member States other than his own, it is essential to remove unfair terms from those contracts;

Whereas sellers of goods and suppliers of services will thereby be helped in their task of selling goods and supplying services, both at home and throughout the internal market; whereas competition will thus be stimulated, so contributing to increased choice for Community citizens as consumers;

Whereas the two Community programmes for a consumer protection and information policy[4] underlined the importance of safeguarding consumers in the matter of unfair terms of contract; whereas this protection ought to be

Notes

[1] OJ No. C73, 24.3.1992, p. 7.

[2] OJ No. C326, 16.12.1991, p. 108 and OJ No. C21, 25.1.1993.

[3] OJ No. C159, 17.6.1991, p. 34.

[4] OJ No. C92, 25.4.1975, p. 1 and OJ No. C133, 3.6.1981, p. 1.

provided by laws and regulations which are either harmonised at Community level or adopted directly at that level;

Whereas in accordance with the principle laid down under the heading 'Protection of the economic interests of the consumers', as stated in those programmes: 'acquirers of goods and services should be protected against the abuse of power by the seller or supplier, in particular against one-sided standard contracts and the unfair exclusion of essential rights in contracts';

Whereas more effective protection of the consumer can be achieved by adopting uniform rules of law in the matter of unfair terms; whereas those rules should apply to all contracts concluded between sellers or suppliers and consumers; whereas as a result *inter alia* contracts relating to employment, contracts relating to succession rights, contracts relating to rights under family law and contracts relating to the incorporation and organisation of companies or partnership agreements must be excluded from this Directive;

Whereas the consumer must receive equal protection under contracts concluded by word of mouth and written contracts regardless, in the latter case, of whether the terms of the contract are contained in one or more documents;

Whereas, however, as they now stand, national laws allow only partial harmonisation to be envisaged; whereas, in particular, only contractual terms which have not been individually negotiated are coverd by this Directive; whereas Member States should have the option, with due regard for the Treaty, to afford consumers a higher level of protection through national provisions that are more stringent than those of this Directive;

Whereas the statutory or regulatory provisions of the Member States which directly or indirectly determine the terms of consumer contracts are presumed not to contain unfair terms; whereas, therefore, it does not appear to be necessary to subject the terms which reflect mandatory statutory or regulatory provisions and the principles or provisions of international conventions to which the Member States or the Community are party; whereas in that respect the wording 'mandatory statutory or regulatory provisions' in Article 1(2) also covers rules which, according to the law, shall apply between the contracting parties provided that no other arrangements have been established;

Whereas Member States must however ensure that unfair terms are not included, particularly because this Directive also applies to trades, business or professions of a public nature;

Whereas it is necessary to fix in a general way the criteria for assessing the unfair character of contract terms;

Whereas the assessment, according to the general criteria chosen, of the unfair character of terms, in particular in sale or supply activities of a public nature providing collective services which take account of solidarity among users, must be supplemented by a means of making an overall evaluation of the different interests involved; whereas this constitutes the requirement of good faith; whereas, in making an assessment of good faith, particular regard shall be had to the strength of the bargaining positions of the parties, whether the consumer had an inducement to agree to the term and whether the goods or services were sold or supplied to the special order of the consumer; whereas the requirement of good faith may be satisfied by the seller or supplier where he deals fairly and equitably with the other party whose legitimate interests he has to take into account;

Whereas, for the purposes of this Directive, the annexed lists of terms can be of indicative value only and, because of the cause of the minimal character of the Directive, the scope of these terms may be the subject of amplification or more restrictive editing by the Member States in their national laws;

Whereas the nature of goods or services should have an influence on assessing the unfairness of contractual terms;

Whereas, for the purposes of this Directive, assessment of unfair character shall not be made of terms which describe the main subject matter of the contract nor the quality/price ratio of the goods or services supplied; whereas the main subject matter of the contract and the price/quality ratio may nevertheless be taken into account in assessing the fairness of other terms; whereas it follows, *inter alia*, that in insurance contracts, the terms which clearly define or circumscribe the insured risk and the insurer's liability shall not be subject to such assessment since these restrictions are taken into account in calculating the premium paid by the consumer;

Whereas contracts should be drafted in plain, intelligible language, the consumer should actually be given an opportunity to examine all the terms and, if in doubt, the interpretation most favourable to the consumer should prevail;

Whereas Member States should ensure that unfair terms are not used in contracts concluded with consumers by a seller or supplier and that if, nevertheless, such terms are so used, they will not bind the consumer, and the contract will continue to bind the parties upon those terms if it is capable of continuing in existence without the unfair provisions;

Whereas there is a risk that, in certain cases, the consumer may be deprived of protection under this Directive by designating the law of a non-Member country as the law applicable to the contract; whereas provisions should therefore be included in this Directive designed to avert this risk;

Whereas persons or organisations, if regarded under the law of a Member State as having a legitimate interest in the matter, must have facilities for initiating proceedings concerning terms of contract drawn up for general use in contracts concluded with consumers, and in particular unfair terms, either before a court or before an administrative authority competent to decide upon complaints or to initiate appropriate legal proceedings; whereas this possibility does not, however, entail prior verification of the general conditions obtaining in individual economic sectors;

Whereas the courts or administrative authorities of the Member States must have at their disposal adequate and effective means of preventing the continued application of unfair terms in consumer contracts,

HAS ADOPTED THIS DIRECTIVE

Article 1

1.   The purpose of this Directive is to approximate the laws, regulations and administrative provisions of the Member States relating to unfair terms in contracts concluded between a seller or supplier and a consumer.

2.   The contractual terms which reflect mandatory statutory or regulatory provisions and the provisions or principles of international conventions to which the Member States or the Community are party, particularly in the transport area, shall not be subject to the provisions of this Directive.

Article 2

For the purposes of this Directive:

(a)   'unfair terms' means the contractual terms defined in Article 3;

(b) 'consumer' means any natural person who, in contracts covered by this Directive, is acting for purposes which are outside his trade, business or profession;

(c) 'seller or supplier' means any natural or legal person who, in contracts covered by this Directive, is acting for purposes relating to his trade, business or profession, whether publicly owned or privately owned.

Article 3

1.   A contractual term which has not been individually negotiated shall be regarded as unfair if, contrary to the requirement of good faith, it causes a significant imbalance in the parties' rights and obligations arising under the contract, to the detriment of the consumer.

2.   A term shall always be regarded as not individually negotiated where it has been drafted in advance and the consumer has therefore not been able to influence the substance of the term, particularly in the context of a pre-formulated standard contract.

The fact that certain aspects of a term or one specific term have been individually negotiated shall not exclude the application of this Article to the rest of a contract if an overall assessment of the contract indicates that it is nevertheless a pre-formulated standard contract.

Where any seller or supplier claims that a standard term has been individually negotiated, the burden of proof in this respect shall be incumbent on him.

3.   The Annex shall contain an indicative and non-exhaustive list of the terms which may be regarded as unfair.

Article 4

1.   Without prejudice to Article 7, the unfairness of a contractual term shall be assessed, taking into account the nature of the goods or services for which the contract was concluded and by referring, at the time of conclusion of the contract, to all the circumstances attending the conclusion of the contract and to all the other terms of the contract or of another contract on which it is dependent.

2.   Assessment of the unfair nature of the terms shall relate neither to the definition of the main subject matter of the contract nor to the adequacy of the price and remuneration, on the one hand, as against the services or goods supplied in exchange, on the other, in so far as these terms are in plain intelligible language.

Article 5

In the case of contracts where all or certain terms offered to the consumer are in writing, these terms must always be drafted in plain, intelligible language. Where there is doubt about the meaning of a term, the interpretation most favourable to the consumer shall prevail. This rule on interpretation shall not apply in the context of the procedures laid down in Article 7(2).

Article 6

1.   Member States shall lay down the unfair terms used in a contract concluded with a consumer by a seller or supplier shall, as provided for under their national law, not be binding on the consumer and that the contract shall continue to bind the parties upon those terms if it is capable of continuing in existence without the unfair terms.

2.   Member States shall take the necessary measures to ensure that the consumer does not lose the protection granted by this Directive by virtue of the choice of the law of a non–Member country as the law applicable to the contract if the latter has a close connection with the territory of the Member States.

Article 7

1.   Member States shall ensure that, in the interests of consumers and of competitors, adequate and effective means exist to prevent the continued use of unfair terms in contracts concluded with consumers by sellers or suppliers.

2.   The means referred to in paragraph 1 shall include provisions whereby persons or organisations, having a legitimate interest under national law in protecting consumers, may take action according to the national law concerned before the courts or before competent administrative bodies for a decision as to whether contractual terms drawn up for general use are unfair, so that they can apply appropriate and effective means to prevent the continued use of such terms.

3.   With due regard for national laws, the legal remedies referred to in paragraph 2 may be directed separately or jointly against a number of sellers or suppliers from the same economic sector or their asociations which use or recommend the use of the same general contractual terms or similar terms.

Article 8

Member States may adopt or retain the most stringent provisions compatible with the Treaty in the area covered by this Directive, to ensure a maximum degree of protection for the consumer.

Article 9

The Commission shall present a report to the European Parliament and to the Council concerning the application of this Directive five years at the latest after the date in Article 10(1).

Article 10

1.   Member States shall bring into force the laws, regulations and administrative provisions necessary to comply with this Directive no later than 31 December 1994. They shall forthwith inform the Commission thereof.
These provisions shall be applicable to all contracts concluded after 31 December 1994.

2.   When Member States adopt these measures, they shall contain a reference to this Directive or shall be accompanied by such reference on the occasion of their official publication. The methods of making such a reference shall be laid down by the Member States.

3.   Member States shall communicate the main provisions of national law which they adopt in the field covered by this Directive to the Commission.

Article 11

This Directive is addressed to the Member States.

Done at Luxembourg, 5 April 1993.
For the Council,
The President
N. HELVEG PETERSEN

ANNEX   TERMS REFERRED TO IN ARTICLE 3(3)

1.   Terms which have the object or effect of:

(a)   excluding or limiting the legal liability of a seller or supplier in the event of the death of a consumer or personal injury to the latter resulting from an act or omission of that seller or supplier;

(b)   inappropriately excluding or limiting the legal rights of the consumer *vis-à-vis* the seller or supplier or another party in the event of total or partial non-performance or inadequate performance by the seller or supplier of any of the contractual obligations, including the option of offsetting a debt owed to the seller or supplier against any claim which the consumer may have against him;

(c)   making an agreement binding on the consumer whereas provision of services by the seller or supplier is subject to a condition whose realisation depends on his own will alone;

(d)   permitting the seller or supplier to retain sums paid by the consumer where the latter decides not to conclude or perform the contract, without providing for the consumer to receive compensation of an equivalent amount from the seller or supplier where the latter is the party cancelling the contract;

(e)   requiring any consumer who fails to fulfil his obligation to pay a disproportionately high sum in compensation;

(f)   authorising the seller or supplier to dissolve the contract on a discretionary basis where the same facility is not granted to the consumer, or permitting the seller or supplier to retain the sums paid for services not yet supplied by him where it is the seller or supplier himself who dissolves the contract;

(g)   enabling the seller or supplier to terminate a contract of indeterminate duration without reasonable notice except where there are serious grounds for doing so;

(h)   automatically extending a contract of fixed duration where the consumer does not indicate otherwise, when the deadline fixed for the consumer to express this desire not to extend the contract is unreasonably early;

(i)   irrevocably binding the consumer to terms with which he had no real opportunity of becoming acquainted before the conclusion of the contract;

(j)   enabling the seller or supplier to alter the terms of the contract unilaterally without a valid reason which is specified in the contract;

(k)   enabling the seller or supplier to alter unilaterally without a valid reason any characteristics of the product or service to be provided;

(l)   providing for the price of goods to be determined at the time of delivery or allowing a seller of goods or supplier of services to increase their price without in both cases giving the consumer the corresponding right to cancel the contract if the final price is too high in relation to the price agreed when the contract was concluded;

(m)   giving the seller or supplier the right to determine whether the goods or services supplied are in conformity with the contract, or giving him the exclusive right to interpret any term of the contract;

(n)   limiting the seller's or supplier's obligation to respect commitments undertaken by his agents or making his commitments subject to compliance with a particular formality;

(o)   obliging the consumer to fulfil all his obligations where the seller or supplier does not perform his;

(p)   giving the seller or supplier the possibility of transferring his rights and obligations under the contract, where this may serve to reduce the guarantees for the consumer, without the latter's agreement;

(q)   excluding or hindering the consumer's right to take legal action or exercise any other legal remedy, particularly by requiring the consumer to take disputes exclusively to arbitration not covered by legal provisions, unduly restricting the evidence available to him or imposing on him a burden of proof which, according to the applicable law, should lie with another party to the contract.

2.   Scope of subparagraphs (g), (j) and (l)

(a)   Subparagraph (g) is without hindrance to terms by which a supplier of financial services reserves the right to terminate unilaterally a contract of indeterminate duration without notice where there is a valid reason, provided that the supplier is required to inform the other contracting party or parties thereof immediately.

(b)   Subparagraph (j) is without hindrance to terms under which a supplier of financial services reserves the right to alter the rate of interest payable by the consumer or due to the latter, or the amount of other charges for financial services without notice where there is a valid reason, provided that the supplier is required to inform the other contracting party or parties thereof at the earliest opportunity and that the latter are free to dissolve the contract immediately.

Subparagraph (j) is also without hindrance to terms under which a seller or supplier reserves the right to alter unilaterally the conditions of a contract of indeterminate duration, provided that he is required to inform the consumer with reasonable notice and that the consumer is free to dissolve the contract.

(c)   Subparagraphs (g), (j) and (l) do not apply to:

— transactions in transferable securities, financial instruments and other products or services where the price is linked to fluctuations in a stock exchange quotation or index or a financial market rate that the seller or supplier does not control;

— contracts for the purchase or sale of foreign currency, traveller's cheques or international money orders denominated in foreign currency;

(d)   Subparagraph (l) is without hindrance to price-indexation clauses, where lawful, provided that the method by which prices vary is explicitly described.

FINANCIAL SERVICES: BANKING AND FINANCE

COUNCIL DIRECTIVE 73/183/EEC OF 28 JUNE 1973 ON THE ABOLITION OF RESTRICTIONS ON FREEDOM OF ESTABLISHMENT AND FREEDOM TO PROVIDE SERVICES IN RESPECT OF SELF-EMPLOYED ACTIVITIES OF BANKS AND OTHER FINANCIAL INSTITUTIONS
[OJ 1973 L194/1]*

THE COUNCIL OF THE EUROPEAN COMMUNITIES,

Having regard to the Treaty establishing the European Economic Community, and in particular Article 54(2) and (3), Article 61(2) and Article 63(2) and (3) thereof;

Having regard to the general programme for the abolition of restrictions on freedom of establishment,[1] and in particular Title IV a thereof;

Having regard to the general programme for the abolition of restrictions on freedom to provide services,[2] and in particular title V C2(b) thereof;

Having regard to the proposal from the Commission;

Having regard to the opinion of the European Parliament;[3]

Having regard to the opinion of the Economic and Social Committee;[4]

Having regard to the opinion of the monetary committee;

Whereas, as regards banks and other financial institutions, the general programmes provide for the abolition, before the end of the second year of the second stage, of restrictions on freedom of establishment and freedom to provide services not linked with capital movements and the abolition, at the same rate as the liberalisation of capital movements, of restrictions on banking services linked with such capital movements;

Whereas, as regards services linked with capital movements, a series of closely specified activities should be liberalised in an initial stage, having regard to the opinion of the monetary committee;

Whereas the list of such activities will be supplemented, particularly on the basis of progress in liberalising capital movements;

Notes
*As corrected by OJ 1974 L17/22.
[1]OJ No. 2, 15.1.1962, p. 36/62.
[2]OJ No. 2, 15.1.1962, p. 32/62.
[3]OJ No. 201, 5.11.1966, p. 3472/66.
[4]OJ No. 224, 5.12.1966, p. 3799/66.

Whereas the provider of a service may, in order to provide his service, temporarily pursue his activity in the country in which the service is supplied under the same conditions as those applied by that country to its own nationals;

Whereas the activities of brokers pose particular problems because of the rules governing the taking-up and pursuit of such activity in the various countries;

Whereas the liberalisation of this activity should be the subject of a future Directive;

Whereas the activities of self-employed intermediaries in the sector of banks and other financial institutions is not covered by the Council Directive of 25 February 1964 relating to the achievement of freedom of establishment and the freedom to provide services in respect of the activities of intermediaries in commerce, industry and small craft industries;[1]

Whereas such activities should therefore be included in this Directive;

Whereas, however, in the present state of the various bodies of legislation, the activities of intermediaries moving to another member state in order to provide services there would pose problems difficult to resolve;

Whereas there should therefore be a further Directive on the liberalisation of the provision of services by such intermediaries;

Whereas, pending co-ordination, this Directive does not alter the provisions of the member states laid down by law, regulation or administrative action which, applicable without condition as to nationality, forbid natural persons and companies or firms constituted in certain forms to pursue any one of the activities covered by this Directive;

Whereas the general programme for the abolition of restrictions on freedom of establishment provides that restrictions on the right to join professional or trade organisations must be abolished where the professional activities of the person concerned necessarily involve the exercise of this right;

Whereas, although the provisions laid down by law, regulation or administrative action relating to the taking-up and pursuit of the activities covered by this Directive should be co-ordinated as soon as possible, restrictions can be abolished without prior or simultaneous reference to this co-ordination;

Whereas it should be guaranteed that there is joint examination of the problems which will face the authorities responsible in the community and the member states for implementing banking regulations, concerning supervision of the activities covered by this Directive and to this end close cooperation should be established between the Commission and the member states and among the latter;

Whereas measures that a member state might take in order to implement joint decisions taken in the framework of monetary cooperation between the member states do not constitute restrictions within the meaning of this Directive,

HAS ADOPTED THIS DIRECTIVE:

Note
[1] OJ No. 56. 4.4.1964, p. 869/64.

Article 1

Member states shall abolish, in respect of the natural persons and companies or firms covered by Title I of the general programmes for the abolition of restrictions on freedom of establishment and freedom to provide services (hereinafter called 'beneficiaries'), the restrictions referred to in Title III of those general programmes affecting the right to take up and pursue the activities specified in Article 2 of this Directive. As regards the provision of services linked with capital movements, this Directive shall only apply to the services listed in Annex I excluding those provided by the managers and trustees of unit trusts. The following services connected with securities and involving the transfer of the provider of the service to the country of the beneficiary shall not be liberalised:

— receipt of orders to buy or to sell,

— participation as intermediary in transfers outside the market and the recording of such transfers,

— information or advice given following a public offer,

— payment of coupons.

Article 2

This Directive shall apply to activities of self-employed persons falling within group 620 of Annex I of the general programme for the abolition of restrictions on freedom of establishment, as set out in Annex II to this Directive, except for the activity of brokers (category 4 of Annex II).

This Directive shall not apply to the provision of services, in connection with banks and other financial institutions, by self-employed intermediaries who move to a member state other than that in which they are established.

Article 3

1.   Member states shall in particular abolish the following restrictions:

(a)   those which prevent beneficiaries from establishing themselves or from providing services in the host country under the same conditions and with the same rights as nationals of that country;

(b)   those existing by reason of administrative practices which result in treatment being applied to beneficiaries that is discriminatory by comparison with that applied to nationals.

2.   The restrictions to be abolished shall include in particular those arising out of measures which prohibit or limit establishment or the provision of services by beneficiaries by the following means:

(a)   in Belgium:

— the obligation imposed by Article 10 of Arrete Royale No. 185 of 9 July 1935 for foreign banks belonging to private individuals or constituted in the form of a partnership to operate in Belgium with a capital of at least 10 million francs required for Belgian banks of the same type is only 2 million francs,

— the reciprocity requirement referred to in Article 8 of the provisions for the control of private savings banks, co-ordinated by the law of 23 June 1967, and in Article 8 of Arrete Royale no 43 of 15 December 1934, as regards private savings banks and financing companies respectively, and in Articles 38 and 44 of Arrete Royale No. 225 of 7 January 1936 as regards mortgage undertakings;

(b)   in Denmark:

— necessity for a special authorisation for foreign banks stipulated by Law No. 122 of 15 April 1930, amended by Laws No. 163 of 13 April 1938 and No. 134 of 29 May 1956,

— the nationality requirements demanded of members of the board of directors and managers of banks and branches located in Denmark, by Article 8(2) of the abovementioned Law,

— the nationality requirement demanded of members of the supervisory board, by Article 8(3) of the abovementioned Law,

— the nationality requirement demanded of the supervisory board and managers of savings banks and branch savings banks by Article 7(6) of Law No. 159 of 18 May 1937, in conjunction with Law No. 327 of 3 July 1950, which were amended by Article 18 of Law No. 286 of 18 June 1951, and by Law No. 343 of 23 December 1959;

(c) in France:

— the obligation to hold a carte d'identité de commerçant pour les étrangers, imposed by the Decret-loi of 12 November 1938 and the Decret of 2 February 1939, as amended by the Law of 8 October 1940,

— the nationality requirement for persons who carry out banking operations, direct, administer or manage a company or firm or an agency for a company or firm which carries out these operations, who sign, on behalf of a bank, with power of attorney, the papers relating to the said operations, laid down by Article 7 of the Law of 13 June 1941, as amended by Article 49 of Law No. 51-592 of 24 May 1951, and by Article 2 of the Decret of 28 May 1946,

— the nationality requirement laid down for the undertakings referred to in Articles 1 and 2 of the Law of 14 June 1941 by Articles 7 and 11 of the same Law which refer to the requirements laid down in banking matters,

— the nationality requirement laid down for auxiliaries of the banking professions, referred to in Article 13 of the Law of 14 June 1941, as amended by the Ordonnance of 16 October 1958,

— the nationality requirement laid down for démarcheurs en valeurs mobilières by Article 8 of the Law no 72-6, 3 January 1972,

— the nationality requirement laid down for auxiliaries of the stock market professions referred to in Article 5 of Law no 72-1128 of 21 December 1972,

— the nationality requirement laid down by Article 11 of Ordonnance no 45-2710 of 2 November 1945 for the Chairman of the board of directors, the managing director and at least two-thirds of the board of any investment Company,

— the registration of foreign banks on a special list, referred to in Article 15 of the Law of 13 June 1941;

(d) in Ireland:

— the requirement to be constituted in Ireland for any company which requests approval for access to banking activity and stipulated by the instructions of the central bank by virtue of the powers conferred upon it by Section 9 of the Central Bank Act, 1971 (No. 24 of 1971), and published in the autumn 1972 number of the 'quarterly bulletin' of the said bank,

— the nationality requirement laid down for the majority of the members to the board of directors, stipulated by the same instructions as above,

— the nationality requirement and, for companies, the requirement that they be Irish-owned, imposed by Section 6(3) of the Moneylenders Act, 1933 (No. 36 of 1933), on those who intend to become moneylenders;

— the obligation to be constituted in Ireland required of any company which intends to exercise the activity of manager and trustee of a unit trust, stipulated by Article 3(1)(b) and (c) of the Unit Trusts Act, 1972 (No. 23 of 1972);

(e) in Italy:

— the reciprocity requirement, referred to in Article 2 of regio decreto no 1620 of 4 September 1919 concerning banks, and the discriminatory

requirements regarding foreigners, which are imposed individually by ministerial Decree when the said Article is implemented;

(f)   in the Grand Duchy of Luxembourg:

— the limited duration of authorisations granted to foreigners, laid down
in Article 21 of the Law of 2 June 1962;

(g)   in the Netherlands:

— the nationality requirement for members of the 'vereniging voor den
effectenhandel te Amsterdam', the 'vereniging van effectenhandelaren te
Rotterdam' and the 'bond voor de geld — en effectenhandel in de provincie te'
S-gravenhage' laid down by their statutes, approved by the ministerial
authorities;

(h)   in the United Kingdom:

— the obligation to be constituted in the United Kingdom imposed on any
company which intends to exercise the activity of manager and trustee of a unit
trust, stipulated by Article 17(1)(a), of title 45 of the law of 23 July 1958,
known as the 'Prevention of Fraud (Investments) Act', and by Article 15(1)(a),
of title 9 of the law of 28 May 1940, known as the 'Prevention of Fraud
(Investments) Act (Northern Ireland)'.

Article 4

1.   Member states shall ensure that beneficiaries have the right to join
professional or trade organisations under the same conditions and with the
same rights and obligations as their own nationals.

2.   The right to join professional or trade organisations shall, in the case of
establishment, entail eligibility for election or appointment to high office in
such organisations. However, such posts may be reserved for nationals where,
in pursuance of any provision laid down by law or regulation, the organization
concerned is involved in the exercise of official authority.

3.   In the Grand Duchy of Luxembourg, membership of the chambre de
commerce shall not give beneficiaries the right to take part in the election of the
administrative organs of that chamber.

Article 5

1.   Where a member state requires of its own nationals, who wish to pursue
one of the activities referred to in Article 2, either an extract from the 'judicial
records' or the production of a specific document, it shall accept, in respect of
nationals of other member states, the production of the document required for
the same purpose in the member state of origin or the state from which the
foreign national comes or, failing this, an equivalent document issued by a
competent judicial or administrative authority in the state of origin or in the
state from which the foreign national comes.

2.   Where a member state takes other information into account in respect
of its own nationals, account may also be taken of facts other than those
which may appear in the documents referred to in paragraph 1 if they can
be substantiated and if they show that the person concerned does not fulfil
all the requirements as to good repute necessary in order to pursue his
activity. Member states shall accord to certificates issued by the competent
judicial or administrative authorities of the country of origin or country
from which the foreign national comes and relating to the existence or
non-existence of certain facts the same recognition as they accord to certificates
issued by their own authorities.

3.   Where a member state requires of its own nationals wishing to take up or pursue any activity referred to in Article 2 proof of no previous bankruptcy, that state shall accept, in respect of nationals of other member states, the production of the certificate usually issued for this purpose by the authorities of the member state of origin or country from which the foreign national comes.

4.   Where the country of origin or the country from which the foreign national comes does not issue one of the documents referred to in paragraphs 1 and 3, such proof may be replaced by a declaration on oath — or, in states where there is no provision for declaration on oath, by a solemn declaration — made by the person concerned before a competent judicial or administrative authority, or, where appropriate, a notary, in the country from which the person comes; such authority or notary will issue a certificate attesting the authority of the declaration on oath or solemn declaration. A declaration in respect of no previous bankruptcy may also be made before a competent professional or trade body in the said country.

5.   Documents issued in accordance with paragraphs 1, 2 and 3 may not be produced more than three months after their date of issue.

6.   Member states shall, within the time limit laid down in Article 8, designate the authorities and bodies competent to issue these documents and shall forthwith inform the other member states and the Commission thereof.

Article 6
Pending co-ordination of the provisions laid down by law, regulation or administrative action relating to legal protection of the title 'bank', 'banker', 'savings bank' or any other equivalent term, unestablished foreign undertakings may provide services under names including such words provided such names are their original ones and that such undertakings leave no doubt as to their status under the national law to which they are subject. To this end, member states may require prior registration on a special list of unestablished foreign providers of services. Such registration may be subject to production of a certificate issued by the authority of the country of origin specifying the status of the undertaking in question under the national legislation applicable.

For public information, the competent authority may publish the list and require foreign providers of services to inform their clients of their legal status and the chief characteristics of and facts about their activity and their financial position.

Article 7
The Commission and the representatives of the authorities responsible in the member states for the supervision of banks and other financial institutions shall meet regularly so that they may facilitate, for the purpose of implementing the Directive, the solution of problems which the authorities might face regarding supervision of the activities covered by this Directive, and shall ensure all appropriate cooperation among themselves within the limits of their respective powers.

Article 8
Member states shall adopt the measures necessary to comply with this Directive within 18 months of its notification and shall forthwith inform the Commission thereof. However, as regards the abolition of the restriction referred to in Article 3(2)(g), the Netherlands shall be allowed a period of four years as from the date of the said notification.

Article 9

This Directive is addressed to the member states.

Done at Luxembourg, 28 June 1973.
For the Council,
The President,
W. de CLERCQ.

ANNEX I

Banking services linked with the capital movements referred to in lists A and B in Annex I to the first Directive of 11 May 1960, as supplemented and amended by the Second Directive of 18 December 1962[1]

List A   Direct investments
— commercial and financial information (soliciting custom, information on solvency of client, statistics, forwarding of accountancy data)
— assistance and representation before the (administrative and judicial) authorities and other competent bodies
— advice and assistance to undertakings with a view to their possible merger (seeking of foreign partners, expert advice etc.)
— aid in large-scale share buying (particularly for take-over bids) in order to obtain a controlling interest in an undertaking (stock exchange formalities, capital financial assessment, etc.)
— physical exchange of securities
— custody of securities
— delivery of securities allotted to the shareholders of a company.
Liquidation of direct investments
— commercial and financial information (soliciting custom etc.)
— assistance and representation before the (administrative and judicial) authorities and other competent bodies
— advice and assistance to undertakings with a view to facilitating liquidation operations
— aid in the large-scale of shares
— physical exchange of securities
— custody of securities. Investments in real estate and liquidation thereof
— commercial and financial information
— assistance and representation before the (administrative and judicial) authorities and other competent bodies
— advice and assistance concerning investments and the liquidation thereof
— administration of estates (assistance and representation in connection with the upkeep of the property, letting, etc.)
— assistance for the building-up and possible liquidation of sureties and guarantees of all kinds not issued by banks.
Personal capital movements
— estate management on the occasion of succession (payment of taxes, search for missing person, etc.). The granting and repayment of short-term and medium-term credits in respect of commercial transactions or provision of services in which a resident is participating

Note
[1]The headings are defined in the explanatory notes annexed to the first Directive for the implementation of Article 67. These definitions have been adopted in this table.

— commercial and financial information (soliciting custom, etc..)

— assistance and representation before the (administrative and judicial) authorities and other competent bodies

— advice on the financial management of an undertaking

— recovery of claims

— collection of bills

— domiciling of bills

— management of documentary credits

— assistance for the building-up and possible liquidation of sureties and guarantees of all kinds not issued by banks

— blocking of cash, bonds or securities belonging to a client and guaranteeing his obligation towards a third party

— canvassing on behalf of third parties

— services in connection with factoring operations.

Sureties, other guarantees and rights of pledge and transfers connected with them (sureties and guarantees issued by banks)

Death duties

— tax information,

— tax deposits.

Other capital transactions in list A from a banking point of view these other transactions only involve transfers.

List B   Operations in securities dealt in on a stock exchange excluding units of unit trusts

— receipt of orders to buy and sell

— assistance in the issue of bearer certificates representing securities previously issued and dealt in on a stock exchange

— servicing of securities (stamping, renewal of coupons, exchange, renewal, regrouping, splitting up, destruction)

— financial services (payment of coupons, redemption of securities, aid in exercising allotment and subscription rights, etc.)

— financial information (current information, analyses, etc.)

— advice on investments in stocks and shares dealt in on a stock exchange

— management of a portfolio of securities dealt in on a stock exchange[1]

— acceptance and implementation of powers of attorney for exercising the rights of holders of securities dealt in on a stock exchange (particularly representation at shareholders' meetings and in court)

— custody of securities

— conversion of securities

— assistance for entry on the official list of securities assigned to the holders of securities dealt in on a stock exchange

— canvassing on behalf of third parties in connection with securities dealt in on a stock exchange

— search for another party with a view to buying or selling securities dealt in on a stock exchange

— acting as a clearing house. The services listed in this Annex are not liberalised if they relate to capital movements other than those in lists A and B. The headings underlined correspond to those in lists A and B of the Directives on the capital movements in question.

Note
[1]These services concern both private and corporate investors.

ANNEX II

Regrouped headings of ISIC group 620[1] referred to in Article 2
Banks and other financial institutions such as:

Category 1: Banks
Banks
Merchant banks
Discounting banks

Category 2: savings and loan undertakings
Instalment sales finance undertakings
Retail sales finance undertakings
Commodity sales finance undertakings
Building and loan associations
Real estate credit agencies
Urban mortgage undertakings
Farm mortgage undertakings
Mortgage guarantee undertakings
Credit undertakings
Short-term-credit undertakings
Agricultural loan institutions
Commercial credit undertakings
Industrial credit undertakings
Personal credit undertakings
Development finance undertakings
Savings banks
Savings and loan banks
Discount and loan
Financial institutions
Rediscount undertakings
Finance companies
Financiers for their own account
Holding companies
Investment companies
Finance-raising holding companies
Financial trustees
Pawnbroking

Category 3: syndicates
Underwriting syndicates
Surety syndicates
Guarantee syndicates

Category 4: brokers
Stock-exchange brokers
Outside brokers
Stock jobbers
Brokers in transferable securities

Notes
[1]Indexes to the international standard industrial classification of all economic activities
(ISIC) — United nations — statistical papers series M, No. 4, rev. 1 add.

Category 5: intermediaries or middlemen
Discount brokers operating on their own account
Bank brokers (courtiers en banque)
Financial intermediaries or middlemen

Category 6: miscellaneous
Foreign exchange offices
Stock exchanges
Precious metals markets
Financial consultancy[2]
Clearing houses
Trust companies[3]

Notes
[2] For the activities covered by this Directive.
[3] Excluding the activities of companies covered by other Directives.

FIRST COUNCIL DIRECTIVE 77/780/EEC OF 12 DECEMBER 1977 ON THE CO-ORDINATION OF THE LAWS, REGULATIONS AND ADMINISTRATIVE PROVISIONS RELATING TO THE TAKING UP AND PURSUIT OF THE BUSINESS OF CREDIT INSTITUTIONS
[OJ 1977 L322/30]*

THE COUNCIL OF THE EUROPEAN COMMUNITIES,

Having regard to the Treaty establishing the European Economic Community, and in particular Article 57 thereof,
  Having regard to the proposal from the Commission,
  Having regard to the opinion of the European Parliament,[1]
  Having regard to the opinion of the Economic and Social Committee,[2]

Whereas, pursuant to the Treaty, any discriminatory treatment with regard to establishment and to the provision of services, based either on nationality or on the fact that an undertaking is not established in the member states where the services are provided, is prohibited from the end of the transitional period;
  Whereas, in order to make it easier to take up and pursue the business of credit institutions, it is necessary to eliminate the most obstructive differences between the laws of the member states as regards the rules to which these institutions are subject;
  Whereas, however, given the extent of these differences, the conditions required for a common market for credit institutions cannot be created by means of a single Directive;
  Whereas it is therefore necessary to proceed by successive stages;

Notes
*As amended by OJ 1979 L291/90, OJ 1985 L302/156, OJ 1994 L241/199 and Directives 85/345 [OJ 1985 L183/19], 86/524 [OJ 1986 L309/15], 89/646 [OJ 1989 L386/1], 95/26 [OJ 1995 L168/7 and 96/13 [OJ 1996 L66/15].
[1] OJ No. C128, 9.6.1975, p. 25.
[2] OJ No. C263, 17.11.1975, p. 25.

Whereas the result of this process should be to provide for overall supervision of a credit institution operating in several member states by the competent authorities in the member state where it has its head office, in consultation, as appropriate, with the competent authorities of the other member states concerned;

Whereas measures to co-ordinate credit institutions must, both in order to protect savings and to create equal conditions of competition between these institutions, apply to all of them;

Whereas due regard must be had, where applicable, to the objective differences in their statutes and their proper aims as laid down by national laws;

Whereas the scope of those measures should therefore be as broad as possible, covering all institutions whose business is to receive repayable funds from the public whether in the form of deposits or in other forms such as the continuing issue of bonds and other comparable securities and to grant credits for their own account;

Whereas exceptions must be provided for in the case of certain credit institutions to which this Directive cannot apply;

Whereas the provisions of this Directive shall not prejudice the application of national laws which provide for special supplementary authorisations permitting credit institutions to carry on specific activities or undertake specific kinds of operations;

Whereas the same system of supervision cannot always be applied to all types of credit institution;

Whereas provision should therefore be made for application of this Directive to be deferred in the case of certain groups or types of credit institutions to which its immediate application might cause technical problems;

Whereas more specific provisions for such institutions may prove necessary in the future;

Whereas these specific provisions should nonetheless be based on a number of common principles;

Whereas the eventual aim is to introduce uniform authorisation requirements throughout the Community for comparable types of credit institution;

Whereas at the initial stage it is necessary, however, to specify only certain minimum requirements to be imposed by all member states;

Whereas this aim can be achieved only if the particularly wide discretionary powers which certain supervisory authorities have for authorising credit establishments are progressively reduced;

Whereas the requirement that a programme of operations must be produced should therefore be seen merely as a factor enabling the competent authorities to decide on the basis of more precise information using objective criteria;

Whereas the purpose of co-ordination is to achieve a system whereby credit institutions having their head office in one of the member states are exempt from any national authorisation requirement when setting up branches in other member states;

Whereas a measure of flexibility may nonetheless be possible in the initial stage as regards the requirements on the legal form of credit institutions and the protection of banking names;

Whereas equivalent financial requirements for credit institutions will be necessary to ensure similar safeguards for savers and fair conditions of competition between comparable groups of credit institutions;

Whereas, pending further co-ordination, appropriate structural ratios should be formulated that will make it possible within the framework of cooperation between national authorities to observe, in accordance with standard methods, the position of comparable types of credit institutions;

Whereas this procedure should help to bring about the gradual approximation of the systems of coefficients established and applied by the member states;

Whereas it is necessary, however, to make a distinction between coefficients intended to ensure the sound management of credit institutions and those established for the purposes of economic and monetary policy;

Whereas, for the purpose of formulating structural ratios and of more general cooperation between supervisory authorities, standardisation of the layout of credit institutions' accounts will have to begin as soon as possible;

Whereas the rules governing branches of credit institutions having their head office outside the community should be analogous in all member states;

Whereas it is important at the present time to provide that such rules may not be more favourable than those for branches of institutions from another member state;

Whereas it should be specified that the community may conclude agreements with third countries providing for the application of rules which accord such branches the same treatment throughout its territory, account being taken of the principle of reciprocity;

Whereas the examination of problems connected with matters covered by Council Directives on the business of credit institutions requires cooperation between the competent authorities and the Commission within an advisory committee, particularly when conducted with a view to closer co-ordination;

Whereas the establishment of an advisory committee of the competent authorities of the member states does not rule out other forms of co-operation between authorities which supervise the taking up and pursuit of the business of credit institutions and, in particular, cooperation within the contact committee set up between the banking supervisory authorities,

HAS ADOPTED THIS DIRECTIVE:

TITLE I   DEFINITIONS AND SCOPE

Article 1

For the purposes of this Directive:

— 'credit institution' means an undertaking whose business is to receive deposits or other repayable funds from the public and to grant credits for its own account;

— 'authorisation' means an instrument issued in any form by the authorities by which the right to carry on the business of a credit institution is granted;

— 'branch' means a place of business which forms a legally dependent part of a credit institution and which conducts directly all or some of the operations inherent in the business of credit institutions; any number of branches set up in the same member state by a credit institution having its head office in another member state shall be regarded as a single branch;

Without prejudice to Article 4(1),

— 'own funds' means the credit institution's own capital, including items which may be treated as capital under national rules;

— 'close links' shall mean a situation in which two or more natural or legal persons are linked by:

(a) 'participation', which shall mean the ownership, direct or by way of control, of 20% or more of the voting rights or capital of an undertaking; or

(b) 'control', which shall mean the relationship between a parent undertaking and a subsidiary, in all the cases referred to in Article 1(1) and (2) of Directive 83/349/EEC,[1] or a similar relationship between any natural or legal person and an undertaking; any subsidiary undertaking of a subsidiary undertaking shall also be considered a subsidiary of the parent undertaking which is at the head of those undertakings. A situation in which two or more natural or legal persons are permanently linked to one and the same person by a control relationship shall also be regarded as constituting a close link between such persons.

Note
[1]OJ No. L193, 18.7.1983, p. 1. Directive as last amended by Directive 90/605/EEC (OJ No. L317, 16.11.1990, p. 60).

Article 2

1.   This Directive shall apply to the taking up and pursuit of the business of credit institutions.

2.   It shall not apply to:

— the central banks of Member States,

— post office giro institutions,

— in Belgium, the 'Institut de Rescompte et de Garantie/Herdisconteringen Waarborginstituut',

— in Denmark, the 'Dansk Eksportfinansieringsfond', the 'Danmarks Skibskreditfond' and the 'Dansk Landbrugs Realkreditfond',

— in Germany, the 'Kreditanstalt fuer Wiederaufbau', undertakings which are recognized under the 'Wohnungsgemeinnuetzigkeitsgesetz' as bodies of state housing policy and are not mainly engaged in banking transactions and undertakings recognized under that law as non-profit housing undertakings,

— in Greece, the 'AA UE aaae aa' (Elliniki Trapeza Viomichanikis Anaptyxeos), the 'aass AE aass' (Tameio Parakatathikon kai Danion) and the 'ae ue aa' (Tahidromiko Tamieftirio),

— in Spain, the 'Instituto de Credito Oficial',

— in France, the 'Caisse des dépôts et consignations',

— in Ireland, credit unions and friendly societies,

— in Italy, the 'Cassa Depositi et Prestiti',

— in the Netherlands, the 'Nederlandse Investingsbank voor Ontwikkelingslanden NV', the 'NV Noordelijke Ontwikkelingsmaatschappij', the 'NV Industriebank Limburgs Instituut voor Ontwikkeling en Finaniering' and the 'Overijsselse Ontwikkelingsmaatschappij NV',

— in Austria, undertakings recognized as housing associations in the public interest and the 'Oesterreichische Kontrollbank AG',

— in Portugal, 'Caixas Economicas' existing on 1 January 1986 with the exception of those incorporated as limited companies and of the 'Caixa Economica Montepio Geral',

— in Finland, the 'Teollisen yhteistyoen rahasto Oy/Fonden foer industriellt samarbete Ab' and the 'Kera Oy/Kera Ab',

—in Sweden, the 'Svenska Skeppshypotekskassan',

—in the United Kingdom, the National Savings Bank, the Commonwealth Development Finance Company Ltd, the Agricultural Mortgage Corporation Ltd, the Scottish Agricultural Securities Corporation Ltd, the Crown Agents for overseas governments and administrations, credit unions and municipal banks.

3.   The Council, acting on a proposal from the Commission, which, for this purpose, shall consult the committee referred to in Article 11 (hereinafter referred to as 'the advisory committee') shall decide on any Amendments to the list in paragraph 2.

4.   (a)   credit institutions existing in the same member state at the time of the notification of this Directive and permanently affiliated at that time to a central body which supervises them and which is established in that same member state, may be exempted from the requirements listed in the first, second and third indents of the first subparagraph of Article 3(2), the second subparagraph of Article 3(2), Article 3(4) and Article 6, if, no later than the date when the national authorities take the measures necessary to translate this Directive into national law, that law provides that:

—the commitments of the central body and affiliated institutions are joint and several liabilities or the commitments of its affiliated institutions are entirely guaranteed by the central body,

—the solvency and liquidity of the central body and of all the affiliated institutions are monitored as a whole on the basis of consolidated accounts,

—the management of the central body is empowered to issue instructions to the management of the affiliated institutions.

(b)   credit institutions operating locally which are affiliated, subsequent to notification of this Directive, to a central body within the meaning of subparagraph (a) may benefit from the conditions laid down in subparagraph (a) if they constitute normal additions to the network belonging to that central body.

(c)   in the case of credit institutions other than those which are set up in areas newly reclaimed from the sea or have resulted from scission or mergers of existing institutions dependent or answerable to the central body, the Council, acting on a proposal from the Commission, which shall, for this purpose, consult the advisory committee, may lay down additional rules for the application of subparagraph (b) including the repeal of exemptions provided for in subparagraph (a), where it is of the opinion that the affiliation of new institutions benefiting from the arrangements laid down in subparagraph (b) might have an adverse effect on competition. The Council shall decide by a qualified majority.

5.   Member states may defer in whole or in part the application of this Directive to certain types or groups of credit institutions where such immediate application would cause technical problems which cannot be overcome in the short-term. The problems may result either from the fact that these institutions are subject to supervision by an authority different from that normally responsible for the supervision of banks, or from the fact that they are subject to a special system of supervision. In any event, such deferment cannot be justified by the public law statutes, by the smallness of size or by the limited scope of activity of the particular institutions concerned. Deferment can apply only to groups or types of institutions already existing at the time of notification of this Directive.

6.   Pursuant to paragraph 5, a member state may decide to defer application of this Directive for a maximum period of five years from the notification thereof and, after consulting the advisory committee may extend deferment once only for a maximum period of three years. The member state shall inform the Commission of its Decision and the reasons therefor not later than six months following the notification of this Directive. It shall also notify the Commission of any extension or repeal of this decision. The Commission shall publish any decision regarding deferment in the Official Journal of the European Communities not later than seven years following the notification of this Directive, the Commission shall, after consulting the advisory committee, submit a report to the Council on the situation regarding deferment. Where appropriate, the Commission shall submit to the Council, not later than six months following the submission of its report, proposals for either the inclusion of the institutions in question in the list in paragraph 2 or for the authorisation of a further extension of deferment. The Council shall act on these proposals not later than six months after their submission.

TITLE II   CREDIT INSTITUTIONS HAVING THEIR HEAD OFFICE IN A MEMBER STATE AND THEIR BRANCHES IN OTHER MEMBER STATES

Article 3

1.   Member states shall require credit institutions subject to this Directive to obtain authorisation before commencing their activities. They shall lay down the requirements for such authorisation subject to paragraphs 2, 3 and 4 and notify them to both the Commission and the advisory committee .

2.   Without prejudice to other conditions of general application laid down by national laws, the competent authorities shall grant authorisation only when the following conditions are complied with:

— the credit institution must possess separate own funds,
— the credit institution must possess adequate minimum own funds,
— there shall be at least two persons who effectively direct the business of the credit institution.

Moreover, the authorities concerned shall not grant authorisation if the persons referred to in the third indent of the first subparagraph are not of sufficiently good repute or lack sufficient experience to perform such duties. Moreover, where close links exist between the financial undertaking and other natural or legal persons, the competent authorities shall grant authorisation only if those links do not prevent the effective exercise of their supervisory functions.

The competent authorities shall also refuse authorisation if the laws, regulations or administrative provisions of a non-member country governing one or more natural or legal persons with which the undertaking has close links, or difficulties involved in their enforcement, prevent the effective exercise of their supervisory functions. The competent authorities shall require financial undertakings to provide them with the information they require to monitor compliance with the conditions referred to in this paragraph on a continuous basis.

2A.   Each Member State shall require that:

— any credit institution which is a legal person and which, under its national law, has a registered office have its head office in the same Member State as its registered office,

— any other credit institution have its head office in the Member State which issued its authorisation and in which it actually carries on its business.

3. (a) the provisions referred to in paragraphs 1 and 2 may not require the application for authorisation to be examined in terms of the economic needs of the market;

(b) where the laws, Regulations or administrative provisions of a member state provide, at the time of notification of the present Directive, that the economic needs of the market shall be a condition of authorisation and where technical or structural difficulties in its banking system do not allow it to give up the criterion within the period laid down in Article 14(1), the state in question may continue to apply the criterion for a period of seven years from notification. It shall notify its decision and the reasons therefor to the Commission within six months of notification.

The Hellenic Republic may continue to apply the criterion of economic need. On a request from the Hellenic Republic, the Commission shall, if appropriate, submit to the Council by 15 June 1989 proposals authorising the Hellenic Republic to continue to apply the criterion of economic need until 15 December 1992. The Council shall act within six months of the submission of those proposals;

(c) within six years of the notification of this Directive the Commission shall submit to the Council, after consulting the advisory committee, a report on the application of the criterion of economic need. If appropriate, the Commission shall submit to the Council proposals to terminate the application of that criterion. The period referred to in subparagraph (b) shall be extended for one further period of five years, unless, in the meantime, the Council, acting unanimously on proposals from the Commission, adopts a decision to terminate the application of that criterion;

(d) the criterion of economic need shall be applied only on the basis of general predetermined criteria, published and notified to both the Commission and the advisory committee and aimed at promoting:

— security of savings,

— higher productivity in the banking system,

— greater uniformity of competition between the various banking networks,

— a broader range of banking services in relation to population and economic activity. Specification of the above objectives shall be determined within the advisory committee, which shall begin its work as from its initial meetings.

4. Member states shall also require applications for authorisation to be accompanied by a programme of operations setting out inter alia the types of business envisaged and the structural organization of the institution.

5. The advisory committee shall examine the content given by the competent authorities to requirements listed in paragraph 2, any other requirements which the member states apply and the information which must be included in the programme of operations, and shall, where appropriate, make suggestions to the Commission with a view to a more detailed co-ordination.

6. Reasons shall be given whenever an authorisation is refused and the applicant shall be notified thereof within six months of receipt of the application or, should the latter be incomplete, within six months of the

applicant's sending the information required for the decision. A decision shall, in any case, be taken within 12 months of the receipt of the application.

7.   Every authorisation shall be notified to the Commission. Each credit institution shall be entered in a list which the Commission shall publish in the Official Journal of the European Communities and shall keep up to date.

Article 4

1.   Member states may make the commencement of business in their territory by branches of credit institutions covered by this Directive which have their head office in another member state subject to authorisation according to the law and procedure applicable to credit institutions established on their territory.

2.   However, authorisation may not be refused to a branch of a credit institution on the sole ground that it is established in another member state in a legal form which is not allowed in the case of a credit institution carrying out similar activities in the host country. This provision shall not apply, however, to credit institutions which possess no separate own funds.

3.   The competent authorities shall inform the Commission of any authorisations which they grant to the branches referred to in paragraph 1.

4.   This Article shall not affect the rules applied by member states to branches set up on their territory by credit institutions which have their head office there. Notwithstanding the second part of the third indent of Article 1, the laws of member states requiring a separate authorisation for each branch of a credit institution having its head office in their territory shall apply equally to the branches of credit institutions the head offices of which are in other member states.

Article 5

For the purpose of exercising their activities, credit institutions to which this Directive applies may, notwithstanding any provisions concerning the use of the words 'bank', 'Savings bank' or other banking names which may exist in the host member state, use throughout the territory of the Community the same name as they use in the member states in which their head office is situated. In the event of there being any danger of confusion, the host member state may, for the purposes of clarification, require that the name be accompanied by certain explanatory particulars.

Article 6

1.   Pending subsequent co-ordination, the competent authorities shall, for the purposes of observation and, if necessary, in addition to such coefficients as may be applied by them, establish ratios between the various assets and/or liabilities of credit institutions with a view to monitoring their solvency and liquidity and the other measures which may serve to ensure that savings are protected. To this end, the advisory committee shall decide on the content of the various factors of the observation ratios referred to in the first subparagraph and lay down the method to be applied in calculating them. Where appropriate, the advisory committee shall be guided by technical consultations between the supervisory authorities of the categories of institutions concerned.

2.   The observation ratios established in pursuance of paragraph 1 shall be calculated at least every six months.

3. The advisory committee shall examine the results of analyses carried out by the supervisory authorities referred to in the third subparagraph of paragraph 1 on the basis of the calculations referred to in paragraph 2.

4. The advisory committee may make suggestions to the Commission with a view to co-ordinating the coefficients applicable in the member states.

Article 7

1. The competent authorities of the member states concerned shall collaborate closely in order to supervise the activities of credit institutions operating, in particular by having established branches there, in one or more member states other than that in which their head offices are situated. They shall supply one another with all information concerning the management and ownership of such credit institutions that is likely to facilitate their supervision and the examination of the conditions for their authorisation and all information likely to facilitate the monitoring of such institutions, in particular with regard to liquidity, solvency, deposit guarantees, the limiting of large exposures, administrative and accounting procedures and internal control mechanisms.

2. The competent authorities may also, for the purposes and within the meaning of Article 6, lay down ratios applicable to the branches referred to in this Article by reference to the factors laid down in Article 6.

3. The advisory committee shall take account of the adjustments necessitated by the specific situation of the branches in relation to national Regulations.

Article 8

1. The competent authorities may withdraw the authorisation issued to a credit institution subject to this Directive or to a branch authorised under Article 4 only where such an institution or branch:

(a)   does not make use of the authorisation within 12 months, expressly renounces the authorisation or has ceased to engage in business for more than six months, if the member state concerned has made no provision for the authorisation to lapse in such cases;

(b)   has obtained the authorisation through false statements or any other irregular means:

(c)   no longer fulfils the conditions under which authorisation was granted, with the exception of those in respect of own funds;

(d)   no longer possesses sufficient own funds or can no longer be relied upon to fulfil its obligations towards its creditors, and in particular no longer provides security for the assets entrusted to it;

(e)   falls within one of the other cases where national law provides for withdrawal of authorisation.

2. In addition, the authorisation issued to a branch under Article 4 shall be withdrawn if the competent authority of the country in which the credit institution which established the branch has its head office has withdrawn authorisation from that institution.

3. Member states which grant the authorisations referred to in Articles 3(1) and 4(1) only if, economically, the market situation requires it may not invoke the disappearance of such a need as grounds for withdrawing such authorisations.

4.   Before withdrawal from a branch of an authorisation granted under Article 4, the competent authority of the member state in which its head office is situated shall be consulted. Where immediate action is called for, notification may take the place of such consultation. The same procedure shall be followed, by analogy, in cases of withdrawal of authorisation from a credit institution which has branches in other member states.

5.   Reasons must be given for any withdrawal of authorisation and those concerned informed thereof; such withdrawal shall be notified to the Commission.

TITLE III   BRANCHES OF CREDIT INSTITUTIONS HAVING THEIR HEAD OFFICES OUTSIDE THE COMMUNITY

Article 9

1.   Member states shall not apply to branches of credit institutions having their head office outside the Community, when commencing or carrying on their business, provisions which result in more favourable treatment than that accorded to branches of credit institutions having their head office in the Community.

2.   The competent authorities shall notify the Commission and the advisory committee of all authorisations for branches granted to credit institutions having their head office outside the community.

3.   Without prejudice to paragraph 1, the Community may, through agreements concluded in accordance with the Treaty with one or more third countries, agree to apply provisions which, on the basis of the principle of reciprocity, accord to branches of a credit institution having its head office outside the Community identical treatment throughout the territory of the Community.

TITLE IV   GENERAL AND TRANSITIONAL PROVISIONS

Article 10

1.   Credit institutions subject to this Directive, which took up their business in accordance with the provisions of the member states in which they have their head offices before the entry into force of the provisions implementing this Directive shall be deemed to be authorised. They shall be subject to the provisions of this Directive concerning the carrying on of the business of credit institutions and to the requirements set out in the first and third indents of the first subparagraph and in the second subparagraph of Article 3(2). Member states may allow credit institutions which at the time of notification of this Directive do not comply with the requirement laid down in the third indent of the first subparagraph of Article 3(2), no more than five years in which to do so. Member states may decide that undertakings which do not fulfil the requirements set out in the first indent of the first subparagraph of Article 3(2) and which are in existence at the time this Directive enters into force may continue to carry on their business. They may exempt such undertakings from complying with the requirement contained in the third indent of the first subparagraph of Article 3(2).

2.   All the credit institutions referred to in paragraph 1 shall be given in the list referred to in Article 3(7).

3.   If a credit institution deemed to be authorised under paragraph 1 has not undergone any authorisation procedure prior to commencing business, a

prohibition on the carrying on of its business shall take the place of withdrawal of authorisation. Subject to the first subparagraph, Article 8 shall apply by analogy.

4.   By way of derogation from paragraph 1, credit institutions established in a member state without having undergone an authorisation procedure in that member state prior to commencing business may be required to obtain authorisation from the competent authorities of the member state concerned in accordance with the provisions implementing this Directive. Such institutions may be required to comply with the requirement in the second indent of Article 3(2) and with such other conditions of general application as may be laid down by the member state concerned.

Article 11

1.   An 'advisory committee of the competent authorities of the member states of the European Economic Community' shall be set up alongside the Commission.

2.   The tasks of the advisory committee shall be to assist the Commission in ensuring the proper implementation of both this Directive and Council Directive 73/183/EEC of 28 June 1973 on the abolition of restrictions on freedom of establishment and freedom to provide services in respect of self-employed activities of banks and other financial institutions[1] in so far as it relates to credit institutions. Further it shall carry out the other tasks prescribed by this Directive and shall assist the Commission in the preparation of new proposals to the Council concerning further co-ordination in the sphere of credit institutions.

3.   The advisory committee shall not concern itself with concrete problems relating to individual credit institutions.

4.   The advisory committee shall be composed of not more than three representatives from each member state and from the Commission. These representatives may be accompanied by advisers from time to time and subject to the prior agreement of the committee. The committee may also invite qualified persons and experts to participate in its meetings. The secretariat shall be provided by the Commission.

5.   The first meeting of the advisory committee shall be convened by the Commission under the chairmanship of one of its representatives. The advisory committee shall then adopt its rules of procedure and shall elect a chairman from among the representatives of member states. Thereafter it shall meet at regular intervals and whenever the situation demands. The Commission may ask the committee to hold an emergency meeting if it considers that the situation so requires.

6.   The advisory committee's discussions and the outcome thereof shall be confidential except when the Committee decides otherwise.

Note

[1] OJ NO L194, 16.7.1973, p. 1.

Article 12

1.   The Member States shall provide that all persons working or who have worked for the competent authorities, as well as auditors or experts acting on behalf of the competent authorities, shall be bound by the obligation of professional secrecy. This means that no confidential information which they

may receive in the course of their duties may be divulged to any person or authority whatsoever, except in summary or collective form, such that individual institutions cannot be identified, without prejudice to cases covered by criminal law.

Nevertheless, where a credit institution has been declared bankrupt or is being compulsorily wound up, confidential information which does not concern third parties involved in attempts to rescue that credit institution may be divulged in civil or commercial proceedings.

2. Paragraph 1 shall not prevent the competent authorities of the various Member States from exchanging information in accordance with the Directives applicable to credit institutions. That information shall be subject to the conditions of professional secrecy indicated in paragraph 1.

3. Member States may conclude cooperation agreements, providing for exchanges of information, with the competent authorities of third countries only if the information disclosed is subject to guarantees of professional secrecy at least equivalent to those referred to in this Article.

4. Competent authorities receiving confidential information under paragraphs 1 or 2 may use it only in the course of their duties:

— to check that the conditions governing the taking-up of the business of credit institutions are met and to facilitate monitoring, on a non-consolidated or consolidated basis, of the conduct of such business, especially with regard to the monitoring of liquidity, solvency, large exposures, and administrative and accounting procedures and internal control mechanisms, or

— to impose sanctions, or

— in an administrative appeal against a decision of the competent authority, or

— in court proceedings initiated pursuant to Article 15 or to special provisions provided for in the Directives adopted in the field of credit institutions.

5. Paragraphs 1 and 4 shall not preclude the exchange of information within a Member State, where there are two or more competent authorities in the same Member State, or between Member States, between competent authorities and:

— authorities entrusted with the public duty of supervising other financial organisations and insurance companies and the authorities responsible for the supervision of financial markets,

— bodies involved in the liquidation and bankruptcy of credit institutions and in other similar procedures,

— persons responsible for carrying out statutory audits of the accounts of credit institutions and other financial institutions, in the discharge of their supervisory functions, and the disclosure to bodies which administer deposit-guarantee schemes of information necessary to the exercise of their functions. The information received shall be subject to the conditions of professional secrecy indicated in paragraph 1.

5a. Notwithstanding paragraphs 1 to 4, Member States may authorise exchanges of information between the competent authorities and:

— the authorities responsible for overseeing the bodies involved in the liquidation and bankruptcy of financial undertakings and other similar procedures, or

— the authorities responsible for overseeing persons charged with carrying out statutory audits of the accounts of insurance undertakings, credit institutions, investment firms and other financial institutions. Member States which have recourse to the option provided for in the first subparagraph shall require at least that the following conditions are met:

— the information shall be for the purpose of performing the task of overseeing referred to in the first subparagraph,

— information received in this context shall be subject to the conditions of professional secrecy imposed in paragraph 1,

— where the information originates in another Member State, it may not be disclosed without the express agreement of the competent authorities which have disclosed it and, where appropriate, solely for the purposes for which those authorities gave their agreement. Member States shall communicate to the Commission and to the other Member States the names of the authorities which may receive information pursuant to this paragraph.

5b.   Notwithstanding paragraphs 1 to 4, Member States may, with the aim of strengthening the stability, including integrity, of the financial system, authorise the exchange of information between the competent authorities and the authorities or bodies responsible under the law for the detection and investigation of breaches of company law.

Member States which have recourse to the option provided for in the first subparagraph shall require at least that the following conditions are met:

— the information shall be for the purpose of performing the task referred to in the first subparagraph,

— information received in this context shall be subject to the conditions of professional secrecy imposed in paragraph 1,

— where the information originates in another Member State, it may not be disclosed without the express agreement of the competent authorities which have disclosed it and, where appropriate, solely for the purposes for which those authorities gave their agreement.

Where, in a Member State, the authorities or bodies referred to in the first subparagraph perform their task of detection or investigation with the aid, in view of their specific competence, of persons appointed for that purpose and not employed in the public sector, the possibility of exchanging information provided for in the first subparagraph may be extended to such persons under the conditions stipulated in the second subparagraph.

In order to implement the final indent of the second subparagraph, the authorities or bodies referred to in the first subparagraph shall communicate to the competent authorities which have disclosed the information, the names and precise responsibilities of the persons to whom it is to be sent. Member States shall communicate to the Commission and to the other Member States the names of the authorities or bodies which may receive information pursuant to this paragraph.

Before 31 December 2000, the Commission shall draw up a report on the application of the provisions of this paragraph.

6.   This Article shall not prevent a competent authority from transmitting:

— to central banks and other bodies with a similar function in their capacity as monetary authorities,

— where appropriate, to other public authorities responsible for overseeing payment systems, information intended for the performance of their task, nor shall it prevent such authorities or bodies from communicating to the competent authorities such information as they may need for the purposes of paragraph 4. Information received in this context shall be subject to the conditions of professional secrecy imposed in this Article.

7. In addition, notwithstanding the provisions referred to in paragraphs 1 and 4, the Member States may, by virtue of provisions laid down by law, authorise the disclosure of certain information to other departments of their central government administrations responsible for legislation on the supervision of credit institutions, financial institutions, investment services and insurance companies and to inspectors acting on behalf of those departments. However, such disclosures may be made only where necessary for reasons of prudential control.

However, the Member States shall provide that information received under paragraphs 2 and 5 and that obtained by means of the on-the-spot verification referred to in Article 15(1) and (2) of Directive 89/646/ EEC[1] may never be disclosed in the cases referred to in this paragraph except with the express consent of the competent authorities which disclosed the information or of the competent authorities of the Member State in which on-the-spot verification was carried out.

8. This Article shall not prevent the competent authorities from communicating the information referred to in paragraphs 1 to 4 to a clearing house or other similar body recognised under national law for the provision of clearing or settlement services for one of their Member States' markets if they consider that it is necessary to communicate the information in order to ensure the proper functioning of those bodies in relation to defaults or potential defaults by market participants. The information received in this context shall be subject to the conditions of professional secrecy referred to in paragraph 1. The Member States shall, however, ensure that information received under paragraph 2 may not be disclosed in the circumstances referred to in this paragraph without the express consent of the competent authorities which disclosed it.

Note
[1] OJ No. L386, 30.12.89, p.1.

Article 12a
1. Member States shall provide at least that:
    (a) any person authorised within the meaning of Directive 84/253/EEC,[1] performing in a financial undertaking the task described in Article 51 of Directive 78/660/EEC,[2] Article 37 of Directive 83/349/EEC or Article 31 of Directive 85/611/EEC or any other statutory task, shall have a duty to report promptly to the competent authorities any fact or decision concerning that undertaking of which he has become aware while carrying out that task which is liable to:
    — constitute a material breach of the laws, regulations or administrative provisions which lay down the conditions governing authorisation or which specifically govern pursuit of the activities of financial undertakings, or
    — affect the continuous functioning of the financial undertaking, or
    — lead to refusal to certify the accounts or to the expression of reservations;

Notes
[1] OJ No. L126, 12.5.1984, p. 20.
[2] OJ No. L222, 14.8.1978, p. 11. Directive as last amended by Directive 90/605/EEC (OJ No. L317, 16.11.1990, p. 60).

(b)   that person shall likewise have a duty to report any facts and decisions of which he becomes aware in the course of carrying out a task as described in (a) in an undertaking having close links resulting from a control relationship with the financial undertaking within which he is carrying out the abovementioned task.

2.   The disclosure in good faith to the competent authorities, by persons authorised within the meaning of Directive 84/253/EEC, of any fact or decision referred to in paragraph 1 shall not constitute a breach of any restriction on disclosure of information imposed by contract or by any legislative, regulatory or administrative provision and shall not involve such persons in liability of any kind.

Article 13
Member states shall ensure that decisions taken in respect of a credit institution in pursuance of laws, Regulations and administrative provisions adopted in accordance with this Directive may be subject to the right to apply to the courts. The same shall apply where no decision is taken within six months of its submission in respect of an application for authorisation which contains all the information required under the provisions in force.

TITLE V   FINAL PROVISIONS

Article 14
1.   Member states shall bring into force the measures necessary to comply with this Directive within 24 months of its notification and shall forthwith inform the Commission thereof.

2.   As from the notification of this Directive, member states shall communicate to the Commission the texts of the main laws, Regulations and administrative provisions which they adopt in the field covered by this Directive.

Article 15
This Directive is addressed to the member states.

Done at Brussels , 12 December 1977.
For the Council,
The President,
A. HUMBLET.

COUNCIL DIRECTIVE OF 17 APRIL 1989 ON THE OWN FUNDS OF CREDIT INSTITUTIONS
[89/299/EEC]*

THE COUNCIL OF THE EUROPEAN COMMUNITIES

Having regard to the Treaty establishing the European Economic Community, and in particular the first and third sentences of Article 57(2) thereof,

Having regard to the proposal from the Commission,[1]
In cooperation with the European Parliament,[2]
Having regard to the opinion of the Economic and Social Committee,[3]

Notes
*As amended by Directives 91/633 (OJ 1991 L339/33), 92/16 (OJ 1992 L75/48), 92/30 (OJ 1992/100/52).
[1]OJ No. C243, 27.9.1986, p. 4.
[2]OJ No. C246, 14.9.1987, p. 72 and OJ No. C96, 17.4.1989.
[3]OJ No. C180, 8.7.1987, p. 51.

Whereas common basic standards for the own funds of credit institutions are a key factor in the creation of an internal market in the banking sector since own funds serve to ensure the continuity of credit institutions and to protect savings; whereas such harmonization will strengthen the supervision of credit institutions and contribute to further coordination in the banking sector, in particular the supervision of major risks and solvency ratios;

Whereas such standards must apply to all credit institutions authorized in the Community;

Whereas the own funds of a credit institution can serve to absorb losses which are not matched by a sufficient volume of profits; whereas the own funds also serve as an important yardstick for the competent authorities, in particular for the assessment of the solvency of credit institutions and for other prudential purposes;

Whereas credit institutions in a common banking market engage in direct competition with each other, and the definitions and standards pertaining to own funds must therefore be equivalent; whereas, to that end, the criteria for determining the composition of own funds must not be left solely to Member States; whereas the adoption of common basic standards will be in the best interests of the Community in that it will prevent distortions of competition and will strengthen the Community banking system;

Whereas the definition laid down in this Directive provides for a maximum of items and qualifying amounts, leaving it to the discretion of each Member State to use all or some of such items or to adopt lower ceilings for the qualifying amounts;

Whereas this Directive specifies the qualifying criteria for certain own funds items, and the Member States remain free to apply more stringent provisions;

Whereas at the initial stage common basic standards are defined in broad terms in order to encompass all the items making up own funds in the different Member States;

Whereas, according to the nature of the items making up own funds, this Directive distinguishes between on the one hand, items constituting original own funds and, on the other, those constituting additional own funds;

Whereas it is recognized that due to the special nature of the fund for general banking risks, this item is to be included provisionally in own funds without limit; whereas, however, a decision on its final treatment will have to be taken as soon as possible after the implementation of the Directive; whereas that decision will have to take into account the results of discussions in international fora;

Whereas, to reflect the fact that items constituting additional own funds are not of the same nature as those constituting original own funds, the amount of the former included in own funds must not exceed the original own funds; whereas, moreover, the amount of certain items of additional own funds included must not exceed one-half of the original own funds;

Whereas, in order to avoid distortions of competition, public credit institutions must not include in their own funds guarantees granted them by the Member States or local authorities; whereas, however, the Kingdom of Belgium should be granted a transitional period up to 31 December 1994 in order to permit the institutions concerned to adjust to the new conditions by reforming their statutes;

Whereas whenever in the course of supervision it is necessary to determine the amount of the consolidated own funds of a group of credit institutions, that calculation shall be effected in accordance with Council Directive 83/350/EEC of 13 June 1983 on the supervision of credit institutions on a consolidated basis;[1] whereas that Directive leaves the Member States scope to interpret the technical details of its application, and that scope should be in keeping with the spirit of this Directive; whereas the former Directive is currently being revised to achieve greater harmonization;

Whereas the precise accounting technique to be used for the calculation of own funds must take account of the provisions of Council Directive 86/635/EEC of 8 December 1986 on the annual accounts and consolidated accounts of banks and other financial institutions,[2] which incorporates certain adaptations of the provisions of Council Directive 83/349/EEC of 13 June 1983 based on Article 54(3)(g) of the Treaty on consolidated accounts;[3] whereas pending transposition of the provisions of the abovementioned Directives into the national laws of the Member States, the use of a specific accounting technique for the calculation of own funds should be left to the discretion of the Member States;

Whereas this Directive forms part of the wider international effort to bring about approximation of the rules in force in major countries regarding the adequacy of own funds;

Whereas measures to comply with the definitions in this Directive must be adopted no later than the date of entry into force of the measures implementing the future directive harmonizing solvency ratios;

Whereas the Commission will draw up a report and periodically examine this Directive with the aim of tightening its provisions and thus achieving greater convergence on a common definition of own funds; whereas such convergence will allow the alignment of Community credit institutions' own funds;

Whereas it will probably be necessary to make certain technical and terminological adjustments to the directive to take account of the rapid development of financial markets; whereas pending submission by the Commission of a proposal which takes account of the special characteristics of the banking sector and which permits the introduction of a more suitable procedure for the implementation of this Directive, the Council reserves the right to take such measures.

HAS ADOPTED THIS DIRECTIVE:

Notes
[1]OJ No. L193, 18.7.1983, p. 18.
[2]OJ No. L372, 31.12.1986, p. 1.
[3]OJ No. L193, 18.7.1983, p. 1.

Article 1:   Scope

1.   Wherever a Member State lays down by law, regulation or administrative action a provision in implementation of Community legislation concerning the prudential supervision of an operative credit institution which uses the term or refers to the concept of own funds, it shall bring this term or concept into line with the definition given in the following Articles.

2.   For the purposes of this Directive, 'credit institutions' shall mean the institutions to which Directive 77/780/EEC,[1] as last amended by Directive 86/524/EEC,[2] applies.

Notes
[1]OJ No. L322, 17.12.1977, p. 30.
[2]OJ No. L309, 4.11.1986, p. 15.

Article 2:   General principles

1.   Subject to the limits imposed in Article 6, the unconsolidated own funds of credit institutions shall consist of the following items:

(1)   capital within the meaning of Article 22 of Directive 86/635/EEC, in so far as it has been paid up, plus share premium accounts but excluding cumulative preferential shares;

(2)   reserves within the meaning of Article 23 of Directive 86/635/EEC and profits and losses brought forward as a result of the application of the final profit or loss. The Member States may permit inclusion of interim profits before a formal decision has been taken only if these profits have been verified by persons responsible for the auditing of the accounts and if it is proved to the satisfaction of the competent authorities that the amount thereof has been evaluated in accordance with the principles set out in Directive 86/635/EEC and is net of any foreseeable charge or dividend;

(3)   revaluation reserves within the meaning of Article 33 of Council Directive 78/660/EEC of 25 July 1978 based on Article 54(3)(g) of the Treaty on the annual accounts of certain types of companies,[1] as last amended by Directive 84/569/EEC;[2]

(4)   funds for general banking risks within the meaning of Article 38 of Directive 86/635/EEC;

(5)   value adjustments within the meaning of Article 37(2) of Directive 86/635/EEC;

(6)   other items within the meaning of Article 3;

(7)   the commitments of the members of credit institutions set up as cooperative societies and the joint and several commitments of the borrowers of certain institutions organized as funds, as referred to in Article 4(1);

(8)   fixed-term cumulative preferential shares and subordinated loan capital as referred to in Article 4(3). The following items shall be deducted in accordance with Article 6:

(9)   own shares at book value held by a credit institution;

(10)   intangible assets within the meaning of Article 4(9) ('assets') of Directive 86/635/EEC;

(11)   material losses of the current financial year;

(12)   holdings in other credit and financial institutions amounting to more than 10% of their capital, subordinated claims and the instruments referred to in Article 3 which a credit institution holds in respect of credit and financial institutions in which it has holdings exceeding 10% of the capital in each case. Where shares in another credit or financial institution are held temporarily for the purposes of a financial assistance operation designed to reorganize and save that institution, the supervisory authority may waive this provision;

Notes
[1]OJ No. L222, 14.8.1978, p. 11.
[2]OJ No. L314, 4.12.1984, p. 28.

(13)   holdings in other credit and financial institutions of up to 10% of their capital, the subordinated claims and the instruments referred to in Article 3 which a credit institution holds in respect of credit and financial institutions other than those referred to in point 12 in respect of the amount of the total of such holdings, subordinated claims and instruments which exceed 10% of that credit institution's own funds calculated before the deduction of items 12 and 13.

Pending subsequent coordination of the provisions on consolidation, Member States may provide that, for the calculation of unconsolidated own funds, parent companies subject to supervision on a consolidated basis need not deduct their holdings in other credit institutions or financial institutions which are included in the consolidation. This provision shall apply to all the prudential rules harmonized by Community acts.

2.   The concept of own funds as defined in points 1 to 8 of paragraph 1 embodies a maximum number of items and amounts. The use of those items and the fixing of lower ceilings, and the deduction of items other than those listed in items 9 to 13 of paragraph 1 shall be left to the discretion of the Member States. Member States shall nevertheless be obliged to consider increased convergence with a view to a common definition of own funds.

To that end, the Commission shall, not more than three years after the date referred to in Article 9(1), submit a report to the European Parliament and to the Council on the application of this Directive, accompanied, where appropriate, by such proposals for amendment as it shall deem necessary. Within five years of the date referred to in Article 9(1), the Council shall, acting by qualified majority on a proposal from the Commission, in cooperation with the European Parliament and after consultation of the Economic and Social Committee, examine the definition of own funds with a view to the uniform application of the common definition.

3.   The items listed in points 1 to 5 must be available to a credit institution for unrestricted and immediate use to cover risks or losses as soon as these occur. The amount must be net of any foreseeable tax charge at the moment of its calculation or be suitably adjusted in so far as such tax charges reduce the amount up to which these items may be applied to cover risks or losses.

Article 3:   Other items referred to in Article 2(1)(6):

1.   The concept of own funds used by a Member State may include other items provided that, whatever their legal or accounting designations might be, they have the following characteristics:

(a)   they are freely available to the credit institution to cover normal banking risks where revenue or capital losses have not yet been identified;

(b)   their existence is disclosed in internal accounting records;

(c)   their amount is determined by the management of the credit institution, verified by independent auditors, made known to the competent authorities and placed under the supervision of the latter. With regard to verification, internal auditing may be considered as provisionally meeting the aforementioned requirements until such time as the Community provisions making external auditing mandatory have been implemented.

2.   Securities of indeterminate duration and other instruments that fulfil the following conditions may also be accepted as other items:

(a)   they may not be reimbursed on the bearer's initiative or without the prior agreement of the supervisory authority;

(b)   the debt agreement must provide for the credit institution to have the option of deferring the payment of interest on the debt;

(c)   the lender's claims on the credit institution must be wholly subordinated to those of all non-subordinated creditors;

(d)   the documents governing the issue of the securities must provide for debt and unpaid interest to be such as to absorb losses, whilst leaving the credit institution in a position to continue trading;

(e)   only fully paid-up amounts shall be taken into account. To these may be added cumulative preferential shares other than those referred to in Article 2(1)(8).

Article 4

1.   The commitments of the members of credit institutions set up as cooperative societies referred to in Article 2(1)(7), shall comprise those societies' uncalled capital, together with the legal commitments of the members of those cooperative societies to make additional non-refundable payments should the credit institution incur a loss, in which case it must be possible to demand those payments without delay.

The joint and several commitments of borrowers in the case of credit institutions organized as funds shall be treated in the same way as the preceding items.

All such items may be included in own funds in so far as they are counted as the own funds of institutions of this category under national law.

2.   Member States shall not include in the own funds of public credit institutions guarantees which they or their local authorities extend to such entities. However, the Kingdom of Belgium shall be exempt from this obligation until 31 December 1994.

3.   Member States or the competent authorities may include fixed-term cumulative preferential shares referred to in Article 2(1)(8) and subordinated loan capital referred to in that provision in own funds, if binding agreements exist under which, in the event of the bankruptcy or liquidation of the credit institution, they rank after the claims of all other creditors and are not to be repaid until all other debts outstanding at the time have been settled. Subordinated loan capital must also fulfil the following criteria:

(a)   only fully paid-up funds may be taken into account;

(b)   the loans involved must have an original maturity of at least five years, after which they may be repaid; if the maturity of the debt is not fixed, they shall be repayable only subject to five years' notice unless the loans are no longer considered as own funds or unless the prior consent of the competent authorities is specifically required for early repayment. The competent authorities may grant permission for the early repayment of such loans provided the request is made at the initiative of the issuer and the solvency of the credit institution in question is not affected;

(c)   the extent to which they may rank as own funds must be gradually reduced during at least the last five years before the repayment date;

(d)   the loan agreement must not include any clause providing that in specified circumstances, other than the winding up of the credit institution, the debt will become repayable before the agreed repayment date.

Article 4a

Denmark may allow its mortgage credit institutions organized as cooperative societies or funds before 1 January 1990 and converted into public limited liability companies to continue to include joint and several commitments of members, or of borrowers as referred to in Article 4(1) claims on whom are treated in the same way as such joint and several commitments, in their own funds, subject to the following limits:

(a) the basis for calculation of the part of joint and several commitments of borrowers shall be the total of the items referred to in Article 2(1), points 1 and 2, minus those referred to in Article 2(1), points 9, 10 and 11;

(b) the basis for calculation on 1 January 1991 or, if converted at a later date, on the date of conversion, shall be the maximum basis for calculation. The basis for calculation may never exceed the maximum basis for calculation;

(c) the maximum basis for calculation shall, from 1 January 1997, be reduced by half of the proceeds from any issue of new capital, as defined in Article 2(1), point 1, made after that date; and

(d) the maximum amount of joint and several commitments of borrowers to be included as own funds must never exceed:

50% in 1991 and 1992,
45% in 1993 and 1994,
40% in 1995 and 1996,
35% in 1997,
30% in 1998,
20% in 1999,
10% in 2000, and
0% after 1 January 2001, of the basis for calculation;

Article 5

Until further coordination of the provisions on consolidation, the following rules shall apply.

1. Where the calculation is to be made on a consolidated basis, the consolidated amounts relating to the items listed under Article 2(1) shall be used in accordance with the rules laid down in Directive 92/350/EEC. Moreover, the following may, when they are credit ('negative') items, be regarded as consolidated reserves for the calculation of own funds:

— any minority interests within the meaning of Article 21 of Directive 83/349/EEC, where the global integration method is used,

— the first consolidation difference within the meaning of Articles 19, 30 and 31 of Directive 83/349/EEC,

— the translation differences included in consolidated reserves in accordance with Article 39 (6) of Directive 86/635/EEC,

— any difference resulting from the inclusion of certain participating interests in accordance with the method prescribed in Article 33 of Directive 83/349/EEC.

2. Where the above are debit ('positive') items, they must be deducted in the calculation of consolidated own funds.

Article 6: Deductions and limits

1. The items referred to in Article 2(1), points 3 and 5 to 8 shall be subject to the following limits:

(a) the total of items 3 and 5 to 8 may not exceed a maximum of 100% of items 1 plus 2 and 4 minus 9, 10 and 11;

(b) the total of items 7 and 8 may not exceed a maximum of 50% of items 1 plus 2 and 4 minus 9, 10 and 11;

(c) the total of items 12 and 13 shall be deducted from the total of the items.

3. The limits referred to in paragraph 1 must be complied with as from the date of the entry into force of the implementing measures for the Council Directive on a solvency ratio for credit institutions and by 1 January 1993 at the latest. Credit institutions exceeding those limits must gradually reduce the extent to which the items referred to in Article 2(1), points 3 and 5 to 8, are taken into account so that they comply with those limits before the aforementioned date.

4. The competent authorities may authorize credit institutions to exceed the limit laid down in paragraph 1 in temporary and exceptional circumstances.

Article 7
Compliance with the conditions laid down in Articles 2 to 6 must be proved to the satisfaction of the competent authorities.

Article 8
1. Without prejudice to the report referred to in the second subparagraph of Article 2(2), technical adaptations to be made to this Directive in the following areas shall be adopted in accordance with the procedure laid down in paragraph 2:
— clarification of the definitions to ensure uniform application of this Directive throughout the Community,
— clarification of the definitions in order to take account in the implementation of this Directive of developments on financial markets, and
— the alignment of terminology on, and the framing of definitions in accordance with, subsequent acts on credit institutions and related matters.

2. The Commission shall be assisted by a committee composed of representatives of the Member States and chaired by a representative of the Commission. The Commission representative shall submit to the committee a draft of the measures to be taken. The committee shall deliver its opinion on the draft within a time limit which the chairman may lay down according to the urgency of the matter. The opinion shall be delivered by the majority laid down in Article 148(2) of the Treaty in the case of decisions which the Council is required to adopt on a proposal from the Commission. The votes of the representatives of the Member States in the committee shall be weighted in the manner set out in that Article. The chairman shall not vote. The Commission shall adopt the measures envisaged if they are in accordance with the opinion of the committee. If the measures envisaged are not in accordance with the opinion of the committee, or if no opinion is delivered, the Commission shall, without delay, submit to the Council a proposal concerning the measures to be taken. The Council shall act by a qualified majority. If, on the expiry of a period of three months from the date of referral to the Council, the Council has not acted, the proposed measures shall be adopted by the Commission, save where the Council has decided against the said measures by a simple majority.

Article 9
1. Member States shall bring into force the laws, regulations and administrative provisions necessary for them to comply with this Directive no later than the date laid down for the entry into force of the implementing measures of the Council directive on a solvency ratio for credit institutions, and by 1 January 1993 at the latest. They shall forthwith inform the Commission thereof.

2. Member States shall communicate to the Commission the texts of the main provisions of national law which they adopt in the field governed by this Directive.

3. The communication referred to in paragraph 2 must also include a statement, accompanied by an explanatory text, notifying the Commission of the specific provisions adopted and the items selected by the Member States' respective competent authorities as comprising own funds.

Article 10
This Directive is addressed to the Member States.

Done at Luxembourg, 17 April 1989.
For the Council
The President
C. SOLCHAGA CATALAN

SECOND COUNCIL DIRECTIVE (89/646/EEC) OF 15 DECEMBER 1989 ON THE COORDINATION OF LAWS, REGULATIONS AND ADMINISTRATIVE PROVISIONS RELATING TO THE TAKING UP AND PURSUIT OF THE BUSINESS OF CREDIT INSTITUTIONS AND AMENDING DIRECTIVE 77/780/EEC
[OJ 1989, No. L386/1]*

THE COUNCIL OF THE EUROPEAN COMMUNITIES,

Having regard to the Treaty establishing the European Economic Community, and in particular the first and third sentences of Article 57(2) thereof,
　　Having regard to the proposal from the Commission,[1]
　　In cooperation with the European Parliament,[2]
　　Having regard to the opinion of the Economic and Social Committee,[3]

Whereas this Directive is to constitute the essential instrument for the achievement of the internal market, a course determined by the Single European Act and set out in timetable form in the Commission's White Paper, from the point of view of both the freedom of establishment and the freedom to provide financial services, in the field of credit institutions;
　　Whereas this Directive will join the body of Community legislation already enacted, in particular the first Council Directive 77/780/EEC of 12 December 1977 on the coordination of laws, regulations and administrative provisions relating to the taking up and pursuit of the business of credit institutions,[4] as last amended by Directive 86/524/EEC,[5] Council Directive 83/350/EEC of 13 June 1983 on the supervision of credit institutions on a consolidated basis,[6]

Notes
*As corrected at OJ 1990 L83/128, OJ 1990 L158/87, OJ 1990 L258/35 and amended by Directive 92/30/EEC [OJ 1992 L110/52].
[1]OJ No. C84, 31.3.1988, p. 1.
[2]OJ No. C96, 17.4.1989, p. 33 and Decision of 22 November 1989 (not yet published in the Official Journal).
[3]OJ No. C318, 17.12.1988, p. 42.
[4]OJ No. L322, 17.12.1977, p. 30.
[5]OJ No. L309, 4.11.1986, p. 15.
[6]OJ No. L193, 18.7.1983, p. 18.

Council Directive 86/635/EEC of 8 December 1986 on the annual and consolidated accounts of banks and other financial institutions[7] and Council Directive 89/299/EEC of 17 April 1989 on the own funds of credit institutions;[8]

Whereas the Commission has adopted recommendations 87/62/EEC on large exposures of credit institutions[9] and 87/63/EEC concerning the introduction of deposit-guarantee schemes;[10]

Whereas the approach which has been adopted is to achieve only the essential harmonization necessary and sufficient to secure the mutual recognition of authorisation and of prudential supervision systems, making possible the granting of a single licence recognised throughout the Community and the application of the principle of home Member State prudential supervision;

Whereas, in this context, this Directive can be implemented only simultaneously with specific Community legislation dealing with the additional harmonization of technical matters relating to own funds and solvency ratios;

Whereas, moreover, the harmonization of the conditions relating to the reorganisation and winding-up of credit institutions is also proceeding;

Whereas the arrangements necessary for the supervision of the liquidity, market, interest-rate and foreign-exchange risks run by credit institutions will also have to be harmonised;

Whereas the principles of mutual recognition and of home Member State control require the competent authorities of each Member State not to grant authorisation or to withdraw it where factors such as the activities programme, the geographical distribution or the activities actually carried on make it quite clear that a credit institution has opted for the legal system of one Member State for the purpose of evading the stricter standards in force in another Member State in which it intends to carry on or carries on the greater part of its activities; whereas, for the purposes of this Directive, a credit institution shall be deemed to be situated in the Member State in which it has its registered office; whereas the Member States must require that the head office be situated in the same Member State as the registered office;

Whereas the home Member State may also establish rules stricter than those laid down in Articles 4, 5, 11, 12 and 16 for institutions authorised by its competent authorities;

Whereas responsibility for supervising the financial soundness of a credit institution, and in particular its solvency, will rest with the competent authorities of its home Member State; whereas the host Member State's competent authorities will retain responsibility for the supervision of liquidity and monetary policy; whereas the supervision of market risk must be the subject of close cooperation between the competent authorities of the home and host Member States;

Whereas the harmonization of certain financial and investment services will be effected, where the need exists, by specific Community instruments, with the intention, in particular, of protecting consumers and investors; whereas the

Notes
[7] OJ No. L372, 31.12.1986, p. 1.
[8] OJ No. L124, 5.5.1989, p. 16.
[9] OJ No. L33, 4.2.1987, p. 10.
[10] OJ No. L33, 4.2.1987, p. 16.

Commission has proposed measures for the harmonization of mortgage credit in order, inter alia, to allow mutual recognition of the financial techniques peculiar to that sphere;

Whereas, by virtue of mutual recognition, the approach chosen permits credit institutions authorised in their home Member States to carry on, throughout the Community, any or all of the activities listed in the Annex by establishing branches or by providing services;

Whereas the carrying-on of activities not listed in the Annex shall enjoy the right of establishment and the freedom to provide services under the general provisions of the Treaty;

Whereas it is appropriate, however, to extend mutual recognition to the activities listed in the Annex when they are carried on by financial institutions which are subsidiaries of credit institutions, provided that such subsidiaries are covered by the consolidated supervision of their parent undertakings and meet certain strict conditions;

Whereas the host Member State may, in connection with the exercise of the right of establishment and the freedom to provide services, require compliance with specific provisions of its own national laws or regulations on the part of institutions not authorised as credit institutions in their home Member States and with regard to activities not listed in the Annex provided that, on the one hand, such provisions are compatible with Community law and are intended to protect the general good and that, on the other hand, such institutions or such activities are not subject to equivalent rules under the legislation or regulations of their home Member States;

Whereas the Member States must ensure that there are no obstacles to carrying on activities receiving mutual recognition in the same manner as in the home Member State, as long as the latter do not conflict with legal provisions protecting the general good in the host Member State;

Whereas the abolition of the authorisation requirement with respect to the branches of Community credit institutions once the harmonization in progress has been completed necessitates the abolition of endowment capital; whereas Article 6(2) constitutes a first transitional step in this direction, but does not, however, affect the Kingdom of Spain or the Portuguese Republic, as provided for in the Act concerning the conditions of those States' accession to the Community;

Whereas there is a necessary link between the objective of this Directive and the liberalisation of capital movements being brought about by other Community legislation; whereas in any case the measures regarding the liberalisation of banking services must be in harmony with the measures liberalising capital movements; whereas where the Member States may, by virtue of Council Directive 88/361/EEC of 24 June 1988 for the implementation of Article 67 of the Treaty,[1] invoke safeguard clauses in respect of capital movements, they may suspend the provision of banking services to the extent necessary for the implementation of the abovementioned safeguard clauses;

Whereas the procedures established in Directive 77/780/EEC, in particular with regard to the authorisation of branches of credit institutions authorised in third countries, will continue to apply to such institutions; whereas those

Note
[1] OJ No. L178, 8.7.1988, p. 5.

branches will not enjoy the freedom to provide services under the second paragraph of Article 59 of the Treaty or the freedom of establishment in Member States other than those in which they are established; whereas, however, requests for the authorisation of subsidiaries or of the acquisition of holdings made by undertakings governed by the laws of third countries are subject to a procedure intended to ensure that Community credit institutions receive reciprocal treatment in the third countries in question;

Whereas the authorisations granted to credit institutions by the competent national authorities pursuant to this Directive will have Community-wide, and no longer merely nationwide, application, and whereas existing reciprocity clauses will henceforth have no effect; whereas a flexible procedure is therefore needed to make it possible to assess reciprocity on a Community basis; whereas the aim of this procedure is not to close the Community's financial markets but rather, as the Community intends to keep its financial markets open to the rest of the world, to improve the liberalisation of the global financial markets in other third countries; whereas, to that end, this Directive provides for procedures for negotiating with third countries and, as a last resort, for the possibility of taking measures involving the suspension of new applications for authorisation or the restriction of new authorisations;

Whereas the smooth operation of the internal banking market will require not only legal rules but also close and regular cooperation between the competent authorities of the Member States; whereas for the consideration of problems concerning individual credit institutions the Contact Committee set up between the banking supervisory authorities, referred to in the final recital of Directive 77/780/EEC, remains the most appropriate forum; whereas that Committee is a suitable body for the mutual exchange of information provided for in Article 7 of that Directive;

Whereas that mutual information procedure will not in any case replace the bilateral collaboration established by Article 7 of Directive 77/780/EEC; whereas the competent host Member State authorities can, without prejudice to their powers of control proper, continue either, in an emergency, on their own initiative or following the initiative of the competent home Member State authorities to verify that the activities of a credit institution established within their territories comply with the relevant laws and with the principles of sound administrative and accounting procedures and adequate internal control;

Whereas technical modifications to the detailed rules laid down in this Directive may from time to time be necessary to take account of new developments in the banking sector; whereas the Commission shall accordingly make such modifications as are necessary, after consulting the Banking Advisory Committee, within the limits of the implementing powers conferred on the Commission by the Treaty; whereas that Committee shall act as a 'Regulatory' Committee, according to the rules of procedure laid down in Article 2, procedure III, variant (b), of Council Decision 87/373/EEC of 13 July 1987 laying down the procedures for the exercise of implementing powers conferred on the Commission,[1]

Note
[1] OJ No. L197, 18.7.1987, p. 33.

HAS ADOPTED THIS DIRECTIVE:

TITLE I   DEFINITIONS AND SCOPE

Article 1
For the purpose of this Directive:
  1.   'credit institution' shall mean a credit institution as defined in the first indent of Article 1 of Directive 77/780/EEC;
  2.   'authorisation' shall mean authorisation as defined in the second indent of Article 1 of Directive 77/780/EEC;
  3.   'branch' shall mean a place of business which forms a legally dependent part of a credit institution and which carries out directly all or some of the transactions inherent in the business of credit institutions; any number of places of business set up in the same Member State by a credit institution with headquarters in another Member State shall be regarded as a single branch;
  4.   'own funds' shall mean own funds as defined in Directive 89/299/EEC;
  5.   'competent authorities' shall mean the national authorities which are empowered by law or regulation to supervise credit institutions;
  6.   'financial institution' shall mean an undertaking other than a credit institution the principal activity of which is to acquire holdings or to carry on one or more of the activities listed in points 2 to 12 in the Annex;
  7.   'home Member State' shall mean the Member State in which a credit institution has been authorised in accordance with Article 3 of Directive 77/780/EEC;
  8.   'host Member State' shall mean the Member State in which a credit institution has a branch or in which it provides services;
  9.   'control' shall mean the relationship between a parent undertaking and a subsidiary, as defined in Article 1 of Directive 83/349/EEC,[1] or a similar relationship between any natural or legal person and an undertaking;
  10.   'qualifying holding' shall mean a direct or indirect holding in an undertaking which represents 10% or more of the capital or of the voting rights or which makes it possible to exercise a significant influence over the management of the undertaking in which a holding subsists. For the purposes of this definition, in the context of Articles 5 and 11 and of the other levels of holding referred to in Article 11, the voting rights referred to in Article 7 of Directive 88/627/EEC[2] shall be taken into consideration;
  11.   'initial capital' shall mean capital as defined in Article 2(1)(1) and (2) of Directive 89/299/EEC;
  12.   'parent undertaking' shall mean a parent undertaking as defined in Articles 1 and 2 of Directive 83/349/EEC;
  13.   'subsidiary' shall mean a subsidiary undertaking as defined in Articles 1 and 2 of Directive 83/349/EEC; any subsidiary of a subsidiary undertaking shall also be regarded as a subsidiary of the parent undertaking which is at the head of those undertakings;
  14.   'solvency ratio' shall mean the solvency coefficient of credit institutions calculated in accordance with Directive 89/647/EEC.[3]

Notes
[1]OJ No. L193, 18.7.1983, p. 1.
[2]OJ No. L348, 17.12.1988, p. 62.
[3]See p. 14 of this Official Journal.

Article 2

1.   This Directive shall apply to all credit institutions.

2.   It shall not apply to the institutions referred to in Article 2(2) of Directive 77/780/EEC.

3.   A credit institution which, as defined in Article 2(4)(a) of Directive 77/780/EEC, is affiliated to a central body in the same Member State may be exempted from the provisions of Articles 4, 10 and 12 of this Directive provided that, without prejudice to the application of those provisions to the central body, the whole as constituted by the central body together with its affiliated institutions is subject to the abovementioned provisions on a consolidated basis.

In cases of exemption, Articles 6 and 18 to 21 shall apply to the whole as constituted by the central body together with its affiliated institutions.

Article 3

The Member States shall prohibit persons or undertakings that are not credit institutions from carrying on the business of taking deposits or other repayable funds from the public. This prohibition shall not apply to the taking of deposits or other funds repayable by a Member State or by a Member State's regional or local authorities or by public international bodies of which one or more Member States are members or to cases expressly covered by national or Community legislation, provided that those activities are subject to regulations and controls intended to protect depositors and investors and applicable to those cases.

TITLE II   HARMONISATION OF AUTHORISATION CONDITIONS

Article 4

1.   The competent authorities shall not grant authorisation in cases where initial capital is less than ECU 5 million.

2.   The Member States shall, however, have the option of granting authorisation to particular categories of credit institutions the initial capital of which is less than that prescribed in paragraph 1. In such cases:

(a)   the initial capital shall not be less than ECU 1 million;

(b)   the Member States concerned must notify the Commission of their reasons for making use of the option provided for in this paragraph;

(c)   when the list referred to in Article 3(7) of Directive 77/780/EEC is published, the name of each credit institution that does not have the minimum capital prescribed in paragraph 1 shall be annotated to that effect;

(d)   within five years of the date referred to in Article 24(1), the Commission shall draw up a report on the application of this paragraph in the Member States, for the attention of the Banking Advisory Committee referred to in Article 11 of Directive 77/780/EEC.

Article 5

The competent authorities shall not grant authorisation for the taking-up of the business of credit institutions before they have been informed of the identities of the shareholders or members, whether direct or indirect, natural or legal persons, that have qualifying holdings, and of the amounts of those holdings.

The competent authorities shall refuse authorisation if, taking into account the need to ensure the sound and prudent management of a credit institution, they are not satisfied as to the suitability of the abovementioned shareholders or members.

Article 6

1. Host Member States may no longer require authorisation, as provided for in Article 4 of Directive 77/780/EEC, or endowment capital for branches of credit institutions authorised in other Member States. The establishment and supervision of such branches shall be effected as prescribed in Articles 13, 19 and 21 of this Directive.

2. Until the entry into force of the provisions implementing paragraph 1, host Member States may not, as a condition of the authorisation of branches of credit institutions, authorised in other Member States, require initial endowment capital exceeding 50% of the initial capital required by national rules for the authorisation of credit institutions of the same nature.

3. Credit institutions shall be entitled to the free use of the funds no longer required pursuant to paragraphs 1 and 2.

Article 7

There must be prior consultation with the competent authorities of the other Member State involved on the authorisation of a credit institution which is:

— a subsidiary of a credit institution authorised in another Member State, or

— a subsidiary of the parent undertaking of a credit institution authorised in another Member State, or

— controlled by the same persons, whether natural or legal, as control a credit institution authorised in another Member State.

TITLE III   RELATIONS WITH THIRD COUNTRIES

Article 8

The competent authorities of the Member States shall inform the Commission:

(a)   of any authorisation of a direct or indirect subsidiary one or more parent undertakings of which are governed by the laws of a third country. The Commission shall inform the Banking Advisory Committee accordingly;

(b)   whenever such a parent undertaking acquires a holding in a Community credit institution such that the latter would become its subsidiary. The Commission shall inform the Banking Advisory Committee accordingly.

When authorisation is granted to the direct or indirect subsidiary of one or more parent undertakings governed by the law of third countries, the structure of the group shall be specified in the notification which the competent authorities shall address to the Commission in accordance with Article 3(7) of Directive 77/780/EEC.

Article 9

1. The Member States shall inform the Commission of any general difficulties encountered by their credit institutions in establishing themselves or carrying on banking activities in a third country.

2. Initially no later than six months before the application of this Directive and thereafter periodically, the Commission shall draw up a report examining the treatment accorded to Community credit institutions in third countries, in the terms referred to in paragraphs 3 and 4, as regards establishment and the

carrying-on of banking activities, and the acquisition of holdings in third-country credit institutions. The Commission shall submit those reports to the Council, together with any appropriate proposals.

3. Whenever it appears to the Commission, either on the basis of the reports referred to in paragraph 2 or on the basis of other information, that a third country is not granting Community credit institutions effective market access comparable to that granted by the Community to credit institutions from that third country, the Commission may submit proposals to the Council for the appropriate mandate for negotiation with a view to obtaining comparable competitive opportunities for Community credit institutions. The Council shall decide by a qualified majority.

4. Whenever it appears to the Commission, either on the basis of the reports referred to in paragraph 2 or on the basis of other information that Community credit institutions in a third country do not receive national treatment offering the same competitive opportunities as are available to domestic credit institutions and the conditions of effective market access are not fulfilled, the Commission may initiate negotiations in order to remedy the situation.

In the circumstances described in the first subparagraph, it may also be decided at any time, and in addition to initiating negotiations, in accordance with the procedure laid down in Article 22(2), that the competent authorities of the Member States must limit or suspend their decisions regarding requests pending at the moment of the decision or future requests for authorisations and the acquisition of holdings by direct or indirect parent undertakings governed by the laws of the third country in question. The duration of the measures referred to may not exceed three months.

Before the end of that three-month period, and in the light of the results of the negotiations, the Council may, acting on a proposal from the Commission, decide by a qualified majority whether the measures shall be continued. Such limitations or suspension may not apply to the setting up of subsidiaries by credit institutions or their subsidiaries duly authorised in the Community, or to the acquisition of holdings in Community credit institutions by such institutions or subsidiaries.

5. Whenever it appears to the Commission that one of the situations described in paragraphs 3 and 4 obtains, the Member States shall inform it at its request:

(a) of any request for the authorisation of a direct or indirect subsidiary one or more parent undertakings of which are governed by the laws of the third country in question;

(b) whenever they are informed in accordance with Article 11 that such an undertaking proposes to acquire a holding in a Community credit institution such that the latter would become its subsidiary.

This obligation to provide information shall lapse whenever an agreement is reached with the third country referred to in paragraph 3 or 4 or when the measures referred to in the second and third subparagraphs of paragraph 4 cease to apply.

6. Measures taken pursuant to this Article shall comply with the Community's obligations under any international agreements, bilateral or multilateral, governing the taking-up and pursuit of the business of credit institutions.

TITLE IV HARMONISATION OF THE CONDITIONS GOVERNING PURSUIT OF THE BUSINESS OF CREDIT INSTITUTIONS

Article 10

1. A credit institution's own funds may not fall below the amount of initial capital required pursuant to Article 4 at the time of its authorisation.

2. The Member States may decide that credit institutions already in existence when the Directive is implemented, the own funds of which do not attain the levels prescribed for initial capital in Article 4, may continue to carry on their activities. In that event, their own funds may not fall below the highest level reached after the date of the notification of this Directive.

3. If control of a credit institution falling within the category referred to in paragraph 2 is taken by a natural or legal person other than the person who controlled the institution previously, the own funds of that institution must attain at least the level prescribed for initial capital in Article

4. 4. However, in certain specific circumstances and with the consent of the competent authorities, where there is a merger of two or more credit institutions falling within the category referred to in paragraph 2, the own funds of the institution resulting from the merger may not fall below the total own funds of the merged institutions at the time of the merger, as long as the appropriate levels pursuant to Article 4 have not been attained.

5. However, if, in the cases referred to in paragraphs 1, 2 and 4, the own funds should be reduced, the competent authorities may, where the circumstances justify it, allow an institution a limited period in which to rectify its situation or cease its activities.

Article 11

1. The Member States shall require any natural or legal person who proposes to acquire, directly or indirectly a qualifying holding in a credit institution first to inform the competent authorities, telling them of the size of the intended holding. Such a person must likewise inform the competent authorities if he proposes to increase his qualifying holding so that the proportion of the voting rights or of the capital held by him would reach or exceed 20%, 33% or 50% or so that the credit institution would become his subsidiary.

Without prejudice to the provisions of paragraph 2 the competent authorities shall have a maximum of three months from the date of the notification provided for in the first subparagraph to oppose such a plan if, in view of the need to ensure sound and prudent management of the credit institution, they are not satisfied as to the suitability of the person referred to in the first subparagraph. If they do not oppose the plan referred to in the first subparagraph, they may fix a maximum period for its implementation.

2. If the acquirer of the holdings referred to in paragraph 1 is a credit institution authorised in another Member State or the parent undertaking of a credit institution authorised in another Member State or a natural or legal person controlling a credit institution authorised in another Member State and if, as a result of that acquisition, the institution in which the acquirer proposes to acquire a holding would become a subsidiary or subject to the control of the acquirer, the assessment of the acquisition must be the subject of the prior consultation referred to in Article 7.

3. The Member States shall require any natural or legal person who proposes to dispose, directly or indirectly, of a qualifying holding in a credit institution first to inform the competent authorities, telling them of the size of his intended holding. Such a person must likewise inform the competent authorities if he proposes to reduce his qualifying holding so that the proportion of the voting rights or of the capital held by him would fall below 20%, 33% or 50% or so that the credit institution would cease to be his subsidiary.

4. On becoming aware of them, credit institutions shall inform the competent authorities of any acquisitions or disposals of holdings in their capital that cause holdings to exceed or fall below one of the thresholds referred to in paragraphs 1 and 3.

They shall also, at least once a year, inform them of the names of shareholders and members possessing qualifying holdings and the sizes of such holdings as shown, for example, by the information received at the annual general meetings of shareholders and members or as a result of compliance with the regulations relating to companies listed on stock exchanges.

5. The Member States shall require that, where the influence exercised by the persons referred to in paragraph 1 is likely to operate to the detriment of the prudent and sound management of the institution, the competent authorities shall take appropriate measures to put an end to that situation. Such measures may consist for example in injunctions, sanctions against directors and managers, or the suspension of the exercise of the voting rights attaching to the shares held by the shareholders or members in question.

Similar measures shall apply to natural or legal persons failing to comply with the obligation to provide prior information, as laid down in paragraph 1. If a holding is acquired despite the opposition of the competent authorities, the Member States shall, regardless of any other sanctions to be adopted, provide either for exercise of the corresponding voting rights to be suspended, or for the nullity of votes cast or for the possibility of their annulment.

Article 12

1. No credit institution may have a qualifying holding the amount of which exceeds 15% of its own funds in an undertaking which is neither a credit institution, nor a financial institution, nor an undertaking carrying on an activity referred to in the second subparagraph of Article 43(2)(f) of Directive 86/635/EEC.

2. The total amount of a credit institution's qualifying holdings in undertakings other than credit institutions, financial institutions or undertakings carrying on activities referred to in the second subparagraph of Article 43(2)(f) of Directive 86/635/EEC may not exceed 60% of its own funds.

3. The Member States need not apply the limits laid down in paragraphs 1 and 2 to holdings in insurance companies as defined in Directive 73/239/EEC,[1] as last amended by Directive 88/357/EEC,[2] and Directive 79/267/EEC,[3] as last amended by the Act of Accession of 1985.

Notes
[1] OJ No. L228, 16.8.1973, p. 3.
[2] OJ No. L172, 4.7.1988, p. 1.
[3] OJ No. L63, 13.3.1979, p. 1.

4. Shares held temporarily during a financial reconstruction or rescue operation or during the normal course of underwriting or in an institution's own name on behalf of others shall not be counted as qualifying holdings for the purpose of calculating the limits laid down in paragraphs 1 and 2. Shares which are not financial fixed assets as defined in Article 35(2) of Directive 86/635/EEC shall not be included.

5. The limits laid down in paragraphs 1 and 2 may be exceeded only in exceptional circumstances. In such cases, however, the competent authorities shall require a credit institution either to increase its own funds or to take other equivalent measures.

6. Compliance with the limits laid down in paragraphs 1 and 2 shall be ensured by means of supervision and monitoring on a consolidated basis in accordance with Directive 83/350/EEC.

7. Credit institutions which, on the date of entry into force of the provisions implementing this Directive, exceed the limits laid down in paragraphs 1 and 2 shall have a period of 10 years from that date in which to comply with them.

8. The Member States may provide that the competent authorities shall not apply the limits laid down in paragraph 1 and 2 if they provide that 100% of the amounts by which a credit institution's qualifying holdings exceed those limits must be covered by own funds and that the latter shall not be included in the calculation of the solvency ratio. If both the limits laid down in paragraphs 1 and 2 are exceeded, the amount to be covered by own funds shall be the greater of the excess amounts.

Article 13

1. The prudential supervision of a credit institution, including that of the activities it carries on in accordance with Article 18, shall be the responsibility of the competent authorities of the home Member State, without prejudice to those provisions of this Directive which give responsibility to the authorities of the host Member State.

2. Home Member State competent authorities shall require that every credit institution have sound administrative and accounting procedures and adequate internal control mechanisms.

3. Paragraphs 1 and 2 shall not prevent supervision on a consolidated basis pursuant to Directive 83/350/EEC.

Article 14

1. In Article 7(1) of Directive 77/780/EEC, the end of the second sentence is hereby replaced by the following: and all information likely to facilitate the monitoring of such institutions, in particular with regard to liquidity, solvency, deposit guarantees, the limiting of large exposures, administrative and accounting procedures and internal control mechanisms.

2. Host Member States shall retain responsibility in cooperation with the competent authorities of the home Member State for the supervision of the liquidity of the branches of credit institutions pending further coordination. Without prejudice to the measures necessary for the reinforcement of the European Monetary System, host Member States shall retain complete responsibility for the measures resulting from the implementation of their monetary policies. Such measures may not provide for discriminatory or restrictive treatment based on the fact that a credit institution is authorised in another Member State.

3.   Without prejudice to further coordination of the measures designed to supervise the risks arising out of open positions on markets, where such risks result from transactions carried out on the financial markets of other Member States, the competent authorities of the latter shall collaborate with the competent authorities of the home Member State to ensure that the institutions concerned take steps to cover those risks.

Article 15
1.   Host Member States shall provide that, where a credit institution authorised in another Member State carries on its activities through a branch, the competent authorities of the home Member State may, after having first informed the competent authorities of the host Member State, carry out themselves or through the intermediary of persons they appoint for that purpose on-the-spot verification of the information referred to in Article 7(1) of Directive 77/780/EEC.
2.   The competent authorities of the home Member State may also, for purposes of the verification of branches, have recourse to one of the other procedures laid down in Article 5(4) of Directive 83/350/EEC.
3.   This Article shall not affect the right of the competent authorities of the host Member State to carry out, in the discharge of their responsibilities under this Directive, on-the-spot verifications of branches established within their territory.

Article 16
Article 12 of Directive 77/780/EEC is hereby replaced by the following:

Article 12
1.   The Member States shall provide that all persons working or who have worked for the competent authorities, as well as auditors or experts acting on behalf of the competent authorities, shall be bound by the obligation of professional secrecy. This means that no confidential information which they may receive in the course of their duties may be divulged to any person or authority whatsoever, except in summary or collective form, such that individual institutions cannot be identified, without prejudice to cases covered by criminal law. Nevertheless, where a credit institution has been declared bankrupt or is being compulsorily wound up, confidential information which does not concern third parties involved in attempts to rescue that credit institution may be divulged in civil or commercial proceedings.
2.   Paragraph 1 shall not prevent the competent authorities of the various Member States from exchanging information in accordance with the Directives applicable to credit institutions. That information shall be subject to the conditions of professional secrecy indicated in paragraph 1.
3.   Member States may conclude cooperation agreements, providing for exchanges of information, with the competent authorities of third countries only if the information disclosed is subject to guarantees of professional secrecy at least equivalent to those referred to in this Article.
4.   Competent authorities receiving confidential information under paragraphs 1 or 2 may use it only in the course of their duties:
— to check that the conditions governing the taking-up of the business of credit institutions are met and to facilitate monitoring, on a non-consolidated or consolidated basis, of the conduct of such business,

especially with regard to the monitoring of liquidity, solvency, large exposures, and administrative and accounting procedures and internal control mechanisms, or

— to impose sanctions, or

— in an administrative appeal against a decision of the competent authority, or

— in court proceedings initiated pursuant to Article 15 or to special provisions provided for in the Directives adopted in the field of credit institutions.

5. Paragraphs 1 and 4 shall not preclude the exchange of information within a Member State, where there are two or more competent authorities in the same Member State, or between Member States, between competent authorities and:

— authorities entrusted with the public duty of supervising other financial organisations and insurance companies and the authorities responsible for the supervision of financial markets,

— bodies involved in the liquidation and bankruptcy of credit institutions and in other similar procedures,

— persons responsible for carrying out statutory audits of the accounts of credit institutions and other financial institutions, in the discharge of their supervisory functions, and the disclosure to bodies which administer deposit-guarantee schemes of information necessary to the exercise of their functions. The information received shall be subject to the conditions of professional secrecy indicated in paragraph 1.

6. Nor shall the provisions of this Article preclude a competent authority from disclosing to those central banks which do not supervise credit institutions individually such information as they may need to act as monetary authorities. Information received in this context shall be subject to the conditions of professional secrecy indicated in paragraph 1.

7. In addition, notwithstanding the provisions referred to in paragraphs 1 and 4, the Member States may, by virtue of provisions laid down by law, authorise the disclosure of certain information to other departments of their central government administrations responsible for legislation on the supervision of credit institutions, financial institutions, investment services and insurance companies and to inspectors acting on behalf of those departments.

However, such disclosures may be made only where necessary for reasons of prudential control. However, the Member States shall provide that information received under paragraphs 2 and 5 and that obtained by means of the on-the-spot verification referred to in Article 15(1) and (2) of Directive 89/646/ EEC[1] may never be disclosed in the cases referred to in this paragraph except with the express consent of the competent authorities which disclosed the information or of the competent authorities of the Member State in which on-the-spot verification was carried out.

Note
[1]OJ No. L386, 30.12.1989, p.1.

Article 17

Without prejudice to the procedures for the withdrawal of authorisations and the provisions of criminal law, the Member States shall provide that their respective competent authorities may, as against credit institutions or those who effectively control the business of credit institutions which breach laws, regulations or administrative provisions concerning the supervision or pursuit of their activities, adopt or impose in respect of them penalties or measures aimed specifically at ending observed breaches or the causes of such breaches.

TITLE V   PROVISIONS RELATING TO THE FREEDOM OF ESTABLISHMENT AND THE FREEDOM TO PROVIDE SERVICES

Article 18

1.   The Member States shall provide that the activities listed in the Annex may be carried on within their territories, in accordance with Articles 19 to 21, either by the establishment of a branch or by way of the provision of services, by any credit institution authorised and supervised by the competent authorities of another Member State, in accordance with this Directive, provided that such activities are covered by the authorisation.

2.   The Member States shall also provide that the activities listed in the Annex may be carried on within their territories, in accordance with Articles 19 to 21, either by the establishment of a branch or by way of the provision of services, by any financial institution from another Member State, whether a subsidiary of a credit institution or the jointly-owned subsidiary of two or more credit institutions, the memorandum and articles of association of which permit the carrying on of those activities and which fulfils each of the following conditions:

— the parent undertaking or undertakings must be authorised as credit institutions in the Member State by the law of which the subsidiary is governed,

— the activities in question must actually be carried on within the territory of the same Member State,

— the parent undertaking or undertakings must hold 90% or more of the voting rights attaching to shares in the capital of the subsidiary,

— the parent undertaking or undertakings must satisfy the competent authorities regarding the prudent management of the subsidiary and must have declared, with the consent of the relevant home Member State competent authorities, that they jointly and severally guarantee the commitments entered into by the subsidiary,

— the subsidiary must be effectively included, for the activities in question in particular, in the consolidated supervision of the parent undertaking, or of each of the parent undertakings, in accordance with Directive 83/350/EEC, in particular for the calculation of the solvency ratio, for the control of large exposures and for purposes of the limitation of holdings provided for in Article 12 of this Directive.

Compliance with these conditions must be verified by the competent authorities of the home Member State and the latter must supply the subsidiary with a certificate of compliance which must form part of the notification referred to in Articles 19 and 20.

The competent authorities of the home Member State shall ensure the supervision of the subsidiary in accordance with Articles 10(1), 11, 13, 14(1), 15 and 17 of this Directive and Articles 7(1) and 12 of Directive 77/780/EEC.

The provisions mentioned in this paragraph shall be applicable to subsidiaries, subject to the necessary modifications. In particular, the words 'credit institution' should be read as 'financial institution fulfilling the conditions laid down in Article 18(2)' and the word 'authorisation' as 'memorandum and articles of association'.

The second subparagraph of Article 19(3) shall read:

'The home Member State competent authorities shall also communicate the amount of own funds of the subsidiary financial institution and the consolidated solvency ratio of the credit institution which is its parent undertaking.'

If a financial institution eligible under this paragraph should cease to fulfil any of the conditions imposed, the home Member State shall notify the competent authorities of the host Member State and the activities carried on by that institution in the host Member State shall become subject to the legislation of the host Member State.

Article 19

1.   A credit institution wishing to establish a branch within the territory of another Member State shall notify the competent authorities of its home Member State.

2.   The Member State shall require every credit institution wishing to establish a branch in another Member State to provide the following information when effecting the notification referred to in paragraph 1:

(a)   the Member State within the territory of which it plans to establish a branch;

(b)   a programme of operations setting out inter alia the types of business envisaged and the structural organization of the branch;

(c)   the address in the host Member State from which documents may be obtained;

(d)   the names of those responsible for the management of the branch.

3.   Unless the competent authorities of the home Member State have reason to doubt the adequacy of the administrative structure or the financial situation of the credit institution, taking into account the activities envisaged, they shall within three months of receipt of the information referred to in paragraph 2 communicate that information to the competent authorities of the host Member State and shall inform the institution concerned accordingly.

The home Member State competent authorities shall also communicate the amount of own funds and the solvency ratio of the credit institution and, pending subsequent coordination, details of any deposit-guarantee scheme which is intended to ensure the protection of depositors in the branch.

Where the competent authorities of the home Member State refuse to communicate the information referred to in paragraph 2 to the competent authorities of the host Member State, they shall give reasons for their refusal to the institution concerned within three months of receipt of all the information. That refusal or failure to reply shall be subject to a right to apply to the courts in the home Member State.

4.   Before the branch of a credit institution commences its activities the competent authorities of the host Member State shall, within two months of receiving the information mentioned in paragraph 3, prepare for the supervision of the credit institution in accordance with Article 21 and if necessary indicate the conditions under which, in the interest of the general good, those activities must be carried on in the host Member State.

5.   On receipt of a communication from the competent authorities of the host Member State, or in the event of the expiry of the period provided for in

paragraph 4 without receipt of any communication from the latter, the branch may be established and commence its activities.

6. In the event of a change in any of the particulars communicated pursuant to paragraph 2(b), (c) or (d) or in the deposit-guarantee scheme referred to in paragraph 3 a credit institution shall give written notice of the change in question to the competent authorities of the home and host Member States at least one month before making the change so as to enable the competent authorities of the home Member State to take a decision pursuant to paragraph 3 and the competent authorities of the host Member State to take a decision on the change pursuant to paragraph 4.

Article 20

1. Any credit institution wishing to exercise the freedom to provide services by carrying on its activities within the territory of another Member State for the first time shall notify the competent authorities of the home Member State of the activities on the list in the Annex which it intends to carry on.

2. The competent authorities of the home Member State shall, within one month of receipt of the notification mentioned in paragraph 1, send that notification to the competent authorities of the host Member State.

Article 21

1. Host Member States may, for statistical purposes, require that all credit institutions having branches within their territories shall report periodically on their activities in those host Member States to the competent authorities of those host Member States.

In discharging the responsibilities imposed on them in Article 14(2) and (3), host Member States may require that branches of credit institutions from other Member States provide the same information as they require from national credit institutions for that purpose.

2. Where the competent authorities of a host Member State ascertain that an institution having a branch or providing services within its territory is not complying with the legal provisions adopted in that State pursuant to the provisions of this Directive involving powers of the host Member State competent authorities, those authorities shall require the institution concerned to put an end to that irregular situation.

3. If the institution concerned fails to take the necessary steps, the competent authorities of the host Member State shall inform the competent authorities of the home Member State accordingly. The competent authorities of the home Member State shall, at the earliest opportunity, take all appropriate measures to ensure that the institution concerned puts an end to that irregular situation. The nature of those measures shall be communicated to the competent authorities of the host Member State.

4. If, despite the measures taken by the home Member State or because such measures prove inadequate or are not available in the Member State in question, the institution persists in violating the legal rules referred to in paragraph 2 in force in the host Member State, the latter State may, after informing the competent authorities of the home Member State, take appropriate measures to prevent or to punish further irregularities and, insofar as is necessary, to prevent that institution from initiating further transactions within its territory. The Member States shall ensure that within their territories it is possible to serve the legal documents necessary for these measures on credit institutions.

5. The foregoing provisions shall not affect the power of host Member States to take appropriate measures to prevent or to punish irregularities committed within their territories which are contrary to the legal rules they have adopted in the interest of the general good. This shall include the possibility of preventing offending institutions from initiating any further transactions within their territories.

6. Any measure adopted pursuant to paragraphs 3, 4 and 5 involving penalties or restrictions on the exercise of the freedom to provide services must be properly justified and communicated to the institution concerned. Every such measure shall be subject to a right of appeal to the courts in the Member State the authorities of which adopted it.

7. Before following the procedure provided for in paragraphs 2 to 4, the competent authorities of the host Member State may, in emergencies, take any precautionary measures necessary to protect the interests of depositors, investors and others to whom services are provided. The Commission and the competent authorities of the other Member States concerned must be informed of such measures at the earliest opportunity.

The Commission may, after consulting the competent authorities of the Member States concerned, decide that the Member State in question must amend or abolish those measures.

8. Host Member States may exercise the powers conferred on them under this Directive by taking appropriate measures to prevent or to punish irregularities committed within their territories. This shall include the possibility of preventing institutions from initiating further transactions within their territories.

9. In the event of the withdrawal of authorisation the competent authorities of the host Member State shall be informed and shall take appropriate measures to prevent the institution concerned from initiating further transactions within its territory and to safeguard the interests of depositors. Every two years the Commission shall submit a report on such cases to the Banking Advisory Committee.

10. The Member States shall inform the Commission of the number and type of cases in which there has been a refusal pursuant to Article 19 or in which measures have been taken in accordance with paragraph 4. Every two years the Commission shall submit a report on such cases to the Banking Advisory Committee.

11. Nothing this Article shall prevent credit institutions with head offices in other Member States from advertising their services through all available means of communication in the host Member State, subject to any rules governing the form and the content of such advertising adopted in the interest of the general good.

TITLE VI   FINAL PROVISIONS

Article 22

1. The technical adaptations to be made to this Directive in the following areas shall be adopted in accordance with the procedure laid down in paragraph 2:

— expansion of the content of the list referred to in Article 18 and set out in the Annex or adaptation of the terminology used in that list to take account of developments on financial markets,

— alteration of the amount of initial capital prescribed in Article 4 to take account of developments in the economic and monetary field,

— the areas in which the competent authorities must exchange information as listed in Article 7(1) of Directive 77/780/EEC,

— clarification of the definitions in order to ensure uniform application of this Directive throughout the Community,

— clarification of the definitions in order to take account in the implementation of this Directive of developments on financial markets,

— the alignment of terminology on and the framing of definitions in accordance with subsequent acts on credit institutions and related matters.

2. The Commission shall be assisted by a committee composed of representatives of the Member States and chaired by a representative of the Commission.

The Commission representative shall submit to the committee a draft of the measures to be taken. The committee shall deliver its opinion on the draft within a time limit which the chairman may lay down according to the urgency of the matter. The opinion shall be delivered by the majority laid down in Article 148(2) of the Treaty in the case of decisions which the Council is required to adopt on a proposal from the Commission. The votes of the representatives of the Member States in the committee shall be weighted in the manner set out in that Article. The chairman shall not vote.

The Commission shall adopt the measures envisaged if they are in accordance with the opinion of the committee.

If the measures envisaged are not in accordance with the opinion of the committee, or if no opinion is delivered, the Commission shall, without delay, submit to the Council a proposal concerning the measures to be taken. The Council shall act by a qualified majority.

If the Council does not act within three months of the referral to it the Commission shall adopt the measures proposed, unless the Council has decided against those measures by a simple majority.

Article 23

1. Branches which have commenced their activities, in accordance with the provisions in force in their host Member States, before the entry into force of the provisions adopted in implementation of this Directive shall be presumed to have been subject to the procedure laid down in Article 19(1) to (5). They shall be governed, from the date of that entry into force, by Articles 15, 18, 19(6) and 21. They shall benefit pursuant to Article 6(3).

2. Article 20 shall not affect rights acquired by credit institutions providing services before the entry into force of the provisions adopted in implementation of this Directive.

Article 24

1. Subject to paragraph 2, the Member States shall bring into force the laws, regulations and administrative provisions necessary for them to comply with this Directive by the later of the two dates laid down for the adoption of measures to comply with Directives 89/299/EEC and 89/647/EEC and at the latest by 1 January 1993. They shall forthwith inform the Commission thereof.

2. The Member States shall adopt the measures necessary for them to comply with Article 6(2) by 1 January 1990.

3. The Member States shall communicate to the Commission the texts of the main provisions of national law which they adopt in the field covered by this Directive.

Article 25

This Directive is addressed to the Member States.

Done at Brussels, 15 December 1989.
For the Council
The President
B R GOVOY

ANNEX   LIST OF ACTIVITIES SUBJECT TO MUTUAL RECOGNITION

1. Acceptance of deposits and other repayable funds from the public.
2. Lending.[1]
3. Financial leasing.
4. Money transmission services.
5. Issuing and administering means of payment (e.g. credit cards, travellers' cheques and bankers' drafts).
6. Guarantees and commitments.
7. Trading for own account or for account of customers in:
   (a) money market instruments (cheques, bills, CDs, etc.);
   (b) foreign exchange;
   (c) financial futures and options;
   (d) exchange and interest rate instruments;
   (e) transferable securities.
8. Participation in securities issues and the provision of services related to such issues.
9. Advice to undertakings on capital structure, industrial strategy and related questions and advice and services relating to mergers and the purchase of undertakings.
10. Money broking.
11. Portfolio management and advice.
12. Safekeeping and administration of securities.
13. Credit reference services.
14. Safe custody services.

Note
[1]Including inter alia:
   — consumer credit,
   — mortgage credit,
   — factoring, with or without recourse,
   — financing of commercial transactions (including forfeiting).

COUNCIL DIRECTIVE OF 18 DECEMBER 1989 ON A SOLVENCY RATIO FOR CREDIT INSTITUTIONS (89/647/EEC)★
[OJ 1989, No. L386/14]

THE COUNCIL OF THE EUROPEAN COMMUNITIES,

Having regard to the Treaty establishing the European Economic Community, and in particular the first and third sentences of Article 57(2) thereof,

Having regard to the proposal from the Commission,[1]
In cooperation with the European Parliament,[2]
Having regard to the opinion of the Economic and Social Committee,[3]

Whereas this Directive is the outcome of work carried out by the Banking Advisory Committee, which, pursuant to Article 6(4) of Council Directive 77/780/EEC of 12 December 1977 on the coordination of laws, regulations and administrative provisions relating to the taking up and pursuit of the business of credit institutions,[4] as last amended by Directive 89/646/ EEC,[5] is responsible for making suggestions to the Commission with a view to coordinating the coefficients applicable in the Member States;

Whereas the establishment of an appropriate solvency ratio plays a central role in the supervision of credit institutions;

Whereas a ratio which weights assets and off-balance-sheet items according to the degree of credit risk is a particularly useful measure of solvency;

Whereas the development of common standards for own funds in relation to assets and off-balance-sheet items exposed to credit risk is, accordingly, an essential aspect of the harmonization necessary for the achievement of the mutual recognition of supervision techniques and thus the completion of the internal banking market;

Whereas, in that respect, this Directive must be considered in conjunction with other specific instruments also harmonizing the fundamental techniques of the supervision of credit institutions;

Whereas this Directive must also be seen as complementary to Directive 89/646/ EEC, which lays out the broader framework of which this Directive is an integral part;

Whereas, in a common banking market, institutions are required to enter into direct competition with one another and whereas the adoption of common solvency standards in the form of a minimum ratio will prevent distortions of competition and strengthen the Community banking system;

Whereas this Directive provides for different weightings to be given to guarantees issued by different financial institutions; whereas the Commission accordingly undertakes to examine whether the Directive taken as a whole significantly distorts competition between credit institutions and insurance companies and, in the light of that examination, to consider whether any remedial measures are justified;

Whereas the minimum ratio provided for in this Directive reinforces the capital of credit institutions in the Community; whereas a level of 8% has been adopted following a statistical survey of capital requirements in force at the beginning of 1988;

Notes
*As amended by Directives 91/31/EEC [OJ 1991 L17/20], 92/30/EEC [OJ 1992 L110/52] and 94/7/EC [OJ 1994 L89/17], Decision 95/1 [OJ 1995 L1/1], Directives 95/15/EC [OJ 1995 L125/23], 95/67/EC [OJ 1995 L314/72] and 96/10/EC [OJ 1996 L85/17]. Annex amended by OJ 1996 L85/19.
[1]OJ No. C135, 25.5.1988, p. 2.
[2]OJ No. C96, 17.4.1984, p. 86 and OJ No. C304, 4.12.1984.
[3]OJ No. C337, 31.12.1988, p. 8.
[4]OJ No. L322, 17.12.1977, p. 30.
[5]See page 1 of this Official Journal.

Whereas measurement of and allowance for interest-rate, foreign-exchange and other market risks are also of great importance in the supervision of credit institutions; whereas the Commission will accordingly, in cooperation with the competent authorities of the Member States and all other bodies working towards similar ends, continue to study the techniques available; whereas it will then make appropriate proposals for the further harmonization of supervision rules relating to those risks; whereas in so doing it will keep a special watch on the possible interaction between the various banking risks and consequently pay particular attention to the consistency of the various proposals;

Whereas, in making proposals for rules for the supervision of investment services and the adequacy of the capital of entities operating in that area, the Commission will ensure that equivalent requirements are applied in respect of the level of own funds, if the same type of business is transacted and identical risks are assumed;

Whereas the specific accounting technique to be used for the calculation of solvency ratios must take account of the provisions of Council Directive 86/635/EEC of 8 December 1986 on the annual accounts and consolidated accounts of banks and other financial institutions,[1] which incorporates certain adaptations of the provisions of Council Directive 83/349/EEC,[2] as amended by the Act of Accession of Spain and Portugal; whereas, pending transposition of the provisions of those Directives into the national laws of the Member States, the use of a specific accounting technique for the calculation of solvency ratios should be left to the discretion of the Member States;

Whereas the application of a 20% weighting to credit institutions' holdings of mortgage bonds may unsettle a national financial market on which such instruments play a preponderant role; whereas, in this case, provisional measures are taken to apply a 10% risk weighting;

Whereas technical modifications to the detailed rules laid down in this Directive may from time to time be necessary to take account of new developments in the banking sector; whereas the Commission will accordingly make such modifications as are necessary, after consulting the Banking Advisory Committee, within the limits of the implementing powers conferred on the Commission by the provisions of the Treaty; whereas that Committee will act as a 'Regulatory' Committee, according to the rules of procedure laid down in Article 2, procedure III, variant (b), of Council Decision 87/373/EEC of 13 July 1987 laying down the procedures for the exercise of implementing powers conferred on the Commission,[3]

HAS ADOPTED THIS DIRECTIVE:

Notes
[1]OJ No. L372, 31.12.1986, p. 1.
[2]OJ No. L193, 18.7.1983, p. 18.
[3]OJ No. L197, 18.7.1987, p. 33.

Article 1 Scope and definitions

1. This Directive shall apply to credit institutions as defined by the first indent of Article 1 of Directive 77/780/EEC.

2. Notwithstanding paragraph 1, the Member States need not apply this Directive to credit institutions listed in Article 2(2) of Directive 77/780/EEC.

3. A credit institution which, as defined in Article 2(4)(a) of Directive 77/780/EEC, is affiliated to a central body in the same Member State, may be exempted from the provisions of this Directive, provided that all such affiliated credit institutions and their central bodies are included in consolidated solvency ratios in accordance with this Directive.

4. Exceptionally, and pending further harmonization of the prudential rules relating to credit, interest-rate and market risks, the Member States may exclude from the scope of this Directive any credit institution specialising in the inter-bank and public-debt markets and fulfilling, together with the central bank, the institutional function of banking-system liquidity regulator, provided that:

— the sum of its asset and off-balance-sheet items included in the 50% and 100% weightings, calculated in accordance with Article 6, must not normally exceed 10% of total assets and off-balance-sheet items and shall not in any event exceed 15% before application of the weightings,

— its main activity consists of acting as intermediary between the central bank of its Member State and the banking system,

— the competent authority applies adequate systems of supervision and control of its credit, interest-rate and market risks.

The Member States shall inform the Commission of the exemptions granted, in order to ensure that they do not result in distortions of competition. Within three years of the adoption of this Directive, the Commission shall submit to the Council a report together, where necessary, with any proposals it may consider appropriate.

Article 2

1. For the purposes of this Directive:

— 'competent authorities' shall mean the national authorities which are empowered by law or regulation to supervise credit institutions,

— 'Zone A' shall comprise all the Member States and all other countries which are full members of the Organization for Economic Cooperation and Development (OECD) and those countries which have concluded special lending arrangements with the International Monetary Fund (IMF) associated with the Fund's General Arrangements to Borrow (GAB). Any country which reschedules its external sovereign debt is, however, precluded from Zone A for a period of 5 years.

— 'Zone B' shall comprise all countries not in Zone A,

— 'Zone A credit institutions' shall mean all credit institutions authorised in the Member States, in accordance with Article 3 of Directive 77/780/EEC, including their branches in third countries, and all private and public undertakings covered by the definition in the first indent of Article 1 of Directive 77/780/EEC and authorised in other Zone A countries, including their branches,

— 'Zone B credit institutions' shall mean all private and public undertakings authorised outside Zone A covered by the definition in the first indent of Article 1 of Directive 77/780/EEC, including their branches within the Community,

— 'non-bank sector' shall mean all borrowers other than credit institutions as defined in the fourth and fifth indents, central governments and central banks, regional governments and local authorities, the European Communities, the European Investment Bank and multilateral development banks as defined in the seventh indent,

— 'multilateral development banks' shall mean the International Bank for Reconstruction and Development, the International Finance Corporation, the Inter-American Development Bank, the Asian Development Bank, the African Development Bank, the Council of Europe Resettlement Fund, the Nordic Investment Bank, the Caribbean Development Bank, the European Bank for Reconstruction and Development, the European Investment Fund, the Inter-American Investment Corporation,

— 'full-risk', 'medium-risk', 'medium/low-risk' and 'low-risk' off-balance-sheet items shall mean the items described in Article 6(2) and listed in Annex I.

2.   For the purposes of Article 6(1)(b), the competent authorities may include within the concept of regional governments and local authorities non-commercial administrative bodies responsible to regional governments or local authorities, and those non-commercial undertakings owned by central governments, regional governments, local authorities or authorities which, in the view of the competent authorities, exercise the same responsibilities as regional and local authorities.

Article 3   General principles

1.   The solvency ratio referred to in paragraphs 2 to 7 expresses own funds, as defined in Article 4, as a proportion of total assets and off-balance-sheet items, risk-adjusted in accordance with Article 5.

2.   The solvency ratios of credit institutions which are neither parent undertakings as defined in Article 1 of Directive 83/349/EEC nor subsidiaries of such undertakings shall be calculated on an individual basis.

3.   The solvency ratios of credit institutions which are parent undertakings shall be calculated on a consolidated basis in accordance with the methods laid down in this Directive and in Directives 83/350/EEC and 86/635/EEC.[1]

4.   The competent authorities responsible for authorising and supervising a parent undertaking which is a credit institution may also require the calculation of a subconsolidated or unconsolidated ratio in respect of that parent undertaking and of any of its subsidiaries which are subject to authorisation and supervision by them. Where such monitoring of the satisfactory allocation of capital within a banking group is not carried out, other measures must be taken to attain that end.

5.   Where the subsidiary of a parent undertaking has been authorised and is situated in another Member State, the competent authorities which granted that authorisation shall require the calculation of a subconsolidated or unconsolidated ratio.

6.   Notwithstanding paragraph 5, the competent authorities responsible for authorising the subsidiary of a parent undertaking situated in another Member State may, by way of a bilateral agreement, delegate their responsibility for supervising solvency to the competent authorities which have authorised and which supervise the parent undertaking so that they assume responsibility for supervising the subsidiary in accordance with this Directive. The Commission shall be kept informed of the existence and content of such agreements. It shall forward such information to the other authorities and to the Banking Advisory Committee.

Note
[1]OJ No. L372, 31.12.1986, p. 1.

7. Without prejudice to credit institutions' compliance with the requirements of paragraphs 2 to 6, the competent authorities shall ensure that ratios are calculated not less than twice each year, either by credit institutions themselves, which shall communicate the results and any component data required to the competent authorities, or by the competent authorities, using data supplied by the credit institutions.

8. The valuation of assets and off-balance-sheet items shall be effected in accordance with Directive 86/635/EEC. Pending implementation of the provisions of that Directive, valuation shall be left to the discretion of the Member States.

Article 4 The numerator: own funds

Own funds as defined in Directive 89/299/EEC[1] shall form the numerator of the solvency ratio.

Note
[1] OJ No. L124, 5.5.1989, p. 16.

Article 5 The denominator: risk-adjusted assets and off-balance-sheet items

1. Degrees of credit risk, expressed as percentage weightings, shall be assigned to asset items in accordance with Articles 6 and 7, and exceptionally Articles 8 and 11. The balance-sheet value of each asset shall then be multiplied by the relevant weighting to produce a risk-adjusted value.

2. In the case of the off-balance-sheet items listed in Annex I, a two-stage calculation as prescribed in Article 6(2) shall be used.

3. In the case of the interest-rate- and foreign-exchange-related off-balance-sheet items referred to in Article 6(3), the potential costs of replacing contracts in the event of counterparty default shall be calculated by means of one of the two methods set out in Annex II. Those costs shall be multiplied by the relevant counterparty weightings in Article 6(1), except that the 100% weightings as provided for there shall be replaced by 50% weightings to produce risk-adjusted values.

4. The total of the risk-adjusted values of the assets and off-balance-sheet items mentioned in paragraphs 2 and 3 shall be the denominator of the solvency ratio.

Article 6 Risk weightings

1. The following weightings shall be applied to the various categories of asset items, although the competent authorities may fix higher weightings as they see fit:

(a) Zero weighting
 1. cash in hand and equivalent items;
 2. asset items constituting claims on Zone A central governments and central banks;
 3. asset items constituting claims on the European Communities;
 4. asset items constituting claims carrying the explicit guarantees of Zone A central governments and central banks or of the European Communities;
 5. asset items constituting claims on Zone B central governments and central banks, denominated and funded in the national currencies of the borrowers;

6.   asset items constituting claims carrying the explicit guarantees of Zone B central governments and central banks, denominated and funded in the national currency common to the guarantor and the borrower;

7.   asset items secured, to the satisfaction of the competent authorities, by collateral in the form of Zone A central government or central bank securities, or securities issued by the European Communities, or by cash deposits placed with the lending institution or by certificates of deposit or similar instruments issued by and lodged with the latter;

(b)   20% weighting

1.   asset items constituting claims on the European Investment Bank (EIB);

2.   asset items constituting claims on multilateral development banks;

3.   asset items constituting claims carrying the explicit guarantee of the European Investment Bank (EIB);

4.   asset items constituting claims carrying the explicit guarantees of multilateral development banks;

5.   asset items constituting claims on Zone A regional governments or local authorities, subject to Article 7;

6.   asset items constituting claims carrying the explicit guarantees of Zone A regional governments or local authorities, subject to Article 7;

7.   asset items constituting claims on Zone A credit institutions but not constituting such institutions' own funds as defined in Directive 89/299/EEC;

8.   asset items constituting claims, with a maturity of one year or less, on Zone B credit institutions, other than securities issued by such institutions which are recognised as components of their own funds;

9.   asset items carrying the explicit guarantees of Zone A credit institutions;

10.   asset items constituting claims with a maturity of one year or less, carrying the explicit guarantees of Zone B credit institutions;

11.   asset items secured, to the satisfaction of the competent authorities, by collateral in the form of securities issued by the EIB or by multilateral development banks;

12.   cash items in the process of collection;

(c)   50% weighting

1.   loans fully and completely secured, to the satisfaction of the competent authorities, by mortgages on residential property which is or will be occupied or let by the borrower and loans fully and completely secured, to the satisfaction of the competent authorities, by shares in Finnish residential housing companies, operating in accordance either the Finnish Housing Company Act of 1991 or subsequent equivalent legislation, in respect of residential property which is or will be occupied or let by the borrower.

2.   prepayments and accrued income: these assets shall be subject to the weighting corresponding to the counterparty where a credit institution is able to determine it in accordance with Directive 86/635/EEC. Otherwise, where it is unable to determine the counterparty, it shall apply a flat-rate weighting of 50%;

(d)   100% weighting

1.   asset items constituting claims on Zone B central governments and central banks except where denominated and funded in the national currency of the borrower;

2.   asset items constituting claims on Zone B regional governments or local authorities;

3.   asset items constituting claims with a maturity of more than one year on Zone B credit institutions;

4.   asset items constituting claims on the Zone A or Zone B non-bank sectors;

5.   tangible assets within the meaning of assets as listed in Article 4(10) of Directive 86/635/EEC;

6.   holdings of shares, participations and other components of the own funds of other credit institutions which are not deducted from the own funds of the lending institutions;

7.   all other assets except where deducted from own funds.

2.   The following treatment shall apply to off-balance-sheet items other than those covered in paragraph 3. They shall first be grouped according to the risk groupings set out in Annex I. The full value of the full-risk items shall be taken into account, 50% of the value of the medium-risk items and 20% of the medium/low-risk items, while the value of low-risk items shall be set at zero. The second stage shall be to multiply the off-balance-sheet values, adjusted as described above, by the weightings attributable to the relevant counterparties, in accordance with the treatment of asset items prescribed in paragraph 1 and Article 7. In the case of asset sale and repurchase agreements and outright forward purchases, the weightings shall be those attaching to the assets in question and not to the counterparties to the transactions.

3.   The methods set out in Annex II shall be applied to the interest-rate and foreign-exchange risks listed in Annex III.

4.   Where off-balance-sheet items carry explicit guarantees, they shall be weighted as if they had been incurred on behalf of the guarantor rather than the counterparty. Where the potential exposure arising from off-balance-sheet transactions is fully and completely secured, to the satisfaction of the competent authorities, by any of the asset items recognised as collateral in paragraph 1(a)(7) or (b)(11), weightings of 0% or 20% shall apply, depending on the collateral in question.

5.   Where asset and off-balance-sheet items are given a lower weighting because of the existence of explicit guarantees or collateral acceptable to the competent authorities, the lower weighting shall apply only to that part which is guaranteed or which is fully covered by the collateral.

Article 7

1.   Notwithstanding the requirements of Article 6(1)(b), the Member States may fix a weighting of 0% for their own regional governments and local authorities if there is no difference in risk between claims on the latter and claims on their central governments because of the revenue-raising powers of the regional governments and local authorities and the existence of specific institutional arrangements the effect of which is to reduce the chances of default by the latter. A zero weighting fixed in accordance with these criteria shall apply to claims on and off-balance-sheet items incurred on behalf of the regional governments and local authorities in question and claims on others and off-balance-sheet items incurred on behalf of others and guaranteed by those regional governments and local authorities.

2.   The Member States shall notify the Commission if they believe a zero weighting to be justified according to the criteria laid down in paragraph 1. The

Commission shall circulate that information. Other Member States may offer the credit institutions under the supervision of their competent authorities the possibility of applying a zero weighting where they undertake business with the regional governments or local authorities in question or where they hold claims guaranteed by the latter.

Article 8

1.   The Member States may apply a weighting of 20% to asset items which are secured, to the satisfaction of the competent authorities concerned, by collateral in the form of securities issued by Zone A regional governments or local authorities, by deposits placed with Zone A credit institutions other than the lending institution, or by certificates of deposit of similar instruments issued by those credit institutions.

2.   The Member States may apply a weighting of 10% to claims on institutions specialising in the inter-bank and public-debt markets in their home Member States and subject to close supervision by the competent authorities where those asset items are fully and completely secured, to the satisfaction of the competent authorities of the home Member States, by a combination of asset items mentioned in Article 6(1)(a) and (b) recognised by the latter as constituting adequate collateral.

3.   The Member States shall notify the Commission of any provisions adopted pursuant to paragraphs 1 and 2 and of the grounds for such provisions. The Commission shall forward that information to the Member States. The Commission shall periodically examine the implications of those provisions in order to ensure that they do not result in any distortions of competition. Within three years of the adoption of this Directive, the Commission shall submit to the Council a report together, where necessary, with any proposals it may consider appropriate.

Article 9

1.   The technical adaptations to be made to this Directive in the following areas shall be adopted in accordance with the procedure laid down in paragraph 2:

— a temporary reduction in the minimum ratio prescribed in Article 10 or the weightings prescribed in Article 6 in order to take account of specific circumstances,

— the definition of 'Zone A' in Article 2,

— the definition of 'multilateral development banks' in Article 2,

— amendment of the definitions of the assets listed in Article 6 in order to take account of developments on financial markets,

— the lists and classification of off-balance-sheet items in Annexes I and III and their treatment in the calculation of the ratio as described in Articles 5, 6 and 7 and Annex II,

— clarification of the definitions in order to ensure uniform application of this Directive throughout the Community,

— clarification of the definitions in order to take account in the implementation of this Directive of developments on financial markets,

— the alignment of terminology on and the framing of definitions in accordance with subsequent acts on credit institutions and related matters.

2.   The Commission shall be assisted by a committee composed of representatives of the Member States and chaired by a representative of the

Commission. The Commission representative shall submit to the committee a draft of the measures to be taken. The committee shall deliver its opinion on the draft within a time limit which the chairman may lay down according to the urgency of the matter. The opinion shall be delivered by the majority laid down in Article 148(2) of the Treaty in the case of decisions which the Council is required to adopt on a proposal from the Commission. The votes of the representatives of the Member States in the committee shall be weighted in the manner set out in that Article. The chairman shall not vote.

The Commission shall adopt the measures envisaged if they are in accordance with the opinion of the committee.

If the measures envisaged are not in accordance with the opinion of the committee, or if no opinion is delivered, the Commission shall, without delay, submit to the Council a proposal concerning the measures to be taken. The Council shall act by a qualified majority.

If the Council does not act within three months of the referral to it the Commission shall adopt the measures proposed, unless the Council has decided against those measures by a simple majority.

Article 10

1.   With effect from 1 January 1993 credit institutions shall be required permanently to maintain the ratio defined in Article 3 at a level of at least 8%.

2.   Notwithstanding paragraph 1, the competent authorities may prescribe higher minimum ratios as they consider appropriate.

3.   If the ratio falls below 8% the competent authorities shall ensure that the credit institution in question takes appropriate measures to restore the ratio to the agreed minimum as quickly as possible.

Article 11

1.   A credit institution the minimum ratio of which has not reached the 8% prescribed in Article 10(1) by the date prescribed in Article 12(1) must gradually approach that level by successive stages. It may not allow the ratio to fall below the level reached before that objective has been attained. Any fluctuation should be temporary and the competent authorities should be apprised of the reasons for it.

2.   For not more than five years after the date prescribed in Article 10(1) the Member States may fix a weighting of 10% for the bonds defined in Article 22(4) of Council Directive 85/611/EEC on the coordination of laws, regulations and administrative provisions relating to undertakings for collective investment in transferable securities (UCITS),[1] as amended by Directive 88/220/EEC.[2] and maintain it for credit institutions when and if they consider it necessary, to avoid grave disturbances in the operation of their markets. Such exceptions shall be reported to the Commission.

3.   For not more than seven years after 1 January 1993, Article 10(1) shall not apply to the Agricultural Bank of Greece. However, the latter must approach the level prescribed in Article 10(1) by successive stages according to the method described in paragraph 1.

Notes
[1] OJ No. L375, 31.12.1985, p. 3.
[2] OJ No. L100, 19.4.1988, p. 31.

4.   By derogation from Article 6(1)(c)(1), until 1 January 1996 Germany, Denmark, Greece and Austria may apply a weighting of 50% to assets which are entirely and completely secured to the satisfaction of the competent authorities concerned, by mortgages on completed residential property, on offices or on multi-purpose commercial premises, situated within the territories of those four Member States provided that the sum borrowed does not exceed 60% of the value of the property in question, calculated on the basis of rigorous assessment criteria laid down in statutory or regulatory provisions.

5.   Member States may apply a 50% weighting to property leasing transactions concluded within ten years of the date laid down in Article 12(1) and concerning assets for business use situated in the country of the head office and governed by statutory provisions whereby the lessor retains full ownership of the rented asset until the tenant exercises his option to purchase.

Article 12

1.   The Member States shall adopt the measures necessary for them to comply with the provisions of this Directive by 1 January 1991 at the latest.

2.   The Member States shall communicate to the Commission the texts of the main laws, regulations and administrative provisions which they adopt in the field covered by this Directive.

Article 13

This Directive is addressed to the Member States.

Done at Brussels, 18 December 1989.
For the Council,
The President,
B R GOVOY

ANNEX I   CLASSIFICATION OF OFF-BALANCE-SHEET ITEMS

Full risk
   — Guarantees having the character of credit substitutes,
   — Acceptances,
   — Endorsements on bills not bearing the name of another credit institution,
   — Transactions with recourse,
   — Irrevocable standby letters of credit having the character of credit substitutes,
   — Asset sale and repurchase agreements as defined in Articles 12(1) and (2) of Directive 86/635/EEC, if these agreements are treated as off-balance-sheet items pending application of Directive 86/635/EEC,
   — Assets purchased under outright forward purchase agreements,
   — Forward forward deposits,
   — The unpaid portion of partly-paid shares and securities,
   — Other items also carrying full risk.
Medium risk
   — Documentary credits issued and confirmed (see also medium/low risk),
   — Warranties and indemnities (including tender, performance, customs and tax bonds) and guarantees not having the character of credit substitutes,
   — Asset sale and repurchase agreements as defined in Article 12(3) and (5) of Directive 86/635/EEC,

— Irrevocable standby letters of credit not having the character of credit substitutes,

— Undrawn credit facilities (agreements to lend, purchase securities, provide guarantees or acceptance facilities) with an original maturity of more than one year,

— Note issuance facilities (NIFs) and revolving underwriting facilities (RUFs),

— Other items also carrying medium risk.

Medium/low risk

— Documentary credits in which underlying shipment acts as collateral and other self-liquidating transactions,

— Other items also carrying medium/low risk.

Low risk

— Undrawn credit facilities (agreements to lend, purchase securities, provide guarantees or acceptance facilities) with an original maturity of up to and including one year or which may be cancelled unconditionally at any time without notice,

— Other items also carrying low risk.

The Member States undertake to inform the Commission as soon as they have agreed to include a new off-balance-sheet item in any of the last indents under each category of risk. Such items will be definitively classified at Community level once the procedure laid down in Article 9 has been completed.

ANNEX II   THE TREATMENT OF OFF-BALANCE-SHEET ITEMS CONCERNING INTEREST AND FOREIGN-EXCHANGE RATES

1.   SCOPE AND CHOICE OF METHOD

Subject to the consent of their competent authorities, credit institutions may choose one of the methods set out below to measure the risks associated with the transactions listed in Annex III. Interest-rate and foreign-exchange contracts traded on recognised exchanges where they are subject to daily margin requirements and foreign-exchange contracts with an original maturity of fourteen calendar days or less are excluded.

2.   METHODS
Method 1: the 'mark-to-market' approach

Step (a): by attaching current market values to contracts (mark to market) the current replacement cost of all contracts with positive values is obtained.

Step (b): to obtain a figure for the potential future credit exposure,[1] the notional principal amounts or underlying values are multiplied by the following percentages:

TABLE 1

Residual maturity	Interest-rate contracts	Foreign-exchange contracts
One year or less	0%	1%
More than one year	0.5%	5%

Step (c): the sum of the current replacement cost and the potential future credit exposure is multiplied by the risk weightings allocated to the relevant counterparties in Article 6.

Method 2: the 'original exposure' approach

Step (a): the notional principal amount of each instrument is multiplied by the percentages given below:

TABLE 2

Original maturity[1]	Interest-rate contracts	Foreign-exchange contracts
One year or less	0.5%	2%
More than one year but not exceeding two years	1%	5%
Additional allowance for each additional year	1%	3%

[1]In the case of interest-rate contracts, credit institutions may, subject to the consent of their competent authorities, choose either original or residual maturity.

Step (b): the original exposure thus obtained is multiplied by the risk weightings allocated to the relevant counterparties in Article 6.

Note
[1]Except in the case of single-currency 'floating/floating' interest-rate swaps in which only the current replacement cost will be calculated.

3. CONTRACTUAL NETTING (CONTRACTS FOR NOVATION AND OTHER NETTING AGREEMENTS)

(a) Types of netting that the competent authorities may recognise
For the purposes of this point 3 'counterparty' means any entity (including natural persons) that has the power to conclude a contractual netting agreement.

The competent authorities may recognise as risk-reducing the following types of contractual netting:

(i) bilateral contracts for novation between a credit institution and its counterparty under which mutual claims and obligations are automatically amalgamated in such a way that this novation fixes one single net amount each time novation applies and thus creates a legally binding, single new contract extinguishing former contracts;

(ii) other bilateral netting agreements between a credit institution and its counterparty.

(b) Conditions for recognition
The competent authorities may recognise contractual netting as risk-reducing only under the following conditions:

(i) a credit institution must have a contractual netting agreement with its counterparty which creates a single legal obligation, covering all included transactions, such that, in the event of a counterparty's failure to perform owing to default, bankruptcy, liquidation or any other similar circumstance, the credit institution would have a claim to receive or an obligation to pay only the net sum of the positive and negative mark-to-market values of included individual transactions;

(ii) a credit institution must have made available to the competent authorities written and reasoned legal opinions to the effect that, in the event of a legal challenge, the relevant courts and administrative authorities would, in the cases described under (i), find that the credit institution's claims and obligations would be limited to the net sum, as described in (i), under:

— the law of the jurisdiction in which the counterparty is incorporated and, if a foreign branch of an undertaking is involved, also under the law of the jurisdiction in which the branch is located,

— the law that governs the individual transactions included, and

— the law that governs any contract or agreement necessary to effect the contractual netting;

(iii) a credit institution must have procedures in place to ensure that the legal validity of its contractual netting is kept under review in the light of possible changes in the relevant laws.

The competent authorities must be satisfied, if necessary after consulting the other competent authorities concerned, that the contractual netting is legally valid under the law of each of the relevant jurisdictions. If any of the competent authorities is not satisfied in that respect, the contractual netting agreement will not be recognised as risk-reducing for either of the counterparties.

The competent authorities may accept reasoned legal opinions drawn up by types of contractual netting.

No contract containing a provision which permits a non-defaulting counterparty to make limited payments only, or no payments at all, to the estate of the defaulter, even if the defaulter is a net creditor (a 'walkaway' clause), may be recognised as risk-reducing.

    (c) Effects of recognition

      (i) Contracts for novation

The single net amounts fixed by contracts for novation, rather than the gross amounts involved, may be weighted. Thus, in the application of Method 1, in

— Step (a): the current replacement cost, and in

— Step (b): the notional principal amounts or underlying values

may be obtained taking account of the contract for novation. In the application of Method 2, in Step (a) the notional principal amount may be calculated taking account of the contract for novation; the percentages of Table 2 must apply.

      (ii) Other netting agreements

In the application of Method 1, in Step (a) the current replacement cost for the contracts included in a netting agreement may be obtained by taking account of the current hypothetical net replacement cost which results from the agreement. In Step (b) the single net amounts may be taken into account only for forward foreign-exchange contracts and other similar contracts, in which notional principal is equivalent to cash flows, in cases where the amounts to be claimed or delivered fall due on the same value date and in the same currency.

In the application of Method 2, in Step (a)

— for forward foreign-exchange contracts and other similar contracts, in which notional principal is equivalent to cash flows, in cases where the amounts to be claimed or delivered fall due on the same value date and in the same currency, the notional principal amount may be calculated taking account of the netting agreement; to all these contracts Table 2 must apply,

— for all other contracts included in a netting agreement, the percentages applicable may be reduced as indicated in Table 3:

TABLE 3

Original maturity[1]	Interest-rate contracts	Foreign-exchange contracts
One year or less	0.35%	1.50%
More than one year but not more than two years	0.75%	3.75%
Additional allowance for each additional year	0.75%	2.25%

[1]In the case of interest-rate contracts, credit institutions may, subject to the consent of their competent authorities, choose either original or residual maturity.

ANNEX III   TYPES OF OFF-BALANCE-SHEET ITEMS CONCERNING INTEREST RATES AND FOREIGN EXCHANGE

Interest-rate contracts
— Single-currency interest rate swaps,
— Basic swaps,
— Forward-rate agreements,
— Interest-rate futures,
— Interest-rate options purchased,
— Other contracts of a similar nature.
Foreign-exchange contracts
— Cross-currency interest-rate swaps,
— Forward foreign-exchange contracts,
— Currency futures,
— Currency options purchased,
— Other contracts of a similar nature.

COUNCIL DIRECTIVE OF 10 JUNE 1991 ON PREVENTION OF THE USE OF THE FINANCIAL SYSTEM FOR THE PURPOSE OF MONEY LAUNDERING (91/308/ EEC)
[OJ 1991, No. L166/77]

THE COUNCIL OF THE EUROPEAN COMMUNITIES,

Having regard to the Treaty establishing the European Economic Community, and in particular Article 57(2), first and third sentences, and Article 100a thereof,

Having regard to the proposal from the Commission,[1]
In cooperation with the European Parliament,[2]
Having regard to the opinion of the Economic and Social Committee,[3]

Notes
[1]OJ No. C106, 28.4.1990, p. 6; and OJ No. C319, 19.12.1990, p. 9.
[2]OJ No. C324, 24.12.1990, p. 264; and OJ No. C129, 20.5.1991.
[3]OJ No. C332, 31.12.1990, p. 86.

Whereas when credit and financial institutions are used to launder proceeds from criminal activities (hereinafter referred to as 'money laundering'), the soundness and stability of the institution concerned and confidence in the financial system as a whole could be seriously jeopardized, thereby losing the trust of the public;

Whereas lack of Community action against money laundering could lead Member States, for the purpose of protecting their financial systems, to adopt measures which could be inconsistent with completion of the single market; whereas, in order to facilitate their criminal activities, launderers could try to take advantage of the freedom of capital movement and freedom to supply financial services which the integrated financial area involves, if certain coordinating measures are not adopted at Community level;

Whereas money laundering has an evident influence on the rise of organized crime in general and drug trafficking in particular; whereas there is more and more awareness that combating money laundering is one of the most effective means of opposing this form of criminal activity, which constitutes a particular threat to Member States' societies;

Whereas money laundering must be combated mainly by penal means and within the framework of international cooperation among judicial and law enforcement authorities, as has been undertaken, in the field of drugs, by the United Nations Convention Against Illicit Traffic in Narcotic Drugs and Psychotropic Substances, adopted on 19 December 1988 in Vienna (hereinafter referred to as the 'Vienna Convention') and more generally in relation to all criminal activities, by the Council of Europe Convention on laundering, tracing, seizure and confiscation of proceeds of crime, opened for signature on 8 November 1990 in Strasbourg;

Whereas a penal approach should, however, not be the only way to combat money laundering, since the financial system can play a highly effective role; whereas reference must be made in this context to the recommendation of the Council of Europe of 27 June 1980 and to the declaration of principles adopted in December 1988 in Basle by the banking supervisory authorities of the Group of Ten, both of which constitute major steps towards preventing the use of the financial system for money laundering;

Whereas money laundering is usually carried out in an international context so that the criminal origin of the funds can be better disguised; whereas measures exclusively adopted at a national level, without taking account of international coordination and cooperation, would have very limited effects;

Whereas any measures adopted by the Community in this field should be consistent with other action undertaken in other international fora; whereas in this respect any Community action should take particular account of the recommendations adopted by the financial action task force on money laundering, set up in July 1989 by the Paris summit of the seven most developed countries;

Whereas the European Parliament has requested, in several resolutions, the establishment of a global Community programme to combat drug trafficking, including provisions on prevention of money laundering;

Whereas for the purposes of this Directive the definition of money laundering is taken from that adopted in the Vienna Convention; whereas, however, since money laundering occurs not only in relation to the proceeds of drug-related offences but also in relation to the proceeds of other criminal activities (such as organized crime and terrorism), the Member States should, within the meaning of their legislation, extend the effects of the Directive to include the proceeds of such activities, to the extent that they are likely to result in laundering operations justifying sanctions on that basis;

Whereas prohibition of money laundering in Member States' legislation backed by appropriate measures and penalties is a necessary condition for combating this phenomenon;

Whereas ensuring that credit and financial institutions require identification of their customers when entering into business relations or conducting transactions, exceeding certain thresholds, are necessary to avoid launderers' taking advantage of anonymity to carry out their criminal activities; whereas such provisions must also be extended, as far as possible, to any beneficial owners;

Whereas credit and financial institutions must keep for at least five years copies or references of the identification documents required as well as supporting evidence and records consisting of documents relating to transactions or copies thereof similarly admissible in court proceedings under the applicable national legislation for use as evidence in any investigation into money laundering;

Whereas ensuring that credit and financial institutions examine with special attention any transaction which they regard as particularly likely, by its nature, to be related to money laundering is necessary in order to preserve the soundness and integrity of the financial system as well as to contribute to combating this phenomenon; whereas to this end they should pay special attention to transactions with third countries which do not apply comparable standards against money laundering to those established by the Community or to other equivalent standards set out by international fora and endorsed by the Community;

Whereas, for those purposes, Member States may ask credit and financial institutions to record in writing the results of the examination they are required to carry out and to ensure that those results are available to the authorities responsible for efforts to eliminate money laundering;

Whereas preventing the financial system from being used for money laundering is a task which cannot be carried out by the authorities responsible for combating this phenomenon without the cooperation of credit and financial institutions and their supervisory authorities; whereas banking secrecy must be lifted in such cases; whereas a mandatory system of reporting suspicious transactions which ensures that information is transmitted to the abovementioned authorities without alerting the customers concerned, is the most effective way to accomplish such cooperation; whereas a special protection clause is necessary to exempt credit and financial institutions, their employees and their directors from responsibility for breaching restrictions on disclosure of information;

Whereas the information received by the authorities pursuant to this Directive may be used only in connection with combating money laundering; whereas Member States may nevertheless provide that this information may be used for other purposes;

Whereas establishment by credit and financial institutions of procedures of internal control and training programmes in this field are complementary provisions without which the other measures contained in this Directive could become ineffective;

Whereas, since money laundering can be carried out not only through credit and financial institutions but also through other types of professions and categories of undertakings, Member States must extend the provisions of this Directive in whole or in part, to include those professions and undertakings whose activities are particularly likely to be used for money laundering purposes;

Whereas it is important that the Member States should take particular care to ensure that coordinated action is taken in the Community where there are strong grounds for believing that professions or activities the conditions governing the pursuit of which have been harmonized at Community level are being used for laundering money;

Whereas the effectiveness of efforts to eliminate money laundering is particularly dependent on the close coordination and harmonization of national implementing measures; whereas such coordination and harmonization which is being carried out in various international bodies requires, in the Community context, cooperation between Member States and the Commission in the framework of a contact committee;

Whereas it is for each Member State to adopt appropriate measures and to penalize infringement of such measures in an appropriate manner to ensure full application of this Directive,

HAS ADOPTED THIS DIRECTIVE:

Article 1
For the purpose of this Directive:

— 'credit institution' means a credit institution, as defined as in the first indent of Article 1 of Directive 77/780/EEC,[1] as last amended by Directive 89/646/EEC,[2] and includes branches within the meaning of the third indent of that Article and located in the Community, of credit institutions having their head offices outside the Community,

— 'financial institution' means an undertaking other than a credit institution whose principal activity is to carry out one or more of the operations included in numbers 2 to 12 and number 14 of the list annexed to Directive 89/646/EEC, or an insurance company duly authorized in accordance with Directive 79/267/EEC,[3] as last amended by Directive 90/619/EEC,[4] in so far as it carries out activities covered by that Directive; this definition includes branches located in the Community of financial institutions whose head offices are outside the Community,

— 'money laundering' means the following conduct when committed intentionally:

— the conversion or transfer of property, knowing that such property is derived from criminal activity or from an act of participation in such activity, for the purpose of concealing or disguising the illicit origin of the property or of assisting any person who is involved in the commission of such activity to evade the legal consequences of his action,

Notes
[1] OJ No. L322, 17.12.1977, p. 30.
[2] OJ No. L386, 30.12.1989, p. 1.
[3] OJ No. L63, 13.3.1979, p. 1.
[4] OJ No. L330, 29. 11.1990, p. 50.

—the concealment or disguise of the true nature, source, location, disposition, movement, rights with respect to, or ownership of property, knowing that such property is derived from criminal activity or from an act of participation in such activity,

—the acquisition, possession or use of property, knowing, at the time of receipt, that such property was derived from criminal activity or from an act of participation in such activity,

—participation in, association to commit, attempts to commit and aiding, abetting, facilitating and counselling the commission of any of the actions mentioned in the foregoing paragraphs. Knowledge, intent or purpose required as an element of the abovementioned activities may be inferred from objective factual circumstances. Money laundering shall be regarded as such even where the activities which generated the property to be laundered were perpetrated in the territory of another Member State or in that of a third country.

— 'Property' means assets of every kind, whether corporeal or incorporeal, movable or immovable, tangible or intangible, and legal documents or instruments evidencing title to or interests in such assets.

— 'Criminal activity' means a crime specified in Article 3 (1)(a) of the Vienna Convention and any other criminal activity designated as such for the purposes of this Directive by each Member State.

— 'Competent authorities' means the national authorities empowered by law or regulation to supervise credit or financial institutions.

Article 2
Member States shall ensure that money laundering as defined in this Directive is prohibited.

Article 3
1. Member States shall ensure that credit and financial institutions require identification of their customers by means of supporting evidence when entering into business relations, particularly when opening an account or savings accounts, or when offering safe custody facilities.

2. The identification requirement shall also apply for any transaction with customers other than those referred to in paragraph 1, involving a sum amounting to ECU 15,000 or more, whether the transaction is carried out in a single operation or in several operations which seem to be linked. Where the sum is not known at the time when the transaction is undertaken, the institution concerned shall proceed with identification as soon as it is apprised of the sum and establishes that the threshold has been reached.

3. By way of derogation from paragraphs 1 and 2, the identification requirements with regard to insurance policies written by insurance undertakings within the meaning of Directive 79/267/EEC, where they perform activities which fall within the scope of that Directive shall not be required where the periodic premium amount or amounts to be paid in any given year does or do not exceed ECU 1,000 or where a single premium is paid amounting to ECU 2,500 or less. If the periodic premium amount or amounts to be paid in any given year is or are increased so as to exceed the ECU 1,000 threshold, identification shall be required.

4. Member States may provide that the identification requirement is not compulsory for insurance policies in respect of pension schemes taken out by virtue of a contract of employment or the insured's occupation, provided that

such policies contain no surrender clause and may not be used as collateral for a loan.

5. In the event of doubt as to whether the customers referred to in the above paragraphs are acting on their own behalf, or where it is certain that they are not acting on their own behalf, the credit and financial institutions shall take reasonable measures to obtain information as to the real identity of the persons on whose behalf those customers are acting.

6. Credit and financial institutions shall carry out such identification, even where the amount of the transaction is lower than the threshold laid down, wherever there is suspicion of money laundering.

7. Credit and financial institutions shall not be subject to the identification requirements provided for in this Article where the customer is also a credit or financial institution covered by this Directive.

8. Member States may provide that the identification requirements regarding transactions referred to in paragraphs 3 and 4 are fulfilled when it is established that the payment for the transaction is to be debited from an account opened in the customer's name with a credit institution subject to this Directive according to the requirements of paragraph 1.

Article 4
Member States shall ensure that credit and financial institutions keep the following for use as evidence in any investigation into money laundering:

— in the case of identification, a copy or the references of the evidence required, for a period of at least five years after the relationship with their customer has ended,

— in the case of transactions, the supporting evidence and records, consisting of the original documents or copies admissible in court proceedings under the applicable national legislation for a period of at least five years following execution of the transactions.

Article 5
Member States shall ensure that credit and financial institutions examine with special attention any transaction which they regard as particularly likely, by its nature, to be related to money laundering.

Article 6
Member States shall ensure that credit and financial institutions and their directors and employees cooperate fully with the authorities responsible for combating money laundering:

— by informing those authorities, on their own initiative, of any fact which might be an indication of money laundering,

— by furnishing those authorities, at their request, with all necessary information, in accordance with the procedures established by the applicable legislation.

The information referred to in the first paragraph shall be forwarded to the authorities responsible for combating money laundering of the Member State in whose territory the institution forwarding the information is situated. The person or persons designated by the credit and financial institutions in accordance with the procedures provided for in Article 11(1) shall normally forward the information.

Information supplied to the authorities in accordance with the first paragraph may be used only in connection with the combating of money laundering. However, Member States may provide that such information may also be used for other purposes.

Article 7

Member States shall ensure that credit and financial institutions refrain from carrying out transactions which they know or suspect to be related to money laundering until they have apprised the authorities referred to in Article 6. Those authorities may, under conditions determined by their national legislation, give instructions not to execute the operation. Where such a transaction is suspected of giving rise to money laundering and where to refrain in such manner is impossible or is likely to frustrate efforts to pursue the beneficiaries of a suspected money-laundering operation, the institutions concerned shall apprise the authorities immediately afterwards.

Article 8

Credit and financial institutions and their directors and employees shall not disclose to the customer concerned nor to other third persons that information has been transmitted to the authorities in accordance with Articles 6 and 7 or that a money laundering investigation is being carried out.

Article 9

The disclosure in good faith to the authorities responsible for combating money laundering by an employee or director of a credit or financial institution of the information referred to in Articles 6 and 7 shall not constitute a breach of any restriction on disclosure of information imposed by contract or by any legislative, regulatory or administrative provision, and shall not involve the credit or financial institution, its directors or employees in liability of any kind.

Article 10

Member States shall ensure that if, in the course of inspections carried out in credit or financial institutions by the competent authorities, or in any other way, those authorities discover facts that could constitute evidence of money laundering, they inform the authorities responsible for combating money laundering.

Article 11

Member States shall ensure that credit and financial institutions:

1. establish adequate procedures of internal control and communication in order to forestall and prevent operations related to money laundering,

2. take appropriate measures so that their employees are aware of the provisions contained in this Directive. These measures shall include participation of their relevant employees in special training programmes to help them recognize operations which may be related to money laundering as well as to instruct them as to how to proceed in such cases.

Article 12

Member States shall ensure that the provisions of this Directive are extended in whole or in part to professions and to categories of undertakings, other than the credit and financial institutions referred to in Article 1, which engage in activities which are particularly likely to be used for money-laundering purposes.

Article 13

1.   A contact committee (hereinafter referred to as 'the Committee') shall be set up under the aegis of the Commission. Its function shall be:

(a)   without prejudice to Articles 169 and 170 of the Treaty, to facilitate harmonized implementation of this Directive through regular consultation on any practical problems arising from its application and on which exchanges of view are deemed useful;

(b)   to facilitate consultation between the Member States on the more stringent or additional conditions and obligations which they may lay down at national level;

(c)   to advise the Commission, if necessary, on any supplements or amendments to be made to this Directive or on any adjustments deemed necessary, in particular to harmonize the effects of Article 12;

(d)   to examine whether a profession or a category of undertaking should be included in the scope of Article 12 where it has been established that such profession or category of undertaking has been used in a Member State for money laundering.

2.   It shall not be the function of the Committee to appraise the merits of decisions taken by the competent authorities in individual cases.

3.   The Committee shall be composed of persons appointed by the Member States and of representatives of the Commission. The secretariat shall be provided by the Commission. The chairman shall be a representative of the Commission. It shall be convened by its chairman, either on his own initiative or at the request of the delegation of a Member State.

Article 14

Each Member State shall take appropriate measures to ensure full application of all the provisions of this Directive and shall in particular determine the penalties to be applied for infringement of the measures adopted pursuant to this Directive.

Article 15

The Member States may adopt or retain in force stricter provisions in the field covered by this Directive to prevent money laundering.

Article 16

1.   Member States shall bring into force the laws, regulations and administrative decisions necessary to comply with this Directive before 1 January 1993 at the latest.

2.   Where Member States adopt these measures, they shall contain a reference to this Directive or shall be accompanied by such reference on the occasion of their official publication. The methods of making such a reference shall be laid down by the Member States.

3.   Member States shall communicate to the Commission the text of the main provisions of national law which they adopt in the field governed by this Directive.

Article 17

One year after 1 January 1993, whenever necessary and at least at three yearly intervals thereafter, the Commission shall draw up a report on the implementation of this Directive and submit it to the European Parliament and the Council.

Article 18
This Directive is addressed to the Member States.

Done at Luxembourg, 10 June 1991.
For the Council
The President
J.-C. JUNCKER

DIRECTIVE 97/5/EC OF THE EUROPEAN PARLIAMENT AND OF THE COUNCIL OF 27 JANUARY 1997 ON CROSS-BORDER CREDIT TRANSFERS

THE EUROPEAN PARLIAMENT AND THE COUNCIL OF THE EUROPEAN UNION,

Having regard to the Treaty establishing the European Community, and in particular Article 100a thereof,
    Having regard to the proposal from the Commission,[1]
    Having regard to the opinion of the Economic and Social Committee,[2]
    Having regard to the opinion of the European Monetary Institute,
    Acting in accordance with the procedure laid down in Article 189b of the Treaty[3] in the light of the joint text approved on 22 November 1996 by the Conciliation Committee,

(1)   Whereas the volume of cross-border payments is growing steadily as completion of the internal market and progress towards full economic and monetary union lead to greater trade and movement of people within the Community; whereas cross-border credit transfers account for a substantial part of the volume and value of cross-border payments;
(2)   Whereas it is essential for individuals and businesses, especially small and medium-sized enterprises, to be able to make credit transfers rapidly, reliably and cheaply from one part of the Community to another, whereas, in conformity with the Commission Notice on the application of the EC competition rules to cross-border credit transfers,[4] greater competition in the market for cross-border credit transfers should lead to improved services and reduced prices;
(3)   Whereas this Directive seeks to follow up the progress made towards completion of the internal market, in particular towards liberalisation of capital movements, with a view to the implementation of economic and monetary union; whereas its provisions must apply to credit transfers in the currencies of the Member States and in ECUs;

Notes
[1]OJ No. C360, 17.12.1994, p. 13, and OJ No. C199, 3.8.1995, p. 16.
[2]OJ No. C236, 11.9.1995, p. 1.
[3]Opinion of the European Parliament of 19 May 1995 [OJ No. C151, 19.6.1995, p. 370], Council common position of 4 December 1995 [OJ No. C353, 30.12.1995, p. 52] and Decision of the European Parliament of 13 March 1996 [OJ No. C96, 1.4.1996, p. 74]. Decision of the Council of 19 December 1996 and Decision of the European Parliament of 19 December 1996 and Decision of the European Parliament of 16 January 1997.
[4]OJ No. C251, 27.9.1995, p. 3.

(4)   Whereas the European Parliament, in its resolution of 12 February 1993,[5] called for a Council Directive to lay down rules in the area of transparency and performance of cross-border payments;

(5)   Whereas the issues covered by this Directive must be dealt with separately from the systemic issues which remain under consideration within the Commission; whereas it may become necessary to make a further proposal to cover these systemic issues, particularly the problem of settlement finality;

(6)   Whereas the purpose of this Directive is to improve cross-border credit transfer services and thus assist the European Monetary Institute (EMI) in its task of promoting the efficiency of cross-border payments with a view to the preparation of the third stage of economic and monetary union;

(7)   Whereas, in line with the objectives set out in the second recital, this Directive should apply to any credit transfer of an amount of less than ECU 50,000;

(8)   Whereas, having regard to the third paragraph of Article 3b of the Treaty, and with a view to ensuring transparency, this Directive lays down the minimum requirements needed to ensure an adequate level of customer information both before and after the execution of a cross-border credit transfer; whereas these requirements include indication of the complaints and redress procedures offered to customers, together with the arrangements for access thereto; whereas this Directive lays down minimum execution require-ments, in particular in terms of performance, which institutions offering cross-border credit transfer services should adhere to, including the obligation to execute a cross-border credit transfer in accordance with the customer's instructions; whereas this Directive fulfils the conditions deriving from the principles set out in Commission Recommendation 90/109/EEC of 14 February 1990 on the transparency of banking conditions relating to cross-border financial transactions;[6] whereas this Directive is without prejudice to Council Directive 91/308/EEC of 10 June 1991 on prevention of the use of the financial system for the purpose of money laundering;[7]

(9)   Whereas this Directive should contribute to reducing the maximum time taken to execute a cross-border credit transfer and encourage those institutions which already take a very short time to do so to maintain that practice;

(10)   Whereas the Commission, in the report it will submit to the European Parliament and the Council within two years of implementation of this Directive, should particularly examine the time-limit to be applied in the absence of a time-limit agreed between the originator and his institution, taking into account both technical developments and the situation existing in each Member State;

(11)   Whereas there should be an obligation upon institutions to refund in the event of a failure to successfully complete a credit transfer; whereas the obligation to refund imposes a contingent liability on institutions which might, in the absence of any limit, have a prejudicial effect on solvency requirements; whereas that obligation to refund should therefore be applicable up to ECU 12,500;

Notes
[5] OJ No. C72, 15.3.1993, p. 158.
[6] OJ No. L67, 15.3.1990, p. 39.
[7] OJ No. L166, 28.6.1991, p. 77.

(12)   Whereas Article 8 does not affect the general provisions of national law whereby an institution has responsibility towards the originator when a cross-border credit transfer has not been completed because of an error committed by that institution;

(13)   Whereas it is necessary to distinguish, among the circumstances with which institutions involved in the execution of a cross-border credit transfer may be confronted, including circumstances relating to insolvency, those caused by *force majeure*; whereas for that purpose the definition of *force majeure* given in Article 4(6) of Directive 90/314/EEC of 13 June 1990 on package travel, package holidays and package tours[8] should be taken as a basis;

(14)   Whereas there need to be adequate and effective complaints and redress procedures in the Member States for the settlement of possible disputes between customers and institutions, using existing procedures where appropriate;

Note
[8] OJ No. L158, 23.6.1990, p. 59.

HAVE ADOPTED THIS DIRECTIVE:

SECTION 1   SCOPE AND DEFINITIONS

Article 1   Scope
The provisions of this Directive shall apply to cross-border credit transfers in the currencies of the Member States and the ECU up to the equivalent of ECU 50,000 ordered by persons other than those referred to in Article 2(a), (b) and (c) and executed by credit institutions or other institutions.

Article 2   Definitions
For the purposes of this Directive:

(a)   'credit institution' means an institution as defined in Article 1 of Council Directive 77/780/EEC,[1] and includes branches, within the meaning of the third indent of that Article and located in the Community, of credit institutions which have their head offices outside the Community and which by way of business execute cross-border credit transfers;

(b)   'other institution' means any natural or legal person, other than a credit institution, that by way of business executes cross-border credit transfers;

(c)   'financial institution' means an institution as defined in Article 4(1) of Council Regulation (EC) No. 3604/93 of 13 December 1993 specifying definitions for the application of the prohibition of privileged access referred to in Article 104a of the Treaty;[2]

(d)   'institution' means a credit institution or other institution; for the purposes of Articles 6, 7 and 8, branches of one credit institution situated in different Member States which participate in the execution of a cross-border credit transfer shall be regarded as separate institutions;

(e)   'intermediary institution' means an institution which is neither that of the originator nor that of the beneficiary and which participates in the execution of a cross-border credit transfer;

Notes
[1] OJ No. L322, 17.12.1977, p. 30. Directive as last amended by Directive 95/26/EC [OJ No. L168, 18.7.1995, p. 7].
[2] OJ No. L332, 31.12.1993, p. 4.

Compensation shall comprise the payment of interest calculated by applying the reference rate of interest to the amount of the cross-border credit transfer for the period from:

— the end of the agreed time limit or, in the absence of any such time limit, the end of the banking business day following the day on which the funds were credited to the account of the beneficiary's institution, to

— the date on which the funds are credited to the beneficiary's account.

3. No compensation shall be payable pursuant to paragraphs 1 and 2 where the originator's institution or, as the case may be, the beneficiary's institution can establish that the delay is attrributable to the originator or, as the case may be, the beneficiary.

4. Paragraphs 1, 2 and 3 shall be entirely without prejudice to the other rights of customers and institutions that have participated in the execution of a cross-border credit transfer order.

Article 7   Obligation to execute the cross-border transfer in accordance with instructions

1. The originator's institution, any intermediary institution and the beneficiary's institution, after the date of acceptance of the cross-border credit transfer for the full amount thereof unless the originator has specified that the costs of the cross-border credit transfer are to be borne wholly or partly by the beneficiary.

The first subparagraph shall be without prejudice to the possibility of the beneficiary's institution levying a charge on the beneficiary relating to the administration of his account, in accordance with the relevant rules and customs. However, such a charge may not be used by the institution to avoid the obligations imposed by the said subparagraph.

2. Without prejudice to any other claim which may be made, where the originator's institution or an intermediary institution has made a deduction from the amount of the cross-border credit transfer in breach of paragraph 1, the originator's institution shall, at the originator's request, credit, free of all deductions and at its own cost, the amount deducted to the beneficiary unless the originator requests that the amount be credited to him.

Any intermediary institution which has made a deduction in breach of paragraph 1 shall credit the amount deducted, free of all deductions and at its own cost, to the originator's institution or, if the originator's institution so requests, to the beneficiary of the cross-border credit transfer.

3. Where a breach of the duty to execute the cross-border credit transfer order in accordance with the originator's instructions has been caused by the beneficiary's institution, and without prejudice to any other claim which may be made, the beneficiary's institution shall be liable to credit to the beneficiary, at its own cost, any sum wrongly deducted.

Article 8   Obligation upon institutions to refund in the event of non-execution of transfers

1. If, after a cross-border credit transfer order has been accepted by the originator's institution, the relevant amounts are not credited to the account of the beneficiary's institution, and without prejudice to any other claim which may be made, the originator's institution shall credit the originator, up to ECU 12,500, with the amount of the cross-border credit transfer plus:

— interest calculated by applying the reference interest rate to the amount of the cross-border credit transfer for the period between the date of the cross-border credit transfer order and the date of the credit, and

— the charges relating to the cross-border credit transfer paid by the originator.

These amounts shall be made available to the originator within fourteen banking business days following the date of his request, unless the funds corresponding to the cross-border credit transfer have in the meantime been credited to the account of the beneficiary's institution.

Such a request may not be made before expiry of the time limit agreed between the originator's institution and the originator for the execution of the cross-border credit transfer order or, in the absence of any such time limit, before expiry of the time limit laid down in the second subparagraph of Article 6(1).

Similarly, each intermediary institution which has accepted the cross-border credit transfer order owes an obligation to refund at its own cost the amount of the credit transfer, including the related costs and interests, to the institution which instructed it to carry out the order. If the cross-border credit transfer was not completed because of errors or omissions in the instructions given by that institution, the intermediary institution shall endeavour as far as possible to refund the amount of the transfer.

2. By way of derogation from paragraph 1, if the cross-border credit transfer was not completed because of its non-execution by an intermediary institution chosen by the beneficiary's institution, the latter institution shall be obliged to make the funds available to the beneficiary up to ECU 12,500.

3. By way of derogation from paragraph 1, if the cross-border credit transfer was not completed because of an error or omission in the instructions given by the originator to his institution or because of non-execution of the cross-border credit transfer by an intermediary institution expressly chosen by the originator, the originator's institution and the other institutions involved shall endeavour as far as possible to refund the amount of the transfer.

Where the amount has been recovered by the originator's institution, it shall be obliged to credit it to the originator. The institutions, including the originator's institution, are not obliged in this case to refund the charges and interest accruing, and can deduct the costs arising from the recovery if specified.

Article 9   Situation of *force majeure*

Without prejudice to the provisions of Directive 91/308/EEC, institutions participating in the execution of a cross-border credit transfer order shall be released from the obligations laid down in the Directive where they can adduce reasons of *force majeure*, namely abnormal and unforeseeable circumstances beyond the control of the person pleading *force majeure*, the consequences of which would have been unavoidable despite all efforts to the contrary, which are relevant to its provisions.

Article 10   Settlement of disputes

Member States shall ensure that there are adequate and effective complaints and redress procedures for the settlement of disputes between an originator and his institution or between a beneficiary and his institution, using existing procedures where appropriate.

SECTION IV FINAL PROVISIONS

Article 11 Implementation

1. Member States shall bring into force the laws, regulations and administrative provisions necessary to comply with this Directive by 14 August 1999 at the latest. They shall forthwith inform the Commission thereof.

When Member States adopt these provisions, they shall contain a reference to this Directive or shall be accompanied by such reference on the occasion of their official publication. The methods of making such reference shall be laid down by Member States.

2. Member States shall communicate to the Commission the text of the main laws, regulations or administrative provisions which they adopt in the field governed by this Directive.

Article 12 Report to the European Parliament and the Council

No later than two years after the date of implementation of this Directive, the Commission shall submit a report to the European Parliament and the Council on the application of this Directive, accompanied where appropriate by proposals for its revision.

This report shall, in the light of the situation existing in each Member State and of the technical developments that have taken place, deal particularly with the question of the time limit set in Article 6(1).

Article 13 Entry into force

This Directive shall enter into force on the date of its publication in the *Official Journal of the European Communities*

Article 14 Addresses

This Directive is addressed to the Member States.

Done at Brussels, 27 January 1997.
For the European Parliament,
The President,
J. M. GIL-ROBLES

For the Council,
The President,
G. ZALM

JOINT STATEMENT — BY THE EUROPEAN PARLIAMENT, THE COUNCIL AND THE COMMISSION

The European Parliament, the Council and the Commission note the determination of the Member States to implement the laws, regulations and administrative provisions required to comply with this Directive by 1 January 1999.

INSURANCE SECTOR DIRECTIVES: NON LIFE

FIRST COUNCIL DIRECTIVE OF 24 JULY 1973 ON THE COORDINATION OF LAWS, REGULATIONS AND ADMINISTRATIVE PROVISIONS RELATING TO THE TAKING-UP AND PURSUIT OF THE BUSINESS OF DIRECT INSURANCE OTHER THAN LIFE ASSURANCE (73/239/EEC)
[OJ 1973 L228/3]*

THE COUNCIL OF THE EUROPEAN COMMUNITIES,

Having regard to the Treaty establishing the European Economic Community, and in particular Article 57(2) thereof;

Having regard to the general programme for the abolition of restrictions on freedom of establishment, and in particular Title IV C thereof;

Having regard to the proposal from the Commission;

Having regard to the opinion of the European Parliament;[1]

Having regard to the opinion of the Economic and Social Committee;[2]

Whereas by virtue of the general programme the removal of restrictions on the establishment of agencies and branches is, in the case of the direct insurance business, dependent on the coordination of the conditions for the taking-up and pursuit of this business;

Whereas such coodination should be effected in the first place in respect of direct insurance other than life assurance;

Whereas in order to facilitate the taking-up and pursuit of the business of insurance, it is essential to eliminate certain divergencies which exist between national supervisory legislation;

Whereas in order to achieve this objective, and at the same time ensure adequate protection for insured and third parties in all the member states, it is desirable to coordinate, in particular, the provisions relating to the financial guarantees required of insurance undertakings;

Whereas a classification of risks in the different classes of insurance is necessary in order to determine, in particular, the activities subject to a

Note

*As amended by OJ 1979 L291/90, OJ 1985 L302/156 & OJ C241/197 and Directives 76/580 [OJ 1976 L189/13], 84/461 [OJ 1984 L339/21], 87/343 [OJ 1987 L185/72], 87/344 [OJ 1987 L185/77], 88/357 [OJ 1988 L172/1], 90/618 [OJ 1990 L330/44], 92/49 [OJ 1992 L228/1] and 95/26 [OJ 1995 L168/7].

[1] OJ 1968 C27/15.

[2] OJ 1967 C158/1.

compulsory authorisation and the amount of the minimum guarantee fund fixed for the class of insurance concerned;

Whereas it is desirable to exclude from the application of this Directive mutual associations which, by virtue of their legal status, fulfil appropriate conditions to security and financial guarantees;

Whereas it is further desirable to exclude certain institutions in several member states whose business covers a very limited sector only and is restricted by law to a specified territory or to specified persons;

Whereas the various laws contain different rules as to the simultaneous undertaking of health insurance, credit and suretyship insurance and insurance in respect of recourse against third parties and legal defence, whether with one another or with other classes of insurance;

Whereas continuance of this divergence after the abolition of restrictions on the right of establishment in classes other than life assurance would mean that obstacles to establishment would continue to exist;

Whereas a solution to this problem must be provided in subsequent coordination to be effected within a relatively short period of time;

Whereas it is necessary to extend supervision in each member state to all the classes of insurance to which this Directive applies;

Whereas such supervision is not possible unless the undertaking of such classes of insurance is subject to an official authorisation;

Whereas it is therefore necessary to define the conditions for the granting or withdrawal of such authorisation;

Whereas provision must be made for a right to apply to the courts should an authorisation be refused or withdrawn;

Whereas it is desirable to bring the classes of insurance known as transport classes bearing Nos 4, 5, 6, 7 and 12 in paragraph A of the Annex, and the credit insurance classes bearing Nos 14 and 15 in paragraph A of the Annex, under more flexible rules in view of the continual fluctuations in conditions affecting goods and credit;

Whereas the search for a common method of calculating technical reserves is at present the subject of studies at Community level;

Whereas it therefore appears to be desirable to reserve the attainment of coordination in this matter, as well as questions relating to the determination of categories of investments and the valuation of assets, for subsequent Directives;

Whereas it is necessary that insurance undertakings should possess, over and above technical reserves of sufficient amount to meet their underwriting liabilities, a supplementary reserve, to be known as the solvency margin, and represented by free assets, in order to provide against business fluctuations; whereas in order to ensure that the requirements imposed for such purposes are determined according to objective criteria, whereby undertakings of the same size are placed on an equal footing as regards competition, it is desirable to provide that such margin shall be related to the overall volume of business of the undertaking and be determined by reference to two indices of security, one based on premiums and the other on claims;

Whereas it is desirable to require a minimum guarantee fund related to the size of the risk in the classes undertaken, in order to ensure that undertakings possess adequate resources when they are set up and that in the subsequent course of business the solvency margin shall in no event fall below a minimum of security;

Whereas it is necessary to make provision for the case where the financial condition of the undertaking becomes such that it is difficult for it to meet its underwriting liabilities;

Whereas the coordinated rules concerning the taking-up and pursuit of the business or direct insurance within the Community should, in principle, apply to all undertakings entering the market and, consequently, also to agencies and branches where the head office of the undertaking is situated outside the Community;

Whereas it is, nevertheless, desirable as regards the methods of supervision to make special provision with respect to such agencies or branches in view of the fact that the assets of the undertakings to which they belong are situated outside the Community;

Whereas it is, however, desirable to permit the relaxation of such special conditions, while observing the principle that such agencies and branches should not obtain more favourable treatment than undertakings within the Community:

Whereas certain transitional provisions are required in order, in particular, to permit small and medium-sized undertakings already in existence to adapt themselves to the requirements which must be imposed by the member states in pursuance of this Directive, subject to the application of Article 53 of the Treaty;

Whereas it is important to guarantee the uniform application of coordinated rules and to provide, in this respect, for close collaboration between the Commission and the member states in this field,

HAS ADOPTED THIS DIRECTIVE:

TITLE I   GENERAL PROVISIONS

Article 1

1.   This Directive concerns the taking-up and pursuit of the self-employed activity of direct insurance, including the provision of assistance referred to in paragraph 2, carried on by undertakings which are established in the territory of a member state or which wish to become established there.

2.   The assistance activity shall be the assistance provided for persons who get into difficulties while travelling, while away from home or while away from their permanent residence. It shall consist in undertaking, against the prior payment of a premium, to make aid immediately available to the beneficiary under an assistance contract where that person is in difficulties following the occurrence of a chance event, in the cases and under the conditions set out in the contract. The aid may consist in the provision of benefits in cash or in kind, the provision of benefits in kind may also be effected by means of the staff and equipment of the person providing them. The assistance activity does not cover servicing, maintenance, after-sales service or the mere indication or provision of aid as an intermediary.

3.   The classification by classes of the activity referred to in this Article appears in the Annex.

Article 2

This Directive does not apply to:

1.   The following kinds of insurance:

(a)   life assurance, that is to say, the branch of insurance which comprises, in particular, assurance on survival to a stipulated age only,

3. Bayerische Landestierversicherungsanstalt, Schlachtviehversicherun, Munich,

4. Braunschweigische Landesbrandversicherungsanstalt, Brunswick,

5. Hamburger Feuerkasse, Hamburg,

6. Hessische Brandversicherungsanstalt (Hessische Brandversicherungskammer), Darmstadt,

7. Hessische Brandversicherungsanstalt, Kassel,

8. Hohenzollernsche Feuerversicherungsanstalt, Sigmaringen,

9. Lippische Landesbrandversicherungsanstalt, Detmold,

10. Nassauische Brandversicherungsanstalt, Wiesbaden,

11. Oldenburgische Landesbrandkasse, Oldenburg,

12. Ostfriesische Landschaftliche Brandkasse, Aurich,

13. Feuersozietaet Berlin, Berlin,

14. Wuerttembergische Gebaeudebrandversicherungsanstalt, Stuttgart.

However, territorial capacity shall not be regarded as modified in the case of a merger between such institutions which has the effect of maintaining for the benefit of the new institution the territorial capacity of the institutions which have merged, nor shall capacity as to the classes of insurance be regarded as modified if one of these institutions takes over in respect of the same territory one or more of the classes of another such institution.

The following semi-public institutions:

1. Postbeamtenkrankenkasse,

2. Krankenversorgung der Bundesbahnbeamten;

    (b) in France

The following institutions:

1. Caisse départementale des incendies des Ardennes,

2. Caisse départementale des incendies de la Côte-d'or,

3. Caisse départementale des incendies de la Marne,

4. Caisse départementale des incendies de la Meuse,

5. Caisse départementale des incendies de la Somme,

6. Caisse départementale grele du Gers,

7. Caisse départementale grele de l'Herault;

    (c) in Ireland

Voluntary health insurance board;

    (d) in Italy

The cassa di previdenza per l'assicurazione degli sportivi (sportass);

    (e) in the United Kingdom

The crown agents.

    (f) In Denmark

'Falcks redningskorps a/s, Koebenhavn.'

    (g) In Spain

The following institutions:

1. Comisaria de Seguro Obligatorio de Viajeros,

2. Consorcio de Compensacion de Seguros,

3. Fondo Nacional de Garantia de Riesgos de la Circulacion.

Article 5

For the purposes of this Directive:

(a) Unit of account means the European unit of account (EUA) as defined by Commission Decision 3289/75/ECSC.[1] Wherever this directive refers to the unit of account, the conversion value in national currency to be adopted shall, as from 31 December of each year, be that of the last day of the preceding month of October for which EUA conversion values are available in all the community currencies.

(b) 'matching assets' means the representation of underwriting liabilities expressed in a particular currency by assets expressed or realisable in the same currency;

(c) 'localisation of assets' means the existence of assets, whether movable of immovable, within a member state but shall not be construed as involving a requirement that movable property be deposited or that immovable property be subjected to restrictive measures such as the registration of mortgages. Assets represented by claims against debtors shall be regarded as situated in the member state where they are to be liquidated.

(d) 'large risks' means:

(i) risks classified under classes 4, 5, 6, 7, 11 and 12 of point A of the Annex;

(ii) risks classified under classes 14 and 15 of point A of the Annex, where the policy-holder is engaged professionally in an industrial or commercial activity or in one of the liberal professions, and the risks relate to such activity;

(iii) risks classified under classes 3, 8, 9, 10, 13 and 16 of point A of the Annex in so far as the policy-holder exceeds the limits of at least two of the following three criteria:

first stage: until 31 December 1992:
— balance-sheet total: 12.4 million ECU,
— net turnover: 24 million ECU,
— average number of employees during the financial year: 500.

second stage: from 1 January 1993:
— balance-sheet total: 6.2 million ECU,
— net turnover: 12.8 million ECU,
— average number of employees during the financial year: 250.

If the policy-holder belongs to a group of undertakings for which consolidated accounts within the meaning of Directive 83/349/EEC[2] are drawn up, the criteria mentioned above shall be applied on the basis of the consolidated accounts.

Each Member State may add to the category mentioned under (iii) risks insured by professional associations, joint ventures or temporary groupings.

Notes
[1] OJ 1975 No. L327/4.
[2] OJ No. L193, 18.7.1983, p. 1.

TITLE II   RULES APPLICABLE TO UNDERTAKINGS WHOSE HEAD OFFICES ARE SITUATED WITHIN THE COMMUNITY

SECTION A   CONDITIONS OF ADMISSION

Article 6
The taking up of the business of direct insurance shall be subject to prior official authorisation. Such authorisation shall be sought from the competent authorities of the home Member State by:

(a) any undertaking which establishes its head office within the territory of that State;

(b) any undertaking which, having received the authorisation referred to in the first subparagraph, extends its business to an entire class or to other classes.

Article 7

1. Authorisation shall be valid for the entire Community. It shall permit an undertaking to carry on business there, under either the right of establishment or the freedom to provide services.

2. Authorisation shall be granted for a particular class of insurance. It shall cover the entire class, unless the applicant wishes to cover only some of the risks pertaining to that class, as listed in point A of the Annex. However:

(a) Member States may grant authorisation for the groups of classes listed in point B of the Annex, attaching to them the appropriate denominations specified therein;

(b) authorisation granted for one class or a group of classes shall also be valid for the purpose of covering ancillary risks included in another class if the conditions imposed in point C of the Annex are fulfilled.

Article 8

1. The home Member State shall require every insurance undertaking for which authorisation is sought to:

(a) adopt one of the following forms:

— in the case of the Kingdom of Belgium: 'société anonyme/naamloze vennootschap', 'société en commandite par actions/commanditaire vennootschap op aandelen', 'association d'assurance mutuelle/onderlinge verzekeringsvereniging', 'société cooperative/cooeperatieve vennootschap';

— in the case of the Kingdom of Denmark: 'aktieselskaber', 'gensidige selskaber';

— in the case of the Federal Republic of Germany: 'Aktiengesellschaft', 'Versicherungsverein auf Gegenseitigkeit', 'Oeffentlich-rechtliches Wettbewerbsversicherungsunternehmen';

— in the case of the French Republic: 'société anonyme', 'société d'assurance mutuelle', 'institution de prévoyance régie par le code de la sécurité sociale', 'institution de prévoyance régie par le code rural' and 'mutuelles régies par le code de la mutualité';

— in the case of Ireland: incorporated companies limited by shares or by guarantee or unlimited;

— in the case of the Italian Republic: 'società per azioni', 'società cooperativa', 'mutua di assicurazione';

— in the case of the Grand Duchy of Luxembourg: 'société anonyme', 'société en commandite par actions', 'association d'assurances mutuelles', 'société cooperative';

— in the case of the Kingdom of the Netherlands: 'naamloze vennootschap', 'onderlinge waarborgmaatschappij';

— in the case of the United Kingdom: incorporated companies limited by shares or by guarantee or unlimited, societies registered under the Industrial and Provident Societies Acts, societies registered under the Friendly Societies Acts, the association of underwriters known as Lloyd's;

— in the case of the Hellenic Republic: 'anonymi etairia', 'allilasfalistikos synetairismos';

—in the case of the Kingdom of Spain: 'sociedad annima', 'sociedad mutua', 'sociedad cooperativa';

—in the case of the Portuguese Republic: 'sociedade annima', 'mutua de seguros'.

—In the case of the Republic of Austria: Aktiengesellschaft, Versicherungsverein auf Gegenseitigkeit

—In the case of the Reublic of Finland: keskinaeinen vakuutusyhtioe/oemsesidigt foersaekringsbolag, vakuutusosakeyhtioe/foersaekringsakti bolag, vakuutusyhdistys/foersaekringsfoerening

—In the case of the Kingdom of Sweden: foersaekringsaktiebolag, oemsesidiga foersaekringsbolag, understoedsfoereningar.

An insurance undertaking may also adopt the form of a European Company (SE) when that has been established. Furthermore, Member States may, where appropriate, set up undertakings in any public-law form provided that such bodies have as their objects insurance operations under conditions equivalent to those under which private-law undertakings operate;

(b)   limit its objects to the business of insurance and operations arising directly therefrom, to the exclusion of all other commercial business;

(c)   submit a scheme of operations in accordance with Article 9;

(d)   possess the minimum guarantee fund provided for in Article 17(2);

(e)   be effectively run by persons of good repute with appropriate professional qualifications or experience. Moreover, where close links exist between the financial undertaking and other natural or legal persons, the competent authorities shall grant authorisation only if those links do not prevent the effective exercise of their supervisory functions. The competent authorities shall also refuse authorisation if the laws, regulations or administrative provisions of a non-member country governing one or more natural or legal persons with which the undertaking has close links, or difficulties involved in their enforcement, prevent the effective exercise of their supervisory functions. The competent authorities shall require financial undertakings to provide them with the information they require to monitor compliance with the conditions referred to in this paragraph on a continuous basis.

1a.   Member States shall require that the head offices of insurance undertakings be situated in the same Member State as their registered offices.

2.   An undertaking seeking authorisation to extend its business to other classes or to extend an authorisation covering only some of the risks pertaining to one class shall be required to submit a scheme of operations in accordance with Article 9. It shall, furthermore, be required to show proof that it possesses the solvency margin provided for in Article 16 and, if with regard to such other classes Article 17(2) requires a higher minimum guarantee fund than before, that it possesses that minimum.

3.   Nothing in this Directive shall prevent Member States from maintaining in force or introducing laws, regulations or administrative provisions requiring approval of the memorandum and articles of association and communication of any other documents necessary for the normal exercise of supervision. Member States shall not, however, adopt provisions requiring the prior approval or systematic notification of general and special policy conditions, scales of premiums and forms and other printed documents which an undertaking intends to use in its dealings with policyholders. Member States may not retain or introduce prior notification or approval of proposed increases

in premium rates except as part of general price-control systems. Nothing in this Directive shall prevent Member States from subjecting undertakings seeking or having obtained authorisation for class 18 in point A of the Annex to checks on their direct or indirect resources in staff and equipment, including the qualification of their medical teams and the quality of the equipment available to such undertakings to meet their commitments arising out of this class of insurance.

4. The abovementioned provisions may not require that any application for authorisation be considered in the light of the economic requirements of the market.

Article 9

The scheme of operations referred to in Article 8(1)(c) shall include particulars or proof concerning:

(a) the nature of the risks which the undertaking proposes to cover;

(b) the guiding principles as to reinsurance;

(c) the items constituting the minimum guarantee fund;

(d) estimates of the costs of setting up the administrative services and the organization for securing business; the financial resources intended to meet those costs and, if the risks to be covered are classified in class 18 in point A of the Annex, the resources at the undertaking's disposal for the provision of the assistance promised and, in addition, for the first three financial years:

(e) estimates of management expenses other than installation costs, in particular current general expenses and commissions;

(f) estimates of premiums or contributions and claims;

(g) a forecast balance sheet;

(h) estimates of the financial resources intended to cover underwriting liabilities and the solvency margin.

Article 10

1. An insurance undertaking that proposes to establish a branch within the territory of another Member State shall notify the competent authorities of its home Member State.

2. The Member States shall require every insurance undertaking that proposes to establish a branch within the territory of another Member State to provide the following information when effecting the notification provided for in paragraph 1:

(a) the Member State within the territory of which it proposes to establish a branch;

(b) a scheme of operations setting out, inter alia, the types of business envisaged and the structural organization of the branch;

(c) the address in the Member State of the branch from which documents may be obtained and to which they may be delivered, it being understood that that address shall be the one to which all communications to the authorised agent are sent;

(d) the name of the branch's authorised agent, who must possess sufficient powers to bind the undertaking in relation to third parties and to represent it in relations with the authorities and courts of the Member State of the branch. With regard to Lloyd's, in the event of any litigation in the Member State of the branch arising out of underwritten commitments, the insured persons must not be treated less favourably than if the litigation had been brought against businesses of a conventional type. The authorised agent must, therefore, possess sufficient powers for proceedings to be taken against him and must in that capacity be able to bind the Lloyd's underwriters concerned. Where the undertaking intends its branch to cover risks in class 10 of point A of the Annex, not including carrier's liability, it must produce a declaration that it has become a member of the national bureau and the national guarantee fund of the Member State of the branch.

3.   Unless the competent authorities of the home Member State have reason to doubt the adequacy of the administrative structure or the financial situation of the insurance undertaking or the good repute and professional qualifications or experience of the directors or managers or the authorised agent, taking into account the business planned, they shall within three months of receiving all the information referred to in paragraph 2 communicate that information to the competent authorities of the Member State of the branch and shall inform the undertaking concerned accordingly. The competent authorities of the home Member State shall also attest that the insurance undertaking has the minimum solvency margin calculated in accordance with Articles 16 and 17. Where the competent authorities of the home Member State refuse to communicate the information referred to in paragraph 2 to the competent authorities of the Member State of the branch they shall give the reasons for their refusal to the undertaking concerned within three months of receiving all the information in question. That refusal or failure to act may be subject to a right to apply to the courts in the home Member State.

4.   Before the branch of an insurance undertaking starts business, the competent authorities of the Member State of the branch shall, within two months of receiving the information referred to in paragraph 3, inform the competent authority of the home Member State, if appropriate, of the conditions under which, in the interest of the general good, that business must be carried on in the Member State of the branch.

5.   On receiving a communication from the competent authorities of the Member State of the branch or, if no communication is received from them, on expiry of the period provided for in paragraph 4, the branch may be established and start business.

6.   In the event of a change in any of the particulars communicated under paragraph 2(b), (c) or (d), an insurance undertaking shall give written notice of the change to the competent authorities of the home Member State and of the Member State of the branch at least one month before making the change so that the competent authorities of the home Member State and the competent authorities of the Member State of the branch may fulfil their respective roles under paragraphs 3 and 4.

Article 11
(Repealed)

Article 12
Any decision to refuse an authorisation shall be accompanied by the precise grounds for doing so and notified to the undertaking in question. Each member state shall make provision for a right to apply to the courts should there be any refusal. Such provision shall also be made with regard to cases where the competent authorities have not dealt with an application for an authorisation upon the expiry of a period of six months from the date of its receipt.

SECTION B   CONDITIONS FOR EXERCISE OF BUSINESS

Article 13

1.   The financial supervision of an insurance undertaking, including that of the business it carries on either through branches or under the freedom to provide services, shall be the sole responsibility of the home Member State.

2.   That financial supervision shall include verification, with respect to the insurance undertaking's entire business, of its state of solvency, of the establishment of technical provisions and of the assets covering them in accordance with the rules laid down or practices followed in the home Member State under provisions adopted at Community level. Where the undertaking in question is authorised to cover the risks classified in class 18 in point A of the Annex, supervision shall extend to monitoring of the technical resources which the undertaking has at its disposal for the purpose of carrying out the assistance operations it has undertaken to perform, where the law of the home Member State provides for the monitoring of such resources.

3.   The competent authorities of the home Member State shall require every insurance undertaking to have sound administrative and accounting procedures and adequate internal control mechanisms.

Article 14

The Member State of the branch shall provide that where an insurance undertaking authorised in another Member State carries on business through a branch the competent authorities of the home Member State may, after having informed the competent authorities of the Member State of the branch, carry out themselves or through the intermediacy of persons they appoint for that purpose on-the-spot verification of the information necessary to ensure the financial supervision of the undertaking. The authorities of the Member State of the branch may participate in that verification.

Article 15

1.   The home Member State shall require every insurance undertaking to establish adequate technical provisions in respect of its entire business. The amount of such technical provisions shall be determined in accordance with the rules laid down in Directive 91/674/EEC.

2.   The home Member State shall require every insurance undertaking to cover the technical provisions in respect of its entire business by matching assets in accordance with Article 6 of Directive 88/357/ EEC. In respect of risks situated within the European Community, those assets must be localised within the Community. Member States shall not require insurance undertakings to localise their assets in any particular Member State. The home Member State may, however, permit relaxations in the rules on the localisation of assets.

3.   If the home Member State allows any technical provisions to be covered by claims against reinsurers, it shall fix the percentage so allowed. In such cases, it may not specify the localisation of the assets representing such claims.

Article 15a

1.   Member States shall require every insurance undertaking with a head office within their territories which underwrites risks included in class 14 in point A of the Annex (hereinafter referred to as 'credit insurance') to set up an equalisation reserve for the purpose of offsetting any technical deficit or above-average claims ratio arising in that class in any financial year.

2.   The equalisation reserve shall be calculated in accordance with the rules laid down by the home Member State in accordance with one of the four methods set out in point D of the Annex, which shall be regarded as equivalent.

3.   Up to the amount calculated in accordance with the methods set out in point D of the Annex, the equalisation reserve shall be disregarded for the purpose of calculating the solvency margin.

4.   Member States may exempt insurance undertakings with head offices within their territories from the obligation to set up equalisation reserves for credit insurance business where the premiums or contributions receivable in respect of credit insurance are less than 4% of the total premiums or contributions receivable by them and less than ECU 2,500,000.

Article 16

1.   The home Member State shall require every insurance undertaking to establish an adequate solvency margin in respect of its entire business. The solvency margin shall correspond to the assets of the undertaking free of any foreseeable liabilities less any intangible items. In particular the following shall be included:

— the paid-up share capital or, in the case of a mutual insurance undertaking, the effective initial fund plus any members' accounts which meet all the following criteria:

(a)   the memorandum and articles of association must stipulate that payments may be made from these accounts to members only insofar as this does not cause the solvency margin to fall below the required level, or, after the dissolution of the undertaking, if all the undertaking's other debts have been settled;

(b)   the memorandum and articles of association must stipulate, with respect to any such payments for reasons other than the individual termination of membership, that the competent authorities must be notified at least one month in advance and can prohibit the payment within that period; and

(c)   the relevant provisions of the memorandum and articles of association may be amended only after the competent authorities have declared that they have no objection to the amendment, without prejudice to the criteria stated in (a) and (b);

— one-half of the unpaid share capital or initial fund, once the paid-up part amounts to 25% of that share capital or fund,

— reserves (statutory reserves and free reserves) not corresponding to underwriting liabilities,

— any profits brought forward,

— in the case of mutual or mutual-type association with variable contributions, any claim which it has against its members by way of a call for supplementary contribution, within the financial year, up to one-half of the difference between the maximum contributions and the contributions actually called in, and subject to a limit of 50% of the margin,

— at the request of and on the production of proof by the insurance undertaking, any hidden reserves arising out of the undervaluation of assets, insofar as those hidden reserves are not of an exceptional nature,

— cumulative preferential share capital and subordinated loan capital may be included but, if so, only up to 50% of the margin, no more than 25% of which shall consist of subordinated loans with a fixed maturity, or fixed-term cumulative preferential share capital, if the following minimum criteria are met:

(a)   in the event of the bankruptcy or liquidation of the insurance undertaking, binding agreements must exist under which the subordinated loan capital or preferential share capital ranks after the claims of all other creditors and is not to be repaid until all other debts outstanding at the time have been settled. Subordinated loan capital must fulfil the following additional conditions:

(b)   only fully paid-up funds may be taken into account;

(c)   for loans with a fixed maturity, the original maturity must be at least five years. No later than one year before the repayment date the insurance undertaking must submit to the competent authorities for their approval a plan showing how the solvency margin will be kept at or brought to the required level at maturity, unless the extent to which the loan may rank as a component of the solvency margin is gradually reduced during at least the last five years before the repayment date. The competent authorities may authorise the early repayment of such loans provided application is made by the issuing insurance undertaking and its solvency margin will not fall below the required level;

(d)   loans the maturity of which is not fixed must be repayable only subject to five years' notice unless the loans are no longer considered a component of the solvency margin or unless the prior consent of the competent authorities is specifically required for early repayment. In the latter event the insurance undertaking must notify the competent authorities at least six months before the date of the proposed repayment, specifying the actual and required solvency margins both before and after that repayment. The competent authorities shall authorise repayment only if the insurance undertaking's solvency margin will not fall below the required level;

(e)   the loan agreement must not include any clause providing that in specified circumstances, other than the winding-up of the insurance undertaking, the debt will become repayable before the agreed repayment dates;

(f)   the loan agreement may be amended only after the competent authorities have declared that they have no objection to the amendment;

—securities with no specified maturity date and other instruments that fulfil the following conditions, including cumulative preferential shares other than those mentioned in the preceding indent, up to 50% of the margin for the total of such securities and the subordinated loan capital referred to in the preceding indent:

(a)   they may not be repaid on the initiative of the bearer or without the prior consent of the competent authority;

(b)   the contract of issue must enable the insurance undertaking to defer the payment of interest on the loan;

(c)   the lender's claims on the insurance undertaking must rank entirely after those of all non-subordinated creditors;

(d)   the documents governing the issue of the securities must provide for the loss-absorption capacity of the debt and unpaid interest, while enabling the insurance undertaking to continue its business;

(e)   only fully paid-up amounts may be taken into account.

2.   The solvency margin shall be determined on the basis either of the annual amount of premiums or contributions, or of the average burden of claims for the past three financial years. In the case, however, of undertakings

which essentially underwrite only one or more of the risks of credit, storm, hail or frost, the last seven financial years shall be taken as the reference period for the average burden of claims.

3.   Subject to the provisions of Article 17, the amount of the solvency margin shall be equal to the higher of the following two results:

First result (premium basis):

— the premiums or contributions (inclusive of charges ancillary to premiums or contributions) due in respect of all direct business in the last financial year for all financial years, shall be aggregated,

— to this aggregate there shall be added the amount of premiums accepted for all reinsurance in the last financial year,

— from this sum there shall then be deducted the total amount of premiums or contributions cancelled in the last financial year, as well as the total amount of taxes and levies pertaining to the premiums or contributions entering into the aggregate. The amount so obtained shall be divided into two portions, the first portion extending up to 10 million units of account, the second comprising the excess; 18% and 16% of these portions respectively shall be calculated and added together. The first result shall be obtained by multiplying the sum so calculated by the ratio existing in respect of the last financial year between the amount of claims remaining to be borne by the undertaking after deduction of transfers for reinsurance and the gross amount of claims; this ratio may in no case be less than 50%.

Second result (claims basis):

— the amounts of claims paid in respect of direct business (without any deduction of claims borne by reinsurers and retrocessionaires) in the periods specified in (2) shall be aggregated,

— to this aggregate there shall be added the amount of claims paid in respect of reinsurances or retrocessions accepted during the same periods,

— to this sum there shall be added the amount of provisions or reserves for outstanding claims established at the end of the last financial year both for direct business and for reinsurance acceptances,

— from this sum there shall be deducted the amount of claims paid during the periods specified in (2),

- from the sum then remaining, there shall be deducted the amount of provisions or reserves for outstanding claims established at the commencement of the second financial year preceding the last financial year for which there are accounts, both for direct business and for reinsurance acceptances. One-third, or one-seventh, of the amount so obtained, according to the period of reference established in (2), shall be divided into two portions, the first extending up to seven million units of account and the second comprising the excess; 26% and 23% of these portions respectively shall be calculated and added together. The second result shall be obtained by multiplying the sum so obtained by the ratio existing in respect of the last financial year between the amount of claims remaining to be borne by the business after transfers for reinsurance and the gross amount of claims; this ratio may in no case be less than 50%. In the case of the risks listed under No 18 in point A of the Annex, the amount of claims paid used to calculate the second result (claims basis) shall be the costs borne by the undertaking in respect of assistance given. Such costs shall be calculated in accordance with the national provisions of the member state in whose territory the head office of the undertaking is situated.

4.   The fractions applicable to the portions referred to in (3) shall each be reduced to a third in the case of health insurance practised on a similar technical basis to that of life assurance, if

— the premiums paid are calculated on the basis of sickness tables according to the mathematical method applied in insurance,

— a reserve is set up for increasing age,

— an additional premium is collected in order to set up a safety margin of an appropriate amount,

— the insurer may only cancel the contract before the end of the third year of insurance at the latest,

— the contract provides for the possibility of increasing premiums or reducing payments even for current contracts.

5.   In the case of Lloyd's, the calculation of the first result in respect of premiums, referred to in Paragraph 3, shall be made on the basis of net premiums, which shall be multiplied by a flat-rate percentage fixed annually by the internal auditor. This flat-rate percentage must be calculated on the basis of the most recent statistical data on Commissions paid. The details, together with the relevant calculations shall be sent to the authorities of the countries where Lloyd's is established.

Article 17

1.   One-third of the solvency margin shall constitute the guarantee fund.

2.   (a)   the guarantee fund may not, however, be less than:

— 1,400,000 ECU in the case where all or some of the risks included in the class listed in point A of the Annex under No 14 are covered. This provision shall apply to every undertaking for which the annual amount of premiums or contributions due in this class for each of the last three financial years exceeded 2,500,000 ECU or 4% of the total amount of premiums or contributions receivable by the undertaking concerned;

— 400,000 ECU in the case where all or some of the risks included in one of the classes listed in point A of the Annex under Nos 10, 11, 12, 13 and 15 and, insofar as the first indent does not apply, No 14.

— 200,000 units of account in the case where all or some of the risks included in one of the classes listed in point a of the annex under Nos 9 and 17 are covered;

(b)   if the business carried on by the undertaking covers several classes or several risks, only that class or risk for which the highest amount is required shall be taken into account;

(c)   any member state may provide for a one-fourth reduction of the minimum guarantee fund in the case of mutual associations and mutual-type associations.

(d)   Where an undertaking carrying on credit insurance is required to increase the fund referred to in subparagraph (a), first indent, to 1,400,000 ECU, the Member State concerned shall allow such undertaking:

— a period of three years in which to bring the fund up to 1,000,000 ECU,

— a period of five years to bring the fund up to 1,200,000 ECU,

— a period of seven years to bring the fund up to 1,400,000 ECU.

These periods shall run from the date from which the conditions referred to in the first indent of subparagraph (a) are fulfilled.

Article 18

1.   Member States shall not prescribe any rules as to the choice of the assets that need not be used as cover for the technical provisions referred to in Article 15.

2.   Subject to Article 15(2), Article 20(1), (2), (3) and (5) and the last subparagraph of Article 22(1), Member States shall not restrain the free disposal of those assets, whether movable or immovable, that form part of the assets of authorised insurance undertakings.

3.   Paragraphs 1 and 2 shall not preclude any measures which Member States, while safeguarding the interests of the insured persons, are entitled to take as owners or members of or partners to the undertakings in question.

Article 19

1.   Each member state shall require every undertaking whose head office is situated in its territory to produce an annual account, covering all types of operation, of its financial situation, solvency and, as regards cover for risks listed under No 18 in point A of the Annex, other resources available to them for meeting their liabilities, where its laws provide for supervision of such resources.

1a.   In respect of credit insurance, the undertaking shall make available to the supervisory authority accounts showing both the technical results and the technical reserves relating to that business.

2.   Member States shall require insurance undertakings with head offices within their territories to render periodically the returns, together with statistical documents, which are necessary for the purposes of supervision. The competent authorities shall provide each other with any documents and information that are useful for the purposes of supervision.

3.   Every Member State shall take all steps necessary to ensure that the competent authorities have the powers and means necessary for the supervision of the business of insurance undertakings with head offices within their territories, including business carried on outwith those territories, in accordance with the Council Directives governing such business and for the purpose of seeing that they are implemented. These powers and means must, in particular, enable the competent authorities to:

(a)   make detailed enquiries regarding an undertaking's situation and the whole of its business, inter alia, by:

— gathering information or requiring the submission of documents concerning its insurance business,

— carrying out on-the-spot investigations at the undertaking's premises;

(b)   take any measures with regard to an undertaking, its directors or managers or the persons who control it, that are appropriate and necessary to ensure that that undertaking's business continues to comply with the laws, regulations and administrative provisions with which the undertaking must comply in each Member State and in particular with the scheme of operations insofar as it remains mandatory, and to prevent or remedy any irregularities prejudicial to the interests of insured persons;

(c)   ensure that those measures are carried out, if need be by enforcement and where appropriate through judicial channels. Member States may also make provision for the competent authorities to obtain any information regarding contracts which are held by intermediaries.

Article 20

1. If an undertaking does not comply with Article 15, the competent authority of its home Member State may prohibit the free disposal of its assets after having communicated its intention to the competent authorities of the Member States in which the risks are situated.

2. For the purposes of restoring the financial situation of an undertaking the solvency margin of which has fallen below the minimum required under Article 16(3), the competent authority of the home Member State shall require that a plan for the restoration of a sound financial situation be submitted for its approval. In exceptional circumstances, if the competent authority is of the opinion that the financial situation of the undertaking will deteriorate further, it may also restrict or prohibit the free disposal of the undertaking's assets. It shall inform the authorities of other Member States within the territories of which the undertaking carries on business of any measures it has taken and the latter shall, at the request of the former, take the same measures.

3. If the solvency margin falls below the guarantee fund as defined in Article 17, the competent authority of the home Member State shall require the undertaking to submit a short-term finance scheme for its approval. It may also restrict or prohibit the free disposal of the undertaking's assets. It shall inform the authorities of other Member States within the territories of which the undertaking carries on business accordingly and the latter shall, at the request of the former, take the same measures.

4. The competent authorities may further take all measures necessary to safeguard the interests of insured persons in the cases provided for in paragraphs 1, 2 and 3.

5. Each Member State shall take the measures necessary to be able, in accordance with its national law, to prohibit the free disposal of assets located within its territory at the request, in the cases provided for in paragraphs 1, 2 and 3, of the undertaking's home Member State, which shall designate the assets to be covered by such measures.

Article 21
(Deleted)

Article 22

1. Authorisation granted to an insurance undertaking by the competent authority of its home Member State may be withdrawn by that authority if that undertaking:

(a) does not make use of that authorisation within 12 months, expressly renounces it or ceases to carry on business for more than six months, unless the Member State concerned has made provision for authorisation to lapse in such cases;

(b) no longer fulfils the conditions for admission;

(c) has been unable, within the time allowed, to take the measures specified in the restoration plan or finance scheme referred to in Article 20;

(d) fails seriously in its obligation under the regulations to which it is subject.

In the event of the withdrawal or lapse of authorisation, the competent authority of the home Member State shall notify the competent authorities of the other Member States accordingly, and they shall take appropriate measures to prevent the undertaking from commencing new operations within their territories, under either the right of establishment or the freedom to provide services. The home Member State's competent authority shall, in conjunction with those authorities, take all measures necessary to safeguard the interests of insured persons and, in particular, shall restrict the free disposal of the undertaking's assets in accordance with Article 20(1), (2), second subparagraph, or (3), second subparagraph.

2. Any decision to withdraw authorisation shall be supported by precise reasons and communicated to the undertaking in question.

TITLE III A   RULES APPLICABLE TO AGENCIES OR BRANCHES ESTABLISHED WITHIN THE COMMUNITY AND BELONGING TO UNDERTAKINGS WHOSE HEAD OFFICES ARE OUTSIDE THE COMMUNITY

Article 23

1. Each member state shall make access to the business referred to in Article 1 by any undertaking whose head office is outside the Community subject to an official authorisation.

2. A member state may grant an authorisation if the undertaking fulfils at least the following conditions:

(a) it is entitled to undertake insurance business under its national law;

(b) it establishes an agency or branch in the territory of such member state;

(c) it undertakes to establish at the place of management of the agency or branch accounts specific to the business which it undertakes there, and to keep there all the records relating to the business transacted;

(d) it designates an authorised agent, to be approved by the competent authorities;

(e) it possesses in the country where it carries on its business assets of an amount equal to at least one-half of the minimum amount prescribed in Article 17(2), in respect of the guarantee fund, and deposits one-fourth of the minimum amount as security;

(f) it undertakes to keep a margin of solvency in accordance with the requirements referred to in Article 25;

(g) it submits a scheme of operations in accordance with the provisions of Article 11(1) and (2).

Article 24

Member states shall require undertakings to establish adequate technical reserves to cover the underwriting liabilities assumed in their territories. Member states shall see that the agency or branch covers such technical reserves by means of assets which are equivalent to such reserves and are, to the extent fixed by the state in question, matching assets. The law of the member states shall be applicable to the calculation of technical reserves, the determination of categories of investments, and the valuation of assets. The member state in question shall require that the assets representing the technical reserves shall be localised in its territory. Article 15(3) shall, however, be applicable.

Article 25

1. Each member state shall require for agencies or branches established in its territory a solvency margin consisting of assets free of all foreseeable liabilities, less any intangible items. The solvency margin shall be calculated in

accordance with the provisions of Article 16(3). However, for the purpose of calculating this margin, account shall be taken only of the premiums or contributions and claims pertaining to the business effected by the agency or branch concerned.

2. One-third of the solvency margin shall constitute the guarantee fund. The guarantee fund may not be less than one-half of the minimum required under Article 17(2). The initial deposit lodged in accordance with Article 23(2)(e) shall be counted towards such guarantee fund.

3. The assets representing the solvency margin must be kept within the country where the business is carried on up to the amount of the guarantee fund and the excess, within the Community.

Article 26

1. Any undertaking which has requested or obtained authorisation from more than one member state may apply for the following advantages which may be granted only jointly:

(a) the solvency margin referred to in Article 25 shall be calculated in relation to the entire business which it carries on within the Community; in such case, account shall be taken only of the operations effected by all the agencies or branches established within the Community for the purposes of this calculation;

(b) the deposit required under Article 23(2)(e) shall be lodged in only one of those member states;

(c) the assets representing the guarantee fund shall be localised in any one of the member states in which it carries on its activities.

2. Application to benefit from the advantages provided for in paragraph 1 shall be made to the competent authorities of the member states concerned. The application must state the authority of the member state which in future is to supervise the solvency of the entire business of the agencies or branches established within the Community. Reasons must be given for the choice of authority made by the undertaking. The deposit shall be lodged with that member state.

3. The advantages provided for in paragraph 1 may only be granted if the competent authorities of all member states in which an application has been made agree to them. They shall take effect from the time when the selected supervisory authority informs the other supervisory authorities that it will supervise the state of solvency of the entire business of the agencies or branches within the community. The supervisory authority selected shall obtain from the other member states the information necessary for the supervision of the overall solvency of the agencies and branches established in their territory.

4. At the request of one or more of the member states concerned, the advantages granted under this Article shall be withdrawn simultaneously by all member states concerned.

Article 27

The provisions of Articles 19 and 20 shall also apply in relation to agencies and branches of undertakings to which this title applies. As regards the application of Article 20, where an undertaking qualifies for the advantages provided for in Article 26(1), the authority responsible for verifying the solvency of agencies or branches established within the Community with respect to their entire business shall be treated in the same way as the authority of the state in the territory of which the head office of a Community undertaking is situated.

Article 28

In the case of a withdrawal of authorisation by the authority referred to in Article 26(2), this authority shall notify the authorities of the other member states where the undertaking operates and the latter supervisory authorities shall take the appropriate measures. If the reason for the withdrawal of the authorisation is the inadequacy of the overall state of solvency as fixed by the member states which agreed to the request referred to in Article 26, the member states which gave their approval shall also withdraw their authorisations.

Article 28a

1.   Under the conditions laid down by national law, each Member State shall authorise agencies and branches set up within its territory and covered by this Title to transfer all or part of their portfolios of contracts to an accepting office established in the same Member State if the competent authorities of that Member State or, if appropriate, of the Member State referred to in Article 26 certify that after taking the transfer into account the accepting office possesses the necessary solvency margin.

2.   Under the conditions laid down by national law, each Member State shall authorise agencies and branches set up within its territory and covered by this Title to transfer all or part of their portfolios of contracts to an insurance undertaking with a head office in another Member State if the competent authorities of that Member State certify that after taking the transfer into account the accepting office possesses the necessary solvency margin.

3.   If under the conditions laid down by national law a Member State authorises agencies and branches set up within its territory and covered by this Title to transfer all or part of their portfolios of contracts to an agency or branch covered by this Title and set up within the territory of another Member State it shall ensure that the competent authorities of the Member State of the accepting office or, if appropriate, of the Member State referred to in Article 26 certify that after taking the transfer into account the accepting office possesses the necessary solvency margin, that the law of the Member State of the accepting office permits such a transfer and that that State has agreed to the transfer.

4.   In the circumstances referred to in paragraphs 1, 2 and 3 the Member State in which the transferring agency or branch is situated shall authorise the transfer after obtaining the agreement of the competent authorities of the Member State in which the risks are situated, where different from the Member State in which the transferring agency or branch is situated.

5.   The competent authorities of the Member States consulted shall give their opinion or consent to the competent authorities of the home Member State of the transferring insurance undertaking within three months of receiving a request; the absence of any response from the authorities consulted within that period shall be considered equivalent to a favourable opinion or tacit consent.

6.   A transfer authorised in accordance with this Article shall be published as laid down by national law in the Member State in which the risk is situated. Such transfers shall automatically be valid against policyholders, insured

persons and any other persons having rights or obligations arising out of the contracts transferred. This provision shall not affect the Member States' right to give policyholders the option of cancelling contracts within a fixed period after a transfer.

Article 29

The Community may, by means of agreements concluded pursuant to the Treaty with one or more third countries, agree to the application of provisions different to those provided for in this title, for the purpose of ensuring, under conditions of reciprocity, adequate protection for insured persons in the member states.

TITLE III B   RULES APPLICABLE TO SUBSIDIARIES OF PARENT UNDERTAKINGS GOVERNED BY THE LAWS OF A THIRD COUNTRY AND TO ACQUISITIONS OF HOLDINGS BY SUCH PARENT UNDERTAKINGS

Article 29a

The competent authorities of the Member States shall inform the Commission:

    (a)   of any authorisation of a direct or indirect subsidiary, one or more parent undertakings of which are governed by the laws of a third country. The Commission shall inform the Insurance Committee to be established by the Council on proposal by the Commission;

    (b)   whenever such a parent undertaking acquires a holding in a Community insurance undertaking which would turn the latter into its subsidiary. The Commission shall inform the Insurance Committee to be established by the Council on proposal by the Commission accordingly. When authorisation is granted to the direct or indirect subsidiary of one or more parent undertakings governed by the law of third countries, the structure of the group shall be specified in the notification which the competent authorities shall address to the Commission.

Article 29b

    1.   Member States shall inform the Commission of any general difficulties encountered by their insurance undertakings in establishing themselves or carrying on their activities in a third country.

    2.   Initially not later than six months before the application of this Directive, and thereafter periodically, the Commission shall draw up a report examining the treatment accorded to Community insurance undertakings in third countries, in the terms referred to in paragraphs 3 and 4, as regards establishment and the carrying on of insurance activities, and the acquisition of holdings in third-country insurance undertakings. The Commission shall submit those reports to the Council, together with any appropriate proposals.

    3.   Whenever it appears to the Commission, either on the basis of the reports referred to in paragraph 2 or on the basis of other information, that a third country is not granting Community insurance undertakings effective market access comparable to that granted by the Community to insurance undertakings from that third country, the Commission may submit proposals to the Council for the appropriate mandate for negotiation with a view to obtaining comparable competitive opportunities for Community insurance undertakings. The Council shall decide by a qualified majority.

4. Whenever it appears to the Commission, either on the basis of the reports referred to in paragraph 2 or on the basis of other information, that Community insurance undertakings in a third country are not receiving national treatment offering the same competitive opportunities as are available to domestic insurance undertakings and that the conditions of effective market access are not being fulfilled, the Commission may initiate negotiations in order to remedy the situation. In the circumstances described in the first subparagraph, it may also be decided at any time, and in addition to initiating negotiations, in accordance with the procedure laid down in the Act establishing the Insurance Committee referred to in Article 29a, that the competent authorities of the Member States must limit or suspend their decisions:

— regarding requests pending at the moment of the decision or future requests for authorisations, and

— regarding the acquisition of holdings by direct or indirect parent undertakings governed by the laws of the third country in question.

The duration of the measures referred to may not exceed three months. Before the end of that three-month period, and in the light of the results of the negotiations, the Council may, acting on a proposal from the Commission, decide by a qualified majority that the measures shall be continued. Such limitations or suspension may not apply to the setting up of subsidiaries by insurance undertakings or their subsidiaries duly authorised in the Community, or to the acquisition of holdings in Community insurance undertakings by such undertakings or subsidiaries.

5. Whenever it appears to the Commission that one of the situations described in paragraphs 3 and 4 has arisen, the Member States shall inform it at its request:

(a) of any request for the authorisation of a direct or indirect subsidiary, one or more parent undertakings of which are governed by the laws of the third country in question;

(b) of any plans for such an undertaking to acquire a holding in a Community insurance undertaking such that the latter would become the subsidiary of the former. This obligation to provide information shall lapse once an agreement is concluded with the third country referred to in paragraph 3 or 4 or when the measures referred to in the second and third subparagraphs of paragraph 4 cease to apply.

6. Measures taken under this Article shall comply with the Community's obligations under any international agreements, bilateral or multilateral, governing the taking-up and pursuit of the business of insurance undertakings.

TITLE IV TRANSITIONAL AND OTHER PROVISIONS

Article 30

1. Member States shall allow undertakings referred to in Title II which at the entry into force of the implementing measures to this Directive provide insurance in their territories in one or more of the classes referred to in Article 1 a period of five years, commencing with the date of notification of this Directive, in order to comply with the requirements of Articles 16 and 17.

2. Furthermore, Member States may:

(a) allow any undertakings referred to in (1), which upon the expiry of the five-year period have not fully established the margin of solvency, a further period not exceeding two years in which to do so provided that such undertakings have, in accordance with Article 20, submitted for the approval of the supervisory authority the measures which they propose to take for such purpose;

(b)   exempt undertakings referred to in (1) whose annual premium or contribution income upon the expiry of the period of five years falls short of six times the amount of the minimum guarantee fund required under Article 17(2) from the requirement to establish such minimum guarantee fund before the end of the financial year in respect of which the premium or contribution income is as much as six times such minimum guarantee fund. After considering the results of the examination provided for under Article 33, the Council shall unanimously decide, on a proposal from the Commission, when this exemption is to be abolished by Member States.

3.   Undertakings desiring to extend their operations within the meaning of Article 8(2) or Article 10 may not do so unless they comply immediately with the rules of this Directive. However, the undertakings referred to in paragraph (2)(b) which within the national territory extend their business to other classes of insurance or to other parts of such territory may be exempted for a period of ten years from the date of notification of the Directive from the requirement to constitute the minimum guarantee fund referred to in Article 17(2).

4.   An undertaking having a structure different from any of those listed in Article 8 may continue, for a period of three years from the notification of the Directive, to carry on their present business in the legal form in which they are constituted at the time of such notification. Undertakings set up in the United Kingdom 'by royal charter' or 'by private act' or 'by special public act' may continue to carry on their business in their present form for an unlimited period.

Undertakings in Belgium which, in accordance with their objects, carry on the business of intervention mortgage loans or savings operations in accordance with No 4 of Article 15 of the provisions relating to the supervision of private savings banks, coordinated by the 'arrete Royal' of 23 June 1967, may continue to undertake such business for a period of three years from the date of notification of this Directive.

The Member States in question shall draw up a list of such undertakings and communicate it to the other Member States and the Commission.

5.   At the request of undertakings which comply with the requirements of Articles 15, 16 and 17, Member States shall cease to apply restrictive measures such as those relating to mortgages, deposits and securities established under present regulations.

Article 31

Member States shall allow agencies or branches referred to in Title III which, at the entry into force of the implementing measures to this Directive, are undertaking one or more classes referred to in Article 1 and do not extend their business within the meaning of Article 10(2) a maximum period of five years, from the date of notification of this Directive, in order to comply with the conditions of Article 25.

Article 32

During a period which terminates at the time of the entry into force of an agreement concluded with a third country pursuant to Article 29 and at the latest upon the expiry of a period of four years after the notification of the

Directive, each Member State may retain in favour of undertakings of that country established in its territory the rules applied to them on 1 January 1973 in respect of matching assets and the localisation of technical reserves, provided that notification is given to the other Member States and the Commission and that the limits of relaxations granted pursuant to Article 15(2) in favour of the undertakings of Member States established in its territory are not exceeded.

TITLE V   FINAL PROVISIONS

Article 33
The Commission and the competent authorities of the Member States shall collaborate closely for the purpose of facilitating the supervision of direct insurance within the Community and of examining any difficulties which may arise in the application of this Directive.

Article 34
1.   The Commission shall submit to the Council, within six years from the date of notification of this Directive, a report on the effects of the financial requirements imposed by this Directive on the situation on the insurance markets of the Member States.
2.   The Commission shall, as and when necessary, submit interim reports to the Council before the end of the transitional period provided for in Article 30(1).

Article 35
Member States shall amend their national provisions to comply with this Directive within 18 months of its notification and shall forthwith inform the Commission thereof. The provisions thus amended shall, subject to Article 30, 31 and 32, be applied within 30 months from the date of notification.

Article 36
Upon notification of this Directive, Member States shall ensure that the texts of the main provisions of a legislative, regulatory or administrative nature which they adopt in the field covered by this Directive are communicated to the Commission.

Article 37
The Annex shall form an integral part of this Directive.

Article 38
This Directive is addressed to the Member States.

Done at Brussels, 24 July 1973,
For the Council,
The President,
I. NOERGAARD

ANNEX

A.   Classification of risks according to classes of insurance
1.   Accident (including industrial injury and occupational diseases)
   — fixed pecuniary benefits
   — benefits in the nature of indemnity
   — combinations of the two
   — injury to passengers

2. Sickness
— fixed pecuniary benefits
— benefits in the nature of indemnity
— combinations of the two
3. Land vehicles (other than railway rolling stock)
All damage to or loss of
— land motor vehicles
— land vehicles other than motor vehicles
4. Railway rolling stock
All damage to or loss of railway rolling stock
5. Aircraft
All damage to or loss of aircraft
6. Ships (sea, lake and river and canal vessels)
All damage to or loss of
— river and canal vessels
— lake vessels
— sea vessels
7. Goods in transit (including merchandise, baggage, and all other goods)
All damage to or loss of goods in transit or baggage, irrespective of the form of transport
8. Fire and natural forces
All damage to or loss of property (other than property included in classes 3, 4, 5, 6 and 7) due to
— fire
— explosion
— storm
— natural forces other than storm
— nuclear energy
— land subsidence
9. Other damage to property
All damage to or loss of property (other than property included in classes 3, 4, 5, 6 and 7) due to hail or frost, and any event such as theft, other than those mentioned under 8
10. Motor vehicle liability
All liability arising out of the use of motor vehicles operating on the land (including carrier's liability)
11. Aircraft liability
All liability arising out of the use of aircraft (including carrier's liability)
12. Liability for ships (sea, lake and river and canal vessels)
All liability arising out of the use of ships, vessels or boats on the sea, lakes, rivers or canals (including carrier's liability)
13. General liability
All liability other than those forms mentioned under Nos 10, 11 and 12
14. Credit
— insolvency (general)
— export credit
— instalment credit
— mortgages
— agricultural credit

15. Suretyship
— suretyship (direct)
— suretyship (indirect)
16. Miscellaneous financial loss
— employment risks
— insufficiency of income (general)
— bad weather
— loss of benefits
— continuing general expenses
— unforeseen trading expenses
— loss of market value
— loss of rent or revenue
— indirect trading losses other than those mentioned above
— other financial loss (non-trading)
— other forms of financial loss
17. Legal expenses
Legal expenses and costs of litigation
18. Assistance
Assistance for persons who get into difficulties while travelling, while away from home or while away from their permanent residence. The risks included in a class may not be included in any other class except in the cases referred to in point C.

B. Description of authorisations granted for more than one class of insurance where the authorisation simultaneously covers:
    (a) classes Nos 1 and 2, it shall be named 'accident and health insurance';
    (b) classes Nos 1 (fourth indent), 3, 7 and 10, it shall be named 'motor insurance';
    (c) classes Nos 1 (fourth indent), 4, 6, 7 and 12, it shall be named 'marine and transport insurance';
    (d) classes Nos 1 (fourth indent), 5, 7 and 11, it shall be named 'aviation insurance';
    (e) classes Nos 8 and 9, it shall be named 'insurance against fire and other damage to property';
    (f) classes Nos 10, 11, 12 and 13, it shall be named 'liability insurance';
    (g) classes Nos 14 and 15, it shall be named 'Credit and suretyship insurance';
    (h) all classes, it shall be named at the choice of the member state in question, which shall notify the other member states and the Commission of its choice.

C. Ancillary risks
An undertaking obtaining an authorisation for a principal risk belonging to one class or a group of classes may also insure risks included in another class without an authorisation being necessary for them if they:
    — are connected with the principal risk,
    — concern the object which is covered against the principal risk, and
    — are covered by the contract insuring the principal risk.
However, the risks included in classes 14, 15 and 17 in point A may not be regarded as risks ancillary to other classes. Nonetheless, the risk included in

class 17 (legal expenses insurance) may be regarded as an ancillary risk of class 18 where the conditions laid down in the first subparagraph are fulfilled, where the main risk relates solely to the assistance provided for persons who fall into difficulties while travelling, while away from home or while away from their permanent residence. Legal expenses insurance may also be regarded as an ancillary risk under the conditions set out in the first subparagraph where it concerns disputes or risks arising out of, or in connection with, the use of sea-going vessels.

D. Methods of calculating the equalisation reserve for the credit insurance class

Method No. 1

1.   In respect of the risks included in the class of insurance in point A No. 14 (hereinafter referred to as 'credit insurance'), the undertaking shall set up an equalisation reserve to which shall be charged any technical deficit arising in that class for a financial year.

2.   Such reserve shall in each financial year receive 75% of any technical surplus arising on credit insurance business, subject to a limit of 12% of the net premiums or contributions until the reserve has reached 150% of the highest annual amount of net premiums or contributions received during the previous five financial years.

Method No. 2

1.   In respect of the risks included in the class of insurance listed in point A No. 14 (hereinafter referred to as 'credit insurance') the undertaking shall set up an equalisation reserve to which shall be charged any technical deficit arising in that class for a financial year.

2.   The minimum amount of the equalisation reserve shall be 134% of the average of the premiums or contributions received annually during the previous five financial years after subtraction of the cessions and addition of the reinsurance acceptances.

3.   Such reserve shall in each of the successive financial years receive 75% of any technical surplus arising in that class until the reserve is at least equal to the minimum calculated in accordance with paragraph 2.

4.   Member States may lay down special rules for the calculation of the amount of the reserve and/or the amount of the annual levy in excess of the minimum amounts laid down in this Directive.

Method No. 3

1.   An equalisation reserve shall be formed for class 14 in point A (hereinafter referred to as 'credit insurance') for the purpose of offsetting any above-average claims ratio for a financial year in that class of insurance.

2.   The equalisation reserve shall be calculated on the basis of the method set out below. All calculations shall relate to income and expenditure for the insurer's own account. An amount in respect of any claims shortfall for each financial year shall be placed to the equalisation reserve until it has reached, or is restored to, the required amount. There shall be deemed to be a claims shortfall if the claims ratio for a financial year is lower than the average claims ratio for the reference period. The amount in respect of the claims shortfall shall be arrived at by multiplying the difference between the two ratios by the earned premiums for the financial year. The required amount shall be equal to six times the standard deviation of the claims ratios in the reference period from

the average claims ratio, multiplied by the earned premiums for the financial year. Where claims for any financial year are in excess, an amount in respect thereof shall be taken from the equalisation reserve. Claims shall be deemed to be in excess if the claims ratio for the financial year is higher than the average claims ratio. The amount in respect of the excess claims shall be arrived at by multiplying the difference between the two ratios by the earned premiums for the financial year. Irrespective of claims experience, 3.5% of the required amount of the equalisation reserve shall be first placed to that reserve each financial year until its required amount has been reached or restored. The length of the reference period shall be not less than 15 years and not more than 30 years. No equalisation reserve need be formed if no underwriting loss has been noted during the reference period. The required amount of the equalisation reserve and the amount to be taken from it may be reduced if the average claims ratio for the reference period in conjunction with the expenses ratio show that the premiums include a safety margin.

Method No. 4

1.   An equalisation reserve shall be formed for class 14 in point A (hereinafter referred to as 'credit insurance') for the purpose of offsetting any above-average claims ratio for a financial year in that class of insurance.

2.   The equalisation reserve shall be calculated on the basis of the method set out below. All calculations shall relate to income and expenditure for the insurer's own account. An amount in respect of any claims shortfall for each financial year shall be placed to the equalisation reserve until it has reached the maximum required amount. There shall be deemed to be a claims shortfall if the claims ratio for a financial year is lower than the average claims ratio for the reference period. The amount in respect of the claims shortfall shall be arrived at by multiplying the difference between the two ratios by the earned premiums for the financial year. The maximum required amount shall be equal to six times the standard deviation of the claims ratio in the reference period from the average claims ratio, multiplied by the earned premiums for the financial year. Where claims for any financial year are in excess, an amount in respect thereof shall be taken from the equalisation reserve until it has reached the minimum required amount. Claims shall be deemed to be in excess if the claims ratio for the financial year is higher than the average claims ratio. The amount in respect of the excess claims shall be arrived at by multiplying the difference between the two ratios by the earned premiums for the financial year.

The minimum required amount shall be equal to three times the standard deviation of the claims ratio in the reference from the average claims ratio multiplied by the earned premiums for the financial year. The length of the reference period shall be not less than 15 years and not more than 30 years. No. equalisation reserve need be formed if no underwriting loss has been noted during the reference period. Both required amounts of the equalisation reserve and the amount to be placed to it or the amount to be taken from it may be reduced if the average claims ratio for the reference period in conjunction with the expenses ratio show that the premiums include a safety margin and that safety margin is more than one-and-a-half times the standard deviation of the claims ratio in the reference period. In such a case the amounts in question shall be multiplied by the quotient or one-and-a-half times the standard deviation and the safety margin.

COUNCIL DIRECTIVE 78/473/EEC OF 30 MAY 1978 ON THE COORDINATION OF LAWS, REGULATIONS AND ADMINISTRATIVE PROVISIONS RELATING TO COMMUNITY CO-INSURANCE
[OJ 1978 L151/25]

THE COUNCIL OF THE EUROPEAN COMMUNITIES,

Having regard to the Treaty establishing the European Economic Community, and in particular Articles 57(2) and 66 thereof,

Having regard to the proposal from the Commission,

Having regard to the opinion of the European Parliament,[1]

Having regard to the opinion of the Economic and Social Committee,[2]

Whereas the effective pursuit of Community co-insurance business should be facilitated by a minimum of coordination in order to prevent distortion of competition and inequality of treatment, without affecting the freedom existing in several Member States;

Whereas such coordination covers only those co-insurance operations which are economically the most important, i.e. those which by reason of their nature or their size are liable to be covered by international co-insurance;

Whereas this Directive thus constitutes a first step towards the coordination of all operations which may be carried out by virtue of the freedom to provide services; whereas this coordination, in fact, is the object of the proposal for a second Council Directive on the coordination of laws, regulations and administrative provisions relating to direct insurance other than life assurance and laying down provisions to facilitate the effective exercise of freedom to provide services, which the Commission forwarded to the Council on 30 December 1975;[3]

Whereas the leading insurer is better placed than the other co-insurers to assess claims and to fix the minimum amount of reserves for outstanding claims;

Whereas work is in progress on the winding-up of insurance undertakings;

Whereas provision must be made at this stage to ensure that, in the event of winding-up, beneficiaries under Community co-insurance contracts enjoy equality of treatment with beneficiaries in respect of the other insurance business, irrespective of the nationality of such persons;

Whereas special cooperation should be provided for in the Community co-insurance field both between the competent supervisory authorities of the Member States and between those authorities and the Commission;

Whereas any practices which might indicate a misuse of the purpose of the Directive are to be examined in the course of such cooperation,

HAS ADOPTED THIS DIRECTIVE:

Notes
[1]OJ No. C60, 13.3.1975, p. 16.
[2]OJ No. C47, 27.2.1975, p. 40.
[3]OJ No. C32, 12.2.1976, p. 2.

TITLE I   GENERAL PROVISIONS

Article 1

1.   This Directive shall apply to Community co-insurance operations referred to in Article 2 which relate to risks classified under point A. 4, 5, 6, 7, 8, 9, 11, 12, 13 and 16 of the Annex to the first Council Directive of 24 July 1973 on the coordination of laws, regulations and administrative provisions relating to the taking-up and pursuit of the business of direct insurance other than life assurance,[1] hereinafter called the 'first coordination Directive'. It shall not apply, however, to Community co-insurance operations covering risks classified under point A. 13 which concern damage arising from nuclear sources or from medicinal products. The exclusion of insurance against damage arising from medicinal products shall be examined by the Council within five years of the notification of this Directive.

2.   This Directive shall apply to risks referred to in the first subparagraph of paragraph 1 which by reason of their nature or size call for the participation of several insured for their coverage. Any difficulties which may arise in implementing this principle shall be examined pursuant to Article 8.

Note
[1] OJ No. L228, 16.8.1973, p. 3.

Article 2

1.   This Directive shall apply only to those Community co-insurance operations which satisfy the following conditions:

(a)   the risk, within the meaning of Article 1(1), is covered by a single contract at an overall premium and for the same period by two or more insurance undertakings, hereinafter referred to as 'co-insurers', each for its own part; one of these undertakings shall be the leading insurer;

(b)   the risk is situated within the Community;

(c)   for the purpose of covering this risk, the leading insurer is authorised in accordance with the conditions laid down in the first coordination Directive, i.e. he is treated as if he were the insurer covering the whole risk;

(d)   at least one of the co-insurers participates in the contract by means of a head office, agency or branch established in a Member State other than that of the leading insurer;

(e)   the leading insurer fully assumes the leader's role in co-insurance practice and in particular determines the terms and conditions of insurance and rating.

2.   Those co-insurance operations which do not satisfy the conditions set out in paragraph 1 or which cover risks other than those specified in Article 1 shall remain subject to the national laws operative at the time when this Directive comes into force.

Article 3

The right of undertakings which have their head office in a Member State and which are subject to and satisfy the requirements of the first coordination Directive to participate in Community co-insurance may not be made subject to any provisions other than those of this Directive.

TITLE II   CONDITIONS AND PROCEDURES FOR COMMUNITY CO-INSURANCE

Article 4

1.   The amount of the technical reserves shall be determined by the different co-insurers according to the rules fixed by the Member State where they are established or, in the absence of such rules, according to customary practice in that State. However, the reserve for outstanding claims shall be at least equal to that determined by the leading insurer according to the rules or practice of the State where such insurer is established.

2.   The technical reserves established by the different co-insurers shall be represented by matching assets. however, relaxation of the matching assets rule may be granted by the Member States in which the co-insurers are established in order to take account of the requirements of sound management of insurance undertakings. Such assets shall be localised either in the Member States in which the co-insurers are established or in the Member State in which the leading insurer is established, whichever the insurer chooses.

Article 5

The Member States shall ensure that co-insurers established in their territory keep statistical data showing the extent of Community co-insurance operations and the countries concerned.

Article 6

The supervisory authorities of the Member States shall cooperate closely in the implementation of this Directive and shall provide each other with all the information necessary to this end.

Article 7

In the event of an insurance undertaking being wound up, liabilities arising from participation in Community co-insurance contracts shall be met in the same way as those arising under that undertaking's other insurance contracts without distinction as to the nationality of the insured and of the beneficiaries.

TITLE III   FINAL PROVISIONS

Article 8

The Commission and the competent authorities of the Member States shall cooperate closely for the purposes of examining any difficulties which might arise in implementing this Directive. In the course of this cooperation they shall examine in particular any practices which might indicate that the purpose of the provisions of this Directive and in particular of Article 1(2) and Article 2 are being misused either in that the leading insurer does not assume the leader's role in co-insurance practice or that the risks clearly do not require the participation of two or more insurers for their coverage.

Article 9

The Commission shall submit to the Council within six years of the notification of this Directive a report on the development of Community co-insurance.

Article 10

Member States shall amend their national provisions so as to comply with this Directive within 18 months of its notification and shall immediately inform the

Commission thereof. The provisions thereby amended shall be applied within 24 months of such notification.

Article 11
Upon notification of this Directive Member States shall ensure that the texts of the main provisions of laws, regulations or administrative measures which they adopt in the field covered by this Directive are communicated to the Commission.

Article 12
This Directive is addressed to the Member States.

Done at Brussels, 30 May 1978.
For the Council,
The President,
I. NOERGAARD.

COUNCIL DIRECTIVE (84/641/EEC) OF 10 DECEMBER 1984 AMENDING, PARTICULARLY AS REGARDS TOURIST ASSISTANCE, THE FIRST DIRECTIVE (73/239/EEC) ON THE COORDINATION OF LAWS, REGULATIONS AND ADMINISTRATIVE PROVISIONS RELATING TO THE TAKING-UP AND PURSUIT OF THE BUSINESS OF DIRECT INSURANCE OTHER THAN LIFE ASSURANCE
[OJ No. L339/21].*

THE COUNCIL OF THE EUROPEAN COMMUNITIES,

Having regard to the Treaty establishing the European Economic Community, and in particular Article 57(2) thereof,
   Having regard to the proposal from the Commission,[1]
   Having regard to the opinion of the European Parliament,[2]
   Having regard to the opinion of the Economic and Social Committee,[3]

Whereas the first Council Directive (73/239/EEC) of 4 July 1973 on the coordination of laws, regulations and administrative provisions relating to the taking-up and pursuit of the business of direct insurance other than life assurance,[4] hereinafter referred to as the 'first directive', as amended by Directive 76/580/EEC,[5] eliminated certain differences between the laws of Member States in order to facilitate the taking-up and pursuit of the above business;
   Whereas considerable progress has been achieved in that area of business involving the provision of benefits in kind;
   Whereas such benefits are governed by provisions which differ from one Member State to another;

Notes
*Only the Articles which are self standing are retained here. All others which made amendments to the first Directive have been removed.
[1] OJ No. C51, 10.3.1981, p. 5; OJ No. C30, 4.2.1983, p. 6.
[2] OJ No. C149, 14.6.1982, p. 129.
[3] OJ No. C343, 31.12.1981, p. 9.
[4] OJ No. L228, 16.8.1973, p. 3.
[5] OJ No. L189, 13.7.1976, p. 13.

Whereas those differences constitute a barrier to the exercise of the right of establishment;

Whereas, in order to eliminate that barrier to the right of establishment, it should be specified that an activity is not excluded from the application of the first directive for the simple reason that it constitutes a benefit solely in kind or one for which the person providing it uses his own staff or equipment only;

Whereas, therefore such provision of assistance consisting in the promise of aid on the occurrence of a chance event should be covered by the above Directive, taking into account the special characteristics of such assistance;

Whereas the purpose of the inclusion, for reasons of supervision, of assistance operations in the scope of the first directive, which does not involve the definition of these operations, is not to affect the fiscal rules applicable to them;

Whereas the sole fact of providing certain forms of assistance on the occasion of an accident or breakdown involving a road vehicle normally occurring in the territory of the Member State of the undertaking providing cover is not a reason for any person or undertaking that is not an insurance undertaking to be subject to the arrangements of the first directive;

Whereas provision should be made for certain relaxations to the condition that the accident or breakdown must occur in the territory of the Member State of the undertaking providing cover in order to take into account either the existence of reciprocal agreements or of certain specific circumstances relating to the geographical situation or to the structure of the organisations concerned, or to the very limited economic importance of the operations referred to;

Whereas an organization of a Member State whose main activity is to provide services on behalf of the public authorities should be excluded from the scope of the first directive;

Whereas an undertaking offering assistance contracts must possess the means necessary for it to provide the benefits in kind which it offers within an appropriate period of time;

Whereas special provisions should be laid down for calculating the solvency margin and the minimum amount of the guarantee fund which such undertaking must possess;

Whereas certain transitional provisions are necessary in order to permit undertakings providing only assistance to adapt themselves to the application of the first directive;

Whereas, having regard to special structural and geographical difficulties, it is necessary to allow a transitional period to the automobile club of a member state for bringing itself into line with the said directive concerning repatriation of the vehicle, possibly accompanied by the driver and passengers;

Whereas it is necessary to keep up-to-date the provisions of the first directive concerning the legal forms which insurance undertakings may assume;

Whereas certain provisions of the said Directive concerning the rules applicable to agencies or branches established within the Community and belonging to undertakings whose head offices are situated outside the Community should be amended in order to make them consistent with the provisions of Directive 79/267/EEC,[1]

HAS ADOPTED THIS DIRECTIVE:

Note
[1]OJ No. L63, 13.3.1979, p. 1.

Article 15

Any Member State may, in its territory, make the provision of assistance to persons who get into difficulties in circumstances other than those referred to in Article 1 subject to the arrangements introduced by the first Directive. If a Member State makes use of this possibility it shall, for the purposes of applying these arrangements, treat such activity as if it were listed in Class 18 in point A of the Annex to the first Directive without prejudice to point C thereof.

The preceding paragraph shall in no way affect the possibilities for classification laid down in the Annex to the first Directive for activities which obviously come under other classes.

It shall not be possible to refuse authorisation to an agency or branch solely on the grounds that the activity covered by this article is classified differently in the Member State in the territory of which the head office of the undertaking is situated.

TRANSITIONAL PROVISIONS

Article 16

1. Member States may allow undertakings which, on the date of notification of this directive, provide only assistance in their territories, a period of five years from that date in order to comply with the requirements set out in Articles 16 and 17 of the first Directive.

2. Member States may allow any undertakings referred to in paragraph 1 which, upon expiry of the five-year period, have not fully established the solvency margin, a further period not exceeding two years in which to do so provided that such undertakings have, in accordance with Article 20 of the first Directive, submitted for the approval of the supervisory authority the measures which they propose to take for that purpose.

3. Any undertaking referred to in Paragraph 1 which wishes to extend its business within the meaning of Article 8(2) or Article 10 of the first Directive may do so only on condition that it complies forthwith with that Directive.

4. Any undertaking referred to in Paragraph 1 which has a form different to those referred to in Article 8 of the first Directive may continue for a period of three years from the date of notification of this Directive to carry on its existing business in the form in which it exists on that date.

5. This Article shall apply mutatis mutandis to undertakings formed after the date of notification of this Directive which take over business already conducted on that date by a legally distinct body.

Article 17

Member States may allow agencies and branches referred to in Title III of the first Directive which provide only assistance in the territories of those Member States a maximum period of five years commencing on the date of notification of this Directive in order to comply with Article 25 of the first Directive, provided such agencies or branches do not extend their business within the meaning of Article 10(2) of the first Directive.

Article 18

During a period of eight years from the date of notification of this Directive, the condition that the accident or breakdown must have happened in the territory of the member State of the undertaking providing cover shall not apply to the operations referred to in the third indent of the first subparagraph of Article

2(3) of the first Directive where these operations are carried out by the ELPA (Automobile and Touring Club of Greece).

FINAL PROVISIONS

Article 19

1. Member States shall amend their national provisions in order to comply with this Directive not later than 30 June 1987. They shall forthwith inform the Commission thereof. The provisions thus amended shall, subject to Articles 16, 17 and 18 of this Directive apply at the latest beginning on 1 January 1988.

2. Member States shall communicate to the Commission the texts of the main provisions laid down by law, regulation or administrative action which they adopt in the field governed by this Directive.

Article 20

The Commission shall report to the Council, within six years of notification of this Directive, on the difficulties arising from the application thereof, and in particular Article 15 thereof. it shall, if appropriate, submit proposals to put an end to them.

Article 21

This Directive is addressed to the Member States.

Done at Brussels, 10 December 1984.
For the Council
The President
A. DUKES

COUNCIL DIRECTIVE OF 22 JUNE 1987 ON THE COORDINATION OF LAWS, REGULATIONS AND ADMINISTRATIVE PROVISIONS RELATING TO LEGAL EXPENSES INSURANCE (87/344/EEC)
[OJ 1987 L185/77]

THE COUNCIL OF THE EUROPEAN COMMUNITIES,

Having regard to the Treaty establishing the European Economic Community, and in particular Article 57(2) thereof,
　　Having regard to the proposal from the Commission,[1]
　　Having regard to the opinion of the European Parliament,[2]
　　Having regard to the opinion of the Economic and Social Committee,[3]

Whereas Council Directive 73/239/EEC of 24 July 1973 on the coordination of laws, regulations and administrative provisions relating to the taking-up and pursuit of the business of direct insurance other than life assurance,[4] as last amended by Directive 87/343/EEC,[5] eliminated, in order to facilitate the taking-up and pursuit of such activities, certain differences existing between national laws;

Notes
[1] OJ No. C198, 7.8.1979, p. 2.
[2] OJ No. C260, 12.10.1981, p. 78.
[3] OJ No. C348, 31.12.1980, p. 22.
[4] OJ No. L228, 16.8.1973, p. 3.
[5] See page 72 of this Official Journal.

Whereas, however, Article 7(2)(c) of Directive 73/239/EEC provides that 'pending further coordination, which must be implemented within four years of notification of this Directive, the Federal Republic of Germany may maintain the provision prohibiting the simultaneous undertaking in its territory of health insurance, credit and suretyship insurance or insurance in respect of recourse against third parties and legal defence, either with one another or with other classes';

Whereas the present Directive provides for the coordination of legal expenses insurance as envisaged in Article 7(2)(c) of Directive 73/239/EEC;

Whereas, in order to protect insured persons, steps should be taken to preclude, as far as possible, any conflict of interests between a person with legal expenses cover and his insurer arising out of the fact that the latter is covering him in respect of any other class of insurance referred to in the Annex to Directive 73/239/EEC or is covering another person and, should such a conflict arise, to enable it to be resolved;

Whereas legal expenses insurance in respect of disputes or risks arising out of, or in connection with, the use of sea-going vessels should, in view of its specific nature, be excluded from the scope of this Directive;

Whereas the activity of an insurer who provides services or bears the cost of defending the insured person in connection with a civil liability contract should also be excluded from the scope of this Directive if that activity is at the same time pursued in the insurer's own interest under such cover;

Whereas Member States should be given the option of excluding from the scope of this Directive the activity of legal expenses insurance undertaken by an assistance insurer where this activity is carried out in a Member State other than the one in which the insured person normally resides and where it forms part of a contract covering solely the assistance provided for persons who fall into difficulties while travelling, while away from home or while away from their permanent residence;

Whereas the system of compulsory specialization at present applied by one Member State, namely the Federal Republic of Germany, precludes the majority of conflicts; whereas, however, it does not appear necessary, in order to obtain this result, to extend that system to the entire Community, which would require the splitting-up of composite undertakings;

Whereas the desired result can also be achieved by requiring undertakings to provide for a separate contract or a separate section of a single policy for legal expenses insurance and by obliging them either to have separate management for legal expenses insurance, or to entrust the management of claims in respect of legal expenses insurance to an undertaking having separate legal personality, or to afford the person having legal expenses cover the right to choose his lawyer from the moment that he has the right to claim from his insurer;

Whereas, whichever solution is adopted, the interest of persons having legal expenses cover shall be protected by equivalent safeguards;

Whereas the interest of persons having legal expenses cover means that the insured person must be able to choose a lawyer or other person appropriately qualified according to national law in any inquiry or proceedings and whenever a conflict of interests arises;

Whereas Member States should be given the option of exempting undertakings from the obligation to give the insured person this free choice of lawyer if the legal expenses insurance is limited to cases arising from the use of road vehicles on their territory and if other restrictive conditions are met;

Whereas, if a conflict arises between insurer and insured, it is important that it be settled in the fairest and speediest manner possible; whereas it is therefore appropriate that provision be made in legal expenses insurance policies for an arbitration procedure or a procedure offering comparable guarantees;

Whereas the second paragraph of point C of the Annex to Directive 73/239/EEC provides that the risks included in classes 14 and 15 in point A may not be regarded as risks ancillary to other classes; whereas an insurance undertaking should not be able to cover legal expenses as a risk ancillary to another risk without having obtained an authorisation in respect of the legal expenses risk; whereas, however, Member States should be given the option of regarding class 17 as a risk ancillary to class 18 in specific cases; whereas, therefore, point C of the said Annex should be amended accordingly,

HAS ADOPTED THIS DIRECTIVE:

Article 1
The purpose of this Directive is to coordinate the provisions laid down by law, regulation or administrative action concerning legal expenses insurance as referred to in paragraph 17 of point A of the Annex to Council Directive 73/239/EEC in order to facilitate the effective exercise of freedom of establishment and preclude as far as possible any conflict of interest arising in particular out of the fact that the insurer is covering another person or is covering a person in respect of both legal expenses and any other class in that Annex and, should such a conflict arise, to enable it to be resolved.

Article 2
1. This Directive shall apply to legal expenses insurance. Such consists in undertaking, against the payment of a premium, to bear the costs of legal proceedings and to provide other services directly linked to insurance cover, in particular with a view to:
— securing compensation for the loss, damage or injury suffered by the insured person, by settlement out of court or through civil or criminal proceedings,
— defending or representing the insured person in civil, criminal, administrative or other proceedings or in respect of any claim made against him.

2. This Directive shall not, however, apply to:
— legal expenses insurance where such insurance concerns disputes or risks arising out of, or in connection with, the use of sea-going vessels,
— the activity pursued by the insurer providing civil liability cover for the purpose of defending or representing the insured person in any inquiry or proceedings if that activity is at the same time pursued in the insurer's own interest under such cover,
— where a Member State so chooses, the activity of legal expenses insurance undertaken by an assistance insurer where this activity is carried out in a Member State other than the one in which the insured person normally resides, where it forms part of a contract covering solely the assistance provided for persons who fall into difficulties while travelling, while away from home or while away from their permanent residence. In this event the contract must

clearly state that the cover in question is limited to the circumstances referred to in the foregoing sentence and is ancillary to the assistance.

Article 3

1. Legal expenses cover shall be the subject of a contract separate from that drawn up for the other classes of insurance or shall be dealt with in a separate section of a single policy in which the nature of the legal expenses cover and, should the Member State so request, the amount of the relevant premium are specified.

2. Each Member State shall take the necessary measures to ensure that the undertakings established within its territory adopt, in accordance with the option imposed by the Member State, or at their own choice, if the Member State so agrees, at least one of the following solutions, which are alternatives:

(a) the undertaking shall ensure that no member of the staff who is concerned with the management of legal expenses claims or with legal advice in respect thereof carries on at the same time a similar activity:

— if the undertaking is a composite one, for another class transacted by it.

— irrespective of whether the undertaking is a composite or a specialized one, in another having financial, commercial or administrative links with the first undertaking and carrying on one or more of the other classes of insurance set out in Directive 73/239/EEC;

(b) the undertaking shall entrust the management of claims in respect of legal expenses insurance to an undertaking having separate legal personality. That undertaking shall be mentioned in the separate contract or separate section referred to in paragraph 1. If the undertaking having separate legal personality has links with an undertaking which carries on one or more of the other classes of insurance referred to in point A of the Annex to Directive 73/239/EEC, members of the staff of the undertaking who are concerned with the processing of claims or with legal advice connected with such processing may not pursue the same or a similar activity in the other undertaking at the same time. In addition, Member States may impose the same requirements on the members of the management body;

(c) the undertaking shall, in the contract, afford the insured person the right to entrust the defence of his interests, from the moment that he has the right to claim from his insurer under the policy, to a lawyer of his choice or, to the extent that national law so permits, any other appropriately qualified person.

3. Whichever solution is adopted, the interest of persons having legal expenses cover shall be regarded as safeguarded in an equivalent manner under this Directive.

Article 4

1. Any contract of legal expenses insurance shall expressly recognise that:

(a) where recourse is had to a lawyer or other person appropriately qualified according to national law in order to defend, represent or serve the interests of the insured person in any inquiry or proceedings, that insured person shall be free to choose such lawyer or other person;

(b) the insured person shall be free to choose a lawyer or, if he so prefers and to the extent that national law so permits, any other appropriately qualified person, to serve his interests whenever a conflict of interests arises.

2. Lawyer means any person entitled to pursue his professional activities under one of the denominations laid down in Council Directive 77/249/EEC of 22 March 1977 to facilitate the effective exercise by lawyers of freedom to provide services.[1]

Note
[1]OJ No. L78, 26.3.1977, p. 17.

Article 5

1. Each Member State may provide exemption from the application of Article 4 (1) for legal expenses insurance if all the following conditions are fulfilled:

    (a) the insurance is limited to cases arising from the use of road vehicles in the territory of the Member State concerned;

    (b) the insurance is connected to a contract to provide assistance in the event of accident or breakdown involving a road vehicle;

    (c) neither the legal expenses insurer nor the assistance insurer carries out any class of liability insurance;

    (d) measures are taken so that the legal counsel and representation of each of the parties to a dispute is effected by completely independent lawyers when these parties are insured for legal expenses by the same insurer.

2. The exemption granted by a Member State to an undertaking pursuant to paragraph 1 shall not affect the application of Article 3 (2).

Article 6

Member States shall adopt all appropriate measures to ensure that, without prejudice to any right of appeal to a judicial body which might be provided for by national law, an arbitration or other procedure offering comparable gaurantees of objectivity is provided for whereby, in the event of a difference of opinion between a legal expenses insurer and his insured, a decision can be taken on the attitude to be adopted in order to settle the dispute. The insurance contract must mention the right of the insured person to have recourse to such a procedure.

Article 7

Whenever a conflict of interests arises or there is disagreement over the settlement of the dispute, the legal expenses insurer or, where appropriate, the claims settlement office shall inform the person insured of
    — the right referred to in Article 4,
    — the possibility of having recourse to the procedure referred to in Article 6.

Article 8

Member States shall abolish all provisions which prohibit an insurer from carrying out within their territory legal expenses insurance and other classes of insurance at the same time.

Article 9

The second subparagraph of point C of the Annex to Directive 73/239/EEC shall be replaced by the following text:

'However, the risks included in classes 14, 15 and 17 in point A may not be regarded as risks ancillary to other classes. Nonetheless, the risk included in class 17 (legal expenses insurance) may be regarded as an ancillary risk of class 18 where the conditions laid down in the first subparagraph are fulfilled, where the main risk relates solely to the assistance provided for persons who fall into difficulties while travelling, while away from home or while away from their permanent residence. Legal expenses insurance may also be regarded as an ancillary risk under the conditions set out in the first subparagraph where it concerns disputes or risks arising out of, or in connection with, the use of sea-going vessels.'

Article 10
Member States shall take the measures necessary to comply with this Directive by 1 January 1990. They shall forthwith inform the Commission thereof. They shall apply these measures from 1 July 1990 at the latest.

Article 11
Following notification[1] of this Directive, Member States shall communicate to the Commission the texts of the main provisions of national law which they adopt in the field governed by this Directive.

Note
[1]This Directive was notified to the Member States on 25 June 1987.

Article 12
This Directive is addressed to the Member States.

Done at Luxembourg, 22 June 1987.
For the Council,
The President,
L. TINDEMANS

**SECOND COUNCIL DIRECTIVE (88/357/EEC) OF 22 JUNE 1988
ON THE COORDINATION OF LAWS, REGULATIONS AND
ADMINISTRATIVE PROVISIONS RELATING TO DIRECT
INSURANCE OTHER THAN LIFE ASSURANCE AND LAYING
DOWN PROVISIONS TO FACILITATE THE EFFECTIVE
EXERCISE OF FREEDOM TO PROVIDE SERVICES AND
AMENDING DIRECTIVE 73/239/EEC
[OJ 1988 L172/1]***

THE COUNCIL OF THE EUROPEAN COMMUNITIES,

Having regard to the Treaty establishing the European Economic Community, and in particular Articles 57(2) and 66 thereof,
 Having regard to the proposal from the Commission,[1]
 In cooperation with the European Parliament,[2]
 Having regard to the opinion of the Economic and Social Committee,[3]

Whereas it is necessary to develop the internal insurance market and, to achieve this objective, it is desirable to make it easier for insurance undertakings having their head office in the Community to provide services in the Member States,

Notes
*As amended by Directive 90/618 [OJ 1990 L330/44] and Directive 92/49 [OJ 1992 L228/1].
[1]OJ No. C32, 12.2.1976, p. 2.
[2]OJ No. C36, 13.2.1978, p. 14, OJ No. C167, 27.6.1988 and Decision of 15 June 1988 (not yet published in the Official Journal).
[3]OJ No. C204, 30.8.1976, p. 13.

thus making it possible for policy-holders to have recourse not only to insurers established in their own country, but also to insurers which have their head office in the Community and are established in other Member States;

Whereas, pursuant to the Treaty, any discrimination with regard to freedom to provide services based on the fact that an undertaking is not established in the Member State in which the services are provided has been prohibited since the end of the transitional period; whereas this prohibition applies to services provided from any establishment in the Community, whether it is the head office of an undertaking or an agency or branch;

Whereas, for practical reasons, it is desirable to define the provision of services taking into account both the insurer's establishment and the place where the risk is situated; whereas therefore a definition of the situation of the risk should also be adopted; whereas, moreover, it is desirable to distinguish between the activity pursued by way of establishment and the activity pursued by way of freedom to provide services;

Whereas it is desirable to supplement the First Council Directive 73/239/ EEC of 24 July 1973 on the coordination of laws, regulations and administrative provisions relating to the taking-up and pursuit of the business of direct insurance other than life assurance,[4] hereinafter referred to as the 'First Directive', as last amended by Directive 87/343/EEC,[5] in order particularly to clarify the powers and means of supervision vested in the supervisory authorities; whereas it is also desirable to lay down specific provisions regarding the taking-up, pursuit and supervision of activity by way of freedom to provide services;

Whereas policy-holders who, by virtue of their status, their size or the nature of the risk to be insured, do not require special protection in the State in which the risk is situated should be granted complete freedom to avail themselves of the widest possible insurance market; whereas, moreover, it is desirable to guarantee other policy-holders adequate protection;

Whereas the concern to protect policy-holders and to avoid any disturbance of competition justifies coordinating the relaxation of the matching assets rules, provided for by the First Directive;

Whereas the provisions in force in the Member States regarding insurance contract law continue to differ; whereas the freedom to choose, as the law applicable to the contract, a law other than that of the State in which the risk is situated may be granted in certain cases, in accordance with rules taking into account specific circumstances;

Whereas the scope of this Directive should include compulsory insurance but should require the contract covering such insurance to be in conformity with the specific provisions relating to such insurance, as provided by the Member State imposing the insurance obligation;

Whereas the provisions of the First Directive on the transfer of portfolio should be reinforced and supplemented by provisions specifically covering the transfer of the portfolio of contracts concluded for the provision of services to another undertaking;

Notes
[4]OJ No. L228, 16.8.1973, p. 3.
[5]OJ No. L185, 4.7.1987, p. 72.

Whereas the scope of the provisions specifically concerning freedom to provide services should exclude certain risks, the application to which of the said provisions is rendered inappropriate at this stage by the specific rules adopted by the Member States' authorities, owing to the nature and social implications of such provisions; whereas, therefore, these exclusions should be re-examined after this Directive has been in force for a certain period;

Whereas, in the interests of protecting policy-holders, Member States should, at the present stage in coordination, be allowed the option of limiting the simultaneous pursuit of activity by way of freedom to provide services and activity by way of establishment; whereas no such limitation can be provided for where policy-holders do not require this protection;

Whereas the taking-up and pursuit of freedom to provide services should be subject to procedures guaranteeing the insurance undertaking's compliance with the provisions regarding both financial guarantees and conditions of insurance; whereas these procedures may be relaxed in cases where the activity by way of provision of services covers policy-holders who, by virtue of their status, their size or the nature of the risk to be insured, do not require special protection in the State in which the risk is situated;

Whereas it is necessary to initiate special cooperation with regard to freedom to provide services between the competent supervisory authorities of the Member States and between these authorities and the Commission; whereas provision should also be made for a system of penalties to apply where the undertaking providing the service fails to comply with the provisions of the Member State of provision of service;

Whereas, pending future coordination, the technical reserves should be subject to the rules and supervision of the Member State of provision of services where such provision of services involves risks in respect of which the State receiving the service wishes to provide special protection for policy-holders; whereas, however, if such concern to protect the policy-holders is unjustified, the technical reserves continue to be subject to the rules and supervision of the Member State in which the insurer is established;

Whereas some Member States do not subject insurance transactions to any form of indirect taxation, while the majority apply special taxes and other forms of contribution, including surcharges intended for compensation bodies; whereas the structure and rate of these taxes and contributions vary considerably between the Member States in which they are applied; whereas it is desirable to avoid a situation where existing differences lead to disturbances of competition in insurance services between Member States; whereas, pending future harmonization, the application of the tax system and of other forms of contributions provided for by the Member State in which the risk is situated is likely to remedy such mischief and whereas it is for the Member States to establish a method of ensuring that such taxes and contributions are collected;

Whereas it is desirable to prevent the uncoordinated application of this Directive and of Council Directive 78/473/EEC of 30 May 1978 on the coordination of laws, regulations and administrative provisions relating to Community co-insurance[1] from leading to the existence of three different systems in every Member State;

Note
[1] OJ No. L151, 7.6.1978, p. 25.

whereas, therefore, the criteria defining 'large risks' in this Directive should also define risks likely to be covered under Community co-insurance arrangements;

Whereas it is desirable to take into account, within the meaning of Article 8C of the Treaty, the extent of the effort which needs to be made by certain economies showing differences in development; whereas, therefore, it is desirable to grant certain Member States transitional arrangements for the gradual application of the specific provisions of this Directive relating to freedom to provide services,

HAS ADOPTED THIS DIRECTIVE:

TITLE I   GENERAL PROVISIONS

Article 1
The object of this Directive is:
(a)   to supplement the First Directive 73/239/EEC;
(b)   to lay down special provisions relating to freedom to provide services for the undertakings and in respect of the classes of insurance covered by that First Directive.

Article 2
For the purposes of this Directive:
(a)   'First Directive' means: Directive 73/239/EEC;
(b)   undertaking':
— for the purposes of applying Titles I and II, means: any undertaking which has received official authorisation under Article 6 or 23 of the First Directive,
— for the purposes of applying Title III and Title V, means: any undertaking which has received official authorisation under Article 6 of the First Directive;
(c)   'establishment': means the head office, agency or branch of an undertaking, account being taken of Article 3;
(d)   'Member State where the risk is situated' means:
— the Member State in which the property is situated, where the insurance relates either to buildings or to buildings and their contents, in so far as the contents are covered by the same insurance policy,
— the Member State of registration, where the insurance relates to vehicles of any type,
— the Member State where the policy-holder took out the policy in the case of policies of a duration of four months or less covering travel or holiday risks, whatever the class concerned,
— the Member State where the policy-holder has his habitual residence or, if the policy-holder is a legal person, the Member State where the latter's establishment, to which the contract relates, is situated, in all cases not explicitly covered by the foregoing indents;
(e)   'Member State of establishment' means: the Member State in which the establishment covering the risk is situated;
(f)   'Member State of provision of services' means: the Member State in which the risk is situated when it is covered by an establishment situated in another Member State.

Article 3

For the purposes of the First Directive and of this Directive, any permanent presence of an undertaking in the territory of a Member State shall be treated in the same way as an agency or branch, even if that presence does not take the form of a branch or agency, but consists merely of an office managed by the undertaking's own staff or by a person who is independent but has permanent authority to act for the undertaking as an agency would.

Article 4

For the purposes of this Directive and the First Directive, general and special policy conditions shall not include specific conditions intended to meet, in an individual case, the particular circumstances of the risk to be covered.

TITLE II PROVISIONS SUPPLEMENTARY TO THE FIRST DIRECTIVE

Article 5

The following is added to Article 5 of the First Directive:

(d) 'large risks' means:

(i)   risks classified under classes 4, 5, 6, 7, 11 and 12 of point A of the Annex;

(ii)   risks classified under classes 14 and 15 of point A of the Annex, where the policy-holder is engaged professionally in an industrial or commercial activity or in one of the liberal professions, and the risks relate to such activity;

(iii) risks classified under classes 8, 9, 13 and 16 of point A of the Annex in so far as the policy-holder exceeds the limits of at least two of the following three criteria:

first stage: until 31 December 1992:

— balance-sheet total: 12.4 million ECU,

— net turnover: 24 million ECU,

— average number of employees during the financial year: 500.

second stage: from 1 January 1993:

— balance-sheet total: 6.2 million ECU,

— net turnover: 12.8 million ECU,

— average number of employees during the financial year: 250.

If the policy-holder belongs to a group of undertakings for which consolidated accounts within the meaning of Directive 83/349/EEC[1] are drawn up, the criteria mentioned above shall be applied on the basis of the consolidated accounts.

Each Member State may add to the category mentioned under (iii) risks insured by professional associations, joint ventures or temporary groupings.

Note
[1] OJ No. L193, 18.7.1983, p. 1.

Article 6

For the purposes of applying the first subparagraph of Article 15(2) and Article 24 of the First Directive, the Member States shall comply with Annex 1 to this Directive as regards the matching rules.

(c) A Member State shall accept, as proof that the insurance obligation has been fulfilled, a certificate, the content of which is in conformity with the second indent of subparagraph (a).

Article 9

1.   The last subparagraph of Article 9 and the last subparagraph of Article 11(1) of the First Directive are replaced by the following:

'However, the information referred to in (a) and (b) concerning the general and special conditions and the scales of premiums shall not be required in the case of risks referred to in Article 5(d).'

2.   Article 8(3) and Article 10(3) of the First Directive are replaced by the following:

'3.   This coordination shall not prevent the Member States from maintaining or introducing laws, regulations or administrative provisions concerning, in particular, the necessity for managers and directors to be technically qualified and the approval of articles of association, the general and special conditions of insurance policies, the scales of premiums and any other document necessary for the normal exercise of supervision.

However, with regard to the risks referred to in Article 5(d), Member States shall not lay down provisions requiring the approval or systematic notification of general and special policy conditions, scales of premiums, or forms and other printed documents which the undertaking intends to use in its dealings with policy-holders. They may require only non-systematic notification of these conditions and other documents, for the purpose of verifying compliance with laws, regulations and administrative provisions in respect of such risks, and this requirement may not constitute a prior condition for an undertaking to be able to carry on its activities.

With regard to the risks referred to in Article 5(d), Member States may not retain or introduce prior notification or approval of proposed increases in premium rates except as part of a general price control system.

This coordination shall also not prevent Member States from subjecting undertakings requesting or having obtained authorisation for class 18 in point A of the Annex to checks on their direct or indirect resources in staff and equipment, including the qualification of their medical teams and the quality of the equipment, available to the undertakings to meet their commitments arising from this class of insurance.'

Article 10

The following paragraph is added to Article 19 of the First Directive:

'3.   Each Member State shall take all steps necessary to ensure that the authorities responsible for supervising insurance undertakings have the powers and means necessary for supervision of the activities of insurance undertakings established within their territory, including activities engaged in outside that territory, in accordance with the Council Directives governing those activities and for the purpose of seeing that they are implemented.

Those powers and means must, in particular, enable the supervisory authorities to:

— make detailed inquiries about the undertaking's situation and the whole of its business, inter alia by:

— gathering information or requiring the submission of documents concerning insurance business,

— carrying out on-the-spot investigations at the undertaking's premises,

— take any measures with regard to the undertaking which are appropriate and necessary to ensure that the activities of the undertaking remain in conformity with the laws, regulations and administrative provisions with which the undertaking has to comply in each Member State and in particular with the scheme of operations in so far as it remains mandatory, and to prevent, or remove any irregularities prejudicial to the interests of policy-holders,

— ensure that measures required by the supervisory authorities are carried out, if need be by enforcement, where appropriate through judicial channels.

Member States may also make provision for the supervisory authorities to obtain any information regarding contracts which are held by intermediaries.'

Article 11

1. Article 21 of the First Directive is hereby deleted.
2-7 (Repealed).

TITLE III   PROVISIONS PECULIAR TO THE FREEDOM TO PROVIDE SERVICES

Article 12

1. This Title shall apply where an undertaking, through an establishment situated in a Member State, covers a risk situated, within the meaning of Article 2(d), in another Member State; the latter shall be the Member State of provision of services for the purposes of this Title.

2. This Title shall not apply to the transactions, undertakings and institutions to which the First Directive does not apply, nor to the risks to be covered by the institutions under public law referred to in Article 4 of that Directive. This Title shall not apply to insurance contracts covering risks classified under the following numbers of point A of the Annex to the First Directive:

— No 1: as regards accidents at work,

These exclusions will be examined by the Council not later than 1 July 1998.

Article 12a

1. This Article shall apply where an undertaking, through an establishment situated in a Member State, covers a risk, other than carrier's liability, classified under class 10 of point A of the Annex to Directive 73/239/EEC which is situated in another Member State.

2. The Member State of provision of services shall require the undertaking to become a member of and participate in the financing of its national bureau and its national guarantee fund.

The undertaking shall not, however, be required to make any payment or contribution to the bureau and fund of the Member State of provision of services in respect of risks covered by way of provision of services other than one calculated on the same basis as for undertakings covering risks, other than carrier's liability, in class 10 through an establishment situated in that Member State, by reference to its premium income from that class in that Member State or the number of risks in that class covered there.

3. This Directive shall not prevent an insurance undertaking providing services from being required to comply with the rules in the Member State of provision of services concerning the cover of aggravated risks, insofar as they apply to established undertakings.

4. The Member State of provision of services shall require the undertaking to ensure that persons pursuing claims arising out of events occurring in its territory are not placed in a less favourable situation as a result of the fact that the undertaking is covering a risk, other than carrier's liability, in class 10 by way of provision of services rather than through an establishment situated in that State. For this purpose, the Member State of provision of services shall require the undertaking to appoint a representative resident or established in its territory who shall collect all necessary information in relation to claims, and shall possess sufficient powers to represent the undertaking in relation to persons suffering damage who could pursue claims, including the payment of such claims, and to represent it or, where necessary, to have it represented before the courts and authorities of that Member State in relation to these claims. The representative may also be required to represent the undertaking before the competent authorities of the State of provision of services with regard to checking the existence and validity of motor vehicle liability insurance policies. The Member State of provision of services may not require that appointee to undertake activities on behalf of the undertaking which appointed him other than those set out in the second and third subparagraphs. The appointee shall not take up the business of direct insurance on behalf of the said undertaking. The appointment of the representative shall not in itself constitute the opening of a branch or agency for the purpose of Article 6(2)(b) of Directive 73/239/EEC and the representative shall not be an establishment within the meaning of Article 2(c) of this Directive.

Article 13
(Repealed)

Article 14
Any undertaking that intends to carry on business for the first time in one or more Member States under the freedom to provide services shall first inform the competent authorities of the home Member State, indicating the nature of the risks it proposes to cover.

Article 15
(Repealed)

Article 16
1. Within one month of the notification provided for in Article 14, the competent authorities of the home Member State shall communicate to the Member State or Member States within the territories of which an undertaking intends to carry on business under the freedom to provide services:

(a) a certificate attesting that the undertaking has the minimum solvency margin calculated in accordance with Articles 16 and 17 of Directive 73/239/EEC;

(b) the classes of insurance which the undertaking has been authorised to offer;

(c) the nature of the risks which the undertaking proposes to cover in the Member State of the provision of services. At the same time, they shall inform the undertaking concerned accordingly. Each Member State within the territory of which an undertaking intends, under the freedom to provide services, to cover risks in class 10 of point A of the Annex to Directive 73/239/EEC other than carrier's liability may require that the undertaking:

— communicate the name and address of the representative referred to in Article 12a(4) of this Directive,

— produce a declaration that the undertaking has become a member of the national bureau and national guarantee fund of the Member State of the provision of services.

2. Where the competent authorities of the home Member State do not communicate the information referred to in paragraph 1 within the period laid down, they shall give the reasons for their refusal to the undertaking within that same period. That refusal shall be subject to a right to apply to the courts in the home Member State.

3. The undertaking may start business on the certified date on which it is informed of the communication provided for in the first subparagraph of paragraph 1.

Article 17
Any change which an undertaking intends in make to the information referred to in Article 14 shall be subject to the procedure provided for in Articles 14 and 16.1.

Article 18
(Repealed)

Article 19
(Repealed)

Article 20
(Repealed)

Article 21
(Repealed)

Article 22
(Repealed)

Article 23
(Repealed)

Article 24
(Repealed)

Article 25
(Repealed)

Article 26
1. The risks which may be covered by way of Community co-insurance within the meaning of Directive 78/473/EEC shall be those defined in Article 5(d) of the First Directive.

2. The provisions of this Directive regarding the risks defined in Article 5(d) of the First Directive shall apply to the leading insurer.

TITLE IV   TRANSITIONAL ARRANGEMENTS

Article 27

1.   Greece, Ireland, Spain and Portugal may apply the following transitional arrangements:

(i)   until 31 December 1992, they may apply, to all risks, the regime other than that for risks referred to in Article 5(d) of the First Directive,

(ii)   from 1 January 1993 to 31 December 1994, the regime for large risks shall apply to risks referred to under (i) and (ii) of Article 5(d) of the First Directive; for risks referred to under (iii) of the abovementioned Article 5(d), these Member States shall fix the thresholds to apply therefor;

(iii)   Spain — from 1 January 1995 to 31 December 1996, the thresholds of the first stage described in Article 5(d)(iii) of the First Directive shall apply,

— from 1 January 1997, the thresholds of the second stage shall apply. Portugal, Ireland and Greece — from 1 January 1995 to 31 December 1998 the thresholds of the first stage described in Article 5(d)(iii) of the First Directive shall apply,

— from 1 January 1999 the thresholds of the second stage shall apply. The derogation allowed from 1 January 1995 shall only apply to contracts covering risks classified under classes 3, 8, 9, 10, 13 and 16 situated exclusively in one of the four Member States benefiting from the transitional arrangements.

2.   Until 31 December 1994, Article 26(1) of this Directive shall not apply to risks situated in the four Member States listed in this Article. For the transitional period from 1 January 1995, the risks defined under Article 5(d)(iii) of the First Directive situated in these Member States and capable of being covered by Community co-insurance within the meaning of Directive 78/473/EEC shall be those which exceed the thresholds referred to in paragraph 1(iii) of this Article.

TITLE V   FINAL PROVISIONS

Article 28

The Commission and the competent authorities of the Member States shall collaborate closely for the purpose of facilitating the supervision of direct insurance within the Community. Every Member State shall inform the Commission of any major difficulties to which application of this Directive gives rise, inter alia any arising if a Member State becomes aware of an abnormal transfer of insurance business to the detriment of undertakings established in its territory and to the advantage of branches and agencies located just beyond its borders. The Commission and the competent authorities of the Member States concerned shall examine these difficulties as quickly as possible in order to find an appropriate solution. Where necessary, the Commission shall submit appropriate proposals to the Council.

Article 29

The Commission shall forward to the Council regular reports, the first on 1 July 1993, on the development of the market in insurance transacted under conditions of freedom to provide services.

Article 30

Where this Directive makes reference to the ECU, the exchange value in national currencies to be used with effect from 31 December of each year shall be the value which applies on the last day of the preceding October for which exchange values for the ECU are available in all Community currencies. Article 2 of Directive 76/580/EEC[1] shall apply only to Articles 3, 16 and 17 of the First Directive.

Note
[1] OJ No. L189, 13.9.1976, p. 13.

Article 31
Every five years, the Council, acting on a proposal from the Commission, shall review and if necessary amend any amounts expressed in ECU in this Directive, taking into account changes in the economic and monetary situation of the Community.

Article 32
Member States shall amend their national provisions to comply with this Directive within 18 months of the date of its notification[1] and shall forthwith inform the Commission thereof. The provisions amended in accordance with this Article shall be applied within 24 months of the date of the notification of the Directive.

Note
[1] This Directive was notified to Member States on 30 June 1988.

Article 33
Upon notification of this Directive, Member States shall ensure that the texts of the main laws, regulations or administrative provisions which they adopt in the field covered by this Directive are communicated to the Commission.

Article 34
The Annexes shall form an integral part of this Directive.

Article 35
This Directive is addressed to the Member States.

Done at Luxembourg, 22 June 1988.
For the Council
The President
M. BANGEMANN

ANNEX 1   MATCHING RULES

The currency in which the insurer's commitments are payable shall be determined in accordance with the following rules:

1. Where the cover provided by a contract is expressed in terms of a particular currency, the insurer's commitments are considered to be payable in that currency.

2. Where the cover provided by a contract is not expressed in terms of any currency, the insurer's commitments are considered to be payable in the currency of the country in which the risk is situated. However, the insurer may choose the currency in which the premium is expressed if there are justifiable grounds for exercising such a choice. This could be the case if, from the time

the contract is entered into, it appears likely that a claim will be paid in the currency of the premium and not in the currency of the country in which the risk is situated.

3. The Member States may authorise the insurer to consider that the currency in which he must provide cover will be either that which he will use in accordance with experience acquired or, in the absence of such experience, the currency of the country in which he is established:

— for contracts covering risks classified under classes 4, 5, 6, 7, 11, 12 and 13 (producers' liability only), and

— for contracts covering the risks classified under other classes where, in accordance with the nature of the risks, the cover is to be provided in a currency other than that which would result from the application of the above procedures.

4. Where a claim has been reported to an insurer and is payable in a specified currency other than the currency resulting from application of the above procedures, the insurer's commitments shall be considered to be payable in that currency, and in particular the currency in which the compensation to be paid by the insurer has been determined by a court judgment or by agreement between the insurer and the insured.

5. Where a claim is assessed in a currency which is known to the insurer in advance but which is different from the currency resulting from application of the above procedures, the insurers may consider their commitments to be payable in that currency.

6. The Member States may authorise undertakings not to cover their technical reserves by matching assets if application of the above procedures would result in the undertaking — whether head office or branch — being obliged, in order to comply with the matching principle, to hold assets in a currency amounting to not more than 7% of the assets existing in other currencies. However:

(a) in the case of technical reserve assets to be matched in Greek drachmas, Irish pounds and Portuguese escudos, this amount shall not exceed:

— 1 million ECU during a transitional period ending 31 December 1992,

— 2 million ECU from 1 January 1993 to 31 December 1998;

(b) in the case of technical reserve assets to be matched in Belgian francs, Luxembourg francs and Spanish pesetas, this amount shall not exceed 2 million ECU during a transitional period ending 31 December 1996. From the end of the transitional periods defined under (a) and (b), the general regime shall apply for these currencies, unless the Council decides otherwise.

7. The Member States may choose not to require undertakings — whether head offices or branches — to apply the matching principle where commitments are payable in a currency other than the currency of one of the Community Member States, if investments in that currency are regulated, if the currency is subject to transfer restrictions or if, for similar reasons, it is not suitable for covering technical reserves.

8. Insurance undertakings may hold non-matching assets to cover an amount not exceeding 20% of their commitments in a particular currency.

9. A Member State may provide that when under the preceding procedures a commitment must be covered by assets expressed in a Member State's currency that requirement shall also be considered as satisfied when the assets are expressed in ECUs.

ANNEX 2A   UNDERWRITING ACCOUNT

1. Total gross premiums earned
2. Total cost of claims
3. Commission costs
4. Gross underwriting result

ANNEX 2B   UNDERWRITING ACCOUNT

1. Gross premiums for the last underwriting year
2. Gross claims in the last underwriting year (including reserve at the end of underwriting year)
3. Commission costs
4. Gross underwriting result

COUNCIL DIRECTIVE 92/49/EEC OF 18 JUNE 1992 ON THE COORDINATION OF LAWS, REGULATIONS AND ADMINISTRATIVE PROVISIONS RELATING TO DIRECT INSURANCE OTHER THAN LIFE ASSURANCE AND AMENDING DIRECTIVES 73/239/EEC AND 88/357/ EEC (THIRD NON-LIFE INSURANCE DIRECTIVE)
[OJ 1992, No. L228/1]*

THE COUNCIL OF THE EUROPEAN COMMUNITIES,

Having regard to the Treaty establishing the European Economic Community, and in particular Articles 57(2) and 66 thereof,

Having regard to the proposal from the Commission,[1]

In cooperation with the European Parliament,[2]

Having regard to the opinion of the Economic and Social Committee,[3]

(1) Whereas it is necessary to complete the internal market in direct insurance other than life assurance from the point of view both of the right of establishment and of the freedom to provide services, to make it easier for insurance undertakings with head offices in the Community to cover risks situated within the Community;

(2) Whereas the Second Council Directive of 22 June 1988 on the coordination of laws, regulations and administrative provisions relating to direct insurance other than life assurance and laying down provisions to facilitate the effective exercise of freedom to provide services and amending Directive 72/239/EEC (88/357/EEC)[4] has already contributed substantially to the achievement of the internal market in direct insurance other than life assurance by granting policyholders who, by virtue of their status, their size or the nature of the risks to be insured, do not require special protection in the Member State in which a risk is situated complete freedom to avail themselves of the widest possible insurance market;

Notes
*As amended by Directive 95/26 [OJ 1995 L168/7]
[1] OJ No. C244, 28.9.1990, p. 28 and OJ No. C93, 13.4.1992, p. 1.
[2] OJ No. C67, 16.3.1992, p. 98 and OJ No. C150, 15.6.1992.
[3] OJ No. C102, 18.4.1991, p. 7.
[4] OJ No. L172, 4.7.1988, p. 1. Last amended by Directive 90/618/EEC (OJ No. L330, 29.11.1990, p. 44).

(3)   Whereas Directive 88/357/ EEC therefore represents an important
stage in the merging of national markets into an integrated market and
that stage must be supplemented by other Community instruments with a
view to enabling all policyholders, irrespective of their status, their size or
the nature of the risks to be insured, to have recourse to any insurer with a
head office in the Community who carries on business there, under the right of
establishment or the freedom to provide services, while guaranteeing them
adequate protection;

(4)   Whereas this Directive forms part of the body of Community legislation already enacted which includes the First Council Directive of 24 July 1973
on the coordination of laws, regulations and administrative provisions relating
to the taking up and pursuit of the business of direct insurance other than life
assurance (73/239/EEC)[5] and the Council Directive of 19 December 1991 on
the annual accounts and consolidated accounts of insurance undertakings
(91/674/EEC);[6]

(5)   Whereas the approach adopted consists in bringing about such
harmonization as is essential, necessary and sufficient to achieve the mutual
recognition of authorisations and prudential control systems, thereby making it
possible to grant a single authorisation valid throughout the Community and
apply the principle of supervision by the home Member State;

(6)   Whereas, as a result, the taking up and the pursuit of the business of
insurance are henceforth to be subject to the grant of a single official
authorisation issued by the competent authorities of the Member State in
which an insurance undertaking has its head office; whereas such authorisation
enables an undertaking to carry on business throughout the Community, under
the right of establishment or the freedom to provide services; whereas the
Member State of the branch or of the provision of services may no longer
require insurance undertakings which wish to carry on insurance business there
and which have already been authorised in their home Member State to seek
fresh authorisation; whereas Directives 73/239/EEC and 88/357/ EEC should
therefore be amended along those lines;

(7)   Whereas the competent authorities of home Member States will
henceforth be responsible for monitoring the financial health of insurance
undertakings, including their state of solvency, the establishment of adequate
technical provisions and the covering of those provisions by matching assets;

(8)   Whereas certain provisions of this Directive define minimum standards; whereas a home Member State may lay down stricter rules for insurance
undertakings authorised by its own competent authorities;

(9)   Whereas the competent authorities of the Member States must have at
their disposal such means of supervision as are necessary to ensure the orderly
pursuit of business by insurance undertakings throughout the Community
whether carried on under the right of establishment or the freedom to provide
services; whereas, in particular, they must be able to introduce appropriate
safeguards or impose sanctions aimed at preventing irregularities and infringements of the provisions on insurance supervision;

Notes
[5]OJ No. L228, 16.8.1973, p. 3. Last amended by Directive 88/357/EEC (OJ No. L172,
4.7.1988, p. 1).
[6]OJ No. L374, 31.12.1991, p. 7.

(10) Whereas the internal market comprises an area without internal frontiers and involves access to all insurance business other than life assurance throughout the Community and, hence, the possibility for any duly authorised insurer to cover any of the risks referred to in the Annex to Directive 73/239/EEC; whereas, to that end, the monopoly enjoyed by certain bodies in certain Member States in respect of the coverage of certain risks must be abolished;

(11) Whereas the provisions on transfers of portfolios must be adapted to bring them into line with the single authorisation system introduced by this Directive;

(12) Whereas Directive 91/674/EEC has already effected the necessary harmonization of the Member States' rules on the technical provisions which insurers are required to establish to cover their commitments, and that harmonization makes it possible to grant mutual recognition of those provisions;

(13) Whereas the rules governing the spread, localisation and matching of the assets used to cover technical provisions must be coordinated in order to facilitate the mutual recognition of Member States' rules; whereas that coordination must take account of the measures on the liberalisation of capital movements provided for in the Council Directive of 24 June 1988 for the implementation of Article 67 of the Treaty (88/361/EEC)[1] and the progress made by the Community towards economic and monetary union;

(14) Whereas, however, the home Member State may not require insurance undertakings to invest the assets covering their technical provisions in particular categories of assets, as such a requirement would be incompatible with the measures on the liberalisation of capital movements provided for in Directive 88/361/EEC;

(15) Whereas, pending the adoption of a Directive on investment services harmonizing inter alia the definition of the concept of regulated market, for the purposes of this Directive and without prejudice to such future harmonization that concept must be defined provisionally; whereas that definition will be replaced by that harmonised at Community level which will give the home Member State of the market the responsibilities for these matters which this Directive transitionally gives to the insurance undertaking's home Member State;

(16) Whereas the list of items of which the solvency margin required by Directive 73/239/EEC may be made up must be supplemented to take account of new financial instruments and of the facilities granted to other financial institutions for the constitution of their own funds;

(17) Whereas within the framework of an integrated insurance market policyholders who, by virtue of their status, their size or the nature of the risks to be insured, do not require special protection in the Member State in which a risk is situated should be granted complete freedom to choose the law applicable to their insurance contracts;

(18) Whereas the harmonization of insurance contract law is not a prior condition for the achievement of the internal market in insurance; whereas, therefore, the opportunity afforded to the Member States of imposing the

Note
[1] OJ No. L178, 8.7.1988, p. 5.

application of their law to insurance contracts covering risks situated within their territories is likely to provide adequate safeguards for policyholders who require special protection;

(19)   Whereas within the framework of an internal market it is in the policyholder's interest that he should have access to the widest possible range of insurance products available in the Community so that he can choose that which is best suited to his needs; whereas it is for the Member State in which the risk is situated to ensure that there is nothing to prevent the marketing within its territory of all the insurance products offered for sale in the Community as long as they do not conflict with the legal provisions protecting the general good in force in the Member State in which the risk is situated, and insofar as the general good is not safeguarded by the rules of the home Member State, provided that such provisions must be applied without discrimination to all undertakings operating in that Member State and be objectively necessary and in proportion to the objective pursued;

(20)   Whereas the Member States must be able to ensure that the insurance products and contract documents used, under the right of establishment or the freedom to provide services, to cover risks situated within their territories comply with such specific legal provisions protecting the general good as are applicable; whereas the systems of supervision to be employed must meet the requirements of an integrated market but their employment may not constitute a prior condition for carrying on insurance business; whereas from this standpoint systems for the prior approval of policy conditions do not appear to be justified; whereas it is therefore necessary to provide for other systems better suited to the requirements of an internal market which enable every Member State to guarantee policyholders adequate protection;

(21)   Whereas if a policyholder is a natural person, he should be informed by the insurance undertaking of the law which will apply to the contract and of the arrangements for handling policyholders' complaints concerning contracts;

(22)   Whereas in some Member States private or voluntary health insurance serves as a partial or complete alternative to health cover provided for by the social security systems;

(23)   Whereas the nature and social consequences of health insurance contracts justify the competent authorities of the Member State in which a risk is situated in requiring systematic notification of the general and special policy conditions in order to verify that such contracts are a partial or complete alternative to the health cover provided by the social security system; whereas such verification must not be a prior condition for the marketing of the products; whereas the particular nature of health insurance, serving as a partial or complete alternative to the health cover provided by the social security system, distinguishes it from other classes of indemnity insurance and life assurance insofar as it is necessary to ensure that policyholders have effective access to private health cover or health cover taken out on a voluntary basis regardless of their age or risk profile;

(24)   Whereas to this end some Member States have adopted specific legal provisions; whereas, to protect the general good, it is possible to adopt or maintain such legal provisions in so far as they do not unduly restrict the right of establishment or the freedom to provide services, it being understood that such provisions must apply in an identical manner whatever the home Member State of the undertaking may be; whereas these legal provisions may differ in

nature according to the conditions in each Member State; whereas these measures may provide for open enrolment, rating on a uniform basis according to the type of policy and lifetime cover; whereas that objective may also be achieved by requiring undertakings offering private health cover or health cover taken out on a voluntary basis to offer standard policies in line with the cover provided by statutory social security schemes at a premium rate at or below a prescribed maximum and to participate in loss compensation schemes; whereas, as a further possibility, it may be required that the technical basis of private health cover or health cover taken out on a voluntary basis be similar to that of life assurance;

(25) Whereas, because of the coordination effected by Directive 73/239/ EEC as amended by this Directive, the possibility, afforded to the Federal Republic of Germany under Article 7(2)(c) of the same Directive, of prohibiting the simultaneous transaction of health insurance and other classes is no longer justified and must therefore be abolished;

(26) Whereas Member States may require any insurance undertakings offering compulsory insurance against accidents at work at their own risk within their territories to comply with the specific provisions laid down in their national law on such insurance; whereas, however, this requirement may not apply to the provisions concerning financial supervision, which are the exclusive responsibility of the home Member State;

(27) Whereas exercise of the right of establishment requires an undertaking to maintain a permanent presence in the Member State of the branch; whereas responsibility for the specific interests of insured persons and victims in the case of third-party liability motor insurance requires adequate structures in the Member State of the branch for the collection of all the necessary information on compensation claims relating to that risk, with sufficient powers to represent the undertaking vis-à-vis injured parties who could claim compensation, including powers to pay such compensation, and to represent the undertaking or, if necessary, to arrange for it to be represented in the courts and before the competent authorities of that Member State in connection with claims for compensation;

(28) Whereas within the framework of the internal market no Member State may continue to prohibit the simultaneous carrying on of insurance business within its territory under the right of establishment and the freedom to provide services; whereas the option granted to Member States in this connection by Directive 88/357/ EEC should therefore be abolished;

(29) Whereas provision should be made for a system of penalties to be imposed when, in the Member State in which a risk is situated, an insurance undertaking does not comply with those provisions protecting the general good that are applicable to it;

(30) Whereas some Member States do not subject insurance transactions to any form of indirect taxation, while the majority apply special taxes and other forms of contribution, including surcharges intended for compensation bodies; whereas the structures and rates of such taxes and contributions vary considerably between the Member States in which they are applied; whereas it is desirable to prevent existing differences' leading to distortions of competition in insurance services between Member States; whereas, pending subsequent harmonization, application of the tax systems and other forms of contribution provided for by the Member States in which risks are situated is likely to

remedy that problem and it is for the Member States to make arrangements to ensure that such taxes and contributions are collected;

(31) Whereas technical adjustments to the detailed rules laid down in this Directive may be necessary from time to time to take account of the future development of the insurance industry; whereas the Commission will make such adjustments as and when necessary, after consulting the Insurance Committee set up by Directive 91/675/EEC,[1] in the exercise of the implementing powers conferred on it by the Treaty;

(32) Whereas it is necessary to adopt specific provisions intended to ensure smooth transition from the legal regime in existence when this Directive becomes applicable to the regime that it introduces, taking care not to place an additional workload on Member States' competent authorities;

(33) Whereas under Article 8c of the Treaty account should be taken of the extent of the effort which must be made by certain economies at different stages of development; whereas, therefore, transitional arrangements should be adopted for the gradual application of this Directive by certain Member States,

Note
[1]OJ No. L374, 31.12.1991, p. 32.

HAS ADOPTED THIS DIRECTIVE:

(**Editor's Note:** All the amendments noted in this directive have been made to previous Directives and removed from here to avoid unnecessary repetition)

TITLE I   DEFINITIONS AND SCOPE

Article 1
For the purposes of this Directive:

(a) 'insurance undertaking' shall mean an undertaking which has received official authorisation in accordance with Article 6 of Directive 73/239/EEC;

(b) 'branch' shall mean an agency or branch of an insurance undertaking, having regard to Article 3 of Directive 88/357/ EEC;

(c) 'home Member State' shall mean the Member State in which the head office of the insurance undertaking covering a risk is situated;

(d) 'Member State of the branch' shall mean the Member State in which the branch covering a risk is situated;

(e) 'Member State of the provision of services' shall mean the Member State in which a risk is situated, as defined in Article 2(d) of Directive 88/357/ EEC, if it is covered by an insurance undertaking or a branch situated in another Member State;

(f) 'control' shall mean the relationship between a parent undertaking and a subsidiary, as defined in Article 1 of Directive 83/349/EEC,[1] or a similar relationship between any natural or legal person and an undertaking;

(g) 'qualifying holding' shall mean a direct or indirect holding in an undertaking which represents 10% or more of the capital or of the voting rights or which makes it possible to exercise a significant influence over the management of the undertaking in which a holding subsists.

Note
[1]OJ No. L193, 18.7.1983, p. 1.

For the purposes of this definition, in the context of Articles 8 and 15 and of the other levels of holding referred to in Article 15, the voting rights referred to in Article 7 of Directive 88/627/EEC[2] shall be taken into account;

(h) 'parent undertaking' shall mean a parent undertaking as defined in Articles 1 and 2 of Directive 83/349/EEC;

(i) 'subsidiary' shall mean a subsidiary undertaking as defined in Articles 1 and 2 of Directive 83/349/EEC; any subsidiary of a subsidiary undertaking shall also be regarded as a subsidiary of the undertaking which is those undertakings' ultimate parent undertaking;

(j) 'regulated market' shall mean a financial market regarded by an undertaking's home Member State as a regulated market pending the adoption of a definition in a Directive on investment services and characterised by:

— regular operation, and

— the fact that regulations issued or approved by the appropriate authorities define the conditions for the operation of the market, the conditions for access to the market and, where the Council Directive of 5 March 1979 coordinating the conditions for the admission of securities to official stock-exchange listing (79/279/EEC)[3] applies, the conditions for admission to listing imposed in that Directive or, where that Directive does not apply, the conditions to be satisfied by a financial instrument in order to be effectively dealt in on the market. For the purposes of this Directive, a regulated market may be situated in a Member State or in a third country. In the latter event, the market must be recognised by the home Member State and meet comparable requirements. Any financial instruments dealt in on that market must be of a quality comparable to that of the instruments dealt in on the regulated market or markets of the Member State in question;

(k) 'competent authorities' shall mean the national authorities which are empowered by law or regulation to supervise insurance undertakings;

(l) 'close links' shall mean a situation in which two or more natural or legal persons are linked by:

(a) 'participation', which shall mean the ownership, direct or by way of control, of 20% or more of the voting rights or capital of an undertaking or

(b) 'control', which shall mean the relationship between a parent undertaking and a subsidiary, in all the cases referred to in Article 1(1) and (2) of Directive 83/349/EEC,[4] or a similar relationship between any natural or legal person and an undertaking; any subsidiary undertaking of a subsidiary undertaking shall also be considered a subsidiary of the parent undertaking which is at the head of those undertakings. A situation in which two or more natural or legal persons are permanently linked to one and the same person by a control relationship shall also be regarded as constituting a close link between such persons.

Notes

[2]OJ No. L348, 17.12.1988, p. 62.

[3]OJ No. L66, 13.3.1979, p. 21. Last amended by Directive 82/148/EEC (OJ No. L62, 5.3.1982, p. 22).

[4]OJ No. L193, 18.7.1983, p. 1. Directive as last amended by Directive 90/605/EEC (OJ No. L317, 16.11.1990, p. 60).

Article 2

1. This Directive shall apply to the types of insurance and undertakings referred to in Article 1 of Directive 73/239/EEC.

2.   This Directive shall apply neither to the types of insurance or operations, nor to undertakings or institutions to which Directive 73/239/EEC does not apply, nor to the bodies referred to in Article 4 of that Directive.

Article 3
Notwithstanding Article 2(2), Member States shall take every step to ensure that monopolies in respect of the taking up of the business of certain classes of insurance, granted to bodies established within their territories and referred to in Article 4 of Directive 73/239/EEC, are abolished by 1 July 1994.

TITLE II   THE TAKING UP OF THE BUSINESS OF INSURANCE

Article 4
Article 6 of Directive 73/239/EEC shall be replaced by the following:

Article 5
Article 7 of Directive 73/239/EEC shall be replaced by the following:

Article 6
Article 8 of Directive 72/239/EEC shall be replaced by the following:

Article 7
Article 9 of Directive 73/239/EEC shall be replaced by the following:

Article 8
The competent authorities of the home Member State shall not grant an undertaking authorisation to take up the business of insurance before they have been informed of the identities of the shareholders or members, direct or indirect, whether natural or legal persons, who have qualifying holdings in that undertaking and of the amounts of those holdings. The same authorities shall refuse authorisation if, taking into account the need to ensure the sound and prudent management of an insurance undertaking, they are not satisfied as to the qualifications of the shareholders or members.

TITLE III   HARMONIZATION OF THE CONDITIONS GOVERNING THE BUSINESS OF INSURANCE

CHAPTER 1

Article 9
Article 13 of Directive 73/239/EEC shall be replaced by the following:

Article 10
Article 14 of Directive 73/239/EEC shall be replaced by the following:

Article 11
Article 19(2) and (3) of Directive 73/239/EEC shall be replaced by the following:

Article 12
1.   Article 11(2) to (7) of Directive 88/357/EEC is hereby repealed.
2.   Under the conditions laid down by national law, each Member State shall authorise insurance undertakings with head offices within its territory to transfer all or part of their portfolios of contracts, concluded either under the right of establishment or the freedom to provide services, to an accepting office established within the Community, if the competent authorities of the home

Member State of the accepting office certify that after taking the transfer into account the latter possesses the necessary solvency margin.

3. Where a branch proposes to transfer all or part of its portfolio of contracts, concluded either under the right of establishment or the freedom to provide services, the Member State of the branch shall be consulted.

4. In the circumstances referred to in paragraphs 2 and 3, the competent authorities of the home Member State of the transferring undertaking shall authorise the transfer after obtaining the agreement of the competent authorities of the Member States in which the risks are situated.

5. The competent authorities of the Member States consulted shall give their opinion or consent to the competent authorities of the home Member State of the transferring insurance undertaking within three months of receiving a request; the absence of any response within that period from the authorities consulted shall be considered equivalent to a favourable opinion or tacit consent.

6. A transfer authorised in accordance with this Article shall be published as laid down by national law in the Member State in which the risk is situated. Such transfers shall automatically be valid against policy-holders, insured persons and any other persons having rights or obligations arising out of the contracts transferred.

This provision shall not affect the Member States' rights to give policy-holders the option of cancelling contracts within a fixed period after a transfer.

Article 13
1. Article 20 of Directive 73/239/EEC shall be replaced by the following:

Article 14
Article 22 of Directive 73/239/EEC shall be replaced by the following:

Article 15
1. Member States shall require any natural or legal person who proposes to acquire, directly or indirectly, a qualifying holding in an insurance undertaking first to inform the competent authorities of the home Member State, indicating the size of his intended holding. Such a person must likewise inform the competent authorities of the home Member State if he proposes to increase his qualifying holding so that the proportion of the voting rights or of the capital he holds would reach or exceed 20, 33 or 50% or so that the insurance undertaking would become his subsidiary.

The competent authorities of the home Member State shall have up to three months from the date of the notification provided for in the first subparagraph to oppose such a plan if, in view of the need to ensure sound and prudent management of the insurance undertaking in question, they are not satisfied as to the qualification of the person referred to in the first subparagraph. If they do not oppose the plan in question, they may fix a maximum period for its implementation.

2. Member States shall require any natural or legal person who proposes to dispose, directly or indirectly, of a qualifying holding in an insurance undertaking first to inform the competent authorities of the home Member State, indicating the size of his intended holding. Such a person must likewise inform the competent authorities if he proposes to reduce his qualifying holding so that the proportion of the voting rights or of the capital he holds

would fall below 20, 33 or 50% or so that the insurance undertaking would cease to be his subsidiary.

3.   On becoming aware of them, insurance undertakings shall inform the competent authorities of their home Member States of any acquisitions or disposals of holdings in their capital that cause holdings to exceed or fall below any of the thresholds referred to in paragraphs 1 and 2.

They shall also, at least once a year, inform them of the names of shareholders and members possessing qualifying holdings and the sizes of such holdings as shown, for example, by the information received at annual general meetings of shareholders or members or as a result of compliance with the regulations relating to companies listed on stock exchanges.

4.   Member States shall require that, where the influence exercised by the persons referred to in paragraph 1 is likely to operate against the prudent and sound management of an insurance undertaking, the competent authorities of the home Member State shall take appropriate measures to put an end to that situation. Such measures may consist, for example, in injunctions, sanctions against directors and managers, or suspension of the exercise of the voting rights attaching to the shares held by the shareholders or members in question. Similar measures shall apply to natural or legal persons failing to comply with the obligation to provide prior information imposed in paragraph 1. If a holding is acquired despite the opposition of the competent authorities, the Member States shall, regardless of any other sanctions to be adopted, provide either for exercise of the corresponding voting rights to be suspended, or for the nullity of votes cast or for the possibility of their annulment.

Article 16

1.   The Member States shall provide that all persons working or who have worked for the competent authorities, as well as auditors and experts acting on behalf of the competent authorities, shall be bound by the obligation of professional secrecy. This means that no confidential information which they may receive while performing their duties may be divulged to any person or authority whatsoever, except in summary or aggregate form, such that individual insurance undertakings cannot be identified, without prejudice to cases covered by criminal law.

Nevertheless, where an insurance undertaking has been declared bankrupt or is being compulsorily wound up, confidential information which does not concern third parties involved in attempts to rescue that undertaking may be divulged in civil or commercial proceedings.

2.   Paragraph 1 shall not prevent the competent authorities of different Member States from exchanging information in accordance with the Directives applicable to insurance undertakings. Such information shall be subject to the conditions of professional secrecy laid down in paragraph 1.

3.   Member States may conclude cooperation agreements, providing for exchanges of information, with the competent authorities of third countries only if the information disclosed is subject to guarantees of professional secrecy at least equivalent to those provided for in this Article.

4.   Competent authorities receiving confidential information under paragraphs 1 or 2 may use it only in the course of their duties:

— to check that the conditions governing the taking up of the business of insurance are met and to facilitate monitoring of the conduct of such business, especially with regard to the monitoring of technical provisions, solvency margins, administrative and accounting procedures and internal control mechanisms,

— to impose sanctions,

— in administrative appeals against decisions of the competent authorities, or

— in court proceedings initiated under Article 56 or under special provisions provided for in the Directives adopted in the field of insurance undertakings.

5. Paragraphs 1 and 4 shall not preclude the exchange of information within a Member State, where there are two or more competent authorities in the same Member State, or, between Member States, between competent authorities and:

— authorities responsible for the official supervision of credit institutions and other financial organisations and the authorities responsible for the supervision of financial markets,

— bodies involved in the liquidation and bankruptcy of insurance undertakings and in other similar procedures, and

— persons responsible for carrying out statutory audits of the accounts of insurance undertakings and other financial institutions, in the discharge of their supervisory functions, or the disclosure to bodies which administer compulsory winding-up proceedings or guarantee funds of information necessary to the performance of their duties. The information received by those authorities, bodies and persons shall be subject to the conditions of professional secrecy laid down in paragraph 1.

5a. Notwithstanding paragraphs 1 to 4, Member States may authorise exchanges of information between the competent authorities and:

— the authorities responsible for overseeing the bodies involved in the liquidation and bankruptcy of financial undertakings and other similar procedures, or

— the authorities responsible for overseeing the persons charged with carrying out statutory audits of the accounts of insurance undertakings, credit institutions, investment firms and other financial institutions, or

— independent actuaries of insurance undertakings carrying out legal supervision of those undertakings and the bodies responsible for overseeing such actuaries. Member States which have recourse to the option provided for in the first subparagraph shall require at least that the following conditions are met:

- this information shall be for the purpose of carrying out the overseeing or legal supervision referred to in the first subparagraph,

— information received in this context will be subject to the conditions of professional secrecy imposed in paragraph 1,

— where the information originates in another Member State, it may not be disclosed without the express agreement of the competent authorities which have disclosed it and, where appropriate, solely for the purposes for which those authorities gave their agreement. Member States shall communicate to the Commission and to the other Member States the names of the authorities, person and bodies which may receive information pursuant to this paragraph.

5b. Notwithstanding paragraphs 1 to 4, Member States may, with the aim of strengthening the stability, including integrity, of the financial system, authorise the exchange of information between the competent authorities and the authorities or bodies responsible under the law for the detection and investigation of breaches of company law. Member States which have recourse to the option provided for in the first subparagraph shall require at least that the following conditions are met:

— the information shall be for the purpose of performing the task referred to in the first subparagraph,

— information received in this context shall be subject to the conditions of professional secrecy imposed in paragraph 1,

— where the information originates in another Member State, it may not be disclosed without the express agreement of the competent authorities which have disclosed it and, where appropriate, solely for the purposes for which those authorities gave their agreement.

Where, in a Member State, the authorities or bodies referred to in the first subparagraph perform their task of detection or investigation with the aid, in view of their specific competence, of persons appointed for that purpose and not employed in the public sector, the possibility of exchanging information provided for in the first subparagraph may be extended to such persons under the conditions stipulated in the second subparagraph.

In order to implement the final indent of the second subparagraph, the authorities or bodies referred to in the first subparagraph shall communicate to the competent authorities which have disclosed the information, the names and precise responsibilities of the persons to whom it is to be sent. Member States shall communicate to the Commission and to the other Member States the names of the authorities or bodies which may receive information pursuant to this paragraph.

Before 31 December 2000, the Commission shall draw up a report on the application of the provisions of this paragraph.

5c. Member States may authorise the competent authorities to transmit:

— to central banks and other bodies with a similar function in their capacity as monetary authorities,

— where appropriate, to other public authorities responsible for overseeing payment systems, information intended for the performance of their task and may authorise such authorities or bodies to communicate to the competent authorities such information as they may need for the purposes of paragraph 4. Information received in this context shall be subject to the conditions of professional secrecy imposed in this Article.

6. In addition, notwithstanding paragraphs 1 and 4, the Member States may, under provisions laid down by law, authorise the disclosure of certain information to other departments of their central government administrations responsible for legislation on the supervision of credit institutions, financial institutions, investment services and insurance companies and to inspectors acting on behalf of those departments.

However, such disclosures may be made only where necessary for reasons of prudential control.

The Member States shall, however, provide that information received under paragraphs 2 and 5 and that obtained by means of the on-the-spot verification referred to in Article 14 of Directive 73/239/EEC may never be disclosed in the cases referred to in this paragraph except with the express consent of the competent authorities which disclosed the information or of the competent authorities of the Member State in which on-the-spot verification was carried out.

Article 16a

1. Member States shall provide at least that:

(a)   any person authorised within the meaning of Directive 84/253/EEC,[1] performing in a financial undertaking the task described in Article 51 of Directive 78/660/EEC,[2] Article 37 of Directive 83/349/EEC or Article 31 of Directive 85/611/EEC or any other statutory task, shall have a duty to report promptly to the competent authorities any fact or decision concerning that undertaking of which he has become aware while carrying out that task which is liable to:

— constitute a material breach of the laws, regulations or administrative provisions which lay down the conditions governing authorisation or which specifically govern pursuit of the activities of financial undertakings, or

— affect the continuous functioning of the financial undertaking, or

— lead to refusal to certify the accounts or to the expression of reservations;

(b)   that person shall likewise have a duty to report any facts and decisions of which he becomes aware in the course of carrying out a task as described in (a) in an undertaking having close links resulting from a control relationship with the financial undertaking within which he is carrying out the abovementioned task.

2.   The disclosure in good faith to the competent authorities, by persons authorised within the meaning of Directive 84/253/EEC, of any fact or decision referred to in paragraph 1 shall not constitute a breach of any restriction on disclosure of information imposed by contract of by any legislative, regulatory or administrative provision and shall not involve such persons in liability of any kind.

Notes

[1] OJ No. L126, 12.5.1984, p. 20.

[2] OJ No. L222, 14.8.1978, p. 11. Directive as last amended by Directive 90/605/EEC (OJ No. L317, 16.11.1990, p. 60).

CHAPTER 2

Article 17

Article 15 of Directive 73/239/EEC shall be replaced by the following:

Article 18

Article 15a of Directive 72/239/EEC shall be replaced by the following:

Article 19

Article 23 of Directive 88/357/ EEC is hereby repealed.

Article 20

The assets covering the technical provisions shall take account of the type of business carried on by an undertaking in such a way as to secure the safety, yield and marketability of its investments, which the undertaking shall ensure are diversified and adequately spread.

Article 21

1.   The home Member State may not authorise insurance undertakings to cover their technical provisions with any but the following categories of assets:

A. Investments

   (a)   debt securities, bonds and other money and capital market instruments;

   (b)   loans;

   (c)   shares and other variable yield participations;

   (d)   units in undertakings for collective investment in transferable securities and other investment funds;

   (e)   land, buildings and immovable property rights;

B. Debts and claims

   (f)   debts owed by reinsurers, including reinsurers' shares of technical provisions;

   (g)   deposits with and debts owed by ceding undertakings;

   (h)   debts owed by policyholders and intermediaries arising out of direct and reinsurance operations;

   (i)   claims arising out of salvage and subrogation;

   (j)   tax recoveries;

   (k)   claims against guarantee funds;

C. Others

   (l)   tangible fixed assets, other than land and buildings, valued on the basis of prudent amortisation;

   (m) cash at bank and in hand, deposits with credit institutions and any other bodies authorised to receive deposits;

   (n)   deferred acquisition costs;

   (o)   accrued interest and rent, other accrued income and prepayments; In the case of the association of underwriters known as Lloyd's, asset categories shall also include guarantees and letters of credit issued by credit institutions within the meaning of Directive 77/780/EEC[1] or by assurance undertakings, together with verifiable sums arising out of life assurance policies, to the extent that they represent funds belonging to members.

   The inclusion of any asset or category of assets listed in the first subparagraph shall not mean that all categories of assets must automatically be accepted as cover for technical provisions. The home Member State shall lay down more detailed rules fixing the conditions for the use of acceptable assets; in this connection, it may require valuable security or guarantees, particularly in the case of debts owed by reinsurers.

   In the determination and the application of the rules which it lays down, the home Member State shall, in particular, ensure that the following principles are complied with:

   (i)   assets covering technical provisions shall be valued net of any debts arising out of their acquisition;

   (ii)   all assets must be valued on a prudent basis, allowing for the risk of any amounts' not being realisable. In particular, tangible fixed assets other than land and buildings may be accepted as cover for technical provisions only if they are valued on the basis of prudent amortisation;

Note
[1]OJ No. L322, 17.12.1977, p. 30. Last amended by Directive 89/646/EEC (OJ No. L386, 30.12.1989, p. 1).

(iii)   loans, whether to undertakings, to State authorities or international organisations, to local or regional authorities or to natural persons, may be accepted as cover for technical provisions only if there are sufficient guarantees as to their security, whether these are based on the status of the borrower, mortgages, bank guarantees or guarantees granted by insurance undertakings or other forms of security;

(iv)   derivative instruments such as options, futures and swaps in connection with assets covering technical provisions may be used in so far as they contribute to a reduction of investment risks or facilitate efficient portfolio management. They must be valued on a prudent basis and may be taken into account in the valuation of the underlying assets;

(v)   transferable securities which are not dealt in on a regulated market may be accepted as cover for technical provisions only if they can be realised in the short term;

(vi)   debts owed by and claims against a third party may be accepted as cover for technical provisions only after deduction of all amounts owed to the same third party;

(vii)   the value of any debts and claims accepted as cover for technical provisions must be calculated on a prudent basis, with due allowance for the risk of any amounts not being realisable. In particular, debts owed by policyholders and intermediaries arising out of insurance and reinsurance operations may be accepted only in so far as they have been outstanding for not more than three months;

(viii)   where the assets held include an investment in a subsidiary undertaking which manages all or part of the insurance undertaking's investments on its behalf, the home Member State must, when applying the rules and principles laid down in this Article, take into account the underlying assets held by the subsidiary undertaking; the home Member State may treat the assets of other subsidiaries in the same way;

(ix)   deferred acquisition costs may be accepted as cover for technical provisions only to the extent that that is consistent with the calculation of the technical provision for unearned premiums.

2.   Notwithstanding paragraph 1, in exceptional circumstances and at an insurance undertaking's request, the home Member State may, temporarily and under a properly reasoned decision, accept other categories of assets as cover for technical provisions, subject to Article 20.

Article 22

1.   As regards the assets covering technical provisions, the home Member State shall require every insurance undertaking to invest no more than:

(a)   10% of its total gross technical provisions in any one piece of land or building, or a number of pieces of land or buildings close enough to each other to be considered effectively as one investment;

(b)   5% of its total gross technical provisions in shares and other negotiable securities treated as shares, bonds, debt securities and other money and capital market instruments from the same undertaking, or in loans granted to the same borrower, taken together, the loans being loans other than those granted to a State, regional or local authority or to an international organization of which one or more Member States are members. This limit may be raised to 10% if an undertaking does not invest more than 40% of its gross technical provisions in the loans or securities of issuing bodies and borrowers in each of which it invests more than 5% of its assets;

(c)   5% of its total gross technical provisions in unsecured loans, including 1% for any single unsecured loan, other than loans granted to credit institutions, assurance undertaking — in so far as Article 8 of Directive 73/239/EEC allows it — and investment undertakings established in a Member State;

(d)   3% of its total gross technical provisions in the form of cash in hand;

(e)   10% of its total gross technical provisions in shares, other securities treated as shares and debt securities, which are not dealt in on a regulated market.

2.   The absence of a limit in paragraph 1 on investment in any particular category does not imply that assets in that category should be accepted as cover for technical provisions without limit. The home Member State shall lay down more detailed rules fixing the conditions for the use of acceptable assets. In particular it shall ensure, in the determination and the application of those rules, that the following principles are complied with:

(i)   assets covering technical provisions must be diversified and spread in such a way as to ensure that there is no excessive reliance on any particular category of asset, investment market or investment;

(ii)   investment in particular types of asset which show high levels of risk, whether because of the nature of the asset or the quality of the issuer, must be restricted to prudent levels;

(iii)   limitations on particular categories of asset must take account of the treatment of reinsurance in the calculation of technical provisions;

(iv)   where the assets held include an investment in a subsidiary undertaking which manages all or part of the insurance undertaking's investments on its behalf, the home Member State must, when applying the rules and principles laid down in this Article, take into account the underlying assets held by the subsidiary undertaking; the home Member State may treat the assets of other subsidiaries in the same way;

(v)   the percentage of assets covering technical provisions which are the subject of non-liquid investments must be kept to a prudent level;

(vi)   where the assets held include loans to or debt securities issued by certain credit institutions, the home Member State may, when applying the rules and principles laid down in this Article, take into account the underlying assets held by such credit institutions. This treatment may be applied only where the credit institution has its head office in a Member State, is entirely owned by that Member State and/or that State's local authorities and its business, according to its memorandum and articles of association, consists of extending, through its intermediary, loans to or guaranteed by the State or local authorities or loans to bodies closely linked to the State or to local authorities.

3.   In the context of the detailed rules laying down the conditions for the use of acceptable assets, the Member State shall give more limitative treatment to:

— any loan unaccompanied by a bank guarantee, a guarantee issued by an insurance undertaking, a mortgage or any other form of security, as compared with loans accompanied by such collateral,

— Ucits not coordinated within the meaning of Directive 85/611/EEC[1] and other investment funds, as compared with Ucits coordinated within the meaning of that Directive,

— securities which are not dealt in on a regulated market, as compared with those which are,

— bonds, debt securities and other money and capital market instruments not issued by States, local or regional authorities or undertakings belonging to Zone A as defined in Directive 89/647/EEC,[2] or the issuers of which are international organisations not numbering at least one Community Member State among their members, as compared with the same financial instruments issued by such bodies.

4. Member States may raise the limit laid down in paragraph 1(b) to 40% in the case of certain debt securities when these are issued by a credit institution which has its head office in a Member State and is subject by law to special official supervision designed to protect the holders of those debt securities. In particular, sums deriving from the issue of such debt securities must be invested in accordance with the law in assets which, during the whole period of validity of the debt securities, are capable of covering claims attaching to the debt securities and which, in the event of failure of the issues, would be used on a priority basis for the reimbursement of the principal and payment of the accrued interest.

5. Member States shall not require insurance undertakings to invest in particular categories of assets.

6. Notwithstanding paragraph 1, in exceptional circumstances and at an insurance undertaking's request, the home Member State may, temporarily and under a properly reasoned decision, allow exceptions to the rules laid down in paragraph 1(a) to (e), subject to Article 20.

Notes
[1]OJ No. L375, 31.12.1985, p. 3. Amended by Directive 88/220/EEC (OJ No. L100, 19.4.1988, p. 31).
[2]OJ No. L386, 30.12.1989, p. 14.

Article 23
Points 8 and 9 of Annex 1 to Directive 88/357/ EEC shall be replaced by the following:

Article 24
Article 16(1) of Directive 73/239/EEC shall be replaced by the following:

Article 25
No more than three years after the date of application of this Directive the Commission shall submit a report to the Insurance Committee on the need for further harmonization of the solvency margin.

Article 26
Article 18 of Directive 79/239/EEC shall be replaced by the following:

CHAPTER 3

Article 27
Article 7(1)(f) of Directive 88/357/EEC shall be replaced by the following:

Article 28
The Member State in which a risk is situated shall not prevent a policyholder from concluding a contract with an insurance undertaking authorised under the conditions of Article 6 of Directive 73/239/EEC, as long as that does not

nature of those measures shall be communicated to the competent authorities of the Member State concerned.

5.   If, despite the measures taken by the home Member State or because those measures prove inadequate or are lacking in that State, the undertaking persists in infringing the legal provisions in force in the Member State concerned, the latter may, after informing the competent authorities of the home Member State, take appropriate measures to prevent or penalise further infringements, including, in so far as is strictly necessary, preventing that undertaking from continuing to conclude new insurance contracts within its territory. Member States shall ensure that within their territories it is possible to serve the legal documents necessary for such measures on insurance undertakings.

6.   Paragraphs 3, 4 and 5 shall not affect the emergency power of the Member States concerned to take appropriate measures to prevent irregularities within their territories. This shall include the possibility of preventing insurance undertakings from continuing to conclude new insurance contracts within their territories.

7.   Paragraphs 3, 4 and 5 shall not affect the powers of the Member States to penalise infringements within their territories.

8.   If an undertaking which has committed an infringement has an establishment or possesses property in the Member State concerned, the competent authorities of the latter may, in accordance with national law, apply the administrative penalties prescribed for that infringement by way of enforcement against that establishment or property.

9.   Any measure adopted under paragraphs 4 to 8 involving penalties or restrictions on the conduct of insurance business must be properly reasoned and communicated to the undertaking concerned.

10.   Every two years, the Commission shall submit to the Insurance Committee set up by Directive 91/675/EEC a report summarising the number and types of cases in which, in each Member State, authorisation has been refused under Article 10 of Directive 73/239/EEC or Article 16 of Directive 88/357/EEC as amended by this Directive or measures have been taken under paragraph 5. Member States shall cooperate with the Commission by providing it with the information required for that report.

Article 41
Nothing in this Directive shall prevent insurance undertakings with head offices in Member States from advertising their services, through all available means of communication, in the Member State of the branch or the Member State of the provision of services, subject to any rules governing the form and content of such advertising adopted in the interest of the general good.

Article 42
1.   Article 20 of Directive 88/357/EEC is hereby repealed.

2.   In the event of an insurance undertaking's being wound up, commitments arising out of contracts underwritten through a branch or under the freedom to provide services shall be met in the same way as those arising out of that undertaking's other insurance contracts, without distinction as to nationality as far as the persons insured and the beneficiaries are concerned.

Article 43

1.   Article 21 of Directive 88/357/EEC is hereby repealed.

2.   Where insurance is offered unter the right of establishment or the freedom to provide services, the policyholder shall, before any commitment is entered into, be informed of the Member State in which the head office or, where appropriate, the branch with which the contract is to be concluded is situated. Any documents issued to the policyholder must convey the information referred to in the first subparagraph. The obligations imposed in the first two subparagraphs shall not apply to the risks referred to in Article 5(d) of Directive 73/239/EEC.

3.   The contract or any other document granting cover, together with the insurance proposal where it is binding upon the policyholder, must state the address of the head office, or, where appropriate, of the branch of the insurance undertaking which grants the cover. Each Member State may require that the name and address of the representative of the insurance undertaking referred to in Article 12a(4) of Directive 88/357/EEC also appear in the documents referred to in the first subparagraph.

Article 44

1.   Article 22 of Directive 88/357/EEC is hereby repealed.

2.   Every insurance undertaking shall inform the competent authority of its home Member State, separately in respect of transactions carried out under the right of establishment and those carried out under the freedom to provide services, of the amount of the premiums, claims and commissions, without deduction of reinsurance, by Member State and by group of classes, and also as regards class 10 of point A of the Annex to Directive 73/239/EEC, not including carrier's liability, the frequency and average cost of claims. The groups of classes are hereby defined as follows:

— accident and sickness (classes 1 and 2),

— motor (classes 3, 7 and 10, the figures for class 10, excluding carriers' liability, being given separately),

— fire and other damage to property (classes 8 and 9),

— aviation, marine and transport (classes 4, 5, 6, 7, 11 and 12),

— general liability (class 13),

— credit and suretyship (classes 14 and 15),

— other classes (classes 16, 17 and 18).

The competent authority of the home Member State shall forward that information within a reasonable time and in aggregate form to the competent authorities of each of the Member States concerned which so request.

Article 45

1.   Article 24 of Directive 88/357/EEC is hereby repealed.

2.   Nothing in this Directive shall affect the Member States' right to require undertakings carrying on business within their territories under the right of establishment or the freedom to provide services to join and participate, on the same terms as undertakings authorised there, in any scheme designed to guarantee the payment of insurance claims to insured persons and injured third parties.

Article 46

1.   Article 25 of Directive 88/357/EEC is hereby repealed.

2.   Without prejudice to any subsequent harmonization, every insurance contract shall be subject exclusively to the indirect taxes and parafiscal charges on insurance premiums in the Member State in which the risk is situated as defined in Article 2(d) of Directive 88/357/EEC, and also, in the case of Spain, to the surcharges legally established in favour of the Spanish 'Consorcio de Compensación de Seguros' for the performance of its functions relating to the compensation of losses arising from extraordinary events occurring in that Member State. In derogation from the first indent of Article 2(d) of Directive 88/357/EEC, and for the purposes of this paragraph, moveable property contained in a building situated within the territory of a Member State, except for goods in commercial transit, shall be a risk situated in that Member State, even if the building and its contents are not covered by the same insurance policy. The law applicable to the contract under Article 7 of Directive 88/357/EEC shall not affect the fiscal arrangements applicable. Pending future harmonization, each Member State shall apply to those undertakings which cover risks situated within its territory its own national provisions to ensure the collection of indirect taxes and parafiscal charges due under the first subparagraph.

TITLE V   TRANSITIONAL PROVISIONS

Article 47

The Federal Republic of Germany may postpone until 1 January 1996 the application of the first sentence of the second subparagraph of Article 54(2). During that period, the provisions of the following subparagraph shall apply in the situation referred to in Article 54(2). When the technical basis for the calculation of premiums has been communicated to the competent authorities of the home Member State in accordance with the third sentence of the second subparagraph of Article 54(2), those authorities shall without delay forward that information to the competent authorities of the Member State in which the risk is situated so that they may comment. If the competent authorities of the home Member State take no account of those comments, they shall inform the competent authorities of the Member State in which the risk is situated accordingly in detail and state their reasons.

Article 48

Member States may allow insurance undertakings with head offices in their territories, the buildings and land of which that cover their technical provisions exceed, at the time of the notification of this Directive, the percentage laid down in Article 22(1)(a), a period expiring no later than 31 December 1998 within which to comply with that provision.

Article 49

The Kingdom of Denmark may postpone until 1 January 1999 the application of this Directive to compulsory insurance against accidents at work. During that period the exclusion provided for in Article 12(2) of Directive 88/357/EEC for accidents at work shall continue to apply in the Kingdom of Denmark.

Article 50

Spain, until 31 December 1996, and Greece and Portugal, until 31 December 1998, may operate the following transitional arrangements for contracts covering risks situated exclusively in one of those Member States other than those defined in Article 5(d) of Directive 73/239/EEC:

(a)   in derogation from Article 8(3) of Directive 73/239/EEC and from Articles 29 and 39 of this Directive, the competent authorities of the Member States in question may require the communication, before use, of general and special insurance policy conditions;

(b)   the amount of the technical provisions relating to the contracts referred to in this Article shall be determined under the supervision of the Member State concerned in accordance with its own rules or, failing that, in accordance with the procedures established within its territory in accordance with this Directive. Cover of those technical provisions by equivalent and matching assets and the localisation of those assets shall be effected under the supervision of that Member State in accordance with its rules and practices adopted in accordance with this Directive.

TITLE VI   FINAL PROVISIONS

Article 51

The following technical adjustments to be made to Directives 73/239/EEC and 88/357/EEC and to this Directive shall be adopted in accordance with the procedure laid down in Directive 91/675/EEC:

— extension of the legal forms provided for in Article 8(1)(a) of Directive 73/239/EEC,

— amendments to the list set out in the Annex to Directive 73/239/EEC, or adaptation of the terminology used in that list to take account of the development of insurance markets,

— clarification of the items constituting the solvency margin listed in Article 16(1) of Directive 73/239/EEC to take account of the creation of new financial instruments,

— alteration of the minimum guarantee fund provided for in Article 17(2) of Directive 73/239/EEC to take account of economic and financial developments,

— amendments, to take account of the creation of new financial instruments, to the list of assets acceptable as cover for technical provisions set out in Article 21 of this Directive and to the rules on the spreading of investments laid down in Article 22,

— changes in the relaxations in the matching rules laid down in Annex 1 to Directive 88/357/EEC, to take account of the development of new currency-hedging instruments or progress made towards economic and monetary union,

— clarification of the definitions in order to ensure uniform application of Directives 73/239/EEC and 88/357/EEC and of this Directive throughout the Community.

Article 52

1.   Branches which have started business, in accordance with the provisions in force in their Member State of establishment, before the entry into force of the provisions adopted in implementation of this Directive shall be presumed to have been subject to the procedure laid down in Article 10(1) to (5) of Directive 73/239/EEC. They shall be governed, from the date of that entry into force, by Articles 15, 19, 20 and 22 of Directive 73/239/EEC and by Article 40 of this Directive.

2. Articles 34 and 35 shall not affect rights acquired by insurance undertakings carrying on business under the freedom to provide services before the entry into force of the provisions adopted in implementation of this Directive.

Article 53
The following Article shall be inserted in Directive 73/239/EEC: 'Article 28a'.

Article 54
1. Notwithstanding any provision to the contrary, a Member State in which contracts covering the risks in class 2 of point A of the Annex to Directive 73/239/EEC may serve as a partial or complete alternative to health cover provided by the statutory social security system may require that those contracts comply with the specific legal provisions adopted by that Member State to protect the general good in that class of insurance, and that the general and special conditions of that insurance be communicated to the competent authorities of that Member State before use.

2. Member States may require that the health insurance system referred to in paragraph 1 be operated on a technical basis similar to that of life assurance where:

— the premiums paid are calculated on the basis of sickness tables and other statistical data relevant to the Member State in which the risk is situated in accordance with the mathematical methods used in insurance,

— a reserve is set up for increasing age,

— the insurer may cancel the contract only within a fixed period determined by the Member State in which the risk is situated,

— the contract provides that premiums may be increased or payments reduced, even for current contracts,

— the contract provides that the policyholder may change his existing contract into a new contract complying with paragraph 1, offered by the same insurance undertaking or the same branch and taking account of his acquired rights. In particular, account must be taken of the reserve for increasing age and a new medical examination may be required only for increased cover. In that event, the competent authorities of the Member State concerned shall publish the sickness tables and other relevant statistical data referred to in the first subparagraph and transmit them to the competent authorities of the home Member State. The premiums must be sufficient, on reasonable actuarial assumptions, for undertakings to be able to meet all their commitments having regard to all aspects of their financial situation. The home Member State shall require that the technical basis for the calculation of premiums be communicated to its competent authorities before the product is circulated. This paragraph shall also apply where existing contracts are modified.

Article 55
Member States may require that any insurance undertaking offering, at its own risk, compulsory insurance against accidents at work within their territories comply with the specific provisions of their national law concerning such insurance, except for the provisions concerning financial supervision, which shall be the exclusive responsibility of the home Member State.

Article 56
Member States shall ensure that decisions taken in respect of an insurance undertaking under laws, regulations and administrative provisions adopted in

accordance with this Directive may be subject to the right to apply to the courts.

Article 57

1.　The Member States shall adopt the laws, regulations and administrative provisions necessary for their compliance with this Directive not later than 31 December 1993 and bring them into force no later than 1 July 1994. They shall forthwith inform the Commission thereof. When they adopt such measures the Member States shall include references to this Directive or shall make such references when they effect official publication. The manner in which such references are to be made shall be laid down by the Member States.

2.　The Member States shall communicate to the Commission the texts of the main provisions of national law which they adopt in the field covered by this Directive.

Article 58

This Directive is addressed to the Member States.

Done at Luxembourg, 18 June 1992.
For the Council,
The President,
Vitor MARTINS

INSURANCE SECTOR DIRECTIVES: LIFE

FIRST COUNCIL DIRECTIVE (79/267/EEC) OF 5 MARCH 1979 ON THE COORDINATION OF LAWS, REGULATIONS AND ADMINISTRATIVE PROVISIONS RELATING TO THE TAKING UP AND PURSUIT OF THE BUSINESS OF DIRECT LIFE ASSURANCE
[OJ 1979 L63/1]*

THE COUNCIL OF THE EUROPEAN COMMUNITIES,

Having regard to the Treaty establishing the European Economic Community, and in particular Articles 49 and 57 thereof,

Having regard to the proposal from the Commission,[1]

Having regard to the opinion of the European Parliament,[2]

Having regard to the opinion of the Economic and Social Committee,[3]

Whereas, in order to facilitate the taking up and pursuit of the business of life assurance, it is essential to eliminate certain divergences which exist between national supervisory legislation;

Whereas, in order to achieve this objective and at the same time ensure adequate protection for policy-holders and beneficiaries in all member states, the provisions relating to the financial guarantees required of life assurance undertakings should be coordinated;

Whereas a classification by class of insurance is necessary in order to determine, in particular, the activities subject to compulsory authorisation;

Whereas certain mutual associations which, by virtue of their legal status, fulfil requirements as to security and other specific financial guarantees should be excluded from the scope of this Directive;

Whereas certain organisations whose activity covers only a very restricted sector and is limited by their Articles of association should also be excluded;

Whereas the member states have different regulations and practices as to the simultaneous carrying on of life assurance and non-life insurance; whereas newly formed undertakings should no longer be authorised to carry on these two activities simultaneously;

Notes

*As amended by the Accession Acts and Directives 90/619 [OJ 1990 L330/44], 92/96 [OJ 1992 No. L360/1] 95/26 [OJ 1995 No. L168].

[1]OJ No. C35, 28.3.1974, p. 9.

[2]OJ No. C140, 13.11.1974, p. 44.

[3]OJ No. C109, 19.9.1974, p. 1.

Whereas member states should be allowed to permit existing undertakings which carry on these activities simultaneously to continue to do so provided that separate management is adopted for each of their activities, in order that the respective interests of life policy-holders and non-life policy-holders are safeguarded and the minimum financial obligations in respect of one of the activities are not borne by the other activity;

Whereas, when one of the undertakings wishes to establish itself in a member state to pursue life assurance in that state, it should set up a subsidiary for that purpose, which may be eligible on a transitional basis for certain facilities;

Whereas, member states should be given the option of requiring those existing undertakings established in their territory which carry on life assurance and non-life insurance simultaneously to put an end to this practice;

Whereas, moreover, specialized undertakings should be subject to special supervision where a non-life undertaking belongs to the same financial group as a life undertaking;

Whereas life assurance is subject to official authorisation and supervision in each member state;

Whereas the conditions for the granting or withdrawal of such authorisation should be defined;

Whereas provision must be made for the right to apply to the courts should an authorisation be refused or withdrawn;

Whereas, as regards technical reserves, including mathematical reserves, the same rules may be adopted as in the case of non-life insurance, namely, they must be localised in the country where activities are carried on and the rules of that country are to govern the methods of calculation, the determination of investment categories and the valuation of assets;

Whereas, although it is desirable that these various subjects should be coordinated, this is not essential for the purposes of this Directive and may be carried out subsequently; where as it is necessary that, over and above technical reserves, including mathematical reserves, of sufficient amount to meet their underwriting liabilities, insurance undertakings should possess a supplementary reserve, known as the solvency margin, represented by free assets and, with the agreement of the supervisory authority, by other implicit assets, in order to provide against business fluctuations;

Whereas, in order to ensure that the requirements imposed for such purposes are determined according to objective criteria whereby undertakings of the same size will be placed on an equal footing as regards competition, it is desirable to provide that this margin shall be related to all the commitments of the undertaking and to the nature and gravity of the risks presented by the various activities falling within the scope of the Directive;

Whereas this margin should therefore vary according to whether the risks are of investment, death or management only;

Whereas it should accordingly be determined in terms of mathematical reserves and capital at risk underwritten by an undertaking, of premiums or contributions received, of reserves only or of the assets of tontines;

Whereas it is necessary to require a guarantee fund, the amount and composition of which are such as to provide an assurance that the undertakings possess adequate resources when they are set up and that in the subsequent course of business the solvency margin in no event falls below a minimum of security;

Whereas the whole or a specified part of this guarantee fund must consist of explicit asset items;

Whereas it is necessary to provide for measures in cases where the financial position of the undertaking becomes such that it is difficult for it to meet its underwriting liabilities;

Whereas the coordinated rules concerning the pursuit of the business of direct insurance within the Community should, in principle, apply to all undertakings operating on the market and, consequently, also to agencies and branches where the head office of the undertaking is situated outside the Community;

Whereas it is nevertheless desirable as regards the methods of supervision to lay down special provisions for such agencies or branches, in view of the fact that the assets of the undertakings to which they belong are situated outside the Community;

Whereas it is desirable to provide for the conclusion of reciprocal agreements with one or more third countries in order to permit the relaxation of such special conditions, while observing the principle that such agencies and branches should not obtain more favourable treatment than Community undertakings;

Whereas certain transitional provisions are required in order, in particular, to permit small and medium-sized undertakings already in existence to adapt themselves to the requirements to be introduced by the member states in pursuance of this Directive, subject to Article 53 of the Treaty applying;

Whereas Article 52 of the EEC Treaty has been directly applicable since the end of the transitional period;

Whereas since that time there has accordingly been no need for the adoption of Directives abolishing restrictions on the freedom of establishment;

Whereas, however, the provisions concerning proof of good repute and no previous bankruptcy contained in Council Directive 73/240/EEC of 24 July 1973, abolishing restrictions on freedom of establishment in the business of direct insurance other than life assurance[1] do not strictly speaking constitute restrictions and are also required in life assurance;.Whereas they should accordingly be included in this coordination Directive;

Whereas it is important to guarantee the uniform application of the coordinated rules and to provide accordingly for close collaboration between the Commission and the member states in this field,

Note
[1]OJ No. L228, 16.8.1973, p. 20.

HAS ADOPTED THIS DIRECTIVE:

TITLE I   GENERAL PROVISIONS

Article 1
This Directive concerns the taking up and pursuit of the self-employed activity of direct insurance carried on by undertakings which are established in a Member State or wish to become established there in the form of the activities defined below:

　　1.　The following kinds of insurance where they are on a contractual basis:

　　　　(a)　life assurance, that is to say, the class of insurance which comprises, in particular, assurance on survival to a stipulated age only, assurance on death only, assurance on survival to a stipulated age or on earlier death, life assurance with return of premiums, marriage assurance, birth assurance;

    (b)   annuities;

    (c)   supplementary insurance carried on by life assurance undertakings, that is to say, in particular, insurance against personal injury including incapacity for employment, insurance against death resulting from an accident and insurance against disability resulting from an accident or sickness, where these various kinds of insurance are underwritten in addition to life assurance;

    (d)   the type of insurance existing in Ireland and the United Kingdom known as permanent health insurance not subject to cancellation.

    2.   The following operations, where they are on a contractual basis, in so far as they are subject to supervision by the administrative authorities responsible for the supervision of private insurance:

    (a)   tontines whereby associations of subscribers are set up with a view to jointly capitalising their contributions and subsequently distributing the assets thus accumulated among the survivors or among the beneficiaries of the deceased;

    (b)   capital redemption operations based on actuarial calculation whereby, in return for single or periodic payments agreed in advance, commitments of specified duration and amount are undertaken;

    (c)   management of group pension funds, i.e. operations consisting, for the undertaking concerned, in managing the investments, and in particular the assets representing the reserves of bodies that effect payments on death or survival or in the event of discontinuance or curtailment of activity;

    (d)   the operations referred to in (c) where they are accompanied by insurance covering either conservation of capital or payment of a minimum interest;

    (e)   the operations carried out by insurance companies such as those referred to in chapter 1, Title 4 of Book IV of the French 'Code des Assurances'.

    3.   Operations relating to the length of human life which are prescribed by or provided for in social insurance legislation, when they are effected or managed at their own risk by assurance undertakings in accordance with the laws of a member state.

Article 2

This Directive shall not concern:

    1.   Subject to the application of Article 1(1)(c) of this Directive, the classes designated in the Annex to first Council Directive 73/239/EEC of 24 July 1973 on the coordination of laws, regulations and administrative provisions relating to the taking-up and pursuit of the business of direct insurance other than life assurance,[1] hereinafter referred to as 'the first coordination Directive (non-life insurance)';

    2.   Operations of provident and mutual-benefit institutions whose benefits vary according to the resources available and which require each of their members to contribute at the appropriate flat rate;

    3.   Operations carried out by organisations other than undertakings referred to in Article 1, whose object is to provide benefits for employed or

Note
[1]OJ No. L228, 16.8.1973, p. 3.

self-employed persons belonging to an undertaking or group of undertakings, or a trade or group of trades, in the event of death or survival or of discontinuance or curtailment of activity, whether or not the commitments arising from such operations are fully covered at all times by mathematical reserves;

4. Subject to the application of Article 1(3), insurance forming part of a statutory system of social security.

Article 3
This Directive shall not concern:

1. Organisations which undertake to provide benefits solely in the event of death, where the amount of such benefits does not exceed the average funeral costs for a single death or where the benefits are provided in kind;

2. Mutual associations, where:

— the Articles of association contain provisions for calling up additional contributions or reducing their benefits or claiming assistance from other persons who have undertaken to provide it, and

— the annual contribution income for the activities covered by this Directive does not exceed 500,000 units of account for three consecutive years. If this amount is exceeded for three consecutive years this Directive shall apply with effect from the fourth year.

Article 4
This Directive shall not concern the 'Versorgungsverband Deutscher Wirtschaftsorganisationen' in Germany or the 'Caisse d'épargne de l'Etat' in Luxembourg unless their statutes are amended as regards the scope of their activities. This Directive shall not concern the pension activities of pension insurance undertakings prescribed in the Employees' Pensions Act (TEL) and other related Finnish legislation provided that:

(a) pension insurance companies which already under Finnish law are obliged to have separate accounting and management systems for their pension activities will furthermore, as from the date of accession, set up separate legal entities for carrying out these activities;

(b) the Finnish authorities shall allow in a non-discriminatory manner all nationals and companies of Member States to perform according to Finnish legislation the activities specified in Article 1 related to this exemption whether by means of:

— ownership or participation in an existing insurance company or group;

— creation or participation of new insurance companies or groups, including pension insurance companies;

(c) the Finnish authorities will submit to the Commission for approval a report within three months from the date of accession, stating which measures have been taken to split up TEL-activities from normal insurance activities carried out by Finnish insurance companies in order to conform to all the requirements of the third life assurance Directive.

Article 5
For the purposes of this Directive:

(a) 'unit of account' means the European unit of Account (EUA) as defined by Article 10 of the financial Regulation of 21 December 1977 applicable to the general budget of the European communities;[1] wherever this Directive refers to the unit of account, the conversion value in national currency to be adopted shall as from 31 December of each year be that of the last day of the preceding month of October for which EUA conversion values are available in all the Community currencies;

(b) 'matching assets' means the representation of underwriting liabilities which can be required to be met in a particular currency by assets expressed or realisable in the same currency;

(c) 'localisation of assets' means the existence of assets, whether movable or immovable, within a Member State but shall not be construed as involving a requirement that movable assets be deposited or that immovable assets be subjected to restrictive measures such as the registration of mortgages; assets represented by claims against debtors shall be regarded as situated in the Member State where they are realisable;

(d) 'capital at risk' means the amount payable on death less the mathematical reserve for the main risk.

Note
[1]OJ No. L356, 31.12.1977, p. 1.

TITLE II   RULES APPLICABLE TO UNDERTAKINGS WHOSE HEAD OFFICES ARE SITUATED WITHIN THE COMMUNITY

SECTION A   CONDITIONS OF ADMISSION

Article 6
The taking-up of the activities covered by this Directive shall be subject to prior official authorisation. Such authorisation shall be sought from the authorities of the home Member State by:

(a) any undertaking which establishes its head office in the territory of that State;

(b) any undertaking which, having received the authorisation required in the first subparagraph, extends its business to an entire class or to other classes.

Article 7
1. Authorisation shall be valid for the entire Community. It shall permit an undertaking to carry on business there, under either the right of establishment or freedom to provide services.

2. Authorisation shall be granted for a particular class of assurance as listed in the Annex. It shall cover the entire class, unless the applicant wishes to cover only some of the risks pertaining to that class.

The competent authorities may restrict authorisation requested for one of the classes to the operations set out in the scheme of operations referred to in Article 9.

Each Member State may grant authorisation for two or more of the classes, where its national laws permit such classes to be carried on simultaneously.

Article 8
1. The home Member State shall require every assurance undertaking for which authorisation is sought to:

(a) adopt one of the following forms:

—in the case of the Kingdom of Belgium: 'société anonyme/naamloze vennootschap', 'société en commandite par actions/commanditaire vennootschap op aandelen', 'association d'assurance mutuelle/onderlinge verzekeringsvereniging', 'société coopérative/cooeperatieve vennootschap',

— in the case of the Kingdom of Denmark: 'aktieselskaber', 'gensidige selskaber', 'pensionskasser omfattet af lov om forsikringsvirksomhed (tvaergaaende pensionskasser)',

— in the case of the Federal Republic of Germany: 'Aktiengesellschaft', 'Versicherungsverein auf Gegenseitigkeit', 'Oeffentlich-rechtliches Wettbewerbsversicherungsunternehmen',

— in the case of the French Republic: 'société anonyme', 'société d'assurance mutuelle', 'institution de prévoyance régie par le code de la sécurité sociale', 'institution de prévoyance régie par le code rural' and 'mutuelles régies par le code de la mutualité',

— in the case of Ireland: incorporated companies limited by shares or by guarantee or unlimited, societies registered under the Industrial and Provident Societies Acts and societies registered under the Friendly Societies Acts,

— in the case of the Italian Republic: 'società per azioni', 'società cooperativa', 'mutua di assicurazione',

— in the case of the Grand Duchy of Luxembourg: 'société anonyme', 'société en commandite par actions', 'association d'assurances mutuelles', 'société coopérative',

— in the case of the Kingdom of the Netherlands: 'naamloze vennootschap', 'onderlinge waarborgmaatschappij',

— in the case of the United Kingdom: incorporated companies limited by shares or by guarantee or unlimited, societies registered under the Industrial and Provident Societies Acts, societies registered or incorporated under the Friendly Societies Acts, the association of underwriters known as Lloyd's,

— in the case of the Hellenic Republic: 'áíþíõiç aaôáéñssá',

— in the case of the Kingdom of Spain: 'sociedad anonima', 'sociedad mutua', 'sociedad cooperativa',

— in the case of the Portuguese Republic: 'sociedade anónima', 'mútua de seguros'.

— in the case of the Republic of Austria: Aktiengesellschaft, Versicherungsverein auf Gegenseitigkeit

— in the case of the Repubic of Finland: keskinaeinen vakuutusyhtioe/oemsesidigt foersaekringsbolag, vakuutusosakeyhtioe/foersaekringsakti bolag, vakuutusyhdistys/foersaekringsfoerening

— in the case of the Kingdom of Sweden: foersaekringsaktiebolag, oemsesidiga foersaekringsbolag, understoedsfoereningar.

An assurance undertaking may also adopt the form of a European company when that has been established. Furthermore, Member States may, where appropriate, set up undertakings in any public-law form provided that such bodies have as their object insurance operations under conditions equivalent to those under which private-law undertakings operate;

(b)   limit its objects to the business provided for in this Directive and operations directly arising therefrom, to the exclusion of all other commercial business;

(c)   submit a scheme of operations in accordance with Article 9;

(d)   possess the minimum guarantee fund provided for in Article 20(2);

(e)   be effectively run by persons of good repute with appropriate professional qualifications or experience.

Moreover, where close links exist between the financial undertaking and other natural or legal persons, the competent authorities shall grant authorisation only if those links do not prevent the effective exercise of their supervisory functions. The competent authorities shall also refuse authorisation if the laws, regulations or administrative provisions of a non-member country governing one or more natural or legal persons with which the undertaking has close links, or difficulties involved in their enforcement, prevent the effective exercise of their supervisory functions. The competent authorities shall require to monitor compliance with the conditions referred to in this paragraph on a continuous basis.

1a. Member States shall require that the head offices of insurance undertakings be situated in the same Member State as their registered offices.

2. An undertaking seeking authorisation to extend its business to other classes or to extend an authorisation covering only some of the risks pertaining to one class shall be required to submit a scheme of operations in accordance with Article 9.

It shall, furthermore, be required to show proof that it possesses the solvency margin provided for in Article 19 and the guarantee fund referred to in Article 20(1) and (2).

3. Member States shall not adopt provisions requiring the prior approval or systematic notification of general and special policy conditions, of scales of premiums, of the technical bases, used in particular for calculating scales of premiums and technical provisions or of forms and other printed documents which an assurance undertaking intends to use in its dealings with policy-holders.

Notwithstanding the first subparagraph, for the sole purpose of verifying compliance with national provisions concerning actuarial principles, the home Member State may require systematic notification of the technical bases used for calculating scales of premiums and technical provisions, without that requirement constituting a prior condition for an undertaking to carry on its business.

Nothing in this Directive shall prevent Member States from maintaining in force or introducing laws, regulations or administrative provisions requiring approval of the memorandum and articles of association and the communication of any other documents necessary for the normal exercise of supervision. Not later than five years after the date of entry into force of Directive 92/96/EEC,[1] the Commission shall submit a report to the Council on the implementation of this paragraph.

4. The abovementioned provisions may not require that any application for authorisation be considered in the light of the economic requirements of the market.

Note
[1] OJ No. L360, 9.12.1992, p. 1.

Article 9
The scheme of operations referred to in Article 8(1)(c) and (2) shall include particulars or proof concerning:

(a) the nature of the commitments which the undertaking proposes to cover;

(b) the guiding principles as to reassurance;

(c)   the items constituting the minimum guarantee fund;

(d)   estimates relating to the costs of setting up the administrative services and the organization for securing business and the financial resources intended to meet those costs; in addition, for the first three financial years:

(e)   a plan setting out detailed estimates of income and expenditure in respect of direct business, reassurance acceptances and reassurance cessions;

(f)   a forecast balance sheet;

(g)   estimates relating to the financial resources intended to cover underwriting liabilities and the solvency margin.

Article 10

1.   An assurance undertaking that proposes to establish a branch within the territory of another Member State shall notify the competent authorities of its home Member State.

2.   The Member States shall require every assurance undertaking that proposes to establish a branch within the territory of another Member State to provide the following information when effecting the notification provided for in paragraph 1:

(a)   the Member State within the territory of which it proposes to establish a branch;

(b)   a scheme of operations setting out inter alia the types of business envisaged and the structural organization of the branch;

(c)   the address in the Member State of the branch from which documents may be obtained and to which they may be delivered, it being understood that that address shall be the one to which all communications to the authorised agent are sent;

(d)   the name of the branch's authorised agent, who must possess sufficient powers to bind the undertaking in relation to third parties and to represent it in relations with the authorities and courts of the Member State of the branch. With regard to Lloyd's, in the event of any litigation in the Member State of the branch arising out of underwritten commitments, the assured persons must not be treated less favourably than if the litigation had been brought against businesses of a conventional type. The authorised agent must, therefore, possess sufficient powers for proceedings to be taken against him and must in that capacity be able to bind the Lloyd's underwriters concerned.

3.   Unless the competent authorities of the home Member State have reason to doubt the adequacy of the administrative structure or the financial situation of the assurance undertaking or the good repute and professional qualification or experience of the directors or managers or the authorised agent, taking into account the business planned, they shall within three months of receiving all the information referred to in paragraph 2 communicate that information to the competent authorities of the Member State of the branch and shall inform the undertaking concerned accordingly.

The competent authorities of the home Member State shall also attest that the assurance undertaking has the minimum solvency margin calculated in accordance with Articles 19 and 20.

Where the competent authorities of the home Member State refuse to communicate the information referred to in paragraph 2 to the competent authorities of the Member State of the branch they shall give the reasons for their refusal to the undertaking concerned within three months of receiving all the information in question. That refusal or failure to act shall be subject to a right to apply to the courts in the home Member State.

4.   Before the branch of an assurance undertaking starts business, the competent authorities of the Member State of the branch shall, within two months of receiving the information referred to in paragraph 3, inform the competent authority of the home Member State, if appropriate, of the conditions under which, in the interest of the general good, that business must be carried on in the Member State of the branch.

5.   On receiving a communication from the competent authorities of the Member State of the branch or, if no communication is received from them, on expiry of the period provided for in paragraph 4, the branch may be established and start business.

6.   In the event of a change in any of the particulars communicated under paragraph 2(b), (c) or (d), an assurance undertaking shall give written notice of the change to the competent authorities of the home Member State and of the Member State of the branch at least one month before making the change so that the competent authorities of the home Member State and the competent authorities of the Member State of the branch may fulfil their respective roles under paragraphs 3 and 4.

Article 11
(deleted)

Article 12
Any decision to refuse an authorisation shall be accompanied by the precise grounds for doing so and notified to the undertaking in question. Each member state shall make provision for a right to apply to the courts should there be any refusal.

Such provision shall also be made with regard to cases where the competent authorities have not dealt with an application for an authorisation upon the expiry of a period of six months from the date of its receipt.

Article 13
1.   Without prejudice to paragraphs 3 and 7, no undertaking may be authorised both pursuant to this Directive and pursuant to Directive 73/239/EEC.

2.   However, Member States may provide that:

—undertakings authorised pursuant to this Directive may also obtain authorisation, in accordance with Article 6 of Directive 73/239/EEC for the risks listed in classes 1 and 2 in the Annex to that Directive,

—undertakings authorised pursuant to Article 6 of Directive 73/239/EEC solely for the risks listed in classes 1 and 2 in the Annex to that Directive may obtain authorisation pursuant to this Directive.

3.   Subject to paragraph 6, undertakings referred to in paragraph 2 and those which at the time of notification of this Directive carry on simultaneously both of the activities covered by this Directive and by Directive 73/239/EEC may continue to do so, provided that each activity is separately managed in accordance with Article 14.

4.   Member States may provide that the undertakings referred to in paragraph 2 shall comply with the accounting rules governing undertakings authorised pursuant to this Directive for all of their activities. Pending coordination in this respect, Member States may also provide that, with regard

to rules on winding-up, activities relating to the risks listed in classes 1 and 2 in the Annex to Directive 73/239/EEC carried on by the undertakings referred to in paragraph 2 shall be governed by the rules applicable to life assurance activities.

5.   Where an undertaking carrying on the activities referred to in the Annex to Directive 73/239/EEC has financial, commercial or administrative links with an undertaking carrying on the activities covered by this Directive, the supervisory authorities of the Member States within whose territories the head offices of those undertakings are situated shall ensure that the accounts of the undertakings in question are not distorted by agreements between these undertakings or by any arrangement which could affect the apportionment of expenses and income.

6.   Any Member State may require undertakings whose head offices are situated in its territory to cease, within a period to be determined by the Member State concerned, the simultaneous pursuit of activities in which they were engaged at the time of notification of this Directive.

7.   The provisions of this Article shall be reviewed on the basis of a report from the Commission to the Council in the light of future harmonization of the rules on winding-up, and in any case before 31 December 1999.

Article 14

1.   The separate management referred to in Article 13(3) must be organised in such a way that the activities covered by this Directive are distinct from the activities covered by the first coordination Directive (non-life insurance) in order that:

— the respective interests of life policy-holders and non-life policy-holders are not prejudiced and, in particular, that profits from life assurance benefit life policy-holders as if the undertaking only carried on the activity of life assurance,

— the minimum financial obligations, in particular solvency margins, in respect of one or other of the two activities, namely an activity under this Directive and an activity under the first coordination Directive (non-life insurance) are not borne by the other activity,

However, as long as the minimum financial obligations are fulfilled under the conditions laid down in the second indent of the first subparagraph and, provided the competent authority is informed, the undertaking may use those explicit items of the solvency margin which are still available for one or other activity.

The supervisory authorities shall analyse the results in both activities so as to ensure that the provisions of this paragraph are complied with.

2.   (a)   accounts shall be drawn up in such a manner as to show the sources of the results for each of the two activities, life assurance and non-life insurance. To this end all income (in particular premiums, payments by re-insurers and investment income) and expenditure (in particular insurance settlements, additions to technical reserves, reinsurance premiums, operating expenses in respect of insurance business) shall be broken down according to origin. Items common to both activities shall be entered in accordance with methods of apportionment to be accepted by the competent supervisory authority.

(b)   undertakings must, on the basis of the accounts, prepare a statement clearly identifying the items making up each solvency margin, in accordance with Article 18 of this Directive and Article 16(1) of the first coordination Directive (non-life insurance).

3. If one of the solvency margins is insufficient, the supervisory authorities shall apply to the deficient activity the measures provided for in the relevant Directive, whatever the results in the other activity. By way of derogation from the second indent of the first subparagraph of paragraph 1, these measures may involve the authorisation of a transfer from one activity to the other.

SECTION B   CONDITIONS FOR CARRYING ON ACTIVITIES

Article 15

1. The financial supervision of an assurance undertaking, including that of the business it carries on either through branches or under the freedom to provide services, shall be the sole responsibility of the home Member State. If the competent authorities of the Member State of the commitment have reason to consider that the activities of an assurance undertaking might affect its financial soundness, they shall inform the competent authorities of the undertaking's home Member State. The latter authorities shall determine whether the undertaking is complying with the prudential principles laid down in this Directive.

2. That financial supervision shall include verification, with respect to the assurance undertaking's entire business, of its state of solvency, the establishment of technical provisions, including mathematical provisions, and of the assets covering them, in accordance with the rules laid down or practices followed in the home Member State pursuant to the provisions adopted at Community level.

3. The competent authorities of the home Member State shall require every assurance undertaking to have sound administrative and accounting procedures and adequate internal control mechanisms.

Article 16

The Member State of the branch shall provide that, where an assurance undertaking authorised in another Member State carries on business through a branch, the competent authorities of the home Member State may, after having first informed the competent authorities of the Member State of the branch, carry out themselves, or through the intermediary of persons they appoint for that purpose, on-the-spot verification of the information necessary to ensure the financial supervision of the undertaking. The authorities of the Member State of the branch may participate in that verification.

Article 17

1. The home Member State shall require every assurance undertaking to establish sufficient technical provisions, including mathematical provisions, in respect of its entire business. The amount of such technical provisions shall be determined according to the following principles:

A. (i) The amount of the technical life-assurance provisions shall be calculated by a sufficiently prudent prospective actuarial valuation, taking account of all future liabilities as determined by the policy conditions for each existing contract, including:

— all guaranteed benefits, including guaranteed surrender values,
— bonuses to which policy-holders are already either collectively or individually entitled, however those bonuses are described — vested, declared or allotted, — all options available to the policy-holder under the terms of the contract,

— expenses, including commissions; taking credit for future premiums due;

(ii)   the use of a retrospective method is allowed, if it can be shown that the resulting technical provisions are not lower than would be required under a sufficiently prudent prospective calculation or if a prospective method cannot be used for the type of contract involved;

(iii)   a prudent valuation is not a 'best estimate' valuation, but shall include an appropriate margin for adverse deviation of the relevant factors;

(iv)   the method of valuation for the technical provisions must not only be prudent in itself, but must also be so having regard to the method of valuation for the assets covering those provisions;

(v)   technical provisions shall be calculated separately for each contract. The use of appropriate approximations or generalisations is allowed, however, where they are likely to give approximately the same result as individual calculations. The principle of separate calculation shall in no way prevent the establishment of additional provisions for general risks which are not individualised;

(vi)   where the surrender value of a contract is guaranteed, the amount of the mathematical provisions for the contract at any time shall be at least as great as the value guaranteed at that time.

B.   The rate of interest used shall be chosen prudently. It shall be determined in accordance with the rules of the competent authority in the home Member State, applying the following principles:

(a)   for all contracts, the competent authority of the undertaking's home Member State shall fix one or more maximum rates of interest, in particular in accordance with the following rules:

(i)   when contracts contain an interest rate guarantee, the competent authority in the home Member State shall set a single maximum rate of interest. It may differ according to the currency in which the contract is denominated, provided that it is not more than 60% of the rate on bond issues by the State in whose currency the contract is denominated. In the case of a contract denominated in ECUs, this limit shall be set by reference to ECU-denominated issues by the Community institutions.

If a Member State decides, pursuant to the second sentence of the preceding paragraph, to set a maximum rate of interest for contracts denominated in another Member State's currency, it shall first consult the competent authority of the Member State in whose currency the contract is denominated;

(ii)   however, when the assets of the undertaking are not valued at their purchase price, a Member State may stipulate that one or more maximum rates may be calculated taking into account the yield on the corresponding assets currently held, minus a prudential margin and, in particular for contracts with periodic premiums, furthermore taking into account the anticipated yield on future assets. The prudential margin and the maximum rate or rates of interest applied to the anticipated yield on future assets shall be fixed by the competent authority of the home Member State;

(b)   the establishment of a maximum rate of interest shall not imply that the undertaking is bound to use a rate as high as that;

(c)   the home Member State may decide not to apply (a) to the following categories of contracts:

— unit-linked contracts,

— single-premium contracts for a period of up to eight years,

— without-profits contracts, and annuity contracts with no surrender value.

In the cases referred to in the last two indents of the first subparagraph, in choosing a prudent rate of interest, account may be taken of the currency in which the contract is denominated and corresponding assets currently held and where the undertaking's assets are valued at their current value, the anticipated yield on future assets.

Under no circumstances may the rate of interest used be higher than the yield on assets as calculated in accordance with the accounting rules in the home Member State, less an appropriate deduction;

(d) the Member State shall require an undertaking to set aside in its accounts a provision to meet interest-rate commitments vis-à-vis policy-holders if the present or foreseeable yield on the undertaking's assets is insufficient to cover those commitments;

(e) the Commission and the competent authorities of the Member States which so request shall be notified of the maximum rates of interest set under (a).

C. The statistical elements of the valuation and the allowance for expenses used shall be chosen prudently, having regard to the State of the commitment, the type of policy and the administrative costs and commissions expected to be incurred.

D. In the case of participating contracts, the method of calculation for technical provisions may take into account, either implicitly or explicitly, future bonuses of all kinds, in a manner consistent with the other assumptions on future experience and with the current method of distribution of bonuses.

E. Allowance for future expenses may be made implicitly, for instance by the use of future premiums net of management charges. However, the overall allowance, implicit or explicit, shall be not less than a prudent estimate of the relevant future expenses.

F. The method of calculation of technical provisions shall not be subject to discontinuities from year to year arising from arbitrary changes to the method or the bases of calculation and shall be such as to recognise the distribution of profits in an appropriate way over the duration of each policy.

2. Assurance undertakings shall make available to the public the bases and methods used in the calculation of the technical provisions, including provisions for bonuses.

3. The home Member State shall require every assurance undertaking to cover the technical provisions in respect of its entire business by matching assets, in accordance with Article 24 of Directive 92/96/EEC. In respect of business written in the Community, these assets must be localised within the Community. Member States shall not require assurance undertakings to localise their assets in a particular Member State. The home Member State may, however, permit relaxations in the rules on the localisation of assets.

4. If the home Member State allows any technical provisions to be covered by claims against reassurers, it shall fix the percentage so allowed. In such case, it may not require the localisation of the assets representing such claims.

Article 18

Each member state shall require of every undertaking whose head office is situated in its territory an adequate solvency margin in respect of its entire business.

The solvency margin shall consist of:

1. the assets of the undertaking free of any foreseeable liabilities, less any intangible items. In particular the following shall be included:

— the paid-up share capital or, in the case of a mutual assurance undertaking, the effective initial fund plus any members' accounts which meet all the following criteria:

(a) the memorandum and articles of association must stipulate that payments may be made from these accounts to members only in so far as this does not cause the solvency margin to fall below the required level, or, after the dissolution of the undertaking, if all the undertaking's other debts have been settled;

(b) the memorandum and articles of association must stipulate, with respect to any such payments for reasons other than the individual termination of membership, that the competent authorities must be notified at least one month in advance and can prohibit the payment within that period;

(c) the relevant provisions of the memorandum and articles of association may be amended only after the competent authorities have declared that they have no objection to the amendment, without prejudice to the criteria stated in (a) and (b),

— one half of the unpaid share capital or initial fund, once the paid-up part amounts to 25% of that share capital or fund,

— reserves (statutory reserves and free reserves) not corresponding to underwriting liabilities,

— any profits brought forward,

— cumulative preferential share capital and subordinated loan capital may be included but, if so, only up to 50% of the margin, no more than 25% of which shall consist of subordinated loans with a fixed maturity, or fixed-term cumulative preferential share capital, if the following minimum criteria are met:

(a) in the event of the bankruptcy or liquidation of the assurance undertaking, binding agreements must exist under which the subordinated loan capital or preferential share capital ranks after the claims of all other creditors and is not to be repaid until all other debts outstanding at the time have been settled. Subordinated loan capital must also fulfil the following conditions:

(b) only fully paid-up funds may be taken into account;

(c) for loans with a fixed maturity, the original maturity must be at least five years. No later than one year before the repayment date the assurance undertaking must submit to the competent authorities for their approval a plan showing how the solvency margin will be kept at or brought to the required level at maturity, unless the extent to which the loan may rank as a component of the solvency margin is gradually reduced during at least the last five years before the repayment date.

The competent authorities may authorise the early repayment of such loans provided application is made by the issuing assurance undertaking and its solvency margin will not fall below the required level;

(d) loans the maturity of which is not fixed must be repayable only subject to five years' notice unless the loans are no longer considered as a component of the solvency margin or unless the prior consent of the competent authorities is specifically required for early repayment. In the latter event the assurance undertaking must notify the competent authorities at least six months before the date of the proposed repayment, specifying the actual and required solvency margin both before and after that repayment. The competent authorities shall authorise repayment only if the assurance undertaking's solvency margin will not fall below the required level;

(e) the loan agreement must not include any clause providing that in specified circumstances, other than the winding-up of the assurance undertaking, the debt will become repayable before the agreed repayment dates;

(f) the loan agreement may be amended only after the competent authorities have declared that they have no objection to the amendment,

— securities with no specified maturity date and other instruments that fulfil the following conditions, including cumulative preferential shares other than those mentioned in the preceding indent, up to 50% of the margin for the total of such securities and the subordinated loan capital referred to in the preceding indent:

(a) they may not be repaid on the initiative of the bearer or without the prior consent of the competent authority;

(b) the contract of issue must enable the assurance undertaking to defer the payment of interest on the loan;

(c) the lender's claims on the assurance undertaking must rank entirely after those of all non-subordinated creditors;

(d) the documents governing the issue of the securities must provide for the loss-absorption capacity of the debt and unpaid interest, while enabling the assurance undertaking to continue its business;

(e) only fully paid-up amounts may be taken into account.

2. In so far as authorised under national law, profit reserves appearing in the balance sheet where they may be used to cover any losses which may arise and where they have not been made available for distribution to policy-holders;

3. Upon application, with supporting evidence, by the undertaking to the supervisory authority of the Member State in the territory of which its head office is situated and with the agreement of that authority:

(a) an amount equal to 50% of the undertaking's future profits; the amount of the future profits shall be obtained by multiplying the estimated annual profit by a factor which represents the average period left to run on policies; the factor used may not exceed 10; the estimated annual profit shall be the arithmetical average of the profits made over the last five years in the activities listed in Article 1. The bases for calculating the factor by which the estimated annual profit is to be multiplied and the items comprising the profits made shall be defined by common agreement by the competent authorities of the member states in collaboration with the Commission. Pending such agreement, those items shall be determined in accordance with the laws of the Member State in the territory of which the undertaking (head office, agency or branch) carries on its activities.

When the competent authorities have defined the concept of profits made, the Commission shall submit proposals for the harmonization of this concept by means of a Directive on the harmonization of the annual accounts of insurance undertakings and providing for the coordination set out in Article 1(2) of Directive 78/660/EEC;[1]

(b)   where zillmerizing is not practised or where, if practised, it is less than the loading for acquisition costs included in the premium, the difference between a non-zillmerized or partially zillmerized mathematical reserve and a mathematical reserve zillmerized at a rate equal to the loading for acquisition costs included in the premium; this figure may not, however, exceed 3.5% of the sum of the differences between the relevant capital sums of life assurance activities and the mathematical reserves for all policies for which zillmerizing is possible; the difference shall be reduced by the amount of any undepreciated acquisition costs entered as an asset;

(c)   where approval is given by the supervisory authorities of the Member States concerned in which the undertaking is carrying on its activities any hidden reserves resulting from the under-estimation of assets and over-estimation of liabilities other than mathematical reserves in so far as such hidden reserves are not of an exceptional nature.

Note
[1] OJ 1978 No. L222/11 as amended by Directive 90/605 OJ 1990 LJ17/60.

Article 19

Subject to Article 20, the minimum solvency margin shall be determined as shown below according to the classes of insurance underwritten:

(a)   for the kinds of insurance referred to in Article 1(1)(a) and (b) other than assurances linked to investment funds and for the operations referred to in Article 1(3), it must be equal to the sum of the following two results:

— first result:

A 4% fraction of the mathematical reserves, relating to direct business gross of re-insurance cessions and to re-insurance acceptances shall be multiplied by the ratio, for the last financial year, of the total mathematical reserves net of re-insurance cessions to the gross total mathematical reserves as specified above; that ratio may in no case be less than 85%;

— second result:

For policies on which the capital at risk is not a negative figure, a 0.3% fraction of such capital underwritten by the undertaking shall be multiplied by the ratio, for the last financial year, of the total capital at risk retained as the undertaking's liability after re-insurance cessions and retrocessions to the total capital at risk gross of re-insurance; that ratio may in no case be less than 50%.

For temporary assurance on death of a maximum term of three years the above fraction shall be 0.1%; for such assurance of a term of more than three years but not more than five years the above fraction shall be 0.15%.

(b)   For the supplementary insurance referred to in Article 1(1)(c), it shall be equal to the result of the following calculation:

— the premiums or contributions (inclusive of charges ancillary to premiums or contributions) due in respect of direct business in the last financial year in respect of all financial years shall be aggregated;

— to this aggregate there shall be added the amount of premiums accepted for all reinsurance in the last financial year;

— from this sum shall then be deducted the total amount of premiums or contributions cancelled in the last financial year as well as the total amount of taxes and levies pertaining to the premiums or contributions entering into the aggregate.

The amount so obtained shall be divided into two portions, the first extending up to 10 million units of account and the second comprising the excess; 18% and 16% of these portions respectively shall be calculated and added together.

The result shall be obtained by multiplying the sum so calculated by the ratio existing in respect of the last financial year between the amount of claims remaining to be borne by the undertaking after deduction of transfers for reinsurance and the gross amount of claims; this ratio may in no case be less than 50%.

In the case of the association of underwriters known as Lloyd's, the calculation of the solvency margin shall be made on the basis of net premiums, which shall be multiplied by flat-rate percentage fixed annually by the supervisory authority of the head-office Member State. This flat-rate percentage must be calculated on the basis of the most recent statistical data on commissions paid. The details together with the relevant calculations shall be sent to the supervisory authorities of the countries in whose territory Lloyd's is established.

(c) for permanent health insurance not subject to cancellation referred to in Article 1(1)(d), and for capital redemption operations referred to in Article 1(2)(b), it shall be equal to a 4% fraction of the mathematical reserves calculated in compliance with the conditions set out in the first result in (a) of this Article.

(d) for tontines, referred to in Article 1(2)(a), it shall be equal to 1% of their assets.

(e) for assurances covered by Article 1(1)(a) and (b) linked to investment funds and for the operations referred to in Article 1(2)(c), (d) and (e) it shall be equal to:

— a 4% fraction of the mathematical reserves, calculated in compliance with the conditions set out in the first result in (a) of this Article in so far as the undertaking bears an investment risk, and a 1% fraction of the reserves calculated in the fashion, in so far as the undertaking bears no investment risk provided that the term of the contract exceeds five years and the allocation to cover management expenses set out in the contract is fixed for a period exceeding five years plus:

— a 0.3% fraction of the capital at risk calculated in compliance with the conditions set out in the first subparagraph of the second result of (a) of this Article in so far as the undertaking covers a death risk.

Article 20

1. One third of the minimum solvency margin as specified in Article 19 shall constitute the guarantee fund. Subject to paragraph 2, at least 50% of this fund shall consist of the items listed in Article 18(1) and (2).

2. (a) the guarantee fund may not, however, be less than a minimum of 800,000 units of account.

(b) any member state may provide for the minimum of the guarantee fund to be reduced to 600,000 units of account in the case of mutual associations and mutual-type associations and tontines.

(c) for mutual associations referred to in the second sentence of the second indent of Article 3(2), as soon as they come within the scope of this Directive, and for tontines, any Member State may permit the establishment of a minimum of the guarantee fund of 100,000 units of account to be increased progressively to the amount fixed in (b) by successive tranches of 100,000 units of account whenever the contributions increase by 500,000 units of account.

(d)   the minimum of the guarantee fund referred to in (a), (b) and (c) must consist of the items listed in Article 18(1) and (2).

3.   Mutual associations wishing to extend their business within the meaning of Article 8(2) or Article 10 may not do so unless they comply immediately with the requirements of paragraph 2(a) and (b) of this Article.

Article 21

1.   Member States shall not prescribe any rules as to the choice of the assets that need not be used as cover for the technical provisions referred to in Article 17.

2.   Subject to Article 17(3), Article 24(1), (2), (3) and (5) and the second subparagraph of Article 26(1), Member States shall not restrain the free disposal of those assets, whether movable or immovable, that form part of the assets of authorised assurance undertakings.

3.   Paragraphs 1 and 2 shall not preclude any measures which Member States, while safeguarding the interests of the lives assured, are entitled to take as owners or members of or partners in the undertakings in question.

Article 22

1.   Member States may not require undertakings to cede part of their underwriting of activities listed in Article 1 to an organization or organisations designated by national regulations.

2.   The Italian Republic shall take all steps to ensure that the requirement that undertakings established in its territory cede part of their underwriting to the 'Istituto Nazionale di Assicurazioni' is abolished no later than 20 November 1994.

Article 23

1.   Each Member State shall require every undertaking whose head office is situated in its territory to produce an annual account, covering all types of operation of its financial situation and solvency.

2.   Member States shall require assurance undertakings with head offices within their territories to render periodically the returns, together with statistical documents, which are necessary for the purposes of supervision. The competent authorities shall provide each other with any documents and information that are useful for the purposes of supervision.

3.   Every Member State shall take all steps necessary to ensure that the competent authorities have the powers and means necessary for the supervision of the business of assurance undertakings with head offices within their territories, including business carried on outside those territories, in accordance with the Council directives governing those activities and for the purpose of seeing that they are implemented. These powers and means must, in particular, enable the competent authorities to:

(a)   make detailed enquiries regarding the undertaking's situation and the whole of its business, inter alia by:

—gathering information or requiring the submission of documents concerning its assurance business,

—carrying out on-the-spot investigations at the undertaking's premises;

(b)   take any measures, with regard to the undertaking, its directors or managers or the persons who control it, that are appropriate and necessary to ensure that the undertaking's business continues to comply with the laws, regulations and administrative provisions with which the undertaking must comply in each Member State and in particular with the scheme of operations in so far as it remains mandatory, and to prevent or remedy any irregularities prejudicial to the interests of the assured persons;

(c) ensure that those measures are carried out, if need be by enforcement, where appropriate through judicial channels.

Member States may also make provision for the competent authorities to obtain any information regarding contracts which are held by intermediaries.

Article 24

1. If an undertaking does not comply with Article 17, the competent authority of its home Member State may prohibit the free disposal of its assets after having communicated its intention to the competent authorities of the Member States of commitment.

2. For the purposes of restoring the financial situation of an undertaking the solvency margin of which has fallen below the minimum required under Article 19, the competent authority of the home Member State shall require that a plan for the restoration of a sound financial position be submitted for its approval.

In exceptional circumstances, if the competent authority is of the opinion that the financial situation of the undertaking will further deteriorate, it may also restrict or prohibit the free disposal of the undertaking's assets. It shall inform the authorities of other Member States within the territories of which the undertaking carries on business of any measures it has taken and the latter shall, at the request of the former, take the same measures.

3. If the solvency margin falls below the guarantee fund as defined in Article 20, the competent authority of the home Member State shall require the undertaking to submit a short-term finance scheme for its approval. It may also restrict or prohibit the free disposal of the undertaking's assets. It shall inform the authorities of other Member States within the territories of which the undertaking carries on business accordingly and the latter shall, at the request of the former, take the same measures.

4. The competent authorities may further take all measures necessary to safeguard the interests of the assured persons in the cases provided for in paragraphs 1, 2 and 3.

5. Each Member State shall take the measures necessary to be able in accordance with its national law to prohibit the free disposal of assets located within its territory at the request, in the cases provided for in paragraphs 1, 2 and 3, of the undertaking's home Member State, which shall designate the assets to be covered by such measures.

Article 25
(Deleted)

SECTION C   WITHDRAWAL OF AUTHORISATION

Article 26

1. Authorisation granted to an assurance undertaking by the competent authority of its home Member State may be withdrawn by that authority if that undertaking:

(a) does not make use of the authorisation within 12 months, expressly renounces it or ceases to carry on business for more than six months, unless the

Member State concerned has made provision for authorisation to lapse in such cases;

(b)   no longer fulfils the conditions for admission;

(c)   has been unable, within the time allowed, to take the measures specified in the restoration plan or finance scheme referred to in Article 24;

(d)   fails seriously in its obligations under the regulations to which it is subject.

In the event of the withdrawal or lapse of the authorisation, the competent authority of the home Member State shall notify the competent authorities of the other Member States accordingly and they shall take appropriate measures to prevent the undertaking from commencing new operations within their territories, under either the freedom of establishment or the freedom to provide services. The home Member State's competent authority shall, in conjunction with those authorities, take all necessary measures to safeguard the interests of the assured persons and shall restrict, in particular, the free disposal of the assets of the undertaking in accordance with Article 24(1), (2), second subparagraph, or (3), second subparagraph.

2.   Any decision to withdraw an authorisation shall be supported by precise reasons and notified to the undertaking in question.

TITLE III A   RULES APPLICABLE TO AGENCIES OR BRANCHES ESTABLISHED WITHIN THE COMMUNITY AND BELONGING TO UNDERTAKINGS WHOSE HEAD OFFICES ARE OUTSIDE THE COMMUNITY

Article 27

1.   Each Member State shall make access to the activities referred to in Article 1 by any undertaking whose head office is outside the Community subject to an official authorisation.

2.   A Member State may grant an authorisation if the undertaking fulfils at least the following conditions:

(a)   it is entitled to undertake insurance activities covered by Article 1 under its national law;

(b)   it establishes an agency or branch in the territory of such Member State;

(c)   it undertakes to establish at the place of management of the agency or branch accounts specific to the activity which it carries on there and to keep there all the records relating to the business transacted;

(d)   it designates a general representative, to be approved by the competent authorities;

(e)   it possesses in the Member State where it carries on an activity assets of an amount equal in value to at least one half of the minimum amount prescribed in Article 20(2)(a) in respect of the guarantee fund and deposits one fourth of the minimum amount as security;

(f)   it undertakes to keep a solvency margin complying with Article 29;

(g)   it submits a scheme of operations in accordance with Article 11(1) and (2).

Article 28

Member States shall require undertakings to establish reserves, referred to in Article 17, adequate to cover the underwriting liabilities assumed in their territories. Member States shall see that the agency or branch covers such reserves by means of assets which are equivalent to such reserves and, to the extent fixed by the Member State in question, matching assets.

The law of the Member States shall be applicable to the calculation of such reserves, the determination of categories of investment and the valuation of assets, and, where appropriate, the determination of the extent to which these assets may be used for the purpose of covering such reserves.

The Member State in question shall require that the assets covering these reserves, shall be localised in its territory. Article 17(3) shall, however, apply.

Article 29

1. Each Member State shall require of agencies or branches set up in its territory a solvency margin consisting of the items listed in Article 18. The minimum solvency margin shall be calculated in accordance with Article 19. However, for the purpose of calculating this margin, account shall be taken only of the operations effected by the agency or branch concerned.

2. One third of the minimum solvency margin shall constitute the guarantee fund. However, the amount of this fund may not be less than one half of the minimum required under Article 20(2)(a). The initial deposit lodged in accordance with Article 27(2)(e) shall be counted towards such guarantee fund.

The guarantee fund and the minimum of such fund shall be constituted in accordance with Article 20.

3. The assets representing the minimum solvency margin must be kept within the Member State where activities are carried on up to the amount of the guarantee fund and the excess within the Community.

Article 30

1. Any undertaking which has requested or obtained authorisation from more than one Member State may apply for the following advantages which may be granted only jointly:

(a)   the solvency margin referred to in Article 29 shall be calculated in relation to the entire business which it carries on within the Community; in such case, account shall be taken only of the operations effected by all the agencies or branches established within the Community for the purposes of this calculation;

(b)   the deposit required under Article 27(2)(E) shall be lodged in only one of those Member States;

(c)   the assets representing the guarantee fund shall be localised in any one of the Member States in which it carries on its activities.

2. Application to benefit from the advantages provided for in paragraph 1 shall be made to the competent authorities of the Member States concerned. The application must state the authority of the Member State which in future is to supervise the solvency of the entire business of the agencies or branches established within the Community. Reasons must be given for the choice of authority made by the undertaking. The deposit shall be lodged with that Member State.

3. The advantages provided for in paragraph 1 may only be granted if the competent authorities of all Member States in which an application has been made agree to them. They shall take effect from the time when the selected supervisory authority informs the other supervisory authorities that it will

supervise the state of solvency of the entire business of the agencies or branches within the Community.

The supervisory authority selected shall obtain from the other Member States the information necessary for the supervision of the overall solvency of the agencies and branches established in their territory.

4.   At the request of one or more of the Member States concerned, the advantages granted under this Article shall be withdrawn simultaneously by all Member States concerned.

Article 31

1.   (a)   subject to point (b), agencies and branches referred to in this title may not simultaneously carry on in a Member State the activities referred to in the Annex to the first coordination Directive (non-life insurance) and those covered by this Directive.

(b)   subject to point (c), Member States may provide that agencies and branches referred to in this title which at the time of notification of this Directive carry on both activities simultaneously in a Member State may continue to do so there provided that each activity is separately managed in accordance with Article 14.

(c)   any Member State which under Article 13 (6)(a) and (b) requires undertakings established in its territory to cease the simultaneous pursuit of the activities in which they are engaged at the time of notification of this Directive must also impose this requirement on agencies and branches referred to in this title which are established in its territory and simultaneously carry on both activities there.

(d)   Member States may provide that agencies and branches referred to in this title whose head office simultaneously carries on both activities and which at the time of notification of this Directive carry on in the territory of a Member State solely the activity covered by this Directive may continue their activity there. If the undertaking wishes to carry on the activity referred to in the first coordination Directive (non-life insurance) in that territory it may only carry on the activity covered by this Directive through a subsidiary.

2.   Articles 23 and 24 shall apply mutatis mutandis to agencies and branches referred to in this title. For the purposes of applying Article 24, the supervisory authority which supervises the overall solvency of agencies or branches shall be treated in the same way as the supervisory authority of the head-office Member State.

3.   In the case of a withdrawal of authorisation by the authority referred to in Article 30(2), this authority shall notify the supervisory authorities of the other Member States where the undertaking operates and the latter authorities shall take the appropriate measures. If the reason for the withdrawal of authorisation is the inadequacy of the solvency margin calculated in accordance with Article 30(1)(a), the supervisory authorities of the other Member States concerned shall also withdraw their authorisations.

Article 31a

1.   Under the conditions laid down by national law, each Member State shall authorise agencies and branches set up within its territory and covered by this Title to transfer all or part of their portfolios of contracts to an accepting office established in the same Member State if the competent authorities of that Member State or, if appropriate, those of the Member State referred to in

Article 30 certify that after taking the transfer into account the accepting office possesses the necessary solvency margin.

2. Under the conditions laid down by national law, each Member State shall authorise agencies and branches set up within its territory and covered by this Title to transfer all or part of their portfolios of contracts to an assurance undertaking with a head office in another Member State if the competent authorities of that Member State certify that after taking the transfer into account the accepting office possesses the necessary solvency margin.

3. If under the conditions laid down by national law a Member State authorises agencies and branches set up within its territory and covered by this Title to transfer all or part of their portfolios of contracts to an agency or branch covered by this Title and set up within the territory of another Member State it shall ensure that the competent authorities of the Member State of the accepting office or, if appropriate, of the Member State referred to in Article 30 certify that after taking the transfer into account the accepting office possesses the necessary solvency margin, that the law of the Member State of the accepting office permits such a transfer and that the State has agreed to the transfer.

4. In the circumstances referred to in paragraphs 1, 2 and 3 the Member State in which the transferring agency or branch is situated shall authorise the transfer after obtaining the agreement of the competent authorities of the Member State of the commitment, where different from the Member State in which the transferring agency or branch is situated.

5. The competent authorities of the Member States consulted shall give their opinion or consent to the competent authorities of the home Member State of the transferring assurance undertaking within three months of receiving a request; the absence of any response from the authorities consulted within that period shall be considered equivalent to a favourable opinion or tacit consent.

6. A transfer authorised in accordance with this Article shall be published as laid down by national law in the Member State of the commitment. Such transfers shall automatically be valid against policy-holders, assured persons and any other persons having rights or obligations arising out of the contracts transferred. This provision shall not affect the Member States' right to give policy-holders the opinion of cancelling contracts within a fixed period after a transfer.

Article 32

The Community may, by means of agreements concluded pursuant to the Treaty with one or more third countries, agree to the application of provisions different from those provided for in this title, for the purpose ensuring, under conditions of reciprocity, adequate protection for policy-holders in the Member States.

TITLE III B   RULES APPLICABLE TO SUBSIDIARIES OF PARENT UNDERTAKINGS GOVERNED BY THE LAWS OF A THIRD COUNTRY AND TO ACQUISITIONS OF HOLDINGS BY SUCH PARENT UNDERTAKINGS

Article 32a

The competent authorities of the Member States shall inform the Commission:

(a)   of any authorisation of a direct or indirect subsidiary one or more parent undertakings of which are governed by the laws of a third country. The Commission shall inform the Committee referred to in Article 32b(6) accordingly;

(b)   whenever such a parent undertaking acquires a holding in a Community insurance undertaking which would turn the latter into its subsidiary. The Commission shall inform the Committee referred to in Article 32b(6) accordingly. When authorisation is granted to the direct or indirect subsidiary of one or more parent undertakings governed by the law of third countries, the structure of the group shall be specified in the notification which the competent authorities shall address to the Commission.

Article 32b

1.   The Member States shall inform the Commission of any general difficulties encountered by their insurance undertakings in establishing themselves or carrying on their activities in a third country.

2.   Initially no later than six months before the date referred to in the second paragraph of Article 30 of Directive 90/619/EEC,[1] and thereafter periodically, the Commission shall draw up a report examining the treatment accorded to Community insurance undertakings in third countries, in the terms referred to in paragraphs 3 and 4, as regards establishment and the carrying on of insurance activities, and the acquisition of holdings in third-country insurance undertakings. The Commission shall submit those reports to the Council, together with any appropriate proposals.

3.   Whenever it appears to the Commission, either on the basis of the reports referred to in paragraph 2 or on the basis of other information, that a third country is not granting Community insurance undertakings effective market access comparable to that granting Community to insurance undertakings effective market access comparable to that granted by the Community to insurance undertakings from that third country, the Commission may submit proposals to the Council for the appropriate mandate for negotiation with a view to obtaining comparable competitive opportunities for Community insurance undertakings. The Council shall decide by a qualified majority.

4.   Whenever it appears to the Commission, either on the basis of the reports referred to in paragraph 2 or on the basis of other information, that Community insurance undertakings in a third country are not receiving national treatment offering the same competitive opportunities as are available to domestic insurance undertakings and that the conditions of effective market access are not being fulfilled, the Commission may initiate negotiations in order to remedy the situation. In the circumstances described in the first subparagraph, it may also be decided at any time, and in addition to initiating negotiations, in accordance with the procedure laid down in Article 32b(6), that the competent authorities of the Member States must limit or suspend their decisions:

—regarding requests pending at the moment of the decision or future requests for authorisations, and

—regarding the acquisition of holdings by direct or indirect parent undertakings governed by the laws of the third country in question.

Note
[1]OJ No. L330, 29.11.1990, p. 50.

The duration of the measures referred to may not exceed three months. Before the end of that three-month period, and in the light of the results of the negotiations, the Council may, acting on a proposal from the Commission, decide by a qualified majority whether the measures shall be continued. Such limitations or suspension may not apply to the setting up of subsidiaries by insurance undertakings or their subsidiaries duly authorised in the Community, or to the acquisition of holdings in Community insurance undertakings by such undertakings or subsidiaries.

5.   Whenever it appears to the Commission that one of the situations described in paragraphs 3 and 4 has arisen, the Member States shall inform it at its request:

(a)   of any request for the authorisation of a direct or indirect subsidiary one or more parent undertakings of which are governed by the laws of the third country in question;

(b)   of any plans for such an undertaking to acquire a holding in a Community insurance undertaking such that the latter would become the subsidiary of the former.

This obligation to provide information shall lapse whenever an agreement is reached with the third country referred to in paragraph 3 or 4 when the measures referred to in the second and third subparagraphs of paragraph 4 cease to apply.

6.   The Commission shall be assisted by a committee composed of the representatives of the Member States and chaired by the representative of the Commission. The representative of the Commission shall submit to the committee a draft of the measures to be taken. The committee shall deliver its opinion on the draft within a time limit which the chairman may lay down according to the urgency of the matter. The opinion shall be delivered by the majority laid down in Article 148(2) of the Treaty in the case of decisions which the Council is required to adopt on a proposal from the Commission. The votes of the representatives of the Member States within the committee shall be weighted in the manner set out in that Article. The chairman shall not vote. The Commission shall adopt the measures envisaged if they are in accordance with the opinion of the committee.

If the measures envisaged are not in accordance with the opinion of the committee, or if no opinion is delivered, the Commission shall, without delay, submit to the Council a proposal relating to the measures to be taken. The Council shall act by a qualified majority. If, on the expiry of a period to be laid down in each act to be adopted by the Council under this paragraph but which may in no case exceed three months from the date of referral to the Council, the Council has not acted, the proposed measures shall be adopted by the Commission, save where the Council has decided against the said measures by a simple majority.

7.   Measures taken under this Article shall comply with the Community's obligations under any international agreements, bilateral or multilateral, governing the taking-up and pursuit of the business of insurance undertakings.

TITLE IV   TRANSITIONAL AND OTHER PROVISIONS

Article 33

1.   Member states shall allow undertakings referred to in Title II which at the entry into force of the implementing measures to this Directive provide

insurance in their territories in one or more of the classes referred to in the Annex, a period of five years from the date of notification of this Directive in order to comply with Articles 18, 19 and 20.

2.   Furthermore, Member States may:

   (a)   allow any undertakings referred to in paragraph 1, which upon the expiry of the five-year period have not fully established the solvency margin, a further period not exceeding two years in which to do so provided that such undertakings have, in accordance with Article 24, submitted for the approval of the supervisory authority the measures which they propose to take for such purpose;

   (b)   except for the mutual associations referred to in the second sentence of the second indent of Article 3(2), exempt undertakings referred to in paragraph 1 of this Article, for which upon the expiry of the five-year period the solvency margin to be established pursuant to Article 19 without deduction for re-insurance does not reach the minimum of the guarantee fund referred to in Article 20(2)(a) and (b), from the requirement to establish this fund before the end of the financial year in respect of which the solvency margin referred to reaches this minimum amount. The maximum period thus granted to these undertakings to establish this minimum amount shall in no case exceed 10 years from the date of notification of this Directive.

3.   Undertakings desiring to extend their business within the meaning of Article 8(2) or 10 may not do so unless they comply immediately with the rules of this Directive.

4.   Undertakings having a structure different from any of those listed in Article 8 may continue, for a period of three years from the notification of this Directive, to carry on their present business in the legal form in which they are constituted at the time of such notification. Undertakings set up in the United Kingdom by Royal Charter or by private act or by special public act may carry on their activity in their present form for an unlimited period. The Member States in question shall draw up a list of such undertakings and communicate it to the other Member States and the Commission.

5.   Undertakings which, in accordance with their objects, carry on the activities of life assurance and savings operations may continue to carry on such activities, with the exception of savings operations, which must cease within three years from the date of notification of this Directive. As an exception, the 'caisse generale d'épargne et de retraite (cger) '/'algemene spoor — en lifrentekas (aslk)' in Belgium, the societies registered under the friendly societies acts in the United Kingdom and the 'banca nazionale delle communicazioni' in Italy may continue the activities they were carrying on when the Directive was notified.

6.   Undertakings which carry on simultaneously both activities in accordance with the terms of Article 13 shall have a period of five years from the date of notification of this Directive to comply with the provisions of Article 14.

7.   At the request of undertakings which comply with the requirements of Articles 17 to 20, Member States shall cease to apply any restrictive measures such as those relating to mortgages, deposits or securities established under their present regulations.

Article 34

Member States shall allow agencies or branches referred to in Title III which, at the entry into force of the implementing measures to this Directive, are carrying on one or more classes referred to in annex I and which do not extend their business within the meaning of Article 10(2), a maximum period of five years from the date of notification of this Directive in order to comply with the conditions in Article 29.

Article 35

(deleted)

Article 36

During a period which terminates at the time of the entry into force of an agreement concluded with a third country pursuant to Article 32, and at the latest upon the expiry of a period of four years after the notification of this Directive, each Member State may retain for undertakings of that country established in its territory the rules applied to them on 1 January 1979 in respect of matching assets and the localisation of technical reserves, including mathematical reserves, provided that notification is given to the other Member States and the Commission and that the limits of relaxations granted pursuant to Article 17(2) in favour of the undertakings of member states established in its territory are not exceeded.

Article 37

1. Where a Member State requires of its own nationals proof of good repute and proof of no previous bankruptcy, or proof of either of these, that State shall accept as sufficient evidence in respect of nationals of other Member States the production of an extract from the 'judicial record' or, failing this, of an equivalent document issued by a competent judicial or administrative authority in the Member State of origin or the Member State whence the foreign national comes showing that these requirements have been met.

2. Where the Member State of origin or the Member State whence the foreign national concerned comes does not issue the document referred to in paragraph 1, it may be replaced by a declaration on oath — or in states where there is no provision for declaration on oath by a solemn declaration — made by the person concerned before a competent judicial or administrative authority or, where appropriate, a notary in the Member State of origin or the Member State whence that person comes; such authority or notary shall issue a certificate attesting the authenticity of the declaration on oath or solemn declaration. The declaration in respect of no previous bankruptcy may also be made before a competent professional or trade body in the said country.

3. Documents issued in accordance with paragraphs 1 and 2 must not be produced more than three months after their date of issue.

4. Member States shall, within the time limit of 18 months from the date of notification of this Directive, designate the authorities and bodies competent to issue the documents referred to in paragraphs 1 and 2 and shall forthwith inform the other Member States and the Commission thereof. Within the same time limit, each Member State shall also inform the other Member States and the Commission of the authorities or bodies to which the documents referred to in this Article are to be submitted in support of an application to carry on in the territory of this Member State the activities referred to in Article 1.

TITLE V   FINAL PROVISIONS

Article 38

The Commission and the competent authorities of the Member States shall collaborate closely for the purpose of facilitating supervision of direct insurance within the Community and of examining any difficulties which might arise in the application of this Directive.

Article 39

1. The Commission shall submit to the Council, within six years from the date of notification of this Directive, a report dealing with the effects of the financial requirements imposed by this Directive on the situation in the insurance markets of the Member States. If necessary, the Commission shall submit interim reports to the Council before the end of the transitional period provided for in Article 33(1).

2. Following a period of 10 years from the notification of this Directive, the Commission shall submit to the Council a report dealing with the operations of the two types of undertakings covered by this Directive: that is to say, those undertakings which carry on simultaneously the activity covered by the first coordination Directive (non-life insurance) in addition to the activity covered by this Directive and those undertakings which carry on only the activity covered by this Directive.

3. The Council, acting on a proposal from the Commission, shall every two years examine and, where appropriate, review the amounts expressed in units of account in this Directive, in the light of how the Community's economic and monetary situation has evolved. The Commission shall submit its first proposal in this connection to the Council at the time as a proposal concerning non-life insurance, as laid down in Article 3 of Directive 76/580/EEC,[1] and not later than four years after the date of notification of this Directive.

Note
[1]OJ No. L189, 13.7.1976, p. 13.

Article 40

Member States shall amend their national provisions to comply with this Directive within 18 months of its notification and shall forthwith inform the Commission thereof. The provisions thus amended shall, subject to Articles 33 to 36, be applied within 30 months from the date of notification.

Article 41

Following notification of this Directive, Member States shall communicate the texts of the main provisions of a legislative, regulatory or administrative nature which they adopt in the field covered by this Directive to the Commission.

Article 42

This Directive is addressed to the Member States.

Done at Brussels, 5 March 1979.
For the Council,
The President,
J. FRANÇOIS-PONCET

ANNEX   CLASSES OF INSURANCE

I.   The assurance referred to in Article 1(1)(a), (b) and (c) excluding those referred to in ii and iii

II.   Marriage assurance, birth assurance

III.   The assurance referred to in Article 1(1)(A) and (b), which are linked to investment funds

IV.   Permanent health insurance, referred to in Article 1(1)(d)

V.   Tontines, referred to in Article 1(2)(a)

VI.   Capital redemption operations, referred to in Article 1(2)(b)

VII.   Management of group pension funds, referred to in Article 1(2)(c) and (d)

VIII.   The operations referred to in Article 1(2)(e)

IX.   The operations referred to in Article 1(3),

COUNCIL DIRECTIVE 90/619/EEC OF 8 NOVEMBER 1990 ON THE COORDINATION OF LAWS, REGULATIONS AND ADMINISTRATIVE PROVISIONS RELATING TO DIRECT LIFE ASSURANCE, LAYING DOWN PROVISIONS TO FACILITATE THE EFFECTIVE EXERCISE OF FREEDOM TO PROVIDE SERVICES AND AMENDING DIRECTIVE 79/267/EEC
[OJ 1990 L330/44]*

THE COUNCIL OF THE EUROPEAN COMMUNITIES,

Having regard to the Treaty establishing the European Economic Community, and in particular Articles 57(2) and 66 thereof,

Having regard to the proposal from the Commission,[1]

In cooperation with the European Parliament,[2]

Having regard to the opinion of the Economic and Social Committee,[3]

Whereas it is necessary to develop the internal market in life assurance and in the operations referred to in First Council Directive 79/267/EEC of 5 March 1979 on the coordination of laws, regulations and administrative provisions relating to the taking-up and pursuit of the business of direct life assurance,[4] hereinafter called the 'First Directive' as last amended by the Act of Accession of Spain and Portugal;

Whereas, in order to achieve that objective, it is desirable to make it easier for assurance undertakings having their head office in the Community to provide services in the Member States, thus making it possible for policy-holders to have recourse not only to assurers established in their own country, but also to assurers which have their head office in the Community and are established in other Member States;

Notes

*Amended by Directive 92/96 [OJ No. L360/1]

[1] OJ No. C38 of 15.2.1989, p. 7 and OJ No. C72 of 22.3.1990, p. 5.

[2] OJ No. C175, 16.7.1990, p. 107, and Decision of 24 October 1990 (not yet published in the Official Journal).

[3] OJ No. C298, 27.11.1989, p. 2.

[4] OJ No. L63, 13.3.1979, p. 1.

Whereas, under the Treaty, any discrimination with regard to freedom to provide services based on the fact that an undertaking is not established in the Member State in which the services are provided has been prohibited since the end of the transitional period; whereas that prohibition applies to services provided from any establishment in the Community, whether it be the head office of an undertaking or an agency or branch;

Whereas, for practical reasons, it is desirable to define provision of services taking into account both the assurer's establishment and the place where the commitment is to be covered; whereas, therefore, commitment should also be defined; whereas, moreover, it is desirable to distinguish between activities pursued by way of establishment and activities pursued by way of freedom to provide services;

Whereas it is desirable to supplement the First Council Directive in order in particular to clarify the powers and means of supervision vested in the supervisory authorities; whereas it is also desirable to lay down specific provisions regarding the taking-up, pursuit and supervision of activity by way of freedom to provide services;

Whereas policy-holders who, by virtue of the fact that they take the initiative applicable to the activities referred to in the First Directive continue to differ; whereas the freedom to choose, as the law applicable to the contract, a law other than that of the State of the commitment may be granted in certain cases, in accordance with rules which take into account specific circumstances;

Whereas the First Directive's provisions on transfer of portfolio should be reinforced and supplemented by provisions specifically concerning the transfer to another undertaking of the portfolio of contracts concluded by way of freedom to provide services;

Whereas, in the interests of protecting policy-holders, Member States should, at the present stage of the coordination process, be given the option of limiting the simultaneous pursuit of activity by way of freedom to provide services and activity by way of establishment; whereas no such limitation can be provided for where policy-holders do not require such protection;

Whereas the taking-up and pursuit of activity by way of freedom to provide services should be subject to procedures guaranteeing the assurance undertaking's compliance with provisions regarding financial guarantees, conditions of assurance and premium rates; whereas those procedures may be relaxed where the activity pursued by way of freedom to provide services covers policy-holders who, by virtue of the characteristics of the commitment they propose to enter into, do not require special protection in the State of the commitment;

Whereas for life assurance contracts entered into by way of the free provision of services the policy-holder should be given the opportunity of cancelling the contract within a period of between 14 and 30 days;

Whereas the First Directive adopted the principle of prohibiting the simultaneous pursuit of the activities covered by Directive 73/239/EEC[1] (called the First Directive on the coordination of non-life insurance) as last amended by Directive 88/357/ EEC[2] and those covered by the First Directive; whereas, while it authorised the continued existence of existing composite

Notes
[1]OJ No. L228, 16.8.1973, p. 3.
[2]OJ No. L172, 4.7.1988, p. 1.

undertakings, it stated that they may not set up agencies or branches for life assurance; whereas the specific nature of the commitments entered into in the insurance field under the freedom of services regime nevertheless justifies, at least on a transitional basis as from notification of this Directive to Member States, the introduction of a degree of flexibility in the application of the above principle;

Whereas nothing in this Directive would prevent a composite undertaking from dividing itself into two undertakings, one active in the field of life assurance, the other in non-life insurance; whereas in order to allow such division to take place under the best possible conditions, it is desirable to permit Member States, in accordance with Community rules of competition law, to provide for appropriate tax arrangements, in particular with regard to the capital gains such division could entail;

Whereas it is necessary to make provision for special cooperation in the sphere of freedom to provide services between the competent supervisory authorities of the Member States and between those authorities and the Commission; whereas provision should also be made for a system of penalties to apply where the undertaking providing the service fails to comply with the provisions of the Member State in which the service is provided;

Whereas the technical reserves, including mathematical reserves, should be subject to the rules of and supervision by the Member State in which the service is provided where the provision of services involves commitments in respect of which the State in which the service is received wishes to provide special protection for policy-holders; whereas, however, if such concern to protect policy-holders is unjustified, the technical reserves, including mathematical reserves, should remain subject to the rules of and supervision by the Member State in which the undertaking is established;

Whereas some Member States do not subject life assurance contracts and the other operations covered by the First Directive to any form of indirect taxation, while others apply special taxes; whereas the structure and rate of those taxes vary considerably between the Member States in which they are applied; whereas it is desirable to avoid a situation where those differences lead to distortions of competition between undertakings in the various Member States; whereas, pending further harmonization, the application of the tax arrangements provided for by the Member State in which the commitment is entered into is a means of remedying such mischief; whereas it is for the Member States to establish a method of ensuring that such taxes are collected;

Whereas the First Directive makes express provision for specific rules concerning the authorisation of agencies and branches of undertakings whose head offices are outside the Community;

Whereas provision should be made for a flexible procedure to make it possible to assess reciprocity with third countries on a Community basis; whereas the aim of this procedure is not to close the Community's financial markets but rather, as the Community intends to keep its financial markets open to the rest of the world, to improve the liberalisation of the global financial markets in other third countries; whereas, to that end, this Directive provides for procedures for negotiating with third countries and, as a last resort, for the possibility of taking measures involving the suspension of new applications for authorisation or the restriction of new authorisations;

Whereas it is desirable to take into account, within the meaning of Article 8c of the Treaty, the extent of the effort which needs to be made by certain economies showing differences in development; whereas, therefore, it is desirable to grant certain Member States transitional arrangements for the gradual application of the specific provisions of this Directive relating to freedom to provide services;

Whereas, in view of the differences in the national legislation, it is also appropriate to grant to those Member States which so wish transitional arrangements enabling them to adapt their legislation before applying in their entirety, as regards group insurance contracts linked to a contract of employment or the intervention of a broker, the provisions of this Directive relating to the case where the policy-holder takes the initiative to conclude a contract by way of provision of services;

Whereas it will be particularly important to allow those Member States who so wish a sufficiently long period to be able to adopt the appropriate provisions in order to ensure the professional qualification and independence of insurance brokers; whereas taking into account the growing role such brokers play in advising those buying insurance and facing an increasing range of products as a result of the freedom to provide services, their professional qualification and independence will become essential elements for protection of the consumer,

HAS ADOPTED THIS DIRECTIVE:*

Note
*In order to avoid unnecessary repetition throughout this Directive, where Articles have been replaced in previous Directives, the text is removed from this Directive.

TITLE I   GENERAL PROVISIONS

Article 1
The object of this Directive is to:
(a)   supplement Directive 79/267/EEC;
(b)   lay down specific provisions relating to freedom to provide services in respect of the activities referred to in the said Directive, such provisions being set forth in Title III of this Directive.

Article 2
For the purposes of this Directive:
(a)   'First Directive': means Directive 79/267/EEC;
(b)   'undertaking':
— for the purposes of Titles I and II, means any undertaking which has received official authorisation under Article 6 or Article 27 of the First Directive,
— for the purposes of Titles III and IV, means any undertaking which has received official authorisation under Article 6 of the First Directive;
(c)   'establishment':
means the head office, an agency or a branch of an undertaking, having regard to Article 3;
(d)   'commitment':
means a commitment represented by one of the kinds of insurance or operation referred to in Article 1 of the First Directive;
(e)   'Member State of the commitment':

means the Member State where the policy-holder has his habitual residence or, if the policy-holder is a legal person, the Member State where the latter's establishment, to which the contract relates is situated;

    (f) 'Member State of establishment':

means the Member State in which the establishment covering the commitment is situated;

    (g) 'Member State of provision of services':

means the Member State of the commitment where the commitment is covered by an establishment situated in another Member State;

    (h) 'parent undertaking':

means a parent undertaking within the meaning of Articles 1 and 2 of Directive 83/349/EEC;[1]

    (i) 'subsidiary':

means a subsidiary undertaking within the meaning of Articles 1 and 2 of Directive 83/349/EEC; any subsidiary undertaking of a subsidiary undertaking shall also be regarded as a subsidiary of the parent undertaking which is at the head of those undertakings.

Note

[1]OJ No. L193, 18.7.1983, p. 1.

Article 3

For the purposes of the First Directive and of this Directive, any permanent presence of an undertaking in the territory of a Member State shall be treated in the same way as an agency or branch, even if that presence does not take the form of a branch or agency, but consists merely of an office managed by the undertaking's own staff or by a person who is independent but has permanent authority to act for the undertaking as an agency would.

TITLE II   PROVISIONS SUPPLEMENTARY TO THE FIRST DIRECTIVE

Article 4

    1.   The law applicable to contracts relating to the activities referred to in the First Directive shall be the law of the Member State of the commitment. However, where the law of that State so allows, the parties may choose the law of another country.

    2.   Where the policy-holder is a natural person and has his habitual residence in a Member State other than that of which he is a national, the parties may choose the law of the Member State of which he is a national.

    3.   Where a State includes several territorial units, each of which has its own rules of law concerning contractual obligations, each unit shall be considered a country for the purposes of identifying the law applicable under this Directive. A Member State in which various territorial units have their own rules of law concerning contractual obligations shall not be bound to apply the provisions of this Directive to conflicts which arise between the laws of those units.

    4.   Nothing in this Article shall restrict the application of the rules of the law of the forum in a situation where they are mandatory, irrespective of the law otherwise applicable to the contract. If the law of a Member State so stipulates, the mandatory rules of the law of the Member State of the commitment may be applied if and in so far as, under the law of that Member State, those rules must be applied whatever the law applicable to the contract.

5. Subject to the preceding paragraphs, the Member States shall apply to the assurance contracts referred to in this Directive their general rules of private international law concerning contractual obligations.

Article 5
The following paragraph is added to Article 23 of the First Directive:

Article 6
1. Article 25 of the First Directive is hereby deleted.
(articles (2) to (7) deleted)
7. A transfer authorised in accordance with this Article shall be published, under the conditions laid down by national law, in the Member State of the commitment. Such transfer shall be automatically valid against policy-holders, assured persons and any other person having rights or obligations arising out of the contracts transferred. This provision shall not affect the right of Member States to provide that policy-holders may cancel the contract within a given period after the transfer.

Article 7
Article 22(2) of the First Directive is replaced by the following:

Article 8
1. The heading of Title III of the First Directive is replaced by the following:
'TITLE III A Rules applicable to agencies or branches established within the Community and belonging to undertakings whose head offices are outside the Community'
2. The following heading is placed after Article 32 of the First Directive:
'TITLE III B Rules applicable to subsidiaries of parent undertakings governed by the laws of a third country and to acquisitions of holdings by such parent undertakings.'

Article 9
The following Articles are added to Title III B of the First Directive:
'**Article 32a and Article 32b**'

TITLE III   PROVISIONS RELATING SPECIFICALLY TO THE FREEDOM TO PROVIDE SERVICES

Article 10
(deleted)

Article 11
Any undertaking that intends to carry on business for the first time in one or more Member States under the freedom to provide services shall first inform the competent authorities of the home Member State, indicating the nature of the commitments it proposes to cover.

Article 12
(deleted)

Article 13
(deleted)

Article 14
1. Within one month of the notification provided for in Article 11, the competent authorities of the home Member State shall communicate to the Member State or Member States within the territory of which the undertaking intends to carry on business by way of the freedom to provide services:

(a) a certificate attesting that the undertaking has the minimum solvency margin calculated in accordance with Articles 19 and 20 of Directive 79/267/EEC;

(b) the classes which the undertaking has been authorised to offer;

(c) the nature of the commitments which the undertaking proposes to cover in the Member State of the provision of services.

At the same time, they shall inform the undertaking concerned accordingly.

2. Where the competent authorities of the home Member State do not communicate the information referred to in paragraph 1 within the period laid down, they shall give the reasons for their refusal to the undertaking within that same period. The refusal shall be subject to a right to apply to the courts in the home Member State.

3. The undertaking may start business on the certified date on which it is informed of the communication provided for in the first subparagraph of paragraph 1.

Article 15
1. Each Member State shall prescribe that a policy-holder who concludes an individual life-assurance contract shall have a period of between 14 and 30 days from the time when he was informed that the contract had been concluded within which to cancel the contract.

The giving of notice of cancellation by the policy-holder shall have the effect of releasing him from any future obligation arising from the contract. The other legal effects and the conditions of cancellation shall be determined by the law applicable to the contract as defined in Article 4, notably as regards the arrangements for informing the policy-holder that the contract has been concluded.

2. The Member States need not apply paragraph 1 to contracts of six months' duration or less, nor where, because of the status of the policy-holder or the circumstances in which the contract is concluded, the policy-holder does not need this special protection. Member States shall specify in their rules where paragraph 1 is not applied.

Article 16
(deleted)

Article 17
Any change which an undertaking intends to make to the information referred to in Article 11 shall be subject to the procedure provided for in Articles 11 and 14.

Article 18
(deleted)

Article 19
(deleted)

Article 20
(deleted)

Article 21
(deleted)

Article 22
(deleted)

Article 23
(deleted)

Article 24
(deleted)

Article 25
(deleted)

TITLE IV   TRANSITIONAL PROVISIONS

Article 26
(deleted)

Article 27

1.   In the case of group assurance contracts entered into by virtue of the insured person's contract of employment or professional activity, any Member State may, until 31 December 1994, limit the commitments for which it is the Member State of provision of services to those entered into in accordance with the arrangements referred to in Article 12.

2.   Member States may, up to three years at the latest after the date of application laid down in the second paragraph of Article 30, consider that the policy-holder shall be deemed to have taken the initiative only in the case provided for in the first indent of Article 13(1).

TITLE V   FINAL PROVISIONS

Article 28

The Commission and the competent authorities of the Member States shall collaborate closely with a view to facilitating the supervision of the kinds of insurance and the operations referred to in the First Directive within the Community.

Each Member State shall inform the Commission of any major difficulties to which application of this Directive gives rise, inter alia any arising if a Member State becomes aware of an abnormal transfer of business referred to in the first Directive to the detriment of undertakings established in its territory and to the advantage of agencies and branches located just beyond its borders.

The Commission and the competent authorities of the Member States concerned shall examine such difficulties as quickly as possible in order to find an appropriate solution.

Where necessary, the Commission shall submit appropriate proposals to the Council.

Article 29
The Commission shall forward to the European Parliament and the Council regular reports, the first on 20 November 1995, on the development of the market in assurance and operations transacted under conditions of freedom to provide services.

Article 30
Member States shall amend their national provisions to comply with this Directive within 24 months of the date of its notification[1] and shall forthwith inform the Commission thereof. The provisions amended in accordance with the first paragraph shall be applied within 30 months of the date of notification of this Directive.

Note
[1]This Directive was notified to the Member States on 20 November 1990.

Article 31
Upon notification of this Directive, Member States shall ensure that the texts of the main laws, regulations or administrative provisions which they adopt in the field covered by this Directive are communicated to the Commission.

Article 32
This Directive is addressed to the Member States.

Done at Brussels, 8 November 1990.
For the Council
The President
P. ROMITA

ANNEX

A.   Statement to be signed by the policy-holder under Article 13(1), second indent:

'I hereby state that I wish (name of intermediary) to provide me with information on assurance contracts offered by undertakings established in Member States other than (Member State of habitual residence of policy-holder). I understand that such undertakings are subject to the supervisory arrangements of the State in which they are established and not to the supervisory arrangements of (Member State of habitual residence of policy-holder).'

B.   Statement to be signed by the policy-holder under Article 13(2)

'I hereby take note that (name of assurer) is established in (Member State of establishment of assurer) and I realise that supervision of that assurer is the responsibility of the supervisory authorities in (Member State of establishment of assurer) and not the responsibility of the authorities in (Member State of habitual residence of policy-holder).'

COUNCIL DIRECTIVE 92/96/EEC OF 10 NOVEMBER 1992 ON THE COORDINATION OF LAWS, REGULATIONS AND ADMINISTRATIVE PROVISIONS RELATING TO DIRECT LIFE ASSURANCE AND AMENDING DIRECTIVES 79/267/EEC AND 90/619/EEC (THIRD LIFE ASSURANCE DIRECTIVE)*
[OJ No. L360/1]

THE COUNCIL OF THE EUROPEAN COMMUNITIES,

Having regard to the Treaty establishing the European Economic Community, and in particular Articles 57(2) and 66 thereof,

Having regard to the proposal from the Commission,[1]

In cooperation with the European Parliament,[2]

Having regard to the opinion of the Economic and Social Committee,[3]

1. Whereas it is necessary to complete the internal market in direct life assurance, from the point of view both of the right of establishment and of the freedom to provide services, to make it easier for assurance undertakings with head offices in the Community to cover commitments situated within the Community;

2. Whereas the Second Council Directive 90/619/EEC of 8 November 1990 on the coordination of laws, regulations and administrative provisions relating to direct life assurance, laying down provisions to facilitate the effective exercise of freedom to provide services and amending Directive 79/267/EEC[4] has already contributed substantially to the achievement of the internal market in direct life assurance by granting policy-holders who, by virtue of the fact that they take the initiative in entering into a commitment with an assurance undertaking in another Member State, do not require special protection in the Member State of the commitment complete freedom to avail themselves of the widest possible life assurance market;

3. Whereas Directive 90/619/EEC therefore represents an important stage in the merging of national markets into an integrated market and that stage must be supplemented by other Community instruments with a view to enabling all policy-holders, irrespective of whether they themselves take the initiative, to have recourse to any assurer with a head office in the Community who carries on business there, under the right of establishment or the freedom to provide services, while guaranteeing them adequate protection;

4. Whereas this Directive forms part of the body of Community legislation already enacted which includes the First Council Directive 79/267/EEC of 5 March 1979 on the coordination of laws, regulations and administrative provisions relating to the taking up and pursuit of the business of direct life assurance[5] and Council Directive 91/674/EEC of 19 December 1991 on the annual accounts and consolidated accounts of insurance undertakings;[6]

Notes

*Amended by Directive 95/26 [OJ No. L168]

[1] OJ No. C99, 16.4.1991, p. 2.

[2] OJ No. C176, 13.7.1992, p. 93; and Decision of 28 October 1992 (not yet published in the Official Journal).

[3] OJ No. C14, 20.1.1992, p. 11.

[4] OJ No. L330, 29.11.1990, p. 50

[5] OJ No. L63, 13.3.1979, p. 1. Directive as last amended by the Second Directive 90/619/EEC [OJ No. L330, 29.11.1990, p. 40]

[6] OJ No. L374, 31.12.1991, p. 7.

5. Whereas the approach adopted consists in bringing about such harmonization as is essential, necessary and sufficient to achieve the mutual recognition of authorisations and prudential control systems, thereby making it possible to grant a single authorisation valid throughout the Community and apply the principle of supervision by the home Member State;

6. Whereas, as a result, the taking up and the pursuit of the business of assurance are henceforth to be subject to the grant of a single official authorisation issued by the competent authorities of the Member State in which an assurance undertaking has its head office;

Whereas such authorisation enables an undertaking to carry on business throughout the Community, under the right of establishment or the freedom to provide services;

Whereas the Member State of the branch or of the provision of services may no longer require assurance undertakings which wish to carry on assurance business there and which have already been authorised in their home Member State to seek fresh authorisation;

Whereas Directives 79/267/EEC and 90/619/EEC should therefore be amended along those lines;

7. Whereas the competent authorities of home Member States will henceforth be responsible for monitoring the financial health of assurance undertakings, including their state of solvency, the establishment of adequate technical provisions and the covering of those provisions by matching assets;

8. Whereas the performance of the operations referred to in Article 1(2)(c) of Directive 79/267/EEC cannot under any circumstances affect the powers conferred on the respective authorities with regard to the entities holding the assets with which that provision is concerned;

9. Whereas certain provisions of this Directive define minimum standards;

Whereas a home Member State may lay down stricter rules for assurance undertakings authorised by its own competent authorities;

10. Whereas the competent authorities of the Member States must have at their disposal such means of supervision as are necessary to ensure the orderly pursuit of business by assurance undertakings throughout the Community whether carried on under the right of establishment or the freedom to provide services;

Whereas, in particular, they must be able to introduce appropriate safeguards or impose sanctions aimed at preventing irregularities and infringements of the provisions on assurance supervision;

11. Whereas the provisions on transfers of portfolios must be adapted to bring them into line with the single legal authorisation system introduced by this Directive;

12. Whereas provision should be made for the specialization rule laid down by Directive 79/267/EEC to be relaxed so that those Member States which so wish are able to grant the same undertaking authorisations for the classes referred to in the Annex to Directive 79/267/EEC and the insurance business coming under classes 1 and 2 in the Annex to Directive 73/239/EEC;[1] whereas

Notes
[1]First Council Directive 73/239/EEC of 24 July 1973 on the coordination of laws, regulations and administrative provisions relating to the taking-up and pursuit of the business of direct insurance other than life assurance [OJ No. L228, 16.8.1973, p. 3]. Directive as last amended by Directive 90/618/EEC [OJ No. L330, 29.11.1990, p. 44].

that possibility may, however, be subject to certain conditions as regards compliance with accounting rules and rules on winding-up;

13. Whereas it is necessary from the point of view of the protection of lives assured that every assurance undertaking should establish adequate technical provisions;

Whereas the calculation of such provisions is based for the most part on actuarial principles;

Whereas those principles should be coordinated in order to facilitate mutual recognition of the prudential rules applicable in the various Member States;

14. Whereas it is desirable, in the interests of prudence, to establish a minimum of coordination of rules limiting the rate of interest used in calculating the technical provisions;

Whereas, for the purposes of such limitation, since existing methods are all equally correct, prudential and equivalent, it seems appropriate to leave Member States a free choice as to the method to be used;

15. Whereas the rules governing the spread, localisation and matching of the assets used to cover technical provisions must be coordinated in order to facilitate the mutual recognition of Member States' rules;

Whereas that coordination must take account of the measures on the liberalisation of capital movements provided for in Council Directive 88/361/ EEC of 24 June 1988 for the implementation of Article 67 of the Treaty[2] and the progress made by the Community towards economic and monetary union;

16. Whereas, however, the home Member State may not require assurance undertakings to invest the assets covering their technical provisions in particular categories of assets, as such a requirement would be incompatible with the measures on the liberalisation of capital movements provided for in Directive 88/361/EEC;

17. Whereas, pending the adoption of a directive on investment services harmonizing inter alia the definition of the concept of a regulated market, for the purposes of this Directive and without prejudice to such future harmoniz- ation that concept must be defined provisionally, to be replaced by the definition harmonised at Community level, which will give the home Member State of the market the responsibilities for these matters which this Directive transitionally gives to the assurance undertaking's home Member State;

18. Whereas the list of items of which the solvency margin required by Directive 79/267/EEC may be made up must be supplemented to take account of new financial instruments and of the facilities granted to other financial institutions for the constitution of their own funds;

19. Whereas the harmonization of assurance contract law is not a prior condition for the achievement of the internal market in assurance;

Whereas, therefore, the opportunity afforded to the Member States of imposing the application of their law to assurance contracts covering commitments within their territories is likely to provide adequate safeguards for policy-holders;

20. Whereas within the framework of an internal market it is in the policy-holder's interest that he should have access to the widest possible range of assurance products available in the Community so that he can choose that which is best suited to his needs;

Note
[2]OJ No. L178, 8.7.1988, p. 5.

Whereas it is for the Member State of the commitment to ensure that there is nothing to prevent the marketing within its territory of all the assurance products offered for sale in the Community as long as they do not conflict with the legal provisions protecting the general good in force in the Member State of the commitment and in so far as the general good is not safeguarded by the rules of the home Member State, provided that such provisions must be applied without discrimination to all undertakings operating in that Member State and be objectively necessary and in proportion to the objective pursued;

21. Whereas the Member States must be able to ensure that the assurance products and contract documents used, under the right of establishment or the freedom to provide services, to cover commitments within their territories comply with such specific legal provisions protecting the general good as are applicable;

Whereas the systems of supervision to be employed must meet the requirements of an internal market but their employment may not constitute a prior condition for carrying on assurance business;

Whereas, from this standpoint, systems for the prior approval of policy conditions do not appear to be justified;

Whereas it is therefore necessary to provide for other systems better suited to the requirements of an internal market which enable every Member State to guarantee policy-holders adequate protection;

22. Whereas, for the purposes of implementing actuarial principles in conformity with this Directive, the home Member State may nevertheless require systematic notification of the technical bases used for calculating scales of premiums and technical provisions, with such notification of technical bases excluding notification of the general and special policy conditions and the undertaking's commercial rates;

23. Whereas in a single assurance market the consumer will have a wider and more varied choice of contracts;

Whereas, if he is to profit fully from this diversity and from increased competition, he must be provided with whatever information is necessary to enable him to choose the contract best suited to his needs;

Whereas this information requirement is all the more important as the duration of commitments can be very long;

Whereas the minimum provisions must therefore be coordinated in order for the consumer to receive clear and accurate information on the essential characteristics of the products proposed to him as well as the particulars of the bodies to which any complaints of policy-holders, assured persons or beneficiaries of contracts may be addressed;

24. Whereas publicity for assurance products is an essential means of enabling assurance business to be carried on effectively within the Community;

Whereas it is necessary to leave open to assurance undertakings the use of all normal means of advertising in the Member State of the branch or of provision of services;

Whereas Member States may nevertheless require compliance with their national rules on the form and content of advertising, whether laid down pursuant to Community legislation on advertising or adopted by Member States for reasons of the general good;

25. Whereas, within the framework of the internal market, no Member State may continue to prohibit the simultaneous carrying on of assurance

business within its territory under the right of establishment and the freedom to provide services;

Whereas the option granted to Member States in this connection by Directive 90/619/EEC should therefore be abolished;

26. Whereas provision should be made for a system of penalties to be imposed when, in the Member State in which the commitment is entered into, an assurance undertaking does not comply with those provisions protecting the general good that are applicable to it;

27. Whereas some Member States do not subject assurance transactions to any form of indirect taxation, while the majority apply special taxes and other forms of contribution;

Whereas the structures and rates of such taxes and contributions vary considerably between the Member States in which they are applied;

Whereas it is desirable to prevent existing differences leading to distortions of competition in assurance services between Member States;

Whereas, pending subsequent harmonization, application of the tax systems and other forms of contribution provided for by the Member States in which commitments entered into are likely to remedy that problem and it is for the Member States to make arrangements to ensure that such taxes and contributions are collected;

28. Whereas it is important to introduce Community coordination on the winding-up of assurance undertakings;

Whereas it is henceforth essential to provide, in the event of the winding-up of an assurance undertaking, that the system of protection in place in each Member State must guarantee equality of treatment for all assurance creditors, irrespective of nationality and of the method of entering into the commitment;

29. Whereas technical adjustments to the detailed rules laid down in this Directive may be necessary from time to time to take account of the future development of the assurance industry;

Whereas the Commission will make such adjustments as and when necessary, after consulting the Insurance Committee set up by Directive 91/675/EEC,[3] in the exercise of the implementing powers conferred on it by the Treaty;

30. Whereas it is necessary to adopt specific provisions intended to ensure smooth transition from the legal arrangements in existence when this Directive becomes applicable to those that it introduces;

Whereas care should be taken in such provisions not to place an additional workload on Member States' competent authorities;

31. Whereas, pursuant to Article 8c of the Treaty, account should be taken of the extent of the effort which must be made by certain economies at different stages of development;

Whereas, therefore, transitional arrangements should be adopted for the gradual application of this Directive by certain Member States,

Note
[3]OJ No. L374, 31.12.1991, p. 32.

HAS ADOPTED THIS DIRECTIVE:*

Note
*In order to avoid unnecessary repetition throughout this Directive, where Articles have been replaced in previous Directives, the text is removed from this Directive.

TITLE I   DEFINITIONS AND SCOPE

Article 1

For the purposes of this Directive:

(a) 'assurance undertaking' shall mean an undertaking which has received official authorisation in accordance with Article 6 of Directive 79/267/EEC;

(b) 'branch' shall mean an agency or branch of an assurance undertaking, having regard to Article 3 of Directive 90/619/EEC;

(c) 'commitment' shall mean a commitment represented by one of the kinds of insurance or operations referred to in Article 1 of Directive 79/267/EEC;

(d) 'home Member State' shall mean the Member State in which the head office of the assurance undertaking covering the commitment is situated;

(e) 'Member State of the branch' shall mean the Member State in which the branch covering the commitment is situated;

(f) 'Member State of the provision of services' shall mean the Member State of the commitment, as defined in Article 2(e) of Directive 90/619/EEC, if the commitment is covered by an assurance undertaking or a branch situated in another Member State;

(g) 'control' shall mean the relationship between a parent undertaking and a subsidiary, as defined in Article 1 of Directive 83/349/EEC,[1] or a similar relationship between any natural or legal person and an undertaking;

(h) 'qualifying holding' shall mean a direct or indirect holding in an undertaking which represents 10% or more of the capital or of the voting rights or which makes it possible to exercise a significant influence over the management of the undertaking in which a holding subsists.

For the purposes of this definition, in the context of Articles 7 and 14 and of the other levels of holding referred to in Article 14, the voting rights referred to in Article 7 of Directive 88/627/EEC[2] shall be taken into consideration;

(i) 'parent undertaking' shall mean a parent undertaking as defined in Articles 1 and 2 of Directive 83/349/EEC;

(j) 'subsidiary' shall mean a subsidiary undertaking as defined in Articles 1 and 2 of Directive 83/349/EEC; any subsidiary of a subsidiary undertaking shall also be regarded as a subsidiary of the undertaking which is those undertakings' ultimate parent undertaking;

(k) 'regulated market' shall mean a financial market regarded by an undertaking's home Member State as a regulated market pending the adoption of a definition in a Directive on investment services and characterised by:

— regular operation, and

— the fact that regulations issued or approved by the appropriate authorities define the conditions for the operation of the market, the conditions for access to the market and, where Council Directive 79/279/EEC of 5 March

Note

[1] Seventh Council Directive 83/349/EEC of 13 June 1983 based on Article 54 (3)(g) of the Treaty on consolidated accounts [OJ No. L193, 18.7.1983, p. 1]. Directive as last amended by Directive 90/605/EEC [OJ No. L317, 16.11.1990, p. 60].

[2] Council Directive 88/627/EEC of 12 December 1988 on the information to be published when a major holding in a listed company is acquired or disposed of [OJ No. L348, 17.12.1988, p. 62].

1979 coordinating the conditions for the admission of securities to official stock-exchange listing[1] applies, the conditions for admission to listing imposed in that Directive or, where that Directive does not apply, the conditions to be satisfied by a financial instrument in order to be effectively dealt in on the market.

For the purposes of this Directive, a regulated market may be situated in a Member State or in a third country. In the latter event, the market must be recognised by the undertaking's home Member State and meet comparable requirements. Any financial instruments dealt in must be of a quality comparable to that of the instruments dealt in on the regulated market or markets of the Member State in question;

(1)   'competent authorities' shall mean the national authorities which are empowered by law or regulation to supervise assurance undertakings.

(m)   'close links' shall mean a situation in which two or more natural or legal persons are linked by:

(a)   Participation, which shall mean the ownership, direct or by way of control of 20% or more of the voting rights or capital of an undertaking; or

(b)   control, which shall mean the relationship between a parent undertaking and a subsidiary, in all the cases referred to in Article 1(1) and (2) of Directive 83/349/EEC,[2] or a similar relationship between any natural or legal person and an undertaking; any subsidiary undertaking of a subsidiary undertaking shall also be considered a subsidiary of the parent undertaking which is at the head of those undertakings. A situation in which two or more natural or legal persons are permanently linked to one and the same person by a control relationship shall also be regarded as constituting a close link between such persons.

Notes
[1]OJ No. L66, 13.3.1979, p. 21. Directive as last amended by Directive 82/148/EEC [OJ No. L62, 5.3.1982, p. 22].
[2]OJ No. L193, 18.7.1983, p. 1. Directive as last amended by Directive 90/605/EEC [OJ No. L317, 16.11.1990, p. 60].

Article 2
1.   This Directive shall apply to the commitments and undertakings referred to in Article 1 of Directive 79/267/EEC.

2.   In Article 1(2) of Directive 79/267/EEC the words 'and are authorised in the country concerned' shall be deleted.

3.   This Directive shall apply neither to classes of insurance or operations nor to undertakings or institutions to which Directive 79/267/EEC does not apply, nor shall it apply to the bodies referred to in Article 4 of that Directive.

TITLE II   THE TAKING-UP OF THE BUSINESS OF LIFE ASSURANCE

Article 3
Article 6 of Directive 79/267/EEC shall be replaced by the following:

Article 4
Article 7 of Directive 79/267/EEC shall be replaced by the following:

Article 5
Article 8 of Directive 79/267/EEC shall be replaced by the following:

Article 6
Article 9 of Directive 79/267/EEC shall be replaced by the following:

Article 7
The competent authorities of the home Member State shall not grant an undertaking authorisation to take up the business of assurance before they have been informed of the identities of the shareholders or members, direct or indirect, whether natural or legal persons, who have qualifying holdings in that undertaking and of the amounts of those holdings. The same authorities shall refuse authorisation if, taking into account the need to ensure the sound and prudent management of an assurance undertaking, they are not satisfied as to the qualifications of the shareholders or members.

TITLE III   HARMONIZATION OF CONDITIONS GOVERNING PURSUIT OF BUSINESS

CHAPTER 1

Article 8
Article 15 of Directive 79/267/EEC shall be replaced by the following:

Article 9
Article 16 of Directive 79/267/EEC shall be replaced by the following:

Article 10
Article 23(2) and (3) of Directive 79/267/EEC shall be replaced by the following:

Article 11
1.   Article 6(2) to (7) of Directive 90/619/EEC shall be deleted.

2.   Under the conditions laid down by national law, each Member State shall authorise assurance undertakings with head offices within its territory to transfer all or part of their portfolios of contracts, concluded under either the right of establishment or the freedom to provide services, to an accepting office established within the Community, if the competent authorities of the home Member State of the accepting office certify that after taking the transfer into account the latter possesses the necessary solvency margin.

3.   Where a branch proposes to transfer all or part of its portfolio of contracts, concluded under either the right of establishment or the freedom to provide services, the Member State of the branch shall be consulted.

4.   In the circumstances referred to in paragraph 2 and 3, the authorities of the home Member State of the transferring undertaking shall authorise the transfer after obtaining the agreement of the competent authorities of the Member States of the commitment.

5.   The competent authorities of the Member States consulted shall give their opinion or consent to the competent authorities of the home Member State of the transferring assurance undertaking within three months of receiving a request; the absence of any response within that period from the authorities consulted shall be considered equivalent to a favourable opinion or tacit consent.

6.   A transfer authorised in accordance with this Article shall be published as laid down by national law in the Member State of the commitment. Such transfers shall automatically be valid against policy-holders, the assured

persons and any other person having rights or obligations arising out of the contracts transferred. This provision shall not affect the Member States' rights to give policy-holders the option of cancelling contracts within a fixed period after a transfer.

Article 12

1. Article 24 of Directive 79/267/EEC shall be replaced by the following:

Article 13

Article 26 of Directive 79/267/EEC shall be replaced by the following:

Article 14

1. Member States shall require any natural or legal person who proposes to acquire, directly or indirectly, a qualifying holding in an assurance undertaking first to inform the competent authorities of the home Member State, indicating the size of the intended holding. Such a person must likewise inform the competent authorities of the home Member State if he proposes to increase his qualifying holding so that the proportion of the voting rights or of the capital held by him would reach or exceed 20, 33 or 50% or so that the assurance undertaking would become his subsidiary.

The competent authorities of the home Member State shall have a maximum of three months from the date of the notification provided for in the first subparagraph to oppose such a plan if, in view of the need to ensure sound and prudent management of the assurance undertaking, they are not satisfied as to the qualifications of the person referred to in the first subparagraph. If they do not oppose the plan in question they may fix a maximum period for its implementation.

2. Member States shall require any natural or legal person who proposes to dispose, directly or indirectly, of a qualifying holding in an assurance undertaking first to inform the competent authorities of the home Member State, indicating the size of his intended holding. Such a person must likewise inform the competent authorities if he proposes to reduce his qualifying holding so that the proportion of the voting rights or of the capital held by him would fall below 20, 33 or 50% or so that the assurance undertaking would cease to be his subsidiary.

3. On becoming aware of them, assurance undertakings shall inform the competent authorities of their home Member States of any acquisitions or disposals of holdings in their capital that cause holdings to exceed or fall below one of the thresholds referred to in paragraphs 1 and 2. They shall also, at least once a year, inform them of the names of shareholders and members possessing qualifying holdings and the sizes of such holdings as shown, for example, by the information received at the annual general meetings of shareholders and members or as a result of compliance with the regulations relating to companies listed on stock exchanges.

4. Member States shall require that, if the influence exercised by the persons referred to in paragraph 1 is likely to operate to the detriment of the prudent and sound management of the assurance undertaking, the competent authorities of the home Member State shall take appropriate measures to put an end to that situation. Such measures may consist, for example, in injunctions, sanctions against directors and managers, or the suspension of the exercise of the voting rights attaching to the shares held by the shareholders or members in question.

Similar measures shall apply to natural or legal persons failing to comply with the obligation to provide prior information, as laid down in paragraph 1. If a holding is acquired despite the opposition of the competent authorities, the Member States shall, regardless of any other sanctions to be adopted, provide either for exercise of the corresponding voting rights to be suspended, or for the nullity of votes cast or for the possibility of their annulment.

Article 15

1. The Member States shall provide that all persons working or who have worked for the competent authorities, as well as auditors or experts acting on behalf of the competent authorities, shall be bound by the obligation of professional secrecy. This means that no confidential information which they may receive in the course of their duties may be divulged to any person or authority whatsoever, except in summary or aggregate form, such that individual assurance undertakings cannot be identified, without prejudice to cases covered by criminal law.

Nevertheless, where an assurance undertaking has been declared bankrupt or is being compulsorily wound up, confidential information which does not concern third parties involved in attempts to rescue that undertaking may be divulged in civil or commercial proceedings.

2. Paragraph 1 shall not prevent the competent authorities of the different Member States from exchanging information in accordance with the directives applicable to assurance undertakings. That information shall be subject to the conditions of professional secrecy indicated in paragraph 1.

3. Member States may conclude cooperation agreements, providing for exchanges of information, with the competent authorities of third countries only if the information disclosed is subject to guarantees of professional secrecy at least equivalent to those referred to in this Article.

4. Competent authorities receiving confidential information under paragraphs 1 or 2 may use it only in the course of their duties:

— to check that the conditions governing the taking-up of the business of assurance are met and to facilitate monitoring of the conduct of such business, especially with regard to the monitoring of technical provisions, solvency margins, administrative and accounting procedures and internal control mechanisms, or

— to impose sanctions, or

— in administrative appeals against decisions of the competent authority, or

— in court proceedings initiated pursuant to Article 50 or under special provisions provided for in the directives adopted in the field of assurance undertakings.

5. Paragraphs 1 and 4 shall not preclude the exchange of information within a Member State, where there are two or more competent authorities in the same Member State, or, between Member States, between competent authorities and:

— authorities responsible for the official supervision of credit institutions and other financial organisations and the authorities responsible for the supervision of financial markets,

— bodies involved in the liquidation and bankruptcy of assurance undertakings and in other similar procedures, and

—persons responsible for carrying out statutory audits of the accounts of assurance undertakings and other financial institutions, in the discharge of their supervisory functions, and the disclosure, to bodies which administer (compulsory) winding-up proceedings or guarantee funds, of information necessary to the performance of their duties. The information received by these authorities, bodies and persons shall be subject to the obligation of professional secrecy laid down in paragraph 1.

5a.   Notwithstanding paragraphs 1 to 4, Member States may authorise exchanges of information between the competent authorities and:

—the authorities responsible for overseeing the bodies involved in the liquidation and bankruptcy of financial undertakings and other similar procedures, or

—the authorities responsible for overseeing the persons charged with carrying out statutory audits of the accounts of insurance undertakings, credit institutions, investment firms and other financial institutions, or

—independent actuaries of insurance undertakings carrying out legal supervision of those undertakings and the bodies responsible for overseeing such actuaries. Member States which have recourse to the option provided for in the first subparagraph shall require at least that the following conditions are met:

—this information shall be for the purpose of carrying out the overseeing or legal supervision referred to in the first subparagraph,

—information received in this context will be subject to the conditions of professional secrecy imposed in paragraph 1,

—where the information originates in another Member State, it may not be disclosed without the express agreement of the competent authorities which have disclosed it and, where appropriate, solely for the purposes for which those authorities gave their agreement. Member States shall communicate to the Commission and to the other Member States the names of the authorities, person and bodies which may receive information pursuant to this paragraph.

5b.   Notwithstanding paragraphs 1 to 4, Member States may, with the aim of strengthening the stability, including integrity, of the financial system, authorise the exchange of information between the competent authorities and the authorities or bodies responsible under the law for the detection and investigation of breaches of company law.

Member States which have recourse to the option provided for in the first subparagraph shall require at least that the following conditions are met:

—the information shall be for the purpose of performing the task referred to in the first subparagraph,

—information received in this context shall be subject to the conditions of professional secrecy imposed in paragraph 1,

—where the information originates in another Member State, it may not be disclosed without the express agreement of the competent authorities which have disclosed it and, where appropriate, solely for the purposes for which those authorities gave their agreement.

Where, in a Member State, the authorities or bodies referred to in the first subparagraph perform their task of detection or investigation with the aid, in view of their specific competence, of persons appointed for that purpose and not employed in the public sector, the possibility of exchanging information provided for in the first subparagraph may be extended to such persons under the conditions stipulated in the second subparagraph. In order to implement the final indent of the second subparagraph, the authorities or bodies referred to in the first subparagraph shall communicate to the competent authorities which have disclosed the information, the names and precise responsibilities of the persons to whom it is to be sent. Member States shall communicate to the Commission and to the other Member States the names of the authorities or bodies which may receive information pursuant to this paragraph.

Before 31 December 2000, the Commission shall draw up a report on the application of the provisions of this paragraph.

5c. Member States may authorise the competent authorities to transmit:

— to central banks and other bodies with a similar function in their capacity as monetary authorities,

— where appropriate, to other public authorities responsible for overseeing payment systems, information intended for the performance of their task and may authorise such authorities or bodies to communicate to the competent authorities such information as they may need for the purposes of paragraph 4. Information received in this context shall be subject to the conditions of professional secrecy imposed in this Article.

6. In addition, notwithstanding paragraphs 1 and 4, Member States may, under provisions laid down by law, authorise the disclosure of certain information to other departments of their central government administrations responsible for legislation on the supervision of credit institutions, financial institutions, investment services and assurance undertakings and to inspectors acting on behalf of those departments.

However, such disclosures may be made only where necessary for reasons of prudential control.

However, Member States shall provide that information received under paragraphs 2 and 5 and that obtained by means of the on-the-spot verification referred to in Article 16 of Directive 79/267/EEC may never be disclosed in the cases referred to in this paragraph except with the express consent of the competent authorities which disclosed the information or of the competent authorities of the Member State in which on-the-spot verification was carried out.

Article 15a

1. Member States shall provide at least that:

(a) any person authorised within the meaning of Directive 84/253/EEC,[1] performing in a financial undertaking the task described in Article 51 of Directive 78/660/EEC,[2] Article 37 of Directive 83/349/EEC or Article 31 of Directive 85/611/EEC or any other statutory task, shall have a duty to report promptly to the competent authorities any fact or decision concerning that undertaking of which he has become aware while carrying out that task which is liable to:

— constitute a material breach of the laws, regulations or administrative provisions which lay down the conditions governing authorisation or which specifically govern pursuit of the activities of financial undertakings, or

Notes
[1] OJ No. L126, 12.5.1984, p. 20.
[2] OJ No. L222, 14.8.1978, p. 11. Directive as last amended by Directive 90/605/EEC [OJ No. L317, 16.11.1990, p. 60].

— affect the continuous functioning of the financial undertaking, or

— lead to refusal to certify the accounts or to the expression of reservations;

(b) that person shall likewise have a duty to report any facts and decisions of which he becomes aware in the course of carrying out a task as described in (a) in an undertaking having close links resulting from a control relationship with the financial undertaking within which he is carrying out the abovementioned task.

2. The disclosure in good faith to the competent authorities, by persons authorised within the meaning of Directive 84/253/EEC, of any fact or decision referred to in paragraph 1 shall not constitute a breach of any restriction on disclosure of information imposed by contract or by any legislative, regulatory or administrative provision and shall not involve such persons in liability of any kind.

Article 16
Article 13 of Directive 79/267/EEC shall be replaced by the following:

Article 17
Article 35 of Directive 79/267/EEC and Article 18 of Directive 90/619/EEC shall be deleted.

CHAPTER 2

Article 18
Article 17 of Directive 79/267/EEC shall be replaced by the following:

Article 19
Premiums for new business shall be sufficient, on reasonable actuarial assumptions, to enable assurance undertakings to meet all their commitments and, in particular, to establish adequate technical provisions. For this purpose, all aspects of the financial situation of an assurance undertaking may be taken into account, without the input from resources other than premiums and income earned thereon being systematic and permanent in such a way that it may jeopardise the undertaking's solvency in the long term.

Article 20
The assets covering the technical provisions shall take account of the type of business carried on by an undertaking in such a way as to secure the safety, yield and marketability of its investments, which the undertaking shall ensure are diversified and adequately spread.

Article 21
1. The home Member State may not authorise assurance undertakings to cover their technical provisions with any but the following categories of assets:

A. Investments

(a) debt securities, bonds and other money- and capital-market instruments;

(b) loans;

(c) shares and other variable-yield participations;

(d) units in undertakings for collective investment in transferable securities and other investment funds;

(e) land, buildings and immovable property rights;

B. Debts and claims

    (f)   debts owed by reassurers, including reassurers' shares of technical provisions;

    (g)   deposits with and debts owed by ceding undertakings;

    (h)   debts owed by policy-holders and intermediaries arising out of direct and reassurance operations;

    (i)   advances against policies;

    (j)   tax recoveries;

    (k)   claims against guarantee funds;

C. Others

    (l)   tangible fixed assets, other than land and buildings, valued on the basis of prudent amortisation;

    (m) cash at bank and in hand, deposits with credit institutions and any other body authorised to receive deposits;

    (n)   deferred acquisition costs;

    (o)   accrued interest and rent, other accrued income and prepayments;

    (p)   reversionary interests.

In the case of the association of underwriters known as Lloyd's, asset categories shall also include guarantees and letters of credit issued by credit institutions within the meaning of Directive 77/780/EEC[1] or by assurance undertakings, together with verifiable sums arising out of life assurance policies, to the extent that they represent funds belonging to members.

Note
[1] First Council Directive 77/780/EEC of 12 December 1977 on the coordination of the laws, regulations and administrative provisions relating to the taking up and pursuit of the business of credit institutions [OJ No. L322, 17.12.1977, p. 30]. Directive as last amended by Directive 89/646/EEC [OJ No. L386, 30.12.1989, p. 1].

The inclusion of any asset or category of assets listed in the first subparagraph shall not mean that all these assets should automatically be accepted as cover for technical provisions. The home Member State shall lay down more detailed rules fixing the conditions for the use of acceptable assets; in this connection, it may require valuable security or guarantees, particularly in the case of debts owed by reassurers.

In determining and applying the rules which it lays down, the home Member State shall, in particular, ensure that the following principles are complied with:

    (i)   assets covering technical provisions shall be valued net of any debts arising out of their acquisition;

    (ii)   all assets must be valued on a prudent basis, allowing for the risk of any amounts not being realisable. In particular, tangible fixed assets other than land and buildings may be accepted as cover for technical provisions only if they are valued on the basis of prudent amortisation;

    (iii) loans, whether to undertakings, to a State or international organization, to local or regional authorities or to natural persons, may be accepted as cover for technical provisions only if there are sufficient guarantees as to their security, whether these are based on the status of the borrower, mortgages, bank guarantees or guarantees granted by assurance undertakings or other forms of security;

    (iv) derivative instruments such as options, futures and swaps in connection with assets covering technical provisions may be used in so far as they contribute to a reduction of investment risks or facilitate efficient portfolio management. They must be valued on a prudent basis and may be taken into account in the valuation of the underlying assets;

(v) transferable securities which are not dealt in on a regulated market may be accepted as cover for technical provisions only if they can be realised in the short term or if they are holdings in credit institutions, in assurance undertakings, within the limits permitted by Article 8 of Directive 79/267/ EEC, or in investment undertakings established in a Member State;

(vi) debts owed by and claims against a third party may be accepted as cover for the technical provisions only after deduction of all amounts owed to the same third party;

(vii) the value of any debts and claims accepted as cover for technical provisions must be calculated on a prudent basis, with due allowance for the risk of any amounts not being realisable. In particular, debts owed by policy-holders and intermediaries arising out of assurance and reassurance operations may be accepted only in so far as they have been outstanding for not more than three months;

(viii) where the assets held include an investment in a subsidiary undertaking which manages all or part of the assurance undertaking's investments on its behalf, the home Member State must, when applying the rules and principles laid down in this Article, take into account the underlying assets held by the subsidiary undertaking; the home Member State may treat the assets of other subsidiaries in the same way;

(ix) deferred acquisition costs may be accepted as cover for technical provisions only to the extent that this is consistent with the calculation of the mathematical provisions.

2. Notwithstanding paragraph 1, in exceptional circumstances and at an assurance undertaking's request, the home Member State may, temporarily and under a properly reasoned decision, accept other categories of assets as cover for technical provisions, subject to Article 20.

Article 22

1. As regards the assets covering technical provisions, the home Member State shall require every assurance undertaking to invest no more than:

(a) 10% of its total gross technical provisions in any one piece of land or building, or a number of pieces of land or buildings close enough to each other to be considered effectively as one investment;

(b) 5% of its total gross technical provisions in shares and other negotiable securities treated as shares, bonds, debt securities and other money- and capital-market instruments from the same undertaking, or in loans granted to the same borrower, taken together, the loans being loans other than those granted to a State, regional or local authority or to an international organization of which one or more Member States are members. This limit may be raised to 10% if an undertaking invests not more than 40% of its gross technical provisions in the loans or securities of issuing bodies and borrowers in each of which it invests more than 5% of its assets;

(c) 5% of its total gross technical provisions in unsecured loans, including 1% for any single unsecured loan, other than loans granted to credit institutions, assurance undertakings — in so far as Article 8 of Directive 79/267/EEC allows it — and investment undertakings established in a Member

State. The limits may be raised to 8 and 2% respectively by a decision taken on a case-by-case basis by the competent authority of the home Member State;

(d)   3% of its total gross technical provisions in the form of cash in hand;

(e)   10% of its total gross technical provisions in shares, other securities treated as shares and debt securities which are not dealt in on a regulated market.

2.   The absence of a limit in paragraph 1 on investment in any particular category does not imply that assets in that category should be accepted as cover for technical provisions without limit. The home Member State shall lay down more detailed rules fixing the conditions for the use of acceptable assets. In particular it shall ensure, in the determination and the application of those rules, that the following principles are complied with:

(i)   assets covering technical provisions must be diversified and spread in such a way as to ensure that there is no excessive reliance on any particular category of asset, investment market or investment;

(ii)   investment in particular types of asset which show high levels of risk, whether because of the nature of the asset or the quality of the issuer, must be restricted to prudent levels;

(iii)   limitations on particular categories of asset must take account of the treatment of reassurance in the calculation of technical provisions;

(iv)   where the assets held include an investment in a subsidiary undertaking which manages all or part of the assurance undertaking's investments on its behalf, the home Member State must, when applying the rules and principles laid down in this Article, take into account the underlying assets held by the subsidiary undertaking; the home Member State may treat the assets of other subsidiaries in the same way;

(v)   the percentage of assets covering technical provisions which are the subject of non-liquid investments must be kept to a prudent level;

(vi)   where the assets held include loans to or debt securities issued by certain credit institutions, the home Member State may, when applying the rules and principles contained in this Article, take into account the underlying assets held by such credit institutions. This treatment may be applied only where the credit institution has its head office in a Member State, is entirely owned by that Member State and/or that State's local authorities and its business, according to its memorandum and articles of association, consists of extending, through its intermediaries, loans to, or guaranteed by, States or local authorities or of loans to bodies closely linked to the State or to local authorities.

3.   In the context of the detailed rules laying down the conditions for the use of acceptable assets, the Member State shall give more limitative treatment to:

— any loan unaccompanied by a bank guarantee, a guarantee issued by an assurance undertaking, a mortgage or any other form of security, as compared with loans accompanied by such collateral,

— UCITS not coordinated within the meaning of Directive 85/611/EEC[1] and other investment funds, as compared with UCITS coordinated within the meaning of that Directive,

Note

[1]Council Directive 85/611/EEC of 20 December 1985 on the coordination of laws, regulations and administrative provisions relating to undertakings for collective investment in transferable securities (UCITS) [OJ No. L375, 31.12.1985, p. 3]. Directive as amended by Directive 88/220/EEC [OJ No. L100, 19.4.1988, p. 31].

— securities which are not dealt in on a regulated market, as compared with those which are,

— bonds, debt securities and other money- and capital-market instruments not issued by States, local or regional authorities or undertakings belonging to Zone A as defined in Directive 89/647/EEC,[2] or the issuers of which are international organisations not numbering at least one Community Member State among their members, as compared with the same financial instruments issued by such bodies.

4. Member States may raise the limit laid down in paragraph 1(b) to 40% in the case of certain debt securities when these are issued by a credit institution which has its head office in a Member State and is subject by law to special official supervision designed to protect the holders of those debt securities. In particular, sums deriving from the issue of such debt securities must be invested in accordance with the law in assets which, during the whole period of validity of the debt securities, are capable of covering claims attaching to debt securities and which, in the event of failure of the issuer, would be used on a priority basis for the reimbursement of the principal and payment of the accrued interest.

5. Member States shall not require assurance undertakings to invest in particular categories of assets.

6. Notwithstanding paragraph 1, in exceptional circumstances and at the assurance undertaking's request, the home Member State may, temporarily and under a properly reasoned decision, allow exceptions to the rules laid down in paragraph 1(a) to (e), subject to Article 20.

Note
[2]Council Directive 89/647/EEC of 18 December 1989 on a solvency ratio for credit institutions [OJ No. L386, 30.12.1989, p. 14].

Article 23
1. Where the benefits provided by a contract are directly linked to the value of units in an UCITS or to the value of assets contained in an internal fund held by the insurance undertaking, usually divided into units, the technical provisions in respect of those benefits must be represented as closely as possible by those units or, in the case where units are not established, by those assets.

2. Where the benefits provided by a contract are directly linked to a share index or some other reference value other than those referred to in paragraph 1, the technical provisions in respect of those benefits must be represented as closely as possible either by the units deemed to represent the reference value or, in the case where units are not established, by assets of appropriate security and marketability which correspond as closely as possible with those on which the particular reference value is based.

3. Articles 20 and 22 shall not apply to assets held to match liabilities which are directly linked to the benefits referred to in paragraphs 1 and 2. References to the technical provisions in Article 22 shall be to the technical provisions excluding those in respect of such liabilities.

4. Where the benefits referred to in paragraph 1 and 2 include a guarantee of investment performance or some other guaranteed benefit, the corresponding additional technical provisions shall be subject to Articles 20, 21 and 22.

Article 24

1.   For the purposes of Articles 17(3) and 28 of Directive 79/267/EEC, Member States shall comply with Annex I to this Directive as regards the matching rules.

2.   This Article shall not apply to the commitments referred to in Article 23 of this Directive.

Article 25

Article 18, second subparagraph, point 1 of Directive 79/267/EEC shall be replaced by the following:

Article 26

No more than three years after the date of application of this Directive, the Commission shall submit a report to the Insurance Committee on the need for further harmonization of the solvency margin.

Article 27

Article 21 of Directive 79/267/EEC shall be replaced by the following:

CHAPTER 3

Article 28

The Member State of the commitment shall not prevent a policy-holder from concluding a contract with an assurance undertaking authorised under the conditions of Article 6 of Directive 79/267/EEC, as long as that does not conflict with legal provisions protecting the general good in the Member State of the commitment.

Article 29

Member States shall not adopt provisions requiring the prior approval or systematic notification of general and special policy conditions, scales of premiums, technical bases used in particular for calculating scales of premiums and technical provisions or forms and other printed documents which an assurance undertaking intends to use in its dealings with policy-holders.

Notwithstanding the first subparagraph, for the sole purpose of verifying compliance with national provisions concerning actuarial principles, the Member State of origin may require systematic communication of the technical bases used in particular for calculating scales of premiums and technical provisions, without that requirement constituting a prior condition for an undertaking to carry on its business.

Not later than five years after the date of application of this Directive, the Commission shall submit a report to the Council on the implementation of those provisions.

Article 30

1.   In the first subparagraph of Article 15(1) of Directive 90/619/EEC the words 'in one of the cases referred to in Title III' shall be deleted.

2.   Article 15(2) of Directive 90/619/EEC shall be replaced by the following:

Article 31

1.   Before the assurance contract is concluded, at least the information listed in point A of Annex II shall be communicated to the policy-holder.

2.   The policy-holder shall be kept informed throughout the term of the contract of any change concerning the information listed in point B of Annex II.

3.   The Member State of the commitment may require assurance undertakings to furnish information in addition to that listed in Annex II only if it is necessary for a proper understanding by the policy-holder of the essential elements of the commitment.

4.   The detailed rules for implementing this Article and Annex II shall be laid down by the Member State of the commitment.

TITLE IV   PROVISIONS RELATING TO RIGHT OF ESTABLISHMENT AND FREEDOM TO PROVIDE SERVICES

Article 32
Article 10 of Directive 79/267/EEC shall be replaced by the following:

Article 33
Article 11 of Directive 79/267/EEC shall be deleted.

Article 34
Article 11 of Directive 90/619/EEC shall be replaced by the following:

Article 35
Article 14 of Directive 90/619/EEC shall be replaced by the following:

Article 36
Article 17 of Directive 90/619/EEC shall be replaced by the following:

Article 37
Articles 10, 12, 13, 16, 22 and 24 of Directive 90/619/EEC shall be deleted.

Article 38
The competent authorities of the Member State of the branch or the Member State of the provision of services may require that the information which they are authorised under this Directive to request with regard to the business of assurance undertakings operating in the territory of that State shall be supplied to them in the official language or languages of that State.

Article 39
1.   Article 19 of Directive 90/619/EEC shall be deleted.

2.   The Member State of the branch or of provision of services shall not lay down provisions requiring the prior approval or systematic notification of general and special policy conditions, scales of premiums, technical bases used in particular for calculating scales of premiums and technical provisions, forms and other printed documents which an undertaking intends to use in its dealings with policy-holders. For the purpose of verifying compliance with national provisions concerning assurance contracts, it may require an undertaking that proposes to carry on assurance business within its territory, under the right of establishment or the freedom to provide services, to effect only non-systematic notification of those policy conditions and other printed documents without that requirement constituting a prior condition for an undertaking to carry on its business.

Article 40
1.   Article 20 of Directive 90/619/EEC shall be deleted.

2. Any undertaking carrying on business under the right of establishment or the freedom to provide services shall submit to the competent authorities of the Member State of the branch and/or of the Member State of the provision of services all documents requested of it for the purposes of this Article in so far as undertakings the head office of which is in those Member States are also obliged to do so.

3. If the competent authorities of a Member State establish that an undertaking with a branch or carrying on business under the freedom to provide services in its territory is not complying with the legal provisions applicable to it in that State, they shall require the undertaking concerned to remedy that irregular situation.

4. If the undertaking in question fails to take the necessary action, the competent authorities of the Member State concerned shall inform the competent authorities of the home Member State accordingly. The latter authorities shall, at the earliest opportunity, take all appropriate measures to ensure that the undertaking concerned remedies that irregular situation. The nature of those measures shall be communicated to the competent authorities of the Member State concerned.

5. If, despite the measures taken by the home Member State or because those measures prove inadequate or are lacking in that State, the undertaking persists in violating the legal provisions in force in the Member State concerned, the latter may, after informing the competent authorities of the home Member State, take appropriate measures to prevent or penalise further irregularities, including, in so far as is strictly necessary, preventing that undertaking from continuing to conclude new assurance contracts within its territory. Member States shall ensure that in their territories it is possible to serve the legal documents necessary for such measures on assurance undertakings.

6. Paragraphs 3, 4 and 5 shall not affect the emergency power of the Member States concerned to take appropriate measures to prevent or penalise irregularities committed within their territories. This shall include the possibility of preventing assurance undertakings from continuing to conclude new assurance contracts within their territories.

7. Paragraph 3, 4 and 5 shall not affect the power of the Member States to penalise infringements within their territories.

8. If an undertaking which has committed an infringement has an establishment or possesses property in the Member State concerned, the competent authorities of the latter may, in accordance with national law, apply the administrative penalties prescribed for that infringement by way of enforcement against that establishment or property.

9. Any measure adopted under paragraphs 4 to 8 involving penalties or restrictions on the conduct of assurance business must be properly reasoned and communicated to the undertaking concerned.

10. Every two years, the Commission shall submit to the Insurance Committee a report summarising the number and type of cases in which, in each Member State, authorisation has been refused pursuant to Article 10 of Directive 79/267/EEC or Article 14 of Directive 90/619/EEC as amended by this Directive or measures have been taken under paragraph 5. Member States shall cooperate with the Commission by providing it with the information required for that report.

Article 41

Nothing in this Directive shall prevent assurance undertakings with head offices in other Member States from advertising their services through all available means of communication in the Member State of the branch or Member State of the provision of services, subject to any rules governing the form and content of such advertising adopted in the interest of the general good.

Article 42

1.   Article 21 of Directive 90/619/EEC shall be deleted.

2.   Should an assurance undertaking be wound up, commitments arising out of contracts underwritten through a branch or under the freedom to provide services shall be met in the same way as those arising out of that undertaking's other assurance contracts, without distinction as to nationality as far as the lives assured and the beneficiaries are concerned.

Article 43

1.   Article 23 of Directive 90/619/EEC shall be deleted.

2.   Every assurance undertaking shall inform the competent authority of its home Member State, separately in respect of transactions carried out under the right of establishment and those carried out under the freedom to provide services, of the amount of the premiums, without deduction of reassurance, by Member State and by each of classes I to IX, as defined in the Annex to Directive 79/267/EEC.

The competent authority of the home Member State shall, within a reasonable time and on an aggregate basis forward this information to the competent authorities of each of the Member States concerned which so request.

Article 44

1.   Article 25 of Directive 90/619/EEC shall be deleted.

2.   Without prejudice to any subsequent harmonization, every assurance contract shall be subject exclusively to the indirect taxes and parafiscal charges on assurance premiums in the Member State of the commitment within the meaning of Article 2(e) of Directive 90/619/EEC and also, with regard to Spain, to the surcharges legally established in favour of the Spanish 'Consorcio de compensación de seguros' for the performance of its functions relating to the compensation of losses arising from extraordinary events occurring in that Member State. The law applicable to the contract pursuant to Article 4 of Directive 90/619/EEC shall not affect the fiscal arrangements applicable.

Pending future harmonization, each Member State shall apply to those undertakings which cover commitments situated within its territory its own national provisions for measures to ensure the collection of indirect taxes and parafiscal charges due under the first subparagraph.

TITLE V   TRANSITIONAL PROVISIONS

Article 45

Member States may allow assurance undertakings with head offices in their territories, and whose buildings and land covering their technical provisions exceed, at the time of the notification of this Directive, the percentage laid down in Article 22(1)(a) a period expiring no later than 31 December 1998 within which to comply with that provision.

Article 46

1. Article 26 of Directive 90/619/EEC shall be deleted.

2. Spain and Portugal, until 31 December 1995, and Greece, until 31 December 1998, may operate the following transitional arrangements for contracts in respect of which one of those Member States is the Member State of the commitment:

(a) by way of derogation from Article 8(3) of Directive 79/267/EEC and from Articles 29 and 39 of this Directive, the competent authorities of the Member States in question may require the communication, before use, of general and special insurance policy conditions;

(b) the amount of the technical provisions relating to such contracts shall be determined under the supervision of the Member State concerned in accordance with its own rules or, failing that, in accordance with the procedures established in that State in accordance with this Directive.

Cover of those technical provisions by equivalent and matching assets and the localisation of those assets shall be effected under the supervision of that Member State in accordance with its rules and practices adopted in accordance with this Directive.

TITLE VI   FINAL PROVISIONS

Article 47

The following technical adjustments to be made to Directives 79/267/EEC and 90/619/EEC and to this Directive shall be adopted in accordance with the procedure laid down in Directive 91/675/EEC:

— extension of the legal forms provided for in Article 8(1)(a) of Directive 79/267/EEC,

— amendments to the list set out in the Annex to Directive 79/267/EEC, or adaptation of the terminology used in that list to take account of the development of assurance markets,

— clarification of the items constituting the solvency margin listed in Article 18 of Directive 79/267/EEC to take account of the creation of new financial instruments,

— alteration of the minimum guarantee fund provided for in Article 20(2) of Directive 79/267/EEC to take account of economic and financial developments,

— amendments, to take account of the creation of new financial instruments, to the list of assets acceptable as cover for technical provisions set out in Article 21 of this Directive and to the rules on the spreading of investments laid down in Article 22 of this Directive,

— changes in the relaxations in the matching rules laid down in Annex I to this Directive, to take account of the development of new currency-hedging instruments or progress made in economic and monetary union,

— clarification of the definitions in order to ensure uniform application of Directives 79/267/EEC and 90/619/EEC and of this Directive throughout the Community,

— the technical adjustments necessary to the rules for setting the maxima applicable to interest rates, pursuant to Article 17 of Directive 79/267/EEC, as amended by this Directive, in particular to take account of progress made in economic and monetary union.

Article 48

1.   Branches which have started business, in accordance with the provisions in force in their Member State of establishment, before the entry into force of the provisions adopted in implementation of this Directive shall be presumed to have been subject to the procedure laid down in Article 10(1) to (5) of Directive 79/267/EEC. They shall be governed, from the date of that entry into force, by Articles 17, 23, 24 and 26 of Directive 79/267/EEC and by Article 40 of this Directive.

2.   Articles 11 and 14 of Directive 90/619/EEC, as amended by this Directive, shall not affect rights acquired by assurance undertakings carrying on business under the freedom to provide services before the entry into force of the provisions adopted in implementation of this Directive.

Article 49

The following Article 31a shall be inserted in Directive 79/267/EEC: Article 31a

Article 50

Member States shall ensure that decisions taken in respect of an assurance undertaking under laws, regulations and administrative provisions adopted in accordance with this Directive may be subject to the right to apply to the courts.

Article 51

1.   Member States shall adopt the laws, regulations and administrative provisions necessary for their compliance with this Directive no later than 31 December 1993 and bring them into force no later than 1 July 1994. They shall forthwith inform the Commission thereof.

When they adopt such measures, the Member States shall include references to this Directive or shall make such references when they effect official publication. The manner in which such references are to be made shall be laid down by the Member States.

2.   The Member States shall communicate to the Commission the texts of the main provisions of national law which they adopt in the field covered by this Directive.

Article 52

This Directive is addressed to the Member States.

Done at Brussels, 10 November 1992.
For the Council,
The President,
R. NEEDHAM

ANNEX I   MATCHING RULES

The currency in which the assurer's commitments are payable shall be determined in accordance with the following rules:

1.   Where the cover provided by a contract is expressed in terms of a particular currency, the assurer's commitments are considered to be payable in that currency.

2.   Member States may authorise undertakings not to cover their technical provisions, including their mathematical provisions, by matching assets if

application of the above procedures would result in the undertaking being obliged, in order to comply with the matching principle, to hold assets in a currency amounting to not more than 7% of the assets existing in other currencies.

3.   Member States may choose not to require undertakings to apply the matching principle where commitments are payable in a currency other than the currency of one of the Community Member States, if investments in that currency are regulated, if the currency is subject to transfer restrictions or if, for similar reasons, it is not suitable for covering technical provisions.

4.   Undertakings are authorised not to hold matching assets to cover an amount not exceeding 20% of their commitments in a particular currency. However, total assets in all currencies combined must be at least equal to total commitments in all currencies combined.

5.   Each Member State may provide that, whenever under the preceding procedures a commitment has to be covered by assets expressed in the currency of a Member State, this requirement shall also be considered to be satisfied when the assets are expressed in ECUs.

ANNEX II   INFORMATION FOR POLICY-HOLDERS

The following information, which is to be communicated to the policy-holder before the contract is concluded (A) or during the term of the contract (B), must be provided in a clear and accurate manner, in writing, in an official language of the Member State of the commitment.

However, such information may be in another language if the policy-holder so requests and the law of the Member State so permits or the policy-holder is free to choose the law applicable.

A. Before concluding the contract

Information about the assurance undertaking
Information about the commitment
(a)   1.   The name of the undertaking and its legal form
(a)   2.   The name of the Member State in which the head office and, where appropriate, the agency or branch concluding the contract is situated
(a)   3.   The address of the head office and, where appropriate, of the agency or branch concluding the contract
(a)   4.   Definition of each benefit and each option
(a)   5.   Term of the contract
(a)   6.   Means of terminating the contract
(a)   7.   Means of payment of premiums and duration of payments
(a)   8.   Means of calculation and distribution of bonuses
(a)   9.   Indication of surrender and paid-up values and the extent to which they are guaranteed
(a)   10.   Information on the premiums for each benefit, both main benefits and supplementary benefits, where appropriate
(a)   11.   For unit-linked policies, definition of the units to which the benefits are linked
(a)   12.   Indication of the nature of the underlying assets for unit-linked policies
(a)   13.   Arrangements for application of the cooling-off period
(a)   14.   General information on the tax arrangements applicable to the type of policy

(a)   15.   The arrangements for handling complaints concerning contracts by policy-holders, lives assured or beneficiaries under contracts including, where appropriate, the existence of a complaints body, without prejudice to the right to take legal proceedings

(a)   16.   Law applicable to the contract where the parties do not have a free choice or, where the parties are free to choose the law applicable, the law the assurer proposes to choose

B. During the term of the contract

In addition to the policy conditions, both general and special, the policy-holder must receive the following information throughout the term of the contract.

Information about the assurance undertaking
Information about the commitment

(b)   1.   Any change in the name of the undertaking, its legal form or the address of its head office and, where appropriate, of the agency or branch which concluded the contract

(b)   2.   All the information listed in points (a)(4) to (a)(12) of A in the event of a change in the policy conditions or amendment of the law applicable to the contract

(b)   3.   Every year, information on the state of bonuses

THE BRUSSELS CONVENTION OF 27 SEPTEMBER 1968 ON JURISDICTION AND THE ENFORCEMENT OF JUDGMENTS IN CIVIL AND COMMERCIAL MATTERS
[OJ 1972 L299/32]*

PREAMBLE
THE HIGH CONTRACTING PARTIES TO THE TREATY
ESTABLISHING THE EUROPEAN ECONOMIC COMMUNITY,

DESIRING to implement the provisions of Article 220 of that Treaty by virtue of which they undertook to secure the simplification of formalities governing the reciprocal recognition and enforcement of judgments of courts or tribunals; ANXIOUS to strengthen in the Community the legal protection of persons therein established; CONSIDERING that it is necessary for this purpose to determine the international jurisdiction of their courts, to facilitate recognition and to introduce an expeditious procedure for securing the enforcement of judgments, authentic instruments and court settlements (2);

Note
*This is the codified and consolidated version as appeared in OJ 1990 C189/2 (Celex number 490Y0728(01) and further amended by the accession of Austria, Finland and Sweden on 29.11.1996 as reproduced in OJ 1997 C15/1 15.1.1997. A previous consolidated version appeared in OJ 1983 C97/2, which amended the original Convention by the Convention of 9 October 1978 on the accession of the Kingdom of Denmark, Ireland and the United Kingdom of Great Britain and Northern Ireland — hereafter referred to as the 1978 Accession Convention and by the Convention of 25 October 1982 on the accession of the Hellenic Republic — hereafter referred to as the 1982 Accession Convention. The previous Legislative Decisions are: 68/927/EEC, 78/884/EEC [OJ 1978 L304/1], 82/972/EEC [OJ 1982 L388/1] and 89/535/EEC [OJ 1989 L285/1].

HAVE DECIDED to conclude this Convention and to this end have designated as their Plenipotentiaries:

HIS MAJESTY THE KING OF THE BELGIANS:
Mr Pierre HARMEL,
Minister for Foreign Affairs;

THE PRESIDENT OF THE FEDERAL REPUBLIC OF GERMANY:
Mr Willy BRANDT,
Vice-Chancellor,
Minister for Foreign Affairs;

THE PRESIDENT OF THE FRENCH REPUBLIC:
Mr Michel DEBRÉ,
Minister for Foreign Affairs;

THE PRESIDENT OF THE ITALIAN REPUBLIC:
Mr Giuseppe MEDICI,
Minister for Foreign Affairs;

HIS ROYAL HIGHNESS THE GRAND DUKE OF LUXEMBOURG:
Mr Pierre GRÉGOIRE,
Minister for Foreign Affairs;

HER MAJESTY THE QUEEN OF THE NETHERLANDS:
Mr. J. M. A. H. LUNS,
Minister for Foreign Affairs;

WHO, meeting within the Council, having exchanged their Full Powers, found in good and due form,

HAVE AGREED AS FOLLOWS:

TITLE I   SCOPE

Article 1

This Convention shall apply in civil and commercial matters whatever the nature of the court or tribunal. It shall not extend, in particular, to revenue, customs or administrative matters.

The Convention shall not apply to:

1.   the status or legal capacity of natural persons, rights in property arising out of a matrimonial relationship, wills and succession;

2.   bankruptcy, proceedings relating to the winding-up of insolvent companies or other legal persons, judicial arrangements, compositions and analogous proceedings;

3.   social security;

4.   arbitration.

Note
[1]Second sentence added by Article 3 of the 1978 Accession Convention.

TITLE II JURISDICTION
SECTION 1   GENERAL PROVISIONS

Article 2

Subject to the provisions of this Convention, persons domiciled in a Contracting State shall, whatever their nationality, be sued in the courts of that State.

Persons who are not nationals of the State in which they are domiciled shall be governed by the rules of jurisdiction applicable to nationals of that State.

Article 3
Persons domiciled in a Contracting State may be sued in the courts of another Contracting State only by virtue of the rules set out in Sections 2 to 6 of this Title. In particular the following provisions shall not be applicable as against them:

— in Belgium: Article 15 of the civil code (Code civil — Burgerlijk Wetboek) and Article 638 of the judicial code (Code judiciaire — Gerechtelijk Wetboek),

— in Denmark: Article 246 (2) and (3) of the law on civil procedure (Lov om rettens pleje),

— in the Federal Republic of Germany: Article 23 of the code of civil procedure (Zivilprozessordnung),

— in Greece, Article 40 of the code of civil procedure (Kvdikass Politikhss Dikonomiass),

— in France: Articles 14 and 15 of the civil code (Code civil),

— in Ireland: the rules which enable jurisdiction to be founded on the document instituting the proceedings having been served on the defendant during his temporary presence in Ireland,

— in Italy: Articles 2 and 4, Nos. 1 and 2 of the code of civil procedure (Codice di procedura civile),

— in Luxembourg: Articles 14 and 15 of the civil code (Code civil),

— in Austria: Article 99 of the Law on Court Jurisdiction (Jurisdiktionsnorm),

— in the Netherlands: Articles 126 (3) and 127 of the code of civil procedure (Wetboek van Burgerlijke Rechtsvordering),

— in Finland: the second, third and fourth sentences of the first paragraph of Section 1 of Chapter 10 of the Code of Judicial Procedure (oikeudenkäymiskaari/rättegångsbalken),

— in Sweden: the first sentence of the first paragraph of Section 3 of Chapter 10 of the Code of Judicial Procedure (rättegångsbalken),

— in Portugal: Article 65 (1)(c), Article 65 (2) and Article 65A (c) of the code of civil procedure (Código de Processo Civil) and Article 11 of the code of labour procedure (Código de Processo de Trabalho),

— in the United Kingdom: the rules which enable jurisdiction to be founded on:

(a)   the document instituting the proceedings having been served on the defendant during his temporary presence in the United Kingdom; or

(b)   the presence within the United Kingdom of property belonging to the defendant; or

(c)   the seizure by the plaintiff of property situated in the United Kingdom.

Article 4
If the defendant is not domiciled in a Contracting State, the jurisdiction of the courts of each Contracting State shall, subject to the provisions of Article 16, be determined by the law of that State. As against such a defendant, any person domiciled in a Contracting State may, whatever his nationality, avail himself in that State of the rules of jurisdiction there in force, and in particular those

specified in the second paragraph of Article 3, in the same way as the nationals of that State.

SECTION 2   SPECIAL JURISDICTION

Article 5

A person domiciled in a Contracting State may, in another Contracting State, be sued:

1.   in matters relating to a contract, in the courts for the place of performance of the obligation in question; in matters relating to individual contracts of employment, this place is that where the employee habitually carries out his work, or if the employee does not habitually carry out his work in any one country, the employer may also be sued in the courts for the place where the business which engaged the employee was or is now situated;

2.   in matters relating to maintenance, in the courts for the place where the maintenance creditor is domiciled or habitually resident or, if the matter is ancillary to proceedings concerning the status of a person, in the court which, according to its own law, has jurisdiction to entertain those proceedings, unless that jurisdiction is based solely on the nationality of one of the parties;

3.   in matters relating to tort, delict or quasi-delict, in the courts for the place where the harmful event occurred;

4.   as regards a civil claim for damages or restitution which is based on an act giving rise to criminal proceedings, in the court seised of those proceedings, to the extent that that court has jurisdiction under its own law to entertain civil proceedings;

5.   as regards a dispute arising out of the operations of a branch, agency or other establishment, in the courts for the place in which the branch, agency or other establishment is situated;

6.   as settlor, trustee or beneficiary of a trust created by the operation of a statute, or by a written instrument, or created orally and evidenced in writing, in the courts of the Contracting State in which the trust is domiciled;

7.   as regards a dispute concerning the payment of remuneration claimed in respect of the salvage of a cargo or freight, in the court under the authority of which the cargo or freight in question:

    (a)   has been arrested to secure such payment, or

    (b)   could have been so arrested, but bail or other security has been given;

provided that this provision shall apply only if it is claimed that the defendant has an interest in the cargo or freight or had such an interest at the time of salvage.

Article 6

A person domiciled in a Contracting State may also be sued:

1.   where he is one of a number of defendants, in the courts for the place where any one of them is domiciled;

2.   as a third party in an action on a warranty or guarantee or in any other third party proceedings, in the court seised of the original proceedings, unless these were instituted solely with the object of removing him from the jurisdiction of the court which would be competent in his case;

3.   on a counter-claim arising from the same contract or facts on which the original claim was based, in the court in which the original claim is pending;

4.   in matters relating to a contract, if the action may be combined with an action against the same defendant in matters relating to rights in rem in

immovable property, in the court of the Contracting State in which the property is situated.

Article 6a
Where by virtue of this Convention a court of a Contracting State has jurisdiction in actions relating to liability from the use or operation of a ship, that court, or any other court substituted for this purpose by the internal law of that State, shall also have jurisdiction over claims for limitation of such liability.

SECTION 3   JURISDICTION IN MATTERS RELATING TO INSURANCE

Article 7
In matters relating to insurance, jurisdiction shall be determined by this Section, without prejudice to the provisions of Articles 4 and 5 point 5.

Article 8
An insurer domiciled in a Contracting State may be sued:
1. in the courts of the State where he is domiciled, or
2. in another Contracting State, in the courts for the place where the policy-holder is domiciled, or
3. if he is a co-insurer, in the courts of a Contracting State in which proceedings are brought against the leading insurer.

An insurer who is not domiciled in a Contracting State but has a branch, agency or other establishment in one of the Contracting States shall, in disputes arising out of the operations of the branch, agency or establishment, be deemed to be domiciled in that State.

Article 9
In respect of liability insurance or insurance of immovable property, the insurer may in addition be sued in the courts for the place where the harmful event occurred. The same applies if movable and immovable property are covered by the same insurance policy and both are adversely affected by the same contingency.

Article 10
In respect of liability insurance, the insurer may also, if the law of the court permits it, be joined in proceedings which the injured party had brought against the insured. The provisions of Articles 7, 8 and 9 shall apply to actions brought by the injured party directly against the insurer, where such direct actions are permitted. If the law governing such direct actions provides that the policy-holder or the insured may be joined as a party to the action, the same court shall have jurisdiction over them.

Article 11
Without prejudice to the provisions of the third paragraph of Article 10, an insurer may bring proceedings only in the courts of the Contracting State in which the defendant is domiciled, irrespective of whether he is the policy-holder, the insured or a beneficiary. The provisions of this Section shall not affect the right to bring a counterclaim in the court in which, in accordance with this Section, the original claim is pending.

Article 12
The provisions of this Section may be departed from only by an agreement on jurisdiction:

1. which is entered into after the dispute has arisen, or
2. which allows the policy-holder, the insured or a beneficiary to bring proceedings in courts other than those indicated in this Section, or
3. which is concluded between a policy-holder and an insurer, both of whom are domiciled in the same Contracting State, and which has the effect of conferring jurisdiction on the courts of that State even if the harmful event were to occur abroad, provided that such an agreement is not contrary to the law of that State, or
4. which is concluded with a policy-holder who is not domiciled in a Contracting State, except in so far as the insurance is compulsory or relates to immovable property in a Contracting State, or
5. which relates to a contract of insurance in so far as it covers one or more of the risks set out in Article 12a.

Article 12a
The following are the risks referred to in point 5 of Article 12:
1. Any loss of or damage to:
   (a) sea-going ships, installations situated offshore or on the high seas, or aircraft, arising from perils which relate to their use for commercial purposes;
   (b) goods in transit other than passengers' baggage where the transit consists of or includes carriage by such ships or aircraft;
2. Any liability, other than for bodily injury to passengers or loss of or damage to their baggage:
   (a) arising out of the use or operation of ships, installations or aircraft as referred to in point 1(a) above in so far as the law of the Contracting State in which such aircraft are registered does not prohibit agreements on jurisdiction regarding insurance of such risks;
   (b) for loss or damage caused by goods in transit as described in point 1(b) above;
3. Any financial loss connected with the use or operation of ships, installations or aircraft as referred to in point 1(a) above, in particular loss of freight or charter-hire;
4. Any risk or interest connected with any of those referred to in points 1 to 3 above.

SECTION 4   JURISDICTION OVER CONSUMER CONTRACTS

Article 13
In proceedings concerning a contract concluded by a person for a purpose which can be regarded as being outside his trade or profession, hereinafter called 'the consumer', jurisdiction shall be determined by this Section, without prejudice to the provisions of point 5 of Articles 4 and 5, if it is:
1. a contract for the sale of goods on instalment credit terms; or
2. a contract for a loan repayable by instalments, or for any other form of credit, made to finance the sale of goods; or
3. any other contract for the supply of goods or a contract for the supply of services, and
   (a) in the State of the consumer's domicile the conclusion of the contract was preceded by a specific invitation addressed to him or by advertising; and
   (b) the consumer took in that State the steps necessary for the conclusion of the contract. Where a consumer enters into a contract with a party who is not

domiciled in a Contracting State but has a branch, agency or other establishment in one of the Contracting States, that party shall, in disputes arising out of the operations of the branch, agency or establishment, be deemed to be domiciled in that State.

This Section shall not apply to contracts of transport.

Article 14

A consumer may bring proceedings against the other party to a contract either in the courts of the Contracting State in which that party is domiciled or in the courts of the Contracting State in which he is himself domiciled. Proceedings may be brought against a consumer by the other party to the contract only in the courts of the Contracting State in which the consumer is domiciled. These provisions shall not affect the right to bring a counter-claim in the court in which, in accordance with this Section, the original claim is pending.

Article 15

The provisions of this Section may be departed from only by an agreement:

1.   which is entered into after the dispute has arisen; or

2.   which allows the consumer to bring proceedings in courts other than those indicated in this Section; or

3.   which is entered into by the consumer and the other party to the contract, both of whom are at the time of conclusion of the contract domiciled or habitually resident in the same Contracting State, and which confers jurisdiction on the courts of that State, provided that such an agreement is not contrary to the law of that State.

SECTION 5   EXCLUSIVE JURISDICTION

Article 16

The following courts shall have exclusive jurisdiction, regardless of domicile:

1.   (a) in proceedings which have as their object rights in rem in immovable property or tenancies of immovable property, the courts of the Contracting State in which the property is situated;

(b) however, in proceedings which have as their object tenancies of immovable property concluded for temporary private use for a maximum period of six consecutive months, the courts of the Contracting State in which the defendant is domiciled shall also have jurisdiction, provided that the landlord and the tenant are natural persons and are domiciled in the same Contracting State;

2.   in proceedings which have as their object the validity of the constitution, the nullity or the dissolution of companies or other legal persons or associations of natural or legal persons, or the decisions of their organs, the courts of the Contracting State in which the company, legal person or association has its seat;

3.   in proceedings which have as their object the validity of entries in public registers, the courts of the Contracting State in which the register is kept;

4.   in proceedings concerned with the registration or validity of patents, trade marks, designs, or other similar rights required to be deposited or registered, the courts of the Contracting State in which the deposit or registration has been applied for, has taken place or is under the terms of an international convention deemed to have taken place;

5.   in proceedings concerned with the enforcement of judgments, the courts of the Contracting State in which the judgment has been or is to be enforced.

SECTION 6   PROROGATION OF JURISDICTION

Article 17
If the parties, one or more of whom is domiciled in a Contracting State, have agreed that a court or the courts of a Contracting State are to have jurisdiction to settle any disputes which have arisen or which may arise in connection with a particular legal relationship, that court or those courts shall have exclusive jurisdiction.

Such an agreement conferring jurisdiction shall be either:

(a)   in writing or evidenced in writing; or

(b)   in a form which accords with practices which the parties have established between themselves; or

(c)   in international trade or commerce, in a form which accords with a usage of which the parties are or ought to have been aware and which in such trade or commerce is widely known to, and regularly observed by, parties to contracts of the type involved in the particular trade or commerce concerned.

Where such an agreement is concluded by parties, none of whom is domiciled in a Contracting State, the courts of other Contracting States shall have no jurisdiction over their disputes unless the court or courts chosen have declined jurisdiction.

The court or courts of a Contracting State on which a trust instrument has conferred jurisdiction shall have exclusive jurisdiction in any proceedings brought against a settlor, trustee or beneficiary, if relations between these persons or their rights or obligations under the trust are involved.

Agreements or provisions of a trust instrument conferring jurisdiction shall have no legal force if they are contrary to the provisions of Articles 12 or 15, or if the courts whose jurisdiction they purport to exclude have exclusive jurisdiction by virtue of Article 16.

If an agreement conferring jurisdiction was concluded for the benefit of only one of the parties, that party shall retain the right to bring proceedings in any other court which has jurisdiction by virtue of this Convention.

In matters relating to individual contracts of employment an agreement conferring jurisdiction shall have legal force only if it entered into after the dispute has arisen or if the employee invokes it to seise courts other than those for the defendant's domicile or those specified in Article 5 (1).

Article 18
Apart from jurisdiction derived from other provisions of this Convention, a court of a Contracting State before whom a defendant enters an appearance shall have jurisdiction. This rule shall not apply where appearance was entered solely to contest the jurisdiction, or where another court has exclusive jurisdiction by virtue of Article 16.

SECTION 7   EXAMINATION AS TO JURISDICTION AND ADMISSIBILITY

Article 19
Where a court of a Contracting State is seised of a claim which is principally concerned with a matter over which the courts of another Contracting State

have exclusive jurisdiction by virtue of Article 16, it shall declare of its own motion that it has no jurisdiction.

Article 20
Where a defendant domiciled in one Contracting State is sued in a court of another Contracting State and does not enter an appearance, the court shall declare of its own motion that it has no jurisdiction unless its jurisdiction is derived from the provisions of the Convention.

The court shall stay the proceedings so long as it is not shown that the defendant has been able to receive the document instituting the proceedings or an equivalent document in sufficient time to enable him to arrange for his defence, or that all necessary steps have been taken to this end.

The provisions of the foregoing paragraph shall be replaced by those of Article 15 of the Hague Convention of 15 November 1965 on the service abroad of judicial and extrajudicial documents in civil or commercial matters, if the document instituting the proceedings or notice thereof had to be transmitted abroad in accordance with that Convention.

SECTION 8   LIS PENDENS — RELATED ACTIONS

Article 21
Where proceedings involving the same cause of action and between the same parties are brought in the courts of different Contracting States, any court other than the court first seised shall of its own motion stay its proceedings until such time as the jurisdiction of the court first seised is established.

Where the jurisdiction of the court first seised is established, any court other than the court first seised shall decline jurisdiction in favour of that court.

Article 22
Where related actions are brought in the courts of different Contracting States, any court other than the court first seised may, while the actions are pending at first instance, stay its proceedings.

A court other than the court first seised may also, on the application of one of the parties, decline jurisdiction if the law of that court permits the consolidation of related actions and the court first seised has jurisdiction over both actions.

For the purposes of this Article, actions are deemed to be related where they are so closely connected that it is expedient to hear and determine them together to avoid the risk of irreconcilable judgments resulting from separate proceedings.

Article 23
Where actions come within the exclusive jurisdiction of several courts, any court other than the court first seised shall decline jurisdiction in favour of that court.

SECTION 9   PROVISIONAL, INCLUDING PROTECTIVE, MEASURES

Article 24
Application may be made to the courts of a Contracting State for such provisional, including protective, measures as may be available under the law of that State, even if, under this Convention, the courts of another Contracting State have jurisdiction as to the substance of the matter.

TITLE III   RECOGNITION AND ENFORCEMENT

Article 25

For the purposes of this Convention, 'judgment' means any judgment given by a court or tribunal of a Contracting State, whatever the judgment may be called, including a decree, order, decision or writ of execution, as well as the determination of costs or expenses by an officer of the court.

SECTION 1   RECOGNITION

Article 26

A judgment given in a Contracting State shall be recognised in the other Contracting States without any special procedure being required.

Any interested party who raises the recognition of a judgment as the principal issue in a dispute may, in accordance with the procedures provided for in Sections 2 and 3 of this Title, apply for a decision that the judgment be recognised.

If the outcome of proceedings in a court of a Contracting State depends on the determination of an incidental question of recognition that court shall have jurisdiction over that question.

Article 27

A judgment shall not be recognised:

1.   if such recognition is contrary to public policy in the State in which recognition is sought;

2.   where it was given in default of appearance, if the defendant was not duly served with the document which instituted the proceedings or with an equivalent document in sufficient time to enable him to arrange for his defence;

3.   if the judgment is irreconcilable with a judgment given in a dispute between the same parties in the State in which recognition is sought;

4.   if the court of the State of origin, in order to arrive at its judgment, has decided a preliminary question concerning the status or legal capacity of natural persons, rights in property arising out of a matrimonial relationship, wills or succession in a way that conflicts with a rule of the private international law of the State in which the recognition is sought, unless the same result would have been reached by the application of the rules of private international law of that State;

5.   if the judgment is irreconcilable with an earlier judgment given in a non-contracting State involving the same cause of action and between the same parties, provided that this latter judgment fulfils the conditions necessary for its recognition in the state addressed.

Article 28

Moreover, a judgment shall not be recognised if it conflicts with the provisions of Sections 3, 4 or 5 of Title II, or in a case provided for in Article 59.

In its examination of the grounds of jurisdiction referred to in the foregoing paragraph, the court or authority applied to shall be bound by the findings of fact on which the court of the State of origin based its jurisdiction.

Subject to the provisions of the first paragraph, the jurisdiction of the court of the State of origin may not be reviewed; the test of public policy referred to in point 1 of Article 27 may not be applied to the rules relating to jurisdiction.

Article 29
Under no circumstances may a foreign judgment be reviewed as to its substance.

Article 30
A court of a Contracting State in which recognition is sought of a judgment given in another Contracting State may stay the proceedings if an ordinary appeal against the judgment has been lodged.

A court of a Contracting State in which recognition is sought of a judgment given in Ireland or the United Kingdom may stay the proceedings if enforcement is suspended in the State of origin, by reason of an appeal.

SECTION 2   ENFORCEMENT

Article 31
A judgment given in a Contracting State and enforceable in that State shall be enforced in another Contracting State when, on the application of any interested party, it has been declared enforceable there.

However, in the United Kingdom, such a judgment shall be enforced in England and Wales, in Scotland, or in Northern Ireland when, on the application of any interested party, it has been registered for enforcement in that part of the United Kingdom.

Article 32
1.   The application shall be submitted:
— in Belgium, to the tribunal de première instance or rechtbank van eerste aanleg,
— in Denmark, to the byret,
— in the Federal Republic of Germany, to the presiding judge of a chamber of the Landgericht,
— in Greece, to the Monomelez Prvtodikeio,
— in Spain, to the Juzgado de Primera Instancia,
— in France, to the presiding judge of the tribunal de grande instance,
— in Ireland, to the High Court,
— in Italy, to the corte dappello,
— in Luxembourg, to the presiding judge of the tribunal d'arrondisse-ment,
— in Austria, to the Bezirksgericht,
— in the Netherlands, to the presiding judge of the arrondissementsrech-tbank,
— in Finland, to the käräjäoikeur/tingsrätt,
— in Sweden, to the Svea hovrätt,
— in Portugal, to the Tribunal Judicial de Círculo,
— in the United Kingdom:
1.   in England and Wales, to the High Court of Justice, or in the case of maintenance judgment to the Magistrates' Court on transmission by the Secretary of State;
2.   in Scotland, to the Court of Session, or in the case of a maintenance judgment to the Sheriff Court on transmission by the Secretary of State;
3.   in Northern Ireland, to the High Court of Justice, or in the case of a maintenance judgment to the Magistrates' Court on transmission by the Secretary of State.

2.   The jurisdiction of local courts shall be determined by reference to the place of domicile of the party against whom enforcement is sought. If he is not domiciled in the State in which enforcement is sought, it shall be determined by reference to the place of enforcement.

Article 33
The procedure for making the application shall be governed by the law of the State in which enforcement is sought.

The applicant must give an address for service of process within the area of jurisdiction of the court applied to. However, if the law of the State in which enforcement is sought does not provide for the furnishing of such an address, the applicant shall appoint a representative ad litem.

The documents referred to in Articles 46 and 47 shall be attached to the application.

Article 34
The court applied to shall give its decision without delay; the party against whom enforcement is sought shall not at this stage of the proceedings be entitled to make any submissions on the application.

The application may be refused only for one of the reasons specified in Articles 27 and 28.

Under no circumstances may the foreign judgment be reviewed as to its substance.

Article 35
The appropriate officer of the court shall without delay bring the decision given on the application to the notice of the applicant in accordance with the procedure laid down by the law of the State in which enforcement is sought.

Article 36
If enforcement is authorised, the party against whom enforcement is sought may appeal against the decision within one month of service thereof. If that party is domiciled in a Contracting State other than that in which the decision authorising enforcement was given, the time for appealing shall be two months and shall run from the date of service, either on him in person or at his residence. No extension of time may be granted on account of distance.

Article 37(1)
1.   An appeal against the decision authorising enforcement shall be lodged in accordance with the rules governing procedure in contentious matters:
— in Belgium, with the tribunal de première instance or rechtbank van eerste aanleg,
— in Denmark, with the landsret,
— in the Federal Republic of Germany, with the Oberlandesgericht,
— in Greece, with the Efeteio,
— in Spain, with the Audiencia Provincial,
— in France, with the cour d'appel,
— in Ireland, with the High Court,
— in Italy, with the corte d'appello,
— in Luxembourg, with the Cour supérieure de justice sitting as a court of civil appeal,
— in Austria with the Bezirksgericht,

— in the Netherlands, with the arrondissementsrechtbank,
— in Finland, with the hovioikeus/hovrätt,
— in Sweden, with the Svea hovrätt,
— in Portugal, with the Tribunal de Relação,
— in the United Kingdom:

(a) in England and Wales, with the High Court of Justice, or in the case of a maintenance judgment with the Magistrates' Court;

(b) in Scotland, with the Court of Session, or in the case of a maintenance judgment with the Sheriff Court;

(c) in Northern Ireland, with the High Court of Justice, or in the case of a maintenance judgment with the Magistrates' Court.

2. The judgment given on the appeal may be contested only:

— in Belgium, Greece, Spain, France, Italy, Luxembourg and in the Netherlands, by an appeal in cassation,

— in Denmark, by an appeal to the hoejesteret, with the leave of the Minister of Justice,

— in the Federal Republic of Germany, by a Rechtsbeschwerde,

— in Ireland, by an appeal on a point of law to the Supreme Court,

— in Austria, in the case of an appeal, by a Revisionskurs and, in the case of opposition proceedings, by a Berufung with the possibility of a revision,

— in Portugal, by an appeal on a point of law,

— in Finland, by an appeal to korkein oikeus/högsta domstolen,

— in Sweden, by an appeal to Högsta domstolen,

— in the United Kingdom, by a single further appeal on a point of law.

Article 38

The court with which the appeal under Article 37(1) is lodged may, on the application of the appellant, stay the proceedings if an ordinary appeal has been lodged against the judgment in the State of origin or if the time for such an appeal has not yet expired; in the latter case, the court may specify the time within which such an appeal is to be lodged.

Where the judgment was given in Ireland or the United Kingdom, any form of appeal available in the State of origin shall be treated as an ordinary appeal for the purposes of the first paragraph.

The court may also make enforcement conditional on the provision of such security as it shall determine.

Article 39

During the time specified for an appeal pursuant to Article 36 and until any such appeal has been determined, no measures of enforcement may be taken other than protective measures taken against the property of the party against whom enforcement is sought. The decision authorising enforcement shall carry with it the power to proceed to any such protective measures.

Article 40

If the application for enforcement is refused, the applicant may appeal:

— in Belgium, to the cour d'appel or hof van beroep,
— in Denmark, to the landsret,
— in the Federal Republic of Germany, to the Oberlandesgericht,
— in Greece, to the Efeteio,
— in Spain, to the Audiencia Provincial,

— in France, to the court d'appel,

— in Ireland, to the High Court,

— in Italy, to the corte d'appello,

— in Luxembourg, to the Cour supérieure de justice sitting as a court of civil appeal,

— in the Netherlands, to the gerechtshof,

— in Austria, to the Bezirksgericht,

— in Portugal, to the Tribunal da Relação,

— in Finland, to hovioikeus/hovrätten,

— in Sweden, to the Svea hovrätt,

— in the United Kingdom:

(a)   in England and Wales, to the High Court of Justice, or in the case of a maintenance judgment to the Magistrates' Court;

(b)   in Scotland, to the Court of Session, or in the case of a maintenance judgment to the Sheriff Court;

(c)   in Northern Ireland, to the High Court of Justice, or in the case of a maintenance judgment to the Magistrates' Court.

2.   The party against whom enforcement is sought shall be summoned to appear before the appellate court. If he fails to appear, the provisions of the second and third paragraphs of Article 20 shall apply even where he is not domiciled in any of the Contracting States.

Article 41

A judgment given on an appeal provided for in Article 40 may be contested only:

— in Belgium, Greece, Spain, France, Italy, Luxembourg and in the Netherlands, by an appeal in cassation,

— in Denmark, by an appeal to the hoejesteret, with the leave of the Minister of Justice,

— in the Federal Republic of Germany, by a Rechtsbeschwerde,

— in Ireland, by an appeal on a point of law to the Supreme Court,

— in Austria, by a Revisionsrekurs,

— in Portugal, by an appeal on a point of law,

— in Finland, by an appeal to korkein oikeus/högsta domstolent,

— in Sweden, by an appeal to Högsta domstolen,

— in the United Kingdom, by a single further appeal on a point of law.

Article 42

Where a foreign judgment has been given in respect of several matters and enforcement cannot be authorised for all of them, the court shall authorise enforcement for one or more of them. An applicant may request partial enforcement of a judgment.

Article 43

A foreign judgment which orders a periodic payment by way of a penalty shall be enforceable in the State in which enforcement is sought only if the amount of the payment has been finally determined by the courts of the State of origin.

Article 44

An applicant who, in the State of origin has benefited from complete or partial legal aid or exemption from costs or expenses, shall be entitled, in the procedures provided for in Articles 32 to 35, to benefit from the most favourable legal aid or the most extensive exemption from costs or expenses provided for by the law of the State addressed.

However, an applicant who requests the enforcement of a decision given by an administrative authority in Denmark in respect of a maintenance order may, in the State addressed, claim the benefits referred to in the first paragraph if he presents a statement from the Danish Ministry of Justice to the effect that he fulfils the economic requirements to qualify for the grant of complete or partial legal aid or exemption from costs or expenses.

Article 45
No security, bond or deposit, however described, shall be required of a party who in one Contracting State applies for enforcement of a judgment given in another Contracting State on the ground that he is a foreign national or that he is not domiciled or resident in the State in which enforcement is sought.

SECTION 3   COMMON PROVISIONS

Article 46
A party seeking recognition or applying for enforcement of a judgment shall produce:
    1.   a copy of the judgment which satisfies the conditions necessary to establish its authenticity;
    2.   in the case of a judgment given in default, the original or a certified true copy of the document which establishes that the party in default was served with the document instituting the proceedings or with an equivalent document.

Article 47
A party applying for enforcement shall also produce:
    1.   documents which establish that, according to the law of the State of origin the judgment is enforceable and has been served;
    2.   where appropriate, a document showing that the applicant is in receipt of legal aid in the State of origin.

Article 48
If the documents specified in point 2 of Articles 46 and 47 are not produced, the court may specify a time for their production, accept equivalent documents or, if it considers that it has sufficient information before it, dispense with their production. If the court so requires, a translation of the documents shall be produced; the translation shall be certified by a person qualified to do so in one of the Contracting States.

Article 49
No legalisation or other similar formality shall be required in respect of the documents referred to in Articles 46 or 47 or the second paragraph of Article 48, or in respect of a document appointing a representative ad litem.

TITLE IV   AUTHENTIC INSTRUMENTS AND COURT SETTLEMENTS

Article 50
A document which has been formally drawn up or registered as an authentic instrument and is enforceable in one Contracting State shall, in another Contracting State, be declared enforceable there, on application made in accordance with the procedures provided for in Article 31 et seq. The

application may be refused only if enforcement of the instrument is contrary to public policy in the State addressed.

The instrument produced must satisfy the conditions necessary to establish its authenticity in the State of origin.

The provisions of Section 3 of Title III shall apply as appropriate.

Article 51

A settlement which has been approved by a court in the course of proceedings and is enforceable in the State in which it was concluded shall be enforceable in the State addressed under the same conditions as authentic instruments.

TITLE V   GENERAL PROVISIONS

Article 52

In order to determine whether a party is domiciled in the Contracting State whose courts are seised of a matter, the Court shall apply its internal law. If a party is not domiciled in the State whose courts are seised of the matter, then, in order to determine whether the party is domiciled in another Contracting State, the court shall apply the law of that State.

Article 53

For the purposes of this Convention, the seat of a company or other legal person or association of natural or legal persons shall be treated as its domicile. However, in order to determine that seat, the court shall apply its rules of private international law. In order to determine whether a trust is domiciled in the Contracting State whose courts are seised of the matter, the court shall apply its rules of private international law.

TITLE VI   TRANSITIONAL PROVISIONS

Article 54

The provisions of the Convention shall apply only to legal proceedings instituted and to documents formally drawn up or registered as authentic instruments after its entry into force in the State of origin and, where recognition or enforcement of a judgment or authentic instruments is sought, in the State addressed.

However, judgments given after the date of entry into force of this Convention between the State of origin and the State addressed in proceedings instituted before that date shall be recognised and enforced in accordance with the provisions of Title III if jurisdiction was founded upon rules which accorded with those provided for either in Title II of this Convention or in a convention concluded between the State of origin and the State addressed which was in force when the proceedings were instituted.

If the parties to a dispute concerning a contract had agreed in writing before 1 June 1988 for Ireland or before 1 January 1987 for the United Kingdom that the contract was to be governed by the law of Ireland or of a part of the United Kingdom, the courts of Ireland or of that part of the United Kingdom shall retain the right to exercise jurisdiction in the dispute.

Article 54a

For a period of three years from 1 November 1986 for Denmark and from 1 June 1988 for Ireland, jurisdiction in maritime matters shall be determined in these States not only in accordance with the provisions of Title II, but also in accordance with the provisions of paragraphs 1 to 6 following. However, upon the entry into force of the International Convention relating to the arrest of sea-going ships, signed at Brussels on 10 May 1952, for one of these States, these provisions shall cease to have effect for that State.

1.   A person who is domiciled in a Contracting State may be sued in the courts of one of the States mentioned above in respect of a maritime claim if the ship to which the claim relates or any other ship owned by him has been arrested by judicial process within the territory of the latter State to secure the claim, or could have been so arrested there but bail or other security has been given, and either:

   (a)   the claimant is domiciled in the latter State; or

   (b)   the claim arose in the latter State; or

   (c)   the claim concerns the voyage during which the arrest was made or could have been made; or

   (d)   the claim arises out of a collision or out of damage caused by a ship to another ship or to goods or persons on board either ship, either by the execution or non-execution of a manoeuvre or by the non-observance of regulations; or

   (e)   the claim is for salvage; or

   (f)   the claim is in respect of a mortgage or hypothecation of the ship arrested.

2.   A claimant may arrest either the particular ship to which the maritime claim relates, or any other ship which is owned by the person who was, at the time when the maritime claim arose, the owner of the particular ship. However, only the particular ship to which the maritime claim relates may be arrested in respect of the maritime claims set out in (5)(o), (p) or (q) of this Article.

3.   Ships shall be deemed to be in the same ownership when all the shares therein are owned by the same person or persons.

4.   When in the case of a charter by demise of a ship the charterer alone is liable in respect of a maritime claim relating to that ship, the claimant may arrest that ship or any other ship owned by the charterer, but no other ship owned by the owner may be arrested in respect of such claim. The same shall apply to any case in which a person other than the owner of a ship is liable in respect of a maritime claim relating to that ship.

5.   The expression 'maritime claim' means a claim arising out of one or more of the following:

   (a)   damage caused by any ship either in collision or otherwise;

   (b)   loss of life or personal injury caused by any ship or occurring in connection with the operation on any ship;

   (c)   salvage;

   (d)   agreement relating to the use or hire of any ship whether by charterparty or otherwise;

   (e)   agreement relating to the carriage of goods in any ship whether by charterparty or otherwise;

   (f)   loss of or damage to goods including baggage carried in any ship;

   (g)   general average;

   (h)   bottomry;

   (i)   towage;

   (j)   pilotage;

   (k)   goods or materials wherever supplied to a ship for her operation or maintenance;

(l)   construction, repair or equipment of any ship or dock charges and dues;

(m) wages of masters, officers or crew;

(n) master's disbursements, including disbursements made by shippers, charterers or agents on behalf of a ship or her owner;

(o) dispute as to the title to or ownership of any ship;

(p) disputes between co-owners of any ship as to the ownership, possession, employment or earnings of that ship;

(q) the mortgage or hypothecation of any ship.

6. In Denmark, the expression 'arrest' shall be deemed as regards the maritime claims referred to in 5(o) and (p) of this Article, to include a 'forbud', where that is the only procedure allowed in respect of such a claim under Articles 646 to 653 of the law on civil procedure (lov om rettens pleje).

TITLE VII   RELATIONSHIP TO OTHER CONVENTIONS

Article 55

Subject to the provisions of the second subparagraph of Article 54, and of Article 56, this Convention shall, for the States which are parties to it, supersede the following conventions concluded between two or more of them:

— the Convention between Belgium and France on jurisdiction and the validity and enforcement of judgments, arbitration awards and authentic instruments, signed at Paris on 8 July 1899,

— the Convention between Belgium and the Netherlands on jurisdiction, bankruptcy, and the validity and enforcement of judgments, arbitration awards and authentic instruments, signed at Brussels on 28 March 1925,

— the Convention between France and Italy on the enforcement of judgments in civil and commercial matters, signed at Rome on 3 June 1930,

— the Convention between the United Kingdom and the French Republic providing for the reciprocal enforcement of judgments in civil and commercial matters, with Protocol, signed at Paris on 18 January 1934,

— the Convention between the United Kingdom and the Kingdom of Belgium providing for the reciprocal enforcement of judgments in civil and commercial matters, with Protocol, signed at Brussels on 2 May 1934,

— the Convention between Germany and Italy on the recognition and enforcement of judgments in civil and commercial matters, signed at Rome on 9 March 1936,

— the Convention between the Kingdom of Belgium and Austria on the reciprocal recognition and enforcement of judgments and authentic instruments relating to maintenance obligations, signed at Vienna on 25 October 1957,

— the Convention between the Federal Republic of Germany and the Kingdom of Belgium on the mutual recognition and enforcement of judgments, arbitration awards and authentic instruments in civil and commercial matters, signed at Bonn on 30 June 1958,

— the Convention between the Kingdom of the Netherlands and the Italian Republic on the recognition and enforcement of judgments in civil and commercial matters, signed at Rome on 17 April 1959,

— the Convention between the Federal Republic of Germany and Austria on the reciprocal recognition and enforcement of judgments, settlements and authentic instruments in civil and commercial matters, signed at Vienna on 6 June 1959,

— the Convention between the Kingdom of Belgium and Austria on the reciprocal recognition and enforcement of judgments, arbitral awards and authentic instruments in civil and commercial matters, signed at Vienna on 16 June 1959,

— the Convention between the United Kingdom and the Federal Republic of Germany for the reciprocal recognition and enforcement of judgments in civil and commercial matters, signed at Bonn on 14 July 1960,

— the Convention between the Kingdom of Greece and the Federal Republic of Germany for the reciprocal recognition and enforcement of judgments, settlements and authentic instruments in civil and commercial matters, signed in Athens on 4 November 1961,

— the Convention between the United Kingdom and Austria providing for the reciprocal recognition and enforcement of judgments in civil and commercial matters, signed at Vienna on 14 July 1961, with amending Protocol signed at London on 6 March 1970,

— the Convention between the Kingdom of Belgium and the Italian Republic on the recognition and enforcement of judgments and other enforceable instruments in civil and commercial matters, signed at Rome on 6 April 1962,

— the Convention between the Kingdom of the Netherlands and the Federal Republic of Germany on the mutual recognition and enforcement of judgments and other enforceable instruments in civil and commercial matters, signed at The Hague on 30 August 1962,

— the Convention between the Kingdom of the Netherlands and Austria on the reciprocal recognition and enforcement of judgments and authentic instruments in civil and commercial matters, signed at The Hague on 6 February 1963,

— the Convention between the United Kingdom and the Republic of Italy for the reciprocal recognition and enforcement of judgments in civil and commercial matters, signed at Rome on 7 February 1964, with amending Protocol signed at Rome on 14 July 1970,

— the Convention between France and Austria on the recognition and enforcement of judgments and authentic instruments in civil and commercial matters, signed at Vienna on 15 July 1966,

— the Convention between the United Kingdom and the Kingdom of the Netherlands providing for the reciprocal recognition and enforcement of judgments in civil matters, signed at The Hague on 17 November 1967,

— the Convention between Spain and France on the recognition and enforcement of judgment arbitration awards in civil and commercial matters, signed at Paris on 28 May 1969,

— the Convention between Luxembourg and Austria on the recognition and enforcement of judgments and authentic instruments in civil and commercial matters, signed at Luxembourg on 29 July 1971,

— the Convention between Italy and Austria on the recognition and enforcement of judgments in civil and commercial matters, of judicial settlements and of authentic instruments, signed at Rome on 16 November 1971,

— the Convention between Spain and Italy regarding legal aid and the recognition and enforcement of judgments in civil and commercial matters, signed at Madrid on 22 May 1973,

—the Convention between Finland, Iceland, Norway, Sweden and Denmark on the recognition and enforcement of judgments in civil matters, signed at Copenhagen on 11 October 1977,

—the Convention between Austria and Sweden on the recognition and enforcement of judgments in civil matters, signed at Stockholm on 16 September 1982,

—the Convention between Spain and the Federal Republic of Germany on the recognition and enforcement of judgments, settlements and enforceable authentic instruments in civil and commercial matters, signed at Bonn on 14 November 1983, and, in so far as it is in force:

—the Treaty between Belgium, the Netherlands and Luxembourg on jurisdiction, bankruptcy, and the validity and enforcement of judgments, arbitration awards and authentic instruments, signed at Brussels on 24 November 1961,

—the Convention between Austria and Spain on the recognition and enforcement of judgments, settlements and enforceable authentic instruments in civil and commercial matters, signed at Vienna on 17 February 1984,

—the Convention between Finland and Austria on the recognition and enforcement of judgments in civil matters, signed at Vienna on 17 November 1986.

Article 56

The Treaty and the conventions referred to in Article 55 shall continue to have effect in relation to matters to which this Convention does not apply.

They shall continue to have effect in respect of judgments given and documents formally drawn up or registered as authentic instruments before the entry into force of this Convention.

Article 57

1. This Convention shall not affect any conventions to which the Contracting States are or will be parties and which in relation to particular matters, govern jurisdiction or the recognition or enforcement of judgments.

2. With a view to its uniform interpretation, paragraph 1 shall be applied in the following manner:

(a) this Convention shall not prevent a court of a Contracting State which is a party to a convention on a particular matter from assuming jurisdiction in accordance with that Convention, even where the defendant is domiciled in another Contracting State which is not a party to that Convention. The court hearing the action shall, in any event, apply Article 20 of this Convention;

(b) judgments given in a Contracting State by a court in the exercise of jurisdiction provided for in a convention on a particular matter shall be recognised and enforced in the other Contracting State in accordance with this Convention.

Where a convention on a particular matter to which both the State of origin and the State addressed are parties lays down conditions for the recognition or enforcement of judgments, those conditions shall apply. In any event, the provisions of this Convention which concern the procedure for recognition and enforcement of judgments may be applied.

3. This Convention shall not affect the application of provisions which, in relation to particular matters, govern jurisdiction or the recognition or

enforcement of judgments and which are or will be contained in acts of the institutions of the European Communities or in national laws harmonised in implementation of such acts.

Article 58

Until such time as the Convention on jurisdiction and the enforcement of judgments in civil and commercial matters, signed at Lugano on 16 September 1988, takes effect with regard to France and the Swiss Confederation, this Convention shall not affect the rights granted to Swiss nationals by the Convention between France and the Swiss Confederation on jurisdiction and enforcement of judgments in civil matters, signed at Paris on 15 June 1869.

Article 59

This Convention shall not prevent a Contracting State from assuming, in a convention on the recognition and enforcement of judgments, an obligation towards a third State not to recognise judgments given in other Contracting States against defendants domiciled or habitually resident in the third State where, in cases provided for in Article 4, the judgment could only be founded on a ground of jurisdiction specified in the second paragraph of Article 3.

However, a Contracting State may not assume an obligation towards a third State not to recognise a judgment given in another Contracting State by a court basing its jurisdiction on the presence within that State of property belonging to the defendant, or the seizure by the plaintiff of property situated there:

1.   if the action is brought to assert or declare proprietary or possessory rights in that property, seeks to obtain authority to dispose of it, or arises from another issue relating to such property; or

2.   if the property constitutes the security for a debt which is the subject-matter of the action.

TITLE VIII   FINAL PROVISIONS

Article 60

(Deleted)

Article 61

This Convention shall be ratified by the signatory States. The instruments of ratification shall be deposited with the Secretary-General of the Council of the European Communities.

Article 62

This Convention shall enter into force on the first day of the third month following the deposit of the instrument of ratification by the last signatory State to take this step.

Article 63

The Contracting States recognise that any State which becomes a member of the European Economic Community shall be required to accept this Convention as a basis for the negotiations between the Contracting States and that State necessary to ensure the implementation of the last paragraph of Article 220 of the Treaty establishing the European Economic Community. The necessary adjustments may be the subject of a special convention between the Contracting States of the one part and the new Member States of the other part.

Article 64
The Secretary-General of the Council of the European Communities shall notify the signatory States of:
- (a) the deposit of each instrument of ratification;
- (b) the date of entry into force of this Convention;
- (c) ... (Deleted);
- (d) any declaration received pursuant to Article IV of the Protocol;
- (e) any communication made pursuant to Article VI of the Protocol.

Article 65
The Protocol annexed to this Convention by common accord of the Contracting States shall form an integral part thereof.

Article 66
This Convention is concluded for an unlimited period.

Article 67
Any Contracting State may request the revision of this Convention. In this event, a revision conference shall be convened by the President of the Council of the European Communities.

Article 68
This Convention, drawn up in a single original in the Dutch, French, German and Italian languages, all four texts being equally authentic, shall be deposited in the archives of the Secretariat of the Council of the European Communities. The Secretary-General shall transmit a certified copy to the Government of each signatory State.

(Signatures omitted)

PROTOCOL[1]

The High Contracting Parties have agreed upon the following provisions, which shall be annexed to the Convention:

Article I
Any person domiciled in Luxembourg who is sued in a court of another Contracting State pursuant to Article 5(1) may refuse to submit to the jurisdiction of that court. If the defendant does not enter an appearance the court shall declare of its own motion that it has no jurisdiction.

An agreement conferring jurisdiction, within the meaning of Article 17, shall be valid with respect to a person domiciled in Luxembourg only if that person has expressly and specifically so agreed.

Article II
Without prejudice to any more favourable provisions of national laws, persons domiciled in a Contracting State who are being prosecuted in the criminal courts of another Contracting State of which they are not nationals for an offence which was not intentionally committed may be defended by persons qualified to do so, even if they do not appear in person.

Note
[1]Text as amended by the 1978 Accession Convention, the 1982 Accession Convention and the 1989 Accession Convention.

However, the court seised of the matter may order appearance in person; in the case of failure to appear, a judgment given in the civil action without the person concerned having had the opportunity to arrange for his defence need not be recognised or enforced in the other Contracting States.

Article III

In proceedings for the issue of an order for enforcement, no charge, duty or fee calculated by reference to the value of the matter in issue may be levied in the State in which enforcement is sought.

Article IV

Judicial and extrajudicial documents drawn up in one Contracting State which have to be served on persons in another Contracting State shall be transmitted in accordance with the procedures laid down in the conventions and agreements concluded between the Contracting States.

Unless the State in which service is to take place objects by declaration to the Secretary-General of the Council of the European Communities, such documents may also be sent by the appropriate public officers of the State in which the document has been drawn up directly to the appropriate public officers of the State in which the addressee is to be found. In this case the officer of the State of origin shall send a copy of the document to the officer of the State applied to who is competent to forward it to the addressee. The document shall be forwarded in the manner specified by the law of the State applied to. The forwarding shall be recorded by a certificate sent directly to the officer of the State of origin.

Article V

The jurisdiction specified in Articles 6(2) and 10 in actions on a warranty or guarantee or in any other third party proceedings may not be resorted to in the Federal Republic of Germany or in Austria. Any person domiciled in another Contracting State may be sued in the courts:

— of the Federal Republic of Germany, pursuant to Articles 68, 72, 73 and 74 of the code of civil procedure (Zivisprozessordnung) concerning third-party notices,

— in Austria, pursuant to Article 21 of the code of civil procedure (Zivilsprozessordnung) concerning third-party notices.

Judgments given in the other Contracting States by virtue of point 2 of Article 6 or Article 10 shall be recognised and enforced in the Federal Republic of Germany and in Austria in accordance with Title III. Any effects which judgments given in those States may have on third parties by application of the provisions in the preceding paragraph shall also be recognised in the other Contracting States.

Article Va

In matters relating to maintenance, the expression 'court' includes the Danish administrative authorities.

In Sweden, in summary proceedings concerning orders to pay (betalningsförelgggände) and assistance (handräcking), the expression 'court' includes the 'Swedish enforcement service' (kronofogdemyndighet).

Article Vb

In proceedings involving a dispute between the master and a member of the crew of a sea-going ship registered in Denmark, in Greece, in Ireland or in

Portugal, concerning remuneration or other conditions of service, a court in a Contracting State shall establish whether the diplomatic or consular officer responsible for the ship has been notified of the dispute. It shall stay the proceedings so long as he has not been notified. It shall of its own motion decline jurisdiction if the officer, having been duly notified, has exercised the powers accorded to him in the matter by a consular convention, or in the absence of such a convention has, within the time allowed, raised any objection to the exercise of such jurisdiction.

Article Vc
Articles 52 and 53 of this Convention shall, when applied by Article 69(5) of the Convention for the European patent for the common market, signed at Luxembourg on 15 December 1975, to the provisions relating to 'residence' in the English text of that Convention, operate as if 'residence' in that text were the same as 'domicile' in Articles 52 and 53.

Article Vd
Without prejudice to the jurisdiction of the European Patent Office under the Convention on the grant of European patents, signed at Munich on 5 October 1973, the courts of each Contracting State shall have exclusive jurisdiction, regardless of domicile, in proceedings concerned with the registration or validity of any European patent granted for that State which is not a Community patent by virtue of the provisions of Article 86 of the Convention for the European patent for the common market, signed at Luxembourg on 15 December 1975.

Article Ve
Arrangements relating to maintenance obligations concluded with administrative authorities or authenticated by them shall also be regarded as authentic instruments within the meaning of the first paragraph of Article 50 of the Convention.

Article VI
The Contracting States shall communicate to the Secretary-General of the Council of the European Communities the text of any provisions of their laws which amend either those articles of their laws mentioned in the Convention or the lists of courts specified in Section 2 of Title III of the Convention.

(Signatures omitted)

JOINT DECLARATION

The Governments of the Kingdom of Belgium, the Federal Republic of Germany, the French Republic, the Italian Republic, the Grand Duchy of Luxembourg and the Kingdom of the Netherlands,

On signing the Convention on jurisdiction and the enforcement of judgments in civil and commercial matters,
  Desiring to ensure that the Convention is applied as effectively as possible,
  Anxious to prevent differences of interpretation of the Convention from impairing its unifying effect,
  Recognising that claims and disclaimers of jurisdiction may arise in the application of the Convention,
  Declare themselves ready:

1.   to study these questions and in particular to examine the possibility of conferring jurisdiction in certain matters on the Court of Justice of the European Communities and, if necessary, to negotiate an agreement to this effect;

2.   to arrange meetings at regular intervals between their representatives.

(Signatures omitted)

PROTOCOL
ON THE INTERPRETATION BY THE COURT OF JUSTICE OF THE CONVENTION OF 27 SEPTEMBER 1968 ON JURISDICTION AND THE ENFORCEMENT OF JUDGMENTS IN CIVIL AND COMMERCIAL MATTERS
(90/C 189/03)[1]

THE HIGH CONTRACTING PARTIES TO THE TREATY ESTABLISHING THE EUROPEAN ECONOMIC COMMUNITY,

Having regard to the Declaration annexed to the Convention on jurisdiction and the enforcement of judgments in civil and commercial matters, signed at Brussels on 27 September 1968,

Have decided to conclude a Protocol conferring jurisdiction on the Court of Justice of the European Communities to interpret that Convention, and to this end have designated as their Plenipotentiaries:

HIS MAJESTY THE KING OF THE BELGIANS:
Mr Alfons VRANCKX,
Minister of Justice;

THE PRESIDENT OF THE FEDERAL REPUBLIC OF GERMANY:
Mr Gerhard JAHN,
Federal Minister of Justice;

THE PRESIDENT OF THE FRENCH REPUBLIC:
Mr René PLEVEN,
Keeper of the Seals, Minister of Justice;

THE PRESIDENT OF THE ITALIAN REPUBLIC:
Mr Erminio PENNACCHINI,
Under Secretary of State in the Ministry of Justice;

HIS ROYAL HIGHNESS THE GRAND DUKE OF LUXEMBOURG:
Mr Eugène SCHAUS,
Minister of Justice,
Deputy Prime Minister;

HER MAJESTY THE QUEEN OF THE NETHERLANDS:
Mr C. H. F. POLAK,
Minister of Justice;

WHO, meeting within the Council, having exchanged their Full Powers, found in good and due form,

HAVE AGREED AS FOLLOWS:

Note
[1]As amended to 1997 OJ 1997 C15/1.

Article 1

The Court of Justice of the European Communities shall have jurisdiction to give rulings on the interpretation of the Convention on jurisdiction and the enforcement of judgments in civil and commercial matters and of the Protocol annexed to that Convention, signed at Brussels on 27 September 1968, and also on the interpretation of the present Protocol.

The Court of Justice of the European Communities shall also have jurisdiction to give rulings on the interpretation of the Convention on the accession of the Kingdom of Denmark, Ireland and the United Kingdom of Great Britain and Northern Ireland to the Convention of 27 September 1968 and to this Protocol.

The Court of Justice of the European Communities shall also have jurisdiction to give rulings on the interpretation of the Convention on the accession of the Hellenic Republic to the Convention of 27 September 1968 and to this Protocol, as adjusted by the 1978 Convention.

The Court of Justice of the European Communities shall also have jurisdiction to give rulings on the interpretation of the Convention on the accession of the Kingdom of Spain and the Portuguese Republic to the Convention of 27 September 1968 and to this Protocol, as adjusted by the 1978 Convention and the 1982 Convention.

The Court of Justice of the European Communities shall also have jurisdiction to give rulings on the interpretation of the Convention on the accession of the Republic of Austria, the Republic of Finland and the Kingdom of Sweden to the Convention of 27 September 1968 and to this Protocol, as adjusted by the 1978 Convention, the 1982 Convention and the 1989 Convention.

Article 2

The following courts may request the Court of Justice to give preliminary rulings on questions of interpretation:

1. — in Belgium: la Cour de Cassation — het Hof van Cassatie and le Conseil d'État — de Raad van State,

   — in Denmark: hoejesteret,

   — in the Federal Republic of Germany: die obersten Gerichtshoefe des Bundes,

   — in Greece: the anvtata dikasthria,

   — in Spain: el Tribunal Supremo,

   — in France: la Cour de Cassation and le Conseil d'État,

   — in Ireland: the Supreme Court,

   — in Italy: la Corte Suprema di Cassazione,

   — in Luxembourg: la Cour supérieure de Justice when sitting as Cour de Cassation,

   — in Austria, the Oberste Gerichtshof, the Verwaltungsgerichtshof and the Verfassungsgerichtshof,

   — in the Netherlands: de Hoge Raad,

   — in Finland, korkein oikeus/hoegsta domstolen and korkein hallintooikeus/hoegsta foervaltningsdomstolen,

   — in Sweden, Hoegsta domstolen, Regeringsraetten, Arbetsdomstolen and Marknadsdomstolen,

   — in Portugal: o Supremo Tribunal de Justiça and o Supremo Tribunal Administrativo,

—in the United Kingdom: the House of Lords and courts to which application has been made under the second paragraph of Article 37 or under Article 41 of the Convention;

2.   the courts of the Contracting States when they are sitting in an appellate capacity;

3.   in the cases provided for in Article 37 of the Convention, the courts referred to in that Article.

Article 3

1.   Where a question of interpretation of the Convention or of one of the other instruments referred to in Article 1 is raised in a case pending before one of the courts listed in point 1 of Article 2, that court shall, if it considers that a decision on the question is necessary to enable it to give judgment, request the Court of Justice to give a ruling thereon.

2.   Where such a question is raised before any court referred to in point 2 or 3 of Article 2, that court may, under the conditions laid down in paragraph 1, request the Court of Justice to give a ruling thereon.

Article 4

1.   The competent authority of a Contracting State may request the Court of Justice to give a ruling on a question of interpretation of the Convention or of one of the other instruments referred to in Article 1 if judgments given by courts of that State conflict with the interpretation given either by the Court of Justice or in a judgment of one of the courts of another Contracting State referred to in point 1 or 2 of Article 2. The provisions of this paragraph shall apply only to judgments which have become res judicata.

2.   The interpretation given by the Court of Justice in response to such a request shall not affect the judgments which gave rise to the request for interpretation.

3.   The Procurators-General of the Courts of Cassation of the Contracting States, or any other authority designated by a Contracting State, shall be entitled to request the Court of Justice for a ruling on interpretation in accordance with paragraph 1.

4.   The Registrar of the Court of Justice shall give notice of the request to the Contracting States, to the Commission and to the Council of the European Communities; they shall then be entitled within two months of the notification to submit statements of case or written observations to the Court.

5.   No fees shall be levied or any costs or expenses awarded in respect of the proceedings provided for in this Article.

Article 5

1.   Except where this Protocol otherwise provides, the provisions of the Treaty establishing the European Economic Community and those of the Protocol on the Statute of the Court of Justice annexed thereto, which are applicable when the Court is requested to give a preliminary ruling, shall also apply to any proceedings for the interpretation of the Convention and the other instruments referred to in Article 1.

2.   The Rules of Procedure of the Court of Justice shall, if necessary, be adjusted and supplemented in accordance with Article 188 of the Treaty establishing the European Economic Community.

Article 6
(Deleted)

Article 7
This Protocol shall be ratified by the signatory States. The instruments of ratification shall be deposited with the Secretary-General of the Council of the European Communities.

Article 8
This Protocol shall enter into force on the first day of the third month following the deposit of the instrument of ratification by the last signatory State to take this step; provided that it shall at the earliest enter into force at the same time as the Convention of 27 September 1968 on jurisdiction and the enforcement of judgments in civil and commercial matters.

Article 9
The Contracting States recognise that any State which becomes a member of the European Economic Community, and to which Article 63 of the Convention on jurisdiction and the enforcement of judgments in civil and commercial matters applies, must accept the provisions of this Protocol, subject to such adjustments as may be required.

Article 10
The Secretary-General of the Council of the European Communities shall notify the signatory States of:
  (a) the deposit of each instrument of ratification;
  (b) the date of entry into force of this Protocol;
  (c) any designation received pursuant to Article 4(3);
  (d) ... (Deleted).

Article 11
The Contracting States shall communicate to the Secretary-General of the Council of the European Communities the texts of any provisions of their laws which necessitate an amendment to the list of courts in point 1 of Article 2.

Article 12
This Protocol is concluded for an unlimited period.

Article 13
Any Contracting State may request the revision of this Protocol. In this event, a revision conference shall be convened by the President of the Council of the European Communities.

Article 14
This Protocol, drawn up in a single original in the Dutch, French, German and Italian languages, all four texts being equally authentic, shall be deposited in the archives of the Secretariat of the Council of the European Communities. The Secretary-General shall transmit a certified copy to the Government of each signatory State.

(Signatures omitted)

JOINT DECLARATION

The Governments of the Kingdom of Belgium, the Federal Republic of Germany, the French Republic, the Italian Republic, the Grand Duchy of Luxembourg and the Kingdom of the Netherlands,

On signing the Protocol on the interpretation by the Court of Justice of the Convention of 27 September 1968 on jurisdiction and the enforcement of judgments in civil and commercial matters,

Desiring to ensure that the provisions of that Protocol are applied as effectively and as uniformly as possible,

Declare themselves ready to organise, in cooperation with the Court of Justice, an exchange of information on the judgments given by the courts referred to in Article 2(1) of that Protocol in application of the Convention and the Protocol of 27 September 1968.

JOINT DECLARATION
OF 9 OCTOBER 1978
(90/C 189/04)

THE REPRESENTATIVES OF THE GOVERNMENTS OF THE MEMBER STATES OF THE EUROPEAN ECONOMIC COMMUNITY, MEETING WITHIN THE COUNCIL,

Desiring to ensure that in the spirit of the Convention of 27 September 1968 uniformity of jurisdiction should also be achieved as widely as possible in maritime matters,

Considering that the International Convention relating to the arrest of sea-going ships, signed at Brussels on 10 May 1952, contains provisions relating to such jurisdiction,

Considering that all of the Member States are not parties to the said Convention,

Express the wish that Member States which are coastal States and have not already become parties to the Convention of 10 May 1952 should do so as soon as possible.

Done at Luxembourg on the ninth day of October in the year one thousand nine hundred and seventy-eight.

(Signatures omitted)

JOINT DECLARATION
OF 26 MAY 1989 CONCERNING THE RATIFICATION OF THE CONVENTION ON THE ACCESSION OF THE KINGDOM OF SPAIN AND THE PORTUGUESE REPUBLIC TO THE 1968 BRUSSELS CONVENTION
(90/C 189/05)

Upon signature of the Convention on the accession of the Kingdom of Spain and the Portuguese Republic to the 1968 Brussels Convention, done at Donostia — San Sebastián on 26 May 1989,

THE REPRESENTATIVES OF THE GOVERNMENTS OF THE MEMBER STATES OF THE EUROPEAN COMMUNITIES, MEETING WITHIN THE COUNCIL,

DESIROUS that, in particular with a view to the completion of the internal market, application of the Brussels Convention and of the 1971 Protocol should be rapidly extended to the entire Community,

WELCOMING the conclusion on 16 September 1988 of the Lugano Convention which extends the principles of the Brussels Convention to those States becoming parties to the Lugano Convention, designed principally to govern relations between the Member States of the European Economic Community (EEC) and those of the European Free Trade Association (EFTA) with regard to the legal protection of persons established in any of those States and to the simplification of formalities for the reciprocal recognition and enforcement of judgments,

CONSIDERING that the Brussels Convention has as its legal basis Article 220 of the Treaty of Rome and is interpreted by the Court of Justice of the European Communities,

MINDFUL that the Lugano Convention does not affect the application of the Brussels Convention as regards relations between Member States of the European Economic Community, since such relations must be governed by the Brussels Convention,

NOTING that the Lugano Convention is to enter into force after two States, of which one is a member of the European Communities and the other a member of the European Free Trade Association, have deposited their instruments of ratification,

DECLARE THEMSELVES READY to take every appropriate measure with a view to ensuring that national procedures for the ratification of the Convention on the accession of the Kingdom of Spain and the Portuguese Republic to the Brussels Convention, signed today, are completed as soon as possible and, if possible, by 31 December 1992 at the latest.

Done at Donostia — San Sebastián on the twenty-sixth day of May in the year one thousand nine hundred and eighty-nine.

(Signatures omitted)

CONVENTION ON THE LAW APPLICABLE TO CONTRACTUAL OBLIGATIONS OPENED FOR SIGNATURE IN ROME ON 19 JUNE 1980 (THE ROME CONVENTION) 80/934/EEC
[OJ 1980 L266/1]*

PREAMBLE

The High Contracting Parties to the Treaty establishing the European Economic Community, anxious to continue in the field of private international law the work of unification of law which has already been done within the

Note

*As corrected by OJ No. L266 of 9 October 1980 and amended by (92/529/EEC) OJ 1992 L33/1. **Editor's Note**: Annexes I & II (Containing the Spanish and Portuguese translations of the Convention, protocol and common declaration) have been omitted. Note also that for the present the Convention was not amended when the First and Second Protocols were added nor when Austria, Finland and Sweden acceeded to it. These were established by separate conventions which are reproduced here after the Convention itself.

Community, in particular in the field of jurisdiction and enforcement of judgments, wishing to establish uniform rules concerning the law applicable to contractual obligations,

Have agreed as follows:

TITLE I   SCOPE OF THE CONVENTION

Article 1   Scope of the Convention

1.   The rules of this Convention shall apply to contractual obligations in any situation involving a choice between the laws of different countries.

2.   They shall not apply to:

(a)   questions involving the status or legal capacity of natural persons, without prejudice to article 11;

(b)   contractual obligations relating to:

—wills and succession,

—rights in property arising out of a matrimonial relationship,

—rights and duties arising out of a family relationship, parentage, marriage or affinity, including maintenance obligations in respect of children who are not legitimate;

(c)   obligations arising under bills of exchange, cheques and promissory notes and other negotiable instruments to the extent that the obligations under such other negotiable instruments arise out of their negotiable character;

(d)   arbitration agreements and agreements on the choice of court;

(e)   questions governed by the law of companies and other bodies corporate or unincorporate such as the creation, by registration or otherwise, legal capacity, internal organization or winding up of companies and other bodies corporate or unincorporate and the personal liability of officers and members as such for the obligations of the company or body;

(f)   the question whether an agent is able to bind a principal, or an organ to bind a company or body corporate or unincorporate, to a third party;

(g)   the constitution of trusts and the relationship between settlors, trustees and beneficiaries;

(h)   evidence and procedure, without prejudice to article 14.

3.   The rules of this Convention do not apply to contracts of insurance which cover risks situated in the territories of the member states of the European economic Community. In order to determine whether a risk is situated in these territories the court shall apply its internal law.

4.   The preceding paragraph does not apply to contracts of re-insurance.

Article 2   Application of law of non-contracting states

Any law specified by this Convention shall be applied whether or not it is the law of a contracting state.

TITLE II   UNIFORM RULES

Article 3   Freedom of choice

1.   A contract shall be governed by the law chosen by the parties. The choice must be express or demonstrated with reasonable certainty by the terms

of the contract or the circumstances of the case. By their choice the parties can select the law applicable to the whole or a part only of the contract.

2.   The parties may at any time agree to subject the contract to a law other than that which previously governed it, whether as a result of an earlier choice under this article or of other provisions of this Convention. Any variation by the parties of the law to be applied made after the conclusion of the contract shall not prejudice its formal validity under article 9 or adversely affect the rights of third parties.

3.   The fact that the parties have chosen a foreign law, whether or not accompanied by the choice of a foreign tribunal, shall not, where all the other elements relevant to the situation at the time of the choice are connected with one country only, prejudice the application of rules of the law of that country which cannot be derogated from by contract, hereinafter called 'mandatory rules'.

4.   The existence and validity of the consent of the parties as to the choice of the applicable law shall be determined in accordance with the provisions of articles 8, 9 and 11.

Article 4   Applicable law in the absence of choice

1.   To the extent that the law applicable to the contract has not been chosen in accordance with article 3, the contract shall be governed by the law of the country with which it is most closely connected. Nevertheless, a severable part of the contract which has a closer connection with another country may by way of exception be governed by the law of that other country.

2.   Subject to the provisions of paragraph 5 of this article, it shall be presumed that the contract is most closely connected with the country where the party who is to effect the performance which is characteristic of the contract has, at the time of conclusion of the contract, his habitual residence, or, in the case of a body corporate or unincorporate, its central administration.

However, if the contract is entered into in the course of that party's trade or profession, that country shall be the country in which the principal place of business is situated or, where under the terms of the contract the performance is to be effected through a place of business other than the principal place of business, the country in which that other place of business is situated.

3.   Notwithstanding the provisions of Paragraph 2 of this Article, to the extent that the subject matter of the contract is a right in immovable property or a right to use immovable property it shall be presumed that the contract is most closely connected with the country where the immovable property is situated.

4.   A contract for the carriage of goods shall not be subject to the resumption in Paragraph 2. In such a contract if the country in which, at the time the contract is concluded, the carrier has his principal place of business is also the country in which the place of loading or the place of discharge or the principal place of business of the consignor is situated, it shall be presumed that the contract is most closely connected with that country. In applying this paragraph single voyage charter-parties and other contracts the main purpose of which is the carriage of goods shall be treated as contracts for the carriage of goods.

5.   Paragraph 2 shall not apply if the characteristic performance cannot be determined, and the presumptions in paragraphs 2, 3 and 4 shall be

disregarded if it appears from the circumstances as a whole that the contract is more closely connected with another country.

Article 5   Certain consumer contracts

1.   This article applies to a contract the object of which is the supply of goods or services to a person ('the consumer') for a purpose which can be regarded as being outside his trade or profession, or a contract for the provision of credit for that object.

2.   Notwithstanding the provisions of article 3, a choice of law made by the parties shall not have the result of depriving the consumer of the protection afforded to him by the mandatory rules of the law of the country in which he has his habitual residence:

—if in that country the conclusion of the contract was preceded by a specific invitation addressed to him or by advertising, and he had taken in that country all the steps necessary on his part for the conclusion of the contract, or

—if the other party or his agent received the consumer's order in that country, or

—if the contract is for the sale of goods and the consumer travelled from that country to another country and there gave his order, provided that the consumer's journey was arranged by the seller for the purpose of inducing the consumer to buy.

3.   Notwithstanding the provisions of Article 4, a contract to which this article applies shall, in the absence of choice in accordance with Article 3, be governed by the law of the country in which the consumer has his habitual residence if it is entered into in the circumstances described in Paragraph 2 of this Article.

4.   This article shall not apply to:

(a)   a contract of carriage;

(b)   a contract for the supply of services where the services are to be supplied to the consumer exclusively in a country other than that in which he has his habitual residence.

5.   Notwithstanding the provisions of Paragraph 4, this Article shall apply to a contract which, for an inclusive price, provides for a combination of travel and accommodation.

Article 6   Individual employment contracts

1.   Notwithstanding the provisions of Article 3, in a contract of employment a choice of law made by the parties shall not have the result of depriving the employee of the protection afforded to him by the mandatory rules of the law which would be applicable under Paragraph 2 in the absence of choice.

2.   Notwithstanding the provisions of Article 4, a contract of employment shall, in the absence of choice in accordance with Article 3, be governed:

(a)   by the law of the country in which the employee habitually carries out his work in performance of the contract, even if he is temporarily employed in another country; or

(b)   if the employee does not habitually carry out his work in any one country, by the law of the country in which the place of business through which he was engaged is situated; unless it appears from the circumstances as a whole that the contract is more closely connected with another country, in which case the contract shall be governed by the law of that country.

Article 7 Mandatory rules

1. When applying under this Convention the law of a country, effect may be given to the mandatory rules of the law of another country with which the situation has a close connection, if and in so far as, under the law of the latter country, those rules must be applied whatever the law applicable to the contract. In considering whether to give effect to these mandatory rules, regard shall be had to their nature and purpose and to the consequences of their application or non-application.

2. Nothing in this Convention shall restrict the application of the rules of the law of the forum in a situation where they are mandatory irrespective of the law otherwise applicable to the contract.

Article 8 Material validity

1. The existence and validity of a contract, or of any term of a contract, shall be determined by the law which would govern it under this Convention if the Contract or term were valid.

2. Nevertheless a party may rely upon the law of the country in which he has his habitual residence to establish that he did not consent if it appears from the circumstances that it would not be reasonable to determine the effect of his conduct in accordance with the law specified in the preceding paragraph.

Article 9 Formal validity

1. A contract concluded between persons who are in the same country is formally valid if it satisfies the formal requirements of the law which governs it under this Convention or of the law of the country where it is concluded.

2. A contract concluded between persons who are in different countries is formally valid if it satisfies the formal requirements of the law which governs it under this Convention or of the law of one of those countries.

3. Where a contract is concluded by an agent, the country in which the agent acts is the relevant country for the purposes of Paragraphs 1 and 2.

4. An act intended to have legal effect relating to an existing or contemplated contract is formally valid if it satisfies the formal requirements of the law which under this Convention governs or would govern the contract or of the law of the country where the act was done.

5. The provisions of the preceding paragraphs shall not apply to a contract to which Article 5 applies, concluded in the circumstances described in Paragraph 2 of Article 5. The formal validity of such a contract is governed by the law of the country in which the consumer has his habitual residence.

6. Notwithstanding paragraphs 1 to 4 of this Article, a contract the subject matter of which is a right in immovable property or a right to use immovable property shall be subject to the mandatory requirements of form of the law of the country where the property is situated if by that law those requirements are imposed irrespective of the country where the contract is concluded and irrespective of the law governing the contract.

Article 10 Scope of the applicable law

1. The law applicable to a contract by virtue of articles 3 to 6 and 12 of this Convention shall govern in particular:

    (a) interpretation;
    (b) performance;

(c) within the limits of the powers conferred on the court by its procedural law, the consequences of breach, including the assessment of damages in so far as it is governed by rules of law;

(d) the various ways of extinguishing obligations, and prescription and limitation of actions;

(e) the consequences of nullity of the contract.

2.   In relation to the manner of performance and the steps to be taken in the event of defective performance regard shall be had to the law of the country in which performance takes place.

Article 11   Incapacity

In a contract concluded between persons who are in the same country, a natural person who would have capacity under the law of that country may invoke his incapacity resulting from another law only if the other party to the contract was aware of this incapacity at the time of the conclusion of the contract or was not aware thereof as a result of negligence.

Article 12   Voluntary assignment

1.   The mutual obligations of assignor and assignee under a voluntary assignment of a right against another person ('the debtor') shall be governed by the law which under this Convention applies to the contract between the assignor and assignee.

2.   The law governing the right to which the assignment relates shall determine its assignability, the relationship between the assignee and the debtor, the conditions under which the assignment can be invoked against the debtor and any question whether the debtor's obligations have been discharged.

Article 13   Subrogation

1.   Where a person ('the creditor') has a contractual claim upon another ('the debtor'), and a third person has a duty to satisfy the creditor, or has in fact satisfied the creditor in discharge of that duty, the law which governs the third person's duty to satisfy the creditor shall determine whether the third person is entitled to exercise against the debtor the rights which the creditor had against the debtor under the law governing their relationship and, if so, whether he may do so in full or only to a limited extent.

2.   The same rule applies where several persons are subject to the same contractual claim and one of them has satisfied the creditor.

Article 14   Burden of proof, etc.

1.   The law governing the contract under this Convention applies to the extent that it contains, in the law of contract, rules which raise presumptions of law or determine the burden of proof.

2.   A contract or an act intended to have legal effect may be proved by any mode of proof recognised by the law of the forum or by any of the laws referred to in Article 9 under which that contract or act is formally valid, provided that such mode of proof can be administered by the forum.

Article 15   Exclusion of renvoi

The application of the law of any country specified by this Convention means the application of the rules of law in force in that country other than its rules of private international law.

Article 16 'ordre public'

The application of a rule of the law of any country specified by this Convention may be refused only if such application is manifestly incompatible with the public policy ('ordre public') of the forum.

Article 17 No retrospective effect

This Convention shall apply in a contracting state to contracts made after the date on which this Convention has entered into force with respect to that state.

Article 18 Uniform interpretation

In the interpretation and application of the preceding uniform rules, regard shall be had to their international character and to the desirability of achieving uniformity in their interpretation and application.

Article 19 States with more than one legal system

1. Where a state comprises several territorial units each of which has its own rules of law in respect of contractual obligations, each territorial unit shall be considered as a country for the purposes of identifying the law applicable under this Convention.

2. A state within which different territorial units have their own rules of law in respect of contractual obligations shall not be bound to apply this Convention to conflicts solely between the laws of such units.

Article 20 Precedence of Community law

This Convention shall not affect the application of provisions which, in relation to particular matters, lay down choice of law rules relating to contractual obligations and which are or will be contained in acts of the institutions of the European Communities or in national laws harmonised in implementation of such acts.

Article 21 Relationship with other Conventions

This Convention shall not prejudice the application of international conventions to which a contracting state is, or becomes, a party.

Article 22 Reservations

1. Any contracting state may, at the time of signature, ratification, acceptance or approval, reserve the right not to apply:
   (a) the provisions of article 7(1);
   (b) the provisions of article 10(1)(e).

2. ... deleted

3. Any contracting state may at any time withdraw a reservation which it has made; the reservation shall cease to have effect on the first day of the third calendar month after notification of the withdrawal.

TITLE III   FINAL PROVISIONS

Article 23

1. If, after the date on which this Convention has entered into force for a Contracting state, that state wishes to adopt any new choice of law rule in regard to any particular category of contract within the scope of this Convention, it shall communicate its intention to the other signatory states through the Secretary-General of the Council of the European Communities.

2. Any signatory state may, within six months from the date of the communication made to the Secretary-General, request him to arrange consultations between signatory states in order to reach agreement.

3. If no signatory state has requested consultations within this period or if within two years following the communication made to the Secretary-General no agreement is reached in the course of consultations, the contracting state concerned may amend its law in the manner indicated. The measures taken by that State shall be brought to the knowledge of the other signatory states through the Secretary-General of the Council of the European Communities.

Article 24

1. If, after the date on which this Convention has entered into force with respect to a contracting state, that state wishes to become a party to a Multilateral Convention whose principal aim or one of whose principal aims is to lay down rules of private international law concerning any of the matters governed by this Convention, the procedure set out in Article 23 shall apply. However, the period of two years, referred to in Paragraph 3 of that Article, shall be reduced to one year.

2. The procedure referred to in the preceding paragraph need not be followed if a contracting state or one of the European Communities is already a party to the Multilateral Convention, or if its object is to revise a Convention to which the state concerned is already a party, or if it is a Convention concluded within the framework of the treaties establishing the European Communities.

Article 25

If a contracting state considers that the unification achieved by this Convention is prejudiced by the conclusion of agreements not covered by Article 24(1), that state may request the Secretary-General of the Council of the European Communities to arrange consultations between the signatory states of this Convention.

Article 26

Any contracting state may request the revision of this Convention. In this event a revision conference shall be convened by the President of the Council of the European Communities.

Article 27

(deleted)

Article 28

1. This Convention shall be open from 19 June 1980 for signature by the states party to the Treaty establishing the European Economic Community.

2. This Convention shall be subject to ratification, acceptance or approval by the signatory states. The instruments of ratification, acceptance or approval shall be deposited with the Secretary-General of the Council of the European Communities.

Article 29

1. This Convention shall enter into force on the first day of the third month following the deposit of the seventh instrument of ratification, acceptance or approval.

2.   This Convention shall enter into force for each signatory state ratifying, accepting or approving at a later date on the first day of the third month following the deposit of its instrument of ratification, acceptance or approval.

Article 30

1.   This Convention shall remain in force for 10 years from the date of its entry into force in accordance with Article 29(1), even for states for which it enters into force at a later date.

2.   If there has been no denunciation it shall be renewed tacitly every five years.

3.   A contracting state which wishes to denounce shall, not less than six months before the expiration of the period of 10 or five years, as the case may be, give notice to the Secretary-General of the Council of the European Communities.

4.   The denunciation shall have effect only in relation to the state which has notified it. The Convention will remain in force as between all other contracting states.

Article 31

The Secretary-General of the Council of the European Communities shall notify the states party to the Treaty establishing the European Economic Community of:

(a)   the signatures;

(b)   the deposit of each instrument of ratification, acceptance or approval;

(c)   the date of entry into force of this Convention;

(d)   communications made in pursuance of Articles 23, 24, 25, 26 and 30;

(e)   the reservations and withdrawals of reservations referred to in Article 22.

Article 32

The protocol annexed to this Convention shall form an integral part thereof.

Article 33

This Convention, drawn up in a single original in the Danish, Dutch, English, French, German, Irish and Italian languages, these texts being equally authentic, shall be deposited in the archives of the Secretariat of the Council of the European Communities. The Secretary-General shall transmit a certified copy thereof to the government of each signatory state.

Done at Rome on the nineteenth day of June in the year one thousand nine hundred and eighty.

(Signatures omitted)

PROTOCOL

The high contracting parties have agreed upon the following provision which shall be annexed to the Convention:

Notwithstanding the provisions of the Convention, Denmark may retain the rules contained in Soeloven (statute on maritime law) Paragraph 169 concerning the applicable law in matters relating to carriage of goods by sea and may revise these rules without following the procedure prescribed in Article 23 of the Convention.

Done at Rome on the nineteenth day of June in the year one thousand nine hundred and eighty.

(Signatures omitted)

JOINT DECLARATION

At the time of the signature of the Convention on the law applicable to contractual obligations, the governments of the Kingdom of Belgium, the Kingdom of Denmark, the Federal Republic of Germany, the French Republic, Ireland, the Italian Republic, the Grand Duchy of Luxembourg, the Kingdom of the Netherlands and the United Kingdom of Great Britain and Northern Ireland,

I.   Anxious to avoid, as far as possible, dispersion of choice of law rules among several instruments and differences between these rules, express the wish that the institutions of the European Communities, in the exercise of their powers under the Treaties by which they were established, will, where the need arises, endeavour to adopt choice of law rules which are as far as possible consistent with those of this Convention;

II.   Declare their intention as from the date of signature of this Convention until becoming bound by Article 24, to consult with each other if any one of the Signatory States wishes to become a party to any Convention to which the procedure referred to in Article 24 would apply;

III.   Having regard to the contribution of the Convention on the law applicable to contractual obligations to the unification of choice of law rules within the European Communities, express the view that any state which becomes a member of the European Communities should accede to this Convention.

(Signatures omitted)

JOINT DECLARATION

The governments of the Kingdom of Belgium, the Kingdom of Denmark, the Federal Republic of Germany, the French Republic, Ireland, the Italian Republic, the Grand Duchy of Luxembourg, the Kingdom of the Netherlands, and the United Kingdom of Great Britain and Northern Ireland,

On signing the Convention on the law applicable to contractual obligations; Desiring to ensure that the Convention is applied as effectively as possible; Anxious to prevent differences of interpretation of the Convention from impairing its unifying effect;

Declare themselves ready:

1.   To examine the possibility of conferring jurisdiction in certain matters on the Court of Justice of the European Communities and, if necessary, to negotiate an agreement to this effect;

2.   To arrange meetings at regular intervals between their representatives.

(Signatures omitted)

FIRST PROTOCOL
ON THE INTERPRETATIN BY THE COURT OF JUSTICE OF THE EUROPEAN COMMUNITIES OF THE CONVENTION ON THE LAW APPLICABLE TO CONTRACTUAL OBLIGATIONS, OPENED FOR SIGNATURE IN ROME ON 19 JUNE 1980 (89/128/EEC) [OJ L048/1]

THE HIGH CONTRACTING PARTIES TO THE TREATY ESTABLISH-ING THE EUROPEAN ECONOMIC COMMUNITY,

HAVING REGARD to the Joint Declaration annexed to the Convention on the law applicable to contractual obligations, opened for signature in Rome on 19 June 1980,

HAVE DECIDED to conclude a Protocol conferring jurisdiction on the Court of Justice of the European Communities to interpret that Convention, and to this end have designated as their Plenipotentiaries:

HIS MAJESTY THE KING OF THE BELGIANS:
Paul DE KEERSMAEKER
State Secretary for European Affairs and Agriculture,
Deputy to the Minister for External Relations

HER MAJESTY THE QUEEN OF DENMARK:
Knud Erik TYGESEN
State Secretary

THE PRESIDENT OF THE FEDERAL REPUBLIC OF GERMANY:
Irmgard ADAM-SCHWAETZER
Deputy Minister for Foreign Affairs

THE PRESIDENT OF THE HELLENIC REPUBLIC:
Théodoros PANGALOS
Deputy Minister for Foreign Affairs

HIS MAJESTY THE KING OF SPAIN:
Francisco FERNANDEZ ORDOÑEZ
Minister for Foreign Affairs

THE PRESIDENT OF THE FRENCH REPUBLIC:
Philippe LOUËT
Ambassador Extraordinary and Plenipotentiary

THE PRESIDENT OF IRELAND:
Brian LENIHAN
Deputy Prime Minister and Minister for Foreign Affairs

THE PRESIDENT OF THE ITALIAN REPUBLIC:
Gianni MANZOLINI
State Secretary for Foreign Affairs

HIS ROYAL HIGHNESS THE GRAND DUKE OF LUXEMBOURG:
Jacques POOS
Vice-President of the Government, Minister for Foreign Affairs, External Trade and Cooperation, Minister for the Economy and the Middle Classes, Minister for the Treasury

HER MAJESTY THE QUEEN OF THE NETHERLANDS:
H. van den BROEK
Minister for Foreign Affairs

THE PRESIDENT OF THE PORTUGUESE REPUBLIC:
Joao de Deus PINHEIRO
Minister for Foreign Affairs

HER MAJESTY THE QUEEN OF THE UNITED KINGDOM OF
GREAT BRITAIN AND NORTHERN IRELAND:
Lynda CHALKER
Minister of State for Foreign and Commonwealth Affairs

WHO, meeting within the Council of the European Communities, having
exchanged their full powers, found in good and due form,

HAVE AGREED AS FOLLOWS:

Article 1
The Court of Justice of the European Communities shall have jurisdiction to
give rulings on the interpretation of:
    (a) the Convention on the law applicable to contractual obligations,
opened for signature in Rome on 19 June 1980, hereinafter referred to as 'the
Rome Convention';
    (b) the Convention on accession to the Rome Convention by the States
which have become Members of the European Communities since the date on
which it was opened for signature;
    (c) this Protocol.

Article 2
Any of the courts referred to below may request the Court of Justice to give a
preliminary ruling on a question raised in a case pending before it and
concerning interpretation of the provisions contained in the instruments
referred to in Article 1 if that court considers that a decision on the question is
necessary to enable it to give judgment:
    (a) — in Belgium: la Cour de cassation (het Hof van Cassatie) and le
Conseil d'Etat (de Raad van State),
    — in Denmark: Hoejesteret,
    — in the Federal Republic of Germany: die obersten Gerichtshoefe des
Bundes,
    — in Greece: Ta anotata Aikastiria,
    — in Spain: el Tribunal Supremo,
    — in France: la Cour de cassation and le Conseil d'Etat,
    — in Ireland: the Supreme Court,
    — in Italy: la Corte suprema di cassazione and il Consiglio di Stato,
    — in Luxembourg: la Cour Supérieure de Justice, when sitting as Cour de
cassation,
    — in the Netherlands: de Hoge Raad,
    — in Portugal: o Supremo Tribunal de Justiça and o Supremo Tribunal
Administrativo,
    — in the United Kingdom: the House of Lords and other courts from
which no further appeal is possible;
    (b) the courts of the Contracting States when acting as appeal courts.

Article 3

1. The competent authority of a Contracting State may request the Court of Justice to give a ruling on a question of interpretation of the provisions contained in the instruments referred to in Article 1 if judgments given by courts of that State conflict with the interpretation given either by the Court of Justice or in a judgment of one of the courts of another Contracting State referred to in Article 2. The provisions of this paragraph shall apply only to judgments which have become res judicata.

2. The interpretation given by the Court of Justice in response to such a request shall not affect the judgments which gave rise to the request for interpretation.

3. The Procurators-General of the Supreme Courts of Appeal of the Contracting States, or any other authority designated by a Contracting State, shall be entitled to request the Court of Justice for a ruling on interpretation in accordance with paragraph 1.

4. The Registrar of the Court of Justice shall give notice of the request to the Contracting States, to the Commission and to the Council of the European Communities; they shall then be entitled within two months of the notification to submit statements of case or written observations to the Court.

5. No. fees shall be levied or any costs or expenses awarded in respect of the proceedings provided for in this Article.

Article 4

1. Except where this Protocol otherwise provides, the provisions of the Treaty establishing the European Economic Community and those of the Protocol on the Statute of the Court of Justice annexed thereto, which are applicable when the Court is requested to give a preliminary ruling, shall also apply to any proceedings for the interpretation of the instruments referred to in Article 1.

2. The Rules of Procedure of the Court of Justice shall, if necessary, be adjusted and supplemented in accordance with Article 188 of the Treaty establishing the European Economic Community.

Article 5

This Protocol shall be subject to ratification by the Signatory States. The instruments of ratification shall be deposited with the Secretary-General of the Council of the European Communities.

Article 6

1. To enter into force, this Protocol must be ratified by seven States in respect of which the Rome Convention is in force. This Protocol shall enter into force on the first day of the third month following the deposit of the instrument of ratification by the last such State to take this step. If, however, the Second Protocol conferring on the Court of Justice of the European Communities certain powers to interpret the Convention on the law applicable to contractual obligations, opened for signature in Rome on 19 June 1980, concluded in Brussels on 19 December 1988,[1] enters into force on a later date, this Protocol shall enter into force on the date of entry into force of the Second Protocol.

Note
[1]See page 17 of this Official Journal.

2. Any ratification subsequent to the entry into force of this Protocol shall take effect on the first day of the third month following the deposit of the instrument of ratification, provided that the ratification, acceptance or approval of the Rome Convention by the State in question has become effective.

Article 7
The Secretary-General of the Council of the European Communities shall notify the Signatory States of:
  (a) the deposit of each instrument of ratification;
  (b) the date of entry into force of this Protocol;
  (c) any designation communicated pursuant to Article 3(3);
  (d) any communication made pursuant to Article 8.

Article 8
The Contracting States shall communicate to the Secretary-General of the Council of the European Communities the texts of any provisions of their laws which necessitate an amendment to the list of courts in Article 2(a).

Article 9
This Protocol shall have effect for as long as the Rome Convention remains in force under the conditions laid down in Article 30 of that Convention.

Article 10
Any Contracting State may request the revision of this Protocol. In this event, a revision conference shall be convened by the President of the Council of the European Communities.

Article 11
This Protocol, drawn up in a single original in the Danish, Dutch, English, French, German, Greek, Irish, Italian, Portuguese and Spanish languages, all 10 texts being equally authentic, shall be deposited in the archives of the General Secretariat of the Council of the European Communities. The Secretary-General shall transmit a certified copy to the Government of each Signatory State.

Done at Brussels on the nineteenth day of December in the year one thousand nine hundred and eighty-eight.

(Signatures omitted)

JOINT DECLARATIONS

Joint Declaration
    The Governments of the Kingdom of Belgium, the Kingdom of Denmark, the Federal Republic of Germany, the Hellenic Republic, the Kingdom of Spain, the French Republic, Ireland, the Italian Republic, the Grand Duchy of Luxembourg, the Kingdom of the Netherlands, the Portuguese Republic and the United Kingdom of Great Britain and Northern Ireland,
    On signing the First Protocol on the interpretation by the Court of Justice of the European Communities of the Convention on the law applicable to contractual obligations, opened for signature in Rome on 19 June 1980,
    Desiring to ensure that the Convention is applied as effectively and as uniformly as possible,
    Declare themselves ready to organise, in cooperation with the Court of Justice of the European Communities, an exchange of information on

judgments which have become res judicata and have been handed down pursuant to the Convention on the law applicable to contractual obligations by the courts referred to in Article 2 of the said Protocol.

The exchange of information will comprise:

— the forwarding to the Court of Justice by the competent national authorities of judgments handed down by the courts referred to in Article 2(a) and significant judgments handed down by the courts referred to in Article 2(b),

— the classification and the documentary exploitation of these judgments by the Court of Justice including, as far as necessary, the drawing up of abstracts and translations, and the publication of judgments of particular importance,

— the communication by the Court of Justice of the documentary material to the competent national authorities of the States parties to the Protocol and to the Commission and the Council of the European Communities.

Done at Brussels on the nineteenth day of December in the year one thousand nine hundred and eighty-eight.

(Signatures omitted)

CONVENTION ON THE ACCESSION OF THE REPUBLIC OF AUSTRIA, THE REPUBLIC OF FINLAND AND THE KINGDOM OF SWEDEN TO THE CONVENTION ON THE LAW APPLICABLE TO CONTRACTUAL OBLIGATIONS, OPENED FOR SIGNATURE IN ROME ON 19 JUNE 1980, AND TO THE FIRST AND SECOND PROTOCOLS ON ITS INTERPRETATION BY THE COURT OF JUSTICE
[OJ 1997 C15/10]

THE HIGH CONTRACTING PARTIES TO THE TREATY ESTABLISH-ING THE EUROPEAN COMMUNITY,

CONSIDERING that the Republic of Austria, the Republic of Finland and the Kingdom of Sweden, in becoming Members of the European Union, under-took to accede to the Convention on the Law applicable to Contractual Obligations, opened for signature in Rome on 19 June 1980, and to the First and Second Protocols on its interpretation by the Court of Justice,

HAVE AGREED AS FOLLOWS:

TITLE I   GENERAL PROVISIONS

Article 1
The Republic of Austria, the Republic of Finland and the Kingdom of Sweden hereby accede to:

(a)   the Convention on the Law applicable to Contractual Obligations, opened for signature in Rome on 19 June 1980, hereinafter referred to as 'the Convention of 1980', as it stands following incorporation of all the adjustments and amendments made thereto by:

— the Convention signed in Luxembourg on 10 April 1984, hereinafter referred to as 'the Convention of 1984', on the accession of the Hellenic Republic to the Convention on the Law applicable to Contractual Obligations,

— the Convention signed in Funchal on 18 May 1992, hereinafter referred to as 'the Convention of 1992', on the accession of the Kingdom of Spain and the Portuguese Republic to the Convention on the Law applicable to Contractual Obligations;

(b)   the First Protocol, signed on 19 December 1988, hereinafter referred to as 'the First Protocol of 1988', on the interpretation by the Court of Justice of the European Communities of the Convention on the Law applicable to Contractual Obligations;

(c)   the Second Protocol, signed on 19 December 1988, hereinafter referred to as 'the Second Protocol of 1988', conferring on the Court of Justice of the European Communities certain powers to interpret the Convention on the Law applicable to Contractual Obligations.

TITLE II   ADJUSTMENTS TO THE PROTOCOL ANNEXED TO THE CONVENTION OF 1980

Article 2

The Protocol annexed to the Convention of 1980 is hereby replaced by the following:

'Notwithstanding the provisions of the Convention, Denmark, Sweden and Finland may retain national provisions concerning the law applicable to questions relating to the carriage of goods by sea and may amend such provisions without following the procedure provided for in Article 23 of the Convention of Rome. The national provisions applicable in this respect are the following:

— in Denmark, paragraphs 252 and 321(3) and (4) of the 'Soelov' (maritime law),

— in Sweden, Chapter 13, Article 2(1) and (2), and Chapter 14, Article 1(3), of 'sjoelagen' (maritime law),

— in Finland, Chapter 13, Article 2(1) and (2), and Chapter 14, Article 1(3), of 'merilaki'/'sjoelagen' (maritime law).'

TITLE III   ADJUSTMENTS TO THE FIRST PROTOCOL OF 1988

Article 3

The following indents shall be inserted in Article 2(a) of the First Protocol of 1988:

(a)   between the 10th and 11th indents:

'— in Austria: the Oberste Gerichtshof, the Verwaltungsgerichtshof and the Verfassungsgerichtshof,';

(b)   between the 11th and 12th indents:

'— in Finland: korkein oikeus/hoegsta domstolen, korkein hallinto-oikeus/ hoegsta foervaltningsdomstolen, markkinatuomioistuin/marknadsdomstolen and tyoetuomioistuin/arbetsdomstolen,

— in Sweden: Hoegsta domstolen, Regeringsraetten, Arbetsdomstolen and Marknadsdomstolen,'.

TITLE IV   FINAL PROVISIONS

Article 4

1.   The Secretary-General of the Council of the European Union shall transmit a certified copy of the Convention of 1980, the Convention of 1984, the First Protocol of 1988, the Second Protocol of 1988 and the Convention of

1992 in the Danish, Dutch, English, French, German, Greek, Irish, Italian, Spanish and Portuguese languages to the Governments of the Republic of Austria, the Republic of Finland and the Kingdom of Sweden.

2. The text of the Convention of 1980, the Convention of 1984, the First Protocol of 1988, the Second Protocol of 1988 and the Convention of 1992 in the Finnish and Swedish languages shall be authentic under the same conditions as the other texts of the Convention of 1980, the Convention of 1984, the First Protocol of 1988, the Second Protocol of 1988 and the Convention of 1992.

Article 5

This Convention shall be ratified by the signatory States. The instruments of ratification shall be deposited with the Secretary-General of the Council of the European Union.

Article 6

1. This Convention shall enter into force, as between the States which have ratified it, on the first day of the third month following the deposit of the last instrument of ratification by the Republic of Austria, the Republic of Finland or the Kingdom of Sweden and by one Contracting State which has ratified the Convention on the Law applicable to Contractual Obligations.

2. This Convention shall enter into force for each Contracting State which subsequently ratifies it on the first day of the third month following the deposit of its instrument of ratification.

Article 7

The Secretary-General of the Council of the European Union shall notify the signatory States of:

(a) the deposit of each instrument of ratification;

(b) the dates of entry into force of this Convention for the Contracting States.

Article 8

This Convention, drawn up in a single original in the Danish, Dutch, English, Finnish, French, German, Greek, Irish, Italian, Portuguese, Spanish and Swedish languages, all 12 texts being equally authentic, shall be deposited in the archives of the General Secretariat of the Council of the European Union. The Secretary-General shall transmit a certified copy to the Government of each signatory State.

Done at Brussels on the twenty-ninth day of November in the year one thousand nine hundred and ninety-six.

(Signatures omitted)

Joint Declaration

The High Contracting Parties having examined the terms of the Protocol annexed to the Convention of Rome of 1980, as amended by the Convention of Accession of the Republic of Austria, the Republic of Finland and the Kingdom of Sweden to the Convention of 1980, and to the First and Second Protocols of 1988, take note that Denmark, Sweden and Finland state their readiness to examine the extent to which they will be able to ensure that any future amendment concerning their national law applicable to questions relating to the carriage of goods by sea complies with the procedure provided for in Article 23 of the Convention of Rome of 1980.

CONVENTION ON JURISDICTION AND THE ENFORCEMENT OF JUDGMENTS IN CIVIL AND COMMERCIAL MATTERS (88/592/EEC) (LUGANO CONVENTION)
[OJ 1988 L319/9]

THE HIGH CONTRACTING PARTIES TO THIS CONVENTION,

ANXIOUS to strengthen in their territories the legal protection of persons therein established,

CONSIDERING that it is necessary for this purpose to determine the international jurisdiction of their courts, to facilitate recognition and to introduce an expeditious procedure for securing the enforcement of judgments, authentic instruments and court settlements,

AWARE of the links between them, which have been sanctioned in the economic field by the free trade agreements concluded between the European Economic Community and the States members of the European Free Trade Association,

TAKING INTO ACCOUNT the Brussels Convention of 27 September 1968 on jurisdiction and the enforcement of judgments in civil and commercial matters, as amended by the Accession Conventions under the successive enlargements of the European Communities,

PERSUADED that the extension of the principles of that Convention to the States parties to this instrument will strengthen legal and economic cooperation in Europe,

DESIRING to ensure as uniform an interpretation as possible of this instrument,

HAVE in this spirit DECIDED to conclude this Convention and

HAVE AGREED AS FOLLOWS:

TITLE I   SCOPE
Article 1

This Convention shall apply in civil and commercial matters whatever the nature of the court or tribunal. It shall not extend, in particular, to revenue, customs or administrative matters.

The Convention shall not apply to:

1.   the status or legal capacity of natural persons, rights in property arising out of a matrimonial relationship, wills and succession;

2.   bankruptcy, proceedings relating to the winding-up of insolvent companies or other legal persons, judicial arrangements, compositions and analogous proceedings;

3.   social security;

4.   arbitration.

TITLE II   JURISDICTION
SECTION 1   GENERAL PROVISIONS
Article 2

Subject to the provisions of this Convention, persons domiciled in a Contracting State shall, whatever their nationality, be sued in the courts of that State.

Persons who are not nationals of the State in which they are domiciled shall be governed by the rules of jurisdiction applicable to nationals of that State.

Article 3

Persons domiciled in a Contracting State may be sued in the courts of another Contracting State only by virtue of the rules set out in Sections 2 to 6 of this Title.

In particular the following provisions shall not be applicable as against them:

— in Belgium: Article 15 of the civil code (Code civil — Burgerlijk Wetboek) and Article 638 of the judicial code (Code judiciaire — Gerechtelijk Wetboek),

— in Denmark: Article 246(2) and (3) of the law on civil procedure (Lov om rettens pleje),

— in the Federal Republic of Germany: Article 23 of the code of civil procedure (Zivilprozessordnung),

— in Greece: Article 40 of the code of civil procedure (Kodikas politikis dikoyomias),

— in France: Articles 14 and 15 of the civil code (Code civil),

— in Ireland: the rules which enable jurisdiction to be founded on the document instituting the proceedings having been served on the defendant during his temporary presence in Ireland,

— in Iceland: Article 77 of the Civil Proceedings Act (loeg um medferd einkamála í héradi),

— in Italy: Articles 2 and 4, Nos. 1 and 2 of the code of civil procedure (Codice di procedura civile),

— in Luxembourg: Articles 14 and 15 of the civil code (Code civil),

— in the Netherlands: Articles 126(3) and 127 of the code of civil procedure (Wetboek van Burgerlijke Rechtsvordering),

— in Norway: Section 32 of the Civil Proceedings Act (tvistemaalsloven),

— in Austria: Article 99 of the Law on Court Jurisdiction (Jurisdiktionsnorm)

— in Portugal: Articles 65(1)(c), 65(2) and 65A(c) of the code of civil procedure (Código de Processo Civil) and Article 11 of the code of labour procedure (Código de Processo de Trabalho),

— in Switzerland: le for du lieu du séquestre/Gerichtsstand des Arrestortes/foro del luogo del sequestro within the meaning of Article 4 of the loi fédérale sur le droit international privé/Bundesgesetz ueber das internationale Privatrecht/legge federale sul diritto internazionale privato,

— in Finland: the second, third and fourth sentences of Section 1 of Chapter 10 of the Code of Judicial Procedure (oikeudenkaeymiskaari/raettegaangsbalken),

— in Sweden: the first sentence of Section 3 of Chapter 10 of the Code of Judicial Procedure (Raettegaangsbalken),

— in the United Kingdom: the rules which enable jurisdiction to be founded on:

(a) the document instituting the proceedings having been served on the defendant during his temporary presence in the United Kingdom; or

(b) the presence within the United Kingdom of property belonging to the defendant; or

(c) the seizure by the plaintiff of property situated in the United Kingdom.

Article 4

If the defendant is not domiciled in a Contracting State, the jurisdiction of the courts of each Contracting State shall, subject to the provisions of Article 16, be determined by the law of that State.

As against such a defendant, any person domiciled in a Contracting State may, whatever his nationality, avail himself in that State of the rules of jurisdiction there in force, and in particular those specified in the second paragraph of Article 3, in the same way as the nationals of that State.

SECTION 2   SPECIAL JURISDICTION

Article 5

A person domiciled in a Contracting State may, in another Contracting State, be sued:

1. in matters relating to a contract, in the courts for the place of performance of the obligation in question; in matters relating to individual contracts of employment, this place is that where the employee habitually carries out his work, or if the employee does not habitually carry out his work in any one country, this place shall be the place of business through which he was engaged;

2. in matters relating to maintenance, in the courts for the place where the maintenance creditor is domiciled or habitually resident or, if the matter is ancillary to proceedings concerning the status of a person, in the court which, according to its own law, has jurisdiction to entertain those proceedings, unless that jurisdiction is based solely on the nationality of one of the parties;

3. in matters relating to tort, delict or quasi-delict, in the courts for the place where the harmful event occurred;

4. as regards a civil claim for damages or restitution which is based on an act giving rise to criminal proceedings, in the court seised of those proceedings, to the extent that that court has jurisdiction under its own law to entertain civil proceedings;

5. as regards a dispute arising out of the operations of a branch, agency or other establishment, in the courts for the place in which the branch, agency or other establishment is situated;

6. in his capacity as settlor, trustee or beneficiary of a trust created by the operation of a statute, or by a written instrument, or created orally and evidenced in writing, in the courts of the Contracting State in which the trust is domiciled;

7. as regards a dispute concerning the payment of remuneration claimed in respect of the salvage of a cargo or freight, in the court under the authority of which the cargo or freight in question:

    (a)   has been arrested to secure such payment, or

    (b)   could have been so arrested, but bail or other security has been given;

provided that this provision shall apply only if it is claimed that the defendant has an interest in the cargo or freight or had such an interest at the time of salvage.

Article 6

A person domiciled in a Contracting State may also be sued:

1. where he is one of a number of defendants, in the courts for the place where any one of them is domiciled;

2.   as a third party in an action on a warranty or guarantee or in any other third party proceedings, in the court seised of the original proceedings, unless these were instituted solely with the object of removing him from the jurisdiction of the court which would be competent in his case;

3.   on a counterclaim arising from the same contract or facts on which the original claim was based, in the court in which the original claim is pending;

4.   in matters relating to a contract, if the action may be combined with an action against the same defendant in matters relating to rights in rem in immovable property, in the court of the Contracting State in which the property is situated.

Article 6A

Where by virtue of this Convention a court of a Contracting State has jurisdiction in actions relating to liability arising from the use or operation of a ship, that court, or any other court substituted for this purpose by the internal law of that State, shall also have jurisdiction over claims for limitation of such liability.

SECTION 3   JURISDICTION IN MATTERS RELATING TO INSURANCE

Article 7

In matters relating to insurance, jurisdiction shall be determined by this Section, without prejudice to the provisions of Articles 4 and 5(5).

Article 8

An insurer domiciled in a Contracting State may be sued:

1.   in the courts of the State where he is domiciled; or

2.   in another Contracting State, in the courts for the place where the policy-holder is domiciled; or

3.   if he is a co-insurer, in the courts of a Contracting State in which proceedings are brought against the leading insurer.

An insurer who is not domiciled in a Contracting State but has a branch, agency or other establishment in one of the Contracting States shall, in disputes arising out of the operations of the branch, agency or establishment, be deemed to be domiciled in that State.

Article 9

In respect of liability insurance or insurance of immovable property, the insurer may in addition be sued in the courts for the place where the harmful event occurred. The same applies if movable and immovable property are covered by the same insurance policy and both are adversely affected by the same contingency.

Article 10

In respect of liability insurance, the insurer may also, if the law of the court permits it, be joined in proceedings which the injured party has brought against the insured. The provisions of Articles 7, 8 and 9 shall apply to actions brought by the injured party directly against the insurer, where such direct actions are permitted. If the law governing such direct actions provides that the policy-holder or the insured may be joined as a party to the action, the same court shall have jurisdiction over them.

Article 11

Without prejudice to the provisions of the third paragraph of Article 10, an insurer may bring proceedings only in the courts of the Contracting State in which the defendant is domiciled, irrespective of whether he is the policy-holder, the insured or a beneficiary. The provisions of this Section shall not affect the right to bring a counterclaim in the court in which, in accordance with this Section, the original claim is pending.

Article 12

The provisions of this Section may be departed from only by an agreement on jurisdiction:

1. which is entered into after the dispute has arisen; or

2. which allows the policy-holder, the insured or a beneficiary to bring proceedings in courts other than those indicated in this Section; or

3. which is concluded between a policy-holder and an insurer, both of whom are at the time of conclusion of the contract domiciled or habitually resident in the same Contracting State, and which has the effect of conferring jurisdiction on the courts of that State even if the harmful event were to occur abroad, provided that such an agreement is not contrary to the law of the State; or

4. which is concluded with a policy-holder who is not domiciled in a Contracting State, except in so far as the insurance is compulsory or relates to immovable property in a Contracting State; or

5. which relates to a contract of insurance in so far as it covers one or more of the risks set out in Article 12A.

Article 12A

The following are the risks referred to in Article 12(5):

1. any loss of or damage to:

(a) sea-going ships, installations situated off shore or on the high seas, or aircraft, arising from perils which relate to their use for commercial purposes;

(b) goods in transit other than passengers' baggage where the transit consists of or includes carriage by such ships or aircraft;

2. any liability, other than for bodily injury to passengers or loss of or damage to their baggage;

(a) arising out of the use or operation of ships, installations or aircraft as referred to in (1)(a) above in so far as the law of the Contracting State in which such aircraft are registered does not prohibit agreements on jurisdiction regarding insurance of such risks;

(b) for loss or damage caused by goods in transit as described in (1)(b) above;

3. any financial loss connected with the use or operation of ships, installations or aircraft as referred to in (1)(a) above, in particular loss of freight or charter-hire;

4. any risk or interest connected with any of those referred to in (1) to (3) above.

SECTION 4   JURISDICTION OVER CONSUMER CONTRACTS

Article 13

In proceedings concerning a contract concluded by a person for a purpose which can be regarded as being outside his trade or profession, hereinafter called 'the consumer', jurisdiction shall be determined by this Section, without prejudice to the provisions of Articles 4 and 5(5), if it is:

1.   a contract for the sale of goods on instalment credit terms; or

2.   a contract for a loan repayable by instalments, or for any other form of credit, made to finance the sale of goods; or

3.   any other contract for the supply of goods or a contract for the supply of services, and

   (a)   in the State of the consumer's domicile the conclusion of the contract was preceded by a specific invitation addressed to him or by advertising, and

   (b)   the consumer took in that State the steps necessary for the conclusion of the contract.

Where a consumer enters into a contract with a party who is not domiciled in a Contracting State but has a branch, agency or other establishment in one of the Contracting States, that party shall, in disputes arising out of the operations of the branch, agency or establishment, be deemed to be domiciled in that State.

This Section shall not apply to contracts of transport.

Article 14

A consumer may bring proceedings against the other party to a contract either in the courts of the Contracting State in which that party is domiciled or in the courts of the Contracting State in which he is himself domiciled. Proceedings may be brought against a consumer by the other party to the contract only in the courts of the Contracting State in which the consumer is domiciled. These provisions shall not affect the right to bring a counterclaim in the court in which, in accordance with this Section, the original claim is pending.

Article 15

The provisions of this Section may be departed from only by an agreement:

1.   which is entered into after the dispute has arisen; or

2.   which allows the consumer to bring proceedings in courts other than those indicated in this Section; or

3.   which is entered into by the consumer and the other party to the contract, both of whom are at the time of conclusion of the contract domiciled or habitually resident in the same Contracting State, and which confers jurisdiction on the courts of that State, provided that such an agreement is not contrary to the law of that State.

SECTION 5   EXCLUSIVE JURISDICTION

Article 16

The following courts shall have exclusive jurisdiction, regardless of domicile:

1.   (a)   in proceedings which have as their object rights in rem in immovable property or tenancies of immovable property, the courts of the Contracting State in which the property is situated;

   (b)   however, in proceedings which have as their object tenancies of immovable property concluded for temporary private use for a maximum period of six consecutive months, the courts of the Contracting State in which the defendant is domiciled shall also have jurisdiction, provided that the tenant is a natural person and neither party is domiciled in the Contracting State in which the property is situated;

2.   in proceedings which have as their object the validity of the constitution, the nullity or the dissolution of companies or other legal persons or associations of natural or legal persons, or the decisions of their organs, the courts of the Contracting State in which the company, legal person or association has its seat;

3.   in proceedings which have as their object the validity of entries in public registers, the courts of the Contracting State in which the register is kept;

4.   in proceedings concerned with the registration or validity of patents, trade marks, designs, or other similar rights required to be deposited or registered, the courts of the Contracting State in which the deposit or registration has been applied for, has taken place or is under the terms of an international convention deemed to have taken place;

5.   in proceedings concerned with the enforcement of judgments, the courts of the Contracting State in which the judgment has been or is to be enforced.

SECTION 6   PROROGATION OF JURISDICTION

Article 17

1.   If the parties, one or more of whom is domiciled in a Contracting State, have agreed that a court or the courts of a Contracting State are to have jurisdiction to settle any disputes which have arisen or which may arise in connection with a particular legal relationship, that court or those courts shall have exclusive jurisdiction. Such an agreement conferring jurisdiction shall be either:

(a)   in writing or evidenced in writing, or

(b)   in a form which accords with practices which the parties have established between themselves, or

(c)   in international trade or commerce, in a form which accords with a usage of which the parties are or ought to have been aware and which in such trade or commerce is widely known to, and regularly observed by, parties to contracts of the type involved in the particular trade or commerce concerned. Where such an agreement is concluded by parties, none of whom is domiciled in a Contracting State, the courts of other Contracting States shall have no jurisdiction over their disputes unless the court or courts chosen have declined jurisdiction.

2.   The court or courts of a Contracting State on which a trust instrument has conferred jurisdiction shall have exclusive jurisdiction in any proceedings brought against a settlor, trustee or beneficiary, if relations between these persons or their rights or obligations under the trust are involved.

3.   Agreements or provisions of a trust instrument conferring jurisdiction shall have no legal force if they are contrary to the provisions of Article 12 or 15, or if the courts whose jurisdiction they purport to exclude have exclusive jurisdiction by virtue of Article 16.

4.   If an agreement conferring jurisdiction was concluded for the benefit of only one of the parties, that party shall retain the right to bring proceedings in any other court which has jurisdiction by virtue of this Convention.

5.   In matters relating to individual contracts of employment an agreement conferring jurisdiction shall have legal force only if it is entered into after the dispute has arisen.

Article 18

Apart from jurisdiction derived from other provisions of this Convention, a court of a Contracting State before whom a defendant enters an appearance shall have jurisdiction. This rule shall not apply where appearance was entered solely to contest the jurisdiction, or where another court has exclusive jurisdiction by virtue of Article 16.

SECTION 7   EXAMINATION AS TO JURISDICTION AND ADMISSIBILITY

Article 19

Where a court of a Contracting State is seised of a claim which is principally concerned with a matter over which the courts of another Contracting State have exclusive jurisdiction by virtue of Article 16, it shall declare of its own motion that it has no jurisdiction.

Article 20

Where a defendant domiciled in one Contracting State is sued in a court of another Contracting State and does not enter an appearance, the court shall declare of its own motion that it has no jurisdiction unless its jurisdiction is derived from the provisions of this Convention.

The court shall stay the proceedings so long as it is not shown that the defendant has been able to receive the document instituting the proceedings or an equivalent document in sufficient time to enable him to arrange for his defence, or that all necessary steps have been taken to this end.

The provisions of the foregoing paragraph shall be replaced by those of Article 15 of the Hague Convention of 15 November 1965 on the service abroad of judicial and extrajudicial documents in civil or commercial matters, if the document instituting the proceedings or notice thereof had to be transmitted abroad in accordance with that Convention.

SECTION 8   LIS PENDENS — RELATED ACTIONS

Article 21

Where proceedings involving the same cause of action and between the same parties are brought in the courts of different Contracting States, any court other than the court first seised shall of its own motion stay its proceedings until such time as the jurisdiction of the court first seised is established. Where the jurisdiction of the court first seised is established, any court other than the court first seised shall decline jurisdiction in favour of that court.

Article 22

Where related actions are brought in the courts of different Contracting States, any court other than the court first seised may, while the actions are pending at first instance, stay its proceedings. A court other than the court first seised may also, on the application of one of the parties, decline jurisdiction if the law of that court permits the consolidation of related actions and the court first seised has jurisdiction over both actions. For the purposes of this Article, actions are deemed to be related where they are so closely connected that it is expedient to hear and determine them together to avoid the risk of irreconcilable judgments resulting from separate proceedings.

Article 23

Where actions come within the exclusive jurisdiction of several courts, any court other than the court first seised shall decline jurisdiction in favour of that court.

SECTION 9   PROVISIONAL, INCLUDING PROTECTIVE, MEASURES

Article 24

Application may be made to the courts of a Contracting State for such provisional, including protective, measures as may be available under the law of that State, even if, under this Convention, the courts of another Contracting State have jurisdiction as to the substance of the matter.

TITLE III   RECOGNITION AND ENFORCEMENT

Article 25

For the purposes of this Convention, 'judgment' means any judgment given by a court or tribunal of a Contracting State, whatever the judgment may be called, including a decree, order, decision or writ of execution, as well as the determination of costs or expenses by an officer of the court.

SECTION 1   RECOGNITION

Article 26

A judgment given in a Contracting State shall be recognised in the other Contracting States without any special procedure being required. Any interested party who raises the recognition of a judgment as the principal issue in a dispute may, in accordance with the procedures provided for in Section 2 and 3 of this Title, apply for a decision that the judgment be recognised.

If the outcome of proceedings in a court of a Contracting State depends on the determination of an incidental question of recognition that court shall have jurisdiction over that question.

Article 27

A judgment shall not be recognised:

1.   if such recognition is contrary to public policy in the State in which recognition is sought;

2.   where it was given in default of appearance, if the defendant was not duly served with the document which instituted the proceedings or with an equivalent document in sufficient time to enable him to arrange for his defence;

3.   if the judgment is irreconcilable with a judgment given in a dispute between the same parties in the State in which recognition is sought;

4.   if the court of the State of origin, in order to arrive at its judgment, has decided a preliminary question concerning the status or legal capacity of natural persons, rights in property arising out of a matrimonial relationship, wills or succession in a way that conflicts with a rule of the private international law of the State in which the recognition is sought, unless the same result would have been reached by the application of the rules of private international law of that State;

5.   if the judgment is irreconcilable with an earlier judgment given in a non-contracting State involving the same cause of action and between the same parties, provided that this latter judgment fulfils the conditions necessary for its recognition in the State addressed.

Article 28

Moreover, a judgment shall not be recognised if it conflicts with the provisions of Sections 3, 4 or 5 of Title II or in a case provided for in Article 59.

A judgment may furthermore be refused recognition in any case provided for in Article 54B (3) or 57(4).

In its examination of the grounds of jurisdiction referred to in the foregoing paragraphs, the court or authority applied to shall be bound by the findings of fact on which the court of the State of origin based its jurisdiction.

Subject to the provisions of the first and second paragraphs, the jurisdiction of the court of the State of origin may not be reviewed; the test of public policy referred to in Article 27(1) may not be applied to the rules relating to jurisdiction.

Article 29

Under no circumstances may a foreign judgment be reviewed as to its substance.

Article 30

A court of a Contracting State in which recognition is sought of a judgment given in another Contracting State may stay the proceedings if an ordinary appeal against the judgment has been lodged.

A court of a Contracting State in which recognition is sought of a judgment given in Ireland or the United Kingdom may stay the proceedings if enforcement is suspended in the State of origin by reason of an appeal.

SECTION 2   ENFORCEMENT

Article 31

A judgment given in a Contracting State and enforceable in that State shall be enforced in another Contracting State when, on the application of any interested party, it has been declared enforceable there.

However, in the United Kingdom, such a judgment shall be enforced in England and Wales, in Scotland, or in Northern Ireland when, on the application of any interested party, it has been registered for enforcement in that part of the United Kingdom.

Article 32

1.   The application shall be submitted:
　　—in Belgium, to the tribunal de première instance or rechtbank van eerste aanleg,
　　—in Denmark, to the byret,
　　—in the Federal Republic of Germany, to the presiding judge of a chamber of the Landgericht,
　　—in Greece, to the monomeles protodikeio,
　　—in Spain, to the Juzgado de Primera Instancia,
　　—in France, to the presiding judge of the tribunal de grande instance,
　　—in Ireland, to the High Court,
　　—in Iceland, to the héradsdómari,
　　—in Italy, to the corte d'appello,
　　—in Luxembourg, to the presiding judge of the tribunal d'arrondissement,
　　—in the Netherlands, to the presiding judge of the arrondissementsrechtbank,
　　—in Norway, to the herredsrett or byrett as namsrett,
　　—in Austria, to the Landesgericht or the Kreisgericht,

—in Portugal, to the Tribunal Judicial de Círculo,

—in Switzerland:

(a)   in respect of judgments ordering the payment of a sum of money, to the juge de la mainlevée/Rechtsoeffnungsrichter/giudice competente a pronunciare sul rigetto dell'opposizione, within the framework of the procedure governed by Articles 80 and 81 of the loi fédérale sur la poursuite pour dettes et la faillite/Bundesgesetz ueber Schuldbetreibung und Konkurs/legge federale sulla esecuzione e sul fallimento;

(b)   in respect of judgments ordering a performance other than the payment of a sum of money, to the juge cantonal d'exequatur compétent/zustaendiger kantonaler Vollstreckungsrichter/giudice cantonale competente a pronunciare l'exequatur,

—in Finland, to the ulosotonhaltija/oeverexekutor,

—in Sweden, to the Svea hovraett,

—in the United Kingdom:

(a)   in England and Wales, to the High Court of Justice, or in the case of a maintenance judgment to the Magistrates' Court on transmission by the Secretary of State;

(b)   in Scotland, to the Court of Session, or in the case of a maintenance judgment to the Sheriff Court on transmission by the Secretary of State;

(c)   in Northern Ireland, to the High Court of Justice, or in the case of a maintenance judgment to the Magistrates' Court on transmission by the Secretary of State.

2.   The jurisdiction of local courts shall be determined by reference to the place of domicile of the party against whom enforcement is sought. If he is not domiciled in the State in which enforcement is sought, it shall be determined by reference to the place of enforcement.

Article 33

The procedure for making the application shall be governed by the law of the State in which enforcement is sought. The applicant must give an address for service of process within the area of jurisdiction of the court applied to. However, if the law of the State in which enforcement is sought does not provide for the furnishing of such an address, the applicant shall appoint a representative ad litem. The documents referred to in Articles 46 and 47 shall be attached to the application.

Article 34

The court applied to shall give its decision without delay; the party against whom enforcement is sought shall not at this stage of the proceedings be entitled to make any submissions on the application. The application may be refused only for one of the reasons specified in Articles 27 and 28. Under no circumstances may the foreign judgment be reviewed as to its substance.

Article 35

The appropriate officer of the court shall without delay bring the decision given on the application to the notice of the applicant in accordance with the procedure laid down by the law of the State in which enforcement is sought.

Article 36

If enforcement is authorised, the party against whom enforcement is sought may appeal against the decision within one month of service thereof. If that party is domiciled in a Contracting State other than that in which the decision authorising enforcement was given, the time for appealing shall be two months and shall run from the date of service, either on him in person or at his residence. No extension of time may be granted on account of distance.

Article 37

1. An appeal against the decision authorising enforcement shall be lodged in accordance with the rules governing procedure in contentious matters:

— in Belgium, with the tribunal de première instance or rechtsbank van eerste aanleg,

— in Denmark, with the landsret,

— in the Federal Republic of Germany, with the Oberlandesgericht,

— in Greece, with the efeteio,

— in Spain, with the Audiencia Provincial,

— in France, with the cour d'appel,

— in Ireland, with the High Court,

— in Iceland, with the héradsdómari,

— in Italy, with the corte d'appello,

— in Luxembourg, with the Cour supérieure de justice sitting as a court of civil appeal,

— in the Netherlands, with the arrondissements rechtsbank,

— in Norway, with the lagmannsrett,

— in Austria, with the Landesgericht or the Kreisgericht,

— in Portugal, with the Tribunal da Relaçao,

— in Switzerland, with the tribunal cantonal/Kantonsgericht/tribunale cantonale,

— in Finland, with the hovioikeus/hovraett,

— in Sweden, with the Svea hovraett,

— in the United Kingdom:

(a)   in England and Wales, with the High Court of Justice, or in the case of a maintenance judgment with the Magistrates' Court;

(b)   in Scotland, with the Court of Session, or in the case of a maintenance judgment with the Sheriff Court;

(c)   in Northern Ireland, with the High Court of Justice, or in the case of a maintenance judgment with the Magistrates' Court.

2.   The judgment given on the appeal may be contested only:

— in Belgium, Greece, Spain, France, Italy, Luxembourg and in the Netherlands, by an appeal in cassation,

— in Denmark, by an appeal to the hoejesteret, with the leave of the Minister of Justice,

— in the Federal Republic of Germany, by a Rechtsbeschwerde,

— in Ireland, by an appeal on a point of law to the Supreme Court,

— in Iceland, by an appeal to the Haestiréttur,

— in Norway, by an appeal (kjaeremaal or anke) to the Hoyesteretts Kjaeremaalsutvalg or Hoyesterett,

— in Austria, in the case of an appeal, by a Revisionsrekurs and, in the case of opposition proceedings, by a Berufung with the possibility of a Revision,
— in Portugal, by an appeal on a point of law,
— in Switzerland, by a recours de droit public devant le tribunal fédéral/staatsrechtliche Beschwerde beim Bundesgericht/ricorso di diritto pubblico davanti al tribunale federale,
— in Finland, by an appeal to the korkein oikeus/hoegsta domstolen,
— in Sweden, by an appeal to the hoegsta domstolen,
— in the United Kingdom, by a single further appeal on a point of law.

Article 38
The court with which the appeal under Article 37(1) is lodged may, on the application of the appellant, stay the proceedings if an ordinary appeal has been lodged against the judgment in the State of origin or if the time for such an appeal has not yet expired; in the latter case, the court may specify the time within which such an appeal is to be lodged.

Where the judgment was given in Ireland or the United Kingdom, any form of appeal available in the State of origin shall be treated as an ordinary appeal for the purposes of the first paragraph. The court may also make enforcement conditional on the provision of such security as it shall determine.

Article 39
During the time specified for an appeal pursuant to Article 36 and until any such appeal has been determined, no measures of enforcement may be taken other than protective measures taken against the property of the party against whom enforcement is sought. The decision authorising enforcement shall carry with it the power to proceed to any such protective measures.

Article 40
1. If the application for enforcement is refused, the applicant may appeal:
— in Belgium, to the cour d'appel or hof van beroep,
— in Denmark, to the landsret,
— in the Federal Republic of Germany, to the Oberlandesgericht,
— in Greece, to the efeteio,
— in Spain, to the Audiencia Provincial,
— in France, to the cour d'appel,
— in Ireland, to the High Court,
— in Iceland, to the héradsdómari,
— in Italy, to the corte d'appello,
— in Luxembourg, to the Cour supérieure de justice sitting as a court of civil appeal,
— in the Netherlands, to the gerechtshof,
— in Norway, to the lagmannsrett,
— in Austria, to the Landesgericht or the Kreisgericht,
— in Portugal, to the Tribunal da Relaçao,
— in Switzerland, to the tribunal cantonal/Kantons gericht/tribunale cantonale,
— in Finland, to the hovioikeus/hovraett,
— in Sweden, to the Svea hovraett,
— in the United Kingdom:

(a) in England and Wales, to the High Court of Justice, or in the case of a maintenance judgment to the Magistrates' Court;

(b) in Scotland, to the Court of Session, or in the case of a maintenance judgment to the Sheriff Court;

(c) in Northern Ireland, to the High Court of Justice, or in the case of a maintenance judgment to the Magistrates' Court.

2. The party against whom enforcement is sought shall be summoned to appear before the appellate court. If he fails to appear, the provisions of the second and third paragraphs of Article 20 shall apply even where he is not domiciled in any of the Contracting States.

Article 41

A judgment given on an appeal provided for in Article 40 may be contested only:

—in Belgium, Greece, Spain, France, Italy, Luxembourg and in the Netherlands, by an appeal in cassation,

—in Denmark, by an appeal to the hoejesteret, with the leave of the Minister of Justice,

—in the Federal Republic of Germany, by a Rechtsbeschwerde,

—in Ireland, by an appeal on a point of law to the Supreme Court,

—in Iceland, by an appeal to the Haestiréttur,

—in Norway, by an appeal (kjaeremaal or anke) to the Hoyesteretts kjaeremaalsutvalg or Hoyesterett,

—in Austria, by a Revisionsrekurs,

—in Portugal, by an appeal on a point of law,

—in Switzerland, by a recours de droit public devant le tribunal fédéral/staatsrechtliche Beschwerde beim Bundesgericht/ricorso di diritto pubblico davanti al tribunale federale,

—in Finland, by an appeal to the korkein oikeus/hoegsta domstolen,

—in Sweden, by an appeal to the hoegsta domstolen,

—in the United Kingdom, by a single further appeal on a point of law.

Article 42

Where a foreign judgment has been given in respect of several matters and enforcement cannot be authorised for all of them, the court shall authorise enforcement for one or more of them. An applicant may request partial enforcement of a judgment.

Article 43

A foreign judgment which orders a periodic payment by way of a penalty shall be enforceable in the State in which enforcement is sought only if the amount of the payment has been finally determined by the courts of the State of origin.

Article 44

An applicant who, in the State of origin, has benefited from complete or partial legal aid or exemption from costs or expenses, shall be entitled, in the procedures provided for in Articles 32 to 35, to benefit from the most favourable legal aids or the most extensive exemption from costs or expenses provided for by the law of the State addressed.

However, an applicant who requests the enforcement of a decision given by an administrative authority in Denmark or in Iceland in respect of a maintenance order may, in the State addressed, claim the benefits referred to in the first paragraph if he presents a statement from, respectively, the Danish Ministry of Justice or the Icelandic Ministry of Justice to the effect that he fulfils the economic requirements to qualify for the grant of complete or partial legal aid or exemption from costs or expenses.

Article 45
No. security, bond or deposit, however described, shall be required of a party who in one Contracting State applies for enforcement of a judgment given in another Contracting State on the ground that he is a foreign national or that he is not domiciled or resident in the State in which enforcement is sought.

SECTION 3 COMMON PROVISIONS

Article 46
A party seeking recognition or applying for enforcement of a judgment shall produce:
    1. a copy of the judgment which satisfies the conditions necessary to establish its authenticity;
    2. in the case of a judgment given in default, the original or a certified true copy of the document which establishes that the party in default was served with the document instituting the proceedings or with an equivalent document.

Article 47
A party applying for enforcement shall also produce:
    1. documents which establish that, according to the law of the State of origin, the judgment is enforceable and has been served;
    2. where appropriate, a document showing that the applicant is in receipt of legal aid in the State of origin.

Article 48
If the documents specified in Articles 46(2) and 47(2) are not produced, the court may specify a time for their production, accept equivalent documents or, if it considers that it has sufficient information before it, dispense with their production.

If the court so requires, a translation of the documents shall be produced; the translation shall be certified by a person qualified to do so in one of the Contracting States.

Article 49
No legalisation or other similar formality shall be required in respect of the documents referred to in Articles 46 or 47 or the second paragraph of Article 48, or in respect of a document appointing a representative ad litem.

TITLE IV AUTHENTIC INSTRUMENTS AND COURT SETTLEMENTS

Article 50
A document which has been formally drawn up or registered as an authentic instrument and is enforceable in one Contracting State shall, in another

Contracting State, be declared enforceable there, on application made in accordance with the procedures provided for in Articles 31 et seq. The application may be refused only if enforcement of the instrument is contrary to public policy in the State addressed.

The instrument produced must satisfy the conditions necessary to establish its authenticity in the State of origin. The provisions of Section 3 of Title III shall apply as appropriate.

Article 51

A settlement which has been approved by a court in the course of proceedings and is enforceable in the State in which it was concluded shall be enforceable in the State addressed under the same conditions as authentic instruments.

TITLE V GENERAL PROVISIONS

Article 52

In order to determine whether a party is domiciled in the Contracting State whose courts are seised of a matter, the Court shall apply its internal law. If a party is not domiciled in the State whose courts are seised of the matter, then, in order to determine whether the party is domiciled in another Contracting State, the court shall apply the law of that State.

Article 53

For the purposes of this Convention, the seat of a company or other legal person or association of natural or legal persons shall be treated as its domicile. However, in order to determine that seat, the court shall apply its rules of private international law. In order to determine whether a trust is domiciled in the Contracting State whose courts are seised of the matter, the court shall apply its rules of private international law.

TITLE VI TRANSITIONAL PROVISIONS

Article 54

The provisions of this Convention shall apply only to legal proceedings instituted and to documents formally drawn up or registered as authentic instruments after its entry into force in the State of origin and, where recognition or enforcement of a judgment or authentic instrument is sought, in the State addressed.

However, judgments given after the date of entry into force of this Convention between the State of origin and the State addressed in proceedings instituted before that date shall be recognised and enforced in accordance with the provisions of Title III if jurisdiction was founded upon rules which accorded with those provided for either in Title II of this Convention or in a convention concluded between the State of origin and the State addressed which was in force when the proceedings were instituted.

If the parties to a dispute concerning a contract had agreed in writing before the entry into force of this Convention that the contract was to be governed by the law of Ireland or of a part of the United Kingdom, the courts of Ireland or of that part of the United Kingdom shall retain the right to exercise jurisdiction in the dispute.

Article 54A

For a period of three years from the entry into force of this Convention for Denmark, Greece, Ireland, Iceland, Norway, Finland and Sweden, respectively, jurisdiction in maritime matters shall be determined in these States not only in accordance with the provisions of Title II, but also in accordance with the provisions of paragraphs 1 to 7 following. However, upon the entry into force of the International Convention relating to the arrest of sea-going ships, signed at Brussels on 10 May 1952, for one of these States, these provisions shall cease to have effect for that State.

1.   A person who is domiciled in a Contracting State may be sued in the courts of one of the States mentioned above in respect of a maritime claim if the ship to which the claim relates or any other ship owned by him has been arrested by judicial process within the territory of the latter State to secure the claim, or could have been so arrested there but bail or other security has been given, and either:

    (a)   the claimant is domiciled in the latter State; or

    (b)   the claim arose in the latter State; or

    (c)   the claim concerns the voyage during which the arrest was made or could have been made; or

    (d)   the claim arises out of a collision or out of damage caused by a ship to another ship or to goods or persons on board either ship, either by the execution or non-execution of a manoeuvre or by the non-observance of regulations; or

    (e)   the claim is for salvage; or

    (f)   the claim is in respect of a mortgage or hypothecation of the ship arrested.

2.   A claimant may arrest either the particular ship to which the maritime claim relates, or any other ship which is owned by the person who was, at the time when the maritime claim arose, the owner of the particular ship. However, only the particular ship to which the maritime claim relates may be arrested in respect of the maritime claims set out under 5(o), (p) or (q) of this Article.

3.   Ships shall be deemed to be in the same ownership when all the shares therein are owned by the same person or persons.

4.   When in the case of a charter by demise of a ship the charterer alone is liable in respect of a maritime claim relating to that ship, the claimant may arrest that ship or any other ship owned by the charterer, but no other ship owned by the owner may be arrested in respect of such claim. The same shall apply to any case in which a person other than the owner of a ship is liable in respect of a maritime claim relating to that ship.

5.   The expression 'maritime claim' means a claim arising out of one or more of the following:

    (a)   damage caused by any ship either in collision or otherwise;

    (b)   loss of life or personal injury caused by any ship or occurring in connection with the operation on any ship;

    (c)   salvage;

    (d)   agreement relating to the use or hire of any ship whether by charterparty or otherwise;

    (e)   agreement relating to the carriage of goods in any ship whether by charterparty or otherwise;

    (f)   loss of or damage to goods including baggage carried in any ship;

    (g)   general average;

    (h)   bottomry;

    (i)   towage;

    (j)   pilotage;

    (k)   goods or materials wherever supplied to a ship for her operation or maintenance;

    (l)   construction, repair or equipment of any ship or dock charges and dues;

    (m) wages of masters, officers or crew;

    (n)   master's disbursements, including disbursements made by shippers, charterers or agents on behalf of a ship or her owner;

    (o)   dispute as to the title to or ownership of any ship;

    (p)   disputes between co-owners of any ship as to the ownership, possession, employment or earnings of that ship;

    (q)   the mortgage or hypothecation of any ship.

6. In Denmark, the expression 'arrest' shall be deemed as regards the maritime claims referred to under 5(o) and (p) of this Article, to include a 'forbud', where that is the only procedure allowed in respect of such a claim under Articles 646 to 653 of the law on civil procedure (lov om rettens pleje).

7. In Iceland, the expression 'arrest' shall be deemed, as regards the maritime claims referred to under 5(o) and (p) of this Article, to include a 'loegbann', where that is the only procedure allowed in respect of such a claim under Chapter III of the law on arrest and injunction (loeg um kyrrsetningu og loegbann).

TITLE VII   RELATIONSHIP TO THE BRUSSELS CONVENTION AND TO OTHER CONVENTIONS

Article 54B

1. This Convention shall not prejudice the application by the Member States of the European Communities of the Convention on Jurisdiction and the Enforcement of Judgments in Civil and Commercial Matters, signed at Brussels on 27 September 1968 and of the Protocol on interpretation of that Convention by the Court of Justice, signed at Luxembourg on 3 June 1971, as amended by the Conventions of Accession to the said Convention and the said Protocol by the States acceding to the European Communities, all of these Conventions and the Protocol being hereinafter referred to as the 'Brussels Convention'.

2. However, this Convention shall in any event be applied:

    (a)   in matters of jurisdiction, where the defendant is domiciled in the territory of a Contracting State which is not a member of the European Communities, or where Article 16 or 17 of this Convention confer a jurisdiction on the courts of such a Contracting State;

    (b)   in relation to a lis pendens or to related actions as provided for in Articles 21 and 22, when proceedings are instituted in a Contracting State which is not a member of the European Communities and in a Contracting State which is a member of the European Communities;

    (c)   in matters of recognition and enforcement, where either the State of origin or the State addressed is not a member of the European Communities.

3. In addition to the grounds provided for in Title III recognition or enforcement may be refused if the ground of jurisdiction on which the judgment has been based differs from that resulting from this Convention and recognition or enforcement is sought against a party who is domiciled in a Contracting State which is not a member of the European Communities, unless the judgment may otherwise be recognised or enforced under any rule of law in the State addressed.

Article 55
Subject to the provisions of Articles 54(2) and 56, this Convention shall, for the States which are parties to it, supersede the following conventions concluded between two or more of them:

— the Convention between the Swiss Confederation and France on jurisdiction and enforcement of judgments in civil matters, signed at Paris on 15 June 1869,

— the Treaty between the Swiss Confederation and Spain on the mutual enforcement of judgments in civil or commercial matters, signed at Madrid on 19 November 1896,

— the Convention between the Swiss Confederation and the German Reich on the recognition and enforcement of judgments and arbitration awards, signed at Berne on 2 November 1929,

— the Convention between Denmark, Finland, Iceland, Norway and Sweden on the recognition and enforcement of judgments, signed at Copenhagen on 16 March 1932,

— the Convention between the Swiss Confederation and Italy on the recognition and enforcement of judgments, signed at Rome on 3 January 1933,

— the Convention between Sweden and the Swiss Confederation on the recognition and enforcement of judgments and arbitral awards signed at Stockholm on 15 January 1936,

— the Convention between the Kingdom of Belgium and Austria on the reciprocal recognition and enforcement of judgments and authentic instruments relating to maintenance obligations, signed at Vienna on 25 October 1957,

— the Convention between the Swiss Confederation and Belgium on the recognition and enforcement of judgments and arbitration awards, signed at Berne on 29 April 1959,

— the Convention between the Federal Republic of Germany and Austria on the reciprocal recognition and enforcement of judgments, settlements and authentic instruments in civil and commercial matters, signed at Vienna on 6 June 1959,

— the Convention between the Kingdom of Belgium and Austria on the reciprocal recognition and enforcement of judgments, arbitral awards and authentic instruments in civil and commercial matters, signed at Vienna on 16 June 1959,

— the Convention between Austria and the Swiss Confederation on the recognition and enforcement of judgments, signed at Berne on 16 December 1960,

— the Convention between Norway and the United Kingdom providing for the reciprocal recognition and enforcement of judgments in civil matters, signed at London on 12 June 1961,

—the Convention between the United Kingdom and Austria providing for the reciprocal recognition and enforcement of judgments in civil and commercial matters, signed at Vienna on 14 July 1961, with amending Protocol signed at London on 6 March 1970,

—the Convention between the Kingdom of the Netherlands and Austria on the reciprocal recognition and enforcement of judgments and authentic instruments in civil and commercial matters, signed at The Hague on 6 February 1963,

—the Convention between France and Austria on the recognition and enforcement of judgments and authentic instruments in civil and commercial matters, signed at Vienna on 15 July 1966,

—the Convention between Luxembourg and Austria on the recognition and enforcement of judgements and authentic instruments in civil and commercial matters, signed at Luxembourg on 29 July 1971,

—the Convention between Italy and Austria on the recognition and enforcement of judgments in civil and commercial matters, of judicial settlements and of authentic instruments, signed at Rome on 16 November 1971,

—the Convention between Norway and the Federal Republic of Germany on the recognition and enforcement of judgments and enforceable documents, in civil and commercial matters, signed at Oslo on 17 June 1977,

—the Convention between Denmark, Finland, Iceland, Norway and Sweden on the recognition and enforcement of judgments in civil matters, signed at Copenhagen on 11 October 1977,

—the Convention between Austria and Sweden on the recognition and enforcement of judgments in civil matters, signed at Stockholm on 16 September 1982,

—the Convention between Austria and Spain on the recognition and enforcement of judgments, settlements and enforceable authentic instruments in civil and commercial matters, signed at Vienna on 17 February 1984,

—the Convention between Norway and Austria on the recognition and enforcement of judgments in civil matters, signed at Vienna on 21 May 1984, and

—the Convention between Finland and Austria on the recognition and enforcement of judgments in civil matters, signed at Vienna on 17 November 1986.

Article 56

The Treaty and the conventions referred to in Article 55 shall continue to have effect in relation to matters to which this Convention does not apply. They shall continue to have effect in respect of judgments given and documents formally drawn up or registered as authentic instruments before the entry into force of this Convention.

Article 57

1.   This Convention shall not affect any conventions to which the Contracting States are or will be parties and which in relation to particular matters, govern jurisdiction or the recognition or enforcement of judgments.

2.   This Convention shall not prevent a court of a Contracting State which is party to a convention referred to in the first paragraph from assuming

jurisdiction in accordance with that convention, even where the defendant is domiciled in a Contracting State which is not a party to that convention. The court hearing the action shall, in any event, apply Article 20 of this Convention.

3.   Judgments given in a Contracting State by a court in the exercise of jurisdiction provided for in a convention referred to in the first paragraph shall be recognised and enforced in the other Contracting States in accordance with Title III of this Convention.

4.   In addition to the grounds provided for in Title III, recognition or enforcement may be refused if the State addressed is not a contracting party to a convention referred to in the first paragraph and the person against whom recognition or enforcement is sought is domiciled in that State, unless the judgment may otherwise be recognised or enforced under any rule of law in the State addressed.

5.   Where a convention referred to in the first paragraph to which both the State of origin and the State addressed are parties lays down conditions for the recognition or enforcement of judgments, those conditions shall apply. In any event, the provisions of this Convention which concern the procedures for recognition and enforcement of judgments may be applied.

Article 58
(None)

Article 59
This Convention shall not prevent a Contracting State from assuming, in a convention on the recognition and enforcement of judgments, an obligation towards a third State not to recognise judgments given in other Contracting States against defendants domiciled or habitually resident in the third State where, in cases provided for in Article 4, the judgment could only be founded on a ground of jurisdiction specified in the second paragraph of Article 3.

However, a Contracting State may not assume an obligation towards a third State not to recognise a judgment given in another Contracting State by a court basing its jurisdiction on the presence within that State of property belonging to the defendant, or the seizure by the plaintiff of property situated there:

1.   if the action is brought to assert or declare proprietary or possessory rights in that property, seeks to obtain authority to dispose of it, or arises from another issue relating to such property, or

2.   if the property constitutes the security for a debt which is the subject-matter of the action.

TITLE VIII   FINAL PROVISIONS

Article 60
The following may be parties to this Convention:

(a)   States which, at the time of the opening of this Convention for signature, are members of the European Communities or of the European Free Trade Association;

(b)   States which, after the opening of this Convention for signature, become members of the European Communities or of the European Free Trade Association;

(c)   States invited to accede in accordance with Article 62(1)(b).

Article 61

1. This Convention shall be opened for signature by the States Members of the European Communities or of the European Free Trade Association.

2. The Convention shall be submitted for ratification by the signatory States. The instruments of ratification shall be deposited with the Swiss Federal Council.

3. The Convention shall enter into force on the first day of the third month following the date on which two States, of which one is a member of the European Communities and the other a member of the European Free Trade Association, deposit their instruments of ratification.

4. The Convention shall take effect in relation to any other signatory State on the first day of the third month following the deposit of its instrument of ratification.

Article 62

1. After entering into force this Convention shall be open to accession by:
   (a)   the States referred to in Article 60(b);
   (b)   other States which have been invited to accede upon a request made by one of the Contracting States to the depositary State. The depositary State shall invite the State concerned to accede only if, after having communicated the contents of the communications that this State intends to make in accordance with Article 63, it has obtained the unanimous agreement of the signatory States and the Contracting States referred to in Article 60(a) and (b).

2. If an acceding State wishes to furnish details for the purposes of Protocol 1, negotiations shall be entered into to that end. A negotiating conference shall be convened by the Swiss Federal Council.

3. In respect of an acceding State, the Convention shall take effect on the first day of the third month following the deposit of its instrument of accession.

4. However, in respect of an acceding State referred to in paragraph 1(a) or (b), the Convention shall take effect only in relations between the acceding State and the Contracting States which have not made any objections to the accession before the first day of the third month following the deposit of the instrument of accession.

Article 63

Each acceding State shall, when depositing its instrument of accession, communicate the information required for the application of Articles 3, 32, 37, 40, 41 and 55 of this Convention and furnish, if need be, the details prescribed during the negotiations for the purposes of Protocol 1.

Article 64

1. This Convention is concluded for an initial period of five years from the date of its entry into force in accordance with Article 61(3), even in the case of States which ratify it or accede to it after that date.

2. At the end of the initial five-year period, the Convention shall be automatically renewed from year to year.

3. Upon the expiry of the initial five-year period, any contracting State may, at any time, denounce the Convention by sending a notification to the Swiss Federal Council.

4. The denunciation shall take effect at the end of the calendar year following the expiry of a period of six months from the date of receipt by the Swiss Federal Council of the notification of denunciation.

Article 65
The following are annexed to this Convention:
— a Protocol 1, on certain questions of jurisdiction, procedure and enforcement,
— a Protocol 2, on the uniform interpretation of the Convention,
— a Protocol 3, on the application of Article 57.
These Protocols shall form an integral part of the Convention.

Article 66
Any Contracting State may request the revision of this Convention. To that end, the Swiss Federal Council shall issue invitations to a revision conference within a period of six months from the date of the request for revision.

Article 67
The Swiss Federal Council shall notify the States represented at the Diplomatic Conference of Lugano and the States who have later acceded to the Convention of:
(a) the deposit of each instrument of ratification or accession;
(b) the dates of entry into force of this Convention in respect of the Contracting States;
(c) any denunciation received pursuant to Article 64;
(d) any declaration received pursuant to Article Ia of Protocol 1;
(e) any declaration received pursuant to Article Ib of Protocol 1;
(f) any declaration received pursuant to Article IV of Protocol 1;
(g) any communication made pursuant to Article VI of Protocol 1.

Article 68
This Convention, drawn up in a single original in the Danish, Dutch, English, Finnish, French, German, Greek, Icelandic, Irish, Italian, Norwegian, Portuguese, Spanish and Swedish languages, all fourteen texts being equally authentic, shall be deposited in the archives of the Swiss Federal Council. The Swiss Federal Council shall transmit a certified copy to the Government of each State represented at the Diplomatic Conference of Lugano and to the Government of each acceding State.

Done at Lugano on the sixteenth day of September in the year one thousand nine hundred and eighty-eight.

For Her Majesty the Queen of the United Kingdom of Great Britain and Northern Ireland

PROTOCOL 1
ON CERTAIN QUESTIONS OF JURISDICTION, PROCEDURE AND ENFORCEMENT

THE HIGH CONTRACTING PARTIES HAVE AGREED UPON THE FOLLOWING PROVISIONS, WHICH SHALL BE ANNEXED TO THE CONVENTION:

Article I
Any person domiciled in Luxembourg who is sued in a court of another Contracting State pursuant to Article 5(1) may refuse to submit to the

jurisdiction of that court. If the defendant does not enter an appearance the court shall declare of its own motion that it has no jurisdiction. An agreement conferring jurisdiction, within the meaning of Article 17, shall be valid with respect to a person domiciled in Luxembourg only if that person has expressly and specifically so agreed.

Article Ia

1. Switzerland reserves the right to declare, at the time of depositing its instrument of ratification, that a judgment given in another Contracting State shall be neither recognised nor enforced in Switzerland if the following conditions are met:

(a) the jurisdiction of the court which has given the judgment is based only on Article 5(1) of this Convention; and

(b) the defendant was domiciled in Switzerland at the time of the introduction of the proceedings; for the purposes of this Article, a company or other legal person is considered to be domiciled in Switzerland if it has its registered seat and the effective centre of activities in Switzerland; and

(c) the defendant raises an objection to the recognition or enforcement of the judgment in Switzerland, provided that he has not waived the benefit of the declaration foreseen under this paragraph.

2. This reservation shall not apply to the extent that at the time recognition or enforcement is sought a derogation has been granted from Article 59 of the Swiss Federal Constitution. The Swiss Government shall communicate such derogations to the signatory States and the acceding States.

3. This reservation shall cease to have effect on 31 December 1999. It may be withdrawn at any time.

Article Ib

Any Contracting State may, by declaration made at the time of signing or of deposit of its instrument of ratification or of accession, reserve the right, notwithstanding the provisions of Article 28, not to recognise and enforce judgments given in the other Contracting States if the jurisdiction of the court of the State of origin is based, pursuant to Article 16(1)(b), exclusively on the domicile of the defendant in the State of origin, and the property is situated in the territory of the State which entered the reservation.

Article II

Without prejudice to any more favourable provisions of national laws, persons domiciled in a Contracting State who are being prosecuted in the criminal courts of another Contracting State of which they are not nationals for an offence which was not intentionally committed may be defended by persons qualified to do so, even if they do not appear in person.

However, the court seised of the matter may order appearance in person; in the case of failure to appear, a judgment given in the civil action without the person concerned having had the opportunity to arrange for his defence need not be recognised or enforced in the other Contracting States.

Article III

In proceedings for the issue of an order for enforcement, no charge, duty or fee calculated by reference to the value of the matter in issue may be levied in the State in which enforcement is sought.

Article IV

Judicial and extrajudicial documents drawn up in one Contracting State which have to be served on persons in another Contracting State shall be transmitted in accordance with the procedures laid down in the conventions and agreements concluded between the Contracting States.

Unless the State in which service is to take place objects by declaration to the Swiss Federal Council, such documents may also be sent by the appropriate public officers of the State in which the document has been drawn up directly to the appropriate public officers of the State in which the addressee is to be found.

In this case the officer of the State of origin shall send a copy of the document to the officer of the State applied to who is competent to forward it to the addressee.

The document shall be forwarded in the manner specified by the law of the State applied to. The forwarding shall be recorded by a certificate sent directly to the officer of the State of origin.

Article V

The jurisdiction specified in Articles 6(2) and 10 in actions on a warranty or guarantee or in any other third party proceedings may not be resorted to in the Federal Republic of Germany, in Spain, in Austria and in Switzerland. Any person domiciled in another Contracting State may be sued in the courts:

— of the Federal Republic of Germany, pursuant to Articles 68, 72, 73 and 74 of the code of civil procedure (Zivilprozessordnung) concerning third-party notices,

— of Spain, pursuant to Article 1482 of the civil code,

— of Austria, pursuant to Article 21 of the code of civil procedure (Zivilprozessordnung) concerning third-party notices,

— of Switzerland, pursuant to the appropriate provisions concerning third-party notices of the cantonal codes of civil procedure.

Judgments given in the other Contracting States by virtue of Article 6(2) or 10 shall be recognised and enforced in the Federal Republic of Germany, in Spain, in Austria and in Switzerland in accordance with Title III. Any effects which judgments given in these States may have on third parties by application of the provisions in the preceding paragraph shall also be recognised in the other Contracting States.

Article Va

In matters relating to maintenance, the expression 'court' includes the Danish, Icelandic and Norwegian administrative authorities. In civil and commercial matters, the expression 'court' includes the Finnish ulosotonhaltija/ oeverexekutor.

Article Vb

In proceedings involving a dispute between the master and a member of the crew of a sea-going ship registered in Denmark, in Greece, in Ireland, in Iceland, in Norway, in Portugal or in Sweden concerning remuneration or other conditions of service, a court in a Contracting State shall establish whether the diplomatic or consular officer responsible for the ship has been notified of the dispute. It shall stay the proceedings so long as he has not been notified. It shall of its own motion decline jurisdiction if the officer, having been duly notified, has exercised the powers accorded to him in the matter by a consular convention, or in the absence of such a convention has, within the time allowed, raised any objection to the exercise of such jurisdiction.

Article Vc
(None)

Article Vd
Without prejudice to the jurisdiction of the European Patent Office under the Convention on the grant of European patents, signed at Munich on 5 October 1973, the courts of each Contracting State shall have exclusive jurisdiction, regardless of domicile, in proceedings concerned with the registration or validity of any European patent granted for that State which is not a Community patent by virtue of the provision of Article 86 of the Convention for the European patent for the common market, signed at Luxembourg on 15 December 1975.

Article VI
The Contracting States shall communicate to the Swiss Federal Council the text of any provisions of their laws which amend either those provisions of their laws mentioned in the Convention or the lists of courts specified in Section 2 of Title III.

PROTOCOL 2
ON THE UNIFORM INTERPRETATION OF THE CONVENTION

PREAMBLE

THE HIGH CONTRACTING PARTIES,

HAVING REGARD to Article 65 of this Convention,

CONSIDERING the substantial link between this Convention and the Brussels Convention,

CONSIDERING that the Court of Justice of the European Communities by virtue of the Protocol of 3 June 1971 has jurisdiction to give rulings on the interpretation of the provisions of the Brussels Convention,

BEING AWARE of the rulings delivered by the Court of Justice of the European Communities on the interpretation of the Brussels Convention up to the time of signature of this Convention,

CONSIDERING that the negotiations which led to the conclusion of the Convention were based on the Brussels Convention in the light of these rulings,

DESIRING to prevent, in full deference to the independence of the courts, divergent interpretations and to arrive at as uniform an interpretation as possible of the provisions of the Convention, and of these provisions and those of the Brussels Convention which are substantially reproduced in this Convention,

HAVE AGREED AS FOLLOWS:

Article 1
The courts of each Contracting State shall, when applying and interpreting the provisions of the Convention, pay due account to the principles laid down by any relevant decision delivered by courts of the other Contracting States concerning provisions of this Convention.

Article 2

1. The Contracting Parties agree to set up a system of exchange of information concerning judgments delivered pursuant to this Convention as well as relevant judgments under the Brussels Convention. This system shall comprise:

— transmission to a central body by the competent authorities of judgments delivered by courts of last instance and the Court of Justice of the European Communities as well as judgments of particular importance which have become final and have been delivered pursuant to this Convention or the Brussels Convention,

— classification of these judgments by the central body including, as far as necessary, the drawing-up and publication of translations and abstracts,

— communication by the central body of the relevant documents to the competent national authorities of all signatories and acceding States to the Convention and to the Commission of the European Communities.

2. The central body is the Registrar of the Court of Justice of the European Communities.

Article 3

1. A Standing Committee shall be set up for the purposes of this Protocol.

2. The Committee shall be composed of representatives appointed by each signatory and acceding State.

3. The European Communities (Commission, Court of Justice and General Secretariat of the Council) and the European Free Trade Association may attend the meetings as observers.

Article 4

1. At the request of a Contracting Party, the depositary of the Convention shall convene meetings of the Committee for the purpose of exchanging views on the functioning of the Convention and in particular on:

— the development of the case-law as communicated under the first indent of Article 2(1),

— the application of Article 57 of the Convention.

2. The Committee, in the light of these exchanges, may also examine the appropriateness of starting on particular topics a revision of the Convention and make recommendations.

PROTOCOL 3
ON THE APPLICATION OF ARTICLE 57

THE HIGH CONTRACTING PARTIES HAVE AGREED AS FOLLOWS:

1. For the purposes of the Convention, provisions which, in relation to particular matters, govern jurisdiction or the recognition or enforcement of judgments and which are, or will be contained in acts of the institutions of the European Communities shall be treated in the same way as the conventions referred to in Article 57(1).

2. If one Contracting State is of the opinion that a provision contained in an act of the institutions of the European Communities is incompatible with the Convention, the Contracting States shall promptly consider amending the Convention pursuant to Article 66, without prejudice to the procedure established by Protocol 2.

DECLARATION by the representatives of the Governments of the States signatories to the Lugano Convention which are members of the European Communities on Protocol 3 on the application of Article 57 of the Convention upon signature of the Convention on jurisdiction and the enforcement of judgments in civil and commercial matters done at Lugano on 16 September 1988,

THE REPRESENTATIVES OF THE GOVERNMENTS OF THE MEMBER STATES OF THE EUROPEAN COMMUNITIES, taking into account the undertakings entered into vis-à-vis the member states of the European Free Trade Association, anxious not to prejudice the unity of the legal system set up by the Convention, declare that they will take all measures in their power to ensure, when Community acts referred to in paragraph 1 of Protocol 3 on the application of Article 57 are being drawn up, respect for the rules of jurisdiction and recognition and enforcement of judgments established by the Convention.

In witness whereof the undersigned have signed this Declaration.

Done at Lugano on the sixteenth day of September in the year one thousand nine hundred and eighty-eight.

For the Government of the United Kingdom of Great Britain and Northern Ireland

DECLARATION by the Representatives of the Governments of the States signatories to the Lugano Convention which are members of the European Communities upon signature of the Convention on jurisdiction and the enforcement of judgments in civil and commercial matters done at Lugano on 16 September 1988,

THE REPRESENTATIVES OF THE GOVERNMENTS OF THE MEMBER STATES OF THE EUROPEAN COMMUNITIES declare that they consider it appropriate that the Court of Justice of the European Communities, when interpreting the Brussels Convention, pay due account to the rulings contained in the case-law of the Lugano Convention.

In witness whereof the undersigned have signed this Declaration.

Done at Lugano on the sixteenth day of September in the year one thousand nine hundred and eighty-eight.

For the Government of the United Kingdom of Great Britain and Northern Ireland

DECLARATION by the Representatives of the Governments of the States signatories to the Lugano Convention which are members of the European Free Trade Association upon signature of the Convention on jurisdiction and the enforcement of judgments in civil and commercial matters done at Lugano on 16 September 1988,

THE REPRESENTATIVES OF THE GOVERNMENTS OF THE MEMBER STATES OF THE EUROPEAN FREE TRADE ASSOCIATION declare that they consider as appropriate that their courts, when interpreting the Lugano Convention, pay due account to the rulings contained in the case law of the Court of Justice of the European Communities and of courts of the Member States of the European Communities in respect of provisions of the Brussels Convention which are substantially reproduced in the Lugano Convention.

In witness whereof the undersigned have signed this Declaration.

Done at Lugano on the sixteenth day of September in the year one thousand nine hundred and eighty-eight.

FINAL ACT

The Representatives of:

THE GOVERNMENT OF THE KINGDOM OF BELGIUM,
THE GOVERNMENT OF THE KINGDOM OF DENMARK,
THE GOVERNMENT OF THE FEDERAL REPUBLIC OF GERMANY,
THE GOVERNMENT OF THE HELLENIC REPUBLIC,
THE GOVERNMENT OF THE KINGDOM OF SPAIN,
THE GOVERNMENT OF THE FRENCH REPUBLIC,
THE GOVERNMENT OF IRELAND,
THE GOVERNMENT OF THE REPUBLIC OF ICELAND,
THE GOVERNMENT OF THE ITALIAN REPUBLIC,
THE GOVERNMENT OF THE GRAND DUCHY OF LUXEMBOURG,
THE GOVERNMENT OF THE KINGDOM OF THE NETHERLANDS,
THE GOVERNMENT OF THE KINGDOM OF NORWAY,
THE GOVERNMENT OF THE REPUBLIC OF AUSTRIA,
THE GOVERNMENT OF THE PORTUGUESE REPUBLIC,
THE GOVERNMENT OF THE KINGDOM OF SWEDEN,
THE GOVERNMENT OF THE SWISS CONFEDERATION,
THE GOVERNMENT OF THE REPUBLIC OF FINLAND,
THE GOVERNMENT OF THE UNITED KINGDOM OF GREAT BRITAIN AND NORTHERN IRELAND,

Assembled at Lugano on the sixteenth day of September in the year one thousand nine hundred and eighty-eight on the occasion of the Diplomatic Conference on jurisdiction in civil matters, have placed on record the fact that the following texts have been drawn up and adopted within the Conference:

   III.   the Convention on jurisdiction and the enforcement of judgments in civil and commercial matters;

   III.   the following Protocols, which form an integral part of the Convention:

    — 1, on certain questions of jurisdiction, procedure and enforcement,
    — 2, on the uniform interpretation of the Convention,
    — 3, on the application of Article 57;

   III.   the following Declarations:

    — Declaration by the Representatives of the Governments of the States signatories to the Lugano Convention which are members of the European Communities on Protocol 3 on the application of Article 57 of the Convention,

    — Declaration by the Representatives of the Governments of the States signatories to the Lugano Convention which are members of the European Communities,

    — Declaration by the Representatives of the Governments of the States signatories to the Lugano Convention which are members of the European Free Trade Association.

In witness whereof, the undersigned have signed this Final Act.

Done at Lugano on the sixteenth day of September in the year one thousand nine hundred and eighty-eight.

   For the Government of the United Kingdom of Great Britain and Northern Ireland.

ANNEX I

TREATY ESTABLISHING THE EUROPEAN ECONOMIC COMMUNITY[1]

CONTENTS

Note

[1]This is the EEC Treaty before its amendment by the Treaty on European Union. Whilst this contents page has been retained in full, all of the Articles of the EEC Treaty which were not amended by the TEU have been removed and only those which were changed are reproduced here.

EXTRACTS FROM THE TREATY ESTABLISHING THE EUROPEAN ECONOMIC COMMUNITY AS AMENDED BY THE TREATY AMENDING CERTAIN FINANCIAL PROVISIONS, THE SINGLE EUROPEAN ACT, THE MERGER TREATY, THE GREENLAND TREATY AND THE ACTS OF ACCESSION

PART ONE   PRINCIPLES

Article 1

By this Treaty, the High Contracting Parties establish among themselves a European Economic Community.

Article 2

The Community shall have as its task, by establishing a common market and progressively approximating the economic policies of Member States, to promote throughout the Community a harmonious development of economic activities, a continuous and balanced expansion, an increase in stability, an accelerated raising of the standard of living and closer relations between the States belonging to it.

Article 3

For the purposes set out in Article 2, the activities of the Community shall include, as provided in this Treaty and in accordance with the timetable set out therein

    (a)   the elimination, as between Member States, of customs duties and of quantitative restrictions on the import and export of goods, and of all other measures having equivalent effect;

    (b)   the establishment of a common customs tariff and of a common commercial policy towards third countries;

    (c)   the abolition, as between Member States, of obstacles to freedom of movement for persons, services and capital;

    (d)   the adoption of a common policy in the sphere of agriculture;

    (e)   the adoption of a common policy in the sphere of transport;

    (f)   the institution of a system ensuring that competition in the common market is not distorted;

    (g)   the application of procedures by which the economic policies of Member States can be coordinated and disequilibria in their balances of payments remedied;

    (h)   the approximation of the laws of Member States to the extent required for the proper functioning of the common market;

    (i)   the creation of a European Social Fund in order to improve employment opportunities for workers and to contribute to the raising of their standard of living;

(j)   the establishment of a European Investment Bank to facilitate the economic expansion of the Community by opening up fresh resources;

(k)   the association of the overseas countries and territories in order to increase trade and to promote jointly economic and social development.

Article 4

1.   The tasks entrusted to the Community shall be carried out by the following institutions:

a European Parliament,

a Council,

a Commission,

a Court of Justice.

Each institution shall act within the limits of the powers conferred upon it by this Treaty.

2.   The Council and the Commission shall be assisted by an Economic and Social Committee acting in an advisory capacity.

3.   The audit shall be carried out by a Court of Auditors acting within the limits of the powers conferred upon it by this Treaty.[1]

Note

[1]Paragraph 3 added by Article 11 of the Treaty amending Certain Financial Provisions.

Article 6

1.   Member States shall, in close cooperation with the institutions of the Community, coordinate their respective economic policies to the extent necessary to attain the objectives of this Treaty.

2.   The institutions of the Community shall take care not to prejudice the internal and external financial stability of the Member States.

Article 7

Within the scope of application of this Treaty, and without prejudice to any special provisions contained therein, any discrimination on grounds of nationality shall be prohibited.

The Council may, on a proposal from the Commission and in cooperation with the European Parliament, adopt, by a qualified majority, rules designed to prohibit such discrimination.[1]

Note

[1]Second paragraph as amended by Article 6(2) of the SEA.

Article 8

1.   The common market shall be progressively established during a transitional period of twelve years.

This transitional period shall be divided into three stages of four years each; the length of each stage may be altered in accordance with the provisions set out below.

2.   To each stage there shall be assigned a set of actions to be initiated and carried through concurrently.

3.   Transition from the first to the second stage shall be conditional upon a finding that the objectives specifically laid down in this Treaty for the first stage have in fact been attained in substance and that, subject to the exceptions and procedures provided for in this Treaty, the obligations have been fulfilled.

This finding shall be made at the end of the fourth year by the Council, acting unanimously on a report from the Commission. A Member State may not, however, prevent unanimity by relying upon the non-fulfilment of its own obligations. Failing unanimity, the first stage shall automatically be extended for one year.

At the end of the fifth year, the Council shall make its finding under the same conditions. Failing unanimity, the first stage shall automatically be extended for a further year.

At the end of the sixth year, the Council shall make its finding, acting by a qualified majority on a report from the Commission.

4.   Within one month of the last-mentioned vote any Member State which voted with the minority or, if the required majority was not obtained, any Member State shall be entitled to call upon the Council to appoint an arbitration board whose decision shall be binding upon all Member States and upon the institutions of the Community. The arbitration board shall consist of three members appointed by the Council acting unanimously on a proposal from the Commission.

If the Council has not appointed the members of the arbitration board within one month of being called upon to do so, they shall be appointed by the Court of Justice within a further period of one month.

The arbitration board shall elect its own Chairman.

The board shall make its award within six months of the date of the Council vote referred to in the last subparagraph of paragraph 3.

5.   The second and third stages may not be extended or curtailed except by a decision of the Council, acting unanimously on a proposal from the Commission.

6.   Nothing in the preceding paragraphs shall cause the transitional period to last more than fifteen years after the entry into force of this Treaty.

7.   Save for the exceptions or derogations provided for in this Treaty, the expiry of the transitional period shall constitute the latest date by which all the rules laid down must enter into force and all the measures required for establishing the common market must be implemented.

Article 8a[1]

The Community shall adopt measures with the aim of progressively establishing the internal market over a period expiring on 31 December 1992, in accordance with the provisions of this Article and of Articles 8b, 8c, 28, 57(2), 59, 70(1), 84, 99, 100a and 100b and without prejudice to the other provisions of this Treaty.

The internal market shall comprise an area without internal frontiers in which the free movement of goods, persons, services and capital is ensured in accordance with the provisions of this Treaty.

Note
[1]Article added by Article 13 of the SEA.

Article 8b[1]

The Commission shall report to the Council before 31 December 1988 and again before 31 December 1990 on the progress made towards achieving the internal market within the time limit fixed in Article 8a.

Note
[1]Article added by Article 14 of the SEA.

The Council, acting by qualified majority on a proposal from the Commission, shall determine the guidelines and conditions necessary to ensure balanced progress in all the sectors concerned.

Article 8c[1]

When drawing up its proposals with a view to achieving the objectives set out in Article 8a, the Commission shall take into account the extent of the effort that certain economies showing differences in development will have to sustain during the period of establishment of the internal market and it may propose appropriate provisions.

If these provisions take the form of derogations, they must be of a temporary nature and must cause the least possible disturbance to the functioning of the common market.

Note

[1]Article added by Article 15 of the SEA.

PART TWO   FOUNDATIONS OF THE COMMUNITY
TITLE III   FREE MOVEMENT OF PERSONS, SERVICES AND CAPITAL
CHAPTER 1   WORKERS

Article 49

As soon as this Treaty enters into force, the Council shall, acting by a qualified majority on a proposal from the Commission, in cooperation with the European Parliament and after consulting the Economic and Social Committee, issue directives or make regulations setting out the measures required to bring about, by progressive stages, freedom of movement for workers, as defined in Article 48, in particular:[1]

(a)   by ensuring close cooperation between national employment services;

(b)   by systematically and progressively abolishing those administrative procedures and practices and those qualifying periods in respect of eligibility for available employment, whether resulting from national legislation or from agreements previously concluded between Member States, the maintenance of which would form an obstacle to liberalisation of the movement of workers;

(c)   by systematically and progressively abolishing all such qualifying periods and other restrictions provided for either under national legislation or under agreements previously concluded between Member States as imposed on workers of other Member States conditions regarding the free choice of employment other than those imposed on workers of the state concerned;

(d)   by setting up appropriate machinery to bring offers of employment into touch with applications for employment and to facilitate the achievement of a balance between supply and demand in the employment market in such a way as to avoid serious threats to the standard of living and level of employment in the various regions and industries.

Note

[1]First sentence as amended by Article 6(3) of the SEA.

CHAPTER 2 RIGHT OF ESTABLISHMENT

Article 54

1. Before the end of the first stage, the Council shall, acting unanimously from the Commission and after consulting the Economic and Social Committee and the European Parliament, draw up a general programme for the abolition of existing restrictions on freedom of establishment within the Community. The Commission shall submit its proposal to the Council during the first two years of the first stage.

The programme shall set out the general conditions under which freedom of establishment is to be attained in the case of each type of activity and in particular the stages by which it is to be attained.

2. In order to implement this general programme or, in the absence of such programme, in order to achieve a stage in attaining freedom of establishment as regards a particular activity, the Council shall, acting on a proposal from the Commission, in cooperation with the European Parliament and after consulting the Economic and Social Committee, issue directives, acting unanimously until the end of the first stage and by a qualified majority thereafter.[1]

3. The Council and the Commission shall carry out the duties devolving upon them under the preceding provisions, in particular:

(a) by according, as a general rule, priority treatment to activities where freedom of establishment makes a particularly valuable contribution to the development of production and trade;

(b) by ensuring close cooperation between the competent authorities in the Member States in order to ascertain the particular situation within the Community of the various activities concerned;

(c) by abolishing those administrative procedures and practices, whether resulting from national legislation or from agreements previously concluded between Member States, the maintenance of which would form an obstacle to freedom of establishment;

(d) by ensuring that workers of one Member State employed in the territory of another Member State may remain in that territory for the purpose of taking up activities therein as self-employed persons, where they satisfy the conditions which they would be required to satisfy if they were entering that State at the time when they intended to take up such activities;

(e) by enabling a national of one Member State to acquire and use land and buildings situated in the territory of another Member State, in so far as this does not conflict with the principles laid down in Article 39(2);

(f) by effecting the progressive abolition of restrictions on freedom of establishment in every branch of activity under consideration, both as regards the conditions for setting up agencies, branches or subsidiaries in the territory of a Member State and as regards the subsidiaries in the territory of a Member State and as regards the conditions governing the entry of personnel belonging to the main establishment into managerial or supervisory posts in such agencies, branches or subsidiaries;

(g) by coordinating to the necessary extent the safeguards which, for the protection of the interests of members and others, are required by Member

Note
[1] Paragraph 2 as amended by Article 6(4) of the SEA.

States of companies or firms within the meaning of the second paragraph of Article 58 with a view to making such safeguards equivalent throughout the Community;

(h) by satisfying themselves that the conditions of establishment are not distorted by aids granted by Member States.

Article 56

1. The provisions of this Chapter and measures taken in pursuance thereof shall not prejudice the applicability of provisions laid down by law, regulation or administrative action providing for special treatment for foreign nationals on grounds of public policy, public security or public health.

2. Before the end of the transitional period, the Council shall, acting unanimously on a proposal from the Commission and after consulting the European Parliament, issue directives for the coordination of the aforementioned provisions laid down by law, regulation or administrative action. After the end of the second stage, however, the Council shall, acting by a qualified majority on a proposal from the Commission and in cooperation with the European Parliament, issue directives for the coordination of such provisions as, in each Member State, are a matter for regulation or administrative action.[1]

Note
[1]Second sentence of paragraph 2 as amended by Article 6(5) of the SEA.

Article 57

1. In order to make it easier for persons to take up and pursue activities as self-employed persons, the Council shall, on a proposal from the Commission and in cooperation with the European Parliament, acting unanimously during the first stage and by a qualified majority thereafter, issue directives for the mutual recognition of diplomas, certificates and other evidence of formal qualifications.[1]

2. For the same purpose, the Council shall, before the end of the transitional period, acting on a proposal from the Commission and after consulting the European Parliament, issue directives for the coordination of the provisions laid down by law, regulation or administrative action in Member States concerning the taking up and pursuit of activities as self-employed persons. Unanimity shall be required for directives the implementation of which involves in at least one Member State amendment of the existing principles laid down by law governing the professions with respect to training and conditions of access for natural persons.[2] In other cases the Council shall act by a qualified majority, in cooperation with the European Parliament.[3]

3. In the case of the medical and allied and pharmaceutical professions, the progressive abolition of restrictions shall be dependent upon coordination of the conditions for their exercise in the various Member States.

Notes
[1]Paragraph 1 as amended by Article 6(6) of the SEA.
[2]Second sentence of paragraph 2 as amended by Article 16(2) of the SEA.
[3]Third sentence of paragraph 2 as amended by Article 6(7) of the SEA.

CHAPTER 4   CAPITAL AND PAYMENTS[1]

Article 67

1. During the transitional period and to the extent necessary to ensure the proper functioning of the common market, Member States shall progressively

abolish between themselves all restrictions on the movement of capital belonging to persons resident in Member States and any discrimination based on the nationality or on the place of residence of the parties or on the place where such capital is invested.

2.   Current payments connected with the movement of capital between Member States shall be freed from all restrictions by the end of the first stage at the latest.

Note
[1]Title as amended by Article G(14) TEU.

Article 68
1.   Member States shall, as regards the matters dealt with in this Chapter, be as liberal as possible in granting such exchange authorisations as are still necessary after the entry into force of this Treaty.

2.   Where a Member State applies to the movements of capital liberalised in accordance with the provisions of this Chapter the domestic rules governing the capital market and the credit system, it shall do so in a non-discriminatory manner.

3.   Loans for the direct or indirect financing of a Member State or its regional or local authorities shall not be issued or placed in other Member States unless the States concerned have reached agreement thereon. This provision shall not preclude the application of Article 22 of the Protocol on the Statute of the European Investment Bank.

Article 69
The Council shall, on a proposal from the Commission, which for its purpose shall consult the Monetary Committee provided for in Article 105, issue the necessary directives for the progressive implementation of the provisions of Article 67, acting unanimously during the first two stages and by a qualified majority thereafter.

Article 70
1.   The Commission shall propose to the Council measures for the progressive coordination of the exchange policies of Member States in respect of the movement of capital between those States and third countries. For this purpose the Council shall issue directives, acting by a qualified majority. It shall endeavour to attain the highest possible degree of liberalisation. Unanimity shall be required for measures which constitute a step back as regards the liberalisation of capital movements.

2.   Where the measures taken in accordance with paragraph 1 do not permit the elimination of differences between the exchange rules of Member States and where such differences could lead persons resident in one of the Member States to use the freer transfer facilities within the Community which are provided for in Article 67 in order to evade the rules of one of the Member States concerning the movement of capital to or from third countries; that State may, after consulting the other Member States and the Commission, take appropriate measures to overcome these difficulties.

Should the Council find that these measures are restricting the free movement of capital within the Community to a greater extent than is required for the purpose of overcoming the difficulties, it may, acting by a qualified majority on a proposal from the Commission, decide that the State concerned shall amend or abolish these measures.

Article 71

Member States shall endeavour to avoid introducing within the Community any new exchange restrictions on the movement of capital and current payments connected with such movements, and shall endeavour not to make existing rules more restrictive.

They declare their readiness to go beyond the degree of liberalisation of capital movements provided for in the preceding Articles in as far as their economic situation, in particular the situation of their balance of payments, so permits.

The Commission may, after consulting the Monetary Committee, make recommendations to Member States on this subject.

Article 72

Member States shall keep the Commission informed of any movements of capital to and from third countries which come to their knowledge. The Commission may deliver to Member States any opinions which it considers appropriate on this subject.

Article 73

1. If movements of capital lead to disturbances in the functioning of the capital market in any Member State, the Commission shall, after consulting the Monetary Committee, authorise that State to take protective measures in the field of capital movements, the conditions and details of which the Commission shall determine.

The Council may, acting by a qualified majority, revoke this authorisation or amend the conditions or details thereof.

2. A Member State which is in difficulties may, however, on grounds of secrecy or urgency, take the measures mentioned above, where this proves necessary, on its own initiative. The Commission and the other Member States shall be informed of such measures by the date of their entry into force at the latest. In this event the Commission may, after consulting the Monetary Committee, decide that the State concerned shall amend or abolish the measures.

TITLE IV   TRANSPORT

Article 75

1. For the purpose of implementing Article 74, and taking into account the distinctive features of transport, the Council shall, acting unanimously until the end of the second stage and by a qualified majority thereafter, lay down, on a proposal from the Commission and after consulting the Economic and Social Committee and the European Parliament:

   (a)   common rules applicable to international transport to or from the territory of a Member State or passing across the territory of one or more Member States;

   (b)   the conditions under which non-resident carriers may operate transport services within a Member State;

   (c)   any other appropriate provisions.

2. The provisions referred to in (a) and (b) of paragraph 1 shall be laid down during the transitional period.

3. By way of derogation from the procedure provided for in paragraph 1, where the application of provisions concerning the principles of the regulatory

system for transport would be liable to have a serious effect on the standard of living and on employment in certain areas and on the operation of transport facilities, they shall be laid down by the Council acting unanimously. In so doing, the Council shall take into account the need for adaptation to the economic development which will result from establishing the common market.

PART THREE   POLICY OF THE COMMUNITY
TITLE 1   COMMON RULES
CHAPTER 1   RULES ON COMPETITION
SECTION 3   AIDS GRANTED BY STATES

Article 92

1.   Save as otherwise provided in this Treaty, any aid granted by a Member State or through State resources in any form whatsoever which distorts or threatens to distort competition by favouring certain undertakings or the production of certain goods shall, in so far as it affects trade between Member States, be incompatible with the common market.

2.   The following shall be compatible with the common market:

(a)   aid having a social character, granted to individual consumers, provided that such aid is granted without discrimination related to the origin of the products concerned;

(b)   aid to make good the damage caused by natural disasters or exceptional occurrences;

(c)   aid granted to the economy of certain areas of the Federal Republic of Germany affected by the division of Germany, in so far as such aid is required in order to compensate for the economic disadvantages caused by that division.

3.   The following may be considered to be compatible with the common market:

(a)   aid to promote the economic development of areas where the standard of living is abnormally low or where there is serious underemployment;

(b)   aid to promote the execution of an important project of common European interest or to remedy a serious disturbance in the economy of a Member State;

(c)   aid to facilitate the development of certain economic activities or of certain economic areas, where such aid does not adversely affect trading conditions to an extent contrary to the common interest. However, the aids granted to shipbuilding as of 1 January 1957 shall, in so far as they serve only to compensate for the absence of customs protection, be progressively reduced under the same conditions as apply to the elimination of customs duties, subject to the provisions of this Treaty concerning common commercial policy towards third countries;

(d)   such other categories of aid as may be specified by decision of the Council acting by a qualified majority on a proposal from the Commission.

Article 94

The Council may, acting by a qualified majority on a proposal from the Commission, make any appropriate regulations for the application of Articles 92 and 93 and may in particular determine the conditions in which Article 93(3) shall apply and the categories of aid exempted from this procedure.

CHAPTER 2   TAX PROVISIONS

Article 99[1]

The Council shall, acting unanimously on a proposal from the Commission and after consulting the European Parliament, adopt provisions for the harmonisation of legislation concerning turnover taxes, excise duties and other forms of indirect taxation to the extent that such harmonisation is necessary to ensure the establishment and the functioning of the internal market within the time-limit laid down in Article 8a.

Note

[1]Article as replaced by Article 17 of the SEA.

CHAPTER 3   APPROXIMATION OF LAWS

Article 100

The Council shall, acting unanimously on a proposal from the Commission, issue directives for the approximation of such provisions laid down by law, regulation or administrative action in Member States as directly affect the establishment or functioning of the common market.

The European Parliament and the Economic and Social Committee shall be consulted in the case of directives whose implementation would, in one or more Member States, involve the amendment of legislation.

Article 100a[1]

1.   By way of derogation from Article 100 and save where otherwise provided in this Treaty, the following provisions shall apply for the achievement of the objectives set out in Article 8a. The Council shall, acting by a qualified majority on a proposal from the Commission in cooperation with the European Parliament and after consulting the Economic and Social Committee, adopt the measures for the approximation of the provisions laid down by law, regulation or administrative action in Member States which have as their object the establishment and functioning of the internal market.

2.   Paragraph 1 shall not apply to fiscal provisions, to those relating to the free movement of persons nor to those relating to the rights and interests of employed persons.

3.   The Commission, in its proposals envisaged in paragraph 1 concerning health, safety, environmental protection and consumer protection, will take as a base a high level of protection.

Note

[1]Article added by Article 18 of the SEA.

4.   If, after the adoption of a harmonisation measure by the Council acting by a qualified majority, a Member State deems it necessary to apply national provisions on grounds of major needs referred to in Article 36, or relating to protection of the environment or the working environment, it shall notify the Commission of these provisions.

The Commission shall confirm the provisions involved after having verified that they are not a means of arbitrary discrimination or a disguised restriction on trade between Member States.

By way of derogation from the procedure laid down in Articles 169 and 170, the Commission or any Member State may bring the matter directly before the

Court of Justice if it considers that another Member State is making improper use of the powers provided for in this Article.

5. The harmonisation measures referred to above shall, in appropriate cases, include a safeguard clause authorising the Member States to take, for one or more of the non-economic reasons referred to in Article 36, provisional measures subject to a Community control procedure.

TITLE II ECONOMIC POLICY
CHAPTER 1[1] COOPERATION IN ECONOMIC AND MONETARY POLICY
(ECONOMIC AND MONETARY UNION)

Article 102a

1. In order to ensure the convergence of economic and monetary policies which is necessary for the further development of the Community, Member States shall cooperate in accordance with the objectives of Article 104. In so doing, they shall take account of the experience acquired in cooperation within the framework of the European Monetary System (EMS) and in developing the ECU, and shall respect existing powers in this field.

2. Insofar as further development in the field of economic and monetary policy necessitates institutional changes, the provisions of Article 236 shall be applicable. The Monetary Committee and the Committee of Governors of the Central Banks shall also be consulted regarding institutional changes in the monetary area.

Note
[1]Chapter as inserted in Title II of Part Three of the Treaty by Article 20 of the SEA.

CHAPTER 2[1] CONJUNCTURAL POLICY

Article 103

1. Member States shall regard their conjunctural policies as a matter of common concern. They shall consult each other and the Commission on the measures to be taken in the light of the prevailing circumstances.

2. Without prejudice to any other procedures provided for in this Treaty, the Council may, acting unanimously on a proposal from the Commission, decide upon the measures appropriate to the situation.

3. Acting by a qualified majority on a proposal from the Commission, the Council shall, where required, issue any directives needed to give effect to the measures decided upon under paragraph 2.

4. The procedures provided for in this Article shall also apply if any difficulty should arise in the supply of certain products.

Note
[1]Renumbering of the Chapter as established by Article 20(2) of the SEA.

CHAPTER 3[1] BALANCE OF PAYMENTS

Article 104

Each Member State shall pursue the economic policy needed to ensure the equilibrium of its overall balance of payments and to maintain confidence in its currency, while taking care to ensure a high level of employment and a stable level of prices.

Article 105

1. In order to facilitate attainment of the objectives set out in Article 104, Member States shall coordinate their economic policies. They shall for this purpose provide for cooperation between their appropriate administrative departments and between their central banks.

The Commission shall submit to the Council recommendations on how to achieve such cooperation.

2. In order to promote coordination of the policies of Member States in the monetary field to the full extent needed for the functioning of the common market, a Monetary Committee with advisory status is hereby set up. It shall have the following tasks:

— to keep under review the monetary and financial situation of the Member States and of the Community and the general payments system of the Member States and to report regularly thereon to the Council and to the Commission;

— to deliver opinions at the request of the Council or of the Commission or on its own initiative, for submission to these institutions.

The Member States and the Commission shall each appoint two members of the Monetary Committee.

Article 106

1. Each Member State undertakes to authorise, in the currency of the Member State in which the creditor or the beneficiary resides, any payments connected with the movement of goods, services or capital, and any transfers of capital and earnings, to the extent that the movement of goods, services, capital and persons between Member States has been liberalised pursuant to this Treaty.

The Member States declare their readiness to undertake the liberalisation of payments beyond the extent provided in the preceding subparagraph, in so far as their economic situation in general and the state of their balance of payments in particular so permit.

2. In so far as movements of goods, services, and capital are limited only by restrictions on payments connected therewith, these restrictions shall be progressively abolished by applying, *mutatis mutandis*, the provisions of the Chapters relating to the abolition of quantitative restrictions, to the liberalisation of services and to the free movement of capital.

3. Member States undertake not to introduce between themselves any new restrictions on transfers connected with the invisible transactions listed in Annex III to this Treaty.

The progressive abolition of existing restrictions shall be effected in accordance with the provisions of Articles 63 to 65, in so far as such abolition is not governed by the provisions contained in paragraphs 1 and 2 or by the Chapter relating to the free movement of capital.

4. If need be, Member States shall consult each other on the measures to be taken to enable the payments and transfers mentioned in this Article to be effected; such measures shall not prejudice the attainment of the objectives set out in this Chapter.

Note

[1] Renumbering of the Chapter as established by Article 20(2) of the SEA.

Article 107

1.   Each Member State shall treat its policy with regard to rates of exchange as a matter of common concern.

2.   If a Member State makes an alteration in its rate of exchange which is inconsistent with the objectives set out in Article 104 and which seriously distorts conditions of competition, the Commission may, after consulting the Monetary Committee, authorise other Member States to take for a strictly limited period the necessary measures, the conditions and details of which it shall determine, in order to counter the consequences of such alteration.

Article 108

1.   Where a Member State is in difficulties or is seriously threatened with difficulties as regards its balance of payments either as a result of an over-all disequilibrium in its balance of payments, or as a result of the type of currency at its disposal, and where such difficulties are liable in particular to jeopardise the functioning of the common market or the progressive implementation of the common commercial policy, the Commission shall immediately investigate the position of the State in question and the action which, making use of all the means at its disposal, that State has taken or may take in accordance with the provisions of Article 104. The Commission shall state what measures it recommends the State concerned to take.

If the action taken by a Member State and the measures suggested by the Commission do not prove sufficient to overcome the difficulties which have arisen or which threaten, the Commission shall, after consulting the Monetary Committee, recommend to the Council the granting of mutual assistance and appropriate methods therefor.

The Commission shall keep the Council regularly informed of the situation and of how it is developing.

2.   The Council, acting by a qualified majority, shall grant such mutual assistance; it shall adopt directives or decisions laying down the conditions and details of such assistance, which may take such forms as:

(a)   a concerted approach to or within any other international organisations to which Member States may have recourse;

(b)   measures needed to avoid deflection of trade where the State which is in difficulties maintains or reintroduces quantitative restrictions against third countries;

(c)   the granting of limited credits by other Member States, subject to their agreement.

During the transitional period, mutual assistance may also take the form of special reductions in customs duties or enlargements of quotas in order to facilitate an increase in imports from the State which is in difficulties, subject to the agreement of the States by which such measures would have to be taken.

3.   If the mutual assistance recommended by the Commission is not granted by the Council or if the mutual assistance granted and the measures taken are insufficient, the Commission shall authorise the State which is in difficulties to take protective measures, the conditions and details of which the Commission shall determine.

Such authorisation may be revoked and such conditions and details may be changed by the Council acting by a qualified majority.

Article 109

1. Where a sudden crisis in the balance of payments occurs and a decision within the meaning of Article 108(2) is not immediately taken, the Member State concerned may, as a precaution take the necessary protective measures. Such measures must cause the least possible disturbance in the functioning of the common market and must not be wider in scope than is strictly necessary to remedy the sudden difficulties which have arisen.

2. The Commission and the other Member States shall be informed of such protective measures not later than when they enter into force. The Commission may recommend to the Council the granting of mutual assistance under Article 108.

3. After the Commission has delivered an opinion and the Monetary Committee has been consulted, the Council may, acting by a qualified majority, decide that the State concerned shall amend, suspend or abolish the protective measures referred to above.

CHAPTER 4[1]   COMMERCIAL POLICY

Article 111

The following provisions shall, without prejudice to Articles 115 and 116, apply during the transitional period:

1. Member States shall coordinate their trade relations with third countries so as to bring about, by the end of the transitional period, the conditions needed for implementing a common policy in the field of external trade.

The Commission shall submit to the Council proposals regarding the procedure for common action to be followed during the transitional period and regarding the achievement of uniformity in their commercial policies.

2. The Commission shall submit to the Council recommendations for tariff negotiations with third countries in respect of the common customs tariff.

The Council shall authorise the Commission to open such negotiations.

The Commission shall conduct these negotiations in consultation with a special committee appointed by the Council to assist the Commission in this task and within the framework of such directives as the Council may issue to it.

3. In exercising the powers conferred upon it by this Article, the Council shall act unanimously during the first two stages and by a qualified majority thereafter.

4. Member States shall, in consultation with the Commission, take all necessary measures, particularly those designed to bring about an adjustment of tariff agreements in force with third countries, in order that the entry into force of the common customs tariff shall not be delayed.

5. Member States shall aim at securing as high a level of uniformity as possible between themselves as regards their liberalisation lists in relation to third countries or groups of third countries. To this end, the Commission shall make all appropriate recommendations to Member States.

If Member States abolish or reduce quantitative restrictions in relation to third countries, they shall inform the Commission beforehand and shall accord the same treatment to other Member States.

Article 113

1. After the transitional period has ended, the common commercial policy shall be based on uniform principles, particularly in regard to changes in tariff

rates, the conclusion of tariff and trade agreeements, the achievement of uniformity in measures of liberalisation, export policy and measures to protect trade such as those to be taken in case of dumping or subsidies.

2. The Commission shall submit proposals to the Council for implementing the common commercial policy.

3. Where agreements with third countries need to be negotiated, the Commission shall make recommendations to the Council, which shall authorise the Commission to open the necessary negotiations.

The Commission shall conduct these negotiations in consultation with a special committee appointed by the Council to assist the Commission in this task and within the framework of such directives as the Council may issue to it.

4. In exercising the powers conferred upon it by this Article, the Council shall act by a qualified majority.

Note
[1]Renumbering of the Chapter as established by Article 20(2) of the SEA.

Article 114
The agreements referred to in Article 111(2) and in Article 113 shall be concluded by the Council on behalf of the Community, acting unanimously during the first two stages and by a qualified majority thereafter.

Article 115
In order to ensure that the execution of measures of commercial policy taken in accordance with this Treaty by any Member State is not obstructed by deflection of trade, or where differences between such measures lead to economic difficulties in one or more of the Member States, the Commission shall recommend the methods for the requisite cooperation between Member States. Failing this, the Commission shall authorise Member States to take the necessary protective measures, the conditions and details of which it shall determine.

In case of urgency during the transitional period, Member States may themselves take the necessary measures and shall notify them to the other Member States and to the Commission, which may decide that the States concerned shall amend or abolish such measures.

In the selection of such measures, priority shall be given to those which cause the least disturbance to the functioning of the common market and which take into account the need to expedite, as far as possible, the introduction of the common customs tariff.

Article 116
From the end of the transitional period onwards, Member States shall, in respect of all matters of particular interest to the common market, proceed within the framework of international organisations of an economic character only by common action. To this end, the Commission shall submit to the Council, which shall act by a qualified majority, proposals concerning the scope and implementation of such common action.

During the transitional period, Member States shall consult each other for the purpose of concerting the action they take and adopting as far as possible a uniform attitude.

TITLE III   SOCIAL POLICY
CHAPTER 1   SOCIAL PROVISIONS

Article 118a[1]

1.   Member States shall pay particular attention to encouraging improvements, especially in the working environment, as regards the health and safety of workers, and shall set as their objective the harmonisation of conditions in this area, while maintaining the improvements made.

2.   In order to help achieve the objective laid down in the first paragraph, the Council, acting by a qualified majority on a proposal from the Commission, in cooperation with the European Parliament and after consulting the Economic and Social Committee, shall adopt, by means of directives, minimum requirements for gradual implementation, having regard to the conditions and technical rules obtaining in each of the Member States.

Such directives shall avoid imposing administrative, financial and legal constraints in a way which would hold back the creation and development of small and medium-sized undertakings.

3.   The provisions adopted pursuant to this Article shall not prevent any Member State from maintaining or introducing more stringent measures for the protection of working conditions compatible with this Treaty.

Note
[1]Article added by Article 21 of the SEA.

CHAPTER 2   THE EUROPEAN SOCIAL FUND

Article 123

In order to improve employment opportunities for workers in the common market and to contribute thereby to raising the standard of living, a European Social Fund is hereby established in accordance with the provisions set out below; it shall have the task of rendering the employment of workers easier and of increasing their geographical and occupational mobility within the Community.

Article 125

1.   On application by a Member State the Fund shall, within the framework of the rules provided for in Article 127, meet 50% of the expenditure incurred after the entry into force of this Treaty by that State or by a body governed by public law for the purposes of:
   (a)   ensuring productive re-employment of workers by means of:
            — vocational retraining;
            — resettlement allowances;
   (b)   granting aid for the benefit of workers whose employment is reduced or temporarily suspended, in whole or in part, as a result of the conversion of an undertaking to other production, in order that they may retain the same wage level pending their full re-employment.

2.   Assistance granted by the Fund towards the cost of vocational retraining shall be granted only if the unemployed workers could not be found employment except in a new occupation and only if they have been in productive employment for at least six months in the occupation for which they have been retrained.

Assistance towards resettlement allowances shall be granted only if the unemployed workers have been caused to change their home within the Community and have been in productive employment for at least six months in their new place of residence.

Assistance for workers in the case of the conversion of an undertaking shall be granted only if:

(a) the workers concerned have again been fully employed in that undertaking for at least six months;

(b) the Government concerned has submitted a plan beforehand, drawn up by the undertaking in question, for that particular conversion and for financing it;

(c) the Commission has given its prior approval to the conversion plan.

Article 126

When the transitional period has ended, the Council, after receiving the opinion of the Commission and after consulting the Economic and Social Committee and the European Parliament, may:

(a) rule, by a qualified majority, that all or part of the assistance referred to in Article 125 shall no longer be granted; or

(b) unanimously determine what new tasks may be entrusted to the Fund within the framework of its terms of reference as laid down in Article 123.

Article 127

The Council shall, acting by a qualified majority on a proposal from the Commission and after consulting the Economic and Social Committee and the European Parliament, lay down the provisions required to implement Articles 124 to 126; in particular it shall determine in detail the conditions under which assistance shall be granted by the Fund in accordance with Article 125 and the classes of undertakings whose workers shall benefit from the assistance provided for in Article 125(1)(b).

Article 128

The Council shall, acting on a proposal from the Commission and after consulting the Economic and Social Committee, lay down general principles for implementing a common vocational training policy capable of contributing to the harmonious devlopment both of the national economies and of the common market.

TITLE IV   THE EUROPEAN INVESTMENT BANK

Article 129

A European Investment Bank is hereby established; it shall have legal personality.

The members of the European Investment Bank shall be the Member States.

The Statute of the European Investment Bank is laid down in a Protocol annexed to this Treaty.

Article 130

The task of the European Investment Bank shall be to contribute, by having recourse to the capital market and utilising its own resources, to the balanced and steady development of the common market in the interest of the Community. For this purpose the Bank shall, operating on a non-profit-making basis, grant loans and give guarantees which facilitate the financing of the following projects in all sectors of the economy:

(a) projects for developing less-developed regions;

(b) projects for modernising or converting undertakings or for developing fresh activities called for by the progressive establishment of the common market, where these projects are of such a size or nature that they cannot be entirely financed by the various means available in the individual Member States;

(c) projects of common interest to several Member States which are of such a size or nature that they cannot be entirely financed by the various means available in the individual Member States.

TITLE V[1] ECONOMIC AND SOCIAL COHESION

Article 130a

In order to promote its overall harmonious development, the Community shall develop and pursue its actions leading to the strengthening of its economic and social cohesion.

In particular the Community shall aim at reducing disparities between the various regions and the backwardness of the least-favoured regions.

Article 130b

Member States shall conduct their economic policies, and shall coordinate them, in such a way as, in addition, to attain the objectives set out in Article 130a. The implementation of the common policies and of the internal market shall take into account the objectives set out in Article 130a and in Article 130c and shall contribute to their achievement. The Community shall support the achievement of these objectives by the action it takes through the structural Funds (European Agricultural Guidance and Guarantee Fund, Guidance Section, European Social Fund, European Regional Development Fund), the European Investment Bank and the other existing financial instruments.

Article 130d

Once the Single European Act enters into force the Commission shall submit a comprehensive proposal to the Council, the purpose of which will be to make such amendments to the structure and operational rules of the existing structural Funds (European Agricultural Guidance and Guarantee Fund, Guidance Section, European Social Fund, European Regional Development Fund) as are necessary to clarify and rationalise their tasks in order to contribute to the achievement of the objectives set out in Article 130a and Article 130c, to increase their efficiency and to coordinate their activities between themselves and with the operations of the existing financial instruments. The Council shall act unanimously on this proposal within a period of one year, after consulting the European Parliament and the Economic and Social Committee.

Note

[1]Title V consisting of Articles 130a, 130b, 130c, 130d and 130e as added to Part Three of the Treaty by Article 23 of the SEA.

Article 130e

After adoption of the decision referred to in Article 130d, implementing decisions relating to the European Regional Development Fund shall be taken by the Council, acting by a qualified majority on a proposal from the Commission and in cooperation with the European Parliament.

With regard to the European Agricultural Guidance and Guarantee Fund, Guidance Section and the European Social Fund, Articles 43, 126 and 127 remain applicable respectively.

TITLE VI[1]   RESEARCH AND TECHNOLOGICAL DEVELOPMENT

Article 130f

1. The Community's aim shall be to strengthen the scientific and technological basis of European industry and to encourage it to become more competitive at international level.

2. In order to achieve this, it shall encourage undertakings including small and medium-sized undertakings, research centres and universities in their research and technological development activities; it shall support their efforts to cooperate with one another, aiming, notably, at enabling undertakings to exploit the Community's internal market potential to the full, in particular through the opening up of national public contracts, the definition of common standards and the removal of legal and fiscal barriers to that cooperation.

3. In the achievement of these aims, special account shall be taken of the connection between the common research and technological development effort, the establishment of the internal market and the implementation of common policies, particularly as regards competition and trade.

Article 130h

Member States shall, in liaison with the Commission, coordinate among themselves the policies and programmes carried out at national level. In close contact with the Member States, the Commission may take any useful initiative to promote such coordination.

Article 130i

1. The Community shall adopt a multiannual framework programme setting out all its activities. The framework programme shall lay down the scientific and technical objectives, define their respective priorities, set out the main lines of the activities envisaged and fix the amount deemed necessary, the detailed rules for financial participation by the Community in the programme as a whole and the breakdown of this amount between the various activities envisaged.

2. The framework programme may be adapted or supplemented, as the situation changes.

Article 130k

The framework programme shall be implemented through specific programmes developed within each activity. Each specific programme shall define the detailed rules for implementing it, fix its duration and provide for the means deemed necessary.

The Council shall define the detailed arrangements for the dissemination of knowledge resulting from the specific programmes.

Note

[1]Title VI consisting of Articles 130f, 130g, 130h, 130i, 130k, 130l, 130m, 130n, 130o, 130p and 130q, as added to Part Three of the Treaty by Article 24 of the SEA.

Article 130l

In implementing the multiannual framework programme, supplementary programmes may be decided on involving the participation of certain Member

States only, which shall finance them subject to possible Community participation.

The Council shall adopt the rules applicable to supplementary programmes, particularly as regards the dissemination of knowledge and the access of other Member States.

Article 130m

In implementing the multiannual framework programme, the Community may make provisions, with the agreement of the Member States concerned, for participation in research and development programmes undertaken by several Member States, including participation in the structures created for the execution of those programmes.

Article 130n

In implementing the multiannual framework programme, the Community may make provision for cooperation in Community research, technological development and demonstration with third countries or international organisations.

The detailed arrangements for such cooperation may be the subject of international agreements between the Community and the third parties concerned which shall be negotiated and concluded in accordance with Article 228.

Article 130o

The Community may set up joint undertakings or any other structure necessary for the efficient execution of programmes of Community research, technological development and demonstration.

Article 130p

1. The detailed arrangements for financing each programme, including any Community contribution, shall be established at the time of the adoption of the programme.

2. The amount of the Community's annual contribution shall be laid down under the budgetary procedure, without prejudice to other possible methods of Community financing. The estimated cost of the specific programmes must not in aggregate exceed the financial provision in the framework programme.

Article 130q

1. The Council shall, acting unanimously on a proposal from the Commission and after consulting the European Parliament and the Economic and Social Committee, adopt the provisions referred to in Articles 130i and 130o.

2. The Council shall, acting by a qualified majority on a proposal from the Commission, after consulting the Economic and Social Committee, and in cooperation with the European Parliament, adopt the provisions referred to in Articles 130k, 130l, 130m, 130n and 130p(1). The adoption of these supplementary programmes shall also require the agreement of the Member States concerned.

TITLE VII[1] ENVIRONMENT

Article 130r

1. Action by the Community relating to the environment shall have the following objectives:

Note

[1]Title VII consisting of articles 130r, 130s and 130t, as added to Part Three of the Treaty by Article 25 of the SEA.

     (i)   to preserve, protect and improve the quality of the environment;
     (ii)   to contribute towards protecting human health;
     (iii) to ensure a prudent and rational utilisation of natural resources.

2.   Action by the Community relating to the environment shall be based on the principles that preventive action should be taken, that environmental damage should as a priority be rectified at source, and that the polluter should pay. Environmental protection requirements shall be a component of the Community's other policies.

3.   In preparing its action relating to the environment, the Community shall take account of:
     (i)   available scientific and technical data;
     (ii)   environmental conditions in the various regions of the Community;
     (iii) the potential benefits and costs of action or of lack of action;
     (iv) the economic and social development of the Community as a whole and the balanced development of its regions.

4.   The Community shall take action relating to the environment to the extent to which the objectives referred to in paragraph 1 can be attained better at Community level than at the level of the individual Member States. Without prejudice to certain measures of a Community nature, the Member States shall finance and implement the other measures.

5.   Within their respective spheres of competence, the Community and the Member States shall cooperate with third countries and with the relevant international organisations. The arrangements for Community cooperation may be the subject of agreements between the Community and the third parties concerned, which shall be negotiated and concluded in accordance with Article 228.

The previous paragraph shall be without prejudice to Member States' competence to negotiate in international bodies and to conclude international agreements.

Article 130s

The Council, acting unanimously on a proposal from the Commission and after consulting the European Parliament and the Economic and Social Committee, shall decide what action is to be taken by the Community.

The Council shall, under the conditions laid down in the preceding subparagraph, define those matters on which decisions are to be taken by a qualified majority.

Article 130t

The protective measures adopted in common pursuant to Article 130s shall not prevent any Member State from maintaining or introducing more stringent protective measures compatible with this Treaty.

PART FIVE   INSTITUTIONS OF THE COMMUNITY
TITLE 1   PROVISIONS GOVERNING THE INSTITUTIONS
CHAPTER 1   THE INSTITUTIONS
SECTION 1   THE EUROPEAN PARLIAMENT

Article 137

The European Parliament, which shall consist of representatives of the peoples of the States brought together in the Community, shall exercise the advisory and supervisory powers which are conferred upon it by this Treaty.

Article 138

(Paragraphs 1 and 2 lapsed on 17 July 1979 in accordance with Article 14 of the Act concerning the election of the representatives of the European Parliament) [*See Article 1 of that Act which reads as follows:*

1. The representatives in the European Parliament of the peoples of the States brought together in the Community shall be elected by direct universal suffrage.]

See Article 2 of that Act which reads as follows:

2. The number of representatives elected in each Member State is as follows:

Belgium	24
Denmark	16
Germany	81
Greece	24
Spain	60
France	81
Ireland	15
Italy	81
Luxembourg	6
Netherlands	25
Portugal	24
United Kingdom	81.][1]

3. The European Parliament shall draw up proposals for elections by direct universal suffrage in accordance with a uniform procedure in all Member States.[2]

The Council shall, acting unanimously, lay down the appropriate provisions, which it shall recommend to Member States for adoption in accordance with their respective constitutional requirements.

Notes

[1] Number of representatives as fixed by Article 10 of the Act of Accession ESP/PORT.
[2] See also Article 7(1) and (2) of the Act concerning the election of the representatives of the European Parliament.

Article 139

The European Parliament shall hold an annual session. It shall meet, without requiring to be convened, on the second Tuesday in March.[1]

The European Parliament may meet in extraordinary session at the request of a majority of its members or at the request of the Council or of the Commission.

Note

[1] First paragraph as amended by Article 27(1) of the Merger Treaty. As regards the second sentence of this Article see also Article 10(3) of the Act concerning the election of the representatives of the European Parliament.

Article 144

If a motion of censure on the activities of the Commission is tabled before it, the European Parliament shall not vote thereon until at least three days after the motion has been tabled and only by open vote.

If the motion of censure is carried by a two-third majority of the votes cast, representing a majority of the members of the European Parliament, the

members of the Commission shall resign as a body. They shall continue to deal
with current business until they are replaced in accordance with Article 158.

SECTION 2   THE COUNCIL

Article 146

(Article repealed by Article 7 of the Merger Treaty)   [*See Article 2 of the Merger
Treaty, which reads as follows:*

The Council shall consist of representatives of the Member States. Each
Government shall delegate to it one of its members.

The office of President shall be held for a term of six months by each member
of the Council in turn, in the following order of Member States:

— for a first cycle of six years: Belgium, Denmark, Germany, Greece, Spain,
France, Ireland, Italy, Luxembourg, Netherlands, Portugal, United Kingdom,

— for the following cycle of six years: Denmark, Belgium, Greece, Germany,
France, Spain, Italy, Ireland, Netherlands, Luxembourg, United Kingdom,
Portugal.][1]

Note
[1]Second paragraph as amended by Article 11 of the Act of Accession ESP/PORT.

Article 149[1]

1.   Where, in pursuance of this Treaty, the Council acts on a proposal from
the Commission, unanimity shall be required for an act constituting an
amendment to that proposal.

2.   Where, in pursuance of this Treaty, the Council acts in cooperation with
the European Parliament, the following procedure shall apply:

(a)   The Council, acting by a qualified majority under the conditions of
paragraph 1, on a proposal from the Commission and after obtaining the
Opinion of the European Parliament, shall adopt a common position.

(b)   The Council's common position shall be communicated to the
European Parliament. The Council and the Commission shall inform the
European Parliament fully of the reasons which led the Council to adopt its
common position and also of the Commission's position.

If, within three months of such communication, the European Parliament
approves this common position or has not taken a decision within that period,
the Council shall definitively adopt the act in question in acordance with the
common position.

(c)   The European Parliament may within the period of three months
referred to in point (b), by an absolute majority of its component members,
propose amendments to the Council's common position. The European
Parliament may also, by the same majority, reject the Council's common
position. The result of the proceedings shall be transmitted to the Council and
the Commission.

If the European Parliament has rejected the Council's common position,
unanimity shall be required for the Council to act on a second reading.

(d)   The commission shall, within a period of one month, re-examine the
proposal on the basis of which the Council adopted its common position, by
taking into account the amendments proposed by the European Parliament.

The Commission shall forward to the Council, at the same time as its
re-examined proposal, the amendments of the European Parliament which it
has not accepted, and shall express its opinion on them. The Council may
adopt these amendments unanimously.

(e)   The Council, acting by a qualified majority, shall adopt the proposal as re-examined by the Commission.
Unanimity shall be required for the Council to amend the proposal as re-examined by the Commission.

(f)   In the cases referred to in points (c), (d) and (e), the Council shall be required to act within a period of three months. If no decision is taken within this period, the Commission proposal shall be deemed not to have been adopted.

(g)   The periods referred to in points (b) and (f) may be extended by a maximum of one month by common accord between the Council and the European Parliament.

3.   As long as the Council has not acted, the Commission may alter its proposal at any time during the procedures mentioned in paragraphs 1 and 2.

Note
[1]Article as replaced by Article 7 of the SEA.

Article 151
(Article repealed by Article 7 of the Merger Treaty)
[*See Articles 5 and 4 of the Merger Treaty, which read as follows:*
Article 5:
The Council shall adopt its rules of procedure.
Article 4:
A committee consisting of the Permanent Representatives of the Member States shall be responsible for preparing the work of the Council and for carrying out the tasks assigned to it by the Council.]

SECTION 3   THE COMMISSION

Article 158
(Article repealed by Article 19 of the Merger Treaty)
[*See Article 11 of the Merger Treaty, which reads as follows:*
The members of the Commission shall be appointed by common accord of the Governments of the Member States. Their term of office shall be four years. It shall be renewable.]

Article 159
(Article repealed by Article 19 of the Merger Treaty)
[*See Article 12 of the Merger Treaty, which reads as follows:*
Apart from normal replacement, or death, the duties of a member of the Commission shall end when he resigns or is compulsorily retired.
The vacancy thus caused shall be filled for the remainder of the member's term of office. The Council may, acting unanimously, decide that such a vacancy need not be filled.
Save in the case of compulsory retirement under the provisions of Article 13[1], members of the Commission shall remain in office until they have been replaced.]

Note
[1]Article 13 of the Merger Treaty. See Article 160 below.

Article 161
(Article repealed by Article 19 of the Merger Treaty)
[*See Article 14 of the Merger Treaty, which reads as follows:*

The President and the six Vice-Presidents of the Commission shall be appointed from among its members for a term of two years in accordance with the same procedure as that laid down for the appointment of members of the Commission. Their appointments may be renewed.[1]

The Council, acting unanimously, may amend the provisions concerning Vice-Presidents.[2]

Save where the entire Commission is replaced, such appointments shall be made after the Commission has been consulted.

In the event of retirement or death, the President and the Vice-Presidents shall be replaced for the remainder of their term of office in accordance with the preceding provisions.]

Note
[1]First paragraph as amended by Article 16 of the Act of Accession ESP/PORT.
[2]Second paragraph added by Article 16 of that Act.

SECTION 4   THE COURT OF JUSTICE

Article 165
The Court of Justice shall consist of thirteen Judges.[1]

The Court of Justice shall sit in plenary session. It may, however, form Chambers, each consisting of three or five Judges, either to undertake certain preparatory inquiries or to adjudicate on particular categories of cases in accordance with rules laid down for these purposes.

Whenever the Court of Justice hears cases brought before it by a Member State or by one of the institutions of the Community or, to the extent that the Chambers of the Court do not have the requisite jurisdiction under the Rules of Procedure, has to give preliminary rulings on questions submitted to it pursuant to Article 177, it shall sit in plenary session.[2]

Should the Court of Justice so request, the Council may, acting unanimously, increase the number of Judges and make the necessary adjustments to the second and third paragraphs of this Article and to the second paragraph of Article 167.

Notes
[1]First paragraph as amended by Article 17 of the Act of Accession ESP/PORT.
[2]Third paragraph as amended by Article 1 of the Council Decision of 26 November 1974 (*Official Journal of the European Communities*, No L318, 28 November 1974).

Article 168a[1]
1. At the request of the Court of Justice and after consulting the Commission and the European Parliament, the Council may, acting unanimously, attach to the Court of Justice a court with jurisdiction to hear and determine at first instance, subject to a right of appeal to the Court of Justice on points of law only and in accordance with the conditions laid down by the Statute, certain classes of action or proceeding brought by natural or legal persons. That court shall not be competent to hear and determine actions brought by Member States or by Community institutions or questions referred for a preliminary ruling under Article 177.

2.   The Council, following the procedure laid down in paragraph 1, shall determine the composition of that court and adopt the necessary adjustments and additional provisions to the Statute of the Court of Justice. Unless the Council decides otherwise, the provisions of this Treaty relating to the Court of Justice, in particular the provisions of the Protocol on the Statute of the Court of Justice, shall apply to that court.

3.   The members of that court shall be chosen from persons whose independence is beyond doubt and who posses the ability required for appointment to judicial office; they shall be appointed by common accord of the Governments of the Member States for a term of six years. The membership shall be partially renewed every three years. Retiring members shall be eligible for reappointment.

4.   That court shall establish its rules of procedure in agreement with the Court of Justice. Those rules shall require the unanimous approval of the Council.

Note
[1]Article added by Article 11 of the SEA.

Article 171
If the Court of Justice finds that a Member State has failed to fulfil an obligation under this Treaty, the State shall be required to take the necessary measures to comply with the judgment of the Court of Justice.

Article 172
Regulations made by the Council pursuant to the provisions of this Treaty may give the Court of Justice unlimited jurisdiction in regard to the penalties provided for in such regulations.

Article 173
The Court of Justice shall review the legality of acts of the Council and the Commission other than recommendations or opinions. It shall for this purpose have jurisdiction in actions brought by a Member State, the Council or the Commission on grounds of lack of competence, infringement of an essential procedural requirement, infringement of this Treaty or of any rule of law relating to its application, or misuse of powers.

Any natural or legal person may, under the same conditions, institute proceedings against a decision addressed to that person or against a decision which, although in the form of a regulation or a decision addressed to another person, is of direct and individual concern to the former.

The proceedings provided for in this Article shall be instituted within two months of the publication of the measure, or of its notification to the plaintiff, or, in the absence thereof, of the day on which it came to the knowledge of the latter, as the case may be.

Article 175
Should the Council or the Commission, in infringement of this Treaty, fail to act, the Member States and the other institutions of the Community may bring an action before the Court of Justice to have the infringement established.

The action shall be admissible only if the institution concerned has first been called upon to act. If, within two months of being so called upon, the institution concerned has not defined its position, the action may be brought within a further period of two months.

Any natural or legal person may, under the conditions laid down in the preceding paragraphs, complain to the Court of Justice that an institution of the Community has failed to address to that person any act other than a recommendation or an opinion.

Article 176

The institution whose act has been declared void or whose failure to act has been declared contrary to this Treaty shall be required to take the necessary measures to comply with the judgment of the Court of Justice.

This obligation shall not affect any obligation which may result from the application of the second paragraph of Article 215.

Article 177

The Court of Justice shall have jurisdiction to give preliminary rulings concerning:

    (a)   the interpretation of this Treaty;

    (b)   the validity and interpretation of acts of the institutions of the Community;

    (c)   the interpretation of the statutes of bodies established by an act of the Council, where those statutes so provide.

Where such a question is raised before any court or tribunal of the Member State, that court or tribunal may, if it considers that a decision on the question is necessary to enable it to give judgment, request the Court of Justice to give a ruling thereon.

Where any such question is raised in a case pending before a court or tribunal of a Member State, against whose decisions there is no judicial remedy under national law, that court or tribunal shall bring the matter before the Court of Justice.

Article 180

The Court of Justice shall, within the limits hereinafter laid down, have jurisdiction in disputes concerning:

    (a)   the fulfilment by Member States of obligations under the Statute of the European Investment Bank. In this connection, the Board of Directors of the Bank shall enjoy the powers conferred upon the Commission by Article 169;

    (b)   measures adopted by the Board of Governors of the Bank. In this connection, any Member State, the Commission or the Board of Directors of the Bank may institute proceedings under the conditions laid down in Article 173;

    (c)   measures adopted by the Board of Directors of the Bank. Proceedings against such measures may be instituted only by Member States or by the Commission, under the conditions laid down in Article 173, and solely on the grounds of non-compliance with the procedure provided for in Article 21(2), (5), (6) and (7) of the Statute of the Bank.

Article 184

Notwithstanding the expiry of the period laid down in the third paragraph of Article 173, any party may, in proceedings in which a regulation of the Council or of the Commission is in issue, plead the grounds specified in the first paragraph of Article 173, in order to invoke before the Court of Justice the inapplicability of that regulation.

CHAPTER 2   PROVISIONS COMMON TO SEVERAL INSTITUTIONS

Article 189
In order to carry out their task the Council and the Commission shall, in accordance with the provisions of this Treaty, make regulations, issue directives, take decisions, make recommendations or deliver opinions.

A regulation shall have general application. It shall be binding in its entirety and directly applicable in all Member States.

A directive shall be binding, as to the result to be achieved, upon each Member State to which it is addressed, but shall leave to the national authorities the choice of form and methods.

A decision shall be binding in its entirety upon those to whom it is addressed.

Recommendations and opinions shall have no binding force.

Article 190
Regulations, directives and decisions of the Council and of the Commission shall state the reasons on which they are based and shall refer to any proposals or opinions which were required to be obtained pursuant to this Treaty.

Article 191
Regulations shall be published in the Official Journal of the Community. They shall enter into force on the date specified in them or, in the absence thereof, on the twentieth day following their publication.

Directives and decisions shall be notified to those to whom they are addressed and shall take effect upon such notification.

CHAPTER 3   THE ECONOMIC AND SOCIAL COMMITTEE

Article 194
The number of members of the Committee shall be as follows:

Belgium	12
Denmark	9
Germany	24
Greece	12
Spain	21
France	24
Ireland	9
Italy	24
Luxembourg	6
Netherlands	12
Portugal	12
United Kingdom	24[1]

The members of the Committee shall be appointed by the Council, acting unanimously, for four years. Their appointments shall be renewable.

The members of the Committee shall be appointed in their personal capacity and may not be bound by any mandatory instructions.

Note
[1] First paragraph as amended by Article 21 of the Act of Accession ESP/PORT.

Article 196

The Committee shall elect its chairman and officers from among its members for a term of two years.

It shall adopt its rules of procedure and shall submit them to the Council for its approval, which must be unanimous.

The Committee shall be convened by its chairman at the request of the Council or of the Commission.

Article 198

The Committee must be consulted by the Council or by the Commission where this Treaty so provides. The Committee may be consulted by these institutions in all cases in which they consider it appropriate.

The Council or the Commission shall, if it considers it necessary, set the Committee, for the submission of its opinion, a time limit which may not be less than ten days from the date which the chairman receives notification to this effect. Upon expiry of the time limit, the absence of an opinion shall not prevent further action.

The opinion of the Committee and that of the specialised section, together with a record of the proceedings, shall be forwarded to the Council and to the Commission.

TITLE II FINANCIAL PROVISIONS

Article 199

All items of revenue and expenditure of the Community, including those relating to the European Social Fund, shall be included in estimates to be drawn up for each financial year and shall be shown in the budget.

The revenue and expenditure shown in the budget shall be in balance.

Article 200

1. The budget revenue shall include, irrespective of any other revenue, financial contributions of Member States on the following scale:

Netherlands	7.9
Germany	28
France	28
Italy	28
Luxembourg	0.2
Netherlands	7.9

2. The financial contributions of Member States to cover the expenditure of the European Social Fund, however, shall be determined on the following scale:

Belgium	8.8
Germany	32
France	32
Italy	20
Luxembourg	0.2
Netherlands	7

3. The scales may be modified by the Council, acting unanimously.

Article 201

The Commission shall examine the conditions under which the financial contributions of Member States provided for in Article 200 could be replaced by the Community's own resources, in particular by revenue accruing from the common customs tariff when it has been finally introduced.

To this end, the Commission shall submit proposals to the Council.

After consulting the European Parliament on these proposals the Council may, acting unanimously, lay down the appropriate provisions, which it shall recommend to the Member States for adoption in accordance with their respective constitutional requirements.

Article 205

The Commission shall implement the budget, in accordance with provisions of the regulations made pursuant to Article 209, on its own responsibility and within the limits of the appropriations.

The regulations shall lay down detailed rules for each institution concerning its part in effecting its own expenditure.

Within the budget, the Commission may, subject to the limits and conditions laid down in the regulations made pursuant to Article 209, transfer appropriations from one chapter to another or from one sub-division to another.

Article 206[1]

1. A Court of Auditors is hereby established.

2. The Court of Auditors shall consist of twelve members.[2]

3. The members of the Court of Auditors shall be chosen from among persons who belong or have belonged in their respective countries to external audit bodies or who are especially qualified for this office. Their independence must be beyond doubt.

4. The members of the Court of Auditors shall be appointed for a term of six years by the Council, acting unanimously after consulting the European Parliament.

However, when the first appointments are made, four members of the Court of Auditors, chosen by lot, shall be appointed for a term of office of four years only.

The members of the Court of Auditors shall be eligible for reappointment.

They shall elect the President of the Court of Auditors from among their number for a term of three years. The President may be re-elected.

5. The members of the Court of Auditors shall, in the general interest of the Community, be completely independent in the performance of their duties.

In the performance of these duties, they shall neither seek nor take instructions from any government or from any other body. They shall refrain from any action incompatible with their duties.

6. The members of the Court of Auditors may not, during their term of office, engage in any other occupation, whether gainful or not. When entering upon their duties they shall give a solemn undertaking that, both during and after their term of office, they will respect the obligations arising therefrom and in particular their duty to behave with integrity and discretion as regards the acceptance, after they have ceased to hold office, of certain appointments or benefits.

7. Apart from normal replacement, or death, the duties of a member of the Court of Auditors shall end when he resigns, or is compulsorily retired by a ruling of the Court of Justice pursuant to paragraph 8.

The vacancy thus caused shall be filled for the remainder of the member's term of office.

Save in the case of compulsory retirement, members of the Court of Auditors shall remain in office until they have been replaced.

8.   A member of the Court of Auditors may be deprived of his office or of his right to a pension or other benefits in its stead only if the Court of Justice, at the request of the Court of Auditors, finds that he no longer fulfils the requisite conditions or meets the obligations arising from his office.

9.   The Council, acting by a qualified majority, shall determine the conditions of employment of the President and the members of the Court of Auditors and in particular their salaries, allowances and pensions. It shall also, by the same majority, determine any payment to be made instead of remuneration.

10.   The provisions of the Protocol on the Privileges and Immunities of the European Communities applicable to the Judges of the Court of Justice shall also apply to the members of the Court of Auditors.

Notes
[1]Text excepting paragraph 2, as amended by Article 15 of the Treaty amending Certain Financial Provisions.
[2]Paragraph 2 as amended by Article 20 of the Act of Accession ESP/PORT.

Article 206a[1]

1.   The Court of Auditors shall examine the accounts of all revenue and expenditure of the Community. It shall also examine the accounts of all revenue and expenditure of all bodies set up by the Community in so far as the relevant constituent instrument does not preclude such examination.

2.   The Court of Auditors shall examine whether all revenue has been received and all expenditure incurred in a lawful and regular manner and whether the financial management has been sound.

The audit of revenue shall be carried out on the basis both of the amounts established as due and the amounts actually paid to the Community.

The audit of expenditure shall be carried out on the basis both of commitments undertaken and payments made.

These audits may be carried out before the closure of accounts for the financial year in question.

3.   The audit shall be based on records and, if necessary, performed on the spot in the institutions of the Community and in the Member States. In the Member States the audit shall be carried out in liaison with the national audit bodies or, if these do not have the necessary powers, with the competent national departments. These bodies or departments shall inform the Court of Auditors whether they intend to take part in the audit.

The institutions of the Community and the national audit bodies or, if these do not have the necessary powers, the competent national departments, shall forward to the Court of Auditors, at its request, any document or information necessary to carry out its task.

4.   The Court of Auditors shall draw up an annual report after the close of each financial year. It shall be forwarded to the institutions of the Community and shall be published, together with the replies of these institutions to the observations of the Court of Auditors, in the *Official Journal of the European Communities*.

The Court of Auditors may also, at any time, submit observations on specific questions and deliver opinions at the request of one of the institutions of the Community.

It shall adopt its annual reports or opinions by a majority of its members.

It shall assist the European Parliament and the Council in exercising their powers of control over the implementation of the budget.

Note

[1]Article added by Article 16 of the Treaty amending Certain Financial Provisions.

Article 206b[1]

The European Parliament, acting on a recommendation from the Council which shall act by a qualified majority, shall give a discharge to the Commission in respect of the implementation of the budget. To this end, the Council and the European Parliament in turn shall examine the accounts and the financial statement referred to in Article 205a and the annual report by the Court of Auditors together with the replies of the institutions under audit to the observations of the Court of Auditors.

Note

[1]Article added by Article 17 of the Treaty amending Certain Financial Provisions.

Article 209[1]

The Council, acting unanimously on a proposal from the Commission and after consulting the European Parliament and obtaining the opinion of the Court of Auditors, shall:

Note

[1]Text as amended by Article 18 of the Treaty amending Certain Financial Provisions.

   (a)   make Financial Regulations specifying in particular the procedure to be adopted for establishing and implementing the budget and for presenting and auditing accounts;

   (b)   determine the methods and procedure whereby the budget revenue provided under the arrangements relating to the Communities' own resources shall be made available to the Commission, and determine the measures to be applied, if need be, to meet cash requirements;

   (c)   lay down rules concerning the responsibility of authorising officers and accounting officers and concerning appropriate arrangements for inspection.

PART SIX   GENERAL AND FINAL PROVISIONS

Article 215

The contractual liability of the Community shall be governed by the law applicable to the contract in question.

In the case of non-contractual liability, the Community shall, in accordance with the general principles common to the laws of the Member States, make good any damage caused by its institutions or by its servants in the performance of their duties.

The personal liability of its servants towards the Community shall be governed by the provisions laid down in their Staff Regulations or in the Conditions of Employment applicable to them.

Article 227

1.   This Treaty shall apply to the Kingdom of Belgium, the Kingdom of Denmark, the Federal Republic of Germany, the Hellenic Republic, the

Kingdom of Spain, the French Republic, Ireland, the Italian Republic, the Grand Duchy of Luxembourg, the Kingdom of the Netherlands, the Portuguese Republic and the United Kingdom of Great Britain and Northern Ireland.[1]

2.   With regard to Algeria and the French overseas departments, the general and particular provisions of this Treaty relating to:
— the free movement of goods;
— agriculture, save for Article 40(4);
— the liberalisation of services;
— the rules on competition;
— the protective measures provided for in Articles 108, 109 and 226;
— the institutions,
shall apply as soon as this Treaty enters into force.

The conditions under which the other provisions of this Treaty are to apply shall be determined, within two years of the entry into force of this Treaty, by decisions of the Council, acting unanimously on a proposal from the Commission.

The institutions of the Community will, within the framework of the procedures provided for in this Treaty, in particular Article 226, take care that the economic and social development of these areas is made possible.

3.   The special arrangements for association set out in Part Four of this Treaty shall apply to the overseas countries and territories listed in Annex IV to this Treaty.

This Treaty shall not apply to those overseas countries and territories having special relations with the United Kingdom of Great Britain and Northern Ireland which are not included in the aforementioned list.[2]

4.   The provisions of this Treaty shall apply to the European territories for whose external relations a Member State is responsible.

5.[3]   Notwithstanding the preceding paragraphs:

Notes
[1]Paragraph (1) as amended by Article 24 of the Act of Accession ESP/PORT.
[2]Second subparagraph of paragraph 3 added by Article 26(2) of the Act of Accession DK/IRL/UK.
[3]Paragraph 5 added by Article 26(3) of the Act of Accession DK/IRL/UK, modified by Article 15(2) of the AD AA DK/IRL/UK.

(a)   This Treaty shall not apply to the Faeroe Islands. The Government of the Kingdom of Denmark may, however, give notice, by a declaration deposited by 31 December 1975 at the latest with the Government of the Italian Republic, which shall transmit a certified copy thereof to each of the Governments of the other Member States, that this Treaty shall apply to those Islands. In that event, this Treaty shall apply to those Islands from the first day of the second month following the deposit of the declaration.

(b)   This Treaty shall not apply to the Sovereign Base Areas of the United Kingdom of Great Britain and Northern Ireland in Cyprus.

(c)   This Treaty shall apply to the Channel Islands and the Isle of Man only to the extent necessary to ensure the implementation of the arrangements for those islands set out in the Treaty concerning the accession of new Member

States to the European Economic Community and to the European Atomic Energy Community signed on 22 January 1972.

Article 228

1. Where this Treaty provides for the conclusion of agreements between the Community and one or more States or an international organisation, such agreements shall be negotiated by the Commission. Subject to the powers vested in the Commission in this field, such agreements shall be concluded by the Council, after consulting the European Parliament where required by this Treaty.

The Council, the Commission or a Member State may obtain beforehand the opinion of the Court of Justice as to whether an agreement envisaged is compatible with the provisions of this Treaty. Where the opinion of the Court of Justice is adverse, the agreement may enter into force only in accordance with Article 236.

2. Agreements concluded under these conditions shall be binding on the institutions of the Community and on Member States.

Article 231

The Community shall establish close cooperation with the Organisation for European Economic Cooperation, the details to be determined by common accord.

Article 236

The Government of any Member State or the Commission may submit to the Council proposals for the amendment of this Treaty.

If the Council, after consulting the European Parliament and, where appropriate, the Commission, delivers an opinion in favour of calling a conference of represenatives of the Governments of the Member States, the conference shall be convened by the President of the Council for the purpose of determining by common accord the amendments to be made to this Treaty.

The amendments shall enter into force after being ratified by all the Member States in accordance with their respective constitutional requirements.

Article 237

Any European State may apply to become a member of the Community. It shall address its application to the Council, which shall act unanimously after consulting the Commission and after receiving the assent of the European Parliament which shall act by an absolute majority of its component members.[1]

The conditions of admission and the adjustments to this Treaty necessitated thereby shall be the subject of an agreement between the Member States and the applicant State. This agreement shall be submitted for ratification by all the Contracting States in accordance with their respective constitutional requirements.

Note

[1]First paragraph as replaced by Article 8 of the SEA.

Article 238

The Community may conclude with a third State, a union of States or an international organisation agreements establishing an association involving reciprocal rights and obligations, common action and special procedures.

These agreements shall be concluded by the Council, acting unanimously and after receiving the assent of the European Parliament which shall act by an absolute majority of its component members.[1]

Where such agreements call for amendments to this Treaty, these amendments shall first be adopted in accordance with the procedure laid down in Article 236.

Note

[1]Second paragraph as replaced by Article 9 of the SEA.

ANNEX II

TREATY OF AMSTERDAM
AMENDING THE TREATY ON EUROPEAN UNION, THE TREATIES ESTABLISHING THE EUROPEAN COMMUNITIES AND CERTAIN RELATED ACTS

HIS MAJESTY THE KING OF THE BELGIANS,
HER MAJESTY THE QUEEN OF DENMARK,
THE PRESIDENT OF THE FEDERAL REPUBLIC OF GERMANY,
THE PRESIDENT OF THE HELLENIC REPUBLIC,
HIS MAJESTY THE KING OF SPAIN,
THE PRESIDENT OF THE FRENCH REPUBLIC,
THE COMMISSION AUTHORISED BY ARTICLE 14 OF THE CONSTITUTION OF IRELAND TO EXERCISE AND PERFORM THE POWERS AND FUNCTIONS OF THE PRESIDENT OF IRELAND,
THE PRESIDENT OF THE ITALIAN REPUBLIC,
HIS ROYAL HIGHNESS THE GRAND DUKE OF LUXEMBOURG,
HER MAJESTY THE QUEEN OF THE NETHERLANDS,
THE FEDERAL PRESIDENT OF THE REPUBLIC OF AUSTRIA,
THE PRESIDENT OF THE PORTUGUESE REPUBLIC,
THE PRESIDENT OF THE REPUBLIC OF FINLAND,
HIS MAJESTY THE KING OF SWEDEN,
HER MAJESTY THE QUEEN OF THE UNITED KINGDOM OF GREAT BRITAIN AND NORTHERN IRELAND,

HAVE RESOLVED to amend the Treaty on European Union, the Treaties establishing the European Communities and certain related acts,
and to this end have designated as their Plenipotentiaries:

HIS MAJESTY THE KING OF THE BELGIANS:
Mr. Erik Derycke,
Minister for Foreign Affairs;

HER MAJESTY THE QUEEN OF DENMARK:
Mr. Niels Helveg Petersen,
Minister for Foreign Affairs;

THE PRESIDENT OF THE FEDERAL REPUBLIC OF GERMANY:
Dr. Klaus Kinkel,
Federal Minister for Foreign Affairs and Deputy Federal Chancellor;

THE PRESIDENT OF THE HELLENIC REPUBLIC:
Mr. Theodoros Pangalos,
Minister for Foreign Affairs;

HIS MAJESTY THE KING OF SPAIN:
Mr. Juan Abel Matutes,
Minister for Foreign Affairs;

THE PRESIDENT OF THE FRENCH REPUBLIC:
Mr. Hubert Védrine,
Minister for Foreign Affairs;

THE COMMISSION AUTHORISED BY ARTICLE 14 OF THE
CONSTITUTION OF IRELAND TO EXERCISE AND PERFORM THE
POWERS AND FUNCTIONS OF THE PRESIDENT OF IRELAND:
Mr. Raphael P. Burke,
Minister for Foreign Affairs;

THE PRESIDENT OF THE ITALIAN REPUBLIC:
Mr. Lamberto Dini,
Minister for Foreign Affairs;

HIS ROYAL HIGHNESS THE GRAND DUKE OF LUXEMBOURG:
Mr. Jacques F. Poos,
Deputy Prime Minister,
Minister for Foreign Affairs, Foreign Trade and Cooperation;

HER MAJESTY THE QUEEN OF THE NETHERLANDS:
Mr. Hans van Mierlo,
Deputy Prime Minister and Minister for Foreign Affairs;

THE FEDERAL PRESIDENT OF THE REPUBLIC OF AUSTRIA:
Mr. Wolfgang Schüssel,
Federal Minister for Foreign Affairs and Vice Chancellor;

THE PRESIDENT OF THE PORTUGUESE REPUBLIC:
Mr. Jaime Gama,
Minister for Foreign Affairs;

THE PRESIDENT OF THE REPUBLIC OF FINLAND:
Ms. Tarja Halonen,
Minister for Foreign Affairs;

HIS MAJESTY THE KING OF SWEDEN:
Ms. Lena Hjelm-Wallén,
Minister for Foreign Affairs;

HER MAJESTY THE QUEEN OF THE UNITED KINGDOM OF
GREAT BRITAIN AND NORTHERN IRELAND:
Mr. Douglas Henderson,
Minister of State,
Foreign and Commonwealth Office;

WHO, having exchanged their full powers found in good and due form,

HAVE AGREED AS FOLLOWS:

PART ONE
SUBSTANTIVE AMENDMENTS

ARTICLE 1

The Treaty on European Union shall be amended in accordance with the provisions of this Article.

(1)   After the third recital the following recital shall be inserted:

'CONFIRMING their attachment to fundamental social rights as defined in the European Social Charter signed at Turin on 18 October 1961 and in the 1989 Community Charter of the Fundamental Social Rights of Workers,'

(2)   The existing seventh recital shall be replaced by the following:

'DETERMINED to promote economic and social progress for their peoples, taking into account the principle of sustainable development and within the context of the accomplishment of the internal market and of reinforced cohesion and environmental protection, and to implement policies ensuring that advances in economic integration are accompanied by parallel progress in other fields,'

(3)   The existing ninth and tenth recitals shall be replaced by the following:

'RESOLVED to implement a common foreign and security policy including the progressive framing of a common defence policy, which might lead to a common defence in accordance with the provisions of Article J.7, thereby reinforcing the European identity and its independence in order to promote peace, security and progress in Europe and in the world,

RESOLVED to facilitate the free movement of persons, while ensuring the safety and security of their peoples, by establishing an area of freedom, security and justice, in accordance with the provisions of this Treaty,'

(4)   In Article A the second paragraph shall be replaced by the following:

'This Treaty marks a new stage in the process of creating an ever closer union among the peoples of Europe, in which decisions are taken as openly as possible and as closely as possible to the citizen.'

(5)   Article B shall be replaced by the following:

'**Article B**

The Union shall set itself the following objectives:

— to promote economic and social progress and a high level of employment and to achieve balanced and sustainable development, in particular through the creation of an area without internal frontiers, through the strengthening of economic and social cohesion and through the establishment of economic and monetary union, ultimately including a single currency in accordance with the provisions of this Treaty;

— to assert its identity on the international scene, in particular through the implementation of a common foreign and security policy including the progressive framing of a common defence policy, which might lead to a common defence, in accordance with the provisions of Article J.7;

— to strengthen the protection of the rights and interests of the nationals of its Member States through the introduction of a citizenship of the Union;

— to maintain and develop the Union as an area of freedom, security and justice, in which the free movement of persons is assured in conjunction with appropriate measures with respect to external border controls, asylum, immigration and the prevention and combating of crime;

—to maintain in full the acquis communautaire and build on it with a view to considering to what extent the policies and forms of cooperation introduced by this Treaty may need to be revised with the aim of ensuring the effectiveness of the mechanisms and the institutions of the Community.

The objectives of the Union shall be achieved as provided in this Treaty and in accordance with the conditions and the timetable set out therein while respecting the principle of subsidiarity as defined in Article 3b of the Treaty establishing the European Community.'

(6) In Article C, the second paragraph shall be replaced by the following: 'The Union shall in particular ensure the consistency of its external activities as a whole in the context of its external relations, security, economic and development policies. The Council and the Commission shall be responsible for ensuring such consistency and shall cooperate to this end. They shall ensure the implementation of these policies, each in accordance with its respective powers.'

(7) Article E shall be replaced by the following:

'**Article E**
The European Parliament, the Council, the Commission, the Court of Justice and the Court of Auditors shall exercise their powers under the conditions and for the purposes provided for, on the one hand, by the provisions of the Treaties establishing the European Communities and of the subsequent Treaties and Acts modifying and supplementing them and, on the other hand, by the other provisions of this Treaty.'

(8) Article F shall be amended as follows:
 (a) paragraph 1 shall be replaced by the following:
'1. The Union is founded on the principles of liberty, democracy, respect for human rights and fundamental freedoms, and the rule of law, principles which are common to the Member States.';
 (b) the existing paragraph 3 shall become paragraph 4 and a new paragraph 3 shall be inserted as follows:
'3. The Union shall respect the national identities of its Member States.'
(9) The following Article shall be inserted at the end of Title I:

'**Article F.1**
1. The Council, meeting in the composition of the Heads of State or Government and acting by unanimity on a proposal by one third of the Member States or by the Commission and after obtaining the assent of the European Parliament, may determine the existence of a serious and persistent breach by a Member State of principles mentioned in Article F(1), after inviting the government of the Member State in question to submit its observations.

2. Where such a determination has been made, the Council, acting by a qualified majority, may decide to suspend certain of the rights deriving from the application of this Treaty to the Member State in question, including the voting rights of the representative of the government of that Member State in the Council. In doing so, the Council shall take into account the possible consequences of such a suspension on the rights and obligations of natural and legal persons.

The obligations of the Member State in question under this Treaty shall in any case continue to be binding on that State.

3.   The Council, acting by a qualified majority, may decide subsequently to vary or revoke measures taken under paragraph 2 in response to changes in the situation which led to their being imposed.

4.   For the purposes of this Article, the Council shall act without taking into account the vote of the representative of the government of the Member State in question. Abstentions by members present in person or represented shall not prevent the adoption of decisions referred to in paragraph 1. A qualified majority shall be defined as the same proportion of the weighted votes of the members of the Council concerned as laid down in Article 148(2) of the Treaty establishing the European Community.

This paragraph shall also apply in the event of voting rights being suspended pursuant to paragraph 2.

5.   For the purposes of this Article, the European Parliament shall act by a two thirds majority of the votes cast, representing a majority of its members.'

(10)   Title V shall be replaced by the following:

'TITLE V
PROVISIONS ON A COMMON FOREIGN AND SECURITY POLICY

Article J.1

1.   The Union shall define and implement a common foreign and security policy covering all areas of foreign and security policy, the objectives of which shall be:

to safeguard the common values, fundamental interests, independence and integrity of the Union in conformity with the principles of the United Nations Charter;

— to strengthen the security of the Union in all ways;

— to preserve peace and strengthen international security, in accordance with the principles of the United Nations Charter, as well as the principles of the Helsinki Final Act and the objectives of the Paris Charter, including those on external borders;

— to promote international cooperation;

— to develop and consolidate democracy and the rule of law, and respect for human rights and fundamental freedoms.

2.   The Member States shall support the Union's external and security policy actively and unreservedly in a spirit of loyalty and mutual solidarity. The Member States shall work together to enhance and develop their mutual political solidarity. They shall refrain from any action which is contrary to the interests of the Union or likely to impair its effectiveness as a cohesive force in international relations. The Council shall ensure that these principles are complied with.

Article J.2

The Union shall pursue the objectives set out in Article J.1 by:

— defining the principles of and general guidelines for the common foreign and security policy;

— deciding on common strategies;

— adopting joint actions;

— adopting common positions;

— strengthening systematic cooperation between Member States in the conduct of policy.

Article J.3

1. The European Council shall define the principles of and general guidelines for the common foreign and security policy, including for matters with defence implications.

2. The European Council shall decide on common strategies to be implemented by the Union in areas where the Member States have important interests in common. Common strategies shall set out their objectives, duration and the means to be made available by the Union and the Member States.

3. The Council shall take the decisions necessary for defining and implementing the common foreign and security policy on the basis of the general guidelines defined by the European Council.

The Council shall recommend common strategies to the European Council and shall implement them, in particular by adopting joint actions and common positions.

The Council shall ensure the unity, consistency and effectiveness of action by the Union.

Article J.4

1. The Council shall adopt joint actions. Joint actions shall address specific situations where operational action by the Union is deemed to be required. They shall lay down their objectives, scope, the means to be made available to the Union, if necessary their duration, and the conditions for their implementation.

2. If there is a change in circumstances having a substantial effect on a question subject to joint action, the Council shall review the principles and objectives of that action and take the necessary decisions. As long as the Council has not acted, the joint action shall stand.

3. Joint actions shall commit the Member States in the positions they adopt and in the conduct of their activity.

4. The Council may request the Commission to submit to it any appropriate proposals relating to the common foreign and security policy to ensure the implementation of a joint action.

5. Whenever there is any plan to adopt a national position or take national action pursuant to a joint action, information shall be provided in time to allow, if necessary, for prior consultations within the Council. The obligation to provide prior information shall not apply to measures which are merely a national transposition of Council decisions.

6. In cases of imperative need arising from changes in the situation and failing a Council decision, Member States may take the necessary measures as a matter of urgency having regard to the general objectives of the joint action. The Member State concerned shall inform the Council immediately of any such measures.

7. Should there be any major difficulties in implementing a joint action, a Member State shall refer them to the Council which shall discuss them and seek appropriate solutions. Such solutions shall not run counter to the objectives of the joint action or impair its effectiveness.

Article J.5

The Council shall adopt common positions. Common positions shall define the approach of the Union to a particular matter of a geographical or thematic nature. Member States shall ensure that their national policies conform to the common positions.

Article J.6

Member States shall inform and consult one another within the Council on any matter of foreign and security policy of general interest in order to ensure that the Union's influence is exerted as effectively as possible by means of concerted and convergent action.

Article J.7

1. The common foreign and security policy shall include all questions relating to the security of the Union, including the progressive framing of a common defence policy, in accordance with the second subparagraph, which might lead to a common defence, should the European Council so decide. It shall in that case recommend to the Member States the adoption of such a decision in accordance with their respective constitutional requirements.

The Western European Union (WEU) is an integral part of the development of the Union providing the Union with access to an operational capability notably in the context of paragraph 2. It supports the Union in framing the defence aspects of the common foreign and security policy as set out in this Article. The Union shall accordingly foster closer institutional relations with the WEU with a view to the possibility of the integration of the WEU into the Union, should the European Council so decide. It shall in that case recommend to the Member States the adoption of such a decision in accordance with their respective constitutional requirements.

The policy of the Union in accordance with this Article shall not prejudice the specific character of the security and defence policy of certain Member States and shall respect the obligations of certain Member States, which see their common defence realised in the North Atlantic Treaty Organisation (NATO), under the North Atlantic Treaty and be compatible with the common security and defence policy established within that framework.

The progressive framing of a common defence policy will be supported, as Member States consider appropriate, by cooperation between them in the field of armaments.

2. Questions referred to in this Article shall include humanitarian and rescue tasks, peacekeeping tasks and tasks of combat forces in crisis management, including peacemaking.

3. The Union will avail itself of the WEU to elaborate and implement decisions and actions of the Union which have defence implications.

The competence of the European Council to establish guidelines in accordance with Article J.3 shall also obtain in respect of the WEU for those matters for which the Union avails itself of the WEU. When the Union avails itself of the WEU to elaborate and implement decisions of the Union on the tasks referred to in paragraph 2 all Member States of the Union shall be entitled to participate fully in the tasks in question. The Council, in agreement with the institutions of the WEU, shall adopt the necessary practical arrangements to allow all Member States contributing to the tasks in question to participate fully and on an equal footing in planning and decision-taking in the WEU. Decisions having defence implications dealt with under this paragraph shall be taken without prejudice to the policies and obligations referred to in paragraph 1, third subparagraph.

4. The provisions of this Article shall not prevent the development of closer cooperation between two or more Member States on a bilateral level, in the framework of the WEU and the Atlantic Alliance, provided such cooperation does not run counter to or impede that provided for in this Title.

5. With a view to furthering the objectives of this Article, the provisions of this Article will be reviewed in accordance with Article N.

Article J.8

1. The Presidency shall represent the Union in matters coming within the common foreign and security policy.

2. The Presidency shall be responsible for the implementation of decisions taken under this Title; in that capacity it shall in principle express the position of the Union in international organisations and international conferences.

3. The Presidency shall be assisted by the Secretary General of the Council who shall exercise the function of High Representative for the common foreign and security policy.

4. The Commission shall be fully associated in the tasks referred to in paragraphs 1 and 2. The Presidency shall be assisted in those tasks if need be by the next Member State to hold the Presidency.

5. The Council may, whenever it deems it necessary, appoint a special representative with a mandate in relation to particular policy issues.

Article J.9

1. Member States shall coordinate their action in international organisations and at international conferences. They shall uphold the common positions in such fora. In international organisations and at international conferences where not all the Member States participate, those which do take part shall uphold the common positions.

2. Without prejudice to paragraph 1 and Article J.4(3), Member States represented in international organisations or international conferences where not all the Member States participate shall keep the latter informed of any matter of common interest.

Member States which are also members of the United Nations Security Council will concert and keep the other Member States fully informed. Member States which are permanent members of the Security Council will, in the execution of their functions, ensure the defence of the positions and the interests of the Union, without prejudice to their responsibilities under the provisions of the United Nations Charter.

Article J.10

The diplomatic and consular missions of the Member States and the Commission Delegations in third countries and international conferences, and their representations to international organisations, shall cooperate in ensuring that the common positions and joint actions adopted by the Council are complied with and implemented.

They shall step up cooperation by exchanging information, carrying out joint assessments and contributing to the implementation of the provisions referred to in Article 8c of the Treaty establishing the European Community.

Article J.11

The Presidency shall consult the European Parliament on the main aspects and the basic choices of the common foreign and security policy and shall ensure that the views of the European Parliament are duly taken into consideration. The European Parliament shall be kept regularly informed by the Presidency and the Commission of the development of the Union's foreign and security policy. The European Parliament may ask questions of the Council or make recommendations to it. It shall hold an annual debate on progress in implementing the common foreign and security policy.

Article J.12

1.   Any Member State or the Commission may refer to the Council any question relating to the common foreign and security policy and may submit proposals to the Council.

2.   In cases requiring a rapid decision, the Presidency, of its own motion, or at the request of the Commission or a Member State, shall convene an extraordinary Council meeting within forty eight hours or, in an emergency, within a shorter period.

Article J.13

1.   Decisions under this Title shall be taken by the Council acting unanimously. Abstentions by members present in person or represented shall not prevent the adoption of such decisions. When abstaining in a vote, any member of the Council may qualify its abstention by making a formal declaration under the present subparagraph. In that case, it shall not be obliged to apply the decision, but shall accept that the decision commits the Union. In a spirit of mutual solidarity, the Member State concerned shall refrain from any action likely to conflict with or impede Union action based on that decision and the other Member States shall respect its position. If the members of the Council qualifying their abstention in this way represent more than one third of the votes weighted in accordance with Article 148(2) of the Treaty establishing the European Community, the decision shall not be adopted.

2.   By derogation from the provisions of paragraph 1, the Council shall act by qualified majority:

—when adopting joint actions, common positions or taking any other decision on the basis of a common strategy;

—when adopting any decision implementing a joint action or a common position. If a member of the Council declares that, for important and stated reasons of national policy, it intends to oppose the adoption of a decision to be taken by qualified majority, a vote shall not be taken. The Council may, acting by a qualified majority, request that the matter be referred to the European Council for decision by unanimity. The votes of the members of the Council shall be weighted in accordance with Article 148(2) of the Treaty establishing the European Community. For their adoption, decisions shall require at least 62 votes in favour, cast by at least 10 members. This paragraph shall not apply to decisions having military or defence implications.

3.   For procedural questions, the Council shall act by a majority of its members.

Article J.14

When it is necessary to conclude an agreement with one or more States or international organisations in implementation of this Title, the Council, acting unanimously, may authorise the Presidency, assisted by the Commission as appropriate, to open negotiations to that effect. Such agreements shall be concluded by the Council acting unanimously on a recommendation from the Presidency. No agreement shall be binding on a Member State whose representative in the Council states that it has to comply with the requirements of its own constitutional procedure; the other members of the Council may agree that the agreement shall apply provisionally to them. The provisions of this Article shall also apply to matters falling under Title VI.

Article J.15

Without prejudice to Article 151 of the Treaty establishing the European Community, a Political Committee shall monitor the international situation in the areas covered by the common foreign and security policy and contribute to the definition of policies by delivering opinions to the Council at the request of the Council or on its own initiative. It shall also monitor the implementation of agreed policies, without prejudice to the responsibility of the Presidency and the Commission.

Article J.16

The Secretary General of the Council, High Representative for the common foreign and security policy, shall assist the Council in matters coming within the scope of the common foreign and security policy, in particular through contributing to the formulation, preparation and implementation of policy decisions, and, when appropriate and acting on behalf of the Council at the request of the Presidency, through conducting political dialogue with third parties.

Article J.17

The Commission shall be fully associated with the work carried out in the common foreign and security policy field.

Article J.18

1.   Articles 137, 138, 139 to 142, 146, 147, 150 to 153, 157 to 163, 191a and 217 of the Treaty establishing the European Community shall apply to the provisions relating to the areas referred to in this Title.

2.   Administrative expenditure which the provisions relating to the areas referred to in this Title entail for the institutions shall be charged to the budget of the European Communities.

3.   Operational expenditure to which the implementation of those provisions gives rise shall also be charged to the budget of the European Communities, except for such expenditure arising from operations having military or defence implications and cases where the Council acting unanimously decides otherwise.

In cases where expenditure is not charged to the budget of the European Communities it shall be charged to the Member States in accordance with the gross national product scale, unless the Council acting unanimously decides otherwise. As for expenditure arising from operations having military or defence implications, Member States whose representatives in the

Council have made a formal declaration under Article J.13(1), second subparagraph, shall not be obliged to contribute to the financing thereof.

4. The budgetary procedure laid down in the Treaty establishing the European Community shall apply to the expenditure charged to the budget of the European Communities.'

(11) Title VI shall be replaced by the following:

'TITLE VI
PROVISIONS ON POLICE AND JUDICIAL COOPERATION IN CRIMINAL MATTERS

Article K.1

Without prejudice to the powers of the European Community, the Union's objective shall be to provide citizens with a high level of safety within an area of freedom, security and justice by developing common action among the Member States in the fields of police and judicial cooperation in criminal matters and by preventing and combating racism and xenophobia. That objective shall be achieved by preventing and combating crime, organised or otherwise, in particular terrorism, trafficking in persons and offences against children, illicit drug trafficking and illicit arms trafficking, corruption and fraud, through:

— closer cooperation between police forces, customs authorities and other competent authorities in the Member States, both directly and through the European Police Office (Europol), in accordance with the provisions of Articles K.2 and K.4;

— closer cooperation between judicial and other competent authorities of the Member States in accordance with the provisions of Articles K.3(a) to (d) and K.4;

— approximation, where necessary, of rules on criminal matters in the Member States, in accordance with the provisions of Article K.3(e).

Article K.2

1. Common action in the field of police cooperation shall include:

(a) operational cooperation between the competent authorities, including the police, customs and other specialised law enforcement services of the Member States in relation to the prevention, detection and investigation of criminal offences;

(b) the collection, storage, processing, analysis and exchange of relevant information, including information held by law enforcement services on reports on suspicious financial transactions, in particular through Europol, subject to appropriate provisions on the protection of personal data;

(c) cooperation and joint initiatives in training, the exchange of liaison officers, secondments, the use of equipment, and forensic research;

(d) the common evaluation of particular investigative techniques in relation to the detection of serious forms of organised crime.

2. The Council shall promote cooperation through Europol and shall in particular, within a period of five years after the date of entry into force of the Treaty of Amsterdam:

(a) enable Europol to facilitate and support the preparation, and to encourage the coordination and carrying out, of specific investigative actions by the competent authorities of the Member States, including operational actions of joint teams comprising representatives of Europol in a support capacity;

(b)   adopt measures allowing Europol to ask the competent authorities of the Member States to conduct and coordinate their investigations in specific cases and to develop specific expertise which may be put at the disposal of Member States to assist them in investigating cases of organised crime;

(c)   promote liaison arrangements between prosecuting/investigating officials specialising in the fight against organised crime in close cooperation with Europol;

(d)   establish a research, documentation and statistical network on cross-border crime.

Article K.3

Common action on judicial cooperation in criminal matters shall include:

(a)   facilitating and accelerating cooperation between competent ministries and judicial or equivalent authorities of the Member States in relation to proceedings and the enforcement of decisions;

(b)   facilitating extradition between Member States;

(c)   ensuring compatibility in rules applicable in the Member States, as may be necessary to improve such cooperation;

(d)   preventing conflicts of jurisdiction between Member States;

(e)   progressively adopting measures establishing minimum rules relating to the constituent elements of criminal acts and to penalties in the fields of organised crime, terrorism and illicit drug trafficking.

Article K.4

The Council shall lay down the conditions and limitations under which the competent authorities referred to in Articles K.2 and K.3 may operate in the territory of another Member State in liaison and in agreement with the authorities of that State.

Article K.5

This Title shall not affect the exercise of the responsibilities incumbent upon Member States with regard to the maintenance of law and order and the safeguarding of internal security.

Article K.6

1.   In the areas referred to in this Title, Member States shall inform and consult one another within the Council with a view to coordinating their action. To that end, they shall establish collaboration between the relevant departments of their administrations.

2.   The Council shall take measures and promote cooperation, using the appropriate form and procedures as set out in this Title, contributing to the pursuit of the objectives of the Union. To that end, acting unanimously on the initiative of any Member State or of the Commission, the Council may:

(a)   adopt common positions defining the approach of the Union to a particular matter;

(b)   adopt framework decisions for the purpose of approximation of the laws and regulations of the Member States. Framework decisions shall be binding upon the Member States as to the result to be achieved but shall leave to the national authorities the choice of form and methods. They shall not entail direct effect;

(c)   adopt decisions for any other purpose consistent with the objectives of this Title, excluding any approximation of the laws and regulations of the Member States. These decisions shall be binding and shall not entail direct effect; the Council, acting by a qualified majority, shall adopt measures necessary to implement those decisions at the level of the Union;

(d)   establish conventions which it shall recommend to the Member States for adoption in accordance with their respective constitutional requirements. Member States shall begin the procedures applicable within a time limit to be set by the Council. Unless they provide otherwise, conventions shall, once adopted by at least half of the Member States, enter into force for those Member States. Measures implementing conventions shall be adopted within the Council by a majority of two-thirds of the Contracting Parties.

3.   Where the Council is required to act by a qualified majority, the votes of its members shall be weighted as laid down in Article 148(2) of the Treaty establishing the European Community, and for their adoption acts of the Council shall require at least 62 votes in favour, cast by at least 10 members.

4.   For procedural questions, the Council shall act by a majority of its members.

Article K.7

1.   The Court of Justice of the European Communities shall have jurisdiction, subject to the conditions laid down in this Article, to give preliminary rulings on the validity and interpretation of framework decisions and decisions, on the interpretation of conventions established under this Title and on the validity and interpretation of the measures implementing them.

2.   By a declaration made at the time of signature of the Treaty of Amsterdam or at any time thereafter, any Member State shall be able to accept the jurisdiction of the Court of Justice to give preliminary rulings as specified in paragraph 1.

3.   A Member State making a declaration pursuant to paragraph 2 shall specify that either:

(a)   any court or tribunal of that State against whose decisions there is no judicial remedy under national law may request the Court of Justice to give a preliminary ruling on a question raised in a case pending before it and concerning the validity or interpretation of an act referred to in paragraph 1 if that court or tribunal considers that a decision on the question is necessary to enable it to give judgment, or

(b)   any court or tribunal of that State may request the Court of Justice to give a preliminary ruling on a question raised in a case pending before it and concerning the validity or interpretation of an act referred to in paragraph 1 if that court or tribunal considers that a decision on the question is necessary to enable it to give judgment.

4.   Any Member State, whether or not it has made a declaration pursuant to paragraph 2, shall be entitled to submit statements of case or written observations to the Court in cases which arise under paragraph 1.

5.   The Court of Justice shall have no jurisdiction to review the validity or proportionality of operations carried out by the police or other law enforcement services of a Member State or the exercise of the responsibilities

incumbent upon Member States with regard to the maintenance of law and order and the safeguarding of internal security.

6. The Court of Justice shall have jurisdiction to review the legality of framework decisions and decisions in actions brought by a Member State or the Commission on grounds of lack of competence, infringement of an essential procedural requirement, infringement of this Treaty or of any rule of law relating to its application, or misuse of powers. The proceedings provided for in this paragraph shall be instituted within two months of the publication of the measure.

7. The Court of Justice shall have jurisdiction to rule on any dispute between Member States regarding the interpretation or the application of acts adopted under Article K.6(2) whenever such dispute cannot be settled by the Council within six months of its being referred to the Council by one of its members. The Court shall also have jurisdiction to rule on any dispute between Member States and the Commission regarding the interpretation or the application of conventions established under Article K.6(2)(d).

Article K.8

1. A Coordinating Committee shall be set up consisting of senior officials. In addition to its coordinating role, it shall be the task of the Committee to:

— give opinions for the attention of the Council, either at the Council's request or on its own initiative;

— contribute, without prejudice to Article 151 of the Treaty establishing the European Community, to the preparation of the Council's discussions in the areas referred to in Article K.1.

2. The Commission shall be fully associated with the work in the areas referred to in this Title.

Article K.9

Within international organisations and at international conferences in which they take part, Member States shall defend the common positions adopted under the provisions of this Title. Articles J.8 and J.9 shall apply as appropriate to matters falling under this Title.

Article K.10

Agreements referred to in Article J.14 may cover matters falling under this Title.

Article K.11

1. The Council shall consult the European Parliament before adopting any measure referred to in Article K.6(2)(b), (c) and (d). The European Parliament shall deliver its opinion within a time limit which the Council may lay down, which shall not be less than three months. In the absence of an opinion within that time limit, the Council may act.

2. The Presidency and the Commission shall regularly inform the European Parliament of discussions in the areas covered by this Title.

3. The European Parliament may ask questions of the Council or make recommendations to it. Each year, it shall hold a debate on the progress made in the areas referred to in this Title.

Article K.12

1.   Member States which intend to establish closer cooperation between themselves may be authorised, subject to Articles K.15 and K.16, to make use of the institutions, procedures and mechanisms laid down by the Treaties provided that the cooperation proposed:

(a)   respects the powers of the European Community, and the objectives laid down by this Title;

(b)   has the aim of enabling the Union to develop more rapidly into an area of freedom, security and justice.

2.   The authorisation referred to in paragraph 1 shall be granted by the Council, acting by a qualified majority at the request of the Member States concerned and after inviting the Commission to present its opinion; the request shall also be forwarded to the European Parliament. If a member of the Council declares that, for important and stated reasons of national policy, it intends to oppose the granting of an authorisation by qualified majority, a vote shall not be taken.

The Council may, acting by a qualified majority, request that the matter be referred to the European Council for decision by unanimity.

The votes of the members of the Council shall be weighted in accordance with Article 148(2) of the Treaty establishing the European Community. For their adoption, decisions shall require at least 62 votes in favour, cast by at least 10 members.

3.   Any Member State which wishes to become a party to cooperation set up in accordance with this Article shall notify its intention to the Council and to the Commission, which shall give an opinion to the Council within three months of receipt of that notification, possibly accompanied by a recommendation for such specific arrangements as it may deem necessary for that Member State to become a party to the cooperation in question. Within four months of the date of that notification, the Council shall decide on the request and on such specific arrangements as it may deem necessary. The decision shall be deemed to be taken unless the Council, acting by a qualified majority, decides to hold it in abeyance; in this case, the Council shall state the reasons for its decision and set a deadline for re-examining it. For the purposes of this paragraph, the Council shall act under the conditions set out in Article K.16.

4.   The provisions of Articles K.1 to K.13 shall apply to the closer cooperation provided for by this Article, save as otherwise provided for in this Article and in Articles K.15 and K.16. The provisions of the Treaty establishing the European Community concerning the powers of the Court of Justice of the European Communities and the exercise of those powers shall apply to paragraphs 1, 2 and 3.

5.   This Article is without prejudice to the provisions of the Protocol integrating the Schengen acquis into the framework of the European Union.

Article K.13

1.   Articles 137, 138, 138e, 139 to 142, 146, 147, 148(3), 150 to 153, 157 to 163, 191a and 217 of the Treaty establishing the European Community shall apply to the provisions relating to the areas referred to in this Title.

2.   Administrative expenditure which the provisions relating to the areas referred to in this Title entail for the institutions shall be charged to the budget of the European Communities.

3.   Operational expenditure to which the implementation of those provisions gives rise shall also be charged to the budget of the European Communities, except where the Council acting unanimously decides otherwise. In cases where expenditure is not charged to the budget of the European Communities it shall be charged to the Member States in accordance with the gross national product scale, unless the Council acting unanimously decides otherwise.

4.   The budgetary procedure laid down in the Treaty establishing the European Community shall apply to the expenditure charged to the budget of the European Communities.

Article K.14

The Council, acting unanimously on the initiative of the Commission or a Member State, and after consulting the European Parliament, may decide that action in areas referred to in Article K.1 shall fall under Title IIIa of the Treaty establishing the European Community, and at the same time determine the relevant voting conditions relating to it. It shall recommend the Member States to adopt that decision in accordance with their respective constitutional requirements.'

(12)   The following new Title shall be inserted:

'TITLE VIa
PROVISIONS ON CLOSER COOPERATION

Article K.15

1.   Member States which intend to establish closer cooperation between themselves may make use of the institutions, procedures and mechanisms laid down by this Treaty and the Treaty establishing the European Community provided that the cooperation:

(a)   is aimed at furthering the objectives of the Union and at protecting and serving its interests;

(b)   respects the principles of the said Treaties and the single institutional framework of the Union;

(c)   is only used as a last resort, where the objectives of the said Treaties could not be attained by applying the relevant procedures laid down therein;

(d)   concerns at least a majority of Member States;

(e)   does not affect the 'acquis communautaire' and the measures adopted under the other provisions of the said Treaties;

(f)   does not affect the competences, rights, obligations and interests of those Member States which do not participate therein;

(g)   is open to all Member States and allows them to become parties to the cooperation at any time, provided that they comply with the basic decision and with the decisions taken within that framework;

(h)   complies with the specific additional criteria laid down in Article 5a of the Treaty establishing the European Community and Article K.12 of this Treaty, depending on the area concerned, and is authorised by the Council in accordance with the procedures laid down therein.

2.   Member States shall apply, as far as they are concerned, the acts and decisions adopted for the implementation of the cooperation in which they participate. Member States not participating in such cooperation shall not impede the implementation thereof by the participating Member States.

Article K.16

1.   For the purposes of the adoption of the acts and decisions necessary for the implementation of the cooperation referred to in Article K.15, the relevant institutional provisions of this Treaty and of the Treaty establishing the European Community shall apply. However, while all members of the Council shall be able to take part in the deliberations, only those representing participating Member States shall take part in the adoption of decisions. The qualified majority shall be defined as the same proportion of the weighted votes of the members of the Council concerned as laid down in Article 148(2) of the Treaty establishing the European Community. Unanimity shall be constituted by only those Council members concerned.

2.   Expenditure resulting from implementation of the cooperation, other than administrative costs entailed for the institutions, shall be borne by the participating Member States, unless the Council, acting unanimously, decides otherwise.

Article K.17

The Council and the Commission shall regularly inform the European Parliament of the development of closer cooperation established on the basis of this Title.'

(13)   Article L shall be replaced by the following:

'Article L

The provisions of the Treaty establishing the European Community, the Treaty establishing the European Coal and Steel Community and the Treaty establishing the European Atomic Energy Community concerning the powers of the Court of Justice of the European Communities and the exercise of those powers shall apply only to the following provisions of this Treaty:

(a)   provisions amending the Treaty establishing the European Economic Community with a view to establishing the European Community, the Treaty establishing the European Coal and Steel Community and the Treaty establishing the European Atomic Energy Community;

(b)   provisions of Title VI, under the conditions provided for by Article K.7;

(c)   provisions of Title VIa, under the conditions provided for by Article 5a of the Treaty establishing the European Community and Article K.12 of this Treaty;

(d)   Article F(2) with regard to action of the institutions, insofar as the Court has jurisdiction under the Treaties establishing the European Communities and under this Treaty;

(e)   Articles L to S.'

(14)   In Article N, paragraph 2 shall be deleted and paragraph 1 shall remain without a number.

(15)   In Article O, the first paragraph shall be replaced by the following:
'Any European State which respects the principles set out in Article F(1) may apply to become a member of the Union. It shall address its application

to the Council, which shall act unanimously after consulting the Commission and after receiving the assent of the European Parliament, which shall act by an absolute majority of its component members.'

(16)   In Article S, a new paragraph shall be added as follows:
'Pursuant to the 1994 Accession Treaty, the Finnish and Swedish versions of this Treaty shall also be authentic.'

ARTICLE 2

The Treaty establishing the European Community shall be amended in accordance with the provisions of this Article.

(1)   In the preamble the following recital shall be inserted after the eighth recital:
'DETERMINED to promote the development of the highest possible level of knowledge for their peoples through a wide access to education and through its continuous updating,'

(2)   Article 2 shall be replaced by the following:

'Article 2

The Community shall have as its task, by establishing a common market and an economic and monetary union and by implementing common policies or activities referred to in Articles 3 and 3a, to promote throughout the Community a harmonious, balanced and sustainable development of economic activities, a high level of employment and of social protection, equality between men and women, sustainable and non-inflationary growth, a high degree of competitiveness and convergence of economic performance, a high level of protection and improvement of the quality of the environment, the raising of the standard of living and quality of life, and economic and social cohesion and solidarity among Member States.'

(3)   Article 3 shall be amended as follows:
  (a)   the existing text shall be numbered and become paragraph 1;
  (b)   in new paragraph 1, point (d) shall be replaced by the following:
    '(d)   measures concerning the entry and movement of persons as provided for in Title IIIa;';
  (c)   in new paragraph 1, the following new point (i) shall be inserted after point (h):
    '(i)   the promotion of coordination between employment policies of the Member States with a view to enhancing their effectiveness by developing a co-ordinated strategy for employment;'
  (d)   in new paragraph 1, the existing point (i) shall become point (j) and the subsequent points shall be renumbered accordingly;
  (e)   the following paragraph shall be added:
    '2.   In all the activities referred to in this Article, the Community shall aim to eliminate inequalities, and to promote equality, between men and women.'

(4)   The following Article shall be inserted:

'Article 3c

Environmental protection requirements must be integrated into the definition and implementation of the Community policies and activities referred to in Article 3, in particular with a view to promoting sustainable development.'

(5)   The following Article shall be inserted:

'**Article 5a**

1.   Member States which intend to establish closer cooperation between themselves may be authorised, subject to Articles K.15 and K.16 of the Treaty on European Union, to make use of the institutions, procedures and mechanisms laid down by this Treaty, provided that the cooperation proposed:

(a)   does not concern areas which fall within the exclusive competence of the Community;

(b)   does not affect Community policies, actions or programmes;

(c)   does not concern the citizenship of the Union or discriminate between nationals of Member States;

(d)   remains within the limits of the powers conferred upon the Community by this Treaty; and

(e)   does not constitute a discrimination or a restriction of trade between Member States and does not distort the conditions of competition between the latter.

2.   The authorisation referred to in paragraph 1 shall be granted by the Council, acting by a qualified majority on a proposal from the Commission and after consulting the European Parliament.

If a member of the Council declares that, for important and stated reasons of national policy, it intends to oppose the granting of an authorisation by qualified majority, a vote shall not be taken. The Council may, acting by a qualified majority, request that the matter be referred to the Council, meeting in the composition of the Heads of State or Government, for decision by unanimity. Member States which intend to establish closer cooperation as referred to in paragraph 1 may address a request to the Commission, which may submit a proposal to the Council to that effect. In the event of the Commission not submitting a proposal, it shall inform the Member States concerned of the reasons for not doing so.

3.   Any Member State which wishes to become a party to cooperation set up in accordance with this Article shall notify its intention to the Council and to the Commission, which shall give an opinion to the Council within three months of receipt of that notification. Within four months of the date of that notification, the Commission shall decide on it and on such specific arrangements as it may deem necessary.

4.   The acts and decisions necessary for the implementation of cooperation activities shall be subject to all the relevant provisions of this Treaty, save as otherwise provided for in this Article and in Articles K.15 and K.16 of the Treaty on European Union.

5.   This Article is without prejudice to the provisions of the Protocol integrating the Schengen acquis into the framework of the European Union.'

(6)   In Article 6, the second paragraph shall be replaced by the following:
'The Council, acting in accordance with the procedure referred to in Article 189b, may adopt rules designed to prohibit such discrimination.'

(7)   The following Article shall be inserted:

'**Article 6a**

Without prejudice to the other provisions of this Treaty and within the limits of the powers conferred by it upon the Community, the Council, acting unanimously on a proposal from the Commission and after consulting the

European Parliament, may take appropriate action to combat discrimination based on sex, racial or ethnic origin, religion or belief, disability, age or sexual orientation.'

(8) The following Article shall be inserted at the end of Part One:

'**Article 7d**

Without prejudice to Articles 77, 90 and 92, and given the place occupied by services of general economic interest in the shared values of the Union as well as their role in promoting social and territorial cohesion, the Community and the Member States, each within their respective powers and within the scope of application of this Treaty, shall take care that such services operate on the basis of principles and conditions which enable them to fulfil their missions.'

(9) Article 8(1) shall be replaced by the following:

'1. Citizenship of the Union is hereby established. Every person holding the nationality of a Member State shall be a citizen of the Union. Citizenship of the Union shall complement and not replace national citizenship.'

(10) Article 8a(2) shall be replaced by the following:

'2. The Council may adopt provisions with a view to facilitating the exercise of the rights referred to in paragraph 1; save as otherwise provided in this Treaty, the Council shall act in accordance with the procedure referred to in Article 189b. The Council shall act unanimously throughout this procedure.'

(11) In Article 8d, the following paragraph shall be added:

'Every citizen of the Union may write to any of the institutions or bodies referred to in this Article or in Article 4 in one of the languages mentioned in Article 248 and have an answer in the same language.'

(12) Article 51 shall be replaced by the following:

'**Article 51**

The Council shall, acting in accordance with the procedure referred to in Article 189b, adopt such measures in the field of social security as are necessary to provide freedom of movement for workers; to this end, it shall make arrangements to secure for migrant workers and their dependants:

(a) aggregation, for the purpose of acquiring and retaining the right to benefit and of calculating the amount of benefit, of all periods taken into account under the laws of the several countries;

(b) payment of benefits to persons resident in the territories of Member States.

The Council shall act unanimously throughout the procedure referred to in Article 189b.'

(13) Article 56(2) shall be replaced by the following:

'2. The Council shall, acting in accordance with the procedure referred to in Article 189b, issue directives for the coordination of the abovementioned provisions.'

(14) Article 57(2) shall be replaced by the following:

'2. For the same purpose, the Council shall, acting in accordance with the procedure referred to in Article 189b, issue directives for the coordination of the provisions laid down by law, regulation or administrative action in Member States concerning the taking-up and pursuit of activities as self-employed persons. The Council, acting unanimously throughout the procedure referred to in Article 189b, shall decide on directives the implementation of which involves in at least one Member State amendment of the existing principles laid down by law governing the professions with respect to training and conditions of access for natural persons. In other cases the Council shall act by qualified majority.'

(15)   The following title shall be inserted in Part Three:

'TITLE IIIa
VISAS, ASYLUM, IMMIGRATION AND OTHER POLICIES RELATED TO FREE MOVEMENTOF PERSONS

Article 73i
In order to establish progressively an area of freedom, security and justice, the Council shall adopt:

(a)   within a period of five years after the entry into force of the Treaty of Amsterdam, measures aimed at ensuring the free movement of persons in accordance with Article 7a, in conjunction with directly related flanking measures with respect to external border controls, asylum and immigration, in accordance with the provisions of Article 73j(2) and (3) and Article 73k(1)(a) and (2)(a), and measures to prevent and combat crime in accordance with the provisions of Article K.3(e) of the Treaty on European Union;

(b)   other measures in the fields of asylum, immigration and safeguarding the rights of nationals of third countries, in accordance with the provisions of Article 73k;

(c)   measures in the field of judicial cooperation in civil matters as provided for in Article 73m;

(d)   appropriate measures to encourage and strengthen administrative cooperation, as provided for in Article 73n;

(e)   measures in the field of police and judicial cooperation in criminal matters aimed at a high level of security by preventing and combating crime within the Union in accordance with the provisions of the Treaty on European Union.

Article 73j
The Council, acting in accordance with the procedure referred to in Article 73o, shall, within a period of five years after the entry into force of the Treaty of Amsterdam, adopt:

(1)   measures with a view to ensuring, in compliance with Article 7a, the absence of any controls on persons, be they citizens of the Union or nationals of third countries, when crossing internal borders;

(2)   measures on the crossing of the external borders of the Member States which shall establish:

(a)   standards and procedures to be followed by Member States in carrying out checks on persons at such borders;

(b)   rules on visas for intended stays of no more than three months, including:

(i)   the list of third countries whose nationals must be in possession of visas when crossing the external borders and those whose nationals are exempt from that requirement;

(ii)   the procedures and conditions for issuing visas by Member States;

(iii)   a uniform format for visas;

(iv)   rules on a uniform visa;

(3)   measures setting out the conditions under which nationals of third countries shall have the freedom to travel within the territory of the Member States during a period of no more than three months.

Article 73k

The Council, acting in accordance with the procedure referred to in Article 73o, shall, within a period of five years after the entry into force of the Treaty of Amsterdam, adopt:

(1)   measures on asylum, in accordance with the Geneva Convention of 28 July 1951 and the Protocol of 31 January 1967 relating to the status of refugees and other relevant treaties, within the following areas:

(a)   criteria and mechanisms for determining which Member State is responsible for considering an application for asylum submitted by a national of a third country in one of the Member States,

(b)   minimum standards on the reception of asylum seekers in Member States,

(c)   minimum standards with respect to the qualification of nationals of third countries as refugees,

(d)   minimum standards on procedures in Member States for granting or withdrawing refugee status;

(2)   measures on refugees and displaced persons within the following areas:

(a)   minimum standards for giving temporary protection to displaced persons from third countries who cannot return to their country of origin and for persons who otherwise need international protection,

(b)   promoting a balance of effort between Member States in receiving and bearing the consequences of receiving refugees and displaced persons;

(3)   measures on immigration policy within the following areas:

(a)   conditions of entry and residence, and standards on procedures for the issue by Member States of long term visas and residence permits, including those for the purpose of family reunion,

(b)   illegal immigration and illegal residence, including repatriation of illegal residents;

(4)   measures defining the rights and conditions under which nationals of third countries who are legally resident in a Member State may reside in other Member States.

Measures adopted by the Council pursuant to points 3 and 4 shall not prevent any Member State from maintaining or introducing in the areas concerned national provisions which are compatible with this Treaty and with international agreements.

Measures to be adopted pursuant to points 2(b), 3(a) and 4 shall not be subject to the five year period referred to above.

Article 73l

1.   This Title shall not affect the exercise of the responsibilities incumbent upon Member States with regard to the maintenance of law and order and the safeguarding of internal security.

2.   In the event of one or more Member States being confronted with an emergency situation characterised by a sudden inflow of nationals of third

countries and without prejudice to paragraph 1, the Council may, acting by qualified majority on a proposal from the Commission, adopt provisional measures of a duration not exceeding six months for the benefit of the Member States concerned.

Article 73m

Measures in the field of judicial cooperation in civil matters having cross-border implications, to be taken in accordance with Article 73o and insofar as necessary for the proper functioning of the internal market, shall include:

(a) improving and simplifying:

— the system for cross-border service of judicial and extrajudicial documents;

— cooperation in the taking of evidence;

— the recognition and enforcement of decisions in civil and commercial cases, including decisions in extrajudicial cases;

(b) promoting the compatibility of the rules applicable in the Member States concerning the conflict of laws and of jurisdiction;

(c) eliminating obstacles to the good functioning of civil proceedings, if necessary by promoting the compatibility of the rules on civil procedure applicable in the Member States.

Article 73n

The Council, acting in accordance with the procedure referred to in Article 73o, shall take measures to ensure cooperation between the relevant departments of the administrations of the Member States in the areas covered by this Title, as well as between those departments and the Commission.

Article 73o

1. During a transitional period of five years following the entry into force of the Treaty of Amsterdam, the Council shall act unanimously on a proposal from the Commission or on the initiative of a Member State and after consulting the European Parliament.

2. After this period of five years:

— the Council shall act on proposals from the Commission; the Commission shall examine any request made by a Member State that it submit a proposal to the Council;

— the Council, acting unanimously after consulting the European Parliament, shall take a decision with a view to providing for all or parts of the areas covered by this Title to be governed by the procedure referred to in Article 189b and adapting the provisions relating to the powers of the Court of Justice.

3. By derogation from paragraphs 1 and 2, measures referred to in Article 73j(2)(b)(i) and (iii) shall, from the entry into force of the Treaty of Amsterdam, be adopted by the Council acting by a qualified majority on a proposal from the Commission and after consulting the European Parliament.

4. By derogation from paragraph 2, measures referred to in Article 73j(2)(b)(ii) and (iv) shall, after a period of five years following the entry into force of the Treaty of Amsterdam, be adopted by the Council acting in accordance with the procedure referred to in Article 189b.

Article 73p

1. Article 177 shall apply to this Title under the following circumstances and conditions: where a question on the interpretation of this Title or on the validity or interpretation of acts of the institutions of the Community based on this Title is raised in a case pending before a court or a tribunal of a Member State against whose decisions there is no judicial remedy under national law, that court or tribunal shall, if it considers that a decision on the question is necessary to enable it to give judgment, request the Court of Justice to give a ruling thereon.

2. In any event, the Court of Justice shall not have jurisdiction to rule on any measure or decision taken pursuant to Article 73j(1) relating to the maintenance of law and order and the safeguarding of internal security.

3. The Council, the Commission or a Member State may request the Court of Justice to give a ruling on a question of interpretation of this Title or of acts of the institutions of the Community based on this Title. The ruling given by the Court of Justice in response to such a request shall not apply to judgments of courts or tribunals of the Member States which have become res judicata.

Article 73q

The application of this Title shall be subject to the provisions of the Protocol on the position of the United Kingdom and Ireland and to the Protocol on the position of Denmark and without prejudice to the Protocol on the application of certain aspects of Article 7a of the Treaty establishing the European Community to the United Kingdom and to Ireland.'

(16) In Article 75(1), the introductory part shall be replaced by the following:

'1. For the purpose of implementing Article 74, and taking into account the distinctive features of transport, the Council shall, acting in accordance with the procedure referred to in Article 189b and after consulting the Economic and Social Committee and the Committee of the Regions, lay down:'

(17) In Article 100a, paragraphs 3, 4 and 5 shall be replaced by the following paragraphs:

'3. The Commission, in its proposals envisaged in paragraph 1 concerning health, safety, environmental protection and consumer protection, will take as a base a high level of protection, taking account in particular of any new development based on scientific facts. Within their respective powers, the European Parliament and the Council will also seek to achieve this objective.

4. If, after the adoption by the Council or by the Commission of a harmonisation measure, a Member State deems it necessary to maintain national provisions on grounds of major needs referred to in Article 36, or relating to the protection of the environment or the working environment, it shall notify the Commission of these provisions as well as the grounds for maintaining them.

5. Moreover, without prejudice to paragraph 4, if, after the adoption by the Council or by the Commission of a harmonisation measure, a Member State deems it necessary to introduce national provisions based on new scientific evidence relating to the protection of the environment or the

working environment on grounds of a problem specific to that Member State arising after the adoption of the harmonisation measure, it shall notify the Commission of the envisaged provisions as well as the grounds for introducing them.

6.   The Commission shall, within six months of the notifications as referred to in paragraphs 4 and 5, approve or reject the national provisions involved after having verified whether or not they are a means of arbitrary discrimination or a disguised restriction on trade between Member States and whether or not they shall constitute an obstacle to the functioning of the internal market. In the absence of a decision by the Commission within this period the national provisions referred to in paragraphs 4 and 5 shall be deemed to have been approved. When justified by the complexity of the matter and in the absence of danger for human health, the Commission may notify the Member State concerned that the period referred to in this paragraph may be extended for a further period of up to six months.

7.   When, pursuant to paragraph 6, a Member State is authorised to maintain or introduce national provisions derogating from a harmonisation measure, the Commission shall immediately examine whether to propose an adaptation to that measure.

8.   When a Member State raises a specific problem on public health in a field which has been the subject of prior harmonisation measures, it shall bring it to the attention of the Commission which shall immediately examine whether to propose appropriate measures to the Council.

9.   By way of derogation from the procedure laid down in Articles 169 and 170, the Commission and any Member State may bring the matter directly before the Court of Justice if it considers that another Member State is making improper use of the powers provided for in this Article.

10.   The harmonisation measures referred to above shall, in appropriate cases, include a safeguard clause authorising the Member States to take, for one or more of the non-economic reasons referred to in Article 36, provisional measures subject to a Community control procedure.'

(18)   Articles 100c and 100d shall be repealed.

(19)   The following Title shall be inserted after Title VI:

'TITLE VIa
EMPLOYMENT

Article 109n

Member States and the Community shall, in accordance with this Title, work towards developing a co-ordinated strategy for employment and particularly for promoting a skilled, trained and adaptable workforce and labour markets responsive to economic change with a view to achieving the objectives defined in Article B of the Treaty on European Union and in Article 2 of this Treaty.

Article 109o

1.   Member States, through their employment policies, shall contribute to the achievement of the objectives referred to in Article 109n in a way consistent with the broad guidelines of the economic policies of the Member States and of the Community adopted pursuant to Article 103(2).

2. Member States, having regard to national practices related to the responsibilities of management and labour, shall regard promoting employment as a matter of common concern and shall coordinate their action in this respect within the Council, in accordance with the provisions of Article 109q.

Article 109p
1. The Community shall contribute to a high level of employment by encouraging cooperation between Member States and by supporting and, if necessary, complementing their action. In doing so, the competences of the Member States shall be respected.
2. The objective of a high level of employment shall be taken into consideration in the formulation and implementation of Community policies and activities.

Article 109q
1. The European Council shall each year consider the employment situation in the Community and adopt conclusions thereon, on the basis of a joint annual report by the Council and the Commission.
2. On the basis of the conclusions of the European Council, the Council, acting by a qualified majority on a proposal from the Commission and after consulting the European Parliament, the Economic and Social Committee, the Committee of the Regions and the Employment Committee referred to in Article 109s, shall each year draw up guidelines which the Member States shall take into account in their employment policies. These guidelines shall be consistent with the broad guidelines adopted pursuant to Article 103(2).
3. Each Member State shall provide the Council and the Commission with an annual report on the principal measures taken to implement its employment policy in the light of the guidelines for employment as referred to in paragraph 2.
4. The Council, on the basis of the reports referred to in paragraph 3 and having received the views of the Employment Committee, shall each year carry out an examination of the implementation of the employment policies of the Member States in the light of the guidelines for employment. The Council, acting by a qualified majority on a recommendation from the Commission, may, if it considers it appropriate in the light of that examination, make recommendations to Member States.
5. On the basis of the results of that examination, the Council and the Commission shall make a joint annual report to the European Council on the employment situation in the Community and on the implementation of the guidelines for employment.

Article 109r
The Council, acting in accordance with the procedure referred to in Article 189b and after consulting the Economic and Social Committee and the Committee of the Regions, may adopt incentive measures designed to encourage cooperation between Member States and to support their action in the field of employment through initiatives aimed at developing exchanges of information and best practices, providing comparative analysis and advice as well as promoting innovative approaches and evaluating experiences, in particular by recourse to pilot projects. Those measures shall not include harmonisation of the laws and regulations of the Member States.

Article 109s

The Council, after consulting the European Parliament, shall establish an Employment Committee with advisory status to promote coordination between Member States on employment and labour market policies. The tasks of the Committee shall be:

— to monitor the employment situation and employment policies in the Member States and the Community;

— without prejudice to Article 151, to formulate opinions at the request of either the Council or the Commission or on its own initiative, and to contribute to the preparation of the Council proceedings referred to in Article 109q.

In fulfilling its mandate, the Committee shall consult management and labour.

Each Member State and the Commission shall appoint two members of the Committee.'

(20)   In Article 113, the following paragraph shall be added:

'5.   The Council, acting unanimously on a proposal from the Commission and after consulting the European Parliament, may extend the application of paragraphs 1 to 4 to international negotiations and agreements on services and intellectual property insofar as they are not covered by these paragraphs.'

(21)   The following Title shall be inserted after Title VII:

'TITLE VIIa
CUSTOMS COOPERATION

Article 116

Within the scope of application of this Treaty, the Council, acting in accordance with the procedure referred to in Article 189b, shall take measures in order to strengthen customs cooperation between Member States and between the latter and the Commission. These measures shall not concern the application of national criminal law or the national administration of justice.'

(22)   Articles 117 to 120 shall be replaced by the following Articles:

'Article 117

The Community and the Member States, having in mind fundamental social rights such as those set out in the European Social Charter signed at Turin on 18 October 1961 and in the 1989 Community Charter of the Fundamental Social Rights of Workers, shall have as their objectives the promotion of employment, improved living and working conditions, so as to make possible their harmonisation while the improvement is being maintained, proper social protection, dialogue between management and labour, the development of human resources with a view to lasting high employment and the combating of exclusion.

To this end the Community and the Member States shall implement measures which take account of the diverse forms of national practices, in particular in the field of contractual relations, and the need to maintain the competitiveness of the Community economy.

They believe that such a development will ensue not only from the functioning of the common market, which will favour the harmonisation of social systems, but also from the procedures provided for in this Treaty and from the approximation of provisions laid down by law, regulation or administrative action.

Article 118

1. With a view to achieving the objectives of Article 117, the Community shall support and complement the activities of the Member States in the following fields:

— improvement in particular of the working environment to protect workers' health and safety;

— working conditions;

— the information and consultation of workers;

— the integration of persons excluded from the labour market, without prejudice to Article 127;

— equality between men and women with regard to labour market opportunities and treatment at work.

2. To this end, the Council may adopt, by means of directives, minimum requirements for gradual implementation, having regard to the conditions and technical rules obtaining in each of the Member States. Such directives shall avoid imposing administrative, financial and legal constraints in a way which would hold back the creation and development of small and medium-sized undertakings.

The Council shall act in accordance with the procedure referred to in Article 189b after consulting the Economic and Social Committee and the Committee of the Regions.

The Council, acting in accordance with the same procedure, may adopt measures designed to encourage cooperation between Member States through initiatives aimed at improving knowledge, developing exchanges of information and best practices, promoting innovative approaches and evaluating experiences in order to combat social exclusion.

3. However, the Council shall act unanimously on a proposal from the Commission, after consulting the European Parliament, the Economic and Social Committee and the Committee of the Regions in the following areas:

— social security and social protection of workers;

— protection of workers where their employment contract is terminated;

— representation and collective defence of the interests of workers and employers, including co-determination, subject to paragraph 6;

— conditions of employment for third country nationals legally residing in Community territory;

— financial contributions for promotion of employment and job-creation, without prejudice to the provisions relating to the Social Fund.

4. A Member State may entrust management and labour, at their joint request, with the implementation of directives adopted pursuant to paragraphs 2 and 3. In this case, it shall ensure that, no later than the date on which a directive must be transposed in accordance with Article 189, management and labour have introduced the necessary measures by agreement, the Member State concerned being required to take any necessary measure enabling it at any time to be in a position to guarantee the results imposed by that directive.

5. The provisions adopted pursuant to this Article shall not prevent any Member State from maintaining or introducing more stringent protective measures compatible with this Treaty.

6. The provisions of this Article shall not apply to pay, the right of association, the right to strike or the right to impose lock outs.

Article 118a

1. The Commission shall have the task of promoting the consultation of management and labour at Community level and shall take any relevant measure to facilitate their dialogue by ensuring balanced support for the parties.

2. To this end, before submitting proposals in the social policy field, the Commission shall consult management and labour on the possible direction of Community action.

3. If, after such consultation, the Commission considers Community action advisable, it shall consult management and labour on the content of the envisaged proposal. Management and labour shall forward to the Commission an opinion or, where appropriate, a recommendation.

4. On the occasion of such consultation, management and labour may inform the Commission of their wish to initiate the process provided for in Article 118b. The duration of the procedure shall not exceed nine months, unless the management and labour concerned and the Commission decide jointly to extend it.

Article 118b

1. Should management and labour so desire, the dialogue between them at Community level may lead to contractual relations, including agreements.

2. Agreements concluded at Community level shall be implemented either in accordance with the procedures and practices specific to management and labour and the Member States or, in matters covered by Article 118, at the joint request of the signatory parties, by a Council decision on a proposal from the Commission.

The Council shall act by qualified majority, except where the agreement in question contains one or more provisions relating to one of the areas referred to in Article 118(3), in which case it shall act unanimously.

Article 118c

With a view to achieving the objectives of Article 117 and without prejudice to the other provisions of this Treaty, the Commission shall encourage cooperation between the Member States and facilitate the coordination of their action in all social policy fields under this chapter, particularly in matters relating to:

— employment;
— labour law and working conditions;
— basic and advanced vocational training;
— social security;
— prevention of occupational accidents and diseases;
— occupational hygiene;
— the right of association and collective bargaining between employers and workers.

To this end, the Commission shall act in close contact with Member States by making studies, delivering opinions and arranging consultations both on problems arising at national level and on those of concern to international organisations.

Before delivering the opinions provided for in this Article, the Commission shall consult the Economic and Social Committee.

Article 119

1. Each Member State shall ensure that the principle of equal pay for male and female workers for equal work or work of equal value is applied.

2. For the purpose of this Article, "pay" means the ordinary basic or minimum wage or salary and any other consideration, whether in cash or in kind, which the worker receives directly or indirectly, in respect of his employment, from his employer. Equal pay without discrimination based on sex means:

(a) that pay for the same work at piece rates shall be calculated on the basis of the same unit of measurement;

(b) that pay for work at time rates shall be the same for the same job.

3. The Council, acting in accordance with the procedure referred to in Article 189b, and after consulting the Economic and Social Committee, shall adopt measures to ensure the application of the principle of equal opportunities and equal treatment of men and women in matters of employment and occupation, including the principle of equal pay for equal work or work of equal value.

4. With a view to ensuring full equality in practice between men and women in working life, the principle of equal treatment shall not prevent any Member State from maintaining or adopting measures providing for specific advantages in order to make it easier for the under-represented sex to pursue a vocational activity or to prevent or compensate for disadvantages in professional careers.

Article 119a

Member States shall endeavour to maintain the existing equivalence between paid holiday schemes.

Article 120

The Commission shall draw up a report each year on progress in achieving the objectives of Article 117, including the demographic situation in the Community. It shall forward the report to the European Parliament, the Council and the Economic and Social Committee.

The European Parliament may invite the Commission to draw up reports on particular problems concerning the social situation.'

(23) Article 125 shall be replaced by the following:

'Article 125

The Council, acting in accordance with the procedure referred to in Article 189b and after consulting the Economic and Social Committee and the Committee of the Regions, shall adopt implementing decisions relating to the European Social Fund.'

(24) Article 127(4) shall be replaced by the following:

'4. The Council, acting in accordance with the procedure referred to in Article 189b and after consulting the Economic and Social Committee and the Committee of the Regions, shall adopt measures to contribute to the achievement of the objectives referred to in this Article, excluding any harmonisation of the laws and regulations of the Member States.'

(25)   Article 128(4) shall be replaced by the following:

'4.   The Community shall take cultural aspects into account in its action under other provisions of this Treaty, in particular in order to respect and to promote the diversity of its cultures.'

(26)   Article 129 shall be replaced by the following:

'Article 129

1.   A high level of human health protection shall be ensured in the definition and implementation of all Community policies and activities.

Community action, which shall complement national policies, shall be directed towards improving public health, preventing human illness and diseases, and obviating sources of danger to human health. Such action shall cover the fight against the major health scourges, by promoting research into their causes, their transmission and their prevention, as well as health information and education.

The Community shall complement the Member States' action in reducing drugs-related health damage, including information and prevention.

2.   The Community shall encourage cooperation between the Member States in the areas referred to in this Article and, if necessary, lend support to their action.

Member States shall, in liaison with the Commission, coordinate among themselves their policies and programmes in the areas referred to in paragraph 1. The Commission may, in close contact with the Member States, take any useful initiative to promote such coordination.

3.   The Community and the Member States shall foster cooperation with third countries and the competent international organisations in the sphere of public health.

4.   The Council, acting in accordance with the procedure referred to in Article 189b and after consulting the Economic and Social Committee and the Committee of the Regions, shall contribute to the achievement of the objectives referred to in this Article through adopting:

(a)   measures setting high standards of quality and safety of organs and substances of human origin, blood and blood derivatives; these measures shall not prevent any Member State from maintaining or introducing more stringent protective measures;

(b)   by way of derogation from Article 43, measures in the veterinary and phytosanitary fields which have as their direct objective the protection of public health;

(c)   incentive measures designed to protect and improve human health, excluding any harmonisation of the laws and regulations of the Member States.

The Council, acting by a qualified majority on a proposal from the Commission, may also adopt recommendations for the purposes set out in this Article.

5.   Community action in the field of public health shall fully respect the responsibilities of the Member States for the organisation and delivery of health services and medical care. In particular, measures referred to in paragraph 4(a) shall not affect national provisions on the donation or medical use of organs and blood.'

(27)   Article 129a shall be replaced by the following:

'Article 129a
1.   In order to promote the interests of consumers and to ensure a high level of consumer protection, the Community shall contribute to protecting the health, safety and economic interests of consumers, as well as to promoting their right to information, education and to organise themselves in order to safeguard their interests.
2.   Consumer protection requirements shall be taken into account in defining and implementing other Community policies and activities.
3.   The Community shall contribute to the attainment of the objectives referred to in paragraph 1 through:
    (a)   measures adopted pursuant to Article 100a in the context of the completion of the internal market;
    (b)   measures which support, supplement and monitor the policy pursued by the Member States.
4.   The Council, acting in accordance with the procedure referred to in Article 189b and after consulting the Economic and Social Committee, shall adopt the measures referred to in paragraph 3(b).
5.   Measures adopted pursuant to paragraph 4 shall not prevent any Member State from maintaining or introducing more stringent protective measures. Such measures must be compatible with this Treaty. The Commission shall be notified of them.'
(28)   In the first subparagraph of Article 129c(1), the first part of the third indent shall be replaced by the following:
    '—may support projects of common interest supported by Member States, which are identified in the framework of the guidelines referred to in the first indent, particularly through feasibility studies, loan guarantees or interest-rate subsidies;'.
(29)   Article 129d shall be amended as follows:
    (a)   the first paragraph shall be replaced by the following:
'The guidelines and other measures referred to in Article 129c(1) shall be adopted by the Council, acting in accordance with the procedure referred to in Article 189b and after consulting the Economic and Social Committee and the Committee of the Regions.';
    (b)   the third paragraph shall be deleted.
(30)   In Article 130a, the second paragraph shall be replaced by the following:
'In particular, the Community shall aim at reducing disparities between the levels of development of the various regions and the backwardness of the least favoured regions or islands, including rural areas.'
(31)   In Article 130e, the first paragraph shall be replaced by the following:
'Implementing decisions relating to the European Regional Development Fund shall be taken by the Council, acting in accordance with the procedure referred to in Article 189b and after consulting the Economic and Social Committee and the Committee of the Regions.'
(32)   In Article 130i(1), the first subparagraph shall be replaced by the following:
    '1.   A multiannual framework programme, setting out all the activities of the Community, shall be adopted by the Council, acting in accordance with

the procedure referred to in Article 189b after consulting the Economic and Social Committee.'

(33)   Article 130o shall be replaced by the following:

'Article 130o
The Council, acting by qualified majority on a proposal from the Commission and after consulting the European Parliament and the Economic and Social Committee, shall adopt the provisions referred to in Article 130n.

The Council, acting in accordance with the procedure referred to in Article 189b and after consulting the Economic and Social Committee, shall adopt the provisions referred to in Articles 130j, 130k and 130l. Adoption of the supplementary programmes shall require the agreement of the Member States concerned.'

(34)   Article 130r(2) shall be replaced by the following:

'2.   Community policy on the environment shall aim at a high level of protection taking into account the diversity of situations in the various regions of the Community. It shall be based on the precautionary principle and on the principles that preventive action should be taken, that environmental damage should as a priority be rectified at source and that the polluter should pay.

In this context, harmonisation measures answering environmental protection requirements shall include, where appropriate, a safeguard clause allowing Member States to take provisional measures, for non-economic environmental reasons, subject to a Community inspection procedure.'

(35)   Article 130s shall be amended as follows:

(a)   Paragraph 1 shall be replaced by the following:

'1.   The Council, acting in accordance with the procedure referred to in Article 189b and after consulting the Economic and Social Committee and the Committee of the Regions, shall decide what action is to be taken by the Community in order to achieve the objectives referred to in Article 130r.';

(b)   The introductory part of paragraph 2 shall be replaced by the following:

'2.   By way of derogation from the decision-making procedure provided for in paragraph 1 and without prejudice to Article 100a, the Council, acting unanimously on a proposal from the Commission and after consulting the European Parliament, the Economic and Social Committee and the Committee of the Regions, shall adopt:';

(c)   The first subparagraph of paragraph 3 shall be replaced by the following:

'3.   In other areas, general action programmes setting out priority objectives to be attained shall be adopted by the Council, acting in accordance with the procedure referred to in Article 189b and after consulting the Economic and Social Committee and the Committee of the Regions.'

(36)   Article 130w(1) shall be replaced by the following:

'1. Without prejudice to the other provisions of this Treaty, the Council, acting in accordance with the procedure referred to in Article 189b, shall adopt the measures necessary to further the objectives referred to in Article 130u. Such measures may take the form of multiannual programmes.'

(37)   In Article 137, the following paragraph shall be added:

'The number of Members of the European Parliament shall not exceed seven hundred.'

(38)   Article 138 shall be amended as follows:

(a)   in paragraph 3, the first subparagraph shall be replaced by the following:

'3. The European Parliament shall draw up a proposal for elections by direct universal suffrage in accordance with a uniform procedure in all Member States or in accordance with principles common to all Member States.';

(b)   the following paragraph shall be added:

'4. The European Parliament shall, after seeking an opinion from the Commission and with the approval of the Council acting unanimously, lay down the regulations and general conditions governing the performance of the duties of its Members.'

(39)   Article 151 shall be replaced by the following:

'**Article 151**

1.   A committee consisting of the Permanent Representatives of the Member States shall be responsible for preparing the work of the Council and for carrying out the tasks assigned to it by the Council. The Committee may adopt procedural decisions in cases provided for in the Council's Rules of Procedure.

2.   The Council shall be assisted by a General Secretariat, under the responsibility of a Secretary-General, High Representative for the common foreign and security policy, who shall be assisted by a Deputy Secretary-General responsible for the running of the General Secretariat. The Secretary-General and the Deputy Secretary-General shall be appointed by the Council acting unanimously.

The Council shall decide on the organisation of the General Secretariat.

3.   The Council shall adopt its Rules of Procedure. For the purpose of applying Article 191a(3), the Council shall elaborate in these Rules the conditions under which the public shall have access to Council documents. For the purpose of this paragraph, the Council shall define the cases in which it is to be regarded as acting in its legislative capacity, with a view to allowing greater access to documents in those cases, while at the same time preserving the effectiveness of its decision-making process. In any event, when the Council acts in its legislative capacity, the results of votes and explanations of vote as well as statements in the minutes shall be made public.'

(40)   In Article 158(2), the first and second subparagraphs shall be replaced by the following:

'2.   The governments of the Member States shall nominate by common accord the person they intend to appoint as President of the Commission; the nomination shall be approved by the European Parliament.

The governments of the Member States shall, by common accord with the nominee for President, nominate the other persons whom they intend to appoint as Members of the Commission.'

(41)   In Article 163, the following paragraph shall be inserted as the first paragraph:

'The Commission shall work under the political guidance of its President.'

(42)   In Article 173, the third paragraph shall be replaced by the following:

'The Court of Justice shall have jurisdiction under the same conditions in actions brought by the European Parliament, by the Court of Auditors and by the ECB for the purpose of protecting their prerogatives.'

(43)   Article 188c shall be amended as follows:

(a)   The second subparagraph of paragraph 1 shall be replaced by the following:

'The Court of Auditors shall provide the European Parliament and the Council with a statement of assurance as to the reliability of the accounts and the legality and regularity of the underlying transactions which shall be published in the *Official Journal of the European Communities.*';

(b)   The first subparagraph of paragraph 2 shall be replaced by the following:

'2.   The Court of Auditors shall examine whether all revenue has been received and all expenditure incurred in a lawful and regular manner and whether the financial management has been sound. In doing so, it shall report in particular on any cases of irregularity.';

(c)   Paragraph 3 shall be replaced by the following:

'3.   The audit shall be based on records and, if necessary, performed on the spot in the other institutions of the Community, on the premises of any body which manages revenue or expenditure on behalf of the Community and in the Member States, including on the premises of any natural or legal person in receipt of payments from the budget. In the Member States the audit shall be carried out in liaison with national audit bodies or, if these do not have the necessary powers, with the competent national departments. The Court of Auditors and the national audit bodies of the Member States shall cooperate in a spirit of trust while maintaining their independence. These bodies or departments shall inform the Court of Auditors whether they intend to take part in the audit.

The other institutions of the Community, any bodies managing revenue or expenditure on behalf of the Community, any natural or legal person in receipt of payments from the budget, and the national audit bodies or, if these do not have the necessary powers, the competent national departments, shall forward to the Court of Auditors, at its request, any document or information necessary to carry out its task.

In respect of the European Investment Bank's activity in managing Community expenditure and revenue, the Court's rights of access to information held by the Bank shall be governed by an agreement between the Court, the Bank and the Commission. In the absence of an agreement, the Court shall nevertheless have access to information necessary for the audit of Community expenditure and revenue managed by the Bank.'

(44)   Article 189b shall be replaced by the following:

'Article 189b

1.   Where reference is made in this Treaty to this Article for the adoption of an act, the following procedure shall apply.

2.   The Commission shall submit a proposal to the European Parliament and the Council. The Council, acting by a qualified majority after obtaining the opinion of the European Parliament,

—if it approves all the amendments contained in the European Parliament s opinion, may adopt the proposed act thus amended;

— if the European Parliament does not propose any amendments, may adopt the proposed act;

— shall otherwise adopt a common position and communicate it to the European Parliament. The Council shall inform the European Parliament fully of the reasons which led it to adopt its common position. The Commission shall inform the European Parliament fully of its position. If, within three months of such communication, the European Parliament:

(a)   approves the common position or has not taken a decision, the act in question shall be deemed to have been adopted in accordance with that common position;

(b)   rejects, by an absolute majority of its component members, the common position, the proposed act shall be deemed not to have been adopted;

(c)   proposes amendments to the common position by an absolute majority of its component members, the amended text shall be forwarded to the Council and to the Commission, which shall deliver an opinion on those amendments.

3.   If, within three months of the matter being referred to it, the Council, acting by a qualified majority, approves all the amendments of the European Parliament, the act in question shall be deemed to have been adopted in the form of the common position thus amended; however, the Council shall act unanimously on the amendments on which the Commission has delivered a negative opinion. If the Council does not approve all the amendments, the President of the Council, in agreement with the President of the European Parliament, shall within six weeks convene a meeting of the Conciliation Committee.

4.   The Conciliation Committee, which shall be composed of the members of the Council or their representatives and an equal number of representatives of the European Parliament, shall have the task of reaching agreement on a joint text, by a qualified majority of the members of the Council or their representatives and by a majority of the representatives of the European Parliament. The Commission shall take part in the Conciliation Committee's proceedings and shall take all the necessary initiatives with a view to reconciling the positions of the European Parliament and the Council. In fulfilling this task, the Conciliation Committee shall address the common position on the basis of the amendments proposed by the European Parliament.

5.   If, within six weeks of its being convened, the Conciliation Committee approves a joint text, the European Parliament, acting by an absolute majority of the votes cast, and the Council, acting by a qualified majority, shall each have a period of six weeks from that approval in which to adopt the act in question in accordance with the joint text. If either of the two institutions fails to approve the proposed act within that period, it shall be deemed not to have been adopted.

6.   Where the Conciliation Committee does not approve a joint text, the proposed act shall be deemed not to have been adopted.

7.   The periods of three months and six weeks referred to in this Article shall be extended by a maximum of one month and two weeks respectively at the initiative of the European Parliament or the Council.'

(45)   The following Article shall be inserted:

'**Article 191a**

1. Any citizen of the Union, and any natural or legal person residing or having its registered office in a Member State, shall have a right of access to European Parliament, Council and Commission documents, subject to the principles and the conditions to be defined in accordance with paragraphs 2 and 3.

2. General principles and limits on grounds of public or private interest governing this right of access to documents shall be determined by the Council, acting in accordance with the procedure referred to in Article 189b within two years of the entry into force of the Treaty of Amsterdam.

3. Each institution referred to above shall elaborate in its own Rules of Procedure specific provisions regarding access to its documents.'

(46) In Article 198, the following paragraph shall be added:
'The Committee may be consulted by the European Parliament.'

(47) In Article 198a, the third paragraph shall be replaced by the following:
'The members of the Committee and an equal number of alternate members shall be appointed for four years by the Council acting unanimously on proposals from the respective Member States. Their term of office shall be renewable. No member of the Committee shall at the same time be a Member of the European Parliament.'

(48) In Article 198b the second paragraph shall be replaced by the following:
'It shall adopt its Rules of Procedure.'

(49) Article 198c shall be amended as follows:
(a) the first paragraph shall be replaced by the following:
'The Committee of the Regions shall be consulted by the Council or by the Commission where this Treaty so provides and in all other cases, in particular those which concern cross-border cooperation, in which one of these two institutions considers it appropriate.';
(b) after the third paragraph, the following paragraph shall be inserted:
'The Committee of the Regions may be consulted by the European Parliament.'

(50) In Article 205, the first paragraph shall be replaced by the following:
'The Commission shall implement the budget, in accordance with the provisions of the regulations made pursuant to Article 209, on its own responsibility and within the limits of the appropriations, having regard to the principles of sound financial management. Member States shall cooperate with the Commission to ensure that the appropriations are used in accordance with the principles of sound financial management.'

(51) Article 206(1) shall be replaced by the following:
'1. The European Parliament, acting on a recommendation from the Council which shall act by a qualified majority, shall give a discharge to the Commission in respect of the implementation of the budget. To this end, the Council and the European Parliament in turn shall examine the accounts and the financial statement referred to in Article 205a, the annual report by the Court of Auditors together with the replies of the institutions under audit to the observations of the Court of Auditors, the statement of assurance referred to in Article 188c(1), second subparagraph and any relevant special reports by the Court of Auditors.'

(52)   Article 209a shall be replaced by the following:

'Article 209a

1.   The Community and the Member States shall counter fraud and any other illegal activities affecting the financial interests of the Community through measures to be taken in accordance with this Article, which shall act as a deterrent and be such as to afford effective protection in the Member States.

2.   Member States shall take the same measures to counter fraud affecting the financial interests of the Community as they take to counter fraud affecting their own financial interests.

3.   Without prejudice to other provisions of this Treaty, the Member States shall coordinate their action aimed at protecting the financial interests of the Community against fraud. To this end they shall organise, together with the Commission, close and regular cooperation between the competent authorities.

4.   The Council, acting in accordance with the procedure referred to in Article 189b, after consulting the Court of Auditors, shall adopt the necessary measures in the fields of the prevention of and fight against fraud affecting the financial interests of the Community with a view to affording effective and equivalent protection in the Member States. These measures shall not concern the application of national criminal law or the national administration of justice.

5.   The Commission, in cooperation with Member States, shall each year submit to the European Parliament and to the Council a report on the measures taken for the implementation of this Article.'

(53)   The following Article shall be inserted:

'Article 213a

1.   Without prejudice to Article 5 of the Protocol on the Statute of the European System of Central Banks and of the European Central Bank, the Council, acting in accordance with the procedure referred to in Article 189b, shall adopt measures for the production of statistics where necessary for the performance of the activities of the Community.

2.   The production of Community statistics shall conform to impartiality, reliability, objectivity, scientific independence, cost-effectiveness and statistical confidentiality; it shall not entail excessive burdens on economic operators.'

(54)   The following Article shall be inserted:

'Article 213b

1.   From 1 January 1999, Community acts on the protection of individuals with regard to the processing of personal data and the free movement of such data shall apply to the institutions and bodies set up by, or on the basis of, this Treaty.

2.   Before the date referred to in paragraph 1, the Council, acting in accordance with the procedure referred to in Article 189b, shall establish an independent supervisory body responsible for monitoring the application of such Community acts to Community institutions and bodies and shall adopt any other relevant provisions as appropriate.'

(55)   Article 227(2) shall be replaced by the following:

'2. The provisions of this Treaty shall apply to the French overseas departments, the Azores, Madeira and the Canary Islands.

However, taking account of the structural social and economic situation of the French overseas departments, the Azores, Madeira and the Canary Islands, which is compounded by their remoteness, insularity, small size, difficult topography and climate, economic dependence on a few products, the permanence and combination of which severely restrain their development, the Council, acting by a qualified majority on a proposal from the Commission and after consulting the European Parliament, shall adopt specific measures aimed, in particular, at laying down the conditions of application of the present Treaty to those regions, including common policies.

The Council shall, when adopting the relevant measures referred to in the second subparagraph, take into account areas such as customs and trade policies, fiscal policy, free zones, agriculture and fisheries policies, conditions for supply of raw materials and essential consumer goods, State aids and conditions of access to structural funds and to horizontal Community programmes.

The Council shall adopt the measures referred to in the second subparagraph taking into account the special characteristics and constraints of the outermost regions without undermining the integrity and the coherence of the Community legal order, including the internal market and common policies.'

(56)   Article 228 shall be amended as follows:

(a)   the second subparagraph of paragraph 1 shall be replaced by the following:

'In exercising the powers conferred upon it by this paragraph, the Council shall act by a qualified majority, except in the cases where the first subparagraph of paragraph 2 provides that the Council shall act unanimously.';

(b)   paragraph 2 shall be replaced by the following:

'2.   Subject to the powers vested in the Commission in this field, the signing, which may be accompanied by a decision on provisional application before entry into force, and the conclusion of the agreements shall be decided on by the Council, acting by a qualified majority on a proposal from the Commission. The Council shall act unanimously when the agreement covers a field for which unanimity is required for the adoption of internal rules and for the agreements referred to in Article 238.

By way of derogation from the rules laid down in paragraph 3, the same procedures shall apply for a decision to suspend the application of an agreement, and for the purpose of establishing the positions to be adopted on behalf of the Community in a body set up by an agreement based on Article 238, when that body is called upon to adopt decisions having legal effects, with the exception of decisions supplementing or amending the institutional framework of the agreement.

The European Parliament shall be immediately and fully informed on any decision under this paragraph concerning the provisional application or the suspension of agreements, or the establishment of the Community position in a body set up by an agreement based on Article 238.'

(57)   The following Article shall be inserted:

'**Article 236**

1. Where a decision has been taken to suspend the voting rights of the representative of the government of a Member State in accordance with Article F.1(2) of the Treaty on European Union, these voting rights shall also be suspended with regard to this Treaty.

2. Moreover, where the existence of a serious and persistent breach by a Member State of principles mentioned in Article F(1) of the Treaty on European Union has been determined in accordance with Article F.1(1) of that Treaty, the Council, acting by a qualified majority, may decide to suspend certain of the rights deriving from the application of this Treaty to the Member State in question. In doing so, the Council shall take into account the possible consequences of such a suspension on the rights and obligations of natural and legal persons.

The obligations of the Member State in question under this Treaty shall in any case continue to be binding on that State.

3. The Council, acting by a qualified majority, may decide subsequently to vary or revoke measures taken in accordance with paragraph 2 in response to changes in the situation which led to their being imposed.

4. When taking decisions referred to in paragraphs 2 and 3, the Council shall act without taking into account the votes of the representative of the government of the Member State in question. By way of derogation from Article 148(2) a qualified majority shall be defined as the same proportion of the weighted votes of the members of the Council concerned as laid down in Article 148(2).

This paragraph shall also apply in the event of voting rights being suspended in accordance with paragraph 1. In such cases, a decision requiring unanimity shall be taken without the vote of the representative of the government of the Member State in question.'

(58) The Protocol on Social Policy and the Agreement on social policy attached thereto shall be repealed.

(59) The Protocol on the Economic and Social Committee and the Committee of the Regions shall be repealed.

ARTICLE 3
The Treaty establishing the European Coal and Steel Community shall be amended in accordance with the provisions of this Article.

(1) In Article 10(2) the first and second subparagraphs shall be replaced by the following:

'2. The governments of the Member States shall nominate by common accord the person they intend to appoint as President of the Commission; the nomination shall be approved by the European Parliament. The governments of the Member States shall, by common accord with the nominee for President, nominate the other persons whom they intend to appoint as Members of the Commission.'

(2) In Article 13, the following paragraph shall be inserted as the first paragraph:

'The Commission shall work under the political guidance of its President.'

(3) In Article 20, the following paragraph shall be added:

'The number of Members of the European Parliament shall not exceed seven hundred.'

(4)   Article 21 shall be amended as follows:
   (a)   in paragraph 3, the first subparagraph shall be replaced by the following:
'3.   The European Parliament shall draw up a proposal for elections by direct universal suffrage in accordance with a uniform procedure in all Member States or in accordance with principles common to all Member States.';
   (b)   the following paragraph shall be added:
'4.   The European Parliament shall, after seeking an opinion from the Commission and with the approval of the Council acting unanimously, lay down the regulations and general conditions governing the performance of the duties of its Members.'
(5)   Article 30 shall be replaced by the following:

'Article 30
   1.   A committee consisting of the Permanent Representatives of the Member States shall be responsible for preparing the work of the Council and for carrying out the tasks assigned to it by the Council. The Committee may adopt procedural decisions in cases provided for in the Council's Rules of Procedure.
   2.   The Council shall be assisted by a General Secretariat, under the responsibility of a Secretary-General, High Representative for the common foreign and security policy, who shall be assisted by a Deputy Secretary-General responsible for the running of the General Secretariat. The Secretary-General and the Deputy Secretary-General shall be appointed by the Council acting unanimously.
   The Council shall decide on the organisation of the General Secretariat.
   3.   The Council shall adopt its Rules of Procedure.'
(6)   In Article 33, the fourth paragraph shall be replaced by the following:
'The Court of Justice shall have jurisdiction under the same conditions in actions brought by the European Parliament and by the Court of Auditors for the purpose of protecting their prerogatives.'
(7)   Article 45c shall be amended as follows:
   (a)   The second subparagraph of paragraph 1 shall be replaced by the following:
'The Court of Auditors shall provide the European Parliament and the Council with a statement of assurance as to the reliability of the accounts and the legality and regularity of the underlying transactions which shall be published in the *Official Journal of the European Communities*.';
   (b)   The first subparagraph of paragraph 2 shall be replaced by the following:
'2.   The Court of Auditors shall examine whether all revenue has been received and all expenditure incurred in a lawful and regular manner and whether the financial management has been sound. In doing so, it shall report in particular on any cases of irregularity.';
   (c)   Paragraph 3 shall be replaced by the following:
'3.   The audit shall be based on records and, if necessary, performed on the spot in the other institutions of the Community, on the premises of any body which manages revenue or expenditure on behalf of the Community and in the Member States, including on the premises of any natural or legal person in receipt of payments from the budget. In the Member States the

audit shall be carried out in liaison with national audit bodies or, if these do not have the necessary powers, with the competent national departments. The Court of Auditors and the national audit bodies of the Member States shall cooperate in a spirit of trust while maintaining their independence. These bodies or departments shall inform the Court of Auditors whether they intend to take part in the audit.

The other institutions of the Community, any bodies managing revenue or expenditure on behalf of the Community, any natural or legal person in receipt of payments from the budget, and the national audit bodies or, if these do not have the necessary powers, the competent national departments, shall forward to the Court of Auditors, at its request, any document or information necessary to carry out its task.

In respect of the European Investment Bank's activity in managing Community expenditure and revenue, the Court's rights of access to information held by the Bank shall be governed by an agreement between the Court, the Bank and the Commission. In the absence of an agreement, the Court shall nevertheless have access to information necessary for the audit of Community expenditure and revenue managed by the Bank.'

(8) In Article 78c, the first paragraph shall be replaced by the following:

'The Commission shall implement the budget, in accordance with the provisions of the regulations made pursuant to Article 78h, on its own responsibility and within the limits of the appropriations, having regard to the principles of sound financial management. Member States shall cooperate with the Commission to ensure that the appropriations are used in accordance with the principles of sound financial management.'

(9) Article 78g(1) shall be replaced by the following:

'1. The European Parliament, acting on a recommendation from the Council which shall act by a qualified majority, shall give a discharge to the Commission in respect of the implementation of the budget. To this end, the Council and the European Parliament in turn shall examine the accounts and the financial statement referred to in Article 78d, the annual report by the Court of Auditors together with the replies of the institutions under audit to the observations of the Court of Auditors, the statement of assurance referred to in Article 45c(1), second subparagraph, and any relevant special reports by the Court of Auditors.'

(10) The following Article shall be inserted:

'Article 96

1. Where a decision has been taken to suspend the voting rights of the representative of the government of a Member State in accordance with Article F.1(2) of the Treaty on European Union, these voting rights shall also be suspended with regard to this Treaty.

2. Moreover, where the existence of a serious and persistent breach by a Member State of principles mentioned in Article F(1) of the Treaty on European Union has been determined in accordance with Article F.1(1) of that Treaty, the Council, acting by a qualified majority, may decide to suspend certain of the rights deriving from the application of this Treaty to the Member State in question. In doing so, the Council shall take into account the possible consequences of such a suspension on the rights and obligations of natural and legal persons.

The obligations of the Member State in question under this Treaty shall in any case continue to be binding on that State.

3.   The Council, acting by a qualified majority, may decide subsequently to vary or revoke measures taken in accordance with paragraph 2 in response to changes in the situation which led to their being imposed.

4.   When taking decisions referred to in paragraphs 2 and 3, the Council shall act without taking into account the votes of the representative of the government of the Member State in question. By way of derogation from Article 28, fourth paragraph, a qualified majority shall be defined as the same proportion of the weighted votes of the members of the Council concerned as laid down in Article 28, fourth paragraph.

This paragraph shall also apply in the event of voting rights being suspended in accordance with paragraph 1. In such cases, a decision requiring unanimity shall be taken without the vote of the representative of the government of the Member State in question.'

ARTICLE 4

The Treaty establishing the European Atomic Energy Community shall be amended in accordance with the provisions of this Article.

(1)   In Article 107, the following paragraph shall be added:

'The number of Members of the European Parliament shall not exceed seven hundred.'

(2)   Article 108 shall be amended as follows:

(a)   in paragraph 3, the first subparagraph shall be replaced by the following:

'3.   The European Parliament shall draw up a proposal for elections by direct universal suffrage in accordance with a uniform procedure in all Member States or in accordance with principles common to all Member States.';

(b)   the following paragraph shall be added:

'4. The European Parliament shall, after seeking an opinion from the Commission and with the approval of the Council acting unanimously, lay down the regulations and general conditions governing the performance of the duties of its Members.'

(3)   Article 121 shall be replaced by the following:

'Article 121

1.   A committee consisting of the Permanent Representatives of the Member States shall be responsible for preparing the work of the Council and for carrying out the tasks assigned to it by the Council. The Committee may adopt procedural decisions in cases provided for in the Council's Rules of Procedure.

2.   The Council shall be assisted by a General Secretariat, under the responsibility of a Secretary-General, High Representative for the common foreign and security policy, who shall be assisted by a Deputy Secretary-General responsible for the running of the General Secretariat. The Secretary-General and the Deputy Secretary-General shall be appointed by the Council acting unanimously.

The Council shall decide on the organisation of the General Secretariat.

3.   The Council shall adopt its Rules of Procedure.'

(4)   In Article 127, the first and second subparagraphs of paragraph 2 shall be replaced by the following:

'2. The governments of the Member States shall nominate by common accord the person they intend to appoint as President of the Commission; the nomination shall be approved by the European Parliament.

The governments of the Member States shall, by common accord with the nominee for President, nominate the other persons whom they intend to appoint as Members of the Commission.'

(5)   In Article 132, the following paragraph shall be inserted as the first paragraph:

'The Commission shall work under the political guidance of its President.'

(6)   In Article 146, the third paragraph shall be replaced by the following:

'The Court of Justice shall have jurisdiction under the same conditions in actions brought by the European Parliament and by the Court of Auditors for the purpose of protecting their prerogatives.'

(7)   Article 160c shall be amended as follows:

(a)   the second subparagraph of paragraph 1 shall be replaced by the following:

'The Court of Auditors shall provide the European Parliament and the Council with a statement of assurance as to the reliability of the accounts and the legality and regularity of the underlying transactions which shall be published in the *Official Journal of the European Communities*.';

(b)   the first subparagraph of paragraph 2 shall be replaced by the following:

'2. The Court of Auditors shall examine whether all revenue has been received and all expenditure incurred in a lawful and regular manner and whether the financial management has been sound. In doing so, it shall report in particular on any cases of irregularity.';

(c)   paragraph 3 shall be replaced by the following:

'3. The audit shall be based on records and, if necessary, performed on the spot in the other institutions of the Community, on the premises of any body which manages revenue or expenditure on behalf of the Community and in the Member States, including on the premises of any natural or legal person in receipt of payments from the budget. In the Member States the audit shall be carried out in liaison with national audit bodies or, if these do not have the necessary powers, with the competent national departments. The Court of Auditors and the national audit bodies of the Member States shall cooperate in a spirit of trust while maintaining their independence. These bodies or departments shall inform the Court of Auditors whether they intend to take part in the audit.

The other institutions of the Community, any bodies managing revenue or expenditure on behalf of the Community, any natural or legal person in receipt of payments from the budget, and the national audit bodies or, if these do not have the necessary powers, the competent national departments, shall forward to the Court of Auditors, at its request, any document or information necessary to carry out its task.

In respect of the European Investment Bank's activity in managing Community expenditure and revenue, the Court's rights of access to information held by the Bank shall be governed by an agreement between the Court, the Bank and the Commission. In the absence of an agreement, the

Court shall nevertheless have access to information necessary for the audit of Community expenditure and revenue managed by the Bank.'

(8)   In Article 170, the following paragraph shall be added:

'The Committee may be consulted by the European Parliament.'

(9)   In Article 179, the first paragraph shall be replaced by the following:

'The Commission shall implement the budget, in accordance with the provisions of the regulations made pursuant to Article 183, on its own responsibility and within the limits of the appropriations, having regard to the principles of sound financial management. Member States shall cooperate with the Commission to ensure that the appropriations are used in accordance with the principles of sound financial management.'

(10)   Article 180b(1) shall be replaced by the following:

'1.   The European Parliament, acting on a recommendation from the Council which shall act by a qualified majority, shall give a discharge to the Commission in respect of the implementation of the budget. To this end, the Council and the European Parliament in turn shall examine the accounts and the financial statement referred to in Article 179a, the annual report by the Court of Auditors together with the replies of the institutions under audit to the observations of the Court of Auditors, the statement of assurance referred to in Article 160c(1), second subparagraph, and any relevant special reports by the Court of Auditors.'

(11)   The following Article shall be inserted:

'**Article 204**

1.   Where a decision has been taken to suspend the voting rights of the representative of the government of a Member State in accordance with Article F.1(2) of the Treaty on European Union, these voting rights shall also be suspended with regard to this Treaty.

2.   Moreover, where the existence of a serious and persistent breach by a Member State of principles mentioned in Article F(1) of the Treaty on European Union has been determined in accordance with Article F.1(1) of that Treaty, the Council, acting by a qualified majority, may decide to suspend certain of the rights deriving from the application of this Treaty to the Member State in question. In doing so, the Council shall take into account the possible consequences of such a suspension on the rights and obligations of natural and legal persons.

The obligations of the Member State in question under this Treaty shall in any case continue to be binding on that State.

3.   The Council, acting by a qualified majority, may decide subsequently to vary or revoke measures taken in accordance with paragraph 2 in response to changes in the situation which led to their being imposed.

4.   When taking decisions referred to in paragraphs 2 and 3, the Council shall act without taking into account the votes of the representative of the government of the Member State in question. By way of derogation from Article 118(2) a qualified majority shall be defined as the same proportion of the weighted votes of the members of the Council concerned as laid down in Article 118(2). This paragraph shall also apply in the event of voting rights being suspended in accordance with paragraph 1. In such cases, a decision requiring unanimity shall be taken without the vote of the representative of the government of the Member State in question.'

ARTICLE 5

The Act concerning the election of the representatives of the European Parliament by direct universal suffrage annexed to the Council Decision of 20 September 1976 shall be amended in accordance with the provisions of this Article.

(1) In Article 2, the following paragraph shall be added:

'In the event of amendments to this Article, the number of representatives elected in each Member State must ensure appropriate representation of the peoples of the States brought together in the Community.'.

(2) In Article 6(1), the following indent shall be inserted after the fifth indent:

'– member of the Committee of the Regions,'.

(3) Article 7(2) shall be replaced by the following:

'2. Pending the entry into force of a uniform electoral procedure or a procedure based on common principles and subject to the other provisions of this Act, the electoral procedure shall be governed in each Member State by its national provisions.'

(4) Article 11 shall be replaced by the following:

'Pending the entry into force of the uniform electoral procedure or the procedure based on common principles referred to in Article 7, the European Parliament shall verify the credentials of representatives. For this purpose it shall take note of the results declared officially by the Member States and shall rule on any disputes which may arise out of the provisions of this Act other than those arising out of the national provisions to which the Act refers.'

(5) Article 12(1) shall be replaced by the following:

'1. Pending the entry into force of the uniform electoral procedure or the procedure based on common principles referred to in Article 7 and subject to the other provisions of this Act, each Member State shall lay down appropriate procedures for filling any seat which falls vacant during the five-year term of office referred to in Article 3 for the remainder of that period.'

PART TWO
SIMPLIFICATION

ARTICLE 6

The Treaty establishing the European Community, including the annexes and protocols thereto, shall be amended in accordance with the provisions of this Article for the purpose of deleting lapsed provisions of the Treaty and adapting in consequence the text of certain of its provisions.

I. TEXT OF THE ARTICLES OF THE TREATY

(1) In Article 3, point (a), the word 'elimination' shall be replaced by 'prohibition'.

(2) Article 7 shall be repealed.

(3) Article 7a shall be amended as follows:

(a) the first and second paragraphs shall be numbered and thus become paragraphs 1 and 2;

(b) in the new paragraph 1, the following references shall be deleted: '7b', '70(1)' and 'and 100b'; before the citation of Article 100a, the comma shall be replaced by the word 'and';

(c)   there shall be added a paragraph 3 with the wording of the second paragraph of Article 7b which reads as follows:

'3.   The Council, acting by a qualified majority on a proposal from the Commission, shall determine the guidelines and conditions necessary to ensure balanced progress in all the sectors concerned.'.

(4)   Article 7b shall be repealed.

(5)   Article 8b shall be amended as follows:

(a)   in paragraph 1 the words 'to be adopted before 31 December 1994' shall be replaced by 'adopted';

(b)   in paragraph 2, first sentence, the reference to 'Article 138(3)' shall be replaced by 'Article 138(4)';

(c)   in paragraph 2, second sentence, the words 'to be adopted before 31 December 1993' shall be replaced by 'adopted'.

(6) In Article 8c, second sentence, the words 'Before 31 December 1993, Member States . . . ' shall be replaced by 'Member States . . .'.

(7)   In Article 8e, first paragraph, the words 'before 31 December 1993 and then,' shall be deleted, as well as the comma after the words 'every three years'.

(8)   In Article 9(2), the words 'The provisions of Chapter 1, Section 1, and of Chapter 2 . . . ' shall be replaced by 'The provisions of Article 12 and of Chapter 2 . . .'.

(9)   In Article 10, paragraph 2 shall be deleted and paragraph 1 shall remain without a number.

(10)   Article 11 shall be repealed.

(11)   In Chapter 1, The Customs Union, the heading 'Section 1 Elimination of customs duties between Member States' shall be deleted.

(12)   Article 12 shall be replaced by the following:

'**Article 12**

Customs duties on imports and exports and charges having equivalent effect shall be prohibited between Member States. This prohibition shall also apply to customs duties of a fiscal nature.'.

(13)   Articles 13 to 17 shall be repealed.

(14)   The heading 'Section 2 — Setting up of the Common Customs Tariff' shall be deleted.

(15)   Articles 18 to 27 shall be repealed.

(16)   Article 28 shall be replaced by the following:

'**Article 28**

Common Customs Tariff duties shall be fixed by the Council acting by a qualified majority on a proposal from the Commission.'.

(17)   In the introductory part of Article 29, the words 'this Section' shall be replaced by 'this Chapter'.

(18)   In the title of Chapter 2, the word 'Elimination' shall be replaced by 'Prohibition'.

(19)   In Article 30, the words 'shall, without prejudice to the following provisions, be prohibited . . . ' shall be replaced by 'shall be prohibited . . .'.

(20)   Articles 31, 32 and 33 shall be repealed.

(21)   In Article 34, paragraph 2 shall be deleted and paragraph 1 shall remain without a number.

(22)   Article 35 shall be repealed.

(23)   In Article 36, the words 'The provisions of Articles 30 to 34' shall be replaced by 'The provisions of Articles 30 and 34'.

(24)   Article 37 shall be amended as follows:

(a)   in paragraph 1, first subparagraph, the word 'progressively' and the words 'when the transitional period has ended' shall be deleted;

(b)   in paragraph 2, the word 'abolition' shall be replaced by 'prohibition';

(c)   paragraphs 3, 5 and 6 shall be deleted and paragraph 4 shall become paragraph 3;

(d)   in the new paragraph 3, the words 'account being taken of the adjustments that will be possible and the specialisation that will be needed with the passage of time.' shall be deleted and the comma after 'concerned' shall become a full stop.

(25)   Article 38 shall be amended as follows:

(a)   in paragraph 3, first sentence, the reference to Annex II shall be replaced by a reference to Annex I and the second sentence, beginning with the words 'Within two years of the entry into force . . . ' shall be deleted;

(b)   in paragraph 4, the words 'among the Member States.' shall be deleted.

(26)   Article 40 shall be amended as follows:

(a)   paragraph 1 shall be deleted and paragraphs 2, 3 and 4 shall become paragraphs 1, 2 and 3;

(b)   (does not concern the English language version)

(c)   in new paragraph 2, the reference to 'paragraph 2' shall become 'paragraph 1';

(d)   in new paragraph 3, the reference to 'paragraph 2' shall become 'paragraph 1';

(27)   Article 43 shall be amended as follows:

(a)   in paragraph 2, third subparagraph, the words 'acting unanimously during the first two stages and by a qualified majority thereafter' shall be replaced by 'acting by a qualified majority';

(b)   in paragraphs 2 and 3, the reference to 'Article 40(2)' shall become 'Article 40(1).

(28)   Articles 44 and 45 and Article 47 shall be repealed.

(29)   In Article 48(1), the words 'by the end of the transitional period at the latest' shall be deleted.

(30)   Article 49 shall be amended as follows:

(a)   in the introductory part, the words 'As soon as this Treaty enters into force, the Council . . . ' shall be replaced by 'The Council . . . ' and the words 'by progressive stages' together with the commas preceding and following those words shall be deleted;

(b)   in points (b) and (c) respectively, the words 'systematically and progressively' shall be deleted.

(31)   The first paragraph of Article 52 shall be amended as follows:

(a)   in the first sentence, the words 'abolished by progressive stages in the course of the transitional period' shall be replaced by the word 'prohibited';

(b)   in the second sentence, the words 'progressive abolition' shall be replaced by the word 'prohibition'.

(32)   Article 53 shall be repealed.

(33)   Article 54 shall be amended as follows:

(a)　paragraph 1 shall be deleted and paragraphs 2 and 3 shall become paragraphs 1 and 2;

(b)　in new paragraph 1, the words 'implement this general programme or, in the absence of such a programme, in order to achieve a stage in attaining' shall be replaced by 'attain'.

(34)　In Article 59, first paragraph, the words 'progressively abolished during the transitional period' shall be replaced by 'prohibited'.

(35)　In Article 61(2), the word 'progressive' shall be deleted.

(36)　Article 62 shall be repealed.

(37)　Article 63 shall be amended as follows:

(a)　paragraph 1 shall be deleted and paragraphs 2 and 3 shall become paragraphs 1 and 2;

(b)　in new paragraph 1, the words 'implement this general programme or, in the absence of such a programme, in order to achieve a stage in' shall be replaced by the word 'achieve' and the words 'unanimously until the end of the first stage and by a qualified majority thereafter' shall be replaced by the words 'by a qualified majority';

(c)　in new paragraph 2, the words 'As regards the proposals and decisions referred to in paragraphs 1 and 2' shall be replaced by 'As regards the directives referred to in paragraph 1'.

(38)　In Article 64, first paragraph, 'Article 63(2)' shall be replaced by 'Article 63(1)'.

(39)　Articles 67 to 73a, Article 73e and Article 73h shall be repealed.

(40)　Article 75(2) shall be deleted and paragraph 3 shall become paragraph 2.

(41)　In Article 76, the words 'when this Treaty enters into force' shall be replaced by 'on 1 January 1958 or, for acceding States, the date of their accession'.

(42)　Article 79 shall be amended as follows:

(a)　in paragraph 1 the words 'at the latest, before the end of the second stage' shall be deleted;

(b)　in paragraph 3, the words 'Within two years of the entry into force of this Treaty, the Council shall' shall be replaced by 'The Council shall'.

(43)　In Article 80(1), the words 'as from the beginning of the second stage' shall be deleted.

(44)　In Article 83, the words 'without prejudice to the powers of the transport section of the Economic and Social Committee.' shall be replaced by 'without prejudice to the powers of the Economic and Social Committee.'.

(45)　In Article 84(2), second subparagraph, the words 'procedural provisions of Article 75(1) and (3)' shall be replaced by 'procedural provisions of Article 75'.

(46)　In Article 87, the two subparagraphs of paragraph 1 shall be merged into a single paragraph. This new paragraph shall read as follows:

'1.　The appropriate regulations or directives to give effect to the principles set out in Articles 85 and 86 shall be laid down by the Council, acting by a qualified majority on a proposal from the Commission and after consulting the European Parliament.'.

(47)　In Article 89(1), the words ',as soon as it takes up its duties,' shall be deleted.

(48)　After Article 90, the heading 'Section 2 — Dumping' shall be deleted.

(49)   Article 91 shall be repealed.

(50)   Before Article 92, the heading 'Section 3' shall be replaced by 'Section 2'.

(51)   In Article 92(3)(c), the second sentence, beginning 'However, the aids granted to shipbuilding . . . ' and ending 'towards third countries;' shall be deleted and the remaining part of point (c) shall end with a semicolon.

(52)   In Article 95, the third paragraph shall be deleted.

(53)   Article 97 and Article 100b shall be repealed.

(54)   In Article 101, second paragraph, the words 'acting unanimously during the first stage and by a qualified majority thereafter' shall be replaced by 'acting by a qualified majority'.

(55)   In Article 109e(2)(a), first indent, the following words shall be deleted: ', without prejudice to Article 73e,'.

(56)   Article 109f shall be amended as follows:

(a)   in paragraph 1, second subparagraph, the words 'on a recommendation from, as the case may be, the Committee of Governors of the central banks of the Member States (hereinafter referred to as "Committee of Governors") or the Council of the EMI' shall be replaced by 'on a recommendation from the Council of the EMI';

(b)   in paragraph 1, the fourth subparagraph which states 'The Committee of Governors shall be dissolved at the start of the second stage.' shall be deleted;

(c)   in paragraph 8, the second subparagraph which states 'Where this Treaty provides for a consultative role for the EMI, references to the EMI shall be read, before 1 January 1994, as referring to the Committee of Governors.' shall be deleted.

(57)   Article 112 shall be amended as follows:

(a)   in paragraph 1, first subparagraph, the words 'before the end of the transitional period' shall be deleted;

(b)   in paragraph 1, second subparagraph, the words 'acting unanimously until the end of the second stage and by a qualified majority thereafter' shall be replaced by 'acting by a qualified majority'.

(58)   In Article 129c(1), first subparagraph, third indent, the words 'Cohesion Fund to be set up no later than 31 December 1993' shall be replaced by 'Cohesion Fund set up'.

(59)   In Article 130d, second paragraph, the words 'The Council, acting in accordance with the same procedure, shall before 31 December 1993 set up a Cohesion Fund to' shall be replaced by 'A Cohesion Fund set up by the Council in accordance with the same procedure shall'.

(60)   In Article 130s, paragraph 5, second indent, the words 'Cohesion Fund to be set up no later than 31 December 1993 pursuant to Article 130d' shall be replaced by 'Cohesion Fund set up pursuant to Article 130d.'.

(61)   In Article 130w, paragraph 3, the words 'ACP EEC Convention' shall be replaced by 'ACP EC Convention'.

(62)   In Article 131, first paragraph, the words 'Belgium' and 'Italy' shall be deleted and the reference to Annex IV shall be replaced by a reference to Annex II.

(63)   Article 133 shall be amended as follows:

(a)   in paragraph 1, the words 'completely abolished' shall be replaced by the word 'prohibited' and the words 'progressive abolition' shall be replaced by the word 'prohibition';

(b)   in paragraph 2, the words 'progressively abolished' shall be replaced by the word 'prohibited' and the references to Articles 13, 14, 15 and 17 shall be deleted with the result that the paragraph ends with the words '... in accordance with the provisions of Article 12.';

(c)   in paragraph 3, second subparagraph, the words 'shall nevertheless be progressively reduced to' shall be replaced by 'may not exceed' and the second sentence beginning 'The percentages and the timetable ...' and ending with 'importing country or territory.' shall be deleted;

(d)   in paragraph 4, the words 'when this Treaty enters into force' shall be deleted.

(64)   Article 136 shall be replaced by the following:

'Article 136

The Council, acting unanimously, shall, on the basis of the experience acquired under the association of the countries and territories with the Community and of the principles set out in this Treaty, lay down provisions as regards the detailed rules and the procedure for the association of the countries and territories with the Community.'.

(65)   Article 138 shall be amended as follows, to include Article 1, Article 2 as amended by Article 5 of this Treaty, and Article 3(1) of the Act concerning the election of the representatives of the European Parliament by direct universal suffrage, annexed to the Council Decision of 20 September 1976; Annex II of that Act shall continue to be applied:

(a)   in the place of paragraphs 1 and 2, which lapsed in accordance with Article 14 of the Act concerning the election of the representatives of the European Parliament, there shall be inserted the text of Articles 1 and 2 of the said Act as paragraphs 1 and 2; the new paragraphs 1 and 2 shall read as follows:

'1.   The representatives in the European Parliament of the peoples of the States brought together in the Community shall be elected by direct universal suffrage.

2.   The number of representatives elected in each Member State shall be as follows:

Belgium	25
Denmark	16
Germany	99
Greece	25
Spain	64
France	87
Ireland	15
Italy	87
Luxembourg	6
Netherlands	31
Austria	21
Portugal	25
Finland	16
Sweden	22
United Kingdom	87.

In the event of amendments to this paragraph, the number of representatives elected in each Member State must ensure appropriate representation of the peoples of the States brought together in the Community.';

(b) after the new paragraphs 1 and 2, there shall be inserted the text of Article 3(1) of the aforesaid Act as paragraph 3; the new paragraph 3 shall read as follows:

'3. Representatives shall be elected for a term of five years.';

(c) the existing paragraph 3 as amended by Article 2 of this Treaty shall become paragraph 4;

(d) paragraph 4 as added by Article 2 of this Treaty shall become paragraph 5.

(66) Article 158(3) shall be deleted.

(67) In Article 166, first paragraph, the words 'as from the date of accession' shall be replaced by 'as from 1 January 1995'.

(68) In Article 188b(3), the second subparagraph, commencing 'However, when the first appointments . . .' shall be deleted.

(69) In Article 197, the second paragraph, commencing 'In particular, it shall . . .' shall be deleted.

(70) In Article 207, the second, third, fourth and fifth paragraphs shall be deleted.

(71) In the place of Article 212 there shall be inserted the text of Article 24(1), second subparagraph, of the Treaty establishing a Single Council and a Single Commission of the European Communities; the new Article 212 shall accordingly read as follows:

'**Article 212**

The Council shall, acting by a qualified majority on a proposal from the Commission and after consulting the other institutions concerned, lay down the Staff Regulations of officials of the European Communities and the Conditions of Employment of other servants of those Communities.'.

(72) In the place of Article 218 there shall be inserted the adapted text of Article 28, first paragraph, of the Treaty establishing a Single Council and a Single Commission of the European Communities; the new Article 218 shall accordingly read as follows:

'**Article 218**

The Community shall enjoy in the territories of the Member States such privileges and immunities as are necessary for the performance of its tasks, under the conditions laid down in the Protocol of 8 April 1965 on the privileges and immunities of the European Communities. The same shall apply to the European Central Bank, the European Monetary Institute, and the European Investment Bank.'.

(73) In Article 221 the words 'Within three years of the entry into force of this Treaty, Member States shall accord . . .' shall be replaced by 'Member States shall accord . . .'.

(74) In Article 223, paragraphs 2 and 3 shall be merged and replaced by the following:

'2. The Council may, acting unanimously on a proposal from the Commission, make changes to the list, which it drew up on 15 April 1958, of the products to which the provisions of paragraph 1(b) apply.'.

(75) Article 226 shall be repealed.

(76) Article 227 shall be amended as follows:

(a) in paragraph 3, the reference to Annex IV shall be replaced by a reference to Annex II;

(b)   after paragraph 4, a new paragraph shall be inserted as follows:

'5. The provisions of this Treaty shall apply to the Åland Islands in accordance with the provisions set out in Protocol No 2 to the Act concerning the conditions of accession of the Republic of Austria, the Republic of Finland and the Kingdom of Sweden.';

(c)   the former paragraph 5 shall become paragraph 6 and point (d) thereof, concerning the Åland Islands shall be deleted; point (c) shall end with a full stop.

(77)   In Article 229, first paragraph, the words 'organs of the United Nations, of its specialised agencies and of the General Agreement on Tariffs and Trade.' shall be replaced by 'organs of the United Nations and of its specialised agencies.'

(78)   In Article 234, first paragraph, the words 'before the entry into force of this Treaty' shall be replaced by 'before 1 January 1958 or, for acceding States, before the date of their accession'.

(79)   The heading preceding Article 241 entitled 'Setting up of the institutions' shall be deleted.

(80)   Articles 241 to 246 shall be repealed.

(81)   In Article 248 a new paragraph shall be added as follows:

'Pursuant to the Accession Treaties, the Danish, English, Finnish, Greek, Irish, Portuguese, Spanish and Swedish versions of this Treaty shall also be authentic.'.

II ANNEXES

(1)   Annex I 'Lists A to G referred to in Articles 19 and 20 of the Treaty' shall be deleted.

(2)   Annex II 'List referred to in Article 38 of the Treaty' shall become Annex I and the reference to 'Annex II to the Treaty' under numbers ex 22.08 and ex 22.09 shall become a reference to 'Annex I to the Treaty'.

(3)   Annex III 'List of invisible transactions referred to in Article 73h of the Treaty' shall be deleted.

(4)   Annex IV 'Overseas countries and territories to which the provisions of Part IV of the Treaty apply' shall become Annex II. It is brought up to date and reads as follows:

'ANNEX II

OVERSEAS COUNTRIES AND TERRITORIES
to which the provisions of Part Four of the Treaty apply
    — Greenland,
    — New Caledonia and Dependencies,
    — French Polynesia,
    — French Southern and Antarctic Territories,
    — Wallis and Futuna Islands,
    — Mayotte,
    — Saint Pierre and Miquelon,
    — Aruba,
    — Netherlands Antilles:
        — Bonaire,
        — Curaçao,

— Saba,
— Sint Eustatius,
— Sint Maarten,
— Anguilla,
— Cayman Islands,
— Falkland Islands,
— South Georgia and the South Sandwich Islands,
— Montserrat,
— Pitcairn,
— Saint Helena and Dependencies,
— British Antarctic Territory,
— British Indian Ocean Territory ,
— Turks and Caicos Islands,
— British Virgin Islands,
— Bermuda.'.

III PROTOCOLS AND OTHER ACTS

(1)   The following protocols and acts shall be repealed:
   (a)   Protocol amending the Protocol on the privileges and immunities of the European Communities;
   (b)   Protocol on German internal trade and connected problems;
   (c)   Protocol on certain provisions relating to France;
   (d)   Protocol on the Grand Duchy of Luxembourg;
   (e)   Protocol on the treatment to be applied to products within the province of the European Coal and Steel Community in respect of Algeria and the overseas departments of the French Republic;
   (f)   Protocol on mineral oils and certain of their derivatives;
   (g)   Protocol on the application of the Treaty establishing the European Community to the non-European parts of the Kingdom of the Netherlands;
   (h)   Implementing Convention on the Association of the Overseas Countries and Territories with the Community;
   — Protocol on the tariff quota for imports of bananas (ex 08.01 of the Brussels Nomenclature);
   — Protocol on the tariff quota for imports of raw coffee (ex 09.01 of the Brussels Nomenclature).
(2)   At the end of the Protocol on the Statute of the European Investment Bank, the list of signatories shall be deleted.
(3)   The Protocol on the Statute of the Court of Justice of the European Community shall be amended as follows:
   (a)   the words 'HAVE DESIGNATED as their plenipotentiaries for this purpose:' and the list of Heads of State and their plenipotentiaries shall be deleted;
   (b)   the words 'WHO, having exchanged their full powers, found in good and due form,' shall be deleted;
   (c)   in Article 3, the adapted text of Article 21 of the Protocol on the privileges and immunities of the European Communities shall be added as a fourth paragraph; this new fourth paragraph shall accordingly read as follows:
   'Articles 12 to 15 and 18 of the Protocol on the privileges and immunities of the European Communities shall apply to the Judges, Advocates-General, Registrar and Assistant Rapporteurs of the Court of Justice, without

prejudice to the provisions relating to immunity from legal proceedings of Judges which are set out in the preceding paragraphs.';

(d)   Article 57 shall be repealed;

(e)   the concluding formula 'IN WITNESS WHEREOF, the undersigned Plenipotentiaries have signed this Protocol.' shall be deleted;

(f)   the list of signatories shall be deleted.

(4)   In Article 40 of the Protocol on the Statute of the European System of Central Banks and of the European Central Bank, the words 'annexed to the Treaty establishing a Single Council and a Single Commission of the European Communities' shall be deleted.

(5)   In Article 21 of the Protocol on the Statute of the European Monetary Institute, the words 'annexed to the Treaty establishing a Single Council and a Single Commission of the European Communities' shall be deleted.

(6)   The Protocol on Italy shall be amended as follows:

(a)   in the last paragraph commencing 'RECOGNISE that in the event . . .', the reference to Articles 108 and 109 shall be replaced by a reference to Articles 109h and 109i;

(b)   the list of signatories shall be deleted.

(7)   The Protocol on goods originating in and coming from certain countries and enjoying special treatment when imported into a Member State shall be amended as follows:

(a)   in the introductory part of point 1:

— the words 'applicable, at the time of the entry into force of this Treaty' shall be replaced by 'applicable on 1 January 1958.';

— after the words 'to imports', the text of point (a) shall follow on immediately; the text resulting therefrom shall read as follows:

'. . . to imports into the Benelux countries of goods originating in and coming from Suriname or the Netherlands Antilles;';

(b)   in point 1, points (a), (b) and (c) shall be deleted;

(c)   in point 3, the words 'Before the end of the first year after the entry into force of this Treaty, Member States . . .' shall be replaced by 'Member States';

(d)   the list of signatories shall be deleted.

(8)   The Protocol concerning imports into the European Community of petroleum products refined in the Netherlands Antilles shall be amended as follows:

(a)   the concluding formula 'IN WITNESS WHEREOF the undersigned Plenipotentiaries have placed their signatures below this Protocol.' shall be deleted;

(b)   the list of signatories shall be deleted.

(9)   In the Protocol on special arrangements for Greenland, Article 3 shall be repealed.

ARTICLE 7

The Treaty establishing the European Coal and Steel Community, including the annexes, protocols and other acts annexed thereto, shall be amended in accordance with the provisions of this Article for the purpose of deleting lapsed provisions of the Treaty and adapting in consequence the text of certain of its provisions.

I   TEXT OF THE ARTICLES OF THE TREATY

(1)   In Article 2, second paragraph, the word 'progressively' shall be deleted.

(2)   In Article 4, in the introductory part, the words 'abolished and' shall be deleted.

(3)   Article 7 shall be amended as follows:

(a)   in the first indent, the words 'a HIGH AUTHORITY (hereinafter referred to as 'the Commission')' shall be replaced by 'a COMMISSION';

(b)   in the second indent, the words 'a COMMON ASSEMBLY (hereinafter referred to as 'the European Parliament')' shall be replaced by 'a EUROPEAN PARLIAMENT';

(c)   in the third indent, the words 'a SPECIAL COUNCIL OF MINISTERS (hereinafter referred to as 'the Council')' shall be replaced by 'a COUNCIL';

(4)   Article 10 (3) shall be deleted.

(5)   In Article 16, the first and second paragraphs shall be deleted.

(6)   Article 21 shall be amended as follows, to include Article 1, Article 2 as amended by Article 5 of this Treaty, and Article 3(1) of the Act concerning the election of the representatives of the European Parliament by direct universal suffrage, annexed to the Council Decision of 20 September 1976; Annex II of that Act shall continue to be applied:

(a)   in the place of paragraphs 1 and 2, which lapsed in accordance with Article 14 of the Act concerning the election of the representatives of the European Parliament, there shall be inserted the text of Articles 1 and 2 of the said Act as paragraphs 1 and 2; the new paragraphs 1 and 2 shall read as follows:

'1.   The representatives in the European Parliament of the peoples of the States brought together in the Community shall be elected by direct universal suffrage.

2.   The number of representatives elected in each Member State shall be as follows:

Belgium	25
Denmark	16
Germany	99
Greece	25
Spain	64
France	87
Ireland	15
Italy	87
Luxembourg	6
Netherlands	31
Austria	21
Portugal	25
Finland	16
Sweden	22
United Kingdom	87

In the event of amendments to this paragraph, the number of representatives elected in each Member State must ensure appropriate representation of the peoples of the States brought together in the Community.';

(b)   after the new paragraphs 1 and 2, there shall be inserted the text of Article 3(1) of the aforesaid Act as paragraph 3; the new paragraph 3 shall read as follows:

'3.   Representatives shall be elected for a term of five years.';

(c)   the existing paragraph 3 as amended by Article 3 of this Treaty shall become paragraph 4;

(d)   paragraph 4 as added by Article 3 of this Treaty shall become paragraph 5.

(7)   In Article 32a, first paragraph, the words 'the date of accession' shall be replaced by '1 January 1995'.

(8)   In Article 45b(3), the second subparagraph commencing 'However, when the first appointments . . .' shall be deleted.

(9)   In Article 50, the adapted text of paragraphs 2 and 3 of Article 20 of the Treaty establishing a Single Council and a Single Commission of the European Communities shall be inserted as new paragraphs 4 and 5; the new paragraphs 4 and 5 shall accordingly read as follows:

'4.   The portion of the expenditure of the budget of the Communities covered by the levies provided for in Article 49 shall be fixed at 18 million units of account. The Commission shall submit annually to the Council a report on the basis of which the Council shall examine whether there is reason to adjust this figure to changes in the budget of the Communities. The Council shall act by the majority laid down in the first sentence of the fourth paragraph of Article 28. The adjustment shall be made on the basis of an assessment of developments in expenditure arising from the application of this Treaty.

5.   The portion of the levies assigned to cover expenditure under the budget of the Communities shall be allocated by the Commission for the implementation of that budget in accordance with the timetable provided for in the financial regulations adopted pursuant to Article 209(b) of the Treaty establishing the European Community and Article 183(b) of the Treaty establishing the Atomic Energy Community.'.

(10)   Article 52 shall be repealed.

(11)   In the place of Article 76 there shall be inserted the adapted text of Article 28, first paragraph, of the Treaty establishing a Single Council and a Single Commission of the European Communities; the new Article 76 shall accordingly read as follows:

'**Article 76**
The Community shall enjoy in the territories of the Member States such privileges and immunities as are necessary for the performance of its tasks, under the conditions laid down in the Protocol of 8 April 1965 on the privileges and immunities of the European Communities.'.

(12)   Article 79 shall be amended as follows:

(a)   in the second sentence of the first paragraph, the part of the sentence which commences 'as regards the Saar . . .' shall be deleted and the semicolon shall be replaced by a full stop;

(b)   after the first paragraph, a second paragraph shall be inserted as follows:

'The provisions of this Treaty shall apply to the Åland Islands in accordance with the provisions of Protocol No 2 of the Act concerning the conditions of accession of the Republic of Austria, the Republic of Finland and the Kingdom of Sweden.';

    (c)   in the existing second paragraph, in the introductory part, the words 'Notwithstanding the preceding paragraph:' shall be replaced by 'Notwithstanding the preceding paragraphs:';

    (d)   in the existing second paragraph, point (d) concerning the Åland Islands shall be deleted.

    (13)   In Article 84, the words 'Treaty and its Annexes, of the Protocols annexed thereto and of the Convention on the transitional Provisions.' shall be replaced by 'Treaty and its Annexes and of the Protocols annexed thereto.'

    (14)   Article 85 shall be repealed.

    (15)   In Article 93, the words 'Organisation for European Economic Cooperation' shall be replaced by 'Organisation for Economic Cooperation and Development'.

    (16)   In Article 95, third paragraph, the words 'If, after the end of the transitional period provided in the Convention on the Transitional Provisions, unforeseen difficulties . . .' shall be replaced by 'If unforeseen difficulties . . .'.

    (17)   In Article 97, the wording 'This Treaty is concluded for a period of 50 years from its entry into force.' shall be replaced by 'This Treaty shall expire on 23 July 2002.'.

II   TEXT OF ANNEX III 'SPECIAL STEELS'

At the end of Annex III, the initials of the plenipotentiaries of the Heads of State and Government shall be deleted.

III   PROTOCOLS AND OTHER ACTS ANNEXED TO THE TREATY

    (1)   The following acts shall be repealed:

    (a)   Exchange of letters between the Government of the Federal Republic of Germany and the Government of the French Republic concerning the Saar;

    (b)   Convention on the Transitional Provisions.

    (2)   The Protocol on the Statute of the Court of Justice of the European Coal and Steel Community shall be amended as follows:

    (a)   Titles I and II of the Protocol shall be replaced by the text of Titles I and II of the Protocol on the Statute of the Court of Justice of the European Community annexed to the Treaty establishing the European Community;

    (b)   Article 56 shall be repealed and the heading 'Transitional provision' which precedes it shall be deleted;

    (c)   the list of signatories shall be deleted.

    (3)   The Protocol on relations with the Council of Europe shall be amended as follows:

    (a)   Article 1 shall be repealed;

    (b)   the list of signatories shall be deleted.

ARTICLE 8

The Treaty establishing the European Atomic Energy Community, including the annexes and protocols thereto, shall be amended in accordance with the provisions of this Article for the purpose of deleting lapsed provisions of the Treaty and adapting in consequence the text of certain of its provisions.

I   TEXT OF THE ARTICLES OF THE TREATY

(1)   In Article 76, second paragraph, the words 'after the entry into force of this Treaty' shall be replaced by 'after 1 January 1958'.

(2)   In the introductory part to the first paragraph of Article 93, the words 'Member States shall abolish between themselves, one year after the entry into force of this Treaty, all customs duties …' shall be replaced by 'Member States shall prohibit between themselves all customs duties …'.

(3)   Articles 94 and 95 shall be repealed.

(4)   In Article 98, second paragraph, the words 'Within two years of the entry into force of this Treaty, the Council …' shall be replaced by 'The Council …'.

(5)   Article 100 shall be repealed.

(6)   Article 104 shall be amended as follows:

(a)   in the first paragraph, the words 'after the entry into force of this Treaty' shall be replaced by 'after 1 January 1958 or, for acceding States, after the date of their accession,';

(b)   in the second paragraph the words 'after the entry into force of this Treaty, within the purview thereof' shall be replaced by 'after the dates referred to in the first paragraph, within the scope of this Treaty'.

(7)   Article 105 shall be amended as follows:

(a)   in the first paragraph, the words 'concluded before its entry into force by a Member State' shall be replaced by 'concluded before 1 January 1958 or, for acceding States, before the date of their accession, by a Member State'. At the end of that paragraph the words 'the entry into force of this Treaty' shall be replaced by 'the aforesaid dates';

(b)   in the second paragraph, the words 'concluded between the signature and the entry into force of this Treaty' shall be replaced by 'concluded between 25 March 1957 and 1 January 1958 or, for acceding States, between the signature of the instrument of accession and the date of their accession'.

(8)   In Article 106, first paragraph, the words 'before the entry into force of this Treaty' shall be replaced by 'before 1 January 1958 or, for acceding States, before the date of their accession'.

(9)   Article 108 shall be amended as follows, to include Article 1, Article 2 as amended by Article 5 of this Treaty, and Article 3(1) of the Act concerning the election of the representatives of the European Parliament by direct universal suffrage, annexed to the Council Decision of 20 September 1976; Annex II of that Act shall continue to be applied:

(a)   in the place of paragraphs 1 and 2, which lapsed in accordance with Article 14 of the Act concerning the election of the representatives of the European Parliament, there shall be inserted the text of Articles 1 and 2 of the said Act as paragraphs 1 and 2; the new paragraphs 1 and 2 shall read as follows:

'1. The representatives in the European Parliament of the peoples of the States brought together in the Community shall be elected by direct universal suffrage.

2.   The number of representatives elected in each Member State shall be as follows:

Belgium	25
Denmark	16
Germany	99
Greece	25
Spain	64
France	87
Ireland	15
Italy	87
Luxembourg	6
Netherlands	31
Austria	21
Portugal	25
Finland	16
Sweden	22
United Kingdom	87.

In the event of amendments to this paragraph, the number of representatives elected in each Member State must ensure appropriate representation of the peoples of the States brought together in the Community.';

(b)   after the new paragraphs 1 and 2, there shall be inserted the text of Article 3(1) of the aforesaid Act as paragraph 3; the new paragraph 3 shall read as follows:

'3.   Representatives shall be elected for a term of five years.';

(c)   the existing paragraph 3 as amended by Article 4 of this Treaty shall become paragraph 4;

(d)   paragraph 4 as added by Article 4 of this Treaty shall become paragraph 5.

(10)   In Article 127, paragraph 3 shall be deleted.

(11)   In Article 138, first paragraph, the words 'the date of accession' shall be replaced by '1 January 1995'.

(12)   In Article 160b(3), the second subparagraph commencing 'However, when the first appointments . . .' shall be deleted.

(13)   In Article 181, the second, third and fourth paragraphs shall be deleted.

(14)   In the place of Article 191 there shall be inserted the adapted text of Article 28, first paragraph, of the Treaty establishing a Single Council and a Single Commission of the European Communities; the new Article 191 shall accordingly read as follows:

'**Article 191**

The Community shall enjoy in the territories of the Member States such privileges and immunities as are necessary for the performance of its tasks, under the conditions laid down in the Protocol of 8 April 1965 on the privileges and immunities of the European Communities.'.

(15)   Article 198 shall be amended as follows:

(a)   after the second paragraph there shall be inserted a third paragraph as follows:

'The provisions of this Treaty shall apply to the Åland Islands in accordance with the provisions set out in Protocol No 2 to the Act concerning the conditions of accession of the Republic of Austria, the Republic of Finland and the Kingdom of Sweden.';

(b)   in the existing third paragraph, point (e) concerning the Åland Islands shall be deleted.

(16)   In Article 199, first paragraph, the words 'and of the General Agreement on Tariffs and Trade' shall be replaced by 'and of the World Trade Organisation'.

(17)   Title VI, 'Provisions relating to the initial period', comprising Section 1, 'Setting up of the institutions', Section 2, 'Provisions for the initial application of this Treaty' and Section 3, 'Transitional provisions' and Articles 209 to 223, shall be repealed.

(18)   In Article 225 there shall be added a new paragraph as follows:

'Pursuant to the Accession treaties the Danish, English, Finnish, Greek, Irish, Portuguese, Spanish and Swedish versions of this Treaty shall also be authentic.'.

II   ANNEXES

Annex V, 'Initial research and training programme referred to in Article 215 of this Treaty' including the table 'Breakdown by main headings . . .' shall be deleted.

III   PROTOCOLS

(1)   The Protocol on the application of the Treaty establishing the European Atomic Energy Community to the non-European parts of the Kingdom of the Netherlands shall be repealed.

(2)   The Protocol on the Statute of the Court of Justice of the European Atomic Energy Community shall be amended as follows:

(a)   the words 'HAVE DESIGNATED as their Plenipotentiaries for this Purpose:' and the list of Heads of State and their plenipotentiaries shall be deleted;

(b)   the words 'WHO, having exchanged their full powers, found in good and due form,' shall be deleted;

(c)   in Article 3, the adapted text of Article 21 of the Protocol on the privileges and immunities of the European Communities shall be added as a fourth paragraph; this new fourth paragraph shall accordingly read as follows:

'Articles 12 to 15 and 18 of the Protocol on the privileges and immunities of the European Community shall apply to the Judges, Advocates-General, Registrar and Assistant Rapporteurs of the Court of Justice, without prejudice to the provisions relating to immunity from legal proceedings of Judges which are set out in the preceding paragraphs.';

(d)   Article 58 shall be repealed;

(e)   the concluding formula 'IN WITNESS WHEREOF, the undersigned Plenipotentiaries have signed this Protocol.' shall be deleted;

(f)   the list of signatories shall be deleted.

ARTICLE 9

1.   Without prejudice to the paragraphs following hereinafter, which have as their purpose to retain the essential elements of their provisions, the Convention of 25 March 1957 on certain institutions common to the European Communities and the Treaty of 8 April 1965 establishing a Single Council and a Single Commission of the European Communities, but with the exception of the Protocol referred to in paragraph 5, shall be repealed.

2. The powers conferred on the European Parliament, the Council, the Commission, the Court of Justice and the Court of Auditors by the Treaty establishing the European Community, the Treaty establishing the European Coal and Steel Community and the Treaty establishing the European Atomic Energy Community shall be exercised by the single institutions under the conditions laid down respectively by the said Treaties and this Article.

The functions conferred on the Economic and Social Committee by the Treaty establishing the European Community and the Treaty establishing the European Atomic Energy Community shall be exercised by a single committee under the conditions laid down respectively by the said Treaties. The provisions of Articles 193 and 197 of the Treaty establishing the European Community shall apply to that Committee.

3. The officials and other staff of the European Communities shall form part of the single administration of those Communities and shall be governed by the provisions adopted pursuant to Article 212 of the Treaty establishing the European Community.

4. The European Communities shall enjoy in the territories of the Member States such privileges and immunities as are necessary for the performance of their tasks under the conditions set out in the Protocol referred to in paragraph 5. The position shall be the same as regards the European Central Bank, the European Monetary Institute and the European Investment Bank.

5. In the Protocol of 8 April 1965 on the privileges and immunities of the European Communities there shall be inserted an Article 23, as laid down in the Protocol amending the said Protocol; that Article reads as follows:

'**Article 23**
This Protocol shall also apply to the European Central Bank, to the members of its organs and to its staff, without prejudice to the provisions of the Protocol on the Statute of the European System of Central Banks and the European Central Bank.

The European Central Bank shall, in addition, be exempt from any form of taxation or imposition of a like nature on the occasion of any increase in its capital and from the various formalities which may be connected therewith in the State where the Bank has its seat. The activities of the Bank and of its organs carried on in accordance with the Statute of the European System of Central Banks and of the European Central Bank shall not be subject to any turnover tax.

The above provisions shall also apply to the European Monetary Institute. Its dissolution or liquidation shall not give rise to any imposition.'.

6. The revenue and expenditure of the European Community, the administrative expenditure of the European Coal and Steel Community and the revenue relating thereto and the revenue and expenditure of the European Atomic Energy Community, except for those of the Supply Agency and Joint Undertakings, shall be shown in the budget of the European Communities, under the conditions laid down respectively in the Treaties establishing the three Communities.

7. Without prejudice to the application of Article 216 of the Treaty establishing the European Community, Article 77 of the Treaty establishing the European Coal and Steel Community, Article 189 of the Treaty establishing the European Atomic Energy Community and the second paragraph of Article

1 of the Protocol on the Statute of the European Investment Bank, the representatives of the Governments of the Member States shall adopt by common accord the necessary provisions for the purpose of dealing with certain problems particular to the Grand Duchy of Luxembourg which arise from the creation of a Single Council and a Single Commission of the European Communities.

ARTICLE 10

1.   The repeal or deletion in this Part of lapsed provisions of the Treaty establishing the European Community, the Treaty establishing the European Coal and Steel Community and the Treaty establishing the European Atomic Energy Community as in force before the entry into force of this Treaty of Amsterdam and the adaptation of certain of their provisions shall not bring about any change in the legal effects of the provisions of those Treaties, in particular the legal effects arising from the time limits laid down by the said Treaties, nor of Accession Treaties.

2.   There shall be no change in the legal effects of the acts in force adopted on the basis of the said Treaties.

3.   The position shall be the same as regards the repeal of the Convention of 25 March 1957 on certain institutions common to the European Communities and the repeal of the Treaty of 8 April 1965 establishing a Single Council and a Single Commission of the European Communities.

ARTICLE 11

The provisions of the Treaty establishing the European Community, the Treaty establishing the European Coal and Steel Community and the Treaty establishing the European Atomic Energy Community relating to the powers of the Court of Justice of the European Communities and to the exercise of those powers shall apply to the provisions of this Part and to the Protocol on privileges and immunities referred to in Article 9(5).

PART THREE
GENERAL AND FINAL PROVISIONS

ARTICLE 12

1.   The articles, titles and sections of the Treaty on European Union and of the Treaty establishing the European Community, as amended by the provisions of this Treaty, shall be renumbered in accordance with the tables of equivalences set out in the Annex to this Treaty, which shall form an integral part thereof.

2.   The cross references to articles, titles and sections in the Treaty on European Union and in the Treaty establishing the European Community, as well as between them, shall be adapted in consequence. The same shall apply as regards references to articles, titles and sections of those treaties contained in the other Community treaties.

3.   The references to the articles, titles and sections of the Treaties referred to in paragraph 2 contained in other instruments or acts shall be understood as references to the articles, titles and sections of the Treaties as renumbered pursuant to paragraph 1 and, respectively, to the paragraphs of the said articles, as renumbered by certain provisions of Article 6.

4.   References, contained in other instruments or acts, to paragraphs of articles of the Treaties referred to in Articles 7 and 8 shall be understood as

referring to those paragraphs as renumbered by certain provisions of the said Articles 7 and 8.

ARTICLE 13
This Treaty is concluded for an unlimited period.

ARTICLE 14
1. This Treaty shall be ratified by the High Contracting Parties in accordance with their respective constitutional requirements. The instruments of ratification shall be deposited with the Government of the Italian Republic.

2. This Treaty shall enter into force on the first day of the second month following that in which the instrument of ratification is deposited by the last signatory State to fulfil that formality.

ARTICLE 15
This Treaty, drawn up in a single original in the Danish, Dutch, English, Finnish, French, German, Greek, Irish, Italian, Portuguese, Spanish and Swedish languages, the texts in each of these languages being equally authentic, shall be deposited in the archives of the Government of the Italian Republic, which will transmit a certified copy to each of the governments of the other signatory States.

IN WITNESS WHEREOF the undersigned Plenipotentiaries have signed this Treaty.

Done at Amsterdam on the second day of October in the year one thousand nine hundred and ninety seven.

(Editor's Note: Signatures omitted)

FINAL ACT

The CONFERENCE OF THE REPRESENTATIVES OF THE GOVERN-MENTS OF THE MEMBER STATES convened in Turin on the twenty ninth day of March in the year nineteen hundred and ninety six to adopt by common accord the amendments to be made to the Treaty on European Union, the Treaties establishing respectively the European Community, the European Coal and Steel Community and the European Atomic Energy Community and certain related Acts has adopted the following texts:

I. The Treaty of Amsterdam amending the Treaty on European Union, the Treaties establishing the European Communities and certain related Acts

II PROTOCOLS

A. Protocol annexed to the Treaty on European Union:
1. Protocol on Article J.7 of the Treaty on European Union
B. Protocols annexed to the Treaty on European Union and to the Treaty establishing the European Community:
2. Protocol integrating the Schengen acquis into the framework of the European Union
3. Protocol on the application of certain aspects of Article 7a of the Treaty establishing the European Community to the United Kingdom and to Ireland
4. Protocol on the position of the United Kingdom and Ireland
5. Protocol on the position of Denmark

C.   Protocols annexed to the Treaty establishing the European Community:
6.   Protocol on asylum for nationals of Member States of the European Union
7.   Protocol on the application of the principles of subsidiarity and proportionality
8.   Protocol on external relations of the Member States with regard to the crossing of external borders
9.   Protocol on the system of public broadcasting in the Member States
10.   Protocol on protection and welfare of animals
D.   Protocols annexed to the Treaty on European Union and to the Treaties establishing the European Community, the European Coal and Steel Community and the European Atomic Energy Community
11.   Protocol on the institutions with the prospect of enlargement of the European Union
12.   Protocol on the location of the seats of the institutions and of certain bodies and departments of the European Communities and of Europol
13.   Protocol on the role of national parliaments in the European Union

III   DECLARATIONS

The Conference adopted the following declarations annexed to this Final Act:
1.   Declaration on the abolition of the death penalty
2.   Declaration on enhanced cooperation between the European Union and the Western European Union
3.   Declaration relating to Western European Union
4.   Declaration on Articles J.14 and K.10 of the Treaty on European Union
5.   Declaration on Article J.15 of the Treaty on European Union
6.   Declaration on the establishment of a policy planning and early warning unit
7.   Declaration on Article K.2 of the Treaty on European Union
8.   Declaration on Article K.3(e) of the Treaty on European Union
9.   Declaration on Article K.6(2) of the Treaty on European Union
10.   Declaration on Article K.7 of the Treaty on European Union
11.   Declaration on the status of churches and non-confessional organisations
12.   Declaration on environmental impact assessments
13.   Declaration on Article 7d of the Treaty establishing the European Community
14.   Declaration on the repeal of Article 44 of the Treaty establishing the European Community
15.   Declaration on the preservation of the level of protection and security provided by the Schengen acquis
16.   Declaration on Article 73j(2)(b) of the Treaty establishing the European Community
17.   Declaration on Article 73k of the Treaty establishing the European Community
18.   Declaration on Article 73k(3)(a) of the Treaty establishing the European Community
19.   Declaration on Article 73l(1) of the Treaty establishing the European Community

50. Declaration relating to the Protocol on the institutions with the prospect of enlargement of the European Union

51. Declaration on Article 10 of the Treaty of Amsterdam

The Conference also took note of the following declarations annexed to this Final Act:

1. Declaration by Austria and Luxembourg on credit institutions

2. Declaration by Denmark relating to Article K.14 of the Treaty on European Union

3. Declaration by Germany, Austria and Belgium on subsidiarity

4. Declaration by Ireland on Article 3 of the Protocol on the position of the United Kingdom and Ireland

5. Declaration by Belgium on the Protocol on asylum for nationals of Member States of the European Union

6. Declaration by Belgium, France and Italy on the Protocol on the institutions with the prospect of enlargement of the European Union

7. Declaration by France concerning the situation of the overseas departments in the light of the Protocol integrating the Schengen acquis into the framework of the European Union

8. Declaration by Greece concerning the Declaration on the status of churches and non-confessional organisations

Finally, the Conference agreed to attach, for illustrative purposes, to this Final Act the texts of the Treaty on European Union and the Treaty establishing the European Community, as they result from the amendments made by the Conference.

Done at Amsterdam on the second day of October in the year one thousand nine hundred and ninety seven.

(Editor s Note: Signatures omitted).

ANNEX
Tables of equivalences referred to in Article 12 of the Treaty of Amsterdam
A.   Treaty on European Union

Previous numbering	New numbering
Title I	Title I
Article A	Article 1
Article B	Article 2
Article C	Article 3
Article D	Article 4
Article E	Article 5
Article F	Article 6
Article F.1(*)	Article 7
Title II	Title II
Article G	Article 8
Title III	Title III
Article H	Article 9
Title IV	Title IV
Article I	Article 10
Title V(***)	Title V
Article J.1	Article 11
Article J.2	Article 12
Article J.3	Article 13
Article J.4	Article 14
Article J.5	Article 15
Article J.6	Article 16
Article J.7	Article 17
Article J.8	Article 18
Article J.9	Article 19
Article J.10	Article 20
Article J.11	Article 21
Article J.12	Article 22
Article J.13	Article 23
Article J.14	Article 24
Article J.15	Article 25
Article J.16	Article 26
Article J.17	Article 27
Article J.18	Article 28
Title VI(***)	Title VI
Article K.1	Article 39
Article K.2	Article 30
Article K.3	Article 31
Article K.4	Article 32
Article K.5	Article 33
Article K.6	Article 34
Article K.7	Article 35
Article K.8	Article 36
Article K.9	Article 37
Article K.10	Article 38
Article K.11	Article 39
Article K.12	Article 40
Article K.13	Article 41
Article K.14	Article 42

Note
(*)   New Article introduced by the Treaty of Amsterdam.
(***)   Title restructured by the Treaty of Amsterdam.

Previous numbering	New numbering
Title VIa(**)	Title VII
Article K.15(*)	Article 43
Article K.16(*)	Article 44
Article K.17(*)	Article 45
Title VII	Title VIII
Article L	Article 46
Article M	Article 47
Article N	Article 48
Article O	Article 49
Article P	Article 50
Article Q	Article 51
Article R	Article 52
Article S	Article 53

Note
(*)   New Article introduced by the Treaty of Amsterdam.
(**)   New Title introduced by the Treaty of Amsterdam.

B.   Treaty establishing the European Community

Previous numbering	New numbering
Part One	Part One
Article 1	Article 1
Article 2	Article 2
Article 3	Article 3
Article 3a	Article 4
Article 3b	Article 5
Article 3c(*)	Article 6
Article 4	Article 7
Article 4a	Article 8
Article 4b	Article 9
Article 5	Article 10
Article 5a(*)	Article 11
Article 6	Article 12
Article 6a(*)	Article 13
Article 7 (repealed)	—
Article 7a	Article 14
Article 7b (repealed)	—
Article 7c	Article 15
Article 7d(*)	Article 16
Part Two	Part Two
Article 8	Article 17
Article 8a	Article 18
Article 8b	Article 19
Article 8c	Article 20
Article 8d	Article 21
Article 8e	Article 22
Part Three	Part Three
Title I	Title I
Article 9	Article 23
Article 10	Article 24
Article 11 (repealed)	—

Note
(*)   New Article introduced by the Treaty of Amsterdam.

Previous numbering	New numbering
Chapter 1	**Chapter 1**
Section 1 (deleted)	—
Article 12	Article 25
Article 13 (repealed)	—
Article 14 (repealed)	—
Article 15 (repealed)	—
Article 16 (repealed)	—
Article 17 (repealed)	—
Section 2 (deleted)	—
Article 18 (repealed)	—
Article 19 (repealed)	—
Article 20 (repealed)	—
Article 21 (repealed)	—
Article 22 (repealed)	—
Article 23 (repealed)	—
Article 24 (repealed)	—
Article 25 (repealed)	—
Article 26 (repealed)	—
Article 27 (repealed)	—
Article 28	Article 26
Article 29	Article 27
Chapter 2	**Chapter 2**
Article 30	Article 28
Article 31 (repealed)	—
Article 32 (repealed)	—
Article 33 (repealed)	—
Article 34	Article 29
Article 35 (repealed)	—
Article 36	Article 30
Article 37	Article 31
Title II	**Title II**
Article 38	Article 32
Article 39	Article 33
Article 40	Article 34
Article 41	Article 35
Article 42	Article 36
Article 43	Article 37
Article 44 (repealed)	—
Article 45 (repealed)	—
Article 46	Article 38
Article 47 (repealed)	—
Title III	**Title III**
Chapter 1	**Chapter 1**
Article 48	Article 39
Article 49	Article 40
Article 50	Article 41
Article 51	Article 42
Chapter 2	**Chapter 2**
Article 52	Article 43
Article 53 (repealed)	—
Article 54	Article 44
Article 55	Article 45
Article 56	Article 46
Article 57	Article 47
Article 58	Article 48

Previous numbering	New numbering
Chapter 3	**Chapter 3**
Article 59	Article 49
Article 60	Article 50
Article 61	Article 51
Article 62 (repealed)	—
Article 63	Article 52
Article 64	Article 53
Article 65	Article 54
Article 66	Article 55
Chapter 4	**Chapter 4**
Article 67 (repealed)	—
Article 68 (repealed)	—
Article 69 (repealed)	—
Article 70 (repealed)	—
Article 71 (repealed)	—
Article 72 (repealed)	—
Article 73 (repealed)	—
Article 73a (repealed)	—
Article 73b	Article 56
Article 73c	Article 57
Article 73d	Article 58
Article 73e (repealed)	—
Article 73f	Article 59
Article 73g	Article 60
Article 73h (repealed)	—
Title IIIa(**)	**Title IV**
Article 73i(*)	Article 61
Article 73j(*)	Article 62
Article 73k(*)	Article 63
Article 73l(*)	Article 64
Article 73m(*)	Article 65
Article 73n(*)	Article 66
Article 73o(*)	Article 67
Article 73p(*)	Article 68
Article 73q(*)	Article 69
Title IV	**Title V**
Article 74	Article 70
Article 75	Article 71
Article 76	Article 72
Article 77	Article 73
Article 78	Article 74
Article 79	Article 75
Article 80	Article 76
Article 81	Article 77
Article 82	Article 78
Article 83	Article 79
Article 84	Article 80
Title V **Chapter 1** **Section 1**	**Title VI** **Chapter 1** **Section 1**
Article 85	Article 81
Article 86	Article 82
Article 87	Article 83
Article 88	Article 84

Note
(*)   New Article introduced by the Treaty of Amsterdam.
(**)   New Title introduced by the Treaty of Amsterdam.

Previous numbering		New numbering	
Article 89		Article 85	
Article 90		Article 86	
	Section 2 (deleted)		—
Article 91 (repealed)		—	
	Section 3		Section 2
Article 92		Article 87	
Article 93		Article 88	
Article 94		Article 89	
Article 95		Article 90	
Article 96		Article 91	
Article 97 (repealed		—	
Article 98		Article 92	
Article 99		Article 93	
Article 100		Article 94	
Article 100a		Article 95	
Article 100b (repealed)		—	
Article 100c (repealed)		—	
Article 100d (repealed)		—	
Article 101		Article 96	
Article 102		Article 97	
	Title VI		Title VII
	Chapter 1		Chapter 1
Article 102a		Article 98	
Article 103		Article 99	
Article 103a		Article 100	
Article 104		Article 101	
Article 104a		Article 102	
Article 104b		Article 103	
Article 104c		Article 104	
	Chapter 2		Chapter 2
Article 105		Article 105	
Article 105a		Article 106	
Article 106		Article 107	
Article 107		Article 108	
Article 108		Article 109	
Article 108a		Article 110	
Article 109		Article 111	
	Chapter 3		Chapter 3
Article 109a		Article 112	
Article 109b		Article 113	
Article 109c		Article 114	
Article 109d		Article 115	
	Chapter 4		Chapter 4
Article 109e		Article 126	
Article 109f		Article 127	
Article 109g		Article 128	
Article 109h		Article 129	
Article 109i		Article 120	
Article 109j		Article 121	
Article 109k		Article 122	
Article 109l		Article 123	
Article 109m		Article 124	

Previous numbering	New numbering
Title VIa(★★)	Title VIII
Article 109n(*)	Article 125
Article 109o(*)	Article 126
Article 109p(*)	Article 127
Article 109q(*)	Article 128
Article 109r(*)	Article 129
Article 109s(*)	Article 130
Title VII	Title IX
Article 110	Article 131
Article 111 (repealed)	—
Article 112	Article 132
Article 113	Article 133
Article 114 (repealed)	—
Article 115	Article 134
Title VIIa(★★)	Title X
Article 116(*)	Article 135
Title VIII Chapter 1(★★★)	Title XI Chapter 1
Article 117	Article 136
Article 118	Article 137
Article 118a	Article 138
Article 118b	Article 139
Article 118c	Article 140
Article 119	Article 141
Article 119a	Article 142
Article 120	Article 143
Article 121	Article 144
Article 122	Article 145
Chapter 2	Chapter 2
Article 123	Article 146
Article 124	Article 147
Article 125	Article 148
Chapter 3	Chapter 3
Article 126	Article 149
Article 127	Article 150
Title IX	Title XII
Article 128	Article 151
Title X	Title XIII
Article 129	Article 152
Title XI	Title XIV
Article 129a	Article 153
Title XII	Title XV
Article 129b	Article 154
Article 129c	Article 155
Article 129d	Article 156
Title XIII	Title XVI
Article 130	Article 157

Note

(*)　New Article introduced by the Treaty of Amsterdam.
(★★)　New Title introduced by the Treaty of Amsterdam.
(★★★)　Chapter 1 restructured by the Treaty of Amsterdam.

Previous numbering	New numbering
Title XIV	Title XVII
Article 130a	Article 158
Article 130b	Article 159
Article 130c	Article 160
Article 130d	Article 161
Article 130e	Article 162
Title XV	Title XVIII
Article 130f	Article 163
Article 130g	Article 164
Article 130h	Article 165
Article 130i	Article 166
Article 130j	Article 167
Article 130k	Article 168
Article 130l	Article 169
Article 130m	Article 170
Article 130n	Article 171
Article 130o	Article 172
Article 130p	Article 173
Article 130q (repealed)	—
Title XVI	Title XIX
Article 130r	Article 174
Article 130s	Article 175
Article 130t	Article 176
Title XVII	Title XX
Article 130u	Article 177
Article 130v	Article 178
Article 130w	Article 179
Article 130x	Article 180
Article 130y	Article 181
Part Four	Part Four
Article 131	Article 182
Article 132	Article 183
Article 133	Article 184
Article 134	Article 185
Article 135	Article 186
Article 136	Article 187
Article 136a	Article 188
Part Five	Part Five
Title I	Title I
Chapter 1	Chapter 1
Section 1	Section 1
Article 137	Article 189
Article 138	Article 190
Article 138a	Article 191
Article 138b	Article 192
Article 138c	Article 193
Article 138d	Article 194
Article 138e	Article 195
Article 139	Article 196
Article 140	Article 197
Article 141	Article 198
Article 142	Article 199
Article 143	Article 200
Article 144	Article 201

Previous numbering	New numbering
Section 2	Section 2
Article 145	Article 202
Article 146	Article 203
Article 147	Article 204
Article 148	Article 205
Article 149 (repealed)	—
Article 150	Article 206
Article 151	Article 207
Article 152	Article 208
Article 153	Article 209
Article 154	Article 210
Section 3	Section 3
Article 155	Article 211
Article 156	Article 212
Article 157	Article 213
Article 158	Article 214
Article 159	Article 215
Article 160	Article 216
Article 161	Article 217
Article 162	Article 218
Article 163	Article 219
Section 4	Section 4
Article 164	Article 220
Article 165	Article 221
Article 166	Article 222
Article 167	Article 223
Article 168	Article 224
Article 168a	Article 225
Article 169	Article 226
Article 170	Article 227
Article 171	Article 228
Article 172	Article 229
Article 173	Article 230
Article 174	Article 231
Article 175	Article 232
Article 176	Article 233
Article 177	Article 234
Article 178	Article 235
Article 179	Article 236
Article 180	Article 237
Article 181	Article 238
Article 182	Article 239
Article 183	Article 240
Article 184	Article 241
Article 185	Article 242
Article 186	Article 243
Article 187	Article 244
Article 188	Article 245
Section 5	Section 5
Article 188a	Article 246
Article 188b	Article 247
Article 188c	Article 248

Previous numbering	New numbering
Chapter 2	**Chapter 2**
Article 189	Article 249
Article 189a	Article 250
Article 189b	Article 251
Article 189c	Article 252
Article 190	Article 253
Article 191	Article 254
Article 191a(*)	Article 255
Article 192	Article 256
Chapter 3	**Chapter 3**
Article 193	Article 257
Article 194	Article 258
Article 195	Article 259
Article 196	Article 260
Article 197	Article 261
Article 198	Article 262
Chapter 4	**Chapter 4**
Article 198a	Article 263
Article 198b	Article 264
Article 198c	Article 265
Chapter 5	**Chapter 5**
Article 198d	Article 266
Article 198e	Article 267
Title II	**Title II**
Article 199	Article 268
Article 200 (repealed)	—
Article 201	Article 269
Article 201a	Article 270
Article 202	Article 271
Article 203	Article 272
Article 204	Article 273
Article 205	Article 274
Article 205a	Article 275
Article 206	Article 276
Article 206a (repealed)	—
Article 207	Article 277
Article 208	Article 278
Article 209	Article 279
Article 209a	Article 280
Part Six	**Part Six**
Article 210	Article 281
Article 211	Article 282
Article 212(*)	Article 283
Article 213	Article 284
Article 213a(*)	Article 285
Article 213b(*)	Article 286
Article 214	Article 287
Article 215	Article 288
Article 216	Article 289
Article 217	Article 290
Article 218(*)	Article 291
Article 219	Article 292
Article 220	Article 293

Note
(*)   New Article introduced by the Treaty of Amsterdam.

Previous numbering	New numbering
Article 221	Article 294
Article 222	Article 295
Article 223	Article 296
Article 224	Article 297
Article 225	Article 298
Article 226 (repealed)	—
Article 227	Article 299
Article 228	Article 300
Article 228a	Article 301
Article 229	Article 302
Article 230	Article 303
Article 231	Article 304
Article 232	Article 305
Article 233	Article 306
Article 234	Article 307
Article 235	Article 308
Article 236(*)	Article 309
Article 237 (repealed)	—
Article 238	Article 310
Article 239	Article 311
Article 240	Article 312
Article 241 (repealed)	—
Article 242 (repealed)	—
Article 243 (repealed)	—
Article 244 (repealed)	—
Article 245 (repealed)	—
Article 246 (repealed)	—
Final Provisions	Final Provisions
Article 247	Article 313
Article 248	Article 314

Note
(*)   New Article introduced by the Treaty of Amsterdam.